THE HISTORY OF PARLIAMENT

THE HOUSE OF COMMONS 1820–1832

Already published:

The House of Commons, 1386–1421, ed. J. S. Roskell, Linda Clark and Carole Rawcliffe (4 vols., 1992)

The House of Commons, 1509–1558, ed. S. T. Bindoff (3 vols., 1982)

The House of Commons, 1559–1603, ed. P. W. Hasler (3 vols., 1981)

The House of Commons, 1660–1690, ed. B. D. Henning (3 vols., 1983)

The House of Commons, 1690–1715, ed. E. Cruickshanks, S. Handley and D.W. Hayton (5 vols., 2002)

The House of Commons, 1715–1754, ed. Romney Sedgwick (2 vols., 1970)

The House of Commons, 1754–1790, ed. Sir Lewis Namier and John Brooke (3 vols., 1964)

The House of Commons, 1790–1820, ed. R. G. Thorne (5 vols., 1986)

In preparation:

The House of Commons, 1422–1504

The House of Commons, 1604–1629

The House of Commons, 1640–1660

The House of Commons, 1832–1868

The House of Lords, 1660–1832

Robert Peel
by Henry William Pickersgill (National Portrait Gallery, London)

THE HISTORY OF PARLIAMENT

THE HOUSE OF COMMONS 1820–1832

D. R. Fisher

VI

MEMBERS

L–R

PUBLISHED FOR THE HISTORY OF PARLIAMENT TRUST
BY CAMBRIDGE UNIVERSITY PRESS
2009

CAMBRIDGE UNIVERSITY PRESS
Cambridge, New York, Melbourne, Madrid, Cape Town, Singapore, São Paulo, Delhi

Cambridge University Press
The Edinburgh Building, Cambridge CB2 8RU, UK

Published in the United States of America by Cambridge University Press, New York

www.cambridge.org
Information on this title: www.cambridge.org/9780521193146

First published 2009

Printed in the United Kingdom at the University Press, Cambridge

A catalogue record for this publication is available from the British Library

ISBN 978-0-521-19317-7 Volume 1 hardback
ISBN 978-0-521-19320-7 Volume 2 hardback
ISBN 978-0-521-19322-1 Volume 3 hardback
ISBN 978-0-521-19325-2 Volume 4 hardback
ISBN 978-0-521-19328-3 Volume 5 hardback
ISBN 978-0-521-19331-3 Volume 6 hardback
ISBN 978-0-521-19334-4 Volume 7 hardback
ISBN 978-0-521-19314-6 7-volume set hardback

Contents

Contributors

S.R.B.	Stephen Bairstow
M.P.J.C.	Martin Casey
R.B.C.	Richard Cockett
M.M.E.	Margaret Escott
S.M.F.	Stephen Farrell
D.R.F.	David Fisher
S.R.H.	Simon Harratt
R.M.H.	Robin Healey
T.A.J.	Terry Jenkins
S.K.	Sharman Kadish
P.J.S.	Philip Salmon
H.J.S.	Howard Spencer

Editorial note

A raised asterisk (*) following a name denotes a Member of the House of Commons during the period covered by these volumes, where such inference is not apparent from the surrounding text. A raised dagger (†) against a name indicates a Member sitting outside the period and for whom an entry is to be found in earlier or later volumes. Where two (or more) Members bear exactly the same name and style they have been differentiated by the addition of roman numerals according to when they first entered Parliament, for instance John Fane I, John Fane II. This numbering is specific to this section of the *History* only, and does not reflect a Member's seniority by age or within his family. For other conventions concerning the arrangement and content of biographies, the reader should refer to the section on 'Method' in Volume I (pp. xxi–xxvi).

Abbreviations

In addition to standard and self-explanatory abbreviations, the following abbreviations are used in this volume.

In the preliminary paragraphs:

abp.	archbishop
adn.	archdeacon
adv.	advocate
att.-gen.	attorney-general
Bar.	Baron
bp.	bishop
called	called to the bar
c.bar. exch.	chief baron of the exchequer
cdr.	commander
ch.	child, children
chan.	chancellor
c.j.	chief justice
coh.	coheir(ess)
commn.	commission
commr.	comissioner
c.p.	common pleas
cr.	created
ct.	court
cttee.	committee
dep.	deputy
d.s.p.	died *sine prole* (without issue)
d.v.p.	died *vita patris* (in the lifetime of his father)
e.	elder, eldest
E.I.	East Indies, East India
exch.	exchequer
f.m.	field marshall
Ft.	Foot regiment
g.s.	grammar school
[GB]	Great Britain

h.	heir(ess)
h.s.	high school
[I]	Ireland, Irish
jt.	joint
k.b.	king's bench
l.c.b.	lord chief baron of exchequer
l.c.j.c.p.	lord chief justice of common pleas
mq.	marquess
o.	only
posth.	posthumous
preb.	prebend, prebendary
q.m.g.	quartermaster general
q. sess.	quarter sessions
rect.	rector
recvr.	receiver
res.	resigned
ret.	retired
[S]	Scotland, Scottish
SCJ	Senator of the College of Justice
s.p.	*sine prole* (without issue)
s.p.m.	(without male issue)
suc.	succeeded
treas.	treasurer
[UK]	United Kingdom
vic.	vicar
vol.	volunteer
w.	wife
W.I.	West Indies, West Indian
wid.	widow
yr.	younger

In the endnotes:

Add.	Additional manuscripts, British Library
AHR	*American Historical Review*
Al. Cant.	*Alumni Cantabrigienses* ed. Venn
Al. Ox.	*Alumni Oxonienses* ed. Foster
Althorp Letters	*Letters of Lord Althorp* (private, 1929)
Ann. Reg.	*Annual Register*
AO	Archive(s) Office
Arbuthnot Corresp.	*The Correspondence of Charles Arbuthnot* ed. A. Aspinall (Camden ser. 3, lxv, 1941)
Arbuthnot Jnl.	*The Journal of Mrs. Arbuthnot, 1820–1832* ed. F. Bamford and the Duke of Wellington, 2vv (1950)

Argyll Mems.	8th Duke of Argyll, *Autobiography and Memoirs* ed. Dowager Duchess of Argyll, 2vv (1906)
Arniston Mems.	*The Arniston Memoirs. Three Centuries of a Scottish House* ed. G.W.T. Omond (1887)
Arnould, *Denman*	Sir J. Arnould, *Memoirs of Thomas, Lord Denman*, 2vv (1873)
AS	Archive Service
Ashley, *Palmerston*	Evelyn Ashley, *The Life of Henry John Temple, Viscount Palmerston*, 2vv (3rd edn. 1877)
Bagot, *Canning and Friends*	*George Canning and his Friends* ed. J. Bagot, 2vv (1909)
Balfour, *Aberdeen*	Lady Frances Balfour, *The Life of George, 4th Earl of Aberdeen*, 2vv (1922)
Baring Jnls.	*Journals and Correspondence of Francis Thornhill Baring, Baron Northbrook, 1808–1852* ed. Earl of Northbrook, 2vv (private, Winchester, 1905)
Bentham Corresp.	*The Correspondence of Jeremy Bentham* ed. T.L.S. Sprigge et *al*, 5vv (1968–81)
Berry Jnls.	*Extracts from the Journals and Correspondence of Miss [Mary] Berry, 1783–1852* ed. Lady Theresa Lewis, 3vv (1866)
BIHR/HR	*Bulletin of the Institute of Historical Research/ Historical Research*
Bk.	*Book*
BL	British Library
Blakiston, *Lord William Russell*	Georgiana Blakiston, *Lord William Russell and his Wife, 1815–1846* (1972)
Bodl.	Bodleian Library, Oxford
Borthwick	Borthwick Institute of Historical Research, York
Brougham, *Life and Times*	*The Life and Times of Henry, Lord Brougham, written by Himself*, 3vv (1871)
Broughton, *Recollections*	Lord Broughton, *Recollections of a Long Life* ed. Lady Dorchester, 6vv (1909–11)
Buckingham, *Mems. Geo. IV*	Duke of Buckingham and Chandos, *Memoirs of the Court of George IV, 1820–1830*, 2vv (1859)
Bulwer, *Palmerston*	Sir Henry Lytton Bulwer, *The Life of Henry John Temple, Viscount Palmerston*, 3vv (1870–4)
Bunbury Mem.	*Memoir and Literary Remains of Sir Henry Edward Bunbury* ed. Sir C.J.F. Bunbury (private, 1868)
Burke Corresp.	*The Correspondence of Edmund Burke* ed. various, 10vv (Cambridge, 1958–78)
Burke LG	*Burke's Landed Gentry*
Burke PB	*Burke's Peerage and Baronetage*
Buxton Mems.	*Memoirs of Sir Thomas Fowell Buxton* ed. C. Buxton (1848)

Cam. Soc.	Camden Society
Canning's Ministry	*The Formation of Canning's Ministry, February to August 1827* ed. A. Aspinall (Camden ser. 3, lix, 1937)
Canning Official Corresp.	*Some Official Correspondence of George Canning* ed. E.J. Stapleton, 2vv (1887)
Castlereagh Corresp.	*Correspondence, Despatches, and Other Papers of Viscount Castlereagh* (ser. 3) ed. Marquess of Londonderry, 4vv (1853)
CB	*Complete Baronetage*
CITR	*Calendar of Inner Temple Records*
CJ	*Journals of the House of Commons*
Cockburn Jnl.	*Journal of Henry Cockburn, 1831–1854*, 2vv (Edinburgh, 1874)
Cockburn, *Jeffrey*	Lord Cockburn, *Life of Lord Jeffrey*, 2vv (Edinburgh, 1850)
Cockburn Letters	*Letters Chiefly Connected with the Affairs of Scotland, from Henry Cockburn to Thomas Francis Kennedy, 1818–1852* (1874)
Cockburn Mems.	Henry Cockburn, *Memorials of His Time* ed. K.F.C. Miller (Chicago, 1974)
Colchester Diary	*The Diary and Correspondence of Charles Abbot, Lord Colchester* ed. Lord Colchester, 3vv (1861)
Countess Granville Letters	*Letters of Harriet, Countess Granville, 1818–1845* ed. F. Leveson Gower, 2vv (1894)
Cowley Diary	*The Diary and Correspondence of Henry Wellesley, First Lord Cowley, 1790–1846* ed. F.A. Wellesley (1930)
CP	*Complete Peerage*
Crabb Robinson Diary	*Diary, Reminiscences and Correspondence of Henry Crabb Robinson* ed. T. Sadler, 2vv (3rd edn. 1872)
Creevey Pprs.	*The Creevey Papers* ed. Sir Herbert Maxwell, 2vv (2nd edn. 1904)
Creevey's Life and Times	*Creevey's Life and Times* ed. J. Gore (1937 edn.)
Croker Pprs.	*The Correspondence and Diaries of John Wilson Croker* ed. L.J. Jennings, 3vv (1884)
CUL	Cambridge University Library
D. Am. B.	*Dictionary of American Biography*
Disraeli Letters	*Benjamin Disraeli Letters* ed. various, 7vv (Toronto, 1982–2004)
DNB	*Dictionary of National Biography*
DWB	*Dictionary of Welsh Biography*
Dyott's Diary	*Dyott's Diary, 1781–1845* ed. R.W. Jeffery, 2vv (1907)

EcHR	*Economic History Review*
Edgeworth Letters	*Maria Edgeworth. Letters from England, 1813–1844* ed. C. Colvin (Oxford, 1971)
Eg.	Egerton mss, British Library
EHR	*English Historical Review*
Ellenborough Diary	Lord Ellenborough, *A Political Diary, 1828–1830* ed. Lord Colchester, 2vv (1881)
Farington Diary	*The Diary of Joseph Farington* ed. various, 16vv (Yale, 1978–84)
Fox Jnl.	*The Journal of Henry Edward Fox, 1818–1830* ed. Lord Ilchester (1923)
Gen. Mag.	*Genealogist's Magazine*
Gent. Mag.	*Gentleman's Magazine*
Geo. IV Letters	*The Letters of King George IV* ed. A. Aspinall, 3vv (Cambridge, 1938)
GL	Guildhall Library
Gladstone Diaries	*The Gladstone Diaries* ed. M.R.D. Foot and H.G.C. Matthew, 14vv (Oxford, 1994)
Glenbervie Diaries	*The Diaries of Sylvester Douglas (Lord Glenbervie)* ed. F. Bickley, 2vv (1928)
Glenbervie Jnls.	*The Glenberve Journals* ed. W. Sichel (1910)
Greville Mems.	*The Greville Memoirs* ed. L. Strachey and R. Fulford, 8vv (1938)
Gronow Reminiscences	*The Reminiscences and Recollections of Captain Gronow,* 2vv (1900 edn.)
Heber Letters	R.H. Cholmondeley, *The Heber Letters, 1783–1832* (1950)
HEHL	Henry E. Huntington Library, San Marino, California
Heron, *Notes*	Sir Robert Heron, *Notes* (2nd edn. 1851)
Highland Lady	*Memoirs of a Highland Lady* ed. Lady Strachey (1911)
HJ	*Historical Journal*
HLB/HLQ	*Huntington Library Bulletin,* later *Huntington Library Quarterly*
HLRO	House of Lords Record Office (Parliamentary Archives)
HMC	*Historical Manuscripts Commission*
Hobhouse Diary	*The Diary of Henry Hobhouse (1820–1827)* ed. A. Aspinall (1947)
Holland, *Further Mems.*	Lord Holland, *Further Memoirs of the Whig Party, 1807–1821* ed. Lord Stavordale (1905)
Holland, *Mems. Whig Party*	Lord Holland, *Memoirs of the Whig Party during My Time* ed. Lord Holland, 2vv (1852)

Holland House Diaries	*The Holland House Diaries* ed. A.D. Kriegel (1977)
Horner Pprs.	*The Horner Papers* ed. K. Bourne and W.B. Taylor (Edinburgh, 1994)
Howard Sisters	*Three Howard Sisters* ed. Lady Leconfield and J. Gore (1955)
HP	*History of Parliament*
Huskisson Pprs.	*The Huskisson Papers* ed. L. Melville (1931)
IGI	International Genealogical Index
IHR	Institute of Historical Research
IR	Death duty registers
JBS	*Journal of British Studies*
JEH	*Journal of Ecclesiastical History*
JMH	*Journal of Modern History*
JRL	John Rylands University Library, Manchester
Lady Holland Jnl.	*The Journal of Elizabeth, Lady Holland (1791–1811)* ed. Lord Ilchester, 2vv (1908)
Lady Holland to Son	*Elizabeth, Lady Holland to her Son, 1821–1845* ed. Lord Ilchester (1946)
Lady-in-Waiting	Lady Charlotte Bury, *The Diary of a Lady-in-Waiting* ed. A.F. Steuart (1908)
Lady Lyttelton Corresp.	*Correspondence of Sarah Spencer, Lady Lyttelton, 1787–1870* ed. Mrs. Hugh Wyndham (1912)
Lady Palmerston Letters	*Letters of Lady Palmerston* ed. T. Lever (1957)
Later Corresp. Geo. III	*The Later Correspondence of George III* ed. A. Aspinall, 5vv (Cambridge, 1962–70)
Le Marchant, *Althorp*	Sir Denis Le Marchant, *Memoir of John Charles, Viscount Althorp, Third Earl Spencer* (1876)
Leveson Gower Corresp.	*Lord Granville Leveson Gower. Private Correspondence, 1781 to 1821* ed. Countess Granville, 2vv (1916)
Lieven Letters	*Letters of Dorothea, Princess Lieven, during her residence in London, 1812–1834* ed. L.G. Robinson (1902)
Lieven-Palmerston Corresp.	*The Lieven-Palmerston Correspondence, 1828–1856* ed. Lord Sudeley (1943)
Lieven-Grey Corresp.	*Correspondence of Princess Lieven and Earl Grey* ed. G. Le Strange, 2vv (1890)
Life of Campbell	*Life of John, Lord Campbell* ed. Mrs. Hardcastle, 2vv (1881)
Life of Wilberforce	R.I. and S. Wilberforce, *Life of William Wilberforce* (1838)
LJ	*Journals of the House of Lords*
LMA	London Metropolitan Archives

Macaulay Letters	*The Letters of Thomas Babington Macaulay* ed. T. Pinney, 6vv (Cambridge, 1974–81)
Malmesbury Letters	*A Series of Letters of the First Earl of Malmesbury, his Family and Friends, from 1745 to 1820* ed. Lord Malmesbury, 2vv (1870)
Malmesbury Mems.	Earl of Malmesbury, *Memoirs of an Ex-Minister*, 2vv (1884)
Martin, *Lyndhurst*	Sir Theodore Martin, *A Life of Lord Lyndhurst* (1883)
Martineau Letters	*Harriet Martineau. Selected Letters* ed. V. Sanders (Oxford, 1990)
Maxwell, *Clarendon*	Sir Henry Maxwell, *The Life and Letters of George William Frederick, Fourth Earl of Clarendon*, 2vv (1913)
Melbourne's Pprs.	*Lord Melbourne's Papers* ed. L.C. Sanders (1889)
Melville, *Cobbett*	L. Melville, *The Life and Letters of William Cobbett*, 2vv (1913)
MI	Monumental Inscription(s)
Mill Works	*Collected Works of John Stuart Mill* ed. various, 33vv (Toronto,1963–91)
Misc. Gen. et Her.	*Miscellanea Genealogica et Heraldica*
Monypenny and Buckle, *Disraeli*	W.F. Monypenny and G.E. Buckle, *The Life of Benjamin Disraeli, Earl of Beaconsfield*, 6vv (1910–20)
Moore Jnl.	*The Journal of Thomas Moore* ed. Wilfrid S. Dowden, 6vv (Newark, Delaware, 1983–91)
Moore Mems.	*Memoirs, Journal and Correspondence of Thomas Moore* ed. Lord John Russell, 8vv (1853–6)
Morley, *Gladstone*	J. Morley, *The Life of William Ewart Gladstone*, 3vv (1903)
Mus.	Museum
NAI	National Archives of Ireland
N and Q	*Notes and Queries*
NAS	National Archives of Scotland
n.d.	no date
NLI	National Library of Ireland
NLS	National Library of Scotland
NLW	National Library of Wales
NLWJ	*National Library of Wales Journal*
NMM	National Maritime Museum
n.s.	new series
O'Connell Corresp.	*The Correspondence of Daniel O'Connell* ed. M.R. O'Connell, 8vv (Dublin, 1972–80)
OIOC	Oriental and India Office Collections, British Library

Oldfield, *Rep. Hist.*	T.H.B. Oldfield, *Representative History of Great Britain and Ireland*, 6vv (1816)
Oldfield, *Key* (1820)	T.H.B. Oldfield, *Key to the House of Commons* (1820)
OR	*Official Return of Members of Parliament* (1878–91)
Overstone Corresp.	*The Correspondence of Lord Overstone* ed. D.P. O'Brien, 3vv (Cambridge, 1971)
Oxford DNB	*Oxford Dictionary of National Biography*
Palmerston-Sulivan Letters	*The Letters of the Third Viscount Palmerston to Laurence and Elizabeth Sulivan, 1804–1863* ed. K. Bourne (Camden ser. 4, xxiii, 1979)
P and P	*Past and Present*
par.	parish
Parker, *Graham*	C.S. Parker, *Life and Letters of Sir James Graham*, 2vv (1907)
Parker, *Peel*	C.S. Parker, *Sir Robert Peel from his Private Papers*, 3vv (1891)
Parl. Deb.	*Hansard's Parliamentary Debates*
Peel Letters	*The Private Letters of Sir Robert Peel* ed. G. Peel (1920)
Peel Mems.	*Memoirs of Sir Robert Peel* ed. Lord Stanhope and E. Cardwell, 2vv (1856)
Pellew, *Sidmouth*	G. Pellew, *The Life and Correspondence of Henry Addington, First Viscount Sidmouth*, 3vv (1847)
PH	*Parliamentary History*
Phipps, *Plumer Ward Mems.*	E. Phipps, *Memoirs of the Political and Literary Life of Robert Plumer Ward*, 2vv (1850)
PP	*Parliamentary Papers*
Prince of Wales Corresp.	*The Correspondence of George, Prince of Wales, 1770–1812* ed. A. Aspinall, 8vv (1963–71)
PROB	Probate Records: wills, administrations and valuations
PRO NI	Public Record Office of Northern Ireland
Raikes Jnl.	*A Portion of the Journal kept by Thomas Raikes from 1831 to 1847*, 4vv (1856–7)
Reid, *Lord Durham*	S.J. Reid, *Life and Letters of the First Earl of Durham*, 2vv (1900)
Reid, *Monckton Milnes*	T.W. Reid, *The Life, Letters and Friendships of Richard Monckton Milnes, First Lord Houghton*, 2vv (1890)
RO	Record Office
Romilly Mems.	*Memoirs of the Life of Sir Samuel Romilly, written by himself; with a Selection from his Correspondence*, 3vv (1840)

Russell Early Corresp.	*Early Correspondence of Lord John Russell, 1805–40* ed. R. Russell, 2vv (1913)
Russell Later Corresp.	*The Later Correspondence of Lord John* Russell ed. G.P. Gooch, 2vv (1925)
Russell Letters	*Letters to Lord G. William Russell*, 3vv (private, 1915–20)
Russell, *Recollections*	Earl Russell, *Recollections and Suggestions* (1875)
Scott Jnl.	*The Journal of Sir Walter Scott* (Edinburgh, 1950 edn.)
Scott Letters	*The Letters of Sir Walter Scott: 1878-1828* ed. H.J.C. Grierson, 10vv (1932-6)
Scottish Electoral Politics	*Papers on Scottish Electoral Politics, 1832–1854* ed. J.I. Brash (Scottish Hist. Soc. ser. 4, xi, Edinburgh, 1974)
ser.	series
Shelley Diary	*The Diary of Frances, Lady Shelley* ed. R. Edgcumbe, 2vv (1912)
SHR	*Scottish Historical Review*
Smith Letters	*The Letters of Sydney Smith* ed. N.C. Smith, 2vv (Oxford, 1953)
Somerset Letters	*Letters, Remains, and Memoirs of Edward Adolphus Seymour, Twelth Duke of Somerset* ed. W. Mallock and Lady G. Ramsden (1893)
Spencer-Stanhope Letter-Bag	A.M.W. Stirling, *The Letter-Bag of Lady Elizabeth Spencer Stanhope, 1806–1873* (1913)
Stirling, *Coke of Norf.*	A.M.W. Stirling, *Coke of Norfolk and his Friends* (1912 edn.)
Taylor Autobiog.	*Autobiography of Henry Taylor, 1800–1875*, 2vv (1885)
Taylor Pprs.	*The Taylor Papers: being a Record of Certain Reminiscences, Letters and Journals in the Life of Sir Herbert Taylor* ed. E. Taylor (1913)
TCD	Trinity College, Dublin
Three Diaries	*Three Early Nineteenth Century Diaries* ed. A. Aspinall (1952)
TNA	The National Archives
Torrens, *Melbourne*	W.M. Torrens, *Memoirs of William, 2nd Viscount Melbourne*, 2vv (1878)
Trans.	*Transactions*
TRHS	*Transactions of the Royal Historical Society*
Twiss, *Eldon*	H. Twiss, *The Public and Private Life of Lord Chancellor Eldon*, 3vv (1844)
Two Brothers	*Correspondence of Two Brothers: Edward Adolphus, Eleventh Duke of Somerset, and his brother, Lord*

	Webb Seymour, 1800–1819 and after ed. Lady G. Ramsden (1906)
Two Duchesses	*The Two Duchesses: Georgiana, Duchess of Devonshire, Elizabeth, Duchess of Devonshire. Family Correspondence, 1777–1859* ed. V. Foster (1898)
UCL	University College, London
UCNW	University College of North Wales (now Bangor University)
VCH	*Victoria County History*
Victoria Letters (ser. 1)	*The Letters of Queen Victoria: a selection from Her Majesty's Correspondence between the years 1837 and 1861* ed. A.C. Benson and Lord Esher, 3vv (1907–11)
Victoria Letters (ser. 2)	*The Letters of Queen Victoria, 1862–1885* ed. G.E. Buckle, 3vv (1926–8)
Victoria Letters (ser. 3)	*The Letters of Queen Victoria, 1886–1901* ed. G.E. Buckle, 3vv (1930–2)
Vis.	*Visitation*
Von Neumann Diary	*The Diary of Philipp Von Neumann, 1819–1850* trans. and ed. E. Beresford Chancellor, 2vv (1928)
Walpole, *Russell*	S. Walpole, *Life of Lord John Russell*, 2vv (1889)
Ward, *Llandaff Letters*	*Letters to the Bishop of Llandaff by the Earl of Dudley* ed. E. Coplestone (1840)
Ward, *Letters to 'Ivy'*	*Letters to 'Ivy' from the First Earl of Dudley* ed. S.H. Romilly (1905)
WCA	Westminster City Archives
Wellesley Mems.	R.R. Pearce, *Memoirs and Correspondence of Richard, Marquess Wellesley*, 3vv (1846)
Wellesley Pprs.	*The Wellesley Papers: Life and Correspondence of Marquess Wellesley*, 2vv (1914)
Wellington and Friends	*Wellington and his Friends* ed. 7th Duke of Wellington (1965)
Wellington Despatches	*Despatches, Correspondence and Memoranda of the Duke of Wellington* ed. 2nd Duke of Wellington, 8vv (1867–80)
Wellington Pol. Corresp.	*The Prime Ministers' Papers: Wellington Political Correspondence I: 1833–November 1834* ed. J. Brooke and J. Gandy (1975); *II: November 1834–April 1835* ed. R.J. Olney and J. Melvin (1986)
WHR	*Welsh History Review*
Wilberforce Corresp.	*The Correspondence of William Wilberforce* ed. R.I. and S. Wilberforce, 2vv (1840)
Wilberforce Priv. Pprs.	*Private Papers of William Wilberforce* ed. A.M. Wilberforce (1897)

William IV-Grey Corresp.	*Correspondence of Earl Grey with King William IV* ed. Lord Grey, 2vv (1867)
Williams Wynn Corresp.	*Correspondence of Charlotte Grenville, Lady Williams Wynn, and her Three Sons, Sir Watkin Williams Wynn, Charles Williams Wynn, and Sir Henry Williams Wynn* ed. R. Leighton (1920)

MEMBERS
L–R

LABOUCHERE, Henry (1798–1869), of 4 Hamilton Place, Piccadilly, Mdx.

MITCHELL	6 Apr. 1826–1830
TAUNTON	1830–July 1859

b. 15 Aug. 1798, 1st s. of Peter Caesar Labouchere of 4 Hamilton Place and Hylands, nr. Chelmsford, Essex and Dorothy Elizabeth, da. of Sir Francis Baring, 1st bt†., of Stratton Park, Hants. *educ.* Winchester 1808-12; Christ Church, Oxf. 1816; L. Inn 1817. *m.* (1) 10 Apr. 1840, his cos. Frances (*d.* 25 May 1850), da. of Sir Thomas Baring, 2nd bt*., 3 da.; (2) 13 July 1852, Lady Mary Matilda Georgiana Howard, da. of George Howard†, 6th earl of Carlisle, *s.p. suc.* fa. 1839; *cr.* Bar. Taunton 18 Aug. 1859. *d.* 13 July 1869.

Ld. of admiralty June 1832-Dec. 1834; master of mint Apr. 1835-Sept. 1841; PC 6 May 1835; vice-pres. bd. of trade May 1835-Aug. 1839, pres. Aug. 1839-Sept. 1841, July 1847-Feb. 1852; under-sec. of state for war and colonies Feb.-Sept. 1839, sec. of state Nov. 1855-Feb. 1858; chief sec. to ld. lt. [I] July 1846-July 1847; PC [I] 4 Sept. 1846.

Commr. on naval and mil. promotion 1838-40, Great Exhibition 1851, London corporation 1853-4, schools 1864-7.

Elder bro. Trinity House 1850-*d.*

Labouchere's father, a Dutchman of Huguenot descent, became a partner in the leading Amsterdam mercantile firm of Hope, established a lucrative business connection by marrying into the Baring family and eventually retired to the life of an English landowner.[1] In 1824-5 Labouchere travelled through North America with the young Members John Evelyn Denison, Edward George Geoffrey Smith Stanley and John Stuart Wortley, acquiring 'a strong liking for American institutions and a genuine affection for the American people', and developing a particular interest in Canadian affairs.[2] Through the patronage of his uncle Alexander Baring, Member for Taunton, he was returned unopposed for Mitchell on the Hawkins interest at a by-election in April 1826.[3] He voted for reform of Edinburgh's representation, 13 Apr., revision of the corn laws, 18 Apr., and parliamentary reform, 27 Apr. 1826. At the general election that summer he was again returned unopposed for Mitchell. His Whig allegiance was confirmed by his admission to Brooks's Club, 25 Feb. 1827.

He voted against the duke of Clarence's grant, 16 Feb. 1827. He divided for Catholic relief, 6 Mar., the spring guns bill, 23 Mar., and further information on the conduct of the Lisburn magistrates, 29 Mar. He voted to postpone the committee of supply pending the formation of a new ministry, 30 Mar. He divided against Canning's coalition ministry to disfranchise Penryn, 28 May, but with them for the grant to improve water communications in Canada, 12 June 1827. Writing to his friend Lord Sandon* at the end of the year, he expressed his willingness to support Lord Goderich's ministry 'without much trusting or esteeming them as a whole, for the sake of Huskisson and Lord Lansdowne'.[4] He divided for repeal of the Test Acts, 6 Feb., and Catholic relief, 12 May 1828. He voted to transfer East Retford's seats to Birmingham, 21 Mar., and for a lower pivot price on the corn duties sliding scale, 22 Apr. In supporting the motion for a select committee on the civil government of Canada (to which he was named), 2 May, he urged the need to allay the fears of French settlers and hoped that in holding on to what Chatham and Wolfe had gained, 'we shall yet achieve a still more glorious victory, and more essentially English, by giving to the country we have conquered ... the advantages of our free and liberal institutions'. He spoke in favour of the grant to the Society for the Propagation of the Gospels in Canada and other colonies, 6 June, because he was unwilling to 'deprive the clergy in those colonies of the means of support', not because he wished 'to make the religion of the Church of England the dominant religion there'. He defended the grant for military works in Canada, 7 July, recognizing the need for prudent precautions against American attack and declaring that 'if we lose Canada, we shall most assuredly lose New Brunswick and Nova Scotia, and with them the whole of our extensive fisheries'. If this happened, 'then must the maritime greatness of England sink ... never again [to] be brought back to its former splendid eminence'. He presented a petition from inhabitants of Lower Canada against the repressive measures taken by the governor general, Lord Dalhousie, 14 July. He voted against the Wellington ministry to omit the salary of the governor of Dartmouth Castle from the garrisons grant, 20 June, condemn the misapplication of public money for building work at Buckingham House, 25 June, and reduce the salary of the lieutenant-general of the ordnance, 4 July. He divided against them on the silk duties, 14 July 1828.

He voted for the government's Catholic emancipation bill, 6, 30 Mar. 1829. However, he opposed the clause requiring statements from Jesuits and members of other resident Catholic monastic orders, 'a paltry and unnecessary measure of security' which marred a bill that 'upon the whole I admire with such fervency', 24 Mar. He regarded it as 'the best colonial measure that ever passed the House', 30 Mar., as it would mollify Irish emigrant communities and ensure that 'no other sentiments prevail amongst the entire population of our colonies than an undivided love for their country'. He pressed ministers to announce their intentions for the reform of Canada's civil government, in the light of the previous year's select committee report, and to avoid disappointing the colonists' expectations, 23 Feb., 6 Apr., 14 May. On 5 June he declared that the Canadians were ready for 'a complete ... system of freedom', which should be 'given them under the shade of the British monarchy and of those admirable institutions which Mr. Pitt gave to Canada', so that Britain might 'outbid America in purchasing the affections of the people'. He again supported the grant to the Society for the Propagation of the Gospels in the colonies, 6 Apr., but warned it to be more cautious in its activities to avoid provoking irritation and suspicion. He voted to transfer East Retford's seats to Birmingham, 5 May, reduce the additional grant for the sculpture of marble arch, 25 May, and lower the hemp duty, 1 June 1829. He divided for Knatchbull's amendment to the address on distress, 4 Feb. 1830, and acted with the revived Whig opposition on most issues during that session. He voted against Lord Blandford's reform scheme, 18 Feb., but for the enfranchisement of Birmingham, Leeds and Manchester, 23 Feb., the transfer of East Retford's seats to Birmingham, 5, 15 Mar., and Russell's reform motion, 28 May, when he was said to be 'pleased with the change and ... strong for reform'.[5] He divided for Jewish emancipation, 5 Apr., 17 May. He demanded a thorough investigation of the pension list and warned that the country was likely to be disappointed at Parliament's failure to 'maintain ... strict economy in the public expenditure', 1 Mar. However, he was against abolishing the treasurership of the navy, 12 Mar., believing this to be tantamount to a censure of the government, although he hoped to see a check on the 'system of extravagance'. He voted to abolish the death penalty for forgery, 7 June, and opposed the Lords' amendments to the forgeries punishment bill, criticizing ministers for not framing the measure properly, 20 July 1830.

Labouchere was active on issues relating to Canada and other colonies throughout that session. He argued that reform of Canadian civil government would allow 'the present enormous military establishments there' to be reduced, 19 Feb. He agreed to put off his resolutions on Canada so as not to retard progress on the estimates, 25 Mar. He was prepared to allow a first reading of the government's Canada bill, as so few Members were present, 29 Apr., but indicated that he would oppose it at a later stage. He declared that 'a complete alteration' in the principle of the bill was needed, as it involved taxation to which the colonists would never submit, 14 June. He brought forward his resolutions on 25 May, justifying his initiative on the ground that few other Members had a specialist interest in Canada. He called for a reduction in the number of placemen in the legislative councils and the removal of judges from the executive councils, arguing that it was necessary to 'strike at the root itself of all abuse, which can only be corrected ... by placing in the hands of the Canadians themselves the unlimited management of their own internal concerns'. He was a teller for the motion, which was defeated by 153-94. He announced that he now favoured phasing out the grant to the Society for the Propagation of the Gospels in Canada and other colonies, 14 June, believing it to be 'decidedly injurious to the Church of England', which was 'fading away through the jealousy and animosity ... excited against her'. That day he argued that the government should end the 'most unchristian' practice of giving presents to the Canadian Indians in order to secure their service as military auxiliaries, maintaining that 'the Indians to whom the advantages of civilization have not yet been extended, are as barbarous in their system of warfare as in their mode of living'. He urged ministers to pledge themselves to a bill on Canadian revenues in the next session, 16 July. He approved of those named as government commissioners to investigate abuses in colonial expenditure, 10 May. He supported the motion for inquiry into the state of Newfoundland, where the 'greatest discontent' existed, 11 May, and was a minority teller. He endorsed a petition from the Cape of Good Hope for a representative system of government, 24 May, deploring the practice of 'sending out men of broken fortunes to occupy situations in the colonies'. In the debate on the civil establishment in the Bahamas, 11 June, he criticized the instinct to inject English ideas about the coexistence of monarchical, aristocratic and democratic elements into colonial constitutions, suggesting that 'our offspring will be more healthy and vigorous if we allow them to depend more on their own strength'; he hastened to add that 'in this country I am no enemy to the aristocracy'. He urged the government to abolish the establishment at Sierra Leone for extinguishing the slave trade, which 'only grievously aggravates ... the horrors of that odious traffic', 20 July 1830. In the absence of co-operation from other countries, he thought Britain should confine itself to 'preventing our own subjects from engaging in that traffic'.

At the general election of 1830 Labouchere offered for Taunton on his uncle's interest and was returned comfortably at the head of the poll. He affirmed his determination to uphold 'the noble institutions of this country', by his 'readiness to apply to every part of them a searching but well-considered reform', to 'alleviate the burthens of the people', by enforcing 'a system of rigid economy in the public expenditure', and support 'a pacific system' of foreign policy 'compatible with the national interests and honour'. He subsequently declared that while he would 'join in no factious opposition' to the ministry, he was 'inclined to watch its conduct with great distrust', as he doubted whether it contained 'enough efficiency and ability adequately to do justice to the great and various interests of this empire'. He also welcomed the 'late glorious events in France', which had opened up 'a new and greater order of things to our view'. Privately, however, he suspected that 'if things get hot abroad it will not fail to produce a rally round the duke, and such language as that which Brougham and Graham have been indulging in will materially assist to produce such an effect'.[6] The ministry of course reckoned Labouchere among their 'foes', and he duly voted against them in the crucial civil list division, 15 Nov. 1830. He had tried unsuccessfully to extract information from them about the awaited report of the commission on finance and expenditure in the colonies, 5 Nov. He presented a Taunton anti-slavery petition and urged Lord Grey's new ministry to face up to this issue, 23 Nov. He supported the grant for the Rideau Canal in Canada, regarding it as 'true economy to undertake these works and fortifications', 6 Dec. 1830. He approved the ministerial resolutions on the government of Canada, 18 Feb. 1831, but wished to see the legislative council elected rather than nominated, arguing that 'our only course of governing Canada well, is not to govern it at all'. He questioned Goulburn, the former chancellor of the exchequer, over the granting of pensions by the Wellington ministry, 9 Dec., and presented a Taunton petition for repeal of the assessed taxes, 17 Dec. 1830. He criticized the spiralling expenditure on Windsor Castle and Buckingham House, 15 Feb. 1831, asserting that 'if one thing more than another has of late shaken the attachment of the people to monarchical institutions, it is these ill-advised buildings'. He was named to the select committee on the East India Company, 4 Feb. (and again, 28 June 1831, 27 Jan., 27 June 1832). In presenting a Taunton petition for parliamentary reform, 14 Feb., he said he was 'much disposed to support a great extension of suffrage, because I am desirous that the lower as well as the other classes should participate in the benefits of the constitution, and believe that their exclusion from the right of suffrage is neither just nor expedient'. He expressed his opposition to a Taunton petition for the ballot, which was likely to 'produce greater evils than it is intended to remove', 28 Feb., but praised the willingness of Taunton's potwallopers to sacrifice their exclusive power by supporting an extended franchise, 7, 19 Mar., 19 Apr. He divided for the second reading of the ministry's reform bill, 22 Mar., and against Gascoyne's wrecking amendment, 19 Apr. 1831. At the ensuing general election he and his Whig colleague Bainbridge received a 'cordial welcome' at Taunton and were returned unopposed. Labouchere denied that the reform bill would destroy the influence of the aristocracy, maintaining on the contrary that it would

> tend to place it on a sounder basis. If the nobility wished to retain that influence, they would find that it was not to be done by secluding themselves, or trusting to their close boroughs, but by mixing with the people, and identifying themselves with the growing spirit and liberal sentiment of the age. He believed that the people of England loved the crown and the constitutional nobility of the land, and considered their own liberties to be inseparably bound up with the just prerogative and privileges of the other orders of the state.[7]

He divided for the second reading of the reintroduced reform bill, 6 July 1831, and steadily for its details, although he was in the minority to transfer Aldborough from schedule B to A, 14 Sept. He presented a petition from certain householders of St. Mary Magdalene, Taunton, for their inclusion in the borough, 8 July. He opposed granting representation at Westminster to the colonies, 16 Aug., arguing that it would be impossible for colonial Members to perform double duties and improper for them to vote on issues relating to English taxation, he denied that a reformed House of Commons would neglect colonial interests. He opposed any alteration of the time for commencing parliamentary business and praised Lord Althorp's handling of the bill, 27 Aug. He divided for the third reading, 19 Sept. Next day he admitted that he had 'belonged to that school which wished reform to take place gradually', but explained that after Wellington's refusal to act 'the time for that course ... passed by'. Grey's ministry had rightly displayed a 'prudent boldness' by introducing 'a measure of a broad and extensive character ... which would give the hope of settling this great question'. He believed that in the future 'we may have a battle to fight between those who look upon all rights as usurpations and those who love and reverence existing institutions', but this could not be 'fought on the ground we now occupy', whereas in a reformed Parliament 'we shall be joined by all the public virtue and ... private worth of the country'. He voted for the bill's passage, 21 Sept., and Lord Ebrington's confidence motion, 10 Oct. 1831.

He supported the grant for salaries and allowances to certain Oxbridge professors for reading courses of lectures, 8 July 1831, as 'the benefits which [they] confer upon the country ... especially upon the poorer classes, are incalculable'. He pressed ministers to name a day for the third reading of the Canadian revenue bill, 8 July. He again recommended phasing out the grant to the Society for the Propagation of the Gospels in the colonies, 25 July, as it tended 'to sow the seeds of religious dissension and civil discord'; he also urged ministers to deal with the question of the clergy reserves and amend the charter of the University of Upper Canada. That day he used a debate on Canadian canals to raise the colonists' discontent at their system of civil government, arguing that the legislative councils must be reformed and pointing to the evils of a situation where an 'oligarchy of placeholders' was able to appropriate executive and judicial offices for its party supporters. He presented petitions from Lower Canada for the extinction of feudal rights in land and complaining of the legislative councils, the judicial system and the clergy reserves, 14 Oct. He supported the motion to grant constitutional government to Newfoundland, which should be 'founded upon those broad principles of British liberty', 13 Sept. He called for generous measures to relieve the people of Barbados and St. Vincent following a hurricane, 13 Oct. He questioned ministers as to whether the bill regulating child factory labour would apply to the silk industry, 6 Aug. He voted in the minority to print the Waterford petition for disarming the Irish yeomanry, 11 Aug. He presented petitions for omnibuses to be taxed as hackney cabs rather than stagecoaches, 16 Aug., and to reduce the duty and relax the regulations on the picking up of passengers, 7 Sept., when he observed that they were 'a great convenience to the lower classes of the metropolis'. He voted to punish only those guilty of bribery at the Dublin election and against censuring the Irish administration, 23 Aug. He divided in the minority for an amendment to the motion for the Liverpool writ, which recognized that there had been gross bribery at the last general election, 5 Sept., but he supported issuing the writ as it would inflict unfair hardship 'on the great trading and commercial interests of that town not to be fully represented in the House'; he hoped the freemen would 'soon be visited with the punishment they deserve'. He voted in the minority against the quarantine duties, 6 Sept 1831.

Writing in late October 1831 from Brighton, where he had gone 'to put myself in complete *repair* after the labours of the session', Labouchere told a Tory friend that he saw no sign of 'reaction' in the country, apart from the southern agricultural counties, and had 'no fear of disturbance from political excitement unless distress comes to its aid'. However, he was 'exceedingly afraid that during the winter political pains and contractions of all kinds will spread over the whole kingdom'.[8] In the debate on the address, 12 Dec., he expressed regret that the ministerial reform proposal did so little for Ireland, and feared that this neglect might 'strengthen the power of agitators and the discontented and afford a handle for still stronger language of complaint'. He ridiculed Sir Robert Peel's argument that the Commons should be grateful to the Lords for giving them a chance to reconsider the reform bill, pointing out that the Lords might simply have amended the previous measure and so avoided provoking the public anger that had damaged respect for the upper House and the Church of England. According to one observer, Labouchere 'spoke remarkably well' and his retort to Peel was 'received with two distinct rounds of applause', while his comments about Ireland prompted other speakers to address that subject 'with still greater warmth'.[9] He divided for the second reading of the revised bill, 17 Dec. 1831, and generally for its details. However, he was in the minority for replacing Gateshead in schedule D with Merthyr Tydfil, 5 Mar. 1832, as he saw no reason to separate Gateshead from Newcastle but was conscious of the 'important interests' at Merthyr, 'which have increased with a rapidity almost unparalleled' and should be recognized as 'a matter of justice'. He divided for the third reading, 22 Mar., and Ebrington's motion for an address asking the king to appoint only ministers committed to carrying an unimpaired measure, 10 May. During the debate on this motion the previous day, he reportedly 'spoke violently',[10] urging the Commons to 'place itself in the front of the battle, for we have arrived at a period when the great battle of reform must be fought and settled'. If a stand was not taken, 'I fear we shall see such scenes in this country as would make every man shudder'. He spoke on the ministerial crisis 'as an Englishman and ... an independent Member', 14 May, hoping that Grey would be reinstated and the 'honour and character' of the country not injured by the spectacle of the Conservatives carrying a bill. He presented a Taunton petition for the Commons to withhold supplies until the bill was passed, 24 May. He voted for the second reading of the Irish bill, 25 May, and paired against increased representation for Scotland, 1 June 1832.

He presented a petition for abolition of the soap duty, which would 'contribute much to the benefit of the lower orders', 9 Dec. 1831, and urged ministers to consider 'making an extensive reduction of those taxes which press most severely on the springs of industry ... substituting in their place others which will fall principally on the richer classes of society', 28 Feb. 1832. He stated that the silk manufacturers felt their case for exemption from Sadler's factory bill had not been fully heard, 15 Dec. 1831, and successfully proposed that Bainbridge be added to the committee on it to represent Somerset interests, 16 Mar. 1832. He sided with ministers on the Russian-Dutch loan, 26 Jan., 12, 16, 20 July. In the debate on the Swan River colony in Australia, 17 Feb., he regretted that it had been founded on 'incorrect principles' and deprecated the 'system of composing the population of English colonies of the scourings of our gaols ... making them receptacles for vice and crime'. He welcomed the proposed relief grant to Barbados, St. Vincent and Grenada, 29 Feb., as these colonies had 'a claim upon the public bounty of the mother country'. He pressed Fowell Buxton to state how much compensation should be given to slave owners after emancipation, 15 Mar., and presented a Taunton anti-slavery petition, 24 May. He remarked on the frequent appointment of unsuitable persons to judicial offices in the colonies, 13 Apr., questioned ministers about reduction in the 'excessive' salary of the governor of Madras, 25 May, and welcomed their plans to dispense with the grant for ecclesiastical establishments in the North American colonies, 23 July. He doubted whether the country would accept the general register bill, but acknowledged its potential benefits, 22 Feb. He opposed the motion to place all English county Members on the resulting select committee, 6 Mar., as he deemed it important to have a proper inquiry. He presented petitions from the conservators of the River Tone and Taunton's inhabitants against the Bridgwater and Taunton Canal bill, 27 Feb., when his motion to reject the second reading was defeated by 97-65; he was a minority teller. He expressed indignation at 'the shameless and faithless conduct of Russia' towards the Poles, which was 'shocking to humanity', 18 Apr., and warned that 'until redress is obtained ... there can be no security for the preservation of the peace of Europe'. He voted to make coroners' inquests public, 20 June 1832.

Labouchere's appointment as a lord of the admiralty in June 1832 marked the beginning of a long ministerial career. He was re-elected unopposed at Taunton, where he hailed the Reform Act as 'a measure of justice ... freedom ... good order ... conciliation and ... peace'.[11] He was again returned unopposed at the general election of 1832 and sat until 1859, when he was raised to the peerage as Baron Taunton. He was said to be 'such a perfect gentleman' that the Commons heard him 'with peculiar favour', and he was 'generally and highly respected' as a 'zealous and able servant of the public', although he never reached 'the first rank of politics'.[12] In 1839 he inherited from his father £200,000 invested in securities, together with properties in Piccadilly and Essex and joint interests with Baring (now Lord Ashburton) in Maine, Pennsylvania and Louisiana; the total value of the estate was reputedly around £500,000.[13] He had purchased an estate at Overstowey near Bridgwater, Somerset, in 1833, and made further acquisitions to consolidate his property, forming the so-called Quantock Lodge estate.[14] He died in July 1869 and his barony became extinct. He left his estates in Somerset and Essex to his elder daughters Mary and Mina respectively. His American estates were dealt with by a separate will, and it was presumably these which passed to his nephew Henry Labouchere (1831-1912), the maverick Radical Member for Windsor, 1865-6, Middlesex, 1867-8 and Northampton, 1880-1906.[15]

[1] A.L. Thorold, *Life of Henry Labouchere*, 1-4, 11-12. [2] Ibid. 13; *The Times*, 14 July 1869. [3] Cornw. RO, Carlyon mss 3226/3, Hawkins to Carlyon, 30 Mar. 1826. [4] Harrowby mss, Labouchere to Sandon, 20 Dec. 1827. [5] Ibid. Lady Bute to Lord D. Stuart, 22 May 1830. [6] *Taunton Courier*, 19 May, 16 June, 11, 18 Aug. 1830; Add. 61937, f. 116. [7] *Taunton Courier*, 27 Apr., 4 May 1831. [8] Cent. Kent. Stud. Stanhope mss U1590/C381/1, Labouchere to Mahon, 27 Oct. 1831. [9] NLS mss 24762, f. 49. [10] Lonsdale mss, Beckett to Lowther, 9 May 1832. [11] *Taunton Courier*, 13 June 1832. [12] Add. 52011, f. 214; *Life of Campbell*, ii. 210; *The Times*, 14 July 1869. [13] PROB 11/1908/167; IR26/1521/149; *Smith Letters*, ii. 683. [14] *VCH Som.* v. 194; vi. 114, 119, 162, 165-6. [15] Thorold, 12.

T.A.J.

LAMB, Hon. George (1784–1834), of Whitehall Yard, Westminster, Mdx. and Richmond, Surr.

WESTMINSTER 3 Mar. 1819–1820

DUNGARVAN 18 Feb. 1822–2 Jan. 1834

b. 11 July 1784, 4th but 3rd surv. s. of Peniston Lamb†, 1st visct. Melbourne [I], and Elizabeth, da. of Sir Ralph Milbanke†, 5th bt., of Halnaby Hall, Yorks.; bro. of Hon. Peniston† and Hon. William Lamb*.[1] *educ.* Eton 1796-1802; Trinity Coll. Camb. 1802; L. Inn 1805, called 1809. *m.* 17 May 1809, Caroline Rosalie Adelaide St. Jules, illegit. da. of William Cavendish, 5th duke of Devonshire (and his future w. Lady Elizabeth Foster), *s.p. d.* 2 Jan. 1834.

Under-sec. of state for home affairs Nov. 1830-*d.*

Capt. 1 Herts. vols. 1803.

Lamb was a good natured, high spirited, noisy man, whose ebullience was often mistaken for coarseness. Sydney Smith took a dim view of him at a dinner party in 1826:

> George Lamb made the usual quantity of noise; his only art in conversation seems to be to contradict plainly and plumply whatever is said upon the opposite side of the table, and then to burst out into a horse laugh, and this supplies the place of wit and sense.[2]

Henry Fox* found him 'always vulgar and noisy', but 'entertaining' and with 'some share of humour'.[3] Less complicated and talented than his eldest brother William, to whom he played second fiddle, he was more immediately likeable, as well as politically more adventurous. His physical bulk concealed a flawed constitution, which he abused with heavy drinking, though he was no soak. His 'home and happiness', as his sister Lady Cowper put it, was in the theatre; but he was an able parliamentary speaker and was capable of spasmodic bouts of hard political work.[4]

Lamb's attempt at the general election of 1820 to retain the Westminster seat which he had spectacularly won for the Whigs against the radicals at the by-election of 1819 ended in failure. With Sir Francis Burdett secure in the other seat, the fight was between Lamb and his opponent of the previous year, John Cam Hobhouse*, who had just been released from his imprisonment for breach of privilege. Lamb's 'imprudent' (as Lord Grey thought) canvassing letter to a Tory voter, in which he equated Hobhouse's supporters with 'the lower classes' and asked for support to prevent the return of 'a rejected candidate ... merely from the circumstance of ... [the Commons] having ventured to punish him for a flagrant insult and libel', fell into enemy hands and was made public on the first day. Lamb, who could scarcely gain a hearing on the hustings throughout, boasted of having seconded Burdett's parliamentary reform motion of 1819 and declared his support for the disfranchisement of 'notoriously rotten' boroughs for the benefit of 'populous places' and a limited extension of the franchise; but he dismissed the 'wild and unintelligible system of reform' advocated by the radicals. An exchange of insults on the fifth day, when Hobhouse called Lamb a liar for alleging that he had deliberately contrived his martyrdom as 'an electioneering trick', led Lamb to demand satisfaction the following morning. A duel seemed likely for several hours, but the affair ended tamely in mutual public retraction. With the Liverpool ministry this time refusing to intervene, Lamb, who failed to see the joke when he was pelted with mud, trailed badly from the start and, despite a late rally, finished almost 450 behind Hobhouse.[5]

A fortnight later Tierney, the Whig leader in the Commons, acknowledged that of men left stranded, Lamb and Richard Sharp* had 'the strongest claims upon anything which party can do', but saw little immediate prospect of accommodating him.[6] Lady Cowper, who found him 'in very good spirits', thought 'the law will be the best speculation for him, but as he has no children to work for', felt 'he should do what amuses him best and Parliament is certainly what he likes'; while William Lamb also judged that though he 'undoubtedly felt at first relieved by getting rid' of his onerous seat, 'in course of time he will begin to miss the importance and the consequence of it'.[7] Lamb, who suffered a 'very long and severe fit of the gout' in the summer of 1820, reluctantly resumed his humdrum career at the bar and amused himself with the completion of a competent but uninspired translation of Catullus, from which he hoped to make some much needed money. It was largely well received on its publication in June 1821, though one critic savaged it in *Blackwood's*. A drinking bout had made him ill again in the spring, when his sister observed, 'What a pity that a *bon vivant* who enjoys all those things so much should not be stronger'.[8]

In February 1822 Lamb secured a seat through the good offices of his wife's half-brother, the 6th duke of Devonshire, who created a vacancy for him at Dungarvan. He reported from Ireland to his brother Frederick, 14 Feb.:

> The newest light that has struck upon me is the different view one takes of the chattering of our patriots, when actually resident on the spot which they are ignorantly prating about. Here I am in a part of the country [western county Waterford] considered quite quiet ...

> which in England would be considered [in] utter warfare and turmoil ... A regular Irish squire, whom I canvassed the other day, said, 'Well, Sir, I like your principles, but I wish you and your party would show a little more consideration for the loyal party ... Our inconveniences never trouble your minds, but directly a man becomes a Whiteboy or a robber he is entitled to every kindness at your hands' ... Want of employment and starvation are the roots of all the present disturbances ... The spirit of hostility ... is principally against tithes.

On his way home through Dublin, where his theatrical connections smoothed his path, Lamb, who had given himself 'a little goutishness' by drinking 'a whole bottle of port' on his arrival in Waterford, had a largely one-sided conversation with the viceroy, Lord Wellesley. He returned to London feeling unable to identify any practical measures to improve the state of affairs in Ireland and inclined, as he facetiously told Frederick, to 'propose that nothing at all should be done [in Parliament] for any part of the empire this session, certainly nothing by me'.[9]

He voted for abolition of one of the joint-postmasterships, 13 Mar., 2 May 1822. On 15 Mar. he chided Williams Wynn for refusing to let sleeping dogs lie on the question of his ministerial colleague Charles Arbuthnot's alleged breach of privilege. He divided with Burdett for the remission of Hunt's gaol sentence, 24 Apr., and for Lord John Russell's motion for parliamentary reform (to which William Lamb was opposed) the following day. He was in the minority of 25 for a fixed 20*s*. import duty on wheat, 9 May. He voted against government on diplomatic expenditure, 15, 16 May, repeal of the salt tax, 3 June (William opposed this on the 28th), Irish tithes, 19 June, the influence of the crown, 24 June, and the lord advocate's dealings with the Scottish press, 25 June. He scolded Richard Martin for accusing Hume of indifference to the Irish poor, 17 May, and secured the adjournment of the debate on the Irish constables bill, 21 June.[10] He voted for the public houses licensing bill, 27 June, but presented petitions against the sale of beer bill, 10, 17 July.[11] He divided against the aliens bill, 1 July, and the Irish insurrection bill, 8 July, and was in small minorities against the orphans' fund bill, 22 July, and the lotteries bill, 24 July 1822. Two weeks later he wrote to Frederick from Richmond, Surrey, where he had a copyhold property:

> We have closed the longest session ever known except only the Rump Parliament. The grumblers of course say that nothing has [been] done and much more wisely abstained from. Certainly as much relief from taxation has been given as could with any prudence be resolved in one session ... So much for politics, which certainly for some inexplicable reason or another was never in my life so flat and little thought of as at present ... I am extremely well, and am now laying in a stock of health by regular living against the next winter campaign.[12]

However, he took 'such flings at the wine' at his parental home at Panshanger in the autumn that gout racked him yet again.[13]

Lamb, whose brother William was now moving quickly towards alignment with the liberal wing of the ministry, voted for reform, 20 Feb., 24 Apr. 1823. He was in the opposition minorities for tax reductions and against the national debt bill, 28 Feb., 3, 6, 17 Mar., when he also voted with Creevey against the Barbados duties and with Hume against the ordnance estimates. He privately denounced William's speech of 16 Apr. against repeal of the Foreign Enlistment Act as 'milk and water', though he was not in the minority.[14] On 22 Apr. he voted for inquiry into the prosecution of the Dublin Orange rioters, which his brother opposed. He divided for inquiries into the state of Ireland, 12 May, and chancery delays, 5 June. He voted for repeal of the usury laws, 17 June (and again, 8 Feb. 1825). He paired for the Scottish juries bill, 20 June, and spoke and voted for Mackintosh's attempt to end capital punishment for certain larcenies, 25 July 1823. He was in small minorities against the Irish glebe houses grant and for reception of the petition against Crosbie, Member for Kerry, 1 July. Next day he was a teller for the majority to consider the conduct of O'Grady, chief baron of the Irish exchequer court, and on the 9th he was in a minority of 16 against the decision to proceed no further against him. He voted with a dozen other Members to have capital offences committed by serving soldiers tried by courts martial, 11 July 1823. He voted for the production of information on Catholic burials, 6 Feb., Catholic office holders, 19 Feb., and the criminal jurisdiction of the Isle of Man, 18 Feb. 1824. He had no strong objection to the home secretary Peel's plan for consolidation of jury regulations, 19 Feb., but warned that 'every new Act of this nature seemed only to create, instead of to remove doubts'. He and William voted on opposite sides on reform of Edinburgh's representation, 26 Feb., and the aliens bill, 23 Mar. He voted in support of a complaint of breach of privilege against lord chancellor Eldon, 1 Mar., against the Welsh judicature bill, 11 Mar., to reduce the colonial services grant, 12 Mar., and to postpone that for Irish Protestant charter schools, 15 Mar., when he was in Hume's minority for the abolition of army flogging. He presented and supported a petition from distressed fishermen of Dungarvan and Dundalk against the proposed reduction of export bounties, 19 Mar.[15] On 6 Apr., after presenting a petition from Old Bailey jurors for felons to have the full benefit of defence by counsel, 6 Apr., he moved for leave to introduce a bill to that effect, having taken over the subject from Martin. He conceded that he was 'running counter to all the prejudices of the profession' (which he had by now given up) and was defeated by 80-50. His renewed attempt to bring in the measure, 25 Apr. 1826, was lost by 105-36. He divided against the grant for new churches, 9 Apr., for an advance of capital to Ireland, 4 May, and for inquiries into the Irish church establishment, 6 May, and the state of Ireland, 11 May 1824. That autumn he and his wife were 'very comfortable' at Melbourne Hall, near Derby, though gout briefly attacked his left hand and wrist.[16]

He was at odds with William over the Irish unlawful societies bill, which he condemned as 'exceedingly obscure and mysterious', 14 Feb., and 'obnoxious', 22 Feb. 1825. He supported a Waterford petition against it, 24 Feb.[17] He voted for Catholic relief, 1 Mar., 10 May, and presented a favourable petition from Kenmare, 10 Mar.[18] He opposed Martin's bill to suppress bear-baiting, which he saw as 'interfering unnecessarily with that, the cure of which should be left to ... education', 11 Mar., and was a teller for the hostile majority. He presented a Derbyshire petition against alteration of the corn laws, 9 May.[19] He voted against the Leith docks bill, 20 May, when he was also in Brougham's minority of 29 on the independence of the judiciary. He divided against the duke of Cumberland's annuity, 6, 9, 10 June. That day he saw no objection to the smuggling prevention bill, arguing that ladies might 'obviate the difficulty' in carrying out searches under it 'by staying at home'.[20] On 13 June 1825 he voted in small minorities with Hume and Burdett against details of the Irish estimates, and the next day he was one of Hume's 37 supporters for inquiry into the Irish church. At a Derbyshire county meeting to petition for the abolition of slavery, 12 Jan. 1826, he spoke cautiously, calling for 'moderation of language' towards the planters and admitting that he had opposed equalization of the East and West Indian sugar duties because he saw no point in alienating them.[21] He voted against government on the promissory notes bill, which William supported, 20 Feb. On 1 Mar. he presented another petition of complaint from Dungarvan fishermen.[22] He divided for army reductions, 3, 7 Mar., but said that he would 'cheerfully vote' for whatever money was necessary to refurbish Windsor Castle, 13 Mar.[23] He opposed the cruelty to cattle bill because it was not based on any 'fixed principle' of legislation, 16 Mar. He voted against government on the salary of the president of the board of trade, 7, 10 Apr., and for Russell's reform motion, 27 Apr., and his resolution condemning electoral bribery, 26 May. He supported the spring guns bill, 27 Apr., and was a teller for the minority for its third reading. Next day he secured the addition to the criminal justice bill of a clause to prevent the annulment of indictments on pleas of misnomer. He divided to reduce the salaries of Irish prison inspectors, 5 May, and for investigation of James Silk Buckingham's† charges concerning press freedom in India, 9 May 1826.

Lady Cowper had reported in February 1826 that 'George dreads his election with this "No Popery" cry'; but in his address to Dungarvan at the general election that summer he asserted that 'the day-star of Ireland's happiness ... must be Catholic emancipation'. He was detained at Shrewsbury by 'a severe illness', but got to Dungarvan in time for his unopposed return.[24] He persuaded Littleton to withdraw, 28 Nov., and modify, 4 Dec. 1826, his proposal for a requirement for £500 security from complainants over private bills. Soon afterwards he was poorly, but on Boxing Day his sister wrote that he was

> still a little lame, and looking thin, but I think looking well, and he has left off wine entirely and seems not to mind this, which I am delighted at ... for it makes the greatest possible difference in him, and he is so good humoured and quiet, instead of being irritable, and disputatious after dinner.[25]

Lamb was, apparently, one of seven Whigs who voted with government for the duke of Clarence's grant, 16 Feb. 1827; and he did so again, 16 Mar.[26] On 26 Feb. he supported Lord Althorp's scheme for a permanent select committee to deal with election petitions alleging bribery and a motion to end the 'degradation' of flogging in the army.[27] He presented, 2 Mar., a Dungarvan petition for Catholic relief, for which he voted on the 6th.[28] He was against opening coroners' inquests to the public, 21 Mar.[29] Next day he voiced reservations about the salmon fisheries bill and voted for information on the Barrackpoor mutiny. He divided for the spring guns bill, 23 Mar. He voted to suspend supply until the ministerial crisis was resolved, 30 Mar., and for inquiry into the Irish miscellaneous estimates, 5 Apr. Later that month his brother became Irish secretary in Canning's ministry. Their sister reported that 'George is ... much pleased, and sits with great satisfaction on the treasury bench'; but they were on opposite sides on the disfranchisement of Penryn, which Lamb supported, 28 May, when Lady Cowper noted that he was 'getting quite stout again'.[30] He was in the government majority on the grant for Canadian canals, 12 June 1827.

When presenting a petition for relief from Dungarvan Catholics, 5 Feb. 1828, Lamb deplored the return to power of Wellington and Peel as a setback to the cause of emancipation. (William stayed in office with his leader Huskisson, whom George apparently regarded as 'an immeasurable villain'.)[31] He presented petitions for repeal of the Test Acts, 20, 25 Feb., but regretted that some Dissenters had not allied themselves with the Catholics; he voted for repeal, 26 Feb. Supporting Brougham's motion for a commission on the common law, 29 Feb., he lamented 'the increase of our ponderous statute book'. He was at a small meeting at Henry Bankes's* 'to see whether we could devise any plan for controlling the follies of the board of works and stopping Nash's devastation of the parks', 7 Mar.[32] He voted against tinkering with the East Retford franchise, 21 Mar., and again, 24, 27 June, after William had seceded from the government with the other Huskissonites. On the proposed transfer of Penryn's seats to Manchester, 24 Mar., he urged Russell to drop the 'cumbersome machinery' of his bill. He thought the right to give evidence on affirmation should be extended beyond Quakers and Moravians, 5 May, when he offered constructive comments on Peel's offences against the person bill. He secured leave to introduce another felons' counsel bill, 15 May, but it got nowhere.[33] He voted for Catholic claims, 12 May. He welcomed Peel's bill to facilitate the recovery of small debts as part of his commendably cautious approach to legal reform, 22 May. He agreed to go into committee on the game bill, 13 June, but on the 24th said that it contained 'a mass of the greatest possible absurdities'. He voted against ministers on the archbishop of Canterbury's bill, 16 June, the expenditure of public money on Buckingham House, 23 June, and Irish church pluralities, 24 June. He saw no merit in Lord Nugent's voters' registration bill, 19 June, and objected to the imposition of excise duty on cider on the pretext of safeguarding morality, 26 June. He was in a minority of 13 against the small notes bill, 27 June. He spoke and voted against the additional churches bill, 30 June, when he made a personal attack on John Calcraft for deserting the Whigs for office. He was in opposition minorities on the ordnance estimates, 4, 7 July, and divided for the corporate funds bill, 10 July 1828.

Long before his death in November 1828, which removed William Lamb from the Commons, Melbourne had confirmed to George and his wife the use of Melbourne Hall 'during their lives'. By his father's will, Lamb received £10,000.[34] Presenting pro-Catholic petitions from Dungarvan and Abbeyside, 20 Feb., he applauded the government's decision to concede emancipation, for which he duly voted, 6, 30 Mar. 1829. He gave 'reluctant' consent to the disfranchisement of Irish 40*s.* freeholders, 26 Mar. He presented a Derbyshire women's petition for action to suppress suttee, 2 Apr. He brought up petitions from East Retford electors for the immediate issue of a new writ and criticized the 'sort of hostile partnership' formed by Charles Calvert and Tennyson in their struggle to decide the fate of the borough, 10 Apr., 5 May, when he voted for the transfer of its seats to Birmingham. He helped to persuade Calvert to postpone his disfranchisement bill until next session, 11 May, and supported an attempt to have a new writ issued, 2 June. He spoke and voted in favour of Daniel O'Connell being allowed to take his seat unhindered, 18 May. He voted against the grant for the marble arch, 25 May, and to reduce the hemp duties, 1 June. He supported a petition for a ban on the staging of plays without the author's consent, 4 June, and on 22 June 1829 gave notice that he would deal with the problem next session. According to Creevey, he backed Lord Durham's bid to talk Grey out of his threats to have nothing more to do with George IV.[35] He and his wife were in Berne in October 1829.[36] The following month his sister's lover Lord Palmerston* met him and William (now Lord Melbourne) in England and found them ready for aggressive political action, though claiming to be 'free and unshackled' in their views.[37]

Lamb voted for the amendment to the address, 4 Feb. 1830, and on the 8th explained that he had done so because it contained 'a true representation of the state of the country, and a pledge of inquiry into measures of relief'. He conceded that some ministers had embraced liberal notions, but said that 'if ... they are Whigs in this country ... in their continental policy they are the veriest Tories in existence', and declared his utter lack of confidence in them. He voted for the transfer of East Retford's seats to Birmingham, 11 Feb., 15 Mar., and the enfranchisement of Birmingham, Leeds and Manchester, 23 Feb. On 5 Mar., however, when he paired on the East Retford question, he said that the secret ballot would create 'a complete system of hypocrisy and bribery'. He divided with Hume for a reduction of taxes, 15 Feb., and against the army estimates, 19, 22 Feb., when he described the yeomanry as 'the worst species of force that can be employed in the suppression of local tumults'; but on 1 Mar. he opposed Hume's attempt to restrict the navy grant to six months. On 22 Feb. he presented another Dungarvan petition for the retention of fishery bounties and got leave to bring in his dramatic writings bill, which foundered on 23 Mar.[38] He seconded Taylor's motion for leave to introduce a bill to revise the lunacy commission system, 2 Mar. He was 'not asked to go' to the Whig meeting which nominated Althorp as Commons leader for the campaign for economy and retrenchment, 3 Mar.[39] He presented a Waterford tanners' petition for repeal of the leather tax, 10 Mar. He divided against government over British interference in the affairs of Portugal that day, and voted with the reviving opposition on most major issues in the following weeks. On 18 Mar. he was a teller with O'Connell for the minority of 12 in favour of adjourning the debate on distress. He presented a Monmouthshire petition against the truck system, 4 May. He deplored the proposed increase in stamp duty on Irish newspapers, 6 May, and presented a hostile constituency petition, 18 June. He voted for Jewish emancipation, 17 May. He was in the minorities on Irish first fruits, 18 May, and for Russell's reform motion, 28 May. He attacked the Northern Roads bill and was a teller for the minority against its second reading, 3 June. He was a teller for the majority for the usury laws repeal bill, 15 June, and presented a petition for repeal of the Irish Vestries Act from Dungarvan Catholics, 1 July 1830.

Lamb had long anticipated trouble from them at the general election the following month, and he was opposed by a Catholic councillor, on the pretext of Devonshire's supposed indifference to the 'misery' of local fishermen. Lamb, who stressed his support for emancipation and 'professed himself friendly to a moderate reform in Parliament [and] modification of the Vestry and Subletting Acts', won easily.[40] Ministers of course listed him among their 'foes', and at Panshanger in September he predicted 'a violent opposition in the approaching session'.[41] He presented a Melbourne petition for the abolition of slavery, 11 Nov. 1830. He divided against government on the civil list, 15 Nov. Melbourne became home secretary in the Grey ministry and appointed George his under-secretary and Commons spokesman.[42] Of pressing concern to the office were the 'Swing' disturbances, which worried Lamb, who was sent by his brother to Francis Place, the influential radical tailor of Charing Cross, in a bid to persuade him to write appeals to the rioters to desist. This Place, who felt patronised by Lamb, refused to do. On reform, which they then discussed, Place 'found that he knew very little of what was really passing' and that 'the information he had secured appeared to be very vague and defective'. When Place lectured him on the course he thought the new ministers should pursue, Lamb kept his counsel, but agreed that they probably lacked the 'courage' to take a bold initiative.[43] His contributions to debate were now largely confined to official business and responses to questions on matters falling within his department's remit. For example, he defended the decision to allow the trades to process to St. James's with an address to the king, 10 Dec., arguing that it would have been 'the height of madness' to keep them back by force. He denied that O'Grady's former prosecutors, such as himself, were being hypocritical in seeking to give him a peerage in order to facilitate the Irish law arrangements, 20 Dec. 1830. On 8 Feb. 1831 he dismissed Hunt's speech for a general pardon for convicted 'Swing' rioters as 'rather an account of his own personal adventures in his tour of the country, than an argument or a statement of facts'. He presented Irish Catholics' petitions against any further grant to the Kildare Place Society, 18 Feb., and one from Melbourne for the ballot, 28 Feb. He lost his temper with Hume over his contrary opposition to the Tower Hamlets militia bill, 15 Mar. He acquiesced in Davies's motion for the appointment of a select committee on secondary punishments, on which he sat, 17 Mar., but warned that 'there are difficulties attaching to the subject much greater than he sees'. He presented a St. Pancras petition for reform of the metropolitan police, 13 Apr. He voted silently for the second reading of the reform bill, 22 Mar., and against Gascoyne's wrecking amendment, 19 Apr. 1831; and at the ensuing general election he was returned unopposed for Dungarvan as a supporter of 'that great measure'.[44]

Lamb, whom Macaulay found 'very diverting' at a dinner party in June 1831, when he opined that the perpetrators of 'extreme cases' of blasphemy should be prosecuted, voted for the second reading of the reintroduced reform bill, 6 July.[45] He was of course a steady supporter of its details in committee, but he was not required to utter a word on it in debate. He justified to Hunt the decision to order troops to open fire on rioters at Merthyr, causing fatalities, 21 June, and on the 27th maintained that in present circumstances the yeomanry were 'absolutely necessary to maintain order and peace'. He was a teller for the ministerial majority against a motion for a reduction of public salaries, 30 June. He endorsed the game bill, 8 Aug. On 11 Aug. he told Hunt what was known of a fatal affray at Bolton, persuaded Lord Duncannon to drop a motion for information on the treatment of a prisoner in Hertfordshire county gaol and presented a Dungarvan Catholics' petition against the grant to the Kildare Place Society. He was a government teller that day for the majority against disarming the Irish yeomanry. He defended magistrates' use of troops to quell disturbances in a colliery wages dispute at Whitehaven. He concurred in a motion for the appointment of a select committee on steamboat accidents (on which he sat) in order to 'satisfy the public', 6 Sept., but said it would achieve nothing. When Hume complained of the chaotic mismanagement of arrangements for the transport of guests after the coronation, 9 Sept., Lamb retorted that he should have followed his own example and walked.[46] He voted for the third reading, 19 Sept., and passage, 21 Sept., of the reform bill, and the second reading of the Scottish bill, 23 Sept. He supported a Lords' amendment to the lunatics bill and was a teller for the minority, 26 Sept. Next day he was a teller for the majority against inquiry into the Deacles' allegations against William Bingham Baring* as a Hampshire magistrate, and on the 28th he was a teller for the majority for proceeding with the bankruptcy bill. He approved modifications to Hobhouse's vestries bill, 30 Sept., and, despite the discovery of a ludicrous clerical error, steered through the Lords' amendments, 19 Oct. He of course voted for the motion of confidence in the administration, 10 Oct. 1831. On the 12th he replied to Hunt's criticisms of their handling of pro-reform meetings, processions and disturbances, defended the home office and denied that his colleagues had 'permitted or connived at the proceedings of the rioters'.

Reporting to Melbourne developments in Grey's negotiations with Lord Wharncliffe and the 'Waverers' in the Lords, 20 Nov. 1831, Lamb commented:

> It would be infinitely better to break up the government than to be party to a proposition more democratic than the last ... if your measure be brought forward and rejected I see nothing but danger, and no remedy. It seems clear that Grey is for moderation, but if nobody stands firmly by him he is sure to give way; and it seems to me that the violent part of the cabinet are put in continued communication upon this subject, and act in concert, while those who ought to check them do not understand each other, and have no mutual reliance or knowledge of each other's sentiments ... It is ... high time that something were done or at least said about these political unions.[47]

He voted for the second reading of the revised reform bill, 17 Dec. 1831, to go into committee on it, 20 Jan., and for various details, 3, 23, 28 Feb., but he was a surprising absentee (presumably because of illness) from the division on its third reading, 22 Mar. 1832. He dismissed Wetherell's complaint at having been omitted, as recorder of Bristol, from the commission of inquiry into the riots which he had provoked there, 6 Dec. 1831. Greville claimed to have it from Melbourne that Lamb lied to the House when denying official knowledge of one of the recently executed burkers' supposed confession to further murders implicating surgeons, 12 Dec. 1831.[48] He described Hobhouse's vestry bill as 'one of the most premature pieces of legislation that ever was attempted', 23 Jan. 1832, and voted in the majority which threw it out. A surprised Hobhouse believed him to have been 'a little tipsy'.[49] On the 'not very interesting subject' of the premature dismissal of two regiments of the Lincolnshire militia, 8 Mar., he resisted a demand for information. He opposed Hunt's motion for inquiry into the Peterloo massacre, 15 Mar., and was a teller for the hostile majority. On 27 Mar. he allowed Ewart to introduce a bill to abolish the death penalty for horse, sheep and cattle stealing and non-violent theft from private houses, though he had personal reservations. By 30 May he had concluded that the measure was sound and that Parliament should 'sweep away the punishment of death in every case in which its infliction is not supported by the public sentiments'. He spoke and voted against an attempt to increase the salary of the Irish registrar of deeds, 9 Apr. He voted for the address calling on the king to appoint only ministers who would carry the reform bill unimpaired, 10 May; and on the 18th assured the House that no unauthorized troop movements had occurred during the recent crisis and suggested that treasonable libels were best left 'to the contempt of the people, who, I hope, are now satisfied with the prospect of public affairs'. He voted for the second reading of the Irish reform bill, 25 May, but, under pressure from his constituents, protested half-heartedly against the disfranchisement of freeholders in Dungarvan, Downpatrick and Newry, 13 June, 2 July. He paired against an opposition amendment to the Scottish bill, 1 June. He said the returns moved for by De Lacy Evans to expose alleged aristocratic interference in municipal affairs were so otiose that he might as well have called for 'a return of every man with a black head of hair'. Opposing the printing of a petition alleging maltreatment of prisoners in Nottingham gaol, 22 June, he dismissed its presenter Hunt's wild assertions that 'a system of persecution exists in our prisons'. He reluctantly acquiesced in Agnew's motion of 3 July for the appointment of a select committee on Sabbath observance, to which he was named. Later that day he mockingly suggested that it might consider the reckless behaviour of cabriolet drivers condemned by Waldo Sibthorp. He played down fears of a revival of the cholera and suggested that most reported cases were nothing more than 'common bowel complaints', 4 July. He told Hume that ministers would review the cost of the metropolitan police, but reminded him of the inefficiency of the former watch system, 24 July. He answered Hume's questions on the election riot at Clitheroe, 10 Aug., stating that 'the chief damage arose from the persons who, in the course of the tumult, were trodden under foot'; and on 15 Aug. 1832 he announced that 'inquiry tends more and more to show that the troops behaved exceedingly well, under circumstances of great provocation'.

Lamb wrote to his brother Frederick from Richmond, 26 Aug. 1832:

> With ... [William's] illness and Phillipps [the permanent under-secretary] in the country, I have the whole office on myself and keep tight to work, but slipping here every night is an amusement that I think keeps me in health and exercise and I don't care how long it continues ... We all as to politics stand ... pretty fair, though nothing can be known with certainty as to the tone and prospects of the country till after the elections. One thing I feel certain of, which is that the Tories are by no means done for by the Reform [Act] ... There ought clearly to be enough Tories when joined with the moderate part of our friends to defeat the Radicals, and then all will be well.[50]

At the general election in December he was returned for Dungarvan after a contest with a Repealer which produced 'terrible rioting'.[51] His health collapsed a year later and he died in Whitehall Yard, after a distressing illness, in January 1834. An anonymous obituarist was kind to him:

> His official duties were executed in an efficient manner, and his speeches in Parliament were delivered in a sensible and intrepid style ... In private society ... [he] was unreserved, communicative, and agreeable; his accomplishments were admitted by all who knew him; his kindness of heart and mildness of temper were proverbial.[52]

Princess Lieven, who knew him 'but slightly', considered him 'a man of great intelligence, with a mind of a very superior order, honest, and frank almost to simplicity, and such an excellent heart'.[53] His widow wrote to Frederick, 20 Jan. 1834:

> You cannot think how miserable I am. I have lost my best, my kindest friend ... I hope he was not aware of his danger, and the doctors assure me he did not suffer, though the difficulty of breathing made it appear as if he did, but that it was from the throat not the chest, and the water getting to the brain produced stupor ... It still seems to me like a horrid dream ... You cannot think how great and general is the regret. He was justly appreciated, and it is looked upon as a public loss. His great popularity and good humour disarmed all malice, and many ill natured attacks. His talents, his gaiety, his unequalled temper made him the most delightful companion.[54]

By his will, dated 27 Oct. 1832, Lamb left the Richmond property and his freehold chambers in Lincoln's Inn to his wife, along with the residue of his personal estate. He devised two sums of £5,000 to which he was entitled under the marriage settlements of his parents and of William, plus his £10,000 inheritance from his father, to Frederick. His effects were sworn under £20,000.[55]

[1] There seems to be no doubt that his real father was George IV, who, as prince of Wales, began a blatantly public affair with the promiscuous Lady Melbourne in 1783. See L.G. Mitchell, *Melbourne*, 6, 16; K. Bourne, *Palmerston*, 185-6. [2] *Smith Letters*, i. 427. [3] *Fox Jnl.* 93, 95. [4] Mitchell, 12; *Lady Palmerston Letters*, 12, 18. [5] *Lady Palmerston Letters*, 27-29; Add. 36458, ff. 191, 203; 56541, ff. 10-20; *The Times*, 10, 11, 13-18, 20-25, 27 Mar.; Grey mss, Grey to Wilson, 13 Mar.; Bessborough mss, same to Duncannon, 9 Apr. 1820. [6] Add. 51586, Tierney to Lady Holland [12 Apr. 1820]. [7] *Lady Palmerston Letters*, 32; Herts. Archives, Panshanger mss D/ELb F78, W. to F. Lamb, 3 May 1820. [8] Panshanger mss F78, W. to F. Lamb, 29 July 1820; F97/2; Lady Airlie, *Lady Palmerston*, i. 64, 88; *Lady Palmerston Letters*, 64-65, 67, 70, 81. [9] *Waterford Chron.* 12, 23 Feb. 1822; *Lady Palmerston Letters*, 93-94; Panshanger mss F87/2, 3. [10] *The Times*, 22 June 1822. [11] Ibid. 11, 18 July 1822. [12] Panshanger mss F87/4. [13] *Lady Palmerston Letters*, 112. [14] Ibid. 123. [15] *The Times*, 20 Mar. 1824. [16] Panshanger mss F87/5, 6. [17] *The Times*, 25 Feb. 1825. [18] Ibid. 11 Mar. 1825. [19] Ibid. 10 May 1825. [20] Ibid. 11 June 1825. [21] *Derby Mercury*, 18 Jan. 1826; Panshanger mss F97/4. [22] *The Times*, 2 Mar. 1826. [23] Ibid. 14 Mar. 1826. [24] *Lady Palmerston Letters*, 146; *Waterford Mail*, 7, 10, 21 June 1826; Lady Airlie, i. 131. [25] *Lady Palmerston Letters*, 154. [26] Add. 51784, Holland to C.R. Fox, 17 Feb. 1827. [27] *The Times*, 27 Feb. 1827. [28] Ibid. 3 Mar. 1827. [29] Ibid. 22 Mar. 1827. [30] *Canning's Ministry*, 296, 316. [31] Add. 48406, f. 147. [32] Northants. RO, Agar Ellis diary. *Lady Holland to Son*, 88-89. [33] *CJ*, lxxxiii. 353, 377, 432. [34] *Lady Holland to Son*, 88-89; PROB 11/1748/660. [35] *Creevey Pprs.* ii. 201. [36] Blakiston, *Lord William Russell*, 197. [37] Bourne, 306. [38] *CJ*, lxxxv. 128, 157, 282. [39] Castle Howard mss, Graham to Morpeth, 3 Mar. 1830. [40] Chatsworth mss, Lamb to Devonshire, 25 June 1829, 8 Aug.; *Waterford Mail*, 31 July, 7, 11 Aug. 1830. [41] *Greville Mems.* ii. 45. [42] P. Mandler, *Aristocratic Government in Age of Reform*, 125, referring to a supposed 'controversy' over Lamb's appointment for which he gives no evidence, unfairly dismisses him as 'an idle fop with a taste for political melodrama' who was unacceptable to both radicals and moderates. [43] *Howard Sisters*, 169; Add. 27789, ff. 207-10; P. Zeigler, *Melbourne*, 131, 134. [44] *Waterford Mail*, 4, 7 May 1831. [45] *Macaulay Letters* ii. 43-44, 80. [46] *Howard Sisters*, 203. [47] *Melbourne Pprs.* 142-5. [48] *Greville Mems.* ii. 230. [49] Add. 56556, f. 44. [50] Panshanger mss F87/7. [51] *The Times*, 18 Dec. 1832. [52] *Gent. Mag.* (1834), i. 437-8; Add. 39949, f. 146. [53] *Lieven-Grey Corresp.* ii. 496. [54] Panshanger mss F88/1. [55] PROB 11/1831/287; IR26/1359/142; Panshanger mss F99/1.

D.R.F.

LAMB, Hon. William (1779–1848), of Brocket Hall, nr. Hatfield, Herts.[1]

LEOMINSTER	31 Jan. 1806–1806
HADDINGTON BURGHS	1806–1807
PORTARLINGTON	1807–1812
PETERBOROUGH	16 Apr. 1816–Nov. 1819
HERTFORDSHIRE	29 Nov. 1819–1826
NEWPORT I.O.W.	24 Apr. 1827–29 Apr. 1827
BLETCHINGLEY	7 May 1827–16 July 1828

b. 15 Mar. 1779, 2nd but 1st surv. s. of Peniston Lamb†, 1st Visct. Melbourne [I], and Elizabeth, da. of Sir Ralph Milbanke†, 5th bt., of Halnaby Hall, Yorks.; bro. of Hon. George Lamb* and Hon. Peniston Lamb†. *educ.* privately by Rev. Thomas Marsham, curate of Hatfield, 1785-8; Eton 1788-96; Trinity Coll. Camb. 1796; by Prof. John Millar at Glasgow 1799-1801; L. Inn 1797, called 1804. *m.* 3 June 1805, Lady Caroline Ponsonby, da. of Frederick Ponsonby†, 3rd earl of Bessborough [I], 1s. surv. *d.v.p.* 1da. *d.v.p. suc.* fa. as 2nd Visct. Melbourne [I] and 2nd Bar. [UK] 22 July 1828. *d.* 24 Nov. 1848.

Chief sec. to ld. lt. [I] Apr. 1827-June 1828; PC [UK] 30 Apr. 1827 and [I] 16 July 1827; sec. of state for home affairs Nov. 1830-July 1834; first ld. of treasury 16 July-17 Nov. 1834, 18 Apr. 1835-3 Sept. 1841.

Capt. Herts. vol. inf. 1803, maj. 1804.

Lord John Russell recalled that Lamb's 'ease of manner and apparent indifference tended to conceal the excellence of his understanding and the warmth of his feelings'.[2] A painfully sensitive man, given to gloomy introspection, he adopted for the world a mask of cynical indifference. Despite the miseries of his private life, which, thanks to his unbalanced and promiscuous wife's recklessness and his own feebleness, were often publicly exposed, he was usually delightful, if quirky company. Greville wrote:

> The vast fund of knowledge with which his conversation was always replete ... mixed up with his characteristic peculiarities, gave an extraordinary zest and pungency to his society ... This richness of talk was rendered the more piquant by the quaintness and oddity of his manner, and an ease and naturalness proceeding in no small degree from habits of self-indulgence and freedom ... He was often paradoxical, and often coarse, terse, epigrammatic, acute, droll, with fits of silence and abstraction, from which he would suddenly break out with a violence and vigour which amused those who were accustomed to him, and filled with indescribable astonishment those who were not.[3]

Lamb had a low estimate of mankind and, though he was one of the best-read and most thoughtful men ever to cut a figure in political life, with a well-stocked mind and formidable memory, he held no strong convictions on politics and religion.[4] Always liable to see merit in both sides of an argument and averse to confronting trouble, he could be indecisive in the extreme, though he was not without ambition and showed himself capable, when in office, of energy and determination. By 1820 the essential conservatism of his Whiggism, which had led him to oppose parliamentary reform and support the suspension of habeas corpus, had distanced him irrevocably from the mainstream of the party, though he gave half-hearted support to its opposition to the repressive legislation which followed the Peterloo agitation. Politically he was adrift, reluctant to commit himself to the liberal, Canningite wing of the Tories, who seemed his natural allies.[5] In January 1820 he wrote to Lord Fitzwilliam (on whose interest he had sat for Peterborough for three and a half years before his return for Hertfordshire, with the support of local ministerialists, in November 1819) indicating that while he considered Russell's proposal to give Grampound's seats to Leeds as 'the commencement of a reformation of the present system of the representation', he was 'not unwilling' to support it, given 'the feeling and opinion of the country upon the subject'. His main object, however, was to encourage Fitzwilliam to ascertain from Lord Grey, the Whig leader, with whom Lamb was 'not much in the habit of communicating', whether his son-in-law John Lambton's anticipated motion for a reform bill based on triennial parliaments, a householder franchise and the disfranchisement of nomination boroughs was to be regarded as 'a party measure':

> It is a distinct declaration on the part of those who profess themselves moderate reformers, that they will be satisfied with nothing cautious and gradual, but that they are determined if they can to adopt at once a large and extensive change ... It has always been my opinion that no circumstances should ever induce an opposition to support measures which they are not convinced they should be able and willing to adopt in administration, and I cannot but think that reasonable men, if they give the matter a fair consideration, must feel themselves inclined at least to pause, before they pledge themselves to so sweeping an alteration of the constitution on the one hand, or expose themselves to the disagreeable alternative of receding from their words and abandoning their own votes, and thus subjecting themselves to all the imputations which are naturally cast upon such conduct.[6]

Lamb, whose wife, after an interlude of something close to rationality, made an exhibition of herself in the county that month, came forward again at the general election, claiming to have pursued such a course as would 'secure the public tranquillity' and at the same time 'preserve the rights of the people from infringement or diminution'. There was no opposition to his return for what he described to his diplomat brother Frederick as 'a very pleasant and independent' seat; but he acknowledged the ever-present threat of 'an expensive contest', a particularly forbidding prospect in view of the age and infirmity of his father, an alcoholic wreck. Immediately after his own election he did what he could, which included asking Arbuthnot, the patronage secretary, and the duke of Wellington for ministerial intervention, to assist his brother George, a thoroughgoing Whig, in his unsuccessful bid to retain the Westminster seat which he had won against the radicals at the by-election of 1819.[7]

Lamb sensed a 'spirit of violence' in the new Parliament, as in the country at large, where economic distress had helped to create 'discontent'. He divided with opposition on the civil list, 3 May, but 'a bad cold' kept him away from the division on the same subject, 5 May 1820, when he anticipated nothing more significant than 'much talk'.[8] He voted against government on the issue, 8 May, the additional baron of exchequer in Scotland, 15 May, and the aliens bill, 1 June. On 19 May he presented a Hertfordshire agriculturists' petition for relief from distress, but declined to comment on the problem, as 'partial and casual discussions ... only tended to keep up ill feeling and irritation'. He divided against Wilberforce's compromise resolution on the Queen Caroline affair, 22 June 1820, but privately deplored the 'shocking scrape' in which it had landed the country, believing that 'it ought to have been kept quiet at all hazards and at any expense'.[9] When Wilberforce sought his support for his notion of calling county meetings to petition the king and Parliament to 'put a stop to the whole inquiry', he replied that it was too late for such a risky step, though he admitted that 'I am too despairing in matters of this nature, and lean too much to the side of doing nothing, and awaiting the course of events'. Fearing 'serious popular tumult and insurrection', but wishing to conceal his alarm from 'those from whom the danger proceeds', he argued against 'an exertion of influence on the part of the property of the country', which might 'create in the disaffected an exaggerated notion of the present peril, and of their own strength'.[10]

Lamb was further aggravated in the autumn of 1820 by Lady Caroline's flaunting of her latest conquest, the young Scottish doctor hired to treat their only child Augustus, who was mentally retarded beyond redemption. He was also afflicted by a succession of minor ailments as the year drew to a close.[11] He thought 'this whole country is gone out of its wits upon the business of the queen' and blamed the king and his ministers for unnecessarily persecuting her and Caroline for her intransigence in refusing the offer of an honourable settlement. He told his brother that he would oppose the insertion of her name in the liturgy, the 'principal' point at issue;[12] but he voted for Hamilton's motion deploring its omission, 26 Jan. 1821. On 31 Jan., supporting the proposal to go into committee on provision for the queen, he expressed regret that ministers had 'agitated the country with the most unfortunate and the most useless question that had ever been proposed', but also attacked Caroline, which earned him a lashing from Henry Brougham. Many other Whigs, according to his sister Emily, Countess Cowper, were 'very angry' with him for this speech; but he voted with them in censure of ministers' conduct, 6 Feb. At the end of the debate on a proposal to restore the queen's name to the liturgy, 13 Feb., he reiterated his view that she had no legal entitlement and that she should have conceded the question for the sake of harmony, but announced that 'in deference to the opinion of a large majority of the people' he would vote for the motion, which he duly did. His sister thought it, as she told Frederick, 'twaddling and foolish, speaking on one side and voting on the other, splitting hairs ... When you differ with *your party* about trifles, it is better to hold your tongue'. Lamb, who was worried by the potentially disruptive effects of serious distress among landowners, told Frederick ten days later that

> the interest respecting the queen seems to be subsiding quietly, as after all everything which is so very foolish must in time. The Whigs blundered the business in my opinion in this. Whilst the trial was going on, there was undoubtedly a strong, real, vivid public feeling; but after the bill was given up, the feeling that was manufactured was for the most part fictitious, belonging to party and excited by the Whigs themselves. If they had remained quiet and adopted the tone of wishing to tranquillize the country out of doors, I think they would have had a better chance of attacking the ministry within. As it was they did what they always will do when they make a manifest reach at power. They called forth a very strong expression on the part of the House of Commons that however much they might disapprove of the ministers, they dreaded the opposition still more.

Lamb's attitude did him no good with the king, ordinarily his admirer, though his snubbing of the couple at a Devonshire House rout in the summer was probably inspired principally by tales of Lady Caroline's ostentatious espousal of the queen's cause.[13]

On 24 Jan. 1821 Lamb urged ministers to undertake 'wise and timely interference' to preserve the integrity of the liberal government in Naples. He was still 'frightened out of my wits at anything like movement or disturbance' there in late February, though he did not vote for Mackintosh's motion on the subject on the 21st.[14] He voted for Catholic relief, 28 Feb. He presented Royston petitions for reform, 26 Feb., and relief from agricultural distress, 3 Apr., and one from county agriculturists to the same effect, 6 Mar.[15] He was not particularly well in March, when his sister blamed Lady Caroline's insistence on his being 'cupped continually' for his recurrent lumbago, which made him 'look fat and white'.[16] He voted for repeal of the additional malt duty, 3 Apr., but with government against the omission of arrears from the duke of Clarence's grant, 18 June. At the county meeting called to petition for relief from agricultural distress, 1 Feb. 1822, he objected to the terms of the radical amendment calling for specific tax cuts and reserved his right to exercise his own judgement on the question. He advised agriculturists not to 'recommit themselves with theorists' on protection and currency reform and said he would support all retrenchment consistent with public welfare, but contended that distress, which the radicals exaggerated, was the inescapable consequence of the late wars. Criticized for his failure to support Hume's campaign for economy in the previous session, he pleaded the excuse of his illnesses; but, to the anger of many of his audience, he added that he had no wish to be associated with many of Hume's motions, as they were 'brought forward in a tone and spirit of opposition in which he could not participate'.[17] He divided with ministers against more extensive tax reductions, 11 Feb., and mitigation of the salt duties, 28 Feb., but was in the minority on the navy five per cents bill, 4 Mar. 1822. He had already given emphatic support to the coercive legislation to deal with Irish disturbances, 8 Feb., when he spoke of his 'confidence' in the government in both countries. Although he did not absolve them from blame for the current problems of Ireland, he argued that many of them were beyond their control and called on the Irish gentry to put their own house in order. The Tory Henry Bankes* thought Lamb's was 'among the speeches which deserved particular commendation'.[18] He refused to support inquiry into the disorder at the queen's funeral, 28 Feb., insisting that there were 'evil-minded persons in this country who aimed to disturb the peace' and that unless breaches of the law in the capital were discountenanced by Members, 'they would sooner or later find that the consequences would be violence and bloodshed'. Mackintosh noted, 19 Feb., that Lamb 'has now openly left us' and 'says that as soon as Tierney resigned the [Commons] leadership [in 1821] he considered himself as free from all party engagements. It is better that he should be an open enemy than a pretended friend'.[19] George Agar Ellis* and Charles Baring Wall* considered trying to 'engage' Lamb in their projected 'new party', but nothing came of this.[20] Lamb's denial of the right of the likes of Denman and Hobhouse to set themselves up as champions of 'the people of England', which Mackintosh considered 'a most insolent and malignant attack on his old friends',[21] earned him a rebuke from Hobhouse, 6 Mar., when he replied that there was a difference between 'the people' and 'a tumultuous rabble', though he criticized ministers over the route selected for the funeral procession. Lamb, who had been named to the select committee on agricultural distress, 18 Feb., presented a Hoddesden petition for relief, 28 Mar.;[22] but he voted, with George, now Member for Dungarvan, in the minority of 25 for the imposition of a fixed duty of 20*s*. on imported wheat, 9 May. His only other known vote that session was against repeal of the salt duties, 28 June 1822. He was harried and distracted by renewed outbursts of lunacy by Lady Caroline, who was drunk for days on end in the summer. His sister recorded a conversation with him on the subject in October, which showed him to be moving, albeit hesitantly, towards a separation:

> He says that he is quite miserable, and does not know what to do about her, that he never has a day's peace, and that her violence increases so much that he is always afraid of her doing some serious mischief to some of her servants ... He says she is the greatest bore in the world, and that there never was such a temper ... He is a *great* ass, for having borne her as he has done, but one cannot help feeling for him, just particularly when it appears that he is not blinded about her, and that he really sees her as she is.

Yet a month later Emily told Frederick, whom she had encouraged to stiffen William's resolve, that she had 'little or no hope of him', for he had fallen silent on the matter: 'I suppose he feels that he has not courage to take any decisive step and is reduced to do what Cobbett advises the farmers to do – grin and bear'.[23]

There was speculation after Lord Londonderry's* suicide in August 1822 that a place might be found in government for Lamb, especially if Canning came in. The duke of Buckingham thought he would be 'a great accession'; but John Croker* was less sure, as he told Peel, the home secretary:

> He is a very respectable man and a good grave speaker for once or twice in a session, but *non tali auxilio* just now; besides his father cannot live many *years*, perhaps not many *months* [and] it would therefore be extremely imprudent to embarrass the *cabinet* with another peer, of which you have already one or two too many. If he would take a privy councillor's office during his father's life, I should like ... to see him by your side.[24]

This ended in smoke, but Lamb, who had initially thought that the anti-Catholics in government would succeed in keeping Canning out, strongly advised his friend John William Ward* to accept Canning's offer of an under-secretaryship at the foreign office.[25] How far Thomas Creevey* was justified in writing in February 1823 that Lamb was 'in Canning's confidence' is not clear. Fifteen years later he was at pains to deny that he had ever been 'a Canningite or a follower of the Canning party', as Brougham would have had the world believe:

> I was acquainted with Canning, liked him, admired him, agreed with him upon some great questions, in his opposition to parliamentary reform and in his support of the Roman Catholic claims, but never acted with him, nor was in his confidence, nor had any political connection with him until I accepted office in 1827.

Indeed, in the latter year, four months after Canning's death, Lamb snobbishly told his brother that he had 'never got rid of' the 'tone' of 'a clerk' and that as 'a schemer' he 'had none of the straightforward simplicity which belongs to a great man, although he could at times assume the appearance of it'. Lamb was, however, increasingly intimate with Canning's close associate William Huskisson*, to whom he was related by marriage, and whom he came to admire as 'the greatest practical statesman he had known'. His sister's adulterous relationship with Lord Palmerston* (whose wife she eventually became) may also have had an influence on Lamb's accelerated gravitation towards the liberal wing of the Liverpool ministry after Canning's return to the cabinet.[26]

Lamb attended the county meeting called to petition for reform, 8 Feb. 1823, and was barracked when he declared that he was 'not prepared to vote for any sudden and extensive changes', including Russell's 'plan of divesting certain boroughs of their franchises, and scattering them over the face of the country'.[27] In the House, he objected to Creevey's attempt to obstruct the supplies, 14 Feb., and voted with government against repeal of the assessed taxes, 18 Mar. On 16 Apr. he opposed repeal of the Foreign Enlistment Act, deploring French aggression against Spain, but denying that Britain was bound to interfere and urging the House not to be 'led away by declamation and invective'. When accused by Dr. Lushington of apostasy, he rather lamely replied that it was the Whig party and not himself that had changed. His brother George told Emily that his speech was 'bad, such milk and water'; she wished he 'would join one side or the other'. Privately Lamb, who told Frederick that no one in Britain wanted war except 'some few who have a sort of blind passion for Spain and the more violent democrats who are anxious to see a general struggle in Europe of people against kings', thought he had done what he could to promote moderation. He considered that Canning had on the whole handled the matter well, though he had perhaps 'condemned the conduct of France too openly, and expressed his hopes for her failure in a manner not quite consistent with a determination to be truly neutral'.[28] He voted against inquiry into the prosecution of the Dublin Orange rioters, 22 Apr., and presented a Hertfordshire agriculturists' petition for an open trade in beer, 7 May.[29] After enjoying the late spring beauties of Brocket for a week, he attended to vote against Scottish reform, 2 June, and inquiries into chancery delays, 5 June, and the currency, 12 June 1823. He presented a petition from Canterbury corporation for repeal of the coal duties, 4 Feb. 1824.[30] He voted against reform of Edinburgh's representation, 26 Feb., but was in the minority of 19 against the grant for the propagation of the gospels in the colonies, 12 Mar. When supporting renewal of the Aliens Act, 23 Mar., he countered the arguments of Hobhouse and Mackintosh and asserted that the disturbed state of Europe was the fault not of despotism but of 'the impracticable designs of that very liberal party, who now lamented over the evils by which the continent was afflicted'. He criticized their 'violent and indefensible language', and went on:

> Before any attempt was made to stir up ill feeling, and excite insurrection, those who wished to make such an attempt ought to consider, whether they would do more for those persons on whose passions they intended to work, than to give them a dinner, a few toasts, a certain portion of violent speeches, some five or six thousand pounds, and an inefficient vote in that House.

Asserting that in all matters of foreign policy it was necessary to give 'extended powers' to the government of the day, he ended by praising Canning, who subsequently confirmed to his wife that 'Lamb is professedly with *me*'. It was at about this time, according to Canning, that the king told him that he wished Lamb to be offered a place at the treasury : 'I stared. William Lamb! Sir, it would surely affront to him to offer it – a lordship of the treasury for a person of his standing and pretensions!' It turned out that the king really wanted the place for his mistress's son Lord Francis Conyngham*; but it seems that cautious overtures may have been made to Lamb by Lord Liverpool.[31] He voted with ministers on the prosecution of the missionary John Smith in Demerara, 11 June, and the Irish insurrection bill, 14 June, having been named to the select committee on Irish disturbances, 11 May 1824.

On the address, 3 Feb. 1825, Lamb, provoked by a personal reference to him by Brougham, warned against taking too sanguine a view of the country's economic prospects and indicated that he would support the bill to suppress the Catholic Association, observing that the cause of emancipation, which he still warmly espoused, was being endangered by 'the imprudence, if not the violence, of some of its advocates'. He duly welcomed the unlawful societies bill, in what Sir John Nicholl* thought 'a good speech',

15 Feb., when Brougham attacked him for 'extreme inconsistency and want of argument'.[32] He voted for Catholic relief, 1 Mar. He divided for the introduction of Onslow's usury laws amendment bill, 8 Feb., the grant to the duke of Cumberland, 30 May, and the spring guns bill, 21 June. On 17 June 1825 he said that although he had opposed inquiry into Sir Robert Wilson's* dismissal from the army, he was as anxious as anyone to see him restored to his rank. Charles Williams Wynn*, president of the board of control, worrying about the inadequacies of Lord Amherst as governor-general of India, told Buckingham that he had occasionally thought of Lamb, who had 'very considerable talents', as a replacement, not least because he would 'probably not be sorry to accept any situation which placed him on the other side of the ocean from Lady Caroline'.[33]

Lamb was indeed largely preoccupied in the spring and summer of 1825 with the problem of effecting a formal separation from his wife, whose behaviour, more outrageous than ever since the death of Byron, her former lover, the previous year, had finally driven him, at the behest of his siblings, to cut the cord.[34] Although he was resolute about the end in view, he dithered over the means, and characteristically shied from grappling with the sordid details, absenting himself in Paris at one stage. Emily, who kept him up to the mark, complained that 'never in my life did I see so irresolute a person: every trifle turns his purpose and makes him waver'. After protracted negotiations, during which Caroline used every trick in her repertoire in an attempt to break Lamb's resolve, a settlement was reached and she finally submitted to it, taking herself off to Paris in early August. Later that month Lamb went to Melbourne Hall in Derbyshire 'as happy as possible', in the words of his sister, though she reflected that the condition of his idiot son, whom he took with him, was bound to be yet another 'drawback to his comfort'. Lady Caroline wrote Lamb an hysterical letter of abuse from Calais in early September, and by mid-October 1825 she was back in London, on the rampage. Lamb, to Emily's delight, acted decisively and had her confined under the care of a Dr. Goddard. Eventually she was allowed to live at Brocket or Brighton, with Goddard usually in attendance, and, broken in health and spirit, she began her rapid decline towards death.[35]

Lamb, aware that his political conduct had cost him the support of most Hertfordshire Whigs, had decided by May 1825 that in view of his father's state of health he was not prepared to risk the expense of a contest in order to retain his seat, and contemplated buying one for a close borough. Although he thought that the rejection of the Catholic relief bill by the Lords and the strong current of anti-Catholic feeling in the country made it unlikely that there would be a dissolution that year, he informed the Tory marquess of Salisbury, who helped to prop him up in the county, that he did 'not feel it to be worth my while to maintain my seat at the expense which will be required', the more so as the terms of his matrimonial separation had imposed a further financial burden on him.[36] When an imminent dissolution was expected in September 1825, Lamb announced his intention to give up the county from 'personal and private considerations', but accepted an invitation to stand for Hertford, where his brother-in-law Lord Cowper had an interest, and whose independent Member, Nicolson Calvert, had offered for the county in Lamb's room. He was forced to deny the allegation that he was only standing as a locum for Cowper's son Lord Fordwich*, who would come of age in 1827.[37] His opponent was Thomas Duncombe*, the heir to a valuable Yorkshire estate, and a reckless and debt-ridden gambler with a dubious private life, who had unsuccessfully contested the borough as an independent against Salisbury's nominee in 1823, and cultivated it ever since. By February 1826 it had become clear that he was 'quite sure' of beating Lamb, whose sister was critical of his typical 'want of energy' and his 'doing the thing by halves', but thought that, however unpleasant the prospect of defeat at such hands, he could not 'give up now without cutting such a foolish figure'. She was not, however, sorry when Lamb gave it up in April 1826 and announced his withdrawal, recommending in his place Henry Lytton Bulwer*, whose brother Edward*, then fresh from Cambridge, had been the victim of Lady Caroline's last major flirtation in 1824.[38]

Lamb approved the government's emergency measures to deal with the financial crash of 1825-6, which he attributed largely to rash speculation in '*convertible* paper' currency, but wondered whether it was possible to go on for much longer without 'depreciation in some mode or other'.[39] He was largely inactive in the House in the 1826 session, but he led the resistance to further investigation of the charges against the Welsh judge William Kenrick†, arguing that formal parliamentary condemnation of him would 'shake the whole system of constitutional law': his motion to drop the matter was defeated by 81-42, 17 Feb. More significantly, he spoke and voted, 'from conviction', against Russell's reform scheme, 27 Apr., when he said that its advocates had failed to demonstrate 'what real benefit could be derived from it' and warned them that although they denied that they wished to create 'democracy', they should remember that men 'did not always want what they got, nor get what they wanted'. William Fremantle* thought 'Lamb's was the only good effective speech'; but Emily Cowper took a dim view of it:

> All the Whigs are furious with him for his speech ... and I think it is a pity that he should always somehow manage to say the strangest things against the people he has left. However, as far as the speaking went all accounts say it was very good, but Canning said I could not say anything after William Lamb, for I could not have gone so far, and it is a pity that he should always take the unpopular side.[40]

By now Lamb had, as he told Frederick, 'made up my mind to have nothing to do with the next Parliament', and he contemplated leaving England after the elections to 'travel leisurely and in my manner through France' in order to spend six weeks with his brother in Spain, returning home by the beginning of September. Emily reported to Frederick in June 1826 that he 'seems well satisfied to be out of Parliament and looks very cheerful and gay'; but soon afterwards he abandoned the Spanish plan, fearing 'the heat of travelling at this time', and talked of making a tour of the Rhine. His sister suspected that his real reason for prevaricating was his reluctance to go abroad while Lady Caroline, unknown to Lord Melbourne, remained in stubborn occupation of Brocket, where Lamb had been 'monstrous foolish' enough to let her take root. He appears to have remained in England, and in February 1827, when Lady Caroline had removed to Hastings, he was 'as amiable as ever and the best company possible' for Emily at Cowper's Hertfordshire residence at Panshanger.[41]

In the early stages of the negotiations of April 1827 which led to the formation of Canning's ministry, Lamb was widely seen as a potential recruit. To his sister's irritation, he was not only 'terribly supine about putting himself forward', but even went off to Derbyshire at a critical juncture: 'I think there is nothing so stupid as not to be on the spot. Seeing you puts people in mind of you.' The negotiations faltered when the moderate Whig Lord Lansdowne, whom Canning wished to be home secretary, insisted that the lord lieutenant of Ireland and his chief secretary should be Catholic. This Canning could not concede, being bound by the king's scruples on the Catholic question. After several false starts, the king agreed to the appointment of Lamb as Irish secretary until a suitable Protestant could be found or he was removed to the Lords by his father's death; and Lansdowne acquiesced in the arrangement as an earnest of good faith. There was a possibility at one point that if Lansdowne declined to come in, Lamb would have the home seals; but Lansdowne, who entered the cabinet without portfolio, agreed to take them at a future date, when the anticipated embarrassment of appointing a Protestant viceroy had been got over. Lamb's return on the Holmes interest for Newport, on 'very reasonable terms', had already been arranged, and within a few days of it he was obliged by his acceptance of office to vacate the seat in order to seek re-election. It was initially hoped that the Holmes trustees would have 'no objection' to facilitating this, but difficulties evidently arose, and he was brought in instead for Bletchingley, whose owner and Member William Russell had made the seat available to Canning before going abroad, on condition that he could reclaim it if desired on his return home.[42]

His sister reported that Lamb, who 'looks more happy and comfortable than I have ever seen him', was

> pleased with his appointment and feels I think comfortable to be fixed in his politics after having been so long no how ... Canning speaks most highly of him [and] told Madame Lieven that he looked upon him not as one, but as *the* cleverest person going. I am afraid he will find Ireland a hornet's nest, but he seems very stout-hearted and well satisfied.[43]

Lamb, who lost no time in making obsequious contact with Lord Wellesley, the lord lieutenant, initially found the pressure of office business and 'constant attendance in the House', which 'loses him his dinner almost every day', a little overwhelming, but he soon warmed to his task and began to thrive on it.[44] When he submitted the Irish miscellaneous estimates which he had inherited, 25 May 1827, he listened to the comments of backbenchers who were willing to accept them as they stood in return for a promise of future economies, but, demonstrating a ready mastery of the techniques of ministerial evasion, gave a vague answer:

> No man was more impressed than himself with the necessity of preserving a strict, but at the same time a prudent economy in the public service. He was anxious to make every reduction in these grants that was consistent with humanity and the responsibility which government had in preserving the health of the people.

He did, however, warn Wellesley that the attitude of these Members laid 'the ground of future difficulty, unless something effectual can be done', and he recommended a curb on additional expenditure by the institutions which had come in for criticism. He conceded a select committee on Irish grand jury presentments, 6 June, but the following day dismissed Moore's proposal for the establishment of a small loans fund to assist needy labourers as a 'dangerous' precedent and departure from the safer practice of relying on private charity.[45] On 28 May he had spoken and voted, with Canning, against the reformers' plan to transfer Penryn's seats to Manchester; and he voted for Lord Althorp's election expenses bill the same day. He was in the government majority on the grant for Canadian canals, 12 June 1827.

On the eve of his departure for Dublin in early July he told Frederick that 'I have a difficult mission, but somehow or other I feel it in me, as if I shall manage it. I may and probably do deceive myself'. He took Augustus with him, which Emily considered to be 'madness'; and a month after his arrival he informed his brother:

> I find myself well enough here and shall bide it for a short time. The business is not much in itself, but it is enough for me, who have been so long used to do nothing, particularly when added to the necessary dining out, which goes on without intermission. There is a good deal of annoyance with impudent applications, and more to do with gaols, police, hospitals, penitentiaries than suits me, being subjects which I have little or no time for.[46]

Before leaving for Dublin Lamb had sent a message to the Catholic leader Daniel O'Connell* to the effect that '*I must for a time be worse than Peel* but when we can we will do all the good we can. Beg of him to have confidence, though we cannot do much, or worse men will come'. O'Connell was unimpressed, and although he later conceded that Lamb was 'perfectly free from guile' and 'honourable', he always felt that he had 'done nothing', even though he had it in his power, to break the Orange supremacy.[47] In truth, Lamb, who retained his office under Lord Goderich after Canning's death, achieved little in Ireland, but he 'gained much credit by his readiness of access and conciliatory manners', as Sir John Newport* and others were happy to admit.[48] He worked hard, set his face against jobbery and attempted to master the great variety of issues which confronted anyone responsible for Ireland.[49] Temperamentally better suited to the identification and analysis of problems than to devising solutions, he soon concluded that pending the concession of Catholic emancipation, which he thought could not be pressed 'in opposition to the wishes of the king', there was little that could be done beyond keeping order and conciliating Catholic opinion as far as possible. He wrote to Brougham:

> As to the Roman Catholics, it is of course better that they should be tranquil and prudent than the contrary, but it is of importance that they should not think that they confer a great obligation upon the government by their tranquillity and forbearance.

He initiated a correspondence with Brougham on the possibility of introducing a general system of education to Ireland, but was discouraged by the 'very great difficulties' which emerged as he studied the subject.[50]

On 18 Nov. 1827 Lamb wrote to Frederick of the general political scene:

> There are competent men enough, but the difficulty in governments is putting men together and making them co-operate. I do not see how this is to be done. They have all got into false positions, the duke of Wellington falsest of all. He made a wrong move [in refusing to serve with Canning], and the consequence is that he never can make a right one after. I have no doubt he had every provocation; but a politician should be, as the thirty nine articles define the deity, *sine passionibus*.[51]

The following month he was informed that William Russell now wanted to resume his seat, but an opening for him presented itself in county Durham and Lamb was allowed to remain undisturbed at Bletchingley.[52] He had known for several weeks that his wife was declining fast, but, though 'harassed to death with domestic calamity', felt it would be 'awkward' if he left Dublin early in January 1828, when he was confronted with the prospect of the simultaneous parochial meetings planned by the Catholic Association after mass on the 13th. He thought they ought to be prevented and urged Wellesley, who was in London to hand over power to his replacement, Lord Anglesey, to press this course on ministers, arguing that the meetings were 'the commencement of a system of combined and concerted movement'. His view was not accepted, and he was ordered to do nothing more than monitor the gatherings.[53] In the negotiations with Wellington after the collapse of the Goderich ministry (which Lamb believed it had been John Herries's* intention to bring about from the moment he took office in it), Huskisson insisted on Lamb's inclusion in the new administration, and the duke accordingly wrote to him, 12 Jan., asking him to stay in his office. Before he received this offer, Lamb commented to Frederick that it was

> more than probable that the arrangement will be such as will make my present situation untenable. In politics tone and impression are everything, and whatever may be the real feelings and merits of the duke of Wellington, Peel, Goulburn, etc., they have got such a damned character for intolerance ... in this country, that their accession to the office would encourage the violent Protestants and depress the Roman Catholics to such a degree, as would make it impossible for me to pursue my course in this country or to continue here with credit and the appearance of consistency.

In reply to Wellington's letter, Lamb asked for time to consult Huskisson and the other Canningites in London. He arrived there on 19 Jan. 1828, after a dreadful sea passage to Holyhead, as he told his mistress, Lady Branden, the estranged wife of the 4th Lord Branden, a worthless clergyman, with whom he had formed an indiscreet, warm and volatile relationship soon after going to Dublin:

> When I got down to the water and saw how it blew, I should have liked to return without going on board, but was ashamed. What would Dublin have said of a secretary who was turned back from the edge of the sea by a gale of wind? I had a melancholy journey, believe me. Behind me deep grief, before me death.[54]

After consultations with Huskisson, Palmerston, Anglesey and others, and interviews with Wellington and Peel, Lamb, whose continuance in Ireland was seen, with Anglesey's appointment, as a guarantee of ministerial neutrality on the Catholic question, had little hesitation in accepting the offer. He told Frederick:

> With respect to the past I could not make out much from any of them. With respect to the future nothing could be more satisfactory or in fact more agreeable to my own opinions than the language and views of Peel and the duke; and under the circumstances in which I stood there was nothing to preclude me from giving them every assistance I could, and if they thought I could serve them best by remaining in my present situation, I was ready to do so, in fact liking it better than any other, except the real efficient places, such as the treasury and the secretaryships of state.[55]

Lady Caroline died on 26 Jan. 1828. Lamb attended her death bed, and was not quite as unmoved as it appeared to his sister, who reported that he was 'hurt at the time and rather low next day, but he is now just as usual, and his mind filled with politics'. 'Nothing but tears and misery here below', he told Lady Branden, to whom he wrote almost every day, and whom he assured that 'the six months we have just passed seem to me as if they were the last sunshine which would gleam upon my life'. He was 'very low and melancholy' before the funeral, but felt 'relieved by it', as 'it seems as if everything had been done that could be and every duty paid'. Yet two weeks later he told her:

> I have had a great blow and have not recovered my spirits. I felt upon that occasion [the funeral] a sort of impossibility of believing that I should never see her countenance or hear her voice again, a sort of sense of desolation, solitude and carelessness about everything, when I forced myself to remember that she was really gone, such as I never experienced before, nor anything like it.

This said, Lamb, who had essentially had a millstone removed from his neck, did not grieve for long; and, politics aside, he had enough to distract him in the importunities of Lady Branden, to whom he wrote, 21 Feb. 1828:

> I have received your letter of the 17th. There is no ground whatever for any suspicion, and my feelings are just the same, as when I left Dublin. Is this distinct enough? Is this satisfactory? Will this do? I am still very low. What I have seen haunts me and returns to my recollection upon every occasion.[56]

In answer to Spring Rice's question in the House, 15 Feb. 1828, as to whether the government intended to renew the Act to curb the activities of the Catholic Association, Lamb, having consulted Wellington, said that nothing had yet been decided. When, in late March, Anglesey strongly recommended allowing the Act to lapse at the end of the session and relying on the ordinary law and the constabulary to maintain order, Lamb was in complete agreement with him; but on discussing the matter with Wellington, he was

> sorry to find ... that his mind was a good deal impressed with the idea of its being necessary to renew the bill ... I stated to him strongly my opinion that the bill could have no other effect than to produce useless and unnecessary exasperation ... He looked staggered and with that air, which he always has, of a man very little accustomed to be differed from or contradicted, and changed the subject.

Lamb forcefully argued the 'conclusive' case against renewal to Peel and Huskisson and eventually carried the point.[57] On calls for repeal of the Irish Subletting Act, 19 Feb., he agreed that the practice of 'minutely dividing land' was one of the fundamental causes of discontent, but he hesitated to legislate to effect sudden changes and called on the resident gentry to exercise moderation. His observation that he was willing to consider any practical modification of the system gave rise to expectations of action, which he was at pains to lower, 21 Mar., when he said that in the last resort he would rather keep the law as it was than abandon its principle. After discussing the problem of general education with Peel, he said on 28 Feb. that as the difficulties in the way of devising such a scheme as would 'give general satisfaction' had been 'greatly augmented', ministers were not prepared to submit one that session. He did, however, as he had known he must, acquiesce in Spring Rice's motion for the appointment of a select committee, 11 Mar., though he made it clear that he expected nothing to come of it, while professing his willingness to do everything to promote education which was 'compatible with the public expenditure, and which will not extinguish private benevolence'.[58] Lamb, who voted silently for repeal of the Test Acts, 26 Feb., introduced bills dealing with jury laws, the lighting and improvement of towns, the appointment of sheriffs, the larceny laws, linen manufactures and the prevention of malicious damage to property, most of which reached the statute book. On 1 Apr. he argued, like Peel, that it was idle to think that a system of poor laws could be successfully introduced to Ireland and urged Members not to be 'too sanguine in their plans' for economic improvement:

> When ... a country is distressed, if we wish to alleviate that distress, the only way is to introduce a system of patient perseverance, of rigid economy, of increasing industry. This may be a hard lesson to learn.

He would not commit himself to abolishing the jurisdiction of the Irish ecclesiastical courts, 25 Apr., but thought the subject worthy of 'a full and solemn inquiry'. His speech of 9 May 1828 in favour of Catholic relief, which, though it would not 'heal all the wounds or remedy all the evils of Ireland', would 'give rise to a general feeling that justice has been done ... [and provide] a ray of light which will illumine the darkest cabin of this country', was applauded by Croker as 'a short and fine burst for conciliation and harmony'.[59]

When the government seemed to be on the verge of breaking up in late March 1828 over Charles Grant's* disagreement with the rest of the cabinet on the revised corn bill, Lamb, though he thought Huskisson was wrong to offer his resignation in sympathy, did not see how he could remain in office if they and Palmerston and Lord Dudley went out.[60] This crisis blew over, but there was no reprieve for Lamb in May, when Huskisson sent his ill-considered letter of resignation to Wellington after finding himself in the minority against throwing the delinquent borough of East Retford into the hundred of Bassetlaw rather than transferring its seats to Birmingham, and the duke, anxious to be rid of him, took it at face value with indecent haste. Lamb, who thought such tinkering with the representative system would only 'hasten and advance' general reform, to which he remained hostile, had voted with Peel in the majority; but after talks with Huskisson, Palmerston and Dudley, he saw no alternative but to show solidarity and go out, as he had come in, with them. He dismissed Dudley's tortured attempts to reconcile staying in with political honour and consistency, and was said to have rejected a personal appeal from the king to remain in his place.[61] It is clear he that made a considerable sacrifice of self-interest and inclination by resigning. To Anglesey, whom he successfully persuaded to continue as lord lieutenant, he explained:

> Having remained in office in January last with Huskisson, being connected with him by the ties of relationship and feeling that though he erred in the first instance, yet that the duke took too hasty an advantage of that error, and acted towards him both harshly and sharply, I felt myself ... bound to resign with him. At the same time I did not take this course with perfect satisfaction to myself. I feel that the ground of difference is too insignificant and even ridiculous, and that I am depriving myself of the power of doing some good and running the risk of doing some evil by producing an unfavourable impression upon the public mind in Ireland for no sufficient reason. On the other hand, if we had acquiesced in the duke's conduct without notice or remonstrance and let Huskisson go, how would he hereafter have treated those who remained, if upon any occasion they had differed from or resisted him?

He elaborated the point a few days later:

> The real cause of my resignation is that under the circumstances I felt that I could not abandon Huskisson. It has always been a maxim with me, that it is more necessary to stand by one's friends when they are in the wrong, than when they are in the right; and though I do not say that he is quite in the former predicament, yet to have let him go out, with circumstances by no means clear in his favour and with the additional blow of being deserted by all his personal and political friends, would have been a course to which I could not have reconciled my feelings. At the same time I must say that I never took a step with deeper regret and less satisfaction, but I think I should have felt even more dissatisfied and uneasy, if I had adopted a contrary line of conduct.

Yet Anglesey told Holland that Lamb was 'probably in some measure influenced [in] his decision' by the '*scrape*' which he had got into with Lady Branden. When Wellington made overtures to Lamb two years later, he suggested to him that the sole reason for his resignation had been that entanglement, 'which made it unpleasant to him to return to Dublin'; but Lamb emphatically and quite justifiably rejected this interpretation of his motives. He was prepared to place 'the most perfect reliance upon the sincerity' of Peel and Wellington in their public professions that they had 'no intention to change the principles upon which the government had been conducted during the last five years and upon which the administration had been formed in January', though he was worried about 'the high opinions and strong prejudices of the duke, fostered, as they are said to be, by those who are about him and have his ear, and not opposed by persons of weight and authority, as they have been'; all the more reason, he thought, for Anglesey to stay in office.[62] In the House, 9 June 1828, Lamb replied to Hume's attack on the Irish estimates with the comment that 'every possible reduction' had been made. According to Croker, who thought it 'a great pity' that he had not been made colonial secretary, for, though he was 'idle and careless', he was 'bold, high-minded and eloquent', Lamb had taken his seat that night 'in his old place on Bankes's bench just *vis a vis* to the Huskisson seats'.[63] On 12 June he defended the generality of the Irish constabulary force against charges of corruption and stressed the importance of its being 'efficiently kept up' and adequately funded. He refused to answer Frankland Lewis's question about the outcome of the Irish revenue board's recommendations for reductions in the establishment, 23 June. Two days later his old adversary Hobhouse sat next to him at dinner, and reflected that his 'abrupt breaker of a laugh and attention to his plate and glass do not bespeak him the clever able man that he certainly is'. As William Russell had come out against the government, Lamb had to surrender his seat for Bletchingley in the third week of July 1828; but it scarcely signified, for his father's long anticipated death on the 22nd sent him to the Lords, where James Abercromby* surmised that he would be 'more at his ease ... than he was in the Commons'. A month later Creevey noted that 'never man was so improved as William Lamb, whether from gaining his title, or losing his wife I know not'.[64]

In May 1828 Lamb, who had developed a taste for flagellation in his sexual relationships, had an action for crim. con. brought against him by Lord Branden. When it came to court the following year, it was thrown out; but it is clear that Lamb had bought Branden off. In 1836, as prime minister, he successfully defended another action brought against him by the hitherto complaisant husband of his current mistress, Mrs. Caroline Norton.[65] As a peer, he scaled the political heights. He took office as home secretary in the Grey ministry and soon, as Greville wrote

> surprised all those about him by a sudden display of activity and vigour, rapid and diligent transaction of business, for which nobody was prepared, and which will prove a great mortification to Peel and his friends, who were in hopes he would do nothing and let the country be burnt and plundered without interruption.[66]

Ever the pragmatist, he swallowed the reform bills when he saw that there was no alternative. The story went that when the king sent for him to ask him to form a government on Grey's resignation in July 1834, he said to his secretary Tom Young that

> 'he thought it a damned bore, and he was in many minds what he should do – be minister or no'. Young said, 'Why, damn it, such a position was never occupied by any Greek or Roman, and, if it lasts two months, it is well worth while to have been prime minister of England'. 'By God that's true', said Melbourne; 'I'll go'.[67]

As the head of two troubled and divided administrations, with the thrust of which he was increasingly out of sympathy, he applied all his arts of cynical passivity to the task of keeping them in power. His greatest achievement perhaps lay in his political education of the young Queen Victoria, who was devoted to him.[68]

Lamb's health began to fail from 1842 and, while at times he came close to recovering his old exuberance, he tended frequently to lapse into 'gloomy silence and reverie', as Lady Holland put it. After his death, following a series of strokes, at Melbourne Hall in November 1848, Hobhouse commented that 'his existence had become painful to himself and others, and the continuance of it was not to be desired'.[69] By his will, dated 31 Jan. 1843, he disposed of his real estate in accordance with the strict settlement imposed in his father's will of 1819. Lamb's original will had not come to light by the time limited administration was granted on the authority of a copy, 19 Mar. 1849, to his executors, Brougham and Edward Ellice*. As the wretched Augustus had died in 1836, Lamb was succeeded in the peerage and estates by his brother Frederick, who had been created Lord Beauvale in 1839, and to whom he left separate instructions making generous financial provision for Lady Branden and Mrs. Norton. Beauvale was not best pleased at the prospect of the scarcely sane Brougham having access to Lamb's correspondence.[70] On Beauvale's death without issue in 1853 the peerages became extinct, and the estates, including Brocket, were inherited by Emily, now Palmerston's wife. They passed from her to the Cowpers.

One of Lamb's obituarists, in a sour piece, wrote disparagingly that his life and career had been shaped by 'the negative enjoyment, which he vastly prized, of avoiding trouble', though he conceded that he had 'many estimable qualities'.[71] Guizot characterized him as 'a judicious epicurean, an agreeable egotist, gay without warmth, and mingling a natural air of authority with a carelessness which he took delight in proclaiming'.[72] Like many others, Lady Holland was captivated by his conversation, which was 'pleasant, rich in matter and full of genius and originality'; and Lord Campbell wrote that

> of all the public men I have ever known, Lord Melbourne was approached with the greatest pleasure and satisfac-

tion ... He seemed to have no reserves, and to make everyone his confidant. Yet without any duplicity or deceit he was exceedingly prudent, and to those only whom he knew he could perfectly trust did he say anything that he wished not to be repeated. Then he had singular rectitude of judgement and much vigour in cases of emergency, his courage always rising with the danger ... His great defect was that he had no fixed system of policy. In his heart he was inclined to Conservatism ... He was contented with indolence and luxury, and cared little about the active exercise of power.[73]

Henry Lytton Bulwer portrayed him in what was perhaps a rather flattering light:

His habits were in appearance those of indolence ... and consequently he was called idle, and for many years of his life decried as idle, by a vast variety of persons who were far less usefully employed than himself. During this time he read more, and thought more, than perhaps any person of his own station and standing ... As a minister ... he had ... many qualities of a first-rate kind ... a temperament cool and courageous; a mind dispassionate and unprejudiced; a manner remarkably good humoured and conciliating; an intellect of a high order, and which had been improved by incessant, though not forced cultivation ... The extent of Lord Melbourne's acquirements, and the comprehensiveness of his understanding, stood in one sense in his way. They made him so well acquainted with all that could be said on one side or the other of every argument ... that the tendency of his judgement was to underrate distinctions; and to deem differences between opinions less wide and less important than they really were ... This habit of mind, while it gave moderation to his judgement, did not infuse irresolution into his conduct ... He never, after having once adopted a policy, faltered in the execution of it.[74]

In a thoughtful and objective assessment of Lamb, Greville, who knew him well, but not intimately, wrote:

He was certainly a very singular man ... good-natured, eccentric, and not nice ... He never was really fitted for political life, for he had a great deal too much candour, and was too fastidious to be a good party man ... And still less was he fit to be the leader of a party and the head of a government, for he had neither the strong convictions, nor the eager ambition, nor the firmness and resolution which such a post requires. No position could be more false than the position in which Melbourne was often placed, and no man ever was more perplexed and tormented than he was by it, for he was remarkably sensitive; and most of the latter years of his administration were passed in a state of dissatisfaction with himself and all about him ... He held office with a profound sense of its responsibilities; there never was a minister more conscientious in the distribution of patronage ... He was perfectly disinterested, without nepotism, and without vanity ... His distinctive qualities were strong sound sense, and an innate taste for what was great and good, either in action or sentiment ... But while he pursued truth, as a philosopher, his love of paradox made him often appear a strange mass of contradictions and inconsistency. A sensualist and a sybarite, without much refinement or delicacy, a keen observer of the follies and vices of mankind, taking the world as he found it, and content to extract as much pleasure and diversion as he could from it, he at one time would edify and astonish his hearers with the most exalted sentiments, and at another would terrify and shock them by indications of the lowest morality and worldly feelings, and by thoughts and opinions fraught with the most cold-hearted mockery and sarcasm. His mind seems all his life long, and on almost every subject, to have been vigorous and stirring, but unsettled and unsatisfied ... During his administration his great object seemed to be to keep a rickety concern together, less from political ambition than from his personal feelings for the queen. He abhorred disputes and quarrels of every description, and he was constantly temporising and patching them up ... by all sorts of expedients ... Such weak and unworthy misrule brought his cabinet, his party, and himself into contempt, and it was unquestionably in great measure owing to his want of judgement and firmness that they became so unpopular, and at last fell with so little credit and dignity ... Taking him altogether, he was a very remarkable man in his abilities and his acquirements, in his character and his career, with virtues and vices, faults and merits, curiously intermingled, and producing as eccentric results as society has beheld.[75]

Lamb once observed that 'neither man nor woman can be worth anything until they have discovered that they are fools';[76] he was no fool, but he had looked inside himself and been unimpressed by what he found.

[1] The best biography is P. Ziegler, *Melbourne* (1976); the 1987 edn. has been used here. L.G. Mitchell, *Lord Melbourne* (1997) offers an updated version of the psychological study by Lord D. Cecil in *The Young Melbourne* (1939) and *Lord M* (1954). See also W.M. Torrens, *Mems. Visct. Melbourne* (1878), *Lord Melbourne's Pprs.* ed. L.C. Sanders (1889) and D. Marshall, *Lord Melbourne* (1975). [2] Russell, *Recollections*, 140. [3] *Melbourne Pprs.* p. vi; *Greville Mems.* vi. 129-30. [4] C.R. Leslie, *Autobiog. Recollections*, i. 170. [5] Ziegler, 63-73. [6] Wentworth Woodhouse mun. F49/76. [7] *Lady Palmerston Letters*, 24, 28; *County Chron.* 29 Feb.; *County Herald*, 11 Mar.; Wentworth Woodhouse mun. F49/77; Add. 38458, f. 323; 45550, f. 17; Herts. Archives, Panshanger mss D/ELb F78, W. to F. Lamb, 3 May 1820. [8] Panshanger mss F78, W. to F. Lamb, 3 May 1820. [9] Ibid. F78, W. to F. Lamb, 29 July 1820; *Life of Wilberforce*, v. 76. [10] *Wilberforce Corresp.* ii. 433-5. [11] Lady Airlie, *Lady Palmerston*, i. 60-61, 65-66; Add. 45550, ff. 52, 78. [12] Panshanger mss F78, W. to F. Lamb, 18 Dec. 1820, 9 Jan. 1821. [13] *Lady Palmerston Letters*, 68, 70, 83; Lady Airlie, i. 84, 91; Add. 45550, f. 110; Buckingham, *Mems. Geo. IV*, i. 122. [14] Panshanger mss F78, W. to F. Lamb, 23 Feb. 1821. [15] *The Times*, 27 Feb., 7 Mar., 4 Apr. 1821. [16] *Lady Palmerston Letters*, 75; Lady Airlie, i. 88; Add. 45550, f. 105. [17] *The Times*, 2 Feb.; *County Chron.* 5 Feb. 1822. [18] Dorset RO, Bankes mss D/BKL, Bankes jnl. 131 (7 Feb. 1822). [19] Add. 52445, f. 50.

[20] Northants. RO, Agar Ellis diary, 21 Feb. [1822]. [21] Add. 52445, f. 63. [22] *The Times*, 29 Mar. 1822. [23] *Lady Palmerston Letters*, 96, 101, 102, 111; Add. 45550, f. 128. [24] Bucks. RO, Fremantle mss, Buckingham to Fremantle, 19 Sept. 1822; NLW, Coedymaen mss 647; Add. 40319, f. 57. [25] Panshanger mss F78, W. to F. Lamb, 16 Aug. 1822; Ward, *Llandaff Letters*, 362-3. [26] Creevey mss, Creevey to Miss Ord, 21 Feb. 1823; Brougham mss, Melbourne to Mrs. G. Lamb, 24 Dec. 1838; Panshanger mss F78, W. to F. Lamb, 16 Aug. 1822, 3 Dec. 1827; *Greville Mems.* ii. 45; Ziegler, 84-86; Torrens, i. 182-4. [27] *The Times*, 10 Feb.; *County Herald*, 15 Feb. 1823. [28] *Lady Palmerston Letters*, 123; Panshanger mss F78, W. to F. Lamb, 6, 20, 30 May 1823. [29] *The Times*, 8 May 1823. [30] Ibid. 5 Feb. 1824. [31] Harewood mss, Canning to wife, 31 Mar., 4 Apr. 1824; Torrens, 187; Ziegler, 85. [32] Merthyr Mawr mss F/2/8; Agar Ellis diary, 15 Feb. [1825]. [33] Buckingham, ii. 272. [34] *Lady Holland to Son*, 28-29, 31; *Shelley Diary*, ii. 121. [35] *Lady Palmerston Letters*, 133-44; Lady Airlie, i. 116-19, 121-3; Panshanger mss F78, W. to F. Lamb, 16, 28 May, 23 July 1825; Add. 45548, f. 159; 45550, f. 176; Ziegler, 80-83; H. Blyth, *Caro. The Fatal Passion*, 209-45. [36] Panshanger mss F78, W. to F. Lamb, 16, 23 May, 23 July 1825. [37] Torrens, i. 207-11; *Herts Mercury*, 3, 24 Sept., 1 Oct. 1825. [38] Torrens, i. 211-15; *Lady Palmerston Letters*, 142, 146-8; Keele Univ. Lib. Sneyd mss SC8/79; *Herts Mercury*, 29 Apr. 1826; Add. 45550, f. 202; 45551, ff. 3, 7. [39] Add. 45548, ff. 161, 163. [40] Buckingham, ii. 300; Lady Airlie, i. 126. [41] Panshanger mss F78, W. to F. Lamb, 13 Apr. 1826; Add. 45551, ff. 39, 43, 45, 47, 77; Lady Airlie, i. 132; *Lady Palmerston Letters*, 154. [42] Coedymaen mss 193, 196; Add. 45551, f. 93; *Canning's Ministry*, 111, 180, 220, 236, 239, 240, 242, 255, 256, 258; *Geo. IV Letters*, iii. 1318; *Arbuthnot Jnl.* ii. 108; Wellington mss WP1/887/48; *Lady Palmerston Letters*, 164-6; Lincs. AO, Tennyson d' Eyncourt mss H1/105. [43] *Canning's Ministry*, 283, 396; *Lady Palmerston Letters*, 169. [44] Add. 37305, ff. 97, 100, 103, 111; 45551, ff. 96, 98. [45] *The Times*, 7, 8 June 1827. [46] *Lady Palmerston Letters*, 169; Add. 45548, f. 165; 45551, ff. 99, 101, 103. [47] *O'Connell Corresp.* iii. 1392, 1394-6, 1398, 1413, 1445. [48] *Geo. IV Letters*, i. 1393; *Lady Palmerston Letters*, 174; *Lady Holland to Son*, 70; Add. 51742, Duncannon to Holland, 29 Sept.; 51833, Newport to same, 15 Aug.; Lansdowne mss, Duncannon to Abercromby, 19 Aug. 1827. [49] NLI, Monteagle mss 548, pp. 4-7, 15. [50] Add. 37305, ff. 163, 173; Brougham mss, Lamb to Brougham, 4, 28 Sept., 14 Oct.; PRO NI, Anglesey mss, same to Anglesey, 9 Sept.; Lansdowne mss, same to Lansdowne, 17, 20 Sept.; (3) 34, Holland to Lansdowne, 2 Dec.; Add. 51724, Duncannon to Holland [Oct.]; Panshanger mss F78, W. to F. Lamb, 11 Oct. 1827; Ziegler, 91-95; Torrens, i. 226-80. [51] Panshanger mss F78. [52] Add. 38753, ff. 3, 4; Grimsby Pub. Lib. Tennyson mss, Gregson to Tennyson, 17 Dec.; Lansdowne mss, Lamb to Lansdowne, 24 Dec.; Panshanger mss F78, W. to F. Lamb, 12 Jan. 1828. [53] *Melbourne Pprs.* 79-80; Torrens, i. 295-6; Add. 37305, ff. 236, 240-3, 246-7, 252, 254, 264. [54] *Geo. IV Letters*, iii. 1461; Wellington mss WP1/913/21; 918/20; Panshanger mss F78, W. to F. Lamb, 11, 12 Jan.; F40, same to Lady Branden, 18, 21 Jan. 1828. [55] Add. 38754, ff. 162, 182, 200, 219; 40395, f. 86; *Huskisson Pprs.* 285; Bulwer, *Palmerston*, i. 215-18; Fitzwilliam mss, Scarlett to Milton [c. 27 Jan.]; Panshanger mss F78, W. to F. Lamb, 28 Jan. 1828. [56] *Howard Sisters*, 107; Lady Airlie, i. 129; *Melbourne Pprs.* 80-81; Panshanger mss F40, Lamb to Lady Branden, 27-29 Jan., 4, 18, 21 Feb. 1828. [57] Wellington mss WP1/917/18; 923/13; Mq. of Anglesey, *One-Leg*, 194; Add. 38755, f. 263; 40396, ff. 90, 109. [58] Add. 40395, ff. 187, 218. [59] *Croker Pprs.* i. 419. [60] Bulwer, i. 239, 244-5; Anglesey mss, Lamb to Anglesey, 28 Mar. 1828; *Ellenborough Diary*, i. 112. [61] Bulwer, i. 272, 275; *Melbourne Pprs.* 117; *Arniston Mems.* 346; Brougham mss, Melbourne to Brougham, 2 Nov. 1838; Wellington mss WP1/933/13; Add. 38756, f. 171; 40322, f. 249; 40397, ff. 14, 15; 51564, Brougham to Lady Holland, 25 May; 51567, Anglesey to Holland, 28 May 1828. [62] Anglesey mss, Lamb to Anglesey, 27 May, 3 June; Add. 51567, Anglesey to Holland, 7 June 1828; Southampton Univ. Lib. Broadlands mss, Palmerston's memo. [June 1830]. [63] Lonsdale mss, Croker to Lowther, 10 June 1828. [64] Broughton, *Recollections*, iii. 280; Lonsdale mss, Lowther to Lonsdale, 5 [?July]; Add. 51574, Abercromby to Holland, 19 Nov. 1828; *Creevey's Life and Times*, 280. [65] See Ziegler, 106-10, 226-39. [66] *Greville Mems.* ii. 75. [67] Ibid. iii. 76. [68] See Ziegler, 127-342; *Oxford DNB*. [69] *Lady Palmerston Letters*, 266, 268-9, 302-3; *Lady Holland to Son*, 203, 205, 226, 230; *Greville Mems.* vi. 8, 128; Broughton, vi. 226-7. [70] Brougham mss, Melbourne to Brougham, 30 Jan. 1843; PROB 11/2090/209; IR26/1841/175; *Greville Mems.* vi. 139-40. [71] *Gent. Mag.* (1849), i. 83-87. [72] *CP*, viii. 639. [73] *Lady Holland to Son*, 158; *Life of Campbell*, ii. 204-5. [74] Bulwer, *Priv. Mem. of Melbourne* (1848), 2, 28-29. [75] *Greville Mems.* vi. 129-36. [76] *Melbourne Pprs.* 91.

D.R.F.

LAMBERT, Henry (1786–1861), of Carnagh, co. Wexford.

CO. WEXFORD 1831–1834

b. 1 Sept. 1786, 1st s. of Patrick Lambert of Carnagh and Mary Anne, da. of George Lattin of Morristown Lattin, co. Kildare. *m.* 11 June 1835, Catharine, da. of William Talbot of Castle Talbot, co. Wexford, 2s. 6da. (1 *d.v.p*). *suc.* fa. 1808. *d.* 20 Oct. 1861.

Lambert, the head of an old Catholic family, had for several years been active in the politics of county Wexford.[1] At the 1818 general election he assisted the return of a second pro-Catholic candidate, Caesar Colclough.[2] Following the 1826 general election, when another pro-Catholic, Arthur Chichester II*, was forced to withdraw, he began working for him and was credited with being chiefly responsible for an improvement in his standing.[3] He was a leading member of the county Liberal Club established in 1828 and a regular attender of county meetings for Catholic emancipation, which he publicly urged the duke of Wellington to concede, 26 Jan. 1829.[4] On 28 Apr. he wrote to Wellington that having done so, there was another 'great measure' open to him:

> The seats of many gentlemen have been demolished as they have been forced to sell their homes. They lost their estates because of a legislative Act. Nothing but misery and desolation can result from a system which decrees that the more successful a manufacturer becomes the more likely is his ruin and that all classes must surrender their property. The changes in the currency have meant that the number of buyers for merchandise has decreased. Overproduction has resulted and producers have become bankrupt. The present financial system is unsatisfactory. Since the end of the war Britain has trebled its national debt. The continuation of peace and this system is leading Britain to bankruptcy.[5]

On the retirement of his friend Robert Shapland Carew at the 1830 dissolution, Lambert offered as a 'thorough-going radical reformer', advocating reform in Parliament, the law, and the church, but condemning the 'mockery of free trade', under which 'commerce is nearly annihilated' and the agricultural interest 'deliberately and obstinately sacrificed'.[6] After a severe contest, in which Colclough and Chichester declined to assist him, he was defeated in third place, but promised to stand again.[7] Complaining that 'certain friendships that I have been for years in the habit of admitting as a matter of fact' had turned out to be 'a matter of farce when put on trial', he turned to Thomas Wyse* for 'advice and direction in the measures best calculated to place me as your zealous co-operator in the House', and for help in securing the Portsmouth interest in county Wexford at the next election.[8]

At the 1831 general election he offered as a reformer with the backing of the Grey ministry, Carew having assured Smith Stanley, the Irish secretary, he could 'depend upon Lambert's support in the House' and in support of the Union, for 'though a Catholic, he is strongly anti-agitation and shares the sentiments of Lord Killeen, Wyse, etc.'[9] On 10 May Lambert informed Smith Stanley that he would be 'quite unable to meet the whole of the heavy expense which must attend the contest' as his estate was 'heavily encumbered', whereupon £500 from the Reform Fund Committee was forthcoming.[10] After a six-day poll he was returned in second place.[11] In the House he campaigned relentlessly for inquiry into the Newtownbarry massacre of 18 June 1831 and for the disbanding of the Irish yeomanry, in support of which he brought up numerous petitions; he voted to print the one from Waterford, 11 Aug. On 30 June he unexpectedly withdrew a motion for information on the yeomanry in order not to 'embarrass' the government. (The previous day Smith Stanley, fearing that he would 'insist' on bringing it forward, had asked the foreign secretary Lord Palmerston* to 'call a cabinet to consider this whole question'.)[12] Lambert maintained that a report about the 'ripping open of the abdomen of a pregnant woman' at Newtownbarry was true and that the yeomanry had later fired over the chapel at the funeral of the victims, 31 Aug.; and on 9 Sept. he complained of having been denounced by the Orange press and warned that 'if justice be denied' the 'most lamentable consequences' would ensue. He voted for the second reading of the reintroduced reform bill, 6 July, at least twice against the adjournment, 12 July, and gave steady support to its detailed provisions, though he was in the minority for the disfranchisement of Saltash, 26 July, when he described reform 'as a new Magna Charta'. He voted against the grant for the Society for the Propagation of the Gospels in the colonies, 25 July. He divided against the disqualification of the Dublin election committee, 29 July, and the issue of a writ, 8 Aug., and with ministers on the controversy, 23 Aug. He voted against the Irish union of parishes bill, 19 Aug., and for legal provision for the Irish poor, 29 Aug. He welcomed the bill to create lord lieutenants of Irish counties, 20 Aug., and congratulated ministers on the 'impartiality' of their appointments, especially Carew for county Wexford, 6 Oct. He divided for the passage of the reform bill, 21 Sept., the second reading of the Scottish bill, 23 Sept., and Lord Ebrington's confidence motion, 10 Oct. He voted for inquiry into the conduct of the Winchester magistrates during the arrest of the Deacles, 27 Sept., and opposed the grant to the Royal Dublin Society, 29 Sept. 1831.

Lambert paired for the second reading of the revised reform bill, 17 Dec. 1831, was granted a fortnight's leave on account of ill health, 26 Jan., but gave steady support to its details and divided for the third reading, 22 Mar. 1832. Speaking against Alexander Baring's bill to exclude insolvent debtors from Parliament, 14 Feb., he said that there was 'scarcely a landed proprietor who has not some judgement debts against him' and asked 'how long Fox and Pitt and many other great men could have remained in the House' under it. He was in the hostile minority of four, 30 May, when he called for inquiry, and was a minority teller against it, 6 June. He spoke regularly against the 'tyrannical and oppressive' system of Irish tithes, presented numerous petitions for their abolition, and voted to print the one from Woollen Grange, 16 Feb. He divided against the Irish tithes bill, 8, 27, 30 Mar., when he implored ministers not to resort to coercion and was a teller for his own hostile amendment, which was lost by 130-25. On 10 July he warned that the bill would 'raise a new class of leaders for repeal of the Union' and complained that 'as in 1819' with the 'change in currency ... so now I shall probably be stripped of a portion of my property, but it shall be seized as I am determined never to pay'; he was again a minority teller, 13 July. He was in the minority of 28 for information on military punishments, 16 Feb. He welcomed the Irish Subletting Act amendment bill, 20 Feb., and supported the Maynooth grant, 11 Apr. That month Daniel O'Connell* was advised that Lambert, who 'deserves well of his county', would probably lose his seat at the next general election if the Conservatives succeeded at the expected by-election.[13] He voted for the address calling on the king to appoint only ministers who would carry reform unimpaired, 10 May, and the second reading of the Irish reform bill, 25 May, but was in the minority for the enfranchisement of Irish £5 freeholders, 18 June. He spoke and voted for a tax on absentee Irish landlords to provide permanent provision for the poor, 19 June. He divided with ministers on the Russian-Dutch loan, 12 July. He was granted a month's leave on 'urgent private business', 16 July. On 5 Sept. 1832 Carew informed Smith Stanley that there might be 'considerable difficulty' in getting 'moderate men' to support Lambert at the next election, as 'the warmth of his zeal' had offended some and

> vexes me, for when I originally supported him, he pledged himself to me to adopt my principles. However, a popular Member has a very difficult card in the present state of Ireland, and I know him to be attached to the British connection and constitution and thoroughly opposed to anarchy or violence.[14]

He stood as a Liberal at the 1832 general election and was comfortably returned in second place. He retired in 1834. In 1832 he published a *Letter on the Currency* to the chancellor of the exchequer Lord Althorp* denouncing the 'absurd' resumption of cash payments, under which Ireland, 'being entirely agricultural and possessing little money capital', had 'suffered even more severely than England' (pp. 7, 13, 28). His anonymous *Memoir of Ireland in 1850 by an ex-MP* (1851) also blamed the 1819 bank restriction for the 'degraded condition of Ireland' and alleged that the Irish Reform Act had created 'a monster borough at the sole disposal of one individual'. Urging Irish Catholics to reject their 'abject submission to the Whig party', he claimed that '*every concession ... from the first dawn of toleration to the repeal of the penal laws in 1829 was the work of Tories exclusively*' (pp. 1, 44, 92-93, 119). In 1852 he unsuccessfully contested New Ross as a Conservative. Lambert died in October 1861, described as 'one of the very few now remaining of the old guard that fought the battle of civil and religious liberty', and was succeeded by his elder son Henry Patrick Lambert (1836-96).[15]

[1] *Wexford Herald*, 28 July, 18 Aug. 1830. [2] NLI, Wyse mss 15024 (1), Lambert to Wyse, 7 Aug. 1830. [3] Ibid. (10), Anthony to Wyse, 3 Aug. 1830. [4] *Wexford Evening Post*, 30 Jan. 1829. [5] Wellington mss WP1/1013/3. [6] Wyse mss (1), Lambert to Wyse, 6 July; *Wexford Herald*, 10 July, 14, 18 Aug. 1830. [7] *Wexford Herald*, 21, 28 Aug.; *Dublin Evening Post*, 17, 19, 21 Aug. 1830. [8] Wyse mss (7), Lambert to Wyse, 26 Aug., 13 Sept. 1830. [9] TCD, Shapland Carew mss 4020/25; Derby mss 920 Der (14) 128/15, Carew to Stanley, 25 Apr. 1831. [10] Derby mss 125/11; Shapland Carew mss 26. [11] *Wexford Independent*, 29 Apr., 3, 13, 17, 20, 24 May 1831. [12] Grey mss, Smith Stanley to Grey, [29 June] 1831. [13] *O'Connell Corresp.* iv. 1885. [14] Derby mss 128/15. [15] *Dublin Evening Post*, 24 Oct. 1861.

P.J.S.

LAMBERT, James Staunton (1789–1867), of Creg Clare, co. Galway.

CO. GALWAY 11 Apr. 1827–1832

b. 5 Mar. 1789, 1st s. of Walter Lambert of Creg Clare and 2nd w. Catherine, da. and coh. of James Staunton of Waterdale, Herts. *educ.* Dr. Thomas Jones's sch. Redland, Bristol, Glos.; Trinity, Dublin 1806; King's Inns 1809. *m.* 25 Sept. 1832, Hon. Camden Elizabeth Maclellan Gray, da. and h. of Camden, 10th Lord Kirkcudbright [S], 5s. (1 *d.v.p.*) 2da. (1 *d.v.p.*). *suc.* fa. 1822. *d.* 1 July 1867.

Sheriff, co. Galway 1814-15.

Lambert, whose family originated in Yorkshire, was the great-grandson of Walter Lambert, who in 1726 acquired the lease of Creg Clare, which passed to his eldest son Charles, and in 1729 purchased Aggard, the residence of his second son John and his descendants; his third (Peter) and fourth (Thomas) sons founded the Castle Ellen and Castle Lambert branches of this county Galway gentry family.[1] James Lambert, whose father may have been the 'Mr. Lambert' admitted to Brooks's in 1801, came briefly to prominence in Galway in 1812, when he was the only Protestant gentleman who refused to sign the county Member Richard Martin's pro-Catholic petition.[2] This seems to have been an aberration, for thereafter he was a minor figure among the liberal freeholders: for example, he was a member of the Whig Denis Bowes Daly's† committee at the 1818 county election, chaired the meeting of independents in the borough in March 1820 and signed requisitions for county meetings to address the new lord lieutenant Lord Wellesley in February and to complain about agricultural distress in November 1822.[3] He succeeded to Creg Clare on the death of his father, 21 Sept. 1822.

In the summer of 1824 Lambert was considered a potential candidate for county Galway or the town, particularly as the nominee of Lord Clanricarde, with whose family he was connected through his father's first wife. Doubts arose about his attitude to Catholic relief, but in early October he wrote to a local newspaper to insist that he supported it and had signed many favourable petitions.[4] He assisted in the promotion of the county's pro-Catholic petition in February and attended separate meetings of its Catholics and Protestants for the same purpose in August 1825.[5] He declined to attend the Catholic Association dinner on 2 Feb. 1826, but that month he again signed another favourable petition from county Galway.[6] His conversion to the Catholic cause was supposed by some to be of recent date and he was attacked over this by Martin, who was reckoned to be vulnerable to him, especially as James Daly, the other sitting Tory Member, was thought to be in league with Clanricarde. Yet he promised the independents in the borough to continue to work for their interests against Daly, the patron of the corporation, and seconded the resolution to this effect at their meeting, 24 May.[7] He duly offered at the general election that summer, when he defended himself from Martin's aspersions on the hustings but was eventually pushed narrowly into third place by him after a desperate contest, during which his brother Thomas accidentally shot dead a rioter. He blamed his defeat on the intimidation used against his voters and the desertion of the key interest belonging to Arthur St. George, with whom he quarrelled, and he missed the Protestants' pro-Catholic county meeting, 4 Sept.[8] His petition was lodged in December 1826, and, despite last ditch opposition, he was seated in place of Martin the following April.

Lambert, who hardly spoke in the House except to bring up petitions, sided with the Canning ministry against the disfranchisement of Penryn, 28 May, and for the grant for water communications in Canada, 12 June 1827. He attended the meeting of the Catholics of county Galway, 19 Aug. 1827, and voted for repeal of the Test Acts, 26 Feb., and Catholic relief, 12 May 1828. He paired for Fyler's motion to repeal the Act prohibiting the use of ribbons at elections, 20 Mar. He voted against the Wellington administration for various economies, 20 June, 4, 7 July, and inquiry into the Irish church, 24 June, and against the additional churches bill, 30 June, and the corporate funds bill, 10 July. He approved the formation of a liberal club in Galway town that autumn, when he signed the Irish Protestants' declaration in favour of Catholic claims.[9] As chairman of the Connaught provincial meeting of the friends of civil and religious liberty, he stated that he had supported Canning but opposed the Wellington administration because of its hostility to the Catholics, 8 Oct. 1828, and he was active in promoting the county's address to the recalled lord lieutenant, Lord Anglesey, in January 1829.[10] He voted for emancipation, 6, 30 Mar., and presented and endorsed the favourable petition from Tuam on the grounds that it would secure 'the peace and prosperity of Ireland', 18 Mar., but he divided against the second reading of the related franchise measure, 19 Mar. He was in minorities for allowing Daniel O'Connell to take his seat unimpeded, 18 May, and against the grant for the marble arch, 25 May 1829.

Lambert chaired the Galway independents' meeting for extending the franchise of the town to Catholics, 30 Aug. 1829, and spoke for this in the House, 4 Mar. 1830.[11] He voted for parliamentary reform, 18 Feb., 28 May, the enfranchisement of Birmingham, Leeds and Manchester, 23 Feb., and (as in the previous two sessions) to transfer East Retford's seats to Birmingham, 5, 15 Mar. He divided for information on Portugal, 10 Mar., and Labouchere's motion on Canada, 25 May. He paired for inquiry into distress, 23 Mar., and voted steadily in the opposition's revived campaign for economies and tax reductions that year. He divided for Jewish emancipation, 5 Apr., 17 May. He voted for alteration of the Irish vestry laws, 27 Apr., and abolition of the Irish lord lieutenancy, 11 May, and joined in the Irish Members' agitation against the increased stamp and spirit duties towards the end of the session. He signed the requisition for a county Galway meeting on this in June 1830, when his parliamentary duties, including those relating to the Galway franchise bill, kept him in London.[12] He offered on the basis of his past conduct at the general election that year, when he received O'Connell's endorsement and may have been the 'James Lambert' who voted for the defeated independent Valentine Blake[†] in the Galway borough contest. On the hustings, where he accepted all the pledges put to the candidates, he stressed his opposition to ministers' inadequate reductions and advocated parliamentary reform, but insisted that he was of no party. He led throughout the ensuing contest and was returned ahead of Clanricarde's uncle Sir John Burke, with whom he was thought to be in collusion; he survived a petition.[13] He signed the resolutions establishing the county's Election Club that autumn.[14]

Lambert voted for O'Connell's motion to repeal the Irish Subletting Act, 11 Nov., and Parnell's for reducing the duty on wheat imported to the West Indies, 12 Nov., and he commented on the Galway town election petition, 6 Dec. 1830. Having been listed by ministers among their 'foes', he divided in the majority against them on the civil list, 15 Nov. 1830. He signed requisitions for (but did not attend) county Galway reform meetings in January and April 1831.[15] He voted for the second reading of the Grey ministry's reform bill, 22 Mar., and against Gascoyne's wrecking amendment, 19 Apr. Blaming the need for the ensuing dissolution on the 'machinations of a factious oligarchy', he stood again and was returned unopposed with Burke as a reformer at the general election that spring, when he seconded the successful liberal candidate John James Bodkin in Galway borough.[16] He voted for the second reading of the reintroduced reform bill, 6 July, at least twice against adjourning proceedings on it, 12 July, and steadily for its details, though he voted against the division of counties, 11 Aug. He was in minorities against two grants, 18, 25 July, and for printing the Waterford petition for disarming the Irish yeomanry, 11 Aug. He sided with ministers for prosecuting those guilty of bribery at the Dublin election, 23 Aug., but apparently did not vote in the division on censuring the Irish government over this that day. He divided for the passage of the reform bill, 21 Sept., and Lord Ebrington's confidence motion, 10 Oct. 1831.

Lambert, of whom one radical publication noted that he 'votes well', left the House before the division on the second reading of the revised bill, 17 Dec. 1831.[17] He explained to his constituents that month that he had done so because of the predominance of manufacturing over agricultural seats and the granting to town freeholders (of counties of towns) the right to vote in the surrounding county, as well as the inadequate number of additional Irish seats; it was also thought to mark his disapproval of the Irish government.[18] However, he voted to go into committee on the bill, 20 Jan., again usually for its details and for the third reading, 22 Mar. 1832. He divided against government on the Russian-Dutch loan, 26 Jan., for inquiry into Peterloo, 15 Mar., to recommit the Irish registrar of deeds bill, 9 Apr., to abolish colonial slavery, 24 May, and reduce the barracks grant, 2 July. He voted for printing the Woollen Grange petition for the abolition of Irish tithes, 16 Feb., Brownlow's motion to adjourn the debate on this until the completion of the select committee's deliberations, 8 Mar., amendments to the ministerial resolutions, 27, 30 Mar., and to postpone the subject to the next session, 13 July. He divided for Ebrington's motion for an address calling on the king to appoint only ministers who would carry reform unimpaired, 10 May, and the second reading of the Irish bill, 25 May, but for O'Connell's amendment to enfranchise £5 freeholders, 18 June. He was overshadowed by his much more active and advanced Whig namesake Henry Lambert, Member for Wexford, with whom he may sometimes have been confused in the parliamentary reports, but he was appointed to the select committee on the recent Irish outrages, 31 May, and it was probably he who vindicated the 40*s*. freeholders of Galway borough as 'a most industrious, respectable and hard working class of persons', 29 June 1832.

Pleading ill health brought on by his laborious parliamentary duties, Lambert, who married the heiress of a recently deceased Scottish peer that autumn, retired at the dissolution in 1832.[19] He proposed the Liberal Martin Joseph Blake† for Galway borough at the general election of 1835, but at that of 1841, when he produced a written protest against the return of Valentine Blake, his family affairs were bandied about in a disgraceful fashion and he was forced to flee the hooting mob by escaping through a back door of the court house.[20] He proposed the Conservative Christopher St. George† for the county at the general election of 1847, and another, Robert Daly, in 1852, when he was shouted down.[21] He sold Creg Clare to Lord Clanmorris for £19,000 in about 1855 and presumably thereafter settled at Waterdale, the Hertfordshire estate which he had inherited from his mother's family, the Stauntons, three of whom had represented Galway borough in the Irish Parliament.[22] He died at his then residence in Budleigh Salterton, Devon in July 1867, leaving six surviving children, of whom the eldest, Captain Walter Maclellan (*b*. 1833), had retired from the 41st Foot in 1860.[23]

[1] J. Fahey, *Hist. and Antiquities of Diocese of Kilmacduagh*, 317-19; *Lamberts of Athenry* ed. F. O'Regan, 41. [2] S. Lynam, *Humanity Dick*, 160, 243. [3] J. Kelly, 'Politics of "Protestant Ascendancy": Co. Galway', *Galway Hist. and Soc.* ed. G. Moran and R. Gillespie, 261; *Dublin Evening Post*, 28 Mar. 1820, 16 Feb.; *Dublin Weekly Reg.* 16 Nov. 1822. [4] *Connaught Jnl.* 20 May, 17, 24 June, 9 Aug., 7 Oct.; *Dublin Evening Post*, 9, 25 Sept. 1824. [5] *Connaught Jnl.* 10 Feb., 28 Mar., 8, 11, 18 Aug. 1825. [6] Ibid. 20 Feb. 1826; *O'Connell Corresp.* iii. 1278. [7] *Connaught Jnl.* 15, 20 Apr., 1, 25 May 1826. [8] Ibid. 12, 22 June, 3, 6, 10, 13, 17 July, 17 Aug., 4 Sept. 1826. [9] Ibid. 29 Sept.; *Dublin Evening Mail*, 8 Oct. 1828. [10] *Dublin Evening Post*, 14 Oct. 1828; *Connaught Jnl.* 26 Jan. 1829. [11] *Connaught Jnl.* 31 Aug. 1829. [12] Ibid. 10 May, 14, 17, 21 June 1830. [13] Ibid. 12, 19 July, 12, 16, 19, 23 Aug. 1830. [14] Ibid. 30 Sept., 4 Oct. 1830. [15] Ibid. 20, 24, 27 Jan., 31 Mar., 4, 7 Apr. 1831. [16] Ibid. 2, 9, 12 May 1831. [17] [W. Carpenter], *People's Bk.* (1831), 311. [18] *Connaught Jnl.* 22, 29 Dec. 1831. [19] Ibid. 6 Aug. 1832. [20] Ibid. 22 Jan. 1835, 10 July 1841. [21] *Galway Vindicator*, 11 Aug. 1847, 24 July 1852. [22] Fahey, 319; P.G. Lane, 'Encumbered Estates Court and Galway Land Ownership', *Galway Hist. and Soc.* 409; *Hist. Irish Parl.* vi. 325-8. [23] *Galway Vindicator*, 3 July 1867; *Gent. Mag.* (1867), ii. 259.

S.M.F.

LAMBTON, John George (1792–1840), of Lambton Hall, Chester-Le-Street, co. Dur.; Wimbledon, Surr., and 13 Cleveland Row, Mdx.[1]

DURHAM CO. 20 Sept. 1813–29 Jan. 1828

b. 12 Apr. 1792, 1st s. of William Henry Lambton† of Lambton and Lady Anne Barbara Frances Villiers, da. of George Bussy Villiers†, 4th earl of Jersey. *educ*. by Dr. Thomas Beddoes at Clifton, Glos. 1798-1805; Eton 1805-8. *m*. (1) 1 Jan. 1812, at Gretna Green, Harriet (*d*. 11 July 1815), illegit. da. of George James Cholmondeley, 4th earl of Cholmondeley, 3da. *d.v.p.*; (2) 9 Dec. 1816, Lady Louisa Elizabeth Grey, da. of Charles Grey†, 2nd Earl Grey, 2s. (1 *d.v.p.*) 3da. *suc*. fa. 1797; *cr*. Bar. Durham 29 Jan. 1828; earl of Durham 23 Mar. 1833; GCB 27 June 1837. *d*. 28 July 1840.

Cornet 1 Drag. 1809, lt. 1810, ret. 1811.

Ld. privy seal Nov. 1830-Mar. 1833; PC 22 Nov. 1830; spec. mission to Prussia, Russia and Austria 1832; ambassador extraordinary to Russia 1835-7; gov.-gen. Canada Jan.-Dec. 1838.

High steward, Hull 1836.

'Radical Jack' Lambton, a handsome, wealthy, talented, unhappy man, whose 17,000-acre estate in north-east County Durham contained a lucrative coalfield, was, with Lord John Russell*, the Whig standard bearer of parliamentary reform in this period.[2] As Lord Grey's son-in-law, his authority in the party was potentially considerable, but arrogance, impetuosity and a vile temper made him unpopular. Princess Lieven thought him 'clever, disagreeable, violent'; Tom Macaulay* referred to his 'bitter, vindictive, pugnacious spirit'; Lord William Lennox* recalled him as 'often ... bursting with passion when thwarted', and Guizot perceived in his 'haughty melancholy a strong imprint of egotism and vanity'.[3] Henry Brougham* acknowledged his 'many good and some great qualities', though they were 'much obscured, and even perverted, by his temper', for which his affliction with agonizing neuralgia was partly responsible.[4] Poor health in general undermined him, for he was haunted by the spectre of the consumption which had killed his father at the age of 33 and his first wife even younger, had laid its mark on himself and was a harrowing threat to the lives of his children.[5]

His notice in December 1819 of a motion for extensive reform had alarmed the Whig hierarchy, notably Lord Holland, and earned him a rebuke, which he returned with interest, from Grey.[6] At the general election of 1820 Lambton, who Grey thought was 'goading his adversaries ... unnecessarily', faced a concerted Tory bid to turn him out of his county seat. At the nomination he denounced the grants to the royal dukes, the imposition of heavy taxes 'for the benefit of placemen and pensioners, and for extending the influence of corruption', the Foreign Enlistment Act and the repressive legislation after Peterloo. He won after a six-day contest which cost him about £30,000 and '31 hours of incessant pain' in the head, and was reckoned to have made himself secure 'for the remainder of his life'.[7] On 28 Apr. he gave notice of his reform motion for 6 June, and on 12 May he endorsed the prayer of the Newcastle merchants' reform petition. At the annual Westminster purity of election dinner, 23 May, the Members Burdett and Hobhouse toasted his health and 'success' to his reform motion.[8] He condemned the aliens bill and was a minority teller against it, 1 June. He divided with Brougham against the ministerial amendment to restrict the scope of the inquiry into agricultural distress, 31 May.[9] On 19 June Sir James Mackintosh*, who realised that Lambton's 'liver complaints [were] so dreadful that they abate my dislike of his temper', recorded that the previous evening he had been overcome 'by headache and giddiness', having 'seen flashes from both his eyes which seemed to run into a ball of fire'.[10] He first postponed and then deferred to next session his reform motion in view of the impending affair of Queen Caroline; he voted against Wilberforce's compromise resolution, 22 June 1820.

Lambton, who was kept abreast of the trial by his friend Sir Robert Wilson*, had planned to go to Paris that October, but in the event stayed in England. He was in the House when Parliament was summarily prorogued, 23 Nov. 1820.[11] Next day he persuaded Tierney, the Whig Commons leader, to write to Grey urging the importance of the party's taking the lead in promoting county meetings in support of the queen. The initially overcautious Grey admired the 'spirit, energy and zeal' with which Lambton organized a Durham meeting, 13 Dec. 1820, when he declared that it was 'a melancholy sign of the times and of the corruption of the [Liverpool] administration ... that every year the nation had to complain of some additional act of oppression' and accused the government, which was 'suspended, like Mahomet's tomb, between the crown and the people', of conniving in the Holy Alliance's suppression of liberal movements on the continent. The conservative Whig William Lamb* thought his denunciation of the 'confederate tyrants at Troppeau' was 'pretty language for the son-in-law of the future secretary of state for foreign affairs to hold in the presence of that expectant minister'.[12] The persecution of Caroline was one of the topics of Lambton's speech at the Edinburgh Fox dinner, 12 Jan. 1821, when he called for reform. He and Grey paid their personal respects to the queen, 28 Jan.[13] Presenting and endorsing the Stockton petition in her support, 24 Jan., he urged the House to 'pay a degree of attention to the sentiments and prayers of the people', most of whom were 'in avowed and open hostility, not to the sovereign, but to his ministers'. He presented similar petitions from Durham, 31 Jan., Yarm, 1 Feb., Barnard Castle, 2 Feb., and Chester-le-Street, 6 Feb.[14] He made a splash as seconder of the opposition censure motion, 5 Feb., when he said that its inevitable defeat would confirm the need to reform the Commons. The radical Whig Henry Grey Bennet* thought it 'a remarkable good speech, moderate and rational' and, though clearly 'of great preparation ... well got up'; while his fellow 'Mountaineer' Thomas Creevey considered it 'a very pretty, natural and ornamental speech, delivered with singular grace and discretion, and in a beautiful voice'.[15] The Tory Henry Bankes* conceded that Lambton 'acquitted himself extremely well, and without any of that arrogance and petulance which he has sometimes wanted taste or temper to conceal'.[16] Grey was pleased with his success and hoped it would have 'a beneficial effect on him, by making him exert himself more than he has yet done'. When commenting on Tierney's inadequacies as leader a few days later he asserted that

> Lambton might do it, if he had industry and ambition. But the last does not excite him beyond the effort of a speech. When he has obtained the applause of having done well he is satisfied, and relaxes into those habits of self-indulgence which by the faults of his education, and being too early his own master he has unfortunately contracted.[17]

There was talk among the Westminster activists of asking Lambton to chair the public meeting called to address Burdett on his imprisonment for seditious libel, from 'a hope that the Whigs would subscribe', but Hobhouse knocked this idea on the head.[18] Lambton divided against the additional malt duty, 14 Feb., and the tax on husbandry horses, 5 Mar., and on 22 Feb. 1821 presented a County Durham petition complaining of agricultural distress, but said he 'did not think that protecting duties would give any relief ... while the present weight of taxation' remained. He presented petitions from Sunderland ship owners for revision of the timber duties and from Stockton corporation for reform of the criminal code, 26 Feb.[19] He voted to deplore the Allies' suppression of the liberal movement in Naples, 21 Feb., and for Catholic relief, 28 Feb. He spoke and voted for reception of Broadhurst's petition complaining of his treatment in Lancaster gaol, 7 Mar., and on the 9th unsuccessfully moved the previous question against a Tory allegation of breach of privilege by the Whig *Morning Chronicle*. Lambton, who was believed by the backbencher Hudson Gurney to be on the 'economical committee of five' which took over direction of the opposition after Tierney's resignation,[20] was in Creevey's minority for a reduction in the number of placemen in the Commons, 9 Mar., and joined in the obstructive resistance to the army estimates, 12 Mar., when his motion to prolong affairs at four in the morning was defeated by 146-38. He cast sporadic votes against the estimates, 14 Mar., 6, 16 Apr., 14, 21 May. At the *London Tavern* reform dinner, 4 Apr., he prefaced his Commons motion by explaining that he had taken the initiative as no other Whig had seemed willing to do so. He asserted that 'every species of corruption ... was vindicated with astonishing effrontery' in the unrepresentative House, called for unity among reformers, sketched the details of his scheme and rejoiced that on the continent liberalism was 'breaking through the dark clouds of ignorance and tyranny'.[21] Presenting a petition from an inhabitant of Sligo alleging that most of its residents were excluded from the franchise, 11 Apr., he said that he 'believed that many other Irish boroughs were similarly circumstanced, and that the burgesses in most of them might be inhabitants of Nova Zembla'.[22] Next day he presented a petition from the resident freeholders of Lyme Regis complaining of Lord Westmorland's electoral control and supported an unsuccessful bid to have it referred to the committee of privileges (of which he was a member). According to Hobhouse, 'many efforts' were made by the Whigs 'to induce Lambton to postpone his [reform] motion [of 17 Apr.] owing to [an] adjourned debate in the Lords [on the Catholic relief bill and] Castlereagh and Burdett's absence', but he would not listen. After describing the 'improved intelligence' of the people and asserting that about 180 individuals returned some 350 Members, he proposed an extension of the franchise to householders in the equal single Member districts with which he wished to replace the existing English boroughs, and to copy and leaseholders in the counties, triennial parliaments and curbs on election expenses. Hobhouse thought he spoke 'well, but detailed his plan too much, and spoke too much on foreign politics'; while George Agar Ellis* felt he 'spoke remarkably well'. The debate was adjourned to the following day, when Canning took advantage of Lambton's absence from the chamber for refreshment to divide a thin House by 55-43 against the motion. When Lambton returned to find the House engaged on other business he was greeted with mocking laughter from the government side, which enraged him and prompted him to accuse the ministers Huskisson and George Dawson of ridiculing him and to move an adjournment, but the Speaker slapped him down.[23] According to Grey Bennet, when he next appeared in the House to vote for Russell's reform motion, 9 May

> he would not sit amongst us, but sat with Burdett on the neutral bench ... His conduct on this subject drives me half wild. With great talents and acquirements, his temper makes them useless and unpredictable, and I foresee that he will ruin himself as a public man unless he changes his whole course and character. He is a spoiled child; unless he has his way he will do nothing; and with many virtues and splendid qualities, his habitual indulgence of passion and his determination to brook no check or control will make him quarrel with his friends, and be of no benefit to the cause he espouses. He openly accuses all of us who voted in the minority upon his ... [motion]

of being in a conspiracy to ruin him ... and that he never more will act with ... us. It is in vain to tell him that he has nobody to blame but himself, and if he had not adjourned the debate and gone out to dinner, nothing of the nature that did happen would have occurred.[24]

He was in Paris in late June 1821. Three months later Creevey, who disliked him, recorded one of his 'sublimities', to the effect that 'he considered £40,000 a moderate income [and] such a one as a man *might jog on with*'; henceforward he was 'King Jog' in Creevey's menagerie.[25] Incensed by the dismissal of Wilson from the army for his involvement in the disturbances at the queen's funeral – 'it is a consolation', he wrote, 'to think that you have experienced the ministerial vengeance in the name of humanity' – he contributed £500 to the relief subscription and advised Wilson during the autumn of 1821.[26] In mid-December he took his wife and Lady Ossulston 'over to Calais on a stormy day *in an open boat*', to the astonishment of Henry Fox*, who noted that 'his insolence to everybody and his tyranny in his family are insufferable' and 'his temper and selfishness pass all credited or permitted bounds'. Grey evidently chastised him by letter for his 'unjustifiable rashness', but Lambton sent an indignant reply from Paris, 2 Jan. 1822, claiming that the trip had been Louisa's idea and that the weather had been fine when they set off. He subsequently apologized for his abrasive tone.[27]

He divided for the amendment to the address, 5 Feb. 1822, but reported to Grey next day that there had been 'a very bad attendance' and that 'amongst the old stagers of what was our party in the House of Commons there seems the greatest apathy', although ministers had 'cut a subservient figure without Canning'. He divided steadily against the Irish insurrection bill, 8 Feb., but was disgusted 'to hear so many of our friends praising Lord Wellesley', the new pro-Catholic viceroy, and 'offering to grant ... supreme powers [to] a man who proved himself in India to be the greatest despot that ever governed that country'. He begged Grey to come to London as it was 'impossible to conceive anything more disunited than the opposition, many anxious to be in action, but not knowing what to do and having no one to point out to them the best mode'.[28] He was one of the 21 Whigs shut out of the division on further tax reductions, 11 Feb., when he was hosting a dinner party;[29] but he was present to vote for a similar motion, 21 Feb. Although he disapproved of Wilson's handling his own case, 13 Feb., he 'supported him as well as I could, but under the disadvantage of one of my *very worst headaches* ... so that I was fitter for bed than the House'; he was a teller for the minority. He cast doubt on the success of the government's plan to relieve agricultural distress, 15 Feb.[30] He voted for inquiry into the Scottish burghs, 20 Feb., and fairly regularly for economy, retrenchment and reduced taxation until Easter. He presented petitions from Malton, 13 Mar., and Sunderland, 2 May, for mitigation of the criminal code.[31] He presented and endorsed one for Henry Hunt's* release from gaol, but dissociated himself from his 'principles and politics', 22 Mar.; he was a teller for the minority of 22 and divided for remission of Hunt's sentence, 24 Apr. He voted silently for Russell's reform motion, 25 Apr. He presented a Durham tanners' petition for repeal of the leather tax, 1 May, and two from the ship owners of Sunderland and North Shields against the navigation bill, 6 May, when he said that while he was not opposed to alteration of the laws, he would resist the measure, despite 'his own sentiments in favour of free trade', unless ministers convinced him that it would do no harm. He brought up a hostile South Shields petition, 20 May.[32] He was in the minority of 36 against the new corn duties, 9 May, and presented petitions in favour of the poor removal bill, 31 May 1822.[33] According to Hobhouse, who had heard that Lambton approved of Burdett's recent conduct and was 'eager' to attend the Westminster anniversary dinner, Lord Tavistock* told him that he was one of the 'many who would have nothing to do with a measure unless they originated it' and was therefore unlikely to back Tavistock's fanciful notion of installing Burdett as opposition leader in the Commons. Lady Grey's illness prevented Lambton from attending the dinner.[34]

Later that summer he put on a show of 'magnificence' to entertain the duke of Sussex at Lambton. At Cantley for the St. Leger in September he ran into Creevey, who reported:

[He] brought with him *nine* race horses ... [and] is in the greatest possible feather, and does not in the least disguise from one that it is *he* and not the duke of Sussex who has received the universal adulation of the north ... He is evidently deeply affected at this probability of Canning staying at home [as foreign secretary], which he is pleased to consider as *fatal* ... Not that he ... wishes ... to see Lord Grey take office; *quite the contrary*, he believes it would be a very bad thing for him and his friends ... He predicts that Canning will carry all before him in the ... Commons, and that the unhappy Whigs are once more removed for ages from their favourite object ... What a victim of temper poor Lambton is! He has been complaining to me of his *unhappiness*. I observed ... that he had a good many of the articles men in general considered as tolerable ingredients for promoting happiness; to which he replied, 'I don't know that; but I *do* know that it's damned hard that a man with £80,000 a year can't

> sleep!' He has not much merit but his looks, his property and his voice and power of public speaking. He has not the slightest power or turn for conversation, and would like to live exclusively on the flattery of toadies.[35]

Fox witnessed more displays of temper at the annual gathering for Lambton races in October.[36] Yet when Lambton travelled with Creevey to Lord Sefton's* home at Croxteth the following month he was 'very amiable ... barring one volcanic eruption against the post boys for losing their way'. He shunned a proposed 'committee of foreigners in distress' because it involved 'four Saints', who he said would 'appropriate part of the money to the use of the blacks at Demerara'. He argued to Creevey (who now called him 'the angry Boy') that 'if ... the Whigs could but arrange our matters between ourselves, the sovereign would be happy to send for us'. After his departure Creevey and Sefton laughed immoderately at his assertion 'in the *strictest* confidence that it is of vital importance' to get Brougham's consent to James Scarlett's* becoming lord chancellor and himself attorney-general in a Whig administration.[37] With Grey's blessing, he sounded Lord Darlington, the lord lieutenant, on the possibility of convening a Durham county meeting to declare 'the necessity of reform', but the idea was given up for lack of time and because, as Lambton admitted, he had 'not been pressed by a single individual in the county to agitate the subject'.[38]

From London in February 1823 he told Grey that in the 'kind of armistice' which prevailed pending the outcome of the Franco-Spanish contretemps, 'nothing is doing in the House worth your hearing'. He took a keen interest in the struggles of the Spanish liberals and with James Macdonald* helped to organize a City dinner in their support.[39] According to Brougham, he was 'ailing' at the beginning of March, when he informed Grey that he did not

> like the way in which we are acting with regard to ministers. I think it will be found that they have taken advantage of the confidence granted to them to strengthen the Spanish cause, in order to intrigue ... to induce the Spaniards to alter their constitution. We have thrown our confidence at their heads without them asking for it and I fear we shall pay the penalty of our folly. I do not like to do anything without your advice and therefore I have not said anything in the House, which I otherwise felt inclined to do.[40]

He remained silent on this subject, but was a regular in the opposition division lobby that month. He presented petitions from Sunderland, 4 Mar., and Darlington, 10 Mar., for repeal of the Insolvent Debtors Act, and one from Sunderland, 27 Mar., for repeal of the coastal coal duties, on which topic he had earlier submitted to Liverpool a memorial from local colliery and ship owners.[41] On 24 Mar. he spoke and voted for the production of papers relevant to the prosecution of the Dublin Orange rioters, arguing that a '*prima facie*' case of 'injustice and unconstitutional conduct had been made out' against the renegade Whig William Plunket*, the Irish attorney-general. He was in the opposition majority for a parliamentary inquiry, 22 Apr. In mid-March he and Lord Duncannon* were said to have written to Brougham 'about some plan of a republican form of government for the opposition'.[42] He put up his brother Henry, who was abroad, to oppose the re-election of the ministerialist Hardinge for Durham in early April, but he was trounced. Lambton divided for repeal of the Foreign Enlistment Act, 16 Apr., and Russell's reform motion, 24 Apr. He presented petitions from the ship owners of South Shields and Newcastle against the warehousing bill, 21 Apr., and one from the former against the imposition of additional duties on account of the rebuilding of London Bridge. 16 May.[43] He went to the Westminster dinner, 23 May, sat at the head of the table next to the chairman Hobhouse and spoke in support of the Spanish and Greek liberals. Hobhouse recorded that he

> had a little sparring with Hume, to which Colonel Torrens* ... drew the attention of the company. Lambton was mightily out of sorts and said a fatality attended him and he would give up public life. I told him no notice would be taken by the press, and so it turned out.[44]

He continued to work for the Spaniards, chairing a meeting of the subcommittee appointed to organize a public meeting, 27 May 1823, and proposing a subscription to finance the sending of arms to Vigo, to which he gave £1,000.[45]

On 7 Jan. 1824 Lambton, who had been 'bilious and nervous' lately, got into a furious row with one Thomas Pemberton, a 'blackguard' under prosecution for excise fraud, at a meeting of the River Wear commissioners. His friends talked him out of the folly of fighting a duel with such a reprobate. He managed to keep the episode from his wife and was convinced by the warmth of his reception at a Newcastle Masonic dinner, 27 Jan., that he had acted honourably. Not anticipating any pressing business in the Commons early in the session, he went to stay with Grey in Devonport and did not reach London until the first week in March, to join a deputation of northern colliery owners who urged Robinson, the chancellor of the exchequer, not to alter the coal duties to their disadvantage. His wife's uncle Edward Ellice* had warned Grey that Lambton would be 'very angry with his political friends' should they attack the 'northern confederacy'.[46] In the House, 1 Apr., he denied that the owners were trying to establish a monopoly. Grey had authorized him to start his eldest son Lord Howick* for Northumberland if the unstable Tory Member Beaumont vacated his seat, as seemed likely. Lambton was keen to finance a campaign to prevent the seat falling to the duke of Northumberland's candidate, but in the event Beaumont remained in place.[47] Lambton presented petitions from the worsted spinners and woollen manufacturers of Darlington against the export of long wool and one from Barnard Castle for the abolition of slavery, 15 Mar., and ten from Durham to the same effect, 16 Mar. He brought up the petition of Sunderland ship owners for an end to drawback on cordage for their Canadian competitors, 25 Mar. He presented petitions from South Shields, Gateshead and Barnard Castle against the hides and skins bill, 29, 31 Mar.[48] He 'could not help but laugh' at Canning's mockery of fat Lord Nugent's* Spanish military exploits, 18 Mar.[49] He persuaded Hobhouse to divide the House on his amendment to the motion to bring in the aliens bill, 23 Mar.[50] On 2 Apr. he 'had some good fun with that vulgar beast Hume' over the grant for the expenses of Sir William Congreve* as inspector-general of gas light companies: when Hume accused him of being an interested party he retorted that 'if he did not absolutely supply the gas companies with the material from which their smoke was produced, they might go to ...[Hume] for the pipes which conveyed it'.[51] He presented petitions against the combination laws from Sunderland boot makers, 5 Apr., and Darlington artisans, 9 Apr., and a Darlington petition for the county courts bill, 8 Apr.[52] On 5 Apr. he told Grey that having been 'so plagued with headache since the first week of my arrival at Devonport' and finding no relief from calomel treatment, he had consulted another doctor, who had subjected him, beneficially, to the 'disagreeable operation' of cupping. At Easter he went to try the waters at Cheltenham, but suffered 'extreme languor, with considerable headache, in addition to a cold in the head'.[53] He voted for repeal of the assessed taxes, 10 May, and inquiry into the state of Ireland, 11 May. At the Westminster dinner, 24 May, as Hobhouse noted, he (like Burdett) 'expatiated on the inutility of attending Parliament', where 'a system of humbug' prevailed, to the silent annoyance of Hume. He added that on reform he wanted 'a free and extended suffrage' of householders at least, and attacked the government's 'arbitrary principles' and 'temporizing measures' which had inflicted 'misery' on Ireland.[54] Next day he presented and endorsed Silk Buckingham's petition alleging infringement of press freedom in India; Hobhouse thought he performed 'very well', as a 'very neat, and indeed finished parliamentary speaker'.[55] He presented a Barnard Castle petition deploring the prosecution in Demerara of the Methodist missionary John Smith, 26 May, and voted thus, 11 June. On 14 June 1824 he presented and endorsed the petition of the artist Benjamin Haydon for the encouragement of historical painting. According to Creevey, the 'ill-fated, ill-conditioned' Lambton got into 'another fighting scrape' in September by calling 'Dandy' Mills a liar, but was persuaded by his friends to apologize. He won £2,300 at Doncaster races that month, but Creevey, who paid his first visit to Lambton Hall in October 1824, thought he was 'infernally damaged in public opinion' because he won '*a great deal too much*' at his own races: he was, despite his current civility, 'a stingy, swindling, tyrannical kip', who allegedly beat his manservant with a stick for failing to respond immediately to his summons.[56] He was 'delighted' by Plunket's 'disgrace' at the hands of the Orange grand jury.[57]

He went to London for the Fox dinner in late January 1825. A few days later he sent Francis Place a donation of £50 for the London Mechanics' Institute.[58] He anticipated 'warmth and violence' in the Commons over the government's bill to suppress the Catholic Association, which he steadily but silently opposed in February. He found Burdett inclined to treat reform as 'a secondary consideration' to Catholic relief in any negotiations for a coalition ministry and strongly urged Grey to come to London to avoid creating an impression that he disapproved of the conduct of the Catholics.[59] He voted for Catholic claims, 1 Mar., and the second reading of the relief bill, 21 Apr., and presented a Cove petition in support of the Association, 16 Mar.[60] He was one of the score of Whigs and radicals who divided against the bill to disfranchise Irish 40*s.* freeholders, 26 Apr., when he criticized Burdett for accepting it. On 9 May he again spoke and voted against the measure and exchanged angry words with Brougham and Hobhouse over his declared intention of not voting for the third reading of the relief bill next day, when he, Sefton, Creevey and a small 'squad' ostentatiously abstained.[61] At the Westminster anniversary dinner, 23 May, he was accused by one Fearon of 'running riot in Parliament respecting Burdett's bill, and of entertaining the duke of York'. Hobhouse recorded that Lambton 'gave him a very temperate and good answer and was well received'.[62] He presented Sunderland petitions for repeal of the coastal coal duties, 23 Feb., and opposed and was a minority teller against the Tees railway bill, 4 Mar.[63]

He brought up petitions for repeal of the assessed taxes from Bishop Auckland, 9 Mar., and Stockton, 24 Mar. He welcomed the government's concession of a select committee on the Combination Acts, to which he was named, 29 Mar., having observed that Hume's 1824 legislation had failed. He wanted to see Peel, the home secretary, to press him to intervene against rioting north-east seamen, but was 'completely' satisfied with his explanation of his 'prompt and judicious ... arrangements'.[64] He condemned the disturbances in the House, 15 Apr. As one of the promoters of the New Zealand Company, he sent to Huskisson, president of the board of trade, a memorial applauding the ministry's 'enlightened system of commercial policy' and asking for a grant of 31 years exclusive trading rights.[65] He presented County Durham petitions against interference with the corn laws, 25 Apr., and one from Swallwell artisans for their revision, 29 Apr. 1825, when he urged government to 'take some steps in order to allay the ... agitation and uncertainty which prevailed upon this subject'.[66]

Creevey reported that Lambton took with surprising 'philosophy' the defeat in the St. Leger of the hitherto unbeaten Cedric, which he had recently bought for 2,500 guineas, but that he was reassuringly abrasive and rude at Lambton races in October 1825.[67] In late November he became 'very unwell', and he remained so for about six weeks; his death was falsely reported in the press on 9 Jan. 1826. He stayed in London under medical supervision, but was too poorly to attend the House. Ellice confided to Grey his belief that 'beyond all these complaints' Lambton had been 'suffering from great anxiety' about his financial affairs, which were becoming problematic. In early March Tierney found him looking 'much worse' and planning to go abroad in May: 'unless climate does wonders for him [he] goes I fear on a very forlorn hope. I am really sorry for him, for with all his faults he has many good qualities, and to me personally he has always been very kind'. Lambton was 'very much better' by early May, and the dissolution delayed his departure to southern Italy.[68] At his unopposed return for his county he applauded the 'very different system' of government from the repressive regime of 1820, praised Canning, who 'had not the support of the Tory aristocracy' but 'had to depend upon ... the co-operation and aid of the people', and called for a continuation of liberal policies, 'a great and important extension of the elective franchise' and Catholic emancipation. He refused to support prohibitive restrictions on corn imports, but acknowledged the need to give domestic producers 'an adequate protection under the artificial state in which they now existed'.[69] Despite still 'suffering in ... head and cheek', he threw himself energetically – 'No more sleep! No more Whig gentryism', he wrote to Grey – into the organization of the Whig campaign in Northumberland. His reception at the county meeting, where he nominated Matthew Bell*, was cool, and some local Whigs felt that as an outsider he was doing Howick 'more harm than good'. His bitter personal attacks eventually goaded Beaumont into accusing him of prompting Howick on the hustings, 30 June 1826, and their ensuing exchange of insults led to their fighting a bloodless duel on Bamburgh sands the following day.[70]

Lambton went with his family to Paris, 23 July, and from there to Naples in late September 1826, when Russell reported that he was 'in good health, but feels the changes of weather, and is bent on his three winters in Italy'. From Naples Lambton wrote to Grey in late January 1827 that Canning's speech of 12 Dec. 1826 announcing British intervention to defend Portugal against Spanish aggression had 'produced a wonderful effect on the continent and raised England about one thousand per cent'.[71] His debts were mounting, the coal trade was depressed and he needed to save money. He had already sold his stud, but in February 1827 Grey, who heard that he was 'quite well and very gay', thought he was still spending too much.[72] When he learned of the formation of Canning's ministry in April Lambton, who was rightly believed by Holland and Ellice to covet a peerage, in which ambition he was encouraged by Brougham and Wilson, hurried back to England to affirm his support. He made the journey 'in ten days, resting five times' and eating 'nothing on the road but tea and biscuits and occasionally fruit and eggs'. His 'adhesion' was strongly rumoured before he arrived, and Grey, who detested the Lansdowne Whigs' coalition with Canning, admitted that it was 'not at all improbable', though he could not believe that 'he should have announced his determination without communicating it to me'. Mackintosh was surprised to hear of his supposed 'love of coalition', as 'political placability was not ... a virtue of his', and suspected that 'what he really rejoices in is ... the destruction of the Whigs as a party'. He could not see how Lambton could 'expect to mollify Grey' and predicted that he would 'get a quarrel and a peerage for his pains'. Lambton called on Grey in London, 1 June, and his father-in-law reported:

> He looks well ... The state of politics brought him home. His opinions are decidedly in favour of the junction with Canning ... Nothing can be more kind than all his expressions and feelings towards me, and he offers to go out of Parliament if the appearance of a difference between us should be painful to me. This of course is out of the question.

Mackintosh, who described him as 'a red hot Canningite', encouraged him to inform the House of the boost given to 'the English character' by 'the landing of troops in Portugal'. He did not do so, but, in his last known act in the Commons he voted with government on the grant for Canadian water communications, 12 June, when he told his wife that despite their political differences he was striving to 'keep well in private with all' his friends, especially her parents.[73] He apparently rejected an approach from the ousted Tory ministers to become 'the head of the opposition in the House of Commons', pursuing 'measures ... as liberal as those of Canning'. On 9 July Canning sounded him 'as to his inclination to accept a peerage', partly to 'counteract Lord Grey in the House of Lords'; and a few day later he informed Grey that 'his peerage is settled', though the timing was still uncertain. Ellice suspected that he had 'taken *gracious* expressions for promises and qualified assurances of a desire to promote his views for arrangements'.[74] He was in Paris when Canning died, 8 Aug. 1827, but dashed to London. He gleaned something of Lord Goderich's attempt to form a coalition ministry, of which he approved, attended the funeral and returned to Paris and thence to Italy on the 17th. He told Ellice that day that 'his great object in returning' had been to seize any chance of 'contributing to a better understanding and co-operation' between the ministers and Grey, and that he believed that 'in the choice of evils before them, the king and the government were determined ... to convince foreign powers that there would be no change in ... Canning's policy respecting Greece and Portugal'. 'All this is mighty well', remarked Ellice, 'but [it] does not make the ultimate formation of a good and strong government an atom less difficult'.[75] Lambton evidently got Lord Lansdowne, home secretary under Canning and engaged in negotiations to remain in office under Goderich, to ensure that his claim to a peerage, to which he felt he had 'a perfect right', was not overlooked. Grey, who heard in September that 'the state of Lambton's affairs is the talk of Italy, where they say he is ruined and can never again live at Lambton', commented sourly that he might well 'get his peerage as a sop to Lansdowne' from his Tory colleagues. From Rome, 18 Oct., Lambton complained to Wilson that since leaving England he had 'not had one line ... from any friend in that country'. Still panting for news of his peerage, he made his way to Paris by late November, when Tierney, a member of the government, was 'sorry but not surprised' to hear that he was 'out of humour'. In Florence he had met Fox, who found him 'in good humour' and seemingly 'satisfied with his English prospects': 'He talked very bigly about the extreme importance of his return to London, as if upon that depended the stability of the present government'. Fox noted that Lady Louisa was 'very much annoyed at the state of her husband's health, and fears it will be necessary to return to Naples, much as she wishes and as he thinks it important that he should be in England. He thinks completely upon politics'.[76] On 19 Nov. Goderich finally overcame the king's reluctance to confer the peerages promised by Canning, and Lansdowne sent the news confidentially to Lambton, who replied by arguing that 'he ought to take a move beyond others and be a viscount at once', on the strength of the antiquity of his family, his wealth and his political influence. Lansdowne feared that this would be 'impracticable'. Lambton made no mention of the peerage when writing to Grey a few days later of his improved health and qualified approval of the destruction of the Turkish fleet at Navarino; but he did acknowledge Holland's congratulations, and wrote of his great anxiety to prevent 'any violent or decided public difference of opinion' with Grey when the ministry met Parliament in the new year. Grey was sorry that he would be gazetted with 'five rank Tories'.[77] Lambton asked Brougham to promote his claim to an earldom, asserting that anything lower would be a degradation, as 'the situation of first commoner is more marked and honourable than that of the last baron', and that his grandfather had declined Pitt's offer of a peerage in 1793. Brougham would not help him, and when sending his letter to Sefton mocked him 'with every species of ridicule for his pretensions'. Sefton and Creevey reckoned both men to be 'perfectly incredible' in their egotism.[78] When Goderich told him in London at the end of December that an earldom was out of the question Lambton gave way. To Grey, of whose disapproval he was painfully aware, he explained lamely that the peerage was 'never considered by me as a "favour received from the administration"', but 'as a matter of right which had been long withheld from my family and which my consenting to receive was more a favour conferred on them than one granted to myself'. He expressed his wish to see Grey installed 'at the head of a strong and liberal administration' and argued that in supporting Goderich's and Canning's he had been trying to advance that object, as well as 'to keep out the old Tories'.[79] A difficulty over his title (his first preference of D'Arcy was objected to by the duke of Leeds) protracted the business beyond Goderich's resignation. Meanwhile he tried to convince Grey that the bulk of the Whig party remained loyal to him. The Wellington ministry, prompted by Goderich, agreed to implement the peerages; but several more days elapsed before it was settled that Lambton should become Baron Lambton of the City of Durham. He told Grey that 'my great consolation in a Tory government is that I shall find myself by your side' in the Lords in opposition to it. He felt obliged to let it be known that the peerage had not been conferred by the new administration. The duke of Bedford snobbishly commented to Lady Holland, 28 Jan. 1828:

> So Mr. Lambton the great commoner and coal man has fallen into the ranks of the mushroom peers ... He certainly has not changed for the better, and was far more respectable as Mr. Lambton of Lambton *Castle* than as my Lord anything ... though as the prince in a principality he may consider himself as a sort of *make-believe* prince ... and having been *King Coal*, he is now *Prince Durham*. Lambton has always appeared to me more like a rich *parvenu* than an English gentleman, as his father and grandfather unquestionably were.[80]

He was appointed lord privy seal in his father-in-law's 1830 administration: he would have preferred 'the occupation of an office', but had placed himself entirely at Grey's disposal. He assured Lord Londonderry that he would

> find the new government as much attached to conservative principles as you could wish. But ... that conservation is to be effected not by a blind and obstinate resistance to the just demands of the intelligence of the age, but by a judicious and yet sufficient concession. Make the middle and lower orders interested in the maintenance of a constitution which guarantees your high principles and at the same time ensures them the possession of their just rights. We shall then have one common interest.[81]

Durham chaired the committee of four which devised the ministerial reform proposals. His preferences for the secret ballot and triennial parliaments were eventually discarded, but he later tried to claim most of the credit for the scheme, to the detriment of Russell.[82] His experience of office was brief and unhappy. As early as 20 July 1831 Holland wrote in his diary of his

> childish ill humour with most of his [cabinet] colleagues and with Grey in particular (to whom he owes his office and seat and such importance and consideration as he enjoys) ... When any individual in our councils differs with him in opinion or criticizes the minutest article of the [reform] bill ... he answers him shortly and petulantly by imputing his opposition to some mean and interested motive or by resenting the observation as a personal reflection upon himself. This, in spite of some very good qualities and yet greater talents, is intolerable and renders him both useless and offensive in council. I am afraid his forward temper will ere long furnish more matter for my diary of ministerial transactions than will be pleasant to witness or record.[83]

So it proved. Durham 'hurt' Grey 'with an unreasonable and unseasonable request' for an earldom in early September 1831. The death from consumption three weeks later of his beloved elder son Charles William, at the age of 13, almost unhinged him. Grief contributed to his 'unprovoked and ungovernable tirade' against Grey, 30 Nov. 1831, over modifications to the reform bill adopted in his absence on a mission to Belgium; the rest of the cabinet were horrified and disgusted by it.[84] He remained a disruptive element in 1832 (when two of the daughters of his first marriage died), until he was sent on a futile special mission to Russia, Prussia and Austria. Problems continued on his return, and in March 1833, in wretched health and unhappy with the government's church policy, he resigned from the cabinet, 'gratified', as Holland noted, 'with an earldom for which, in spite of all his understanding, and his half republican principles, he had long panted with childish vanity'.[85] He quarrelled irrevocably with Brougham in 1834, manoeuvred unsuccessfully as self-styled leader of the advanced Whigs for the succession to Grey, was deliberately excluded from his cabinet by Lord Melbourne in April 1835 and in July was got out of the way as ambassador to Russia. A third daughter died in December.[86] Early in 1838 he was sent as governor-general to Canada, but his regime was disastrous and he resigned precipitately and unjustifiably after nine months. The *Report* with which his name is associated, a blueprint for subsequent colonial policy, has now been largely discredited.[87] Consumption overtook him and he died at Cowes, Isle of Wight in July 1840. By his will, dated 29 Apr. 1837, he left all his property to his wife, who followed him to the grave sixteen months later. His personalty was sworn under £250,000 in the province of York and under £12,000 in that of Canterbury, but he left mortgage debts of about £635,000. He was succeeded in his estates and the peerage by his only surviving son George Frederick D'Arcy (1828-79), under whom coal profits increased and debts were reduced by over £500,000.[88] Hobhouse wrote that he was

> in the main, a kind and friendly man. Whatever defects he had were on the surface, and he took no pains to conceal them ... He had cultivated his understanding with more assiduity than is usually bestowed upon intellectual qualities by young men of his position. He was a good and fluent speaker ... [and] had an abundance of political courage, sometimes, perhaps, a little approaching to rashness; but, in his intercourse with his friends, he was by no means overbearing, nor excepting in public controversy, arrogant ... He did not attach so much value to his character, or opinions, as to give himself a sufficient amount of self-confidence in matters of importance. With all his manifest defects, he was much beloved in his own country.[89]

Despite their rift, Brougham judged him generously:

> He was in the best sense of the word high-spirited. He was generous, open, and incapable of falsehood or meanness ... His abilities were great ... When he spoke in Parliament ... he distinguished himself very much, and ... at public meetings more than almost anybody. He was very modest respecting his own merits ... He really was chiefly fond of exalting his wealth and family ... He ... overrated greatly his parliamentary weight in Durham ... [He was] very active in political matters ... and very much misunderstood ... Always a strong party man, he had violent personal prejudices, and strong dislikes and dislikings.[90]

Sydney Smith, who had a soft spot for him, observed to Lady Grey that 'in spite of his defects, which were apparent, there was a great deal of excellence in him'; but Benjamin Disraeli* commented that his 'death makes no sensation. He was found out before his last illness – a dull charlatan'.[91]

[1] See S.J. Reid, *Life and Letters of Lord Durham* (1906) and C.W. New, *Lord Durham* (1929). L. Cooper, *Radical Jack* (1959) draws heavily on these and adds little. See also Oxford DNB. [2] D. Spring, 'Earls of Durham and Great Northern Coalfield', *Canadian Hist. Rev.* xxxiii (1952), 237-42. [3] *Lieven Letters*, 276; *Macaulay Letters*, iii. 262; Lord W.P. Lennox, *Celebrities I Have Known* (ser. 2), i. 99; *CP*, iv. 559-60. [4] Brougham, *Life and Times*, iii. 500. [5] Cooper, 82-85. [6] *HP Commons, 1790-1820*, iv. 369; Reid, i. 128-33; Grey mss, Lambton to Grey [7], 10 Jan. 1820. [7] Reid, i. 136-8; New, 59-63; Grey mss, Grey to Wilson, 6 Feb., 13 Mar., Tierney to Grey, 22 Feb., 22 Mar., Ellice to same, 16 Mar.; Add. 38458, f. 294; *The Times*, 13, 17 Mar. 1820. [8] Add. 56541, f. 37; *The Times*, 24 May 1820. [9] Brougham mss, Brougham to Grey [1 June 1820]. [10] Add. 52444, f. 160. [11] Grey mss, Grey to Lady Grey, 9, 18, 20, 23, 26 Oct.; Add. 51579, Morpeth to Lady Holland, 19 Oct. 1820; *Creevey Pprs.* i. 342; Reid, i. 139-41 [12] A. Mitchell, *Whigs in Opposition*, 151-2; Grey mss, Tierney to Grey, 24 Nov., 13 Dec.; Add. 30109, f. 140; Bessborough mss F138; *The Times*, 18 Dec. 1820; *Speech of Lambton at Dur. County Meeting* (1820); Herts. Archives, Panshanger mss D/Elb F78. [13] *The Times*, 17 Jan. 1821; *Creevey Pprs.* ii. 7. [14] *The Times*, 3, 7 Feb. 1821. [15] HLRO, Hist. Coll. 379, Grey Bennet diary, 12; *Creevey Pprs.* ii. 12. [16] Dorset RO D/BKL, Bankes jnl. 123 (5 Feb. 1821). [17] Grey mss, Grey to wife, 6, 10 Feb. 1821. [18] Add. 56542, f. 1. [19] *The Times*, 23, 27 Feb. 1821. [20] Trinity Coll. Camb. Dawson Turner mss DT2/K2/3. [21] *The Times*, 5 Apr. 1821. [22] Ibid. 12 Apr. 1821. [23] Broughton, *Recollections*, ii. 146, 148-9; Northants. RO, Agar Ellis diary, 17, 18 Apr. [1821]; Heron, *Notes*, 127; Reid, i. 146-9. [24] Grey Bennet diary, 76-77. [25] *Creevey Pprs.* ii. 31-32. [26] Ibid. ii. 32; Add. 30109, ff. 225, 258, 331; 30111, f. 262. [27] *Fox Jnl.* 90, 93; Grey mss, Ellice to Grey [23 Dec. 1821, 4 Feb.], Lambton to same, 2, 22 Jan. 1822. [28] Grey mss, Lambton to Grey, 6, 11 Feb. 1822. [29] *Creevey Pprs.* ii. 34. [30] Grey mss, Lambton to Grey, 11, 14 Feb. 1822. [31] *The Times*, 14 Mar., 3 May 1822. [32] Ibid. 2, 7, 21 May 1822. [33] Ibid. 1 June 1822. [34] Add. 56545, ff. 5-7. [35] *The Times*, 3, 6, 10 Sept. 1822; *Creevey's Life and Times*, 158-60, 162; *Creevey Pprs.* ii. 49-50. [36] *Fox Jnl.* 146-7. [37] *Creevey Pprs.* ii. 56-57; Add. 36459, f. 320. [38] Grey mss, Lambton to Grey, 7, 15 Dec. 1822. [39] Ibid. Lambton to Grey, 13 Feb. 1823. [40] Bessborough mss F53, Brougham to Duncannon [2 Mar.]; Grey mss, Lambton to Grey [5 Mar. 1823]. [41] *The Times*, 5, 11, 28 Mar. 1823; Add. 38293, f. 150. [42] Add. 76369, Althorp to Brougham, 17 Mar. 1823. [43] *The Times*, 22 Apr., 17 May 1823. [44] Add. 56548, ff. 2-3; *The Times*, 24 May 1823. [45] Reid, i. 159-60; Add. 30110, f. 184; 36460, f. 86; 51832, Wilks to Holland, 28 May 1823. [46] Grey mss, Ellice to Grey [25 Nov. 1823], Lambton to same [29 Jan.], 23 Mar.; Northumb. RO, Ridley mss ZRI 25/45, Grey to Ridley, 4 Mar. 1824. [47] Ridley mss 25/45, Grey to Ridley, 21 Mar.; Grey mss, Lambton to Grey, 16-18 Mar. [1824]. [48] *The Times*, 15, 16, 26, 30 Mar., 1 Apr. 1824. [49] Grey mss, Lambton to Grey, 30 Mar. [1824]. [50] Add. 56548, f. 62. [51] Grey mss, Lambton to Grey, 3 Apr. [1824]. [52] *The Times*, 6, 9, 10 Apr. 1824. [53] Grey mss, Lambton to Grey, 5, 19, 24, 28 Apr. 1824. [54] Add. 56548; *The Times*, 25 May 1824. [55] Broughton, iii. 44. [56] *Creevey's Life and Times*, 201, 203; *Creevey Pprs.* ii. 80-82; Broughton, iii. 80; Add. 47226, f. 74. [57] Grey mss, Lambton to Grey, 6 Jan. 1825. [58] Ibid. Lambton to Grey, 21 Jan. 1825; Add. 27823, ff. 360, 361. [59] Grey mss, Lambton to Grey, 9 [12], 16 [20] Feb. [1825]. [60] *The Times*, 17 Mar. 1825. [61] Buckingham, *Mems. Geo. IV*, ii. 242, 247. [62] Add. 56549, f. 124; *The Times*, 24 May 1825. [63] *The Times*, 24 Feb., 5 Mar. 1825. [64] Add. 40375, ff. 301, 303. [65] Add. 38761, f. 175. [66] *The Times*, 26, 30 Apr. 1825. [67] *Creevey's Life and Times*, 217-18; *Creevey Pprs.* ii. 91. [68] Grey mss, Lambton to Grey, 26 Dec. [1825], 30 Jan., Ellice to same [21 Jan.]; *The Times*, 9 Jan.; Add. 36461, f. 398; 40386, f. 105; 51580, Carlisle to Lady Holland, 27 Mar; 51584, Tierney to Holland, 12 Mar., 10 Apr.; 51586, same to Lady Holland, 3 Mar.; 51668, Bedford to Lady Holland [12 May]; Creevey mss, Creevey to Miss Ord, 23 Feb. 1826. [69] *The Times*, 30 May, 19, 26 June; *Newcastle Chron.* 17 June 1826; Reid, i. 172; New, 91. [70] Reid, i. 170-2; Grey mss, Lambton to Grey, 29, 31 May, 1, 3 [6], 25 June, 13 [22] July, Ellice to same, 29 May; *Newcastle Chron.* 17 June; *The Times*, 6 June, 3, 4 July 1826; Brougham, iii. 505-7; Add. 30111, f. 231. [71] Grey mss, Lambton to Grey, 22 July 1826, 29 Jan. 1827; Add. 51679, Russell to Lady Holland, 24 Sept. [1826]. [72] *Creevey Pprs.* ii. 120; Grey mss, Ellice to Grey [20 Nov. 1826]; NLS, Ellice mss, Grey to Ellice, 7 Feb. 1827. [73] *Canning's Ministry*, 247, 334; Grey mss, Ellice to Grey [28 May]; Ellice mss, Grey to Ellice, 31 May, 1 June; Add. 51655, Mackintosh to Lady Holland, 27 May, 1 June 1827; Add. 52447, f. 70; *Creevey Pprs.* ii. 120. [74] *Canning's Ministry*, 331; Brougton, iii. 208, 209; Ellice mss, Grey to Ellice, 13 July; Grey mss, Ellice to Grey, 19 July 1827. [75] Grey mss, Ellice to Grey [4], 17 Aug., Lambton to same, 11, 13, 15, 16 Aug.; *Wellington Despatches*, iv. 91; Lambton mss, Wilson to Lambton, 12 Aug. 1827; Add. 40394, f. 189. [76] *Creevey Pprs.* ii. 126; Ellice mss, Grey to Ellice, 8 Sept., 22 Oct.; Add. 30111, f. 308; 51586, Tierney to Lady Holland, 8 Nov. [1827]; *Fox Jnl.* 234-6. [77] *Geo. IV Letters*, iii. 1423; Landsdowne mss, Lambton to Lansdowne, 24 Nov.; Add. 51687, Lansdowne to Holland, 26 Nov., 1 Dec.; 51833, Lambton to same, 3 Dec.; Grey mss, Lambton to Grey, 29 Nov.; Ellice mss, Grey to Ellice, 7 Dec. 1827. [78] Brougham, iii. 50-4; *Creevey Pprs.* ii. 141-2. [79] Grey mss, Lambton to Grey [27 Dec. 1827]. [80] *Geo. IV Letters*, iii. 1448, 1453; Grey mss, Lambton to Grey [8, 12, 17], 18 Jan. 1828; *Wellington Despatches*, iv. 185-6, 188-90, 196-7; Broughton, iii. 236; Add. 51669. [81] Dur. RO, Londonderry mss D/Lo/C86/16. [82] M. Brock, *Great Reform Act*, 136, 140-1; J. Cannon, *Parliamentary Reform*, 204-11. [83] *Holland House Diaries*, 8. [84] Ibid. 44, 88-89; *Three Diaries*, 134; *Greville Mems.* ii. 228-9; Le Marchant, *Althorp*, 374-4; Reid, i. 261-96. [85] *Creevey's Life and Times*, 346; *Three Diaries*, 217; *Lieven Letters*, 328, 329, 337; *Greville Mems.* ii. 331-2; Reid, i. 297-321; New, 200-43; *Holland House Diaries*, 207. [86] Reid, ii. 1-135; New, 244-300; *Holland House Diaries*, 294; Broughton, v. 161-2; I. Newbould, *Whiggery and Reform*, 177-8. [87] Reid, ii. 136-305; New, 301-474; G. Martin, *The Durham Report and British Policy*, p. vii. [88] *Gent. Mag.* (1840), ii. 316-20; *The Times*, 22, 29, 30 July, 12, 18 Aug., 5 Oct. 1840; PROB 8/233 (3 Oct. 1840); PROB 11/1934/692; Reid, ii. 343-76; Spring, 250-3. [89] Broughton, v. 291-2. [90] Brougham, iii. 500, 504-5. [91] *Smith Letters*, ii. 704; *Disraeli Letters*, iii. 1082.

D.R.F.

LANE FOX, George (1793–1848), of Bramham Park, nr. Tadcaster, Yorks.

BEVERLEY 1820–1826

BEVERLEY 1837–15 Jan. 1840

b. 4 May 1793, 1st s. of James Fox Lane† of Bramham and Hon. Maria Lucy Pitt, da. of George Pitt†, 1st Bar. Rivers; bro. of Sackville Walter Lane Fox*. *educ.* Westminster; Emmanuel, Camb. 1811. *m.* 20 Sept. 1814, Georgiana Henrietta, da. of Edward Pery Buckley of Minestead Lodge, Hants, 1s. 2da. *suc.* fa. 1821. *d.* 15 Nov. 1848.

Lane Fox's wealthy but spendthrift father, a friend of George IV as prince of Wales who liked to regard himself as the first commoner of England, had inherited the extensive Bramham estate in 1773 from his uncle George Fox†, 1st Baron Bingley. He was an inconspicuous Member for Horsham in the 1796 Parliament.[1] Lane Fox, an irresponsible young man, was addicted to horse racing and 'gambled away half his fortune': a few months after he succeeded his father in 1821, Edward Littleton* visited Bramham, which was 'laid out in the old French style, like St. Cloud', and discovered that Lane Fox was 'too poor to live there and occupies a smaller house adjoining'.[2] A member of Brooks's Club (like his father) since 1816, at the general election of 1820 he offered for the venal and open borough of Beverley as a third man. After spending lavishly, keeping his political views to himself and amusing his opponents with his stumbling oratory, he was returned at the head of the poll by a considerable margin. He refused to supply the customary bull for baiting, which he denounced as a 'cruel and barbarous' amusement.[3]

Lane Fox, a very lax attender who is not known to have spoken in debate, seems to have given general but not slavish support to the Liverpool ministry when present. He was in the opposition minority against Wilberforce's compromise resolution on the Queen Caroline affair, 22 June, but divided with government against economies in revenue collection, 4 July 1820. He voted against the opposition censure motion on ministers' conduct towards the queen, 6 Feb., but for restoration of her name to the liturgy, 13 Feb., and inquiry into the conduct of the sheriff of Dublin at the local meeting in her support, 22 Feb. 1821. He voted to condemn the Allies' suppression of liberalism in Naples, 21 Feb. Although he voted against Catholic relief, 28 Feb., and presented a hostile petition from the corporation and burgesses of Beverley, 12 Mar., he was reported to have declared his intention of 'not voting in the committee' on the relief bill, and in fact voted with the pro-Catholic majority for the first clause, 23 Mar. 1821.[4] He voted for the second reading of the new Catholic relief bill, 21 Apr. 1825. He divided with government against repeal of the additional malt duty, 21 Mar., and was given a month's leave of absence on account of his father's death, 7 May 1821. He was in the minority for Hume's amendment to the address, 5 Feb., but the ministerial majorities for the aliens bill, 19 July 1822, and against inquiry into chancery delays, 5 June 1823. On 20 Feb. 1823 he brought up a Beverley petition for repeal of the Insolvent Debtors Act.[5] He voted in defence of the prosecution of the Methodist missionary John Smith in Demerara, 11 June 1824. He was in the ministerial majorities for the duke of Cumberland's annuity, 6, 10 June 1825, and paired against revision of the corn laws, 18 Apr. 1826. He presented constituency petitions for the abolition of slavery, repeal of the window tax and an end to the practice of quartering soldiers in inns, 15 Feb. 1826.[6] In the autumn of 1825 he had indicated his willingness to stand again for Beverley at the next general election; but when the dissolution came in June 1826 he retired and recommended a successor.[7]

By then his private life was in disarray. In 1822 he decided to separate from his wife, a society figure of dubious virtue, whose mother had been a lady of the bedchamber to the royal princesses. He had accomplished this by early 1824, but two years later he sought a reconciliation. Mrs. Arbuthnot, who considered Lane Fox to be 'an odious man', advised her to 'accept his offer but to contrive some money arrangement which may be beneficial to her children, and also to secure some provision to her should she be again driven away by him'.[8] Nothing seems to have come of this, and in the late 1820s Mrs. Fox had a 'notorious' and indiscreet affair with the 6th earl of Chesterfield, who ruthlessly ditched her in 1830 to marry Anne Weld Forester.[9] On 29 July 1828 the mansion at Bramham and its valuable contents were almost totally destroyed by fire, and it remained in a state of dereliction for many years.[10] Lane Fox successfully contested Beverley as a Conservative in 1837, but he retired from Parliament on health grounds in 1840. A keen promoter in his later years of agricultural improvement, he died in November 1848.[11]

[1] *HP Commons, 1790-1820*, iii. 824. [2] Hatherton diary, 3 Oct. [1821]. [3] *Yorks. Gazette*, 26 Feb., 4, 11 Mar.; *The Times*, 6, 10 Mar. 1820; Hull Univ. Lib. DDMM/2/18; G. Oliver, *Hist. Beverley*, 422. [4] *The Times*, 13 Mar. 1821; Buckingham, *Mems. Geo. IV*, i. 135, 142; Keele Univ. Lib. Sneyd mss SC17/20. [5] *The Times*, 21 Feb. 1823. [6] Ibid. 16 Feb. 1826. [7] Fitzwilliam mss, Wood to Milton, 7 Oct.; *Yorks. Gazette*, 22 Oct. 1825; *Hull Advertiser*, 2 June; Hull Univ. Lib. Hotham mss DDHO/8/4, Hall to Hotham, 4 June 1826. [8] *Arbuthnot*

Jnl. i. 167, 286, 300; ii. 2-3; *Peel Letters*, 52. [9] *Arbuthnot Jnl*. ii. 301, 391-2. [10] *The Times*, 31 July, Aug. 1828; W.H. White, *Hist. W. Riding* (1837-8), ii. 304. [11] *Yorks. Gazette*, 25 Nov. 1848.

M.P.J.C.

LANE FOX, Sackville Walter (1797–1874).

HELSTON	1831–1834
BEVERLEY	24 Jan. 1840–1841
IPSWICH	17 Aug. 1842–1847
BEVERLEY	1847–1852

b. 24 Mar. 1797, 2nd s. of James Fox Lane† of Bramham, Yorks. and Hon. Maria Lucy Pitt, da. of George Pitt†, 1st Bar. Rivers; bro. of George Lane Fox*. *educ*. Eton 1811. *m*. 22 June 1826, Lady Charlotte Mary Anne Osborne, da. of George, 6th duke of Leeds, 2s. 2da. *d*. 18 Aug. 1874.

Ensign and lt. 1 Ft. Gds. 1814, lt. and capt. 1820, ret. 1822.

Like his elder brother George, Lane Fox was an inveterate and largely unsuccessful gambler. His ceremonial army career was brief. His marriage to the only daughter of the 6th duke of Leeds was the key to his first return to Parliament, for it was on Leeds's commanding interest that he came in unopposed for Helston at the general election of 1831. He voted against the second reading of the Grey ministry's reintroduced reform bill, 6 July, and presented a hostile petition from the corporation and inhabitants of Helston, 12 July. He divided for using the 1831 census to determine the disfranchisement schedules, 19 July, to postpone consideration of Chippenham's inclusion in B, 27 July, and against the passage of the bill, 21 Sept. He voted against the second reading of the Scottish reform bill, 23 Sept. He was in the minority for O'Connell's motion for swearing the depleted Dublin election committee, 29 July. A devoted supporter of the Church of England, he voted in the diehard minority of 47 against the Maynooth grant, 26 Sept. He divided against the second, 17 Dec. 1831, and third reading of the revised reform bill, 22 Mar. 1832. He voted against the second reading of the Irish bill, 25 May, and for an attempt to preserve the voting rights of Irish borough freemen, 2 July. He divided against government on the Russian-Dutch loan, 26 Jan., 12 July, and in a minority of 29 against the Irish party processions bill, 25 June 1832. He is not known to have spoken in debate in this period.

At the general election of 1832 Lane Fox was returned unopposed as a Conservative for the one seat retained by Helston under the Reform Act.[1] He stood down in 1834, but subsequently sat for Beverley and Ipswich. His defence of the Church became increasingly obsessive and eccentric: for example, he wrote to Peel in 1843 to inform him of the imminence of the second coming.[2] He died in August 1874. His elder son Sackville George, an army officer, inherited the baronies of Darcy and Conyers from his uncle the 7th duke of Leeds in 1859.

[1] *West Briton*, 14 Dec.; *R. Cornw. Gazette*, 29 Dec. 1832. [2] Add. 40528, f. 200.; K.J. Atton, 'Municipal and Parl. Politics in Ipswich' (London Univ. Ph.D. thesis, 1980), 214, 242.

M.P.J.C.

LANGSTON, James Haughton (?1797–1863), of Sarsden House, Chipping Norton, Oxon. and 143 Piccadilly, Mdx.

NEW WOODSTOCK	1820–1826
OXFORD	1826–1834
OXFORD	1841–19 Oct. 1863

b. ?1797, o.s. of John Langston† of Sarsden and Sarah, da. of John Goddard of Woodford Hall, Essex. *educ*. Eton 1811; Christ Church, Oxf. 23 May 1814, aged 17. *m*. 6 July 1824, Hon. Julia Moreton, da. of Thomas Reynolds, 4th Bar. Ducie, 1da. *suc*. fa. 1812. *d*. 19 Oct. 1863.

Sheriff, Oxon. 1819-20; verderer, Wychwood Forest.

On coming of age in about 1818 Langston took possession of a handsome inheritance from his father, a second generation London banker turned Oxfordshire squire, whose personal estate had been sworn under £250,000 after his death while Langston was still at school. The residue was calculated for duty at £192,611.[1] Langston also inherited his father's Whig politics, and on 22 Jan. 1819 he was admitted to Brooks's, sponsored by his future father-in-law, Lord Ducie, and Sir Ronald Ferguson*. Soon afterwards he became sheriff of Oxfordshire, and as such he sanctioned and chaired the county meeting called to vote a loyal address in the aftermath of Peterloo, 12 Nov. 1819.[2] At the general election of 1820 he made an opportunistic intervention at Woodstock, which lay about 12 miles from Sarsden, against the interest of the impecunious 5th duke of Marlborough, having apparently been alerted to the possibility of an opening in a 'chance' encounter in London with General John Michel†. Marlborough's son Lord Blandford* withdrew after an unpromising canvass, and Langston was returned unopposed with a nominee of the Liverpool ministry. He subsequently told the disgruntled Marlborough that he had never 'entertained for a single moment the idea of wantonly opposing your interest, or setting up any pretensions of my own'.[3] He may have complied with Marlborough's demand for a payment of £2,500 to help defray his local debts.

In the House, he acted consistently with the Whig opposition, but he was an indifferent attender, and is not known to have spoken in debate in this period. He voted against government on the civil list, 3, 5, 8 May, economies in revenue collection, 4 July, and the barrack agreement bill, 17 July 1820. He was in the minority against the appointment of a secret committee on Queen Caroline's activities, 26 June 1820. Lord Jersey told Lord Holland, 20 Nov. 1820, that Langston might be 'the best person' to consult about the possibility of organizing an Oxfordshire meeting in support of the queen, although 'caution' was required as he had 'expressed himself rather in a *touchy* manner upon being courted by Whig ladies'.[4] He joined in the parliamentary campaign in Caroline's support in the first weeks of the 1821 session. He voted for ordnance reductions, 16 Feb., and in condemnation of the Allies' suppression of the liberal regime in Naples, 21 Feb. He was one of the few Whigs who were hostile to Catholic relief, and he voted in that sense, 28 Feb. After an apparent absence from the House of about two months he resurfaced in May 1821 to vote for various economies (he was in minorities of 27 on 7 May and of 29 on the 28th). He divided for repeal of the Blasphemous Libels Act, 8 May. He voted for parliamentary reform, 9 May, and for reform of the Scottish county representation the following day; and he was later a supporter of reform in the divisions of 20 Feb., 25 Apr. 1822, 20 Feb., 24 Apr., 2 June 1823, and 27 Apr. 1826. He voted for the forgery punishment mitigation bill, 23 May, against the duke of Clarence's grant, 18 June, and for Hume's motion for economy and retrenchment, 27 June 1821.

Langston divided for more extensive tax reductions to relieve distress, 21 Feb. 1822, but his only recorded votes for retrenchment were for abolition of one of the joint-postmasterships, 13 Mar., 2 May, to pay naval and military pensions from the sinking fund, 3 May, and for cuts in diplomatic expenditure, 15, 16 May. He voted against Canning's bill to relieve Catholic peers of their disabilities, 30 Apr. He was in the minority of 25 for Ricardo's proposal for a fixed duty of 20*s*. on wheat imports, 9 May. He voted to limit the duration of the Irish insurrection bill, 8 July 1822. His only known votes in the 1823 session, besides those on reform, were for inquiries into the legal proceedings against the Dublin Orange rioters, 22 Apr., the state of Ireland, 12 May, and chancery delays, 5 June. After a long period of inactivity, he turned up to present a Woodstock petition for repeal of the house and window taxes, 14 Apr.,[5] and to vote for inquiries into the Irish church establishment, 6 May, Ireland, 11 May, and Irish first fruits revenues, 25 May, and for repeal of the leather tax, 18 May 1824. He was a defaulter on a call of the House, 28 Feb. 1825, and did not vote in the division on Catholic claims the following day. He was granted a fortnight's sick leave, 14 Apr., and missed the divisions on the relief bill, 21 Apr., 10 May; he later claimed that he had been 'confined from the effects of an accident'.[6] Yet he was listed in a minority of 23 for repeal of the beer duties, 5 May. He voted against the duke of Cumberland's annuity, 6, 10 June 1825. In 1826 he voted for inquiry into the corn laws, 18 Apr., and for the introduction of defence by counsel to felony trials, 25 Apr.

Langston had stood his ground at Woodstock in September 1825 when, with an early dissolution expected, Blandford and an aristocratic kinsman declared their joint candidature. He offered again at the general election of 1826, and at the nomination denied a report that he had voted for Catholic relief in 1825, but he seems to have been knocked out of his stride by heckling. The more overt anti-Catholicism of Blandford and his colleague was probably decisive, and Langston was narrowly beaten into third place.[7] He immediately went to Oxford, in response to a request from some of the leading resident freemen, resentful of the intrusion of a wealthy stranger, William Hughes Hughes*, who was expected to walk over with one of the sitting Members, Lockhart. It was suggested that Langston's 'great popularity and property in the county must make him a very formidable rival', and so it proved, for he easily topped the poll, receiving support from two-thirds of those who voted. He proclaimed himself 'the champion of public principles'.[8] He was in the minority of 39 against the Clarence annuity bill, 2 Mar. 1827. He voted against Catholic relief, 6 Mar. He voted with the Whig opposition to postpone going into committee of supply, 30 Mar., and for inquiries into the Irish miscellaneous estimates and chancery delays, 5 Apr., when he was appointed to the select committee on borough polls. He presented an Oxford parish petition for repeal of the Test Acts, 7 June 1827.[9] He presented several more petitions on this subject, 21, 26 Feb. 1828, when he voted for repeal. He voted against sluicing the delinquent borough of East Retford, 21 Mar. He presented Oxford corporation's petition against Catholic claims, 2 May, and voted accordingly, 12 May. He voted against the Wellington ministry for inquiry into civil list pensions, 20 May, and on the archbishop of Canterbury's bill, 16 June, the grant for the Royal Cork Institution, 20 June, the misapplication of public money on Buckingham House, 23 June, and the ordnance estimates, 4 July 1828. At the annual Oxford mayoral feast, 1 Oct. 1828, Langston stated his view that the time had arrived for ministers to take decisive action on the Catholic question.[10] In February 1829 he was asked to present an Oxford petition against emancipation. In a reply subsequently made public, he agreed to do so if it was entrusted to him (it was not), but said that he felt unable to support its prayer, having concluded that concession was essential to avert rebellion in Ireland, and being confirmed in this view by his awareness, 'above all, of the utter impossibility of forming what is called a Protestant government, the united talent of the country being arrayed against it'.[11] Planta, the patronage secretary, expected him to vote 'with government', and he duly did so, 6, 30 Mar. He voted for the transfer of East Retford's seats to Birmingham, 5 May, and against the grant for the marble arch, 25 May. At the Oxford mayoral dinner, 30 Sept. 1829, he defended and explained his turnabout on Catholic emancipation, to the apparent satisfaction of his audience.[12] In the 1830 session, Langston was more active in the lobbies than had been his habit. He voted for the amendment to the address, 4 Feb. He divided for the transfer of East Retford's seats to Birmingham, 11 Feb., 15 Mar., and the enfranchisement of Birmingham, Leeds and Manchester, 23 Feb., but against Blandford's reform plan, 18 Feb. He voted for Russell's reform motion, 28 May. He voted against government in most of the major divisions forced by the reviving opposition, including those on the Bathurst and Dundas pensions, 26 Mar., the Terceira incident, 28 Apr., the treasury establishment, 10 May, abolition of the Irish lord lieutenancy, 11 May, privy councillors' emoluments, 14 May, South American missions, 7 June, and consular services, 11 June. He was listed in the minority in favour of Jewish emancipation, 17 May, but let it be known in Oxford that he had in fact voted against it.[13] He voted against abolition of the death penalty for all forgery offences, 7 June 1830.

Langston offered again for Oxford at the 1830 general election, when he made much of his recent support for tax reductions, economy and retrenchment and 'every measure of constitutional liberty', but claimed that he had 'lent his support to ministers when he conceived they were aiming to advance the public good, and ... had never countenanced a factious opposition to them'. He again topped the poll after a contest in which Hughes Hughes defeated Lockhart.[14] Ministers numbered him among the 'bad doubtfuls', and he voted against them on the civil list, 15 Nov. 1830. Two days later he presented an Oxford Dissenters' petition for the abolition of slavery. He did not attend the Oxford meeting to endorse the Grey ministry's reform bill, 15 Mar., but he presented its petition, 19 Mar. 1831. He voted for the second reading of the bill, 22 Mar., and against Gascoyne's wrecking amendment, 19 Apr. 1831. He was returned unopposed for Oxford at the ensuing general election, when he said that he 'could not hesitate to support the main principle of the bill', believing that

> the diminution of influence, and the extension of the elective franchise, will bind a powerful class of the community to all that is good and sacred, and that the sound sense of Englishmen will not be led to adopt wild theories or revolutionary opinions.[15]

He voted for the second reading of the reintroduced reform bill, 6 July, at least twice against the adjournment, 12 July, and was a fairly steady supporter of the measure's details. He was listed in the ministerial minority against the enfranchisement of £50 tenants-at-will, 18 Aug., but later claimed that he had in fact voted with Hughes Hughes for it. However, he was at odds with his colleague by voting with government against attempts to preserve the voting rights of freemen, 27, 30 Aug.[16] He voted for the passage of the reform bill, 21 Sept., the second reading of the Scottish bill, 23 Sept., and the motion of confidence in the Grey ministry, 10 Oct. He was in the majority in favour of the Irish union of parishes bill, 19 Aug. He voted for the second reading of the revised reform bill, 17 Dec. 1831, could again be relied on to support its details and divided for its third reading, 22 Mar. 1832. He voted for the address calling on the king to appoint only ministers who would carry the measure unimpaired, 10 May, and the second reading of the Irish reform bill, 25 May. He divided with government on the Russian-Dutch loan, 26 Jan., 12, 16, 20 July, relations with Portugal, 9 Feb., and the navy civil departments bill, 6 Apr. 1832.

He stood again for Oxford, declaring that reform was 'essential to the honest administration of public affairs, and the establishment of ... mutual confidence between the government and the people', at the 1832 general election, and easily headed the poll.[17] He did not stand at the next two general elections, but came in again in 1841, and occupied the seat, as a Liberal in favour of the ballot, franchise extension and 'rational progress', for the rest of his life.[18] He died at Sarsden in October 1863. It was rather lamely said of him that he 'stood very high in the estimation even of his political opponents, and he was also favourably known as a good landlord and an active magistrate'. In 1826 he had entirely subsidized, to the tune of at least £14,000, the building of 'a new gothic church', with a tower 'exactly copied from Magdalen tower, Oxford', at his neighbouring village of Churchill.[19] By his will, dated 3 Aug. 1850, he devised his London house in Piccadilly to his wife, along with a life annuity of £1,000, and confirmed the settlement of his Oxfordshire estates on his only child Julia, at the time of her marriage in 1849 to her cousin Lord Moreton (1827-1921), later 3rd earl of Ducie.

[1] *Gent. Mag.* (1812), i. 196; PROB 11/1531/130; IR26/551/171. [2] *Jackson's Oxford Jnl.* 30 Oct., 13 Nov. 1819. [3] *VCH Oxon.* Xii. 404; *Jackson's Oxford Jnl.* 4, 11 Mar.; St. Deiniol's Lib. Glynne-Gladstone mss 290, Langston to Marlborough, 8 Mar., reply, 9 Mar., Marlborough to J. Gladstone, 13 Mar. 1820. [4] Add. 51729. [5] *The Times*, 15 Apr. 1824. [6] *Jackson's Oxford Jnl.* 10 June 1826. [7] Ibid. 10 Sept. 1825, 29 Apr., 3, 10, 17 June 1826; *VCH Oxon.* Xii. 404-5. [8] *Oxford University and City Herald*, 10, 17 June 1826. [9] *The Times*, 8 June 1827. [10] *Oxford University and City Herald*, 4 Oct. 1828. [11] Ibid. 28 Feb. 1829. [12] Ibid. 3 Oct. 1829. [13] *Jackson's Oxford Jnl.* 5 June 1830. [14] Ibid. 10, 31 July 1830. [15] *Oxford University and City Herald*, 30 Apr., 7 May 1831. [16] Ibid. 20, 27 Aug. 3 Sept. 1831. [17] *Jackson's Oxford Jnl.* 30 June, 1, 8, 15 Dec. 1832. [18] *Dod's Parl. Companion* (1855), 220; (1857), 230. [19] *Gent. Mag.* (1863), ii. 779-80; Northants. RO, Agar Ellis diary, 17 Oct. [1826]; *Buildings of England: Oxon.* ed. J. Sherwood and N. Pevsner (1974), 363.

D.R.F.

LANGTON *see* GORE LANGTON

LASCELLES, Hon. Henry (1797–1857), of Goldsborough Hall, Knaresborough, Yorks. and 14 Hanover Square, Mdx.

NORTHALLERTON 1826–1831

b. 11 June 1797, 2nd but 1st surv. s. of Henry Lascelles†, 2nd earl of Harewood, and Henrietta, da. of Lt.-Gen. Sir John Saunders Sebright†, 6th bt., of Beechwood, Herts.; bro. of Hon. William Saunders Sebright Lascelles*. *m.* 5 July 1823, Lady Louisa Thynne, da. of Thomas Thynne†, 2nd mq. of Bath, 7s. (2 *d.v.p.*) 6da. *styled* Visct. Lascelles 17 Dec. 1839-41; *suc.* fa. as 3rd earl of Harewood 24 Nov. 1841. *d.* 22 Feb. 1857.

Ensign 1 Ft. Gds. 1814, half-pay 1820, ret. 1831.

Ld. Lt. Yorks. (W. Riding) 1846-*d.*

Lt. Yorks. Hussars yeomanry 1820.

Lascelles, who joined the army at the age of 17, was slightly wounded by an exploding shell while bearing the standard of the second battalion of the Grenadier Guards at Waterloo. He was injured again in 1823 when a gun burst in his hands as he was shooting sea fowl off Cowes. By September that year he had reportedly recovered and was accompanying his younger brother William on a 'drawing expedition' to Switzerland.[1] At the general election of 1826 he was returned for Northallerton on his Tory father's interest, somewhat to the surprise of the brother of Lord Carlisle, who 'thought that he entertained a dislike of being in Parliament'.[2]

He was certainly a very lax attender, who cast no recorded votes in the 1827 session. He presented a petition complaining of the Malt Act, 22 Feb. 1828. In his only known speech, 3 Mar., he urged the rejection of the Wakefield and Ferrybridge canal bill, maintaining that the House was bound to do so as long as the Aire and Calder Canal Company 'perform their contract'. He divided against Catholic relief, 12 May. He voted with the duke of Wellington's government against reduction of the salary of the lieutenant-general of the ordnance, 4 July 1828. In February 1829 Planta, the patronage secretary, listed him as one who was 'opposed to the principle' of Catholic emancipation, but he gave no recorded votes that session. His name does not appear in the lists compiled that autumn by the Ultra leader Sir Richard Vyvyan*. He was granted three weeks' leave on account of illness in his family, 10 Mar. 1830. He returned to vote against Jewish emancipation, 5 Apr., 17 May. He divided for abolition of the death penalty for forgery, 7 June 1830. He was again returned for Northallerton at the general election that summer. The ministry regarded him as one of their 'friends', but he was absent from the crucial division on the civil list, 15 Nov. 1830. He divided against the second reading of the Grey ministry's reform bill, 22 Mar., and for Gascoyne's wrecking amendment, 19 Apr. 1831. At the ensuing general election he made way for William at Northallerton. According to the Whig Thomas Creevey*, he had intended to contest Yorkshire but his father had withdrawn him.[3]

Lascelles may have been the 'son of Lord Harewood' whom the Conservatives of Pontefract had reportedly 'been trying to prevail on ... to *bleed* ... without success' in the autumn of 1832.[4] He never returned to the Commons. The death of his elder brother in 1839 made him heir to his father's earldom, and he succeeded to the title in 1841. He tendered his resignation of the lord lieutenancy of the West Riding of Yorkshire in 1846 because of his opposition to repeal of the corn laws, but was assured by the prime minister Sir Robert Peel that the office did not oblige him to support the government. He died in February 1857, four weeks after a hunting accident which had left him with a fractured skull and other injuries. He was succeeded by his eldest son, Henry Thynne Lascelles (1824-92); his second son Egremont William Lascelles (1825-92) was Conservative Member for Northallerton, 1866-8.[5]

[1] *Gent. Mag.* (1815), i. 633; (1857), i. 490; Add. 52011, John Stuart Wortley to H. E. Fox, 10 Sept. 1823. [2] Castle Howard mss, Lord William Howard to Carlisle, 10 June 1826. [3] Creevey mss, Creevey to Miss Ord, 30 Apr. 1831. [4] Staffs. RO, Stafford Jerningham mss D641/3/P/3/14/68. [5] *Gent. Mag.* (1857), i. 490.

M.P.J.C.

LASCELLES, Hon. William Saunders Sebright (1798–1851), of Harewood House, Yorks. and 13 Hanover Square, Mdx.

NORTHALLERTON	1820–1826
EAST LOOE	1826–1830
NORTHALLERTON	1831–1832
WAKEFIELD	1837–1841
WAKEFIELD	21 Apr. 1842–1847
KNARESBOROUGH	1847–2 July 1851

b. 29 Oct. 1798, 3rd s. of Henry Lascelles†, 2nd earl of Harewood (*d.* 1841), and Henrietta, da. of Lt.-Gen. Sir John Saunders Sebright†, 6th bt., of Beechwood, Herts.; bro. of Hon. Henry Lascelles*. *m.* 14 May 1823, Lady Caroline Georgina Howard, da. of George Howard†, 6th earl of Carlisle, 7s. (3 *d.v.p.*) 5da. *d.* 2 July 1851.

Ensign 1 Ft. Gds. 1817, half-pay 1818, ret. 1837.

PC 22 July 1847; comptroller of household July 1847-*d.*

Lascelles, who supposedly joined the navy at an early age before transferring to the army,[1] was returned for the family seat at Northallerton in 1820 in the room of his father, who succeeded as 2nd earl of Harewood shortly afterwards. He was an occasional attender and a silent Member who, like his father, gave general support to Lord Liverpool's ministry. He voted in defence of their conduct towards Queen Caroline, 6 Feb., and against Maberly's resolution on the state of the revenue, 6 Mar., and parliamentary reform, 9 May 1821. He was absent from the division on Catholic relief, 28 Feb. 1821, but voted against relieving Catholic peers of their disabilities, 30 Apr. 1822. He divided against more extensive tax reductions, 11, 21 Feb., reduction of the junior lords of the admiralty, 1 Mar., and abolition of one of the joint-postmasterships, 13 Mar. 1822. That autumn, the Whig Thomas Creevey* described him as being 'of the most Tory cast', and in January 1823 the patronage secretary Arbuthnot mentioned him as a possible mover or seconder of the address, observing that he was 'very presentable' but 'probably not to be got at'; nothing came of this.[2] He voted against inquiries into the prosecution of the Dublin Orange rioters, 22 Apr., and delays in chancery, 5 June 1823.

That spring he married into the Howard family, earls of Carlisle, whose politics and connections were largely Whig. Although Lord Harewood accepted the marriage, relations between him and the couple were strained at times, and the situation was no doubt exacerbated by the necessity of their living with him at Harewood and in London, as they could not afford to set up on their own. Lascelles had some heated exchanges, too, with his brother-in-law Lord Morpeth*, although his views became more tempered than those of his father and brother Henry. John Stuart Wortley* learned that 'the old earl [his wife's grandfather] is gracious and civil to him, which from what I had heard I hardly expected'.[3] Lascelles presented a petition from Northallerton curriers against the combination laws, 16 Mar., and was added to the select committee on artisans and machinery, 2 Apr. 1824. He divided in the minority for repeal of the usury laws, 8 Apr. 1824, and paired against the grant for new church building the next day. He was named to the select committee on the export of machinery, 24 Feb., and added to that on the combination laws, 17 May 1825. In February he received a letter from his brother-in-law George Agar Ellis* urging him to attend the forthcoming debate on Catholic relief. Before the division on 1 Mar., according to Lady Spencer, he 'went out declaring he could not vote with government and would have voted with us but for his father'. Edward Littleton* claimed that he had been converted by Plunket's speech and that 'he wrote to his father to announce himself a rat and ... though admonished, as I was told, on his conduct, refused to vote against the motion'.[4] In fact, he became bolder and voted for relief, 21 Apr., 10 May 1825. In the spring of 1826, after a particularly heavy loss, he gave up gambling on horses, which had been his chief weakness.[5] He paired against reducing the salary of the president of the board of trade, 12 Apr. 1826, and voted against reform of Edinburgh's representation the next day. It was reported at the beginning of May that he had 'just gone off to Yorkshire to command his troop of yeomanry, in case of its being wanted to suppress riots'.[6] At the general election that summer he vacated Northallerton for Henry, possibly on account of disagreements with his father, but was returned for East Looe with the patron, James Buller Elphinstone. Around this time he joined the London debating society set up by John Stuart Mill.[7]

In October 1826 Agar Ellis advised Lord Harewood to seek a government appointment for his son. Lascelles's wife was keen on the idea, believing that it 'might open a career for him', but she had 'no hope of any result, as all [Harewood's] feelings are against it'. This hostility apparently stemmed not from any political disagreement, but from the earl's distaste for political life and official men, which was such that 'it would make him very uncomfortable to think of William in the midst of it'.[8] Lascelles was listed as dividing both for and against Catholic relief, 6 Mar. 1827, but he presumably maintained his favourable stance. He voted to go into committee on the spring guns bill, 23 Mar. The following month he welcomed the resignations of the duke of Wellington, Peel and other Protestant Tories, and his father-in-law, now Lord Carlisle, was one of the Whigs who took office in Canning's ministry.[9] Nevertheless, he voted in the minority against the Penryn disfranchisement bill, 28 May 1827. Early in January 1828 his wife was told that William Huskisson* had considered asking him to move or second the address on behalf of Lord Goderich's ministry, but had not done so 'as it might have been disagreeable to Lord Harewood'. Shortly afterwards Thomas Macaulay* reported that Lascelles was one of a number of men he had met in Leeds who shared 'the universal opinion that none but a coalition ministry can stand or can deserve to stand'.[10] He voted for repeal of the Test Acts, 26 Feb., and Catholic relief, 12 May. He divided against extending East Retford's franchise to Bassetlaw freeholders, 21 Mar. He was absent from the East Retford division which prompted Huskisson's resignation from Wellington's ministry, 19 May, but was subsequently listed as one of the Huskissonite group by Lord Palmerston*. He voted in the minority against the East Retford bill, 27 June 1828. In February 1829 Planta, the patronage secretary, listed him as being 'with government' in favour of Catholic emancipation, and he voted accordingly, 6, 30 Mar. That autumn the Ultra leader Sir Richard Vyvyan* numbered him among the supporters of emancipation whose sentiments on a possible coalition ministry were unknown. He divided in the opposition minority on the incident at Terceira, 28 Apr. 1830, his only recorded vote of that session. At the dissolution that summer he did not stand again at East Looe, where a change of patron had occurred, and rumours that he might contest Pontefract came to nothing. He later wrote to Lady Carlisle congratulating her on Morpeth's 'glorious success' in Yorkshire.[11]

At the general election of 1831 Lascelles replaced his brother as Member for Northallerton. He divided against the second reading of the Grey ministry's reintroduced reform bill, 6 July. He voted for use of the 1831 census to determine the disfranchisement schedules, 19 July, and against the partial disfranchisement of Chippenham, 27 July, and the bill's passage, 21 Sept. He paired against the second reading of the revised bill, 17 Dec. 1831, and voted against going into committee on it, 20 Jan 1832. He agreed with Wrangham that Northallerton rather than York should be the polling place for the North Riding of Yorkshire, 24 Jan., and added that Beverley would prove most inconvenient for the East Riding. He divided against the enfranchisement of Tower Hamlets, 28 Feb., and the bill's third reading, 22 Mar., and paired against the second reading of the Irish bill, 25 May. He voted against ministers on the Russian-Dutch loan, 26 Jan., 12 July 1832. The opening of Northallerton by the Reform Act meant that he was left without a seat at the general election later that year, though he may have been the Lascelles who was reportedly pressed by the Conservatives to contest Pontefract.[12] He returned to the House as a Conservative in 1837 and supported repeal of the corn laws in 1846, but the following year he came in as a Liberal and received a household appointment. He died in July 1851 and left all his real and personal estate to his wife.[13]

[1] *Howard Sisters*, p. x. [2] Creevey mss, Creevey to Miss Ord, 19 Sept. 1822; Add. 38744, f. 49. [3] *Howard Sisters*, 32, 70, 97, 104; Add. 52011, Stuart Wortley to H.E. Fox, 10 Sept. 1823. [4] Add. 75938, Lady to Lord Spencer, 4 Mar. 1825; TNA 30/29/6/3/93. [5] *Howard Sisters*, 54. [6] Northants. RO, Agar Ellis diary, 1 May 1826. [7] *Macaulay Letters*, i, 232. [8] *Howard Sisters*, 58-59. [9] Ibid. 66, 68. [10] Ibid. 97; *Macaulay Letters*, i. 232. [11] *Leeds Mercury*, 10 July; Castle Howard mss, Lascelles to Lady Carlisle, 7 Aug. 1830. [12] Staffs. RO, Stafford Jerningham mss D641/3/P/3/14/68. [13] *Gent. Mag.* (1851), ii. 193; PROB 11/2136/574; IR26/1906/477.

M.P.J.C.

LATOUCHE, Robert (1773–1844), of Harristown, co. Kildare.

CO. KILDARE 1802–1830

b. Oct. 1773, 1st s. of John Latouche†, MP [I], of Harristown and Gertrude, da. of Robert Uniacke Fitzgerald of Corkbeg, co. Cork; bro. of John Latouche†. *educ.* Kildare; Harrow 1785-8; Eton 1788-90; Trinity, Dublin 8 Nov. 1790, aged 17. *m.* 17 Apr. 1810, Lady Emily Le Poer Trench, da. of William, 1st earl of Clancarty [I], 3s. 3da.(2 *d.v.p.*). *suc.* fa. 1810. *d.* 22 May 1844.[1]

MP [I] 1794-1800.

Sheriff, co. Kildare 1797-8.

Commdt. Kilcullen yeoman cav. 1798.

Dir. Farming Soc. of Ireland 1815-24, Barrow Navigation Co. 1837.

Latouche continued to sit undisturbed for county Kildare on the combined interest of his family and the duke of Leinster, who had sponsored his election to Brooks's, 5 Apr. 1804. In 1810 he had succeeded to his father's partnership in the family bank and substantial estates in Kildare, to which he had added property at Narraghmore in 1813, acquired from the Keating family for £93,000.[2] At the 1820 general election he was again returned unopposed.[3] A regular but mostly silent attender, he voted with the Whig opposition to the Liverpool ministry on most major issues, especially economy, retrenchment and reduced taxation.[4] He voted for Catholic relief, 28 Feb. 1821, 21 Apr., 10 May 1825. He was granted six weeks' leave on urgent private business, 1 May 1821. He divided for parliamentary reform, 25 Apr. 1822, 24 Apr. 1823, and inquiry into the parliamentary franchise, 20 Feb. 1823.

At the 1826 general election he stood on 'the same liberal principles' and was returned unopposed.[5] He voted for Catholic claims, 6 Mar. 1827, 12 May 1828. On 19 Mar. 1827 he wrote to John Hely Hutchinson I* asking him to support the passage of two presentments for road making at the next assizes, one of which was to finish a road from Latouche's colliery at Slieve-nar-Man, county Tipperary.[6] He was granted a month's leave to attend the Kildare assizes, 23 Mar. 1827. He presented petitions for Catholic emancipation, 23 Feb., 13 Mar., and voted accordingly, 6, 30 Mar. 1829. He presented petitions for repeal of the Irish Subletting and Vestry Acts, 13 Mar., 3 Apr. In October 1829 the Ultra leader Sir Richard Vyvyan* numbered him among those who had voted in favour of emancipation whose attitude towards a putative coalition government was 'unknown'. On 24 Dec. 1829 Lord Anglesey was informed that Daniel O'Connell's* endeavours to 'make the Society for the Improvement of Ireland a debating club' had resulted in 'the loss of the duke of Leinster, La Touche and some others of our best members'.[7] He was granted three weeks' leave to attend the assizes, 11 Mar. 1830. He divided for the abolition of the Irish viceroyalty, 11 May, and information on privy councillors' emoluments, 14 May. That day, in his only known spoken intervention, he presented and briefly endorsed a petition from the Provincial Bank of Ireland for abolition of the death penalty for forgery, for which he voted, 7 June. He divided for Jewish emancipation, 17 May, and parliamentary reform, 28 May. His only other recorded votes of the 1830 session were for reduction of the grants for South American missions, 7 June, consular services, 11 June, and Novia Scotia and Prince Edward Island, 14 June. On 21 June 1830 he presented a county petition against increased Irish stamp and spirit duties.

At the 1830 general election Latouche offered again, but 'abruptly' withdrew three days later, explaining that he found the attendance required of a Member 'incompatible' with his arrangements in 'business and in personal life'. His actions were widely condemned. 'It is very unexpected', complained the *Dublin Evening Post*, and he 'has not acted with frankness towards his late constituents'. In the ensuing contest he 'positively' denied charges of attempting to bring in a 'nominee'.[8] Latouche died at 27 Merrion Square, Dublin in May 1844 and was succeeded by his son John (1814-1904).[9]

[1] *Dublin Evening Post*, 28 May 1844. *Hist. Irish Parl.* v. 70 gives 19 May. [2] *Hist. Irish Parl.* v. 70. [3] *Dublin Evening Post*, 9, 25 Mar. 1820. [4] *Black Bk.* (1823), 169; *Session of Parl. 1825*, p. 466. [5] *Dublin Evening Post*, 10, 17, 20, 29 June 1826. [6] PRO NI, Donoughmore mss G/6/10. [7] PRO NI, Anglesey mss 32/A/3/1/267. [8] *Dublin Evening Post*, 15, 20, 29 July, 14, 19 Aug. 1830. [9] Ibid. 28 May 1844.

P.J.S.

LAWLEY, Francis (1782–1851), of Middleton Hall, nr. Tamworth, Staffs. and 18 Grosvenor Square, Mdx.

WARWICKSHIRE 7 Nov. 1820–1832

bap. 13 Sept. 1782,[1] 3rd but 2nd surv. s. of Sir Robert Lawley†, 5th bt. (*d.* 1793), of Spoonhill, Salop and Canwell Priory, Staffs. and Jane, da. of Beilby Thompson of Escrick, Yorks.; bro. of Sir Robert Lawley †, 6th bt. and Paul Beilby Thompson*. *educ.* Rugby 1792; Christ Church, Oxf. 1800; fellow, All Souls 1803-15. *m.* 18 May 1815, Mary Anne, da. of George Talbot of Temple Guiting, Glos., *s.p. suc.* bro. Robert as 7th bt. and to estates in Salop, Staffs. and Warws. 10 Apr. 1834. *d.* 30 Jan. 1851.

Cornet Warws. yeoman cav. 1803, capt. 1805, maj. 1818, lt.-col. 1845, res. 1848.

Lawley's father, who represented Warwickshire 'under Whig auspices', died in 1793, having entrusted the care of his younger sons Francis and Beilby, then aged ten and eight, to their mother (*d.* 1816), a Yorkshire heiress, and directed their brother Robert, his heir, to provide for them.[2] Thwarted in Wenlock and Warwickshire, Robert represented Newcastle-under-Lyme as a Whig, 1802-6, before leaving for Italy, where he devoted himself to art collecting. He complained in April 1820 that he had spent £50,000 on his brothers and of their enmity, neglect and ingratitude towards him.[3] Francis Lawley remained at Oxford, where he graduated in law, until he married, when his sister Jane, Lady Middleton, made Middleton Hall, near Tamworth on the Staffordshire-Warwickshire border, available to him.[4] A keen agriculturist and yeomanry officer, the Tory Sir Charles Mordaunt* considered him popular 'as a farmer, yeoman and *fox-hunter*, and of straightforward independence ... not, as his two brothers, radical'.[5] He inherited a town house in Grosvenor Square and £200,000 on the death of his maternal uncle Richard Thompson in September 1820 and successfully contested Warwickshire, which Mordaunt vacated, at a by-election in November.[6] Supporters of his opponent, the radical Birmingham banker Richard Spooner*, denied him a hearing on the hustings, but at the nomination meeting, 19 Oct., he declared for the 'church and the constitution', refused to give pledges and expressed support for 'temperate reform'.[7] Squibs highlighted 'Frank's fortune' and love of the chase.[8] Spooner failed with a petition on behalf of the Coventry freeholders, whose votes, if accepted, could have cost Lawley his victory.[9] He now lobbied successfully with his brothers to prevent Cecil Weld Forester† taking the title Baron Wenlock (which Robert coveted) when he became a coronation peer.[10]

Lawley attended the House frequently, spoke and voted sparingly and gained respect for his independence, common sense and readiness to promote Warwickshire interests. He was named to few major committees prior to that on the Bank of England's charter, 23 May 1832, but he was a busy Member and his appointment to ones on county business (highways, 25 Feb. 1821, the game laws, 13 Mar. 1823, prisons, 18 Mar. 1824, county rates, 19 May 1824, 9 Mar. 1825, 2 Mar. 1826, clerks of the peace, 23 Feb. 1830) and especially those on artisans and machinery, 13 Feb. 1824, 24 Feb. 1825, the combination laws, 10 May 1825, and Irish vagrants, 12 Mar. 1828, which materially affected Birmingham and the silk towns, was considered important locally, as was the part he played in the passage of numerous transport and enclosure bills.[11] He is not known to have voted on Queen Caroline's case (or with the Liverpool ministry on any issue), but he presented a petition from Southam for restoration of her name to the liturgy, 13 Feb. 1821.[12] He delayed voting for Catholic relief, which his colleague Dugdale Stratford Dugdale and most Warwickshire squires opposed, until 1825 (1 Mar., 21 Apr., 10 May).[13] A radical publication that year noted that he 'appeared to attend frequently and to vote with the opposition'.[14] He divided for parliamentary reform, 9 May 1821, 25 Apr. 1822, 20 Feb., 24 Apr., 2 June 1823, 13 Apr. 1826.

In his maiden speech, 8 Feb. 1821, Lawley endorsed the prayer of the banker Thomas Attwood's† Birmingham distress petition and asserted that the 'experience of Birmingham' did 'not bear out the improvements in trade outlined by ministers'. He presented the farmers' distress petitions, 20 Feb., 5 Mar.,[15] and testified to the 'general and strong opposition' in Warwickshire to Scarlett's poor bill, 24 May 1821. To the annoyance of some of his 1820 supporters, he divided with opposition for extensive tax cuts, 11, 21 Feb., admiralty reductions, 1 Mar. and abolition of one of the joint-postmasterships, 2 May, and failed to comment on the agriculturists' distress petitions he presented, 1 Mar., and others criticizing remedies proposed by the political economist David Ricardo*, 8 May, and the foreign secretary Lord Castlereagh, 21 May 1822.[16] He voted for gradual abolition of the salt duties, 28 Feb., against the Irish constables bill, 7 June 1822, and for inquiry into the prosecution of the Dublin Orange rioters, 22 Apr. 1823. Representing Birmingham interests, in 1824 he brought up petitions for repeal of the excise licence duties, 12 Mar., and combination laws, 15 Mar., against the Bristol town dues bill, 13 Apr., and the sale of beer bill, 11, 13 May, and took charge of the assay office's petition and bill regulating the hallmarking of wrought silver plate, 19 Feb., 15 Mar., and the contentious Birmingham gas light bill, which he withdrew, 6 May 1824, and carried amended in 1825.[17] He voted to repeal the usury laws, 8 Apr. 1824, 8 Feb. 1825, and to condemn the indictment in Demerara of the Methodist missionary John Smith, 11 June 1824. During the recess he consulted the home secretary Peel at Drayton concerning the dispute between the Coventry ratepayers and the corporation and made a comparative study of corporations in counties corporate.[18] He called for a select committee and presented Birmingham's petition for lower duties on metals, 11 Mar., and endorsed complaints of the 'mischief' caused by the repeal of the combination laws, 29 Apr., 11 May 1825.[19] He paired against the duke of Cumberland's annuity bill, 6 June.[20] He indicated that the manufacturers would support the proposed increases in board of trade salaries, 14 June 1825, but divided against receiving the report on its president's, 10 Apr. 1826.[21] He voted for military reductions, 10 Mar., and to abolish flogging, 15 Mar. 1826. He presented and endorsed anti-slavery petitions, 26 Apr., 5 May, carried the Rugby School estates bill and contributed £100 to the Coventry weavers' distress fund.[22] Before the dissolution, Birmingham Chamber of Manufactures and Commerce, whose deputations to the Bank of England he had assisted during the 1825-6 crisis, carried a resolution commending his conduct.[23] His return was not opposed. At the nomination meeting, 13 June 1826, he acknowledged the controversy caused by his pro-Catholic and opposition votes and defended his right to sit unfettered. On corn, he expressed regret at endeavours to separate agricultural and commercial interests 'so interwoven ... that they must both flourish or decay together' and predicted that the discredited system of taking corn price averages would be done away with in the next Parliament and the ports opened at a restrictive price.[24] His brother Beilby, who had taken the name Thompson on succeeding to Escrick, came in for Wenlock.

Lawley divided for Catholic relief, 6 Mar., kept a low profile pending the appointment of a successor to Lord Liverpool as premier and presented petitions for repeal of the Test Acts, 31 May, 8 June 1827. Presenting the Birmingham ratepayers' petition for the transfer of East Retford's seats to Birmingham, 29 June 1827, he said that the town deserved to be represented by men familiar with its diverse and complex manufacturing interests and emphasized that the petitioners left it to Parliament to determine Birmingham's franchise and electoral regulations – a sticking point in the proposed Grampound-Leeds and Penryn-Manchester transfers. He was directed with Charles Tennyson to introduce a bill effecting the transfer, 31 Jan., and had copies 'served on the returning officer of East Retford and high bailiff of Birmingham', 4 Feb. 1828. He divided against sluicing at East Retford, 21 Mar. He presented petitions, 25, 26, 28 Feb., 1 Apr., and voted to repeal the Test Acts, 26 Feb., and for Catholic relief, 12 May, having brought up favourable petitions from Catholics of the Midland counties, 24 Apr., and Coventry, 1 May. He presented numerous petitions for repeal of the 1827 Malt Act, 12 Mar., and the Small Notes Act, 15 July, and against the friendly societies bill, 24 Apr., and slavery, 11 July. Contributing to the discussion provoked by the Warwickshire magistrates' petition, 6 Mar., he criticized the 'pre-trial imprisonment of young offenders, often for three months, where they became educated in crime' and cited Eardley Wilmot's corroborative statistics. Introducing a petition from the guardians and gunbarrel and arms manufacturers of Birmingham for repeal of the Foreign Enlistment Act, 3 July, he explained, in what he termed a 'rare speech', how the Act, by authorizing customs officers to seize arms destined for export or to protect unlicensed vessels, had assisted manufacturers in Hamburg and elsewhere to Birmingham's detriment. He promised to revive the issue should ministers fail to act and ridiculed Huskisson's arguments that the matter was adequately dealt with through orders in council. He divided with opposition for ordnance reductions, 4 July 1828.

With opinion in Warwickshire and the House divided on the rival Napton and Oxford canal bills, the Birmingham poor bill, the Catholic question and distress, the 1829 session was a difficult one for Lawley. As the patronage secretary Planta had predicted, he voted 'with government' for Catholic emancipation, 6, 30 Mar., and presented and endorsed Birmingham's favourable petitions, 9, 27 Mar. He testified to the distress referred to in the Nuneaton ribbon weavers' petition, but rejected its plea for protective tariffs, 20 Mar. Nor would he, as bid by the meeting,[25] support Attwood's 8,000-signature Birmingham petition attributing distress to overtrading and currency change, 4 June. He explained:

> I am firm in my conviction that no such change as they seem to desire can take place in the currency without diffusing the most wide-spreading injustice among all classes of the community ... I do not think the state of the currency is the cause of the prevailing distress, which I lament as much as any man ... It is an acknowledged fact that bankers are ready in all directions to advance money upon receiving good and adequate security. Is not this a more wholesome state of affairs than when persons of no capital could command paper money for every kind of ill-advised speculation? There are other reasons ... to account for the present distress, besides this supposition of the altered currency. Great overproduction is ... one of them.

He voted to transfer East Retford's seats to Birmingham, 5 May 1829, 5 Mar. 1830.

Denis Le Marchant† recalled Lawley, 'a country gentleman ... of high standing and consideration in the House', as one of the instigators of the meeting held on 3 Mar. 1830 'to endeavour to form a party under the guidance of Lord Althorp with a view to take off some of the most oppressive taxes', which heralded the revival of the Whig opposition.[26] He naturally divided steadily with them for the remainder of that Parliament, including for Jewish emancipation, 17 May (when he also presented Birmingham's favourable petition), and to end capital punishment for forgery, 24 May, 7 June. He confirmed the Warwickshire petitioners' distress and welcomed the chancellor of the exchequer Goulburn's retrenchment proposals, 17 Mar. He took charge of many local petitions and bills, including Birmingham Chamber of Commerce's petition for equalization of the sugar duties, 14 June; but his chief concerns were the fate of the London-Birmingham canal bill, beleaguered following revelations of fraud and the culpable neglect of the attorney Eyre Lee, on which he commented, 11 Mar., 20 May, and the proposed closure of the ordnance proof house at Birmingham. He opposed this as a member of the Birmingham delegation, and complained on presenting their petition how the gunsmiths and arms manufacturers had been goaded to overproduction, 25 Mar. On 2 Apr., drawing heavily on the 1828 finance committee report, he argued that the manufacture of arms by government at Enfield, Middlesex was 'expensive and unnecessary', criticized ministers for directing the East India Company to buy their arms there instead of from Birmingham, and vainly sought reductions in the ordnance factory grants. With a further motion in mind, he ordered accounts itemizing production costs at Enfield, 26 May. Nothing came of a rumoured opposition at the general election in August, but Attwood's Birmingham Political Union members fêted Sir Francis Burdett* and mustered in force to cross-examine Lawley on the hustings, 6 Aug. 1830. Angry but undaunted, he defended his record, protested at Birmingham's ingratitude, refused to be tied down by pledges, and criticized Attwood's currency theories and support for Lord Blandford's* 'absurd' reform scheme.[27]

Ministers listed Lawley among their 'foes', and he helped to vote them out on the civil list, 15 Nov. 1830. He presented numerous anti-slavery petitions, 12 Nov. 1830, 19 Mar. 1831. The St. Martin's (Birmingham) burial ground bill was successfully rushed through, but bills entrusted to him for the proposed Birmingham-Basford railway, 21 Mar., 20 Apr., the Birmingham poor, 21 Mar., and the King Edward VI grammar school, 18 Apr., became casualties of the dissolution. He divided for the Grey ministry's reform bill at its second reading, 22 Mar., confirmed his support for it at the county meeting, 4 Apr., brought up favourable petitions from Warwick, 18 Apr., and voted against Gascoyne's wrecking amendment, 19 Apr. 1831.[28] His failure to present the county reform petition before the dissolution attracted notice, but his return at the general election, when the reformer Sir Gray Skipwith replaced Dugdale as his colleague, was never in doubt.[29] He praised the bill and the decision to award Birmingham two Members, but his insistence on sitting unfettered irked the political unions and ensured that his parliamentary conduct was critically reviewed in the *Midland Representative*.[30] Lawley goaded Hunt, the reluctant presenter of the Stockport reform petition, by promising to oppose its reception if Hunt doubted its merits, 30 June 1831. He divided for the second reading of the reintroduced reform bill, 6 July, and supported it steadily in committee, where his only wayward vote, for the enfranchisement of £50 tenants-at-will, 18 Aug., was attuned to local interests.[31] Contradicting the anti-reformer Mackworth Praed's claim that Birmingham returned the Warwickshire Members, 24 Aug., he attributed his victory in 1820 to support from the eastern hundreds, 'chiefly because my opinions coincided with the agricultural interest'. He cast doubt on Hunt's unsubstantiated claims of waning support for the bill without the ballot, 30 Aug. The Beilby Thompson estate bill had received royal assent, 23 Aug., Robert was created Baron Wenlock at the coronation and the three brothers attended a party meeting at Lord Ebrington's, 21 Sept.[32] Travelling between London and Warwick during the annual yeomanry training, Lawley voted for the reform bill at its third reading, 19 Sept., and passage, 21 Sept., rallied his troop with a rousing speech at Warwick bowling green, 22 Sept., and divided for the second reading of the Scottish measure, 23 Sept., and for Ebrington's confidence motion, 10 Oct.[33] At the Warwickshire meeting, 8 Nov., he thanked his constituents for praising his conduct and petitioning in protest at the bill's defeat.[34] He voted for the revised bill at its second reading, 17 Dec. 1831, consistently for its details, and for the third reading, 22 Mar., and the address requesting the king to appoint only ministers who would carry it unimpaired, 10 May 1832. He voted for the second reading of the Irish bill, 25 May, and against a Conservative amendment to the Scottish measure, 1 June 1832. He divided with government on the Dublin election controversy, 23 Aug. 1831, Portugal, 9 Feb., the navy civil departments bill, 6 Apr., and the Russian-Dutch loan, 12, 16, 20 July, and voted to make coroners' inquests public, 20 June 1832.

He brought up numerous petitions on local legislation and private bills on his constituents' behalf and successfully handled the revived bills for the grammar school and the Birmingham poor. As committee chairman, he was obliged to withdraw the 1831 Birmingham-Basford railway bill, which Edward Littleton and certain Birmingham and Castle Bromwich landowners opposed, 6 July. He and Skipwith secured the passage of the Birmingham-London railway bill after a severe struggle during which they carried the division on 18 June by 125-46, but it foundered in the Lords, 12 July 1832.[35] Qualifying remarks by the chairman of the Lords select committee on the bill, Lord Wharncliffe, at a meeting of the scheme's promoters at London's *Thatched House Tavern* next day, Lawley asserted that diligent attendance in committee to hear evidence for and against it had convinced him that the fears and objections of landed proprietors were unfounded, 'otherwise he could not have supported the measure as he had done'.[36] Irked by delays, disruptions to the business of the House and procedural changes pending the reform bill's passage, he exposed the system of 'parallel lists' for presenting petitions operated by the Speaker's office, 23 Feb. 1832. That day he succeeded in calling up Warwickshire petitions against the importation of French ribbons, testified to the petitioners' forbearance and the great hardship caused by the partial introduction of free trade, but declined to endorse their plea for prohibitory tariffs.

Lawley was admitted to Brooks's, 29 Jan. 1832. He announced his impending retirement on health grounds, 22 June 1832, and ceased to play an active part at elections. A personal friend and hunting companion of Peel, he declined an invitation to stand for Tamworth in 1847.[37] In 1834 he succeeded Robert, who had no legitimate issue, as 8th baronet and to the Lawley estates, where he promoted cattle breeding and spent £40-50,000 repairing dilapidated farm buildings and cottages. He died without issue at Middleton Hall in January 1851, recalled as a patron of Birmingham School of Design and the Midland Counties and Royal shows, and as one of the last aristocrats to pronounce 'goold for gold, woold for would'.[38] He was succeeded in the baronetcy and estates by Beilby (since 1839 Baron Wenlock) and his heirs. His will provided generously for his widow (*d.* 21 Dec. 1878).[39]

[1] IGI (Warws.). [2] PROB 11/1230/159. [3] Hull Univ. Lib. Forbes Adams mss DDFA/39/45/22. [4] Ibid. 44/56. [5] Norf. RO, Wodehouse of Kimberley mss KIM6/37, Walton to J. Wodehouse, 7 Nov. 1820. [6] CUL, Buxton of Shadwell Court mss 117/61; Salop Archives, Corbett of Longnor mss 1066/125, diary of Katherine Plymley, 2 Nov.; *Coventry Herald*, 3, 10, 17 Nov. 1820. [7] *Warwick Advertiser*, 23 Oct. 1820. [8] Warws. RO, election handbills CR1886; 2023/1/4. [9] *The Times*, 4, 6-9, 16 Nov. 1820. [10] Forbes Adams mss 39/45/21-27; Add. 38369, f. 332. [11] *The Times*, 8 Apr. 1826. [12] Ibid. 13 Feb. 1821. [13] *Warwick Advertiser*, 17 June 1826. [14] *Session of Parl. 1825*, p. 472. [15] *The Times*, 21 Feb., 6 Mar. 1821. [16] *Creevey Pprs.* ii. 34; A. Mitchell, *Whigs in Opposition*, 163; *The Times*, 2 Mar., 9, 21 May 1822; *Warwick Advertiser*, 17 June 1826. [17] *The Times*, 13, 16 Mar., 14 Apr., 12, 14 May 1824. [18] Add. 40369, ff. 89, 91, 298, 300; 40371, f. 4. [19] *The Times*, 30 Apr., 12 May 1825. [20] Ibid. 10 June 1825. [21] Ibid. 15 June 1825. [22] Ibid. 27 Apr., 6, 9 May; *Coventry Herald*, 12 May 1826. [23] *The Times*, 8 Apr. 1826. [24] *Warwick Advertiser*, 10, 17 June; *The Times*, 17 June 1826. [25] *The Times*, 11 May 1829. [26] Grey mss, Howick jnl. 3 Mar.; Castle Howard mss, Graham to Morpeth [3 Mar. 1830]; Le Marchant, *Althorp*, 244; Mitchell, 226-7. [27] *Coventry Mercury*, 11 July; *Warwick Advertiser*, 24 July, 7 Aug. 1830. [28] *Warwick Advertiser*, 9 Apr. 1831. [29] *Coventry Herald*, 22 Apr.; *Midland Representative*, 30 Apr.; St. Deiniol's Lib. Glynne-Gladstone mss 454, G. Nicholls to T. Gladstone, 2 May; Brougham mss, Philips to Brougham, 5 May; *Warwick Advertiser*, 7, 14 May 1831; Warws. RO MI 247, Philips Mems. ii. 124-5. [30] *Midland Representative*, 14 May; *Coventry Mercury*, 15 May 1831. [31] *The Times*, 18, 19 Aug. 1831. [32] *Greville Mems.* ii. 283. [33] *Warwick Advertiser*, 24 Sept., 15 Oct. 1831. [34] Ibid. 29 Oct., 12 Nov. 1831. [35] *LJ*, lxiv. 374. [36] *The Times*, 17 July 1832. [37] *Birmingham Jnl.* 30 June 1832; *The Times*, 6 Dec. 1847. [38] *Warwick Advertiser*, 8 Feb.; *Gent. Mag.* (1851), i. 433; *N and Q* (ser. 3), x. 456. [39] PROB 11/2134/491; IR26/1906/364.

M.M.E.

LAWSON, Marmaduke (1792–1823), of Boroughbridge Hall, Yorks.

BOROUGHBRIDGE 1818–22 Mar. 1819

BOROUGHBRIDGE 30 Mar. 1819–7 June 1820

b. 10 July 1792,[1] 1st s. of Rev. Marmaduke Lawson, rect. of Sproatley, and Barbara Isabella, da. of John Wilkinson of the M. Temple, h. of Rev. James Wilkinson of Boroughbridge Hall. *educ.* Shrewsbury; St. John's, Camb. 1811; fellow, Magdalene, Camb. 1815. *unm. suc.* fa. 1814. *d.* 10 Mar. 1823.

Capt. N. regt. W. Riding yeomanry 1817.

Lawson, whose family controlled the Wilkinson interest at Boroughbridge through his mother's inheritance, had successfully challenged the duke of Newcastle's domination of that borough in 1818 and at a by-election in 1819. Though his contemporaries regarded him as an amusing eccentric, some passages in letters to his old headmaster, Dr. Butler, suggest that he may have been prone to mental instability: an illness that had affected his academic career at Cambridge caused him to 'set the college on fire' and walk naked 'at noon day'. His deep-seated conservatism led him to rail against some 'blackguard discontented stocking weavers' who were 'abusing' the government in 1812, and six years later he referred dismissively to a 'surly democrat'. Yet until Peterloo he voted against Lord Liverpool's government.[2] In 1820 he offered again for Boroughbridge with Richard Spooner, against Newcastle's nominees. Both parties elected their own bailiffs, who conducted separate polls, but it was Lawson and Spooner's return that was accepted by the sheriff of Yorkshire. All four candidates were chaired and in the ensuing affray Lawson narrowly escaped injury.[3] He is not known to have spoken in the House in this period and his only recorded vote was against government on the appointment of an additional baron of exchequer in Scotland, 15 May 1820. Three weeks later, as Lawson had anticipated, he and Spooner were unseated on petition. He died, politically unfulfilled, in March 1823. No will has been found. His brother Andrew became the heir to their mother's estate.

[1] IGI (Yorks.). [2] Add. 34583, ff. 371, 405; 34584, f. 330. [3] T. Lawson-Tancred, *Recs. of a Yorks. Manor*, 335-41.

R.M.H.

LEADER, Nicholas Philpot (1773–1836), of Dromagh Castle, Kanturk, co. Cork.

Kilkenny 1830–1832

b. 19 Jan. 1773, 1st s. of William Leader of Mount Leader and Margaret, da. of Wareham St. Leger of Heyward's Hill. *educ.* by Mr. Lee; Trinity, Dublin 1789; King's Inns 1791; M. Temple 1793, called [I] 1798. *m.* 2 Nov. 1807, Margaret, da. and coh. of Andrew Nash of Nashville, 3s. 2da. *suc.* fa. 1828. *d.* 7 Feb. 1836.

Leader was the first member of his family to start coal mining on their 'vast' estates in county Cork, which included Mount Leader, purchased by his father from his cousin John Leader. His funds 'being limited during his father's lifetime', he obtained a loan of £10,000 at five per cent from government, to be paid off by instalments according to his profits, and 'his first step was to open an access to the exhaustless collieries around him'.[1] In 1812 he stood unsuccessfully for county Cork as a supporter of Catholic claims in a junior partnership with a prominent Whig.[2] Next year he interceded at the Catholic Association to prevent a duel between Maurice Magrath and Daniel O'Connell*, whose brother-in-law later complained of how the affair had been 'patched up by that miserable meddler in Catholic affairs'.[3] In a letter to Peel, the home secretary, submitting plans for a railroad from his colliery at Dromagh to the market at Cork, 26 July 1822, he explained that 'in consequence of the Acts passed' by Peel as Irish secretary and his successor Charles Grant*, 'my establishment in the centre of the distressed and disturbed districts has ... been able to bear up against two famines', and that he could 'devote my time ... to the wants of others, having the ... satisfaction of knowing that my workmen are fully able to supply themselves'.[4] In December that year he spoke at the meeting of Catholics in Dublin called to vote an address to the Irish viceroy Lord Wellesley. He declined to attend the Association dinner for the 'friends of civil and religious liberty', 2 Feb. 1826. He was a founder member of the Society for the Improvement of Ireland established in 1828 and a regular speaker at its meetings.[5] In September 1828 he was nominated at the Tralee by-election at the instigation of O'Connell, on account of his local residence and commercial expertise, in a token challenge to the corporation's control. Next month he and O'Connell attended a meeting of the independents called to open the borough.[6] He was received with 'long and continued cheering' at the Association's meeting for a petition in support of emancipation, 20 Jan. 1829, when he praised Protestants and Catholics for their co-operation, paid tribute to the Irish Catholics for their services to the Protestant constitution and moved that the petition be sent to Parliament: 'He would not count the hours that the battle would last, but he would proclaim that the victory was won'.[7] That month Maurice O'Connell* chaired a Tralee meeting at which resolutions were passed thanking Leader for his 'great exertions and splendid subscription towards the opening of this borough'.[8] He was again nominated ineffectually at the by-election of June, providing the basis for a petition against the return, which in the event lapsed.[9]

Shortly before the 1830 general election it was reported that he was 'ready to start' for Carlow if the independents decided 'everything was clear and certain', which they were unable to do. 'I greatly regret that if it was Leader's serious intention to contest this borough', one of them informed O'Connell, 'he did not see the propriety of making you the organ of conveying his wishes', whereupon 'every effort ... would have been made'.[10] After declining an offer to stand for Clare, where he later claimed to have 'sent my friend O'Connell in my place', he accepted an invitation from the independents of Kilkenny. With O'Connell's support he offered as a 'Liberal', vowing to reform the corporation, which had hitherto dominated the representation. Leader has 'sometimes appeared *ad captandum* as a wild and visionary theorist', reported the *Kilkenny Moderator*, 'but we happen to know that, setting aside these chimerical and political aberrations, he is really, as a county gentleman ... and resident landlord, one of the most excellent persons'. He was returned after a four-day struggle, amidst allegations of intimidation and outrage by his supporters. At his election dinner, which was attended by O'Connell, 11 Oct. 1830, toasts were drunk to repeal of the Union.[11]

He was listed by the Wellington ministry among their 'foes' and as 'opposed to government' by Henry Brougham*. He will be 'most useful', an informant advised Maurice Fitzgerald*, by 'calling the attention of the public, out of the House, to the enormous abuses that are suffered to exist' in Ireland.[12] In his maiden speech, 3 Nov. 1830, he criticized the lack of government measures to relieve the 'mass of misery, distress and destitution' in Ireland, which would only increase support for repeal. He objected to the martial language of Sir Henry Hardinge, the Irish secretary, declaring that the Irish had 'uniformly showed a disposition to submit to the laws', 5 Nov. He voted for repeal of the Irish Subletting Act, 11 Nov., and reduction of West Indian wheat import duties, 12 Nov., when he presented Athlone petitions for Jewish emancipation and inquiry into its corporation, which had 'diverted' its poor relief funds to other purposes. He divided against government on the civil list, 15 Nov. On the 19th he presented and endorsed a Galway petition against 'corporate usurpation in Ireland and the conversion of public funds to private purposes', adding that he had similar ones from Galway and Kilkenny, where lands worth £10,000 per annum had been 'converted to any purpose but that of sheltering the poor as originally intended'. He presented them, 14 Dec., when he contemplated introducing a bill 'for a practical redress of admitted abuses' in Kilkenny and the 'prevention of the malversation of the public revenue of the city'. (No bill was forthcoming.) He supported a motion for returns of Irish freeholder electors, 2 Dec. That day he welcomed Wyse's bill for employment of the Irish poor, which would do 'more to repress disturbances than all the exertion of military strength'. 'Your friend Mr. Leader made an excellent speech on the subject', Wyse was informed by his agent.[13] He demanded greater ministerial attention to the problems of Ireland, 11, 23 Dec. On 17 Dec. he moved for a new writ for Bere Alston where the Member had succeeded to the earldom of Beverley but had yet to transfer to the Lords, insisting that 'the first duty of this House is to fill up the vacancies in their own body'; but he waived his motion following the intervention of the Speaker. He defended the Grey ministry's Irish legal appointments, 20 Dec. 1830. On 8 Feb. 1831 he denied that the Irish were ready to use force to obtain repeal, saying that he had recently attended without being 'afraid' a meeting of 30,000 Catholics, at which he had advocated the 'advantages to be derived from English connection' and received a 'unanimous vote of confidence'. He presented repeal petitions from Dublin, 14 Feb., when he explained that his desire to 'act with moderation' prevented him from endorsing it, and Kilkenny, 30 Mar. He objected to the withdrawal of grants to Irish charities 'at a time of ruin and misery', 23 Feb., and to the cessation of Irish public work schemes, 1 Mar. He argued for Irish first fruits to be applied to relief of the people, 14 Mar., and for more employment schemes, 18 Mar., and welcomed proposals to issue exchequer bills for 'local and temporary' relief, 30 Mar. On 13 Apr. he denounced the 'abstract theories' and 'new doctrines of the economical reformers' and demanded greater attention to 'the wants of the Irish'. He supported the Irish vestries bill, 18 Apr., and called for curbs on the 'corrupt and infamous practices' of Irish sheriffs, 20 Apr. He believed the ministry's English reform bill would give 'general satisfaction', 9 Mar., and voted for its second reading, 22 Mar. On the 24th he presented factual evidence showing that Ireland was underrepresented and demanded additional Members for Irish counties with more than 250,000 inhabitants and a second Member for Kilkenny city. He denied that reform would give an 'undue preponderance' to Catholics and presented a favourable petition, 30 Mar. He divided against Gascoyne's wrecking amendment, 19 Apr. 1831.

At the ensuing general election Leader stood again as a reformer, promising to oppose the Irish Subletting Act and introduce a motion against the 'monstrous tyranny' of Irish tithes. He was returned unopposed.[14] He voted for the second reading of the reintroduced reform bill, 6 July, at least twice against the adjournment, 12 July 1831, and gave steady support to its details. He divided for its third reading, 19 Sept., and passage, 21 Sept., and voted for the second reading of the Scottish bill, 23 Sept., though he advocated an increase in the Scottish representation, 4 Oct. He divided for Lord Ebrington's confidence motion, 10 Oct. He demanded more Members for Ireland on account of its population, 17 Oct., 12 Dec., when he asserted that London's claims to additional representatives were not sufficient 'to warrant the House excluding some more distant parts of the empire from any share in the representation'. He presented petitions for repeal of the Irish Vestry Acts and the abolition of tithes, but regretted that the Tithes Composition Act had not been more generally applied as it had produced 'peace in many places', 22 June. Next day he condemned the Newtownbarry massacre, saying that 'calling out the yeomanry to enforce the payment of tithes ... ought never to be resorted to', and voted for printing the Waterford petition for disarming the Irish yeomanry, 11 Aug. He defended the Irish board of public works, 30 June, and grants for Irish roads and bridges, 5 July. He argued against repeal of the corn laws and any further 'sacrifice Ireland may be doomed to make to a free trade system', 25 July. He presented three petitions for Irish poor laws that day, upbraiding his fellow Irish Members for having done so little 'to alleviate the wants or meet the wishes of their constituents'. In an article published that month Richard Sheil* commended him as a 'most useful Member':

> He has a minute knowledge of Ireland, and possesses perhaps more acquaintance with its statistics than any other of its representatives. He never speaks without conveying information, and on that account he is always attended to, although it must be owned, that he sometimes displays so much vivacity, and animates his oratorical physique with so much impetuosity of emotion, that he gives the Saxon temperament of his hearers a start.[15]

He voted against disqualification of the Dublin election committee, 29 July, and to postpone the issue of a new writ, 8 Aug., when he called for inquiry, but with ministers on the controversy, 23 Aug. He opposed the union of Irish parishes bill, 10, 17 Aug., when he contended that Ireland was 'overrun with churches', and 19 Aug., when he divided against it. On 11 Aug. he clashed with Spring Rice, the treasury secretary, over the delayed Irish estimates. He expressed 'great alarm' at the powers conferred on the new lord lieutenants of Irish counties, which would give them 'the nomination to seats in Parliament' and 'defeat the benefit expected from the reform bill', 15 Aug., and warned that abolition of the Irish viceroyalty would damage the economy, 31 Aug. He defended grants to the Hibernian Society for Soldiers' Children, 22 Aug., and the Royal Dublin Society, of which he had 'been a member for the last 29 years', 29 Aug. That day he spoke and voted for Sadler's proposal for legal provision for the Irish poor. On the 31st he defended a grant for Irish legal proceedings which been opposed by Hume, protesting that 'the system of economy some persons wish to pursue seems to pauperise one half of the empire, in order to bring all the wealth to the other'. He presented and endorsed petitions against the grant to the Kildare Place Society, maintaining that education funds should be 'distributed generally throughout the country without reference to religion', 6 Sept. He was in the minority of 24 against the truck bill, 12 Sept., when he said its extension to Ireland would not work because in some areas there was 'no money at all in circulation'. (He had earlier informed James Emerson, the sponsor of extending the bill to Ireland, that he would prefer to 'let any experiment be had in England' first rather than 'interfere in the present state of Ireland with employment'.)[16] He denounced the 'atrocious system of jobbing' in Irish vestries, 20 Sept. He presented and endorsed a Kilkenny petition for the construction of a railway to the sea, 28 Sept. He contended that renewal of the Irish Arms Acts was most 'tyrannical and unjust' to the 20 undisturbed counties and expressed 'great anxiety' about the Irish grand jury amendment bill, 29 Sept. The following day he suggested that the establishment of an Irish board of trade might lessen the agitation for repeal. He declared that he had 'pledged himself' to introduce a measure for the abolition of Irish tithes, 18 Oct., and warned that while they remained there would be no peace, 6 Dec. He presented and endorsed a petition against the nomination of Irish grand juries and the 'great severity' of their local taxation, 9 Dec. He attacked the Irish Subletting Act as 'inexpedient and injudicious', 12 Dec. On 15 Dec. 1831 he asserted that the maintenance of a 'gorgeous Protestant church' was 'amongst the undisputed causes' of 'hostility to the laws and institutions' of Ireland, and successfully moved for the 'whole state of the Irish church' to be considered by the Irish tithes committee, to which he was appointed that day.

Leader voted for the second reading of the revised reform bill, 17 Dec. 1831, for going into committee on it, 20 Jan., 20 Feb. 1832, and again steadily supported to its details. He divided for the third reading, 22 Mar. On 19 Jan. he demanded that something be done about Ireland's 'rotten boroughs', which like those of England were 'a mockery of representation', and resumed his campaign for additional Irish Members, for which he spoke regularly thereafter. He demanded limits on the cost of election booths, 15 Feb. He voted for the address calling on the king to appoint only ministers who would carry reform unimpaired, 10 May. On 23 May he divided for the Liverpool disfranchisement bill. That day he presented 16 petitions for the Irish reform bill and one from Kilkenny for a second Member and destruction of the nomination boroughs, which he endorsed. He voted for the second reading of the Irish bill, 25 May, but protested that under its terms 'many towns which are now open' would 'become close boroughs', 6 June, and spoke at great length against the proposed boundaries and the comparatively small increase in the number of Irish electors, which would 'inflame' calls for repeal, 13 June. On the 18th he regretted that the provisions of the bill fell so 'lamentably short of the expectations raised by the pompous preamble', voted in the minority for the enfranchisement of £30 occupiers, and argued and was a minority teller for O'Connell's motion to extend the county franchise to £5 freeholders. He spoke in similar terms, 2 July. On 27 June he endorsed a Mallow petition protesting that the bill would reduce its electorate from 800 to 200, which made a 'mere mockery of reform'. He was in the minority of 26 for a system of representation for New South Wales, 28 June. Next day he divided against the liability of Irish electors to pay municipal taxes before they could vote. He condemned the proposed division of Irish counties into polling districts, 18 July. He disapproved of a Lords' amendment to the Irish bill preventing certain types of borough freeholders from qualifying after 31 Mar. 1831, but waived his opposition, 3 Aug. 1832.

He presented petitions for the abolition of Irish tithes, 17 Jan., 16 Feb., when he moved and was a minority teller for printing the one from Woollen Grange, 15 Mar., 5 July. On 8 Mar. he spoke at length against the Irish tithes bill, which had caused 'considerable embarrassment' to those Irish Members who had hitherto been the 'steady and undeviating supporters of every measure of liberal policy', not one of whom considered it had the 'slightest chance of success'. He voted against it that day, 27 Mar., when he opposed the introduction of further coercive measures to enforce collection, and again, 30 Mar., 6 Apr., 13, 24 July, 1, 2 Aug. He warned of the 'disorder and violence' and 'immense expenditure' it would entail, 2 Apr., and spoke regularly against it thereafter, but was one of the Members 'usually opposing ministers' who supported Crampton's amendment regarding the payment of arrears, 9 Apr.[17] On 2 Aug. he challenged its details in committee one by one, but denied charges of throwing 'unnecessary delay in the way of the business of the House'. He argued for the reception of an anti-tithes petition from the peasantry couched 'in very coarse language' that day. He voted with government on the Russian-Dutch loan, 26 Jan., 12, 16 July, and the navy civil departments bill, 6 Apr., but was in the minorities for information on military punishments, 16 Feb., and the immediate abolition of slavery, 24 May. He contended that greater army reductions would be possible if attention was paid to the causes of Irish disturbances, 17 Feb. He condemned the Irish Subletting Act that day and 20 Feb. He argued that the 'benefits of an English jury system should be extended to Ireland', 22 Feb., demanded compensation for Irish tobacco traders, 29 Feb., and welcomed the new Irish education plan, 2 Mar. He opposed Irish military increases, 23 May, and insisted that it was 'worse than useless to talk of Insurrection Acts' and establish committees on the suppression of Irish outrages while the 'evils' of absenteeism and lack of legal provision for the Irish poor remained unremedied, 31 May. He was a minority teller against the King's County assizes bill, 30 May, and next day opposed a motion for inquiry into the state of Queen's County.[18] He divided for permanent provision of the Irish poor by a tax on absentee landlords, 19 June, and for inquiry into the inns of court, 17 July. On the 18th he asked for the office of Irish secretary to be placed on a proper footing and for greater access to official information to be given to Irish Members. That day he contended that if more were spent on the employment of the Irish poor, crime would decrease. He called for the bill excluding the Dublin recorder from sitting in Parliament to be extended to all recorders, 24 July. He endorsed a petition from Blarney, county Cork, against the recent suppression of a public meeting on Irish manufactures, 27 July, condemned it as 'a most wanton exercise of military power', 2 Aug., and demanded inquiry, 10 Aug. He believed that abolition of the viceroyalty would be 'disastrous', as 8,000,000 people 'cannot be governed without there being an executive power on the spot', and warned that it would increase agitation for repeal of the Union, 30 July 1832.

At the 1832 general dissolution Leader retired from Parliament, after refusing to take O'Connell's pledge in support of repeal. *The Times* noted that 'there has come forth from Ireland perhaps no popular representative, not being of the desperado faction, who has more generally thrown aside all compromise in pursuing his own straightforward course'.[19] He died at Nashville, county Cork, in February 1836, and was succeeded by his eldest son and namesake (1808-80), Conservative Member for the county, 1861-68.[20]

[1]PRO NI, Leader mss D3653. [2]*HP Commons, 1790-1820*, ii. 634-5. [3]*O'Connell Corresp*. i. 437; ii. 515. [4]Add. 40611, f. 39. [5]*O'Connell Corresp*. ii. 982; iii. 1278; iv. 1672; Leader mss 16/3/42. [6]*Dublin Evening Post*, 16 Sept., 23 Oct. 1828; *O'Connell Corresp*. viii. 3409. [7]*The Times*, 24 Jan. 1829. [8]Leader mss 16/3/37. [9]*Dublin Evening Post*, 13 June 1829. [10]*O'Connell Corresp*. iv. 1681. [11]*Kilkenny Moderator*, 31 July, 11, 14, 18, 21 Aug., 20 Oct. 1830; G. Burtchaell, *MPs for Kilkenny*, 209-10; *O'Connell Corresp*. iv. 1700, 1716; NLI, Wyse mss 15024 (3). [12]PRO NI, Fitzgerald mss MIC/639/13/7/77/116. [13]Wyse mss 15024 (2). [14]*Dublin Evening Post*, 28 Apr.; *Kilkenny Moderator*, 27, 30 Apr., 7 May 1831. [15]*Sketches, Legal and Political* ed. M. Savage, ii. 341. [16]PRO NI, Emerson Tennant mss D2922/C/1A/4. [17]*The Times*, 10 Apr. 1832. [18]*O'Connell Corresp*. iv. 1899. [19]*The Times*, 4 Oct. 1832. [20]*Gent. Mag*. (1836), i. 444.

P.J.S.

LEADER, William (1767–1828), of 14 Queen Square, Westminster, Mdx. and Lower House, Putney Hill, Surr.[1]

CAMELFORD	1812–1818
WINCHELSEA	20 Feb. 1823–1826

b. 8 Nov. 1767,[2] o.s. of William Leader, coachmaker to the prince of Wales,[3] of 37 Liquor Pond Street, St. Andrew's, Holborn and 32 Bedford Row, Mdx. and w. Mary.[4] (His sis. Mary Rose *m*. John Maberly*.) *educ*. Eton 1779-81. *m*. 1 Mar. 1792, Mary *née* Bond (*d*. 7 May 1838, aged 72),[5] 2s. (1 *d.v.p*.) 4da. *suc*. fa. 1798. *d*. 13 Jan. 1828.

Leader, like his father, prospered handsomely in business. He was a partner with John Falconer Atlee and James Langdale in a malt distillery at Wandsworth and had a stake in the firm of Pellatt and Green, china, glass and earthenware dealers, of 16 St. Paul's Churchyard.[6] In February 1823 he was returned on a vacancy for Winchelsea by the 3rd earl of Darlington, under whose aegis he had sat during his previous membership of the House. As before, he aligned himself with opposition, generally acting with its radical fringe in conjunction with his brother-in-law John Maberly, though he was not the most dedicated of attenders. Like Maberly he never joined Brooks's Club. He voted for large tax reductions, 28 Feb. 1823, and cast occasional further votes for economy and retrenchment throughout the session. He divided for repeal of the Foreign Enlistment Act, 16 Apr., parliamentary reform, 24 Apr., 2 June, mitigation of the penal code, 21 May, 25 June, and inquiries into the malt and beer taxes, 28 May, chancery delays, 5 June, and the coronation expenses, 9 June. He voted for investigations of the legal proceedings against the Dublin Orange rioters, 22 Apr., and the state of Ireland, 12 May, against the Irish tithes composition bill, 16, 19 June, and in support of Irish Catholics' complaints against the administration of justice, 26 June 1823.

In 1824 he divided for repeal of the usury laws, 27 Feb., 8 Apr., as he did again, 8, 17 Feb. 1825. He voted to get rid of the window tax, 2 Mar., and to transfer the duty from beer to malt, 15 Mar. 1824. He divided against military flogging, 15 Mar., and naval impressment, 10 June, and opposed the aliens bill, 23 Mar., 12 Apr. He favoured Scottish judicial reform, 30 Mar., and allowing counsel for defendants in cases of felony to address the jury on the evidence, 6 Apr. He voted in condemnation of the trial of the missionary John Smith, 11 June. He supported an advance of capital to Ireland, 4 May, and reform of her church establishment, 6, 25, 27 May, but he divided with government for the Irish insurrection bill, 14 June. His son recalled that Leader never spoke in the House 'except to present a petition from his constituents': he produced one in support of the county courts bill, 14 Apr. 1824.[7] He voted against the bill to suppress the Catholic Association, 15, 18, 21 Feb., for Catholic relief, 1 Mar., 21 Apr., 10 May, and for proposals to ameliorate the problems of Ireland, 13, 14 June 1825. He favoured repeal of the assessed taxes, 3 Mar., 17 May, and of the beer duties, 5 May. He voted for relaxation of the corn laws, 28 Apr., and action on chancery delays, 7 June, and was in small minorities for attempts to modify the combination bill, 27 June. He voted against the duke of Cumberland's grant, 27 May, but supported it in the divisions of 2, 6, 7 June 1825. His only recorded votes in the 1826 session were for revision of the corn laws, 18 Apr., reform, 27 Apr., and inquiries into the state of the nation, 4 May, and curbs on press freedom in India, 9 May. He retired from Parliament at the dissolution.

Leader, whose elder son William was killed, at the age of 24, in a carriage accident in Oxford, 28 Feb. 1826, made a will on 2 Aug. of that year. He left his wife £1,000 and an annuity of £1,500. He had secured to his four daughters £10,000 each by their marriage settlements, and he now bequeathed an additional sum of £10,000 each to three of them, having provided the other with the same amount by bond. Various other legacies to relatives and his executors amounted to some £14,500. He left the residue of his personalty and all his real estate to his surviving son John, who was to receive £1,000 a year until he attained his majority.[8] In September 1827 Leader fell ill with 'a liver complaint' and decided to make a fresh disposition of his property. He replaced John Maberly as an executor with his son William Leader Maberly*; added some new legacies and amended some existing ones; increased his son's allowance to £1,500 a year, and made new provisions for the disposal of the residue in the event of his son's death during his nonage. He planned to pay all his daughters' legacies by bond and to invest on their behalf a sum of £30,000 due to him from Atlee. He approved the final draft of the new will early in January 1828, but wished to delay its execution until his solicitor returned to London. Yet the clerk, perceiving Leader's worsening state, thought it prudent to have the instruments engrossed. On 11 Jan. Leader became 'alarmingly ill'. He rallied the following day, but on 13 Jan. 1828, when he was 'evidently sinking', was advised by his doctor to complete his worldly business:

> The will was brought to him; he attempted to sit up, but was unable; a pen was given to him, and he was lifted up in the bed, but at the very instant he was about to sign the paper, he expired.[9]

The will of 1826 was proved under £300,000 on 1 Feb. 1828, but this probate was revoked by interlocutory decree, 13 Jan. 1829, when judgment was given in favour of the second will and its annexed bonds as representing the clear intention of the deceased. It too was proved under £300,000 on 24 Mar. 1829. The personalty amounted to almost £200,000, in addition to real estate worth about £100,000.[10] Leader's son John Temple Leader (1810-1903) sat as a radical for Bridgwater, 1835-7, and Westminster, 1837-47, spent most of his subsequent life abroad and made a name for himself as a connoisseur of the fine arts.[11]

[1] See J.T. Leader, *Rough and Rambling Notes Chiefly on My Early Life* (Florence, 1899), 9-24; Manning and Bray, *Surr.* iii. 298. [2] IGI. [3] *Gent. Mag.* (1798), i. 449; *Prince of Wales Corresp.* ii. 665. [4] He left £100 by his will to Robert Lucas, 'my wife's relation and now my partner' (PROB 11/1308/417). [5] They *m.* at St. Martin-in-the Fields, Mdx. (IGI); *Gent. Mag.* (1838), i. 666. [6] *VCH Surr.* ii. 393, 396; P. Mathias, *Brewing Industry in England* 75. [7] Leader, 25; *The Times*, 15 Apr. 1824. [8] Leader, 24; PROB 11/1737/111. [9] PROB 11/1753/167; *The Times*, 16 Jan. 1828, 14 Jan. 1829; *Ann. Reg.* (1829), Chron. pp. 8-10. [10] IR26/1168/51; 1200/62. [11] Leader, 41-42, 61-73.

D.R.F.

LEAKE, William (?1771–1852), of 20 Devonshire Street, Portland Place, Mdx. and Mount Ararat, Wimbledon, Surr.

MITCHELL	1818–1820
MALMESBURY	27 June 1820–1826
MITCHELL	1826–1830

b. ?1771,[1] s. of William Leake (*d.* ?1795) of St. Martin's Lane, Mdx.[2] *m.* 3 June 1792, Sarah Fresselicque of St. George, Holborn, Mdx., *s.p.*; ?1da. illegit. *d.* 21 Apr. 1852.

Vol. London and Westminster light horse 1795; capt. Loyal Britons vol. inf. 1803.

Leake, a king's bench attorney with a flourishing practice, was put up at Grampound by his client and patron Sir Christopher Hawkins* at the general election of 1820, but the attempt was unsuccessful.[3] Two months later he wrote to Lord Morley, the friend of George Canning*, who was president of the India board in Lord Liverpool's administration:

> I am very sensible of your lordship's kind attention to my wishes in mentioning my name to Mr. C[anning] and, in the event of my succeeding in the object I have in view either at P. or elsewhere, I shall be most happy ... to endeavour, by devoting myself solely and exclusively to his individual line of conduct, to prove myself not wholly undeserving his future protection, and I can with truth assure your lordship that had you been in England when I first went into Parliament I should have made to you the same avowal of my political and personal feelings towards your distinguished friend which I now do.

Canning professed to be 'exceedingly flattered' by Leake's declaration, but asked Morley to tell him 'without incivility, though without disguise or reserve', that he was not interested in acquiring a 'separate following'.[4] Penryn may have been the borough on which Leake had his eye, but as it turned out he found an opening at Malmesbury on the interest of Joseph Pitt* in June 1820.

Leake, seemingly a very lax attender in this period, voted against ministers on the omission of Queen Caroline's name from the liturgy, 26 Jan., probably rallied to them on the Whig censure motion, 6 Feb., but again deserted them on the liturgy question, 13 Feb. 1821. He was named to the select committee on the laws governing the admission of attorneys and solicitors, 14 Feb., and took leave to attend to private business, 18 May 1821. He divided against government for tax reductions and economies, 11, 21 Feb., 1, 13 Mar., and was said to have voted for Canning's bill to relieve Catholic peers of their disabilities, 30 Apr. 1822.[5] On 10 July 1823, observing that delays in chancery had lately increased 'to an extent amounting in its effects and consequences almost to a denial of justice', he gave notice of his intention to introduce legislation to regulate the appointment of clerks and reform administration of the bankruptcy laws. He abandoned this plan, 25 Feb. 1824, after ministers agreed to the appointment of a commission of inquiry into chancery procedure. Later that session he brought forward a bill designed to improve the examination of witnesses in the equity courts, but it foundered at the report stage, 11 June.[6] He voted for repeal of the usury laws, 8 Feb., and for the bill to suppress the Catholic Association, 25 Feb. 1825, but (as in 1821) he apparently missed the divisions on Catholic relief that year. In the absence of Sir Gerard Noel Noel, another of his fashionable clients, he presented a Rutland petition against Catholic relief, 19 Apr. 1825.[7] He sided with government on the president of the board of trade's salary, 10 Apr. 1826.

Leake was returned for Mitchell, his former seat, by Hawkins at the general election of 1826. He left little trace of activity in that Parliament, though he was evidently a practised purveyor of political gossip in the London coffee houses.[8] He was in the minority of five in the Berwick election committee against unseating John Gladstone for treating, 19 Mar. 1827.[9] He paired against Catholic relief, 6 Mar. 1827, and reportedly paired again on the next division on the same issue, 12 May 1828, but on which side is not clear.[10] He handled the petition of the freeholders of county Clare for permission to renew their challenge to the return of Daniel O'Connell, 5, 9 Feb. 1829. He was listed by Planta, the Wellington ministry's patronage secretary, as likely to be 'with government' for emancipation, but although he brought up anti-Catholic petitions, 20 Mar. 1829, he is not known to have voted in any of the major divisions on the question that year. He divided against the transfer of East Retford's seats to Birmingham, 11 Feb., and may have been the 'J. Leech' who was listed as voting with government for the grant for South American missions, 7 June 1830. He retired from the House at the dissolution soon afterwards. Perhaps he had been a more active parliamentarian than his voting record suggests, for in January 1831 Lord Lowther*, now in opposition to the Grey ministry, commended him as 'a very well disposed person' who had been 'a constant attender' and 'a good voter'.[11]

Leake appears to have retired from legal practice in 1833, and later moved his London home from Devonshire Street to 45 Upper Harley Street. He died, aged 81, in April 1852, at his then residence of

Moorcroft House, Hillingdon, Middlesex.[12] He had evidently separated from his wife, who died on 28 June 1833, in the mid-1820s, and he thereafter lived with Madame Virginie Levasseur, his 'highly valued and much esteemed friend'. By his will, dated 17 Aug. 1846, he left her £3,000. He bequeathed an annuity of £150 to Emily Smith, 'commonly known by the name of Emily Leake', possibly a natural daughter, and perhaps the lady of that name who told Benjamin Disraeli† in 1832 that his novel *Contarini Fleming* was 'the finest work ever produced'. Two other women, both married, received annuities of £100 and £50. Leake's executor and residuary legatee, John William Bury of Charles Street, the author of an obscure study of the Leake family of Bedlington, Durham, predeceased him. His 'lawful cousins german once removed and only next of kin', Thomas Clement Jones and Alfred, Mary and William Henry Savage, having renounced their claims, administration was granted to Emily Leake, now married to Isaac Thomas Welchman of Belmore Lodge, South Lambeth.[13]

[1] Unless he was the William, son of William and Mary Leake, *b.* 9 Sept., who was baptized at St. Anne, Soho, 30 Sept. 1769: IGI (London). [2] His fa. was possibly the 'surgeon and apothecary' (*d.* 18 Feb. 1795), the bro. of Dr. John Leake (1729-92), founder of Westminster maternity hospital (*Gent. Mag.* (1795), i. 348; PROB 11/1222/437; *Oxford DNB*). [3] *The Times*, 7 Mar. 1820. [4] Add. 48221, ff. 67, 69. [5] *Black Bk.* (1823), 169. [6] *The Times*, 15 Apr., 19 May 1824; *CJ*, lxxix. 381-2, 405, 442, 455, 478. [7] 20 Apr. 1825. [8] *Arbuthnot Corresp.* 90. [9] St. Deiniol's Lib. Glynne-Gladstone mss 194, T. to J. Gladstone, 19 Mar. 1827. [10] *The Times*, 19 May 1828. [11] Lonsdale mss, Lowther to Lonsdale, 13 Jan. 1831. [12] *Gent. Mag.* (1852), i. 635. [13] Ibid. (1833), i. 650; PROB 11/2157/646; IR26/1939/639; *Disraeli Letters*, i. 207; *HP Commons, 1790-1820*, iv. 398.

D.R.F./S.M.F.

LEE, John Lee (1802–1874), of Orleigh Court, nr. Bideford, Devon.

WELLS 1830–1837

b. 11 Dec. 1802, o.s. of William Hanning of Dillington House, nr. Ilminster, Som. and Harriett, da. of Edward Lee of Pinhoe, Devon. *educ.* Westminster 1813; Christ Church, Oxf. 1821. *m.* (1) 18 Feb. 1834, Jessy (*d.* 1 Mar. 1836), da. of John Edwards Vaughan*, 1s.; (2) 17 Aug. 1841, Hon. Mary Sophia Hood, da. of Samuel Hood†, 2nd Bar. Bridport [I], 2s. 2da. (1 *d.v.p.*) *suc.* uncle Maj. Edward Lee to Orleigh 1823 and took name of Lee by royal lic. 21 Mar. 1825; fa. 1834. *d.* 16 Aug. 1874.

Sheriff, Som. 1845-6.

John Lee Hanning inherited his maternal uncle's property on coming of age in 1823 and took the name of Lee two years later in accordance with his instructions.[1] His early Tory proclivities were shown by his nomination of Sir Thomas Lethbridge* at the Somerset election of 1826.[2] His father, William Hanning, was a key figure in the 'church and king' party which seized control of Wells corporation in 1828, and Lee stood there at the general election in 1830 in alliance with John Edwards Vaughan; their joint address was noteworthy only for the absence of any expressions of political principle. To his detractors, Lee was a 'mumbudget automaton', devoid of talent and incapable of impromptu public speaking, but corporation influence ensured that he and Edwards Vaughan were comfortably returned.[3]

The Wellington ministry listed him as one of their 'friends', though they knew nothing of him. His name appeared both in the majority and minority lists on the crucial civil list division, 15 Nov. 1830, but he informed *The Times* that he had voted against government, and he privately expressed the hope that Lord Grey's new ministry would prove to be 'more popular than the last'.[4] In presenting a Wells petition for repeal of the assessed taxes, 15 Dec. 1830, he observed that the house and window duties were especially onerous and that the 'poor and middle classes' were entitled to relief. He presented petitions from Ilminster and Hindon for parliamentary reform, 28 Feb., and after serving on an election committee was granted a week's leave for urgent private business, 14 Mar. He voted for the second reading of the ministerial reform bill, 22 Mar., and against Gascoyne's wrecking amendment, 19 Apr. 1831. At the Somerset county meeting in March he expressed his 'decided approbation' of the measure.[5] He stood again for Wells at the ensuing general election, issuing a separate address from Edwards Vaughan's in which he trusted that his 'assiduity and constant attendance in Parliament' and 'independent' conduct would commend him to his constituents. He condemned Gascoyne's amendment, believing that 'a side blow was an unfair way of upsetting a measure fraught with such advantage as ... amending the abuses of the rotten borough system'. However, he wished to see the reform bill amended in detail, particularly as to the £10 householder franchise, which reflected his sense of obligation to defend 'all vested interests' affecting the electors of Wells. Expressing general confidence in ministers, who had made 'progress in economy and retrenchment and ... the reduction of useless expenditure', he was finally spared a contested election.[6]

He presented petitions from Wells for repeal of the Beer Act, 14 July, and Ilminster for a small debts recovery bill, 17 Aug. He briefly advocated the extension of free trade principles to Ireland, 25 July, and voted in defence of the Irish administration's conduct during the Dublin election, 23 Aug. He divided for the second reading of the reintroduced reform bill, 6 July, and generally supported its details in committee, notifying *The Times* that he had voted against the use of the 1831 census for the purpose of scheduling boroughs, 19 July, a matter of some significance for Wells.[7] He advocated increased representation for Cambridgeshire, 12 Aug. However, he voted for the Chandos amendment to enfranchise £50 tenants-at-will, 18 Aug. After dividing for the third reading, 19 Sept., he moved an amendment to clause 22, to secure the voting rights of sons of freeholders currently under-age who would have qualified under the old system, which was accepted by ministers. He voted for the bill's passage, 21 Sept., the second reading of the Scottish bill, 23 Sept., and Lord Ebrington's confidence motion, 10 Oct. 1831. He was absent from the division on the second reading of the revised reform bill, 17 Dec. 1831, but supported it in committee and voted for the third reading, 22 Mar 1832. He divided for Ebrington's motion for an address asking the king to appoint only ministers committed to carrying an unimpaired measure, 10 May. He voted for the second reading of the Irish bill, 25 May, and presented an Ilminster petition to withhold supplies until the reform bill was passed, 30 May. He divided with ministers on relations with Portugal, 9 Feb., but was in the minorities for inquiry into distress in the glove trade, 31 Jan., and against the Russian-Dutch loan, 26 Jan., 12 July 1832. Following this last vote, he wrote that 'I am *glad* to say ministers had a majority ... although I voted against them', which he had done for the sake of consistency, having no intention of supporting any further attempt to 'annoy them' on this issue.[8]

Although Lee's support for reform had alienated many of the corporators at Wells, local reformers were also critical of him for being 'inattentive and neglectful of his duties'. It was claimed that he had missed the second reading division in December 1831 in order to attend a ball and had absented himself from several other important divisions in favour of '*sporting occasions*'. He tried to excuse his absences to a meeting of reformers in June 1832, but 'also stated that he did not approve of going into the House as a pledged representative'.[9] He was opposed by two staunch reformers at the general election in December 1832, but was narrowly returned in second place.[10] He sat as an advocate of 'moderate Whig principles' until his retirement in 1837.[11] He belatedly joined Brooks's on 29 Nov. that year. He died in August 1874 and was succeeded by his son from his first marriage, Vaughan Hanning Vaughan Lee (1836-82), Conservative Member for West Somerset, 1874-82.

[1] *Bristol Mirror*, 20 Dec. 1823. The will was proved under £30,000, 17 July 1819 (PROB 11/1618/335; IR26/791/570). [2] *Taunton Courier*, 21 June 1826. [3] *Bristol Mirror*. 10 July; *Keene's Bath Jnl.* 19, 26 July, 9 Aug. 1830. [4] *The Times*, 20 Nov. 1830; Wells City RO 189/8, Lee to Davies, 19 Nov. 1830. [5] *Bristol Mirror*, 2 Apr. 1831. [6] Ibid. 30 Apr., 7 May 1831. [7] *The Times*, 21 July 1831. [8] Wells City RO 189/8, Lee to Davies, 13 July 1832. [9] *Keene's Bath Jnl.* 30 Jan., 2 Apr., 25 June 1832. [10] *Bristol Mirror*, 15 Dec. 1832. [11] *Dod's Parl. Companion* (1833), 133.

T.A.J.

LEFEVRE *see* **SHAW LEFEVRE**

LEFROY, Anthony (1800–1890), of Newcastle, co. Longford.

Co. Longford	1830–1832
Co. Longford	2 Apr. 1833–1837
Co. Longford	18 Apr. 1842–1847
Dublin University	27 Mar. 1858–Feb. 1870

b. 21 Mar. 1800, 1st s. of Thomas Langlois Lefroy* of 12 Leeson Street, Dublin and Carrickglass, co. Longford and Mary, da. and h. of Jeffrey Paul of Silverspring, co. Wexford. *educ.* Trinity, Dublin 1816; King's Inns 1820; L. Inn 1822. *m.* 19 July 1824, Hon. Jane King, da. of Robert Edward King, MP [I], 1st Visct. Lorton [I], 1s. *d.v.p.* 2da. *suc.* fa. 1869. *d.* 11 Jan. 1890.

Sheriff, co. Longford 1849-50.

Lefroy followed his father, a distinguished lawyer who was appointed Irish first serjeant in 1822, to Trinity, but unlike him and his younger brother Thomas, he never practised law. In April 1827 Daniel O'Connell* reported that Lefroy's father, who had been 'most actively canvassing the College' for himself, had 'announced his son for Dublin city for the next vacancy on the strongest Orange principles'.[1] Two months before the 1830 general election, however, Lefroy started for county Longford as the second nominee of the dowager Lady Rosse, his wife's maternal grandmother, prompting complaints that it was not 'handsome of a man' to 'canvass during the sitting Member's absence in Parliament'.[2] At the election he denied that a 'coalition had been formed' in his favour and that his family's opposition to emancipation should be 'a reason for the Catholics opposing my present claims'. One of the sitting Members retired and he was returned unopposed. At the declaration he urged the Wellington government to 'take warning' from the 'state of things' in France and welcomed the defeat of their Irish 'placemen', especially at Dublin University, where his father had been returned.[3]

He was listed by the Irish agent Pierce Mahony† as 'neutral', by ministers as one of the 'moderate Ultras' and by Henry Brougham* as anti-ministerial, and he voted against government on the civil list, 15 Nov. 1830. He presented petitions for the abolition of slavery, 16 Nov., 2, 21 Dec. In his maiden speech, 6 Dec., he protested that a Longford petition for repeal of the Union was unrepresentative and contended that Ireland had a much better chance of relief from distress under a united Parliament. He defended the Kildare Place Society against an attack by O'Connell, observing that it educated 'upwards of 120,000 children of Catholic and Protestant parents' and was 'better calculated to benefit the people ... than any other in existence', 10 Dec. 1830, and objected to a hostile petition from Waterford, 16 Feb. 1831. He insisted that the recorder of Dublin Frederick Shaw had 'performed all the duties of his office and discharged all the prisoners remaining for trial' before attending as Member for Dublin, 20 Dec. 1830. He defended the conduct of the archbishop of Dublin in making a return of Irish church livings, 17 Feb. 1831. His subsequent speeches were not always clearly distinguished in the parliamentary reports from those of his father, who arrived from Ireland later that month, but it was probably he who presented a petition in support of the Kildare Place Society and called for the London coal bill to 'be extended to the coalmeters of Dublin', 16 Mar., and insisted that the landed proprietors of Ireland had 'done their utmost to relieve' distress, 18 Mar. Like his father he divided against the second reading of the Grey ministry's English reform bill, 22 Mar., and for Gascoyne's wrecking amendment, 19 Apr. 1831.

At the ensuing general election he offered again, denouncing the bill as a 'traitorous conspiracy', but professing to favour 'such constitutional measures' as would 'strengthen and purify the representation'. He was returned in second place after a three-day poll.[4] He defended the Irish yeomanry and police against the 'misstatements' of O'Connell, noting that the 'unfortunate incidents' at Castle Pollard and Newtownbarry had 'not yet been fully investigated', 27 June. He voted against the second reading of the reintroduced reform bill, 6 July, and at least four times to adjourn the debates, 12 July. He divided for use of the 1831 census to determine the disfranchisement schedules, 19 July, and to postpone consideration of the inclusion of Chippenham in B, 27 July. He voted against the bill's passage, 21 Sept., and the second reading of the Scottish bill, 23 Sept. He supported the compensation claim of the former king's stationer in Ireland, Sir Abraham Bradley King, 11, 18 July, when he insisted that 'a positive contract' had been entered into by the previous government. He again rebutted criticism of the Kildare Place Society, 14 July, and presented petitions in its support, 26 July, when he clashed with O'Connell, and 2 Sept. On 8 Aug. he insisted that there was no case for removing the 'privilege of voting' from the Dublin freemen, of whom he was one, and demanded the immediate issue of a new writ. He denounced the 'vain declarations and groundless assertions of those self-styled popular representatives' from Ireland who had 'indulged in most violent attacks upon the yeomanry', 10 Aug., and criticised Sheil for 'finding fault with the mode' by which Irish juries were selected, 16 Aug. He voted for the motion of censure against the Irish government for using undue influence in the Dublin election, 23 Aug., and defended the character of one of the witnesses examined by the committee, 25 Aug. He argued against reducing the grant to the Royal Dublin Society, which had a 'beneficial' influence 'in promoting the arts and sciences', 29 Aug. He divided for inquiry into the effects of renewal of the Sugar Refinery Act on the West India interest, 12 Sept. Speaking in defence of Irish tithes, 14 Sept., he maintained that the Catholics of Ireland should 'contribute to the support of that religion which is still as much the established religion of Ireland as of England'. He objected to a constituency petition presented by O'Connell for repeal, which 'all the gentry in the county' were against, 26 Sept. He voted to end the Maynooth grant that day, saying it was 'inconsistent as a member of the Protestant church' to 'contribute to the support of an institution which not only maintains, but educates and sends forth through the country, the ministers of a religion which I believe to be erroneous'. He condemned the government's appointment of non-resident lord lieutenants to counties Carlow, Cavan, Donegal, Leitrim, Limerick, Waterford and Wexford as a 'great injustice' and unwarranted 'departure from principle', 6 Oct. 1831.

Lefroy was absent from the division on the second reading of the revised reform bill, 17 Dec. 1831, but voted against the enfranchisement of Tower Hamlets, 28 Feb., and the third reading, 22 Mar. 1832. He divided against the second reading of the Irish bill, 25 May, which he argued would not 'give peace to the country', 14 June, and was in the minority of 39 for preserving the voting rights of Irish freemen, 2 July. He presented petitions against the new plan of Irish education, 5, 19 Mar., when he warned that Protestants would not permit 'national education to be made subservient to a Popish priesthood', and promised to oppose steadily 'a plan so unscriptural', 5 June. He presented and endorsed further hostile petitions, 20 June, 2 July, and voted against the grant for Irish education, 23 July.

He insisted that the payment of Irish tithes should be enforced, accused ministers of advancing money to pay 'a legal debt owed by the people of Ireland to the clergy', and complained that since taking office they had 'exercised their influence to the prejudice of Protestant institutions and in a way insulting to Protestant feelings', 30 Mar. He was in his father's minority of 13 against Crampton's amendment to the arrears of Irish tithes bill, 9 Apr. He had no doubt that a breach of privilege had been committed by the newspaper responsible for publishing the report of the tithes committee, but believed that the Irish secretary Smith Stanley was wrong to prosecute this case when he had ignored others, 31 May. Greville later recorded a conversation about the 'views of the Protestants' and 'the Lefroys' on tithes, in which Lord John Russell* had stated that they

> begin to admit the necessity of change ... and were willing where there was a large parish consisting entirely of Catholics that the tithes should be taken from the rector of such parish and given to one who had a large Protestant flock, an arrangement which would disgust the Catholics ... and be considered a perfect mockery.[5]

In a speech in which he denied using the 'tone or language attributed' to him by Henry Grattan, 14 June, he complained that the party processions bill did not extend to anti-tithe meetings, which 'too frequently cause the shedding of blood', but prevented 'processions of the Orangemen' who 'meet as loyal subjects to support the laws and constitution of the country'. He spoke in similar terms, 25 June, when he voted against the measure, and 29 June. Either he or his father divided against a tax on absentee landlords to provide permanent provision for the Irish poor, 19 June. He voted for Baring's bill to exclude insolvent debtors from Parliament, 27 June. He presented Protestant petitions from county Longford for repeal of Catholic emancipation, 6 July. He voted against ministers on the Russian-Dutch loan, 12 July, but divided for their Irish tithes composition bill the following day and 1 Aug. It was probably his father who was a minority teller against the bill to disqualify the recorder of Dublin from Parliament, 24 July 1832.

At the 1832 general election he was defeated for county Longford as a Conservative, but he was seated on petition the following year. He was re-elected in second place in 1835, defeated in 1837 and 1841, reseated on petition the following year, and lost his seat in 1847. He came in for Dublin University in 1858 and sat until his retirement in 1870. Lefroy died at Carrickglass in January 1890.[6] The family estates passed to his brother Thomas Paul Lefroy, who died the following year.

[1] Lansdowne mss, O'Connell to Knight of Kerry, 24 Apr. 1827. [2] NLI, Farnham mss 18613 (4), C. Fox to H. Maxwell, 22 June 1830. [3] *Dublin Evening Post*, 29 July, 14, 19 Aug.; *Roscommon and Leitrim Gazette*, 14, 21 Aug. 1830. [4] *Roscommon and Leitrim Gazette*, 30 Apr., 7, 14 May; *Dublin Evening Post*, 3, 5, 12 May 1831. [5] *Greville Mems*. ii. 310. [6] *The Times*, 15 Jan. 1890.

P.J.S.

LEFROY, Thomas Langlois (1776–1869), of 12 Leeson Street, Dublin and Carrickglass, co. Longford.[1]

DUBLIN UNIVERSITY 1830–Nov. 1841

b. 8 Jan. 1776, 1st s. of Capt. Anthony Peter Lefroy of Limerick and Anne, da. of Col. Thomas George Gardner of Doonass, co. Clare. *educ*. private tutors; Trinity, Dublin 1790, BA 1795, LLB and LLD 1827; L. Inn 1793; King's Inns 1794, called [I] 1797. *m*. 16 Mar. 1799, Mary, da. and h. of Jeffrey Paul of Silverspring, co. Wexford, 4s. 3da. *suc*. fa. 1819. *d*. 4 May 1869.

KC [I] 1816; 3rd sjt. [I] 1818, 2nd 1820, 1st 1822, res. 1830; bencher, King's Inns 1819; PC [I] 29 Jan. 1835; bar. exch. [I] 1841-52; c.j.q.b. [I] 1852-66.

Lefroy's ancestors were Huguenots who in the late sixteenth century migrated from Cambrai in the Spanish Netherlands to Canterbury, where they practised as silk dyers and obtained the freedom of the borough. In the early eighteenth century, the only remaining male member of the family, Anthony, became a banker and merchant in Leghorn, where he made and lost a fortune, but was a notable art collector. In 1738 he married Elizabeth, daughter of his business partner Pierre L'Anglois, a Languedoc Huguenot who had been naturalized in 1702 and whose son Benjamin Langlois, Member for St. Germans, 1768-74, was under-secretary of state for the Southern department, 1779-82. Their two sons, who were sent back to England to be educated at the King's School, Canterbury, were Isaac Peter George, who became rector of Ashe in Hampshire, and his elder brother Anthony Peter, who joined the army as ensign in the 33rd Foot in 1763 and was stationed in Limerick. At Killaloe on 15 Nov. 1765 he contracted a clandestine marriage to the daughter of a penurious local squire, with whom he had three daughters, but the marriage was resolemnized in Limerick Cathedral in 1774, with the apparent blessing of his childless uncle Benjamin Langlois, the patron of the Irish branch of the family. The following year he was promoted from his lieutenancy in the 49th Foot to be a captain in the 13th Dragoons, and the eldest of his five sons, Tom, was born in 1776. On the death of his widowed mother in 1781, he divided his father's estate with his brother, which enabled him to purchase the command of another cavalry regiment, the 9th Dragoons, in 1785. He retired in 1791, when he sold his remaining English property to his brother, but he later regretted his inactivity, especially during the Rebellion.[2] Tom Lefroy was admitted to Trinity, Dublin in November 1790, when his great-uncle Benjamin Langlois, who had ambitions for him to study at the English bar and enter Parliament, commented that his 'parts are so promising, and his character so winning', in the first of a series of complimentary letters to his father. His time there, which included the award of several gold medals and his appointment as auditor of the refounded History Society, was glittering and on his departure in 1795 his tutor the Rev. Robert Burrowes reported to his father that 'within my memory, no young man has left our college with a higher character'.[3]

Yet he had overworked himself and in the winter of 1795 he was dispatched to recuperate at Ashe, where his aunt was a friend of the young and then unknown Jane Austen, the daughter of the rector of neighbouring Steventon.[4] Evidently replying to an admonition from her elder sister Cassandra, Jane, who thought that Tom had 'only *one* fault, which time will, I trust, entirely remove – it is that his morning coat is a great deal too light', wrote teasingly of the previous night's ball, 9 Jan. 1796, that

> I am almost afraid to tell you how my Irish friend and I behaved. Imagine to yourself everything most profligate and shocking in the way of dancing and sitting down together. I *can* expose myself, however, only *once more*, because he leaves the country soon after next Friday, on which day we *are* to have a dance at Ashe after all. He is a very gentlemanlike, good-looking, pleasant young man, I assure you. But as to our having ever met, except at the last three balls, I cannot say much; for he is so excessively laughed at about me at Ashe, that he is ashamed of coming to Steventon, and ran away when we called on Mrs. Lefroy a few days ago.

In the same flippant tone of playful indifference, which was possibly meant to disguise anxious expectation, she wrote on the 14th, of the following night's party, that

> I look forward with great impatience to it, as I rather expect to receive an offer from my friend in the course of the evening. I shall refuse him, however, unless he promises to give away his white coat ... Tell Mary that I make over Mr. Heartley and all his estate to her for her sole use and benefit in future, and not only him, but all my other admirers into the bargain wherever she can find them, even the kiss which C. Powlett wanted to give me, as I mean to confine myself in future to Mr. Tom Lefroy, for whom I do not care sixpence.

The next evening, when she added that 'at length the day is come on which I am to flirt my last with Tom Lefroy, and when you receive this it will be over – my tears flow as I write, at the melancholy idea', was possibly the last time they ever met. Quite how far each had become attracted or committed to the other is not known, but evidently Mrs. Lefroy, aware of the family weakness for contracting improvident marriages, hurried away Tom, who soon began his legal studies in London. Two years later, Jane reported to Cassandra about a visit from Mrs. Lefroy

> with whom, in spite of interruptions both from my father and James, I was enough alone to hear all that was interesting, which you will easily credit when I tell you that of her nephew she said nothing at all, and of her friend [the Rev. Samuel Blackall, another potential suitor] very little. She did not mention the name of the former to *me*, and I was too proud to make any enquiries; but on my father's afterwards asking where he was, I learnt that he was gone back to London in his way to Ireland, where he is called to the bar and means to practise.[5]

The unhappy affair, perhaps among others, no doubt informed her novels, but one commentator has speculated that he meant much more to her than is usually supposed and in fact remained the central focus of her romantic life, serving as the model for Henry Tilney in *Northanger Abbey* and Frederick Wentworth in *Persuasion*; the argument is certainly suggestive, her young Irishmen being, for example, invariably figures of ease, charm and gentleness. That there was a lasting sense of bitterness is shown by the coolness that thereafter subsisted between the two families, even after the wedding of Tom's cousin Benjamin Lefroy and Jane's niece Anna Austen, which took place in glacial circumstances in 1814.[6] As for Lefroy, who married the sister of a short-lived College friend three years after he had left Hampshire, he risked being blamed (as some Janeites have subsequently done) for throwing her over. It was perhaps for this reason that, in the year of his death, his sister Caroline wrote forcefully to James Edward Austen-Leigh, the discreet first biographer of his aunt Jane, that

> I think I need not warn *you* against raking up that old story of the still living chief justice. That there was something in it, is true – but nothing out of the common way (as *I* believe). Nothing to call ill usage, and no very serious sorrow endured. The *York* Lefroys [their brother Anthony, with whom they differed over family settlements, was barrack master at York] got up a very strong version of it all, and spread their own notions in the family – but they were for years very angry with their kinsman, and rather delighted in a proof as *they* thought, of his early heartlessness. I have *my* story from my mother, who

was near at the time. It was a disappointment, but Mrs. Lefroy sent the gentleman off at the end of a *very* few weeks, that no more mischief might be done. If *his* love had continued a few more years, he *might* have sought her out again – as he was *then* making enough to marry on – but who can wonder that he did *not*? He was settled in Ireland, and he married an Irish lady, who certainly *had* the convenience of *money* – there was *no* engagement, and never *had* been.

Soon afterwards one of Lefroy's nephews confirmed that in later life his uncle often alluded to his admiration of Jane, with whom he had apparently had no more than a holiday flirtation: 'he did not state in what her fascination consisted, but he said in so many words that he was in love with her, although he qualified his confession by saying it was a boyish love'.[7] Whatever he really at that time thought of Jane, after whom he was said to have named his eldest and favourite daughter (although it was also his mother-in-law's name), her real feelings were (and, to some extent, remain) hidden behind the private language employed in what are her earliest surviving letters. Yet if the suggestion is correct that these were written in the style of 'Catharine, or the Bower', a work of juvenilia with which only her sister was familiar, that would confirm that she was genuinely in love with him.[8]

Lefroy, who led a blameless life with his wife Mabs, the great-granddaughter of Jeffrey Paul, Member for county Carlow, 1725-30, did not start to practise law in Ireland until a year or so after his marriage, but proved an instant success and soon earned a substantial income. In November 1801, arguing a writ of error in an intractable exchequer case, he was praised by the lord chancellor Lord Clare. In 1802 he published a pamphlet on *Proceedings by Elegit*, which was well received, and, with his friend John Schoales, he compiled the valuable *Reports of Cases in the Court of Chancery in Ireland during the time of Lord Redesdale*, an early patron. He served with distinction on the Munster circuit for many years and took silk in 1816, the year, as he wrote in one of his numerous Evangelical memoranda, 'when I first began to have any view of God's true method of salvation for a sinner'. He expounded his pious attitude to life, and explained his refusal to court favour by pandering to the fripperies of Castle society, in letters to his father, who died at his house in George's Street, Limerick, 9 Sept. 1819.[9] By then he had been appointed third serjeant and although he rose to be first serjeant in May 1822, in the early 1820s he three times declined offers of puisne judgeships; his belief that his leading position in equity questions destined him for higher office was attested by the lord lieutenant Lord Wellesley, who admired his striking address to the grand jury of county Limerick at the spring assizes of 1822 following the agrarian outrages there. A firm believer in the importance of education as a cure for social and economic ills, he was closely involved in the Kildare Place Society and took a leading role in other charitable organizations. In 1823 his suave and saintly look at Bible meetings, at which he was a fixture, was contrasted by Richard Sheil* with his hawk-like appearance in chancery, where

instead of eyes alternately veiled in the humility of their long and downcast lashes, or lifted up in visionary devotion, you behold them fixed upon the chancellor, and watching with a subtle intensity all the shiftings of expression with which the judicial countenance intimates its approval or dissent. The whole face of the vigilant and wily pleader is overspread with craft. There is a lurking design in every feature of his sharp and elongated visage.[10]

Lefroy, who was given the freedom of Cork in 1825, owned property in several southern counties and eventually rebuilt the ruined mansion at Carrickglass in county Longford, where his eldest son Anthony had political ambitions, but mostly resided at his house in Dublin, where he devoted much of his time to gardening.[11]

He was brought forward as the Ascendancy candidate for Dublin University in May 1827, at the by-election caused by the new Canning ministry's decision to grant a peerage to William Plunket, the pro-Catholic Member. As Lefroy explained to Peel, the recently resigned home secretary

it never was my intention to have engaged in parliamentary pursuits but called upon as I was by so respectable a portion of that body (including its heads) I felt myself bound to forego my own inclinations and to afford our only Protestant university an opportunity of being represented according to its great charter principle.

He was too late in the field to gain sufficient promises and, after an ugly contest in which he was dismissed as 'sophism personified' and the 'silky serjeant', he finished in third place behind the government candidate, John Croker, and another pro-Catholic barrister, John Henry North*.[12] Despite there having been some sort of promise from Wellesley, Lefroy was passed over on the appointment of law officers that month, although Canning conceded that he might have changed his mind if Lefroy had been in Parliament.[13] In May 1828 the new lord lieutenant Lord Anglesey, who described him as 'an extremely sensible gentlemanlike man', noted Lefroy's claim to be the next Irish solicitor-general, but later that year the duke of Wellington, the prime minister, disavowed any informal promise given by his elder brother.[14] Lefroy, who was active in the national and university Brunswick Clubs in the autumn of 1828, seconded the resolution damning the Wellington administration's emancipation bill at the grand anti-Catholic meeting in Dublin, 19 Feb. 1829.[15] Rebuffing further applications on his behalf, in April Peel, the reinstated home secretary, commented that Lefroy had

> made a wrong cast in politics ... After the part Lefroy has lately been taking (very much I believe out of a mistaken calculation of his own interests) it requires some assurance to present himself as a candidate for confidential employment or high judicial office.[16]

To the delight of the staunch Protestants, including those who at this time asked him to stand for Cork, in early 1830 he sensationally resigned as first serjeant in protest at the Castle's attempt to prevent him going the circuit in place of the indisposed Baron McClelland.[17]

Considered 'the darling object of the Brunswickers and Ultra Tories', Lefroy had powerful backing within the Protestant College and, as Croker rightly feared, North's persistence in the contest divided the ministerialist support, so allowing Lefroy to win the university seat by three votes at the general election of 1830.[18] He and his son Anthony, whose return for Longford he also paid for, were listed as 'neutrals' in Pierce Mahony's† analysis of the Irish elections, but the Castle expected him to be hostile and in the patronage secretary Planta's list, his name, which was entered among the 'moderate Ultras', was annotated, 'said he was not opposed to government – will oppose'.[19] He was credited with voting in the majority against ministers on the civil list, 15 Nov. 1830, but he apparently remained in Dublin all that winter to attend to his clients' legal business. During that time, when he intervened to try to obstruct the appointment of a Whig as the new provost of Trinity, he wrote often to one of the Ultra leaders, Lord Farnham, urging Tory unity in order to preserve Protestant principles in Ireland in the face of the reinvigorated Catholic challenge, though he did draw comfort from his hopes that the Grey ministry would soon collapse under the weight of its own ineptitude.[20] After his friends had failed to secure him leave from the Commons, 9 Feb., he confided to Farnham on the 17th that, in spite of the impending call of the House, he was determined not to abandon certain important cases, and he did not finally leave Ireland until 21 Feb. 1831.[21] He argued strongly against the ministerial reform bill on the grounds that it transgressed the constitution and would end in democracy, 8 Mar., after which Henry Goulburn* commented to his wife that 'at an advanced period of the debate the House will not listen to constitutional law declared in rather a drowsy tone'.[22] Among a number of minor contributions which may have been by him or his son, whose speeches were not always clearly distinguished in the parliamentary reports, it was probably he who defended the Kildare Place Society, 14, 29 Mar., objected to the appropriation of the Irish first fruits fund, 14 Mar., criticized the Catholic charities bill, 15 Mar., and reserved his position relative to the College franchise under the Irish reform bill, 24 Mar. He divided against the second reading of the reform bill, 22 Mar., and for Gascoyne's wrecking amendment, 19 Apr. 1831.

On 4 and 6 Apr. 1831 Lefroy lamented to Farnham the lack of Protestant activism and added, in an apparent reference to the restrained official Tory opposition to the reform bill, that

> I agree with you as to the sad disembodied state in which an overwhelming opposition (for such it really is) now stands. No head, because none in whom, even the bulk of them, would or can confide, but more and worse, nobody appears willing to put himself at the head of the *whole*; those to whom you allude as standing off are playing an unaccountable game and seem to be only looking to their own old party, and this appears so to others as an influence from the stand-off system which they have perceived, as well as yourself.[23]

Nevertheless, he set an example by retaining his university seat at the ensuing general election, defeating Philip Crampton*, the Irish solicitor-general, by eight votes in a bitter contest, during which he opposed reform and raised the spectre of its securing 40 or 50 Catholic Members for Irish seats.[24] He also, apparently at Farnham's suggestion, played a major role in the organization and financing of the Irish elections on behalf of the central Tory committee in London.[25] Of his involvement in handling the expenses of the petition against the Dublin election and the canvassing of the anti-reform candidates at the subsequent by-election that summer, the Tory whip William Holmes* noted, 9 Aug., that Lefroy, 'who begs lustily from Englishmen', had not subscribed a penny, but Wellington was assured by his confidant Charles Arbuthnot*, 10 Aug. 1831, that 'I think you may employ Holmes advantageously in negotiation with Mr. Lefroy, for I have found him perfect in all our joint transactions'.[26]

Lefroy vindicated the conduct of the clergyman and yeomanry at the centre of the Newtownbarry affair, 23 June, 1 July, and clashed with Daniel O'Connell over the unrest in Ireland, 27, 30 June 1831, when he presented the Trinity College petition for its franchise to be assimilated to that of Oxford and Cambridge. He insisted that the wealth and intelligence of Ireland were against reform, 1 July, and voted against the second reading of the reintroduced reform bill, 6 July, at least twice to adjourn proceedings on it, 12 July, for using the 1831 census, 19 July, and to postpone consideration of the partial disfranchisement of Chippenham, 27 July. He joined in the complaints about the condemned boroughs being refused permission to represent their cases by counsel, 4 Aug., brought up Dublin guild petitions against reform, 5 Aug., when he denied that the College electorate was exclusive in character, and divided for preserving the right of voting to non-resident freemen for their lives, 30 Aug. He vindicated the role of Frederick Shaw as both recorder of and Member for Dublin, 12 Aug., justified the presence of clergymen in the commissions of the peace in Ireland, 15 Aug., and spoke and acted as a teller for the minority for the Irish union of parishes bill, 19 Aug. He accused Irish officials of direct interference in the Dublin election, 20, 23 Aug., when he joined Robert Gordon as teller for the minority for his amendment to this effect, and reiterated his views on this topic, 25, 26, 31 Aug. He voted for Benett's successful amendment to the motion to issue the Liverpool writ alleging gross bribery at the previous election, 5 Sept., and for inquiry into how far the Sugar Refinery Act could be renewed with due regard to the interests of the West Indies and against going into committee on the truck bill, 12 Sept. Among several other short contributions to debate, he defended the established church in relation to the Irish Vestry Acts, 29 Aug., complaints about non-residence and pluralities, 14 Sept., and the necessity of collecting tithes, 6 Oct., when he condemned the party political appointments of lord lieutenants in several Irish counties. He spoke at length in defence of the Kildare Place Society, 9 Sept., and spoke and voted against the Maynooth grant, 26 Sept. He divided against the third reading, 19 Sept., and passage of the reform bill, 21 Sept., and the second reading of the Scottish bill, 23 Sept. 1831.

Lefroy, who was one of the requisitionists for the Protestant meeting in Dublin that month, was appointed to the select committee on Irish tithes, 15 Dec., and paired (with O'Connell) against the second reading of the revised reform bill, 17 Dec. 1831.[27] He used the debate on 14 Feb. 1832, when Sheil welcomed the speech of the Irish secretary Smith Stanley as presaging the abolition of tithes, to announce his withdrawal in protest from the committee, at which Smith Stanley dryly pointed out that Lefroy had attended it for the first time only two days earlier. Despite this rebuff, he pointedly expatiated on his opposition to Smith Stanley's plan for national education in Ireland as not only unprotestant but unchristian, 6, 16 Mar., and reverted to the subject of tithes and distress, 20, 27 Mar. On 9 Apr. he spoke and acted as teller for the minorities against Crampton's amendment disallowing payments to clergy in compensation for legal costs under the Irish tithes bill and, after having by his own amendment secured the recommittal of the Irish registry of deeds bill in order to restore the salary of the former Dublin Member George Moore to £1,500, against Hume's amendment to refer this question to a select committee. Having voted against the enfranchisement of Tower Hamlets, 28 Feb., and the third reading of the reform bill, 22 Mar., he was entrusted with moving the wrecking amendment to the second reading of the Irish bill, 25 May. He argued that there was no necessity for reform as since 1801 up to 83 of the 100 seats had been filled by men standing on the popular interest and the remaining 17 single Member boroughs had hardly departed from their franchises to the extent of the schedule A boroughs in England, while the effect of the bill, by allowing an influx of Catholic Members, would be effectively to breach the Protestant constitution and open the way for repeal of the Union. He was a teller for the minority that day and continued to oppose the bill, except on 13 June, when he defended the granting of a second seat to Dublin University, and 9 July, when he declined to comment on the proposal to extend its franchise to the masters of arts. He presented and endorsed the hostile petition of the Protestant Conservative Society of Ireland, which he was active in promoting as an electoral counterweight to O'Connell, 18 June, unsuccessfully moved an amendment to alter the franchise qualification from the 'clear yearly value' to the 'beneficial interest' test, 25 June, and divided to preserve the voting rights of Irish freemen, 2 July.[28] He voted for Alexander Baring's bill to exclude insolvent debtors from Parliament, 27 June 1832.

Lefroy, who made numerous interventions and sat on a handful of select committees on Irish matters that session, called for firm action to suppress outrages, 31 May, and divided (unless it was Anthony) against making permanent provision for the Irish poor by a tax on absentees, 19 June 1832. Vindicating the conduct of the Irish Orangemen, he unsuccessfully moved the amendment (and acted as teller) against the Irish party processions bill, 25 June, and he clashed with Smith Stanley over this, 29 June, and the latter's suggestion that he was stirring up religious animosity by airing allegations of a conspiracy against Protestant landlords, 9 July. He voted against government on the Russian-Dutch loan, 12 July, but with them against postponing the Irish tithes bill to the reformed Parliament, 13 July, when, however, he gave notice that he would resist all attempts to appropriate church revenues. He again vaunted the superiority of the Kildare Place Society scheme on dividing against the grant for the plan of national education, 23 July, and the following day it was probably he, not Anthony, who spoke and was a teller for the minority against Hume's bill to exclude Shaw from the Commons. He objected to the retrospective character of the ecclesiastical courts bill, 1 (when either he or Anthony was in the majority against Blake's amendment to the Irish tithes bill) and 3 Aug. (when he was in the minority for going into committee on crown colonies relief). Wrongly believing that the party processions bill would no longer be pursued that session, he left London in early August and, emphasizing his constant rearguard efforts in defence of Protestant education and the established church, was again returned for Trinity College in December 1832.[29] He sat until 1841, when he finally accepted a junior position on the bench, although it was another 11 years, by which time he was in his mid-70s, before his Conservative allies at last rewarded him with a senior judgeship. He retired, ignominiously without a peerage, in May 1866 and died, 'a thorough impersonation of the better class of Tory of the old school', three years later, when he was succeeded by Anthony Lefroy, who since 1858 had occupied his former seat for Dublin University.[30]

[1] Largely based on T. Lefroy, *Mem. of Chief Justice Lefroy* (1871) and J.A.P. Lefroy, 'Jane Austen's Irish Friend', *Procs. Huguenot Soc. of London*, xxiii (1977-82), 148-65. [2] *Herald and Genealogist*, vi. 125-31; Sir J.H. Lefroy, *Notes and Documents relating to Fam. of Loffroy* (1868), 2, 42, 44, 79-85, 104-5; J.A.P. Lefroy, 'Anthony Lefroy, 1703-1779', *Procs. Huguenot Soc. of London*, xxiii (1977-82), 240-51. [3] Lefroy, *Mem.* 3-14. [4] For accounts of this affair, see W. and R.A. Austen-Leigh, *Jane Austen* (1989), 85-87; *Collected Reports of Jane Austen Soc. 1976-1985*, pp. 208-13, 336-8; P. Honan, *Jane Austen*, 105-12; C. Tomalin, *Jane Austen: A Life*, 112-20; J. Spence, *Becoming Jane Austen*, 95-116; H. O'Carroll, 'Jane Austen's Limerick Romance', in *Georgian Limerick* ed. D. Lee and C. Gonzalez, ii. 310-15. [5] *Jane Austen's Letters* ed. D. Le Faye, 1-4, 19. [6] N. Radovici, *A Youthful Love: Jane Austen and Tom Lefroy?*, 1, 4-5, 18-20, 24, 29-30, 48-49, 53. [7] J.E. Austen-Leigh, *Mem. of Jane Austen* (1926), 56; R.W. Chapman, *Jane Austen: Facts and Problems*, 57-58; J.K. Ray, 'The Truth about Jane Austen and Tom Lefroy', *N and Q*, ccli (2006), 311-14. [8] See the interpretation given in L.R. Walker, 'Jane Austen and Tom Lefroy: Stories', *Persuasions On-Line*, xxvii, 1 (2006) [www.jasna.org/persuasions/on-line/vol27no1/walker.htm]. [9] Lefroy, *Mem.* pp. i-iii, 20-68, 340-72; A.R. Hart, *Hist. King's Serjeants at Law in Ireland*, 191-4; *General Advertiser or Limerick Gazette*, 10 Sept. 1819; D. Lee, 'House of Lefroy' in *Georgian Limerick*, ii. 316-17. [10] Lefroy, *Mem.* 70-79, 87-98; R. L. Sheil, *Sketches of Irish Bar* (1854), i. 216-31. [11] Lefroy, 'Jane Austen's Irish Friend', 155-6, 160. [12] Add. 40394, f. 73; *Dublin Evening Post*, 8, 15, 17, 22 May 1827. [13] *Canning's Ministry*, 313, 320. [14] Add. 37310, f. 307; PRO NI, Anglesey mss D619/31F, pp. 84-88; Wellington mss WP1/952/20; 957/10. [15] *Dublin Evening Mail*, 27 Aug., 10 Nov. 1828; *Report of Speech delivered by Lefroy* (1829), 3-15. [16] Add. 40336, f. 266. [17] Lefroy, *Mem.* 111-19; *Warder*, 3, 13 Mar. 1830. [18] Add. 40320, ff. 166, 170; 40338, f. 223; Wellington mss WP1/1127/2; 1133/5; *Warder*, 12 June, 7 Aug.; *Dublin Evening Post*, 29 July, 5 Aug. 1830. [19] NAI, Leveson Gower letter bks. M738, Leveson Gower to Peel, 25 July 1830. [20] NLI, Farnham mss 18611 (1), Lefroy to Farnham, 2, 5, 7, 25 Dec. 1830, 15, 22 Jan. 1831; TCD, Prior mss 3369, p. 177. [21] Farnham mss 18611 (1). [22] Surr. Hist. Cent. Goulburn mss 304/67B. [23] Farnham mss 18611 (1). [24] *Dublin Evening Post*, 3, 10 May 1831. [25] Farnham mss 18606 (1), Farnham to Arbuthnot, 11 May, replies, 14, 18, 25 May; 18611 (1), Lefroy to Farnham, 1, 8 June 1831. [26] Ibid. 18611 (2), Lefroy to Farnham, 1, 9, 18 Aug. 1831; Wellington mss. [27] *Dublin Evening Post*, 29 Nov., 13 Dec. 1831. [28] Farnham mss 18611 (3), Lefroy to Farnham, 4 June 1832. [29] *Macaulay Letters*, ii. 173; *Dublin Evening Post*, 13, 20 Dec. 1832. [30] *Dublin Evening Post*, 5 May; *The Times*, 6 May 1869; *Ann. Reg.* (1869), Chron. pp. 171-2; Lefroy, *Notes and Documents*, 105-6; *DNB*; *Oxford DNB*.

S.M.F.

LEGGE, Hon. Arthur Charles (1800–1890), of 12 Berkeley Square, Mdx.

BANBURY 10 Feb. 1826–1830

b. 25 June 1800, 3rd s. of George Legge†, 3rd earl of Dartmouth (*d.* 1810), and Lady Frances Finch, da. of Heneage Finch†, 3rd earl of Aylesford; bro. of Hon. Heneage Legge*. *educ.* Eton 1814. *m.* (1) 14 June 1827, Lady Anne Frederica Catherine Holroyd (*d.* 31 Aug. 1829), da. of John Baker Holroyd†, 1st earl of Sheffield [I], 1s. *d.v.p.*; (2) 29 Aug. 1837, Caroline, da. of James Charles Bouwens of Welbeck Street, Mdx., 1s. 1da. *d.* 18 May 1890.

Ensign 28 Ft. 1816; ensign and lt. 2 Ft. Gds. 1817, half-pay 1818; lt. 1 Life Gds. 1820, capt. 1822, half-pay 1837; major, army 1837; lt.-col. 1851; col. 1854; maj.-gen. 1865; lt.-gen. 1874; gen. 1877.

Lt.-col. Staffs. rifle vols. 1860; col. S. Staffs. Regt. 1868-*d.*

Legge, whose father had succeeded as 3rd earl of Dartmouth in 1801 and died as lord chamberlain in 1810, had an uneventful career in the Guards. In the autumn and winter of 1819-20 he was in Paris with his younger brother Charles. He had an 'encounter with so unpleasant a gentleman as the rheumatism', and was quite ill for a time, but on 10 Jan. 1820 told his mother:

> I gain strength much faster this frosty weather, than I did in the warm damp weather which we had a fortnight ago, though the sudden change did not agree with me at first. I have taken quantities of bark, and continue to take some daily; and feel as well as possible.[1]

He joined the Life Guards in July 1820. From the family home in Staffordshire he wrote to Charles, who was with his ship in South America, 14 Dec.:

> The queen is doing her best to create a revolution in the country, and I should not be very much surprised if the radicals were to gain ground through her; hitherto small parties of our men have kept London tolerably quiet; but I hate to talk about the 'Jezebel'. You will be glad to hear that I 'carry on' well with my new regiment and like it much.[2]

In February 1826 Legge quietly replaced his elder brother Heneage, who had been appointed a commissioner of customs, as Member for Banbury on the interest of their kinsman, the 5th earl of Guilford.[3] He voted with the Liverpool ministry against reform of Edinburgh's representation, 13 Apr., and came in again without incident at the 1826 general election.[4] He made no mark in the House, where he is not known to have spoken in debate. He voted against repeal of the Test Acts, 26 Feb. 1828. He presented a Banbury petition against Catholic claims, 6 May, and voted against relief, 12 May 1828. Planta, the Wellington ministry's patronage secretary, predicted in February 1829 that he would vote 'with government' for Catholic emancipation, but he opposed it, 6, 18, 30 Mar. He lost his first wife, a niece of Guilford, in July that year. He presented petitions from Banbury corporation for repeal of the beer and malt taxes, 11 Feb., and from the inhabitants for mitigation of the severity of the criminal code, 30 Mar. 1830. He voted for abolition of the death penalty for forgery, 24 May, but apparently reversed this vote in the division of 7 June, when he also sided with government in defence of the grant for South American missions. He voted against Jewish emancipation, 5 Apr., 17 May 1830. Guilford had died in 1827, and at the 1830 general election his successor as patron of Banbury, the 2nd marquess of Bute, replaced Legge with a kinsman of his own.

He remarried in 1837, shortly after going on the captain's half-pay on which he still remained when seniority saw him attain the rank of general 40 years later. He died at his then residence at Caynton, Shropshire, in May 1890. By his will, dated 24 Feb. 1880, he left all his property to his wife and only surviving son, the Rev. Alfred Arthur Kaye Legge (1839-1906).

[1] Staffs. RO, Dartmouth mss D 1778/V/1044, Legge to Lady Dartmouth, 24 Oct. [1819], 1, 10 Jan. 1820. [2] Ibid. V/1047. [3] *Jackson's Oxford Jnl.* 11 Feb. 1826. [4] Ibid. 17 June 1826.

D.R.F.

LEGGE, Hon. Heneage (1788–1844), of Putney House, Richmond, Surr.

BANBURY 22 Nov. 1819–Feb. 1826

b. 29 Feb. 1788, 2nd s. of George Legge†, 3rd earl of Dartmouth (*d.* 1810), and Lady Frances Finch, da. of Heneage Finch†, 3rd earl of Aylesford; bro. of Hon. Arthur Charles Legge*. *educ.* Eton 1799; Christ Church, Oxf. 1805; fellow, All Souls 1812-28, BCL 1812, DCL 1818; L. Inn 1809, called 1815. *m.* 19 July 1827, Mary Gregory, 1da.[1] *d.* 12 Dec. 1844.

Gent. usher to the king 1822-37, sen. gent. usher to Queen Victoria 1837-*d.*

Commr.of customs Feb. 1826-d.

Capt. R. Staffs. militia 1820.

Legge was again returned unopposed for the corporation borough of Banbury on the interest of his kinsman the 5th earl of Guilford at the general election of 1820, when a murderous stone-throwing mob besieged the town hall, and he 'escaped with his life' only by 'being dragged over the top of some of the houses and let down into the inn yard, from whence he made his escape in the disguise of a post boy'.[2] He gave general support to the Liverpool ministry, but was not a particularly assiduous attender. He voted against economies in revenue collection, 4 July 1820. He was one of the 'most remarkable' of the deserters who joined the opposition minority deploring the omission of Queen Caroline's name from the liturgy, 26 Jan. 1821;[3] but he returned to the government fold to vote in defence of their general conduct towards her, 6 Feb. 1821. His only reported speech was against the restoration of her name to the liturgy, 13 Feb., when he explained his apparent volte face on the grounds that her 'pertinacious attempts of late to set the people in hostile array against both Houses of Parliament' justified the exclusion, which he had originally considered 'ill advised' and provocative. He also changed his mind over Catholic relief, voting for it, 28 Feb. 1821, but subsequently opposing it, 30 Apr. 1822, 1 Mar., 21 Apr, 10 May 1825. He divided against the Irish franchise bill, 26 Apr. 1825. He voted against repeal of the additional malt duty, 3 Apr. 1821, and tax reductions, 21 Feb. 1822, 3, 18 Mar. 1823. He opposed parliamentary reform, 20 Feb. 1823. He presented a petition for the abolition of slavery, 5 May 1823,[4] but paired against Brougham's motion condemning the trial of the Methodist missionary John Smith for inciting insurrection among slaves in Demerara, 11 June 1824. He voted for the duke of Cumberland's annuity, 30 May, 6, 10 June 1825. Legge's brother Lord Dartmouth had been pestering Lord Liverpool to accommodate him as a commissioner of customs or excise since 1822, when he had been given a minor household post; and in March 1824, following false reports of the resignation of Lord Francis Conyngham* as under-secretary at the foreign office, Robert Wilmot* told Lord Granville that 'Heneage Legge is very anxious to get something, I don't mean that he would look to that post, but to some advantage arising out of the move'.[5] In February 1826 he was appointed a commissioner of customs, at £1,200 a year, and necessarily vacated his seat.

The following year he made what was evidently an unsuitable marriage, at least in the eyes of his mother. In January 1829 George Fortescue* told a mutual friend:

> I had a letter ... from Heneage Legge telling me that his mother had at last allowed him to 'declare his marriage, explaining his history to his friends and nearest relations, with an understanding that the subject should not be talked about or the marriage supposed to be acknowledged' ... He has too at last been made acquainted with his wife's name and genealogy, and though he cannot divulge it, seems to derive comfort from finding it respectable and ancient beyond what from former conversations with me, he appeared to expect.

Soon afterwards Fortescue reported that at a dinner at their club Legge 'did not quite *look* as he used to in a merry party of friends and was more silent than ever'.[6] He died in December 1844, leaving all his real and personal property to his trustees, whom he had instructed to sell it for the benefit of his wife and daughter.[7]

[1] At St. James, Paddington, Mdx. (IGI). Successive editions of *Burke PB* state that he *m.* 19 July 1821, Mary, da. of Maj. Johnstone; but it has not proved possible to verify this from other sources. [2] S. Beesley, *My Life* 18; Devon RO, Sidmouth mss, Sheffield to Sidmouth, 17 Mar. 1820. [3] Lonsdale mss, Lowther to Lonsdale, 27 Jan. 1821. [4] *The Times*, 6 May 1823. [5] Add. 38295, f. 231; TNA 30/29/9/6/18. [6] Keele Univ. Lib Sneyd mss SC10/87, 89. [7] *Gent. Mag.* (1845), i. 109; PROB 11/2012/136.

H.J.S.

LEGH, Thomas (1793–1857), of Lyme Hall, Cheshire and Haydock Lodge and Golborne Park, Lancs.

NEWTON 16 Apr. 1814–1832

b. 1793, 1st illegit. s. of Thomas Peter Legh† of Golborne and Lyme. *educ.* Brasenose, Oxf. 15 June 1810, aged 17. *m.* (1) 14 Jan. 1828,[1] Ellen (*d.* 17 Jan. 1831), da. and h. of William Turner† of Shrigley Park, Cheshire, 1s. *d.v.p.* 1da.; (2) 3 Oct. 1843, Maud, da. of Gorges Lowther of Hampton Hall, Som., *s.p. suc.* fa. 1797. *d.* 8 May 1857.

Legh, his father's eldest illegitimate son, had succeeded him as head of the family and from 1808 bore their arms. The rental of his estates was estimated in 1824 at £27,000.[2] A distinguished traveller in early life, he served the duke of Wellington as an extra aide-de-camp at Waterloo and represented the family borough of Newton unopposed from his coming of age until its disfranchisement in 1832. He generally supported the Liverpool ministry, casting very occasional wayward votes, and made no reported parliamentary speeches. Early in 1820 he became involved in a minor dispute with Lord Liverpool, who had refused to allow his brother-in-law Thomas Claughton* preferential treatment in the purchase of some royal manors in Cardiganshire.[3] He divided against Catholic relief, 30 Apr. 1822, 21 Apr., 10 May, and the attendant Irish franchise bill, 26 Apr. 1825; according to a radical publication of that session, he 'attended occasionally, and appeared to vote with ministers'.[4] He voted against them on the appointment of an additional baron of exchequer in Scotland, 15 May 1820, received six weeks' leave on urgent private business, 9 Apr., and divided with them on economy and retrenchment, 27 June 1821, the Foreign Enlistment Act, 16 Apr. 1823, and for the duke of Cumberland's annuity, 10 June 1825.

Claughton's bankruptcy in March 1824 embroiled Legh in a number of legal actions. He was sued early in 1825 for the £3,500 value of a bill of exchange drawn on him in 1821 by Claughton, which the attorney-general Sir John Singleton Copley*, representing him, successfully contended had come into the plaintive (Usher's) hands by fraudulent means.[5] On 11 Feb. 1825 a creditors' meeting put Claughton's debt to Legh at £100,000, and he was found liable and ordered to pay the value of a promissory note worth £8-9,000 when sued in 1826.[6] He divided against Catholic relief, 6 Mar. 1827. In January 1828 he married Ellen Turner, the daughter of a neighbouring landowner and heiress to the Shrigley estate, who in 1826 had been abducted and inveigled into marriage (later annulled) by Edward Gibbon Wakefield.[7] As the Wellington ministry's patronage secretary anticipated, Legh remained opposed to the concession of Catholic emancipation and voted accordingly, 6 Mar. 1829. He received three weeks' leave on account of his wife's illness, 15 Apr. 1830. After the general election that summer ministers listed him among the 'moderate Ultras', which they endorsed to 'friend', but he voted to bring them down on the civil list, 15 Nov. 1830. He was granted three weeks' leave, 14 Feb. 1831, following his wife's death, and another fortnight on account of illness in his family, 9 Mar. 1831. He did not vote on the second reading of the Grey ministry's reform bill, which proposed Newton's disfranchisement, 22 Mar., but he divided for Gascoyne's wrecking amendment, 19 Apr. 1831. He voted against the reintroduced reform bill at its second reading, 6 July, but apparently with government against making the 1831 census the determinant of English borough disfranchisements, 19 July 1831. He divided against the bill's third reading, 19 Sept., and passage, 21 Sept., the second reading of the Scottish reform bill, 23 Sept. 1831, and the third reading of the revised reform bill, 22 Mar. 1832. He left Parliament at the dissolution that year.

Legh died at Milford Lodge, Lymington, Hampshire, in May 1857, having bequeathed the family estates to his nephew and heir Captain William John Legh (1828-98) of Lyme, Conservative Member for South Lancashire, 1859-65, and East Cheshire, 1868-85, who in 1892 was created Baron Newton. He left his second wife, for whom he established a trust, the rents of his leasehold properties and his personal effects, including jewellery, to the value of £1,373, and created separate trusts for his daughter and her son.[8]

[1] *Gent. Mag.* (1828), i. 80; J.P. Earwaker, *E. Cheshire*, ii. 306. [2] *The Times*, 27 Feb. 1824. [3] Add. 38281, f. 240, 362; 38282, f. 84, 192, 229, 280, 360; *HP Commons, 1790-1820*, iv. 404. [4] *Session of Parl. 1825*, p. 472. [5] *The Times*, 2 Mar. 1825. [6] *London Gazette*, 18 Jan. 1825; *The Times*, 22 Dec. 1826 [Knight *v.* Legh]. [7] W. Beamont, *House of Lyme*, 200; *Oxford DNB sub* Wakefield, Edward Gibbon. [8] *Preston Guardian*, 16 May; *Liverpool Mercury*, 20 May 1857; PROB 11/2253/476; IR26/2104/523.

S.R.B./M.M.E.

LEGH KECK, George Anthony (1774–1860), of Stoughton Grange, nr. Leicester, Leics. and Bank Hall, nr. Preston, Lancs.

LEICESTERSHIRE 25 Oct. 1797–1818

LEICESTERSHIRE 1820–1831

b. 15 July 1774, 3rd but 2nd surv. s. of Anthony James Keck† (*d.* 1782) of Stoughton and Elizabeth, da. and h. of Peter Legh† of Lyme, Cheshire. *educ.* Eton 1785-90; Christ Church, Oxf. 1791. *m.* 18 May 1802, his cos. Elizabeth, da. of Robert Vernon Atherton of Atherton, Lancs., *s.p.* Took name of Legh bef. Keck under will of maternal grandfa. by royal lic. 31 July 1792. *suc.* bro. Peers Anthony Keck to Stoughton 1797. *d.* 4 Sept. 1860.

Cornet, Loyal Leicester yeomanry (afterwards Prince Albert's own regt. of yeomanry cav.) 1798, lt. 1801, commdt. 1803, lt.-col. commdt. 1803-*d.*

Legh Keck, the owner of a substantial inherited Leicestershire estate, had abandoned the county seat which he had occupied for over 20 years in 1818 in the face of popular hostility to his firm stand against radicalism in the distressed manufacturing districts.[1] Encouraged by a reaction in his favour in the alarmist response to the Peterloo massacre and its aftermath, he came forward again at the 1820 general election on the 'true Blue' independent interest. He was returned unopposed with his former colleague Lord Robert Manners, a brother of the 5th duke of Rutland. Returning thanks, he referred to his past parliamentary conduct 'in the place of professions'.[2] A somewhat lax attender, he resumed his general but far from slavish support of the Liverpool ministry.[3]

He voted against them on the appointment of an additional Scottish exchequer judge, 15 May, but was in their majority against economies in revenue collection, 4 July 1820. He presented petitions for the restoration of Queen Caroline's name to the liturgy, 26 Jan., 8 Feb., but divided against the opposition censure motion, 6 Feb. 1821.[4] He brought up a petition against Catholic relief, 23 Feb., and voted thus, 28 Feb.[5] On 27 Mar. he obtained leave to introduce a bill to validate certain indentures of apprenticeship and certificates of settlement, which became law on 28 May (1 & 2 Geo. IV, c. 32).[6] He cast wayward votes for repeal of the additional malt duty, 3 Apr., admiralty reductions, 4 May, and the omission of arrears from the duke of Clarence's grant, 18 June, but sided with government against a cut in the army estimates, 11 Apr., and parliamentary reform, 9 May 1821. He presented petitions complaining of agricultural distress in Rutland and Leicestershire, 18 Feb., 24 Apr., when he assured the House that the graziers' grievances were genuine, as 'distress equally pervaded all parts of the country'.[7] Although he mustered for the division against more extensive tax reductions, 21 Feb., he divided for relaxation of the salt duties, 28 Feb., admiralty economies, 1 Mar., and abolition of one of the joint-postmasterships, 2 May 1822. He voted against Canning's bill to relieve Catholic peers of their disabilities, 30 Apr., and presented hostile petitions, 13, 16 May.[8] He delivered Leicester petitions against the poor removal bill, 24 May 1822.[9] In 1823 he voted for tax reductions, 28 Feb., 18 Mar., inquiry into the prosecution of the Dublin Orange rioters, 22 Apr., and equalization of the East and West Indian sugar duties, 22 May, but divided with ministers against repeal of the Foreign Enlistment Act, 16 Apr., and Scottish parliamentary reform, 2 June. He presented petitions from Lord Stamford against the Marriage Act, 21 Feb., and from his constituents in favour of a bill to facilitate the recovery of small debts, 14 Mar. 1823.[10] He voted for repeal of the window tax, 2 Mar., and presented petitions to that effect, 15 Mar., 5 Apr. 1824.[11] He brought up anti-slavery petitions, 4, 17, 25 Mar., 6 Apr., and one for repeal of victuallers' licence duties, 18 Mar. 1824.[12] He was granted a month's leave on account of ill health, 14 Feb., and again, 15 Apr.; but he was present to vote against Catholic relief, 21 Apr. 1825. He paired for the division of 10 May 1825. He presented petitions for revision of the corn laws, 28 Feb., 1 Mar., and for an increase in coroner's allowances, 10 Apr. 1826, when he voted against government on the president of the board of trade's salary.[13]

Legh Keck was returned unopposed for Leicestershire at the general election of 1826, when he 'flattered himself that a service of nearly 30 years would preclude the necessity of making any assurances as to his future conduct'.[14] He was absent from the division on Catholic relief, 6 Mar. 1827. Opposing Sykes's motion for inquiry into the allegations of improper electoral interference by Leicester corporation, 15 Mar. 1827, he denied that they had misapplied their revenues or created honorary freemen to secure the return of their candidate at the last election. He received the thanks of the corporation, 20 Mar.[15] He chaired the Penryn election committee, appointed on 27 Feb., and reported its findings to the House, 9 Mar.: evidence had emerged of 'gross acts of bribery and corruption', which the committee wished to have investigated.[16] On 8 May he proposed to bring in a bill to restrict the franchise to the possessors of land within the borough and extend it to the freeholders of two neighbouring hundreds. He dismissed the prevalent notion of disfranchising Penryn and transferring its seats to Leeds or Manchester. He pressed for the prosecution of offenders and was given leave to bring in his bill. On 28 May he defended it and resisted Russell's amendment to give the seats to Manchester as 'an evil precedent' which would threaten the parliamentary 'balance' between the manufacturing and landed interests.[17] He was a teller for the minority in the ensuing division. He was reported as saying that he would vote for the third reading of the amended bill, 7 June, even though it was 'at variance with the measure which he himself had proposed', but he was listed in the hostile minority.[18] He presented petitions for repeal of the Test Acts, 30 May, 6 June 1827.[19] In reply to the home secretary Peel's solicitation of his support for the duke of Wellington's new ministry, 23 Jan. 1828, Legh Keck stated that 'no one would more rejoice in the practical reassertion of the principles of Lord Liverpool than myself, and ... no one will be more ready to co-operate with yourself'.[20] He did not act up to these professions. He presented more petitions for repeal of the Test Acts in February, but absented himself from the division when it was carried on the 26th. He presented a Leicester petition against the Malt Act, 28 Feb., and secured a return of information on its operation, 7 Mar. He presented a petition against Catholic relief, 1 May, and voted accordingly, 12 May. He divided against the provision for Canning's family, 13 May, and on the 20th, as an 'independent' Member of long standing, defended this action, observing that 'no motives of delicacy towards any man ... shall induce me to decline what I conceive to be a painful but unavoidable duty'. He refuted Otway Cave's charges against Leicester corporation, 14 May, and repudiated his accusation of hypocrisy over the Penryn bill, 10 June, but disclaimed any responsibility for the petition which Abney Hastings, the Tory Leicester Member, had tried to present in vindication of the corporation. He voted for Hume's motion for information on civil list pensions, 20 May, and against the government's proposal to restrict the circulation of small notes, 5 June; he presented petitions on this subject, 12, 16 June. He divided against the archbishop of Canterbury's estate bill, 16 June, and brought up anti-slavery petitions, 17, 24 June 1828.

In February 1829 Planta, the bungling patronage secretary, predicted that Legh Keck would side 'with government' for their concession of Catholic emancipation. However, he was 'red-hot' against it and, presenting the hostile Leicestershire petition, 3 Mar., he delivered what Manners described as a 'flaming speech'.[21] He deplored the measure, which ran counter to the views of most of his constituents, and spoke in 'fearless independence' of the consequent 'diminution' in his confidence in the ministry. In a clash with Otway Cave, he denied that he had compromised his vaunted independence by accepting patronage from the Goderich administration. He presented more anti-Catholic petitions, 9, 10 Mar. 1829, and was one of the diehard voters against emancipation that month. Alienated from the ministry by this episode, he voted against them on the treasurership of the navy, 12 Mar., the Bathurst-Dundas pensions, 25 Mar., the ordnance estimates, 29 Mar., privy councillors' emoluments, 14 May, and the grant for South American missions, 11 June 1830. On 4 May he presented Leicester petitions against the sale of beer bill and spoke and voted against its second reading, commenting that 'as a magistrate I must disclaim all responsibility whatever for any scenes of disorder or confusion which may arise'. He presented petitions against renewal of the East India Company's charter, 4 May, 29 June, and the Maynooth grant, 25 June. He divided against Jewish emancipation, 17 May 1830.

Legh Keck topped the poll at the contested general election of 1830, when he stressed his independence and said that 'it was not in the power of government to make him swerve from what he considered the strict line of duty, by anything which it could bestow'.[22] Ministers listed him as one of the 'moderate Ultras', and he helped to vote them out of office on the civil list, 15 Nov. 1830. He brought up anti-slavery petitions, 15, 16 Nov. On 8 Dec. he presented one from Hinckley for a reduction in the window tax and urged the Grey ministry to give 'serious attention' to the subject. He presented petitions for parliamentary reform and the ballot, 26 Feb. 1831. When he produced petitions in support of the ministerial reform bill, 17 Mar., he stated that he would act on it 'as I think right, upon seeing the alterations made to it in the committee'. He accordingly divided for the second reading, 22 Mar., but for Gascoyne's wrecking amendment, 19 Apr. 1831. He retired from Parliament at the ensuing dissolution.

Thereafter he 'employed himself either in attending to his vast estates, or in maintaining the efficiency of his yeomanry corps'.[23] He restored and enlarged Bank Hall and devised it, together with his Leicestershire property, to his nephew, Henry Littleton Powys (1812-63), who took the additional name of Keck.[24] He died at Bank Hall in September 1860.

[1] *HP Commons, 1790-1820*, iv. 406. [2] *Leicester Jnl.* 3, 10, 17 Mar. 1820. [3] *Session of Parl. 1825*, p. 471. [4] *The Times*, 27 Jan., 9 Feb. 1821. [5] Ibid. 24 Feb. 1821. [6] Ibid. 28, 29 Mar. 1821. [7] Ibid. 19 Feb., 26 Apr. 1822. [8] Ibid. 14, 17 May 1822. [9] Ibid. 25 May 1822. [10] Ibid. 22 Feb., 15 Mar. 1823. [11] Ibid. 16 Mar., 6 Apr. 1824. [12] Ibid. 5, 18, 19, 26 Mar., 7 Apr. 1824. [13] Ibid. 1, 2 Mar., 11 Apr. 1826. [14] *Leicester Jnl.* 16 June 1826. [15] *Leicester Borough Recs.* v. 474. [16] *The Times*, 10 Mar. 1827 [17] Ibid. 12, 29 May 1827. [18] Ibid. 8 June 1827. [19] Ibid. 31 May, 7 June 1827. [20] Add. 40395, f. 87. [21] Aberdeen Univ. Lib. Arbuthnot mss, Rutland to Mrs. Arbuthnot, 3 Mar.; Rutland mss (History of Parliament Aspinall transcripts), Manners to Rutland [Mar. 1829]. [22] *Leicester Chron.* 14, 21 Aug. 1830. [23] *Gent. Mag.* (1860), ii. 554. [24] *VCH Lancs.* vi. 106.

S.R.H.

LEIGH, Francis (1758–1839), of Rosegarland, co. Wexford.

WEXFORD	1801–1 Feb. 1801
NEW ROSS	9 Feb. 1821–9 Feb. 1824

bap. 18 Jan. 1758, 1st s. of Robert Leigh†, MP [I], of Rosegarland and Arabella, da. of Robert Leslie of Glasslough, co. Monaghan. *educ.* by Rev. Benjamin Hobart, Carlow; Trinity, Dublin 10 Feb. 1775, aged 17. *m.* Dec. 1788, Grace, da. of Richard Baldwin, 3s. (1 *d.v.p.*) 3da. (1 *d.v.p.*). *suc.* fa. 1803. *d.* 1839.

MP [I] 1785-97, Feb.-Dec. 1800.

Collector of excise, co. Wexford c.1791-9, co. Dublin 1801-18.

Sovereign, New Ross 1796-8.

Col. Wexford militia.

In the summer of 1818 Leigh applied to government for permission to retire with a pension from his excise collectorship. He was 'past sixty years of age', had complied with the requirements of the Superannuation Act, and was anxious, above all, to take his ailing wife 'to a climate more suited to her constitution'.[1] His wish was granted, and he was later reckoned to be in receipt of a pension of £1,384 per annum.[2] Leigh was co-patron with Charles Tottenham† of the borough of New Ross. It was his turn to nominate the Member at the 1820 general election but, for whatever reason, he did not exercise his right until early the following year, when he returned himself as a supporter of government. An inconspicuous Member, who is not known to have spoken in debate, he was inaccurately described by a radical commentary of 1823 as an 'absentee'.[3] He voted against Catholic relief, 28 Feb. 1821, 30 Apr. 1822. On 6 Mar. 1821 he was granted six weeks' leave on account of the death of his second son. He divided against tax reductions, 21 Feb., and presented a petition for repeal of the Irish window tax, 17 Apr. 1822.[4] He was credited with a vote in a minority of 16 against a clause of the London Bridge bill, 20 June 1823. In 1824 he retired to accommodate a prominent Irish barrister.

Leigh, who lost his eldest son in 1827, died in 1839, when he was succeeded by his grandson, Francis Augustus Leigh (1822-1900).

[1] Add. 40277, f. 263; 40279, f. 242; *PP* (1822), xiii. 904, 908. [2] *PP* (1822), xiii. 904, 908; *Extraordinary Black Bk.* (1832), 550. [3] *Black Bk.* (1823), 169. [4] *The Times*, 18 Apr. 1822.

D.R.F.

LEIGH, James Henry (1765–1823), of Adlestrop, Glos. and Stoneleigh Abbey, Warws.

MARLBOROUGH	1802–1806
GREAT BEDWYN	1806–12 Mar. 1818
WINCHESTER	18 Mar. 1818–30 Jan. 1823

b. 8 Feb. 1765, o. surv. s. of James Leigh of Adlestrop and Lady Caroline Brydges, da. of Henry Brydges†, 2nd duke of Chandos. *educ.* ?Harrow 1779; Christ Church, Oxf. 1782. *m.* 8 Dec. 1786, Hon. Julia Judith Twistleton, da. of Thomas, 7th Bar. Saye and Sele, 1s. 4da. *suc.* fa. 1774; cos. Hon. Mary Leigh to Stoneleigh estates of her bro. Edward, 5th Bar. Leigh, 1806. *d.* 28 Oct. 1823.

High Steward, Winchester until 1819.

'Bunny' Leigh, who had inherited the extensive family estates of the extinct barony of Leigh in 1806, had been returned for Winchester in 1818 on the old

Chandos interest revived by his cousin's husband, the 2nd marquess of Buckingham. He was intended as a stopgap for his only son Chandos Leigh, a rake and versifier who frequented Holland House, but it was Leigh himself who came in again at the 1820 general election.[1] It is not clear whether he regarded himself as one of Buckingham's parliamentary allies, the remnant of the old Grevillite party, but the marquess, who considered him a 'reluctant' politician whose political ideas required a 'little polishing', does not seem to have taken him very seriously.[2] A lax attender, who is not known to have spoken in debate, soon after his election he unsuccessfully pressed his claims to a peerage on Lord Liverpool, the premier, with the support of Buckingham and his kinsman Lord Ailesbury.[3] In contrast to the Grenvillites, he voted against Catholic relief, 28 Feb. 1821, 30 Apr. 1822, and presented a hostile Winchester petition, 2 Apr. 1821.[4] He was in the ministerial majorities against repeal of the additional malt duty, 3 Apr., military reductions, 11 Apr., and the omission of arrears from the duke of Clarence's grant, 18 June, but was in the minority for parliamentary reform, 9 May. He divided for criminal law reform, 4 June 1821, 4 June 1822. He voted with ministers against further tax reductions, 11 Feb., and repeal of the salt duties, 28 June, but was in the protectionist minority of 24 for a 40*s*. fixed duty on imported corn, 8 May 1822. That November his retirement was announced at a corporation dinner given by Buckingham's son Lord Chandos*.[5] In accordance with Buckingham's wishes, he duly vacated his seat for the father-in-law of his daughter Caroline at the start of the 1823 session.[6]

Leigh's retirement from public life was short-lived, for he was found dead in his bed in October 1823. An obituary described him as 'a man who, from the excellence of his private life, the extent of his charities, and his universal philanthropy, will long be embalmed in the recollection of a numerous circle of friends'.[7] By his will, dated 28 June 1819, his leasehold properties in Portman Square, London passed to his wife, with remainder to his eldest son Chandos, who was created Baron Leigh by the Melbourne ministry in 1839. The residue of his personal estate, which was sworn under £50,000, was divided equally among his five children.[8]

[1] *HP, Commons 1790-1820*, ii. 194-5. [2] NLW, Coedymaen mss 20, Buckingham to Williams Wynn [n.d.]. [3] *Black Bk.* (1823), 169; Add. 38285, f. 98. [4] *The Times*, 3 Apr. 1821. [5] *Salisbury Jnl.* 11 Nov. 1822. [6] Bucks. RO, Fremantle mss D/FR/46/11/67. [7] *Gent. Mag.* (1824), i. 87. [8] PROB 11/1679/698; IR26/968/1575.

D.R.F./P.J.S.

LEIGH, Thomas Charles (1801–1863), of 35 Dover Street, Piccadilly, Mdx.

WALLINGFORD 21 Sept. 1831–1832

b. 5 Feb. 1801, 1st s. of Charles Hanbury Tracy*. *educ.* privately; European tour 1818; Christ Church, Oxf. 1819. *m.* 25 Aug. 1831, Emma Elizabeth Alicia, da. and coh. of George Hay Dawkins Pennant*, 6s. (1 *d.v.p.*) 6da. (1 *d.v.p.*). Took name of Leigh by royal lic. 11 Apr. 1806; resumed patronymic of Hanbury Tracy by royal lic. 30 Mar. 1839; *suc.* fa. as 2nd Bar. Sudeley 10 Feb. 1858. *d.* 19 Feb. 1863.

Ld. lt. Mont. 1858 – *d.*

Leigh was so named at the age of five in deference to the memory of his maternal grandfather, to whose estates in Gloucestershire, Montgomeryshire and Shropshire he was his father's heir.[1] The year before he went to Oxford he undertook a four month tour of Switzerland and Italy.[2] He shared his father's advanced Whig politics and was elected to Brooks's on 12 Feb. 1826, sponsored by his father's friends and associates Sir Francis Burdett* and William Lewis Hughes, Member for Wallingford. In August 1831 he married an heiress worth £70,000. When Hughes was raised to the peerage as Lord Dinorben by the Grey ministry the following month he recommended Leigh to his supporters at Wallingford. (The story was that Dinorben had offered his support in the first instance to Hanbury Tracy, but he had irons in the fire at Tewkesbury, where he came in on a vacancy the following January.) Leigh, who was chaperoned by his father, was opposed by a local Tory put up by the corporation-backed Blue party dedicated to ending the systematic bribery by which Hughes's interest had largely been sustained. According to a hostile newspaper report, he was given a hard time on the hustings, where his opponents denounced him as Dinorben's nominee and 'a mere tool of ministers'. The extreme brevity of his speech, in which he promised to 'adhere to the liberal principles in which I have been brought up, and lend my aid in reforming every species of abuse in church and state', was seized on as evidence of a lack of talent, and his silence when asked to renounce electoral corruption was construed as a refusal. It was asserted that his 'assumed nonchalance of a modern exquisite' was 'shattered' by his critics, whose attacks reduced him to 'a perfect specimen of suffering meekness'. For all this, he was easily returned on the poll. Emboldened, perhaps, by his success, he denounced as 'useless and absurd' the question thrown at him by one of his tormentors as to whether he would support the ministerial bill to outlaw bribery: 'How is it possible for a man who has promised to vote for every species of reform to do otherwise? The question answers itself'. The petition alleging bribery which was lodged against his return was not pursued.[3]

Leigh revealed no hidden talents in the House, where he is not known to have opened his mouth in debate and provided reliable lobby fodder for the ministry. He voted for the second reading of the Scottish reform bill, 23 Sept., and Lord Ebrington's confidence motion, 10 Oct. 1831. He divided for the second reading of the revised English reform bill, 17 Dec. 1831, was a steadfast supporter of its details, and voted for its third reading, 22 Mar. 1832. He rallied to ministers on the Russian-Dutch loan, 26 Jan., 12, 16 July, relations with Portugal, 9 Feb., and the navy civil departments bill, 6 Apr. He voted for the address calling on the king to appoint only a government which would carry the reform bill unimpaired, 10 May, and for the second reading of the Irish bill, 25 May, and against a Conservative amendment to the Scottish measure, 1 June. He voted to make coroners' inquests public, 20 June 1832. He retired from the Commons at the dissolution of 1832.

Leigh, who resumed the names of Hanbury Tracy after his father's ennoblement as Lord Sudeley in 1838, enjoyed the dignity himself for only five years before dying at Pau, in the South of France in February 1863. By his will, dated 17 June 1862, he left his wife £2,000, an annuity of £3,000, and his house at Eastern Terrace, Brighton. Having settled £25,000 on each of his three married daughters, he devised the same sum to their two spinster sisters, and left £20,000 each to his four surviving younger sons. He was succeeded in the peerage by his eldest son, Sudeley Charles George Hanbury Tracy (1837-77). He was succeeded by his next brother, Charles Douglas Richard Hanbury Tracy (1840-1922), who, compounding the problems created by an encumbered inheritance with a succession of failures in business and speculation, was twice declared bankrupt and lost all the family estates.[4]

[1] *Williams Wynn Corresp.* 272. [2] *The Sudeleys, Lords of Toddington* ed. Lord Sudeley (1987), 215. [3] E.A. Smith, 'Bribery and Disfranchisement', *EHR*, lxxv (1960), 628-9; *Reading Mercury*, 19, 26 Sept.; *Berks. Chron.* 24 Sept. 1831. [4] *The Sudeleys*, 253-67.

D.R.F.

LEMON, Sir Charles, 2nd bt. (1784–1868), of Carclew, nr. Penryn, Cornw. and 37 Sackville Street, Mdx.

PENRYN	1807–1812
PENRYN	1830–1831
CORNWALL	1831–1832
CORNWALL WEST	1832–1841
CORNWALL WEST	16 Feb. 1842–1857

b. 3 Sept. 1784,[1] 2nd but o. surv. s. of Sir William Lemon, 1st bt.*, of Carclew and Jane, da. of James Buller† of Morval. *educ.* Harrow 1798-1803; Christ Church, Oxf. 1803. *m.* 5 Dec. 1810, Lady Charlotte Anne Fox Strangways, da. of Henry Thomas Fox Strangways†, 2nd earl of Ilchester, 2s. 1da. all *d.v.p. suc.* fa. as 2nd bt. 11 Dec. 1824. *d.* 13 Feb. 1868.

Sheriff, Cornw. 1827-8; dep. warden of the stannaries 1852.

Cornet, Dorset yeoman cav. 1813.

On his father's death in 1824 Lemon inherited all his Cornish property, including interests in several copper mines, and was the residuary legatee of the personal estate, which was sworn under £70,000.[2] In 1830 he was returned at the head of the poll for the venal borough of Penryn, which he had represented in the 1807 Parliament and where he possessed 'considerable property', apparently with support from the corporation.[3] Although he had previously voted with the Whig opposition, like his father, he had apparently taken no part in the Cornish reform movement. The duke of Wellington's ministry regarded him as one of their 'foes', but he was absent from the crucial division on the civil list, 15 Nov. His Whig affiliation was confirmed by his admission to Brooks's Club, 5 Dec., which was sponsored by his friend Lord Lansdowne. He presented several Cornish anti-slavery petitions, 5, 11 Nov., 6 Dec. 1830. Early in March 1831 he informed Lansdowne of 'some important mistakes in the Cornish returns' relating to the Grey ministry's reform bill, and was asked to 'make a statement of them'.[4] He divided for the bill's second reading, 22 Mar., and against Gascoyne's wrecking amendment, 19 Apr. 1831. At the ensuing general election he withdrew from Penryn when the opportunity arose to stand for Cornwall, as 'a candidate zealously interested in the cause of reform but a man of no party'. He declared that he 'should not pledge himself to the details' of the bill but that its main principle, 'the disfranchisement of insignificant and nomination boroughs, admitted of no compromise', and he called for 'a national effort ... to throw off from our institutions the burthen with which time has encumbered them'. He was returned with the Whig sitting Member Wynne Pendarves after a notable contest in which he ousted the Ultra Tory, Sir Richard Vyvyan.[5]

He divided for the second reading of the reintroduced reform bill, 6 July 1831, and generally for its details. However, he voted against Downton's inclusion in schedule A, 21 July, and for the Chandos amendment to enfranchise £50 tenants-at-will, 18 Aug. He contradicted Wetherell's assertion that the population of Appleby was equal to that of Truro, 19 July, and commended the 'most desirable' union of Penryn with Falmouth, which were 'both ports increasing in importance', 9 Aug. He divided for the bill's passage, 21 Sept., the second reading of the Scottish bill, 23 Sept., and Lord Ebrington's confidence motion, 10 Oct. Following the Lords' rejection of the reform bill he attended a county meeting, 26 Oct., when he expressed confidence that the people would avoid 'violent passions' as it was 'a question of time only' before the measure was carried. He maintained that it would 'remedy' the antagonism between the manufacturing and agricultural interests, while ensuring that the latter retained its 'due weight in the representation'. On the other hand, he was grateful that he had not been asked to pledge support to all its details, as he 'should have felt great embarrassment in some votes which I have given, departing from the original bill and I think introducing great improvements into it'.[6] He voted to punish only those guilty of bribery at the Dublin election, 23 Aug. When presenting a petition from the parochial clergy of Cornwall against the Beer Act, 27 Aug., he denied Hume's imputation that they had a vested interest in maintaining magisterial control over the granting of public house licenses. He divided for the second reading of the revised reform bill, 17 Dec. 1831, and generally for its details, but he was against the enfranchisement of Tower Hamlets, 28 Feb., and Gateshead, 5 Mar. 1832. He was mentioned by Grey that January as 'standing amongst the list of those whose claims are the strongest if new creations [of peers] should take place'.[7] He voted for the bill's third reading, 22 Mar., and the motion for an address asking the king to appoint only ministers committed to carrying an unimpaired measure, 10 May. He divided for the second reading of the Irish bill, 25 May, and against the Conservative amendment for increased Scottish county representation, 1 June. He voted with ministers on the Russian-Dutch loan, 26 Jan., 12, 16, 20 July, and relations with Portugal, 9 Feb. He divided with the minority for inquiry into colonial slavery, 24 May 1832.

At the general election of 1832 Lemon was returned unopposed for West Cornwall, after pledging support for agricultural protection and the commutation of tithes, and he sat as an advocate of 'Whig principles', with one brief interruption, until his retirement in 1857.[8] He published a number of pamphlets on mining subjects and had a 'passion for scientific pursuits', cultivating a 'collection of exotic trees and shrubs' in his gardens. He was elected a fellow of the Royal Society in 1822 and helped to found the Statistical Society in 1834. He was also 'a zealous freemason' and served as 'provincial grandmaster of Cornwall for many years'.[9] On his death in February 1868 the baronetcy became extinct; he left his estates to his nephew, Colonel Arthur Tremayne (1827-1905).

[1] IGI (Cornw.). [2] PROB 11/1698/208; IR26/1050/249. [3] *West Briton*, 9 July, 6 Aug. 1830. [4] Grey mss, Lansdowne to Grey, 5 Mar. 1831. [5] *West Briton*, 29 Apr., 6, 13, 20 May 1831. [6] Ibid. 28 Oct. 1831. [7] Lansdowne mss, Grey to Lansdowne, 16 Jan 1832. [8] *R. Cornw. Gazette*, 25 Aug., 22 Dec. 1832; *Dod's Parl. Companion* (1833), 133. [9] *Gent. Mag.* (1868), i. 389-90; Boase, *Modern Eng. Biog.* ii. 386.

T.A.J.

LEMON, Sir William, 1st bt. (1748–1824), of Carclew, nr. Penryn, Cornw. and Whitehall Yard, Westminster, Mdx.

PENRYN	17 Jan. 1770–Dec. 1772
PENRYN	28 Dec. 1772–1774
CORNWALL	1774–11 Dec. 1824

b. 11 Oct. 1748, 1st s. of William Lemon of Carclew (who *d.v.p.*) and Anne, da. of John Willyams of Carnanton, Cornw. *educ.* Christ Church, Oxf. 1765; grand tour 1768. *m.* 3 Apr. 1771, Jane, da. of James Buller† of Morval, 2s. (1 *d.v.p.*) 9da. (3 *d.v.p.*) *suc.* grandfa. William Lemon 1760; *cr.* bt. 24 May 1774. *d.* 11 Dec. 1824.

Capt. R. Cornw. militia 1770, maj. 1780., lt.-col. 1798, col. 1803-7.

Lemon had inherited his grandfather's fortune, which was based on copper mining interests, and during the late eighteenth century he made several additions to his Cornish estates.[1] He had sat for the county since 1774 and had shared the representation since 1806 with his Tory son-in-law, John Hearle Tremayne. He was again returned unopposed in 1820, after promising to 'discharge [his] public duty ... conscientiously and independently', and became Father of the House.[2] According to Cornish Tory sources he was 'warmly attached from principle to the politics of ... Fox' and seemed to be 'just as systematic an opposer of the measures of government, whether right or wrong, as the most devoted tool of administration is in favour of them'.[3] He continued to attend regularly and voted with the Whig opposition to Lord Liverpool's ministry on most major issues, including parliamentary reform, 9 May 1821, 25 Apr. 1822, 24 Apr. 1823. He divided for inquiry into the Peterloo massacre, 16 May 1821. A radical publication of 1823 noted approvingly of him that he 'attends well and votes well'.[4] However, apparently for constituency reasons, he continued to vote against Catholic relief, 28 Feb. 1821, although he was also against the Irish constables bill, 7 June 1822. He made no known speeches in this period, but he was active in presenting petitions from Cornwall on various issues, including relief from agricultural distress in 1820 and 1821, and ones from county meetings which also called for retrenchment and reform, 9 Apr. 1821, 22 Apr. 1822.[5] He presented several petitions for restoring Queen Caroline's name to the liturgy and voted in this sense, 23, 26 Jan., 13 Feb. 1821.[6] He was reportedly absent in the early part of the 1822 session, owing to a 'very severe indisposition', but that October he attended a county meeting where he seconded the resolutions by which he hoped the government would be 'apprised of the disastrous consequences' of removing the packet service from Falmouth; they had the desired effect.[7] In 1824 he presented numerous petitions for repeal of the coal duties,[8] and several for the abolition of slavery.[9] His death that December was apparently unexpected, although he had been 'for some time in a rather declining state of health'. It was said of him that he was 'neither an orator nor, in the vulgar acceptation of the term, a statesman', but he exhibited 'a rare combination of private and public virtue' and was 'an excellent citizen and patriot' whose 'every vote ... had for its object to uphold the liberties and to diminish the burthens of the country'.[10] He was succeeded in his title and estates by his only surviving son Charles, who became a county Member in 1831.[11]

[1] *Gent. Mag.* (1824), ii. 641-2. [2] *West Briton*, 25 Feb., 24 Mar. 1820. [3] Cornw. RO, Rashleigh mss DD/R/5313, Canon Rogers to Rashleigh, 24 Jan. 1820; *R. Cornw. Gazette*, 18 Dec. 1824. [4] *Black Bk.* (1823), 169. [5] *The Times*, 10, 19 May 1820, 21, 28 Feb., 2 Mar., 10 Apr. 1821, 23 Apr. 1822. [6] Ibid. 27 Jan., 3, 6, 13 Feb. 1821. [7] *West Briton*, 1 Mar., 1 Nov., 6 Dec. 1822. [8] *The Times*, 5, 14, 17, 19, 20, 24, 27 Feb. 1824. [9] Ibid. 13, 16, 17 Mar. 1824. [10] *West Briton*, 17 Dec. 1824. [11] PROB 11/1698/208; IR26/1050/249.

T.A.J.

LENNARD *see* **BARRETT LENNARD**

LENNOX, Lord Arthur (1806–1864), of 5 Upper Portland Place, Mdx.

CHICHESTER	1831–3 Feb. 1846
GREAT YARMOUTH	1847–14 Feb. 1848

b. 2 Oct. 1806, 7th s. of Charles Lennox†, 4th duke of Richmond (*d.* 1819), and Lady Charlotte Gordon, da. of Alexander, 4th duke of Gordon [S]; bro. of Lord John George Lennox* and Lord William Pitt Lennox*. *m.* 1 July 1835, Adelaide Constance, da. of John Campbell† of Shawfield and Islay, Argyll, 1s. 3da. *d.* 15 Jan. 1864.

Ensign 71 Ft. 1823, lt. 1825, capt. (half-pay) 1826; returned to regt. 1834; maj. 1838; lt.-col. (half-pay) 72 Ft. 1842, 60 Ft. 1845; ret. 1854.

Lt.-col. R. Suss. light infantry 1854, lt.-col. commdt. 1860-*d.*

Ld. of treasury May 1844-Aug. 1845; clerk of ordnance Aug. 1845-July 1846.

Lennox's brother William recalled how the duke of Wellington, a family friend, 'took ... [him] by the hand and forwarded his military career', which was nevertheless an unremarkable one.[1] In April 1831 his elder brother the 5th duke of Richmond, who had joined Lord Grey's ministry, expected him to be returned for Chichester after the passage of the government's reform bill, but in the event a vacancy occurred immediately. He promised Richmond that 'when I am in Parliament I will do my best to meet your approbation and that of my constituents'. The family interest in the city and their recent conversion to the cause of reform ensured that he was comfortably returned at the head of the poll.[2]

He made no reported contribution to debate in this period. He divided for the second reading of the reintroduced reform bill, 6 July, and steadily for most of its details, though he joined his brother George in the minority for the total disfranchisement of Aldborough, 14 Sept. 1831. He voted for the bill's passage, 21 Sept., the second reading of the Scottish bill, 23 Sept., and Lord Ebrington's confidence motion, 10 Oct. He divided against the motion censuring the Irish administration for using undue influence at the Dublin election, 23 Aug. On 10 Nov. he asked Richmond to divulge when Parliament was due to reassemble so that he might assess the feasibility of a trip to Islay, the Scottish seat of his future wife's family. He apparently delayed the visit and voted for the second reading of the revised reform bill, 17 Dec. 1831, before requesting that his mail be forwarded north.[3] He had returned by early February 1832 to vote for the bill's details, and he obeyed Richmond's specific instruction to attend the division on the 28th for the enfranchisement of Tower Hamlets.[4] He divided for the third reading, 22 Mar., and Ebrington's motion for an address asking the king to appoint only ministers committed to carrying an unimpaired measure, 10 May, paired for the second reading of the Irish bill, 25 May, and voted against increased representation for Scotland, 1 June. He divided with the minority, chiefly composed of Scottish Members, against the malt drawback bill, 2 Apr. He joined his brothers in the majority for the Liverpool franchise bill, 23 May, and in the minority next day for the immediate abolition of slavery; the latter vote apparently displeased Richmond.[5] He divided with ministers on the Russian-Dutch loan, 12, 16, 20 July 1832.

At the general election of 1832 Lennox was again returned for Chichester, but his frequent absences in Scotland caused some annoyance to his supporters in the years that followed. Lord William Pitt Lennox expressed surprise that his youngest brother's 'poverty' did not spur Richmond to find him a place in the Whig ministry. He eventually followed Richmond over to the Conservatives and held junior office in Peel's second ministry, but he was obliged to resign his seat in 1846 owing to his support for repeal of the corn laws.[6] He was elected the following year for Great Yarmouth, only to be unseated for bribery. He died in January 1864.

[1] Lord W.P. Lennox, *My Recollections*, ii. 37. [2] W. Suss. RO, Goodwood mss 1433, f. 113; 1486, f. 28. [3] Ibid. 1451, f. 416; 1497, f. 101. [4] Ibid. 1455, f. 543. [5] Ibid. 1489, f. 118. [6] D.A. Smith, 'The Richmond Interest and Party Politics, 1834-41', *Suss. Arch. Colls.* cxvii. (1979), 205, 208-9; Goodwood mss 1455, f. 545; *Dod's Parl. Companion* (1847), 196.

H.J.S.

LENNOX, Lord John George (1793–1873), of 79 South Audley Street, Mdx.

CHICHESTER	22 Nov. 1819–1831
SUSSEX	1831–1832
SUSSEX WEST	1832–1841

b. 3 Oct. 1793, 2nd s. of Charles Lennox†, 4th duke of Richmond (*d.* 1819), and Lady Charlotte Gordon, da. of Alexander, 4th duke of Gordon [S]; bro. of Lord Arthur Lennox* and Lord William Pitt Lennox*. *educ.* Westminster until 1811. *m.* 29 June 1818, Louisa Frederica, da. of Hon. John Rodney† of Armsworth, Hants, 5s. (2 *d.v.p.*) 3da. (2 *d.v.p.*). *d.* 10 Nov. 1873.

Cornet 13 Drag. 1811, 9 Drag. 1812; lt. 9 Drag. 1813; capt. 3 garrison batt. 1815, 9 Drag. 1816; maj. 1817; lt.-col. 1823 (half-pay); lt.-col. 6 Drag. 1830; ret. 1832.

Ld. of bedchamber to Prince Albert 1840-61.

In 1812 Lennox's great aunt noted of him that 'he has been very unwisely, in my mind, kept at Westminster school till 18 and ... I suspect there is a great deal to amend in his ideas, which have been allowed to run their own way as a full grown man at school in a metropolis'. He appeared to be 'handsome [and] pleasant', but was 'a little sudden and too tenacious of his opinions for good company, having a horror of being advised or directed'. Recalling his subsequent army career, which was distinguished by service in the Peninsula and at Waterloo, his brother William wrote that 'George was truly respected and beloved by all his brother officers for his downright honest John Bull manner, his sterling qualities [and] his kindly nature under rather a rough aspect'.[1] He was returned for Chichester on the family interest following his eldest brother's succession as 5th duke of Richmond in 1819, and he was again returned unopposed in 1820 with the Tory minister Huskisson.[2]

He was an occasional attender who gave general but silent support to Lord Liverpool's ministry. He presented a Chichester petition in favour of restoring Queen Caroline's name to the liturgy, 24 Jan.,[3] but voted in defence of ministers' conduct towards her, 6 Feb. 1821. He divided against Catholic relief, 28 Feb. He voted against repeal of the additional malt duty, 3 Apr., and Hume's economy and retrenchment motion, 27 June. He divided against parliamentary reform, 9 May, and the forgery punishment mitigation bill, 23 May 1821. His only known opposition vote in this Parliament was for Sir Robert Wilson's motion complaining of his dismissal from the army, 13 Feb. 1822. He voted against abolition of one of the joint-postmasterships, 14 Mar. He paired against relieving Catholic peers of their disabilities, 30 Apr. 1822. His placement on the army half-pay list in January 1823 had little apparent effect on his parliamentary attendance. He divided against repeal of the Foreign Enlistment Act, 16 Apr., and inquiry into the prosecution of the Dublin Orange rioters, 22 Apr. 1823. He voted against the abolition of flogging in the army, 5 Mar. 1824. He divided for the Irish unlawful societies bill, 25 Feb., and against Catholic relief, 1 Mar., 21 Apr., 10 May, presenting a hostile petition from Chichester's archdeacon and clergy, 18 Apr. 1825. On 16 Feb. 1826 he presented two Welsh anti-slavery petitions and one from West Sussex landowners against revision of the corn laws.[4] At the general election that summer he was returned for Chichester at the head of the poll, as a friend of the government's 'liberal and enlightened' policies.[5]

He took a slightly more prominent role in the 1826 Parliament. He presented a Sussex petition against alteration of the corn laws, 8 Feb., and voted accordingly, 2 Apr. 1827. He presented a West Sussex landowners' petition against the importation of wool, 12 Feb.[6] He divided against Catholic relief, 6 Mar. In his first recorded contribution to debate, 2 Apr., he decried as 'a measure most injurious to the town of Chichester and the western part of Sussex' the proposal to hold county elections in Lewes. He maintained that 'no riot or disorder' had occurred at the last county election, 9 May. He was granted two weeks' leave for urgent business, having served on an election committee, 3 Apr. 1827. He divided against repeal of the Test Acts, 26 Feb., and Catholic relief, 12 May 1828. He voted with the duke of Wellington's ministry against reduction of the salary of the lieutenant-general of the ordnance, 4 July 1828. In February 1829 Planta, the patronage secretary, listed him as being 'opposed to the principle' of Catholic emancipation, and he duly divided against it, 6, 18 Mar., paired against it, 27 Mar., and presented numerous hostile petitions. He clashed with his Whig colleague Poyntz over the division of opinion on the subject at Chichester, 9 Mar., and denied that he and Richmond had orchestrated the anti-Catholic petitioning there. He was a minority teller against the bill to disfranchise 40*s.* freeholders in Ireland, 19 Mar. 1829. His name does not appear in Sir Richard Vyvyan's* list of Ultra Tories that autumn. On 9 Feb. 1830 he introduced a bill to oblige smugglers sentenced to serve in the navy to maintain their families, rather than having them thrown on the parish; it gained royal assent, 8 Apr. (11 Geo. IV & 1 Gul. IV, c. 10). He voted against the transfer of East Retford's seats to Birmingham, 11 Feb. However, he opposed ministers by voting to restrict the grant for the army, 19 Feb., and against the Bathurst and Dundas pensions, 26 Mar. He presented a Chichester petition against the sale of beer bill, 27 Apr., and voted to prohibit on-consumption in beer houses, 21 June. He divided against Jewish emancipation, 17 May 1830. Contrary to speculation that his resumption of an active army career with a regiment in Ireland might cause him to retire from the Commons, he offered again for Chichester at the general election that summer. He pledged support for 'a very limited degree' of parliamentary reform, consistent with the security of traditional ruling institutions, the 'gradual emancipation' of colonial slaves, reform of the game laws and abolition of the death penalty for forgery, but he betrayed no great disaffection with Wellington's government; he was returned at the head of the poll.[7]

The ministry listed Lennox as one of the 'moderate Ultras', but it was noted that he 'always votes with us'. In fact, he voted against them in the crucial civil list division, 15 Nov. 1830. About this time Lord George Cavendish Bentinck* praised his 'firmness, skill and celerity' in helping to 'restore peace and good government in the Chichester district' following the 'Swing' riots.[8] He was named to the Evesham election committee, 2 Dec., and called for the evidence of bribery and corruption to be presented to the House, 13 Dec., observing that this had made him 'a reformer to a large extent'. The fact that Richmond, who shared his disappointment at the passage of Catholic emancipation and his concern about agricultural unrest, had joined Lord Grey's ministry, doubtless also influenced his change of opinion. He declared that if the corruption at Evesham was 'as extensive as there is reason to believe, the franchise should be ... transferred to some other town', 16 Dec. 1830. He was granted three weeks' leave for urgent private business, 11 Feb. 1831, which he apparently used to visit his regiment in Ireland. He returned, as he had promised his brother,[9] to praise the government's 'efficient' reform bill, 4 Mar., and expressed the hope that if it was rejected ministers would 'throw themselves upon the country and manfully appeal to it for support'. He presented a friendly petition from Chichester, 9 Mar., voted for the bill's second reading, 22 Mar., spoke at the Sussex county meeting convened in its support, 7 Apr.,[10] and divided against Gascoyne's wrecking amendment, 19 Apr. He presented a Chichester petition for repeal of the coal duties, 9 Feb., called for the closure of a military riding establishment near Maidstone, 14 Mar. 1831, but warned next day that repeal of the timber duties would 'strike a fatal blow to one-fifth of our shipping interest and alienate the affections of our colonists'. At the general election that May he offered for the Sussex seat vacated by the death of Walter Burrell, which Richmond had long wanted him to fill, and the family's standing in the county and pro-reform stance ensured his unopposed return.[11]

In May 1831 Lennox, piqued at being overlooked for military promotion, unsuccessfully pressed on Richmond his claim to be appointed an aide-de-camp to the king, pointing out that he had seen service in 'seven general actions for which medals were given'. He also mentioned that he had voted for the reform candidates at the Dublin election and predicted their comfortable return.[12] He divided for the second reading of the reintroduced reform bill, 6 July, and steadily for most of its details, though he diverged from the government line by voting for the complete disfranchisement of Aldborough, 14 Sept. He gained something of a reputation as a heckler of opponents, and one such incident, 19 July, sparked a furious row with George Bankes over who was more able to vote according to the dictates of his conscience. Next day he expressed support for the sweeping borough disfranchisements proposed for Sussex and stated that his recent extensive canvass there had shown overwhelming support for reform. He opposed giving two Members to Brighton on the ground that its population included many transients, 5 Aug. He informed *The Times* that he had voted with ministers on their proposed division of counties, 11 Aug.[13] He ridiculed Hunt's claim to represent public opinion in his radical critique of the bill, 30 Aug. He divided for its third reading, 19 Sept., its passage, 21 Sept., the second reading of the Scottish bill, 23 Sept., and Lord Ebrington's confidence motion, 10 Oct. He spoke in favour of a close scrutiny of the pensions list, 19 July. He voted in the minorities to swear in the Dublin election committee, 29 July, and suspend the issue of a new writ, 8 Aug., when he denied that this would impugn the entire electorate. However, he voted to punish only those guilty of bribery and against the motion censuring the Irish administration, 23 Aug. He divided with the minority against issuing the Liverpool election writ, 5 Sept. He expressed sympathy for the plight of labourers thrown out of work as a result of the use of threshing machines, 13 Sept., but confessed himself 'at a loss ... to point out any effectual way of relieving them'. Writing from Dublin, where he was stationed with his regiment, 25 Nov., he told Richmond that he considered the early reconvening of Parliament to be 'a great bore',[14] and he was absent from the division on the second reading of the revised reform bill, 17 Dec. 1831. He was in place to vote steadily for its details, and he divided for the third reading, 22 Mar. 1832, after being advised by Richmond that it would not be 'safe' to miss Parliament for the Lewes assizes.[15] He was absent from the division on Ebrington's motion for an address asking the king to appoint only ministers committed to carrying an unimpaired measure, 10 May, but voted for the second reading of the Irish bill, 25 May, and against increased county representation for Scotland, 1 June. He voted with government on the Russian-Dutch loan, 26 Jan., paired with them on this issue, 12, 16 July, and voted with them on relations with Portugal, 9 Feb. He divided in the minority for printing a petition in favour of the abolition of Irish tithes, 16 Feb. Next day he pledged himself to introduce a bill to enable farmers to receive compensation for riot-damaged threshing machines, as manufacturers did in comparable circumstances. The bill was duly introduced, 1 Mar., and gained royal assent, 1 Aug. (2 & 3 Gul. IV, c. 72). He presented a Sussex petition calling for a rate to be levied to stimulate the employment of labourers, 10 Apr. He was added to the select committee on the renewal of the East India Company's charter, 23 Feb. On 23 May 1832 he voted for the Liverpool franchise bill and questioned the arbitrary manner in which the Sussex assizes had been moved from Horsham to Lewes. Next day he and his brothers voted for the immediate abolition of slavery, apparently to Richmond's displeasure.[16]

At the end of July 1832 Lennox retired from the army, his ambitions for promotion having been disappointed. This may have influenced his decision not to abandon his parliamentary career, as Richmond had earlier thought he might, and he was returned at the general election later that year for the western division of Sussex, which he represented until Richmond's heir came of age. After 1832 he displayed a greater degree of loyalty to the Liberal governments than did Richmond, which led to occasional friction in their relations.[17] He died in November 1873.

[1] *Life of Lady Sarah Lennox* ed. Lady Ilchester, ii. 256-7; W.P. Lennox, *Drafts upon my Memory*, i. 109. [2] *Suss. Advertiser*, 13 Mar. 1820. [3] *The Times*, 25 Jan. 1821. [4] Ibid. 17 Feb. 1826. [5] *Brighton Gazette*, 8, 15 June 1826. [6] *The Times*, 9, 13 Feb. 1827. [7] *Chichester Election Procs. 1830*, pp. 132-3. [8] Nottingham Univ. Lib. Portland mss PwH 150, Bentinck to Portland, 22 Nov. 1830; E. Hobsbawm and G. Rudé, *Captain Swing* (1985), 85. [9] W. Suss. RO, Goodwood mss 1433, f. 156. [10] *The Times*, 9 Apr. 1831. [11] Goodwood mss 1433, ff. 202, 218. [12] Ibid. f. 274. [13] *The Times*, 16 Aug. 1831. [14] Goodwood mss 1451, f. 366. [15] Ibid. 1457, f. 236. [16] Ibid. 1455, f. 543. [17] Ibid. 1486, f. 28; D.A. Smith, 'The Richmond Interest and Party Politics, 1834-41', *Suss. Arch. Colls.* cxvii. (1979), 213-15.

H.J.S.

LENNOX, Lord William Pitt (1799–1881), of Regent Street, Mdx.

KING'S LYNN 1831–1834

b. 20 Sept. 1799, 4th s. of Charles Lennox†, 4th duke of Richmond (*d.* 1819), and Lady Charlotte Gordon, da. of Alexander, 4th duke of Gordon [S]; bro. of Lord Arthur Lennox* and Lord John George Lennox*. *educ.* Westminster 1808-13; privately by Rev. James Knollis of Littlewick Green, Maidenhead Thicket, Berks. 1813-14. *m.* (1) 7 May 1824, Mary Anne (*div.* 26 Feb. 1831), da. of George Paton, schoolmaster, of Edinburgh, 1da. *d.v.p.*;[1] (2) 1854, Ellen (*d.* 3 Nov. 1859), da. of John Smith, 1s.; (3) 17 Nov. 1863, Maria Jane, da. of Rev. Capel Molyneux, incumbent of St. Paul's, Onslow Square, Mdx. *s.p. d.* 18 Feb. 1881.

Cornet R. Horse Gds. 1813, lt. 1814, capt. 1822, out of service 1829.

Although Lennox never achieved the political eminence of the godfather after whom he was named, he emerges from his published memoirs as the most colourful of the three brothers of the 5th duke of Richmond who sat in the Commons in this period. His early education, 'neither systematic nor strict', took place near the family seat of Goodwood, Sussex, and with holidays at Phoenix Park, Dublin, where his father lived as lord lieutenant of Ireland, it inspired his interest in horse riding and the theatre.[2] A semi-autobiographical work entitled *Percy Hamilton* (1851) documents his experiences of Westminster School, which he left (after playing truant to see a stage performance) to be coached for the army, the usual career of his family.[3] After Buonaparte's first defeat he accompanied the duke of Wellington as an aide-de-camp to Paris, the Netherlands and the Congress of Vienna. He was similarly attached to General Sir Peregrine Maitland at Waterloo, but he missed the battle owing to a freak riding accident, which cost him the sight of an eye.[4] He subsequently rejoined Wellington's staff in England before linking up with his father, then governor-general of Canada, in 1818. On the latter's untimely death from hydrophobia the following year he returned to his regiment, then quartered at Windsor.[5] Off duty he acquired a reputation as a fashionable young man-about-town, a 'strange, wild thing' whose 'quickness and drollery' impressed Henry Edward Fox* when he met him in 1822. He owned and rode racehorses, frequented gambling houses and, though he later claimed never to have fallen into debt, he was, like many peers' younger sons, perennially short of money.[6]

Lennox's love of the stage brought him into the society of Mary Anne Paton, a celebrated singer. An unkind contemporary biographer wondered if her 'brilliant eye, fair complexion and ... fine figure may offer an apology for the disproportioned size of that mouth from which such enchanting notes have often pleased the ear'.[7] She initially spurned his advances, but accepted his proposal after he pursued her to Edinburgh, where they were discreetly married, despite opposition from both families. Thereafter Lady William continued her stage career under her maiden name, an arrangement which, though apparently made at her own insistence, must have suited her husband, as 'the profits of her benefit amounted to more, by a third, than his annual income'.[8] Newspapers and cartoonists were quick to censure this, and to query the validity of the marriage, particularly after the birth of a child early in 1825.[9] Their spotlight again fell on Lennox in August 1826 when, finding himself suspected of contributing to Westmacott's scurrilous newspaper *The Age*, he asked the 2nd earl of Glengall to investigate these allegations. Glengall declined to exonerate Lennox, who made the affair a matter of honour, and they fought a bloodless duel at Cowes.[10] The original accusation later featured in Disraeli's *Vivian Grey* (1827), in which Lennox appears as Lord Prima Donna.[11]

The disintegration of his marriage, occasioned by his wife's desertion in May 1830, prompted much prurient interest and comment.[12] Reports stated that they had been 'living together very unamiably' for some time, and blamed Lennox for 'looseness of habits and indifference to the pleasures and comforts of a domestic life'. The coverage highlighted the disparity of the couple's backgrounds and incomes, which *The Times* concluded 'almost necessarily led to catastrophe'. The paper recounted a public exchange in Covent Garden, in which Lennox's reference to his wife's indebtedness to him for 'rank' prompted the riposte, 'When I knew you, you had not a decent coat to your back'. The commentators' tone changed when it emerged that Lady William had eloped with her leading man, the 'bewitchingly handsome' singer Joseph Wood, with whom she fled to Dublin. Details were published of her numerous premarital affairs, and it was alleged that she had initiated and carried on the liaison with Wood for some time before the separation.[13] Lennox (dubbed 'Blinking Billy' by the cartoonists) failed to effect a reconciliation, and consented to a divorce. To provide the evidence of adultery necessary to dissolve a Scottish marriage, Lennox, it was later claimed, spent three nights in an Edinburgh brothel where, 'having made up his mind to go through with the business, he did in Rome as Rome does and frolicked and whisked about ... like any other wanton bacchanal'. He stated that he had acquiesced in the arrangement 'from a feeling that this course is the best for Lady William's interest', but financial motives and a desire to avoid publicity lay closer to his heart.[14] The Scottish lord ordinary dissolved the marriage, 26 Feb. 1831, but, contrary to assertions made in *Burke's Peerage* and elsewhere, the judgment was never ratified by Act of Parliament. This had implications for the validity of the divorce if (as one source claims) the couple went through a second marriage ceremony in England in 1828, and may explain why details of Lennox's remarriage in 1854 remain obscure.[15] Lady William and Joseph Wood were married on 3 Mar. 1831.[16]

Lennox was reputed to have sold his commission for £8,000 in 1829 on a hint from Wellington concerning the incompatibility of his army rank with his wife's occupation, but, as with all matters pertaining to his marriage, this is glossed over in his memoirs, which ascribe his decision to frustration at lack of promotion opportunities and his wish to embark on a political career.[17] He had always been politically at odds with his Tory family, displaying liberal, even radical, tendencies. Byron was a hero of his youth, he had canvassed for John Cam Hobhouse* at the Westminster election of 1820 and was on friendly terms with the *bête noire* of the Sussex landed interest, Sir Godfrey Webster†.[18] He later recollected 'chaffing' over politics with his brother Richmond, although by 1831 they were united in support of the Grey ministry's reform bill.[19] On 7 Apr. Lennox issued a ringing denunciation of the unreformed system at the Sussex county meeting, where he seconded a pro-reform petition to the Lords.[20] Two days later Richmond, the Grey ministry's postmaster-general, hoped that Lennox, who he predicted would 'distinguish himself in Parliament', might take his brother John George's seat at Chichester if the latter was elected for Sussex.[21] In the event, at the general election that month he was delighted to come in for King's Lynn as a reformer with Richmond's racing colleague and friend Lord George Cavendish Bentinck.[22]

Lennox prefaced his vote for the second reading of the reintroduced reform bill, 6 July 1831, with what Thomas Spring Rice* called a 'pointed and effective' maiden speech that countered the chief arguments of the anti-reformers.[23] It was too pointed for one of them, Charles Waldo Sibthorp, who according to Lennox took offence at his injunction to him 'not to use the House as a foundling hospital for his illegitimate theories' (which he may have misheard) and demanded an apology via John Cheesement Severn. This was delivered later in the debate, and its acceptance rendered 'a call to arms' unnecessary.[24] Lennox divided fairly steadily for the bill's details in committee, and joined Cavendish Bentinck in pressing for Brighton to be awarded two Members, 5 Aug. He wrote to *The Times*, 3 Sept., to explain that contrary to the published list, he had not voted in the ministerial majority against the preservation of freemen's voting rights, 30 Aug., adding that 'if present' he would have supported the amendment, for he regretted that this class of electors 'will not be enabled to hand down to their posterity the right they have so disinterestedly exercised'. He divided for the bill's passage, 21 Sept., the second reading of the Scottish measure, 23 Sept., and Lord Ebrington's confidence motion, 10 Oct. A borough meeting at King's Lynn, 1 Oct., commended his parliamentary conduct, and addressing them, he urged the bill's passage in the country's interest and praised the schedule A disfranchisements.[25] He voted for the revised bill at its second reading, 17 Dec. 1831, having previously deplored the Lords' rejection of the bill and condemned its opponents for their apocalyptic vision of its consequences: 'The ... Commons is a safety valve through which complaints and grievances find vent; its enlargement will assuredly prevent explosion'. He voted to proceed with it in committee, 20 Jan. gave its details steady but silent support, and divided for its third reading, 22 Mar., and the address calling on the king to appoint only ministers who would carry it unimpaired, 10 May 1832. The following day he expressed indifference as to the composition of a new ministry, as 'no government could exist unpledged to the measure', but he deprecated a call for non-payment of taxes until the bill was passed. He reiterated his support for ministers and an 'unmutilated' reform bill when attempting to present his constituents' petition in this vein, 18 May, and again when he succeeded in doing so on the 22nd.[26] He would hear no excuse for those who had cheered false reports of Wellington's assassination, though he confessed to relief that he had not returned to office, 23 May. He paired for the Irish reform bill at its second reading, 25 May, and presented the Flintshire petition for withdrawal of supplies pending the reform bill's passage, 30 May.[27] He voted against a Conservative amendment to the Scottish measure, 1 June, and to go into committee on the privileges of Parliament bill, which sought to remove Members' immunity from prosecution for debt, 27 June 1832. He divided in the minority for appointing 11 of its original members to the reconstituted Dublin election committee, 29 July, but with ministers against censuring the Irish government for electoral interference, 23 Aug. 1831. He voted with government on the Russian-Dutch loan, 26 Jan., 12 July, and relations with Portugal, 9 Feb., but he was listed (with his brother John George) in the minority for printing the radical Woollen Grange petition for the abolition of Irish tithes, 16 Feb., and divided against the government amendment to Buxton's motion for a select committee on colonial slavery, 24 May. A growing rift between the brothers over Lennox's parliamentary conduct caused him to write to Richmond, 14 June 1832:

> I was greatly annoyed to hear last night from George Bentinck 'that you were much displeased at many of my votes' and that it was a breach of honour and faith towards you to vote against the government. Now my inclination is to support the present government, and had I not been disposed so to do, questions during the reform bill and the 'Russian loan' would have afforded me ample grounds to go against them. On the West India question [Buxton's motion, 24 May] I own I voted according to the best of my judgement, and this is the only vote I think you can find fault with. It is my wish to be guided by your better judgements, and on every occasion to follow your

wishes. But I wish to acquit myself of having acted dishonourably towards you, and I only trust that in future you will yourself communicate to me your sentiments.[28]

As requested by the corporation of King's Lynn, Lennox called for the removal of quarantine duties, 6 Sept. 1831.[29] He opposed the anatomy bill, because he did not believe it would curb body-snatching, 27 Feb., 27 Mar., 11 Apr., 11 May 1832, when he complained that its rushed passage constituted 'an additional proof that the feelings of the lower orders are never consulted when they come into contact with the interests of the higher'. He spoke in favour of Lord John George's bill to secure compensation for owners of threshing machines destroyed in rural unrest, 1 Mar., and for abolition of the merchant seamen's contribution to Greenwich Hospital, in which his constituents had a vested interest, 8 Mar. His fine words in support of Sadler's factories regulation bill, 16 Mar. – 'whilst we all wish to ameliorate the state of the foreign slave, we should not be wholly unmindful of the condition of our ones' – irritated the brewer John Kearsley, whose reply, that Lennox knew 'nothing whatever about cotton mills, nor indeed about anything else', surprisingly drew no rebuke from the Speaker. As a member of the select committee on postal communications between Britain and Ireland (17 Mar.), he gave assurances on the continuance of the Liverpool-Dublin packet, 4 Apr., and he defended Richmond when arrangements for newspaper conveyancing, 11 Apr., and his public conduct were criticized, 30 July. Later he recalled how he had accompanied his brother to the general post office 'two or three times a week' to qualify him to make an informed response.[30] He voted for the Liverpool disfranchisement bill at its second reading, 23 May, and spoke the same day against transferring the Norfolk assizes from Thetford to Norwich. As requested, he presented petitions from King's Lynn in favour of the Maynooth grant and against the general register bill, 30 May, and against the Irish and Scottish vagrants removal bill, 13 July, and military flogging, 30 July 1832.[31]

Fraternal relations worsened after the 1832 general election, when, standing as a Liberal, Lennox was again returned for King's Lynn.[32] On 22 Apr. 1833 he angrily denied Richmond's charge that he had leagued with radicals in 'repeatedly and factiously opposing the government', but, after facing similar complaints at King's Lynn, he retired at the dissolution in 1834.[33] Expressing a hope that their quarrel was now at an end, he wrote forlornly to Richmond, 19 Dec. 1834:

If you ever wish me to come into Parliament and like to bring me in, I will pledge myself, and guarantee the fulfilment of my promise by a bond of £4,000 to vote according to your wishes. I mention this confidentially and wish *no* answer to it, as I am aware that nothing but dire necessity would make you wish to have me in.[34]

He did not stand for Parliament again. An obituarist wrote that he 'preferred the easy life of a man about town' to the duties of a Member.[35] Financial necessity propelled him into the secondary careers of miscellaneous writer and paid lecturer. He contributed to several periodicals and edited *The Review* in 1858, while the first of several 'feeble novels' was published in 1841.[36] Pride and disappointed ambition marked his recollection of his parliamentary career:

I took my fair share of duty in the House of Commons and out of it. I neither professed too much, nor promised too largely. I contributed as far as I was able to the great success the Whigs achieved when they ousted their rivals from place and power, but I cannot say that I profited materially by their success.

Anxious to stress that he had been no radical, he noted that 'I put forward no extravagant propositions and steadily opposed mischievous legislation'. He remembered the chamber itself as 'small and ill-ventilated, and the coffee room abominable'. Speeches were 'often long and tedious', though this observation did not deter him from quoting the *Parliamentary Debates* record of his own efforts in full.[37] Lennox died in February 1881, leaving two-thirds of his personal estate to his third wife (*d.* 1916), and the remainder to his son William Robert Lennox (1855-1907), who unsuccessfully contested the will three years later. In response to the plaintiff's claims to the contrary, it was stated that Lennox had been in full possession of his mental faculties until days before his death, and had dictated an article for the *Court Journal* on 10 Feb. 1881.[38]

[1] A report in *The Times*, 2 June 1830, alleged that she bore Lennox three children and was pregnant with their fourth child at the time of their separation. [2] Lord W.P. Lennox, *50 Years of Biographical Reminiscences*, i. 83, *Drafts upon my Memory* (1866), i. 9 and *My Recollections* (1874), i. 33, 47, 151. [3] *Biog. Reminiscences*, i. 83, 123-6; *Drafts upon my Memory*, i. 9; *My Recollections*, i. 33, 47, 151. [4] *My Recollections*, i. 55; *Drafts upon my Memory*, i. 76; *Biog. Reminiscences*, i. 222-6. [5] *HP Commons, 1790-1820*, iv. 414-5; *Drafts upon my Memory*, i. 59; *Biog. Reminiscences*, ii. 5, 69-73, 117-8. [6] *Drafts upon my Memory*, i. 60; *Biog. Reminiscences*, ii. 129; *Fox Jnl.* 131, 147-8; *Creevey Pprs.* ii. 75; *Gronow Reminiscences*, i. 134. [7] *Highly Interesting Life of Lady William Lennox* [BL 1203. k. 6(3).]. [8] *Authentic Mems. of Mr. and Mrs. Wood* (1843), 23-47. [9] *The Times*, 16 May 1826; M.D. George, *Cat. of Pol. and Personal Satires*, x. 14872-3, 15170. [10] *The Times*, 15 Aug. 1826; *Lady Holland to Son*, 48, 52. [11] *Oxford DNB*. [12] Hopetoun mss 167 f. 142. [13] *Mems. of Mr. and Mrs. Wood*, 27-60; *Life of Lady William Lennox*; *The Times*, 25, 28, 29, 31 May, 1, 2, 7, 14, 29 June 1830. [14] George, xi. 16420-4; *Mems. of Mr. and Mrs. Wood*, 65-66, 72-76. [15] *Burke PB* (1939), ii. 2073; L.

Stone, *The Road to Divorce*, 336; *Mems. of Mr. and Mrs. Wood*, 26. [16] *Mems. of Mr. and Mrs. Wood*, 77. [17] *Biog. Reminiscences*, ii. 152-4. [18] *Drafts upon My Memory*, i. 29, 51-52; *The Times*, 31 May 1830. [19] *Drafts upon My Memory*, ii. 372. [20] *The Times*, 9 Apr. 1831; D.A. Smith, 'The Richmond Interest and Party Politics, 1834-41', *Suss. Arch. Colls.* cxvii. (1979), 202. [21] W. Suss. RO, Goodwood mss 1486, f. 28. [22] *My Recollections*, i. 230; *Biog. Reminiscences*, ii. 157-68. [23] Add. 51579, Rice to Holland [6 July 1831]. [24] *My Recollections*, i. 239-41; Lord W.P. Lennox, *Fashion Then and Now*, ii. 186-7. [25] *The Times*, 3 Oct. 1831. [26] Ibid. 19, 23 May 1832. [27] Ibid. 31 May 1832. [28] Goodwood mss 1459, f. 541. [29] *Norf. Chron.* 24 Sept., 8 Oct. 1831. [30] *Drafts upon My Memory*, ii. 53-54. [31] *Norf. Chron.* 24 Mar., 14 Apr., 28 July 1832. [32] Ibid. 15 Dec. 1832. [33] Goodwood mss 1459, f. 541-3; *The Times*, 3, 9 Jan. 1835. [34] Goodwood mss 1455, ff. 543-7. [35] *The Times*, 19 Feb. 1881. [36] *Oxford DNB*. [37] *Biog. Reminiscences*, 168-71; *My Recollections*, i. 232, 298-9. [38] *The Times*, 8 July 1884.

H.J.S./M.M.E.

LESLIE, Charles Powell (?1767–1831), of Glasslough, co. Monaghan.[1]

CO. MONAGHAN	1 Dec. 1801–1826
NEW ROSS	1830–1831

b. ?1767,[2] 1st s. of Charles Powell Leslie, MP [I], of Glasslough and 1st w. Hon. Prudence Hill Trevor, da. of Arthur, 1st Visct. Dungannon [I]. *educ.* Christ Church, Oxf. 30 Apr. 1784, aged 17. *m.* (1) Oct. 1791, Anne (*d.* Jan. 1813), da. and coh. of Rev. Dudley Charles Ryder of Merrion Square, Dublin, rect. of Streamstown, co. Leitrim, 3da. (at least 1 *d.v.p.*); (2) 24 May 1819, Christiana, da. of George Fosbery of Clorane, co. Limerick, 3s. 4da. *suc.* fa. 1800. *d.* 15 Nov. 1831.

Sheriff, co. Monaghan 1788-9, gov. 1802-*d.*

Trustee, linen board [I] 1807.

Col. Monaghan militia 1797-*d.*; capt. Glasslough inf. 1805.

Leslie, whose family came originally from Aberdeenshire, was a descendant of the 'fighting bishop', John Leslie of Clogher.[3] A well-connected country gentleman (he was cousin to Lord Wellesley and the duke of Wellington), he was thought to be disappointed that his brother John was promoted from Dromore to Elphin and not to the see of Clogher, which contained the family estates, in 1819. But he continued to be reckoned favourable to the administration of Lord Liverpool, on the rare occasions when he attended Parliament.[4] At the general election of 1820 he was again returned unopposed for Monaghan, where, as a governor of the county and colonel of its militia, he wielded enormous influence in the early 1820s. This dominance was much to the disgust of his wary colleague Henry Westenra, Lord Rossmore's son, who nevertheless reflected that he was too powerful to disturb and hoped that he might be removed by the award of a peerage.[5] He voted against making economies in revenue collection, 4 July 1820, and in defence of ministers' conduct towards Queen Caroline, 6 Feb. 1821. He was granted two weeks' leave on urgent private business, 15 Feb., but was present to divide against Catholic relief, 28 Feb. He voted against abolition of the additional malt duty, 3 Apr. 1821. He divided against the Catholic peers bill, 30 Apr. 1822, and presented the Monaghan anti-Catholic petition, 16 Apr. 1823.[6] He voted against parliamentary reform, 20 Feb., and repeal of £2,000,000 of taxes, 3 Mar., but for inquiry into the legal proceedings against the Dublin Orange rioters, 22 Apr. 1823. On 11 May 1824 he brought up a petition from the freemasons of Ballybay against the Secret Societies Act, the only instance of parliamentary activity which has been traced for that session.[7] Having voted for the Irish unlawful societies bill, 15 Feb., he divided against Catholic claims, 1 Mar., 21 Apr., 10 May, and the related franchise measure, 26 Apr. 1825. His only other known votes were for the duke of Cumberland's annuity bill, 10 June 1825, and against the emergency admission of foreign corn, 8 May 1826.

A leading Orangeman, who joined the committee of the Grand Orange Lodge in September 1824, Leslie was encouraged then and in the autumn of 1825, when a dissolution was expected, to stand again for Monaghan, with Protestant and Tory support. Reported to be 'more fond of money than ever', so that he apparently would 'not spend a stiver upon elections', he was advised to avoid a contest by allying with the new interest of Evelyn Shirley*, hitherto an absentee landlord, who ostensibly favoured Catholic relief.[8] This was set in train, but in February 1826, when he was admitted to the York Club, a prominent Irish Protestant organization, doubts were raised about his vulnerability to Westenra, whose reluctance to back the Catholics was counteracted by his father's advocacy of their cause.[9] Having offered on the basis of his past conduct after the dissolution that summer, he was criticized for attempting to preserve his undue ascendancy over the county by means of an unprincipled junction.[10] He was also made the target of the Catholic Association and, in a circular letter to local priests, Daniel O'Connell* described him as having 'grown old in the principles of bigotry' and as 'one of the most uncompromising enemies of his Catholic countrymen'.[11] Desperate to stop the second votes of his and Shirley's tenants going to the liberally inclined Westenra, who in the end was backed by his disgruntled patron Lord Cremorne, Leslie issued an address explaining his recent absences on the ground of illness and claiming that only he could guarantee the independence of the county by holding the other interests in check.[12]

Lucky to escape without injury during the ugly scenes which greeted his arrival on the hustings, Leslie was forced to resign on the sixth day of the poll. His defeat, largely owing to the spirited opposition of the Catholic freeholders, was one of the spectacular reverses suffered by the Protestant interest at the general election of 1826.[13] In reply to an address of thanks for his parliamentary service from the county's leading Tory landowners, he blamed his defeat on the influence of the Catholic clergy; he reiterated this at dinners in Armagh, 5 Oct. 1826, and Enniskillen, 2 Jan. 1827.[14] His petition, which recited O'Connell's letter, was couched in the same terms, but he allowed it to lapse, preferring, as he made clear in another address, to hold out the illusory hope of a wider Commons inquiry.[15] In mid-1828 Wellesley, the recently retired lord lieutenant, recommended Leslie to Wellington, the new prime minister, as 'a very proper person for the favour of the king's government in Ireland whenever you may be enabled to confer the dignity of a peerage upon him', but nothing ever came of this.[16] Active in opposition to the Westenras in local politics, he attended the county anti-Catholic meeting, 10 Oct. 1828, became a vice-president of the ensuing Monaghan Brunswick Club (as well as of the Ulster Club) and was chosen for the presidency of the branch at Glasslough.[17]

It was at first asserted that Leslie would offer again for Monaghan at the general election of 1830, but he ruled himself out as sick. He apparently thought his position was too weak to risk another rebuff and gave his interest to the like-minded Lord Blayney's son, who was returned with the now ministerialist Shirley, a result which was thought likely to strengthen his future interest.[18] Instead, he was brought in for New Ross by his cousin Francis Leigh* of Rosegarland, county Wexford, whose turn it was to nominate the Member.[19] Listed by Pierce Mahony† as 'pro-government' and by ministers among their 'friends', he was absent from the division on the civil list which led to their resignation, 15 Nov. 1830. He also missed the vote on the second reading of the Grey ministry's reform bill, 22 Mar., but sided with opposition for Gascoyne's wrecking amendment, 19 Apr. 1831; he was deprived of his seat at the subsequent dissolution. He died, at his then London residence of 3 Upper Harley Street, in mid-November.[20] By his will, dated 1 Nov. 1831, he left the bulk of his estates and personal wealth, which was sworn under £184,000 in Ireland and under £18,000 in England, to his eldest son Charles Powell Leslie (1821-71), Conservative Member for Monaghan, 1842-71.[21] He was in turn succeeded by his brother John Leslie the painter (1822-1916), Conservative Member for Monaghan, 1871-80, who was awarded a baronetcy in 1876.

[1] See also A. Doyle, *Charles Powell Leslie (II)'s Estates at Glaslough* (2001). [2] The catalogue of the Leslie of Castle Leslie mss gives 1769 (*Co. Monaghan Sources*, 58). [3] E.P. Shirley, *Hist. Co. Monaghan*, 140-53; [W.] S. Leslie, *Of Glaslough* (1913), 15-26, and *Jerome Connexion*, 26-29. [4] Add. 38279, f. 375; 40296, f. 36; PRO NI, Rossmore mss T2929/3/74; *Black Bk.* (1823), 170; *Session of Parl. 1825*, p. 472; *HP Commons, 1790-1820*, iv. 416-18. [5] Rossmore mss 3/4, 10, 14, 19, 33, 36, 37. [6] *The Times*, 17 Apr. 1823. [7] Ibid. 12 May 1824. [8] PRO NI, Leslie mss MIC606/3/J/7/14/1-2, 4-5, 11-12, 14, 23-24; 21/2; Rossmore mss 3/110. [9] Leslie mss 3/J/7/14/31-32, 37-39, 50-51, 53-54, 56, 66-67. [10] *Dublin Evening Post*, 8 June; *Newry Commercial Telegraph*, 16 June 1826; Rossmore mss 10B/1A, 8. [11] PRO NI, Clogher Diocesan mss DIO(RC)1/6/2; Leslie mss 3/J/7/14/111-12. [12] Leslie mss 3/J/7/14/104, 108-9, 117-19, 120-1, 123-4. [13] *Belfast Commercial Chron.* 26, 28 June, 3 July; *Newry Commercial Telegraph*, 30 June, 4, 11 July 1826. [14] *Dublin Evening Post*, 11 July; *Belfast Commercial Chron.* 11 Oct. 1826; *Enniskillen Chron.* 4 Jan. 1827; Doyle, 37. [15] *CJ*, lxxxii. 67-68; Leslie mss 3/J/7/14/147-8, 158-9, 161-2. [16] Wellington mss WP1/938/31; 944/1. [17] *Belfast Guardian*, 30 Sept., 17 Oct.; *Enniskillen Chron.* 6 Nov.; *The Times*, 17 Dec. 1828. [18] PRO NI, Barrett Lennard mss MIC170/3, Ellis to Barrett Lennard, 3 July, Westenra to same, 9 July 1830; Leslie mss 3/J/7/17/6-7, 12-14, 20-21, 26-27, 31-33, 37, 49-50. [19] Leslie mss 3/J/7/17/23-24. [20] *Belfast Guardian*, 22 Nov. 1831; *Gent. Mag.* (1832), i. 563. [21] PROB 11/1794/31; IR26/1295/61.

S.M.F.

LESTER, Benjamin Lester (1779–1838), of 65 High Street, Poole and Stone Cottage, nr. Poole, Dorset.

POOLE 14 Feb. 1809–1834

b. 18 Dec. 1779, 1st s. of George Garland†, Newfoundland merchant, of Leeson House, Purbeck, Dorset and Amy, da. of Benjamin Lester†, Newfoundland merchant, of Poole. *unm.* ?2s. ?2da. illegit. *suc.* mat. grandfa. 1802; changed name to Lester 15 May 1805; *suc.* fa. 1825. *d.* 16 July 1838.

Sheriff, Poole 1804-5, mayor 1815-16.

Capt. Poole vol. inf. 1803, Dorset vol. inf. 1804, maj. 1805-8; capt. E. Dorset militia 1813.

Lester came from one of the prosperous dynasties of Poole Newfoundland merchants, who between them dominated the corporation and largely controlled the representation. He was the grandson and heir of Benjamin Lester, Member for Poole, 1790-6, and eldest son of George Garland, who sat for the borough, 1801-7.[1] Elected a free burgess of Poole in 1801,[2] his father contrived to bring him into Parliament at a contested by-election in 1809, with tacit government support, though in the House he was inactive and independent.[3] He had a difficult relationship with his father, particularly over money, perhaps because of the downturn in the fortunes of the Newfoundland trade. Garland censured his son's extravagance, writing to him, 9 Feb. 1821, that

> you must be aware if you reflect a moment that what I allow you one way or another and the necessary repairs of your houses, etc., etc., is little if any thing short of £1,600 per year, which with your own is equal to a tolerably well conditioned estate of £2,500 per year. I do not wish to point out here, but you must alter some of your plans and live at less expense. Do not therefore put it off, for I can consent to no further advance, nor will I pay any more debts; and if you were not in Parliament, I would not allow you so largely.

Nothing came of his father's plan in May 1822 to set him at the head of a country bank in Poole.[4]

At the general election of 1820 Lester was again returned unopposed for Poole, from whose inhabitants he often brought up petitions. He was granted ten days' leave on urgent private business, 27 June 1820. He voted to reinstate Queen Caroline's name in the liturgy, 26 Jan., 13 Feb., but divided against condemning the Liverpool administration's conduct towards her, 6 Feb. 1821.[5] He paired for Catholic claims, 28 Feb. He sided with ministers against disqualifying civil officers of the ordnance from voting in parliamentary elections, 12 Apr., but divided against them on the forgery punishment mitigation bill, 23 May 1821. He voted several times for reduced expenditure and taxation, though the radical John Ward commented that he 'did not vote for any popular motion' that session.[6] He was listed in the minority for parliamentary reform, 25 Apr. 1822, and voted for abolition of one of the joint-postmasterships, 2 May, inquiry into the civil list, 15 May, and reduction of the cost of the embassy to the Swiss Cantons, 16 May. He spoke in favour of repealing the salt tax, 11 June 1822.[7] He supported the prospective candidacy of the Tory Henry Bankes* for Dorset at the by-election in February 1823.[8] He voted with ministers against Hume's amendment to limit the sinking fund to the real surplus of revenue not exceeding £5,000,000, 13 Mar., and repeal of the Foreign Enlistment Act, 16 Apr., but with opposition for inquiry into the legal proceedings against the Dublin Orange rioters, 22 Apr., and parliamentary reform, 24 Apr. Unless it was Ralph Leycester, Member for Shaftesbury, with whom he was sometimes confused, he seconded the motion for leave for the jurors' qualification bill, 19 June, and voted for the introduction of trial by jury under the New South Wales jurisdiction bill, 7 July 1823. He urged repeal of the salt tax, 4 Mar., 9 Apr. 1824.[9] He voted in the minority for securing proper use of the Irish first fruits fund, 25 May, but in the government majority against condemning the trial of the Methodist missionary John Smith in Demerara, 11 June 1824. He divided to repeal the usury laws, 17 Feb. 1825. He voted for Catholic relief, 1 Mar., 21 Apr., 10 May. He voted for repeal of the assessed taxes, 3 Mar., and revision of the corn laws, 28 Apr., and against the window tax, 17 May, and the duke of Cumberland's grant, 6, 10 June. His father died, as the result of a road accident, 28 Dec. 1825, leaving a large estate, which included personalty sworn under £120,000. Lester inherited his personal effects, £16,000 and properties in Poole and elsewhere, but the residue, including his father's ships, was divided between his brothers.[10] He suggested that distressed manufacturers could be relieved by allowing corn in hand to be released to general circulation, 14 Apr., and voted for inquiry into the corn laws, 18 Apr., parliamentary reform, 27 Apr., and Maberly's clause in the alehouses licensing bill to permit adjourned meetings for granting licenses, 12 May 1826.[11] The expectation that if he stood singly for Poole he would be re-elected was borne out at the general election that summer, when he plumped for himself and topped the poll in a contest against two local country gentlemen.[12]

Lester voted against the Clarence grant, 16 Feb., for inquiry into the allegations against Leicester corporation, 15 Mar., to condemn chancery administration, 5 Apr., and for the disfranchisement of Penryn, 28 May 1827. He divided for repeal of the Test Acts, 26 Feb. 1828, and Catholic claims, 6 Mar. 1827, 12 May 1828. He voted against extending the franchise of East Retford to the freeholders of the hundred of Bassetlaw, 21 Mar., but was credited with dividing with the Wellington ministry against inquiry into chancery administration, 24 Apr.; he voted for various economies, 20, 23 June, 4 July 1828. He was listed by Planta, the patronage secretary, as likely to be 'with government' on the Catholic question, and duly divided in favour of emancipation, 6, 30 Mar. 1829. He voted to transfer East Retford's seats to Birmingham, 5 May, against an additional grant for the sculpture of the marble arch, 25 May, and for reduction of the hemp duties, 1 June 1829. Later that year Sir Richard Vyvyan*, the Ultra leader, listed him among 'those who voted in favour of the third reading [of the Catholic bill] but whose sentiments are unknown' on the possible formation of a coalition ministry. He voted for Knatchbull's amendment to the address complaining of distress, 4 Feb. 1830, and divided steadily in favour of retrenchment and lower taxation that year. He voted to transfer East Retford's seats to Birmingham, 11 Feb., 5, 15 Mar., and for the enfranchisement of Birmingham, Leeds and Manchester, 23 Feb., and paired for parliamentary reform, 28 May. He voted for Jewish emancipation, 5 Apr., 17 May. He was listed in the minority on the motion of his father's former partner, George Richard Robinson, for inquiry into the state of Newfoundland, 11 May, and voted for inquiry into Ceylon, 27 May 1830.

As no alternative candidates in the end materialized, he was returned unopposed for Poole at the general election that summer, when he told the electors that he had some sympathy with the cause of the unfranchised commonalty and boasted that for 21 years he 'had acted in the House in the most independent manner'. In September he provided the land for a new library in Poole and having (like all the other electors) nominated two additional freemen, 16 Sept., he attended a celebratory dinner there, 28 Sept. 1830, when he promised to vote for economies.[13] Later that year he privately expressed concern about the spread of the 'Swing' riots to Dorset.[14] He was listed by ministers among their 'foes', and voted in the majority against them on the civil list, 15 Nov. He brought up reform petitions from Poole, 17 Dec. 1830, 14 Mar. 1831, and voted for the second reading of the Grey ministry's reform bill, 22 Mar., and against Gascoyne's wrecking amendment, 19 Apr. He was thanked for his reform votes at a public dinner in Poole, 7 Apr., when he congratulated the inhabitants on obtaining the franchise and spoke in favour of reform, retrenchment, and civil and religious liberties. In his address, he claimed that 'independence and liberality I have attempted to make the mainsprings of my parliamentary conduct', and he was again returned unopposed with the reformer William Ponsonby at the ensuing general election.[15] In the Dorset contest he split for the reformers Edward Berkeley Portman* and John Calcraft*.[16]

He divided for the second reading of the reintroduced reform bill, 6 July, at least twice against adjourning proceedings on it, 12 July, and steadily in favour of its details, though he was in the minority for the total disfranchisement of Aldborough, 14 Sept., when government allowed it to retain one seat. He voted in favour of the third reading, 19 Sept., and passage of the bill, 21 Sept. He sided with ministers on the Dublin election, 23 Aug., and for Lord Ebrington's confidence motion, 10 Oct. He voted for Ponsonby in the Dorset by-election that month.[17] He complained of the curtailment of debate on the bankruptcy court bill, 13 Oct., when he replied to the Tory George Bankes's jibe that those on the other side of the chamber were asleep, by retorting that 'it is only for the last few minutes that I have sat upon this side of the House. For three hours I sat on the same side with the honourable gentleman ... patiently expecting that something would be said to the purpose'. He divided for the second reading of the revised reform bill, 17 Dec. 1831, regularly for its details, and for the third reading, 22 Mar. 1832. In January he was reported to be ready to join the putative Dorset Whig Club.[18] He voted with government against the production of information on Portugal, 9 Feb., and military punishments, 16 Feb., and against amendment of the navy civil departments bill, 6 Apr. He divided for Ebrington's motion for an address calling on the king to appoint only ministers who would carry the reform bill unimpaired, 10 May, and for the second reading of the Irish bill, 25 May, and against increasing the representation of Scotland, 1 June. He voted for Baring's bill to exclude insolvent debtors from Parliament, 27 June. His only other known votes that session were with ministers for the Russian-Dutch loan, 26 Jan., 12, 16, 20 July. He made representations to ministers about their plans for the administration of Newfoundland,[19] and in the House, 23 July 1832, he denied that the grant for its civil establishment included charges for conveying the governor from post to post.

Lester was returned as a Liberal at the top of the poll at the general election in December 1832.[20] He retired from Parliament two years later and perhaps moved abroad, though he retained his roughly 50 properties in Poole, which brought him rent of £649 in 1837. He died in Paris in July 1838, and the French death certificate, dated 25 July, described him as a '*rentier*', resident in the Avenue de Neuilly. By his will, dated 10 May 1838, he divided his estate, which included personal wealth sworn under £16,000, between his siblings and their children, and left £10,000 and the residue in trust to his brother, Augustus Lester Garland, a Leghorn merchant.[21] Lester evidently had at least two illegitimate children in Newfoundland, as on 3 June 1820 he wrote to his brother John Bingley Garland (who was later speaker of the assembly there), that 'with respect to the boys, my only wish is that they should be brought up to that situation which is likely best to suit their capacity'. He probably also had two illegitimate daughters, as his will made provision for Miss Jane Moore, the mistress of the Parkstone boarding school near Poole, and her daughters Eliza and Mary Ann.[22]

[1] C.N. Cullingford, *Hist. Poole*, 124, 129-36; D. Beamish, J. Hillier and H.F.V. Johnstone, *Mansions and Merchants of Poole and Dorset*, 85-114; *Dict. of Canadian Biog.* vi. 490-2; PROB 11/1370/123. [2] Dorset RO, Poole borough recs. DC/PL RMP3. [3] *HP Commons, 1790-1832*, iv. 419. [4] Dorset RO, Lester-Garland mss D/LEG F23, ff. 39, 69, 70, 87. [5] *Salisbury Jnl.* 26 Feb. 1821. [6] *Black Book* (1823), 170, where some of Ralph Leycester's votes are credited to Lester. [7] *The Times*, 12 June 1822. [8] Dorset RO, Bankes mss D/BKL, Lester to Bankes, 11 Feb. 1823. [9] *The Times*, 5 Mar., 10 Apr. 1824. [10] *Dorset Co. Chron.* 29 Dec. 1825; PROB 11/1707/18;

IR26/1082/27. [11] *The Times*, 15 Apr. 1826. [12] Lester-Garland mss F23, f. 113; *Dorset Co. Chron.* 22 Sept. 1825, 1, 15 June 1826; Poole borough recs. S1666. [13] *Dorset Co. Chron.* 5 Aug., 9, 23, 30 Sept. 1830. [14] Lester-Garland mss F60, Lester to Garland, 12 Nov. 1830. [15] *Dorset Co. Chron.* 14, 21 Apr., 5 May 1831. [16] *Dorset Pollbook* (1831), 42. [17] Ibid. (Sept.-Oct. 1831), 36. [18] Dorset RO, Fox-Strangways mss D/FSI 332, Parry Okeden to Ilchester, 14 Jan. 1832. [19] *Dorset Co. Chron.* 2 Feb. 1832; Beamish, Hillier and Johnstone, 119. [20] *Dorset Co. Chron.* 13 Dec. 1832. [21] Ibid. 26 July 1838; *Gent. Mag.* (1838), ii. 343; Lester-Garland mss E4; F32-34; PROB 11/1899/539; IR26/1490/487. [22] Lester-Garland mss F38; PROB 11/1899/539.

S.M.F.

LETHBRIDGE, Sir Thomas Buckler, 2nd bt. (1778–1849), of Sandhill Park, nr. Taunton, Som. and 20 Whitehall Place, Westminster, Mdx.

SOMERSET 16 June 1806–1812

SOMERSET 1820–1830

b. 21 Feb. 1778, o.s. of Sir John Lethbridge, 1st bt.†, of Sandhill Park and Dorothea, da. and coh. of William Buckler of Boreham, Wilts. *educ.* Oriel, Oxf. 1794. *m.* (1) 14 May 1796, Jacintha Catherine (*d.* 31 Aug. 1801), da. of Thomas Hesketh of Rufford Hall, Lancs., 1s. 1da. (*d.v.p.*); (2) 14 May 1803, Anne, da. of Ambrose Goddard† of Swindon, Wilts., 2s. 4da. *suc.* fa. as 2nd bt. 15 Dec. 1815. *d.* 17 Oct. 1849.

Capt. 2 Som. militia 1798, maj. 1803, lt.-col. commdt. 1808, col. 1819.

Lethbridge, who was known as 'Leatherbreeches' by his opponents, had retired as Tory Member for Somerset in 1812 fearing disinheritance by his father, with whom he had quarrelled. The latter died intestate, having reputedly torn up his will after being reconciled to his son on his deathbed; Lethbridge and his sisters were granted administration of the estate.[1] He was thereafter free to attempt to regain the county seat, and in 1818 he unsuccessfully challenged the sitting Members, William Dickinson and William Gore Langton*. The following year he was active in arousing anti-Catholic feeling among the freeholders, and he used this at the dissolution in 1820 to force Gore Langton's retirement. He declared himself to be a 'firm friend to our excellent constitution in church and state', yet 'far from ... inimical to the Dissenters', and said he was prepared to allow Catholics 'every possible liberty of worship' but not to remove the restraints on their political power, 'since whenever they possessed power they never failed to abuse it'. He was returned unopposed with Dickinson, who had shifted his ground on the Catholic question, and rested his claim for future support on his 'independence of mind, I mean that genuine independence which, unswayed by either hopes or fears of any sort, rests upon conviction, anxiously and deliberately formed'.[2]

His conduct, as in the past, was unpredictable, and he often acted with the Whig opposition to Lord Liverpool's ministry. He voted in the minority to defer the civil list report, 8 May, presented a Somerset petition for agricultural relief, 17 May,[3] and was granted a month's leave on account of family illness, 16 June 1820. He was satisfied that the Lords' proceedings against Queen Caroline had shown her to be 'guilty of the charges brought', 1 Feb. 1821, and was so appalled by the reports of how money previously granted to her had been spent that, in what a radical Whig Member described as 'an effusive, furious and ungentlemanlike speech', he seconded Holme Sumner's amendment to reduce the new grant from £50,000 to £30,000.[4] He voted in defence of ministers' conduct towards the queen, 6 Feb. He criticized the Whigs' 'vexatious' opposition to the additional malt duties, 14 Feb., yet voted with them for repeal, 3 Apr. He presented Somerset petitions for relief from agricultural distress, 21, 26 Feb., and was named to the subsequent select committee, 7 Mar. (and again, 18 Feb. 1822).[5] He divided with ministers against Maberly's revenue motion, 6 Mar., but supported repeal of the agricultural horse tax as a 'small boon', 5 Apr., and voted for inquiry into the currency, 9 Apr. He divided against Catholic claims, 28 Feb. On 26 Mar. he warned that if the relief bill was carried Parliament must logically also repeal the Test Acts, 'and then indeed there would be an end to the constitution'. He recalled 'the evils which England had suffered under Catholic domination and trembled at the repeal of laws which provided against their recurrence'. He had no objection to Catholics being made silks, but 'could not suffer them upon the bench'. He was confident that an inquiry into Ilchester gaol would find that it was run 'in a most perfect manner', 9 Mar., and argued that whatever the truth concerning the gaoler's conduct 'not the slightest blame could be attributed to the visiting magistrates', 11 Apr. He introduced a charitable establishments bill allowing such foundations to alienate land by way of exchange, 15 Mar.; it was later withdrawn and a charitable lands exchange bill brought in, which received royal assent, 10 July. He believed the *John Bull* newspaper to be guilty of a breach of privilege, which was 'disgraceful to the press, injurious to morality, and inconsistent with the existence of society', 10 May 1821, and called for a general inquiry into the press, which had 'grown up into a fearful engine of mighty mischief'.

In January 1822 he attended the Taunton meeting on agricultural distress and supported the proposed petition, while doubting whether the situation was so bad that it could not be 'remedied by the manly character of the British nation'. He initially seemed to reject calls for reform as a remedy, but then promised to give it his 'dispassionate attention' as he was well aware 'how time corrodes and impairs the most valued institutions'; even the British constitution was no exception to 'this truth'.[6] In the ensuing session he was one of the country gentlemen who, as a Tory Member put it, 'literally seem to have run wild'.[7] He found it his 'painful duty' to support Hume's amendment to the address for retrenchment, 5 Feb., as he feared ministers were 'unacquainted with the frightful ravages' of 'individual and collective distress'. He voted with ministers against Brougham's motion on distress, 11 Feb., but was in the minorities for more extensive tax reductions, 21 Feb., and reduction of the salt duties, 28 Feb., when he argued that taxation 'must be regarded as an auxiliary cause of ... distress'. He emphasized his faith in the character and general policy of ministers, who still possessed the confidence of the people, by which he meant 'the legitimate people ... the manly yeomanry' as distinct from 'a certain unfortunate portion of the population which inhabited great manufacturing towns', but he warned that if they persisted in 'sacrificing the landed to the monied interest' he would be obliged to withdraw his support. He divided for retrenchment, 1, 13 Mar., 2, 16 May, 3 June, and inquiry into diplomatic expenditure, 15 May. He presented numerous Somerset petitions for relief that session, and declared on 6 May that 'nothing less than the most efficient duties upon the importation of every kind of agricultural produce could restore prosperity to the cultivators of the United Kingdom'.[8] Next day he moved resolutions specifying higher duties on a wide range of agricultural commodities, including a 40*s.* fixed duty on corn, argued that without increased protection 'it was in vain to expect that the agriculturists could maintain their station in society', blamed the resumption of cash payments for the existing distress and urged Members not to be 'led away by false speculations and the abominable theories of political economists'. He was a teller the following day when his resolutions were defeated by 243-24.[9] In presenting a Somerset petition for a tax on absentees, 16 May, he pointed out that the revenue from it could be used to finance relief measures for agriculture. He admitted that the leader of the Commons, Lord Londonderry's proposals for relief seemed on balance to be the 'most eligible', 24 May, but 'clearly this was not the opinion of the country at large'. He opposed Canning's amendment to the corn bill, allowing warehoused foreign corn to be ground for flour and exported, 3, 10 June, complaining that 'the agriculturists had been ... completely ground already' and that the proposal would encourage further imports. He argued that the navigation bill and other board of trade measures were 'undigested and would produce great mischief', 4 June, and observed that government policies were 'now ensuring parliamentary reform', as 'the yeomanry were beginning to be reformers from one end of the country to the other'. He was 'a convert to that doctrine' and would in future support any proposition from Lord John Russell, who 'would advocate nothing unconstitutional or dangerous'.[10] He initially maintained that the radical agitator Henry Hunt* had not been improperly treated in Ilchester gaol, 8, 20 Feb., but was forced to admit that some of the revelations in the commissioner's report 'excite ... indignation' and must not happen again, 27 Feb. He agreed that Hunt's treatment provided grounds for remitting his sentence, 13 Mar. He voted for revision of the criminal code, 4 June. He thought the people were too preoccupied with their 'own distresses' to organize petitions against Catholic claims, but they 'still continued decidedly hostile to the question', 30 Apr.; he voted that day against the Catholic peers bill. He recognized that it could not be stopped in the Commons, but was thankful that 'there were three estates of this realm', 17 May 1822. Later that year there were local reports that Lethbridge was personally feeling the financial effects of the agricultural depression and had a large number of unlet farms.[11]

He attended both county meetings at Wells in January 1823. At the first, he supported the petition for agricultural relief and emphasized his desire to see 'an equal distribution of the public burthens' through tax cuts, which would most benefit the poor, but he was cautious about committing himself to tithe commutation. At the second meeting on reform, he acknowledged that the people must have their rights but would 'not ask for more than the constitution granted', adding that 'it would first become them to correct such decays as might have crept in' since 1688. He was willing to support a measure to increase the representation of 'the landed interests', but 'could not go further'. The meeting carried Hunt's amendment in favour of universal suffrage and the secret ballot.[12] Lethbridge regretted the absence from the king's speech of any indication of ministerial intentions regarding agricultural relief and pressed for a statement, 14 Feb., declaring that 'the landed interest had become depressed by no fault of their own, but by the impolitic conduct of the legislature' in allowing cheap imports and cash payments. He urged ministers to give a 'decided negative' to Whitmore's plan to amend the corn laws, as a gesture of support for the agriculturists, 26 Feb. He refused to put off his intended motion, 13 Mar., as the government had failed to act. He supported West Indian petitions against misuse of the four-and-a-half per cent duties, in the belief that 'the whole of the landed interest of this country was bound to support the colonial interests', 19 Mar. On 21 Mar. he claimed that he had only been prevented from introducing his motion by 'the thin attendance of Members last night'. He presented the Somerset county petition on distress, 16 Apr., but regretted that owing to Hunt's 'fascinating powers' there was 'scarcely one paragraph in it which contained opinions that he could advocate'; he brought forward more conventional petitions from Cirencester and Gloucestershire, 29 Apr.[13] In presenting a petition from butchers at Leadenhall market for a higher duty on imported tallow, 12 May, he said it was 'monstrous' that Russian produce was being allowed to flood the British market. However, he announced that he was withdrawing his motion on the advice of 'many able friends of the agricultural interests', 2 June, and pointed to 'the contrast of circumstances between the present time ... and that in which he gave notice of it' as offering 'hope of great alleviation'. He divided for more extensive tax reductions, 28 Feb., against the national debt reduction bill, 6, 13, 17 Mar., and for repeal of the assessed taxes, 18 Mar. He urged that 'every measure of reduction and economy should be adopted that could be resorted to with safety', 7 Mar., and advocated further cuts in the army estimates and public salaries; he voted against the grant for colonial agents, 24 Mar. He supported petitions against the Insolvent Debtors Act, 17, 18 Feb., but denied that he intended to act on the matter.[14] He voted for inquiry into the parliamentary franchise, 20 Feb., and Russell's reform motion, 24 Apr., which would 'have the necessary effect of bringing into the House, through the medium of county representation, a different class ... of persons to those who now composed it' and 'discourage those absurd and visionary doctrines which were held out to the country by specious and designing characters'. He presented petitions complaining of Jesuit activities in Ireland, 5 Mar., and calling for inquiry into Papist establishments there, 17 Apr., when he was a minority teller against Catholic claims. He divided for inquiry into the prosecution of the Dublin Orange rioters, 22 Apr. He introduced a division of counties bill enabling magistrates at quarter sessions to define these more exactly, 7 Mar. 1823; it passed but did not reach the Lords.

He 'entirely approved' of the king's speech, 4 Feb. 1824, finding that 'a considerable amendment had taken place in the state of agriculture' which he hoped would be permanent, and he urged Members to 'give ... ministers all the support in their power'. He believed that in the field of foreign policy 'this country stood high in the opinion of Europe and of every other part of the world', and that ministers were right not to interfere over the French invasion of Spain. He complained of the burden on landowners of paying for the administration of criminal justice in the counties, arguing that the whole nation should share the cost, 19 Feb. He warned that petitioners for repeal of the coal duties were ignoring the consequent injury to colliers in Somerset and elsewhere, 19 Feb., and said he would prefer to see repeal of the malt or window taxes, 1 Apr.[15] He presented numerous petitions that session for repeal of the assessed taxes,[16] and voted against the window and leather taxes, 2 Mar., 18 May. He urged the government to reconsider its plan to remove the prohibitory duty on French silks, 5 Mar., maintaining that the industry 'would continue to do well, so long as it was protected from that free trade on which the ministers and the House were running wild'. He presented Taunton and Shepton Mallet petitions against the proposed regulations for the industry, 11, 12 Mar.[17] He explained that he had changed his mind and would oppose the wheat warehousing bill, 4 May.[18] He voted against the usury laws repeal bill, 27 Feb., which he thought would 'place borrowers at the mercy of lenders', 31 Mar. He voted to reform Edinburgh's representation, 26 Feb. He warned that the Cheltenham water works bill would cut off supplies to some land and mill owners in Gloucestershire, and was a minority teller against its second reading, 25 Mar. He was a majority teller for the second reading of the Bristol and Taunton canal bill, 30 Mar. He presented a petition against the use of the treadmill in prisons and asserted that 'such a mode of punishment was unknown to the constitutional jealousy of our forefathers', 5 May 1824.

Lethbridge congratulated ministers on their intention to suppress the Catholic Association, 4 Feb. 1825, declaring that 'a body which trenched so much on the spirit of the constitution ought no longer to be permitted to exist'. He voted for the third reading of the unlawful societies bill, 25 Feb. He considered it was 'high time to hold firm and strong language with respect to the demands of Roman Catholics', 15 Feb., presented numerous petitions during the session against their claims,[19] and voted accordingly, 1 Mar. In opposing the first reading of the relief bill he regretted 'the apathy which at this moment prevailed throughout the country', 23 Mar., but he retracted this complaint in the light of subsequent petitions, which would hopefully 'excite a similar spirit in the House', 18 Apr., and voted against the second reading, 21 Apr. He dismissed the evidence taken before the select committee as '*ex parte*', 26 Apr. On the motion to go into committee, 6 May, he asked the clerk to read aloud the oath of supremacy taken by Members and denounced 'a most vicious piece of legislation', which 'could never be passed without a violation of that solemn engagement which they had entered into ... with the country'; he also asserted that 'no honourable and conscientious Catholic' could take the proposed new oath. He divided against the third reading, 10 May, and dismissed complaints about the 'clamour' against it in the country, 26 May. He thought the Irish franchise bill would deprive Catholics of a more valuable privilege than that conferred by the relief bill, 22 Apr., and voted against the second reading, 26 Apr. He said it would be 'niggardly in the extreme' to withhold the grants to Irish charitable institutions, 18 Mar., as there was 'nothing ... so important, in the present state of Ireland, as to provide permanent establishments for the education of the lower orders'. He divided against the usury laws repeal bill, 17 Feb. He voted for repeal of the assessed taxes, 3 Mar., and of the window tax, 17 May. He pressed ministers to take the initiative in revising the corn laws, 25 Apr., observing that 'he never wished to see prices higher than they were at that moment, and should be happy to see the old principle of open ports and fixed duties again acted upon'. He introduced the Western ship canal bill to link Seaton Bay with the Bristol Channel, 3 Mar.; it gained royal assent, 6 July 1825. It was said of him at this time that he 'spoke often, but more solemnly than well'.[20] That summer he was at the forefront of the 'no Popery' campaign in Somerset, forcing the Members for Taunton, where he had substantial propertied influence, to announce their forthcoming retirements, and encouraging a similar but less successful movement at Wells, where he was a freeman. He confidently predicted to the home secretary Peel, to whom 'the church of England and the Protestant part of the community look up', that 'anti-Catholic principles will ... be triumphant whenever the election comes'.[21]

He welcomed the government's decision to defer action on the corn laws, 3 Feb. 1826, arguing that the currency question must first be settled and recommending the establishment of joint-stock banks. He favoured the return to a metallic circulation, which would help to 'remove the want of confidence which prevailed in money matters' and 'secure to the poor man the full produce of his industry in a coin which could not be depreciated', 14 Feb. He feared that ministers still planned to alter the corn laws, 9 Feb., and declared that while low prices were desirable 'high prices there must be ... kept up by an import duty, amounting to an absolute prohibition, so long as the interest of the national debt was to be paid'. He doubted the political economists' assumption that free importation of corn would create foreign demand for British manufactures, 2 Mar. He opposed the motion to go into committee on the laws, 2 May, rejecting the 'fallacy' that high food prices were the cause of distress and claiming that this was merely 'a pretext for coming at the landed interest ... and destroying them at one blow'; the 'real object was ... to get rid of the whole system of corn laws by a side wind'. He maintained that industrial labourers were 'bred in habits of luxury and had acquired wants which they found it difficult to divest themselves of', but they had more cause for complaint about other taxes than that on bread. He therefore moved for a select committee to inquire into the causes of distress in the manufacturing districts, which was rejected by 214-82; he was a minority teller. He saw no case for the ministerial proposal to admit foreign corn at a low duty, 5 May, dismissing the argument about possible famine as 'a piece of reasoning contrary to common sense and real facts', and warning that the new duty would 'always be a precedent to the prejudice of the landed interest'. He denied that the price of labour was high because corn prices were high, insisting that the real reason was that 'taxes were high', 8 May, and he pledged himself to pursue 'the most rigid economy' if returned to the next Parliament. He voted that day against empowering the government temporarily to admit foreign corn. He wished to take the sense of the House by forcing a division against the second reading of the corn bill, 11 May, but was defeated by 189-65, acting as a minority teller. He recognized that further opposition was futile, 17 May, but was determined to register his 'solemn protest', which he did 'in spite of all the intimidations he had received from quarters which he despised from the very bottom of his heart'. In February he presented several petitions from silk weavers and glovers for the restoration of protective duties.[22] He voted with opposition for inquiry into the treasurership of the navy, 7 Apr., against the report on the salary of the president of the board of trade, 10 Apr., for reform of Edinburgh's representation, 13 Apr., and Russell's resolutions to curb electoral bribery, 26 May 1826. At the dissolution that summer he and Dickinson joined forces to repel a challenge from Hunt. Professing 'an inward consciousness of having done his duty to the freeholders ... [and] to his country', he was easily returned in second place after a contest marked by semi-comic personal clashes with his radical opponent.[23]

Lethbridge advocated inquiry to procure 'full and complete information' before action was taken over the corn laws, 22 Nov. 1826. He resented Lord Milton's 'high tone' on this issue, 21 Feb. 1827, protested against 'any attempt to destroy what he must always consider the most important interest of the state' and asserted that it would be better to encourage agricultural improvements, which would enable farmers to support 'thousands thrown out of employment by the use of machinery'. He admitted that the proposed new duties were better than he had expected, 1 Mar., but said they still afforded 'no protection whatever to the landed interest' and argued that 64*s*. was the minimum possible duty on wheat, 8 Mar. He was grateful for modifications to the proposed duties on barley and oats, although they were still too low, 13 Mar. He vindicated the conduct of the country gentlemen, who were 'there upon their defence', 19 Mar. He denounced the corn bill as a measure for 'the more effectual encouragement of speculation in the corn trade ... the more rapid diminution of the growth of grain in Great Britain and ... the better encouragement of the growth of grain in other counties', 2 Apr. He suspected that ministers were divided on the issue and predicted a formidable opposition in the Lords; he was a minority teller against the second reading. He supported the London ship owners' petition against the new navigation laws, which he claimed were causing their distress, 19 Mar., and added that it was 'impossible for this highly-taxed country to follow up the system of free trade'. He divided against Catholic relief, 6 Mar. On 3 Apr., with the arrangements for a new ministry to replace Liverpool's still unsettled, Lethbridge put down a motion calling for the formation of a government united on the main areas of policy, by which he meant the Catholic question.[24] He told Lord Colchester that 'he was tired, and the country was tired, of a see-saw government here and in Ireland', and that he would rather have 'any *decided* government than none ... even if it were Roman Catholic ... especially as a Roman Catholic government would not last six weeks'. The Whigs were deeply divided on this motion, some fearing that by supporting it they might pave the way for 'an ultra Tory and Orange government'.[25] On the advice of his fellow anti-Catholics, Sir Edward Knatchbull and Sir Thomas Gooch, who feared that the motion might offend the king, Lethbridge indicated his willingness to withdraw it, 6 Apr., but said he could only do so if Canning confirmed that a new ministry was in the process of being formed. Canning, who wanted Lethbridge to persist for the same reason that it might alienate the king, 'answered very drily', ridiculing his logic. He was stung into announcing that he must press the motion, but withdrew it later that evening. Canning reportedly believed that the anti-Catholics had 'completely cut their own throats'.[26] Lethbridge welcomed Peel's decision not to join Canning's coalition government, 1 May, believing that this would 'lead the country to a real and just view of the great and leading public principles upon which the present administration was made up'. He trusted that the Catholic question would 'now come before the House in a decided form' and demanded that Canning give a plain statement of intent 'instead of continuing to temporize'. He deplored the provisional state of the government, in which certain offices were left unfilled and no clear principles enunciated, 4 May, and thought this 'looked like ... greediness for the loaves and fishes'. He maintained that it was desirable to have 'two different parties in the country professing opposite principles', and boasted that while he was 'only a plain country gentleman' who was 'not able to speak well', he 'had the courage to do his duty' despite the ridicule he suffered. Canning described this speech to the king as a 'foolish and furious ebullition ... which produced nothing but laughter', and confided that his own object was to 'force the *new* opposition to come to a regular attack'.[27] Lethbridge accused Canning of 'un-Torying Toryism and un-Whigging Whiggism', 11 May, and suspected that he had come to a private understanding with the Whigs before the demise of the previous government. He unsuccessfully pressed Canning for a reply to this charge, 18 May. According to the diary of an independent Whig, however, Lethbridge's attacks may have had some effect: 'Canning looking very ill, and very foolishly excited by some foolish questions of Leatherbreeches'.[28] He returned to the attack, 25 May, when he argued that no supplies should be granted and prophesied that the government would 'end in great disappointment, if not in serious injury, to the empire'. He introduced the General Turnpike Act amendment bill, 1 Mar., and 'repelled with some warmth' Alexander Baring's insinuation that he was actuated by selfish motives in wanting to close an old road on his property, 27 Mar.; it received royal assent, 14 June. He applauded Lord Althorp's plan for reforming the mode of taking polls at county elections, which would 'open a wider door for more numerous county candidates, in the same proportion as the expense of a contest would be diminished', 15 Mar. He voted for the Clarences' annuity bill, 16 Mar. 1827. It appears that before the session ended Lethbridge had gone abroad, 'disgusted ... with the perverseness of his age and country'.[29]

In January 1828 he wrote to Wellington and Peel expressing relief that the duke had been asked to form a government which, he trusted, would act on 'fixed and unshaken principles ... Protestant to the full extent of that term'. He told Peel that 'I verily believe you will be another *Mr. Pitt* and ... the country will support you, as they did him'. At the opening of the session, he reportedly sat on the treasury bench.[30] On 6 Feb. he expressed his 'highest respect and confidence' in the new premier, whose foreign policy would 'support the dignity, honour and fair fame of the British character', unlike the 'wholly inefficient and ... totally imbecile' Goderich ministry. He presented petitions for repeal of the Test Acts, 20 Feb., but did not vote in the division of 26 Feb. Two days later he stated that he had come down intending to vote for repeal, 'contrary to my own opinion', because of the surprisingly strong feeling in its favour, but that Milton's unconciliatory speech displaying 'party hostility' had caused him to change his mind. In presenting a Wells clergy petition against Catholic relief, 10 Mar., he denied that repealing the Test Acts had any bearing on the Catholic case, as the Dissenters had no divided allegiance. He presented further anti-Catholic petitions that session and voted thus, 12 May. However, on 12 June, in a vague speech possibly foreshadowing his dramatic change of opinion in the next session, he lamented that 'the greatest misfortune this country labours under' was having a government divided on this vital issue, when he had supposed it would be 'formed on an united ... intelligible and ... clear principle'. While the Catholic Association deserved to be suppressed for its 'violent and unconstitutional' actions, he now wished 'from the bottom of my heart that the Catholic question could be settled with satisfaction to all parties'. He noticed 'as a circumstance of great importance' that the issue had 'latterly been received more favourably than ... in other times', and though he would 'resist intimidation', he believed that with 'calm temper and cool deliberation' the matter would 'make its way fairly to the minds and feelings of the people of England and ... will then be carried'. He declared that 'the increase of crime' was 'so alarming in all parts' of Britain that some measure to check it was 'absolutely necessary', 6 Mar. He presented a Chard magistrates' petition against the low duty on cider, 28 Mar., and Wincanton and Wells petitions for licensing of cider sales, 2 June, when he noted that 'great demoralization had already taken place in that part of the country ... in consequence of the defective state of the law'. He presented petitions against private turnpike trusts, which he argued should be controlled by responsible public boards, 17 Mar., and the excessive fees incurred in passing turnpike bills, 25 Mar. He considered the ministerial resolutions on the corn laws preferable to those of last session, although he would ideally have liked a prohibition on foreign imports and a drawback for exports, 31 Mar. He presented petitions for protection against imported wool, 17, 28 Apr., 9 June. He regretted having latterly been obliged to oppose Canning's policies, 14 May 1828, and in what was described as a 'very gentlemanlike speech' supported financial provision for his family, as he would not 'grudge to pay this tribute of respect' to the memory of 'one of the most eminent of statesmen'.[31] The following month he assured Wellington of the country's 'unbounded confidence' in his government and expressed admiration for the manner in which he had received the resignations of the Huskissonite ministers.[32]

Early in 1829 Lethbridge reportedly offered his services to Peel as seconder of the address, under the impression that the recall of the lord lieutenant of Ireland, Lord Anglesey, meant that the government was adhering to a Protestant line.[33] He spoke at the Devon county meeting on the Catholic question, 18 Jan., when he agreed that 'things cannot remain as they are', but called for the suppression of the Catholic Association and of the power of the 'Popish priests'.[34] In presenting a Chew Magna petition against relief, 6 Feb., he stated this 'his opinions were unchanged ... he would vigilantly watch and, if necessary, oppose all measures likely to infringe upon our Protestant constitution in church and state'. However, in the debate on the address later that day, he announced that he was prepared to consider the issue, now that it was a 'recommendation from the crown', adding that while he was determined to safeguard the interests of Protestant institutions he was also 'aware that the settlement of this question, even if it were settled in a way contrary to my wishes ... would be a far more desirable thing than the leaving those parts of the community in the state in which they exist at the present moment'. He subsequently explained, in a published letter, that he had changed his position after arriving in London on 4 Feb. to find that ministers planned to recommend concession, and that with no alternative policy to offer he had felt obliged to support them. He wrote to Peel, 8 Feb. assuring him of his continued 'esteem, regard and attachment', promising to do all he could to 'tranquillize the public disappointment, not ... irritate it', and trusting in his '*superior knowledge and judgement*':

> Although differing from you in this measure I do most entirely confide in you on all others and *rejoice* that you have held your office in spite of the difficulties you must have had to contend with, for I know into what arms we must fall if you should not remain where you are. I hope and trust the country will submit to the great change that is contemplated and that you may be able to effect your objects with safety to our Protestant institutions.[35]

Five days later he asked the duke to recommend him for a peerage, which had been a family object since his father's application to the Regent in 1811, resting his claim on his long parliamentary service, consistent support for the monarchy and extensive landholdings. Wellington, however, eventually replied that it was undesirable to increase the number of peers and that he could make no promises.[36] Lethbridge presented numerous Somerset anti-Catholic petitions in February and March. Planta, the patronage secretary, still regarded him as 'doubtful' in late February, but he spoke and voted in favour of emancipation, 6 Mar. He regretted having to differ from old friends, but maintained that public opinion was now moving in favour of settling the issue and that adequate securities had been provided for the Protestant establishment, which was safe as long as Wellington and Peel were in office. He complained that 'the privileges of Parliament have been grossly outraged by a malignant and venal press', 23 Mar., and insisted that 'I never gave a vote with more mental satisfaction than the one ... I gave to maintain the great and vital interests of the country'. He paired for the third reading of the relief bill, 30 Mar. He confirmed the 'dreadful distress' suffered by the Somerset, Dorset and Wiltshire silk-throwsters, 9 Apr. 1829. He informed Wellington in June that his course on the Catholic question had so alienated his supporters in Somerset that he would retire at the next general election, and he renewed his application for a peerage so that he might continue to be politically useful, but without success.[37]

In February 1830 it was reported that Lethbridge had purchased the Basing Park estate in Hampshire and intended to use it as his 'permanent residence'.[38] He wrote to Wellington that month repeating his request for a peerage.[39] He corroborated the claims made in a Taunton petition about the general state of distress in Somerset, 8 Mar., asserting that 'at no previous time, within the memory of any person living, have all classes suffered more severely', hoping that ministers would offer relief from taxation and increased protection for agriculture, and adding his personal opinion that reform of the banking system was needed, as credit was not forthcoming. He was one of a group of Members who met with Wellington, 20 Mar., to ascertain the government's intentions regarding banking reform.[40] He paired against the Jewish emancipation bill, 17 May 1830. He announced his retirement at the dissolution that summer, claiming that poor health prevented him from giving the 'unceasing attendance ... which I have been accustomed to do', and he again solicited Wellington for a peerage.[41] In November he welcomed the duke's anti-reform speech, declaring that this would increase the peoples' confidence in him, and after the government's resignation he made a final fruitless attempt to obtain a peerage through Wellington, whom he assured of his continued support whatever was decided.[42] In fact, as the reform crisis unfolded, Lethbridge underwent an extraordinary political metamorphosis becoming, in the words of the Somerset parson Sydney Smith, 'the most reforming reformer we have in these parts'.[43] This new volte face was similarly connected to familial ambition, as he had applied to Lords Grey and Brougham for their support in promoting his legally tenuous claim to the extinct barony of Fitzwarine. He explained to Brougham in August 1831 that

> I am the more anxious for this favour, that the remainder of my days – being now 53 only – should not be wholly useless to the country, and my eldest son having married into a family, by which his successors will in all probability derive great wealth, I feel that such an advance would be in character therewith ... Should you think proper to effect this object, you shall not find me either an indifferent or ungrateful supporter.

He renewed his application during the constitutional crises of autumn 1831 and May 1832, hopeful that he might benefit from the need for a large creation of peers, and he persisted in later years, but his wish was never granted.[44] There is an unavoidable suspicion that throughout his career, private interests were a prime determinant of his erratic political course. At the general election of 1832 he nominated Charles Kemeys Tynte*, the successful Liberal candidate for the Western division of Somerset, and published a letter calling for an 'extensive and deep-searching corrective of the abuses in the church'.[45] He made an ill-judged attempt to return to Parliament as a Liberal at the Bridgwater by-election of August 1837, having been duped by a requisition organized by venal electors determined to force a contest; he received just five votes.[46] In February 1846 he wrote to Peel offering his 'heartfelt gratitude and admiration' for his free trade policies.[47] Sydney Smith thought him 'as absurd in his political capacity as he is amiable and obliging in all the relations of private life, in which he shines'.[48] He died in October 1849 and was succeeded by his eldest son, John Hesketh Lethbridge (1798-1873), who inherited most of his Somerset estates and all his properties in Devon, Dorset and Monmouthshire; certain Somerset properties and the Cornish estates went to his other sons, Ambrose and Thomas, respectively.[49]

[1] The personalty was sworn under £60,000 (PROB 6/192/191).
[2] Som. RO, Drake mss DD/NE/12, Lethbridge to Drake, 12 Mar., 20 Apr. 1819, 1 Feb.; *Bristol Mirror*, 12, 19, 26 Feb., 11, 18, 25 Mar.

1820. [3] *The Times*, 18 May 1820. [4] HLRO, Hist. Coll. 379, Grey Bennet diary, 9. [5] *The Times*, 22, 27 Feb. 1821. [6] *Bristol Mirror*, 19 Jan. 1822. [7] *Colchester Diary*, iii. 251. [8] *The Times*, 16 Feb., 1 Mar., 18 Apr., 3, 7 May 1822. [9] B. Hilton, *Corn, Cash, Commerce*, 152. [10] *The Times*, 5 June 1822. [11] *Bristol Mirror*, 6 July, 14 Dec. 1822. [12] Ibid. 25 Jan., 1 Feb. 1823. [13] *The Times*, 14, 19 Mar., 17, 30 Apr. 1823. [14] Ibid. 18, 19 Feb. 1823. [15] Ibid. 20 Feb., 2 Apr. 1824. [16] Ibid. 24 Feb., 13, 19 Mar., 13, 15 Apr., 5 May 1824. [17] Ibid. 12, 13 Mar. 1824. [18] Ibid. 5 May 1824. [19] Ibid. 26, 30 Mar., 22, 23 Apr., 5, 10 May 1825. [20] *Session of Parl. 1825*, p. 472. [21] *Bristol Mirror*, 11 June, 16, 23, 30 July 1825; Add. 40381, f. 385. [22] *The Times*, 7, 11, 16, 24 Feb. 1826. [23] *Bristol Mirror*, 10, 17, 24 June, 1 July 1826. [24] *The Times*, 4 Apr. 1827. [25] *Colchester Diary*, iii. 476; Brougham mss, Allen to Brougham, 4 Apr.; Castle Howard mss, Holland to Carlisle, [Apr. 1827]; A. Mitchell, *Whigs in Opposition*, 197-8. [26] G.I.T. Machin, *Catholic Question in English Politics*, 98-99; Nottingham Univ. Lib. Denison diary, 6 Apr. 1827. [27] *Geo. IV Letters*, iii. 1324. [28] Gurney diary, 21 May 1827. [29] BL OIOC mss Eur. C. 247/3, R.P. to C. Smith, 13 June 1827. [30] Wellington mss WP1/913/22; Add. 40395, f. 50; Keele Univ. Lib. Sneyd mss SC17/34. [31] Harewood mss, Backhouse to Lady Canning, 15 May 1828. [32] Wellington mss WP1/938/15. [33] *Ellenborough Diary*, i. 312. [34] *Taunton Courier*, 21 Jan. 1829. [35] *Bristol Mirror*, 21 Mar. 1829; Add. 40398, f. 206. [36] Wellington mss WP1/996/7, 1001/23, 1007/6; *Prince of Wales Corresp.* vii. 3035. [37] Wellington mss WP1/1024/3; *Bristol Mirror*, 14 Mar., 4 July, 5, 12, 19 26 Sept., 3 Oct. 1829, for the local reaction. [38] *Bristol Mirror*, 13 Feb. 1830. [39] Wellington mss WP1/1095/22. [40] Add. 38758, f. 138. [41] *Bristol Mirror*, 3 July 1830. [42] Wellington mss WP1/1150/10, 1152/1. [43] *Smith Letters*, ii. 623. [44] Brougham mss, Lethbridge to Brougham, 15 Aug., 9 Oct., 17 Nov. 1831, 8 May 1832, 7 June 1833, 6 Sept. 1834, 10 Nov. 1836. [45] *Bristol Mirror*, 1 Dec.; *Taunton Courier*, 19 Dec. 1832. [46] S.G. Jarman, *Hist. Bridgwater*, 151. [47] Parker, *Peel*, iii. 340-1. [48] *Smith Letters*, ii. 539. [49] PROB 11/2104/944; IR26/1844/871.

T.A.J.

LEVESON GOWER, Lord Francis (1800–1857), of 12 Albemarle Street, Mdx.

BLETCHINGLEY	19 Feb. 1822–1826
SUTHERLAND	1826–1831
LANCASHIRE SOUTH	1835–6 July 1846

b. 1 Jan. 1800, 2nd surv. s. of George Granville Leveson Gower†, 2nd mq. of Stafford, and Elizabeth, *s.j.* countess of Sutherland [S], da. and h. of William, 18th earl of Sutherland; bro. of George Granville Leveson Gower, Earl Gower†. *educ.* Eton 1811-14; Christ Church, Oxf. 1817. *m.* 18 June 1822, Harriet Catherine, da. of Charles Greville of Wilberry, Wilts., 5s. (1 *d.v.p.*) 2da. *suc.* fa. by reversion to estates of gt.-uncle Francis Egerton, 3rd duke of Bridgwater, 1833 and took name of Egerton by royal lic. 24 Aug. 1833; *cr.* earl of Ellesmere 6 July 1846; KG 7 Feb. 1855. *d.* 18 Feb. 1857.

Cornet 10 Drag. 1821-3.

Ld. of treasury Apr.-Sept. 1827; under-sec. of state for war and colonies Feb.-May 1828; chief sec. to ld. lt. [I] June 1828-July 1830; PC 28 June 1828; PC [I] 9 Aug. 1828; sec. at war July-Nov. 1830.

Rect. King's Coll. Aberdeen 1837-*d*; ld. lt. Lancs. 1856-*d*.

Lt. Staffs. yeomanry 1819, capt. 1819.

Leveson Gower's father possessed valuable landed-industrial estates in Staffordshire and his mother was the largest landowner in northern Scotland. He was described at the age of 11 by his aunt, Lady Granville, as 'quite a little *heros de roman*', being 'handsome, intelligent [with] the most perfect manners' and having a 'grave, unaffected sort of zeal, a look and voice of inquiry about anything that interests and a scornful smile when he does not believe or approve of what is said'; she was sure 'he must be something wonderful in time'.[1] As a young man he 'displayed a taste for literature and the fine arts', publishing poems, which were 'at least respectable', and translations of works by Goethe, Schiller and others.[2] In 1822 Lady Granville noted that he was 'very large, upright and handsome', though unfortunately 'he speaks ... little'. His decision to marry Harriet Greville, the daughter of Lady Charlotte Greville (and niece of the 4th duke of Portland) was resisted by his family, but they were eventually reconciled to it. Lady Granville found Harriet to be a 'very loveable person' and thought her nephew had 'improved, chiefly by her ease and straightforwardness, the two things he wants'. George Agar Ellis* was less charitable, dismissing Harriet as 'foolish in conversation and uncultivated to a degree rarely to be met with', whereas Leveson Gower showed 'talent in conversation' but 'wants character and above all common sense'.[3] He had briefly embarked on an army career, but was returned at a by-election for Bletchingley in February 1822 on Portland's interest, which had been secured through the influence of the duke's brother-in-law George Canning.*[4]

He was an occasional attender who supported Lord Liverpool's ministry. He divided against more extensive tax reductions, 21 Feb., and abolition of one of the joint-postmasterships, 13 Mar. 1822. He welcomed Canning's Catholic peers bill as 'an act of justice' and rejected the 'fears of those who resisted the Catholic claims generally' as 'altogether chimerical', 30 Apr. 1822. That autumn he informed Canning, now foreign secretary, that he had 'decided upon leaving the army' and was 'very desirous to employ my time to ... more purpose than I have hitherto been able to do [in] politics'. His mother apparently hoped that he might become Canning's under-secretary, but he accepted Canning's advice that 'his position in Parliament and chance of success as a speaker would not be improved by being connected with office'; he therefore planned to 'shoot and hunt till the meeting of Parliament ... then ... try his powers in the ... Commons'.[5] In fact, early in 1823 he accompanied Lord Fitzroy Somerset* on an 'expedition of observation' to Spain.[6] He returned to vote against repeal of the Foreign

Enlistment Act, 16 Apr., and inquiry into the prosecution of the Dublin Orange rioters, 22 Apr. He drew on his first-hand knowledge in the debate on Spain, 28 Apr., when he defended the conduct of ministers, who had merely advised the Spaniards that making concessions was the only way of avoiding war with France. The Tory Henry Bankes* recorded that the speech was 'deservedly taken notice of, as indicating facility and fluency and good judgement in selecting ... topics'. Hudson Gurney, a Whiggish independent, was less impressed, noting that 'Lord Francis Gower's is a very bad *manner*, and was an ill-judged attempt at oratory, instead of [taking] his vantage ground in a plain story'; nevertheless, 'he *may* speak after a little practice'.[7] He welcomed the government's plan to raise the duty on barilla in order to assist the kelp manufacturers, 13 June 1823. He divided against the motion condemning the trial of the Methodist missionary John Smith in Demerara, 11 June 1824. Selected to move the address, 3 Feb. 1825, he said he was partly 'at a loss how to proceed', as economic distress had 'vanished' together with its 'concomitants ... exasperation and sedition'. Even in Ireland, 'tranquillity ... reigns ... to a degree ... unparalleled in our recollection', and this had encouraged 'British enterprise ... to exercise a salutary operation'. As a friend to Catholic relief, he expressed an 'ardent wish for [the] speedy annihilation' of the Catholic Association, which, with the 'equally pernicious virulence of Orange insanity', threatened to check Ireland's progress. He approved of the proposed increase in military forces to protect India and other colonies, praised ministers' efforts to promote worldwide abolition of the slave trade, welcomed the commercial treaties with the new South American states and declared that 'our commerce is now happily in the process of being freed from many restrictions, which, bottomed upon false principles, impeded its free course'. Canning told his wife that the speech was 'eminently good and showed *very* considerable powers', and noted how 'he made a little reply ... to Brougham, who had been rather saucy to him, which was remarkable for spirit as well as for readiness, and was exceedingly well received by the House'. On the other hand, Agar Ellis thought he 'spoke indifferently', and William Fremantle* judged that the speech was 'not first rate, though sensible and well-delivered'.[8] He divided for the Irish unlawful societies bill, 25 Feb., and Catholic relief, 1 Mar., 21 Apr., 10 May. On 29 Apr. 1825 he moved a resolution to make provision from state funds for the maintenance of the secular Catholic clergy in Ireland, which he estimated would apply to about 2,000 priests and cost £250,000. He argued that this was 'inseparably connected with the welfare and ... good government of Ireland', as it would help to give Britain a 'strong and unalienable hold on the affection and the duty of the Catholic priests and population'. He hoped that a 'competent provision' would encourage a greater 'mixture of the higher classes of the community' within the ranks of the Catholic clergy, as well as making them less 'dependent upon the people' in times of tumult, but he denied that his object was to undermine the Catholic religion. He was a teller for the resolution, which was carried by 205-162. Henry Hobhouse, the home office under-secretary, described him as 'an intimate friend of ... Canning' and claimed that the resolution had been 'contrived by Lord Grenville and Lord Wellesley's agent, Mr. Blake, as the only mode in which the question could be agitated without a breach of privilege', since the king had not consented to the issue being raised.[9] That summer Leveson Gower wrote to John Evelyn Denison*, an old school friend, expressing disillusionment with his position:

> As to politics, the course of last session has entirely obliterated any taste I ever had for them. I think there was a time, now utterly gone, when there was a kind of royal road to influence, place, etc., but I do not think now that the education of a gentleman at large suffices to raise him to any distinction in this country, and I am quite sure that to attain it a regular apprenticeship either legal or scientific is absolutely necessary. This I have never had and no one hardly in my situation can have, and I am therefore perfectly contented to go on for the rest of my life reading *les belles lettres* ... as it is not in my power to be of use to others. I do not speak in any disgust, as in anything I have attempted in the ... Commons I consider myself to have succeeded to the full extent of my expectations.[10]

He voted against the motion condemning the Jamaican slave trials, 2 Mar., and reform of Edinburgh's representation, 13 Apr. 1826. He opposed Lord John Russell's reform motion in a flowery and verbose speech, 27 Apr. 1826, in which he recognized that the constitution contained 'some antique peculiarities and grotesqueness of detail', but nevertheless 'shuddered to approach, with the intention of repair, a composition which ... I must look at with reliance and admiration'. At the general election that summer, while he was in St. Petersburg attending the tsar of Russia's coronation, he was returned for Sutherland, where his mother controlled the nomination.[11]

He criticized Hume for making the grant to the duke of Clarence a 'matter of obloquy in the eyes of a great portion of the distressed' population, 19 Feb. 1827. He divided for Catholic relief, 6 Mar. He presented a petition from Sutherland landholders and inhabitants against revision of the corn laws, 3 Apr.[12] Later that month he deliberated as to whether to accept any offer he might receive to serve in Canning's coalition ministry. He explained to Charles Arbuthnot* that he regretted the secession of the duke of Wellington, 'to whose invariable kindness and condescension ... I owe more than I can ever repay', and other anti-Catholic ministers, but felt that 'with my general political principles and decided ... opinions on the Catholic question, I do not see how I can act otherwise than support the new government, though it contains no friend of mine'. If there was one minister 'to whom I should wish to attach myself and whose motions I should be inclined to watch as a guide ... to my own', that was Frederick Robinson*, whom he knew to be 'well inclined' towards him. He thought it unlikely that he would be offered anything more than a lordship of the treasury and was 'very doubtful whether that would answer my purpose, which is ... to obtain practice and information ... not salary'. Wellington, on being directly approached, advised him not to allow personal considerations to influence a decision affecting his public career. Denison recorded in his diary, 21 Apr., that he and Leveson Gower went together to see Canning, who 'saw him first and offered him a lordship of the treasury, saying that he was the first person but one for whom he wished to provide in his new administration'; this was accepted.[13] In the House, 29 June, he dismissed the charges of corruption made against Lord Charles Somerset†, governor of the Cape of Good Hope, as 'utterly groundless'. Following Canning's death and the appointment of Robinson (now Lord Goderich) as premier, Leveson Gower resigned but pledged his 'zealous support' for the new government. Goderich recognized that 'such a post as ... lord of the treasury must be as irksome to you as it is below your proved ... qualifications', and assured him that 'there is no person whose claims and fitness for efficient office are more cordially acknowledged'. Huskisson, the new colonial secretary, wrote that he hoped soon to be able to tempt him with 'efficient business and full employment' as his under-secretary, once certain other individuals had been provided for. However, his mother, who thought he had 'a wish for employment in the foreign office', regretted his decision and feared that he might 'by this fanciful sort of unsteady way put himself out of ... consideration'.[14] On the formation of Wellington's administration in January 1828 Leveson Gower was offered the colonial under-secretaryship, at Huskisson's request, but he initially declined it owing to objections from his father, who was politically hostile to the duke. To Arbuthnot, he expressed exasperation with his position, which obliged him 'whenever ... difference occurs ... to give up my own opinion without discussion or defence, both of which in the state of my father's health are impossible'; he had therefore 'requested my father to find a successor for my seat' and intended to 'retire from public life'. In the event his brother, Lord Gower, at ministerial behest, persuaded Lord Stafford to relent, and Leveson Gower was allowed to join a government which, as he told Huskisson, 'rather comes up to my notion of the greatest perfection attainable'. He believed that 'as long as ... Wellington and yourself can honourably act together, no form of government could be deemed so well calculated to carry this country through its difficulties'.[15] He of course divided against repeal of the Test Acts, 26 Feb., but said that 'if the question between repeal or suspension came to a vote, he would undoubtedly vote for repeal', 28 Feb. He introduced the passenger regulation bill, which applied to merchant ships, 6 Mar.; it gained royal assent, 23 May. He explained, 24 Mar., that while he was 'opposed ... generally ... to questions of parliamentary reform', he believed a case had been 'fully and substantially made out' for disfranchising Penryn, which should serve as 'an example and warning to ... others'. He declared that 'equal rights, producing equal interests, are the bond of our connection and form, at once, the safeguard and glory of our state', 8 May, and concluded that 'every consideration ... of safety as well as of expediency' pointed towards Catholic relief. The power of 'the printing press' afforded 'the best security against the revival and general prevalence of bigotry and superstition', and he doubted whether 'the absurd tenets' of the Catholic faith could 'bear the light of discussion and investigation'. He voted for relief, 12 May. Lord Seaford reported that on the night of the debate on the East Retford disfranchisement bill, 19 May, Leveson Gower had 'told Huskisson ... he should have a quarrel with his father if he voted with Peel', and been advised to 'leave the House before the division'. It was therefore assumed that he would resign if the other Canningite ministers went out. He attempted to act as a peacemaker, sending Wellington a lengthy statement of Huskisson's intentions in offering to resign, but without effect. He adhered to office when Huskisson and his friends departed, assuring the duke of his 'readiness to give your government any assistance in my power, as long as ... the changes which it is to undergo and its subsequent measures authorize me to do so', but he was subsequently obliged to resign at his father's insistence. He wrote to James Loch* that 'the world I know will accuse me of the despicable course of endeavouring to keep well with both parties and of watching my opportunity of joining either', but 'the fact is I am deliberately renouncing all claim upon both'.[16] However, the following month he was allowed to accept the Irish chief secretaryship, a volte face which the cabinet minister Lord Ellenborough attributed to family 'ambition'. Harriet Arbuthnot recorded that he was 'in the third heaven with delight'. Lord Anglesey, the lord lieutenant, had tried to resist the appointment, arguing that he needed 'some steady and experienced person on whom I can place implicit reliance', but Wellington pressed it. To the Whig Lord Holland, Anglesey confided that Leveson Gower was 'certainly not a man after my heart', explaining that 'he is cold, reserved, distant'. Nevertheless, the receipt of a 'very modest yet very manly and satisfactory letter' from him raised Anglesey's hopes that 'everything will go on smoothly'.[17] Among the Canningites, bemusement and disgust was expressed at his 'undecided' and 'ignoble' conduct in resigning his place then 'being [un]able to resist the offer of a better one'.[18]

In July 1828 Leveson Gower warned Peel, the home secretary, that if next session the opposition moved a 'temperately and judiciously worded' address for early consideration of Catholic claims, it was 'at least possible that I might be called upon to support it'.[19] He wrote to Loch that he hoped 'the interest of all parties will concur in keeping Ireland from boiling over during the recess' and that he would 'esteem myself very fortunate if I can contribute anything to keeping it in that gentle simmer which is the utmost we can expect from such a cauldron'. He anticipated a 'harder task with the Protestants than the [Catholic] Association', as 'some of the latter I know are well inclined to me individually'. For the rest, 'I must trust to my cook and my cellar'.[20] On visiting Ireland that summer he reported to Wellington his favourable impression of the Irish solicitor-general, John Doherty*, and his admiration for Anglesey's 'ways of business', but observed that the lord lieutenancy 'exposes a man more perhaps than any other [post] to ... political mistakes which arise from want of official experience', and urged the duke to maintain an 'unreserved communication' with Anglesey in order to 'prevent any ... misunderstanding'. He added that 'I find the business here very constant, and it is necessary to pay very unrelaxing attention to it, but I leave no arrears and get through it, I hope well, at least somehow'.[21] Lord Palmerston*, who visited Dublin that autumn, noted that Leveson Gower 'appeared well pleased with his duties and relaxes his coldness and reserve as much as the most vigorous efforts to conquer nature can enable him to do'. However, Palmerston also learned that 'Anglesey and F. Gower do not quite harmonize', because 'the former wants to act without check or control, and the latter considers himself as more immediately in the confidence of the duke'.[22] Despite a proclamation in October banning political meetings, which Leveson Gower believed would have a beneficial effect, as 'the check ... given to Catholic violence will cause Protestant exasperation to subside', Wellington remained dissatisfied with what he regarded as the inaction of the Irish administration. Early in November he complained to Peel that Anglesey and Leveson Gower were increasing his difficulties with the king 'by their unwillingness to carry into execution the measures necessary to ... preserve the peace of the country, by the partiality to everything that is connected with opposition to the government, and by the company which they keep and the society in which they live in Ireland'. Later that month, Leveson Gower wrote to assure the duke that there was 'no systematic reluctance' on Anglesey's part to 'act with decision against the agitators of this country'.[23] Nevertheless, when Anglesey's indiscreet letter to the archbishop of Armagh regarding Catholic emancipation led to his recall at the end of the year, Leveson Gower made clear his disapproval of his chief's action and acceded to Wellington's request that he should remain in office, observing that 'I have seen nothing in the conduct of government ... which is not perfectly consistent with your present expressions as to the system of government which ought to be pursued in Ireland'.[24] Whig opinion was unanimous in condemning his 'shabby' and 'disgraceful' behaviour.[25] He responded with 'interest and satisfaction' to Peel's confidential communication, 17 Jan. 1829, that the king had consented to allow ministers to consider Catholic emancipation.[26] He defended the suppression of the Catholic Association as an essential 'preliminary' step, 6 Feb., describing it as 'the very *elixir vitae* of Ireland', an 'act of justice ... granting to the Protestant population ... that protection and security' to which they were entitled. He praised Wellington and Peel as 'the saviours of their country and the regenerators of Ireland', 12 Feb. He attended the cabinet meeting which considered the emancipation bill, 1 Mar., but 'said nothing'.[27] He viewed with 'suspicion and distrust' calls for more time to consider the issue, 9 Mar., and observed that those who wanted to force a dissolution seemed to 'prefer consulting with those ... [who were] incapable of drawing the most simple deduction' from history. He was pleased by reports that the Irish Catholics were displaying none of the 'insolence of triumph', 13 Mar., claimed that a hostile petition from Irish Protestants had been got up by the Brunswick clubs, 17 Mar., and opposed Moore's amendment to exclude Catholics from being colonial governors, 24 Mar. He attended a meeting of ministers at Peel's house which agreed to set the Irish county franchise at £10, 17 Feb., and was present at cabinet, 9 Mar., when he warned that 'the franchise bill may lose all the support which has been promised it, if the writs are to be suspended till the new registry is completed'. He noted with satisfaction, 23 Mar., that 'our large majorities' on the bill were 'useful'.[28] He guided several pieces of Irish legislation through the House that session. He accepted Spring Rice's request for a select committee on the Irish estimates, 4 Apr., and moved its appointment, 9 Apr., when he explained that the grants for Maynooth College, the Kildare Place Society and the Society for Discountenancing Vice were being postponed for further consideration, owing to their controversial nature. He hoped the House would 'leave the government unfettered' as to its course on education grants in the next session, 22 May, and denied having pledged himself to support the resolutions of last session's select committee on the subject (of which he had been a member), although he had 'felt very favourable' to them at the time. He defended the grant for the Royal Canal Company of Ireland, even if it was 'perhaps ... erroneous in point of law', 7 Apr. In response to a petition criticizing the mode of appointing sub-sheriffs, 14 Apr., he stated that government was not prepared with further measures to improve the law and suggested that 'much more good may be confidently expected ... from the improvement in the general state of society now going on in Ireland'. He moved the previous question against Villiers Stuart's motion for the introduction of an Irish poor law, 7 May, as more information was required and it would be 'inconvenient' if the House pledged itself; the motion was withdrawn. He advised Wellington, 15 May, that the Irish Army Act, which was about to expire, was 'defective and useless', but there was insufficient time to carry an amending bill that session and the Act should be renewed for one year; this was the course taken.[29] He observed to the Irish attorney-general Henry Joy, 22 May, that the recent Commons debate on Scottish judges' salaries 'proves ... how little chance we should have had of carrying through a measure this session for either Irish judges or assistant barristers'.[30] Early in July he sent from Dublin a favourable report to Wellington about the effects of emancipation, which had 'separated the Catholic gentry to a man from the seditious faction'. He also thought the Court of the lord lieutenant, the duke of Northumberland, was 'doing very well', observing that 'it is impossible that the duchess should not become very popular and the household appears to me to be on a very eligible footing'. On the other hand, the cabinet was informed a few days later that he 'despairs' of settling the poor law and education questions.[31] Later that month he wrote to Wellington to refute rumours of his wish to resign, explaining that while 'I depend less than many people on politics for excitement or amusement', he would feel 'disgraced in shrinking' from his present office if his services were required. He professed satisfaction with the position he had achieved in the Commons, where 'the peculiar course which the last session took afforded me no fair opportunity of showing that I was competent to my duties'. He also believed that 'if people do not avail themselves of the accidental advantages of birth and station to interfere in the affairs of the country, they run the risk of losing these advantages by a revolution'. Wellington, who wanted to keep him, suspected that he was 'tired of his office'. Northumberland testified at this time to his 'unlimited confidence in the zeal and talents' of his chief secretary.[32] However, during the summer and autumn there were signs of doubt among senior ministers as to his capacity and judgement. His proposal to disband the yeomanry alarmed Wellington, who wrote a firm letter reminding him that this was the only loyal force available in Ireland. The duke complained about his extensive autumn tour of the south and west of the country, telling Mrs. Arbuthnot that 'Lord Francis is doing us great mischief' by 'going only to the most Catholic and liberal houses, which excites great indignation'. He also told Peel that he regretted to find Leveson Gower 'a little in dread of [Daniel] O'Connell*', remarking that 'I cannot bear to see a young man afraid of anybody or anything, he should work to render himself a match for him'. On being shown some of Leveson Gower's letters to Peel, Ellenborough noted that they were 'in an odd style, rather affected occasionally, and his ideas are almost always such as to require to be overruled'. Ellenborough concluded that 'he is a forward boy; but I see nothing of the statesman in him'. A little later, Ellenborough added that 'he has as yet proposed *nothing* worthy of adoption' and had often been saved from 'errors' by Peel's advice, as in the case of his plan to appoint stipendiary magistrates in every county, 'the effect of which would have been to disgust all the gentleman magistrates and ... lead them to the abandonment of their duty'.[33] Following a number of murders in Tipperary in October 1829, Leveson Gower observed to Arbuthnot:

> Be the government what it may and its measures what they may, you will have considerable crime among the overcrowded population of this country during the winter. The currency is contracting, prices low and the rent will be hard to raise ... Remember that our crimes are part of a system which has subsisted since the English conquest and cannot be reversed in a day'.[34]

In the debate on Knatchbull's amendment to the address on distress, 4 Feb. 1830, Leveson Gower acknowledged the 'universality of ... distress in Ireland' but denied that it was 'greater ... than it usually is', adding that emancipation had 'saved us from ... contending against moral distress in addition to physical distress'. The Whig Lord Howick* was 'quite sorry to see [him] fail so egregiously'.[35] He acknowledged the 'compliment' of being asked to present the Irish Catholic bishops' petition for measures to educate the Irish poor, 26 Feb., but said he 'could have wished [it] had found its way into other hands'. He 'cordially concurred' in Spring Rice's motion for inquiry into the state of the Irish poor, 11 Mar., but warned against placing additional burdens on landlords and rejected the 'fallacy' that a poor law would stop Irish migration to Britain. He privately hoped that Davenport's motion on the state of the nation would be 'damaged past recovery' by the favourable reception of the budget, 15 Mar. After three nights of debate he reported, 20 Mar., that 'with the exception of Peel and Huskisson [it] has been wretched'.[36] In his own contribution, 23 Mar., he pointed to the payment of rents, the growth of steam navigation and the ready availability of credit to prove that distress in Ireland had not increased relative to the size of its population, and he recommended that 'we should leave Ireland to exert her own mighty energies for her own improvements'. He was confident that 'one of the first great results' of emancipation would be an 'influx of British capital'. He dismissed Sadler's motion for an Irish poor law as a 'mere resolution', which ignored all of the practical difficulties, 3 June, and said he would move the previous question; it was negatived. He introduced the Irish subletting bill, to clarify the existing law, 16 Feb.; it did not get beyond the committee stage. He said he would oppose any motion for immediate reduction of the Irish yeomanry corps, 22 Feb., but did not rule out supporting 'a moderate and temperate proposition for reduction' in future, provided it did not 'endanger the peace of the country'. He introduced the Irish Constabulary Act amendment bill, to transfer from magistrates to the government the power of appointing constables, 30 Mar., and had 'no doubt' that if this had been done in the first place, 'we should have prevented the occurrence of many evils'; it made no further progress. He opposed O'Connell's motion for papers regarding the Cork special commission trials and was a majority teller against it, 12 May. He explained that the Irish arms bill imposed reduced penalties and that he had no objection to renewing it for just one year, 30 June, but the 'weight of responsibility' meant that he could not abandon it altogether; it gained royal assent, 16 July. He promised to give his 'best consideration' to the Galway franchise bill, 4 Mar., as he believed that 'no civil disabilities ought to be allowed to remain on account of religious opinions'. In the debate that day on Newport's Irish church motion he observed that the 'operation of time and events has been most salutary' in bringing about the removal of abuses, and he proposed an amended motion for inquiry by a royal commission in order to 'judge more accurately ... the real state of the church'; this was agreed. He reported afterwards that 'we got satisfactorily out of Newport's motion ... by granting him his commission and refusing his other demands', and added that 'the debate was languid and innoxious'.[37] He successfully resisted O'Connell's Irish vestries regulation bill, to introduce a ratepayer franchise, 27 Apr., observing that the existing law 'rather admits than urgently requires amendment' and that it was not 'a case of remarkable failure and grievance'. He felt that 'the tone of feeling in Ireland' on this subject made it undesirable to act 'at ... present'. He reserved judgement on O'Connell's Catholic marriages bill, 4 May. He opposed Newport's resolutions on Irish first fruits, 18 May, as he was not prepared to concede that the church was 'established for the benefit of the clergy and not for that of the country', and declared that 'burdened as it is with the crimes, errors and follies of preceding generations', the church 'may yet be considered in a state of probation'. He moved the previous question, which was carried by 94-69. He resisted O'Connell's parish vestries bill, 10 June, on the ground that 'if an established church is to be maintained ... the existing law must be upheld', but he indicated that the government would legislate on the matter in the next session; he was a majority teller. In moving the second reading of the Irish deserted children bill, 26 Apr., he stated that the question of provision for illegitimate children had been omitted; it did not get beyond the committee stage. That day he advised Wellington that the proceedings in a Commons committee against Sir Jonah Barrington, judge in the Irish admiralty court, for alleged defalcation was too advanced to be stopped, and that such action would cause more embarrassment than any disclosures Barrington might make about the Act of Union.[38] He carried resolutions declaring that Barrington was guilty and unfit to hold office, 6 May, and a motion for an address to the king to remove him, 22 May. He deplored Hume's motion for inquiry into the lord lieutenancy so soon after emancipation, 11 May, and denied that the Irish people regarded themselves as subjects of a 'colonial government'; he was a teller for the majority. That day he opposed Lord

Tullamore's motion for inquiry into the grant for the Royal Canal Company and rejected claims that 'jobbery' had been involved. He maintained that the Irish administration no longer exercised control over the press through expenditure on the printing of proclamations, 2 July, and expressed his opinion that it was 'absolutely necessary' to establish an Irish office in London, which should be placed under the home secretary's control. He hoped that the Ellenborough divorce case would prompt 'some amendment of the law', which was 'highly disgraceful and prejudicial to the interests of society', 6 Apr. He defended the policy of neutrality adopted by the government in the incident at Terceira, 28 Apr., and carried the previous question against a hostile motion by 191-78. He reported later that the 'strong division' was attributable to the 'hostility of the Whigs and Brunswickers to Huskisson's party, and to a decided *waiting on providence* on the part of the former, in the present state of the king's health'. He added that 'the question was a pinching one, and I had some reason to regret having undertaken to take part in it, as I made a speech very defective in argument and very disproportioned in all respects to the place I took in the debate'. However, 'my opponents behaved with singular forbearance towards me, which is a proof of the general inclination of the House'.[39] After attending the privy council meeting, 28 June, he was satisfied that William IV's 'confidence ... is cordially and substantially given to the duke' and that rumours of a 'sudden change' in the ministry were 'unfounded'. On 2 July he reported that 'we had a very pleasant night in the ... Commons', with 'Hume and the Mountain assisting us against the Whigs to get through our vote of credit'. He attributed this to the fact that 'Hume with a view to the county of Middlesex is anxious that Parliament should be up as soon as possible'.[40] In late March he had informed Wellington that, from 'considerations purely of a personal and domestic nature', he was ready to leave 'this office' at a convenient time, and in late May it was agreed that he should switch places with the secretary at war, Sir Henry Hardinge*; the change took place in July. Ellenborough thought that 'there cannot be a better thing ... for the government and for Ireland', as Leveson Gower was 'quite unequal to the situation' of chief secretary.[41] At the general election in August 1830 he was returned unopposed for Sutherland.[42]

In September 1830 he intimated to Arbuthnot that he would 'with pleasure resign' if this would help facilitate a reconstruction of the government, although he emphasized that 'he liked his office' and only made the offer so that 'additional strength [might] be obtained'; his sacrifice was not required.[43] Responding to Whig criticism of the absence of any mention of parliamentary reform in the king's speech, 3 Nov., he felt impelled to declare that his own views were 'unchanged ... at present' and that any future change would arise not from 'any jingling of the cabinet key' but from 'sincere and honest conviction that circumstances or events rendered a change necessary'. He expressed 'admiration not unmingled with regret' at the revolution in France, admitting that the French people were 'justified in the resistance ... they made' to a 'bigoted' monarch. He hoped that his successor would reintroduce the Irish subletting bill, 11 Nov. Two days later Sir John Walsh* noted that he 'breathed nothing but war against the incendiaries' responsible for the agricultural disturbances in southern England.[44] He of course voted in the government minority in the crucial civil list division, 15 Nov., and resigned with his colleagues. He supported the Grey ministry's motion to adjourn the House as a 'matter of common justice', 23 Dec. 1830, but could not 'pledge myself to support them'. Presenting a county Galway magistrates' petition against reduction of the barilla duties, 17 Feb. 1831, he said that he had advised them not to expect this, but he hoped ministers might find some alternative means of assisting the kelp manufacturers. He saw 'no ground of objection' to the army estimates, 21 Feb. In the debate on the ministerial reform bill, 1 Mar., he spoke 'in defence of the existing institutions of the country' and condemned the 'dangerous delusion' that economic distress was a product of the representative system. He declared that 'this country possesses all that share of liberty which it could possibly wish to possess' and that 'every principle of liberty has been introduced into our constitution, which is consistent with the permanency and stability of our government and the security of the peace and happiness of society'. He maintained that the Scottish representative system was 'much more efficient than is generally supposed' and that under its auspices 'the country has rapidly advanced in prosperity'; he dreaded the reintroduction of religious strife into that country if the clergy again became involved in politics. He also deplored the 'language of dictation ... assumed ... by the advocates of reform' and the 'reiterated display ... of the tricoloured flag', and trusted that the House would not bend to popular pressure. According to Thomas Gladstone*, he 'rose far above what I had any conception of his being capable of ... he was occasionally too poetic, but often extremely eloquent and forcible, and proved himself a decidedly able man'.[45] He divided against the second reading, 22 Mar., when he expressed 'astonishment' that the Irish bill had not been laid before the House and complained that 'the whole measure is the most ... sweeping ... since the revolution of 1688'. He voted for Gascoyne's wrecking amendment, 19 Apr. He warned that a dissolution would be 'pregnant with future evils' in Ireland, where the 'measure of reform is inapplicable', 21 Apr., and said he feared 'for the welfare of the Protestant interests'. He observed that the 'suicidal' English bill 'unites among its advocates the majority of those who wish ill to our best institutions, and who are seeking for the subversion of the monarchy'. His opposition to reform caused a political breach with his family and he did not offer for Sutherland at the general election in May 1831. The Gladstones held him in reserve as a possible second Tory candidate for Liverpool, but nothing came of this.[46]

In November 1831 Leveson Gower cautioned against the plan to form a loyal association in Berkshire, fearing that this would be 'too near a preparation for civil war'.[47] That month his wife, presumably at his instigation, tried to elicit information from Wellington about the progress of the negotiations between ministers and the Tory 'Waverers'. Two months later, Ellenborough listed him as a likely member of a Harrowby-Wharncliffe administration.[48] In fact, he did not return to the Commons until 1835, when he was elected for South Lancashire as a Conservative, and he never held office again, although Peel, on forming his government in 1841, professed to have 'the highest opinion' of him and thought he 'would have filled the office of chancellor of the duchy [of Lancaster] with great eclat'.[49] On his father's death in 1833 a substantial part of the fabulously wealthy estates of his great-uncle, the 3rd duke of Bridgwater, reverted to him, comprising land in Shropshire, Lancashire and Northamptonshire, yielding an annual income of £90,000, and an art collection valued at £150,000; he thereupon assumed the surname of Egerton.[50] He was raised to an earldom in 1846. He continued to pursue his literary interests and remained an active figure in public life. His death in February 1857 prompted a glowing tribute from his brother-in-law, the diarist Charles Greville, who noted:

> He was most estimable in every relation of life, and as such enjoyed universal respect and regard ... He had no taste for the turmoil of political life, and his temper was too serene and his love of repose too great to allow him to plunge deeply into political warfare. His abilities were not of a very high order, but he had a good understanding, a cultivated mind, and an inquisitive disposition ... Though not profound in any branch of literature or science, he loved to wander over the vast fields of knowledge ... His taste was good both in literature and art; he was an elegant poet, and a fair writer of his own tongue ... In political opinions he was the very type and model of a Liberal Conservative, and the statesman to whom he gave all his allegiance ... was ... Wellington ... He was sincerely religious, without intolerance [or] austerity.[51]

He was succeeded by his eldest son, George Egerton (1823-62), Liberal-Conservative Member for North Staffordshire, 1847-51.

[1] *Countess Granville Letters*, i. 19. [2] *Gent. Mag.* (1857), i. 358-9. [3] *Countess Granville Letters*, i. 220, 225; Northants. RO, Agar Ellis diary, 5, 11, 18 May, 28 Nov. 1822. [4] TNA 30/29/8/6/285. [5] Harewood mss WYL 250/8, Leveson Gower to Canning, 28 Oct., Granville to same, 10, 14 Nov. 1822. [6] Nottingham Univ. Lib., Portland mss PwH 128, Lord G. Cavendish Bentinck to Portland, 30 Dec. 1822; Bucks. RO, Fremantle mss D/FR/46/10/46. [7] Dorset RO D/BKL, Bankes jnl. 144 (28 Apr.); Gurney diary, 30 Apr. 1823. [8] Harewood mss 250/8, Canning to wife, 3 Feb.; Agar Ellis diary, 3 Feb. 1825, Buckingham, *Mems. Geo. IV*, ii. 217. [9] *Hobhouse Diary*, 113-14. [10] Nottingham Univ. Lib. Ossington mss OsC 17, Leveson Gower to Denison, 14 Aug. 1825. [11] *Inverness Courier*, 10 May, 5 July 1826. [12] *The Times*, 4 Apr. 1827. [13] *Canning's Ministry*, 148, 183; Wellington mss WP1/887/31; 888/13; Nottingham Univ. Lib. Denison diary, 21 Apr. 1827. [14] Add. 38750, ff. 22, 34, 229, 231, 235, 264, 270; 38751, ff. 71, 84. [15] Add. 38754, ff. 215, 300, 313, 317, 325, 327; Wellington mss WP1/914/35, 37; *Arbuthnot Corresp.* 104. [16] TNA 30/29/9/5/69; Wellington mss WP1/933/4; 934/1, 9, 10; 935/35, 50; NAS GD268/346/1; *Ellenborough Diary*, i. 118-19, 122, 124; A. Aspinall, 'Canningite Party', *TRHS* (ser. 4), xvii. (1934), 224-5. [17] Wellington mss WP1/936/22; 937/25; 939/14; Add. 51567, Anglesey to Holland, 20, 21, 23 June 1828; *Ellenborough Diary*, i. 145-6; *Arbuthnot Jnl.* ii. 193. [18] Agar Ellis diary, 14 June 1828; *Palmerston-Sulivan Letters*, 202; Add. 38757, f. 91. [19] Parker, *Peel*, ii. 52-53. [20] NAS GD268/240/16. [21] Wellington mss WP1/948/28; 952/20. [22] *Palmerston-Sulivan Letters*, 216-17. [23] Wellington mss WP1/953/3; 959/5; 960/6; 961/12; 967/20; Parker, ii. 73-4. [24] Wellington mss WP1/973/26; 975/30; 988/1; *Arbuthnot Corresp.* 115; *Colchester Diary*, iii. 589, 593-4. [25] Add. 51574, Abercromby to Holland, 4 Jan.; 51599B, Lady Cowper to same, 28 Jan.; Agar Ellis diary, 6 Jan. 1829. [26] Parker, ii. 82-4. [27] *Ellenborough Diary*, i. 370. [28] Ibid. i. 348-9, 385; NAI, Leveson Gower letterbks. M. 736, Leveson Gower to Singleton, 23 Mar. 1829. [29] Wellington mss WP1/1018/2. [30] Leveson Gower letterbks. M. 736, Leveson Gower to Joy, 22 May 1829. [31] Wellington mss WP1/1030/16; *Ellenborough Diary*, ii. 68. [32] Wellington mss WP1/1032/13, 17; 1035/65; 1037/11. [33] Ibid. WP1/1040/4; 1048/1; 1054/64; *Arbuthnot Jnl.* ii. 301, 308; *Ellenborough Diary*, ii. 79-80, 134-5, 160. [34] *Arbuthnot Corresp.* 126. [35] Grey mss, Howick jnl., 4 Feb. 1830. [36] Leveson Gower letterbks. Leveson Gower to Singleton, 16, 20 Mar. 1830. [37] Ibid. same to same, 5 Mar. 1830. [38] Wellington mss WP1/1109/16. [39] Leveson Gower letterbks. Leveson Gower to Singleton, 29 Apr. 1830. [40] Ibid. M. 738, same to same, 29 June, 3 July 1830. [41] Wellington mss WP1/1103/16; 1114/19; *Ellenborough Diary*, ii. 260. [42] *Inverness Courier*, 18 Aug. 1830. [43] Add. 40340, f. 230. [44] NLW, Ormathwaite mss FG/1/5, p. 132. [45] St. Deiniol's Lib. Glynne Gladstone mss 197, T. to J. Gladstone, 2 Mar. 1831. [46] Staffs. RO, Sutherland mss D593/K/1/5/27, Loch to Gunn, 16 Mar.; Brougham mss, Shepherd to Brougham, 2 May 1831. [47] Ormathwaite mss FG/1/5, p. 223. [48] Wellington mss WP1/1200/1; 1203/19; *Three Diaries*, 177. [49] *Arbuthnot Corresp.* 226. [50] *CP*, v. 54-55; his father's will was proved under £350,000 (PROB 11/1823/659; IR26/1337/571). [51] *Greville Mems.* vii. 269-72.

T.A.J.

LEWIS, **Thomas Frankland** (1780–1855), of Harpton Court, Rad.

Beaumaris	1812–1826
Ennis	1826–Apr. 1828
Radnorshire	9 Apr. 1828–1834
New Radnor Boroughs	1847–22 Jan. 1855

b. 14 May 1780, o.s. of John Lewis† of Harpton Court and 2nd w. Anne, da. of Adm. Sir Thomas Frankland†, 5th bt., of Thirkleby, Yorks. *educ.* Croydon 1788-92; Eton 1792-8; Christ Church, Oxf. 1798. *m.* (1) 12 Jan. 1805, Harriet (*d.* 11 Aug. 1838), da. of Sir George Cornewall†, 2nd bt., of Moccas Court, Herefs., 2s.; (2) 15 Oct. 1839, Mary Anne, da. of John Ashton, capt. Horse Gds., *s.p. suc.* fa. 1797; mother 1841; *cr.* bt. 11 July 1846. *d.* 22 Jan. 1855.

Commr. revenue [I] 1821, [UK] 1822-4, education [I] 1824-8; sec. to treasury Sept. 1827-Feb. 1828; vice-pres. bd. of trade Feb.-May 1828; PC 5 Feb. 1828; treas. of navy Feb.-Nov. 1830; chairman, poor law commission 1834-9; charity commr. 1835-7; roads commr. 1839, commr. S. Wales turnpikes ('Rebecca' riots in Wales) 1843-4.

Sheriff, Rad. 1804-5; recorder, New Radnor 1819.

Maj. Rad. vols. 1803, lt.-col. 1803-5, (militia) 1808.

Lewis, whose father and grandfather had represented New Radnor Boroughs, aimed to re-establish his family's political supremacy in Radnorshire, where enclosures and crown land sales enabled him to increase his holdings.[1] After early unsuccessful forays there, in 1812 he had been promised support in the county at the next vacancy by Richard Price*, provided he refrained from opposing him in New Radnor Boroughs. He accordingly arranged to sit for Beaumaris, which he represented until 1826 on the interest of its patron, the 7th Viscount Bulkeley, a Grenvillite peer. In the Commons he had generally acted with the third party, led by Lord Grenville's nephew Charles Watkin Williams Wynn, but, like Bulkeley's half-brother Sir Robert Williams*, he had preferred to sit with the Whig opposition in the 1818 Parliament.[2] He had a reputation as a frequent debater, useful parliamentary spokesman and consummate and ambitious man of business attracted to political economy.[3] He sat on the 1817 and 1819 finance committees, and had been accorded the sobriquet 'Louis le Devisant' ['Lewis the Currency'] on account of his strong support for the resumption of cash payments in 1819.[4] He habitually devoted time to legislation on canals and turnpikes, in which he had a vested interest, and had drafted several select committee reports, including those on the assize of bread (1815) and poverty (1817), which he wrote with William Sturges Bourne*.[5] Being outspoken and pro-Catholic, his great ambition to become Irish secretary had eluded him, despite his wife's close family connection with the premier Lord Liverpool.[6] Addressing Beaumaris corporation at his election in 1820, he delivered an hour-long critique of Robert Owen of New Lanark's plan for the poor, in which he lauded the advantages of the Scottish over the English relief system.[7]

Lewis was included on select committees on issues associated with poverty, including the employment of agricultural labourers, vagrancy and emigration, as a matter of course throughout the 1820s. On questions of trade and finance he shared Grenville's tendency to strict economic liberalism, and generally aligned with Canning, John Herries, William Huskisson and Thomas Wallace I. He intervened briefly 'in the interests of trade and navigation' to support the call for government action over London Bridge, 4 May 1820, and advocated concessions for the Baltic trade under the 1821 Timber Act, 5 Apr., and deregulation of the colonial woollen trade, 14 June 1821. He was appointed to the select committees on foreign trade, 1821-4, and on the combination laws and protective legislation prohibiting tools and machinery exports, 1824-5. He believed that the agriculture committee conceded to Holme Sumner, to which he was appointed, 31 May, was unlikely to realize the expectations of the petitioners complaining of distress, and had said so when justifying his opposition to its establishment, 30 May 1820. He shared Holme Sumner's commitment to extended inquiry and improved means of regulating the corn laws, but he recommended a duty of 20*s.* a quarter on corn, when Holme Sumner proposed 40*s.*, and warned that protection and overregulation of the currency would themselves induce distress and higher taxes.

He presented the Berkshire freeholders' petition for shorter polls, 19 June, and chaired the investigative committee, 29 June, 3, 4 July 1820, bringing up its report, 13 July.[8] As previously, he divided against parliamentary reform, 9 May 1821, 25 June 1822, 22 Feb. 1823, and for Catholic relief, 28 Feb. 1821, 1 Mar., 21 Apr., 10 May 1825. He did not speak on the Queen Caroline case, which exposed differences among the Grenvillites, but he divided against the opposition motion censuring her treatment by ministers, 6 Feb. 1821. Reinforcing Huskisson's arguments against the Hull poor rates bill, 20 Feb. 1821, he declared that its proposal to make the port chargeable confirmed 'the acknowledged tendency of the poor laws to swallow up all the property in the kingdom'. He added that he 'did not mean to throw out the wild notion that the system could be entirely got rid of'; the subject was one to be 'touched with gentleness', but 'one great misfortune in the system of poor rates was that it wore the appearance of humanity whilst it produced real hardship and severity'. He was against including Irish corn averages in those for the United Kingdom, because of their inferior grain, 26 Feb. 1821. The following day, when certain London merchants petitioned against renewal of the West India Dock Company's charter, he referred to the frequent abuse of loopholes in commercial legislation and called for it to be subjected to better parliamentary scrutiny. His speech on bank cash payments, 19 Mar., which according to *The Times* was 'for some time inaudible in the gallery', stressed the crippling effect of forged pound notes on the poor, who were least able to detect them or sustain losses. It also set out the advantages of increasing the circulating coinage and taking steps to prevent bullion exports destabilizing currencies.[9] He spoke similarly when endorsing the Irish Bank cash payments bill, 11 Apr., and suggested that Irish, like Scottish banking legislation, should set 'no limit to the number of partners'. He paired against making forgery a non-capital offence, 23 May. He was 'particularly averse' to the malt duty repeal bill, promoted by the Whig opposition, and claimed that reducing the tax would 'necessarily affect the sinking fund ... and shake the security of the country', without affording 'relief to the extent of one farthing in the pot of porter', 3 Apr. He was a majority teller for Tennyson's gamekeepers bill, 15 May. Speaking on the vagrancy laws amendment bill, 24 May, he defended the laws of settlement and conceded the difficulty of dealing with part of the poor law system without considering the whole. Commenting later that day on Scarlett's poor relief bill, he reiterated his belief that

> the meaning of the statute [of 1601] ... was to inflict compulsory labour by way of punishment, not to afford labour for the mere purpose of maintenance. It was anything but in the nature of giving the poor personal property.

He agreed with the bill's 'great objects', but joined Calcraft in pressing for its deferral, 20 June, arguing, in what Williams Wynn described as 'an extremely good speech',[10] evocative of the 1817 report, that the 'present system would in time destroy the foundations of our national prosperity'. He did not see the remedy in new enactments, but in a strict examination of the law as it now stood and an understanding of how it had been perceived formerly and what it ought to provide in future. On 15 June Lewis was appointed to the Irish revenue commission, a salaried post which he accepted after first consulting Grenville. The radical Joseph Hume alleged in the House that day that the appointment was a bribe held out by government for Grenvillite support, but Calcraft extolled Lewis's abilities and independence, and an amendment blocking his appointment was defeated by 81-23. As a placeman he aligned with the liberal Tories in government and divided steadily with them. On 2 July 1821, as a member (since 20 June) of the select committee on the extra post bill, he defended the decision not to bring up their report.[11] He gave Bulkeley £100 for the Beaumaris corporation improvement fund in December 1821.[12]

Lewis's overture to Lord Londonderry* when the Grenvillites went over to government in January 1822 brought no definite promise of office, but he congratulated Peel on his appointment as home secretary and sought Lord Harrowby's patronage for a cousin.[13] Like Williams Wynn, now president of the India board, on 22 Feb. he voted against reducing the additional duties on salt, which he had previously advocated. When Wiltshire petitioned for government action to combat agricultural distress, 3 Apr., he defended the purely investigative role of the agriculture committee (to which he had been reappointed, 18 Feb.), and announced that it 'did not seek to increase restrictions on foreign corn imports'. He presented Beaumaris's petition for repeal of the leather tax, 1 May. The revenue commission 'proceeded upon the principle of removing if possible every remaining distinction between the revenue regulators of Ireland' and the United Kingdom, a policy that Lewis defended when the Irish calico printers petitioned, 15 May.[14] He was appointed to the select committee on the Irish linen trade, 18 May, which the commission, whose powers were extended to England and Scotland, 24 June, also investigated.[15] He spoke and voted in Canning's minority of 21 for allowing warehoused foreign corn to be ground for flour and exported, 10 June 1822.

Having chaired and drafted the report of the 1820 select committee on turnpikes and highways,[16] and been instrumental in placing those of the metropolis and Scotland under scrutiny, Lewis was granted leave on 11 Feb. 1823 to bring in a consolidating bill for England and Wales, but it made little headway that session.[17] Supporting the introduction of an *ad valorem* duty on beer, he pointed out that quality could be ascertained accurately with a saccharometer and duties apportioned accordingly, 24 Mar. He endorsed the St. Marylebone petition against the coal duties, which he steadfastly opposed, 27 Mar. He gave noncommittal replies to questions on the Irish linen bounty, 25, 29 Apr. He voted against inquiry into the currency, 12 June, and to receive the report on the usury laws repeal bill, 27 June 1823, and supported similar measures, 27 Feb., 8 Apr. 1824. When he and his wife visited Beaumaris on their way from Ireland in December 1823, he contributed £400 to the corporation's funds.[18] Control of the constituency, which the Grenvillite duke of Buckingham still hoped to use to 'enlarge *our* phalanx', had passed to Bulkeley's widow, who made it known that Lewis's return 'depended on the footing on which ... [he] stood.'[19]

He was one of several supporters of Catholic relief to vote against Newport's motion on Catholic burials, 6 Feb. 1824.[20] Deputizing for the master of the mint, he succeeded in deferring a motion on the feasibility of switching to a decimal currency, 16 Feb.[21] He spoke against Hume's abortive amendment on the sugar duties, 8 Mar., and ordered an account of British exports to France under the Commercial Trade Acts, 12 Mar.[22] He was named to the committee on the assize of bread, to which his 1815 report had been referred, 22 Mar.[23] He was busy steering the troubled Radnor and Hereford roads bill through the Commons, when Cripps, by proposing a general turnpike bill, made him concede that his own measure was delayed because of the 'complexity' of the task; this Peel confirmed, 25 Mar.[24] Later that day, possibly to safeguard his Radnorshire interests, he tried to alter the game laws amendment bill to ensure that certain tenants of manorial lords 'legally qualified to kill game' did not lose that right. He summarily dismissed petitioners' grievances against the beer bill, 17 May, and again advocated fiscal changes to end tariff differences between Ireland and the United Kingdom, 26, 27 May.[25] He voted against condemning the indictment in Demerara of the Methodist missionary John Smith for encouraging slaves to riot, 11 June. His appointment to the Irish education commission on Peel's recommendation, 14 June, brought his revenue commission work to a close, and meetings with Dr. Patrick Curtis, the Catholic archbishop of Armagh, and archbishop John Magee of Dublin took up much of his time during the recess.[26] In December 1824 Lady Bulkeley confirmed that Beaumaris would be available to him at the next election, their intermediary Richard Neville* having assured her that Lewis did 'not object to the terms of £8,020, by £500 [£500 annually] with all election expenses and annual dinners paid'.[27]

In January 1825 Williams Wynn received and circulated 'a long, most interesting and satisfactory letter from Frankland Lewis on his recent visit to Ireland, which I thought showed so much observation and good sense that I sent it down to Bath to Lord Liverpool'. The Grenvilles remained personally and politically committed to doing all they could to bring about Lewis's appointment as Irish secretary, and, commending him to Buckingham, Wynn wrote:

> He mentions that he has been himself in 22 counties, and that with his colleagues, he may say that they have really been in every corner of Ireland, and that they all agree in the opinion that there is no ground for immediate alarm and that the Catholics are too well aware of the advantage which they enjoy from Lord Wellesley's government to hazard his recall and the revival of the high Orange system, which would be the probable effect of any insurrection.[28]

Grenville acknowledged the value of such 'local information, which I have not, and which is so necessary for a right judgement', when assessing policy on the Catholic Association.[29] Lewis's testimony in February before the Lords select committee on the state of Ireland was highly praised.[30] He agreed with the petitioner, John Kirby of Kerry, that the catechizing practices of Catholic priests in Irish schools were deplorable, 1 May, but defended the government's policy of non-interference while the education commission had the matter in hand. Replying to Peel, 15 Feb., he made it clear that he could not bring in consolidating legislation on turnpikes that session and suggested that until he could do so, the matter should be referred to the select committee on the metropolitan trusts proposed by Lord Lowther, to which he was named, 17 Feb.[31] He presented the Belfast cotton traders' petition against the coal duties, 25 Mar.[32] When London petitioned for a fixed duty on corn, 25 Apr., and Huskisson intimated that government might introduce corrective legislation next session, he announced that he now regretted his vote for the 1815 law, 'being convinced that the alteration between a free importation on the one hand, and the entire exclusion of corn on the other, was a most injudicious and erroneous regulation'. To forestall a private bill, he warned that it 'could only be safely and satisfactorily treated by the united consideration of the government and legislature'. He pointedly 'disclaimed all concurrence in' the Aberdeen whalers' petition for protection and the oil-gas bill, with which he had previously been associated, 6 May.[33] His report from the education commission criticized the proselytizing tendencies of Irish charter schools, but he cautioned against using it to justify postponing their funding, 30 May, and strongly opposed Newport's motion for an address to the king regretting the commission's findings, 9 June.[34] He had to delay his departure for Ireland with the commission in September 1825 because of family illness and begged his colleagues 'to proceed without me from Dublin to Belfast in the hope that I may be able to join them there or at all events to meet them at their return'.[35]

Newport's motion for accounts of the previous session's grants for Irish education, 7 Mar. 1826, brought an admission from Goulburn that government policy was undecided, and Lewis now promised that all the commission's reports except that on Maynooth College would be presented in time. He was against confining Spring Rice's local jurisdiction bill to Ireland, 9 Mar., and, explaining that Radnorshire was similarly short of suitable magistrates, he suggested that the shortfall could be remedied by using crown appointees, provided 'chartered and corporation rights' were also honoured. He defended the commission and the Kildare Place Society when the Irish estimates were voted, and saw off attempts to reduce their funding and transfer administration to the lord lieutenant in Dublin, 20, 22 Mar. As teller for the government majority on the corn importation bill, 8 May, he stressed his reliance on 'income from the land' and refuted charges that the measure had been hurriedly adopted and would harm the landed interest. 'Gold', he added, 'it was true, must go out for corn; but as we have no gold for that purpose in this country, we must send goods abroad in order to purchase it'. He opposed the abortive freeholders in districts bill, 2 May, and Russell's resolutions denouncing electoral bribery, 26 May 1826. Lady Bulkeley's death on 3 Feb. had left him searching for a safe seat at the impending general election. He started canvassing Radnorshire, but soon realized that his interests would be better served if he adopted a higher local profile and refrained from challenging the ailing and elderly Walter Wilkins, so he went to Ireland to be returned for Ennis on the O'Brien interest.[36] Before Parliament met he attended to patronage matters and education commission business.[37]

On 3 Feb. 1827 he warned Peel that the education commission would submit two reports and enclosed that adopted and 'signed only by Grant, Blake and myself – Foster and Gladstone having declined to put their names to it'. He attributed their differences

> to *animism*. We could not agree either as to the extent to which it is promoted or disseminated by the [Belfast] Institution ... [or on] the arrangements which were necessary to guard against it. I kept back the report as long as I could in the hopes of our agreeing, but finding it was not likely to take place, I have taken the only step which was open to us.[38]

He endorsed the Irish bishops' petition, expressed continued support for Catholic relief, 2 Mar., and divided for it, 6 Mar. When he represented the Canningite John Gladstone on the Berwick-upon-Tweed election committee which voided his election, 19 Mar., his opponent Lord Howick repeatedly complained to his father Earl Grey that Lewis's 'experience in the House and plausible manner give him great influence over the other members of the committee'.[39] Grey agreed that Howick 'could not have had a more dangerous adversary. I know him well. He is one of those smooth tongued flammable fellows, who, making the greatest professions of candour, are ready for any roguery'.[40] On 2 Apr. Lewis urged Robert Grant to withdraw the petition against the return of George Spence for Reading.[41] In committee on the Corn Trade Acts, 19 Mar., he spoke of the scarcity of 1801 and called for a system which would work equally well at times of dearth and plenty, warning that if Parliament left the public exposed to combinations of capitalists (corn factors and millers), 'they would have occasion to rue it'. He reaffirmed the need for a select committee and legislation to amend and consolidate the General Turnpike Act, pointing out that commissioners of roads could levy over £1,500,000 annually in tax, 27 Mar. His consolidating bill was referred to a select committee appointed by the Canning ministry, 16 May, and enacted.[42] He cautioned against accepting the Lords' amendments to the spring guns bill, 17 May. Though unsuccessful, Newport's attempt to have the education commission's reports referred to a select committee, 5 Apr., put pressure on Lewis to explain their delayed production. He made no comment on the differences between them, and referred instead to the reductions in expenditure which his majority report recommended. He later (25 May) tried to allay fears about the Maynooth grant, and used statistics to confirm the findings of the Irish revenue commission presented by Spencer Perceval, 18 June.[43] As a speaker for the Canning ministry's warehoused corn bill that day, he referred to the 'appalling position in which the country was placed' by the failure of the Liverpool ministry's measure.[44] Many, including the patronage secretary Planta, had wished to see Lewis '*fly aloft*' when Canning formed his ministry. He had again been passed over for the Irish secretaryship and, with his work on the education commission almost over, he wrote to Canning, 25 June, pledging support and seeking further employment.[45] Promising to recall him 'when I can', Canning claimed to be

> glad you have made the enquiry; because while I rather wished that you should be apprized of the existence of the disposition towards you which I have here declared, I felt that in the absence of all power on my part to specify

> the *when* or the *how*, the time or place of the probable occurrence of such an opportunity, the *gratuitous* expression of such a disposition might have appeared but a cheap and barren compliment.[46]

'At the desire of Lord G[oderich]', and briefed by Williams Wynn, Lewis remained in London during the ministerial negotiations which followed Canning's death in August 1827. He was nervous lest he should be offered the treasury secretaryship under Herries, and informed his wife, 20 Aug., that he considered bringing

> my political matters to a crisis, and having it distinctly understood that either I must now know what I have to depend upon, or at once retire. To go into the House of Commons to support Herries and Tom Courtenay as finance ministers (and if Huskisson was ill they would be effectively managers of the business) would be too degrading, and I for one have no wish to undergo it. I intend to see Planta today and I will endeavour to explain myself fully to him; and I will also try to see Lord Lansdowne, to spirit him up if I can, to put his wits upon Herries. All this is very disagreeable. I will write again in the course of the day if any thing occurs.

He also had doubts about accepting a place on the India board 'that by the good will of Lord Goderich and of Charles Wynn I presume I might fill', although 'several of my friends have told me I ought not to refuse it, as it is more easy to be promoted with an office in hand than without, and that it is in all respects on a par with the other secretaryships'.[47] John Fazakerley*, who would have preferred to see Lewis at the board of trade, viewed his appointment as treasury secretary in the Goderich ministry as a necessary step in the perpetuation of the Canningite system.[48] He accepted it and was duly congratulated by the Grenvilles and Lord Lansdowne, with whom, according to Lord Lowther*, 'if he has any connection ... I am sure it must have been these six weeks'. Lowther added:

> I have by chance been thrown into business with him three or four time in committees of the House of Commons, etc., etc., and after Huskisson and Herries I should esteem him as the best man of business amongst all the Commons and far superior to many holding places in the cabinet, [such] as Palmerston, Wynn, C. Grant. However, time will show, and in my opinion I think he will be soon thought qualified to hold a higher situation.[49]

Lady Williams Wynn saw the appointment, with its income of £3,000-£4,000 a year, as one of several gains for 'the House of Cornewall ... the only people who have profited in the late storms'.[50] Noting the Tory ascendancy, Grey observed: 'Will they quote as a set off the appointment of [the pro-Catholic] Frankland Lewis, whom it would have surprised one a good deal some time ago to hear described as a Whig'.[51] By November 1827, he was said to be first in line for the next privy council vacancy.[52]

Lewis made way for George Dawson at the treasury when the duke of Wellington formed his coalition ministry in January 1828.[53] Now ready to be 'ruled' by Huskisson, he was made a privy councillor and appointed vice-president of the board of trade under another Canningite, Charles Grant. Grenville made much of his being in neither the cabinet nor a post 'where your opinion will be counted or even asked on the fate and subject of Ireland', and placed little faith in his efforts to secure a pension for Williams Wynn, who was left unplaced.[54] His re-election for Ennis, 11 Feb., posed no immediate problem. Herries (now master of the mint) considered him a suitable government nominee for the 1828 finance committee, but he was not appointed to it.[55] As agreed in cabinet, he divided against repealing the Test Acts, 26 Feb. On Irish issues, he approved the principle of the landlord and tenant bill, which he perceived as a useful step towards assimilating Irish with English land tenure and establishing a 'wealthy, decorous and orderly occupying tenantry', 25 Feb. He defended the education commission when the hostile Grange Corman petition was received on the 28th. The cabinet was divided on the disfranchisement of East Retford and, assisted by Williams Wynn, Lewis vainly tried to defer the issue by preventing counsel being summoned, 7 Mar. He faced tough questioning in the House on a loophole in the corn bill permitting imports through the Isle of Man, 10 Mar., and strove to defend the decision to continue levying stamp duty on transactions under 6*d.* when the tradesmen of Hull petitioned against it, 11 Mar. Opposing the appointment that day of a select committee on the franchise in counties corporate, because it 'would introduce the consideration of the entire state of the representation of this country', he noted the peculiar characteristics of each and cited Fox's analogy between the elective franchise and 'a house built at various times, which though an odd piece of patchwork, that could not be explained on any system of architecture, was yet far better and more convenient than if devised as a whole on any regular plan of science'. (He raised similar objections to the freeholders bill, 16 May 1828.)

Wilkins's death, 17 Mar., gave Lewis his opportunity in Radnorshire, and he resigned his seat and declared his candidature, 21 Mar. 1828, having first ensured that Wilkins's son would not stand.[56] He was returned unopposed and resumed his seat,

17 Apr., notwithstanding a counter-campaign led by the Whig diplomat, Sir Harford Jones Brydges of Boultibrook and Kentchurch Court, who criticized his recent 'anti-protection' speeches and his management of the New Radnor tithes, and maintained that Radnorshire would not be adequately represented should he remain in office.[57] Sir Edward O'Brien had turned down his request to nominate a replacement for Ennis and refunded him 'less than £700'. As agreed at his election, Lewis took charge of the Rhayader enclosure bill. He also faced a further challenge from Jones Brydges, in the shape of a strongly worded Radnorshire petition for protective tariffs on wool.[58] He defended the government's trade policy when the Spitalfields silk weavers petitioned similarly, 21 Apr. He spoke and was a majority teller for the resolutions on corn, 29 Apr., and took charge of the bill prohibiting the importation of corn through the Isle of Man, 30 Apr., 7 May, playing an active part in debate when opposition amendments to it were defeated, 20, 21, 23 May. He voted for Catholic relief, 12 May. He ordered detailed returns of metal exports and imports, 19 May, and was a majority teller for the government's Pensions Act amendment bill, 22 May. His ministerial future had been uncertain since Huskisson had first threatened resignation over East Retford in March. Ellenborough, the lord privy seal, had then professed 'no doubt of his staying, and he will do the business [of the board of trade] better than Grant'. However, though annoyed at the turn of events, when Huskisson, Grant and William Lamb resigned in May, Lewis declined the Irish secretaryship and joined the exodus.[59] He informed Wellington, 29 May:

> By undertaking to discharge the arduous duties which devolve upon the chief secretary to the lord lieutenant of Ireland, I should be placed in a situation of so much embarrassment in consequence of the withdrawal of so many persons with whom I have been to a certain degree politically connected, that I feel it politically incumbent upon me to decline.[60]

Ellenborough noted, 30 May, 'I find Frankland Lewis resigns too. He mars his fortune at the very moment when it would have been made'.[61] Lewis described his own misgivings in a letter to his brother-in-law, the Kington banker James Davies, 7 June:

> I decided not to hold office with the present ministry. I trust I have done right, though it is certainly not so clear a point as I could wish, considering how important a decision it has been. Certainly, it would have been in my power to prevent much mischief in Ireland, and if a Tory lord lieutenant and secretary are sent there the evils will be very great. Again there is nothing to look forward to. The Whigs are divided and no one confides in them as a mass. We who are now gone out are an important and respectable body, but not now strong enough to do much *alone*, and with whom are we to unite? Time and chance however are open, and at all events we shall have might enough in the House to prevent the government from being influenced to any great extent by their Tory supporters. If the government had held together six months longer we should have gone on very well. For myself, I own that every day increased my good opinion of the duke. His worst quality is that he sometimes thinks he understands things of which he knows nothing but he listens to the practical people who are brought before him, and governs himself by their statements. I was very much struck with this at the meeting with the governors of the Bank on the last day of my official existence ... I was tired of Ireland and felt that it would absent me so much from home that in addition to other considerations I could not bring myself to like the idea of taking the office. It is however a great sacrifice considering the position in which I started, the change it will make, and the prospects which it opened. All this honour must now be set aside and there is nothing now but to attend to what is going on and to look forward.[62]

Lord Palmerston* observed privately on 19 June how the appointment of Lord Francis Leveson Gower (as Irish secretary) and Calcraft (as paymaster to the forces)

> have struck with bitter repentance the breast of Frankland Lewis. He feels about Ireland as a capricious young lady when she sees a more interested and less romantic fair led to the hymenal altar by the wealthy young squire whom she had lately rejected. He told [Lord] Minto the other day that if he had known what he now knows (God knows what that is) he should certainly not have left government. 'Well', said Minto, 'but you know if you had not left the government you might have kept your office, but you could not have kept your character, and so on the whole it is as well as it is'. Whether Lewis agreed in this he did not say, but he was sitting all last night on the treasury bench as if to recall to his recollection happiness gone by, or to preface the way for happiness to come.[63]

In the Commons, 2 June, Lewis claimed that he had supported and voted 'from the first' for sluicing the franchise at East Retford with the neighbouring hundred, disfranchising only those voters found guilty of corruption, and said he would do so again 'in the same sense and with the same object as I did before'. He remained hostile to transferring East Retford's seats to Birmingham, and when challenged in debate by Tennyson and Williams Wynn, 27 June, he confirmed his preference, as previously stated, taking New Shoreham and Cricklade as his precedents. Later that day, justifying his support, as a majority teller, for the borough polls bill, which he had previously opposed, at its third reading, he claimed that 90 per cent of the original bill had been 'taken away'. Proposing an amendment to his 1827 General Turnpike Act in order to reduce the personal liability of trustees, 3, 26 June, he argued that without it the whole turnpike system would be put at risk, as trustees stood only to gain the market rate of interest on their investments whereas liabilities could total £11,000,000. He defended the policy of abolishing the tariffs on foreign wool when Lincolnshire petitioned for protective duties, 3 June. However, on presenting a similar petition from Radnorshire, 12 June, he suggested doubling the current import levy to a penny a pound and reducing that on exports to 6*d.* a hundredweight. Knatchbull congratulated the wool producers on changing his mind, but Lewis said that he still believed that high duties would not work. On 4 July 1828 he carried an amendment to the customs bill, making the duty on wool nominal. As a speaker for the bill restricting the circulation of low denomination Scottish banknotes in England, 3 June 1828, he cited statistical evidence from the 1825-6 crisis, endorsing the 1819 Act, and repeated his arguments in favour of gold coinage and against a paper, silver or dual standard. He approved the £80,000 Windsor Castle grant, 6 June, and the game bill, 13 June. Heartened by the tone of Wellington's speech on Catholic relief, and ever anxious for office, he flaunted his knowledge of Irish affairs when supplies were voted, 23 June, catching the former secretary Lamb unprepared with a detailed question on the Cork Institution, and launching into a staunch defence of the Belfast Academy's right to government funding.[64] Responding to the Colne handloom weavers' petition, 1 July, he defended free trade and argued against minimum wages. He drew attention to inconsistencies in the savings banks bill, 3 July, spoke of its relevance to poor law policy and the national debt and, taking the chancellor of the exchequer Goulburn by surprise, proposed an amendment, which he later withdrew at Goulburn's request. Highlighting the dangers of permitting banks to hold deposits of £15,000,000 to £17,000,000 redeemable at any time, he vainly renewed his attempt to have corrective clauses inserted when the bill was reported, 10 July. He argued that 'government can never interfere with the money market without producing a certain quantity of mischief, because the interest paid upon the deposits of savings banks is above the market rate of interest'. He also defended the corporate funds bill, which Poulett Thomson's adjournment motion failed to kill, 4 July. He voted in the government's majority that day on ordnance salaries. In committee on the customs bill, 10 July, he spoke of his regret at hearing Members 'speaking of the corn law as a measure intended as a protection to the landed interest', and agreed with Goulburn that there should be no backtracking. He later rallied to his own defence in committee on the Irish butter trade bill, which closed a loophole whereby Dublin had been excluded from the provisions of his 1827 Act. His attempt to rescue the bill failed, 15 July. John Evelyn Denison* complained privately that Lewis's report from the committee on civil government in Canada was 'very ill drawn', 14 July 1828.[65]

As the patronage secretary Planta predicted in February, Lewis voted for Catholic emancipation, 6, 30 Mar. 1829. He also refused to endorse Radnorshire's anti-Catholic petition, 9 Mar.[66] Voicing his opposition to the attendant changes in the Irish freeholder franchise, he made it clear that he sanctioned them only as a means of carrying emancipation, 20 Mar., and deplored the absence of a middle class and genuine freeholders in Ireland, which the measure would help to remedy. He maintained that the threat posed by Jesuits to national security was exaggerated and had already been adequately dealt with in the relief bill, 23, 27 Mar. Opposing the county bridges bill, 12 May, he said that its proposal to transfer maintenance costs from the county to the turnpike trusts was particularly unsuitable for Wales, where trust revenues were low and there was great risk of damage from mountain torrents. He attributed the distress in the wool trade referred to in the county Meath petition to the 'evils of smuggling', not insufficient protection as stated, 11 May. Later that day he failed (with Peel and Monck), to prevent the committal of the justices of the peace bill. He decided against voting on the Clare election on the 19th 'because it would be putting on the records of this House, matter contradictory and unintelligible without that explanation which will not be affixed to it'. Although he was no longer a member of the commission or the select committee, his views on Irish education featured in the Rev. William Lee of Cashel's correspondence with Wellington in April 1829.[67] When he was pressed to counter allegations made in the Commons that the commission had recommended a plan based on the exclusion of the Scriptures, 22 May, Peel did nothing to assist him. His professions of support for John Nash, whom he had commissioned to refurbish Harpton Court, did not preclude Lewis from sitting on the investigative committee on the Buckingham House contract, 27 May, 19 June, of which he wrote, 'Colonel Davies is his opponent. Lowther and Croker his real enemies. There is no case of fraud against him'.[68] He spent much of the 1829 summer recess abroad and in September became deputy chairman of the Economic Life Assurance

Society, chaired by Sir James Mackintosh*.[69] In December Peel consulted him over the Radnorshire memorial against the proposed abolition of the courts of great sessions and remodelling of the Welsh assize system.[70]

Prompted by William Vesey Fitzgerald's* illness he consulted Charles Arbuthnot* and Planta in January 1830, fuelling speculation that he would go to the mint or return to the board of trade; but he had to be content with the treasurership of the navy, then targeted (as a sinecure) for attack by the radicals.[71] *The Times*, copied by the provincial press, judged him 'an able man, well acquainted with business and on the score both of talent and integrity thoroughly worthy of ministerial and public confidence'; but Lord Durham thought it 'a strange appointment. He brings no one and has a sinecure'.[72] He voted against transferring East Retford's seats to Birmingham, 11 Feb. His re-election, at a cost of about £240, was a formality despite attempts to isolate him and encourage hostility to government.[73] After being sworn in, 5 Mar., he observed privately, 'it is an anxious session, and the position of the government is a very odd one'.[74] As the South Wales industrialist Walter Coffin observed in March, Lewis's presence on the London coal trade committee made it a government matter, and he successfully countered amendments to extend its scope to 'other ports', 11 Mar. He brought up their report, for which he was responsible, 13 July, together with those from the select committees on Irish tolls.[75] He countered Spring Rice's motion for a select committee on the Irish poor by calling for a similar inquiry for England and an end to policy differences between the two countries, 11 Mar. As usual, he warned against hasty abolition of the cess or taking an optimistic view of Irish unemployment, and spoke of the evils of absenteeism and the merits of the Scottish poor relief system. He was not included on the committee. Drawn into the debate on the state of the nation, 23 Mar., he pointed out that Hume's pamphlet assumed an increasing, not a depreciating currency, claimed that Burdett's arguments 'in favour of paper' were based on a misinterpretation of John Horne Tooke†, and criticized the inadequacies of the Bank Restriction Act. He remained convinced that

> those mischievous dreamers who propose not a fixed, but some fluctuating standard, which the government and this House may change at their pleasure, would by such a measure hazard the safety of all descriptions of property, but would also never be able to avert the distress whenever it threatened any particular interest. I am convinced their opinions are founded in error and, therefore, I hope never to see them adopted in this country.

He ordered a detailed breakdown of accounts of London's wool exports and imports, 30 Mar. He attributed the rise in imports complained of in the Colchester flour manufacturers' petition to 'Ireland', rather than defects in the corn bill, 28 May. He divided against Jewish emancipation, 5 Apr., 14 May. Ever scornful of Owenite ideas, in committee on the poor law amendment bill, 26 Apr. 1830, he was among the many who argued strongly on humanitarian grounds against the clause empowering parishes to remove children from parents unable to support them, which was defeated by 91-9. He agreed that 'the procreation of children without the means of supporting them is a very great evil', but he did not consider a retarding system appropriate and reiterated his preference for the Scottish relief system. Although critical of the government's cavalier attitude, 27 Apr., he refused to make common cause with his constituents or Welsh Members opposed to the administration of justice bill, by which the Welsh judicature and courts of great sessions were abolished, and had backed similar proposals since 1817. Its provision for holding joint-assizes for 'Welsh' Breconshire and Radnorshire, however, grieved him, for he had hoped for an arrangement with Hereford.[76] Attending to his department's business in the Commons, where he frequently acted as a government teller, he did much to counter allegations of wasteful naval expenditure (22 Mar.). As announced, 10 Mar., and despite being repeatedly outmanoeuvred by Hume, he successfully steered through consolidating legislation on naval pay, 10 May. Earlier, in the committee of supply, he had spoken against salary reductions. He faced tough questioning from Hume when he introduced his bill to consolidate and regulate the navy treasurership, 7 June, but succeeded in rushing it through before the dissolution precipitated by George IV's death. He also defended the navy commissioners' policy when the parish of Greenwich petitioned alleging underpayment of rates by the Hospital, 2 July 1830. He now looked to Planta for patronage and was mentioned as a 'possible' for the war office or as a replacement for Leveson Gower as Irish secretary in the event of a reshuffle. Sir Henry Hardinge* considered Robert Wilmot Horton* a better choice for either post.[77]

According to the 5th Earl of Oxford's heir Lord Harley, Lewis had no money to fight a contest when he came in for Radnorshire unopposed at the 1830 general election.[78] On the hustings he defended the government's record on taxation, allayed fears of war with France and praised amendments made by Spence to the administration of justice bill.[79] He attended the meeting convened by Herries on 25 Aug. to review the outcome of the elections nationally.[80] In September, when political realignments were considered following Huskisson's death, Lewis's loyalty to Wellington was not in doubt, but Ellenborough, who met him at a pre-session dinner, 30 Oct., noted:

> He longs for the Grants. I told him it would not do, and what sort of man Charles Grant was. Frankland Lewis does not seem to like his office, but he says he shall bring it into order if he remains there, and make it a privy councillor's office without drudgery. He and indeed all seem to wish they were better and more boldly led in the House of Commons.[81]

Lewis divided with his ministerial colleagues on the civil list when they were brought down, 15 Nov. 1830, and resigned with them. He briefed Lord Grey, as premier, on the problems of combining the navy treasurership and vice-presidency of the board of trade, 24 Nov. 1830;[82] and expressed confidence in Poulett Thomson's right to hold both posts concurrently, when the House considered the matter, 25 Feb. 1831. Yet he also suggested awarding clerks in those departments higher salaries to ensure future competence. Referring to the Irish trade commissioner's report, 'the last public business ... [Huskisson] ever prosecuted with me', 10 Mar., he supported Warburton's bill to prevent tobacco growing in Ireland, arguing that the House should pause before throwing away £3,000,000 in easily collected revenue; he offered to introduce compensatory legislation should the bill fail. The London coal bill took up much of his time this session. Having been accused of abusing his position as committee chairman by including information in the 1830 report without his colleagues' authorization, 14 Dec., he announced his bill as a private Member's measure, 23 Dec. 1830, and carried its first and second readings, 28 Mar., 18 Apr. 1831, before it became a casualty of the dissolution.[83] He voted against the ministry's reform bill at its second reading, 22 Mar., and questioned the basis on which franchise decisions had been taken, 25 Mar., when, citing the return for Radnorshire, he called for publication of a table of all results collated from the home office's questionnaires. This brought a defensive response from Lord John Russell, who admitted that different procedures had been followed in England and Wales. At the Radnorshire reform meeting, 5 Apr., Lewis said he would support 'a well arranged measure', but opposed the government's because it would deprive England of 60 Members and showed 'undue preference for Ireland'. He failed to carry a counter-petition which expressed general agreement with the principle of the bill and the decision to enfranchise Presteign, but opposed any change in the proportion of Members 'fixed at the respective Unions with Scotland and Ireland'.[84] He insisted that he did not vote for Gascoyne's wrecking amendment with the objective of ousting the government, 19 Apr. 1831. Seeing off a challenge in Radnorshire at the ensuing general election from the reformer Edward Romilly, son of the late Whig lawyer, he said:

> I distrust a measure which at once blows hot and cold ... I dislike it because I find it popular in places where bribery habitually, systematically and shamelessly prevails amongst electors with whom the receipt of money for their votes has not been confined to the low or the needy. The provisions of the bill not only do not provide an efficient remedy for this species of corruption, they tend, I fear very materially to enforce it.

His failure to present the Radnorshire petition before the dissolution was resented and, though eventually unopposed, he faced intense pressure to represent his constituents' views on reform.[85]

Speaking with 'candour and sincerity', before dividing for the reintroduced reform bill at its second reading, 6 July 1831, he said that as he had supported the original bill before learning its details, he felt 'bound in deference ... to go as far as I can in support of this bill, consistently with the free exercise of my own judgement, which I can never consent to surrender'. He made it clear that although he intended voting to consider it in committee, 'it must wear a different and a fairer shape than at present, before I can give it my vote that it shall pass into a law'. He pointed to disfranchisements proposed 'not for the purpose of improving, but of destroying' – a principle he could never approve – and argued against applying the same voting qualifications nationwide. He confirmed that he had voted for Gascoyne's amendment as a fair proposition, not anticipating that it would cause the bill to be abandoned, and warned of the threat which additional Irish Members would pose to the Union. The minister Spring Rice noted, 'We have gained an unexpected recruit in Frankland Lewis'.[86] He voted to hear counsel on the Appleby petition, 12 July, possibly also to delay the bill's committal by adjournment that day, and to make the 1831 census the determinant of English borough disfranchisements, 19 July. He was listed among the bill's supporters absent from the divisions on Downton, 20 July, and St. Germans, 26 July. The same day, following discussions with Wellington, he declined Russell's offer of an unsalaried place on the boundary commission.[87] Peel thought he would have taken it had he been able to 'place the responsibility for acceptance on others'.[88] He criticized the decision to enfranchise Tower Hamlets, which he claimed erroneously assumed that the interests of London and Middlesex freemen were the same, 4 Aug., and succeeded in restricting Presteign's franchise to the part of the town which lay wholly in Wales, 9, 10 Aug. However, his campaign to include landholding in assessments of £10 householders in rural areas failed, 9, 10, 20 Aug., 2 Sept. He considered the condition (in clause 21) requiring all rents, rates and taxes to be paid before a £10 householder could vote inoperable, as rents were commonly paid six months in arrears, and said it would encourage the poor to join electoral clubs, 'accept bribes and to be corrupted', 25 Aug. He voted against disfranchising non-resident freemen in the hundreds of Aylesbury, Cricklade, East Retford and New Shoreham, 2 Sept. Ministers conceded minor alterations which he suggested in the wording of clauses 48 and 53, 6 Sept.; but arguing that little substantial change had been achieved, he divided against the bill's passage, 22 Sept. 1831.

Lewis was named to the select committee on Windsor Castle and Buckingham House, 23 June 1831, and corresponded with the colonial secretary Goderich on the 'irregularity' of Nash's subcontracting policy.[89] He disapproved of the wording of Poulett Thomson's motion for a select committee on the use of molasses in United Kingdom breweries and distilleries, but after speaking in defence of the corn growers, whose interests he felt were threatened, he was appointed to it, 30 June. He was also named to committees on steam carriages, 20 July, civil list expenditure, 12 Aug., and drawback duties on malt and spirits, before which he testified, 23 Sept.[90] Despite Wellington's fears that Herries, Goulburn or others connected with the coal trade would wreck Lewis's London coal trade bill in committee, he successfully steered it though the Commons, carrying its third reading with only minor alterations, 12 Sept.[91] He had supported the decision to give the administration in Dublin control of the education grant and called for a single system which attempted no religious instruction, 9 Sept. He urged the House to suspend judgement pending 'an explanation from a proper authority' when Colraine petitioned against the dismissal of two British army officers for refusing to participate in Catholic ceremonies in Malta, 12 Oct. 1831.

Lewis was at Gorhambury with Lord Harrowby and moderate anti-reformers early in September, and he reported regularly to Williams Wynn in Montgomeryshire on the bill's progress in the Lords. He considered Lord Ebrington's confidence motion of 10 Oct. '*little less than seditious*' and wished it 'had never appeared, as it binds the House to something like the old bill'.[92] He declined attendance at the Radnorshire meeting which addressed the king urging the reform bill's speedy passage, 1 Nov. Like Lord Clive, with whom he conferred, he deliberately left town before the division on the second reading of the revised reform bill, 17 Dec. 1831.[93] He voted against its committal, 20 Jan. 1832. When opposition sought to 'clog' the £10 householder franchise 'with *et ceteras*', he pointed to apparent anomalies giving county voters burgess or householder votes in boroughs, 2 Feb. He voted against the enfranchisement of Tower Hamlets, 28 Feb., and the bill's third reading, 22 Mar. When in May 1832 a government headed by Wellington was in contemplation, he included Lewis on his list of cabinet members, but it is not clear whether he would have accepted, or what his post would have been, had the ministry been formed.[94] He did not vote when party strength was tested on the Russian Dutch loan. Hyde Villiers had offered Lewis a place on the East India committee, 21 Dec. 1831, to which he was named, 27 Jan. 1832, possibly after a meeting with Lord Althorp.[95] He was named to several other select committees that session, including that on slavery, 30 May. His comments on the coroners bill were mainly critical, but he refused to support amendments making inquests public and medical and legal qualifications obligatory, arguing that in view of the low salaries offered the office would never attract the best professional men. In the summer of 1832 Lewis sent his elder son George Cornewall Lewis† (1806-63) to Paris with Nassau Senior to study poverty, and despite local opposition, he had his younger son Gilbert (*b.* 1808) presented to the living of Gladestry.[96] He attended the assizes at Presteign in August as foreman of the grand jury, but left before the reform festival on the 11th.[97]

After an arduous canvass, Lewis came in unopposed for Radnorshire at the general election in December 1832 and assisted the Conservatives at Hereford and Ludlow, which were 'sharply fought'.[98] He was refused dispensation to keep his seat when appointed to the poor law commission in 1834 and did not contest the county subsequently. In 1847, after his service as a commissioner had terminated, he came in for the New Radnor district with a view to reserving the seat for George, retaining it until his death at Harpton Court in January 1855.[99] His estates had, since 1844, largely been settled as part of his marriage settlement on George, his successor in the baronetcy conferred on him by Peel in 1846 in recognition of their joint public service. Lewis left his second wife Marianne (*d.* 1868) his London house in Grafton Street with its contents and her property previous to their marriage (£40,000), and his Radnorshire tithes reverted to Frederick Calvert and Sir Walter Cornewall. His will made no mention of his younger son, on whom the baronetcy and Harpton Court devolved in 1863.[100]

[1] *Oxford DNB*; K. Parker, 'Parl. Enclosure in Rad.' and 'Sale of Crown Lands in Rad. in 19th Cent.' *Trans. Rad. Soc.* lxxiii (2003),127-47; lxxv (2005), 153-73. [2] *HP Commons, 1790-1820*, iv. 433-4; J.J. Sack, *Grenvillites*, 166, 175, 179, 183; UCNW, Beaumaris mss v. 58. [3] P.J. Jupp, 'Landed Elite and Political Authority in Britain c. 1760-1850', *JBS*, xxix (1990), 53-71. [4] B. Hilton, *Corn, Cash, Commerce*, 32, 41-42; *Williams Wynn Corresp.* 245. [5] J.R. Poynter, *Society and Pauperism* (1969), 246-7; A. Brundage, *Making of New Poor Law*, 9; P. Mandler, 'Tories and Paupers: Christian Political Economy and the Making of the New Poor Law', *HJ*, xxxiii (1990), 93. [6] Torrens, *Melbourne*, 93. [7] *N. Wales Gazette*, 16 Mar. 1820. [8] *PP* (1820), ii. 330-63; *CJ*, lxxv. 449. [9] *The Times*, 20 Mar. 1821. [10] NLW, Coedymaen mss 608. [11] *The Times*, 3 July 1821. [12] Beaumaris mss iv. 319. [13] NLW, Harpton Court mss C/487; Add. 40344, f. 181. [14] *PP* (1822), xiii. 1214-15. [15] *The Times*, 2, 16 May 1822; *PP* (1823), vii. 239-52, 747. [16] *PP* (1820), ii. 317. [17] *The Times*, 12, 20 Feb., 19 Apr. 1823. [18] Beaumaris mss iv. 319. [19] Bucks. RO, Fremantle mss, Buckingham to Fremantle, 11 Jan. 1824; Buckingham, *Mems. Geo. IV*, ii. 33. [20] *The Times*, 7 Feb. 1824. [21] Ibid. 17 Feb. 1824. [22] Ibid. 13 Mar. 1824. [23] *PP* (1824), vi. 467-84. [24] Ibid. 667-84; *CJ*, lxxix. 148, 154, 191, 247, 393, 451. [25] *PP* (1824), xi. 1-773; *The Times*, 18, 27, 28 May 1824. [26] Add. 40511, f. 231; *PP* (1825), xiii; Harpton Court mss 495; Wellington mss WP1/798/8; 800/24; 801/12. [27] Harpton Court mss C/377. [28] Coedymaen mss 1012; Harpton Court mss C/589; Buckingham, ii. 192. [29] Buckingham, ii. 213; Coedymaen mss 414. [30] Buckingham, ii. 218; *LJ*, lvii. 39. [31] Add. 40373, ff. 124, 140; 40378, ff. 39, 297. [32] *The Times*, 26 Mar. 1825. [33] Ibid. 7 May 1825. [34] Ibid. 31 May 1825; *PP* (1825), xii. 1-881. [35] Add. 40382, f. 406; *Williams Wynn Corresp.* 333. [36] Harpton Court mss C/397, 595-6; P. Parris, 'Shire Hall Presteign', *Trans. Rad. Soc.* li (1981), 40-41; *Hereford Jnl.* 17 Jan. 1827. [37] Harpton Court mss C/584-5; *PP* (1826-7), xii. [38] Add. 40391, f. 198; *PP* (1826-7), xiii. 1137-42. [39] Grey mss, Howick to Grey, 6, 12, 20 Mar.; St. Deiniol's Lib. Glynne-Gladstone mss 194, T. to J. Gladstone, 16 Mar. 1827. [40] Grey mss, Grey to Howick, 14 Mar. 1827. [41] *The Times*, 3 Apr. 1827. [42] *Carmarthen Jnl.* 27 Apr. 1827. [43] *The Times* 19 June 1827. [44] Ibid. 19 June 1827. [45] Duke Univ. Lib. Fazakerley mss, Ord to Fazakerley, 17 Apr. 1827; Harpton Court mss C/523, 593. [46] Harpton Court mss C/379. [47] Coedymaen mss 712, 715; BL, Fortescue mss, Lewis to Grenville, 22 Aug. 1827; Add. 40394, f. 170; Harpton Court mss C/621. [48] Harpton Court mss C/405. [49] Ibid. C/416, 419; Buckingham, ii. 350; Lonsdale mss, Lowther to Lonsdale, 10 Sept. 1827. [50] *Williams Wynn Corresp.* 361. [51] NLS, Ellice mss, Grey to Ellice, 8 Sept. 1827. [52] Harpton Court mss C/513. [53] TNA 30/29/9/3/37. [54] Harpton Court mss C/417, 418; Add. 38754, f. 179; 59406, f. 14; Wellington mss WP1/915/46; 920/5; *Ellenborough Diary*, i. 18; Coedymaen mss 448, 466, 736. [55] Add. 40395, f. 221. [56] Harpton Court mss C/3044; *Hereford Jnl.* 26 Mar. 1828. [57] Harpton Court mss 2160, 2161; C/597; *Cambrian*, 29 Mar., 5, 12 Apr.; *Hereford Jnl.* 2, 9, 16 Apr. 1828; MacLeod of MacLeod mss 1062/12. [58] Harpton Court mss C/598-601; *Hereford Jnl.* 28 May, 4, 18 June, 30 July, 3 Sept. 1828, 4 Mar. 1829. [59] *Ellenborough Diary*, i. 71, 112, 130; Harpton Court mss C/403, 600; *Hereford Jnl.* 4 June 1828; *HMC Bathurst*, 654; TNA 30/29/9/5/71; N. Gash, *Secretary Peel*, 472-3; *Croker Pprs.* i. 421. [60] Wellington mss WP1/943/19. [61] *Ellenborough Diary*, i. 130-1. [62] Harpton Court mss C/601. [63] Southampton Univ. Lib. Broadlands mss BR2 3AA/5/3. [64] *Greville Mems.* i. 212. [65] Nottingham Univ. Lib. Denison diary, 12 July 1828. [66] *The Times*, 10 Mar. 1829; Harpton Court mss C/398. [67] Wellington mss WP1/1011/16. [68] Harpton Court mss C/606. [69] Ibid. C/492, 602; *Hereford Jnl.* 19 Aug. 1829. [70] Harpton Court mss C/517; *Hereford Jnl.* 22 Apr., 26 Oct.; *Chester Courant*, 3 Nov. 1829. [71] Harpton Court mss C/359, 524; Coedymaen mss 976; Add. 51680, Lord J. Russell to Lady Holland [Jan.]; 51785, Holland to C.R. Fox, 11 Jan.; *Greville Mems.* i. 350, 352; Lonsdale mss, Lowther to Lonsdale, 4 Feb. 1830; Wellington mss WP1/1098/16. [72] *The Times*, 15 Feb.; *Hereford Jnl.* 17 Feb., *Cambrian*, 19 Feb.; Grey mss, Durham to Grey [15 Feb. 1830]. [73] *Hereford Jnl.* 10, 17, 24, Feb., 3, 10, 17 Mar.; *Cambrian*, 19 Feb., 5 Mar.; *Shrewsbury Chron.* 19 Mar. 1830; Harpton Court mss 2625-7. [74] Harpton Court mss C/603. [75] NLW, Bute mss L73/29. [76] Harpton Court mss C/399, 604-6. [77] Ibid. C/498; *Ellenborough Diary*, ii. 306; PRO NI, Anglesey mss D619/31, pp. 95-99. [78] NLW, Ormathwaite mss G36, f. 19. [79] Harpton Court mss 2626; *Hereford Jnl.* 30 June, 21 July; *Shrewsbury Chron.* 13 Aug. 1830; D.R.Ll. Adams, 'Parl. Rep. Rad. 1536-1832' (Univ. of Wales M.A. thesis, 1969), 457-9. [80] Harpton Court mss C/430. [81] *Ellenborough Diary*, ii. 407-8. [82] Harpton Court mss C/421. [83] *Hereford Jnl.* 30 Mar. 1831. [84] 30 Mar., 13 Apr. 1831; Adams, 464-5. [85] Harpton Court mss 2161-4; C/535, 536, 579; *Hereford Jnl.* 27 Apr., 4, 11, 18 May; *Cambrian*, 30 Apr. 1831. [86] Add. 51573, Spring Rice to Lady Holland [6 July 1831]. [87] Wellington mss WP1/1190/5, 11; Harpton Court mss C/581. [88] Wellington mss WP1/1190/25. [89] Harpton Court mss C/407-9. [90] *PP* (1831), vii. 452-3. [91] Wellington mss WP1/1197/4. [92] *Greville Mems.* ii. 190; Harpton Court mss C/590; Coedymaen mss 1014-20. [93] *Hereford Jnl.* 26 Oct., 16, 23 Nov. 1831; Coedymaen mss, bdle. 19, Clive to Williams Wynn, 23 Dec. 1831. [94] Wellington mss WP1/1224/2. [95] Harpton Court mss C/368, 571. [96] Ibid. C/367-9, 400; Brougham mss, Lewis to Brougham, 27 Feb., 4 May 1831. [97] Harpton Court mss C/401; *Hereford Jnl.* 13 June, 8, 22 Aug. 1832. [98] Harpton Court mss 2165, 2628; Add. 40879, f. 344. [99] NLW, Maybery mss 6615; Ormathwaite mss FG1/7, p. 203; Add. 40511, ff. 231-2. [100] PROB 11/2210/336; IR26/2038/305; Add. 40595, f. 209; Harpton Court mss C/520-1.

M.M.E.

LEWIS, Wyndham (1780–1838), of Greenmeadow, Tongwynlais, Glam. and Grosvenor Gate, Mdx.

CARDIFF BOROUGHS	1820–1826
ALDEBURGH	22 May 1827–19 Feb. 1829
MAIDSTONE	1835–14 Mar. 1838

b. 7 Oct. 1780, 4th but 3rd surv. s. of Rev. Wyndham Lewis (*d.* 1781), rect. of Newhouse, Glam., and Mary, da. and coh. of Samuel Price of The Park and Coity, Glam. *educ.* L. Inn 1812, called 1819. *m.* 22 Dec. 1815, Mary Ann, da. of Capt. John Viney Evans, RN, of Brampford Speke, Devon, *s.p.*; 1 da. illegit. *d.* 14 Mar. 1838.

'A thin, narrow, pale man' lampooned as Timothy Weasel, Wyndham Lewis was the second son so named of the Rev. Wyndham Lewis. He shared a common ancestry and could draw on family connections with the earls of Plymouth, the Windsor family and the radical Richard Price, while as a direct descendant of the Lewises of Newhouse, Llanishen and Y Fan, he inherited shares in the Dowlais Iron Company and substantial estates in Glamorgan, Monmouthshire and Gloucestershire.[1] The estates became his in trust on his father's death in 1781, but transfer of the six-sixteenth share in the Dowlais works he inherited jointly with his brother, the Rev. William Price Lewis, was delayed until the death in 1810 of their uncle, William

Lewis of Pentyrch Forge.[2] Lewis was intended to play an active role in the management of the family estate and foundries. The running of the latter was overseen by the other major shareholders, Josiah John Guest* and his brother Thomas Revel Guest; and Lewis, who was credited with 'acute business acumen', was primarily concerned with accounts and managing the company's leases, contracts, property, transport and banking, including the Cardiff and Merthyr Bank.[3] This brought him into contact with the 2nd marquess of Bute, whose agent Peter Taylor Walker he regularly accompanied on business to Bristol and London where, in November 1819, after attending the legal proceedings against the town clerk of Cardiff's sons, Frederick and Nichol Wood, for insulting Walker (as constable of Cardiff Castle), he stayed on to fulfil his ambition of being called to the bar.[4] Like other ironmasters and landowners, he had invested in turnpike and canal companies, served in the county militia (as major) and was an active magistrate and deputy lieutenant; while as sheriff of Glamorgan, 1819-20, his partner Josiah Guest officiated at the county's hard-fought election in 1820.[5] Lewis's late opportunity to contest Cardiff Boroughs in 1820 derived from Walker's decision to caution Bute against offering his brother, the pro-Catholic Whig Lord James Crichton Stuart*, for re-election there and the marquess's reluctance to back the 6th duke of Beaufort's nominee, his agent Ebenezer Ludlow.[6] Lewis's success in the fierce contest has been attributed to the ironmasters, local opposition to representation by 'an outsider', the ease with which new voters could be created in Cardiff, Cowbridge and Llantrisant, where Bute was strongest, and the backing of the Margam trustees, whose Kenfig voters turned the election. Margam in return secured county votes for the successful candidate Sir Christopher Cole, whom Lewis had supported since 1817.[7] He was, according to another potential candidate, Lewis Weston Dillwyn† of Penlle'rgaer, 'so obviously under the thumb of the marquess, that I cannot consider him as much more than a *locum tenens*'.[8] He took his seat 'on the independent benches of the ministerial side', for he was 'not determined as to my politics' and strove to sit unfettered, committed only to opposing Catholic relief and to promoting his commercial interests.[9] On the latter, he wrote to Josiah Guest of the proposed curbs on emissions from industrial furnaces, 2 May 1820:

> As it may possibly affect the iron works in Wales, I called on Sir Charles Morgan, Lord G. Somerset, Mr. Benett, etc., to apprize them of the great injury which the works would sustain if they were compelled to put up any expensive apparatus for consuming the smoke, and they have all promised to watch the proceedings and oppose any measure which they find may be prejudicial to the ironworks. Will you be good enough to mention the business to the ironmasters that may be prepared to take the necessary steps to oppose it, if it should be considered prudent?[10]

The ironmasters' success in restricting the new standards to new furnaces pleased him.[11] However, from July 1822, 'Unus Populi', writing in the *Cambrian*, accused him of abusing his membership of the House to procure dockyard contracts for Guest and Dowlais.[12]

He divided against Catholic relief, 28 Feb. 1821, 30 Apr. 1822, 1 Mar., 21 Apr., 10 May, and the attendant Irish franchise bill, 26 Apr. 1825. A radical publication of that year noted that he 'appeared to attend frequently and to vote sometimes with, and sometimes against ministers'.[13] He divided with them on Queen Caroline's case, 6 Feb., the additional malt duty, 3 Apr., and the voting rights of civil ordnance officers, 12 Apr., and voted to retain the death penalty for forgery, 23 May 1821.[14] He divided against more extensive tax reductions, 21 Feb. 1822. His reports to Bute on constituency issues now became defensive in tone.[15] Sir John Nicholl*, observing Lewis's critical vote on the peacetime appointment of Canning's ally Beresford as lieutenant-general of the ordnance, 19 Feb. 1823, wrote to his son:

> Lewis, the Member for our Boroughs, was inserted in the minority on the ordnance question, and the fact of his having so voted is repeated in the *Cambrian*. I very much doubt it, but if it is true, he could not have selected a more fortunate occasion for '*showing his independence*', *Mr. Hume's motion being shown to be so unfounded in allegation*, as well as inexpedient in its proposition, that some of the Whigs proposed an amendment to it, and several of them voted against it. Yet this was the motion which a *wise* and *honest* Member chooses as the first to support in order to prove that he is not uniform in voting with government.[16]

He divided with opposition on the Barbados revenues, 17 Mar., but was against repealing the assessed taxes, 18 Mar. 1823. Bute, Dowlais and the Glamorgan Canal Company were in dispute over the extension of the Western Union Canal and the engineer Thomas Telford's plans for Cardiff when in May 1823 Lewis discussed his political future with Bute, who asked him to vacate in Crichton Stuart's favour at the dissolution.[17] An exchange of letters on 1 Mar. 1824 formalized their breach.[18] Lewis voted for the usury laws repeal bill, 8 Apr. 1824. He divided with administration on the Foreign Enlistment Act, 16 Apr., and the duke of Cumberland's award, 10 June, but against increasing it, 27 May 1825. He voted against the president of the board of trade's proposed salary, 10 Apr. 1826.

Assisted by his Cowbridge agent Thomas Williams and by the philanthropy and entertainments showered on constituents by his petite and vivacious wife Mary Ann, he had been canvassing for re-election for Cardiff Boroughs since February 1824, despite strenuous opposition from Bute, with whom he and Dowlais remained in dispute on business matters.[19] He reported favourably to his wife and others in July 1824 on his overtures to the Margam trustees and Beaufort, but his inability to get government money for Swansea and the western boroughs during the 1825-6 banking crisis, which his own firm survived, distanced him from Dillwyn and Christopher Rice Mansel Talbot* of Penrice and Margam, who in February 1826 declared for Crichton Stuart.[20] He hoped 'No Popery' and a thorough canvass of the Bristol and London out-voters would carry him through, but Bute's manipulation of his erstwhile supporters made his cause hopeless and, after informing Bute, 31 May, he renounced his candidature in an open letter from London, 2 June 1826.[21] Although denied Cardiff Boroughs, Lewis's wealth, anti-Catholicism and professed 'disposition to support the ministers' brought him an opportunity to contest Camelford with Sir Henry Frederick Cooke* on the 3rd marquess of Hertford's interest in a costly close-fought contest at the general election of 1826, when the result, a quadruple return, was settled by a scrutiny in favour of Lord Darlington's candidates.[22] He had also, over an eight-month period, negotiated with the London freemen of Maidstone, where he proposed buying a mansion and the mayor accused him of issuing 'anonymous addresses' in a 'selfish and designing attempt to destroy the ancient rights of this borough'.[23] Standing on the 'Pink' interest, he polled a poor third there in 1826. On the hustings he described himself as a country gentleman connected with commercial affairs through Dowlais, 'the largest [iron enterprise] in the world', said that he supported ministers 'no further than I considered their measures right' and claimed that despite his continued opposition to Catholic relief, he was 'a steady friend to civil and religious liberty, particularly as it respects Protestant Dissenters'.[24] By arrangement with Hertford and his man of business John Croker, he was substituted for the latter on a vacancy at Aldeburgh in May 1827. He sat '*during pleasure*' and his parliamentary conduct was dictated by Croker and the marquess.[25] He divided against repeal of the Test Acts, 26 Feb., and Catholic relief, 12 May 1828. In February 1829, ostensibly on account of his opposition to conceding Catholic emancipation, which Hertford instructed his Members to support, Lewis, who did not vote on the issue, 6 Mar., had to make way at Aldeburgh for the duke of Wellington's heir Lord Douro.[26] False reports circulated in Glamorgan that Wellington would compensate him with a baronetcy.[27]

Despite his retiring nature, Lewis had tried hard while in Parliament to make the most of social and political contacts, who now included the Speaker and his wife, and he and Mary Anne retained these connections following his 'retirement'.[28] He did not stand for Parliament in 1830 or in 1831, when he had misgivings over the Grey ministry's reform bill; but he worked with Josiah Guest towards securing the enactment in 1830 of the amended Bute canal bill, and also for the separate representation of Merthyr Tydfil under the 1832 Reform Act.[29] He was defeated at Maidstone in 1832, when uncertainty concerning his political allegiance and stance on reform and the truck system went against him, but he was returned there as a Conservative in 1835.[30] He died suddenly in March 1838, while writing at his desk. In business his most recent concern had been development of the Dyffryn Llynfi and Porthcawl Railway Company. He had formed a close friendship with Benjamin Disraeli†, his colleague at Maidstone since 1837, who, on 28 Aug. 1839 married his widow.[31] Mary Ann (*d.* 1872) retained the Grosvenor Gate mansion and a life interest in Lewis's Glamorgan, Monmouthshire, Gloucestershire and Somerset estates, which passed to the heirs of his brother William. Lewis also provided for another nephew and niece, his 'natural daughter Frances' (Mrs. May), and 'Thomas the son of Mary Jenkins' of St. Marylebone, 'formerly of Cardiff'.[32]

[1] NLW ms 6569E; G.T. Clark, *Limbus Patrum Morganiae*, i. 58. [2] PROB 11/1084/530; J. Lloyd, *Early Hist. Old S. Wales Iron Works*, 33, 45. [3] M. Elsas, *Iron in the Making*, pp. vii, viii. [4] TNA IND1/4584, p. 91; J.H. Matthews, *Cardiff Recs.* ii. 60; iii. 260, 262, 265; v. 503-7; Bodl. Hughenden Dep. D/I/D/39-43; L. Hargest, 'Cardiff's "Spasm of Rebellion" in 1818', *Morgannwg*, xxi (1977), 69-88. [5] R.D. Rees, 'Parl. Rep. S. Wales, 1790-1830' (Reading Univ. Ph.D. thesis, 1962), ii. 394-5; Hughenden Dep. D/I/D/39-43, 189; D/II/A/21-30; E. Ball, 'Glam. Members During the Reform Bill Period', *Morgannwg*, x (1966), 5-30. [6] R. Grant, *Parl. Hist. Glam. 1542-1976*, p. 250; Glam. RO DA/8/11; Christ Church, Oxf. Phillimore mss, Crichton Stuart to Phillimore, 17 Oct. 1824. [7] Glam. RO D/DA12/2/22; NLW, Bute mss L63/20, 25, 26; *Diaries of John Bird of Cardiff* ed. H.M. Thomas (S. Wales Rec. Soc. v), 38-41. [8] Rees, i. 247; NLW, Penllergaer mss B, 11/21, 19/13. [9] Grant, 21-22, 34, 148-9; Ball, 6-7. [10] Elsas, 216-17. [11] Hughenden Dep. D/I/D/190. [12] *Cambrian*, 20 July 1822. [13] *Session of Parl. 1825*, p. 473. [14] *Seren Gomer*, iv (1821), 154. [15] Bute mss L64/22, 35, 37. [16] Merthyr Mawr mss F/51/4. [17] Bute mss L66/2-7, 13, 15-20; L67/22. [18] Ibid. L67/11. [19] Glam RO D/DA11/2, 8-14, 18, 19, 22, 42; 12/6, 118; Bute mss L67/11, 19, 32-35, 38, 42; *Cambrian*, 31 Dec. 1825, 11 Mar.,

13, 27 May 1826. [20] Glam. RO D/DA11/47; 12/35; Hughenden Dep. D/I/D/47, 49, 50, 53-55, 57, 58, 60, 63-67, 70-73; Bute mss L67/23; L68/17; NLW, Penrice and Margam mss 9235, Lewis to T. Llewellyn, 23 Sept. 1825. [21] Hughenden Dep. D/I/D/68, 74-79; Glam. RO D/DA/12/17, 24, 104; Bute mss L69/39, 40; *Cambrian*, 3, 10 June 1826. [22] *The Times*, 6, 20 June; *R. Cornw. Gazette*, 10, 17 June 1826; Add. 60287, ff. 201, 205. [23] Hughenden Dep. D/II/B/64-66, 77; D/II/C/1-19; *Maidstone Jnl.* 13 June 1826. [24] *The Times*, 13, 20 June 1826. [25] Add. 60287, ff. 250-96; Hughenden Dep. D/I/D/97, 102; *Suff. Chron.* 19, 26 May 1827. [26] Add. 60288, ff. 22-30, 107, 125; Elsas, 225-7; Lloyd, 41-45. [27] Bute mss L72/15. [28] Hughenden Dep. D/I/D/93; *Oxford DNB sub* Disraeli, Mary Anne. [29] Hughenden Dep. D/I/D/115-17, 124, 133. [30] Ibid. 135, 139-47, 153-6; *Maidstone Gazette*, 27 Nov., 4, 11, 18 Dec.; *Maidstone Jnl.* 11, 18 Dec. 1832. [31] *Maidstone Jnl.* 20 Mar.; *Cambrian*, 24 Mar. 1838. [32] PROB 11/1894/255; IR26/1489/157; Hughenden Dep. D/II/B/1-28.

M.M.E.

LEYCESTER, Ralph (1763–1835), of Toft Hall, Cheshire and 65 Portland Place, Mdx.

SHAFTESBURY 12 Sept. 1821–1830

b. 17 Dec. 1763, in Calcutta,[1] 1st s. of Ralph Leycester, E. I. Co. service (Bengal), and Charlotte, da. of Rev. Henry Lushington, vic. of Eastbourne, Suss. *educ.* Eton 1775; Trinity Coll. Camb. 1781; L. Inn 1786, called 1791. *m.* 28 Sept. 1797,[2] his 1st cos. Susanna, da. of Ven. Egerton Leigh, adn. of Salop, 3s. (2 *d.v.p.*) 5da. (3 *d.v.p.*). *suc.* fa. 1822. *d.* 29 May 1835.

Capt. earl of Chester's vol. cav. 1803.

The Leycesters, many called Ralph or Rafe, had been settled at Toft since the twelfth century.[3] This Member's father, who was born on 4 Sept. and baptized on 29 Sept. 1737 at Nether Knutsford, was the second son and namesake of Ralph Leycester of Toft (1699-1777) and brother of the Welsh judge Hugh Leycester, Member for Milborne Port, 1802-12. He was appointed a writer in the East India Company in 1753, and married in Calcutta, 20 Nov. 1762, the sister of one of his colleagues, Henry Lushington.[4] Soon after the birth of Ralph junior, the family returned to England and later took up residence at Hall Grove, near Bagshot, Surrey. As well as three daughters, there were three other sons: Henry (*d.* 1796),[5] a captain in the navy, George (*d.* 1827), a fellow of King's College, Cambridge, and William (*d.* 1831), another Bengal civil servant. This Member, who was a scholar at Cambridge and was awarded the chancellor's medal in 1786, qualified and probably practised as a barrister. In 1797 he married into a related Cheshire gentry family, and in 1809 his father succeeded to Toft on the death of his unmarried elder brother George. He played a minor role in Cheshire politics; for instance, he signed the requisition to the sitting independent Member Davies Davenport at the general election of 1820.[6] He attended the turbulent county meeting at Northwich, 11 Jan. 1821, and added his personal statement to the Whig address complaining of the sheriff's refusal to put the question on Lord Grosvenor's amendment in favour of Queen Caroline.[7] On a vacancy later that year, Grosvenor had him returned unopposed as a Whig for Shaftesbury, one of his pocket boroughs.[8]

He voted in condemnation of the Whig Sir Robert Wilson's* removal from the army, 13 Feb., and for more extensive tax reductions to relieve distress, 21 Feb. 1822; thereafter he divided regularly for opposition motions, notably for lower expenditure and taxation. He called for an increase in the number of gaol deliveries, 27 Mar., in order to shorten the time that prisoners had to await trial. He voted for parliamentary reform, 25 Apr., and to condemn the present influence of the crown, 24 June. He criticized ministerial proposals for relieving agricultural distress as futile, 6 May, and divided with the agriculturists for a permanent 18*s.* bounty on wheat exports, 9 May. He presented and endorsed the Manchester and Salford petition for reform of the criminal laws, 4 June, when he voted in this sense. He spoke in praise of his friend Western's motion for a select committee on the resumption of cash payments, 12 June, and paired in its favour.[9] On the death of his father, 31 Dec. 1822, he inherited Toft and the bulk of his personal wealth, which was sworn under £7,000.[10] He again voted for parliamentary reform, 20 Feb., 24 Apr. 1823. He urged reduction in taxes, 24, 26 Feb., and objected to the chancellor's financial resolutions, 3 Mar.[11] He criticized ministers for failing to warn France against invading Spain, 30 Apr., when he voted for the abolition of punishment by whipping. He condemned the 'moral pestilence' of the lottery, 23 June. It was probably he, not Lester, who seconded the motion for leave for the jurors' qualification bill, 19 June. On 14 July he was elected to Brooks's, and on 9 Oct. 1823 he joined the Cheshire Whig Club, at whose meetings he was an habitual attender.[12]

In what Hudson Gurney* described as a 'heavy' speech, he seconded Western's motion for leave for the jurors' qualification bill, 11 Feb. 1824, when he also called for the introduction of a third assize.[13] He seconded motions for information on the grant for building new churches, 14 Apr., and against the ensuing bill's report stage, 4 June.[14] Again objecting to payments to the sinking fund, he spoke and voted for repeal of the assessed and leather taxes, 10, 18 May. He presented a Shaftesbury petition against colonial slavery, 25 May, and voted in condemnation of the trial of the Methodist missionary John Smith in

Demerara, 11 June 1824.[15] He voted against the Irish unlawful societies bill, 15, 18, 21, 25 Feb., when he defended the Catholic Association, and for Catholic relief (which he advocated on 19 Apr.), 1 Mar., 21 Apr., 10 May 1825. He spoke and voted to repeal the assessed taxes, 3 Mar., and the window tax, 17 May, and seconded Wodehouse's motion for information on the prices of foreign corn, 2 June 1825.[16] Blaming the recent financial crisis on excessive speculation, he praised ministers for reducing the scope of country banks to issue notes, 13 Feb., but criticized the introduction of joint-stock status, as he did again, 14 Apr. 1826. He expressed his doubts about the chancellor's proposals on promissory notes, 27 Feb., when he voted to maintain their convertibility into gold. As he had on 26 Feb. 1824, he voted to reform the representation of Edinburgh, 13 Apr., and he sided with opposition for parliamentary reform, 27 Apr. 1826. He divided for revising the corn laws, 18 Apr., and made interventions on the level of the corn duty, 27 Apr., 4, 5, 8 May.[17] As expected, he was returned unopposed for Shaftesbury at the general election of 1826.[18]

Leycester seconded Western's amendment to the address on distress, 22 Nov. 1826, speaking at length for revising the corn laws, reduced taxation and relief for the agricultural interest. He divided against the grant for the duke of Clarence, 16 Feb., and spoke against it, 16 Mar. 1827, but sided that day with the majority for the committal of the annuity bill. He voted for Catholic relief, 6 Mar. He urged the abolition of the 'barbarous practice' of corporal punishment in the army, 12 Mar., and criticized the corn bill, 9, 12 Apr. On 15 May, when he called for repeal of the sugar duties, he declared himself 'favourable to the present administration', under Canning's leadership, because he hoped that it would introduce Catholic emancipation. He voted for the disfranchisement of Penryn, 28 May, and the grant for improved water communications in Canada, 12 June. He seconded his colleague Davenport's motion for inquiry into the distress of the commercial classes, 14 June, but the fact that his call for further restrictions on the issue of banknotes conflicted with Davenport's views was adversely noticed in the debate. He chaired the annual meeting of the Cheshire Whig Club, 9 Oct., when he advocated Catholic relief.[19] His name was included on George Tierney's* list of the proposed finance committee in November 1827.[20]

Leycester attacked the newly appointed ministry of the duke of Wellington, 6 Feb. 1828, especially as its head opposed the Catholic cause. He voted for repeal of the Test Acts, 26 Feb., and Catholic relief, 12 May. He opposed plans to promote emigration, 4, 27 Mar., and again called for reduced taxation and the abolition of the sinking fund, 11 Mar. He voted against extending East Retford into the hundred of Bassetlaw, 21 Mar. He seconded Wilbraham's motion for inquiry into the administration of justice in Cheshire (to which he later submitted written evidence),[21] 22 Apr., and Davenport's motion for greater uniformity of prison discipline, 14 May. He approved of the corn law resolutions, 25 Apr., but then and on the 28th he objected to the scale of duties. He spoke and voted against the additional churches bill, 30 June, stating that it was 'impossible to force and cram religion down the throats of the people in this way'. He welcomed government's decision to repeal the Military and Naval Pensions Act, 10 July, and to abolish the sinking fund, 'that inglorious piece of nonsense and humbug', 11 July, but he condemned the national debt reduction bill, 17 July, on the ground that it would still require borrowing to meet the interest payments. He voted for Fyler's amendment about silk duties in the committee on the customs bill, 14 July, and advocated free trade in silk, 15, 16 July 1828. He opposed alteration of the game laws, 17 Feb. 1829. He praised ministers for their change of policy in favour of Catholic emancipation, 19 Feb., and called it 'the best, the purest and the most beneficent measure since the revolution'. He rebutted the claims of hostile petitions, 24 Feb., 12 Mar., and voted for emancipation, 6, 30 Mar. He seconded Warburton's motion for leave to introduce the anatomy bill, 12 Mar., and moved, but then withdrew, a wrecking amendment against the Cheshire constabulary bill, 13 Apr. He argued that agricultural distress could best be dealt with not by alteration of the currency but by scrapping the sinking fund, 4 June 1829. This effectively marked the end of his parliamentary career because early in 1830 he suffered a paralytic stroke.[22] He was granted six weeks' leave on this account, 3 Mar., and on 26 Apr. John Whishaw informed Lady Holland that Leycester, 'a reasonable and liberal man', had 'lately fallen into very bad health'; he added that 'his wife and daughter, I am sorry to say, are very Evangelical and intolerant, and much given to *conversion*'.[23] He probably never attended again, but he paired in favour of Jewish emancipation, 17 May, and parliamentary reform, 28 May 1830.

In an address dated 16 July 1830, he informed his constituents that 'the heavy blow that fell upon me last winter has rendered me quite unequal to give such attendance in Parliament as would be satisfactory to my feelings'. He therefore withdrew from Shaftesbury at the dissolution, recommending his first cousin Edward Penrhyn* as his successor.[24] In the expected contest in

Cheshire, he offered his support to George Legh and Grosvenor's eldest son Lord Belgrave*.[25] His name headed the requisition for the Cheshire county meeting in support of the Grey ministry's reform bill, but he was prevented by sickness from attending it on 17 Mar. 1831. He was a member of Wilbraham's committee in the county contest at the general election of 1831, and signed the requisition for another county meeting following the defeat of the reform bill in the Lords later that year. He proposed the Liberal Edward John Stanley* for Cheshire North at the general elections of 1832 and 1834.[26] He died at Toft in May 1835. By his will, dated 23 Jan. 1834, he left an annuity of £1,000 to his wife (who died, aged 61, 10 Mar. 1837), and £25,000 each, in three per cent stocks, to his daughters Charlotte and Emma Theodosia. The residue of his estate, which included personal wealth sworn under £70,000 in the province of Canterbury and under £10,000 in that of York, was inherited by his only surviving son, Ralph Gerard (1817-51).[27]

[1] His birth year is usually given as 1764, but if 17 Dec. is correct, it must have been 1763 as he was baptized in Calcutta, 4 Feb. 1764 (BL OIOC N/1/2, f. 53). [2] *Gent. Mag.* (1797), 980. [3] For peds. see *Burke Commoners* (1833), i. 73-75; G. Ormerod, *Cheshire*, i. 507; iii. 893. [4] BL OIOC J/1/2, f. 112. [5] *The Times*, 30 Mar. 1796. [6] *Macclesfield Courier*, 18 Mar. 1820. [7] *The Times*, 18 Jan. 1821. See CHESHIRE. [8] His parliamentary speeches were sometimes confused with those of Benjamin Lester Lester, Member for Poole. [9] *The Times*, 5, 13 June 1822. [10] PROB 11/1668/154; IR26/964/316. [11] *The Times*, 25 Feb. 1823. [12] *Chester Chron.* 17 Oct. 1823. [13] Gurney diary. [14] *The Times*, 15 Apr. 1824. [15] Ibid. 26 May 1824. [16] Ibid. 3 June 1825. [17] Ibid. 28 Apr., 5, 6 May 1826. [18] *Dorset Co. Chron.* 8, 15 June 1826. [19] *The Times*, 12 Oct. 1827. [20] Add. 38761, f. 269. [21] *PP* (1829), ix. 369-70. [22] *Smith Letters*, ii. 518. [23] Add. 51659. [24] *Hist. Shaftesbury Election 1830*, p. 12; *Dorset Co. Chron.* 22 July 1830. [25] Grosvenor mss 12/4, Leycester to Belgrave, n.d. [1830]. [26] *Chester Courant*, 15, 22 Mar., 3 May, 18 Oct. 1831, 25 Dec. 1832, 20 Jan. 1835. [27] Ibid. 2 June 1835; *Gent. Mag.* (1837), i. 554; PROB 11/1849/437; IR26/1393/363.

S.M.F.

LIDDELL, Hon. Henry Thomas (1797–1878).

NORTHUMBERLAND	1826–1830
DURHAM NORTH	1837–1847
LIVERPOOL	9 July 1853–8 Mar. 1855

b. 10 Mar. 1797, 1st s. of Sir Thomas Henry Liddell†, 6th bt., 1st Bar. Ravensworth, of Ravensworth Castle, co. Dur. and Eslington Hall, Northumb. and Maria Susannah, da. and coh. of John Simpson of Bradley Hall, co. Dur. *educ.* Eton 1808; St. John's, Camb. 1814. *m.* 9 Nov. 1820, Isabella Horatia, da. of Lord George Seymour†, 6s. (3 *d.v.p.*) 4da. (1 *d.v.p.*). *suc.* fa. as 2nd Bar. Ravensworth 8 Mar. 1855; *cr.* Earl Ravensworth 2 Apr. 1874. *d.* 19 Mar. 1878.

Attaché and chargé d'affaires at Wurttemberg Mar.-June 1820; supernumerary clerk, foreign office Feb.-Apr. 1824, jun. clerk Apr. 1824-Jan. 1826; asst. priv. sec. to sec. of state for foreign affairs Nov. 1826-July 1827.

The son of a leading northern coal owner and court favourite, Liddell was heir to extensive estates in Northumberland and Durham, and the baronetcy conferred in 1642 on the royalist Thomas Liddell for his defence of Newcastle-upon-Tyne against the Scots. An excellent scholar and classicist, he was intended for a political or diplomatic career and left Cambridge without taking his degree. Overtures to the premier Lord Liverpool by his father, who represented county Durham as a Grenvillite, 1806-7, seeking treasury assistance for Liddell's candidature in 1818 for Northumberland and in 1820 for county Durham, brought too little reassurance on which to proceed, and, lacking funds to fight independently, he had to bide his time.[1] He served briefly at the Stuttgart embassy and was party to the resettlement of the Ravensworth estates in October 1820, prior to his marriage to a granddaughter of the 1st marquess of Hertford.[2] At the Durham county meeting in support of Queen Caroline, 13 Dec. 1820, he boldly and 'foolishly' defended the king and his ministers, refused to concede the queen's innocence and announced that he would 'always attend' meetings and 'say what he thought'.[3] He was appointed to the Florence legation when his father became a coronation peer in 1821 and was recalled in October 1823 to the foreign secretary Canning's office, where he remained until 1826. He oversaw arrangements for Canning's visit to Ireland in 1824 and corresponded closely with his private secretary Stapleton and daughter Lady Clanricarde during his illness in the summer of 1825.[4] Promising to reside at his family's subsidiary seat of Eslington Hall, near Whittingham, he declared early for Northumberland when the death of the Tory Charles Brandling created a vacancy in February 1826, but the Whig aristocracy were anxious to improve the prospects of Lord Grey's son Lord Howick* at the general election and coalesced with the anti-Catholic Tory Matthew Bell to defeat him in a 13-day poll he had insufficient means to finance.[5] He was ridiculed during it as the 'Ravensworth puppy', an effeminate scholar and a stranger, and caricatured as a passive and insignificant participant in his own canvass. The Whig Thomas Creevey* (Bell's uncle by marriage) wrote that he 'made himself the damnedest fool possible' on the hustings, where he declared his support for Liverpool and Canning and appealed for the votes of pro and anti-Catholics.[6] Fêted in defeat, he accepted a requisition to stand on subscription and entered the fray against Bell, Howick and the sitting Whig 'madman' Thomas Wentworth Beaumont at the ensuing general election. His canvass, a continuation of his February campaign, was fraught with allegations and recriminations between him and Bell, who challenged him to direct his opposition against Lord Grey's son-in-law, the Whig John Lambton*, in county Durham.[7] Obscuring his views on the Catholic question until his canvass was almost complete, Liddell stated at North Shields, 8 May, and again on the hustings, 13, 20 June 1826, that he would support concessions 'on the broad basis of the national welfare only, not for the sake of the Roman Catholic church, but for the sake of the empire at large'. He conceded the necessary exclusion of Catholics from 'certain high offices of state', but 'refused to make a public pledge as to his future conduct'. He declared against both slavery and its 'precipitate' abolition, was 'not yet for free trade' and advocated a 'low and steady' remunerating price for corn growers.[8] He topped the poll and came in with Bell. According to Grey's brother-in-law Edward Ellice*, he spent £50,000 on both elections. He refused to draw on his £4,000 subscription fund.[9]

Liddell returned to London and Canning's private office in November 1826.[10] Moving the address in a maiden speech 'of considerable ability and great promise' on the 21st, he presented himself as a 'friend to the present administration ... pledged neither to men nor measures'.[11] He justified the recent relaxation of the corn laws to ease distress in manufacturing areas, projected the end of the Burmese war and Canning's 'prompt and decided' recognition of the South American republics as a boon for commerce, and advocated support for representative government in Spain and Portugal and assistance for Greece. The editor of the *Durham Chronicle* caustically questioned his 'liberal' intentions and the Whig James Abercromby* commented: 'Liddell has plenty of words, but very few thoughts. When he has instructions to speak for any portion of his constituents, he may do it fluently and respectably, but I expect nothing beyond that'.[12] He presented his constituents' petitions for increased coroners' fees, 30 Nov. 1826.[13] His obligations to ministers, Canningites, and the agriculturists and ship owners who had secured his election made his position an extremely difficult one and placed him under considerable personal strain. He forwarded a draft scheme for 'moderate' protection for corn, in which he drew on the letters of Sir Claude Scott† as his 'authority', to Canning with an explanatory letter, 18 Jan. 1827. He lobbied for inquiry into the increased use of foreign ships in the carrying trade following relaxation of the navigation laws, in 'language' which the home secretary Peel felt 'obliged' to draw to Canning's attention, 14 Feb., and, troubled and unwell with a venereal complaint which he asked Stapleton to pass off as a 'violent cold and sore throat', he joined Bell in endorsing and presenting their constituents' petitions for protection, 21, 26, 27 Feb., 29 Mar., 3 May 1827.[14] He privately suggested 64*s.* a quarter as an acceptable remunerating price for the grower and was also prepared to see foreign corn admitted 'at all times on paying a duty of 32*s.*', with reductions when domestic prices reached 72*s.*, and concessions made for Canadian wheat.[15] Defending government policy, 9 Mar., he claimed that he had voted silently for Canning's resolutions based on a 60*s.* pivot price, because it was 'an improvement on the existing system'; and he accused Whitmore, who sought to reduce it by 10*s.*, of stealing and perverting Tory ideas. Although it placed him in opposition to the new Canning ministry, he had 'no hesitation' in seconding Gascoyne's motion (withdrawn after Huskisson 'turned the debate') for the appointment of a select committee on the distressed state of shipping, 7 May. His speech, which to avoid 'misrepresentation' he published and dedicated to the 'ship owners and seamen of the ports of Northumberland', incorporated arguments from the Tyne ship owners' petition presented by Cuthbert Ellison, 3 May, and Henry Brougham's* *Enquiry into the Colonial Policy of European Powers*, and drew also on the statistics he had previously sent to Peel. He dismissed reciprocity as fanciful talk and called for protection, yet he took pains to state that he did not oppose free trade as such, but only 'the means of going about it'.[16] He voted for Catholic relief, 6 Mar., and presented petitions from Northumberland for repeal of the Test Acts, 7 June.[17] He supported and was named to the select committee on pauper lunatics, 13 June. He left Canning's service in July 1827, a month before his death.

Speaking on the recent ministerial changes, 4 Feb. 1828, Liddell expressed qualified and conditional support for the duke of Wellington's administration, asserted that Canning 'alone was the main strength and stay' of the late ministry he had adhered to and that 'its dissolution ... was as much a relief to its friends as ... a measure of satisfaction to its opponents'.[18] He deemed Wellington 'better placed as head of the armed forces' than as premier and welcomed Peel's return to the home office, but not his anti-Catholic views. He expressed confidence in the Canningites Lord Palmerston* (secretary at war) and Charles Grant* (president of the board of trade), who remained in office, but not the colonial secretary Huskisson, and called for 'conciliation and concession' in Ireland.[19] Knowing that he would be away when Lord John Russell moved for repeal of the Test Acts, 25 Feb., he declared for it when presenting favourable petitions from North Shields and Braunton, 18 Feb. (He divided for Catholic relief, 12 May 1828.) He found 'much to agree with' in Portman's resolutions on the corn laws, 22 Apr., but denied that Wellington's importation bill gave less protection to farmers than Canning's had done, and, citing examples of corn imported at 24*s*. in Northumberland, he warned of the dangers of 'unfettered importation' in terms which Grant found difficult to contradict. Presenting a hostile petition from Newcastle, 5 May, he criticized the small notes bill as a harbinger of distress, fraught with practical problems for the Tyne ship owners and Newcastle's 'efficient bankers', who stood to lose business by it to Scotland. He echoed Alexander Baring's vain plea for inquiry into the currency, 22 May, and seconded that proposed by the Whig Sir James Graham, 5 June; but he carefully projected himself on doing so as a reluctant opponent of government, who was acting from 'public duty' to his constituents. He also emphasized his differences with Graham on the currency. He presented and endorsed petitions against the small notes bill from certain Derbyshire and Yorkshire ironmasters and Nottinghamshire colliers, 13 June. Supporting Gascoyne in the debate on shipping, 17 June, he rejected Grant's assumption that recent improvements in orders and employment signalled an end to the crisis and reiterated his belief that competition could not be sustained effectively without protection. He warmly praised Canning when provision was made for his family, 22 May 1828. In the Canningite lists drawn up following the resignation of the 'rump' from Wellington's administration that month, he was included as a 'probable' by Palmerston, but omitted by Lord Colchester.

The 3rd duke of Northumberland's 'supposed conversion' to the Catholic cause prompted empty speculation that Liddell would join the Wellington administration directly emancipation was conceded.[20] However, he approved their address, 6 Feb., divided for emancipation, 6, 30 Mar., and criticized his constituents' hostile petitions, 3, 4, 17 Mar., including several he presented, 4 Mar. 1829. After hoping to see the East Retford disfranchisement bill deferred, 5 May, he gave what he termed a reluctant wayward vote to transfer its seats to Birmingham, but added that he would remain a committed opponent of parliamentary reform. On 2 June 1829, a week before leaving town, he requested an interview with Wellington to discuss the electoral influence of the Greenwich Hospital estate in Northumberland, but he received no formal offer of support.[21] Liddell delayed his return to London for the 1830 session and, deliberately following the example of Graham in Cumberland, he personally instigated a requisition for a county distress meeting, convened for him by his political ally Sanderson Ilderton as sheriff, 15 Feb. In the absence of the Whigs and Ultras and opposed only by the Whig renegade and former county Member Sir Charles Monck, he carried a petition for inquiry, which attributed distress to the restoration of the gold standard in 1819, compounded by the Small Notes Act, and called for retrenchment and cuts in taxes 'most affecting the poor'. He also professed personal support for Wellington, but proclaimed himself 'independent of all administrations'.[22] In the House, 5 Mar., he endorsed the Suffolk petitioners' call for 'some protection' against Irish imports. Bringing up the Northumberland distress petition, 12 Mar., he reiterated his remarks at its adoption and insisted that any inquiry into distress should include the currency and the introduction of Scottish banking practices in its remit. He presented and endorsed two petitions from Durham that day for repeal of the Small Notes Act, and paired for Graham's critical motion on the appointment as navy treasurer of the erstwhile Canningite Thomas Frankland Lewis*. He quibbled over the estimates, 15 Mar. Contributing to the state of the nation debate, 18 Mar., he said he felt compelled by the Northumberland distress petition to support Edward Davenport; but he remained unsure how to vote and, when the debate was held over, he disclosed that he would have preferred to see the motion killed by adjournment, rather than postponed, 19 Mar. He was one of the delegation who waited on Wellington the next day to lobby for an investigative committee.[23] He divided with government to retain the 'necessary post' of lieutenant-general of the ordnance, 29 Mar. He presented and endorsed protectionist petitions from Northumberland ship owners, 6 May, lead miners and tobacco manufacturers, 25 May. Like Graham, whose remarks he praised, he maintained that manufacturers had the same rights to protection as agriculture, 25 May. He voted to abolish the death penalty for forgery, 7 June, having presented a favourable petition from Newcastle, 3 May 1830.

Liddell reaffirmed his opposition to reform before voting to transfer East Retford's seats to Birmingham, 5 Mar. 1830, which concessions, he maintained, afforded the 'best argument' against the 'sweeping reformers'. He said he would also have voted to enfranchise Birmingham, Leeds and Manchester (23 Feb.) had he been in London. Representing the northern coal owners, he called for inquiry into the London coal trade and was named to the committee, 11 Mar., backed the parliamentary campaign for repeal of the coastwise coal duties, 17 Mar., and brought up petitions for it, 3 May. An opponent, to his cost, of the Newcastle-Carlisle railway, he spoke, 3, 4 June, and voted, 3 June, for the Northern Roads bill, which the Lowthers bitterly opposed and was now held over.[24] His opposition to the sale of beer bill was confined to its provisions for on-consumption, 21 June, which he deemed suitable for remedial legislation, and he did not want to see the measure sacrificed, 1 July. Describing himself as an 'independent county Member' and consistent supporter of ministers, he joined in the Whig protest at the deferral of the regency question to the next Parliament, 30 June. In his canvassing address of the previous day, he defended his voting record and conduct and sought financial assistance for the anticipated contest against Bell and Beaumont. He withdrew from lack of funds, 14 July 1830.[25] Disturbed by reports that Canning's friend Lord Carlisle had backed him, the Newcastle barrister Losh complained that Liddell was 'not a very good politician, nor likely to adhere very steadily to the principles of civil and religious liberty'.[26] He was forced to deny speculation that he was to second the upstart John Hodgson* for Newcastle.[27]

Liddell reluctantly accepted that some reform was necessary and, projecting himself as a candidate in waiting, he delivered what the 1831-2 boundary commissioner William Henry Ord† termed a 'sort of half speech which suited neither one side nor the other, being ... like his [parliamentary] speeches intended to suit both' at the Newcastle meeting of 23 Dec. 1830. Speaking similarly, he again failed miserably at the Durham county meeting, 1 Feb., and in Northumberland, 9 Feb. 1831. He declared against wholesale disfranchisement, but was for transferring single Members from small, depopulated places to manufacturing towns and an extended franchise. He was unexpectedly absent from the Northumberland meeting of 16 Mar.[28] Arrangements to start him as a Tory for county Durham in 1831 and as a Conservative for Northumberland North in 1832 and 1835 were abandoned, but he famously outshone Howick on the hustings at Alnwick, 16 Dec. 1832, when, with what the Conservative *Newcastle Journal* termed 'his usual polished and nervous eloquence', he claimed that satisfaction with the Reform Act would be short-lived. He also criticized the campaigns for the ballot and tithe reform, warned of the dangers of any precipitate abolition of slavery and an 'expensive currency' and opposed intervention in Holland and Belgium and financing war in Portugal.[29] He successfully contested county Durham in 1837, resigned over protection in 1847, and, having failed at South Shields in 1852, was elected in 1853 for Liverpool, which he represented until he succeeded his father to the peerage in March 1855. An ardent protectionist opposed to church disestablishment, he was created an earl in 1874, for services to the Derby and Disraeli ministries.[30] He died at Ravensworth Castle in March 1878, predeceased in 1856 by his wife, and recalled as a statesman and poet. In addition to his epic *The Wizard of the North* (1833) and *Poems* (1877), he published translations of Classical verse (*The Odes of Horace* (1858), *Carmina* (1865), *Virgil's Ænid* (1872)), and several studies for *Archaeologia Aeliana*.[31] He made provision by his will (proved in London, 21 May 1878) for his younger children, executors and trustees, and was succeeded in turn in his barony, earldom and estates by his sons Henry George Liddell (1821-1903), Lord Eslington, Conservative Member for Northumberland South, 1852-78, and Atholl Liddell (1833-1904), on whose death without issue the earldom became extinct.[32]

[1] Add. 38258, f. 266; 38458, ff. 318, 320; Castle Howard mss, Lady to Lord Morpeth [1 Feb.]; *Tyne Mercury*, 21 Mar. 1820. [2] Durham CRO, Clayton and Gibson mss D/CG16/6-9. [3] *The Times*, 18 Dec. 1820; Sheffield Archives, Wharncliffe mss WLM/T.E24. [4] W. Yorks. AS (Leeds), Stapleton mss 1/42, Liddell to Canning, 1 Nov. 1823, to Stapleton, 22 Apr. 1824-20 July 1825; 1/47, Lady Clanricarde to Stapleton, undated letters, 1824-5. [5] Creevey mss, Creevey to Miss Ord, 11 Feb.-9 Mar.; *Durham Chron.* 11, 18, 25 Feb.; Fitzwilliam mss 124/5, 9; Keele Univ. Lib. Sneyd mss SC17/28; *The Times*, 27 Feb.-10 Mar. 1826. [6] Creevey mss, Creevey to Grey, 21 Feb.; *The Times*, 15 Mar. 1826; M.D. George, *Cat. of Pol. and Personal Satires*, x. 15120-2. [7] *Northumb. Pollbook and Election Pprs. June-July 1826* (W. Davison, Alnwick edn. 1827), 21-32, 37-39, 44-45, 48-51. [8] Creevey mss, Creevey to Miss Ord, 9, 11 Mar.; *Durham Chron.* 18 Mar.; Liddell, *Speech at George Tavern, N. Shields* (1826). [9] *The Times*, 23, 30 June, 19 Sept.; *The Globe*, 23 June 1826; *Procs. and Poll, N. Dur.* (1837), 8-9, 11; NLS, Ellice mss, Grey to Ellice, 7 Feb. 1827. [10] Stapleton mss 1/42, Liddell to Stapleton [Aug.] 1826. [11] *Geo. IV Letters*, ii. 1271; Dorset RO D/BKL, Bankes jnl. 158 (21 Nov.); Castle Howard mss, Morpeth to Lady Carlisle [25 Nov.] 1826. [12] Castle Howard mss, Abercromby to Carlisle [22 Nov.] *Durham Chron.* 25 Nov., 2 Dec. 1826. [13] *The Times*, 1 Dec. 1826. [14] Stapleton mss 1/42, Liddell to Canning, 18 Jan., to Stapleton, 23 Feb.; Add. 38749, ff. 74, 76; *The Times*, 22, 27, 28 Feb., 30 Mar., 4 May 1827. [15] Stapleton mss 1/42, Liddell to Canning, 18 Jan. 1827. [16] Liddell, *Speech ... for a committee to take into consideration the depressed state of shipping* (1827); Nottingham Univ. Lib. Acc 636, Denison diary, 7 May 1827. [17] *The Times*, 8 June 1827. [18] A. Aspinall, 'The Last of the Canningites', *EHR*, l (1935), 650. [19] Sneyd mss SC17/34. [20] Nottingham Univ. Lib. Ossington mss OsC 67a, Sandon to Denison, 22 Jan. 1829. [21] Wellington mss WP1/1023/15, 16. [22] Ellice mss, Grey to Ellice, 24 Jan.; *Newcastle Chron.* 13, 20 Feb.; *Durham Chron.* 20 Feb. 1830. [23] Add. 38758, f. 138. [24] Cumbria RO (Carlisle), Howard (Corby Castle) mss D/HC/1/21, Losh to H. Howard, 13 July 1830; Wellington mss WP1/1119/11. [25] Northumb. RO, Ridley (Blagdon) mss ZRI25/59, Stable to Ridley, 31 May, Donkin to same, 5 July; *Newcastle Chron.* 3, 10, 17, 24 July; *Corresp. of James Losh* ed. E. Hughes (Surtees Soc. cclxxiv), ii. 94; Add. 40401, f. 140. [26] Howard (Corby Castle) mss, Losh to H. Howard, 13 July 1830. [27] Ridley (Blagdon) mss 59, Stable to Ridley, 31 May; *Newcastle Chron.* 5,

12, 26 June 1830. [28] Northumb. RO, Blackett-Ord (Whitfield) mss NRO324/A/36, W.H. Ord to fa. [23 Dec.]; *Durham Chron.* 25 Dec. 1830, 6 Feb. 1831; *The Times*, 30 Dec. 1830; *Tyne Mercury*, 8 Feb. 1831. [29] *Durham Chron.* 6 Feb. 1831; Wellington mss WP1/1182/25; 1184/3; *Tyne Mercury*, 18 Dec.; *Newcastle Jnl.* 22 Dec. 1832; *Greville Mems.* iii. 122. [30] *The Times*, 1, 2 Apr. 1874. [31] Ibid. 20 Mar. 1878; *Oxford DNB*. [32] *The Times*, 31 May 1878; Clayton and Gibson mss 16/25-39; M.H. Dodds, *Hist. Northumb.* xiv. 518-19.

M.M.E.

LINDSAY, Hon. Hugh Primrose (1765–1844), of Plaistow Lodge, Bromley, Kent and 22 Berkeley Square, Mdx.

PERTH BURGHS 1820–1830

b. 31 Oct. 1765,[1] 8th but 5th surv. s. of James Lindsay, 5th earl of Balcarres [S] (*d.* 1768), and Hon. Anne Dalrymple, da. of Sir Robert Dalrymple of Castleton, Berwick. *m.* 14 Jan. 1799, Jane, da. of Hon. Alexander Gordon (Lord Rockville SCJ), 1s. 1da. *d.* 23 Apr. 1844.

Entered RN 1779, lt. 1782; E.I. Co.'s marine service by 1787, capt. 1793.[2]

Dir. E.I.Co. 1814-*d.*, dep. chairman 1826-7, chairman 1827-8.

Marshall of admiralty ct. 1815-*d.*; metropolitan lunacy commr. 1827-*d.*

Lindsay was in his infancy when his father died and spent much of his childhood with his mother's relations, the Dalrymples, at Bargany, Ayrshire. His chosen career in the royal navy was, he recalled in maturity, curtailed 'by the entire stop to promotion which took place at the close of the American war in the year 1782'.[3] His sister Lady Anne Lindsay, however, wrote that he left the navy in disgust after Lord Howe objected to his promotion by Lord Rodney, under whom he had served with distinction in the West Indies.[4] He joined the East India Company's marine service and in 1793, on the recommendation of the captain of the *Melville Castle*, Philip Dundas†, he was appointed captain of the *Rockingham*. The new-built *Lady Jane Dundas* trading to Bengal and Madras was entrusted to him (1799) and in 1811 he successfully escorted a valuable fleet home from Canton, where the Hoppo, to whom he headed a delegation, had threatened to bar their passage.[5] After settling with his family at Plaistow Lodge, on the outskirts of London, he leased a house in Berkeley Square and in 1814 became a director of the East India Company, with responsibility for shipping. He received a £300 salary, but later maintained that 'the general opinion of the day seems to have been that the worth of each directorship amounted to no less than £10,000 *per annum* in one form or another'.[6] Assisted by his brother the 6th earl of Balcarres (whose heir Lord Lindsay now came in for Wigan) and the Liverpool ministry's Scottish manager Lord Melville, Lindsay offered for the venal Perth district of burghs at the general election of 1820, with a view to promoting East Indian interests, and saw off his rivals Sir David Moncrieff† and George Simson† to come in unopposed.[7] It was evident during the canvass that the conflicting patronage demands of Lindsay, whose constituency included the Fifeshire burghs of Cupar and St. Andrews, and the new Fifeshire Member James Wemyss could pose problems for ministers, and so it proved in the winter of 1824-5, when, in an acrimonious trial of strength, Lindsay failed to secure the appointment of Dr. Fleming as second minister of Cupar.[8]

Parliamentary reporters occasionally confused Lindsay, a pro-Catholic Tory, who divided fairly steadily with the ministry, with his anti-Catholic nephews Lord Lindsay (from 1825 7th earl of Balcarres) and Colonel James Lindsay. Petitions were regularly entrusted to him, and in the 1820 Parliament he represented his constituents' interests in select committees on salmon fisheries (1824, 1825), the linen trade (1825) and local legislation. He voted for Catholic relief, 28 Feb. 1821, 30 Apr. 1822, 1 Mar., 21 Apr., but to outlaw the Catholic Association, 25 Feb. 1825. He divided consistently with government on the revenue and retrenchments, 1820-3. He declined to comment on a petition he presented from the mayor and council of Dundee countering one from the burgesses accusing them of malversation, 17 Apr. 1821, or on one against the lord advocate's burghs regulation bill from the corporation of Perth, 30 May 1822.[9] He presented a petition from Perth for continuation of the linen bounties, 16 June 1820.[10] He brought up several from Perth and elsewhere for restoration of Queen Caroline's name to the liturgy, 26 Jan., but divided against censuring ministers' handling of the affair, 6 Feb. 1821.[11] He presented petitions from the brewers of Dundee and Perth for amendment of the excise laws, 28 June 1821.[12] In July, replying to a request from the duke of Gordon, he claimed that he had recently given up 'the whole' of his East India Company patronage to establish his son Hugh Hamilton Lindsay as a merchant in China.[13] He presented a petition from the ship owners of Dundee against relaxation of the navigation laws, 14 May,[14] and voted against inquiring into Irish tithes, 19 June, and the lord advocate's treatment of the Scottish press, 25 June 1822.

Lindsay was listed in the government majority against producing papers on the plot to murder the Irish viceroy, 24 Mar., and their minority against inquiring into the subsequent prosecutions, 22 Apr.

1823. He divided with them against repealing the Foreign Enlistment Act, 16 Apr., and on chancery arrears, 5 June, but against them on the Irish tithes composition bill, 16 June, and for equalizing the duties on East and West Indian sugars, 22 May. The 1823 Tay ferries amendment bill was entrusted to him, and he presented and endorsed numerous Fifeshire and Forfarshire petitions against proposed changes in the laws regulating the linen trade, 7, 15, 21, 23, 27 May 1823.[15] He brought up petitions for trading concessions from certain flax spinners and linen manufactures, 15 Mar., and for the reintroduction of yarn inspectors, 25 Mar. 1824. He presented several against the Tay salmon fisheries regulation bill, 8, 12 Mar., for legislation to facilitate small debt recovery, 18 Mar., and against the notaries' tax, 29 Mar., 1 Apr. 1824, 14 Feb. 1825. Dundee's petition in favour of the London and Westminster oil-gas bill was entrusted to and presented by him, 12 Apr., as were their petitions for deregulation of the trade in hides and skins, 3, 28 May, and repeal of the beer retail bill, 12 May 1824.[16] He also presented petitions for repeal of the duties on fire insurance policies (in which as a manager of the Sun Alliance Company he had a vested interest), 4 Mar., and of the assessed taxes, 7, 22 Mar. 1825. He called on ministers to postpone proposed tariff reductions affecting linen, which the trade viewed with alarm, 25 Mar., and presented petitions advocating this, 18, 25 Apr., 3, 19 May.[17] In a rare intervention on the estimates, 7 Mar., he declared that the accommodation for conveying troops on East India Company ships, where men were allocated 18-inch berths and deck space, was better than that provided on naval vessels, and urged that the *Kent* East Indiaman be fully repaired. He presented petitions from the whale fishery of Dundee against the proposed tariff reduction on rapeseed oil, 18 Apr., from the corporations of Perth, 28 Apr., and Forfar, 5 May, for corn law revision, and from Perth against the salmon fisheries bill, 19 May 1825.[18] He voted to kill the 'jobbing' Leith docks bill, 20 May, and steadily for the duke of Cumberland's annuity bill, 30 May-10 June 1825.[19] Adhering as usual to government policy when chairing meetings at East India House, he cautioned his fellow directors against dismissing Lord Amherst as governor of Bengal for allegedly mishandling the Burmese war and Barrackpoor mutiny, and was probably in the minority of nine (to 12) against sending out Lord Elphinstone to replace him.[20] He voted in a minority of four against authorizing the return to India of George Lamb, a former partner in William Palmer and Company, 14 Dec. 1825.[21]

On 25 Feb. 1826 Lindsay, who divided against reform of the Scottish representation, 20 Feb., 18 Apr., strongly endorsed and urged ministers to heed the provost and council of Perth's petition criticizing the changes in the Scottish banking system contemplated in the wake of the 1825-6 crisis. He presented petitions from Forfar for corn law revision, 28 Feb., from the ship owners of Dundee complaining of the high collection costs of the northern lighthouse dues, 17 Apr., and several against slavery, 13 Feb.-7 Apr.[22] Contradicting Trant, he joined the president of the India board Charles Williams Wynn in praising the education offered to East India Company cadets at Haileybury College, 16 Mar.[23] He voted to receive the report on Huskisson's board of trade salary, 10 Apr. Lindsay's relations looked to him for East India patronage and had considered making Wigan or the Anstruther Burghs available to him if his return for the Perth district was doubtful.[24] However, boosted by his recent appointment as the East India Company's deputy chairman, he came in there *in absentia* and unopposed at the general election in June 1826, notwithstanding his refusal to accede to a demand from the corporation of Dundee that he pledge himself to support corn law reform, which, as an advocate of the 80*s*. pivot price, he privately opposed.[25] Before Parliament met, he submitted memorials to Williams Wynn and Huskisson explaining the Company's decision to 'suspend for the present season ... making any provision of goods and stores for sale at the several residencies of India' on account of 'the unexampled commercial distress of the past year' and bullion losses of almost 'two million sterling'.[26] He was elected to the committee of Lloyd's, 13 Dec. 1826.[27]

Lindsay paired for Catholic relief, 6 Mar. 1827, 12 May 1828. Sir John Malcolm's* plan for the government of India preoccupied him early in 1827, when the abortive Perth harbour bill was entrusted to him;[28] but he presented petitions from the provost and council urging consideration of the corn laws, 12 Feb., and from certain Perth landowners recommending the admission of foreign corn on payment of a small protective tariff, 19 Mar.[29] He also brought up the Dundee ship owners' petition for inquiry into their distressed trade, 15 Mar. 1827.[30] After being installed as East India Company chairman in April he adopted a higher public profile and (although some uncertainty remains) it was probably he and not his nephew James who announced in the House on 25 May that he was withholding his support from the Canning ministry, 'the most extraordinary sort of alliance or coalition that could be imagined', until he had 'seen more of their measures' and could ascertain 'whether they did or did not mean to adhere to those principles which they had formerly professed'.[31] Following a business meeting with Canning early in July, he chaired several turbulent ones at East India House before Lord William Cavendish Bentinck's* departure to India as governor-general was approved and he presided at his farewell dinner on 17 Oct. 1827.[32] In November he wrote to the Goderich ministry's home secretary Lord Lansdowne offering to make bullion available to government notwithstanding the Company's depleted stocks.[33]

Lindsay was one of 20 pro-Catholic Members who voted in the ministerial minority against considering repeal of the Test Acts, when the duke of Wellington as prime minister made it a government question, 26 Feb. 1828.[34] He welcomed inquiry but disputed the claims in a petition presented by Sir James Mackintosh on the 18th from Captain Myles O'Reilly of Dublin, who blamed the Company's directors for financial losses suffered by his family after depositing money with the Company's treasurer at Madras, Samuel Ricketts. (He was appointed to the investigative committee, 5 May 1829.) Supporting increased naval expenditure, 19 May 1828, he referred to his experience on 12 Apr. 1782, under Lord Rodney's command, when 'we had not enough midshipmen in the whole fleet, which consisted of 36 ships of the line, qualified to fill the vacancies in the rank above them'. He presented a petition for lower duties on fire insurances from the Forfarshire chamber of commerce, 17 Apr., and was a majority teller, 23 May 1828, for the Scottish salmon fisheries bill enacted that session. The abilities of his nephews Charles and Colin Lindsay, promoted during his chairmanship, were widely praised, but Lindsay, who had also obtained a pension for the superintendent of the Bombay marine, Thomas Buchanan, and an increased trust fund for the marquess of Hastings, had difficulty countering charges of nepotism, made against him and his predecessor Sir George Robinson*, when he campaigned for re-election to the direction in April 1829.[35] As the patronage secretary Planta had predicted, he divided 'with government' for Catholic emancipation, 6, 30 Mar., but he called for the provisions of the attendant bill disfranchising 40*s.* freeholders to be extended to Scotland, 24 Mar. 1829. He presented petitions from Dundee for and against emancipation, 9 Mar., but is unlikely to have presented those credited to him on 24, 30 Mar., which were almost certainly introduced by James Lindsay or the Perthshire Member Sir George Murray (24 Mar.). He voted to permit Daniel O'Connell to take his seat for county Clare without swearing the oath of supremacy, 16 May. He brought up petitions against the Fifeshire roads bill, 24 Mar., and the Scottish gaols bill, 11, 12 May. He had been removed from the select committee on the Perth waterworks bill at the request of Robert Dundas, 23 Mar. 1829.

No votes on national issues can safely be attributed to Lindsay in 1830. His constituents now made no secret of their opposition to the East India Company's trading monopoly and forwarded hostile petitions for presentation to Archibald Campbell and Lord Kinnoull.[36] Local legislation was also largely entrusted to others, but on 28 May, acting for the corporation, Lindsay failed, by 59-76, to prevent Hume carrying the amendment which ensured the appointment of three ship owners as commissioners under the 1830 Perth harbour bill. Declaring the measure 'completely changed', the *Perthshire Courier* added: 'The London papers, presuming that the usual fate attended this as Hume's other motions, reported the majority of 17 to be against his amendment, but the fact is as we have stated it'.[37] He presented a petition from the lord provost, magistrates and town council of Perth against taxing Scottish probate inventories, 5 July 1830. Citing ill health, he reluctantly relinquished the representation of the Perth Burghs at the dissolution that month and did not stand for Parliament again.[38]

Lindsay, who gave his name to a steam ship, remained a lifelong director of the East India Company and an active member of their shipping, finance and home committees. He died at his home in Berkley Square in April 1844, shortly after his re-election to the direction had been confirmed.[39] By his will, dated 28 Mar. 1839, he left his daughter, the wife of Sir Edmund Antrobus†, his 'kindest love and blessing' and everything else to his wife (*d.* 1862). His son Hugh Hamilton Lindsay (1800-81), Conservative Member for Sandwich, 1841-7, and founder of Lindsay and Company of Hong Kong, the banking and shipping concern bankrupted in 1865, was the 'default legatee'.[40]

[1] *Burke PB*; *Farrington's Biog. Index of EI Co. Maritime Service Officers, 1660-1834*, IGI (Fife) and *Scottish Peerage* give 1763. Lindsay's reported age at death was 78. [2] *Farrington*, 476. [3] Lord Lindsay, *Lives of the Lindsays* (1858 edn.), iii. 479. [4] Ibid. ii. 340-1. [5] Ibid. ii. 479-86; *Farrington*, 370, 447-8, 563, 570, 708. [6] C.H. Philips, *E.I. Co.* 336; C. Northcote Parkinson, *Trade in Eastern Seas*, 13. [7] NAS GD51/1/198/10/82; 198/21/65-68; GD51/5/749/1, f. 182; NLS mss 1054, f. 177; *Perth Courier*, 17 Feb., 2 Mar.; *The Times*, 24 Feb. *Dundee, Perth and Cupar Advertiser*, 24, 31 Mar., 7 Apr. 1820. [8] NAS GD51/5/749/1, ff. 199-202; Add. 40370, ff. 235-8; 40371, ff. 53, 59, 294; 40372, ff. 43, 45, 140, 170-84, 208-9; 40373, ff. 3-5. [9] *The Times*, 18 Apr. 1821, 31 May 1822. [10] Ibid. 17 June 1820. [11] Ibid. 27 Jan. 1821. [12] Ibid. 29 June 1821 [13] NAS GD44/43/355. [14] *The Times*, 15 May 1822. [15] Ibid. 25 Apr., 8, 16, 22, 24, 28 May 1823. [16] Ibid. 9, 13, 16, 19, 26, 30 Mar., 2, 13 Apr., 4, 13, 29 May 1824. [17] Ibid. 15 Feb., 5, 8, 23 Mar., 19, 26 Apr., 4, 20 May 1825. [18] Ibid. 19, 29 Apr., 6, 20 May. 1825. [19] Ibid. 20 May 1825. [20] Philips, 252; *The Times*, 23 July 1826. [21] BL OIOC

mss Eur D960. [22] *The Times*, 14, 25 Feb., 1, 15, 17, 21 Mar., 8 Apr. 1826. [23] Ibid. 17 Mar. 1826. [24] NLS, Crawford mss 25/1/363-4, 417-19. [25] Add. 35652, f. 328; *Perthshire Courier*, 25 May, 8, 15 June, 6 July 1826. [26] Add. 38748, ff. 175-82. [27] *The Times*, 14 Dec. 1826. [28] *Dundee, Perth and Cupar Advertiser*, 21 Dec. 1826; Wellington mss WP1/912/4. [29] *The Times*, 13, 20 Mar. 1827. [30] Ibid. 16 Mar. 1827. [31] Ibid. 26 May 1827; *Parl. Deb.* (n.s.), xvii. 1034. [32] Crawford mss 24/1/422; *The Times*, 27 July; 13 Sept., 18 Oct. 1827. [33] TNA HO44/10. [34] G.I.T. Machin, 'Resistance to Repeal of Test and Corporation Acts: 1828', *HJ*, xxii (1979), 123-4. [35] *Corresp. of Lord William Cavendish Bentinck* ed. C.H. Philips, i. 122-4; *The Times*, 27 Sept., 10 Oct., 20 Dec. 1827, 20 Mar., 12, 15 Nov. 1828. [36] *Perthshire Courier*, 4, 11, 25 Mar. 1830. [37] Ibid. 3 June 1830. [38] *Dundee, Perth and Cupar Advertiser*, 15 July 1830. [39] *E.I. Reg.* 1814-44; *Ann. Reg.* (1844), App. to Chron. p. 233. [40] PROB 11/2000/473; IR26/1681/368; Staffs. RO D(W)1920/5/3/1-20.

M.M.E.

LINDSAY, James, Lord Lindsay (1783–1869), of Muncaster Castle, Cumb.; Haigh Hall, nr. Wigan, Lancs., and 21 Berkeley Square, Mdx.

WIGAN 1820–27 Mar. 1825

b. 23 Apr. 1783, 1st s. of Alexander, 6th earl of Balcarres [S], and his cos. Elizabeth, da. and h. of Charles Dalrymple of North Berwick, Haddington. *m.* 21 Nov. 1811, Hon. Maria Frances Margaret Pennington, da. and h. of John Pennington†, 1st Bar. Muncaster [I], 4s. 1da. *d.v.p. suc.* fa. as 7th earl of Balcarres [S] and *de jure* 24th earl of Crawford [S] 27 Mar. 1825; *cr.* Bar. Wigan [UK] 5 July 1826. *d.* 15 Dec. 1869.

Lt. 83 Ft. 1795; capt. army 1796; capt. 20 Drag. 1797, maj. 1803, ret. 1804; a.d.c. to ld. lt. [I] 1801-4.

Maj. Wigan loyal vols. 1806.

The Lindsays were an old Fifeshire family with an estate at Balcarres and a tradition of support for the Stuarts. The 5th earl of Balcarres (1691-1768) fought with the Pretender at Sheriffmuir in 1715, but was pardoned on account of his youth and obtained a commission in the British army. He distinguished himself at Dettingen in 1743 but, having been refused promotion by George II, retired in 1745 and devoted the rest of his life to agricultural improvement and literature. He did not marry until he was 57 and died when the youngest of his 11 children, who included eight sons, was only two. He was resigned to the fact that his eldest son Alexander, who became 6th earl of Balcarres at the age of 16, after joining the army, would have to part with the Fifeshire estate, as he told his eldest child Lady Anne (the composer, as Lady Anne Barnard, of the ballad 'Auld Robin Gray'):

> Your brother will not find it possible to keep Balcarres unless he marries a woman of large fortune, and I should be sorry if my boy were to sell himself for this purpose. I do not reckon it the family estate of our ancestors; that passed away from us long ago ... Balcarres has not been 200 years in our family, and never was an estate of value; I shall leave it loaded with debt for the portions of my younger children, though they are but small, and my son must be obliged to sell it.

He had advised his heir in 1765:

> As your nine brothers and sisters must be provided, and as you will have two jointures to pay, your condition will be but mean at first, and will require good management ... But if you can learn to be temperate and frugal, you may be easy and happy in body and mind. When your circumstances become better, never save your money when justice, charity, or honour, require you to part with it.[1]

On succeeding to the peerage Balcarres, who later claimed that his patrimony yielded him an income of only £150 a year, spent two years at the University of Gottingen before resuming his military career. He served under Burgoyne in North America, was wounded at Ticonderoga and was in American hands until 1779. The following year he married his cousin Elizabeth Dalrymple, the heiress of the former Bradshaigh estate at Haigh, near Wigan, which, though neglected and dilapidated, and, thanks to the feudal basis on which its farms were rented, yielded virtually no annual income, held potentially lucrative deposits of top grade cannel and coal.[2] In 1784 and 1790 Balcarres, a pro-Catholic Tory, was elected a Scottish representative peer; and in 1789 he obtained the colonelcy of the 63rd Foot, which he held until his death.[3] At about this time he gave up his struggle to retain the Balcarres estate and sold it to his younger brother Robert, who had prospered in the Bengal civil service, in order to pay debts and, with the modest surplus, to finance his operations at Haigh. He also borrowed £4,000 from the 3rd earl of Hardwicke, who had married his sister Elizabeth in 1782.[4] On the outbreak of war in 1793 he was appointed to the command in Jersey, where he carried on communications with the army of La Vendée. His appointment as lieutenant-governor of Jamaica in 1795 came to his financial rescue, enabling him to liquidate his debt to Hardwicke and invest more heavily at Haigh. During his six years in Jamaica he suppressed, not without controversy at home, a serious rebellion by the Maroons.[5] Lady Nugent, the wife of his successor, was nauseated by his filthy habits at table:

> I wish ... [he] would wash his hands, and use a nail-brush, for the black edges of his nails really make me sick. He has, besides, an extraordinary propensity to dip his fingers into every dish.

Tales of the 'profligate and disgusting scene' which marked his '*domestic* conduct' convinced her that he was 'more than half mad'.[6] Returning home 'ready for anything and anywhere' and with a pension of £300 a year, he was chosen again as a representative peer in 1802 and at the five subsequent general elections. He settled at Haigh and applied himself to the exploitation of its coal, buying hundreds of small plots of land to monopolise mining in the vicinity. He established an 'aggrandising fund' to accumulate capital and interest for his descendants. Twenty years later he was making £5,000 a year from the mines and their associated ironworks, which manufactured pit and cotton factory machinery, steam pumps and, later, locomotives, and paying £20,000 in wages; he boasted in 1822 of having restored his family to 'a handsome competence'.[7]

He secured the nominal entry of his eldest son Lord Lindsay to the army at the age of 11, and in 1797 obtained for him a company in the 20th Dragoons, who were then stationed in Jamaica; it is not clear whether Lindsay went out there.[8] In 1801 he was made an extraordinary aide-de-camp to his uncle, Hardwicke, as viceroy of Ireland; and in December 1803 he purchased a majority in the 20th. Soon afterwards the question arose of whether he should join the regiment, which was now at home, or give up the majority in order to raise a hundred men for the rank of lieutenant-colonel. His father strongly favoured the former course, pointing out that apart from the expense of the latter, it would bind him to the army for life, whereas at present he was

> possessed of a majority in an old regiment of dragoons with a prospect of being eldest major in a short period of time. What a situation for a young man ... a pleasant service, a delightful and interesting command, a handsome income arising from it, not liable to be sent to noxious climates, on the *spot* to follow out any object in life to which either your interest or turn of mind may direct you, a situation peculiarly valuable to you, as ... you have not that fixed and robust constitution to be dashed about the world as I have been.

He had in any case, as an 'effective field officer', to relinquish his duties as aide-de-camp. Balcarres, feeling that the attempt to raise men would be 'extremely difficult and hazardous', presented him with the choice between joining the 20th and taking a lieutenant-colonelcy in one of the six new regiments. He opted for the former, left Ireland in March 1804 and eventually located his regiment in Dorset. He retired altogether from the army at the end of the year.[9]

In 1811 he married the only child of the 1st Baron Muncaster, who was apparently not without misgivings over the extent to which the Lindsays' wealth was dependent on 'commercial speculation'. A year later Lindsay became embroiled in a squabble with his uncle Robert, who evidently thought he could have made more effort to persuade Muncaster to give Balcarres some financial assistance, and was accused in turn of having 'by some unwarrantable transaction debarred you from the right of succession to the family estate'.[10] On her father's death in 1813 Lady Lindsay inherited a life interest in the rents of his Cumberland estates and was confirmed in the 21-year lease on Muncaster Castle granted on her marriage, though it may have been technically invalid; and in March 1820 they were legally obliged to 'leave Muncaster'.[11] Lindsay took a close interest in the Haigh coal mining enterprise, and in 1821 clashed with his father over its financial management, in which he seems to have wanted a greater say. His apparent threat to withhold supplies of coal from Haigh to the ironworks was countered with a warning that 'a clause has always stood in my will that if you refused to furnish such supply ... my destination of the personal capital goes from you immediately'. Balcarres argued that to draw more than the £3,000 a year which he took from the pits 'would very shortly kill the hen that lays the precious egg'.[12] Their differences seem to have been resolved.

Lindsay had staked his future claim to a seat for Wigan on the former Bradshaigh interest in 1806, and Balcarrres subsequently cultivated good relations with the sitting Members, Robert Holt Leigh, a local squire, and John Hodson, a cotton manufacturer.[13] Both retired at the dissolution in 1820, when Lindsay stood with Hodson's nephew. They were returned after a contest forced by an attempt to revive the Bradford interest.[14] A very poor attender, who is not known to have spoken in debate, Lindsay supported the Liverpool ministry when present.[15] He voted in defence of their conduct towards Queen Caroline, 6 Feb. 1821. Soon afterwards he sought treasury patronage for some constituents, 'myself and family being firm supporters of ... government'.[16] He was absent from the division on Catholic relief, 28 Feb., but divided against Canning's bill to relieve Catholic peers of their disabilities, 30 Apr. 1822. He was given six weeks' leave to attend to urgent private business, 7 May 1821. The following year he went to live at Haigh Hall, and his father advised him:

> Your residence there will be the best guarantee for the success of our objects ... The strong claim which you have to two seats in Parliament will afford to your pretensions a more respectable position in the empire than any other which you can otherwise acquire, provided, however, that you are successful in maintaining your interest and weight in the corporation of Wigan. This is of high importance because your elective seat in the House of

> Lords would be much endangered if you were to lose the hold which we will have of this borough. Your residence here will be delightful to yourself and the pleasing reflection that we have extricated ourselves from the mire of corroding poverty and acquired independence in fortune, without which all is dark and dismal.[17]

Lindsay voted against abolition of one of the joint postmasterships, 13 Mar. 1822, repeal of the Foreign Enlistment Act, 16 Apr., and inquiry into the prosecution of the Dublin Orange rioters, 22 Apr. 1823. Later that session he contemplated making way at the prorogation or the next dissolution for his uncle Robert or his youngest uncle, Hugh Lindsay, Member for Perth Burghs.[18] No trace of parliamentary activity has been found for 1824. He was given a month's leave for private business, 17 Feb., but attended to vote for the Irish unlawful societies bill, 28 Feb., and against Catholic claims, 1 Mar. 1825. He presented a Wigan petition for repeal of the assessed taxes, 3 Mar. 1825.[19]

Balcarres's death later that month removed Lindsay from the Commons. In July 1826 he obtained the British peerage, as Baron Wigan, for which his father had unsuccessfully applied eight years earlier.[20] As a peer he took little active part in national politics, but he remained attached to the Conservative party of Wellington and Peel. The reform crisis of 1831 overturned his electoral interest at Wigan, but it was restored by the return of his son in 1845.[21] He devoted most of his energies to the expansion, consolidation and modernisation of the Haigh coal and iron businesses, on which he laid his personal stamp as a practically minded and enterprising owner. In 1865, when his collieries produced over 1,000,000 tons of coal a year, he merged his interests with those of other local proprietors in the Wigan Coal and Iron Company.[22] He rebuilt Haigh Hall and acquired a Scottish estate at Dunecht, 12 miles west of Aberdeen. On the death in 1808 of the 22nd earl of Crawford the senior branch of the Lindsays had become extinct in the male line. Lindsay's father had then become *de jure* 23rd earl of Crawford, but had never assumed that title. Lindsay's claim to it was admitted by the Lords in 1848, but his subsequent attempt to establish his right to the dukedom of Montrose was unsuccessful.

He died at Dunecht in December 1869. By his will, dated 8 Mar. 1849, and proved under £70,000, 14 Mar. 1870,[23] he left his wife £5,000 and an annuity of £1,700. He bequeathed £25,000 to his second son James Lindsay (1815-74), a soldier and Conservative Member for Wigan, 1845-57, 1859-65. He devised legacies totalling £28,000 and £31,000 respectively to his third and fourth sons, Charles Hugh (1816-89), Conservative Member for Abingdon, 1865-74, and Colin (1819-92), who became a Catholic in 1868. He was succeeded in the earldom and settled estates by his eldest son Alexander William Crawford Lindsay (1812-80), a bibliophile, genealogist and family historian, who in 1846 married his second cousin Margaret Lindsay. Their son, the 26th earl of Crawford (1847-1913), bought back the Balcarres estate for £150,000 in 1886.

[1] *Oxford DNB*; Lord Lindsay, *Lives of the Lindsays* (1858), ii. 342-3, 364-5. [2] D. Anderson and A.A. France, *Wigan Coal and Iron*, 9, 52. [3] Lindsay, ii. 343-53; *Geo. III Corresp.* i. 78. [4] Lindsay, ii. 364; Add. 35645, f. 213. [5] Lindsay, ii. 357-9; Anderson and France, 52; *Colchester Diary*, i. 46; *Farington Diary*, ii. 619-30. [6] *Lady Nugent's Jnl.* ed. F. Cundall (1939), 18, 19, 22, 53-54. [7] Add. 33109, f. 266; 35730, f. 97; Lindsay, ii. 360-1; *Crawford Pprs.* ed. J. Vincent, 4-5; Anderson and France, 54-60, 200-1. [8] Add. 35916, f. 207. [9] Add. 35746, ff. 163, 165; 35747, f. 273. [10] Add. 35649, ff. 246, 332; NLS, Crawford mss 25/1/608, 610, 611. [11] PROB 11/1551/28; Crawford mss 25/1/644; Northumb. RO, Middleton mss ZMI/576/35/1. [12] Crawford mss 25/1/182, 185, 186, 190, 191. [13] *HP Commons, 1790-1820*, ii. 239. [14] *Liverpool Mercury*, 18 Feb., 3, 10 Mar. 1820. [15] *Black Bk.* (1823), 170. [16] Crawford mss 25/13/219. [17] Anderson and France, 53. [18] Crawford mss 25/1/415, 416, 418. [19] *The Times*, 4 Mar. 1825. [20] Add. 38271, ff. 358, 414; 38371, ff. 162, 165. [21] Add. 40392, f. 210; 40575, f. 427; Wellington mss WP1/1010/12; 1100/19; 1102/7; 1149/12; *Wellington Pol. Corresp.* i. 444. [22] *Crawford Pprs.* 5; Anderson and France, 60-69. [23] Not under £7,000, as stated in *CP*, iii. 524.

S.R.B./D.R.F.

LINDSAY, James (1791–1855), of Balcarres and Leuchars, Fife and 14 Lower Berkeley Street, Mdx.

WIGAN	6 Apr. 1825–1831
FIFESHIRE	1831–1832

bap. 22 Apr. 1791,[1] 1st s. of Hon. Robert Lindsay of Balcarres and Elizabeth, da. of Sir Alexander Dick, 3rd bt., of Prestonfield, Edinburgh. *m.* (1) 16 Feb. 1819, Mary Ann (*d.* 14 July 1820), da. of Francis Grant of Kilgraston, Perth, *s.p.*; (2) 2 Apr. 1823, Anne, da. and coh. of Sir Coutts Trotter, 1st bt., of Westville, Lincs., 2s. 2da. surv. *suc.* fa. 1836. *d.* 5 Dec. 1855.

Ensign 1 Ft. Gds. 1807, lt. and capt. 1812, capt. and lt.-col. 1823; half-pay 1830; col. army 1838; maj.-gen. 1851; lt.-gen. 1855.

Lindsay's father, the second of the eight sons of the 5th earl of Balcarres, who died in 1768, recalled in his maturity that he had been 'flung into the wide world at the age of 13 upon my father's death before my education was well begun', and that 'pursuits of the most active nature, not sedentary ones, afterwards engrossed my attention'. His eldest sister later wrote that while he was 'less handsome' than his next brother Colin

> his countenance had much of the *bon ami* in it. He possessed sound sense without quick abilities, kind attachments and benevolence without parade, bluntness and sweetness, with a natural mercantile genius.

His elder brother, the 6th earl of Balcarres, a professional soldier, whose modest and encumbered inheritance created severe financial problems, described him as 'a lad sound and solid in his judgement, having in his line the quickness of a projector, with an excellent understanding, to limit his undertakings'.[2] On his father's death his uncle William Dalrymple, a merchant at Cadiz, took him into his business; and when Dalrymple's affairs became temporarily embarrassed he was taken on by his cousin James Duff, who encouraged him to learn Spanish. In 1772 he obtained a writership in the East India Company's Bengal civil service. He prospered in India, where he attained the position of superintendent of Sylhet, near the Burmese border: a local monopoly of the capture of elephants and trade in oranges to Calcutta enhanced his fortune. He was generous with it, and gave his mother an annuity of £250 a year and his brother money towards payment of the heavy debts on the family's estate at Balcarres in southern Fifeshire.[3] On his return from India in 1788 he married, acquired an estate at Leuchars, near Balcarres, and bought the latter from his brother, who needed capital to exploit the coal and mineral deposits on the Haigh estate at Wigan, which had come to him on his marriage. Robert Lindsay offered Balcarres back to him soon after his return from his spell as lieutenant-governor of Jamaica in 1801, but he declined to take it.[4]

James Lindsay, the eldest of Robert's six sons, visited his uncle, the 3rd earl of Hardwicke, with his next brother Alexander in January 1807, when their father wrote:

> You will find them lads of a good disposition with affable manners ... Take an opportunity of sounding them as to their progress in general learning ... You will find them greatly behind boys of their own age who have had all the advantages of a regular English education. Were I to begin again I certainly would either take up my residence in England or be satisfied with such education as Scotland affords ... James is ... a decided soldier. Between 17 and 18 I propose giving him a commission in the Guards, and in the meantime to improve his education, in such branches [as are] best suited to the line he has chosen.[5]

In the event Lindsay joined the Grenadiers in December that year, at the age of 16. He served on the Walcheren expedition in 1809 and contracted fever after his return. At one point his life was despaired of, but his aunt, Lady Anne Barnard, who ran a literary salon in London, nursed him back to health. He was at the siege of Cadiz in 1811, distinguished himself at the capture of Seville and went home after Salamanca. He returned to active service in Holland in 1813, but was invalided home after being badly wounded at Bergen-op-Zoom.[6]

Lindsay lost his first wife, who died at Clay Hall, near Windsor, in July 1820, after only 17 months of marriage.[7] He was a spectator at the Lords debate on the second reading of the bill of pains and penalties against Queen Caroline, 4 Nov. 1820, when he detected 'a direct division amongst ministers'.[8] In 1823 he married one of the daughters of the wealthy London banker Sir Coutts Trotter, a native of Berwickshire, who settled £20,000 on the children of the marriage, while Robert Lindsay contributed the same amount.[9] In June 1823 he was sounded about standing on the next vacancy for Anstruther Easter Burghs, which lay close to Balcarres. He gave it serious thought, but concluded that, leaving aside the potential cost, such a seat was not especially 'desirable', and directed his attention to Wigan, where his cousin Lord Lindsay, Balcarres's heir, Member since 1820, was contemplating retirement.[10] As it happened, Balcarres's death in March 1825 created a vacancy, which was quietly filled by James Lindsay, who the previous year had paid £5,000 for the lease of a London house at 14 Lower Berkeley Street.[11] On 21 Apr. 1825 he voted against Catholic relief, which his uncle, Hugh Lindsay, Member for Perth Burghs since 1820, supported. He voted against the Irish franchise bill, 26 Apr. He divided with the Liverpool ministry for the duke of Cumberland's annuity, 2, 6 June 1825, and against reform of the representation of Edinburgh, 13 Apr. 1826.

Returned unopposed for Wigan at the 1826 general election,[12] he divided against Catholic relief, 6 Mar. 1827. It was probably his uncle who on 25 May withheld his support from the Canning ministry until he had 'seen more of their measures'.[13] He condemned the sending of British troops to Portugal, which had 'placed the peace of the country in a very precarious situation', 8 June 1827. He presented a petition from Wigan for repeal of the Malt Act, 22 Feb. 1828. He voted against repeal of the Test Acts, 26 Feb. He argued for the retention of corporal punishment in the army, the 'most uncontrollable body of men in the community', 10 Mar. He voted against Catholic claims, 12 May. He defended the appointment of Sir George Murray*, a former soldier, as colonial secretary against Hume's criticisms, 30 May. He opposed an amendment to the salmon fisheries bill intended to permit the Sinclairs of Ulbster to fish the River Thurso, and was a teller for the hostile majority, 23 June. He divided with the Wellington ministry on the ordnance estimates, 4 July 1828. In February 1829 Planta, the patronage secretary, predicted that Lindsay, who was considered as a possible mover or seconder of the address,[14] would vote 'with government' for Catholic emancipation. Lindsay, having approved Wellington's recall of Lord Anglesey from Ireland, and reassured by the 'security' offered by the proposal to disfranchise Irish 40*s*. freeholders, which would 'effectively break down the power of the priesthood', took a pragmatic view, as he explained to an initially dubious Balcarres:

> We have the choice between two evils ... either a civil war fomented by religion immediately before us, or the granting these concessions with the hope of being able to adopt measures to avert the impending evil ... He who stems this current must be swept away ... [but] the able and skilful minister may cautiously direct the stream and prevent mischief.

He conceded that emancipation

> will not quiet Ireland in the sudden manner which visionary enthusiasts have supposed, but it will strengthen the hands of government, it will remove the nominal cause of grievance, it will unite England, and gain over all the moderate and well disposed Catholics.

With Balcarres's blessing, he voted for the motion to consider emancipation, 6 Mar., and on 23 Mar. declared in the House that it was 'calculated to improve, and not to deteriorate the constitution', for 'if we are to contend with the Roman Catholics, it is much better that the contest should be carried on within the walls of Parliament, than without'. He presented a favourable petition from Wigan, 17 Mar. He thought that any discontent which his vote might excite there would evaporate in six months; but, unlike Hugh, he did not vote for the third reading of the relief bill, 30 Mar. 1829, after being informed that his support for emancipation had indeed roused angry feelings. He nevertheless canted to one correspondent that 'had the loss of my seat ... been the *immediate* result, which may hereafter be the alternative, I would not for a moment have hesitated in following that course which I thought the best for the welfare of the country'.[15]

He voted against the enfranchisement of Birmingham, Leeds and Manchester, 23 Feb. 1830. On the Scottish judicature proposals, 1 Apr., he said that judges' salaries should be raised because 'the remuneration to all public men in high office are, at this time, scarcely sufficient'. He divided against Jewish emancipation, 5 Apr., 17 May. He presented petitions from Wigan publicans against opening the retail beer trade, 7 Apr., and voted for an amendment to the beer bill to prohibit on-sales, 21 June. He presented a petition from Linlithgowshire farmers against any increase in the duty on spirits manufactured in Scotland, 7 Apr. Lindsay, who had solicited government patronage for constituents in February, agreed with Balcarres in May that Wellington's refusal of his request for an army promotion was not 'that return which you merit', but pointed out that the duke 'has a number of most urgent applications [and] has made promises which must be complied with'.[16] He voted against abolition of the death penalty for forgery, 7 June. On 24 June he criticized the Medway Navigation Company for setting a high dividend and failing to maintain the waterway. In the debate on William IV's message on his accession, 30 June 1830, he expressed his continued confidence in ministers.

On the eve of the general election the following month, when he stood again for Wigan, Lindsay received a declaration signed by 40 Wigan burgesses condemning the East India Company's trade monopoly and a letter from the mayor urging him to denounce it. His reply, that he considered monopoly to be 'injurious' in principle and that, though reluctant to give a pledge as to his future conduct, he would support the opening of the trade, was deemed by some to be 'evasive'. At the nomination, when two radical manufacturers who had been put up by local dissidents seeking to widen the franchise came forward, he was attacked as a neglectful Member and aristocratic nominee by his colleague Hodson's cousin, John Kearsley*, a local brewer, who unexpectedly announced his own candidature. Lindsay defended himself, argued that the Wellington administration had 'effected great reductions in the expenditure, and done more than any other ministry for the people'; proclaimed, to general derision, his 'independence', and petulantly agreed, under pressure, that he was pledged to oppose the East India Company's monopoly. He was returned in second place behind Hodson.[17]

Lindsay, who retired from the army on half-pay in November 1830, was listed by ministers as one of their 'friends', and he voted with them on the civil list, 15 Nov. He presented a petition from the merchants and manufacturers of Wigan for repeal of the duty on calicos and cotton goods, 10 Feb. 1831. The following day he wrote to Balcarres:

> These are *momentous* times and if the House of Commons does not show *independence* of their constituents and act openly and honestly in support of existing

establishments and the maintenance of the constitution, I think we shall see some fearful changes ... My notion is that when the great question of reform comes before the House in the shape of alterations of existing laws, ministers will find that they have sadly miscalculated the opinion of the Commons.

Later in the month Lindsay, who was confirmed in his seat by the decision of the election committee on his opponents' petition, flattered himself that the Grey ministry was 'every day losing the confidence of the House' and 'losing ground more and more'.[18] He attended meetings of the West India merchants and planters committee, 24 Feb., 13 Apr.[19] He was '*decidedly* of opinion' that the reform bill would be 'thrown out [on] the second reading', but feared that 'much mischief must arise from it' and was not 'quite satisfied that the House will divide so decidedly as to stop further discussion on the subject'.[20] He divided against the second reading, 22 Mar., and on the 25th declared that he would 'most heartily and zealously' resist the Scottish bill 'in every one of its stages' and that 'four-fifths of the wealth and influence of Scotland are opposed to it'. Supporting a petition from Anstruther Easter Burghs against their proposed disfranchisement, 28 Mar., he said that

the general system of the whole bill, with regard to reform in Scotland, appears to me to be most objectionable ... I have no intention, whatever, to oppose a moderate reform in Scotland as respects the burghs – indeed I think some reform is justly necessary; but it appears to me that the present plan is so completely at variance with every principle of justice and expediency, that I cannot give my support to it.

He insisted that the Scottish people did not want reform, which might damage their 'flourishing' economy, 14 Apr., and voted for Gascoyne's wrecking amendment to the English bill, 19 Apr. 1831. At the ensuing general election he abandoned Wigan, where popular support for reform was very strong, and stood for Fifeshire against the incumbent, Wemyss, a reformer. At the election meeting, he admitted under interrogation that he was opposed to the reform bill, which sought to establish 'a new constitution', but claimed to be a supporter of 'moderate' reform: 'the man who stands on the quicksands of expediency must take the consequences'. He defeated Wemyss by 85-68.[21]

He presented and supported a petition from the council of Cupar asking for the burgh to be joined with St. Andrews, Crail, Kilrenny, the Anstruthers and Pittenweem to return a Member, 30 June 1831, observing that the existing Anstruther district had over 6,000 inhabitants and that in the proposed new arrangement the Fife district would be dominated by the urban and manufacturing interests. He voted against the second reading of the reintroduced reform bill, 6 July, and for the first adjournment motion of 12 July. Next day he accused ministers of reneging on pledges to reduce expenditure and of fostering the delusion that reform would lead to lower taxation. Claiming again to be 'a moderate reformer', he praised the existing constitution, which conferred 'liberty without licentiousness, and power without despotism', and predicted that if the bill became law 'anarchy and confusion' would result. On the 14th he denied having defended pocket boroughs, as reported in *The Times*, but endorsed the way in which the 'democratic principle' was 'checked by the aristocratic influence that enters into this House, through the close boroughs and the corporate towns'. He voted to postpone consideration of the partial disfranchisement of Chippenham, 27 July. On 6 Aug. he presented Fifeshire and Linlithgowshire petitions against the use of molasses in breweries and distilleries, and one from Anstruther Easter against the disfranchisement of its group, supporting it on the grounds of the district's population and the injustice of grouping Cupar and St. Andrews with Perth, which deserved separate representation. He told Balcarres that 'we got up a very lusty attack, and debate, against ministers on the disfranchisement of the Fife Eastern Burghs', which had been of 'great service to *my cause* there' should an opportunity arise.[22] He joined in calls on Tom Duncombe to retract his allegation that Lord Durham's influence had secured preferential treatment for that county's representation, 9 Aug. He divided in the minority of ten for Hunt's amendment to make proven payment of rent a qualification for voting, 25 Aug. The following day he claimed that as the occupiers of £10 houses 'neither represent the feelings nor intelligence of the people of this country', the new franchise would 'lead to the grossest corruption' and fraud and would create 'almost universal suffrage' in the large towns, while 'in the small boroughs, you will exclude hundreds who formerly enjoyed the franchise'. He gave notice that in the committee on the Scottish bill he would move that 'the eastern district of Fife burghs shall continue to return a Member', 31 Aug. He voted against the passage of the English reform bill, 21 Sept. He presented a petition from Kilrenny against the disfranchisement of the Anstruther district, 23 Sept. when he spoke and voted against the second reading of the Scottish bill, contrasting the solid achievements of Wellington's administration with the incompetence of Grey's, who used reform to mask their inadequacies.

He argued that the 'preposterous and unjust' measure, quite apart from giving Scotland inadequate representation, would deprive Scots of the chance to come in for English seats, turn the sheriffs into partisans and give the manufacturing interest the preponderance. He alleged that the bill would 'lead to universal suffrage', 1 Oct. As a vestryman of Marylebone, he repudiated Hume's charge that they had set an illegal rate, 30 Sept. 1831, and contended that while Hobhouse's bill to open vestry elections was sound in principle, some of its details were 'inappropriate to metropolitan parishes'. He supported Lord Althorp's amendment to increase the proportion of ratepayers required to sanction the local adoption of the measure and Hume's to increase the quorate figure.

He admitted that the revised reform bill contained some improvements, notably its regulation of the £10 franchise and preservation of resident freemen's voting rights, 17 Dec. 1831; but he complained that by it 'the agricultural interest will be completely crushed' and drew a parallel between contemporary Britain and France on the eve of the Revolution. He voted against the second reading that day. He supported Inglis's attempt to have a reference to Providence inserted in the preamble to the Scottish cholera prevention bill, 16 Feb. 1832. He voted against the enfranchisement of Tower Hamlets, 28 Feb. On 2 Mar. he reprimanded Adam for his 'obsequious' and misguided assurance that majority opinion in Scotland was satisfied with the number of Members now proposed for that country. He divided against the third reading of the English bill, 22 Mar. He disagreed with Boldero's plan to embody veterans on half-pay in order to save money, 28 Mar. He said that the malt drawback bill would drive Scottish distillers out of the market, 30 Mar., and voted against its third reading, 2 Apr. He presented and endorsed a petition from the synod of Fife against the use of public money to educate Irish Catholics, but denied that he wished to promote intolerance, 7 May; and on 21 May alleged that the scheme would lead to 'the exclusion of Protestant children'. He objected to the threatened creation of peers to carry the reform bill, 17 May. He condemned the Scottish bill as 'nothing more than a new constitution', of which most Scots remained ignorant, 21 May. On 25 May he presented a petition from Auchtermuchty for the burgh to be added to the revised district composed of St. Andrews, Cupar, the Anstruthers, Kilrenny and Pittenweem (Perth having been given its own Member) and voted against the second reading of the Irish reform bill. On 1 June he urged Lord Milton not to put off his proposed motion on the corn laws. Later that day, notwithstanding the changes made in the Scottish reform bill, he insisted that Scotland was entitled to at least 11 more Members than the 53 proposed. He begged Johnston to drop his amendment to debar Scottish clergymen from voting, 6 June. He was granted a month's leave to attend to urgent business, 10 July. On 25 July 1832 he asked Althorp if ministers intended to introduce a bill to establish a provincial police force.

Lindsay offered himself again for Fifeshire in June 1832 as the opponent of 'those speculative theories, which, advocating change for the sake of trial, unsettle men's minds, diminish public and private confidence, and may lead into those fearful results we have so lately witnessed in other countries'. A week before the election in December, however, he withdrew, 'finding my chance of success quite hopeless'. He told Peel that Fifeshire had been particularly affected by the Reform Act, as a result of which 'the £10 constituency has entirely swamped the agricultural interests in Scotland', and that 'possibly I might have been returned for Wigan, but after three successive contests which I have had, I require to recruit a little for a future occasion, and consequently determined not to attempt it'.[23] Congratulating Peel on his accession to office in December 1834, he wrote:

> In ... [Scotland] the name of the duke [of Wellington] is still unpopular ... connecting it with the cry of no reform; but they readily accept of you and some of the Whigs consider you as belonging to them; and this will be the general feeling amongst them ... if any declaration of reform is made by you. The people in the burghs are still very radical. The agricultural population are now all Conservative. If you decide on a dissolution of Parliament you will have a better return from Scotland than last time, but the change of opinion in favour of Conservative measures is certainly not so great as it is in England.

He stood for Fifeshire against Wemyss at the general election the following month, when he professed his 'Tory's creed' of opposition to the ballot and unwavering support for church establishments. He explained his humiliating defeat, by 467 votes in a poll of 1,635, to Peel:

> Nine tenths of the landed interest ... supported me and nearly all the tenantry, but all our exertions could not avail. Above one half of our constituency in Fife are manufacturers, £10 voters. These and the Dissenters coalesced and with the assistance of the mob, the character of which was the most brutal I ever saw, they carried on ... [a] system of intimidation ... Our prophecies when debating the reform bill have proved too true in the alteration it would make in the character of the people in Scotland. Instead of that quiet and contented spirit

> which existed at least in our rural population, and also to a certain extent amongst our manufacturing, at present all are discontented and restless, occupied exclusively on politics and anxious for further changes but not knowing what these should be.[24]

On his father's death, aged 82, in May 1836, Lindsay inherited Balcarres, which he turned into a social and intellectual centre of 'refinement and high tone', Leuchars and other property in the vicinity.[25] He could not be persuaded to stand for Wigan in 1837 and in Fifeshire stepped aside for Lord Bruce, who fared even worse against Wemyss than he had. In 1841, he considered any Conservative attempt on the county to be 'hopeless'.[26] Between 1839 and 1843 he travelled extensively with his family in France and Italy. On his return he placed his services in Fifeshire, where he was now convener and believed that he possessed 'more influence ... than any other individual', at the disposal of Peel and his party, and applied unsuccessfully for a share of county patronage. He subsequently kept Peel informed of local opinion on proposed alterations to the Scottish banking system and the 1845 budget.[27] In his last years, he took great interest and pride in the military career of his younger son Robert James (1832-1901), whose valour at Alma and Inkerman earned him the Victoria Cross.[28] In the last year of his life Lindsay wrote to his wife from London:

> I did not know till this morning that I was troubled with tender feelings, or delicate sympathies, or liable to make a fool of myself from such causes. But I went today to see the panorama of the Alma, and as I first looked upon the representation of that bloody field, the Guards in the foreground, and so many of them lying prostrate ... and our gallant boy the prominent figure in the foreground, raising the standard of England in the midst of the fight, looking boldly aloft in contempt of the danger surrounding him, I began to see *indistinctly*, and walked away to the other side of the room.

In the autumn of 1855 he defied sickness to set out for Florence. After falling ill at Avignon he managed to reach Genoa, where he died in early December 1855.[29] By his will, dated 28 Sept. 1853, he left his wife their London house and the lands of her family, which came in 1894 to their elder son Sir Coutts Lindsay (1824-1913), a soldier, who had succeeded to the Trotter baronetcy under a special remainder in 1837. Lindsay devised to him Balcarres and Leuchars, along with £20,000 in cash, £3,106 worth of shares in the Newcastle Railway Company and personal effects worth an estimated £2,000. He bequeathed an annuity of £300 to his elder daughter Margaret, who in 1846 had married her second cousin, the future 25th earl of Crawford. Her son, the 26th earl, restored the Balcarres estate to the senior branch of the Lindsays by buying it from Sir Coutts in 1886 for £150,000. Robert James Lindsay, who received an annuity of £300 and a legacy of £6,000, was Conservative Member for Berkshire, 1865-85, and was created Lord Wantage in 1885.[30]

[1] IGI (Fifeshire). He was presumably *b.* 17 Apr. 1791, not 1793, as stated in *Burke PB*. [2] Lord Lindsay, *Lives of the Lindsays*(1858), ii. 309, 353. [3] Ibid. ii. 340, 354-5; iii. 149-226; C.A. Bayley, *Indian Society and Making of British Empire*, 53. [4] Lindsay, ii. 354-5, 364-5. [5] Add. 35648, f. 115. [6] *Gent. Mag.* (1856), i. 83; Lady Wantage, *Lord Wantage*, 2-5. [7] *Gent. Mag.* (1820), ii. 281. [8] NLS, Crawford mss 25/1/410. [9] Ibid. 25/1/414. [10] Ibid. 25/1/415, 416. [11] Ibid. 25/13/11; 40/7/27; 40/8/7. [12] *Liverpool Mercury*, 16 June 1826. [13] *The Times*, 26 May 1827. [14] Add. 40389, f. 85. [15] Crawford mss 25/1/430, 432-5; 40/7/12, 13. [16] Ibid. 25/1/440, 443. [17] Ibid. 40/7/1; *Manchester Guardian*, 31 July, 7 Aug. 1830; *Account of Wigan Election* (1830), 33-35, 50-52, 53-59. [18] Crawford mss 25/1/448, 449, 453. [19] Inst. of Commonwealth Stud. M915/4/2. [20] Crawford mss 25/1/456-8. [21] Ibid. 40/7/32; *Caledonian Mercury*, 23, 30 Apr., 7, 28 May; *Manchester Guardian*, 30 Apr. 1831. [22] Crawford mss 25/1/460. [23] *Caledonian Mercury*, 30 June, 15 Dec. 1832; Add. 40403, f. 140. [24] *Scottish Electoral Politics*, 224; Add. 40404, ff. 312, 314; 40412, f. 13; *The Times*, 1, 27, 31 Jan. 1835. [25] *Gent. Mag.* (1836), i. 678; PROB 11/1864/434; IR26/1426/729; Wantage, 6-8. [26] Crawford mss 40/7/14; Add. 40423, f. 342; 40487, f. 389. [27] Wantage, 9, 88; Add. 40553, ff. 15, 17, 195-203; 40561, ff. 70-76. [28] *Oxford DNB*. [29] Wantage, 111, 125-6; *Gent. Mag.* (1856), i. 83. [30] PROB 11/2229/217; IR26/2073/317; *Oxford DNB*.

S.R.B./D.R.F.

LITTLETON (formerly **WALHOUSE**), **Edward John** (1791–1863), of Teddesley Park, Staffs. and 45 Grosvenor Place, Mdx.

STAFFORDSHIRE	6 June 1812–1832
STAFFORDSHIRE SOUTH	1832–11 May 1835

b. 18 Mar. 1791, o.s. of Moreton Walhouse of Hatherton, Staffs. and Anne Cracroft, da. of Abraham Portal of Ludgate Hill, London. *educ.* Chiswick 1798-1800; Brewood 1800-6; Rugby 1806-7; Brasenose, Oxf. 1809-12; L. Inn 1810. *m.* (1) 21 Dec. 1812, Hyacinthe Mary (*d.* 4 Jan. 1849), illegit. da. of Richard Colley Wellesley†, 1st Mq. Wellesley [I], 1s. 3da. (2 *d.v.p.*); (2) 11 Feb. 1852, Caroline Anne, da. of Richard Hurt of Wirksworth, Derbys., wid. of Edward Davies Davenport*, *s.p. suc.* gt.-uncle Sir Edward Littleton†, 4th bt., to Teddesley 1812 and took name of Littleton by royal lic. 23 July 1812; fa. 1821; *cr.* Bar. Hatherton 11 May 1835. *d.* 4 May 1863.

PC [GB] 12 June 1833, [I] 21 Sept. 1833; chief sec. to ld. lt. [I] May 1833-Nov. 1834.

Maj. Staffs. yeomanry 1814, lt.-col. 1819, lt.-col. commdt. 1829.

Ld. lt. Staffs. 1854-63.

Chairman, Staffs. and Worcs. Canal Co. 1816-63.

Dubbed 'that marplot Littleton' by Thomas Creevey*, but considered 'a man of good understanding and considerable acquirement, with a large share of vanity accompanied with pride and pomp' by his Staffordshire neighbour William Dyott, Littleton continued to sit on the former interest of his great-uncle Sir Edward Littleton, whom he had succeeded in the representation.[1] Described by Mrs. Arbuthnot as 'a determined Canningite', he continued to vote 'sometimes with, and sometimes against' the Liverpool ministry.[2] The keeper of a detailed journal, which he sometimes 'omitted for a long time to fill up' (explaining, 'when you are in the way of seeing and hearing a great deal, you are too much occupied to record it'), he later recalled that he had

> generally voted with the government, opposing it however occasionally on some questions ... of economy, but especially on questions relating to the improvement of criminal law. The great battle of succeeding years was the Catholic question, on which I for several years witnessed with admiration Canning's unrivalled oratorical powers, and in favour of which I always gave a zealous vote, and something more than a formal support both in Parliament and in my county, where I had on that account much prejudice to encounter.[3]

The Staffordshire industrialist Sir Robert Peel† abhorred his 'Catholic politics', but thought him 'an excellent *commercial* Member'.[4] In the House, where he aspired to the chair, he fostered a reputation as an authority on procedure and made regular technical interventions. He proposed and served on committees on several private bills, and campaigned for reform of the regulations governing the constitution of such committees, which were adopted by the House, 19 Apr. 1826, 15 Feb. 1827, 26 Feb. 1830. An incessant presenter of petitions, on subjects including the Staffordshire pottery trade, coal duties, malt and beer taxes, Catholic claims, the East India Company's monopoly, truck and slavery, he steadily opposed 'any attempt, by the introduction of a standing order, to restrict' the practice, defending it as a privilege 'warmly cherished not only by my constituents, but by the public at large', 21 May 1829.

At the 1820 general election Littleton pledged to continue his support for the 'extensive manufacturing districts of our county' in a declaration sent from Vienna, where he was detained on account of his wife's illness, and deputed his uncle John Walhouse to campaign on his behalf. The controversial decision of the other sitting Member Lord Gower to relinquish his family's traditional seat rather than face an expensive contest allowed Littleton to come in unopposed.[5] Welcoming the collapse of the Trentham interest, the Whig Lord Anson hoped that Littleton would 'take the hint, and become a better politician than before'.[6] He condemned the Western Union canal bill as a 'gross violation of private property', 15 May 1820. At a dinner with the duke of Wellington, 19 May, he expressed approval for Lord John Russell's bill to disfranchise Grampound and transfer its seats to Yorkshire, which 'occasioned them to immediately stigmatise me as a reformer'.[7] He spoke in support of Lord Althorp's insolvent debtors bill, 26 May. On 1 June he obtained leave for a bill to abolish the 'oppressive effects' of the truck system, which he read a second time 'to the joy of the Staffordshire nail makers, at whose request I introduced it', 23 June.[8] He argued for hearing inquiry evidence before the introduction of trade bills and was appointed to the select committee on the subject, 14 June. That day he spoke and voted for inquiry into Anglo-Irish trade, claiming that abolition of the ten per cent duties 'would be of infinite advantage to the starving manufacturers'. He was a minority teller for exempting the potteries from them, 10 July 1820, and endorsed a petition for their repeal, 16 Feb. 1821. He voted with opposition for economies, 4 July 1820.

He ignored the government's 'expresses' urging his attendance at a meeting on the Queen Caroline affair, 21 Aug. 1820; but Huskisson informed Canning, 30 Jan. 1821, that 'many of our friends (Littleton for one) who had come down to vote for Lord Archibald [Hamilton] turned against him', and he divided in defence of ministers' conduct, 6 Feb.[9] Supporting a Birmingham petition complaining of distress, 8 Feb., he admitted that it had partly resulted from what had been 'very properly done by government with respect to the currency', but also blamed the 'system of taxation' and suggested that 'a tax bearing equally on funded and landed property' would prove 'a great relief to the farmer, as well as the manufacturer'. Apprehending that his views might have been misinterpreted (the radical Whig Henry Grey Bennet, for example, recorded in his diary that Littleton 'called the fundowner a monster and recommended an attack upon him') he explained that he favoured taxes both 'on land and on the national debt', 12 Feb. The Whig Henry Labouchere* nevertheless considered that 'the speeches of Littleton and still more of Curwen' were 'a declaration of war against the fundholders'.[10] On 12 Feb. he called for the redistribution of Grampound's seats, arguing that it was 'most improper and impolitic, that so many large and populous towns ... should remain unrepresented'. He was absent from the division lists on Catholic claims, 28 Feb., but present to vote with ministers on the revenue, 6 Mar. He was appointed to select committees on agricultural distress, 7 Mar. 1821, 18 Feb. 1822. He recommended changes to the regulations governing the sale of bread and was appointed to the related select committee, 15 Mar. 1821. He spoke and voted for repeal of the additional malt duty, 21 Mar., but abstained on 3 Apr. He supported calls for country banks to provide 'either legal coin or bank of England pound notes' in exchange for 'their larger notes', 13 Apr. He divided for the forgery punishment mitigation bill, 4 June 1821.

Littleton divided with government against more extensive tax reductions, 11, 21 Feb., but with opposition for naval reductions, explaining that 'the altered situation of the country warranted an alteration of his vote', 1 Mar., and abolition of one of the joint-post-masterships, 13 Mar. 1822. He condemned the salt tax as 'grievous and impolitic', 28 Feb., but opposed immediate repeal as 'inconsistent' with recent measures 'to support public credit with a sinking fund'. He welcomed the vagrancy laws amendment bill, 29 Mar. 1822, and testified to the success of its operation, 4, 10 Feb. 1824. He spoke in favour of a clause proposed to be added to the licensing bill 'encouraging the sale of beer of a diminished strength', 24 May 1822. He divided for criminal law reform, 4 June, and presented two petitions against the truck system, 17 June 1822. He voted with government on the sinking fund, 5 Mar., and against tax reductions, 10 Mar., and warned that 'too sudden a repeal' of the coal duties would 'very materially' injure investors, 27 Mar. 1823. He divided against repeal of the Foreign Enlistment Act, 16 Apr., and inquiry into the prosecution of the Dublin Orange rioters, 22 Apr. He condemned the French invasion of Spain, 30 Apr., but discountenanced war as 'our commerce and manufactures were now in a flourishing state' and should not be risked in 'a quarrel which was not ... our own'. He criticized the combination bill's 'minute and vexatious regulations', which 'no man connected with the manufacturing districts could possibly approve of', 27 May. He voted with government on the currency, 12 June 1823. He divided against reform of Edinburgh's representation, 26 Feb., and the usury laws repeal bill, 26 Feb., 8 Apr., which he described as 'impolitic', 9 Apr. 1824. He condemned proposals to encourage importation of foreign silks as a 'menace' to which his constituents were 'unanimously opposed', 5 Mar., but three days later announced that 'his opinion on the question had been altered' by the ministerial explanation. On 18 Mar. he endorsed the government's 'wise and prudent' policy of 'keeping out of war' with France, and 'at the request' of Canning, the foreign secretary, moved a successful amendment to the opposition censure motion. George Agar Ellis* thought it 'a very good speech' to which 'the House did not pay all the attention that it deserved'.[11] Littleton again opposed proposals to revise the coal duties, 29 Mar., 1 Apr. He voted with government against condemning the trial in Demerara of the Methodist missionary John Smith, 11 June 1824.

He divided for suppression of the Catholic Association, 26 Feb., and for Catholic relief, 1 Mar., 21 Apr., 10 May 1825. On 28 Mar. he gave notice of 'a measure for the regulation of the franchise in Ireland', which he hoped would provide 'an indispensable accompaniment to Catholic concession'. Next day, however, Canning wrote to complain of his fixing the first reading for 14 Apr., 'the day on which the House meets after the recess', and entreated him 'to reconsider' and 'not to moot that question, till the Catholic bill had passed a second reading'. Wilmot Horton protested in similar terms that Burdett had postponed the relief bill 'specially on account of the inconvenience accruing to Members from attendance on that day', but Spring Rice advised him to 'adhere to your present resolutions' as 'I am sure we should do well on that day'. Littleton postponed until the 22nd when, as Canning had promised, he experienced 'no difficulty' in obtaining leave to bring in the bill.[12] On the second reading, 2 Apr., he explained that the bill, 'in every respect his own measure', was intended to remove 'fictitious votes' from the Irish registers and raise the minimum freehold qualification from 40*s.* to £10, which would 'take from the Catholic population an influence in elections which was neither useful to their interests nor safely exercised'. Sir John Nicholl* noted in his diary that the measure, which was carried by 233-185, was 'opposed by the ultra-Whigs as a disfranchisement and abandoning [of] popular rights', but 'supported by those who supported Catholic claims, as tending to help in the Catholic bill'.[13] Littleton defended the disfranchisement of freeholders who 'exercised the elective franchise by a fraud on the constitution', 9 May, and 'could not conceive on what principle those who supported parliamentary reform could oppose this measure', 12 May; but following the Lords' rejection of Catholic relief he withdrew it, 27 May. On 10 Mar. he opposed a motion to prevent interested Members from voting on private bills, observing in his diary that he 'carried the House so completely ... that Hume did not divide'.[14] He endorsed a Birmingham petition against the iron, copper and metal duties, 11 Mar., and warned that Staffordshire manufacturers would be 'seriously affected' by a proposed reduction of the china duties,

25 Mar. He voted to revise the corn laws, 28 Apr., but for the duke of Cumberland's annuity bill, 6 June. He presented and endorsed a Nottingham petition against the exportation of machinery, 14 June 1825, and spoke thus, 11 May 1826. He called for the restoration of Sir Robert Wilson* to his army rank, 17 June 1825.

Rumours of an impending dissolution that September prompted Littleton to ask Sir Robert Peel to second his nomination, as a representative of 'the manufacturing body'. William Peel* told his brother the home secretary that the letter 'is (as I think the writer also) a perfect piece of humbug', but added that their father intended to 'second the nomination, stating that he does not approve of Littleton's Catholic politics'. Littleton welcomed the subsequent postponement of a dissolution, informing the home secretary that it 'cannot fail to be regarded by those who have compromised their interests with their constituents on the Catholic question as a gracious act on the part of the government'; and Canning observed that 'your constituents will not have an opportunity of throwing your disfranchisement bill in your face, on the hustings, this *year*'.[15] Littleton duly lost his £50 wager with the Speaker that Parliament would be dissolved before 1 Nov. 1825.[16] He voted for inquiry into silk trade petitions, 24 Feb. He was a majority teller for the resolutions governing the passage of private bills, 19 Apr., and against a proposed amendment to the licensing bill, 12 May. He was not unduly concerned by the circulation of Staffordshire handbills urging the electors to choose anti-Catholic Members, telling his agent:

> The mass of the people are seldom unjust, and I cannot think that after 14 years' zealous devotion to the county representation and parliamentary business, during which period my vote on the Catholic question has always been the same ... they would now be influenced to turn around upon me, and tell me I am unworthy of their confidence.[17]

He spoke in similar terms at the 1826 general election, when he also contended that Canning's foreign policy afforded the 'best hopes for an enduring peace' and that distress had 'arisen mainly from natural causes', but advocated a 'gradual' alleviation of the tax burden. Rumours of an anti-Catholic candidate came to nothing and he was returned unopposed.[18]

Writing to Canning to support his claims to the premiership, 22 Feb. 1827, Littleton described 'a meeting of the opposition' at which Lord John Russell, James Abercromby 'and several others' had agreed that 'your accession to the principal post in the administration' would be 'a great advantage to the principles they support in common with yourself' and 'a great gain to their own views as a party'.[19] He was 'one of the most earnest and active members' of the '*petit comité*' which met at Norfolk House in support of Catholic relief, for which he voted, 6 Mar. 1827.[20] He presented petitions and spoke against the game laws, 28 Mar. He boasted privately that the Canning ministry had 'the entire confidence of the king, and the heir presumptive, and the best understanding with the Whigs', and hoped that 'the old Tories will be kept out for ever', 23 Apr.; but he reassured his agent that there was 'not the *slightest ground*' for the widespread reports that he would be made a peer, noting that he would 'never ask for such a thing, much less intrigue for it', 28 Apr.[21] He argued for the transfer of East Retford's seats to Birmingham, 2 July. On 19 May he had informed his agent that he could 'not see how even the Catholic question is to turn out the government' since they were not pledged 'to it as a *cabinet* measure', but warned of other 'defects in its construction which endanger its continuance, for instance were Canning to die, there is not a soul on the treasury bench who could succeed him'. He returned from Holland to attend his funeral, when he 'saw more men of character and talent in tears than I had ever expected to have seen on any occasion'.[22] Lord Londonderry informed Wellington of having been 'long since told by Littleton that if Canning's health failed, Robinson [Lord Goderich] would succeed him'.[23] According to Sir Henry Hardinge*, Littleton believed that Goderich's ministry was the 'best that could possibly be formed', that it would 'gradually be strengthened by the old Tory interests, excepting a small band who will adhere to the ex-ministers' and that Wellington 'must accept the army'.[24] Writing to Peel, 6 Dec. 1827, he 'contradicted the calumnious report' that 'Huskisson had declared it impossible for him to continue in the cabinet, if you were restored to it', and later claimed that 'this correspondence was the means of smoothing the negotiations that brought the parties together in the [Wellington] cabinet in the month following'.[25] He considered a 'union' of Peel and Huskisson as 'the most desirable of all things in the present state of the country' and wrote to congratulate Peel 'on the realisation of that event', 23 Jan. 1828.[26] Meeting Wellington, 29 Jan., he informed him that 'as the last administration could not hold together it was evident no one party was strong enough to form one alone' and that he would support the government 'as long as a liberal system should be persevered in'. On being asked if he 'had noticed in the ... Commons any symptom of organization of opposition', he replied, 'none whatever. How could there be any? Every leading man of every party had been in some of the governments of the last year, and all had been parties to the same measures'.[27]

Littleton, who considered the inclusion of Lords Londonderry and Aberdeen to be 'the only discreditable part of the new cabinet arrangements', was appointed to the finance committee, 15 Feb. 1828, 'on a distinct understanding that I shall vote on each question as I think proper', but he was not made its chairman, as had been widely rumoured.[28] Elected to Brooks's the following day, he recalled how he had been blackballed the previous year 'when I was supporting a government more than half Whiggish, and now the Whigs are out, they have elected me!'[29] Giving 'the House an extempore effusion' of his opinions, 18 Feb., he pledged support for the administration, defended Huskisson's acceptance of office and pronounced his 'perfect confidence in the declaration of the duke, that he will have a bona fide neutrality observed in the cabinet with reference to Catholic claims'. That day, however, Wellington told Peel that he was 'a little uneasy about the composition' of the finance committee, as he could not 'consider Mr. Littleton and Mr. Wilmot Horton as friends'.[30] He was part of a deputation to Wellington, 22 Feb., to put the case for transferring East Retford's seats to Birmingham rather than extending its franchise to Bassetlaw, against which he spoke, 25 Feb., and voted, 21 Mar.[31] Commenting that he was 'not a friend to the general question of reform in Parliament', 19 May, he explained that he was 'anxious for the success of this bill, as no measure is better calculated to prevent anything like violent innovation'. He presented numerous petitions against the Test Acts, 20, 22 Feb., and voted for their repeal, 26 Feb., observing in his diary that although he was 'undecided even to the last', the 'government spoke so feebly, and all the arguments the other way were so ably put, that it was impossible to resist'.[32] He spoke against infusing the issue with 'party spirit', 28 Feb. He divided for the spring guns bill, 23 Mar. He called for turnpike bills to be exempted from parliamentary fees, arguing that they were 'unjust' as 'every one has an interest in the improvement of public roads', 21 Apr. He was appointed to the committee for their amendment, 19 May, and on 11 July introduced new resolutions which were adopted early the next session. He voted against condemning chancery delays, 24 Apr. He was added to the committee on the Catholic land tax, 6 May, and voted for relief, 12 May. On 16 May he informed the Irish viceroy Lord Anglesey of his hope that Burdett's tactic of 'abstaining hereafter from discussing details till the concurrence of the Lords' would 'finally lead to that concurrence between the two Houses which will force on the government the settlement of the question', and added that 'the duke's government increases in strength daily ... founded on an almost universal belief of his *fitness for his post*' and that 'no administration in my time has ever stood so well with the public'.[33] Following the resignation of the Huskissonites in May, he told Huskisson, 'I don't know what the devil to do. I have been going into opposition rapidly, especially in the finance committee, where the government has not acted up to its early professions'.[34] He was one of the 'ejected liberals' identified by Lord Palmerston*, 4 June, and his name appears in the other lists of Huskissonites that month. He presented petitions against bull-baiting but cautioned against any 'positive enactment' that would 'deprive the poor and working classes of this species of amusement', 6 June. He enquired about the government's policy on the expiring silk duties and presented petitions for their reduction, 12 June. He called for 'some delay' to the additional churches bill, 23 June. He supported the cider excise licensing bill, 26 June. Next day he asked whether Peel would support the transfer of East Retford's franchise 'to a great town like Birmingham or Manchester', but got no reply. He expressed sympathy with British claimants seeking compensation for loss of property during the Napoleonic wars and attacked the conduct of the commissioners responsible for handling their claims, 1 July 1828, 4, 28 May 1829. He condemned the Foreign Enlistment Act for its 'most injurious influence upon the shipping and manufacturing interests', 3 July, and voted for ordnance reductions, 4 July 1828.

Littleton, who had observed in his diary, 7 Feb., that the 'Speaker told me seriously that he had heard me mentioned as likely to succeed him in the chair', dismissed a fresh rumour that he 'was likely to be elected Speaker' in a letter to Robert Percy Smith*, 10 Sept. 1828:

> How it originated I cannot conceive ... That I would take the office, all conscious as I am of my unfitness for it, and would fearlessly face that family of disease (piles, fistulae, stone, gravel, strangury, and constipation) for the sake of such an honour, I will not conceal from you. But depend on it, it is an honour not reserved for me ... I have disregarded my connection with the duke's family, and have followed the remnants of the Canning party to 'honest corner'; while I lost no opportunity last session of giving Peel such kicks as a country gentleman could give, on the East Retford question. He was more than angry with me: and no doubt dislikes me for it ... It cannot be that I stand well at Downing Street.[35]

Lord Bathurst informed Wellington, 29 Sept. 1828, that 'there is a silent canvass going on in the favour of Mr. Littleton being Speaker, on the supposition that there will be a vacancy', and that 'he will be supported by the Whigs and the Canningites, and have some friends among the country gentlemen and will therefore be a formidable rival to Sir John Beckett if, as it is imagined, Sir John should be proposed'.[36] No vacancy occurred.

On 8 Sept. 1828 Littleton informed Huskisson that he was convinced that Wellington meant 'to propose some arrangement on the Catholic question', noting 'some strange changes of sentiment among many of the [Protestant] party' which would make him 'indifferent about risking a difference with Peel'. Writing from Ireland, 29 Oct. 1828, where his visit to 'nine or ten counties' had 'rather altered' his hostile 'feeling about the *Brunswickers* of the north', he predicted that the duke himself 'would propose nothing, but that if a bill were sent up by a large majority next session he would make what he could of it'.[37] He and John Fazakerley* were 'satisfied that the duke is honest' about the question and concurred in thinking that 'it looks as if he means waiting for a vote of ... Commons', 27 Jan. 1829.[38] Writing to his wife, 5 Feb., Littleton rejoiced 'at the prospect of an early and complete settlement of the question', but thought that 'after Peel's speech in 1827 in which he declared his *sole* motive for quitting Canning was his certain advocacy of the Catholic question, his facility in turning now is rather strange'. 'We liberals are dying with laughter at the just confusion and shame, to which roguery, selfishness and intolerance are at length put', he commented in his diary, 6 Feb., adding to his wife four days later:

> It is to me, for who for 17 years have fought in the ranks of the friends of religious liberty, nuts and sugar to see the men who from selfish and unchristian like motives have been struggling to keep the Catholics down politically, at length left to do their own dirty work alone, without one name of respectability to help themselves with ... They are all now in shame and confusion ... Peel has done himself great honour, and should be stoutly supported.[39]

He duly assisted Peel in his contest against Sir Robert Inglis*, 'the prince of bigots', at Oxford University, although he felt that Peel had been 'wrong to resign' and 'having resigned ... wrong to offer himself again, and put his friends to a test under awkward circumstances'.[40] He presented petitions against emancipation with which he differed, 23, 27 Feb., 6, 26 Mar., and in favour, 9, 26 Mar., and voted accordingly, 6 Mar., when he congratulated the House, and again, 30 Mar. On 19 Mar. he welcomed the Irish freeholders bill, 'having offered ... in 1825 a measure similar in principle' as a 'necessary accompaniment to the measure of relief', and argued that without it 'we shall have, not Catholic equality, but Catholic ascendancy'. Writing to his agent, 29 Apr., he claimed to

> have given myself great pains by inquiring among the best informed Irish to ascertain how many Roman Catholics might ... get into Parliament from Ireland under the present modification of the electors' franchises: I am assured universally *not ten*. I know that there are not more who could get returned from England. Here endeth my first epistle to the Romans.[41]

He argued against the issue of the East Retford writ and voted for the transfer of its seats to Birmingham, 5 May 1829, 11 Feb. 1830. He contended that the restriction of small notes had 'considerably increased' the 'evil' of the truck system, 11 May 1829. He presented and endorsed petitions against renewal of the East India Company's charter, 12, 14 May, having advised his agent that he was ready 'to join with the public in its efforts to completely destroy that monopoly'.[42] He argued against allowing Daniel O'Connell to take his seat unhindered as he had been 'elected eleven months ago, under the old law' and had 'no claim to the benefit of the new', 21 May. (On hearing that O'Connell was to pass through Bilston early the following year, he told his agent, 'catch him, and burn him alive!')[43] He opposed the Rotherhithe poor bill and refuted 'imputations' circulated against him by its parliamentary agent, 28 May 1829.

Littleton spoke in favour of the lunatic licenses bill, 9 Feb. 1830, when he was appointed to the select committee on the East India Company. Informing his wife of the government's difficulties and their small minority on the address, 10 Feb., he observed, 'there is no certainty for them on any point, party being dissolved, they do not know their opponents. Neither do they know their friends ... Questions will continually arise incidentally in debates, on they will find themselves basketted'.[44] On 17 Feb. he sought leave to introduce his truck bill, and he inveighed against the 'policy and expediency of connecting this subject with the currency' the following day. After postponing his motion for 25 Feb. and abortive bids to obtain leave, 17, 18 Mar., it was introduced by Benson, 1 Apr. On 3 May Littleton appealed for its 'consideration' by a select committee, of which he was appointed chairman that day. He sought clarification of the government's attitude at the end of May, but was warned by Herries, president of the board of trade, that 'there may be a greater difference even with respect to the principle than you supposed'.[45] Littleton, a majority teller for the amendments to the second reading of the bill, 23 June, 1 July, condemned the delaying tactics of Hume, its chief opponent. On 9 July he was forced to abandon it, but hoped that the next Parliament would sanction 'some effective measures for the repeal of the most baneful system that ever afflicted the manufacturing body of this or any other nation'. He voted against Lord Blandford's parliamentary reform scheme, 18 Feb., but for the enfranchisement of Birmingham, Leeds and Manchester, 23 Feb., and the transfer of East Retford's seats to Birmingham, 5 Mar. He divided against ministers on the interference of British troops in the internal affairs of Portugal, 10 Mar., and the treasurership of the navy, 12 Mar. He welcomed their proposed remission of beer duties, which would 'not only be an assistance to the labourer, but to the agriculturist', 16 Mar, but he condemned ordnance monopolies and voted for a revision of taxation, 25 Mar., and against the estimates, 29 Mar. He opposed the Scottish and Irish poor removal bill, 26 May, urging either inquiry or repeal of 'the whole law of removal'. He voted for abolition of the death penalty for forgery, 7 June 1830.

At the 1830 general election Littleton offered again, stressing his support for 'transferring the franchise from convicted boroughs to the large towns', hostility to slavery and the East India Company's monopoly and campaign to end truck. Observing that 'violent party distinctions were more nearly obliterated than they had been, for a long series of years' and that 'every honest man' now ought to exercise 'private judgement', he promised to 'join any party, in whatever quarter of the House it might sit, for the purpose of obtaining some remission of the public burdens'. He was again returned unopposed. 'He is such a favourite with his constituents', remarked his wife, 'that there is no danger of his being turned out, like so many county Members have been this time'.[46] Writing to Lord Wharncliffe, 12 Sept., Littleton hoped that 'the new reign, and the notoriety of the present king's opinions being more liberal, or at all events more flexible than his predecessor's', would provide 'an honourable ground for an attempt to improve the construction of the government' and remedy its 'extreme weakness in talent', adding that 'if from long connection with the old Canningite party I can be of any assistance ... my regard for the duke ... and my cordial respect for Peel would make me a most willing agent'.[47] That month he was listed by ministers as one of 11 members of the 'Huskisson party'. He believed that by 'the calamity' of Huskisson's fatal accident, which he witnessed, 'an obstacle was removed', whereupon he, Wharncliffe and 'several other independent parties, not so inveterately hostile to the duke, urged on various members of his government the importance of renewing his efforts to effect a junction'.[48] Agar Ellis, however, distrusted Littleton, who 'wants to be Speaker', believing that he and Wharncliffe 'would gladly coalesce with Wellington, but if the Canning party can be kept together, I doubt their impudence enough to go over alone'.[49] Following the breakdown of private negotiations between Palmerston and Wellington, Littleton

> regretted so much that they should not have come to a more close understanding, both as to men and measures, and was so convinced that on the latter point the duke could at that moment make great concessions, without inconsistency, that I was determined to talk to [Charles] Arbuthnot* on the subject. Accordingly I called on him ... [31 Oct.] and found that he and the duke were under an idea that Palmerston's friends would insist on the introduction of [Henry] Brougham*. I disabled his mind on this point, and told him that Graham and Stanley were, in my belief, the only Whigs in the ... Commons Palmerston would care for, and perhaps Lord Grey in the House of Lords, that it appeared to me these parties might honourably join the government on the following terms: the duke of Kent to be regent, a reduced civil list, a bill to abolish pluralities in civil offices, abolition of the China monopoly, two Members to be given to three or four large towns, with a positive engagement that every future case of convicted borough should be a case of transfer.[50]

According to Mrs. Arbuthnot, Littleton hoped that 'Pal[mersto]n and Co.' might drop all their demands except parliamentary reform, of which 'the *most moderate* would satisfy them, that is to say, representatives for four great towns to be obtained by taking *one* from eight rotten boroughs and some alterations in county voting'.[51] He accordingly deplored Wellington's declaration against reform, which had made 'all amalgamation of parties ... now hopeless', telling his agent, 11 Nov., 'never was there greater folly':

> What makes the duke's conduct more silly, is that men's minds were attuned to moderation on the subject of reform. They were united in temperate views, and would have thought representation given to a *few* great towns, as many rotten boroughs extinguished, and a reform of the Scotch franchise a great thing. Now we must fight for it.[52]

On 9 Nov. Littleton accused O'Connell of deliberately misrepresenting his remark that he 'did not care about Ireland' in terms of his truck bill, which had appeared out of context in the *Dublin Evening Post* of 23 Oct., and repudiated the charge. James Hope Vere recalled that he 'never saw in the House such a storm or heard such cheering'.[53] Littleton helped to vote the Wellington ministry out of office on the civil list, 15 Nov. Writing to Wellesley, 19 Nov. he reported that Palmerston

> had no sooner received a letter from Lord Grey informing him he had just left the king ... than he came to me to tell me what had passed between Grey and himself, and concluded by asking me what objects I had for myself. I of course stammered out 'none', and then slipped in a ...

> suggestion others had frequently made to me, re[garding] the anticipated vacancy of the Speaker's chair. I told him I would not ask for a peerage but through the chair, I should value the attainment of that distinction. He commended my ambition and promised his support.[54]

On 26 Nov., however, he observed that 'the Speaker will I fear hold on', not wanting to '*ask* to be removed', adding, 'I must devise means of making him or others think of it in the course of this session. At all events I should think a coronation would carry him off'. He duly asked Grey for the government's support whenever Manners Sutton retired, 6 Dec. 1830, claiming that 'many of the Members who now occupy minor departments' had 'voluntarily expressed' their preference for him, that he had the backing of Palmerston and Graham and some leading backbenchers, and that 'pecuniary compensation either now or hereafter is no object to me'. Grey, however, declined 'to enter into any engagement' in advance of a vacancy.[55]

On 14 Dec. 1830 Littleton resumed his campaign against the truck system and secured leave to reintroduce his bill by 167-27. He moved its second reading, 11 Feb., but its commitment was repeatedly deferred until 22 Mar. 1831, when the provisions prohibiting truck and the repeal of earlier Acts were divided into two separate bills. The repeal bill passed its third reading, 20 Apr., but both measures were overtaken by the dissolution that month. Reintroduced in the Lords by Wharncliffe, 28 June, they passed their third reading, 5 Aug., and after being steered through the Commons by Littleton, they were read a third time, 5 Oct., the repeal bill without opposition, and the prohibition bill with amendments which passed 61-4, with Littleton as teller. That day he noted in his diary:

> Passed my truck bills after 20 months incessant attention, and correspondence of more than 1,000 letters, constant interviews, daily attendance in the House to watch opportunities of bringing on the different stages. My mind is quite relieved.

The bills received royal assent (as 1 & 2 Gul. IV, cc. 36, 37), 15 Oct. 1831, and Littleton later claimed that 'in the Potteries the practice has ceased' and in Gloucestershire was 'waging an unequal war with the law, which I am told will put it down'.[56] He criticized the game laws, 8, 15 Feb. 1831, when he approved a bill to regulate the employment of cotton factory apprentices. He contended that 'great dissatisfaction' existed 'amongst the agricultural and manufacturing interests at the immunity from taxes conceded to the fundholder', 14 Feb. He defended the government's 'very trifling augmentation' of the army, 21 Feb., and their grant of £25,000 to the queen, 25 Mar. He endorsed petitions from the Potteries for repeal of the duty on boric acid, 30 Mar. 1831, explaining that use of its cheaper alternative, white lead, meant that workers 'seldom live beyond the age of forty'.

Littleton had opposed Lord Chandos's motion to disfranchise Evesham, 16 Dec. 1830, insisting that his support for a full measure of reform was not the 'result of any new-born zeal'. By now, as he informed Wellesley, 20 Dec. 1830, he was convinced that

> nothing short of an extensive and almost republican basis of franchise will satisfy the country. We can still have a milder measure of reform than we could if reform were resisted six months longer, but already it is a problem how the monarchy and the peerage can coexist with the independent House of Commons we are about to construct ... Retford and the duke's speech occurring about the same time with the French revolution have brought us to this crisis.[57]

Citing the numerous reform petitions from Staffordshire which he had been asked to present, 28 Feb. 1831, he noted that they were 'signed by Whig and Tory, poor and rich, and by persons of all classes and conditions' and that he had never seen 'so much unanimity on any public question before'. Littleton, who had privately expressed to Hume 'very grave doubts of the possibility of carrying reform with this present House', 29 Dec. 1830, commended the ministerial reform bill's 'comprehensiveness and its *perfect* safety' to his agent, 4 Mar. 1831, hoping that the country might 'be roused from one end to the other, if the bill be rejected, for its only chance will be to get a dissolution'.[58] He voiced his 'indignation' at seeing 'the term "revolutionary" applied to a measure' which would 'produce great benefit' and insisted that Huskisson would have supported it, 9 Mar. He voted for its second reading, 22 Mar., spoke again in its support, 18 Apr., and divided against Gascoyne's wrecking amendment the following day. 'Thank God we are prorogued', he informed his agent, 22 Apr. 1831.[59] At the ensuing general election he declared his 'firm support' for the 'strictly conservative' reform bill, which was 'indispensable for the health and preservation of the constitution, and the peace and welfare of the country'. He instructed his agent to work 'elsewhere in promoting the cause of reform', as 'you are too good a man to employ in a pageant (for such I hope the Staffordshire election will be)'. Rumours of opposition by Peel came to nothing and he was returned unopposed.[60]

Littleton presented the Turnpike Acts continuance bill, 27 June 1831, and was reappointed to the East India committee the following day. He demanded more time to consider the register of deeds bill, 30 June. He opposed withholding the Liverpool writ since 'under the present system there is not a borough in England and Wales in which we can expect an election to take place without some kind of corruption', 8 July. He voted for the second reading of the reintroduced reform bill, 6 July, at least twice against an adjournment, 12 July, and steadily supported its details, although he objected to 'taking the amount of assessed taxes as the tests of the prosperity of the manufacturing districts' on the ground that 'their capital is employed in trade', 5 Aug., and was a leading campaigner for giving representatives to the Potteries. In an undated memorandum, he claimed to have submitted plans for the enfranchisement of Stoke in December 1830 to Althorp, who 'told me he had read it to Grey's cabinet', and that when he 'subsequently found that Gateshead was to have Members' he had 'insisted on the equal claim of Walsall'. On 3 July he complained to Althorp that despite his firm belief that the Potteries should be allocated two Members rather than one

> at the earnest and very just remonstrance of the government and the friends of the reform bill, I had consented not to move the transfer of Stoke from schedule D to schedule C ... I receive greater unpopularity by it than by any act of my parliamentary life. Judge of my surprise when I heard ... Gisborne give notice that he should move to bring Stockport from schedule D to C, and when he further informed me that Lord John Russell had consented to the measure. My constituents will hardly think when they see this motion that I am acting fairly by them ... I hope I may be released from my engagement ... The cases of Stockport and Stoke are so precisely the same, that the 60,000 of my constituents in the latter place will condemn my conduct.[61]

He presented and strongly endorsed a Stoke petition for 'two representatives', 12 July, and after being informed by Russell that the government would not relent, gave notice of a motion to that effect, 29 July. After attending a meeting at Althorp's where it was 'agreed to waive all minute differences of opinion', 3 Aug., he told his agent that he did not intend 'without further instructions from my constituents' to press it; but the following day he voted in committee for giving Stoke two Members, having

> made, to my great pain (for I feared embarrassing the government, but was compelled by an engagement made to my constituents) a motion for bringing the Potteries out of schedule D (one Member) and inserting it in schedule C. After a short debate it was negatived, though I think my statement was a strong one.[62]

The agent handling Stoke's campaign, however, was far from mollified and in a series of letters to the local press condemned Littleton's handling of the business, especially his failure to inform the government that 'Peel and his friends would support the motion', of which Littleton insisted he had 'had no knowledge' until 'the last minute', 19 Aug. 'Had our case been circulated at the time you presented our petition', the agent remonstrated, 12 Sept., 'and had you then moved the transfer of Stoke into schedule C, as it was expected you would have done, *the Potteries would have had two representatives*, or had it been allowed to circulate and the motion made but *ten days earlier* than it was, the result would have been the same'.[63] On 26 July Littleton had advised his agent:

> We march slowly in the reform bill. All sorts of unfair tricks are practised to clog and defeat it. Sir Robert Peel affects to dislike it, but never tells his friends privately not to delay it, this is always his way, and gets him the character of a Jesuit. He wishes to upset the bill and defeat the government ... I have had the best constituents for twenty years that ever man had, and hope to repay them by taking a share, by unfailing presence in the House of Commons, in the accomplishment of a measure which shall shut the door of the temple forever to mere dandies, young lifeguardsmen, jobbing lawyers, and money changers.

He later boasted that he had 'been present in every division except two, and on those I *paired*. It is sharpish work, and many Members are ill'. 'Reform, Reform', he complained in another diary entry, 27 Aug., 'the dullness of the committee is dreadful'.[64] He defended the proposed registration system, 2 Sept., and voted for the bill's passage, 21 Sept., when he was one of the organizers of a backbenchers' meeting to oppose the resignation of ministers in the event of defeat.[65] He urged the necessity of 'reasserting the principle of the bill' with 'as little delay as possible' following its rejection by the Lords, 10 Oct., declaring that 'if I am to be blamed for having become a convert to the necessity of introducing at once an extensive measure of reform, the country at large must share in the censure, for my opinions have changed with those of the country'. Privately he confessed that 'I omitted half of what I meant to say through want of self-possession', brought on by seeing 'Peel taking notes, and Croker smiling, which annoyed me'.[66] He voted (as a teller) for Lord Ebrington's confidence motion that day, and for the revised bill's second reading, 17 Dec. 1831.

Littleton, who had been asked by Russell to assist with the boundary commission, 21 July, defended the arrangements proposed for Wolverhampton and

Walsall during a 'little skirmish with Croker', 4, 6 Aug. 1831, and again, 8, 28 Feb., 5, 7 Mar. 1832. He privately urged Althorp to appoint a select committee to 'suggest satisfactory divisions of most of the counties', 25 July, and spoke at length in defence of the proposed division, 11 Aug. 1831, commenting in his diary that 'this was a question of infinite delicacy and difficulty' whose 'tendency and object was aristocratic and designed to please the Tories and the Lords'. He was 'employed daily in keeping the government to their colours' on it and after a 'capital division' that day, which he attributed to 'Ebrington and myself solely', he remarked, 'I was so happy, I could not sleep'. 'The division of Worcestershire is the only blot in the whole scheme', he later informed his agent, 'all other counties divide easily and advantageously'.[67] On 1 Sept. he was officially

> proposed with 30 others as a commissioner [unpaid] for dividing counties and giving limits to boroughs, and selecting the chief towns for the courts to be held. Some of the opposition objected to Mr. D. Gilbert and myself as being Members, but no division.[68]

On 28 Oct. he 'set to work on the borough reports' under the supervision of Lieutenant Thomas Drummond of the Royal Engineers. 'I am hard at work here at the limits for boroughs', he reported to his agent, 10 Nov., 'and not a holiday now have I had a chance of over this year'.[69] Having discovered 'some clear cases of fraud on the part of the returning officers of small boroughs', 11 Nov., the commissioners met with ministers, 15 Nov., when 'it was thought that the number of houses, and the amount of assessed taxes together would furnish a better test of respectability of each place than the arbitrary line of population proposed in the late bill'; they 'were accordingly instructed to prepare tables'.[70] Littleton warned Russell against Lord Sandon's attempts to restrict urban voters 'to the borough elections, and shut them out from counties', which would 'lead to a division of the country and of the Members of Parliament into two parties, a town party, and a country party, and jealousy and hatred would thus be engendered, and would endure till one party destroyed the other'.[71] He and Ebrington later pledged 'to die on the benches of the House of Commons sooner than allow town influence to be shut out of county elections'.[72] On hearing of ministers' plans to 'give two Members to ten places in schedule D', 8 Dec. 1831, Littleton

> rejoiced to find the Potteries was one place, and, though there was some doubt about it, Dudley was agreed upon as another. The Potteries have not behaved well to me, they owe to me entirely, to my early and continued insistence with the government, their construction as a borough, and they now owe to me another Member. They are no borough in fact, and the government would never have thought of making them one.[73]

He continued to work on the boundary arrangements 'from 11 till 7' for much of December and January, observing that 'nothing can be more dull and flat than the House of Commons', 8 Dec., and complaining that Russell had produced 'a fresh set of instructions respecting the boundaries to be given to boroughs containing less than 300 qualifying tenants', which amounted to 'a complete *bouleversement* of all our proceedings' and meant that 'many of their reports must be torn, and reconstructed, and many of them must revisit their boroughs in the frost and snow', 19 Dec. 1831.[74]

On 29 July 1831 he had voted for O'Connell's motion to swear in the original Dublin election committee. He presented and endorsed a petition for repeal of the stamp duty on fire insurances, 18 Aug., commended the Irish public works bill as 'a material improvement upon the old system', 16 Sept., and was appointed to the select committee on Irish tithes, 15 Dec. He retained his ambitions for the Speakership, promising his wife to 'do all in my power to create claims on Stanley and all the rest for the chair', and writing a 'long letter' to Palmerston about his claim, 15 Oct. 1831, on account of James Abercromby* being 'likely to come into Parliament again' and 'the Whigs preferring him, as it is natural they should'.[75] He divided for going into committee on the reform bill, 20 Jan. 1832, and again supported its detailed provisions. Next day Russell asked him to make himself 'master of all such details relating to the numbers of houses counted, as *forming the towns* disfranchised' and to 'sit behind him' and 'furnish him with them if wanted'. 'Tired to death with the reform committee', he paired off, 8 Feb.[76] He spoke regularly in defence of the boundary bill's details and the work of the commissioners, insisting that 'we never in any one instance in the course of our labours, made any inquiries as to the owners of property, or their political opinions', 5 Mar. When Russell demanded that he 'give up Walsall' the following day, he 'positively refused unless Gateshead and five or six others were given up too', but he left it to Wrottesley, his county colleague, to argue 'the claims of Walsall to one representative' against the protests of Croker, 9 Mar.[77] He voted for the third reading of the reform bill, 22 Mar., the address calling on the king to appoint only ministers who would carry it unimpaired, 10 May, the second reading of the Irish bill, 25 May, and against a Conservative amendment to the Scottish bill, 1 June.

On 17 May he noted in his diary that 'any attempt at amelioration' had been 'rendered hopeless by the prejudice and recklessness of the House of Lords', who by rejecting the bill had 'become odious to the nation'.[78] He presented and endorsed Staffordshire petitions for the supplies to be withheld until the bill was passed, 23, 24 May. He rejected Croker's allegations of impropriety over the new boundaries for Tamworth and Exeter, 7 June, asserting that he knew of no instance where 'the boundary line has been carried one yard to the right, or one yard to the left, for the accommodation or in favour of any particular interest'. The following day he spoke in support of the allocation of county polling places and defended the boundaries for Arundel. That day

> the boundary bill went through a committee, not occupying altogether more than 10 hours. It had been universally supposed early in the session that a month at least would have been occupied at this stage, every line being debatable matter. But by much previous labour in satisfying objections, and by having observed throughout most scrupulously the fairest and most impartial conduct much opposition was got over before we entered the House.[79]

He was a majority teller at least three times for the bill, 22 June, when it passed 'after only three nights' discussion' and 'no very important alterations'. 'Thank God the boundary bill is now out of my hands', he wrote to his agent the following day.[80] Warning that 'considerable anxiety prevails ... on the part of the borough and parochial authorities, as to the duties that will devolve on them under the English reform bill', he urged ministers to ensure a wide circulation of the Act, 25 June 1832.

He voted with government on the Russian-Dutch loan, 26 Jan., 12, 20 July, and relations with Portugal, 9 Feb. 1832. On 8 Feb. he argued for a select committee on the register of deeds bill, to which he was appointed, 22 Feb. He supported a bill to regulate the election of coroners, 16 Feb., and voted to make their inquests public, 20 June. He proposed measures to expedite the processing of 'the immense quantity of private business', 2 Mar. He was appointed to the select committees on petitions, 9 Mar., and slavery, 30 May. He favoured postponing discussion of the corn laws, 1 June, and presented and endorsed a petition for hearing the complaints of country banks, 4 June. He expressed 'great satisfaction at the reductions which have been made by the government', 25 July, noting that their repeal of the borax duties would prevent 'great loss of life' in the Potteries. He called for a 'complete statement of the imports and exports of the country', 30 July. That day he complimented the work of the Speaker, who was expected to retire. On 2 Nov. he advised Fazakerley that he had made up his mind 'to accept the support of my friends as Manners Sutton's successor', adding that Grey 'earnestly desired to see my election' and 'Althorp's feelings were the same, so were Dartmouth's and Palmerston's'.[81] He 'did us such good service in the boundary bill' and 'knowing as we did before ... what he aimed at, we are bound to him unless it was very odious to our friends', Althorp informed Earl Fortescue, 21 Nov.[82] That day Agar Ellis noted in his diary that Abercromby was 'not to be the new Speaker, Althorp having used him very ill, in favour of Littleton', who in private boasted to Mrs. Huskisson that he had been 'assured that all will go right' and might 'consider it as all but settled'.[83] Russell, however, preferred Abercromby and considered that 'Littleton ought to be a peer', conjuring the prospect of a contest which Edward Ellice*, who hated Littleton 'most cordially', believed he would lose, as 'the most unpopular man in the House'. Greville felt that Littleton had 'no claims to be Speaker compared with those of Abercromby (having been half his life in opposition to the present government)', but observed that 'he obstinately insists upon the expectations held out to him being realised'.[84] As Dyott noted:

> No schoolboy was ever more vain of a school prize than my friend ... It was certainly driving at a post of high distinction, but the vain ostentation exhibited, betrayed rather a want of the proper feeling of a great mind ... He wants temper; he is deficient in acquirement; he is haughty and peevish in manner, with a want of suavity in general deportment.[85]

Fearing a rift in the party, the government opted to re-elect Manners Sutton.[86] Annoyed at this decision, the radicals put Littleton up for the Speakership at the beginning of the 1833 session, when he was nominated by Hume and seconded by O'Connell, but he declared himself an 'unwilling candidate' and they lost the division by 241-31.[87]

At the 1832 general election Littleton was returned unopposed for the new division of Staffordshire South, where he was re-elected in 'a short but inexpensive contest' with the local Tories following his appointment as Irish secretary in May 1833. His unauthorized proffering of alterations to the Irish coercion bill during negotiations with O'Connell, which he later admitted to have been 'a gross indiscretion', initiated the political crisis which led to Grey's retirement in July 1834. He was derided by many, including Greville, as 'the instrument of breaking up this government'; as Dyott put it, his 'conduct was highly censured and deservedly, his motive was vanity and an effort to appear of supreme consequence'. After the 1835 general election, when he was returned unopposed, he was passed over by Russell as the Liberal candidate for the Speakership, and on the formation of the second Melbourne ministry was elevated to the Lords, where he spoke 'rarely'.[88] Unsuccessful in his attempts to influence the outcome of the ensuing Staffordshire South by-election, Littleton, who Dyott believed had 'lost the respectable situation he once held in the county by his unsteadiness as a political character', took 'a great interest' in agriculture and the improvement of his own estates.[89] Commenting on the decline of the landed interest, 26 Dec. 1856, he boasted to Croker, 'here I still am, well; once the county's Member, now its lord lieutenant and its father with a vengeance ... I am only the fifth proprietor of my property since the time of James I. I believe I am the only peer of whom that can be said'.[90] *Hatherton's Memoir and Correspondence relating to Political Occurrences in June and July 1834*, published posthumously in 1874, went some way towards vindicating his conduct in the O'Connell affair and correcting his unflattering portrayal in Brougham's *Memoirs* of 1871, although it was criticized in Denis Le Marchant's† *Memoir of Lord Althorp* (1876).[91] He died at Teddesley Park in May 1863. By his will the family estates passed to his only son and successor in the barony, Edward Richard (1815-88), Liberal Member for Walsall, 1847-52, and Staffordshire South, 1853-7.

[1] *Creevey Pprs.* ii. 305; *Dyott's Diary*, ii. 45. [2] *Arbuthnot Jnl.* ii. 96; *Session of Parl. 1825*, p. 473. [3] Hatherton diary, intro., 21 Nov. 1821, 27 June 1831. [4] Add. 40381, f. 342. [5] Hatherton mss D260/M/7/5/11, ff. 1, 30, 36, 40; *Staffs. Advertiser*, 26 Feb., 4, 11, 18, 25 Mar., *Lichfield Mercury*, 10 Mar. 1820. [6] Add. 51830, Anson to Holland, 19 Mar. 1820. [7] Hatherton diary. [8] Ibid. [9] Add. 38742, f. 171. [10] HLRO, Hist. Coll. 379, Grey Bennet diary, 16; Harrowby mss, Labouchere to Sandon, 12 Feb. 1821. [11] Hatherton diary, Mar. 1824; TNA 30/29/9/5/22. [12] Hatherton mss 27/2, ff. 70, 72-74; Bagot, *Canning and Friends* ii. 282. [13] Merthyr Mawr mss, Nicholl diary, 26 Apr. 1825. [14] Hatherton diary, 13 Mar. 1825. [15] Hatherton mss 27/2, ff. 82, 85; Add. 40381, ff. 342, 381. [16] Hatherton mss 27/2, f. 53. [17] Ibid. 27/52, ff. 36-37. [18] *Staffs. Advertiser*, 10, 17 June 1826. [19] Hatherton mss 27/4, f. 3. [20] *Gent. Mag.* (1863) i. 101-2; *Canning's Ministry*, 40, 43; Hatherton mss 27/4, f. 8. [21] Hatherton mss 27/52, ff. 58, 62; Duke Univ. Lib. Fazakerley mss, Ord to Fazakerley, 17 Apr. 1827. [22] Hatherton mss 27/52, ff. 64, 68. [23] Wellington mss WP1/895/18. [24] Ibid. WP1/895/25. [25] Hatherton mss 27/4, ff. 115-17; Parker, *Peel*, ii. 23-25. [26] Hatherton mss 27/5, f. 13. [27] Hatherton diary, 29 Jan. 1828. [28] Ibid. 11, 15 Feb.; Keele Univ. Lib. Sneyd mss SC12/85; 17/36. [29] Hatherton diary, 16 Feb. 1828. [30] Add. 40307, f. 50. [31] Hatherton diary, 22 Feb.; Lincs. AO, Tennyson D'Eyncourt mss 2 Td'E M85/9, C. to G. Tennyson, 27 Feb. 1828. [32] Hatherton diary, 26 Feb. 1828. [33] PRO NI, Anglesey mss D619/31B/1. [34] Add. 38756, f. 198. [35] Hatherton diary; Hatherton mss 27/5, f. 44. [36] Wellington mss WP1/955/15. [37] Add. 38757, ff. 44, 91. [38] Hatherton mss 27/5, f. 84. [39] Hatherton mss, Littleton to wife, 5, 10 Feb.; diary, 6 Feb. 1829. [40] Hatherton mss 27/52, f. 110. [41] Ibid. f. 121. [42] Ibid. f. 124. [43] Ibid. 27/53, f. 46. [44] Hatherton mss. [45] Ibid. 27/6, ff. 24, 62. [46] *Staffs. Advertiser*, 17, 24, 31 July, 7, 14 Aug.; *Staffs. Mercury*, 14 Aug.; Hatherton mss, Hyacinthe Littleton to G. Wellesley, 9 Sept. 1830. [47] Hatherton mss 27/6, f. 45. [48] Ibid. f. 80. [49] Brougham mss, Agar Ellis to Brougham, 4 Oct. 1830. [50] Hatherton mss 27/6, f. 80. [51] *Arbuthnot Jnl.* ii. 398. [52] Hatherton mss 27/53, f. 40. [53] Hopetoun mss 167, f. 183. [54] Hatherton mss 27/6, f. 66B. [55] Ibid. ff. 71, 74, 77. [56] Ibid. 27/53, f. 141. [57] Ibid. 27/6, f. 80. [58] Ibid. 27/6, f. 84; 27/53, f. 52. [59] Ibid. 27/53, f. 85. [60] *Staffs. Advertiser*, 30 Apr., 7 May 1831; Hatherton mss 27/53, f. 98. [61] Hatherton mss 27/7, ff. 38, 40. [62] Hatherton diary, 29 July, 4 Aug.; Hatherton mss 27/53, f. 116. [63] Hatherton mss 27/7, ff. 41, 45, 51. [64] Ibid. 27/53, ff. 112, 116; Hatherton diary, 27 Aug. 1831. [65] M. Brock, *Great Reform Act*, 236. [66] Hatherton diary, 11 Oct. 1831. [67] Ibid. 21, 25 July, 11 Aug. 1831; Hatherton mss 27/53, f. 141. [68] Hatherton diary, 1 Sept. 1831. [69] Hatherton mss 27/53, f. 136. [70] Hatherton diary 26/7. [71] Ibid. 7-8 Dec. 1831. [72] Ibid. 29 Feb. 1832. [73] Ibid. 7-8 Dec. 1831. [74] Ibid. 7-8, 19-20 Dec. 1831. [75] Hatherton mss 27/7 f. 94; Hatherton diary, 15 Oct. 1831. [76] Hatherton diary, 21 Jan., 8 Feb. 1832. [77] Ibid. 6, 9 Mar. 1832. [78] Ibid. [79] Ibid. 7-8 June 1832. [80] Hatherton mss 27/53, f. 165. [81] Fazakerley mss. [82] Devon RO, Earl Fortescue mss. [83] Northants. RO, Agar Ellis diary, 21 Nov. 1832; Add. 39948, f. 145. [84] Add. 51680, Russell to Lady Holland, 2 Dec. 1832; 40403, f. 115; *Greville Mems.* ii. 332. [85] *Dyott's Diary*, ii. 145-6. [86] Earl Fortescue mss, Althorp to Ebrington, 30 Dec. 1832. [87] *Gent. Mag.* (1863), i. 102; *Oxford DNB*. [88] *Staffs. Advertiser*, 22 Dec. 1832; *Greville Mems.* iii. 61-2; *Dyott's Diary*, ii. 179; Torrens, *Melbourne*, ii. 82; *Holland House Diaries*, 387. [89] *Dyott's Diary*, ii. 203; *Gent. Mag.* (1863), i. 102. [90] *Croker Pprs.* iii. 369. [91] Hatherton mss D1121/P/1/1; D4028/6/1/6; Le Marchant, *Althorp*, 512-16.

P.J.S.

LLOYD, Sir Edward Pryce, 2nd bt. (1768–1854), of Pengwern, Flint and Bodfach, Mont.

FLINT BOROUGHS	1806–1807
BEAUMARIS	10 Dec. 1807–1812
FLINT BOROUGHS	1812–10 Sept. 1831

b. 17 Sept. 1768, 1st s. of Bell Lloyd of Bodfach, recvr.-gen. for Flint, and Anne, da. and h. of Edward Pryce of Bodfach. *educ.* Westminster 1777-85. *m.* 11 Feb. 1794, Elizabeth, da. of Sir Roger Mostyn†, 5th bt., of Mostyn, 2s. 2da. *suc.* fa. 1793; gt.-uncle Sir Edward Lloyd, 1st. bt., to Pengwern and as 2nd bt. by spec. rem. 26 May 1795; to estates of bro.-in-law Sir Thomas Mostyn, 6th bt.*, 17 Apr. 1831;[1] *cr.* Bar. Mostyn 10 Sept. 1831. *d.* 3 Apr. 1854.

Sheriff, Flint 1796-7, Caern. 1797-8, Merion. 1804-5, Card. 1825-6.

Capt. Flints. fusiliers 1803, maj. 1805; lt.-col. commdt. Flints militia 1813.

By 1820 Lloyd's return for Flint Boroughs was assured and he could command considerable influence in the county, which was represented by his brother-in-law and fellow Whig Sir Thomas Mostyn. Lloyd had small estates and commercial interests, chiefly in lead mines, in most North Wales counties and, like his constant hunting companion Mostyn, he spent much of his time in Oxfordshire, where he rented property at Stratton Audley. However, he invariably returned to

Flintshire for county functions, at which his bilingualism and skill as a public speaker were major assets. He also took charge of most local legislation and undertook much county business in Parliament.[2] His own and Mostyn's agents had acted with those of another brother-in-law, Sir Robert Williames Vaughan*, on enclosures, and together they promoted supplementary bills for the parishes of Newmarket (1828) and Tremeirchion (1831).[3]

Lloyd made no mention of his political views in his addresses at the 1820 general election, when he gave his customary support to the Plas Newydd (Paget) candidates in Caernarvonshire and Anglesey and the Chirk Castle interest of the Myddelton Biddulphs in Denbigh Boroughs.[4] He divided against the Liverpool ministry on most major issues in the 1820 Parliament, including parliamentary reform, 25 Apr. 1822, 24 Apr. 1823, 27 Apr. 1826, and voted for Catholic relief, 28 Feb. 1821, 1 Mar., 21 Apr., 10 May 1825. A radical publication of that year noted that he 'attended regularly and voted in general with the opposition'.[5] As in 1817, he was named to the 1820 and 1821 select committees on the administration of justice in Wales. As vice-president, he addressed the Flintshire Agricultural Society at Mold, 27 Oct. 1820.[6] He supported the 1820-1 parliamentary campaigns on Queen Caroline's behalf and his Flintshire tenantry illuminated their windows when her prosecution was abandoned in November 1820.[7] He was granted a month's leave because of 'illness in the family', 16 May 1821. Distress was acute in Flintshire in January 1822, when a correspondent to the *Chester Chronicle* wrote an open letter to Lloyd urging improvements in poor law administration.[8] He did not vote on Lord Althorp's resolutions criticizing the ministry's inadequate relief proposals, 21 Feb., but divided steadily against government, 27 Feb.-17 Apr. 1822, when at the Flintshire meeting he carried a petition calling for further government action to combat distress and regretting the 'total inadequacy of the measures proposed by ministers'.[9] He voted for remission of Henry Hunt's* gaol sentence, 24 Apr., and consistently with opposition until 25 June 1822. He delayed returning to the House in 1823 until the Pont Blyddyn roads bill was considered in March,[10] and his only reported votes in 1824 were against the aliens bill, 23 Mar., and for reallocating Irish first fruit revenues, 24 May. He took charge of the Denbigh-Pentre Foelas road bill during the illness of John Wynne Griffith in February 1825.[11] He paired for repeal of the window tax, 17 May, and divided against the duke of Cumberland's annuity bill, 2, 6, 13 June, and for inquiry into chancery delays, 7 June 1825. He was probably the 'Sir E. Lynd' listed in the minority for prior inquiry pending the award of grants to encourage Irish emigration to Canada, 13 June 1825. Before the 1826 general election, when he was again returned unopposed, he presented an anti-slavery petition from Holywell, 20 Apr., and voted for Hume's state of the nation motion, 4 May, and Lord John Russell's resolutions to curb electoral bribery, 26 May.[12] After the election he promoted the interests of the River Dee commissioners with Mostyn.[13]

Lloyd seems to have been lax in his attendance early in the 1826 Parliament, but Lord William Paget, Member for Caernarvon Boroughs, attributed the failure in committee in May 1827 of the Caernarvon improvements bill to his 'officious and uncalled for interference with the duties of the Members for the county and Boroughs of Caernarvon'.[14] He voted to disfranchise Penryn, 28 May, and presented a petition from Flint for repeal of the Test Acts, 8 June 1827, but apparently failed to vote on the issue in 1828. He divided for Catholic relief, 12 May. He was against the provision for Canning's family, 13 May, and voted for the associated motion on the misapplication of public funds, 23 June. He voted for inquiry into the circulation of Scottish and Irish pound notes, 5 June, and presented Flintshire petitions against restricting small bank notes, 7 May, 27 June. He presented the Holywell silk throwers' petition against reducing the protective tariffs on silks, 25 June, and ordered detailed returns on lead imports, 30 June. He voted for ordnance reductions, 4, 7 July 1828. Lloyd divided for Catholic emancipation, 6, 30 Mar., presented a favourable petition from Holywell, 9 Mar., and voted to permit Daniel O'Connell to sit without swearing the oath of supremacy, 18 May 1829. That October the Ultra Commons leader Sir Richard Vyvyan included him on his list of supporters of emancipation whose attitude to a putative coalition government was 'unknown'. He chaired celebrations to mark the coming of age of John Douglas of Gyrn in August, and on 15 Sept. 1829 attended the Denbighshire county meeting that petitioned against the justice commission's proposals for abolishing the Welsh judicature and court of great sessions. He is not known to have spoken publicly or voted on the 1830 administration of justice bill which effected the change, but Lord Cawdor's agent R.B. Williams directed the Anglesey bench to forward any pro-abolition petitions to Lloyd for presentation.[15] The birth of his grandson Thomas, 'the heir apparent to Pengwern', was celebrated throughout his estates, and notably in Denbigh, where plans were made to oust the sitting Tory Frederick Richard West at the first opportunity. Local newspapers reported the event alongside accounts of meetings to petition for action to combat distress in 'agriculture, commerce, manufactures and mines', and at the Flintshire meeting in Mold, 8 Feb. 1830, Lloyd promised the petitioners his own and Mostyn's support and claimed that he already advocated these sentiments in Parliament.[16] He presented their petition with another from Holywell, 15 Mar. He was probably the 'Sir C. Lloyd' who voted in the minority against the East Retford disfranchisement bill that day, and he divided steadily with the revived Whig opposition until 11 June, including for parliamentary reform, 28 May 1830. He was foreman of the Flintshire grand jury when the fraud action against the Mold Mining Company was heard in April,[17] and presented a Flintshire miners and smelters' petition for higher protective tariffs on foreign lead, 26 May. On the hustings at the August 1830 general election, he promised to promote the reform of all abuses in the state, 'notably in the representation of the people in Parliament'. Although toasted at dinners marking the return of Robert Myddelton Biddulph for Denbigh Boroughs, he now held aloof from Denbigh politics and stayed in Flintshire for the assizes.[18]

The Wellington ministry counted Lloyd among their 'foes', but he was absent from the division on the civil list which brought them down, 15 Nov. 1830. He presented the landowners' petition of complaint by which the passage of the Ffestiniog railway bill was delayed, 18 Mar. 1831. He divided for the Grey ministry's reform bill at its second reading, 22 Mar., and presented favourable petitions from Flintshire, Flint, Holywell and Mold, 29 Mar., another that day from St. Asaph seeking enfranchisement, and several for the abolition of colonial slavery.[19] He paired against Gascoyne's wrecking amendment to the reform bill, 19 Apr. Mostyn, whose estates he inherited in trust, had died on the 17th, vacating the Flintshire seat, and to counter a challenge by Sir John Hanmer† of Bettisfield, Lloyd and his agents immediately promoted the candidature of his son Edward, who, as Mostyn's eventual heir, now adopted his name and arms.[20] At the general election of 1831 Lloyd stood again for the Boroughs, promising to attend to 'local interests and to all the great questions of general policy', especially the reform bill, neither constituency was polled and Lloyd's election dinner served to rally support for Lloyd Mostyn in the county.[21] Lloyd had declined a requisition from the reformers of Montgomeryshire, but he directed his own and the Mostyn tenants to support reformers in contests there and in Caernarvon Boroughs.[22]

Lloyd and his son divided for the reintroduced reform bill at its second reading, 6 July 1831, and steadily throughout July and August for its details. Lloyd voted for the disfranchisement of Saltash, which ministers no longer pressed, 26 July, and, unlike most Welsh Members, he endorsed the decision to make Merthyr a contributory of Cardiff, 10 Aug. Applied to by reformers throughout North Wales, he supported local campaigns to enfranchise Abergele, St. Asaph and Llanrwst, and, when the addition of Holywell and Mold to Flint Boroughs was considered, 10 Aug., he intervened, apparently with Althorp's support, and had the franchise confined to the township of Mold and extended to the parish of Holywell.[23] He divided with administration on the Dublin election controversy, 23 Aug. The Mostyn baronetcy had been extinguished by Sir Thomas's death and Lloyd was awarded the title Baron Mostyn when he became a coronation peer in September 1831.[24] Addressing his constituents, he urged them to return another reformer at the ensuing by-election, but he decided against putting forward his younger son Thomas and tacitly supported the Glynnes of Hawarden.[25] Friends assumed that he did so to reduce the risk of opposition to Edward in the county and to promote reform in Denbighshire, which had been conceded a second seat.[26]

Mostyn's estates and difficult financial legacy preoccupied the new Lord Mostyn over the following months, but Lloyd Mostyn, who sought his assistance on 'small notes', the Caernarvon roads bill and arrangements for Maelor Sais and the Montgomery Boroughs constituency, briefed him regularly on proceedings in the Commons, while entreating him to attend the Lords.[27] In March 1832 he wrote:

> I would not urge you coming up for the second reading if it were not my conscientious opinion that you ought not in justice to the opinion you have always held on the subject of reform, in justice to your former constituents, and in justice to Lord Grey, absent yourself on so vital and important an occasion.[28]

He voted to secure the reform bill's passage, 7 Oct. 1831, 9 May 1832, and, as they were to do throughout his life, his sons championed the Liberal cause in North Wales at the 1832 general election, and assisted with subsequent petitions.[29] Financial setbacks arising from overspeculation, high election costs, his reluctance to sell land and difficulties in executing Sir Thomas Mostyn's will and dealing with his impoverished and overmortgaged estates almost bankrupted the family in 1844 and 1853, when Lord Mostyn was said to owe £192,300 and his estates were valued at £189,932.[30] He died at Pengwern in April 1854 and was buried in the family vault at Llanrhos. His will, though later acknowledged by his heirs and agents, was not now proved, but on 16 Nov. 1854 administration of his personalty, sworn under £300, was granted as 2nd baronet to Edward Mostyn Lloyd Mostyn.[31]

[1] *DWB*. [2] T.A. Glenn, *Fam. of Mostyn of Mostyn*, 173-5; *Y Gwyliedydd*, ii (1924), 58; *HP Commons, 1790-1820*, ii. 497-9; iv. 437-8. [3] Flint RO, Mostyn mss D/M/3318-34; A.H. Dodd, 'Enclosure Movement in North Wales', *Bull. Bd. Celtic Stud.* iii (1926), 210-38. [4] *Chester Chron.* 25 Feb., 3, 10, 17, 24 Mar. 1820. [5] *Session of Parl. 1825*, p. 473. [6] Ibid. 27 Oct. 1820. [7] *Shrewsbury Chron.* 24 Nov. 1820. [8] *Chester Chron.* 18 Jan. 1822; Flint RO, Leeswood mss D/LE/1352. [9] *Salopian Jnl.* 24 Apr. 1822. [10] *CJ*, lxxviii. 152, 267, 334. [11] Ibid. lxxx. 94, 95, 336, 401, 411, 518. [12] *N. Wales Gazette*, 12 Jan., 29 June; *Chester Courant*, 6, 13, 20 June; *Chester Chron.* 9, 23 June 1826. [13] *Chester Courant*, 15 Aug. 1826. [14] UCNW, Porth-yr-aur mss 12497, 12498; *CJ*, lxxxii. 109-10, 252, 304, 426, 452; *N. Wales Gazette*, 31 May, 14 June 1827. [15] *Chester Courant*, 11 Aug., 22 Sept.; *Shrewsbury Chron.* 25 Sept. 1829; Lord Cawdor, *Letter to Lord Lyndhurst*; *Cambrian Quarterly Mag.* (1829), 16-20; UCNW, Plas Newydd mss i. 740-1. [16] *Chester Courant*, 9, 23 Feb. 1830; Flint RO D/KK/467-8. [17] *Chester Courant*, 13 Apr. 1830. [18] *Chester Chron.* 16, 31 Aug. 1830. [19] Mostyn of Mostyn mss 7902, 7903. [20] *The Times*, 22 Apr. 1831; Flint RO, Mostyn mss D/M/3869, 3870; Mostyn of Mostyn mss 7904-8085, Warws. RO, Pennant mss CR2017/TP483/1. [21] Flint RO D/KK/461; Mostyn of Mostyn mss 572; *Chester Courant*, 3, 10 May; *Morning Chron.* 3 May 1831. [22] Plas Newydd mss i. 599, 609; Mostyn of Mostyn mss 7845-50; NLW, Coedymaen mss 239. [23] Mostyn of Mostyn mss 7871. [24] *Chester Courant*, 13 Sept.; *Macclesfield Courier and Herald*, 17 Sept. 1831. [25] *Chester Courant*, 13, 20 Sept. 1831; Mostyn of Mostyn mss 8128-31, 8133, 8134, 8136, 8137, 8139-45; NLW, Glynne of Hawarden mss 5392, 5404. [26] Mostyn of Mostyn mss 8132, 8135, 8138. [27] Ibid. 265, *passim*, 7471; Coedymaen mss 984. [28] Mostyn of Mostyn mss 265, Lloyd Mostyn to fa. Mar. 1832. [29] Ibid. 7876-80; Plas Newydd mss iii. 3609, 3618, 3737, 3753; *N. Wales Chron.* 1 Jan. 1833; B. Ellis, 'Parl. Rep. Mont. 1728-1868', *Mont. Colls.* lxiii (1973), 84-88; T.M. Bassett, 'Y Bedyddwyr yng Ngwleidyddiaeth Sir Gaernarfon', *Trans. Caern. Hist. Soc.* xlii (1981), 129-34. [30] Mostyn of Mostyn mss 265-71; Flint RO, Mostyn mss D/M/3305. [31] *Chester Chron.* 8, 15 Apr. 1854; Mostyn of Mostyn mss 593; PROB 6/230.

M.M.E.

LLOYD, James Martin (1762–1844), of Lancing, Suss.

STEYNING	1790–7 Mar. 1791
STEYNING	24 Mar. 1791–7 May 1792
STEYNING	1796–14 Feb. 1806
STEYNING	1806–1818
NEW SHOREHAM	1818–1826

b. 21 May 1762, o.s. of James Lloyd of Lancing and Elizabeth, da. of Rev. Edward Martin of Lancing. *educ.* Univ. Coll. Oxf. 1780. *m.* (1) 20 Jan. 1785, Rebecca (*d.* 7 Feb. 1812), da. of Rev. William Green of Eccles Hall, Norf., 3da. (2 *d.v.p.*); (2) 10 Nov. 1812, Elizabeth Anne, da. of Rev. Colston Carr of Ealing, Mdx., *s.p. cr.* bt. 30 Sept. 1831. *d.* 24 Oct. 1844.

Maj. Suss. militia 1783, 1st maj. 1798, lt.-col. 1803.

Clerk of deliveries, ordnance 1806-7.

After sitting for a number of years as Member for Steyning on the interest of the dukes of Norfolk, Lloyd transferred in 1818 to New Shoreham, where he had his own local base as well as the ducal interest. The contest there in 1820 was not aimed at him, and he topped the poll.[1] He was a silent Member who attended fairly regularly in the first two sessions of the new Parliament and continued to vote with the Whig opposition to Lord Liverpool's ministry. He divided against the civil list, 8 May, and the additional baron of exchequer in Scotland, 15 May 1820. He was granted a month's leave owing to a family illness, 30 June 1820. He voted to condemn the omission of Queen Caroline's name from the liturgy, 23, 26 Jan., 13 Feb., and ministers' conduct towards her, 6 Feb., and for inquiry into the conduct of the sheriff of Dublin, 22 Feb. 1821. He voted against renewal of the sugar duty, 9 Feb., and for Maberly's resolution on the state of the revenue, 6 Mar., military retrenchment, 14, 15 Mar., repeal of the additional malt duty, 21 Mar., 3 Apr., and Hume's economy and retrenchment motion, 27 June. He divided for Catholic relief, 28 Feb. He voted for the enfranchisement of Leeds as a scot and lot borough in lieu of Grampound, 2 Mar., and the general parliamentary reform motion, 18 Apr. He was granted a month's leave owing to ill health, 4 May 1821. Thereafter his attendance lapsed sharply, and he does not appear to have voted at all during the 1822 session: a source which places him in the government majority against more extensive tax reductions, 11 Feb., is almost certainly in error.[2] He paired for Russell's reform motion, 24 Apr. 1823. He was probably the 'W. Lloyd' recorded as voting against the Irish tithes composition bill, 16 June 1823, and the 'T.M. Lloyd' who was for repeal of the window tax, 2 Mar. 1824. He paired for inquiry into the state of Ireland, 11 May, and voted for repeal of the leather duty, 18 May. The 'J.S. Lloyd' listed in the government majority against Brougham's motion condemning the prosecution of the Methodist missionary John Smith in Demerara, 11 June 1824, is more likely to have been Samuel Loyd. He paired in favour of Catholic relief, 1 Mar., 21 Apr., 10 May 1825. Either he or Samuel Loyd divided for revision of the corn laws, 18 Apr. 1826. He retired at the dissolution that summer, having signified his intention of doing so a year earlier.[3]

In 1827 Lloyd purchased the manor of Lancing, where his family had owned land since the early eighteenth century, and by 1834 he owned four-fifths of the parish. Lord Grey's ministry made him a baronet in 1831. He died in October 1844 and his title expired with him; his estate passed to his only child, Rebecca, and reverted on her death two years later to his second wife.[4]

[1] *Suss. Advertiser*, 13 Mar. 1820. [2] *The Times*, 13 Feb. 1822. [3] Arundel Castle mss FC 251; *Brighton Gazette*, 1 June 1826. [4] *VCH Suss.* vi. (2), 42; T.W. Horsfield, *Hist. Suss.* ii. 206; PROB 11/2009/912.

H.J.S.

LLOYD, Thomas (?1771–1829), of Beechmount, nr. Rathkeale, co. Limerick and 1 Merrion Square East, Dublin.

Co. LIMERICK 1826–18 Dec. 1829

b. ?1771, 2nd but 1st surv. s. of Col. Thomas Lloyd of Beechmount and Ellen, da. of Thomas Lloyd, ?MP [I], of Kildromin and Drumsallagh, co. Limerick.[1] *educ.* Trinity, Dublin aged 15, 4 July 1786; G. Inn 1791; King's Inns 1791, called [I] 1794. *m.* 1797, Catherine, da. of Eyre Evans of Miltown Castle, co. Cork, 2s. 2da. *d.* 18 Dec. 1829.

Asst. barrister, co. Limerick ?1804-25; KC [I] 1816.

Lloyd, whose family was of Welsh origin, was descended from the Thomas Lloyd of Tower Hill, county Limerick, whose brother Charles was awarded a baronetcy in 1661. This Thomas's grandson, the Rev. Thomas Lloyd, chancellor of Cashel and chanter of Limerick, whose will was proved in 1746, had, with his second wife Frances, a fourth son, another Thomas, this Member's father, who was a colonel in the army and purchased Beechmount in 1805. He, like his half-brother William of Tower Hill, had married one of his second cousins, the daughters of his namesake, who owned the estates of Kildromin and Drumsallagh. This Thomas Lloyd, who was called to the Irish bar in 1762 and became recorder of Limerick in 1782, was probably the lawyer of that name who sat in the Irish Commons for Tralee, 1777-83.[2] This Member, who thus shared his name with his father and both his grandfathers, married the daughter of Eyre Evans, who was no doubt the son of Thomas Evans of Miltown Castle, Member for Castlemartyr, 1737-53, and nephew of the 1st Baron Carbery. Like his maternal grandfather, he became a barrister, serving on the Munster circuit, and from about 1804 he held the office of assistant barrister, or chairman of quarter sessions, for his native county.[3] Lloyd, whose elder brother William, a naval lieutenant, was drowned at sea in 1805, at some point thereafter succeeded his father to Beechmount. His next younger brother Richard, lieutenant-colonel of the 84th Foot, was killed at the Nive in 1813 and was mentioned as a promising young officer in Wellington's subsequent dispatch.[4] Three of Lloyd's other brothers served in the army, while a fourth, John, was rector of Cashel.

Lloyd occasionally participated in county Limerick politics, for instance in seconding the candidacy of the unsuccessful independent challenger Standish O'Grady* at the general election of 1818, and he had a substantial territorial interest.[5] Nevertheless, he caused considerable surprise by his decision to resign as assistant barrister in the autumn of 1825, by which time he had established a local reputation amounting almost to veneration, in order to contest the county. He staked his claim as a supporter of Catholic relief at the Munster provincial meeting of Catholics in Limerick, 24 Oct., and Daniel O'Connell* thought he was certain to throw out O'Grady.[6] In January 1826, when he received addresses of thanks from the magistrates of the Limerick and Rathkeale divisions of the county on his retirement after 22 years' assiduous service, he declined to attend the Dublin dinner to the friends of civil and religious liberty got up by O'Connell.[7] That April he clashed with O'Grady at a county meeting, insisting that Limerick should petition against the suppression of small Irish banknotes, and he stood against him at the general election that summer, when he claimed his local record of service as an indicator of how he would carry out the 'honest and anxious performance' of his parliamentary duties. Having given cautious support to the Liverpool government, he was returned in second place after a severe contest at the expense of O'Grady, largely because of the territorial interests arrayed in his favour.[8] He survived a petition.

Lloyd presented several county Limerick petitions for Catholic claims, 9 Feb. (as he did in the following session), and voted for them, 6 Mar. 1827.[9] He was one of the liberal Protestant Irish Members who was threatened with O'Connell's retribution if he failed to back the pro-Catholic Canning in his attempt to form a government early that year.[10] He was appointed to the select committee on Irish grand jury presentments, 6 June 1827. He divided for repeal of the Test Acts, 26 Feb., and Catholic relief, 12 May 1828. He supported the salmon fisheries bill at the request of his constituents, 30 Mar., and brought up their petition for protection from foreign wool, 7 May. He sided with opposition for reducing the grant to the Royal Cork Institution, 20 June 1828. Seconding the motion for a petition at the Irish Protestants' pro-Catholic meeting in Dublin, 20 Jan. 1829, he declared that its success 'would destroy a system of monopoly, which had been too long suffered to exist, to the injury of the many for the benefit of the few, and which was most detrimental to the power and the happiness of the empire'.[11] He presented petitions for repeal of the Irish Subletting and Vestry Acts from Newcastle, county Limerick, 13 Feb., and Rathkeale, 24 Feb., and rebutted allegations of electoral interference by Catholic priests, 3 Mar. He supported relief as a means of providing Ireland with peace and prosperity, 26 Feb., when he denied that most of the Protestants of his own county were hostile to it. He had been listed by Planta, the Wellington ministry's patronage secretary, as likely to be 'with government' on Catholic emancipation, and duly voted for it, 6, 30 Mar. He explained that he had been against the disfranchisement of the Irish 40*s*. freeholders, but was willing to defer to the opinion of others in its favour, 26 Mar., when, however, he objected to its being applied to such county boroughs as Limerick. His only other known votes were for transferring East Retford's seats to Birmingham, 5 May, and allowing O'Connell to take his seat unimpeded, 18 May 1829.

In mid-December 1829 he was reported to have recovered from a dangerous and painful illness, but he died suddenly, aged 58, that month, when it was suggested that his constitution had never really recovered from the severe shock it had received during the general election campaign.[12] He was succeeded by his eldest son Thomas (1798-1873), an army officer, who briefly offered as a Conservative for county Limerick in 1841, but never entered Parliament.[13]

[1] The Thomas Lloyd who was this Member's father was an army officer, so it is unlikely that he was the man of this name who sat in the Dublin Parliament (as conjectured in *Hist. Irish Parl.* v. 101); as the Thomas Lloyd who briefly represented Tralee was evidently a barrister, he was quite possibly this Member's maternal grandfather. [2] Ibid.; *Burke Irish LG* (1904), 343; *Burke Irish Fam. Recs.* (1976), 727-9. [3] *Limerick Chron.* 19 Dec. 1829. [4] J.A. Hall, *Hist. Peninsular War*, viii. 349. [5] *General Advertiser and Limerick Gazette*, 3, 7 July 1818; NLI mss 14118, 14119. [6] *Dublin Evening Post*, 22 Sept., 27, 29 Oct. 1825; *O'Connell Corresp.* iii. 1253. [7] *Limerick Chron.* 28 Jan. 1826; *O'Connell Corresp.* iii. 1278. [8] *Limerick Chron.* 12 Apr., 7, 10, 24, 28 June, 1, 5, 12 July 1826. [9] *The Times*, 10 Feb. 1827. [10] *O'Connell Corresp.* iii. 1364. [11] *The Times*, 24 Jan. 1829. [12] *Limerick Chron.* 12, 19 Dec.; *Limerick Evening Post*, 18, 22 Dec. 1829; *Gent. Mag.* (1830), i. 381. [13] *O'Connell Corresp.* vii. 2895.

S.M.F.

LLOYD MOSTYN, Edward Mostyn (1795–1884), of Mostyn Hall, Flint and 14 Park Place, Mdx.

FLINTSHIRE	1831–1837
FLINTSHIRE	1841–23 May 1842
LICHFIELD	31 Jan. 1846–1847
FLINTSHIRE	1847–3 Apr. 1854

b. 13 Jan. 1795, 1st s. of Sir Edward Pryce Lloyd, 2nd bt.*, of Pengwern, Flint and Bodfach, Mont. and Elizabeth, da. of Sir Roger Mostyn†, 5th bt. *educ.* Westminster 1807-12; Christ Church, Oxf. 1813. *m.* 20 June 1827, Lady Harriet Margaret Scott, da. of Thomas Scott†, 2nd earl of Clonmell [I], 5s. (2 *d.v.p.*) 5da. (1 *d.v.p.*). *suc.* fa. as 2nd Bar. Mostyn and 3rd bt. and to estates of his maternal uncle Sir Thomas Mostyn, 6th bt*, 3 Apr. 1854, having taken the additional name of Mostyn by royal lic. 7 May 1831. *d.* 17 Mar. 1884.

Sheriff, Merion. 1839, Flint 1840; ld. lt. Merion. 1840-*d.*

Col. Merion. militia 1847-52; v.-adm. N. Wales 1854-*d.*

Mostyn Lloyd, as he was first known, was born at his maternal grandfather's Flintshire seat of Mostyn, and was referred to by close friends and relations as 'Taff', on account of his bilingualism and pride in his Welsh ancestry and the bardic tradition of the house of Pengwern. After leaving Oxford without taking a degree, he became a magistrate and indulged his love of hunting and horse racing. His horses won the Oaks and St. Leger in 1825 and at Doncaster races in 1830.[1] When he married in 1827, his paternal grandmother's Montgomeryshire estates near Llanidloes, parcels of land in Bodfari, Cwm, Rhuddlan, St. Asaph, Tremeirchion and Whitford, Flintshire, and £10,000 were settled on him; and his bride had a portion of £3,750.[2] The birth of their first son, 'the heir apparent to Pengwern', 23 Dec. 1829, was widely celebrated, but there was little substance in rumours then current that he would stand for Denbigh Boroughs at the next election on the Whig or Chirk Castle interest of Robert Myddelton Biddulph*.[3] He lost no time in mobilizing support and declaring his candidature for Flintshire in 1831, when the dissolution precipitated by the defeat of the Grey ministry's reform bill followed closely on the death of his uncle Sir Thomas Mostyn, whose vast estates in Caernarvonshire, Cheshire, Flintshire, Merioneth and Montgomeryshire his father inherited in trust for him with an assured annual income of £3,000.[4] Drawing on the emotive appeal of the name of Mostyn, which Sir Thomas had directed him to take, he adopted it throughout his canvass, although the change had not been gazetted. He professed to be a reformer, 'a friend of religious toleration' and advocate of retrenchment and 'the final extinction of slavery ... born, brought up and resident in the county', and promised to promote all local interests.[5] Assisting him, on 27 Apr. his kinsman, the Tory Edward Lloyd of Rhagatt, observed that 'the reform question has been of wonderful advantage to you, also the circumstance of young [Sir Stephen] Glynne* [of Hawarden] being sheriff. I really augur most favourable things'.[6] He canvassed assiduously notwithstanding the retirement of his declared opponent, Sir John Hanmer† of Bettisfield, 28 Apr., mustered his supporters in a show of strength before his father's election for Flint Boroughs, 4 May, and, with the major interests in the county supportive or neutral, he was returned at Flint on the 10th with a great display of largesse.[7] He and his father gave Sir Charles Paget* their interest in Caernarvon Boroughs, and he was later sworn in as mayor of its out-borough of Pwllheli, a hereditary office which had passed to Mostyn through the Vaughans of Corsygedol.[8] His father endorsed St. Asaph's petition for enfranchisement as a contributory of Flint, and Lloyd Mostyn agreed to support Denbigh's campaign to add Abergele and Llanrwst to its contributories, 20 May 1831. However, he ensured that petitions entrusted to him from Llanrwst for enfranchisement and from Merioneth for additional representation were presented by Members less committed than he to supporting the 'whole bill'.[9]

Generally with his father, he divided for the reintroduced reform bill at its second reading, 6 July 1831, and steadily for its details. His wayward vote for Lord Chandos's amendment to enfranchise £50 tenants-at-will, 18 Aug., was attuned to local interests. He divided for the bill's third reading, 19 Sept., and passage, 21 Sept., for the second reading of the Scottish reform bill, 23 Sept., and for Lord Ebrington's confidence motion, 10 Oct. In September 1831 he had co-operated with Glynne to ensure that Flintshire petitioned urging the Lords to pass the reform bill.[10] His father's elevation to the Lords as Baron Mostyn at the coronation that month created a vacancy for Flint Boroughs, where, on their agents' advice, they acquiesced in the return of Henry Glynne as locum for his brother during his term as sheriff; Lloyd Mostyn moved the writ for the by-election to bring in Sir Stephen Glynne, 16 Feb. 1832.[11] He divided for the revised reform bill at its second reading, 17 Dec. 1831, steadily for its details, its third reading, 22 Mar., and the address calling on the king to appoint only ministers who would carry it unimpaired, 10 May 1832. He repeatedly urged his father to support it in the Lords.[12] He abstained when most Welsh Members voted for the amendment awarding separate representation to Merthyr Tydfil, 5 Mar. 1832.

The enfranchisement of Llanidloes and Newtown as contributories of Montgomery increased his family's interest there and Lloyd Mostyn ensured that he was well briefed to forestall attempts by Charles Watkin Williams Wynn* to increase the electorate in the rival Tory boroughs of Llanfyllin and Welshpool.[13] In the autumn of 1832 he forwarded Williams Wynn's request for his vote in his bid for the Speakership to his father with the endorsement, '*I don't* like the Right Honourable C.W.W.W. What shall I say to the application? Please to turn the matter over in your mind'.[14] Acting with the Ultra Lloyd Kenyon of Gredington and Frederick Richard Price of Bryn-y-Pys, whose estates and interests it affected, he opposed the unpopular proposal to transfer Maelor Sais (which included the borough of Overton) from Flintshire to Shropshire and discussed the matter with the leader of the House Lord Althorp, who had the decision reversed.[15] He voted in the radical minority to reduce public salaries to 1797 levels, 30 June 1831, but divided with government on the Dublin election controversy, 23 Aug. 1831, and the Russian-Dutch loan, 26 Jan., 12, 16, 20 July 1832. He received an 'unexpected summons to a meeting in the foreign office' to rally support for the government's resolutions on Irish tithes, 9 Mar.[16] He abstained on the government's temporizing amendment to Buxton's motion for a select committee on colonial slavery, 24 May 1832. He presented Flintshire's petition against the use of molasses in brewing and distilling, 13 Aug.,[17] and one from towns on the North Wales coast for tougher regulation of passenger steam ships following the *Rothsay Castle* disaster, 20 Sept. 1831, when he was added to the investigative committee. Taking over from his father, he met the local agents and served on parliamentary committees on the 1832 Ffestiniog railway and Caernarvon roads bills and reported back favourably to them.[18] After presenting a hostile petition from Holywell, he was added to the committee on the factory regulation bill, 24 July 1832.

His agents urged him to spend on voter registration, warning, 9 Aug., that Kenyon (anticipating failure in Denbighshire) was '*slyly*' targeting Flintshire.[19] Adopting a high local profile, Lloyd Mostyn became foreman of the grand jury that month, presided over dynastic celebrations in September to mark the coming of age of his Catholic kinsman Pyers Mostyn of Talacre, and came in for Flintshire unopposed as a Liberal at the December 1832 general election.[20] Seeking his urgent assistance with Denbighshire's Llanrwst voters, 12 Dec., Myddelton Biddulph asked him to

> tip them a few words of Welsh on the hustings (if there are any). It would do wonders in this neighbourhood. As your own election will be over by the 21st, our polling day, this will not interfere with your own business or subject you to any remarks should any of the Flintshire Tories be so disposed.[21]

He also canvassed for Sir Charles Paget* in Caernarvon Boroughs and provided documents to substantiate claims in subsequent pro-Paget petitions that the pre-1832 franchise there had been 'scot and lot',[22] and supported the Liberal John Edwards† when his return for Montgomery Boroughs was petitioned against.[23] Problems arising from Sir Thomas Mostyn's mortgage debts, bequests and reclaiming his property caused friction between Lloyd Mostyn and his father, who was reluctant to authorize the land sales necessary to balance the accounts.[24] Amid deepening financial crises, Lloyd Mostyn retained his Flintshire seat until defeated by Sir Stephen Glynne in 1837, was unseated on petition after regaining it in 1841, and by 1843 faced bankruptcy proceedings. He sat briefly for Lichfield as his young cousin Viscount Anson's locum before regaining Flintshire for the Liberals in 1847.[25] His debts were estimated at £838,604 and his estates valued at £493,011, 12 Jan. 1853, and some of his property was distrained in January 1857; but he recouped by facilitating the development of the seaside resort of Llandudno on his Gloddaeth estate and promoting the Cambrian Coast (Shrewsbury-Pwllheli) railway. In 1883 he held 8,390 acres in Caernarvonshire, Denbighshire and Flintshire.[26] He died at Mostyn in March 1884, having succeeded his father there in 1854, and was buried at Llanrhos.[27] His eldest son Thomas Edward Mostyn Lloyd Mostyn (1829-61), Liberal Member for Flintshire, 1854-61, had predeceased him and he left 'everything to my dear wife [*d.* 1892] absolutely' and land to his brother Thomas and younger son Roger. He was succeeded in the baronetcy and as 3rd Baron Mostyn by his grandson (Thomas's son) Llewelyn Nevill Vaughan Lloyd Mostyn (1856-1929).

[1] *Y Gwyliedydd*, ii (1824), 58; *Chester Chron.* 23 Aug. 1825; UCNW, Nannau mss 757, 758. [2] Flint RO, Mostyn mss D/M/3415, 3716, 3717; *Gent. Mag.* (1827), i. 641. [3] UCNW, Mostyn of Mostyn mss 258; *Chester Courant*, 9 Feb., 13 Apr.; *Salopian Jnl.* 10, 17 Feb. 1830. [4] Mostyn mss D/M/3869; Mostyn of Mostyn mss 5470-2. [5] Flint RO D/KK/459-62; Mostyn of Mostyn mss 572, 7904; *Chester Chron.* 22, 29 Apr.; *Chester Courant*, 26 Apr., 3 May; *London Gazette*, 13 May 1831. [6] Mostyn of Mostyn mss 7906. [7] Ibid 7905-8081, 8151, 8152; *Chester Courant*, 3, 10, 17 May; *Morning Chron.* 3 May; *Y Gwyliedydd*, viii (1831), 221-3. [8] UCNW, Plas Newydd mss i. 599; UCNW, Porth-yr-aur mss 12583; Mostyn of Mostyn mss 7848, 7851; *Caernarvon Herald*, 26 May, 9 June 1832. [9] Mostyn of Mostyn mss 7871, 7872; *Salopian Jnl.* 22 June; *The Times*, 25 June 1831. [10] Mostyn of Mostyn mss 8438-40; *Chester Chron.* 30 Sept.; *Chester Courant*, 4, 11, 18 Oct. 1831. [11] *Chester Courant*, 13, 20 Sept. 1831, 21, 28 Feb. 1832; Mostyn of Mostyn mss 8128-45, 8155-8; NLW, Glynne of Hawarden mss 5392, 5404; *Chester Chron.* 2 Mar. 1832. [12] Mostyn of Mostyn mss 265, Lloyd Mostyn to fa., 28 Jan. [13], 17 [28] Mar. 1832. [13] NLW, Coedymaen mss 984; Mostyn of Mostyn mss 265, Lloyd Mostyn to fa. 9 Mar. 1832. [14] Mostyn of Mostyn mss 8422. [15] Ibid. same to same Feb., 28 Mar.; 8159-62. [16] Ibid. 265, Lloyd Mostyn to fa., 9 Mar. 1832. [17] *Chester Courant*, 12 July, 23 Aug. 1831. [18] *CJ*, lxxxvi. 858; lxxxvii. 331-2; Mostyn of Mostyn mss 265, Lloyd Mostyn to fa. 16 Dec. 1831, 16 Feb., 9 Mar. 1832. [19] Mostyn of Mostyn mss 8163-8, 8435, 8842. [20] *Chester Chron.* 10 Aug., 29 Sept., 6 Oct. 1832; *N. Wales Chron.* 1 Jan. 1833. [21] Mostyn of Mostyn mss 7876-80. [22] Plas Newydd mss iii. 3609, 3618, 3735, 3737; K. Evans, 'Caernarfon Borough', *Trans. Caern. Hist. Soc.* viii (1947), 64; T.M. Bassett, 'Y Bedyddwyr yng Ngwleidyddiaeth Sir Gaernarfon', ibid. xlii (1981), 129-34; Gwynedd Archives (Caernarfon RO), Poole mss 5510, 5534, 5535, 5545, 5548; *CJ*, lxxxvii. 146, 398, 428, 479. [23] B. Ellis, 'Parl. Rep. Mont. 1728-1868', *Mont. Colls.* lxiii (1973), 84-88. [24] Mostyn of Mostyn mss 265, 266, *passim.* [25] *Staffs. Mercury*, 10, 17 Jan., 7 Feb. 1846. [26] Mostyn of Mostyn mss 270, 271, 292. [27] *Chester Courant*, 19, 26 Mar.; *Chester Chron.* 22 Mar. 1884.

M.M.E.

LOCH, James (1780–1855), of 23 Hart Street, Bloomsbury, Mdx.

ST. GERMANS	7 June 1827–1830
TAIN BURGHS	1830–1832
WICK BURGHS	1832–1852

b. 7 May 1780, 1st s. of George Loch of Drylaw, Edinburgh and Mary, da. of John Adam of Blair Adam, Kinross; bro. of John Loch*. *educ.* L. Inn 1796, called 1806; Edinburgh Univ. 1797; adv. 1801. *m.* (1) 4 Jan. 1810, Ann (*d.* 28 Jan. 1842), da. of Patrick Orr of Bridgeton, Kincardine, 7s. (1 *d.v.p.*) 2da. *d.v.p.*; (2) 2 Dec. 1847, Elizabeth Mary, da. of John Pearson of Tettenhall Wood, Staffs., wid. of Maj. George Macartney Greville, *s.p. suc.* fa. 1788. *d.* 28 June 1855.

Loch's ancestors migrated in the late fifteenth century from Gloucestershire to Edinburgh, where they prospered in the Baltic trade, became prominent in municipal affairs and acquired the Drylaw estate in 1641. His grandfather James Loch (1698-1759) was a Jacobite sympathizer who donated £10,000 to the Stuart cause, thereby compounding the debts with which his general prodigality had saddled the family property. His father, who was described as being of 'a gentle nature, much given to art and generally accomplished', married the sister of William Adam†, a rising Scottish lawyer and Whig Member of Parliament, and followed his brother-in-law's advice by selling Drylaw for £24,000, in order to 'secure a good competency to my children'. Loch was raised, after his father's death, by his mother in the family's town house in Edinburgh, which he inherited on coming of age in 1801. He also spent much time with his uncle, an improving landlord, at Blair Adam.[1] At Edinburgh University, where he studied law, he was one of the intellectual circle dominated by Henry Brougham*, Francis Horner† and Francis Jeffrey*, and as a member of the Speculative Society he espoused egalitarian and anti-Trinitarian views. During vacations he supervised improvements at Blair Adam and stayed for spells with his uncle in London, where he attended parliamentary debates. Although he was admitted as a Scottish advocate in 1801, he had already decided to forge a career at the English bar, for which he started serious study the following year. He was an early contributor to the *Edinburgh Review*, but an article in July 1804 caused a temporary rift with Brougham, who considered its gratuitous attack on the East India Company's monopoly to be ill-advised, especially as Adam was counsel to the Company. Brougham also chided him for his 'raffish' conduct in canvassing for Sir Francis Burdett* at the Middlesex by-election that summer.[2] Under the aegis of his uncle, Loch established himself with the leaders of the Whig party as a reliable factotum, dividing his time between Edinburgh, London and Blair Adam. In 1806 he was employed by George Tierney*, president of the board of control in Lord Grenville's ministry, as his private secretary. Unsure where his future lay, Loch completed his legal studies and established himself as a conveyancing barrister, while retaining his political connections. Early in 1808 Adam and Tierney recommended him to Grenville, now leader of the opposition, who was keen to find 'some person on whose secrecy, integrity and capacity and knowledge of the state of things ... he could depend ... [and] who could communicate with the confidential editors of newspapers his ideas on leading points'. Adam observed that the post would 'bring about most confidential communication with [Grenville] and, on a change, lead to a situation of permanent provision', but that it was ultimately 'a matter of taste'. Loch, who was an enthusiast for the Spanish cause, seems to have demurred, but he was involved in the abortive Whig attempts to secure the allegiance of the *British Press* and *Globe* newspapers in 1809. The following year, he supplied Grenville and the prince of Wales with calculations of the likely outcome of the Commons clash on the Walcheren expedition.[3]

In January 1810 Loch informed his uncle that, 'look[ing] upon politics as they are in fact' and given his equally unpromising professional prospects, he had decided to concentrate on estate management and property law, and to 'hold myself out as a candidate ... for the auditorship of any estate'. Two years later Adam negotiated his appointment as auditor (at £1,500 per annum) of the English estates, centred on Staffordshire, of the 2nd marquess of Stafford. Loch implemented a long-term programme of rational improvements, applying the principles of political economy and the techniques of scientific management. He also became increasingly involved in the management of the vast estates in Sutherland belonging to Stafford's wife, and he assumed general control of them in 1816. He gained notoriety by continuing and intensifying the policy, begun in 1807, of removing the crofting population to the coast and turning over the vacant land to sheep farming, the profits of which were theoretically to be invested in fishing, harbour construction and kelp manufacture, to create employment for the displaced population. Allotments were provided for growing food, coal and salt workings were set on foot at Brora, and the entire scheme of regional development was underpinned by improvements in transport communications. Loch never lost faith in this programme, which he supervised for almost 40 years, but he eventually had to concede that the coastal fishing economy could not support the population and that there was no alternative to emigration on a considerable scale. He replied to criticism of the clearances in an anonymous *Account of the Improvements on the Estate of Sutherland* (1815), which he published under his own name five years later in a greatly expanded version, as a retort to 'unfounded slanders'. It was an able, if less than frank *apologia* for the policy, which Brougham considered to be 'excellent and ... useful to all large proprietors'.[4] With his rapidly growing family causing him problems, Loch was taken on in 1823 as estate manager by the 5th earl of Carlisle, and he subsequently became responsible for the Bridgwater, Dudley, Egerton and Keith estates. He perceived the long-term implications of the development of railways and sought, by intelligent planning and co-operation with their promoters, to minimize the impact on those of his employers, notably the Staffords, with vested interests in canals. Although he was a convinced free trader, he favoured a gradual diminution of agricultural protection 'to keep the squires in good humour'. A firm believer in the ethos of improvement, he was a council member of London University and played an active part in the affairs of the Society for the Diffusion of Useful Knowledge.[5]

If the pace of social change sometimes alarmed Loch, he was nevertheless a committed supporter of moderate and concessionary parliamentary reform. He drew up Lord John Russell's bill of 1820 for the disfranchisement of Grampound. Later that year he showed to Adam and Lord Grey a plan of reform designed to deal with the four major developments which he thought had undermined the representative system: the 'vast additional influence obtained by the treasury', which had increased government control over elections; the 'great creation of peers' initiated by Pitt (that 'wretched, rash and shallow adventurer'), which had augmented aristocratic influence in the Commons, where the great landowners, now ennobled, had been replaced by 'their lawyers or needy younger children'; the 'great increase of the manufacturing towns and their want of representation'; and, most important of all, the spread of the 'superior education of the bulk of the people', based on the 'extension and influence of the press' in its widest sense. He proposed to deprive of one Member every borough with less than 5,000 inhabitants, and to give two to every unrepresented town with over 10,000 and one to the next six largest; the remaining surplus Members were to be distributed among the counties, where he also contemplated an extension of the franchise and the establishment of polling districts. On submitting the plan to Russell, who used it as the basis of the scheme which he presented to the Commons in April 1822, Loch commented:

> There is one thing we Whigs must acknowledge, which is that not only has the constitution retrograded somewhat ... and to that extent ought to be brought back, but that there has also sprung up a new and powerful and growing influence in the country and the world, making large and incessant demands for attention and influence which must be acceded to ... [an] influence and power in some degree more at variance with ... the old Whig feelings, prejudices and aristocracy than with the powerless, inconsequential influence of the present placemen, who exist only for a season ... If the old Whigs would acknowledge to themselves the truth of this fact and become the sincere and active and zealous promoters of a moderate reform they would, as they ought from the liberality and consistency of their public conduct, and their great wealth and distinguished names, become the real and effective leaders of the people.[6]

In April 1827 Loch told Adam that if Stafford offered to return him to the Commons to support Canning's new administration, he saw no reason to refuse. The next month he accordingly came in on a vacancy for St. Germans on the interest of the 2nd earl of St. Germans, whose deceased first wife had been Stafford's half-sister. The duke of Bedford echoed Loch's earlier strictures, now conveniently forgotten, on the intrusion of the employees of the aristocracy into the House, remarking that 'it will be a bad thing for him' and that he '*was* a good Whig and ... ought not to be converted into a *Staffordite*'.[7] Loch was disturbed by reports that the government planned to revive the 'grievous and mischievous' post of minister for Scotland, 'that fruitful source of misgovernment, oppression and jobbing'. He privately sought to persuade the home secretary Lord Lansdowne of the importance of continuing the practice established by his predecessor, Peel, of dealing directly with Scottish patronage and ignoring 'the extremes of both Edinburgh parties'. In this way, he argued, it would be possible to 'understand the actual circumstances and position of the country' and 'attend to its just claims'. His views were made known to Canning, who commissioned him to set them out at length on paper.[8] That autumn Adam introduced him to Huskisson, who had assumed Canning's mantle following the latter's death.[9] Loch was so uneasy about the duke of Wellington's accession to the premiership early in 1828 that he considered leaving Parliament, not, as he told Adam, 'because Lord Stafford and I differed on any essential point', but 'because I was determined not to mix myself up with keen party politics on their side, but to support those measures that seemed to me beneficial to the country'. In the event, he retained his seat and endorsed Huskisson's participation in the government.[10] He was absent from the division on repeal of the Test Acts, 26 Feb., but voted for Catholic relief, 12 May 1828. He divided against extending East Retford's franchise to Bassetlaw freeholders, 21 Mar. That day he gave evidence before the select committee on the Scottish entails bill, of which he was a member.[11] He recognized that Peel, the leader of the Commons, was in difficulties with the more reactionary Tories, and after the resignation of the Huskissonites from the ministry in May he feared that the outcome of these 'strange proceedings' would be a return to 'the age of restrictions, monopolies and non-intercourse with foreign powers'.[12] He was duly listed, with Stafford, as one of the Huskissonite parliamentary group. In presenting an Axminster petition in favour of the circulation of small bank notes, 13 June 1828, he asserted that 'the branch establishments of the Bank of England were unnecessary'.[13] That autumn, fresh from a visit to Huskisson's constituency of Liverpool, he reported the prevalent view, which he shared, that ministers had no clear Irish policy and that the fate of Catholic relief would 'depend on the first division in the ... Commons'.[14] He naturally voted for the government's emancipation bill, 6, 30 Mar. 1829. He was named to the select committee on Scottish entails, 27 Feb., and assisted Thomas Kennedy in preparing further legislation to reform the current laws.[15] Late in 1829 he tried to persuade ministers to intervene to curb the proliferation of speculative railway projects, until the Liverpool and Manchester experiment had 'proved what this mode of conveyance was equal to'. Politically, he thought there was 'a great chance, by the time ... Parliament meets, that the agriculturists will alone be the complaining body'.[16] He divided against Lord Blandford's reform plan, 18 Feb. (he thought it 'not a little singular' to see Daniel O'Connell and Blandford 'as brother radicals'),[17] but for the transfer of East Retford's seats to Birmingham, 5 Mar., and Jewish emancipation, 5 Apr. 1830. It is uncertain whether it was he or his brother John, recently returned for Hythe, who voted with government on the grant for South American missions, 7 June. He divided that day against abolition of the death penalty for forgery. He was privately critical of the rejuvenated Whig opposition, 'under the well regulated tempers of Lords Durham and Grey', for giving ministers 'the opportunity of closing the session with the only considerable majority of the year' on the regency question, 6 July 1830.[18] At the general election that summer Stafford returned him for Tain Burghs. In a speech at a subsequent dinner, he 'stated his approbation' of the government, explaining that 'he had gone into Parliament to support ... Mr. Canning' but had found Wellington and his colleagues 'so desirous to abridge every expense and to alleviate the burdens of the people', that 'no ministry since the Revolution seemed better entitled to support'. He also 'eulogized the exertions' of Peel in 'ameliorating the criminal law and effecting other useful reforms'.[19]

The ministry listed Loch among the 'doubtful doubtfuls', with the comment that 'he should be a favourable doubtful at least'. After an excursion on the Liverpool and Manchester railway in October 1830 he predicted that it was 'destined to produce the most important and serious change in the condition of the world'.[20] He was astounded by Wellington's 'ill-advised' declaration against reform, 2 Nov. 1830, and promptly informed Peel that, like Stafford, he felt obliged to support a reform measure and would vote accordingly in the anticipated showdown in the Commons. He probably absented himself from the crucial civil list division, 15 Nov., though it is just possible that it was he rather than John who sided with government.[21] He applauded the Grey ministry's decision to take up reform, assuring one doubting correspondent that the issue was 'impossible to avoid' and 'the sooner it is conceded the less will be required'.[22] According to the Scottish judge James Abercromby*, Loch told him in early December that 'the subject' of reform in Scotland 'has fallen into his hands [and] he is in association with Lord Duncannon and John Russell', two of the committee of four deputed to draft the ministry's reform bills. He sent Abercromby 'his plans', which were based on the principles of enfranchising the larger towns as part of the burgh representation, rather than throwing them into the counties, and of ensuring that the county voting qualification was higher than that for the burghs. Abercromby regarded it 'one of undisguised distrust towards the people', its 'main object being to maintain the monopoly of the landed proprietors' and 'give nothing, at least in counties, to the people'.[23] According to Brougham's unreliable account, Durham, another of the reform committee, by-passed the Scottish law officers in confiding the ministerial scheme directly to Loch, who was thus encouraged to indulge in 'jobbing and mischievous activity' and to try to 'smuggle through a *Stafford job against reform*'.[24] Loch, who presented three Scottish petitions for reform, 3 Feb. 1831, was initially disappointed with the government's plan for Scotland, which, he told a friend, was 'most inadequate for its purpose'. On reflection, however, he decided not to 'throw more difficulties in their way', as the scheme went some distance towards meeting his views, and he complied with the agreement that 'the friends of the measure' should suggest amendments in private. He made a number of such proposals, some of which were accepted, including one to allow the eldest sons of Scottish peers to sit for Scottish constituencies. He paired for the second reading of the English reform bill, 22 Mar., having broken his collar bone nine days earlier, but was present to vote against Gascoyne's wrecking amendment, 19 Apr.[25] It was reported in February 1831 that he was 'strongly pressing' the board of trade to repeal the kelp duty, 'as a compensation for the reduction on barilla'.[26] He was again returned for Tain Burghs at the general election that spring.

He divided for the second reading of the reintroduced reform bill, 6 July 1831, and steadily for its details. He voted for its passage, 21 Sept., the second reading of the Scottish bill, 23 Sept., and Lord Ebrington's confidence motion, 10 Oct. It is not clear whether it was he or his brother who voted with ministers on the Dublin election dispute, 23 Aug. He divided for the second reading of the revised reform bill, 17 Dec. 1831, though he believed that government had little backing in the country on any other issue. His support for the measure cost him his job as auditor of the insane Lord Dudley's estates.[27] He again voted steadily for the bill's details and for the third reading, 22 Mar. 1832. When it faced defeat in the Lords he expressed the fear that 'we are on the brink of a tremendous crisis, not for this country but the world at large'.[28] He presented a Tain petition in favour of minor amendments to the Scottish bill, 13 Apr., and was in the ministerial majorities on that measure, 1, 15 June. He voted for the second reading of the Irish bill, 25 May. He divided with government on the Russian-Dutch loan, 26 Jan., relations with Portugal, 9 Feb., and the navy civil departments bill, 6 Apr. On 16 Apr. he introduced a bill to empower Scottish burghs to establish police forces; it gained its second reading, 15 May, but foundered at the report stage. Either he or his brother divided against the exclusion of insolvent debtors from the House, 6 June, and to make coroners' inquests public, 20 June 1832.

At the general election of 1832 Loch was returned for what had now become Wick Burghs, and he sat until his defeat in 1852. He died in June 1855 and left his freehold property and London house in Albemarle Street to his eldest son, William Adam Loch, who recalled him as being

> a man of various accomplishments, of powerful intellect ... [whose] judgement was sound, well read and an excellent converser. He was strict, even perhaps stern in the discharge of his duty, and yet he had a gentle heart ... He had a commanding presence, tall and well made, his face very handsome, with a profile like that of the first Napoleon.[29]

[1] G. Loch, *Loch Fam.* pp. xii-xv, 138, 143, 145, 235-7 (quoted); E. Richards, *Leviathan of Wealth*, 19-22; Add. 40885, ff. 238-42. [2] *Brougham and His Early Friends* ed. R.B. Atkinson and G.A. Jackson, i. 11, 39, 51, 173-5, 211, 261, 265, 281, 289, 346; ii. 3, 77-79, 83, 143-6, 149-50 (quoted), 161-4; iii. 278-83; *Horner Mems.* (1843), i. 203-5, 211-14. [3] *Brougham and Early Friends*, ii. 269-71, 295-6 (quoted); iii. 280; *Horner Mems.* ii. 424; A. Aspinall, *Politics and the Press*, 291, 298; *Geo. III Corresp.* v. 4122. [4] Blair Adam mss (NRA 9954), Loch to Adam, 7 Jan. 1810; Richards, pp. ix-xviii, 88-105, 195-7; D. Spring, *English Landed Estate in 19th Cent.* 89-95; E. Richards, *Highland Clearances*, i. 182, 306, 331, 337-8 (quoted); ii. 52-56, 380-2, 387-8, 405; *Sutherland Estate Management Pprs.* ed. R.J. Adam (Scottish Hist. Soc. ser. 4. viii-ix), *passim.* [5] Loch, 243; Spring, 93-94; Richards, *Leviathan*, 28 (quoted); Blair Adam mss 2/269, 290, 297; Brougham mss, Loch to Brougham, 19 Aug. 1825, 1 Jan. 1827, 4, 6 Oct., to James Brougham, 15 July 1828. [6] Richards, *Leviathan*, 27-28, 30; Staffs. RO, Sutherland mss D593/K/1/5/10, Loch to Abercromby, 20 Apr., to Russell, 16 Oct. 1821. [7] Blair Adam mss 2/332; Add. 51669, Bedford to Lady Holland, 23 May 1827. [8] Blair Adam mss 2/333; *Canning's Ministry*, 277. [9] Add. 38751, f. 103. [10] Blair Adam mss 2/339; Add. 38755, f. 58. [11] *PP* (1828), vii. 237-49. [12] Blair Adam mss 2/341; Add. 38756, f. 224. [13] *The Times*, 13 June 1828. [14] Brougham mss, Loch to Brougham, 30 Sept. [1828]; Add. 38757, f. 81. [15] Add. 51574, Abercromby to Holland [Mar. 1829]. [16] Add. 38758, ff. 52, 76. [17] Blair Adam mss 2/362. [18] Ibid. 2/366. [19] *Inverness Courier*, 18 Aug. 1830. [20] Loch, 249. [21] Sutherland mss K/1/5/27, Loch to Innes, 25 Mar. 1831; *Countess Granville Letters*, ii. 62; *Howard Sisters*, 164. [22] Blair Adam mss 2/370; Sutherland mss K/1/5/26, Loch to Dempster, 25 Dec. 1830. [23] Add. 52182, f. 21. [24] Brougham mss, autiobiog. fragment. [25] Sutherland mss K/1/5/27, Loch to Laing, 16, Gunn, 16, Sellar, 18, Russell, 24, Innes, 25 Mar. 1831; J. Cannon, *Parl. Reform*, 206. [26] Orkney Archives, Balfour mss D2/8/9, Traill to Balfour, 5 Feb. 1831. [27] Blair Adam mss 2/383-4. [28] Ibid. 2/386. [29] PROB 11/2218/706; IR26/2039/639; Loch, 238-9, 250-3.

D.R.F.

LOCH, John (1781–1868), of 18 Upper Bedford Place, Russell Square, Mdx.

Hythe 26 Mar. 1830–1832

b. 8 Sept. 1781, 2nd s. of George Loch (*d.* 1786) of Drylaw, Edinburgh and Mary, da. of John Adam of Blair Adam, Kinross; bro. of James Loch*. *m.* 17 Feb. 1820, Rabina Marion, da. of Archibald Cullen of 23 Old Square, L. Inn, Mdx., 1s. *d.v.p.* 1da. *d.* 19 Feb. 1868.

Cdr. E.I. Co. marine service 1806.

Dir. E.I. Co. 1821-54, dep. chairman 1828-9, 1836-7, chairman 1829-30, 1833-4.

Between voyages to Bombay and China in the marine service of the East India Company, Loch served as a volunteer with the navy. He was in Lord St. Vincent's flagship during the blockade of Brest in the summer of 1800, and later that year went on the Ferrol expedition as aide-de-camp to Sir Edward Pellew†: one of his Adam cousins deemed it 'labour lost', as he had nothing to do.[1] From the *Chiffone*, off Le Havre, 21 May 1805, he wrote to his brother James of the defeat, 'by a much larger majority than I expected', of the Roman Catholic petition: 'the English are terrible fellows in sticking by old prejudices'. Although a political opponent, he was 'almost a little sorry' for Lord Melville in his humiliation.[2] In 1808, commanding the *Scaleby Castle* on her return from China, he beat off a French frigate near the Nicobar Islands.[3] He made 'a considerable fortune' in the East, where he seems to have been involved in private trade with China, but 'delicate' health forced him to return home prematurely.[4] In 1817 he began to canvass for a seat in the court of directors of the East India Company. He was elected four years later, became one of the leaders of the dominant private trading interest and was twice chairman, though his abilities in that capacity were modest.[5] In February 1830, during his first spell in the chair, he was rescued from the threat of being examined before the Lords select committee on the Company's affairs by the intervention of Lord Ellenborough, president of the board of control.[6] A month later he stood on a vacancy for Hythe, where his third cousin Stewart Marjoribanks, the brother of a fellow director, was the other sitting Member. A rumoured opposition did not materialize and Loch, who promised to 'support economy in all its branches' and to promote the interests of the shipping industry, was returned as a self-styled 'independent man'.[7]

Loch, whose brother was at this time associated with the Huskissonites, took his seat on 1 Apr. 1830 and four days later voted for Jewish emancipation. He voted for parliamentary reform, 28 May. It is not clear whether it was he or James who divided with ministers on the grant for South American missions, 7 June. He probably voted against the abolition of the death penalty for forgery the same day. On 19 June he opposed Mackintosh's bill to compensate sufferers by the defalcation of the registrar of Madras, disputing the validity of its premise that 'the state is answerable for the delinquencies of its officers'. He was in minorities for amendments to the sale of beer bill, 21 June,

1 July 1830. He stood again for Hythe at the 1830 general election and survived the resident ratepayers' attempt to open the borough. He was described by one reporter as a supporter of the Wellington ministry 'from principle';[8] but ministers listed him among the 'Good Doubtfuls', with the comment that he would be a 'friend except on parliamentary reform'. He probably voted with them on the civil list, 15 Nov. 1830, though it is possible that it was he rather than James who abstained.[9] Three months later Ellenborough noted him as being 'violent' against the Grey ministry and scornful of their budget;[10] but, like his brother, he voted for the second reading of their reform bill, 22 Mar., and against Gascoyne's wrecking amendment, 19 Apr. 1831. At the ensuing general election he was returned unopposed for Hythe as a reformer.[11]

Loch was named to the select committees on the East India Company, 28 June 1831, 27 Jan. 1832. He voted for the second reading of the reintroduced reform bill, 6 July 1831, but was rather less assiduous than James in his support of its details. He only paired for the passage of the bill, 21 Sept., and was not present to vote for the motion of confidence in the ministry, 10 Oct. It is uncertain whether it was he or his brother who voted with government on the Dublin election dispute, 23 Aug. He divided for the second reading of the revised reform bill, 17 Dec. 1831, and was in the majorities for its borough disfranchisement schedules, 20, 23 Jan., and third reading, 22 Mar. 1832. He voted for the address asking the king to appoint only ministers who would carry undiluted reform, 10 May. He sided with government on the Russian-Dutch loan, 26 Jan., 12, 20 July. Either he or James voted against Baring's bill to exclude insolvent debtors from Parliament, 6 June, and in favour of public inquests, 20 June 1832. He retired from the House at the dissolution later that year.

When Marjoribanks's brother resigned as chairman of the East India Company in protest at the new Charter Act in October 1833 Loch replaced him. He hoped to salvage some of the company's independence and succeeded in regaining the directors' unrestricted use of patronage.[12] On 15 Mar. 1837 he was attacked and stabbed at East India House by one Kearney, a disgruntled former employee of the Company, who soon afterwards committed suicide in custody.[13] Loch left the direction in 1854. His only son, George Loch, joined the navy but died of fever at Martinique, aged 25, in 1848. His daughter Marion Finella, whose birth in 1823 proved fatal to his wife, married Edward Marjoribanks, the nephew of his former colleague at Hythe. It was at his son-in-law's home at Bushey Grove, Hertfordshire that Loch died in February 1868.[14] By his will, made on 27 Apr. 1852 and proved on 3 Feb. 1870, he left all his property to his daughter. His nephew William Adam Loch remembered him as 'a man of strong masculine sense', who 'possessed a sweet temper and warm affections combined with a calm and remarkably sound judgement'.[15]

[1] C. Hardy, *Reg. E.I. Co. Ships, 1760-1810*, pp. 208, 228; *Gent. Mag.* (1868), i. 679; G. Loch, *Loch Fam.* 254-5; *Brougham and Early Friends*, i. 194, 221; ii. 27, 63. [2] *Brougham and Early Friends*, ii. 233-4. [3] Hardy, 259, 275. [4] Blair Adam mss at Blair Adam, Loch to Adam, 1 Aug. 1807. [5] Blair Adam mss 2/176, Loch to Adam, 18 Mar. 1817; 2/197, same to same, 31 May 1818; Brougham mss, James Loch to Brougham, 31 Mar. 1817; C.H. Philips, *E. I. Co.* 243, 247, 263, 277. [6] *Ellenborough Diary*, 202-3. [7] *Kentish Chron.* 23, 30 Mar. 1830. [8] *Kentish Gazette*, 6 Aug. 1830. [9] *Howard Sisters*, 164. [10] *Three Diaries*, 51. [11] *Kentish Gazette*, 6 May 1831. [12] Philips, 297. [13] *Ann. Reg.* (1837), Chron., p. 26. [14] Loch, 255-6. [15] Ibid. 256.

D.R.F.

LOCKHART, John Ingram (1765–1835), of Sherfield House, Romsey, Hants and Great Haseley House, Oxon.

OXFORD	1807–1818
OXFORD	1820–1830

b. 5 Sept. 1765, yr. s. of James Lockhart, merchant banker, of St. Dunstan's, London and Melchett Park, Wilts. and w. Mary Harriot Gray of St. Benet and St. Peter, Paul's Wharf, London.[1] *educ.* Eton 1779-83; Univ. Coll. Oxf. 1783; L. Inn 1783, called 1790. *m.* 14 Jan. 1804, Mary, da. and h. of Francis Wastie of Cowley and Haseley, *s.p.* Took name of Wastie by Act of Parliament 23 May 1832 to hold estates for life following *d.* of w. (12 Oct. 1831). *d.* 13 Aug. 1835.

Recorder, Romsey to 1834; dep. recorder, Oxford 1830-5, recorder Mar. 1835-*d.*

Vol. London and Westminster light horse 1794-8; capt. Mdx. vol. cav. 1797.

Lockhart, a loquacious, talented and successful barrister, and conscientious parliamentarian, was defeated at Oxford in 1818 by the resurgent Blenheim interest, which he had himself overturned in 1812. He had weakened his own position in the constituency through his support for the corn laws, the property tax and repressive legislation, and by failing to pay his election bills.[2] At the Oxfordshire county meeting called to vote a loyal address to the regent, 12 Nov. 1819, he likened 'the secret conspiracies of the radical reformers, and the mysterious and concerted watchwords by means of which their innovating counsels were carried into effect, to the kindred operation of the *Black Tribunal* which had heretofore operated in

Germany'. He argued that annual parliaments and universal suffrage would make stable government impossible, and dramatically recalled the horrors of the French Revolution:

> It was not unusual to tie a virgin back to back with her lover, and then, after every indignity and abomination that could sicken the heart and revolt our nature, to throw them together into the Loire – and this, in the wretched slang of this polluted nation, was denominated *a republican marriage*![3]

At the general election of 1820, when one of the Members for Oxford retired, he offered again, professing independence and resting his pretensions on his previous parliamentary conduct. He became involved in a contest with the sitting Blenheim Member and a leading equity lawyer of extreme Tory views. On the hustings, he deplored 'the blasphemous, seditious, and assassinating temper of the times' and declared that he would

> strive to direct his political conduct in the spirit of that temperate, constitutional wisdom which aims at the security of liberty, not the infringement of it, and which might preserve our rights and privileges by guarding them from the canker of licentious abuse.

He finished in second place, well behind the newcomer, but comfortably ahead of the Blenheim man, who retired after three days.[4]

Lockhart pursued an independent and idiosyncratic line in the 1820 Parliament, where he frequently intervened in debate, especially on legal subjects. He hoped that Lord Althorp's proposed bill to amend the Insolvent Debtors Act, 2 May 1820, would deal harshly with offenders guilty of inflicting 'severe personal injuries'. He saw no reason to bring prisoners confined in the Fleet for contempt of chancery under the review of an inferior judge, 31 May; but on 20 June he objected to the Liverpool ministry's king's bench proceedings bill, designed to extend *nisi prius* hearings, arguing that it would create ruinous expense for litigants and overwhelm the chief justice. He was a teller for the minority of eight against the measure. He called for the exchequer court to be opened to all attorneys, 7 July.[5] On 16 June he advocated the establishment of a 'vigorous police force' to take a tougher line with loiterers and complained that conditions in Millbank penitentiary were too luxurious: 'when he saw that with improved prisons and new charities, crimes were increasing, he felt that the country was losing its way on an amiable system'. He linked the cost of Millbank, which he put at £100 per prisoner, with the argument that 'Parliament, unless in cases of urgent necessity, ought not to vote an additional shilling to increase the burdens of the people', 19 June. He had no patience with Maxwell's motion for inquiry into distress among cotton weavers, 29 June, when he said that it would 'only serve to hold out false hopes' and encourage equally deserving groups, especially the agriculturists, to make impossible demands, dismissed the proposal to tax absentees and all 'plans of spade-husbandry' and contended that 'time alone and patience' would bring respite. He promised support for Parnell's proposed bill to deal with Irish tithes, 5 July. On the report of the Grantham election committee, 12 July, he thought that a resolution declaring the illegality of payments to out-voters under the fiction of expenses was unnecessary and would not bind the courts. Next day he presented and endorsed petitions against any alteration of the timber duties and approved the offences at sea bill, which would 'prevent much inhumanity'.[6] On 18 July 1820 he came out strongly against the barrack agreement bill, of which he had previously approved:

> In the present dense state of the population, when the activity of the public mind was increased through the medium of the press, and when the extension of education had opened inlets to general knowledge, and the pressure of taxation had created discontent, he thought it was absolutely necessary for the safety of the metropolis, that an armed force of some kind should be kept on foot.

Yet he saw no reason why that force should be provided exclusively by the army, housed in permanent barracks, and put the case for the creation of armed bands of respectable citizens. He unsuccessfully divided the House against the third reading.

On 17 Oct. 1820 Lockhart condemned the bill of pains and penalties against Queen Caroline as

> a flagrant violation of Magna Charta, a proceeding fatal to the liberty and security of the country ... vexatiously protracted, when no doubt could remain of Her Majesty's innocence, like a wounded snake, 'dragging its slow length along', unfit to live, and yet unwilling to die.

He may have been at the Oxfordshire meeting called to vote a loyal address to the king, 22 Jan. 1821, when a Whig amendment was carried; but if so he remained silent.[7] In the House, 24 Jan., he demanded the restoration of the queen's name to the liturgy as an act of justice and 'healing':

> He had hitherto in general supported ministers. He had supported them throughout the war, which by their wisdom, fortitude, and perseverance, they had brought to so triumphant a conclusion ... but he doubted whether they understood the arts of peace as well as those of war.

He voted for the restoration, 26 Jan., 13 Feb., when he again spoke on the subject; but he abstained from the division on the opposition censure motion, 6 Feb. On 9 Feb. he said that 'the most rigid economy on the part of ministers' was the only solution to distress, assuming that a reversion to the old currency system or a redistribution of taxes were out of the question. That day he was in the minority against renewal of the sugar duties, and he presented further petitions against interference with the timber duties, 23 Feb.[8] He could not see how a change in the method of taking the corn averages would relieve agricultural distress, 26 Feb. He presented petitions for relief from Richmond, Yorkshire, 1 Mar., and Hereford, 6 Mar.[9] He spoke and voted for repeal of the tax on husbandry horses, 5 Mar., warning ministers that if they did not acknowledge the severity of distress, 'they would be obliged at last to yield by necessity, what they were not now disposed to concede as a boon'. He voted for Maberly's resolution on the state of the revenue, 6 Mar., and to reduce the army by 10,000 men, 15 Mar., observing that 'the House acted with regard to the public expenditure like a prodigal, who first determined to spend a certain sum, and then proceeded to consider how he should get it'. He voted for repeal of the additional malt duty, 21 Mar., 3 Apr., and on the latter occasion condemned the system whereby fundholders did not pay their fair share of the tax burden and mocked Vansittart's maladroit financial expedients: 'he was speaking on behalf of helpless millions, who must be reduced to the depths of misery unless saved by the wisdom of Parliament'. He did not object to the disfranchisement of Grampound, 12 Feb., but was hostile to the proposal to give Leeds, its possible replacement, a scot and lot franchise, which would be 'injurious to the mixed monarchical form of the British government'. At the same time, he 'felt that the representation ... stood upon too narrow a basis to shield the people, or support the just rights and dignity of the crown; and he should support any plan which had a tendency to give greater effect to individual property'. He defended Justice Best† against Davison's charges, 23 Feb., but spoke and voted for the reception of Broadhurst's petition complaining of his treatment in Lancaster gaol, 7 Mar. He saw 'many solid objections' to Martin's proposed capital crimes defence bill, 26 Feb. That day he chaired a London meeting called to establish a Society for the Prosecution of Felons.[10] He gave a cautious welcome to Althorp's bill to remove litigation over trifling sums from the main courts, 15 Mar., but was unhappy with the plan to create new county tribunals to deal with work which he thought could be entrusted to quarter sessions. He supported the Irish tithes leasing bill later that day.[11] He paired against Catholic relief, which was anathema to most of his constituents, 28 Feb., and on 16 Mar. presented Oxford council's hostile petition.[12] He approved indemnification of genuine American loyalists, but not of mere speculators, 21 Mar. He was against any alteration of the game laws, as proposed by Lord Cranborne, 5 Apr. After an apparent absence from the House of several weeks, Lockhart voted in minorities on the Barbados pension fund, 24 May, to equalize the rates of interest on Irish and British treasury bills, 30 May, and to reduce the barracks grant, 31 May, when he again accused ministers of disregarding agricultural distress. The following day he voted against the lottery proposals and returned to his themes of retrenchment and a fairer distribution of taxation. He voted against the appointment of Thomas Frankland Lewis* to the Irish revenue commission, 15 June, and spoke and voted against making any additional grant to the duke of Clarence, 18 June. On 24 May he said that Chetwynd's proposed vagrancy bill would only continue the present 'destructive system', which overlooked the need to inculcate principles of self-reliance in beggars. He saw no prospect of a reduction in poor rates under the current laws, and on 20 June argued that their effect was to demoralize the poor. He blamed chancery delays on the mechanism of the court and called for inquiry into means of speeding up the processing of minor disputes, 30 May. He objected to the exceptions made in the forgery punishment mitigation bill for offences against the Bank of England, which would make the notes of country banks more tempting targets, 4 June. He presented a petition against alteration of the navigation laws, 18 June 1821.

On the address, 7 Feb. 1822, Lockhart, claiming that he 'did not attribute any callosity of heart to ministers, but [that] he believed their judgement was unsound', repeated his appeal for 'speedy measures of relief' to avert 'the total ruin of the agricultural interest', which might end in unrest on the Irish scale: as ever, he specified economy and retrenchment, but now dwelt also on the need to keep up protection. He presented and endorsed agriculturists' petitions calling for relief, 18, 20, 21 Feb., 6, 7 Mar., and objected to voting the navy estimates on inadequate information, 22 Feb.;[13] but he did not vote for the general opposition motions for more extensive tax reductions, 11, 21 Feb. He was in the minority of 39 for postponing a clause of the navy five per cents bill, 4 Mar. He supported the Irish insurrection bill and related measures because 'their merits overbalanced their defects', 8 Feb. He favoured investigation of Henry Hunt's* complaints of his treatment in Ilchester gaol, on the ground that aggravated punishment was unacceptable, 20 Feb., 4 Mar. He approved Denison's plan to reduce the cost of actions for recovery of damages inflicted by riotous mobs, 5 Mar.: this and similar measures 'might save the people from being law-ridden as they now were – their best blood being sucked up by this vampire'. He gave notice of a motion for leave to introduce a bill of his own to facilitate the recovery of small debts from tenants, but did not pursue it.[14] He deplored laxity in the licensing regulations for public houses, 24 Apr., and spoke and voted for Bennet's licensing bill, 27 June.[15] Returning to the subjects of agricultural distress, taxation and protection, he presented petitions and promised to support repeal of the leather and other taxes which had been increased 'by a side wind' through the change of currency, 29 Apr.[16] He brought up more agricultural distress petitions, 2, 3 May, and on the first occasion criticized Ricardo's proposition to allow foreign corn in bond into the market above 65*s*. He accused ministers of trying to shift the responsibility for dealing with distress onto the select committee, 7 May, but stood aside when Lord Londonderry intervened with a promise of ministerial action. The following day, when he presented an Oxfordshire agriculturists' petition, Lockhart argued that Wyvill's plan for a remission of £20,000,000 in taxation went too far, again challenged Ricardo's identification of protection and overproduction as the causes of distress, and, apparently now pinning his own hopes on protection, applauded Londonderry's assurance that it would be provided against sudden imports of foreign corn: 'all that the agricultural classes wished was that they might be allowed to live, to pay their taxes, and to support government'.[17] Yet he was in the protectionist minority of 24 against the resolutions based on the committee's report that day, and on 9 May was in that of 36 against the revised corn duties, after explaining that 'he did not desire such an amount of taxes taken off, as would endanger the safety of the public creditor; but ... unless such a degree of protection was afforded, as would remunerate the cultivator of the soil, the ruin of the agricultural interest was inevitable'. On 10 June he opposed a clause of the corn bill dealing with the import of ground grain.[18] Frustrated in his hopes of adequate protection, he resumed his pursuit of tax reductions, voting for cuts in diplomatic expenditure, 15, 16 May. On 14 June he said that whatever the faults of the paper currency, the French wars could not have been successfully waged without it, and again pressed ministers to consider means of redistributing the tax burden more equitably. He was, however, in the ministerial majority against repeal of the salt duties, 28 June, and concurred in the chancellor's argument that repeal of the Scottish cottage tax would achieve little, 9 July.[19] He did vote for repeal of the window tax, 2 July. He spoke and voted for inquiry into the lord advocate's dealings with the Scottish press, 25 June, and opposed the aliens bill, 1, 19 July, when he was in the small minority for an amendment to its preamble.[20] He threatened to move next session for a standing order to prevent any bill concerning taxation being read a second time without being printed, 2 July. He voted for investigation of the Calcutta bankers' grievances, 4 July. He suggested the appointment of inspectors to help improve the quality of Bank of England notes, 8 July. He supported the beer retail bill, 10, 18 July. He objected to a £400 pension for one of the late queen's servants, 12 July 1822.[21]

Lockhart, who explained his parliamentary conduct at the annual Oxford mayor's feast, 30 Sept. 1822,[22] was barely in evidence in the House in 1823, when illness evidently put him out of action: he was granted a month's sick leave, 14 Apr. He said that Wood's proposal to amend the settlement regulations would 'produce as much litigation as the existing law', 4 June. He voted against the grant for the new London Bridge, 16 June, and deplored the repeated resurrection of the charges against chief baron O'Grady, 3 July 1823. On 11 Feb. 1824, in a speech which the backbencher Hudson Gurney considered 'hard-headed and original, as usual', Lockhart warned that Western's qualification of jurors bill required careful consideration, lest it excluded the 'sturdy' yeoman with his 'common stock of common sense'.[23] He advised John Williams to withdraw for the moment his motion for inquiry into chancery administration, 24 Feb., contending that it would be improper to give the lord chancellor the nomination of a commission. He voted in small minorities to reduce the grants for the barracks department, 27 Feb., and colonial services, 12 Mar., and divided for repeal of the window tax, 2 Mar. Later that month he encouraged the promotion of an Oxford petition to that effect.[24] He voted against repeal of the usury laws, 27 Feb., and spoke in that sense, 8 Apr., when he praised ministers for not making it government policy and reminded Members that it would deprive the poor of their protection against the 'extortion of pawnbrokers'. He said that Stuart Wortley's reform of the game laws would 'set the people by the ears', 11 Mar., and he was a teller for the majority against it, 31 May. He tried unsuccessfully to amend the county courts bill to raise the limit on debts recoverable under it from £10 to £20, 26 Mar. He thought that legatees could be saved money if the archbishop of Canterbury appointed standing commissioners in every county, 1 Apr. He did not want the bankruptcy bill discussed in isolation from the insolvent debtors bill, 5 Apr., and on the third reading, 31 May, he secured the addition of a clause empowering the commissioners to report cases of gross fraud to the lord chancellor.[25] He approved the principle of Althorp's bill to abolish settlement by hiring and service, which would 'cut off one great head of litigation', 30 Mar. He was a teller for the minority against the second reading of the hides and skins bill, 3 May, and he presented hostile petitions from Oxford and Cheltenham, 4, 12 May, as he did ones in favour of the equitable loans bank bill, 7 May, and (from Oxford inhabitants) for repeal of the assessed taxes, 13 May.[26] He did not see why Quakers should be required to take oaths, 12 May. On 17 May he predicted that if the warehoused wheat bill became law, it would 'deteriorate considerably the security of the landed proprietor and cultivator, and destroy altogether their dependence on any future legislative protection'. As chairman of the committee on the beer duties bill, he explained that they had sought to benefit the poor by recommending magistrates to license free houses to counter brewers' local monopolies, 24 May. He opposed Hume's motion for a return of recent commitments and convictions, 27 May. He supported the marine insurance bill, 28 May, and objected to the provision for punishment by whipping under the vagrancy bill, 3 June 1824.

Lockhart presented Oxford parish petitions for repeal of the laws concerning small debts, 14 Feb. 1825.[27] He supported the Irish unlawful societies bill, 15, 25 Feb., having no doubt that 'the notoriety of the system was quite sufficient to justify that House in putting down the [Catholic] Association'. He said that Catholic claims ought not to be conceded under duress, and he voted against them, 1 Mar., 21 Apr. He voted against the usury laws repeal bill, 17 Feb., and renewed his opposition to interference with the game laws, 17 Feb., 7 Mar., when he moved an unsuccessful wrecking amendment to the bill. He supported the Oxford parochial petitioning campaign for repeal of the house and window taxes, 25, 28 Feb., and voted to that effect, 3 Mar., 17 May, when 'a very severe cold' prevented him from speaking at length.[28] He opposed as 'injurious' and 'inapplicable' Hume's attempt to prevent Members from voting on matters in which they had a pecuniary interest, 10 Mar. He disapproved of the bill to promote the Peruvian Mining Company, 16 Mar., and of grants for various Irish charities, which only increased the number of paupers and the quantum of misery, 18 Mar. He called for reform of the settlement laws, 22 Mar.[29] On 24 Mar. he cautioned Martin against weakening the effects of his measure to prevent cruelty to animals by 'perpetual legislation' on the subject and applauded Peel's criminal law reforms, though he thought that the felonies pardons bill perhaps went too far. He feared that the proposed new government buildings in Whitehall would lead to higher official salaries, greater remoteness from the public and an increase in expenditure: 'this he should the more lament, inasmuch as ... ministers had certainly shown more feeling for the people, than any he had ever known'. When opposing abolition of the prohibitory duties on colonial corn, 2 May, he cited Tacitus as an authority on the dangers of extending too much reciprocal protection to colonies. He was credited with a vote in favour of the duke of Cumberland's annuity bill, 6 June, but it was subsequently asserted in the local press that he had voted against the grant of £6,000 for the education of Prince George.[30] He thought that Burdett was not justified in calling for the evidence to the inquiry into chancery delays to be made public until its work had been completed, 7 June. At this time he conveyed to Peel, the home secretary and Member for Oxford University, the 'lively apprehensions' which many of his constituents entertained over the proposed universities police bill.[31] He voted for the spring guns bill and supported an amendment to the church lands bill designed to protect collegiate interests, 21 June. On the Kenrick† case, 28 June 1825, he wanted an end to be put to the practice of including judges in commissions of the peace.

Lockhart made light of the recent commercial crisis, 3 Feb. 1826, for he 'considered occasional paroxysms of that nature as inseparable from the enlarged and growing bulk of the trade and resources of this great nation'. Nor was he disposed to blame the Bank, though he would not oppose the proposed measures for 'opening the traffic to other adventurers'. He was in the minority of nine against the third reading of the promissory notes bill, 7 Mar. He said that the bill dealing with the arrangements between debtor and creditor did not go far enough, 27 Feb., and on 7 Mar. suggested that if the power to commit to the Fleet for contempt was done away with, the usefulness of chancery jurisdiction would be destroyed. He presented an Oxford petition for the abolition of slavery, 2 Mar.[32] He again praised Peel's work at the home office, 9 Mar., but said that outside the metropolis the only significant check on crime was provided by parental influence, which had been weakened by the poor laws. He supported Russell's bill to curb electoral bribery, 14 Mar., and spoke and voted for his resolution on the subject, 26 May, though he thought it failed to deal with the practice of paying voters after elections. He repeated his misgivings over the extension of Martin's humane legislation, 16 Mar. He opposed Newport's motion for regulation of Irish first fruits revenues, 21 Mar., but was in minorities of six and four for Hume's resistance to grants for Irish charities, 23 Mar. His votes against the proposal to give the president of the board of trade a ministerial salary, 7, 10 Apr., earned him praise in an Oxford paper as 'the most active, useful, and independent' Member the city had ever had.[33] He was shocked by Hume's attack on lord chancellor Eldon, whom he exonerated from any personal blame for chancery delays, 18 Apr. 1826.

Lockhart stood again for Oxford at the 1826 general election, when he boasted of his support for his constituents' campaigns for the abolition of slavery and repeal of the window tax. Another contest occurred, in which he finished a comfortable second.[34] A serious deterioration in his health undermined him in the new Parliament. He had something to say on fictitious election returns, 24 Nov. 1826. On Hervey's motion for details of excise informations and prosecutions, 1 Dec., he reiterated his call for the court of exchequer to be thrown open. He welcomed Shadwell's plan to amend the law of dower, 14 Feb. 1827. He did not vote in the division on Catholic relief, 6 Mar. It is not clear whether it was he or William Eliott Lockhart who voted for the Clarence annuity bill, 16 Mar. He was given a month's sick leave, 26 Mar. 1827. He was in Paris in early October that year, reportedly in improving health.[35] He may have voted in the Wellington ministry's majority on chancery delays, 24 Apr. 1828. He divided against Catholic relief, 12 May. He spoke at some length in support of investigation of the complaint by Baron de Bode of inadequate compensation for loss of property in Alsace in 1793, 1 July. At the Oxford mayor's dinner, 1 Oct. 1828, he explained why he had lately hardly attended Parliament:

> He might plead as his excuse a long and serious illness; but he should add ... another cause ... that very few questions of great national importance had been there discussed, in consequence of the numerous changes which had taken place in the ministry. The House had been occupied by contentions for power and place, by matters of mere personal and party interest, with which he never chose to mix himself.

He claimed that he would have voted for repeal of the Test Acts if his support had been crucially necessary. On Catholic relief, he announced that he had now decided to remain neutral until ministers, whom he strongly criticized for their 'disunion at this momentous crisis', when 'demagogues' were threatening revolution in Ireland, had made up their collective mind one way or the other.[36] Planta, the patronage secretary, expected him to vote 'with government' for emancipation, and he duly did so, 6, 30 Mar. 1829. On the 23rd he asked if the second clause of the relief bill could be adjusted to make it 'clear and explicit' that Catholic clergymen could not sit in the House, but Peel assured him that this contingency was covered elsewhere. The Speaker did not sanction his demand for action against an individual who had struck out names from an anti-Catholic petition, 27 Mar. On 12 Mar. he expressed worries about dispensing with jury trial for juveniles, as Davenport proposed, and approved Warburton's anatomy bill, though he wanted the safeguard of the coroner's warrant to be retained. He was critical of Stuart Wortley's new game bill, 6 Apr. At the mayor's feast, 30 Sept. 1829, when he was said to be in 'most excellent health', he explained and justified, to an apparently sympathetic audience, his conversion to Catholic emancipation as a means of averting disaster in Ireland.[37] On the presentation of an Oxford parish petition for repeal of the malt and beer duties, 17 Mar. 1830, Lockhart blamed distress largely on the alteration of the currency, which had 'thrown down every species of property':

> We have been wandering in search of foreign markets, and by our improvident measures at home, have put it out of the power of our own people to consume our manufactures. Perhaps it is scarcely possible to go back to the currency to which the country has been accustomed, and by which all transactions were measured during the war, but that is no reason why we should obstinately persevere in our present course of conduct, without endeavouring to adopt some measures to counteract, in the language of Burke, 'the most gigantic swindling transaction of which any state was ever guilty'.

He supported Davenport's motion for inquiry into the state of the nation, 19 Mar., declaring that 'the evil rankling in the very core of the heart of our social system' could no longer be ignored. From the opposition benches, 23 Mar., he tried to prevent the reception of a Drogheda petition for repeal of the Union, but eventually yielded to the sense of the House. His only recorded vote in the 1830 session was against Jewish emancipation, 17 May 1830.

He stood again for Oxford at the general election that year, and was forced to defend himself against criticism of his absenteeism, which he said his critics had exaggerated and which he ascribed mostly to poor health: 'surely, at the age of 70 [*sic*], and after 23 years arduous service in their cause, he might be allowed a little indulgence, to enable him to recruit his health sufficiently to resume his duties'. He could not get a hearing on the hustings and was beaten into third place by the man whom he had kept out in 1826. He petitioned, but, still handicapped by poor health, did not follow it up.[38] At an Oxford dinner to present him with a commemorative plate, 4 Oct. 1830, he described himself as

> the friend of freedom, but it is freedom of a rational kind; and I am the enemy of every doctrine and practice tending to loosen the links or subvert the order of society, whether it be the tyranny of the rich over the poor, or the attempts of the lower to degrade or destroy the upper classes.[39]

In October 1831 it was revealed that he had approved the principle of the Grey ministry's reform bill earlier in the year, having spent his life 'in active opposition to all unconstitutional influence, as well as to base and lawless corruption'.[40] He declined an invitation to stand for Oxford, of which he was now deputy recorder, at the general election of 1832.[41]

He died, as John Ingram Wastie, at Great Haseley in August 1835, five months after becoming recorder of Oxford. An obituary reckoned that 'his great legal knowledge, sterling independence, and sound constitutional principles, deservedly secured to him the respect of the Senate, and the confidence of his constituents'.[42] By his will, dated 7 Aug. 1835, he distributed property in Oxfordshire, Berkshire, Buckinghamshire, Hampshire, Lancashire, Suffolk and Wiltshire among numerous relatives and friends, including his nephew James Lockhart. His personalty was sworn under £20,000, and the residue calculated for duty at £1,434.[43]

[1] *HP Commons, 1790-1820*, iv. 441, following L. Inn admiss. reg., describes him as yst. s.; but his bro. Samuel was *bap.* in London, 8 Apr. 1767. His parents *m.* 17 Oct. 1762 (*Reg. St. Bene't and St. Peter, Paul's Wharf, London* ed. W.A. Littledale, 217). [2] *HP Commons, 1790-1820*, ii. 327. [3] *Jackson's Oxford Jnl.* 13 Nov. 1819. [4] Ibid. 26 Feb., 4, 11 Mar. 1820. [5] *The Times*, 8 July 1820. [6] Ibid. 14 July 1820. [7] Ibid. 23 Jan.; *Jackson's Oxford Jnl.* 27 Jan. 1821. [8] *The Times*, 24 Feb. 1821. [9] Ibid. 2, 7 Mar. 1821. [10] *Oxford University and City Herald*, 3 Mar. 1821. [11] *The Times*, 16 Mar. 1821. [12] Ibid. 17 Mar. 1821. [13] Ibid. 19, 21-23 Feb., 6, 8 Mar. 1822. [14] Ibid. 6 Mar. 1822. [15] Ibid. 25 Apr., 28 June 1822. [16] Ibid. 30 Apr. 1822. [17] Ibid. 3, 4, 8 May 1822. [18] Ibid. 11 June 1822. [19] Ibid. 10 July 1822. [20] Ibid. 20 July 1822. [21] Ibid. 11, 19, 20 July 1822. [22] *Jackson's Oxford Jnl.* 5 Oct. 1822. [23] Gurney diary, 11 Feb. [1824]. [24] *Jackson's Oxford Jnl.* 27 Mar. 1824. [25] *The Times*, 6 Apr., 1 June 1824. [26] Ibid. 5, 8, 13, 14 May 1824. [27] Ibid. 15 Feb. 1825. [28] Ibid. 26 Feb., 1 Mar.; *Jackson's Oxford Jnl.* 19 Feb., 21 May 1825. [29] *The Times*, 23 Mar. 1825. [30] *Jackson's Oxford Jnl.* 18 June 1825. [31] Add. 40379, f. 20. [32] *The Times*, 3 Mar. 1826. [33] *Oxford University and City Herald*, 15 Apr. 1826. [34] Ibid. 3, 10, 17 June 1826. [35] Ibid. 6 Oct. 1827. [36] Ibid. 4 Oct. 1828. [37] Ibid. 3 Oct. 1829. [38] Ibid. 10, 17, 24, 31 July, 7 Aug. 1830. [39] *Jackson's Oxford Jnl.* 9 Oct. 1830. [40] *Oxford University, City and County Herald*, 1 Oct. 1831. [41] *Jackson's Oxford Jnl.* 23 June, 14 July 1832. [42] *Gent. Mag.* (1835), ii. 432. [43] PROB 11/1854/684; IR26/1406/667.

D.R.F.

LOCKHART *see also* **ELIOTT LOCKHART**

LOMBE (formerly **BEEVOR**), **Edward** (?1800–1852), of Great Melton, Norf.

ARUNDEL 1826–1830

b. ?1800, o.s. of Edward Beevor (who took name of Lombe for himself and issue by Act of Parl. 7 July 1817), attorney, of Norwich and w. Sylvia. *m.* in Berne, 21 Nov. 1831, Marie Rozer de St. Julien of St. Julien, Meuse, France,[1] *s.p. suc.* fa. 1847. *d.* 1 Mar. 1852.

Lombe's father, who took this surname when he inherited Sir John Lombe's Great Melton estate in 1817, was probably the latter's illegitimate son with the wife of John Beevor, a Norwich doctor. If so, this Member was descended from an old Norfolk family, the most notable of whom were the brothers Thomas and John Lombe, textile manufacturers, who had introduced the technique of silk throwing to England in the early eighteenth century.[2] In February 1822 Lombe told Sir James Mackintosh*, who was trying to find a seat for him, that he had 'been at every debate' in the Commons and 'means to attend regularly'.[3] It was through Mackintosh's influence that he joined Brooks's Club, 11 July 1823, sponsored by the duke of Norfolk, on whose interest he came in for Arundel in 1826 'with a distinct promise to vote for Catholic relief'.[4]

He duly acted with the Whig opposition to Lord Liverpool's ministry. He presented a petition from Arundel farmers for maintenance of the corn laws, 12 Feb.,[5] but divided for a 50*s.* rather than 60*s.* import price for corn, 9 Mar. 1827. He illustrated his opposition to naval impressment with examples of desertion 'which could only be traced to something faulty in the management of that service', 13 Feb. That day he endorsed Hume's call for economies in expenditure and particularly objected to that incurred in Sierra Leone; he announced his intention of submitting a motion on maladministration there, 21 Mar., but took the matter no further.[6] He divided against the duke of Clarence's annuity, 16 Feb., 2 Mar., yet voted for the bill's passage into committee, 16 Mar. He spoke and voted against the army estimates, 20 Feb., specifically objecting to the lack of explanation in the accounts.[7] He voted for a select committee on the Irish miscellaneous estimates, 5 Apr. He seconded an amendment criticizing the reappointment of the committee on emigration as an inadequate response to distress, 15 Feb., and ascribed Ireland's economic plight to lack of investment resulting from the unrest there, which could be ended by granting Catholic relief; he voted accordingly, 6 Mar. He voted for inquiry into the allegations against Leicester corporation, 15 Mar., and information about the mutiny at Barrackpoor, 22 Mar., and the conduct of Lisburn magistrates regarding an Orange procession, 29 Mar. He divided against Canning's ministry for inquiry into delays in chancery, 5 Apr., separation of bankruptcy cases from that court's jurisdiction, 22 May, and the disfranchisement of Penryn and Lord Althorp's election expenses bill, 28 May. He successfully moved that the appendix to a report on the Cape of Good Hope administration be printed, 30 May 1827.[8] Next day he voted for repeal of the Blasphemous and Seditious Libels Act. He paired for Catholic relief, 12 May 1828, having been 'prevented by illness from attending the House'.[9] That autumn he made preparations to contest Norwich at the next general election, but a year later he abandoned this plan.[10] He voted for Catholic emancipation, 6 Mar. 1829. Although he was granted a month's leave on account of ill health, 10 Mar. 1830, a radical newspaper subsequently alleged that 'instead of attending to his parliamentary duties' he had 'lately been rendering himself not a little conspicuous in the fashionable circles at Bath'.[11] He retired at the dissolution that summer.

Lombe apparently spent the remainder of his life abroad, and he died in Florence in March 1852. He left his entire personal estate to his wife, with remainder to the treasurer of University College Hospital for 'the general purposes of that institution'. His Norfolk estate passed to his uncle, Charles Beevor, in accordance with Sir John Lombe's will, and it eventually reverted to a legitimate branch of the family.[12]

[1] GL 20/926/2. [2] G.A. Carthew, *Hist. Launsditch*, iii. 401. [3] Add. 52445, ff. 24, 40, 62. [4] Ibid. f. 57; W.D. Cooper, *Parl. Hist. Suss.* 7. [5] *The Times*, 13 Feb. 1827. [6] Ibid. 14 Feb., 22 Mar. 1827. [7] Ibid. 21 Feb. 1827. [8] Ibid. 31 May 1827. [9] Ibid. 15 May 1828. [10] *Norwich Mercury*, 4 Oct. 1828, 21 Nov. 1829. [11] *Brighton Guardian*, 7 Apr. 1830. [12] PROB 11/1593/314; 2149/232.

H.J.S.

LONDONDERRY, 2nd mq. of [I] *see* **STEWART, Robert**

LONG, Charles (1760–1838), of Bromley Hill Place, Kent.

RYE	13 Jan. 1789–1796
MIDHURST	1796–1802
WENDOVER	1802–1806
HASLEMERE	1806–1826

bap. 29 Jan. 1760, 4th but 3rd surv. s. of Beeston Long (*d.* 1785), W.I. merchant, of Carshalton Park, Surr. and Sarah, da. and h. of Abraham Cropp of Richmond, Surr.; bro. of Samuel Long†. *educ.* Greenwich Sch.; Emmanuel, Camb. 1779; I. Temple 1779. *m.* 28 May 1793, Amelia, da. of Abraham Hume†, 2nd bt., of Wormleybury, Herts., *s.p.*; GCB 20 May 1820; *cr.* Bar. Farnborough 8 July 1826. *d.* 17 Jan. 1838.

Sec. to treasury Feb. 1791-Apr. 1801; PC [GB] 13 Jan. 1802; member, bd. of trade Feb. 1802; ld. of treasury May 1804-Feb. 1806; chief sec. to ld. lt. [I] Sept. 1805-Mar. 1806; PC [I] 5 Oct. 1805; jt. paymaster-gen. Apr. 1807-Aug. 1817, paymaster-gen. Aug. 1817-July 1826.

Dir. Greenwich Hosp. 1799-1829; trustee, British Museum 1812-*d.*, National Gallery 1824-*d.*

Lt.-col. commdt. Lewisham and Lee vols. 1803.

By 1820 Long was comfortably settled in the various roles which gave him a place close to the centre of affairs: departmental minister and party organizer; personal friend of the new king and arbiter of his taste in the fine arts, and confidant of the 1st earl of Lonsdale, on whose interest he was again returned unopposed for Haslemere, after some alarms, at the general election. Two months later, to his surprise and delight, he received a civil knighthood of the Bath as a personal favour from George IV.[1] With his wife, a discerning judge of *objets d'art* and skilled horticulturist, Long devoted his moments of leisure to the creation of a shrine of good taste and centre of hospitality at their Italianate villa at Bromley Hill. His activities in this sphere were financed by an inheritance of £19,000 from his long dead father, the spoils of some 25 years of political employment, which currently brought him £2,000 a year, and a pension of £1,500 on the four and a half per cent Leeward Island duties, with remainder of £700 to his wife, which had been obtained for him by his mentor Pitt in 1801.[2] Reviewing the elections, from which he reckoned that the Liverpool ministry had marginally gained, Long observed that 'the country is fast dividing itself into the friends of government and radicals; the Whigs will, I am satisfied, soon disappear from the stage'. Lord Gower's abandonment of Staffordshire was 'one of the worst symptoms', for 'we are arrived at times when, if the rich will not fight the battles, we shall be overwhelmed by the rabble and the wild doctrines by which they are guided'.[3] In the House, he of course voted steadily with his ministerial colleagues, and very occasionally acted as a government teller. He was an infrequent speaker. He opposed inquiry into military expenditure, 16 May 1820, when he defended his own record in clearing arrears of unsettled accounts, reducing the expenses of the pay office and eliminating sinecures.

In December 1820 he commented to Lonsdale of Canning's resignation from the board of control that 'the course he has steered ... is not always quite intelligible to plain men'. On the approaching 'hard battle in the House of Commons' over Queen Caroline, he thought 'we have nothing to do but to fight, and many of our country gentlemen I know are stout and firm'. He took no part in the debates on the issue, but was 'much satisfied' with the majority of 101 on the liturgy question, 26 Jan. 1821. A month later he was confident that 'the queen is going down hill very fast'. He asked Holmes, the whip, to 'be upon the alert' for the impending division on Catholic relief, of which he was an inveterate opponent; he was a teller for the hostile minorities, 28 Feb., 30 Mar.[4] As a trustee of the British Museum, he defended restrictions on public access to the reading room, 16 Feb., 11 Apr. He did not resist Hume's motion for information on public expenditure, 2 Mar., insisting that all ministers were willing to submit their departments to 'the minutest inquiries'. He defended the composition of the select committee on receivers general of taxes against Hume's allegation that it was packed with ministerialists, and deplored his 'misrepresentations with respect to the possibility of retrenchment', which were 'eagerly received out of doors', 22 Mar. At the same time, he suggested six additional names, in which Hume ('one of the most troublesome Members in the House', in Long's private opinion) acquiesced.[5] He had again to defend his own office, 30 Mar., when Hume demanded its eventual abolition. He denied Creevey's charge that government intended to get rid of large numbers of lower grade clerks, 30 Apr., justified application of the Barbados repair fund to other purposes, 21 May, and on 24 May answered Creevey's attack on this, complaining of 'anonymous slanders circulated against him'. His salary and pension were the subjects of satirical comment at this time.[6] He defended the grant for Millbank penitentiary, 31 May, and the proposed inquiry into Irish revenue, 15 June.[7] On Hume's call for economy and retrenchment, 27 June 1821, he stated that the commission of inquiry into the customs, of which he had been head since 1817, had produced 'very great benefits'. He had drafted the amendment which he helped to persuade the respected backbencher Henry Bankes to move.[8]

Long was not unduly perturbed by reports in September 1821 that the king, influenced by Lady Conyngham, was determined to turn out Lord Liverpool: 'the ship has righted so often when she appeared to be sinking that I expect the same will happen again'. He was relieved to learn that the Catholics had 'gained no step whatever' from Canning's recent visit to Ireland, which 'in other respects has done good'. In mid-November, after the king's return from Hanover, he told Lonsdale that 'every difference is reconciled', and 'there appears much more prospect of cordiality than has been the case for some time past'. When Lord Buckingham, keen to have Vansittart removed from the exchequer before committing himself to a junction with government, wondered if Long might replace him, Lord Londonderry* told him that Long was 'too old to go to school under Liverpool and could not act with him like Vansittart'. For his own part Long welcomed the alliance with the Grenvillites, especially after lengthy conversations at Brighton with the king and Lord Wellesley had satisfied him that the latter's appointment as Irish viceroy was not intended to encourage the agitation for Catholic relief.[9] On the eve of the 1822 session Long submitted to Liverpool a memorandum proposing that, as the customs commission had largely had its recommendations for economies blocked by the treasury (not quite what he had professed in the House six months earlier), the more powerful parliamentary commission of inquiry into the Irish revenue boards should be extended to those of England and Scotland which had not yet been scrutinized. If the premier decreed that the customs commissioners should press on 'I will do my best; but I assure you it will be under feelings more nearly approaching to despair, than those with which I ever undertook any task before in my life.' There was no reprieve, and Long's commission continued its work until 1823.[10] In the House, 12 Mar. 1822, he opposed Davies's motion for economies in revenue collection, arguing that the present complement of customs commissioners was irreducible, though he admitted that superannuations had got out of hand. He had to defend his own department against renewed attack, 20 Mar., when he observed that for all the reductions he had made, opposition 'approved of nothing which was done by gentlemen in office'. He denied responsibility for allowing a continuance of half-pay to officers who had taken holy orders, 22 Mar., and handled routine pay office business, 4, 28 June, 17 July. He was a teller for the minority against Canning's bill to relieve Catholic peers, 30 Apr. He replied to criticisms of the receivers general bill, 9 July 1822.[11]

In early September 1822 the king gave Long several 'very long audiences' in which he rehearsed his worries over the problem of replacing the dead Londonderry. Long thought the only solution was to make a fair offer to Canning: there were drawbacks, but 'the objections to not making the proposition are still stronger'. The arrangement finally reached was, in his opinion, 'the most desirable' one. A dim view of his fitness as an adviser to the king was taken by George's secretary, Sir William Knighton, who, according to Charles

Arbuthnot*, accused him of 'indecision of character'.[12] Long anticipated 'a stormy session' in 1823; and early in the year, at Liverpool's behest, he made an unsuccessful bid to resolve the conflict between Lord Palmerston*, the secretary at war, and the duke of York, the commander-in-chief, over staff reductions in foreign garrisons. Palmerston later wrote Long off as 'a servile toady of the duke'.[13] He again defended the application of the Leeward Islands duties, 17 Mar., and presented an anti-Catholic petition from the dean of St. George's Chapel, Windsor, 14 Apr. On the motion to refer papers on George III's library, a gift to the nation, to a committee, 18 Mar., he explained George IV's wishes for the fullest possible public access and its separate housing. He answered carping criticisms from Hobhouse and Croker, 18 Apr., 20 June, emphasizing that the decision to accommodate the library in an extension to the British Museum accorded with the king's desires.[14] As a man who recognized rubbish when he saw it, he brushed aside a petition from Benjamin Haydon for greater encouragement of historical painting, 25 June 1823. He had refused to handle it himself because Haydon would not specify what he wanted; and he taunted its presenter, Brougham, with his opposition to the purchase of the Elgin marbles.

By the will of his wife's uncle, the 7th earl of Bridgwater, who died in October 1823, Long received a life annuity of £4,000, and he consequently surrendered his pension.[15] At about this time he placed his expertise at the disposal of Liverpool in the negotiations for the purchase of the Angerstein collection of pictures as a basis for a national gallery;[16] and of the king, over the extensive and costly alterations and improvements at Windsor Castle, in which he played a central directing role. At the turn of the year he commented to Lonsdale:

> We look well I think ... both internally and externally. No petitions complaining of grievances, and the country gentlemen silent, if not satisfied, from finding perhaps that clamour has done them no good. The only black spot is the West Indies, of which we shall hear a good deal in the next session.[17]

He voted against the production of information on Catholic office-holders, 19 Feb. 1824. In response to a tribute from his ministerial colleague Robinson, chancellor of the exchequer, to the work of the customs commission, 25 Feb., he boasted, for public consumption, that 'their exertions had been deemed most useful' and all their suggestions 'adopted with entire success'. (He was privately cursed by Lonsdale's son Lord Lowther* for causing almost all customs patronage to be removed from the treasury.)[18] Long justified the grant for the new Westminster law courts, 1 Mar., though he concurred in criticism of Soane's designs, 23 Mar., when he was named to the select committee. He dismissed charges of incompetence levelled against the trustees of the Museum, 29 Mar., explained the Angerstein purchase and future policy on such matters, 2 Apr., and defended the Windsor Castle grant, 5 Apr. 1824. Not without difficulty, he secured for £10,000 from 'Chin' Grant* the lease of a house at 5 Whitehall Gardens, next to Peel's: his wife had 'always set her heart upon my getting a house at Whitehall'. 'In point of architecture', he deemed it 'very meagre', but he was confident that 'in the interior arrangements we shall make it good'. His purchase prompted idle speculation that he was about to crown his 'political and *dilettante* life' with retirement and a peerage.[19] He visited Paris in the autumn of 1824, partly to inspect the Soult collection of paintings with a view to their purchase. On his return he reviewed the progress of the Windsor improvements and, with Liverpool's blessing, acceded to the king's request that he should act as the channel of communication between them on the subject of the furnishing.[20] Long, who thought that 'if those who have supported the Catholic claims do not see the danger now of admitting them, nothing can open their eyes', hoped for strong measures to curb agitation in Ireland on the eve of the 1825 session.[21] He divided against relief, 1 Mar., 21 Apr., 10 May, and the Irish franchise bill, 26 Apr. He agreed to arrange for wounded soldiers' allowances to be paid quarterly, 4, 7 Mar., and explained a departure from the normal practice of succession by rotation among the clerks at Chelsea Hospital, 8 June.[22] He raised difficulties when Colborne proposed the establishment of a national gallery separate from the British Museum, 28 Mar., pointing out that the Angerstein collection had been left to the Museum's trustees. He welcomed the provision of funds to buy the Rich collection, 25 Apr. 1825.

Long and his wife visited Paris in September 1825 and executed 'some commissions' for the king, whom he found on his return 'very anxious that the dissolution should not take place' that autumn. Personally, he was 'glad that the evil day ... is put off', though he hoped that 'care will be taken not to bring forward questions that are unnecessary in the next session, and which may place us in a less favourable condition for a general election than that in which we now stand'. In particular, he was concerned that the vexed question of the corn laws should not be agitated. At about this time Mrs. Arbuthnot, whose husband, as commissioner of woods and forests, was in dispute with

George IV over the ownership of a piece of Green Park, condemned Long as 'a complete courtier', who 'always acquiesces in anything the king says and never dares contest a point with him'.[23] In the commercial crisis of early 1826 he welcomed the measures taken to 'restore the confidence among mercantile men', but privately wished his colleagues had followed Pitt's example in restricting cash payments:

> I am sorry to say there appears to me a disposition in many persons to think all that Mr. Pitt did was wrong, and that we are much wiser now. The cash restriction bill passed in 1797 is said to have been a very unwise measure. Does any rational man believe that we could have carried on the war without it; and where should we now be, if at that time we had been at the mercy of France? And what besides would have been the state of the country, if the Bank (as certainly would have been the case) had stopped payment? I am of the old school. I venerate all Mr. Pitt did, and I have not seen more wisdom displayed in later times than there was by him in the midst of unparalleled difficulties.[24]

Long, who in 1826 published *Short Remarks and Suggestions* on the improvements in hand in the west end of London, introduced a bill to consolidate the regulations governing Chelsea and Kilmainham Hospitals, 3 Mar. He absolved government from blame for the increase in the grant for Chelsea pensioners, 6 Mar. On 15 Mar. he explained the consolidation bill, which became law, 11 Apr. (7 Geo. IV, c. 16).[25] On the subject of a national gallery, 19 Apr., he stressed that 'none but first-rate works should have a place' in it. He also said that he had decided to refuse all future invitations to view and value potential acquisitions, a 'thankless task' in which it was too easy to cause offence. It was known by then that Long, who, as he later wrote, 'had always determined when I reached the age of 65 that I would quit all busy life', intended to retire from office at the end of the current session. He duly did so, 'with as much eagerness and delight as any man ever accepted the highest object of his ambition', and took a peerage, which the odious duke of Newcastle considered 'a prostitution' of the dignity.[26]

Although he devoted his retirement largely to his artistic pursuits, he remained utterly hostile to Catholic relief, dismissing all notion of 'compromise', because 'if seats in Parliament are given to the Catholics everything is given'. He was one of the Protestants who peremptorily declined Canning's offer of the home secretaryship in April 1827.[27] In 1829, when he opposed emancipation in the Lords, he was suspected of abetting the duke of Cumberland's attempts to turn the king against it. His intimacy with George IV earned him the dubious honour of selection as keeper of the royal signet during his fatal illness in 1830.[28] He did 'not like the political atmosphere' in the autumn of 1830, as he told his friend, the engraver George Cumberland: 'the influence of revolution is very catching. I trust we shall escape the contagion'. The Grey ministry's reform bill, which he opposed in the Lords, appalled him, and he could only hope that 'those who have lighted up the inflammable spirit which now rages everywhere may be able to put out the fire they have kindled when it has burned as long as they wished, but I doubt it'. He blamed reform for the decline in British artistic activity in the early 1830s, in that 'the wild theories which have been advocated have induced many persons to think property insecure' and so to curb expenditure on 'superfluities'. Yet the arts remained his 'great solace and amusement', while the British Museum had become 'a principal object of my care and attention'.[29] He died at Bromley Hill in January 1838. By his will, dated 14 Feb. 1837 and proved under £120,000, he devised Bromley, 5 Whitehall Gardens and property in Westminster to his nephew Samuel Long, and real estate at Duxford and Whittlesford, Cambridgeshire, plus £5,000 to his nephew William Long. He left other legacies amounting to about £21,000, and bequeathed pictures by Canaletto, Poussin, Reynolds, Rubens and others to the trustees of the Museum for deposit in the National Gallery.[30]

[1] *Oxford DNB*; *Arbuthnot Corresp.* 14; Lonsdale mss, Long to Lonsdale, 11 Mar. [1820]; *Farington Diary*, xvi. 5515, 5696. [2] *Farington Diary*, xi. 4020-1; *Arbuthnot Jnl.* i. 113; PROB 11/1125/32; *Geo. III Corresp.* iii. 2339; *PP* (1822), iv. 41. [3] Lonsdale mss, Long to Lonsdale, 11, 21, 23 Mar. [1823]. [4] Ibid. same to same, 21 Dec. [1820], 27 Jan., 22 Feb. 1821. [5] *The Times*, 2, 23 Mar. 1821; Lonsdale mss, Long to Lonsdale, 20 Mar. [1820]. [6] *The Times*, 22 May 1821; M.D. George, *Cat. of Pol. and Personal Satires*, x. 14195. [7] *The Times*, 1, 16 June 1821. [8] Dorset RO D/BKL, Bankes jnl. 129. [9] Lonsdale mss, Long to Lonsdale, 7, 19 Sept., 8, 13, 19 Nov., 22, 28 Dec.; BL, Fortescue mss, Buckingham to Grenville, 2 Dec. [1821]. [10] Add. 38290, ff.254-60; *PP* (1823), vii. 175. [11] *The Times*, 21, 23 Mar., 5, 29 June, 10, 18 July 1822. [12] Lonsdale mss, Long to Lonsdale, 15 Aug., 4, 7, 12 Sept. 1822; Add. 38290, f. 233; 40351, f. 31. [13] Lonsdale mss, Long to Lonsdale, 2 Feb. [1823]; K. Bourne, *Palmerston*, 173, 180; *Palmerston-Sulivan Letters*, 156-7; Add. 38370, f. 224. [14] *The Times*, 15, 19 Apr. 1823. [15] On *d.* of 8th earl of Bridgwater in 1830, Mrs. Long, as a residuary legatee, came into £63,821. See PROB 11/1678/670; IR26/1185/175; *Gent. Mag.* (1829), i. 560; (1838), i. 426. [16] Northants. RO, Agar Ellis diary, 24 Dec. [1823]. [17] Add. 38297, ff.84, 321, 324, 337; 38298, ff.64, 66; 38371, ff.1-8; *Wellington and Friends*, 39; *Arbuthnot Corresp.* 47-51; Lonsdale mss, Long to Lonsdale, 1 Jan. 1824. [18] Lonsdale mss, Lowther to Lonsdale, 19 Dec. 1823. [19] Add. 36510, f. 103; 40362, f. 214; 40605, ff. 168, 171, 228, 240, 271, 311; *Survey of London*, xiii. 196; Buckingham, *Mems. Geo. IV*, ii. 143; Grey mss, Tierney to Grey, 31 Jan. 1825. [20] Add. 38299, ff.150, 152, 180, 198, 199. [21] Lonsdale mss, Long to Lonsdale, 6 Dec. [1824], 2 Jan. [1825]. [22] *The Times*, 9 June 1825. [23] Lonsdale mss, Long to Lonsdale, 23 Sept., 1 Oct. [1825]; *Arbuthnot Jnl.* ii. 419. [24] Lonsdale mss, Long to Lonsdale, 25 Feb. [1826]. [25] *The Times*, 4, 7, 16 Mar. 1826.

[26] *Arbuthnot Jnl.* ii. 17; Add. 36513, f. 176; 38301, f. 185; *Colchester Diary*, iii. 436; Nottingham Univ. Lib. Newcastle mss Ne2 F2/1/139. [27] Lonsdale mss, Long to Lonsdale, 21 Aug., 10 Sept. [1826]; *Palmerston-Sulivan Letters*, 187; *Canning's Ministry*, 168, 182, 210. [28] Add. 40394, f. 210; *Greville Mems.* i. 260; *Colchester Diary*, iii. 610; *Wellington Despatches*, v. 488; vii. 66-67; *Arbuthnot Jnl.* ii. 361. [29] Add. 36512, f. 326; 36513, ff. 64, 249, 273. [30] PROB 11/1893/238; IR26/1481/154.

D.R.F.

LONG NORTH, Dudley (1748–1829), of Little Glemham Hall and Hurts Hall, Suff.

ST. GERMANS	1780–1784
GREAT GRIMSBY	1784–11 Apr. 1793
GREAT GRIMSBY	17 Apr. 1793–1796
BANBURY	1796–1806
NEWTOWN I.O.W.	1807–Feb. 1808
BANBURY	16 Feb. 1808–Feb. 1812
RICHMOND	1812–1818
HADDINGTON BURGHS	1818–1820
NEWTOWN I.O.W.	1820–1 Feb. 1821

bap. 14 Mar. 1748, 2nd s. of Charles Long of Hurts Hall and Mary, da. and coh. of Dudley North† of Little Glemham. *educ.* Bury St. Edmunds g.s.; Emmanuel, Camb. 1766; L. Inn 1769. *m.* 6 Nov. 1802, Hon. Sophia Anderson Pelham, da. of Charles Anderson Pelham†, 1st Bar. Yarborough, *s.p. suc.* aunt Anne, wid. of Hon. Nicholas Herbert†, to Little Glemham 1789 and took name of North by royal lic. 2 May 1789; bro. Charles to Hurts Hall and resumed name of Long in addition to North 1812. *d.* 21 Feb. 1829.

Long North, a veteran Foxite, was in a 'shocking state' of depression in late 1819 and had to be 'closely watched'. By early 1820, however, he was 'getting quite well'.[1] On 21 Feb. his father-in-law reported:

> North is certainly much better. He writes letters, and draughts upon his banker, but his spirits [are] low and [he] cannot yet touch on the state of his affairs without showing he considers them in a very different state from what they really are. Till that delusion subsides can we consider him ... himself again?[2]

At that year's general election his brother-in-law Charles Anderson Pelham* returned him for Newtown, as he had in 1807. He is not known to have spoken or voted in this period, was granted a month's leave, 1 July 1820, and retired from the House at the opening of the 1821 session. A 'gentleman of distinguished and accomplished manners, and a consistent Whig of the old school', he died at Brampton, 'aged 80', in February 1829.[3] By his will, dated 25 July 1814 and proved under £18,000, 2 Apr. 1829, he left annuities of £2,792 to his cousins Jane and Susannah Long, £100 to Lord George Augustus Henry Cavendish*, one of his executors, a £50 annuity to the poor of Little Glemham, and bequests ranging from £24 to £40 to various servants. The residue passed to his widow.[4]

[1] Grey mss, Tierney to Grey, 5 Nov. 1819, 22 Jan. 1820. [2] Wentworth Woodhouse mss F48/161. [3] *Gent. Mag.* (1829), i. 208. [4] PROB 11/1754/232; IR26/1204/139.

D.R.F./P.J.S.

LOPES *see* **FRANCO** and **MASSEH LOPES**

LOTT, Harry Baines (1781–1833), of Tracey House, Awlescombe, Devon.

HONITON	1826–1830
HONITON	1831–1832

bap. 9 Oct. 1781, o.s. of Samuel Lott, banker, of Honiton and w. Elizabeth Baines.[1] *educ.* Blundell's, Tiverton 1792-7. *m.* 30 Apr. 1804, Mary Ann Buckland, 8s. (3 *d.v.p.*) 6da. (1 *d.v.p.*). *suc.* fa. 1819. *d.* 20 June 1833.

Lott, whose father had originally been a stationer, insurance agent and postmaster in Honiton, succeeded him in 1819 as a partner in the local bank and was the residuary legatee of his estate, which was sworn under £20,000.[2] He accepted a requisition to stand for that venal borough at the general election of 1826 and was returned in second place, declaring that his 'attachment to our glorious constitution is well known' and that he was 'unfettered by any pledge'. He was commended to Robert Peel, the home secretary in Lord Liverpool's ministry, as 'a thorough Protestant' who 'in all public matters seems inclined to put faith in your judgement'.[3]

He divided against Catholic relief, 6 Mar., and for the duke of Clarence's annuity bill, 16 Mar., and the spring guns bill, 23 Mar. 1827. He was granted one month's leave for urgent business, having served on an election committee, 3 May 1827. In presenting a petition from Honiton Baptists for repeal of the Test Acts he declared that 'their continuance was improper and inexpedient', 13 Feb.; he voted accordingly, 26 Feb. 1828. He divided against Catholic relief, 12 May. He voted with the duke of Wellington's ministry against the motion condemning delays in chancery, 24 Apr. He argued that the system of alehouse licensing was 'productive of great inconvenience and ... ought to be remedied', 19 June 1828. In February 1829 Planta, the patronage secretary, listed him as being 'opposed to the principle' of Catholic emancipation. He presented a hostile petition from East Devon, 23 Feb., and explained that he opposed concession 'as a friend to civil and religious liberty', believing that 'the tenets of the Catholic church were likely to lead to despotism and tyranny'. However, as a 'supporter of the general measures of the present ministry' he was prepared to 'suspend his opinion' until he had seen the emancipation bill, which had to 'provide for the safety ... of the established church'. He claimed next day that the signatories to the Protestant petition arising from the Devon county meeting, at which he had been present the previous month, were mainly resident freeholders, unlike the supporters of the pro-Catholic petition. He voted against emancipation, 6, 18, 23, 27, 30 Mar. He favoured the abolition of imprisonment for debt, 19 Feb., but also wished to see a 'summary mode of proceeding for the recovery of small sums' in order to protect the 'poorer class of creditors'. He believed that the poor employment bill would 'produce an immense benefit to the country' by reducing the burden of the poor rate on small farmers, 24 Feb. He objected to a provision in the justices of the peace bill that only the magistrates who had issued the summons could hear a case, 25 Mar. He presented an East Devon petition for repeal of the duty on coals and culm, 3 June 1829. He divided for Hume's amendment to restrict the vote for the volunteers, 9 Mar. 1830. Next day he was granted one month's leave on urgent private business. He paired against Jewish emancipation, 17 May, and voted to abolish the death penalty for forgery, 7 June 1830.[4] At the dissolution that summer he retired, possibly because he feared the expense of a contested election.[5]

Lott was among the speakers at an anti-slavery meeting in Honiton, 18 Nov. 1830.[6] When Parliament was dissolved in April 1831 he accepted an invitation to stand for the borough, free of expense, made by voters who were hostile to the Grey ministry's reform bill, which proposed to deprive Honiton of one of its seats. Poor health prevented him from canvassing, but he claimed to have 'no connection with any party'. He was returned in second place, helping to oust the sitting Whig Member, and while his own views were unclear it was said that he might be 'termed [a] moderate reformer'.[7] He was absent from the division on the second reading of the reintroduced reform bill, 6 July, and cast no recorded votes on this or any other issue. He was granted six weeks' leave, 23 Sept., when he was said to be 'suffering from great debility, the effect of a long ... and most dangerous illness'. He 'ventured his life' the following month in order to vote for the anti-reformer, Lord Ashley*, in the Dorset by-election, but in February 1832 it was reported that 'continued indisposition' prevented him from attending to his parliamentary duties.[8] In September 1832 he announced that ill health precluded him from standing again for Honiton.[9] He died in June 1833 and left the residue of his estate to his eldest son, Harry Buckland Lott, who succeeded him as a partner in the Honiton Bank; his personalty was sworn under £70,000.[10]

[1] IGI (Devon). [2] PROB 11/1620/430; IR26/791/765; A. Farquharson, *Hist. Honiton*, 61-62. [3] *Trewman's Exeter Flying Post*, 15, 22 June; *Honiton Election Placards*, Lott's address, 16 June 1826; Add. 40389, f. 260. [4] *Western Times*, 19 June 1830. [5] Ibid. 10 July 1830; *Besley's Exeter News*, 7 May 1831. [6] *Western Times*, 27 Nov. 1830. [7] W. Country Stud. Lib., Exeter Sf/324.61/HON/COL U, Lott's addresses, 24, 28 Apr.; *Trewman's Exeter Flying Post*, 5 May 1831. [8] *Western Times*, 1 Oct.; *The Times*, 13 Oct. 1831; *Woolmer's Exeter and Plymouth Gazette*, 25 Feb. 1832. [9] *The Times*, 20 Sept. 1832. [10] PROB 11/1833/517; IR26/1329/471.

T.A.J.

LOUGHBOROUGH, Lord *see* **ST. CLAIR ERSKINE**

LOVAINE, Lord *see* **PERCY, George**

LOWRY CORRY, Armar, Visct. Corry (1801–1845).

CO. FERMANAGH 8 Mar. 1823–1831

b. 23 Dec. 1801, 1st s. of Somerset Lowry Corry†, 2nd Earl Belmore [I], and Lady Juliana Butler, da. of Henry Thomas, 2nd earl of Carrick [I]; bro. of Hon. Henry Thomas Lowry Corry*. *educ.* Christ Church, Oxf. 1820. *m.* 27 May 1834, Emily Louise, da. and coh. of William Shepherd of Brabourne, Kent, 4s. 4da. *styled* Visct. Corry 1802-41; *suc.* fa. as 3rd Earl Belmore [I] 18 Apr. 1841. *d.* 17 Dec. 1845.

Sheriff, co. Fermanagh 1832-3.

Corry's father, an opponent of the Union who represented Tyrone at Dublin and Westminster for five years from 1797, succeeded as 2nd Earl Belmore and to the magnificent Castle Coole, near Enniskillen, in Fermanagh in 1802. An influential magnate in both counties, he at last gained his desired Irish representative peerage in 1819 and thereafter supported Lord Liverpool's government in the Lords.[1] On a vacancy occurring in Fermanagh (once represented by his Corry ancestors) in the autumn of 1822, Corry, abandoning his studies at Oxford, was put forward by Belmore, who, in the absence of a suitable member of the Cole family, secured the tacit approval of their powerful neighbour and kinsman Lord Enniskillen, but not that of the independent former candidate Sir Henry Brooke. Despite being unknown to the electors, which his proposer excused on the ground of his having travelled extensively on the continent with his father, Corry was narrowly elected ahead of Brooke at the by-election in March 1823, when he denied that he had benefited from a coalition with Enniskillen.[2] An inactive ministerialist, he served at least once on the committee of the Grand Orange Lodge.[3]

Corry presented anti-Catholic petitions from Fermanagh, 16 Apr., when he voted against repeal of the Foreign Enlistment Act, but he divided for inquiry into the legal proceedings against the Dublin Orange rioters, 22 Apr. 1823.[4] He voted against condemning the trial of the Methodist missionary John Smith in Demerara, 11 June 1824. He divided for the Irish unlawful societies bill, 15, 25 Feb., and against Catholic relief, 1 Mar., 21 Apr., 10 May 1825. He voted against the related franchise measure, 26 Apr., but conceded that it would at least greatly mitigate the evil of emancipation, 9 May 1825. No evidence of parliamentary activity has been traced for the 1826 session. With Enniskillen's backing and no opponent coming forward, Corry was returned unopposed at the general election that summer.[5] He signed the requisitions for, but apparently did not attend, the Fermanagh and Tyrone Protestant meetings in October and December, although he did represent his brother Henry, now Member for Tyrone, at an Orange dinner in Omagh, 6 Nov. 1826, and speak at another in Enniskillen, 2 Jan. 1827.[6] He signed the anti-Catholic petition of the noblemen and gentlemen of Ireland in February and voted against Catholic relief, 6 Mar., but his father's past pro-Catholic votes were held against him at an Orange gathering in his constituency, 13 Aug. 1827.[7] Corry voted against repeal of the Test Acts, 26 Feb., and, despite having brought up at least one Irish petition for Catholic claims, 7 Mar., against relief, 12 May 1828. He divided with the Wellington ministry against reduction of the salary of the lieutenant-general of the ordnance, 4 July. At an Orange celebration in Enniskillen, 12 Aug., he declared that no one 'could be more steadfast in supporting our ancient constitution than he was', yet he seems to have absented himself from the occasions when Brunswick Clubs were established in Fermanagh and Tyrone that autumn and from the meetings in both counties that winter.[8] His reticence, like that of his brother, was probably owing to the situation of their father, who was appointed governor of Jamaica that year and who informed the duke of Wellington in December 1828 that he favoured Catholic relief if accompanied by sufficient securities.[9] Listed by Planta, the patronage secretary, as likely to be 'with government' on emancipation, he was approached to second the address. According to Lord Ellenborough, he was 'a little taken aback' to find that this recommended settling the religious question, but nonetheless agreed to do it, only 'reserving his judgement as to details'. He duly praised ministers' handling of foreign and financial matters and welcomed Catholic relief insofar as it would not trench upon the Protestant constitution, 5 Feb. 1829, when John Cam Hobhouse* recorded that he 'spoke well and liberally'.[10] However, he retracted this, citing the securities as inadequate, and voted against emancipation, 6 Mar. He divided against the second and third readings of the bill, 18, 30 Mar., the franchise bill, 26 Mar., and allowing Daniel O'Connell to take his seat unimpeded, 18 May; by contrast, Belmore's proxy was given in the Lords in favour of emancipation, 4, 10 Apr. 1829.

Corry voted against parliamentary reform, 18 Feb., and the enfranchisement of Birmingham, Leeds and Manchester, 23 Feb. 1830. He obtained three weeks' leave to attend the assizes, 15 Mar., and that month signed the requisition for a Fermanagh meeting to petition in favour of amending the grand jury laws.[11] He divided against Jewish emancipation, 17 May, presented his county's petition for the introduction of turnpike laws to Ireland, 21 May, and voted against abolition of the death penalty for forgery, 7 June. Corry, who had acted as his father's representative in negotiations with Wellington and Lord Aberdeen, the foreign secretary, relative to Tyrone politics earlier in the year, was expected to face a contest at the general election that summer in Fermanagh, where he was wrongly thought to have capitulated to ministers on the Catholic issue.[12] But, nominated by Enniskillen's eldest son Lord Cole*, who was now of age, he and his Orange colleague Archdall defeated Brooke and his son after a six-day poll.[13] He was listed by ministers among their 'friends' and divided with them on the civil list, 15 Nov. 1830, which led to their downfall. His last known votes in the Commons were against the second reading of the Grey ministry's reform bill, 22 Mar., and for Gascoyne's wrecking amendment, 19 Apr. 1831.

Despite being an anti-reformer, he was said to be unpopular with the Ultras and distrusted by the gentry, so allowing Enniskillen, who was concerned to safeguard his future interest by providing for his own son, to abandon his allies, regardless of the trouble and expense to which they had been put in cultivating the seat. Corry therefore resigned and was replaced by Cole at the Fermanagh election of 1831, when he was praised for his services to the county. Belmore was impotently furious at this mistreatment, but Corry seems to have acted with more equanimity and did not apparently attempt to organize any independent opposition to Cole as a means of marking his resentment. Nothing came of the request for a United Kingdom peerage for him that year, which his father wished could be made to descend via his brother, given Corry's '*vows of celibacy*'.[14] Having played little further part in local politics, he succeeded his father, who was recalled from Jamaica in 1832, as 3rd Earl Belmore in April 1841. He died at Castle Coole in December 1845. He made substantial provision for his younger children, including Henry William (1845-1927), Conservative Member for Tyrone, 1873-80, and was succeeded in his Irish estates by his eldest son, Somerset Richard (1835-1913), 4th Earl Belmore, a Conservative junior minister and colonial governor, who wrote several electoral, family and local studies.[15]

[1] *HP Commons, 1790-1820*, iv. 459-60. [2] *Hist. Irish Parl.* iii. 515-17; Lord Belmore, *Parl. Mems. of Fermanagh*, 83; PRO NI, Belmore mss D3007/H/7/8; 14/4-6, 11, 16, 23, 26; *Enniskillen Chron.* 27 Feb., 6, 13 Mar. 1823. [3] *Session of Parl. 1825*, p. 458; PRO NI, Leslie mss MIC606/3/J/7/21/4. [4] *The Times*, 17 Apr. 1823. [5] *Enniskillen Chron.* 8, 15, 29 June 1826. [6] *Impartial Reporter*, 26 Oct., 16, 30 Nov. 1826; *Belfast News Letter*, 9 Jan. 1827. [7] Add. 40392, f. 5; *Enniskillen Chron.* 16 Aug. 1827. [8] *Impartial Reporter*, 14 Aug., 25 Sept., 2, 9 Oct., 11 Dec. 1828, 8 Jan. 1829. [9] Wellington mss WP1/971/19. [10] *Ellenborough Diary*, i. 329; Broughton, *Recollections*, iii. 301. [11] *Enniskillen Chron.* 8 Apr. 1830. [12] Add. 43234, ff. 80, 82, 364; Wellington mss WP1/1096/14; Leslie mss 3/J/7/17/31-33. [13] *Enniskillen Chron.* 15, 22 July, 12, 19, 26 Aug. 1830. [14] Ibid. 28 Apr., 12, 19 May 1831; Belmore mss G/30; H/7/19-23; 14/21-26. [15] *Impartial Reporter*, 18 Dec.; *The Times*, 20 Dec. 1845; *Gent. Mag.* (1846), i. 310, 658; PROB 11/2033/244; IR26/1728/206.

S.M.F.

LOWRY CORRY, Hon. Henry Thomas (1803–1873).

Co. Tyrone 27 June 1825–5 Mar. 1873

b. 9 Mar. 1803, 2nd s. of Somerset Lowry Corry†, 2nd Earl Belmore [I] (*d.* 1841), and Lady Juliana Butler, da. of Henry Thomas, 2nd earl of Carrick [I]; bro. of Armar Lowry Corry, Visct. Corry*. *educ.* Christ Church, Oxf. 1820; I. Temple 1824. *m.* 18 Mar. 1830, Lady Harriet Anne Ashley Cooper, da. of Cropley Ashley Cooper†, 6th earl of Shaftesbury, 2s. 2da. *d.* 5 Mar. 1873.

Comptroller of household Dec. 1834-May 1835; PC 23 Feb. 1835; ld. of admiralty Sept. 1841-Feb. 1845, sec. Feb. 1845-July 1846, Mar. 1858-June 1859; chairman, R. commn. on tidal harbours 1845, commr. 1845-6; commr. of charities 1866-7; vice-pres. cttee. of PC for education July 1866-Mar. 1867; first ld. of admiralty Mar. 1867-Dec. 1868.

Lowry Corry, who graduated from Oxford in 1823, joined his elder brother Lord Corry, Member for Fermanagh, in the Commons in the summer of 1825, when their father Lord Belmore put him up on his family's significant, if latterly dormant, interest for the neighbouring county of Tyrone. (Not only Belmore, but this Member's grandfather and great-grandfather had previously occupied the seat.)[1] Nothing came of a possible contest and, described as 'a young man of affable manners and of great promise in point of talent and qualification', he was returned unopposed at a by-election held within a fortnight of the end of the session; Ahenis, the address given in the *Returns*, was his qualifying property, not his residence.[2] He was an inactive supporter of Lord Liverpool's administration, like Corry, whose voting record he almost exactly replicated, although it was he, not his brother, who divided against the emergency admission of foreign corn, 11 May 1826. As his potential challengers again stood aside, he was returned unopposed with his colleague William Stewart at the general election the following month.[3]

Lowry Corry missed the Protestant dinner and county meeting in Omagh, 6 Nov. and 1 Dec. 1826, but signed the anti-Catholic petition of the noblemen and gentlemen of Ireland in February and voted against Catholic relief, 6 Mar. 1827.[4] He divided against repeal of the Test Acts, 26 Feb., and, having brought up his county's hostile petition, 5 May, again against Catholic claims, 12 May 1828. He voted with the Wellington ministry against reducing the salary of the lieutenant-general of the ordnance, 4 July, and for Fyler's amendment on silk duties which was carried with government support, 14 July. He professed that 'none could be more firmly attached to Protestantism than he' at the Orange celebration in Enniskillen, 12 Aug., and was expected to attend the meeting for the establishment of the Tyrone Brunswick Club, 26 Sept., but he apparently missed this and another county meeting, 2 Dec.[5] To suggestions by the cabinet minister Lord Ellenborough in May and Belmore in December 1828 that he be considered for office, the duke of Wellington replied that it was hopeless to appoint ineffectual young men who were 'unaccustomed to business'.[6] Listed by Planta, the patronage secretary, as likely to be 'with government' for Catholic emancipation, he was considered as a possible mover or seconder of the address and was said by Ellenborough to be delighted with the king's speech in February 1829.[7] However, under pressure from his constituents, he presented hostile petitions from Tyrone and elsewhere, 18 Feb., 3, 11, 16 Mar., and voted against emancipation, 6, 18, 30 Mar., and allowing Daniel O'Connell to take his seat unimpeded, 18 May 1829.[8] His parliamentary conduct was praised by a meeting of the leading interests of the county in January 1830.[9] He voted against transferring East Retford's seats to Birmingham, 11 Feb., parliamentary reform, 18 Feb., and the enfranchisement of Birmingham, Leeds and Manchester, 23 Feb. He divided against Jewish emancipation, 17 May, paired against abolition of the death penalty for forgery, 7 June, and presented the Tyrone petition against the increased Irish stamp and spirit duties, 9 July. After the withdrawal of another contender, he was again returned unopposed at the general election that summer, this time with Sir Hugh Stewart, who replaced his retiring kinsman with Belmore's blessing.[10]

Listed by ministers among their 'friends', Lowry Corry voted in their minority on the civil list, 15 Nov. 1830, which led to Wellington's resignation. He divided against the second reading of the Grey ministry's reform bill, 22 Mar., and for Gascoyne's wrecking amendment, 19 Apr. 1831. With the approval of his father, who was allowed to remain as governor of Jamaica despite his opposition to government, he was returned unopposed as an anti-reformer at the ensuing general election.[11] He voted against the second reading of the reintroduced reform bill, 6 July, to postpone consideration of the partial disfranchisement of Chippenham, 27 July, and against the passage of the bill, 21 Sept., and the second reading of the Scottish bill, 23 Sept. 1831. He divided against the Maynooth grant, 26 Sept. 1831, 27 July 1832. He voted against the second, 17 Dec. 1831, and third readings of the revised reform bill, 22 Mar., the enfranchisement of Tower Hamlets, 28 Feb., the second reading of the Irish bill, 25 May, and to preserve the voting rights of Irish freemen, 2 July 1832. In his only other known votes in this period, he sided against government on the Russian-Dutch loan, 26 Jan., 12 July, but with it for the Irish tithes bill, 13 July. In June 1832 he was considered a potential member of the Protestant Conservative Society of Ireland.[12] An acknowledged expert on naval affairs, Lowry Corry, who served in several spells as a junior minister and entered the cabinet under Benjamin Disraeli† in 1867, continued to sit as Conservative Member for Tyrone until his death in March 1873.[13] He was presumably succeeded in his estate by his elder son, Armar Henry (1836-93). His younger son, Montagu William (1838-1903), Disraeli's influential private secretary, was created Baron Rowton in 1880.

[1] *Hist. Irish Parl.* v. 123-7; *HP Commons, 1790-1820*, iv. 459-60. [2] *Enniskillen Chron.* 9, 30 June 1825; Lord Belmore, *Parl. Mems. of Fermanagh and Tyrone* (1887), 326. [3] *Belfast Commercial Chron.* 10, 24 June 1826. [4] Ibid. 11 Nov., 9 Dec. 1826; Add. 40392, f. 5. [5] *Impartial Reporter*, 14 Aug., 25 Sept., 2 Oct., 11 Dec. 1828. [6] *Ellenborough Diary*, i. 132; Wellington mss WP1/971/19; 974/27. [7] Add. 40398, f. 86; *Ellenborough Diary*, i. 334. [8] *Impartial Reporter*, 5 Mar. 1829. [9] PRO NI, Stewart of Killymoon mss D3167/2/310. [10] *Enniskillen Chron.* 15, 22, 29 July, 12, 26 Aug. 1830. [11] Ibid. 5, 26 May 1831; PRO NI, Belmore mss D3007/G/30/18; *O'Connell Corresp.* iv. 1854. [12] NLI, Farnham mss 18611 (3), Lefroy to Farnham, 4 June 1832. [13] *The Times*, 7 Mar.; *Impartial Reporter*, 13 Mar. 1873; *Ann. Reg.* (1873), Chron. p. 131; *DNB*; *Oxford DNB*.

S.M.F.

LOWTHER, Hon. Henry Cecil (1790–1867), of Barleythorpe, Rutland.

WESTMORLAND 1812–4 Dec. 1867

b. 27 July 1790, 2nd s. of William Lowther†, 1st earl of Lonsdale (*d.* 1844), and Lady Augusta Fane, da. of John Fane†, 9th earl of Westmorland; bro. of William Lowther, Visct. Lowther*. *educ.* Westminster. *m.* 19 May 1817, Lady Eleanor Sherard, da. of Philip Sherard†, 5th earl of Harborough, 3s. (1 *d.v.p.*) 4da. (2 *d.v.p.*). *d.* 4 Dec. 1867.

Cornet 7 Drag. 1807, lt. 1808, capt. 1810; maj. 41 Ft. Apr. 1814, maj. 10 Drag. Nov. 1814; lt.-col. 12 Ft. 1817, half-pay 1818, ret. 1830.

Maj. commdt. Westmld. yeoman cav. 1819, lt.-col. commdt. 1821; col. commdt. R. Cumb. militia 1830.

Lowther, a fine horseman and career soldier who had served with distinction under Moore and Wellington in the Peninsular war, had represented Westmorland on his father Lord Lonsdale's interest since 1812. Popularly known as the 'silent Colonel', he was no public speaker and since 1813 had dutifully followed the political leadership of his elder brother Lord Lowther, voting in support of Lord Liverpool's administration and against Catholic relief.[1] At the general election of 1820 the brothers faced a renewed challenge from the Whig Henry Brougham*, whom they had defeated in 1818.[2] Reports that Lonsdale would seat Henry elsewhere to avoid a contest were dispelled by the prompt announcement of his candidature, and he was re-elected with his brother after an exhaustive seven-day poll, after trailing in third place for the first five days.[3]

Lowther, who made no reported speeches before 1831, was detained as a defaulter, 20 July 1820. He voted against parliamentary reform, 9 May 1821, 20 Feb. 1823, 13 Apr. 1826, and Catholic relief, 28 Feb. 1821, 1 Mar., 21 Apr., 10 May, and the attendant Irish franchise bill, 26 Apr. 1825. A radical publication of 1825 described him correctly as a Member who 'attended occasionally and voted with ministers'.[4] He divided with them on their handling of Queen

Caroline's case, 6 Feb., the additional malt tax repeal bill, 3 Apr., and the duke of Clarence's grant, 18 June 1821. He voted against more extensive tax reductions to relieve distress, 11 Feb., abolition of one of the joint-postmasterships, 2 May, and inquiry into Irish tithes, 19 June, and for the aliens bill, 19 July, and the grant for publishing Irish government publications, 22 July 1822. He voted against investigating chancery arrears, 2, 12 June 1823, and against condemning the indictment in Demerara of the Methodist missionary John Smith for inciting slaves to riot, 11 June 1824. He divided against the spring guns bill, 27 Apr. 1826. At the general election in June he contested Westmorland successfully with his brother, canvassing arduously despite the extreme heat and making a valiant effort to contribute to the nightly close of poll speeches.[5] Bingley Broadhead, a lieutenant in the 80th Foot who recognized him shortly afterwards in Manchester, wrote:

> Such a figure you can hardly conceive. His face had come in contact with the mountain wind and sun, and no skin was left. Indeed, the old comparisons of a chapped face being like the bark of a plum tree was not the least exaggerated.[6]

Lowther divided against Catholic relief, 6 Mar. 1827, 12 May 1828, and with his brother in the Tory minority against the Coventry magistracy bill, 18 June 1827, and the Wellington ministry's majority against ordnance reductions, 4 July 1828. Their patronage secretary Planta noted that he was 'opposed to the principle' of Catholic emancipation in 1829, and he presented hostile petitions, 4 Mar., and divided against it, 6, 18, 30 Mar., having paired against admitting Catholic Members, 23 Mar., and against bringing up the report, 27 Mar. His wife had a reputation for showing off at society gatherings;[7] and Mrs. Arbuthnot, who met the couple in January 1830 at Cottesmore, where Lowther led the hunt, described her as 'a fat ugly woman of seven or eight and thirty' flirting with a dandy, while he 'does not seem to care'.[8] He voted against transferring East Retford's seats to Birmingham, 11 Feb. His brother, a government minister suspected of disloyalty by his colleagues, was embarrassed by Lonsdale's decision to ordered Lowther back to London to vote for the production of *ex-officio* informations involving the *Morning Chronicle*, 2 Mar., which government opposed, but there was no division.[9] He voted against Jewish emancipation, 17 May, and abolition of the death penalty for forgery, 7 June 1830. Although a compromise left Cumberland and Westmorland uncontested at the general election of 1830, Lowther proceeded with a precautionary canvass and chaired the party dinner at Cockermouth prior to his return.[10]

Ministers counted him among their 'friends', but he was absent from the division on the civil list by which they were brought down, 15 Nov. 1830. The Grey administration's reform bill threatened Lonsdale's electoral influence at Appleby, Cockermouth and Haselmere. As directed, Lowther voted against its second reading, 22 Mar., and for Gascoyne's wrecking amendment, 19 Apr. 1831.[11] He refused to moderate his opposition to the bill, and his uncontested return for Westmorland at the ensuing election was secured through a pre-poll pact with the reformers, whose candidates defeated Lord Lowther in Cumberland.[12] He divided against the reintroduced reform bill at its second reading, 6 July 1831. Representing Lonsdale's interests in the Commons until his brother was seated for Dunwich in February 1832, he presented and endorsed Appleby's petition against disfranchisement, 22 June, called in vain for its referral to a select committee to be heard by counsel, 12 July 1831, and brought up another on the 14th against the suggested boundaries for the new Whitehaven constituency, which he rightly complained had been drawn to minimize Lowther influence. On 6 Aug. he ridiculed the first lord of the admiralty Sir James Graham's explanation that Harrington had been added to Whitehaven because they were neighbouring seaports, pointing out that Harrington, being one-and-a-half miles inland, was 'no more a seaport than the Regent's Park'. He voted to make the 1831 census the determinant of borough disfranchisement, 19 July, against taking a seat from Chippenham, 27 July, and to preserve freemen's voting rights, 30 Aug. He divided against the bill's passage, 21 Sept., and for the second reading of the Scottish reform bill, 23 Sept. He voted against the second reading of the revised reform bill, 17 Dec. 1831, the enfranchisement of Tower Hamlets, 28 Feb., and the third reading, 22 Mar., and against the Irish reform bill at its second reading, 25 May. He divided against government on the Russian-Dutch loan, 26 Jan., 12 July, and the malt drawback bill, 29 Feb. 1832. He voted to reduce civil list expenditure, 18 July, against the Maynooth grant 26 Sept. 1831, and for Sadler's scheme to tax absentee landlords to provide for the Irish poor, 19 June 1832. He presented petitions from Westmorland for the alienation of tithes, 30 July 1831.[13]

Lowther directed the Conservatives' canvass of the new Cumberland and Westmorland constituencies at the general election of 1832, when his brother was abroad, came in for Westmorland with him, and represented the county for life.[14] He was Father of the

House when he died in December 1867, recalled for the good sense and brevity of his rare utterances and his prowess as a huntsman and cricketer.[15] His successor at Barleythorpe and the principal beneficiary of his will, proved on 26 Feb. 1868, was his eldest son Henry Lowther (1818-76), Conservative Member for Cumberland West from 1847 until he succeeded his uncle as 3rd earl of Lonsdale in 1872.

[1] H. Owen, *Lowther Fam.* 395-6; *HP Commons, 1790-1820*, ii. 405-8; iv. 460. [2] W.A. Hay, *The Whig Revival, 1808-1830*, pp. 67-87. [3] Lonsdale mss, W. Hodgson to Lonsdale, 18 Feb.; Clwyd RO, Lowther mss DD/L/178, J. Lowther to same [1820]; *Cumb. Pacquet*, 15, 29 Feb., 7 Mar. 1820; J.R. McQuiston, 'The Lonsdale Connection and its Defender', *Northern Hist.* xi (1975), 143-60. [4] *Session of Parl. 1825*, p. 473. [5] *Cumb. Pacquet*, 13 June-11 July 1826; *Wordsworth Letters* ed. M. Moorman and A.G. Hill (1970), iii. 456; McQuiston, 163-6. [6] Northumb. RO, Middleton mss ZM1/S/76/52/2. [7] Lonsdale mss, Lonsdale to Lowther, 23 Sept. 1829. [8] *Arbuthnot Jnl.* ii. 325. [9] *Greville Mems.* i. 363-4; Lonsdale mss, Lonsdale to Lowther, 1 Mar., reply, 3 Mar. 1830. [10] Lonsdale mss, Lowther to Lonsdale, 22 June; *Carlisle Jnl.* 17 July, 7, 14 Aug.; *Cumb. Pacquet*, 10 Aug. 1830; McQuiston, 176. [11] Lonsdale mss, Lowther to Lonsdale, 25 Feb. 1831. [12] McQuiston, 177-8; *Westmld. Advertiser*, 2, 30 Apr., 7, 14 May; Lowther mss 167, J.H. to J. Lowther, 29 Apr. 1831. [13] Lonsdale mss, Lowther to Lonsdale, 27 Jan. 1832. [14] Ibid. H.C. Lowther to J. Benn, 18 June, 7, 17 July, 27 Nov., 1, 4 Dec.; Brougham mss, W. Crackanthorpe to J. Brougham, 21 July, 11 Aug.; *Carlisle Patriot*, 22 Dec. 1832. [15] *The Times*, 7, 9, 16 Dec.; F. Lillywhite, *Cricket Scores and Biogs.*(1860), i. 399; *Sporting Gazette*, 14 Dec. 1867; *Gent. Mag.* (1868), i. 108.

M.M.E.

LOWTHER, John (1759–1844), of Swillington, nr. Leeds, Yorks.

COCKERMOUTH	1780–Mar. 1786
CARLISLE	10 Apr. 1786–31 May 1786
HASLEMERE	13 June 1786–1790
CUMBERLAND	1796–1831

b. 1 Apr. 1759, 2nd s. of Rev. Sir William Lowther, 1st bt. (*d.* 1788), rect. of Swillington, and Anne, da. of Rev. Charles Zouch, vic. of Sandal. *educ.* Westminster 1771-3; Trinity Coll. Camb. 1776; L. Inn 1780. *m.* 4 Sept. 1790, Lady Elizabeth Fane, da. of John Fane†, 9th earl of Westmorland, 3s. (1 *d.v.p.*) 3da. (2 *d.v.p.*). *cr.* bt. 3 Nov. 1824. *d.* 11 May 1844.

Lowther, who bore a strong physical resemblance to his brother and close confidant the 1st earl of Lonsdale, had been confirmed in possession of Swillington and Yorkshire estates worth £4,000 a year on the death in 1802 of their cousin Lord Lonsdale. Subsequently his interests focused increasingly on that county and the rebuilding of his castle at Wilton, near Middlesbrough, to the design of Smirke. Despite his growing disenchantment with parliamentary life, he remained one of the Lowther 'ninepins' for over 50 years, voting steadily with successive Tory ministries and against parliamentary reform and Catholic relief.[1] His loyalty to his brother was severely tested at the general election of 1820, for Lonsdale threatened to refuse to seat his son and heir John Henry, Member for the family borough of Cockermouth since 1816. Lowther's hopes of making way for him in Cumberland were thus dashed, and his fifth return for the county, where his non-residence was increasingly resented, was secured only after a three-day poll.[2]

Lowther was briefed personally on policy by Lonsdale as hitherto, but his votes were now directed by his nephew Lord Lowther*, whom he had advised to play a more prominent part in organizing the family Members.[3] He voted against parliamentary reform, 9 May 1821, 20 Feb. 1823, and divided against Catholic relief, 28 Feb. 1821 (paired), 1 Mar., 21 Apr., 10 May, and the attendant Irish franchise bill, 26 Apr. 1825. A radical publication of that session observed that he 'attended frequently and voted with government'.[4] He divided against censuring their handling of the Queen Caroline case, 6 Feb., abolition of the death penalty for forgery, 23 May, and Hume's call for economy and retrenchment, 27 June 1821. He divided against more extensive tax reductions, 21 Feb., to retain the salt tax, 28 Feb., for the public accounts bill, 13 Mar, and against abolishing one of the joint-postmasterships, 2 May, and investigating the lord advocate's treatment of the Scottish press, 25 June 1822. He was in the ministerial minority against inquiring into the prosecution of the Dublin Orange rioters, 22 Apr., and voted against investigating chancery arrears, 2, 12 June 1823. That autumn, with Lonsdale's backing, he applied to Lord Liverpool for a peerage to pass on to his son, but had to be content with a promise of the Swillington baronetcy, eventually conferred on him on 3 Nov. 1824.[5] He presented several anti-Catholic petitions, 25 Apr., and others that day and on the 28th against amending the corn laws.[6] He voted against the spring guns bill, 21 June 1825. For want of a suitable replacement, Lonsdale prevailed on him to change his mind about retiring and he came in unopposed for Cumberland at the general election of 1826.[7]

Lowther, who received a month's leave on urgent business, 16 Mar. 1827, remained one of his brother's closest political confidants in the 1826 Parliament.[8] He presented and endorsed constituency petitions for agricultural protection, 19 Feb. 1827.[9] He voted against Catholic relief, 6 Mar. 1827, 12 May 1828, brought up petitions for repeal of the Small Notes Act, 6 May, and the abolition of colonial slavery, 3,

30 June, and divided with the Wellington ministry against ordnance reductions, 4 July 1828. They were right to doubt his support for Catholic emancipation in 1829, when he presented hostile petitions, 23, 26 Feb., 4 Mar., and divided against it, 6, 18, 30 Mar. (paired).[10] He presented and supported his constituents' petitions for relief from distress, 5, 23 Mar., and voted against Jewish emancipation, 17 May, and abolishing the death penalty for forgery, 7 June 1830. Afterwards, he helped to secure the compromise which left Cumberland and Westmorland uncontested at the general election of 1830 and, with a view to persuading Lonsdale to relent and bring John Henry forward for Cumberland at a future date, he made him accompany him to the Carlisle assizes and the election at Cockermouth, where the radical mob was out in force.[11] The Wellington ministry counted Lowther among their 'friends', but, though summoned 'for the trial of strength' by Lord Lowther, he was absent from the division on the civil list by which they were brought down, 15 Nov. 1830.[12] He presented petitions for the abolition of colonial slavery from Whitehaven and Shap, 17 Nov. 1830, before returning to Swillington, where John Henry sent him regular reports of the progress of Lord Grey's administration.[13] He divided against their reform bill at its second reading, 22 Mar., and for Gascoyne's wrecking amendment, 19 Apr. 1831. There was 'no hope' of his standing for Cumberland at the ensuing general election, and as Lonsdale rejected his offer to sit for Cockermouth, he retired.[14]

Out of Parliament Lowther retained a keen interest in Yorkshire politics and John Henry's career as Member for York, and he encouraged his son Charles Hugh, who was blind from infancy, to establish a library of embossed books for the blind. He died at Swillington in May 1844, eight days before his wife.[15] He was succeeded in the baronetcy and estates by John Henry, who, with his grandchildren and Charles, was the main beneficiary of his will, dated 21 Feb. 1838 and proved under £45,000, 2 July 1844, but resworn at £10,000, 31 Oct. 1845.[16]

[1] H. Owen, *Lowther Fam.* 364-8; *HP Commons, 1754-90*, iii. 60; *HP Commons, 1790-1820*, iv. 462; *VCH Yorks. N. Riding*, ii. 375, 378. [2] Clwyd RO, Lowther mss DD/L/178, J. Lowther to Lonsdale and replies, 26 Jan.-24 Mar., W.P. Johnston to J. Lowther, 27 Feb., E. Stanley to same, 6 Mar.; Lonsdale mss, Lord Lowther to Lonsdale, 8 Feb., J. Lowther to same, 12 Feb.; *Cumb. Pacquet*, 14 Mar.; *Whitehaven Gazette*, 20 Mar.; *The Times*, 21 Mar. 1820. [3] Lowther mss 161, Lonsdale to J. Lowther, 4 Dec.; 178, J. Lowther to Lowther, n.d. [1820]; Lonsdale mss, Lowther to Lonsdale, 23 Feb. 1821. [4] *Session of Parl. 1825*, p. 473. [5] Lowther mss 67, 79, *passim.*; Add. 38298, f. 82; 38299, f. 108; Lonsdale mss, Liverpool to Lonsdale, 23 Dec. 1823, 8 Aug. 1824. [6] *The Times*, 26, 29 Apr. 1825. [7] Lonsdale mss, Lowther to Lonsdale, 23 Mar. 1825, W. Hodgson to same, 1 June, P. Musgrave to same, 14 June; Lowther mss, Lonsdale to J. Lowther, 10 Mar.; *The Times*, 20 June 1826. [8] Lowther mss 164, 165, *passim.* [9] *The Times*, 20 Feb.; *Carlisle Patriot*, 24 Feb. 1827. [10] Lowther mss 179, Lonsdale to J. Lowther, 3 Mar.; Lonsdale mss, Lowther to Lonsdale, 24 Feb.; Add. 76369, Althorp to Brougham, 18, 19 Mar. 1829. [11] Lowther mss 178, J.H. to J. Lowther, 22 July 1830; 179, Lonsdale to same, 5 Feb. 1829, J.H. Lowther to same, 20 July, 28 Aug., Lowther to same, n.d., J. Lowther to wife, n.d.; Lonsdale mss, Lauderdale to J. Lowther, 6 June, 5 July 1830. [12] Lowther mss 166, Lowther to J. Lowther, 16 Oct. 1830. [13] Lowther mss 166, 167, *passim.* [14] Lonsdale mss, Lowther to Lonsdale, 28 Dec. 1830, 5 Apr.; Lowther mss 167, E. Stanley to J. Lowther, 28 Apr., J.H. Lowther to same, 29 Apr. 1831. [15] *Leeds Intelligencer*, 18, 25 May; *The Times*, 22 May 1844. [16] PROB 11/2002/560; IR26/1681/454.

M.M.E.

LOWTHER, John Henry (1793–1868), of Swillington, Yorks.

COCKERMOUTH	1 Mar. 1816–1826
WIGTOWN BURGHS	1826–1831
COCKERMOUTH	1831–1832
YORK	1835–1847

b. 23 Mar. 1793, 1st s. of John Lowther* of Swillington and Lady Elizabeth Fane, da. of John Fane†, 9th earl of Westmorland. *educ.* Westminster 1808-10; Trinity Coll. Camb. 1811. *unm. suc.* fa. as 2nd bt. 11 May 1844. *d.* 23 June 1868.

Sheriff, Yorks. 1852-3.

Capt. Cumb. militia 1820; lt.-col. 1st W. Yorks. militia 1830.

By the general election of 1820, when he was absent touring the northern European courts, Lowther had forfeited the confidence of his uncle and patron the 1st earl of Lonsdale, and he owed his third return for the family borough of Cockermouth to his father's supplications on his behalf and usefulness to Lonsdale as Member for Cumberland.[1] It was agreed that he would 'not accept of a seat with any other view than that of supporting the measures of government' and see Lonsdale on his return to discuss his future.[2] He left Russia for England in late July 1820.[3]

In 1821 and for the remainder of the 1820 Parliament Lowther, of whom a radical publication of 1825 noted that he 'attended frequently and voted with ministers', divided steadily with his father at his cousin Lord Lowther's* direction.[4] He voted against parliamentary reform, 9 May 1821, 20 Feb. 1823, and Catholic relief, 28 Feb. 1821, 1 Mar., 21 Apr., 10 May, and the attendant Irish franchise bill, 26 Apr. 1825. He voted against censuring ministers' handling of the Queen Caroline case, 6 Feb., and abolition of the death penalty for forgery, 23 May, and was in the government majorities on retrenchment, 27 June 1821, tax reductions, 21 Feb., the salt tax, 28 Feb., and the public accounts bill, 13 Mar. 1822. He divided against abolishing one of the joint-postmasterships, 2 May, and investigating the lord advocate's treatment of the Scottish press, 25 June 1822. He was in the ministerial minority against inquiring into the prosecution of the Dublin Orange rioters, 22 Apr., and voted against investigating chancery arrears, 2, 12 June 1823, and the spring guns bill, 21 June 1825. He had yet to speak in debate, and Lord Lowther cautioned Lonsdale against putting him forward for Cumberland in place of his father at the general election of 1826, 'as I believe his political inclinations are opposed to us and he does not seem disposed to give us any assistance'.[5] He turned down a requisition to stand for York and, under an exchange agreed by Lonsdale, made way for Lord Garlies at Cockermouth and came in for Wigtown Burghs in 1826 on the Galloway interest.[6]

Lowther, who received three weeks' leave on urgent business after serving on the Dover election committee, 16 Mar. 1827, divided with his father as previously in the 1826 Parliament, against Catholic relief, 6 Mar. 1827, 12 May 1828, and with the duke of Wellington's ministry against ordnance reductions, 4 July 1828. Their patronage secretary Planta correctly doubted his support for Catholic emancipation in 1829, and he divided against it, 6, 18, 30 Mar. He joined Lord Lowther in opposing the Northern Roads bill, 3 June 1830. Condemned as 'an ass ... or worse' by Lonsdale's son-in-law, the judge advocate Sir John Beckett*, for proposing a toast to the Whig lawyer Henry Brougham* at the assize ball in Carlisle shortly before the 1829 by-election, he was again rejected for Cumberland by Lonsdale, who suggested him for Plympton at the general election of 1830.[7] However, when the arrangement with Garlies was belatedly revived, Lonsdale acquiesced in his preference to sit for Wigtown Burghs. He accompanied his father to the elections at Carlisle, Cockermouth and Whitehaven, where his speeches were 'very well received', particularly by the Ultras who felt 'let down' by the recent electoral pact between Brougham and Lonsdale.[8]

Though counted by the Wellington ministry among their 'friends', Lowther, like his father, was absent from the division on the civil list by which they were brought down, 15 Nov. 1830. Lonsdale, who anticipated an immediate dissolution, dismissed him as lazy, ineffective and of no use 'beyond that of attending a committee of the House of Commons', and was as reluctant as ever to seat him for Cumberland, though his father's retirement was now certain.[9] He remained in London, dined regularly at the Travellers' Club and wrote regularly to his father of Lord Althorp's shortcomings as chancellor of the exchequer, dissension within Lord Grey's administration and their reform bill, which he thought would ultimately be carried.[10] He voted against it at its second reading, 22 Mar., and for Gascoyne's wrecking amendment, 19 Apr. 1831. He canvassed with Lonsdale's sons at the ensuing general election and was seated for Cockermouth, which the bill threatened to deprive of a Member. On the hustings he refused to give any pledges, but conceded the need for some reform.[11] Much to his embarrassment, for his relations suspected him of complicity, he was also requisitioned to stand for Cumberland, where Lord Lowther stood uninvited and was defeated by two reformers.[12]

Lowther found the constant attendance required of him as an opponent of 'the odious reform bill' in 1831-2 particularly irksome.[13] He voted against the reintroduced bill at its second reading, 6 July, and committal, 12 July, to make the 1831 census the criterion for English borough disfranchisements, 19 July, and to postpone consideration of the partial disfranchisement of Chippenham, 27 July 1831. He intervened briefly next day to protest at the summary dismissal by ministers of all arguments in favour of Cockermouth's retaining two seats, and joined in the protest against the intended boundaries for the new Whitehaven constituency, which he rightly surmised were calculated to minimize the Lowther influence, 6 Aug. He was one of only 15 anti-reformers to vote in favour of the proposed division of counties, 11 Aug. He was in the minority for preserving freemen's voting rights, 30 Aug., when he backed the call for maximum electorates of 4,000. He divided against the bill's passage, 21 Sept., and for the second reading of the Scottish reform bill, 23 Sept. He voted against the revised reform bill at its second reading, 17 Dec. 1831, against its committal, 20 Jan., the enfranchisement of Tower Hamlets, 28 Feb., and the third reading, 22 Mar., having, in view of his local interest, voiced support for Stockton's petition for separate enfranchisement, 5 Mar. 1832. He divided against the Irish reform bill at its second reading, 25 May. 1832. When the Irish government was implicated in bribery at the Dublin election, he defended the conduct of his kinsman Edward Smith Stanley as Irish secretary, but voted for the opposition censure motion, 23 Aug. 1831. He divided against issuing the Liverpool writ, 5 Sept., with the West India lobby for a select committee on the sugar trade, 12 Sept., and against the Maynooth grant, 26 Sept. He had 'no qualms' in opposing the bankruptcy court bill, 15 Oct. 1831. Lord Lowther noticed the effort he made to be present to vote against government on the Russian-Dutch loan, 26 Jan., 12 July 1832.[14] Mindful of his interests in the North East, he opposed the South Shields-Monkwearmouth railway bill, 26 Mar. 1832.

Lowther ceased to act with the Lonsdale Lowthers and was defeated at York on the Conservative interest in 1832 and again at the 1833 by-election, when he declined nomination and went abroad. He topped the poll there in 1835, 1837 and 1841 and was cleared by the parliamentary inquiry of 1835 of personal involvement in bribery.[15] In May 1844 he succeeded to the estates and the baronetcy conferred 20 years previously on his father. He retired from Parliament at the dissolution of 1847. He developed the 16-foot ironstone seam discovered under his Wilton estate in 1850, served as sheriff of Yorkshire in 1852-3 and died unmarried and without issue at his London home in Portland Street, Grosvenor Square in June 1868. A personal friend since 1833 of Benjamin Disraeli†, he was recalled as a patron of the opera and the Turf, and as a staunch high church Tory.[16] His will, dated 12 Dec. 1863, was proved at Wakefield, 17 July 1868, and administered by his blind brother Charles (1803-94), his successor in the estates and baronetcy.[17]

[1] *HP Commons, 1790-1820*, iv. 462; Clwyd RO, Lowther mss DD/L/178, J. Lowther to Lonsdale and replies, 26 Jan.-24 Mar.; Lonsdale mss, Lord Lowther to Lonsdale, 8 Feb.; J.R. McQuiston, 'The Lonsdale Connection and its Defender', *Northern Hist.* xi (1975), 155-6; *Cumb. Pacquet*, 14 Mar. 1820. [2] Lonsdale mss, J. Lowther to Lonsdale, 12 Feb.; Lowther mss 178, Lonsdale to J. Lowther, 4 Mar. 1820. [3] Lowther mss 161, J.H. Randolph to J. Lowther, 16 July 1820. [4] *Session of Parl. 1825*, p. 473. [5] Lonsdale mss, Lowther to Lonsdale, 23 Mar. 1825. [6] *York City Poll ... Account of General Election of 1826* (1830), 95; Lonsdale mss, Lowther to Lonsdale, 23 May 1825; *Cumb. Pacquet*, 13 May 1826; *Westmld. Advertiser*, 2 Apr. 1831. [7] Lonsdale mss, Beckett to Lowther, n.d. [1829], Lonsdale to same, 20 July; Lowther mss 178, J.H. to J. Lowther, 20 July 1830; 179, Lonsdale to same, 3, 5 Feb. 1829. [8] Lowther mss 178, J.H. to J. Lowther, 22 July; 179, same to same, 28 Aug., Lowther to same, n.d., J. Lowther to wife, n.d.; Lonsdale mss, Lowther to Lonsdale, 24 July 1830; McQuiston, 176-7. [9] Lonsdale mss, Lowther to Lonsdale, 29 Dec., reply, 30 Dec. 1830. [10] Lowther mss 166, 167, *passim*. [11] *Westmld. Advertiser*, 2, 30 Apr., 7 May 1831. [12] Lonsdale mss, Lonsdale to Lowther, 29 Apr.; Lowther mss 167, E. Stanley to J. Lowther, 28 Apr., J.H. to J. Lowther, 29 Apr. 1831. [13] Hants RO, Carnarvon mss 75M91/M12/7. [14] Lonsdale mss, Lowther to Lonsdale, 27 Jan. 1832. [15] Lowther mss 149, 168, *passim*; *The Times*, 18 Sept. 1832, 12 Sept. 1835, 1 July 1841; *CJ*, xc. 401, 457, 511-12, 560, 655; Add. 40422, f. 260; 40558, ff. 102-4; H. Owen, *Lowther Fam.* 369-71. [16] *Yorks. Post*, 25, 27 June 1868; *Disraeli Letters*, i. 228, 242; *Shelley Diary*, ii. 296; *VCH Yorks. N. Riding*, ii. 405, J.S. Jeans, *Pioneers of the Cleveland Iron Trade*, 75-81. [17] *The Times*, 22 Aug. 1868.

M.M.E.

LOWTHER, William, Visct. Lowther (1787–1872).

COCKERMOUTH	11 July 1808–Nov. 1813
WESTMORLAND	22 Nov. 1813–1831
DUNWICH	2 Feb. 1832–1832
WESTMORLAND	1832–8 Sept. 1841

b. 30 July 1787, 1st s. of William Lowther†, 1st earl of Lonsdale, and Lady Augusta Fane, da. of John Fane†, 9th earl of Westmorland; bro. of Hon. Henry Cecil Lowther*. *educ.* Harrow 1796-1803/4; 'under the roof of the Rev. John Stonard', 1804;[1] Trinity Coll. Camb. 1805. *unm. styled* Visct. Lowther 1807-41. *summ.* to the Lords in his fa.'s barony as Bar. Lowther 8 Sept. 1841; *suc.* fa. as 2nd earl of Lonsdale 19 Mar. 1844. *d.* 4 Mar. 1872.

Ld. of admiralty Nov. 1809-July 1810; commr. bd. of control July 1810-June 1818; ld. of treasury Nov. 1813-Apr. 1827; PC 30 May 1828; chief commr. of woods, forests and land revenues June 1828-Dec. 1830; vice-pres. bd. of trade and treas. of navy Dec. 1834-May 1835; postmaster-gen. Sept. 1841-Dec. 1845; ld. pres. of council Feb.-Dec. 1852.

Dir. Greenwich Hosp. 1819.

Lt.-col. Whitehaven militia 1809.

Ld. lt. Cumb. and Westmld. 1844-68.

A well-connected Tory with a penchant for office, Lowther was heir to the vast Northern estates and electoral influence of his father, Lord Lonsdale, whose ability to return nine Members (two for Westmorland, Cockermouth and Haslemere and one for Appleby, Carlisle and Cumberland) was severely challenged in this period.[2] His transfer from Cockermouth to Westmorland had been opposed by Henry Brougham* for the Whigs at the general election of 1818; and with further contests threatened, he had lately attended closely to local issues and promoted the anti-Catholic cause in the Commons.[3] His private life was governed by his love of opera, the Turf and Paris, where his daughter Marie Caroline was born, 2 May 1818, and which he eulogized in January 1820 as the only place

> where I attend dinners without suffering in my health; where I am well received and my acquaintance courted; greeted with confidence by men of all ranks and situations, ministers of France, ambassadors, bankers; where *ennui* is quickly banished; where novelty cheers; time most plenty; little left to desire.[4]

His absence there when George III died, coupled with dissension between his uncle John Lowther* and Lonsdale, disrupted planning at the general election of 1820, when he and his brother Henry only narrowly defeated Brougham in Westmorland after an exhaustive poll. Cumberland and Carlisle were also contested and trouble was threatened at Appleby and Haslemere.[5]

Lowther was regarded as a placeman and his father's 'party manager', although Lonsdale also turned to his brother John, his son-in-law John Beckett*, the government whip William Holmes* and trusted agents for advice and to do his bidding.[6] He was appointed to many select committees, including those on privilege, 30 Mar. 1821, public accounts, 18 Apr. 1822, the metropolitan police, 14 Mar. 1822, 28 Feb. 1828, 15 Apr. 1829, the civil list, 16 Nov. 1830, and on numerous public and private bills. He also sat on the 1828 finance committee on William Huskisson's* recommendation, and was regarded as an excellent Tory nominee on election committees.[7] He mustered support for the anti-Catholics and, dismayed by their defeat, 28 Feb. 1821,[8] he deliberately absented himself from the division of 17 Apr. 1823.[9] As agreed with Lonsdale, he voted but refused to speak against relief, 1 Mar., 21 Apr., 10 May, and divided against the attendant Irish franchise bill, 26 Apr. 1825.[10]

Acting for his constituents, he presented petitions for repeal of the wool duties, 1 May, and government action to combat distress, 17 May, and expressed support for the posthorse duties bill, 11 July 1820.[11] He failed to dispel unease at the deployment of troops to restore order at the Carlisle election or to prevent the new Member William James's motion summoning the Carlisle magistracy being held over, 3 July. As a treasury spokesman, he indicated that ministers would reconsider the French General Desfourneaux's right to compensation for loses resulting from the capture of Guadeloupe in 1794, 15 July 1820.[12] He was instrumental in drawing the king's attention to the 'difficulty about praying for the queen', privately doubted the wisdom of prosecuting her,[13] and had no qualms about making financial provisions for her, 1 Feb. 1821.[14] His attempts to kill James's motion alleging improper interference by the military at the Carlisle election also failed, 15 Mar., but the anodyne report of the investigative committee saved him from further embarrassment, 3 Apr.[15] He spoke and was a majority teller against appointing select committees on the game laws, 5 Apr., and the Lyme Regis franchise, 12 Apr., and poured scorn on its presenter Curwen's endorsement of the Cumberland petition suggesting parliamentary reform as a remedy for distress, 17 Apr.[16] He paired against mitigation of the death penalty for forgery, 23 May. He presented petitions against the timber duties, 23 Feb., and the tax on wool, 12 Apr.[17] He was appointed to the select committee on the extra post bill, 13 June, for which he was a minority teller, 2 July. He stayed at Windsor for the Ascot races in June, and spent November and December 1821 in Paris, whence his return was delayed by bad weather.[18]

As requested at the county meetings, Lowther presented Westmorland petitions for action to combat distress, 11, 13 Feb. 1822.[19] Before leaving London for the obligatory autumn round of meetings and functions in Westmorland, he gave his opinion on the political consequences of the foreign secretary Lord Londonderry's* suicide in a letter to the king's secretary Sir William Knighton, in which he observed that 'barkers and worriers' apart, opposition had 'but Brougham and Mackintosh fit for everyday service', and Canning 'such sudden twists and quirks I know not whether he is most to be dreaded as *friend* or *foe*'; but he accepted the need to 'yield to circumstances and take him' as foreign secretary.[20] He advised Lonsdale to 'remain neuter' at the Cambridge University by-election in November 1822 when the anti-Catholic William Bankes defeated Lord Hervey* and James Scarlett*.[21] Lowther predicted a 'quiet session' in 1823, but was soon embroiled in the protracted negotiations surrounding Robert Ward's appointment as civil list auditor in April, and replacing him at Haslemere with his relation George Lowther Thompson.[22] He presented a petition against Catholic relief, 11 Apr. 1823.[23] He was appointed to the select committee on the game laws, 13 Mar., and was a teller for the minority against legalizing sales, 2 June. On 13 June he was named to the select committee on gas lighting, an issue that was to cost him electoral support in Lancashire after he refused to back the first 1824 Manchester gas bill.[24] He presented petitions against the wool duties, 21 May, and for abolishing colonial slavery, 28 May, 23, 25 June.[25] In November 1823 he was a party to the negotiations which led to the conferral of a baronetcy on John Lowther a year later.[26] Lowther's ability to summon the Swillington Lowthers and Lowther Thompson for the 1824 session was sorely tested, but they mustered to vote against reforming the representation of Edinburgh, 26 Feb.[27] He had much constituency business to attend to, and presented petitions against wool imports, 10 Feb., taxes on sheepdogs and coal, 25 Feb., colonial slavery, 11, 16, 23, 31 Mar., 5, 14 Apr., the hides regulation bill, 17 Mar., 18 May, and the excise license duties, 23 Mar., and in favour of the proposed legislation for the recovery of small debts, 30 Mar.[28] Calling for an end to the monopolies enjoyed by bridge companies, he expressed qualified support for the Hammersmith bridge bill and dismissed the compensation claims of rival companies as a matter to be dealt with by the select committee, 13 Apr. 1824.[29] He supported the abortive Dublin coal trade bill, 13 Apr., notwithstanding Curwen's criticism and petitions against it from Whitehaven, where Lowther control of the harbour was resented. As a majority teller for recommitting the Tees and Weardale railway bill, in which the Swillington Lowthers had a vested interest, 3 May, he claimed that its opponents greatly exaggerated the detrimental effect it would have on Lord Londonderry's estates. (He promoted the bill again when it was reintroduced in 1825.)[30] He was a majority teller for the Equitable Loan Company bill, later rejected by the Lords, in both divisions, 1 June 1824.

Having urged close scrutiny of the London turnpike trusts when William Cobbett† petitioned, 5 May 1824, Lowther (a member of the 1821 and 1827 select committee) moved for and was appointed to chair that on their revenues, 17 Feb. 1825. He voted against the usury laws repeal bill that day, and also presented a petition for the county courts bill. He corresponded with Lonsdale about the Carlisle by-election occasioned by the death in March of Sir James Graham, and presented petitions from Kirkby Lonsdale and Carlisle against amending the corn laws, 28 Apr.[31] He voted against the spring guns bill, 21 June. He was at Newmarket for the July races, but with a dissolution in contemplation, constituency arrangements took up much of his time and he joined Beckett, Holmes, Lord Lauderdale and Sir John Lowther in negotiations calculated to secure the neutrality of Lord Thanet in Westmorland, where Lonsdale was 'in a terrible fright about a contested election'. With an eye to commercial investment in mining and quarrying, he also toured Wales for six weeks with Alderman William Thompson* before returning to London on 11 Sept.[32] Knowing that the Whigs planned to oppose them on all fronts, he encouraged his father to spend to protect their strongholds of Cumberland, Westmorland and Carlisle at the next general election, and suggested selling their borough seats through the treasury to finance the expected contests.[33] He privately criticized Lord Liverpool's decision to patch up his ministry and avoid a dissolution that autumn, and dallied in London and Brighton where he enjoyed the low life with Holmes and Henry de Ros, who had found him a compliant woman.[34] The 'awkward' Cambridge University election, the December 1825 banking crisis, and trouble at Haslemere spurred him to political activity.[35] He privately considered treasury intervention on behalf of the country banks in the aftermath of the crisis counter-productive.[36] He steered the successful Middlesex turnpike trust bill through the Commons with Brogden, and advised making tarred roads a proviso of the 1826 Westminster improvement bill, 1 May.[37] He presented anti-slavery petitions, 22 Feb., 10 Mar., 19 Apr., chose not to divide on the Jamaican slave trials, 2 Mar., but voted against reforming Edinburgh's representation, 13 Apr. 1826.[38] His Westmorland committee insisted that he direct them personally at the general election in June, when he and his brother defeated Brougham at an estimated cost of £50,000. They were repeatedly castigated for exploiting the anti-Catholic vote and 'mushroom' freeholds and 'inventing' and circulating speeches giving the 'false' impression that Lowther had outshone Brougham.[39] Afterwards he organized the requisite payments, appealed against the court ruling on the charitable status of St. Bees School, which had gone against Lonsdale, and arranged for William Carus Wilson to be replaced at Cockermouth by Lawrence Peel.[40]

Lowther viewed the death of the duke of York as

> a severe national calamity; his influence balanced or checked the effects of the present system of liberalism. What is to happen now no one can predict. Our country gentlemen are sore even now and grumble they have to divide in company with the radicals. All must depend upon the views of Canning; if he is as ambitious as some of his followers a short time can only elapse before some separation must take place.[41]

Pleased to see election petitions resolved 'fortunately ... to the advantage of the Protestants and the government', he mustered support against Burdett's motion for Catholic relief, which he denounced as trickery 'concocted by Canning', and rejoiced in its defeat, 6 Mar. 1827.[42] He presented anti-Catholic petitions, 2 Apr.[43] He had little confidence in Canning's corn bill, but he had advised Lonsdale against encouraging petitioning and he chose not to endorse the hostile ones he presented, 26 Feb.[44] He introduced several complaining of depressed trading conditions following the relaxation of the navigation laws, 23 Mar.[45] When inquiry into county polls was sought, 15 Mar., he said that he 'had had his share of contested elections' and refuted Lord Althorp's criticism of land tax based registration. His motion for printing membership lists of committees on private bills was carried without a division, 21 Mar.[46] After Liverpool's stroke, Lowther's preference was for a ministry headed by the duke of Wellington, with his schoolfellow Robert Peel as home secretary and leader of the Commons.[47] On Lonsdale's advice, he took 'no part whatever' in politics and stayed away from the House while confusion attended the appointment of the pro-Catholic Canning as premier. He was one of the 'shoals of underlings' who resigned with Peel when it was effected.[48] Mistrusting 'Whig men and ultra liberal measures', after talks involving Lord Lyndhurst, Beckett and the king, he turned down Canning's conditional offer to make him chief commissioner of woods and forests.[49] The clerk of the ordnance Sir Henry Hardinge* recalled in January 1828 that

> Lord Lowther is still more selfish [than Lord Hertford], but his father is no means so, and last year [1827], when Lowther was consulting with Canning, told him he might vote as he pleased, but the family strength should oppose Canning, if he L. accepted the woods and forests.[50]

To Lonsdale, 23, 24 Apr., Lowther predicted that the Canning ministry would be unstable, adding that there would be 'little opportunity of trying the division of parties' that session. He depicted the Commons as

> the strangest jumble and mixture of parties that ever assembled in one room. There will be: the actual government; the seceders opposed; the seceders supporting government; some late supporters of government who will not vote at all. There will be: Whigs supporting government; Whigs against the government and the Mountain against all government. How to calculate upon the relative numbers of these different bodies is quite impossible at this time.[51]

He moved the third reading of the Marylebone vestry bill, 22 May, voted against disfranchising Penryn, 28 May, and joined Lord Hertford's Members in opposing the Coventry magistracy bill, 11 June, to which he failed to add a rider limiting the concurrent jurisdiction of county magistrates in the borough during parliamentary elections, 18 June.[52] He presented an anti-Catholic petition from the deanery of Richmond, 7 June. He voted for the Canadian waterways grant, 12 June. He called in vain for the deferral of the East Retford disfranchisement bill, 22 June, but, by threatening a division, he precipitated the withdrawal on the 29th of Lord Nugent's voters' registration bill.[53] A difficult by-election for Carlisle, where his nominee the East India Company director James Law Lushington eventually prevailed, kept him away from London during the first flurry of negotiations following Canning's death in August.[54] The king advised Canning's successor Lord Goderich to appoint Lowther to woods and forests in order to secure the Lonsdale interest, but no cabinet place was offered and Lonsdale, who saw the king on 31 Aug., reiterated his preference for Wellington and Peel and refused to compromise.[55] Writing to his friend John Croker*, 14 Aug. 1827, Lowther, who was disappointed not to be offered a peerage in return for his support, rightly predicted that the ministry would be short-lived, as 'Goderich has not talent, nerve or audacity to conduct or regulate so large a machine'. He remained convinced that it would not be propped up by a middle party.[56]

Lonsdale cautiously welcomed the appointment of the Wellington ministry in January 1828, but Lowther warned of the impossibility of mixed government without Canning and strongly criticized the arrangement, especially the appointment of Goulburn as chancellor of the exchequer in preference to Herries. Having turned down the vice-presidency of the board of trade as incompatible with the representation of agricultural counties opposed to free trade, he was furious to be passed over in favour of Charles Arbuthnot* for woods and forests, and declined a place on the privy council.[57] As a member of the 1828 finance committee, he was, according to Philip Pusey*, 'the most active reformer'.[58] He took charge of the Scottish vagrants bill, 19 Feb., divided (as the cabinet had agreed) against repealing the Test Acts, 26 Feb., and by arrangement with ministers, he and his colleagues voted in defence of East Retford, 7 Mar.[59] Now unusually voluble in debate, in speeches and interventions (21 Feb., 3, 6, 11, 20, 25, 31 Mar., 15, 16 May) he admitted that better regulation of elections was desirable and conceded that there might be advantages in providing additional polling facilities, particularly in boroughs such as Carlisle, where safe conduct to the poll was an issue; but he vehemently opposed each of the five remedial bills introduced by the opposition that session and expressed his mistrust of voter registration and short polls and continued confidence in the land tax based system. He used similar arguments against the transfer of Penryn's seats to Manchester, 24 Mar. Despite his previous criticisms, on 27 June, as a member of the select committee, he successfully moved the third reading and was a teller for the borough polls bill, from which 'all the parts which I thought objectionable were removed'. He expressed himself wholly dissatisfied with the salmon fisheries bill that day and was a majority teller against it, 20 Mar. He presented protectionist petitions from the Cumberland lead miners, 1 Apr., and Kirkby Lonsdale wool producers, 13 May, and another that day for repeal of the Bank Restriction Act. He divided against Catholic relief, 12 May. The Canningite exodus later that month facilitated his appointment as chief commissioner of woods and forests.[60] He was re-elected with only token opposition.[61] He took charge of the Regent's Park and Charing Cross improvement bills, previously drafted for his department, carrying both that session.[62] Having declared that the corporate funds bill was flawed in principle, 1 July, he opposed it to the last by brief interventions and as a minority teller, 4, 10 July. He divided with his colleagues against ordnance reductions, 4 July, and against amending the duties on silk, 14 July 1828. As

George Agar Ellis* observed, Lowther was 'really interested' in his work and he continued to correspond with Goulburn and Wellington on departmental business during the recess, also briefing Peel on likely allies among the Middlesex vestry clerks and magistrates.[63] He proposed 'steering clear and unconnected' at the Cumberland by-election of January 1829, when the Whig Sir James Graham succeeded Curwen, and reluctantly acquiesced in the candidature of Sir William Scott* of Ancrum for the Carlisle seat thus vacated, on which Lonsdale refused to spend.[64]

By 15 Jan. 1829 the Lowthers knew through Holmes of the negotiations that fixed Wellington's determination to concede Catholic emancipation.[65] Lonsdale was belatedly briefed by the duke, and on 2 Feb. Peel saw Lowther and, according to Lord Ellenborough, found him 'quiet, but not favourable', and reluctant to 'take a different line from that which his family and himself had acted for so long, and on which their interest was supported'.[66] Lowther informed Lonsdale, who backed him throughout, that he had 'abstained from committing myself', but that, being determined to avoid 'any charge of inconsistency', he 'was not disposed to be dragged in to sanction the principle'. He surmised that 'no effectual opposition' could be made and by 9 Feb. had concluded that to support emancipation or to betray Wellington on other issues would amount to an unacceptable 'loss of all political character'.[67] Holmes and Croker, who saw him on 11 Feb., claimed that they were hard pressed to prevent his precipitate resignation.[68] In late February the patronage secretary Planta predicted that Lowther would go 'with government' for emancipation, and classified his relations as 'hostile' or 'doubtful'; but there was also speculation that he would join any new anti-Catholic ministry.[69] In the event the 'ninepins' voted together against emancipation, 6 Mar., and Lowther tendered his resignation with Beckett, the judge advocate, the next day.[70] He presented hostile petitions, 10 Mar., and voted against the relief bill, 18, 30 Mar., knowing that it had the king's approval notwithstanding ministers' unease at the duke of Cumberland's visits to Windsor.[71] Wellington, anxious not to irritate the king and to keep his supporters together, neither replied to Lowther's resignation letter nor replaced him, and amidst speculation over his future, and as to whether he was 'in', 'out', or 'sacked', he kept a low profile until the measure was enacted.[72] He commented briefly when required to on turnpikes, 27 Feb., 31 Mar., lighthouses, 3 Mar., county bridges, 25 Mar., public compensation, 18 Mar., 6 Apr. and the Clarence railway bill, of which he had charge, 19 Mar., 2 Apr. He was also forced to defend his decisions on Charing Cross, 7 Apr., and as a director of Greenwich Hospital, 9, 14 Apr. Wellington summoned him on the evening of 15 Apr. and by the 18th his reinstatement had been settled. No formalities were necessary, as his resignation had not been accepted by the king.[73] Holmes, Beckett and Lonsdale were among the first to congratulate him on his conduct.[74] Acting with the chairman of ways and means, Sir Alexander Grant, he promoted the 1829 Land Revenues Act and the Charing Cross Improvements Act, and fended off criticism of the Buckingham House improvements in committee, 12, 14, 19, 28 May.[75] John Nash's leases, the royal residences and the proposed road through Windsor Great Park remained difficult issues for his department, and decisions were increasingly referred to Wellington.[76] According to the duke's confidante Mrs. Arbuthnot, Lowther had been 'attacking Mr. Nash' but 'totally failed in his object of proving Mr. Nash to have been a cheat', 14 June.[77] In August he rallied behind the Ultra editors of the Lowther newspapers, which had served him so well at elections, and was criticized by Brougham and Michael Sadler* for doing so.[78] So furious was he with the prevarications of the Haslemere electors that by November 1829 he contemplated selling the borough.[79]

Lowther acknowledged the severity of the economic distress against which a Whig meeting in Cumberland petitioned in January 1830. Deeming the petitioners' plight to be well known and not easily remedied, he expected them to gain nothing thereby and he was irked by the fuss generated by the signature of a Lonsdale agent on the requisition, which Wellington asked him to explain.[80] He divided with his colleagues on the address, 4 Feb., but testified to the severity of the depression in their trade when the Cumberland lead workers' petitioned for protection, 16 Feb.[81] Departmental business proved difficult and Wellington now privately doubted his loyalty and ability.[82] However, he was committed to supporting government until the end of the session, and was annoyed and embarrassed by Lonsdale's decision to back Wetherell's motion for the production of *ex-officio* informations involving the *Morning Chronicle*, which government opposed, 2 Mar.[83] He made light of an opposition motion for inquiry into crown land revenues, 30 Mar.; but the Haymarket removal bill which he promoted (8, 15, 26 Mar., 2 Apr.) was powerfully opposed and referred to counsel before being passed, 7 Apr.[84] The approach road to Waterloo Bridge and proposed entrance to St. James's Park were quibbled over at Court and in Parliament, 6 May, 4 June.[85] He also had to answer regular complaints about the Charing Cross and Strand improvements and other matters relating to the metropolis, and the Dean Forest bill he tried to steer through the Commons was repeatedly deferred and timed out, 5 Apr., 13 May, 4, 11, 14, 18 June.[86] On 5 July he succeeded in confining the scope of a motion for returns on crown lands to 'existing papers'. He reaffirmed his mistrust of any measure of parliamentary reform, 11 Feb., divided against the enfranchisement of Birmingham, Leeds and Manchester, 23 Feb., and, as briefed by the duke of Newcastle's agents, spoke strongly against referring the Newark petition condemning his electoral interference there to a select committee, 1 Mar.[87] He divided against Jewish emancipation, 5 Apr., 17 May, and abolition of the death penalty for forgery, 7 June. He was bitterly opposed to the Northern Roads bill, which he regarded as a potential financial drain on government, 20, 28 May, 4, 7 June, and was a minority teller against its committal, 3 June. Knowing it would be overtaken by the dissolution following the king's death, he ordered returns with further opposition in mind, 8 July, and warned Wellington accordingly.[88] Rumours that he would stand for Cambridge University as an Ultra were soon discounted.[89] At the general election in August 1830 his return for Westmorland was made 'perfectly safe' by a compromise agreed to by his father and Brougham. However, the return of the radical Lord Radnor's son Philip Pleydell Bouverie for Cockermouth and of James Brougham for Radnor's borough of Downton caused comment and he had to act swiftly to quell opposition at Carlisle, Cockermouth, Cumberland and Haslemere, where he was pleased to return Holmes.[90]

Lowther was in the government's minority on the civil list when they were brought down, 15 Nov. 1830, and resigned with them, co-operating briefly with his successor Agar Ellis while his patent was authorized.[91] Though irked by the defections and apathy which had contributed to their defeat, he privately acknowledged that the 'commanding talent for the *times*' was 'nowhere to be found in the Tory ranks ... We are lamentably deficient in debaters, and that is perhaps the real reason for our failure'.[92] 'Half glad' to be out of office, he became a regular guest at Tory dinners where opposition policy and tactics were discussed, and considered the future representation of their constituencies with his father, who suggested transferring him to Cumberland.[93] He presented constituency petitions for the eradication of West Indian slavery, 13 Dec. He repudiated Hume's criticisms of the government of the Isle of Man and the management of the signet office, 21 Dec., and was a minority teller for printing Sir Harcourt Lees's petition against the oaths in Parliament bill, 23 Dec. 1830. Defending his former department and his own record, he had the commissioners' returns printed, 9 Feb., justified his decisions to create an entrance to St. James's Park from Waterloo Place, 15 Feb., and criticized changes to his proposals for the Forest of Dean, 11 Mar., and Waterloo Bridge New Street, 18 Apr. Anticipating a division 'of some moment' when the Grey ministry's reform bill was introduced and dissolution in the event of its defeat, 1 Mar., he summoned his Members and was disappointed when Peel failed to divide the House.[94] Denis Le Marchant†, believing that Lowther, 'a very adroit intriguer', had learnt on 28 Feb. of the boroughs to be disfranchised, which included Appleby and Haslemere in schedule A and Cockermouth in schedule B, held him personally responsible for failing to brief Peel adequately, but realized afterwards that this was not the case.[95] The Lowther newspapers now mounted strong attacks on the first lord of the admiralty Sir James Graham and the chancellor of the exchequer Althorp, and Lowther criticized the likely loss of revenue if legislation preventing tobacco cultivation in Ireland was carried, 10 Mar. Opposing the corporate funds bill at its second reading, 11 Mar., he protested that it imputed corruption to every borough and claimed that redress was already available through the court of chancery. He presented petitions against the timber duties, 17 Mar., and the general registry bill, 30 Mar., and another that day for the abolition of capital punishment for property offences. He acknowledged privately that his initial confidence that the Ultras would all join them in opposition was misplaced, and by 7 Mar. he doubted whether the reform bill could be defeated; contemplating compromise, he resented the cost of an additional and expensive election to carry reform.[96] He nevertheless voted against the bill at its second reading, 22 Mar., obtained detailed population returns for the places it enfranchised, 30 Mar., and divided for Gascoyne's wrecking amendment, 19 Apr. 1831. Amid great publicity the Lowthers were 'attacked everywhere' at the ensuing general election and forfeited seats for Westmorland and Carlisle to the Blues. Lacking a suitable candidate, Lowther stood for Cumberland himself, demanded a poll, when the show of hands was decidedly against him, and came a poor third behind the reformers Graham and William Blamire.[97] His claims that he was a moderate reformer were ridiculed and he was taken to task on the hustings for accommodating the turncoat Scarlett at Cockermouth and for the 'disgraceful' Westmorland compromise.[98] Lonsdale observed:

> Had you not come to a poll both you and your friends would have remained under a delusion, which is now dissipated. What has occurred under your own eyes, and

which indeed has pervaded the whole empire, shows how little the influence of property can resist popular clamour.[99]

He had his first success in the Derby in May 1831 with Spaniel.[100] Dependent on his brother and their friends to represent their constituency interests, he attended party meetings and encouraged opposition to test opinion and ministerial resolve by arranging for petitions to be sent up from Appleby, Westmorland's county town, requesting to be heard by counsel concerning its disfranchisement, 12 July. He canvassed for the anti-reformers at the October 1831 by-elections in Dorset and Cambridgeshire, and was regarded as a contender for cabinet office in the event of Lords Wharncliffe or Harrowby forming a ministry following the reform bill's defeat in the Lords.[101] Anxious to return to the Commons, he was suggested by Holmes for Ennis, defeated at Bandon Bridge, 22 July 1831, considered for Newark by Newcastle, whose offer he 'wisely declined', and eventually accommodated at Dunwich by Michael Barne* for £1,000 a year, 2 Feb. 1832.[102] He divided against the enfranchisement of Tower Hamlets, 28 Feb., and the third reading of the revised reform bill, 22 Mar., and voted against the Irish reform bill at its second reading, 25 May. He hoped in vain to see Wellington return to office that month, and was appointed to the committees established by the Conservatives to manage the English elections and a partisan press.[103] He divided against government on the Russian-Dutch loan, 12 July 1832.[104]

Lowther set out on a lengthy tour of France and Italy in September 1832, leaving his brother Henry in charge of the first post-reform elections in Cumberland and Westmorland.[105] After much wrangling he successfully contested Cumberland West and Westmorland *in absentia* and chose to sit for the latter, which he represented without interruption until summoned to the Lords in September 1841.[106] Unsuited for high office by his poor debating skills, he was a shrewd and cool political observer, who remained loyal to the Conservatives, filling places under Peel and Lord Derby, and regularly hosted party and business meetings at his Carlton Terrace residence, noted for its Louis XV style and 'profusion of fine old Sèvres china'.[107] After succeeding his father as earl of Lonsdale and to the county lord lieutenancies in 1844, he took pride in instigating land drainage schemes and patronising London and provincial opera, but he spent little time at Lowther Castle. He died at Carlton Terrace in March 1872, remembered for his wealth, love of the arts and electioneering, and as the inspiration for Lord Eskdale in Benjamin Disraeli's† novels *Coningsby* (1844) and *Tancred* (1847).[108] Despite his father's admonitions and testamentary provisions, Lowther, who acknowledged three illegitimate children by three opera singers, never married, and the main beneficiary of his will, proved on 28 Mar. 1872, was his nephew Henry Lowther (1818-76), Conservative Member for Cumberland West, 1847-1872, his successor in the earldom and Lonsdale estates. He provided £125,000 each for his daughter Frances Broadwood (*d.* 1890) and son Francis William (1841-1908), a naval captain.[109]

[1] *Heber Letters*, 196. [2] H. Owen, *Lowther Fam.* 395-6; J.R. McQuiston, 'The Lonsdale Connection and its Defender', *Northern Hist.* xi (1975), 143-97; *The Times*, 13 Sept. 1819. [3] *HP Commons, 1790-1820*, ii. 405-8; iv. 462-5; W.A. Hay, 'Henry Brougham and the 1818 Westmorland Election: A Study in Provincial Opinion and the Opening of Constituency Politics', *Albion*, xxxvi (2004), 28-51, and *The Whig Revival, 1808-1830*, pp. 67-87. [4] Owen, 393; Lonsdale mss, Lowther's diary, January 1820. [5] Clwyd RO, Lowther mss DD/L/178, J. Lowther to Lonsdale and replies, 26 Jan.-24 Mar.; Lonsdale mss, Lowther to Lonsdale and replies, Feb.-Apr., Ward to Lonsdale, 6, 23 Mar., Long to Lowther, 14, 20, 23 Mar., J. Lowther to same, 12 Feb.; *The Times*, 20-23, 25 Mar.; *Whitehaven Gazette*, 27 Mar. 1820. [6] Lowther mss DD/L/178, J. Lowther to Lowther [1820]. [7] Add. 40395, f. 221; St. Deiniol's Lib. Glynne-Gladstone mss 276, Huskisson to J. Gladstone, 10 Dec. 1826; 350, J. Gladstone's pprs. on the 1825 Liverpool-Manchester railway bill. [8] Lowther mss 178, J. Lowther to Lowther, 23, 27 Feb. 1821. [9] *The Times*, 12 Apr.; Lonsdale mss, Lowther to Lonsdale, 12 Apr. 1823. [10] Lonsdale mss, Lowther to Lonsdale, 21-28 Mar. 1825. [11] *The Times*, 2, 18 May, 12 July 1820. [12] Ibid. 17 July 1820. [13] *Croker Pprs.* i. 159; Lonsdale mss, Lowther's diary, 9, 16 Nov. 1820. [14] Lonsdale mss, Lowther to Lonsdale, 27 Jan. 1821. [15] Ibid. Lowther to Lonsdale, 27 Feb.; Brougham mss, Sir J. Graham to Brougham, 15 Mar.; *The Times*, 16 Mar., 4 Apr. 1821; *CJ*, lxxvi. 230. [16] *The Times*, 13, 18 Apr. 1821. [17] Ibid. 24 Feb., 13 Apr. 1820. [18] *Croker Pprs.* i. 194; Lonsdale mss, Lowther's diary, 16 Nov.-20 Dec. 1821; *Von Neumann Diary*, i. 89. [19] *The Times*, 12, 14 Feb. 1822. [20] *Geo. IV Letters*, ii. 1043. [21] Lonsdale mss, Lowther to Lonsdale, n.d. Oct., 12 Nov. 1822. [22] Ibid. same to same, 24 Jan.-9 Apr. 1823. [23] *The Times*, 12 Apr.; Lonsdale mss, Lowther to Lonsdale, 12 Apr. 1823. [24] Northumb. RO, Middleton mss ZM1/S/76/52/2, 3; *The Times*, 19, 25 Sept. 1826. [25] *The Times*, 23, 29 May 1823. [26] Lonsdale mss, Lowther to Lonsdale, 18 Nov., 8 Dec. 1823. [27] Ibid. same to same, 15 Jan., 11, 17 Feb. 1824. [28] *The Times*, 11, 26 Feb., 12, 16, 24, 31 Mar., 6, 15 Apr., 19 May 1824. [29] Ibid. 14 Apr. 1824. [30] Ibid. 14 Apr., 4 May 1824, 5 Mar. 1825. [31] Lonsdale mss, Lowther to Lonsdale, 21-28 Mar.; *The Times*, 29 Apr. 1825. [32] Lonsdale mss, A. Stewart to Lowther, 23 May, Lowther to Lonsdale, 12 July, 12, 14 Sept., 18 Oct., Lowther's diary, 2 July-18 Sept. 1825; Gwynedd Archives, Caernarfon XD/8/2/215; McQuiston, 160-2. [33] Lonsdale mss, Lowther to Lonsdale, 19, 24, 29 Sept., 12 Oct. 1825. [34] *Arbuthnot Jnl.* i. 414; *Hobhouse Diary*, 119; Lonsdale mss, Lowther's diary, 20 Sept.-2 Dec. 1825. [35] Lonsdale mss, Lowther's diary, 2 Dec. 1825-2 Jan. 1826; Lowther to Lonsdale, 12 Nov.-28 Dec. 1825. [36] Lonsdale mss, Lowther to Lonsdale, 9 Feb. 1826. [37] *The Times*, 15 Mar., 2 May 1826; *CJ*, lxxxi. 202, 252, 310, 391. [38] *The Times*, 23 Feb., 11 Mar., 20 Apr. 1826. [39] McQuiston, 162-6; R.S. Ferguson, *Cumb. and Westmld. MPs*, 245-50; *The Times*, 11 Apr., 1, 12, 20-23, 26, 30 June, 1, 13, 18 July 1826; *Baring Jnls.* i. 48. [40] Lonsdale mss, Lowther to Lonsdale, 1 Aug., 25 Oct., 27 Nov. 1826, 3, 7, 17 Jan. 1827. [41] Lonsdale mss, Lowther to Lonsdale, 5 Jan. 1827. [42] *Geo. IV Letters*, ii. 1289; Lonsdale mss, Lowther to Lonsdale, 7 Mar. 1827. [43] *The Times*, 3 Apr. 1827. [44] Lonsdale mss, Lowther to Lonsdale, 27

Nov. 1826; *The Times*, 27 Feb. 1827. [45] *The Times*, 24 Mar. 1827. [46] Ibid. 22 Mar. 1827. [47] N. Gash, *Secretary Peel*, 42, 430; *Geo. IV Letters*, ii. 1289. [48] Lonsdale mss, Lonsdale to Lowther, 25 Apr.; Nottingham Univ. Lib. Denison diary, 14 Apr. 1827. [49] Lonsdale mss, Lyndhurst to Beckett, n.d., Beckett to Lowther, 14 Apr., Canning to same, 4 May, Lonsdale to same, 13 May 1827; *Croker Pprs.* i. 372-4; Add. 48406, ff. 118, 121. [50] Durham CRO, Londonderry mss D/Lo/C83/25 (1). [51] Lonsdale mss. [52] *The Times*, 19 June 1827. [53] Ibid. 30 June 1827. [54] Lonsdale mss, Lowther to Lonsdale, 21 July-17 Aug. 1827; McQuiston, 168-73. [55] *Geo. IV Letters*, iii. 1381; Wellington mss WP1/895/15, 22, 25, 44; Add. 40394, f. 189; Lonsdale mss, Lonsdale to Lowther, 6 Sept. 1827. [56] *Croker Pprs.* i. 392-4; Grey mss, Ellice to Grey, 15 Aug.; Lonsdale mss, Lowther to Lonsdale, 7 Sept., 5, 10 Oct. 1827. [57] Wellington mss WP1/903/20; 915/21; *Geo. IV Letters*, iii. 1454; Lonsdale mss, Lowther to Lonsdale and replies, 10 Jan.-3 Feb. 1828; Buckingham, *Mems. Geo. IV*, ii. 363; Add. 38754, f. 215; *Ellenborough Diary*, i. 11. [58] Cent. Kent. Stud. Stanhope mss U1590 C335, Pusey to Mahon, 8 Apr. 1828. [59] Lonsdale mss, Lowther to Lonsdale [1828]. [60] Wellington mss WP1/933/11; 980/30; *Ellenborough Diary*, i. 125; *Arbuthnot Jnl.* ii. 189. [61] *Carlisle Jnl.* 7, 14, 21 June 1828. [62] *CJ*, lxxxiii. 418-19, 473, 481, 491, 504, 535, 544. [63] Wellington mss WP1/935/24; 951/65; 952/19; 953/15; 956/25; Add. 40397, f. 326; Northants. RO, Agar Ellis diary, 7 July 1828. [64] Lonsdale mss, Lowther to Lonsdale, 22 Dec.-4 Feb. 1829. [65] Ibid. Lowther's memo. 15-17 Jan. 1829. [66] Wellington mss WP1/994/28; 995/4; 1000/12, 13; Grey mss, Ellice to Grey, 6 Feb. 1829; N. Gash, *Secretary Peel*, 556; *Ellenborough Diary*, i. 333, 340. [67] Lonsdale mss, Lowther to Lonsdale, 3-7 Feb.; Grey mss, Howick jnl. 8 Feb. 1829. [68] *Croker Pprs.* ii. 7-11; Lonsdale mss, Lowther to Lonsdale, 11 Feb. 1829. [69] *Ellenborough Diary*, i. 365. [70] *Croker Pprs.* iii. 159; *Ellenborough Diary*, i. 382, 385; Wellington mss WP1/1002/8; Lonsdale mss, Lowther to Wellington, 9 Mar. 1829. [71] Lonsdale mss, Lowther to Lonsdale, 12-31 Mar. 1829. [72] Wellington mss WP1/996/18; *Arbuthnot Jnl.* 250-1; Howick jnl. 10 Mar.; Keele Univ. Lib. Sneyd mss, Ellis to Sneyd, 16 Mar., Lady Bathurst to same [19 Mar.]; Add. 76369, Althorp to Brougham, 18 Mar.; Lonsdale mss, Lowther to Lonsdale, 24 Mar.; Brougham mss, Lord J. Russell to Brougham, 25 Mar. 1829. [73] Wellington mss WP1/1011/9, 10; 1014/15, 16; Lonsdale mss, Lowther to Lonsdale, 16 Apr. 1829. [74] Lonsdale mss, Lonsdale to Lowther, 17, 19, 21 Apr., Holmes to same, 25 Apr., Beckett to same, 25 Apr. 1829. [75] *CJ*, lxxxiv. 365, 399, 416. [76] Wellington mss WP1/1036/31; 1039/28; 1042/21, 54, 62; 1100/18. [77] *Arbuthnot Jnl.* ii. 283. [78] Add. 51562, Brougham to Holland [14 Aug.]; Lonsdale mss, Sadler to Lowther, 22 Oct. 1829. [79] Lonsdale mss, Lowther to Lonsdale, 22 Sept., 2 Nov., 22 Dec. 1829, 11 Jan. 1830. [80] Ibid. bdle. for Cumb. meeting (1830), Lowther to Lonsdale, 18-28 Jan. 1830. [81] Ibid. Lowther to Lonsdale, 4, 6 Feb. 1830. [82] *Greville Mems.* i. 363-4; Lincs. AO, Ancaster mss 3Anc 9/2/20, Valletort to Heathcote, 9 Feb. 1830. [83] Lonsdale mss, Lowther to Lonsdale, 22 Feb., 1, 3 Mar. 1830. [84] Howick jnl. 30 Mar., 6 Apr. 1830; *CJ*, lxxxv. 151, 180, 184, 209-10, 253, 278, 355. [85] Wellington mss WP1/1102/3; 1122/46. [86] *CJ*, lxxxv. 548, 565, 569, 576, 579. [87] Notts Archives, Tallents mss, Clinton to Tallents, 23 Feb. 1830. [88] Wellington mss WP1/1139/1. [89] *Palmerston-Sulivan Letters*, 240. [90] Lonsdale mss, bdles. for 1830 election, Lowther to Lonsdale, 18 July-21 Sept.; Wilts. RO, Radnor mss 490/1374, Radnor's memo. 9 July; Nottingham Univ. Lib. Ne2 F3/1/248; *Carlisle Jnl.* 17, 24 July, 7, 14 Aug. 1830; McQuiston, 176-7. [91] Agar Ellis diary, 23, 27 Nov. 1830. [92] Lonsdale mss, Lowther to Lonsdale, 16, 17 Nov. 1830; *Three Diaries*, 2. [93] Add. 40340, f. 250; *Three Diaries*, 27, 37, 45, 47, 56-57, 63; Lonsdale mss, Lowther to Lonsdale, 22 Nov. 1830-24 Jan. 1831. [94] Lonsdale mss, Lowther to Lonsdale, 25 Feb., 2 Mar. 1831. [95] *Three Diaries*, 13; Le Marchant, *Althorp*, 297. [96] Lonsdale mss, Lowther to Lonsdale, 22 Nov. 1830, 7 Mar., 3, 4 Apr.; Grey mss, Ellice to Grey, 6 Apr. 1831. [97] Lonsdale mss, Lowther to Lonsdale, 28, 29 Apr.; Lowther mss, J.H. to J. Lowther, 28 Apr.; Sir James Graham mss (IHR microfilm XR 80),1, bdle. 5, Graham to Grey, 5 May; *The Times*, 28, 29 Apr., 11, 12, 14, 24 May; *Westmld. Advertiser*, 30 Apr., 7, 14 May 1831; *Three Diaries*, 7, 90; Northumb. RO, Hope-Wallace mss ZHW/2/12, 14, 15, *Greville Mems.* ii. 147. [98] *The Times*, 10 May 1831. [99] Lonsdale mss, Lonsdale to Lowther, 16 May 1831. [100] *Von Neumann Diary*, i. 124, 248. [101] NLW, Ormathwaite mss FG1/5, pp. 183, 240; Lonsdale mss, Lowther to Lonsdale, 11, 22 July, 29 Sept.-29 Oct.; Sheffield Archives, Wharncliffe mss, Harrowby to Wharncliffe, 22 Nov. 1831; *Macaulay Letters*, ii. 17, 143; *Three Diaries*, 93, 100, 177, 250; Wellington mss WP1/1199/13. [102] Add. 40402, f. 183; *Westmld. Advertiser*, 30 July, 20 Aug.; Tallents mss, Newcastle to Tallents, 2 Nov., 2 Dec.; Lonsdale mss, Lowther to Lonsdale, 13 Dec. 1831, 21 Jan.; Sneyd mss SC17/68; *Ipswich Jnl.* 18, 25 Feb. 1832. [103] Add. 57370, Arbuthnot to Herries, 11 June 1832; *Three Diaries*, 257, 266, 269. [104] *The Times*, 14 July 1832. [105] Lonsdale mss, H.C. Lowther to Benn, June-Dec. 1832. [106] Sir James Graham mss 2, bdle. 14, Graham to Rev. E. Stanley, 7 July, 21 Aug.; Brougham mss, Crackanthorpe to J. Brougham, 21 July, 11 Aug., 1 Dec., J. Brougham to Atkinson, 15, 21 Nov., 19 Dec.; Lonsdale mss, bdles. for 1832 election. [107] N. Gash, *Sir Robert Peel*, 458, 563; J.R. Vincent, *Disraeli, Derby and the Conservative Party*, 76; *Greville Mems.* iii. 104; v. 14; vi. 283; *Raikes Jnl.* ii. 353; iv. 198-9; *Von Neumann Diary*, ii. 145. [108] *The Times*, 6, 11, 13 Mar.; *Cumb. Pacquet*, 12 Mar. 1872; *Ann. Reg.* (1872), Chron. p. 145. [109] *The Times*, 6 Apr. 1872; Owen, 376-8, 391-2; *Oxford DNB*.

M.M.E.

LOYD, Samuel Jones (1796–1883), of 22 New Norfolk Street, Park Lane, Mdx.[1]

HYTHE 20 May 1819–1826

b. 25 Sept. 1796, o.s. of Lewis Loyd, banker, of 43 Lothbury, London and 1st w. Sarah, da. of John Jones, banker, of Manchester. *educ.* Kentish Town 1804; Chiswick (Rev. Thomas Horne) 1809; Eton 1809-13; Trinity Coll. Camb. 1814. *m.* 10 Aug. 1829, Harriet, da. of Ichabod Wright, banker, of Mapperley Hall, Notts., 1s. *d.v.p.* 1da. *cr.* Bar. Overstone 5 Mar. 1850; *suc.* fa. 1858. *d.* 17 Nov. 1883.

Sheriff, Warws. 1838-9.

Loyd was returned unopposed for Hythe in 1820, having established himself there on the 'independent' interest ten months earlier with the aid of the wealth provided by his family's flourishing banking business. He made no mark in the House, where he was a very infrequent attender, and neither side could rely on his consistent support.[2] He voted with opposition to establish parliamentary control over the droits of the crown, 5 May 1820, and against the exclusion of Queen Caroline's name from the liturgy, 26 Jan. 1821, but sided with the Liverpool government in defence of their general conduct towards her, 6 Feb. 1821. He voted for Catholic relief, 28 Feb. He was in the ministerial majority against cuts in expenditure, 6 Mar., but voted to reduce the army by 10,000 men, 14 Mar. 1821. On 17 May 1821 Loyd was granted six weeks' leave of absence, and a month later he embarked on a foreign tour which took him to France, Switzerland and Italy. From Berne he wrote to his mother, 31 July:

> Moralists and philosophers may argue as much as they like about the nature of happiness and the mode of obtaining it; but I know from experience that my path to happiness lies up the side of a mountain and that true felicity is always to be found at the summit.

More soberly, he reported to his father from Florence, 18 Oct. 1821:

> The Tuscans are perhaps at present in the enjoyment of the best possible government, an absolute monarchy administered by a mild and humane prince, who is really anxious to increase the happiness and prosperity of his subjects, and he is amply repaid by their devoted attachment.

Soon afterwards, news of his mother's illness (she had in fact died on 1 Oct. 1821) brought him prematurely home.[3]

Loyd resumed his desultory parliamentary career, voting with ministers against more extensive tax cuts, 11 Feb., abolition of one of the joint-postmasterships, 13 Mar. 1822, and the repeal of the Foreign Enlistment Act, 16 Apr. 1823, but against them in favour of inquiry into the prosecution of the Dublin Orange rioters, 22 Apr. 1823. He voted to end flogging in the army, 15 Mar., and he may have been the 'J.J. Lloyd' who was listed in the majority against Brougham's condemnation of the conviction of the Methodist missionary John Smith for exciting insurrection among the slaves in Demerara, 11 June 1824. (Eight years later he was publicly accused, on the strength of this evidence, of favouring slavery, but he strongly denied the charge.)[4] His only recorded votes in 1825 were for Catholic relief, 1 Mar., 10 May. The following year he was listed in minorities for taking securities for notes of issue, 27 Feb., against giving the president of the board of trade a ministerial salary, 10 Apr. (as 'S.G. Lloyd'), and (once more as 'J.J. Lloyd') for relaxation of the corn laws, 18 Apr. His friend William Prescott later wrote that 'notwithstanding his facility of expression' in private, Loyd 'was always averse to public speaking';[5] he is not known to have uttered a syllable in debate. He retired at the dissolution of 1826, possibly under pressure from his father, who seems to have regarded politics as a distraction from the essential business of increasing the family fortune.[6]

This Loyd, who became active in the firm in the early 1820s, helped him to do with outstanding success. In 1842, John Cam Hobhouse* visited the London bank and found 'these masters of millions ... in their little back room as hard at work as if they had their bread to gain by it'.[7] Two years later Loyd took over as head of the bank, which he sold in 1864. The family acquired several landed estates, notably Overstone in Northamptonshire and Lockinge in Berkshire, which at the time of Loyd's death were worth over £58,000 per annum, supplementing a personal fortune in excess of £2,000,000.[8] Loyd unsuccessfully contested Manchester in 1832 as a moderate reformer independent of party ties. He made no further attempts to re-enter the Commons, but rose to prominence as a leading authority on banking and finance, who exercised considerable influence on the fiscal policy of Victorian governments. His views, expressed in his evidence before select committees in 1832 and 1840 and in a series of pamphlets, did much to shape the Bank Charter Act of 1844, which he steadfastly defended thereafter. He had the ear of Charles Wood*, chancellor of the exchequer in the Russell administration (1846-52), which rewarded him with a peerage (only hesitatingly accepted). An infrequent speaker in the Lords, but active in committees, he later became a Conservative in politics.[9]

Prescott wrote of him in 1863:

> His characteristics, as a banker, in addition to his wealth, were his thorough comprehension of the principles of business and his consistent application of them to his own affairs ... He was perhaps too cautious to have *created* the business, but his judgement in managing the banks ... was unrivalled ... I have always regarded him as one of the most upright minded and honourable men I have ever known; scrupulous and sensitive even to a fault ... He is a first rate adviser both as a friend, and as a man of business, capable of taking rapid and clear views of any matter submitted to him. His ability in conversational discussion is remarkable. He is a close reasoner, quick in detecting and exposing the fallacy of an argument, ready to give the reasons for his own opinions, and capable of expressing himself with unusual clearness and vigour. Strictly just himself he is not tolerant of shift or subterfuge in others and from feeling his own strength he does not make much allowance for the weakness or the ignorance of an adversary.[10]

A widower for the last 19 years of his life, Loyd died in November 1883.

[1] See *The Correspondence of Lord Overstone* ed. D.P. O'Brien, 3 vols. (1971). [2] *Black Bk.* (1823), 172; *Session of Parl. 1825*, p. 474. [3] *Overstone Corresp.* i. 155, 166, 183, 187. [4] Ibid. i. 21. [5] Ibid. iii. 1025. [6] Ibid. i. 231. [7] Broughton, *Recollections*, vi. 53. [8] See *Overstone Corresp.* i. 17-47 and R.C. Michie, 'Income, expenditure and investment of a Victorian millionaire', *BIHR*, lxiii (1985), 59-77. [9] *Oxford DNB.* [10] *Overstone Corresp.* iii. 1024-5.

D.R.F.

LUCY, George (1789–1845), of Charlecote House, Warws.

FOWEY 1818–5 Mar. 1819
FOWEY 1820–1830

b. 8 June 1789, 1st s. of Rev. John Lucy (formerly Hammond) of Charlecote and Maria, da. of John Lane of Bentley Hall, Staffs. *educ.* Harrow 1804-5; Christ Church, Oxf. 1807; continental tour. *m.* 2 Dec. 1823, Mary Elizabeth, da. of Sir John Williams, 1st bt., of Bodelwyddan, Flints., 5s. (1 *d.v.p.*) 2da. *suc.* fa. 1823. *d.* 30 June 1845.

Maj. 3 Warws. militia 1808; cornet, Warws. yeoman cav. 1814.

Recorder, Fowey 1819-27.

Sheriff, Warws. 1831-2.

Lucy, the heir to a Warwickshire landed estate, had had an interest at Fowey purchased for him by his father in 1818, and 'never ... [knew] real peace of mind again'. He was returned at the general election that year but unseated on petition the following March. He subsequently agreed to share the representation with his rival Joseph Austen, and was returned in 1820 after a threatened opposition evaporated.[1] He was an occasional attender who gave general but silent support to Lord Liverpool's ministry. He divided against economies in revenue collection, 4 July 1820. That October he expressed to a friend his suspicion that the government regretted having initiated legal proceedings against Queen Caroline, for although 'every unbiased person must be clear of her guilt', the case against her had been 'so badly got up' that she was likely to 'escape'. Ministers should have been 'satisfied they were going on sure ground before making a trial'. He later wrote to Austen that the proposed allowance of £50,000 to the queen was 'too much' and that an opposition attempt to insert her name in the liturgy would 'try the strength of ... government', but he thought the outcome of the debate on 26 Jan. 1821 had helped to 'keep ... ministers in their places'.[2] He voted in defence of their conduct, 6 Feb. He divided against Catholic relief, 28 Feb. 1821. He voted against more extensive tax reductions, 21 Feb., but for abolition of one of the joint-postmasterships, 2 May 1822. He divided against removing Catholic peers' disabilities, 30 Apr., and inquiry into the lord advocate's conduct towards the Scottish press, 25 June 1822. In April 1823 he was named as the residuary legatee of his father's estate, which included personalty sworn under £18,000 and resworn under £20,000 in 1825.[3] He voted against the motion condemning the trial of the Methodist missionary John Smith in Demerara, 11 June, and for the Irish insurrection bill, 14 June 1824. That autumn he wrote to Austen that 'having seen what Parliament is ... I am grown indifferent about it and would prefer ... a pecuniary return to a seat'.[4] He divided for the Irish unlawful societies bill, 25 Feb., and against Catholic relief, 21 Apr., 10 May 1825. At the general election in 1826 he was returned for Fowey after a troublesome contest and survived a subsequent petition.[5] He voted against Catholic relief, 6 Mar. 1827, and repeal of the Test Acts, 26 Feb. 1828. He divided against extending the East Retford franchise to Bassetlaw freeholders, 21 Mar. 1828. He presented a Fowey petition for continuation of the export bounty on pilchards, 17 Feb. 1829. That month Planta, the Wellington ministry's patronage secretary, predicted that he would side 'with government' on Catholic emancipation, but in fact he voted against their bill, 6, 27, 30 Mar. He divided with the minority to transfer East Retford's seats to Birmingham, 5 May 1829, but was against the enfranchisement of Birmingham, Leeds and Manchester, 23 Feb. 1830. At the general election that summer it was reported that he had retired 'in consequence of family arrangements, which will necessarily occasion his absence from this country, which ... he does not consider to be compatible with his parliamentary duties'.[6]

In the summer of 1831 Lucy observed to his successor, John Severn, that there seemed little prospect of saving Fowey from the disfranchisement proposed by the Grey ministry's 'abominable' reform bill, which the Commons was certain to pass as the government would not 'dare to flinch' from the details 'as given out to the public'. He believed that if the Lords rejected the measure 'the people finding their hopes dashed ... may grow desperate and ... a revolution may be the consequence in six months', but added that 'they would never have thought of getting so much, and would have been contented with far less, if the ministers had not put it into their heads'. He feared that 'in the excited state of the country and under the influence of the innovating spirit of the time', there was 'little ... doubt' that the bill's passage 'must fast pave the way to a republican form of government'. When the bill was carried, he wrote to Austen:

> I suppose it will be impossible hereafter for idle men like myself to get seats in Parliament, and that none can enter Parliament who have not local interests in the places they sit for ... so that this greater diffusion of the elective franchise actually contracts the number of those out of which MPs can be chosen, and many interests, such as the East and West Indian, may have none in Parliament to watch over and protect them. The future governments ... of the country ... must be at the mercy of the fluctuating opinions of the people and mob law hereafter we must

submit to be governed by. How upon earth men in their senses could propose such a scheme, is to me perfectly incomprehensible.[7]

He devoted much of his retirement to the 'renovation and embellishment' of the 'fine Elizabethan mansion of Charlecote', on which he 'expended large sums' and which showed him to be 'a man of polished mind and refined taste'. He died in June 1845 and was succeeded in turn by his eldest son William Fulke Lucy (1824-48) and his second son Henry Spencer Lucy (1830-90).[8]

[1] A. Fairfax-Lucy, *Charlecote and the Lucys*, 252-3, 281; *West Briton*, 3, 10 Mar. 1820. [2] CUL, Buxton of Shadwell Court mss 117/69, Lucy to Buxton, 17 Oct.; Treffry mss (Aspinall transcripts), Lucy to Austen, 12 Dec. 1820, 27 Jan. 1821. [3] PROB 11/1669/222; IR26/964/327. [4] Treffry mss, Lucy to Austen, 1 Oct. 1824. [5] *West Briton*, 9, 30 June 1826. [6] Ibid. 30 July 1830. [7] Cornw. RO AD 275/17-18; Treffry mss, Lucy to Austen, 23 July 1832. [8] *Gent. Mag.* (1845), ii. 534-5; PROB 6/221/247; 11/2014/246.

T.A.J.

LUMLEY, John Savile (1788–1856), of 95 Park Street, Mdx.

NOTTINGHAMSHIRE	1826–1832
NOTTINGHAMSHIRE NORTH	1832–21 Feb. 1835

b. 18 July 1788, 2nd but o. surv. s. of Rev. John Lumley (later 7th earl of Scarbrough), preb. of York, and Anna Maria, da. of Julines Herring of Heybridge, Essex. *educ.* Eton 1805; St. John's, Camb. 1808; Trinity Hall, Camb. 1809. *unm.*; 5s. (1 *d.v.p.*) 1da. illegit. *styled* Visct. Lumley 17 June 1832-5; *suc.* fa. as 8th earl of Scarbrough 21 Feb. 1835 and took additional name of Savile. *d.* 29 Oct. 1856. Ld. lt. Notts. 1840-*d.*

This Member's paternal grandfather was the Rockinghamite Whig 4th earl of Scarbrough of Sandbeck Park, Yorkshire, who married the sister of the childless Sir George Savile† of Rufford, Nottinghamshire, a prominent independent country gentleman. On Scarbrough's death in 1782 his eldest son, a former Lincoln Member, became the 5th earl, while two years later, when Savile died, the Rufford estate descended to the second son, Richard, who had also once sat for Lincoln, as the next in line to the earldom, pursuant to Savile's will. In 1807 Richard succeeded as 6th earl and relinquished the entailed Savile estates to his next surviving brother, John, this Member's father, who changed his surname to Lumley Savile, as prescribed by his uncle's bequest.[1] The ramifications of this complex family arrangement lay behind the bitter, long-lasting quarrel between this Member, who was also sometimes referred to as 'John Lumley Savile', and his psychopathic father, 'Black Jack'. According to one report, the latter was

a most singular character and of the most peculiar habits, and very little intimacy existed between himself and his son; indeed, it is pretty well ascertained that it was through his father's violent conduct towards him, when a boy, that he was a cripple through life.[2]

It was only owing to the perseverance of his advisers that Lumley was allowed to go up to Cambridge, and even then his father initially baulked at the idea of granting him an allowance. Too impetuous for his own good, he jeopardized his hopes of parental approval by absenting himself, which may have been why he changed colleges, and, as one correspondent warned him, by 'idling away your time, as before'.[3] A keen sportsman, he was reproached for his appalling extravagance by his mother, who feared he would ruin himself and lectured him, 1 Feb. 1810, that

you cannot expect to support yourself on *any* income if you give way to that foolish and extravagant propensity of buying up every horse you happen to take a fancy to. I hear too with great concern that you gave 350 for a horse of Lord Monson's, nearly a fourth of your yearly income.

Distressed by the escalation of this family feud, which was exacerbated by her husband's intransigence and her son's negligence, she wrote to him, 14 Dec. 1811:

How it will end, God only knows; I dread any law proceedings on your account, for you are no match for your father *there*, as I am convinced he is laying by 1,000s every year to enable him to defray the expenses of a chancery suit, which he says must be the consequence of your withholding your signature from the deeds relating to settlements. I beg for heaven's sake that you will inform yourself most accurately upon this head.[4]

This state of affairs evidently continued throughout the 1810s, during which Lumley several times travelled abroad. Captain Gronow recollected seeing him in Paris in the winter of 1816, when he, 'notwithstanding his lameness, was one of the gayest of the gay'. Gronow also recorded that Madame de Staël, on being informed of Lumley's name, exclaimed, 'L'homme laid! Quelle drôle de nom! Mais c'est vrai. Il n'est pas joli garçon!'[5] Some years earlier he had formed a liaison with a married French woman, known simply as Agnes Lumley, with whom he had several children. Heavily indebted, he resented his father's parsimony and sought to resolve his monetary difficulties by raising capital on his reversionary interest in the Rufford estate. Following the failure of negotiations in the late 1810s, when his father offered to grant him £20,000, presumably in exchange for assurances that he would limit his future liabilities on their properties, the duke of Portland, acting as a family friend, attempted to reconcile their differences. In 1820 he requested the assistance of Lumley's maternal uncle, Lord Middleton, who, however, replied that 'knowing them both, I have every reason to apprehend any effort of mine would meet with very little encouragement from either side'.[6] Like his first cousin Frederick, Lumley, who early that year lodged £5,000 at a Nottingham bank, had parliamentary ambitions, and, notwithstanding his father's opposition, he made a bid for the county against the Tory sitting Member, Frank Sotheron, at the general election of 1820.[7] Although a stranger, he came forward on the strength of his family's landed interest and Whig politics. Yet, unprepared for a contest, he reluctantly withdrew, explaining to the electors that

> had I followed my own inclinations I should have proceeded to a poll ... Allow me to hope, in the interval which will elapse before another election occurs, you will keep in view the promotion of an interest for securing the independence of the county.[8]

His decision to pull out shortly before the election was probably owing to Middleton's intervention.[9]

In 1821, when there was a threat of imminent legal proceedings, Portland was unflagging in his efforts to resolve the deadlock, although his endeavours foundered on the vehement mutual recrimination of old grievances.[10] Lumley's father damned him for being unco-operative and dishonest, particularly in failing to abide by earlier agreements and in progressively raising his selfish financial claims, even after the entail had been barred, which was 'to *his unspeakable* benefit'. He informed Portland that he would increase his offer to his 'extravagant, undutiful son' to £27,000, but that he would be just as willing to turn the whole dispute over to the lord chancellor as to 'subject myself to the repeated unreasonable avaricious demands of an unworthy son, who has disturbed my peace for nearly the last 20 years'. Lumley also came under pressure from his mother, who was alarmed at the prospect of his losing Rufford to one of his scheming uncles, so endangering not only his own future, but that of her and her daughters. She pleaded with him not to continue 'under that fatal error of supposing you can do what you please with the estate', not least because 'in case your uncle Scarbrough should die before your father ... it would go to another remainder man, for a life, before it came to you'. In one of her clandestine letters to him, she confided: 'that your father is highly to blame in many instances of his conduct towards you, I am fully sensible and with real sorrow have I felt it ... but I must own, at the same time, that I think you also to blame'.[11] Although Portland, who himself put up a loan of £27,000 secured on the family estates, to cement the settlement, was thanked by Lumley for his unsuccessful mediation, 18 June 1821, he must ultimately have triumphed, since he was congratulated by his son Lord George Cavendish Bentinck*, 26 Dec. 1822, for having by then finally 'prevented the civil war threatened in Nottinghamshire'.[12]

Lumley, who joined Brooks's in February 1822, failed in his bid to persuade the Nottinghamshire grand jury to sign a requisition for a reform meeting in March 1823.[13] John Smith* informed Henry Brougham*, 19 Sept. 1825, that Lumley, who 'with some faults is at bottom a *most excellent man*', would offer for the county at the next opportunity, but would be unlikely to succeed in a contest.[14] He was, however, returned unopposed at the general election the following summer, a vacancy having been created by the resignation of Lord William Henry Cavendish Bentinck. On the hustings, he declared his belief that Members 'cannot be too strictly the representatives of the people', opposed agricultural protection by urging the admittance of foreign corn at a duty of 12*s*., and stated that he was a sworn advocate of religious toleration. The duke of Newcastle, who thought he cut a poor figure beside Sotheron, noted laconically in his diary that 'Lumley gave general offence', in that he 'did not even thank the electors and slunk away without giving them any refreshment'.[15] He divided for Catholic relief, 6 Mar. 1827. He voted against the duke of Clarence's annuity, 2 Mar., and to relax the corn laws, 9, 12 Mar. He divided for information on the mutiny at Barrackpoor, 22 Mar., and the committal of the spring guns bill, 23 Mar. He voted to condemn chancery administration, 5 Apr., and to separate bankruptcy jurisdiction from it, 22 May. He was in the minority against the Canadian canals grant, 12 June 1827.

Lumley divided for repeal of the Test Acts, 26 Feb. 1828. He defended the witness Jonathan Fox against the imputation of withholding evidence relating to election expenses at East Retford, 3, 4 Mar., and, following Fox's committal to Newgate, briefly moved for his immediate release, 6 Mar. On the 7th, when he proposed that Fox be admonished and discharged, he spoke and voted in the minority against finding another witness, William Leadbeater, guilty of perjury, and on the 10th he opposed a move to call Samuel Crompton* to answer questions about electoral bribery, 10 Mar. He divided for repealing the law which prohibited the use of ribbons in elections,

20 Mar. He voted to lower the pivot price of foreign corn, 22 Apr., and the duty on it, 29 Apr. He again divided against chancery administration, 24 Apr., and to rationalize the law relating to customs and excise prosecutions, 1 May. He presented constituency petitions for Catholic relief, 5, 9 May, and voted for this, 12 May. He announced that he might move a new writ for East Retford, 7 May, and justified extending its seats to the hundred of Bassetlaw, which he denied was under aristocratic domination, 19 May. He divided against the grant for the Society for the Propagation of the Gospels, 6 June, and to condemn the misapplication of public money on Buckingham House, 23 June. He voted for the Irish lessors bill, 12 June, and the usury bill, 19 June. He was in minorities for inquiry into the Irish church establishment, 24 June, and against the additional churches bill, 30 June. He missed the division on Calvert's proposal to exclude the corrupt voters of East Retford, 24 June, but was present to oppose the modified bill, which would only 'disfranchise some old men, many of whom are now dead', 27 June. Deprecating the endless East Retford debates, which had 'virtually disfranchised' the borough for almost two years, he censured the conduct of its leading protagonist, Tennyson, 27 June 1828.

He presented and endorsed the pro-Catholic petition from Newark, 10 Feb., and brought up another from Worksop, 9 Mar. 1829. He voted for emancipation, 6, 30 Mar., and proposed adjourning the long discussion on how to frame a new oath of allegiance, 23 Mar. On 10 Apr. he again urged the issuing of a new writ for East Retford, arguing that the continued suspension of its representation was unconstitutional and demanding that progress be made with the proposed legislation, in order that 'the borough should at once be pronounced either innocent or guilty'. He repeated these points, 5 May, 2 June 1829, when he was in the minority for moving the writ, and 11 Feb. 1830, when he voted against the transfer of East Retford's seats to Birmingham, but with Lord Howick against its bribery prevention bill. Lumley, who divided for Knatchbull's amendment to the address on distress, 4 Feb., was said by Howick to have 'made a fool of himself' in speaking in favour of ministerial attempts to suppress £1 bank notes and to make greater economies, 12 Feb.[16] Despite this ostensible declaration of support, he divided for tax reductions, 15 Feb., 25 Mar., and retrenchment, 26, 29, 30 Mar., 7, 11, 14 June. He voted for Lord Blandford's parliamentary reform motion, 18 Feb., and to refer the Newark petition complaining of Newcastle's electoral influence to a select committee, 1 Mar. He supported the Nottinghamshire petition complaining of distress, 23 Mar. He divided for Jewish emancipation, 17 May. He voted for reform of the divorce laws, 3 June, and paired for abolishing the death penalty for forgery, 7 June 1830.

Since John Evelyn Denison*, whose ambitions were opposed by Newcastle, did not persist in his candidacy, Lumley was again returned unopposed at the general election that summer, when he largely confined himself to the uncontroversial issue of tax reductions.[17] The Wellington ministry listed him among their 'foes' and he duly voted against them on the civil list, 15 Nov. He divided for reducing the duty on wheat imported to the West Indies, 12 Nov., and rejected calls for increased agricultural protection, 17 Dec. 1830, declaring that 'one of the principal causes of that distress is the high price labourers are paying for the necessaries of life', and criticizing the 'fallacy of the averages'. He attended the Nottinghamshire reform meeting, 17 Mar., and, declaring himself a moderate reformer, praised the resulting petition, which he presented, 28 Mar. 1831.[18] He brought up other favourable petitions from his county, 26 Feb., 15 Apr., and objected to the hostile one from Cambridge University, 22, 30 Mar. He voted for the second reading of the Grey ministry's reform bill, 22 Mar., and against Gascoyne's wrecking amendment, 19 Apr. 1831. At the ensuing general election, when he was apparently sent by Newcastle in a vain attempt to persuade Sotheron to stand again, he was returned unopposed with Denison as a supporter of reform, which he depicted not as 'a struggle whether Whig or Tory should have power and patronage', but as whether 'the country should be really and honestly represented'.[19] He divided for the second reading of the reintroduced reform bill, 6 July 1831, and generally for its details, though he voted against the disfranchisement of Downton, 21 July, and for the total disfranchisement of Saltash, which ministers allowed to retain one seat, 26 July. He divided against censuring the Irish government over the Dublin election, 23 Aug. He voted for the passage of the reform bill, 21 Sept., the second reading of the Scottish bill, 23 Sept., and Lord Ebrington's confidence motion, 10 Oct. He divided for the second reading of the revised reform bill, 17 Dec. 1831, again steadily for its details, and the third reading, 22 Mar. 1832. He voted for Ebrington's motion for an address calling on the king to appoint only ministers who would carry it unimpaired, 10 May, for the second reading of the Irish reform bill, 25 May, and against increasing the county representation of Scotland, 1 June. He defended the Nottingham magistrates from the imputation of having mistreated the reform rioters in their custody, 22 June. His only other known votes were with government against the production of information on Portugal, 9 Feb., and for the Russian-Dutch loan, 26 Jan., 12, 16, 20 July 1832.

His father, who succeeded as 7th earl of Scarbrough in June 1832, described himself as a 'staunch Whig', but angrily denied that he had any partisan electioneering influence.[20] His heir, now styled Viscount Lumley, was, as Lord Titchfield* put it, 'guilty of his usual indiscretion' in August over the candidacy of one of Portland's family.[21] He was, however, returned for Nottinghamshire North as a Liberal after a contest at the general election of 1832, and sat until inheriting the peerage in February 1835. Of the late earl, who was killed in a fall from his horse, Newcastle commented that 'there never was a more odious or more detested character. Poor man, he was truly unfit to appear suddenly before his maker, but his death, awful as it is, must be a blessing to all those who had anything to do with him'.[22] Lumley, who died in October 1856, successfully established in law his right to hold both the Sandbeck and Rufford estates, which had previously been held by peer and heir respectively. The former passed, with the earldom, to his kinsman, Richard George Lumley (1813-84), but the latter was bequeathed to his illegitimate sons and eventually finished in the hands of the eldest surviving of them, John Savile Lumley (1818-96), a diplomat, who took the name of Savile only in 1887 and was created Baron Savile in 1888.[23]

[1] T. Bailey, *Notts.* 4. [2] *Nottingham Jnl.* 14 Nov. 1856. [3] Notts. Archives, Savile mss DD/SR/221/83, White to Lumley, 21 July 1808, Dixon to same, n.d. [4] Ibid. 221/83. [5] *Gronow Reminiscences*, i. 327. [6] Savile mss 221/69/4, 9; Nottingham Univ. Lib. Portland mss PwH 1172, 2636, 2638. [7] Wentworth Woodhouse mun. F49/69, 71; Nottingham Univ. Lib. Newcastle mss NeC 6275. [8] *Nottingham Rev.* 10, 17, 21 Mar.; *Nottingham Jnl.* 11 Mar. 1820. [9] Newcastle mss NeC 6277. [10] Portland mss PwH 2634-56. [11] Ibid. 2643, 2647; Savile mss 221/69/2, 20; 221/83, A.M. to J. Lumley, 19 Mar., 3 Apr. [?1821]. [12] Portland mss PwH 125, 2651, 2657. [13] *Unhappy Reactionary* ed. R.A. Gaunt (Thoroton Soc. rec. ser. xliii), 42. [14] Brougham mss. [15] *Nottingham Rev.* 2, 16 June; Glos. RO, Sotheron Estcourt mss F789, Newcastle to Sotheron, 17 June 1826; *Unhappy Reactionary*, 52. [16] Grey mss, Howick jnl. [17] Newcastle mss NeC 7561-2; Nottingham Univ. Lib. acc. 636, Denison diary, 26 June; *Nottingham Jnl.* 31 July; *Nottingham and Newark Mercury*, 7 Aug. 1830. [18] *Nottingham Rev.* 18 Mar. 1831. [19] *Unhappy Reactionary*, 78; *Nottingham Jnl.* 7 May; *Lincoln and Newark Times*, 11 May 1831. [20] Notts. Archives, Thoroton Soc. mss DD/TS/6/2/13. [21] Portland mss PwH 359. [22] *Unhappy Reactionary*, 104. [23] *Retford Advertiser*, 4 Nov.; *Notts. Guardian*, 6 Nov. 1856; *Gent. Mag.* (1856), ii. 770-1; *CP*, xi. 461-2, 514; *Oxford DNB sub* John Savile, 1st Bar. Savile.

S.R.H./S.M.F.

LUSHINGTON, James Law (1780–1859), of 14 Portman Square, Mdx.

PETERSFIELD	2 Apr. 1825–1826
HASTINGS	15 Dec. 1826–12 Apr. 1827
CARLISLE	16 Aug. 1827–1831

bap. 24 July 1780, 3rd. s. of Rev. James Stephen Lushington (*d.* 1801) of Rodmersham, Kent, vic. of Newcastle-upon-Tyne and preb. of Carlisle, and 2nd w. Mary, da. of Rev. Humphrey Christian of Docking, Norf.; bro. of Stephen Rumbold Lushington*. *educ.* ?Durham.[1] *m.* 1836, Rosetta Sophia Costen, *s.p.* CB 17 Oct. 1818; KCB 10 Mar. 1837; KGCB 20 July 1838. *d.* 29 May 1859.

Cadet, E.I. Co. (Madras) 1796, ensign 1797; lt. 4 cav. batt. 1799, adj. 1800, capt. 1804, maj. 1812, lt.-col. 1819; col. 1829; maj.-gen. 1837; lt.-gen. 1849; gen. 1854.

Dir. E.I. Co. 1827-54, dep. chairman 1837-8, 1841-2, 1847-8, chairman 1838-9, 1842-3, 1848-9.

Lushington, the younger son of a clergyman with strong East India Company connections, entered their army in 1796 and was sent as an infantryman to Madras, where his elder brother Stephen was private secretary to the commander-in-chief. He transferred to the cavalry on his arrival in 1797 and served at Malavilly and the siege of Seringapatam during the Mysore war, becoming a brigade major under the future duke of Wellington, 1800-02. After an extended leave in England, he commanded a troop against Bungurb Bawn in 1807 and was suspended, 1810-13, for alleged misconduct at the battle of Travancore (1809). Later he served with distinction under Sir Thomas Hislop against the Marathas and was made a commander of the Bath for his part in leading the relief charge at the Battle of Maheidpoor in December 1817.[2] In October 1824 he left India, intending to promote the Company's interests in Parliament in order to become one of its directors, and he was returned for Petersfield in April 1825 as the paying guest of the Jolliffes, through Stephen's influence as the Liverpool ministry's patronage secretary.

Lushington accepted his brother's political leadership and confined his few reported remarks to East Indian matters. He divided against Catholic relief, 21 Apr., 10 May, the attendant Irish franchise bill, 26 Apr. 1825, and parliamentary reform, 13 Apr., 26 May 1826. He voted for the duke of Clarence's award, 30 May, 2, 10 June, and defended the conduct of Wellington and Charles Arbuthnot* as trustees of the Deccan Prize money, 1, 5 July 1825.[3] He voted to receive the report on the president of the board of trade's salary, 10 Apr., and was one of ten ministerialists added to the select committee on James Silk Buckingham's† petition on freedom of the press in India, 11 May 1826. He was left without a seat at the general election in June, but was returned for Hastings as a treasury nominee in December 1826. He voted against Catholic relief, 6 Mar., and to consider the spring guns bill, 23 Mar. 1827, before making way in April for Joseph Planta, his brother's replacement as patronage secretary in Canning's administration.

Lushington defeated Sir William Young by 798 votes to 694 in a 'sharp' contest for a place on the direction of the East India Company, 25 July 1827.[4] Next month he won a closely fought by-election at Carlisle, where the Tory whip William Holmes* had negotiated his candidature on the Lonsdale interest for £2,000 down and up to £2,000 in costs.[5] He was described as 'about 45 years of age, of very prepossessing exterior, firmness, sincerity and good humour', a Tory Protestant and experienced parliamentarian, and caricatured as an 'Indian juggler' and a stranger.[6] On the hustings he promised to promote commercial interests and oppose Catholic relief and maintained (but it could not be proved) that he had voted with Canning to relax restrictions on corn imports.[7] He divided with the Wellington ministry against repeal of the Test Acts, 26 Feb., Catholic relief, 12 May, the corporate funds bill, 10 July, and amending the duties on silk, 14 July 1828. Planta, as their patronage secretary, predicted that he would vote 'with government' for Catholic emancipation in 1829, but he divided against it with the Lowthers, 6, 18, 30 Mar. On 6 May, in his only reported speech that session, he defended his brother's decision to go to Madras as governor without resigning his Canterbury seat (the target of an opposition motion by Alexander Baring) and affirmed that he was prepared to stand down should a majority of his constituents or the House so wish. He voted against transferring East Retford's seats to Birmingham, 11 Feb., Lord Blandford's reform proposals, 18 Feb., the enfranchisement of Birmingham, Leeds and Manchester, 23 Feb., and Jewish emancipation, 17 May 1830. He voted for the grant for South American missions, 7 June, and against abolishing the death penalty for forgery the same day. Deliberately targeted on account of his prominence in the East India Company, whose trading monopoly he was keen to preserve in a new charter, he had to canvass assiduously in Carlisle and among the out-voters to secure re-election at the general election in August 1830.[8] Ministers counted him among their 'friends' and he divided with them on the civil list when they were brought down, 15 Nov. 1830. He heeded the Lowthers' request to vote against the Grey ministry's reform bill at its second reading, 22 Mar., presented and 'fully endorsed' three hostile petitions from guilds of Carlisle, and protested at the proposed disfranchisement of resident hereditary freemen, 29 Mar. He divided for Gascoyne's wrecking amendment, 19 Apr. 1831.[9] His prospects at the ensuing general election were blighted by illness and the popularity of reform. His retirement at Carlisle after a one-day poll was tactical and calculated to void the reformers' election on petition for voter intimidation. Though presented, his supporters' petition was not proceeded with.[10] A squib writer claimed that he had desisted to avoid provoking government resentment which could jeopardize the Company's charter negotiations.[11]

Lushington did not stand for Parliament again. He remained a director of the Company until 1854, serving as deputy chairman and chairman. Although initially hostile, he accepted the Company's 1833 charter vesting power in the crown, in preference to paralyzing business by repeatedly opposing it.[12] He died without issue at his London home in Dorset Square in May 1859, remembered for his service to the Company and as founder of the Addiscombe scholarship at Cheltenham College.[13] By his will, dated 9 July 1849 and proved in London, 6 July 1859, he left everything to his wife (*d.* 1867) for life, with reversion to his nephew Charles Hugh Lushington (1813-74) of the Bengal Civil Service.

[1] According to Carlisle supporters. Though not listed, it seems likelier that he was educated at Rugby like his brothers Stephen Rumbold and William John Lushington. [2] BL OIOC L/Mil//11/38, f. 133; E.I. Co. ct. minutes 1811-12, pp. 876, 1381; 1812-13, pp. 179, 603, 665, 987. [3] *The Times*, 6 July 1825. [4] Cent. Kent. Stud. Harris mss U627 C264. [5] Lonsdale mss, Lowther to Lonsdale, 28, 31 July, 6 Aug.; NLW, Powis mss (History of Parliament Aspinall transcripts), Holmes to Powis, 31 July; *Carlisle Jnl.* 4, 18 Aug. 1827. [6] Reading Univ. Archives Printing coll. (Folio 324.4285 SQU), Carlisle Elections, ff. 49, 58, 64; J.R. McQuiston, 'The Lonsdale Connection and its Defender', *Northern Hist.* xi (1975), 170-1. [7] *Carlisle Jnl.* 11 Aug. 1830. [8] Lonsdale mss, Lowther to Lonsdale, 22, 24 July; *Carlisle Jnl.* 31 July 1830. [9] Lonsdale mss, Lowther to Lonsdale, 25 Feb. 1831. [10] *Carlisle Jnl.* 30 Apr., 7 May 1831. [11] Carlisle Elections, f. 210. [12] C.H. Philips, *E.I. Co.* 284, 286. [13] *Gent. Mag.* (1859), ii. 91; *Oxford DNB sub* S.R. Lushington.

M.M.E.

LUSHINGTON, Stephen (1782–1873), of Meryhill, nr. Watford, Herts. and 2 Great George Street, Mdx.

GREAT YARMOUTH	1806–20 June 1808
ILCHESTER	1820–1826
TREGONY	1826–1830
WINCHELSEA	4 Apr. 1831–1831
ILCHESTER	1831–1832
TOWER HAMLETS	1832–1841

b. 14 Jan. 1782, 2nd surv. s. of Stephen Lushington† (*d.* 1807) of South Hill Park, Berks. and Hester, da. of John Boldero, banker, of Aspenden Hall, Herts. *educ.* Eton 1789; Christ Church, Oxf. 1797, BA 1802, fellow, All Souls 1802-21, MA 1806, BCL 1807, DCL 1808; L. Inn 1801; I. Temple 1801, called 1806. *m.* 8 Aug. 1821, Sarah Grace, da. of Thomas William Carr of Frognal, Mdx., 5s. (1 *d.v.p.*) 5da. *d.* 19 Jan. 1873.

Adv. Doctors' Commons 3 Nov. 1808; charity commr. 1818-34; commr. for building new churches 1825; chanc. dioc. of Rochester 1826-56, dioc. of London, judge of consistory ct. 1828-58; judge of ct. of admiralty 1838-67; PC 5 Nov. 1838 (member of jud. cttee.); bencher, I. Temple 1840, reader 1850, treas. 1851; dean of the arches 1858-67.

Capt. Blickling and Gunton vols. 1803.

Lushington, the younger son of an East India Company chairman,[1] began his parliamentary career at the age of 24, but it ended abruptly after less than two years as his determinedly independent course alienated his patron, Lord Suffield, who obliged him to vacate his Great Yarmouth seat for a ministerialist. He concentrated on building a reputation as a civil and ecclesiastical lawyer and rose to prominence in 1816, when he acted with Henry Brougham* for Lady Byron in her separation case.[2] He maintained his interest in various aspects of reform politics, campaigning from 1813 for the abolition of the death penalty, joining the committee of the Prison Discipline Society in 1816 and urging the importance of county meetings to denounce the Peterloo massacre.[3] Identified by the Whig leadership as a talented man worth bringing back into Parliament, he informed George Tierney* in January 1820 that his desire to return had 'been in great measure subdued', as he doubted his ability to adapt to the Commons after so long an absence; it therefore seemed 'not worth a pecuniary sacrifice'. His reluctance was overcome and at the 1820 general election he was returned for Ilchester, after a contest, on Lord Darlington's interest. Brougham, another of Darlington's clients, who may well have been instrumental in arranging the seat for Lushington, declared that he was 'a host in himself' besides all the other Whig gains.[4]

He quickly emerged as an active figure in the opposition to Lord Liverpool's ministry on all major issues, including parliamentary reform, 18 Apr., 31 May 1821, 25 Apr., 24 June 1822, 20 Feb., 2 June 1823, 13, 27 Apr., 26 May 1826. He voted for Catholic relief, 28 Feb. 1821, 1 Mar., 21 Apr., 10 May 1825. He regularly served on select committees. He criticized the admiralty for issuing instructions to naval commanders which had resulted in the country being 'burthened with an enormous sum of money to be paid' in compensation to Portuguese vessels arrested by British warships for engaging in the slave trade, 16 June 1820. That day he supported the grant for the refuge for the destitute, which had 'saved the country a very considerable sum' by dealing with juvenile delinquents who would otherwise have 'spread vice and crime'. He 'reluctantly' supported the financial assistance given to Irish country banks, 16 June, as the distress there was so bad that he feared 'the most dreadful results might occur' if nothing was done. He moved to recommit the Marriage Act amendment bill and was a minority teller, 30 June. He called for papers regarding the alleged negotiation between France and Buenos Aires for the establishment of a Bourbon dynasty in South America, 11 July 1820, declaring that Britain was 'imperiously called upon to acknowledge the independence of the states of South America' and warning of the lost commercial opportunities that would occur if 'a more ambitious rival' was allowed to move in first; the motion was withdrawn.

During the latter part of the 1820 session he became a central figure in the Queen Caroline affair. He urged that the coronation be delayed, 3 July, as it was not constitutionally necessary, would be 'improper' while the queen was unable to attend and would 'rouse ... the feelings of the people'. Observing the military preparations being made to suppress disorder, he believed that 'whatever excesses the people might commit they had been driven to' by the government's 'arrogant and oppressive conduct' and 'contempt of public feeling'. He was granted leave to act as counsel for the queen before the bar of the Lords, 12 July.[5] In the absence of her solicitor-general, Thomas Denman*, he moved an address to the king requesting the return of her service of plate, 15 July, and complained of 'the numberless insults ... and indignities that had been heaped on Her Majesty'. The motion was postponed until 17 July, when it was negatived after he had denied that he was trying to 'inflame the passions of the people'. A Grenvillite Member heard that he 'got a most handsome and proper dressing' from Lord Castlereagh, the leader of the Commons.[6] He was disinclined to take notice of the 'atrocious paragraph' about the queen in *Flindell's Western Luminary*, 25 July, but blamed ministers for creating a climate of opinion in which such calumnies could be published. According to a civilian rival, writing in August

> Lushington ... now very much presides over the councils of Her Majesty ... in many respects he is well calculated to please her, for he is good-natured and obliging in his demeanour, rash in his advice, and a lover to excess of popular applause. He is everywhere with her now: airs with her, assists her in receiving addresses, etc.[7]

While the Lords' proceedings on the bill of pains and penalties were under way, Lushington privately expressed the view that it would be passed 'whatever may be the evidence produced for the queen', as 'ministers ... think they have their places at stake'. However, he believed it could be stopped by systematic obstruction in the Commons: 'if only a few Members will cordially unite, it is impossible this bill can pass ... it must be a most determined union ... very few would be sufficient to move adjournment upon adjournment, amendment upon amendment, and to divide the House unceasingly until ministers have wearied out'.[8] In fact, his largely forensic speech to the peers in his capacity as third counsel to the queen, 26 Oct. 1820, made an important contribution to the defence team's success in stalling the proceedings there. Brougham, the queen's principal law officer, reported that a powerful oration by Denman had

> made Lushington's task to follow very difficult. But I was obliged to make him do so, because Denman had made one or two great omissions. Lushington's was a most admirable speech and has had a great effect. The style was chaste and there were no false ornaments ... His great merit was the wonderful originality of his remarks on so trite a matter, after three speeches. He adhered strictly to directions and even passed from some half dozen topics, changed others as he went on, under my hand. He once kicked when I forced him to leave a point handled to a turn by Denman ... but I brought him to, and he left it.

All three counsellors were subsequently given the freedom of the City of London.[9] Lushington was active on the queen's behalf during the 1821 session, when he effectively assumed the role of her chief legal advisor. In presenting an Ilchester petition to restore her name to the liturgy, 24 Jan., he warned that Parliament must attend to the wishes of the people 'before the day came ... when a reform would be most hastily resorted to'. He denounced the refusal of the sheriff of Kent to summon a county meeting for similar petitioning purposes, 8 Feb. He presented petitions in support of the queen from King's Lynn and ten Anglican churchmen, 13 Feb., and observed that if the crown was to be allowed to alter the form of divine worship, 'who could tell whether [just as James II tried to restore Popery] some future king, in his latter days, having spent his youth in profligacy and debauchery, might not be wheedled and deluded by that class of religious enthusiasts called Methodists' into introducing dangerous new doctrines. On the vote for the expenses of the Milan commission, 19 Mar., he stated that it would be impossible for the queen to furnish details of all the expenditure she had incurred, adding that 'some of the items it might be unfit to submit to the public'.[10] He was present when the queen died, 7 Aug. 1821, was named as an executor of her will and made the arrangements with ministers for the funeral procession, accompanying the body to Brunswick.[11]

He criticized the mode of voting for the employment of seamen before the estimates had been submitted, 2 Feb., unsuccessfully moved to reduce the grant for the judge advocate general and his subordinates, 11 Apr., and disapproved of the sums expended in presents to foreign ambassadors on the occasion of the king's accession, 28 May 1821.[12] He was a minority teller against the third reading of the Irish revenue inquiry bill, 26 June. He moved that Thomas Ellis, Member for Dublin, could not adequately discharge his parliamentary duties and act as an Irish master in chancery, 5 Mar., and on being opposed by ministers he reportedly 'made a very bitter reply and said many things of Mr. Ellis that went near the wind, to say the least';[13] his motion was defeated by 112-52. On 27 Mar. he introduced a bill to exclude all higher Irish judicial officers from sitting in Parliament in future, which gained royal assent, 28 May (1 & 2 Geo. IV, c. 44).[14] He described the Newington vestry bill as 'one of the most objectionable ever introduced into that House', 5 Mar., as it gave arbitrary powers of patronage, taxation and punishment.[15] He persuaded Stuart Wortley to withdraw his motion condemning the *Morning Chronicle* for breach of privilege in publishing a minority division list, 9 Mar.[16] He was a steward of the *London Tavern* reform dinner, 4 Apr., when he delivered what the radical Whig Henry Grey Bennet* considered to be 'the most violent' of the speeches, arguing that reform was 'the all important question', for 'if it failed, every popular measure failed'.[17] He presented a petition for inquiry into Peterloo, while doubting that anything would be done, 15 May.[18] He made what Grey Bennet thought 'a very good speech' in presenting a petition from Thomas Dolby, a Strand bookseller, complaining of persecution by the Constitutional Association,

6 June.[19] He reportedly made 'a violent speech' in support of a petition against the Association's activities, 3 July, but his incidental 'abuse of the Society for the Suppression of Vice called up Wilberforce, who made an able and vigorous defence ... and was very bitter against Lushington, saying more than once "he ought to be ashamed of himself"'.[20] He supported the motion that day to stop all indictments brought against individuals by the Association, which caused 'nothing but dissension and ill will'. He thought the magistrates at Ilchester 'would come purified' out of an inquiry, 11 Apr., but was inclined to 'suspend opinion' about the gaoler's conduct. He supported Mackintosh's forgery punishment mitigation bill, 23 May, believing that 'the punishment of death did not ... produce that salutary terror which some individuals supposed' and that it encouraged perjury by juries, which 'acquitted prisoners of capital charges, rather than subject them to the severity of the law'; he was a majority teller. He suggested that the punishment for forgery 'ought never to be less than confinement to hard labour for ten years', with no discretionary power to the judge, 25 May; Mackintosh adopted this as an amendment, which was agreed to. Lushington was a majority teller for the third reading, 4 June, and a minority teller against the subsequent amendment to exclude cases involving banknotes. He was infuriated when ministers engineered the bill's defeat on the motion that it should pass, and he reportedly threatened that 'he would come into no arrangement to facilitate business, on the contrary ... he would throw all impediments in the way to punish the government for the base manoeuvre they had practised'.[21] He supported the Newfoundland petition for reform of its courts of justice, 28 May. He complained of the ineffectiveness of the London police forces, 29 June, and of 'the great mischief done ... by the fairs in and about the metropolis', which were 'nurseries of vice'. He warned that if the government did not act in the next session to abolish them, he would bring in his own bill.[22] He supported a Manchester chamber of commerce petition against an additional duty on East Indian sugar to protect West Indian growers, 4 May, maintaining that the system of slavery 'must ever be productive of human misery'. He supported Wilberforce's motion for government action to put pressure on other countries to end the slave trade, 26 June. That day he described Robert Owen's plan for a colony at New Lanark as 'the most visionary and the most impracticable he had ever met with'. He opposed the extra post bill, 29 June, as it gave unfair preference to certain places and travelling at 11 miles per hour would lead to accidents; he was a minority teller.[23] He approved of Scarlett's decision to withdraw his poor relief bill, 2 July, when he argued that 'the effect of the present laws was to oblige the industrious and prudent to support the improvident and thoughtless'; emigration was the only solution. He noted that the Peace Preservation Act was in force in 14 Irish counties and regretted that during the session no time had been found to inquire into the state of that country, 3 July 1821.[24] He was present in December at a poorly attended meeting at the *Freemasons' Tavern* to organize a public meeting in support of the Greeks.[25]

He denounced the 'obnoxious' Irish insurrection bill, 8 Feb. 1822, arguing that outrages would be better dealt with by the 'prompt interposition' of special commissions, which would 'vindicate the power of the law by the immediate conviction of its transgressors', and calling for a 'searching investigation' of the underlying causes of the disturbances. He introduced a slave trade laws consolidation bill, 12 Feb., explaining that the existing statutes were 'much at variance' with each other and created problems for legal tribunals in the colonies and for naval officers, but that no change was proposed to the principle behind them; it was put off at the report stage, 27 June. He condemned Portugal for failing to fulfil its obligations to stop the trade under a treaty of 1815 and demanded effective measures to prevent 'such foul enormities', 27 June.[26] He briefly stated his recollections of the tumultuous events surrounding Queen Caroline's funeral procession, in support of Sir Robert Wilson's motion regarding his removal from the army, 13 Feb., and supported the motion complaining of the subsequent assault by troops on Alderman Robert Waithman*, 28 Feb. On Bennet's motion concerning the funeral arrangements, 6 Mar., he gave a long account of his own involvement in negotiations with the authorities and agreed that the preparations had been inadequate: 'too much had been left to chance ... proper respect had not been paid and the feelings of the country had been grossly outraged'. He expressed regret that no pensions had been given to those holding high offices in the queen's service, 12 July.[27] He presented an Ilchester petition for relief of the restrictions imposed on the radical Henry Hunt*, a prisoner there, 4 Mar., and advised that the local magistrates should draw up new regulations.[28] He supported a petition from Essex grand jury for the speedier administration of justice, 27 Mar., hoped that Parliament would consent to appoint more judges if necessary and opined that their salaries 'were not sufficient to support the dignity of the office'. He moved a successful amendment to the prison laws consolidation bill to allow every prisoner under sentence of death to receive spiritual ministration from a Dissenting minister, 21 June.[29] He initially supported the Marriage Act amendment bill, as the grievances arising from the current law were 'so numerous and so glaring', 20 May, but he condemned the Lords' amendments, which rendered parts of the bill 'wholly unintelligible' and would produce a 'train of evils', 12 July; he moved a hostile amendment and was a minority teller. In response to a London ship owners' petition complaining of the piracy resulting from Spain's war with its South American colonies, he renewed his demand for British recognition of their independence, 30 July 1822.

Lushington presented a Sligo petition accusing Lord Kingston of improper interference in the recent county by-election, 11 Feb. 1823.[30] He supported the Catholic franchise bill and expressed 'warm ... feelings in favour of the Catholics generally', 30 June. He secured an unopposed second reading for the Marriage Act amendment bill from the Lords, 13 Mar., on the understanding that it would be debated in committee;[31] it received royal assent, 26 Mar. He supported the motion for papers concerning the prosecution of the Dublin Orange rioters, 24 Mar., as he harboured 'strong doubts' whether justice had been done. He was a minority teller that day for the motion for information regarding the plot to murder the lord lieutenant. He pressed for further information about the grant to defray expenses incurred by colonial governors to promote abolition of the slave trade, which was promised, 19 Mar.[32] He reintroduced his Slave Trade Acts consolidation bill, 10 Apr., which passed the Commons but did not reach the Lords, and supported Wilberforce's motion for inquiry into the condition of slaves and free Indians in the Honduras, 11 July.[33] He approved the Newfoundland laws bill, as 'there never had been a colony so neglected', 25 Mar. That day he introduced a bill to facilitate the examination of witnesses in foreign countries, which did not reach the Lords,[34] and one to make certain forgery acts penal, which was postponed until the next session. He strongly supported repeal of the Foreign Enlistment Act, 16 Apr., expressing indignation at the 'slavish doctrine' that Britain should avoid doing anything to antagonize France, when public opinion was outraged at her intervention in Spain. He supported the abolition of punishment by whipping, 30 Apr., claiming that the victims' 'feelings become blunted and their moral characters degenerated in proportion'. He was a minority teller against the Lords' amendment to the prisons bill to continue flogging, 7 July 1823.

On 6 Feb. 1824 he gave notice of the reintroduction of the slave trade laws consolidation bill, which passed, with another bill for making trafficking in slaves piracy incorporated into it, and gained royal assent, 24 June (5 Geo. IV, c. 113).[35] During this session he became immersed in the revived campaign against slavery, which preoccupied him for the remainder of his parliamentary career. He enjoyed a 'peculiarly close connection' with Thomas Fowell Buxton, becoming a member of his 'anti-slavery cabinet', and 'every idea ... every plan, was originated and arranged between them'. He was also a vice-president of the Anti-Slavery society and a director of the African Institution.[36] With Wilberforce, he waited on the foreign secretary, Canning, 14 Feb., only to be disappointed by the government's unambitious plan of action, and the following month he privately urged Buxton to expose their vacillation and broken promises.[37] He welcomed the statement of ministerial intentions for ameliorating the condition of slaves in the West Indies, 16 Mar., but urged Canning to hold out the prospect of emancipation in the near future, doubted whether colonial legislatures would co-operate with the ameliorative measures and repudiated the claim that the abolitionists were responsible for the recent insurrections; these were entirely owing to 'the melancholy condition of the negroes'. He objected to the principle of the bill to incorporate the West India Company, 10 May, and was a teller for the minority. He presented a petition from Lecesne and Escoffery, coloured freemen of Jamaica who had been seized and transported to St. Domingo without trial, 21 May, and declared that he 'would not rest until he had rescued the character of the British nation from the foul disgrace of having participated in an act of such odious oppression'. He presented several petitions denouncing the prosecution of the Methodist missionary John Smith in Demerara, 1 June.[38] A Whig Member recorded that he 'spoke for two hours ... argumentatively but dully' in support of Brougham's motion on this subject, 11 June 1824, when he was a minority teller.[39]

He welcomed Peel's jury laws consolidation bill, 19 Feb. 1824, observing that 'the multiplicity and confusion of our statutes constituted one of the greatest grievances conceivable'. He supported the county courts bill, 4 Mar., as he was concerned about the practice of selling offices to unsuitable persons. He secured a select committee on the consolidation of the criminal law in England and Wales, 16 Mar. He gave his 'cordial support' to George Lamb's motion to permit defence by counsel in felony cases and was a minority teller, 6 Apr. He supported the cattle ill-treatment bill as 'a necessary adjunct' to previous legislation aimed at stopping 'atrocities which had so long disgraced the national character', 9 Mar. He thought that ministers had made out 'a clear case of necessity' for financial assistance to the civil establishment in Upper Canada, 12 Mar. As 'a determined advocate for unfettering trade in every branch to the greatest possible limit', 28 May, he was a majority teller for the marine insurance bill. He recommended the Equitable Loan Company bill as 'advantageous to the public', 1 June, but said he would not vote as he was a vice-president.[40] He supported the proposed grant for building churches as 'a measure of justice' to the established church, 9 Apr.; but he successfully opposed the Londonderry Cathedral bill, 10 May, seeing no reason why Parliament should pay for the 'criminal neglect' of the responsible authorities. He approved of the superannuation fund bill and incidentally agreed with the claim that 'the chief officers of state were underpaid', 17 June 1824.

Lushington moved for details of the committal of two Catholics and two Presbyterians to gaol in Londonderry for alleged violation of the Irish Marriage Acts, 8 Feb. 1825, as he was anxious to ensure that the 'sacred institution of marriage ... was no longer perverted into a source of national disquietude and party exasperation'. He was a minority teller for two adjournment motions against the introduction of the bill to suppress the Catholic Association, 11 Feb. He declared amid much interruption that the bill would be 'productive of great mischief' in Ireland and that emancipation was the only antidote, 14 Feb. According to one account, he had not originally intended to speak 'but stood up at an unfavourable moment' and 'did not do himself justice'.[41] He warned that the grant to the Irish linen board would 'create a factitious trade and finally leave many hands out of employment', 18 Mar., but refrained from pressing a division. He supported the 'extremely necessary' attempt to limit plurality of benefices in Ireland, 14 Apr., as non-residence was 'a great cause of the increase of Dissenters' there. He supported inquiry into the Norfolk assizes, seeing no reason for holding them in Thetford, 24 Feb. He welcomed Peel's juries regulation bill, 9 Mar. He supported the Dissenters' marriages bill, allowing Unitarians to take a modified oath, 25 Mar., and observed that the general subject of marriage law required consideration: 'some civil form should be adopted'. He regretfully differed from many of his usual friends by supporting the proposed increase in judges' salaries, which would raise the 'dignity of the bench' by allowing them to retire at an appropriate age and by making the judiciary attractive to barristers, 16 May, 2 June. He defended the delay in producing the report of the commission inquiring into delays in chancery, of which he was a member, 31 May, and warned that too much should not be expected from it as its remit was only to consider the practices of the court, not the law governing its decisions. He supported the motion to publish the evidence already taken in order to stimulate public discussion, 7 June. He supported the grant to the commission for suppressing the slave trade, commending its work at Sierra Leone, 11 Mar., and said that he would oppose the ministerial plan to amend his Slave Trade Act unless a clause was inserted to prevent refugee slaves from being returned to their colony, 15 Mar.[42] He urged the government to end the 'rank injustice' of differential sugar duties between the East and West Indies, 'upon the obvious principles of political economy', and denied that he was motivated by hostility to the West India planters, 21 Mar. He opposed the West India Company bill, fearing that the slaves would be 'subjected to many new sufferings', 16 May. He moved for inquiry into the deportation of Lecesne and Descoffery, 16 June, but withdrew in the hope of a full investigation next session. He supported Buxton's motion condemning the expulsion of the Methodist missionary Shrewsbury from Barbados, 23 June. He strongly supported the cotton mills regulation bill, which would 'remove a most crying evil', 16 May, arguing that children needed to be protected from excessive hours of labour although 'adults might be permitted to do as they pleased'. He opposed the grant for the duke of Cumberland's son unless he was educated in England, 27 May, and objected to the way Parliament was conceding control of the money to the king, 30 May. In the debate on the smuggling prevention bill, 10 June, he warned that if Britain claimed the right to search foreign vessels near her shores other countries would do the same, causing 'much trouble and inconvenience'.[43] He accused the duke of Wellington, a trustee of the Deccan prize money, of showing 'contempt and disregard' for the claimants, 28 June, 1 July 1825. His absence through illness in the early part of the 1826 session contributed, in Peel's opinion, to the slackness of the opposition.[44] He supported Denman's motion condemning the Jamaican slave trials, 2 Mar., and pleaded with the House to abide by 'those principles laid down by eternal providence for the good government of man' and 'endeavour to impart to the negro a sense of justice and a knowledge of his God'. He denied Alexander Baring's charges that the abolitionists were guilty of exaggeration, 20 Apr. He supported Brougham's motion on colonial slavery, 19 May, and expressed concern that ministerial indecision was encouraging the planters to resist change; he was a minority teller. He defended the work of the chancery commissioners, 18 May, but was not 'sanguine' that the recommended reforms would greatly facilitate business, although they were a prudent first step from which 'bolder remedies' might follow. He personally favoured separating the bankruptcy business, which caused 'infinite delay'. At the general election that summer he stood for Tregony, a borough supposedly controlled by Darlington. There was a double return, settled in favour of Lushington and James Brougham, 29 Nov. 1826.[45]

He divided for Catholic claims, 6 Mar. 1827. He voted for a 50*s.* import duty on corn, 9 Mar., against increased protection for barley, 12 Mar., and for reduction of the corn duty to 10*s.* by 1833, 27 Mar. He supported a motion to abolish corporal punishment in the army, 12 Mar., declaring that the subject was one requiring agitation 'until we should arrive at that *minimum* of human suffering which would be compatible with the preservation of discipline'. On 13 Mar. he drew attention to the case of an Anglican clergyman in Jamaica who had incited an attack on the meeting house of a Methodist missionary, which showed that 'the spirit of illiberality was spreading'. He voted for information about the Barrackpoor mutiny, 22 Mar. He divided for the spring guns bill, 23 Mar., and urged acceptance of the Lords' amendments, 17 May, as 'justice and humanity called for the total abolition of the practice'. He welcomed the writ of right bill, which offered 'some amelioration in the practice of transferring real property', 27 Mar. He pronounced a 'most decided negative' to Taylor's motion to separate bankruptcy cases from chancery jurisdiction, 22 May, arguing that it would 'destroy ... uniformity of decision on all points relating to the property of the subject'; some specific measure of procedural reform should have been proposed. He voted for information regarding the Lisburn Orange procession, 29 Mar. He firmly opposed a petition from Norwich weavers and master manufacturers for wage regulation, 31 May. He presented petitions from Jamaica and Honduras for coloured freemen to be given the legal rights and privileges of British subjects, 12 June 1827. During the recess he devoted much of his time to aspects of the slavery question, meeting regularly to discuss tactics with Buxton, Brougham, Zachary Macaulay and others, and communicating with ministers on the issue of coloured freemen. He wrote to Buxton in November:

> We have had warm work since you left London, and it seems likely to continue; however, I am high in spirits. We have Brougham in full energy, strength and determination, and we have a case in all points impregnable. Would I had more leisure! for my appetite is whetted by all the follies and iniquities of the planters.[46]

Brougham was furious that the king's hostility had apparently prevented Lushington from being offered a judicial appointment by Lord Goderich's coalition ministry, and thought he had behaved 'admirably' in the circumstances by promising his continued support, although he felt his exclusion 'bitterly', as 'an insult as well as a wrong', and '*hate[d] them properly*'.[47]

He voted to repeal the Test Acts, 26 Feb., and paired in favour of Catholic relief, 12 May 1828. He supported the motion for copies of all the public Acts of colonial assemblies and the orders in council issued for regulating the colonies, 27 Feb., as Parliament and the country were being kept in a 'state of ignorance'. He maintained that Parliament and the government were already committed to the 'ultimate abolition' of slavery, 5 Mar., and thought no one could 'refuse the expense consequent upon maintaining a police, even for the whole world', to combat the trade, when they remembered 'the debt we contracted in consequence of the enormities [committed] in times past ... by ourselves'. He said he would not oppose the Slave Trade Act continuance bill, 1 July, on the understanding that the Wellington ministry would adhere to the principles of their predecessors until the whole issue had been properly considered. On the home secretary Peel's motion for inquiry into police and crime in the metropolis, 28 Feb., he suggested that the Old Bailey sessions should be extended to deal with cases in Kent and Surrey to achieve a speedier administration of justice. He introduced a rights of executors bill to define their powers over the undisposed residues of personal estates, 2 Apr.; it passed but did not reach the Lords. He gave an 'unexpected' vote against the pension for Canning's widow, 13 May,[48] and supported the motion for information on civil list pensions, 20 May, warning of the threat to the judiciary's independence if judges were partially dependent on financial favours from the crown. He expressed his 'hearty concurrence' in Peel's bill to abolish church briefs, 22 May, as 'the mischief will be infinite and beyond all calculation' if more places were not provided for the poor. He supported the additional churches bill, 30 June, and opposed the benefices resignation bill, 17 July, arguing that every clergyman should hold his living independently of another person's favour and warning that it would 'tend to multiply pluralities' and 'have the effect of loosening the bond which ought to subsist between the pastor and his flock'. That day he made a vigorous defence of Sir John Nicholl*, judge in the prerogative court of Canterbury, against 'unfounded, frivolous and malicious ... charges', telling Hume that he was being made the tool of 'disappointed suitors'. He praised Canning's achievement in recognizing the South American republics, which 'marked his attachment to the cause of right and liberty', 3 July 1828.

Lushington defended the Catholics of England and Scotland from 'false and unfounded aspersions' cast by certain Members and praised the 'unexampled patience' with which they had borne their exclusion from public life, 16 Feb. 1829. He extolled Peel's courage and sincerity in recognizing that circumstances in Ireland had changed and that Catholic emancipation was the best means to 'preserve the integrity of the Protestant church'. He voted for emancipation, 6, 30 Mar. He rejected the demand for an immediate dissolution, 9 Mar., declaring that ministers would 'deserve impeachment' if they complied. He had qualms about the bill to disfranchise Irish 40*s.* freeholders, 20 Mar., but felt it was justified 'on the principle of reciprocal advantage', as their loss would mean that 'the gates of the constitution are open for the admission of the whole people of Ireland'. He supported the proposed new oath for Catholic Members, 23 Mar., and opposed the amendment requiring Catholics to disavow the doctrine of having no faith with heretics, 27 Mar. He approved of the rights of executors bill, 10 Mar., and hoped that lord chancellor Lyndhurst would carry out an extensive reform of chancery, including its bankruptcy proceedings, 25 May. He supported the ecclesiastical courts bill, 21 May, acknowledging as a judge himself (since 1826) that they were not conducted in a satisfactory way. He did not oppose a motion for information on them, 12 June, but warned that procedural reform 'cannot be accomplished by any effort of human wisdom' and that it was 'extremely dangerous to pull down before we are prepared to build up'. He thought the government should be accountable in the courts for vessels damaged by the king's ships, 22 May. He supported the bill requiring Members to vacate their seats if appointed to East India Company posts in India, but saw difficulties in making it retrospective, 6 May. He presented a Jamaica petition for the extension of the order in council removing the disabilities of the coloured population of Trinidad, 1 June. He believed that an inquiry into the condition of the slaves in Mauritius was 'absolutely necessary', 3 June. He was consulted by the foreign secretary, Lord Aberdeen, on the proposal to extend the deadline for ending the Brazilian slave trade in return for a right to seize ships equipped for the trade, but he reportedly feared that Britain would thereby 'permit the transportation of a very large number of slaves, of whom many might be destroyed by ill-treatment'; this view was accepted by ministers.[49] He gave notice, 19 June 1829, that next session he would introduce a bill providing that slaves brought to Britain should thereafter be free in all British dominions.

He divided for Knatchbull's amendment to the address on distress, 4 Feb. 1830, explaining next day that his real objection was to the government's foreign policy, including its apparent intention of recognizing Dom Miguel's usurpation of the Portuguese throne and its failure to prevent Spain from threatening Mexico. He was 'averse' to war, but considered it 'the duty of England, when called upon by the ties of treaty and of public honour, to assume the attitude of defiance and ... unfurl the banners of war'. He paired for the enfranchisement of Birmingham, Leeds and Manchester, 23 Feb., after stating that his experience in the House since 1806 had 'fully strengthened [his] early impressions respecting the propriety of parliamentary reform', warning that 'a heavy pressure of distress has come upon the country and ... measures infinitely wider in their extent and more severe in their operation ... must be speedily adopted', and advising ministers to 'appeal to the well-educated, the well-informed, the moral people of this country' for support. He paired for the transfer of East Retford's seats to Birmingham, 5 Mar., and voted for Russell's reform motion, 28 May. He supported the Jewish emancipation bill, acting as a majority teller, 5 Apr., and voted for the second reading, 17 May. He supported Lord Ellenborough's divorce bill, 6 Apr., explaining that he had presided over the case, had no doubt that Lady Ellenborough had committed adultery and believed that Ellenborough's 'general unpopularity' was the cause of Members' hostility towards him. He advised against burdening the ecclesiastical courts commissioners, of whom he was one, with the task of considering the question of allowing divorce for adultery in the law courts, 3 June, and suggested that a practical proposal should be submitted so that the complicated issues involved could be debated. He defended the established churches in England and Ireland, 27 Apr., declaring that he could 'never consent' to a redistribution of church property in England and arguing that the Irish church was now performing its duties 'more decorously and more beneficially than before', though he admitted the need to end pluralism and non-residence. He voted for Mackintosh's amendments to abolish the death penalty for forgery, 24 May, 7 June. He judged the time was not yet ripe for granting representative government to the Cape of Good Hope, 24 May, as Britain needed to retain 'efficient control' in order to ensure that steps were taken to improve the condition of the African natives. He was 'perfectly satisfied' with the 'utility' of the settlement at Sierra Leone, 15 June, maintaining that 'no other place could be fixed upon which is so favourable for our benevolent purpose' of ending the slave trade. He voted to reduce the grants for diplomatic missions, 7, 11 June, and against the pension for the governor of Prince Edward Island, 14 June. At the dissolution that summer he was obliged to find a new seat, as his patron, now marquess of Cleveland, had deserted the Whigs for the government. He offered at Chichester in early July, but withdrew after a disappointing canvass. He stood for Reading, where he focused on economy and retrenchment, linking these to the need for reform, but was attacked for supporting subsidies for church buildings and the anatomy bill. He ostentatiously refused to resort to bribery and came bottom of the poll after a 'desperate' contest in which, he told Brougham, 'the church and a large portion of the party called semi-Evangelicals ... united against me', although 'the old Dissenters ... stood firm by my side'.[50] His abolitionist supporters backed a petition against the result, which was presented, 16 Nov. 1830, but not pursued.[51]

On the formation of Lord Grey's ministry in November 1830 Lushington urged Buxton to resume his public duties, as he foresaw

> a fearful crisis for many of the great objects you have at heart. Without great exertion both slavery and capital punishment will be almost unaltered. I have but little confidence in the merely voluntary good will of the new government, and feel strongly that they should be taught that the voice of the people will not admit of dilatory or half measures.[52]

His own opportunity to return to Parliament came early in April 1831, when Cleveland, who had reverted to the Whigs in the hope of obtaining a dukedom, created a vacancy for him at Winchelsea.[53] He delivered what a Tory West India Member considered an 'excessively violent and *malignant*' speech for Buxton's slavery motion, 15 Apr., contending that 'the introduction of slavery into our colonies has been the cause of the demoralisation and distress which prevail there' and that 'the present situation of the colonists is a punishment inflicted upon them by Providence for their departure from good principles'.[54] He divided against Gascoyne's wrecking amendment to the ministry's reform bill, 19 Apr., and two days later made a rousing speech in favour of an immediate dissolution to strengthen the hand of 'those who have advocated the great measure of national restoration'. He was returned unopposed for both Winchelsea and Ilchester at the ensuing general election, but chose to sit for the latter. He divided for the second reading of the reintroduced reform bill, 6 July 1831, and voted steadily for its details in committee. He defended the use of the 1821 census for the purpose of scheduling boroughs, 14 July, observing that the bill was based on the simple principle of 'the annihilation of all those boroughs in which nomination prevails'. He voted for the bill's passage, 21 Sept., and Lord Ebrington's confidence motion, 10 Oct. On 23 Aug. he opposed the punishment for bribery of Dublin voters, many of whom were ignorant and 'poor wretches', but argued that 'the person who offers a bribe assails the very foundation of the morals of the poorer voters and is guilty of a trespass upon all the laws of justice and honour'; he was a teller for the successful government amendment that only those found guilty of bribery should be punished. He voted to print the Waterford petition for disarming the Irish yeomanry, 11 Aug. He argued that Parliament was bound to pay compensation to Lecesne and Escoffery and deplored the long delay involved in another inquiry, 18 Aug. In his capacity as a church building commissioner, he took charge of the Church Building Act amendment bill, 26 Sept., 3 Oct., and the augmentation of benefices bill, 26 Sept., 4 Oct. 1831.

He divided for the second reading of the revised reform bill, 17 Dec. 1831, and voted for its details, the third reading, 22 Mar., and Ebrington's motion for an address asking the king to appoint only ministers committed to carrying an unimpaired measure, 10 May 1832. He voted for the second reading of the Irish bill, 25 May. On 15 Mar. he supported an inquiry into Peterloo, which would 'teach a great moral lesson to persons in possession of political power', that 'they shall ever be answerable for their misdeeds'. He was aware that he had 'spoken with some degree of warmth on this subject, as ... I do on most occasions'. He opposed Herries's resolution against the use of public money to repay the Russian-Dutch loan, 26 Jan., concluding that Britain was clearly bound by its treaty obligation regardless of the conduct of the Netherlands. He accused Herries of 'consummate cunning' in his mode of reviving the issue, 12 July, and again sided with ministers, 16, 20 July. He voted with them on relations with Portugal, 9 Feb. He declared that Britain should not interfere in the affairs of other nations 'unless we are justified by the law of nations and by treaties', 18 Apr., but felt that the people's 'utter detestation and abhorrence' of Russia's conduct in Poland must be clearly expressed. He gave the government his 'zealous support' for their course on slavery, 9 Mar. In May he and Buxton were privately urged by ministers not to embarrass them and obstruct the progress of the reform bill by pressing the issue, but he encountered fierce resistance from campaigners outside Parliament to the idea of showing restraint. Fearing that a 'violent' anti-slavery motion might drive ministers into the arms of the West India interest and persuade them to 'suspend or revoke the orders in council', he used his 'utmost personal influence with Buxton to induce him to adopt a wiser course', that of moving for an inquiry into the means of facilitating the early abolition of slavery.[55] He divided against the government's temporizing amendment to Buxton's motion, 24 May, vindicating the abolitionists' campaign, pressing for the implementation of the resolution of 1823 and denying that emancipation would lead to the destruction of the sugar plantations. He approved of the grant to compensate West Indian islands for hurricane damage, 29 June, but protested at the assistance also being offered to the Jamaican colonists in the aftermath of the insurrection, which they had brought on themselves. He supported financial relief for the West Indian crown colonies, 3 Aug., since they were subject to direct authority from the British government, unlike the chartered colonies, and were therefore obliged to respond to the order in council on slavery. He supported the bill to abolish capital punishment for certain forms of theft, 27 Mar., and pressed ministers to abolish the death penalty for forgery, 17 May. He supported their determination to uphold the law in Ireland by enforcing the payment of tithes, 30 Mar., arguing that 'the whole frame of society will be disturbed' if nothing was done to combat the present conspiracy. However, he recognized that tithes were unjust to the Catholic population, thought they should be commuted in some way and indicated his support for lay appropriation of surplus Irish church revenues. He supported the motion for information on plurality of benefices in England and Wales, 8 May, rejecting the claim that church property was private on the ground that 'tenure subjects the holders to the performance of certain duties'. He supported the ecclesiastical courts contempts bill, extending the courts' jurisdiction to cover peers and Members, 3 Aug. 1832.

At the general election of 1832 Lushington was returned at the head of the poll for Tower Hamlets. He sat as 'a reformer ... in favour of the immediate abolition of slavery, the repeal of the taxes on knowledge and of the Septennial Act', who also supported 'the ballot ... revision of the corn laws and general reform', until his enforced retirement in 1841. He was deeply involved in issues of church reform and the continuing campaign against world-wide slavery.[56] A parliamentary journalist noted in 1836 that he had 'no pretensions to genius' and 'seldom delights his audience by anything brilliant or original', but his speeches were 'always argumentative and forcible' and rarely relied on 'declamation'. Unfortunately, his voice was 'shrill' and 'his elocution ... somewhat impaired by his inability to pronounce the letter *r*'.[57] He retired from the bench in July 1867, having become 'one of the old landmarks of legal and political life'.[58] He died in January 1873.

[1] Who left him £1,000 and £4,000 to be invested in securities; 'a larger sum of money' had already been 'advanced' to him (PROB 11/1456/130). [2] S.M. Waddams, *Law, Politics and the Church of England: the career of Stephen Lushington*, 4-5, 100-34. [3] Ibid. 27-30; Add. 51584, Lushington to Tierney, 19 Sept. 1819. [4] Hants RO, Tierney mss 47; Add. 38284, f. 28. [5] *The Times*, 13 July 1820. [6] Buckingham, *Mems. Geo. IV*, i. 51-52. [7] Ibid. i. 66. [8] Add. 30109, f. 129. [9] NLS mss 1036, ff. 70-73; Waddams, 135-46; C. New, *Life of Brougham*, 260. [10] *The Times*, 20 Mar. 1821. [11] Waddams, 147-59. [12] *The Times*, 29 May 1821. [13] HLRO, Hist. Coll. 379, Grey Bennet diary, 30a. [14] *The Times*, 28 Mar. 1821. [15] Ibid. 6 Mar. 1821. [16] Grey Bennet diary, 33. [17] Ibid. 50; *The Times*, 4, 5 Apr. 1821. [18] *The Times*, 16 May 1821. [19] Grey Bennet diary, 97. [20] Ibid. 115. [21] Ibid. 96. [22] *The Times*, 30 June 1821. [23] Ibid. 30 June 1821. [24] Ibid. 4 July 1821. [25] Add. 36459, f. 183. [26] *The Times*, 28 June 1822. [27] Ibid. 13 July 1822. [28] Ibid. 5 Mar. 1822. [29] Ibid. 22 June 1822. [30] Ibid. 12 Feb. 1823. [31] Ibid. 14 Mar. 1823. [32] Ibid. 20 Mar. 1823. [33] Ibid. 11 Apr., 12 July 1823. [34] Ibid. 26 Mar. 1823. [35] Ibid. 7, 19 Feb., 6, 15 May 1824. [36] *Buxton Mems.* 152-3; Waddams, 63-99. [37] Bodl. MS Wilberforce c. 39, f. 61; Buxton, 145. [38] *The Times*, 2 June 1824. [39] Northants. RO, Agar Ellis diary, 11 June 1824. [40] *The Times*, 2 June 1824. [41] Merthyr Mawr mss F/2/8, Nicholl's diary, 14 Feb. 1825. [42] *The Times*, 12, 16 Mar. 1825. [43] Ibid. 11 June 1825. [44] Wellington mss WP1/850/9. [45] *R. Cornw. Gazette*, 17 June; Brougham mss, Lushington to Brougham, 27 Aug. 1826. [46] Brougham mss, Buxton to Brougham, 3 Oct. 1827; New, 297; Buxton, 205. [47] NLS mss 24748, f. 47. [48] Harewood mss, Backhouse to Lady Canning, 15 May 1828. [49] *Ellenborough Diary*, ii. 47. [50] *Chichester Election of 1830*, pp. 34-35, 92; *Reading Mercury*, 2, 9, 16 Aug.; Brougham mss, Lushington to Brougham, 12 Aug. 1830. [51] Bodl. MS. Eng. lett. c. 160, ff. 188, 227. [52] Buxton, 255. [53] Creevey mss, Creevey to Miss Ord, 29, 30 Mar. 1831. [54] St. Deiniol's Lib. Glynne-Gladstone mss 198, T. to J. Gladstone, 16 Apr. 1831. [55] Buxton, 287; Brougham mss, Lushington to Brougham [May 1832]. [56] *Dod's Parl. Companion* (1833), 136; Waddams, 15-22, 41-43, 73-99, 249-69. [57] [J. Grant], *Random Recollections of Commons*, 265-7. [58] *The Times*, 21 Jan. 1873.

T.A.J.

LUSHINGTON, Stephen Rumbold (1776–1868), of Norton Court, nr. Faversham, Kent.

RYE	1807–1812
CANTERBURY	1812–1830
CANTERBURY	26 Mar. 1835–1837

b. 6 May 1776, 2nd s. of Rev. James Stephen Lushington (*d.* 1801) of Rodmersham, Kent, vic. of Newcastle-upon-Tyne and preb. of Carlisle, and 2nd w. Mary, da. of Rev. Humphrey Christian of Docking, Norf.; bro. of James Law Lushington*. *educ.* Rugby 1785; Linton acad. *m.* (1) 9 Dec. 1797, Anne Elizabeth (*d.* 25 Mar. 1856), da. of Gen. George Harris, *cr.* Bar. Harris, 6s. (5 *d.v.p.*) 2da. (1 *d.v.p.*); (2) 8 May 1858, Marianne, da. of James Hearne of Great Portland Street, Mdx., *s.p. d.* 5 Aug. 1868.

Writer, E.I. Co. (Madras) 1790; asst. to sec., military, pol. and secret dept. 1792; asst. to translator, bd. of revenue 1793, Persian translator 1794; dep. sec. bd. of revenue 1796, sec. 1798; under searcher, Sea Gate 1796, collector, Ramnad 1799, Tinnevelly 1801; registrar, sadr and faujdari adalat 1803; at home 1803, res. 1807.

Chairman of ways and means 1810-13; sec. to treasury Jan. 1814-Apr. 1827; PC 30 June 1827; gov. Madras Oct. 1827-Oct. 1832.

Capt. Lath of Scray vols. 1805; maj. 2 E. Kent militia 1810.

Lushington was appointed financial secretary to the treasury in 1814 and became an established, if unimpressive, second-ranking official in the Liverpool administration. Firmly entrenched at Canterbury, he offered again at the general election of 1820 and, 'animated in my loyalty to the crown', as he put it, was returned just ahead of the leading Whig candidate, Lord Clifton, after a contest.[1] He continued to fulfil several basic managerial functions in the House and, of course, voted with his colleagues on all major issues, and was frequently a ministerial teller and committeeman, especially on matters relating to finance and economic policy. He was not an able speaker and was sometimes inaudible in the reporters' gallery.[2] He rarely spoke at any length, limiting his contributions to attempts to parry embarrassing opposition motions and questions, or postponing business in the absence of the chancellor or other ministers.[3] Much of his time was taken up with routine departmental affairs, though he was sometimes also involved with the patronage and whipping functions of his office.[4] He counted his fellow treasury secretary as the chief architect of his good fortune. As he wrote to his father-in-law Lord Harris in 1821:

> I should be very sorry that you did any thing harsh towards [Charles] Arbuthnot*: he is irregular, but has many excellent qualities. When thinking of him you should always bear this in your remembrance – that the very particulars of which you complain led to my intimacy with him, to my appointment to the treasury, and to any other person of the family in whose prosperity or fame I have been in any shape instrumental, or may hereafter succeed in being so.[5]

He was also connected with Robert Peel* and wanted to see him return to the cabinet in 1820.[6] For his part Peel enjoyed what he described in 1835 as 'those friendly and confidential habits of intercourse in which we so long lived'.[7] Lushington's relations with his senior colleagues were cordial, but he was viewed as merely adequate in the execution of his duties.[8]

He spoke against Hume's resolutions on revenue collection, 4 July 1820, condemning them as unnecessary and statistically inaccurate. He objected to the reception of a petition criticizing the role of peers in elections, 15 July.[9] In August he refused to present a laudatory address from Canterbury to the queen.[10] He was named to a select committee appointed to examine the *Lords Journals* on the bill of pains and penalties against her, 18 Sept., and privately commented that 'we had as stupid a night of it as could be wished in our House', 17 Oct. 1820, owing to the partisan proceedings on this in the Lords that evening.[11] He opposed printing the Nottingham petition for the impeachment of ministers over the affair, 20 Feb. 1821. On 6 Mar. he made a long intervention in defence of the inhabited house and window taxes, which Ricardo wanted abolished, arguing that the opposition plan would disrupt the chancellor's budget, fail to relieve agricultural distress and endanger public credit. He spoke against Hume's motion for reducing expense and maladministration in the system of revenue collection, 22 Mar., and defended the corn bill, which he claimed was designed only to prevent fraud, not to raise prices, 29 Mar.[12] He voted against Mackintosh's forgery punishment mitigation bill, 23 May, and spoke in favour of the unlawful associations bill, 6 June 1821.[13]

Lushington maintained a close connection with Harris, and encouraged him to support the government by sending in a proxy, 3 Jan. 1822.[14] He spoke against tax reductions, which would damage public credit, 7 Feb., and defended the administration of hackney coaches, 27 Feb.[15] He rebutted Davies's allegations about the enormous expense of collecting revenues, 12 Mar., and justified the system of laying public accounts before Parliament, 14 Mar.[16] Writing to Henry Goulburn* in March, he insisted that smugglers be given exemplary punishments in order to ensure the successful protection of the revenue; in the House he claimed that receipts had been increased and smuggling diminished, 12 June.[17] He spoke against leniency towards the imprisoned Henry Hunt*, 22 Apr. He moved the third reading of the malt duties repeal bill and assured the House that the chancellor intended to equalize the duties on Irish and English distilleries, 18 May, but he opposed further changes in the laws relating to hop-bags, 13 June.[18] He spoke against repeal of the salt duties, 28 June, stating that a diminution of the coal or candle taxes would be preferable.[19] He defended the system of receivers-general against Hume's criticisms, 9 July, and recommended to him 'the consideration of a passage in Mr. Burke's writings, in which he points out the danger and folly of crude and clumsy reforms in such subjects as this'.[20] He managed to raise a laugh in the House when he supported the receivers-general bill, 18 July, and asked – by way of a rider – that no more than three of them be obliged to travel together.[21] He proposed paying off the late queen's debts, 24 July, but only those owing to British creditors, 31 July 1822.[22]

During the discussions of ministerial changes in late 1822 Liverpool objected to Lushington replacing Arbuthnot as patronage secretary to the treasury. The new foreign secretary George Canning*, Arbuthnot reported to William Huskisson*, also disliked the idea 'for various reasons and particularly because he considers him as not having his heart in the cause'.[23] However, while Lushington continued to carry out much the same role in the government, he replaced Arbuthnot as senior secretary, and John Charles Herries* became the junior, 7 Feb. 1823. He was immensely busy at the start of the 1823 session because of the absence of both his colleagues with gout, the Deccan prize case and the problem of the kelp manufacturers of Scotland.[24] In addition, he oversaw the passage of financial measures and boasted to Harris that

> we have done an immense quantity of public business since we met. I have actually *completed* what Arbuthnot had not done last year in the month of July. This is no disparagement on him, but it shows how the temper of the House is altered from the expectation of European war, and at least we have this credit of having taken advantage of this tide as it flowed.[25]

Apart from dealing with the inevitable departmental business, Lushington was less active in the Commons from this time onwards. He was mistakenly thought to have intrigued for his son to replace Robert Ward as Member for Lord Lonsdale's borough of Haslemere in March 1823, but was later acquitted of the allegation.[26] He was, however, involved in suggesting candidates for the by-election at Eye that summer.[27] He took the opportunity of a debate on colonial supplies to point out the extent of government economies, 12 Mar. 1824.[28] Ever active on local affairs, he moved for leave to introduce a bill to repeal the hides and skins duties, 14 Apr., spoke and was a teller for this, 3, 31 May, chaired it in committee in early May, and was praised in Canterbury as the principal architect of its success.[29] He introduced a bill for the erection of a new corn and hop market in Canterbury, 4 May, but was unable to attend the ceremony of laying the foundation stone on 29 July 1824 because of the illness of one of his sons.[30]

Lushington had previously served in the East India Company and still cherished his early ambition of a lucrative Indian appointment. In January 1824 the government received the news that Sir Thomas Munro intended to resign the governorship of Madras, which would create a vacancy there, or at Bombay if Mountstuart Elphinstone was promoted to Madras. Lushington began canvassing the opinion of the directors about his going to Madras, but was not encouraged by the result.[31] William Wigram*, the chairman, was not personally hostile to Lushington, but was invincibly opposed to the appointment of someone connected with government. Lushington also thought him embittered by the disappointed aspirations of his family to a peerage, and by the new silk and wool arrangements.[32] Although Charles Williams Wynn*, the president of the India board, opined that ridding the government of 'a bad secretary to the treasury' would be worth the appearance of 'a *job*', he doubted the directors would ultimately swallow what was hardly a '*dainty*' pill.[33] Liverpool threw his weight behind Lushington, but thought the climate of Bombay was preferable and that allowing the directors' choice for the Madras posting would make them more likely to accept a former government official for Bombay.[34] He also wanted to prevent the Company having the nomination to both positions and was in any case unimpressed with the directors' preference for Sir John Malcolm*.[35] Meanwhile, Canning was in favour of Lushington leaving the treasury so that he could be replaced by his own protégé Joseph Planta*: 'Lushington has behaved perfectly well, but his connections are ultra and he is no way mine. Planta will be wholly so and will make the House of Commons much easier and pleasanter than it is'.[36] Lushington was in doubts whether to push it to a contest, and thus first became reconciled to the idea of Bombay rather than Madras and then declined the attempt altogether in mid-May.[37] However, against the views of several of his colleagues, Liverpool twice asked the king to veto Malcolm's nomination by the Company, and so the speculation continued that Lushington might be appointed.[38] With both directors and ministers split and the prime minister indecisive, the duke of Wellington and the king, who certainly favoured Lushington staying at the treasury in order to keep out Planta, insisted on Malcolm, while Arbuthnot thought that the government was committed to sending Lushington to Bombay.[39]

Everything changed when it became clear that Sir Charles Stuart required the governorship as compensation for leaving the embassy in Paris. Canning and Liverpool jumped at the chance to appease him, although, according to Williams Wynn, the premier was affronted that Wigram had not considered Lushington to be 'of a rank of sufficient *cal-*

liber (to use his phrase)'.[40] Liverpool therefore wrote to Lushington, lamenting that the hoped for support from the directors had not been forthcoming and that the king was antagonistic to the move. The communication left him to understand, *inter alia*, that the government would no longer support his pretensions. Lushington made a bland reply, pledging his 'anxious desire to act in entire conformity to your wishes'.[41] But in private he revealed his knowledge of, and anger at, Liverpool's abrupt about-face:

> In his letter of the 15th of October, after my friends have shown their firmness and attachment to me by rejecting Malcolm and are prepared to propose me substantively and without a doubt of succeeding, he (the said lord) turns suddenly around, and thinks they (the government) have done enough and ought not to force upon the directors a person they are unwilling to receive. Since I came to town I have found out that this is all humbug. He and Canning wish to avoid two things. He will not consent to make Sir Charles Stuart, the Paris ambassador, a peer because his profligate private character would make him a disgrace to the peerage, and Canning having turned him out of the embassy at Paris will not consent to employ him (as the king wishes) at The Hague.

However, apart from insisting upon a pension for himself and his son, Lushington was prepared to be placatory towards Liverpool:

> I feel conscious of nothing but honourable feelings and useful co-operation in all the measures of his administration during the ten years in which I have acted under him, and though he has never said 'thank you' or shown the least particle of interest in any one of my family, I shall go on in the strict discharge of my duty and leave the rest to Providence, not suffering myself hereafter to be annoyed by that coldness of heart which freezes almost every object that approaches it.[42]

In the end he was glad to be rid of the constant anxiety that the months of negotiations had occasioned.[43] The outbreak of the Burmese war delayed the retirement of Munro and allowed the government to put the whole embarrassing episode on ice. Indian employment would, however, have cured Lushington's recurring financial problems. He had an official salary of £4,000, and now received a pension of £1,500, but by the beginning of 1825 he was in debt to Harris to the tune of £8,000, with no prospect of any improvement.[44] Perhaps this was one reason for the speculation that he might move to the pay office.[45]

Lushington voted against Catholic relief, 28 Feb., was involved in the promotion of an anti-Catholic petition from Canterbury to the Lords in early April, and was a teller for the majority against allowing Catholics to hold the offices of governor and director of the Bank of Ireland, 13 June 1821.[46] He was a teller against allowing Catholic peers to sit in the Lords, 30 Apr., 10 May, when he declared that he would rather vote for emancipation in full than this small measure of it; he presented a petition from Canterbury against the proposal, 16 May 1822.[47] He was heavily committed to the government's policy of putting down the Catholic Association at the start of the 1825 session.[48] He voted for repeal of the usury laws, 8 Feb., and the following day, in a rare example of drawing attention to himself in debate, mentioned the merits of an infamous book by the prostitute Harriette Wilson.[49] In late February he was not sure that the government would succeed in thwarting Catholic relief, but described to Harris how the previously divided Canning and Liverpool had become united on the necessity of paying the Catholic clergy. He added:

> For my own part I would rather see 50 Catholic laymen sitting in Parliament after the priests are in the pay of the state, than five of them coming amongst us as the bearers of all the just complaints of the priesthood and the ready instruments of a factious opposition, or of a weak government, or the subversion of the titles of property in Ireland.[50]

He voted against relief, 1 Mar., 21 Apr. He was unable to leave London while the question was undecided, because Liverpool was so anxious about the outcome, and he wrote:

> I own that I agree with Lord L. in thinking that after 150 years of religious calm, we are about to enter upon a revival of religious warfare by concession to this mockery of worship.[51]

He presented a petition from St. Andrew's, Canterbury, against relief, 26 Apr., when he voted against the Irish franchise bill, and was a teller for the minority against the third reading of the relief bill, 10 May 1825.

Lushington received the freedom of Sandwich for his assistance in the passage of the Stour Navigation and Sandwich Harbour bill, 28 June 1825.[52] In May he had complained to Mrs. Arbuthnot of Huskisson's rashness and 'said he thought he had put Mr. [Frederick John] Robinson* up to stop him in his career; for really, with his resolutions and his trade regulations, he was setting all law at defiance and all the merchants were expecting to be bankrupts'.[53] He told Lord Darlington in September 1825 that 'Lady Anne threw herself, husband and child over in an open carriage, but no essential harm except *her miscarriage*'.[54] He was inclined to blame the Bank of England for the financial crisis late that year, and he wrote to Peel in February 1826 that it was

> vain to argue against the non-existence of a great and growing pressure upon all classes of the community, and however induced, the evil will gather hourly strength until confidence between the bankers, the merchants, and the manufacturers be re-established.[55]

In one of his few speeches that session, he defended Haileybury College as a training school for the East India Company, 28 Apr. He had been involved in preparations for a general election the previous autumn, when his own position at Canterbury was considered secure, as he was generally well regarded.[56] However, criticisms were now voiced among the electors that he had voted against repeal of the corn laws, was a placeman and held a pension.[57] He canvassed actively in the city in May and received the support of many of the Canterbury freemen in London.[58] Having given the customary pledges to uphold the constitution in church and state, and 'to watch over the local interests of the city of Canterbury, with the utmost attention and kindness', he easily headed the poll, being more than 200 votes in front of Clifton.[59] As on former occasions, his official involvement in elections elsewhere was not wholly admired; for example, he treated John Norman Macleod*, who had hopes of a Scottish burgh, with appalling incivility.[60] According to the anti-Catholic Mrs. Arbuthnot, he 'uses the influence of government any way Mr. Canning pleases; and that, in many instances, has been in favour of the opposition candidates'.[61] Yet Sir Robert Heron* afterwards complained that 'this experienced jobber spared no exertions to expel from the treasury boroughs, or any others where government had influence, every man who would not declare himself' against Catholic relief.[62] He helped John Evelyn Denison*, who had been promised Hastings by the government, though in the event he withdrew and was not returned until an arrangement was made in November.[63] One major embarrassment was the loss of the safe treasury seat at Queenborough, despite Wellington's repeated warnings about the decline of the government's interest there.[64]

During July 1826 speculation began again that Lushington would be appointed to one of the Indian governorships, 'the directors having shown a disposition to change their opinions upon that question'.[65] Rumours circulated in the Canterbury papers to this effect, and once the nomination was provisionally confirmed in January 1827 there was a general expectation that he would soon have to resign his seat.[66] Mrs. Arbuthnot noted in February that Lushington had found the treasury odious and was glad to escape to Madras, but the appointment only officially began in the autumn, leaving him to play a limited role within the government until his resignation in July.[67] In late February he acted as a conduit between Canning and members of opposition over the timing of motions.[68] He gave a silent vote against Catholic relief, 6 Mar., after which he and his likeminded colleague Herries were blamed for the narrow defeat of the question.[69] Although differing with Canning over this, he enthusiastically supported his claim to take over the premiership after Liverpool's stroke, rather than face the alternative of a 'Protestant' cabinet under Wellington or Peel. As he wrote to the king's secretary Sir William Knighton:

> Of the rejection of the Catholic claims I felt the fullest confidence, and that there would be no immediate conflict in the cabinet; whilst the plan for altering the corn laws seemed so manifestly advantageous to the landed interest, without pressing unjustly upon other classes of the community, that I contemplated no feelings but those of restored contentment and satisfaction towards Mr. Canning on the part of the landed interest. To him I looked as the person who would be selected by the king as Lord Liverpool's successor and every act and every thought of mine has had this object in view.[70]

In June 1827 he was made a privy councillor, but (as was made clear to Malcolm, who had similar pretensions as the new governor of Bombay) this was not because of his promotion, but as a reward for his services at the treasury.[71]

A Canterbury petition to enforce his resignation from Parliament was presented by Clifton, 12 June 1827. In the debate that followed, Lushington claimed that all its 54 signatories were political opponents, that they represented less than one-fortieth of his constituents and that he would resign if so requested by a sufficient number of his supporters. He added that his absence from Parliament had been occasioned by his wife's serious illness and not by any hostility to Canning's ministry, of which he approved.[72] As the time approached for him to sail to India, even his friends began to realize that he had no intention of giving up his seat. An excuse was circulated that he intended to test the climate of Madras before deciding whether or not to stay for any length of time, but the atmosphere was evidently too tense for him to risk attending a public dinner in Canterbury which was to have been given in his honour.[73] Perhaps his financial problems were partly behind his decision to go to India. At the mayor's dinner in September 1827 his son William commented that Lushington, 'compelled as he had been from prudential reasons to quit for a time his native shore', yet retained his affection for his constituents.[74] Once the 1828 session began, there were renewed attempts by the Canterbury freemen to secure Lushington's removal. It was argued that it was illegal for him to continue to serve as Member whilst he was absent at such a distance, and he was also attacked for allegedly siphoning off £140,000 of public money to his own purse and for having taken 'French leave' of his constituents. A petition calling for his removal was brought up, 27 Mar., but stalemate was reached in June 1828 when Clifton refused to move a new writ because legally Lushington was under no obligation to resign.[75] Further meetings followed to formulate other petitions for redress the following year, but his brother James Law Lushington defended his conduct in the Commons, 6 May 1829, stating that he would have resigned had his constituents wished it and had he been approached in a reasonable and amicable manner, and he escaped legislative sanction.[76] As the next general election approached, increasing criticisms were voiced of Lushington in Canterbury, where two Whig candidates were eventually elected.[77]

In late 1828 the president of the India board Lord Ellenborough, who was a first cousin of Lushington's half-brother Edmund, was disgusted to learn that Lushington had stupidly written to Williams Wynn 'that he could not express his anxiety for the success of the Goderich government', the continuation of Canning's administration, but had later congratulated the pro-Catholic Lord Melville on 'the retreat of the Whigs and the establishment of a *Protestant government*, which he hopes will last forever', under Wellington.[78] His administration of Madras was not satisfactory to the government at home, especially because he dismissed an official who had to be re-instated and spent too much of his time trying to establish a British colony in the Neilgherry Hills.[79] His unpopularity among the Indian population led to an assassination attempt by a disaffected Indian soldier: he was grazed on the head by a shot from close range as he returned home in his carriage from the New Year's Day festivities in January 1831.[80] He unsuccessfully contested Canterbury as a Conservative in 1835, but was seated on petition and sat until his retirement in 1837. He wrote a laudatory account of the *Life and Services of General Lord Harris* (1840), was embroiled in a controversy over his refusal to pay church rates and enjoyed 'a green old age'.[81] He died in August 1868, outliving all his sons, including Charles Manners (1819-64), Member for Canterbury, 1854-7, except for Richard Henry, who inherited his annuity, while the rest of his estate was bequeathed in trust to his grandson James Lushington Wildman (1825-78), the son of his daughter Mary Ann and James Beckford Wildman*.

[1] *Kentish Gazette*, 25, 29 Feb., 3, 10 Mar.; *Kentish Chron.* 10 Mar. 1820. [2] For example, *Geo. IV Letters*, ii. 895; *The Times*, 27 June 1820, 16 June 1821. [3] For example, *The Times*, 8 Mar., 8, 9 May, 6 Aug. 1822, 10 Mar. 1826. [4] Add. 38299, f. 80; 40379, ff. 190, 320-1; 40382, ff. 248, 285; 40392, f. 72; Wellington mss WP1/768/5; 773/12; 789/18; 830/6; Lonsdale mss, Lowther to Lonsdale, 19 Dec. 1823. [5] Cent. Kent. Stud. Harris mss U624 C67/120. [6] Add. 40406, f. 205. [7] Add. 40344, f. 75. [8] Add. 38743, f. 262. [9] *The Times*, 17 July 1820. [10] *Kentish Chron.* 8, 11 Aug. 1820. [11] Northumb. RO, Middleton mss ZMI/S76/31/11. [12] *The Times*, 23, 30 Mar. 1821. [13] Ibid. 7 June 1821. [14] Harris mss C67/121. [15] *The Times*, 28 Feb. 1822. [16] Ibid. 13 Mar. 1822. [17] Add. 37298, f. 324; *The Times*, 13 June 1822. [18] *The Times*, 20 May, 14 June 1822. [19] Ibid. 29 June 1822. [20] Ibid. 10 July 1822. [21] Ibid. 19 July 1822. [22] Ibid. 25 July, 1 Aug. 1822. [23] *Arbuthnot Jnl.* i. 195; Add. 38743, f. 262. [24] Harris mss C249, Lushington to Harris, 11, 16 Jan. 1823; Add. 40354, ff. 101-3. [25] Harris mss C249, Lushington to Harris, 26 Mar. 1823. [26] Lonsdale mss, Ward to Lonsdale, 26 Mar., 1 Apr. 1823. [27] Add. 38296, f. 68; 40357, f. 305. [28] *The Times*, 13 Mar. 1824. [29] Ibid. 4 May; *Kentish Chron.* 2, 16 Apr.; *Kent Herald*, 3 June 1824; *PP* (1824), vii. 183-301. [30] *Kentish Gazette*, 7 May, 30 July; *Kent Herald*, 29 July, 5 Aug.; *Kentish Chron.* 30 July 1824. [31] BL OIOC Robinson mss Eur.F.142.26, Lushington to Robinson, 15, 25, 28 Mar. 1824. [32] Add. 38411, f. 233. [33] Buckingham, *Mems. Geo. IV*, ii. 48, 66. [34] Robinson mss Eur.F.142.26, Liverpool to Lushington, 19 Mar. 1824. [35] Ibid. Lushington to Robinson, 30 Mar. 1824; Wellington mss WP1/791/2; *Arbuthnot Jnl.* i. 297. [36] Harewood mss, Canning to his wife, 4, 6 Apr. 1824. [37] Harris mss C67/123; Add. 40365, ff. 152-4; TNA, Granville mss, Howard de Walden to Granville, 14 May; *Kent Herald*, 17, 24 June 1824. [38] C.H. Philips, *E.I. Co.* 251-2. [39] Buckingham, ii. 112, 114-16, 120-3; Wellington mss, Wellington to Mrs. Arbuthnot, 1 Sept. 1824; Add. 38746, f. 32. [40] Add. 38193, f. 200; 38411, f. 240; *Arbuthnot Jnl.* i. 360-1; Philips, 253; Buckingham, ii. 133, 145. [41] Add. 38411, ff. 238, 247. [42] Harris mss C67/120. [43] Add. 40368, f. 304; 40369, ff. 105-6, 240. [44] *Black Bk.* (1832), 551; Harris mss C67/133. For Lushington's financial problems, see Harris mss C67/125, 127, 128; C242; C257. [45] Grey mss, Tierney to Grey, 31 Jan. 1825. [46] *Kentish Chron.* 10 Apr. 1821. [47] *The Times*, 11, 17 May 1822. [48] Harris mss C67/126. [49] *Arbuthnot Jnl.* i. 378. [50] Harris mss C67/129. [51] Ibid. C242, Lushington to Harris, 15, 16 Apr. 1825. [52] *Kentish Chron.* 1 July 1825. [53] *Arbuthnot Jnl.* i. 392. [54] Grey mss GRE/B10/9/25. [55] Add. 40385, f. 271. [56] *Arbuthnot Corresp.* 70; *Kentish Chron.* 12 July, 9 Aug., 23 Sept., 1 Nov. 1825. [57] Ibid. 3, 14 Mar., 2 June; *Kentish Gazette*, 2 June 1826. [58] *Kentish Chron.* 16, 19, 23, 26 May; *Kentish Gazette*, 16, 19 May 1826. [59] *Kentish Chron.* 13 June; *Kentish Gazette*, 13 June 1826. [60] Macleod mss 1055/1, 1061/2. [61] *Arbuthnot Jnl.* ii. 31. [62] Heron, *Notes*, 164. [63] Nottingham Univ. Lib. Ossington mss, Denison diary, 6 June, 15, 17 Nov. 1826. [64] Wellington mss WP1/822/20; 825/12; 826/11; 857/9. [65] Lonsdale mss, Ward to Lonsdale, 25 July 1826; Philips, 260. [66] *Kentish Chron.* 17 Nov. 1826, 16, 30 Jan., 13 Feb., 27 Mar., 3, 6, 10, 20, 27 Apr., 4 May; *Kentish Gazette*, 26 Jan., 3, 20 Apr., 4 May 1827. [67] *Arbuthnot Jnl.* ii. 75-76. [68] *Canning's Ministry*, 12, 27. [69] G.I.T. Machin, *Catholic Question in English Politics*, 92. [70] *Geo. IV Letters*, iii. 1296. [71] Wellington mss WP1/893/3. [72] *The Times*, 13 June; *Kentish Chron.* 12 June; *Kentish Gazette*, 15 June 1827, 6 Mar. 1829. [73] *Kentish Chron.* 8, 26 June, 3 July; *Kentish Gazette*, 3, 13 July 1827. [74] *Kentish Gazette*, 2 Oct. 1827. [75] Ibid. 22 Feb., 11, 18 Mar., 15 Apr., 10 June; *Kentish Chron.* 26 Feb., 11, 18 Mar., 1, 8, 15 Apr., 10 June 1828; see CANTERBURY. [76] *Kentish Chron.* 6, 20, 24 Feb., 3, 24 Mar., 12, 19, 26 May, 9 June; *Kentish Gazette*, 10, 24 Feb., 3, 13, 24 Mar., 8, 12, 15, 19, 22, 26 May, 5, 9 June 1829. [77] *Kentish*

Chron. 29 June, 6, 13 July; *Kentish Gazette*, 25, 29 June, 2, 6, 13 July 1830. [78] *Ellenborough Diary*, i. 278-80. [79] Ibid. i. 222-3; ii. 181-2; Wellington mss WP1/937/18; 964/17; 974/32; *Bentinck Corresp.* ed. C.H. Philips, 30-31, 34-35, 50-53, 66, 108, 156, 434, 539-40, 641-5, 649-50; *Government of Madras under Lushington* (1831). [80] *Kentish Gazette*, 25 Mar. 1831. [81] *Account of Refusal of Church Rates by Lushington* (1841); *The Times*, 8 Aug. 1868; *DNB*; *Oxford DNB*.

S.M.F.

LUTTRELL, Henry Lawes, 2nd earl of Carhampton [I] (1737–1821), of Painshill, Surr.

BOSSINEY	1768–Apr. 1769
MIDDLESEX	15 Apr. 1769–1774
BOSSINEY	1774–1784
PLYMPTON ERLE	1790–24 Jan. 1794
LUDGERSHALL	28 June 1817–25 Apr. 1821

b. 7 Aug. 1737,[1] 1st s. of Simon Luttrell†, 1st earl of Carhampton [I], and Judith Maria, da. and h. of Sir Nicholas Lawes, gov. Jamaica; bro. of Hon. James Luttrell†, Hon. John Luttrell† and Hon. Temple Simon Luttrell†. *educ.* Westminster 1751; Christ Church, Oxf. 1755. *m.* 25 June 1776, Jane, da. of George Boyd of Dublin, *s.p.*; 1s. illegit. *styled* Lord Luttrell 1785-7. *suc.* fa. as 2nd earl of Carhampton [I] 14 Jan. 1787. *d.* 25 Apr. 1821.

MP [I] 1783-7.

Ensign 48 Ft. 1757; lt. 34 Ft. 1759; capt. 16 Drag. 1759, maj. 1762; dep. adj.-gen. in Portugal and local rank as lt.-col. 1762; lt.-col. 1 Horse 1765; adj.-gen. [I] 1770-83; col. 1777; maj.-gen. 1782; col. 6 Drag. Gds. 1788; col. en second R. Regt. Artillery [I] 1789-97, col. 1797-1800; lt.-gen. 1793; c.-in-c. [I] 1796-7; gen. 1798.

PC [I] 16 Aug. 1786; lt.-gen. of ordnance [I] 1789-97, master-gen. 1797-1800.

Patent customer, Bristol c.1770-1813; paving commr. Dublin 1784; foreman of grand jury, co. Dublin 1784, gov. 1789-*d.*, custos rot. 1792-*d.*

Carhampton, one of a wild, cynical and unscrupulous Irish family, was a parliamentary relic of the days of Wilkes, his Commons career far outlasting those of his brothers.[2] His army duties kept him mainly in Ireland, where he also held various non-professional appointments, at least until the late 1790s, when he sold Luttrellstown, county Dublin, to Luke White*.[3] Having been out of the House for over 23 years, he was brought in for Ludgershall in 1817 on the interest of Sir James Graham* of Kirkstall, Yorkshire, and, aged 82, he was again returned by him at the general election of 1820. Goaded by the Liverpool administration's rejection of his high-handed demands for a United Kingdom peerage, which he claimed as a belated reward for his support of the Union, he was generally in opposition, although he had approved of government's stern response to radical agitation in 1819.[4] He seems to have sided, nominally at least, with opposition on the Queen Caroline affair at the start of the 1821 session. Charles Williams Wynn* noted, 14 Feb., that 'on a preceding night' Carhampton and White, who is known to have paired with the Whigs in the divisions on 26 Jan. and 6 Feb., 'paired off and went comfortably to bed, without finding out that they were on the same side'.[5] No other trace of parliamentary activity has been found before his death in April 1821. His illegitimate son, Henry Luttrell (1768-1851), who had briefly sat for Clonmines in the last Irish Parliament, became an habitué of Holland House and enjoyed a high reputation as a wit and conversationalist. The peerage passed to Carhampton's brother John (c.1745-1829), Member for Stockbridge, 1774-5 and 1780-5, and latterly a commissioner of excise, on whose death it became extinct. The Jamaican plantation was devised to a nephew, subject to the 3rd earl's life interest, but the rest of his real and personal estate, which was sworn under £60,000, went to his wife (*d.* 1831).[6]

[1] *Gent. Mag.* (1737), 514. [2] *CP*, iii. 23-25; *HP Commons, 1754-90*, iii. 65-71. [3] *Hist. Irish Parl.* v. 141-3. [4] Lonsdale mss, Long to Lonsdale, 24 Feb. 1820; *HP Commons, 1790-1820*, iv. 476-8. [5] Buckingham, *Mems. Geo. IV*, i. 122. [6] *Gent. Mag.* (1821), i. 468, 648; PROB 11/1643/262; IR26/856/446; *DNB*; *Oxford DNB*.

D.R.F./S.M.F.

LUTTRELL *see also* **FOWNES LUTTRELL**

LYGON, Hon. Edward Pyndar (1786–1860), of 12 St. James's Square, Mdx.

CALLINGTON	1818–12 June 1820

bap. 3 Apr. 1786,[1] 4th s. of William Lygon†, 1st Earl Beauchamp (*d.* 1816), and Catherine, da. of James Denn; bro. of Hon. Henry Beauchamp Lygon*. *educ.* Westminster until c.1802. *unm.* CB 22 June 1815. *d.* 11 Nov. 1860.

Cornet 2 Life Gds. 1803, lt. 1805, capt. 1808, maj. and lt.-col. 1815, lt.-col. 1818, col. 1822; maj.-gen. 1837; col. 13 Drag. 1845-*d.*; lt.-gen. 1846; gen. 1854.

Lygon, a Guards officer and veteran of the Peninsular campaign and Waterloo, received £16,000 and an annuity of £3,000 from his father's estate in 1816.[2] He was returned for Callington in 1818 on Lord Clinton's precarious interest and gave silent support to Lord Liverpool's ministry. He was elected again in 1820 but unseated on petition three months later, before he could make any mark in the House. He concentrated thereafter on his military career and served as inspector general of cavalry 'for some years' until his death in November 1860.[3]

[1] IGI (Worcs.) [2] PROB 11/1591/169; IR26/697/320 [3] *Gent. Mag.* (1860), ii. 685.

R.M.H./T.A.J.

LYGON, Hon. Henry Beauchamp (1784–1863), of Springfield, Worcs. and 16 Grosvenor Place, Mdx.

WORCESTERSHIRE	5 Dec. 1816–1831
WORCESTERSHIRE WEST	1832–22 Jan. 1853

b. 5 Jan. 1784, 3rd s. of William Lygon†, 1st Earl Beauchamp (*d.* 1816), and Catherine, da. of James Denn; bro. of Hon. Edward Pyndar Lygon* and Hon. William Beauchamp Lygon†. *educ.* Westminster 1797; Christ Church, Oxf. 1803. *m.* 8 July 1824, Lady Susan Caroline Eliot, da. of William Eliot†, 2nd earl of St. Germans, 4s. (2 *d.v.p.*) 3da. (2 *d.v.p.*). *suc.* bro. John Reginald Pyndar as 4th Earl Beauchamp 22 Jan. 1853. *d.* 8 Sept. 1863.

Cornet 13 Drag. 1803, lt. 1804; capt. 16 Drag. 1807, maj. 1812, brevet lt.-col. 1815; maj. 1 Life Gds. 1815, lt.-col. 1821-37; brevet col. 1822; maj.-gen. 1837; col. 10 Drag. 1843-63; lt.-gen. 1846; gen. 1854; col. 2 Life Gds. and gold stick 1863.

Lygon, who had distinguished himself as a cavalry commander in the Peninsula, continued to sit for Worcestershire on the family interest, headed since 1816 by his eldest brother William, 2nd Earl Beauchamp. Like him he had given general support to the Liverpool ministry. At the 1820 general election he offered again, despite the fears of his brother who, having reported that Lygon was 'very unwell' a month before, worried whether he would be 'stout enough to bear the fatigues of his election or even a contest, should one unfortunately arise'. He was returned unopposed.[1] A regular but generally silent attender, who steadily brought up petitions of local concern, he continued to support ministers on most major issues, although he sided with the opposition for admiralty reductions in 1822.[2] He presented a Kidderminster petition for repeal of the import restrictions on foreign wool, 15 May 1820, and a county petition complaining of agricultural distress, 27 Feb. 1821.[3] He was absent from the division on Catholic relief, 28 Feb. 1821, but voted against it, 30 Apr. 1822, 1 Mar., 21 Apr., 10 May 1825. He attended a Worcestershire county meeting in support of agricultural relief and parliamentary reform, 8 Feb., when he promised to 'readily concur in any measures which appeared to be capable of mitigating the present distresses of the country', and he brought up the resulting petition, 4 Mar. 1822.[4] On 28 Feb. he rebutted the claims of a London corporation petition complaining of an alleged attack on Robert Waithman* by soldiers under his command at Knightsbridge barracks in the aftermath of Queen Caroline's funeral procession, saying that 'the more the matter was inquired into, the more the good temper and forbearance of the troops would be made evident'.[5] The House divided against inquiry into the incident. He was in the opposition majority for admiralty reductions, 1 Mar. He presented a petition from the silk manufacturers of Blockley against the navigation bill, 30 May 1822.[6] He voted against parliamentary reform, 20 Feb 1823. He brought up petitions for repeal of the Insolvent Debtors Act, 18 Mar. 1823, and the removal of excise licenses, 5 Apr., 5, 26 May 1824.[7] He divided for the Irish unlawful societies bill, 25 Feb. 1825. He presented constituency petitions for repeal of the corn laws, 25 Apr. 1825, 21 Feb. 1826.[8] He brought up one from the silk throwsters of Worcester against the importation of French silks, 13 Feb., and voted for inquiry into the subject, 24 Feb. 1826. He presented a Shipston petition for the abolition of slavery, 7 Apr. 1826.[9]

At the 1826 general election Lygon was returned unopposed.[10] He voted against Catholic relief, 6 Mar. 1827, 12 May 1828. He presented a petition from the Protestant Dissenters of Kidderminster against the Test Acts, 15 Feb., but divided against their repeal, 26 Feb. 1828. He brought up petitions from Evesham against the Malt Act, 14 Mar., and from Stourbridge against bull-baiting, 28 Mar. On 2 May he presented two petitions from the carpet manufacturers of Kidderminster against the discontinuation of promissory notes under £5 and the tax on wool imports. He presented one from the silk throwsters of Blockley against reducing the duty on foreign silk, 12 June 1828. Despite his earlier hostility to Catholic claims, in January 1829 he was listed by Planta, the Wellington ministry's patronage secretary, as a possible mover or seconder of the address announcing their concession of emancipation. He presented hostile petitions from 6,000 Worcester Protestants, 19 Feb., Evesham, 27 Feb., and the Worcester clergy, 30 Mar. At the end of February he was listed by Planta as 'opposed to the principle' of emancipation and he duly voted against it, 6, 18 (as a pair), 27, 30 Mar. He presented petitions from the merchants and manufacturers of Kidderminster against renewal of the East India Company's charter, 11 May 1829, 17 Mar. 1830. He divided against the transfer of East Retford's seats to Birmingham, 11 Feb., and the enfranchisement of

Manchester, Birmingham, and Leeds, 23 Feb. 1830. He presented parish petitions against the Kidderminster road bill, 24 Feb. He was granted ten days' leave on urgent private business, 1 Mar. On 9 Mar. he presented a Stourbridge petition against the truck system. He was in the minority against the appointment of a navy treasurer, 12 Mar. He presented a petition from the farmers of Lower Sapey complaining of distress that day, and another in similar terms from the grand jury of Worcestershire, 16 Mar. He presented and endorsed a petition from Worcestershire farmers against the additional duty on corn spirits, 27 Apr. He brought up petitions against the sale of beer bill from Kidderminster, 28 Apr., and Dudley, 6 May, and voted for a continuation of the restrictions, 1 July. He divided against Jewish emancipation, 17 May. Next day he presented a Kidderminster petition against the insolvent debtors bill. He voted for abolition of the death penalty for forgery, 7 June 1830.

At the 1830 general election Lygon offered again for Worcestershire, where rumours of a third candidate came to nothing and he was returned unopposed.[11] He was listed by the Wellington ministry as one of their 'friends', but was absent from the crucial division on the civil list, 15 Nov. 1830. He presented an anti-slavery petition, 5 Nov. On 14 Dec. 1830 he endorsed a Stourbridge petition against the truck system. He presented a petition for the removal of impediments to the study of anatomy, 9 Feb. 1831. On 14 Mar. he presented and endorsed a petition against the proposed disfranchisement of Evesham, whose electors, he claimed, regretted that 'in consequence of the misconduct of certain out-voters, a stigma should be attached to the whole borough'. He voted against the second reading of the Grey ministry's reform bill, 22 Mar., presented petitions in its favour from Horsley, Repton and Normanton two days later, and divided for Gascoyne's wrecking amendment, 19 Apr. 1831. Next day, when moving the second reading of the Worcester county hall bill, he argued that any objections raised by the borough Member should be dealt with in committee. Later that day he protested that a petition from Stourbridge in favour of the reform bill did 'not express the opinion of the county' and presented a counter-petition from the magistrates of Worcestershire with which he entirely concurred, observing that although 'the decision to which the House came this morning [about preserving the rights of freeman voters] will divest the bill of one of its objectionable features, yet even that which remains is so objectionable, that I cannot give it my consent'.

At the ensuing general election Lygon stood again, denouncing the reform bill as 'violent in principle' and 'hazardous to our well balanced constitution', but insisting that he was 'by no means an enemy to such reform as time and change of circumstances may have rendered necessary'. After a heated contest lasting one week, during which he was assaulted twice by an 'infuriated mob', he conceded defeat, regretting 'to find that the way I voted has lost me the good wishes and support of some of my constituents'. A 'numerous county meeting' was held in honour of his services, 21 May 1831.[12] He was a founder member of the Carlton Club in March 1832. At that year's general election he came forward for the new division of Worcestershire West, where he was returned unopposed without being proposed or seconded, the crowd's cries of 'Foley and Lygon' being taken by the sheriff as sufficient. He sat there as a Conservative who opposed repeal of the corn laws until he succeeded to his brother's peerage in 1853.[13]

Lygon died at his seat at Madresfield Court in September 1863.[14] By his will, dated 2 Mar. 1861, he left legacies of £10,000 to his only surviving daughter Georgiana, Lady Raglan, and her two sons. A trust fund of £25,000 was established for his son Frederick, which was augmented by two codicils of the same date granting him additional sums of £15,000 and £6,000. The remaining estate, including Madresfield, passed to his eldest surviving son and successor in the peerage Henry Lygon (1829-66), who had succeeded him as Conservative Member for Worcestershire West in March 1853.

[1] Worcs. RO, Lechmere mss, Beauchamp to Sir A. Lechmere, 17 Feb.; *Berrow's Worcester Jnl.* 2 Mar. 1820. [2] *Black Bk.* (1823), 173; *Session of Parl. 1825*, p. 474. [3] *The Times*, 16 May 1820, 28 Feb. 1821. [4] Ibid. 11 Feb., 5 Mar. 1822. [5] Ibid. 1 Mar. 1822. [6] Ibid. 31 May 1822. [7] Ibid. 6 Apr., 6, 27 May 1824. [8] Ibid. 26 Apr. 1825, 22 Feb. 1826. [9] Ibid. 14 Feb., 8 Apr. 1826. [10] Ibid. 5, 20 June; *Worcester Herald*, 10, 17 June 1826. [11] *Worcester Herald*, 10, 17, 24, 31 July, 7 Aug. 1830. [12] *The Times*, 29 Apr., 28 May; *Worcester Herald*, 30 Apr., 7, 14, 21, 28 May 1831. [13] T.C. Turberville, *Worcs. in 19th Cent.* 22-24; *Dod's Parl. Companion* (1833), 136. [14] *Gent. Mag.* (1863), ii. 506-7.

P.J.S.

LYNE STEPHENS, Stephens (?1800–1860), of 32 Portman Street, Mdx.

BARNSTAPLE 1830–1831

b. ?1800, o.s. of Charles Lyne (afterwards Lyne Stephens) of Pole Vellyn, Cornw. and Wilhelmina Augusta, da. of William Tonkin of Lisbon. *educ.* by Mr. Ruddock, Fulham Park, Mdx.; Trinity Coll. Camb. 10 May 1819, aged 18. *m.* 14 Oct. 1845,[1] Yolande Marie Louise, da. of Jean Louis Duvernay, *s.p. suc.* fa. 1851. *d.* 28 Feb. 1860.

Sheriff, Norf. 1858-9

Lyne Stephens's Lyne ancestors had long been resident in Cornwall. In 1826 his father, whose occupation is unknown, took the additional name of Stephens in memory of his cousin, John James Stephens, a merchant at Lisbon, who had named him as the residuary legatee of his will, which was proved under £600,000.[2] It was rumoured in 1830 that Lyne Stephens would stand for Kingston-upon-Hull, but in the event he offered for the venal borough of Barnstaple on 'perfectly independent principles', professing 'a firm attachment to our excellent constitution' and promising 'a strict regard to retrenchment and economy'. He was returned at the head of the poll.[3] The duke of Wellington's ministry listed him among their 'friends', but with a query, which proved justified as he voted against them in the crucial civil list division, 15 Nov. 1830. He ignored a request to support the Barnstaple reform petition, forwarded from a public meeting,[4] and he divided against the second reading of the Grey's ministry's bill, 22 Mar., and for Gascoyne's wrecking amendment, 19 Apr. 1831. He is not known to have spoken in debate, and retired at the ensuing dissolution. He stood for Sudbury as a Conservative in 1835, but came bottom of the poll. A devotee of the Turf, he was the residuary legatee of his father's estate in 1851; the personalty was sworn under £180,000.[5] In 1856 he purchased and rebuilt Lynford Hall, near Brandon, Norfolk. He died in February 1860 and left his property, including personalty sworn under £700,000, to his French wife, a former ballet dancer and noted beauty.[6]

[1] *Gent. Mag.* (1845), ii. 416. [2] PROB 11/1719/657; IR26/1106/1177. [3] Lincs. AO, Ancaster mss, Denison to Heathcote [July]; *N. Devon Jnl.* 22 July, 5 Aug. 1830. [4] *N. Devon Jnl.* 10 Mar. 1831. [5] PROB 11/2135/510; IR26/1914/389. [6] N. Pevsner and B. Wilson, *Buildings of England: Norf.* ii. 531-2; W. Rubinstein, *Men of Property*, 253.

T.A.J.

LYON, David (?1794–1872), of 34 Grosvenor Square, Mdx.

BERE ALSTON 11 Jan. 1831–1832

b. ? 1794, 3rd s. of David Lyon (*d.* 1827), W.I. merchant, of Mincing Lane, London and Isabella, da. of John Read of Cairney, Forfar; bro. of William Lyon*. *educ.* Harrow 1809. *m.* 1848, Blanche, da. of Rev. Edward John Bury, rect. of Lichfield, Hants, *s.p. d.* 8 Apr. 1872.

Sheriff, Suss. 1851-2

Lyon was a descendant of Sir Thomas Lyon of Auldbar, Forfarshire, the master of Glamis and lord high treasurer of Scotland, who died in 1608. His grandfather John Lyon lived at Castle Lyon, Perthshire and Kinnaird, Forfarshire, and married Jane Ochterlony of Pitforthy, Forfarshire, the aunt of General Sir David Ochterlony (1758-1825), the conqueror of Nepal. His father was in business in London as a West India merchant, with interests and property in Jamaica. Lyon seems to have been the only one of five brothers to have participated in the family business, and he was listed in the directories as a merchant at 5 Lime Street Square until 1831. He was appointed to the standing committee of the London West India merchants and planters in 1822, but played little part in their proceedings.[1] He was named as the residuary legatee of his father's estate in 1827, and apparently benefited to the tune of about £171,000.[2] His subsequent political conduct suggests that he was not the David Lyon who joined Brooks's Club, 23 May 1829. In January 1831 he was returned *in absentia* on a vacancy for Bere Alston on Lord Beverley's controlling interest, after an attempt to open the borough by extending the franchise beyond the burgage holders had been thwarted.[3]

He took his seat, 10 Feb. 1831, but is not known to have spoken in debate during his brief parliamentary career. He divided against the second reading of the Grey ministry's reform bill, 22 Mar., and paired for Gascoyne's wrecking amendment, 19 Apr. 1831. At the ensuing general election he came in again for Bere Alston with Beverley's son, after a token contest organized on behalf of two members of the government.[4] He divided against the second reading of the reintroduced reform bill, 6 July 1831. He voted for an adjournment motion, 12 July, to use the 1831 census for the purpose of determining the disfranchisement schedules, 19 July, and to postpone consideration of Chippenham's inclusion in schedule B, 27 July. However, he voted with government to include St. Germans in schedule A, 26 July. He divided against the bill's passage, 21 Sept. He presented a local landowners' petition against the Llanelli tithes bill, 18 July 1831. His only other recorded votes were against ministers on the Russian-Dutch loan, 26 Jan., 12 July, and the third reading of the revised reform bill, 22 Mar. 1832. He took a pair for a week in May 1832.[5]

Bere Alston was disfranchised by the Reform Act and Lyon was never again in the House. On the eve of the general election of 1835 he reported the prospects of Conservative success at Arundel to Francis Bonham*, the election manager, with whom he was on friendly enough terms to feel able to advise him that William Holmes*, the whip, appeared to be '*excessively* angry' with him.[6] Not long after retiring from Parliament he purchased the estate and castle at Goring, near Worthing, Sussex,[7] and he also bought Balintore Castle in Forfarshire, not far from Glamis. In 1848 he married the daughter of the novelist Lady Charlotte Bury (*née* Campbell) and her second husband. He died in Nice 'aged 77', in April 1872, and left Goring and Balintore to his only surviving brother William, and other property in Sussex to his nephew Arthur James Fremantle.[8]

[1] Inst. of Commonwealth Stud. M915/4/1/10. [2] The personalty was sworn under £600,000 (PROB 11/1728/438; IR26/1135/590). [3] *R. Devonport Telegraph*, 15 Jan. 1831. [4] Ibid. 30 Apr., 7 May 1831. [5] *The Times*, 14 May 1832. [6] Add. 40405, f. 98; 40617, f. 11. [7] *Suss. Arch. Coll.* xvi. (1864), 187. [8] *The Times*, 13 Apr., 6 July 1872.

D.R.F.

LYON, William (1807–1892).

SEAFORD 7 Mar. 1831–1832

bap. 7 July 1807,[1] 5th s. of David Lyon (*d.* 1827), W.I. merchant, and Isabella, da. of John Read of Cairney, Forfar; bro. of David Lyon*. *educ.* Harrow 1820. *m.* 28 June 1860, Louisa Maria Sporle, da. of Henry Valentine Smith (*alias* Swanborough) of Albert Terrace, Mdx., 3s. *suc.* bro. David to Goring, Suss. and Balintore Castle, Forfar 1872. *d.* 5 Apr. 1892.

Cornet 8 Drag. 1823, lt. 1825, capt. 1826; capt. (half-pay) 6 W.I. Regt. 1833; maj. (ret.) 67 Ft. 1841-*d.*

Lyon, who inherited £100,000 from his father on coming of age, had a brief army career.[2] At the general election of 1830 he and William Williams, sheriff of Glamorgan, stood jointly for Seaford, apparently in response to an invitation from a group of electors in rebellion against the patron Lord Seaford, whose son Augustus Ellis and coadjutor John Fitzgerald were the sitting Members. While Lyon and Williams, who claimed to favour 'retrenchment and reform of abuses', stressed their championship of electoral 'independence', the contest had strong political overtones: Seaford, his son and Fitzgerald were followers of Canning's political heir Huskisson; and the intrusion of Lyon and Williams, who were said by their opponents to have been sent down and subsidized by the treasury, was seen as part of the Wellington ministry's vendetta against the Canningite rump. Five votes tendered for Lyon and Williams were rejected by the returning officer, leaving Lyon four behind Ellis in third place. Although he failed to enter into recognizances in support of his own petition, that lodged in the names of five electors was pursued to a successful conclusion, 7 Mar. 1831, when Lyon was seated in place of Ellis.[3] In his maiden speech, 9 Mar., he condemned the Grey ministry's 'revolutionary' reform bill, which infringed chartered rights and, in the case of Seaford, passed 'a sentence of annihilation'. He voted against the second reading, 22 Mar., and for Gascoyne's wrecking amendment, 19 Apr. 1831.

At the ensuing general election he came in unopposed for Seaford. At the nomination he stated his belief that

> no reform was necessary. If populous towns ought to be represented, then give them the Members from those boroughs which were disfranchised for their venality and corruption, and give them also the Members for those nomination boroughs which the nominees [sic] were willing to resign. He thought that the Members who were returned for close boroughs had the interest of Birmingham, Manchester and such other towns as much at heart as any Members would have if returned for those places, because they would not be fettered by local prejudices.[4]

He voted against the second reading of the reintroduced reform bill, 6 July, and for use of the 1831 census as a basis for disfranchisement, 19 July. On the proposal to disfranchise Seaford, 26 July, he cited his own success as proof that it was not 'under nomination'; his suggestion that it be united with Hastings on the model of Sandwich and Deal was disregarded. He voted in favour of allowing the freeholders of the four sluiced boroughs to retain their votes, 2 Sept. He divided against the passage of the bill, 21 Sept., and the second reading of the revised measure, 17 Dec. 1831. His only other known vote against it was on the enfranchisement of Tower Hamlets, 28 Feb. 1832. He voted against government on the Russian-Dutch loan, 26 Jan., 12 July, and was in the minority of 16 against the Greek loan, 6 Aug. 1832.

By his own later account, Lyon 'retired into private life, living chiefly abroad', after the disfranchisement of Seaford.[5] He was in England in 1837, when he unsuccessfully contested Lewes as a Conservative at the general election; and Benjamin Disraeli† encountered him in London in 1841.[6] Five years later he had taken up residence at 22 Park Lane. By then he had undergone a political transformation, converted by his belated recognition of 'the errors of a system of restriction and protection' into 'a free trader and a Liberal'. It was in this guise that he stood in 1859 on a vacancy for Marylebone, where his recent work as member for St. George's, Hanover Square on the metropolitan board of works had made him widely known. He advocated neutrality in the Italian conflict, economy in the public departments and an end to 'the corrupting process of nepotism', abolition of church rates and a 'full and entire' reform of the electoral system, with the ballot a *sine qua non*. He voiced his objections to 'political clubs', which thrived on 'hocus-pocus and confusion', and was comfortably beaten by a more outspoken Liberal critic of the new Palmerston ministry, who was supported by Cobden.[7]

The following summer he married, at St. Margaret's Westminster, the actress daughter of Henry Swanborough, a failed and bankrupt accountant, who in 1861 became lessee and manager of the Strand theatre. (He cut his throat two years later in a fit of 'temporary insanity' and was succeeded in the management by his widow.)[8] In March 1862 Lyon, who was then living at 4 Grosvenor Gate, Park Lane, came within a whisker of returning to Parliament as 'a thorough Liberal and practical reformer', losing the Canterbury by-election by three votes in a poll of 1,385. At the general election of 1865 he was confident of a quiet return there by tacit agreement with the Conservatives, but he was dished when a section of the local Liberals started a second man and provoked an unsuccessful contest.[9]

On the death of his only surviving brother David in 1872 Lyon inherited his properties at Goring, Sussex and Balintore, Forfarshire, as well as his London house in South Street, Park Lane. He subsequently sold his own house in Upper Grosvenor Street. He stood for Shoreham as a Liberal at the general election of 1874, but finished a very distant third. In 1886 he moved his London home to 1 Hill Street, Berkeley Square, which cost him £5,600. He died at Goring in April 1892. By his will, dated 8 Mar. 1863 he provided his wife with an annuity of £1,400 and legacies of £5,400. He left £70,000 to his second son Fitzroy David Lyon (1862-1914) and £58,000 to his youngest son Nathaniel John Lyon (1865-1907), with an additional sum of £12,000 to be invested in a life trust fund. He was succeeded at Goring by his eldest son William Francis Lyon (1861-1925), on whose death the estate passed to Fitzroy Lyon's daughter Joy Betty Marina.

[1] At St. Giles, Camberwell (IGI). [2] PROB 11/1728/438. [3] *Brighton Guardian*, 7, 14, 21, 28 July, 4, 11 Aug. 1830, 9 Mar. 1831. [4] *Suss. Advertiser*, 2 May 1831. [5] *The Times*, 23 June 1859. [6] Ibid. 5, 18, 21, 25-27 July 1837; *Disraeli Letters*, iv. 1156X. [7] *The Times*, 21-25, 27 June, 6-8 July 1859. [8] Ibid. 29 May 1863; *Ann. Reg.* (1863), Chron. pp. 87-88. [9] *The Times*, 3, 7 Mar. 1862, 3, 6, 12, 13 July 1865.

D.R.F.

MABERLY, John (c.1775–c. 1840), of Shirley House, Croydon, Surr.

RYE 10 May 1816–1818

ABINGDON 1818–1832

b. c. 1775, 1st s. of Stephen Maberly of London and Reading, Berks. and w. Mary Herbert. *m.* (1) 31 Mar. 1796, Mary Rose (*d.* ?14 Apr. 1810),[1] da. of William Leader, coachmaker to the prince of Wales, of Bedford Row, Holborn, Mdx., 2s. (1 *d.v.p.*) 2da.; (2) 13 Apr. 1813,[2] Anne Bailie, 2s. 3da. *suc.* fa. 1831. *d.* by 25 Feb. 1840.

Cornet London and Westminster light horse vols. 1800, lt. 1803, capt. 1804, maj. 1814.

Maberly, a hard-bitten, forceful and abrasive entrepreneur, self-confident to the point of arrogance, had prospered initially as a London contractor for army clothing, and subsequently as the owner of the Broadford linen and sailcloth factory in Aberdeen and founder of the Exchange and Deposit Bank in Edinburgh, with branches eventually established in Aberdeen, Dundee, Glasgow and Montrose. As Member for Rye from 1816 to 1818 he had supported the Liverpool ministry, but he had fallen out with them in somewhat mysterious circumstances at the time of the dissolution of the 1812 Parliament. After he had secured an unopposed return for the single Member borough of Abingdon, which he had been cultivating for several months, his politics underwent a complete transformation, as he moved into uncompromising opposition, though he never joined Brooks's. There were suggestions that his conversion owed more to disappointed ambition, possibly for a peerage or to supplant the existing government-backed patron of Rye, than to conviction; but on the hustings in 1830, while hinting that there was some truth in the latter story, he attributed it largely to his disgust at the government's failure to reform the fiscal system and promote economy and tax reductions.[3] These, indeed, became his pet subjects, which, as a member of the opposition's parliamentary awkward squad and a frequent though rarely a lengthy speaker, he pursued remorselessly.

His unopposed return for Abingdon at the general election of 1820 was a foregone conclusion.[4] He secured returns of information on the national finances and linen export bounties, 2 May 1820.[5] On 11 May, moving for an account of outstanding exchequer bills and Irish treasury bills, he called for an end to chancellor Vansittart's system of 'temporary expedients' and 'the adoption of a permanent system of finance'. In an argument which he was to repeat ad nauseam, he put the case for the creation a genuine sinking fund from a real surplus of revenue over expenditure, the repeal of taxes on raw materials and of the assessed taxes and their replacement by a tax on landed property, and, to underpin and facilitate these reforms, 'the most rigid economy in every branch of public expenditure'. He was critical of Vansittart's bargain with the Bank for a loan of £7,000,000 in exchequer bills and of the proposal to enable the Bank to secure repayment out of the revenue, 30,[6] 31 May, and damned his budget statement of 19 June with the faint praise that it was the best he had ever presented, though he warned that it would only realise half the amount of sinking fund anticipated. He was successful in having the linen export bounties reconsidered, 1, 30 June, but not in his attempt to have the duty charged on the importation of foreign yarn. A bill to continue the Act of 1756 became law on 15 July 1820.

On 18 Sept. 1820 he spoke and voted, in the minority of 12, for Hobhouse's motion for a prorogation of Parliament, explaining that he had divided in good faith for Wilberforce's compromise resolution of 22 June, but that ministers had since proceeded with the prosecution of Queen Caroline in the teeth of public opinion. As the owner of a 'charming' property at Croydon, he signed the requisition for and attended the Surrey county meeting to petition in her support, 2 Feb. 1821, when he called for economies and tax reductions and attacked the county Member, Holme Sumner, for his assertion of the queen's guilt.[7] He joined fully in the parliamentary campaign on her behalf, and renewed his criticism of Holme Sumner when presenting the petition, 8 Feb. Unlike his eldest son William, who had been returned for Northampton, Maberly was at this stage hostile to Catholic relief, as were most of his constituents, and he duly voted against it, 28 Feb. He broached the subject of the national finances, with particular emphasis on the savings which he thought could be made in the cost of revenue collection, 1 Feb., and again badgered ministers on the problem of the linen bounties, 27 Feb.[8] On 6 Mar., appealing to disgruntled agricultural backbenchers for support, he made what the 'Mountaineer' Henry Grey Bennet considered 'a clear, good, and convincing case' for a 50 per cent reduction in the window tax from 1822, and was only beaten by 109-83;[9] but his subsequent resolution for the repeal of almost £2,000,000 in taxes was negatived without a division. Thereafter he was a regular voter for economy, retrenchment and tax reductions. Among his several interventions in debate on these topics, he denied that his scheme for tax savings was 'an attempt to delude the public', 12 Mar.; said that 'the wanton extravagance of ministers was not to be endured', 18 May; argued in favour of ordnance rationalizations, 25 May; spoke in favour of repeal of the tax on husbandry horses, 14 June; and clashed with Lord Londonderry over government's failure to implement the recommendations of the agricultural distress committee for economies, 25 June.[10] On 12 Apr. he was excused further attendance at the Callington election committee on account of gout, to which he was a martyr. He attacked ministers for borrowing at great expense from the Bank of Ireland, 10 May, moved unsuccessfully to equalize the interest paid on Irish treasury and exchequer bills, 30 May, and tried in vain to veto certain appointments to the Irish revenue commission, 15 June. He peddled his usual nostrums on the budget statement, 1 June, and on 8 June complained that ministers had yet again brought in the ways and means before the supplies had been voted.[11] He supported Hume's accusations of jobbery in the purchase of the new stamp office in Edinburgh, 27 June, when he also spoke and voted for his call for economy and retrenchment. (Grey Bennet, reflecting on Hume's verbosity, observed that Maberly, 'as a rival artist in the same line, is no bad evidence of what can be done in the way of economy'.)[12] Maberly had a clause added to the audit of accounts bill for the production of an annual comparison of income and expenditure, 1 July.[13] He was no radical reformer, but he voted silently for parliamentary reform, 18 Apr., 9 May, and for reform of the Scottish county representation, 19 May. He paired for the forgery punishment mitigation bill, 23 May, and commented that a forger would be mad to copy Bank notes when, by this bill, he could forge those of country banks at much less risk, 25 May. He endorsed Hume's complaint of numerous delays and failures in the production of information, 10 July 1821.[14]

At the Surrey county meeting to petition for relief from agricultural distress, 4 Feb. 1822, Maberly urged the reformers not to create discord: 'though parliamentary reform was the most desirable thing they could have, it was inexpedient to connect it with the present petition'.[15] At the meeting which petitioned for tax reductions and reform, 18 Feb., he attacked Holme Sumner for failing to support the former in the House.[16] He spoke and voted for inquiry into the Scottish burghs, 20 Feb., contending that an overwhelming majority of burgesses wanted reform. He voted silently for Russell's reform motion, 25 Apr., and for Hume's amendment to the royal burghs accounts bill, 19 July. He voted for more extensive tax reductions to relieve distress, 21 Feb., and went on to support various proposals to that end. He asserted that economies in revenue collection could finance repeal of the salt tax, 28 Feb., and he spoke and voted for it again, 28 June.[17] On the army estimates, 15 Mar., he betrayed his frustration by advising Hume, who had 'undoubtedly done more good for the country than any man who had sat in Parliament for the last 20 years', to give up

> the useless task of disputing the estimates, item by item, since all exertions were rendered unavailing by the overwhelming majorities of ministers. He entreated ... [Hume] not to exhaust his own strength, and that of his friends, night after night, but to propose at once a reduction of taxation to the amount which he considered fair and reasonable, and then to leave the country to decide between him and ministers.

On the budget, 1 July, when he called for greater economies, he observed that 'the country would go on increasing in prosperity, not in consequence of its good government, but in spite of its bad one'. Next day, supporting repeal of the house and window taxes, he denied that in attacking the 'delusion' of the sinking fund, the opponents of ministers were seeking to undermine public credit. He supported amendments to the navy five per cents bill, 25 Feb., 4, 8 Mar. He made some progress in his campaign to secure an improvement in the way the public accounts were presented, explaining on 1 Mar., when he gave notice of a motion and expressed his pleasure that ministers intended to act, that he had recently gone to the treasury himself to point out an error. His demands for the production of large quantities of relevant papers, 4, 13 Mar., ruffled ministerial feathers. When he moved for the appointment of a select committee of inquiry into the means of simplifying the accounts, 14 Mar., government moved a restrictive amendment; but when Vansittart offered to take up the question at a later date, Maberly withdrew his motion. On 27 Mar. he complained that accounts ordered the previous May had not yet been produced.[18] Welcoming the government's proposal to set up a public accounts committee, to which he was named, 18 Apr., he extolled the virtues of the balance sheet, which even thick-headed country gentlemen would be able to understand. He voted against Canning's bill to relieve Catholic peers of their disabilities, 30 Apr. He was contemptuous of the ministerial plan to relieve the immediate burden of naval and military pensions by granting contractors a fixed annuity of 45 years, 1 May: it was 'a perfect delusion', which amounted to a new loan. He supported amendments to safeguard the sinking fund, 3, 24 May. He was anxious that when the Bank's charter was renewed, steps should be taken to curb its excessive profits, 7, 14 May, 20 June. He presented an Abingdon petition for revision of the criminal code, 9 May, when he also voted for a 20*s.* duty on wheat.[19] He was appointed to the select committee on the Irish linen trade, 18 May, and presented a petition against the beer retail bill, 17 July.[20] In his parting shot of the session, 31 July 1822, he criticized ministers for only tinkering with tax reductions and for throwing 'additional burdens upon posterity' in the form of massive interest on the public debt and additional expenditure of £25,000,000.

Maberly attended the Surrey reform and distress meeting, 10 Feb. 1823, but evidently remained silent while William Cobbett† created trouble.[21] In the House that day, and on 14 Feb., he secured the production of a variety of financial accounts. He presented an Abingdon merchants' petition for reform of the laws dealing with insolvent debtors, 12 Feb.[22] He voted for inquiry into the parliamentary franchise, 20 Feb., parliamentary reform, 24 Apr., and reform of the Scottish representative system, 2 June. On the government's proposal to raise £20,000,000 in exchequer bills, 21 Feb., he disputed the new chancellor Robinson's argument that the only way to support public credit was to apply the £5,000,000 excess of taxation revenue to redemption of the debt, and put his own case for dealing with the debt through redemption and purchase of the land tax, thus allowing £7,000,000 of oppressive taxes to be repealed. He moved resolutions to this effect, 28 Feb., when Ricardo supported the scheme, though he would have preferred to restrict the tax remissions to £5,000,000; the plan was rejected by 157-72. Two days later Mrs. Arbuthnot alleged that Maberly and Ricardo had taken advantage of advance knowledge of Canning's speech to the effect that hopes of staying neutral in the Franco-Spanish conflict had diminished to sell out of the funds 'to a large amount, anticipating a fall'.[23] He supported Hume's amendment to the national debt reduction bill, 13 Mar., pressing ministers to limit the sinking fund to a real surplus of revenue and, at all events, not to proceed immediately with the measure and so nullify in advance the various motions for tax remissions of which notice had been given.[24] He voted against the third reading, 17 Mar., and the next day was defeated by 94-48 on his motion for a repeal of assessed taxes. He questioned the sense of and voted against the military and naval pensions bill, 11, 14 Apr., and on the 18th seconded Hume's unsuccessful wrecking amendment to its third reading.[25] On 30 Apr. he was one of the opposition Members who were trapped in the House to form part of the nominal minority against Stuart Wortley's pacific amendment to Macdonald's motion on the negotiations with Spain, though it was known that he had intended to vote for it.[26] He welcomed the government's plan to remove restrictive regulations on Scottish linen manufacturing, 9 May, but he regretted the continuance of the 'useless' stamp commissioners. He denounced the beer duties bill as 'most unjust towards the brewer', arguing that the impost should be levied on the malt instead, 12 May; and on 28 May he moved for an inquiry into this proposition, but was beaten by 119-27. He repeated his objections to the measure, 13 June, and divided the House against its third reading, 17 June. He called for repeal of the hemp duties, 12 June.[27] He thought the grant for the British Museum should be placed in the hands of a committee, 20 June. On 2 July he generously congratulated Robinson on his unprecedentedly candid financial statement, which seemed to hold out good prospects of future tax reductions, and applauded the 'liberal principles' which he and his colleagues had applied to trade. At the same time, he encouraged them to reduce the land tax and lower Irish taxes. His motion for printing the petition of Thomas Hazard, who had been taken up on suspicion of involvement in the Cato Street conspiracy, 7 July, was rejected by 60-31.[28] He advised Hume to withdraw his resolutions concerning the collection of the land tax, 8 July 1823, because they were founded on 'an erroneous assumption'.

Maberly secured the return of another clutch of financial papers at the start of the 1824 session.[29] He voted for reform of Edinburgh's representation, 26 Feb. He demanded inquiry into the Bank's profit from its management of the public debt and denounced the 'most wanton bargain' with it over the dead weight of half-pay and pensions, 19 Feb. He repeated his criticism of this contract, which was reminiscent of Vansittart's fumbling expedients, 23 Feb., but he welcomed the 'enlarged and liberal principles' of tax remissions outlined by Robinson, even though he carped at their exact application. The following day he presented a petition for repeal of the assessed taxes, giving notice of his intention of renewing the subject later in the session.[30] He called for even-handed justice for England, Ireland and Scotland on the linen bounties, 26 Feb., when he was not disposed to back Hume's motion for information on the Austrian loan, the recovery of which he regarded as a 'God-send'. He spoke and voted for reductions on the ordnance estimates, 27 Feb. Seconding Hobhouse's motion for repeal of the window tax, 2 Mar., he spoke at some length in his usual terms about the sinking fund and redemption of the land tax, though he promised to support the ministry's tax reductions, as far as they went. He said that their intention to implement a graduated relaxation of the linen bounties was 'highly satisfactory' to the Scottish manufacturers, 5 Mar.;[31] but on 12 Mar. he complained that the ill-digested plan to rescind the low scale Irish bounties, without at the same time repealing the duty on hemp, had caused much unemployment. He spoke in the same vein on 18 Mar., and the next day, contesting the wisdom of repealing the bounties on fish, argued that if Ireland was not treated as an exception to the application of liberal commercial principles, many of her people must starve.[32] He deprecated the ignorant clamour against the government's 'most politic' proposal to relax prohibitory duties on imports of foreign silk, 8 Mar. On 15 Mar. he again moved for inquiry into transferring the beer duty to malt, but he mustered only 26 votes against 130; and he repeated his strictures on the bill, which had caused 'almost unparalleled' anger in the country, 13 May. When Robinson said that he would not press that part of the measure which imposed a new scale of duties, 21 May, Maberly protested that the retailing provisions were its most obnoxious feature, and he duly divided the House against the bill and tried in vain to amend it in committee, 24 May.[33] He supported the prayer of a Canterbury petition for repeal of the assessed taxes, 25 Mar., presented one from Abingdon to the same effect, along with one for the abolition of slavery, 29 Mar., and called for repeal of all the coal duties, 29 Mar., 5 Apr.[34] Robinson would not countenance his motion for redemption of the land tax as it stood, 6 Apr., but encouraged him to embody it in a bill. He presented it on 21 May, but it was thrown out at the report stage, 14 June, despite his boast that it would liberate £34,000,000 to be applied to the unfunded debt and permit £5,000,000 of tax reductions. He was not happy with the ministerial proposal to repeal the Hides and Skins Acts, 14 Apr., when he was a teller for the minority of six against its introduction. He presented three petitions against it, 4 May, and one from Dartmouth for repeal of the house and window taxes, for which he moved in a long and wide-ranging speech, 10 May, when his scheme was rejected by 171-78.[35] On

4 May 1824 he spoke and voted for his son's motion for an advance of capital to Ireland: 'if the people were not employed, rebellion would break out again'.

Maberly endorsed Hume's criticism of the navy estimates, 14 Feb. 1825.[36] He voted steadily against the bill to suppress the Catholic Association that month, presented a petition from Meath Catholics against it, 23 Feb.,[37] and, for the first time, voted for Catholic relief, 1 Mar., and did so again, 21 Apr., 10 May. The presentation of an Abingdon petition for tax reductions enabled him to bring out his usual old chestnuts, 17 Feb.[38] On the budget statement, 28 Feb., he pointed out that the vaunted increase in revenue was the natural result of the application of 'sound commercial principles'. He deplored the 'thin state of the House' which rejected his motion for a repeal of assessed taxes by 11-64, 3 Mar., when he asserted that the government 'must give way to the petitions of the people', another one of which he presented himself, 30 Mar.[39] He wanted prior and thorough investigation before the duties on iron and copper were considered, 11 Mar. He suggested that the select committee on the Irish linen trade, to which he was appointed, 14 Apr., should consider the 'ruinous' protecting duties; but, while he concurred in the 'wisdom' of the government's general commercial policy, he thought it 'desirous that they should travel by degrees' as far as Ireland was concerned. He called for relaxation of the corn laws, which impaired the beneficial effects of commercial liberalization, 29 Apr. Yet on the presentation of petitions for reform of the Combination Acts he wore his factory master's hat, stating that while workers were entitled to bargain for wages to keep pace with prices, they had no right to combine to dictate to employers, as had some Aberdeen operatives over the apprentices issue. He later voted for amendments to the combination bill dealing with intimidation and jury trial, 27 June. Another indifferent House voted down his motion for repeal of the beer duties by 88-23, 5 May. He supported Hobhouse's attack on the window tax, in resisting which ministers were 'in opposition to the sentiments of the whole country', 17 May. His only known vote against the grant to the duke of Cumberland was on 10 June. On the 17th he defended the government's customs consolidation proposals against Parnell's strictures and praised Huskisson, the president of the board of trade, but voted against the judicial salaries bill. He clashed with Hume over a petition complaining of country bank notes not being honoured in gold, which he thought should be thrown out, 27 June. Maberly's campaign for tax reductions was very popular with most of his constituents, and at the annual visitation feast of the Abingdon free school, 7 Aug. 1825, he was lavishly praised by the mayor.[40] The following month John Smith, Member for Midhurst, whose nephew was married to Maberly's daughter, told Henry Brougham* that Maberly had refused to subscribe to the planned London University:

> It is hinted to me that he considers he ought to have been invited to our committee and has taken offence. He hinted that the original idea of a metropolitan institution came from himself. As he is by no means an agreeable man to act with I hope you will agree with me that he is not worth conciliating. His claim of originality in this scheme is equally unfounded and ridiculous.[41]

On the address, 2 Feb. 1826, Maberly joined in praise of the Bank for its conduct during the recent financial panic, though he carped that it would have done even better if it had not been 'crippled ... by the dead weight of mortgages'. He thought that the difficulties had been exacerbated by the government's deluging the country with bank notes. He secured the production of a series of accounts, as usual, 6, 7, 10 Feb.[42] He asked why small notes should be suppressed only in England, 13 Feb., when he voted against going into committee on the Bank Charter Acts. He called for greater openness in transactions between the Bank and the government and urged legislation to force the Bank to give distressed merchants longer discounts on the security of deposited goods. He spoke and voted against the government's proposal to exempt the Bank from the provisions of the promissory notes bill, 20 Feb., and moved an unsuccessful amendment to extract more disclosures from the Bank, 24 Feb., but he opposed Hume's amendment requiring deposits with the exchequer equal in amount to notes issued, 27 Feb. On 10 Mar. he argued at some length that the Bank had 'added greatly to the previously existing causes of distress' by mismanaging the unfunded and funded debts. On 13 Mar. he said that Robinson's budget statement contained some 'complete fallacies', especially concerning the diminution of the charge on the public debt; but he approved of the scheme to fund £10,000,000 of exchequer bills and apply the sinking fund to the unfunded as well as the funded debt, and rejoiced at the improved prospects held out by the chancellor. He presented Abingdon petitions for relief from the assessed taxes and the burdensome mode of poor rate collection, 22 Mar., complained that although half the former had been taken off, the intolerable expense of collection still remained, 10 Apr., and on 28 Apr. moved for returns to illustrate their 'severe pressure'.[43] He thought the president of the board of trade should have the same salary as the secretaries of state, 6 Apr., but only if the treasurership of the navy was got rid of; he seconded Hume's amendment to that effect, and paired on the same side, 10 Apr. He voted to revise the corn laws, 18 Apr., and on 12 May demanded an assurance that they would be properly dealt with in the next Parliament, as the government's 'vacillating and uncertain policy' had created universal dissatisfaction. On 4 May Maberly, who three days earlier had given evidence to the Lords committee on the currency, came out against any alteration to the Scottish banking system.[44] Supporting Hume's motion on the state of the nation later that day, he said that the national debt had not really been reduced and offered his assistance to ministers in the execution of their plan to produce a thorough examination of the public accounts. His bid to add a clause to Estcourt's alehouses licensing bill to provide a regular adjournment day for applications, 12 May, was moved in his temporary absence from the House by Hume; it was defeated by 40-12.[45] He voted for reform of Edinburgh's representation, 13 Apr., parliamentary reform, 27 Apr., and Russell's resolutions to curb electoral bribery, 26 May 1826. (He later claimed that he and his son had gone up from Epsom races to vote for them and so ensure their success.)[46]

On 10 May 1826 Maberly, confident of an unopposed return for Abingdon at the approaching general election, had treated a dinner gathering of 280 of his constituents to an elaborate and boastful explanation and defence of his conduct in the expiring Parliament. Claiming to be attached to no party, he stressed his campaign for tax reductions, reform of the sinking fund, an improvement in public accounting and 'just and fair corn laws'. On parliamentary reform, he declared his strong preference for a ratepayer franchise to anything approaching universal suffrage; and, justifying his conversion to support of Catholic relief, for which 'the proper time was then come', he promised to be bound by his constituents' views on the subject in the next Parliament. The appearance of a local Tory challenger a few days later sent him hastily back to the borough to canvass again; but the opposition collapsed after a fortnight. At his uncontested election, Maberly repeated his account of his 'stewardship', denied having 'pursued a systematic opposition to government', whose recent implementation of liberal commercial policies he applauded, and repeated his pledge to take the 'instructions' of his constituents on the Catholic question. After the formalities he rushed off to Northampton, where his son was involved in a fierce but ultimately successful struggle against a Tory backed by the corporation. From a window of the *Peacock* inn he angrily denounced their alleged misappropriation of corporate funds.[47]

Maberly had taken one Richards into partnership with him in the Aberdeen linen works in March 1825, and in about 1826, when his long-running dispute with the older Scottish banks over the time in which a draft on a London bank could be cashed came to a temporary end, he seems to have established a branch of his own bank in London, initially in Upper Thames Street and later in Bread Street.[48] He supported Hume's amendment to the address, 21 Nov. 1826, because the king's speech had made no reference to distress, the corn laws or the reduction of heavy taxation, 'the great disease under which they laboured'. He threatened to resist the voting of all grants of public money until he had submitted his planned motions for tax cuts. He was called to order, 28 Nov., when he digressed from a notice of motions for accounts into a commentary on trade and Bank issues.[49] Later that day he agreed with Littleton that some change in the regulations governing Members' conduct in private bill committees was necessary, but thought it absurd to prohibit them from voting on subjects which they had not heard discussed. He pressed Waithman to lay the charges concerning James Brodgen's* involvement in the Arigna Mine Company fairly before the House, 30 Nov. He supported Graham's call for an advance of public money to relieve distress, 7 Dec. 1826. On 12 Feb. 1827 he backed Hume's demands for a candid statement of the national balance sheet before voting the navy estimates, but, having divided with ministers for sending troops to Portugal, felt that he could not fairly oppose the provision for 30,000 seamen. He was less accommodating on the ordnance estimates, 16 Feb., and the army estimates, 19, 20 Feb. On the latter day, he said that although he had advised Hume not to persevere in his detailed objections, because the estimates could be examined more effectively in a finance committee, for the appointment of which he devoutly wished, he conceded that in doing so Hume was providing 'a wholesome check to the expenditure'. He complained of the way in which ministers had dealt with the currency problem, creating a paper monopoly without prior inquiry, 22 Feb. He voted for Catholic relief, 6 Mar. He divided for a 50*s.* corn import price, 9 Mar., and for Hume's proposal to reduce the duty in stages to 10*s.*, 27 Mar. Supporting petitions from Bolton cotton manufacturers for lower wheat prices, 26 Mar., he criticized the government's revision of the laws, contending that the landed interest had no right to be exclusively protected.[50] He called for abolition of the linen board, 12 Mar.,[51] and the hackney coach office, 14 Mar., but approved the new arrangements for the post of solicitor to the customs, 13 Mar. He voted for inquiry into Leicester corporation's supposed application of their funds to electoral purposes, 15 Mar. He had voted against the resolutions on the duke of Clarence's grant, 16 Feb.; but on 16 Mar., pleading that his action had been misunderstood and arguing that the heir presumptive to the throne must be adequately provided for, he voted to go into committee on his annuity bill; he admonished Hume for putting forward the sufferings of the working classes as a reason for withholding the grant. He supported investigation of the mutiny at Barrackpoor, to which he hinted there was more than met the eye, 22 Mar. He opposed going into committee of supply in the 'deranged state' of the national finances, 26 Mar., and voted to withhold supplies until the ministerial uncertainty had been resolved, 30 Mar. He divided for inquiries into the Irish miscellaneous estimates and chancery delays, 5 Apr. 1827.

Maberly presented petitions from retail brewers of Gloucestershire for alteration of the licensing laws and from Blackburn cotton spinners for a minimum wage, 9 Apr. 1827.[52] On 7 May he declared his support for Canning's ministry, repudiating taunts that he had abandoned his struggle for reform of the sinking fund and the appointment of a finance committee. He strongly and successfully urged Canning to appoint such a committee early the next session, and thereby 'completely establish the government' in the 'eyes of the country'. He declared his undiminished enthusiasm for parliamentary reform and repeal of the Test Acts, but made it clear that he would not support them merely to gratify any 'factious' opposition to the government. On 11 May he announced that he had postponed all his financial notices until next session and would not oppose any of that year's estimates, even though he had strong objections to that for Millbank penitentiary, and urged Hume to follow suit, in view of Canning's promise of a finance committee. However, when repeating these remarks on 25 May, he implored Canning not to be too lavish in his demands on the public purse.[53] He dismissed as misguided a Glasgow manufacturers' petition against the use of machinery, 8 May.[54] He seconded Wilmot Horton's motion for inquiry into the administration of Lord Charles Somerset† at the Cape, 17 May, praising Donkin's preceding regime, after which there had occurred 'insecurity, murder, plunder, dissatisfaction, and ... utter ruin'. He expressed regret that the inquiry had been abandoned, 29 June. He was in the minority for separating bankruptcy jurisdiction from chancery, 22 May. He presented petitions for repeal of the Test Acts, 7 June.[55] On Davenport's motion for inquiry into industrial and commercial distress, 14 June, he said that there could be no sound system of currency while the Bank was free to expand and contract the circulation as it pleased. He called for examination of the beer duties, 15 June, and presented a petition from an individual who wanted permission to grind foreign corn, 21 June 1827.[56] The following day he withdrew his planned motion to outlaw the application of corporate funds to electoral purposes, but warned Northampton and other errant corporations to watch their steps in future, and complained of misrepresentation of his son's conduct in the dispute. Maberly was friendly with his fellow banker John Herries*, whose appointment as chancellor of the exchequer by Goderich after Canning's death in August, which almost drove the Lansdowne Whigs in government to resignation, he was reported to have described as 'a very proper one'. He subsequently tried to root out the author of hostile articles in the Whig *Morning Chronicle*.[57] His connection with Herries gave him advance knowledge of the impending collapse of the Goderich ministry in January 1828 and of the shape of the duke of Wellington's administration which succeeded it.[58]

Maberly began the 1828 session in belligerent mood, pressing for economies in the estimates and threatening to oppose 'every grant of money' unless proper and full accounts were first laid before the House, 1, 4, 6 Feb. On 11 Feb. he voiced his suspicion that Peel, the new home secretary, would not go into the business of the finance committee, for full details of which Maberly was desperate, with the same 'fairness' as would Canning. In committee on the navy estimates, he attacked the sinking fund in its present guise as a permanent charge on the consolidated fund, and demanded to know whether the finance committee would be allowed to go beyond 'a bare examination of accounts' and to recommend future levels of expenditure: if not, he was determined to divide against every supply proposal, which he now did on the grant for 30,000 seamen, being defeated by 48-15. The next day he expressed pleasure that Peel, contradicting Huskisson, had given assurances that the committee would have the same remit as that of 1817, but he was still suspicious enough to hope that it was 'not intended as a delusion, to amuse and gull the public'. He recommended Poulett Thomson to drop his opposition to the navy estimates, but was in a minority of eight for Hume's amendment for economies. In drawing up lists of candidates for the finance committee, to which Maberly was duly appointed, 15 Feb., Peel and Herries had been at pains to achieve a balance between safety and appearance. Maberly and Hume were included among five 'reformers'; but, so Herries hoped, they would 'in some material points counteract each other. Maberly will support establishments and run at the sinking fund, while Hume will be ultra violent against both'.[59] On 19 Feb. Maberly suggested that the expense of producing returns of information could be reduced if all papers likely to be of interest during a session could be laid on the table at its start. He cautioned the House against accepting the large army estimates on the mistaken assumption that they could be reduced by the recommendation of the finance committee, 22 Feb. John Croker*, the secretary to the admiralty, who was examined by the committee that day, was predictably contemptuous of the 'blockheads' Hume and Maberly: 'The latter asked me if the entry books and records of the office could not be copied by a *machine* to save clerks! And all his other questions were of the same force'.[60] Maberly voted for repeal of the Test Acts, 26 Feb. He presented an Abingdon maltsters' petition against the Malt Act and called for the system of army promotions to be referred to the finance committee, 12 Mar. He said that the penalties for infringing the laws governing the retailing of beer were already severe enough, 2 Apr. On behalf of manufacturers, he dismissed a demand for increased protection for British wool producers, 17 Apr., arguing that restrictions damaged all interests, not least the agricultural. He attacked the corn laws, 28, 29 Apr., when he voted for a fixed duty of 15*s*. He divided for inquiry into chancery delays, 24 Apr. He spoke and voted for Hume's bid to wreck the Aberdeen harbour bill, 5 May, and expressed surprise that agriculturists should resist repeal of the usury laws, 15 May. He voted for Catholic claims, 12 May. On 16 May he was involved in a tetchy running battle with ministers on the navy estimates, complaining that they had been brought on without reference to the findings of the finance committee. Croker reflected:

> We see now the folly, as we before saw the cowardice, of putting Hume and Maberly on this committee. They are more troublesome than ever, because being placed on the committee has redeemed their characters, and increased their information ... I whispered this to Peel, whose act it was, and he was very little pleased with the remark.[61]

Maberly kept up his refrain of the need for better information and an extension of the powers of the finance committee on the navy estimates, 19 May, the vote for civil contingencies, 30 May, when he called for an annually renewable select committee to examine details before they were submitted to the House, the vote for volunteer corps, 13 June, and the governorship of Dartmouth Castle, 20 June, when he voted for a reduction in the salary. On 19 May he presented a petition from Abingdon corporation against the alehouses licensing bill, which he spoke against, 19 June. He objected to the bill to restrict the circulation of Scottish bank notes in England, 3 June, and voted for inquiry into the question, 5 June. He divided to postpone consideration of the grant for missionary work in the colonies, 6 June, and in favour of the Irish assessment of lessors bill, 16 June, and on 30 June opposed the additional churches bill, against which he presented a petition from Westminster, 3 July. The following day he explained the grounds on which the finance committee had recommended reduction of the salary of the lieutenant-general of the ordnance, for which he now voted, and later supported Hume's adjournment motion, complaining that it was unfair to keep hard-working members of the committee up late on these 'most extravagant of all' estimates. He demanded further reductions, 7 July, when his own motion to halve the cost of the ordnance survey was rejected by 126-9, and he voted against the grant for Canadian military canals. On 8 July, however, he acknowledged the government's willingness to implement all the recommendations of the finance committee except that concerning the lieutenant-general's salary, as well as accepting their bill to regulate public pensions and salaries. On 10 July he expressed his hope that the projected 30 per cent maximum duty on East Indian silk would be strictly adhered to, and protested against a surreptitious attempt to bring forward the date for repeal of the linen bounties. He had more to say on the silk duties, 15, 16 July, when he supported Poulett Thomson's amendment to limit the duty to 30 per cent and urged ministers to drop the measure. He voted for the corporate funds bill, 10 July, and on 17 July supported Otway Cave's call for inquiry into the conduct of Leicester corporation. He voted against the archbishop of Canterbury's registrar bill, 16 June. He would have been one of the majority who voted by 10-9 in the finance committee, 23 June, to recommend the application of a real surplus of revenue rather than a fixed sum to the sinking fund;[62] and on 11 July he welcomed chancellor Goulburn's announcement that ministers had at last decided to adopt this principle, though he stated his own preference for allocating half the surplus to the remission of taxes. In a clash with Herries, he denied having opposed in the committee any reduction of the national debt by the sinking fund. He approved the subsequent national debt reduction bill, 15, 17 July 1828.

In January 1829 a public meeting at Cheltenham voted thanks to Maberly for his efforts to secure a reduction of the assessed taxes. In reply, he doubted whether any minister would lower taxation sufficiently 'until he shall be convinced of its necessity by the *manifestations of the people*, through their representatives'.[63] That month his second son died at Naples.[64] In the House, 13 Feb., he attacked Goulburn for refusing to deal with the potentially ruinous debt. On 20 Feb. he opposed proceeding to consider the army estimates in order to register his bitter protest against the extinction of the finance committee, by which the country would 'lose considerably' and 'all chance of reduction of taxation will be put an end to'. He observed that 'the government never will, constituted as it is', with each department fighting for its own interests, 'form any consistent plan of retrenchment'. He called for considerable reductions in the navy estimates, in line with the committee's recommendations, 27 Feb., though he gave credit to Hardinge, the secretary at war, for doing his best to make economies. He carped at details of the ordnance estimates, 2 Mar., while admitting the futility of such protests. He silently presented an Abingdon inhabitants' petition against Catholic emancipation, 2 Mar., but he voted for the measure, 6 Mar., and on 9 Mar. said that none of the talentless Members who had blindly opposed it, among whom he included Pallmer of Surrey, had offered 'a single remedy in any way applicable to the disease' of Irish unrest and looming insurrection. Later that day he presented the hostile petition of Abingdon corporation, which he had earlier referred back to them, on the advice of the Speaker, after being clandestinely informed by the two bailiffs, who were nominally included among its authors, that they in fact dissented from its prayer; he now brought it up as the petition of the individual signatories and dissociated himself from it. The episode provoked a row in his constituency.[65] He presented a favourable petition from Abingdon, 16 Mar., when he also approved the government's plan to suspend militia balloting. At the Surrey anti-Catholic meeting, 21 Mar., he criticized Denison, the other county Member, but was howled down after stating that without emancipation 'they would have a rebellion in Ireland in less than six months'.[66] Maberly, whose eccentric and rabidly anti-Catholic brother Frederick Herbert, curate of Bourn, near Cambridge, was foaming at the mouth over the measure, voted for the third reading of the relief bill, 30 Mar. 1829.[67]

Returning to financial questions, he said that revival of the finance committee would check the potential increase in expenditure, 2 Apr., when he moaned that without it, individuals such as himself were powerless to prevent the voting of vast sums of public money by thin and indifferent Houses. He welcomed ministers' agreement to refer the Irish miscellaneous estimates to a select committee, 4 Apr. He again complained that without proper accounts and information, 'we are granting money in the dark', 6 Apr. He had reservations about details of the assessed taxes composition bill, 9 Apr. On 13 Apr. he moved for the continued production of accounts of the national debt, with the object of demonstrating that its redemption had last year cost £157,000. He gave 'warm support' to the silk trade bill and countered Sadler's protectionist arguments, 1 May. He voted to transfer East Retford's seats to Birmingham, 5 May, and for Lord Blandford's parliamentary reform scheme, 2 June. On the budget, 8 May, he again applauded ministers' change of heart on the sinking fund, but also deplored the loss of the finance committee and denounced the issue of £3,000,000 in exchequer bills as 'a profligate waste of the public money'. He returned to the latter theme, 11, 14, 22 May, when he estimated the loss at £480,000 and, regretting that Goulburn had adopted this tortured course after seeming to be on the right track, commented that 'there is ... something in the constitution of a chancellor of the exchequer which leads him out of the straight road into complicated ways'. On 21 May he joined in Hume's opposition to the ecclesiastical courts bill which Peel, the home secretary, reeling after eighteen hours unbroken labour, denounced at three in the morning as 'the most vaxatious within the memory of the House'; Maberly was in Hume's minority of three. He voted to reduce the grant for the marble arch, 25 May. He supported the appointment of as select committee, to which he was named, to investigate the conduct of the architect John Nash over the leasing and sale of crown lands, 27 May; but he thought its sponsor, Davies, went too far in making allegations before it had reported, 19 June. He voted to reduce the duties on hemp, 1 June, considering the ministerial proposal a dereliction of the principle of removing imposts on raw materials. On the presentation of a Blackburn petition complaining of manufacturing distress, 12 June, he said that the best remedy was a programme of tax reductions and called for mass petitioning on the subject if ministers did not act in the next session. At the August 1829 school visitation feast at Abingdon, where there were increasing mutterings about distress and unemployment in the local hemp and flax manufacturing industries as a result of competition from Scotland, Maberly pledged to continue to work for tax reductions.[68]

He duly did so, with implacable determination, in the 1830 session, when he set the tone by supporting the amendment to the address, 4 Feb. His remarks on the currency, which he wanted to see established on a sound paper system, drew some satirical comment the next day from Sir Joseph Yorke, from whom Maberly extracted an apology. He described the 'monopoly' created by the corn laws as 'a law to starve the people', 8 Feb. Supporting Hume's motion for a revision and reduction of taxation, 15 Feb., when he went into considerable detail in his 'long and dull' review of the national finances, he repeated his lament for the finance committee, as he did on several more occasions during the session.[69] He voted to postpone going into committee of supply that day, and objected to proceeding with the army estimates without due consideration, 16 Feb. He supported economies in them, 19, 22, 26 Feb., though on the 22nd he conceded that 'as the finance committee has been abolished, the time for making any useful opposition to extravagant expenditure has gone by', and advised Hume to give up dividing the House in vain. He attacked the admiralty and the navy board for failing to economize after the French wars and voted to halve the grant for the Royal Military College, a particular *bete noir* of his, 26 Feb. Supporting cuts in the navy estimates, 1 Mar., he drew attention to the threat posed to the country by the massive pension fund; but on 8 Mar. he praised Hardinge for savings made in this area, though he did not neglect to observe that the system of exchequer fees was 'a disgrace to the country'. In a further concession, 9 Mar., he admitted that ministers had given every indication of wanting 'a full and fair inquiry into the public expenditure'. He exposed the fallacies which he detected in the London merchants' anti-free trade petition, 12 Mar., when he voted against giving the treasurer of the navy a ministerial salary. He commended the new budget as 'the best I ever heard', 15 Mar., approving particularly of the proposed reductions in the beer and leather taxes and increase in that on spirits. Yet he still called for greater reductions in the estimates, and spoke and voted to that effect on the naval establishment, 22 Mar. He supported Poulett Thomson's motion for a wholesale revision of taxation, 25 Mar., though he had no time for his notion of a vote of credit to indemnify the government against any deficiency, and disliked a property tax. Believing that ministers had been 'driven' into lowering taxes by the pressure of public opinion, he called for redoubled efforts to push them further. He denounced pluralism in civil offices, suggested that Cockburn, a lord of the admiralty, was being prevented by senior ministers from fully implementing his wish to economize, and opposed the Bathurst and Dundas pensions, 26 Mar. He supported abolition of the lieutenant-generalship of the ordnance, 29 Mar., and recommended a merger of the Tower Hill and Pall Mall offices and closure of the arms factory at Enfield, 2 Apr. He urged ministers not to persist with the bill to grant bounties on Irish tobacco, 8 Apr. He now refused to support Blandford's reform bill, 18 Feb., because it was 'full of inconsistencies';[70] but he professed his continued support for practical reform, and voted for the enfranchisement of Birmingham, Leeds and Manchester, 23 Feb., investigation of the Newark petition of complaint against the duke of Newcastle, 1 Mar., and the transfer of East Retford's seats to Birmingham, 5, 15 Mar., when he was in O'Connell's minority of 21 to incorporate provision for the ballot in the East Retford bill. He voted against government on relations with Portugal, 10 Mar., and divided for Jewish emancipation, 5 Apr., 17 May. He spoke and voted against the grant for the Woolwich Academy, 30 Apr., and voted against that for public buildings, 3 May. That day he divided for Hume's motion for a bill to deal with a demise of the crown. He wanted decent colonial accounts to be furnished, 10 May, when he supported reduction of the salary of the assistant secretary to the treasury. He voted for abolition of the Irish lord lieutenancy, 11 May, and repeal of the Irish coal duties, 13 May, and almost certainly divided for the production of information on privy councillors' emoluments, 14 May. He backed Hume's motion for production of the law officers' opinion on the customs duty payable in discharge of the four and a half per cent duties and condemned the waste of money on Millbank penitentiary, when hulks were available, 21 May. He welcomed changes to the coinage system which relaxed the Bank's monopoly, 4 June. He spoke and voted for reductions in the grant for South American missions, 11 June, and for the Canadian colonies, 14 June. He took exception to Littleton's bill to end payment in truck as an interference with trade, 23 June, 1 July, though he admitted that it was 'an experiment to put down an objectionable system'. He thought West India proprietors were entitled to complain about the rum duties, but not those on sugar, 30 June, 1 July, when he voted for greater reductions in the latter than those proposed by government. He generally approved of the principle of the sale of beer bill, 4 May, but had misgivings over the effects on publicans who had invested considerable capital in the trade of opening it suddenly and completely. Accordingly, he moved on 1 July to add a clause to postpone for two years the option to sell beer for consumption on the premises; he was beaten by 133-91. On 2 July 1830 he thanked Sir James Graham for moving an amendment concerning the financial surplus, which had aired an important question, but advised him to withdraw it because he had misunderstood the accounts. He went on to explain why he intended to vote for various estimates which had been criticized by Brougham: speaking as one of the few Members who had that year 'discussed the voting away the public money', whereas Brougham and others had only lately joined in, he said that as the two crucial issues of the regency and the civil list had now been settled, opposition to individual items was pointless. He vowed to return to the attack in the next Parliament.[71]

At the general election of 1830 he was challenged by the Tory Ebenezer Fuller Maitland*, a Berkshire squire, whose backers sought to blame Maberly, as a Scottish manufacturer, for the decline in the local fabric industries. He had already denied responsibility for these problems, bluntly blaming the Abingdonians' own lack of enterprise and offering to pay for a delegation to go to study the improved techniques used in Scotland, and he made an elaborate defence of his parliamentary conduct at a dinner on 6 July. He boasted of his determined campaign for tax reductions and economies, declared his support for 'gradual reform' of Parliament, particularly by enfranchising large towns, stood by his opposition to restrictive duties on trade and high protection and took credit for having secured the adoption by ministers of a proper national balance sheet and the appointment of the finance committee. As for Catholic emancipation, he said that if his constituents had censured him for his vote at the time he would have resigned his seat, but that as they had remained silent they could not fairly impugn him retrospectively. He largely repeated this performance on the hustings, adding some *ad hominem* jibes at his opponent and alleging bribery and interference by the corporation. He had a comfortable victory at the poll.[72] At the Surrey election at Guildford, 5 Aug. 1830, he attacked Hylton Jolliffe, the unsuccessful Tory candidate, for having opposed every proposition for reform and retrenchment as Member for Petersfield, and called for abolition of the county's four rotten boroughs.[73] He intervened by letter and address in Aberdeen Burghs on behalf of the candidature of his son-in-law, Robert George Smith, a London banker, but they gave it up before the elction meeting.[74]

At a party meeting before the opening of the new Parliament, 31 Oct. 1830, Maberly was reported to have put and end to 'a good deal of talking which came to very little' by asserting that 'a party could only act upon some principle', whereupon it was 'agreed that reform and retrenchments were to be our great objects'. However, his advocacy of 'opposition to every sort of monopoly' cut little ice.[75] In the House, 3 Nov., he suggested that two days in the parliamentary week be devoted exclusively to ministerial business. On the report of the address later that day, he registered his protest against the 'extraordinary' speech from the throne, which had ignored the two burning issues of tax reductions and reform. He argued that if the finance committee had been continued, the entire financial system would have been renewed and streamlined, and that

> tranquillity will not continue without reform. There is no disaffection abroad; the people are well inclined, and all they want is that to which they are fairly and honestly entitled. If that is not conceded to them, I fear a state of things will arise which we shall regret.

He thought Hume was wasting valuable time by pressing for information on the official printers, 5 Nov. He was an absentee from the decisive division on the civil list, 15 Nov., when, according to a local newspaper, he was 'accidentally shut out'.[76] He was appointed to the resultant select committee. He paid tribute to Peel for his introduction of the metropolitan police force, 18 Nov. He spoke in defence of Lord Exeter's influence at Stamford, which he deemed to be limited and legitimate, 30 Nov., 14 Dec. On 6 Dec. he cautioned Althorp, chancellor in the new Grey ministry, not to fall into the trap of laying out public money one day and borrowing it the next, and encouraged him to do all in his power to reduce expenditure and abolish useless offices. He foreswore his opposition to the scandalous Canadian waterways grant because ministers had indicated their willingness to curb it in future. His assertion that Irish petitions for repeal of the Union were 'frequently got up by designing persons', and his advice to nationalists to discourage rather than stir up agitation, in order to create the calm conditions necessary for economic improvement, led to heated exchanges with O'Connell and the O'Gorman Mahon, 11 Dec. On 13 Dec. he again warned ministers that they 'cannot expect the support of the friends who now sit behind them' unless they fulfilled their pledges on 'reform and retrenchment'; and as far as the former was concerned, he said that they 'cannot rely upon the support of the aristocracy, but must look to the people', by dissolving Parliament if they were defeated. When the Evesham election was declared void that day, he issued an address declaring the candidature of his absent son who, though currently out of the House, was in line for an ordnance place. The success of an opposition bid to have the writ suspended on account of the blatant bribery which had been uncovered forced Maberly to explain himself in the House, 16 Dec.; the suspicion of 'a most corrupt job' having been thwarted stayed with Croker.[77] On 17 Dec. Maberly called for petitions for 'a general modification' of the tax system rather than against specific items and opposed high protection of the Irish cotton trade, as he did that of the barilla industry, 20 Dec. 1830.

When Althorp, who at the turn of the year was reported to be 'coaxing' Maberly, Hume and others of the same stamp 'in small select parties', revealed his plans to deal with the civil list, Maberly applauded his innovative plan to take out diplomatic and other expenses and put them under parliamentary control, but was not happy with the proposals touching the granting of pensions. Lord Ellenborough thought that he had expressed his reservations 'doubtingly' on account of his son's appointment as surveyor-general of the ordnance.[78] He supported the government's reduction of the barilla duties and clashed again with Sadler over free trade, 7 Feb., advocated repeal of the duty on printed calico, 8 Feb., and on 10 Feb. welcomed the belated appointment of a select committee on the Canadian waterways, the subsidization of which he held out as a warning to the House never again to sanction such outlays of money without access to full information. He gave Althorp's first budget a mixed reception, 11 Feb.: he was not displeased with its sinking fund proposals and approved the reductions of the tobacco and newspaper taxes and the repeal of the coal duties; but he jibbed at the imposition of an import duty on raw cotton and the controversial levy on transfers of funded property. At the same time, he indicated that if necessary he would swallow it whole to keep ministers in place. He thought the reductions in sugar duties, though necessarily limited by current circumstances, would be beneficial, 11 Mar., but wondered if ministers might not allow the use of sugar in distilleries. On 17 Feb., when he was named to the revived finance committee, he repudiated a Tory description of Abingdon as a corrupt borough. He presented and endorsed petitions from Croydon and Wallington for reform of Surrey's proprietary boroughs, 28 Feb., along with one from Abingdon in favour of general reform. He supported the corporate funds bill, 11 Mar., having no doubt that Northampton corporation's guilt had been conclusively proved. On the 17th he was at an Abingdon meeting called to express approval of the ministerial reform bill, whose petition he presented, evidently without comment, 21 Mar.[79] Later that day he hoped that the 'disjointed' estimates would be made 'more complete in future'. He voted silently for the second reading of the reform bill, 22 Mar. He again opposed Littleton's truck bill, founded as it was 'on a most erroneous principle', 12 Apr. He was pleased with the government's plan to abolish the lieutenant-generalship of the ordnance and praised their willingness to economize, 13 Apr. The next day he defended their civil list proposals. He voted against Gascoyne's wrecking amendment to the reform bill, 19 Apr. His return for Abingdon at the ensuing general election was unopposed and largely unreported; but at a celebration dinner, 6 May 1831, he endorsed the reform bill, which 'struck at the very root of corruption' without endangering the constitution, and called on its supporters to rally behind the government in the work of further reforms which lay ahead.[80]

Maberly, whose father died on 3 June 1831, voted for the second reading of the reintroduced reform bill, 6 July, and was a steady supporter of its details, though he paired for the divisions of 5 and 17 Aug. He deplored the opposition's obstructive tactics, 12 July, and ascertained that they were adopted in defiance of Peel's prior agreement with ministers. Five days later he privately confided to Goulburn 'his apprehension that the radical party were beginning to object to the bill and would be very troublesome'.[81] He spoke for the disfranchisement of Bletchingley, which, along with the other closed boroughs of Surrey, 'override all the interests of the people', 20 July, and saw no compelling reason for allowing Chippenham (Fuller Maitland's former seat) to retain two Members, 27 July. On 24 Aug. he took the reformer Davies of Worcester to task for suggesting that public support for the bill had declined and that many on the government back benches were getting cold feet. On 30 June he opposed limitations on the factory hours of children and the use of steam driven machinery as recipes for unemployment and said that all public salaries should 'indiscriminately' be fixed at the standard of 1797, though he again praised ministers for acting up to their promises on retrenchment. He commended George Robinson's scheme to levy an equitable tax on real property and halve the duties on sugar and tea and the remaining assessed taxes, 1 July. He contrasted ministers' appointment of an inquiry into the way in which exchequer accounts were kept with the inertia of their predecessors, 8 July, when he called for the grants for professors at Oxford and Cambridge to be discontinued or extended to other universities. He urged government to produce an intelligible, printed colonial budget, as recommended by the finance committee, and pressed Hobhouse to set aside, at least temporarily, the parts of his cotton factories apprentices bill dealing with Scotland and Ireland, 18 July. After Hobhouse had agreed to exclude wool and flax factories, 28 Sept., Maberly, who was against 'meddling interference with the production of any article', commented that if he had not done so the manufacturers of linen would have been 'up in arms'. He could see no reason to suspend the issue of the Dublin writ, 8 Aug., and voted twice with government on the controversy surrounding the late election there, 23 Aug. His attempts to extend the benefits of the game bill beyond lords of the manor to the owners of a minimum of 300 acres, 8 Aug., 2 Sept., were thwarted. He opposed reception of a Preston petition for repeal of the corn laws because its language was disrespectful, 12 Aug., and deprecated the 'principle of petty legislation, namely interfering with anything', which informed the bill to regulate steam vessels, 19 Aug. On 6 Sept. he argued that the ministry had acted fairly on the subject of quarantine fees on ships and should not be badgered to reduce it before the planned date, even though he was a personal sufferer as things stood, and later expressed pleasure that the Bank of Scotland's new charter would allow it to sue and be sued by its officials. He approved the proposed increase in the duties on Cape wines in proportion to those on French and Spanish produce, 7 Sept. He asked Hume to abandon his opposition to the grant for the works at Windsor Castle and Buckingham House, 28 Sept., as it was now simply a question of justice to the contractors who were owed money. He went on to support the government's proposals for the sugar duties, asserting that while the West Indians did have a case for some protection, they would gain nothing from the inquiry which they sought. He advocated consolidation of the victualling and navy boards and the withdrawal of direct government involvement in the manufacturing of goods for the public service, 30 Sept. He gave his blessing to ministers' course on the sinking fund and dismissed the criticisms of Goulburn, who when in office had blundered by taking only a retrospective view of the problem, 3 Oct. He called for the half-pay regulations to be thoroughly investigated so that equal justice could be done to all public servants, 7 Oct. 1831.

Maberly voted for the third reading, 19 Sept., and passage of the reform bill, 21 Sept. 1831. He voted for the second reading of the Scottish bill, 23 Sept., and on 4 Oct. declared that in neither counties nor burghs was 'a single man ... fairly represented under the existing system'. On 10 Oct. he and Hume addressed a Marylebone parish meeting held in the grounds of his house in Regent's Park: he said that in throwing out the reform bill the Lords had defied the wishes of the people, who should now assert their rights, and promised that 'under no circumstances would he accept of any measure of reform from the detestable Tories'.[82] He voted for the motion of confidence in the Grey ministry later that day. On 12 Oct. he defended the government's low profile policing of the London parochial procession to St. James's, in which the participants had 'exercised their rights quietly and peaceably'. He disapproved of attempts by Hunt, 11 Oct., and Hume, 18 Oct., to turn the Commons into a tribunal for investigating the grievances of individuals who had fallen foul of the law. At the Surrey meeting called to address the king in support of the government and the reform bill, 20 Oct., Maberly, who urged rejection of Cobbett's amendment specifically condemning the bishops, declared that 'public opinion was now too strong any longer to be resisted by anybody', expressed confidence that ministers would not compromise on reform, and quoted Ricardo, 'the greatest man who had written on the subject', in an attempt to dispel the notion that the bill would injure the agricultural interest. He took the same line at a Croydon meeting, 9 Nov., though he turned his face against violence and disorder.[83] He moved for returns of information on the flax, hemp and linen trades, 9 Dec. 1831, when he got nowhere with his suggestion that the duties of the board of works should be transferred to the ordnance rather than to woods and forests, as ministers proposed. He later voiced his hope that in compensating the auditors of the land revenue, they would not, as in the case of the lottery commissioners, grant large sums to well paid and undeserving officials. In his last known intervention in debate, 12 Dec., he backed Hume's request for an inquiry into the question of how best to reorganize the board of works. He was present to vote for the second reading of the final reform bill, 17 Dec. 1831.

On 3 Jan. 1832 news broke that Maberly's bank had failed, though the linen manufacturing business was unaffected. It soon afterwards emerged that he had in fact withdrawn from the latter, which overnight was restyled Richards and Company, the previous May. The failure was largely attributed to misguided transactions on the stock exchange and some disastrous foreign loans, which, according to Edward Ellice*, had forced Maberly to live from hand to mouth for the past two years. His fall elicited little sympathy, and indeed gave pleasure to many.[84] Although his Abingdon supporters initially proclaimed that his difficulties were only temporary and would not prevent a speedy resumption of his parliamentary duties, his political career was finished, and rivals for his seat were almost immediately in the field.[85] He was granted a nominal two month's leave to attend to 'urgent business', 19 Jan. At the first meeting of his creditors, 10 Feb., which he did not attend, his debts were put at only £30,000, but the amount owing on account of deposits in the Scottish banks was reckoned at just under £110,000. He attended for the examinations of 9 Mar. and 6 and 19 Apr., when additional debts were proved, and details emerged of his indebtedness to his late brother-in-law William Leader†, and to his own son, to the trustees of whose marriage settlement of late 1830 he had been obliged to assign the Regent's Park property as security. Ironically, for a man who had campaigned so persistently for simplicity and clarity in the public accounts, the court was far from satisfied with the state of his own; but a malicious story that a fire in his house in John Street, Berkeley Square on 28 Jan. had been started by his burning incriminating papers was discounted. He promised on 19 Apr. not to take advantage of his parliamentary privilege, and soon afterwards it was rumoured in Abingdon that he was about to resign the seat. Yet, as Ellice had predicted, he retained it until the dissolution in December 1832.[86]

By then he was in the Netherlands, having gone to The Hague in August armed, at his own request, with a letter of introduction and recommendation from his friend the duke of Richmond to the prince of Orange.[87] In November 1832 his assignees, having ratified debts of £200,000 and assets of £20,000, declared a dividend of 2*s.* in the pound on his estate. The bankruptcy proceedings dragged on for several years, and in 1835 an additional dividend of 1*s.* 6*d.* was declared on debts of £158,000.[88] In April 1834 he was said to be living in Brussels.[89] The last trace which has been found of him alive is his involvement in a duel with a journalist of *The Times* in Madrid in September 1834, when he was evidently working as a foreign correspondent for the *Morning Chronicle*.[90] The date of his death, which almost certainly occurred abroad, has not been ascertained; but according to a marginal note on the registered copy will of the fashionable London attorney Evan Foulkes, who had named Maberly as one of his executors in 1824, it had taken place by 25 Feb. 1840.[91]

[1] *Gent. Mag.* (1810), i. 495. [2] At St. James's, Westminster, Mdx. (IGI). [3] *HP Commons, 1790-1820*, iv. 483-5; *Full Report of Speeches and Other Proceedings connected with Abingdon Election* (1830), 43-44. [4] *Jackson's Oxford Jnl.* 12 Feb., 11 Mar. 1820. [5] *The Times*, 3 May 1820. [6] Ibid. 31 May 1820. [7] *Von Neumann Diary*, i. 73, 102; *The Times*, 3 Feb. 1821. [8] *The Times*, 2, 28 Feb.; *Reading Mercury*, 5 Feb. 1821. [9] HLRO, Hist. Coll. 379, Grey Bennet diary, 31 [10] *The Times*, 26 June 1821. [11] Ibid. 9 June 1821. [12] Grey Bennet diary, 106. [13] *The Times*, 28 June, 2 July 1821. [14] Ibid. 11 July 1821. [15] Ibid. 5 Feb. 1822. [16] Ibid. 19 Feb. 1822. [17] Ibid. 29 June 1822. [18] Ibid. 2, 5, 14, 28 Mar. 1822. [19] Ibid. 8, 10, 15 May, 21 June 1822. [20] Ibid. 18 July 1822. [21] Ibid. 11 Feb. 1823. [22] Ibid. 11, 13, 15 Feb. 1823. [23] *Arbuthnot Jnl.* i. 221. [24] *The Times*, 14 Mar. 1823. [25] Ibid. 19 Apr. 1823. [26] Ibid. 1 May 1823. [27] Ibid. 13 June 1823. [28] Ibid. 8 July 1823. [29] Ibid. 7, 10, 12, 13 Feb. 1824. [30] Ibid. 25 Feb. 1824. [31] Ibid. 6 Mar. 1824. [32] Ibid. 20 Mar. 1824. [33] Ibid. 14, 18, 22, 25 May 1824. [34] Ibid. 30 Mar., 6 Apr. 1824. [35] Ibid. 5 May 1824. [36] Ibid. 15 Feb. 1825. [37] Ibid. 24 Feb. 1825. [38] Ibid. 18 Feb. 1825. [39] Ibid. 4, 31 Mar. 1825. [40] *Berks. Chron.* 13 Aug. 1825. [41] Brougham mss, Smith to Brougham, 6 Sept. 1825. [42] *The Times*, 7, 8, 11 Feb. 1826. [43] *Berks. Chron.* 25 Feb., 25 Mar.; *The Times*, 23 Mar., 11, 29 Apr. 1826. [44] *Colchester Diary*, iii. 426. [45] *The Times*, 13 May 1826. [46] *Reading Mercury*, 12 June 1826. [47] *Berks. Chron.* 13, 20 May, 3, 10, 17, 24 June; *Reading Mercury*, 22 May, 5, 12, 26 June; *The Times*, 20 June 1826. [48] *The Times*, 25 Jan., 7 Apr. 1832; J.M. Bulloch, 'Father of Maberly Street' in *Bon Accord*, 24 May 1930. [49] *The Times*, 29 Nov. 1826. [50] Ibid. 27 Mar. 1827. [51] Ibid. 13 Mar. 1827. [52] Ibid. 10 Apr. 1827. [53] Ibid. 12, 26 May 1827. [54] Ibid. 9 May 1827. [55] Ibid. 8 June 1827. [56] Ibid. 16, 22 June 1827. [57] Parker, *Peel*, ii. 21; E. Herries, *Life of Herries*, i.167, 201; Add. 40394, f. 216; 57419, ff. 68, 70, 88, 90. [58] Bucks. RO, Buckinghamshire mss, Lansdowne to Goderich, 6 Jan. 1828; Wellington mss WP1/914/40. [59] B. Hilton, *Corn, Cash, Commerce*, 247; Add. 40395, ff. 219-21. [60] *Croker Pprs.* i. 407. [61] Ibid. i. 419. [62] Hilton, 253-4. [63] *Berks. Chron.* 31 Jan. 1829. [64] *Gent. Mag.* (1829), i. 382. [65] *Berks. Chron.* 7, 14 Mar.; *Reading Mercury*, 27 Apr.; *Jackson's Oxford Jnl.* 2, 16, 23 May 1829. [66] *The Times*, 23 Mar. 1829, [67] See CAMBRIDGESHIRE and *Oxford DNB*. [68] *Reading Mercury*, 10 Aug.; *Berks. Chron.* 22 Aug. 1829. [69] Grey mss, Howick jnl. 15 Feb. [1830]. [70] Ibid. 18 Feb. [1830]. [71] Ibid. 11 July [1830]. [72] *Berks. Chron.* 10, 24, 31 July, 7 Aug.; *Reading Mercury*, 12, 19, 26 July, 2 Aug.; *Full Report of Speeches and Other Proceedings connected with Abingdon Election* (1830), 22-51. [73] *The Times*, 6 Aug. 1830. [74] *Aberdeen Jnl.* 28 July, 4, 18 Aug. 1830. [75] A. Mitchell, *Whigs in Opposition*, 236; Howick jnl. 31 Oct. [1830]. [76] *Reading Mercury*, 20 Nov. 1830. [77] *Croker Pprs.* ii. 106. [78] Aberdeen Univ. Lib. Arbuthnot mss, Herries to Arbuthnot, 3 Jan. 1831; *Three Diaries*, 46. [79] *Jackson's Oxford Jnl.* 19 Mar. 1831. [80] *Reading Mercury*, 2, 9 May 1831. [81] Surr. Hist. Cent. Goulburn mss Acc 304/67B, Goulburn to wife, 17 June 1831. [82] *The Times*, 11 Oct. 1831; *Wellington Despatches*, vii. 561. [83] *The Times*, 21 Oct., 10 Nov. 1831. [84] Ibid. 4, 25, 28 Jan., 11 Feb.; *Reading Mercury*, 9 Jan.; *London Gazette*, 27 Jan.; Brougham mss, Ellice to Brougham [Jan. 1832]; *Raikes Jnl.* i. 11. [85] *Reading Mercury*, 16 Jan.; *Berks. Chron.* 4, 11, 18 Feb. 1832. [86] *The Times*, 31 Jan., 11 Feb., 10 Mar., 7, 20 Apr.; *Berks. Chron.* 21 Apr.; Brougham mss, Ellice to Brougham [Jan. 1832]. [87] W. Suss. RO, Goodwood mss, Richmond to Orange, 5 Aug. 1832. [88] Add. 28673, f. 19; *The Times*, 30 Aug., 19 Nov. 1832, 21 Dec. 1833, 26 Mar. 1834, 16 Apr. 1834, 29 June 1835, 1 July 1836, 18 Mar., 28 July 1837. [89] *The Times*, 16 Apr. 1834. [90] Ibid. 1 Sept. 1834; *Raikes Jnl.* i. 281. [91] PROB 11/1705/572.

D.R.F.

MABERLY, William Leader (1798–1885), of Shirley House, Croydon, Surr.

WESTBURY 1 May 1819–1820

NORTHAMPTON 1820–1830

SHAFTESBURY 19 Apr. 1831–1832

CHATHAM 1832–June 1834

b. 7 May 1798, 1st s. of John Maberly* (*d.* c. 1840) and 1st w. Mary Rose, da. of William Leader, coachmaker to the prince of Wales, of Bedford Row, Mdx. *educ.* Eton 1811; Brasenose, Oxf. 1815. *m.* 11 Nov. 1830, Katherine Charlotte, da. of Hon. Francis Aldborough Prittie*, at least 1s. *d.v.p.*[1] *d.* 6 Feb. 1885.

Lt. 7 Ft. 23 Mar., 7 Drag. 20 Apr. 1815, 9 Drag. 1817; half-pay capt. 100 Ft. 1818-24; capt. 84 Ft. 1824; maj. 72 Ft. 1825; lt.-col. 96 Ft. 1826, 76 Ft. 1827; half-pay 1832; ret. 1881.

Surveyor-gen. of ordnance Jan. 1831-Nov. 1832; clerk of ordnance Nov. 1832-June 1834; commr. of customs 1834-6; jt.-sec. post office 1836, permanent sec. 1846-54; commr. of audit 1854-67.

Maberly stood for Northampton at the general election of 1820, having continued to cultivate the borough since his aborted attempt on it in 1818. In the view of Lord Althorp* he showed 'great skill' in throwing all the 'odium' of his own unpaid bills on Lord Compton, the sitting Member, whom he relegated to third place after a lively contest.[2] He had joined his formidable father in steady opposition to the Liverpool ministry during his brief membership of the 1818 Parliament, and he continued in the same line, but, partly perhaps on account of the distractions of his army career, he never remotely matched his father in volubility and doggedness.

He participated in the parliamentary campaign in support of Queen Caroline, to whom he had presented the Northampton loyal address, 1 Dec. 1820, at the opening of the 1821 session, though he was a little less pertinacious than his father. He endorsed his constituents' petition for restoration of her name to the liturgy, 1 Feb., and on 8 Feb. declared that 'ministers ought to have resigned their places rather than have instituted the proceedings against the queen'.[3] He voted on the opposite side to his father in favour of Catholic claims, 28 Feb., when he also presented a Northamptonshire petition for relief from agricultural distress.[4] He spoke and voted for his father's motion for repeal of the house and window taxes, 6 Mar. A founder member but not particularly dedicated attender of the Political Economy Club, from which he resigned in 1829,[5] he divided rather spasmodically for economy and retrenchment during the 1821 session. He supported Lambton's parliamentary reform motion, 18 Apr., but made clear his hostility to the specific plan, contending that to 'make property the basis' of the franchise 'and then proceed on a principle of equality, was an objection not to be overcome':

> He had no hesitation in declaring himself to be a reformer, but one of the most moderate description; and therefore he could only approve of such a plan of reform as was moderate and temperate in its principle ... On the whole, he would prefer that that House should be connected with the peers and the crown, and be in some measure under the direction of secret influence, than that it should be controlled by the harsh and overbearing power of popular clamour.

He also voted for Russell's reform proposals, 9 May 1821. Soon afterwards he went to Paris, whence he travelled with Samuel Jones Loyd, Member for Hythe, to Switzerland and Italy.[6]

At the Surrey county meeting, 4 Feb. 1822, Maberly ascribed agricultural distress to low prices, the return to the gold standard and, above all, the 'enormous pressure of taxation'; echoing his father, he asserted that immediate abandonment of the ruinous sinking fund would facilitate reductions of £7,000,000.[7] He voted for the amendment to the address, 5 Feb., and for more extensive tax reductions to relieve distress, 11, 21 Feb., but was again not the most assiduous of attenders in support of detailed cuts. He presented a Wellingborough petition for repeal of the leather tax, 29 Apr.[8] He voted for inquiry into the Scottish royal burghs, 20 Feb., and Russell's parliamentary reform motion, 25 Apr. On 25 Feb. he was admitted to Brooks's, which his father never joined. On 14 Mar., when he voted for investigation of the duties of officers of the board of control, he supported his father's motion for a select committee on public accounts. He voted against the government's scheme to relieve the immediate burden of naval and military pensions, 3, 24 May, when he spoke briefly in support of Hume's amendment deploring its invasion of the sinking fund. On 31 May 1822 he presented two Northampton parish petitions against Scarlett's poor removal bill, which he said made 'too violent an alteration' to the existing system and would be 'exceedingly oppressive to the rich'.

Maberly voted for inquiry into the parliamentary franchise, 20 Feb. 1823. He had attended the Surrey county meeting to petition for relief from distress and reform, 10 Feb.; and when Denison, the county Member, presented its petition, 26 Feb., he signified his dissent from the proposition that the adjustment of the currency had created serious problems. He voted against inquiry into the currency, 12 June. He spoke and voted for his father's motion for tax remissions of £7,000,000, 28 Feb., replying to objections to the scheme, which he reckoned would create a genuine sinking fund 'perfectly secure from the rapacity of ministers'. He divided for parliamentary reform, 24 Apr., and reform of the Scottish representative system, 2 June. On Macdonald's motion concerning the negotiations with Spain, 29 Apr., when he also presented a Daventry petition for repeal of the leather tax,[9] he expressed 'considerable dissatisfaction' at their 'whole tone and character', feeling that they had achieved only a 'temporary cessation of hostilities rather than ... a permanent and durable peace'; he and his father were trapped in the House to form part of the nominal minority of 20 against Stuart Wortley's pacific amendment, which they had intended to support, the following day.[10] Maberly supported repeal of the usury laws on account of their 'total inefficacy and impolicy', 17 June 1823, 16, 27 Feb. 1824, when he deplored Robertson's 'very remote and barbarian retrospect' in opposing Onslow's bill. He questioned the need for the proposed augmentation of the navy, 16 Feb.

He presented a Northampton butchers' petition against the leather tax, 24 Feb.[11] On the presentation of a petition for protection for the silk trade, 5 Mar., he 'deprecated the clamour which had been raised against the endeavours of ... government to introduce a sounder system of commercial policy, by the very parties whose interests these measures were essentially calculated to promote'. He spoke and voted for his father's motion to transfer the tax on beer to malt, 15 Mar. On 4 May, according to George Agar Ellis*, he 'spoke well' in moving at some length for an advance of £1,000,000 to Ireland to provide employment for the poor and curb the evil of 'excessive population'.[12] In reply he complained that Robinson, the chancellor, had misunderstood his intentions, explaining that he meant the money to be deposited with manufacturers and traders who could furnish adequate security. He admitted the force of many of the objections raised against the scheme, which was rejected by 85-33. He was named to the select committee on the current Irish disturbances, 11 May. He voted for his father's call for a repeal of assessed taxes, 10 May, and for repeal of the leather tax, 18 May, which he noted would be facilitated by adoption of his father's proposal to tax malt instead of beer. He presented a constituency petition against the beer duties bill, 21 May, and voted against the measure, 24 May 1824.[13] On 11 Feb. 1825 he voiced the 'deepest indignation' at the introduction of the 'ruinous' Irish unlawful societies bill 'on the flimsiest pretext', and warned that if Catholic emancipation was not graciously conceded as a matter of justice, it might one day be 'extracted from them by a sanguinary rebellion'. He voted against the measure, 15, 18, 21, 25 Feb., and was appointed to the renewed select committee on the state of Ireland, 17 Feb. He divided for Catholic relief (which his father now supported), 1 Mar., 21 Apr., 10 May. He suggested substituting the treadmill for the whip as an instrument of military punishment, 11 Mar. He opposed calls for enhanced protection for West Indian sugar, 18 Mar., arguing that the sooner those expensive colonies were got rid of the better; and voted for revision of the corn laws, 28 Apr. Like his father, he cast only one recorded vote against the grant to the duke of Cumberland, his own being on 27 May. He objected to the vagueness of a clause of the combination bill, 27 June 1825, when he voted for amendments dealing with intimidation and jury trial.

On 10 Feb. 1826 Maberly, speaking on the government's plans to deal with the financial and commercial crisis, dismissed Baring's bimetallic crotchet, paid tribute to the Bank of England's recent conduct and argued that the basic causes of the difficulties were 'overtrading' and the 'mania for speculation'. Although he had hoped to be able to support ministers on all commercial subjects, given their adoption of enlightened principles, he felt obliged to oppose their proposed restriction of the circulation of small notes, as he duly did on 13 Feb. Agar Ellis considered it

> one of the most luminous and ingenious speeches I ever heard in Parliament, of course on the most purely politico-economical principles, and therefore according to my view too theoretical in some things; but his explanation of the causes of the late panic and present distress was admirable.

John Evelyn Denison* also thought that Maberly 'spoke well', even though he 'did not hit the mark' in his analysis.[14] He voted for reform of Edinburgh's representative system, 13 Apr., parliamentary reform, 27 Apr., and Russell's resolutions to curb electoral bribery, 26 May. He spoke and voted for investigation of the corn laws, 18 Apr., complaining of the 'inconsistency' of ministers and urging the adoption of 'a judicious legislative enactment' to stop wild fluctuations in price and end the current high protection, which 'exposed the country to disorder and distress on the one hand, while it operated as a severe check upon our wealth and prosperity on the other'. On 12 May he contended that the laws as they stood encouraged the cultivation of bad land and so made it 'impossible to know what was a remunerating price for the agriculturist'. On 11 May 1826 he persuaded Hume to drop his plan to introduce a bill to promote the export of machinery. At the general election the following month he stood again for Northampton, where the Tory corporation had publicly pledged to finance his opponent to the tune of £1,000. Althorp reported that his effective oratory and strong support among 'the back lane gentry' gave him an edge over Gunning, the corporation man; and he was returned comfortably in second place after a turbulent contest in which his father joined after his own re-election for Abingdon.[15]

Maberly obtained a lieutenant-colonelcy at the end of the year. On 14 and 21 Feb. 1827 he presented petitions from electors of Northampton complaining of the corporation's application of corporate funds to electoral purposes; and on the latter date, when he detailed and denounced this 'palpable abuse', in what the backbencher Hudson Gurney thought a 'very good' speech, he moved that they be referred to a select committee. Before the close of the debate he altered the terms of his motion to make it one for general inquiry into the corporation's payment of or engagement to pay election expenses.[16] He was named to the committee, which reported on 9 Mar. He voted for inquiry into alleged electoral malpractice by Leicester corporation, 15 Mar., and on 10 Apr. got leave to introduce a bill to prevent the use of municipal funds for electoral purposes. The next day he said that he would not obstruct a threatened inquiry into the claim of some Northampton residents that their names had been fraudulently attached to the anti-corporation petition. His bill passed the Commons, 21 May, but was rejected on its third reading in the Lords, 13 June.[17] He supported Althorp's motion for inquiry into the possibility of reducing the duration and expense of county polls, 15 Mar., but urged him to extend its scope to include boroughs, pointing out that the Northampton poll had dragged on for eight days. He was appointed to the select committee, 5 Apr. He voted for Catholic relief, 6 Mar., and for the production of information on the Lisburn Orange procession, 29 Mar. On 9 Mar. he supported as the lesser of two evils Wolryche Whitmore's proposal for a protecting price for corn of 50*s*. rather than 60*s*., though he preferred a fixed duty; and on 27 Mar. he was in Hume's minority of 16 for a gradual reduction of the duty to 10*s*. He voted for investigation of the mutiny at Barrackpoor, 22 Mar., the opposition motion to withhold supplies until the uncertainty over a new ministry had been resolved, 30 Mar., and inquiries into the Irish miscellaneous estimates and chancery delays, 5 Apr. 1827. He was in the minority of 15 against the Wellington ministry's proposed vote for 30,000 seamen, 11 Feb. 1828. On 21 Feb. he gave qualified support to Davies's election polls bill: while he did not think it would provide 'a complete and practical remedy', he had not wished to risk his silence, as a member of the committee, being construed as an admission of the validity of the objections raised to it. He urged Davies to postpone the second reading, 3 Mar., though he said he was prepared to put the case for the bill in committee. He voted for repeal of the Test Acts, 26 Feb., presented three favourable petitions from Dissenters, 11 Mar., and voted for Catholic relief, 12 May. He was in the minorities on chancery delays, 24 Apr., recovery of penalties under the customs and excise regulations, 1 May, and civil list pensions, 20 May. Soon afterwards the duke of Wellington, seeking to strengthen his ministry in the Commons after the defection of the Huskissonites, sought to recruit Maberly as clerk of the ordnance. The king was agreeable, and Maberly was sounded, but he must have declined the offer.[18] He presented Northampton petitions against the friendly societies bill, 30 May, and voted for the Irish assessment of lessors bill, 12 June, and inquiry into the Irish church, 24 June, and against the additional churches bill, 30 June 1828. Maberly's only known votes in the 1829 session were for Catholic emancipation, 6, 30 Mar., and the transfer of East Retford's seats to Birmingham, 5 May. He was scarcely more active in the following session, when he voted against the grant for the navy pay office, 22 Mar., the Bathurst and Dundas pensions, 26 Mar., and the ordnance estimates, 29 Mar.; for Jewish emancipation, 5 Apr., 17 May, and for reform of Irish vestries, 27 Apr. It was almost certainly his father who voted for the production of information on privy councillors' emoluments, 14 May 1830.

Maberly did not seek re-election for Northampton at the 1830 general election, and failed to find a seat elsewhere.[19] Shortly before the fall of the Wellington ministry, when he was in Ireland with his regiment, he married Katherine Prittie, a member of the Irish Whig aristocracy, and a kinswoman of Lord Duncannon*, the opposition whip; she brought him an Irish estate. The Grey administration wished to appoint him to a place at the ordnance, but were at a loss to find him a seat. As soon as the Evesham election was declared void, 13 Dec. 1830, John Maberly issued an address declaring his son a candidate for the anticipated by-election as a supporter of the new ministry 'in all its measures tending to promote economy, reduction of taxation, reform of Parliament, and non-interference in the domestic affairs of other states'. However, the Tory opposition exploited in the House the blatant corruption exposed by the election committee's investigation, and the issue of a new writ was cancelled, 16 Dec. 1830.[20] Maberly was nevertheless appointed surveyor-general of the ordnance in January 1831, when John Hobhouse*, noting that his and other ordnance appointments were 'generally disapproved', uncharitably surmised that he must have solicited the place, for 'how else would he have had it'.[21] At the end of March he was approached by the corporation of Queenborough to stand there at the next general election on the ordnance interest; but a few days later the 2nd Earl Grosvenor contacted Duncannon offering to bring him in on a vacancy for Shaftesbury. He was returned unopposed, 19 Apr. 1831, too late to be able to vote against Gascoyne's wrecking amendment to the reform bill that night. Parliament was dissolved only four days later, and at the general election Maberly was returned again for Shaftesbury after a contest.[22]

As a minister, he voted steadily for the reintroduced reform bill, though he was in the minority for the disfranchisement of Saltash in the confused division of 26 July 1831. When speaking in favour of the passage of the bill, 20 Sept., he answered objections raised to its provisions for the mechanics of polling, defended it as a necessary and final corrective to the defects which time had wrought on the constitution and argued that far from being 'democratic and revolutionary', it was 'quite aristocratic in principle', and would be found to be so in practice from 'being framed with a view rather to property than to numbers'. On departmental business, he joined in tributes to the 'ability and economy' of the previous board of ordnance, 27 June. He had something to say on the Irish miscellaneous estimates, 18 July. He voted with his colleagues on the Dublin election controversy, 23 Aug., and for Lord Ebrington's confidence motion, 10 Oct. 1831. He was appointed to the renewed select committee on the East India Company, 27 Jan. 1832. He was a steady, though silent supporter of the revised reform bill in the 1832 session, when he also divided with his fellow ministers on the Russian-Dutch loan, 26 Jan., 12, 16, 20 July, relations with Portugal, 9 Feb., the navy civil departments bill, 6 Apr., the motion for an address asking the king to appoint only ministers who would carry undiluted reform, 10 May, and the Irish, 25 May, and Scottish reform bills, 1 June. On the navy estimates, 13 Feb., he defended the state of the buildings in the Cork depot. He explained the government's attempt to present the ordnance estimates 'in a constitutional and efficient manner', 22 Feb.; corrected Hume's misapprehension about the role of the Royal Military College, 28 Mar.; advocated a reduction in the enormous dead weight burden of military pensions, 2 Apr., and apportioned all the credit for reductions in the Irish ordnance establishment to the Grey ministry, 2 July. He was appointed to the committee of secrecy on the Bank, 22 May 1832.

In November 1832 Maberly, who was showing an interest in church reform 'for the sake of the church itself', was made clerk of the ordnance. At the general election the following month he was returned with government backing for Chatham after a contest with a disgruntled Liberal. He was also nominated for Abingdon by the supporters of his now financially ruined father in a vain attempt to prevent the seat falling into Conservative hands.[23] He vacated his Chatham seat in 1834 to take a customs place, and two years later was appointed joint-secretary to the post office, where he remained for 18 years before being moved to the audit office. At the post office he was frequently at loggerheads with Rowland Hill†, whom he despised, and for whose reforming schemes he had little time; but he was hardly unique in his resistance to the introduction of the penny postage, and in fact helped to implement a number of improvements in the office and had an ability to select talented men for executive positions.[24] Trollope, who crossed his path there, did not get on with him; but the novelist and journalist Edmund Yates, who was appointed to a clerkship in his department in 1847, denied that he was 'cruel and unjust':

> Though he was always pleasant to me after a fashion, his chief characteristic was ... indifference. He liked his station at the post office, he liked the salary which it gave him, he was fond of money, and he went through the work; but he was an Irish landlord ... married to a beautiful and brilliant lady, who wrote fashionable novels and went into society, so he had much besides the post office to occupy his thoughts ... [He was] a clear-headed man of business, inclined to let matters run in their ordinary groove, detesting all projects of reform, and having an abiding horror of Rowland Hill ... He was with me generally easily good-natured, but he could assume an air of *hauteur* and be uncommonly unpleasant sometimes.[25]

Maberly's lively and indiscreet wife, who published half a dozen novels, was sometimes an embarrassment to him, never more so than in 1846-7, when the 'ridiculous and unbecoming', though apparently platonic liaison into which her charms had betrayed Duncannon (then 4th earl of Bessborough and old enough to know better) caused tongues to wag and threatened to interfere with his ability to perform his duties as Irish viceroy in the new Russell ministry. His premature death in May 1847 possibly prevented a scandal over Mrs. Maberly's suspected meddling in government business and patronage.[26]

She died in 1875. Maberly himself, who enjoyed pensions from both the post office and the audit office, died at his London home at 23 Gloucester Place, Portman Square in February 1885. By his will, dated 31 Mar. 1876, he left all his property to his brother Evan Maberly. By a second codicil (15 Apr. 1879), he left annuities of £50 to two married women in Paris and the daughter of one of them, and to Emma Rosanna Harding (usually known as Bingham) of 353 Edgware Road.

[1] William Anson Robert, *bap.* 21 Sept. 1838 at St. Marylebone, Mdx. (IGI). [2] *Althorp Letters*, 101-2; *Northampton Borough Recs.* ii. 510; *Northampton Mercury*, 5, 12 Feb., 4, 11, 18 Mar.; *Leicester Jnl.* 11 Feb. 1820. [3] *Northampton Mercury*, 2 Dec. 1820, 20 Jan.; *The Times*, 2 Feb. 1821. [4] *The Times*, 1 Mar. 1821. [5] *Pol. Economy Club* (1921), 2, 5, 6, 12, 15. [6] *Overstone Corresp.* i. 158, 160, 165, 173, 179, 184. [7] *The Times*, 5 Feb. 1822. [8] Ibid. 30 Apr. 1822. [9] Ibid. 30 Apr. 1823. [10] Ibid. 1 May 1823. [11] Ibid. 25 Feb. 1823. [12] Northants. RO, Agar Ellis diary. [13] *The Times*, 22 May 1824. [14] Keele Univ. Lib. Sneyd mss SC8/79; Nottingham Univ. Lib. Denison diary, 10 Feb. 1826. [15] *Northampton Borough Recs.* ii. 510-11; *Althorp Letters*, 128-9; *Northampton Mercury*, 10, 17, 24 June 1826. [16] *The Times*, 15, 22 Feb.; Gurney diary, 21 Feb. 1827; Add. 40392, f. 303; 40393, ff. 60, 62. [17] *The Times*, 11, 12 Apr. 1827; *CJ*, lxxxii. 405, 422; *LJ*, lix. 403. [18] *Wellington Despatches*, iv. 455; *Arbuthnot Jnl.* ii. 189-91; Add. 40307, f. 138. [19] *The Times*, 20 July 1830. [20] Add. 76373, Althorp

to Grey [12 Dec.]; Lonsdale mss, Lowther to Lonsdale, 12 Dec.; *The Times*, 15 Dec. 1830; *Croker Pprs.* ii. 106. [21] Add. 56555, f. 80. [22] *Three Diaries*, 46; St. Deiniol's Lib. Glynne-Gladstone mss 197, T. to J. Gladstone, 29 Mar.; 521, Capel to T. Gladstone, 1 Apr.; Grey mss, Durham to Grey, 8 Apr.; *Dorset Co. Chron.* 21 Apr., 5 May 1831. [23] Brougham mss, Maberly to unknown, 19 Nov.; *The Times*, 14, 28 Dec.; *Berks. Chron.* 15 Dec. 1832. [24] H. Robinson, *Britain's Post Office*, 136, 143, 155, 157, 163, 171; *British Post Office*, 287, 325, 327, 335, 336, 363-4; cf. *Oxford DNB*. [25] A. Trollope, *Autobiog.* (1883), i. 59; E. Yates, *Mems. of a Man of the World*, 63-65. [26] *Oxford DNB*; *Lieven-Palmerston Corresp.* 70; *Disraeli Letters*, iv. 1284; v. 1784, 1975, 1981; *Greville Mems.* v. 338, 339-40, 356, 446, 448; D. Howell-Thomas, *Duncannon*, 263, 314-16.

D.R.F.

MACAULAY, Colin Campbell (?1759–1836), of Lowesby, Leics.[1]

SALTASH 19 Dec. 1826–1830

b. ?1759, ?4th but 2nd surv. s.[2] of Rev. John Macaulay (*d.* 1789), minister of Lismore, Argyll, and 2nd w. Margaret, da. of Colin Campbell of Inveresragan, Argyll. *unm. d.* 20 Feb. 1836.

Cadet, E.I. Co. (Madras) 1777, ensign 1778, lt. 1782, capt. 1796, maj. 1799, lt.-col. 1803, col. 1812, maj.-gen. 1814, lt.-gen. 1830.

Resident at Travancore 1800-10.

Macaulay's father John (1720-89) and his grandfather Aulay (?1673-1758) were both Presbyterian ministers who, according to family tradition, had been involved in an attempt to turn the fugitive Charles Edward Stuart over to the authorities in 1746. His uncle Kenneth Macaulay (1723-79), another Presbyterian minister, had a prickly encounter with Samuel Johnson during the latter's Hebridean excursion in 1773. The Doctor called Kenneth, to his face, 'a *bigot* to laziness', and privately scorned him as 'the most ignorant booby and the grossest bastard'; John Macaulay was also sneered at for his 'rusticity'.[3] Colin Macaulay, who was one of 12 children, entered the Indian army and was one of the officers captured by Hyder Ali in 1780 and imprisoned for almost four years in conditions of great barbarity and squalor. In 1799 he was secretary to the political and diplomatic mission, headed by Arthur Wellesley†, which accompanied General Harris on the invasion of Mysore; he was present at the capture of Seringapatam. Wellesley's brother Lord Wellesley, the governor-general of Bengal, appointed Macaulay political resident at the court of the rajah of Travancore in January 1800. He had his knuckles rapped four years later for making an 'unguarded' and 'imperfect statement' of a transaction concerning tobacco, but Wellesley was anxious that such 'an honest and deserving servant of the public', who subscribed to 'good principles of government in India', should not be made to suffer unduly for this indiscretion. He was involved in the controversy surrounding the dismissal of George Vaughan Hart*, commissary of grain to the army of Mysore, for alleged peculation, and later sought to vindicate his conduct in *Two Letters to Lord Harris* (1816). In 1808 he faced a revolt by the dewan of Travancore and survived an attempt on his life; the following year he commanded an army of 15,000 men in a successful campaign against the rebels.[4] He left India for the sake of his health in April 1810.[5] On his return to England Hannah More described him as 'a first-rate man' of 'the gentlest manners', who had 'brought home, after all his hairbreadth escapes, an ample fortune and a sober mind'. After visiting his brother-in-law Thomas Babington in Leicestershire, where he later acquired a property, he spent several months at Clapham with his younger brother Zachary, the leading abolitionist and friend of William Wilberforce*; he took a keen interest in the development of his nephew Thomas Babington Macaulay*, a child prodigy.[6] In January 1811 he wrote that 'if I could support sitting up at night I would become a Member of the House of Commons, but I must relinquish all thoughts of this during the winter'.[7] He welcomed the replacement in India of Minto and Barlow by Moira and Abercromby in 1812. He remained a devotee of Wellesley, now duke of Wellington, and was in Paris in 1814, where his command of several European languages (learnt in India) made him useful to the duke in the negotiations for suppression of the foreign slave trade. In 1822 he accompanied Wellington to the Congresses of Vienna and Verona, as his advisor on the slave trade.[8]

He was sufficiently recovered from a recent 'severe illness' to take a seat for Saltash on the Russell interest in December 1826. However, his health remained 'feeble' and he rarely attended the House.[9] He is not known to have spoken in debate. He voted against Canning's ministry for the disfranchisement of Penryn, 28 May 1827. He divided against Catholic relief, 12 May 1828, and privately urged Wellington, now prime minister, to settle the issue as soon as possible.[10] Soon afterwards a relapse drove him to Rome, where he almost certainly still was when the government carried Catholic emancipation in 1829 (he was named as a defaulter, 5, 10 Mar.). That October he was at Clifton, 'subject to severe coughs', but 'on the whole ... better than he was last year'.[11] He attended the House to vote for the transfer of East Retford's seats to Birmingham, 5 Mar. 1830. He divided against government for a reduction in the salary of the assistant secretary of the treasury, 10 May, abolition of the Irish viceroyalty, 11 May, and against an increase in the recognizances required by the libel law amendment bill, 9 July 1830. He rejoiced in the brilliance of his Whig nephew's parliamentary debut, but decided to leave the House at the dissolution that summer as it was 'too laborious a duty for any but a hale, hearty man'.[12]

Macaulay headed for the south of France, whence he wrote to Henry Brougham*, lord chancellor in Lord Grey's new government, to congratulate him on

> the recent happy change of ministry, and *that*, notwithstanding my unabated personal attachment to ... [Wellington]. But the change was called for, and ... it has taken place in a mode the best calculated to satisfy in these eventful times the fair demands of the well wisher to the true interests of England internally and externally. And I must say, had the Castlereagh politics not received some such check we might have been drawn into that Serbonian bog into which a war would only have plunged us deeper and deeper.[13]

He returned to England in the spring of 1831, when Thomas Macaulay noted: 'What an excellent old man he is. I cannot tell you how kind he has been in his expressions and demeanour towards me'.[14] The following year he gave evidence before the select committee inquiring into the claim by the descendants of John Hutchinson, commercial resident at Anjengo, for payment of the balance of a debt due to his estate from the rajah of Travancore. He published a defence of his own part in the affair, during his time at Travancore, in his *Desultory Notes*. The committee's report recommended settlement of the debt, but exonerated Macaulay from the Hutchinsons' charge that he had been guilty of 'repeated and vexatious interference' to prevent the claim from being settled. John Briscoe* brought in a bill to facilitate settlement of the debt, but Grey's ministry decided that the claim was fraudulent and defeated the measure on its second reading, 31 May 1833. Thomas Macaulay, now secretary to the India board, spoke against it, and took satisfaction in the reflection that 'it was by our uncle ... that the rascality of the transaction was originally exposed', and 'it was by me that the *coup de grace* was given'.[15] Macaulay was in Italy in 1834, as he found 'the climate of England becoming less and less tolerable to me'. Nevertheless, it was at Clifton that he died in February 1836, 'aged 76'.[16] He directed that his real estate be sold and left £10,000 to Thomas (which helped to set him up for the rest of his life) and the residue to Zachary; his personalty was sworn under £8,000.[17]

[1] He was baptized thus, according to his will (PROB 11/1859/178). [2] *Mems. of Clan 'Aulay'*, 10-11. [3] *Oxford DNB sub* Kenneth and Zachary Macaulay; *Fasti Ecclesiae Scoticanae* (new edn.), iii. 336; iv. 12, 99, 107, 120; vii. 189; F. Thomas, 'Traditions of Macaulays of Lewis', *Procs. Soc. Antiquaries of Scotland*, xiv. (1879-80), 363-430; G.O. Trevelyan, *Macaulay* (1908 edn.), 3-7; *Boswell's Life of Johnson* ed. L.F. Powell, v. 120, 505-7, 561, 563. [4] *Fort William-India House Corresp.* ed. H. Heras, xviii. 529, 533; *Wellington Despatches*, i. 6, 1362; Lady Knutsford, *Zachary Macaulay*, 282, 284; *Macaulay Letters*, ii. 224; iii. 51. [5] London Univ. Lib. Booth mss 797/1/5464, 5622. [6] Knutsford, 283-4; *Life of Wilberforce*, iv. 213, 215. [7] Booth mss 797/1/5467. [8] Ibid. 5468; Add. 38410, ff. 359, 361; *Macaulay Letters*, i. 39; *Life of Wilberforce*, v. 152-3; Knutsford, 379-80. [9] Booth mss 5661-3. [10] Knutsford, 380. [11] Booth mss 5665, 5667. [12] Ibid. 5471. [13] Ibid. 5669; Brougham mss, Macaulay to Brougham, 2 Dec. 1830. [14] *Macaulay Letters*, ii. 50. [15] Ibid. ii. 247; *PP* (1831-2), v. 445-51. [16] Booth mss 5473a; *Gent. Mag.* (1836), i. 443. [17] PROB 8/230 (21 Jan. 1837); 11/1859/178; *Macaulay Letters*, iii. 182.

D.R.F.

MACAULAY, Thomas Babington (1800–1859), of 8 South Square, Gray's Inn, Mdx.[1]

CALNE	15 Feb. 1830–1832
LEEDS	1832–4 Feb. 1834
EDINBURGH	4 June 1839–1847
EDINBURGH	1852–Jan. 1856

b. 25 Oct. 1800, 1st s. of Zachary Macaulay (*d.* 1838), merchant and philanthropist, of 26 Birchin Lane, London and Selina, da. of Thomas Mills, bookseller and stationer, of Bristol, Glos. *educ.* William Greaves's sch. Clapham, Surr. ?1806; Rev. Matthew Morris Preston's sch. Little Shelford, Cambs. 1813 and Aspenden Hall, Herts. 1814; Trinity Coll. Camb. 1818, fellow 1824-52; L. Inn 1822, called 1826. *unm. cr.* Bar. Macaulay 10 Sept. 1857. *d.* 28 Dec. 1859.

Commr. of bankrupts 1828-32; commr. bd. of control June-Dec. 1832, sec. Dec. 1832-Dec. 1833; member, supreme council of India 1833-38; PC 30 Sept. 1839; sec. at war Sept. 1839-Sept. 1841; paymaster-gen. July 1846-Apr. 1848.

Rect. Glasgow Univ. 1848-50; bencher, L. Inn 1849; high steward, Camb. Univ. 1857-*d.*

Macaulay's family was Scottish in origin, his father Zachary being the next younger brother of Colin Campbell Macaulay, who, late in life, became Member for Saltash in the 1826 Parliament.[2] Zachary, who was born in 1768, spent his early years as a plantation manager in Jamaica and returned to England with a hatred of colonial slavery. Under the influence of Thomas Babington, Member for Leicester, 1800-18, who had married his sister Jean, he became a convinced acolyte of the Evangelicals, and it was under their auspices that he served from 1793 to 1799 as governor of Sierra Leone, an experimental colony for emancipated slaves. He married, 26 Aug. 1799, Selina Mills, the daughter of a Bristol Quaker, who lived as a companion of the More sisters, the eldest of whom,

Hannah, was the noted Evangelical blue-stocking. Thereafter he acted as secretary of the Sierra Leone Company and, with his nephew Thomas Gisborne Babington, he founded a London firm of African merchants at 26 Birchin Lane, which moved to 16 George Street, Mansion House, in about 1820. Yet he bent most of his considerable energies to the anti-slavery cause, and assisted in numerous other religious and charitable activities. A self-taught man of iron will, who displayed a formidable intelligence and an unrelenting capacity for business, he was recognized as one of the leading members of the Clapham Sect.[3]

It was in Clapham, to which the family moved in 1802 or 1803, that Tom Macaulay soon began to display signs of his alarmingly prodigious abilities. Not only did he read widely from an early age, but he could recall much of it almost verbatim, added to which his acknowledged habit of indulging in day-dreams and fantasies endowed him with a highly developed creative faculty. Educated locally and then at the school of an Evangelical minister, he excelled in his private studies and inevitably grew up something of a man apart.[4] This was despite the best efforts of his parents, who sought to prevent him from becoming conscious of his rare abilities; and so it was with delight that Hannah More recorded in 1815 that

> his fine promise of mind expands more and more and, what is extraordinary, he has as much accuracy in his expression as spirit and vivacity in his imagination. I like, too, that he takes a lively interest in all passing events and that the *child* is still preserved ... Several men of sense and learning have been struck with the union of gaiety and rationality in his conversation.[5]

With these talents he proved a great success at Cambridge, where he was known as 'Beast' Macaulay to distinguish him from his cousin, John Heyrick 'Bear' Macaulay. He revelled in the intellectual and social climate, won several prizes and scholarships, dominated the Union in 1822 and 1823, and gained a fellowship at Trinity College.[6]

Macaulay was unlucky in his relations with his father, who, imbued with the rigidities of his Evangelical principles, set impossibly high standards even for so gifted a man as his son. Slovenliness and laziness, even novel reading, were regarded as faults, and criticized as such, because they indicated a lack of self-discipline and awareness of a higher purpose.[7] Zachary was thus deeply disappointed when Macaulay took only an ordinary degree, having failed to apply himself sufficiently to the mathematical part of the tripos.[8] He had also set his heart on his son making a splendid career in the church, and was grieved that he displayed no signs of Evangelical fervour.[9] There was never a breach between them, but Macaulay, who, after university, lived at 50 Great Ormond Street, with the rest of the family (who had moved there in 1823 after five years in Cadogan Place), was always under a constraint in his father's presence. It was with his affectionate mother, and especially when at ease in the company of his doting and beloved sisters Hannah and Margaret, upon whom he was emotionally dependent, that he could be unselfconsciously happy.[10] As Zachary himself once remarked, 'I am glad to see Tom retain all his exquisite relish for the domestic circle. He seems to seek no other pleasures as a relaxation from graver pursuits than are to be found there'.[11]

Brought up in an atmosphere dominated by public affairs, Macaulay soon immersed himself in politics.[12] At Cambridge he had witnessed the borough election in 1820, when he received a dead cat in his face having ventured out into a mêlée, and had taken a lively interest in the university by-election in 1822.[13] It was also there that his political views began to be transformed from a passive acceptance of the prevailing Tory outlook of the Evangelicals to approval of an increasingly reformist Whiggism.[14] His father was concerned that he was too ready to condemn the events at Peterloo in 1819, and to express a measure of sympathy for Queen Caroline the following year, though at the time of the disturbances after her funeral in late 1821, his son wrote that 'the conduct of the rabble, of the jury, and of Sheriff [Robert] Waithman*, sometimes turns me for a few hours into a Tory. I now and then fear I shall be a perfect *jure-divino* if these things go on'.[15] While this hardly amounted to a radical interlude, he was certainly influenced by the lawyer Charles Austin, one of his brilliant Cambridge friends, into a brief flirtation with Utilitarianism.[16] He declared at that time that 'I have been a Tory; I am a Radical; *but I will never be a Whig*'.[17] Yet, he was already beginning to move towards an avowedly Whig position, as can be seen in his 1822 prize essay on William III, which revealed the first intimations of his famous history of William's reign and his admiration for the triumph of progress.[18] But the decisive factor in his change of mind was the gradual realization, in line with that experienced by the Evangelicals generally, that the best hope of abolishing slavery lay with the Whig opposition. In the same way, he came to believe that they offered the best chance of preserving the peace and stability of existing society from the dangers posed by Tory or radical extremes.[19]

It was through his writings that Macaulay confirmed his Whig credentials and first achieved celebrity. He had written a good deal of juvenile prose and verse, and in 1816 he outwitted his father by inducing him to print an anonymous letter in defence of novel reading in his *Christian Observer*. This was one of his earliest publications, and it was followed by a variety of other miscellaneous writings.[20] In 1823 and 1824 he was (as 'Tristram Merton'), with his Cambridge friend and rival Winthrop Mackworth Praed*, among others, one of the main contributors to *Knight's Quarterly Magazine*. Although these were largely incidental pieces, in the first issue (June 1823) an essay appeared 'On West Indian Slavery', probably in order to please his father, who nevertheless expressed considerable disquiet at the nature of the journal.[21] He was a member of the committee of the Anti-Slavery Society, which Zachary had helped to found with Thomas Fowell Buxton* in 1823, and at its first anniversary meeting, 25 June 1824, his speech was given an ecstatic ovation by the distinguished audience, and his generally unbending father was left hardly able to bear his feelings of paternal pride.[22] Although the exact details of the transaction are unclear, it was almost certainly the leading Whig lawyer Henry Brougham*, an anti-slavery colleague of Zachary's, who in early 1823 had written to advise him on his son's education, who now urged Francis Jeffrey*, editor of the *Edinburgh Review*, to commission an article from Macaulay. His essay on 'The West Indies', closely modelled on the *Knight's* article, duly appeared in January 1825.[23] In August that year there appeared the essay which brought him almost instant fame. As Sir James Mackintosh* commented to Lady Holland, 8 Oct. 1825, Macaulay 'has written a most splendid panegyric on the genius, writing and politics of Milton'. Not only was it an outstanding critical study, but, by identifying with the poet against Charles I, he had placed himself firmly in the Whig tradition. Jeffrey, who thought Macaulay 'more nearly a universal genius than any man of our time', told him that 'the more I think the less I can conceive where you picked up that style'.[24] In 1826 the writer Henry Crabb Robinson described Macaulay as

> one of the most promising of the rising generation I have seen for a long time ... He has a good face – not the delicate features of a man of genius and sensibility, but the strong lines and well knit limbs of a man in sturdy body and mind. Very eloquent and cheerful. Overflowing with words and not poor in thought. Liberal in opinion, but no radical. He seems a correct as well as a full man. He showed a minute knowledge of subjects not introduced by himself.[25]

Early that year he was called to the bar and, although he never had a practice to speak of, he joined the northern circuit, on which he met Thomas Flower Ellis, his only close male friend.[26] He was praised for his activity as counsel to William Evans* during the Leicester contest at the general election of 1826, which involved him in legal argument and writing handbills.[27] He also used his anti-slavery influence against the Irish secretary, Henry Goulburn*, at the Cambridge University election that year.[28] He was present for the university by-election in 1827, when he had some verses printed in *The Times* (as he did on two other occasions), and voted for Sir Nicholas Conyngham Tindal*.[29] He was instrumental in having a university anti-Catholic petition defeated by bringing some London lawyers up to oppose it, 11 Feb. 1829, and later that year he voted for William Cavendish* to replace Tindal in another by-election.[30]

Apart from electoral affairs, he busied himself with attending the Commons, speaking at debating societies and other literary activities.[31] He wrote regularly for the *Edinburgh*, to which he contributed essays on critical and historical subjects until 1845. In the June 1827 issue, in a rare piece of party polemic, he defended the 'Present Administration', and stressed the importance of holding a middle path:

> We are convinced that the cause of the present ministers is the cause of liberty, the cause of toleration, the cause of political science, the cause of the people, who are entitled to expect from their wisdom and liberality many judicious reforms, the cause of the aristocracy, who, unless those reforms be adopted, must inevitably be the victims of a violent and desolating revolution.

He wrote to his father that he was 'extremely shocked' by the death of George Canning, the prime minister, later that year, but that he believed the government would continue, if anything strengthened by it.[32] Although this prediction proved to be false, he benefited from the influence of Brougham, who persuaded Lord Lyndhurst, the lord chancellor, to appoint him a commissioner of bankrupts. The position was financially important to Macaulay because his father's fortunes had been in decline for some time and his partnership was finally dissolved in December 1828. Macaulay now had to support himself and to assist his family, which he managed to do with the income from his fellowship, place and articles.[33] He would have accepted the editorship of the *Edinburgh* on Jeffrey's resignation in late 1829, if its offices had been moved to London, but he did not in any case relish working under Brougham's tutelage.[34] He gained a reputation for being a dangerous man to cross with his savage reviews of Mill's 'Essay on Government' (March, June and October 1829),[35] and similarly aggressive attacks on Robert Southey*, the poet laureate (January 1830), and Michael Thomas Sadler* (July 1830 and January 1831).

Lord Lansdowne, who had served as home secretary in Canning's government and had praised Macaulay's article in support of it (among others), was particularly impressed by his arguments against the Utilitarians. As a result, in early 1830 he offered to bring him in for Calne, his pocket borough, where there was a vacancy which his eldest son, Lord Kerry†, was as yet too young to fill. Macaulay accepted, having warned Lansdowne, who had a high opinion of his moral character, that he wished to vote as he himself determined, and in particular that he would follow his father's line in any division on slavery.[36] He visited the town for the first time, and was elected unopposed, after making a speech, in which he

> denominated Dr. Southey, Mr. Sadler and Mr. [William] Cobbett† three *quacks*, and observed that it must be by a continuance of peace, by great economy in our ministers and by industry and frugality on the part of the people, that the country would be enabled to surmount its present difficulties.[37]

Zachary, thanking Lansdowne by letter that month, wrote of his son that the

> sphere of usefulness thus opened to him I trust he will labour so to occupy as to justify your lordship's choice, and I am ready to believe that it is not merely the blind partiality of parental affection but my intimate acquaintance with his mind and habits which persuades me that he will at least leave no means unattempted to prove himself not undeserving of it.[38]

According to his sister Selina, Macaulay, who had recently taken lodgings in Gray's Inn, returned to London on 17 Feb., but having neglected some necessary forms, he was unable to take his seat that day, as intended. He therefore took the oaths the following day, at the same time as Brougham, newly elected for Knaresborough, who immediately turned his back on him and cut him dead. This behaviour was attributed to his jealousy of Macaulay's successes in the *Edinburgh*. He was also angry that he had not been consulted by Lansdowne, and that the more deserving and senior Whig lawyer Thomas Denman* had been overlooked.[39] Macaulay voted for reducing the grant for the army, 19, 22 Feb., and the enfranchisement of Birmingham, Leeds and Manchester, 23 Feb. 1830.

As early as 1824 Hannah More had wished that Macaulay 'was rich enough to be in Parliament; he would eclipse them all'; and Lord Dudley, the former foreign secretary, who thought him 'a *very* clever, *very* educated and *very* disagreeable man', reckoned that he would 'cut some considerable figure' there.[40] Benjamin Disraeli† wrote in *The Young Duke* (book v, chapter 6), which was published the following year:

> I hear that Mr. Babington Macaulay is to be returned. If he speaks half so well as he writes, the House will be set in fashion again. I fear that he is one of those who, like the individual whom he has most studied [Edmund Burke†], will 'give up to party what was meant for mankind'.[41] At any rate, he must get rid of his rabidity. He writes now on all subjects, as if he certainly intended to be a renegade and was determined to make the contrast complete.

Macaulay was therefore a man of whom great things were expected and, although he had been advised to speak as soon as possible, in order to gain the indulgence of the House, he did not do so.[42] He told his father that he would wait to see how his political career progressed before deciding about his future at the bar, but in fact he never practised again after going on the northern circuit that year, for which he took one month's leave, 10 Mar. 1830.[43] He made what George Agar Ellis* described as 'an ingenious maiden speech', 5 Apr., arguing that, on moral and pragmatic grounds, Jews ought to be admitted to the same rights as had recently been granted to Catholics.[44] Mackintosh, who had given way to him at the start of his speech, praised his performance, as did Sugden, the solicitor-general. Its main fault was the speed of the delivery, and Hannah commented that the report in *The Times*, 'though a good abstract, gives no idea ... of its spirit and power'. Macaulay himself, who when asked by his family how he had felt on making his first intervention, had replied 'oh, desperate, you know! quite desperate', informed a friend, probably the former Member Richard Sharp*, that 'as far as I can learn, the impression that I made was far more favourable than I at all anticipated, as I carefully abstained from everything like display. Your advice has been of great use to me'.[45] The Commons clerk John Rickman informed Southey, who found Macaulay 'in league with the sinners by principle ... and with the saints by blood', that he 'threw off with a good specimen speech, rather too epigrammatic I thought for good taste, but showing ability and dexterity of thought'.[46] Macaulay voted for Jewish emancipation that day, and again, 17 May, and, urged on by the Jewish lobby, he prepared an article in its favour for the *Edinburgh*, which appeared in January 1831.[47] He voted with the Irish Catholic leader Daniel O'Connell for alteration of the laws relating to select vestries in Ireland, 27 Apr., for the production of papers on the affair at Terceira, 28 Apr. 1830, and several times that session in favour of further economies and reductions in taxation. He spoke against slavery at a meeting of the Anti-Slavery Society, 15 May.[48] He voted in favour of parliamentary reform, 28 May, and revision of the divorce laws, 3 June. He divided for abolition of the death penalty for forgery, 24 May, 7 June, when he argued that the severity of the law reduced its effectiveness. A few days later Selina recorded (perhaps in reference to 5 Apr.) that the

> speech was extremely admired as to matter, but all who heard it agree in saying that he speaks far too rapidly, and thus weakens very much the effect of what he says. Mr. O'Connell said to him it was the best speech he had heard since he had been in Parliament, but said he, 'Your delivery is not suited to the House', and a host of other persons have given the same opinion. Lord Nugent* said to him that it was impossible for the reporters to follow him, and that consequently the speech was given extremely ill. He also said Tom's style of speaking was one which particularly required time to be given to weigh the arguments, and that by the present manner the effect of these was in a great measure lost. Tom seems determined to speak more slowly, but he says he shall find it exceedingly difficult to do so when he is animated in debate.[49]

On 6 July, answering Sugden, he gave his 'most earnest and hearty support' to, and promised to vote for, an address to the new king to recommend regency proposals. He voted for Brougham's motion against colonial slavery, 13 July. He was elected to the Athenaeum, 12 June 1830.[50] His uncle, Colin, who commented that 'Tom attracts notice in Parliament, as was to be looked for if ever he got in there', left the House at the dissolution that summer, but Macaulay was returned for Calne, despite a contest and a petition.[51] In early September he began a visit to Paris, to collect materials for a history of the recent revolution there, but he had to cut short his stay because of the death of his sister Jean, 22 Sept. Brougham, who had already irritated Macaulay by asking him to 'puff' his latest speech against slavery, insisted that Macvey Napier, the new editor of the *Edinburgh*, replace Macaulay's intended article with his own account. Macaulay had already prepared some of the text and, although he hoped to have it published elsewhere, it was not printed during his lifetime.[52]

Macaulay, who in August thought that the duke of Wellington and his 'ministers are clearly in a scrape' and that they could not possibly stand until Christmas, was listed by them among their 'foes', and duly voted against them on the civil list, 15 Nov. 1830. On 23 Nov. he acknowledged that some praise was due to Wellington, who made way for Lord Grey, especially on Catholic emancipation, 'which I believe saved the country from civil war'. That day he came to the defence of Brougham, who, despite promises that he would not join the coalition ministry, had just left the Commons to become lord chancellor, against John Wilson Croker, for whom he had already formed a mutual dislike. Although he 'speaks like a gentleman', as John James Hope Vere* put it, he was called to order for saying of Croker, that he 'would have sooner burned his tongue last week, than have made the attack which he has done this day'.[53] He advocated the abolition of slavery accompanied by the payment of compensation to planters, 13 Dec., and the next day Thomas Gladstone*, wrote to his father John Gladstone*, a West India merchant, that he wished 'all the emancipators were as moderate'.[54] He presented and endorsed over 200 anti-slavery petitions, 15 Dec., when, in the absence of Fowell Buxton, he also moved for information on the subject. He was elected to Brooks's, 18 Dec. 1830, sponsored by Lansdowne and Lord King. Zachary reported to Brougham, 24 Feb. 1831, that Robert Gordon*, another bankruptcy commissioner

> appears to have spared anyone the pains of drubbing him. Tom I believe would have been quite ready to do his best to make him regret any attack he might have made on you. He has been sadly baffled by circumstances in his purposes of speaking, though he has been on the watch for fair opportunities.[55]

Macaulay, who in February 1831 briefly contemplated writing an article on parliamentary reform, made an early intervention on the ministry's reform proposals, 2 Mar.[56] He called it 'a great, noble and comprehensive measure, a medicine most skilfully prepared for removing a dangerous distemper, a plan excellently contrived for uniting and knitting together all orders in the state'. He pledged his support for it, 'not merely as a measure of reform, but as a measure of conservation', which, by enfranchising the middle classes, though stopping well short of a universal franchise, would prevent revolution. He added that 'we must not adhere to what our ancestors did, but must do what, under similar circumstances, it is probable they would have done'. His speech, which, like most of those on reform he revised for publication,[57] caused a sensation, not least because of the passion that he lent to his historical examples and the sense of urgency that he injected into the proceedings. As he said in his peroration (which was apparently modelled on the conclusion of Brougham's speech in defence of Queen Caroline, 4 Oct. 1820):

> Let me then implore you to take counsel, not from prejudice or party, but from the history of past events, the

knowledge of what is passing around you. It is yet time to save the country from risk, to save the multitude from its own ungovernable power and passion, to save it from that danger to which even a few days may expose it.

He was answered by his friend and fellow historian Lord Mahon, who, as others were often to do, pointed out that, despite Macaulay's arguments to the contrary, he had provided eloquent testimony in favour of the retention of rotten boroughs as seats for talented young men. Later that day Denman, now attorney-general, said that it was 'a speech which is yet tingling in our ears, and which will dwell in our memories as long as memory lasts'. Margaret, who noted that Mackintosh relieved her poorly brother with oranges during the speech, recorded that 'his voice from cold and overexcitement got quite into a scream towards the last part, and some of his opponents were inclined to titter at his having got into [Charles Williams] "Wynn's* scream", which was drowned in applause'. Indeed, except for the fact that he again spoke too fast, most observers were united in their praise, and the Speaker summoned him to compliment him on his success.[58] However, Sir Henry Bunbury* felt that although the 'matter and language' were 'very fine', his delivery was bad, 'his manner vulgar, and there was a sort of Methodistical rant which marred the effect'. This opinion was echoed by Maria Edgeworth, who decided that his speech

reads better than it was spoken. Quite marred in the delivery and he does not *look* the orator well, a mean whitey looking man, of the Babbage sort but more forward-vivacity of air and yellow hair all any-how except the right way, not with the inspiration-electrico look of [Thomas] Spring Rice*. But no matter for all this, in spite of his outside, his inside will get him on.[59]

Years later Macaulay described that day as an epoch in his life, and it certainly made him a political and literary lion in London, for instance at Holland House, to which he was soon invited.[60] His letters, particularly the informal ones to his sisters, contain some fascinating anecdotes and many brilliant vignettes of his contemporaries. Perhaps the most famous is his description of the second reading of the reform bill, 22 Mar., which was written to Ellis, 30 Mar. 1831. He first confided that 'till we had a majority, I was half inclined to tremble at the storm which we had raised. At present I think that we are absolutely certain of victory, and of victory without commotion'. He continued:

Such a scene as the division of last Tuesday I never saw, and never expect to see again. If I should live 50 years the impression of it will be as fresh and sharp in my mind as if it had just taken place. It was like seeing Caesar stabbed in the Senate House, or seeing Oliver take the mace from the table, a sight to be seen only once and never to be forgotten.

He vividly depicted the telling of the 302 votes in favour of the bill, of which he was of course one, and dwelt on the speculation on the size of the opposition:

We were all breathless with anxiety, when Charles Wood who stood near the door jumped on a bench and cried out, 'They are only 301'. We set up a shout that you might have heard to Charing Cross, waving our hats, stamping against the floor and clapping our hands. The tellers scarcely got through the crowd: for the House was thronged up to the table, and all the floor was fluctuating with heads like the pit of a theatre. But you might have heard a pin drop as Duncannon read the numbers. Then again the shouts broke out, and many of us shed tears; I could scarcely refrain. And the jaw of Peel fell, and the face of Twiss was as the face of a damned soul, and Herries looked like Judas taking his neck-cloth off for the last operation.[61]

Macaulay was vexed by Buxton's notice for an anti-slavery motion, and even offered Lansdowne to resign his seat, as he expected, for his father's sake, to have to act against ministers on it. Lansdowne left him free to decide his own course of action and, in the end, no division occurred on the question, 15 Apr.[62] He voted against Gascoyne's wrecking amendment to the reform bill, 19 Apr. 1831, which brought about the dissolution.

Macaulay again faced the threat of an opposition at Calne at the general election of 1831 and in order, as he wished, to keep up Lansdowne's interest for Kerry, he was forced to engage in extensive canvassing and to defend the rights of the corporators on the hustings, 2 May, when he was again re-elected.[63] He returned to London the following day to discover, from a newspaper, that his mother had died.[64] Although he remarked that 'the fury of the minority surpasses all description', he believed that 'our blood is up and we know our strength'. He thought it 'foolish to throw away my fire' on the address, but obeyed the summons from Lord Althorp, the chancellor, to attend, 24 June, when he went with the procession to St. James's Palace, and thereafter he was 'at the House every evening'.[65] He made another successful reform speech on the second reading of the reintroduced bill, 5 July, when he denied either that disfranchisement was an invasion of property rights, or that it would lead to moves for further changes, still less to revolution. He argued that

the whole of history shows that all great revolutions have been produced by a disproportion between society and

> its institutions; for while society has grown, its institutions have not kept pace and accommodated themselves to its improvements ... The very reason that the people of England are great and happy is that their history is the history of reform.

He differed with Lord Porchester, Mahon's colleague at Wootton Bassett, by saying that it was not reforms as such which had led to revolution in France, but reforms offered too late to satisfy the raised expectations of the people. Amid shouts of disapprobation, he insisted that 'we are now all reformers', and that the bill had 'passed its crisis ... this second Bill of Rights, the great charter of the liberties of the people of England; the country, our children, will hereafter call it so'. Althorp, who twice told him privately that it was the best speech he had ever heard, said in the chamber that he had 'electrified the House with his eloquence'. According to John Cam Hobhouse*, he 'made a most effective oration, and was applauded to the skies, particularly towards the end of his speech, when he said that if this bill was defeated, Peel would bring in a reform bill of his own'. Some aspersive comments were made by opposition speakers, but it was largely left to Peel, the former home secretary, who 'winced a good deal' at this last point, to answer him. As before, Macaulay received an enormous number of compliments on his triumph, as well as an invitation to dine with Grey.[66] He claimed to have delivered his speech more slowly than usual, but others thought differently. They also believed that the reports misrepresented it, a view with which he agreed (though he declined to correct it for publication).[67]

With this speech Macaulay's reputation reached new heights. Jeffrey, now lord advocate, wrote that he had

> surpassed his former appearance in closeness, fire and vigour, and very much improved the effect of it by a more steady and graceful delivery. It was prodigiously cheered, as it deserved, and I think puts him clearly at the head of the great speakers, if not the debaters, of the House.

Mackintosh called Macaulay 'the orator of his time', and Lord Holland, the chancellor of the duchy of Lancaster, opined that he and Edward Smith Stanley, the Irish secretary, would soon learn the art of keeping Peel in order, now that Brougham had been removed.[68] However, Wilson's appraisal, which appeared in *Blackwood's Magazine*, used a tactic which was soon picked up by the Tories, of applauding Macaulay's performances, while denying that there was any substance to them. Macaulay, he wrote,

> is an ugly, cross-made, splay-footed, shapeless little dumpling of a fellow, with a featureless face too, except indeed a good expansive forehead, sleek puritanical sandy hair, large glimmering eyes and a mouth from ear to ear. He has a lisp and a burr, moreover, and speaks thickly and huskily for several minutes before he gets into the swing of his discourse: but after that nothing can be more dazzling than his whole execution. What he says, is substantially of course, mere stuff and nonsense; but it is so well worded, and so volubly and forcible delivered – there is such an endless stream of epigram and antithesis, such a flashing of epithets, such an accumulation of images – and the voice is so trumpet-like and the action so grotesquely emphatic that you might hear a pin drop in the House. Manners Sutton himself listens. It is obvious that he has got the main parts at least by heart, but for this I give him the more praise and glory. Altogether, the impression on my mind was very much beyond what I had been prepared for, so much so that I can honestly and sincerely say I felt for his situation most deeply, when Peel was skinning him alive the next evening, and the sweat of agony kept pouring down his well bronzed cheeks under the merciless affliction.[69]

Later in July Hobhouse recorded that

> Brougham was anxious that the attorney-general should be put forward ... It seems he depreciates Macaulay and always extols the attorney as having made the best speech on the bill. Sydney Smith says it is because Macaulay is not content with being a moon, but 'wants to do a little bit in the *solar line*'.[70]

Yet at some point the two seem to have buried their differences. As Sir George Philips*, a friend, put it:

> When Macaulay first obtained a seat in Parliament, Brougham went about telling people that he had quite failed, and that there was no chance of his ever distinguishing himself as a speaker in the House of Commons. His jealousy was so extreme that he ceased for a long time speaking to him, or even recognizing him in the streets. All at once he altered his conduct, laid hold of him by the arm, called him Tom and enquired affectionately after his health. He talked to some of Macaulay's friends, who asked him what Tom he meant. He said there was only one Tom, and that was Tom Macaulay.[71]

Macaulay, who voted for the second reading of the bill, 6 July, divided at least twice against adjourning the proceedings on it, 12 July, but he 'left the House at about three, in consequence of some expressions of Lord Althorp's which indicated that the ministry was inclined to yield', and he afterwards 'much regretted' that he had gone away.[72] He voted steadily in favour of the bill's details, and kept up a regular attendance, except when illness or fatigue induced by long debates (he likened the crowd and heat in the chamber to the compression in a slave ship) forced him to pair, as he did on at least one occasion both with Mahon and

Samuel Smith, Member for Wendover.[73] He made an impromptu speech on the enfranchisement of Greenwich, 3 Aug., when he advocated extending the representation of the metropolis in order to provide an outlet for the influential and wealthy classes to vent their grievances. Croker taunted him by saying that now that 'the question of Calne is set at rest [controversially, it was to retain its two seats], I hope we shall see [him] more frequently among us'. Macaulay himself informed Hannah that his few words

> were not ill received. I feel that much practice will be necessary to make me a good debater on points of detail. But my friends tell me that I have raised my reputation by showing that I was quite equal to the work of extemporaneous reply. My manner, they say, is cold and wants ease. I feel this myself. Nothing but strong excitement and a great occasion overcomes a certain reserve and *mauvaise honte* which I have in public speaking; not a *mauvaise honte* which in the least confuses me or makes me hesitate for a word, but a *mauvaise honte* which keeps me from putting any fervour into my tone or my action. This is perhaps in some respects an advantage. For when I do warm, I am the most vehement speaker in the House, and nothing strikes an audience so much as the animation of an orator who is generally cold.[74]

He voted in the minorities on the issuing of writs for Dublin, 8 Aug., and Liverpool, 5 Sept. 1831.

Looking forward to visiting his relatives, he wrote to Hannah, 12 Aug. 1831, that

> I shall not be sorry to be out of the way of the miserable proceedings in the House of Commons. One is ashamed to support such a government and, in my situation, I cannot attack it. The weakness, dullness, cowardice and tergiversation of the ministers, those I mean who sit in the House of Commons, have begun to disgust their most devoted friends. I will tell you instances of their fatuity and infirmity of purpose ... which are absolutely astounding ... But nothing can save them from ruin if they do not speedily alter their course ... it is no business of mine whether they stand or fall. There is not one of them in the House of Commons except Lord Althorp who is not either useless or worse than useless, and I do not see that it would be either for my interest or my honour to thrust myself between them and the public contempt.

At the end of that month he reiterated that 'my opinion of Lord Althorp is extremely high. In fact his character is the only stay of the ministry'.[75] In mid-September Lansdowne, the lord president, told a genuinely alarmed Macaulay that the bill would probably be lost in the Lords and that ministers would then resign. He insisted to his patron, who demurred, that enough peers must be created to carry the bill, and that 'if nobody else will move an address to the crown against a Tory ministry, I will'. In a letter to Lady Holland of about this date, he explained that

> the question is this: if the reform bill is lost, ought the ministers to resign? I have conversed on this subject with people of different ranks and of different shades of opinion; and I have heard only one answer. The unanimous sentiment is this: that if the ministers resign they will prove themselves to be men unfit for their station, small men unhappily called to power at a great crisis, that they will act unfairly towards the king, and towards the people who have supported them. A very distinguished Member of the House of Commons, a county Member, the heir to a peerage, said to me a few days ago, 'You know my personal attachment to the ministers. You know my public conduct. I have stood by them for 20 years. If they resign in consequence of the decision of the Lords, I have done with them. My confidence in them is at an end for ever'. This is but a single instance. I have heard expressions as strong from at least 20 Members for populous places. In fact it is difficult to convince the ministerial Members of the House of Commons that the ministers can possibly think of resigning at such a crisis as this.

He added that government 'might, by a very moderate exercise of the undoubted prerogative of the crown, secure a majority in the Lords'.[76]

His reservations about ministers probably heightened the passion he brought to his speech in favour of the passage of the bill, 20 Sept. 1831, when he spoke of the benefits that would accrue to national prosperity, denied that there was any public reaction against it, rebutted the argument that it would destroy the privileges of peers and urged Members to place themselves at the head of the people and ensure its success. Denman noted that he was 'divine', though 'perhaps a little too severe in his censure of the ex-ministers', while William Henry Fremantle* considered him the only reformer worth listening to.[77] He was answered by Croker, who, hinting that he would soon obtain office, insultingly referred to him as a mere 'practising barrister'; it was this occasion that provoked the long-running quarrel between them in Parliament and the press.[78] Also intent on attacking him were Wetherell, the former attorney-general, who, like Croker, argued that it was concessions, not resistance, by the nobility that had caused the French Revolution; and Peel, who according to Greville, 'cut Macaulay to ribbands ... Macaulay is very brilliant, but his speeches are harangues and never replies'.[79] He, of course, voted for the passage of the bill, 21 Sept., and for the second reading of the Scottish bill, 23 Sept., and the following day he spoke at a dinner in honour of Althorp and Lord John Russell in the City.[80] Having stated his opposition to excessive expenditure and taxation, monopolies, slavery and interference in the affairs of foreign states, and his grudging approval of the ballot, he received a requisition to stand for Leeds at the first opportunity, and accepted it, 5 Oct.[81] He was appointed to the select committee on the West Indies, 6 Oct. Despite his stated reluctance to get involved, he had in fact been active in defence of the bill behind the scenes. On 15 Sept. he wrote to Hannah that

> I have been very busy since I wrote last [13 Sept.], moving heaven and earth to render it certain that, if our ministers are so foolish as to resign in the event of a defeat in the Lords, the Commons may be firm and united: and I think that I have arranged a plan that will secure a bold and instant declaration on our part, if necessary. Lord Ebrington* is the man whom I have in my eye as our leader. I have had much conversation with him and with several of our leading county Members. They are all staunch: and I will answer for this, that if the ministers should betray us, we will be ready to defend ourselves.[82]

His former colleague at Calne, Sir James Macdonald, now Member for Hampshire, contemplating a reinforced ministry, confirmed that Macaulay was '*bold* and *ambitious* and quite ready to take his line. The Leeds overture has roused him'.[83] Two days after the Lords threw out the bill, Ebrington moved his confidence motion, 10 Oct. 1831, and Macaulay, though expected to wait until he could answer Peel, spoke quite early, to try to bring the debate to a conclusion. He made a strong plea for immediate action over the bill, given that the legislature would be powerless to enforce the laws of the country if it lost the support of the people, and that it must bend to the popular will: 'I know only two ways in which societies can permanently be governed: by public opinion, and by the sword'. He emphasized that

> the circumstances admit of no delay. Is there one among us who is not looking with breathless anxiety for the next tidings which may arrive from the remote parts of the kingdom? Even while I speak the moments are passing away, the irrevocable moments, pregnant with the destiny of a great people. The country is in danger; it may be saved; we can save it. This is the way, this is the time. In our hands are the issues of great good and great evil, the issues of life and death of the state.

His speech was much attacked as an incitement to violence, and Hobhouse thought 'he went somewhat near the wind on the intimidation side; and I told him so, and I saw he was not pleased'. Peel criticized him, but Edward John Littleton* observed that 'an allusion of Macaulay's to his having bowed his head into the dust, when he recanted his error on the Catholic question, seemed to *combler* him with suffering ... His speech was one of almost unconditional surrender'.[84] Croker also attacked him, largely because of Macaulay's devastating review of his edition of Boswell's *Life of Johnson*, which had just appeared in the *Edinburgh*. Macaulay, who was motivated more by critical opinion than by a desire for retribution for former attacks on him, nevertheless commented that Croker 'looks across the House of Commons at me with a leer of hatred which I repay with a gracious smile of pity'.[85] He voted in the majority in favour of ministers, and boasted to Ellis (in an otherwise uncorroborated statement) that

> *entre nous* they would have made a poor hand of it without me. Our meeting at Willis's rooms and Lord Ebrington's motion were wholly brought about by me. I really believe that, but for the stir which I made among our county Members, the ministers would have resigned. This is all in the strictest confidence.[86]

Macaulay approved of, and by his own account voted for (on 28 Sept. and/or 13 Oct. 1831), Brougham's bankruptcy court bill, by which his commissionership was to be abolished.[87] He privately expressed great anger against Brougham for seeming to go back on his promise, which was eventually kept in December, to place his father on the commission of public charities.[88] He himself had ambitions for high office, and was widely expected to receive something, so he was not surprised to be summoned by Grey on 13 Nov. According to Margaret 'his scale' was this:

> He will refuse a lordship of the treasury, a lordship of the admiralty, and the mastership of the ordnance. He will accept the secretaryship of the board of control, but will not thank them for it; and would not accept that, but that he thinks it would be a place of importance during the approaching discussions on the East India monopoly. Anything above that he would be glad to have.

He was disappointed, therefore, merely to be asked to prepare a cabinet paper, which was probably on Wellington's complaint about the arming of the Birmingham Political Union, a subject that was considered by the cabinet the following day.[89] Macdonald offered to resign from the board of control to make room for Macaulay, and although Brougham thought that Mackintosh was more deserving of promotion, ministers were anxious to bring him in, as Grey's eldest son, Lord Howick*, explained to him at the end of December. The real obstacle, however, was Lansdowne's refusal to risk the necessary election at Calne, where, the borough now being scheduled to lose one seat in the revised bill, his interest was being challenged by the corporation.[90]

On the second reading of the revised reform bill, 16 Dec. 1831, Macaulay made another great speech, even though, prompted by Mahon's references to Leeds and the ballot, 'it was spoken a day sooner than was intended and the last touches were not put to it'. He reiterated his opinions on the unjustifiable anomaly of rotten boroughs, the history of gradual and concessionary reforms, the role of the middle classes and his animosity to levelling doctrines. As was his habit, he castigated the conduct of the former ministers: 'I allow that there is danger in legislating in times of excitement; but reformers are compelled to reform at last, because bigots would not reform at first'. In particular, he was even more than usually vitriolic in his attack on Peel, condemning him for changing his principles and stealing the reformers' thunder on emancipation. Littleton left this description of his 'brilliant' speech

> which carried the House away in the same furious whirlwind of mixed passions which seemed to seize himself. Never was a more extraordinary compound of deep philosophy, exalted sentiments and party bitterness, enunciated with a warmth, a vigour and rapidity inconceivable. The public can collect but little of it from the papers. It is like the course of a meteor, never to be forgotten by those who have the fortune to see it, but seen but by a few, and to be known to others only by description. A paragraph of his speech, which he concluded by a denunciation of the late administration as 'one that would be known to posterity only for its recantations', was followed by a crash of cheers, which pained me, from my respect for the motive which induced Peel to accomplish the passing of the Catholic bill.

Rice called this personal attack 'a caustic as severe as [the convicted empiric John] St. John Long's. Enough indeed to blister a rhinoceros'; and Hobhouse noted that Peel 'looked as if sweating blood. I never saw him so scalded, not even in the days of Brougham'. Croker rose immediately in his defence, but made so many factual errors that Macaulay drew up a list of them, which Smith Stanley used to demolish him the following day. On 17 Dec. 1831 Peel was still 'so nettled by Macaulay's sarcasms', that he 'for three-quarters of an hour made a very lame and laboured defence of himself'.[91] Macaulay, who voted for the second reading that day, observed that 'we had a glorious majority, and as great a superiority, I think, in the debate as in the division'.[92] Richard Lalor Sheil*, who considered him 'the most extraordinary person in either House except one, to whom he is not sufficiently like to be compared – I mean the chancellor', reckoned that he had 'the power of coming forward on great occasions with a speech that commands the House and ... I hope to see him soon in office'.[93] Holland, echoing this sentiment, opined that 'he is clearly of the young ones the most remarkable and most rising man'.[94]

Macaulay ceased to fulfil his time-consuming duties on the bankruptcy commission on its abolition, 11 Jan. 1832.[95] He was still in hopes of office, and especially that the proposed 'creation of new peers will leave a government borough open', but he was again disappointed. Littleton recorded, 2 Feb., that Macaulay, who was perhaps also dispirited by a bout of illness

> said he would not speak in the House [on relations with Belgium and Holland]. 'He had his doubts about our foreign policy'. In short I found he was sulky and thought himself slighted, on account of Hobhouse's being made secretary at war. He did not say this; but I am sure it is so, and accordingly gave the government the hint.[96]

On 12 Feb. Macaulay met Lansdowne, who explained about Calne, but asked him whether he would accept office, if one were available. He replied that

> he was a poor man, but he had as much as he wanted and, as far as he was personally concerned, had no desire for office. At the same time, he thought that after the reform bill had passed it would be absolutely necessary that the government should be strengthened, that he thought he could do it good service, that he approved of its general principles and should not be unwilling to join it. Lord Lansdowne said that, indeed, they all, and particularly mentioned Lord Grey, felt of what importance to them his help was.

At that time ministers were trying to find another position for Robert Grant* in order to make a vacancy for Macaulay at the board of control.[97] He voted for going into committee on the reform bill, 20 Jan. 1832, and again divided steadily in favour of its details. He voted against the production of information on Portugal, 9 Feb., and spoke for the anatomy bill, 27 Feb. He again defended the increased representation of the capital, 28 Feb., when he also presented, but dissented from, a petition from the inhabitants of Calne to be allowed to retain two Members. He spoke in favour of the third reading of the bill, 19 Mar., when, arguing that its purpose was to retain the part of the constitution which had made the country happy and prosperous, and to amend the part which had contributed to the current distress and discontent, he declared that

> we are legislating not for a republic, but for the England of the present day. I do not support this bill because I think democratical institutions are calculated for all ages and all countries, but because I think that a more democratical system of representation than now exists would, in this country and in this age, produce a good government.

He pointed out the inconsistency of Tories who argued against any reform as a breach of the prescriptive constitution but tacitly accepted the need for moderate alterations, and also had an exhortation for ministers, of whom he said that 'in their situation they see and feel, that to abandon their country would be to abandon themselves'. Peel again had to justify his conduct and made clear that he would never take responsibility for bringing in a reform bill, and Littleton thought that 'it was amusing to observe the extreme deference with which he treated Macaulay; paid him compliments with evidently great pain [and] showed him much very distant civility'.[98] According to his sister, Macaulay had intended to speak a day later, but

> hearing that Miss --- was to be in the House today, he did not wish, after the reports that have even reached the newspapers about her engagement to him, to countenance them by speaking when she was known to be there. He says, 'the House is thoroughly tired of the interminable bill'. The report he hears from Mr. [John] Fazakerley* is, that the young men say, 'Macaulay was not so effective tonight', but that ministers were highly pleased, and say he helped them very much.[99]

He divided with ministers on the third reading, 22 Mar. 1832.

With the bill in the Upper House, Macaulay feared that they 'evidently shrank from taking the only means [the creation of peers] by which they could make sure of a majority' there. He was in despair at the prospect of the disastrous consequences of the ministry's fall, and stated that he would resign his seat if that happened, 'for I never will consent to follow their lead more'. He had heard of one possibility, however:

> Lord --- has lately been keeping very quiet; apparently he is ill. If the bill is lost he may come forward at the head of the sturdy reformers, who would carry the bill at all risks, say that he disapproved of the conduct of his colleagues, has had nothing to do with it, and put himself at the head of a new ministry of strong Whigs and carry the bill.[100]

As in late 1831, he may have been involved in attempts to strengthen the nerve of the government from the inside. In the House, 9 May 1832, after Grey had resigned, he denied that Members who 'speak with approbation of the conduct of ministers, or who say that they regret the advice given by the ministers was not adopted and acted upon', were casting a slur on the king. The following day, Ebrington moved for an address, written by Macaulay, calling on the king to appoint only ministers who would carry the bill unimpaired.[101] Macaulay, speaking unusually late in the debate, laid great weight on the necessity of the Commons asserting its just authority in favour of ministers, and of the king's right to create peers to carry the bill (especially as over the previous 30 years a Tory majority had gradually been built up in the Lords). He doubted that there could be any future for an anti-reform Tory ministry, which would have a 'constant struggle against the mind and will of a whole people', or for one pledged to introduce a moderate measure of reform: 'the discussion is too recent, the lapse of time too short, the inconsistency would be too glaring, the motive too obvious'. He was answered by Wetherell, and by Henry Hunt, who, not for the first time, complained that Macaulay was not a sufficiently radical reformer. His speech was again acclaimed as 'magnificent', though Sir Francis Burdett* thought it 'too like Coachmakers' Hall', and William Ord* found it 'a little overdone at the end'.[102] According to Margaret, Macaulay, who voted in the majority in favour of Ebrington's motion that day, was

> in extremely good spirits and thinks the Whigs will be firmer to their places than ever before the week is out. I should like a month of opposition for him very much. It would be a stirring time for him. He describes the excitement and indignation felt on his side of the House to be immense. Mr. [Henry] Gally Knight* said to him, 'I would drink hot blood'.[103]

On 14 May Macaulay rounded on Wellington for inconsistency in countenancing a measure of reform after having opposed disfranchisement in the Lords. According to Denis Le Marchant†, he

> expressed himself with his usual energy and the House went with him in every word, one part especially where he said, 'I am willing to let others have *infamy and place*, only leave us honour and the bill'. The effect was electrical. Poor Hardinge's face seemed swollen with rage. He jumped up as if to enter into some personal conflict, and vehemently complained of such language. His complaints were coldly received and Macaulay's explanation was if possible worse than his charge.[104]

Another exchange between the two occurred the following day.

Macaulay spoke and voted in the minority for Buxton's motion for a select committee on colonial slavery, 24 May 1832. This was a decision taken against the reinstated ministers, but it did not harm his relations with them, probably because, as Althorp explained to him a few days later, the depth of support for an inquiry had persuaded them of its inevitability.[105] He voted for the second reading of the Irish reform bill, 25 May, and against increasing the county representation of Scotland, 1 June. A few days after the death of Mackintosh, 30 May, he succeeded him as a commissioner of the board of control, with a salary of £1,200. Although Althorp suggested that he might take advantage of a possible vacancy at Chipping Wycombe, he was returned unopposed for Calne, 13 June, when he spoke in favour of reform, and two days later he was well received at a reform dinner in Leeds.[106] He took a deep interest in Indian affairs and, having taken his seat (probably on 19 June), he was added to the select committee on the East India Company, 22 June, and attended many of its sittings on political matters.[107] He justified the continued payment of the Russian-Dutch loan, 12 July, and of course sided with ministers on this, 12, 16, 20 July. He voted in the majority for inquiry into the Inns of Court, 17 July, when the House was found to be inquorate. Now one of the government's payroll vote, he was obliged to give much of his time to the chamber, as he complained to his sisters, 26 July:

> The House is still sitting, and sitting 12 hours out of the 24. I am forced to be there almost without intermission: for so few Members are left that we are in constant danger of being counted out. There is a snug party of 40 of us who lay on taxes and pass laws in the quietest manner in the world.[108]

He defended Brougham against a charge of nepotism brought by Sugden, 27 July. Citing the situation in Leeds, he denied the suggestion in a petition from Manchester that the Reform Act would enfranchise an insufficient number of inhabitants, 15 Aug. 1832, and that day he voted with government, in 17 divisions, in favour of the bill prohibiting processions of Orangemen.[109] Having left the remaining seat at Calne to Kerry at the general election in December 1832, Macaulay, who that month succeeded Thomas Hyde Villiers* as secretary to the board of control, was elected with the industrialist John Marshall* for Leeds, defeating the Conservative Sadler after an intense contest.[110]

Macaulay dressed carelessly, and, being short with a tendency to fatness, was generally remarked for his ugliness, except when the strongly marked features of his face accentuated the overwhelming flow of his speech.[111] *The Times* once referred to him as 'Mr. Babbletongue Macaulay', and he was notorious for what Sydney Smith, who thought him 'a book in breeches', termed his 'waterspouts of talk'. Smith later joked that 'there are flashes of silence in his conversation which are very agreeable', but insisted to Maria Edgeworth that 'Macaulay bursts like a beer barrel and it all comes over you, but he can't help it. He really has no wish to show off'.[112] Greville, who met Macaulay at Holland House without being introduced to him, 'settled that he was some obscure man of letters or of medicine, perhaps a cholera doctor'. Disabused of this misapprehension, he was astounded at the

> vulgarity and ungainliness of his appearance; not a ray of intellect beams from his countenance; a lump of more ordinary clay never enclosed a powerful mind and lively imagination. He had a cold and a sore throat, the latter of which occasioned a constant contraction of the muscles of the thorax, making him appear as in momentary danger of a fit. His manner struck me as not pleasing, but it was not assuming, unembarrassed, yet not easy, unpolished, yet not coarse; there was no kind of usurpation of the conversation, no tenacity as to opinion or facts, no assumption of superiority, but the variety and extent of his information were soon apparent, for whatever subject was touched upon he evinced the utmost familiarity with it; quotation, illustration, anecdote, seemed ready in his hands for every topic.[113]

Apart from his extraordinary memory and depth of knowledge, he was also notable for other legacies of his Clapham upbringing, such as his burning desire to expose falsehood and proclaim truth, his amazing confidence in the making of moral judgements and his strong sense of his own importance in the progress of mankind.[114]

These factors help to account for the sensational effect of his speeches. His sister Margaret recalled, 10 Oct. 1831, that

> we talked of eloquence, which he has often compared to fresco painting, the result of long study and deep meditation, but at the moment of execution thrown off with the greatest rapidity; what has *apparently* been the work of a few hours to last for ages. Today, he said that in really eloquent displays there must be plan and order, the right thing said in the right place, but it must be done with apparent carelessness and unconsciousness: 'a mighty maze, but not without a plan'.[115]

It was not so much that he learned his speeches by rote, but that he worked them up by long hours of preparation, contemplation and rehearsal. That he achieved something like the effect he sought is shown by Rice's comment, 16 Dec. 1831, that 'Caravaggio never painted more broadly and more powerfully. It was like the Gamblers at the Sciarra'.[116] Macaulay, who acknowledged what a difficult place the Commons was to succeed in as a speaker, once told Edward Lytton Bulwer*, 'the great secret of speaking: you must never bore for a moment'; and no doubt his rapidity assisted him in this respect.[117] He was always more impressive when giving a set speech than a reply, and was never reckoned to be a debater as such, but although he was at a disadvantage in appearance and delivery, he usually electrified the House and left its Members mesmerized.[118] As James Grant put it:

> He was an excellent speaker withal; not forcible or vehement, carrying you away, as it were, by force; but seducing you, taking you a willing captive, if I may so speak, by his dulcet tones and engaging manner, wherever he chose to go. Time after time has the House listened to him as if entranced.[119]

Macaulay, who is credited with introducing the words 'constituency' and 'fourth estate' into contemporary usage, played a highly significant part in the passage of the Reform Act.[120] For a while during the reform debates he was one of the leading speakers on the government side, and 'pitted' against Tories like Mackworth Praed and Croker, he was of invaluable assistance to ministers.[121] His interpretation of history, of the nature of progress and the importance of warding off revolution, together with his emphasis on the need to enfranchise the middle class and to integrate it into governing society, added a terrifying sense of urgency and immediacy, as well as of historical legitimacy, to the arguments in favour of reform, which must have influenced many Members.[122] If his letters are to be believed, he was crucial to the behind-the-scenes agitation that led to Ebrington's confidence motion on 10 Oct. 1831, which shored up support for ministers, at a time of intense pressure, and he may have been similarly active in May 1832. Finally, insofar as his stinging attacks contributed to Peel's declaration that he would never assist in the passage of a reform bill, and given that it was for this reason that Peel refused to serve in, and thereby aborted, the putative Wellington ministry, he ensured that the bill would pass in the form that the Whigs desired.[123]

Macaulay, having sat for Leeds until early 1834, returned financially secure from a spell in office in India in time to administer the estate of his father, who died in 1838, leaving personalty of under £5,000.[124] He subsequently represented Edinburgh as a Liberal and became a member of Russell's first cabinet. He filled numerous academic, literary and honorary positions, but is known to posterity for his immensely popular *History of England*, which was published in five volumes between 1849 and 1861. As earlier in his career, his success was largely due to the fact that his enormous intellect was allied to great communicative abilities, though he was said to lack that emotional confidence which would have given him a sureness of touch with his fellow man and a greater insight into human character.[125] In his youth, he was romantically linked with his cousin Mary Babington and Sharp's ward Maria Kinnaird, but he never married. After the death of his sister Margaret in 1834, he lived mostly with his other favourite, Hannah, the wife of the Indian administrator Sir Charles Edward Trevelyan† of Wallington, Northumberland. Indeed, it was Hannah's imminent departure for India to rejoin her husband that may have precipitated Macaulay's final decline.[126] He died in December 1859, when the peerage awarded to him two years earlier became extinct, leaving Hannah the bulk of his estate.[127] Her only son George Otto Trevelyan (1838-1928), a Liberal Member and statesman, wrote an acclaimed life of Macaulay. His third son, George Macaulay Trevelyan (1876-1962), was another eminent historian.

[1] Based on G. O. Trevelyan, *Life and Letters of Lord Macaulay* (1876), which was republished, slightly enlarged, in 1908; *The Letters of Thomas Babington Macaulay* ed. T. Pinney (1974-81); and J. Clive, *Thomas Babington Macaulay, The Shaping of the Historian* (1973), the best modern biography. [2] *Mems. of Clan 'Aulay'*, 10-11; Trevelyan, i. 4-8; W. Anderson, *Scottish Nation*, iii. 718-19. [3] Lady Knutsford, *Life and Letters of Zachary Macaulay*; C. Booth, *Zachary Macaulay*; *Oxford DNB*. [4] *Greville Mems.* iii. 279; London Univ. Lib. Booth mss 797/1/5467; Add. 51655, Mackintosh to Lady Holland, 24 Jan. 1829; Trevelyan, i. 26-36, 38-39, 50-51; Clive, 17, 21-29. [5] Knutsford, 278-80, 288; *Letters of Hannah More* ed. A. Roberts, 83-85. [6] J.M.F. Wright, *Alma Mater*, ii. 218; *Laws and Trans. of Union Soc.* (1829), 20-27; Trevelyan, i. 72-92; Clive, 36-39. [7] Trevelyan, i. 47-49, 65-67; Clive, 15, 23-35, 45-46, 50-54, 59-60, 248-51. [8] *Macaulay Letters*, i. 169; Clive, 50-51. [9] *Macaulay Letters*, i. 173; Clive, 30-32, 44-45. [10] Trevelyan, i. 59-60, 127-36, 285-6; Clive, 34-35, 39-41, 246-8, 256-88. This was attested by some of Macaulay's sisters: Selina in 'Selina Macaulay's Diary', *Bull. of New York Pub. Lib.* lxvi (1962), 440; Frances in an 'Unpublished Mem. of Lord Macaulay', *N and Q*, ccxxiii (1978), 240-2; and Margaret in her important recollections, which are printed in *Mems. of Clan 'Aulay'*, 183-264 [hereafter cited as Margaret Macaulay, *Recollections*]. [11] Knutsford, 366. [12] Trevelyan, i. 43; *Macaulay Letters*, i. 21, 30, 85. [13] Trevelyan, i. 72-73; *Macaulay Letters*, i. 181. [14] Trevelyan, i. 76, 120; W. Thomas, *Quarrel of Macaulay and Croker*, 60-92. [15] *Macaulay Letters*, i. 132-4, 148, 163-4. [16] Clive, 61-65. [17] Trevelyan (1908), 56. [18] *Times Lit. Supp.* 1 May 1969. [19] Clive, 41-44, 67, 125-6; *Macaulay Letters*, i. pp. xix-xx; J. Hamburger, *Macaulay and Whig Tradition*, p. x. [20] For a full list of Macaulay's published works, see *Allibone's Dict. of Eng. Literature* (1870), ii. 1156-61; *Macaulay Letters*, i. 321-2; vi. 289-302. Several of his articles were revised by himself and published in his *Essays, Critical and Misc.* (1843); others, including many of his early pieces, were reprinted in *Misc. Writings of Lord Macaulay* ed. T.F. Ellis (1860). [21] C. Knight, *Passages of a Working Life*, i. 298, 303, 307; *Macaulay Letters*, i. 187-8; Clive 54-59. [22] CUL, Add. 7621/15, pp. 13-14; *Report of Cttee. of Soc. for Mitigation and Gradual Abolition of Slavery* (1824), 70-79; Trevelyan (1908), 721-2; *Macaulay Letters*, i. 202. [23] Hants RO, Malmesbury mss 9M73/403, Brougham to Z. Macaulay, 20 Mar. 1823; *Greville Mems.* iii. 280; *Macaulay Letters*, i. 185-6, 203; Clive, 67-74, 92-95; J. Millgate, 'Father and Son: Macaulay's *Edinburgh* Debut', *Rev. Eng. Stud.* xxi (1970), 159-67. [24] Add. 51655; Trevelyan, i. 117-18; J. A. Greig, *Jeffrey of the Edinburgh Review*, 7-8; Clive, 74-92. [25] *Crabb Robinson Diary*, ii. 41. [26] *Macaulay Letters*, i. pp. xxii, 171-2. [27] Ibid. i. 198, 211-12; vi. 301; *The Times*, 15 June 1826; R. Read, *Modern Leicester*, 244-6; *Mems. of 'Clan Aulay'*, 71; 'Selina Macaulay's Diary', 440-1. [28] K. Bourne, *Palmerston*, 246. [29] *The Times*, 17 Apr. 1827, 18 Mar., 14 May 1828; *Camb. Univ. Pollbook* (1827), 24. [30] Trevelyan, i. 146; *Camb. Univ. Pollbook* (1829), 29. [31] *Macaulay Letters*, i. 322-3; Clive, 96, 98-99. [32] *Macaulay Letters*, i. 224, 226. [33] Ibid. i. 230, 252-3; Trevelyan, i.

125-7, 138-9; Clive, 99-100. [34] Trevelyan, i. 186; *Macaulay Letters*, i. 253-4. [35] Clive, 126-33, 138-9. [36] Lansdowne mss, Lansdowne to Rice, 26 Dec. [1828]; Add. 51690, to Lady Holland, 8 Feb. 1830; *Macaulay Letters*, i. 224, 263-5; Trevelyan, i. 139-40; 'Unpublished Mem.' 242; 'Selina Macaulay's Diary', 441-2. [37] *Devizes Gazette*, 18, 25 Feb. 1830. [38] Lansdowne mss. [39] 'Selina Macaulay's Diary', 442-3; Broughton, *Recollections*, iv. 327; *Creevey Pprs.* ii. 208; Brougham, *Life and Times*, iii. 35; Trevelyan, i. 186-8; Knutsford, 450. [40] *Letters of Hannah More*, 193; Ward, *Letters to 'Ivy'*, 347. [41] O. Goldsmith, *Retaliation* (1774). [42] 'Selina Macaulay's Diary', 442. [43] *Macaulay Letters*, i. 265, 277. [44] Northants. RO, Agar Ellis diary. [45] *Macaulay Letters*, i. 272; Margaret Macaulay, *Recollections*, 193; Trevelyan, i. 159-60. [46] *Life and Letters of John Rickman* ed. O. Williams, 254. [47] *Macaulay Letters*, i. 273, 311. [48] *Anti-Slavery Monthly Reporter*, ii (1831), 242-6. [49] 'Selina Macaulay's Diary', 442. [50] *Macaulay Letters*, i. 294-5. [51] Ibid. i. 273, 276, 279, 312; Booth mss 797/5471; *Devizes Gazette*, 7 July, 5 Aug. 1830. [52] *Macaulay Letters*, i. 281-2, 286, 287, 298-300, 307, 309-10, 323-4; T.B. Macaulay, *Napoleon and Restoration of Bourbons* ed. J. Hamburger (1977). [53] *Macaulay Letters*, i. 286-7, 312-13; Trevelyan, i. 124, 170-1; Hopetoun mss 167, f. 195. [54] St. Deiniol's Lib. Glynne-Gladstone mss 196. [55] Brougham mss. [56] *Macaulay Letters*, i. 319. [57] Ibid. ii. 376; iv. 225. [58] Ibid. ii. 5-7; vi. 275; Margaret Macaulay, *Recollections*, 204-5; 'Selina Macaulay's Diary', 442; Add. 51655, Mackintosh to Lady Holland, 3 Mar.; *The Times*, 3 Mar. 1831; Broughton, iv. 89; *Greville Mems.* ii. 124; *Howard Sisters*, 191; Trevelyan, i. 172; Clive, 161-2. [59] *Bunbury Mem.* 158-60; *Edgeworth Letters*, 488. [60] *Macaulay, Selected Writings* ed. J. Clive and T. Pinney, 166; *Macaulay Letters*, ii. 11, 20; Trevelyan, i. 175-9; Clive, 206-18. [61] *Macaulay Letters*, ii. 9-11. [62] Ibid. ii. 22; Margaret Macaulay, *Recollections*, 209. [63] *Macaulay Letters*, ii. 8-9, 12-13; *Devizes Gazette*, 28 Apr., 5 May 1831. [64] *Macaulay Letters*, ii. 14. [65] Ibid. ii. 45, 49, 51-53, 55, 59. [66] Ibid. ii. 56, 62, 64; Le Marchant, *Althorp*, 327-8; Broughton, iv. 119; *Three Diaries*, 100; *Greville Mems.* ii. 159. [67] *Macaulay Letters*, ii. 63, 69; Hatherton diary. [68] Trevelyan, i. 192-3; PRO NI, Anglesey mss D619/27A/122; Add. 51655, Mackintosh to Lady Holland, 28 July 1831. [69] *Wilson's Noctes Ambrosianae* ed. R.S. Mackenzie, iv. 356. [70] Broughton, iv. 124-5. [71] Warws. RO MI 247, Philips's Mems. i. 371-2. [72] *Macaulay Letters*, ii. 70. [73] Ibid. ii. 73, 75, 78, 80, 83, 86-87, 89. [74] Ibid. ii. 83-84. [75] Ibid. ii. 87-88, 90. [76] Ibid. ii. 99-100; vi. 275-6. [77] Ibid. ii. 105-6; *Three Diaries*, 130; Hatherton diary; Arnould, *Denman*, i. 350; Bucks. RO, Fremantle mss D/FR/139/20/32. [78] Thomas, 8-12. [79] *Greville Mems.* ii. 201, 203. [80] *Macaulay Letters*, ii. 101. [81] Ibid. ii. 92-94, 103-4; A. S. Turberville, 'Leeds and Parl. Reform', *Pubs. Thoresby Soc.* xli (1954), 40-43. [82] *Macaulay Letters*, ii. 100-1. [83] Add. 61937, f. 125. [84] Cornw. RO, Hawkins mss 10/2172; Hants RO, Carnarvon mss 75M91/l12/14; Le Marchant, 356; *Three Diaries*, 150; Hatherton diary; Broughton, iv. 138-9; *Greville Mems.* ii. 207, 225; *Howard Sisters*, 215. [85] *Macaulay Letters*, ii. 106; E. S. De Beer, 'Macaulay and Croker', *Rev. of Eng. Stud.* x (1959), 388-97. [86] *Macaulay Letters*, ii. 101, 105-6. [87] Trevelyan, i. 175. [88] Ibid. ii. 101-2; Margaret Macaulay, *Recollections*, 219-20, 222-3. [89] Margaret Macaulay, *Recollections*, 215-17; Clive, 200-1. The paper may have been 'Lord Grey's observations on the correspondence', which is mentioned by Holland (*Holland House Diaries*, 74-78). [90] Add. 51563, Brougham to Holland [bef. 27 Oct.]; Brougham mss, reply, 27 Oct.; Lansdowne mss, Grey to Lansdowne, 27 Dec.; Grey mss, reply, 28 Dec. 1831; *Holland House Diaries*, 97, 106; *Baring Jnls.* i. 92; Margaret Macaulay, *Recollections*, 225-6. [91] Margaret Macaulay, *Recollections*, 225; *Three Diaries*, 169, 171-2; Le Marchant, 382; Hatherton diary; Broughton, iv. 155-7; *Greville Mems.* ii. 230-1; Add. 51569, Ord to Lady Holland [16 Dec.]; 51573, Rice to same [16 Dec. 1831]; *William IV-Grey Corresp.* ii. 39; *Cockburn Letters*, 365; Cockburn, *Jeffrey*, ii. 242; Trevelyan, i. 193. [92] *Macaulay Letters*, ii. 109. [93] *Three Diaries*, 169. [94] Anglesey mss 27A/143. [95] *Macaulay Letters*, i. 271-2. [96] Ibid. ii. 113; Margaret Macaulay, *Recollections*, 227-9; *Holland House Diaries*, 120; Hatherton diary. [97] Margaret Macaulay, *Recollections*, 231-2, 233-4. [98] Ibid. 241; Hawkins mss 10/2190; *Three Diaries*, 213, 215; Hatherton diary. [99] Margaret Macaulay, *Recollections*, 241. [100] Ibid. 241-2, 244-5. [101] Ibid. 264. [102] Add. 51569, Ord to Lady Holland [10 May 1832]; Hatherton diary; Broughton, iv. 222; Le Marchant, 428. [103] Margaret Macaulay, *Recollections*, 264. [104] Broughton, iv. 225; *Croker Pprs.* ii. 165; *Three Diaries*, 255. [105] *Buxton Mems.* 296. [106] *Macaulay Letters*, ii. 122-3, 129-33; BL, Althorp mss, Althorp to Smith [?June]; *Devizes Gazette*, 7, 14 June 1832; Turberville, 54-57. [107] *Macaulay Letters*, ii. 134; Clive, 219-21; *PP* (1831-2), xiv. 11. [108] *Macaulay Letters*, ii. 153, 158, 160, 171-2. [109] Ibid. ii. 173-4. [110] Ibid. ii. 114-20, 162-7, 175-9, 186, 188-91, 193, 198-212; Turberville, 40-87; *Leeds Mercury*, 15 Dec. 1832. [111] Margaret Macaulay, *Recollections*, 207-8; *Lady Holland to Son*, 108; *Life of Wilberforce*, v. 249-50; Clive, 238-40. [112] H. Herd, *March of Journalism*, 196; *Greville Mems.* ii. 419; *Smith Letters*, ii. 763; *Edgeworth Letters*, 592, 600; Trevelyan, i. 120-5; Clive, 243-6. [113] *Greville Mems.* ii. 247-9, 317; iii. 280-1, 480. [114] *Macaulay Letters*, i. p. xvii; Clive, 30. [115] Margaret Macaulay, *Recollections*, 215. [116] Add. 51573. [117] *Macaulay Letters*, i. 317-18; *Corresp. of Abraham Hayward* ed. H.E. Carlisle, ii. 63. [118] Margaret Macaulay, *Recollections*, 237; G.H. Francis, *Orators of the Age* (1847), 78-100; *Life of Campbell*, i. 525; *Baring Jnls.* ii. 187; *Three Diaries*, 310, 346; *Macaulay Letters*, ii. 5; Trevelyan, ii. 139-41; Clive, 157-65. [119] [J. Grant], *Random Recollections of Commons* (1837), 176-8. [120] *Macaulay Letters*, ii. 13, 22; *OED*; Clive, 124-5. [121] *Macaulay Letters*, i. 190, 317; *Croker Pprs.* ii. 46-49; Clive, 189-96. [122] Clive, 103-5, 125-6, 133-8, 165-89; Hamburger, 4-13, 116-22, 144-58; D. Wahrman, *Imagining the Middle Class*, 306, 356-8; J. Cannon, *Parl. Reform*, 244. [123] Clive, 197-200; N. Gash, *Sir Robert Peel*, 26. [124] PROB 6/214. [125] *Corresp. of Abraham Hayward*, ii. 62-63; J.H. Plumb, *Making of an Historian*, i. 258-61; *Macaulay Letters*, i. p. vii; Clive, 251-5. [126] Trevelyan, ii. 269-80; Clive, 256-7. [127] *The Times*, 31 Dec. 1859, 23 Jan. 1860; *DNB*; *Oxford DNB*.

S.M.F.

McCLINTOCK, John (1769–1855), of Drumcar, co. Louth.

ATHLONE	1820–May 1820
CO. LOUTH	1830–1831

b. 14 Aug. 1769, 1st s. of John McClintock, MP [I], of Drumcar and Patience, da. of William Foster of Rosy Park, co. Louth. *educ.* Drogheda sch.; Trinity, Dublin 1787; L. Inn 1790. *m.* (1) 11 June 1797, Jane (*d.* 28 Apr. 1801), da. and h. of William Bunbury, MP [I], of Moyle, co. Carlow, 2s. 1da. *d.v.p.*; (2) 15 Apr. 1805, Lady Elizabeth Trench, da. of William Power Keating, 1st earl of Clancarty [I], 5s. (2 *d.v.p.*) 3da. (1 *d.v.p.*). *suc.* fa. 1799. *d.* 12 July 1855.

Dep. sjt.-at-arms of House of Commons [I] 1794-1800. Sheriff, co. Louth 1798-9.

McClintock's father, Member of the Irish Parliament for Enniskillen, 1783-90, and Belturbet, 1790-99, came from a well-established family of Scottish Protestant settlers. In 1766 he married a first cousin of John Foster* who, as Irish Speaker, appointed him chief serjeant-at-arms of the Commons and his two eldest sons John and William as deputies, for which they later received a joint pension of £2,545. McClintock, who had been present at the battles of Arklow and Vinegar Hill in June 1798, was reported to be the last person with the Speaker to leave the Irish House following enactment of the Union, to which he had been 'consistently opposed'.[1] In 1815 he wrote twice to Peel, the Irish secretary, to recommend a man for a vacancy as a boatman 'at the little port of Annagassan near my house'.[2] On 27 Jan. 1817 he warned William Gregory, the Irish under-secretary, of the 'alarming state of the country':

> If we do not partake of the benefit likely to result from an Insurrection Act, you may expect to hear of dreadful results ... As government refused us the advantage of this law, the general observation among the people is that it will never be resorted to. We must have it, as every hour the lawless and diabolical spirit becomes worse.[3]

At the 1820 general election he served as a locum at Athlone for its patron Lord Castlemaine, a kinsman by his second marriage. He did not take his seat and by 16 May 1820 had vacated.[4] A Protestant proselytizer, throughout the 1820s he and his brother Henry, collector of revenues at Dundalk, regularly attended the local Bible meetings of Robert Jocelyn*, 3rd earl of Roden, with their kinsman John Leslie Foster*.[5]

At the 1830 general election McClintock came forward for Louth on the Foster interest, headed since 1828 by the 2nd Baron Oriel, with the support of Roden, who was now vice-president of the Protestant Reformation Society. He described himself as a 'constant resident in the county', where his 'ancestors had been long established', and a 'constitutional representative, anxious to improve every description of oppressive taxation'.[6] On learning of his candidature the Wellington ministry's Irish secretary, Lord Francis Leveson Gower, notified the popular Catholic candidate Richard Sheil* that 'as a representative of the Foster interest', government would have to give McClintock 'such support as it has to give'.[7] After a turbulent three-day contest, in which the Catholic vote was split between two 'belligerent' candidates, McClintock finished in second place, his brother Henry noting that it was 'rather a remarkable circumstance that ... John is 61 years old this very day on which he is returned'.[8] Following the widespread circulation of a list of 'Brunswick Papists' who had voted against Sheil, McClintock subscribed £30 towards the fund established to 'protect and assist ... the individuals named'.[9] Speculation that he would be 'turned out' on petition came to nothing.[10]

He was, of course, listed by the Wellington ministry as one of their 'friends', although this was later queried. He presented a petition for the abolition of slavery from the Wesleyan Methodist Society of Dundalk, 5 Nov. 1830. In his only known speech, 11 Nov., he rejected the charges contained in a petition presented by Daniel O'Connell against the Dundalk magistracy, who he insisted were 'extremely active and zealous in discharging their duty in a proper manner'. He voted in the ministerial minority on the civil list, 15 Nov. He was granted a month's leave on urgent private business, 2 Dec. 1830. He divided against the second reading of the Grey ministry's reform bill, 22 Mar., and for Gascoyne's wrecking amendment, 19 Apr. 1831. At the ensuing dissolution he retired from Louth, where the Catholics had reunited, without explanation. Expectations that he would be Roden's nominee at Dundalk proved to be false.[11] McClintock died at Drumcar in July 1855 and was succeeded by his eldest son John (1798-1879), Conservative Member for Louth, 1857-9, who was created Baron Rathdonell [I] in 1868.[12]

[1] W. Abbott, *McClintock Fam.* 1-3; A. Malcomson, *John Foster*, 267; *Extraordinary Black Bk.* (1832), 552; *Gent. Mag.* (1855), ii. 204-5. [2] Add. 40248, f. 258; 40249, f. 80. [3] Add. 40203, f. 169. [4] PRO NI, Redhall mss MIC 582/1/20, McClintock diary, 29 Mar. 1820. [5] Malcomson, 152; Redhall mss MIC 582/2/2. [6] *Drogheda Jnl.* 20, 24 July 1830. [7] NAI, Leveson Gower letterbks. 7. B.3. 33, Leveson Gower to Sheil, 17 May 1830. [8] *Drogheda Jnl.* 14, 17 Aug., *Dublin Evening Post*, 12, 14 Aug. 1830. [9] PRO NI, Anglesey mss D.619/32C/12. [10] Ibid. 32C/14, Flanagan to Anglesey, 1 Dec. 1830. [11] *Drogheda Jnl.* 30 Apr., 3, 7 May; *Dublin Evening Post*, 7, 14 May 1831. [12] *Gent. Mag.* (1855), ii. 204-5.

P.J.S.

MACDONALD, James (1784–1832), of East Sheen, Surr. and Woolmer Lodge, nr. Liphook, Hants.

Tain Burghs	26 June 1805–1806
Newcastle-under-Lyme	1806–1812
Sutherland	1812–1 Feb. 1816
Calne	23 Feb. 1816–1831
Hampshire	1831–June 1832

b. 14 Feb. 1784, o. surv. s. of Sir Archibald Macdonald†, 1st bt., of East Sheen and Lady Louisa Leveson Gower, da. of Granville Leveson Gower†, 1st mq. of Stafford. *educ.* Westminster 1797; Christ Church, Oxf. 1801; L. Inn 1804. *m.* (1) 5 Sept. 1805, Elizabeth (*d.* 4 Jan. 1818), da. of John Sparrow of Bishton, Staffs., *s.p.*; (2) 10 Aug. 1819, Lady Sophia Keppel (*d.* 29 Sept. 1824), da. of William Charles, 4th earl of Albemarle, 2s. (1 *d.v.p.*); (3) 20 Apr. 1826, Anne Charlotte, da. of Rev. John Savile Ogle of Kirkley Hall, Northumb., preb. of Durham, *s.p.* *suc.* fa. as 2nd bt. 18 May 1826; GCMG 22 June 1832. *d.* 29 June 1832.

Principal clerk of privy seal 1806-30; commr. bd. of control May 1827-Jan. 1828, Dec. 1830-June 1832; high commr. Ionian Islands 2 June 1832-*d.*

'Descended from that ancient family, formerly kings of the Isles', Macdonald's father, Archibald, was the third son of Sir Alexander Macdonald, 7th baronet, of Sleat, Skye, and younger brother of Alexander, who was given the Irish barony of Macdonald in 1776. Archibald, whose political and legal career under Pitt was advanced by the influence of his father-in-law, created marquess of Stafford in 1786, was appointed chief baron of the exchequer in 1793, from which he retired with a baronetcy in 1813. James, his first and only surviving son, was brought into Parliament by the 2nd marquess in 1805.[1] He supported the Grenville ministry, and thereafter was usually an active member of opposition, being elected to Brooks's, 11 Feb. 1810, and acting as a list-maker and parliamentary manager. Following a difference of political opinion with his family connections, he transferred in 1816 to Calne, the pocket borough of the leading Whig magnate, the 3rd marquess of Lansdowne.[2] 'One of the clever agreeable diners-out of London',[3] he was listed in the directories as having lived at several addresses there, including his father's house at 20 Duke Street. He sometimes resided at Loudham Hall, Suffolk, after his second marriage, into the Keppel family, which took place in 1819. That year he was an assiduous opponent in the House of the Liverpool ministry's coercive legislation, which he urged his colleague James Abercromby to resist as 'the most fatal experiment ever attempted', and which he denounced at the Norfolk Fox Club dinner, 24 Jan. 1820.[4] He also eulogized his political mentor there, but confided to Fox's nephew Lord Holland, 30 Jan., his

> hope that nothing fell from me on the subject ... that you will not approve. I have always thought that the least popular parts of Mr. Fox's career ought not to be kept out of view, but that the people should be told that if there was any fault at all it had its origin in the lukewarmness of their support of him on many trying occasions.[5]

Despite admitting privately that retaining his seat was 'a matter of total indifference, except in so far as I must ever feel a deep interest in Lansdowne's political credit', he was returned unopposed for Calne, with Abercromby, at the general election of 1820.[6] He continued to attend meetings of the Whig managers,[7] and, esteemed by his colleagues, his opinions carried weight in party counsels; but it was with increasing rarity that he played any prominent role in Parliament, where he, of course, divided solidly with opposition on most major issues, occasionally acting as a teller.

On 24 Apr. 1820 Macdonald wrote to Edward Davies Davenport*, whose proposed article on Peterloo he still hoped would appear, that

> things are in so extraordinary a state between the king and ministers that we have resolved for the first few days of the session to leave them to settle their matters together, and to await the bringing forward the civil list next week before we open our campaign.

He added that he had little hope of George IV 'having *nerve* to change his ministers, which implies a change of system', although 'the women who are about him ... are hard at work to effect it'.[8] He sided silently with opposition on the civil list, 3, 8 May, and was a teller for the minority against considering the droits of the crown and admiralty as sources of revenue for it, 5 May, when he criticized government for reneging on a former pledge to review the question on the accession of a new king, and declared that

> this system of giving money to the sovereign held out a strong temptation to the minister to barter the public money for royal favour, and the crown to depend not on Parliament for support but, to a certain extent, on the corrupt obsequiousness of the minister.

He spoke briefly in favour of reducing the costs of trying insolvent debtors, 26 May, and against serving Irish masters in chancery becoming Members, 30 June. He divided against Wilberforce's compromise motion on Queen Caroline, 22 June, and for adjourning debate on the appointment of a secret committee, 26 June, but left the House before the division on Hobhouse's motion for an address to the king to prorogue Parliament, 18 Sept.[9] In early October 1820 he believed Henry Brougham's* speech for her defence in the Lords would 'shake not only the case, but the administration also to its foundations'. Yet he remained doubtful of opposition success, even if the bill never reached the Commons, confiding to Davenport:

> I am not sanguine as to the result of a change of ministry, for I have my fears *it is too late*; however, it is worth trying, for to go from bad to worse will with the present men and this wretched system must be ruin. The Whigs are too much afraid of committing themselves and, therefore, too backward in giving the public to understand what they will really and what thy will not do, but I am convinced they would enter office (for the first time) with a thorough knowledge of the state of the public feelings and expectations, and would set themselves honestly to work to do good and not to job ... If, then, it is any object to get rid of the present men, should this opportunity be lost? I think not and I am, therefore, clear that every county should be stirred *immediately* after the defence.[10]

He ridiculed the proceedings against the queen at the Fox Club dinner in Norwich, 19 Jan., and at the end of the Surrey county meeting, 2 Feb. 1821, he made 'a good speech, well lashing' George Holme Sumner's conduct on the issue and successfully moved that the petition to the Commons in her favour should be entrusted only to the other county Member, William Joseph Denison.[11] In the House on the 8th he defended his actions on that occasion, and he divided steadily in the Whig campaign on Caroline's behalf that month.

The marquess of Buckingham, leader of the Grenvillites, advised William Henry Fremantle*, 4 Feb. 1821, that 'Macdonald's conversation was a *pumping* one, and meant to impress you with the idea that there is no alternative but the present government or opposition and that we had better join the latter'.[12] He voted to make Leeds, proposed for enfranchisement in place of Grampound, a scot and lot borough, 2 Mar., and for parliamentary reform, 9 May. He attacked the army estimates, 12 Mar., arguing that certain salaries should be reduced, that the colonies could provide for their own defence and that a large peacetime standing army was not necessary for the preservation of public order. As promised, he moved an amendment to reduce the size of the land forces by 10,000 men, 14 Mar., when he explained how sufficient defences could be maintained by the voluntary services and insisted that the country's future ability to wage war depended on its first recovering its economic strength. The veteran Sir Richard Hussey Vivian, in reply, set the tone for the debate by stating that the amendment would not guarantee adequate security, and Macdonald, who acted as teller, was defeated by 211-115. Charles Williams Wynn* reported to Buckingham the following day that opposition Members 'are outrageous against each other and, according to Macdonald's report, may be expected by the next session to split into three or more distinct parties', though he 'did not specify either the persons likely to form these or the points in dispute'.[13] He congratulated Lansdowne on escaping from the 'spirit of intrigue' at Court by visiting France, 19 Aug. 1821, as

> never was it so difficult to foresee what will be the course of political events at home as at this moment. The death of the queen must loosen the ties that bind the king to his present ministers as a body; his momentary popularity will turn his head; and there will be a much wider field for a favourite's influence to act upon than heretofore.

He added that he gave some credence to the rumour that ministers would try to increase their strength against Lady Conyngham 'by a desperate attempt to get the king to marry'.[14]

He attended the Norfolk Fox Club dinner, 24 Jan., and the Suffolk county meeting on agricultural distress, 29 Jan. 1822.[15] According to John Cam Hobhouse*, he and a few others divided 'against us' on Sir Francis Burdett's amendment to delay consideration of the address, 5 Feb., but he voted for Hume's subsequent amendment to it, on distress, that day.[16] He criticized Lord Londonderry, the foreign secretary, for an ill-timed pleasantry against Coke, Member for Norfolk, 7 Mar., when he condemned Thomas Gooch, on his presenting the petition from the Suffolk meeting, for inconsistency between his then stated preference for economies and his subsequent voting behaviour in the House. He divided steadily for opposition motions for retrenchment that session, including in the majority for abolition of one of the joint-postmasterships, 2 May, when he pressed the case for economies. He voted for receiving the Greenhoe, Norfolk, petition for parliamentary reform, 3 June, to condemn the present influence of the crown, 24 June 1822, again for reform, 20 Feb., and information on Inverness elections, 26 Mar. 1823. Macdonald, whose financial position was never strong, held the sinecure office of clerk of the privy seal, though the salary of £400 was 'all given by him to his deputy', according to a report of the Commons of July 1822.[17] Following a long bout of rheumatic fever, he wrote to James Alexander Stewart Mackenzie*, 3 Aug., that he was inclined to make his elder infant son 'an Highland laird rather than an English squire eat up with tithes and poor rates, if I could find a good opportunity, but am in no hurry as I could not conveniently diminish my income just at present'.[18] In a letter to Lansdowne from Loudham, 18 Aug., he speculated on the possibility of the ministry collapsing after Londonderry's suicide:

> Indeed when one considers the state of Liverpool's health and constitution it is not very irrational to conjecture that he might not feel equal to attempt to remodel his cabinet, and I think it just possible that if the event had happened prior to the Grenville accession he would not, but my opinion of Liverpool has always been that the public are quite wrong in supposing him indifferent to office, that on the contrary he is personally disposed to cling to it with the utmost tenacity.

He also complained that

> having abandoned the Norfolk Fox dinner I am now met with another almost at my door ... Though I think I am rather more inclined to favour the kind of communication out-of-doors than you are I have my doubts whether, as things now stand, they are very desirable, for those celebrations to which they were first opposed are rapidly falling away.[19]

He duly attended the Suffolk Fox dinner, 21 Aug., when he noted the declining number of dinners honouring Pitt, and ridiculed his reputation as 'the pilot who weathered the storm', adding that the despots of Europe could expect popular upheavals unless they introduced the 'safety valve of popular representation'.[20] He wrote to Thomas Kennedy*, 16 Oct. 1822, that he had put off his visit to Scotland because of his wife's illness, and, condemning Canning's abandonment of the Catholic cause in his speech at Liverpool, commented that if the new foreign secretary succeeded in removing Manners Sutton from the Speaker's chair to make room for Williams Wynn, he would propose either William Holmes, the Tory whip, or Henry Swann, the convicted briber, Member for Penryn, against him.[21]

On Hume's motion against the appointment of a lieutenant-general of the ordnance, 19 Feb. 1823, Macdonald, despite having a 'disposition to save every farthing that could be spared consistently with the efficient management of the several public departments', said that 'he felt himself, in common with sundry friends around him, somewhat embarrassed by the wording of the present motion'. Arguing that the office should only be suppressed as part of a general review, he urged Hume to call instead for a select committee, and did not divide in the minority with him. However, he sided with opposition on lowering taxation by £7,000,000, 28 Feb., against reducing the national debt by as much as £5,000,000, 6, 17 Mar., and against the military and naval pensions bill, 14, 16 Apr. He seconded Hamilton's amendment to shorten the length of the Easter adjournment, 27 Mar., in order to take into early consideration the French invasion of Spain. Calling this an attack on the 'independence of nations', he asserted that Canning had been negligent in not exerting Britain's influence to prevent France's 'unprincipled aggression'. He acknowledged that hostilities might become inevitable, but appealed to the House whether

> any man who looked at the enormous amount of our public debt, of which five-sixths was incurred in putting down the Bourbons, and then in restoring them to the throne of which they had subsequently shown themselves unworthy – any man who looked to that stupendous memorial of the Tory governments which had ruled the country for the last 60 years, could not but pray that we might be spared as long as possible the necessity of again going to war.

Responding to Brougham's comments on party tactics,[22] he wrote to him lamenting his decision not to take the lead of 'our ragamuffin forces ... for a leader makes his party respected in debate as a good general does his army in a campaign and you may be sure none of us young lords will attempt what we manifestly cannot succeed in'. Expressing 'great anxiety' about Brownlow's intended motion on the disturbances in Dublin and Irish *ex-officio* informations, he stated that 'I cannot and will not side with the Orangemen to restore their cursed supremacy, and I do not think the establishment question one of great importance'. He suggested that it should be met by the previous question, and presumably welcomed this, 15 Apr., but he divided for Burdett's motion for inquiry into the legal proceedings against the Dublin rioters, 22 Apr. He was also grateful that Brougham thought 'I did no harm' (on 27 Mar.) and, suggesting that their friend Sir James Mackintosh should open the case against Canning after the recess, nevertheless hinted that 'if I were of sufficient importance there is no task I should like so well as moving'.[23] He duly moved for an address to the king condemning ministers' handling of the crisis, 28 Apr., when he blamed their conduct on subservience to the Allies and disregard for liberal constitutions. William Lamb* thought this, Macdonald's last major speech, worse

> than he usually has done for his speeches, though always in a bad style and taste, have generally had something of liveliness and force in them, but this was dull and unmanly. At the same time, the motion had put him upon such very narrow ground that it was very difficult to make anything of a speech ... He employed two hours, I believe, in saying nothing, and saying it very heavily and confusedly.[24]

James Stuart Wortley moved, as an amendment, the Lords' address praising ministers for avoiding war, and Canning vindicated himself so well, that at the end of three days of debate, as the Tory diarist Mrs. Arbuthnot recorded

> Macdonald said that the amendment was *so nearly what he approved of*! that he would withdraw his motion and adopt it, satisfied with having drawn from the House an unanimous vote of censure upon *the conduct of France*! Mr. Canning refused to allow this; the opposition then attempted to leave the House, but were so hissed and hooted that they stopped short amidst the laughter of the whole House. At last they divided, most of the opposition voting *with us* as a means of concealing their own defeat.[25]

Twenty Members trapped in the House formed a purely nominal minority, while Macdonald was among the majority of 372 who voted with ministers for the amendment, 30 Apr. 1823.[26]

He divided in favour of reforming the representation of Edinburgh, 26 Feb. 1824, and was a fixture in opposition minorities that year up to and including Brougham's motion condemning the trial of the

Methodist missionary John Smith in Demerara, 11 June. Had Monmouth been opened that session against the duke of Beaufort's interest, the seat would apparently have been offered to him.[27] He divided against the Irish unlawful societies bill, 15, 18, 21, 25 Feb., and (as he had on 28 Feb. 1821) for Catholic relief, 1 Mar., 21 Apr., 10 May 1825. He entered the House after the doors had been closed for the division on reforming the representation of Edinburgh, 13 Apr., but voted for a bill against non-resident voters in Irish boroughs, 9 Mar., and parliamentary reform, 27 Apr. 1826. His wife died in childbed, 29 Sept. 1824, 'sincerely regretted by her family and friends'.[28] Shortly afterwards his father moved from East Sheen to an estate in Hampshire, once owned by the former Member Sir Thomas Miller, where he built Woolmer Lodge.[29] He died in May 1826, a month after his son's third marriage, and by his will, dated 19 May 1825, he gave his wife a life interest in his entire estate, which included shares in the Trent and Mersey canal and personal wealth sworn under £18,000. She died, 29 Jan. 1827, leaving Sir James Macdonald, as he had become, one of his parents' main beneficiaries.[30] At the general election of 1826 he nearly lost his seat at Calne, where the supporters of an increasingly powerful independent interest only backed off from a contest at the last moment, but in the guildhall he declared that he was proud to be returned as the '*unsold representative of unbought men*'.[31] He was a teller for the minority for a second amendment to the address, for inquiry into the state of Ireland and further economies, 21 Nov. 1826. He voted against the grant for the duke of Clarence, 16 Feb. 1827. A member of the '*petit comité*' of party managers who met to discuss tactics after Liverpool's stroke, he was in favour of putting off the intended motion on Catholic relief, but divided in its favour, 6 Mar.[32] He voted in the majority for going into committee on the spring guns bill, 23 Mar. He divided for information on the Orange procession and Lisburn magistrates, 29 Mar., and chancery administration, 5 Apr., and for postponing the committee of supply, 30 Mar. 1827.

He was one of several supporters of Lansdowne, now the recognized leader of the moderate Whigs, who urged him to overcome his scruples and join Canning in a pro-Catholic ministry, perhaps even with himself as first lord of the treasury. On 14 Apr. 1827 he wrote:

> It is right I should state to you that, with the exception of some crochets of Lord Grey's which vary every hour, there seems to exist hardly any difference among those called the opposition, of the necessity of your doing more than giving your support to a government that should be formed *without any restrictions* on the Catholic question. Duncannon ... tells me ... that the opposition ... may be fairly taken at 200 ... No slight body this to bring into any negotiation. Of these the most eager, perhaps, for something more than support to Canning under his present circumstances are the Members for the populous places and the Irish Members – the latter indeed would be in perfect despair if, when all that is Orange and illiberal is arrayed against Canning, a mistrust of the man were to limit your powerful aid to a mere support. The opposition tender you their unqualified confidence if you shall see grounds for assisting in the formation of the new ministry. Ireland will tender you hers the moment they see you so embarked, and what if the king should mean to make Canning his dupe? May you not then prove too strong for him, or if you do not, shall you suffer for the part you have thus honestly and gallantly taken, either in public reputation or in self-satisfaction?[33]

Although he expressed willingness to step aside in favour of Mackintosh, he was delighted that he and Abercromby were to accept office, so long as Lansdowne was ultimately also to come in. He stated a preference for the India board

> because it would induce me to devote myself to the thorough understanding of the great subjects that in the course of a few years must come under discussion with reference to the empire, and to which I might look to obtain some little credit, and compensate for some years of illness.[34]

Since he was not deemed to be qualified as an under-secretary for home affairs, 'which is a very laborious office and must be filled by an active lawyer fresh from practice', he was granted his wish and the salary of £1,500, and was returned unopposed for Calne at the same time as Abercromby, 25 May.[35] He was noticed by Thomas Creevey* as being absent from the House on the disfranchisement of Penryn, 28 May,[36] but he voted with ministers for the grant to improve water communications in Canada, 12 June. Following Canning's death in early August, Macdonald imagined that the king would soon send for the duke of Wellington, and 'doubted whether the government could go on, for although Lord Lansdowne had no objection to men, provided the same principles were to be acted upon ... he saw the leaning was to a decided Tory administration'.[37] On 21 Oct. 1827 he urged Lansdowne, who in fact remained in place under Lord Goderich despite the fracas caused by the Whigs' hostility to the appointment of John Herries* as chancellor of the exchequer, not to vacate the home office, as 'I cannot help thinking that where a man feels that he is succeeding and giving general satisfaction he may reconcile himself to duties otherwise uncongenial to him'.[38]

Macdonald left office with Lansdowne on the appointment of Wellington as prime minister in January 1828. In the House, 21 Feb., he denied an allegation made by Herries that the Whigs who had lately been his colleagues had schemed to break up the government. He spoke in favour of the army estimates, 22 Feb., but emphasized that he was 'particularly anxious to guard myself against the supposition that I grant it from any confidence in the present administration', because he saw in the new cabinet 'men acting together in concert, between whom an irreconcilable difference recently existed'. He also defended the last government's practice of referring the estimates to a committee, and its record in cutting expenditure. He voted to repeal the Test Acts, 26 Feb., and for Catholic relief, 12 May. He divided against extending the right of voting in East Retford to the freeholders of Bassetlaw, 21 Mar., and recommitting the disfranchisement bill, 27 June. He acted as teller for the majority against instructing the committee on the Penryn disfranchisement bill to consider extending the borough to the neighbouring hundreds, 24 Mar. As John Fazakerley* reported to Edward Littleton*, 20 Sept., while on holiday that autumn Macdonald

> was seized by a paralytic attack at Lausanne, which has deprived him of the use of all below his waist. I had a long letter from him yesterday written with great composure, and even cheerfulness: he is assured by the medical men that his intellects are in no danger, nor his life threatened immediately. This to a man who for some days thought that a *coup de grace* was hanging over him is naturally a great relief. There seems even a chance of partial recovery.[39]

His case was initially despaired of, and, for example, Abercromby wrote that 'I have for some time been aware that his constitution, not strong by nature, has been materially shaken', and blamed the attack on a recent complaint in one of his legs having been 'injudiciously treated'. However, by early October he was in much better health.[40] He recorded for Fazakerley, 10 Nov. 1828, his delight at visiting Genoa, and his unwillingness to contemplate returning to England until after Easter:

> Indeed, the state of things at home makes me regret the less my inability to do so, for what good is to be expected? England is fast sinking in the scale of nations under the administration of the duke of Wellington. It is thrown in one's teeth at every step one takes on the continent. His conduct in permitting the British empire to be distracted, as it seems to be, and verging towards a civil war, from a base fear of the basest of factions, the English Tory aristocracy, must damn him to all posterity. A liberal party surely must be formed, I care not under whom, to prevent as far as in themselves (and it must be a bold-spirited, uncompromising party) to prevent our further degradation abroad, and our dissolution at home.[41]

He was absent in France during the early part of the following year, but was present to vote for Catholic emancipation, 6 Mar. 1829, the only evidence of parliamentary activity that session.[42]

He voted for Knatchbull's amendment to the address on distress, 4 Feb. 1830, and divided steadily in favour of economies and lower taxes during the following months. He asked Peel, the home secretary, for a 'very extensive and efficient committee' to be appointed on the East India Company, 9 Feb., and that the regulations governing the trade and the welfare of the people of India be considered. He also objected to the method of naming committees, whereby 'the list is read rather rapidly, and we are immediately called on to say, whether it is considered sufficient'. Avoiding the invidiousness of naming individuals, he thought the committee should contain more Members representing 'great commercial and manufacturing interests', and not just 'those persons who are called great Indian authorities' or those, like the directors, who 'have too great an interest in the question'. He voted for East Retford's seats to be transferred to Birmingham, 11 Feb., 15 Mar. He divided in favour of enfranchising Birmingham, Leeds and Manchester, 23 Feb., and parliamentary reform, 28 May. He was absent from the party meeting in early March at which Lord Althorp was chosen as leader.[43] He sided with opposition against British interference in Portugal, 10 Mar., and on the affair at Terceira, 28 Apr., and the civil government of Canada, 25 May. He divided in favour of Jewish emancipation, 5 Apr. He voted for altering the laws respecting Irish vestries, 27 Apr., and to abolish the Irish lord lieutenancy, 11 May. He was in the majority for abolishing the death penalty for forgery, 7 June, and the minority against increasing recognizances in cases of libel, 9 July. At the general election the following month, he was returned with his new colleague Tom Macaulay for Calne, despite a contest and a petition.[44] Having declined to stand himself, he was enthusiastically active on behalf of Lord Porchester*, elder son of the 2nd earl of Carnarvon, and John Ogle, his brother-in-law, in their attempt to open Petersfield. They lost the contest, but 'that most sanguine man', as Harriet Stapleton called Macdonald, was very hopeful that they would be seated on petition.[45] With Sir Thomas Baring*, he conveyed to Carnarvon the news that Porchester had been nominated for Hampshire, and he subsequently explained to the freeholders why Porchester had declined, 8 Aug. 1830. He also attacked the Tory Member John Fleming as no true friend of reform, seeing that

> the time was come when people would look about them, and should the House of Commons continue to act on such bigoted, intolerant and antiquated notions, as it had hitherto pursued, if they did not timely reform themselves, it would soon be too late and they would place the crown in jeopardy.[46]

Blaming Wellington and the 1815 settlement for the recent revolution in France, Macdonald lamented to Lansdowne, 22 Oct. 1830, that he felt 'everything has been put at risk by the wicked and atrocious policy of this country in departing from her ancient policy to please the despots and the "late king", in support of the "monarchical principle".' He admitted that however desirable it was for Wellington to be replaced, he did not wish the task on anyone

> for the public mind is in a state not easily to be satisfied, discontent the most indefinite prevails and expectations the most extravagant are entertained. That great changes at home are at hand no rational man can doubt, but who is to direct them and can they be effected peaceably? There is no disguising from ourselves that we are not in the right, that the system whether in church or state is vicious, and above all that the constitution of the House of Commons has failed for many years to give the people a fair control over the expenditure of the government. But having postponed rectifying positive and grievous abuses at a fit season, we are now called upon to do so at a period of unexampled excitement.

He believed the only solution was for 'all men who think rightly and mean well' to take counsel and act together; specifically that

> a party ought to be formed upon the basis of *certain things which they require to be done*. Confidence in any body of public men no longer exists, mere vague professions or known good intentions no longer pass current. Unless means be found to fix public confidence somewhere, an explosion will take place. Now I conceive this can only be effected by an intelligible creed on the points which the greatest portion of the public deem indispensable. In giving such pledges we are bound to see that what we proposed shall be *practicable*, and within this limit, the object being to satisfy all the reasonable portion of the community, we are bound frankly to go at once to the utmost extent. The next object must be to avoid more detail than is necessary, as details naturally lead to differences.

He promised to be at his post at the start of the session, and duly attended pre-session meetings of the party leaders, including ones to discuss Brougham's intended reform motion.[47] Listed by ministers among their 'foes', he voted against them on the civil list, 15 Nov., which led to the formation of the Grey ministry. He wrote to Porchester 'speaking in desponding terms of the actual crisis but saying that Lord Grey's government offers the only hope of safety', and Wellington later asserted that Macdonald was one of those who had overruled Grey in making his appointments.[48] Although again considered for other offices, he returned to his former position at the India board, much to Lord Sandon's* disappointment.[49] It was apparently also at this time that he, at least temporarily, relinquished his sinecure office, without compensation, though he continued to be listed as clerk to the privy seal in the *Royal Kalendar*.[50] Thomas Gladstone* informed his father, 2 Dec., that Macdonald was to 'strike for' Kirkman Finlay* that day on his petition against the Glasgow Burghs election return.[51] He was safely re-elected for Calne, 10 Dec. 1830.

Corresponding with Lansdowne about a scheme for parliamentary reform, he explained, 17 Jan. 1831, that

> all that we can have to rely upon must be qualification, whether with ballot or without it: if with it, so entirely is the public mind centred in that one point, that I doubt if the amount of qualification would create any sensation; if without it, I much fear that universal suffrage would not satisfy. I am disposed to compromise for a fair qualification with the *alternative* of ballot at the option of electors in *towns only*. In counties, no case of grievance has occurred, nor has there been any demand for it.

He outlined how, if the ballot was made voluntary, it would speedily fall into disuse, especially as some places 'will *pique* themselves on their boldness in preferring open voting, and that will give the *ton* in the end'. He concluded that a £10 householder qualification in boroughs, with a £10 freeholder and £20 leaseholder franchise in counties, would give a wide and sufficiently propertied electorate.[52] He was appointed to the select committee on the affairs of the East India Company, 4 Feb. Having expressed himself willing, 8 Mar., he was granted permission to give evidence to the Lords about the 3rd Baron Macdonald's right to vote in Irish peerage elections. He presented reform petitions from Calne, which he denied was a venal borough, and Havant, 14 Mar. At the Hampshire county meeting, 17 Mar., he praised the 'short and simple', 'comprehensive and efficacious' ministerial reform bill, the reception of which, with 'curses loud and deep by half the House of Commons', proved its necessity. He strongly condemned the Tory speakers, hailed the measure as a 'death-blow to the faction which had derived its power for the last 60 years from that system which the bill went to overthrow', and called it 'a great healing measure, which will pour balm into the wounds of society, and which will restore that confidence which has long ceased to exist between the rulers and the ruled'. Boasting that he had supported every proposition for reform ever made in the Commons, he declared: 'The mode of reform pleased him, so did the time, and they might depend upon what he now said to them, "it was now or never".'[53] Despite his efforts, the Petersfield election was eventually decided against the petitioners, 22 Mar.[54] He, of course, voted for the second reading of the reform bill, 22 Mar., and against Gascoyne's wrecking amendment, 19 Apr. 1831, which precipitated a dissolution.

Macdonald had issued a joint address with Macaulay to the electors of Calne, 19 Mar. 1831, when a future opposition had threatened to arise. But having received, with Charles Shaw Lefevre*, a requisition to stand for Hampshire as a reformer against the sitting Members, Fleming and Sir William Heathcote, he duly announced his candidature, 21 Apr., and embarked on an extensive canvass of the county.[55] He was also involved with the independent interest at Petersfield, and seconded the nomination of Ogle at the election there, but again without success.[56] He received extensive popular support, and the county Members withdrew rather than face an expensive contest; Wellington noted that, in any case, Macdonald's success 'would have cost him nothing but time and breath in making seditious speeches'. At the election, 6 May 1831, he denied that he was a pensioner, pledged that he would only remain in office as long as the government promoted measures he agreed with and spoke forcefully in support of parliamentary reform to root out the 'illegitimate power grown up in this country, acting against the king and his people'. Fleming thought that he had gone too far in having said, as he understood, that

> if the gentlemen of the county made a party against the people (which he inferred from the very scanty attendance of influential gentlemen) and he saw an overpowering aristocracy oppressing the people, *he* would put himself at their head to claim their rights.[57]

He was not made a magistrate of the county until this year, though he had been originally recommended in 1826.[58]

He was again appointed to the select committee on the East India Company, 28 June 1831, when he agreed that it could best put its own case by preparing a petition for consideration by the committee. He spoke against the Llanelli tithes bill, 11 July, only withdrawing his wrecking amendment against its second reading on being assured that it was not the same measure as had been introduced the previous session. A member of the payroll vote, he divided for the second reading of the reintroduced reform bill, 6 July, and regularly for its details. However, he voted against the total disfranchisement of Saltash, 26 July, when ministers allowed it to be transferred to schedule B, and for Daniel O'Connell's motion that the original Dublin committee be sworn, 29 July. Having an 'intimate connection with Gosport', he denied Croker's suggestion that Portsea and Gosport wished to be represented separately from Portsmouth, 3 Aug., and told him, 11 Aug., that he ought to welcome the decision to grant a seat to the Isle of Wight, as well as two extra ones to Hampshire, because it would help to counteract what he saw as the bill's over-emphasis on the North and the manufacturing interest. He voted against government for Lord Chandos's amendment to enfranchise £50 tenants-at-will, 18 Aug. He reckoned that every effort should be made to ensure that the Lords did not defeat the bill, and admitted to Fazakerley that

> my alarm is for *ministers*. Some things that have dropped from Lansdowne, and even from [Charles] Grant* make me doubt more than ever whether they are equal to the crisis. I know he would prefer *resignation* to the *coup d'état* of another batch of 30 or 40 peers, and I much doubt if the premier could make up his mind to such a blow (and no doubt it would be a severe blow) to his order. But if Grey retires lost in public estimation the consequence will be an attempt at a Tory ministry which will be the signal for the non-payment of taxes, in other words a revolution, and then the accession to power of a violent ultra liberal but able set of men to the utter extinction of all that have been or are. Resignation would now be the height of baseness and poltroonery, but I tremble.[59]

He voted for Lord Ebrington's confidence motion, 10 Oct. His was the first name on the requisition for another county meeting in Hampshire, at which, 26 Oct. 1831, he lauded the reform bill 'as the charter of their restored rights and liberties', damned the opposition to it of peers and 'so formidable a *levée en masse* of lawn sleeves', condemned William Cobbett's† interventions as encouraging divisions amongst the reformers and urged the bill's eventual passage through Parliament.[60]

That autumn he advocated bringing Macaulay into office in order to strengthen the ministry, and even offered to resign his own place for him, which Holland thought handsome but of which Brougham disapproved.[61] Granville Southwell, Macdonald's younger son, 'a peculiarly interesting and affectionate child', died unexpectedly, aged ten, 4 Dec. 1831, but two days later he confided to Holland, that 'I hope by the time there comes any pinch in the reform bill to be again in a state to find myself in my place'.[62] He was present to vote for the second reading of the revised bill, 17 Dec. 1831, and to go into committee on it, 20 Jan. 1832. The *Mirror of Parliament* reported him, presumably erroneously, as opposing the partial disfranchisement of 30 boroughs in schedule B, but he did, in fact, vote for this, 23 Jan., and the third reading, 22 Mar. He was reappointed to the select committee on the affairs of the East India Company, 27 Jan., when he once more called for it to be given a wider remit. He served as chairman of the subcommittee on public and miscellaneous matters at its many meetings before the Easter recess.[63] That session he sided regularly with government and among his last known votes were those for Ebrington's motion for an address calling on the king to appoint only ministers who would carry the reform bill unimpaired, 10 May, the second reading of the Irish bill, 25 May, and against increasing the county representation of Scotland, 1 June 1832.

Macdonald issued an address, dated 1 June 1832, indicating that he had been persuaded to retire from the House and live abroad, as governor of the Ionian Islands, because of the precarious state of his health.[64] The appointment was made on the 2nd, and he must have left the House almost immediately, as the Hampshire writ was moved four days later. His departure was lamented at the subsequent election, 22 June, and by Carnarvon, who had intended Porchester to replace Macdonald on his expected retirement at the next general election.[65] Macdonald dined at Lord Albemarle's on the 27th, was taken ill the following day and died, of cholera, 29 June 1832, to the great shock of his friends.[66] Macaulay, now at the India board himself, wrote that day:

> Poor Macdonald is dead, suddenly, yet not suddenly. He has for years been so ill that I never reckoned on his living three months ... He was a very kind and very useful friend to me. I shall always remember him with affection. Poor fellow! The table at which I am writing was his a few weeks ago.[67]

By his will, which had been written in Lausanne, 20 Sept. 1828, he made various bequests to his wife, noting that 'I only regret that the state of my finances renders it impossible for me to mark more strongly my sense of her attachment to me without doing injustice to others'. He also left numerous gifts, including one of a Poussin to Lansdowne, and 'the antique wig usually worn by me' to his friend Robert Wilmot Horton.* He left the bulk of his estate, which included landed property, shares in the Birmingham and Liverpool Junction Company and personalty sworn under £12,000, to his only surviving son, Archibald Keppel (1820-1901), an army officer, who succeeded him as the 3rd baronet.[68]

[1] Rev. A. Macdonald, *Clan Donald*, iii. 548-50; *Gent. Mag.* (1826), i. 561-3; *Oxford DNB*. [2] *HP Commons, 1790-1820*, iv. 487-9. [3] *Edgeworth Letters*, 270. [4] NLS mss 24770, f. 1; *Norf. Chron.* 29 Jan. 1820. [5] Add. 51830. [6] NLS mss 24770, f. 1. [7] For example, *Cockburn Letters*, 12. [8] JRL, Bromley Davenport mss. [9] Essex RO, Barrett Lennard mss D/DL C60, T. to Sir T. Barrett Lennard, 19 Sept. 1820. [10] Bromley Davenport mss, Macdonald to Davenport, 4 Oct. 1820. [11] *Norf. Chron.* 27 Jan.; *The Times*, 3 Feb.; HLRO, Hist. Coll. 379, Grey Bennet diary, 10-11. [12] Bucks. RO, Fremantle mss D/FR/46/11/45. [13] Buckingham, *Mems. Geo. IV*, i. 131. [14] Lansdowne mss. [15] *Norf. Chron.* 26 Jan.; *The Times*, 31 Jan. 1822. [16] Add. 56544, f. 61. [17] *CJ*, lxxvii. 1364-5. [18] NAS GD46/4/61. [19] Lansdowne mss. [20] *The Times*, 23 Aug. 1822. [21] *Cockburn Letters*, 67-69. [22] Bessborough mss, Brougham to Duncannon, 2 Mar. 1823. [23] Brougham mss, Macdonald to Brougham, 1, 3 Apr. [1823]. [24] Herts. Archives, Panshanger mss D/ELb F78, W. to F. Lamb, 20 May 1823. [25] *Arbuthnot Jnl.* i. 230-1. [26] Gurney diary. [27] Add. 51832, Goodwin to Holland, 18 Oct. 1824. [28] *Gent. Mag.* (1824), ii. 466. [29] R.C. Gill, *Dict. of Local Celebrities.* (Barnes and Mortlake Hist. Soc. 1980), 16; *VCH Hants*, ii. 493. [30] *Gent. Mag.* (1826), i. 561; (1827), i. 186-7; PROB 11/1713/336; IR26/1093/483. [31] Lansdowne mss, Macdonald to Lansdowne, 7 June; *Devizes Gazette*, 8, 15 June 1826. [32] *Canning's Ministry*, 32, 40, 43. [33] Ibid. 117. [34] Ibid. 265, 276. [35] Add. 52447, ff. 101, 107; *Devizes Gazette*, 31 May 1827. [36] *Creevey Pprs.* ii. 120. [37] Wellington mss WP1/895/10, 16. [38] Lansdowne mss; Add. 57419, ff. 88, 90. [39] Hatherton mss. [40] Duke Univ. Lib. Fazakerley mss, Abercromby to Fazakerley, 13 Sept., Littleton to same, 22 Sept.; Add. 51576, Fazakerley to Lady Holland, 20 Sept.; 51580, Carlisle to same, 9 Oct.; 51659, Whishaw to same, 6 Oct. 1828. [41] Fazakerley mss. [42] Add. 51574, Abercromby to Holland, 20 Jan.; 51687, Lansdowne to same, 23 Jan. 1829. [43] Castle Howard mss, Graham to Morpeth [3 Mar. 1830]. [44] *Devizes Gazette*, 29 July, 5 Aug., 2 Dec. 1830. [45] Hants RO, Carnarvon mss 75M91/E4/28-30, 81; J3/17; L14/3; L17/1. [46] Ibid. E4/80; *Hants Chron.* 9, 30 Aug. 1830. [47] Lansdowne mss; Add. 51564, Brougham to Holland, 8 Nov. 1830; 56554, f. 42; A. Mitchell, *Whigs in Opposition*, 242-4. [48] Carnarvon mss J3/18; *Three Diaries*, 42. [49] Grey mss, Lansdowne to Grey [19 Nov.]; Harrowby mss, Sandon to Harrowby, 19, 25 Nov. 1830. [50] *Hants Chron.* 16, 23 May 1831; *Gent. Mag.* (1832), ii. 178; *Black Bk.* (1832), 552. [51] St. Deiniol's Lib. Glynne-Gladstone mss 196. [52] Lansdowne mss. [53] *The Times*, 18 Mar. 1831. [54] Carnarvon mss E4/96, 99; *Hants Chron.* 28 Mar. 1831. [55] *Devizes Gazette*, 24 Mar., 14, 28 Apr.; *Hants Chron.* 25 Apr., 2 May; *Hants Advertiser*, 7 May 1831. [56] W. Suss. RO, Goodwood mss 1433, f. 238; 1486, f. 36. See PETERSFIELD. [57] Wellington mss WP4/3/4/17, 22, 23; *Hants Chron.* 9 May 1831. [58] Wellington mss WP1/848/15; Hants RO, q. sess. recs. Q27/3/297. [59] Add. 61937, f. 125. [60] *Hants Chron.* 24, 31 Oct.; *The Times*, 28 Oct. 1831. [61] Add. 51563, Brougham to Holland, bef. 27 Nov. 1831; *Holland House Diaries*, 72, 106; Broughton, *Recollections*, iv. 165; J. Clive, *Macaulay*, 201-2. [62] *Gent. Mag.* (1831), ii. 571; Add. 51836. [63] *PP* (1831-2), ix. 21. [64] *Hants Chron.* 4 June, 2 July; *Salisbury Jnl.* 11 June 1832. [65] *The Times*, 25 June 1832; Wellington mss WP1/1229/24. [66] Fazakerley mss, Lansdowne to Fazakerley, 29 June; Add. 51575, Abercromby to Holland, 1 July 1832; *Gent. Mag.* (1832), ii. 178; *Raikes Jnl.* i. 57-58; *Wilts. Parson and his Friends* ed. G. Greever, 109. [67] *Macaulay Letters*, ii. 143, 145. [68] Fazakerley mss, Lansdowne to Fazakerley, 3 July 1832; PROB 11/1804/526; IR26/1296/391.

S.M.F.

MACDONALD, Ranald George (1788–1873), of Seamore Place, Mdx.

PLYMPTON ERLE 1812–28 Feb. 1824

b. 29 Aug. 1788, 2nd but 1st surv. s. of John Macdonald, 18th chief of Clanranald, and 1st w. Katherine, da. of Robert Macqueen, SCJ (Lord Braxfield), of Braxfield, Lanark. *educ.* Edinburgh; Eton 1799; European tour. *m.* (1) 13 Feb. 1812, Lady Caroline Anne Edgcumbe (*d.* 10 Apr. 1824), da. of Richard Edgcumbe†, 2nd earl of Mount Edgcumbe, 1s. 5da.; (2) 30 June 1826, Anne Selby (*d.* 8 July 1835), da. of William Cunninghame of Lainshaw, Ayr, wid. of Richard Barre Dunning, 2nd Bar. Ashburton, *s.p.*; (3) Nov. 1855, Elizabeth Rebecca Newman, *s.p. suc.* fa. 1794. *d.* 11 Mar. 1873.

Lt.-col. commdt. 4 Inverness militia 1809.

Macdonald, the 19th chief of Clanranald, was again returned for Plympton Erle on his father-in-law's interest in 1820. He was an occasional attender whose few recorded votes were all with Lord Liverpool's ministry. He did not vote in this Parliament on the question of Catholic relief, which he had supported before 1820. He voted in defence of ministers' conduct towards Queen Caroline, 6 Feb., and against repeal of the additional malt duty, 3 Apr., and Hume's economy and retrenchment motion, 27 June 1821. He divided against more extensive tax reductions, 21 Feb., and for the Canada bill, 18 July 1822. He 'expressed his disapprobation' of the bill to lower the barilla duties, which was seen as a threat to the makers of kelp, 29 July 1822, and welcomed the government's proposal, made in deference to these fears, to increase the duties for a limited period, 13 June 1823.[1] He vacated his seat early in 1824. In April 1831 he sent a letter to the Inverness county meeting expressing his 'zealous and unconditional good wishes' for the Grey ministry's reform bill.[2]

His second marriage, to a wealthy widow, did not arrest the steady decline of his fortunes, which forced him to sell almost all his inherited property in Inverness-shire by 1838. While Macdonald blamed his difficulties on the mismanagement and depredations of the trustees responsible for his inheritance during his minority, it seems clear that they were caused largely by his own folly and extravagance. In 1844, 'forced into retirement by circumstances I could not control', he used the pretext of urging the need to introduce coroners' inquests and legislation against cruelty to animals into Scotland to beg the prime minister, Sir Robert Peel, for financial assistance to rescue him from his 'unmerited privation'. He was 'now in the most painful straits imaginable' and trusted that 'such a wreck of the interests of a family, such alienation of property handed down to me from remote years, must excite regret'. Peel, however, was unmoved, observing that he 'might with more propriety' address his application to the 'many parties in affluent circumstances connected with you by the ties of relationship or intimate friendship, and cognisant of the circumstances which you mention as having led to your embarrassments'.[3] Macdonald died in March 1873 and was succeeded as chief of Clanranald by his only son, Admiral Sir Reginald Macdonald (1820-99).

[1] *The Times*, 30 July 1822, 14 June 1823. [2] *Inverness Courier*, 6 Apr. 1831. [3] Rev. C. Macdonald, *Moidart*, 238-9; Rev. A. Macdonald, *Clan Donald*, ii. 363-4; Add. 40554, ff. 1-10.

D.R.F.

MACKENZIE, Sir James Wemyss, 5th bt. (1770–1843), of Scatwell and Suddie, Ross.

ROSS-SHIRE 20 Dec. 1822–1831

b. 10 Aug. 1770, 2nd but o. surv. s. of Sir Roderick Mackenzie, 4th bt., of Scatwell and Catherine, da. of James Colquhoun (formerly Grant) of Rossdhu, Luss, Dunbarton. *educ.* privately; Perth acad. (Alexander Gibson) 1784-5. *m.* 26 Mar. 1810, Henrietta Wharton, da. and eventual h. of William Mackenzie of Suddie, wid. of Capt. Robert Pott of Gallalaw, Roxburgh, 1s. *suc.* fa. as 5th bt. 11 June 1811. *d.* 5 Mar. 1843.[1]

Paymaster 55 Ft. 1808-11.

Ld. lt. Ross 1826-*d.*

Mackenzie's family was a senior branch of the Mackenzies of Kintail. Kenneth Mackenzie of Scatwell (*d.* 1730), who sat for Ross-shire in the Union Parliament, 1702-7, was created a baronet in 1703. His successors were Sir Roderick (?1687-1750) and Sir Lewis (1715-56). The latter's son Roderick, this Member's father, was about 16 when he succeeded to the baronetcy. He had a brief army career and in the 1790s rebuilt Rosehaugh House, near Fortrose and removed his family to it from Findon, on the other side of the Black Isle. With Catherine Colquhoun (whose father was created a baronet shortly before his death in 1786) he had two sons, Lewis and James Wemyss, the junior by five years. The first 40 years of James Mackenzie's life seem to have been almost uniformly wretched. Sir Roderick, a stingy and overbearing father, was at a loss to find a suitable career for him, particularly as most of such money as he was prepared to spend went on buying Lewis, his favourite, a commission in the army. Lewis, who served in the 73rd and 21st Foot, before exchanging into the 6th Dragoon Guards in 1787, eventually became a colonel of militia. He was frequently in hot water for dissipation and heavy spending. He did not mend his ways even after his marriage in 1794, and he was only rescued from arrest for debt by a loan from his uncle Colin Mackenzie, a London insurance broker. James was sent to school in Perth just before his 14th birthday, being, as his father's agent Alexander Mackenzie of Portmore put it, 'rather too advanced in life for a public school, and not sufficiently qualified for a university'. He wanted to follow his brother into the army, and 'did not relish' Portmore's attempts to dissuade him: 'It will be difficult if not in vain to oppose his choice. He is a spirited, fine boy, and unless he changes his mind soon, the earlier he gets into the army ... the better for him'.[2] In this ambition he was frustrated, and in the autumn of 1786 he was furnished with an allowance of £40 a year and entrusted to his uncle Colin, with the intention that he should be trained to make him fit to seek a writership in the East India Company. This scheme collapsed when it emerged that 'nothing less than parliamentary interest can obtain a berth for him to that chosen quarter for fortune'. Nor did anything come of Portmore's hope that Lord Gower's uncle, Admiral John Leveson Gower, might provide an opening for him in the navy.[3] Early in 1787 Sir Roderick received 'discouraging accounts' of James, and his agent commented:

> I still hope that when he has sown his wild oats he will act differently. A good *education* is the great foundation for good conduct through life and I fear poor James has been unfortunate in that respect, and he should still make up for it as much as possible.[4]

Later that year Portmore tried unsuccessfully to place him with a Wiltshire cloth manufacturer.[5] Eventually 'poor Jamie' was packed off to Jamaica to work for one Mackay, a plantation owner in the parish of Trelawny; and there he stayed for almost 18 years.[6] On 8 Oct. 1794 Andrew Fowler, who had concerns in Jamaica, reported to Sir Roderick:

> I visited your son ... and ... I found him doing well, making plenty of good sugar ... and pleasing his employer. From your kind intention to James and the handsome manner you expressed yourself to push him in life when I had the honour of being at Rosehaugh House, I have procured him a lease of a piece of land from a friend of mine *gratis* ... This land is for a residence for James's negroes and will give him provisions to feed them in abundance. In consequence of this promising prospect I advised him to add to his gang of negroes and he has actually purchased 11 healthy seasoned negroes for the sum of £700 ... [and] has drawn on you for the purchase money in my favour.

It was apparently with reluctance that Sir Roderick parted with the cash, under pressure from Portmore, who thought 'it may be the means of making his fortune, and the not honouring it would be undoing all you have done and ruin him'.[7]

Mackenzie returned to Scotland in the summer of 1806, but was back in Jamaica by March 1807.[8] The chief object of his visit, it seems, was to press his suit with the widow Henrietta Pott, an old flame of 20 years standing, who had married a soldier in 1792. More pertinently, she was the only sister of Colonel John Randoll Mackenzie, who was returned for Tain Burghs in 1806 and whose Suddie estate lay near the Scatwell property. While Suddie had reservations, he was not hostile to the match; but Sir Roderick had strong objections, based chiefly, though not exclusively, on financial grounds. On his arrival in Jamaica James Mackenzie, who, in return for the sum of £1,877 which his father had advanced him over the years, had waived all his claims on Sir Roderick's estate, sought Suddie's help. Although he was determined to marry Henrietta regardless of his father's views, he felt the way would be smoothed if he could secure a regular income; and he asked Suddie to get him a place in the Jamaican customs, 'worth at *least* £2,000 per annum' or, as a preferable alternative, an equivalent permanency in Britain. As a Member of Parliament supporting government, and politically connected with the Staffords and Seaforth, Suddie, he naively believed, could 'easily procure' such provision for him. Pending Suddie's reply, he promised to 'enter into no speculation of lands of any sort, or purchasing slaves', but to 'keep perfectly clear of encumbrance of any kind, ready to march at a moment's notice'. By the time his letter arrived the Grenville ministry had fallen and Suddie was in opposition, unable 'to assist him in the way he alluded to', but still kindly disposed towards him.[9]

In the spring of 1808 Suddie, who was about to transfer to the Sutherland county seat, secured Mackenzie the vacant paymastership of the 55th regiment, which was currently stationed in Jamaica. He and General Alexander Mackenzie, Member for Ross-shire, who had been given the nomination, stood surety for £1,000 each. The post was doubly attractive to Mackenzie because the regiment was expected to return to Britain within a few months. Calculating that it would produce a guinea a day, and banking on receiving overdue payment for his slaves, 'long since' sold, he assured Henrietta that 'we have no occasion to care as to ... [Sir Roderick's] will and pleasure now', as her brother had 'made us independent so far':

> I trust ... that a few months will now complete all we ever wished for. Oh, happy day, how my heart at this moment beats with raptures of joy on the thoughts of being united to my Dearest Hen ... I am figuring to myself Sir Roderick's astonishment when he reads my appointment gazetted. It may produce a good effect. A bad one it can't. I know he likes gain, now the paymastership is equal to your bringing me £10,000 portion at least. Money or bank notes, you know, was declared before you was born his psalm book; indeed, I might well add his God, for all I have seen of him.

At the same time, he warned her to be careful lest his father, whose 'spies are everywhere', got wind of her clandestine correspondence with his sister Kate. As it happened, he was far from being out of the wood. Not only did his Jamaican debtors continue to default, but the prospects of his regiment's early return to Britain rapidly receded. All his attempts to obtain leave of absence failed, and he was equally unsuccessful in his application to have his commission as paymaster antedated by two months. Relief came through tragedy. Suddie was killed in action at Talavera, 28 July 1809, and, thanks to the recent death of his niece Mrs. Ramsay, his estates devolved on Henrietta Pott. Through the intervention of his kinsman Sir George Mackenzie of Copul, Mackenzie obtained a year's leave. He left Jamaica in January 1810, having set in train legal proceedings for the recovery of his debts there.[10]

He reached London on 1 Mar. 1810, called on his uncle Colin and, coached by Portmore's successor William Mackenzie of Muirton, wrote a fawning letter to his father in which he expressed filial piety, announced his intention of marrying Henrietta forthwith, and asked for Sir Roderick's blessing.[11] Before the marriage took place in Edinburgh later that month Mackenzie, concerned at the prospect of having to find fresh securities (and perhaps having something to hide in his administration of the 55th's accounts), sought Seaforth's intervention with the premier Spencer Perceval to get him 'some government situation ... where the responsibility is less', but which would 'bring in a comfortable subsistence'.[12] Nothing came of this, but Muirton encouraged Mackenzie, who was pursuing through Seaforth a pension for Henrietta on account of her father's military services, to be optimistic 'of such an arrangement being formed as to enable you with prudent economy to remain at home'. There was a debt of £5,000 on the Suddie estate, to which Henrietta Mackenzie's right was unexpectedly disputed by Thomas Mackenzie of Ord. Muirton took legal advice, which suggested that her title was 'unchallengeable', and Ord dropped his claim.[13] In August 1810 the harassed Mackenzie was pressed by the commanding officer of the 55th to come to a final decision on the paymastership, which he still wished to be rid of; otherwise, he was to rejoin the regiment at headquarters.[14] In the end, his father insisted that he should return to Jamaica, and in his chagrin Mackenzie expressed himself strongly to his uncle, who betrayed him to a furious Sir Roderick. After an unsatisfactory attempt to explain himself verbally, Mackenzie wrote, 17 Sept. 1810:

> I do confess that being obliged to go to Jamaica for a second time after expectations from various quarters, that through their interests I would be under no such necessity, did rouse my feelings, and in confidence [I] might in opening my mind express with too much warmth that had you chose, there was no necessity for my return to that fell climate. But ... the very supposed friends who used to ... condole with me that nothing could be done to prevent my recrossing the Atlantic were ... the very first who roused your passions against me by holding out my expressions of you as undutiful, ungrateful, and in every degree unworthy of a son ... The whole you have been told is a mass of falsehood and lies ... Give that matter a fair and impartial hearing ... but don't condemn me otherwise and withdraw your countenance from me undeservedly.[15]

Mackenzie was dramatically saved by the death without issue of his brother Lewis only three days later. On the advice of Muirton he raised no objections to the terms of his father's resettlement of his affairs, which entailed on him and his heirs not only the Scatwell estates, but those acquired by Sir Roderick since his marriage. Yet he resented his father's refusal to lend him £2,500 to pay off the outstanding debt on the Suddie estate (such a gesture, he complained, 'would cut too deep in his confined ideas of friendship'); and he considered himself entitled to at least half as much again of his proposed allowance of £200 a year. He was disappointed, too, by the amount of the pension conferred on his wife in December 1810: at £100 a year, it was worth only £70 after stoppages. Seaforth shared his 'indignation' and was hopeful of doubling it by creating a public fuss; but Mackenzie decided that 'situated as we are at present, that pension secured is a good lift up', and settled for what was offered.[16] His tortured relationship with his father was ended by Sir Roderick's death in June 1811. Even so Mackenzie, who resigned his paymastership, discovered that, in a last act of vindictiveness, his father had severely restricted his access to the personal estate and obliged him to support his sister to the tune of £200 a year: he was, he moaned, 'left stripped of everything which Sir Roderick could take, even of the rents for 18 months after his death'. For some years he was 'a good deal pinched', but matters slowly improved as rents came in, and in 1816 he was able to fulfil a pledge to his widowed sister-in-law by providing her with an annuity of £100. When his sister died in 1819 Mackenzie, still perturbed by the 'beggarly jointure' left by Sir Roderick to his wife in the event of her surviving him, was astonished by her 'extraordinary' and 'reproachable' bequests, totalling £1,105, to various relatives: 'nothing can account for them, and many other odd acts of her life, but that her mind was from *inebriety never correct*'.[17]

In November 1819 Mackenzie was one of the promoters of a Ross-shire meeting to vote a loyal address to the regent in the wake of Peterloo, but he was unable to attend it.[18] He came in unopposed for his county on a vacancy in December 1822. Two months later his second cousin George Sinclair* introduced him to Peel, the home secretary, as 'one of the most respectable and excellent men whom Scotland ever sent to Parliament'.[19] He proved to be a consistent, if silent supporter of the Liverpool ministry, though he was not the most assiduous of attenders. He divided with them on the national debt reduction bill, 3, 13 Mar., and the assessed taxes, 10 Mar., and against repeal of the Foreign Enlistment Act, 16 Apr., and inquiry into the prosecution of the Dublin Orange rioters, 22 Apr. 1823. In the autumn he asked Peel, to whom he particularly attached himself, for a piece of church patronage in Cromarty, but it is not clear whether he was successful.[20] On the eve of the 1824 session he sought Peel's permission to linger in Scotland to deal with 'a considerable acquisition' to his property, though he was prepared, when required, to 'leave all private business, and attend Parliament for the express purpose of giving the present administration my firmest support'. Peel indulged him, but, as he later reported, 'seeing that your majorities were not so large as I could wish', he set out for London on 23 Feb., only to be struck down at Perth 'with the severest fever I ever had'; he was forced to return to Rosehaugh. He anticipated being able to attend after Easter, was in London by 5 May, and voted with government on the case of the prosecution of the Methodist missionary John Smith in Demerara, 11 June.[21] Peel could not personally comply with his request of 20 Sept. 1824 for promotion in the excise for an influential constituent, but he passed it on the patronage secretary.[22] In 1825 Mackenzie went up early to vote for the Irish unlawful societies bill, 25 Feb. He was threatened with an opposition in Ross-shire at the next election, and again sought a favour for a constituent from Peel, who could only refer him to the treasury.[23] He presented petitions for an extension of the jurisdiction of magistrates in the recovery of small debts and for amendment of the Scottish judicature bill, 15 Mar., and against any relaxation of the corn laws, 26 Apr., 5 May.[24] He voted against the Catholic relief bill, 21 Apr., and paired against its third reading, 10 May. He was in the minority for the Leith docks bill, 20 May. A week later he punctiliously sought, and duly received, Peel's permission to return to Scotland.[25] He was in pursuit of provision for a cousin, possibly his uncle Colin's son, to whom he wrote in December 1825 that there was

> no question as to my success next Parliament ... It might be wise was I not so; a deal of money, and nothing for it but the honour. I want nothing for myself ... the ministry are but a time-serving set, and they keep their loaves and fishes for those who support them. I have done so and will continue to do so, if they deserve it ... My former application ... [for you] will be attended with more effect (if ever to have any at all) after I take my seat again.[26]

Early next month he received Canning's circular requesting attendance but, not wishing to go up so soon, on account of his wife's 'delicate health', he asked Peel whether '*you* really wish for the attendance of *your* supporters immediately as Parliament opens':

> May I ask if the first week of March will be suited to your purpose; but if you wish me earlier please say so, and I shall attend. There are two questions which may be brought on early (the Catholic question and the corn bill). From neither of them would I like to be absent ... Although my county don't at all interfere with my hostile views to the former ... [it is] deeply interested in the latter.

While Peel did not press him, Mackenzie 'proceeded a considerable way' towards London in mid-February, but he was again taken ill and forced back to Ross-shire.[27] He was present to bring up petitions against alteration of the Scottish banking system, 7, 10, 25 Apr.,[28] and to vote against reform of Edinburgh's representative system, 13 Apr. 1826. Shortly before the general election, when the threatened opposition came to nothing, he was appointed lord lieutenant of his county.[29]

Mackenzie, for whatever reason, had become a convert to Catholic relief by the time of the division of 6 Mar. 1827. He voted for the duke of Clarence's annuity, 16 Mar., and presented county petitions for increased agricultural protection, 19 Mar., 2 Apr. 1827.[30] He voted against repeal of the Test Acts, 26 Feb.,[31] but paired in favour of Catholic relief, 12 May 1828. He divided with the Wellington ministry on chancery delays, 24 Apr., the ordnance estimates, 4 July, and the silk duties, 14 July. He presented Ross-shire petitions against the revised corn duties and the Scottish entail bill, 6 May, and for further protection against foreign wool, 30 June 1828. His only known vote in 1829 was for Catholic emancipation, 30 Mar. He sided with government against the enfranchisement of Birmingham, Leeds and Manchester, 23 Feb., and for the grant for South American missions, 7 June 1830. He voted against Jewish emancipation, 17 May, and abolition of the death penalty for forgery, 7 June. He presented petitions against the proposed increase in spirit duty, 24 May, and in favour of the Scottish court of session bill and repeal of the inventory duty, 8 June 1830. Four days later the Irish secretary informed Wellington that Mackenzie, 'one of the most sedentary and steady supporters of government', was engaged to give up his seat at the next election to Colin Mackenzie of Kilcoy, who 'would forego the benefit of this engagement if, through Sir James's influence, he could obtain a baronetcy'. Although he did not expect Wellington to comply, he pointed out that

> the advantage to your administration would be the retaining Sir James Mackenzie, who would be a safer supporter than a gentleman whose politics are now of the same stamp, but who will probably come into Parliament with the full intention of trafficking for the attainment of this particular object of his ambition and perhaps of some others.[32]

As it happened, Kilcoy and two other potential candidates stood aside for Mackenzie at the general election.[33] Ministers of course listed him among their 'friends', and he was in their minority on the civil list, 15 Nov. 1830. He was granted periods of leave to attend to militia business, 8 Feb., 15 Mar., and was absent from the divisions on the Grey ministry's reform bill, 22 Mar., 19 Apr. 1831. Even before the dissolution he announced his intention of retiring, ostensibly because of ill health; and at the 1831 general election he unsuccessfully backed Kilcoy, a very moderate reformer, against James Stewart Mackenzie of Seaforth, an enthusiastic advocate of reform.[34] When Peel asked him to support Hugh Munro of Novar against Seaforth in 1832 Mackenzie, still plagued by illness, professed his unbroken allegiance to 'the Conservative cause', but made difficulties on account of his wife's close family friendship with the Seaforths.[35]

He was mortally ill by the summer of 1842, and he died in March 1843.[36] His son and successor Sir John James Randoll Mackenzie (1814-84), the defeated candidate for Inverness Burghs in 1837, found the Suddie estates encumbered with debts of £21,000, which had mostly been spent on improvements. In return for settling these and other fee simple estates on the heirs of entail, he secured the passage in 1843 of a private Act enabling him to borrow money on the security of the entailed estates to pay off the debt. He subsequently disentailed the Scatwell estates and alienated or sold them.[37]

[1] Add. 39193, f. 171. *CB* and *Burke PB* incorrectly give 8 Mar. [2] Add. 39191, ff. 29, 81, 92, 100, 104, 106, 108. [3] Add. 39191, ff. 131, 133, 148. [4] Add. 39191, f. 143. [5] Add. 39191, ff. 149, 151, 153. [6] Add. 39191, ff. 155, 157. [7] Add. 39191, ff. 171, 173, 175; 39192, f. 112. [8] Add. 39192, f. 52; 38198, ff. 10, 54. [9] Add. 39198, ff. 10, 14, 54, 75; 39200, f. 82. [10] Add. 39192, ff. 69, 73; 39198, ff. 165, 166; 39199, ff. 198, 200; 30204, ff. 20-31. [11] Add. 39192, ff. 75, 77, 78. [12] Add. 39192, ff. 79, 80, 81; 30204, ff. 32, 33. [13] Add. 39192, ff. 81, 87, 94, 96. [14] Add. 39192, f. 92. [15] Add. 39192, f. 98. [16] Add. 39192, ff. 100-115; 39199, ff. 207, 210. [17] Add. 39192, ff. 116, 119, 121, 128, 130, 137, 139, 146, 162, 164, 186, 192; *Geo. III Corresp.* iv. 4229. [18] *Inverness Courier*, 4, 11 Nov. 1819. [19] Add. 40354, f. 184. [20] Add. 40358, ff. 306, 307. [21] Add. 40360, f. 247; 40362, 256; 40364, f. 265. [22] Add. 40368, ff. 236-8 [23] Add. 39192, ff. 56, 57; 40374, f. 401. [24] *The Times*, 16 Mar., 27 Apr., 6 May 1825. [25] Add. 40378, f. 279. [26] Add. 39193, f. 76. [27] Add. 40385, ff. 40, 261. [28] *The Times*, 8, 11, 26 Apr. 1826. [29] *Inverness Courier*, 5 July 1826. [30] *The Times*, 20 Mar., 3 Apr. 1827. [31] Ibid. 3 Mar. 1828. [32] Wellington mss WP1/1119/10. [33] *Inverness Courier*, 21, 28 July, 4, 18 Aug. 1830. [34] Ibid. 30 Mar., 6, 13 Apr., 4 May, 1 June 1831. [35] Add. 40403, f. 54. [36] Add. 39193, ff. 156, 171, 173. [37] Add. 39193, ff. 126, 199, 210; A. Mackenzie, *Clan Mackenzie*, 389, 429-30.

D.R.F.

MACKENZIE, Thomas (1789–1822), of Applecross, Ross.

ROSS-SHIRE 1818–19 Oct. 1822

b. 28 May 1789,[1] o. surv. s. of John Mackenzie, adv., of Applecross and Locharron and Jean, da. of Alexander Elphinstone of Glack, Aberdeen. *unm. suc.* fa. 1820. *d.* 19 Oct. 1822.

When Mackenzie was first returned for Ross-shire in 1818 the Liverpool ministry, who remained neutral in the contest, considered him 'a very uncertain card'; but he made a good impression as a conscientious Member and a 'steady' but 'independent' supporter of the government, which earned him a promise of their full backing for his re-election.[2] Moving the loyal address to the regent at the county meeting, 12 Nov. 1819, he condemned the 'pernicious doctrines' being disseminated by radicals in the Lowlands and England, as a result of which 'people were incited to demand, under the name of reform ... such alterations as would totally change the constitution'.[3] At the general election four months later, when a threatened opposition petered out, he made no reported reference to national politics.[4]

He presented a Ross-shire petition against the additional malt duty, 2 June 1820.[5] On the 26th he secured a month's leave of absence on account of his father's death, which took him to Scotland for the funeral.[6] He was prevented by 'a sudden attack of illness' from attending the Ross-shire loyal meeting, 4 Jan. 1821.[7] He brought up a petition from Dingwall praying for the restoration of Queen Caroline to all her rights, 26 Jan. 1821,[8] but he divided with ministers in defence of their conduct towards her, 6 Feb. He voted for Catholic relief, 28 Feb. 1821. A member of the select committee of inquiry into petitions for Scottish burgh reform appointed on 4 May 1820 and renewed on 16 Feb. 1821, he took 'a very active part' in their deliberations;[9] and on 12 Mar. 1821 he criticized the Whig Sir Ronald Ferguson for asking to be removed from it because he could make no impression with his reforming views, arguing that he ought to remain and promote his case.[10] He showed his independence by seconding and voting for the successful motion for the repeal of the additional malt duty, 21 Mar. 1821, when he maintained that it offered no increase in revenue to counterbalance its bad effects, which in Scotland included the encouragement of smuggling. He stood firm when ministers, threatening resignation, mustered support to defeat the repeal bill, 3 Apr.; but he denied Ferguson's allegation that the select committee appointed to consider Scottish petitions against the duty, 12 Apr., was only offered as an inducement to Scottish Members to vote with government. He was a member of the committee. On 4 May 1821 he complained of a report of a speech by Henry Grey Bennet which had offended his 'near relation' Charles Hope†, lord president of the court of session, but was satisfied with Grey Bennet's explanation;[11] and on 8 May he endorsed Bennet's charge of breach of privilege over subsequent comments on their exchange in *John Bull*. Mackenzie led the opposition to Hamilton's proposals for reform of the Scottish county representation, 10 May:

> He could not consent to vote for any abstract proposition, or even for the matter of fact stated in the resolution ... knowing that it was to be followed by others intended to form the basis of practical measures

He argued that these would not significantly increase the number of freeholders and would be 'a direct violation of the Union'. He presented petitions against the Whig Kennedy's Scottish juries bill, 18, 21 May 1821.[12]

From this point Mackenzie's attendance seems to have lapsed, although he was nominated to the select committee on Scottish turnpikes, 20 Mar. 1822. A sickly individual since boyhood, he was reported to have been 'detained' in Edinburgh 'for six weeks by indisposition' in mid-March 1822.[13] He died a bachelor in London 'of consumption' seven months later.[14]

[1] *Scots Mag.* (1789), 258. [2] NAS GD46/4/124/12; GD51/5/749, p. 170; NLS mss 11, f. 44; 1054, f. 174. [3] *Inverness Courier*, 18 Nov. 1819. [4] NLS mss 11, f. 14; *Inverness Courier*, 16, 23 Mar. 1820. [5] *The Times*, 3 June 1820. [6] Macpherson Grant mss 466, C. Mackenzie to G. Macpherson Grant, 30 June 1820. [7] *Inverness Courier*, 11 Jan. 1821. [8] *The Times*, 27 Jan. 1821. [9] Macpherson Grant mss 489, Macpherson Grant to Lady Stafford, 18 Mar. 1822. [10] *The Times*, 13 Mar. 1821. [11] Ibid. 5 May 1821, [12] Ibid. 19, 22 May 1821, [13] Macpherson Grant mss 489, Macpherson Grant to Lady Stafford, 18 Mar. 1822. [14] *Highland Lady*, 280.

D.R.F.

MACKENZIE *see also* STEWART MACKENZIE

MACKILLOP, James (1786–1870), of 4 Montagu Square, Mdx.

TREGONY 1830–1832

bap. 17 July 1786,[1] 1st s. of John Mackillop and Mary, da. of Robert Downie of Kilmadock, Perth. *unm.* *d.* 27 Jan. 1870.

Little is known of Mackillop's family background, other than that his parents were married at Kilmadock in 1781.[2] His baptismal record and the matriculation record of George Mackillop, almost certainly his younger brother, at Glasgow University in 1807, indicate that their father was a farmer at St. Ninians, Stirling. By then James Mackillop was in Calcutta, working in the agency house in which his uncle Robert Downie* was a partner. When Downie left India in 1811, Mackillop became a partner with George Cruttenden, and the agency of Cruttenden, Mackillop and Company was one of the half-dozen firms which dominated the economy of Bengal in the early nineteenth century. By 1824 Mackillop's active partners were his brother George, their uncle James Cullen, and David Bryce.[3] He returned to Britain at about this time and joined the London mercantile house and East India agency of Palmer's, Mackillop and Company (formerly Palmer, Wilson and Company) of 11 King's Arms Yard, Coleman Street. His chief partners were the brothers John Horsley Palmer, a director of the Bank of England, and George Palmer, later Member for Essex South. At the general election of 1826 he joined James Adam Gordon in a bid to overturn the Whig 3rd earl of Darlington's interest at Tregony. After a three-day contest, rival returning officers each sent in returns, but the House declared the indenture naming Gordon and Mackillop invalid, 29 Nov. 1826; their subsequent petition was unsuccessful.[4] However, Gordon later purchased Darlington's property and in 1830 he returned himself and Mackillop, after a contest; they survived a petition.[5]

The Wellington ministry listed Mackillop as one of their 'friends', and he voted with them in the crucial division on the civil list, 15 Nov. 1830. He divided against the second reading of the Grey ministry's reform bill, which proposed to disfranchise Tregony, 22 Mar., and for Gascoyne's wrecking amendment, 19 Apr. 1831. At the ensuing general election he was again returned for Tregony, after a contest. He divided against the second reading of the reintroduced reform bill, 6 July. He voted for use of the 1831 census in determining the disfranchisement schedules, 19 July, against the inclusion of Chippenham in schedule B, 27 July, and making proven payment of rent a prerequisite for voting, 25 Aug., and to preserve the freeholder franchise of the four sluiced boroughs, 2 Sept. He divided against the bill's passage, 21 Sept. He voted for inquiry into the state of the West India interest, 12 Sept. He divided against the second reading of the revised reform bill, 17 Dec. 1831, going into committee, 20 Jan., the enfranchisement of Tower Hamlets, 28 Feb., and the third reading, 22 Mar. 1832. He voted for inquiry into the glove trade, 3 Apr., and an Irish absentee tax, 19 June. He divided against government on the Russian-Dutch loan, 12 July 1832. He is not known to have spoken in debate. Having been a member of the committee appointed by the London East India merchants in 1830 to consider the impending renewal of the Company's charter, he had returned written answers to questions on Indian trade from the board of control the following year, and was added to the select committee on the Company's affairs, 22 Feb. 1832.[6]

At the general election of 1832 Mackillop made a late entry into the field at Southampton, where another Conservative was challenging two reformers. He stressed his credentials as a commercial man, whose expertise would enable him to 'fill your port with shipping, and your town with trade'. He claimed that he 'belonged to no political party' and 'had always been independent', but promised to 'oppose rash innovations' and support 'the most rigid economy' and the elimination of abuses. He finished a very distant fourth.[7] The Calcutta agency, which in 1831 was being run by Cullen, Thomas Hutton and Robert Browne, was the last of the major houses to fail, going under in January 1834.[8] Mackillop appears to have returned briefly to Bengal, perhaps to set up the new mercantile business of Mackillop, Stewart and Company, of which he was listed as a partner, with Cullen, John Carrington Palmer and J. Stewart in 1838. By 1840 his place had been taken by John Storm, and he had presumably returned home. Mackillop, Stewart and Company were still in operation at 13 Old Court House Street, Calcutta in 1862. The extent of Mackillop's continued involvement in the London agency is not clear: it was styled Palmer's, Mackillop, Dent and Company by 1838, and remained as such until the early 1860s, when it became Dent, Palmer and Company. Mackillop died at Nice in January 1870, aged '83'. Unaccountably, he was described on his death certificate, issued in the British consulate, as a retired lieutenant-colonel (full pay) of the 17th regiment; but no trace of him has been found in the army lists. He left his London house and the residue of his estate to his nephew, Charles William Mackillop, an Indian civil servant; his personalty was sworn under £250,000.

[1] IGI (Stirlingshire). [2] IGI (Perthshire). [3] *Scots Abroad* ed. R.A. Cage, 199; S.B. Singh, *European Agency Houses in Bengal*, 12, 33, 123-4; A. Tripathi, *Trade and Finance in Bengal*, 143. [4] *West Briton*, 26 May, 2, 9, 16 June 1826. [5] Ibid. 6 Aug. 1830. [6] *PP* (1831-2), vi. 506, 516, 518, 520, 531, 541, 567, 572, 574, 576. [7] *Hants Advertiser*, 24 Nov., 1, 8, 15 Dec. 1832. [8] Singh, 293; Tripathi, 238, 240.

D.R.F.

MACKINNON, Charles (1773–1833), of Camden Hill, Kensington and 38 Grosvenor Place, Mdx.

IPSWICH 23 Feb. 1827–1831

b. 1773.[1] *educ.* Aberdeen Univ. 1790. *m.* 19 Dec. 1807, Sophia, da. William Burn of 7 George Street, Hanover Square, Mdx.,[2] 2da. *d.* 20 Oct. 1833.[3]

Surgeon, E.I. Co. naval service 1794; 2nd surgeon Canton 1800-5; head surgeon, Prince of Wales Island 26 Feb. 1808, suspended 27 Oct. 1808, reinstated 29 Mar. 1811, ret. 1821.

Mackinnon's pedigree is not recorded in the annals of Clan Fingon, but it is clear from references in his will to his 'brother' General Henry Mackinnon (*d.* 1812), and the conduct of the head of the clan, William Alexander Mackinnon*, as his executor, that he was one of the Mackinnons of Skye.[4] When facing allegations of commercial malpractice as a servant of the East India Company in Canton, he claimed in a dispatch, 5 Dec. 1804:

> I have been brought up with as high a sense of honour as most men; my education and principles, such as they are, have been taught me in two different universities (I left my parents at an early period of life, perhaps an unfortunate circumstance) and by some of the most eminent professors of the present day, whose correspondence, friendship and good opinion, I have hitherto had the honour to enjoy. By them I have been taught to despise, on all occasions, the low chicanery of artifice and criminal complaisance.[5]

He became a junior member or student of the Medico-Chirurgical Society of Aberdeen in 1790 and entered the East India Company's service in 1794 as a surgeon on the *Duke of Buccleugh*, 1794-5, and the *Nottingham*, 1796-8. His son Charles, who may have been illegitimate, was born at Strathmore, Skye, 22 Jan. 1799. In January 1800 Mackinnon was appointed assistant surgeon at Canton, an unsalaried post that left him financially dependent on profits from agencies in the rhubarb and opium trades.[6] A dispute with Messrs. Harrington, Burnaby and Cockburn caused the governor, James Drummond, to take disciplinary action against him in 1803; and despite receiving support from some members of the Canton Committee, notably Samuel Peach and George Sparkes, he was recalled to London to defend his conduct. He resigned on health grounds in January 1805 and on his return to London lodged with a Dr. Mackenney at 2 Upper Grosvenor Street. He was granted access to Company records and in February 1806 published a memorial in defence of his conduct.[7] He was largely exonerated and remained at Upper Grosvenor Street until his marriage, departing for a new posting as head surgeon of Prince of Wales Island shortly afterwards. A quarrel with Drummond over the time he spent trading, instead of practising medicine, led to his suspension in 1808 for disrespect to the governor and council, but he remained on the island (his daughters Maria Sophia and Sophia Jane were born there in 1808 and 1811) and was reinstated on orders from Canton. In 1818 he returned to England on sick leave and settled in Kensington, retiring formally in November 1821, shortly after his wife's death.[8] His son Charles was by now an assistant surgeon on the Bengal establishment, while Mackinnon registered as an honorary member of the Medico-Chirurgical Society of Aberdeen in 1820 and subscribed to the Royal College of Surgeons.[9] He joined the Union Club, and intended using his East India fortune and contacts to secure a directorship of the Company and a seat in Parliament. In 1826 he put down £7,000 to stand on the Blue or Tory interest at Ipswich with a fellow Scot Robert Adam Dundas, a kinsman of the first lord of the admiralty, the 2nd Viscount Melville.[10] They benefited from admiralty patronage and the local clergy's hostility to concessions to Catholics and Dissenters and, although defeated at the poll, were returned on petition.[11] Mackinnon claimed during his canvass that he would soon be able to bring patronage to Ipswich as a director of the East India Company, as he had already secured 700 (stockholders') votes. His opponent Robert Torrens* and the *Suffolk Chronicle* countered that he was 'endeavouring to obtain a seat in Parliament to further his ambitious views with regard to that directorship' and maintained that 'his fate is already sealed: an effectual determination against him is formed and not even parliamentary voting could reverse the decree'.[12]

Mackinnon made no major speeches in the House and was not an assiduous attender, but Dundas relied on him to deal with constituency business and he generally attended borough elections and dinners at Ipswich, where he acquired a reputation for 'trimming between the two parties'.[13] He divided with government for the duke of Clarence's annuity, 16 Mar., and voted against the spring guns bill 'because he felt conscious he was doing right', 30 Mar. 1827. At the Ipswich chairing, which, because he had been ill, was postponed to 18 Apr., he declined to comment on the pro-Catholic Canning's forthcoming appointment as premier, but spoke of his regret at the anti-Catholic Peel's resignation as home secretary.[14] Canning's successor Lord Goderich informed him in November 1827 that the government patronage necessary to secure an East India Company directorship could only be obtained through the president of the board of control. Finding Charles Williams Wynn* hostile, he welcomed Melville's appointment to the India board in January 1828 in the duke of Wellington's ministry and asked Dundas to transmit a letter to him through his uncle, the lord register William Dundas*, in which he maintained that his previous request had failed '*from political motives* (although the duke of Buckingham and Lord Chandos* support me)'. He added, 'we cannot keep Ipswich without patronage, but with good management and a seat in the direction I have no doubt we shall be able to retain our seats at a moderate expense'.[15] He presented a favourable petition from Ipswich, 22 Feb., but voted against repealing the Test Acts, 26 Feb., and presented others for repeal of the Malt Act, 1 Apr., against the friendly societies bill, 24 Apr., and slavery, 2 June 1828. He paired against Catholic relief, 12 May.[16] He divided with ministers against ordnance reductions, 4 July, and on the silk duties, 14 July. He divided for the corporate funds bill, 10 July 1828. During the recess he became concerned at the extortionate sums of money demanded as 'printing costs' by his Ipswich committee, and renewed his campaign for support in the forthcoming Company elections. Wellington referred his request back to Melville, but no decision seems to have been taken before September, when Lord Ellenborough took over the India board.[17] After consultations with Wellington, Peel and the patronage secretary Planta, who all professed alarm at the promises Mackinnon had made at Ipswich, he was turned down.[18] Despite this, Ellenborough noted in his diary, 5 Feb. 1829:

> Received a letter from Mr. Mackinnon thanking me for a supposed promise to support him on the next vacancy. I never gave any such promise, nor did I use any words from which it could be deduced that I did. I have written to tell him how surprised I am at the interpretation he has put on my letter, and to say, if possibly more distinctly than I did before, that I will not pledge myself.[19]

Mackinnon, like Dundas, opposed Catholic emancipation in 1829, believing that it would increase the pressure for tithe reform. He spoke of his regret at voting against ministers on presenting an anti-Catholic petition from Ipswich, 11 Mar., and deliberately congratulated Peel on 'the firmness he has displayed in pursuing his course', 12 Mar., but divided against the measure, 18, 23, 30 Mar. He is not known to have been active in the House again until after the East India Company election of 6 Apr. 1830, when he lost by 1,009-554 to John Forbes.* On 20 Apr. he sold over £7,000 of his holdings in Company stock in five lots, keeping enough to qualify for one vote.[20] He paired, 5 Apr., and voted personally for Jewish emancipation, 17 May. He voted against reducing the grant for South American missions, 7 June, to make forgery a non-capital offence, 7 June, and to restrict licensing for on-consumption under the sale of beer bill, 21 June 1830, a matter of concern to Ipswich brewers. A late challenge from the Essex Whig John Disney increased the cost of his return for Ipswich with Dundas at the general election, but their success was never in doubt.[21] The liberal merchant John May complained to Gilbert Heathcote* before the election that Mackinnon

> has made a most infamous use of [Thomas Barrett] Lennard's* letters of introduction to myself and brother, so that the general feeling is both amongst the Blues and Orange that Mr. *Lennard* has promised his support to Mackinnon in case of a contest, and really whether there is a contest or not.[22]

The ministry counted Mackinnon among their 'friends' and he divided with them when they were brought down on the civil list, 15 Nov. 1830. He received a week's leave on account of ill health, 2 Dec. 1830. He was added to the select committee on the East India Company's charter, 15 Feb. 1831. Before voting against the Grey ministry's reform bill at its second reading, 22 Mar., he presented but spoke against favourable petitions from Ipswich, commended another recently adopted by resident freemen anxious that their sons and apprentices should not forfeit the franchise, and described himself as 'unfriendly to close boroughs, which have but few constituents, and favourable to the extension of the elective franchise to the large unrepresented manufacturing towns as well as to the respectable householders of open boroughs'. The speech was circulated and commented on in Ipswich, where initially the Blues projected themselves as moderate reformers, and Mackinnon did not vote on Gascoyne's wrecking amendment, 19 Apr.[23] He presented an anti-reform petition from Ipswich's London freemen for protection of their voting rights and testified to the valuable contribution they had made to his own return, 20 Apr. 1831. He contested Ipswich at the general election that month with a new colleague, the Whig 4th duke of Grafton's nephew Robert Fitzroy, but they lost to two reformers. On the hustings Mackinnon spoke against reform, which he predicted would restrict the access of those involved in shipping, commerce, and finance to Parliament, but he again acknowledged the need to enfranchise the growing industrial towns.[24]

Mackinnon contested Ipswich at the general election of 1832, but, having alienated both, he was denied the support of the town's Wellington Club and of the Conservative party and came bottom of the poll in a five-man contest.[25] He maintained his interest in East India Company affairs and printed and circulated his speech at East India House on the China trade, 16 Apr. 1833, in which he declared against monopoly, but defended 'exclusive privilege where freedom of trade is impracticable and where that privilege protects great and important interests'.[26] His elder daughter Maria died, 3 June 1833, and in September he went to France to recuperate, but he died, 'aged 60', at Beauvais on his homeward journey in October.[27] His will, dated 22 Mar. 1831, with an unwitnessed codicil of 14 Sept. 1833 in favour of his daughter Sophia, was proved under £80,000. He entrusted William Alexander Mackinnon and his former East India Company colleagues John Fullarton Elphinstone, Charles Peach and John Spicer to provide annuities of £1,200 for Sophia, £100 for his son Charles, who also received his gold watch, chain and seals, £50 each for his mother's three unmarried daughters, £20 each for his two married sisters, Mrs. W. Maclean and Mrs. J. Matheson. Other beneficiaries were his nephew Charles Mackinnon, 'now at Mr. Slate's school', and George and Donald, the sons of his late 'brother' Henry Mackinnon, to whom the estate was to revert should his own children die without issue.[28] Sophia, who married Henry Dundas Drummond (1812-67) in December 1838 and retained the use of her father's Grosvenor Place house, had to secure a judgement in chancery against William Alexander Mackinnon and Peach, 5 Dec. 1839, to ensure payment of her legacy.[29]

As Mackinnon had wished, she erected a tablet in St. Mary Abbot's church, Kensington in memory of her parents and sister.[30]

[1] Memorial inscriptions and obituaries specify 1773. According to P.J. and R.V. Wallis, *Eighteenth Cent. Medical Practitioners*, 385, Mackinnon was *b.* in 1775 and apprenticed as a surgeon in 1793. [2] *Gent. Mag.* (1807), ii. 1172. [3] Not 19 Nov., as stated in *Ann. Reg.* (1834), Chron. p. 201. [4] D. Mackinnon, *Mem. Clan Fingon* (1899); PROB 11/1825/769; TNA C33/893, f. 539 (Mackinnon *v.* Peach). [5] C. Mackinnon, *Mem. to E.I.Co.* (1806), 49. [6] D.G. Crawford, *Indian Medical Service, 1615-1930*, p. 624; BL OIOC L/MIL/9/371, f. 165. [7] *Mem. to E.I.Co.* (1806). [8] *E.I. Reg.* (1807), ii. 305; Crawford, 626; [9] OIOC L/MIL/9/371, ff. 161, 164; Crawford, 79; *Regulations of Medico – Chirurgical Soc. Aberdeen* (1833), p. xv; *RCS Membership List* (1825), 56. [10] J. Glyde, *New Suff. Garland*, 454. [11] *The Times*, 23, 29 May, 5, 19, 20 June 1826; *Ipswich Jnl.* 24 Feb.; *Suff. Chron.* 24 Feb. 1827. [12] *Ipswich Jnl.* 3 June; *Suff. Chron.* 10 June 1826. [13] *Ipswich Jnl.* 7 Oct. 1826, 12 Sept. 1829; Lincs. AO, Ancaster mss, J. May and C.C. Western to G.J. Heathcote [July 1830]. [14] *Suff. Chron.* 21 Apr.; *Ipswich Jnl.* 21 Apr.; *Colchester Gazette*, 21 Apr. 1827. [15] NAS GD51/3/611/1-2. [16] *The Times*, 19 May 1828. [17] Suff. RO (Ipswich), J. Glyde, 'Materials for Parl. Hist. Ipswich', ff. 101-2; Wellington mss WP1/948/7. [18] *Ellenborough Diary*, i. 268-9, 306-7, 330. [19] Ibid. i. 336. [20] *The Times*, 2, 5, 7, 8 Apr. 1830; OIOC L/AG/14/5/154, f. 77. [21] *Ipswich Jnl.* 10, 24 July, 7 Aug.; Ancaster mss, W. May to Heathcote, 5 Aug. 1830. [22] Ancaster mss, May and Western to Heathcote [July 1830]. [23] *Ipswich Jnl.* 19, 26 Mar.; *Suff. Chron.* 26 Mar. 1831; K.J. Atton, 'Municipal and Parl. Politics in Ipswich, 1818-1847' (London Univ. Ph.D. thesis, 1980), 182-5. [24] *Ipswich Jnl.* 30 Apr., 7 May; *Suff. Chron.* 7 May 1831. [25] *Suff. Chron.* 3 Nov.; *Ipswich Jnl.* 10, 17 Nov. 15 Dec. 1832. [26] Brougham mss, Mackinnon to Brougham, 13 May 1833. [27] *Gent Mag.* (1833), i. 571; (1834); i. 656. [28] PROB11/1825/769; IR26/1300/669. [29] *Gent Mag.* (1839), i. 203; TNA C33/893, f. 539. [30] Mdx. M.I. iv. 39 (Soc. of Genealogists Lib. MX/M/46248D, viii).

M.M.E.

MACKINNON, William Alexander (1784–1870), of Portswood House, nr. Southampton, Hants.

DUNWICH	20 Feb. 1819–1820
LYMINGTON	1831–1832
LYMINGTON	1835–1852
RYE	23 May 1853–1865

b. 2 Aug. 1784,[1] 1st s. of William Mackinnon of Antigua and Harriet, da. of Francis Frye of Antigua. *educ.* St. John's, Camb. 1799; L. Inn 1802. *m.* 3 Aug. 1812, Emma Mary, da. and h. of Joseph Budworth Palmer of Palmerston, co. Mayo, 3s. (1 *d.v.p.*) 3da. *suc.* grandfa. William Mackinnon 1809. *d.* 30 Apr. 1870.

Colonisation commr. for S. Australia 1835; chairman, UK Insurance Office and chairman, Society Against Cruelty 1842.

Capt. Eling troop, S. Hants yeoman cav. 1821-5;[2] Lymington yeoman cav. 1834.

Mackinnon, who had sat briefly before 1820, was spoken of as a local candidate for Southampton at that year's general election, but declined to stand.[3] Thereafter he was out of the House for eleven years, during which he wrote his pioneering treatise *On the Rise, Progress and Present State of Public Opinion in Great Britain and Other Parts of the World* (1828). Passages of this ambitious work revealed his essentially Tory outlook. The 'organ of the public opinion of the community' was Parliament as presently constituted, whereas an assembly elected by universal suffrage 'could only represent the lower class, and not follow public opinion, which ... depends chiefly on the middle class'. While uneducated 'popular clamour' might welcome such an assembly, he was sure that informed, middle class 'public opinion' would countenance nothing more than a return to triennial parliaments. The *Gentleman's Magazine*, to which he was an occasional contributor, applauded his view that the civilizing influence of public opinion had been impeded by the priesthood in Catholic states, so leading, in France, to revolution.[4] The book's kudos probably assisted his eventual return to politics, though on meeting him in May 1832, Benjamin Disraeli† judged him 'an ass'.[5] At the 1826 general election he was narrowly defeated at St. Ives, from where a petition in his favour was lodged but not pursued. In 1830 he unsuccessfully contested Boroughbridge, where he was billed as 'the author', in opposition to the interest of the Ultra Tory 4th duke of Newcastle, who supposed that he had been sent by the Wellington government.[6] His petition against the return failed. His high standing with the former ministry was made plain at the 1831 dissolution, when Sir Harry Neale* sought Sir Robert Peel's* recommendation for a vacancy at Lymington:

> It has been suggested that Mr. Mackinnon's return would be very acceptable to Sir Robert. Should this choice be confirmed, Sir H. would feel much pleasure in putting him in nomination.[7]

Peel evidently approved and Mackinnon was returned unopposed for the borough, which lay some twelve miles from his residence.

He voted against the second reading of the Grey ministry's reintroduced reform bill, 6 July 1831. On 19 July he moved an amendment for using the latest population figures to determine the disfranchisement schedules instead of the 1821 data, which would produce legislation based 'on an *ex post facto* principle'. As he had anticipated, Lord John Russell replied that the 1821 census was more impartial than that gathered under the shadow of the reform bill, and his amendment was defeated by 224-169. He divided against the partial disfranchisement of Chippenham, 27 July, and considered it a 'peculiar hardship' that Lymington should also lose one Member, 29 July. He warned that political impartiality would be compromised by giving county sheriffs the right of selecting returning officers for some newly enfranchised boroughs, 10 Aug., and complained of having received no answer to this, 19 Aug. On 25 Aug. he opposed the introduction of a uniform borough franchise, noting that the 'respectability' of a £10 householder depended on the size of the town, and proposed to raise the minimum qualification to £15 in towns with between 500 and 1,000 houses and to £20 in those with more. Though negatived without a division, 26 Aug., his amendment received some verbal support, unlike his proposal that day to deny the vote to all tenants paying less than £20 per annum who sublet their houses, which he quietly withdrew. He voted against the issue of the Liverpool writ, 5 Sept., and presented a petition from London merchants against an increase in duty on Cape wine, 7 Sept. He divided against the third reading of the reform bill, 19 Sept., and its passage, 21 Sept. 1831.

Mackinnon voted against the second reading of the revised reform bill, 17 Dec. 1831, and going into committee on it, 26 Jan. 1832. Noting with approval the new bill's adoption of most of his proposals on the census and appointment of returning officers, 3 Feb., he resubmitted his motion for a graded household qualification based on the size of towns, but without success; he did not redeem his promise to try again. He refuted assertions that signatures on a Hertfordshire anti-reform address had been obtained fraudulently, 10 Feb. On 23 Feb. he supported Chelmsford's claim for inclusion in schedule C and, harking back to his contest at St. Ives, testified to its 'thriving condition', notwithstanding its position in schedule B. He divided against the enfranchisement of Tower Hamlets, 28 Feb. Speaking at length in terms reminiscent of his book, 20 Mar., he conceded the necessity of reform but denounced the bill as a product of 'popular clamour' rather than 'public opinion', objected to reducing the number of English and Welsh Members, and protested that the disfranchisement schedules and the criteria that determined them were destructive of the influence of property and wealth. His privately printed version of the speech concluded with a metaphoric vision of Parliament in flames, which was seized on by cartoonists.[8] He voted against the bill's third reading, 22 Mar., and moved an amendment for a £20 household franchise for all boroughs in schedule C and for Liverpool, which was negatived without a division, 23 Mar. He divided for Sibthorp's amendment to the proposed division of Lincolnshire that day, and presented two petitions from Lymington against a further boundary extension, 31 May 1832.

Mackinnon supplied a point of information concerning the fees paid by Irish magistrates on renewal of their commissions, 17 Jan. 1832. He presented a petition for improving the laws against cruelty to animals, 20 Jan., introduced a bill to that effect, 18 Apr., and secured and was appointed to a select committee, 30 May. He presented their report, 1 Aug., but there was no time for the bill to progress further. (He subsequently revived it in the reformed House.) On 23 Jan. he denounced the Vestry Act amendment bill as an 'attack on the church' and complained that its provisions for broadening the franchise were 'quite the prototype of the reform bill', which would encourage 'ever more popular measures, leading to universal suffrage and ballot'. He presented Marylebone petitions against the metropolis cemetery bill, 9 Apr., 8 May. That day he obtained leave to introduce a bill to reform the usury laws, which was given a first reading, 24 May, but lost out to other business thereafter. He voted against ministers on the Russian-Dutch loan, 26 Jan., 12 July 1832.

From a passage in his published speech on the reform bill, it is clear that Mackinnon expected to be returned for the reformed constituency of Lymington at the next general election. Writing in similar terms to Neale, 23 Oct., he observed that 'the impression in my mind was that your influence was sufficient to retain a seat or to transfer it, and that you might give me the preference', but in the event the patron had other ideas.[9] On 10 Dec. Lord Stuart de Rothesay, former ambassador to France, advised the duke of Wellington that 'after consultation' with Francis Bonham*, Mackinnon's candidacy for Newry had been suggested to Lord Londonderry and William Holmes* and that he had agreed to 'pay £2,000 towards expenses if elected'.[10] Nothing came of this, however, and he was out of Parliament until 1835, when he was returned unopposed for Lymington on Neale's retirement. At about this time he adopted nearby Newton Park as his main residence. In his subsequent career he supported first Peel, then Lord Palmerston*, and according to a family historian, refused a peerage from both.[11] Latterly he was classed as a Liberal and won renown for his legislative efforts in the fields of public health and industrial relations.[12] In 1846 he published the modestly entitled *History of Civilization*, a substantial revision of his previous work, which went through several editions and was translated into French, German and Italian.

Mackinnon died intestate at Broadstairs in April 1870.[13] His Kent estates at Acryse Park and Belvedere, Broadstairs passed to his eldest son William Alexander

Mackinnon (1818-1903), Liberal Member for Rye, 1852-3, and Lymington, 1857-68, to whom administration was granted. (His second son Lauchlan Bellingham Mackinnon (1815-77) sat for Rye as a Liberal, 1865-8.) Mackinnon never realised his ambition, conceived on a visit in 1812 to the Scottish Isles in the company of Sir Walter Scott, to repurchase his clan's lands. There are indications that his failure to do so may have caused some resentment among some native clansmen. A genealogy published in 1883 cast doubt on the ancestry of the Antiguan branch of the family, and so called into question Mackinnon's right to the title of 33rd head of the clan. The authors were reluctant to do so, for they had never known 'a man who had a higher sense of honour or a more correct appreciation of right than he'. The dispute was settled at the inauguration of the Clan Mackinnon Society in 1892, when William Alexander Mackinnon junior was acknowledged as the undisputed chief.[14]

[1] See *Admissions to St. John's, Camb.* iv. 369 and V.L. Oliver, *Hist. Antigua*, ii. 226. *Burke LG* and other sources give 2 Aug. 1789, which is clearly erroneous. D. Mackinnon, *Mem. Clan Fingon* (1899), 118 states that he was born 'about the year 1782'. [2] Wellington mss WP1/663/7; 823/1. [3] *Hants Chron.* 14, 21 Feb. 1820. [4] Mackinnon, *Public Opinion*, 17-18, 40, 143, 184-200, 230-1; *Gent. Mag.* (1828), ii. 248-50; *Nichols File of Gent. Mag.* ed. J.M. Kuist, 90. [5] *Disraeli Letters*, i. 188. [6] Nottingham Univ. Lib. Newcastle mss Ne2 F3/1/248; *The Times*, 3 Aug. 1830. [7] Hants RO 27M74/F102, Neale to Peel [Apr. 1831]. [8] *Speech of W.A. Mackinnon ... on Third Reading of Reform Bill*; D. Mackinnon, *Mem. Clan Fingon* (1884), 82. [9] Hants RO 27M74/F93. [10] Wellington mss WP1/1239/19, 27. [11] *Mem. Clan Fingon* (1899), 121-9, 210. [12] G.S. Butler, *Mackinnon ... A Sketch* (1863), *passim.* [13] *The Times*, 3 May 1870. [14] A.M. Downie and A. D. Mackinnon, *Mackinnon Fam.* (1883), pp. iii, xi-xii; *Mem. Clan Fingon* (1884), 81; (1899), 66-67, 118-21.

H.J.S./P.J.S.

MACKINTOSH, Sir James (1765–1832).[1]

NAIRNSHIRE	25 June 1813–1818
KNARESBOROUGH	1818–30 May 1832

b. 24 Oct. 1765, 1st s. of Capt. John Mackintosh of Kyllachie, Inverness and Marjory, da. of Alexander Macgillivray.[2] *educ.* Fortrose acad. 1775; King's Coll. Aberdeen 1780; Edinburgh Univ. 1784, MD 1787; L. Inn 1790, called 1795. *m.* (1) 8 Apr. 1789, Catherine (*d.* 8 Apr. 1797), sis. of Daniel Stuart, editor of the *Morning Post*, 1s. *d.v.p.* 3da.; (2) 10 Apr. 1798, Catherine, da. of John Bartlett Allen of Cresselly, Pemb., 2s. (1 *d.v.p.*) 2da. (1 *d.v.p.*). *suc.* fa. 1788; kntd. 21 Dec. 1803. *d.* 30 May 1832.

Recorder, Bombay 1803-11; judge of vice admiralty ct. Bombay 1806-11; professor of law, Haileybury Coll. 1818-24; PC 16 Nov. 1827; commr. bd. of control Dec. 1830-*d.*

Rect. Glasgow Univ. 1823-5.

'I can no more play the game of life than I can play the game of whist', admitted Mackintosh.[3] His intellectual gifts were immense, but his grasp of practicalities was tenuous and his lack of purpose notorious. After his death Sydney Smith, who considered that 'his conversation was more brilliant than that of any human being I ever had the good fortune to be acquainted with', told Mackintosh's son that 'he never knew the use of red tape, and was utterly unfit for the business of life'.[4] Lord John Russell* wrote that 'conversation was his favourite employment and his chief seduction'; and Tom Moore went so far as to say that he 'sacrificed himself to conversation ... read for it, thought for it, and gave up future fame for it'.[5] Torn between the attractions of scholarship and politics, he fell short in both, promising much but delivering little. Indolence and indecision were largely responsible for this, but he was undermined by poor health, particularly an unreliable stomach, a legacy of his singularly unprofitable stay in India. It was real enough, but hypochondria and morbid self-absorption enhanced its debilitating effects. Shortage of money and an unhappy second marriage to an intelligent, waspish woman whose ill concealed disappointment in him had destroyed their intimacy, were further sources of anxiety to him.[6]

At the start of this period Mackintosh combined his parliamentary career, in which he occupied a position of some eminence among the Whig opposition, with his undemanding role as professor of law at the East India Company's training college at Haileybury, Hertfordshire, occupying a rented house, described by Henry Fox* as 'lamentable', at Mardocks, near Ware. There he tried also to advance his too numerous and ambitious literary and historical projects, which included a continuation of Hume's and Fox's history of Britain from 1688.[7] In the spring of 1819 the American George Ticknor met him at Holland House, where he was a great favourite, and found him

> a little too much made up in his manners and conversation, but ... at the same time very exact, definite, and logical in what he says ... As a part of a considerable literary society ... he discourses most eloquent music, and in private he is mild, gentle, and entertaining. But he is seen to greatest advantage, and in all his strength, only in serious discussion, to which he brings a great disciplined acuteness and a fluent eloquence, which few may venture to oppose, and which still fewer can effectually resist.

After visiting him at Mardocks, Ticknor concluded that 'on the whole, I have never met with an Englishman [*sic*] whose conversation was more richly nourished with knowledge, at once elegant and profound'.[8] Later in the year the Whig attorney James Losh privately questioned the view of James Scarlett*, who thought Mackintosh 'the ablest speaker in the House of Commons' (though he was reputed to take opium for courage before major speeches)[9], that he would be 'the fittest leader for opposition' there if George Tierney's health failed:

> I knew Sir James well in former times and cannot agree in his fitness as a leader. He has neither sufficient confidence in himself, nor sufficient energy and independence of spirit ... [He is] mild, liberal and with just and enlarged views on almost every subject; but without much dignity or firmness of mind. Indeed he has several times lamented his want of firmness and resolution.[10]

Mackintosh had offended the radicals, for whom he had no time, and even some Whigs by failing to oppose root and branch the coercive legislation introduced by the Liverpool ministry in the aftermath of Peterloo. He disputed Lord Holland's assertion that the Cato Street conspiracy of February 1820 could be attributed to anger and frustration at repression, as 'the disposition to assassinate must have existed long before the passing of the seditious meetings bill'.[11] Yet, while his Whiggism was of an essentially conservative, thoughtful cast, he remained committed to the cause of moderate, restorative parliamentary reform.[12] He was worried in early 1820 about the potentially damaging consequences for opposition of the Queen Caroline affair 'if a single person of importance among us were to espouse one side with great warmth'.[13] At the general election of 1820 he was returned again, with Tierney, for Knaresborough by the 5th duke of Devonshire, to whom he wrote that 'it will be a great satisfaction to both of us if we can contribute in the least degree to render the inhabitants ... more inaccessible to the seductions of the radicals who surround them'.[14] He travelled there with Tierney for their uneventful election. In the course of their journey Tierney told him that 'he could no longer attend regularly or even frequently in the hot weather, that as I had the same illness with himself he had no choice but the appointment of [Henry] Brougham to act in his stead'. Mackintosh, whose tentative suggestion that the leadership might be put 'into commission' was scouted by Tierney, wrote to his wife, with typically mixed feelings:

> In examining the case calmly I cannot pretend to deny to myself that his determination was right. But to be deprived of so great a distinction which seems to have been brought within reach by a most unexpected concurrence of circumstances must be felt to be painful even while it is acknowledged not to be unreasonable. The state of my health during the present journey compels me to own the justice of the present exclusion, but it is not an agreeable ground of conviction ... From Tierney I have experienced no kindness. He has never trusted or consulted me, nor did he tell me this important determination till it was no longer a secret.[15]

It is safe to say that he would have been a broken man within weeks had he become leader.

Unwell with persistent 'nausea' after his return, he promised his absent wife 'whenever you are pleased to come ... a still more complete forbearance from offence and a more unresisting submission to any censure which you may deem still to be necessary'.[16] Soon afterwards he made what was probably the worst decision of his life. On 2 Apr. 1820 he told Lady Holland that 'my health and spirits are improved and ... I have now no fear of being unable to encounter the toils and conflicts of the session'.[17] Yet three days later he asked his Edinburgh friend Adam Gillies, whom he told that 'circumstances partly connected with my own health and fortune, partly arising out of the state of the country and of our party have of late often made me feel an inclination to steal out of public life', to make discreet soundings as to the possibility of his being appointed to the newly vacant chair of moral philosophy at Edinburgh University. Gillies and other influential Edinburgh Whigs urged him to put himself forward, but he was wracked with indecision, as he told his wife, who was against the idea from the start:

> It is a question in which better health, perhaps longer life, ease in my private affairs and the probability of completing my history are placed on one side; on the other side political importance and parliamentary reputation. These last objects are so dazzling that it would probably [be] difficult to compare them calmly ... [with] those for which they would be sacrificed if it were not for the peculiarly uneasy circumstances of my parliamentary situation. Our party is in a state of the greatest division and dissension and ... there seems little doubt of final schism.

He was still miffed at Tierney's casual rejection of his pretensions to leadership, and the prospect of acting as second string to a headstrong Brougham, determined to involve the party in the queen's cause, did not appeal, particularly as Brougham was currently 'at war' with Devonshire and his family. Yet he feared that if he turned his back on the professorship he 'must lay my account with having no position of that sort to fall back on when the time comes (which probably will come) of Parliament becoming too uneasy to remain in it'. Holland and Lansdowne, whom he consulted, were utterly hostile to the idea of his leaving Parliament, the latter urging him not to sacrifice 'a situation of great authority independent of all official situation [and]

... no inconsiderable share of following and popularity both in and out of Parliament'. Even though Mackintosh complained to his wife that Lansdowne, 'the best example of sincerity without frankness of any man I know', had 'said nothing explicit about the place which he wished me to fill in the House of Commons', these views were decisive with him, the more so when Lansdowne reacted with 'unwonted frankness and even warmth' to dismiss the fanciful notion, held out to him by his Edinburgh friends, that he might take the chair and retain his seat, attending Parliament for only the last three months of each session after completing his lectures, 'which though not enough for the leader leaves room for a respectable situation'.[18]

In early May 1820 Mackintosh was pressed by a deputation from Gibraltar to take steps to become their London agent, which opened to him the enticing prospect of an income of £600, possibly £1,000, a year with an office and a clerk; nothing came of it.[19] In the House, 4 May, when he was named to the select committee on the Scottish royal burghs (as he was again, 16 Feb. 1821), he defended ministers against Hume's attack on the Gibraltar duties, but challenged Vansittart's interpretation of the law of nations. The following day he spoke at length and voted for Brougham's motion on the civil list. He voted against government on the same subject, 8 May, and on the appointment of an additional baron of exchequer in Scotland, 15 May 1820. He voted in the combined government and opposition majority for the resolution restricting the inquiry into agricultural distress which had been carried unexpectedly against ministers and which, in his view, 'held out false hopes to the agriculturists and threatened the rest of the country with instant ruin', 31 May.[20] On 1 June he did not object to the introduction of Littleton's labourers' wages bill, but said that the 'best remedy' would be the abolition of all restrictions. At the request of Sir Robert Wilson, he stayed late at the House for the debate on the aliens bill. Wilson would not let him answer Lord Castlereagh, and he 'gave up all intention of speaking'; but he was eventually provoked by Copley into attacking the measure after midnight 'for three quarters of an hour with unusual energy and universal applause', as he told his wife. He paid for his exertions with a sleepless night and a debilitating headache.[21] He presented and supported a petition from the inhabitants of Galway complaining of abuses in the management of the corporation, 12 June. On the 14th, in the absence of Sir John Newport, who had suffered a bereavement, he moved the new writ for Dublin and delivered a formal eulogy of Henry Grattan I, the late Member. His extreme nervousness beforehand was increased by his receipt of

> an angry letter from Brougham complaining that I should do that for Grattan which I thought in general a bad practice and which we had agreed not to do for [Sir Samuel] Romilly†. I answered him mildly that I was too far advanced to retreat and stated ... the difference between a recent death where the praise might be natural and a death some time before the motion when it must seem cold and studied. I spoke for about half an hour with more than usual satisfaction to myself and with evidently strong impression on the House.

He had written plaintively to his wife the previous day that 'I go on journalising, though you don't vouchsafe to give me any signs that you are satisfied with my attempts to amuse you'.[22] He was 'strongly for impartiality and calmness' by opposition on the queen's case and was alarmed by the determination of the Whig 'Mountaineers' to 'act as her furious partizans': 'We ought not to court [Matthew] Wood's* mob and since the ministers have consented to prosecute the queen we have nothing to expect from the Court even if we were base enough to make sacrifices for Court favour'. Although he professed to have 'little expectation' of the Whigs profiting from the feelers put out by the king in mid-June, he admitted to his wife that 'I am in a flurry on this occasion, the first in my life in which I have been so very near negotiations for forming a government'. Plagued by 'much pain and fullness in the side' and 'a severe cold', he reflected that while the case against Caroline was clearly 'not indefensible', the 'popular current has now set too strongly to be safely resisted'. On 22 June he voted against Wilberforce's 'peace making address, which it was natural for me in my character of Mr. Harmony to support', on the pretext that if it was rejected by the queen the House would be 'exposed to a very great indignity'. Two days later he wrote:

> It seems to me that a dangerous spirit spreads among the soldiery ... Full of these really alarming stories I went to bed at one and had a disturbed night with dreams of revolutionary horrors soothed only by visions of kindness from those from whom I dare not hope for it in my waking hours.

Despite having diarrhoea, he attended 'a Whig council at John Lambton's* beautiful house' next day, when he confided to his wife, 'I often sigh for the professorship'. He voted with his friends against the appointment of a secret committee on the queen's case, 26 June.[23] He made 'a little observation which was well received' in support of Brougham's proposals for promoting the education of the poor, 28 June, when he said that 'though he might be considered a speculist, yet he was no visionary on the subject'.[24] He supported the bill to exclude Thomas Ellis, Grattan's successor as Member for Dublin, from the House as an Irish master in chancery, 30 June. He voted for Hume's 'eternal motion about finance' (for economies in revenue collection), 4 July 1820.

Mackintosh had assumed Romilly's mantle as the parliamentary champion of criminal law reform. On 9 May 1820 he secured the reappointment of his select committee of 1819 and, on the basis of its report, got leave to introduce four bills, which he presented that day, to abolish capital punishment for a variety of offences. On 19 May he introduced two general bills to repeal the whole or part of certain statutes imposing the death penalty, withdrew his original measure relating to the punishment for forgery and brought in an amended one. After consultations with the crown law officers, he withdrew the latter and his measures dealing with robberies in dwelling houses and on navigable rivers, which they would have opposed. On 4 July Mackintosh, who had earlier that day made an unsuccessful personal appeal to Lord Sidmouth, the home secretary, for clemency for a young man sentenced to death for uttering forged notes (Sidmouth pointed out that 'though a married man he had uttered one in a brothel', which prompted in Mackintosh the silent reflection that the miscreant was 'thus in part hanged for adultery'), secured the third reading of the two general bills and the privately stealing in shops bill. He had been forced to modify all of them and felt no personal elation but, as he told his wife, he still felt that if the Lords sanctioned them he would have achieved a significant mitigation of the severity of the criminal code. After passing 'two hours very tiresomely' at the Scottish burghs committee, 5 July, he went to the Lords with his bills, 'and felt more nervous in delivering them to the chancellor than I have of late been used to do on public occasions'. The measures were further emasculated by the Lords, but became law on 25 July 1820 as 1 Geo. IV, c. 115 (capital felonies punishment); c. 116 (capital felonies repeal); and c. 117 (privately stealing in shops).[25] Mackintosh had wanted to speak again against 'the threatened perpetual aliens bill', but, as he told Holland, was 'disheartened by the tone of the last debate in which we seemed to receive C[anning]'s threat as a favour'. He found no opportunity to speak on 7 July, when he voted against the second reading, but on the motion to go into committee on the bill, 10 July, he moved three instructions intended to curb the power of the authorities, including one to protect foreign witnesses in the queen's trial. All were negatived without a division, and he moaned to Lady Holland that he had been 'ill supported by my friends'.[26] He thought it likely at this time that the trial would result in 'the death of the English monarchy', with which would perish the aristocracy. On a visit to London in early August 1820 he found 'more rumours and alarms of military disaffection than ever', though he cynically observed that 'the alarms of the ministerialists are so loud that I could almost fancy that they had it in view to frighten the king into immediate and unlimited submission'.[27]

Soon afterwards he fell ill, but he recovered during the autumn with the aid of a lengthy course of Cheltenham waters, to the extent that in late October he could 'begin to think myself a new man'. However, Lansdowne, with whom he stayed at Bowood a month later, was far from convinced that he was 'well'.[28] Moore had a conversation with Russell at this time about

> Mackintosh's want of observation in common life, and his helplessness in the House of Commons from that circumstance. Tierney ... has rather a slighting opinion of his consequence; and says he is a 'very good historical man, and may be relied upon for a sound opinion about Cardinal Wolsey or so; but for anything of the present day', etc.[29]

Tierney and Lord Grey were accordingly happy to exploit Mackintosh's literary skills, which he applied to the composition for the *Edinburgh Review* of an article advocating a measure of parliamentary reform. Tierney observed to Grey that 'if you like the whole, or any part of his suggestions, you will have the means of drawing up what you may avow as your own creed, and if you disapprove of his project it can be considered only as the speculation of the writer, and binds no one'. Writing the piece, which was ostensibly a review of Russell's speech of 14 Dec. 1819 advocating the transfer of the franchise from corrupt boroughs to unrepresented large towns, convinced Mackintosh, as he told Holland, that

> something substantial and serious must be proposed. Without such a plan I doubt whether the country can be kept quiet and whether you can become ministers. I am sure you cannot without a measure of that sort continue ministers.[30]

He advocated the immediate addition to the Commons of 20 Members for unrepresented large towns, to be elected by 'a widely diffused franchise' adapted to local conditions. He proposed the adoption of more effectual machinery for the disfranchisement of 'delinquent boroughs': the first ten such forfeitures were to be used to restore the membership of the House to its current size; and thereafter transfers of the franchise were to be made piecemeal as necessary. He wanted a significant widening of the Scottish county franchise and an unspecified reduction in the duration of Parliaments. To Losh, the article, which earned Mackintosh some credit, 'looks like feeling the pulse of the reformers, by proposing a plan which might suit what is called the Whig faction'.[31]

Mackintosh voted against the omission of the queen's name from the liturgy, 23 Jan., and spoke and voted in the same sense, 26 Jan. 1821, when the Whig George Howard*, a spectator in the gallery, thought he was 'very good and able, but his voice and lungs were unequal', while the ministerialist Lord Ancram* admitted that his speech was 'excellent'. The 'Mountaineer' Henry Grey Bennet wrote that his 'very able, clever and eloquent speech ... made mincemeat' of the attorney-general Gifford.[32] Supporting the opposition censure motion, 5 Feb., for which he duly voted the following day, he was called to order and rebuked by the Speaker for asserting that 'the majority of the House of Commons had declared war against the people of England'. He spoke after and, according to Grey Bennet, 'scarified' the Tory Henry Bankes, who noted that Mackintosh had 'exerted himself with great acrimony and ingenuity to expose and turn into ridicule most of the topics which were urged'.[33] He was in the opposition minorities on the liturgy, 13, 15 Feb., when he spoke in support of Hamilton's motion for a copy of the order in council to the Scottish church, and on the conduct of the sheriff of Dublin, 22 Feb., when he called for inquiry. John Whishaw informed Sydney Smith that Mackintosh 'has been most successful, and has shown powers of regular debate which he was not supposed to possess'.[34] On 21 Feb. he brought on his eagerly anticipated motion for an address to the king for the production of information on the British government's attitude towards the Allies' suppression of the liberal regime in Naples. Grey Bennet thought 'his speech was of the most brilliant character, very forcible, eloquent and learned, and his invective against the king was in the bitterest tone'; while Bankes conceded that it was 'executed with uncommon ingenuity, variety and brilliancy'.[35] His motion was defeated by 194-125, but he told Sismondi, the Italian economist and historian who was married to his wife's sister and who kept him abreast of European affairs, that it had been attended 'with such success that in the opinion of many, if the discussion had occurred two months earlier it might have produced some effect at Troppau'.[36] He supported the Neapolitan Captain Romeo's petition for redress of his grievances and condemned the secret Austrian treaty, 20 Mar., when, replying to Canning's comments, he said that 'the only opinion which he had ever asserted on this subject was not that the Neapolitan constitution was a good one, but that the independence of nations had been attacked by the flagitious conduct which the allied powers had exhibited towards the Neapolitans'. He spoke and voted for Catholic relief, 28 Feb., after urging Catholics to persevere in their petitioning campaign. On 16 Mar. he questioned the validity of a petition from Staffordshire Catholics against the relief bill, the second reading of which he then supported. The anti-Catholic Bankes wrote that he 'twisted and turned all the arguments with his usual ingenuity of conversion and perversion'.[37] He was believed in some quarters to have been responsible for 'harmoniously' incorporating the veto clauses into the original bill.[38] He spoke on details of the measure, 23, 26, 27 Mar. (subsequently lamenting his 'folly in speaking ... when the House was unwilling to listen and thereby incurring more disagreeable manifestations of their impatience than have usually fallen on me of late'), 2 Apr. Hobhouse reckoned that he expected it to pass the Lords.[39] He was in the minority for the repeal of the duty on husbandry horses, 5 Mar., but only paired for repeal of the additional malt duty, 3 Apr. On 17 Mar. the backbencher Hudson Gurney, noting Tierney's recent resignation of the leadership, observed that Mackintosh had 'sat in Tierney's place the last night or two – whether [as] a sort of leader I know not'.[40] (In fact there was no clear leadership for several sessions.) Mackintosh supported Martin's bill to allow defence by counsel in capital cases, 30 Mar. During the Easter holiday he reflected that

> perhaps there never was a session in which the balance turns out so much against our party as the present. The queen and the Neapolitans have proved wretched adventures, and the Catholic question, which has had a partial success, is not all our own.

He was 'very much perplexed' as to what to do on Lambton's planned parliamentary reform motion, feeling that if it was for inquiry he would be obliged to vote for it to 'avoid being thought an enemy of reform', but that it was 'very difficult' for him to speak on the issue. Relieved to find that Lambton intended to 'open his motion in such a way as to deliver us moderate reformers from the necessity of speaking merely to disavow his plan', he voted silently for it, 18 Apr.[41] He voted with Hume to disfranchise civil officers of the ordnance, 12 Apr. He divided for Russell's reform motion, 9 May, when he also voted in protest at delays in the proceedings of the commission of judicial inquiry, and for reform of the Scottish county representation, 10 May. He voted for repeal of the Blasphemous and Seditious Libels Act, 8 May, and inquiry into Peterloo, 16 May 1821.

On 11 Apr. 1821 he introduced a bill to abolish capital punishment for all forgery offences except that of Bank of England notes, the defence of which he largely entrusted to his coadjutor Fowell Buxton. He had a 'glorious' victory, 23 May, when, to his own great surprise, he carried his motion to go into committee on the measure against ministerial resistance by 118-74.[42] He was subsequently forced to make substantial alterations to the bill, conceding the death penalty for the forgery of wills, country bank notes, marriage entries and stock transfers. Grey Bennet, who liked the principle of the measure, believed that these concessions 'to make friends' had rendered the bill a nullity.[43] Mackintosh carried the third reading, 4 June, by 117-11, but Lord Londonderry dished it by unexpectedly dividing the House against its formal passage, by 121-115.[44] Mackintosh presented a petition from the inhabitants of St. John's, Newfoundland, for judicial reforms, 28 May, spoke and voted for inquiry into the administration of justice in Tobago, 6 June, and was appointed to the select committee on the report of the Irish judicial commission, 26 June. He voted to equalize the rates of interest on Irish treasury bills and British exchequer bills, 30 May, and, in rare votes for economy, for cuts in the ordnance estimates, 31 May; but, with Brougham and Tierney, he left the House before the division on Grey Bennet's motion for a reduction in the number of placemen in the Commons.[45] The next day he supported Maxwell's slaves removal bill. On 21 June, replying to Londonderry, 'but by no means as he ought to have done', as Grey Bennet saw it, he backed Lord William Cavendish Bentinck's motion criticizing the government's indifference to Sicilian independence and denounced the Laybach declaration.[46] He endorsed Wilberforce's motion for an address to encourage suppression of the foreign slave trade, 26 June, observing that 'the principle of reformation in this country of reason and liberty ... would always ultimately triumph, and that from this country it would spread to others'; Wilberforce thought he 'spoke capitally', and Grey Bennet that he 'made, as usual, a splendid speech'.[47] He pressed Londonderry to clarify the British position on the French trade, 2 July.[48] He was credited with a speech in opposition to the grant for the alien office, 29 June, but was not listed in the minority of 27. He voted for Hume's general motion for economy and retrenchment, 27 June, but incurred a rebuke from Lord Grey and a private censure from Grey Bennet, who lamented that all session he and Scarlett had taken 'every occasion to separate themselves from the few combatants who fought on the third bench for public economy', for his failure to speak.[49] Mackintosh, who went to London in mid-July 1821 for the first meeting of the commission on public records, of which he was a assiduous member, told Lady Holland, who had asked how he felt about his recent speeches, that

> I did not satisfy myself on criminal law, but ... I thought I did tolerably on Sicily and the French slave trade. I had however no great reason to believe that others thought so, for as I never before was so scurrilously treated by the enemy, so on the other hand I never received so little countenance and civility from those whom the world calls my political friends. *John Bull* and a villainous paper at Edinburgh called the *Beacon* have pursued me with libels.

He could not 'catch at such straws' as the belief of some Whigs that ministerial conflict with the king would bring them down, though he was 'vulgar enough to wish that the Whigs were in power (by any means) if it were only for a few months and to do two or three things', notably carry Catholic emancipation. He had little interest in the coronation, which he nevertheless attended, and the dispute over the queen's right to be crowned, preferring to dwell instead on the death of Buonaparte, 'the greatest of conquerors and nearly the best': 'No one who forced himself into the supreme power from a private station and conquered so great a part of the bravest and most intelligent of mankind ever did so little evil'. On a personal note, he found it painful to 'recollect how little of the business of life has been accomplished' in the last 20 years. In early August 1821 he felt that 'the Whigs in London are doing all they can by their present clamour to frustrate all good intentions which the king may feel'. Later in the month he observed to Lansdowne, 'I am displeased with the sublimities of some of our friends who seem to think that if once in half a century a favourable breeze should spring up at Court the Whigs should take no advantage of it'.[50]

In October Mackintosh's son-in-law Claudius Rich, the husband of his daughter Mary, died suddenly in Persia. Mackintosh secured a pension of £200 a year from the East India Company for Mary (who eventually came home and contributed to his domestic unease by not getting on with his wife) and negotiated the sale of Rich's papers to the British Museum for £7,000.[51] In mid-December he was irritated by renewed allegations in the Tory press of his supposed appropriation of £20 of the fund collected for the radical Joseph Gerrald, who had been transported for sedition in 1795, even though Samuel Parr and James Perry, the originators of the smear in 1806, when Mackintosh's loyalty to Fox had been called in question, had recently issued public retractions. To Holland, who advised him to ignore the libels, he wondered whether he might not, if the next session proved, as he expected, to be neither 'busy' nor 'important', 'dedicate a great deal more time than formerly to my history', which was well behind schedule. He added:

> I do not think the Whig affairs were in so bad a state since Mr. Fox was first a leader as they are now. We have lost such help as we received from the radicals and the queen. The odium of both connections remains.[52]

At the end of the month he commented to Lansdowne that by accommodating the Grenvillites 'the ministers have considerably secured themselves by taking off all those with whom opposition might have coalesced to make a government'. He considered Peel's appointment as home secretary to be

> a step to a higher Toryism and consequently to a more undistinguishing resistance of all novelties. With that opinion I am perplexed about my criminal law. On the one hand it is not advisable to damp the spirit of the friends of those measures by inactivity. On the other it is dangerous to multiply parliamentary decisions against them.[53]

Three weeks later Whishaw found him

> remarkably well [at Mardocks] and seriously engaged upon his history, in which he is now more in earnest than I have ever known him. He works at it regularly some hours every day, and his conversation shows that his mind is full of the subject. He is inclined to give only an occasional attendance in Parliament.

Yet the same day Mackintosh, seeking instruction from Holland House as to what line opposition intended to take at the opening of the session, prophetically observed that although 'history occupies every hour ... I often have painful misgivings that after all I only collect materials for some man of greater powers who will begin the arduous work in a season of more leisure, cheerfulness and strength'.[54] Maria Edgeworth was a guest at Mardocks at this time:

> Mackintosh is much improved in the art of conversation since we saw him. Mixing more with the polished world and being engaged in great affairs and with great men and women has perfected him in the use and management of his wonderful natural powers and vast accumulated treasures of knowledge. His memory now appears to work less, his eloquence is more easy, his wit more brilliant, his anecdotes more happily introduced. The whole is brought into better compass and proportion and he has the high-bred touch and go of the man of the world as well as the classical high and deep advantages of the scholar and orator. Altogether his conversation is the most delightful I ever heard.[55]

He went to London on 1 Feb. 1822 and occupied lodgings in Cork Street, found for him by the Hollands. Almost immediately he was afflicted with deafness and stomach trouble. He felt that 'the parliamentary prospect is very disheartening', for 'we are no longer a party', and 'every man is in a great measure left to act according to his own judgement or according to his want of it'. Unsure what line to take on Hume's anticipated amendment to the address on 5 Feb., Mackintosh, who thought that the 'Mountaineers look rather adversely on me' and that he was 'weakened' by Brougham's current 'inactivity', consulted Lansdowne 'about speaking'. Lansdowne seemed 'well pleased that the dissolution of the party should clearly distinguish the moderates from the Mountain'; but in the event Hume gave up his amendment and opposition decided to keep quiet. Mackintosh apparently attended on the opening day, although he was ill, and described it as 'one of the most suffering days of the last eleven years of ill health'. He voted against the Irish insurrection bill, 7 Feb.[56] An eruption of cold sores and intermittent bouts of diarrhoea confined him to his quarters for a fortnight and prevented him from attending to support Sir Robert Wilson's motion complaining of his dismissal from the army, 13 Feb. He was better by 21 Feb., when he voted for more extensive tax reductions to relieve distress.[57] He was in the House on 27 Feb., but did not vote for Hume's motion on the estimates. The following day he went to a meeting at Brooks's 'convened for the purpose of trying to patch up a treaty or a truce between us and the Mountain', but the attempt was abandoned as 'vain'. He voted for a gradual reduction of the salt duties (but not in support of the complaint against the assault on Robert Waithman* at the queen's funeral), 28 Feb., and was in the opposition majority for admiralty reductions, 1 Mar. Yet he 'went to bed unwell and little elated by our victory', and returned next day to Mardocks, where he reflected on the 3rd that

> in the course of 12 years suffering I have not had so vexatious an interruption to my usefulness as during the last month. The rude have expressed and even the more refined have betrayed their surprise at my silence in Parliament.[58]

He was in the House on 6 and 7 Mar., when he broke his silence with a few unreported words on the records of Parliament. He was appointed to the select committee on that subject, 12 Mar., and to the one on the police of the metropolis, 14 Mar. He spoke and voted for abolition of one of the 'totally and absolutely useless' joint-postmasterships, 13 Mar., delivering what the Whig backbencher Moulton Barrett considered 'a most brilliant speech'.[59] The following day he witnessed Creevey's vicious attack on the Grenvillites in the guise of a motion for inquiry into the board of control. After hearing the 'Billingsgate and brutality' of Creevey's reply to the debate he was a reluctant voter for the motion, but felt obliged to stand by Tierney, who had earlier committed himself to vote for it. On 25 Mar. 1822 he made a speech in support of Romeo's petition as 'an act of justice to him'. He remained 'very low and in momentary apprehension of stomach complaint'.[60]

At Brooks's on 22 Apr. 1822 Mackintosh 'lamented the irreparable injury done to the Catholic cause by such animosities among its supporters' as the one anticipated in the Commons that day between Plunket, recently appointed Irish attorney-general, and Newport. Like most of the Whigs, he was won over by Plunket's brilliant performance in the debate. He paid the price of his late night with

> a very miserable day of constant headache and languor, frequent efforts to prepare my parliamentary business and very melancholy apprehensions that after having sacrificed so much to it I shall be under the sad necessity of relinquishing it altogether.

He was well enough to speak in support of the remission of Henry Hunt's* prison sentence, 24 Apr., deploring 'the maxim that any illegal severity could be practised upon any individual because he was odious'.[61] He voted silently for Russell's parliamentary reform motion the following day. He was in the majority for Canning's motion for a bill to relieve Catholic peers, 30 Apr., when he was lost in admiration of Canning's 'extraordinary ingenuity and resource'.[62] On 2 May he 'wasted three hours in vexatious and unprofitable talk' at the colonial office about 'the objects of the African Institution' with Wilberforce and Buxton.[63] Later that day he voted in the majority for abolition of one of the joint-postmasterships. He spoke and voted for cuts in diplomatic expenditure, 15, 16 May. He supported the Marriage Act amendment bill, 20 May. On his brother-in-law John Allen's motion to consider the select committee reports on the Welsh judicature, 23 May, he suggested adding two judges to the courts of common law rather than appointing inferior ones. He voted for Hume's motion to pay naval and military pensions from the sinking fund, 3 June. The following day he moved, after prior consultation with Peel, for early consideration next session of the criminal laws, with a view to making them more effective by reducing their severity. He was cheered on both sides of the House and, though opposed by ministers, his motion was carried by 117-101.[64] He was later said to be 'in great spirits at his success'.[65] On 5 June, despite feeling unwell, he fortified himself with 'aromatic vinegar' to attend the debate on the aliens bill, when, enraged by Peel, he made 'a vehement though I hear a very good speech against him'. Taken ill again later in the evening, he made a pair and, as he told his wife, 'was violently sick in the coach the whole way to Holland House. I never remember to have retched and vomited so much'. On 6 June he returned to the Commons for a debate on Ireland, but failed to catch the Speaker's eye.[66] He led the opposition to the second reading of the aliens bill, 14 June, in what Hudson Gurney* described as 'a very long speech of outrageous exaggeration'; and he voted silently against the measure, 1, 19 July, when he was in minorities of 32 and 20.[67] He spoke – 'I think as well as on most occasions' – for the second reading of Thomas Kennedy's Scottish juries bill, 20 June, when he also declared his hostility to the Canada bill.[68] He attended the debate on the Catholic question in the Lords, 21 June.[69] He voted in condemnation of the influence of the crown, 24 June, and spoke and voted for inquiry into the lord advocate's dealings with the Scottish press, 25 June. Supporting Wilberforce's address on the foreign slave trade, 28 June, he gave credit to the British government for their attempts to suppress it, but lamented the 'perfidy' and 'hypocrisy' of the Allies. He voted for repeal of the salt duties that day. On 2 July he voted 'in a minority of *four*' against the bill to authorize the Bank to issue notes of £1 and £2, which were the great temptation to forgery.[70] He quizzed Londonderry about infractions of British maritime rights, 5 July, inadvertently revealing as he did so the foreign secretary's unprecedented state of mental distraction, which presaged his suicide a few weeks later.[71] He supported the Marriage Act amendment bill and was a teller for the majority in favour of the Lords' amendments, 12 July. He presented a petition in support of the Greeks in their struggle with Turkey, 15 July.[72] He failed to draw Londonderry on the question of recognition of the independent South American states, 17 July.[73] Grey and his son-in-law Edward Ellice* had failed to persuade him to drop his opposition to the Canada bill, which he voted against, as one of a minority of 14, 18 July.[74] On 23 July 1822 he took issue with Burdett on the subject and supported calls for the recognition of the South American states. The following day he seconded the government motion for the publication of an edition of the ancient historians of Britain.

Mackintosh, who claimed to 'find industry the best remedy against depression' caused by the ailing state of his daughter Elizabeth and his worries for the safety of Mary Rich, whose ship from the East was overdue, considered the death of Londonderry a 'great blow' to the Catholic cause, and did not think Canning's admission to the cabinet would restore the balance.[75] There was a rumour, discounted as nonsense by John Croker*, of 'an intended overture' from ministers to Mackintosh and Lansdowne.[76] Russell visited him at Mardocks in mid-October 1822, and found him

> looking unwell and old, but ... in better spirits than I expected. He is however too much cast down by the crises and afflictions he has had lately to think of leaving home ... He seems to be living indolently and quietly, feeding himself as usual with new books.

As for his history

> he ... [seemed] more worried by study and the responsibility of an historian than anything else. He seems to have advanced very much ... Five or six years is after all not much for such a work considering he has had a liver, and risen to great fame as an orator and reformer of laws within the same time. To say nothing of reviewing, a species of eminence not easily classified.[77]

At the same time Whishaw reported that Mackintosh, who was additionally distracted by having been given notice to quit Mardocks at next Lady Day [25 Mar. 1823] and by recent disturbances at Haileybury, was 'altogether much better than I expected', though he 'complains of the effects of constant anxiety upon his health, and has lately had some returns of the giddiness which affected him two years ago'. He feared that the history had been neglected for an article on foreign politics for the *Edinburgh*: 'It is become an unpleasant subject, and I could not press him upon it'.[78] The Hollands, Lord Morpeth†, Tierney and James Abercromby* were also very concerned for Mackintosh's physical and emotional welfare; he was 'touched' by the Hollands' 'kindness', and resumed work on the history 'under great depression of spirits'. He was more cheerful by late November, having heard that Mary Rich was safe, and 'tickled' at his election, over Sir Walter Scott, as rector of Glasgow University, where he was to be installed on 3 Jan. 1823.[79] Meanwhile, he was in touch with Lord Ellenborough on the Marriage Act, worried about the French threat to Spain, 'the only independent part of the continent', and fretted over his future accommodation and its effects on the progress of his history:

> I am indeed daily frightened about finishing the history at all. I despair of doing it well. Yet I cannot relinquish it and as I have at last got into the habit of daily application to it I am very anxious that the habit should be interrupted as rarely and shortly as possible.

After Christmas he was at Althorp, where Agar Ellis greatly enjoyed 'his most agreeable and instructive conversation': 'I know no man whose society gives me so high an admiration for his talents ... such clearness of expression, such cultivation of intellect, such memory, wit, everything in short that gives grace and amusement and dignity to social intercourse'.[80] For his Scottish jaunt, Holland talked him out of his notion of asking Lord Lauderdale and William Adam† to act as his minders and as 'a sort of Tory vouchers against Tory calumny in this last public visit to my native country'. He reluctantly accepted a pressing invitation to speak at the Fox dinner in Edinburgh a few days after the Glasgow ceremony.[81] There were conflicting accounts of his speech on that occasion. Henry Cockburn deemed it

> an utter and inconceivable failure. I cannot tell whether the conception or the execution of it was worst [*sic*]. It has baffled all my speculative powers to discover how such an absolute want of tact and effect could be evinced by such a master.

A correspondent of Fox informed him:

> The speech was brilliant in some passages and very Mackintoshian in all. The spirit just and philosophic, the expression copious and refined, but the manner nothing better than the parliamentary see-saw and sing-song. The chief fault was length and a total misconception of the audience. He never seemed to recollect that the great majority of his hearers were almost boys and could not be interested in long details and historical allusions. But on the whole it was well received, though I must not conceal from you that disappointment was the general impression.[82]

He did rather better at the Fox dinner, 14 Jan. 1823. Cockburn thought he was 'didactic' but 'good', while Abercromby wrote that he 'did on the whole very well', though he doubted 'the taste and judgement of having made his speech not only a eulogy of Mr. Fox but also an attack on Mr. Pitt'. Grey, on whom he called at Howick on his way south, noted, with some slight misgivings, 'how deeply he and all our friends pledged themselves to the question of reform'. Mackintosh also descended on Sydney Smith at Foston:

> About half after five in the evening (3 feet of snow on the ground and all communication with Christendom utterly cut off) a chaise and four drove up to the parsonage and from it issued Sir James and his appendages. His letter of annunciation arrived the following morning ... Mackintosh is always agreeable, but is a little older than he was 20 years ago. His daughter [Frances, his favourite] is a pleasant girl, rather overpraised. The most valuable gift Providence could have presented him with, would have been a daughter addicted to arithmetic, and needlework, a cunning sempstress and one who could cast up a bill. Unfortunately this young woman is as helpless as her

father, without having I am afraid so valid an excuse for the deficiency ... Mackintosh had 70 volumes in his carriage; none of the glasses would draw down or let up but one. He left his hat behind him at our house.[83]

On the address, 4 Feb. 1823, he applauded 'many of the just principles' enunciated in the king's speech, but deplored Allied aggression against Spain and held out the spectre of 'a Muscovite army lining the shores of the continent, from Amsterdam to Cadiz'; as Gurney saw it, he 'proved we ought to go to war out of Cicero and the speeches of William III'.[84] He gave himself a 'perplexed and disturbed day', 9 Feb., by yielding to 'the temptation of the Speaker's great variety of wines' at the opposition dinner.[85] He recommended Phillimore to postpone his Marriage Act amendment bill, 14 Feb.[86] He fell ill again,[87] and no further trace of his parliamentary activity has been found until 18 Mar., when he questioned Canning, now foreign secretary, about negotiations to avert war between France and Spain; he and Lansdowne were now said to be 'in favour of peace against the more violent party of the Whigs'.[88] His speech at a public meeting in support of the Spaniards, 7 Mar., when he proposed 'the preservation of the peace of Europe', did not impress Lord Duncannon*, to whose comments Brougham, away on the circuit, replied: 'I could easily suppose it bad, for he was quite sure to overdo that sort of thing, and to do it badly, but it don't signify. The reporters always puff him and so it goes out to the public as a good speech, and that is the same thing'. The duke of Bedford, prompted by Lady Holland's 'just and candid opinion of Mackintosh', agreed that he was 'too prone' to 'pervert almost every feeling to the most unfavourable side of the question'.[89] Russell reported that he had been 'blarneying too much, but he is likewise too much laughed at'.[90] Devastated by the death of his daughter Elizabeth the following month, he set up home at 42 Cadogan Place at about this time.[91] On 22 Apr., after challenging those who alleged that Catholic priests had interfered in the Leitrim election to produce hard evidence, he voted in the majority for inquiry into the prosecution of the Dublin Orange rioters.[92] He voted for Russell's reform motion, 24 Apr., and spoke and voted for reform in Scotland, where there was 'no popular election whatever', 2 June. He spoke at length in support of the opposition motion criticizing British policy on Spain, 29 Apr., condemning 'the unprincipled and atrocious aggression of France'. At this juncture Coleridge assessed Mackintosh as

the king of the men of talent. He is a most elegant converser ... He is uncommonly powerful in his own line; but it is not the line of a first-rate man. After all his fluency and brilliant erudition, you can rarely carry off anything worth preserving. You might not improperly write on his forehead, 'Warehouse to let!' He always dealt too much in generalities for a lawyer. He is deficient in power in applying his principles to the points in debate.[93]

He was in a minority of 14 for an attempt to prevent the reappointment of insolvent collectors under the Irish county treasurers bill, 2 May. He contributed to the Dublin inquiry, 2, 5, 6, 8, 9 May, arguing that witnesses should not be compelled to dispense with their previous oaths. On 21 May he questioned Canning about Russian threats to British maritime rights, before moving nine resolutions for extensive revision of the criminal code. Although Peel secured their defeat by 86-76, he made it clear that ministers intended to introduce reforms, which Mackintosh recognized as the best chance of achieving significant results. He supported Lord Nugent's proposal to place British and Irish Catholics on the same footing as regarded civil rights, 28 May, when he said that the refusal to concede emancipation had the appearance of 'one of those acts of infatuation which had sometimes preceded the downfall of empires'; and he presented a petition for legalizing Catholic marriages by Catholic clergy, 12 June. He voted in condemnation of the lord advocate's treatment of the Scottish press, 3 June, and for inquiry into chancery delays, 5 June. He spoke and voted in favour of referring the silk manufacture bill to a select committee, 9 June, when he was in the opposition minorities on the Leeward Islands duties and the coronation expenses. He spoke at a *London Tavern* meeting in support of the Spanish liberals, 13 June.[94] On 20 June, when Wilberforce thought he 'spoke beautifully', he expressed his preference for housing the late king's library in a new building near Hyde Park rather than in the British Museum.[95] He spoke and voted for the Scottish juries bill that day,[96] and on its third reading, 30 June, endorsed its proposal for selection by ballot. His amendment to the larcenies bill to exempt from capital punishment the crime of stealing from a shop which was part of a dwelling house was defeated by 35-19, 25 June. He unsuccessfully divided the House on the application of an individual to be heard by counsel against certain provisions of the New South Wales jurisdiction bill, 2 July; and on 7 July his attempt to introduce trial by jury into the measure was rejected by 41-30. He persisted in his opposition to the bill, 8, 9 July.[97] He voted for investigation of the Irish Catholics' petition complaining of abuses in the administration of justice, 26 June, and against the grant for Irish glebe houses, 1 July. He said that slave removals in the West Indies were tantamount to a renewal of the trade, 4 July.[98] He voted in the minority of 22 to end flogging in prisons, 7 July 1823.

Later that month Mackintosh, who contrived, with the assistance of Brougham, to keep out of the press reports of the scandal involving his daughter Catherine, who had abandoned her husband Sir William Wiseman for another man, went on a tour of private archives, seeking material for his history, which took him to Welbeck, Netherby and Brougham. In early August, even 'especially abominable heartburn' did not diminish his pleasure at 'the good accounts from Spain'.[99] Three months later Whishaw told Lady Holland that he had 'had another attack of his complaint, which prevented him from going last week to the College, where his lectures have now been suspended near a month'; and Mackintosh confirmed that he had 'passed an ailing time ... free from sharp attacks but seldom applicable to any useful or agreeable purpose'. By the end of 1823, however, he claimed to be very 'eager about the part of history on which I am engaged'.[100] He was 'very ill' again in January 1824, after 'a regular bilious fever', and it was becoming increasingly difficult for him to cope with travelling from London to fulfil his duties at Haileybury. Unfortunately, as Whishaw commented, the professorship was 'a considerable object to him' financially. Bedford was so worried about his 'melancholy state ... both as to health and finances' that he suggested to Lady Holland the possibility of getting up a subscription, under the nominal aegis of Lord Spencer, to 'secure to him a comfortable competence for the remainder of his life'; but nothing seems to have come of the idea. Mackintosh was staying at Holland House at the end of the month, 'better ... and of course agreeable', as Lady Holland noted: 'How full and ready he is with his knowledge'. At the Speaker's opposition dinner, however, the mischievous Creevey mocked to Hobhouse his 'mean-looking face and figure' and assured him that the story of his having made off with Gerrald's money was true. More charitably, Wilberforce recorded a week later that at dinner 'I drew the highest prize in the lottery; I sat by Sir J. Mackintosh'.[101] He voted for information on Catholic burials, 6 Feb. He spoke and voted for the production of papers on the criminal jurisdiction of the Isle of Man, 18 Feb., voted for reform of Edinburgh's representation. 26 Mar., and, speaking 'at no small personal inconvenience' on account of illness, supported the charge of breach of privilege against lord chancellor Eldon, 1 Mar. That day he regretted the 'almost sacrilegious' destruction of historic buildings in Westminster; and on 24 Mar. he supported the appointment of a select committee, to which he was named, on the construction of the new law courts there. He was in a small minority in favour of inquiry into the beer and malt taxes, 15 Mar. He was named to the select committee on the criminal laws, 16 Mar. On 13 Feb. he had given notice for early March of 'a conditional motion of a very extensive nature' concerning relations between Britain and the independent Spanish American states. In doing so, he was acting in concert with Lansdowne, and to the displeasure of Grey.[102] He was in Nugent's minority of 30 censuring the conduct of government towards Spain, 17 Feb. He questioned Canning on the subject, 5 Mar., and said that he would persevere with his own motion. On 18 Mar., after explaining that he 'highly approved' of ministers' policy on the silk duties as a limited but welcome adoption of the 'self-evident principles' of free trade, he supported Russell's unsuccessful motion for information on the occupation of Spain by the French army, replying 'indifferently' to Canning and disclaiming any attempt to impugn the British government.[103] The Canningite member Charles Ellis reported that he was 'very heavy' and 'not at all listened to'; but it seems that there were mitigating circumstances, for Mackintosh told Lady Holland that 'I was so unqualified for exertion as to be attacked in the middle of my speech by the sickness of stomach which has not quite ceased to torment me'. The discomfiture of the Whigs on this occasion prompted him to consult Holland:

> I see more clearly ... that attempts to question our foreign policy are at present unseasonable and serve only to exalt Canning. Shall I for that reason withdraw my notice about South America? It might perhaps be done on the avowed ground of Canning having said on ...[the 18th] that he should consider a Spanish armament against America while the occupation lasts as being in effect French. Do you think that it might be thought shabby after Canning's triumph? I lay no stress on my own bad speech for I think myself rather entitled to credit for having thrown myself into the breach when I was very unwell and when I was not only unprepared to speak but had resolved not to speak. Neither do I say anything of some from whom I expected more friendly treatment and who I think would have done better to have dissuaded myself from the motion than to have run it down in the world.

He accordingly withdrew his notice on that pretext, 25 Mar. 1824. Bedford commented that it was 'a pity' that Mackintosh, 'with all his great talents and lofty mind, should injure himself by fulsome and ridiculous compliments to such a man as Canning'.[104]

Speaking early in the evening because he was still not well, he opposed the aliens bill, 23 Mar. 1824. He voted silently against it, 2, 12 Apr. He voted to refer the reports of the Scottish justice commission to a committee of the whole House, 30 Mar. He spoke and voted for George Lamb's bill to permit defence by counsel in felony cases, 6 Apr. The previous November Fowell Buxton had pressed him to give his '*full, hearty*, and unreserved co-operation' to the abolitionist cause; and he presented an anti-slavery petition, 25 Mar., and welcomed the slave trade piracy bill and the pending treaty with America, 26 Mar. He presented a petition from the London Missionary Society complaining of the prosecution of the Methodist missionary John Smith in Demerara, 13 Apr., and supported Brougham's motion on the subject, 11 June, when Wilberforce wrote that his speech was 'most beautiful, his mind teemed with ideas'.[105] He paired against the grant for the building of new churches, 9 Apr. Mackintosh, who was seen as a likely recruit for Canning should he succeed an ailing Lord Liverpool as premier, presented petitions from Knaresborough both for and against the hides regulation bill, 3 May, and one from Inverness in favour of the Scottish juries bill, 7 May.[106] He voted for inquiry into the state of Ireland, 11 May. On 15 June he presented and, in a long speech which was subsequently published, endorsed the London merchants' petition for recognition of the independent South American states, disclaiming party motives, though he was 'and ever shall be a member of a party associated, as I conceive, for preserving the liberties of the kingdom'. He presented a similar petition from Manchester, 21 June. Before presenting a Perth petition for the gradual abolition of slavery, 17 June, he gave notice that next session he would raise two subjects which 'severe indisposition' had prevented him from pressing in the current one: amendment of the law of copyright and relaxation of the curbs on the licensing of plays. He presented petitions for the removal of restrictions on Church of Scotland marriage ceremonies, 22 June 1824.[107]

That month, still afflicted by poor health which 'not only deprives me of enjoyments, but either hinders or enfeebles the performance of duties, and often crowds with indispensable business the intervals when it is itself more tolerable', he gave up the Haileybury professorship and took a pension of £200.[108] From late August until early October 1824 he was abroad, touring the Low Countries and Germany and finishing in Paris.[109] Towards the end of the year Lady Davy told Henry Fox 'proofs of Sir James Mackintosh's selfishness and cunning combined, which was not much to his credit'; presumably this was a rehash of the Gerrald story.[110] Hazlitt at about this time assessed him as

> one of the ablest and most accomplished men of the age, both as a writer, a speaker, and a converser. He is, in fact, master of almost every known topic ... He has lived much in society, and is deeply conversant with books. He is a man of the world and a scholar; but the scholar gives the tone to all his other acquirements and pursuits ... By education and habit ... [he is] a college man; and perhaps he would have passed his time most happily and respectably, had he devoted himself entirely to that kind of life ... In company he talks well, but too much ... In writing he overlays the original subject and spirit of the composition by an appeal to authorities and by too formal a method ... In public speaking the logician takes the place of the orator ... and he fails to give effect to a particular point or to urge an immediate advantage home ... As a political partisan, he is rather the lecturer than the advocate ... The chief characteristics of his mind are retentiveness and comprehension, with facility of production; but he is not equally remarkable for originality of view, or warmth of feeling, or liveliness of fancy. His eloquence is a little rhetorical; his reasoning chiefly logical ... He is distinguished more as a man of wonderful and variable talent than as a man of commanding intellect ... He makes a respectable ally, but not a very formidable opponent.[111]

Mackintosh denounced the Irish unlawful societies bill and attacked Plunket to 'loud cheers', 14 Feb. 1825; Sir John Nicholl* thought it a 'fine speech ... though not much grappling with the real question; but the biased Bankes was scathing:

> Mackintosh ... laboured at it with tiresome and curious infelicity, applying all the subtleties and discriminations of metaphysical sophistry to the interpretation of a sentiment addressed to the most common and least educated understanding. Never was indeed a more wretched failure than the whole of his long speech.[112]

He voted against the measure, 15, 21, 25 Feb. He presented a Knaresborough petition in favour of the county courts bill, 25 Feb.[113] He supported Martin's cruelty to animals bill, 11 Mar. Having voted silently for Catholic relief, 1 Mar., when he was excused after being named as a defaulter the previous day, he was involved in discussions with Burdett, Newport and Plunket as to how best to proceed with the bill. Believing that the simultaneous measures of the disfranchisement of Irish 40*s.* freeholders and payment of the Irish Catholic clergy were 'the only means by which, short of imminent danger from abroad the Catholic question can be forced', he acquiesced in the decision that Newport should give notice of such measures while Burdett pressed on with the relief bill, though as regarded the payment of priests he made it clear that he would 'not assent to any measure that was not founded on the principle of giving assistance without gaining influence'.[114] On 22 Mar. he opposed the introduction of the 'curse' of the poor laws to Ireland. The following day he set off for Glasgow for a dinner to mark the end of his period as rector of the University. He was taken ill while preparing for the event, but, fortified by 'a grain of opium', he attended, with disastrous consequences, as he told his wife:

> I soon felt a whirl in the head and in about ten minutes I was compelled (in spite of brandy and water) to rush out into an adjoining room where I retched and vomited for twenty minutes over or into an immense pail (used for washing decanters, plates, etc.), surrounded by fifty servants, till I was carried home in a chair and put to bed where I gradually got into a quieter state.[115]

On 21 Apr. he presented and endorsed a Glasgow petition in favour of Catholic claims and voted for the relief bill. He paired for its third reading, 10 May 1825.

His health was by now so poor (he made his will on 30 Jan. 1826, having on the 1st noted that he was 'unwell on the first morning of perhaps *the last day of my life*)[116] that, on doctor's orders, he absented himself from the rest of the 1820 Parliament. In the late summer of 1825 he derived some benefit from the 'nauseous waters' of Harrogate, before going for a while to Brougham's home in Westmorland.[117] On 15 Oct. 1825 he wrote to Lansdowne of speculation that the anticipated dissolution had been put off as a result of the pro-Catholic liberals in the cabinet having over-ruled Eldon. He expected the Whigs to lose 'several seats' at the next general election, though not as a result of anti-Catholic feeling, though 'they will all be ascribed to it'.[118] Early in 1826 Whishaw reported that 'his countenance and manner show more of the marks of age', and that his relaxed and reclusive regime was 'very unfavourable to any material progress in the history', which had 'become an unpleasant and almost painful topic to himself and his friends'. Mackintosh himself claimed in mid-February that 'my present condition is tolerable', but complained that 'too much abstemiousness in study is still enjoined – a great deal more than suits what I have to do and the little time that remains to do it'.[119] He retained his interest in the Catholic question, the abolition of slavery, criminal law reform and the Greek cause, but studiously avoided all political engagements, though he composed four articles for the 1826 *Edinburgh*. He was said to be indulging in 'abuse' of Grey's speech in support of the corn laws in May 1826. He had 'no thoughts of giving up his seat', and at the general election the following month was returned again unopposed for Knaresborough, where Abercromby stood in for him at the formalities.[120]

That summer, when Lady Holland reckoned that he was 'better, but ... still tremulously alive to any symptom that denotes a change in health or sensations', he was in agonies of indecision as to whether to go to Switzerland or Belgium or his brother-in-law's residence at Cresselly in Pembrokeshire for a lengthy period of seclusion. Apart from wishing to devote himself to his flagging history, he needed to economize, having lost money in some unwise speculations as a result of the commercial crash of 1825-6. The Hollands came to his rescue by placing Ampthill at his disposal as a temporary retreat offering 'a very agreeable and undisturbed retirement' within easy reach of London, where he could attend meetings of two obscure insurance companies, for his chairmanship of which he received modest fees. He moved in there with his books and household goods at the beginning of September 1826.[121] He was plagued with toothache and biliousness in the autumn, but claimed that 'my ink ... flows and I think that I can finish four or five quarto pages of print a day, which allowing me a bad day a week would do a great deal in six months'. Yet Scarlett commented that 'he reads too much ever to write much and is more fastidious than he owns himself to be. If he wishes to make sure of accomplishing his work he should put out his eyes'.[122] It had been decided that as his health was still 'feeble', he would attend the new Parliament in the first instance only for the Catholic question. In late February 1827 he told Lady Holland:

> My time is spent in exercise, writing and struggling with my megrim, which, if I could trust appearances which have already deceived, I should almost think subdued. I know that the few who will think of me for a moment when I am dead will call me a hypochondriac. If they knew my whole condition in mind and body and estate they would rather wonder at my cheerfulness.

He was worried that he might be obliged to appear in the Commons to defend the ill-fated Colombian Association, of which he was chairman, against the petition of disgruntled settlers sent out under its aegis, but nothing came of this. He was present to vote, despite being tormented by headache and toothache, for Catholic relief, 6 Mar., resting in a committee at intervals during the debate. Disappointed at the defeat of the motion, and fearful that 'the high Tories if they become rulers' in the aftermath of Liverpool's stroke would 'ruin the country', he attended a meeting at the duke of Norfolk's, 8 Mar., at which it was decided to 'do nothing till the administration is formed'. After further dental treatment he returned to Ampthill. He was given three weeks' leave on account of ill health, 23 Mar., when he complained of 'frequent fits of weakness and languor', but talked optimistically of going to press with the first volume of his history by October 1827. A week later he observed that 'had I begun this continued labour ten years ago unseduced by a little transient and accidental success of another kind, I should have had better faculties as well as more leisure for my undertaking'.[123]

He was at Ampthill when he heard of the negotiations for the formation of Canning's ministry. By his own account, composed three months later, he was initially 'presumptuous enough' to think that if Canning offered the Whigs three cabinet places in the Commons, he would have one of them, along with Tierney and Lord Althorp. He was 'withheld by a perhaps foolish delicacy' from going to London, but wrote to Holland and Lansdowne to express his view, as a professedly 'disinterested spectator', that however circumscribed Canning might be by the king's known aversion to Catholic relief, the Whigs should coalesce in government with him as perhaps 'their last chance of contributing to the pacification of Ireland and mitigating Toryism in this country'.[124] As it turned out, Canning had comparatively little to offer the Lansdowne Whigs in the way of offices. Mackintosh received a number of letters congratulating him on his reported appointment as judge advocate, of which he had heard nothing from his friends in London. In fact the place was first offered to Abercromby, who hesitated, for personal reasons, and suggested that Mackintosh deserved it. When Lansdowne mentioned his name to Canning, the premier insisted that the office required constant attendance in Parliament, and that in any case the king had stipulated that Abercromby was the only Whig whom he was prepared to have in it. Time was short, and Lansdowne and Tierney took it upon themselves to answer for Mackintosh's inability to give regular attendance. Abercromby accepted the post. Lansdowne would not countenance a 'scheme of making way for Mackintosh' suggested, at the instigation of Tierney, by James Macdonald*, who was in line for a place at the board of control, and, as Mackintosh later saw it, 'too easily persuaded himself that there would be a vacancy at the end of the session and that an appointment *then* would better suit my health than one in the hurry and heat of the session'.[125] Mackintosh went to London on 1 May to appear in the House and mark his adhesion to the new ministry by sitting on the treasury benches, and also 'to show by my appearance that I am not at all piqued and not wholly disabled'. Macdonald told him what had occurred regarding his own claims to office, and assured him that 'there was ... the greatest anxiety to do something and he had no doubt that it would be done'. The following day Mackintosh saw Lansdowne and, after his explanation, told him that

> I was not ashamed to own how much office was desirable to me; that I was ambitious of it through him as a public token of the satisfaction of my friends with my public services; that for adequate office I would undertake to attend some part of every night and live within call; that I was aware this rule might stand in my way in almost every department; but that I placed my hopes in obtaining a relaxation of rule in one case when he was bringing so great an accession of strength as the whole Whig party to Canning.

Lansdowne assured him that he would press this on Canning and that 'if a vacancy occurred at the board of control which might be soon he thought means might be found of making matters easy to me'. Mackintosh privately objected to the reported suggestion of Lord Lyndhurst, the new lord chancellor, of a barony of the exchequer, because of 'the great occasional fatigue and exertion of circuit'; but he rejected nothing out of hand, and hinted to Lansdowne that he might after all prefer a diplomatic appointment. After sleeping on the matter he told his wife:

> My prospects seem to be that I am likely to be offered a seat at the board of control with £1,500 a year about the end of the session. For this I must sacrifice much leisure and some health. I must live six months of the year within reach of a message from the House of Commons and I must obey every message. I say nothing of the humiliation. But the expense of that London residence is a material consideration. I am at present determined to prefer an envoyship and doubtful whether I should accept the other.

Through Lansdowne he wrote to Canning in the second week of May to stake his claim and preference for a diplomatic posting, though without ruling himself out for domestic employment; but in passing the letter on to Canning Lansdowne commented that 'it appears to be the opinion of his friends, that if it is found practicable, a situation connected with the legal, would probably suit him better than that which he designates for himself in the diplomatic service'. On 20 May Mackintosh wrote to Lansdowne in an attempt to make it clear that he had not intended to give the impression that he did not want a place on the Scottish bench or a domestic political appointment: 'I pretend to no exclusion and only venture to mention preference'. Desperate for office, he was in fact extremely sore at his treatment, and admitted to Lady Holland, with Lansdowne in mind, that he would have been 'less mortified with the result whatever it may be if I had been informed of the suggestions relating to myself as they passed and if there had been some appearance of consulting me on them as far as circumstances allowed'. 'In a further outburst at the end of May he told her:

> The want of forethought which has helped to keep me poor has the good effect of lessening the ills of poverty to me. I did not suspect myself of much pride and perhaps I have not much. But a sharp mortification has found out a proud corner and I feel the smart more because I cannot divert it into another channel by harbouring dissatisfaction with those who (I am sure) were full of good will towards me. Whatever may be done below and long after everyone else must be merely a personal provision without any disguise. That is my main reason for wishing to pass the remainder of my days out of England, or at least at a distance from the scenes where the last 14 years of my useful life have been misspent.

The filling up of a vacancy at the board of control without a word to him a few days later prompted another complaint to Lady Holland, in which, despite having received assurances of Canning's 'desire to consult my wishes and of his readiness to communicate with me as soon as he was released from the session', he moaned that 'the moment which would have rendered an appointment at home gratifying to me has been missed and will probably not return':

> In the secret of my thoughts I may sometimes doubt whether a little less precipitancy, modesty and facility might not have saved me from being lowered so very much. I am therefore obliged to countenance that opinion of my bodily inability of which I am not convinced. If the whole of the administration were driven into opposition I should then honourably try to confute it by parliamentary exertion and such a trial I should in that case certainly make at any risk.[126]

Two weeks later Whishaw, whom Lady Holland had evidently reproved for failing to make Mackintosh's feelings clear to Lansdowne, defended himself, claiming that 'it was with great surprise I heard by your note early last week that he was seriously annoyed and mortified by what had taken place'.[127]

He had expressed on 20 May 1827 'some desire of speaking in Parliament', having 'been so well ... for the last two months', perhaps for repeal of the Test Acts, when, as he told Lansdowne, 'I could take the oath of allegiance to your government very naturally in such a speech'. He added that 'a man's first appearance after two years' silence is of importance to himself'; but a week later he confessed to Lansdowne that 'my fancy for speaking has rather gone off or at any rate would without watering it'. At the same time, he professed to be 'perfectly satisfied to put off whatever related to myself', in terms of office.[128] He was subsequently dissuaded by Holland and Lord Carlisle from going to the House for the debate on the Penryn election bill, 7 June, 'thinking it ungracious in me to take my first division against Canning'; but, prompted by Holland, who was 'very adverse' to his going abroad and thought that 'as I have nothing specific to propose I should not break in on Canning before his own time', he spoke in defence of the vote of credit to Portugal, 8 June, taking the opportunity to declare his general support for the ministry. He told his wife:

> I had a headache but I brushed up my matters as best I could and went to the House, took my seat on the treasury bench and ... rose at eight o'clock and spoke for three quarters of an hour, for the first few minutes with some nervousness, but afterwards easily and agreeably to myself and with fair success. The House heard me very handsomely and seemed not displeased to renew their acquaintance with an old friend. I was not exhausted and sat down with my nerves strengthened. The sound of my own voice gave me courage. Canning took me by the hand with very kind congratulations on success and enquiries after health. I went home and suffered nothing worse than an entirely sleepless night, which a speech in my best times has sometimes inflicted on me.

Canning told the king that Mackintosh had 'made a splendid speech'. Encouraged by his doctor to believe that 'moderate exertion in public may be more serviceable than hurtful and that at present I need nothing but great attention to eating, drinking and exercise', he went to the House to say 'a few words' in favour of the disfranchisement of East Retford, 11 June. He was present to vote for the ministerial corn bill, 18, 21 June.[129] After weeks of anxious anticipation he had his interview with Canning on 13 July 1827, when, asked whether he wished to remain in Parliament or preferred a more permanent situation out of it, he said that he now believed himself to be physically equal to the duties of any office to which he could aspire, but that 'permanency was undoubtedly a very great object': 'I went through foreign missions and the Scottish exchequer and political office, hinting at a new jurisdiction in colonial appeals which Brougham has I believe on no authority given out that I am to have'. He left 'persuaded' that Canning would 'do all he can whenever an opportunity offers'. A 'curious' interview immediately afterwards with Croker, the secretary to the admiralty, who seems to have engaged to put in a word for him with Canning, led to nothing. The following day Mackintosh wrote that 38 years previously (the day of the taking of the Bastile) he had been 'eight thousand pounds richer than I am now. If the other objects of living had been better obtained this paltry failure would inspire little regret'. A week later he reflected on his interview with Canning:

> I believe that if the administration and my life last something will be done for me. They are much fettered, they must wait for vacancies, and often fill them up with a view to strengthen the government. I thought it absurd to affect resentment though I did not profess to be satisfied and I shall not now throw away such hold as I have. Had the Whigs come in on a footing of reasonable equality, had Lord Holland not been actuated by an ill requited regard for the capricious and unamiable feelings of Lord Grey [towards junction with Canning], had I been in town at the first negotiation, had I then entertained as tolerable an opinion of my health as the trial in the House of Commons helped to give me I should probably have been in some respectable office. I am as sincere an adherent of the present government as if I were a cabinet minister ... I think it honourable as well as prudent to take all proper means of obtaining office. I by no means despair of being placed in a situation somewhat proportioned to my former place in Parliament, if the ministers succeed in withstanding the very formidable combination or conspiracy of peers against them.[130]

He wrote that Canning's death soon afterwards was 'deplored as that of a guardian by every friend of liberty from Philadelphia to Athens'. He attended his funeral with an eye to 'the possibility of advantage besides propriety'. In mid-August 1827, unwell once more, he went with his wife and Frances to stay for several months with their Wedgwood relatives at Maer, Staffordshire, from where he wrote to Lady Holland, 27 Aug., that 'I am neither well nor cheerful' and was worried by rumours that the Lansdowne Whigs were about to resign from the fledgling Goderich ministry; the same day he wrote to Lansdowne encouraging him to stay in office with his associates if decently possible.[131] In the negotiations which confirmed the ministry in office Lansdowne stipulated that Mackintosh was to replace Phillimore at the board of control as soon as the latter could be provided with a legal office, and that in the meantime he was to be made a privy councillor.[132] He accepted this, but only as 'a public pledge of the speedy performance of a specific engagement' to provide him with paid employment as soon as practicable. He admitted that

> I am not sorry at the end of five mortifying months to receive some mark of distinction which may a little conceal from the vulgar the estimate formed of me by the most competent judges. I wish the lesson against conceit had been given when I had more life left to profit by it.

At the same time, he did

> not like the provision intended for me. But my claim would be so strengthened by the public pledge that it might be considered as distinct enough to be the subject of negotiation; and it appears to me that if a vacancy in the Scotch exchequer should occur it would be more easy to promote me to it in my surrender of the promise than professional etiquette might allow it to be after an actual appointment to a political office.[133]

Being 'in the highest degree desirous of bringing my first volume to a conclusion', but ready with a litany of excuses, including 'autumnal bile', for his lack of progress, he was unable to fulfil a tentative agreement with Brougham to supply tracts for the Useful Knowledge Society. Anticipating a summons to London in November to be sworn in to the privy council, he fretted about where he was to settle between then and the opening of Parliament, and asked Lady Holland for permission to use Ampthill. It was given, but he still hesitated between moving there lock, stock and barrel or remaining in Staffordshire.[134] When he went to be sworn in, 16 Nov. 1827, he stayed at Lansdowne House, but he decided to take Ampthill, thereby irritating his wife. His defence was that 'I am now more convinced that I ought to be within hearing of the bell and particularly at a time when there may be unforeseen changes either adverse or prosperous'. He was in some respects disappointed to learn that Lord Stowell, whose retirement from the admiralty court to make way for Phillimore had been daily expected, was now insisting on a pension, which would require an act of Parliament:

> This will delay my poor appointment perhaps for a month after the opening of the session ... There is one advantage ... If I were now to be appointed I should vacate my seat and so be disabled from taking a part in defence of the measures of government for the Greeks. Perhaps I may gain an opportunity of usefully and creditably discharging an important duty.[135]

He was worried by the 'formidable' opposition forming against government in defence of the Turks and in condemnation of Navarino; but two days spent in reading the relevant correspondence in the foreign office files convinced him that 'we have a case which I should not fear to defend'. He had 'some thoughts of showing myself at the opening of Parliament' and of returning to Ampthill until the Greek question came on, and thereafter waiting until 'constant attendance became my official duty or till the hope of it was destroyed by the Turks of England and Constantinople'.[136] He became increasingly alarmed in December at signs of ministerial disarray and weakness, still believing that they had 'an opportunity of re-establishing themselves if they open the session with boldness'. He was planning to go up for the opening when the government collapsed, and he decided to stay away until the Greek question came on, resisting his son's pressure on him to put in an appearance in London 'for the chances of advantage in the confusion':

> I now consider my ship as just about to sink and I cannot enter in another. I can neither prevent nor profit by the fall of my friends. I see no object for striving.

He felt that his only hope lay in the remote possibility of the formation of 'an universal coalition'; and when this was dashed by the duke of Wellington's accession to power he told Lady Holland that 'as my last card is trumped I am turning my thoughts to some retreat suitable to my income and where I am not likely to be disturbed or drawn away'. He elaborated on this in a letter to Allen:

> I cannot pretend that I have not been a good deal vexed ... These vexations have sunk through my spirits into my health and have brought back some of my former uneasinesses, though not in their worst state. I am once more at sea with respect to a plan of residence for my little remaining life. At my age and with my health and income it would be madness to think of regular attendance and active opposition in Parliament. All that I should even wish to do would be to attend say six times in the session on great questions and when I was well. To do that with ease my residence should be within a short ... [distance] of London ... On the other hand it is question[able] whether it would not be more conducive to health, peace of mind, and to some chance of being able to publish some part of my history, if I were to go to some distant retirement either in England or abroad where I should be beyond the reach of all temptation to intermeddle with public broils. The choice is so difficult that it has little chance of being prudently made.[137]

On 14 Feb. 1828 he defended the Treaty of London of July 1827, welcomed ministers' promise to implement it and argued that 'the intervention in favour of the Greeks was an office of humanity to them'. He backed Wilson and Burdett in their denunciation of the Turkish treatment of the Greeks, 3 Apr., when he also approved Williams Wynn's proposals to revise the laws governing controverted elections. He voted silently for repeal of the Test Acts, 26 Feb., and belatedly presented petitions to that effect, 1 Apr. He spoke and voted for the transfer of East Retford's seats to Birmingham, 21 Mar. He presented and endorsed a petition from New South Wales for the introduction there of popular representation and jury trial, 18 Apr., and on 1 May he secured papers concerning the state of the colony in 1822; he moved but did not press amendments to the New South Wales bill, 20 June. He presented and warmly supported the prayer of a petition from Edinburgh University for relaxation of the restrictions on dissection, 21 Apr., and brought up a similar one from British students in Paris, 4 July. He presented two petitions of grievance from the inhabitants of Lower Canada, 1 May, and on Huskisson's motion for inquiry into its civil government the following day spoke at length in favour of a liberal colonial policy; he was named to the select committee. He presented petitions in favour of Catholic relief, 8 May, spoke for it, 9 May, when Croker thought he was 'long and laborious, and puzzled himself and tired us with references to papers', and voted for it, 12 May.[138] He evidently supported the provision for Canning's family, 13 May, but was ignored by the chairman of the committee (Planta) in his several attempts to defend it.[139] He got his chance on 22 May, when he praised Canning and said that 'his friendship was the only favour that I ever received from him'. He presented petitions for redress from the former president of the supreme court of Demerara, 15 May, and an individual who had suffered losses as a result of the insolvency of the registrar of Madras, 22 May, when he confirmed Hume's allegations that the evils of the system of imprisonment for debt in India were 'very great'. He presented a petition for the more effectual suppression of bull-baiting, 6 June. Supporting reception of the Liverpool petition for extension of the local franchise to householders, 9 June, he denied that it constituted 'the purest specimen of radical reform'. Later that day he welcomed Peel's assurances that the government had broken off diplomatic relations with the present regime in Portugal and got him to disavow Dom Miguel; but on 30 June he complained that ministers had 'departed from a neutral temper and spirit, so as to favour the party condemned by every moral principle and natural feeling'. He presented petitions for the abolition of slavery, 17 June, when he moved to refer a petition from Calcutta complaining of hardships inflicted by the stamp duty to a select committee, but was persuaded to withdraw it in the light of the 'liberal sentiment' evinced by ministers. He was in a minority of 22 for reducing the grant to the Royal Cork Institution, 20 June. He again spoke and voted for the transfer of East Retford's seats to Birmingham, 27 June. He paired for reduction of the salary of the lieutenant-general of the ordnance, 4 July,[140] and voted against the grant for North American fortifications, 7 July. On 14 July he welcomed the 'conciliatory' language of the colonial secretary towards Canada, but spoke and voted against government on the silk duties. He presented more anti-slavery petitions, 15, 25 July 1828, when he defended the inactivity that session of the abolitionists in general and Brougham in particular, and promised action in the next; he was inclined to attribute the distorted account in *The Times* to 'corruption or personal animosity in the reporter'.[141]

That month he moved to Clapham Common. Soon afterwards he contracted with Macvey Napier to write for his *Encyclopaedia Britannica* a history of ethical philosophy, which allowed him not only to set aside his onerous history but to borrow money in advance to ease his financial difficulties. Almost immediately he was put out of action for two months by a recurrence of illness. (He told Lady Holland in September 1828 that 'my health has been so unprosperous since I saw you as to render my life equally joyless and useless.') He continued to miss deadlines, the project got out of hand and there was a misunderstanding as to exactly what was required. It was eventually published as a somewhat perfunctory *Dissertation on the Progress of Ethical Philosophy* in 1830.[142] Whishaw reported to Lady Holland, 21 Nov. 1828, that Mackintosh

> seemed tolerably well in health, but not in very good spirits, though he talked with all his usual powers about the books he had been lately reading, which I was sorry to observe had no reference to his historical work. Reading, indeed, and collecting information from books, is become his principal literary pleasure. Composition, except on the spur of an occasion or to answer some temporary purpose, seems no longer to give him any delight.[143]

He agreed with Brougham that 'there should be a general call of our friends from all quarters for the first day and the most vigorous opposition if the speech be silent or unsatisfactory on Ireland'. After recovering from 'a pain in my face and cough', he spoke on the address, 4 Feb. 1829, when, welcoming the announcement that government intended to concede Catholic emancipation, he said that 'I have felt greater joy at the transactions of this day, than I yet have at any public event'.[144] At the same time, he indicated his 'great doubts' over ministerial policy on Portugal, and on 9 Feb. he gave notice of a motion for the 19th for papers on that subject. At Althorp's private request, he postponed it, 16 Feb., until the Catholic question had been dealt with, and put it off until after Easter, 23 Mar.[145] He presented petitions in favour of emancipation, 20 Feb., 4 Mar., when he also brought up one for colonial reform, 25 Mar. He voted silently for emancipation, 6 Mar. According to Hobhouse, some Whigs wanted him to answer Wetherell's violent speech against the measure, 18 Mar.; but 'he went across the House to ask Peel what his wishes were' and found that the minister wished to do it himself.[146] Like many Whigs, he had initially been worried as to what line to take on the security measure of the disfranchisement of Irish 40*s*. freeholders; but he fell in with the decision to swallow it, and he justified it in the House, 20 Mar. He defended the oaths clause of the relief bill, 24 Mar. On 26 Mar., when he was beginning to 'suffer a good deal from these late nights', he presented and endorsed an Edinburgh petition for emancipation, with 7,000 respectable signatures, which he had asked to be put into his hands. He presented a petition from members of regular orders in Ireland against their suppression by the bill, and one for the measure from the Protestant Society for the Protection of Religious Liberty, 30 Mar. He had planned a speech 'from which I expected some credit' on the third reading that day; but he made 'the paltry sacrifice' of giving it up in order to 'expedite the measure'. He subsequently reflected:

> I have felt the great fatigue more yesterday and today than when the exertions were going on. But I am very thankful for my escape from more serious consequences. We (Whigs) have performed a great duty which is its own best, and will probably be its only reward ... Distant generations will I trust pronounce that we have employed our strength for the preservation of our country without any angry remembrance of the past or selfish expectations from the future.[147]

He presented a pro-emancipation petition from Glasgow University students, 8 Apr. 1829.

'Three weeks of a more fatiguing parliamentary attendance than I believe ever was encountered with impunity by a man of my health' took its toll, and he was confined to his house for most of the rest of the month, complaining to Lady Holland that 'my indispositions are embittered by the necessity of employing every half hour of remission in drudgery. This is the punishment of idle youth'.[148] Having recovered, he secured the appointment, 5 May, of a select committee to investigate the financial claims on the registrar of Madras. He got leave to introduce a relief bill, 25 May, but on 3 June set it aside for that session because of lack of time. He opposed the Smithfield market bill, 15 May, and supported the petition of the Church of Scotland requesting the restoration of records currently in the keeping of Sion College, 20 May. He did not vote in the minority in favour of allowing Daniel O'Connell to take his seat for Clare unhindered, 18 May, and on the 21st, supporting the government motion for the issue of a new writ, argued that his temporary exclusion was an unavoidable sacrifice for the achievement of emancipation. He welcomed Peel's plans for the metropolitan police and his hints that he would mitigate the severity of the criminal code, 25 May, when he was also pleased with the ministerial statement that the evidence of slaves was to be made admissible in West Indian courts. He was in a minority of 40 for reduction of the hemp duties, 1 June. That day he successfully pressed his motion for papers on relations with Portugal in a lengthy speech, later polished and published, disclaiming 'any spirit of party opposition' to ministers, but demanding an explanation of the 'aggravated treachery' by which that country had been reduced to 'the lowest level of degradation'. He supported Fowell Buxton's motion for information on the Madras slave trade, 3 June, presented petitions for the suppression of suttee, 4 June, and on 5 June 1829 supported Hume's call for papers on the fees of proctors in Doctors' Commons and endorsed an petition in favour of native Indians being allowed to sit on grand juries. He told Lady Holland that he had 'seen no symptoms' of any approach by the beleaguered Wellington ministry to the Whigs 'if I must not number amongst them a shake of the hand with unwonted kindness which I had in St. James's Park from the great captain'. The following month he was 'a good deal vexed by my old enemy the brow ague', which had him 'stretched on the bed or the sofa' for a week.[149]

In the autumn of 1829 Mackintosh's wife left him for the last time, travelling first to Paris and on to the Sismondis near Geneva. Mackintosh, who had contracted to write a popular *History of England* for *The Cabinet Cyclopaedia*, went with Frances to visit the duc de Broglie in Normandy. On his return he told Lady Holland that 'I began to grow well almost as soon as we landed and have ever since been improving in strength, spirits and appetite'. He accepted her offer of a room at Holland House during the next session, although he could not 'afford many days to Parliament'.[150] In November Greville was in his company at Roehampton:

> It was uncommonly agreeable ... I never was more filled with admiration. His prodigious memory and the variety and extent of his information remind me of all I have heard and read of Burke and Johnson; but his amiable, modest, and unassuming character makes him far more agreeable ... while he is probably equally instructive and amusing ... I do not know of a greater treat than to hear him talk ... I could not help reflecting what an extraordinary thing success is in this world, when a man so gifted ... has failed completely in public life, never having attained honours, reputation, or wealth, while so many ordinary men have reaped an abundant harvest of all ... His virtues are obstacles to his success; he has not the art of pushing or of making himself feared; he is too *doucereux* and complimentary, and from some accident or defect in the composition of his character, and in the course of events which have influenced his circumstances, he has always been civilly neglected.[151]

Wilberforce, a Clapham neighbour, who regarded him as 'a paragon of a companion', heard at this time that he

> spends ... much of his time in the circulating library room at the end of the Common, and chats with the utmost freedom to all the passengers in the Clapham stage as he goes and comes from London. It is really to be regretted that he should thus throw away time so valuable. But he is at everybody's service, and his conversation is always rich and sparkling.[152]

Holland told Russell in December 1829 that Mackintosh had 'settled the state of our friends as usual in a phrase: "He never saw, he will not say, such difference of opinion, but such strong divergences of inclination among them"'.[153] He was present to vote for the amendment to the address, 4 Feb. 1830. The following day he attacked Lord Ellenborough, the president of the board of control, over his leaked letter concerning the renewal of the East India Company's charter. He was named to the select committee on the subject, 9 Feb. He supported Russell's motion calling for a fair and final settlement of Greece as 'the triumph of common sense and natural feeling over the worldly wise', 16 Feb. He voted for the transfer of East Retford's seats to Birmingham, 5 Mar. Feverish illness laid him low soon afterwards, but he attended to speak and vote for Jewish emancipation, 5 Apr.: 'Let us love our neighbours as ourselves, and not withhold any benefit or franchise from them, though they may happen to be as odious to us as the Samaritans were to the Jews'.[154] He was in O'Connell's minority of 47 for Irish vestry reform, 27 Apr., and the next day he supported the opposition motion condemning the government's conduct over the Terceira incident, a 'most flagrant violation' of the law of nations. Mackintosh, who does not seem to have been unduly affected by his wife's sudden death in Switzerland, 6 May 1830, presented an Edinburgh petition for abolition of the death penalty for forgery, 13 May, and on the 24th moved an amendment to Peel's forgery punishment bill to substitute transportation or hard labour for the death penalty for the forgery of bank notes and exchequer bills. It was defeated by 128-113; but on the third reading of the bill, 7 June (after voting against the grant for South American missions), he moved and carried broadly the same amendment, having, against his better judgement, excluded the forgery of wills, by 151-138. It was rejected by the Lords, reinstated by the Commons but not passed. Mackintosh paired for Russell's reform motion, 28 May. On 19 June he handled the second reading of the reintroduced Madras registrar bill, which, after he had conceded modifications, 9 July, became law on the 23rd. He secured a return of droits of the crown during the French wars in connection with a planned motion on the claims of British subjects on Denmark, 9 July 1830.

The first volume of Mackintosh's popular *History of England* was published that summer. It sold well, as did the second volume, which appeared in 1831, and had the approval of Russell, who thought its observations on European history were 'masterly'.[155] Devonshire offered him another return for Knaresborough, which he accepted, though his doctors deemed him to be too sickly to attend the election; he got Brougham to deputise for him.[156] Buoyed by events in France, he went at the beginning of September to Cresselly, where his health temporarily improved. He was at first reluctant to return to London for parliamentary attendance before 'absolute duty requires', feeling that a longer stay would help him to become 'better ... than I had ever hoped to be this side of the grave'; but he yielded to the blandishments of Lady Holland and went up for the opening, even though he professed that 'if I had courage I ought to cut the tie that binds me to Westminster'.[157] On 3 Nov. 1830, when he gave notice that he would present a petition from claimants on the Danish government, he witnessed Brougham's 'splendid speech':

> Many such triumphant displays of superiority in an opposition will be a trying test to the House of Commons ... Nevertheless I believe they [ministers] will try to swim ... The Tories seem to be dispirited and divided ... In the meantime the state of Europe is very alarming. We have lost in Guizot and Broglie our best security for the pacific character of the French government. Their successors are all what we should call a party between Whigs and Radicals ... They will not desire war. But the world is a step nearer to the danger of war since their promotion.[158]

He presented petitions for the abolition of slavery, 9, 10 Nov. He voted in the majority against the Wellington ministry on the civil list, 15 Nov. He wanted to be judge advocate in the Grey administration, but heard nothing definite and agonized in his suspense. Holland assured him that there were 'circumstances unknown to you which might if you had the option, alter your present preference ... to board of control'. This was what he was offered (at £1,500 a year) and accepted, apparently satisfied, as Holland reported, 'though aware that the other was £1,000 better'. Grey, who privately thought that 'with all his extraordinary talents and acquirements he was, practically, quite useless', disingenuously assured him that he had 'wished to offer you a situation more suited to your views and expectations, and I should have done so, had I found the spirit of accommodation which I had a right to expect in others'.[159] At the time Brougham told Holland that he thought that Mackintosh, who had 'very high claims indeed', even though he 'may not be up to much work', had been 'scurvily and I will add shamefully treated'. He later wrote that 'Grey and Co. never could bear him' and that Holland and Lansdowne, 'his sworn friends ... treated him as they always do their friends'.[160] When Croker attacked Brougham's appointment as lord chancellor in the House, 23 Nov., Mackintosh on 'impulse', and in the absence of senior ministers, repudiated his 'insinuations'. He went to Knaresborough for his re-election, 2 Dec., when there was a token show of opposition. Later in the month he observed bitterly to Lady Holland that 'nobody would tell anything to a man who has such a badge of inferiority as my office is at my age and parliamentary standing'. He was further irked to find that 'by the petty expedient of placing Macdonald above me in our commission (against routine) somebody has not only lowered me a peg but pointed me out as the commissioner to be reduced' if the finance committee so decided. He was worried about the political prospects of the new ministry, fearing that if the Tory opposition beat them on reform they would be placed in 'such a situation that by dissolving in such a temper they will frighten all the rich and by not dissolving they will lose all the influence over the reformers which is their only and slender chance of doing good'. He took a house in Great Cumberland Street, Westminster, at the end of the year.[161] Mackintosh, who was of course named to the revived East Indian select committee, 4 Feb., presented Scottish petitions for the abolition of slavery and for reform, 23 Feb. 1831. He presented and endorsed London corporation's reform petition, 4 Mar., taking the opportunity to defend the ministerial bill as 'the best safeguard of the liberties of the country'. He claimed that he bore the 'very close attendance' on the reform bill debates 'better than I could have hoped'. He voted silently for the second reading, 22 Mar. He was 'rather severely seized' on 15 Apr. 1831 'by one of my (of late very infrequent) bilious attacks', but was well enough to attend for the debate on Gascoigne's wrecking amendment on the 19th, though he was under orders 'not to try speaking or long sitting till I get a little stronger'. He voted against the amendment, but would have preferred the government not to have made their defeat 'decisive of the fate of the bill', which he thought 'extremely impolitic on all suppositions but one, namely that there is danger in delay which gives time for the play of intrigue'.[162]

He was obliged to go to Knaresborough for the 1831 general election, when he was returned unopposed and his speech was 'very well received'. He told Lady Holland that he had been led to believe by some of the electors that

> there is no doubt of my having one of the Knaresborough seats after the reformation. But it is hard to foresee the movements of the popular mind for a year or two which in these times may be equal to as many centuries in times of quiet. It would I suppose be best for me to retire and I am disposed to wish that I had done so in November.

He subsequently took the waters at Harrogate, claiming to be 'better than I have been for eight years', and promising to be in London in the first week of June:

> Notwithstanding our numbers we shall have no strength in the House of Commons for any purpose but the bill. We shall continue to be outspoken there. We are outweighed in respectable opinion out of doors. All the most faithful and old reformers of this country are I suspect more alarmed at the extent of the bill than they choose to confess. I believe that the more decent radicals would have liked the banquet better if there had been less of it. Those who are forced by the popular tide to vote for this reform may I fear take their revenge on other matters.[163]

Early in the new Parliament he wrote to Lady Holland from the Commons that 'I had no idea how unpleasant a parliamentary life that of a subaltern placeman is and I am not sure that it is worth while to continue it'.[164] He supported the petition of British merchants resident at Canton for better protection of their interests by the East India Company, 28 June. On 4 July he spoke for two hours in support of the second reading of the reintroduced reform bill, arguing that it sought to restore the balanced relationship between the three elements of the constitution and that the question was one of a choice between 'concession and bloodshed'. Hobhouse thought that he did 'very well indeed – rather "caviare to the general", but sound and profound'. Denis Le Marchant[†] described it as 'one of the last efforts of a philosophical and highly cultivated mind, and not unworthy of his brilliant reputation', though he 'looked very ill, and his voice was too weak to be heard with effect'. The minister Spring Rice considered it 'a very long, learned and well reasoned dissertation in favour of the bill, but it was rather too cold and abstract for our temperature. It was however extremely good indeed'. Henry Lytton Bulwer* recalled the performance as

> remarkable. Overflowing with thought and knowledge, containing sound general principles as to government, undisfigured by the violence of party spirit, it pleased and instructed those who took the pains to listen to it attentively; but it wanted the qualities which attract or command attention ... The speaker's person ... was gaunt and ungainly, his accent Scotch, his voice monotonous, his action (the regular and graceless vibration of two long arms) sometimes vehement, without passion, and sometimes almost cringing, through good nature and civility.[165]

The following day Mackintosh corrected the impression given by press reports that he had stated that 'political privileges were property': he had said exactly the opposite. He was in the majority for the bill, 6 July. He had taken a pair for the all-night divisions on adjournment motions, 12 July.[166] On the 28th, when he was 'recovering rather slowly' from 'an attack of sick headaches', he told Lady Holland that he was required to be present for 'almost every division' on the details of the bill, but that 'I pass the greater part of the evening in an adjoining room ... [where] I read novels'. He was not entirely happy with the performance of the ministers in the front line, who were

> far from rising in general estimation. Most people own to their intimate friends that the campaign in the committee has shown no generalship. They have neither firmly adhered to their rules nor liberally relaxed them with an equal hand. I and many others when we voted with them in some cases were obliged to consider the votes as given to protect them from the consequences of their own fluctuation.[167]

He was in the ministerial majorities on the 1831 census, 19 July, St. Germans and Saltash, 26 July, Dorchester, 28 July, Guildford, 29 July, and Greenwich, 3 Aug.; but a 'stomach attack' which turned out to be 'a bilious fever' and, so he claimed, endangered his life, put him out of action for the rest of that month; he was sent 'by medical advice and political permission' to Ramsgate on the 21st 'in hopes of quickening my recovery by change and by the sea'.[168] He was present to vote in the minority of 20 against the quarantine duties, 6 Sept. He divided for the passage of the reform bill, 21 Sept., and on the 23rd spoke and voted for the second reading of the Scottish bill, which he again defended, as bestowing for the first time 'a popular representation', 4 Oct. He voted for Lord Ebrington's confidence motion, 14 Oct. He supported the prayer of a petition from Lower Canada for redress of grievances, 14 Oct. He remained extremely interested in the problem of Portugal, advised the exiled Palmella, and at the end of October 1831 wrote to Holland recommending recognition of Donna Maria's regency and the offer of a joint mediation with France.[169]

He remained 'weary' of his junior situation at the board of control, and told Lady Holland that he had applied 'in strict confidence' to his chief Charles Grant* for the vacant office of chief justice of Bengal: 'as I rather expected he for reasons perfectly satisfactory to me declined to appoint me'. In late October 1831 Macdonald told Brougham that he was willing to retire from the board of control to accommodate the rising star Tom Macaulay* if ministers wished to bring him in. Brougham, informing Holland, said that any promotion of Macaulay over Mackintosh's head would be 'preferring *interest* to *gratitude*', and was 'not to be thought of'. Holland replied:

> I quite agree in all you say about Mackintosh. You had better say as much to Grey, who is himself well prepared, for he asked me if Robert Grant* [the judge advocate] would not like to go chief justice to Bengal, and if you would approve such an appointment, to which I could only answer from conjecture, not knowledge, that I thought and hoped both would approve of such an arrangement if, as he had before hinted, it was for the purpose of making Mackintosh king's advocate, and introducing Macaulay into the board of control. Grey dropped something about Mackintosh's health or want of energy, but you and I and above all the truth can remove that impression, for Mackintosh is more than equal to the business of king's advocate, which he would do admirably, and *being pleased* would be infinitely more active and useful in the Commons than he is now, and to the full as much as Robert Grant.[170]

Nothing came of this.

Mackintosh, who moved his London residence to Langham Place at the end of the year, voted for the second reading of the final reform bill, 17 Dec. 1831, and for the borough disfranchisement clauses, 20, 23 Jan. 1832. He was in the ministerial majority on the Russian-Dutch loan, 26 Jan. He supported the principle of restricting factory hours for children, 1 Feb., placing considerations of humanity above devotion to the principles of political economy. He voted for clause 27 of the reform bill, 3 Feb. In his last speech in the Commons, 9 Feb., he opposed Courtenay's motion for papers on Portugal, defended the British and French governments and condemned Dom Miguel. After leaving the House on the evening of Friday the 17th he had an accident while 'hurrying through a lonely dinner', as he explained to Allen:

> I unwarily suffered a large morsel of chicken containing a pointed bone to go over almost unchecked or rather unscratched by teeth. I was nearly suffocated and ... I continued very ill Saturday and Sunday. But [Dr.] Kennedy ... with the help of well mixed coaxing and command on Monday got me to take a mustard emetic which produces its effect in three or four minutes and removes the contents of the stomach without an instant's loathing. In my case it brought up immediately one of the largest pieces of flesh and bone which has been commonly removed from a living gullet. This mishap has caused a complete salivation which is very much better today. But I am advised not to venture abroad till it quite ceases.

Mackintosh, who was still privately 'very anxious about the determination of our leaders', was able to vote for the enfranchisement of Tower Hamlets, 28 Feb.[171] But the wound in his throat became infected and inflammation spread eventually to his spine and brain. He struggled on for a few weeks, able to conduct minimal departmental business and to visit Holland House; but in May he took to his death bed in Langham Place, finding consolation in a 'declaration of religious belief ... when he had never believed at all during his life'. He died at the end of the month, 'a great public and private loss', as Whishaw saw it, and, in the view of Holland, 'some loss in politics and much greater in society, and the greatest of all in literature, where his knowledge, good nature and talents rendered him most useful and delightful'.[172] He was buried in the family plot at Hampstead on 4 June. A subscription set up by friends of both parties paid for a memorial to him in Whigs' Corner, Westminster Abbey.[173] By his brief will of January 1826 (which, typically, he forgot to have witnessed) he had left such property as he possessed to his wife, with remainder to his daughter Frances. On 5 July 1832 administration of his estate, which was proved under £8,000, was granted to her, Mackintosh's only surviving son and future biographer Robert James, a fellow of New College, Oxford, and his niece Elizabeth Wedgwood. The residue was assessed for duty at £1,888, but debts and expenses left only £863 to be shared among his five surviving children. His library, which proved to be 'not a very valuable or important collection', was sold over nine days in November 1832.[174] A third volume of his *History of England* was published posthumously that year, while William Wallace completed and published his *History of the Revolution of 1688* in 1834. His massive collection of notes passed to Macaulay, who made better use of it than he had.

Macaulay had a soft spot for Mackintosh, who had been kind to him in his early days in Parliament, and wrote that

> his proper place was his library, a circle of men of letters, or a chair of moral and political philosophy. He distinguished himself highly in Parliament. But nevertheless Parliament was not exactly the sphere for him. The effect of his most successful speeches was small when compared with the quantity of ability and learning which was expended on them.

He observed that Mackintosh was 'a man who would have done something if he had concentrated his powers instead of frittering them away':

> He halted between two opinions. He fell between two stools. He attended too much to politics for a man engaged in a great literary work, and too much to literature for a man who aimed at great influence in politics. Society, too ... stole away too much of his time both from Parliament and from his study.[175]

Lytton Bulwer wrote perceptively of Mackintosh:

> Though it was difficult to fix on any one thing in which he was first-rate, it was generally maintained that he was a first-rate man ... Though mixing in the action of a great and stirring community ... [he] never arrived at an eminence in law, in letters, or in politics that satisfied the expectations of those who, living in his society, were impressed by his intellect and astonished at his acquirements ... [He] was not fit for the daily toil and struggle of Parliament; he had not the quickness, the energy, the hard and active nature of those who rise by constant exertions in popular assemblies ... He was ... inclined by his nature rather to repose than to strife ... His striking, peculiar, and unrivalled merit ... was that of a conversationalist. Great good nature, great and yet gentle animation, much learning, and a sound, discriminating, and comprehensive judgement, made him this ... He knew everything and could talk of everything without being tedious ... He ever remained the *man of promise*; until, amidst hopes which his vast and various information, his wonderful memory, his copious elocution, and his transitory fits of energy, still nourished, he died ... universally admired and regretted, though without a high reputation for any one thing, or the ardent attachment of any particular set of persons.[176]

[1] The latest biography is P. O'Leary, *Sir James Mackintosh: the Whig Cicero* (1989), which, though useful in many respects, is weak on politics and carries no scholarly apparatus. See also *Mems. of Sir James Mackintosh* ed. R.J. Mackintosh (1836) and J. Rendall, 'The Political Ideas and Activities of Sir James Mackintosh (1765-1832): a Study in Whiggism between 1789 and 1832' (London Univ. Ph.D. thesis, 1972). This article draws extensively on Mackintosh's journals, which are in the form of letters to his wife, 1820, 1821-3, 1825-8 (Add. 52444, 52445, 52447). [2] *HP Commons, 1790-1820*, iv. 498 incorrectly describes him as the only son of John Mackintosh; but he had a younger brother John (1769-1800). [3] B. and H. Wedgwood, *The Wedgwood Circle*, 153. [4] *Mackintosh Mems.* ii. 500-2. [5] *Moore Mems.* vi. pp. xi-xii, 292. [6] O'Leary, 181-5; Wedgwood, 159, 163, 171. [7] *Fox Jnl.* 84. [8] *Life, Letters and Jnls. of George Ticknor* ed. G.S. Hillard, i. 265, 289-90. [9] Reid, *Monckton Milnes*, i. 100. [10] *Losh Diaries* ed. E. Hughes (Surtees Soc. clxxi), i. 95. [11] Add. 51653, Mackintosh to Holland, 27 [29] Feb. 1820. [12] *Russell Early Corresp.* i. 205. [13] Ibid. i. 210. [14] Chatsworth mss, Mackintosh to Devonshire, 29 Feb. 1820. [15] Add. 52444, ff. 87-88, 93. [16] Ibid. f. 106. [17] Add. 51654. [18] *Althorp Letters*, 106; *Cockburn Mems.* 348; O'Leary, 144; Add. 51653, Mackintosh to Holland, 18, 24 Apr.; 51659, Whishaw to Lady Holland, 24 Apr. 1820; 52444, ff. 109-13, 116-17; 52453, ff. 30-38, 42-49. [19] Add. 52444, f. 114. [20] Ibid. f. 122. [21] Ibid. ff. 125-7. [22] Ibid. ff. 149-51. [23] Ibid. ff. 120, 133, 146, 174-7. [24] Ibid. f. 180. [25] Ibid. ff. 118, 121, 158, 177, 183, 185, 188, 190-1; *CJ*, lxxv. 173-4, 229, 325-6, 355-6, 394-5, 467, 469, 470-1, 477. [26] Add. 51653, Mackintosh to Holland [2 July]; 51654, to Lady Holland [11 July 1820]; 52444, f. 192. [27] Add. 51653, Mackintosh to Holland, 6 Aug. 1820; 52444, ff. 197-8, 203-4. [28] Add. 51654, Mackintosh to Lady Holland, 8 Sept., 15, 23 Oct., 3 Nov.; 51686, Lansdowne to Holland, 27 Nov. [1820]. [29] *Moore Mems.* iii. 177. [30] Grey mss, Tierney to Grey, 7 Dec.; Add. 51653, Mackintosh to Holland, 22 Dec. [1820]. [31] *Edinburgh Rev.* xxxiv (1820), 464-501; *Russell Early Corresp.* i. 217; *Losh Diaries*, i. 126; Ward, *Llandaff Letters*, 276-7. [32] Castle Howard mss, Howard to Lady Morpeth, 28 [Jan. 1821]; Add. 43212, f. 180; HLRO, Hist. Coll. 379, Grey Bennet diary, 6. [33] Grey Bennet diary, 13; Dorset RO D/BKL, Bankes jnl. 123. [34] *'Pope' of Holland House* ed. Lady Seymour, 234. [35] Grey Bennet diary, 26; Bankes jnl. 124. [36] Add. 51653, Mackintosh to Holland, 31 Jan. 1821; Rendall, 249. [37] Bankes jnl. 126. [38] Add. 51667, Bedford to Holland [16 Mar. 1821]. [39] *The Times*, 24, 27 Mar., 3 Apr.; Agar Ellis diary, 23 Mar.; Add. 51654, Mackintosh to Lady Holland [28 Mar. 1821]; Broughton, *Recollections*, ii. 144. [40] Trinity Coll. Camb. Dawson Turner mss DT2/K2/3. [41] Add. 52182, Mackintosh to Allen, 10 [11] Apr. 1821. [42] Add. 51659, Whishaw to Lady Holland, 30 May; 51679, Russell to same, 24 May 1821. [43] Grey Bennet diary, 86. [44] *The Times*, 18, 26 May, 1, 5 June 1821; *CJ*, lxxvi. 250, 354-5, 402, 413. [45] Grey Bennet diary, 93. [46] Ibid. 103. [47] *Life of Wilberforce*, v. 101; Grey Bennet diary, 105. [48] *The Times*, 3 July 1821. [49] Grey Bennet diary, 107-8, 121. [50] Add. 51654, Mackintosh to Lady Holland, 15, 30 July; 52182, to Allen, 15 July; 52445, ff. 7, 12, 17; Lansdowne mss, Mackintosh to Lansdowne, 23 Aug. 1821. [51] Wedgwood, 190, 193; Add. 51586, Tierney to Lady Holland, 11, 13 Oct. [1821]. [52] Add. 51653, Mackintosh to Holland, 18 Dec., reply, 20 Dec. 1821; Add. 52445, f. 7; O'Leary, 31-33, 84-85, 145-6. [53] Lansdowne mss, Mackintosh to Lansdowne, 28 Dec. 1821. [54] Add. 51659, Whishaw to Lady Holland, 20 Jan.; 52182, Mackintosh to Allen, 20 Jan. 1822. [55] *Edgeworth Letters*, 332. [56] Add. 51654, Mackintosh to Lady Holland, 27 [29] Jan. 1822; 52445, ff. 25-38. [57] Add. 30115, f. 26; 52445, ff. 39-54; *Edgeworth Letters*, 354. [58] Add. 52445, ff. 56-61. [59] Ibid. ff. 63-64; HLRO, HC Lib. Ms89, Moulton Barrett diary, 13 Mar. 1822. [60] Add. 52445, ff. 66-73. [61] Ibid. ff. 78-81; *Fox Jnl.* 113. [62] Add. 52445, ff. 82-83. [63] Ibid. ff. 84-85. [64] Agar Ellis diary, 4 June [1822]. [65] Add. 40347, f. 169; *Fox Jnl.* 123. [66] Add. 52445, f. 86. [67] Gurney diary, 14 June 1822; Add. 52445, ff. 90-91. [68] Add. 52445, f. 88. [69] *Fox Jnl.* 127. [70] Add. 52445, f. 92. [71] Ibid. f. 94. [72] Ibid. f. 100. [73] *The Times*, 18 July 1822. [74] Add. 52445, f. 93. [75] Add. 51654, Mackintosh to Lady Holland, 13, 15, 20 Aug. 1822. [76] Add. 40319, f. 57. [77] Add. 51679, Russell to Lady Holland [18, 20 Oct. 1822]. [78] Add. 51659, Whishaw to Lady Holland, 22 Oct. 1822. [79] Add. 34613, ff. 112, 115; 51579, Morpeth to Lady Holland, 26 Oct.; 51586, Tierney to same, 28 Oct.; 51653, Mackintosh to Holland, 27 Oct., 10 Nov.; 51654, to Lady Holland, 23 Oct.; 51659, Whishaw to same, 29 Oct. [8 Nov.] 1822; *Fox Jnl.* 149. [80] Agar Ellis diary, 28 Dec. [1822]. [81] Add. 51653, Mackintosh to Holland, 4, 8, 12 Dec., reply, 6 Dec.; 52445, ff. 107-8, 110-11. [82] *Cockburn Letters*, 76; *Fox Jnl.* 152. [83] *Cockburn Mems.* 378; Add. 51574, Abercromby to Holland [21 Jan.]; Grey mss, Grey to same, 22 Jan. 1823; *Smith Letters*, i. 394-5. [84] Gurney diary, 4 Feb. [1823]. [85] Add. 52445, f. 112. [86] *The Times*, 15 Feb. 1823. [87] Christ Church, Oxf. Phillimore mss, Mackintosh to Phillimore, Mon., Fri. [Mar.], 13 Mar. 1823. [88] Ibid. 19 Mar.; Wellington mss, Wellington to Mrs. Arbuthnot, 18 Mar. [1823]. [89] *The Times*, 8 Mar.; Bessborough mss, Brougham to Duncannon [10 Mar.]; Add. 51667, Bedford to Lady Holland, 25 Mar. [1823]. [90] Brougham mss, Russell to Brougham [23 Mar. 1823]. [91] O'Leary, 152-3. [92] *The Times*, 23 Apr. 1823. [93] *Specimens of the Table Talk of Coleridge* (1835), i. 24-25. [94] *Von Neumann Diary*, i. 124-5; *The Times*, 14 June 1823. [95] *Life of Wilberforce*, v. 186. [96] *The Times*, 21 June 1823. [97] Ibid. 10 July 1823. [98] Ibid. 5 July 1823. [99] O'Leary, 154-5; Add. 51659, Whishaw to Lady Holland, 20 July 1823; 52445, ff. 116-38. [100] Add. 51654, Mackintosh to Lady Holland, 8 Nov. 19 Dec.; 51659, Whishaw to same, 3 Nov.; 51579, Morpeth to same, 25

Dec. 1823. [101] Add. 51659, Whishaw to Lady Holland, 22 Jan.; 51668, Bedford to same [18 Jan. 1824]; *Lady Holland to Son*, 25; Broughton, iii. 30; *Life of Wilberforce*, v. 213. [102] Add. 51667, Bedford to Lady Holland [16 Mar. 1824]. [103] Agar Ellis diary, 18 Mar. [1824]. [104] TNA 30/29/9/5/22, 24; Add. 51653, Mackintosh to Holland, 20 Mar.; 51654, to Lady Holland [20 Mar.]; 51667, Bedford to same [28 Mar.] 1824. [105] *Buxton Mems.* 135-6; *The Times*, 26 Mar. 1824; *Life of Wilberforce*, v. 222. [106] *Croker Pprs.* i. 266; *The Times*, 4, 8 May 1824. [107] *The Times*, 18, 23 June 1824. [108] Lady Knutsford, *Life and Letters of Zachary Macaulay*, 421-2; O'Leary, 157. [109] Add. 30115, f. 28; 51654, Mackintosh to Lady Holland, 3, 29 Aug.; 51679, Russell to same, 4 Oct. [1824]; 52446A and B. [110] *Fox Jnl.* 198. [111] W. Hazlitt, *Spirit of the Age* ed. E.D. Mackerness (1969), 151-3. [112] Merthyr Mawr mss F/2/8 (14 Feb. 1825); Bankes jnl. 153. [113] *The Times*, 26 Feb. 1825. [114] Brougham mss, Mackintosh to Brougham, 16, 17 Mar. 1825. [115] Add. 52447, ff. 1-6; O'Leary, 161-2. [116] PROB 11/1803/453; Add. 52448, f. 17. [117] Add. 51655, Mackintosh to Lady Holland, 18, 27 Aug., 8 Oct. 1825; 52447, ff. 11-25. [118] Lansdowne mss. [119] Add. 51655, Mackintosh to Lady Holland, 23 Jan., 18 Feb.; 51659, Whishaw to same, 26 Jan. 1826; *Russell Early Corresp.* i. 246. [120] Add. 36462, f. 170; 40385, f. 177; 51659, Whishaw to Lady Holland, 14 May; 51668, Bedford to same, 27 May 1826; 52453, f. 109; Chatsworth mss 6DD/GPI/1263. [121] *Lady Holland to Son*, 43, 49-50; Add. 51653, Mackintosh to Holland [Aug.]; 51655, same to Lady Holland [24], 29 Aug., 1 Sept. 1826; 52447, ff. 27-29; O'Leary, 165-9. [122] Add. 51653, Mackintosh to Holland, 1 Oct.; 51655, to Lady Holland, 24 Oct., 12 Nov., 6 Dec.; 51813, Scarlett to same, 5 Sept. 1826. [123] Add. 51655, Mackintosh to Lady Holland, 21 [27] Feb., 23, 30 Mar. 1827; 52447, ff. 39-60. [124] Add. 51653, Mackintosh to Holland, 19 Apr.; 52182, to Allen, 20 Apr.; 52447, f. 105; Lansdowne mss, Mackintosh to Lansdowne, 22 Apr. 1827. [125] Add. 51655, Mackintosh to Lady Holland, 29 Apr. 1827; 52447, ff. 105-7; *Canning's Ministry*, 241, 265, 276. [126] Add. 51655, Mackintosh to Lady Holland [1] [6], 11, 27 May, 1 June; 52447, ff. 61-68, 107-8; 52453, ff. 132, 134; *Canning's Ministry*, 299; Lansdowne mss, Mackintosh to Lansdowne, 20 May 1827. [127] Add. 51569, Whishaw to Lady Holland, 16 June 1827. [128] Lansdowne mss, Mackintosh to Lansdowne, 20, 27 May 1827. [129] Add. 52447, ff. 69-77, 81-82, 84; *Geo. IV Letters*, iii. 1348. [130] Add. 52447, ff. 85-97, 108-10; 52453, f. 146. [131] Add. 51655; 52447, ff. 113-14, 146; Lansdowne mss. [132] Bucks. RO, Fremantle mss D/FR/138/21/2/17. [133] Add. 38750, f. 180; 51655, Mackintosh to Lady Holland, 7, 20 Sept.; 51687, Lansdowne to Holland, 2, 5 Sept.; 51690, to Lady Holland, 16 Sept. 1827; *Greville Mems.* i. 189. [134] Brougham mss, Mackintosh to Brougham, 4 Oct.; Add. 51655, to Lady Holland, 8 Oct. [15 Nov.] 1827. [135] Add. 51655, Mackintosh to Lady Holland [19 Nov. 1827]; 52447, ff. 117-18, 127, 140-1. [136] Add. 51653, Mackintosh to Holland, 3 Dec.; 51655, to Lady Holland [19], 26 Nov., 14 Dec. 1827; 52447, ff. 117-18. [137] Add. 36464, f. 212; 51653, Mackintosh to Holland, 1 Feb.; 51655, to Lady Holland [5], 23 Jan.; 52182, to Allen, 11 Jan. 1828; 52447, ff. 146-7; 52453, f. 172. [138] *Croker Pprs.* i. 418. [139] Harewood mss, Cavendish Bentinck to Lady Canning, 14 May 1828. [140] *The Times*, 9 July 1828. [141] Brougham mss, Mackintosh to Z. Macaulay, 26 July 1828. [142] Add. 34613, ff. 402, 415, 419, 428, 446, 450; 34614, ff. 1, 5, 12, 14-17, 19, 22, 55, 57, 67, 77, 94, 105, 119, 131, 138, 154, 160, 225, 263, 375; 51655, Mackintosh to Lady Holland [Sept.] [6 Nov. 1828]. [143] Add. 51659. [144] Add. 51655, Mackintosh to Lady Holland, 17 Dec. [Dec.] 1828 [23], 24 Jan. 1829. [145] Add. 76369, Althorp to Brougham, 14 Feb.; Brougham mss, Abercromby to Brougham [c. 16 Mar. 1829]. [146] Broughton, iii. 311. [147] Add. 52447, ff. 148-51; *Cockburn Letters*, 211. [148] Add. 34614, f. 50; 51655, Mackintosh to Lady Holland, 30 Apr. [1829]. [149] Add. 34614, f. 138; 51655, Mackintosh to Lady Holland [5 June], 31 July 1829. [150] O'Leary, 178; *Greville Mems.* i. 325-6; Add. 51655, Mackintosh to Lady Holland, 20 Oct. [1829]. [151] *Greville Mems.* i. 328-30. [152] *Life of Wilberforce*, v. 314-15. [153] *Russell Early Corresp.* i. 297. [154] Add. 51655, Mackintosh to Lady Holland [4 Apr. 1830]. [155] O'Leary, 190-1; Add. 51655, Mackintosh to Lady Holland [July]; 51677, Russell to Holland [26 July 1830]. [156] Add. 51655, Mackintosh to Lady Holland [July]; Brougham mss, to Brougham, 31 July 1830; Chatsworth mss 6DD/GPI/1997. [157] Add. 34614, f. 375; 51655, Mackintosh to Lady Holland, 27 Aug., 26 Sept., 3, 15 Oct.; 51659, Whishaw to same, 12 Sept.; 52182, Mackintosh to Allen, 7 Oct. 1830. [158] Add. 51655, Mackintosh to Lady Holland, 3 Nov. 1830; 52453, f. 194. [159] Add. 51655, Mackintosh to Lady Holland [Nov.]; 52453, ff. 196, 198; Grey mss, Lansdowne to Grey [19 Nov.], Holland to Grey [20 Nov. 1830], Grey to Holland, 2 Nov. 1835; Harrowby mss, Sandon to Harrowby, 19, 25 Nov. 1830. [160] Add. 51562, Brougham to Holland [?29 Nov. 1830]; *Corresp. of Macvey Napier* ed. M. Napier, 251. [161] Add. 51655, Mackintosh to Lady Holland, 2 [18, 22] Dec. 1830. [162] Ibid. Mackintosh to Lady Holland [3, 8, 21 Mar., 19 Apr. 1831]. [163] Ibid. Mackintosh to Lady Holland [24 Apr.], 4, 18 May 1831. [164] Ibid. Mackintosh to Lady Holland, Mon. [?6 June 1831]. [165] Broughton, iv. 119; Le Marchant, *Althorp*, 328; Add. 51573, Rice to Lady Holland [4 July 1831]; Bulwer, *Hist. Characters*, ii. 51. [166] *The Times*, 16 July 1831. [167] Add. 51655. [168] Ibid. Mackintosh to Lady Holland, 25 Aug. 1831. [169] *Holland House Diaries*, 61, 72-73; Add. 51653, Mackintosh to Holland, 31 Oct. 1831. [170] *Holland House Diaries*, 72; Add. 51563, Brougham to Holland [bef. 27 Oct.]; 51655, Mackintosh to Lady Holland, Sat. [Oct.]; Brougham mss, Holland to Brougham, 27 Oct. [1831]. [171] Add. 51565, Mackintosh to Lady Holland [19 Feb.]; 52182, to Allen [22 Feb. 1832]. [172] *Mackintosh Mems.* ii. 484-9; Eg. 3718, f. 22; Add. 51655, Mackintosh to Lady Holland [26 Apr. 1832]; *Losh Diaries* (Surtees Soc. clxxiv), ii. 138; Broughton, iv. 237; *Greville Mems.* iii. 266; *'Pope' of Holland House*, 258; *Holland House Diaries*, 190; *Gent. Mag.* (1832), ii. 81-83. [173] *Althorp Letters*, 157; *Gent. Mag.* (1832), ii. 660; O'Leary, 204-5, 207. [174] PROB 11/1803/453; IR26/1296/319; O'Leary, 207; *Gent. Mag.* (1832), ii. 560. [175] *Edinburgh Rev.* lxi (1835), 268; *Macaulay Letters*, iii. 151; iv. 23, 96. [176] Bulwer, ii. 3-4, 59, 91-92.

D.R.F.

MACKWORTH PRAED, Winthrop (1802–1839), of 2 Brick Court, Temple, Mdx.[1]

ST. GERMANS	17 Dec. 1830–1832
GREAT YARMOUTH	1835–1837
AYLESBURY	1837–15 July 1839

b. 26 July 1802, 3rd surv. s. of William Mackworth Praed (*d.* 1835) of John Street, Bedford Row, Mdx. and Bitton Court, Teignmouth, Devon and Elizabeth, da. of Benjamin Winthrop, gov. Bank of England. *educ.* Langley Broom sch., Colnbrook, Bucks. (Mr. Atkins) 1810; Eton 1814-21; Trinity Coll. Camb. 1821, BA 1825, fellow 1827, MA 1828; M. Temple 1825, called 1829. *m.* 7 July 1835, Helen, da. of George Bogle of Effingham House, Surr., 2da. *d.* 15 July 1839.

Jt.-sec. to bd. of control Dec. 1834-Apr. 1835.

In Parliament I fill my seat,
With many other noodles;
And lay my head in Jermyn Street,
And sip my hock at Boodles.
But often, when the cares of life
Have set my temples aching,
When visions haunt me of a wife,
When duns await my waking ...
I wish that I could run away

From House, and Court, and Levee,
Where bearded men appear today
Just Eton boys, grown heavy;
That I could bask in childhood's sun,
And dance o'er childhood's roses,
And find huge wealth in one pound one,
Vast wit in broken noses;
And play Sir Giles at Datchet Lane,
And call the milk-maids Houris;
That I could be a boy again,
A happy boy, at Drury's.[2]

So wrote Praed in his best known poem, *School and Schoolfellows*, a homage to Eton, which in spirit he never left. There was some substance to Thomas Macaulay's* comment that Praed, his friend at Cambridge, but his opponent in Parliament, had 'gone forth into the world a schoolboy and [was] doomed to be a schoolboy to the last'.[3]

His father (1756-1835) was the son of a partner in the family banks at Falmouth and Truro and first cousin of William Praed† (1747-1833), founder of the London bank of Praed's and Company. He pursued a legal career, enjoyed a lucrative chancery practice, became a serjeant-at-law in 1801 and from 1806 until his retirement on a pension of £1,000 in 1821 was chairman of the audit board. Winthrop, his fourth child, was precocious but delicate and showed an early talent for poetry. At Eton he gained a brilliant reputation as a scholar, writer and debater. In 1820 he produced a manuscript magazine, *Apis Matina*, which ran to six issues. It was printed by the Windsor publisher Charles Knight, who later wrote:

> I was more and more astonished by the unbounded fertility of his mind and the readiness of his resources ... the kindness that lurks under sarcasm; the wisdom that wears the mask of fun; the half-melancholy that is veiled by levity; – these qualities very soon struck me as far out of the ordinary indications of precocious talent ... The Etonian of 1820 was natural and unaffected in his ordinary talk; neither shy nor presuming; proud, without a tinge of vanity; somewhat reserved, but ever courteous ... a pale and slight youth, who had looked upon the aspects of society with the keen perception of a clever manhood; one who had, moreover, seen in human life something more than follies to be ridiculed by the gay jest or scouted by the sarcastic sneer.[4]

Praed enhanced his reputation at Cambridge, where the highest academic honours eluded him but his verses won him an unprecedented haul of medals. With Macaulay, two years his senior, and Charles Austin he dominated debates in the revived union. His contemporary, Edward Lytton Bulwer*, recalled:

> There was a fascination in the very name of this young man which eclipsed the repute of all his contemporaries ... The outlines of his genius were not definitely marked. They vanished away when you sought to seize them ... A political career seemed to be his natural destiny. With all these high animal spirits and strong tendencies, Praed's moral habits were singularly pure ... And yet ... there were touches in his character, tones in his mind, which ... chilled the sympathy, checked the affection, and sometimes even lowered the estimation, with which I regarded him.

He was noted for mild 'republican' tendencies, though his political opinions were probably lightly worn. Of his oratory Bulwer wrote:

> First in readiness and wit, in extempore reply, in aptness of argument and illustration, in all that belongs to the 'stage play' of delivery was unquestionably Praed; but he wanted all the higher gifts of eloquence: he had no passion, he had little power; he confided too much in his facility, and prepared so lightly the matter of his speeches, that they were singularly deficient in knowledge and substance.[5]

Praed had a quick temper, and he almost fought a duel with a fellow undergraduate after an argument over the date of the battle of Bunker Hill. His literary output continued unabated: he was the chief contributor to Knight's *Quarterly Magazine* in 1822, published *Lillian, a Fairy Tale* the following year, worked with Knight on the short-lived *Brazen Head* weekly paper in 1826 and contributed numerous verses, some on political themes, to the *Morning Chronicle*.[6]

In 1825 Praed returned to Eton as private tutor to Lord Ailesbury's second son and began studying for the bar. He won a fellowship at Trinity in 1827, became a pupil in chambers in January 1829 and was called five months later. He went the Norfolk circuit, with scant initial success, but was bent on a parliamentary career. Although he worked for the Whigs in the Cambridge University by-election of June 1829 he was increasingly out of sympathy with the more extreme aspects of their politics. The passage of Catholic emancipation, which he had always strongly supported, removed the only major obstacle to his alignment with the liberal Tories, which was probably also encouraged by his friendship with Edward Fitzgerald, private secretary to the home secretary Peel's close friend William Vesey Fitzgerald*, president of the board of trade in the duke of Wellington's ministry.[7] In February 1830, just after Macaulay's return to Parliament on the opposition side, Praed told his sister that the two ministers had sounded Fitzgerald as to his willingness to be 'pitted against' Macaulay in the House:

> Fitzgerald answered as I should have done, that my friendship with Macaulay was the closest possible; and that I should certainly refuse to occupy any post in which I should be expected to place myself in personal collision with any man. Then, as to my general principles and opinions, he said he had not observed anything in them which should prevent me from giving generally my support to the present administration.

A seat for Wenlock was said to be intended for him, but by 2 Mar. 1830 the negotiations were at an end, and his planned introduction to the party leaders got no further than Vesey Fitzgerald's successor John Herries*. Praed did not find an opening at the general election, but in December 1830 he was offered through Herries a vacant seat for Lord St. Germans's pocket borough, guaranteed for two years at a cost of £1,000. He had misgivings over the financial risk, the wisdom of joining a party now in opposition and his elder brothers' lack of enthusiasm, but decided to take the plunge, as he told his sister:

> All my friends have been dinning in my ears for the last five years, 'Go into Parliament; that is your sphere of action'. If they are wrong the sooner I know the better. I shall get rid of the vexatious feeling 'I might, I might, I might', which is the stumbling-block in the way of all progress.

To his father he explained:

> I am to hold myself at liberty to take in all questions such a line as appears good to my own discretion, it having been previously recognized that my sentiments in most of the matters likely to be discussed are in unison with those of the men who bring me into notice.[8]

After his election he was detained for a few days by 'a trifling but very troublesome disorder' at his father's Devon residence, whence he wrote to Herries, 25 Dec. 1830:

> Until you first honoured me by your notice I never dreamed of being where I am ... I am very grateful for all you have done for me, and ... my old longings after distinction become doubly eager from the desire I feel to show myself not quite unworthy of your good word. I have always told my friends, and I have said as much to you, that I have been an overrated man, and that my services are likely to be scarcely worthy the asking. If it should prove so, I hope people will forget that you ever took up a blockhead ... If I have better fortune than my fears prophecy, I shall hold myself your debtor for the larger half [sic] of whatever success may be my lot in the career you have opened to me.[9]

On his arrival in London Praed gave Herries his ideas for the improvement of the Tory opposition's connections with the press and offered personally to 'grapple with the *Morning Chronicle* as the organ of the government'. He had already made contributions in verse to the *Albion* evening paper, started in the week of Wellington's resignation.[10] He was soon dismayed by the parliamentary scene, as he told his friend Derwent Coleridge:

> The House appears to me day by day more awful ... I begin to find that, after all, I must have recourse to the trite old motive, the hope of doing good ... Personal distinction or profit, even if either were of probable acquirement in the road I travel, would scarcely support me through the horrors of a debut.

Haunted by the fear of failure, he was uncomfortable under the common assumption that he had been returned to take on Macaulay, with its concomitant insinuation that he was a political turncoat, and sought in private to establish his credentials as a free agent. To one correspondent he denied that he had been returned 'for the purpose of serving the views of any particular party' or 'of opposing any particular *man*':

> I pay quite enough for my honour and glory, to be quite independent of any chief or patron; and what sins I may commit must be taxed on my own free will, and on the dictation of no peer or patronage.

He assured another correspondent that, contrary to the story that he was 'pledged to vote against the Whigs'

> there is no man in the House more at liberty to follow his own inclinations. My old college opinions have, however, been considerably modified by subsequent acquaintance with the world ... I am not going to stem a torrent, but I confess I should like to confine its fury within some bounds. I am in no small degree an alarmist ... So my part in political matters will probably expose me to all sorts of abuse for ratting ... I abandon the party, if ever I belonged to it, in which my friends and my interests are both to be found, and I adopt one where I can hope to obtain nothing but a barren reputation, and the consciousness of meaning well. If all I hear be correct ... the Whigs find the machine going a little too fast, and are not sorry that some should be found to put on the drag.[11]

Praed made his carefully prepared maiden speech, for which Macaulay was 'impatient', on the Grey ministry's budget, 14 Feb. 1831, when he criticized the proposal to substitute a duty on raw cotton for that on printed calicoes.[12] Greville reckoned it 'very good', Herries said that Praed 'understood his subject perfectly' and Mrs. Arbuthnot was told that 'everybody considered the speech excellent' and 'the most promising debut ... for years'.[13] Some had reservations: the

Whig Denis Le Marchant† wrote that 'it was thought promising, though his manner is priggish and his voice monotonous'; and on Praed's side of the House, Lord Henry Cholmondeley considered it was 'not perhaps well suited to a new Member', as he '*set the House right* too much about taxes'.[14] Thomas Gladstone* observed that the speech was 'good', but

> evidently *got up*, for he handled his words and names of places as if they were far from being familiar to him. He was brought into the House to *speak*, and that on the side opposed to his own declared opinions; so that it will be rather uphill work with him.[15]

Praed told his sister that he had been 'engrossed by gratulatory notes, visits and meetings', but he was afraid of 'the expectations I seem to have excited'.[16] His next effort, on the ministerial reform bill, 8 Mar., was less happy. He declared his willingness to accept a degree of reform, particularly the enfranchisement of large manufacturing towns, but argued that the measure would 'pull down about our ears the fabric of our time-honoured constitution'. He was handicapped by a cold, a tired House would not hear him out, and he was reckoned to have failed.[17] The Tory ex-minister Henry Goulburn* reported that he had 'evinced great facility in debate, but ... made one or two mistakes incident to want of knowledge of the House and did not know when to conclude'.[18] Macaulay commented:

> A more terrible audience there is not in the world. I wish that Praed had known to whom he was speaking. But with all his talent, he has no tact, no perception of the character of his audience, and he has fared accordingly.[19]

Praed voted against the second reading of the reform bill, 22 Mar., endorsed the hostile Cambridge University petition, 30 Mar., and voted for Gascoyne's wrecking amendment, 19 Apr. 1831.

He divided against the second reading of the reintroduced reform bill, 6 July, and spoke in support of the Appleby petition against disfranchisement, 12 July. In the first three of the obstructive divisions on the question of adjournment which followed he voted with government, but thereafter divided with the diminishing minorities until dawn because of ministers' 'marked indisposition to listen to any suggestion from this side of the House'. His own motion, the sixth in the series of seven, was defeated by 187-25. His opponents condemned him for his part in this episode, and Macaulay wrote that 'Praed and I become colder every day. His silly, conceited, factious conduct has disgraced him even more than his bad speaking'.[20] He took a prominent role in the summer's committee proceedings on the bill, risking serious damage to his health; but, as he told Mrs. Coleridge, he now had a taste for parliamentary combat:

> Losing a dinner now and then, and listening to Mr. Hume till five in the morning, are things which do as much good to me as air and exercise and natural *materia medica* to wiser and soberer men.[21]

He supported Mackinnon's proposal to use the 1831 rather than the 1821 census as a basis for disfranchisement, 19 July, and asserted that the bill's opponents had 'a right to go to the end of their tether in endeavouring to defeat it'. He opposed the total disfranchisement of St. Germans, 26 July, defended his friends against charges of factiousness, 29 July, and on 3 Aug., speaking after Macaulay, argued that the enfranchisement of Greenwich and other metropolitan districts would create 'a self-government of the people'. On 11 Aug., however, he was one of the anti-reformers who voted with government in favour of the proposed division of counties. On 13 Aug. he moved an amendment to restrict electors in the three-Member counties to two votes each, seeking thereby to ensure representation for significant minorities. He had been unable to interest any of the opposition leaders in this 'novel' idea, which he thought 'very important': 'people will consider nothing', he told his sister, 'which does not seem calculated to serve one or other of our conflicting parties'. A thin Saturday attendance showed little enthusiasm for his somewhat abstruse argument and he did not divide the House; but he was satisfied with his performance and encouraged by the subsequent interest shown in his theory to consider presenting it again.[22] He was in the minority in favour of the Irish union of parishes bill, 19 Aug., and voted in censure of the Irish government for interference in the Dublin election, 23 Aug. He opposed, as a further dilution of the landed interest, government's proposals to admit certain borough freeholders to county electorates, 20, 24 Aug. He successfully moved to exclude from the borough franchise persons in receipt of parochial relief within the last year, 26 Aug. He voted against the issue of a new writ for Liverpool, 5 Sept., and to protect the West Indian sugar interest, 12 Sept. He divided against the passage of the reform bill, 21 Sept., and the second reading of the Scottish measure, 23 Sept. He criticized the bankruptcy court bill, 14 Oct., but disclaimed any personal animosity towards its author lord chancellor Brougham. Soon afterwards Henry Crabb Robinson met him on the circuit, where his income had trebled, and noted that he 'spoke fluently, and not ill against the bill'.[23] His first attempt to speak from the hustings at the Cambridgeshire by-election, 29 Oct. 1831, was shouted down; but two days later he declared that had he been given a hearing, he would have explained why he, 'who was always an advocate for reform in Parliament, had so strenuously opposed the late bill'. He now declined to do so.[24]

Praed secured returns of the number of voters polled at the last contested election for each borough and of the number of freemen in every corporate town, 12 Dec. 1831. His speech in opposition to the second reading of the revised reform bill, 17 Dec., was essentially a reply to Macaulay's effort of the previous evening, when he had failed to catch the Speaker's eye. He voted against going into committee on the bill, 20 Jan. 1832, when he persuaded Croker to modify his amendment to the proposal to disfranchise 56 boroughs. He voted against Hobhouse's vestry reform bill, 23 Jan., and against government on the Russian-Dutch loan, 26 Jan. He again supported the division of counties, 27 Jan., on the same principle which had informed his scheme for the three Member counties. On 1 Feb. he moved an amendment to exclude all borough freeholders from the county franchise, which was defeated by 181-91. The success of this speech, which was subsequently published as a pamphlet, bemused him for, having expected to leave the leading role to Goulburn, who in the event could not attend, he had 'bestowed even less study than usual upon the arrangement of my arguments or the structure of my sentences'. 'Nothing that I have before done', he told his sister, 'has earned me half the praise of this':

> I was pleased to be told yesterday, by one of our friends, that Sir R. Peel speaks of *liking* me better (without reference to his estimate of my abilities) than any other of his young recruits ... I fancied there was more of friendliness in his manner to me than he is said to use towards all men. I do not forget his advice to me to 'go home and get to bed' when others whom the world would call kinder were complimenting me on what did not deserve compliments.[25]

He castigated the voters' residential requirements as a sop to the political unions, 7 Feb., mocked the inflexibility of the criteria for disfranchisement, 23 Feb., voted silently against the third reading of the bill, 22 Mar., spoke for preservation of the existing rights of burgesses and freemen and was in the minority of 27 on the freeholders of Lincoln, 23 Mar. A founder member of the Carlton Club, he endorsed a Devon petition against the plan of national education in Ireland, 11 May. On 14 May he denied that anyone on his side of the House had given currency to the notion that the anti-reformers in the Lords would capitulate if Lord Grey was recalled to power. The following day he told Lord Ellenborough that 'the case was not as desperate as was supposed'; but by the 17th he was predicting that 60 peers would be created to pass the bill. He was a member of the committee formed by opposition to manage their campaign in the forthcoming general election in England.[26] In the House, 5 June, he denounced the forcing of the reform bill through the Lords as a 'crime' and became involved in a bad-tempered exchange with Hume. He spoke against the Scottish reform bill, 15 June, and on the Irish, 18 June, produced statistics to ridicule O'Connell's contention that Ireland was entitled to more Members. He supported Baring's bill to exclude insolvent debtors from the House, 27 June. He again voted against government on the Russian-Dutch loan, 12 July, but the following day, like Peel, he welcomed their proposals for reform of Irish tithes and condemned the abolitionists. His last reported speech in this period was against the Russian-Dutch loan, 16 July 1832, when he declared:

> If it supports ministers, this reforming House of Commons will give a vote that will go further to show the necessity of reform in Parliament than any argument I have yet heard.

In the summer of 1832 the *Morning Post* printed the first of Praed's many contributions to that newspaper, of which he subsequently became the leader writer. His efforts greatly improved its reputation and increased its circulation.[27] At the general election of 1832 he was beaten at St. Ives, having complained bitterly (and unreasonably, so Charles Arbuthnot* thought) during his canvass of the refusal of the Maitland family to intervene on his behalf against his Whig opponent, the manager of their mining concerns in the area.[28] He re-entered the House in 1835, when Peel gave him junior office in his first ministry, but his later parliamentary career was not conspicuously distinguished. His talents were too superficial to be first-rate and his reputation always outweighed his achievements. His cousin Emily Shore described him in 1837 as

> a very clever and agreeable man ... as thin as a lath and almost ghastly in countenance; his pallid forehead, haggard features, and the quick glances of his light blue eyes are all indications, I fear, of fatal disease. He seems ... sinking into a consumption which his parliamentary exertions are too likely to hurry forward, if indeed he be not in one already. The profile of Winthrop's face is very like that of Lord Byron, and at times there is a sort of wildness in his look, but the usual expression of his countenance is remarkably sweet.[29]

Macaulay, soured by Praed's public attack on him during his period in India, wrote that 'he was a wonderful boy at seventeen; and a wonderful boy he continued to be till he died' of rapid consumption, aged 36, in July 1839.[30]

[1] See D. Hudson, *A Poet in Parliament* (1939); *Oxford DNB*. [2] *Poems of Winthrop Mackworth Praed* ed. D. Coleridge (1864), ii. 234-5. [3] *Macaulay Letters*, iv. 169. [4] C. Knight, *Passages of a Working Life* (1873), i. 282-3. [5] Earl Lytton, *Life, Letters and Literary Remains of Lord Lytton* (1883), i. 234. [6] Hudson, 3-100. [7] Ibid. 101-69. [8] *Pol. and Occasional Poems of Winthrop Mackworth Praed* ed. G. Young, pp. xiv-xvi. [9] Add. 57420. [10] Aberdeen Univ. Lib. Arbuthnot mss, Herries to Mrs. Arbuthnot, 31 Dec. 1830; A. Aspinall, *Politics and the Press*, 333; *Oxford DNB*. [11] Hudson, 170-2; *Poems*, i. pp. xlv-xlvi. [12] *Macaulay Letters*, i. 317. [13] *Greville Mems*. ii. 117; *Arbuthnot Corresp*. 143; Arbuthnot mss 1029/2/1/27. [14] *Three Diaries*, 9; *Arbuthnot Corresp*. 142-3. [15] St. Deiniol's Lib. Glynne-Gladstone mss 197, T. to J. Gladstone, 15 Feb. [1831]. [16] Hudson, 173. [17] *Three Diaries*, 65-66; *Bunbury Mem*. 160. [18] Surr. Hist. Cent. Goulburn mss Acc 304/67B, Goulburn to wife, 9 Mar. 1831. [19] *Macaulay Letters*, ii. 12. [20] Hatherton diary, 13 July; Add. 51569, C. Wood to Lady Holland, 30 July [1831]; *Macaulay Letters*, ii. 70. [21] Hudson, 176-81. [22] *Pol. Poems*, p. xvii. See J. Hart, *Proportional Representation*, 9-11. [23] *Crabb Robinson Diary*, i. 118. [24] *The Times*, 31 Oct., 1 Nov. 1831. [25] Hudson, 182-7; *Pol. Poems*, p. xviii. [26] *Three Diaries*, 256-7, 263, 266. [27] *Oxford DNB*; Hudson, 189-239; *Pol. Poems*, 180; W. Hindle, *Morning Post*, 148-9. [28] Add. 57370, ff. 91, 94, 96, 98; 57420, ff. 111, 113, 121. [29] *Jnl. of Emily Shore*, 210. [30] *Macaulay Letters*, v. 81-82.

D.R.F.

MACLEOD, John Norman (1788–1835), of Dunvegan Castle, Skye, Inverness and Great Cumberland Street, Mdx.

SUDBURY 9 Apr. 1828–1830

b. 3 Aug. 1788, at Cawnpore, 1st. surv. s. of Norman Macleod† of Dunvegan and 2nd w. Sarah, da. of Norman Stackhouse, second member of council of Bombay. *educ*. Univ. Coll. Oxf. 1804. *m*. 16 Nov. 1809, Anne, da. of John Stephenson, banker, of Great Ormond Street, Mdx. and Mersham, Kent, 3s. 6da. *suc*. fa. as 23rd chief of Macleod 1801. *d*. 25 Mar. 1835.

Cornet 12 Drag. 1807, lt. 1808.

Macleod was born at Cawnpore towards the end of his father's posting there with the East Indian army. The family returned to Scotland with an estimated £100,000 in time for Norman Macleod, the 'laird of the Isle of Skye', to contest Inverness-shire successfully at the 1790 election. His subsequent breach with Pitt and Dundas, defeat at Milborne Port at the general election of 1796, forced sales, drunken excesses, depression and sudden death in 1801 left Macleod heir to estates encumbered with debts of over £33,000.[1] He made his early career in the army, and the family's historian recounts that he fulfilled his obligations as a highland chief to supply a band of men to fight in the Peninsula, and permitted his bride to make extensive improvements to Dunvegan Castle.[2] His burning ambition was to represent Inverness-shire. Financial constraints deterred him from standing there at the general election of 1812 and in 1818 he deferred to Charles Grant*, the namesake son of the purchaser (for £90,000) of his Glenelg estate, who in turn promised to use his influence with the Liverpool government to press Macleod's case for 'some mark of distinction' commensurate with his 'status as a highland chieftain'.[3] The Macleods were claimants to the Lovat peerage.[4] Writing to the premier Lord Liverpool shortly before the general election of 1820, when Macleod's Scottish prospects remained bleak, Grant, then Irish secretary, provided the following account of him:

> He is a young man and had himself entertained views to the county of Inverness, which his father represented, but at the last election he behaved in a very handsome manner towards me, withdrawing his own pretensions and proposing me to the freeholders. Afterwards he represented to me the mortifying situation in which he found himself, as the head of an old distinguished family with a considerable estate, left without a rank which many of his clan had obtained.[5]

Macleod was already in London in search of a parliamentary seat, but Bishop's Castle and Boston, suggested by the government's election managers, proved inappropriate.[6] On 5 Mar. 1820 he informed his wife:

> My politics I am sorry to say do not thrive. Young Charles Grant has done a great deal in the way of recommending me to the proper authorities, but I am yet in as much uncertainty as I ever was and quite as insane as Don Quixote about Dulcina. However, if I fail, I shall endeavour to bear my disappointment like a hero and do as many other people have done before me, 'wait till the next time'.[7]

Combining politics with business and family visits to Edinburgh, where he was pursued at law by Captain Neil Macleod, his former tenant at Gesto, Skye,[8] he waited on George IV with his clansmen at Sir Walter Scott's request in August 1822, vainly pressed his claims to a Scottish constituency in the event of a by-election vacancy and in 1824 leased Culloden House with a view to boosting his prospects in the Inverness Burghs and Inverness-shire, where his relations with the Grants had deteriorated.[9] Hampered, however, by his opposition to Catholic relief, which Melville advocated, and the duplicity of his 'friend' Evan Baillie† of Dochfour, he postponed his challenge and went south to seek a seat at the dissolution in 1826.[10] He discovered that his brother-in-law Spencer Perceval* had failed to mention him to the treasury secretary John Herries*, 'as Nancy said he would', and, finding 'these treasury folks ... very tiring', he obtained an interview with the 5th marquess of Queensberry's brother Keith Douglas* at the admiralty, which brought late offers of the treasury interest in 'Coventry, Worcester or Hull, all three very undesirable with more than a fair chance of defeat'.[11] Before returning to Skye, he instructed the London attorney Robert Broughton, an acquaintance of his roguish brother-in-law Rowland Stephenson*, to contact him in the event of a vacancy (Ayr Burghs, St. Ives and Sudbury were mentioned), and made it known that he would pay up to £4,000 for a safe seat.[12] After failing to secure a nomination against Grant in Inverness-shire at the by-election in February 1828, he gave up Culloden House and took a town house in London, where he lobbied on behalf of the distressed kelp trade.[13] His prospects of a seat were boosted in March by Stephenson, who brokered the purchase of a letter relinquishing the representation of Sudbury from the discredited rogue John Wilks II* in Bruges, to 'use or keep back' at his discretion'.[14] Thus empowered, and assisted by Sir Lachlan Maclean and Dr. McQueen, two Skyemen resident in Sudbury, Macleod canvassed the corporation and the borough's London freemen as a 'No Popery' candidate. Standing on the locally denigrated 'Scotch Melville interest', he defeated the young banker John Abel Smith* at the by-election in April at a cost of £5,000.[15] He sent his first frank to his wife, and disclosed that when he took his seat, 17 Apr. 1828, sponsored by Perceval and Sir James Mackenzie, the Speaker remarked that 'he hoped I should find the air of the House more pure than that of Sudbury – very fractious wasn't it?'[16] His family hurried to London to assist with entertainments commensurate with his new status. The *Book of Dunvegan* records that Count d'Albaine, Henry Brougham*, Robert Peel* and the composer Mendelssohn were among their early guests.[17]

Macleod, as a Presbyterian, had agonized over entrusting his daughters to a Catholic governess, and being too late to vote in the Commons, he listened intently to debates in the Lords on repeal of the Test Acts.[18] He voted with the Wellington ministry on the corn laws, 22 Apr. 1828,[19] and chancery delays, 24 Apr., but cast wayward votes on the ordnance estimates, 4 July, and the silk bill, in which, as he explained on presenting their petitions, Sudbury and the merchant Alexander Macduff had vested interests, 14 July. Making his main contribution on Scottish issues, he praised the salmon fisheries bill, 19 June, and seconded O'Neill's abortive motion for protection for the kelp industry, 15 July. He voted against Catholic relief, 12 May 1828, and as the patronage secretary Planta predicted, he remained a committed opponent of emancipation in 1829. He presented and endorsed hostile petitions from Sudbury, 16 Feb., and Tain, 6 Mar., divided against the measure, 6, 18, 23, 30 Mar., and presented anti-Catholic petitions from Inverness, 25 Mar.[20] He ordered returns on kelp imports, 16 Feb., and was appointed to the committee on Scottish entails, 2 Mar. He testified to the desperate state of the silk trade in Sudbury, Long Melford and Glemsford on bringing up their protectionist petitions, 6 Apr. Macleod's only parliamentary action that attracted widespread publicity arose in consequence of a summons he received on 10 June 1829 to attend the court of common pleas as a juror. Believing that Members were exempt from service, he had refused to attend, and he raised the matter as a breach of privilege motion, 12 June, which he withdrew on hearing that the summons had been issued when the House was not in session and was consequently valid. He voted against transferring East Retford's seats to Birmingham, 11 Feb., Lord Blandford's parliamentary reform scheme, 18 Feb., and the enfranchisement of Birmingham, Leeds and Manchester, 23 Feb. He voted against Robert Grant's Jewish emancipation bill, 5 Apr., 17 May, making forgery a non-capital offence, 7 June, and reduction of the grant for South American missions, 7 June 1830. He toyed with attempting Sudbury at the general election that summer, but the ministry agreed before the dissolution to endorse his candidature against the Huskissonite Charles Grant in Inverness-shire.[21] They had denied him the 'weight ... attached to office' which he had told Melville and Peel were essential to his success, and his prospects were further blighted by the refusal of the duke of Gordon and others to oppose Grant, whom they predicted Wellington would soon re-appoint to office. After trailing by 34-25, he did 'not press the election committee to a vote'.[22] Reporting on 3 Sept. 1830 to Melville, he concluded:

> I am a considerable sufferer by my bad fortune. I lose my seat for Sudbury, where I might have been returned at a moderate expense; I have spent a great deal of money without effect; I have been obliged to take upon myself other men's debts to some amount, and I have entailed on myself the vexation of three lawsuits to make good my rejected votes. It will be no little consolation to me in all my trouble to be assured that I retain the good opinion of your Lordship and that you are satisfied that no exertion has been wanting on my part to strengthen the hands of an administration the principles of which I most cordially approve.[23]

Commenting on Macleod's request for continued government support, Planta observed to Peel that he was 'sure no good inclination or exertion was wanting on his part to obtain success. What I doubt in him is his judgement, and of any mention of that I steer clear'.[24]

Macleod's attempts to return to the Commons failed. He vainly tested his strength in Inverness-shire in November 1830, when Grant's appointment as the Grey's ministry's president of the board of control produced a by-election,[25] and went to Sudbury at the dissolution in April 1831, but desisted there after the sitting anti-reformer Sir John Benn Walsh, who privately dismissed him as a 'slow, cautious, pottering man [who] wants decision and is much afraid of expense', refused to agree to a coalition.[26] Walsh informed their party's election managers in Charles Street that Macleod's refusal to engage the 'Goody or low party' had risked sacrificing a seat to the reformers.[27] He was narrowly defeated in Cromartyshire the following month, and in Inverness-shire in 1832 and December 1834, when he finished only seven votes behind Grant.[28] Grant had previously rejected a plea that both parties should absent themselves from the election on account of Macleod's illness. Macleod attended, his health deteriorated and he died less than three months later. His eldest son Norman Macleod (1812-95), who inherited Dunvegan with debts of £64,161, succeeded him as clan chief. He refused an offer from Grant, on his elevation to the Lords as Baron Glenelg in May 1835, of an uncontested return for Inverness-shire.[29]

[1] R.C. Macleod, *Macleods, the Hist. and Traditions* (1929), 97, 99, 105, 110-11; *HP Commons, 1790-1820*, ii. 543-4; iv. 504-8; *Oxford DNB sub* Norman Macleod. [2] Macleod, 110-11. [3] Macleod mss 1019/1-3; Add. 38272, ff. 105-7. [4] Macleod mss 1189/1-52; *The Times*, 11 May 1885. [5] NAS GD23/6/745/125; Add. 38282, ff. 107-8. [6] Macleod mss 1055/1, 2. [7] Ibid. 1055/3. [8] Ibid. 286/1-6; NAS CS271/975, 58306, 65180, 66177, 66188, 73733. [9] NAS GD23/6/583/3; 600/1; 746/87; Macleod mss 909; 932/1; 933/1; 1056/1-9; 1059/1-5. [10] NAS GD23/6/583/4, 8; 601/2; 612; 746/85; Macleod mss 1061/1. [11] Macleod mss 1061/2, 3, 5. [12] Ibid. 936-8; 1061/6-9. [13] Ibid. 1062/2, 3, 5, 13. [14] Ibid. 1062/7, 9, 10; *The Times*, 8 Apr. 1828. [15] *The Times*, 27, 28 Mar., 12 Apr.; *Suff. Chron.* 12 Apr; *Suff. Herald*, 16 Apr. 1828; NLW, Ormathwaite mss FG1/5, p. 76; G36, f. 17; Suff. RO (Bury St. Edmunds), handbill P581/5; 'Sudbury Borough' (ms *penes* A.T. Copsey in 1991). [16] Macleod mss 1062/9-13. [17] Ibid. 1062/14, 15; Macleod, 108; *Bk. of Dunvegan* ed. R.C. Macleod, ii. 26-30. [18] Macleod mss 1061/4; 1062/13. [19] Ibid. 1062/13. [20] Suff. RO (Bury St. Edmunds), Sudbury borough recs. EE 501/2/16b. [21] Ormathwaite mss G35, f. 98; G37, f.8; Macpherson Grant mss 690; Wellington mss WP1/1130/49; NAS GD23/6/613/3/1; 659/1. [22] Macleod mss 1066/1-4; NLS mss 2, ff. 153-66; Wellington mss WP1/1134/11; 1135/21; 1138/9; 1139/19; *The Times*, 1, 2 Sept. 1830. [23] NLS mss 2, f. 168. [24] Add. 40401, f. 169. [25] NAS GD23/6/583/27; 614/5/1, 2; 746/131/1, 2. [26] Ormathwaite mss FG/1/5, pp. 177-8; *Ipswich Jnl.* 30 Apr. 1831. [27] Ormathwaite mss G39, f. 45. [28] NAS GD23/6/683; *The Times*, 7 June 1831, 4 Dec. 1834. [29] Macleod, 108, 111-13; *The Times*, 7 Feb. 1895.

M.M.E.

MACLEOD, Roderick (1786–1853), of Cadboll and Invergordon Castle, Ross and Cromarty.

CROMARTYSHIRE	1818–1820
SUTHERLAND	14 Sept. 1831–1837
INVERNESS BURGHS	1837–21 Feb. 1840

b. 24 Nov. 1786,[1] o.s. of Robert Bruce Aeneas Macleod† of Cadboll and Invergordon and Elizabeth, da. of Alexander Macleod of Harris. *educ.* Eton 1799; adv. 1810. *m.* 10 July 1813, Isabella, da. of William Cunninghame, merchant, of Lainshaw, Ayr, 2s. 3da. *suc.* fa. 1844. *d.* 13 Mar. 1853.

Ld. lt. Cromarty 1833-*d.*

At the Ross-shire county meeting called to vote a loyal address to George IV in the context of the Queen Caroline affair, 4 Jan. 1821, Macleod, the Whig son of a staunchly Tory father, failed to find a seconder for his amendment for the dismissal of the Liverpool ministry.[2] He was one of the committee appointed to promote Scottish parliamentary reform at a county meeting in December 1830, when his political friends had come to power in Lord Grey's ministry; and he sent an open letter extolling their reform scheme as 'moderate and efficient' to the anti-reform county meeting, 24 Mar. 1831.[3] He resumed his parliamentary career, after an interval of 11 years, when he was nominated by Lord and Lady Stafford to fill a vacancy for Sutherland in September 1831.[4] He voted for the passage of the English reform bill, 21 Sept., the second reading of the Scottish bill, 23 Sept., and Lord Ebrington's motion of confidence in ministers, 10 Oct. On 7 Oct. he spoke for reform of the Scottish exchequer court. He divided for the second reading of the revised reform bill, 17 Dec. 1831, was a reliable supporter of its details and voted for its third reading, 22 Mar. 1832. He divided with government on the Russian-Dutch loan, 26 Jan., 12, 16, 20 July, relations with Portugal, 9 Feb., and the navy civil departments bill, 6 Apr., but was in minorities against the malt drawback bill, 29 Feb., 2 Apr. That day he argued against compensating vested interests in Scotland for financial losses occasioned by the abolition of superiorities. He was one of the many Members who crammed into the House of Lords to witness the debate on the second reading of the English reform bill, 13/14 Apr. The lord advocate Francis Jeffrey* reported:

> Between four and five, when the daylight began to shed its blue beams across the red candlelight, the scene was very picturesque, from the singular grouping of forty or fifty of us sprawling on the floor, awake and asleep, with all sorts of expressions and wrappings. 'Young Cadboll', who chose to try how he could sleep *standing*, jammed in

a corner, fell flat down over two prostrate Irishmen on the floor, but no mischief was done.[5]

Macleod voted for the address asking the king to appoint only ministers who would carry undiluted reform, 10 May, the second reading of the Irish reform bill, 25 May, and against Conservative amendments to the Scottish bill, 1, 15 June. He divided for opening coroners' inquests, 20 June 1832.

The Macleods developed Invergordon, which was acquired during the minority of Roderick's father, as a town and flourishing port, but the cost of the enterprise laid a heavy burden on their Cadboll estates.[6] Thanks to his father's longevity, Macleod enjoyed only nine years as head of the family, dying in March 1853, when he was succeeded by his elder son, Robert Bruce Aeneas (1818-88). His second son, Henry Dunning Macleod (1821-1902), became a distinguished writer on political economy.[7]

[1] *Scots Mag.* (1786), 569. [2] *Inverness Courier*, 11 Jan. 1821. [3] Ibid. 26 Dec. 1830, 30 Mar. 1831. [4] *Scottish Electoral Politics*, 225. [5] Cockburn, *Jeffrey*, i. 329-30. [6] A. Morrison, *Macleods*, 79-81, 103-5; *Third Statistical Account of Scotland* (1987), xiii. 157, 159. [7] *Oxford DNB*.

D.R.F.

MACNAGHTEN, Edmond Alexander (1762–1832), of Beardiville, co. Antrim and Duke Street, St. James's, Mdx.

CO. ANTRIM	1801–1812
ORFORD	1812–1820
ORFORD	23 May 1820–1826
CO. ANTRIM	1826–1830

b. 2 Aug. 1762,[1] 1st s. of Edmund MacNaghten of Beardiville and 2nd w. Hannah, da. of John Johnstone of Belfast. *educ.* Glasgow Univ. 1778; L. Inn 1781. *unm.* 2s. 1da. with Mary Anne Fitzsimmons. *suc.* fa. 1781; *cr.* by patent chief of Clan MacNaghten 1818. *d.* 15 Mar. 1832.

MP [I] 1797-1800.

Ld. of treasury [I] 1813-17, [UK] Mar. 1819-July 1830.

Trustee, linen board [I] 1810.

Sheriff, co. Antrim 1793-4.

An influential ally of the 2nd marquess of Hertford in county Antrim, where his father had prospered as the manager of the 5th earl of Antrim's estates, MacNaghten had been one of the principal pro-Union speakers in the Dublin Parliament and liveliest Members of the Westminster one, and had been appointed to the consolidated treasury board in 1819 in recognition of his services to Lord Liverpool's ministry.[2] He had represented Hertford's borough of Orford since relinquishing the representation of county Antrim in 1812 and intended trying for the county again at the general election of 1820, but he demurred to Hertford's nephew Hugh Seymour* and came in late for Orford on their interest.[3]

An anti-Catholic Tory opposed to parliamentary reform, MacNaghten observed privately in 1823 that 'Nothing annoys me so much as not being well enough to attend the Catholic question'.[4] He voted against Catholic relief, 28 Feb. 1821, 30 Apr. 1822, 1 Mar., 21 Apr., 10 May, and the Irish franchise bill, 9 May 1825, when, breaking his deliberate silence in the House, he criticized it as 'unconstitutional ... absurd and unjust'. Drawn later in the debate by the Whig Lord Milton's claim that his failure to contest county Antrim in 1812 and 1820 proved that the proposed change was necessary, he replied:

> It was not the fact that he ceased to be a Member for the county of Antrim when the heir of a noble family came of age. He ceased to be a Member for county Antrim on grounds best known to himself; and which had been approved of by all his friends.

He voted against reforming the Scottish electoral system, 2 June 1823, 26 Feb. 1824, 13 Apr. 1826.

MacNaghten used his access to patronage as a treasury placeman to further the careers of his sons, Charles and Robert, and divided steadily and consistently with his colleagues in government on English and Irish issues until April 1823, when he informed Lord Liverpool that, like Colonel Barry, he would relinquish his office to 'be at liberty to vote for Mr. Brownlow's motion' criticising the decision to proceed with prosecutions arising from the Dublin Orange theatre riot, on 'information filed *ex-officio* after bills of indictment against them for the same offence had been thrown out by a grand jury'.[5] The home secretary Peel took the matter seriously, since 'an Irishman's resignation of a good office is an unusual proof of sincerity', and Liverpool summoned MacNaghten for discussions.[6] In the event, Brownlow's motion was withdrawn without a division, 15 Apr., in anticipation of Sir Francis Burdett's for inquiry into the prosecution of the rioters, on which government were defeated, 22 Apr. 1823. MacNaghten did not vote that day, nor did he resign or cast wayward votes that Parliament. He retained his seat on the Irish linen board as a trustee of the 'Linen and Hempen Manufactures of Connaught', and was appointed to the select committee on laws regulating that trade, 14 Apr. 1825. Following Hugh Seymour's death, he had been instrumental in securing the return of Lord Beauchamp for county Antrim in 1822, and was returned there unopposed as the 3rd marquess of Hertford's candidate with the 2nd Viscount O'Neill's brother and heir, John Bruce Richard O'Neill, at the general election of 1826.[7]

MacNaghten cast his customary votes against Catholic relief, 6 May 1827, 12 May 1828, and divided with government for the grant to the duke of Clarence, 16 Mar. 1827. He retained his place when the short-lived Canning and Goderich ministries succeeded Liverpool's in 1827, and was kept on when the duke of Wellington became premier in 1828. He divided with his colleagues against Test Act repeal, 26 Feb., on the ordnance estimates, 4 July, and the silk duties, 14 July 1828. The patronage secretary Planta rightly classified him as a Protestant Irishman opposed to Catholic relief in January 1829, when Hertford, Peel and Wellington found the case for conceding emancipation overwhelming. His brother Sir Francis Workman MacNaghten (1763-1843), a lawyer who rose to prominence through service in India, now published a pro-emancipation pamphlet, *A View of the Catholic Question as it Relates to Ireland*.[8] MacNaghten presented a 9-10,000-signature anti-Catholic petition from the barony of Kilconway, county Antrim, 12 Mar. 1829, and faced strong constituency pressure to oppose emancipation, but predictions by Lord Camden and others that he would vote against the bill at its second reading proved incorrect, and he deliberately refrained from voting on the measure.[9] Hertford generally engineered the retirement of his nominees who failed to support emancipation in 1829, but doubting 'how far MacNaghten can without blowing up our power in Antrim support any concessions', he wrote urging him not to resign his seat unless he felt compelled to do so 'from strong private feelings of Orangeism' and expressed the hope, as proved to be the case, that Wellington would 'not turn him out'.[10] He explained to John Croker*:

> I know *out of office* MacN[aghten] at his age would go out of Parl[iamen]t – he has told me so. I have nobody to put up attached to me and I had rather have an uphill race *with* MacN[aghten] than walk over the course with Mr. A. B. or C.[11]

MacNaghten voted against permitting Daniel O'Connell to take his seat for county Clare without swearing the oath of supremacy, 18 May 1829. He received a month's leave on account of his failing health, 10 Mar. 1830, and is not known to have spoken in debate or voted personally that session. He was paired in the minority against the libel laws amendment bill, 6 July 1830. Despite a recent improvement in his health and spirits and entreaties from Hertford, who promised 'never during the Parliament to solicit his attendance in the House for a single hour', he resigned from the treasury and stood down at the dissolution that month.[12] Hertford, whose arrangement with the O'Neills in county Antrim had lapsed, bemoaned the loss of a placeman, who, in Canning's time, had been 'a mighty clog on my leg'.[13] MacNaghten vainly gave his dwindling interest in the county to the marquess's nominee, the countess of Antrim's husband Edmund McDonnell.[14] Nothing came of Hertford's plan to field Sir Francis MacNaghten for county Antrim in 1831.[15]

MacNaghten interrupted his retirement in 1831 to testify on the treasury's behalf in the case of Burnell *v.* the duke of Wellington (alleging underpayment for work carried out at York House).[16] He died in March 1832 at Beardiville, where he lived with his housekeeper Mrs. Fitzsimmons and their daughter Mary Anne.[17] Hertford said he was 'sorry for him because I loved him – as to my political loss in his interest I now feel little'.[18] According to the family's historian, Angus MacNaghten, his will, dated 15 Jan. 1827, made no reference to his sons; but Mrs. Fitzsimmons received a £500 annuity for life and he made his 'reputed daughter, Mary Anne' his joint residuary legatee with his brother Francis, his successor as titular head of the clan.[19]

[1] IGI (Ireland). [2] *HP Commons, 1790-1820*, iv. 513-14. [3] *Dublin Jnl.* 3, 8, 24 Mar.; *Dublin Weekly Reg.* 4, 11 Mar.; *Belfast News Letter*, 25, 29 Feb., 3, 7, 10, 14, 24, 31 Mar. 1820. [4] PRO NI, Perceval Maxwell mss D3244/G/1/21. [5] Wellington mss WP1/824/17; 826/17; Add. 37301, f. 13A. [6] Add. 40304, f. 122; 40329, f. 62; Wellington mss WP1/824/7. [7] PRO NI, McGildowney mss D1375/3/38/45; *The Times*, 31 May 1826; Add. 60287, ff. 117, 119, 120, 190, 212. [8] Add. 60288, f. 110; Wellington mss WP1/955/17; 997/13. [9] Add. 60288, f. 76; Wellington mss WP1/1003/1; *The Times*, 1 Apr. 1829. [10] Add. 60288, ff. 101, 107, 110-16, 128, 133, 139, 144-54. [11] Add. 60288, f. 136. [12] PRO NI, Johnson Smyth mss D2099/5/8-11; *Dublin Morning Post*, 8, 19, 20 July; *Belfast News Letter*, 9 July 1830. [13] Add. 60288, ff. 161, 265, 270. [14] Johnson Smyth mss 5/16, 22; McGildowney mss 3/38/52; Add. 60288, f. 282; *The Times*, 27 July 1830. [15] Add. 60288, ff. 372-3; A.P.W. Malcomson, *John Foster*, 331; *Croker Pprs.* i. 373; *Ellenborough Diary*, ii. 323; *Gent. Mag.* (1832), i. 563. [16] Wellington mss WP1/1187/7. [17] *Belfast News Letter*, 27 Mar. 1832. [18] Add. 60289, f. 36. [19] A.I. Macnachtan, *Chiefs of Clan Macnachtan*, 85-87; *Annual Biog. and Obit.* (1833), 436.

M.M.E.

MACNAMARA, William Nugent (?1776–1856), of Doolin, co. Clare.

CO. CLARE 1830–1852

b. ?1776, 1st s. of Francis Macnamara, MP [I], of Doolin and Moyriesk and Jane, da. of George Stamer of Carnelly. *m.* 1798, Susannah, da. and coh. of Mathias Finucane, j.c.p. [I], of Lifford, 1s. 4da. (1 *d.v.p.*). *suc.* fa. 1815. *d.* 11 Nov. 1856.

Sheriff, co. Clare 1798-9.

Maj. Clare militia.

Macnamara, a descendant of an ancient Milesian family, was the eldest son of Francis Macnamara of Moyriesk, who inherited Doolin through his mother Catherine Sarsfield. Francis, a barrister who had extensive though 'involved' estates, sat as an independent for Ardee, 1776-83, and was sheriff of his county, 1789-90. As Member for Clare in the 1790 Parliament, he supported government and was rewarded with the comptrollership of customs at Dingle, county Kerry, in 1795. He represented Killybegs, 1798-1800, and, by then a colonel in the British army, supposedly received a pension in lieu of the compensation of £400 he might have expected at the Union, for which he had twice voted.[1] William was educated at a Dublin seminary and entered the local militia as a captain of grenadiers, later gaining promotion to major. He may have differed politically with his father since, during his spell as sheriff of Clare, 1798-9, he convened a meeting to petition against the Union. He preserved good order in the county during the Rebellion by the force of his kindly and gentle personality and, having been appointed to the commission of the peace in 1803, he earned a reputation for humanity and impartiality as 'the people's magistrate'.[2]

Macnamara stood for Clare at the general election of 1807 with the support of local Catholics, but, lacking government endorsement, withdrew, apparently under the pretence of not being able to sit because of the place he was reported (perhaps in confusion with his father) to hold.[3] He undertook various travels on the continent between 1814 and 1816, but was in Dublin in early 1815, when he served as second to Daniel O'Connell* in his fatal duel with D'Esterre. Known as 'Fireball' Macnamara for his own duelling expertise, the firmness with which he made the arrangements and the precautions in which he coached his charge, were credited with having saved the life of the future Liberator and consequently raised his own standing.[4] He proposed William Vesey Fitzgerald*, the former chancellor of the Irish exchequer, for Clare at the general election of 1818, and, having declined invitations to come forward himself, did so again two years later.[5] In January 1821 he intervened at a county meeting to force an amendment criticizing the Liverpool ministry over the Queen Caroline affair, but he acquiesced in the approval of a loyal address to the king on his visit to Ireland that summer. He signed the requisition for, and presumably attended, the county meeting on agricultural distress in January 1823 and, as a supporter of their claims, he was thanked by the Catholics of Clare at their gathering in July 1825.[6] Yet he did not attend the O'Connellite dinner to the friends of civil and religious liberty in Dublin, 2 Feb. 1826.[7]

He was reported to be a candidate on the independent interest at the general election that year, when the other Clare Member, the Tory Sir Edward O'Brien, commented that he did not 'think he will persevere, although I am fully aware he would be desirous of giving as much opposition as he could and endeavour to raise himself in to importance by making a noise in the county'.[8] Despite refusing to offer, he was put up by the O'Gorman Mahon* for Ennis, 16 June, and for the county, 23 June 1826, when he again nominated Vesey Fitzgerald. He subsequently explained that he had withdrawn in order to preserve the cause of independence, but promised to stand again, and he was present at the county's Catholics' meeting the following month.[9] Having declared himself a friend and supporter of O'Connell at the Clare Liberal Club meeting in April 1828, he was the first choice of the Catholic Association to oppose Vesey Fitzgerald, the new president of the board of trade, on his standing for re-election that summer. But he hesitated and then, in the face of gentry opposition, excused himself as being under personal obligations to Vesey Fitzgerald and also, as he later wrote, to please his only son Francis Macnamara†, an officer in the 8th Hussars, who was concerned about the expense that would be incurred.[10] He was praised for his refusal, which, like that of other liberal Protestants, opened the way for O'Connell's triumphant candidacy at the by-election, from which he absented himself (though at one point it was thought that he would be put up as a security for him).[11] From London that autumn he sympathized with the efforts of the O'Gorman Mahon to counter the activities of the local Brunswick clubs, agreeing to sign a Protestant petition for Catholic relief and promising that 'when I arrive in Clare I will attack the Brunswickers from the bench'; he regretted his young friend's removal from the magistracy in December 1828.[12]

On O'Connell being sent back for re-election in May 1829, Macnamara, who O'Connell considered would be a better Clare Member than his inactive colleague

Lucius O'Brien, was briefly rumoured to be about to stand, perhaps in opposition to O'Connell himself.[13] Francis, who avoided writing directly to his father, 'lest he should think for a moment that I was about to interfere', observed to his uncle John Macnamara of Moher on the 25th that 'my opinions are now with respect to his standing the same as they always were: what business can a man without money or talents have in standing for a county'.[14] Actually, Macnamara had on the 10th suggested to the O'Gorman Mahon that Vesey Fitzgerald might be welcomed back, especially as, with the passage of the Emancipation Act, 'the occasion has been removed that induced the men of Clare to depart from the course pursued by this and every other county of returning none but gentlemen having property and connections in them'. Rebuked by his correspondent, who only wished that Macnamara was already seated, for even contemplating such an approach to the O'Briens and other Tory proprietors, he replied:

> The shoneens [Clare landlords] are down and I hope for ever. When they imagined they had me, I communicated that any offer from them would be rejected with indignation, that I would support and propose Dan and that myself and the Boys, with O'Gorman Mahon and [Tom] Steele, would return him. In fact the humbugging fellows will not be able, by everything I hear, to even come to the hustings.[15]

He was not granted his wish to propose O'Connell on his unopposed return, 30 July 1829, but he explained his 'most liberal principles' that day and soon afterwards announced his intention of offering at the next election, apparently with O'Connell's blessing. He chaired a meeting of the inhabitants of Ennis for the purpose of improving the state of the town, 29 Sept. 1829.[16]

He headed the list of requisitionists for a county Clare meeting, 2 June 1830, when he secured a petition against the increased Irish stamp and spirit duties, and that day he issued an address denying that he would stand aside at the expected general election.[17] By this time a major misunderstanding had developed between Macnamara, who was said to be short of money and too liberal for the landlords, and O'Connell, for the latter, who still hoped for some amicable arrangement, was very reluctant to fulfil his apparent obligation to support his pretensions and had it put about that Macnamara would not enter. Despite O'Connell's endeavours to resolve the situation, including by indicating to the Wellington administration that Vesey Fitzgerald might possibly be brought back in exchange for a baronetcy for Macnamara and an army promotion for his son, Macnamara remained obstinate; he purportedly had documentary proof that O'Connell had agreed to bring him in as the price of securing his withdrawal at a former election. At Steele's instigation, O'Connell's second son Morgan O'Connell† offered to fight a duel, but Macnamara rebuffed the challenge and, on O'Connell conceding that he was bound too strictly to their undertaking, he emerged as the candidate with the strongest territorial interest.[18] Francis Macnamara, whose father had declared that he was 'determined to fight it out to the last' and was supposedly 'making speeches every day to his *horse* and greyhounds, keeping in practice for Ennis', had feared that 'not only O'Connell but that party in Clare would send my father over board', but was doubtless pleased that O'Connell's withdrawal gave his father greater room for manoeuvre as an independent.[19] Having stated that he was not a party to any coalition and pledged himself for lower taxes, parliamentary reform and the introduction of poor laws, he topped the poll in the ensuing week-long contest.[20]

Although he may only have had to pay the usual fees, Macnamara evidently had difficulty meeting his election expenses in September 1830.[21] Francis, who once wrote to his uncle that, 'God knows I ought not to be surprised at any thing my father does, knowing his intellect to be weak', was furious at being approached for a contribution to the costs:

> I allow his outgoing expenses are heavy, but still he has a good income to spend [which] is not spent on *himself* or *family* for he has not the house or establishment of a gentleman of moderate income. His income therefore goes in some private manner. If not, there is some very gross mismanagement on his part, since the money is not spent on keeping an establishment suitable to his rank or making a family place at Doolin or in any one thing that I can see ... You should not ask me to join him in money, a man that does nothing but live in cabins and prefers the society of the common people to that of gentlemen. You know this has been his mode of life for the last ten years. He must have the money somewhere, so let it come out from under some *stone* at Doolin. Only fancy a man of his property *wanting* a thousand pounds. I look on him as mean in all money matters and not over fond of paying.

A fortnight later he repeated his refusal to assist his father, declaring that 'I am decided on never joining him in anything. I shall have nothing to say to him in money matters, politics, domestic concerns or any thing else. This is the only course I have of keeping on terms with him'.[22]

Having taken lodgings at 108 Jermyn Street, Macnamara, who was concerned about the possibility of a petition, reported to his brother John that on 2 Nov. 1830 'O'Connell and I met in the House of

Commons. The passages going to the benches are so narrow that two cannot pass almost. He bowed to me which I returned. Without any explanation further or interference we shook hands'. He gave his brother permission to state publicly that he and O'Connell were reconciled, but added that 'I need not tell you it is time for me now not to place much or any confidence in him'; a week later he claimed to be thriving on the late sittings.[23] He voted in O'Connell's minority for repeal of the Irish Subletting Act, 11 Nov., and in Parnell's for reducing the duties on wheat imported into the West Indies, 12 Nov. He had been listed among the 'neutrals' in Pierce Mahony's† analysis of the Irish elections, but ministers counted him with their 'foes' and he divided in the majority against them on the civil list, 15 Nov. He presented the Ennis petition against the Union, 25 Nov., but his colleague, the O'Gorman Mahon, warned that he would lose his seat if he were not more supportive of repeal, 23 Dec. In a manner typical of the infrequent and short interventions to which he confined himself in the House, he supported the alteration of the Galway franchise and the extension of religious liberty to Jews and Quakers, 2, 15 Dec. He voted for Hume's amendment to refer the truck bill to a select committee, 14 Dec. 1830.[24]

Following the O'Gorman Mahon's Commons quarrel with Sir James Graham in late February 1831, Macnamara was prepared to act as his second, but no duel transpired.[25] Early the following month he reported to his brother that this had brought on an attack of bile and remarked that 'if vexation and repentance is of any use I have had enough of it'. He several times vowed to take no part in the by-election, caused by the unseating of the O'Gorman Mahon, that took place that month in Clare, and denied that he had promised O'Connell that he would support his son Maurice in his successful campaign. He privately brought the disturbed state of his county to the attention of the Irish secretary Smith Stanley, and adverted to this in the House, 14 Mar.[26] He brought up the county's reform petitions, 21 Mar., and voted for the second reading of the Grey ministry's reform bill, 22 Mar. He boasted to John on the 23rd that 'since my return to Parliament I have not been absent from a single division and every vote I gave was for the benefit of my country', though he admitted that he had little money to spare for a contest in case of a dissolution. On the 26th he noted that after reform was passed, he would apply for a month's leave so as to avoid attending the rest of the session. His opposition to the application of the Insurrection Act on Smith O'Brien's motion on the unrest in Clare, 13 Apr., was an observation made at 'the wish of government', as he put it in an undated letter to his brother.[27] He backed O'Connell in a dispute with Henry Hunt over whether the former had promised to introduce a bill to re-enfranchise the Irish 40*s.* freeholders, 14 Apr., and divided against Gascoyne's wrecking amendment to the reform bill, which precipitated a dissolution, 19 Apr. 1831.

He complained to his brother, 13 Apr. 1831, about the 'lowness and despondency of spirits' brought on by the O'Gorman Mahon affair and other grievances, including the fact that his son (evidently nicknamed Pedro) was pressurizing him to relinquish his seat to him. On the 23rd he lamented that

> truly, if I would not go to great expense in a contest, how could Francis do it? As to my involving myself in joining him, unless he is much changed he would not like to spend money on an election. I am aware of his many honourable and good qualities, but that of his being a kind and affectionate son is not one of them. When I am in error, no person acknowledges it sooner than I do, but when my own family express it in a taunting, insulting way, as I conceive, though it may not be intended, I feel it exceedingly. You know every human being scarcely without any exception have their faults, and God knows I have more than once thought to get rid of all my anxiety in this world by committing suicide, particularly after my daughter Jane's death, and since I came here I never was in such a state of mind.

He concluded that if he was not re-elected, he would resign as a magistrate and grand juror and go to live in a quiet frame of mind at Doolin: 'then there will be an end to all jealousies about votes and presentments and reproaches and finding fault for not doing such and such things'.[28] He cold shouldered O'Connell on his attempting to sound him about the election and asked his brother to prepare an address that stressed his constant attendance and voting record, for which he received praise from radical quarters. He had no time to undertake a personal canvass, but found his freeholders ready to back him against the O'Gorman Mahon and was considered certain to retain his seat.[29] Having pledged to oppose the turnpike bill and declared himself a reformer, he was returned ahead of Maurice O'Connell after a contest with the O'Gorman Mahon, who made an abusive (but ineffectual) verbal attack on him in an Ennis street.[30]

He served as foreman of the jury at the special commission in Clare in June 1831 and in the Commons on the 21st he remarked that this process had had a salutary effect in re-establishing order in the county.[31] Writing to his uncle, 2 July, Francis, who saw Macnamara's recent quarrel with John as 'part of his usual extraordinary conduct on every subject', observed that 'I never saw my father looking so well.

They have had hard work at the House. Several Members are done up by it. The late hours agree with him'.[32] He voted for the second reading of the reintroduced reform bill, 6 July, at least twice against adjourning the proceedings on it, 12 July, and steadily for its details in committee. He divided for reducing the grant for civil list services, 18 July, printing the Waterford petition for disarming the Irish yeomanry, 11 Aug., and making legal provision for the Irish poor, 29 Aug. He was listed in the minority for O'Connell's motion for swearing the original Dublin election committee, 29 July, but sided with ministers in both divisions on motions of censure, 23 Aug.; he voted against Benett's amendment against issuing the Liverpool writ, 5 Sept. He denied allegations made about the Clare elections in 1828, 10 Aug., and 1830, 25 Aug., and on 6 Oct. Maurice O'Connell regretted that he had not been appointed as their county's lord lieutenant. He divided for the third reading, 19 Sept., and passage of the reform bill, 21 Sept., the second reading of the Scottish bill, 23 Sept., and Lord Ebrington's confidence motion, 10 Oct. 1831. He was reported to have returned to Ireland later that month in excellent health despite his arduous parliamentary duties.[33]

He paired for the second reading of the revised reform bill, 17 Dec. 1831, but from London, 6 Jan. 1832, he issued an address excusing himself from O'Connell's putative assembly of Irish Members on the ground that 'my past political life will be sufficient pledge for the future'.[34] He voted for the abolition of 56 boroughs in schedule A, 20 Jan., again generally for the bill's details, and for its third reading, 22 Mar. He sided with ministers against the production of information on Portugal, 9 Feb., and an amendment to the navy civil departments bill, 6 Apr., but with the radicals for inquiry into Peterloo, 15 Mar. He voted for printing the Woollen Grange petition against Irish tithes, 16 Feb., Brownlow's amendment to postpone the debate until the select committee had completed its enquiry, 8 Mar., and radical Irish amendments to Smith Stanley's resolutions, 27, 30 Mar. He commented that only altering the system of tithes would tranquillize Ireland, 3 Apr., and divided against the arrears bill, 6, 9 Apr.; he spoke and voted for postponing the subject to the reformed Parliament, 13 July, and divided against the composition bill, 24 July, 1 Aug., when he stated that he would actively support resistance to the payment of tithes, even if he was threatened with dismissal as a magistrate. He voted for Ebrington's motion for an address calling on the king to appoint only ministers who would carry the reform bill unimpaired, 10 May, and the second reading of the Irish bill, 25 May, though he was in the O'Connellite minority for extending the Irish franchise to £5 freeholders, 18 June. He divided in minorities against Alexander Baring's bill to exclude insolvent debtors from Parliament, 30 May, 6 June, and for Blamire's amendment relating to the boundaries of Whitehaven, 22 June. He blamed past unrest in Clare on the proselytising activities of the Kildare Place Society, 31 May, and differed with the Evangelical James Edward Gordon about Irish education, 5 June, 23 July. Apart from the one in the majority for making coroners' inquests public, 20 June, his only other known votes were with government for the Russian-Dutch loan, 12, 16, 20 July 1832.

Surprisingly, considering that Francis judged his father 'to have as little mind as any man in Bedlam' and that he was himself reluctant to risk the expense of standing for Parliament, Macnamara and his son were returned, after costly contests, as repealers for Clare and Ennis, respectively, at the general election of 1832.[35] Suspected of cultivating a similarity in appearance to George IV, Richard Sheil* described him (in 1828) as having

> by the turn of his coat, the dilation of his chest and an aspect of egregious dignity, succeeded in producing in his person a very fine effigy of his sovereign. With respect to his moral qualities, he belongs to the old school of Irish gentlemen; and from the facility of his manners, and his graceful mode of arbitrating a difference, has acquired a very eminent character as 'a friend'. No man is better versed in the strategies of Irish honour ... In the county of Clare he does not merely enact the part of a sovereign. He is the chief of the clan of the Macnamaras and ... the moment he arrives on the coast of Clare ... becomes 'every inch a king'. He possesses great influence with the people, which is founded upon far better grounds than their hereditary reverence for the Milesian nobility of Ireland. He is a most excellent magistrate. If a gentleman should endeavour to crush a poor peasant, Major Macnamara is ready to protect him, not only with the powers of his office, but at the risk of his life. This creditable solicitude for the rights and the interests of the lower orders had rendered him most deservedly popular.[36]

He retired in 1852 and died, aged 80, in November 1856, being succeeded by Francis (*d.* 1873), who had sat in Parliament until 1834.[37]

[1] *Hist. Irish Parl.* v. 172; *Viceroy's Post-Bag* ed. M. MacDonagh, 47, 50. [2] F.B. Hamilton, *Picture of Parl.* (1831), 55. [3] Wellington mss WP1/166/113; 168/22; *HP Commons, 1790-1820*, ii. 632. [4] NLI, Stacpoole Kenny mss 18889 (3); J. Kelly, *'That Damn'd Thing Called Honour'*, 263; S. O'Faolain, *King of the Beggars* (1970), 197-8; P. White, *Hist. Clare*, 333-4. [5] K. Sheedy, *Clare Elections*, 124, 128-9; Stacpoole Kenny mss 18889 (7), W. to J. Macnamara, 7 Dec. 1819; (8), same to same, 24 Feb. 1820. [6] *Dublin Weekly Reg.* 20 Jan, 10 Feb.; *Dublin Evening Post*, 16 Aug. 1821, 18, 30 Jan. 1823, 30 July, 2 Aug. 1825. [7] *O'Connell Corresp.* iii. 1278. [8] *Morning Reg.* 27, 31 May; NLI,

Inchiquin mss T25/3627, O'Brien to wife, 30 May 1826. [9] *Dublin Evening Post*, 22, 27, 29 June, 18 July 1826. [10] Ibid. 19 Apr.; *The Times*, 27 June 1828; Stacpoole Kenny mss 18889 (15), W. to J. Macnamara, 4 Nov. 1830; R. L. Sheil, *Sketches of Irish Bar* (1854), ii. 268-70. [11] *Dublin Evening Post*, 24, 26 June, 3, 8 July 1828; PRO NI, Anglesey mss D619/32A/2/81. [12] Stacpoole Kenny mss 18889 (12), W. to J. Macnamara, 9, 11, 20 Oct., 10 Dec. 1828. [13] *Dublin Evening Post*, 26 May, 13 June 1829; Anglesey mss 32A/3/166; *O'Connell Corresp.* iv. 1593. [14] Stacpoole Kenny mss 18888 (4). [15] D. Gwynn, *O'Gorman Mahon*, 83-84, 97-101. [16] *Clare Jnl.* 16, 27, 30 July, 3 Aug., 1, 5 Oct. 1829. [17] Ibid. 31 May, 3 June 1830. [18] Ibid. 5, 19 July 1830; *O'Connell Corresp.* iv. 1668, 1670, 1678-9, 1684, 1687, 1689-90, 1692. [19] Stacpoole Kenny mss 18888 (5), F. to J. Macnamara, 2, 8 [9] July; 18889 (14), W. Macnamara to same, 30 June, 11, n.d. [July] 1830. [20] *Clare Jnl.* 12, 19 Aug. 1829. [21] Stacpoole Kenny mss 18891 (10), Woulfe to J. Macnamara, 7 Sept.; 18889 (14), W. Macnamara to same, 13 Sept. 1830. [22] Ibid. 18888 (2), F. to J. Macnamara, 28 Feb. [n.y.]; (5), same to same, 9, 23 Sept., 2 Oct. 1830. [23] Ibid. 18889 (15), W. to J. Macnamara, 4, 11 Nov. 1830. [24] Ibid. W. to J. Macnamara, 15 Dec. 1830. [25] *Clare Jnl.* 28 Feb. 1831. [26] Stacpoole Kenny mss 18889 (16), W. to J. Macnamara, 2 [11], 13, 26 Mar.; (17), same to same, n.d. [Mar.] 1831. [27] Ibid. (16); (17). [28] Ibid. (18). [29] Ibid. W. to J. Macnamara [21 Apr.], 2 May; *Clare Jnl.* 28 Apr., 9 May 1831; [W. Carpenter], *People's Bk.* (1831), 321. [30] *Clare Jnl.* 16, 19, 23 May 1831; *O'Connell Corresp.* iv. 1811. [31] *Clare Jnl.* 2 June 1831. [32] Stacpoole Kenny mss 18888 (6). [33] *Clare Jnl.* 31 Oct. 1831. [34] Ibid. 12 Jan. 1832. [35] Ibid. 22 Nov., 10, 17, 20, 24 Dec.; Stacpoole Kenny mss 18888 (7), F. to J. Macnamara, 15 Aug. [n.d.]; 18891 (12), Woulfe to same, 26 Dec. 1832. [36] Sheil, ii. 266-8. [37] *Clare Jnl.* 27 Nov. 1856; *Gent. Mag.* (1857), i. 118.

S.M.F.

MACPHERSON GRANT, George (1781–1846), of Ballindalloch, Banff. and Invereshie, Inverness.

SUTHERLAND 29 Sept. 1809–1812

SUTHERLAND 6 Mar. 1816–1826

b. 25 Feb. 1781, 1st s. of Capt. John Macpherson and Isabella, da. of Thomas Wilson of Witton Gilbert, co. Dur. *educ.* Edinburgh h.s. 1795.[1] *m.* 26 Aug. 1803, Mary, da. of Thomas Carnegy of Craigo, Forfar, 3s. 3da. *suc.* fa. 1799; gt.-uncle Gen. James Grant† to Ballindalloch and took name of Grant 5 June 1806; uncle William Macpherson to Invereshie 1812; *cr.* bt. 25 July 1838. *d.* 24 Nov. 1846.

Capt. commdt. Invereshie vols. until 1808; maj. Strathspey vols. 1808.

Macpherson Grant, laird of Ballindalloch since 1806, was again returned for Sutherland in 1820 on the interest of Elizabeth, countess of Sutherland, and her Grenvillite husband, George Leveson Gower†, 2nd marquess of Stafford. He was an occasional attender who continued to give general support to Lord Liverpool's ministry, though initially at least he displayed a modest degree of independence which had not been apparent in the previous four years. He was granted a month's leave to attend to urgent private business, 30 June 1820. He presented a Wick petition in support of Queen Caroline, 26 Jan. 1821, when he voted for Hamilton's motion condemning the omission of her name from the liturgy. Explaining this action to Lady Stafford, he observed that 'I have never concealed my opinion from the commencement of the proceedings against the queen that in whatever way they might terminate they were calculated to prove injurious to the dignity of the crown and prejudicial to the interests of the country'. He had trusted the government to make its case for the proceedings, but had been 'astonished' by its 'fatal and unfortunate error' in resolving to take a stand on the matter of the liturgy, 'instead of removing every question which placed the higher orders and the mass of the people in a state of conflict'. He emphasized that his opposition was confined to the 'isolated question of the impolicy of the proceedings against the queen', and he saw 'no inconsistency' in otherwise backing ministers because, 'if they weather this [storm], the interests of the country will require that they should receive every support which independent men can give them'. The Staffords appeared satisfied with this account.[2] He voted against the opposition motion censuring ministers' conduct towards the queen, 6 Feb., but was again in the minority for restoring her name to the liturgy, 13 Feb. He divided for Catholic relief, 28 Feb. He voted against government for repeal of the tax on agricultural horses, 5 Mar., and of the additional malt duty, 21 Mar., 3 Apr., but with them against Maberly's motion on the state of the revenue, 6 Mar. He was granted periods of leave, 12 Apr., 7 May, but was present to vote against parliamentary reform, 9 May 1821. Later that year he suffered an accident, which kept him 'confined' for a 'long' period of time.[3] His only recorded vote in the next session (if indeed this was he rather than Francis William Grant) was against abolition of one of the joint-postmasterships, 13 Mar. 1822. That month he warned Lady Stafford that the lord advocate's proposed bill to reform the Scottish burghs had been so extended in scope as to risk 'overturn[ing] the representation of half' of them, and he hoped that the government would 'consider the danger of thus laying the foundation of parliamentary reform'.[4] He was named to the select committee on the consolidation of the Scottish turnpike laws, 20 Mar., and introduced a bill for that purpose, 30 Apr.; it foundered at the report stage, 7 June 1822. He secured the appointment of a new committee, 28 Feb., and reported its findings, 25 Mar., when he introduced a revised measure which gained royal assent, 4 July 1823 (4 Geo. IV, c. 49).[5] He divided against Hume's motion on the sinking fund, 3 Mar., the repeal of assessed taxes, 10, 18 Mar., and inquiry into the currency, 12 June. He voted for the grant for Irish churches, 11 Apr. He divided against repeal of the Foreign Enlistment Act, 16 Apr., and two weeks later was one of the minority of 20 who 'remained in the House' during the division on British neutrality towards the French invasion of Spain.[6] He voted for Mackintosh's motion to abolish the death penalty for larceny, 21 May. He presented petitions complaining of agricultural distress, 14 Apr. 1823, and against any alteration in the wool duties, 29 Mar. 1824.[7] In the autumn of 1823 the Whig George Agar Ellis*, on a visit to Sutherland, noted that Macpherson Grant, 'a toad of Lady Stafford's', arrived unexpectedly, but added three days later that he had left, 'which made us very happy'.[8] His vote for repeal of the usury laws, 8 Apr. 1824, was the only one recorded for that session. He divided for the Irish unlawful societies bill, 25 Feb., but for Catholic relief, 1 Mar., 21 Apr., 10 May (paired) 1825. He was in the majority against the Leith docks bill, 20 May. He voted for the financial provision for the duke of Cumberland, 30 May 1825. His last known vote was against reform of Edinburgh's representation, 13 Apr. 1826. That month he presented several petitions against revision of the Scottish banking system.[9] At the dissolution that summer he was obliged to vacate his seat in order to accommodate the Staffords' son, and it proved impossible to provide for him in the Tain Burghs; he apparently submitted with a good grace.[10]

At the general election of 1830 Macpherson Grant explained to the Tory candidate for Inverness-shire that 'personal regard' obliged him to support Charles Grant*, but that this did not imply a want of confidence in the duke of Wellington's government.[11] The following spring he described himself as 'a supporter' of the Grey ministry's reform bill, but said that 'neither my health nor my private concerns' would permit him to stand for Banffshire. He demurred again in 1832.[12] He received a baronetcy in the coronation honours of 1838. He died in November 1846 and was succeeded by his eldest son John Macpherson Grant (1804-50).

[1] Macpherson Grant mss 345, Macpherson to Grant, 12 Jan., 27 Apr. 1795. [2] *The Times*, 27 Jan.; Macpherson Grant mss 361, Macpherson Grant to Lady Stafford, 27 Jan., reply, 1 Feb. 1821. [3] Macpherson Grant mss 475, Gardyne to Macpherson Grant, 3 Nov. 1821. [4] Ibid. 489, Macpherson Grant to Lady Stafford, 18 Mar.; 516, reply, 22 Mar. 1822. [5] Ibid. 499, 540, 611; Add. 40367, f. 82; *The Times*, 27 Feb. 1823. [6] *The Times*, 1 May 1823. [7] Ibid. 15 Apr. 1823, 30 Mar. 1824. [8] Northants. RO, Agar Ellis diary, 3, 6 Sept. 1823. [9] *The Times*, 8, 11, 14, 19 Apr. 1826. [10] Macpherson Grant mss 417, Macpherson Grant to Lady Stafford, 20 Apr.; 512, reply, 21 Apr. 1826. [11] Ibid. 690, Macpherson Grant to J. N. Macleod, 14 July 1830. [12] Ibid. 118, Macpherson Grant to son, 27 Apr. 1831; 361, same, 6 Aug. 1832.

D.R.F.

MACQUEEN, Thomas Potter (1792–1854), of Ridgmont House, nr. Woburn, Beds.[1]

EAST LOOE	15 Apr. 1816–1826
BEDFORDSHIRE	1826–1830

b. 28 May 1792, 1st s. of Malcolm Macqueen,[2] MD (Edinburgh), of St. Luke's, Norwich and Mariana, da. and event. h. of Thomas Potter† of Ridgmont, 2nd justice of Anglesey. *educ.* at Dr. Roberts's, Camberwell; at Mr. Nicholson's, St. Albans; Caius, Camb. 1810; L. Inn 1813. *m.* 26 Oct. 1820, Anne, da. of Sir Jacob Henry Astley†, 5th bt., of Melton Constable, Norf., 2s. 2da. *suc.* fa. 1829. *d.* 31 Mar. 1854.

Capt. Beds. yeoman cav. 1817, maj. commdt. 1817, lt.-col. 1820.

Macqueen's father, a Scottish doctor who retired in 1807 and took up agricultural improvement on the south Bedfordshire estate brought to him by his wife, was credited with the following aphorism on

> the character of the people of different countries in respect of economy. He said it is in this proportion: of ten men who possess this disposition, there may, perhaps, be found one Irishman; there will be two Englishmen, and seven Scotchmen.[3]

He settled his property in Bedfordshire and Kent on Macqueen before his marriage into a prominent Norfolk family in 1820. Macqueen, the sole executor and residuary legatee of his will, which he proved under £5,000, a month after his death, 24 July 1829, was no chip off the old block, for he spent copiously and carelessly in pursuit of the restless ambition which drove him to eventual ruin.[4] He was credited in 1830 with having on the occasion of his first return to Parliament in 1816 written and sent to his London address a letter to himself reminding him to take the oaths before he tried to vote.[5]

In November 1819 he wrote to his friend John Macarthur in New South Wales of the 'bad spirit among the lower classes and the idle poor', and his hope that any insurrection would be 'as little sanguinary as possible'. He contemplated going one day to Sydney as a 'rural settler'.[6] Two months later, claiming that no other Member was 'equally conversant in the affairs of the colony', he tried to interest Goulburn, under-secretary at the colonial office, in his plans for the promotion of Scottish emigration to the Cape. He saw systematic and subsidised emigration as one solution to the problems of over-population, rural poverty and rising poor rates, of which his own locality furnished many 'deplorable' examples:

> I yesterday presided at a bench of magistrates at Ampthill, and it was heartrending to witness the clamorous entreaties of the paupers on one side, and on the other, the loud remonstrances of the farmers, who declare their utter inability to provide employment and support for the people, when they get about 6*s*. 6*d*. per bushel for their corn. At this moment, we have nearly 2,000 young men between 16 and 25 years of age who are actually existing upon 4*s*. per week. Of course where there is misery there is seldom morality. Early and improvident marriages are constantly taking place without mutual regard, but with the view to obtain a larger rate of relief from the parish. This is one of the leading causes of the increase of population.[7]

At the general election of 1820 he was again returned for East Looe by Sir Edward Buller†, who, informing the premier Lord Liverpool of the fact as evidence of his own loyalty, commented that it was not necessary to say more of Macqueen, as he was 'a particular friend of your Lordship's'.[8] At the contested county election, he seconded the nomination of the sitting Member, Sir John Osborn*, a junior minister, who was defeated. His father had subscribed £500 to Osborn's election fund.[9] While Macqueen clearly continued to support the Liverpool administration, he had an appalling record of attendance during the 1820 Parliament, in which his only known votes were against more extensive tax reductions, 11, 21 Feb., abolition of one of the joint-postmasterships, 13 Mar. 1822, and inquiry into the prosecution of the Dublin Orange rioters, 22 Apr. 1823. He was given ten days' leave to deal with urgent private business, 12 Mar. 1821. Late in 1820 he tried and exhausted Liverpool's patience on the subject of one Major Williams, whose information of 'very little value and importance' on a supposed conspiracy was out of all proportion to his financial and other demands.[10] He signed the Bedfordshire loyal address to the king, adopted by the local Tories to counter the Whig campaign in support of Queen Caroline, 15 Jan. 1821.[11] When Lord Tavistock, the duke of Bedford's son and one of the two Whig county Members, presented the Bedfordshire reform petition, 26 Apr. 1822, Macqueen, in an intervention barely audible to the reporters, claimed on secondhand authority that anti-reformers had been forcibly excluded from the meeting, and stated his belief that 'the majority of England, like the majority of the county of Bedford, looked upon the taxation which burdened the country as the price of its redemption from foreign slavery'.[12] On 26 June 1822 Hume, making an allegation which was repeated in a radical publication the following year, suggested that the surprisingly high expenses of the Bedfordshire yeomanry cavalry represented a covert means of lining the pockets of Macqueen, their proud and self-important commander; Macqueen was adamant that all the sums granted were '*bona fide* expended for the service of the corps'.[13] He presented petitions from Dunstable and Luton protesting at the importation of foreign straw hats, 3 July 1823.[14] In 1825, when it was asserted in a contemporary review that he had 'attended occasionally, and voted with government', he introduced a bill to regulate the Provincial Bank of Ireland, which did not progress beyond its first reading, 21 Mar., and presented a Woburn petition in favour of the county courts bill, 25 Feb.[15] He brought up a petition from Bedfordshire coroners for an increase in their allowances, 14 Mar. 1826.[16]

In August 1820 Macqueen applied to Liverpool through Osborn to be appointed the first civil governor of New South Wales, who would take out with him 'a very large body of most valuable settlers' as part of his scheme to 'lessen the expenses, to promote the commerce, and to increase the prosperity of the colony'. He boasted that he was qualified by his 'knowledge of the principles of the law of the land, of commerce and of agriculture, energy of mind and activity of disposition, and above all independence of circumstances'. He told Osborn:

> With my prospects and intentions you are well acquainted, that I am disposed to exert the best efforts of my family and connections in support of government in our own county and elsewhere, but to enable me to do this with effect and safety, it is absolutely necessary that I be supported on this occasion. I have no mercenary end to gratify, but the increase of estate and property which might take place in my absence would permit me to adopt measures on my return which would materially assist our political views.[17]

He was passed over, but in July 1823, after the enactment of the New South Wales bill, he successfully applied to government for a grant of 10,000 acres in the interior, with a provisional reserve of 10,000 more, on condition that he invested his own capital in the settlement, cultivation and exploitation of the land, appointed resident agents and overseers, employed convict labour and encouraged emigration by the respectable poor. He appointed as his chief agent Peter McIntyre, who arrived in Australia in April 1825 with a party of carefully selected emigrants, plus livestock, agricultural equipment and tools. On his behalf McIntyre selected 10,000 acres on the River Hunter in the Newcastle area, and the estate which was developed there was called Segenhoe, after the Bedfordshire manor which formed part of the Ridgmont property. Macqueen failed, however, to obtain the ten acres on Sydney Cove which he wanted for the erection of warehouses, and in 1826 he applied, again without success, for an equivalent at Newcastle harbour. Claiming at the end of that year to have invested over £12,000 and to have settled 25 families plus numerous convicts, he called on government to grant him the reserved 10,000 acres, which, after the resolution of a dispute between McIntyre and a colonial official, were handed over to him in June 1827. Later that year, when he put his total investment at over £23,000 and promised the immediate injection of a further £5,000, he was given another small grant of 'inferior land' to consolidate his holding, and allowed to purchase an additional 2,000 contiguous acres which contained a good river ford. His project was the first significant experiment in controlled emigration to New South Wales, and his property there was the most important estate in this phase of the colony's development.[18]

Macqueen aspired to a county seat, and in September 1825, when a dissolution was anticipated, he declared his candidature for Bedfordshire at the next general election. In his canvass of the Luton area in late November he stressed his hostility to Catholic relief and stated that he was 'disposed to support the government, so long as he conceived [its] public conduct to merit his confidence'.[19] Tavistock, who offered on strict purity of election principles, reported in January 1826, when the announced retirement of his colleague Pym and the inability of the county Whigs to find another candidate prepared to stand a poll seemed certain to give Macqueen a walkover, that he had 'been telling a lie about his vote on the Catholic question [on which he is not known to have voted during ten years in the House], and has got into a scrape by it from which he will not easily extract himself'.[20] In fact it did him no harm, for although Pym was nominated in desperation, Macqueen finished comfortably at the head of the poll, over 200 votes above Tavistock. On the hustings, he reiterated his opposition to Catholic claims (his opponents made pointed references to his Catholic mother) and his general support for the ministry, though, under questioning, he said that he would oppose them, as he untruthfully claimed to have done already, if they interfered with the current level of agricultural protection.[21] It was no secret that he had spent very heavily, and there was talk of a petition against him alleging bribery and treating; his total expenditure was later said by the Whigs to have been in excess of £30,000.[22] At one of a series of dinners to celebrate his success, 20 July 1826, he denied that he was 'a tax-loving Tory' and mocked the Whigs' record on this subject during their mercifully brief period in office 20 years earlier.[23] In September, when Macqueen was still lording it in the county, the duke of Bedford explained to Lady Holland, who of course regarded him as 'a contemptible fellow', that

> the splendid equipage which you saw (under permission) pass through Ampthill Park to the races, consisted of four grey horses, which are more usefully employed on ordinary days, in the plough on the old doctor's farm, and his two plough or stable boys to drive them, dressed out in some cast off lord mayor's jackets, which the venerable doctor purchased for the last county contest in 1820.[24]

In November 1826 a hostile newspaper mischievously reported that Macqueen was spreading the story that he was to move the address at the opening of Parliament; in the event, he did no more than secure a return of the number of recent appeals from quarter sessions to king's bench, 29 Nov.[25] Early in 1827 Macqueen, whose wife sustained burns to her face and neck in an accident at Ridgmont, rented Osborn's residence at Chicksands Priory, where he subsequently entertained Tory ministers with shooting parties.[26] It was reported locally that he had voted for the duke of Clarence's allowance, 19 Feb., but a statement that he had done likewise on 2 Mar. was afterwards emphatically refuted.[27] He voted against Catholic relief, 6 Mar. When presenting the Redbournstoke petition against any alteration of the corn laws, 20 Feb., he argued that 'it could be readily shown, that those evils which had so severely afflicted the country, were referable to very different causes than the operation of the present system'. He presented a number of similar petitions, 14, 23, 30 Mar.[28] He voted against the second reading of the new corn bill, 2 Apr., and at the county meeting to petition the Lords against it, 23 May, complained that it did not offer sufficient protection to farmers, who were unfairly burdened with taxation. He attended an agriculturists' dinner to celebrate its defeat in the Upper House, 28 June 1827.[29]

In this Parliament Macqueen took up the vexed subject of the law of settlement. He did not proceed with the amendment bill of which he gave notice, 13 Feb. 1827, but he drew attention to the problem at the Bedfordshire agricultural show in October and tackled it in the House in 1828.[30] Moving successfully for the appointment of a select committee of inquiry, 21 Feb., he warned that 'there might be somewhat of novelty in his views' on the 'harsh and evil policy of the present law'. He advocated abolition of the current regulations affecting settlement by hiring and service, which produced a huge number of expensive appeals from sessions and had a bad moral effect on the poor, and changes to those governing settlement by marriage. On 18 Mar. he introduced a bill to deal with hiring and servitude, which he had printed for the consideration of Members and other interested parties. When he moved its second reading, 29 Apr., he explained that the committee had decided, though not yet formally reported, that revision of the law of settlement was an essential prerequisite of poor law reform. He argued that it was the 'paramount duty of every government to provide and encourage the providing of employment for its population, as the means of their subsistence', and that this employment 'ought to comprehend a sufficiency of the necessaries, and a moderate share of the enjoyments of life'. After detailing his personal experience of the level of rural poverty and unemployment in Bedfordshire, where rates were soaring, he predicted that

> if the progress of pauperism proceeded as it had done during the last twelve months, the time was not far distant when the whole of the produce of the country would be absorbed, not in adding to the comfort and happiness, but in ensuring the degradation and misery, of the poorer classes.

If a domestic solution was not found, he concluded, resort must be had to controlled emigration. The measure had a mixed reception, but Peel, the home secretary, thought the balance of argument was marginally in its favour. Macqueen, who presented a petition from the Society for the Encouragement of Industry for amelioration of the condition of agricultural labourers, 9 May, was named to the select committees on parochial accounts, 15 May, and the poor laws, 22 May. On 9 June 1828 he brought up the report of his select committee and postponed his bill until the next session. He duly brought it in, 18 Feb. 1829, but it encountered strong opposition in committee, 3 Mar., and made no further progress after 4 May. Macqueen did not attempt to revive it in 1830.

He voted against repeal of the Test Acts, 26 Feb., and, after presenting anti-Catholic petitions, 7 May, against relief, 12 May 1828. Presenting a petition for agricultural protection from 400 Bedfordshire landowners and 600 shopkeepers, 25 Apr., he described it as the 'first instance of a body of tradesmen coming forward to advocate the necessity of fair remunerating prices to the farmer'. He brought up a petition from Wixamtree against the revised scale of corn duties, 19 May. He divided with the Wellington ministry against ordnance reductions, 4 July 1828. He had ingratiated himself with the 2nd marquess of Salisbury and his acolyte Samuel Grove Price*, and shared in their financial support of the Tory and anti-Catholic *Herts Mercury*. Writing to Salisbury in Vienna in September 1828, he anticipated the Catholic question coming to a head in the next session:

> It is said that the duke of Wellington and the lord chancellor have an idea of proposing securities to be given by the Catholics. I am disposed to smile at this plan as proceeding from those who are not aware of the leading attribute of Popery, namely *submission to the infallible church* ... Although they have accepted of every liberality, they have conceded nothing ... The duke of Wellington I consider *firm in power*. If any measures be adopted to give further concessions I fully expect Peel to retire.

Salisbury, who deplored the alarmism of the Brunswickers, counselled 'shrewdness and moderation', qualities for which Macqueen was not especially noted.[31] He did, however, give only silent opposition to Catholic emancipation, 6, 18 Mar., and did not vote in the divisions of 23, 27, 30 Mar., being forced to take a pair on the latter occasion on account of his father's terminal illness.[32] He presented hostile petitions, 12, 18 Mar. At the Cambridge University by-election of June 1829 he voted for the anti-Catholic Bankes.

Macqueen, who in the autumn of 1828 claimed to be clearing £1,000 a year from the stock of his pedigree bull at Segenhoe and £300 from that of each stallion, and hoped soon to make an annual profit of £1,500 from wool, tried to interest Salisbury in investing in land in New South Wales. He seems to have exceeded his authority and to have caused himself some financial embarrassment by making a purchase which Salisbury refused to endorse.[33] In November 1828 he joined three other men in applying to government for a large grant of land on the Swan River, where they hoped to cultivate tobacco, cotton, flax and sugar, in return for paying for the cost of sending out 10,000 British settlers, but he soon withdrew from the scheme.[34] In the summer of 1829 he resumed his futile bid to secure a warehouse site at Newcastle.[35] He visited Scotland and Paris in the autumn of 1829, when, following his father's death, he had the house at Ridgmont rebuilt.[36]

At the county meeting to petition for repeal of the malt tax, 16 Feb. 1830, he criticized ministers for the 'unguarded expression' concerning distress which they had inserted in the speech from the throne; asserted that 'at no former period did such an intense degree of misery and wretchedness exist'; advocated 'an equitable adjustment' of the currency to 'meet the interests both of the fundholder and the landlord' and 'render justice to the working classes', and called for due protection for domestic agriculture, observing that 'the essence and real meaning of free trade he always considered to be reciprocity'.[37] He presented the meeting's petition, 18 Mar., with a similar one from Caddington. On 17 Mar. presented a petition from the Bedfordshire authorities for revision of the vagrancy laws and seconded Portman's motion to refer it to the select committee on the Irish poor, to which he had been appointed on the 11th. He was reported in the press to have paired on the ministerial side against the enfranchisement of Birmingham, Leeds and Manchester, 23 Feb., but with opposition against the Bathurst and Dundas pensions, 26 Mar.[38] He voted against government for a reduction of the grant for volunteers, 9 Mar., and the production of information on British interference in the internal affairs of Portugal, 10 Mar., and in condemnation of the appointment of a treasurer of the navy, 12 Mar. He presented a Bedfordshire petition for an increase in the import duty on foreign flour, 27 May. He was in the minority for an amendment to the beer bill which sought to prohibit on-sales, 21 June. In May 1830 he published *Thoughts and Suggestions on the Present State of the Country*, in which he elaborated his arguments in favour of emigration and colonization as a solution to the problems of rural poverty, unemployment and crime. It attracted favourable notice in *The Times*.[39] Earlier in the year it had been thought unlikely that he could afford another contest for the county; and when a second Tory, William Stuart*, a kinsman of Lord Bute with a deep pocket, offered at the general election following the king's death, Macqueen announced his retirement. He initially did so with a good grace, claiming that he did not wish to subject the county to a divisive contest and that it was desirable, in the present state of affairs, where party distinctions had become blurred, even obsolete, that it should have a balanced representation. On 26 July, however, he produced a sour address in which he accused Stuart and Bute of having persuaded ministers to interfere against him as an act of vengeance for his recent wayward votes. There was some speculation that he might be put in nomination, but he went on an excursion to the continent and was out of the way when the election occurred. Ministers reckoned his replacement by Stuart as a gain.[40]

He claimed 2*s.* each for 63 special constables enrolled to keep order in his Bedfordshire parish during the period of rural unrest at the end of 1830.[41] Soon afterwards he published a pamphlet on *The State of the Nation at the Close of 1830*, in which he attacked the Wellington ministry for its failure to deal with distress and poverty. He advocated a partial repeal of the 1819 Currency Act, in conjunction with abolition of the Bank of England's monopoly and the adoption in England of the Scottish banking system, and, above all, his favourite nostrum of managed emigration to Australia, which should cease to be a penal colony. *The Times* liked it less than his previous tract, but gave it generous coverage. Some of his figures on the current cost of administering New South Wales were later shown to be wildly exaggerated.[42] At the contested Bedfordshire election of 1831 he did what he could to assist Tavistock and a fellow reformer, who defeated Stuart.[43] In his evidence to the Commons select committee on secondary punishments, 5, 9 Aug. 1831, he recommended a revision of the transportation system, which was inhibiting respectable emigration to New South Wales; but he could not say how the punishment, which in practice offered the starving labourer a veritable incentive to commit crime, could be made more effectively severe. Sydney Smith commented that 'the ancient profession of picking pockets will certainly not become more discreditable from the knowledge that it may eventually lead to the possession of a farm of a thousand acres on the River Hawkesbury'.[44]

In 1832 Macqueen tried again to obtain land on the Sydney sea frontage, but, despite the colonial secretary Lord Goderich's endorsement of his application, the New South Wales authorities turned it down. He also clashed with them and the home government over a demand for quit-rent on his additional land acquisitions, from which he unsuccessfully claimed exemption by agreement with previous ministries. He complained to the colonial under-secretary that 'it is particularly to be lamented that the practical part of Australian government is so very different from the theoretical assurances held forth in Downing Street', and moaned that 'I have not had fair play in the colony'.[45] That year he unleashed on the world a gloomy assessment of *The State of the Country*, in which he added repeal of the usury laws to his well rehearsed list of solutions. Financial problems were crowding in upon Macqueen, who sold his Bedfordshire property to the duke of Bedford in 1832 and 1833. His wife died in the latter year.[46] He played a leading role in the negotiations with the treasury which led to the formation of the Bank of Australasia in 1832-3, though he had little influence in its affairs thereafter, despite briefly holding a seat on its provisional board.[47] In 1834 he went out to take personal charge of Segenhoe, which falling prices and inefficient management had made unprofitable. He was prominent in the formation of the Commercial Banking Company of Sydney, a rival to the Bank of Australasia, and during the next four years cut a conspicuous figure in colonial society. However, his repeated attempts to secure a harbour site were in vain, as was his bid for an additional land grant in compensation. His claims that he had invested over £42,000 in the colony, employed 160 convicts and rehabilitated 20 of them, encouraged respectable settlers and erected churches and a hospital cut no ice with the Melbourne ministry, who insisted on strict adherence to the regulations governing additional grants. A sale of Segenhoe stock was reported in January 1838, and in August Macqueen left the colony, having leased the estate and placed its affairs in the hands of a Sydney agent.[48] On his journey back to England by way of India, Ceylon, Egypt, Malta, Italy and France, he studied all the agricultural products capable of cultivation in Australia, as he explained in his 1840 pamphlet, *Australia as She is and as She may be*, a protest against the 'extraordinary and unforeseen' report of the recent parliamentary inquiry, which, if implemented, would 'stultify all the progress of the last few years'. He recommended the combination of 'large free immigration' with a revised and more lenient system of transportation, the encouragement of varied cultivation, the establishment of a House of Assembly, with control over internal revenues, and the banishment of the Aborigines to the interior, where there was plenty of room for them to die out. In the Commons debate on transportation, 5 May 1840, Lord John Russell cited with approval Macqueen's views on the remedial effects of transportation on convicts with 'skill and talent'.

He was by now in deep financial trouble. In 1845 he was living at Caen, and by 1852 he was resident at Banbury. He died of apoplexy at the *Queen's Hotel*, Oswestry in March 1854.[49] By his will, dated 23 Jan. 1853, he tried to provide for his three younger children, Henry Archibald, Flora Georgina and Anne, through the sale of his remaining property in England and Australia, having catered for his elder son, John Potter, by the sale of Ridgmont 20 years earlier. But the will was not proved until 22 Mar. 1856, when administration was granted to the legal representative of a creditor, and the personal estate was sworn under a derisory £20.[50]

[1] See *Australian Dict. of Biog.* ii. 195-6. [2] There is an account of him in W. Munk, *Roll R. Coll. Physicians*, ii. 446, under the Latinised name of Columbus Macqueen. [3] *Farington Diary*, xiv. 4917. [4] PROB 11/1759/497; IR26/1201/347; *Gent. Mag.* (1829), ii. 188. [5] Hopetoun mss 167, f. 149. [6] J.J. Eddy, *Britain and the Australian Colonies, 1818-1831*, pp. 39-40. [7] *Cape Recs.* xiii. 2-3. [8] Add. 38283, f. 228. [9] *Cambridge and Hertford Independent Press*, 18 Mar. 182; Beds. RO, Wrest mss L 30/11/204/9. [10] Add. 38288, ff. 80, 82, 245, 253. [11] *Northampton Mercury*, 20 Jan. 1821. [12] *The Times*, 26 Apr. 1822. [13] *Cambridge and Hertford Independent Press*, 25 May; *The Times*, 27 June 1822; *Black Bk.* (1823), 175. [14] *The Times*, 4 July 1823. [15] *Session of Parl. 1825*, p. 475; *The Times*, 19, 26 Feb., 22 Mar. 1825; *CJ*, lxxx. 237. [16] *The Times*, 15 Mar. 1826. [17] Add. 38286, ff. 371, 372. [18] *Hist. Recs. of Australia* (ser. 1), xi. 141-3, 250, 381-2; xii. 794-5; xiii. 150, 156, 623-3; xiv. 239; xv. 78-79; Eddy, 61, 224; J.F. Campbell, 'Genesis of Rural Settlement on Hunter', *R. Australian Hist. Soc. Jnl. and Procs.* xii (1926-7), 84, 91-93; W.J. Goold, 'These Old Homes', *Newcastle and Hunter District Hist. Soc. Jnl. and Procs.* v (1950-1), 158-9. [19] *Herts. Mercury*, 17 Sept., 3 Dec. 1825; TCD, Jebb mss 6396/238. [20] *The Times*, 19 Dec.; Add. 36461, f. 385; 51749, Holland to H.E. Fox, 30 Dec. 1825; 51766, Lady Holland to same, 18 Jan. [1826]. [21] *The Times*, 19, 23, 24, 27 June; *Herts Mercury*, 10, 17, 24 June; *Cambridge and Hertford Independent Press*, 8 July 1826. [22] *Althorp Letters*, 129; Fitzwilliam mss, Tavistock to Milton, 3 Dec. [1826], 5 July 1830. [23] *Herts Mercury*, 22, 29 July, 5, 12, 19 Aug. 1826. [24] Add. 51669, Bedford to Lady Holland, 7 Sept.; 51766, Lady Holland to H.E. Fox, 18 Jan. [1826]. [25] *Cambridge and Hertford Independent Press*, 11 Nov.; *The Times*, 30 Nov. 1826. [26] *Cambridge and Hertford Independent Press*, 3 Feb.; *Herts Mercury*, 17 Feb. 1827, 19 Dec. 1829; *Russell Letters*, i. 115; Hatfield House mss 2M/Gen., Macqueen to Salisbury, 11 Sept. 1828. [27] *Cambridge and Hertford Independent Press*, 24 Feb.; *Herts Mercury*, 3, 10 Mar. 1827. [28] *Herts Mercury*, 24 Feb.; *The Times*, 21 Feb., 24, 29, 30 Mar. 1827. [29] *Cambridge and Hertford Independent Press*, 26 May, 7 July 1827. [30] *The Times*, 14 Feb., 31 May; *Herts Mercury*, 19 May; *Cambridge and Hertford Independent Press*, 13 Oct. 1827. [31] Hatfield House mss 2M/Gen., Macqueen to Salisbury, 20 July, 11 Sept., Sun. [Dec.], reply [Dec. 1828]. [32] *Herts Mercury*, 21 Mar., 11 Apr. 1829. [33] Hatfield House mss 2M/Gen., Macqueen to Salisbury, 11 Sept., Sun. [Dec.] 1828, 4 Jan., reply, 9 Jan. 1829. [34] *Hist. Recs. of Australia* (ser. 3), vi. 588-90, 610. [35] Ibid. (ser. 1), xv. 78. [36] *Herts Mercury*, 24 Oct. 1829. [37] Ibid. 20 Feb. 1830. [38] *The Times*, 1 Mar.; *Herts Mercury*, 17 Apr. 1830. [39] *The Times*, 6, 20 May 1830; *Some Beds. Diaries* (Pubs. Beds. Hist. Rec. Soc. xl), 132-3; J. Godber, *Hist. Beds.* 420-1. [40] Bodl. MS. Eng. lett. c. 160, f. 134; *Herts Mercury*, 10, 31 July; *Althorp Letters*, 151; Beds. RO AD 1081; Add. 40401, f. 132; 51670, Bedford to Lady Holland, Fri. [July 1830]. [41] A.F. Cirket, '1830 Riots in Beds.', *Pubs. Beds. Hist. Rec. Soc.* lvii (1978), 101. [42] *The Times*, 3 Jan. 1831; *Hist. Recs. of Australia* (ser. 1), xvi. 303. [43] Beds. RO, Russell mss R3/3676; R 767, Macqueen to Tavistock's cttee. [1831]. [44] *PP* (1831), vii. 610-15; E. Stockdale, *A Study of Bedford Prison, 1660-1877* (Pubs. Beds. Hist. Rec. Soc. lvi), 155. [45] *Hist. Recs. of Australia* (ser. 1), xvi. 507; xvii. 8-13. [46] *Diary of a Beds. Squire* ed. R. Morgan (Pubs. Beds. Hist. Rec, Soc. lxvi), 1; *Cambridge and Hertford Independent Press*, 31 Mar. 1832; *VCH Beds.* iii. 293, 321; *Gent. Mag.* (1833), ii. 90. [47] S.J. Butlin, *Australia and New Zealand Bank*, 21-23, 33, and *Foundations of Australian Monetary System*, 251, 259; *Hist. Recs. of Australia* (ser. 3), xviii. 12-14. [48] Campbell, 93-94; Butlin, *Foundations*, 251; *Hist. Recs. of Australia* (ser. 1), xvii. 713-14; xviii. 164-5, 252, 265-6, 448, 498, 513, 623; xix. 540-4; xx. 61, 575-8. [49] W. Cathrall, *Oswestry*, 147; *Gent. Mag.* (1854), i. 558. [50] PROB 11/2229/226; IR26/2070/233.

D.R.F.

MADOCKS, William Alexander (1773–1828), of Tan-yr-allt and Morva Lodge, Caern, and Tregunter Hall, Brec.

BOSTON	1802–1820
CHIPPENHAM	1820–1826

b. 17 June 1773,[1] 3rd. surv. s. of John Madocks† of Fron Yw, Denb. and Frances, da. of Joseph Whitchurch, London merchant, of Twickenham, Mdx. *educ.* Charterhouse 1784-9 (expelled); Christ Church, Oxf. 1790, fellow, All Souls 1794-1818; L. Inn 1790; I. Temple 1797. *m.* 2 Apr. 1818,[2] Amelia Sophia, da. and coh. of Samuel Hughes, land agent (who *m.* the Harris heiress of Tregunter Hall), wid. of Roderick Gwynne of Buckland, Brec., 1da. *suc.* fa. to estate in Denb. 1794. *d.* 29 Sept. 1828.

Dir. Hope Insurance Co. 1811-14.

Chamberlain to Queen Caroline 1820-1.

A member of a well-established Denbighshire family, Madocks directed his considerable energies towards the extraordinary engineering projects that became known as 'the Wonder of Wales'. During this period, despite financial problems and poor health, he sought to exploit the area of land between Caernarvonshire and Merionethshire which he had enclosed from the sea, and where he had founded Tremadoc, by the establishment of a harbour at Porthmadog to export slate from the interior.[3] However, he was clearly more or less bankrupt in practice, even though he was never formally declared to be so. In 1820 he was saddened by the death of his brother Joseph, known to the *beau monde* as 'the gayest of the gay', whose will revealed that, like many others, he held a mortgage on part of Madocks's property.[4] Thomas Love Peacock, who accused him of 'complicated villainy and lying' after he refused to return some books belonging to Percy Bysshe Shelley that had been left in his safekeeping as collateral for a debt, informed his fellow poet, 28 Feb. 1822, that Madocks was

> determined to stand an action, with which he has been menaced, thinking perhaps that I shall not be willing to incur so great an expense; more especially as he is insolvent, and all the expenses would thereupon fall upon me, whether I should gain or lose the cause.[5]

Forced to rent out Tan-yr-allt, he lived mostly at Tregunter Hall.[6] Although he afterwards claimed that he could have come in again for Boston at the general election of 1820, he failed to redeem a promise to his constituents to stand, no doubt because the expense would have been too high. (Indeed, he appealed to Lord Darlington for financial assistance.) Instead he purchased a seat for Chippenham, which he thought would prove to be less troublesome, and he was duly elected unopposed, probably on the interest of Anthony Guy, a local solicitor.[7] Formerly a man of sound radical credentials – Charles James Fox and the 11th duke of Norfolk were once 'great *private* and *political* friends' – by 1820 he had largely drifted into obscurity.[8] With his business affairs in a parlous state and demanding all the attention he could give them, it is not surprising that he made no reported speeches during this period and was generally inactive in Parliament.

He voted with opposition on the civil list, 5 May, but on 3 July 1820 was granted a month's leave of absence on account of an attack of jaundice, which he described as 'a miserable complaint'.[9] In a letter printed in *The Times*, 26 June, he claimed that 'severe indisposition' had prevented him from dividing against Wilberforce's compromise motion on the Queen Caroline affair four days earlier. Initially wary of presenting her with an address from Brecon,[10] he came under local pressure to do so, and relented on the grounds that it was couched in respectful language and was such that 'any friend of the House of Brunswick' might safely sign. In a published letter he wrote that he was afraid that

> whenever Members of Parliament become the slavish tools of power, whenever they cease to hold connection with the people and feel no interest in public liberty ... what you dread will really take place, namely the downfall of the greatness of your country; but on the other hand, if the representatives of the people respect and observe the sacred principles of the constitution, if they keep a vigilant eye on the public expenditure and maintain a constant jealousy of power, if they control extravagance, promote economy and keep down taxation, the confidence of the people in their rulers will then place our envied institutions on a rock, where they will long survive the storms and shocks which corrupt and arbitrary governments periodically suffer.[11]

Addresses from Brecon and Chippenham were among those which he therefore felt it was his duty to present to the queen.[12] He signed the requisition for a Breconshire meeting on the issue, which he attended, 20 Jan. 1821. His close involvement in it was described by Thomas Wood, the county Member, as a vain attempt to strengthen the local Whig influence.[13] He voted to restore Caroline's name to the liturgy, 26 Jan., 13 Feb., and in condemnation of ministers' conduct towards her, 6 Feb. His appointment as her chamberlain drew the scorn of Lady Williams Wynn, who observed that it was 'certainly making one step towards having a brilliant Court'.[14] He was sometimes involved in the promotion of Welsh interests and legislation in the House: for example, in attempts to reduce the duties on Welsh coal.[15] It was in pursuance of his own concerns, however, that he was most active. His petition for a bill to allow the construction of Porthmadog harbour was presented, 2 Feb., and was supported by other Welsh Members. It survived technical problems, local opposition from the guardians of the young Lord Newborough, and Lords' amendments, to be given royal assent, 15 June.[16] Madocks was listed as a steward for, but apparently did not attend, the *City of London Tavern* reform dinner, 4 Apr.[17] He divided in favour of inquiry into Peterloo, 16 May 1821.

Having crossed to Le Havre in September 1821, Lord Palmerston* informed his sister that

> our party was not very large but somewhat comical. The principal personages were Bob Heathcote without his Columbine, and William Madocks with a portly dame who passed among the passengers for Lady Madocks but

> who was better qualified for Falstaff than Columbine. But both Heathcote and Madocks are entertaining people.[18]

Madocks voted for Hume's amendment to the address, 5 Feb., further tax reductions to relieve distress, 11 Feb., and the inclusion of a clause in the Irish insurrection bill to require trial by jury, 8 Feb. 1822. No evidence of parliamentary attendance has been traced for the following session. He voted to condemn the trial of the Methodist missionary John Smith in Demerara, 11 June 1824. He was again given a month's leave on medical grounds, 18 Feb. 1825, and later that year he consulted a celebrated liver doctor, 'in order that I may know how to regulate my medicine, diet, etc'.[19] By the mid-1820s he was in 'mild despair' over his plans to link Ffestiniog and Porthmadog by rail, especially because a rival set of interests had decided that the line between the slate mines and the coast should be established along an alternative route. After the necessary legal preparations, his petition for a bill was presented, 18 Feb. 1825, but it was not proceeded with. He tried again the following year, amid much bustle and with anxious hopes for support. His petition was presented, 13 Feb. 1826, and he wrote to his agent, John Williams, 24 Feb., urgently requesting him to meet him at the office of Richard Jones, a clerk of the House, before the committee on 3 Mar., 'so that we may give up our minds to the *most important [?]æra* in our lives'. However, an opposition was again raised, and his scheme collapsed.[20]

In May 1824 there was a possibility that about 20 properties in Chippenham, a burgage borough, might have been sold to Madocks by Guy for £14,000, but they were purchased instead by the Maitlands, who thereby gained a controlling interest.[21] Madocks, who had failed to cultivate any influence of his own in the constituency and had hardly ever visited it, was forced to turn elsewhere.[22] In September 1825, anticipating a dissolution, he briefly canvassed East Retford, and issued an address in favour of free trade and independence. Surprisingly, he came forward with the support of the duke of Newcastle as an opponent of Catholic relief, for which he had formerly voted. Yet he almost immediately withdrew, apparently in disgust at having failed to gain a single promise, and was ridiculed as a 'Mad Ox' and pilloried for his reluctance to re-enter the fray.[23] He sided with ministers against receiving the report on the salary of the president of the board of trade, 10 Apr. 1826. This, his last recorded vote, was the only one he is known to have given against his Whig friends, and it may indicate that he felt an increasing degree of sympathy with the government's more liberal policies. Hudson Gurney* recorded in his diary, 7 May, that at a ministerial dinner given by the foreign secretary Canning, 'Madocks the radical reformer, Sir Charles Forbes and myself [were] the only ones not dead votes'. Having failed to find an alternative seat, he left the Commons at the dissolution in 1826.

As a result of his precarious finances and deteriorating health he left England with his family in May that year, and travelled via France and Switzerland to Naples, from where he continued to issue lengthy and exhortative instructions to Williams. It was always his intention to return, so he must have believed that his business affairs were retrievable, and on 5 July 1827 he wrote that 'in November I am to come in for a borough in *Ireland*. All is arranged for that purpose'. Nothing, however, came of this plan.[24] He looked upon 1828 as the year for the salvation of his fortunes, though he was at times disheartened by numerous setbacks, particularly to his recovery, which delayed his journey home. In characteristic style, he complained, 14 Feb., that

> I have had the fatigue, and anxiety for 17 years of keeping all together, and preserving for others what would all have gone to the Devil and Tremadoc returned to a mere wilderness. How then could those who can now get something, ever have got anything except for the efforts I have made to *keep the property together*, and *where* would the persons be now, who now are flourishing upon the property and enjoying and turning it to account to their own benefit, while I individually, notwithstanding such *undiminished* efforts, and getting friends to come forward from time to time, am only repaid by constant mortification, vexation and breach of all arrangements that are made for the great end, that is *equally* the interest of *all*, whether they have claims on the property that can *produce anything only by my arrangements* and exertions or whether they reside on the property, and are now doing well upon it?[25]

He died in Paris in September, while on his way back to Wales. That his efforts were recognized there was shown by an obituary in the *Carmarthen Journal*, 3 Oct. 1828, which noted that he had 'spent a princely fortune in useful improvements and set an example, which it would be wished that every gentleman of wealth, property and influence would follow'. The Ffestiniog Railway, which was completed in 1836, owed much to his inspiration, and his other schemes prospered.[26] A limited administration was granted in May 1834, but without a valuation, and it is doubtful that he left much of an estate.[27] His wife, generally known as Eliza Ann, who may have enjoyed a family income of her own, had personalty valued at under £8,000 on her death in 1859. Their only child,

Eliza Anne Maria Ermine, married Roderick Gwynne Holford (*d.* 1849), and then John Webb Roche (*d.* 1869) of Rochemount, County Cork, with whom she had four children. John Madocks (*d.* 1837) of Glan-y-wern and Fron Yw, Denbighshire, who was sometimes mistakenly referred to by contemporaries as Madocks's son, but was in fact his nephew, served as Liberal Member for Denbigh Boroughs, 1832-4.[28]

[1] NLW mss 10590. [2] IGI (Brec.). [3] E. Beazley, *Madocks and the Wonder of Wales* (1967). Madocks's business corresp. is in NLW, Porthmadoc mss and Gwynedd (Caern.) RO, Madocks mss XD/8/2. [4] Porthmadoc mss 287; *Cambrian*, 19 Feb. 1820; PROB 11/1636/626; IR26/833/1066; Beazley, 213. [5] *Peacock Letters* ed. R. Garnett (1910), 42, 62, 93-94. [6] Porthmadoc mss 285, 289. [7] Ibid. 290; Grey mss GRE/B10/9/18; *Lincoln, Rutland and Stamford Mercury*, 10 Mar.; *Devizes Gazette*, 23 Mar. 1820; Beazley, 209. [8] NLW mss 20575B, f. 26; *HP Commons, 1790-1820*, iv. 519-21. [9] Porthmadoc mss 292. [10] *Shrewsbury Chron.* 20 Oct. 1820. [11] *Cambrian*, 28 Oct. 1820. [12] Ibid. 4 Nov. 1820; Devizes Mus. Cuttings, xii. 31. [13] *Hereford Jnl.* 10, 24 Jan.; NLW, Maybery mss 6545, Wood to Jones, 17 Jan. 1821. [14] *Williams Wynn Corresp.* 206. [15] P.K. Crimmin, 'William Alexander Madocks and removal of Welsh coal duties', *Trans. Caern. Hist. Soc.* xliii (1982), 125-8. [16] Porthmadoc mss 279; *CJ*, lxxvi. 25, 37, 47, 118, 303, 331, 396, 401, 427, 430, 442; Beazley, 215-17. [17] *The Times*, 4, 5 Apr. 1821. [18] Countess of Airlie, *Lady Palmerston and her Times*, i. 95. [19] Madocks mss XD/8/2/210. [20] Ibid. XD/8/2/201, 210, 215; Porthmadoc mss 312, 318, 319, 322, 335; *CJ*, lxxx. 74; lxxxi. 36, 143, 159, 226, 248; Beazley, 217-22; J.I.C. Boyd, *Ffestiniog Railway*, i. 15-22. See CAERNARVONSHIRE. [21] Wilts. RO, Bevir mss 1171/9, 'Mem. in London', 24 May 1824; 1171/15, 'Some mems. on treating with Mr. Fuller Maitland', June 1824. [22] *Devizes Gazette*, 22 Sept. 1825; NLW mss 20575B, f. 12. [23] Madocks mss XD/8/2/220; Porthmadoc mss 332; *Nottingham Rev.* 23 Sept. 1825; *Electionana Retfordiensis* (1825), 3-9, 39-40, 54, 105. [24] Beazley, 225-33; Madocks mss XD/8/2/247. [25] Madocks mss XD/8/2/253, 256, 264, 270, 275. [26] Beazley, 233-7; *Oxford DNB*. [27] PROB 6/210. [28] Griffith, *Peds. of Anglesey and Caern. Fams.* 315.

S.M.F.

MADRYLL CHEERE, Charles (?1772–1825), of Papworth Hall, Caxton, Cambs. and 18 Charles Street, Berkeley Square, Mdx.

CAMBRIDGE 1820–10 Jan. 1825

b. ?1772. *m.* (1) 10 Nov. 1795, Charlotte Price (*bur.* 12 Feb. 1797) of St. Anne, Soho, Mdx., 1s.[1]; (2) 20 Aug. 1799, Frances, da. of Charles Cheere of Westbourne Green, Paddington, Mdx., 10s. (2 *d.v.p.*) 4da. (2 *d.v.p.*)[2]. Took additional name of Cheere by royal lic. 12 Feb. 1808. *d.* 10 Jan. 1825.

This Member's origins remain obscure, though his early connections seem to have been with London. In 1794, as Charles Madryll, he bought from Matthew Holworthy the estate of Papworth Everard on the western edge of Cambridgeshire, about 12 miles from Cambridge and adjoining the Ermine Street Roman road between Royston and Huntingdon.[3] His first wife died in February 1797, a few days after the birth of their only child, Charles Price Madryll, who was not baptized until 20 July 1799.[4] In August that year Madryll married the 17-year-old niece and co-heiress (with her sister Emma, who remained a spinster) of the Rev. Sir William Cheere, 2nd baronet, of White Roding, Essex. Cheere was the eldest son and successor of Sir Henry Cheere (1703-81), the leading statuary of his day. At his marriage Madryll settled the whole of the Papworth estate on his wife and her issue. It is not known why Charles Price Madryll, who was still alive in 1828, was excluded.[5] When Sir William Cheere died unmarried in February 1808 all his property, which included real estate in Westminster (at Charing Cross) and was reckoned to be worth £150,000, was divided equally between his nieces.[6] In anticipation of this inheritance Madryll took for himself and his wife the additional name of Cheere; their children were to bear the name of Cheere only.

Madryll Cheere's wish to extend the grounds of the old manor house at Papworth led him into conflict with the trustees of the Ermine Street turnpike. In 1798 he was fined for refusing to allow stones to be gathered from his land for road repairs; and the following year he defied an order to remove a hedge and ditch which he had placed too close to the highway. In 1800, however, he lent the trustees £200 towards road repairs, and soon afterwards joined the board. He was no longer a trustee in 1818, when his proposal for the road to be diverted round the eastern edge of his estate was dismissed out of hand.[7] In 1808 he commissioned George Byfield to design a new mansion house in the classical style, which was completed in 1810. Madryll Cheere spent a considerable portion of his wife's fortune on building and furnishing it in sumptuous fashion.[8] His attempt of 1819, which was supported by the 5th duke of Rutland, to have the Cheere baronetcy revived in the person of his son and heir, William Henry Cheere (*b.* 1800), was unsuccessful.[9] Madryll Cheere was a deputy lieutenant and magistrate of Cambridgeshire, but he was not popular in the county, where he had a reputation for moroseness and stinginess. In January 1822 William Cobbett†, travelling from London to Huntingdon, wrote at Royston:

> Between this place and Huntingdon is the village of Caxton, which very much resembles almost a village of the same size in *Picardy*, where I saw the women dragging harrows to harrow in the corn. Certainly this village resembles nothing English, except some of the rascally rotten boroughs in Cornwall and Devonshire, on which a just Providence seems to have entailed its curse. The land just about here does seem to be really bad ... All is bleak and comfortless ... Not far from this is a new house,

> which, the coachman says, belongs to a Mr. Cheer, who, if report speaks truly, is not, however, notwithstanding his name, guilty of making people either drunkards or gluttons. Certainly the spot, on which he has built his house, is one of the most ugly that I ever saw. Few spots have everything that you could wish to find; but this, according to my judgement, has everything that every man of ordinary taste would wish to avoid.[10]

At the general election of 1820 Madryll Cheere stood for Cambridge on Rutland's controlling interest, pledging 'loyalty to our king, and attachment to our excellent constitution'. According to the editor of a hostile newspaper

> the appearance of Mr. Madryll Cheere among us excites no small degree of contemptuous merriment in the good folks of Westminster: did the minister think that he possessed gumption enough, Mr. M. C. would have stood in the court interest for that city; as it is, he is put in for Cambridge in consideration of his influence over eleven hundred Westminster tenants.

At the nomination he was reported to have announced his 'determination to support the present government, to whom we are indebted for the peaceable possession of our property, and the security of our lives, from desperate and misguided men'. He professed to be 'an advocate for economy', prompting a wag in the audience to shout, 'So you lock up your small beer'. Madryll Cheere and the other Rutland nominee won the poll forced by the local independents, whose petition was not pursued.[11] He was one of the prominent supporters of Rutland's brother at the county election nine days later.[12]

Although he is not known to have spoken in debate, he was an assiduous attender who gave, as promised, general support to the Liverpool ministry. He divided with them against economies in revenue collection, 4 July 1820, and in defence of their conduct towards Queen Caroline, 6 Feb. 1821. He voted against Catholic relief, 28 Feb. 1821, 30 Apr. 1822. He was in the minority for repeal of the duty on agricultural horses, 5 Mar. 1821, but voted with government on the state of the revenue the following day, as he did on repeal of the additional malt duty, 3 Apr., the disfranchisement of ordnance officials, 12 Apr., parliamentary reform, 9 May, the duke of Clarence's grant, 18 June, and Hume's call for economy, 27 June. He opposed abolition of the death penalty for forgery, 23 May 1821. He divided with ministers against more extensive tax reductions, 11, 22 Feb., and abolition of one of the joint-postmasterships, 13 Mar. 1822. He was in the protectionist minority of 36 against the revised duties on imported corn, 9 May, but sided with government against inquiry into Irish tithes, 19 June, and for the aliens bill, 19 July 1822. He voted against inquiry into the parliamentary franchise, 20 Feb., reductions of £2,000,000 in taxes, 3 Mar., and repeal of the Foreign Enlistment Act, 16 Apr. 1823. He divided against government for inquiry into the prosecution of the Dublin Orange rioters, 22 Apr., but with them on chancery delays, 5 June, and the currency, 12 June. He was in the minorities of 26 against the beer duties bill and 15 against the usury laws repeal bill, 17 June. He voted with ministers against the Scottish juries bill, 20 June 1823. His only known votes in 1824 were against the abolition of flogging in the army, 5 Mar., and with ministers on the trial of the Methodist missionary John Smith in Demerara, 11 June.

In May 1824 he transmitted to Peel, the home secretary, a bill for the establishment of an office for the registration of births, marriages and deaths in England, which had been drawn up by George White, the town clerk of Cambridge.[13] That year he was given permission to take preliminary steps for the implementation of his scheme to divert the turnpike road, but nothing had been accomplished before he died at Papworth Hall, aged 52, in January 1825.[14] By his will, dated 24 Jan. 1823, he left all his real estate in Cambridgeshire, Bedfordshire, Huntingdonshire, London, Middlesex and Westminster to his wife. He devised a nominal 20*s.* to each of his ten surviving children, 'being sure' of his wife's 'attention to each and every [one] of them'. His personalty was sworn under £8,000.[15] His widow settled the Papworth estate on William Henry Cheere in 1831. On her death in June 1849 her personal estate was sworn under £7,000; it was resworn under £9,000 later in the year. The residue, which she had directed to be equally divided among her children, was assessed at £2,364.[16] William Henry Cheere died unmarried in March 1867 and his brother and successor at Papworth, the Rev. George Cheere, died without surviving issue less than a month later. Papworth was successively in the hands of their brothers the Rev. Frederick Cheere (*d.* 1872), Robert Cheere (*d.* 1876), and the Rev. Edward Cheere, whose death in April 1891 ended the male line. After the death of his only surviving sister, Frances Cheere, in December that year, the estate was sold. In 1917 the Hall became part of the Tuberculosis Colony.[17]

[1] IGI (London); Papworth Everard parish reg. [2] *Gent. Mag.* (1799), ii. 716; Papworth reg. [3] *VCH Cambs.* ix. 360; R. Parker, *On the Road: The Papworth Story*, 90-91. [4] Parker, 91. [5] *Oxford DNB* (Sir Henry Cheere) *N and Q* (ser. 4), vi. 525-6; Parker, 94. [6] *Gent. Mag.* (1808), i. 274, 362; PROB 11/1475/184; Parker, 96. [7] Parker, 91-93; *VCH Cambs.* ix. 361. [8] Parker, 97, 104; *VCH Cambs.* ix. 361. [9] Add. 38277, ff. 21, 27, 122, 337. [10] *Cobbett's Rural Rides* ed. G.D.H.

and M. Cole, i. 76; Parker, 98-100. [11] *Cambridge and Hertford Independent* Press, 4, 11 Mar. 1820. [12] *Cambridge Chron.* 24 Mar. 1820. [13] Add. 40365, ff. 225-42. [14] Parker, 94. [15] PROB 11/1696/123; IR26/1033/172. [16] PROB 11/2096/504; IR26/1831/522. [17] *VCH Cambs.* ix. 360; Parker, 110-13, 126.

D.R.F.

MAGENIS, Richard (c.1763–1831), of Chanter Hill, nr. Enniskillen, co. Fermanagh.

ENNISKILLEN 1812–21 Jan. 1828[1]

b. c.1763, 1st s. of Richard Magenis, MP [I], of Waringstown, co. Down and 2nd w. Elizabeth, da. and coh. of Col. William Berkeley. *educ.* ?Westminster 1778. *m.* (1) 6 Sept. 1788, Lady Elizabeth Anne Cole (*d.* 26 Apr. 1807), da. of William Willoughby, 1st earl of Enniskillen [I], 5s. (1 *d.v.p.*) 4da.; (2) 19 Apr. 1815, Elizabeth, da. of James Callander (afterwards Campbell) of Craigforth, Stirling and Ardkinglas, Argyll, wid. of Col. George Dashwood, 1s. *suc.* fa. 1807. *d.* 6 Mar. 1831.

MP [I] 1790-7.

Collector, Cavan 1797-1801; commr. of accts. [I] 1800-12.

Lt.-col. co. Fermanagh militia 1803.

The Magenis (or Maginnis) family claimed to be a sub-branch of the extinct lords of Iveagh (Viscounts Magenis). Richard Magenis senior, who married the sister of the philosopher Dr. George Berkeley, bishop of Cloyne, was Member for Bangor, 1783-90, Fore, 1794-7, and Carlingford, 1798-1800, and left his Down and Antrim estates to his elder son and namesake in his will, which was proved in 1807.[2] This Member had joined his father in the Irish Parliament in 1790, when he was given a seat for Enniskillen by his father-in-law. A placeman and Orangeman, he was again returned for that borough, of whose corporation he was a member, at the general election of 1812, this time by his brother-in-law, the Tory 2nd earl of Enniskillen.[3] In 1815 he married the daughter of the self-styled baronet, Sir James Campbell of Ardkinglas. He was an inactive supporter of Lord Liverpool's administration, which was reluctant to condone his non-residence in Ireland by acceding to his wish for a place on the linen board.[4]

Returned unopposed at the general elections of 1818, 1820 and 1826, Magenis made no reported speeches in this period. No trace of parliamentary activity has been found for the 1820 session, and he missed the division on ministers' conduct towards Queen Caroline, 6 Feb. 1821, perhaps under pressure from his patron, who had temporarily broken with them on this issue. However, he was probably the 'McKinnies' who (like his brother-in-law Sir Galbraith Lowry Cole) was described by Lord Lowther* as one of the remarkable 'deserters' from government on the failed opposition motion for reinstating Caroline's name in the liturgy, 26 Jan.[5] Magenis divided against Catholic relief, 28 Feb. 1821, and the Catholic peers bill, 30 Apr. 1822. He voted against repeal of the additional malt duty, 3 Apr., Hume's motion for economy and retrenchment, 27 June 1821, and more extensive tax reductions to relieve distress, 11, 21 Feb. 1822. He was in the government majority against abolition of one of the joint-postmasterships, 13 Mar., and paired for its minority on this, 2 May 1822. He divided against parliamentary reform, 20 Apr. 1823, and alteration of the representation of Edinburgh, 26 Feb. 1824. He voted against repeal of the Foreign Enlistment Act, 16 Apr. 1823, and for the duke of Cumberland's annuity bill, 10 June 1825. He divided against government for inquiry into the legal proceedings against the Dublin Orange rioters, 22 Apr. 1823, but for the Irish unlawful societies bill, 15, 25 Feb., and against Catholic claims, 1 Mar., 21 Apr., 10 May 1825. Although in February 1826, presumably following a bout of illness, Lord Belmore commented that he 'looks twenty years younger than he did last year', he apparently missed the whole of that session.[6] His last known vote was against Catholic relief, 6 Mar. 1827.

Magenis vacated his seat at the start of the 1828 session to accommodate another of his wife's brothers, Arthur Henry Cole, and he never returned to the Commons, although he was considered as a possible stopgap candidate for Antrim on the Hertford interest in 1830.[7] He died, at his new London residence of 39 Grosvenor Place, in March 1831. Despite having already settled property on him, by his will, dated 9 Oct. 1826, he left his residuary estate, which included personal wealth sworn under £40,000, to his eldest son Richard William (1789-1863), who had lost an arm at the battle of Albuera. Noting in a third codicil of 3 Dec. 1829 that he now found himself in improved circumstances, he made additional bequests, notably of £5,000 to his third son Henry Arthur Cole Magenis (1793-1852), through whom the family descended, and his fifth son Sir Arthur Charles Magenis (*d.* 1867), a diplomat.[8]

[1] Not 29 Jan., the date of the new writ, as given in *HP Commons, 1790-1820*, iv. 521. [2] *Hist. Irish Parl.* v. 173-4; Sir A. Vicars, *Index to Prerogative Wills of Ireland*, 311. [3] *Hist. Irish Parl.* v. 174-5; *HP Commons, 1790-1820*, iv. 521; Lord Belmore, *Parl. Mems. of Fermanagh*, 73-74; P. Livingstone, *Fermanagh Story*, 142. [4] Add. 40296, f. 40; 40298, f. 18; *Black Bk.* (1823), 175; *Session of Parl. 1825*, p. 475. [5] Lonsdale mss, Lowther to Lonsdale, 27 Jan. 1821. [6] PRO NI, Belmore mss D3007/H/14/18. [7] Eg. 3261, f. 248. [8] *Enniskillen Chron.* 10 Mar. 1831; PROB 11/1783/165; IR26/1263/129; Belmore, 74.

S.M.F.

MAHON, James Patrick, *alias* the **O'Gorman Mahon** (1802–1891), of Mahonburgh, co. Clare.[1]

CO. CLARE	1830–4 Mar. 1831
ENNIS	1847–1852
CO. CLARE	15 May 1879–1885
CO. CARLOW	24 Aug. 1887–15 June 1891

b. 17 Mar. 1802,[2] 1st s. of Patrick Mahon of Snugville and Newpark and Barbara, da. and h. of James O'Gorman of Ennis. *educ.* Clongowes Wood Coll. 1815; Trinity, Dublin 1819; G. Inn 1825; King's Inns 1828, called [I] 1834. *m.* bef. June 1830, Christina Maria, da. and coh. of John O'Brien of 12 Fitzwilliam Square North, Dublin, 1s. *d.v.p.* 1da. *d.v.p. suc.* fa. 1821. *d.* 15 June 1891.

Capt. Clare militia.

The O'Gorman Mahon, a grotesque character even by the exotic standards of some of the Irish Members in this period, was a figure of pure self-invention. Possibly descended from the medieval MacMahons of county Clare, he shared a common ancestor (Bryan the elder of Loughrea, county Galway) with Thomas Mahon of Corbally, county Clare, and Sir Ross Mahon of Castlegar, county Galway, who briefly sat for Ennis in 1820.[3] His father (Bryan's great-grandson), a Catholic who married a local heiress in 1798, was a respectable Ennis merchant and Clare magistrate, although his grandfather was apparently a poor farmer and his father a tithe proctor, while later gossip would have it that Patrick himself was once imprisoned for sheep-stealing.[4] This Member's personal details seem to have been obscured by his own delusions of grandeur: he gave his birth year as 1803, which would make him an exact contemporary of his school friend Maurice O'Connell*, but he was probably born in 1802.[5] The birth date of 17 March, St. Patrick's Day, although possibly accurate, he may have adopted in honour of his patronymic; his adopted first name Charles would appear to be a later genuflection to the cult of Charles James Fox† since he was christened James Patrick; and the addition of O'Gorman as an extra surname was doubtless an erroneous usage derived from the confusing status of his chosen title. This last, the O'Gorman Mahon, was a preposterous conceit; unlike, for instance, the O'Conor Don's*, it had no precedent in historical practice and was perhaps only begun in imitation of one of his late uncles, who had pretentiously called himself 'the O'Gorman'.[6] Yet, with all the pride of an impulsive duellist and all the vanity of a Regency dandy, he insisted on being correctly addressed, even to the extent of making this a point of honour, a peculiarity which sometimes exposed him to ridicule.[7] As Thomas William Coke I* of Norfolk used to relate, he once pompously told the usher in the royal antechamber, 'Pray, be careful – THE O'Gorman Mahon!', but the king's attendant announced him in a stentorian voice as 'Mr. Ōr man Mahōōun!'[8]

Patrick Mahon, a rebel in 1798, was evidently concerned about the rights of his co-religionists; for example, he and his father-in-law were appointed to the committee of the Catholics of Ireland at the county's gathering in Ennis, 3 Aug. 1811. Their cause was also strongly backed by his brother-in-law, the barrister and activist Nicholas Purcell O'Gorman, who for several years was secretary to the Catholics of Ireland, though in 1824 Mary O'Connell, reflecting her husband's sentiments, found him and his uncle Nicholas Mahon too moderate for her liking.[9] The O'Gorman Mahon, who succeeded to a substantial estate on the death of his father in 1821 and was later, like him, a captain in the Clare militia, inherited this family interest in the Catholic cause, although he was very much on the radical wing of the movement. He attended Sir Francis Burdett's* Westminster reform dinner in May 1825, as part of Daniel O'Connell's* delegation to London that spring, when he was entered at Gray's Inn. Through his friend Thomas Steele, he became active in the Catholic Association, for instance serving as secretary, 7 Dec. 1825, and condemning the anti-clerical measures of the Spanish Cortes, 11 Feb. 1826.[10] Although not a burgess, he interrupted proceedings to propose William Nugent Macnamara* for the corporation borough of Ennis at the general election that summer, when he also unsuccessfully attempted to nominate him as a pro-Catholic candidate for Clare. He issued an address to promote the independent interest in the county, 20 June, and was prominent at gatherings of its Catholics in July and August 1826.[11] He chaired his county's Catholic meeting to protest against the defeat of the latest relief bill, 11 Mar., and, at an aggregate meeting of the Irish Catholics in Dublin, he criticized the Irish lord chancellor Lord Manners's refusal to appoint more Catholic magistrates, 5 July 1827. Having spoken condescendingly in praise of O'Connell at the Louth Independent Club dinner, 7 Jan. 1828, he received a sarcastic dressing down from him at the Association on the 15th and differed with him during other debates that month.[12]

Anxious that William Vesey Fitzgerald, the new president of the board of trade, should be opposed on his standing for re-election for Clare in June 1828, the O'Gorman Mahon entreated Macnamara to offer and, having failed in the attempt, was so desperate that he even called on the lord lieutenant Lord Anglesey's son Lord William Paget* to ask him to stand, but Paget 'laughed in his face'. On O'Connell entering, he returned to Clare to canvass extensively for him with other prominent members of the Association and he correctly forecast that the Catholic tenants would desert their landlords.[13] Dressed in the uniform of O'Connell's order of liberators and suspended above the crowd at the front of the gallery, he crushed the querulous objections of the sheriff to this extraordinary behaviour by threatening that

> this gentleman ... tells that gentleman ... that if that gentleman presumes to touch this gentleman, this gentleman will defend himself against that gentleman, or any other gentleman, while he has got the arm of a gentleman to protect him.

After Vesey Fitzgerald had been proposed, the O'Gorman Mahon, who later revealed that he had himself declined to offer, paused dramatically before nominating O'Connell as the only real friend to the Catholic cause.[14] He was active throughout the ensuing contest and, according to the recollections of a junior army officer on peace-keeping duties, he one night invited himself into the mess: he was

> the *right* arm, at least so I believe he styled himself, of Daniel O'Connell. He sat down with us and delighted us with his brilliant jokes and truly amusing conversation. He was the very antithesis to the Agitator's *left* arm, Tom Steele, who was certainly, though very clever and well read, one of the dullest and most melancholy companions.

In attempting to make arrangements for preventing disturbances on the last day of the poll, he had the temerity to treat the commanding officer 'with all the effrontery of a rival general'; but he met his match in Sir Charles William Doyle, who told him, in relation to the forces at his disposal, that in the event of his being involved in any disorder, 'you will find them exactly *at your elbow*, Mr. Mahon, *wherever you are*', at which he 'for once appeared abashed'.[15] As Richard Sheil* wrote of him at the time:

> He has a very striking physiognomy, of the corsair character ... His figure is tall and he is peculiarly free and *dégagé* in all his attitudes and movements. In any other his attire would appear singularly fantastical. His manners are exceedingly frank and natural, and have a character of kindliness as well as of self-reliance imprinted upon them ... His talents as a popular speaker are considerable. He derives from external qualifications an influence over the multitude, which men of a diminutive stature are somewhat slow of obtaining ... When O'Gorman Mahon throws himself out before the people, and, touching his whiskers with one hand, brandishes the other, an enthusiasm is at once produced, to which the fair portion of the spectators lend their tender contribution. Such a man was exactly adapted to the excitement of the people of Clare; and it must be admitted, that by his indefatigable exertions, his unremitting activity and his devoted zeal, he most materially assisted in the election of Mr. O'Connell.[16]

Apparently enraptured by the reception he received, he joined in efforts to prevent landlord retaliation against their tenants and was reimbursed with £700 by the Association for his expenses during the election.[17]

His antics had been reported by Doyle to the Irish administration, and Anglesey wrote to Peel, the home secretary, 20 July 1828, that, among other Catholic agitators who 'are carried away by their feelings and thirst for popularity, and are very unguarded', the O'Gorman Mahon, 'if rebellion should break out, will be a very prominent character in the field'.[18] He continued to act provocatively that autumn, when dinners were held in his honour in Killarney and Limerick, but what proved too much for Peel's patience was his deliberate disruption of the inaugural meeting of the Clare Brunswick Club in Ennis, when he urged the attendant troops to resist the orders of the sheriff, an Orangeman, 20 Oct., and his furious declamations at the Catholic Association, which allegedly included a declaration that that assembly was the real government of the country, 18 Nov.[19] It was perhaps on the latter occasion that a visiting German prince observed, presumably in relation to him, that a 'handsome young man with enormous whiskers and an "*outré*" dress (the dandy of the Association) sprang on the table and uttered a thundering speech which obtained great applause'; while, according to Macnamara, 'it was a speech Mahon made at the Association that broke him. O'Connell several times interrupted him and said he was sure Mahon meant differently ... but he persevered'.[20] Anglesey, upheld by the Irish lord chancellor, Hart, who feared further unrest if he was punished, at first cleared him of any wrongdoing, but he was overruled by the furious prime minister, the duke of Wellington, who ordered him to be dismissed from the magistracy in December 1828; this row was one of the factors behind Anglesey's recall soon afterwards.[21] The following month the O'Gorman Mahon chaired a meeting of the Catholics of Clare and was named to the delegation to accompany their new Member to Westminster.[22] As John Cam Hobhouse* observed in relation to the home secretary's standing for re-election as an advocate of Catholic emancipation, in February 1829 the O'Gorman Mahon 'actually came down to Oxford [University] in one of Peel's coaches. Luckily he was not discovered, or he would have lost Peel many votes and perhaps his own life'.[23] He attended the *Thatched House* meeting to petition in defence of the Irish 40*s*. freeholders, 7 Mar., and was sent by O'Connell to Henry Hunt* in an unavailing attempt to gain the support of other English radicals in this matter.[24] At the *London Tavern* meeting to address the king in gratitude for emancipation, 6 May 1829, he moved the resolution for a grandiose scheme to list all the past friends of the Catholic cause on the pedestal of the statue which was to be erected in Wellington's honour.[25]

O'Connell, who had been sent back to be re-elected for Clare, wrote to him on 14 June 1829 that if (which was not yet clear) 'there is to be a *battle*, we cannot go to *battle* without you', and encouraged him in his own ambitions to represent the county.[26] About that time he replied to the timid Macnamara, who had contemplated a compromise with the Tory proprietors, by commanding him to

> retrieve this unintentional blunder at once by declaring from your own knowledge of me that the Devil himself could not deter your friend O'Gorman Mahon from proposing the president of Irish liberators in the teeth of all the shoneens [Clare landlords] in or out of Christendom.

He also requested Macnamara to nominate him for Clare at the next opportunity, unless there should offer

> any man old or young better acquainted with the real state of the county, its wants and capabilities, the feelings and interests of its inhabitants, or more capable of securing attention to the necessity of redressing the wrongs of the people ... I shall thereby best effect my primeval and dearest object – the welfare of our country.[27]

Before leaving London, he acted as second to Steele in his duel with William Smith O'Brien*, 30 June, when so tense was the atmosphere that he nearly ended up fighting Smith O'Brien himself.[28] Describing Ireland as in a state of suppressed rebellion, he proposed O'Connell at his unopposed return, 30 July, and formally offered himself for the county at the following election, 1 Aug.[29] Later that month O'Connell's then associate Pierce Mahony†, commenting on the O'Gorman Mahon's 'most foolish canvass', wrote that it 'is strange that a man in his circumstances should dream of such a thing but he is so eaten up with inordinate vanity!'[30] By September the O'Gorman Mahon had broken with O'Connell, who announced that he intended to continue to represent Clare, although on the 29th at the town meeting in Ennis, where he moved the resolution condemning the unrepresentative state of the franchise, he denied the existence of any such obstacle to his pretensions.[31] Despite the now disaffected Mahony's statement in December 1829 that he 'disavows and disowns' the Liberator over the latter's dubious behaviour towards the Beresfords in Waterford, O'Connell, urging Nicholas Purcell O'Gorman to stand for that county that month, wrote that 'surely O'Gorman Mahon will come forward; what he saved from [the money he would have spent on a contest in] Clare, he should give now'.[32]

In January 1830 O'Connell was assured by one supporter that 'the Gag would not get a single vote' in Clare and in March his wife, who noted that the O'Gorman Mahon was constantly with the Misses O'Brien in Dublin, wrote that he would make no headway, as he was 'so fallen in the estimation of the people and of the aristocracy of that county'. Similar statements were made that spring, but his marriage to Christine O'Brien, an heiress with £60,000 who had at one point been thought of for Maurice O'Connell*, rehabilitated his fortunes.[33] The Irish secretary Lord Francis Leveson Gower*, who believed that her £500 a year would help return him as a self-proclaimed supporter of the administration, reported to Peel that summer that he had seen him

> in Kensington Gardens and nothing but the New Jerusalem, which you never saw, or the lord mayor's coach, which you may have seen, could give you a notion of the generous splendour of his appearance. His dress was all the colours of the rainbow, his materials, for he had several, starred and striped like the American flag, and he had a sort of halo in glory of bright hair round his face. This is the Drawcansir [a character in a burlesque] who is to enter and kill them all on both sides in Clare.[34]

He applied to Leveson Gower to make his brother a magistrate in compensation for his own supersession, but failed to secure this or the backing of the Irish government at the forthcoming general election.[35] By mid-June Steele had apparently effected a reconciliation between him and O'Connell, whose agent feared that, with Macnamara certain to be returned first, he risked coming third to the O'Gorman Mahon, who in any case could choose to exploit O'Connell's verbal promise to stand down in his favour.[36] The O'Gorman Mahon replied to rumours that he might not stand by issuing from the Windham Club in London, 28 June 1830, an affected address ('Feeling that the hour of my birth was but the registered epoch of my enrolment in the service of Ireland'), in which he promised to enter and made suggestions on how to agitate for the relief of distress.[37]

On O'Connell, who had already announced his retreat to county Waterford, attempting to make a grand entry into Ennis, 18 July 1830, the O'Gorman Mahon spitefully manoeuvred his followers into the way and recklessly clambered on to O'Connell's carriage in a largely successful effort to derail his triumphant procession. Although Steele took grave exception to this, O'Connell, who called his conduct unwise and unnecessary, declined to show any resentment, partly because it was in his own interest to appeal to his Clare supporters to, as he put it, 'give O'Gorman Mahon *at least* vote for vote for any his friends give me in Waterford'.[38] Having intervened aggressively in Ennis to try to prevent the return of Smith O'Brien on his and his family's interest there, he repeated his attack on their territorial influence in opposing his brother Lucius O'Brien* at the county election, when he agreed to pledges for lower taxes, parliamentary reform and the introduction of a poor law. He was elected in second place behind Macnamara after a week-long contest, at the end of which he again urged radical Irish reforms and expressed his sense of commitment to the electors, but was threatened with a petition.[39] His expenses were reported to be at least £8,000 and by September, when he privately declared that 'from the beginning of the election up to the present moment I have not given a single sixpence to any human being, nor will I', his printer and agent began to press for payment of their costs under threat of exposing his electoral malpractices.[40] On the 15th he attended the Dublin liberal meeting arranged to welcome the recent revolution in France, but his behaviour, in seconding a vote of thanks to Lafayette, only exposed further his rift with O'Connell. As Sir Henry Hardinge*, the new Irish secretary, reported to Mrs. Arbuthnot, the O'Gorman Mahon, 'on some pretence, called upon me and said he should support the duke against the libels of the Liberator O'Connell, and did so manfully at the meeting. In short, nothing could have terminated so well to convert the great meeting of the Irish people into a farce'.[41] The imbroglio involved him in a quarrel with the press, but he vindicated his conduct in a letter to the people of Ireland, 5 Oct., and, despite the ridicule of the Tory *Clare Journal*, travelled to France that autumn to present the meeting's congratulatory address in the chamber of deputies.[42] In his absence, he was added to the Ennis committee of independence on its formation, 11 Oct. 1830.[43]

He was listed with the 'neutrals' in Mahony's analysis of the Irish elections, but government counted him among its 'foes' in September 1830. Writing to his brother John from London, 4 Nov., Macnamara noted that 'O'G. M. is here. He told me he would support ministers though he came shortly after and sat next [to] me on the opposition bench. In fact, he is insincere and deceitful. He does not seem to know anyone here'.[44] Attacked in Clare and Dublin for being inactive, he attempted to explain his behaviour and stated in a published letter that had he been in the House he would have voted against O'Connell's minority for repeal of the Irish Subletting Act, 11 Nov., but reluctantly for Parnell's motion for reducing the duties on wheat imported to the West Indies, 12 Nov.[45] Believing that he had plenty of time to dine, he was accidentally shut out from the division on the civil list which led to Wellington's resignation, 15 Nov., when a petition alleging the use of bribery and party emblems was entered against him. He made his maiden speech on presenting a local repeal petition, 9 Dec., when he indicated that he would probably have divided against ministers on the civil list. He angrily rebutted the printed allegations of an unnamed Member that he had been in the pay of the previous administration, even thanking O'Connell for coming to his defence over this; and he was lavish in his praise of Peel's statesmanship, but insisted that he was consistent in his parliamentary politics and emphasized his support for reform, retrenchment and non-interference abroad. Displaying his argumentative and short-tempered character, he justified the current agitation for repeal and urged the relief of Irish distress, 11 Dec., and he was in sarcastic form about English Members' attitudes to his country, 13 Dec. According to Macnamara, who thought him 'a most extraordinary man', he told O'Connell that he would vote for Hume's amendment to refer the truck bill to a select committee, 'after which he voted against it', 14 Dec.[46] He moved for a return of bankrupt Irish magistrates, many of whom he considered inadequate, 15, 23 Dec., pinned the blame for distress in Ireland on its absentee proprietors, 17 Dec., and complained of the improper conduct of Frederick Shaw* as recorder of Dublin, 20, 23 Dec. His withering attack on Inglis over tithes was met with the counting out of the House, 21 Dec., and, on his again being denied the opportunity to make interventions on Irish affairs, he condemned the Commons for crushing the voice of truly representative Irish Members, 23 Dec. 1830. As a potential seconder of O'Connell's expected repeal motion, he that day menaced his colleague and the Grey ministry with reprisals should they fail to support it.

The O'Gorman Mahon, who again travelled to France that month, rallied to the defence of the arrested O'Connell at a repeal meeting in Dublin, 25 Jan. 1831.[47] Anglesey, the reinstated lord lieutenant, informed Lord Melbourne, the home secretary, on the 28th that 'there is not one respectable man who sticks to him [O'Connell]. O'Gorman Mahon is the nearest approach to the character, and he is in low estimation and only playing a game for the county [of Clare]; he, however, detests O'Connell'.[48] To the initial jeers of the House, Hughes Hughes's complaint about his frequent use of the exclamation 'Gracious God!' and the indignation of the Speaker at having to restore order, 8 Feb., he delivered a ferocious tirade against the recent proclamations preventing repeal agitation; during it he revealed that he and Sheil had been the only two Irishmen to vote for Hunt's motion for an amnesty for the English 'Swing' rioters earlier that day. He read a litany of Irish grievances, begged ministers to grant repeal before the Irish pressure for total separation from Britain became irresistible and declared, of the unjustly prosecuted O'Connell, that 'the moment you consign him to a dungeon, the connection between the two countries is at an end'.[49] Not least because of his revelation that for over 11 years he had been a member of a secret society in Ireland, as well as owing to his ludicrous propensity to threaten duels in the chamber, the speech left 'Ogreman', as he was nicknamed in Parliament, generally discredited.[50] Maria Edgeworth, whose source was Sir James Mackintosh*, related that

> he first wanted to challenge the [former] attorney-general [Sir Charles Wetherell*] and then to challenge the Speaker – with the whole House at his [the Speaker's] back! The House resolved to hear him with the utmost patience and cold silence. *He* felt this ... O'Gorman [Mahon] felt that he was *undone* when he had [been] heard out and expressed this as he left.[51]

Edward Smith Stanley, the Irish secretary, considered that by disgusting the Commons he had played into ministers' hands: 'The repealers got a complete set down, and Mr. O'Gorman Mahon is gone. The general opinion is that he is quite mad'.[52] Although a relative reported to him from Dublin that 'the honest anti-Unionists (with scarce one exception) highly approve of it and the public in general admire the matters of fact it exposes so manfully', even he warned that it had been counterproductive in that an idle rumour had circulated that O'Connell had been constrained to plead guilty on 12 Feb. 1831, 'in consequence of the *O'G. M.'s speech*, which they say was calculated to injure him in the minds of the court and jury'.[53] He was privy to attempts by Ellen Courtenay to expose O'Connell's alleged mistreatment of her, but it is not clear that he took any part in the unsuccessful endeavour to smear O'Connell over it at this time.[54]

In the Commons, where his appetite for controversy was unabated, he resumed his attack on Shaw, 10 Feb., and raised matters of Dublin concern, 14, 17 Feb. 1831. He created uproar, 11 Feb., by accusing ministers of sanctioning bloodshed in the suppression of repeal demonstrations and was again called to order by the Speaker. He condemned the legal proceedings against O'Connell that day and on the 14th, when he objected to increased taxes, denied that English Members took any interest in Irish questions and complained about being interrupted. He supported attempts to raise the issue of Irish distress, 16, 18 Feb. On the 17th, when he advocated Jewish emancipation, he insisted on dividing the House on Lord Ebrington's censure motion about the Bridport election (it was lost by 55-38). He made a furious attack on Sir James Graham, the first lord of the admiralty, 18 Feb., for diverting attention from what he saw as the government's poor record by making an easy hit against Irish demagogues who supposedly favoured the dismemberment of the empire; amid derisory laughter, he called on Graham to name names and declared that he would never give up the struggle for repeal. He privately demanded an explanation from, but did not in the end fight, Graham, who on the 21st shabbily stated that he had had O'Connell in mind; by this he was considered to have put himself needlessly in the wrong, as he had clearly intended the remark to apply to the O'Gorman Mahon, whom Thomas Gladstone* called 'a wild, turbulent fellow'.[55] He was in the minority of six for Hume's amendment to reduce the army by 10,000 men, 21 Feb., and was presumably the solitary voter in the minority of one for Ruthven's bill to relieve Irish smallholders of the potato tithe, on which he made the House divide, 22 Feb. He criticized the expenditure on the Kildare Place Society and other such grants, given that the engagements made at the Union had still not been met, 23 Feb., when he again lost his temper at being impeded from pursuing matters of Irish concern. Damning both government and O'Connell for hypocrisy in denying that they had compromised over his trial, 28 Feb. 1831, he assailed the former for prohibiting peaceable gatherings and praised the latter for furthering the cause of repeal. James Joseph Hope Vere* reported that day that the O'Gorman Mahon and the lord advocate Jeffrey 'are similar in one respect – the talent of speaking a cataract of words'.[56]

To the disappointment of Mary O'Connell, who commented that 'now he has taken the honest side, I should regret his losing his seat', and of her husband, who remarked that 'at present it would be a triumph to our enemies that he should be turned out', the O'Gorman Mahon was unseated, 4 Mar. 1831.[57] In Tom Macaulay's* words:

> O'Gorman [Mahon] fell greatly. Caesar in the senate did not die with more attention to the proprieties of character. He came to hear, what few people care to hear, his own sentence read at the bar by the chairman of the committee. To make the matter better he was expelled for bribery by his agents. The fellow sat on the treasury bench, heard the report and never stirred. 'Sir', said the Speaker, 'you must withdraw'. Up he got and swaggered off as fast as he could with his acre of ruff and his three bushels of dirty hair.[58]

Despite being short of money, the O'Gorman Mahon, who was incapacitated from standing again during that Parliament, announced that his brother William Richard Mahon would offer for Clare at the ensuing by-election as his *locum*. O'Connell, who privately confided to his wife that he 'is *not* to be relied on and his absence from the House is *not* a subject of regret', hesitated to start his son Maurice against his erstwhile friend's interest, but the O'Gorman Mahon, lacking popularity and resources, capitulated and supported the young O'Connell's successful candidacy on the hustings, 21 Mar. 1831.[59] He was advised by one supporter in Ennis to show more deference to respectable opinion and to liquidate his 'nasty election debts' in order to secure his success at the general election that spring, when he offered again and wrote confidently to his sister-in-law Kate O'Brien that 'you need have no doubt of my return, no matter what you hear. Do not mind what you see in the rascally papers. We will beat them, the whole county is with me!'[60] By this he was probably referring to the allegations, which involved him in a quarrel with Steele, that he was using the agrarian rioters known as Terry Alts to intimidate voters in his favour. O'Connell, who was bent on removing him from the scene, gleefully informed on the O'Gorman Mahon, who was said to be in hopes of fermenting a revolution so as to prove himself another Lafayette, to Smith Stanley.[61] He in turn reported to Lord Grey, who was frustrated that it in fact led to nothing, that O'Connell 'distinctly declares that he [the O'Gorman Mahon] is at the head of the whole insurrectionary movement in Clare, and he has offered most respectable evidence to *convict* him of *spoken treason*'.[62] On the hustings, he justified his early absences from the Commons and attacked the editor of the O'Connellite *Pilot* newspaper, 13 May 1831, but he trailed throughout the poll, which he kept open as long as possible, apparently in order to exploit his various nefarious electoral practices. He finally accepted defeat on the 19th, when he complained of being ill rewarded for his significant contribution to O'Connell's former victory there. His vituperative personal abuse of Macnamara nearly ended in a challenge, while his brother William came close to fighting the other re-elected Member Maurice O'Connell. He only escaped from an ugly mob in Limerick through O'Connell's intervention a few days later, and in July he was forced to respond to a virulent printed attack by Steele over his supposed conduct at the election.[63]

The O'Gorman Mahon created a frightful scene at the county Dublin reform meeting in December 1831, when he was flung out of the room and prosecuted by O'Connell's son-in-law Christopher Fitzsimon†, and he continued to be involved in judicial disputes and the subject of the O'Connells' displeasure for several years.[64] He had been invited by Hunt to stand for Preston in 1831, but nothing came of that then (or later), nor does it appear that he pursued a requisition the following year to offer for the newly enfranchised borough of Oldham, where William Cobbett† was returned. It was thought that he would stand as a Repealer for Clare at the general election of 1832, but O'Connell kept him out.[65] Two years later Lady Glengall reported to Wellington, the acting chief minister in Peel's putative administration, that the O'Gorman Mahon, who desired a seat as a supporter of government, 'is O'Connell's furious enemy and only wants to get into Parliament to fly at him for his monstrous conduct in trying to have him arrested as a Terry Alt', although she added that he intended to advocate repeal of the Union and was untrustworthy.[66] In May 1835 Robert Graham of Redgorton recorded of the O'Gorman Mahon, 'a hot, lively, pugilistic kind of fellow', that he, now a Liberal, 'was originally closely connected with O'Connell, but was not subservient enough to continue of the Tail and at the last [*sic*] election, O'Connell supported one of his own sons against O'Gorman Mahon and threw him out'.[67]

Later that year he began to travel in Europe and visited several other continents, but he sat for Ennis as a repealer in the 1847 Parliament. After another period in Paris, where he was a journalist and financial speculator, he resumed his quixotic adventures abroad in the 1850s and 1860s; among other tales that he later told, he supposedly served as a lieutenant in the tsar of Russia's bodyguard, as a general in the government forces in Uruguay, as a commander of a Chilean fleet, as a colonel under the emperor of Brazil and as an officer on the Union side in the American civil war. His always tottering financial situation had collapsed by 1872, but he re-entered Parliament as Home Rule Member for Clare in 1879, acting with Charles Stewart Parnell†, to whom he delivered O'Shea's challenge in 1881.[68] He was the original of 'the Mulligan' in Thackeray's *Mrs. Perkins' Ball* (1881). Alluding to his reputation as a duellist, William Ewart Gladstone† wrote of him in 1889 that the 'Commons is now familiar with the stately figure of an Irish gentleman advanced in life, who carries with him the halo of an extraordinary reputation in that particular, but who is conspicuous among all his contemporaries for his singularly beautiful and gentle manners'.[69] As Member for county Carlow, he was, after the death of Christopher Rice Mansel Talbot* in 1890, the last surviving Member of the unreformed House to hold a seat in the Commons, although several others outlived him, including the longest survivor of all, John Charles George Savile, Viscount Pollington (the 4th earl of Mexborough). He died in June 1891, a throwback to an imagined ideal of Irish chieftainship.[70]

[1] Denis Gwynn, *The O'Gorman Mahon: Duellist, Adventurer and Politician* (1934), the only biography, is inaccurate, ramshackle, repetitive and unsatisfactory. [2] Authorities vary, though most (following Gwynn, 34-35) give ?1800 (e.g. *Oxford DNB*); but *King's Inns Admission Pprs.* ed. E. Keane, P. B. Phair and T. U. Sadleir, 323, states 1802, which is confirmed by *Al. Dub.* 548, where it is noted that he was admitted to Trinity, aged 16, 1 Mar. 1819. [3] E. MacLysaght, *Irish Fams.* 217-18; NLI, O'Gorman Mahon coll. 8491 (5), ped. [4] P. White, *Hist. Clare*, 335-6; H. Weir, *Houses of Clare*, 209, 249; Gwynn, 31-34; *Gladstone Autobiog. Memoranda* ed. J. Brooke and M. Sorenson, 38. [5] *O'Connell Corresp.* ii. 640, 643; P. Costello, *Clongowes Wood*, 80. See n. 2. [6] Gwynn, 9, 13, 31, 34. [7] Ibid. 7-8, 36, 109; J. Kelly, *'That Damn'd Thing Called Honour'*, 254, 263-4. [8] Stirling, *Coke of Norf.*, 301-2. [9] *Oxford DNB*; *O'Connell Corresp.* i. 310, 342; iii. 1107. [10] *O'Connell Corresp.* iii. 1236; *Dublin Evening Post*, 8 Dec. 1825; O. MacDonagh, *Hereditary Bondsman*, 223. [11] *Dublin Evening Post*, 22, 29 June, 18 July, 15 Aug.; *Morning Reg.* 1 July 1826. [12] *Dublin Evening Post*, 15 Mar., 7 July 1827, 10, 15, 19, 26 Jan. 1828. [13] *Dublin Evening Post*, 19, 26, 28 June, 1 July; *The Times*, 27, 28 June; Add. 40334, f. 211; 51567, Anglesey to Holland, 1 July 1828; Gwynn, 40-46. [14] *Dublin Evening Post*, 3, 5, 8 July 1828; R. L. Sheil, *Sketches of Irish Bar* (1854), ii. 284-7; Gwynn, 21-30. [15] H. R. Addison, *Recollections of Irish Police Magistrate*, 65, 70-73. [16] Sheil, ii. 274-5. [17] Gwynn, 58-61. [18] PRO NI, Anglesey mss D619/32A/2/87; Add. 40325, f. 127. [19] *Dublin Evening Post*, 2, 26 Aug., 16 Sept., 11 Oct.; *Dublin Evening Mail*, 22, 24, 27 Oct. 1828; Wellington mss WP1/961/27; 965/15. [20] *Tour by a German Prince*, ii. 131; NLI, Stacpoole Kenny mss 18889 (12), W. to J. Macnamara, 10 Dec. 1828. [21] *Dublin Evening Mail*, 8 Dec. 1828; Anglesey mss 32A/2/153, 159, 160; Wellington mss WP1/966/13; 968/14, 18, 26, 31; 969/7, 11; Gwynn, 63-71, 74. [22] *Dublin Evening Post*, 10, 12 Feb. 1829. [23] Broughton, *Recollections*, iii. 306. [24] *O'Connell Corresp.* iv. 1533, 1536. [25] M.D. Jephson, *Anglo-Irish Misc.* 186. [26] *O'Connell Corresp.* iv. 1585. [27] Gwynn, 83-84, 97-101. [28] Ibid. 85-94; *Clare Jnl.* 6, 9, 13 July 1829; NLI, Smith O'Brien mss 426/39. [29] *Dublin Evening Post*, 1 Aug., 10, 17 Sept. 1829. [30] *O'Connell Corresp.* iv. 1601. [31] NLI, Monteagle mss 549, Rice to Vesey Fitzgerald, 23 Sept.; *Clare Jnl.* 1, 5 Oct. 1829. [32] Anglesey mss 32A/3/1/254; Gwynn, 110-11; *O'Connell Corresp.* iv. 1624. [33] *O'Connell Corresp.* iv. 1550a, 1629, 1642, 1668, 1670, 1678; Gwynn, 110. [34] Add. 40338, f. 207. [35] NAI, Leveson Gower letter bks. Leveson Gower to Hart, 7 July 1830. [36] *Dublin Evening Post*, 13 May, 10 June, 8 July 1830; *O'Connell Corresp.* iv. 1679, 1687. [37] Add. 40338, f. 209. [38] *Clare Jnl.* 15, 19, 22, 29 July 1830; W. Fagan, *Life and Times of O'Connell*, ii. 49; Gwynn, 112-15; *O'Connell Corresp.* iv. 1696; viii. 3420. [39] *Clare Jnl.* 5, 12, 19 Aug., 2, 30 Sept. 1830; Gwynn, 115-19. [40] Stacpoole Kenny mss 18891 (10), Woulfe to Macnamara, 7 Sept. 1830; Gwynn, 120-6. [41] *Dublin Evening Post*, 16, 19 Sept. 1830; *Arbuthnot Corresp.* 139. [42] *Clare Jnl.* 30 Sept., 4, 11 Oct. 1830; Gwynn, 140-2. [43] *Clare Jnl.* 14 Oct. 1830; Gwynn, 120. [44] Stacpoole Kenny mss 18889 (15). [45] *Clare Jnl.* 25 Nov., 2 Dec. 1830; Gwynn, 119-20, 133-7. [46] Stacpoole Kenny mss 18889 (15), W. to J. Macnamara, 15 Dec. 1830. [47] *Clare Jnl.* 10, 31 Jan. 1831. [48] Anglesey mss 29B, pp. 49-51. [49] Dorset RO, Bankes mss D/BKL, Bankes jnl. Feb. 1831; Broughton, iv. 83; *Three Diaries*, 48. [50] Hants RO, Carnarvon mss 75M91, Howard to Lady Porchester, 16 Feb. 1831; *O'Connell Corresp.* iv. 1766; *Moore Jnl.* iv. 1384; *Unrepentant Tory* ed. R.A. Gaunt, 138. [51] *Edgeworth Letters*, 480. [52] Anglesey mss 31D/15, 18. [53] O'Gorman Mahon coll. 8491 (8), Vance to O'Gorman Mahon, 14 Feb. 1831. [54] Gwynn, 127-32. [55] St. Deiniol's Lib. Glynne-Gladstone mss 197, T. to J. Gladstone, 19, 22, 23 Feb.; *Clare Jnl.* 28 Feb. 1831; *Three Diaries*, 56, 58. [56] Hopetoun mss 167, f. 222. [57] *'My Darling Danny'* ed. E.I. Bishop, 45; *O'Connell Corresp.* viii. 3424. [58] *Macaulay Letters*, ii. 6-7; M.D. George, *Cat. of Pol. and Personal Satires*, xi. 16628. [59] *O'Connell Corresp.* iv. 1780-2, 1787; Stacpoole Kenny mss 18889 (16), W. to J. Macnamara, 2 Mar.; Derby mss 920 Der (14) 121/1/2, Gosset to Smith Stanley, 10 Mar.; *Clare Jnl.* 10, 17, 21 Mar. 1831. [60] Gwynn, 135, 143-6; *Clare Jnl.* 2 May 1831. [61] Derby mss 121/2, Gosset to Smith Stanley, 28 Apr.; 125/12, O'Connell to Gosset, 6 May; *Clare Jnl.* 9 May 1831; *O'Connell Corresp.* iv. 1800, 1808-9. [62] Grey mss, Smith Stanley to Grey, 9, 14 May; Derby mss 117/5, replies, 11, 18 May 1831. [63] *Clare Jnl.* 16, 19, 23, 26, 30 May, 21 July, 1 Aug. 1831; *O'Connell Corresp.* iv. 1811, 1813-14, 1816. [64] *Dublin Evening Post*, 6 Dec. 1831; *Clare Jnl.* 6 Aug. 1832, 7 Jan. 1833; *'My Darling Danny'*, 76; Fagan, ii. 210-14; Gwynn, 148-50. [65] *Clare Jnl.* 3 Sept., 5 Nov. 17 Dec. 1832; Gwynn, 146-8. [66] *Wellington Pol. Corresp.* ii. 78. [67] *Scottish Whig in Ireland* ed. H. Heaney, 23, 33. [68] O'Gorman Mahon coll. 8491 (4), 'Mem. of James Patrick Mahon'; Gwynn, *passim*; *DNB*; *Oxford DNB*. [69] W.E. Gladstone, 'Daniel O'Connell', *19th Cent.* xxv (1889), 160. [70] *Freeman's Jnl.* 17 June; *The Times*, 17 June 1891; *Ann. Reg.* (1891), Chron. p. 169.

S.M.F.

MAHON, Sir Ross, 1st bt. (1763–1835), of Castlegar, co. Galway.

ENNIS 1820–June 1820

b. 2 Sept. 1763, 1st s. of Ross Mahon of Castlegar and Lady Anne Browne, da. of John, 1st earl of Altamont [I]. *educ.* Trinity, Dublin 1780. *m.* (1) 6 Aug. 1786, his cos. Lady Elizabeth Browne (*d.* 24 Feb. 1795), da. of Peter, 2nd earl of Altamont [I], 5da. (1 *d.v.p.*); (2) 1 Sept. 1805, Diana (*d.* 2 Dec. 1807), da. of Edward Baber of Park Street, Grosvenor Square, Mdx., *s.p.*; (3) 1 Oct. 1809, Mary Geraldine, da. of James Fitzgerald† of Inchicronan, co. Clare, 5s. 7da. *suc.* fa. 1788; *cr.* bt. 14 Apr. 1819. *d.* 10 Aug. 1835.

MP [I] 1798-1800.

The Mahons were in possession of the Castlegar property by 1696. Bryan Mahon (*d.* 1719) was for many years the *homme d'affaires* of the earls of Clanricarde. His son and heir Ross Mahon died in 1767 and was succeeded by his eldest son and namesake, who had married into the Browne family, subsequently earls of Altamont (1771) and marquesses of Sligo (1800). Two years before his death in 1788 his eldest son Ross, this Member, strengthened the alliance by marrying a daughter of his maternal uncle, the 2nd earl. His next brother John married her sister, while his sister Anne married Denis Browne*, Altamont's younger son. After the death of his first wife Mahon sat for Granard for two years in the Irish Parliament as a pro-Union ministerialist.[1] A brief and childless second marriage followed. In 1809 he married the sister of William Vesey Fitzgerald*, subsequently the close friend and ministerial colleague of Robert Peel*, who was Irish secretary from 1812 to 1818. In January 1816 Peel accepted Mahon's invitation to stay at Castlegar during his break from business in Dublin, but he declined to repeat the experience the following year.[2] Mahon, whose annual rental was about £10,000 in 1809, about a quarter of which may have come from his Galway property, received a baronetcy in 1819.[3] At the general election the following year he was returned in his absence, apparently as a seat-warmer, for the close borough of Ennis, where it was the Fitzgeralds' turn to nominate the Member.[4] It seems unlikely that he took his seat, for only three months later he made way for one of the Wellesleys. He died in August 1835. His eldest son Ross, an army officer, died unmarried in 1842, as did his second son James, a lawyer, in 1852, when the baronetcy passed to his third son William Vesey Mahon (1813-93), rector of Rawmarsh, Yorkshire.

[1] *Hist. Irish Parl.* v. 180. [2] Add. 40250, ff. 182, 184; 40261, ff. 248-9. [3] *Hist. Irish Parl.* v. 180; *Analecta Hibernica*, xxv (1967), 91. [4] *Dublin Weekly Reg.* 25 Mar. 1820.

S.M.F.

MAHON, Hon. Stephen (1768–1828), of Strokestown, co. Roscommon.

CO. ROSCOMMON 1806–1826

b. 6 Feb. 1768, 2nd s. of Maurice, 1st Visct. Hartland [I] (*d.* 1819), and Hon. Catherine Moore, da. of Stephen, 1st Visct. Mountcashell [I]; bro. of Hon. Thomas Mahon†. *unm. d.* 27 May 1828.

MP [I] 1800.

Ensign 47 Ft. 1786, lt. 1790; capt. 5 Drag. 1791; maj. 7 Drag. 1793, brevet lt.-col. 1796; lt.-col. 7 Drag. 1797, brevet col. 1805; lt.-col. 8 Drag. 1808; maj.-gen. 1810; lt.-gen. 1819.

At the death in January 1819 of his father, who had been created Baron Hartland in 1800, Mahon inherited a property at Strokestown, with an annual income of £4,000. Like his elder brother Thomas, who had briefly represented Roscommon at the time of the Union and now succeeded to the title and principal estates, he was promoted lieutenant-general that August, but this sop failed to dispel their disgruntlement at their stalled military careers and the 2nd baron's thwarted ambition for promotion in the Irish peerage. Mahon, who had held the county seat on the family interest since 1806 as an inactive pro-Catholic ministerialist, was again returned unopposed at the general election of 1820, but now voted with opposition, for instance on economies and reduced taxation, on his infrequent appearances in the Commons.[1] He voted against Wilberforce's compromise motion on the Queen Caroline affair, 22 June 1820, and to censure ministers' conduct towards her, 6 Feb. 1821. He paired for inquiry into Peterloo, 16 May 1821, and was in the majority for abolition of one of the joint-postmasterships, 2 May 1822. He divided for parliamentary reform, 24 Apr. 1823, and inquiry into the state of Ireland, 11 May 1824. He voted against the Irish unlawful societies bill, 15, 18, 21, 25 Feb., and (as he had on 28 Feb. 1821) for Catholic relief, 1 Mar., 21 Apr., 10 May 1825. No trace of parliamentary activity has been found for the 1826 session. Mahon, who is not known to have spoken in debate, had been expected to stand a contest against the Tory Robert King, the son of the county's leading anti-Catholic proprietor Lord Lorton, at the general election that year. But, to the impotent fury of the Catholics and their supporters, he withdrew too late (apparently on account of ill health) to allow a suitable replacement to offer and his Roscommon seat was taken by King.[2] He died in London in May 1828. By his will, dated 31 Mar. 1819, he left his Roscommon property and personal wealth sworn under £9,000 to his mother (*d.* 1834) as sole legatee and executrix. Following the deaths of the 2nd baron in 1835 and his brother Maurice, an insane clergyman, in 1845, the Strokestown estates passed to their first cousin Major Denis Mahon, a heavy-handed landlord who was murdered during the Famine in 1847.[3]

[1] *Hist. Irish Parl.* v. 179, 181; *HP Commons, 1790-1820*, iv. 522; Add. 40296, f. 40; *Black Bk.* (1823), 175; *Session of Parl. 1825*, p. 475. [2] *Dublin Evening Post*, 8, 10, 15, 17, 20, 22 June 1826. [3] PROB 11/1743/426; IR26/1170/419; *Gent. Mag.* (1828), ii. 272-3; (1848), i. 679; *Famine Diary* ed. B. Ó Cathaoir, 150-1.

S.M.F.

MAHON, Visct. *see* **STANHOPE, Philip Henry**

MAITLAND, Hon. Sir Anthony (1785–1863), of Thirlstane Castle, Berwick.

HADDINGTON BURGHS 16 July 1813–1818

BERWICKSHIRE 1826–1832

b. 10 June 1785, 2nd s. of James Maitland†, 8th earl of Lauderdale [S] and 1st Bar. Lauderdale [UK] (*d.* 1839), and Eleanor, da. and h. of Anthony Todd, sec. to the GPO, of Walthamstow, Essex; bro. of James Maitland, Visct. Maitland*. *unm.* CB 19 Sept. 1816; KCMG 26 Feb. 1820; KCB 6 Apr. 1832; GCB 10 Nov. 1862. *suc.* bro. James as 10th earl of Lauderdale [S] and 3rd Bar. Lauderdale [UK] 22 Aug. 1860. *d.* 22 Mar. 1863.

Entered RN 1795, midshipman 1798, lt. 1805, cdr. 1806, capt. 1806, half-pay 1821, r.-adm. 1841, v.-adm. 1862; naval a.d.c. to the sovereign 1830-41.

Maitland, a naval captain whose father Lord Lauderdale was the acknowledged leader of the Scottish Whigs until he veered to Toryism early in the Parliament of 1820, had been brought in for Haddington Burghs on the family interest in 1813 as the replacement for his uncle Sir Thomas Maitland†, the governor of Malta and (from 1816) the Ionian Isles. Toeing the family line, he had joined Brooks's, divided silently against Lord Liverpool's administration and for Catholic relief and stood down at the 1818 dissolution to facilitate the return for Richmond of his elder brother James, on the interest of Lord Dundas. The *Glasgow*, which he had commanded with distinction at Algiers in 1816, was recommissioned and he captained her in the Mediterranean under Sir Thomas's command, 1818-21, liaising also with the envoy to Naples Sir William A'Court† during Lauderdale's abortive mission to Leghorn in April 1820 to negotiate with Queen Caroline. (He later approved her prosecution.) He paid off his crew and went on half-pay in June 1821.[1] Returning to the family home in Dunbar, where Lauderdale notoriously confined his wife and children, Maitland established a soap factory and took an interest in agricultural improvements and mining enterprises on their Berwickshire and Haddingtonshire estates.[2] With the support of Lord Melville and the government for his candidature for Berwickshire assured, he came in there unopposed at the general election of 1826, when Lord Lonsdale returned James for Appleby.[3] Professions by Lauderdale 'preparatory to ... [his] appearance in Parliament as a government vote', that he had 'no influence over his son Anthony's politics', were naturally ignored.[4]

Though privately less retiring than James and their brother-in-law James Balfour, with whom he generally voted, Maitland made no significant speech in the House before 1831.[5] He divided for Catholic relief, 6 Mar. 1827, the award to the duke of Clarence, 16 Mar., and the spring guns bill, 23 Mar., but against the corn bill, 2 Apr. (the subject of a hostile Berwickshire petition he had presented, 26 Feb.), and for information on chancery delays, 5 Apr.[6] He was in Hume's minority of ten for repeal of the Blasphemous and Seditious Libels Acts, 31 May 1827. Lauderdale, a contender for office, opposed the short-lived ministries of Canning and Lord Goderich and failed in 1828 to persuade the duke of Wellington, whose appointment as premier he had urged, to endorse the future candidature for Stirling Burghs of his son John, an army officer.[7] Maitland, according to Lady Holland, was 'blackballed' at the Travellers' Club that season.[8] He presented petitions for agricultural protection, 28 Apr., and the Scottish gaols bill, 2 May 1828. He divided for Catholic relief, 12 May, and against the pension proposed for Canning's family, 13 May 1828. In November his reputation and devotion to his father and brothers were tested by scurrilous and politically motivated allegations of improper homosexual advances by John to fellow officers.[9] Lauderdale welcomed Wellington's decision to concede Catholic emancipation in 1829 and sent Maitland from Dunbar to vote for it, 6, 30 Mar.[10] He presented a petition against the Berwick-Roxburgh road bill, 23 Mar. 1829. He divided against Lord Blandford's reform scheme, 18 Feb., and enfranchising Birmingham, Leeds and Manchester, 23 Feb. He was in the minority against the Galway franchise bill at its third reading, 25 May, and voted against reducing the grant for South American missions, 7 June 1830. He presented petitions from Haddington for abolition of the Scottish commissary courts, 26 Apr., and repeal of the additional duty on corn spirits, 3 May. His appointment as a naval aide to William IV was gazetted, 22 July 1830, and his return at the general election the following month unopposed.[11]

The Wellington ministry counted Maitland among their 'friends', and he divided with them on the civil list when they were brought down, 15 Nov. 1830. On 17 Mar. 1831, the eve of the Berwickshire reform meeting, he spoke against the Grey ministry's proposals and promised to take up the cause of the Berwick-upon-Tweed out-voters to be disfranchised by the English bill. He divided against its second reading, 22 Mar., presented and endorsed the hostile Berwickshire petition, 24 Mar., and voted for Gascoyne's wrecking amendment, 19 Apr.[12] Lauderdale was instrumental in securing the return of 12 anti-reformers among the 16 Scottish representative peers at the general election in May, and Maitland, whose election for Berwickshire was assured, attended their candidate Augustus

John Dalrymple* throughout the riotous contest for Haddington Burghs.[13] On the hustings at his own election, 17 May 1831, he defended his 'church and state' politics and opposition to the reform bill and praised the moderation shown by his father's tenants during the Lauder riots.[14]

The Times's survey of anti-reformers in the 1831 Parliament noted the 'filial duty' with which Maitland 'attends to his father's directions'.[15] He divided against the reintroduced reform bill at its second reading, 6 July, and committal, 12 July, voted to make the 1831 census the criterion for English borough disfranchisements, 19 July, to postpone consideration of the partial disfranchisement of Chippenham, 27 July, and to preserve non-resident freemen's voting rights, 30 Aug. 1831. He divided against the bill's passage, 21 Sept., and the second reading of the Scottish reform bill, 23 Sept. He divided with opposition against renewing the Sugar Refinery Act, 12 Sept. An early requisitionist for the Berwickshire meeting of 20 Dec. that declared against any reform prejudicial to the landed interest, he voted against the revised reform bill at its second reading, 17 Dec. 1831, and committal, 20 Jan. 1832, and against enfranchising Tower Hamlets, 28 Feb., and the third reading, 22 Mar. His was one of several Scottish abstentions on the third reading of the malt drawback bill, 2 Apr. Later that month he was knighted in recognition of his naval services. He divided against the second reading of the Irish reform bill, 25 May 1832, but no votes or speeches by him on the Scottish measure were reported. Unlike James, he did not divide against government on the Russian-Dutch loan.

At the 1832 general election Maitland declared early for Berwickshire as a Conservative, but was defeated by the nabob Sir Charles Marjoribanks.[16] He did not stand for Parliament again. Following his father's death in 1839 he became a co-partner with James and the attorney F.W. Vizzard in mining enterprises in Yorkshire and Cornwall and patron of several agricultural societies.[17] He succeeded James in the family estates and titles in 1860, and died unmarried at Thirlstane Castle in March 1863, when the English barony became extinct. His nephew Thomas Maitland (1803-78), the only surviving son of his youngest brother William, succeeded him in the Scottish earldom and estates.[18]

[1] W.R. O'Byrne, *Naval Biog.* ii. 712; Addl. Thirlstane mss (NRA 10211), vol. 265; Add. 41536, ff. 20, 34, 40; *British Gazette and Berwick Advertiser*, 15 Apr.; Lauderdale, *Speech ... 2 Nov. 1820*. [2] *Highland Lady*, 314; Thirlstane mss box 34. [3] NLS mss 2, ff. 53-59; NAS GD267/23/8A/8-12; *Berwick Advertiser*, 10 June, 1 July; *Scotsman*, 5 July; *The Times*, 13 July 1826. [4] Lansdowne mss, Minto to Lansdowne, 25 Dec. 1824. [5] Grey mss, Howick jnl. 18 Mar. 1830; *Scotsman*, 24 Mar. 1863. [6] *The Times*, 27 Feb. 1827. [7] *Arbuthnot Jnl.* ii. 119, 274; A. Mitchell, *Whigs in Opposition*, 207; J.J. Sack, *The Grenvillites*, 185, 210; Wellington mss WP1/921/1. [8] *Lady Holland to Son*, 77. [9] Wellington mss WP1/966/17. [10] Add. 40395, f. 85; Wellington mss WP1/995/13. [11] *The Times*, 23 July; *Berwick Advertiser*, 21 Aug. 1830. [12] *Berwick Advertiser*, 26 Mar. 1831. [13] Ibid. 14 May; *Cockburn Jnl.* 17; *Scotsman*, 21, 28 May 1831. [14] *Berwick Advertiser*, 21 May 1831. [15] *The Times*, 25 Aug. 1831. [16] NAS GD267/23/8; *Berwick Advertiser*, 23, 30 June, 7 July, 8, 22 Dec.; *The Times*, 26 Dec. 1832. [17] Doncaster Archives DD/COV/8; Sheffield Archives, Hoyland Nether mss SY/603/B/1-2; Thirlstane mss boxes 33, C146. [18] *Gent. Mag.* (1860), ii. 431.

M.M.E.

MAITLAND, James, Visct. Maitland (1784–1860).

CAMELFORD	1806–1807
RICHMOND	1818–1820
APPLEBY	1826–1832

b. 12 Feb. 1784, 1st s of James Maitland†, 8th earl of Lauderdale [S] and 1st Bar. Lauderdale [UK], and Eleanor, da. and h. of Anthony Todd, sec. to the GPO, of Walthamstow, Essex; bro. of Hon. Sir Anthony Maitland*. *educ.* Eton 1791; Edinburgh Univ. *unm. suc.* fa. as 9th earl of Lauderdale [S] and 2nd Bar. Lauderdale [UK] 15 Sept. 1839. *d.* 22 Aug. 1860.
Ld. lt. Berwick 1841-60.

Maitland was overshadowed by his illustrious Foxite father Lord Lauderdale, a 'violent tempered, shrewd, eccentric man, with a fluent tongue, a broad Scottish accent and a taste for political economy'. He was also the acknowledged leader of the Scottish Whigs until he veered towards Toryism from about 1820 and instrumental in securing the election of 12 anti-reformers among the 16 Scottish representative peers in 1831.[1] Fever and rheumatism had curtailed Maitland's attendance in the 1818 Parliament, when he sat for Richmond on the interest of his distant kinsman Lord Dundas, and he had yet to address or make an impression in the House when he stood down at the dissolution in 1820.[2] Lauderdale chose not to return his sons to the 1820 Parliament and prepared to bring them in at the next opportunity as supporters of the Liverpool ministry. Thus Maitland, a deputy lieutenant of Haddingtonshire since 1822, became Member for Appleby in 1826 under a reciprocal arrangement with Lord Lonsdale, whose nominee General Adolphus Dalrymple was returned for Haddington Burghs on the Dalrymple and Lauderdale interests. His brother Anthony came in for Berwickshire.[3]

Assisting with his family's constituency business, Maitland presented petitions from Lauder and West

Berwickshire against altering the corn laws, 26 Feb. 1827.[4] He divided with his brother for Catholic relief, 6 Mar., the award to the duke of Clarence, 16 Mar., and the spring guns bill, 23 Mar., but against the corn bill, 2 Apr., and for information on chancery delays, 5 Apr. 1827. He also voted against the Coventry magistracy bill, which Lonsdale's Members strenuously opposed, 18 June 1827. Predictions that Lauderdale would back an aristocratic Whig coalition that year remained largely untested, and Lord John Hay* observed privately that Lord Binning*, who had aspired to manage Scotland for Canning's ministry, 'goes against his near political friends ... to overthrow the Maitlands'.[5] He presented and endorsed petitions for repeal of the Test Acts, 27 Mar., and divided for Catholic relief, 12 May, and against the proposed pension for Canning's family, 13 May 1828. He also manoeuvred in vain to secure the new Wellington ministry's backing for the future candidature of his brother John in Stirling Burghs.[6] The concession of Catholic emancipation in 1829 'delighted' Lauderdale, and Maitland, who was considered as a possible mover of the address, was sent from Dunbar to vote for it, 6, 30 Mar.[7] He divided to transfer East Retford's seats to Birmingham, 15 Mar., and for Jewish emancipation, 5 Apr., but refrained from voting on the latter when government intervention secured its defeat, 17 May 1830.[8] Before the general election that summer Lauderdale asked Lonsdale to return Maitland for Cockermouth instead of Appleby, under the 'Westmorland Treaty' negotiated between the Whig Henry Brougham*, Lonsdale and Lord Thanet; but Lonsdale preferred the 1826 arrangement and Maitland retained his Appleby seat.[9]

The Wellington ministry counted him among their 'friends' and he divided with them on the civil list when they were brought down, 15 Nov. 1830. He presented Scottish petitions for the abolition of colonial slavery, 23 Nov. 1830, 14 Apr. 1831. He privately expressed support for 'peace and a paper currency', but the prospect of a 'ministry formed upon the principles of reform', which threatened to curtail his father's electoral influence, alarmed him. He divided against the second reading of the Grey ministry's English reform bill, which proposed Appleby's disfranchisement, 22 Mar., and for Gascoyne's wrecking amendment, 19 Apr. 1831.[10] He came in again for Appleby at the ensuing general election and attended Dalrymple at great personal risk throughout the riotous contest for Haddington Burghs, where the Lauder baillie was abducted despite their endeavours, and a reformer returned.[11] The Tory 5th duke of Buccleuch was informed in June 1831 that Maitland, who helped to secure Dalrymple's return for Haddington Burghs on petition, 10 Aug., adhered to his father's politics and well understood the details of the Scottish reform bill and the political implications of changing the burgh districts.[12] He voted against the reintroduced English reform bill at its second reading, 6 July, and when the opposition met at Peel's on the 11th, he agreed to 'move the question of hearing the Appleby petitioners by the counsel' to test party strength and jeopardize the bill.[13] Doing so next day, he reiterated the petitioners' case, based on the exclusion of the parish of St. Lawrence from the population total for Appleby in the 1821 census, but lost the division by 284-187. The Lowther press praised and the radical *Carlisle Journal* vilified his conduct.[14] He voted against the bill's committal, 12 July, and to make the 1831 census the criterion for English borough disfranchisements, 19 July, when, assisted by Croker and Peel, he moved for the transfer of Appleby from schedule A to B. Certain Whigs sympathized with his argument that the jurisdiction of the mayor and corporation applied to both the parishes of St. Michael and St. Lawrence, but Lord John Russell pointed to the difference between boroughs 'including' and 'extending into' two parishes and defeated the proposal by 302-228. Maitland voted against the partial disfranchisement of Chippenham, 27 July, and to preserve non-resident freemen's voting rights, 30 Aug. He divided against the bill's third reading, 19 Sept., and passage, 21 Sept., and the second reading of the Scottish reform bill, 23 Sept. 1831.

Maitland was the promoter of an anti-reform address from Berwickshire in December 1831.[15] He voted against the revised English reform bill at its second reading, 17 Dec., and committal, 20 Jan. 1832, when he brought up another Appleby petition for its transfer to schedule B. Sir John Hobhouse* wrote that when he joined the ministry soon afterwards his friend

> Maitland was the only man who did not seem pleased, but he gave the reasons, for, he said, 'Of *course* you could not take the place were you not convinced of the permanence of the administration'. Now this showed his cause of vexation, for the Tories have announced the speedy dissolution of government and certainly my taking office would seem to point the other way.[16]

Maitland's last-ditch attempt to refer Appleby's case to a select committee failed by 256-143, 21 Feb., when, protesting at its 'wanton' disfranchisement, he attributed Appleby's fate to the failure to define the limits of the borough when burgage tenure became the acknowledged franchise, errors by the boundary commissioners, and ministerial bias. He voted against the English bill at its third reading, 22 Mar., and the second reading of the Irish reform bill, 25 May. He divided against administration on the Russian-Dutch loan, 26 Jan., and would have done so on the sugar duties, 7 Mar., but he and his friends at dinner at Charles Baring Wall's* arrived too late.[17] He presented petitions from Haddington against the Maynooth grant and the use of molasses in brewing and distilling, 20 July (and one from Dunbar on the latter issue, 18 Aug. 1831), and another from Dunbar against the Haddington court house bill, 28 Feb. 1832.

The prospect of defeat made Maitland relinquish his attempt to come in for Haddington Burghs at the general election of 1832 and he did not stand for Parliament again.[18] He succeeded to his father's estates and titles in 1839 and became a co-partner with Anthony and the attorney F.W. Vizzard in mining enterprises in Yorkshire and Cornwall.[19] He died unmarried at his Berwickshire seat, Thirlestane Castle, in August 1860, recalled as a 'well-made, square, strong and athletic man' who could outwalk his gamekeepers but 'took very little part in public affairs'. His estates and titles passed to Anthony.[20]

[1] *Oxford DNB*; *Cockburn Jnl.* 17. [2] Add. 51692, Lauderdale to Holland [1819]. [3] Addl. Thirlstane mss (NRA 10211) 67/12; Wentworth Woodhouse mun. WWM F48/160; Lansdowne mss, Minto to Lansdowne, 25 Dec. 1824; *Westmld. Advertiser*, 17 June; *Scotsman*, 5 July 1826. [4] *The Times*, 27 Feb. 1827. [5] NLS mss 14441, f. 24. [6] A. Mitchell, *Whigs in Opposition*, 207; J.J. Sack, *The Grenvillites*, 185, 210; Wellington mss WP1/921/1. [7] Add. 40395, f. 85; Wellington mss WP1/995/13. [8] Wellington mss WP1/1127/6; *Scotsman*, 17 July 1830. [9] Lonsdale mss, bdle. on 1830 election; *Westmld. Gazette*, 7 Aug. 1830. [10] Add. 51835, Maitland to Holland [1830]. [11] *Scotsman*, 26 Mar., 2, 27, 30 Apr., 4, 7, 28 May; Wellington mss WP1/1184/18; NAS GD224/580/3/1/3/9; G.B.A.M. Finlayson, 'Note on Employment of Military in Haddington, 1831', *Trans. E. Lothian Antiq. Soc.* x (1966), 17-21. [12] NAS GD224/581/4. [13] Lonsdale mss, Lowther to Lonsdale, 11 July 1831. [14] *Carlisle Jnl.* 16 July; *Westmld. Gazette*, 16 July 1831. [15] *Berwick Advertiser*, 17 Dec. 1831. [16] Wilts. RO, Hobhouse mss 145/2/b, Hobhouse to wife, 1 Feb. 1832. [17] NLW, Ormathwaite mss FG/1/6, p. 34. [18] *Berwick Advertiser*, 16 June, Add. 51644, J.A. Murray to Holland, 17 June 1832; 57370, f. 94; J.I. Brash, 'Conservatives in the Haddington District of Burghs', *Trans. E. Lothian Antiq. Soc.* xi (1968), 46. [19] Thirlstane mss, 'wooden box' 34, 'deed box' C146; Doncaster Archives DD/COV/8; Sheffield Archives, Hoyland Nether mss SY/603/B/1-2. [20] PROB 11/1917/1839; IR26/1524/957; *The Times*, 25 Aug.; *Gent. Mag.* (1860), ii. 431; *Haddington Courier*, 31 Aug. 1860.

M.M.E.

MAITLAND *see also* **FULLER MAITLAND**

MALCOLM, Sir John (1769–1833), of Warfield, nr. Wokingham, Berks.[1]

LAUNCESTON 9 Apr. 1831–1832

b. 2 May 1769, 4th s. of George Malcolm (*d.* 1803) of Burnfoot, nr. Langholm, Dumfries and Margaret, da. of James Pasley of Craig, Dumfries. *educ.* Westerkirk (Archibald Graham); in London by Mr. Allen 1781. *m.* 4 July 1807, at Mysore, Charlotte, da. of Col. Alexander Campbell of Ballede, Perth, 1s. 4da. kntd. 15 Dec. 1812; KCB 7 Apr. 1815; GCB 20 Nov. 1819. *d.* 30 May 1833.

Cadet, E.I. Co. (Madras) 1780, ensign 1781, lt. 1788, capt. 1798, maj. 1802, lt.-col. 1804, col. 1813, maj.-gen. 1819.

Pol. resident, Mysore 1802-12; gov. Bombay 1827-30.

Malcolm's grandfather Robert Malcolm (*d.* 1761), who was descended from a junior branch of a Fifeshire family, was minister of Ewes, near Langholm, and had the tenancy of a sheep farm at Burnfoot. His son George was intended for the church, but a speech impediment put paid to this. He took over Burnfoot and the adjoining farm of Douglan, but got himself into financial difficulties through unwise speculations. His son John, the seventh of his 17 children, was taken to London in 1781 by his maternal uncle John Pasley, a merchant at 23 Surrey Street, who managed to place him in the East India Company's service, despite his extreme youth. He sailed for India in the autumn of 1782 and arrived at Madras in April 1783.[2] In 1788 he joined the forces of the nizam of Hyderabad in the Mysore war. He was, as one observer noted, 'quite illiterate' in terms of formal education, but 'possessed of an intellect which only required to be set a-going, either for good or evil'. His ambitions turned to a diplomatic career, and he made himself master of the Persian language. Illness forced him to return to Britain on furlough in February 1794, but the voyage completely restored him. While at home he attracted the attention of Henry Dundas†, president of the board of control, with a paper on the grievances of Indian army officers. He was appointed to the staff of Sir Alured Clarke, the new commander-in-chief in Madras, and returned with him to India in May 1795, after a winter in Edinburgh where he casually attended university lectures.[3]

He served as private secretary to Clarke and his successor General Harris, but remained a frustrated diplomat. In the Mysore war of 1799, when he formed a lifelong friendship with the governor-general Lord Wellesley's brother Arthur, the future duke of Wellington, he acted as the controlling political officer of the army, and became first secretary to the commission appointed to settle the Mysore territories after the taking of Seringapatam. Soon afterwards Wellesley sent him to Persia, as the first British envoy since the sixteenth century, with the aims of diverting the Afghans, checking French influence and promoting British trade. The mission, which lasted from December 1799 to early 1801, was dogged by difficulties of protocol, but Malcolm was at last presented to the shah, 16 Nov. 1801, and concluded commercial and political treaties. He reflected that he had 'done *as much as I was able*' in 'a first negotiation with a government not two stages removed from a state of barbarism'. The outcome of the mission displeased the Company but found favour with Wellesley, who made Malcolm his private secretary and ambassador at large. His expectation of a nomination to a lucrative Indian post was thwarted by his employment on a succession of special missions, but in 1803 he secured the residency at Mysore, though he was hardly ever there. By 1806 he was out of pocket as a result of his special missions and feeling threatened by the opprobrium which was heaped on Wellesley on his return to England. The following year, when he married, he was advised by Arthur Wellesley not to be 'in a hurry' to go home, because he was 'not yet sufficiently rich'. For his own part, Malcolm now contemplated retirement after 18 months of quiet residence at Mysore to recoup his finances. Late in 1807 he accepted the new governor-general Lord Minto's commission to undertake another mission to Persia, but the Company made difficulties and he went to the Gulf merely as an observer with a small force of ships and marines. The enterprise was negated by French influence and Malcolm was back in India by August 1808, when he looked towards retirement in two years, being 'tired of wasting my life in exertions which, from the virulence of party in England, are unlikely either to be appreciated or rewarded'. In 1810 he returned to Persia on a mission which was dogged by internecine British squabbles and accomplished little. Although he was censured for its extravagance, he was given money and assistants to advance his planned history of Persia, to which he turned his attention after the publication in 1811 of his *Sketch of the Political History of India*. He also dashed off *Disturbances in the Madras Army*, a defence of his suppression of the 1809 rebellion in Masulipatam, which was published in England just before his arrival on furlough in July 1812.[4]

Malcolm accepted an invitation from Lord Buckinghamshire, the new head of the board of control, to discuss Indian affairs with him. He also met and befriended Sir Walter Scott, who thought him 'a fine fellow', distinguished by 'frankness' and 'sound ideas of morality and policy'. He gave evidence on Indian matters before the committee of the whole House, 5, 7 Apr., and the Commons select committee, 7 May 1813. He obtained a grant of £5,000 from the Company in recognition of his services and pressed on with his literary projects, but he still coveted high diplomatic employment. Wellington advised him to get into Parliament if possible, in order to advance this ambition, but also recommended him to 'be nobody's man but your own' and to confine his pretensions to India. He became a literary celebrity on the publication of his successful *History of Persia* in the summer of 1815, after which he visited Wellington with the army of occupation in Brussels and Paris. Concluding that his prospects at home were bleak, he sailed again for India in October 1816. As the governor-general Lord Hastings's agent and a brigadier in the Deccan army, he plunged into a welter of diplomatic and military activity. On 21 Dec. 1817, impetuously commanding an advance guard of cavalry, he scored a spectacular but bloody victory over Holkar's forces at Mehidpoor. While furious at being passed over for Elphinstone as governor of Bombay in March 1819, he was persuaded by Hastings to stay on, in the vague expectation of becoming lieutenant-governor of the central territories, the administration and settlement of which now occupied most of his time. This proved illusory, and his chagrin was intensified when he learned early in 1820 that Sir Thomas Munro had been preferred to him as governor of Madras. Slightly mollified by promotion to major-general and a GCB, he stayed in India to complete his *Report on the Province of Malwa* and *Notes of Instructions* for his successors, both published in 1822. He left for England in December 1821 and travelled via Egypt, Corfu and Italy, where he visited his friend John William Ward*, who reported that 'his Herculean frame has ... yielded in some degree to the effects of climate and fatigue', but that 'his spirits' were 'unabated'.[5]

He published a *Memoir of Central India* in 1823, when a proposal from the Company that he should undertake a fresh mission to Persia foundered on his insistence on having credentials from the crown. Later that year he visited Wellesley in Ireland and returned with reports of its 'improving state', notwithstanding the continuing atrocities there. He toured Scotland in 1824, and the next year went to France to attend the coronation of Charles X.[6] He still thought an Indian governorship was the least he deserved, and in March 1824 he applied to succeed Munro at Madras, only to find ministers committed, at Lord Liverpool's insistence, to supporting the pretensions of Stephen Rumbold Lushington*, the secretary to the treasury.

Although Wellington warned him that he had 'no chance' of attaining his object, Malcolm persisted and, to meet the objection that his father-in-law's holding the command at Madras made his own appointment inappropriate, he persuaded a faction at East India House to press for his appointment to Bombay and Elphinstone's transfer to Madras. Against all the advice of Wellington and Charles Williams Wynn*, president of the board of control, who urged him to settle for a compensatory pension, Malcolm dug in his heels; the affair dragged on for months and ended in disappointment, though he did get the pension. In 1826, when he published his *Political History of India*, he considered but thought better of the idea of bidding for a seat on the direction of the East India Company.[7] At the general election that year he had hopes of a seat at Rochester, where the treasury encouraged him to stand, 'first, I really believe, on my own account, and next, because it will give them a second Member who, though not a Downing Street Member, is not in opposition'. However, he was dished by the intervention of the first lord of the admiralty on behalf of his son. He claimed to have declined 'several' invitations to stand elsewhere, because 'they either do not suit my purse or my sentiments on *the doctrine of free will*'. He later confided to his brother Gilbert that the 'ultimate object' of his ambition was to be governor-general of India.[8] In December 1826 he accepted the government of Bombay in succession to Elphinstone, deluding himself, as Wellington told him he was, that it might lead to the supreme office, if only as provisional successor to Lord Amherst. He secured from the Indian authorities at home what he regarded as an implied promise that he would be given overall responsibility for the administration of central India. Yet nothing had been settled by the time he sailed, with instructions to confine his activities to Bombay, in July 1827. His *Sketches of Persia* was published that year. His governorship was marked by a prolonged dispute with Sir John Grant, one of the puisne judges, over the rights of jurisdiction claimed by the supreme court, and by his policy of stringent economy and retrenchment. He initially retained hope of securing the administration of the central territories, but when this was dashed by the new governor-general Lord William Cavendish Bentinck*, to whom the Company had passed the buck, he decided to abide by his original resolution to leave India for ever at the end of 1830. As he told Bentinck, he had 'an independent fortune' and 'a seat in Parliament awaiting my arrival', which he intended to occupy principally in order to participate in the forthcoming discussions on the renewal of the East India Company's charter.[9] Lord Ellenborough, president of the board of control, was minded in November 1829 to name him as Bentinck's provisional successor, not with the intention that he should actually take up the post, but in order to bring the wayward Bentinck to heel. Wellington and the chairs of the Company saw some merit in the ploy, but Ellenborough had no convincing answer to their objection that going to Calcutta would kill Malcolm, who 'would stay till he died in order to be governor-general one day'. Though disappointed in his main ambitions and vexed at the rejection of his application to be made a privy councillor, he returned to England, so he assured Wellington, 'a very contented man'.[10]

Soon after his arrival in London in February 1831 Maria Edgeworth, whose invitation he accepted, found Malcolm 'as entertaining and delightful as his *Persian Sketches* and as instructive as his *Central India*'. The following month Elphinstone attended a dinner for him at Ellenborough's, in company with Wellington and several of the late ministers:

> Malcolm rattled away precisely as he would have done at his own table in Bombay, kept everybody in good humour, though he took all the talk to himself, and really commanded my admiration for his ease and independence among a class of people for whom I know him to entertain so excessive a respect. He made no attempt to adapt his conversation to them, or please anybody but himself ... I can now account for his popularity with all people of note whom I have heard talk of him. It could never have been gained by mere courting of favour, or sustained by any one who had less frankness, good humour and talent.[11]

Early in April he was returned for Launceston by the 3rd duke of Northumberland, who had turned out one of the sitting Members for supporting the Grey ministry's reform bill. He declared that 'he had not an acre of land' and had been 'returned by the patron ... free of expense', but he 'could vote as he pleased' on all measures except reform, to which he was 'most decidedly opposed'.[12] He planned to concentrate on Indian affairs in the House, and was added to the select committee on the renewal of the East India Company's charter, 18 Apr. (and reappointed, 28 June 1831, 27 Jan. 1832). He was also determined to have his say on what he privately described as 'this goddess reform', which was 'twin-sister to the goddess of reason, who troubled Europe 40 years ago'. To a friend, he wrote:

> I am no enemy ... to reform; but that, to be safe, should be very moderate and very gradual ... The consequences my experience leads me to anticipate may not be immediate, but they are, in my mind, certain; and the option appears to be between our fighting the battle or leaving a sad inheritance of a deteriorated and broken constitu-

tion to our children. My practical education makes me an unbeliever in these new political lights. I cannot think that the mantle of Francis Bacon has descended upon Jeremy Bentham. I would not consult men in a fever on their own case.[13]

On 19 Apr. 1831 he made his maiden speech in support of Gascoyne's wrecking amendment to the reform bill, for which he voted. He defended the 'borough-mongering system', in so far as it enabled the interests of India to be represented by providing a way into Parliament for men such as himself; typically, he talked at length of his own services in the East. He subsequently denied, unconvincingly, an allegation across the floor that he had been returned not on account of his Indian expertise, but because he was willing to fall in with Northumberland's views on reform. Nevertheless, Thomas Gladstone* reported that he had spoken 'with great animation and manliness'.[14] Having written a pamphlet on the subject in the form of a *Letter to a Friend in India*, he came in again for Launceston at the ensuing general election.[15]

He threw cold water on Stuart Wortley's idea of setting up several subsidiary committees to investigate various aspects of the East India Company's affairs, 28 June 1831. He favoured allowing native Indians to serve on grand juries and act as magistrates, 1 Sept., but opposed Hume's call for radical reform of the Indian judicial system. He supported a petition for abolition of the Indian pilgrim tax, 14 Oct., but warned of the dangers of exciting Indian passions through careless pronouncements in Parliament. He condemned the reintroduced reform bill as a 'concession to the clamorous demands of the people', 5 July, and voted against the second reading next day. He supported Agnew's attempt to give the doomed boroughs a share in elections as parts of wider constituencies, 15 July. He voted for use of the 1831 census to determine the disfranchisement schedules, 19 July, deplored the extinction of Midhurst and Old Sarum, which would remove three Indian pundits from the House, 26 July, and voted against the partial disfranchisement of Chippenham, 27 July. He put the case for Launceston being allowed to keep two Members, 29 July, but did not divide the House. Next day he taunted the reformer De Lacy Evans for his bid to save both seats at Rye. He foresaw problems arising from the increase in London Members, 4 Aug., and spoke against the enfranchisement of Gateshead, 5 Aug. He agreed in principle with Hume's call for colonial representation, 16 Aug., and supported Estcourt's attempt to perpetuate the corporation and freeman franchises, 27 Aug. In all this, as he told his brother Charles, he saw himself as

fighting the revolutionary battle ... The evil in this country lies deep. The whole of the lower and numbers of the middle classes have been sedulously taught to regard their superiors not only with envy but hostility, as men that sleep and fatten on their labour and hard earnings. Knowledge without religion or principle has been universally disseminated, and the desire to better their condition through chance or spoliation excited. The designing, who seek change, and the ignorant, who are deceived by them, are active and loud, whilst those who desire the tranquillity of the country are hitherto silent and inert. But the period has come when they must be roused, or England will change her character as well as her constitution.

He remained obsessed with India and her problems:

I am ... working sometimes fifteen hours a day, and always eight or ten ... India and its services are threatened by prejudice, ignorance, and the attacks of bodies of men deeply interested in change ... There is not the smallest borough in England that has been disfranchised or enfranchised that does not excite more interest ... than our whole empire of India ... I desire to retire and to complete much useful work, and to take care of my health; but having begun by filling a certain place in public estimation, and believing that one year more will decide the fate of India, I have hitherto refused to listen to the entreaties of my good lady and ... mean ... to go through with the work in which I have perhaps imprudently engaged.[16]

On the third reading of the reform bill, 19 Sept., he attacked the 'political puritans' who deluded themselves that 'a constituency of 20,000, including voters paying only 3*s.* 10*d.* a week for lodgings, will be free, independent and virtuous'. He also dismissed Hume's plan for direct representation for India as impractical, and suggested instead the creation of a 'constituency' from the 2,000 or so proprietors of the East India Company. He voted against the bill later that day, and divided against its passage, 21 Sept., and the second reading of the Scottish bill, 23 Sept. He was in the majority against issuing the Liverpool election writ, 5 Sept. 1831. That autumn he visited Paris and returned convinced that France, 'where you hear nothing but the voice of reason and political wisdom, and see nothing but distrust and distress', was on the verge of chaos. He hoped that, thanks to the stand made by the Lords, Britain would 'not be hurried down that precipice, to the very brink of which we have been driven by ignorance, violence, inexperience and ambition'.[17]

Malcolm had recently bought a house with 235 acres in Berkshire, and he added supervision of its improvement to his already crowded schedule. He toured Scotland in November, visited the duke of

Northumberland at Alnwick, and returned to London to divide against the second reading of the revised reform bill, 17 Dec. 1831. During the Christmas recess he was in Shropshire and North Wales.[18] He voted against going into committee on the bill, 20 Jan. 1832. He gave notice of his intention of proposing the formation of a constituency to embody Indian interests, 27 Jan., but later abandoned the idea. He paired in favour of preserving the franchise for freemen by marriage, 7 Feb.,[19] and voted against the enfranchisement of Tower Hamlets, 28 Feb. Seconding the wrecking amendment to the bill's third reading, 19 Mar., he welcomed some of the modifications made to it, but warned that 'under its operation, no administration will have sufficient strength to carry on the government of the country', much less that of India, and he exhorted the Lords to reject it; he divided in the minority, 22 Mar. He backed Murray's amendment to increase Scotland's county representation, 1 June. He voted against ministers on the Russian-Dutch loan, 26 Jan. He supported the cholera prevention bill, 15 Feb., but counselled against exciting alarm which, so his Indian experience had convinced him, promoted the spread of the disease. He presented a Launceston petition in favour of the factory bill, 20 Feb. He opposed inquiry into the claims of the Hutchinsons on the rajah of Travancore, 10 Apr., and begged to be excused from serving on the committee, being 'already engaged every day on committees'. As a member of the Indian military subcommittee, he complained to Ellenborough that the chairman, Byng, was 'incapable'; but he was in turn criticized by his colleague Fergusson, who observed that he 'could talk only of himself'. He gave evidence to the general committee on military affairs, 5, 8 Mar., and on India's foreign relations, 12, 17 Apr.[20] He forced ministers to admit that there was room for improvement in the current procedure for adjudicating on such claims as that of the Hutchinsons, 14 June. He approved the Indian juries bill, which opened the way for natives to serve on grand juries, 18 June. He favoured inquiry into the Deccan prize money claims, 6 Aug., and defended Elphinstone and other company officials from allegations of their depredations against the peishwah of the Pindarees, 10 Aug. 1832.

Malcolm had no hope of coming in for the one Launceston seat spared by the Reform Act and, 'being tied to no party', he saw 'a pretty fair prospect of making a salaam to the old walls of St. Stephen's'. However, he was encouraged by the duke of Buccleuch and others to come forward for the Dumfries district of burghs and 'attempt to stem ... the tide of radicalism now flowing, unhappily, with little less violence through our sequestered valleys, than through the streets of Birmingham'. He meant 'neither ... to brook pledge nor to disburse cash' and, having 'the mark of an anti-reformer upon my brow', he had little expectation of success. Following the dissolution in November 1832 two days of canvassing convinced him that, in the divided state of the local Conservative interest, he had no chance, and he withdrew. On his way south at Carlisle he was 'literally taken out of a coach and asked to head an attack against that revolutionary emblem, the tri-coloured flag', but it was generally reckoned that he had allowed himself to be 'the cat's paw' of a corporation rump and he gave up after an hour's polling left him well in arrears of a Radical and a Whig. He nevertheless claimed that his intervention had 'lowered' the 'Whig influence'.[21] Early in 1833 he saw his *Government of India* through the press and, ignoring continued illness, delivered a two-hour speech at a special general court of proprietors, 15 Apr., criticizing the government's proposal to end the East India Company's commercial monopoly; he afterwards collapsed, but attended later sessions without speaking. He subsequently suffered a stroke and died in May 1833.[22] He left his wife an annuity and his one-third share in her late father's estate, and instructed that the Warfield property should be sold for the benefit of his son George Alexander, who also received £5,000 to go towards the purchase of army commissions and the residue of personalty sworn under £40,000.[23] His *Life of Clive* was finished by William Erskine and published in 1836, and he was commemorated by a Chantrey statue in Westminster Abbey and an obelisk on Langholm hill.

Malcolm rose from humble origins to become one of the most distinguished administrators of British India. However, he was not a success in Parliament, where he engaged himself in a lost cause and where 'neither voice nor delivery were much in his favour'. Physically and mentally resilient, he was energetic, versatile and decisive, but was sometimes betrayed by his excessive self-confidence. Thomas Macaulay*, an inveterate political opponent, loathed him, and considered him 'the greatest egotist now living', but others saw past his irritating habit of engrossing every conversation to his winning candour and generosity of spirit. Elphinstone, for one, praised his 'natural abilities' of 'quickness of apprehension' and 'boldness', and wrote that he possessed 'in an eminent degree, the power of gaining the attachment of those with whom he associated', thanks to 'his unbounded good nature ... a temper which nothing could ruffle and spirits which nothing could depress'.[24]

[1] J.W. Kaye, *Life and Corresp. of Sir John Malcolm*, 2 vols. (1856), is monumental but uncritical. R. Pasley, '*Send Malcolm!*' (1982), is a sketch, but pays more attention to Malcolm's writings. [2] Kaye, i. 1-9; Pasley, 6-8. [3] Kaye, i. 9-40; Pasley, 9-14. [4] Kaye, i. 43-512; Pasley, 20-74. [5] Kaye, ii. 70-352; Pasley, 75-122; *PP* (1812-13), vii. 53-60, 61-71, 407-17; Ward, *Llandaff Letters*, 311. [6] Kaye, ii. 415-57; Pasley, 123-30; Harewood mss, Canning to Williams Wynn, 1, 7 Apr., reply, 7 Apr.; Add. 51534, T. Grenville to Holland, 22 Sept. 1823. [7] Kaye, ii. 458-74; Pasley, 127-35; *Arbuthnot Jnl.* i. 297, 360; Buckingham, *Mems. Geo. IV*, ii. 48, 112, 114-15, 123; *Wellington Despatches*, ii. 244-6; Add. 38193, f. 200. [8] Add. 41963, ff. 302, 304; Kaye, ii. 474-6. [9] Kaye, ii. 477-558; Pasley, 136-49; *Bentinck Corresp.* ed. C.H. Philips, i. 10, 26-27, 54-60 (quoted), 74-75, 80, 294-7, 467-8; *Ellenborough Diary*, i. 227, 326; ii. 56; *Wellington Despatches*, vii. 226-9. [10] *Ellenborough Diary*, ii. 146, 149, 151; *Wellington Despatches*, vii. 261-4. [11] *Edgeworth Letters*, 486-7; T.E. Colebrooke, *Elphinstone*, ii. 300. [12] *West Briton*, 15, 22 Apr. 1831. [13] Kaye, ii. 559-63; Add. 41963, f. 292. [14] St. Deiniol's Lib. Glynne-Gladstone mss 198, T. to J. Gladstone, 20 Apr. 1831. [15] *Wellington Despatches*, vii. 459. [16] Kaye, ii. 564-71. [17] Add. 41964, f. 100. [18] Kaye, ii. 572-80. [19] *The Times*, 10 Feb. 1832. [20] *Three Diaries*, 189; *PP* (1831-2), xiii. 38-50; xiv. 27-41. [21] Kaye, ii. 581-97; *Carlisle Jnl.* 15 Dec.; *The Times*, 15, 18 Dec. 1832. [22] Kaye, ii. 598-613; Pasley, 155-62; *Bentinck Corresp.* ii. 1042, 1068. [23] PROB 11/1819/463; IR 26/1727/372. [24] *Gent. Mag.* (1833), ii. 83; *Macaulay Letters*, ii. 107, 250; Colebrooke, ii. 331.

D.R.F.

MALCOLM, Neill (1797–1857), of 1 Princes Street, Hanover Square, Mdx.

BOSTON 1826–1831

b. 5 Nov. 1797, 1st s. of Neill Malcolm of Poltalloch, Argyll and Mary Anne, da. and h. of David Orme of Lamb Abbey, Kent. *educ.* Harrow 1815-16; Christ Church, Oxf. 1817; L. Inn 1818. *m.* (1) 14 July 1831, Harriet Mary (*d.* 21 May 1837), da. of Sir Samuel Clarke Jervoise, 1st bt., of Idsworth Park, Hants, 1s. *d.v.p.* 4da. (1 *d.v.p.*); (2) 2 Sept. 1843, Louisa, da. of Evelyn John Shirley*, *s.p. suc.* fa. 1837. *d.* 2 Oct. 1857.

The Malcolm family had long been established in Argyllshire as lairds of Poltalloch. Malcolm's grandfather, the 11th laird, a West India merchant, introduced extensive changes on their Scottish estates and was involved in the cutting of the Crinan canal. Either he or his son was one of the London merchants who signed the loyal declaration in 1795. Malcolm's father, a member of the standing committee of West India planters and merchants by 1800, acquired Lamb Abbey in Kent through his marriage. He was a deputy lieutenant for Argyllshire and obtained heraldic arms at the Lyon office in 1818, but the mainstay of the family's wealth remained their Argyll estate in Jamaica. The *People's Book* described Neill Malcolm junior, as he was known until his father's death, as a merchant and an East and West India proprietor. He was elected to the standing committee of West India planters in February 1824.[1]

At the 1826 general election he came forward on the Pink or corporation interest for the venal borough of Boston. According to the *Boston Gazette*, he stood under the auspices of Henry Ellis, the corporation's former Member, who had been unseated on petition in 1821. On the hustings he made some deferential allusion to Ellis, but presented himself as 'totally unconnected with any party', denied that he represented the West India interest and was opposed to the abolition of slavery, and professed to favour religious liberty, though he believed it inexpedient to grant further concessions to Catholics. After a two-day contest he was returned in second place. According to *Drakard's Stamford News*, his political opinions were opposed to those of the majority of the freemen, and he cut short his chairing in view of the violence which occurred.[2] He voted against Catholic relief, 6 Mar. 1827, 12 May 1828, and brought up a hostile Boston corporation petition, 1 Apr. 1828. He presented a petition for repeal of the Test Acts, 12 June 1827, and against, 25 Feb., and voted to retain them, 26 Feb. 1828.[3] He divided against inquiry into chancery delays, 24 Apr. 1828. In February 1829, Planta, the Wellington ministry's patronage secretary, predicted that he would vote 'with government' for their concession of Catholic emancipation, but he declared that he 'saw no reason for changing his opinion', 18 Feb., presented hostile petitions that day, 4, 10 Mar., and divided against the measure, 18, 27, 30 Mar. He presented a Boston petition for repeal of the window tax, 14 Apr. 1829. He later told the local press that he had voted for Knatchbull's amendment to the address, 4 Feb. 1830, as he was convinced that distress was more general than ministers had allowed and was anxious for inquiry into means of alleviating it, but he does not appear in the minority lists.[4] He divided against Lord Blandford's parliamentary reform scheme, 18 Feb. He was credited with a vote against government on the treasurership of the navy, 12 Mar. He presented a Boston petition against relaxation of the retail beer trade, 30 Mar. He had attended the meetings of the West Indian merchants' committee with fair regularity after his election to Parliament, and was present at the meeting of Members interested in the West India colonies, 2 June. He was subsequently one of the delegates appointed by the West India merchants' committee to press their case for relief over rum duties with the board of trade, 5 June.[5] He voted against Jewish emancipation, 17 May, abolition of the death penalty for forgery, 7 June, and to amend the sale of beer bill, 21 June 1830.

At the 1830 general election Malcolm offered again for Boston, where he was stigmatized by *Drakard's Stamford News* as a 'ministerialist, anti-reformist and slave-possessor', who was hand in glove with the corporation and a 'wretched speaker'. On the hustings he was censured for his lax attendance, his conduct over the beer bill and his extra-parliamentary support for the West India interest, but in his defence he challenged anyone to say that he had not attended to his constituents' interests and claimed to have 'voted against ministers on many great questions, and so I will again if I think they are wrong'. He supported retrenchment, but would have shirked his responsibilities had he voted for 'wild expedients' and an 'inconsiderate reduction of taxation'. Barracked over his hostility to universal suffrage and the ballot, he doubted whether in America 'anything like the freedom you enjoy exists'. He was no advocate of slavery, but he condemned the libels of the anti-slavery societies and the impracticable measures advocated by their adherents. After a violent contest he was returned at the head of the poll. At his celebratory dinner he denied that the privileges of the corporation were at variance with the interests of the people, conceded that his confidence in the administration had been shaken by the passage of emancipation, but renounced 'factious opposition'.[6]

Malcolm was listed by ministers among the 'moderate Ultras' and he voted against them in the crucial division on the civil list, 15 Nov. 1830. He continued to attend the standing committee of the West India interest and was in the minority of 39 to relax duties on the import of wheat to the West Indies, 12 Nov.[7] He was applauded by the *Gazette* for his 'liberal conduct' on the civil list but his popularity was short-lived. In response to a request to support the Boston reform petition, 3 Dec., he told James Staniland, the chairman of the meeting appointed to promote it, that an extended franchise and shorter parliaments would not improve the constitution and that he was strongly opposed to the ballot and therefore compelled to withhold his support. However, on 16 Dec. 1830, when his colleague presented the petition, he agreed that their constituents were suffering from heavy taxation and conceded that reform to 'a certain extent is desirable', though he could not countenance sweeping changes. That day he challenged the assertion of Sir William Amcotts Ingilby, one of the county Members, that the petition represented the feelings of the county at large. He declined to endorse a further Boston reform petition and defended the mayor's refusal to comply with a requisition to convene a public meeting, 19 Mar. 1831. Shortly afterwards, in a more explicit public letter to his constituents, he declared that although he was not opposed to all attempts to remedy the 'acknowledged defects' in the representative system, he considered the Grey ministry's reform bill to be a 'hazardous experiment', which sanctioned the most 'flagrant violation of all chartered rights'. He duly voted against its second reading, 22 Mar., and, in a published reply to a vote of thanks from an anti-reform meeting at Boston, 7 Apr., assured them that reform was not only 'subversive of their rights and privileges', but also dangerous to the 'best institutions of the country'.[8] Speaking in similar terms, he presented and endorsed a Boston anti-reform petition and promised 'to offer all the opposition in my power to this measure, which I think most unwise and uncalled for', 28 Mar. Declaring himself 'undismayed by popular clamour', he voted for Gascoyne's wrecking amendment, 19 Apr. 1831.

At the ensuing general election Malcolm, who had treated the freemen with coals in the winter of 1830-1, started again for Boston as the corporation candidate, promising to defend the freemen's rights and citing his vote on the civil list as proof of his support for 'practicable retrenchment and economy'. Faced with escalating unrest and taunted as an anti-reformer, he withdrew, 28 Apr., following a 'violent attack' on Thomas Broughton's house in Bargate, where he had been dining. He fled early on the following morning in a carriage and four driven at great speed. The corporation mostly held aloof thereafter, and such was the tumult when Malcolm was proposed *in absentia* by two diehards, that the hustings were completely destroyed. After a token contest he was defeated in third place.[9] Malcolm married in July 1831 and appears to have resumed his business career, though he rarely attended the meetings of the West India committee over the next few years.[10] His only son died in July 1835, followed a month later by his second daughter. His first wife died in 1837, as did his father, whose personal estate was proved at under £500,000 in England and valued at £49,955 in Scotland. After making provision for his daughters and younger son, all the family property, including his lands in England and the West Indies, passed to Malcolm. Among other bequests, including one to his factor in Argyllshire, he left £5,000 to an infant, Charles Temple, more often known as Charles McCullum Campbell, on the understanding that Malcolm would supervise his education and secure his future.[11] Malcolm unsuccessfully contested Oxford as a Conservative in 1841.[12] He continued the tradition of agricultural improvement on the Poltalloch estate and restored Duntroon Castle. Kilmartin House was his principal Scottish residence, though he retained the family properties in London and Kent. He remarried in 1843.[13]

Malcolm died at Brighton in October 1857. By his will, dated 18 July 1851, he devised £20,000 to each of his three surviving daughters and made ample provision for his second wife. He possessed estates in British colonies other than Jamaica, including Australia, and he directed his executors to sell these in order to purchase additional land in Britain. When the will was made Malcolm still hoped for an heir, but in the absence of male issue many of its provisions were void and the family estates passed to his brother John Malcolm (1805-93), whose son and heir John Wingfield Malcolm (1833-1902), was Member for Boston, 1860-78, and Argyllshire, 1886-92. He was created Baron Malcolm of Portalloch in 1896, but the peerage became extinct on his death.[14]

[1] Inst. of Commonwealth Stud. M915, reel 9, cttee. of standing members; [W. Carpenter], *People's Bk.* (1831), 323. [2] *Boston Gazette*, 9, 16 May, 6, 13 June; *Drakard's Stamford News*, 12 May; *The Times*, 27 May 1826; [3] *The Times*, 13 June 1827. [4] *Boston Gazette*, 3 Aug. 1830. [5] M915, reel 4 (minutes 1822-29), 175, 352, 357, 375, 381; mins. 1829-34, 11, 27, 75-78, 97; M915, reel 11, meeting, 2 June 1830. [6] *Boston Gazette*, 29 June, 20, 27 July, 3 Aug.; *Drakard's Stamford News*, 9, 16, 30 July 1830. [7] M915, reel 4 (minutes 1829-34), 130, 149, 157, 164, 169. [8] *Boston Gazette*, 23 Nov., 7, 28 Dec. 1830, 22 Mar., 15 Apr. 1831. [9] Ibid. 26 Apr., 3 May 1831; G.S. Bagley, *Boston*, 203-4. [10] M915, reel 4 (minutes 1829-34), 231, 327. [11] PROB 11/1873/56-7; IR26/1456/45-6. [12] *The Times*, 1 July 1841. [13] *New Statistical Account of Scotland* (1845), vii. 552, 559, 561-3; *Ordnance Gazetteer of Scotland* (1895), vi. 214. [14] PROB 11/2260/288; IR26/2106/957; *Gent. Mag.* (1857), ii. 573.

S.R.H./P.J.S.

MANDEVILLE, Visct. *see* **MONTAGU, George**

MANGLES, James (1762–1838), of Woodbridge, nr. Guildford, Surr.

GUILDFORD 1831–1837

b. 26 July 1762,[1] 2nd or 3rd s. of Robert Mangles (*d.* 1788), ship chandler and oilman, of Wapping, Mdx. and Wanstead, Essex and w. Ann. *m.* 22 July 1791, Mary, da. of John Hughes of Guildford, 6s. (2 *d.v.p.*) 6da. (3 *d.v.p.*). *d.* 25 Sept. 1838.

Sheriff, Surr. 1808-9.

Mangles's father may have been the Robert Mangles who was baptized at Tynemouth in March 1733; he certainly had property in the north-east of England, although he was for many years engaged in trade at Wapping.[2] Mangles and his brother John were partners in their father's chandlery business, which was bequeathed to them in 1788, but they were not relieved of their debts to him at that time.[3] Trade directories indicate that their business (which another brother, Robert, had joined by 1805) subsequently expanded across the Thames to Rotherhithe, where they were listed as shipwrights in 1817 and as Mangles and Company, wharfingers, in 1820. Mangles signed the London merchants' loyal declaration in 1795, when he was apparently resident in Hackney, but he had established himself as a landed proprietor at Woodbridge, Surrey, by 1803.[4] While he maintained an interest in the mercantile concern at Rotherhithe, he was last named in the Wapping partnership in 1821. That year he was appointed deputy chairman of the Wey-Arun Junction Canal Company, and he assumed responsibility for the day-to-day running of this concern during its most profitable period, becoming chairman the year before his death.[5] By the marriage of his daughter Caroline to the Rev. Arthur Onslow in 1815, Mangles became connected to a family with an established electoral interest at Guildford. He reportedly declined several invitations to contest the borough, but at the general election of 1831 he came forward as a supporter of the Grey ministry's reform bill and was returned at the head of the poll, supplanting George Holme Sumner, an anti-reformer and spokesman for the agricultural interest (to whom he had given a plumper at the 1826 county election). He subsequently recorded his sense of 'obligation' at his election and said he would 'feel bound to give up all his time and exertions for the service of the town and every individual in it'.[6]

He divided for the second reading of the reintroduced reform bill, 6 July, and generally for its details, although he voted for the complete disfranchisement of Saltash, on which ministers failed to provide a clear lead, 26 July, and against the partial disfranchisement of Guildford, 29 July 1831. On the latter occasion he read extracts from his constituents' petition to support his argument that a town 'largely increasing both in population and in wealth' should be permitted to retain both its Members. He voted for the bill's third reading, 19 Sept., its passage, 21 Sept., the second reading of the Scottish bill, 23 Sept., and Lord Ebrington's confidence motion, 10 Oct. He divided in the minorities for O'Connell's motion to swear in the 11 members of the Dublin election committee, 29 July, and to postpone the issue of a new writ, 8 Aug., but voted to prosecute only those guilty of bribery and against the motion censuring the Irish administration for use of undue influence, 23 Aug. He supported a petition calling for the regulation of steam vessels, 3 Sept., and was in the minority for protection of the West Indian sugar trade, 12 Sept. He divided for the second reading of the revised reform bill, which afforded Guildford a total reprieve, 17 Dec. 1831, and later gave an 'elegant entertainment' to members of the borough's corporation.[7] He voted steadily for the bill's details, but was absent from the division on the third reading, 22 Mar. 1832. He voted for an address asking the king to appoint only ministers committed to carrying an unimpaired measure, 10 May, the second reading of the Irish bill, 25 May, and against the Conservative amendment to increase Scotland's county representation, 1 June. He divided against Hobhouse's Vestry Act amendment bill, 23 Jan., and with ministers on the Russian-Dutch loan, 26 Jan., 12 July, relations with Portugal, 9 Feb., and military punishments, 16 Feb. He voted to make coroners' inquests public, 20 July 1832.

Mangles was returned for Guildford at the general election of 1832 and sat as a Liberal until his defeat in 1837. He died in September 1838. It appears that he had acquired more real estate in Surrey, which he left to his wife with provision for his sons to exercise a right of purchase. Ross Donnelly Mangles (1801-77), Liberal Member for Guildford, 1841-58, and chairman of the East India Company, 1857-8, took up the option on the Woodbridge property, while Charles Edward Mangles (1798-1873), Liberal Member for Newport, 1857-9, took on the Poyle Park estate near Farnham. Mangles's personal estate was sworn under £25,000.[8]

[1] *Ex. inf.* Stephen Lees. [2] Ibid.; IGI (Northumb.). [3] PROB 11/1172/550. [4] IGI (Mdx., Surr.). [5] P.A.L. Vine, *London's Lost Route to the Sea*, 91, 94, 114, 154, 253, 258. [6] *Gent. Mag.* (1815), i. 641; *Brighton Herald*, 7 May, 22 Oct. 1831. [7] *Brighton Herald*, 14 Jan. 1832. [8] PROB 11/1902/655; IR26/1491/697; *VCH Surr.* iii. 20.

H.J.S.

MANNERS, Lord Charles Henry Somerset (1780–1855), of Belvoir Castle, Leics. and 28 Sackville Street, Mdx.

CAMBRIDGESHIRE	1802–1830
LEICESTERSHIRE NORTH	29 Dec. 1835–1852

b. 24 Oct. 1780, 2nd s. of Charles Manners†, 4th duke of Rutland (*d.* 1787), and Lady Mary Isabella Somerset, da. of Charles Noel Somerset†, 4th duke of Beaufort; bro. of Lord Robert William Manners*. *unm.* CB 4 June 1815; KCB 20 Apr. 1838. *d.* 25 May 1855.

Cornet 10 Drag. 1798, lt. 1799, capt. 1800, maj. 1808; lt.-col. 23 Drag. 1811, 3 Drag. 1812-25; brevet col. and extra a.d.c. to prince regent 1817; maj.-gen. 1825; lt.-gen. 1838; col. 3 Drag. 1839-*d.*; gen. 1854.

When a contest was threatened for Cambridgeshire at the approaching 1820 general election Manners advised his brother, the 5th duke of Rutland, on whose interest he sat, to withdraw him if it materialized.[1] In the event there was no disturbance and Manners, who promised to work to 'secure the liberty and independence of his constituents' and to safeguard the interests and agriculture of the county, and declared his attachment to 'the constitution in church and state', came in again with the other sitting Member, the Whig Lord Francis Osborne. It was not entirely plain sailing, for he was attacked for his 'blind support for every measure of administration' by adherents of the independent party opposed to the Rutland interest in both county and borough. He was questioned as to whether he approved of the perpetuation of corrupt electoral influence such as that exercised by his brother in Cambridge; whether he would vote for or against the civil list; whether he had voted for the grant of £10,000 to the duke of York, and whether he would support Lord John Russell's Grampound disfranchisement bill. He 'declined giving any pledge of future conduct' and claimed that at the time of the proceedings on the ducal grant he had been 'on a bed of sickness'.[2]

Manners continued to support the Liverpool ministry, though he was an unenthusiastic politician and an indifferent attender, who was even keener than his brother, Member for Leicestershire, on hunting and riding. (He used a whip with an eyeglass fitted in the handle.)[3] He presented a petition from the occupiers of 70,000 acres in the Isle of Ely for amelioration of agricultural distress, 31 May 1820.[4] He voted in defence of ministers' conduct towards Queen Caroline, 6 Feb. 1821. Taking the family line, he divided against Catholic relief, 28 Feb., and he presented a hostile petition from the dean and chapter of Ely cathedral, 23 Mar.[5] He presented two Cambridgeshire petitions complaining of agricultural distress, 2 Mar.,[6] but paired with government against repeal of the additional malt duty, 3 Apr. He was in their majorities for the duke of Clarence's grant, 18 June, and against Hume's call for economy and retrenchment, 27 June 1821. Manners voted against more extensive tax reductions to relieve distress, 11 Feb. 1822, though the next day he presented a Wisbech agriculturists' petition for remedial measures.[7] He voted against abolition of one of the joint-postmasterships, 13 Mar. At the county reform meeting, 4 Apr., what amounted to a vote of censure on him was carried when it was resolved that its petition should be presented by Osborne and the Whig Lord Tavistock, the duke of Bedford's son.[8] Manners voted against Canning's bill to emancipate Catholic peers, 30 Apr., and in defence of the lord advocate's dealings with the Scottish press, 25 June 1822. On 20 Feb. 1823 he presented a petition from owners and occupiers of Linton parish for relief from agricultural distress, observing that the petitioners had confidence in the Commons 'as at present constituted', and that none of them had attended the unruly county meeting of 14 Feb. which had supported a radical reform programme.[9] Later that day he voted against parliamentary reform; and he divided with government against inquiry into the prosecution of the Dublin Orange rioters, 22 Apr., Scottish parliamentary reform, 2 June, and investigation of chancery delays, 5 June 1823. The only known traces of his parliamentary activity in 1824 are his presentation of an Isle of Ely publicans' petition against the Beer Acts, 12 May,[10] and his vote in defence of the prosecution of the Methodist missionary John Smith in Demerara, 11 June. He was a defaulter on a call of the House, 28 Feb. 1825, but attended and was excused the next day, when he divided against Catholic relief, as he did on 21 Apr. and 10 May. He voted against the Irish franchise bill, 26 Apr. He presented three Cambridgeshire petitions against any alteration in the corn laws, 22 Apr., but he was criticized in the county for failing to attend to support the Manea enclosure bill.[11] He divided against the spring guns bill, 27 Apr. He voted for the duke of Cumberland's grant, 30 May, 6, 10 June, but was in the protectionist minorities against the relaxation of restrictions on the importation of foreign corn, 8, 11 May 1826.

A week before the 1826 general election Manners, anticipating 'a very unpleasant day' at best and an expensive contest at worst, advised Rutland to give up his interest in Cambridgeshire in the latter eventuality. A few days later, notwithstanding his awareness of their 'very great unpopularity' with some elements, he had come, as he told his brother, to

> presume we must go to a poll, and I will go on until our committee recommend to give up. Believe me, I feel very little on my own account, for you must be aware that my personal ambition would never have led me to ask you to spend a farthing to get me returned for this county, or any other place whatever. I chiefly regret my situation on account of the additional harass[ment] and annoyance which this will cause your mind already overwhelmed with affliction [Rutland's wife had died seven months earlier].[12]

At the nomination, he declared his support for undiminished agricultural protection and the existing constitution, 'the envy of surrounding nations'. When asked by Samuel Wells, the radical Huntingdon attorney, if he would vote for reform, he 'declined answering the question, as he considered it the business of a representative to be guided by the arguments which might be adduced when any question came under discussion'. After a diatribe against Manners, Rutland and their numerous family connections who held lucrative places, Wells nominated Henry Adeane*, a local squire, who had turned down a requisition to stand earlier that day. Even though Adeane declined the nomination and said he would vacate the seat if returned, his radical promoters forced a seven-day poll, principally to create trouble and expense for Rutland. They achieved that object, but posed no threat to the return of Manners who, polling mainly plumpers, finished at the head of the poll, almost 500 above Osborne.[13]

He presented an anti-Catholic petition from the authorities of Ely cathedral, 5 Mar. 1827, and voted against relief the following day.[14] He obtained three weeks' leave ostensibly to attend to urgent private business, 20 Mar.; but according to one of his Cambridgeshire critics his real object was hunting, and he was attacked for thus absenting himself when two important drainage bills were before the House.[15] He attended to vote against the corn bill, 2 Apr. In May 1827 Rutland, lamenting Canning's accession to power, told Mrs. Arbuthnot that Manners and their brother Robert were 'enthusiastic' in their attachment to their fellow soldier the duke of Wellington.[16] Manners was the guest of his close friend Sir Watkin Williams Wynn* at his Denbighshire home in September 1827.[17] Although Rutland told Wellington, the new premier, in January 1828, that his brothers were 'ready to attend in their places, whenever you think their presence desirable', Manners was inconspicuous in the House that session, when he presented the Ely cathedral anti-Catholic petition, 29 Apr., and divided against relief, 12 May 1828.[18] Rutland, informed by Wellington in early February 1829 of the government's decision to concede Catholic emancipation, declined to commit himself either way before the details were revealed, though he doubted whether he would be able to support it. At the same time, he had no difficulty in confirming, as Wellington requested, that whatever 'insulated difference of opinion' he might have with ministers on this issue, he would still 'be *generally* as warm and strenuous in their support as heretofore'.[19] Planta, the patronage secretary, thought that Manners, who presented petitions against Catholic claims from Ely cathedral and Wenlock corporation, 10 Feb., would side 'with government'; but Rutland told Mrs. Arbuthnot that his brothers would probably be obliged to 'go with the current of public feeling'. Manners duly voted with his brother against consideration of relief, 6 Mar. They did so, according to Rutland, 'from the dictates of their own opinions (having no time to communicate again with me) and from a deference to the strong feeling in their respective counties'; they seemed 'very uncomfortable' in opposing Wellington.[20] Manners was less persistent than Robert in his opposition: he presented a dozen hostile Cambridgeshire petitions, 9, 20 Mar., and voted against the relief bill at its report stage, 27 Mar.; but he only paired for the division of 23 Mar., and was absent from those on the second and third readings, 18, 30 Mar. Rutland, whose relations with Wellington remained thoroughly cordial, voted for the second reading in the Lords, 4 Apr., but sent his proxy against the third, 10 Apr. 1829, to mark his reservations about the adequacy of the securities.[21]

Manners attended the county meeting called to petition for repeal of the beer and malt taxes and revision of the licensing regulations, 23 Jan. 1830. Forced by clamour to speak, he as usual evaded the issue:

> He was fully sensible of the existence of ... great distress ... and of the urgent necessity of applying some relief, if it could be effected without an infraction of the public credit. He should be ready to lay their petition before Parliament, but at the same time he should reserve to himself the privilege of fully examining every part of the question, and acting in that manner as he believed would best conduce to the interests of the country.

His obvious 'mental reservation' did not escape his critics, who secured the passage of a resolution instructing him and Osborne to promote the objects of the petition and a 'general repeal of taxes'.[22] On 8 Feb. he seconded his colleague's formal motion to have the petition brought up and acknowledged the 'unexampled distress' which prevailed; but he declined to divulge his own opinion on the subject. He divided against parliamentary reform proposals, 11, 18, 23 Feb. Either he or his brother voted against Jewish emancipation, 5 Apr.; and he definitely did so, 17 May. He presented petitions from Wisbech brewers against, 4 May, and the inhabitants of Ely for, 10 May, the sale of beer bill; and he voted in the minorities for attempts to restrict the extent to which it opened the trade, 21 June, 1 July 1830.

Adeane's acceptance of a requisition to stand at the 1830 general election did not unduly alarm Manners who, 'perfectly well in health, though still disabled in my arm' (presumably after a riding accident), was initially confident of victory, though concerned over the likely cost.[23] At the nomination, he expressed 'the greatest confidence' in the Wellington ministry; said that he had, 'on every occasion when it could be consistent with the safety of the institutions of the country, supported a reduction of taxation', and, seeking to portray himself as a Member who would not give 'a blind or servile support' to government, claimed to have resisted the 1828 corn bill 'by every means in his power' (no trace of such activity has been found) and stressed his opposition to Catholic emancipation. He ignored Wells's demands to know if he would vote for tax reductions, and during the contest refused to pledge himself to support the abolition of slavery. The transfer of the Hardwicke interest to Adeane, the defection of a number of Tory men of influence and a massive increase in turnout, which gave anti-Rutland feeling an electoral impact, overwhelmed Manners. By the end of the second day he was significantly in arrears, and he gave up early on the fifth, almost 230 behind Adeane.[24] A local observer blamed his defeat, which was generally seen as a symptom of ministerial weakness, on 'a combination of untoward circumstances' and the inadequacies of his agents and committee men; but Lord Lowther*, a junior member of the government, attributed it in no small measure to Manners's own feebleness and 'inability and unwillingness to transact the common county business'.[25]

At the general election of 1831 Manners, now backed by Hardwicke, was put up for Cambridgeshire as an opponent of the Grey ministry's 'wild and sweeping' reform bill, a friend to 'any safe and constitutional measure of reform' and the champion of the agricultural interest. Even though Adeane, who had expressed reservations about details of the bill, seemed vulnerable, a week's canvassing revealed that Manners had no chance, and he withdrew.[26] He came in for Leicestershire North on his brother's death in 1835, went on to oppose repeal of the corn laws and retired 'on account of declining health' in 1852. For the last 20 years of his life Manners, who in 1839 obtained the colonelcy of one of his old regiments, had rooms in the Albany. He died in London in May 1855.[27]

[1] Rutland mss (History of Parliament Aspinall transcripts), Manners to Rutland, 16 Mar. 1820. [2] *Cambridge Chron.* 18 Feb., 10, 17, 24 Mar. 1820. [3] T.F. Dale, *Belvoir Hunt*, 122. [4] *The Times*, 1 June 1820. [5] Ibid. 24 Mar. 1821. [6] Ibid. 3 Mar. 1821. [7] Ibid. 13 Feb. 1822. [8] *Cambridge Chron.* 5, 12 Apr. 1822. [9] *The Times*, 21 Feb. 1823. [10] Ibid. 13 May 1824. [11] Ibid. 23 Apr.; *Cambridge and Hertford Independent Press*, 7 May 1825. [12] Rutland mss, Manners to Rutland, 16-19 June 1826. [13] *Cambridge and Hertford Independent Press*, 24 June, 1 July; Rutland mss, Manners to Rutland [24], 26 June, 9 July 1826. [14] *The Times*, 6 Mar. 1827. [15] *Cambridge and Hertford Independent Press*, 31 Mar. 1827. [16] *Canning's Ministry*, 284. [17] *Williams Wynn Corresp.* 361. [18] Wellington mss WP1/914/13, 38. [19] *Wellington Despatches*, v. 489-94; *Ellenborough Diary*, i. 362. [20] Rutland mss, Rutland to Mrs. Arbuthnot, 3, 10 Mar. 1829. [21] *Wellington Despatches*, v. 583-4; Wellington mss WP1/1003/3. [22] *Cambridge and Hertford Independent Press*, 23 Jan. 1830. [23] Rutland mss, Manners to Rutland, 25 July 1830. [24] *Cambridge and Hertford Independent Press*, 7, 14, 21 Aug. 1830. [25] *Cambridge Chron.* 20 Aug.; Lonsdale mss, Lowther to Lonsdale, 14, 20 Aug. 1830. [26] *Cambridge and Hertford Independent Press*, 30 Apr., 7 May 1831. [27] *The Times*, 29 May 1855.

D.R.F.

MANNERS, Lord Robert William (1781–1835), of Belvoir Castle, Leics.

Scarborough	1802–1806
Leicestershire	1806–1831
Leicestershire North	1832–15 Nov. 1835

b. 14 Dec. 1781, 3rd s. of Charles Manners, 4th duke of Rutland (*d.* 1787), and Lady Mary Isabella Somerset, da. of Charles Noel Somerset†, 4th duke of Beaufort; bro. of Lord Charles Henry Somerset Manners*. *unm.* CB 1815. *d.* 15 Nov. 1835.

Cornet 10 Drag. 1798, lt. 1800, capt. 1803, maj. 1810; lt.-col. 2 Ft. 1811, 23 Drag. 1812, 10 Drag. 1814, half-pay 1819; brevet col. 1821; lt.-col. 3 Drag. 1825; maj.-gen. 1830.

Manners, a cavalry officer who had been wounded at Waterloo, came forward again for Leicestershire on the family interest, headed by his brother, the 5th duke of Rutland, at the general election of 1820. He declared his devotion to 'the Protestant establishment' as 'the palladium of liberty and toleration' and promised to

> use his utmost exertions in support of such measures as were best calculated to remove the sad distresses which had unhappily prevailed throughout the country. He would never, however, lend himself to those wild theories, which, if acted upon, would produce that species of horrid revolutionary frenzy that would habituate the minds of the people to assassination and every species of public as well as private vice.

He was returned unopposed.[1] He continued to support the Liverpool ministry, but he was not the most assiduous of attenders, preferring field sports, in which he was a 'hard rider', to politics.[2]

He voted in defence of ministers' conduct towards Queen Caroline, 6 Feb. 1821. He divided against Catholic relief after presenting the hostile Leicestershire petition, 28 Feb. 1821.[3] He voted against Canning's attempt to relieve Catholic peers, 30 Apr. 1822, brought up more anti-Catholic petitions, 16 Apr. 1823, 18 Apr. 1825,[4] and voted against relief, 1 Mar., 21 Apr., 10 May, and the Irish franchise bill, 26 Apr. 1825. He divided against parliamentary reform, 9 May 1821, 20 Feb., 2 June 1823, and paired against mitigation of the forgery laws, 23 May 1821. He mustered for the divisions against more extensive tax cuts, 11 Feb., abolition of one of the joint-postmasterships, 13 Mar., and repeal of the salt duties, 28 June, and for the aliens bill, 19 July 1822. He was in the ministerial minority against inquiry into the prosecution of the Dublin Orange rioters, 16 Apr., and majority against investigation of chancery delays, 5 June 1823. He presented Leicester petitions for the abolition of slavery, 18 May,[5] and voted for the Irish insurrection bill, 14 June 1824. He divided for the duke of Cumberland's grant, 30 May, 6 June 1825. He voted against attempts to restrict the use of spring guns, 21 June 1825, 27 Apr. 1826.

Manners was returned unopposed at the general election of 1826, when he expressed his 'pity and admiration' for the stoicism of the distressed 'working classes' and his 'hopes that the clouds which had caused so much trouble and dismay were fast disappearing', and reiterated his hostility to concessions for Catholics.[6] He voted against their claims, 6 Mar. 1827, 12 May 1828, and repeal of the Test Acts, 26 Feb. 1828. After serving on an election committee, he was given a fortnight's leave to attend to urgent private business, 3 Apr. 1827. Following the formation of Canning's ministry, Rutland told the duke of Wellington's confidante Mrs. Arbuthnot that he expected no good from it and that his brothers were 'enthusiastic respecting the gentleman whom they know by the nickname of the "Beau" ... [and say] "Whatever happens, we'll stick by "*the Beau*"'.[7] Manners duly supported the duke's ministry from January 1828; he was in their majority on the ordnance estimates, 4 July 1828. He presented a Loughborough anti-slavery petition, 11 July 1828. In February 1829 Planta, the patronage secretary, predicted that he would side 'with government' for their concession of Catholic emancipation, but he was wrong. On 3 Mar. Rutland told Mrs. Arbuthnot that Manners had gone to the Commons that day 'to fulfil the wishes of the county' by presenting with his colleague Legh Keck the hostile Leicestershire petition:

> It is a fearful moment altogether, for I foresee that whatever part I might take, my brothers cannot do otherwise than go with the current of public feeling, unless when the measures are detailed they are such as to create a pacification in the spirit of the country.[8]

Chided by Rutland for remaining silent on this occasion, Manners replied:

> I always told you I was not fit to represent the county ... You say ... you wish I had courage to speak, but you must first give me the ability. I wished much to have said something, but I had not two words to put together, so I sat like a log of wood ... I cannot help it, if they turn me out for it.[9]

He presented petitions against emancipation, 18, 23 Mar., and voted steadily against the measure throughout the month, though Rutland (who voted for the second reading of the bill in the Lords, but sent in his proxy against the third) noted that both he and his brother Lord Charles were 'very uncomfortable at giving a vote in opposition to the duke'.[10] When Rutland's Member Frederick Trench was appointed storekeeper of the ordnance in June 1829, some observers believed that Wellington 'might as well previously have made that offer' to Manners or his brother.[11] Emancipation did not permanently alienate him from the administration, and he divided with them against the transfer of East Retford's seats to Birmingham, 11 Feb., and the enfranchisement of Birmingham, Leeds and Manchester, 23 Feb. 1830. He presented a petition for the abolition of truck payments, 17 Mar. It is not clear whether it was he or Lord Charles who voted against Jewish emancipation, 5 Apr., but he definitely did so on 17 May. He was in minorities for amendments to the sale of beer bill, 21 June, 1 July 1830.

He was returned in second place in the contested election for Leicestershire the following month, but Rutland feared for his future hold on the seat.[12] Ministers listed him as one of their 'friends', and he was in their minority in the decisive division on the civil list, 15 Nov. 1830. He brought up a petition for the abolition of slavery, 3 Nov. 1830. He divided against the second reading of the Grey ministry's reform bill, 22 Mar., and for Gascoyne's wrecking amendment, 19 Apr. 1831. He initially planned to stand at the ensuing general election, but the prospect of another contest, this time against two reformers, prompted him to abandon the seat.[13] A year later he was reported as saying that if he ever recovered it 'he supposed he should be under the necessity of supporting Lord Grey' against the radical extremists.[14] He came in for the northern division of the county at the 1832 and 1835 general elections, but died a bachelor, intestate and in harness, aged only 53, in November 1835.[15] Administration of his personal estate, which was sworn under £1,600, 10 Aug. 1836, was granted to Rutland.

[1] *Leicester Chron.* 26 Feb.; *Leicester Jnl.* 17 Mar. 1820. [2] *Session of Parl. 1825*, p. 475; T. F. Dale, *Belvoir Hunt*, 122. [3] *The Times*, 1 Mar. 1821. [4] Ibid. 17 Apr. 1823, 19 Apr. 1825. [5] Ibid. 19 May 1824. [6] *Leicester Jnl.* 16, 23 June 1826. [7] *Arbuthnot Corresp.* 284. [8] Aberdeen Univ. Lib. Arbuthnot mss. [9] Rutland mss (History of Parliament Aspinall transcripts), Manners to Rutland [Mar. 1829]. [10] Arbuthnot mss, Rutland to Mrs. Arbuthnot, 10 Mar. 1829. [11] Rutland mss, Douglas to Rutland, 25 Aug. 1829. [12] *Arbuthnot Corresp.* 138. [13] *Leicester Jnl.* 29 Apr., 6 May 1831. [14] *Three Diaries*, 264. [15] *Gent. Mag.* (1836), i. 89.

S.R.H.

MANNERS SUTTON, Charles (1780–1845), of Palace Yard, Westminster, Mdx. and Mistley Hall, Manningtree, Essex.[1]

SCARBOROUGH	1806–1832
CAMBRIDGE UNIVERSITY	1832–10 Mar. 1835

b. 29 Jan. 1780, 1st s. of Most Rev. Charles Manners Sutton, abp. of Canterbury, and Mary, da. of Thomas Thoroton† of Screveton, Notts. *educ.* Eton 1793-6; Trinity Coll. Camb. 1798; L. Inn 1802, called 1806. *m.* (1) 8 July 1811, Lucy Maria Charlotte (*d.* 7 Dec. 1815), da. of John Denison† of Ossington, Notts., 2s. 1da.; (2) 6 Dec. 1828, Ellen, da. of Edmund Power of Curragheen and Clonea, co. Waterford, wid. of John Purves Home, 1da. *suc.* fa. 1828; GCB 31 Aug. 1833; *cr.* Visct. Canterbury 10 Mar. 1835. *d.* 21 July 1845.

Judge adv.-gen. Nov. 1809-June 1817; PC 8 Nov. 1809; bencher, L. Inn 1817; commr. for building new churches 1818; charity commr. 1818-34; registrar of ct. of faculties 1827-34; high commr. for adjusting claims of Canada 1835.

Speaker of the House of Commons 2 June 1817-29 Dec. 1834.

To what Lord Althorp* called the 'necessary humbug' of the Speakership, Manners Sutton, the grandson of the 3rd duke of Rutland, brought 'a commanding presence, sonorous voice, imperturbable temper, and ... winning grace of manner', but only a modicum of talent and no flair: he was 'wholly deficient in that extraordinary perspicuity of diction and clearness of mind' which had characterized his distinguished predecessor Charles Abbot. He picked Abbot's brains and quickly mastered the forms and procedures of the House, which he supervised in a tolerant spirit.[2] A 'tall and robust' man with a 'very dark' complexion and 'a strong squint in one of his eyes', he became generally respected and liked, although some on the left were naturally indisposed towards his strong anti-Catholic Tory politics. A personal friend of the leading Tory Protestant Robert Peel*, he usually kept his party prejudices in abeyance when in the Chair, but his impartiality (as well as his physical stamina) was severely tested during the reform crisis of 1831-2.[3]

According to John Croker*, Manners Sutton agreed with his father the primate that Queen Caroline's name should be specified in prayers and did 'not approve' of the contrary line which the Liverpool ministry adopted.[4] He was reported to be 'well and in spirits' a week after his unopposed return for Scarborough on the secure interest of his cousin the 5th duke of Rutland at the general election of 1820.[5] On his re-election to the Chair, proposed by Sir William Scott and seconded by George Holme Sumner, 21 Apr. 1820, he referred to the recent doubling of business and 'new embarrassments arising out of the times in which we lived'. An obituary credited him with an aptitude for the facilitation of the vast increase in private bill legislation which was one of the features of his time in the Chair; but Edward John Littleton, a frustrated aspirant to that place, reckoned that he 'had never sat on a committee on a private bill and seemed totally thoughtless about the principles on which that important part of the House of Commons work ... should be governed'.[6] This charge seems unfair, for Manners Sutton clearly addressed his mind to the subject. On 6 Apr. 1821 he observed that it was necessary to reach 'a fair and temperate decision' on procedure in private bill committees, which he felt ought as far as possible to follow the established practice of the House. In 1824 a standing orders committee was established, and that session and in 1825 and 1826-7 select committees were appointed to investigate means of improving the conduct of private business. Their reports exposed the many deficiencies in current practice, but few of the changes which they recommended were implemented in this period: on the initiative of Littleton, 1826-7, new county lists were ordered to be drawn up and a committee of appeals was constituted. More effective reforms were implemented under Manners Sutton's aegis, 1833-4.[7] When a number of Members raised the problem of a lack of accommodation for committees upstairs and Littleton criticized his having allowed private bill committees to use the chamber before the House convened because it had created 'an unwholesome air', 22 Mar. 1825, Manners Sutton explained that he had had no choice on this occasion and said that as no remedy could be implemented that session he would continue the practice for the time being. In response to Littleton's report that the committee on the Welch Mining Company bill had twice failed to meet, 18 May 1825, he observed:

> He had paid great attention to the private business, in order, if possible, to remedy the inconvenience arising from the great pressure of it this session, and that it might be better regulated. But ... if the gentlemen who constituted the committee absented themselves, and never attended ... it was quite idle to think that any regulations could remedy the present grievances ... Nothing was more degrading to the character of the House, in whose hands was vested such a mass of business, than that such a proceeding should take place.

Prompted by Littleton and others, on 15 Apr. 1829 he gave a resume of the principles of private bill committee procedure. On 8 Mar. 1830 he reported that he had 'taken considerable pains' to investigate the fees charged by the private bill office and committee clerks with the aim of making them 'perspicuous' and laid before Members a revised and simplified list for consideration. He had these made into standing orders, 22 July, when he also repealed the order which required an interval of 21 days between the first and second readings of Irish private bills, abolished the maximum scale of 5 inches to the mile for the maps required for turnpike bills and ordered the rearrangement of the standing order book for private legislation to make it easier to use. At the start of the 1830 Parliament, in conjunction with Peel, the leader of the House, he announced that in future he would take the chair at three o'clock rather than four in order to expedite private business. When Littleton raised the problem of obstructive petitions to private bills which, by alleging a failure to comply with standing orders forced the revival of the standing orders committee, he agreed that the practice was getting out of hand and urged Members to 'look cautiously and narrowly' at such petitions and 'not suffer parties, by a side-wind, to impede the progress of bills': he was keen to 'compel parties to come forward at once to oppose a measure, and to state the grounds of their opposition, instead of allowing them to endeavour to obtain their object in an underhand manner'. In response to complaints from Members of the 'uncertainty' of having their names called for the presentation of private bill petitions, 20 Feb. 1832, he announced that he had directed a clerk to attend the chamber each morning at ten o'clock to take down names 'in rotation'. He appealed for 'a general feeling of accommodation' when sharp practice by some Members was revealed, 23 Feb. 1832.

Turning now to some of the most interesting episodes of Manners Sutton's Speakership in this period, he required Canning and Burdett to explain after their exchange of 'coarse and harsh words', 9 May 1820, but took no notice of Burdett's observation that Canning 'appeared drunk with insolence'.[8] He was involved in the discussions which ended in the ministerial decision to proceed against the queen by a bill in the Lords, 25 June.[9] When he checked Hobhouse for alluding to the divisions there, 18 Sept., Hobhouse, considering that he was within his rights, 'appeared to yield, but continued my topics'.[10] Manners Sutton told Mrs. Arbuthnot in October that his father was 'decidedly for' the royal divorce and that he himself thought 'it would be more difficult to pass' the bill of pains and penalties through the Commons 'without the [divorce] clause than with it'; but she did not 'pay much attention to what the Speaker says as he is very apt to take up wrong notions'.[11] On 2 Nov. 1820 there was an unseemly outburst in the House when he was 'hooted' by opposition

Members as he left the chamber to obey Black Rod's summons to the Lords for the prorogation, so denying Denman the opportunity to deliver a communication from the queen. The Whig Commons leader Tierney noted that this was 'not well thought of' even by some ministerialists, and told Lord Grey that 'if you ever saw a pickpocket on his way to be ducked you may have a tolerable idea of the Speaker's walk from the Chair to the door'. He did not return to the House.[12] Tierney did not think that his being 'a great deal' with Peel in the first week of January 1821 necessarily meant that the latter was in negotiation for a return to office, as the two had always been 'great friends'.[13] The Tory independent Member Henry Bankes privately blamed his 'inadvertence and mismanagement' for giving rise to an unexpected debate and division on the queen's affair, 23 Jan; and two months later Joseph Jekyll[†] observed that the House 'disgraces itself by perpetual vulgar tumult', for 'the Speaker is no disciplinarian'.[14] On 26 Mar. he availed himself of the Speaker's privilege of speaking in committee of the whole House to oppose the clause of the Catholic relief bill which allowed Catholics to sit in Parliament as a threat to 'the safety of the constitution'. He congratulated Julia Peel on her husband's 'most powerful' speech against the third reading, 2 Apr.[15] Next day he gave his casting vote against the second reading of the Blackfriars bridge repair bill without giving a reason.[16] In June 1821 Croker found him 'vexed that, in consequence of the prorogation', he could not take his place in the coronation procession as the first commoner and 'more vexed that he must walk, as he says five degrees below his rank as a privy councillor'. The following month he was still out of sorts at the state of affairs.[17] When Hume proposed to lop £1,000 off the vote for the judge advocate's office, 20 Mar. 1822, Manners Sutton, who had held that post for over seven years before becoming Speaker, defended it as one of 'great difficulty' and 'extensive practice', claiming that during his first two years in the place he had 'not been absent from his office for the space of five weeks altogether, and at no one period for a single fortnight'. He privately assured Peel (now home secretary) that there was no modern precedent for the House's addressing the crown for a remission of Henry Hunt's* gaol sentence and that Burdett's motion to that effect (24 Apr. 1822) could be confidently opposed.[18]

At the end of August 1822 he asked Peel (as a matter of personal interest) if he was willing to accept Canning as a cabinet colleague and leader of the House after Lord Londonderry's suicide. Peel indicated that he was.[19] After taking the foreign secretaryship, Canning schemed to have Manners Sutton sent to India as governor-general, to be replaced in the Chair (in which he considered him to be below par) by Charles Williams Wynn, whose cabinet office as president of the board of control would go to Canning's acolyte William Huskisson. Manners Sutton got wind of this and told friends that while he hoped no such offer would be made to him, he felt that if it was he would be obliged to accept it on account of the financial 'duty he owes to his family'. Williams Wynn thought that he was unequal to a 'post of so much importance' and that 'a man naturally indolent would in so indolent a climate be wholly inefficient'. Peel advised him not to take India if it was offered, and in the event he was not required to make a decision, for Canning's plan foundered in the first week of October. He was reported by Peel's brother-in-law George Dawson* to have been in a state of 'anxiety and fidget' and to be 'hurt' and 'very sore' at the appointment of Lord Amherst 'without any communication with him', though at bottom not 'disappointed' at being passed over.[20] Later in the month a vacancy arose for Cambridge University. Among others, the attorney-general John Singleton Copley* was interested, but he told Dawson that he would only start if Manners Sutton, whose credentials as an anti-Catholic Trinity man, related to Rutland, who had a commanding electoral interest in Cambridge, were strong, did not do so. At Copley's request Dawson reported this to Manners Sutton, who was tempted but initially demurred on account of supposed legal obstacles to his re-election as Speaker if he vacated his seat during a Parliament.[21] Copley duly declared himself, but on 26 Oct. Manners Sutton told Lord Liverpool that having been 'strongly urged' to follow suit by several friends and having decided that 'the difficulties as to any public inconvenience in vacating the Chair at this time' were 'so much less ... than I had at first conceived them', he was inclined to stand provided this would not embarrass the government or impede his re-election as Speaker. Liverpool, who was committed to support his nephew Lord Hervey*, gave him no encouragement and advised him to consult Lord Sidmouth and Lord Colchester (Abbot) as the authorities 'most competent to form a correct judgement' on the supposed legal obstacles.[22] To Liverpool's vexation he ignored this advice and declared his candidature on 29 Oct., whereupon Copley withdrew and his supporters rallied to Manners Sutton, who seemed almost certain to succeed. However, Williams Wynn, astonished and cross that Manners Sutton, in an 'extraordinary' act of disrespect towards 'those ministers who are in the House of Commons', should 'commit himself as a candidate ... without ever learning their opinion on a question of so much delicacy and difficulty', alerted Canning and Liverpool to the possible ramifications. He cited a precedent of 1801, which seemed to establish the 'inability of any Member to be chosen Speaker at the meeting of Parliament, who had not already taken the oaths in the House'. Neither Manners Sutton nor Colchester was entirely convinced that it held water, but 'after requiring a day to consider', he withdrew his candidature on 2 Nov. 1822.[23] Manners Sutton, whose 'absurd' conduct caused considerable annoyance in some ministerial circles, remained a candidate for the University at the next general election; but in late August 1825 he abandoned the notion and settled for his Scarborough berth for the rest of this period.[24]

In February 1823 some Whigs believed that to boost Peel, who was supposed to be at loggerheads with Canning, Manners Sutton had 'spread ... a report in the House, that Canning was going to form an administration with Lords Holland and Lansdowne ... and [Henry] Brougham*'.[25] He was 'haunted' by the prospect of Brownlow's motion condemning the Irish attorney-general William Plunket's* *ex-officio* prosecution of the Dublin Orange rioters, 15 Apr., which he urged Peel to meet with a '*direct negative*' as 'a direct unqualified charge against the first law officer of the crown in Ireland'.[26] Two days later, he broke the 'perfect silence' which followed Canning's retort that Brougham's charge against him of 'political tergiversation' was 'false' with a request, delivered in 'a low tone', for Canning to 'retract the expression he had used ... [which was] a complete violation of the customs and of the orders of the House'. Canning refused, forcing Manners Sutton to appeal twice to the House for support for the 'authority' of the Chair. He interpreted Frederick Robinson's assertion that Brougham had provoked Canning and should be called on to apologize as an insinuation that he had been guilty of 'inattention' and was partly to blame for the incident. In the end he seized on Sir Robert Wilson's suggestion of a semantic way out of the impasse. On 12 Aug. 1823, at the request of the king, he laid the first stone of the new buildings of Trinity.[27] In the House, 22 Apr. 1825, asked to rule on a dispute over one Member's reference to the words of another in an earlier debate on the Irish franchise bill, he stated that while it was strictly disorderly to mention the 'express words of a debate', it was usual to 'allow great latitude' to references to the 'subject matter':

> In his opinion ... nothing could be so inconvenient to the progress of business ... as for the Speaker strictly to watch every violation of the letter of their orders. He therefore commonly left such subjects to be regulated by the general sense of the House, taking from them the hint, and declining himself to interfere, unless under circumstances likely to obstruct the public business.

He prefaced his brief speech in committee of the whole House against the Catholic relief bill, 6 May 1825, with an apology for intruding his personal opinion.[28] Later that month he informed Peel of his 'wish to bring in a bill' to abolish the sale of Commons offices and empower the Speaker to tax 'the costs on private sales, if applied to'; he had, after talking to the chancellor of the exchequer, abandoned his idea of a provision to pay his trainbearer's salary 'out of the House of Commons fund instead of out of the Speaker's pocket'.[29] The measure became law as 6 Geo. IV, c. 123 on 5 July 1825. He was unwell in early February 1826, but fears that his life was in danger proved to be groundless.[30] In the first week of May he warned Peel that 'the country gentlemen' were 'all roused again and more hostile than ever' to the government's plans for the emergency admission of bonded corn; and a fortnight later he sent Peel a communication from a constituent about a possible opening for a ministerialist at Beverley at the impending general election.[31] When the House divided 62-62 on Lord John Russell's resolution condemning electoral bribery, 26 May 1826, Manners Sutton gave his casting vote for it on the ground that it was 'merely declaratory of what are the powers and ... duty of the House'. He calculated that the general election had reduced the number of pro-Catholic Members by nine.[32] The king gave him permission to 'remain in Palace Yard till the meeting of the new Parliament'.[33]

On 21 Nov. 1826 he was proposed for re-election to the Chair by William Sturges Bourne and Edward Berkeley Portman II. The Whig Member George Agar Ellis commented that 'they were both rather embarrassed what to say, because he is notoriously a very bad Speaker, though a good natured and popular man'; but Henry Goulburn* reported that he 'seemed very well satisfied to be again in the Chair'.[34] The Whig James Abercromby*, who had a low opinion of Manner's Sutton's abilities, told Lord Carlisle in December 1826 that the committee on the Arigna Mining Company scandal was 'in all sorts of difficulties as to their procedure' and had 'referred to the Speaker, that is a slender reed, in some respects, that is in essentials', for 'we never had a worse, and never stood more in need of a good one'.[35] His indisposition, 22 Feb. 1827, 'occasioned the breaking up of the House' at an early hour.[36] A fortnight later he told Wilson that he 'thought changes had become imperatively necessary' following Liverpool's incapacitating stroke. When

Canning was forming his ministry in April he offered Manners Sutton the home secretaryship (vacated by Peel, in a move of which the Speaker approved), possibly with the promise of a peerage for himself or his father, but, though tempted, he declined it for fear of losing the pension for himself and his elder son of which he was virtually guaranteed on his retirement from the Chair.[37] In June he amused dinner parties with comments on Hume's struggles with the English language, including his 'use of the word "liable" as if it meant telling a lie', and the anecdote of how, in that wet summer, he had been dressing one 'morning, in a bright sunshine and perfect white-trousers weather', when he 'heard a noise of music on the river, and on inquiry from his servant found that the corporation [of London] were going on the water for a day's pleasuring'. He immediately asked for 'a pair of cloth pantaloons', and before long the heavens duly opened. He was brought down to earth by a fall from his horse, which left 'his face much bruised and disfigured' and 'covered with black patches': he looked 'as if he had been a [prize fight] performer at Moulsey Hurst'.[38] He interrupted his seaside holiday at Worthing to attend, 'by invitation', Canning's funeral, 16 Aug. 1827, but gleaned no political news for Peel. He thought the Goderich ministry would 'stand if they don't blow themselves up by internal explosives', which they did in January 1828, when he and his father wrote to the duke of Wellington to express their confidence in his new administration.[39] There had been recent talk of Littleton as his successor in the Chair, whenever he chose to retire, but when he mentioned this in conversation Littleton disingenuously 'ridiculed the idea', but reflected that 'it would not have been difficult to have rivaled him in anything except the extraordinary amenity of his temper and manners'.[40]

Manners Sutton prepared 'a speech to usher in his vote' in case the House divided equally on the Catholic question, 12 May 1828, but the majority of six for relief spared him.[41] He was mentioned as a possible recruit for the ministerial front bench after the resignation of the Huskissonites in May, but nothing came of this.[42] On 17 July he was obliged five times to 'name' the truculent Robert Otway Cave for refusing to retract his accusation of lying against Peel – the only occasion on which he had to resort to this sanction in this period. Next day, when Hume quibbled at the proposed grant for an index to the 14 reports of the charity commissioners, Manners Sutton, an unpaid member, explained its importance. Three days later his father died. It was reported that he would 'have a good reversion in cash' as a result, and by the archbishop's will of 11 July 1826, which he proved under £180,000, Manners Sutton stood to inherit the principal of £50,000 in three per cent consols after his mother's death, as well as his share in the residue of the estate, which realized £92,000.[43] In September there was renewed speculation of his leaving the Chair, perhaps for cabinet office, but Wellington had 'heard nothing upon the subject since his father's death', though Manners Sutton had previously 'more than once complained ... that his office was ruining him' financially. Wellington thought it 'very possible that having now an income as I understand he has, besides that of Speaker [about £6,000 a year], he may not choose to sacrifice it in the public service or to pass his time in the Chair', but could not 'think that he can have determined to give up the Chair and the claims which he has arising out of several years service in it without communicating with any of us'. Althorp could not see him resigning 'unless they will give him his pension', which Wellington was supposed to be reluctant to endorse. Yet his case for reward did not appear to have been strengthened by his second marriage on 6 Dec. 1828, at the age of 48, to the 'very beautiful' widow Mrs. Purves, sister of the notorious Lady Blesington: she had lived before her first marriage with William Stewart* of Killymoon, with whom she had three illegitimate children, and had cohabited with Manners Sutton during her husband's lifetime, but, as Greville recalled, 'they managed their matter with great skill or else good luck, for she had no children by him till after they were married'. She was a hearty hostess at the Speaker's official functions, but she remained for the time an outcast from the Court, though according to an outraged Mrs. Arbuthnot, George IV received her in September 1829.[44] On 23 Feb. 1829 Manners Sutton proposed that proceedings in committee of the whole House should be entered in the journals. He coined a *bon mot* in observing that in the disheveled Wetherell's drunken rant against Catholic emancipation, 18 Mar., 'the only lucid interval he had was that between his waistcoat and his breeches'.[45] He held his peace on the measure (of which Peel was one of the authors), but confided to Hobhouse his hope that 'the bill in the Lords would be carried *not* by a large majority as it would lower that House too much considering the past votes of the peers'.[46] He was obliged to dismiss Daniel O'Connell from the chamber when he refused to swear the oath of supremacy in order to take his seat for Clare, 15, 19 May. On 28 May, prompted yet again by Littleton, he deplored the increasing activity of 'parliamentary agents' masquerading as 'officers of the House' for the purpose of promoting private bills and urged Members 'to consider whether some means ought not to be adopted to bring them within its control, without having recourse to the *dernier resort* of calling them to the bar and visiting on them that punishment which is the result of a distinct breach of privilege'. There was 'a strong report' in June 1829 that he was to be made a peer and replaced by Goulburn, but it had no substance. In the second week of November 1829, however, he reminded Wellington of what he had stated in June 1828, that he would like to resign the Chair in the not too distant future, partly on account of its effect on his health, and hinting at what he considered his due, but he promised that he would not leave the government and the House in the lurch. Wellington's reply was, as Manners Sutton told Peel, 'discouraging', and seemed to set 'the question ... at rest for the present'.[47] Abercromby was told in February 1830 that at one of his regular Sunday dinners for Members Manners Sutton had 'held language ... very hostile to the ministers'; and in May Hobhouse heard that Mrs. Manners Sutton was predicting that when the duke of Clarence succeeded his dying brother George on the throne he would 'turn out the duke of Wellington, that is Mr. Speaker wishes it I suppose'.[48] The cabinet concluded in March that Manners Sutton would 'not resign now, as he would not get a good pension in the present temper of the House'; and two months later Croker could detect 'no symptoms of a change in the Chair': 'the Speaker looks, and what is more important, says he is, tolerably well, and with the present jealousy of pensions, I do not think that he or ... the government would be mad enough to risk a new embarrassment of that nature'. In mid-July 1830, on the eve of the general election, Manners Sutton saw Wellington and confirmed his intention of remaining Speaker in the next Parliament.[49]

He asked Sir John Nicholl to propose him for re-election, as he had in 1817, but Nicholl could not oblige, and in the event, 26 Oct. 1830, his sponsors were Sir Edward Hyde East and Nicolson Calvert.[50] A 'most severe and painful return of my old attack' of the 'gravel' restricted his attendance at the House in the last week of November 1830. This prompted more speculation about his impending retirement, and Williams Wynn and Littleton vied for the support of the new Grey ministry as his successor; but the premier assured Littleton that there was no immediate likelihood of Manners Sutton's departure.[51] Croker told Peel in the first week of January 1831 that he was 'in great force and *very Tory*'.[52] He had his hands full with the O'Gorman Mahon, a preposterous and intemperate new Irish Member, 8, 11 Feb., and required the support of 'the whole House' to bring him under control. He was unseated on petition, 4 Mar., but even then Manners Sutton had to order him to leave the chamber.[53] In collusion with Althorp, the leader of the House, he agreed to take the chair at noon on Saturday, 26 Feb. in an attempt to reduce the backlog of reform petitions. He reiterated his willingness to do the same if necessary, 15 Mar., but when Hume proposed on 18 Mar. that the House should convene next day, a Saturday, for the same purpose, Manners Sutton replied that the previous experiment had failed because the effect of fixing on only one type of business had been to keep many Members away and prompt the immediate departure of those present as soon as they had presented their petitions. He suggested meeting for the dispatch of general business, including reform petitions, and this course was adopted. In response to a complaint of the continued difficulty of getting names on the Speaker's list for the presentation of petitions before the normal start of general business at seven in the evening, he said that he was always willing to receive petitions in the small hours after the end of routine business. Immediately before Russell unveiled the government's reform scheme to a packed House, 1 Mar., Manners Sutton remarked on 'a most unusual occurrence', namely that when he had come down to the House that afternoon he had found it 'unusually full', but 'after prayers had been said, and before the ballots were made', the slips of paper with Members' names fixed 'on the backs of the seats were more numerous than the Members in them'. The scale and scope of the plan must have horrified him. The Tory ex-minister Lord Ellenborough noted in mid-March that he thought ministers 'would not gain by a dissolution'.[54] According to the Whig Denis Le Marchant†, as the numbers for the division on the second reading of the English reform bill were being told, with every appearance of a close call, 22 Mar., Manners Sutton was 'frightened exceedingly at the prospect of having to give the casting vote'. He was spared this ordeal by the majority of one for the measure. Eleven months later he told a government dinner party that he would have 'voted for the bill on the principle of giving the House a opportunity of deciding the question itself'; but few present believed him, for, according to Littleton, it had been 'well known that he meant to have voted against it, on the fanciful ground that it was a courtesy due to Members not to vote for the extinction of the privileges of any of their body'.[55] In committee on the bill, 15 Apr., he endorsed Russell's view that the disfranchisement schedules must be worked through borough by borough before a division could be taken on the clause itself, which promised a protracted deliberation. Hobhouse felt he was 'manifestly partial to the anti-reformers'; and next day the backbencher Hudson Gurney noted that he 'appears to wish everybody to vote for Gascoyne's motion to keep up the numbers of the English Members', arguing that 590 men will get on no better nor faster than 658.[56] Manners Sutton for once lost his temper in the chaotic and rowdy scene which marked the dissolution of Parliament after the defeat of the reform bill, 22 Apr. 1831. He protected Sir Richard Vyvyan in his rant against reform, disputing cries of 'order' and expressing his 'hope that ... Members will be good enough to compute the laws of order in the House as I have laid them down'. Vyvyan gave up at the sound of the guns signaling the king's approach, and Manners Sutton, 'not quite fairly', as Hobhouse thought, called Peel in preference to Burdett, and, in response to the outraged clamour of ministerialists, observed that when Members asked him to decide on questions of order and he had 'endeavoured to give my opinion impartially and satisfactorily, it is not perfectly consistent with the respect which is due to the Chair to proceed further with the matter'. When Black Rod curtailed Peel's apoplectic speech, Manners Sutton, 'with a face equally red and quivering with rage, rose, and, followed by many Members, went to the Lords'. He returned to read the king's speech at the table of the Commons. Seven months later, according to Littleton, the ministers Graham and Smith Stanley laughed about Manners Sutton's 'rage' and his vexation at not having received an advance copy of the king's speech, which had only been dashed off at the last minute.[57]

This episode encouraged speculation that some on the government side would like to oppose Manners Sutton's re-election as Speaker in the next Parliament, though it was also rumoured that senior ministers were willing to grant him a pension and a peerage if he would retire. Peel, enraged by the dissolution, told Wellington that the Speaker must be protected.[58] Manners Sutton consulted Peel and, aware of conflicting reports about the likelihood of his being opposed for 'undisguised partiality in the Chair', drafted and sent to Althorp a letter asking him to declare the intentions of the government. At the same time, he encouraged Tory efforts to muster support for himself in case of a contest. After laying the matter before the cabinet, Althorp told Manners Sutton that they wished him to continue as Speaker. He persuaded Williams Wynn (who had recently resigned from the cabinet because he could not support the reform bills) and Sir Matthew White Ridley (who had seconded Williams Wynn's nomination against him in 1817) to sponsor him, which they duly did on 14 June. Manners Sutton, who was at a Tory dinner of 'political and party men', 3 June, felt that he owed his 'security more to the staunchness of my friends than to the good inclination, or even fair dealing of the government side', and detected the hand of Littleton in the 'stirring and striving' which had taken place.[59] The Whig John Campbell II was tempted to disturb the ostensible harmony of proceedings by making 'a speech against him, for his conduct in the last session was anything but impartial'; but the radical Hunt, whose ignorance and impertinence tried Manners Sutton's patience on several occasions, thought 'it would have been a great loss if he had not been elected again. He is firm, courteous, and truly impartial [and] for this the Whigs hate him'.[60]

On 24 June 1831, dressed in 'a gown flowered with gold and a long lace ruff' and riding in a gilded coach, he led the procession of the Commons to St. James's to present the address to the king.[61] When Hume asked for a ruling after having his designated seat stolen, 4 July, Manners Sutton explained that the essential rule was that places could only be reserved by Members who were present at prayers and condemned the recent practice of men entering the House before it opened at ten in the morning to fix their names to the back of seats. He again appealed for 'general complaisance and good feeling' to avoid abuse. He was in the Chair for '13 hours and a half without quitting and seemed to suffer greatly' as the Tory opposition forced a succession of divisions for the adjournment throughout the night, 12 July; he was 'almost fainting' by eight the next morning.[62] He was clear in his mind that William Long Pole Wellesley could not claim breach of privilege to annul his committal to prison for contempt of court.[63] On 5 Aug., when the House was in committee on the reform bill, he entered the chamber and, 'sitting on the treasury bench, put on his hat, and gave his opinion' on the dispute which had arisen over the right of Members arriving after the question had been put to divide on it.[64] Ellenborough did not share his belief that if the Lords rejected the reform bill Lord Grey would 'propose terms' to Wellington.[65] He was hard pressed to maintain order during the bad tempered debates which followed the bill's defeat, 12, 13 Oct. 1831. He listened in astonishment as Hume stated that after strangers had been cleared from the gallery before Spencer Perceval began his rant for a general fast, 26 Jan. 1832, he had made notes of the performance and handed them to a man outside the House, whence they had found their way into the report of parliamentary proceedings in *The Times*. Hume was unabashed by his assertion that every step of this constituted a flagrant breach of privilege, but Manners Sutton gave him a 'lecture'.[66] On 29 Feb., after consultation with Littleton, who had placed a motion on the order book, he decided, rather than enter a resolution in the journal concerning the priority of names to be called for the presentation of petitions on public business, to continue the attendance of a clerk from ten o'clock to take names, but to introduce a ballot to determine the order; Hunt sarcastically applauded this sudden enthusiasm for the ballot, a striking omission from the reform bills. He defended the overworked Commons printer against insinuations of dilatoriness in the production of the tithes committee report, 1 Mar. His mother's death, 10 Mar. 1832, by which he profited financially, meant that there was no House on the 12th. According to John Heywood Hawkins*, on 23 Mar. 1832 Manners Sutton 'stood for five minutes before his chair laughing, before he could summon a sufficient command of countenance to call ... to order' John Hodson Kearsley, the uncouth Member for Wigan, whose uproarious denunciation of the reform bill reduced the House to hysterics.[67]

Manners Sutton was centrally involved in the abortive attempt to form a Conservative ministry to carry a measure of reform after the resignation of the Grey administration, 9 May 1832. As the only ostensibly uncommitted man in the House and therefore, unlike Wellington, not tainted by previous hostility to all reform, he had some credentials for taking a leading role, as Peel, who refused to serve in any such ministry, realized and pointed out. Lord Lyndhurst, whom the king charged with the task of brokering an arrangement, seems to have confused the issue by giving both Wellington and Manners Sutton the impression that they were to be prime minister. In an audience on 12 May the king made it clear to an embarrassed Manners Sutton, who had been linked with the home office and the Commons lead and a report that his reward for acceptance would be the 'bitter pill' (as the queen put it) of his wife's acceptance at Court, that he would have only the duke as first minister. Manners Sutton, like Alexander Baring*, declined to serve under him on the ground that he was hopelessly compromised on reform. On the afternoon of 13 May Wellington, unable to find enough men of sufficient calibre to occupy the Commons front bench, asked Manners Sutton to become premier, promising his own support and that of Baring. Manners Sutton showed 'much weakness and uncertainty' and rambled at such inordinate length about his feelings and misgivings that he exasperated Lyndhurst, who later declared that he would have nothing to do 'with such a *damned tiresome old bitch*' and observed to the duke that 'this man can never get on – he is nothing but a verbose ninny'. Wellington was said to have been 'quite astonished at the poverty of abilities he displayed', but agreed to his request for further time to make up his mind.[68] On the morning of 14 May Manners Sutton consulted Peel and William Vesey Fitzgerald*, who advised him to accept the premiership, and he informed Wellington by note that he would do so, subject to final confirmation at a meeting that night after the House had risen. He took the Chair as usual, and when Hume questioned him as to why no answer had been received from the king to the address of 10 May asking him to appoint only a ministry which would carry undiluted reform, he disingenuously replied that perhaps William, 'not having any responsible minister or confidential adviser, thinks it better to delay sending an answer till he has such a minister'. The debate of that evening finally dashed all hope of the formation of a viable Conservative reform ministry, and at a midnight meeting of party leaders at Apsley House, which Manners Sutton attended, the notion of his 'intended administration was dropped in silence'.[69] When Littleton heard from Grey that Manners Sutton had been 'seriously proposed' as prime minister, he was predictably scathing: 'If there is a public man whose mind is utterly incapable of conducting a department, it is the Speaker. A perfect old woman!'[70]

When the leaking of the draft report of the Irish tithes committee to the *Dublin Evening Post* was considered, 1 June 1832, Manners Sutton directed that in future committee clerks should notify the Members concerned as soon as any confidential papers were ready to be put into their hands. On 27 June he 'majestically' led the Commons procession to St. James's with the address to the king after the stone throwing incident at Ascot, but he 'made a mistake on entering' the Palace by going into the 'general levee room' rather than the 'entrée room'.[71] That day in the House he interfered 'dexterously', as Greville thought, to allow Sugden to continue his technically invalid rejoinder to lord chancellor Brougham's personal insult to him in the Lords.[72] His intention to retire from the Chair at the dissolution of the 1831 Parliament had been long anticipated, and on 30 July 1832 he announced this to the House. Althorp, Goulburn, Littleton, Burdett, Murray, Russell and Wetherell paid tribute to him, and the House unanimously carried a vote of thanks and a resolution to address the king to confer on him 'some signal mark of his royal favour'. Hobhouse, who noted that he 'could be partial at a pinch', but was 'a gentleman, and we shall not like his successor as well, let him be who he will', thought he was 'somewhat moved' by these compliments. Yet on speaking to him afterwards he was surprised to be told that 'he did not consider his adieu as definitive', as he had 'had two or three communications with Lord Grey, and not being certain of his return to the new Parliament, had thought it right to take leave; but the House might choose him again'. Next day, having reported the king's favourable response to the address, Althorp recommended a committee of the whole House to consider the most appropriate action. On 1 Aug. he proposed to give Manners Sutton a pension of £4,000 a year (to be reduced by half if he later took an office of equivalent value) and his eldest male heir, Charles John Manners Sutton (1812-69), one of £3,000, which was to cease when he came into his reversion to the 'valuable sinecure office' of registrar of wills (worth an estimated £10,000 a year), currently held by the Moores. Hume quibbled but acquiesced, and Hunt, as 'the only avowed radical', praised Manners Sutton and said he had 'taken for his maxim that the House should be rode with a snaffle-bridle, and not with a curb'. The pensions were enshrined in a bill, which became law on 15 Aug. It was common knowledge, however, that Grey, who wanted Manners Sutton to remain in the Chair of the first reformed Commons, would not sanction the customary granting of a peerage, considering that he had behaved 'very infamously to the government' during the May crisis.[73] Grey confirmed this to Manners Sutton's face in late August 1832, claiming to be 'embarrassed about peerages' and frankly admitting that he did not want him in the Lords as a 'formidable opponent to government'.[74] It was thought that the king wished to reward him at the first opportunity, but, having declared his candidature for Cambridge University at the impending general election, he followed Peel's advice and decided not to be 'a supplicant' and to 'remain quite quiet' and await events.[75] The Conservatives prepared to put up Williams Wynn as their candidate for the Chair against the government nominee, thought to be Littleton or perhaps Abercromby, but there were also rumours that they would back Manners Sutton. After his unopposed return for the University, 12 Dec., ministers asked him to stand for the Chair, with their support, in the new Parliament, and he agreed. Althorp explained to Lord Ebrington*, 30 Dec. 1832:

> The question of the Speakership was one of great difficulty. I believe we are now relieved from it in rather a comical way after what happened last session. It appeared not impossible ... that the Tories would put forward Sutton again ... if this had been done it would have been impossible for us after our language on his resignation to have objected ... [for] it would have been said that for the purpose of giving a good place to one of our own friends we were saddling the country with Sutton's pension unnecessarily ... The best course for us to take was to 'propose' it to him ourselves; if he refused it the Tory manoeuvre was defeated; if he accepted it we get a good Speaker, and we are relieved from the difficulty of a contest between Abercromby and Littleton.[76]

Manners Sutton was elected for the seventh successive time by 241-31 over Littleton, who was put up as a token gesture of protest by some disgruntled radicals. The king gave him a knighthood of the Bath in August 1833. Suspicions (which were largely unfounded) of his involvement in the events leading to the king's dismissal of the Melbourne ministry and the formation of Peel's Conservative government in late 1834 prompted the Liberals in opposition to oppose his re-election to the Chair in the 1835 Parliament, and he was defeated by Abercromby by only ten votes in a division of 622 Members. Peel secured him a viscountcy (one step up from the normal rank for a retiring Speaker) before he was turned out of office, but he seldom spoke in the Lords. He died in July 1845, three days after suffering a stroke on a Paddington-bound train just east of Slough. He was succeeded in the peerage by his son Charles, whose 'prodigality' as well as Manners Sutton's own 'carelessness' were thought by Littleton to have been responsible for his financial embarrassments; his personal estate was sworn under a meagre £3,000.[77] Littleton, who had an axe to grind, recorded a harsh verdict on his Speakership:

> [He] had been lifted by the influence of his connections in the unreformed Tory times into the Chair ... for which he was never well qualified ... He was very gentlemanlike, but lengthy and prosing, and let down the discipline of the House by his love of ease ... He was strongly addicted to party, and lost the Chair by it. His honourable character and very open and courteous manner made him generally beloved.[78]

A more dispassionate observer was much kinder in his assessment, emphasizing the positive qualities which Manners Sutton brought to his onerous position:

> He was a great favourite with men of all parties ... A man of more conciliating, bland, and gentlemanly manners never crossed the threshold of St. Stephen's. He was at all times accessible, and to every Member ... He never suffered his political prejudices, strong as they were, to interfere with the amenities of gentlemanly intercourse. The perfect gentleman was visible in everything he said and did.[79]

[1] See J.A. Manning, *Lives of Speakers of House of Commons*, 484-8; A.I. Dasent, *Speakers of House of Commons*, 303-17; *Oxford DNB*. [2] P. Laundy, *The Office of Speaker*, 298; *The Times*, 22 July 1845; *HP Commons, 1790-1820*, iv. 538-9. [3] [J. Grant], *Random Recollections of Commons* (1837), 84-87; *Oxford DNB*. [4] *Croker Pprs*. i. 160. [5] Nottingham Univ. Lib. Ossington mss OsC 7, J. to J.E. Denison, 17 Mar. 1820. [6] *The Times*, 22 July 1845; Hatherton mss, memo. 25 July 1845. [7] O.C. Williams, *Private Bill Procedure*,

i. 47-57. [8] Dorset RO D/BKL, Bankes jnl. 117. [9] *Arbuthnot Jnl.* i. 25. [10] Add. 56541, f. 73. [11] *Arbuthnot Jnl.* i. 39. [12] *Hobhouse Diary*, 41; Buckingham, *Mems. Geo. IV*, i. 79; *Arbuthnot Jnl.* i. 54; Grey mss, Tierney to Grey, 24 Nov. 1820. [13] Grey mss, Tierney to Grey, 10 Jan. 1821. [14] Bankes jnl. 122 (23 Jan.); Dorset RO, Bond mss D/BoH C16, Jekyll to Bond, 20 Mar. 1821. [15] Add. 40344, f. 102. [16] Laundy, 90; *CJ*, lxxvi. 229. [17] *Croker Pprs.* i. 194, 198. [18] Add. 40345, f. 324. [19] Add. 40350, f. 248; Parker, *Peel*, i. 332-3. [20] Harewood mss, Canning to wife, 8 Sept., to Liverpool, 14 Sept., reply, 14 Sept.; Add. 38743, f. 236; 40351, ff. 138, 160, 167, 199; 40352, ff. 26, 30; NLW, Coedymaen mss 377; TNA 30/29/9/5/17; Bucks. RO, Fremantle mss D/FR/46/11/64; Buckingham, i. 381-2, 384, 386; *Greville Mems.* i. 136. [21] Add. 40352, ff. 109, 111; 40353, f. 92; 51653, Mackintosh to Holland, 27 Oct.; 51659, Whishaw to Lady Holland, 25 Oct. 1822. [22] Add. 38291, ff. 149, 150. [23] Coedymaen mss 653; Suff. RO (Bury St. Edmunds), Hervey mss Acc 941/11a, Liverpool to Bristol, 1, 2 Nov, A. Baring to same, 1 Nov.; *Colchester Diary*, iii. 260-1; Buckingham, i. 392-4; Add. 38291, ff. 158, 160; 40328, f. 184; 40352, f. 162. [24] Buckingham, 392, 393; Add. 40328, f. 194; 40331, f. 143; 51659, Whishaw to Lady Holland [8 Nov. 1822]; *HMC Var.* ii. 346. [25] Grey mss, Lambton to Grey, 13 Feb. 1823. [26] Add. 40355, ff. 287, 289, 290. [27] Add. 38295, ff. 251, 253; 38296, f. 118. [28] Laundy, 295. [29] Add. 40378, f. 127. [30] Nottingham Univ. Lib. Acc 636, Denison diary, 5 Feb. [1826]. [31] Add. 40386, f. 26; 40387, f. 1. [32] Fremantle mss, Buckingham to Fremantle, 9 July 1826. [33] Add. 40387, f. 48. [34] Northants. RO, Agar Ellis diary, 14 Nov.; Surr. Hist. Cent. Goulburn mss Acc 304/67A, Goulburn to wife, 20 Nov. 1826. [35] Castle Howard mss. [36] *Canning's Ministry*, 27. [37] Ibid. 47, 98, 182, 192, 226; *Raikes Jnl.* i. 89-90; Add. 36463, f. 378; 40394, f. 35; *Creevey's Life and Times*, 241. [38] Broughton, *Recollections*, iii. 204; *Croker Pprs.* i. 377-8; Agar Ellis diary, 29 June 1827. [39] Add. 40394, ff. 179, 222; Hatherton mss, Manners Sutton to Littleton, 13 Sept. 1827; Wellington mss WP1/914/6, 26. [40] Hatherton diary, 7 Feb. 1828. [41] *Life of Campbell*, i. 456. [42] *Ellenborough Diary*, i. 111. [43] *Gent.Mag.* (1828), ii. 173-5, 194; PROB 11/1744/459; IR26/1158/538; Hatherton mss, Warrender to Littleton, 31 Aug. 1828. [44] Grey mss, Ellice to Grey, 6 [Sept.]; Hatherton mss, Fazakerley to Littleton, 20 Sept. 1828; *Cockburn Letters*, 204; Wellington mss WP1/958/50; *Von Neumann Diary*, i. 194; *Greville Mems.* iii. 178; *Arbuthnot Jnl.* ii. 306. [45] *Greville Mems.* i. 278. [46] *Colchester Diary*, iii. 609; Add. 56553, f. 155. [47] *Greville Mems.* i. 298; Wellington mss WP1/1056/5; 1059/37; Add. 40399, ff. 397, 399. [48] Bessborough mss, Abercromby to Duncannon, 16 Feb. [1830]; Add. 56554, f. 91. [49] *Ellenborough Diary*, ii. 208, 315; *Croker Pprs.* ii. 59; Wellington mss WP1/1130/39. [50] Merthyr Mawr mss L/206/12. [51] Ibid. L/209, Manners Sutton to Nicholl, 6 Dec. 1830; Coedymaen mss 758; Hatherton mss, Palmerston to Littleton, Sunday [Dec.], Littleton to Grey, 6 Dec., reply, 8 Dec. 1830. [52] Add. 40320, f. 173. [53] *Three Diaries*, 48; *Macaulay Letters*, ii. 6. [54] *Three Diaries*, 66. [55] Ibid. 17; Goulburn mss 304/67B, Goulburn to wife [23 Mar. 1831]; *Greville Mems.* ii. 135; *Baring Jnls.* i. 84; Hatherton diary, 11 Feb. [1832]. [56] *Three Diaries*, 78; Add. 56555, f. 123; Gurney diary, 16 Apr. [1831]. [57] Broughton, iv. 104; *Greville Mems.* ii. 137; *Baring Jnls.* i. 86; Hatherton diary, 1 Dec. 1831. [58] Wellington mss WP1/1184/22; Fremantle mss 139/20/25, 26. [59] Add. 40402, ff. 53, 61, 73, 75, 78, 79, 80, 92; NLI, Farnham mss 18612 (11), Somerset to Farnham, 24, 28 May; NLW, Ormathwaite mss FG 1/5, p. 183 (3 June 1831); *Arbuthnot Jnl.* ii. 426. [60] *Life of Campbell*, i. 516; Lancs. RO DDX 113/28, Hunt to Foster, 17 June 1831. [61] *Macaulay Letters*, ii. 52-53. [62] Hatherton diary, 13 July [1831]; *Macaulay Letters*, ii. 70. [63] Hatherton diary, 23 July [1831]. [64] Ibid. 5 Aug. [1831]. [65] *Three Diaries*, 128. [66] Keele Univ. Lib. Sneyd mss SC17/68. [67] Cornw. RO, Hawkins mss 10/2190. [68] *Croker Pprs.* ii. 156, 161-4, 167; *Three Diaries*, 247-8, 249-50, 252, 254; *Greville Mems.* ii. 294; Hatherton diary, 12 May [1832]; Wellington mss WP1/1224/2-4; *Wellington Despatches*, viii. 306, 312, 314, 316; Add. 75941, Althorp to Spencer, 19 May; Hatfield House mss, memo. of conversation with Wellington, 24 May 1832. [69] Wellington mss WP1/1224/5, 8; *Wellington Despatches*, viii. 315-16, 325; *Three Diaries*, 253-5; *Holland House Diaries*, 178-9; *Croker Pprs.* ii. 164-7; *Baring Jnls.* i. 98; *Greville Mems.* ii. 298-9; N. Gash, *Sir Robert Peel*, 31-32; M. Brock, *Great Reform Act*, 294, 300-2. [70] *Three Diaries*, 266. [71] *Macaulay Letters*, ii. 142; Hatherton diary, 27 June [1832]. [72] *Greville Mems.* ii. 313. [73] Hatherton diary, 17 Nov. [1831], 29 May; Broughton, iv. 249; Lonsdale mss, Beckett to Lowther, 31 July; Coedymaen mss 228; *CJ*, lxxxvii. 534-5, 550, 555, 560, 565, 57, 586; *The Times*, 31 July 1832. [74] *Croker Pprs.* ii. 186-7; *The Times*, 13 Sept. 1832; Add. 40403, f. 70. [75] Add. 40403, ff. 79, 91, 117, 126. [76] Devon RO, Earl Fortescue mss 1262M/FC 88; Coedymaen mss 234, 236; *Raikes Jnl.* i. 135; *Greville Mems.* ii. 342. [77] *The Times*, 21-23 July; Hatherton mss, memo. 25 July 1845; IR26/1765/132. [78] Hatherton mss, memo. 25 July 1845. [79] Grant, 82-83.

D.R.F.

MANNING, William (1763–1835), of Coombe Bank, nr. Sevenoaks, Kent.

PLYMPTON ERLE	14 Feb. 1794–1796
LYMINGTON	1796–1806
EVESHAM	1806–1818
LYMINGTON	1818–1820
LYMINGTON	5 June 1821–1826
PENRYN	1826–1830

b. 1 Dec. 1763, o. surv. s. of William Manning, W.I. merchant, of 15 St. Mary Axe, London and Elizabeth, da. and h. of John Ryan of St. Kitts and Santa Cruz. *m.* (1) 23 Oct. 1786, Elizabeth (*d.* 29 Mar. 1789), da. of Abel Smith†, banker, of Nottingham, 2da. (1 *d.v.p.*); (2) 12 July 1792, Mary, da. of Henry Lannoy Hunter, barrister, of Beech Hill, Reading, Berks., 4s. (1 *d.v.p.*) 4da. (1 *d.v.p.*). *suc.* fa. 1791. *d.* 17 Apr. 1835.

Dir. Bank of England 1792-1810, 1814-31, dep. gov. 1810-12, gov. 1812-14; agent, St. Vincent 1792-1806, Grenada 1825-31; pres. London Life Assurance 1817-30.

Vol. London and Westminster light horse 1797; capt. Bank of England vols. 1798, maj. 1801, lt.-col. 1803.

Manning, a West India proprietor, headed the leading mercantile house of Mannings and Anderdon of 3 New Bank Buildings, where his partners in 1823 were his son-in-law John Lavincount Anderdon and his eldest son Frederick Manning.[1] Throughout the 1820s he was an assiduous attender of West India merchants and planters' committee meetings, and his business concerns accounted for much of his Commons activity. His other parliamentary preoccupation was the Bank of England, of which he was a director and former governor. His youngest son Henry Edward Manning, subsequently Cardinal Manning, the Roman Catholic primate, recalled

> hearing him speak once in the House, from the second bench below the gangway, I fancy, on the opposition side; but how I cannot explain, for he supported the Tory

> government ... He spoke with arms folded, with perfect fluency, never recalling a word, with great clearness, and ... was listened to with great attention. It was very high speaking, but not oratory ... He was too refined, modest, and sensitive to make a display, or to overdo anything.[2]

At the dissolution in 1820 Manning was left without a seat, but he resumed his parliamentary career in June the following year, when he was again returned for Lymington by its patron Sir Harry Neale*. He took the oaths, 8 June, and voted with the Liverpool ministry against the omission of arrears from the duke of Clarence's grant, 18 June, and a motion for economy and retrenchment, 21 June 1821.[3] On 24 Jan. 1822 he told a meeting of West India merchants that the goverment's proposed alteration to the sugar duties would 'have the effect of a considerable tax upon a large proportion of the sugars imported' and joined a delegation of protest to ministers, who in the event offered no more than a reduction in the duty on molasses.[4] He voted against greater tax reductions, 11, 21 Feb., and abolition of one of the joint-postmasterships, 13 Mar. On 16 Feb. he presented the duke of Wellington with a silver shield recording his military triumphs, on behalf of an admiring coterie of bankers and merchants.[5] He rebutted the complaints of agriculturists against the resumption of cash payments by the Bank, 18 Feb., and declared that if left free of government interference, the directors would have made the move earlier, 8 Mar. Since the Bank underwrote the risk of forgery, he thought it entitled to profit from dealing in public stocks, 11 Mar, and assured the House of the directors' anxiety to take all precautions against counterfeiting of notes, 14 Mar.[6] On 31 May he refuted a charge of 'tyranny' levelled against the Bank in a petition opposing the renewal of its charter. He blamed agricultural distress on overproduction, 1 Apr., and insisted that the privations of this interest paled into insignificance in comparison with the sufferings of those connected with the West Indies, for whom he sought relief, 17 May. On 26 Apr. he advised a meeting of the West India committee that a bill for the renewal of the West India Dock Company's charter was unlikely to become law that session.[7] He was in the minority against referral of the Calcutta bankers' petition to a select committee, 4 July 1822.

Manning again justified the Bank's monopoly, 18 Feb., and the terms on which it funded the military and naval pensions bill, 18 Apr. 1823.[8] He secured returns from the trustees of Ramsgate harbour and defended Sir William Curtis* from a related charge of financial misconduct, 27 Feb. He voted against a reduction in the sinking fund, 13 Mar., repeal of the Foreign Enlistment Act, 16 Apr., and inquiry into the prosecution of the Dublin Orange rioters, 22 Apr. He presented petitions from the St. Vincent colonial assembly complaining of distress, 19 Mar., and from Antigua against proposed alterations to the sugar duties, 25 Mar., when he presented another from his constituency complaining of the duty on coals.[9] He was appointed to a West India planters' subcommittee to implement resolutions for improving slave conditions, 25 Apr.[10] On 9 June he was among those delegated to lobby the premier for a £5,000,000 government loan to support the plantations, which was refused.[11] He presented a petition against the bill for consolidating the Slave Trade Acts, 11 June.[12] He divided against reform of the Scottish representative system, 2 June, inquiry into the currency, 12 June, and the reciprocity of duties bill, 4 July 1823. He denied that the Bank of England was obliged to provide figures for the number of notes in circulation, 11, 19 Feb. 1824, and characterized a subsequent call for such accounts as interference, 6 May 1825.[13] He presented a petition from Lloyd's underwriters against the marine insurance bill, 27 May 1824, and endorsed it the following day.[14] He was appointed to a subcommittee of West India planters on the sugar duties, 21 Jan 1824, and called for that commodity to be admitted for use in distilleries in preference to foreign grain, as 'no class was more depressed' than the West India proprietors, 8 Mar.[15] He secured accounts of bounties and drawbacks on all British exports, 11 Mar.[16] On 16 Mar. he contended that West India slaves were 'a contented and happy people ... much better off than the lower class in England', but indicated his support for a gradual extension of their rights. He insisted that he had never seen 'exorbitant punishment' used on the plantations, 10 June, and voted against inquiry into the prosecution of the Methodist missionary John Smith for inciting a slave rebellion in Demerara, 11 June 1824. Regarding the expulsion of another missionary from Barbados, he denied that colonists were opposed to slaves receiving religious instruction, 28 June 1825. He moved the second reading of a bill to incorporate the West India Company, 10 Mar. 1824, and after it had foundered in committee, reintroduced it, 21 Mar. 1825.[17] When it ran into opposition from Fowell Buxton, he complained that the anti-slavery lobby had 'paralysed the whole of the transactions between Great Britain and the West Indies', 29 Mar. He secured its third reading by 103-25, 16 May, and it received royal assent, 5 July 1825 (6 Geo. IV, c. 197). He presented petitions from the London Dock Company (of which his son Charles was a director) against the St. Katharine's Docks bill, 30 Mar., 5 Apr., and the South London Docks bill, 3 May 1824, brought up others in similar terms, 11 Mar. 1825, and unsuccessfully divided the House against the former, 24 Mar. 1825.[18] He voted for suppression of the Catholic Association, 25 Feb., paired against Catholic relief, 1 Mar., 21 Apr., and divided against it, 10 May 1825. In a rare stand against ministers, he voted for repeal of the assessed taxes, 3 Mar., but he was back in their majorities in support of the duke of Cumberland's annuity bill, 30 May, 6, 10 June 1825. In January 1826 he was appointed to a planters' defence committee for resisting anticipated legislation against the West Indies.[19] He endorsed a London merchants' petition on distress and urged an exchequer bill issue, 23 Feb. He believed that a general return of the amount of notes in circulation 'would tend rather to mislead than inform the House', 27 Feb, but welcomed a commission to investigate commercial distress the following day. On 20 Mar. he secured a return on lunatic asylums.[20] He drew attention to the efforts of the Antiguan colonial assembly to ameliorate conditions for slaves, 14 Apr., and rejected the claims of an abolitionist pamphleteer as an exaggeration, 20 Apr. 1826.

At the 1826 general election Manning was expected to offer for Wallingford, but he lost interest before he had even made a canvass.[21] Instead he came forward for the venal borough of Penryn, where he was introduced by his son-in-law partner Anderdon, who had been an unsuccessful candidate in 1818. After a contest he was returned with another London merchant, but it did not prove to be a secure berth.[22] In a petition lodged by a defeated rival, 27 Nov., Manning was accused of bribery and treating, and although a committee cleared him and confirmed his return, they found sufficient evidence of corruption to justify proceedings against the borough, 9 Mar. 1827. He protested at the borough's proposed disfranchisement on account of the 'misconduct of a few individuals', 28 Mar., and campaigned steadily for a reprieve thereafter. He presented a constituency petition in these terms, 18 May, and complained that the electors were being made to suffer for the sins of their forebears, 28 May, when he voted against the second reading of the disfranchisement bill.[23] He successfully moved that a constituent incarcerated in Newgate for giving false evidence to the Penryn election committee receive a reprimand at the bar of the House, 1 June, and thereby secured his release, 6 June.[24] Next day he seconded a wrecking amendment and was a minority teller against the third reading of the disfranchisement bill, which subsequently foundered in the Lords. He paired against Catholic relief, 6 Mar. 1827, 12 May 1828. On behalf of the Bank directors, he disclaimed responsibility for an 'extraordinary circular letter', 30 May 1827.[25] On 7 Jan. 1828 Sir Henry Hardinge* informed Wellington that Manning, though 'more disposed to support than oppose' the ailing Goderich administration, was conscious of the premier's 'great loss of character' and desirous of 'a reconciliation or change by which your grace and Mr. Peel may be at the head of affairs'.[26] He spoke against the reintroduction of the bill to disfranchise Penryn, 28 Jan., and presented a hostile inhabitants' petition, 7 Mar. He contended that by the admission of one of its framers, the original petition against his return had been nothing more than a 'base conspiracy' and complained that the proposed transfer of its seats to Manchester had prejudiced their case, 14 Mar. He called for an extension of the borough's franchise to the neighbouring hundred, 24 Mar., and protested against its fate being linked to that of East Retford, 12 May. After the bill fell in the Lords, he called for an account of the costs incurred by the investigation, 17 July. (Wellington had refused his request for treasury assistance for witnesses' expenses, 7 July.)[27] Manning was named to a planters' delegation to urge the case for a reduction in the sugar duties on the new ministry, 8 Feb.[28] He moved that correspondence concerning slavery in India be placed before the House, 12 Mar., and when Brougham suggested a bill to render slave evidence admissible in West Indian courts, 9 June, asserted that such was already the case. He spoke in support of the continuation of the Slave Consolidation Act governing the traffic in slaves between islands, 1 July. Alarmed at the number of anti-slavery petitions calling for a commercial boycott, he portrayed the West India trade as 'an extensive and valuable nursery for seamen', 17 July. He voted against repeal of the Test Acts, 26 Feb. He wanted the circulation of Scottish banknotes to be restricted to that country, 16 June, and secured information on the number of prosecutions for coin counterfeiting during the previous decade, 1 July. He divided against ordnance reductions, 4 July 1828.

In late February 1829 Planta, the patronage secretary, predicted that Manning would vote 'with government' for Catholic emancipation, and he paired accordingly, 6 Mar. No other parliamentary activity has been found for that year, which may have been owing to business difficulties. In making a provision of £1,000 for his son Henry on his coming of age, 18 Aug. 1829, he regretted that 'from the very unfavourable alteration in West India affairs I cannot at present do more for you' and advised, 'Your future success in life must depend upon your own exertions'.[29] Shortly before this he had joined the council of King's College, London.[30] He was back in the House to vote against the transfer of East Retford's seats to Birmingham,

11 Feb., and paired against the enfranchisement of Birmingham, Leeds and Manchester, 23 Feb. 1830. He moved for returns of customs duties on West Indian sugar and other merchandise, 30 Mar., and rum imports, 29 Apr. He voted against reduction of the grant for South American missions, 7 June. On 14 June he complained of government indifference to the tribulations of the West India interest and warned that the measures of relief in contemplation would come too late for many. He ruefully reminded Huskisson of his decision to allow the import of sugar from Mauritius during his spell as president of the board of trade, but nonetheless supported his motion for a general reduction in the duties, 21 June. Describing the package of relief offered by Goulburn, the chancellor of the exchequer, as 'very inadequate', he announced that he would vote for Lord Chandos's motion for a larger remission of the sugar duties, 30 June. On 13 July he denounced Brougham's attempt to agitate the question of colonial slavery so late in the session and suggested that he go the West Indies to view at first hand 'the comforts which the negro population enjoy and the protection that is afforded to their persons and property'. He objected to the printing of an anti-slavery petition and suggested that many of their proponents knew little of the subject, 20 July 1830.

At the 1830 dissolution Manning retired from Penryn. He did not seek election elsewhere. A note to his son Henry on 19 June 1830 had referred, somewhat obliquely, to 'the trials to which I may be exposed in the remainder of my life' and his hope 'that our prospects may improve'.[31] His difficulties were rooted in the long term decline of the West India trade. Henry later observed that

> from 1820 to 1830 he had great cares, which ended at last in complete ruin. During those years he was in London most days in the week. When he came down to Coombe Bank he was worn and weary. He was fond of fishing, and would stand for hours by the water at Coombe Bank. He used to tell me that his chief delight was the perfect quiet after the strain and restlessness of London.[32]

Apparently Mannings's house had first run into trouble in 1823, when they obtained a loan of £60,000 from Smith, Payne and Smith, the banking firm to which he was connected through his first marriage.[33] Diversification and expansion was his formula for commercial survival, and he became deputy governor of the Australian Agricultural Association in 1826 and was one of a syndicate of leading merchants who lobbied Huskisson for exclusive trading rights with New Zealand at around the same time.[34] In 1828 Mannings and Anderdon speculatively purchased estates on St. Kitts, prompting the planter Charles Pinney to observe that 'they may make a considerable sum by this ... but unless one of the firm come out to judge of local circumstances, etc., they may lose considerably'. Less equivocally, he predicted that a similar acquisition on Nevis would 'never return one shilling'.[35] In April 1831 Manning was reported by Maria Edgeworth to be seeking a buyer for his 'beautiful' Coombe Bank estate and it was sold later that year.[36] As he explained to his daughter Mary Carey, 27 July 1831, the price of sugar had fallen by two-thirds since he had purchased the property in 1813. 'Could I have foreseen all this', he lamented, 'I would have lived in a nutshell rather than have exposed my family to their present difficulties'.[37] To his wife's niece Mary Sargent he confided that his annual income had stood at £25,000 in 1810 and blamed his subsequent descent to the brink of 'calamity' on 'the total neglect of the West India colonies by every succeeding administration, and their allowing the foreign slave trade to be carried on'. His outgoings for the previous year, he added defensively, 'did not exceed £2,700'.[38] Mannings and Anderdon ceased trading, 30 July, and were declared bankrupt, 5 Sept. 1831, when their balance sheets revealed debts of at least £374,372. Their chief creditors were the brokers Kemble and Son of Mincing Lane, on whose behalf the commissioners uncovered considerable assets, including property in Antigua, Monserrat, St. Kitts, Nevis, Trinidad and St. Croix, and debts due to the bankrupts of £187,395.[39] Henry, who witnessed his father's surrender of his gold watch and seals, recalled that he felt the humiliation 'like a wound' and had once told him, 'I have belonged to men with whom bankruptcy was synonymous with death'.[40] Relatives subscribed to provide him with an income and in his reduced circumstances he found solace in religion.[41] In October 1832 he made a convalescent trip to Bath and reported that his finances were reasonably stable.[42] He lived for a time at Tillington, Sussex, but died in London in Upper Gower Street in April 1835.[43] In his will, dated 20 Oct. 1832, he left £500 to his wife and the same sum to her brother in repayment of an advance, and registered 'deep regret' that 'since my misfortunes in trade it has become impossible for me to add to the provision already made for my dear children', to whom he bequeathed £50 each to purchase a ring as a memento.[44] His sons Frederick and Charles nevertheless both died in relative prosperity in 1880, while Henry, prevented from pursuing an intended career in politics, eventually wore a cardinal's hat.[45]

[1] V.L. Oliver, *Hist. Antigua*, ii. 232-3. [2] E.S. Purcell, *Life of Cardinal Manning*, i. 7-8. [3] *The Times*, 9 June 1821. [4] Inst. of

Commonwealth Stud. M915/2/2. [5] Bodl. MS. Eng. lett. c. 651, ff. 368, 370. [6] *The Times*, 15 Mar. 1822. [7] Inst. of Commonwealth Stud. M915/4/1. [8] *The Times*, 19 Apr. 1823. [9] Ibid. 20, 26 Mar. 1823. [10] Inst. of Commonwealth Stud. M915/4/1. [11] Ibid. M915/2/2. [12] *The Times*, 12 June 1823. [13] Ibid. 7 May 1825. [14] Ibid. 28 May 1824. [15] Inst. of Commonwealth Stud. M915/4/1. [16] *The Times*, 12 Mar. 1824. [17] Ibid. 22 Mar. 1825. [18] Ibid. 31 Mar., 6 Apr., 4 May 1824, 12, 25 Mar. 1825. [19] Inst. of Commonwealth Stud. M915/4/1. [20] *The Times*, 21 Mar. 1826. [21] *Berks. Chron.* 25 Mar.; *Reading Mercury*, 10, 17 Apr. 1826; Berks. RO, Wallingford borough recs. W/AEp 8, election handbills, 22 Mar.-6 Apr. 1826. [22] *West Briton*, 2, 9 June; *R. Cornw. Gazette*, 3, 10, 17 June 1826. [23] *The Times*, 19 May 1827. [24] Ibid. 1, 2, 7 June 1827. [25] Ibid. 31 May 1827. [26] Wellington mss WP1/913/8. [27] Bodl. MS. Eng. lett. c. 651, f. 378. [28] Inst. of Commonwealth Stud. M915/4/1. [29] Bodl. MS. Eng. lett. c. 651, f. 388. [30] W.R. Williams, *Worcs. MPs*, 155. [31] Bodl. MS. Eng. lett. c. 651, f. 392. [32] Purcell, i. 8. [33] Bodl. MS. Eng. lett. c. 651, f. 405. [34] Add. 38763, f. 99. [35] R. Pares, *West Indian Fortune*, 310-11. [36] *Edgeworth Letters*, 517; Purcell, i. 71. [37] Bodl. MS. Eng. lett. c. 651, f. 396. [38] Ibid. f. 402. [39] Oliver, ii. 235; R.B. Sheridan, 'West India Sugar Crisis and British Slave Emancipation, 1830-1833', *Jnl. Econ. Hist.* xxi (1961), 543-4. [40] Bodl. MS. Eng. lett. c. 652, f. 62; Purcell, i. 71. [41] Bodl. MS. Eng. lett. c. 651, ff. 399, 400. [42] Ibid. c. 652 f. 1. [43] Purcell, i. 71; *Gent. Mag.* (1835), i. 667. [44] PROB 11/1847/308; IR26/1391/156. [45] *The Times*, 17 Jan., 30 Nov., 4 Dec. 1880.

H.J.S./P.J.S.

MANSFIELD, John (1778–1839), of Birstall House, nr. Leicester, Leics.

LEICESTER 1818–1826

b. 13 Mar. 1778, 2nd but 1st surv. s. of John Mansfield, banker, of Leicester and Mary, da. of William Pank. *m.* (1) 16 Feb. 1797, Sarah (*d.* 6 July 1813), da. and h. of Henry Ward of Stamford, Lincs., 7da. (2 *d.v.p.*); (2) 16 Mar. 1815,[1] Hannah Mary, da. and h. of Thomas Harper of Barne Hill, Stamford, *s.p. suc.* fa. 1798. *d.* 9 Jan. 1839.

Maj. commdt. Leicester vols. 1779, lt.-col. commdt. 1803, 1 batt. militia 1809-11; receiver-gen. land tax, Leics. 1804-18; mayor, Leicester 1815; sheriff, Leics. 1833-4.

Mansfield, a partner in the Leicester bank of Boultbee, Mansfield and Boultbee, came forward again as the corporation candidate for the borough at the general election of 1820. He withdrew briefly following an intrigue against him by the editor of the *Leicester Journal*, but in the event was returned unopposed.[2] He continued to give general but not slavish support to the Liverpool ministry. He described Holme Summer's motion for inquiry into agricultural distress, 30 May 1820, as a pretext to increase the 'present protecting duties on corn'; and as 'the representative of a place of large manufacturers' he regretted that their 'much greater' distress was not to be taken into account and could not therefore give his 'entire support' to the agriculturists. He objected to the proposal to submit all bills for the regulation of trade to inquiry before their introduction, 14 June, but failed to prevent the appointment of a select committee on the issue, to which he was named. He was granted a fortnight's leave of absence on account of ill health, 27 June 1820. He voted in defence of government's conduct towards Queen Caroline, 6 Feb., and stated his resentment of opposition's implication that the House had 'voted against the wishes of the people', 14 Feb. 1821. He opposed the printing of the Nottingham petition calling for the impeachment of ministers, 20 Feb., and complained of Sir Ronald Ferguson's 'personal allusions' to them over the proceedings of the Milan commission, 21 Feb.[3] He objected to the levy of additional charges on county rates to provide judicial salaries, but stressed that few other 'burden[s] on the public [were so] light', 15 Mar.[4] He voted against Catholic relief, 28 Feb. 1821, 30 Apr. 1822, 1 Mar., 21 Apr., 10 May 1825, and the Irish franchise bill, 26 Apr. 1825. He divided against inquiry into expenditure, 6 Mar., repeal of the additional malt duty, 3 Apr., parliamentary reform, 9 May, reduction of the barracks grant, 28 May, and economy and retrenchment, 27 June 1821. He presented a petition against Scarlett's poor relief bill, 6 June, and opposing the measure, 20 June 1821, claimed that despite the 'great distress' prevalent in Leicester, the local poor 'had not voluntarily thrown themselves on the rates'.[5]

He mustered for the divisions against more extensive tax reductions to relieve distress, 11, 21 Feb., but voted for admiralty economies, 1 Mar. 1822. When opposing the Newcastle petition on behalf of Henry Hunt*, which imputed 'notorious corruption' to the House, 22 Mar., he denied that ministerialists were 'influenced by corrupt motives':

> He, for one, sat in that House, not by the influence of corruption, but by the unanimous choice of a large number of most respectable constituents; and though his vote had often been given in opposition to the opinions of gentlemen opposite, yet he had given that vote unbiassed by any undue influence or corrupt motive.

He presented petitions for relief on behalf of the woollen manufacturers of Leicester, 22 Apr., and from his constituents against the poor removal bill, 21 May. On 31 May 1822 he argued that the measure was 'likely to prove as injurious to the poor ... as to those who were obliged to contribute to their support'; his wrecking amendment was carried by 82-66.[6] He presented constituency petitions against the Marriage Act, 17 Feb., and the hawkers and pedlars bill, 24 Mar. 1823.[7] He voted against reform, 20 Feb., tax reductions, 3, 13, 18 Mar., repeal of the Foreign Enlistment Act, 16 Apr., and inquiry into chancery delays, 5 June 1823; but he was in the minority for the re-committal of the silk manufacture bill, 9 June 1823. On 12 May 1823 he said that Leicestershire petitioners for the abolition of slavery were willing to 'submit to any burdens which it might be necessary to impose to make up for the loss to the proprietors of slaves'. He presented Leicester abolitionist petitions, 12, 16 Mar. 1824.[8] He presented petitions from Leicester wool staplers against the warehousing bill, 21 May 1823.[9] He presented a Leicester petition against the beer duties bill, 14 May, but approved subsequent modifications to it, 24 May 1824, since 'it would enable the labouring classes to drink a better commodity at a greatly reduced price'.[10] He brought up constituency petitions for repeal of the Combination Acts, 11 June 1823, 11, 25 Mar., 6 Apr., and spoke for this measure, 14 Apr. 1824.[11] He presented a petition against restoration of the laws, 22 Apr., and on 6 May 1825 craved the 'indulgent consideration' of the House for a similar one from the framework knitters of Leicester, who had 'conducted themselves extremely well, even in periods of greatest manufacturing distress'. He protested that the report of the select committee was 'founded on the representations and observations of the masters, while no opportunity was allowed to the workmen to counteract them', 16, 17 June. He declared his hostility to the revised combination bill and expressed his hope that 'the power of enforcing it would be left to the discretion of the magistrates', 27 June 1825, when he divided in two small minorities for opposition amendments.[12] On 11 Mar. 1824 he presented and endorsed a petition from the merchants, wool dealers and worsted manufacturers of Leicester against the plan to repeal the ban on the export of long wool;[13] and he was in the minority of 20 who voted against this proposal, 21 May 1824. He voted for the Irish unlawful societies bill, 25 Feb., and the grant for the duke of Cumberland, 6, 10 June 1825. He presented a Leicester petition for relaxation of the corn laws, 22 Apr., paired in favour of this step, 28 Apr. 1825, brought up another repeal petition, 21 Feb., and voted in that sense, 8 Apr. 1826. Replying to Peel's private inquiry as to the state of public credit in Leicestershire following the failure of three local banks, 21 Dec. 1825, Mansfield noted that 'though the panic [was] ... greatly abated ... great difficulty and distress [would] be felt for some time to come [by the] manufacturing and trading establishments'.[14] As a 'practical man', he approved the government's legislation to regulate country banks and spoke in favour of the promissory notes bill, 27 Feb. 1826. He presented more anti-slavery petitions, 10 Mar., 19 Apr. 1826.[15] He was named to the select committees on poor rate returns in 1821 and 1826 and county rates in 1824 and 1826.

Mansfield, whose two elections for Leicester had cost him a total of £5,200, retired from Parliament at the dissolution in 1826, as he had planned to do for some time.[16] In view of the expense of the ensuing contested election, Hudson Gurney* thought him 'well out of it'.[17] He devoted the remainder of his life to his business, but was 'ever ready to relieve the poor and afflicted'.[18] The intimate friend of the 5th duke of Rutland, treasurer of the Leicester Infirmary and an active promoter of the Leicester music festival of 1827, he 'considerably enlarged' Birstall House.[19] He died in January 1839.[20] By his will of 9 Mar. 1830 he set up trust finds for his second wife and five surviving daughters.[21]

[1] IGI. [2] *Leicester Jnl.* 18, 25 Feb., 3, 10, 17 Mar. 1820. [3] *The Times*, 21, 22 Feb. 1821. [4] Ibid. 16 Mar. 1821. [5] Ibid. 7, 21 June 1821. [6] Ibid. 23 Apr., 22 May, 1 June 1822. [7] Ibid. 18 Feb., 25 Mar. 1823. [8] Ibid. 13 May 1823, 13, 17 Mar. 1824. [9] Ibid. 22 May 1823. [10] Ibid. 15 May 1824. [11] Ibid. 12 June 1823, 12, 26 Mar., 7 Apr. 1824. [12] Ibid. 23 Apr., 7, 16, 18, 28 June 1825. [13] Ibid. 12 Mar. 1824. [14] Add. 40384, ff. 65, 80. [15] *The Times*, 11 Mar., 20 Apr. 1826. [16] Add. 40381, f. 345; 40385, f. 333; *Leicester Jnl.* 2, 9, 16 June 1826. [17] Gurney diary, 23 Sept. 1826. [18] *Roll of Mayors of Leicester* ed. H. Hartopp, 185. [19] C. J. Billson, *Leicester Mems.* 9, 12, 29. [20] *Gent. Mag.* (1839), i. 319. [21] PROB 11/1913/449; IR26/1522/472.

S.R.H.

MARCH PHILLIPPS, Charles (1779–1862), of Garendon Park, nr. Loughborough, Leics.

LEICESTERSHIRE	1818–1820
LEICESTERSHIRE	1831–1832
LEICESTERSHIRE NORTH	1832–1837

b. 28 May 1779, 1st. s. of Thomas March Phillipps (formerly March) of More Critchell, Dorset and his cos. Susan, da. of Charles Lisle of Moyles Court, Hants. *educ.* Dorchester; Sherborne until 1791; Eton 1793-6; Sidney Sussex, Camb. 1800. *m.* 14 Dec. 1807, Harriet, da. of John Gustavus Ducarel of Walford, Som., 2s. 1da. *d.v.p. suc.* fa. 1817. *d.* 24 Apr. 1862.

Capt. Leics. yeomanry 1803-7; sheriff, Leics. 1825-6.

March Phillipps, who had inherited a lucrative Leicestershire estate from his father, had secured the county seat in contentious circumstances in 1818 and, although he never joined Brooks's Club, had acted with the Whig opposition to the Liverpool ministry in that Parliament.[1] At the dissolution in 1820 he stood down in the face of a Tory backlash and restoration of the coalition which he had broken in 1818, and he declined an invitation to stand for Nottinghamshire.[2] He spent some time in Paris and Rome and in the autumn of 1828 went back to Italy, where he stayed until the following year.[3] At the 1830 general election he supported the unsuccessful attempt of the reformer Thomas Paget* to overturn the Rutland interest in Leicestershire, and he was toasted at a dinner of independent freeholders in November.[4] At the county meeting called to express support for the Grey ministry's reform scheme, 29 Mar. 1831, he said that

> he felt confident that the ... measure ... would ... give great satisfaction, while its rejection would be received with disapprobation from one end of the kingdom to the other. A preceding speaker had an objection to the measure, and so had he; but on the whole he considered it ... well calculated to steer clear of the two extremes of high monarchical principles ... and of republican principles.[5]

At the general election precipitated by the bill's defeat he stood for the county with Paget. After their unopposed return, he declared:

> I shall not attempt to amuse and at the same time deceive you with a long tissue of sentimental declamation. I cannot promise that any effort of mine can feed the hungry, and also clothe the naked ... but I ... promise ... to assist in removing every burden of taxation that impedes the free action of the springs of national industry, that I will adopt all the means proposed for invigorating the productive energies of the nation, and for unfettering the commercial policy of the government.

He reiterated his support for the reform proposals, with some reservations as to details, but warned his audience not to expect instant 'miracles' from it. He declined a subsequent invitation to attend a celebratory dinner.[6]

March Phillipps, who is not known to have spoken in debate in this period, divided for the second reading of the reintroduced reform bill, 6 July 1831. He gave steady general support to its details, but cast wayward votes for the disfranchisement of Saltash, 26 July, to give Stoke-on-Trent two Members, 4 Aug., against the proposed division of English counties, 11 Aug., to preserve the voting rights of freemen, 30 Aug., and to disfranchise Aldborough, 14 Sept. He voted for the passage of the bill, 21 Sept., was granted three weeks' leave on account of a family illness, 23 Sept., but was present to divide for Lord Ebrington's motion of confidence in the government, 10 Oct. He was in the two ministerial majorities on the Dublin election controversy, 23 Aug. He incurred some criticism from the pro-reform press by attending Leicester corporation's annual feast, 17 Nov. 1831, when he deplored a recent disturbance at Loughborough and expressed disapproval of the political unions:

> He was satisfied that unanimity, both in religion and government, was unattainable; but he would assert that by *concord* the most important measures were always carried into effect, whilst by discord every blessing was inevitably lost ... Public opinion, and not popular clamour, must ever be considered as the rule and measure of government.[7]

He voted for the second reading of the revised reform bill, 17 Dec. 1831, consistently supported its detailed provisions and voted for the third reading, 22 Mar. 1832. He divided with government on the Russia-Dutch loan, 26 Jan., and relations with Portugal, 9 Feb., but was in Hunt's minority of 31 for inquiry into the Peterloo massacre, 15 Mar. He presented petitions against the Leicester poor bill, 15 Feb. He voted for the address asking the king to appoint only ministers who would carry undiluted reform, 10 May, and on 17 May presented a Loughborough petition for supplies to be withheld until reform was secured. He was in the minority against the government's temporizing amendment to Fowell Buxton's motion for the immediate abolition of slavery, 24 May. He divided for the second reading of the Irish reform bill, 25 May, but voted for an amendment to enfranchise £5 freeholders, 18 June. He sided with government against Conservative amendments to the Scottish reform bill, 1, 15 June. He was in the minority of 29 against Baring's bill to exclude insolvent debtors from Parliament, 6 June, and paired in defence of the Russian-Dutch loan arrangement, 12, 16 July 1832, having been given three weeks leave for urgent private business on the 6th.

March Phillipps sat for Leicestershire North as a Liberal in the 1832 and 1835 Parliaments. His elder son, Ambrose Lisle March Phillipps (1809-78), claimed that 'few men possessed a larger measure of political sagacity' or were capable of 'a more accurate calculation of political probabilities'; but his parliamentary career was unremarkable. Steady accumulation of landed property made him one of the 'wealthiest commoners' in England. Ambrose's conversion to Catholicism in 1825 was a 'heavy aggravation' to his 'other sorrows', but he devised his estates to him.[8] He died at Great Malvern, Worcestershire in March 1862. Ambrose, who was characterized by Disraeli as Eustace Lyle in *Coningsby*, took the additional name of Lisle in 1863.

[1] *HP Commons, 1790-1820*, ii. 241; iv. 545. [2] *Althorp Letters*, 101, 102; *Leicester Chron.* 12, 26 Feb.; *Nottingham Rev.* 3 Mar. 1820. [3] E.S. Purcell, *Life and Letters of Ambrose Phillipps de Lisle*, i. 5, 12, 36. [4] *Leicester Jnl.* 27 Aug.; *Leicester Chron.* 27 Nov. 1830. [5] *Leicester Chron.* 2 Apr. 1831. [6] Ibid. 7, 14, 21, 28 May 1831. [7] *Leicester Jnl.* 18 Nov.; *Leicester Chron.* 19 Nov. 1831. [8] Purcell, i. 13; ii. 295, 343; *Gent. Mag.* (1862), i. 788.

S.R.H.

MARJORIBANKS, Sir John, 1st bt. (1763–1833), of Lees, Berwick.

BUTESHIRE 1812–1818

BERWICKSHIRE 1818–1826

b. 13 Jan. 1763, 1st s. of Edward Marjoribanks of Hallyards and Lees and Grizel, da. of Archibald Stewart† of Edinburgh and Mitcham, Surr.; bro. of Stewart Marjoribanks*. *m.* 15 Apr. 1791, Alison, da. of William Ramsay, banker, of Barnton, Edinburgh, 4s. 5da. *suc.* fa. 1815;[1] *cr.* bt. 6 May 1815. *d.* 5 Feb. 1833.

Ensign 18 Ft. 1779; ensign 1 Ft. Gds. 1780, lt. and capt. 1785, ret. 1792.

Ld. provost, Edinburgh 1814-15.

Marjoribanks was a leading figure in the commercial life of Edinburgh, where he was a partner in his father-in-law's banking house. His election for Berwickshire in 1818 had been approved by the Liverpool ministry's Scottish manager Lord Melville and was widely resented, and plans were made to oppose him at the next election. However, he came in unopposed in 1820, when he was joined in the House, as Member for Hythe, by his brother, the Whig banker Stewart Marjoribanks.[2] Marjoribanks failed to dissuade the Berwickshire landowners' meeting at Greenlaw, 1 May 1820, from petitioning for changes in calculating corn averages.[3] In the House, where he remained a poor attender, he voted consistently with the Liverpool ministry on the revenue and retrenchments, 1820-3, and divided for Catholic relief, 21 Apr., 10 May 1825. A radical publication of that year noted that he 'attended occasionally and voted with government'.[4]

He echoed his constituents' pleas for repeal of the additional Scottish malt duty, which he complained had been rushed through in the absence of most of the Scottish Members, 5 July, and proposed an amendment to extend the scope of the Scottish malt allowance bill, but it was ruled out of order, 13 July 1820. (On 19 Apr. 1823 he was added to the select committee on Scottish petitions against the duty, which he said had been 'very injuriously felt', 20 June 1823).[5] The Marjoribanks listed in the minority for the indefinite postponement of the secret committee of inquiry into Queen Caroline's conduct, 26 June 1820, was almost certainly Stewart. Sir John went to Greenlaw to promote the adoption of Berwickshire's loyal address to the king, 28 Dec. 1820, divided against censuring ministers' handling of the affair, 6 Feb., and, amidst impatient calls for a division, spoke against restoring her name to the liturgy 13 Feb. 1821.[6] He was granted a month's leave because of illness in his family, 12 Mar. He voted against criminal law reform, 23 May, and on 29 June 1821 expressed his hope that the extra post bill would not be extended to Scotland.[7] He voted against reforming the Scottish county representation, 10 May 1823. No record has been found of a vote by him in the next two sessions. He divided against condemning the indictment in Demerara of the Methodist missionary John Smith, 11 June 1824. A motion to grant him six weeks' leave to attend to urgent private business was withdrawn, 14 Apr. 1825, and he was awarded ten days' leave the next day. He presented a Berwickshire petition against alteration of the corn laws, 28 Apr. When provisions for the education of the children of the dukes of Cumberland and Kent were considered, 27 May, Marjoribanks (as he had done in 1815) extolled the virtues of their brother the duke of York and called for payment of his debts. As on the earlier occasion, his introduction of this subject irritated ministers and he was rebuked by Canning.[8] He voted for the Cumberland annuity bill, 30 May-10 June 1825. Confusion with his brother probably accounts for the presence of his name on the list of opponents of the president of the board of trade's salary, 7 Apr., but he certainly divided against the bonded corn bill, 11 May 1826.

Marjoribanks's involvement in urban development in Edinburgh twice landed him in scrapes in the House. On 27 June 1821 he was accused by Joseph Hume of complicity in a dubious transaction with the treasury over the sale of the site, which he had acquired, selected for the construction of a new stamp office. In an 'indistinct manner and tone' he denied that there had been any 'dirty work', professed that he 'could not have been more astonished to find himself in a watch-house on a charge of picking a pocket', and complained that he 'had been detained in London, while his family was in Scotland, merely to wait the commands and pleasure' of his accuser.[9] On 11 May 1825 he refuted opposition allegations of jobbery in the committee on the Leith docks bill: 'if there were, he might be considered the chief jobber, as he had a great property embarked in the Leith docks'. His minority vote in favour of the bill, 20 May, was challenged by Hume, on the ground that he had a direct pecuniary interest in its success, and his plea of 'inadvertence' was disallowed. He had, since 1824, been repeatedly obliged by his Berwickshire constituents to confirm his retirement at the next dissolution, and plans had been laid to return the 8th earl of Lauderdale's second son Sir Anthony Maitland* as his replacement.[10] On 4 June 1825, with his failure to carry the Edinburgh-Leith water bill paramount, he wrote to the Member for Edinburgh William Dundas, accusing him of publicly snubbing and insulting him following their disagreement over the water bill, and announced that he would oppose his return for Edinburgh at the first opportunity. Dundas forwarded the letter to Melville, who had already been warned of a likely application for support from Marjoribanks, whom he considered 'very ill qualified'; and Melville helped the future provost of Edinburgh William Trotter and the council to thwart Marjoribanks's scheme.[11] Peeved at Melville's reaction and refusal to support him, he wrote to him on 14 June, defending his parliamentary conduct, and praising his election successes in Berwickshire and achievements as an Edinburgh businessman, but to no avail.[12] With no prospect of a third return, he went abroad and left the House at the dissolution of 1826, having promised his interest in Roxburghshire to Henry Francis Hepburne Scott*. Maitland duly replaced him as Member for Berwickshire.[13]

Marjoribanks did not stand for Parliament again. He aligned with the reformers in Berwickshire and Roxburghshire in 1831, displayed largesse as a local benefactor and, assisted by his brother, successfully promoted the candidature for Berwickshire of his son Charles, a banker and East India Company official in Canton. Charles returned to Scotland during the campaign and outpolled Maitland at the 1832 general election.[14] Marjoribanks died in February 1833, a few days after his eldest son Edward. His will incorporated a family settlement of 31 Dec. 1832 and was proved in Edinburgh, 21 Feb., and London, 18 Apr. 1833. He provided for his wife, relations and business partners. The baronetcy and entailed estates intended for Edward passed to his second son William, who survived only until 1834, when he was succeeded by his infant son John (1830-84).[15] It was extinguished by the death of the latter's brother William in 1888. Marjoribanks's fourth and youngest son David, who took the name of Robertson in 1834, was created Lord Marjoribanks, 12 June 1873, but died childless seven days later.

[1] *Scots Mag.* (1815), 557 [2] *HP Commons, 1790-1820*, ii. 523-5; iv. 545-6; NAS GD267/23/8A/3. [3] *Berwick Advertiser*, 7 May 1820. [4] *Session of Parl. 1825*, p. 475 [5] *The Times*, 14 July 1820. [6] *Caledonian Mercury*, 1 Jan. 1821. [7] *The Times*, 21, 30 June 1821. [8] Ibid. 29 Apr., 28 May 1825. [9] Ibid. 28 June 1821. [10] NAS GD157/2961/1/8; GD267/23/8A/3-8. [11] NAS GD51/1/198/16/43; GD51/5/3; NLS mss 2, ff. 75-91. See EDINBURGH. [12] NLS mss 2, ff. 93-100. [13] NAS GD157/2962/31; 2963/4. [14] NAS GD157/3007; GD267/23/8/1-5, 13-17; *Berwick Advertiser*, 29 Jan., 19 Feb., 15 Oct. 1831, 23, 30 June; *Caledonian Mercury*, 21 June, 30 July; *The Times*, 19, 21 Dec. 1832. [15] PROB 11/1814/237.

M.M.E.

MARJORIBANKS, Stewart (1774–1863), of Bushey Grove, nr. Watford, Herts.

Hythe	1820–9 May 1837
Hythe	1841–1847

b. 1774, 3rd s. of Edward Marjoribanks (*d.* 1815) of Hallyards and Lees, Berwick and Grizel, da. of Archibald Stewart† of Edinburgh and Mitcham, Surr.; bro. of Sir John Marjoribanks, 1st bt.* *m.* (1) 19 Feb. 1798,[1] Eleanor (*d.* 14 Dec. 1799), illegit. da. of Archibald Paxton, wine merchant, of Buckingham Street, Strand, Mdx. and Watford Place, Herts., 1s. *d.v.p.*; (2) 2 Feb. 1841, Lucy, da. of Edward Roger Pratt of Ryton Hall, Norf., wid. of Rev. William Thellusson, 3rd Bar. Rendlesham [I], *s.p. d.* 31 Aug. 1863.

Dir. E.I. Dock Co. 1824-35, Australian Agricultural Co. 1824-53.

Marjoribanks's maternal grandfather Archibald Stewart, Member for Edinburgh, 1741-7, and his son John Stewart, Member for Arundel, 1771-4, were in business in London as wine merchants, with premises in Buckingham Street, Strand. By 1768 Archibald Paxton who, like Marjoribanks and Stewart, came from a Berwickshire family, was operating a similar but apparently separate enterprise from the same address, and he took over the whole concern after the deaths of the Stewarts in the early 1780s.[2] Marjoribanks was presumably sent to work for Paxton, with whom he was in partnership by 1798. That year he married one of Paxton's daughters, who was almost certainly illegitimate. She died in 1799, after giving birth to a son, Archibald John Marjoribanks, who was at Harrow, 1810-15, received £5,000 by Paxton's will and died in 1826.[3] On Paxton's death in 1817 Marjoribanks continued in the wine business with his son William Gill Paxton*. John Stewart had been active in East India Company politics and Marjoribanks's elder brother Campbell Marjoribanks was elected a director of the company in 1807 and served three times as its chairman. Marjoribanks may have been involved in the East India agency of Paxton's brother Sir William Paxton†. Certainly by 1817 he was pursuing this line on his own account, initially from premises at 6 Great Winchester Street, then at 3 Copthall Buildings, and at King's Arms Yard, Coleman Street from about 1820. He became an East Indian ship owner on a considerable scale.[4]

At the general election of 1820 Marjoribanks stood for Hythe, where wealthy merchants were popular with the numerically dominant out-voters. A threatened opposition came to nothing and, with the aid of money and East India Company patronage, he made himself virtually impregnable there. 'I am not a Whig', he told his kinsman James Loch* on the eve of the election; and at the nomination, according to one report, he said that he

> did not hesitate to declare himself favourable to government, but he was not what is called 'a thick and thin man'. Whenever administration proposed measures, which to his unbiased judgement appeared for the welfare of the country, they should have his support; but measures which he conceived to be of a contrary tendency, he would as firmly oppose; in short, he should look to measures and not to men.[5]

Yet, in marked contrast to the conduct of his eldest brother Sir John Marjoribanks, almost all his known votes in the 1820 Parliament were with the Whig opposition on most major issues, though it was not until 3 May 1823 that he joined Brooks's Club.

He divided for Catholic relief, 28 Feb. 1821, 1 Mar., 21 Apr., 10 May 1825. He voted routinely for economy, retrenchment and reduced taxation throughout the Parliament, but on 18 June 1821 he joined his brother in siding with ministers against the omission of arrears from the duke of Clarence's grant. (They were on opposite sides over the duke of Cumberland's annuity in 1825.) He was granted three weeks' leave to attend the Stirlingshire by-election, 17 May 1821. His first known vote for parliamentary reform was on 25 Apr. 1822: thereafter he supported it in the divisions of 3 June 1822, 20 Feb., 24 Apr., 2 June 1823, 26 Feb. 1824, 13, 27 Apr. 1826. Marjoribanks, of whom James Abercromby* wrote in 1824 that he had 'a very odd temper, which makes it difficult to deal with him', was one of the few mercantile Members to vote in the ministerial majority for the restriction of bank note circulation, 13 Feb. 1826.[6] In his only known contribution to debate in this period, 3 Mar. 1825, he remarked that wine merchants 'would act, not only unjustly, but inconsistently with their own interests, if they did not reduce the prices of all their wines after a ratio at least equal to the reduction of duties upon them'.

He was unopposed at Hythe at the general election of 1826, when he boasted of his 'independence'.[7] He voted against the Clarences' grant, 16 Feb., and for Catholic relief, 6 Mar., information on the Irish government's handling of the Lisburn Orange procession, 29 Mar., and for supplies to be withheld until a strong ministry was formed, 30 Mar. 1827. He voted for chancery reform, 5 Apr., and the disfranchisement of Penryn, 28 May 1827. He presented petitions for repeal of the Test Acts, 25 Feb. 1828, and voted for that measure the next day. He opposed the extension of the East Retford franchise to freeholders of the hundred of Bassetlaw, 21 Mar., and was in minorities for a reduced duty on corn imports, 22 Apr., action on chancery delays, 24 Apr., and the establishment of efficient control over crown proceedings for the recovery of customs and excise penalties, 1 May. He voted for Catholic relief, 12 May, and for the provision for Canning's family, 13 May: 'I feel quite *conceited*', he told Loch the next day, 'in being in *majorities* for *two successive* nights'.[8] He was in the small minorities on civil list pensions, 20 May, bank restriction, 5 June, the archbishop of Canterbury's bill, 16 June, Irish church reform and East Retford voters, 24 June, and the additional churches bill, 30 June; as well as the larger ones on the misappropriation of public funds for work at Buckingham House, 23 June, and for reduction of the ordnance estimates, 4 July 1828. He voted for the Wellington ministry's concession of Catholic emancipation, 6, 30 Mar., and for O'Connell to be allowed to take his seat without hindrance, 18 May 1829. He voted to reduce the grant for Buckingham House works, 25 May, and was in the minorities of 40 and 44 for Lord Blandford's parliamentary reform resolutions and the issue of a new writ for East Retford, 2 June 1829. He divided for the amendment to the address, 4 Feb., and a reduction of taxation, 15 Feb., 25 Mar. 1830. He voted for army economies, 19, 22 Feb., 9 Mar., and divided with the reviving Whig opposition in most of the major divisions which it forced on retrenchment. He again supported Blandford's reform scheme, 18 Feb., and he voted for the enfranchisement of Birmingham, Leeds and Manchester, 23 Feb., inquiry into the duke of Newcastle's electoral interference at Newark, 1 Mar., the transfer of East Retford's seats to Birmingham, 5, 15 Mar., and Russell's reform motion, 28 May. He supported Jewish emancipation, 5 Apr., 17 May, and abolition of the death penalty for forgery, 24 May, 7 June. He divided against government on the Terceira incident, 28 Apr., abolition of the Irish lord lieutenancy, 11 May, and Irish first fruits, 18 May, and was in minorities for amendments to the sale of beer bill, 21 June, 21 July 1830.

When Marjoribanks and his third cousin John Loch, chairman of the East India Company, sought re-election for Hythe in 1830, they encountered an attempt to open the borough. They were returned in defiance of it, and survived a subsequent petition.[9] Soon after the election he expressed to the ministry's patronage secretary Planta 'an anxious wish' that James Redsull of Dover, a kinsman of one of his constituents, should be made a Cinque Ports pilot, a place in the gift of the duke of Wellington as lord warden. Planta commented:

> Now though Mr. Marjoribanks is a Whig and has as yet voted against us, yet his Whiggery is very much modified (I think) of late, and if he chooses to come forward and ask this as a favour, it would perhaps (if it be a small favour) be a good thing to give it to him.

He added that Marjoribanks had 'behaved ... civilly' when they had considered putting up one of Wellington's sons for Hythe on a vacancy earlier in the year. Wellington felt 'some difficulty in acceding to the request', and no immediate decision was taken. When Marjoribanks renewed the request two weeks later Planta, who had hoped he 'would have properly understood my silence to him', asked the duke for his 'formal orders'. It was decided that Marjoribanks's recommendation should be duly considered 'at the proper time' but that, as there was to be no appointment of pilots that year, the matter 'must stand over until another'. Nothing seems to have come of it.[10] Marjoribanks was described in the press as 'a Wellington Whig',[11] but ministers numbered him among their 'foes', and he voted against them in the crucial division on the civil list, 15 Nov. 1830. He presented a Hythe petition for repeal of the coal duties, 8 Feb. 1831. He voted for the second reading of the Grey ministry's reform bill, 22 Mar., and against Gascoyne's wrecking amendment, 19 Apr. 1831, and was returned unopposed for Hythe as a reformer at the ensuing general election.[12] He voted for the second reading of the reintroduced reform bill, 6 July, and was a steady supporter of its details in committee, though he voted in the majority for the Chandos amendment to enfranchise tenants-at-will, 18 Aug. He divided with government on the Dublin election controversy, 29 July, 23 Aug., but voted for inquiry into the grievances of West Indian sugar producers, 12 Sept. He voted for the passage of the reform bill, 21 Sept., and the motion of confidence in the ministry, 10 Oct. 1831. He voted for the second reading of the revised reform bill, 17 Dec. 1831, and supported most of its details, but was in the minority against the separate enfranchisement of Gateshead, 5 Mar. 1832. He voted for the third reading, 22 Mar. He divided for the address asking the king to appoint only ministers who would carry undiluted reform, 10 May, and the second reading of the Irish reform bill, 25 May, and against a Conservative amendment to the Scottish measure, 1 June. He supported vestry reform, 23 Jan. He divided with ministers on the Russian-Dutch loan, 26 Jan., 13, 16, 20 July, and their dealings with Portugal, 9 Feb., but voted to recommit the Irish registry of deeds bill, 9 Apr. He divided against Hunt's call for inquiry into military punishments, 16 Feb. 1832.

At the general election in December 1832 Marjoribanks, who expressed cautious support for the abolition of slavery and, though neither 'a republican, nor a radical', said he was 'ready to vote against and assist in reforming any abuse', stood for the single seat to which Hythe had been reduced. He beat one of his opponents of 1830 and subsequently took up residence at Cliffe House, Folkestone, which formed part of the enlarged constituency.[13] He seems to have withdrawn from the wine business in about 1832.[14] The East India agency, in which he was partnered from the late 1820s by one William Ferrers, moved its premises to 13 Bishopsgate Street in about 1835. By 1838 it was located at 25 Bucklersbury, and Marjoribanks seems to have sold out to his partner about two years later. In 1850 he received a quarter share in the residual estate of his brother-in-law Paxton.[15] He died in August 1863, leaving legacies in excess of £33,000. He divided the residue of his estate, which included property in Tasmania, equally between his nephews Edward Marjoribanks (1814-79), who succeeded him at Bushey, and Dudley Coutts Marjoribanks (1820-94).

[1] *Gent. Mag.* (1798), i. 169. [2] *HP Commons, 1715-54*, ii. 447; *HP Commons, 1754-90*, iii. 480-1. [3] PROB 11/1598/593. [4] G. Wilks, *Barons of Cinque Ports*, 123; Add. 38763, f. 99. [5] *Kentish Chron.* 11, 18, 29 Feb., 3, 7, 10, 14 Mar.; UCL, Loch mss Add. 131, Marjoribanks to Loch, 23 Feb. 1820. [6] Chatsworth mss, Abercromby to Devonshire, 10 Nov. 1824; Add. 56550, f. 49. [7] *Kentish Chron.* 6 June 1826. [8] Loch mss. [9] *Kentish Gazette*, 3, 10 Aug. 1830. [10] Wellington mss WP2/215/31-33, 35. [11] *Kentish Gazette*, 3 Aug. 1830. [12] Ibid. 8 Apr., 6 May 1831. [13] *Kent Herald*, 13 Dec. 1832; Wilks, 122-3. [14] *Creevey Pprs.* ii. 316. [15] PROB 11/2115/461.

D.R.F.

MARKHAM, John (1761–1827), of Ades, nr. Lewes, Suss.

PORTSMOUTH	12 Nov. 1801–1818
PORTSMOUTH	1820–1826

b. 13 June 1761, 2nd s. of Rev. William Markham (*d.* 1807), head master of Westminster Sch. and later abp. of York, and Sarah, da. of John Goddard, English merchant of Rotterdam; bro. of Osborne Markham†. *educ.* Westminster 1768-75. *m.* 27 Nov. 1796, Hon. Maria Rice, da. of George Rice† of Newton, Carm. and Cecil, 2nd Baroness Dinevor, 3s. 1da. *d.* 13 Feb. 1827.

Entered RN 1775, capt. 1783, half-pay 1786-93, r.-adm. 1804, v.-adm. 1809, adm. 1819.

Ld. of admiralty Feb. 1801-May 1804, Feb. 1806-Apr. 1807.

Markham's ancestors were originally from Nottinghamshire and claimed descent from the

Markhams of Markham and Cotham. After three generations of straitened circumstances in Kilkenny, Markham's father, a future church leader and tutor to the prince of Wales, had begun to restore the family fortunes through his own endeavours and a prudent marriage to a wealthy heiress. The second of his 13 children was born within the precincts of Westminster School, of which he was headmaster, 1753-64, and automatically became a pupil at the age of eight. Following a dazzling naval career and important service as a lord of the admiralty, in 1807 Markham more or less retired to the back benches of the Commons, where as Member for Portsmouth on the interest of the Carter family he voted with opposition when present.[1] In 1818 he had withdrawn in face of a challenge with from the admiralty candidate Sir George Cockburn*, but at the 1820 general election he was persuaded out of retirement by John Carter* and returned after a contest.[2] A very lax attender, inaccurately described as having 'attended regularly' by a commentary of 1825, his only known votes in this period were in the opposition minorities for the reception of Nathan Broadhurst's petition protesting against his treatment in Lancaster gaol, 7 Mar. 1821, for further tax reductions, 21 Feb., returns on naval pay, 11, 22 Feb., and in the majority for abolition of one of the joint-postmasterships, 2 May 1822.[3] He paired for parliamentary reform, 25 Apr. 1822, 24 Apr. 1823, and Catholic relief, 1 Mar., 21 Apr. 1825. He is not known to have spoken in debate in this period and he retired from Parliament at the 1826 dissolution, the last naval officer to represent Portsmouth until 1910.

Markham lived out his remaining days on his estate at Ades, near Lewes, which he had purchased in July 1802 for £9,826. In April 1826 his doctors ordered him to winter in a milder climate. He left on 16 Sept., accompanied by his eldest son John and daughter, and, travelling by easy stages, in January 1827 reached Naples, where he died next month with his daughter at his bedside.[4] His will, dated 4 May 1826, provided legacies of £8,000 for his sons William and Frederick and his daughter Maria, presumably charged on landed property, since his personal estate was valued under £7,000. His Sussex house and the residue passed to his son John.[5]

[1] C.R. Markham, *Markham Mems.* ii. 64-75; D. F. Markham, *Hist. Markham Fam.* (1854), 70-73. [2] Hants RO, Bonham Carter mss 94M72 F33, Markham to Carter, 4 Mar. 1820. [3] *Black Bk.* (1823), 176; *Session of Parl. 1825*, p. 475. [4] *Oxford DNB.* [5] PROB 11/1727/376; IR26/1134/472.

S.K./P.J.S.

MARRYAT, Joseph I (1757–1824), of Wimbledon House, Surr. and 6 Great George Street, Mdx.

Horsham	26 Feb. 1808–1812
Sandwich	1812–12 Jan. 1824

b. 8 Oct. 1757, 1st s. of Thomas Marryat (*d.* 1792), Presbyterian minister, of Southwold, Suff. (afterwards physician of Bristol) and Sarah, da. of John Davy of Southwold. *m.* 17 Dec. 1788 at Boston, Mass., Charlotte, da. of Frederick von Geyer of Boston, 9s. (3 *d.v.p.*) 6da. (3 *d.v.p.*). *d.* 12 Jan. 1824.

Agent, Trinidad 1805-15, Grenada 1815-*d.*; chairman of Lloyd's 1811-*d.*

Marryat, a self-made man, had prospered as a West India merchant and ship owner, with London premises at 2 Laurence Pountney Lane and plantations in Grenada, Jamaica and Trinidad. He was a forceful and innovative chairman of Lloyd's, and in 1819 became a partner in (and soon afterwards head of) the London banking house of Marryat, Kay, Price and Coleman at 1 Mansion House Street. His parliamentary conduct had always been markedly independent, and neither government nor opposition could confidently claim him as their own.[1] Following his selective opposition to details of the repressive legislation of December 1819 his application for a Cinque Ports place for a constituent was ignored; and Arbuthnot, the patronage secretary, deemed him to be 'steadily opposed to government'.[2] At the 1820 general election he was again returned unopposed for Sandwich on the independent interest.[3] In 1821 and 1822 he exerted himself to ensure that a proposal to remove the Sandwich customs establishment to Ramsgate was not implemented and to forestall abolition of the annual payment of £300 from the trustees of Ramsgate harbour on account of silt damage to Sandwich haven.[4]

Marryat voted against government on the droits of the crown because of its confiscations in Trinidad and other crown colonies, 5 May, the civil list, 8 May, and the additional Scottish baron of exchequer, 15 May 1820. On the presentation of a London merchants' petition calling for the removal of purely protective import duties, 8 May, he put the case for colonial preference. On 5 June he presented a London shipbuilders' petition against remission of the duties on Baltic timber, which he said would ruin the Canadian trade. He then expanded on this theme in support of a similar London ship owners' petition, delivering a lengthy speech (subsequently published by the Society of Shipowners) in defence of 'those wise and salutary restrictions upon foreigners' which safeguarded colonial interests. He presented and endorsed a London merchants' petition on the timber duties, 20 June. He approved neither of Wilberforce's compromise resolutions, 'a sort of pious fraud', on the Queen Caroline affair, nor of the Whig opposition's amendment for the restoration of her name to the liturgy; and so left the House before the division, 22 June. On the 26th, believing that 'justice could not be done between the parties till the truth was ascertained', but objecting to inquiry by secret committee, he supported the government motion for a further short postponement. He asserted that 'revolutions were ... generally preceded by infatuated councils, but ... also ... by inflammatory speeches, which the ministers loudly cheered'.[5] He protested against the sale of spirits bill, 6, 10 July 1820.[6]

He voted for the restoration of the queen's name to the liturgy, 23, 26 Jan., but divided with government against the opposition censure motion, 6 Feb. 1821: as he explained when supporting the last motion on the liturgy, 13 Feb., this concession would quell public excitement and 'restore the queen to her place without driving ministers from theirs'. He did not vote in the division on Catholic relief, 28 Feb. He supported the navy estimates, 2 Feb., and voted with government on the revenue, 6 Mar., and against repeal of the additional malt duty, 3 Apr., and the disfranchisement of ordnance officials, 12 Apr. Continuing his campaign against reduction of the foreign timber duties, he presented a New Brunswick petition, 9 Feb., and appealed for support to the British landowner by forecasting repeal of the corn laws as the inevitable corollary of free trade in timber:

> Let him ... adhere to that system to which he owes his present opulence ... and let him beware of encouraging those plausible but delusive theories, which would involve him, as well as the other classes of the community, in one common ruin, only leaving him the consolation of being the last devoured.

He presented more petitions on the same issue, 16, 26 Feb., 14, 16, 19, 21 Mar.[7] On the introduction of the government's proposals to open the trade, 29 Mar., he denounced this sacrifice of the colonial and shipping interests at the behest of 'the disciples of the new school of political economy'. His attempt to lessen the reduction was defeated by 71-17, 5 Apr., when he defied 'these philosophers' to 'take off two legs from a three-legged stool, and make it stand on the remaining leg more firmly than it did on all three'. Marryat, a member of the West India Committee's subcommittee on the renewal of the West India Dock Company's charter, presented a London merchants' petition against it, 27 Feb., when he criticized the 'impolicy' and 'injustice' of such monopolies.[8] He moved a successful wrecking amendment against Curwen's bill to establish an Antimephitic Company, 20 Mar., but supported Taylor's measure to curb emissions from steam engine furnaces, 7 May, as 'no man had a right to annoy or poison his neighbours'. He presented a Dorset bankers' petition for repeal of the usury laws, 15 May, called for judicial reform in the colonies, 28 May, supported Hume's motion for papers on the government of the Ionian Islands, 30 May, and objected to Maxwell's slave removal bill, 31 May.[9] He considered the exemption of Bank of England notes from the provisions of the forgery punishment mitigation bill to be 'subversive of all fairness and justice', 4 June. On Lord Nugent's motion for inquiry by select committee into the administration of justice in Tobago, 6 June, he denied that West Indian justice was inherently partial and stated his preference for a commission. He voted with government for the duke of Clarence's grant, 18 June, but against them on Hume's call for economy and retrenchment, 27 June. When they unveiled their plans to relax the navigation laws, 25 June, he 'sounded the alarm', renewed his attack on the exponents of 'the new, but delusive and dangerous doctrines of free trade', described the existing laws, which applied 'the greatest possible extent of human wisdom to the widest possible range of human action', as 'the sheet anchor of our greatness' and predicted 'national bankruptcy and a revolution' if they were infringed.[10] On 26 June 1821 he denied that slaves were better treated in the East than the West Indies and argued that Britain and other countries anxious to eradicate the slave trade should impose commercial sanctions on Portugal.

As chairman of the Committee of Landholders of Trinidad, Marryat had continued his vendetta against the governor, Sir Ralph Woodford, who had forced his resignation of the agency over financial irregularities in 1815. Woodford, in Britain on leave in 1821, successfully refuted Marryat's allegations that he had confiscated lands already granted on lease. Marryat also failed to convince ministers that Woodford had run up excessive expenses in the prosecution of some runaway slaves. On the eve of the 1822 session he informed them of his intention of submitting fresh evidence to substantiate his case against Woodford, which he had been unable to prove in 1819, over the massacre of Colombian refugees refused sanctuary in Trinidad. On the pretext of trying to safeguard British commercial relations with the newly independent South American states, he urged government to terminate Woodford's governorship, but he was again frustrated.[11]

He voted for Hume's amendment to the address, 5 Feb. 1822, because distress was widespread and the tax reductions called for would not violate the sinking fund. He divided with government against more extensive retrenchment, 11, 21 Feb., but voted for admiralty reductions, 1 Mar., 'to convince the public that it was the disposition of the House to make a reasonable abatement of the public burthens', and for abolition of one of the joint-postmasterships, 13 Mar., 2 May. He was in the opposition minority on Sir Robert Wilson's* dismissal from the army, 13 Feb. He applauded the ministerial plan to convert the five per cents, 8 Mar.,[12] but was unimpressed by their superannuation bill, 11 Mar.: he 'knew no right they had to force men to adopt a system of economy', for 'individual morals were not the object of legislative interference'. On 13 Mar. he presented and supported a petition from the assembly of Canada complaining of distress caused by tariff reforms, and one from the assembly of Grenada attributing their economic problems to the increased penetration of the British market by sugar from the East Indies and foreign colonies where the slave trade still flourished. In this instance, he was prepared to accept a modification of the navigation laws to encourage colonial trade with America; and he welcomed the colonial trade bill as a substantial boon, 1 Apr., and defended it on its second reading, 17 May. He declined to oppose the grant for Barbados fortifications, but made clear his hostility to the misapplied four and a half per cent fund, 27 Mar. He voted for parliamentary reform, 25 Apr. He presented petitions against renewal of the West India Dock Company's charter, 2 May, 3 June, and the navigation bill, 10 May, though on the 17th he expressed his approval of the latter.[13] He voted for reductions in diplomatic expenditure, 15, 16 May. He criticized the alehouses licensing bill as a threat to brewers, 24 May, opposed Bankes's attempt to make the duty on corn payable at the time of importation, 3 June, and voted against the Irish constables bill, 7 June. He was a member of the delegation appointed by the West India Committee to lobby Lord Liverpool for immediate relief measures, 20 June;[14] and in the House, 27 June, he demanded enhanced protection of British colonial planters against foreign ones who benefited from the slave trade. On the subject of piracy, a universal issue between 'the commerce of the world' and 'the enemies of the human race', he pressed, as he had in his capacity as chairman of Lloyd's, for the British navy to be allowed to protect neutral ships, 23, 30 July. He opposed the Canada bill, 23 July.[15] In a renewed attack on Woodford's 'arbitrary system of government', 25 July, he supported Hume's amendment to extend to Trinidad the commission of inquiry into the Cape, Mauritius, Ceylon and the Leeward Islands. He detailed the heavy tax burden on the planters, denounced the crown's land policy and advocated the introduction of British laws and institutions. When Hume withdrew his amendment on a government promise to produce papers to elucidate the subject, 26 July, Marryat reluctantly acquiesced.[16] In another implied censure of Woodford, 5 Aug. 1822, he secured a return of information on emigrants from the Spanish Main imprisoned in Trinidad.[17] Three weeks later the minister Croker named him as one of the Members 'inclined to' Canning who would probably follow him into opposition if he opted for that course.[18]

Early in 1823 Marryat published extensive *Observations* on the renewal of the West India Dock Company's charter and a *Reply to the Arguments ... recommending an Equalization of the Duties on East and West Indian Sugar*, of which 1,000 copies were ordered for propaganda purposes by the West India Committee.[19] In the House, 3 Mar., he denied that government was pledged to equalize the duties.[20] Ministers resisted his motion for documents to prove that the admiralty had misled Lloyd's over precautions taken to protect shipping the previous autumn, 4 Mar., but he dropped it in response to Canning's appeal for mutual forbearance. He condemned the coal duties, 10 Mar., but supported the government's warehousing bill, 21 Mar., and merchant vessels apprenticeship bill, 24 Mar., 18 Apr.: 'the political economists ... were ready to grind the navy and shipping interests to powder, rather than abandon their favourite theories'.[21] He opposed the naval and military pensions bill, 14 Apr.,[22] but sided with ministers against repeal of the Foreign Enlistment Act, 16 Apr., arguing that while it was undoubtedly a restraint on liberty, its abandonment might encourage a breach of British neutrality in the Franco-Spanish war. He again voted for parliamentary reform, 24 Apr., and for reform of the Scottish representative system, 2 June. He had doubts about putative changes in the law merchant to protect brokers from the consequences of their own folly, 15 May, but acquiesced in the motion for a select committee, to which he was named.[23] Later that day he supported the government's temporizing amendment to Buxton's motion for the immediate abolition of slavery, reading from colonial governors' reports to support his contention that there had been great improvements in the treatment and conditions of slaves. He was a member of the West India subcommittee on amelioration and of the literary committee set up in June 1823 to publicize their case on this and other issues. After presenting petitions on the subject, 22 May, he spoke against Whitmore's motion for equalization of the sugar duties and answered Ricardo's arguments.[24] He initially accepted, with reservations on points of detail, the reciprocity bill, 6 June, as it was 'the duty of this country to act upon liberal principles', but he denounced it on its third reading, 4 July, as an infraction of the navigation laws, though he was not listed in the hostile minority of 15. He opposed the increase in barilla duty, 13 June, because the 'variable policy ... out of which this proposition arose ... put all property to hazard, and sported with the capital of the country'. Later that day he spoke and voted against the beer duties bill. He presented a Trinidad petition for the introduction of a British form of government, 11 June; and in answer to his question, 19 June, ministers confirmed that the West Indian commissioners would after all extend their inquiry to Trinidad.[25] He doubted the wisdom of including provision for jury trial in the New South Wales bill, 2 July, and supported the appeal of its opponents to be heard by counsel against the measure, which seemed to him to give the governor too much power: 'the question for the House to determine was, whether they would see with their own eyes or with the eyes of the executive government'. He supported a petition for recognition of the independence of Colombia, 8 July 1823.[26]

Marryat attended meetings of the West India Committee, 21 Nov., 30 Dec. 1823.[27] On the morning of Monday, 12 Jan. 1824 he travelled as usual to London from his Wimbledon residence. He left his carriage at Southwark and 'walked heartily towards the City'. Soon after reaching his office at the bank, 'whilst in the act of writing a frank ... he fell on the floor and instantly expired, without speaking a word'.[28] By his will, dated 18 Aug. 1818, he provided his wife with £10,000 and a life annuity of £4,500 and his three surviving daughters with £20,000 each. He directed that his real estate, including plantations in Grenada and Jamaica, should be sold as necessary to fund those bequests. In a codicil of 24 July 1819 he devised the Wimbledon property to his eldest son and partner, subject to the life interest of his widow, whose legacies he now made conditional on her renouncing right of dower in the plantations. His personalty was sworn under £250,000 within the province of Canterbury; and it was generally reckoned that he was worth at least twice that sum.[29] According to an obituary, Marryat, a devout believer in the 'the awfulness' and 'the consolations of revealed religion'

> possessed a great deal of general information [and] a clear, powerful and businesslike manner of speaking, which gave him great ascendancy in all public meetings connected with his own pursuits, and procured him an attentive hearing in the House of Commons.[30]

[1] *HP Commons, 1790-1820*, iv. 549-53. [2] Add. 38282, ff. 92-95. [3] *Kentish Chron.* 8 Feb., 3, 10 Mar. 1820. [4] Cent. Kent. Stud. Sa/C2, mayor of Sandwich to Marryat, 17, 24 May 1821, 4 July 1822, replies, 28 May, 2, 13 June 1821, 21 June, 2, 13 July 1822. [5] Add. 52444, f. 177. [6] *The Times*, 11 July 1820. [7] Ibid. 17, 27 Feb., 15, 17,20-22 Mar. 1821. [8] Inst. of Commonwealth Stud. W.I. cttee. archives M915/3/4/457. [9] *The Times*, 16, 31 May, 1 June 1821. [10] HLRO, Hist. Coll. 379, Grey Bennet diary, 104a. [11] L.M. Frazer. *Hist. Trinidad*, ii. 32-39, 61, 126-30, 140-3; G. Carmichael, *Hist. Trinidad*, 112-17; *PP* (1823), xvii. 325-673. [12] *The Times*, 9 Mar. 1822. [13] Ibid. 3, 11, 18 May, 4 June 1822. [14] W.I. cttee. archives M915/4/1/33. [15] *The Times*, 24, 31 July 1822. [16] Ibid. 27 July 1822; Frazer, ii. 134-40. [17] *The Times*, 6 Aug. 1822; *PP* (1823), xvii. 675-96. [18] Add. 40319, f. 57. [19] W.I. cttee. archives M915/4/1/74, 96. [20] *The Times*, 4 Mar. 1823. [21] Ibid. 11 Mar., 19 Apr. 1823. [22] Ibid. 15 Apr. 1823. [23] Ibid. 16 May 1823. [24] D. Hall, *W.I. Cttee.* 22; *The Times*, 23 May 1823. [25] *The Times*, 12, 20 June 1823. [26] Ibid. 9 July 1823. [27] W.I. cttee. archives M915/4/1/138, 148. [28] *Kentish Gazette*, 13, 16 Jan. 1824; *Gent.Mag.* (1824), i. 372-3. [29] PROB 11/1681/99; IR26/1007/169; *Kentish Chron.* 23 Jan. 1824. [30] *Gent. Mag.* (1824), i. 374; *Kentish Gazette*, 13 Jan. 1824.

D.R.F.

MARRYAT, Joseph II (1790–1876), of Wimbledon House, Surr. and 6 Richmond Terrace, Whitehall, Mdx.

SANDWICH 1826–1834

b. 7 Oct. 1790, at Grenada,[1] 1st s. of John Marryat I* and Charlotte, da. of Frederick von Geyer of Boston, Mass. *m.* 19 Oct. 1819, Mary, da. of James Lindsay of Queen Street, Mdx., *s.p.*[2] *suc.* fa. 1824. *d.* 24 Sept. 1876.
Agent, Grenada 1831-51.

It is not clear whether Marryat attended Mr. Freeman's school at Ponder's End, Middlesex with his next brother Frederick, the future author of *Peter Simple* and *Mr Midshipman Easy*. On coming of age he became his father's partner in his London West India mercantile business in Laurence Pountney Lane, taking a one-third share of the profits.[3] On his father's sudden death in January 1824 he became its head, as well as a member of the committee of Lloyd's.[4] The following year he joined, in his father's room, the bank of Kay, Price, Marryat and Coleman at 1 Mansion House Street. He did not make an immediate bid for his father's seat at Sandwich, but in September 1825 announced his intention of standing at the next general election.[5] When he came forward in 1826 he promised to promote the new harbour scheme and to follow 'the independent line of conduct pursued by my ... father in considering measures themselves, without reference to the parties by whom they are proposed'. He was returned unopposed with the admiralty candidate.[6]

Marryat voted for Catholic relief, 6 Mar. 1827. He voted for the disfranchisement of Penryn, 28 May, and supported a London merchants' petition for reduction of the duties on marine insurance, 21 June 1827.[7] He voted for repeal of the Test Acts, 26 Feb., and Catholic relief, 12 May, and was in the Wellington ministry's majority against inquiry into chancery delays, 24 Apr. 1828. He welcomed the New South Wales bill in the hope that the new council would 'restrain those acts of arbitrary power which have too generally characterized the governors of our distant colonies', 18 Apr. Taking up his father's campaign against Sir Ralph Woodford, governor of Trinidad, he went on to demand compensation for proprietors penalized by Woodford's harsh land and taxation policies, which had been exposed by the 1823 commission of inquiry, and to press government to adopt a 'new and improved system of colonial administration'. (Woodford died at sea on his way home a month later.) On 6 May Marryat secured a return of information on Trinidad. He was listed in both the majority and minority in the division on the silk duties, 14 July 1828.[8] His only known vote in the 1829 session was for Catholic emancipation, 6 Mar.; and he thanked ministers for the Spanish claims bill, 10 Apr. He was a member of the streamlined West India acting committee formed in May 1829.[9]

He voted against the transfer of East Retford's seats to Birmingham, 11 Feb., and Lord Blandford's parliamentary reform scheme, 18 Feb., but for the enfranchisement of Birmingham, Leeds and Manchester, 23 Feb. 1830. He voted against government on the treasurership of the navy, 12 Mar., the Bathurst-Dundas pensions, 26 Mar., the ordnance estimates, 29 Mar., and privy councillors' emoluments, 14 May. He divided for Jewish emancipation, 5 Apr. He supported abolition of the death penalty for forgery, 13, 24 May, 7 June, because bankers were reluctant to prosecute: 'if we affix a mitigated penalty, certain of infliction ... we secure an effectual protection to the public'. He voted for parliamentary reform, 28 May. He argued that it was 'not possible to grant effectual relief' to distress in the shipping industry 'by legislative measures', 2 Apr., and defended colonial preference in the spirit duties,7 Apr. On the presentation of a petition for the introduction of representative government to the Cape, 24 May, he observed that a 'vicious system' of gubernatorial tyranny existed in all the crown colonies. At the same time, he praised the colonial secretary Murray for his evident willingness to resume the work of reform in Trinidad which had been abandoned on Huskisson's resignation two years earlier. He attended the meeting of West India Members which resolved to support the ministerial proposals on the rum duties but to press for a substantial reduction in the duties on colonial sugar, 2 June. Seconding Lord Chandos's motion to this effect, 14 June, he declared that 'the case of the West India planter is one not of mere distress but of absolute annihilation'; he was a teller for the minority of 23. He spoke in the same terms in support of Chandos's unsuccessful bid to double the reduction conceded by government, 30 June 1830, when he complained of their 'vacillating conduct' on West Indian relief.

At the general election of 1830 Marryat came forward again for Sandwich, stressing his 'independent' conduct and support for 'measures ... for alleviating the burthens of the people'.[10] After his unopposed return the government head-counters listed him as one of the 'doubtful doubtfuls', with the additional comment that he was 'surely a friend'. After dividing for a reduction in the duty on wheat imported to the West Indies, 12 Nov., he voted in the ministerial minority in the crucial division on the civil list, 15 Nov. 1830. That month the resident Trinidad planters and merchants, anticipating the British response to their pressure for constitutional change, appointed Marryat their honorary (and unpaid) agent. He subsequently corresponded with the Grey ministry in their modest reform proposals for the colony.[11] On 30 Dec. 1830 he supported the petition of the West India planters and merchants against a precipitate abolition of slavery and accused the abolitionists of reneging on the agreement over the policy of amelioration and of circulating the 'grossest calumnies' against the proprietors. He urged the new ministers to avoid their predecessors' 'apathy and indecision' and called for a commission of inquiry. He voted for the second reading of the reform bill, 22 Mar. 1831, but three days later said that unless its proposed disfranchisement of most freemen, which would affect a majority of his constituents, was modified, he would be 'compelled to vote against it'. He nevertheless voted with government against Gascoyne's wrecking amendment, 19 Apr. 1831. At the ensuing general election he stood for Sandwich as 'a friend to reform' in principle, though he reiterated his determination to oppose the wholesale disfranchisement of freemen. 'No effectual retrenchment of expenditure or diminution of labour', he declared, 'can be expected from the House of Commons as at present constituted.' He comfortably topped the poll after a three-day contest.[12]

Marryat voted for the second reading of the reintroduced reform bill, 6 July, and steadily for most of its details in committee, although he was in the minority for the preservation of freemen's rights, 30 Aug. 1831. On 9 Aug. he welcomed the proposal to unite Sandwich with Deal as a two Member constituency and denied Tory allegations that it would thus become a snug admiralty borough. He voted for the third reading, 19, and passage of the bill, 21 Sept., but was not in the majority for the motion of confidence in the ministry, 10 Oct. He voted for the second reading of the revised reform bill, 17 Dec. 1831, for schedule A, 23 Jan., and to go into committee, 20 Feb., but against the enfranchisement of Tower Hamlets, 28 Feb. 1832. He opposed a Tory bid to add Ramsgate to the Sandwich constituency, 14 Mar. He voted for the third reading of the bill, 22 Mar., and for the address asking the king to appoint only ministers who would carry it unimpaired, 10 May. He divided with government on the Russian-Dutch loan, 26 Jan., and relations with Portugal, 9 Feb. He presented a Sandwich petition against the general register bill, 6 Apr., and voted to make coroners' inquests public, 20 June 1832.

Marryat, who was added to the select committee on the use of molasses in brewing, 8 July, voted in the minority for inquiry into the effects of the Sugar Refinery Act on the West Indian colonies, 12 Sept. 1831. Two months later he was appointed the official agent for Grenada; and in giving evidence to the select committee of inquiry into the commercial state of the West Indies, 13 Feb. 1832, he described himself as a proprietor in Grenada, St. Lucia and Trinidad.[13] He obtained a return of papers on the administration and finances of Trinidad, 9 Feb., and on the 29th thanked ministers for the grant to alleviate the problems caused by hurricane damage in Barbados, St. Lucia and St. Vincent, trusting that it would be 'followed up by a plan of general relief'. He came under pressure from Trinidad slave proprietors to recruit parliamentary support for their resistance to the order in council of November 1831 concerning the amelioration of slavery, compliance with which was to be made a condition for the receipt of financial aid.[14] In the House, 9 Mar. 1832, he defended the disaffected merchants and planters of St. Lucia and denied Lord Howick's allegation that he had expressed approval of the order: on the contrary, he had 'strongly protested' against it in his communications with government. Yet he did not sign the formal West India merchants' protest against it and remained silent at the public meeting of 5 Apr.[15] He was named to the select committee on slavery, 30 May, when he presented a Grenada petition for a reduction in the sugar duties and caution on abolition. He also presented petitions from St. Lucia and Trinidad for the introduction of representative government and repeal of the order; but he conceded that the government had done much to assist the crown colonies and distanced himself from the call for repeal, preferring modification. He denied the assertion of Fowell Buxton (who in the Commons, 15 Apr. 1831, had quoted Marryat's father as having admitted that slaves in Trinidad died off 'like rotten sheep')[16] that the West Indian slave population was rapidly diminishing. On the government proposal to offer £58,000 in relief to the crown colonies, 3 Aug. 1832, Marryat, trying to obtain the best possible terms for Trinidad, read a letter from his planter brother Charles to the effect that the order was now working well there. Accused by the Tory Burge and the radical Hume of betraying the West India interest, he replied that while he had initially remonstrated with ministers against details of the order, he had 'always advocated measures of amelioration' and had not felt justified in recommending the colonists to indulge in 'a contumacious resistance' to the order. The next day, seeking to explain his conduct to the delegate from Trinidad, he wrote that he had been 'unprepared for this opposition to the grant on the part of the West India Members', whose 'objections appear to me to be frivolous and unfounded and very much dictated by the spirit of party feeling against the government'. There was much anger in Trinidad, where it was said that his 'treachery' had been purchased with the promise of a baronetcy; and he was stripped of his honorary agency at a public meeting of proprietors.[17]

Marryat successfully contested Sandwich at the 1832 general election but retired from Parliament at the next dissolution. In 1835 the bank, now styled Price, Marryat and Company, moved to 3 King William Street, where it remained until it stopped payment in 1866. The West Indian firm of Marryat and Sons continued in Laurence Pountney Lane until after his death, but the extent of his later personal involvement in it is not clear. In the mid-1840s he had a residence at Little Heath Lodge, Barnet, Hertfordshire (his mother occupied Wimbledon House until her death in 1854); and he appears to have given up his London house in Richmond Terrace in the early 1850s. He made a name for himself as a pundit on pottery and porcelain with the publication of *Collections towards a History* (1850). His *History of Pottery and Porcelain, Mediaeval and Modern* went through three editions. He spent some of his later years at Maes-y-dderwen, Swansea Vale, Breconshire; but it was in London, at 61 Warwick Street, Pimlico, that he died childless in September 1876. By his brief will, dated 17 July 1866, he left all his property to his wife, his sole executrix.

[1] *Misc. Gen. et Her.* (ser. 4), iii. 341, citing the inscription on his coffin; but ibid. 340 gives 1789. [2] *The Times*, 20 Oct. 1819. [3] F. Marryat, *Life and Letters of Capt. Marryat*, i. 12-13. [4] PROB 11/1681/99; C. Wright and C. E. Fayle, *Hist. Lloyd's*, 293. [5] *Kent Herald*, 22 Sept. 1825. [6] *Kentish Chron.* 19 May, 9, 13 June 1826. [7] *The Times*, 22 June 1827. [8] Ibid. 15 July 1828. [9] Inst. of

Commonwealth Stud. W.I. cttee. archives M915/4/2/22; 5/2/1. [10] *Kentish Gazette*, 2, 16, 27, 30 July, 3 Aug. 1830. [11] L.M. Frazer, *Hist. Trinidad*, ii. 243-4; F. Carmichael, *Hist. Trinidad*, 165,168-9. [12] *Kent Herald*, 21, 28 Apr., 5 May; Hatfield House mss 2M/Gen., S.G. Price to Salisbury, 23 Apr. 1831. [13] *PP* (1831-2), xx. 800. [14] W.I. cttee. archives M915/2/3/106-11. [15] *The Times*, 6, 9 Apr. 1832. [16] *Buxton Mems.* 259. [17] Frazer, ii. 252-60, 291-300; Carmichael, 165-6.

D.R.F.

MARSHALL, John (1765–1845), of Headingley House, nr. Leeds, Yorks.; Hallsteads, Westmld. and 4 Grosvenor Square, Mdx.[1]

YORKSHIRE 1826–1830

b. 27 July 1765, 3rd but o. surv. s. of Jeremiah Marshall, draper, of Leeds and Mary, da. of John Cowper of Crowtrees, Rawdon, Yorks. *educ.* Hipperholme, Halifax; privately by Mr. Astley, Derbys. *m.* 5 Aug. 1795, Jane, da. of William Pollard, manufacturer, of Ovendon Hall, Halifax, 5s. (1 *d.v.p.*) 7da. (2 *d.v.p.*). *suc.* fa. 1787. *d.* 6 June 1845.

Sheriff, Cumb. 1821-2.

Marshall's family originated from Yeadon, near Leeds, where the earliest known trace is that of another John, a clothier, in around 1600. The family remained there until Marshall's father married his grandmother's niece Mary Cowper, who brought him £1,200. He used the money to open a draper's shop at 1 Briggate, Leeds. They were originally Baptists, but with no chapel in Leeds they joined the Unitarians of Mill Hill. His parents' only surviving child, Marshall fell seriously ill after a smallpox vaccination when five years old and was sent away to live with his maternal aunt Sarah Booth at Rawdon, near Bradford, where he remained for five years, receiving a rudimentary education from the local minister. When he was eleven, his father decided his future lay as a merchant and sent him to Hipperholme school for 18 months, after which he returned to Leeds for a further year and a half before being dispatched to a Mr. Astley in Derbyshire to continue his education. Once back in Leeds he learnt French and accounting before entering his father's business aged 17. When his father died in December 1787, he left the 22-year-old Marshall an estate worth £9,000, including £7,500 invested in the business, which produced an annual profit of £500. In the first week of 1788 Marshall visited Darlington where his attention was 'accidentally turned to spinning of flax by machinery, it being a thing much wished for by the linen manufacturers.' Reasoning that it would be 'a new business, where there would be few competitors', he was inspired to try his hand, motivated, he claimed, not by the lure of financial gain, but by 'the ambition of distinguishing myself'. Borrowing £3,000 from Sarah Booth and raising more by taking on two partners, that summer he began attempting to spin flax by machine. The first three years were difficult as he struggled to overcome technological problems. In 1790 he risked all by selling the drapery business and investing in a new mill. As the enterprise prospered he bought out his original investors and in 1793 went into partnership with Thomas and Benjamin Benyon*, woollen merchants of Shrewsbury. He later recalled that 'I set my shoulder to the wheel in good earnest. I was at the mill from six in the morning to nine at night and minutely attended to every part of the manufactory'. In 1796 he started to write an autobiography in order 'to form a better judgement of my own prospects'. The key, he decided, was 'perseverance, hard work and judgement'. In 1804, he concluded that his partners were gaining more from the business than he was and, confident of his own abilities, he bought them out. By now he was worth about £40,000. He appointed two of his experienced managers as junior partners, who were later joined by a third, and saw his business dramatically expand. The war with France made his fortune and by the end of it he was worth an estimated £400,000. He had started to diversify his business interests in 1813 by investing in exchequer bills, and he soon moved into American bonds and South American stock: his holding in the United States alone amounted to £212,000 in 1822.

Marshall's wealth inevitably drew him towards improving his social position. In Leeds, as a Dissenter, he had never been accepted by the town's elite, and he therefore looked further afield. In 1815 he bought Hallsteads, an estate at the head of Ullswater, for £11,800, where his wife could be near her childhood friend Dorothy Wordsworth, sister of the poet. Marshall's acceptance was shown by his appointment as sheriff of Cumberland in 1821. By 1826 he owned properties worth £66,000 in the Lake District. In an effort to broaden his own perspective and social acceptance, in 1821 he leased a house in London, where he was drawn to the developing Utilitarian circle. He also pursued an interest in optics and astronomy, but it was the study of geology and political economy that gave him the greatest satisfaction, and he later gave lectures on these topics. In 1828 he produced a booklet, *The Economy of Social Life*, which attempted to explain political economy in simple terms. Philanthropy and education also played a significant part in his life: he helped to establish the Lancasterian school in Leeds and provided a range of schooling for his employees and their children. He was a generous benefactor of charities in the town and had a part in founding the Leeds Literary and Philosophical Society, where he often spoke, and the Leeds Mechanics' Institute. From 1825-8 he was one of a group of similarly minded men who provided money for the *Parliamentary History and Review*, which was established to promote the ideas of Bentham and Mill, and in 1834 he gave money for the foundation of the *London Review*.[2] In 1826, he proposed the establishment of a university at Leeds and the same year was a subscriber to the new University College of London, becoming a member of its first council.

Marshall had long sought a seat in Parliament, for which his 'chief motive' was

> a wish to see the mechanism by which the affairs of a great nation are conducted and to study the characters of the men who take the lead in public life, and the principles on which they act. I also desire it as being creditable to my family and an introduction to good society ... These measures would be ... obtained by a seat for a close borough, which involves but little of labour or attendance upon business.

An abortive attempt to secure a berth at Rye left him 'so disgruntled with the manoeuvring and jobbing' that he 'determined to give up all thoughts of it', but in 1825 his Lake District neighbour James Brougham* secured him a deal with Hylton Jolliffe* for a seat at Petersfield for 5,000 guineas. Meanwhile, Marshall had come to the attention of Earl Fitzwilliam's son Lord Milton*, who in support of Lord Morpeth's* proposed candidacy for one of the county's new additional seats, suggested that

> with respect to the seconder ... if a proper commercial man could be prevailed upon, I think much advantage would be derived ... There is a Mr. Marshall of Leeds who might perhaps be prevailed upon, a man of great property and the highest character, but I do not suppose you have any knowledge of him.

Following the withdrawal of Morpeth a Whig meeting was held at Wakefield, 13 Jan. 1826, at which Marshall was mooted as a possible candidate.[3] Next week the *Leeds Mercury*, which Marshall had helped to finance, suggested that he would 'ably maintain the interests of trade and commerce, and support the principles of civil liberty'.[4] Milton sought the opinion of Lord Althorp*, who told him, 11 Feb., 'if Marshall's standing will do you no harm I have nothing to say against it'.[5] Early in May Marshall received a deputation requesting him to stand for Pontefract, which he declined, saying that he wanted to be available to contest the county if asked, and was not afraid of the expense. The Whig *York Herald* hoped that he 'could neither be so foolish nor presumptuous as to set up for an honour to which nothing gave him the slightest title, except the acquisition of wealth'; but the leading local Whig Sir Francis Wood of Hemsworth advised Milton, 20 May, that if he did stand, 'we must all heartily join in his support and fight the battle, however hazardous'.[6] The opinion of Thomas Tottie, Fitzwilliam's agent, that he 'would bring the support from the trading towns', persuaded Fitzwilliam to back Marshall, who after some hesitation agreed to offer on the understanding that 'when in Parliament, I should act upon my own opinion respecting parliamentary reform and the corn laws, which I apprehend are somewhat different from those of the party'.[7] On 29 May he formally declared, citing his support for Catholic emancipation 'as the best means of safeguarding the Church of England and quietening Ireland', a 'return to a free trade in grain', the abolition of slavery and repeal of the game laws. On reform he argued that great changes had taken place 'in the population, the wealth, and above all, in the intelligence of the country, and the representation ought to be adapted to them'.[8] The Tory *Leeds Intelligencer* condemned his politics, his profession, and his interests, asking, 'Can the Whig aristocracy themselves bear the humiliation?'.[9] On 6 June Sir John Lowther* reported to Lord Lonsdale that 'Lord Harewood ... and others were furious' and were 'moving heaven and earth ... to oust Marshall'.[10] The *Mercury* was of course delighted and the Cloth Halls of Leeds prepared a formal declaration of support.[11] Marshall's committee met with Milton's in York, 5 June, and they commenced a joint canvass, throughout which Marshall struggled to be heard, being neither a natural public speaker nor the possessor of a powerful voice. At the nomination, 12 June 1826, he dismissed criticism of his status and asserted, 'I do claim that rank and station for the manufacturers as to them is justly due'.[12] Following the late withdrawal of a liberal Tory candidate he was returned unopposed. 'It is not to the humble exertions of individuals, but the exertions of the manufacturers of the county ... that Mr. Marshall owes his election', Edward Baines, editor of the *Mercury*, told the Whig victory dinner, at which Marshall proposed the toast, 'A free, full, and fair representation of the people ... in Parliament'.[13] He gave his Petersfield seat to his eldest son William. On 20 June 1826 Sir John Beckett* warned Peel, the home secretary, that Marshall was 'an avowed radical and leveller', but added, 'he is a great invalid turned 60 and will probably die of it before long'.[14]

In his maiden speech Marshall seconded Hume's amendment to the address, 21 Nov. 1826. Speaking in Utilitarian terms, he argued that after a considerable period of peace the people 'had a right to expect a diminution of the country's burdens and an increase of general happiness and prosperity'. Instead, there was 'an equal degree of want and suffering', from which 'the higher ranks were relieving themselves ... by a monopoly of the great necessity of life, wheat'. The only solution, he declared, was a revision of the corn laws. He was in the minority of 24 for the amendment. Morpeth reported that the speech was 'inaudible and asthmatic', while James Abercromby* observed that 'all agree [he] will do nothing. His sense and being Member for Yorkshire may sustain him, but his speaking power will not'.[15] Marshall presented constituency petitions for repeal of the corn laws, 30 Nov. 1826, 20, 27 Feb., and spoke in the same terms, 21 Feb. 1827.[16] He voted against the grant to the duke of Clarence and presented a York petition from distressed persons for financial aid towards emigration, 16 Feb. 1827.[17] He was in the minority to reduce the import price of corn to 50*s.* rather than 60*s.*, 9 Mar., and seconded and voted for Hume's motion for a gradual reduction to 10*s.*, 27 Mar. He divided for Catholic relief, 6 Mar., inquiry into Leicester corporation, 15 Mar., and to withhold the supplies, 30 Mar. Next month he fell seriously ill and convalesced in Brighton, where he decided that at the next dissolution he would not seek re-election. He later wrote of his early impression of Parliamentary business:

> It occupies a considerable proportion of a man's time, but to one accustomed to the management of extensive commercial transactions, is not likely to be either difficult or oppressive, and I should rather wish for the employment than not when I do attend.

He had recovered sufficiently to present Bradford and Halifax petitions for repeal of the Test Acts, 6 June.[18] Lord Lowther* expressed relief that Marshall and his son were already in the House when the Carlisle by-election occurred that summer. Otherwise, he told Lonsdale, 30 July 1827, 'they might have been formidable if one offered ... as it was once talked about'.[19]

Marshall brought up numerous Yorkshire petitions for repeal of the Test Acts in February and early March and voted accordingly, 26 Feb. 1828, when he protested that the Acts were 'revolting to the spirit of the age'. He secured accounts of the stamp duties on bills of exchange between 1805 and 1826, 21 Feb., and was probably appointed to the select committee on criminal commitments, 5 Mar. He voted against extending the East Retford franchise to the freeholders of Bassetlaw, 21 Mar., 30 June. He moved the second reading of the Leeds and Hunslet road bill, 21 Mar. During the debate on the second reading of the freeholders registration bill, 25 Mar., Sir James Graham alleged that Marshall had spent £120,000 on his election, which Marshall denied, noting that the bill would 'very materially lessen the expenses of the candidates'. On 28 Apr. he objected to a Yorkshire petition against Catholic relief presented by his colleague William Duncombe, as it gave a 'very erroneous opinion' of the opinions of the inhabitants. He brought up a York counter-petition that day and voted accordingly, 12 May. He spoke against the imposition of a duty on imported wool, which would 'materially affect a numerous body of his constituents' and 'enable the foreign manufacturers to compete with ours', 28 Apr., and voted for a reduction of the corn duties, 29 Apr. He presented a petition from the wool staplers of Leeds against the East London railway bill, 1 May, and from Hartished-cum-Clifton against the friendly societies bill next day. He brought up constituency petitions against the restrictions on the circulation of pound notes, 12 May, 5 June, and for the abolition of slavery, 3, 6, 10 June. He was in the minority of 13 for revision of civil list pensions, 10 June, and divided against the third reading of the archbishop of Canterbury's bill, 16 June. He voted for repeal of the usury laws, 19 June. He presented a Leeds petition against the practice of suttee, 23 June, and later that day was in the minority condemning the use of public money for renovating Buckingham House. He divided against the additional churches bill, 30 June, and presented a hostile Sheffield petition containing 'upwards of 10,000' signatures, 3 July. At a meeting of Leeds Dissenters to discuss the bill, 7 July 1828, he explained that he and several other Members had done their best to filibuster on the second reading and had partly succeeded as Goulburn, the chancellor of the exchequer, had agreed to withdraw the clause in the bill giving the power of assessment to churchwardens. However, he warned that power would still rest with the vestries:

> If this law were to pass, then we in Leeds, instead of having one parish church, would have four, and our rates would quadruple ... This obnoxious measure cannot be thrown out without the entire and hearty concurrence of the public of England.

Such parliamentary tactics, he insisted, were the only way to defeat the bill as long as

> we have a House of Commons pretending to represent the people of England [when] it is in fact little more than the nomination of the aristocracy ... I hope and trust that the time is not far distant when these great trading towns will consider it their duty, their indispensable duty, to combine together to demand that share of the representation which is unjustly withheld from them.[20]

After Milton had presented a Sheffield petition for Catholic relief, 27 Feb. 1829, Marshall urged the House to look at the evidence provided by the 'great commercial towns', citing his recent attendance at a Leeds meeting of 16-18,000 people, at which the 'decided majority' were in favour of emancipation. He was of course expected by Planta, the Wellington ministry's patronage secretary, to side 'with government' for their concession of emancipation, and he voted accordingly, 6 and (as a pair) 30 Mar. He brought up a favourable Tadcaster petition, 12 Mar., and questioned the validity of a hostile one from Leeds, 23 Mar. He presented and endorsed petitions from the Bradford, Leeds and Wakefield Gas Light Companies against Crosely's gas apparatus bill, 7, 10, 28 Apr., and brought up petitions from tenement owners in Leeds and Sheffield against the labourers' wages bill, 4, 19 May. He seconded and divided for Tennyson's motion to transfer East Retford's seats to Birmingham, 5 May 1829, when he criticized the proposed extension of the franchise to the hundred as simply handing over the borough to the landed interest and again advocated the enfranchisement of the industrial towns of the North. He voted again in the same sense, 11 Feb., 5 Mar. 1830. He divided for Daniel O'Connell to be allowed to take his seat unhindered, 18 May 1829. Next day he was in a minority of 12 for a fixed duty on corn. In December 1829 he was appointed to a subcommittee of the Society for the Propagation of Useful Knowledge which was formed to draw up a report on the state of the country.[21]

Marshall voted for the amendment to the address, 4 Feb, tax cuts, 15 Feb., and a £500,000 reduction of the army estimates, 22 Feb. 1830. He presented and endorsed a Leeds petition against the renewal of the East India Company's charter, 16 Feb., and brought up similar Yorkshire petitions, 4, 16, 25 Mar., 1 Apr. He voted for Lord Blandford's parliamentary reform scheme, 18 Feb., endorsed a Sheffield petition calling for its own representation and voted for the enfranchisement of Birmingham, Leeds and Manchester, 23 Feb. He chaired a Leeds meeting for retrenchment and reform, 18 Mar., and endorsed the ensuing petition, 11 May. He was in the minority of 13 for O'Connell's motion for a radical reform bill including universal suffrage, 28 May, but later that day voted for Lord John Russell's more conventional motion. He voted to refer the Newark petition against the duke of Newcastle to a select committee, 1 Mar. He moved the second reading of the Leeds and Selby railway bill, dismissing objections as 'slight and frivolous', 4 Mar., and presented multiple petitions in its favour, 22, 25 Mar. On 23 Mar. he brought up a petition from Sheffield surgeons and physicians for the removal of obstacles to 'the science of anatomy', hoping that the 'subject will be taken up as it ought to be, without any desire to provoke popular excitement'. He successfully moved the second reading of the Dewsbury road and bridge bill, 25 Mar., but presented the earl of Cardigan's petition against it, 1 Apr. He divided for Jewish emancipation, 5 Apr., 17 May, when he presented a favourable Leeds petition. He brought up a petition of the inhabitants against the Sheffield waterworks bill, 5 Apr., and a Craven petition for a duty on imported lead, 8 Apr. He was in O'Connell's minority to alter the law on Irish vestries, 27 Apr. He presented petitions from Bradford and Sheffield publicans against the sale of beer bill, 27 Apr., 4 May, and one from Leeds for the poor law amendment bill that day. He was a majority teller for bringing up the report on the Hull and Hedon road bill, 10 May. He divided for abolition of the Irish lord lieutenancy and for inquiry into the state of Newfoundland, 11 May. He seconded Slaney's motion for a select committee on the condition of the poor, 13 May. He voted for information on privy councillors' emoluments, 14 May. He presented a petition from Leeds Dissenters for the abolition of slavery, 24 May, and divided for abolition of the death penalty for forgery that day, and 7 June. He was in the minorities against the grant for South American missions, 7 June, for a reduction in consular services, 11 June, and for inquiry into the conduct of church commissioners in the St. Luke's case, 17 June. He was added to the select committee on manufacturing employment, 3 June, and presented a petition from Leeds merchants for compensation for the losses they had suffered after the 1807 sacking of Copenhagen, 1 July 1830.

At the 1830 dissolution Marshall retired from Yorkshire, declining a request from the Whig gentry to reconsider. Dorothy Wordsworth told his wife:

> Another Parliament would have been too much to look forward to ... When I consider the variety of his tastes, and multiplicity of his affairs and connections, it seems to me that he will have more than enough of salutary employment to satisfy the craving of any mind ... I can fancy Mr. Marshall the gladdest of the glad on retiring to his beautiful home among the mountains.

In the ensuing election he was instrumental in persuading the county Whigs to support Henry Brougham*, whom he considered to be a 'man of business' capable of representing the manufacturing and commercial interests of the West Riding.[22] In December 1830, he became the chairman of the newly formed Leeds Association, whose purpose was to promote the return of liberal candidates at the next election, and in February 1831 he chaired the Leeds reform meeting which agreed to petition Parliament.[23] He played an active role in choosing the four reform candidates at the 1831 general election, subscribing £5,000 to their election fund.[24] He opposed much of the later factory legislation and took an active part in Leeds against Michael Sadler*, but 'in these respects he did not follow the general bent of the manufacturing interest'.[25] At the 1832 election he used his influence to secure a seat at Leeds for his second son John, who with his third son James had assumed control of the family business, although Marshall supervised all their dealings. He continued to place his money into stocks and shares and by 1840 it was estimated that he had over half a million pounds invested in various funds, including £100,000 in railway shares. The capital gains on these amounted to about a million pounds. He was generous with his wealth and in the last 30 years of his life distributed over one million pounds, including gifts to his family worth over £350,000. He divided his time between Hallsteads, Leeds, London and health resorts such as Leamington and Bath. Six or seven weeks before his death he suffered 'a serious attack of both apoplexy and paralysis'. After another attack in June 1845 'he gradually sank and died'. An obituary in the *Mercury* remarked that 'Marshall might have had a title when his political friends were in power, had he being willing to accept it'.[26] His total wealth was estimated to be between one and a half and two and a half million pounds.[27] By his will, dated 19 Oct 1844 and proved under £160,000, he left his wife £60,000, Hallsteads and his London house, in addition to an annuity of £3,000. To his unmarried daughter Ellen he bequeathed £30,000. His eldest daughter Mary, who had married Lord Monteagle, received £20,000, as did his other daughters. His sons with interests in the business received nothing further than the existing stock they held and the houses they lived in. The residue passed to his eldest son.[28] Marshalls and Company, flax spinners, closed in 1886.

[1] Unless otherwise stated this biography is based on W.G. Rimmer, *Marshalls of Leeds*. [2] *Mill Works*, xii. p. 202. [3] Fitzwilliam mss 124/4. [4] E. Baines, *Life of Edward Baines*, 41; *Leeds Mercury*, 21 Jan. 1826. [5] Fitzwilliam mss 124/8. [6] *York Herald*, 20 May 1826; Fitzwilliam mss. [7] Wentworth Woodhouse mun. F 137; *Yorks. Election 1826*, p. 78. [8] *Yorks. Election 1826*, p. 80. [9] *Leeds Intelligencer*, 1 June 1826. [10] Lonsdale mss. [11] *Yorks. Election 1826*, p. 83. [12] Ibid. 135. [13] *Leeds Mercury*, 24 June 1826 [14] Add. 40387, f. 207. [15] Castle Howard mss, Morpeth to Lady Carlisle, 25 Nov., Abercromby to same, 22 Nov. 1826. [16] *The Times*, 1 Dec. 1826, 21, 28 Feb. 1827. [17] Ibid. 17 Feb. 1827. [18] Ibid. 7 June 1827 [19] Lonsdale mss. [20] *Leeds Intelligencer*, 10 July 1828. [21] Add. 38758, f. 52. [22] *Leeds Intelligencer*, 29 July 1830. [23] *Leeds Mercury*, 18 Dec. 1830, 12 Feb. 1831. [24] *The Times*, 3 May 1831. [25] *Gent. Mag.* (1845), ii. 201. [26] *Leeds Mercury*, 14 June 1845. [27] *Leeds Times*, 14 June; *Leeds Intelligencer*, 14 June 1845. [28] PROB 11/2021/581; IR26/1713/459.

M.P.J.C.

MARSHALL, William (1796–1872), of Patterdale Hall, Westmld.

PETERSFIELD	1826–1830
LEOMINSTER	1830–1831
BEVERLEY	1831–1832
CARLISLE	1835–1847
CUMBERLAND EAST	1847–1868

b. 26 May 1796, 1st s. of John Marshall* and Jane, da. of William Pollard of Halifax, Yorks.; bro. of James Garth Marshall† and John Marshall†. *educ.* privately by Dr. Thomas Whitaker of Holme, Lancs.; St. John's, Camb. 1814; L. Inn 1819, I. Temple 1824, called 1824. *m.* 16 June 1828, Georgiana Cristiana, da. of George Hibbert†, W.I. merchant, of Munden, Herts., 4s. 4da. *suc.* fa. 1845. *d.* 16 May 1872.

Marshall had no direct involvement in his family's Leeds flax-spinning and linen business, but he reaped the rewards of its success. On his 28th birthday in 1824 his father gave him the estate of Patterdale, on the southern tip of Ullswater, in the shadow of Helvellyn, which was worth £13,000. He may briefly have gone the northern circuit after his call to the bar that year, but mostly he lived in style in London, drawing £700 a year in pin money from his father. In 1830 he was given £5,000, and he received £20,000 of Louisiana stock in 1832 and by 1839 had been furnished with other property valued at £15,000.[1] At the general election of 1826 his father, having unexpectedly secured the nomination as the second Whig candidate for Yorkshire, gave William the seat for Petersfield on the Jolliffe interest which he had bought for himself the previous year.

Marshall shared his father's politics (though he was not admitted to Brooks's Club until 1846) and interest in Utililitarian doctrine. He was not the most assiduous of attenders in the 1826 Parliament. He was in the minority of 24 for Hume's amendment to the address, 21 Nov. 1826, and voted against the duke of Clarence's grant, 16 Feb. 1827. He divided for Catholic relief, 6 Mar. 1827, 12 May 1828. He voted in small minorities for relaxation of the corn laws, 9, 12, 27 Mar. 1827, and again, 22, 29 Apr. 1828. He divided for information on the Lisburn Orange procession, 29 Mar. 1827, but not for the opposition motion to withhold supply next day, when he was named as a defaulter. He was in the minorities for inquiry into the Irish estimates and information on chancery delays, 5 Apr. He spoke and voted for the Penryn disfranchisement bill, 28 May 1827. He was one of Hume's minority of eight for reductions in the navy estimates, 12 Feb. 1828. That day and on 15 and 21 Feb. he presented petitions for repeal of the Test Acts, for which he voted, 26 Feb. He divided against the Wellington ministry on chancery delays, 24 Apr., and crown proceedings for the recovery of excise penalties, 1 May 1828. He divided for Catholic emancipation, 6, 30 Mar. 1829. He was in the minorities for transferring East Retford's seats to Birmingham, 5 May, and allowing O'Connell to take his seat without swearing the oath of supremacy, 18 May 1829. Next day he spoke and was a minority teller for Hume's motion for a fixed duty on corn imports. He was one of the Whigs who voted with government against the amendment to the address, 4 Feb., but he sided against them for tax reductions, 15 Feb., and cuts in the army estimates, 19, 22, 23 Feb. 1830. He again divided to give East Retford's seats to Birmingham, 11 Feb., 5, 15 Mar., when he was in O'Connell's minority to adopt the ballot there. He voted for Lord Blandford's parliamentary reform scheme, 18 Feb., to enfranchise Birmingham, Leeds and Manchester, 23 Feb., and to investigate the Newark petition complaining of the duke of Newcastle's electoral interference, 1 Mar. He was appointed to the select committee on the East India Company, 6 Feb. 1830 (and again, 28 June 1831, 27 Jan. 1832). He voted to ban Members from voting in committee on bills in which they had a personal stake, 26 Feb.; against the appointment of a treasurer of the navy, 12 Mar.; to reduce the ordnance estimates, 29 Mar., the army estimates, 30 Apr., and the public buildings grant, 3 May; to condemn the government's involvement in the Terceira episode, 28 Apr.; to cut the salary of the assistant treasury secretary, 10 May; to consider abolition of the Irish lord lieutenancy, 11 May, and to repeal the Irish coal duties, 13 May. He voted for Jewish emancipation, 17 May 1830.

At the general election that summer he was returned for the venal borough of Leominster after a token contest. Ministers listed him among their 'foes', and he voted to bring them down on the civil list, 15 Nov. 1830. He was in the minority of 39 for reducing the duty on wheat imported to the West Indies, 12 Nov. He presented a constituency petition for the abolition of slavery, 17 Nov. 1830. On 7 Mar. 1831 he secured a return of stamp duties on bills of exchange. He divided for the second reading of the Grey ministry's reform bill, 22 Mar., and against Gascoyne's wrecking amendment, 19 Apr. 1831. At the ensuing general election he stood as a reformer for the venal borough of Beverley with the backing of the retiring Member Daniel Sykes. On the hustings, he asked:

> What kept up all the monopolies? The interest which Members of the House of Commons had in them. Why were expensive colonies maintained? Because they promoted the interests of a small body who had parliamentary influence. Many of his hearers were engaged in trade: did they want a greater trade? ... Do away with the East India monopoly, and they would be allowed to trade with 30 millions of fellow subjects. Would that be brought about by reform? To be sure it would.

He overcame the initial hostility of the out-voters, who were to be disfranchised by the reform bill, and was returned at the head of the poll.[2]

Marshall voted for the second reading of the reintroduced reform bill, 6 July, at least twice against the adjournment, 12 July 1831, and steadily for the details of the measure, though he was in the minority for the total disfranchisement of Saltash, 26 July. On 14 July he presented the petition of resident householders of the Beverley out-parish of St. John asking to be admitted to the borough franchise. He divided for the passage of the bill, 21 Sept., and for the motion of confidence in the ministry, 10 Oct. He was in the minority for printing the Waterford petition for disarming the Irish yeomanry, 11 Aug. He voted for the second reading of the revised reform bill, 17 Dec. 1831. He again generally supported its details in the lobbies, but he was in the minority of 32 who voted to expunge the clause enfranchising £50 tenants in the counties, 3 Feb. 1832. He divided for the third reading, 22 Mar., for the address asking the king to appoint only ministers who would carry undiluted reform, 10 May, for the second reading of the Irish bill, 25 May, and against a Conservative amendment to the Scottish measure, 1 July. He was in the minority for Hobhouse's vestry reform bill, 23 Jan. He divided with government on the Russian-Dutch loan, 26 Jan., 12, 20 July, relations with Portugal, 9 Feb., and the navy civil departments bill, 6 Apr., but against them to reduce the barracks grant, 2 July 1832.

Marshall did not seek re-election in 1832, but sat as 'a radical reformer' from 1835 until his defeat in 1868, at the age of 72.[3] He profited handsomely from his father's death in 1845 and died a wealthy man in May 1872.[4]

[1] W.G. Rimmer, *Marshalls of Leeds*, 114. [2] *Hull Packet*, 3 May 1831. [3] *Dod's Parl. Companion*. [4] *The Times*, 20 May 1872.

M.P.J.C.

MARTIN, John (1774–1832), of Overbury, Worcs. and 68 Lombard Street, London.

TEWKESBURY 1812–4 Jan. 1832

b. 27 Nov. 1774, 1st s. of James Martin† of Overbury and Penelope, da. of Joseph Skipp of Upper Hall, Ledbury, Herefs. *m.* 5 Mar. 1803, Frances, da. of Richard Stone, banker, of Lombard Street and Chislehurst, Kent, 5s. (2 *d.v.p.*) 2da. *suc.* fa. 1810. *d.* 4 Jan. 1832.

Martin, who became senior partner in the London banking firm of Martin, Stone and Foote in 1807, inherited his father's property in Worcestershire three years later.[1] He was the fifth member of his family to represent Tewkesbury, which was close to the Overbury estate, and it was apparently 'the pride of his political life' to exhibit the same spirit of 'tenacious and uncompromising integrity' as his father.[2] In 1820, on being returned unopposed for the third time with the Tory John Edmund Dowdeswell, he recommended economy, tax reductions and 'a disposition ... to redress every real and substantial grievance', as the remedies for distress and popular discontent.[3]

He was a regular attender who continued to vote with the Whig opposition to Lord Liverpool's ministry on all major issues, including parliamentary reform, 9 Mar., 18 Apr., 9, 10, 31 May 1821, 25 Apr., 24 June 1822, 20 Feb., 24 Apr., 2 June 1823, 26 Feb. 1824, 13, 27 Apr., 26 May 1826. He divided for Catholic relief, 28 Feb. 1821, 1 Mar., 21 Apr., 10 May 1825. On 9 May 1820, during the debate on the motion for inquiry into the evidence against George Edwards, the government spy among the Cato Street conspirators, his adjournment motion was 'immediately negatived'.[4] He argued that the chancellor of the exchequer, Vansittart, had 'violated' statute in the way he had borrowed from the consolidated fund, 9 June 1820. He declared that he would not 'vote away any more of the public money until a more clear mode of keeping the accounts should be adopted', 14 Feb. 1821. He said he regarded it as 'a more sacred obligation to consult the privations and distresses of the people than to vote superfluities to any branch of the royal family', 18 June, when he was a minority teller against receiving the report of the committee on the duke of Clarence's grant. He accused ministers of a 'violation of faith' towards public creditors during the years of depreciated currency, 5 Mar.[5] He was listed as a steward of the City of London Tavern reform dinner, 4 Apr. He advocated Sunday postal deliveries, 17 May.[6] He warned of future opposition to the forgery punishment mitigation bill 'unless the punishment ... in all cases was transportation for life', 25 May, and was a majority teller for the amendment to except promissory notes, bills of exchange and money orders drawn on bankers, 4 June 1821. He divided for Brougham's motion for more extensive tax reductions, 11 Feb., but against Lord Althorp's similar resolution, 21 Feb. 1822; he continued to vote for economy and retrenchment that session. He supported reduction of the salt duty 'on the principle of economy', insisting that 'it would not interfere with his former vote', 28 Feb. He advocated conversion of the navy five per cents into four-and-a-half per cent stock rather than adding to the national debt, 25 Feb., and complained that the government was rushing its plan through without giving Members time to consider the amendments made in committee, 8 Mar.[7] On 18 Apr. he expressed the hope that if the select committee on public accounts, to which he had been named, was unable to execute its duties fully that session it would be reappointed.[8] He condemned the ministerial plan for funding naval and military pensions, which proved that 'they were determined not to reduce the expenditure ... they had made up their minds to continue the employment of useless postmasters-general and expensive clerks', 1 May. He supported the amendment to use the sinking fund to pay these pensions, 24 May, observing that 'it was a palpable juggle to talk of having a sinking fund at a time [when] we were borrowing money to defray the expenses of our ordinary establishments'. He moved to abolish the lottery tax, 1 July 1822, but was defeated by 74-34.

He divided against Hume's call for further tax reductions, 3 Mar. 1823, explaining three days later that he thought the government had done 'as much as could be done in the present circumstances of the country', although he lamented the 'state of inexplicable confusion' in the public accounts.[9] He 'objected to some of the charges incurred by junior branches of the royal family', 9 June 1823.[10] He denounced the usury laws as 'injurious to all classes ... especially ... the agricultural interest', 16 Feb. 1824. He presented, without comment, a Tewkesbury mechanics' petition for repeal of the combination laws, 9 Mar.[11] He supported the game laws amendment bill in principle, but warned that he would oppose it if a clause allowing landowners to kill game without the tenant's permission was added, 25 Mar. He urged referral of the hides and skins repeal bill to a select committee, 14 Apr., and said he could not vote for repeal of the leather duty as he 'entirely approved of the measures taken by ministers for the reduction of taxes', 18 May 1824. He considered the new game laws amendment bill 'exceedingly objectionable' in its present form but was willing to support the second reading in the hope of modifying it in committee, 7 Mar. 1825. He moved an amendment to give property rights in game to the tenant, 24 Mar., which was defeated by 33-4.[12] He dismissed the large anti-Catholic petition from London, Westminster and Southwark, 21 Apr., observing that such petitions were often improperly got up. He favoured the issue of silver *3d.*s for their 'very general convenience', 12 May. He believed he would have 'grossly violated his duty to his constituents' by supporting the financial provision for the duke of Cumberland, but he had 'far less objection' in the case of the duchess of Kent, 27 May 1825. He complained that 'much unmerited odium had been thrown upon the country bankers', 7 Mar. 1826, when he was a minority teller against the third reading of the promissory notes bill. He moved next day for an account of how many commissions of bankruptcy issued against country bankers since 1816 had been proceeded with.[13] At the general election that summer he was again returned unopposed for Tewkesbury.[14]

Martin gave a 'decided negative' to the financial provision for the duke of Clarence, 16 Feb., voting against the annuity bill, 2, 16 Mar. 1827. He divided for Catholic relief, 6 Mar. He presented a Tewkesbury petition for retrenchment and reform, 8 Mar., and ones from Dissenters for repeal of the Test Acts, 25 May, 7 June.[15] He voted against increased protection for barley, 12 Mar. He divided for inquiry into the allegations against Leicester corporation, 15 Mar., for the spring guns bill, 23 Mar., and to postpone the committee of supply, 30 Mar. He voted against Canning's coalition government to disfranchise Penryn, 28 May 1827. He divided against the Wellington ministry for naval retrenchment, 11 Feb., against the grant for the Society for Propagation of the Gospels in the colonies, 6 June, to reduce civil list pensions, 10 June, condemn the misapplication of public money for work on Buckingham House, 23 June, cut the salary of the lieutenant-general of the ordnance, 4 July, and omit the grant for North American fortifications, 7 July 1828. He voted to repeal the Test Acts, 26 Feb., and criticized the proposed new oath, which would exclude Quakers and Jews, as 'not creditable to the good sense or sound policy of the country', 2 May. He divided for Catholic claims, 12 May. He voted against extending the East Retford franchise to Bassetlaw freeholders, 21 Mar., and recommitting the disfranchisement bill, 27 June. He divided for a lower pivot price for the corn duties, 22 Apr., and a smaller protective duty, 29 Apr. He voted to condemn delays in chancery, 24 Apr. He moved an amendment to the offences against the person bill providing for stronger penalties in cases involving aggravated cruelty towards children, 5 May, but withdrew it at the request of the home secretary, Peel, who considered it impracticable, 23 May. He described the usury laws as beneficial only to 'low attornies and an inferior description of agents', 20 May, and was a majority teller for the second reading of the repeal bill, 19 June. He divided for inquiry into the circulation of small bank notes in Scotland and Ireland, 5 June, and against the bill on this subject, 16, 27 June. In the debate on the savings banks bill, 3 July, he confirmed from his own experience that high interest rates were attracting money from those who were not poor. He voted for the corporate funds bill, 10 July. He divided against the archbishop of Canterbury's bill, 16 June, the additional churches bill, 30 June, and for inquiry into the Irish church, 24 June. He opposed the cider and perry excise licences bill, 26 June, arguing that 'public houses in which gin was consumed' were the real source of immorality. He unsuccessfully attempted to add a clause to the sale of game bill giving occupiers rather than owners of land the power to grant sporting licenses, 27 June 1828.

He divided for Catholic emancipation, 6, 30 Mar., expressed 'heartfelt pleasure' at the ministry's conduct, 9 Mar., and condemned the 'inflammatory language' used by peers, clergymen and magistrates in encouraging anti-Catholic demonstrations, 16 Mar. 1829. He voted to allow O'Connell to take his seat without swearing the oath of supremacy, 18 May. He thought 'a reduction of our unfunded debt' was 'very desirable', 11 May 1829. He voted to transfer East Retford's seats to Birmingham, 11 Feb., 5 Mar. 1830, when he opposed voting by secret ballot as he did not believe it would 'diminish bribery or corruption, or even intimidation' and was 'satisfied that a great moral good is effected when an individual comes forward boldly and openly ... and votes against what appears to be his pecuniary interest'; he voted against the disfranchisement bill, 15 Mar. He divided for Lord Blandford's reform plan, 18 Feb., the enfranchisement of Birmingham, Leeds and Manchester, 23 Feb., and Russell's reform motion, 28 May. He regularly voted with the revived Whig opposition that session on retrenchment motions. He had been unable to 'make up my mind as to the propriety of ever abolishing the punishment of death' in cases of forgery, 1 Apr., but concluded on 24 May that since the prospect of execution was deterring prosecutions, 'we should try the experiment of a mitigated punishment'; he voted in that sense, 24 May, 7 June. He was 'flattered at the honour' of being asked to present a Worcester Catholics' petition for Jewish emancipation, which was 'a complete answer to the charges of bigotry and illiberality' made against them, and voted accordingly, 17 May. He divided for reform of the civil government of Canada, 25 May, and of the divorce laws, 3 June, and repeal of the Irish Vestries Acts, 10 June. He voted to prohibit sales for on-consumption in beer houses, 21 June, and to delay it for two years, 1 July. He divided against the increased recognizances required of printers by the libel law amendment bill, 6, 9 July 1830. At the general election that summer he was again returned unopposed for Tewkesbury after assuring his constituents of his 'abhorrence' of slavery.[16]

The ministry of course listed Martin among their 'foes', and he voted against them in the crucial civil list division, 15 Nov. 1830. He presented and 'cordially advocated' a Tewkesbury anti-slavery petition, 19 Nov. He supported the suspension of Evesham's writ, as it was 'one of the most corrupt boroughs in existence ... where the grossest bribery was carried on at every election', 16 Dec. 1830. He warned that the proposed tax on the transfer of property would be 'highly injurious to the public' without greatly benefiting the exchequer and entered a 'protest' against the alternative suggestion of a property tax, 15 Feb. 1831. He expressed his 'entire concurrence' in the motion for inquiry into more efficient modes of secondary punishment, 17 Mar. That day he presented a Tewkesbury petition in favour of the Grey ministry's reform bill, observing that 'I approve of the measure not only for what it contains but also for what it does not, namely, a proposition for annual parliaments, vote by ballot and universal suffrage'. He divided for the second reading, 22 Mar., and against Gascoyne's wrecking amendment, 19 Apr. 1831. At the ensuing general election he headed the poll at Tewkesbury as 'the advocate ... of economy, retrenchment and reform, the enemy of colonial slavery, in whatever state and under whatever modification existing', and as 'the warm and devoted friend of civil and religious liberty'.[17]

He drew attention to the 'disgraceful state' of Westminster Hall, 1 July 1831. He divided for the second reading of the reintroduced reform bill, 6 July, and generally supported its details, although he voted against the proposed division of counties, 11 Aug., and for the Chandos amendment to enfranchise £50 tenants-at-will, 18 Aug. He divided for the bill's passage, 21 Sept., and Lord Ebrington's confidence motion, 10 Oct. He voted to punish only those guilty of bribery at the Dublin election, 23 Aug. He voted to reduce the grant for civil list services, 18 July, and while supporting that for building work already done at Windsor Castle and Buckingham House, 28 Sept., he was 'not ... prepared to vote ... any further sums'. He divided with the minority against the truck bill, 12 Sept. He was prevented by 'severe illness' from voting on the second reading of the revised reform bill, 17 Dec. 1831.[18] His death in January 1832 was attributed to his 'close attendance during the whole of the protracted and harassing debates on reform'.[19] He left freehold property in Herefordshire and Warwickshire to his eldest son John and other freehold property in Herefordshire to his second son James; his personalty was sworn under £90,000.[20] All of his sons served as partners in the family bank.[21] John Martin (1805-80) was Liberal Member for Tewkesbury, 1832-5, 1837-59, and James Martin (1807-78) similarly represented the borough, 1859-65.

[1] The will was sworn under £35,000 (PROB 11/1508/94; IR26/156/260); J.B. Martin, *'The Grasshopper' in Lombard Street*, 100-1. [2] J. Bennett, *Tewkesbury Yearly Reg.* (1840), 82. [3] *Gloucester Jnl.* 13 Mar. 1820. [4] *The Times*, 10 May 1820. [5] Ibid. 6 Mar. 1821. [6] Ibid. 18 May 1821. [7] Ibid. 26 Feb., 9 Mar. 1822. [8] Ibid. 19 Apr. 1822. [9] Ibid. 7 Mar. 1823. [10] Ibid. 10 June 1823. [11] Ibid. 10 Mar. 1824. [12] Ibid. 25 Mar. 1825. [13] Ibid. 9 Mar. 1826. [14] *Gloucester Jnl.* 5, 12 June 1826. [15] *The Times*, 9 Mar., 26 May, 8 June 1827. [16] *Gloucester Jnl.* 10, 24, 31 July 1830. [17] Ibid. 30 Apr., 7 May 1831. [18] Ibid. 24 Dec. 1831. [19] *Gent Mag.* (1832), i. 80-81. [20] PROB 11/1796/102; IR26/1295/49. [21] Martin, 102.

T.A.J.

MARTIN, Richard (1754–1834), of Dangan and Ballynahinch, co. Galway and 16 Manchester Buildings, Mdx.[1]

CO. GALWAY	1801–1812
CO. GALWAY	1818–11 Apr. 1827

b. Feb. 1754, 1st s. of Robert Martin of Dangan and 1st w. Hon. Bridget Barnewall, da. of John, 11th Bar. Trimleston [I]. *educ.* Harrow 1769; by Rev. Joseph Gunning of Sutton, Suff.; Trinity Coll. Camb. 1773; travelled in Europe, Jamaica, America; L. Inn 1776; King's Inns 1781, called [I] 1781. *m.* (1) 1 Feb. 1777, Elizabeth (sep. 1 Mar. 1793 and *d.* c. 1795), da. of George Vesey of Lucan, co. Dublin, 2s. (1 *d.v.p.*) 1da.; (2) 5 June 1796, Harriet, da. of Hugh Evans, army surgeon, wid. of Capt. Robert Hesketh, RN, 2s. (1 *d.v.p.*) 3da. *suc.* fa. 1794. *d.* 6 Jan. 1834.

MP [I] 1776-83, 1798-1800.

Commr. of stamps [I] 1800, of accts. [I] 1800-2; collector, hearth tax [I] 1806, ?gauger [I] 1807; commr. of fisheries [I] 1819-30.

Sheriff, co. Galway 1782-3; col. Galway vols. 1779, maj.-gen. 1784; capt. Ballynahinch yeomanry ?1796.

'Humanity Dick', the animals' friend or the 'Wilberforce of hacks', as Thomas Hood called him, was the great-grandson of 'Nimble Dick', who, by wresting possession of the ancient Clan O'Flaherty territory of Connemara, raised the originally Anglo-

Norman Martin family from its status as one of the old tribes of Galway town to that of the dominant landowners of the eastern half of the county. Martin, whose father became a 'Protestant of convenience' in 1745, was educated in England, but retained the unmistakeable characteristics of a Galway country gentleman throughout his life.[2] A keen actor, who established theatres in Dublin and Galway, a renowned duellist, who well deserved the nickname 'Hairtrigger Dick', and, as 'King of Connemara', a virtual law unto himself on his vast, desolate and encumbered estates, he was one of Ireland's great and perhaps underestimated eccentrics. Hardy, pugnacious and cavalier, he had an over fine sense of honour, tempered only by a ludicrous talent for the bathetic, and a deep disgust for the unconscious barbarities perpetrated against the brutes of creation, abuses which he was always ready to resent in the highest terms. One of the most sensitive of men, he was grief-stricken by the death of his friend and cousin James Jordan following their pointless duel, by the loss of several of his children in pregnancy or early infancy and by the desertion of his first wife, who took a lover in Paris in 1790 (they were separated by ecclesiastical decree in 1793, but she died before a divorce bill could reach the statute book).[3] He could never abide to observe suffering in any form and his love of animals, first instilled in him by his mother, was of a piece with this all encompassing kindness, a universal benevolence which his daughter Harriet (a child and namesake of his second wife, and like her a novelist) could only sum up by the single word, 'fatherliness'.[4]

Martin sat as a Patriot for Jamestown, 1776-83, and as a friend to the proposed Union for Lanesborough, 1798-1800, before being returned for county Galway just before the demise of the Irish Parliament. He continued to represent the county at Westminster until 1812, joining opposition in 1805 in protest at government's failure to reward him with a much needed place, but otherwise acting as an idiosyncratic independent, and again from 1818, when he was elected as an acknowledged supporter of the Liverpool administration, although he remained a consistent advocate of Catholic claims.[5] In the House, where he had a habit of making short and acerbic interjections, he could be a surprisingly effective speaker. According to one description:

> Martin is not a very learned man, neither is he, in the language of the schools, eloquent, but he has a most winning way with him. He holds the House by the very test of the human race, laughter, and while their sides shake, their opposition is shaken and falls down at the same instant. There is a beautiful symmetry, a perfect keeping, as it were, in the whole man ... every limb of his body and every feature of his face is round and solid. He lets drive at the House like a bullet and the flag of truce is instantly flung out upon all sides.[6]

His pugnacious temperament and disarming wit produced a number of anecdotes, some of them possibly apocryphal. In one, he was supposed, on being interrupted by coughing, to have said that 'some honourable Member appears to be afflicted with a bad cold: I have no doubt I can cure his cough with a *single pill*'.[7] According to another, on being jeered with a satirical 'hare, hare', he crossed the floor and demanded to know the name of the culprit; but, when a City Member was surreptitiously pointed out, he contented himself by remarking, with a deliberately Irish intonation, 'Oh, it was only an alderman'. Unable to contain his penchant for humour and his delight in affecting an exaggerated brogue, he was often misunderstood as an inconsequential joker by his fellow Members and misreported in the press.[8] On one occasion, complaining to Nicholas Byrne of the *Morning Post* about being misrepresented in its columns, he deflated a tense confrontation by pointing to the offending passage and asking, 'Sir, did I ever spake in italics?'[9] On another, when he felt himself to have been lampooned, as he sometimes was, in being made to spout obvious nonsense sprinkled with indications of laughter, he (entirely unsuccessfully) forbade the reporter from *The Times* to cover his speeches under threat of bringing an official complaint before the parliamentary authorities.[10] So, in advancing the campaign with which his name became associated in the 1820s, Martin, who largely neglected his own affairs and had long since transferred the management of his Connemara estates to his eldest son Thomas, had to overcome handicaps of his own creating, as well as the ingrained prejudices of politicians and the public.

Having been awarded a commissionership of Irish fisheries, in breach of the pledge he had taken in 1812 not to accept office until Catholic relief had been granted, he was returned unopposed as a ministerialist at the general election of 1820, when he criticized the sanguinary nature of the criminal code.[11] He defended Charles Warren* against the attacks on him for adhering to government as the newly appointed chief justice of Chester, 1 June, but supported the clause to exclude Thomas Ellis, the anti-Catholic Member for Dublin, if he chose to continue as an Irish master in chancery, 30 June. He declared himself proud to be a party man, but backed Wilberforce's amendment to adjourn proceedings on the Queen Caroline affair, 7 June. He stated that George IV could not be expected to have to concede the restoration of her name to the liturgy, 22 June, when he presumably divided with ministers for Wilberforce's compromise motion, but on the 26th, when he remarked that government was bound to press on with the legal proceedings against the queen (and no doubt voted for the secret committee), he suggested that Caroline's name could be reinstated provided she accepted that the king's bargaining position was unchanged. Yet, he styled himself a friend of the queen, when commenting on how the foreign witnesses at her trial would be affected by the aliens bill, 10 July. He defended the size of the army as a safeguard against rebellion, 14 June, but was admonished by the Speaker for his contemptuous treatment of John Cam Hobhouse, Member for Westminster; and he objected to his colleague James Daly's motion for a select committee on the recent disturbances in Ireland, 28 June, when he denied that Galway was in a state of unrest. He gave evidence to the select committee on sheriffs' election expenses, of which he was a member, 19 June, and served on a handful of other Irish select committees during this Parliament.[12] He voted against Hume's motion for economies in revenue collection and criticized Sir James Mackintosh's capital felonies commutation bill because it reduced the punishment for mistreatment of animals, 4 July.[13] At a county Galway meeting, 19 Aug. 1820, he advocated precautionary security measures short of recourse to an insurrection bill and denied Daly's assertion that his intervention in the Commons had prevented him renewing the Act.[14]

Martin, whose attempt to promote a loyal address to the king in county Galway was thwarted early that year, joined ministers in opposing restoration of the queen's name to the liturgy, 26, 31 Jan., 13 Feb. (when he was locked out of the division), and voted against censuring their conduct towards her, 6 Feb. 1821.[15] He objected to the Grampound disfranchisement bill, 12, 13 Feb., 2, 19 Mar., spoke against Lambton's reform proposals, 17 Apr., and divided against disqualifying civil officers of the ordnance from voting in parliamentary elections, 12 Apr., and Russell's reform motion, 9 May.[16] He voted against repeal of the additional malt duty, 14 Feb, 3 Apr., Maberly's motion on the state of the revenue, 6 Mar., and reducing the grant for the adjutant-general's office, 11 Apr., when Hume, with whom he had clashed over the size of the army, 12, 15 Mar., and stamp receivers, 22 Mar., accused him of being willing to side with ministers no matter what financial measures they proposed.[17] He obtained leave for his bill to permit defence by counsel in cases of felony, 27 Feb., and presented it, 1 Mar., but it was negatived on its second reading, 30 Mar., while his Irish coroners bill, which he introduced on 23 Mar., also failed that session.[18] He spoke and voted for Catholic relief, 28 Feb., countered the objections of Lethbridge, Member for Somerset, 26 Mar., and insisted that he would respect his constituents' wishes in supporting the ensuing bill, even though under it Galway would be likely to return Catholic Members, 28 Mar. He brought up a petition from metropolitan coach proprietors against cruelty to horses, 9 May, complained of the post office's ill usage of them, 17 May, and presented the first reading of a bill to outlaw such practices, 18 May. He was a teller for receiving the report of the committee (by 34-31), 1 June, and again, after the House had divided 26-26, on the Speaker's casting vote, 14 June, and secured the third reading against repeated adjournment motions, 20, 25, 29 June. It was taken to the Lords (where it failed), 2 July, when, ever alert to such tactics, he suggested making cruelty to animals an offence under the poor relief bill.[19] He spoke for Mackintosh's forgery punishment mitigation bill, 23 May, 4 June, but only voted for it on the first occasion (unless the vote attributed to John Martin, Whig Member for Tewkesbury, on the second was in fact by him); he proposed his own measure on this subject, 21 June, but withdrew it because of the lateness of the session, 28 June.[20] He divided against omitting the arrears from the grant to the duke of Clarence, 18 June, and Hume's motion for economy and retrenchment, 27 June. At a levee in Dublin, 22 Aug. 1821, the king, who had been angered by his partial support for the queen, joyfully greeted Martin, who had been believed lost in the sinking of the *Earl of Moira* that month, and their friendship was resumed.[21]

Martin moved the address to Lord Wellesley on his appointment as lord lieutenant of Ireland at the county Galway meeting, 25 Feb. 1822, when he declared himself satisfied with the recent coercive legislation given the new viceroy's known pro-Catholic sentiments.[22] In April he wrote to Henry Goulburn, the Irish secretary, about his disagreement with Daly and the borough Member Michael Prendergast over the appointment of a new assistant barrister in their county and demanded 'an immediate decision on the question, which has kept me for upwards of two months, and deprived your friends during that time of my support'.[23] He spoke for the Catholic peers bill, 30 Apr., 10 May. He opposed abolition of one of the joint-postmasterships as an opposition ploy, 2 May, and thanked government for providing employment for the Irish poor, 17 May, when he condemned Hume for his lack of interest in this matter. He spoke against Thomas Spring Rice's Irish grand jury presentments bill, 21 May, and for Goulburn's Irish constables bill, 7 June.[24] He voted for Mackintosh's motion for reform of the criminal law, 4 June, but against James Abercromby's for censuring the conduct of the lord advocate relative to the Scottish press, 25 June. He spoke and voted against Sir John Newport's amendment for inquiry into Irish tithes, 19 June, and repeal of the salt duties, 28 June. He approved of the insurrection bill as it 'would not inflict any injury on the people of Ireland', 15 July, and voted for the Canada bill, 18 July, and the aliens bill, 19 July. He divided for the grant for printing proclamations in Irish newspapers, 22 July, when he complained of the partisan attacks made on him in the *Connaught Journal*. Having opposed the barilla duties bill because of its disadvantageous effects on local kelp producers, 29 July, he denied, amid opposition jeers, that he was a placeman, 31 July 1822.[25]

He obtained leave for his felons' counsel bill, 1 May, and his Irish coroners bill, 12 June, neither of which made progress that year, but he was successful with his cruelty to horses bill, which he reintroduced, 7 May 1822.[26] Known (because it specified a list of farm animals '... and other cattle') as the ill treatment of cattle bill, he moved its second reading (and was a teller for the majority of 29-18), 24 Mar., reported from the committee, 4 June, and secured its third reading against unexpected opposition, 7 June.[27] It received royal assent on 22 July and, as 'Martin's Act' (3 Geo. IV, c. 71), has long been acclaimed as the first legislative provision for the protection of animals in the civilized world. Martin, who had previously attempted to start prosecutions in order to raise public awareness, was swift to use the new law to bring convictions: on 9 Aug. 1822 he had two men from Smithfield Market taken before magistrates and had the satisfaction of seeing them each fined 20*s*.[28] Thereafter he was constantly on the prowl in the streets of London, remonstrating with wrongdoers, initiating unprecedented criminal proceedings, often as a principal, and almost single-handedly changing the climate of public opinion. These escapades not only involved him in occasionally violent altercations, but also brought him into frequent conflict with magistrates, who only with difficulty managed to keep him under control in court, and opened him to widespread popular ridicule. Yet his natural sensitivity was such that he was not infrequently led to appeal for lenient treatment towards those who genuinely repented of their cruelty and he sometimes even paid the fine of contrite but penniless offenders. Of the myriad of similar cases to which he was linked, the most iconic but misleading was that of the itinerant greengrocer Thomas Worster, who had chastised his donkey with an iron buckle at the end of a strap; Martin was inclined to forgive the offence, but Worster, who received a token fine, had brought the donkey along with him to prove it was uninjured and the story went round that Martin, who was sometimes depicted in cartoons with a pair of outsize ass's ears or riding on an ass, had brought it before the bench to be examined. Another affray, in which he knocked down a boy for refusing to stop beating his donkey with a stick, produced a sustained campaign against him in the press and Martin, who ultimately laughed it off as good publicity, was forced to take steps against the *Morning Chronicle* for reproducing a paragraph from *Blackwood's* which almost amounted to incitement to murder ('That Irish jackass Martin throws an air of ridicule over the whole matter by his insufferable idiotism. I hope to see his skull, thick as it is, cracked one of these days').[29] Although his subsequent legislative efforts to improve the condition of animals came to nothing, the implementation of his Act was in itself a major reform.

Martin, who carried another county Galway address to Wellesley, congratulating him on escaping unhurt from the Orange attack upon him in a Dublin theatre, in January 1823, was again reported to have been lost at sea in the *Alert* that spring, when the duke of Bedford commented that 'I am glad to see old Dick Martin of Galway is dead: he has long been a general nuisance, public and private'.[30] Martin, who voted against repeal of the Foreign Enlistment Act, 16 Apr., spoke for Catholic relief, 17 Apr., and denied improper involvement by priests in the recent county Dublin contest, 22 Apr., when he divided in the minority against inquiry into the legal proceedings against the Dublin Orange rioters.[31] He opposed parliamentary reform, but made the mischievous suggestion that Whig patrons could strengthen their case by voluntarily opening their boroughs of Knaresborough and Tavistock to demonstrate whether reform would work, 24 Apr., and he divided against alteration of the Scottish representative system, 2 June. He spoke and voted to end punishment by whipping, 30 Apr., and to abolish the death penalty for larceny, 21 May, and he divided silently to remove the capital penalty from cases of stealing from shops attached to houses, 25 June. He unsuccessfully moved for leave for a bill to prohibit bull-baiting and dog-fighting, 21 May, when, in reply to the frequent criticism that he sought to outlaw only poor men's sports, he answered in his usual pithy style that 'it was as much to say, that if 500 persons were cast upon a rock on a desolate island and all could not be saved, that the attempt should not be made to save any of them'. He forced a futile division against the committal of Daly's

Irish joint tenancy bill on the ground that it would disfranchise many Catholic 40*s.* freeholders, 27 May, and argued that the Irish tithes composition bill should include adequate compensation for the clergy, 30 May. He voted against inquiries into chancery administration, 5 June, and the currency, 12 June, and objected to Parnell's amendment for one into the state of the Ireland prior to the renewal of the Insurrection Act, 24 June. He justified the continued presence of a resident lord lieutenant in Dublin, 25 June, and branded the Irish Catholics' petition, complaining of partiality in the administration of justice, as inflammatory, 26 June 1823.

Martin, who promised to oppose Daly's Galway (borough) tolls bill that session, requested leave to bring in his Ill Treatment of Cattle Act amendment bill, 11 Feb. (when he also briefly called for a bill against bear-baiting); he obtained its first reading, 16 Feb., and overcame the opposition shown on the second reading, 9 Mar. 1824, but the bill was lost in the Lords.[32] Demonstrating that he had popular support, he presented petitions against cruelty to animals from Manchester, 24 Feb., Liverpool, 27 Feb., St. James's, 1 Apr., and Rotherham, 22 June, but gave up his motion for a select committee on this in the face of solid opposition, 26 Feb.[33] He voted against reform of the representation of Edinburgh, 26 Feb. (and 13 Apr. 1826). He divided against the abolition of flogging in the army, 5 Mar., a vote which he justified on the ground of maintaining discipline, 11 Mar., when he objected to the production of information on amnesties granted to ribbonmen. He was granted leave to bring in a bill to prevent unnecessary expenses in Irish legal prosecutions that day, and spoke and voted to permit defence by counsel in felony cases, 6 Apr., but failed to find a seconder for his motion to increase judges' salaries, 13 May.[34] The following day, when he attended the select committee on Ireland, he wrote to his friend Canning, the foreign secretary, in relation to the home secretary, that 'since Peel's conduct to me last night I begin to be in charity with him'.[35] He advocated his (unsuccessful) horses slaughtering bill, 4 June, and again sought leave for a bear-baiting bill, 9 June.[36] He voted against condemning the trial of the Methodist missionary John Smith in Demerara, 11 June, and for the Irish insurrection bill, 14 June. On 16 June 1824 he was present at the meeting, chaired by Thomas Buxton, Member for Weymouth, in *Old Slaughter's* coffee house in St. Martin's Lane, at which his Irish heartiness and determination were instrumental in carrying the decision to establish the Society for the Prevention of Cruelty to Animals (it received its royal imprimatur from Victoria in 1840). Although he always disclaimed being its founder, he was a stalwart in its early activities, including as a member of its subcommittee for inspecting the condition of slaughter houses, as he was in other good causes, such as the campaign for the abolition of colonial slavery.[37] While 'A Casuist from Connemara' criticized him for assisting the animal kingdom at the expense of neglecting his poor tenants, *The Times*, which accused him of being master of a vast army of bootless freeholders to whom he issued brogues only when driving them into vote at elections, called him a Brahmin for his apparent belief in the transmigration of souls: 'Only conceive for a moment', it commented in a rather too realistic satire, 'how Mr. Martin would look were he transformed into a huge, surly mastiff, chained to a kennel'.[38]

Martin, who was thought that year to have united his interest with Daly in order to preserve their seats and to bring his son Tom Martin† in for the borough, asked Canning to use his influence with his future son-in-law Lord Clanricarde against disturbing the peace of county Galway at the next election.[39] He had used his credibility as a long-standing advocate of their claims to warn the Catholics against resorting to excesses at a meeting of the Association, 25 Sept., and wrote to Canning, 1 Dec., that 'I mean to preserve the right of speaking to them, and I think I may be able to expose and put down that arch traitor [Daniel] O'Connell* and his gang', and again, 26 Dec. 1824, that

> we shall divide worse than on any former occasion on the Catholic question. This too will bring into great contempt the labours of the Catholic Parliament. I think however the argument in favour of emancipation stronger than ever as it will disappoint the expectations of the agitators.[40]

Having got up a pro-Catholic petition from the Protestants of his county early the following year, he again wrote to Canning, 5 Feb. 1825, to inform him that he had paid his Catholic rent and that, for electoral purposes, 'I take shame but I shall vote against the bill to put the Association down'.[41] Having vindicated the activities of the Association on the address, 4 Feb., he duly spoke against the Irish unlawful societies bill, 11 Feb., and voted in this sense, 15, 21, 25 Feb., the hypocrisy of which was not lost on Canning.[42] He divided for Catholic relief, 1 Mar., 21 Apr., 10 May, and defended the Irish franchise bill, 26 Apr., 9, 12 May, and the proposed state payments to Catholic priests, 29 Apr., as means to this end, though he believed neither was acceptable without emancipation, to which he again alluded on 26 May. He shocked the House by his graphic descriptions of the French surgeon Majendie's public dissections of live dogs in London, 24 Feb., and obtained leave (by 41-29) for his bear-baiting and dog-fighting bill that day, after receiving the backing of Buxton, who noted that there was 'much disposition to sneer at and make game of Martin'.[43] He presented the bill, 2 Mar., but, opposed by Peel and others, it was lost on its second reading (by 50-32), and he withdraw the notice for his motion for a select committee on bear-baiting, the session being too advanced, 23 June.[44] One of his bills to amend the Ill Treatment of Cattle Act was lost at the first attempt (by 33-23), 24 Mar., while another, for which he obtained leave on 6 May, was defeated by the attorney-general, Sir John Copley (by 27-18), 21 June, and yet another was briefly initiated, 28 June. He voted for the grant for the duke of Cumberland, 30 May, 10 June. He urged higher salaries for judges, 17 June, and threatened to divide the House on the merchant law bill, 28 June 1825.[45]

He congratulated Canning for having made some progress within the cabinet on the Catholic question that autumn and urged him to complete this victory by providing for Goulburn 'anywhere out of Ireland'. He assisted in efforts to prevent the promotion of pro-Catholic petitions in the forthcoming session, which was known to be the last before the general election, but his toadying attempts to secure Canning's backing as a restraining influence on Clanricarde in county Galway were met by stony silences and blank refusals.[46] On 8 Feb. 1826 he moved for leave for a bill to amend the Irish election laws by enabling freeholders to vote if they possessed a certificate showing their rent had been fully paid; this, he argued, would end the legal shenanigans associated with the registration process, though he admitted that it had no hope of being passed. He insisted that borough tolls, like those at Galway, were too high, 16 Feb., when he opposed extending the poor laws to Ireland, and he spoke and voted for the bill to disfranchise non-resident freemen in Irish boroughs, 9 Mar., when he approved of Rice's bill to improve local jurisdiction in corporations. He was a minority teller for his bear-baiting bill, 21 Feb., while another Ill Treatment of Cattle Act amendment bill, which he presented on 24 Feb., was defeated on its second reading, 16 Mar. He made another forlorn attempt to introduce a measure to prohibit cruelty to dogs, 20 Apr., when, as he had on 27 Feb., he squabbled with Hume. He divided for receiving the report on the salary of the president of the board of trade, 10 Apr., and, as one of the supposedly only two county Members in the ministerial majority, vigorously denied that he was a placeman, 27 Apr., when he opposed Lord John Russell's reform motion. He spoke and voted for George Lamb's bill to allow felons to be defended by counsel, 25 Apr., and proposed a law to prevent sick debtors having their lives put at risk by being removed to prison, 9 May. The most credibly pro-Catholic of the candidates spoken of for county Galway, Martin addressed his constituents in April to deny reports that he would retire at the dissolution and spoke at the Catholic Association in early June 1826, when he received O'Connell's endorsement. He duly stood again, as an opponent of Daly and James Lambert*, Clanricarde's nominee, at the general election that summer, when Tom Martin briefly canvassed Galway as an independent.[47] His bitter complaints to Canning about Clanricarde's use of government influence having fallen on deaf ears, Martin exposed the coalition against him on the hustings and, employing desperate measures to bring in his vote during a violent and expensive contest, he gradually overtook Lambert to be elected in second place behind Daly.[48] In a conciliatory letter to Canning on the morning of the declaration, 5 July, he commented that

> it never occurred to my waking thoughts or to my dreams, that either directly or indirectly you sanctioned any engagement entered into at this election. I write this from my bed after a very disturbed rest. At 3 o'clock this contest must terminate and I have to address the county at some length and to appear most joyous though I have not what will pay 10*s*. in the pound of what this contest must cost.[49]

He was bound over after quarrelling with his cousin John D'Arcy, whose tenants had voted for Lambert, 1 Aug., but attended the pro-Catholic gathering of the county's Catholics the following day, and that of its Protestants, 4 Sept. 1826.[50]

Martin complained of the absence of any mention of Ireland in the address, 21 Nov. 1826, when he presumably divided in the minority for Henry Grattan's amendment to this effect. He commented on the Arigna Mining Company affair, 5, 7, 8 Dec., and, on unfurling the several yards of signatures on the Tuam pro-Catholic petition on the 7th he declared, 'There, Sir ... the manner in which this petition is signed will prove that the Irish people are not so ignorant as they are said to be'.[51] Petitions against his return on the grounds of personation and intimidation having been lodged, 4 Dec. 1826, he again failed to enlist Canning's assistance that month, but in January 1827 he issued an address expressing his determination to persist.[52] Giving grudging support to Lord Althorp's resolutions on electoral bribery, 26 Feb., he launched a furious pre-emptive attack against Clanricarde, but he succeeded only in raising the laughter of the House. He denied, as previously, that the Catholic clergy were guilty of any improper conduct in the recent elections, 5 Mar., when he stated that 'the Catholic interest sent him to Parliament in opposition to the influence of government, in whose service he had grown grey and to whom he had given his vote for 40 years'. Alluding to the original intention to grant Catholic claims at the time of the Union, he said that day that 'emancipation was a debt due from the government to the people of Ireland', and he voted for this, 6 Mar. He gave notice of a motion for inquiry into Clanricarde's role in the Galway election, 8 Mar., and insisted on proceeding with it, 13 Mar., but nothing transpired on the 15th, perhaps partly because Peel, who doubted that Canning would have taken offence over it, refused to get involved.[53] His last known vote was in the minority for Brownlow's motion for information on the Orange procession and Lisburn magistrates, 29 Mar. He had failed in his bid to drag Clanricarde before the election committee and, having already travelled to Dover, whence he would abscond to the continent to avoid being arrested for debt once his parliamentary immunity was lifted, he was unseated on 11 Apr.[54] Nothing came of his petition complaining of Clanricarde's conduct, which was brought up by his old enemy, Hume, 13 June 1827.[55] As the son of the revered 'Colonel Martin', Tom was considered a suitably popular candidate for the Wellington ministry to put up against Richard Sheil* and the influence of the Catholic Association in the summer of 1828, when it was thought that Daly's proposed peerage would create a vacancy; the Irish secretary Leveson Gower remarked at that time to the premier that 'it is impossible, I am sure, to commit yourself in any way whatever with the father', who was, indeed, given the brush-off by Peel on his attempting to interfere.[56] It was rumoured that he would canvass the town at the election of 1830, when his son did offer for the county, but Martin, who the following November welcomed the prospect of a limited and constitutional measure of parliamentary reform from the newly appointed Grey ministry, never sat again.[57]

Martin, who was thought to have twice refused a peerage, wrote to the Society for the Prevention of Cruelty to Animals in 1832 giving advice about a bill to amend his famous Act and continued his indefatigable efforts to stamp out unthinking brutality even in exile at Boulogne; the story is told of a young Englishman, who, on being collared by him for giving his mount a wanton beating on the seafront, was prepared to show his resentment by challenging him to a duel, only to recoil and apologize when he was informed of the notorious name of his assailant. According to the Society's secretary Lewis Gompertz's account of his death in January 1834, Martin's 'anxiety to comfort the minds of his affectionate family, and that his favourite dog should be taken care of, are truly characteristic of the man whose motives were so pure'.[58] To the journalist William Jerdan, who was once shown Martin's duelling scars ('not very pleasant to receive or to look at'), he was, as an amalgam of courage, charisma and drollery, 'an Irishman all over':

> With all his eccentricities, Dick Martin was gifted with an abundant fund of sound common sense. His observation was acute and his conversation agreeable, polite and entertaining ... He was nearly, if not quite, the last of his species – a remarkable, an extravagant, a strange, but not what is commonly called a bad man.[59]

Indeed, apart from his son and heir Thomas Barnewall Martin (1786-1847),[60] Liberal Member for county Galway from 1832 until his death from famine fever in 1847, whose only child, the novelist Mary Laetitia (*d.* 1850), witnessed the enforced sale of their estates, he was the last of the Irish branch of the family. Maria Edgeworth, who experienced the 'brusque cordiality and hospitality' offered by Tom, another larger than life Connemara gentleman, at Ballynahinch, 'a white-washed, dilapidated mansion ... very low and ruinous ... with a cow house and pig sty and dunghill adjoining', on a visit in 1834, reported to her brother about the lately deceased proprietor, that 'I once saw him, and remember that my blood crept slow and my breath was held when he first came into the room, a pale little insignificant-looking mortal he was, but he still kept his hold of my imagination'.[61] Gallant and impetuous, generous to a fault and remarkable as a fighter of lost causes, he was said to be the model for the character of uncle Godfrey O'Malley in Lever's *Charles O'Malley* (1841). Almost unique among the reformers of his day for being neither an Evangelical Tory of the type of Buxton or Wilberforce, nor a socially advanced liberal of the style of Hume or Mackintosh, still less an Irish radical like O'Connell or Sheil, his achievements could nevertheless be said to rank nearly as high as theirs.[62] As the parliamentary reporter Samuel Carter Hall later recorded, he was a

> short, thick-set man, with evidence in look and manner, even in step and action, of indomitable resolution. He blundered his way into a reform, blessed in its influences and mighty in its results ... Thus the wild, energetic, heedless and usually unreasoning Irishman is for this Act classed, and rightly so, among the benefactors of his country and all the countries of the Old World and the New.[63]

[1] Based on S. Lynam, *Humanity Dick: Biog. of Richard Martin MP* (1975); P. Phillips, *Humanity Dick: Eccentric Member for*

Galway (2003). See also *Oxford DNB*; S. Farrell, 'Richard Martin: Humanity Dick', *History Today*, liv (June 2004), 60. [2] *Convert Rolls* ed. E. O'Byrne, 195. [3] Phillips, 88-89, 100. [4] E.G. Fairholme and W. Pain, *A Century of Work for Animals*, 47-48. [5] *Hist. Irish Parl.* v. 196-9; *HP Commons, 1790-1820*, iv. 562-5. [6] Fairholme and Pain, 27-28. [7] Hants RO, Carnarvon mss 75M91, Howard to Lady Porchester, 16 Feb. 1831. [8] Lynam, 183-4, 197, 258; Phillips, 48-49, 146, 153-4, 156. [9] W. Jerdan, *Men I have Known*, 317-18. [10] See, e.g., *The Times*, 12 July 1820, 11 May 1821; Lynam, 210-11. [11] Add. 40296, f. 40; 40297, f. 29; 40298, f. 21; *Dublin Evening Post*, 14 Mar., 4 Apr. 1820; *Black Bk.* (1823), 176. [12] *PP* (1820), iii. 279-80. [13] *The Times*, 5 July 1820. [14] *Dublin Evening Post*, 31 Aug. 1820. [15] *Dublin Weekly Reg.* 27 Jan. 1821. [16] *The Times*, 14 Feb., 20 Mar. 1821. [17] Ibid. 13, 23 Mar., 12 Apr. 1821. [18] Ibid. 2, 24 Mar. 1821. [19] Ibid. 10, 18 May, 2, 15, 21, 26, 30 June, 3 July 1821. [20] Ibid. 22, 29 June 1821. [21] Lynam, 202-3. [22] *Dublin Evening Post*, 28 Feb. 1822. [23] Add. 37299, f. 68. [24] *The Times*, 22 May 1822. [25] Ibid. 23, 30 July, 1 Aug. 1822. [26] Ibid. 2, 8 May, 13 June 1822. [27] *CJ*, lxxvii. 242, 243, 297, 320, 327, 446. [28] *The Times*, 12 Aug. 1822; Fairholme and Pain, 25-32. [29] Fairholme and Pain, 34-43; M. D. George, *Cat. of Pol. and Personal Satires*, x. 14674, 14798-9; Lynam, 207-9, 219-25, 246-7, 251-60; Phillips, 166-73. [30] *Dublin Evening Post*, 14, 16 Jan.; Add. 51663, Bedford to Holland, 27 Mar. 1823. [31] *The Times*, 23 Apr. 1823. [32] *Connaught Jnl.* 23 Feb. 1824. [33] *The Times*, 28 Feb., 2 Apr., 23 June 1824. [34] Ibid. 12 Mar. 1824. [35] Harewood mss WYL 250/8/87. [36] *The Times*, 10 June 1824. [37] Fairholme and Pain, 49-50, 54-58, 173; Lynam, 211-12, 231-2, 250. [38] *Dublin Evening Mail*, 9 July; *The Times*, 16 July, 9 Oct. 1824. [39] *Connaught Jnl.* 24 June, 13, 20 Sept.; Harewood mss 8/87, Martin to Canning, 25 Nov. 1824. [40] Lynam, 238-9; Harewood mss 8/87. [41] *Connaught Jnl.* 10 Jan., 10 Feb. 1825; Harewood mss 8/87. [42] *Canning Official Corresp.* i. 242, 246. [43] *Buxton Mems.* 176. [44] *The Times*, 24 June 1825. [45] Ibid. 18, 29 June 1825. [46] Harewood mss 8/87, Martin to Canning, 26 Sept., 2 Oct., 21 Dec. 1825, 28 Jan., 17, 18 Feb. Mar. 1826, replies, 22 Dec. 1825, 2, 3 Mar. 1826. [47] *Dublin Evening Post*, 15 Apr., 18 May, 10, 13 June; *Connaught Jnl.* 20 Apr., 18, 25, 29 May, 5, 12 June 1826. [48] Harewood mss 8/87, Martin to Canning, 9, 16, 25 June, replies, 19, 30 June; *Connaught Jnl.* 22, 29 June, 3, 6 July 1826. [49] Harewood mss 8/87. [50] *Dublin Evening Post*, 1, 3 Aug., 9 Sept. 1826. [51] *The Times*, 6, 8, 9 Dec. 1826. [52] *CJ*, lxxxii. 61-65; Harewood mss 8/87, Martin to Canning, 12 Dec., reply, 15 Dec. 1826; *Dublin Evening Post*, 18 Jan. 1827. [53] *The Times*, 9 Mar. 1827; Add. 40392, ff. 242-7, 250-1. [54] *Dublin Evening Mail*, 6 Apr.; *Dublin Evening Post*, 10, 14 Apr. 1827; *PP* (1826-7), iv. 955, 993. [55] *CJ*, lxxxii. 555; *Connaught Jnl.* 18 June 1827. [56] Add. 40334, f. 246; 40297, ff. 91, 223; Wellington mss WP1/938/12; 949/10. [57] *Connaught Jnl.* 19 July; Brougham mss, Martin to Brougham, 25 Nov. 1830. [58] Fairholme and Pain, 43-44, 48; *The Times*, 10 Jan.; *Dublin Evening Post*, 14 Jan. 1834; *Gent. Mag.* (1834), i. 554-5. [59] Jerdan, 312-17, 320. [60] Not to be confused with Thomas Byam Martin*. [61] M. Edgeworth, *Tour in Connemara* (1950), 4, 39, 44, 66, 80, 111; *Oxford DNB*. [62] Fairholme and Pain, 45-46, 49; E.S. Turner, *All Heaven in a Rage*, 125-34; Lynam, 273-83; Phillips, 121, 123, 199-201. [63] S.C. Hall, *Retrospect of a Long Life*, i. 227, 229.

S.M.F.

MARTIN, Sir Thomas Byam (1773–1854), of 8 Somerset Place, Mdx.

PLYMOUTH 1818–1832

b. 26 July 1773,[1] 4th but 3rd surv. s. of Henry Martin† (*d.* 1794) of Little Farm, nr. Tooting, Surr. and Elizabeth Anne, da. of Harding Parker of Passage West, co. Cork. *educ.* by Mr. Batchelor, Freshford, nr. Bath 1780; Southampton g.s. 1781; by Mr. Coles, Guildford 1782; Portsmouth naval acad. 1785. *m.* 22 Aug. 1798,[2] Catherine, da. of Robert Fanshawe† of Stone Hall, nr. Plymouth, Devon, commr. of Plymouth dockyard, 3s. (1 *d.v.p.*) 3da. KCB 2 Jan. 1815; GCB 3 Mar. 1830. *d.* 21 Oct. 1854.

Entered RN 1786, lt. 1790, cdr. 1793, capt. 1793, r.-adm. 1811, v.-adm. 1819, adm. 1830, v.-adm. of UK 1847-9, adm. of the fleet 1849-*d.*

Controller of navy 1816-31.

Martin, who inherited £3,000 from his father in 1794,[3] served with distinction throughout the French wars and was appointed controller of the navy at £2,000 a year in 1816. He was elected for Plymouth on the admiralty interest in 1818 and was returned unopposed with Sir William Congreve in 1820, when he declared himself to be 'sincerely and ardently attached to the constitution'.[4] He gave steady support to Lord Liverpool's ministry in the 1820 Parliament, speaking in defence of the naval estimates. He maintained that, contrary to radical complaints, the government was more open to the charge that it had been 'too hasty in diminishing the strength of our navy', 9 June 1820. He offered explanations concerning seamen's wages, 6 Feb., private contracts for the disposal of old stores, 20 Feb., the working hours of dockyard employees, 4 May, and the 'great danger' of postponing ship repairs, 7 May 1821.[5] He divided against Catholic claims, 28 Feb. 1821, 30 Apr. 1822, 1 Mar. (as a pair), 21 Apr., 10 May, and the Irish franchise bill, 26 Apr. 1825. He presented constituency petitions against the corn averages bill, 26 Mar. 1821, the coastwise coal duty, 9 Feb. 1824, and in favour of the debtor and creditor bill, 10 Apr. 1826.[6] He pointed to the large reduction in the naval estimates and claimed that the opposition was 'quibbling about trifles', 18 Mar. 1822. He declared that 'the British navy had never been in a more efficient state than ... at the present moment', 14 Mar.,[7] and defended the system of promotion, which was 'unconnected with parliamentary influence', 19 June 1823. He asserted that there was 'less dry rot in the navy at present than at any former period', 20 Feb. 1824, and argued that it would be impossible to carry out the work of the navy office with fewer staff, 21 Feb. 1825.[8] At the general election of 1826 he was again returned unopposed for Plymouth.[9]

He 'utterly denied' that the unpopularity of naval service made impressment necessary, 13 Feb. 1827. He divided against Catholic claims, 6 Mar., and presented a hostile Plymouth petition, 16 Mar.,[10] when he voted for the Clarence annuity bill. He divided with Canning's ministry against the disfranchisement of Penryn, 28 May, 7 June 1827. He warned that the service would suffer if the grant for seamen was delayed any longer, 12 Feb. 1828, but thought the debate provided an opportunity for 'correcting the exaggerations' of Hume; he was a teller for the Wellington ministry's majority against reduction. He maintained that great progress had been made in reducing naval salaries, 16 May, and voted against reducing that of the lieutenant-general of the ordnance, 4 July. He divided against repeal of the Test Acts, 26 Feb., and paired against Catholic claims, 12 May. He voted against the Whig motion condemning delays in chancery, 24 Apr. 1828. In February 1829 Planta, the patronage secretary, predicted that he would side 'with government' on Catholic emancipation, and he voted accordingly, 6, 30 Mar. He said he was at a loss to know when the navy estimates would be low enough to satisfy Hume, 27 Feb., and argued that comparisons with the position in 1792 were misleading because of 'the immense increase of business' in the navy departments and the effects of high food prices on dockyard wages. He presented petitions from Plymouth tradesmen against renewal of the East India Company's charter, 28 Apr. 1829, 12 Feb. 1830. He voted against transferring East Retford's seats to Birmingham, 11 Feb., Lord Blandford's reform motion, 18 Feb., the enfranchisement of Birmingham, Leeds and Manchester, 23 Feb. and the Galway franchise bill, 25 May. He strongly refuted the implication in a pamphlet published by Sir Henry Parnell, chairman of the finance committee, that he and the navy board had obstructed admiralty attempts to achieve economies, 26 Feb., and claimed that the estimates would 'reflect credit upon the government for its moderation', 26 Mar. He presented Plymouth petitions against the death penalty except for murder, 17 Mar., and the death penalty for forgery, 26 Apr., and voted in this sense, 7 June. He divided against Jewish emancipation, 17 May 1830. At the general election that summer he was returned unopposed for Plymouth with Sir George Cockburn, a lord of the admiralty.[11]

Ministers of course listed Martin among their 'friends' and he voted with them in the crucial civil list division, 15 Nov. 1830, but he remained in office when Lord Grey's ministry was formed. However, he privately complained that he was 'much harassed by the disingenuous conduct' of the new first lord of the admiralty, Sir James Graham, who 'from political animosity towards those who are gone out has made me in a great degree personally the object of an attack ably drawn up but full of acrimony and ill-intended views', which would 'no doubt come before Parliament although he has told me he does not intend to force it forward'.[12] Following Graham's intimation of a scheme of naval reorganization, 25 Feb., Martin defended the navy board's practice of applying money voted by Parliament for specific purposes to other branches of the service where needed, and on 25 Mar. 1831 he urged the minister to refute the 'scandalous and slanderous falsehood' in the newspapers that improper use had been made of public money; he was only partially successful. He dutifully voted for the second reading of the government's reform bill, 22 Mar., and against Gascoyne's wrecking amendment, 19 Apr. 1831. At the ensuing dissolution he declined Graham's suggestion that he should stand for Plymouth with a government candidate against Cockburn and stated that he could not pledge himself to an unqualified support of ministerial measures, claiming that he was 'no party man' and that his office had 'never been changed with the change of ministers'. He subsequently rejected a request for him to stand down in favour of the government candidate and retain his office without a seat (a solution approved of by his old naval friend William IV), although letters to his wife suggest that he might have accepted this arrangement had he not felt irrevocably committed to his supporters at Plymouth. He was clearly anxious about the heavy expense of a contested election and, according to his son, was 'at times very much out of sorts' and needed encouragement to 'keep him up to the mark'. He publicly promised to support the 'principle of reform' but 'would not consent to be bound hand and foot' to 'any measure which might be proposed', hinting that he considered the £10 borough franchise qualification too low and that the rights of freemen's sons should be protected. He was returned at the head of the poll, despite the fact that government influence was turned against him.[13] He afterwards wrote that he did not consider it necessary to resign his office immediately but that he would 'gladly take the first opening to make my escape, with as little damage in point of income as may be consistent with a due consideration of ... character and credit'.[14]

He voted for the second reading of the reintroduced reform bill, 6 July, but Graham complained of his 'perpetual absence' from the divisions in committee;[15] he paired for the bill's passage, 21 Sept. 1831. The final straw for ministers was his refusal to attend the division on Lord Ebrington's confidence motion, 10 Oct., and the king reluctantly consented to his dismissal a week later. He reportedly retired with a pension of £830 in addition to his half-pay of two guineas a day.[16] He was absent from the division on the second reading of the revised reform bill, 17 Dec. 1831, but voted against the enfranchisement of Tower Hamlets, 28 Feb., the third reading, 22 Mar., the second reading of the Irish bill, 25 May, and for the preservation of

Irish freemen's rights, 2 July 1832. He was alarmed by the state of the country during the constitutional crisis in May and relieved when Grey and his colleagues returned to office, believing that there would otherwise have been 'an immediate explosion', such was the 'desire of the lower orders to come to blows'.[17] He defended the old navy board against Graham's charges of disobedience and obstruction, 14 Feb., and said his navy civil departments bill was 'aiming at economy, and overlooking much more important matters'. He made detailed criticisms of the measure, 27 Feb., declaring that he could 'conceive nothing more completely at variance with every known principle of utility and simplicity' and warning against the 'introduction of machinery which will be utterly incapable of working in time of war'. On 6 Apr. he observed that 'we are putting down that system which ... had been maintained throughout all the naval glory and success of this ... country', expressed the 'earnest hope ... that England may outlive this insanity' and supported Cockburn's proposed alternative scheme. He added that his dismissal had come as a relief, since he had 'no desire to associate with the present government' and 'did not think that the policy they were pursuing was calculated to promote the interests of the country'. He 'heard with great astonishment' Graham's statement regarding the appointment of a surveyor of the navy who had 'no practical knowledge of the building of a ship', 29 June. He 'heartily agreed' with a ship owners' petition against the Gravesend pier bill, 10 Apr., and moved to reject the third reading; he was defeated by 41-26, acting as a teller. He voted for reduction of the sugar duties, 7 Mar., Baring's bill to exclude insolvent debtors from Parliament, 27 June, and against government on the Russian-Dutch loan, 12 July 1832.

At the general election of 1832 Martin, 'contrary to expectation', offered again for Plymouth, which had been opened by the Reform Act, in the hope that 'the intelligent electors' would 'join ... in the moderated feeling fast spreading through the country'. He repeated his 'determination never to degrade myself, or the Parliament, by going there pledged to the support of any specific measures', but admitted that his prospects were 'less cheering' and withdrew before the poll.[18] In 1833 he declined the post of commander-in-chief in the Mediterranean owing to his 'great mistrust in the ... government, and more particularly ... Graham', and to the 'probability of being obliged to call upon the government for a greater force than a miserable reformed Parliament would have the spirit or the patriotism to allow'.[19] He died in October 1854 and left an estate at Grovewich, near Wantage, Berkshire, to his eldest son, Admiral Sir William Fanshawe Martin (1801-95), who succeeded a cousin to the Martin baronetcy in 1863.[20]

[1] Add. 41364, f. 23; *Oxford DNB* states 25 July. [2] IGI (Devon). [3] PROB 11/1248/424. [4] *Trewman's Exeter Flying Post*, 16 Mar. 1820. [5] *The Times*, 7, 21 Feb., 5, 8 May 1821. [6] Ibid. 27 Mar. 1821, 10 Feb. 1824, 11 Apr. 1826. [7] Ibid. 15 Mar. 1823. [8] Ibid. 22 Feb. 1825. [9] *Alfred*, 13 June 1826. [10] *The Times*, 17 Mar. 1827. [11] *R. Devonport Telegraph*, 31 July, 7 Aug. 1830. [12] Add. 41368, ff. 5-10. [13] *Martin Letters* (Navy Recs. Soc. xix), 239-62; Add. 41368, ff. 40, 56, 58, 67, 71-72; *Plymouth Herald*, 30 Apr., 7 May 1831. [14] Add. 41368, f. 87. [15] Sir James Graham mss (IHR microfilm XR80), Graham to Grey, 28 July 1831. [16] *Holland House Diaries*, 69-70; *Martin Letters*, 262-5; *Plymouth Herald*, 29 Oct. 1831. [17] Add. 41369, ff. 7-9. [18] Ibid. f. 14; *Woolmer's Exeter and Plymouth Gazette*, 1, 15 Dec. 1832. [19] *Martin Letters*, 110-17. [20] PROB 11/2200/844; IR26/2005/982.

T.A.J.

MASSEH LOPES (formerly **LOPES**), **Sir Manasseh**, 1st bt. (1755–1831), of Maristow House, Devon; Market Place, Westbury, Wilts. and 3 Arlington Street, Mdx.

NEW ROMNEY	1802–1806
EVESHAM	1807–22 Feb. 1808
BARNSTAPLE	1812–9 Mar. 1819
WESTBURY	29 Nov. 1820–23 Feb. 1829

b. 27 Jan. 1755, in Jamaica, o.s. of Mordecai Rodriguez Lopes and Rebecca, da. of Manasseh Pereira of Jamaica. *m.* 19 Oct. 1795, Charlotte, da. of John Yeates of Mon., 2da. (1 *d.v.p.*). *suc.* fa. 1796; *cr.* bt. 5 Oct. 1805;[1] took name of Masseh before Lopes by royal lic. 15 Oct. 1805. *d.* 26 Mar. 1831.

Sheriff, Devon 1810-11; recorder, Westbury 1810-*d.*

Dir. Rock Life Assurance Office 1808-13.

Lt.-col. commdt. Roborough vols. 1803, 4 Devon militia 1808.

Masseh Lopes, an ill-fated Sephardic Jew turned Christian, was much ridiculed as the caricature of a corrupt boroughmonger, whose miserliness and naivety led to the frustration of his better intentions and the destruction of his electoral ambitions. Several versions exist of a telling anecdote, in which, moved to give financial assistance to a pauper, he was nevertheless impelled to offer to cash his own bank draft, so that, as Greville put it, 'he gave the money, but first calculated and deducted the discount, thus at once exercising his benevolence and his avarice'.[2] Having inherited his father's Jamaican sugar fortune in 1796,[3] purchased a large Devon estate two years later, and bought his first seat in Parliament in 1802, he received a baronetcy from Pitt, but never secured acceptance by the political establishment. In 1810 he acquired the borough of Westbury, where, as recorder, he subordinated the exercise of the burgage franchise to the small corporation and returned supporters of the Liverpool administration.[4] Yet his interests in other constituencies were thwarted, and he was unseated from the representation of Evesham in 1808, and in 1819 from Barnstaple, where he had indulged in blatant electoral bribery. It was, however, for his notorious indiscretions at Grampound that, on 13 Nov. 1819, king's bench handed down an exemplary sentence of two years' imprisonment and a fine of £10,000.[5] Giving details of a later legal case, brought by Masseh Lopes against a neighbouring mining company from which he drew considerable profits, *The Times* commented that he 'is a baronet: he possesses immense wealth and he has acquired respect and consideration on account of his rank and property exactly in the same proportion which he has maintained the one and made proper use of the other'.[6]

As he had promised, Lord John Russell, who soon secured the disfranchisement of Grampound, moved for an address to the king to shorten the duration of Masseh Lopes's sentence, 11 July 1820, arguing that his age and poor health warranted mitigation of the severity of the punishment. Walter Burrell, the Sussex Member, added that following the death of one of his daughters in 1819,[7] he was 'overwhelmed with domestic affliction, which, with his confinement, had made a deep impression on his health and constitution, and brought him near to the grave'. Several Tories objected to the proposed precedent of overturning the sentence and, after Lord Castlereagh, the foreign secretary, had told the House that it could not interfere with the king's prerogative of mercy, Russell followed the advice of Canning, the president of the India board, and withdrew the motion rather than prejudice the matter further. Masseh Lopes's nephew and heir Ralph Franco* then privately asked the prime minister, Lord Liverpool, for clemency, as 'my uncle's is a case truly worthy of the most humane consideration':

> I do it not to create an effect when I state that, eye-witness as I have been of all his sufferings, there has been no one part more truly hurtful to himself and more painful to those around him, than the unceasing agitation of mind to which a state of suspense and uncertainty has subjected him, so that next to an actual release, the earliest possible intimation of what he may venture to expect, would be a greater relief and kindness than I can possibly describe.[8]

On the advice of ministers, Masseh Lopes was released in September 1820, after serving less than a year of his sentence.[9] It was alleged by radicals, who condemned Whig support for his case, that he had threatened to withdraw the stopgap pro-government Members for Westbury, but had come to a deal whereby he would relinquish one of the seats to ministers in exchange for his freedom.[10] He had himself returned unopposed for Westbury, with the Bristol merchant Philip John Miles, at a by-election later that year.

Not surprisingly, Masseh Lopes was inactive in the House, where he continued to give ministers his silent support.[11] He was not listed as having voted on Catholic relief, 28 Feb. 1821. The Lords requested his attendance, 6 Apr. 1821, to give evidence on the Grampound disfranchisement bill, which passed that session, but he apparently did not do so.[12] He voted against the Catholic peers bill, 30 Apr. 1822, and repeal of the Foreign Enlistment Act, 16 Apr. 1823. He divided to abolish the usury laws, 8 Feb., and was given three weeks' leave on urgent private business, 18 Feb. 1825. He voted against Catholic relief, 21 Apr. He presumably persisted in his forlorn hopes of electoral empire building, and was prosecuted in common pleas for reneging on his promise to pay the legal expenses of the independent interest in East and West Looe, 10 Dec. 1825, when Serjeant Thomas Wilde* observed that he was

> well known to the public as a Member of Parliament, and one who took a very particular interest in the affairs of certain boroughs, and supporting what were alleged to be the rights of particular persons who claimed a right of voting in those boroughs. Whether Sir M. Lopes's interference was dictated purely by the spirit of patriotism, or whether he wished to secure the *gratitude* of those individuals, he would not say, but certain it was that whatever was his motive, he had shown himself very active in the affairs of the boroughs of East and West Looe.[13]

He voted to receive the report on the salary of the president of the board of trade, 10 Apr. 1826. He again returned himself for Westbury, this time with the Canningite Sir George Warrender, at the general election that year. He was granted a month's sick leave, 21 Feb. 1827. His last known vote was against the second reading of the corn bill, 2 Apr. 1827. No trace of parliamentary activity has been found for the 1828 session.

He attended the Devon Protestant county meeting, 16 Jan. 1829, but apparently stood on the pro-Catholic side.[14] In February he was listed by Planta, the Wellington ministry's patronage secretary, as likely to side 'with government' on Catholic emancipation. Later that month he resigned his seat to accommodate Peel, the home secretary, after his defeat at Oxford University, and he proposed him at the ensuing by-election, 2 Mar. He only narrowly maintained control of his interest and had the windows of his house broken.[15] A radical newspaper noted that the

> populace assembled in the hope of receiving some of the worthy baronet's money, arrested him in his progress and, though he threw among them some handfuls of silver, yet, not satisfied with this proof of his *liberality*, some able-bodied men in frock-smocks bore him back again to the entrance to the hall, that he might start afresh and give them a better proof of his *bounty*.[16]

Masseh Lopes was paid £7,000,[17] and eventually secured a consulship for a relative from Peel, who complained to Planta, 'what a torment this Jew is!' Peel balked, however, at granting his request for an English peerage, though the *Devizes Gazette*, 26 Mar. 1829, retailed a rumour that he was be created Lord Roborough (the name of another of his Devon seats), and commented that 'we presume this is an abbreviation of Rottenborough'.[18]

At the general election of 1830 Masseh Lopes returned ministerial candidates for Westbury. Early the following year he became dangerously ill with paralysis and lost the use of his faculties. He died in March 1831. An obituary notice recorded that 'with many eccentricities in minor things, he possessed much excellence of character and benevolence of heart, and his loss will be lamented by his numerous tenantry and dependants'.[19] By his will, dated 21 Nov. 1829, he made provision for his wife, who died in March 1833, and gave bequests to many of his relatives. He left the bulk of his estate, which was estimated to be worth about £800,000, including land in Devon, Somerset and Wiltshire, East India stock and South Sea annuities, and personal wealth sworn under £160,000, to Franco, who succeeded as 2nd baronet and changed his name to Lopes.[20]

[1] *London Gazette*, 1-5 Oct. 1805. [2] C. Redding, *50 Years' Recollections* (1858), i. 158-62; *Devizes Gazette*, 24 Nov. 1825; *Greville Mems.* ii. 58. [3] PROB 11/1272/134. [4] Sir R.C. Hoare, *Wilts.* Westbury, 6. [5] *The Times*, 15 Nov. 1819; *HP Commons, 1790-1820*, ii. 60-61; iv. 455-7. [6] *The Times*, 29 July 1827. [7] Ibid. 28 June 1819. [8] Add. 38286, ff. 98, 117. [9] *Gent. Mag.* (1820), ii. 269. [10] *Black Bk.* (1823), 171, 177; *Cobbett's Rural Rides* ed. G.D.H. and M. Cole, i. 118, 121, 137. [11] *Black Bk.* (1823), 171; *Session of Parl. 1825*, p. 473. [12] *Lords Sess. Pprs.* cxxvii. 1. [13] *The Times*, 12 Dec. 1825. [14] *Western Times*, 17 Jan. 1829. [15] Add. 40399, ff. 25, 27; *Peel Mems.* i. 342; Parker, *Peel*, ii. 104; W.G. Hoskins and H.P.R. Finberg, *Devon Studs.* 414-18. [16] *Keenes' Bath Jnl.* 9 Mar. 1829. [17] Glos. RO, Sotheron Estcourt mss D1571 X114, Long to Bucknall Estcourt, 3 Mar. 1829. [18] Add. 40312, ff. 65, 73, 74; 40399, ff. 361, 370, 371, 374. [19] *Salisbury Jnl.* 28 Mar., 4 Apr.; *Western Times*, 2 Apr. 1831. [20] PROB 11/1785/283; IR26/1263/214; *Gent. Mag.* (1831), i. 465-6; (1833), i. 379; *DNB*; *Oxford DNB*.

S.M.F.

MASSY (afterwards **MASSY DAWSON**), **James Hewitt** (1779–1834), of Ballynacourte, co. Tipperary and 87 Gloucester Place, Mdx.

CLONMEL	1820–2 Jan. 1830
CO. LIMERICK	3 May 1830–1830

b. 13 Sept. 1779, 1st s. of Hon. James Massy Dawson of Dublin and Ballynacourte and Mary, da. of John Leonard of Carha, co. Galway and Brownestown, co. Kildare. *educ.* Exeter, Oxf. 1796. *m.* 11 Mar. 1800, Eliza Jane, da. of Francis Dennis of Jamaica, 5s. 7da. *suc.* fa. 1790. Took additional name of Dawson by royal lic. 4 Apr. 1827. *d.* 2 Oct. 1834.

Massy described his Tipperary family as having 'been for many generations highly considered and respected as well for their loyalty as property and character'.[1] His father, the second son of Hugh Massy, 1st Baron Massy, had assumed the additional surname of Dawson on succeeding to the substantial estates of his mother Mary Dawson, the daughter and heiress of James Dawson of Ballynacourte. At the 1820 general election Massy came forward for Clonmel as the nominee of its patron William Bagwell, Member for county Tipperary, whose nomination he had proposed. He was returned unopposed.[2] A lax and mostly silent attender, when present he generally supported the Liverpool ministry, who incorrectly listed him as Bagwell's 'brother-in-law'.[3] It was certainly he, rather than George Dawson, who joined Bagwell in voting 'with opposition' against the appointment of an additional Scottish baron of exchequer, 15 May 1820.[4] He divided with ministers on their conduct of the Queen Caroline affair, 6 Feb. 1821. He voted for Catholic claims, 28 Feb. 1821. He divided against repeal of the additional malt duty, 3 Apr. 1821. He welcomed a motion for inquiry into the poor relief scheme of Robert Owen, which had not received the 'attention which any proposition for the improvement of the country deserved', 26 June 1821. He voted against further tax reductions, 21 Feb. 1822, 18 Mar. 1823, but with opposition for military economies, 1 Mar. 1822. He divided against parliamentary reform, 20 Feb. 1823. He voted for the grant for Irish churches and glebe houses, 11 Apr. He divided against ministers for inquiry into the prosecution of the Dublin Orange rioters, 22 Apr., and was probably the 'H. Dawson' who spoke in their defence, 26 May 1823. He presented a petition for Irish freemasons to be placed 'in the same situation' as those of England, 5 May, and brought up constituency petitions for Catholic claims, 24 May, and against negro slavery, 27 May.[5] He divided against condemnation of the trial in Demerara of the Methodist missionary John Smith, 11 June. He voted for the Irish insurrection bill, 14 June. Next month he applied to Peel, the home secretary, for a baronetcy, citing the 'respectable standing' of his family and the peerages of his grandfather and 'great-uncle' Lord Clarina. He is 'a good attendant and regular supporter ... and he has a fortune amply sufficient to support it', observed Peel to Lord Liverpool later that year, adding that 'it would be advisable not to discourage a hope of success'. 'I should have no objection ... to your saying to Mr. Massy Dawson that there was no intention of making any baronets at present, but that if there were any recommendations hereafter of gentlemen connected with Ireland, I would bring his name before the king', replied Liverpool. Enclosing Liverpool's response, 9 Nov. 1824, Peel advised, 'I have an impression on my mind that independently of your Irish property, you have a considerable landed estate in this country. If I am right I will state this to Lord Liverpool when I see him. If my impression is ... erroneous ... you will perhaps write either to Lord Wellesley or Mr. Goulburn'.[6] In February 1825 Massy reapplied to Goulburn, the Irish secretary, hoping that

> I shall not be thought too ambitious ... though I feel myself as well entitled to higher honours as many of those who have been made peers. I have been told I am considered an *absentee* which is a bar to my prospects ... in reply to which I wish briefly to inform you that being in Parliament I am obliged to have a house in London, but I assure you I spend nearly six months of every year in Ireland and I have ... never missed attending both assizes in my county town ... besides which I keep in my own hands a considerable part of my own property consisting of large woods, and employ many hands of the labouring classes.

Passing the application to Wellesley, the Irish viceroy, Goulburn observed that he did not 'know enough of the extent of his property or of his family to be able to express an opinion'.[7] The baronetcy eluded him. He presented a Tipperary petition for Catholic claims, 22 Feb.[8] He voted for suppression of the Catholic Association, 15 Feb., but was listed on both sides in the division on Catholic relief, 21 Apr., probably owing to confusion with George Dawson, a hostile teller, whose supposed favourable vote of 1 Mar. was surely also Massy's. He was in the pro-Catholic majority on 10 May 1825. He divided with ministers on the Jamaican slave trials, 2 Mar., but was in the protectionist minorities against the emergency admission of foreign corn, 8, 11 May 1826.

At the 1826 general election he offered again for Clonmel and was returned unopposed. In the county Tipperary contest he seconded the nomination of John Hely Hutchinson I*, in whose favour Bagwell had retired.[9] It was later claimed by one of the Hely Hutchinsons that he voted with their family's head, the 2nd earl of Donoughmore.[10] He presented constituency petitions against the import of foreign flour, 16 Feb., and the duties on imported coal, 27 Feb. 1827.[11] He voted for Catholic relief, 6 Mar. 1827, 12 May 1828, and presented a favourable petition, 15 Feb. 1828. In February 1829 Planta, the Wellington ministry's patronage secretary, predicted that he would vote 'with government' for Catholic emancipation, and he divided accordingly, 6 Mar. 1829. There is no other trace of parliamentary activity that year. In December 1829 he started for a vacancy for county Limerick on the combined interest of his kinsman Baron Massy and Lord Kingston.[12] (He vacated Clonmel in favour of his son-in-law Eyre Coote, 2 Jan. 1830.) 'There can be no doubt that we should support Massy Dawson, the more eagerly as he seems quite sure of his return', Peel informed Leveson Gower, the Irish secretary, 31 Dec. 1829.[13] Faced with an unexpected campaign in support of his opponent by Daniel O'Connell* and the Catholic clergy, whose interference he denounced as unconstitutional, Massy Dawson (as he was now styled) demanded military assistance to protect his freeholders from the 'unfortunate deluded peasantry' and pressed ministers for a baronetcy for Joseph Barrington of Limerick, in order to secure his 'considerable interest', much to the annoyance of Leveson Gower and Peel, who observed that 'to gratify Barrington's peculiar itch for a baronetcy, there being already one in his family ... would be a singular proceeding'.[14] 'Dawson and his friends have acted in a manner unworthy of their rank and fortune', noted William Gregory, the Irish under-secretary.[15] 'I am sorry to see Massy Dawson is contesting the county of Limerick', commented another observer, 'it is a pity to waste so much money in [an] election, with a family of 12 children'.[16] After a severe contest, in which he suffered a nearly murderous assault, he was defeated, but he was seated on petition three months later.[17] He was sworn in, 3 June 1830. He continued to press ministers unsuccessfully for a baronetcy for Barrington.[18] (It was later conferred by the Grey ministry in 1831.) He voted for the grant for South American missions, 7 June, but was in the minority for consular service reductions, 11 June 1830.

At the 1830 general election he offered again for county Limerick, having solicited and secured the support of government. Faced with a junction between his two opponents, however, he withdrew shortly before the expected contest, citing the likely expense.[19] In county Tipperary he again seconded the nomination of Hely Hutchinson.[20] He was listed by Brougham as one of those who had backed 'the duke in the last session'.

Rumours that he would start for county Tipperary at the 1831 general election came to nothing.[21] He died in October 1834. By his will, dated 9 Apr. 1834 and proved under £14,000, he left annuities of £1,000 to each of his seven daughters in a trust controlled by Coote. He was succeeded in the family estates by his eldest son James (1802-37), an army officer.[22]

[1] Add. 37303, f. 208. [2] *Dublin Evening Post*, 11, 21 Mar. 1820. [3] *Black Bk.* (1823), 151; *Session of Parl. 1825*, p. 460. [4] *Williams Wynn Corresp.* 243. [5] *The Times*, 6, 25, 28 May 1824. [6] Add. 40367, ff. 20, 22; 40304, ff. 269-70, 272. [7] Add. 37303, ff. 206, 208. [8] *The Times*, 23 Feb. 1825. [9] *Southern Reporter*, 22 June 1826; TCD, Donoughmore mss F/13/152. [10] Wellington mss WP1/1083/19. [11] *The Times*, 17, 28 Feb. 1827. [12] *Dublin Evening Post*, 29, 31 Dec. 1829. [13] Add. 40337, f. 348. [14] Add. 40334, ff. 309, 311; 40338, ff. 23, 31. [15] Add. 40334, f. 308. [16] Wilts. RO, Poore mss WRO 1915/58. [17] Add. 40338, f. 41; *The Times*, 1, 2 Feb., 1, 4 May 1830. [18] Wellington mss WP1/1112/13; NAI, Leveson Gower letter bks. Leveson Gower to Singleton, 15 July 1830; Add. 40338, f. 223. [19] Leveson Gower letter bks., Leveson Gower to Wellington, 6 July; *Limerick Evening Post*, 13 July, 3 Aug.; *Dublin Evening Post*, 12 Aug. 1830. [20] *Tipperary Free Press*, 18 Aug. 1830. [21] *Clonmel Herald*, 30 Apr. 1831. [22] PROB 11/1842/78; IR26/1379/205, 207.

P.J.S.

MAULE, Hon. William Ramsay (1771–1852), of Panmure and Brechin Castle, Forfar.

FORFARSHIRE 24 Apr. 1796–1796

FORFARSHIRE 24 June 1805–10 Sept. 1831

b. 27 Oct. 1771, 2nd. s. of George Ramsay, 8th earl of Dalhousie [S], and Elizabeth, da. of Andrew Glen; bro. of Hon. John Ramsay†. *educ.* Edinburgh h.s. 1780-4. *m.* (1) 1 Dec. 1794, Patricia Heron (*d.* 11 May 1821), da. of Gilbert Gordon of Hallseaths, Dumfries, 3s. 7da. (2 *d.v.p.*); (2) 4 June 1822, Elizabeth, da. of John William Barton of Hospitalfield, Forfar, *s.p. suc.* fa. under entail in 1787 to Panmure estates of his gt.-uncle William Maule†, 1st earl of Panmure [I] (*d.* 1782), having taken name of Maule in 1782; *cr.* Bar. Panmure 10 Sept. 1831. *d.* 13 Apr. 1852.

Cornet 11 Drag. 1788; capt. Ind. Co. Ft. 1791 (disbanded same year); half-pay 1791; ret. 1825.

Lt. W. Lowland fencibles 1793, capt.-lt. 1793, capt. 1794; maj. commdt. Forfar fencible cav. 1794.

Reviewing Maule's Commons career in 1852, *The Brechin Advertiser* commented: 'Mr. Maule's displays to Parliament, where he but seldom took part in debates, were more useful than ostentatious, and it was chiefly in committees that his shrewd business talent and strong sagacity rendered him useful as a Member'.[1] Renowned by 1820 for the wild excesses of his youth, his violent temper, lavish hospitality and Foxite politics, he had also succeeded in re-establishing the supremacy of the Panmure interest in Forfarshire and its influence in neighbouring counties, and Aberdeen and Perth Burghs; he was a formidable opponent at elections. Despite rumblings of discontent, no Melvillite Tory had been prepared to stand against him since he became Member for Forfarshire in 1805.[2] The break-up of his marriage (his wife had left him in 1817 on account his debauchery and adultery) had highlighted his soured and dysfunctional family life, but he stewarded at the Edinburgh dinner to Lord Erskine as usual, 21 Feb. 1820, and was unopposed at the general election in March, when he also promoted the candidature of his political allies Sir Alexander Ramsay* in Kincardineshire and Joseph Hume* in Aberdeen Burghs.[3]

Maule's spasmodic attendance in the 1820 Parliament was often attributable to his domestic difficulties: the defiance of his son-and-heir Fox Maule (1801-74) in siding with his mother, who died in May 1821; the elopement and marriage, 1820-4, of four of his daughters; his occasional ill health, and the demands of litigation brought by relations and tenants. He made no major speeches, generally voted with the main Whig opposition on major issues, aligning also occasionally with Hume and the 'Mountain' on retrenchment, taxation and certain radical causes, and, according to Guthrie of Craigie, his seconder in Forfarshire in 1826, with the liberal Tories on trade.[4] He arrived late for the 1820 session, but divided with Hume for economies in revenue collection, 4 July, and voted against the aliens bill, 7 July 1820. Brechin, which he normally commanded, petitioned on behalf of Queen Caroline, 28 Feb. 1821, but the only record of Maule's attendance that session is his vote for Catholic relief, 28 Feb. Attending more often in 1822, he voted for a gradual reduction in the salt duty, 28 Feb., and divided steadily with opposition for the next three months, when he was also listed in radical minorities on the estimates, 4, 12, 25 Mar., 1 Apr., and for large tax remissions, 8 May, and voted to receive a Newcastle petition for clemency for Henry Hunt*, which imputed corruption to the House, 22 Mar., and for remission of Hunt's gaol sentence, 24 Apr. He presented petitions from Forfarshire and Kincardineshire complaining of agricultural distress and the export restrictions imposed on Scottish breweries and distilleries, 25 Apr., 6 May.[5] He voted for parliamentary reform, 25 Apr., and Brougham's motion condemning the influence of the crown, 24 June 1822. His marriage to Elizabeth Barton that month was clandestine. He sent ten 'fat bucks' for the king's table during his Scottish visit and in September 1822 accompanied Hume to a party dinner at Montrose, where their parliamentary conduct was commended.[6]

No votes by Maule are recorded for the next two sessions. Fox, having come of age, had brought his refusal to grant him settled funds before the court of session, of which Sir Walter Scott gave the 5th duke of Buccleuch's guardian Lord Montagu the following account, 14 Feb. 1823:

> To amuse us within doors we have the cause of young Maule against his father praying for aliment which Cranstoun is just now pleading in my hearing. The liberality of his father has bestowed on him an ensign's commission and one hundred pounds a year and having thus far discharged his duty to his son he denies the right of the court to take the matter farther into their consideration. The young man's case is stated with much feeling and delicacy but I doubt, considering the dogged and obstinate temper of the Whiggish tyrant, he had not better have gone to the duke's place for the necessary money for the unfortunate consequence will be that his father will make waste on the estate, cut down and dispark [disbark] and do twenty times the mischief which old Q. [Queensberry] made at Drumlanrig ... Is it not odd that so generous fine and honourable a character as Dalhousie [the 9th earl (1770-1838)] should have been brother to this he-wolf who would eat his own issue if law would not solemnize such a banquet of Theystes by a hanging match? So much for living with toad-eaters and parasites in the untempered exercise of every whim that comes uppermost till the slightest contradiction becomes an inexpiable crime in those around him.[7]

The court ruled in favour of Fox, 9 June, but Maule, who appealed to the Lords, 25 June 1823, had the verdict quashed, 1 June 1825. A separate case brought by William Maule of Edinburgh, heir to his father Thomas, the rival claimant by entail to Panmure in 1782, also failed.[8] Maule had mixed success with requests to the home secretary Peel in 1824 and 1825 for church patronage for his partisans, an issue with overtones in his theological differences with Fox, who supported the 'Free Kirk'.[9] After receiving three weeks' leave on account of ill health, 17 Feb., he was present to vote for Catholic relief, 21 Apr., 10 May, paired for repealing the window tax, 17 May, and almost certainly voted to kill the Leith docks bill, 20 May 1825. He divided steadily against the duke of Cumberland's annuity bill, 30 May-10 June, and for inquiry into chancery delays, 7 June 1825, when he was also in Hume's minority for information on an appointment to the committee of stationery in Bengal. In 1826 he voted to enforce payment in specie under the promissory notes bill, 27 Feb., presented and endorsed Forfarshire petitions against altering the Scottish banking system, 6, 13 Mar., 13 Apr.,[10] paired for the abolition of military flogging, 10 Mar.,[11] and voted to reform the representation of Edinburgh, 13 Apr. and in condemnation of electoral bribery, 26 May 1826. On the hustings at the general election, he stated that his political views had not changed for over 20 years and refused to guarantee his future conduct beyond supporting 'the dignity of the crown, the independence of Parliament, and the rights of the people.[12]

Maule did not comment on the Forfarshire petitions against corn law revision he presented, 9, 13 Feb. 1827, and is not known to have he voted on the issue.[13] He divided for Catholic relief, 6 Mar., information on the magistrates' handling of the Lisburn Orange marchers, 29 Mar., and inquiries into chancery delays, 4 Apr., and the Irish miscellaneous estimates, 6 Apr. 1827. Realizing that the duke of Wellington's appointment as premier in January 1828 made his own to the vacant lord lieutenancy of Forfarshire which he coveted impossible, he tactically waived his claim in favour of the Whig moderate Lord Duncan, but failed to prevent the appointment of the Tory 4th earl of Airlie.[14] Airlie sounded Wellington about making Maule a deputy lieutenant, but nothing came of it.[15] He ordered returns on warehoused spirits in Scotland, 13 Feb., and divided for Catholic relief 12 May 1828. In 1829 he referred fresh claims against him by William Maule and others to the Lords.[16] He voted as expected for Catholic emancipation, 6, 30 Mar., and to permit Daniel O'Connell to sit for county Clare without swearing the oath of supremacy, 18 May. He had a petition against the Fifeshire roads bill referred to the select committee and counsel ordered, 25 Mar. His attendance remained lax and he received a month's sick leave, 9 Mar. 1830. He voted to amend the libel law amendment bill, 6 July, in Hume's minority of 11 to reduce judges' salaries under the administration of justice bill, 7 July, and for the abolition of colonial slavery, 13 July 1830. He decided against backing Hume in Aberdeen Burghs at the general election, when Hume came in for Middlesex and his own return was a formality.[17]

Maule was listed among the Wellington ministry's 'foes' but was absent from the division on the civil list which brought them down, 15 Nov. 1830. From Brechin Castle, 4 Dec., he wrote to the cabinet minister Lord Holland confirming his support for the Grey ministry and requesting a peerage:

> I wonder how you could doubt for a moment my warmest support for a ministry of which you, Lord Grey and Lord Lansdowne form a part. To you and them I have invariable [*sic*] looked as the supporters of the principles of your immortal uncle [Fox], which alone can save the country at the present critical moment. With these principles I started, without fear of punishment, or hope of reward,

and with them I shall die, trusting always that you and your friends will never compromise them ... In my grand-uncle's (the late earl of Panmure) settlements, there is a clause which recommends to me my best endeavours to regain the family titles ... I had nearly asked this favour of the ministry of 1806, but I considered then that I had not given sufficient proof of my attachment to Whig principles to enable me to make such a proposal. This objection, I hope you will allow, is pretty well removed. At the same time, I can assure you, that (barring the clause in Lord Panmure's settlement) I feel quite content with holding one of the most independent seats in the ... Commons.[18]

He divided for the government's English reform bill at its second reading, 22 Mar., and against Gascoyne's wrecking amendment, 19 Apr. At the ensuing general election he declared unreservedly 'for the bill', sponsored reform candidates, and scotched the anti-reformers' bid to oppose his return.[19] He insisted that the Forfar anti-reform petition presented on 27 June 1831 did not represent his constituents' views. He voted for the second reading of the reintroduced reform bill, 6 July, and consistently for its details until 3 Sept. 1831, when Holland notified him that he would be a coronation peer.[20] He had served briefly on the Glasgow Burghs election committee from which he contrived to be excused attendance on account of gout in his left foot, 25 July, and divided with government on the Dublin election controversy, 23 Aug. 1831.[21]

His elevation to the Lords, where Belhaven and Dover introduced him (not Holland, as he intended) as Baron Panmure, 13 Sept. 1831, attracted hostile comment on account of his bad character; and his 'bulky form' was caricatured being tossed up from a farm wagon by the king to Grey.[22] Anti-reformers delighted in his nominee Douglas Gordon Hallyburton's defeat at the ensuing Forfarshire by-election, but, encouraged by Panmure, Hallyburton succeeded on petition and retained the seat until 1841.[23] His influence in Forfarshire and the Montrose Burghs endured and he regularly briefed the Whigs on Forfarshire politics and voted mainly by proxy.[24] In a letter to Holland, the patronage secretary Ellice confirmed that Maule's case for promotion in the peerage to safeguard his estates was genuine: 'No friend of Mr. Pitt's would have been allowed to lose an estate of £50,000 a year for want of promotion in the peerage, and Maule has been as steady an adherent of ours, as any of Mr. Pitt's marquesses were, or those raised by the late king'.[25] It was not granted, and he died at Brechin Castle in April 1852 after a long illness, possessed of Forfarshire estates worth an estimated £53,447, and recalled by the Liberal *Dundee Advertiser* and on the Panmure monument erected in his honour in 1839 as a generous sponsor of local causes.[26] Hearing of his death Lord Cockburn, who was staying nearby, observed:

[Panmure was] popular with those who chose to be submissive and to such was never close in the fist. But the virtues were a different matter. To his unfriends – and he made many – he was insanely brutal. His wife, his daughters, and at least two of his three sons, he compelled to fly from his house, his daughters at midnight, and ever after shut his door and heart against them; neither time nor their worth ever abating his mad and savage hatred. And so it was with everyone who incurred the ineffaceable guilt of daring to resist the capricious and intolerant despotism of his will. He would have roasted every soul of them, and their bodies too. A spoiled beast from his infancy. His oldest son, who presumed to save his sisters by helping them out of the house, was the object of his particular hatred: a hatred which the public eminence of the son rather aggravated than lessened.[27]

Fox, then Liberal Member for Perth and lord lieutenant of Forfarshire, succeeded him as 2nd (and last) Baron Panmure, but was barred from inheriting the estates and 'all moveables', which passed, as second son, to Colonel Lauderdale Maule Ramsay† (1807-54). He was killed in the Crimea, having willed his estates to his brother Fox, who in 1860 succeeded their cousin, the Indian viceroy James Andrew Broun Ramsay†, as 11th earl of Dalhousie.[28]

[1] *Brechin Advertiser*, 20 Apr. 1852. [2] *HP Commons, 1790-1820*, ii. 539-41; iv. 571-2; R.P. Gillies, *Mems. of a Literary Veteran*, i. 72. [3] NLS mss 11, f. 7; *Caledonian Mercury*, 19, 26 Feb., 3 Apr. 1820. [4] *The Times*, 5 July 1826. [5] Ibid. 26 Apr., 7 May 1822. [6] Ibid. 7 Aug., 25 Sept. 1822. [7] *Scott Letters*, vii. 331-2. [8] *Panmure Pprs.* ed. G. Douglas and G.D. Ramsay (1908), i. 5-9; *LJ*, lvi. 1113; lxvii. 15, 18, 30, 32, 949, 962, 1035, 1199. [9] Add. 40360, ff. 185-72; 40363, f. 24; 40374, ff. 33, 34; I.F. Maciver, 'Cockburn and the Church', in *Cockburn, a Bicentenary Celebration* ed. A. Bell (1979), 75. [10] *The Times*, 7, 14 Mar., 14 Apr. 1826. [11] Ibid. 15 Mar. 1826. [12] Ibid. 5 July; *Kelso Mail*, 6 July 1826. [13] *The Times*, 10, 14 Feb. 1827. [14] Bucks. RO, Buckinghamshire mss O.33, Lansdowne to Goderich, 1 Jan.; O.24, Maule to Duncan, 3 Jan.; Add. 51637, Lansdowne to Holland, 4 Jan. 1828. [15] NLS mss 2, f. 123. [16] *LJ*, lxi. 9, 97, 205, 216, 475, 481. [17] *Stirling Advertiser*, 13 Aug.; *Scotsman*, 14 Aug. 1830. [18] Add. 51835. [19] NAS GD224/525/18/2; *Perthshire Courier*, 2 June 1831. [20] Add. 51836, Maule to Holland, 3 Sept. 1831. [21] *CJ*, lxxxvi. 681, 689. [22] Add. 51836, Maule to Holland, 13 Sept.; 69364, Sneyd to Fortescue, 12 Sept. 1831; *LJ*, lxiii. 920, 972; *Arbuthnot Jnl.* ii. 429; M.D. George, *Cat. of Pol. and Personal Satires*, xi. 16979. [23] NLW, Coedymaen mss 1014; Dundee City Archives, Camperdown mss GD/Ca/Tin Box EC/12/11. [24] Add. 51836, Panmure to Holland, 30 Nov. 1831, 22 Dec. 1832; Brougham mss, Panmure to Brougham, 13 July 1837, 12 Jan. 1838. [25] Add. 51587. [26] *Brechin Advertiser*, 20 Apr. 1852. [27] Cockburn, *Circuit Journeys* (1983 edn.), 236. For a similar view see *Ann. Reg.* (1852), App. pp. 272-3. [28] PROB 8/245; 11/2156/582; IR26/1943/614; *Oxford DNB sub* Maule, William Ramsay and Maule, Fox.

M.M.E.

MAXWELL, Henry (1799–1868), of Farnham, co. Cavan.

CO. CAVAN 24 Feb. 1824–19 Oct. 1838

b. 9 Aug. 1799, 1st s. of Rev. Henry Maxwell (later 6th Bar. Farnham [I]), rect. of Annagh, co. Cavan and Lady Anne Butler, da. of Henry Thomas, 2nd earl of Carrick [I]; bro. of Hon. James Pierce Maxwell† and Hon. Somerset Richard Maxwell†. *educ.* Fortland sch.; Trinity Coll. Camb. 1818; Trinity, Dublin 1820; King's Inns 1823; L. Inn 1824. *m.* 3 Dec. 1828, Hon. Anna Frances Esther Stapleton, da. of Thomas, 12th Bar. Le Despenser, *s.p. suc.* fa. as 7th Bar. Farnham [I] 19 Oct. 1838; KP 12 Nov. 1845. *d.* 20 Aug. 1868.

Rep. peer [I] 1839-*d.*

Grand sec. Orange Order [I].

Capt.-commdt. Fortland yeomanry corps.

Ultimately descended, like his distant kinsman John Waring Maxwell* of Finnebrogue, county Down, from the clan of Calderwood, Lanarkshire, Maxwell's ennobled Farnham branch of the family had long been the dominant territorial and electoral force in county Cavan. Henry's father and namesake, the younger son of another Henry Maxwell, bishop of Meath, whose elder brother was the 1st earl of Farnham, entered the church but apparently resided permanently in northern France, perhaps for financial reasons; Peel, the home secretary, commented derisively in 1823 that 'such men as Mr. Henry Maxwell, drawing enormous sums from Irish livings, and leading a profligate life at Boulogne, are the real enemies of the establishment', but a legal connection remarked to this Member in 1830 that 'your father could, in my opinion, return home and *appear*, if there was one man in London who would take some trouble and reason with the English creditors'.[1] Maxwell, who was educated at universities and inns of court in both Ireland and England, was therefore taken care of by his uncle, the bishop's elder son, John, who took the surname of Barry on inheriting extensive estates in county Wexford and sat for Cavan in the United Kingdom Parliament. When Barry, an inveterate opponent of Catholic relief, succeeded his cousin (the 2nd earl of Farnham) as 5th Baron Farnham in July 1823, his nephew was brought forward in his place. Declaring his principles to be those of his predecessor, he was duly returned at a by-election the following February, when nothing came of a threatened contest.[2] He survived a petition and vindicated the conduct of the sheriff, 11 May 1824, when he declared that he was not himself an Orangeman, although he must soon afterwards have become one.[3]

Maxwell brought up his county's anti-Catholic petition, 10 Feb., and was appointed to the select committee on the state of Ireland, 17 Feb. 1825. He voted for the Irish unlawful societies bill, 15, 25 Feb., and against Catholic relief, 1 Mar., 21, 26 Apr., 10 May. He pointed out that it was not he, but John Waring Maxwell, who had made the earlier Commons intervention that was (in fact, erroneously) interpreted as implying his conversion to the Catholic cause, 22 Apr., 9 May.[4] He divided with ministers for the grant to the duke of Cumberland, 30 May, 6 June 1825, but no trace of parliamentary activity has been found for the 1826 session. Farnham, who in September 1825 considered his return as certain, coached him through the technicalities of the canvass that followed the dissolution in 1826, warning him to 'take particular care always to speak in your own name and never to use mine respecting the election'.[5] Emphasizing his local associations and speaking strongly against Catholic relief, he was returned with his future brother-in-law Alexander Saunderson after a severe contest against two liberal and emancipationist candidates, whose campaign was promoted by the Catholic Association and supported by many of the mostly Catholic 40*s.* freeholders. He denounced the electoral interference of the priesthood in his final address and at the dinner for the defeated county Waterford Member Lord George Beresford in Cavan, 30 Aug. 1826, and again saw off a petition which alleged intimidation on Farnham's part.[6]

He spoke at county meetings to address the king on the death of the duke of York and to petition Parliament against Catholic relief, 25 Jan. 1827, and gave his support to his uncle's scheme to promote the Protestant Reformation in Cavan the following day.[7] Having signed the anti-Catholic petition of the Irish noblemen and gentlemen, he presented numerous hostile petitions from his county, 14 Feb., 2 (when he reiterated his criticisms of the priests) and 5 Mar., and voted against relief, 6 Mar.[8] He took six weeks' leave on urgent business, 8 Mar. He voted in the Canning ministry's minority against the Penryn election bill, 7 June 1827. Between 17 Apr., when he asked Peel if negotiations were under way with Rome, and 23 June, when he objected to the Maynooth grant, he brought up numerous anti-Catholic petitions and he divided in this sense, 12 May 1828. He voted with the Wellington administration against inquiry into chancery administration, 24 Apr., and reduction of the salary of the lieutenant-general of the ordnance, 4 July. On 13 Oct. 1828 he moved the resolution for establishing a subscription for the Brunswick Club at the county meeting in Cavan and that autumn he was prominent in Protestant activities there and in Dublin, where he had by now become secretary of the Orange Order.[9] In January 1829 Maxwell was considered as a possible mover or seconder of the address by Planta, the patronage secretary, who, however, rightly listed him among those 'opposed to the principle' of the emancipation bill. He condemned it out of hand, 5 Feb., and, predicting on the 9th that Parliament would be deluged by hostile petitions from Britain and Ireland, he on that and many subsequent days brought up an enormous number of them. He voted against emancipation, 6, 18, 27, 30 Mar., and divided for a higher £20 franchise under the related franchise bill, 26 Mar. He spoke and was teller for the minority against the Maynooth grant, 22 May. In October 1829 the Ultra leader Sir Richard Vyvyan* listed him with the 'Tories strongly opposed to the present government'. He was granted leave on urgent private business for a month, 8 Feb., and again, for three weeks, 8 Mar. 1830. He voted against Jewish emancipation, 17 May. Having presented a Newtownbarry petition on the subject, 18 May, he obtained leave for his own (unsuccessful) bill to regulate Irish county rates, 20 May 1830.

At the general election of 1830, when Maxwell was advised not to ensnare himself with his friend Anthony Lefroy's* ambitions in county Longford, he maintained a studied neutrality in the muted Cavan contest between his colleague, who was again returned with him despite having voted for the Catholics, and Sir William Young, another local Protestant.[10] On 11 July Leveson Gower, the Irish secretary, had floated the idea of backing Southwell with Young, 'for the purpose of excluding Maxwell', in a letter to Planta, who listed him among the 'violent Ultras' that autumn.[11] He duly voted in the majority against ministers on the civil list, 15 Nov. He was in the minority of four for Quintin Dick's motion that the petition of Sir Harcourt Lees for repeal of the Act of Abjuration be printed, 23 Dec. 1830. He was presumably the 'Mr. Maxwell' who, on 4 Feb. 1831, moved for a call of the House on the 18th in order to secure a full attendance for what he considered to be such an important session. He brought up petitions from Cavan for the grant to the Kildare Place Society, 16 Mar., and, following his votes against the second reading of the Grey ministry's reform bill, 22 Mar., and for Gascoyne's wrecking amendment, 19 Apr., from Newtownbarry and elsewhere against parliamentary reform, 20 Apr. 1831. A stout anti-reformer, he was returned at the ensuing general election, this time with Young's son John, following another contest with Southwell.[12]

Maxwell vindicated the conduct of the magistracy and yeomanry of county Wexford over the Newtownbarry affray, 23 June, and was forced to return to this topic, 12 July, 26, 27, 31 Aug., 9, 13 Sept. 1831. He voted against the second reading of the reintroduced reform bill, 6 July, at least five times to adjourn the proceedings on it, 12 July, for using the 1831 census to determine the boroughs in schedules A and B, 19 July, and to postpone consideration of the partial disfranchisement of Chippenham, 27 July. He divided against the Irish union of parishes bill, 19 Aug., to censure the Irish government over the Dublin election, 23 Aug., for preserving the voting rights of non-resident freemen, 30 Aug., and for Waldo Sibthorp's complaint of a breach of privilege against *The Times*, 12 Sept. He voted against the third reading, 19 Sept., and passage of the reform bill, 21 Sept., and the second reading of the Scottish bill, 23 Sept. He again divided against the Maynooth grant, 26 Sept., and on 6 Oct. criticized Farnham's being passed over for the lord lieutenancy of Cavan on partisan grounds. He was present at Protestant meetings in Dublin, 7 Dec. 1831, and Cavan, 13 Jan., and was granted leave to attend the assizes, 27 Feb., and again, 5 July 1832.[13] He paired against the second reading of the revised reform bill, 17 Dec. 1831, but voted in person against the third reading, 22 Mar., and for Waldo Sibthorp's amendment relating to Lincoln freeholders, 23 Mar. 1832. Convinced, as he wrote in an address from the Grand Orange Lodge in March, that reform would only pave the way for a Catholic ascendancy in Ireland, he became a founder member of the Carlton Club in London that month.[14] He divided against the second reading of the Irish reform bill, 25 May, and to preserve the voting rights of Irish freemen, 2 July. His only other known votes were against Crampton's amendment to the Irish tithes bill, 9 Apr., Sadler's motion for permanent provision for the Irish poor by a tax on absentees, 19 June, and, having brought up the Orange Order's petition against it that day, the Irish party processions bill, 25 June 1832.

Described as 'Orange to the core', Maxwell was again returned for Cavan at the general election of 1832 and sat as a Conservative until 1838, when he succeeded to the barony which his father had recently inherited from his brother.[15] A lifelong defender of the Irish church and an accomplished genealogist, he was killed with his wife, and about 30 others, in the Abergele railway disaster in August 1868. They had joined the front carriage of the London to Holyhead express at Chester, and it was this portion of the train which bore the brunt of a collision with the accidentally detached rear wagons of a goods train, one of which was carrying petroleum. Their incinerated remains, only identifiable from their pocket watches, were interred with those of the other victims in Abergele.[16] He was succeeded in his title and estates by his brothers, both former Conservative Members for Cavan, Somerset Richard (1803-84) and James Pierce (1813-96), who in 1885 was considered by some to have succeeded to the baronetcy of Maxwell of Calderwood.

[1] Add. 40329, f. 188; N. Gash, *Secretary Peel*, 375; NLI, Farnham mss 18613 (4), Fox to Maxwell, 22 June 1830. [2] Farnham mss 18602 (3), Maxwell to Blackwood, to Bective, 28 Feb.; *Belfast News Letter*, 2 Mar. 1824. [3] *The Times*, 12 May 1824; PRO NI, Leslie mss MIC606/3/J/7/21/4. [4] *The Times*, 23 Apr., 10 May 1825. [5] Add. 40381, f. 367; Farnham mss 18602 (17), Farnham to Maxwell, 26, 29 May 1826. [6] *Dublin Evening Post*, 8, 10, 20, 29 June, 8 July; *Impartial Reporter*, 29 June, 3 July, 7 Sept. 1826. [7] *Enniskillen Chron.* 1, 8 Feb. 1827. [8] Add. 40392, f. 5; *The Times*, 15 Feb., 3, 6 Mar. 1827. [9] *Impartial Reporter*, 23, 30 Oct., 13, 20 Nov.; *Belfast News Letter*, 18 Nov. 1828. [10] Farnham mss 18613 (4), Fox to Maxwell, 22, 28 June 1830; 18602 (41), Maxwell to Southwell, 13 Aug.; *Enniskillen Chron.* 29 July, 19 Aug. 1830. [11] NAI, Leveson Gower letter bks. M738. [12] *Enniskillen Chron.* 19, 26 May 1831. [13] *Belfast Guardian*, 16 Dec. 1831; *Ballyshannon Herald*, 20 Jan. 1832. [14] *Belfast Guardian*, 31 Mar. 1832. [15] *Enniskillener*, 27 Dec. 1832; *Gent. Mag.* (1838), ii. 546, 658. [16] *Cavan Weekly News*, 21, 28 Aug.; *The Times*, 21, 22 Aug.; *Ann. Reg.* (1868), Chron. pp. 106-11.

S.M.F.

MAXWELL, John (1791–1865), of Pollok House, Renfrew and 10 Duke Street, St. James's, Mdx.

RENFREWSHIRE	1818–1830
LANARKSHIRE	1832–1837

b. 12 May 1791, o.s. of Sir John Maxwell†, 7th bt., of Pollok and Hannah Anne, da. of Capt. Richard Gardiner of Aldeburgh, Suff. *educ.* by Rev. Dr. MacLetchie of Mearns 1798; Market Rasen 1802-5; Westminster 1806-9; Christ Church, Oxf. 1809; Edinburgh Univ. 1812; foreign tour 1813-15. *m.* 14 Oct. 1839, Lady Matilda Harriet Bruce, da. of Thomas, 7th earl of Elgin [S], *s.p. suc.* fa. as 8th bt. 30 July 1844. *d.* 6 June 1865.
Lt.-col. Renfrew militia 1813-18.

Maxwell, whose family had been established at Pollok since the fourteenth century, joined Brooks's Club, 10 May 1815, and was returned for Renfrewshire in 1818 as the nominee of the triumvirate of Whig families who controlled the county's representation. He was praised by the 10th duke of Hamilton for the 'Roman virtue that you determine to manifest in this corrupt age', and was described by another Whig friend as having spoken in the House with the 'free and unembarrassed air of a high bred gentleman'.[1] He was again returned in 1820, defeating a Tory opponent, and promised to pursue the same 'independent' course, resisting 'inroads on the constitution' by the crown, which should be 'beloved ... not dreaded', helping to restrain the 'wild and ruinous movements' into which the people had been led by radical agitators and working for the 'real welfare and comfort of the labouring classes'.[2] In a pamphlet published at this time, addressed to 'the honest reformers of Scotland', he warned that 'a few bad men' were busy 'preaching up revolution, equality and atheism', by means of 'infidel publications and the demoralisation of youth'. He believed the chief causes of discontent were 'the neglect of external religion amongst the wealthy, the profuse misapplication of the public money and the poor rate'. If Britain's 'religious and legislative establishments' had 'collected dirt and rust', it would nevertheless be 'folly' to 'destroy the best constitution in the world', when 'it only requires cleaning'. To 'give every knave and beggar a vote' would 'not make honest Members', and the 'purification of Parliament' was best achieved by disfranchising venal boroughs. He maintained that 'the law of nature has no language but one ... inequality of ranks', and the wealth and distinctions enjoyed by the aristocracy were 'for the interest of all classes and of political necessity', as they 'stimulate to activity, and turn to the use of the state, the talents ... of all the country'. He asserted that 'all property comes out of the soil, a mine that is inexhaustible', and if Britain was to 'continue great, good and free', a corn law was required to protect the agricultural interest; the export trade in manufactures was 'temporary and little more than speculation'. Ultimately, the 'one guide ... alone for man' was 'the word of God' and the 'steadfast observation of the principles of Christianity', in the hope of finding 'a more sublime destiny'.[3]

He was a regular attender and continued to vote with the Whig opposition to Lord Liverpool's ministry on all major issues, including parliamentary reform, 9, 10 May 1821, 20 Feb., 24 Apr., 2 June 1823, 26 May 1826. He paired for Catholic relief, 28 Feb. 1821, divided against the Irish unlawful societies bill, 15 Feb., and voted for relief, 1 Mar., 21 Apr., 10 May 1825. He presented a petition from a 'large number of distressed persons' in Renfrewshire who lacked the means to emigrate, 19 May 1820.[4] He said that he had asked to be removed from the select committee on agricultural distress, 31 May, as its 'avowed object was to adhere to the principle of prohibition' when he believed the only 'just [and] efficacious' measure was a 'protecting duty'. The condition of the 'manufacturing classes' in Renfrewshire was 'more deplorable and more afflicting' than anywhere else, and his personal interests were 'essentially affected' by their plight. Yet he was 'not so ignorant of the real interests of the state' and accepted the need to protect agriculture, which constituted 'the great market for manufactures' and was 'the great interest of the empire', though he knew his stance would provoke 'unpopularity and dislike' among his constituents. He presented a Paisley mechanics' petition for assistance to emigrate, 1 June, and implored the government to do 'an act of humanity becoming a Christian country', warning that the petitioners 'in their misery ... might be operated upon to engage in plans of reform, and even risings to any extent'. In moving for a select committee to inquire into distress among the cotton weavers, 29 June, he urged the House to consider whether power loom factories derived an unfair advantage from tax exemptions and condemned the injustice of the combination laws, which enabled employers to 'combine ... for depressing the wages of the labourer', who was 'liable to punishment if he attempted to raise them'. He favoured the 'application of public money' to provide land for the surplus population, and was 'alarmed to see taxation arrive at such an extent as to endanger the existence of our institutions'. After a brief discussion, he postponed his motion until the next session. In a private letter he argued that at a time of national crisis a 'great and disinterested effort of the rich' was required, in the form of a 'one per cent property tax for transferring labour from manufacture to husbandry', which '*reproduces* capital for the maintenance of itself'. He also believed that the 'mad and impious although well meant' Scottish poor law should be abolished.[5] While he had initially supported the aliens bill he opposed the second reading, 7 July, explaining that circumstances had changed with the proceedings against Queen Caroline and the 'barbarous indifference' displayed by ministers towards the distressed labourers. He now feared that government would use the powers it sought to 'obstruct witnesses from abroad', whose testimony might benefit the queen. He supported punishing the editor of *Flindell's Western Luminary* for libelling her, 25 July 1820. He advised his mother at this time to spend the winter abroad, pointing to the 'probability of more or less disturbance on the decisions about the queen's future rank and residence', and he confessed that 'I do not like to have numbers of houses and of servants at a time when so many poor people around me are almost in a state of starvation'.[6] He attended the Renfrewshire county meeting, 4 Jan. 1821, when he unsuccessfully moved an amendment to a loyal address, calling for the removal of ministers.[7] He 'strenuously supported the principle' of the Grampound disfranchisement bill, which would 'give the manufacturing classes their due weight in the state', 12 Feb., and said next day that he might 'put in a claim' for Glasgow.[8] He supported Lord Archibald Hamilton's motion criticizing the Church of Scotland's decision to remove the queen's name from the liturgy, 15 Feb., as it was 'prejudging' the issue. He was granted one month's leave for urgent private business, 16 Feb., and another two months on account of ill health, 13 Mar. He supported the petition of James Turner, a Glasgow rioter arrested for treason but not tried or compensated, whose case was 'more severe than it ought to have been', 2 May. He explained on 8 May that he had accepted the Seditious Meetings Act in 1819 as a temporary measure, and would therefore 'consider himself guilty of a breach of faith' if he voted for repeal, although he thought it was no longer necessary. However, he 'laboured under no such difficulty' with regard to the Seditious and Blasphemous Libel Act. He warned that unless 'the work of machinery was subject to the revenue laws and ... the poor rates', unemployment and poverty would continue to increase, 7 June. Next day he complained that the West of Scotland was being 'inundated' with Irish labourers, who 'received lower wages than the rest of the population and could live upon them because they disregarded all the decencies and comforts of life'. It was essential for 'some guarantee' to be 'given by the manufacturer out of his profits in times of prosperity', to maintain 'those whom he could not employ' when trade declined.[9] In a flowery speech, 26 June, he moved for a committee to examine Robert Owen of New Lanark's plan (presented at a Lanarkshire meeting which he had attended, 9 Apr.)[10] to provide permanent employment for the working classes. He admitted that it was 'impossible to say' whether the scheme could be applied generally, but he believed its 'tendency' was to 'increase the consumption of the poor and ... augment the value of all articles of home production'. He complained that Parliament had neglected the interests of the labourers, who had seen their common land, 'the life-rent property of successive generations', taken by enclosure to 'become the haunt of the pettifogging attorney or the unsightly villa of some sordid money lender', while they were forced into 'crowded assemblies of manufacture'. They felt 'deeply injured by the privileged and influential classes of society', who had imposed high taxes and the corn and combination laws on them, and the 'degradation of human nature' had driven many to crime and violence. At least in him they had 'a feeble but ... sincere advocate', who would endeavour to save the country from the 'undue influence of the crown and ... misgovernment'. He said that he would not divide the House, and his motion was negatived; a radical Whig Member described his speech as 'wild' and 'absurd'.[11] He seconded Hamilton's motion to repeal the clause in the Beer Duties Act requiring accounts of beer sales, 29 June, observing that 'the error which pervaded this measure' was 'apparent in other measures connected with Scotland', such as the malt tax and the proposed duty on herring fishing, 'each of which tended to destroy a portion of the trade of the country'.[12] At the Michaelmas head court in Renfrewshire, 9 Oct., he raised the corn law question, declaring that it 'operated to the hurt of the commercial classes' and suggesting a 'fair and moderate duty' of 5-6*s*. to allow for the local expenses borne by landowners. He chaired a subsequent county meeting, 10 Dec. 1821, when he advocated setting the duty at a level to keep the price of wheat at 30*s*. a quarter; he defended his position in two letters published in the local press.[13]

He presented a Renfrewshire petition for relief from agricultural distress, 29 Apr., and argued that 'all restrictions on the consumption of grain by prevention of distilling ought to be revised', 7 May 1822.[14] His remedy was 'protecting duties and reduction of taxes ... until the labourer can live as cheaply as the Frenchman or the Belgian', 13 May. He was 'satisfied that the *eau medicinale* brought forward by the government in the shape of Peel's [1819 currency] bill had created the existing distress by throwing the burden on the producer', 2 July 1822. He was instrumental in summoning a Renfrewshire meeting on distress, 16 Jan. 1823, when he called for 'very great retrenchments' and relief from the 'great pressure of taxes', which would increase consumption, cheapen labour costs and enable landowners to reduce rents. He presented the resulting petition, 20 Feb., but regretted the prevailing mood of 'total indifference' in the House.[15] He seconded Peter Moore's motion to amend the combination laws, which gave 'protection to wealth and power by withdrawing it from poverty and weakness', 3 Mar. Next day he advocated repeal of the Scottish cottage window tax, which was 'viewed in the most unpopular light' as revenue officers often pocketed the money.[16] He admitted that he now doubted the wisdom of imposing taxes on machinery, 25 Apr., but he thought 'some regulations ... fixing ... minimum' wages in the silk industry would be 'serviceable to the community at large', 21 May, and maintained that labourers, 'whether agricultural or manufacturing', should 'be protected as much as possible from the effects of machinery', 30 May. That day he presented a petition from Middlesex inhabitants for higher wages. He seconded Hamilton's motion for reform of Scotland's representation, 2 June, maintaining that the people were 'extremely dissatisfied with the existing system', which was responsible for Parliament's neglect of the labourers, excessive taxation, 'vice and general discontent'. He paired with the majority for the Scottish juries bill, 20 June 1823. In notes on Christianity made about this time, he observed that it 'inculcates the love of our neighbour and pleads the cause of the poor', but he feared these values were being lost in 'pomp and pageantry' and wished to see the abolition of 'those human abuses which disfigure our form of communication with the Supreme Being'.[17] He presented a Glasgow petition against the combination laws, 12 May 1824.[18] He was 'decidedly opposed to approximating the Scotch poor laws to those ... in England', 14 May.[19] He favoured 'the principle' of extending the Small Debts Act to Scotland, 10 June 1824, but wished to end imprisonment in such cases. That month he wrote to the home secretary, Peel, in support of a memorial from the Glasgow Episcopalians requesting financial aid from government. He observed that 'the Tweed and the Solway seem insurpassable obstacles to enlightened statesmanship in advancing the salutary reign of the English liturgy, and their energy seems impaired in proportion to the necessities of those who claim its exercise'.[20] He approved of Richard Martin's ill-treatment of animals bill, 24 Mar. 1825, believing that 'no duty' was 'more imperative upon the House than that of affording protection to animals'. He clarified his position on the corn laws, 2 May, explaining that farmers deserved protection 'to the extent of the poor rates and the particular duties drawn from agriculture', but that they were 'not ... entitled to the same protection against foreign competition as other manufacturers received'. He presented a Renfrewshire cotton spinners' petition for reduced working hours, 31 May, and one from weavers in the West of Scotland against re-enactment of the combination laws, 21 June, when he suggested that they might be 'bound by indentures ... to ensure ... good workmanship'.[21] He voted for Hume's amendment to the combination bill to prevent factory masters from enforcing the law as justices, 27 June, and declared that 'combinations must be rendered legal, or a minimum of wages established', 30 June 1825. He attended the Renfrewshire meeting, 28 Feb. 1826, and carried modified resolutions on the Scottish banking system, recommending that the withdrawal of small notes be deferred until the superiority of the metallic substitute had been 'demonstrated by the projected alteration in the currency of England'.[22] He maintained that it was 'impossible to keep faith with the public creditor and ... continue a metallic currency' without tax reductions, 26 May. That day he presented a petition from a 'vast number' of unemployed artisans at Pollokshaws asking for assistance to emigrate. Shortly afterwards the chancellor of the exchequer, Robinson, wrote expressing regret that he and the premier had not been able to meet with

Maxwell on this subject.[23] At the general election that summer he was returned unopposed for Renfrewshire, after giving a detailed account of his parliamentary stewardship and explaining that, while he had 'formerly advocated the cause of the farmer', he believed the 'case was now different' and that the price of corn 'should be regulated by the wages of the manufacturers'. He rejoiced at the triumph of 'liberal opinions', through the 'all-powerful force of moral truth', and acknowledged that there was 'in the popular part' of Liverpool's government 'a desire for improvement, and an anxiety to educate the people, which would do honour to the Whigs themselves'. He pledged to do 'all ... in his power to remove the shackles which had so long been laid on human nature'; 'they should have free thought as well as free trade'.[24]

He attended the Lanarkshire meeting on distress, 23 Sept. 1826, when he urged the need to 'strike at the root of the evil', as the 'great mass of the inhabitants' had been 'reduced to a state of mendicity from the effects of war and misrule', and everything should be done to help them even if it involved 'trenching on the property of the county or the kingdom'.[25] Early in 1827 he presented several petitions from Scottish operatives for assistance to emigrate, and he expressed the hope, 16 Feb., that ministers might 'take advantage of the feeling which at present prevailed in the House on the subject'. He again complained of the 'inundation' of Irish into Scotland, 9 Mar. That month he sent Peel details of a scheme to help 300 families emigrate to Canada, with some accompanying remarks on the 'abuse of the poor law in Scotland'. However, his requests to the new prime minister, Canning, for the coalition government to make a £50,000 donation to the emigration relief committee fund were finally disappointed, 18 May.[26] Presenting a petition from the 'productive classes' of Renfrewshire for free trade in corn and parliamentary reform, 22 Feb., he observed that the former would 'partly indemnify the artisan and labourer for the evils induced by the rivalry of mechanical labour without disturbing the general law for agricultural protection', and declared that 'the genius and spirit of the constitution' justified extending the franchise to 'those who paid taxes', which would in turn 'produce greater economy in government'. He presented a Rutherglen petition for revision of the corn laws, 12 Mar., and stated that 'it was his intention to vote for the lowest duties'.[27] He paired for Catholic relief, 6 Mar. He divided against Canning's ministry to separate bankruptcy jurisdiction from the court of chancery, 22 May. He voted with the majorities to disfranchise Penryn, 28 May, and for Lord Althorp's election expenses bill, 28 May 1827. He divided against the duke of Wellington's ministry for more efficient control over crown proceedings for the recovery of penalties under the customs and excise laws, 1 May, to condemn the misapplication of public money for building work at Buckingham House, 23 June, inquire into the Irish church establishment, 24 June, refer the additional churches bill to a committee, 30 June, and reduce the salary of the lieutenant-general of the ordnance, 4 July 1828. However, he voted 'with pleasure' for the financial provision for Canning's family, as his services to the country were 'well deserving of reward', 22 May. He presented three Glasgow petitions for repeal of the Test Acts, which reflected 'the sentiments of the whole body of Dissenters in Scotland', 2 May. He divided for Catholic relief, 12 May. He hoped that government would pass the 'anxiously looked for' Scottish parochial settlements bill, 6 May, and argued that the Irish, who 'benefit by a low price of labour', should 'partake of the burdens which its introduction imposes upon Scotland'; he added that the poor law system 'diminishes the real value of the union between the three countries'. He considered the usury laws amendment bill 'somewhat objectionable in a moral point of view, and on the principle of justice', 20 May, and cautioned against making it retrospective, as many would be 'involved in ruin'. He declared his 'decided feeling in favour of a silver currency', 16 June. He supported an inquiry into the Colne handloom weavers' petition for wage regulation, 1 July 1828, warning that 'the question is not yet set at rest'.

He voted for the government's Catholic emancipation bill, 6, 30 Mar. 1829, when he claimed that the Scottish people were 'nearly divided upon it', with the 'lower classes' being mostly hostile, whereas 'the more intelligent' were 'happy to see the legislature following the lights of the age and spreading blessings over the kingdom'. He concurred with a friendly petition from Paisley, 7 Apr., that 'the principles of the constitution are attacked' by the Irish disfranchisement bill, on which he had not voted from 'fear of having it used as a precedent in cases of future votes upon corrupt boroughs'. Nevertheless, he believed that Irish 40*s.* freeholds were a 'great encouragement to those hovel establishments, which send out constant swarms of poor, uneducated labourers ... into England and Scotland'. That day he favoured referring petitions from the silk trade to a committee, observing that outside Parliament 'there prevails the greatest possible disbelief of the advantages of the free trade system'. He presented a Renfrewshire freeholders' petition for inquiry into distress, 7 May, but said he had refrained from submitting the desired motion for wage regulation because of the 'strong feeling' in the House against it. However, when presenting a Renfrewshire weavers' petition for such regulation, 1 June, he announced that if no inquiry was granted he would move for one next session. He voted for a fixed duty on imported corn, 19 May. On 28 May he and the deputy advocate, Henry Home Drummond, introduced the Scottish landward parishes assessment bill, to give magistrates discretionary powers to vary the poor rate in certain districts, 'so as to preserve the distinction between the local poor and the hordes who flock in upon them'. It permitted a higher rate of assessment to be imposed on 'those bringing in [Irish] migrants', who had spread the 'same improvident spirit among the lower classes of the Scotch people'; his measure sought to 'uphold those distinctions of character which it is ... important to maintain among the poor and the unfortunate'. The bill gained its second reading, 1 June, but made no further progress.[28] He thought it was 'now obvious', 12 June, that the resumption of cash payments ought to have been accompanied by tax reductions on the necessaries of life, but the 'unequal management of the public concerns' had 'operated ... injuriously upon prices and given a stimulus to machinery, so as to affect the wages of labour'. He urged ministers to consider a levy 'even ... at the rate of 25 per cent upon real capital', and favoured 'some arrangement' to encourage employers and workmen to fix wage rates monthly. He was surprised that the government's seisins bill did not 'put an end to these forms altogether', 31 Mar. He supported the Scottish gaols bill, 27 May, but reiterated his desire to see an end to imprisonment for small debts. He voted to reduce the grant for the sculpture of the marble arch, 25 May, and for Lord Blandford's reform resolutions, 2 June. He presented a Renfrewshire petition against renewal of the East India Company's charter, 3 June 1829. In January 1830 he approved of the planned county meeting on distress and advised against any appearance of hostility to ministers, who had 'already shown so much political resolution, when the general good required it' and might be persuaded to 'speedily introduce a more equitable system of finance'. He chaired the meeting, which carried resolutions in favour of tax reductions and public works, 4 Feb.[29] He said he would not oppose the second reading of the poor removal bill, 26 May, but warned that 'some apprehension is felt on the subject in Scotland'. He reintroduced his landward parishes bill, 7 June, and secured its second reading, 24 June, but he agreed to postpone it until another session, 8 July. He supported Attwood's currency motion, 8 June, as the silver standard was 'merely ... a restoration of our ancient system' and would promote employment and better wages. He welcomed the government's 'most proper and just' Scottish judicature bill, to create a more 'expeditious and economical' system, 1 Apr., and praised their conduct in 'giving up so much patronage'. He was pleased that it was 'only an incipient bill', 18 June, but noted with regard to judges' salaries that 'even in these pinching times ... [the] question of expense ought not to be too closely looked at', as 'first-rate talent ... must be liberally paid'. He voted to reduce the grant for public buildings, 3 May, and for Labouchere's motion regarding the civil government of Canada, 25 May. He divided against abolition of the death penalty for forgery, 7 June. He had 'very serious objections' to the usury laws repeal bill, which would 'tend to produce great confusion' with respect to public works contracts, 14 June. He paired against additional securities in the libel law amendment bill, 6 July 1830. At the dissolution that summer he made way for Sir Michael Shaw Stewart, Member for Lanarkshire, in accordance with an arrangement made in December 1828, and he chose not to contest Lanarkshire as originally envisaged, leaving it to his father. Intriguingly, before making this decision he had communicated with Lord Rosslyn, a prominent Scottish Tory, who assured him 'respecting the Lanark election' that 'the support you have afforded to ... government in the late questions of the session will be acknowledged with thanks'.[30] He delivered a farewell address at Renfrew, where he observed that last session he had 'been seen supporting ministers more than on any former occasion'. He endorsed Shaw Stewart as an 'independent' who would 'keep himself ... free from the wiles of Court and ... the patronage of ministers' and not support 'any rash or visionary wars ... to interfere with the liberties of other countries'. One who heard him speak did 'not desire to hear him again' and was 'not surprised the H. of C. would not listen to him'.[31]

Maxwell offered for Lanarkshire at the general election in May 1831 as a supporter of the Grey ministry's 'great and efficacious' reform bill. He maintained that 'the people ... were entitled to the ... franchise from their education and intellectual capacities', and was confident that reform would 'strengthen' the constitution. He was defeated by the Tory sitting Member after a riotous contest.[32] On 17 Oct. he spoke at a Renfrewshire meeting in favour of an address to the king for the creation of new peers, to facilitate the passage of reform, and at a similar meeting in Lanarkshire, 7 Nov., he expressed confidence that Grey would be 'the deliverer of this country'. A letter from him was read to a meeting of the Renfrewshire Political Union, 13 Nov. 1831, stating that he had been in communication with Lord John Russell to suggest improvements to the voter qualification clauses of the Scottish bill, but he declined an invitation to act as the union's London representative.[33] At the general election of 1832, when his father was returned for Paisley, he accepted a requisition to stand for Lanarkshire, as one who was 'favourable disposed' to the Whig ministry and prepared 'in some questions, such as the emancipation of slaves, free trade, East India and Bank charters ... to defer to their knowledge and integrity'; he was comfortably returned and sat until his retirement in 1837.[34] He succeeded to his father's title and 'large estates' in Lanarkshire and Renfrewshire in 1844. He died in June 1865 and was succeeded by his nephew William Stirling Maxwell (1818-78).[35]

[1] Glasgow City Archives, Maxwell mss T-PM 116/184; 117/2/60. [2] *Glasgow Herald*, 6, 24 Mar. 1820. [3] Maxwell mss T-PM 117/3/225. [4] *The Times*, 20 May 1820. [5] Maxwell mss T-PM 117/2/81; 117/3/33. [6] Ibid. 116/213. [7] *Glasgow Herald*, 5, 8 Jan. 1821. [8] *The Times*, 14 Feb. 1821. [9] Ibid. 8, 9 Apr. 1821. [10] *Glasgow Herald*, 13 Apr. 1821. [11] HLRO, Hist. Coll. 379, Grey Bennet diary, 105. [12] *The Times*, 30 June 1821. [13] *Glasgow Herald*, 12 Oct., 14 Dec. 1821, 4, 8 Feb. 1822. [14] *The Times*, 30 Apr., 8 May 1822. [15] *Glasgow Herald*, 10, 17, 24 Jan.; *The Times*, 21 Feb. 1823. [16] *The Times*, 5 Mar. 1823. [17] Maxwell mss T-PM 117/5/34. [18] *The Times*, 13 May 1824. [19] Ibid. 15 May 1824. [20] Add. 40364, f. 125. [21] *The Times*, 1, 22 June 1825. [22] *Glasgow Herald*, 3 Mar. 1826. [23] *The Times*, 27 May 1826; Maxwell mss T-PM 117/2/22. [24] *Greenock Advertiser*, 4 July 1826. [25] *Glasgow Herald*, 25 Sept. 1826. [26] *The Times*, 13, 17 Feb., 11, 12 Apr., 9 May 1827; Add. 40392, ff. 281-93. [27] *The Times*, 13 Mar. 1827. [28] P. Jupp, *British Politics on Eve of Reform*, 176-7. [29] *Glasgow Herald*, 22 Jan., 5 Feb. 1830. [30] Maxwell mss T-PM 117/1/179; 117/3/1. [31] *Glasgow Herald*, 13 Aug. 1830; Hopetoun mss 167, f. 161. [32] *Glasgow Herald*, 16 May 1831. [33] Ibid. 21 Oct., 11, 18, 21 Nov. 1831. [34] Ibid. 30 July, 24, 31 Dec. 1832. [35] *Gent. Mag.* (1865), ii. 244-5.

T.A.J.

MAXWELL, Sir William, 5th bt. (1779–1838), of Monreith, Wauphill, Wigtown.

WIGTOWNSHIRE	15 Apr. 1805–1812
WIGTOWNSHIRE	30 July 1822–1830

b. 5 Mar. 1779, 1st s. of Sir William Maxwell, 4th bt., of Monreith and Katherine, da. and h. of David Blair of Adamton, Ayr. *m.* 23 Apr. 1803, his cos. Catharine, da. of John Fordyce† of Ayton, Berwick, 3s. 6da. (1 *d.v.p.*). *suc.* fa. as 5th bt. 17 Feb. 1812. *d.* 22 Aug. 1838.

Maj. army 1802, 26 Ft. 1803; maj. Wigtown vol. inf. 1803-7; lt.-col. army 1805, ret. 1811; col. commdt. Wigtown militia 1814; maj. Wigtown yeoman cav. 1817.

Maxwell lost his left arm when commanding the Cameronians at Corunna and was wounded in the knee at Walcheren. He was an intelligent, bombastic, God-fearing man and an affectionate but overbearingly fussy father to his eldest son and heir William, born in 1805, who was briefly at Harrow but hankered after an army career. His great passion was the breeding and racing of horses, and he had a large string in training at Middleham, Yorkshire.[1] As Member for his county of Wigtownshire, 1805-12, he had supported the Tory ministries of Pitt, Portland and Perceval, though his father, whom he succeeded in 1812, was a Foxite Whig; but he regarded himself as the man who, when not out of his teens, had 'established a political independency' in the county in defiance of the powerful Galloway interest. On the sudden death of the independent sitting Member Hunter Blair in July 1822 he came forward, as he claimed eight years later, to uphold 'the independent interest' against a 'long formed' plot by a small group of related lairds to fill the seat in rotation, even though a resumption of his parliamentary career was 'entirely unsuited to my inclination and habits'. He easily defeated the son of one of these men, his former ally, having assured Lord Melville, the Liverpool ministry's Scottish manager, who remained neutral, that 'every day affords new proofs of the wisdom of present measures and matter to confirm my already settled principles'.[2]

He divided with government on the sinking fund, 3 Mar., against repeal of the house tax, 10 Mar., and for the grant for Irish glebe houses, 11 Apr. 1823. It was surely not he who voted in the Whig opposition minority for inquiry into the Irish church establishment, 4 Mar., or their majority for the Scottish juries bill, 20 June 1823. In September he agreed to let his son leave his clerical tutor in Northamptonshire and 'remain at home and become my pupil', but warned him that he would 'have an instructor requiring as much instruction as you yourself do'. In February 1824 he described Edinburgh as 'the most infernal place I ever was in'.[3] He apparently returned smartly to Wigtownshire, and no trace of parliamentary activity has been found for that session, during which his son got a commission in the cavalry. In 1825, when he was reckoned to have 'attended seldom', he voted for the Irish unlawful societies bill, 25 Feb., and against the Irish franchise bill, 26 Apr., and the Catholic relief bill, 10 May.[4] He seems to have been inactive in 1826, when he was returned unopposed for Wigtownshire at the general election. He was a cypher in the 1826 Parliament, where he divided against Catholic relief, 6 Mar. 1827, 12 May 1828. In November 1828 he amicably acquiesced in his removal from the office of vice-lieutenant of Wigtownshire, which he had held since 1812, by the new lord lieutenant, Lord Garlies*, son of the 8th earl of Galloway.[5] Two months later Planta, the Wellington ministry's patronage secretary, predicted that he would side 'with government' for the concession of Catholic emancipation, but he evidently did not vote on the issue. Maxwell, who by his own admission was always too nervous to speak in debate, though he possessed a fluent enough tongue in less forbidding circumstances, went abroad for the sake of his and his wife's health and for financial reasons at some point in 1829: they were at Bagneres in southern France in September and had settled in Nice by early November.[6] Maxwell remained there, apart from summer excursions to Switzerland and northern Italy, for almost five years. In April 1830 he confided to his son that 'I never mean to offer myself as a candidate [again], nor should I last election had it not been with a view to your future success'. Warning William, who seemed to be 'careless' about standing, to keep this quiet and not be seduced by the Galloway family's blandishments, he observed that if he did aspire to the county representation it could not be attained

> without pains and troubles, listening without hot reply to a great deal of nonsense you will hear. In short, make as far as you are concerned every man pleased with himself. You must eat at their houses what you hate, drink when not but appear to be thirsty, flatter their wives, kiss bubbly children, and make love to the daughters. Join no party if any such exist ... I am happy to think I never did or said a thing to gain my return which I would not do again, without very much regret. To be sure I have eat[en] two large plates of broth stuffed full of parsnips, my abhorrence ... when canvassing drunk more bumpers of bad port to success to the independent interest than was according to Hoyle, but this gained my point, and perhaps left a pleasing remembrance of me.[7]

On 12 July 1830, having learnt of the dissolution necessitated by the death of George IV, he privately informed his son-in-law and preferred successor Hugh Hathorn of his intention of retiring and lectured William, who had evidently shown some inclination to stand:

> I think you mistake the best place to become fit to make a figure in Parliament. Little is to be picked up there but severe colds and a certainty that most men's speeches are better when said than listened to. The preparation ought to be an extended view of men, a knowledge of foreign courts and enlarged acquaintance of the world, which in London as relating to Europe or the other three quarters of the globe is seen far more obscurely than even through the medium of books, which can only teach in theory.

He advised William to stress his wish to 'support the independence of the county' while reserving his candidature for a future opportunity, and, on his professed political leanings, commented:

> I fear ... if you have incautiously stated your determination to be an *oppositionist* your chance is cut ... A declared man who enlists to one side or the other is equally a slave as he who would lose a salary, who said yes when the minister expected, no when opposition is made ... No man has any right to talk of conscience who does not vote for one or the other side according to circumstances ... I have no doubt that had I stood pledged to any party, a declared ministerial candidate would have sometimes beat me ... My bias was strongly ... to ministry except on Fox's [1806] administration, by a firm belief that had they [Whigs] come into power or longer remained, Britain would never have attained its present rank among nations.

He announced his retirement publicly soon afterwards.[8]

Maxwell, who alienated Hathorn by pressing him to stand, was not best pleased to hear of the return of Sir Andrew Agnew of Lochnaw, whom he regarded as a potential Galloway 'vassal'. When the Grey ministry came to power in late 1830 he observed sarcastically to William that 'now that the patriotic Whigs, your favourites, have got in I suppose we shall have *no taxes* [and] they of course will all give up for the public good their salaries'.[9] His son's costly entanglement with more than one 'artful worthless female' caused him great but temporary vexation in 1831, when he toyed with the idea of dashing to Scotland to vote for Hathorn, an avowed opponent of the ministerial reform scheme, against Agnew, its equivocal supporter, but stayed put because Hathorn (who lost by one vote) did not request his aid.[10] In July 1831 he wrote:

> I look to the reform bill being passed, the excitement subsided and ministers in the exercise of their diplomatic functions supporting those necessary measures in our foreign and domestic policy, which difficult times produce ... Above all I wait to see with what tinsel they will adorn and make pleasing to their friends of the gutter the downfall of all the utopian promises this reform was to bring about ... I prophesy they will not be in office two sessions.[11]

Five months later he condemned the evils of 'bigotry' of all types and, conceding that a degree of reform was now unavoidable and necessary, lamented the duke of Wellington's rash declaration against any change in November 1830, which had

> lost Britain its fittest statesman and which I can't think was expressed with thought. Had he flattered a little and offered to discuss a moderate reform he might have given what reform he liked. He would now have been England's idol and its pilot and the tumult and scenes of devilment which are now passed ... would have been avoided and those men whose bigotry to new fashioned theories are

turning away from old friendly allies ... would now be reaping the neglect they deserve.[12]

The spread of Dissent and lapse from piety in his own parish also appalled him:

> What was, when I left home, a delightful society of friends, all striving along the same path to enter at the same gate, is now a bear garden, father divided against son, mother against daughter, all the worst passions in full operation, and can it be supposed that bigotry and total irreligion could so soon have spread its baneful influence even to the cottage fireside, blinding men's eyes to such a degree that the hour dedicated to the lessons of wisdom of our Creator and Redeemer on the Sabbath evening is now spent by the youths in idleness and mischief.[13]

His wife died in December 1832 and was buried at Nice.[14] He returned to Scotland in August 1834, by which time William had married and settled down, though financial worries continued to harass him. On the eve of the general election of 1835 he tried unsuccessfully to talk William out of his resolution 'never' to stand for Wigtownshire and encouraged him at least to exert himself to keep up the family interest.[15] In June 1835, about to go abroad again and anticipating death there, he disposed of 'some trifles of personal property' and assured his son, who he hoped would 'find my affairs so managed as to give you little trouble', that 'if ever I have said or ever done a harsh or unkind thing to you it was not done from want of love'.[16] He did return, but he died at Monreith in August 1838. By his brief will, dated 5 Apr. 1825, he left all his property to William, his sole executor. His personalty was sworn under £1,500 in the province of Canterbury, but his Scottish estate was proved under £10,688.[17]

[1] NLS, Maxwell mss Acc 7043/8, Maxwell to son [1821], 28 May, 29 Aug., 22 Sept. 1822; *HP Commons, 1790-1820*, iv. 573-4. [2] Maxwell mss, Maxwell to son, 6 Apr., 12 July 1830, 8 Sept. 1832; NAS GD46/4/127; GD51/1/198/28/15; *Glasgow Herald*, 5 Aug. 1822. [3] Maxwell mss, Maxwell to son, 18 Sept. 1823, 7 Feb. 1824. [4] *Session of Parl. 1825*, p. 476. [5] NLS Acc 6604/1, Garlies to Maxwell, 11 Nov., reply, 16 Nov. 1828. [6] Maxwell mss, Maxwell to son, 18 Sept., 6 Nov. 1829. [7] Ibid. Maxwell to son, 6 Apr. 1830. [8] Ibid.; *Caledonian Mercury*, 26 July 1830. [9] Maxwell mss, Maxwell to son, 26 Aug., 10 Sept., 2 Dec. 1830. [10] Ibid. Maxwell to son, 13, 22 May, 10, 19 June 1831. [11] Ibid. Maxwell to son, 14 July 1831. [12] Ibid. Maxwell to son, 5 Dec. 1831. [13] Ibid. Maxwell to son, 5 Jan., 3 Mar. 1832. [14] *Gent. Mag.* (1833), i. 95. [15] Ibid. Maxwell to son, 26 June, 21 Aug., 17 Dec. 1834. [16] Ibid. Maxwell to son, 25 June 1835. [17] *Gent. Mag.* (1838), ii. 441-2; PROB 11/1904/770; IR26/1492/943.

D.R.F.

MAYHEW, William (1788–1855), of 54 Crutched Friars, London and Coggeshall, Essex.

COLCHESTER 9 Apr. 1831–1832

bap. 2 Mar. 1788, 1st s. of William Mayhew of Coggeshall and w. Hannah.[1] *m.* Sophia, 1s. and other issue.[2] *d.* 26 Apr. 1855.

Mayhew belonged to a family who had established themselves in eastern Essex and southern Suffolk by the early eighteenth century. He was descended from Augustine Mayhew (1622-93), an attorney and lord of the manors of Great and Little Coggeshall. Another of his ancestors was William Mayhew (?1736-87), of Colchester, a barrister and a bencher of Gray's Inn, high steward and recorder of Colchester and recorder of Ipswich and Aldeburgh, who died without legitimate issue.[3] His father, a freeman of Colchester, lived at Coggeshall, where he evidently earned his living as a woolcomber before becoming a victualler and innkeeper around the turn of the century. His sons William, Thomas Eaton (*b.* 1790) and James (*b.* 1792) and his daughter Anne (*b.* 1797) were baptized at Great Coggeshall Independent chapel.[4] Thomas Eaton Mayhew became a cabinet maker in Coggeshall, while William and James migrated to London. James was described as a brandy merchant there in 1818, and was probably in partnership with William, who by 1816 was operating as a wine, spirit and beer merchant from 106 Fenchurch Street.[5] In about 1827 he moved to 54 Crutched Friars.

The Mayhews plumped for the ministerialist sitting Member standing on the True Blue corporation interest at the 1820 general election in Colchester.[6] William chaired the anniversary dinner of the Chelmsford Pitt Club, 28 May 1823, and at the Colchester celebration of the return of the True Blue Sir George Smyth in 1826 either he or James was toasted.[7] At the by-election of April 1829 precipitated by Smyth's retirement in disgust at the Wellington ministry's concession of Catholic emancipation the Mayhew brothers, protesting that his replacement Richard Sanderson had been foisted on the electors by the corporation, made the gesture of having William proposed as the champion of 'independent principles'. He did not go to a poll, but announced the imminent creation of a new London freemen's club to promote the cause of 'independence' and to challenge the hegemony of the corporation and the radical sitting Member Daniel Harvey, who had defied most of his constituents by supporting emancipation.[8] This London club flourished during the next year, and at the general election of 1830 William Mayhew was put up as its candidate against Harvey and the corporation nominee Andrew Spottiswoode, a supporter of administration. Mayhew described himself as 'a liberal Blue', who had he been in Parliament would invariably have voted with Harvey, attacked Spottiswoode as 'a cat's paw of the corporation' and insisted on his own independence. He finished a distant third after keeping the poll open for six days, at considerable personal cost.[9] Mayhew, who was involved in the formation of the New Colchester Independent Club in London in November 1830, had Spottiswoode's election declared void the day before the second reading of the Grey ministry's reform bill, 22 Mar. 1831, on the ground of his ineligibility as king's printer.[10] He came forward at the ensuing by-election as 'ever the enemy of corruption, profligacy and oppression, and the fearless advocate of the people's rights'. At a meeting of his London supporters, 28 Mar., he said:

> There was a time when I was against reform. I allude to that reform which was advocated when Mr. [Henry] Hunt* was lord of the ascendant. I have all along thought that some reform must take place, and the plan of reform brought forward by ministers is an exceedingly good one ... I think, however, that the clause which takes away the franchise of the present burgesses ought not to stand in its present form ... He could not vote for the measure as it now stood without first endeavouring to maintain the rights of all the freemen. He did not think the independent out-voters should be disfranchised.

He resisted pressure to pledge himself to support the bill without reserve, arguing that disfranchisement of non-resident freemen was 'little short of a robbery'; but he gave an assurance that he 'would not endanger the bill by persevering in his opposition to the objectionable clause'. The corporation, whom he accused on the hustings of corruption and misappropriation of municipal revenues, vindictively put up an absentee candidate against him and challenged his qualification. After an eight-day poll, which further drained his resources, Mayhew, whose brother died during the election, was comfortably returned. He proclaimed himself 'the friend of the people, not only from principle, but because he prided himself in belonging to the middle class'.[11] He took his seat in time to vote in the ministerial minority against Gascoyne's wrecking amendment to the reform bill, 19 Apr. 1831.

At the subsequent general election enthusiasm for reform temporarily masked the differences between Mayhew and Harvey and their supporters and produced an uneasy coalition which enabled them to defeat the corporation nominee. As well as reiterating his support for the bill, on the same terms as before, Mayhew renewed his attack on corporation 'corruption'.[12] He voted for the second reading of the reintroduced reform bill, 6 July 1831, and was for the most part a steady silent supporter of its details, though he voted for the total disfranchisement of Saltash, 26 July, against the proposed division of counties, 11 Aug., for the enfranchisement of £50 tenants-at-will, 18 Aug., and, in accordance with his election pledge, to preserve freemen's voting rights, 30 Aug.[13] He voted for the passage of the measure, 21 Sept. He divided with government on the Dublin election controversy, 23 Aug., but was in the minority for ending the Maynooth grant, 26 Sept. He rallied to ministers on the vote of confidence after the reform bill's defeat in the Lords, 10 Oct. 1831. Mayhew, who signed the requisition for a county meeting to support the government, 10 Dec., but evidently did not attend it,[14] voted for the second reading of the revised reform bill, 17 Dec. 1831, divided for its details and voted for the third reading, 22 Mar. 1832. He voted against government on the Russian-Dutch loan, 26 Jan., 12 July, and for inquiry into distress in the glove trade, 31 Jan.; but he was in their majority on relations with Portugal, 9 Feb. He presented Coggeshall petitions against the factories regulation bill, 8, 16 Mar. He divided for the address calling on the king to appoint only ministers who would carry the reform bill unimpaired, 10 May, and the second reading of the Irish bill, 25 May, and paired against a Conservative amendment to the Scottish measure, 1 June. He was in minorities for the immediate abolition of slavery, 24 May, an Irish absentee tax, 19 June, and representation for New South Wales, 28 June. He voted to make coroners' inquests public, 20 June 1832. He lost his seat at the general election in December, when he finished a poor third behind Harvey and a Conservative.[15]

Nothing has been discovered of his subsequent life until he was declared bankrupt on 9 Jan. 1843, when he had an address at 2 De Crespigny Place, Camberwell, Surrey, as well as that of his business in Crutched Friars. A second and final dividend of one halfpence in the pound was declared on 15 Feb. 1844.[16] Mayhew died intestate at the home of one Edward Mayhew at 7 Park Terrace, Old Ford Road, Bow, London in April 1855, leaving a widow and an unknown number of 'natural and lawful children'. Administration of his estate, which was sworn under a derisory £20, was granted to his son William.[17]

[1] IGI (Essex). [2] PROB 6/232/386. [3] *Gent. Mag.* (1787), ii. 1128; PROB 11/1161/32. [4] *Colchester Pollbook* (1781), 8; (1788), 10; (1790), 8; (1796), 8; (1806), 9; (1807), 8; (1812), 20; IGI (Essex). [5] *Colchester Pollbook* (1812), 20; (1818), 22; (1820), 31. [6] Ibid.

(1820), 31. [7] *Colchester Gazette*, 31 May 1823, 22 July 1826; M.E. Speight, 'Politics in Colchester' (London Univ. Ph.D. thesis, 1969), 147. [8] *Colchester Gazette*, 25 Apr. 1829. [9] Ibid. 31 July, 7 Aug. 1830; Speight, 192-3. [10] *Colchester Gazette*, 12 Nov., 11 Dec. 1830, 1 Jan., 12, 26 Mar. 1831; *CJ*, lxxxvi. 110-2, 411. [11] *Colchester Gazette*, 26 Mar., 2, 9 Apr. 1831; Speight, 48-49, 103-4, 236. [12] *Colchester Gazette*, 30 Apr. 7, 14 May 1831. [13] *The Times*, 13 Aug.; *Colchester Gazette*, 3, 24 Sept. 1831. [14] *Colchester Gazette*, 3, 17 Dec. 1831. [15] Ibid. 15, 22 Dec. 1832. [16] *London Gazette*, 17 Jan., 17 Mar., 25 Apr., 19 May, 26 Dec. 1843, 23 Feb. 1844. [17] *Gent. Mag.* (1855), ii. 216; PROB 6/232/286.

D.R.F.

METCALFE, Henry (1780–1822), of Laurence's Street, Drogheda, co. Louth and Fludyer Street, Mdx.

DROGHEDA 1820–11 Feb. 1822

b. 20 Aug. 1780, 3rd s. of James Metcalfe, attorney, of Drogheda and w. Elizabeth Richards. *educ.* by Mr. Crawford; Trinity, Dublin, 1796-1800; King's Inns 1800; I. Temple 1800. *m. s.p. d.* 11 Feb. 1822.

Mayor, Drogheda 1808.

Metcalfe's father, who from 27 Nov. 1766 was an attorney of the Irish court of exchequer, had in 1783 acquired a highly favourable lease on 'premises at West Gate' from Drogheda corporation, of which Metcalfe became a leading alderman, serving as mayor in 1808.[1] At the 1820 general election he came forward to succeed the retiring Member with the support of the corporation. After a venal five-day contest against a Catholic backed independent he was returned with a large majority.[2] The Countess de Salis later wrote of the town's 'disgrace' at 'being bought by an attorney', but a petition against his return on the ground of bribery came to nothing.[3] In a move probably designed to compensate him for his expenditure, on 13 Nov. 1820 Drogheda corporation granted him a 'parcel of land' at Duleek Gate on very advantageous terms.[4] He was listed by the Liverpool ministry as seeking public office for Peter Van Homrigh*, Drogheda's recorder, and as having 'strongly recommended' one John Dardis as an inspector of fisheries.

Metcalfe voted for Catholic claims, 28 Feb., and was credited with arguing in its favour in his only known speech, which was delivered in such a 'low tone' as to be inaudible, 16 Mar. 1821.[5] He divided with ministers against revenue cuts, 6 Mar., repeal of the additional malt duty, 3 Apr., military reductions, 11 Apr., and the disfranchisement of ordnance officials, 12 Apr. He was granted ten days' leave on account of ill health, 11 May. He divided against further economies and retrenchment, 27 June 1821. He died 'at Dublin' in February 1822, leaving a widow, who expired at Rathmines, county Dublin, that September and was interred in the same tomb in St. Mary's churchyard.[6]

[1] J. D'Alton, *Hist. Drogheda*, i. 257; *PP* (1835), xxviii. 412. [2] *Dublin Evening Post*, 2, 14, 18, 28 Mar., 11 Apr.; *Belfast News Letter*, 8, 18 Feb., 3, 21 Mar. 1820. [3] PRO NI, Foster mss D562/357, Salis to J.L. Foster, 1 Mar. 1822. [4] *PP* (1835), xxviii. 412. [5] *The Times*, 17 Mar. 1821. [6] *Belfast News Letter*, 15 Feb., 13 Sept. 1822; *Gent. Mag.* (1822), i. 478.

P.J.S.

METGE, John (c.1750–1823), of Athlumney, Navan, co. Meath.

DUNDALK 1806–Jan. 1807
DUNDALK 1812–Dec. 1812
DUNDALK 1820–June 1820

b. c.1750, 2nd s. of Peter Metge of Athlumney and Warrenstown and Anne Lyon. *m.* (1) 1 Aug. 1777, Hon. Mary Bermingham, da. of Francis, 21st Bar. Athenry [I], wid. of Edmund Costello; (2) c. 1798, Henrietta, da. of Henry Cole Bowen of Bowen's Court, co. Cork, 3s. 2da. *suc.* bro. Peter Metge, MP [I], bar. of exch. [I], 1809. *d.* 28 Sept. 1823.

MP [I] 1783-1800.

Lt. 5 Drag. 1775-9.

Dep. auditor gen. [I] 1805-23.

Metge was agent and deputy at the Irish treasury to the 2nd earl of Roden, for whom he again served as a stopgap at Dundalk at the 1820 general election. He did not take his seat and by 19 June 1820 had vacated for another man.[1] He died at 'the residence of Mrs. Thompson', St. Valori, county Wicklow, in September 1823, and was succeeded by his eldest son Peter (*d.* 1873).[2]

[1] *CJ*, lxxv. 324. [2] *Belfast News Letter*, 30 Sept. 1823.

P.J.S.

MEYNELL, Henry (1789–1865), of 35 Grosvenor Street, Mdx.

LISBURN 1826–1847

b. 24 Aug. 1789, 2nd s. of Hugo Meynell (*d.* 1800) of Quorndon Hall, Leics. and Hon. Elizabeth Ingram Shepheard, da. and coh. of Charles Ingram†, 9th Visct. Irvine [S]. *educ.* Harrow 1797. *unm. d.* 24 Mar. 1865.

Vol. RN 1803, midshipman 1805, lt. 1809, cdr. 1813, capt. 1816, half-pay 1838, r.-adm. 1851, v.-adm. 1857, adm. 1862.

Gentleman usher to George IV 1820-30, to William IV 1830-1; groom in waiting to Victoria 1841-5.

Meynell's grandfather, Hugo Meynell of Bradley, Derbyshire, who was ministerialist Member for Lichfield, 1762-8, Lymington, 1769-74, and Stafford, 1774-80, was 'long esteemed the first fox-hunter in the kingdom'. Having had a son, Godfrey, with his first wife (Ann Gell), he married Ann, daughter of Thomas Boothby Skrymsher, and had two more. The elder of these, another Hugo, married on 2 Aug. 1782 one of the five daughters of the last Lord Irvine (*d.* 1778), another of whom was the wife of the 2nd marquess of Hertford.[1] Hugo Meynell junior died on 17 May 1800, following a fall from his horse while hunting; he left his property in trust to his wife, although Quorndon Hall, which his father had already made over to him, was sold at this time to Lord Sefton*.[2] The elder Hugo Meynell died on 14 Dec. 1808 and, by his will, his only surviving son Charles was the sole executor and residual legatee of his estate, which included personalty sworn under £7,500. However, it was said that most of the landed property, worth £11,000 a year, was inherited by his eldest grandson, Hugo Charles Meynell of Hoar Cross, Staffordshire.[3] He had already come into the estates of Templenewsam, Yorkshire, on the death of Viscountess Irvine in 1807, and was described by Sydney Smith as 'a gentlemanlike man, by which I mean a silent and supercilious man ... He is fond of dogs and horses and perhaps other things'.[4]

Henry Meynell, who was Hugo Charles's next brother, was educated at Harrow, where he remembered his contemporary Lord Althorp* as a republican.[5] He entered the navy in 1803, serving as a first class volunteer on the *Isis* at Newfoundland until early 1805. For the next year, during which he was promoted midshipman, he served on the *Pomone* and the *Captain* on the Lisbon and Home stations, and between 1806 and 1809 he saw action on board the *Boreas* and the *Lavinia* in British waters and in the Mediterranean. Promoted to lieutenant in November 1809, he joined the *Theban* early the following year, assisting at the capture of a French merchant brig near Dieppe on 2 Feb. 1811. Having survived the wreck of the *Theban* in a storm in September 1812, on its passage to India, he was nominated acting commander of the *Arrogant* at Bombay, and was made commander of the *Cornwallis* there in August 1813. He was acting captain of the *Jupiter* from August, and of the *Newcastle* from November 1815, and was confirmed in his captaincy of the latter, Sir Pulteney Malcolm's flagship at St. Helena, 10 Apr. 1816. It was while he held this command that he was said to have attracted the attention of Buonaparte, of whom he recorded some memoranda, by his 'refined manners and gentlemanly bearing, joined with the frankness and openness of a sailor'.[6] He was apparently paid off in September 1817 and, although in 1821 he expressed a general anxiety to continue his profession, he never again served at sea.[7]

Presumably through the influence of Hertford, the lord chamberlain, and his wife, the regent's mistress, Meynell was appointed a gentleman usher quarterly waiter on the prince's accession as George IV in 1820. At the general election of 1826 Hertford's son, the 3rd marquess, Meynell's first cousin, brought him in for Lisburn, his Irish pocket borough, as a supporter of Lord Liverpool's administration. He presented the Lisburn petition for assisted emigration, 22 Feb. 1827, but is not otherwise known to have spoken in the House in this period.[8] He voted against Catholic relief, 6 Mar. That summer, when he visited Berlin,[9] he may have been part of Hertford's entourage for his Garter mission to Russia; he certainly was one of Hertford's family supporters, being, for instance, placed on the corporations of the Suffolk boroughs of Aldeburgh, in September 1827, and Orford, in 1830.[10] He divided against repeal of the Test Acts, 26 Feb., and Catholic relief, 12 May 1828. He was listed by Planta, the Wellington ministry's patronage secretary, as a 'Protestant' who was likely to side 'with government' for Catholic emancipation, presumably because his patron had thrown in his lot with the prime minister in its favour. In fact, he voted against it, 18, 27, 30 Mar., and paired for Henry Bankes's motion to prevent Catholics sitting in Parliament, 23 Mar. 1829. Hertford, who had called on him to support government, apologized to John Croker* that he

> should have had any vexation about my *parliamentary* army, which I in one instance (Meynell) neglected from the wonderful violence of my mother on this question, to whom he is under great obligations – had I ever thought I should myself have taken this line I would not have brought him into Parliament.[11]

He divided against Lord Blandford's reform motion, 18 Feb., the enfranchisement of Birmingham, Leeds and Manchester, 23 Feb., and Jewish emancipation, 17 May 1830.

Returned unopposed for Lisburn at the general election of 1830, he was listed by ministers among their 'friends', but was absent from the division on the civil list which led to their resignation, 15 Nov. 1830. He told Sir John Benn Walsh* that he was sure 'in fact the ministers did not wish to carry it, that they were very slack in their exertions to get votes and that it was a ruse to go out on this, rather than on the reform question' the following day.[12] He voted against the second reading of the Grey ministry's reform bill, 22 Mar. 1831, and as a result was immediately stripped of his household appointment, which had been continued under the new king.[13] He divided for Gascoyne's wrecking amendment, 19 Apr., which provoked a dissolution. Nothing came of a rumour that he intended to offer himself for Antrim and he was returned for Lisburn as an anti-reformer.[14] He voted against the second reading of the reintroduced bill, 6 July, for using the 1831 census to determine the boroughs in schedules A and B, 19 July, and for postponing consideration of the partial disfranchisement of Chippenham, 27 July. He was in the majority for Benett's amendment for a bill to deal with electoral bribery at Liverpool, 5 Sept. He divided against the passage of the reform bill, 21 Sept., and the second reading of the Scottish bill, 23 Sept. He voted against the second reading of the revised reform bill, 17 Dec. 1831, going into committee on it, 20 Jan., the enfranchisement of Tower Hamlets, 28 Feb., the third reading, 22 Mar., and the second reading of the Irish reform bill, 25 May 1832. His only other known votes that session were with opposition against the Russian-Dutch loan, 26 Jan., 12 July 1832.

Popular for his resistance to religious and constitutional changes, Meynell was returned for Lisburn as a Conservative at the general election of 1832.[15] He retired from Parliament at the dissolution in 1847 and thereafter lived 'a quiet, unobtrusive life'. He died at the Grand Hotel du Louvre in Paris in March and was buried in the family vault at Ashley, Staffordshire, 1 Apr. 1865. He presumably divided his estate between his surviving brother, Hugo Charles Meynell, who had taken the additional name of Ingram in 1841 (and whose son Hugo Francis was Conservative Member for Staffordshire West, 1869-71), and his only remaining sister, Frances Adeline, the wife of William Beckett, Conservative Member for Leeds, 1841-52, and Ripon, 1852-7.[16]

[1] J. Nichols, *Leicester*, vol. iii. pt. i. pp. 101-2; J. Foster, *Yorks. Peds.* i. *sub.* Ingram of Temple Newsam. [2] *The Times*, 20 May 1800; *Gent. Mag.* (1800), i. 493; PROB 11/1342/389. [3] *Gent. Mag.* (1808), ii. 1134, 1186; PROB 11/1490/977; IR26/142/131. [4] *Gent. Mag.* (1807), ii. 1086; *Smith Letters*, i. 334-6. [5] *Dyott's Diary*, ii. 117. [6] W.R. O'Byrne, *Naval Biog.* ii. 757-8; H. Meynell, *Memoranda of Conversations with Napoleon, St. Helena, 1816* (1909), 1-42; R.V. Taylor, *Biographia Leodiensis* (1865), 529. [7] Add. 60286, f. 226. [8] *The Times*, 23 Feb. 1827. [9] *Geo. IV Letters*, iii. 1373. [10] *PP* (1835), xxvi. 2086, 2510. [11] Add. 60288, ff. 122, 139, 163. [12] NLW, Ormathwaite mss FG/1/5, p. 135. [13] *Creevey Pprs.* ii. 225. [14] *Belfast News Letter*, 3, 17 May 1831. [15] Ibid. 21 Dec. 1832. [16] *Staffs. Advertiser*, 1, 8 Apr. 1865; *Gent. Mag.* (1865), i. 663-4; Taylor, 528-30.

S.M.F.

MILBANK, Mark (1795–1881), of Thorpe Perrow and Barningham Park, Yorks. and 25 Bruton Street, Mdx.

CAMELFORD	1818–8 Apr. 1819
CAMELFORD	1820–1832

b. 2 May 1795, 1st s. of William Milbank of Thorpe Perrow and Dorothy, da. of John Wise of Woolston, Devon. *educ.* Harrow 1805-13; Oriel, Oxf. 1813. *m.* 2 June 1817, Lady Augusta Henrietta Vane, da. of William Harry Vane†, 3rd earl of Darlington, 4s. (1 *d.v.p.*) 3da. (2 *d.v.p.*). *suc.* fa. 1802. *d.* 21 Oct. 1881.

Capt. 4 N. Riding militia 1814; lt. W. Riding yeomanry June 1819, capt. Dec. 1819, res. Apr. 1820.

Sheriff, Yorks. 1837-8.

Milbank, who had inherited his father's estates in North Yorkshire in 1802 and been elected to Brooks's Club, 7 Feb. 1818, was returned for the venal borough of Camelford later that year on his father-in-law Lord Darlington's interest, but unseated on petition. He was returned unopposed in 1820 following a compromise with Lord Yarmouth's rival interest, which was intended to forestall another attempt to disfranchise the borough.[1] He was a regular attender but an almost silent Member, who continued to vote with the Whig opposition to Lord Liverpool's ministry on all major issues, including parliamentary reform, 25 Apr. 1822, 24 Apr., 2 June 1823, 13 Apr. 1826. He was absent from the division on Catholic relief, 28 Feb. 1821. He was named as a defaulter, 28 Feb., but attended next day to vote for relief, and did so again, 21 Apr., 10 May 1825. He was granted three weeks' leave for urgent private business, 14 Feb. 1821, and another two weeks on account of illness in his family, 18 Feb. 1823. He voted against empowering the government to admit foreign corn, 8 May 1826. At the general election that summer he and another Darlington nominee were returned for Camelford ahead of two clients of Yarmouth (now marquess of Hertford).[2]

He divided for Catholic relief, 6 Mar. 1827. He was granted one month's leave for 'urgent private business ... being petitioned against', 12 Mar., but was declared duly elected, 4 May, after Hertford had sold his interest at Camelford to Darlington.[3] He voted against Canning's ministry for the disfranchisement of Penryn, 28 May 1827. He divided for repeal of the Test Acts, 26 Feb., and Catholic relief, 12 May 1828. He voted for more efficient control over crown proceedings for the recovery of excise penalties, 1 May, against the small notes bill, 5 June, to condemn the misapplication of public money for building work at Buckingham House, 23 June, and to reduce ordnance officials' salaries, 4 July 1828. He was absent from the call of the House, 5 Mar., apparently did not attend next day, but voted for Catholic emancipation, 30 Mar., and to allow Daniel O'Connell to take his seat unhindered, 18 May 1829. It was presumably owing to the fact that Darlington (now marquess of Cleveland) had switched his allegiance to the duke of Wellington's ministry that Milbank took no part in the revived Whig opposition on economy and retrenchment issues during the 1830 session. He voted to transfer East Retford's seats to Birmingham, 11 Feb., and enfranchise Birmingham, Leeds and Manchester, 23 Feb., but was against Lord Blandford's reform plan, 18 Feb., and Jewish emancipation, 17 May. He was granted one month's leave for urgent private business, 4 Mar. 1830. He was returned unopposed for Camelford at the general election that summer.[4]

The ministry regarded Milbank as one of their 'friends', and he voted with them in the crucial civil list division, 15 Nov. 1830. However, Cleveland subsequently transferred his support to Lord Grey's ministry, and Milbank divided for the second reading of their reform bill, 22 Mar., and against Gascoyne's wrecking amendment, 19 Apr. 1831. He was returned unopposed at the ensuing general election, although Camelford was scheduled for disfranchisement.[5] He voted for the second reading of the reintroduced bill, 6 July, and steadily for its details, except for a vote with the minority to transfer Aldborough from schedule B to A, 14 Sept. In his only known parliamentary speech, 20 July, he maintained that his constituents were prepared to sacrifice their privileges 'for the benefit of their country'. He divided for the bill's third reading, 19 Sept., and passage, 21 Sept., the second reading of the Scottish bill, 23 Sept., and Lord Ebrington's confidence motion, 10 Oct. He voted to punish only those guilty of bribery at the Dublin election and against the censure motion on the Irish administration, 23 Aug. He divided for the second reading of the revised reform bill, 17 Dec. 1831, steadily for its details, and for the third reading, 22 Mar. 1832. He was absent in the country at the time of Ebrington's motion for an address asking the king to appoint only ministers committed to carrying an unimpaired measure, 10 May.[6] He voted for the second reading of the Irish reform bill, 25 May, and against increased county representation for Scotland, 1 June. He divided with ministers on the Russian-Dutch loan, 26 Jan., 12, 16, 20 July, and relations with Portugal, 9 Feb. 1832. His parliamentary career ended with the demise of Camelford.

In November 1825 Thomas Creevey* visited the Milbanks at Thorpe Perrow and recorded in his diary that

> their house is in every way worthy of them – a great big fat house three stories high ... a very handsome [living room] about 50 feet long, with a great bow furnished with rose coloured satin, and the whole furniture of which cost £4,000. Everything is of a piece – excellent and plentiful dinners, a fat service of plate, a fat butler, a table with a barrel of oysters and a hot pheasant, etc., wheeled into the drawing room every night at half past ten.[7]

Milbank, an accomplished horseman, died in October 1881. His estates passed in turn to his eldest son, Mark Milbank (1819-83), and his second son, Frederick Acclom Milbank (1820-98), Liberal Member for the North Riding of Yorkshire, 1865-85, who was created a baronet in 1882.

[1] *West Briton*, 10, 17 Mar. 1820. [2] Ibid. 9, 16 June 1826. [3] *CJ*, lxxxii. 431; *R. Cornw. Gazette*, 5 May 1827. [4] *R. Cornw. Gazette*, 31 July 1830. [5] *West Briton*, 29 Apr., 6 May 1831. [6] *The Times*, 14 May 1832. [7] *Creevey Pprs.* ii. 92-93.

T.A.J.

MILDMAY *see* ST. JOHN MILDMAY

MILES, Philip John (1774–1845), of Leigh Court, Abbots Leigh, Som.

WESTBURY	29 Nov. 1820–1826
CORFE CASTLE	6 Mar. 1829–1832
BRISTOL	1835–1837

b. 1 Mar. 1774, 2nd but 1st surv. s. of William Miles, merchant, of Bristol and Clifton, Glos. and w. Sarah Berrow of Clifton.[1] *m.* (1) 1795, Maria (*d.* 26 July 1811), da. of Dr. John Whetham, dean of Lismore, 1s. 4da. (2 *d.v.p.*); (2) 11 May 1813, Clarissa, da. of Samuel Peach Peach of Tockington, Glos., 7s. 4da. *suc.* fa. 1803. *d.* 24 Mar. 1845.

Miles's father, the eldest son of Robert Miles (*d.* 1737) of Ledbury, Herefordshire, went early in life to Jamaica, where he prospered. On his return to England he settled in Bristol, set up in business as a West India merchant and acquired a house at Clifton.[2] He was active in municipal affairs, becoming a member of Bristol corporation in 1766 and, having served as mayor, 1780-1, being elected an alderman in 1782.[3] He was the first chairman of the Bristol West India Association, a ginger group formed in 1782, and was admitted to the Society of Merchant Venturers the following year.[4] His eldest son William died, aged 23, in 1790, leaving his second, Philip John Miles, to benefit handsomely as his residuary legatee on his death in 1803. (He also provided his widow with £40,000 and his four daughters with £50,000 each.)[5]

Miles became a Merchant Venturer in 1795, but declined to serve on the corporation the following year.[6] He carried on the business, subsequently taking in his nephew Thomas Kington as a partner, at 61 Queen Square, and later built Leigh Court on the Somerset bank of the Avon as his residence. In 1794 he became the senior partner in the Bristol bank (founded in 1752) of Vaughan and Baker at 29 Corn Street, which became known as Miles and Company. In 1820 the business amalgamated with the banking house of Harford and Company of 8 Corn Street and was thereafter styled Miles, Harford and Company.[7] At the general election early that year, the ministerialist *White Lion* Club invited him to stand for Bristol, but his candidacy was not considered credible and, after some prevarication, he declined on the ground of poor health.[8] Eight months later he came in for Westbury as the paying guest of Sir Manasseh Masseh Lopes*.

Miles made no mark in the House, where he is not known to have spoken in this period. He gave general support to the Liverpool ministry when present, but was a lax attender. He voted in defence of their conduct towards Queen Caroline, 6 Feb., and against parliamentary reform, 9 May 1821, but cast a wayward vote for abolition of one of the joint-postmasterships, 13 Mar. 1822. It is not clear whether it was he or Charles Mills who voted for investigation of the Calcutta bankers' claims on the East India Company, 4 July 1822. He divided with government against parliamentary reform, 20 Feb., repeal of the assessed taxes, 18 Mar., and of the Foreign Enlistment Act, 16 Apr., and inquiry into chancery administration, 5 June 1823. His only known vote in 1824 was against reform of Edinburgh's representative system, 26 Feb., which he again opposed, 13 Apr. 1826. He divided against Catholic relief, 30 Apr. 1822, 1 Mar., 21 Apr., and the Irish franchise bill, 26 Apr. 1825. He was in the ministerial majority on the Jamaican slave trials, 2 Mar. 1826.

Miles did not find a seat in 1826, but in March 1829 he was returned on the Bond interest for Corfe Castle, where he sat until it was disfranchised. His four votes that month against the Wellington ministry's policy of Catholic emancipation, which he was brought in to oppose, are the only traces which have been found of his activity in this Parliament. He took a month's leave to attend to urgent private business, 9 Mar. 1830. After the general election that year ministers numbered him among the 'moderate Ultras' who were essentially 'friends', but, like his son William, who had now returned to the Commons, he failed to rally to them on the civil list, 15 Nov. 1830. The Grey ministry's reform bill returned him to his former allegiance, and he voted against the second reading, 22 Mar., and for Gascoyne's wrecking amendment, 19 Apr. 1831. He divided against the second reading of the reintroduced bill, 6 July, and was in the minorities against the partial disfranchisement of Chippenham, 27 July, the third reading, 19 Sept., and the passage of the bill, 21 Sept. 1831. His only known votes against the revised reform bill were against the enfranchisement of Tower Hamlets, 28 Feb., and the third reading, 22 Mar. 1832. He voted against the second reading of the Irish bill, 25 May. He divided against government on the Russian-Dutch loan, 26 Jan., 12 July 1832.

Miles re-entered Parliament as Conservative Member for Bristol in 1835, and was replaced on his retirement in 1837 by his second son Philip William Skynner Miles (1816-81). In 1833 he bought the De Clifford estate at Kings Weston on the edge of Bristol for £210,000, and he formed 'a most celebrated collection' of pictures at Leigh Court.[9] Noted for 'his kindness of heart, his mental ability, and comprehensive grasp of mind', he died in March 1845, his personalty being sworn considerably in excess of £1,000,000.[10] He devised Leigh Court and his Jamaican plantations to the only son of his first marriage, William (1797-1878), Conservative Member for Somerset East, and made handsome provision for his other sons, who continued the family's banking, West India and cotton spinning concerns. In 1877 the bank amalgamated with the Bristol Old Bank at 35 Corn Street and became Miles, Cave, Baillie and Company.[11]

[1] She was probably da. of William Berrow, linen draper, of Bristol and Stoke Bishop (*d.* 1765), of whose will Miles was an executor (PROB 11/910/244). [2] C.H. Cave, *Hist. Banking in Bristol*, 244-5; *Caribbeana*, ii. 330; iii. 122-3. [3] A.B. Beaven, *Bristol Lists*, 302. [4] *Trade of Bristol in 18th Cent.* ed. W. E. Minchinton (Bristol Rec. Soc. xx), p. xvi; *Politics and Port of Bristol in 18th Cent.* ed. W.E. Minchinton (Bristol Rec. Soc. xxiii), 125, 162, 215; P. McGrath, *Merchant Venturers*, 158. [5] *Gent. Mag.* (1790), ii. 864; PROB 11/1391/389; IR26/74/156. [6] *Politics and Port of Bristol*, 216; Beaven, 302. [7] Cave, 10, 72-78, 99; *Recs. Bristol Ships* ed. G.E. Farr (Bristol Rec. Soc. xv), 33, 36, 55, 100, 152, 207. [8] Wilts. RO, Benett mss 413/485, Buckland to Benett, 5 Feb.; *The Times*, 29 Feb., 9 Mar. 1820; Beaven, 177; J. Williams, 'Bristol in General Election of 1818 and 1820', *Bristol and Glos. Arch. Soc. Trans.* lxxxvii (1968), 193-5. [9] Cave, 74; *Macaulay Letters*, v. 283-4; J. Young, *Cat. of Pictures at Leigh Court* (1822). [10] *Gent. Mag.* (1845), i. 657; IR26/1713/253; B. English, 'Probate Valuations and Death Duty Regs.', *BIHR*, lvii (1984), 88. [11] Cave, 36, 81-84; *Studs. in Business Hist. of Bristol* ed. C.E. Harvey and J. Press, 14.

D.R.F./S.M.F.

MILES, William (1797–1878), of Leigh Court, Abbots Leigh, Som.

CHIPPENHAM	1818–1820
NEW ROMNEY	1830–1832
SOMERSET EAST	3 Feb. 1834–1865

b. 13 May 1797, 1st s. of Philip John Miles* of Leigh Court and 1st w. Maria, da. of Dr. John Whetham, dean of Lismore. *educ.* Eton 1811; Christ Church, Oxf. 1815; L. Inn 1818. *m.* 12 Sept. 1823, Catherine, da. of John Gordon of Clifton, Glos., 5s. (2 *d.v.p.*) 7da. (2 *d.v.p.*). *suc.* fa. 1845; *cr.* bt. 19 Apr. 1859. *d.* 17 June 1878.

Lt.-col. N. Som. yeoman cav. 1839, col. 1843-67.

Miles, the eldest son of an immensely wealthy Bristol banker and West India merchant, declined to contest Chippenham in 1820 and was out of the House for ten years. At the general election of 1830, when his address was given in the *Official Return* as Beesthorpe Hall, Nottinghamshire, he came in for New Romney on the Dering interest, after a token contest. He was unopposed in 1831. The Wellington ministry listed him with his father among the 'moderate Ultras' who were at bottom 'friends', but he was absent from the division on the civil list which brought them down, 15 Nov. 1830. He voted against the second reading of the Grey ministry's reform bill, 22 Mar., presented a New Romney petition against it, 24 Mar., and voted for Gascoyne's wrecking amendment, 19 Apr. 1831. On 5 July he attacked the reintroduced bill as a 'a speculative' and 'dangerous reform', by which 'every enthusiast sees a path opened ... to the long-cherished political utopia of his ardent but distempered imagination': it was, he said, 'the prelude to greater concessions, and an incentive to more democratic demands'. He voted against the second reading the following day, for an adjournment, 12 July, and against the partial disfranchisement of his former constituency, 27 July. He was one of the minority of ten who voted for Hunt's amendment to the borough franchise proposals, 25 Aug. He voted against the passage of the bill, 21 Sept., and the second reading of the Scottish reform bill, 23 Sept. He divided against government on the Dublin election controversy, 23 Aug. On 30 Sept. he objected to the 'lowness' of the qualification proposed by Hobhouse in his bill to reform select vestries and, claiming to be the spokesman of the Bristol vestries, moved the exemption of such bodies as had sole control over church charities. The sense of the House was against him and he did not press the issue.

Miles, who was evidently not the most assiduous of attenders, was absent from the division on the second reading of the revised reform bill, 17 Dec. 1831. He voted against the enfranchisement of Tower Hamlets, 28 Feb., and the third reading 22 Mar. 1832. He divided for the Liverpool disfranchisement bill, 23 May, against the second reading of the Irish reform bill, 25 May, for a tax on Irish absentee landlords, 19 June, and in censure of ministers over the Russian-Dutch loan, 12 July. On the boundary bill, 22 June 1832, he strongly objected to the proposal to include in the Bristol constituency large areas previously belonging to Gloucestershire and Somerset, but his protests were disregarded.

Miles unsuccessfully contested Somerset East at the 1832 general election, but he came in there unopposed on a vacancy in 1834 and held the seat, with only one contest, for over 30 years. He emerged in the 1840s as one of the leading Protectionist backbenchers and was rewarded by Lord Derby with a baronetcy in 1859.[1] By then he was a very rich man, having succeeded his father to a handsome personal fortune, in addition to his Somerset estates and Jamaican sugar plantations, in 1845.[2] He was a partner in the family's Bristol bank and West India mercantile house from that date until his death in June 1878.[3]

[1] *Disraeli Letters*, iv. 1399A, 1503, 1529-30, 1552. [2] PROB 11/2016/318. [3] C. H. Cave, *Hist. Banking in Bristol*, 81.

D.R.F.

MILLER, William Henry (1789–1848), of Craigentinny House, North Leith, Edinburgh; 12 Brompton Row, Mdx., and Britwell Court, nr. Burnham, Berks.

NEWCASTLE-UNDER-LYME	1830–1841

b. 13 Feb. 1789, o. s. of William Miller of Craigentinny and 3rd w. Martha, da. of Henry Rawson of Yorks. *educ.* Jesus, Camb. 1805. *unm. d.* 31 Oct. 1848.

Miller's father, a Scottish Quaker and nurseryman of Edinburghshire, was described in 1788 as 'rich and independent'. His antecedents are obscure, but his sister Mary married John Christy (1707-61), of Ormiston Lodge, Edinburgh, which gave this Member a cousin Miller Christy (1748-1820), of Stockwell, Surrey, a noted London hatter, whose 'great manufacturing house' at 35 Gracechurch Street and 113 and 170 Bermondsey Street continued under his sons Thomas (1776-1846), William (1778-1858) and John (1781-1873) and their heirs. By 1812 Miller had succeeded to his father's freehold estates.[1]

At the 1830 general election Miller came forward as an 'independent' Tory for Newcastle-under-Lyme, where the withdrawal of Lord Stafford and the legal proceedings against the corporation, in which he had assisted, had opened the representation. 'A candidate whose name had been before mentioned', he promised to vote for free trade, reductions of public expenditure, the abolition of slavery, and against renewal of the East India Company's monopoly. His supporters stressed his 'near connections with the greatest hat manufacturers in Europe', who had 'long been a main support of our staple trade' and might 'be induced to send us a larger share of their orders', but he was ridiculed by his opponents for his 'hesitating utterances' and 'want of words' as a public speaker. 'Miller is a young man, and has had but little experience in the art of speaking', conceded one admirer, but 'give him time and he may make, if not an accomplished orator, at least an effective debater'. After a three-day poll he was returned in second place behind the popular independent candidate. 'When Miller found that genius was denied, a Christie's hat the want of wit supplied', ran one broadside.[2]

Miller was listed by the Wellington ministry as one of their 'friends' and divided in their minority on the civil list, 15 Nov. 1830. In his maiden speech, 19 Mar. 1831, he protested that 'unconstitutional means' had been employed 'to influence the minds and feelings of the people' in support of the Grey ministry's reform bill, citing the circulation of handbills claiming that the king supported the proposed plan. He presented and endorsed a hostile Newcastle petition that day, when, in a reference to the proposed abolition of the freeman franchise, he warned that

> many of those Members who represent large towns, and who support this measure, will risk their re-election, for how can they expect to receive the support of those who, by their vote, they have attempted to disfranchise? If this measure were to be carried ... it would prove the first step towards plunging this country into all those evils which the desire of change has brought upon so many other nations.

He divided against the second reading of the bill, 22 Mar., and for Gascoyne's wrecking amendment, 19 Apr. 1831. He presented a Newcastle petition against truck payments, 30 Mar. 1831. At the ensuing general election Miller offered again with the support of 'a very numerous body of the working class', claiming to have 'fearlessly defended' his constituents' elective rights. He professed to be 'friendly to the extension of the franchise', even to houses of 'as low as £5' rental value, but 'did not understand' how it could be expected that the freemen would vote 'against their own rights', which he promised to protect 'with the last shilling in his purse, and the last drop of blood in his veins'. He denied that the vote on the civil list had 'involved the question of retrenchment', insisting that it was 'a manoeuvre of a set of men, who having long been out of office were hungry for its honours and emoluments'. After a violent contest he was returned in second place with a substantially reduced majority. At the declaration he denounced the government, which he was determined to oppose, as the 'most incompetent he had ever known', and 'procured to himself the permanent respect of the females, by expressing an ardent wish that he could marry them all'.[3]

Miller voted against the second reading of the reintroduced reform bill, 6 July, at least four times to adjourn the debates, 12 July, and was in the minorities for use of the 1831 census to determine the redistribution of seats, 19 July, and against Chippenham's inclusion in schedule B, 27 July 1831. He was in a minority of ten for Hunt's amendment against making proven payment of rent a qualification for voting in boroughs, 25 Aug. He voted to preserve the electoral rights of all existing voters, 27 Aug., and non-resident freemen, 30 Aug., when he declared his 'hearty concurrence' in the amendment for a 'permanent continuance' of the freeman franchise proposed by his colleague Edmund Peel. He had hitherto given 'a silent vote against its provisions', but now attacked this 'most iniquitous bill' and its 'utter disregard' for his constituents' rights, arguing that

> the greatest boast of the supporters of the bill is that it will so much extend the elective franchise. In many places, however, its operation will be directly contrary ... [In Newcastle] the electors ... would be reduced from eight or nine hundred to less than half that number.

He voted to preserve the electoral rights of non-resident freeholders in the four sluiced boroughs, 2 Sept. He divided against ministers on the Dublin election controversy, 23 Aug. He voted for inquiry into the effects of the Sugar Refinery Act on the West India interest, 12 Sept., and against the Maynooth grant, 26 Sept. He voted against the third reading of the reform bill, 19 Sept., and its passage, 21 Sept. He divided against the second reading of the Scottish bill, 23 Sept., and was one of the Members 'connected with Scotland' in the minority of 61 for increasing Scottish representation, 4 Oct.[4] He divided against the second reading of the revised reform bill, 17 Dec. 1831, going into committee on it, 20 Jan., the enfranchisement of Tower Hamlets, 28 Feb., and the third reading, 22 Mar. 1832. Next day he was in the minority of 27 for alterations to Lincolnshire's internal boundary divisions.

He divided against ministers on the Russian-Dutch loan, 26 Jan., 12 July 1832. At the 1832 general election Miller was again returned as a Conservative for Newcastle-under-Lyme, where he sat until his defeat in 1841. His opponent's election was declared void on petition the following year, but he declined to stand at the ensuing by-election. He unsuccessfully contested Berwick-upon-Tweed in 1847.

Miller was a renowned bibliophile, whose unrivalled collection of early English poetry included some of the rarest works acquired from the library of Richard Heber*. An eccentric figure, he was known at book sales as 'Measure Miller', from his habit of carrying around a foot rule 'in order to ascertain whether a so-called fine tall copy' had 'the 'legitimate number of inches'.[5] He died a bachelor at Craigentinny House in October 1848. By his will, dated 30 Dec. 1847, he left entrusted property in England and Scotland estimated to be worth £300,000, including his library at Britwell Court, to his cousin Sarah Marsh, with whom he resided. (From her it passed to Miller Christy's grandson Samuel Christy (1810-89), Liberal-Conservative Member for Newcastle-under-Lyme, 1847-59, who took the name and arms of Miller in 1862.) Instructions were left for the erection of a romanesque mausoleum at Craigentinny in which to house his body, which was completed in 1866.[6]

[1] *Pol. State of Scotland 1788*, p. 113; (1812), 56; *Gent. Mag.* (1849), i. 98. [2] *Staffs. Advertiser*, 3, 17 July, 7 Aug. 1830; *Language, Print and Electoral Politics, 1790-1832* ed. H. Barker and D. Vincent, 293, 301, 311, 320. [3] *Staffs. Advertiser*, 30 Apr., 7 May 1831. [4] *Perthshire Courier*, 13 Oct. 1831. [5] *Gent. Mag.* (1849), i. 98. [6] Ibid.; PROB 11/2093/369; IR26/1842/259; *Oxford DNB*.

P.J.S.

MILLS, Charles (1755–1826), of 8 Manchester Square, Mdx. and Barford, Warws.

WARWICK 1802–29 Jan. 1826

b. 13 July 1755, 2nd s. of Rev. John Mills, rect. of Barford and Oxhill, and Sarah, da. of Rev. William Wheeler, vicar of Leamington Hastings, Warws. *educ.* Rugby 1763. *m.* 21 Mar. 1810, his sister-in-law Jane, da. of Hon. Wriothesley Digby of Meriden, Warws., *s.p. d.* 29 Jan. 1826.

Dir. E.I. Co. 1785-1815, dep. chairman 1801, chairman Sept. 1801-2; dir. London Dock Co. 1803-9; asst. Lead Co. 1805.

Lt.-col. 1 R.E.I. vols. 1796, col. 1803; capt. Marylebone vols. 1803; commr. of lieutenancy, London 1808-*d.*

Mills, a partner in the family bank of Glyn, Mills and Company of London since 1777 and a former East India Company chairman, was an anti-Catholic Tory in Parliament, where he attended infrequently, and a reformer of convenience in Warwick, which he had represented on the independent interest since 1802.[1] His sixth return in 1820 was unopposed despite mounting criticism of his politics, which he conceded on the hustings were 'church and state'.[2]

In the House, 2 May 1820, he praised the worsted manufacturer John Parkes's invention for reducing emissions from industrial furnaces, which he had seen in use at Warwick, and advocated its adoption in 'the country at large'. He was appointed to the select committee on the subject later that day. He had refused to comment on reports of Parkes's bankruptcy, which he knew were correct.[3] In his only other reported speech in this Parliament, he criticized the 'inauspicious' timing of the forgery punishment mitigation bill, 4 June 1821. He voted against Catholic relief, 28 Feb. 1821, 1 Mar., 21 Apr., 1825. He divided with government on the revenue, 4 July 1820, their handling of the queen's case, 6 Feb., and the additional malt duty repeal bill, 3 Apr. 1821, and against more extensive tax reductions to relieve distress, 11, 21 Feb. 1822. He also voted with them against abolishing one of the joint-postmasterships, 13 Mar., but may have been the 'J. Mills' in the minority on the Calcutta bankers' petition, 4 July 1822. He divided against the usury laws repeal bill, 27 Feb., and presented the Warrington victuallers' petition against the excise licence duty, 6 May 1824.[4] He voted to outlaw the Catholic Association, 25 Feb. 1825. Certain of opposition, Mills announced in September 1825 that he would stand down at the next dissolution, but died before it in January 1826, recalled as a 'straight man of business' in the City and a generous benefactor in Warwick.[5]

Mills had no children and by his will, dated 3 Jan. 1826, and proved under £120,000, he left his London house to his wife and his Warwickshire estates to his clergyman brother Francis and his heirs. His nephew Charles, an East India Company director since 1822, succeeded to his banking interests. Another nephew, Arthur, declared but desisted at Warwick in 1832.[6]

[1] *HP Commons, 1790-1820*, iv. 590-1; *Oxford DNB sub* Mills family. [2] *Warwick Advertiser*, 19 Feb., 11 Mar. 1820. [3] *VCH Warws.* viii. 436. [4] *The Times*, 7 May 1824. [5] *Warwick Advertiser*, 24 Sept. 1825, 4 Feb. 1826. [6] Ibid. 31 Aug. 1822; PROB 11/1710/166; IR26/1092/149; Warws. RO, Moore and Tibbits mss CR 1097/330/371.

H.J.S./M.M.E.

MILLS, John (1789–1871), of 22 Hill Street, Mdx and Bisterne, Hants.

ROCHESTER 1831–1834

b. 11 Aug. 1789, 1st s. of William Mills† of Bisterne and Elizabeth, da. of Hon. Wriothesley Digby of Coleshill and Meriden Hall, Warws. *educ.* Harrow 1801; Christ Church, Oxf. 1807. *m.* 25 July 1835, Sarah Charlotte, da. of Nathaniel Micklethwait of Taverham Hall, Norf., 3s. (1 *d.v.p.*). *suc.* fa. 1820. *d.* 28 Feb. 1871.

Ensign Coldstream Gds. 1809, lt. and capt. 1814, ret. 1814.

Verderer, New Forest 1820-*d.*; capt. S. Hants yeoman cav. 1824.

Mills was the eldest of the six sons of William Mills, Whig Member for St. Ives, 1790-6, and Coventry, 1805-12, who was descended from an old Warwickshire family and settled at Bisterne in 1792. He inherited the estate there under his father's will, dated 1 Dec. 1819, in March 1820, as well as a share of his personalty, which was sworn under £120,000.[1] His uncle Charles Mills, Member for Warwick, and his brothers Charles, who took over the business on his namesake's death, and Edward Wheler were partners in the highly successful London banking firm of Glyn, Mills and Company, which moved from Birchin Lane to Lombard Street in 1826.[2] He entered the Guards and fought in the Peninsula at Fuentes d'Onoro, Salamanca and the sieges of Ciudad Rodrigo and Burgos. He then served in Holland and retired from the regular army in 1814, but at the duke of Wellington's request he was given a commission in the Hampshire militia in 1824 and the command of the newly amalgamated Avon valley squadron in 1831.[3] At Oxford he had been one of several Harrovians who had moved in Robert Peel's* circle, but his political sympathies lay more with the Whigs and he may well have been the Mr. Mills who was elected to Brooks's, 20 Feb. 1810.[4] He was presumably '*Dandy* Mills', the friend of Thomas Creevey*, who acquired notoriety for his eccentricities of dress and behaviour; for instance, he nearly fought a duel with John George Lambton* over a horse race in 1824 and he at some point fell in love with the courtesan Harriette Wilson 'merely to prove himself a fashionable man'. She described him as 'rather well informed, but a stiff, bad imitation of Meyler's gentlemanly carriage and manner; a sort of man who would rather have died than not been a member of White's club'.[5] He did, indeed, belong to White's (though he could hardly have been the John Mills who was admitted in 1800), and, among many other examples, he lost bets made on 18 Apr. and 14 May 1825 that there would have been a dissolution by the end of October that year.[6]

Mills was introduced at Rochester two days before the poll at the general election of 1830, against the Tory Lord Villiers* and the Whig Ralph Bernal*. This was supposedly in order to replace William Hughes Hughes*, who had retreated to Oxford, on the Pink or Ultra interest, but he actually stood as an independent and spoke against slavery and in favour of economies and parliamentary reform.[7] He retired on the third day, complaining that his opponents had split votes between them, but boasting of 265 plumpers.[8] One correspondent in the local newspaper wrote of the dark subtleties of the Ultras who had inveigled the innocent Mills to offer so as to divide the Whig interest. His 48 hours' amusement had cost him an estimated £1,200, but the corporation of Rochester agreed to make him an honorary freeman, 23 Aug., and after the ceremony, 15 Nov. 1830, he was presented with a snuff box by his friends there, 'as a token of their admiration of his manly and independent conduct'.[9] He was adopted, with Bernal, as a pro-reform candidate for the forthcoming general election at a meeting, 25 Apr. 1831. No contest was seriously expected and Villiers withdrew as a consequence of his re-appearance.[10] He declared that he had supported reform for 20 years, and that the Grey ministry's bill was necessary in order to stem the influence of the aristocracy over elections and to reconcile the middle and labouring classes who had been set against each other by the ruling oligarchy. He hinted, however, that he might wish to oppose some of its details and that he could not agree with the voters on every question.[11] He was returned unopposed and without expense. He seconded the nomination of the Whig James Macdonald* for Hampshire the following month and, at a reform dinner in Rochester, 8 June, he stated:

> I do consider the reform bill of such paramount importance, that unwilling as I am that any of the privileges of my constituents should be lessened, yet I have a *stern duty to perform* and no vote of mine shall in any way interfere with the success of the bill.[12]

Mills's maiden speech, on the occasion of his vote in favour of reducing the grant for the civil service, 18 July 1831, contained a similar declaration: 'I am returned here to do my duty, and no power on earth shall tempt me to vote a shilling unless it be clearly shown that the party to whom it is granted deserves it'. He also complained of the degeneracy of the people, who no longer had the 'proud stubbornness' to refuse parochial relief. However, he confined his activities in his first session almost wholly to reform. He paired for the second reading of the reintroduced bill, 6 July, and voted at least twice against adjourning debate on it,

12 July, and fairly regularly for its details. However, he was listed as absent, 3 Aug., on the enfranchisement of Greenwich, whose two dockyards, arsenal and hospital he deemed good material for the creation of a new rotten borough.[13] He moved an amendment to keep Rochester separate from Chatham and Strood, 9 Aug., on the grounds that his constituency had sufficient £10 houses already to justify its independent representation, would be swamped by the much larger Chatham and was under a recognizably distinct jurisdiction. He was a teller for the minority against uniting the boroughs, and at the end of the session he was thanked by the corporation of Rochester for his exertions on its behalf.[14] On the same principle, he voted against combining Merthyr Tydfil and Cardiff, 10 Aug. He divided for Lord Chandos's motion to enfranchise £50 tenants-at-will, 18 Aug., as he believed they deserved the vote if it was also to be given to £10 borough householders. He voted with government in favour of giving copyholders and leaseholders who had votes in boroughs the right of voting in county elections, 20 Aug., and twice on the Dublin election controversy, 23 Aug.; but he divided for the total disfranchisement of Aldborough, 14 Sept., which had been the original intention, as he could conceive of no reason for the new proposal to retain one seat there and wanted the bill to be as perfect as possible. He voted for the passage of the bill, 21 Sept., the second reading of the Scottish bill, 23 Sept., and Lord Ebrington's confidence motion, 10 Oct. 1831.

Mills voted for the second reading of the revised reform bill, 17 Dec. 1831, its disfranchisement clauses, 20, 23 Jan., and again usually for its details. However, he divided against the enfranchisement of Tower Hamlets, 28 Feb., as he thought that the lowest dwelling in the metropolis was valued at over £10, whereas many respectable houses elsewhere were worth less. He voted for the third reading, 22 Mar., but angered his constituents by leaving the House before the division on Ebrington's motion for an address calling on the king to appoint only ministers who would carry the bill unimpaired, 10 May, because, as he later argued, it 'declared positively that they placed all confidence in His Majesty's ministers and, as he during the progress of the details of the bill frequently voted against them, he could not conscientiously support it'.[15] He objected to the grant of £25,000 for the new Liverpool customs house, 8 Feb., and secured accounts of recent expenditure on Hampton Court and Kensington Palace, 23 Feb. He voted with ministers against producing information on Portugal, 9 Feb., and for the navy civil departments bill, 6 Apr. He again promised to defend his constituency's interests in Parliament, 10 Feb.[16] He voted against Buxton's motion for a select committee on colonial slavery, 24 May, and presented a Bristol petition against its abolition without compensation, 20 June. On 20 July he explained that he had divided against Herries's amendment against the Russian-Dutch loan, 12 July, as it 'seemed to me that the object of his motion was to pass a broad censure at once upon the government, in which I was not prepared to acquiesce', but had voted for Baring's motion for papers, 16 July, because, 'being convinced that the demand was not just, I wished for further information to satisfy my mind that we really were bound in honour to pay the money'; he moved to resume the House and was a teller for the minority that day. His popularity declined in Rochester as a result of his hostile votes on this and reform, but, after having given a lengthy defence of his conduct, he survived a contest at the general election of 1832.[17] At the end of that Parliament, he retired to his Hampshire estate, which, at his death in February 1871, passed to his elder surviving son, John (1836-99).

[1] PROB 11/1628/227; IR26/831/270. [2] E.G. Browne, *Glyn, Mills and Co.* 36-46; R. Fulford, *Glyn's*, 73-75, 80-81; *Oxford DNB sub* Mills fam. [3] Wellington mss WP1/799/2; 1175/21. [4] N. Gash, *Secretary Peel*, 54, 79. [5] *Gronow Reminiscences*, i. 33; ii. 70; *Creevey's Life and Times*, 201, 309; *Harriette Wilson's Mems.* (1929), 602. [6] *Hist. White's*, ii. pt. i. pp. 194-5; pt. ii. p. 62. [7] *Rochester Gazette*, 3 Aug. 1830. [8] *Maidstone Jnl.* 10 Aug.; *Maidstone Gazette*, 10 Aug. 1830. [9] *Rochester Gazette*, 31 Aug., 16 Nov. 1830; *Kentish Gazette*, 21 Jan. 1831; Medway Archives and Local Stud. Cent. Rochester city recs. RCA/A1/6, 621. [10] *Rochester Gazette*, 26 Apr.; *The Times*, 30 Apr.; Add. 51836, Barnett to Holland, 23 Apr.; Creevey mss, Creevey to Miss Ord, 30 Apr. 1831. [11] *Rochester Gazette*, 3 May 1831. [12] *Maidstone Jnl.* 3, 10 May, 14 June; *Hants Chron.* 9 May 1831. [13] Mills's motives for this and later votes against government are taken from his speech at the 1832 general election (*Rochester Gazette*, 18 Dec. 1832). [14] Rochester city recs. A1/6, 676, 688. [15] *Rochester Gazette*, 18 Dec. 1832. [16] Rochester city recs. A1/6, 698. [17] *Kentish Gazette*, 29 June; *Maidstone Jnl.* 21 Aug.; *Rochester Gazette*, 24 July, 11, 18 Dec. 1832.

S.M.F.

MILLS, Robert William (1777–1851), of Willington, co. Dur.

BLETCHINGLEY 1830–10 Feb. 1831

bap. 9 May 1777, 2nd s. of Henry Mills (*d.* 1807) of Willington and Elizabeth, da. of Robert Fenwick of Lemington, Northumb. *m.* 16 Dec. 1806, Jane, da. of George Robinson of Hendon Lodge, co. Dur., 3s. (1 *d.v.p.*) 4da. *d.* 9 Mar. 1851.

Ensign 86 Ft. 1795, lt. 1795, capt. 1798; capt. 36 Ft. 1805, 45 Ft. 1809; brevet maj. 1810; capt. 82 Ft. 1810, 9 Ft. 1813, half-pay 1815-*d.*; brevet lt.-col. 1819; col. 1837; maj.-gen. 1846.

Mills's ancestors included members of the Forster family, aldermen of Durham in the eighteenth century. His father was at one time in business in that city as a wine merchant, in partnership with one of his Forster kinsmen, and by 1787 he was senior partner in the Durham banking house of Mills, Hopper and Company, which ceased trading in 1802; by then he had acquired some land and a house at Willington in the parish of Brancepeth, near Bishop Auckland.[1] Mills pursued an uneventful army career, becoming a brigade major on the staff of the eastern district in 1809 and 1810. On his father's death in 1807 he received £500, charged on a freehold farm at High Close, Willington, in addition to £1,500 already advanced to him from a legacy by his mother's half-sister Isabella (Forster) Widdrington of Hawksly.[2] At the general election of 1830, when he was described as the 'steward' of William Russell*, lord of the manor of Brancepeth, he was returned for Bletchingley on the latter's interest. However, this was said to be 'merely ... a temporary arrangement', until Russell could find an 'efficient' nominee from among his Whig friends.[3]

The duke of Wellington's ministry listed Mills as one of their 'foes', and he duly voted against them in the crucial civil list division, 15 Nov. 1830. He is not known to have spoken in debate, and he vacated early in 1831 to accommodate Sir William Horne, the Grey ministry's solicitor-general.[4] He lived in comparative obscurity at Willington until his death there in March 1851. He divided his modest estate between his children.[5]

[1] H.C. Surtees, *Hist. Willington and Crook*, 5, 10, 12; M. Phillips, *Hist. Banking in Northumb.* 45, 52-53, 57, 64, 69, 307-10, 354; *Gent. Mag.* (1807), ii. 1089. [2] IR26/327/183. The personalty was sworn under £100. [3] *Brighton Guardian*, 4 Aug.; Lincs. AO, Tennyson D'Eyncourt mss 2 Td'E H89/8, C. to G. Tennyson, 9 Aug.; Brougham mss, Durham to Brougham, 7 Sept. 1830. [4] NLS, Ellice mss, Ellice to Russell, 25 Dec., reply, 27 Dec. 1830. [5] IR26/1906/296.

D.R.F.

MILNE, Sir David (1763–1845), of Inveresk, Edinburgh.

BERWICK-UPON-TWEED 1820–3 July 1820

b. 25 May 1763, 1st s. of David Milne of Campie House, Musselburgh, Edinburgh and Susan, da. of Robert Vernor of Musselburgh. *educ.* Edinburgh h.s.[1] *m.* (1) 16 Apr. 1804, Grace (*d.* 4 Oct. 1814), da. of Sir Alexander Purves, 5th bt., of Purves Hall, Eccles, Berwick, 2s.; (2) 19 Sept. 1819, Agnes, da. of George Stephen of Grenada, *s.p.* KCB 20 Sept. 1816; GCB 4 July 1840; *suc.* fa. 1818. *d.* 5 May 1845.

Entered RN 1779, paid off 1783; ship's officer, E.I. Co. (Bombay and Bengal) 1783-93; re-entered RN 1793, lt. 1794, cdr. 1795, capt. 1795, r.-adm. 1814; c.-in-c. N. America 1816-19; v.-adm. 1825, adm. 1841; c.-in-c. Plymouth 1842-5.

Capt. commdt. Firth of Forth sea fencibles c.1803-11.

Milne, whose lifelong motto was *res non verba*, was born and educated in Edinburgh, where his father was a silk merchant. He entered the navy at the age of 16 on Captain Hugh Dalrymple's ship *Canada*, saw action at the siege of Gibraltar and in the West Indies during the American War of Independence and, being paid off, joined the East India Company's vessel *General Elliot*. Resuming his naval career at the outbreak of war in 1793, he returned to African and West Indian waters, where he repeatedly distinguished himself, notably in the capture of the *Pique* (5 Jan. 1795), in which as captain he conducted merchant ships stranded at St. Kitts to Spithead. Attached afterwards to the Channel fleet, he abandoned and burnt the damaged *Pique* after capturing the 40-gun French frigate *Seine*, which he commanded in the West Indies and Gulf of Mexico until the peace of 1802. He was exonerated from blame after the *Seine* was wrecked off the Texel, 21 July 1803, but relegated in 1804 to command the Forth district of sea fencibles for attempting to protect the *Seine*'s pilots and for his insubordination to the board at their court martial. That year he married the daughter of a Berwickshire baronet, with whom he had two sons, the advocate and founder of the Scottish Meteorological Society David Milne Home (1805-90) and Admiral Sir Alexander Milne (1806-96). From 1811-15 Milne commanded vessels in European and North American waters. He was ordered, as commander designate of the Halifax station, to join the expedition against Algiers as Lord Exmouth's second-in-command, and his conduct in battle, 27 Aug. 1816, was rewarded with a knighthood, honours from several European powers, the freedom of the City of London and a vote of thanks from Parliament.[2] He aspired to a baronetcy, but Exmouth, who in 1817 and 1818 vainly pleaded his case at the admiralty, suggested that the first lord, the 2nd Viscount Melville, might be of more assistance to Milne in his role as the Liverpool ministry's Scottish election manager.[3] Milne returned from Halifax in 1819 via Bermuda, where he received a 'very flattering address from the merchants', married for the second time that autumn and took a house in Edinburgh for the winter.

On 4 Feb. 1820 he was requisitioned to stand for the venal and open borough of Berwick-upon-Tweed, where the sitting Tory Alexander Allen was expected to resign.[4] He accepted and, confident of success, turned down the lord advocate Sir William Rae's* offer of government sponsorship against Sir Hew Dalrymple Hamilton* in Haddington Burghs, assuring Melville at the same time that his conduct in the House would be 'entirely guided' by his 'recommendations'.[5] When the late docking of a steamer bringing his London supporters hazarded his return, he contrived to adjourn the poll pending their arrival, and by using the same tactic during the weekend break, he defeated the sitting Tory Henry Heneage St. Paul* to come in with the Whig Lord Ossulston.[6] Milne is not known to have voted or contributed to debate before his election was voided on St. Paul's petition, 3 July 1820. His wife commented:

> My dear Sir David, had you gained, I must have written to congratulate *you*, as it is I most cheerfully congratulate *myself* as I shall now I hope have you with me, or be with you, which is the same thing, *except* you go to Berwickshire, then I shall be tempted to retaliate and stay at home, at *Inveresk I mean*, as I will not acknowledge a Berwickshire home ... Although it may displease you I must acknowledge I feel relieved today to know that this election is over, and you are no longer MP. As to the money, let it go, we can do without it.[7]

Milne, who spent almost £5,000 on Berwick elections, 1820-3, assisted the 8th earl of Lauderdale's son-in-law James Balfour* at the July and November 1820 by-elections and purchased the Berwickshire estate of Milne Graden in 1821, notwithstanding his second wife's wishes.[8] He refrained from opposing the Tory Sir John Poo Beresford* at Berwick in 1823, and from 10 May-20 June 1824 canvassed Berwickshire, where Sir John Marjoribanks was expected to stand down and he could depend on the support of Sir William Purves Hume Campbell and the Homes of Paxton. However, he deferred there to his fellow sailor, Lauderdale's son Captain Anthony Maitland*, whom Melville endorsed, and in 1825 he was promoted to vice-admiral.[9] Milne supported the wealthy Liverpool merchant John Gladstone at Berwick in 1826-7 and was nominated there after Gladstone was unseated, with a view to coming in on petition and restricting the borough's franchise, but the scheme foundered.[10] He applied to the duke of Wellington as premier for a baronetcy in 1828, but the honour (conferred on his son Alexander in 1871) eluded him.[11] He campaigned on behalf of the Berwick out-voters and strenuously supported the Berwickshire anti-reformers, 1831-2.[12] Thwarted there when the Liberal Charles Marjoribanks's death in December 1833 created a vacancy, he confided to his friend, the inspector-general of marines Sir James Cockburn:

> As for our Scottish politics, I am quite disgusted with them. Sir Hugh Campbell is standing for the county. His politics are he says a *moderate* Conservative, that is to vote with ministers when *convenient*, but there is a complete collusion with the Tories and Whigs. I meant to oppose Sir Hugh myself if he had come forward as a Whig, which I had reason to suspect (and still suspect), but the word *moderate* is attached, and I called a few days ago on the lord lieutenant to know his sentiments about so young a man (not yet of age) coming forward and of suspected politics. I found he had his lordship's support of course, and the support of all that party. His Lordship said it was thought necessary *now* to *support* ministers to hinder them being turned out by the radicals in the House of Commons. This is the politics of Scotland at present. I cannot admire it, but I have seen for two years past what has been going on. The Buccleuchs, Lauderdales, Dundases and all their connections are thus linked together.[13]

Milne was soundly defeated as the Conservative candidate for the Leith district of burghs at the 1835 by-election, and subsequently concentrated on promoting the careers of his sons.[14] Assisting Alexander, whom he made his flag-captain, he applied successfully for promotion to admiral and hoisted his flag on the *Caledonia*, 27 Apr. 1842.[15] He died in May 1845 on board the steamer *Clarence*, which was carrying him home in poor health to Scotland after paying off his crew, and was buried in the kirkyard at Inveresk. Contemporaries recalled him as a 'handy seaman' with a remarkable memory for detail. He provided for his widow (*d.* 1862) and left Inveresk to Alexander and Milne Graden to David, whose namesake son represented Berwick as a Conservative, 1874-85.[16]

[1] NMM MLN/41/1/3, *Biog. Sketch of Sir David Milne* (Extracted from the *Edinburgh Post and Record*, 1845), 1-3. [2] Ibid. 5-16; W.R. O'Byrne, *Naval Biog.* ii. 763; *Oxford DNB sub* Milne, David Milne Home and Sir Alexander Milne. [3] NMM MLN/36/1, Exmouth to Milne, 9 Mar. 1817, Milne to Exmouth, 30 July 1819. [4] *Oxford DNB*; *Berwick Advertiser*, 5 Feb. 1820. [5] *Berwick Advertiser*, 12 Feb. 1820; NAS GD51/1/200/43; NLS mss 11, f. 25. See HADDINGTON BURGHS. [6] *Berwick Advertiser*, 19 Feb.; *Newcastle Courant*, 18 Mar. 1820; G. Milne Home, *Biog. Sketch of David Milne Holme*, 15-16. [7] NAS GD267/23/9, Lady Milne to Milne, 6 July 1820. [8] Ibid.; GD267/23/8A/13,14; *Berwick Advertiser*, 8, 15 July, 9 Dec. 1820. [9] *Edinburgh Advertiser*, 18 Feb. 1823; NAS GD267/23/8A/1-12, 19-22. See also BERWICK-UPON-TWEED and BERWICKSHIRE. [10] *Berwick Advertiser*, 10, 17 June 1826; NAS GD267/23/9, letters to Milne, 19 Mar.-9 May 1827. [11] Wellington mss WP1/920/73; *Oxford DNB sub* Sir Alexander Milne. [12] *Edinburgh Evening Courant*, 21, 26 Mar. 1831; NAS GD267/23/8/8-48. See BERWICKSHIRE. [13] NMM MLN36/10, Milne to Cockburn [n.d.]. [14] *Biog. Sketch*, 29-30; *The Times*, 6 May 1835. [15] *Biog. Sketch*, 22. [16] Ibid. 25-27; *Oxford DNB*.

R.M.H./M.M.E.

MILTON, Visct. *see* **FITZWILLIAM, Charles William Wentworth**

MITCHELL, John (?1781–1859), of Richmond, Surr. and Wimpole Street, Mdx.

KINGSTON-UPON-HULL 1818–1826

b. ?1781, 1st s. of David Mitchell of Jamaica, later of Carshalton House, Surr. and w. Anne Hewitt Smith. *educ.* Westminster; Christ Church, Oxf. 5 Feb. 1800, aged 18; L. Inn 1803, called 1808. *m.* 11 Sept. 1824, Eliza, da. of John Elliott, porter brewer, of Pimlico Lodge, Mdx., 2s. 2da.[1] *suc.* fa. 1804; uncle William Mitchell† 1823. *d.* 29 Aug. 1859.

Vol. London and Westminster light horse 1803-16.

Mitchell, a former barrister who had allegedly been sent to Hull by the Liverpool ministry in 1818, offered again at the 1820 general election. He was greeted on his arrival by 'a party of people who treated him with great cruelty and unmerited indignity', and a mob 'broke his carriage and burnt it and all his clothes'. Undeterred, in his address he declared that such action merely illustrated the axiom 'violence ever defeats its purpose', since he had received many promises given in sympathy and indignation.[2] After a rowdy nomination, in which he was refused a hearing, he was returned unopposed, but violence prevented his chairing. The local press found this hostility inexplicable, as he had been 'a great favourite' in 1818, but the Rev. Richard Sykes, brother of his Whig colleague, was in no doubt as to the reason for his unpopularity:

> One grand cause of this, is an improvement in the minds of the people. Severity is an able schoolmistress. The duke of York's pension, the immense prodigality of ministers, the increase of the army, the refusal of all inquiry into the Manchester affair, and the five bills passed last session, have been brought home to the ... lower classes by the pressure of the times. Mr. Mitchell amiable, pleasing and respectable, was assailed by bitter cries of abuse for having supported these obnoxious measures.[3]

A lax attender, when present Mitchell took an independent line, but is not known to have participated in debate, although a contemporary recalled that he was 'a good speaker, fluent, eloquent and expressive, rather rapid in his manner of delivery, but never at a loss for words. He was polite and gentlemanly in his demeanour, tall, and moderately stout'.[4] He presented a Hull petition against any alteration of the timber import duties, 13 June 1820. He voted with ministers on the Queen Caroline affair, 6 Feb. 1821. He divided against Catholic claims, 28 Feb. 1821, 30 Apr. 1822, 1 Mar., 25 Apr. 1825. He voted against Hume's motion for economy and retrenchment, 21 June 1821, and the calls for more extensive tax cuts, 11, 21 Feb., but was in the opposition majority for admiralty reductions, 1 Mar. 1822. He divided against repeal of the Foreign Enlistment Act, 16 Apr., and inquiry into the prosecution of the Dublin Orange rioters, 22 Apr. 1823. He was in the minority for Stuart Wortley's amendment concerning events in Spain, 30 Apr., and voted for inquiry into chancery delays, 5 June 1823. He divided for repeal of the usury laws, 8 Apr., and paired against condemning the trial of the Methodist missionary John Smith for inciting slave riots in Demerara, 11 June 1824. He presented a Hull petition from the manufacturers of tobacco and snuff praying for a reduction of duties, 24 Feb. 1826.

At the 1826 dissolution Mitchell, who was said to be 'strongly aware of his own unpopularity' and afraid of worse treatment in Hull, stepped down.[5] He had inherited his uncle's Jamaican estates and sugar plantations in 1823 and apparently made no other attempt to enter the house. He died at Torquay in August 1859, 'aged 77'.[6]

[1] J.J. Abraham, *Lettsom*, 467. [2] *Hull Rockingham*, 4 Mar. 1820; Hull Univ. Lib. Hotham mss DDHO/8/2, J. Hall to Hotham, 5 Mar. 1820; DDCV/85/10. [3] *Hull Advertiser*, 10 Mar.; *Hull Rockingham*, 11 Mar. 1820; Wentworth Woodhouse mun. F49/27, R. Sykes to Fitzwilliam, 27 Mar. 1820. [4] W.A. Gunnell, *Hull Celebrities*, 445. [5] Hull RO, Corporation letters, BRL 2337, 2338; Fitzwilliam mss, F.S. Wood to Milton, 7 Oct. 1825. [6] *Gent. Mag.* (1859), ii. 432.

M.P.J.C.

MOLYNEUX, William Philip, 2nd earl of Sefton [I] (1772–1838), of 21 Arlington Street, Piccadilly, Mdx.; Croxteth Hall, nr. Liverpool, Lancs. and Stoke Farm, nr. Windsor, Berks.

DROITWICH 2 Apr. 1816–1831

b. 18 Sept. 1772, o.s. of Charles William Molyneux†, 1st earl of Sefton [I], and Lady Isabella Stanhope, da. of William Stanhope†, 2nd earl of Harrington. *educ.* Dr. Glass's sch. Greenford, Mdx. 1783; Christ Church, Oxf. 1789. *styled* Visct. Molyneux until 1795. *m.* 1 Jan. 1792, Hon. Maria Margaretta Craven, da. of William, 6th Bar. Craven, 4s. 6da. (1 *d.v.p.*). *suc.* fa. as 2nd earl of Sefton [I] 31 Jan. 1795; *cr.* Bar. Sefton [UK] 20 June 1831. *d.* 22 Nov. 1838.

Master of the Quorn 1800-5.

Maj. commdt. Croxteth vols. 1803.

Sefton, whom Greville found 'irresistibly comical', was widely noted for his 'liveliness, persiflage and good humour, his hunting, racing, gaming and gastronomy'.[1] Considered 'a complete radical' by Mrs.

Arbuthnot, he continued to sit unchallenged for Droitwich on the interest of his cousin, the 3rd Baron Foley.[2] A mostly silent member of the Whig 'Mountain', whose 'parliamentary attendance never abridged the hours or nights which were devoted to Crockford's', where it was alleged he 'broke the bank' and 'carried off £7,000' in 1829, he was an intimate associate of Thomas Creevey*, to whom he was both patron and allegedly half-brother, and a close confidant of Henry Brougham*. Greville noted how Sefton 'watches him incessantly' and 'rows him unmercifully for all the humbug, nonsense, and palaver he hears him talk'.[3] Despite the handicap of 'a frame somewhat deformed' by a hunchback, Sefton 'was a capital horseman' and 'one of the leaders of the Four in Hand Club'.[4]

He voted steadily with the Whig opposition to the Liverpool ministry on most major issues, including economy, retrenchment and reduced taxation. On 12 May 1820 he presented and endorsed a petition from the merchants of Liverpool complaining of distress and the 'lavish and indiscriminate manner' in which pensions had been bestowed. He played a leading part in the opposition campaign in support of Queen Caroline, although he declined to act with Lord Fitzwilliam on her behalf in the talks with ministers. Greville later commented that he was a 'queer choice', and 'totally unfit for the office of negotiator in a grave matter'.[5] He was 'known to be so strongly against' the bill of pains and penalties that the fact of his having 'betted Lord Thanet 10 to 1' that it would 'pass the Lords' was taken as 'quite convincing' grounds for optimism by the king.[6] According to Sir James Mackintosh*, 3 July, he was much to blame for the 'feud between Grey and Brougham' during the negotiations, and 'immediately reported' back to Brougham Grey's comments implying 'that he had sold the queen for his own silk gown'.[7] Lady Sefton later told the radical Whig Henry Grey Bennet* that 'having for near eight years come daily to their house, and lived in it as one of the family', Brougham no longer 'comes near them'.[8] During July 1820 it was reported that Sefton, Douglas Kinnaird†, Sir Robert Wilson and other 'Mountaineers' were 'exulting in the prospect of mutiny and civil war' at Brooks's over the affair.[9] He presented and endorsed a petition from 10,000 inhabitants of Liverpool calling for the restoration of Caroline's 'rights and dignities', inquiry 'into the outrages at Manchester' and reduced taxation and parliamentary reform, 2 Feb. 1821. He divided steadily in her support early in that session, but was one of the six opposition Members 'at Taylor's supping' who were 'shut out' of the division for restoring her name to the liturgy, to the 'great amusement' of Charles Williams Wynn*, 13 Feb.[10] He was a member of the committee at Brooks's for the management of her subscription and, with Lord Thanet, 'advanced the deposit' of £3,000 for her purchase of Cambridge House in South Audley Street, 24 Feb. 1821.[11]

Sefton voted for Catholic relief, 28 Feb. 1821, 1 Mar., 21 Apr. (as a pair), but he and Creevey joined Lambton's 'seceders' and abstained from the third reading of the bill, there having 'been a great schism in the opposition on the whole matter', 10 May 1825.[12] On 17 Apr. 1823, when Plunket, the renegade Whig Irish attorney-general, rose to open the debate on the Catholic question, Sefton was among those opposition Members who pointedly left the chamber in protest.[13] He divided in favour of Leeds becoming a scot and lot borough if it received Grampound's seats, 2 Mar., and for parliamentary reform, 9 May 1821, 25 Apr. 1822, 20 Feb., 2 June 1823, but was absent from the division on the issue, 27 Apr. 1826. Congratulating Creevey on his 'conversion to reform', 2 Oct. 1825, he declared, 'I have been long convinced that nothing else will bring down taxation and tithes, and therefore would not give a farthing for any other remedy'.[14] On 13 Sept. 1821 he disagreed with Creevey over the conviction of Life Guards accused of murder in the Colchester riots following the queen's death, protesting that 'they are always infamously treated by the mob' and that it was the government which 'ought to be impaled'.[15] On 27 Feb. 1822 Creevey recorded that during his lengthy speech on pensions, 'Brougham and Sefton were amongst my bottle holders in the front row'.[16] Sefton declined an offer to stand against Huskisson at the 1823 Liverpool by-election, but did all he could to 'assist' his son Lord Molyneux†, whom he persuaded the deputation to adopt instead.[17] Having joined Creevey in opposing the Liverpool and Manchester railway bill in March 1825, he was said to be in 'ecstasies' at its being 'strangled' in committee, 1 June 1825.[18] He was in the minorities for revising the corn laws, 28 Apr. 1825, and against the corn bill, 11 May 1826.

Following his return at the 1826 general election Sefton confided to Grey that the recent death of his daughter Georgiana had left 'a blank which can never be filled up'.[19] He voted against the Clarences' grant, 16 Feb. 1827. He divided for Catholic claims, 6 Mar. 1827, 12 May 1828 (as a pair). He voted for inquiry into electoral interference by Leicester corporation, 15 Mar., and for the spring guns bill, 23 Mar. 1827. That month he put up bail for Brougham, who had been arrested for his part in a duel.[20] Following the accession to power of Canning, Sefton commented to Creevey, 13 Apr., that the Tories 'all declare their motive for resigning' to be 'strictly personal' and 'that the Catholics have nothing to do with it', and hoped that 'if opposition support, Canning may stand, and they certainly ought to keep out these villains'. The following day James Macdonald* reported that '[Lord] Duncannon*, backed by Lord Sefton and some of the most unlikely men', were urging 'the necessity' of Lord Lansdowne's accepting office in 'a government that should be formed *without any restrictions* on the Catholic question'.[21] Brougham explained that their 'prime object' was 'to keep out the Ultras and not let them back' and reported that 'Sefton (no friend of Canning or coalitions) is full of this and has written strongly': his letters, Brougham informed Creevey, 'would put life into a wheelbarrow, or anything but a superannuated Whig'.[22] Lady Cowper observed, 24 Apr., that pressure on Lansdowne, who 'does not much like coming into office at this moment', came from 'even those who are in general the greatest democrats – Lord Sefton, Lord Tankerville, Brougham, Wilson. They feel it is everything for the Catholics and that by a refusal the House of Commons must fall back upon the Tories'.[23] On 28 May Sefton defended his conduct to Creevey, who had firmly opposed the coalition:

> I *do say* the junction is justified by the exclusion of Eldon, Wellington, Peel and Bathurst. It could have been brought about by no other means ... As to the 'baseness of the junction', and the rest of your apple-blossom twaddle ... I don't stand up for Canning, but I think the junction with him is a chance for the country ... Don't forget that Grey, whose opposition is solely personal, once preferred him to Whitbread ... I don't care a damn – nor do you – for the Catholics; but I say their chance is a hundredfold better under the new cabinet than under the old; and so do they.[24]

On 13 June Mrs. Arbuthnot noted that Lord Palmerston* 'provoked me very much by boasting of Lord Sefton being the prime supporter of government'.[25] Following Canning's death and his replacement by Lord Goderich, Lord Cassillis advised Peel to 'depend upon it, Brougham and such will break out upon ministers ere long. *Words* won't do with Lambton, Sefton, etc. They want peerages perhaps, which the king will never give them'.[26] Sefton, however, continued to give ministers his support, although privately admitting to Creevey that the 'Navarino business must destroy them'. According to Grey, 13 Dec. 1827

> Sefton's conduct can only be explained on the supposition that he feels himself bound not to abandon, in their difficulties, an administration which he originally promised to support; but I do not think this feeling can prevail long against his own opinion and the increasing opinion of the public.[27]

On 1 Jan. 1828 Lord Tavistock* reported that he had received a letter 'from Sefton anxious to know what we mean to do, as his new friends have tried him too high'.[28] Following the collapse of the ministry, however, and the Canningites' acceptance of office under Wellington, Huskisson was informed by Sir George Warrender* that

> Sefton came to White's obviously for the purpose of contradicting your accession to the new arrangement, and he read to me a letter dated 8th, last evening, which I feel certain was from Brougham, entreating and desiring Sefton everywhere to deny and contradict the sinister reports about you as most injuriously tending to weaken and dishearten their party (i.e. the Whigs).[29]

Sefton presented a petition from Toxteth against the Test Acts, 19 Feb., and paired for their repeal, 26 Feb. 1828. He voted against extending the franchise of East Retford to the freeholders of Bassetlaw, 21 Mar., and the additional churches bill, 30 June. Writing to Creevey, 7 Sept., he doubted that Wellington had 'the slightest intention of doing the smallest thing for the Catholics, or that he ever thinks about them', and warned that 'when the time comes, he will send troops to Ireland'.[30] On 29 Dec. 1828 he told Brougham that he considered

> the duke's letter to Curtis [the Irish Catholic primate] ... as the signal for rebellion. At least it ought to be. It causes a stormy session and I hope you will be at your post and take the field in earnest. What a letter! To be sure he's a great fellow for a prime minister! Surely Grey cannot stand this. He certainly had indignant feelings towards ... [Wellington] and would have forgiven trifles, but he is not the man I take him for, if he quits now.[31]

On hearing of the ministry's proposals to concede emancipation, 6 Feb. 1829, however, Sefton, 'owned that the business is very handsomely done'.[32] He presented a favourable petition, 17 Feb., and voted accordingly, 6, 30 Mar. (as a pair), despite being convinced that Grey 'must and will come into office' before the issue could be settled.[33] (James Abercromby* had incorrectly predicted that 'Sefton and Co.', taking their cue from Grey, would 'not vote for the third reading' on account of the disfranchisement of Irish 40*s.* freeholders.)[34] That June Greville 'set about making a reconciliation between the king and Lord Sefton'. The cause of their quarrel, he explained, was 'very old'. George IV had 'pimped' for Arthur Paget†, who 'was in love with Lady Sefton ... by taking Sefton out on some expedition and leaving the lovers to amuse themselves'. Sefton had 'found out' and 'revenged himself by a thousand jokes at the king's expense', and they had 'been at daggers drawn ever since'.[35] Sefton divided against Lord Blandford's parliamentary reform scheme, 18 Feb., but for the enfranchisement of Birmingham, Leeds and Manchester, 23 Feb., to refer the Newark petition complaining of the duke of Newcastle's electoral interference to a select committee, 1 Mar., and for the transfer of East Retford's seats to Birmingham, 15 Mar. 1830. He voted for Jewish emancipation, 17 May, and for proper use of Irish first fruits revenues, 18 May 1830.

In July 1830 Greville noted that William IV was 'very civil' at his levee, 'particularly to Sefton, who had quarrelled with the late king'.[36] Commenting on Wellington's determination to continue in office, 27 Aug., Sefton warned Brougham:

> If we are not organized, his miserable weakness will still prevail. For God's sake, concert with Grey for a regular place for our union of parties and don't put it off till it is too late. I have a very bad opinion of Huskisson, but he and his people are necessary and are anxious to join you ... An avowed party in opposition is indispensable and will prevent desertion and mischief ... There never was such a moment. You supported ministers as long as you could, but their imbecility and rotten incapacity for conducting the government has become so obvious that it is impossible to support them or even tolerate them any longer. The whole country sees this and has spoken pretty plainly in the elections.[37]

At his Berkshire seat three days later, Sefton boasted to Greville that 'Brougham and Grey were prepared for a violent opposition and that they had effected a formal junction with Huskisson, being convinced that no government could be formed without him'; but Greville was sceptical and later ascertained from George Agar Ellis* that 'there was not a word of truth in the reported junction'.[38] Sefton continued to press on Brougham the importance of keeping options open, commenting on 8 Sept. that 'I don't think there is any occasion to mind the Ultras. You cannot expect to conceal from them co-operation with Huskisson. However, for God's sake don't let the Huskissonites slip through you fingers'. On hearing of Huskisson's accidental death on the Liverpool and Manchester railway, 21 Sept., he wrote:

> What a lucky fellow this duke is! Nothing else could have saved him ... One ought to believe anything, but I cannot believe that the remnant will consent to bolster him ... Surely after his treatment of them at their elections the Grants are out of the question. Granville hates the duke and Palmerston must hate him too ... I have reason to *know* that there is no truth whatsoever in his having made any overtures to Palmerston and Melbourne ... Notwithstanding all you philosophers may say, the locomotive is an uncontrollable machine and if it is used as a conveyance for passengers thousands of horrible accidents will happen.[39]

Sefton, according to Greville, refused Brougham's entreaties 'to go to the Liverpool dinner and attack the duke of Wellington ... face to face' at the ensuing by-election.[40] As Lord John Russell* explained to Lady Holland, 13 Oct., Sefton 'is in great spirits at the prospect of a November Parliament, but he quite agrees with me that we ought to begin quietly'.[41] He was, of course, listed by the Wellington ministry as one of their 'foes', and he voted against them in the division on the civil list which brought them down, 15 Nov. 1830, when, despite being told 'not to cheer', his 'yell was heard triumphant in the din'.[42] The incoming Grey ministry asked him 'to settle the conditions of Brougham's accession to office, and to appease the wrath which had been stirred up in his mind by the offer of being made attorney-general'. This, as Sefton explained to Creevey, 18 Nov., was 'very difficult' as Brougham was 'in a state of insanity' on the subject; but the following day he informed Creevey of Brougham's appointment as lord chancellor. At dinner with Grey and Greville, 22 Nov., Sefton, who found the appointment highly amusing, 'bantered' Brougham 'from the beginning to the end' and afterwards 'walked out before him with the fire shovel for the mace, and left him no repose all the evening'.[43] By December, Sefton felt that 'things are looking awkward' and could not 'be allowed to go on as they are at Manchester', where there had been 'parading with arms and flags'; he believed that 'force must be used'. Having 'done all I can to ascertain the truth about Manchester and its neighbourhood', however, he became more sanguine, telling Grey, 26 Dec. 1830:

> I am quite convinced things are not so bad as represented. [Lord] Derby does not seem alarmed and says the proclamation against procession with offensive flags, placards, etc. was completely successful. He does not believe that they have carried arms to *any extent*. The worst is they are all in a *union* and have a great accumulation of money from their weekly subscriptions, *certainly* above £100,000, so that they can hold out a long time. The marchers are determined not to give way but still I am convinced a compromise will take place.[44]

According to Creevey, when Parliament met Sefton complained that the government 'cut a very sorry figure ... upon the civil list and upon the *pensions* part of it in particular, and ... he was going to blow up Grey about it'.[45] To Greville he observed that Lord Althorp was 'wretched' and 'leading the House of Commons without the slightest acquaintance with the various subjects under discussion'.[46] He presented a petition from the landowners of West Derby against the revived Liverpool and Manchester railway bill, 25 Feb. That month he again used his influence with Brougham, urging him to do all he could to temper the attacks on Grey in *The Times*.[47] He voted for the second reading of the ministerial reform bill, 22 Mar., and against Gascoyne's wrecking amendment, 19 Apr. On 21 Apr. 1831 he asserted that the 'grossest bribery and corruption were practised at Liverpool' in 'former elections', but denied Thomas Gladstone's accusation that he was 'impugning the conduct of Canning', claiming that he was speaking of contests in which he himself had taken 'a very active part'.

At the ensuing general election Sefton made way for another of Foley's cousins at Droitwich, amidst rumours that he was 'shortly to have an English peerage'. He declined an offer to stand for Lancashire, prompting Creevey to complain that 'considering Sefton's connection with Grey, and that he is to be his first peer, he ought to have made some demonstration in favour of the government during this eventful battle'.[48] The results of the election prompted Sefton to remark to Lord Durham and Greville that 'the county Members are tumbling about like ninepins'.[49] As one of five new peers created in June 1831, he perpetually urged Grey and Brougham to create sufficient peers to carry the reform bill.[50] On 20 Aug. Greville noted:

> Sefton ... talks blusteringly of the peers that are to be made, no matter at what cost to the House of Lords, anything rather than be beaten; but I am not sure that he *knows* anything. In such matters as these he is (however sharp) no better than a fool, no knowledge, no information, no reflection or combination; prejudices, partialities, and sneers are what his political wisdom consists of; but he is Lord Grey's *âme damnée*.[51]

During the days of May 1832 Sefton's face, according to Raikes, was 'a true barometer' and 'picture of despair'; and on William IV holding a Jockey Club dinner, 'Sefton, who was indignant at the resignation of his friends the ministers, and most clamorous at what he called the duplicity of the king, in a fit of pique and vexation erased his name from the list of members and sent an excuse to the dinner as no longer belonging'.[52] Later that year Princess Lieven noted that his 'digestion is beginning to trouble him' and that 'he looks ill'.[53]

Sefton died in November 1838, having been for the last six months 'reduced to a state of deplorable imbecility'.[54] By his will, dated 10 Nov. 1836 and proved under £35,000, all his property passed to his wife. He was succeeded in the peerage by his eldest son Charles William (1796-1855), Liberal Member for Lancashire South, 1832-5.[55]

[1] *Greville Mems.* iv. 144; *Smith Letters*, i. 334. [2] *Arbuthnot Jnl.* ii. 125. [3] *Creevey Pprs.* ii. 195; *Greville Mems.* ii. 150-1; iv. 102, 145. [4] Maxwell, *Clarendon*, i. 43; *Gronow Reminiscences*, ii. 110. [5] *Arbuthnot Jnl.* i. 23; *Creevey Pprs.* i. 303; *Greville Mems.* i. 97; ii. 420-1. [6] *Creevey Pprs.* i. 328. [7] Add. 52444, f. 183. [8] HLRO, Hist. Coll. 379, Grey Bennet diary, 83. [9] Add. 52444, f. 202. [10] Grey Bennet diary, 19; Buckingham, *Mems. Geo. IV*, i. 122. [11] Grey Bennet diary, 24; *Creevey Pprs.* ii. 15. [12] Gurney diary, 10 May; TNA 30/29/9/2. [13] Northants. RO, Agar Ellis diary, 17 Apr. 1823. [14] *Creevey Pprs.* ii. 93. [15] Ibid. ii. 32. [16] Ibid. ii. 35. [17] Add. 51836, Sefton to Holland [early 1823]. [18] *Creevey Pprs.* ii. 88. [19] Grey mss GRE/B52/2/4, Sefton to Grey, 7 July 1826. [20] T. Ford, *Brougham and his World*, 426. [21] *Creevey Pprs.* ii. 112-13; *Canning's Ministry*, 117. [22] Add. 51562, Brougham to Holland [Apr. 1827]; *Creevey Pprs.* ii. 114. [23] *Canning's Ministry*, 240. [24] *Creevey Pprs.* ii. 117-18. [25] *Arbuthnot Jnl.* ii. 125. [26] Add. 40394, f. 189. [27] *Creevey Pprs.* ii. 139, 142. [28] *Russell Letters*, ii. 223. [29] Add. 38754, f. 114. [30] *Creevey Pprs.* ii. 170. [31] Brougham mss. [32] *Greville Mems.* i. 248. [33] *Creevey Pprs.* ii. 199. [34] Add. 51574, Abercromby to Holland [?Mar. 1829]; G.I.T. Machin, *Catholic Question in English Politics*, 56. [35] *Greville Mems.* i. 297. [36] Ibid. ii. 11. [37] Brougham mss, Sefton to Brougham, 27 Aug. 1830. [38] *Greville Mems.* ii. 32-33, 39. [39] Brougham mss. [40] *Greville Mems.* ii. 45. [41] Add. 51680. [42] *Greville Mems.* ii. 60. [43] Ibid. ii. 112, 67-8; *Creevey Pprs.* ii. 214. [44] Add. 51835, Sefton to Holland [Dec. 1830]; Grey mss GRE/B52/2/7. [45] Creevey mss, Creevey to Miss Ord, 5 Feb. 1831. [46] *Greville Mems.* ii. 118. [47] *Creevey Pprs.* ii. 219-20. [48] *Worcester Herald*, 23 Apr.; Add. 51680, Russell to Lady Holland [May]; Creevey mss, Creevey to Miss Ord, 4 May 1831. [49] Reid, *Lord Durham*, i. 259-60; *Greville Mems.* ii. 141. [50] *Holland House Diaries*, 42; Grey mss GRE/B52/2/6, Sefton to Grey, 17 Nov. 1831. [51] *Greville Mems.* ii. 186. [52] *Raikes Jnl.* i. 27-28, 36. [53] *Lieven-Palmerston Corresp.* 38. [54] *Gent. Mag.* (1838), ii. 657; *Raikes Jnl.* iii. 341; *Greville Mems.* iv. 143. [55] PROB 11/1907/122; *CP*, xi. 593-4.

P.J.S.

MONCK, John Berkeley (1769–1834), of Coley Park, Reading and Aldworth, Berks.

READING 1820–1830

bap. 19 Sept. 1769, 2nd s. of John Monck (*d.* 1809) of 20 Marlborough Buildings, Bath and Emilia, da. of John Snee, merchant, of Aldermanbury, London.[1] *educ.* Eton 1778-88; L. Inn 1790; I. Temple 1796, called 1797. *m.* 4 May 1810, Mary da. of William Stephens of Aldermaston, Berks., 2s. 2da. *d.* 13 Dec. 1834.

Monck belonged to a branch of an old Devonshire family, of which General George Monck, the celebrated duke of Albemarle, was a member. His more recent antecedents were Irish. Charles Monck, joint surveyor-general of customs in Ireland in 1627, bought property in Westmeath. His son Henry Monck was attainted by James II, but restored in his estates by William III, and married into the Stanley family of Grange Gorman, county Dublin. Of his three sons, Charles (1705-72), the second, was the grandfather of Charles Stanley Monck (?1754-1802), who succeeded to the main family estates in 1787 and sat in the Irish Parliament as Member for Newborough, 1790-7, when he was created Baron Monck in the Irish peerage. He was made a viscount of the British peerage on the Union. His son and successor Henry Stanley Monck (1785-1845) was created earl of Rathdowne in 1822. William Monck, the fifth son of Henry, and grandfather of this Member, was born in 1692. He was called to the bar from the Middle Temple in 1728, prospered as a lawyer, became a bencher and reader of his Inn and died in 1763. With his wife Dorothy Bligh, the sister of the 1st earl of Darnley, he had a son, John Monck, who was born in 1734. He was educated at Westminster and Christ Church and called to the bar from the Middle Temple. In the 1760s he moved from London to Bath, where he lived for over 40 years, and was a generous patron of local hospitals and charitable institutions. According to an obituary, he was distinguished by 'the urbanity of his manners, his cultivated taste and his various and extensive attainments in literary pursuits'.[2] With his wife Emilia Snee he had five sons. The eldest, William Bligh Monck, born in 1768, was educated at Oxford and died unmarried in 1814.[3] Charles (1772-1833), the third, was a barrister on the Western circuit and a fellow of New College, Oxford for many years. Henry Dutton, born in 1795, also went to Oxford, but subsequently lapsed into a state of imbecility.[4] George (1777-1846) entered the church and married a daughter of the 5th Viscount Boyne.

John Berkeley Monck, the second and evidently favourite son, was educated for the bar, but 'very delicate' health forced him to give up living in London at around the time of his call. He settled in Reading, where he was said to have 'pursued his professional duties with industry, honour and integrity', involved himself in the civic affairs of the town, and became friendly with Mary Russell Mitford and Charles Shaw Lefevre, who sat for the borough initially as an Addingtonian and later as an independent supporter of the Whig opposition.[5] In April 1807, 'having much leisure on my hands, in consequence of confinement from illness', he wrote *General Reflections on the System of the Poor Laws*, a subject which deeply interested him, as did Malthusian population theory in general. He contended that the existing laws did far more harm than good and were the main reason why 'the poor are such as we find them, swarming, indolent, improvident, discontented, dispirited, oppressed, degraded, vicious'. While abolition was 'the only radical cure', he accepted that such drastic action was impractical, and suggested a number of reforms to improve the education of poor children, reward the deserving and discourage the idle from claiming relief. He expressed approval of Samuel Whitbread's current bill to reform the system. When his father made his will in June 1808, he left only £4,000 from a trust fund of £27,000 created by his marriage settlement to his eldest son. He devised £6,000 of it to John Berkeley Monck, along with all his unspecified Irish real estate, his jewels, *objets d'art* and household goods and his Bath house. He also made provision from the residue of his personal estate, which was proved at a handsome £125,000 after his death in November 1809, for Monck to purchase real estate, to be settled on himself and his issue in tail male.[6] The following year, when he married the sister of a Reading alderman, Monck bought the manor of Coley, which lay in the southwest of the town, within St. Mary's parish. In 1812 he acquired the Berkshire estate of Aldworth, nine miles north-east of Newbury.[7]

In February that year he published *A Letter to Spencer Perceval on the Present State of the Currency*, in which he stressed the importance of maintaining the circulating medium 'pure and unimpaired', denounced the current metallic currency as 'a debased specie', reflected on the folly of making bank notes legal tender and proposed the issue by the Bank of England of gold guinea tokens as a prelude to prohibiting the issue of notes under £5 in value. To meet a local currency crisis, he issued large amounts of tokens, in gold for 40*s*., and in silver for 2*s*. 6*d*. and 1*s*. 6*d*., which were redeemable in notes on application to the Reading bank of Marsh, Deane and Company.[8] At the general election in October 1812 he stood for Reading as the advocate of parliamentary reform in opposition to Shaw Lefevre's ministerialist colleague Simeon, but finished a distant third.[9] At the Berkshire county meeting of 17 May 1814 he deplored the continuing blockade of Norway and called for petitions against it; and at the borough sessions of January 1816 he appealed unsuccessfully against the poor rate levied on his property, arguing that land was unfairly charged one third more than houses. He subsequently instigated an experiment designed to discourage the able-bodied poor from seeking relief by having those in the workhouse whom he had assisted distinguished by the letters 'M.P' (Monck's Poor) sewn on their sleeves.[10] After the war he spent much time in France, for the good of his health.[11] He was there when the death of George III in January 1820 precipitated a general election. Initially Shaw Lefevre, who was also in France for the sake of his health, offered again, as did his

Whig colleague Charles Fyshe Palmer; but when he decided that he was not well enough his leading supporters issued an invitation to Monck, who had earlier indicated his willingness to stand if either sitting Member retired. Monck hurried home, and a contest ensued when the Tory Blues put up John Weyland*. On the hustings Monck, who was nominated by the leading radical activist Henry Marsh, and whose committee, chaired by his brother-in-law William Stephens, formed the nucleus of the newly established Association for the Purity and Independence of Elections, advocated reform, specifying triennial parliaments and an extension of the franchise in 'decayed boroughs'. He attacked 'excessive taxation' and the corn laws. After a protracted and tight contest he topped the poll.[12] He apparently returned briefly to Paris before the meeting of Parliament.[13]

In the House he was one of the most active of the group of radical Whigs who associated with Joseph Hume, a dedicated attender, never afraid to open his mouth in debate, and a persistent critic of the lavish expenditure and high taxation. He complained of the 'extravagant and enormous' allowances paid to British senior diplomats, 19 May. On 12 July he depicted the aliens bill as part of 'a mysterious and undefined attempt to hunt down the liberal-minded men – the Whigs of the continent – who were deserving of an asylum in this country'. Opposing the appointment of a select committee on agricultural distress, 31 May, he said that the corn laws 'affected the poor in a cruel and disproportionate manner' by driving up the price of food and reducing many of them to 'the dreadful alternative of starvation or pauperism'. He voted with opposition in the divisions on Queen Caroline's case, 22, 26 June, and may have been a member of the Reading deputation which presented her with a loyal address in September.[14] He attended the dinner of the Purity of Election Association, 9 Nov.[15] His name headed the list of requistionists for a town meeting to congratulate the queen on the abandonment of the bill of pains and penalties and call for the dismissal of ministers. When it took place, 7 Dec. 1820, he denounced the 'inexpedient, unnecessary and unconstitutional' prosecution, and attacked the king in savage personal terms. He attributed Caroline's sometimes coarse demeanour to nothing more sinister than lax European habits, which offended 'English reserve':

> Those who have travelled, and those who have seen the common engravings of the Swiss costumes, well know that the peasants in many parts of Switzerland wear petticoats that do not descend even to the knees; and that these mountaineers expose the lower part of their persons as constantly and innocently as some ladies nearer home, from the most amiable of all motives – a desire to please, or frequently without any motive, in obedience only to the sway of fashion – expose the upper part of their persons, the arms and shoulders, the well-turned neck and rising bosom.

Returning to the point, he called for nationwide parish meetings to bring popular opinion to bear on ministers, and to

> demand indemnity for the past, security for the future; to demand a change not of ministers only but of measures; to demand a system of conciliation to be pursued towards a most meritorious but suffering people, instead of coercion; to demand a reduction of all those taxes that press hardest upon national industry and on the labouring class of society; to demand, in lieu of those taxes, a system of economy and retrenchment; if this be not sufficient for the revenue, to demand sacrifices ... of the rich; and above all to demand a reform of Parliament, as the only means of rebuilding the fabric of our constitution on its ancient basis, and of opening to ourselves new sources of wealth and strength, of internal prosperity, and of external power.

He chaired the county meeting on the same subject, 8 Jan. 1821.[16]

Monck presented and endorsed petitions for restoration of Caroline's name to the liturgy from Wantage, 26 Jan., and Hungerford and Newbury, 8 Feb. 1821. On 21 May, pressing ministers to say whether or not she would be admitted to the coronation, he said that it would be shameful if 'a grand national fête was to be converted into an engine for ... [her] humiliation and degradation'.[17] He was a dedicated voter for economy, retrenchment and reduced taxation, often appearing in tiny minorities with Hume. When supporting repeal of the tax on husbandry horses, 5 Mar., he argued, in his familiar refrain, that the interests of agriculture would be best served not by high protecting duties but by a reduction of the burden of domestic taxation and allowances being made for the difficulties created by the resumption of cash payments. He said that the House must be persuaded to insist on 'retrenchment and reform', 9 Mar., as he did when supporting repeal of the additional malt duty, 21 Mar., in what his associate Henry Grey Bennet deemed 'the best [speech] of the night'.[18] However, he opposed and was a teller for the minority against inquiry into Scottish petitions on the duties, 12 Apr. He complained that the enhanced timber duties taxed the whole community taxed the whole community for the benefit of ship-owners, 19 Apr.[19] He backed Hume's call for a revision of salaries increased and inflated by the currency adjustment of 1797, 30 Mar.,[20] and on the bill to accelerate cash resumption, 9 Apr., said that inquiry as proposed by Baring would do no good, although he did not pretend to have a ready answer to the problems arising from the 'return from a false and fictitious, to a sound currency'. On the same theme, 13 Apr., he argued that the Ricardo system, which 'substituted payments in bullion for the ancient currency', was 'a cheat and a fraud upon the public creditor'. He took particular exception to the grant to the duke of Clarence in June, criticizing it severely on the 8th. He voted for Catholic relief, 28 Feb. 1821, as he did again, 1 Mar., 21 Apr., 10 May 1825. He approved the proposal to give Leeds a scot and lot franchise if it received Grampound's seats, 2 Mar., observing that 'the great defect in the constitution was, that the poorer classes were not represented'. He was a steward for the City reform dinner, 4 Apr., when he declared that the corn laws, Peterloo and the prosecution of the queen 'were not calculated to reclaim him from the error of being a reformer'.[21] He spoke and was a teller for the minority of 33 in favour of referring the Lyme Regis petition on the franchise to the committee of privileges, 12 Apr., and voted for Lambton's reform motion, 18 Apr., Russell's, 9 May, reform of the Scottish county representation, 10 May, and Grey Bennet's attempt to reduce the number of placemen in the Commons, 31 May. He spoke for repeal of the usury laws, which he constantly supported, 12 Apr. He voted for inquiry into Peterloo, 16 May, having the previous day, when presenting a petition from a victim, stated that 'never was human blood poured out more wantonly, more lavishly, and more unnecessarily'. He criticized the poor laws, 8 May, and called for a repeal of taxes to benefit the poor and so reduce rates; and on 8 June asserted that if such action was taken the laws would 'die a natural death'.[22] He condemned them as 'an ingenious device for obtaining the greatest quantity of labour at the least expense', 2 July, but admitted that abolition was not feasible. On the vagrancy bill, 24 May, he said that the destitute must be given some relief and that he was not prepared to subject vagrants to 'an eternal round of punishments'. He opposed attempts to legislate to prevent cruelty to animals, 1, 25 June. He was, surprisingly, one of the 'creditable' minority of six against reducing the grant for General Desfourneaux, 28 June 1821.[23]

Monck spoke at length at a Reading meeting to vote thanks to Hume for his parliamentary exertions, 14 Jan. 1822, when he advocated cuts in expenditure and tax remissions in his usual terms and dwelt of the 'monstrous absurdity' of the agriculturalists' selfish demands for increased protection. He called for parliamentary reform at the annual dinner of the Purity of Election Association, 16 Jan.[24] He voted regularly and stubbornly for tax cuts, economy and retrenchment throughout the session. He aired his views on the problems caused by the changes in the currency, 8 Mar., 1 Apr., 2, 31 May, 14 June, and voted for Western's motion for inquiry, 12 June. Although he was 'directly opposed to the principle' of the sinking fund, he initially welcomed the government's scheme to pay naval and military pensions from it, 1 May, 'because it went to effect a reduction of taxation'; but he voted against the measure, 3, 24 May, 3, 26 June. On the presentation of the report of the agricultural distress committee, 8 May, he spoke and voted for Wyvill's amendment calling for retrenchment and tax remissions. He again declared undying hostility to the corn laws as 'a tax for the exclusive benefit of the landed interest', 4 June.[25] He supported repeal of the house and window taxes, 2 July, but thought that abolition of the beer tax would be more beneficial. He welcomed, as 'calculated to effect considerable savings to the public', the bill to regulate the office of receiver general of taxes, 18 July. He voted for inquiry into the Scottish burghs, 20 Feb., and parliamentary reform, 25 Apr., 3 June. On 15 July he said of the Irish insurrection bill that he 'saw nothing in it of a remedial nature' for the problems of a country bedeviled by overpopulation, where 'the state of society was half civilized, half savage'. He called for reform of the oppressive licensing system, 24 Apr., when he censured the autocratic powers vested in magistrates and 'that strait-laced morality which, by forbidding public houses, drove the people of England from their ancient, wholesome, good manly beverage, beer, to drink that nasty, meagre infusion of foreign herbs, tea'. He spoke in the same vein, 6, 20 May, when he asserted that Reading contained not a single free house, supported Grey Bennet's licensing bill, 27 June, and approved a beer retail bill, 10 July, presenting constituency petitions in its favour, 17 July.[26] He presented Reading petitions against Scarlett's poor removal bill, 13 May, and argued that the measure, for all its author's good intentions, would make a bad system worse, 31 May 1822.[27]

At the Berkshire county reform meeting, 27 Jan. 1823, Monck, admitting that 'they might as well ask the wolf to give up its prey' as request a corrupt Commons to reform itself, recommended a nationally organized boycott of the consumption of 'superfluous articles' to 'starve the enemy into compliance'.[28] At the Purity of Election dinner, 16 Jan., he had declared for 'radical reform', and promised that in the approaching session he would be found 'advocating purity of election, reform, and retrenchment' and denouncing 'paper, extravagance and corruption'.[29] He was as good as his word, voting as usual for economy, retrenchment and tax reductions, and speaking for repeal of the tax on tallow candles, 21 May, and of the malt and beer duties, 28 May. On the proposals for reduction of the national debt, 6 Mar., he denounced the sinking fund as 'not only useless, but decidedly mischievous', and urged the application of surplus revenue to tax cuts. He voted for inquiry into the parliamentary franchise, 20 Feb., endorsed the Berkshire reform petition, 27 Feb.,[30] and voted for Russell's reform scheme, 24 Apr., though he missed the division on reform of the Scottish representative system, 2 June. On 26 Feb., when he identified the dislocation of the currency as the basic cause of the 'unparalleled distress which overwhelmed the productive industry of the country', he spoke and voted to reduce the import price of corn to 60*s*. He was one of the 27 Members who voted for inquiry into the currency, 12 June, having told ministers that they were wrong to measure depreciation by simply comparing gold with paper. He supported Hume's motion for inquiry into the Irish church establishment, 4 Mar., distinguishing between 'spoilation' and a reallocation of revenues; he was a teller for the minority. On 23 June he supported the grant to subsidize Irish emigration to Canada as a gesture of goodwill, but argued that Irish absentees should be make to contribute substantially to the economic development of their country. He approved the removal of restrictions on the conduct of marriage services by Catholic priests, 12 June. He was friendly to the principle of the silk manufacture bill, but did not wish it to become law without a repeal of the Combination Acts, and therefore voted for its recommittal, 9 June. He was named to the select committee on poor returns, 23 Feb., as he was on its renewal in the next three sessions. He said a reduction of poor rates was 'indispensably necessary, to prevent them from swallowing up the landed interest', 12 May,[31] and that their 'total but gradual extinction' was the only solution to the problem, 4 June. He was a stern critic of the beer duties bill, which he said would be 'cruel to the public brewer, and not advantageous to the public', as the poor man was entitled to 'a beverage which would neither disagree with his head nor with his stomach', 25 Apr.[32] He called for modifications to it, 12 May, and again denounced it, 17 June, when he was a teller for the minority against the third reading. He supported his colleague Palmer's unsuccessful attempt to legislate to permit brewers to retail beer in small quantities, 28 May 1823.

Monck began his attendance in the 1824 session slightly later than previously, but was present to call for full inquiry into the concerns of the Bank of England and express his hope that its charter would not be renewed as a matter of course, 19 Feb. His customary support for economy, retrenchment and reduced taxation included a vote in a minority of ten against any increase in the standing army, 20 Feb., and a denunciation of the grant for the Society for the Propagation of the Gospels in the colonies as 'a great waste of money', 12 Mar. He would not, however, support John Maberly's motion to transfer the tax on beer to malt alone, 15 Mar., for he thought the agricultural interest deserved some compensation for its heavy burdens; and he only reluctantly supported his motion for inquiry into redemption of the land tax, 6 Apr., believing the scheme to be 'mischievous'. On 14 June, when the measure was abandoned, he opined that it would have entailed too great a sacrifice. He voted for reform of Edinburgh's representation, 26 Feb. On William Maberly's motion for an advance of capital to Ireland, for which he did not vote because it offered only an inadequate solution, at the expense of the taxpayers of England and Wales, 4 May, he argued that the problems of Ireland 'arose from an excessive and redundant population, and from a want of the means to afford employment'. He outlined a remedial programme to check population growth and create work by prohibiting the building of cottages without land attached, taxing absentees and introducing English farming methods. He supported the prayer of an Armagh petition for a fixed import duty on corn, 7 May, when he said that one of the greatest causes of Irish distress was the export of her wheat to England.[33] He presented a Reading petition for immediate execution of the government proposals for the silk duties, 9 Mar.[34] He voted for inquiry into the prosecution of the Methodist missionary John Smith in Demerara, 11 June, having brought up a Reading petition on the subject, 31 May.[35] He presented a Berkshire yeoman's petition against Stuart Wortley's bill to reform the game laws, 25 Mar., but expressed personal approval of its principle, though he carped at the severity of some of its clauses, 1, 12 Apr.[36] On 4 June he opposed the new churches bill, because 'the Church of England had not, at present, its root in the affections of the people'. On 21 May he welcomed the beer retail bill, on which he congratulated the government, 24 May, after presenting a Berkshire parish petition in its favour.[37] He was named to the committee on the vagrancy bill, 6 May, and, as he explained on 3 June, emerged from it a convert to the proposal to give a single magistrate the power to commit for indecent exposure. He was, however, opposed to the whipping of 'incorrigible rogues'. He remarked on the cost to Berkshire of passing on Irish vagrants, 18 June.[38] He spoke and was a teller for the minorities for Hume's attempts to obtain returns of Irish and Scottish commitments and convictions, 27 May. On 1 June 1824 he opposed the Equitable Loan Company bill as 'Jewish in principle, as the object of the speculators was to monopolize the profits which the Jews at present enjoyed'.

Monck presented a Reading petition for repeal of the assessed taxes, 28 Feb.,[39] and spoke and voted for that proposal, 3 Mar. 1825. He supported repeal of the beer duties, 5 May, and voted for that of the window tax, 17 May. On 22 Mar. he confessed that he had recently revised his opinion on the poor laws, having decided that without them the English poor would have been 'quite as turbulent' as their Irish counterparts during the winter. He obtained leave to introduce a bill to prohibit in certain cases the payment of any part of labourers' wages from the poor rates, 12 May, but he withdrew it on 14 June.[40] He voted against the bill to disfranchise Irish 40*s.* freeholders, 26 Apr., 9 May, and on 12 May explained that he objected to the Irishman being deprived of his vote 'on account of evils which were not of his own making', while seats were 'sold openly and notoriously to the highest bidder' in England. He divided for prior inquiry before granting money to subsidize Irish emigration, 13 June, and was a teller for the minority in favour of inquiry into the Irish church, 14 June. He voted for revision of the corn laws, 28 Apr., after presenting a Reading petition to that effect,[41] and on 2 May attacked the laws as a tax on 14,000,000 people for the benefit of a few landowners. He again called for reform of the licensing system, 4 May.[42] He spoke against the grant to the duke of Cumberland, 27 May, and voted steadily against it thereafter. He ridiculed the idea of trying to curb blasphemy by prosecution, 2 June. On 17 June he said that he would have no objection to the new judicial salaries if they were coupled with an assurance that puisne judges would not be promoted; but he was subsequently a teller for the minority for an amendment to the proposals. Like Palmer, he opposed the Newbury improvement and Berkshire and Hampshire canal bills.[43] At the annual Reading mayoral feast, 3 Oct. 1825, he was reported as saying that much good had been accomplished that session 'by a judicious reduction of taxes and many other useful measures', notably the Jury Act, but to have reiterated his demand for 'some material alteration' of the corn laws.[44]

On 9 Feb. 1826 Monck 'condemned the mystery on the part of the Bank' over publication of its accounts, but praised the government measure to restrict the issue of small notes, on which ministers 'had not led, but followed the public mind'. He would not support Hume's motion for a select committee on the banking and currency system, 20 Feb., but he did vote against a ministerial adjustment to the promissory notes bill that day, supported Maberly's call for the Bank to give regular information of the number of notes in circulation, 24 Feb., and was in minorities of nine and 19 for amendments to the measure, 27 Feb., when he pressed ministers to end once and for all the worthless paper issues of country banks, most of which were crooked. His own attempt to ensure that in the event of a banker's failure the holders of one pound notes would have priority in proving debts was negatived. He spoke and voted for Hume's bid to secure regular returns of note issues from country banks, 7 Mar. He denounced the Bank charter amendment bill as 'a positive nuisance', 14 Apr., and on 4 May, endorsing the prayer of a petition on the dangers of a paper currency, rehearsed his argument on the difficulties created by having to pay in gold debts contracted in depreciated paper: the lesser evil was 'to adjust our difficulties to our currency, instead of endeavouring to adjust our currency to our difficulties'. He now advocated the introduction of a system of poor laws to Ireland, 16 Feb., voted for the extirpation of non-resident voters from Irish boroughs, 9 Mar., and supported Grattan's attempt to empower Irish vestries to assess parishes for relief, 27 Apr. He presented a Reading silk weavers' petition for protection against foreign competition, 21 Feb.,[45] but did not vote for inquiry into the trade, 24 Feb. On 6 Mar. he deplored the cost of the Royal Military College. He defended petitions calling for revision of the corn laws or 'bread tax', and called for more of the same, 10 Mar.[46] He voted for inquiry into the laws, 18 Apr., and on 12 May applauded ministers' decision to postpone general discussion of the problem to the next Parliament: 'he trusted that now, when country gentlemen saw that ministers could not, or would not, protect them in their high prices, they would direct their attention to a more legitimate source of wealth – a reduction of the burthens of the country'. He voted for reform of Edinburgh's representation, 13 Apr., and general reform, 25 Apr. He again urged reform of the licensing system, 21, 26 Apr., and spoke and voted for a clause to provide for adjourned sittings to be added to the licensing bill, 12 May 1826.[47]

Monck stood again for Reading at the general election in June, when he and Palmer were opposed by two candidates on the Blue, or Tory interest. He declared himself to be 'the steady friend of a just economy in the public expenditure, of a temperate reform in the representation of the people, and respecting the corn laws, a decided enemy to any system, which, like the present, was calculated for the supposed benefit exclusively on one class, to raise the price of food at the expense of all others'. He confirmed his undiminished support for

Catholic relief. He comfortably topped the poll after a desperate contest, which saw Palmer turned out by four disputed votes. (He was subsequently seated on petition.)[48] At the mayoral dinner in October 1826 he attributed 'the present distress and depression ... to the operation of the corn laws and the hocus-pocus tricks which had been played with the currency'.[49] He voted for the amendment to the address, 21 Nov. 1826. He spoke and voted against the Clarences' grant, which was 'most unseemly in the present state of public distress', 16 Feb., 2, 16 Mar. 1827. He complained of the 'growing charge on the country' imposed by military widows' pensions, 16 Feb., and supported reduction of the grant for the Royal Military College, 16, 19, 20 Feb. On 3 Mar. he at last joined Brooks's, sponsored by Sir Francis Burdett* and Sir Ronald Craufurd Ferguson*. Mary Russell Mitford described him in rather fanciful terms to Benjamin Haydon:

> I am sure you will be pleased with his frankness and originality. He is a great Grecian, and a great political economist – a sort of Andrew Marvell in Parliament; living in a lodging close to the House [15 College Street], with an old woman who cooks him alternately a beef steak, a mutton chop, or a veal cutlet; he does not indulge in a lamb chop until after Easter. He votes sometimes with one party and sometimes with another, as he likes their measures; he is respected by all, notwithstanding his independence, and he is idolized here in the country for his liberalilty, his cheerfulness, his good humour and his unfailing kindness.[50]

He voted for Catholic relief, 6 Mar., as he did again, 12 May 1828. On 9 Mar. and 25 May 1827 he aired his views on the need to provide for the poor in Ireland.[51] He voted for a 50*s.* corn import price, 9 Mar., and on 12 Mar. opposed the increased duty on barley, which he said had been 'conceded to the threats held out to ministers ... by those who ought to be the natural protectors of the people, but who would make themselves their masters'. He was one of Hume's minority of 16 in favour of a reduction in duty to 10*s.* over the next six years, 27 Mar., and on 9 Apr. failed in an attempt to add a clause to the corn bill authorizing the holders of leases granted after 1815 to pay up to two thirds of their rent in corn.[52] He voted for inquiry into the allegations against Leicester corporation, 15 Mar., and the production of information on the mutiny at Barrackpoor, 22 Mar., and the Orange procession at Lisburn, 29 Mar.; but he was not in the opposition minority on Tierney's motion to postpone going into committee of supply until the ministerial crisis was resolved, 30 Mar., even though he spoke and voted, as a teller, for the spring guns that day, as he had on the 23rd.[53] On 3 Apr. 1827 he advised Hume to leave in the hands of ministers his proposed inquiry into debtors' prisons, but to persevere with his attempts to have an end put to arrests for debts of under £20; and on 9 Apr. he endorsed the prayer of petitions for reform of county courts. He voted for inquiry into the Irish miscellaneous estimates and chancery delays, 5 Apr. He divided for the disfranchisement of Penryn, 28 May, was in the minority of ten for repeal of the Blasphemous and Seditious Libels Act, 31 May, and said that Hume's suggestion that Stanley should incorporate the ballot in his bill to regulate Preston elections was 'entitled to consideration', 14 June 1827.

Monck was in Hume's minorities of 15 and eight against the navy estimates, 11, 12 Feb. 1828, when he asserted that 'if such extravagant establishments were maintained, they would lead, at no very distant period, to some dreadful explosion, in which the credit of the country must suffer'. On the army estimates, 22 Feb., he cited with approval the example of France, where retired officers never got full pay. He presented petitions for repeal of the Test Acts, 19, 25, 26 Feb., when he voted for it. He denounced the 'fatal and improvident system of sub-letting' operated by the Irish gentry, 19 Feb., and agreed with Hume that the increase in crime was largely attributable to oppressive taxation, 28 Feb. He presented Reading and Abingdon petitions for repeal of the recent Malt Act, 29 Feb., 7 Mar. He voted against the proposal to extend the franchise at East Retford to the freeholders of the Hundred of Bassetlaw, 21 Mar., 24 June, and later divided for attempts to transfer its seats to Birmingham, 5 May 1829, 5 Mar. 1830. He approved the Wellington ministry's life annuities repeal bill, 25 Mar. 1828, because it gave security for liquidation of a proportion of the national debt, but he stressed the importance of applying any surpluses to tax reductions rather than to the sinking fund. On 31 Mar. he described the debt as 'the root of all our misfortunes' and attacked the new corn bill; he voted for a pivot price of 60*s.*, 22 Apr., and denounced the measure as 'perfectly useless and idle', 23 May. On 1 and 17 Apr. he elaborated his views on the need to introduce a system of poor relief to Ireland, which had 'the most numerous, increasing, unemployed, and desperately wretched population on the face of the earth'; but he saw no merit in refusing relief to the able-bodied in England, as Slaney proposed, and advocated 'the adoption of a minimum of wages', which might 'make a minimum of human misery and human degradation'. On 1 May, however, he pointed out that to ensure fair wages without harming manufacturing industry it was necessary to have a moderate corn law and a remission of taxes on necessities. He supported the principle of Macqueen's settlement by hiring bill, thinking that it would be 'productive of more caution, circumspection and prudence in the lower classes', 29 Apr. He pressed for legislation to fix wages in the stricken silk industry, 26 June, and on 1 July presented and endorsed a petition from Manchester calling for wage regulation and suggested the appointment of an arbitration body to intervene in disputes. He was named on 2 Apr. to the committee on the bill to regulate borough polls, which he supported, 15, 23 May. He divided in the minority on excise penalties, 1 May. He voted against the provision for Canning's family, 13 May, and seconded Hume's bid to have it rejected out of hand, 22 May. Earlier that day, though, he had dissented from Hume's advocacy of a paper currency convertible to gold. He voted for information on civil list pensions, 20 May, and spoke and voted for Hume's motion for reductions, 10 June. He was a teller for the minority against the report stages of the pensions bill, 22 May. He spoke and voted against the grant for the Society for the Propagation of the Gospels in the colonies, 12 June, opposed charitable grants to Ireland, the least taxed country in Europe, 9, 20 June, and voted for the Irish assessment of lessors bill, 12 June, and for inquiry into abuses in the Irish church, 24 June. When complaining again of the 'peculiarly extravagant' dead weight charge of military pensions, 13 June, he declared:

> This House, instead of being a security to the people, and a check upon a lavish expenditure, itself affords the means of excessive expenditure ... Nothing has been done in the way of reduction. We have been employed in voting money into our own pockets. The only way of attending speedily to the wishes of the country is, by making a large reduction. Not a single successful vote has been given by the opposition for reduction this session. What has the finance committee done in the way of reduction? Nothing; on the contrary, in my opinion, they have added, by their vote on the currency, ten per cent to the burdens of the country.

He accordingly voted against the grant for the improvement of Buckingham House, 23 June, the additional churches bill, which would 'impose an unlimited taxation upon the public', 30 June, and the ordnance estimates, 4, 7 July, protesting on the 8th that ministers had made only paltry savings. On 3 June he asked them to consider imposing a standard excise duty of 5*s.* on beer and allowing brewers to produce whatever strength of beer they wished. He supported a clause of the licensing bill which aimed to curb the power of magistrates, 19 June, voted against imposing licenses on cider retailers, 26 June, and on 8 July argued that retail brewers should be allowed to remain open until ten at night. He wanted restrictions placed on savings banks as to interest paid and size of individual deposits allowed, 3 July, but on 10 July asked for the measure to be given a fair trial. He voted for the bill to prevent the application of municipal funds to electoral purposes, 10 July 1828. On the budget the following day, he agreed with Hume in condemning the folly of borrowing money to redeem the national debt and likened the government to 'a young spendthrift dealing with an usurer'.

When he called for army reductions, 20 Feb. 1829, Monck stressed the vital necessity of parliamentary reform, for the Commons as at present constituted had 'a decided interest in the creation and multiplication of places and pensions of all sorts'. He was a guest of the annual Westminster Purity of Election dinner, 25 May.[54] He voted for Lord Blandford's reform scheme, 2 June. He played down the significance of a Reading petition against Catholic emancipation, which he congratulated ministers for conceding, 26 Feb. While he thought the anti-Catholic petition of the Cobbetite William Hallett was drivel, 19 Mar., he agreed with its prayer for provision to be made for the poor in Ireland, without which emancipation would do little good. He duly voted for relief, 6, 30 Mar., though he was unhappy with the severity of the relief bill's restrictions on Jesuits in England, 24, 27 Mar. He thought the disfranchisement of Irish 40*s.* freeholders might be beneficial, but was sure that it would not, as was claimed, create 'a substantial yeomanry'. He presented a Dublin petition for the emancipation of Jews in Ireland, 10 Apr., and voted for O'Connell to be allowed to take his seat without hindrance, 18 May. He spoke and voted against the silk trade bill, which he saw as the death blow to the industry, 1 May, when he called for a property tax to replace taxes on necessities. Supporting inquiry into the beer and malt duties, 12 May, he demanded an end to the 'absurd regulations' affecting the brewing trade and appealed to the country gentlemen for support. He approved Davenport's juvenile offenders bill that day, but wanted it to provide for the use of juries. On 15 May he supported Slaney's labourers' wages bill as 'the first great measure of amelioration', but warned that its clause allowing overseers to contract for the employment of the poor would nullify it by 'degrading the labourers ... to the state of galley-slaves'. He voted for a fixed duty on corn imports, 19 May, and urged ministers to revise them when presenting a Stockport manufacturers' petition complaining of distress, 28 May. On 2 June he pressed for their 'total repeal' next session, along with a significant adjustment of tithes. Like Hume, he deplored the exchequer bills funding bill, 22 May, and he voted for reduction of the grant for the Marble Arch, 25 May, and of the hemp duties, 1 June 1829.

Monck was one of the 28 opposition Members credited with supporting the address, 4 Feb. 1830, after which his first known vote was for Blandford's reform plan, 18 Feb. He voted for the enfranchisement of Birmingham, Leeds and Manchester, 23 Feb., and for investigation of the Newark petition against the duke of Newcastle's electoral interference, 1 Mar., against the East Retford disfranchisement bill, but for O'Connell's proposal to incorporate the ballot in it, 15 Mar.; he had spoken for this on 5 Mar., contending that the time had come to give it a trial in order to uphold the 'legitimate influence' of property. He voted for Russell's reform motion, 28 May. He was a persistent critic of the army estimates in February, demanding on the 22nd cuts of £3,000,000 in expenditure to facilitate essential tax reductions. He again linked retrenchment with a reform of Parliament, 8 Mar., when he said that 'we represent not the people but ourselves, and we help ourselves as well as we can to the contents of the public purse'. He divided 'against the opposition motion for information on relations with Portugal, 10 Mar.[55] He voted regularly for economies and tax cuts as the opposition to the ministry revived; but he declined to support Davenport's motion on the state of the nation, 23 Mar., believing that such an inquiry would be 'unprofitable'. He reiterated his criticisms of the burden of military pensions, 29 Mar., 29 Apr., when he secured returns of information. He preferred repeal of the beer duties to that of the assessed taxes, 28 May. He supported inquiry into the state of the poor in Ireland, 11 Mar., 3 June, and on 17 May exhorted Irish Members to consider resuscitating the system of county asylums. He divided for the Irish vestry reform, 27 Apr., 10 June, abolition of the lord lieutenancy, 11 May, repeal of the coal duties, 13 May, and inquiry into Irish first fruits, 18 May. He presented another petition for the emancipation of Irish Jews, 23 Mar., and voted for the wider measure proposed by Robert Grant, 5 Apr., 17 May. He supported Lord Ellenborough's divorce bill, 6 Apr. He presented a Reading petition for abolition of the death penalty for forgery, 11 May, and voted for that measure, 7 June. He favoured the establishment of a permanent court in London to deal with insolvent debtors, 14 May, objected to the lord chamberlain's powers of censorship over plays, 25 May, and voted to modify the libel law amendment bill, 6, 9 July, and to reduce the new judicial salaries, 7 July. On 30 Apr. he questioned the chancellor of the exchequer on the sale of beer bill, on which he found himself at odds with the majority of his constituents. He described it as a measure for 'the spoliation and confiscation' of brewers' property, 3 May, and the following day he presented petitions against it from the brewers, magistrates and licensed victuallers of Reading. When Palmer brought up the inhabitants' petition in favour of the bill, 11 May, Monck claimed also to favour the opening of the trade, but said that he could not accept that 'the sale of beer should be so extensive, as to enable every man who might so think fit, to turn his house into an ale-house for drinking'. His attempt to prevent consumption on premises licensed under the bill, 21 May, was defeated by 143-118' and he failed in bids to limit the licenses to houses rated at a specified amount, 3 June, and to have third case appeals decided by juries, 4 June. He divided for unsuccessful amendments seeking to restrict on-sales, 21 June, 1 July 1830, when he deplored the 'mischievous' tendency of the bill.

It was initially assumed in Reading that Monck would stand again at the 1830 general election, but on 9 July he made an 'unexpected' announcement of his retirement, claiming that 'I find the regular attendance on parliamentary business, becoming every year, as I grow older, more fatiguing and more inconvenient'. He recommended as his replacement and formally proposed on the hustings the eminent Whig civilian Stephen Lushington*, who was narrowly beaten by a Blue.[56] He had chaired a Reform Association meeting in London, 16 July 1830, when he urged reformers not to 'weaken themselves by internal division'.[57] He remained active in borough and county politics. He addressed a town meeting which petitioned for a repeal of assessed taxes, 12 Oct., and a reform dinner, 21 Oct., when he declared that 'the effect of time had made him a radical reformer', now strongly in favour of the ballot. He was one of the promoters of a petition in favour of lord chancellor Brougham's plan for the establishment of courts of local jurisdiction in early December 1830.[58] He supported the campaign to obtain clemency for the 'Swing' rioters condemned to death by the Reading special commission at the turn of the year.[59] At the county reform meeting, 17 Jan. 1831, he had to abandon for lack of support a proposal for about one sixth of the Commons to be elected by universal suffrage, but he carried a resolution in favour of the ballot. He took prominent roles at the town reform meeting, 31 Jan., and the borough and county meetings to endorse the Grey ministry's reform bill, 14, 16 Mar.; on the 14th he stated that it was

> not an innovation, but a *restoration.* It was objected that the bill took away the power from the aristocracy. It deprived them, certainly, of tyrannical power; but wealth and rank, combined with probity, would always maintain their influence ... The measure was safe, practical and efficient.

In April 1831 he was pressed by Lord Radnor, the leader of the Berkshire reformers, to stand for the county in the event of a dissolution, but he declined, recommending instead the young Catholic, Robert Throckmorton, for whose successful campaign he worked at the ensuing general election, and whose nomination he seconded. In the borough he proposed Palmer as an uncompromising supporter of the bill.[60] He spoke at the county meeting to petition the Lords to pass the bill, 5 Oct., and was the leading spirit behind the town meeting called in response to its defeat, 10 Oct., when he deprecated such measures as refusing to pay taxes and appealed for confidence to be shown in ministers.[61] On 22 Nov. 1831 he was fêted in Reading and was presented with an ornate, inscribed candelabrum in recognition of his public services. Returning thanks, he called on the people to support ministers with 'that moral power which ... is derived from reason, from discussion, from combination, from political union for good, peaceful and lawful purposes'.[62] He again advocated peaceful demonstrations and the formation of unions at the Reading meeting called to discuss the political crisis after the dismissal of the reform ministry, 14 May 1832; and he spoke in the same vein at the county meeting called to address the king and petition the Lords, 25 May.[63] At the county by-election of late May 1832 he seconded and worked for Hallett, the unsuccessful candidate, forecasting that within a year of the passage of the reform bill there would be 'an equitable commutation of tithes'; and at the general election in December he proposed Palmer as the advocate of the abolition of slavery, triennial parliaments and reform of tithes and municipal corporations.[64]

Monck died at Coley Park in December 1834. His funeral at St. Mary's, Reading was marked by civic mourning.[65] In his will, dated 5 June 1815, he confirmed the settlement of his real estate laid down by his father. He left his wife £300, plus selected books and artifacts, and an annual allowance of £150 from the rents of his property. To his elder son, John Bligh Monck (1811-1903), who succeeded him in the Coley estate, he devised diamonds, *objets d'art* and furniture, on condition that on coming of age he should pay £3,000 for them. He directed that the residue of his estate should be sold and the proceeds added to the £10,000 fund created on his marriage settlement. He left £10 a year to one Jane May, 'an infant under my protection'. By a codicil of 14 Aug. 1834 he left modest annuities to a brother, sister and nephew and suits of mourning to all the tenants and labourers on the Coley and Aldworth estates, and to the inmates of local almshouses. His personalty was sworn under £20,000.[66]

[1] She was *bap.* 22 Sept. 1742 (IGI). [2] *Gent. Mag.* (1809), ii. 1236. [3] Ibid. (1814), i. 516. [4] PROB 11/1506/888. [5] *Gent. Mag.* (1835), i. 432; *Friendships of Mary Russell Mitford* ed. A.G.K. L'Estrange, i. 7-9. [6] PROB 11/1506/888; IR26/154/114; *Gent. Mag.* (1809), ii. 1236. [7] *VCH Berks.* iii. 365; iv. 4. [8] *Gent. Mag.* (1835), i. 432; J. Doran, *Hist. Reading*, 265-6; [W. Turner], *Reading 70 Years Ago* ed. P.H. Ditchfield, 33. [9] *HP Commons, 1790-1820*, ii. 12; *Reading Mercury*, 5, 12 Oct. 1812. [10] *Reading 70 Years Ago*, 19, 47; 'Octogenarian', *Reminiscences of Reading*, 133. [11] *Gent. Mag.* (1835), i. 432. [12] *Reading Mercury*, 21, 28 Feb., 6, 13 Mar. 1820. [13] *Friendships of Mary Russell Mitford*, i. 22-23; *Letters of Mary Russell Mitford* (ser. 2) ed. H.F. Chorley, i. 99. [14] *Life of Mary Russell Mitford* ed. A.G.K. L'Estrange, ii. 109-10. [15] *Reading Mercury*, 13 Nov. 1820. [16] Ibid. 4, 11 Dec. 1820, 15 Jan. 1821; *The Times*, 11 Dec., 9 Jan. 1821. [17] *The Times*, 22 May 1821. [18] HLRO, Hist. Coll. 379, Grey Bennet diary, 41. [19] *The Times*, 20 Apr. 1821. [20] Ibid. 31 Mar. 1821. [21] Ibid. 4, 5 Apr. 1821. [22] Ibid. 9 June 1821. [23] Grey Bennet diary, 111. [24] *The Times*, 16, 19 Jan. 1822. [25] Ibid. 5 June 1822. [26] Ibid. 25 Apr., 21 May, 11, 18 July 1822. [27] Ibid. 14 May, 1 June 1822. [28] *Reading Mercury*, 3 Feb. 1823. [29] *The Times*, 18 Jan. 1823. [30] Ibid. 28 Feb. 1823. [31] Ibid. 13 May 1823. [32] Ibid. 26 Apr. 1823. [33] Ibid. 8 May 1824. [34] Ibid. 10 Mar. 1824. [35] Ibid. 1 June 1824. [36] Ibid. 26 Mar., 2 Apr. 1824. [37] Ibid. 25 May 1824. [38] Ibid. 19 June 1824. [39] Ibid. 1 Mar. 1825. [40] *CJ*, lxxx. 407, 416, 483, 538. [41] *The Times*, 29 Apr. 1825. [42] Ibid. 5 May 1825. [43] Ibid. 6 May, 21 June 1825. [44] *Berks. Chron.* 8 Oct. 1825. [45] *The Times*, 22 Feb. 1826. [46] Ibid. 11 Mar. 1826. [47] Ibid. 22, 27 Apr., 13 May 1826. [48] *Reading Mercury*, 12, 19, 26 June 1826. [49] *Berks. Chron.* 8 Oct.; *Reading Mercury*, 9 Oct. 1826. [50] J.J. Cooper, *Worthies of Reading*, 122. [51] *The Times*, 26 May 1827. [52] Ibid. 10 Apr. 1827. [53] Ibid. 31 Mar. 1827. [54] Ibid. 26 May 1829. [55] Grey mss, Howick jnl. 10 Mar. [1830]. [56] *Reading Mercury*, 12, 19 July 1830. [57] Add. 56554, f. 133; *The Times*, 17 July 1830. [58] *Reading Mercury*, 18, 25 Oct. 1830; Bodl. MS. Eng. lett. c. 160, ff. 199, 252. [59] 'Octogenarian', 39-40; Bodl. MS. Eng. lett. d. 153, f. 8. [60] Warws. RO, Throckmorton mss CR 1998/tribune/folder/10/1, 9; *Reading Mercury*, 9, 16 May 1831. [61] *Reading Mercury*, 10, 17 Oct. 1831. [62] Ibid. 28 Nov. 1831. [63] Ibid. 21, 28 May 1832. [64] *The Times*, 29 May, 1 June, 11 Dec. 1832. [65] *Gent. Mag.* (1835), i. 432-3. [66] PROB 11/1841/33; IR26/1391/16.

D.R.F.

MONEY, William Taylor (1769–1834), of Walthamstow, Essex.

WOOTTON BASSETT	8 July 1816–1820
MITCHELL	1820–Mar. 1826

bap. 4 Sept. 1769,[1] 1st s. of Capt. William Money of Wood End House, Walthamstow, dir. E.I. Co. 1789-96, and Martha, da. of James Taylor, merchant chandler, of Carmarthen. *m.* 8 June 1797, Eugenia, da. of William Money of Homme House, Much Marcle, Herefs., 7s. (2 *d.v.p.*) 2da. (1 *d.v.p.*). *suc.* fa. 1796; KH 1831. *d.* 3 Apr. 1834.

Capt. E.I. Co. navy 1793-1801; supt. marine board, Bombay 1803-10.

Dir. E.I. Co. 1818-26.

Consul gen. at Venice and Milan 1826-*d.*

Money, who had been long in the service of the East India Company and was appointed a director to represent the shipping interest,[2] was connected with William Wilberforce*, Zachary Macaulay, Hannah

More and other members of the Clapham Sect, and actively supported such Evangelical causes as the abolition of slavery and the promotion of Christian missions abroad.[3] At the general election of 1820 he abandoned his precarious seat at Wootton Bassett and was returned unopposed for Mitchell on the interest of Sir Christopher Hawkins*.

He continued to attend regularly and give general support to Lord Liverpool's ministry. On 11 July 1820 he favoured a reduction of the prison sentence on Henry Swann, Member for Penryn, who had 'two children at death's door, upon whom he was incapacitated ... from bestowing his attention'. That day he defended the East India Company volunteers bill, explaining that the force in question was not new and was 'composed of men who were under the obligation of self-interest to unite the character of good citizens and good soldiers'. He voted in defence of ministers' conduct towards Queen Caroline, 6 Feb. 1821. He divided, as in the past, for Catholic relief, 28 Feb. He paired against repeal of the additional malt duty, 3 Apr., and voted against the disfranchisement of civil officers of the ordnance, 12 Apr., and Hume's economy and retrenchment motion, 27 June. He divided for the forgery punishment mitigation bill, 23 May. He believed that 'after their long sufferings' American loyalists were 'entitled to the sympathy and consideration of Parliament', 6 June. That day he voted in the minority for inquiry into the administration of justice in Tobago, but on the 7th he dismissed attempts to censure the conduct of the former lord commissioner of the Ionian islands, Sir Thomas Maitland†, who had 'acted only as the agent' of the existing regulations. He supported Fowell Buxton's motion for papers regarding the practice of suttee, 20 June, and hoped Parliament would unite with the 'friends of humanity' to help 'extirpate these dreadful sacrifices'.[4] In the debate on Wilberforce's motion against the slave trade, 26 June 1821, he stated on the 'best authority' that the 'trade was now carrying on at the eastern coast of Africa by the Portuguese with unceasing cruelty'.[5] He voted against more extensive tax reductions, 11, 21 Feb., and opposed abolition of one of the joint-postmasterships, 2 May 1822, as it involved 'considerable duties and great responsibility' and he did not believe 'the immense patronage connected with the office ... should rest in the hands of one person'. He was added to the select committee on foreign trade, 27 Feb. (and reappointed, 12 Feb. 1823, 4 Mar. 1824). On 17 May he complained that East India merchants had been 'treated with injustice and partiality' by Parliament, which had imposed a prohibitive duty on Indian cotton manufactures while allowing British goods to be exported to India freely. He thought the 'main allegations' made in the Calcutta bankers' petition against the East India Company had been 'disproved', and voted against its referral to a committee, 4 July. He divided in the minority to permit the export of bonded corn as flour, 10 June. He voted for the licensing bill, 27 June, and the aliens bill, 19 July. He 'most cordially concurred' in Wilberforce's motion regarding slavery at the Cape, 25 July 1822, as he believed 'the continuance of what was evil in principle and cruel in operation' could not be 'justified by any view to private or public advantage', and in this case it would be 'impolitic and dangerous' as the slaves might join with the Kaffirs in an uprising. He gave examples, from his 'considerable stay' there, to show the brutality of Dutch colonial rule, which Britain was not 'bound to follow'.

He supported the 'most reasonable' petitions from the East India Company and Calcutta merchants for equalization of the East and West Indian sugar duties, 22 May 1823, noting from his 'experience derived from a long residence in India' that 'the effect of our very general employment of machinery at home had been to render the looms of India useless ... and to make the native weavers beggars'. He urged that India be allowed to export sugar on fair terms in exchange for British manufactures.[6] He complained of the 'injustice ... inflicted on the Lascars' by the East India trade bill, 7 July.[7] He supported the clause in the East India mutiny bill empowering the governor of Bombay to summon general courts martial, 11 July.[8] He voted for repeal of the usury laws, 17, 27 June. He opposed the petition of Christian ministers for the free discussion of religious opinions, 1 July, observing that 'since Parliament and different societies had done all in their power to disseminate the blessings of education, care ought to be taken that those blessings should not be abused'. However, he defended Robert Owen from accusations that he disbelieved in a future state of rewards and punishments. He divided in the minorities to introduce trial by jury in New South Wales, 7 July, and continue proceedings against chief baron O'Grady, 9 July 1823. It was reported in March 1824 that Money sided with the East India Company chairs and the government against those directors who wished to appoint Mountstuart Elphinstone as governor of Madras.[9] He emphasized the importance of the coal trade as a 'nursery of seamen and ... one of the chief sources of the strength of the British navy', 1 Apr. He again voted to repeal the usury laws, 8 Apr. He divided for the motion condemning the trial of the Methodist missionary John Smith in Demerara, 11 June. He 'highly approved' of the East

India possessions bill, 17 June 1824, as the acquisition of Dutch colonial territories removed possible places of refuge for 'disaffected subjects' and provided new trading opportunities. That day, according to Canning, the leader of the Commons, Money supported the suggestion that the ten per cent reduction of ministers' and officials' salaries, imposed two years before, should be abolished.[10] He was abroad in late 1824 and early 1825 to recruit his health, but returned to divide for Catholic relief, 21 Apr., 10 May.[11] He maintained that it was in the government's power to suppress suttee without offending the natives and referred to several instances where 'local magistrates had, by mere persuasion, prevented the burnings', 6 June 1825.

By early 1825 Money was seeking an appointment in the consular service, which may have been prompted by financial losses resulting from the dishonest conduct of the agents of his estate in Java.[12] He vacated his seat in March 1826 on being appointed consul to the Lombard states. He died of cholera in Venice in April 1834. He left all his property to his wife in trust for their children, but it was necessary to sell the Javan estate to clear his debts; his personalty was finally sworn under £3,000.[13] Several of his children and grandchildren served in the Indian army or civil service.[14]

[1] IGI (Essex). [2] C.H. Philips, *E. I. Co.* 337. [3] Lambeth Palace Lib. ms 4243, letters to Money. [4] *The Times*, 21 June 1821. [5] Ibid. 27 June 1821. [6] Ibid. 23 May 1823. [7] Ibid. 8 July 1823. [8] Ibid. 12 July 1823. [9] BL OIOC Mss Eur.F.142.26, S.R. Lushington to Robinson, 25 Mar. 1824. [10] *Geo. IV Letters*, iii. 1169. [11] Lambeth Palace Lib. ms 4243, ff. 98, 147. [12] Ibid. f. 25; Harrowby mss, Money diary, 4 Feb. 1830. [13] PROB 11/1858/111; IR26/1423/61. [14] *Geneal. Mag.* vi (1932), 294-5.

T.A.J.

MONTAGU, George, Visct. Mandeville (1799–1855), of Brampton Park, Hunts. and Melchbourne Park, Beds.

HUNTINGDONSHIRE 1826–1837

b. 9 July 1799, 1st s. of William, 5th duke of Manchester, and Lady Susan Gordon, da. of Alexander, 4th duke of Gordon [S]. *educ.* Eton 1811. *m.* (1) 8 Oct. 1822, Millicent (*d.* 21 Nov. 1848), da. and h. of Brig.-Gen. Robert Bernard Sparrow of Brampton, Hunts., 3s. (1 *d.v.p.*) 1da.; (2) 29 Aug. 1850, Harriet Sydney, da. of Conway Richard Dobbs of Castle Dobbs, co. Antrim, 1s. 1da. *suc.* fa. as 6th duke of Manchester 18 Mar. 1843. *d.* 18 Aug. 1855.

Vol. RN 1812, midshipman 1814, lt. 1818, ret. 1822.

Mandeville, whose mother ran off with a footman before formally separating from his father in 1813, entered the navy direct from Eton in 1812, but he was later reported to be unhappy in the profession.[1] He served on the home and Halifax stations before his transfer in 1818 to the *Larne* at Jamaica, where his father had been governor since 1808. He was in the West Indies for the remainder of his career. In 1822 he accompanied his relatives Lord and Lady Huntly to Geneva and Paris, and by the time of his last promotion in July he was engaged to the Huntingdonshire heiress Millicent Sparrow. Her mother, the formidable Evangelical Lady Olivia Sparrow, was keen on the marriage, but left nothing to chance over the settlement. Manchester had little or no disposable capital with which to provide an allowance, but he agreed to settle the Kimbolton estates on Mandeville, who did not return to sea, though he remained on the reserve half-pay list until his death.[2] His Whig cousin Lord John Russell, Member for Huntingdonshire, commented to Lady Holland, 'I suppose Mandeville's marriage will turn me out ... but I don't much care. It is a very good thing for him, and the lady is agreeable and good and will give him some sense'.[3] Her Irish property at Tanderagee, county Armagh, was thought to be worth £10,000 a year. The marriage took place in October 1822, but contrary to Lady Olivia's wishes the couple made their home at Kimbolton as well as Brampton. Mandeville visited the Irish property for the first time in the summer of 1823, and in November 1824 he secured the lease to Melchbourne Park, Bedfordshire.[4]

He shared his mother-in-law's Evangelical zeal and supported a number of Protestant societies, but his abiding passion was the exegesis of apocalyptic texts. He corresponded with clergy and laymen of various denominations, including Henry Drummond and Edward Irving. He regularly attended their conferences for the study of unfulfilled prophecy at Albury Park, Surrey, but it is uncertain whether he became a member of their Holy Catholic Apostolic Church.[5] He addressed its 1829 gathering with great effect; and Irving, who was not always in agreement with him, told his wife:

> Lord Mandeville is truly sublime and soul-subduing in the views he presents. I observed a curious thing, that while he was reading a paper on Christ's office of judgement in the millennium everybody's pen stood still, as if they felt it a desecration to do anything but listen.[6]

He had already ventured into print on behalf of the Continental Society; but it was his elaborate essay *On the New Covenant*, published that year in *Morning*

Watch, which established his reputation as an amateur theologian.[7]

In September 1824 it was reported that Mandeville, who was described as 'a liberal', would offer for county Armagh at the next general election, but nothing came of this.[8] He had little taste for politics, although he was annoyed at the ease with which Russell had secured the county seat in 1820 by taking advantage of his father's absence and his own minority.[9] A preliminary canvass was undertaken in the summer of 1825, and subsequent rumours of an impending dissolution prompted him to declare for the county in coalition with the Tory sitting Member William Fellowes at the Huntingdon mayor's feast in late September. He was reported to have proclaimed his hostility to the 'importation of corn and Catholics', but by early December 1825 he was tormented by doubts and religious scruples. His uncle Lord Frederick Montagu†, perplexed by his pusillanimity, urged him not to disappoint his wife and father:

> Pray do not give way to such mistaken feelings of religion, but consider how much your own importance and character are at stake by your representing the county ... I think on reflection your scruples about the people getting drunk must vanish. If your notions are correct, the whole 600 [sic] Members ... must be culpable, and in fact according to such ideas we ought to have no Parliament.[10]

Shortly afterwards Mandeville changed his mind again and, much to Lord Frederick's approval, took up the cause 'with spirit and energy', though he retained his misgivings about entertaining the freeholders.[11] His inexperience and 'innate modesty' were easy targets for criticism: the *Huntingdon Gazette* sneered at his incompetence as a grand juryman and mocked his 'pathetic zeal' at Bible meetings.[12] His final decision to stand, which was formally announced on 19 Dec. 1825, perhaps owed more to a sense of Christian duty than to his uncle's exhortations. He was reluctant to discuss tactics, and Montagu, convinced that his 'irrational notions of religion' made him miserable, encouraged his wife to persuade him to abandon his rural retreat at Melchbourne, for 'if he can be induced to go into society, and live as other young men of his rank and age do, I am sure he will be much happier'. However, Mandeville perversely went to Ireland until mid-January 1826, leaving his campaign under the direction of his wife.[13] A bitter contest was inevitable once Russell decided to stand his ground. Mandeville duly came forward at the general election in June 1826, though he remained diffident and viewed the prospect of the hustings with some trepidation, since, as Lady Millicent told Montagu, he was 'not fond of being stared at, or made to speak in public'.[14] He was unable to get a hearing at the nomination, but he headed the poll and was returned with Fellowes after a four-day contest.[15] At a Huntingdon agricultural meeting in October 1826 he condemned tithes as an obstacle to improvement, though 'his objection was to the manner in which tithes were collected, and not so much to the abstract principle'.[16]

Mandeville was excused further attendance on an election committee, 20 Feb. 1827, on account of the death of his youngest sister. He voted against Catholic relief, 6 Mar. He was granted three weeks' leave, 27 Mar. In May he was elected as the first president of the non-political British Society for Promoting the Religious Principles of the Reformation.[17] On the appointment of his wife's uncle Lord William Cavendish Bentinck* as governor-general of Bengal in July 1827 it was rumoured that Mandeville was keen to go out with him, but fears for his wife's health soon put this out of the question.[18] He presented petitions for repeal of the Test Acts, 2 Feb., and voted accordingly, 26 Feb. 1828. In his maiden speech, 2 May, he criticized the Lords' amendments to the securities and called for the insertion of an unequivocally Trinitarian declaration in the repeal bill. He presented petitions for the open circulation of small bank notes, 7 May, and the abolition of slavery, 30 June. He brought up anti-Catholic petitions, 8 May, and divided against relief, 12 May 1828. In October 1828 he became president of the newly formed Armagh Brunswick Club.[19] He was surprisingly listed as 'doubtful' by Planta, the Wellington ministry's patronage secretary, in his prediction of Members' conduct on the concession of Catholic emancipation in February 1829. A correspondent of Lady Mandeville envisaged an alliance between Mandeville and the 10th earl of Winchilsea 'to fight the battle inch by inch'.[20] He presented several hostile petitions, 17, 24 Feb., 2, 9 Mar., and on the 7th highlighted one from an assembly of London Dissenting ministers. He divided steadily against emancipation throughout the month, and on the 19th defended anti-Catholic petitioners against the aspersions of Waithman. On the Irish franchise bill, he was in the minority of 20 for the reregistration of Irish 40*s.* freeholders, 20 Mar. He voted in the minority of 14 against the Maynooth grant, 22 May 1829, after arguing that it violated the principle of emancipation and would incur divine judgement. He was not much in evidence in the 1830 session, when he presented petitions against the malt tax, 16 Mar., 11 June, and the northern roads bill, 24, 29 June. He voted to consider Jewish emancipation, 5 Apr., but divided against it, 17 May 1830.

At the general election of 1830, when he topped the poll after a short contest, Mandeville claimed to be motivated by a desire to 'let the oppressed go free' and said he would support ministers only when he judged them to be right.[21] The government listed him among the 'moderate Ultras', and he voted against them in the division on the civil list which brought them down, 15 Nov. 1830. On 30 Nov. 1830 he was given a week's leave on account of the spread of incendiarism to Huntingdonshire. He presented a county petition in favour of a general fast, 14 Feb. 1831. He voted against the second reading of the Grey ministry's reform bill, 22 Mar., and for Gascoyne's wrecking amendment, 19 Apr. 1831. At the ensuing general election he finished in second place behind a reformer, though his return was never in doubt. He claimed to have voted against the Wellington ministry on the civil list from motives of economy and went on:

> Although he was opposed to the reform measure, it was not because he wished to perpetuate a system of corruption, but he could not think that House of Commons very corrupt which had voted out two different administrations, and believed that the present distress did not arise from misrepresentation, but from taxation.

He dismissed the reform bill as 'not a renovation, but a revolution of the constitution'. Pressed to be more explicit, he conceded that £10 householders in Huntingdon might reasonably be enfranchised; but with respect to the country at large, he said that he feared the augmentation of Catholic power and that Daniel O'Connell* would be able to nominate as many Members 'as the borough mongers are said to return'.[22]

Mandeville presented petitions against the Maynooth grant from Scotland and Ireland, as well as constituency petitions against slavery and the coal duties, 23 June 1831. He denounced the grant and questioned the propriety of all such subsidies in the wake of emancipation, 19 July. Having been criticized by O'Connell on account of the bigoted wording of the June petitions, he assured the House, 20 July, that the petition he was about to present contained no inflammatory language. He spoke and voted against the grant, 26 Sept., when, aware that he was an easy target for derision from the treasury benches, he declared, 'I would rather subject myself even to their ridicule than I would say or do anything which could have the effect of hurting the church of which I am a member'. He divided against the second reading of the reintroduced reform bill, 6 July, and in the opposition minorities for using the 1831 census as a basis for disfranchisement, 19 July, and against the partial disfranchisement of Chippenham, 27 July. He voted against the bill's passage, 21 Sept. He was granted three weeks' leave to attend to urgent business, 29 Sept. He was absent from the division on the second reading of the revised reform bill, 17 Dec. 1831. On the 28th he was prominent at the Armagh county meeting which addressed the king on the threatened state of the Protestant interest in Ireland.[23] He voted against the enfranchisement of Tower Hamlets, 28 Feb., the third reading of the reform bill, 22 Mar., and the second reading of the Irish bill, 25 May 1832. He divided against government on the Russian-Dutch loan, 26 Jan., 12 July. He was associated with the revival of the Orange Order and addressed meetings in Armagh and Dublin in January.[24] He spoke at a public meeting at Exeter Hall on the government's plans for interdenominational education in Ireland, 8 Feb., when he said that 'the only remedy for the evils of Ireland was the spread of the word of peace'.[25] He criticized the scheme in the House, 6 Mar. 1832.

Mandeville, who continued to sit for Huntingdonshire until 1837 and succeeded to the dukedom in 1843, was a 'consistent Tory' and active promoter of the Protestant cause throughout his life. He died in August 1855.[26]

[1] Hunts. RO, Manchester mss ddM 21a/8, Bedford to Lord F. Montagu, Wed. [Mar. 1820]. [2] Ibid. 67/2, B.C. Williams to Lady O. Sparrow, 25 July, 16, 20 Aug., replies, 16, 24 July, 7 Aug. 1822. [3] Add. 51679, Russell to Lady Holland [July 1822]. [4] *Huntingdon, Bedford and Peterborough Gazette*, 30 Aug. 1823, 6 Nov. 1824. [5] F.K. Brown, *Fathers of the Victorians*, 259; B. Hilton, *Age of Atonement*, 94; Manchester mss 10a/10/1, 4-9, 11-13; J. Wolffe, *Protestant Crusade in Britain*, 36. [6] M.O.W. Oliphant, *Edward Irving*, 273. [7] *Morning Watch* (1829), i. 187-24, 354-91. [8] TCD, Courtown mss P/33/14/11. [9] Manchester mss 21a/8, Bedford to Mandeville, 27 July, 7 Aug., reply, 1 Aug. 1825. [10] *Huntingdon, Bedford and Peterborough Gazette*, 9 July, 24 Sept.; Manchester mss 21a/8, Maltby to Lady Mandeville, 28 Sept., Montagu to Mandeville, 9 Dec. 1825. [11] Ibid. 21a/8, Montagu to Lady Mandeville, 19, 24 Dec. 1825, 13 Jan. 1826. [12] *Huntingdon, Bedford and Peterborough Gazette*, 12, 26 Nov., 3 Dec. 1825. [13] Manchester mss 21a/8, Montagu to Lady Mandeville, 24 Dec. [1825], 13, 16, 23 Jan. [1826]. [14] Ibid. 49/15, Lady Mandeville to Montagu, 23 May [1826]. [15] *Huntingdon, Bedford and Peterborough Gazette*, 3 June; *The Times*, 17, 22 June 1826. [16] *Drakard's Stamford News*, 27 Oct. 1826. [17] Wolffe, 36. [18] Add. 51669, Bedford to Lady Holland, 26 Oct.; Fitzwilliam mss, Russell to Milton, 11 Nov. 1827. [19] *Belfast News Letter*, 14 Oct. 1828. [20] Manchester mss 10a/7/21, Loftie to Lady Mandeville, 24 Feb. 1829. [21] *Huntingdon Bedford and Peterborough Gazette*, 7 Aug. 1830. [22] Ibid. 7, 14 May 1831. [23] *Belfast News Letter*, 30 Dec. 1831. [24] Wolffe, 73-74; *Huntingdon, Bedford and Peterborough Gazette*, 7, 21 Jan. 1832. [25] *The Times*, 9 Feb. 1832. [26] Wolffe, 210; *The Times*, 20 Aug. 1855; *Gent. Mag.* (1855), ii. 426-7.

S.R.H.

MONTEITH, Henry (?1764–1848), of Westbank, Renfrew Road, Glasgow and Carstairs House, Lanark.

LINLITHGOW BURGHS	1820–1826
SALTASH	1826–12 Dec. 1826
LINLITHGOW BURGHS	1830–1831

b. ?1764, 6th s. of James Monteith, weaver and merchant, of Anderston, Glasgow and Rebecca, da. of John Thomson of Anderston. *educ.* Glasgow Univ. 1776. *m.* (1) 22 June 1788,[1] Christian, da. of John Cameron of Over Carntyne, Lanark, 1s. 1da.; (2) 20 Dec. 1826, Sarah, da. of George Fullerton of Carstairs, *s.p. d.* 14 Dec. 1848.
Ld. provost, Glasgow 1814-16, 1818-20.

Monteith's great-grandfather James Monteith was a small Perthshire laird in the Aberfoyle area, whose livelihood was under constant threat from the depredations and blackmailing of Highland reivers. After his death his son Henry moved south and set up as a market gardener at Anderston, then a village near Glasgow. He fought against the Jacobites at Falkirk and died 'a staunch Presbyterian of the old school'. His eldest son James Monteith, who was born in 1734, took up handloom-weaving. He prospered, especially when he began to import fine French and Dutch yarns, and became a cambric manufacturer on a large scale, with a bleach field near his house and warehouse in Bishop Street. Three of his sons joined him in the cotton manufacturing business, which expanded dramatically with the introduction of power looms. John Monteith, the eldest, formed his own company in 1801 and established the first Scottish power loom factory at Pollokshaws. James Monteith, the second, was initially a dealer in cotton twist at Cambuslang and in 1792 bought David Dale's Blantyre cotton mill. The start of the French wars the following year threatened disaster, but he averted it by adopting the fashionable London method of selling linen and cotton cloth by public auction, which made him £80,000 in five years.[2] He died in 1802. Henry Monteith, the youngest son and the subject of this biography, took the family business to new heights of success and prosperity. He was trained early in the art of weaving, and by 1785, when he was not quite of age, he was running a large cotton weaving mill, Henry Monteith and Company, at Anderston. The story went that during a period of unrest caused by wage reductions, disgruntled workers assaulted him and cut off his queue. Though regarded with disdain by the Glasgow tobacco barons (whose days of high prosperity were over), he played a major role in securing the supremacy of the cotton trade in the city's economy and became a powerful figure in municipal politics. In 1802 he established at Barrowfield a factory for producing bandana handkerchiefs, and on the death of James that year he took on the principal management of the business, which encompassed bleaching, turkey red dyeing and calico printing, as well as cotton spinning and weaving. He told a House of Lords select committee in 1826 that by about 1804 his workforce had reached 6,000, but that it currently stood at about 4,000 after the firm had given up tambouring and needlework.[3] He bought the Fullerton estate of Carstairs, four miles from Lanark, and from 1824 had a mansion built there.[4]

Unlike his father and brothers, Monteith was a staunch church and king Tory.[5] At the general election of 1818 he stood belatedly for Linlithgow Burghs against a Whig, with the backing of the Buccleuch interest. He secured the votes of Lanark and Peebles, but was beaten by the casting vote of the returning burgh, Selkirk.[6] On the death of George III in late January 1820 he declared his renewed candidature for the district and gave Archibald Campbell* of Blythswood 'authority' to assure Lord Melville, the Liverpool ministry's Scottish manager, that he would 'prove as steady and zealous a friend as any we have'. He narrowly won Selkirk, whose vote, together with those of Lanark and Peebles, gave him victory (at the age of 66) over Robert Owen, the socialist cotton master of New Lanark.[7] Two days after his return he was obliged, as lord provost of Glasgow, to lead the magistrates in their co-operation with the military in the adoption of measures to deal with the anticipated insurrection of the working classes. He chaired the merchants' and employers' public meeting of 11 Apr., which adopted a resolution not to employ persons found guilty of involvement in the disorder. He later refused to accept and present to the Commons a petition praying for clemency for the three men condemned to death for treason; and in his official capacity he attended the last rites and execution of James Wilson, 30 Aug. 1820.[8]

Monteith gave general but not entirely slavish support to the ministry.[9] He voted in their majorities against economies in revenue collection, 4 July 1820, and the opposition censure of their conduct towards Queen Caroline, 6 Feb. 1821. He was named to the select committees on the royal burghs, 4 May 1820, 16 Feb. 1821, and added to that on steam engines in factories, 26 May 1820. He divided against Catholic relief, 28 Feb. 1821, 30 Apr. 1822, 1 Mar., 25 Apr. and (as a pair) 10 May 1825. He voted against government for repeal of the additional malt duty, 21 Mar., but reversed this vote when they exerted themselves to defeat the proposal, 3 Apr. He divided for the army estimates, 11 Apr., and against disfranchising ordnance officials, 12 Apr. On 16 Apr. he repudiated as 'most unfounded' Hume's allegation that the Glasgow rising had been fomented by the government spy Franklin. When the Whig Lord Archibald Hamilton presented the petition of a Glasgow tobacconist complaining that he had been arrested for treason but never tried, 2 May, Monteith defended himself and the magistrates, observing that they had acted with commendable restraint and discrimination when faced with masses of dubious information about the activities of individuals.[10] He voted against more extensive tax reductions, 21 Feb., but was in the minority of 36, which included a number of Whigs, against the ministerial corn resolutions, 9 May 1822. He voted to uphold the integrity of the sinking fund, 3, 13 Mar., and against a general repeal of assessed taxes, 18 Mar., but cast a wayward vote for repeal of the levy on houses rated at below £5, 10 Mar. 1823. He divided for the grant for Irish churches and glebe houses, 11 Apr., and against repeal of the Foreign Enlistment Act, 16 Apr., reform of the Scottish electoral system, 2 June, and inquiry into chancery delays, 5 June 1823. His attempts the following year to obtain church preferment and employment for friends were unsuccessful.[11] His only known votes in 1824 were against reform of Edinburgh's representation, 26 Feb. (he repeated this, 13 Apr. 1826), and for repeal of the usury laws, 27 Feb. (and again, 17 Feb. 1825). He presented a Linlithgow petition for equalization of the duties on Scottish and Irish spirits, 18 May 1824.[12] He voted for the Irish unlawful societies bill, 25 Feb. 1825. On 18 Mar. he got leave to introduce a bill for the repair of Glasgow harbour and the improvement of the Clyde navigation, which provoked considerable local opposition but became law on 10 June 1825.[13] On 23 Feb. 1826 he asserted that distress was 'making rapid and alarming progress' in Scotland and that Glasgow was suffering severely. Although he 'valued the principles upon which the government acted so highly', he urged them as a matter of 'absolute necessity' to sanction an issue of exchequer bonds in order to avert a 'frightful train of evils'. He presented a Peebles petition against interference with the Scottish banking system, 10 Apr., and in his evidence to the Lords select committee on small Scottish notes spoke forcefully for their retention.[14] He divided against condemnation of the Jamaican slave trials, 2 Mar. 1826.

At the general election of 1826 he was defeated in Linlithgow Burghs, but he had already been returned unopposed for Saltash on the Russell interest.[15] He presented a petition from the lord provost of Glasgow for relaxation of the corn laws, 28 Nov., and one from Paisley emigration associations for financial assistance, 6 Dec. 1826.[16] A week later he vacated his seat, for reasons unknown. At the general election of 1830 he stood again for Linlithgow Burghs and defeated a radical reformer by three votes to one.[17] The Wellington ministry listed him among their 'friends' and he was in their minority in the division on the civil list which brought them down, 15 Nov. 1830. He was given a fortnight's leave on urgent private business, 14 Feb. 1831. He voted against the second reading of the Grey ministry's English reform bill, 22 Mar., presented a Lanark trades' petition against the Scottish bill, 30 Mar., and was in the opposition majority for Gascoyne's wrecking amendment to the English measure, 19 Apr. 1831. He initially stood for the burghs at the ensuing general election, but, after much ambivalent 'vacillation', which greatly annoyed local Tories, including the 5th duke of Buccleuch, who blamed him for the loss of the seat, he belatedly and reluctantly gave up when his opponent of 1830 gained three of the four.[18]

Monteith retired to private life. He died at Carstairs House in December 1848, 'in his 85th year', and was succeeded by his only son Robert Joseph Ignatius Monteith (1812-84), a Roman Catholic.[19]

[1] IGI (Scotland). [2] G. Stewart, *Curiosities of Glasgow Citizenship*, 54, 72, 93-96, 110-11, 133; G. Eyre-Todd, *Hist. Glasgow*, iii. 310-13. [3] Stewart, 114-15; *PP* (1826-7), vi. 540; *Colchester Diary*, iii. 426; *Glasgow Dir.* (1843-4), 177. [4] Stewart, 115. [5] Ibid. 108. [6] *HP Commons, 1790-1820*, ii. 613. [7] NAS GD51/1/198/15/29; 198/27/11; NLS mss 11, f. 14; *Caledonian Mercury*, 12 Feb., 18, 25 Mar., 3 Apr. 1820. [8] P. Berresford Ellis and S. Mac a' Ghobhainn, *Scottish Insurrection of 1820* (1989), 34, 150, 191, 206-8, 268, 272-4; *The Times*, 17 Apr. 1820. [9] *Black Bk.* (1823), 178; *Session of Parl. 1825*, p. 476. [10] *The Times*, 3 May 1821. [11] Add. 40360, f. 229; 40362, ff. 52, 184; 40363, f. 36; 40366, f. 238. [12] *The Times*, 19 May 1824. [13] Ibid. 19 Mar., 11, 20 May 1825. [14] Ibid. 11 Apr. 1826; *PP* (1826-7), vi. 540-6. [15] *Caledonian Mercury*, 6 July 1826. [16] *The Times*, 29 Nov., 7 Dec. 1826. [17] *Glasgow Herald*, 27 Aug. 1830. [18] NAS GD224/581/4, A. Pringle to Buccleuch, 2, 3, 4 May, reply, 21 May; *Caledonian Mercury*, 2, 5, 26 May 1831. [19] *Glasgow Herald*, 18 Dec. 1848.

D.R.F.

MONTGOMERIE, James (1755–1829), of Wrighthill, Ayr.

AYRSHIRE 1818–13 Apr. 1829

b. 26 Feb. 1755, 6th s. of Alexander Montgomerie of Coilsfield and Lilias, da. and h. of Sir Robert Montgomerie, 11th bt., of Skelmorlie. *m.* 1 June 1824,[1] Isabella Harriet, da. of Thomas Jackson of Westbury, Glos., *s.p. d.* 13 Apr. 1829.

Ensign 51 Ft. 1773 (to Minorca 1774), 13 Ft. 1775; adj. to Gen. Sir James Murray, home 1776; lt. 13 Ft. 1779;

capt. 93 Ft. 1780; brigade maj. to Maj.-Gen. Bruce at home 1794, brevet maj. 1794; lt.-col. 6 W.I. regt. 1795 (Martinique), 31 Drag. 1796; in command at St. Kitts 1796-8; 45th regt. 1798, invalided home; brevet col. 1802; lt.-col. 64 Ft. 1804, brig.-gen. W.I. 1804; commander, Tobago 1804-5; gov. Demerara and Berbice 1805-8, Dominica 1808-12 (home 1809); maj.-gen. 1809; col. 74 Ft. 1813; lt.-gen. 1814; col. 30 Ft. 1823-*d.*

Montgomerie, a professional soldier and former colonial governor, was returned unopposed for Ayrshire for the second time in 1820, supported by his great-nephew, the 13th earl of Eglinton.[2] He was a fairly regular attender who gave a mainly silent support to Lord Liverpool's ministry. Votes attributed to 'J. Montgomery' in the sessions of 1821-3 were almost certainly his, not those of Sir James Montgomery, the virtually inactive Member for Peeblesshire. In April 1820, at the time of the Scottish insurrection, he reported to the government's Scottish manager Lord Melville that, 'hearing of the very unsettled state of the county', he had returned to Ayrshire 'to offer any services in my power'; he evidently shared the opinion of 'many of the best informed gentlemen' that 'martial law for a time would have a very good effect'.[3] He voted to defend ministers' conduct towards Queen Caroline, 6 Feb. 1821. He paired against Catholic relief, 28 Feb. He presented the Ayrshire freeholders' petition against the Scottish juries bill, 10 May 1821.[4] He divided against more extensive tax reductions, 21 Feb. 1822. In his only reported speech, 29 Mar. 1822, he argued that 'change of circumstances and manners' required the sheriff of Glasgow to be permanently resident, like his Edinburgh counterpart.[5] He presented a petition from the planters of Dominica, where he had been governor, against equalizing the East and West Indian sugar duties, 19 Mar. 1823.[6] He voted against repeal of the Foreign Enlistment Act, 16 Apr., parliamentary reform in Scotland, 2 June, and inquiry into delays in chancery, 5 June. However, he divided with the minority to abolish the death penalty for larceny, 21 May 1823. He voted for the Irish unlawful societies bill, 25 Feb., against Catholic claims, 1 Mar., and paired against the relief bill, 21 Apr., 10 May 1825. He divided with the minority against the Leith docks bill, 20 May 1825. It was said of him at this time that he 'attended frequently and voted with ministers'.[7] He voted against the motion to condemn the Jamaican slave trials, 2 Mar. 1826. He presented Ayrshire and Kilmarnock petitions against any alteration to the Scottish banking system, 9, 10 Mar.[8] He divided against Russell's resolutions to curb electoral bribery, 26 May 1826. At the general election that summer he was returned unopposed.[9]

He attended the county meeting on distress, 9 Aug. 1826, when he lamented the 'long continued want of regular employment among the operative manufacturers' and moved that a subscription be raised for their relief.[10] He was granted six weeks' leave on account of illness, 23 Mar. 1827, and appears to have been an invalid for the remainder of his life. A visitor that summer found him 'much better in health than I [expected] from the accounts I had heard', but it was thought unlikely that he would offer again at the next general election.[11] He paired against Catholic relief, 12 May 1828. In February 1829 Planta, the Wellington ministry's patronage secretary, listed him as being 'absent'. He died that April at Bath and left all his property to his wife, whom he had married late in life; his personalty was sworn under £15,000.[12]

[1] IGI (London). [2] *Glasgow Herald*, 31 Mar. 1820. [3] NAS GD51/5/102. [4] *The Times*, 11 May 1821. [5] Ibid. 30 Mar. 1822. [6] Ibid. 20 Mar. 1823. [7] *Session of Parl. (1825)*, p. 477. [8] *The Times*, 10, 11 Mar. 1826. [9] *Glasgow Herald*, 7 July 1826. [10] Ibid. 14 Aug. 1826. [11] NLS mss 2, f. 103. [12] *Gent. Mag.* (1829), ii. 82; PROB 11/1754/232; IR26/1200/130.

T.A.J.

MONTGOMERY, Sir George, 2nd bt. (1765–1831), of Macbie Hill, Peebles.

PEEBLESSHIRE 4 Mar. 1831–10 July 1831

b. 1765, 2nd but 1st surv. s. of Sir William Montgomery, 1st bt., of Macbie Hill and Dublin, MP [I], and 2nd w. Anne, da. of Humphrey Evatt of Mount Louise, co. Monaghan. *unm. suc.* fa. as 2nd bt. 25 Dec. 1788. *d.* 10 July 1831.

Lt. 68 Ft. 1778; capt. army 1783; capt. 14 Drag. 1786; ret. 1790.

Montgomery's family was a cadet branch of that of the earls of Eglinton, based in Ayrshire. His grandfather William bought Coldcoat in Peeblesshire in the early eighteenth century and renamed it Macbie Hill. William's elder son and namesake, who was born in 1777, migrated to Dublin, where he prospered as an army contractor. He sat in the Irish Parliament for Ballynakill, Queen's County, from 1768 until his death in 1788, and was created a baronet in 1774. With his first wife, Hannah Tomkyns of Londonderry, he had a son, William Stone Montgomery, who entered the army and died in 1777 of wounds sustained in the American war. His second wife bore him two sons, George and Robert, who both joined the army. Robert, lieutenant-colonel of the 9th Foot, was killed on 6 Apr. 1803 by Captain Macnamara of the navy in a duel on Primrose Hill, which arose from a minor altercation earlier that day in Hyde Park, where their Newfoundland dogs had started fighting.[1]

George Montgomery retired from the army soon after being served heir to his father, who in 1767 had, with the consent of the Irish viceroy Lord Townshend (his future son-in-law), bought for £2,300 the office of auditor of impressed accounts, with reversion to George. On his father's death Pitt's ministry got his agreement to a recall of the patent, on condition that he was given an office of £800 a year. Soon afterwards he was made clerk of the head permit office, with an engagement to have the salary supplemented to £800. On 23 July 1789 Montgomery had one William Matthews named as his trustee in the office. On his death in 1796 Matthews was replaced by one Joseph Webb, who continued to pay the emoluments to Montgomery until July 1808, when the Portland ministry's Act (48 Geo. III, c. 56) abolished the fees. In 1810 Montgomery went to Dublin and memorialised the viceroy, the duke of Richmond. His claim for compensation was referred to the commissioners of customs, who ruled that the fees were his legal property. He received regular quarterly payments amounting to £492 a year until 5 Apr. 1812, when the Liverpool ministry removed him from the compensation list, after Webb had been given another office and persuaded to relinquish his trust. Montgomery laid his case before Robert Peel, the new Irish secretary, in July 1813, complaining that 'a series of injuries not easily reconciled under the term of inadvertancy' had caused him 'much trouble and inconvenience', and pressing for legislation to amend the Act of 1808 so as to make a compensatory pension payable to the person for whom the trust was held. Peel told Richmond that 'this case certainly calls for redress', but that it would be preferable to avoid recourse to Parliament. Montgomery persisted, and on Peel's advice Richmond personally assured him, on the eve of his departure from Ireland in August 1813, that he would do his utmost to obtain 'satisfaction' for him. He was subsequently offered a compensatory pension, but in January 1814 he rejected it as falling 'very far short of my claim'. Both Peel and the new lord lieutenant, Lord Whitworth, who thought he was being 'unreasonable', were ready to call his bluff of taking legal action. The outcome is unclear, but Montgomery was evidently pacified in some fashion.[2]

He offered for Peeblesshire, promising to 'promote the safety of the king and constitution', when his first cousin Sir James Montgomery, who had held the seat for over 30 years, retired in January 1831. A threatened challenge came to nothing and he was returned unopposed.[3] While Montgomery was connected through two of his sisters' marriages to the Tory Beresfords, his sister Harriet was married to George Byng, the veteran Foxite Whig Member for Middlesex. An Edinburgh Whig had reported that he was 'quite right in politics, supports ministers, reform, retrenchment and economy';[4] but he did not vote on the second reading of the Grey ministry's reform bill, 22 Mar., and divided for Gascoyne's wrecking amendment, 19 Apr. 1831. He came in unopposed at the ensuing general election, when his address ignored the reform issue.[5] Montgomery, who is not known to have spoken in debate, paired against the second reading of the reintroduced reform bill, 6 July 1831, and died, a bachelor, four days later.[6] By his will, dated 24 June 1805, he devised Macbie Hill to his nephew, John Isaac Beresford, son of his sister Emilia, to whom he left £700 and leasehold properties in counties Dublin and Westmeath. His housekeeper Ann Bennet received £500 and an annuity of 20 guineas. His personalty was sworn under £3,000 in the province of Canterbury, at £3,667 in the Edinburgh commissary court and under £4,615 in Ireland.[7]

[1] *Hist. Peebles* ed. J.W. Buchan, iii. 50-51; *The Times*, 8, 9, 11, 15, 21 Apr. 1803; *Gent Mag.* (1803), i. 372; *Raikes Jnl.* iii. 42, 204. [2] Add. 40228, ff. 151, 153; 40229, f. 177; 40233, ff. 29, 31. [3] *Caledonian Mercury*, 22, 24 Jan., 3, 7 Mar. 1831. [4] *Cockburn Letters*, 299. [5] *Caledonian Mercury*, 28, 30 Apr., 21 May 1831. [6] *Gent. Mag.* (1831), ii. 177. [7] PROB 11/1791A/590; IR26/1265/554.

D.R.F.

MONTGOMERY, Sir James, 2nd bt. (1766–1839), of Stobo Castle, Stanhope, Peebles.

PEEBLESSHIRE 23 Dec. 1800–26 Jan. 1831

b. 9 Oct. 1766, 2nd but 1st surv. s. of Sir James Montgomery†, 1st bt., of Stanhope and Margaret, da. and h. of Robert Scott of Killearn, Stirling. *educ.* Edinburgh h.s.; Edinburgh Univ. 1784; adv. 1787. *m.* (1) 1 Aug. 1806, Lady Elizabeth Douglas (*d.* 28 Oct. 1814), da. of Dunbar, 4th earl of Selkirk [S], 1s. *d.v.p.* 2da.; (2) 13 May 1816,[1] Helen, da. of Thomas Graham† of Kinross House, Kinross, 3s. 2da. (1 *d.v.p.*). *suc.* fa. as 2nd bt. 2 Apr. 1803. *d.* 27 May 1839.

Ld. advocate [S] Dec. 1804-Mar. 1806; presenter of signatures in exch. [S] for life.

Capt. R. Edinburgh vols. 1797, Peebles yeoman cav. 1803; dep. gov. British Linen Co. 1817.

Montgomery, the son and heir of a lord chief baron, who had been the last resident of Queensberry House in Edinburgh's Canongate and kept a black servant called Hannibal, was an undistinguished lord advocate in Pitt's second ministry, the possessor of a sinecure worth £610 a year and a 'steady adherent' of the 1st and 2nd Lords Melville.[2] He built Stobo Castle, 1805-11. Like his father, he was on intimate terms with 'Old Q', the degenerate 4th duke of Queensberry, who on his death in 1810 left him a legacy of £20,000. In 1818 Montgomery successfully petitioned chancery for confirmation of his entitlement to the sum of £10,000, plus interest, which Queensberry had bequeathed to his late first wife. As one of Queensberry's trustees he was nominally involved in a series of lawsuits over the administration of his contentious will.[3]

Montgomery continued to sit unopposed for Peeblesshire on the family interest. Melville thought he had 'a fair claim as an active and resident vice-lieutenant' to the vacant lord lieutenancy in October 1820, but he was not appointed.[4] He was a virtual cipher in the House in this period, when his only certain known votes were with the Liverpool ministry against repeal of the assessed taxes, 10 Mar. 1823, and the Wellington administration for Catholic emancipation, 6 Mar. 1829. It is not clear whether it was he or James Montgomerie who voted against the production of papers on the attack on the Irish viceroy, 24 Mar. 1823. He presented constituency petitions for repeal of the duty on notaries' licences, 5 Apr., and against interference with the Scottish banking system, 7 Apr. 1826.[5] He took three weeks' leave to attend to urgent private business, 17 Feb. 1825; it was noted that session that he had 'attended seldom, and voted with ministers'.[6] At his election dinner in 1830 he was reported to have proposed the toast, 'The French revolution, and may the French nation finish in the same spirit what they have so nobly begun'.[7] Ministers counted him among their 'friends'. He gave up his seat in January 1831 'on account of his health'.[8] Montgomery, who was said to have a paranoid dread of being overtaken by poverty, despite his very considerable wealth, died in May 1839.[9] By his will, dated 10 Dec. 1838, he left all his property to his eldest son, successor and residuary legatee, Graham Montgomery (1823-1901), Conservative Member for Peeblesshire, 1852-68, and Selkirkshire and Peeblesshire, 1868-80. He gave £10,000 to his daughter Mary Fleming, £1,200 to his second son John Basil, £20,000 to his third son Thomas Henry and £1,000 to his brother Robert. His personalty was sworn under £18,000 in the province of Canterbury.[10]

[1] *Gent. Mag.* (1816), i. 466. [2] *Cockburn Mems.* 176-7; *HP Commons, 1790-1820*, iv. 623-4. [3] *Hist. Peebles* ed. J.W. Buchan, iii. 495-9; *The Times*, 24 Aug. 1814, 23 May, 25 Dec. 1818, 26, 27 July, 3 Aug. 1820, 20 Apr. 1821, 24 Dec. 1823, 22 May 1824, 26 July 1825, 4 Aug. 1827, 7 Nov. 1828. [4] NAS GD51/5/749/1, pp. 287-8. [5] *The Times*, 6 Apr. 1824, 8 Apr. 1826. [6] *Session of Parl. 1825*, p. 476. [7] *Caledonian Mercury*, 12 Aug. 1830. [8] Ibid. 22 Jan. 1831. [9] *Hist. Peebles*, iii. 499; *Gent. Mag.* (1839), ii. 314. [10] PROB 11/1921/45; IR26/1553/73.

D.R.F.

MOORE, Abraham (1766–1822), of 8 King's Bench Walk, Temple, London.

SHAFTESBURY 1820–20 Apr. 1822

bap. 2 July 1766, 4th s. of Rev. William Moore (*d.* 1799), vicar of South Tawton, Devon, and w. Elizabeth. *educ.* Eton 1778; King's, Camb. (adm. 1780, matric. 1785), BA 1790, MA 1794, fellow 1798; L. Inn 1790, called 1802. *m.* 6s. at least. *d.* 1822.

Commr. of lunatics, chancery 1799-1821; steward of courts, Eton 1803-21.

Recorder, Gravesend, Rochester.

Capt. London and Westminster yeoman cav. 1799-1807.

Moore, whose personal details are largely unknown, came from a Devon family of clergymen. His grandfather was probably one of the Francis Moores of South Tawton whose wills were proved in Exeter in 1739 and 1750.[1] His father, who was for many years vicar of his native parish, died in 1799, leaving his estate to be divided among his several surviving children.[2] These included Francis (?1756-95), rector of Inwardleigh, and William (1759-1819), who was described as 'one of the most dissipated and extravagant men in the university' of Cambridge, rector of Chagford, Devon.[3] Abraham followed William to Eton, where he became a king's scholar in 1778, and King's, Cambridge, where he won the Browne Medal in 1786-7 and was later awarded a fellowship. Latin 'verses received from A. Moore on the birth of my son in June 1793' appear, with some other poems by Moore, in the commonplace book of the writer Sir Frederick Morton Eden.[4]

Moore seems to have entered the service of the 1st Earl Grosvenor in the mid-1790s. He was responsible for agricultural and mining concerns on Grosvenor's Cheshire and Flintshire estates, and according to his account books, which were begun in July 1796, he then received a salary of £200.[5] Having been called to the bar, he went on the western circuit, worked as a special pleader and held other legal offices in Kent and London. He was retained as agent and auditor by the 2nd Earl, who succeeded his father in 1802, and carried on extensive estate correspondence with his patron.[6] He was also employed on election business: for example, giving advice on Grosvenor's difficulties at Chester at the general election of 1812 and acting as counsel during the 1818 contest there.[7] At the general election of 1820, when he was described by John Beckett, Member for Cockermouth, as 'a facetious barrister', he helped oversee his own and Edward Harbord's return for Shaftesbury.[8] Grosvenor had just purchased the electoral interest there and possibly considered Moore merely as a stopgap until his younger son Robert came of age.

Moore, who was expected to follow his patron's Whig line in the Commons, divided with opposition on the civil list, 5, 8, 15 May 1820. Urging the committal of the Grampound disfranchisement bill, 19 May, he commented that whether it was extended into the neighbouring hundreds or had its seats transferred to Leeds 'the principle of parliamentary reform was equally recognized'. He divided against the appointment of a secret committee on the allegations against Queen Caroline, 26 June, and on 5 July 1820 was granted leave to go the circuit. He voted steadily in the opposition campaign on behalf of the queen at the start of the following session; on 20 Feb. 1821, in his only other known speech, he called for inquiry into the conduct of the sheriff of Cheshire. He divided for Catholic relief, 28 Feb., and was expected to be back from the circuit (for which he had again been given leave, 14 Mar.) to vote against Henry Bankes's motion to exclude Catholics from Parliament on 26 Mar.[9] He voted for the second reading of the malt duty repeal bill, 3 Apr., reduction of the admiralty grant, 4 May, and to prohibit further pensions on the four-and-a-half per cent Barbados fund, 24 May. He divided for repeal of the Blasphemous and Seditious Libels Act, 8 May, parliamentary reform, 9 May, inquiry into Peterloo, 16 May, and the forgery punishment mitigation bill, 23 May. His only other known vote was in condemnation of the conduct of the Holy Alliance towards the newly independent states, 20 June 1821.

At the beginning of August 1821 Moore fled to America having, as Grosvenor put it, 'turned one of the greatest scoundrels in existence' by leaving his patron in debt for the 'frightful amount' of about £80,000.[10] Grosvenor confided to his friend Professor John Hailstone, 22 Aug.:

> I hardly know what I wrote to you [two days earlier], I have had such *a multiplicity of communication and conflicting considerations on this horrid* business. I see in the account just prepared and actually sent in to me this very moment ... he made himself my debtor only to the amount of about £1,600 when it should have been above £100,000. I may add indeed considerably to this from former *defraudings* but at the time of his absconding where he did soon after the discovery he left me to pay the above to lead merchants, besides forfeiture to the amount of £20,000 more. The latter only I have some hopes of reducing. The fraud (or *felony on his part*) was most *injurious*, as much as infamous – he got the money by absolutely *selling lead* which *I did not possess* ... One of the dealing partners is strongly suspected of connivance, but only suspected as yet – his clerk and he had took a place in a coach for Devonshire.

Moore's accounts for 1821, when his salary had risen to £500, did indeed record a figure for cash in hand of less than £2,000, so he had evidently concealed the embezzlement in the yearly balances of several tens of thousands of pounds. Grosvenor, who noted that 'everybody is equally astonished at Moore's delinquency', concluded his letter to Hailstone by writing that 'the origin of his malpractices was in unsuccessful speculation in mines and I really believe of all the money he has got he has not a great deal left!'[11] Moore did not resign his parliamentary seat until early the following year, when he was replaced by Robert Grosvenor.

He died of yellow fever in New York, some time in September or October 1822. His wife, whose identity has not been established, also succumbed during the epidemic, and left 'six sons, helpless orphans; the eldest of whom is an idiot, and the next a youth of about 17 years of age'.[12] In his lifetime Moore had published law reports and at least one of his poems,[13] and after his death his friends brought out his translation of the *Odes of Pindar* as a means of supporting the surviving children. One review judged that the work, which 'comes into the world with singular plainness and want of pretence, an orphan child', 'bespeaks a man of scholarlike acquirements and tasteful mind, deeply impressed by the beauty and subtlety of his original; but there is nothing in it which shows native poetical genius'.[14] No will has been found, but in London in December 1824 limited administration was granted of his estate, which was proved under £50.[15] According to the journal of Tom Moore:

> In speaking of Abraham Moore and his irregular life [Henry Alworth] Merewether said that it was a frequent saying of Moore's that he was sure he should 'die in a ditch' – and so he actually did, somewhere in America.[16]

[1] *Devonshire Wills* ed. E.A. Fry (British Recs. Soc. xxxv), 481, 483. [2] PROB 11/1330/670. [3] *Al. Cant.* pt. ii, vol. iv, p. 457; *Gent. Mag.* (1819), i. 186. [4] Add. 43702, ff. 2, 11-12. [5] M.J. Hazelton-Swales, 'Urban Aristocrats' (London Univ. Ph.D. thesis, 1981), 445; WCA, Grosvenor estate mss 1049/6/6. [6] Grosvenor estate mss 10/23-27; Grosvenor mss vol. 4, box 42/6 (NRA 13470). [7] Grosvenor estate mss 9/9; J. Hemingway, *Hist. Chester*, ii. 417. [8] Keele Univ. Lib. Sneyd mss SC17/17; Norf. RO, Gunton mss GTN/1/3, Grosvenor to Harbord, 7 Feb.; 1/7, Moore to same, 5 Mar. 1820; R.M. Bacon, *Mem. of Bar. Suffield*, 110-11. [9] Buckingham, *Mems. Geo. IV*, i.

143. [10] Ibid. i. 196-7; Bucks. RO, Fremantle mss, Sir T.F. to W.H. Fremantle, 2 Sept. 1821; Grosvenor estate mss 15/2/9. [11] Grosvenor estate mss 6/7; 15/2/10. [12] *The Times*, 12 Nov. 1822; *Gent. Mag.* (1822), ii. 569-70. [13] *Reports of Cases in Common Pleas ...from Easter Term 36 Geo. III to Hilary Term 37 Geo. III* (1800); *Niagara, a poem, by A.M.* (1822). [14] *Gent. Mag.* (1822), ii. 570; *Quarterly Rev.* xxviii (1823), 419. [15] PROB 6/200. [16] *Moore Jnl.* v. 1921.

S.M.F.

MOORE, George (*b.* 1778), of 14 Hume Street, Dublin.

DUBLIN 1826–1831

b. 13 Oct. 1778, 5th but 4th surv. s. of John Moore (*d.* 1799) of Summerhill, co. Dublin and w. Mary Anne.[1] *educ.* Trinity, Dublin 1792, scholar 1796, BA 1797, LLD 1808; G. Inn 1798; King's Inns 1800, called [I] 1800. *m.* bef. 1799, Eliza Armstrong,[2] at least 2s. *suc.* uncle George Ogle† to Belview, Enniscorthy, co. Wexford 1814.

Dep. registrar of deeds [I] 1799-1830, registrar 1830-46; KC [I] ?1827/8.

Moore, much of whose personal life remains obscure, was the grandson of William Moore of Tinraheen, county Wexford, whose son Lorenzo (c.1741-1804), colonel of the Battle-Axe Guards, was ministerialist Member for Dungannon, 1783-90, and Ardfert, 1798-1800.[3] His father John was deputy registrar of deeds in Ireland, and presumably owed his appointment to his brother-in-law George Ogle, Member for county Wexford, who was awarded the place of registrar by government in 1784 and thereafter, except on the regency and the Union, by which time he represented Dublin, was a staunch supporter of the Pitt ministry and the Protestant ascendancy. On the death in 1799 of John, whose will was proved in Dublin that year, he was succeeded as deputy registrar by George Moore, who the following year was called to the bar and began to practise. By his will of 1798 Ogle, who died in August 1814, bequeathed his Wexford estates to Moore, his executor, who apparently sold them; since he was sometimes referred to as George Ogle Moore, it may have been at this time that he took the additional name of Ogle.[4] Under a reversionary grant of 1795, the position of registrar passed to the 2nd Viscount Kilwarden, former Member for Ardee, but under a separate agreement of 1806, whose legality was challenged in 1814, Moore undertook to fulfil all the duties of registrar on the payment of 1,000 guineas and the yearly sum of £500 above the usual fees to his nominal superior. The eighth report of the commission on the Irish courts of justice was critical of this arrangement, calling for the abolition of the sinecure of registrar and for the other offices to require permanent attendance. Moore, who gave oral evidence to the commission on many occasions between November 1817 and December 1819, claimed that he was present at least for a short time on most days, so justifying his fees of over £1,000 a year, but the real work was clearly done by his assistants Oliver Moore and Francis Armstrong (both presumably relations).[5] Moore, who had unsuccessfully applied for patronage for his brother from the Irish secretary Robert Peel* in 1814, failed in his bid to become recorder of Dublin in 1821.[6]

In early 1825 and again a year later, when it was explained in the anti-Catholic press that he was a barrister specializing in ecclesiastical law and an Orangeman of his uncle's stamp, he was considered a possible candidate for Dublin University.[7] However, at the general election of 1826, when James Abercromby* described him as 'an Orange lawyer of doubtful fame', he was at the last minute brought forward for the city on the corporation and Protestant interest, and, with the public endorsement of George Dawson*, Peel's brother-in-law and under-secretary at the home office, was returned with the Whig Henry Grattan II after a brief contest.[8] It was more a case of his being knocked up late one night to fill an unexpected vacancy, according to the tale told by Richard Sheil*, who later described him as

> a man distinguished at the Irish bar for the urbanity of his manners, set off by a sweet smile, a look of ruddy juvenility at 48, a formidable flow of tautology and a great charm and gentleness of demeanour, which rendered him an agreeable companion and endeared him to all those who mixed with him in the intercourse of private life. He was known to be a strong politician, but his aspect, intonations and his address made those who differed from him pay little regard to any acerbity in his opinions.[9]

At the new lord mayor's inaugural dinner, which he made a habit of attending each year, he stated that he had been elected to help defend the Protestant constitution, 30 Sept. 1826.[10]

Moore made his maiden speech on the address, the first of many occasions when he took issue with his colleague on the Catholic question, 21 Nov., and brought up a petition complaining about the influence of Catholic priests, 6 Dec. 1826. He signed the anti-Catholic petition of the landed proprietors of Ireland early the following year.[11] As he was frequently to do, he presented hostile petitions, including from Dublin, 2, 5 Mar. 1827, when he spoke strongly but 'badly', according to John Evelyn Denison*, against Catholic relief; he voted in the hostile majority next day.[12] He divided for the duke of Clarence's annuity bill,

16 Mar., and urged protection for Irish milling interests, 19 Mar. He chaired the select committee of inquiry into the allegedly forged signatures appended to the Athlone election petition, 21, 23 May, and called for publication of the Irish education commission's evidence on Maynooth, 25 May.[13] He was in the majority for the grant to improve water communications in Canada, 12 June, but in the minority against the third reading of the Coventry magistracy bill, 18 June 1827. He was praised for his parliamentary conduct, including in an address from the cutlers' guild, that year, when he was denied his silk gown because it was mistakenly thought that this would vacate his seat; the rank of king's counsel was apparently awarded slightly later.[14]

Moore, who was in receipt of the newly appointed Wellington ministry's circular requesting its supporters' attendance in January 1828 and was considered a possible substitute on the intended finance committee the following month, continued to be active on constituency business and in overseeing minor legislation that session.[15] He raised concerns about the growing population of Ireland in relation to the Subletting Act, 19 Feb., the Kildare Place Society, 28 Feb., and economic distress, 5 June. He voted against repeal of the Test Acts, 26 Feb. Lord Anglesey, the lord lieutenant, considered him almost certain to succeed if he stood for the recordership of Dublin, but he lost to Frederick Shaw* at the election in March, when he blamed the Irish government for using its influence against him.[16] Having denied that the treaty of Limerick conferred any greater rights on Catholics, 6 Mar., and damned the Catholic Association as 'an independent Catholic republic in the very heart of a Protestant constitution', 25 Apr., he spoke at length against relief as a dangerous infringement of the constitution which would prove no panacea for Ireland's ills, 8 May, and voted in this sense, 12 May. He divided against inquiry into chancery administration, 24 Apr., and reduction of the salary of the lieutenant-general of the ordnance, 4 July. He took no part in the passage of the Irish registry of deeds bill, which was introduced on the basis of the commission's findings, 27 Mar., and attracted some criticisms of his office, 26 June; it received royal assent on 15 July and provided for the restructuring of the registry's organization on Kilwarden's eventual departure.[17] He called for Protestants to be active in defence of their interests at the Dublin dinner in his honour, 14 Aug., and, as well as serving on the management committee of the Brunswick Club of Ireland that year, he proposed the formation of a branch in Trinity College, 28 Oct., and chaired the meeting which approved the establishment of another for the city, 10 Dec.[18] On 26 Dec. 1828 he informed Wellington of his constituents' doubts about the authenticity of many of the signatures on the Protestants' declaration in favour of the Catholics.[19]

Listed by Planta, the patronage secretary, among those 'opposed to the principle' of the emancipation bill, he denounced ministers' capitulation in the face of what he believed was the Brunswick majority in Ireland, 5 Feb. 1829. He reiterated his long-standing objections to granting Catholic claims, 9, 10, 12 Feb., and thereafter either brought up or supported numerous adverse petitions. On 3 Mar., when he questioned the signatures on the sympathetic Irish Protestant petition, Lord Howick* privately recorded that he was 'very violent and very tiresome'; on 13 Mar., when he presented the hostile petitions of the corporation and inhabitants of Dublin, he was ridiculed by Doherty, the Irish solicitor-general, who complained that 'night after night, has my honourable and learned friend dinned into my ears the words 1688; 1688 has been his everlasting cry ... for 1688 forms the beginning, middle and termination of [his] every speech'.[20] He condemned emancipation as 'an utter subversion of the fundamental principle of the Protestantism of the British constitution', 6 Mar., when, as throughout that month, he divided against it, and he expressed his dread at the Catholic hegemony that would quickly and ruthlessly be established in its wake on bringing up the monster Irish Protestants' petition, 17 Mar. He voted for excluding Catholics from Parliament, 23 Mar., when he suggested alterations to the oaths, and the following day unsuccessfully moved to prevent Catholics being appointed governors of overseas colonies. On 26 Mar., when he tried to have the franchise bill extended to include freeholder boroughs like Dublin and to exclude Protestant 40*s*. freeholders from its provisions, he divided in the minority (of 16-112) for his own amendment to raise the voting qualification from £10 to £20. He seconded (and was a minority teller for) the wrecking amendment against the third reading of the emancipation bill, 30 Mar., when he entered his solemn protest against it. He voted against allowing Daniel O'Connell to take his seat unimpeded, 18 May, and the Maynooth grant, 22 May. Moore, who sought treasury approval for a bill to increase employment in Ireland that session, was rebuffed in an application for government patronage in June 1829, but was well received in Dublin for his exertions in the causes of Protestantism and relief from distress.[21] His name found no place in the list compiled by Sir Richard Vyvyan*, the Ultra leader, later that year.

Moore, who missed the opening of the session through illness, was named to the select committee on the East India Company's affairs, 9 Feb. 1830 (and again, 4 Feb. 1831).[22] He voted against transferring East Retford's seats to Birmingham, 11 Feb., and the enfranchisement of Birmingham, Leeds and Manchester, 23 Feb., but for the Ultra Lord Blandford's motion for parliamentary reform, 18 Feb. On 16 Feb. he obtained leave for his Dublin improvement bill, which was given royal assent, 17 June. He spoke in defence of the Irish church, 4, 16 Mar., 27 Apr., one of the many times when he differed with O'Connell in the chamber. He divided against Jewish emancipation, 5 Apr., 17 May. After objecting to higher taxes on Irish tobacco, 11 May, he complained of the terrible distress prevalent in Dublin while opposing the motion to abolish the Irish lord lieutenancy that day. He spoke and voted for repeal of the Irish coal duties, 13 May, and for the rest of the session devoted most of his parliamentary energies to presenting and endorsing his constituents' petitions against the increased Irish stamp and spirit duties, on which topic he attended meetings of the Irish Members.[23] He divided against the Galway franchise bill, 25 May, for the grant for South American missions and against the abolition of the death penalty for forgery, 7 June, and reducing judges' salaries, 7 July 1830.

Having succeeded Kilwarden, who had died on 22 May 1830, as Irish registrar of deeds, presumably during the dissolution that summer in order to avoid the necessity of a by-election, Moore was attacked for being a placeman who was given leave to make occasional opposition sallies but was otherwise required to toe the administration line, for example on the unpopular tax increases.[24] He had the blessing of government and at least gained credit for his constant parliamentary activity at the general election, when he and Shaw defeated the Whig Grattan in a hard-fought contest.[25] He was listed by ministers among their 'friends', but was absent from the division on the civil list that led to their resignation, 15 Nov. He agreed with O'Connell for extension of the Insolvent Debtors Act to Ireland, 5 Nov., but opposed him in strongly criticizing agitation for repeal of the Union, 19 Nov. 1830. He attended a Dublin meeting to provide relief from distress for the poor, 5 Feb. 1831, and the following month a former fellow of Trinity published a 'Letter to George Moore' against parliamentary reform.[26] He was granted a month's leave on account of ill health, 16 Feb. He voted against the second reading of the Grey ministry's reform bill, 22 Mar., and on the 24th called the Irish bill 'illegal, unconstitutional, immoral and inequitable, and not a measure of restoration, but of destruction'. He complained that house assessments were inadequate in Ireland and that a £10 householder qualification would lead to almost universal suffrage in Dublin, 25 Mar., and he presented and endorsed Dublin common council's petition against reform, especially as an invasion of freeman rights, 29 Mar. He divided for Gascoyne's wrecking amendment, which precipitated a dissolution, 19 Apr. 1831.

For the radical William Carpenter, Moore was 'intolerant in religion and illiberal in politics', while Sheil, who emphasized the contrast between his 'mild manners and violent opinions', commented that 'it was pleasant to see him in the House of Commons delivering himself of the most ferocious conceptions in the gentlest and most simpering fashion: he was happily called Sir Forcible Feeble'.[27] He offered again as an anti-reformer at the general election of 1831, when Anglesey, the reinstated lord lieutenant, advised the prime minister that he 'has a very lucrative office, during pleasure, and if he stands and acts against the government (which he will certainly do) ... surely he ought to be removed'.[28] He came fourth, behind two reformers and Shaw, for whom he plumped, in the bitter contest that ensued, after which he blamed his defeat on the improper influence wielded by the Irish government.[29] He refused either to contribute to the cost of the subsequent election petition or, once the election had been voided, to enter again, as Wellington had wished.[30] Perhaps, as was suspected, he had decided not to endanger his official position by antagonizing ministers, but in any case he retired by issuing a face saving address, 12 Aug., and received votes of thanks for his services from the merchants' guild and the corporation. He proposed his replacement Lord Ingestre at the by-election that month and presided at the dinner for him and Shaw after their victory over another pair of reformers. He attended the grand meeting of Protestants in Dublin in December 1831 and continued to be active in their cause.[31] He voted for Thomas Lefroy* and Shaw in the Dublin university election of 1832 and for the like-minded high Tory candidates in the city contest that year and at the following two general elections.[32]

A bill to amend the 1828 Irish Registry of Deeds Act was introduced by Charles Jephson, Member for Mallow, on 21 July 1831 and got as far as the report stage before the prorogation that autumn.[33] It was reintroduced, 2 Feb. 1832, by Jephson, who again oversaw its preliminary stages. On 3 Apr., when he explained that, by a treasury blunder, warrants had been issued for the registrar's salary to be both £1,200 and £1,500, he justified the higher figure as what Moore had been led to expect and as due recompense for his now obligatory attendance at the office, but Sheil carried an amendment in favour of substituting the lower figure by 23-21. Against the opposition of Sheil and Hume, Lefroy, who had the support of Shaw and ministers, secured the recommittal of the bill by 69-62 in order to reverse this decision, but once in committee Jephson acquiesced in Hume's call for a select committee on the confusion over the two warrants and this was agreed by 91-25. Jephson reported from the select committee, 10 July, but, at the insistence of the radicals, the bill was again sent back to the second reading committee, from which, after further debates on 24 and 25 July, the amended bill was finally reported on the 26th. Given royal assent on 4 Aug. 1832, the new Act confirmed the salary of £1,500 but also explicitly incapacitated the registrar from being in Parliament.[34] Hinting at his political friendship, which he said had been cut short by his opponents' having inserted a clause to prevent him sitting, in January 1835 Moore unsuccessfully requested Peel, now prime minister, to appoint one of his sons as assistant registrar.[35] In July 1843 his own application, on the basis of his long practice in the ecclesiastical courts, for the vacant position of judge of the Irish prerogative court met with a similarly curt negative.[36] O'Connell noted in August 1846 that Moore, 'who has been no less than 48 years at the head of the office, seems much disposed to devote the rest of his life to ease and a more southern climate', but was willing for O'Connell's son Morgan O'Connell†, the deputy registrar, to succeed him provided he was granted a full pension. Although no legislative measure was proceeded with to this effect, the arrangement was apparently facilitated that year and Moore duly retired.[37] His date of death, which possibly took place abroad, has not been traced. Of his two known sons, William Ogle Moore (1799-1874) was consecutively dean of Cashel and Clogher, and James (*b.* 1807) was a barrister, who emigrated to Melbourne, Australia in 1840.[38]

[1] *King's Inns Admission Pprs.* ed. E. Keane, P.B. Phair and T.U. Sadleir, 347. [2] Ibid. (*sub* James Moore). [3] *Hist. Irish Parl.* v. 302. [4] Ibid. v. 392, 394; *DNB sub* Ogle; *Index to Prerogative Wills of Ireland* ed. Sir A. Vicars, 334. [5] *PP* (1820), viii. 423-9, 442, 470, 479-83, 498-535, 593, 595; R. B. McDowell, *Irish Administration*, 280. [6] Add. 40235, f. 25; *Dublin Evening Post*, 4 Jan. 1821. [7] *Dublin Evening Post*, 1 Feb. 1825; *Dublin Evening Mail*, 29 Mar., 7 Apr. 1826; Add. 40319, ff. 167, 171. [8] *Dublin Evening Post*, 8, 10, 13 June; Brougham mss, Abercromby to Brougham, 12 July 1826; Add. 40387, f. 98. [9] R.L. Sheil, *Sketches of Irish Bar* (1854), ii. 357-8; *New Monthly Mag.* (1831), ii. 1-2. [10] *Dublin Evening Mail*, 2 Oct. 1826. [11] Add. 40392, f. 5. [12] *The Times*, 3, 6 Mar.; Nottingham Univ. Lib. Ossington mss acc. 636, Denison diary, 5-6 Mar. 1827. [13] *PP* (1826-7), iv. 1095-1101; *The Times*, 26 May 1827. [14] *Dublin Evening Mail*, 29 June, 20 July, 17 Oct. 1827; Add. 40394, f. 152. [15] NLI mss 8148 (xvii); Add. 40395, f. 221. [16] PRO NI, Anglesey mss D619/31F, pp. 20-23; *Dublin Evening Post*, 20, 22 Mar. 1828. [17] *CJ*, lxxxiii. 208, 480, 535. [18] *Dublin Evening Post*, 16, 26 Aug.; *Dublin Evening Mail*, 29 Oct., 10 Dec. 1828. [19] Wellington mss WP1/972/41. [20] Grey mss, Howick jnl. [21] Wellington mss WP1/1004/37; NAI, Leveson Gower letter bks. M736, Leveson Gower to Moore, 4 June; *Warder*, 25 Apr.; *Dublin Evening Post*, 26 Sept., 1 Oct. 1829. [22] *Dublin Evening Post*, 13 Feb. 1830. [23] Ibid. 8 May, 1 June 1830. [24] *Warder*, 24 Apr., 26 June, 3, 7, 17 July, 20 Nov.; *Freeman's Jnl.* 27 July, 3 Aug. 1830. [25] Add. 40327, f. 194; *Dublin Evening Post*, 6, 13, 22 July, 5, 12, 14 Aug. 1830. [26] *Dublin Evening Post*, 8 Feb.; *Dublin Evening Mail*, 21 Mar. 1831. [27] [W. Carpenter], *People's Bk.* (1831), 327; Sheil, ii. 357; *New Monthly Mag.* (1831), ii. 1-2. [28] *Dublin Evening Post*, 28 Apr.; *Dublin Evening Mail*, 29 Apr., 2 May 1831; Anglesey mss 28C, pp. 106-8. [29] *Dublin Evening Post*, 7, 21 May 1831. [30] NLI, Farnham mss 18611 (2), Lefroy to Farnham, 9 Aug.; Wellington mss, Holmes to Arbuthnot, 9 Aug. 1831. [31] *Dublin Evening Post*, 11, 20 Aug.; *Dublin Evening Mail*, 12, 15, 17, 26 Aug., 12 Dec. 1831. [32] *Dublin Univ. Pollbook* (1832), 20; *Dublin Pollbook* (1837), 132. [33] *CJ*, lxxxvi. 683, 889. [34] Ibid. lxxxvii. 67, 153, 194, 246, 261, 265, 481, 519-20, 526, 532, 555; *PP* (1831-2), xviii. 751; McDowell, 280-1. [35] Add. 40412, ff. 36, 40. [36] Add. 40531, f. 389; NLI mss 8148 (xviii). [37] *O'Connell Corresp.* viii. 3258. [38] *Clergy of Dublin and Glendalough*, 904; *ex. inf.* Mrs. M.B. Wickham of Dunsborough, Western Australia.

S.M.F.

MOORE, Peter (1753–1828), of Edward Street, Mdx.

COVENTRY 30 Mar. 1803–1826

b. 12 Feb. 1753, 2nd s. of Rev. Edward Moore, LLB, vic. of Over, Cheshire (*d.* 1755), and w. Mary. *educ.* Sedbergh. *m.* at Patna, 8 or 10 Jan. 1774, Sarah, da. and coh. of Lt.-Col. Richmond Webb of Bandon, co. Cork, 5s. (4 *d.v.p*) 2 da. *d.* 5 May 1828.

Writer, E.I. Co. (Bengal) 1768; asst. in collector gen.'s office 1770, dep. collector 1771; factor and sec. to bd. of revenue 1774; member, bd. of revenue 1776; jun. merchant 1777; first in council, Murshidabad 1780; sen. merchant 1780; collector, Calcutta 1782; commr. of police 1783-4; home 1785.

Vilified by William Cobbett† in Coventry in 1820 as 'a clerk in *mind*, though a Member of Parliament in name and rank', Moore's Commons and business careers derived from the East Indian one he owed to his elder brother Edward, a well-connected 'alphabet (indexing) clerk' in the *Journals* office, who had secured him the patronage of the 1st Baron Holland.[1] Elections at Tewkesbury and Coventry, which he had represented as a self-professed Foxite Whig since 1803, had eroded his nabob's fortune, but his reputation as an able debater and manager of local and private bills was assured and he retained the support of his wealthy colleague Edward Ellice, to whom he polled second in 1820.[2] Like Ellice, he strenuously supported the return of Samuel Whitbread* for Middlesex.[3] He was a popular figure at the Beefsteak Club and in the House, where he commanded attention and could sense when to give way or seek adjournment. He divided steadily with Hume and the 'Mountain',

1820-3, but seems subsequently to have adhered to the main Whig opposition. He opposed the Irish insurrection bill as a minority teller, 7 Feb. 1822, and again, 7, 8 Feb., 8 July 1822, 12 May 1823. He had failed to secure devaluation when the gold standard was restored in 1819, and he divided for inquiry into the currency, 12 June 1822, and for corn law revision, 18 Apr. 1826.[4] As befitted a Coventry Member, he was named to the select committee on standing orders affecting trade, 14 June 1820, spoke regularly on commercial issues and initiated legislation and undertook much select committee work on private bills.

Moore joined in the opposition to the Western Union Canal bill with a droll speech mocking alterations to its intended course secured by Eton College to safeguard 'the boys' morals', 15 May 1820.[5] He brought up petitions from Andrew Beckwith, 12 June, and the self-styled duchess of Cumberland, Olive Serres, 14 July, and pressed the leader of the House Lord Castlereagh on the cases of other aggrieved persons, 14, 17 July, 18 Sept. 1820.[6] His support for the parliamentary and extra-parliamentary campaigns on behalf of Queen Caroline was unstinting, and he was portrayed with Sir Gerard Noel* and Whitbread as one of the 'three itinerant graces' addressing meeting after meeting in Middlesex on her behalf.[7] He denounced the bill of pains and penalties as a 'dark and foul' conspiracy 'derogatory to the crown', before voting for an address urging prorogation, 18 Sept., and seconded an abortive adjournment motion, 17 Oct. 1820. Bringing up petitions from Monmouth, 26 Jan. 1821, he called for the restoration of the queen's name to the liturgy, and he again criticized her treatment by ministers, 1, 6 Feb. He presented Birmingham's petition for their impeachment, 30 Apr.[8] He voted for Catholic relief, 28 Feb., and provoked laughter by claiming the credit for its consideration, 28 Mar., but nevertheless presented the Coventry clergy's hostile petition, 21 Apr. 1821.[9] He divided for relief, 1 Mar., 21 Apr., 10 May 1825. Moore's support for parliamentary reform was compromised by his obligations to the Coventry outvoters, who jealously guarded their privileges, and the ribbon weavers employed in making election favours. He voted to make Leeds a scot and lot borough under the Grampound disfranchisement bill, 2 Mar. 1821, and divided for reform proposals, 9 May 1821, 25 Apr. 1822, 24 Apr., 2 June 1823, 13, 27 Apr. 1826. He voted to receive the radical Greenhoe petition linking reform and distress, 3 June 1822, and endorsed the '*objectives*' of the contentious Devon petition, 2 June 1823.

Moore joined in the clamour for retrenchment and tax reductions throughout 1821 and 1822, and fulfilled his declared intention of sparing Members by moving adjournments to 'arrest all business after midnight', 11, 14, 18, 25 May 1821, 11, 29 Mar. 1822.[10] His stated objections to the 'unnecessary' award for the duke of Clarence, 18 June 1821, were procedural and based on the revival of a 'vote of a previous Parliament ... without a previous message from the crown'. He pressed for the production of comprehensive estimates early in the session to facilitate 'proper debate', 10 July 1821, 11 Feb., 1, 4, 11 Mar., 18 Apr. 1822. Preferring 1798 or 1799, he urged his 'Mountain' colleagues in vain against making 1797, the first year for which details of government expenditure were available, their standard for measuring inflation, 18 Apr. 1822.[11] He failed to delay the superannuation bill, 11 Mar., or the finance bill, 1 July 1822. Londonderry (Castlereagh) rejected his plea for detailed discussion of the latter – 'that species of enjoyment pointed out by the Hon. Member for Coventry' – and ensured that his amendment restricting the bill's duration (to the fist six weeks of the 1823 session) was defeated, 155-55, 1 July.[12] Neither ministers nor the 'Mountain' would take up Moore's complaint against the Austrian ambassador Frederic Von Gentz, the author of a memorial to the Lords criticizing him and Sir Robert Wilson*, but the chancellor of the exchequer Vansittart made it known that the treasury 'lent no credence' to its claims, 31 May 1822.

Moore endorsed Wilson's opposition to the Stoke Newington vestry bill, 5 Mar., 6 Apr., and secured the recommittal of the metropolitan gas light bill, in which they had vested interests, 24 May 1821.[13] He brought up petitions against and criticized Scarlett's poor relief bill on his constituents' behalf, 28 May, 6 June; likewise the extra post bill, 2 July 1821, 3 Apr., Henry Hunt's* treatment in Ilchester gaol, 1 Mar., 2 Apr., the poor removal bill, 13 May, and the beer bill, 18 July 1822.[14] He enlivened debates with interventions in favour of the vagrancy bill, 29 Mar., and the Salford hundred courts bill, 13 May, and condemned the receivers-general (customs) bill, which he had previously backed.[15] He voted against referring the Calcutta bankers' petition to a select committee, 4 July, and defended the East India Company's handling of the affair, 4, 29 July.[16] On 5 Aug. 1822 he announced that he would seek to repeal the combination laws the following session and requested ministerial backing.[17] Despite objections from the home secretary Peel and the president of the board of trade Huskisson, who criticized the 'short notice' and Moore's private Member status, he received leave to introduce it, 3 Mar. 1823. It 'drew on 28 Acts' and he defined its objectives as: 'First, to bring back a great number of eminent artificers from the continent; secondly, to effect a better distribution of the profits of labour between the employers and the employed; and thirdly, to facilitate the means of recovering debts and deciding suits between artificers and their employers'. He also projected it as a means of reducing poor rates. Its reception and the petitions it attracted were mixed, 22, 27 May, 11, 30 June. Littleton and the Warwickshire Member Dugdale testified to Coventry's opposition to the measure and Huskisson quashed it as too complex, 27 May. However, the bill was printed and circulated, and Moore promised to revive it in 1824, together with his 1819 schemes for regulating the clock-making trades and consolidating the apprenticeship laws, 18 July 1823.[18]

He attributed the failure of his 1823 Insolvent Debtors Act repeal bill, for which Coventry petitioned, 13 Mar., and his masters and servants bill to lack of support from other manufacturing towns.[19] Coventry silkmasters relied on import restrictions and protective tariffs and resisted any relaxation in the navigation laws, and Moore supported their campaign against the 1823 silk manufacture bill, by which the Spitalfields Acts were repealed. His speeches (22 May, 9, 11 June) condemned it as a harbinger of mass unemployment and poverty and he welcomed the three-year adjustment period secured by a late Lords' amendment.[20] He presented and endorsed petitions against the importation of foreign silks, 4, 15 Mar. 1824, and was caricatured by Cruikshank being borne towards the Speaker by the Coventry weavers, holding a placard inscribed 'petitioners shall ever weave' and arguing that 'Coventry is the barometer of the [commercial] world'.[21] As one of the trade's parliamentary spokesmen in 1826, he presented petitions alleging distress and seeking inquiry, 13, 23 Feb., 10 Mar., and advocated their referral to a select committee, 23 Feb. He reiterated their plea in a major speech the following day and criticized Huskisson for ignoring the petitions and the distress and misery his policies had brought to the manufacturing districts and for refusing to accept that 'people mattered more than the Navigation Acts'.[22]

Moore was named to the 1824 and 1825 select committees on artisans and machinery and presented petitions from Coventry and elsewhere for repeal of the combination laws, 29, 31 Mar., 8, 15 Apr. 1824, and from Lancashire against their re-enactment, 28 Apr., 11 May 1825.[23] He decided against proceeding with his own bill, announced on 26, 31 Mar. 1824, and Hume rushed repeal through in a measure denounced by the Coventry silkmasters, who held Moore responsible for it, as a disastrous and costly failure.[24] He continued to divide fairly regularly with opposition and to present petitions, but henceforward most of his time in and out of the House was devoted to promoting and safeguarding his business interests. A major shareholder in at least two coal-gas companies (the Metropolitan and the Imperial), he strove to defeat the bills of the rival London Oil Gas Company in which Ellice had a stake (12 Apr., 3 May 1824, 23 Feb. 1825). The presence of the Coventry Members as rival tellers, 12 Apr. 1824, 22 Feb. 1825, prompted Hume to demand the annulment of the votes of interested Members, and Moore's proprietorial interest was recorded in the *Journal*.[25] The failure of the 1824 Equitable Loan Company bill again compromised Moore, for although his work in committee and in the chamber, 15, 23, Mar. 1825, secured its passage in the Commons (39-12), 24 Mar., its fate rested with the Lords, who rejected it, 25 Mar., and king's bench, where lord chancellor Eldon's ruling of 4 Feb. 1825 in the Joseph *v.* Pebrer case that the 'Equity' was 'illegal within the operation of the Bubble Act' prompted alarm in the City and a spate of protective joint-stock legislation.[26] On 29 Mar. Moore made but subsequently withdrew a motion for leave to bring in a bill to repeal the Bubble Act, but the attorney-general Copley and Huskisson condemned it as ill-prepared. He defended the companies he was associated with, called on the board of trade to take immediate action and reinforced claims that the 'Bubble Act, being so full of penalties and contradictory enactments ... [was] a dead letter'. He protested also that 'various companies possessing a capital of £250 million were left at sea, without rudder or compass, not knowing whether they were acting right or wrong'. Assisted by Grenfell, he proposed but agreed to postpone his revised repeal bill, 30 Mar., 18 Apr., secured its first reading, 30 Apr., but effectively abandoned it, 13 May, when a government measure was known to be imminent.[27] His prosecution in the court of chancery as chairman of the British Annuity Company did not deter the Ffestiniog Railway Company, the Welch Mining Company and others from soliciting his parliamentary services with share offers, which he foolishly accepted after the Bubble Act was repealed in June 1825.[28] He secured leave for a bill enabling the Aegis Insurance Company to sue and be sued, 23 Feb. 1826, but new legislation he promoted on behalf of the 'Equitable' and the Welch Iron and Coal Company failed – the latter through the intervention on 22 Mar. 1826 of Littleton and of the Breconshire Member Wood (as spokesman for Coventry's London out-voters).[29] The silkmasters and corporation had been campaigning to oust Moore since August 1825, and they secured their objective when he polled fourth at the general election of 1826, unable to make himself heard above the mob, which mocked him as 'Pope Peter'.[30]

Defeat cost Moore the House's protection, and the collapse of his businesses following the rejection of his appeal in the British Annuity Company case of Van Sandau *v.* Moore and others, 15 Aug. 1826, induced him to make over his assets, which included East India Company stock, to his creditors and to take refuge in France. His subsequent recovery actions were non-suited.[31] On 16 Aug. 1827, now 74, he vainly wrote to the 3rd Baron Holland, whom he anticipated would become foreign secretary in the reshuffle following Canning's death:

> I anxiously look at the progress of the *Whigs*, as we are called, from this coast and cordially rejoice at the expulsion from office and power of the old sordid leaven so long keeping misery and disgracefully lowering the dignity of our country. I trust that my 35-year support of the Whig cause from which I never spared personal exertion or purse will not be lost sight of, nor the seat for Queenborough which placed ... Romilly in Parliament to strengthen your administration in 1806, for which I never received the promised return: no, not even the return of the fees paid for the Chiltern Hundreds ... I shall be happy to serve under you, either at home or abroad. You cannot have more sincere attachment near you.[32]

'The scapegoat for the slurs of a multitude of jobbers', he died in May 1828 at his home in St. Valery sur Somme, near Abbeville, 'broken', according to the *Times*, by his speculation in the ill-fated Devonshire and Cornwall Mining Company, in which several ministers and Members had invested.[33] He was recalled as a friend and sponsor of the dramatist Richard Brinsley Sheridan†, the author William Thackeray and the Charing Cross tailor Francis Place, and as a casualty of his high profile 'Bubble company' investments.[34] By his will, dated 11 May 1827, and proved under £300, he left everything to his unmarried daughter and housekeeper Maria Sarah, subject to a token payment of £100 to his 'beloved son Macartney Moore' (*d.* 1831), an East India army officer.[35]

[1] *Pol. Reg.* 25 Mar. 1820. [2] *Coventry Herald*, 25 Feb. 10, 24 Mar.; Grey mss, Ellice to Grey [4, 16 Mar. 1820]. [3] *The Times*, 8, 28, 30 Mar. 1820. [4] B. Hilton, *Corn, Cash, Commerce*, 47. [5] *The Times*, 16 May 1820. [6] Ibid. 15, 18 July, 19 Sept. 1820. [7] M.D. George, *Cat. of Pol. and Personal Satires*, x. 13989; *Ann. Reg.* (1821), Chron. pp. 417-20. [8] *The Times*, 27 Jan., 2 Feb., 1 May, 1821. [9] Ibid. 13 Apr. 1821. [10] Ibid. 12, 19, 26 May 1821, 12, 30 Mar. 1822. [11] Ibid. 11 July 1821, 12 Feb., 2, 5, 12 Mar., 19 Apr. 1822. [12] Ibid. 2 July 1822. [13] Ibid. 6 Mar., 7 Apr., 25 May 1821. [14] Ibid. 29 May, 7 June, 3 July 1821, 2 Mar., 3 Apr., 14 May, 19 July 1822. [15] Ibid. 30 Mar., 19 July 1822. [16] Ibid. 30 July 1822. [17] Ibid. 6 Aug. 1822. [18] Ibid. 23 May, 12 June, 1, 19 July 1823. [19] Ibid. 14, 19 Mar., 23 Apr. 1823. [20] P. Moore, 'Letters on the Repeal of the Combinations Laws' (1825) [Coventry Local Stud. Lib. *Coventry Pamphlets*, V]. [21] *The Times*, 5, 16 Mar. 1824; George, x. 14673. [22] *The Times*, 14, 24, 25 Feb., 11 Mar. 1826. [23] Ibid. 30 Mar., 1, 9, 16 Apr. 1824, 29 Apr., 12 May 1825. [24] Ibid. 30 Mar., 1, 9, 16 Apr. 1824; Moore, 'Letters'. [25] *CJ*, lxxx. 110. [26] *The Times*, 27 May 1824, 5 Feb. 16, 24, 25 Mar. 1825; R. Harris, 'Political economy, interest groups and repeal of Bubble Act in 1825', *EcHR*, l (1997), 679-83. [27] *The Times*, 31 Mar., 19 Apr., 14 May 1825; Harris, 688-9. [28] *The Times*, 7, 10 Mar. 1825, 27 Apr., 6, 9 May 1826; NLW, Porthmadoc mss 330; Gwynedd Archives (Caernarvon) XD/8/2/210; *Lawyers and Legislators* (1826), 78. [29] *The Times*, 18, 24 Feb.; *Coventry Herald*, 24 Feb. 1826. [30] *The Times*, 2, 12, 17, 21 June; *Coventry Herald*, 5 June 1826. [31] *The Times*, 16 Aug. 1826, 1, 7 May; *Coventry Mercury*, 18 Mar., 6 May 1827. [32] Add. 51811. [33] *The Times*, 15 May; *Coventry Herald*, 16 May 1828. [34] *Oxford DNB*. [35] PROB 11/1742/368; IR26/1169/364.

M.M.E.

MORDAUNT, Sir Charles, 8th bt. (1771–1823), of Walton, Warws. and 6 Portman Square, Mdx.

WARWICKSHIRE 1 Oct. 1804–7 Oct. 1820

b. 5 Jan. 1771, o. surv. son of Sir John Mordaunt, 7th bt.†, of Walton and Elizabeth, da. and coh. of Thomas Prowse† of Compton Bishop, Som. *educ.* Eton 1779-88; Christ Church, Oxf. 1788. *m.* 31 Jan. 1807, Marianne, da. of William Holbech† of Farnborough Hall, Warws., 1s. 2da. *suc.* fa. as 8th bt. 18 Nov. 1806. *d.* 30 May 1823.

Capt. (Vols.) Warws. militia 1794; cornet Warws. yeoman cav. 1798, capt. 1801, maj. 1802.

Recorder, Stratford-upon-Avon 1807-*d.*[1]

Despite his failing health Mordaunt, a pro-Catholic Whig who had long adapted his politics to appease his constituents, stood again for his county at the general election of 1820 and was returned unopposed.[2] He apologized on the hustings for his absence from Parliament throughout 1819 and explained that, if present, he would have supported the Bank Act and the repressive legislation after Peterloo. He added that he would 'exert all the power he possessed' in the new Parliament to combat the depression in trade and agriculture.[3] Although his name appears in no surviving division list, he was not entirely inactive in his last parliamentary session. He supported inquiry with a view to curbing emissions from industrial furnaces, commended the 'ingenious' and 'effectual' device used by John Parkes at his Warwick factory, where the furnaces 'consumed their own smoke' and was named to the committee, 2 May 1820. The next day he and his colleague Dugdale Stratford Dugdale requested an interview with Lord Liverpool on behalf of a Birmingham deputation seeking inquiry into the causes of distress in manufacturing.[4] He was named to the select committee on restricting the use of capital punishment for felony, which he had long advocated, 9 May 1820.

Mordaunt, whose devoted wife (*d.* 1842) conceded that he was 'never perhaps sufficiently attached' to the duties of public life, preferring 'enjoyment of nature' and 'domestic affection', fell so grievously ill later that year that he resigned his seat.[5] It was supposed that the candidature of the radical Richard Spooner* at the ensuing by-election would 'send him without more delay out of the world with a groan that the whole county will hear', but his preferred candidate, the pro-Catholic Whig Francis Lawley, prevailed.[6] Mordaunt died at Walton in May 1823, worth an estimated £90,000 at probate, having entrusted the care of his 15-year-old son John (1808-45), his heir in the baronetcy and estates in Warwickshire, Norfolk, Bedfordshire, Buckinghamshire and Kent, to his widow and her brothers.[7] Sir John Mordaunt represented Warwickshire South as a Conservative, 1835-45.

[1] Shakespeare Birthplace Trust RO, Stratford borough recs. BRU15/19/27, ff. 57-58; *Aris's Birmingham Gazette*, 16 June 1823. [2] *HP Commons, 1790-1820*, iv. 631-2. [3] Warws. RO CR1368/6; *Coventry Herald*, 17 Mar. 1820. [4] Add. 38284, f. 259. [5] E. Hamilton, *The Mordaunts*, 251-2, 254. [6] *Lady Lyttelton Corresp.* 230; Norf. RO, Wodehouse of Kimberley mss KIM6/37, Walton to J. Wodehouse, 7 Nov. 1820. [7] *Aris's Birmingham Gazette*, 2 June 1823; PROB 11/1673/424; IR26/965/673; Warws. RO, Stoneleigh (Mordaunt) mss DR18/28/1.

M.M.E.

MORETON *see* REYNOLDS MORETON

MORGAN (formerly GOULD), Sir Charles, 2nd bt. (1760–1846), of Tredegar Park, Mon. and Pall Mall, Mdx.

BRECON 6 Dec. 1787–1796

MONMOUTHSHIRE 1796–1831

b. 4 Feb. 1760, 1st s. of Sir Charles Gould†, 1st bt., of Tredegar and Jane, da. of Thomas Morgan† of Tredegar. *educ.* Westminster 1771-4. *m.* 6 Apr. 1791, Mary Margaret, da. of Capt. George Stoney, RN, 4s. (1 *d.v.p.*) 4da. (2 *d.v.p.*). Took name of Morgan 16 Nov. 1792 and *suc.* mother to Tredegar estate of her bro. John Morgan† 1797; fa. as 2nd bt. 6 Dec. 1806. *d.* 5 Dec. 1846.

Ensign 2 Ft. Gds. 1777, lt. and capt. 1781, capt. and lt.-col. 1790, ret. 1792; lt.-col. commdt. Tredegar and Ruperra vol. inf. 1798; col. Mon. vols. 1803; lt.-col. commdt. W. Mon. militia 1818-*d.*

Dir. Equitable Assurance Co. 1804, pres. 1807.

Recorder, Newport 1807-35.

Morgan, according to one of his Monmouthshire critics, was 'a handsome little man ... possessed of great power', which he deployed solely to further his own dynastic interests.[1] By 1820 the Dderw, Ruperra and Tredegar estates from which his political influence in the counties and boroughs of Brecon, Glamorgan and Monmouth derived were worth about £40,000 a year in rentals, revenue from coal and iron workings at his new town of Tredegar, and investments in the Brecon and Monmouth canal, Newport docks and turnpikes. He had supported these enterprises by promoting and scrutinizing local and private bills in the Commons, where he had generally supported Lord Liverpool's ministry and opposed Catholic relief.[2] He controlled the representation of Brecon, reserving it since 1806 for his sons, and chose to sit for Monmouthshire, making his interest in Monmouth's contributory borough of Newport, where he was recorder, available to the lord lieutenant, the 6th duke of Beaufort, whose relations occupied the second Monmouthshire seat. He had failed, despite Beaufort's assistance, to bring in his son and heir Charles Morgan Robinson Morgan* for Breconshire in 1818; and popular opposition to his family was also manifested in Brecon, which his second son George Gould Morgan represented, and in Monmouthshire, where Beaufort-Morgan co-operation was resented.[3] In 1820 he adhered to the arrangement with Beaufort in Monmouthshire and its boroughs, returned George for Brecon, left Breconshire undisturbed, and came in unopposed.[4] Differing from Beaufort in Glamorgan, Morgan and his brother-in-law, the industrialist Samuel Homfray, paraded with their tenants in support of the defeated sitting Member John Edwards* of Rheola.[5] Turning down a requisition to Charles from an unnamed constituency, 13 Feb., he informed its conveyor, Sir John Nicholl*, that he looked forward to

> leaving my son the county of Monmouth without an opposition, and my second son the borough of Brecon – an ambition beyond which I am by no means desirous of aspiring to; leaving my sons and daughters independent of seeking from administration.[6]

After the election Morgan was pressed to sign and support a strongly worded petition complaining of agricultural distress and the inadequate protection afforded by the corn laws, and his agents attended to the Great Forest of Brecon enclosure, and urged him to dine his supporters and create further freeholds in Monmouthshire, where 'a regularly organized opposition' threatened.[7] He also devoted time early in the 1820 Parliament to securing a new house of correction for Usk and opposing legislation regulating steam engine emissions and clauses in the Western Union Canal bill that jeopardized his interests.[8]

He signed the Breconshire loyal address to the king, sponsored by Thomas Wood*, Lord Camden and Beaufort, when Queen Caroline's cause attracted popular support in Brecon and Newport in January 1821, and voted against the censure motion criticizing government's handling of the affair, 6 Feb.[9] He divided against Catholic relief, 28 Feb. 1821, 30 Apr. 1822, 21 Apr., 10 May 1825 (having paired, 1 Mar. 1825), and inquiry into voting rights in parliamentary elections, 20 Feb. 1823.[10] As requested at the meeting, he presented Monmouthshire's petition for lower taxes and the abolition of 'useless places' to combat distress, 15 May 1822, but observed on doing so that the remedies sought would be ineffectual.[11] He presented his constituents' petitions against the Insolvent Debtors Act, 10 Mar., and truck payments, 23 May 1823; for the Rhumney railway and Dyffryn Llynfi tramroad bills, 4 Feb., 21 Mar. 1825, and for the abolition of West Indian slavery, 10 Feb. 1826. He confirmed his support for Beaufort at the October 1821 Monmouth dinner, presided annually over the Gwent Cambrian Society and Brecon eisteddfod, and remained a prominent patron of race meetings, Newport charities, the London Cymmrodorion and Tredegar cattle shows, which, like Thomas William Coke I's* sheep shearings at Holkham, had a political dimension. Morgan's large family served as his entourage, and he provided generous settlements for them, sanctioned by a private Act of 17 June 1824 enabling him to issue leases on property in Stepney, Middlesex.[12] His business and industrial concerns prospered, but his right to claim 'wharf money' in Newport was disputed, and the 1826 Newport Improvement Act he steered through the Commons made him and his agent, the town clerk Thomas Prothero, targets of the vitriolic pen of the pamphleteer and future Chartist John Frost, who also criticized the sinecures held by Morgan's brother-in-law, Rowley Lascelles of Catherel, and son-in-law, the 3rd Baron Rodney.[13] Morgan had failed to secure government patronage for another son-in-law, Francis Miles Milman.[14] The prospect of opposition to Tredegar evaporated before the dissolution in 1826. Breconshire, where Morgan had quarrelled with his local agent Hugh Bold, remained quiet, and he and George were returned unopposed.[15]

Morgan presented a petition for agricultural protection from some Monmouthshire landowners, 14 Feb., divided against Catholic relief, 6 Mar., and presented his constituents' petitions for repeal of the Test Acts, 9 May, 6 June 1827. He was prosecuted that summer over gaming rights in Breconshire Great Forest, where he had exchanged allotments with Charles Kemeys Kemeys Tynte*; and the Rev. Thomas Vaughan Watkins of Penoyre disputed his claim to land in the borough of Brecon.[16] His generosity at the Tredegar show and races and in clothing the poor in December 1827 was unsurpassed.[17] He welcomed Peel's return to the home office in the duke of Wellington's coalition ministry in January 1828, and promised that 'a government formed on the principles of Lord Liverpool's will ever meet with the support of myself and family'.[18] He presented numerous Monmouthshire petitions for repeal of the Test Acts, 11, 18, 25 Feb., 1 Mar., but divided with ministers against the measure, 26 Feb.[19] He presented and endorsed others for repeal of the 1827 Malt Act, 4, 7 Mar., and hostile to the friendly societies bill, 21 Apr., and Catholic relief, 6 May, which he voted against, 12 May 1828. As the patronage secretary Planta had predicted, Morgan's diehard views remained unchanged when Wellington and Peel conceded emancipation in 1829, and he divided, 6, 18, 30 Mar., and presented petitions against it, 16 Mar. He voted against Lord Blandford's parliamentary reform proposals, 18 Feb., and presented a petition from John Hodder Moggeridge, the defeated candidate in Monmouth boroughs in 1820, against paying wages 'in goods', 4 Mar. 1830. He had failed to secure a Welsh judgeship on the Brecon circuit for his kinsman by marriage Sir William Owen in 1828, and afterwards allowed his name to be added to the list of Glamorgan magistrates favourable to the abolition of the Welsh court of great sessions. However, he held aloof from constituency meetings and Commons proceedings on the 1830 administration of justice bill by which the change was enacted.[20] His opposition to the 1830 Monmouth canal bill left him at odds with Capel Hanbury Leigh of Pontypool and others who had supported him hitherto despite their political differences, but they posed no threat to his return at the general election that summer, when, as arranged in 1829, he substituted Charles for George as Member for Brecon.[21]

Ministers listed Morgan among their 'friends' in the new Parliament, but he was absent from the division on the civil list when they were brought down, 15 Nov. 1830. He was granted two weeks' leave because of illness in his family, 25 Nov., and was at Tredegar when rioting and incendiarism broke out there in December. He chaired a meeting at Newport, 6 Dec. 1830, 'to adopt measures for the effectual preservation of the peace and property'; but the fixed wage of 8*s*. a week he introduced for his workers failed to please, and a local campaign for lower taxes, universal suffrage, fair and equal representation and shorter parliaments gathered momentum. He was also taken to task by Frost, who claimed that he had everything to gain and nothing to lose by supporting reform.[22] Meetings in Breconshire and Monmouthshire, where arrangements to field reform candidates were already in place, passed resolutions thanking Morgan and his son for dividing for the Grey ministry's reform bill at its second reading, 22 Mar. 1831. Morgan protested when the Staffordshire reform petition was presented, 19 Apr., that its sole signatory, the marquess of Cleveland, a political turncoat, was guilty of corrupt borough management, and his vote that day for Gascoyne's wrecking amendment put a severe tussle between him and Lord Granville Somerset for the second Monmouthshire seat in prospect. Morgan was 72, and, after establishing that Charles did not wish to take his place, he decided to stand down at the dissolution rather than risk the ignominy of defeat.[23] 'Very much mortified at ... the ingratitude of the county gentlemen' and his own inability to rally support through the local press, he announced his retirement, 20 Apr. 1831, and dismissed Prothero, whom Charles had long mistrusted and who now backed the reformers.[24]

Morgan returned Charles for Brecon in 1831, giving his interests in Monmouth Boroughs and Breconshire to the anti-reformers Lord Worcester* and Wood. He was fêted on his return to Tredegar in July and dined by his supporters.[25] Addressing him, Prothero's legal partner, the Newport attorney and reformer Thomas Phillips, stated:

> We are afraid if in future Parliaments gentlemen like yourself should either be drawn from their seats or through distaste or disgust on their part retire from the ... Commons, then that House will more resemble the French convention, or a House of republican delegates than the high and independent branch of the legislature which in spite of all that has been said to the contrary we maintain to have been the chief glory of our constitution and the admiration and envy of the world.[26]

Morgan refused to stand for Parliament again. Business interests, including the Risca Level dispute (a long and costly case concerning mineral rights that he pursued against Prothero) preoccupied him; and he also sponsored a new race course and paid regular visits to Brecon, where Charles was defeated in 1832 but returned as a Conservative in 1835. The difficult task of canvassing Newport was delegated to his son Charles Augustus Morgan, rector of Machen and future dean of Llandaff.[27] He refused to allow his sons to contest Glamorgan, but he co-operated with Lord Bute in the establishment of the Conservative *Glamorgan, Monmouth and Brecon Gazette and Merthyr Guardian*, and delighted in the success of his fourth son Charles Octavius Swinnerton Morgan (1803-88) in recapturing the second Monmouthshire seat in an 1841 by-election coup.[28] Morgan died at Tredegar in December 1846, after receiving the last rites from Charles Augustus, and was buried in the family vault at Bassaleg and commemorated by a bronze statue in Tredegar Park.[29] His estates and baronetcy passed to Charles and, as he had willed, a family settlement of 1844 was perpetuated.[30]

[1] J. Frost, *Letter to Sir Charles Morgan* (1821), 1. [2] D. Williams, *John Frost* (1939), 21; *Wraxall Mems.* ed. H.B. Wheately, v. 328-30; NLW, Tredegar Park mss 191, *passim.*; NLW, Tredegar mss 45/1445-77, 1510; J.B. Hilling, 'Britain's First Planned Industrial Town? The Development of Tredegar, 1800-1820', *Gwent Local Hist.* xciv (2003), 55-76; *HP Commons, 1790-1820*, iv. 46. [3] W.T. Morgan, 'Mon. Elections', *NLWJ*, x (1957), 170-4; Tredegar mss 45/1478; 121/852-4. [4] Tredegar mss 45/1506-7; 135/764-7, 775, 778; *Bristol Mercury*, 21 Feb., 20 Mar. 1820. [5] Tredegar mss 135/765-9, 773, 803; NLW, Bute mss L63/22; NLW, Penrice and Margam mss 10223, 10226, 10232-3, 10240; H.M. Williams, 'Geographic Distribution of Pol. Opinion in Glam. Parl. Elections, 1820-1950' (Univ. of Wales M.A. thesis, 1951), 21-23. [6] Tredegar mss 135/771. [7] Ibid. 45/1457, 1497, 1516-17; 135/782-3, 795. [8] Ibid. 45/1497, 1520; M. Elsas, *Iron in the Making*, 216. [9] Tredegar mss 141/1-6; NLW, Maybery mss 6545, 6919; *Seren Gomer*, iii (1820), 383, 387; iv (1821), 28-29; *The Times*, 27 Dec. 1820; *Courier*, 31 Jan. 1821. [10] *Seren Gomer*, v (1822), 187; *The Times*, 4 Mar. 1825. [11] *The Times*, 16 May; *Bristol Mercury*, 18 May 1822. [12] *Bristol Mercury*, 20 Oct. 1821; *Seren Gomer*, iv (1821), 374; v (1822), 187, 346-9; Tredegar mss 20/34; 57/35, 37, 42, 48-53, 58-60, 451; 72/134; *Cambrian*, 16 Oct. 1824, 1, 8 Oct. 1825; *LJ*, lvi. 211, 301, 364, 372, 426; *CJ*, lxxix. 476, 488, 497, 504; lxxx. 229, 282, 518. [13] Tredegar mss 57/43; 84/3, 19-20, 228-31; D. Williams, 21-56; Frost, *passim*; NLW ms 17104 D (Llangibby Castle Letters, f. 7), A.M. Hawkins to T. Cooke, 24 June 1826; *CJ*, lxxxi. 10, 17, 29, 39, 40, 92, 109, 118, 165, 198. [14] Add. 40383, ff. 325, 329. [15] Tredegar mss 57/44-47, 68; *Cambrian*, 3, 10, 17 June 1826. [16] Tredegar mss 124/106, 302; 146/101-4; Glam. RO D/DKT/232, 246, 251. [17] *Cambrian*, 12 Jan. 1828. [18] Add. 40395, f. 91. [19] *Cambrian*, 16 Feb. 1828. [20] Wellington mss WP1/928/2; 943/8; *PP* (1829), ix. 387. [21] Bute mss L73/43; *Hereford Jnl.* 30 Sept., 7 Oct. 1829; *Cambrian*, 3, 10 Oct. 1829, 16 Jan. 1830. [22] D. Williams, 60-62; *Mon. Merlin*, 11, 18, 25 Dec. 1830, 12 Feb.; *Cambrian*, 21 Jan. 1831; Frost, *A Christmas Box to Sir Charles Morgan* (1833), *passim.* [23] *Cambrian*, 19 Mar., 16 Apr.; *Hereford Jnl.* 23 Mar.; *Mon. Merlin*, 26 Mar., 2, 9 Apr. 1831; Bute mss L74/34; Morgan, *NLWJ*, x. 176-7. [24] Tredegar mss 1/205-6; C. Williams, 'The Great Hero of the Newport Rising: Thomas Philips, Reform and Chartism', *WHR*, xxi (2003), 488-92; *Cambrian*, 9 July 1831. [25] Tredegar mss 1/205-6; *Cambrian*, 9 July 1831. [26] Tredegar mss 1/204. [27] Ibid. 24/121-6; 84/210-13; 137/346-64; M. Cragoe, *Culture, Politics, and National Identity in Wales, 1832-1886*, pp. 51, 53; *Mon. Merlin*, 8 Oct. 1831, 31 Mar., 4, 11 Aug., 6 Oct., 1 Dec. 1832. [28] Cardiff Pub. Lib. Bute estate letterbks. iii. 36; Bute mss L75/101, 122; Tredegar mss 84/810-29; Cragoe, 17-18. [29] *Mon. Merlin*, 12, 19 Dec. 1846, 15 Jan. 1847; Tredegar mss 86/20-21. [30] PROB 11/2049/56; IR26/1777/36.

M.M.E.

MORGAN, **Charles Morgan Robinson** (1792–1875), of Ruperra, Glam. and Tredegar, Mon.

BRECON	1812–1818
BRECON	1830–1832
BRECON	1835–1847

b. 10 Apr. 1792, 1st s. of Sir Charles Morgan (formerly Gould), 2nd bt.*, and Mary Margaret, da. of Capt. George Stoney, RN; bro. of Charles Octavius Swinnerton Morgan† and George Gould Morgan*. *educ.* Harrow; Westminster; Christ Church, Oxf. 1811. *m.* 6 Oct. 1827, Rosamund, da. of Gen. Godfrey Basil Mundy, 5s. (1 *d.v.p.*) 6da. *suc.* fa. as 3rd bt. 5 Dec. 1846; *cr.* Bar. Tredegar 16 Apr. 1859. *d.* 16 Apr. 1875.

Sheriff, Mon. 1821-2, Brec. 1850-1; ld.-lt. Mon. 1866-*d.*

Capt. W. Mon. militia 1812, N. Hants 1819, E. Glam. 1824, Central Glam. 1829-32; lt.-col. commdt. W. Mon. militia 1846-*d.*

In 1818 Morgan, who was groomed to inherit the family's 40,000-acre estates in south-east Wales and his father's Monmouthshire seat, had relinquished the representation of their borough of Brecon with a view to recapturing Breconshire for Tredegar, but he had been defeated there by the foreign secretary Lord Castlereagh's* brother-in-law Thomas Wood*.[1] Notwithstanding rumours that he might contest Glamorgan or Monmouth Boroughs in 1820, he remained out of Parliament until his father substituted him at Brecon for his brother George in 1830.[2] In the intervening years he regularly accompanied Sir Charles at elections, the assizes and county occasions, and was a signatory with him of the Breconshire loyal address of January 1821 and the Glamorgan magistrates' 1828 memorial in favour of abolishing the Welsh courts of great sessions.[3] His return to Ruperra with his bride in 1827 was widely celebrated, and every endeavour was made to ensure that the lord lieutenant, the 2nd marquess of Bute, who resented Sir Charles's intervention on behalf of John Edwards* in Glamorgan in 1820 and the 6th duke of Beaufort's candidates in Cardiff Boroughs in 1820 and 1824, did not obstruct Morgan's entry into county society as a militia commander and magistrate.[4] In 1829 he succeeded John Nicholl† as captain of the Central Glamorgan yeoman cavalry, and worked hard on behalf of his men.[5] Commenting that year on the alleged antipathy between him and his father's agent Thomas Prothero, the land agent A.T. Hawkins observed:

> I hear Mr. Morgan and T.P. are not very good friends – *that Mr. M. hates him.* I can scarcely believe it, as the good quality of an agent is to bring in the rents, no matter how, and I know Mr. M. never intends to give himself any trouble about representing the county, therefore will care very little what enemies P. makes on that score.[6]

As Member for Brecon in the 1830 Parliament, Morgan was listed among the Wellington ministry's 'friends', but he failed to vote on the civil list when they were brought down, 15 Nov. 1830. He presented anti-slavery petitions, 17 Nov., and accompanied his father to difficult meetings in Newport and Brecon when industrial unrest coincided with clamour for parliamentary reform in 1830-1.[7] He divided for the Grey ministry's reform bill at its second reading, 22 Mar., but, unlike Sir Charles, he chose not to vote on Gascoyne's wrecking amendment, 19 Apr. 1831. He encouraged his father to stand down rather than risk a costly defeat in Monmouthshire at the ensuing general election and came in for Brecon unopposed.[8] He was summoned to Merthyr with his troop to quell the June uprising, and was commended afterwards as a popular officer suitable for promotion. However, the corps being found inadequate, they were disbanded in 1832, a decision he interpreted as a 'sacrifice to prevent the annoyance of others'.[9] He was absent when the reintroduced reform bill was carried at its second reading, 6 July, voted for its adjournment, 12 July 1831, but cast no known vote on it subsequently. He divided against the third reading of the revised measure, 22 Mar. 1832.[10] Having assumed a higher profile at the assizes and county functions in Breconshire and Monmouthshire, in June 1832 he commenced canvassing as a Conservative for Brecon, which he lost in December to a Liberal, after a violent contest.[11] The Dowlais ironmaster John Josiah Guest* observed: 'As a gentleman no man can be more respectable, but Mr. Morgan certainly did not shine as an MP'.[12] Bute, who in July 1832 had approached him about standing for Glamorgan, noted that 'his behaviour to many of the Glamorganshire gentlemen at Tredegar and also at his hunting meetings' was 'considered rather cool', and there was 'no probability of ... [his] wishing it or of Sir Charles permitting *his* standing'; but he proved assiduous in registering the Ruperra tenantry and made an excellent speech at the Glamorgan dinner in which he accused Watkins of winning through bad votes.[13]

A diehard Conservative popular at Queen Victoria's court, Morgan contested Brecon successfully in 1835, helped his brother Charles Octavius (1803-88) to victory in Monmouthshire in 1841, his eldest son Charles Rodney Morgan (1828-54) in Brecon in 1852, and his second son Godfrey Charles Morgan (1831-1913) in Breconshire, which he recaptured in 1858.[14] He was raised to the peerage as Baron Tredegar in

1859 on the Derby ministry's recommendation, and in 1866 became lord lieutenant of Monmouthshire. He died at Tredegar in April 1875 and was buried in the family vault at Bassaleg, having by his will confirmed the 1844 family settlement and made additional provisions for his widow and children, including Godfrey Charles, his successor in the barony and estates.[15]

[1] *HP Commons, 1790-1820*, ii. 482-3; iv. 632-3. [2] NLW, Tredegar mss 135/771; *Mon. Merlin*, 7 Aug. 1830. [3] *Cambrian*, 21 Jan. 1821, 20 Oct. 1827, 22 Nov. 1828; *PP* (1829), ix. 387. [4] *Cambrian*, 20 Oct. 1827; NLW, Bute mss L65/34; L67/21, 34; L71/15, 32, 42; Glam. RO D/DA11/49-50; Cardiff Pub. Lib. Bute estate letterbks. ii. 5. [5] Bute mss L72/85; L73/49-50, 56-58; Bute estate letterbks. ii. 199-200. [6] NLW ms 17104 D, A.M. Hawkins to T. Cooke, 12 Aug. 1829. [7] *Cambrian*, 12 Feb. 1831. [8] *Mon. Merlin*, 23, 30 Apr.; *Hereford Jnl.* 4 May 1831; Bute mss L74/34. [9] *Mon. Merlin*, 18 June 1831; Bute mss L74/34, 145, 163, 204; L75/45. [10] *Carmarthen Jnl.* 25 Nov. 1831; *Welshman*, 15 June; *Cambrian*, 16 June 1832. [11] *Mon. Merlin*, 16 July 1831, 31 Mar., 4, 11 Aug., 6 Oct., 3 Nov., 18 Dec.; *Cambrian*, 16 June, 8, 15, 22 Dec. 1832; Tredegar mss 137/149, 368; Bute estate letterbks. iii. 71. [12] NLW, Maybery mss 6600. [13] Bute mss L75/101, 107, 122; Bute estate letterbks. iii. 6-10, 36; Maybery mss 6603; Tredegar mss 84/810. [14] M. Cragoe, *Culture, Politics, and National Identity in Wales, 1832-1886*, pp. 17-18, 51, 53, 129-30. [15] *Brecon Co. Times*, 24 Apr.; *Illustrated London News* (1875), i. 402, ii. 70.

M.M.E.

MORGAN, George Gould (1794–1845), of Tredegar, Mon.

BRECON 1818–1830

b. 12 July 1794, 2nd s. of Sir Charles Morgan (formerly Gould), 2nd bt.* (*d.* 1846), and Mary Margaret, da. of Capt. George Stoney, RN; bro. of Charles Morgan Robinson Morgan* and Charles Octavius Swinnerton Morgan†. *educ.* Westminster. *m.* 7 July 1824, Eliza Anne, da. of Rev. William Beville of King Street, Portland Square, Mdx., 3da. *d.v.p.* 25 Aug. 1845.

Ensign 2 Ft. Gds. 1811, lt. and capt. 1815, half-pay 1819.

Sheriff, Herts. 1842-3.

Morgan, an anti-Catholic Tory, had been brought in for Brecon by his father in 1818, when his elder brother Charles stood unsuccessfully for Breconshire. He had supported Lord Liverpool's administration with Sir Charles, but spoke against the proposed equalization of the coal duties that threatened their vested interests in the Monmouthshire borough of Newport. His brother choosing to remain out of Parliament, he came in again for Brecon in 1820 at a cost of £388 9*s*.[1] Toeing the family line, he divided with ministers against censuring their treatment of Queen Caroline, 6 Feb. 1821, and voted against Catholic relief, 28 Feb. 1821, 30 Apr. 1822, 1 Mar, 21 Apr., 10 May 1825, and parliamentary reform, 20 Feb. 1823. He paired against the malt duty repeal bill, 3 Apr. 1821, divided with government on distress and taxation, 11, 21 Feb. 1822, 20 Feb., 18 Mar. 1823, and against condemning the trial in Demerara of the Methodist missionary John Smith, 11 June 1824. His marriage the following month, against which his father received an anonymous letter of protest, followed closely on the passage of their private estate bill, and the Clarke family's Brickendonbury property, inherited by his grandmother Jane Morgan in 1792, was thus settled on him and his bride.[2] They accompanied Sir Charles to county and borough functions in Brecon in 1825, and Morgan was re-elected with great ceremony in June 1826, returning in September for the assizes and corporation dinner, and to patronize the eisteddfod and races.[3] He divided against Catholic relief, 7 Mar. 1827, 12 May 1828, and with the duke of Wellington's ministry against repealing the Test Acts, 26 Feb., and ordnance reductions, 4 July 1828. Opposing the concession of Catholic emancipation with his father in 1829, he presented and endorsed a hostile petition from Brecon, 3 Mar., and voted or paired against the relief bill, 6, 18, 23, 27, 30 Mar.[4] He divided against Lord Blandford's reform proposals, 18 Feb., and Jewish emancipation, 17 May 1830. Calling for the committal of the administration of justice bill, by which Wales's separate judicature and courts of great sessions were abolished, 18 June 1830, he declared that he would support any measure he considered 'favourable to the interests' of the Principality. At the dissolution the following month he stood down to make way for his brother.

Morgan did not stand for Parliament again. In August 1845 he died intestate at Brickendonbury, where he had planted a magnificent avenue of trees known as 'Morgan's Walk'. He was buried in the Clarke family vault at All Saints, Hertford. Administration of his personal estate, sworn under £5,000, was granted to his widow, who in 1855 married Captain Claridge, the promoter of hydrotherapy. His nephew the 2nd Baron Tredegar sold Brickendonbury in lots between 1878 and 1883.[5]

[1] *HP Commons, 1790-1820*, iv. 633; *Bristol Mercury*, 21, 28 Feb., 13 Mar. 1820; NLW, Tredegar mss 45/1704, 1705-26. [2] R.D. Rees, 'Parl. Rep. S. Wales, 1790-1830' (Reading Univ. Ph.D. thesis, 1962), 415; Tredegar mss 20/34; 57/48-53, 451. [3] *Cambrian*, 1, 8 Oct. 1825, 3, 17 June, 30 Sept.; *Hereford Jnl.* 3, 21 June; *Bristol Mercury*, 9 Oct. 1826. [4] *Cambrian*, 21, 28 Feb. 1829. [5] *Hertford Mercury*, 30 Aug., 6 Sept. 1845; *VCH Herts.* iii. 409; PROB 6/222.

M.M.E.

MORISON, John (?1757–1835), of Auchintoul, nr. Aberchirder, Banff. and 16 New Burlington Street, Mdx.

BANFFSHIRE 2 Apr. 1827–1832

b. ?1757, 2nd s. of Alexander Morison (*d.* 1801) of Bognie, nr. Forgue, Aberdeen and Katharine, da. of John Duff of Cowbin. *m.* 1s.; at least 11 illegit. ch. *suc.* bro. Theodore Morison to Bognie and Frendraught 1834. *d.* 12 Feb. 1835.

Morison was descended from a family which had been established in north-west Aberdeenshire since at least the mid-seventeenth century. His great-grandfather George Morison (*d.* 1699) was the third husband of Christian, widow of the 2nd Lord Rutherfurd and the 2nd Viscount Frendraught. After the death of her unmarried only son, the 3rd Viscount Frendraught, she conveyed to George Morison the lands of Bognie and Frendraught in the parish of Forgue, near Huntly. Morison was succeeded by his only son Theodore (*d.* 1760), and he in turn by his son Alexander (*b.* ?1723), the father of this Member. His eldest son Theodore succeeded him as owner of the Aberdeenshire estates on his death in September 1801.[1] His third son, George, died in London in 1820. The youngest, James Morison (1770-1840), achieved wealth and notoriety as the self-styled 'hygeist', the inventor and purveyor of 'Morison's Pills', a drastic purgative made mostly of gamboges, which became very popular as a universal medicine in the 1820s but was often lethal when taken in excessive quantities by the infirm or seriously ill.[2] John Morison's life before he became a parliamentary candidate remains largely obscure, but he is known to have been sometime a merchant at Riga, on the Baltic, in partnership with his brother James and one Drachenham. It was there that his 'only legitimate son' Alexander (who entered Trinity College, Cambridge in 1820 and Lincoln's Inn in 1822) was born in about 1802.[3] By Michaelmas 1811 he was on the freeholders' roll of Banffshire as the proprietor (by purchase) of the estate of Auchintoul.[4] In April 1825 he declared his intention of standing for the county at the next election, and he duly did so when Parliament was dissolved in June 1826, backed by the Tories Colonel Francis Grant* and the 4th duke of Gordon. He made no reported political pronouncements and was defeated by the sitting Member Lord Fife, but was seated on his petition claiming a majority of legal votes in April 1827.[5]

Morison was almost entirely inconspicuous in the 1826 Parliament. He voted with the Wellington ministry against inquiry into chancery delays, 24 Apr., and presented a constituency petition for the continuance of the herring bounties, 12 May 1828. As expected, he divided for the government's concession of Catholic emancipation, 30 Mar. 1829, though he was reported to have stated in the House earlier that day that he would 'vote against' it. He was returned unopposed at the 1830 general election, after which ministers listed him as one of their 'friends'. It was almost certainly James Morrison rather than he who voted in Parnell's minority of 39 for reduction of the duty on wheat imported to the West Indies, 12 Nov. He was absent from the division on the civil list three days later which brought down the government.[6] He also absented himself from the divisions on the second reading of the Grey ministry's English reform bill, 22 Mar., and Gascoyne's wrecking amendment, 19 Apr. 1831. According to his constituent John Macpherson Grant, the son of George Macpherson Grant* of Ballindalloch, on the first occasion

> he was actually in the House ... but went home ... on the pretence of age and indifferent health ... The real cause ... I suspect to be a fear of offending by his vote whichever way it was given. Colonel Grant had been attacking him warmly for some time, which terrified him from voting for the bill, and the knowledge that ... many of his constituents were favourable to it had made him afraid of voting against it. I had a note from him next morning expressing a wish to see me ... He seemed to be all in a *fidget* ... and ready to speak on any subject but the bill. I ... let him know what I thought of the measure and of his own shilly shally conduct and sounded the alarm of an early dissolution in his ears.[7]

George Ferguson† of Pitfour, who had the support of Colonel Grant and the 5th duke of Gordon, declared his candidature for the next election in the second week of April, but Morison's wife (whose identity is unknown) told him that her husband had 'no intention of giving up'; he publicly confirmed this a week later. John Macpherson Grant, a reformer, speculated that if Morison, 'a perfect cipher' in Parliament, lost Colonel Grant's backing, he might start his 'indolent and careless' son Alexander, who had moved the resolutions approving reform at the recent county meeting (Morison presented its petition on 20 Apr.)[8] When Parliament was dissolved a few days later Morison stood his ground and claimed the support of local reformers. On 4 May he wrote to *The Times* to contradict its designation of him as being 'against' reform: 'I never voted against the reform bill, but, on the contrary, I am decidedly in favour of it'. In a riposte the following day Ferguson, who also claimed to be 'a reformer', commented that this would come as a surprise to Morison's constituents, whose interests had gone effectively unrepresented in the last Parliament.[9]

Morison secured the support of John Macpherson Grant and other reformers, declared under questioning at the election meeting that he was 'a favourer of the bill' and approved of the disfranchisement of 'rotten boroughs', the enfranchisement of large towns and an extension of the franchise, but said he disliked the proposed £10 Scottish county voting qualification. He defeated Ferguson by seven votes in a poll of 33.[10]

Morison was barely more active than previously in the 1831 Parliament. He paired for the second reading of the reintroduced English reform bill, 6 July, for its details in at least three divisions and for its passage, 21 Sept. He was present to vote against use of the 1831 census to determine the disfranchisement schedules, 19 July, and for clause 15, giving urban freeholders a county vote, 17 Aug. 1831. His next known votes were not until those for the enfranchisement of Tower Hamlets, 28 Feb., and Gateshead, 5 Mar., and the third reading of the revised English reform bill, 22 Mar. 1832. He was in the minorities for a reduction in the West Indian sugar duties, 7 Mar., and against the malt drawback bill, 2 Apr. He voted for the address calling on the king to appoint only ministers who would carry reform unimpaired, 10 May. He divided against increasing the Scottish county representation, 1 June, and presented a Banff reform petition, 4 June. He was in the government majorities on the Russian-Dutch loan, 12, 20 July 1832.

By then he was in severe financial trouble, with 'great' debts, which forced him to sell his Banffshire property. He retired from Parliament at the 1832 dissolution. His much altered will of 25 July 1830 reveals a notably unconventional and disordered private life. He left all his real and personal estate, except his 'small remaining property in Russia', to Alexander, but made provision for a battery of his bastards produced by various women: five by Sarah Cole of Southampton Row, Marylebone, whom he was thinking of 'perhaps legitimating by acknowledging a marriage' with her; a 'natural son Alexander', currently thought to be at Riga; two children with Menzies Munro; two with Matilda Palmer of Fordyce, and one with Mary White of Brompton, Middlesex. His personalty was sworn under £4,000 in the province of Canterbury, 23 July 1835, but a marginal note of 1846 on the death duty register entry indicates that liabilities amounted to £18,254.[11] Morison nominally succeeded his brother Theodore to the entailed Aberdeenshire estates in October 1834, but he died four months later and it was his legitimate son Alexander who was served heir of line to Bognie on 4 Dec. 1835.

[1] A. Jervise, *Epitaphs and Inscriptions from North East Scotland*, ii. 170, 172, 180. [2] Ibid. ii. 180; *Gent. Mag.* (1840), ii. 437-8; *The Times*, 28 Nov., 1 Dec. 1835, 19 Feb., 8 Nov. 1836, 3, 4 Sept. 1838, 11 May 1840; *Oxford DNB*. [3] Jervise, ii. 180; PROB 11/1849/441; *Admissions to Trinity Coll. Camb.* iv. 179. [4] *Pol. State of Scotland 1811*, p. 26. [5] *Aberdeen Jnl.* 20 Apr. 1825, 14, 21 June, 5 July 1826; *Caledonian Mercury*, 5 Apr. 1827. [6] *The Times*, 22 Nov. 1830. [7] Macpherson Grant mss 361, J. to G. Macpherson Grant, 2/4 Apr. 1831. [8] Ibid. 118, Ferguson's circular, 10 Apr.; 361, J. to G. Macpherson Grant, 19 Apr.; *Aberdeen Jnl.* 27 Apr. 1831. [9] *The Times*, 4-6 May 1831. [10] *Aberdeen Jnl.* 25 May 1831. [11] Jervise, ii. 180; PROB 11/1849/441; IR26/1392/331.

D.R.F.

MORLAND, Sir Scrope, 4th bt. (1758–1830), of Kimble and Nether Winchendon, Bucks. and 50 Pall Mall, Mdx.

AYLESBURY	16 Feb. 1789–1802
ST. MAWES	1806–14 Apr. 1808
ST. MAWES	28 Feb. 1809–18 Apr. 1830

b. 1 Oct. 1758, in New Jersey,[1] 3rd s. of Sir Francis Bernard, 1st bt. (*d.* 1779), of Nettleham, Lincs, gov. New Jersey, 1758-60, and Amelia, da. of Stephen Offley of Norton Hall, Derbys. *educ.* Harrow 1774-5; Christ Church, Oxf. 1775, BA 1779, MA 1781, DCL 1788. *m.* 26 July 1785, Hannah, da. and h. of William Morland† of Lee, Kent, 5s. (2 *d.v.p.*) 2da. Took name of Morland by royal lic. 15 Feb. 1811; *suc.* bro. Sir Thomas Bernard, 3rd bt., of Nether Winchendon as 4th bt. 1 July 1818. *d.* 18 Apr. 1830.

Private sec. to ld. lt. [I] Sept. 1782-Apr. 1783, Nov. 1787-June 1789; sec. to commn. of inquiry into public offices 1785-6; gentleman usher of black rod [I] 1787-9; under-sec. of state for home affairs June 1789-Aug. 1792; adv. Doctors' Commons 1789-1801; chan. eccles. ct. of Durham 1795-1818.

Capt. Bucks. militia 1786, Aylesbury vols. 1803.

Trustee, County Fire Office 1807, Provident Life Office 1812.

From 1819 Morland, a substantial Buckinghamshire landowner, was head of the London banking house of Morlands, Auriol and Company at 50 Pall Mall, after the dissolution of his partnership in his father-in-law's establishment of Ransom, Hammersley and Morland. His new partners were James Peter Auriol and George Duckett, former Member for Lymington and Plympton. From 1825, when Morland took in his then second surviving son Thomas as a partner, the firm was styled Morlands and Company.[2] Morland was a member of the small Grenvillite parliamentary squad, having acted as secretary, banker and factotum to his county neighbour the 1st marquess of Buckingham for over 30 years until his death in 1813. The 2nd marquess, who virtually inherited Morland as a family heirloom, hypocritically commented in 1823 that his 'sole object has been ... to fasten ... [his] family on the country for the longest possible space of time'. On his retirement as under-secretary at the home office in 1792 he had received a pension of £554, which he transferred to his wife; and his period of service under Buckingham in Ireland had furnished him with the Irish half-pay agency, worth £600 a year, which he made over to Thomas and his elder brother Francis.[3]

Buckingham returned him again for his borough of St. Mawes at the general election of 1820, when, as usual, he was obliged to attend the formalities.[4] His 'few words' on a patents bill, 14 June, were inaudible in the gallery.[5] The death of his eldest son William at Caen in November 1820 hit him hard; and at this time he watched nervously from the bank, where he was alone with a skeleton staff, the mobs celebrating the abandonment of the bill of pains and penalties against Queen Caroline.[6] He voted in defence of ministers' conduct towards her, 6 Feb. 1821. His comments on the Grampound disfranchisement bill, 12 Feb., escaped the reporters.[7] He divided, as previously, for Catholic relief, 28 Feb. He voted with the Liverpool ministry against repeal of the additional malt duty, 3 Apr., and parliamentary reform, 9 May, for the duke of Clarence's grant, 18 June, and against a call for economy and retrenchment, 27 June; but he was in the minority, with other Grenvillites, for Buckingham's brother Lord Nugent's motion for inquiry into the administration of justice in Tobago, 6 June, when he also spoke in support of compensation for American loyalists. He voted against mitigation of the punishment for forgery, 23 May. On his pet subject, the national lottery, he advocated reducing the number of tickets and restricting draws to two a year, 29 June 1821.[8] At the county quarter sessions in October 1821 he was one of the Grenvillite majority who defeated a proposal to place advertisements in the newly founded Whig *Buckinghamshire Chronicle*.[9]

Morland divided against more extensive tax reductions, 11, 21 Feb. 1822, by when the Grenvillites had coalesced with the ministry, earning Buckingham a dukedom. He suffered a further personal tragedy with the death of his wife on 4 Mar.[10] The following month his son Thomas went to Ireland in a futile bid to secure redress from the viceroy, Lord Wellesley, for his and his brother's loss of income following reform of the half-pay regulations.[11] Resuming parliamentary attendance late in the session, Morland voted against repeal of the salt tax, 28 June, for the Canada bill, 18 July, and, in accordance with Buckingham's directive, for the aliens bill, 19 July.[12] He divided for abolition of the lottery tax, 1 July, and in the minority of 11 against the third reading of the lottery bill, 24 July. On 22 July 1822 he spoke and voted for items in the Irish estimates.[13] He voted with government against inquiry into the parliamentary franchise, 20 Feb., and on the sinking fund, 3, 13 Mar. 1823. That month he got himself in 'a great pucker', as Buckingham put it, for fear that he had gone too far in telling the duke's toady William Fremantle* of his objections to being involved in direct dealings with his nephew White, to whose ailing newspaper Buckingham wished his friends to subscribe. The duke told Fremantle:

> I believe the poor fellow's greatest crime (and a greater crime cannot exist in Morland's eyes) is his owing said Morland money ... If I am disappointed in White and he turns out a *dishonest* man or anything except an *extravagant* man (a very murderer in the eyes of Bernard would be more innocent) I shall be surprised.[14]

Morland presumably complied with Buckingham's request for his attendance to oppose inquiry into the game laws, 13 Mar., though in the event there was no division.[15] He divided with administration for the grant for Irish glebe houses, 11 Apr., and against repeal of the Foreign Enlistment Act, 16 Apr., and inquiry into the prosecution of the Dublin Orange rioters, 22 Apr. He was one of the minority of 16 who opposed the decision to drop proceedings against O'Grady of the Irish exchequer court, 9 July 1823. He voted against the production of information on Catholic office-holders, 19 Feb., and reform of Edinburgh's representation, 26 Feb. 1824. He spoke in defence of the grant for propagation of the gospels in the colonies, 12 Mar. He divided for repeal of the usury laws, 8 Apr. 1824, 17 Feb. 1825. Like other Grenvillites, he was an 'accidental' absentee from the division on the state of Ireland, 11 May.[16] He voted against inquiry into the prosecution of the Methodist missionary John Smith in Demerara, 11 June 1824. At the end of the year he evidently got the impression that Buckingham was disposed to 'blame' him, as the 'principal creditor' of distressed fishermen at St. Mawes, for any discontent which might occur there; but the duke disclaimed any such intention.[17] Morland welcomed Fyshe Palmer's bill to empower magistrates to effect exchanges of land between counties for administrative purposes, 22 Feb. 1825.[18] He voted for the Irish unlawful societies bill, 25 Feb., Catholic claims, 1 Mar., 21 Apr., 10 May, and the duke of Cumberland's annuity bill, 10 June 1825. His only known votes in 1826 were for the president of the board of trade's ministerial salary, 10 Apr., and against the spring guns bill, 21 Apr. Buckingham brought him in again for St. Mawes at the general election that year.[19]

Morland voted for Catholic relief, 6 Mar., and the Clarence annuity bill, 16 Mar. He was in the minority of 18 against the spring guns bill, 30 Mar. He voted against the corn bill, 2 Apr., and in the small Tory minority against the Coventry magistracy bill, 11 June 1827. He was one of the half dozen Members who Buckingham was anxious to see muster '*en masse*' against a threatened 'side wind' strike against Catholic relief that month.[20] He voted for repeal of the Test Acts, 26 Feb., and Catholic relief, 12 May 1828. That session he successfully opposed, on behalf of the Irish Society of London, the salmon fisheries bill, which sought to impose nationally uniform open seasons.[21] On 28 Mar. he urged the speedy passage of the steam-boat passengers regulation bill to forestall evasion by unscrupulous operators. He was in the minority of nine for repeal of the 1827 Act prohibiting the use of ribbons at elections, 20 Mar. He voted against throwing the corrupt borough of East Retford into the hundred of Bassetlaw, 21 Mar., and with the Wellington ministry on the ordnance estimates, 4 July 1828. In November 1828 he was the recipient of a letter from Buckingham, who was in Rome, expressing approval of his Members' political conduct in the last session and warning them not to be seduced into following the line of his rabidly anti-Catholic son Lord Chandos*. He showed it '*in confidence*' to Fremantle. Before the month was out his health, which had been indifferent for some time, took a momentarily alarming turn for the worse, but he recovered.[22]

In mid-January 1829 Morland, who was now almost 'the only remnant of the Grenville party in Parliament', received from Buckingham a letter stating that

> the mode of conduct will please me best as pursued by my friends which will lead in the straightest ... manner to the speediest removal of the Catholic disabilities. There are certain points, which I shall be glad to see joined to the measure as *securities*, but I will not endanger the loss of the measure on account of them ... You are authorized and I request you to state to my friends that such are my wishes ... and that such is the line which I am most desirous of seeing acted upon.

Passing the letter on to Sir Thomas Fremantle*, whom he asked to keep its contents to himself, Morland commented that it showed

> how strongly and entirely it is wished that we should support the Catholic question. Upon foreign politics we are free to oppose if we choose, where *weak* measures are the consequence of our situation with Ireland. Upon all other topics we may give general support, using our discretion as last winter.[23]

The following month he was instructed by Buckingham to assure the duke of Wellington that he had not been party to Chandos's assertion of his pretensions to the Irish lord lieutenancy.[24] He of course voted for Catholic emancipation, 6, 30 Mar. He presented Cornish petitions for retention of the export bounty on pilchards, 26 Mar., 2 June. He supported inquiry into the regulations concerning patents, 9 Apr., presented a Rotherhithe petition against the local poor rates bill, 15 Apr., and seconded a wrecking amendment to Hobhouse's bill to reform St. James's vestry, 21 May 1829. By now Morland, turned 70 and in declining health, had largely left the affairs of the bank in the hands of others.[25] He voted against Lord Blandford's reform scheme, 18 Feb., and the enfranchisement of Birmingham, Leeds and Manchester, 23 Feb. 1830. He was, however, 'much harassed by the incessant late hours to which the debates extended', and, after a short illness, he died at 50 Pall Mall in April 1830.[26] According to a rather fanciful obituary

> his abilities were of a very superior order. He was a sound classical scholar, and possessed a fund of practical knowledge, which ... was always ready to be communicated with singular affability and promptitude ... Unassuming and unostentatious, Sir Scrope passed much of his time, and more particularly in the evening of his days, in retirement: but, if he felt no anxiety to distinguish himself in the bustle of public life, he was ever ready to devote his services to the public advantage.[27]

He left no completed extant will, having made and cancelled at least three during his life, and 'left one commenced at his death'. In an amicable suit in the prerogative court, 27 July 1830, the validity of a will of 1788 was tested: it was ruled invalid and Morland deemed to have died intestate. His personalty was put at £10,000 and his real estate at £16,000.[28] He was succeeded in the latter and the baronetcy by his son Francis (1790-1876), whose partnership with Duckett in the bank ended in its failure in March 1832.[29] Francis was succeeded by his brother Thomas Tyringham (1791-1883), who retained the family's original surname of Bernard and was Conservative Member for Aylesbury, 1857-65. On his death the baronetcy became extinct.

[1] Bucks. RO, Spencer Bernard mss D/SB OE 10/1(b). [2] *VCH Bucks*. ii. 301, 305, 332; iv. 120-1; G. Lipscomb, *Bucks*. i. 530; ii. 351; S.E. Napier Higgins, *Bernards of Abington and Nether Winchendon*, iii. 78, 148, 159; iv. 247-8, 307; F.G. Hilton Price, *London Bankers*, 118, 135. [3] J.J. Sack, *The Grenvillites*, 43; Higgins, iv. 279; *Black Bk.* (1823), 178. [4] Spencer Bernard mss PF1/2(a), diary, 3, 11 Mar.; *West Briton*, 17 Mar. 1820. [5] *The Times*, 15 June 1820. [6] *Gent. Mag.* (1820), ii. 571; Spencer Bernard mss PF1/2(a), diary, 20, 28 Nov., 22, 25 Dec. 1820; Higgins, iv. 265. [7] *The Times*, 13 Feb. 1821. [8] Ibid.

30 June 1821. [9] Bucks. RO, Fremantle mss D/FR/46/9/9. [10] Ibid. 46/10/18. [11] Higgins, iv. 268, 275, 279-87. [12] Fremantle mss 46/12/77. [13] *The Times*, 23 July 1822. [14] Fremantle mss 46/11/71, 72, 75. [15] Ibid. 46/11/78. [16] Buckingham, *Mems. Geo. IV*, ii. 73-75. [17] Spencer Bernard mss PFD8/5, 7. [18] *The Times*, 23 Feb. 1825. [19] Fremantle mss 46/11/118; *West Briton*, 9 June 1826. [20] Fremantle mss 138/28/5. [21] Spencer Bernard mss PF8. [22] Fremantle mss 139/2/2, 4; 139/8/8, 9. [23] Sack, 216; Fremantle mss 139/10/4. [24] Wellington mss WP1/998/13; 1000/29; Higgins, iv. 311. [25] Higgins, iv. 312-13. [26] Spencer Bernard mss P30/42; Higgins, iv. 314. [27] *Gent. Mag.* (1830), i. 466. [28] Ibid. (1830), ii. 98; *The Times*, 28 July 1830. [29] Higgins, iv. 315; Hilton Price, 118.

D.R.F.

MORRISON, James (1789–1857), of Balham Hill, Surr. and The Pavilion, Fonthill, nr. Hindon, Wilts.

ST. IVES	1830–1831
IPSWICH	1831–1834
IPSWICH	19 June 1835–1837
INVERNESS BURGHS	4 Mar. 1840–1847

bap. 6 Sept. 1789, 2nd s. of Joseph Morrison (*d.* 1804), innkeeper of *The George*, Middle Wallop, Wilts., and Sarah, da. of Thomas Barnard, yeoman, of Shapwick, Som. *m.* 6 Aug. 1814, Mary Ann, da. of Joseph Todd, haberdasher, of Fore Street, Cripplegate, London, 7s. (1 *d.v.p.*) 4da. (1 *d.v.p.*). *d.* 30 Oct. 1857.

Sir John Bowring†, a fellow liberal and merchant, recalled how Morrison, who at his death was almost certainly the nineteenth century's richest commoner

> told me that he owed all his prosperity to the discovery that the great art of mercantile traffic was to find out sellers rather than buyers; that if you bought cheap, and satisfied yourself with only a fair profit, buyers – the best sort of buyers, those who have money to buy – would come of themselves. He said he found houses engaged with a most expensive machinery, sending travellers about in all directions to seek orders and to effect sales, while he employed travellers to buy instead of to sell, and, if they bought well, there was no fear of his effecting advantageous sales. So, uniting this theory with another, that small profits and quick returns are more profitable in the long run than long credits with great gains, he established one of the largest and most lucrative concerns that has ever existed in London, and was entitled to a name which I have often heard applied to him, 'the Napoleon of shopkeepers'.[1]

Morrison grew up in Middle Wallop, where his paternal grandfather, a Scot by origin, had settled in the early eighteenth century. His mother died in 1803 and his father, then aged 73, the following year, leaving personal estate valued at under £400 for his four children. The family remained in Middle Wallop but James is said to have been sent to his mother's kin in Somerset before being apprenticed to a watchmaker and moving to 'his relatives the Flints', ready-money haberdashers in London.[2] There, according to John Louis Mallet, he

> remodelled the whole system of the shop in a way so advantageous in its results that he naturally expected to become a partner. The Flints would not, however, do it, so he quitted them and went into a house of the same description, the Todds in Fore Street, Cripplegate. There, being a handsome as well as a clever man, he soon made himself necessary, and captivated Miss Todd, whom he married, and was taken in partnership.[3]

In 1817 he travelled in France, where he made useful contacts in the glove and silk trades; and in 1818, when Todd, Morrison and Company's annual turnover was over £650,000, he became the sole managing partner.[4] He bought and made Balham Hill his home in 1821; and following a legal battle with John Todd in 1824 he bought out his father-in-law 'by instalments', re-establishing the firm as James Morrison and Company in partnership (until 1829) with George Crow, John Dillon and Richard Pearson.[5] Although largely self-taught, he made time to read and to associate with other radicals and liberals in the City and at the Charing Cross tailor Francis Place's library, and he subscribed to and gave advice on the Greek loans.[6] When the poet Robert Southey*, who described him as the 'most interesting stranger who has found his way here', met him in the Lake District in 1823, he was on his way to New Lanark, 'with the intention of investing £5,000 in [Robert] Owen's experiment'. Southey noted that he had already 'realised some £150,000 in trade' and was

> well acquainted with the principal men among the free thinking Christians. He likes the men, but sees reason to doubt their doctrine. He seems to be searching for truth in such a temper of mind that there is good reason for thinking he will find it.[7]

He remained a lifelong member of the Church of England.[8]

He first became a parliamentary candidate in September 1825, when the radical Joseph Hume*, who turned it down, recommended him and another liberal merchant, Charles Poulett Thomson*, for Dover.[9] They canvassed avidly, paying particular attention to the London voters, to whom Morrison was introduced as 'a man of business like themselves, who by mere force of talent and intellect had raised and directed one of the most extensive businesses which this kingdom or perhaps the world could produce'.[10] In a joint address, he and Poulett Thomson promised that 'our public conduct will be guided by the endeavour to produce the greatest sum of happiness to our fellow men', by promoting civil and religious freedom, reform of abuses and retrenchment. They praised liberal Toryism and the president of the board of trade Huskisson's commercial policy.[11] Morrison's withdrawal from Dover in April 1826 was attributed to illness from pressure of work compounded by the 1825-6 banking crisis (which his business interests survived), the appearance of new candidates and a growing awareness that the return of two liberals was unlikely. His announcement specified ill health.[12] Nothing came of invitations to stand for Canterbury and Worcester and, declining Norwich, on 6 June 1826 he made a state entry to Great Marlow, where Thomas Wooler, editor of the *Black Dwarf*, had spotted a late opportunity to undermine the Williams interest.[13] He hoped that his business connections with Barclay, Gurney and Young would procure him votes through their influence on Marlow's local brewers Wethered; but, branded an atheist because he supported religious liberty, and denied access to the *Crown* inn, he came bottom of the poll.[14] He supported Waithman's candidature for the City and continued to cultivate an interest at Marlow, where he denounced the 'monopoly of local power' exercised by the Williamses 'to the prejudice of the electors'.[15]

Combining mercantile interests with the pursuit of knowledge and self-improvement, Morrison took his family to Naples in January 1827 and Carlsbad in 1828, paid £16,500 that year for a 400-acre estate and oyster bed at Wallasea, Essex and rented The Pavilion at Fonthill from George Mortimer for the summer of 1829.[16] He had recently been appointed to the council and the buildings, library and hospital committees of University College, London, and he also joined the Society of Useful Knowledge's publications committee.[17] Anticipating a dissolution, he canvassed Marlow in May and June 1830, but 'his principles as a radical and a reformer' were 'fighting a losing battle with his political enthusiasms and his political ambitions', and he withdrew when consultations with the London constituency broker Isaac Sewell revealed a better prospect at St. Ives, where William Pole Tylney Long Wellesley* had purchased Sir Christopher Hawkins's* properties with a view to returning himself and a candidate able to advance most of the purchase price as a mortgage.[18] The precise cost of Morrison's election is not known, but after legal action had been taken against Hawkins (because there was a contest), he held mortgages 'for some £50,000 on various Wellesley estates'.[19] He had toyed with Sudbury, where he could rely on the support of the silk merchant Alexander Duff, but appears to have offered his influence there to the Tory Sir John Benn Walsh*, whose pamphlet on Irish poverty he admired.[20] On 17 Aug. 1830, he attended the meeting at the *London Tavern* and made a donation to the revolutionary party in France.[21] He negotiated the purchase of the Fonthill Pavilion that autumn, and bought a 1,912-acre estate at Cholsey, near Wallingford for £50,400.[22]

The Wellington ministry counted Morrison, who sat close to but did not vote slavishly with Hume, among their 'foes', and he divided against them when they were brought down on the civil list, 15 Nov. 1830. He spoke infrequently and tended to overburden his speeches with financial detail, but he was respected from the outset as an expert on trade, manufacturing and finance, attended policy meetings in the chancellor of the exchequer Lord Althorp's private rooms and was appointed to the public accounts select committee, 17 Feb. 1831.[23] In his maiden speech, on the barilla duties, 7 Feb. 1831, he defended free trade, described the improvements in the glove and silk trades since restrictions had been lifted under the 1824 Act and referred to the current absence of weavers in Spitalfields workhouse among its benefits. He criticized Waithman's trade resolutions, which assumed that government figures on imports and exports, 1799-1830, did not represent the real value of manufactured goods, 15 Feb. Countering them, he attributed current difficulties to the 'present impolitic system of corn laws', complained that Members consistently failed to distinguish between articles of commerce and manufacture and said that too little attention had been paid to the seasonality of distress and inevitable fluctuations in trade. He also maintained that the manufacturing districts were doing better than at any time since the Napoleonic wars, that there was less insolvency among the middle classes and that 'the return to cash payments was one of the most stupendous undertakings ever devised'. 'The proper question,' he added, 'is not whether the people can pay the taxes, but whether the ministers can do without them'. He condemned the prohibition of machinery exports as 'a bounty on the manufacture of foreign machinery'; argued that domestic manufacture had not been harmed by the importation of quality silks from Lyons and that lower taxes on wine would not help the poor while tea and sugar were 'taxed heavily in every cottage in England', and called for a penny in the pound reduction in the sugar duties to assist the poor. The Member for London William Ward and Poulett Thomson praised the speech, but the radical Henry Hunt, while admitting that Morrison's 'experience in commerce is very great', ridiculed his claim that there was less distress. Morrison replied: 'My observations were not general, but merely directed to certain great branches of trade'.[24] He favoured paying wages in cash, but stressed that while he was no apologist for the truck system, he doubted whether it was 'practicable or politic to put an end to ... [it] by legislative enactment', 12 Apr. His votes for the Grey ministry's reform bill at its second reading, 22 Mar., and against Gascoyne's wrecking amendment, 19 Apr. 1831, were criticized in the Cornish press and encouraged opposition to him at St. Ives, which was set to lose a Member by it.[25] Accordingly, after consulting Sewell, who arranged the appropriate introduction to the Quaker banker Henry Alexander, he stood at Ipswich at the general election in May as 'an independent reformer', and came in at a cost of only £1,395, paid through his firm by Dillon, with the barrister Peter Rigby Wason.[26] Mary Ann Morrison had recently complained: 'I shall tire of the House of Commons, it is a great drawback on domestic comforts. With a home in town it might be rather less objectionable'. The only property Morrison purchased that year was the 645-acre Ton Mawr estate near Neath, for £7,740, but early in 1832 he bought a long lease of 95 Upper Harley Street.[27]

He voted for the second reading of the reintroduced reform bill, 6 July, against adjournment, 12 July 1831, and divided steadily for its details. He voted for the bill's passage, 21 Sept., and Lord Ebrington's confidence motion, 10 Oct. 1831. Unlike Wason, one of its chief advocates, he voted in the minority against suspending the Liverpool writ, 5 Sept. He divided for the second reading of the revised reform bill, 17 Dec. 1831, its details and its third reading, 22 Mar. 1832. He voted for the address calling on the king to appoint only ministers who would pass the bill unimpaired, 10 May, and celebrated its enactment with a reform festival at Fonthill.[28] He voted against a Conservative amendment to the Scottish reform bill, 1 June, but in a minority of 23 for amending the boundary bill to neutralize Lord Lonsdale's influence in Whitehaven, 22 June. He was in the government majority on the Russian-Dutch loan, 26 Jan., for which he also paired, 12 July, but voted against them on the malt drawback bill, 29 Feb., and paired against their amendment to Buxton's motion for a select committee on colonial slavery, 24 May. He voted against Baring's privileges of Parliament bill, 6 June. On the coroners' bill, he was in a minority of 11 for Hume's amendment requiring coroners to be medically qualified, 20 June 1832, and voted the same day for inquests to be made public.

Morrison was appointed to select committees on the East India Company, 27 Jan., the silk trade, 5 Mar., and renewal of the Bank of England's charter, 23 May 1832. His contributions to debate again reflected his trading interests and mercantile expertise. He repeated his support for fixed duties on corn when Lord Milton called for a report on foreign prices, 24 June. He spoke for inquiry into distress in the glove trade, which he attributed to the change in fashion from beaver to kid, lower exports to America and greater use of cotton gloves, 31 Jan. According to Thomas Raikes, when later that evening he asked the Tory whip William Homes for a 'pair', the latter quipped, 'Of what ... gloves or stockings?'[29] He did not vote for inquiry into the effect of smuggling on the glove trade, which Hume advocated and Poulett Thomson opposed, 3 Apr., but he said that he considered the trade a 'good market for the manufacturer' as payments could be expected at the end of each month, saw little advantage for smugglers as stock levels were satisfactory and that the problem lay in the duty imposed on French dressed leather: if this was removed, 'we should fairly be able to compete with the foreign glover; and yet, strange enough, this is a thing that our manufacturers have never asked for'. Hume agreed, but Waithman sought to belittle his remarks by recalling how he had been advised by Morrison to buy French gloves at *12s.6d.* or *13s.* a dozen and sell them at a shilling a pair as a means of advertising; this Morrison naturally denied.[30] He spoke briefly in praise of the Scottish practice when the House considered the regulation of child labour, 1 Feb., and briefly backed Wason's proposal for a bill giving Ipswich the right to hold the Suffolk assizes alternately with Bury St. Edmunds, 3 July 1832.

Standing as a Liberal, Morrison topped the poll at Ipswich in 1832, and he was returned there again at a by-election in 1835 after the poll at the general election was voided.[31] Nominated by James Ramsay McCulloch, he joined the Political Economy Club in March 1834, and became a founder committee member in 1836 of the Reform Club with William Ewart*, whose commitment to establishing a school of industrial design and a national gallery he shared.[32] He decided against contesting Ipswich and Hull in 1837, was defeated at the Sudbury by-election in December that year, but returned to the House in 1840 as Member for Inverness Burghs, where he stood at the invitation of Edward Ellice*.[33] Now a spokesman for railway regulation, Morrison published *Observations Illustrative of the Defects of the English System of Railway Legislation* (1846) and *The Influence of English Railway Legislation on Trade and Industry* (1848).[34] He had established the merchant bank Morrison, Cryder and Company in 1836 and the family partnership of Morrison, Sons and Company in 1841, with his eldest son Charles Morrison

(1817-1909), the senior partner in their American business ventures. In 1850 he made over the Fonthill estate to his second son Alfred Morrison (1821-97).[35] He died in October 1857 at Basildon Park, his 2,500-acre estate near Reading, purchased for £76,000 (plus £21,000 for the timber) in 1838, having provided generously for his widow, large family and McCulloch.[36] Contemporaries and historians have estimated Morrison's wealth at death at between £4,000,000 and £6,000,000. In addition to personalty of £942,106 bequeathed to Charles Morrison, London property, a valuable art collection and over £800,000 in American securities, he owned over 100,000 acres in estates in Berkshire, Buckinghamshire, Essex, Glamorgan, Hampshire, Kent, Middlesex, Oxfordshire, Surrey, Sussex, Wiltshire, Yorkshire and Scotland.[37] According to his obituary in *The Times*:

> His great merit was that he made the fortunes of many other City men ... There was no trade of which he did not find out the trickery and guard himself against its consequences.[38]

[1] W.D. Rubinstein, 'British Millionaires, 1809-1949', *BIHR*, xlvii (1974), 207 and 'Victorian Middle Classes' *EcHR* (ser. 2), xxx (1977), 610-11; M.J. Daunton, 'Gentlemanly Capitalism and British Industry, 1820-1914', *P and P*, cxxii (1989), 138-40; Bowring, *Autobiog. Recollections*, 58. [2] R. Gatty, *Portrait of a Merchant Prince, James Morrison, 1790-1857*, pp. 1-9, 16. [3] *Pol. Economy Club* (1921), 255. [4] Ibid. 9-20; *Dict. Business Biog.* iv. 341-5 (Charles Morrison). [5] Gatty, 20, 28-30; *The Gazette*, 18 Dec. 1829. [6] Gatty, 55. [7] *Southey's Life and Corresp.* (1849), v. 144-5. [8] *Oxford DNB*. [9] *Kentish Chron.* 9, 23, 30 Sept.; *Kentish Gazette*, 20 Sept. 1825. [10] *The Times*, 27, 29 Sept.; *Morning Chron.* 29 Sept.; *Kent Herald*, 29 Sept. 1825. [11] *Kent Herald*, 22 Sept. 1825. [12] Ibid. 20, 27 Apr. 1826 [13] *Kentish. Chron.* 4 Apr.; *Norwich Mercury*, 3, 10 June; *Bucks. Beds. and Herts. Chron.* 10 June 1826; Add. 40387, ff. 78, 88, 90. [14] *The Times*, 12, 13, 20, 22 June; *Bucks. Beds. and Herts. Chron.* 17 June, 1 July 1826; Gatty, 66-70. [15] *The Times*, 12 May; *Bucks. Beds. and Herts. Chron.* 4 Aug. 1827. [16] Gatty, 88-101, 307. [17] Univ. Coll. London Archives, College corresp. 915 (28 Dec. 1828); Add. 38758, f. 52. [18] Gatty, 70, 104-5; *West Briton*, 23, 30 July, 13 Aug.; *R. Cornw. Gazette*, 24, 31 July, 7, 14 Aug. 1830, 26 Mar. 1831. [19] Gatty, 106-7; *R. Cornw. Gazette*, 26 Mar. 1831. [20] NLW, Ormathwaite mss FG1/5, p. 87. [21] *The Times*, 18 Aug. 1830. [22] Gatty, 108-121, 307. [23] *Althorp Letters*, 239; *Three Diaries*, 378. [24] *The Times*, 19 Jan., 16 Feb. 1831. [25] *R. Cornw. Gazette*, 26 Mar., 25 Apr. 1831. [26] *The Times*, 28 Apr.; *Suff. Chron.* 7 May 1831; R. Wason, *A short and sure way of preventing bribery at elections*, 4. [27] Gatty, 122-3, 307. [28] Ibid. 117. [29] *Raikes Jnl.* i. 11-12. [30] Gatty, 76. [31] *Ipswich Jnl.* 15 Dec. 1832; N. Gash, *Politics in Age of Peel*, 156. [32] Gatty, 155-7; *Pol. Economy Club*, 360. [33] Gatty, 195-9; 'Sudbury Borough' (ms *penes* A.T. Copsey in 1991). [34] F.W. Fetter, 'Influence of Economists in Parliament on British Legislation', *Jnl. of Pol. Econ.* lxxxiii (1975), 1051-64. [35] Gatty, 185, 307. [36] *Gent. Mag.* (1857), ii. 681-3; *Illustrated London News*, xxxi (1857), 458. [37] IR26/2138/65-72; W.D. Rubinstein, 'New Men of Wealth and the Purchase of Land in 19th Cent. Britain', *P and P*, xcii (1981), 125-47. [38] *The Times*, 2 Nov. 1857.

M.M.E.

MOSTYN, Sir Thomas, 6th bt. (1776–1831), of Mostyn, Flint. and Gloddaeth, Caern.

FLINTSHIRE	8 Nov. 1796–12 June 1797
FLINTSHIRE	8 Nov. 1799–17 Apr. 1831

b. 20 Oct. 1776, o.s. of Sir Roger Mostyn†, 5th bt., of Mostyn and Gloddaeth and Margaret, da. and h. of Rev. Hugh Wynn, DD, preb. of Salisbury, h. of her uncles Robert Wynne† of Bodysgallen, Caern. and Evan Lloyd Vaughan† of Corsygedol, Merion. *educ.* Westminster bef. 1793; Christ Church, Oxf. 1793. *unm.* 1da. illegit. *suc.* fa. as 6th bt. 26 July 1796. *d.* 17 Apr. 1831.

Sheriff, Caern. 1798-9, Merion. 1799-1800.

Lt.-col. commdt. Flint fusiliers 1803.

Mostyn was one of Wales's largest landowners, with estates and influence in Caernarvonshire, Flintshire, Merioneth and elsewhere. His life had long been governed by his passion for the chase, which he pursued in the company of his brother-in-law Sir Edward Pryce Lloyd* and their kinsman, the hunting parson Griffith Lloyd, in North Wales and the Wirral, and as master of the Bicester Hounds in Gloucestershire, Oxfordshire and Warwickshire.[1] His engagement books record more visits to operas and London theatres than to the Commons, where he had represented Flintshire almost continuously since 1796, but he noted the debates and divisions he considered important, dined regularly at Boodle's, and was attuned to the needs of his constituents, whose petitions and business he either attended to quickly himself or delegated to Lloyd. He made no major speeches.[2]

Mostyn apparently failed to sign the requisition for a Flintshire county meeting to mark the death of George III and remained in London until shortly before his election at Flint, 16 Mar. 1820. His addresses contained no statements of policy, but his Whiggism and support for Catholic relief were well known. He afterwards headed the requisition for a meeting to petition for a St. Asaph enclosure bill, and announced a 25 per cent reduction in his rents.[3] In Parliament he divided consistently but sporadically with the Whig opposition to the Liverpool ministry, doing so on the civil list, 5, 8 May, and the appointment of an additional Scottish baron of exchequer, 15 May 1820. He was named to the 1820 and 1821 select committees on the administration of justice in Wales. He remained central to Whig activity in Flintshire, where he presided at the Agricultural Society dinner in October 1820 and attended the assizes and militia exercises.[4] He supported the 1821 parliamentary campaign on behalf of Queen Caroline, divided as hitherto for Catholic relief, 28 Feb. 1821, 21 Apr., 10 May

1825, and paired, 22 Apr. 1822, and voted for parliamentary reform, 2 June 1823. He received a month's leave on account of ill health, 13 Apr. 1821. He voted to omit arrears from the duke of Clarence's grant, 2 July 1821. Later that month Dr. William Browne accused him of abusing his position as a family friend by violating his daughter. Possibly though the intervention of Lord Jersey, Mostyn avoided both marriage and legal action. A bachelor of nearly 45, he already had a 12-year-old daughter, Elizabeth, tucked away at Catherine Cruickshanks's establishment in Boulogne.[5]

He failed to attend the Flintshire agricultural distress meeting, 17 Apr., but he presented their petition for government action, 24 Apr., and voted to repeal the salt tax, 28 June 1822. He had recently divided for reductions in diplomatic expenditure, 16 May, to condemn the growing influence of the crown, 24 June, and for inquiry into the lord advocate's treatment of the Scottish press, 25 June 1822.[6] During the recess he paid the customary £200 a year for Elizabeth's care and prepared for the hunting season, which was marred for him by 'shoulder lameness'.[7] He paired in condemnation of the indictment of the Methodist missionary John Smith in Demerara, 11 June, and divided against the Irish insurrection bill, 18 June 1824, and the duke of Cumberland's annuity, 6 June 1825. He presented the grand jury of Flintshire's petition against repealing the usury laws, 18 Apr. 1826. His return at the general election in June was unopposed, and he afterwards saw to River Dee Company business, in which as the proprietor of the loss making Mostyn Quay, he had a vested interest.[8] He had given his interest in Caernarvon Boroughs to Lord Anglesey, and was to do so again in 1830.[9]

Increasingly troubled by gout, Mostyn now rarely attended the Commons. He presented his constituents' petitions for repeal of the Test Acts, 7 June 1827, 19 Feb. 1828, but is not known to have spoken or voted on the issue. He paired for Catholic relief, 12 May 1828, and presented petitions against restricting the circulation of one and two pound notes, 2 June, and for an increase in coroners' allowances, 7 June 1828. Ill with rheumatism, he ordered Mostyn to be closed and returned to London in February 1829 to monitor the progress of Catholic emancipation, for which he voted, 30 Mar. He frequented the Welsh Club, attended the Commons, 24 Feb., 18 Mar., and presented, but refused to endorse Flintshire anti-Catholic petitions, 26 Feb. Citing 'pressure of business', he declined to attend anti-Catholic meetings, 20 Mar., and the Flintshire Ultras accordingly turned to his brother-in-law Sir Robert Williames Vaughan* for support.[10] Both were distressed by the death following a hunting accident of their nephew Griffith Lloyd, 26 Mar. 1829.[11] Silt had become a persistent problem at Mostyn docks, and Mostyn hoped that the contentious Dee Ferry road, for which he presented petitions, 6 May 1829, would improve the profitability of his iron works and coal and lead mines. The Ultra Commons leader Sir Richard Vyvyan listed him among the supporters of Catholic emancipation whose attitude to a putative coalition government in October 1829 was 'unknown'.

Mostyn spent the summer of 1829 in London and at the races, often in the company of the sisters of William Lewis Hughes*: Mary, with whom his name was now linked, and Martha, the widow of his friend Cynric Lloyd, who later married Colonel Wyatt.[12] He borrowed an additional £120,000 from the Law Life Assurance Society as security for his mortgage debts to Thomas Coutts and Company, 26 Aug., and when he returned to Mostyn in September he found much county business awaiting him and came under pressure to make new arrangements for Elizabeth, who was 21 in November.[13] Before leaving for Leamington, where he took a house for the hunting season, he contributed to local charities and celebrated the birth in December 1829 of his great-nephew, Lloyd's grandson Thomas Edward Mostyn Lloyd (*d.*1861).[14] He was a requisitionist for the Flintshire distress meeting, 8 Feb., and supported their petition; but another adopted by the Holywell vestry troubled him, and he discussed the case with the home secretary Peel before arranging for Lloyd to present both petitions on 15 Mar. 1830.[15] He voted against the proposed expenditure on Woolwich Academy, 30 Apr., and public buildings, 3 May, and for information on privy councillors' emoluments, 14 May. He was said to favour abolition of the Welsh judicature and reform of the assize system, but when the administration of justice bill that effected it was introduced he presented and endorsed Flintshire's hostile petition for continuation of the assizes as hitherto, 12 May. On the hustings at the general election in August 1830 he referred to the 'unpleasant impression' the bill had given and said that he hoped it would prove better than expected.[16] Mostyn's finances remained troubled, and after meetings with his executors, Sir Edward Pryce Lloyd and Richard Parry, and the bankers William Hughes and Owen Williams*, he took out a modified deed to cover an aggregate mortgage debt of £420,000, to which the attorney-general Sir James Scarlett* contributed £60,000, the barrister Thomas Atkinson £45,000 and the queen's solicitor J.W. Farrer £15,000, 30 June.[17] Before the dissolution precipitated by George IV's death, he attended a meeting of the revived Whig opposition at Lord Althorp's*, 5 July, and presented Flintshire's petition against renewing the East India Company's charter, 9 July 1830. On the hustings at Flint, 7 Aug., when he was returned unopposed and every public house was thrown open, he said that he shared local concern over the monopolies of the Bank of England and the East India Company, supported the abolition of slavery, and advocated tax cuts and rigid economy as the only means of bringing back 'the good old times'.[18] After visiting the county sheriff and the bishop of St. Asaph, he attended the opening of the Liverpool-Manchester railway before returning to London, having apparently thwarted his daughter's plan to visit him there while she was in England that summer.[19]

The Wellington ministry listed Mostyn among their 'foes', but he was absent from the division on the civil list which brought them down, 15 Nov. 1830. By February 1831, when Martha Wyatt protested that Mostyn had encouraged gossip that she had colluded in making her sister his resident mistress, he was too ill and dependent on opiates to consider going to the opera or to attend to parliamentary business, which then included the Holyhead roads bill.[20] He had delegated his Flintshire concerns, including reform petitions, to Lloyd; but he went to the Commons, 22 Mar., to vote for the second reading of the Grey ministry's reform bill. His engagement book records his intention of being there when it was considered in committee on 18 Apr., but he died at 10 pm on the 17th of 'gout in the stomach and head'. He had used his seat in church for the first time, 27 Mar. 1831. His body was taken to the family vault at Llanrhos for burial.[21] Prices realized from the sale of his racing stud in July proved disappointing.[22] His will and settlement, dated 26 Aug. 1829, were proved under £60,000 in Flint and London and administered by Richard Parry and Lloyd, to whom he left his estates in trust. Lloyd's eldest son Edward, to whom he left £3,000, succeeded him as Member for Flintshire and took the name of Mostyn as directed. Bequests of £20,000 to his daughter, who married Charles Clements Brooke of Leamington Priors, Warwickshire, £15,000 to Cynric Lloyd, and £10,000 each to his executors, sisters and named nephews and nieces overburdened the Mostyn estates, which were already encumbered by half – yearly mortgage interest payments of £2,400.[23] The baronetcy being extinct, Lloyd was raised to the peerage at the coronation in September 1831 as Baron Mostyn.

[1] T.A. Glenn, *Fam. of Mostyn of Mostyn*, 173-7. [2] UCNW, Mostyn of Mostyn mss 251-64; *HP Commons, 1790-1820*, iv. 641. [3] *Chester Chron.* 25 Feb., 3, 10, 17, 24, 31 Mar., 7 Apr.; Mostyn of Mostyn mss 7898; *Gent. Mag.* (1820), i. 555. [4] *Tracts on Agriculture: Flint Agric. Soc.* (1825), *passim*; *Chester Chron.* 20, 27 Oct. 1820. [5] Mostyn of Mostyn mss 7424-8, 7433. [6] *Salopian Jnl.* 10, 24 Apr. 1822. [7] Mostyn of Mostyn mss 251, 7431. [8] Ibid. 251, 7431. [9] UCNW, Plas Newydd mss i. 228, 248, 287, 382, 410, 434, 457; Mostyn of Mostyn mss 7451. [10] Mostyn of Mostyn mss 256, 7450; *N. Wales Chron.* 26 Feb. 1829. [11] *Shrewsbury Chron.* 3 Apr. 1829. [12] Mostyn of Mostyn mss 257; NLW ms 2795 D, C. to H. Williams Wynn [1826]. [13] Mostyn of Mostyn mss 258, 3417, 7453-5. [14] Ibid. 258; *Chester Courant*, 1, 8 Dec. 1829. [15] Flint RO D/KK/467-9; Mostyn of Mostyn mss 7456-8; *Chester Courant*, 2, 9 Feb. 1830. [16] *PP* (1829), ix. 413; *N. Wales Chron.* 23 Apr. 1829; *Chester Courant*, 10 Aug. 1830. [17] Mostyn of Mostyn mss 263, 3418. [18] Ibid. 263; *Chester Courant*, 10 Aug. 1830. [19] Mostyn of Mostyn mss 7459-61. [20] Ibid. 264, 7464. [21] Ibid. 264, 7902, 7903; *Caernarvon Herald*, 23 Apr.; *Chester Courant*, 26 Apr. 1832. [22] *Chester Courant*, 5 July 1831. [23] PROB 11/1788/407; IR26/1264/316; Mostyn of Mostyn mss 265, 266, 3305, 7477-88; Flint RO, Mostyn mss D/M/3596-9, 3869, 3879, 3870.

M.M.E.

MOSTYN *see also* LLOYD MOSTYN

MOULTON BARRETT, Samuel Barrett (1787–1837), of Carlton Hall, nr. Richmond, Yorks. and 67 Baker Street, Mdx.

RICHMOND 1820–15 Nov. 1827

b. 31 Mar. 1787, in Jamaica, 2nd s. of Charles Moulton, merchant, of Hammersmith, Mdx. and New York and Elizabeth, da. of Edward Barrett of Cinnamon Hill, Jamaica. *educ.* Harrow 1797-8. *m.* (1) 20 Mar. 1823,[1] Mary Clementina (*d.* 3 June 1831), da. of Rev. Henry Cay Adams of Shrewsbury, Salop, *s.p.*; (2) 23 Apr. 1833, Anne Eliza, da. of Hon. William Gordon, *s.p.* Took additional name of Barrett by royal lic. 6 Jan. 1798; *suc.* fa. 1819. *d.* 23 Dec. 1837.

Moulton Barrett's family could trace their origins to Norfolk in the early seventeenth century: one Henry Moulton had established himself as a merchant at Great Yarmouth by 1633. His grandfather Charles Moulton was a captain in the West Indian navy and his maternal grandfather Edward Barrett was the owner of extensive estates in Jamaica, including Cinnamon Hill, where he was born and spent his early years. His family left Jamaica for England when he was eight so that he and his elder brother Edward (1785-1857) could be educated. The brothers inherited the Jamaican estates of Edward Barrett (*d.* c. 1799) and other property in the island from their uncle George Goodin Barrett, who stipulated that they should assume the name of Barrett. From about 1811 Samuel, being more a man of business than his brother, 'shuttled to and fro between England and Jamaica' and became 'the indispensable custodian of the Moulton Barrett interests'. When their father died in July 1819 Samuel was named as his sole heir, on condition that he paid an annuity to his reputed half-sister Frances Petite.[2] Meanwhile, he had purchased Carlton Hall, near Richmond, Yorkshire, where he took up residence in June 1814. He subsequently 'developed rapidly in the public life of Richmondshire', becoming fast friends with Thomas Dundas, Member for Richmond and grandson of the borough's Whig patron Lord Dundas, who nominated him for Brooks's Club, 18 May 1815. In 1818 he and Thomas Dundas undertook a trip to France together, and by the following year he was hopeful that he would be one of the nominees for Richmond at the next general election. He and his friend were duly returned in 1820.[3]

He was a silent Member but an assiduous attender, who voted with the opposition to Lord Liverpool's ministry on all major issues, including parliamentary reform, 9 May 1821, 25 Apr. 1822, 20 Feb., 24 Apr. 1823, 27 Apr. 1826. He divided for Catholic relief, 28 Feb. 1821, 1 Mar., 21 Apr., 10 May 1825. He presided at a Darlington meeting to celebrate the withdrawal of the bill of pains and penalties against Queen Caroline, 14 Nov. 1820, when he 'entered upon an able, comprehensive and animated retrospect of the circumstances in which Her Majesty had been placed since her alliance with the present king'.[4] He briefly kept a parliamentary diary, which he started on 5 Feb. 1822, the opening day of that session, and abandoned in mid-sentence on 18 Apr.[5] It chiefly consists of a précis of each day's main business, listing speakers and the outcome of divisions. Besides commenting on the merits of some speeches, he only occasionally offered any of his own opinions or recorded his reasons for voting as he did. Although he voted against the suspension of habeas corpus, 7 Feb., and the Irish insurrection bill the next day, he noted on the 7th that 'I did not vote throughout with my party, particularly on the clause "for making imperative a trial by jury"', as he was 'of opinion that if the two Acts were necessary any delay that occurred would rather be injurious than beneficial'. He attended 'a great dinner' at Brooks's, given 'in consequence of the secession of the duke of Buckingham ... from the club', 6 Mar., and a week later was present at the Middlesex county meeting, where Sir Francis Burdett* delivered a 'brilliant speech'. On 14 Mar. he recorded that a discussion on public accounts had taken up 'so much time', and left him feeling 'so particularly stupid', that he 'went to dinner at Taylor's' and missed the whole of Creevey's speech on the motion for inquiry into the duties of the board of control. He managed to return to vote in the minority for the motion, but confessed that he had

> felt much inclined ... to have voted against my friends, 1st upon the ground that even upon the shewing of Tierney (formerly president of the board) ... the office required the number of commissioners complained of, and 2nd that the expenses incurred for the maintenance of the board should not fall upon the country, but upon the East India Company. It was mentioned as one of the inducements for consenting to the motion, that the commissioners having seats in the House were a great source of royal influence. Had a distinct proposition been made to disqualify commissioners from having seats, I could have cheerfully supported it, but worded as the motion was, I regretted to give my assent to it, which I only did because Mr. Tierney voted for it.

He presented a petition against the Edinburgh police bill from the tradesmen of the city, 8 Mar. 1822, a York petition against the Insolvent Debtors Act, 14 Mar. 1823, and one from York comb makers against the combination laws, 16 Mar. 1824.[6]

Problems with his Jamaican estates consumed an increasing amount of Moulton Barrett's time. In 1822 he was obliged to take out a mortgage of £30,000 to cover debts on the estates he had inherited from his uncle, and a dispute with his cousins over this inheritance in 1824 cost him a further £20,000. As his position worsened he realized that he needed to take personal charge, and during the recess of 1825-6 he and Edward visited Jamaica.[7] He was returned again for Richmond at the general election of 1826, but his only known vote in the new Parliament was in the minority for inquiry into Leicester corporation, 15 Mar. 1827. Further complications forced his return to Jamaica, and in November 1827 he resigned his seat. The dilemma of being a slave-owning Whig never weighed lightly with him, and he reformed the regime under which his estates were run. He abolished the whip, appointed a negro overseer, built decent houses, schools and churches for his 1,100 slaves, and encouraged Nonconformist missions. As a result, his property survived almost intact during the uprisings of 1831-2.[8] Throughout his life he maintained a close relationship with his niece Elizabeth Barrett Browning, the poet.[9] He died at Cinnamon Hill in December 1837. He left his house at Montego Bay and an annuity to his wife and the remainder of his Jamaican and English estates to his brother. Limited probate was granted on his estate in England, which was sworn under £9,000.[10] After his death his friend Peter Duncan wrote that he was 'a gentleman of great intelligence and liberality, and also a true friend to the religious instruction of the slaves'.[11]

[1] IGI (Glos.). [2] J. Marks, *Fam. of Barrett*, 224, 238, 282, 308-9, 537. [3] Ibid. 346. [4] *The Times*, 20 Nov. 1820. [5] HLRO HC/LB/1/89. [6] *The*

Times, 9 Mar. 1822, 15 Mar. 1823, 17 Mar. 1824. [7] Marks, 347-8. [8] Ibid. 60, 309, 355-8, 445. [9] Ibid. 283. [10] PROB 11/1893/216; IR26/1473/212. [11] Marks, 408.

M.P.J.C.

MOUNT, William (1787–1869), of Wasing Place, Thatcham, Berks.

YARMOUTH I.O.W. 1818–27 Feb. 1819

NEWPORT I.O.W. 1831–1832

b. 21 Nov. 1787, o.s. of William Mount of Postern Row, Tower Hill, London and Wasing Place and his cos. Jane, da. of Thomas Page of East Sheen and Poynters, Surr. *educ.* Eton 1802-5; Oriel, Oxf. 1805. *m.* 27 June 1818, Charlotte, da. and coh. of George Talbot of Temple Guiting, Glos., 2s. 2da. (1 *d.v.p.*). *suc.* fa. 1815. *d.* 10 Apr. 1869.

Sheriff, Berks. 1826-7.

Mount's ancestors were in business as stationers in the vicinity of Tower Hill, London from the late seventeenth century. His grandfather John Mount established himself as a Berkshire squire by purchasing the Wasing estate in 1760. He served as sheriff of the county in 1770 and died in 1786, after bequeathing £13,500 to his wife, an annuity of £1,000 plus £8,000 to his son John, and a total of £30,000 to his sons Edmund, Harry and Richard, and daughters Harriet, Jane, Louisa and Mary Christian. His residuary legatee and sole executor was his eldest son William Mount, who inherited landed property in Berkshire, Hampshire and Surrey, and a house, shop and warehouse at Tower Hill. He seems to have continued the family business, which was styled Mount and Davidson during the 1790s, until about the turn of the century. He extended and consolidated his holdings of land in the Thatcham area of Berkshire and became captain commandant of a corps of volunteer cavalry raised in 1803. In his will, dated 8 June 1809, he left his wife £2,000 and an annuity of £1,500, and his daughters Emily, Laura and Maria legacies totalling £21,000. The residue of his personalty, which was sworn under £70,000, and all his real estate, including property at Tower Hill, passed to his only surviving son William.[1] A year after coming into this inheritance in 1815 Mount went on an extensive European tour. In 1818 he was returned for Yarmouth by his close friend Sir Leonard Thomas Worsley Holmes*, with whom he had been at Eton. He vacated nine months later to accommodate government. Worsley Holmes made him a guardian of his under-age daughters, an executor of his will, and a trustee of his Isle of Wight property. Immediately after Worsley Holmes's death in January 1825 Mount, on behalf of the trustees and in compliance with his friend's wishes, placed the vacant seat for Newport at the disposal of the Liverpool ministry. In conjunction with Lord Yarborough, a fellow trustee, he had to fend off the importunity of one Charles Rushworth, who pestered them to fulfill his kinsman Worsley Holmes's alleged promise to secure his promotion from the tax to the excise office.[2]

At the 1830 Berkshire election Mount proposed the re-election of Robert Palmer, an 'independent' Member who had served 'with honour' on the finance committee.[3] In April 1831 he signed the Berkshire declaration against the Grey ministry's reform bill, which called for a more moderate measure.[4] At that month's dissolution it was reported that Yarborough, the dominant trustee, had sold the Worsley Holmes seats for Newport and Yarmouth to ministers.[5] Three of the four Members elected were supporters of the reform bill (as was Yarborough's nominee for Newtown), but Mount returned himself for Newport as an opponent of the measure. He voted against the second reading of the revised bill, 6 July, and presented and endorsed a petition calling for an additional Member to be given to the Isle of Wight, 13 July 1831. He voted for use of the 1831 census as a basis for disfranchisement, 19 July, against the inclusion of Chippenham in schedule B, 27 July, and against the passage of the bill, 21 Sept. He was in the minority for inquiry into the grievances of West Indian sugar producers, 12 Sept. He voted against the second reading of the revised reform bill, 17 Dec. 1831, the enfranchisement of Tower Hamlets, 28 Feb., and the third reading, 22 Mar. 1832. On 20 Mar. he presented a petition from Isle of Wight hoteliers for relief from their liability to compensate guests for loss of property. He voted against the second reading of the Irish reform bill, 25 May, and against ministers on the Russian-Dutch loan, 12 July 1832. Earlier that year he was badgered, as one of the Worsley Holmes trustees, to obtain 'long promised provision' for the son of a constituent, who complained that an associate of Yarborough had received preferential treatment. Mount, reporting the failure of his approaches to government, remarked that 'unfortunately ministers forget to fulfil arrangements which they are ready enough to make when it suits them'.[6] He retired from Parliament at the 1832 dissolution.

Mount died in April 1869. By his will, dated 21 Jan. 1858, he settled £1,000 a year on his wife and left £24,000 to his two surviving younger children. He was succeeded by his elder son William George Mount (1824-1906), Conservative Member for South Berkshire, 1885-1900.

[1] *Stationers' Co. Apprentices, 1641-1700* ed. D. McKenzie (Oxf. Bibl. Soc. n.s. xvii), 57, 117 and *1701-1800* (n.s. xix), 243, 244, 258; C.R. Rivington, *Recs. Stationers' Co.* 51; R. Myers, *Stationers' Co. Archive*, 215; *VCH Berks.* iii. 313, 314, 319; iv. 59, 115; S. Barfield, *Thatcham*, i. 64, 67-68, 360; PROB 11/1144/394; 1146/484; 1570/386; IR26/649/443. [2] Berks. RO, Mount mss D/EMt F13, 14, *passim*. [3] *The Times*, 9 Aug. 1830. [4] Ibid. 9 Apr. 1831. [5] *Three Diaries*, 90; *Greville Mems.* ii. 140. [6] Mount mss F15, Faquett to Mount, 7 Feb., 22 Mar., replies, 11 Feb., 23 Mar. 1832.

D.R.F./P.J.S.

MOUNT CHARLES, earl of *see* **CONYNGHAM, Francis Nathaniel** *and* **Henry Joseph**

MULLINS, Frederick William (1804–1854), of Beaufort House, co. Kerry.

CO. KERRY 1831–1837

b. 29 June 1804, 1st s. of Hon. and Rev. Frederick Ferriter Mullins of Beaufort House, rect. of Killiney, co. Kerry, and Elizabeth, da. and h. of William Croker of Johnstown, co. Cork. *educ.* Trinity, Dublin 1822; King's Inns 1827. *m.* 30 Sept. 1826,[1] Lucia, da. of Capt. William Robert Broughton, RN, col. of marines, *s.p. suc.* fa. 1832; took name of De Moleyns (as descendant of 1st Bar. Ventry [I]) by royal lic. 16 Feb. 1841. *d.* 17 Mar. 1854.

It was another Frederick William Mullins (*d.* 1712), an English colonel, who established this branch of the family in Kerry, settling at Burnham House, near Dingle, in about 1666 and serving as Member for Dingle, 1692-3, and Tralee, 1695-6. His great-grandson Thomas (1736-1824), who was awarded a baronetcy in 1797, was created Baron Ventry in the Irish peerage, 31 July 1800, as a reward for his eldest son's support for the Union in the Dublin Parliament, in which he sat briefly for Dingle that year. Ventry, one of the three major electoral patrons in Kerry, shied away from bringing forward his son Thomas, an army officer, in 1801, and thereafter usually backed the ministerialist James Crosbie*, partly in the hope of extracting a step in the peerage from Lord Liverpool's administration.[2] However, the 2nd baron supported the successful interloper William Hare against Crosbie at the general election of 1826, when his brother Major Edward Mullins was one of the magistrates responsible for the massacre that occurred on troops being ordered to fire into the crowd.[3] The 3rd Baron Ventry, who succeeded his uncle to the title in 1827, was said to have come off badly from the disfranchisement of the 40*s.* freeholders in 1829, when Edward Mullins was mentioned as a possible future candidate.[4]

This Member, whose father was the sixth son of the 1st baron, was described by Daniel O'Connell* in 1823 as 'a fine young man of 19', who was then apparently intent on making a disadvantageous marriage with a daughter of 'black Arthur's' (possibly one of the several Blennerhassetts of that name).[5] A trainee barrister, he spoke strongly against the proposed increases in the Irish stamp and spirit duties at the Kerry meeting in May 1830, when it was rumoured he would stand for the county.[6] His or his uncle Edward's pretensions were swept aside by the entry of Lord Kenmare's brother William Browne, whose candidacy he seconded in purposeful style at the general election that summer.[7] He signed the requisition for, but may not have attended, the county meeting in favour of the recent revolution in France in October 1830.[8] On the retirement of Browne, he defied expectations to come in unopposed under the wing of O'Connell, who forced the withdrawal of the other sitting Member, at the general election of 1831. Speaking for parliamentary reform and against colonial slavery, he alluded to O'Connell, who considered him a dependant, as his future parliamentary guide.[9]

Mullins made what one local paper considered a paltry maiden speech, unsuccessfully moving for a return of the number of Protestants in each Irish parish, 30 June 1831; although he obtained a return of the amount of vestry assessments, 25 July, his promised bill to rectify abuses in vestry taxation did not materialize that session.[10] He voted for the second reading of the Grey ministry's reintroduced English reform bill, 6 July, at least twice against adjourning proceedings on it, 12 July, and regularly for its details, except when dividing against the proposed division of counties, 11 Aug. He sided with opposition against the grants for civil list services, 18 July, and the Society for the Propagation of the Gospels in the colonies, 25 July. He briefly urged inquiry into the Castlepollard affair, 3 Aug., and voted for printing the Waterford petition for disarming the Irish yeomanry, 11 Aug. He was in the minority for postponing the Dublin writ, 8 Aug., but divided with ministers in both divisions on the Dublin election controversy, 23 Aug. He voted against the second reading of the Irish union of parishes bill, 19 Aug., was a minority teller for an amendment to the Scottish turnpike roads bill, 26 Aug., and divided against the committal of the truck bill, 12 Sept. Having failed to adjourn the discussion on account of the absence of many Irish Members, he voted for Sadler's motion to make legal provision for the Irish poor, but in his first major speech, during which he declared himself 'the friend of innovation' in all beneficial cases, he expressed his delight at the grant for national education in Ireland, 9 Sept. He divided for the passage of the reform bill, 21 Sept., the second reading of the Scottish bill, 23 Sept., and Lord

Ebrington's confidence motion, 10 Oct. 1831. Later that month he signed the requisition for the Kerry reform meeting.[11]

By a pre-session address to 'the people of Kerry', 4 Dec. 1831, he called for petitions to be forthcoming against the inadequate Irish reform bill, specifically for an extension of the franchise to leaseholders, more Irish seats and a different system of registration; he raised these same points in the House on the Irish measure being presented by Smith Stanley, the Irish secretary, 19 Jan. 1832.[12] He had apparently missed the division on the second reading of the revised English bill, 17 Dec. 1831, but he voted for going into committee on it, 20 Jan., again generally for its details, and the third reading, 22 Mar. 1832. He divided against the Russian-Dutch loan, 26 Jan. (although he was with government on this, 12, 16, 20 July), for inquiry into the glove trade, 31 Jan., and for the production of information on military punishments, 16 Feb.; he did, however, vote with ministers on Portugal, 9 Feb. As he intervened to oppose adjourning the discussion just before the division on Irish tithes, 27 Mar., he was probably in the radical Irish minority for Ruthven's amendment for the appropriation of the revenues of the Irish church. The following day, stating his regret at having to differ from the deserving ministers, he urged Smith Stanley to proceed with the promised legislative abolition of Irish taxes, and on the 30th he divided for Lambert's amendment against the payment of arrears. He voted against the second reading of the Irish tithes arrears bill, 6 Apr., but for the government amendment to it, 9 Apr. 1832.

He divided for Ebrington's motion for an address calling on the king to appoint only ministers who would carry the reform bill unimpaired, 10 May 1832. He voted for Buxton's anti-slavery motion, 24 May, against excluding insolvent debtors from Parliament, 30 May, to make permanent provision for the Irish poor by a tax on absentees, 19 June, and for coroners' inquests to be held in public, 20 June. He divided for the second reading of the Irish reform bill, 25 May, but on 18 June, when he was in the minority for his colleague's motion to enfranchise Irish £5 freeholders, he introduced his own amendment to give the vote to £30 Irish leaseholders of at least 19 years' standing. Passionately insisting that his aim was to give Ireland as extensive, effective and advantageous a reform as England would receive, he argued in detail for this change as the proportional equivalent of the English £10 freeholder and £50 tenant-at-will franchise. He was assisted by O'Connell, but the debate degenerated into a squabble involving the latter, and the motion, for which he was a teller, was defeated by 161-9. He divided for Sheil's amendment against the liability of electors to pay their municipal taxes before being allowed to vote, 29 June, and vainly attempted to secure two other technical alterations to the franchise, 18 July. He objected to Smith Stanley resuming the debate on tithes when so many Irishmen were absent, but was defeated in his attempt to postpone it, 10 July. Advocating a justly distributed general land tax as the best means of securing the state's revenues, he condemned the second report of Smith Stanley's tithes select committee as an inadequate representation of the evidence brought before it, 13 July. Utterly opposed to the commutation of tithes, he voiced the Irish view that the intended alterations would not be sufficient to solve the problem and voted in the minority to postpone the issue to the reformed Parliament. He presented petitions for the total abolition of Irish tithes, 18, 28 July 1832.

With the endorsement of O'Connell, who wrote that 'he has done his duty by the country and the country ought not to desert him', Mullins, whose father died that month, was re-elected as a Liberal and a Repealer at the general election in December 1832.[13] Two years later O'Connell stood by him for tactical reasons, although one of his correspondents observed that 'his conduct in private life exceeds in turpitude his political recreancy, and in Killarney he is regarded as the most perfect exemplification of everything that is dishonourable and mean'. By 1837 his parliamentary absenteeism and wayward behaviour had become unforgivable and he was defeated in that year's general election.[14] His prosecution over a bill of exchange in the bail court in June 1839 may indicate a certain financial precariousness in his subsequent life.[15]

On 8 Mar. 1854 De Moleyns, as he had become at the instigation of the 3rd Baron Ventry in 1841, appeared in the police court in London charged with having forged a signature to a power of attorney with a view to defrauding the Bank of England of £1,500. He indignantly pleaded his innocence, the lord mayor having made several disparaging remarks about a man of his position falling so low, but had insufficient funds to mount bail and was ordered to Newgate. He died there, suddenly, of natural causes, just over a week later.[16] His will, dated 22 Nov. 1843, was not proved until 29 June 1891, when his personalty only amounted to £750. His designated heir, a nephew named Frederick Henry Phillips, refused to accept his inheritance, since he would have had to change his name to De Moleyns and to have resided at least one in every four years in Kerry, so it passed to University

College, London with the intention of establishing a professorship in electrical science. The estate was evidently insufficient for this purpose, but a trust known as the 'De Moleyns Fund' (which still exists) was formed to provide grants for the purchase of electrical equipment.[17] A devoted follower of science, in 1841 he had obtained a patent for the production of electricity and its applications for illumination and motion.[18]

[1] IGI (Glos.). [2] *Hist. Irish Parl.* ii. 244; v. 330; *HP Commons, 1790-1820*, ii. 659-61. [3] *Freeman's Jnl.* 20 June; *Dublin Evening Post*, 27, 29 June, 1, 13, 18 July 1826. [4] *Dublin Evening Post*, 2 July 1829. [5] *O'Connell Corresp.* ii. 988. [6] *Western Herald*, 27, 31 May 1830. [7] PRO NI, Fitzgerald mss MIC639/13/7/58; *Western Herald*, 16 Aug. 1830. [8] *Western Herald*, 4, 11 Oct. 1830. [9] Ibid. 28 Apr., 14, 19 May 1831; *O'Connell Corresp.* iv. 1810, 1815; Fitzgerald mss 14/7/22, 26. [10] *Western Herald*, 5 July 1831. [11] Ibid. 27 Oct. 1831. [12] Ibid. 13 Dec. 1831; *O'Connell Corresp.* iv. 1859. [13] *O'Connell Corresp.* iv. 1923; *Kerry Evening Post*, 24 Nov., 29 Dec. 1832, 2 Jan. 1833; *Gent. Mag.* (1833), i. 186, 386. [14] *O'Connell Corresp.* v. 2174; O. MacDonagh, *Emancipist*, 118, 160. [15] *The Times*, 14 June 1839. [16] Ibid. 9, 21 Mar. 1854; *Gent. Mag.* (1854), i. 555. [17] F. Boase, *Mod. Eng. Biog.* v. 70; *ex. inf.* the administrator, dept. of electrical engineering, UCL. [18] B. Woodcraft, *Alphabetical Index of Patentees of Inventions* (1854), 152, 383.

S.M.F.

MUNDY, Edward Miller (1750–1822), of Shipley Hall, nr. Ilkeston, Derbys.

DERBYSHIRE 1784–18 Oct. 1822

b. 18 Oct. 1750, o.s. of Edward Mundy and Hester, da. of Humphrey Miller of Shipley Hall. *educ.* Eton 1762. *m.* (1) 23 Dec. 1772,[1] Frances (*d.* 28 Oct. 1783), da. and coh. of Godfrey Meynell of Yeldersley, 5s. 1da. *d.v.p.*; (2) 14 Jan. 1788, Lady Georgiana (*d.* 29 June 1789), da. and event. coh. of Col. Evelyn Chadwick of West Leake, Notts., wid. of Thomas Willoughby, 4th Bar. Middleton, 1da.; (3) 19 Oct. 1811, Catherine, da. of Nathaniel Coffin of Bristol, Glos., wid. of Richard Barwell† of Stansted Park, Suss., 1s. *suc.* fa. 1767; mother 1767. *d.* 18 Oct. 1822.

Cornet Derbys. vol. cav. 1794, maj. 1798; col. 2 regt. Derbys. militia 1803.

Mundy, an inconspicuous and entirely silent county Member, was usually a supporter of the Liverpool administration by this period.[2] He was returned for the ninth time for Derbyshire after a token contest at the general election of 1820, when he deprecated the candidacy of his spurious opponent and commended the conduct of his kinsman Francis Mundy* as sheriff.[3] He presented Derbyshire petitions complaining of agricultural distress, 20 Feb. 1821, 26 Apr. 1822.[4] He divided against Catholic relief, 28 Feb. 1821, and paired against the Catholic peers bill, 30 Apr. 1822. Unless it was given to his more active son George, Member for Boroughbridge since 1818, he was granted a month's leave on urgent private business, 30 Apr. 1821; he was reckoned by one radical source to be almost wholly 'an *absentee*'.[5] He died, on his 72nd birthday, in October 1822, when his seat was taken over by Francis Mundy. He was remembered for having the 'elegant manners and accomplishments of the perfect gentleman' and to have been 'zealously attentive' to his county's interests.[6] By his will, he left the bulk of his estate, and personal wealth sworn under £16,000, to his eldest son Edward Miller (*d.* 1834), whose son and namesake (1801-49), was Conservative Member for Derbyshire South, 1841-9.[7]

[1] IGI (Derbys.). [2] *HP Commons, 1790-1820*, iv. 642-3. [3] *Derby Mercury*, 1, 22 Mar. 1820. [4] *The Times*, 21 Feb. 1821, 27 Apr. 1822. [5] *Black Bk.* (1823), 178. [6] *Derby Mercury*, 23 Oct., 6 Nov. 1822; *Gent. Mag.* (1822), ii. 472; (1823), i. 26-27. [7] PROB 11/1669/227; IR26/964/321.

S.R.H./S.M.F.

MUNDY, Francis (1771–1837), of Markeaton Hall, Derbys. and 44 Queen Anne Street, Mdx.

DERBYSHIRE 25 Nov. 1822–1831

b. 29 Aug. 1771, 1st s. of Francis Noel Clarke Mundy of Markeaton and 2nd w. Elizabeth, da. of Sir Robert Burdett†, 4th bt., of Foremark Hall, Derbys. *educ.* ?Eton 1786; Christ Church, Oxf. 1788. *m.* 16 Dec. 1800, Sarah, da. of John Leaper Newton of Mickleover, 1s. 4da. *suc.* fa. 1815. *d.* 6 May 1837.

Cornet Derbys. vol. cav. 1794, lt. 1798; lt.-col. 2 regt. Derbys. militia 1803.

Sheriff, Derbys. 1820-1.

Mundy's ancestors had long been prominent in local politics, frequently serving as sheriff of Derbyshire, and his grandfather, Wrightson Mundy, had sat for Leicestershire, 1747-54. His father, who was a much admired public figure and poet, died in October 1815, leaving him the bulk of his estate, which included personalty sworn under £3,000.[1] At the general election of 1820 his kinsman (Wrightson's second cousin) Edward Miller Mundy, the county Member, recommended him as a future Member by drawing attention to his creditable conduct as sheriff, which gave ample proof of his suitability for 'every public station to which he may be called'.[2] As chairman of the turbulent Derbyshire county meeting on the Queen Caroline affair in January 1821, when a Whig amendment in her favour was agreed, his role was said to have been 'distinguished by the most inflexible firmness and impartiality, and the most conciliating moderation and urbanity'.[3] He offered for Derbyshire on the death of

Edward Mundy in October 1822, when his first cousin Sir Francis Burdett*, who considered that a 'contest would be ruinous to him' and that 'my only surprise is that he should be desirous of being in Parliament', rightly predicted that none of his rumoured opponents would persist, even though the Tories were still smarting from his supposed impartiality at the previous year's county meeting. Mundy was duly returned unopposed at the by-election the following month, when he boasted of his independence: 'my judgement may err, but I will never give a vote contrary to that judgement, nor from any corrupt or unworthy motive'.[4] An active county Member, he regularly presented constituency petitions and served on several select committees.

Mundy, whose votes are not always easily distinguishable from those of his kinsman George Mundy, ministerialist Member for Boroughbridge, divided against parliamentary reform, 20 Feb. 1823. He voted to reduce taxation by £7,000,000, 28 Feb., which suggests that he was not the 'Munday' who was in the majority against a motion, also moved by Maberly, to repeal the assessed taxes, 18 Mar. He became an honorary freeman of Leicester, 5 Mar.[5] He sided with the Liverpool government against repeal of the Foreign Enlistment Act, 16 Apr., but voted for Burdett's motion for inquiry into the legal proceedings against the Dublin Orange rioters, 22 Apr. He was in the minority for inquiry into the sugar duties, 22 May, but in the majority against criticizing chancery administration, 5 June. He voted (as 'E. Mundy') to recommit the silk manufacture bill and for inquiry into the coronation expenses, 9 June. He divided for the beer duties bill, 13 June, and the reciprocity of duties bill, 4 July 1823. He was in minorities against the usury bill, 17 June 1823, 27 Feb. 1824. He voted for repeal of the window tax, 2 Mar., and spoke for further easing the silk trade, 19 Mar., when he acknowledged that the alarm formerly prevailing in Derbyshire on this had subsided. He divided to condemn the trial of the Methodist missionary John Smith in Demerara, 11 June, but with ministers for the Irish insurrection bill, 14 June 1824, and the Irish unlawful societies bill, 25 Feb. 1825. He voted against Catholic relief, 1 Mar., 21 Apr., 10 May, and the Irish franchise bill, 26 Apr. He went against government on the grant to the duke of Cumberland, 2, 10 June. One contemporary source had it that he 'attended occasionally and appeared to join with the opposition'.[6] On 28 Sept. 1825 he wrote to acknowledge the 'very handsome' compliment which Peel, the home secretary, had paid him in response to his request for patronage and to advise him of the local disadvantages of his Jury Act, under which the number of qualified jurors in Derbyshire 'will be rather diminished than increased ... [and] some very respectable and proper persons, in point of intellect, etc., will be excluded'.[7] He declared that he 'yielded to no man in detestation of slavery' at the Derbyshire county meeting, 12 Jan. 1826, when he indicated that he was ready to endorse the 'combined wishes of his constituents' with his vote.[8] In the House, he observed that it was uncommon for Derbyshire banking houses to make their bills payable in London, 27 Feb.[9] He voted in opposition minorities against providing a separate ministerial salary for the president of the board of trade, 7, 10 Apr. 1826. Stating that it was his intention to vote 'conscientiously and to the best of my judgement' and that he had 'no bigoted attachment to the corn laws', he was returned unopposed for the county at the general election that year.[10]

He may have been the Mundy who endorsed the proposal to restrict voting on private bills in committee and spoke of the great 'mischief' which arose from Members voting who had not 'attended to the details', 20 Feb. 1827. He voted against Catholic relief, 6 Mar., but for the disfranchisement of Penryn, 28 May. He brought up Derby petitions in favour of repeal of the Test Acts, 6, 8 June 1827.[11] He would have voted for this had not the effects of illness caught up with him and obliged him to leave the House, 26 Feb. 1828.[12] He called for the appointment of a committee to review and amend the Malt Act, 17 Mar., successfully moved to postpone the turnpike trusts bill, 15 Apr., and voted against reducing the salary of the lieutenant-general of the ordnance, 4 July. He again divided against Catholic relief, 12 May 1828. Listed by Planta, the Wellington ministry's patronage secretary, among those 'opposed to the principle' of the 1829 emancipation bill he confided to one of his local supporters that its opponents 'appear to be rapidly on the increase, and at least we shall make a respectable minority, but I hope for *even better still*'.[13] Claiming that he had 'constantly' opposed Catholic relief and had 'heard no reasons alleged, which would justify me in departing from the opinions I have hitherto held', he presented and endorsed hostile petitions from Derbyshire and Derby, 9, 27 Feb., 4, 12 Mar., clashing with his colleague Lord George Cavendish over their validity, 12, 23 Mar. He divided against emancipation, 6 Mar., and, having said on the 12th that he had given his vote 'not from party feelings, but from principle', did so again, 18, 23, 27, 30 Mar., arguing on the 23rd that the 'admission of Catholics to political power would be fatal to the British constitution'. He expressed his support for the principle of the labourers' wages bill, 4 May 1829, but believed that its details should be 'fully discussed and considered' in committee. One of the Derbyshire magistrates who had addressed Wellington over the prevailing level of distress, he voted for Knatchbull's amendment to the address on this, 4 Feb. 1830.[14] He divided against the transfer of East Retford's seats to Birmingham, 11 Feb., and the enfranchisement of Birmingham, Leeds and Manchester, 23 Feb. He spoke for the introduction of a poor law to Ireland, 9 Mar., calling for the abolition of 'so serious an evil'. He divided against Jewish emancipation, 5 Apr., and paired against this, 17 May. He voted in minorities against the sale of beer for on-consumption, 21 June, 1 July 1830. Speaking of his detestation of slavery and his desire for 'retrenchment and proper economy', he was again returned unopposed at that summer's general election.[15]

Mundy, who on 9 Nov. deprecated the 'enormous expense' incurred by the printing of petitions, had been listed by ministers among their 'friends', and he voted with them in the division on the civil list which brought them down, 15 Nov. 1830. According to the Derby Member Edward Strutt, 'a few hours before he [had] told me he disapproved much of [chancellor of the exchequer Henry] Goulburn's speech and was decidedly of opinion that the civil list should be confined to the king's personal expenses!'[16] Mundy was discharged from an election committee on account of illness, 8 Dec. 1830. He supported a Derbyshire petition for relief from distress, 16 Feb. 1831. On 9 Mar. Strutt confided to his wife that

> Mundy tells me with infinite simplicity that he is in the greatest possible difficulty and anxiety about his vote. He approves of reform, but objects to a considerable part of the [Grey ministry's reform] bill, and wishes to know what is thought of it in Derbyshire.[17]

He announced that he would vote for the bill, 'on the understanding that I shall not feel bound to any of the clauses in it', 19 Mar., stating that he had 'always been satisfied ... that some reform was necessary', and rebutting the argument that a vote for the second reading was a 'pledge' to support the 'whole measure'. He accordingly voted for the second reading, 22 Mar., but, since he deemed any reduction in Members 'most fatal to the interests of this country', he spoke and voted for Gascoyne's wrecking amendment, 19 Apr. He claimed that he did not vote from any 'party motive' nor for the purpose of 'ejecting any ministry ... I hope, indeed, that ministers will not think it necessary to abandon the bill ... but that the bill will be so modified ... that it will be made acceptable to the majority of the House'. However, Grey obtained a dissolution, and Mundy, facing rejection by the county's Tories, on 25 Apr. reluctantly issued a farewell address, in which he vindicated his vote on the civil list. According to the *Derby Mercury*, his retirement was regretted by the landed gentry, especially as he had been 'accessible to the freeholders ... without regard to party or influence', but one radical publication sweepingly denounced him as a 'thick and thin Tory, whose votes are uniformly bad'.[18] His perceived hostility to reform was probably one of the reasons why Markeaton was targeted by the violent mob during the Derby riots in October 1831.[19] The following year he was reported as describing Derbyshire as 'such a disagreeable county to live in!'[20] He died at Markeaton in May 1837, leaving, by his will of 17 Dec. 1836, most of his property and personal wealth sworn under £12,000 to his son William (1801-77), who was Conservative Member for Derbyshire South, 1849-57 and 1859-65.[21]

[1] J. T[illey], *The Old Halls, Manors and Fams. of Derbys.* iv. 129-30; PROB 11/1576/35; IR26/680/18. [2] *Derby Mercury*, 22 Mar. 1820. [3] *The Times*, 11 Jan. 1821. [4] *Derby Mercury*, 23 Oct., 13, 27 Nov.; Wilts. RO, Burdett mss 1883/229-77, bdle. 4, Burdett to Crabtree, 27 Oct. 1822; Chatsworth mss 6DD 739. [5] *Leicester Borough Recs.* vii. 55. [6] *Session of Parl. 1825*, p. 477. [7] Add. 40381, f. 410. [8] *Derby Mercury*, 18 Jan. 1826. [9] *The Times*, 28 Feb. 1826. [10] *Derby Mercury*, 31 May, 21 June 1826. [11] *The Times*, 7, 9 June 1827. [12] *Derby Mercury*, 5 Mar. 1828. [13] Derbys. RO, FitzHerbert mss D239 M/F 8703, 8710. [14] *The Times*, 28 Jan. 1830. [15] *Derby Mercury*, 7 July, 11 Aug. 1830. [16] Derby Local Stud. Lib. Strutt mss, E. to F. Strutt, 19 Nov. 1830. [17] Ibid. [18] FitzHerbert mss 8849; *Derby Mercury*, 27 Apr. 1831; [W. Carpenter], *People's Bk.* (1831), 329. [19] *The Times*, 14 Oct. 1831; *Jnl. of Mary Frampton* ed. H. G. Mundy, 386-94. [20] Strutt mss, E. to F. Strutt, 14 Apr. 1832. [21] *Gent. Mag.* (1837), ii. 99.

S.R.H./S.M.F.

MUNDY, George (1777–1861), of Shipley Hall, Derbys. and 9 Cork Street, Mdx.

BOROUGHBRIDGE 1818–1820

BOROUGHBRIDGE 7 June 1820–1830

b. 3 Mar. 1777, 3rd s. of Edward Miller Mundy* (*d.* 1822) and 1st w. Frances, da. of Godfrey Meynell of Yeldersley. *educ.* Eton 1788; Portsmouth naval acad. 1789-92. *unm.* CB 4 June 1815; KCB 28 Feb. 1837. *d.* 9 Feb. 1861.

Midshipman RN 1792, lt. 1796, cdr. 1798, capt. 1801, r.-adm. 1830, v.-adm. 1841, adm. 1849.

Capt. E. Derbys. vol. cav. 1817-24.

Mundy, a naval officer and son of the Tory Member for Derbyshire, stood again for Boroughbridge at the general election of 1820 on the interest of his brother-in-law, the 4th duke of Newcastle. He again faced a contest and campaigned actively in the constituency. There was a double return in favour of Newcastle's opponents, but Mundy was seated on petition.[1] It is sometimes difficult to distinguish Mundy's votes from those of his father, until the latter's death in 1822, but he was evidently a fairly regular attender who continued to give general support to Lord Liverpool's ministry. He voted in defence of their conduct towards Queen Caroline, 6 Feb. 1821. He divided against Catholic relief, 28 Feb. He voted against parliamentary reform, 9 May, reduction of the barracks grant, 28 May, and Hume's economy and retrenchment motion, 27 June 1821. He divided against abolition of one of the joint-postmasterships, 13 Mar., and for the grant to place government proclamations in Irish newspapers, 22 July 1822. He voted against relieving Catholic peers of their disabilities, 30 Apr., and inquiry into Irish tithes, 19 June. Even after his father's death some difficulty exists in differentiating his votes from that of the new Derbyshire Member, his kinsman Francis Mundy. It was probably George who divided against repeal of the assessed taxes, 18 Mar., and he was certainly with government against inquiry into the currency, 12 June 1823. *The Times* listed him in both the majority and the minority on the Scottish juries bill, 20 June 1823.[2] He voted against reform of Edinburgh's representation, 26 Feb. 1824, and repeal of the usury laws the next day. He made his first known intervention in debate on the silk trade, 5 Mar., when he stated that the proposed repeal of the duty on silk had 'created alarm in the counties of Chester and Stafford, as well as ... Derby'. He spoke again on the game laws, 12 Apr., when he proposed that those liable to transportation if convicted should be given a choice between trial at the quarter sessions or the assizes; he was fearful of the prejudice which magistrates, who were often sportsmen, might have against poachers. He voted against the motion condemning the trial of the Methodist missionary John Smith in Demerara, 11 June 1824. He divided for the Irish unlawful societies bill, 25 Feb. 1825. He was absent from the call of the House, 28 Feb., but attended next day to vote against Catholic relief, and did so again, 21 Apr., 10 May 1825. He voted against the disfranchisement of Irish 40*s*. freeholders, 26 Apr. He may have been the Mundy who presented a petition from Holborn against the Metropolitan Water Company bill, 11 Mar. He divided for the financial provision for the duke of Cumberland, 10 June 1825. In January 1826 Newcastle recorded in his diary how Mundy, while out shooting, had accidentally 'killed a Newfoundland dog led by one of my keepers and wounded the man a good deal in the thigh'.[3] He voted against reform of Edinburgh's representation, 13 Apr. 1826. He was returned unopposed for Boroughbridge at the general election that summer.

It is possible that he was the Mundy who seconded Robert Bransby Cooper's successful resolution to prevent Members from voting on private bills in committees which they had not attended, 20 Feb. 1827. In the Berwick election committee, 24 Mar., he reportedly voted to find John Gladstone* guilty of treating.[4] He divided against Catholic relief, 6 Mar. 1827, 12 May 1828. At the end of that year he was appointed captain of the yacht *Royal George*. In February 1829 Planta, the Wellington ministry's patronage secretary, listed him as one who was 'opposed to the principle' of Catholic emancipation, like his patron, and he voted accordingly, 6, 18, 23, 30 Mar. In affirming his continued opposition to concession, 12 Mar. 1829, he expressed his 'decided disapprobation' of the 'late change of opinion that has taken place in the minds of some gentlemen', who 'appear to have turned round at the beck of a finger held up by a single individual'; such a 'weathercock system ... would never influence me'. However, his name does not appear in the lists compiled that autumn by the Ultra Tory leader, Sir Richard Vyvyan*. His last known vote was against the transfer of East Retford's seats to Birmingham, 11 Feb. 1830. In May Newcastle noted that 'poor George Mundy has had a paralytic stroke and lost his speech and the use of his right side'. He retired at the dissolution that summer, owing to continued 'ill health'.[5] He was replaced about this time as captain of the *Royal George*, but promoted to rear-admiral. It appears that he subsequently regained some of his faculties: in October 1845 he described himself as being in 'tolerable health', and the following March Newcastle found him 'looking surprisingly well, better than I have seen him for years'.[6] He died in February 1861 and divided his property among his nephews.

[1] T. Lawson-Tancred, *Recs. of a Yorks. Manor*, 336. [2] *The Times*, 21 June 1823. [3] Nottingham Univ. Lib. Newcastle mss Ne2 F2/1/90. [4] St. Deiniol's Lib. Glynne-Gladstone mss 277, J. Gladstone to Huskisson, 24 Mar. 1827. [5] Newcastle mss Ne2 F2/1/224; F3/1/245. [6] Add. 38048, f. 428; *Unhappy Reactionary* ed. R.A. Gaunt (Thoroton Soc. rec. ser. xliii), 262.

M.P.J.C.

MURRAY, Sir George (1772–1846), of Bleaton, Perth and 5 Belgrave Square, Mdx.[1]

PERTHSHIRE	6 Apr. 1824–1832
PERTHSHIRE	5 May 1834–1834

b. 6 Feb. 1772, 2nd s. of Sir William Murray, 5th bt. (*d.* 1800), of Ochtertyre, Perth and Lady Augusta Mackenzie, da. of George, 3rd earl of Cromarty [S]; bro. of Sir Patrick Murray, 6th bt.† *educ.* privately; Edinburgh h.s. 1781-5; Edinburgh Univ. 1785; Geneva. *m.* 28 Apr. 1825,[2] Lady Louisa Paget, da. of Henry, 1st earl of Uxbridge, estranged w. and wid. of Maj.-Gen. Sir James Erskine, 3rd bt., of Torriehouse, Fife, 1da. (*b.* 1822). KB 11 Sept. 1813; GCB 2 Jan. 1815; GCH 1816. *d.* 28 July 1846.

Ensign 71 Ft. Mar. 1789, 34 Ft. June 1789; ensign 3 Ft. Gds. 1790, lt. and capt. 1794, capt. and lt.-col. 1799; sen. asst. q.m.g. on Helder expedition 1799, Egyptian expedition 1800-2; adj.-gen. W.I. 1802-3; asst. q.m.g. at Horse Gds. 1803-4; dep. q.m.g. [I] 1804-12, q.m.g 1812-14; dep. q.m.g. Hanover expedition 1805; q.m.g. Baltic army 1807, Stockholm mission 1808, Portugal 1808-9; col. army 1809; q.m.g. Peninsula and France 1809-12, 1813-14; brig.-gen. 1811; maj.-gen. 1812; col. 60 Ft. 1813; adj.-gen. [I] 1814; gov. Canada 1814-15; chief of staff of Allied armies and q.m.g. of British contingent in France 1815-18; col. 72 Ft. 1817; col. 42 Ft. 1823; lt.-gen. 1825; c.-in-c. [I] 1825-8; gen. 1841; col. 1 Ft. 1843-*d.*

Lt.-gen. of ordnance Mar. 1824-Feb. 1825; sec. of state for war and colonies May 1828-Nov. 1830; PC 30 May 1828; master-gen. of ordnance Dec. 1834-May 1835, Sept. 1841-July 1846.

Gov. Edinburgh Castle 1818-19, RMC, Sandhurst 1819-24, Fort St. George, Inverness 1829-*d.*

Murray's parents, setting him a fine example, were divorced in 1791 over his mother's adultery with a Crieff physician. (They had an illegitimate son who was enrolled in the Indian army and died in 1831.)[3] His elder brother Patrick Murray, who was trained as an advocate, succeeded their father to the baronetcy and the family's Perthshire estate in 1800. Murray was carefully educated (becoming fluent in French) before being started on his distinguished army career by his maternal uncle Lord Macleod at the age of 17. As a subaltern in the Scots Guards he served in the Low Countries campaigns of 1793-5, was forced home from the West Indies by ill health in 1795 and was on the staff in Belfast during the Irish rebellion of 1798. His friends and comrades Robert Anstruther and Alexander Hope* (whose sister was married to Patrick) interested him in the quartermaster's aspect of staff work and, following the Austrian and Prussian models, groomed him as one of the new 'Scientifics'. In 1799 Anstruther took him as his senior assistant on the Helder expedition, but he was wounded in the ankle on the first day. Anstruther employed him again in Egypt, where he was present at all the actions, 1800-2. After five months' study at the new Royal Military College in 1802 he was taken as adjutant-general to the West Indies by General Grinfield. He filled an assistant quartermaster's post at Horse Guards, 1803-4, when General Brownrigg sent him to Ireland to remodel the quartermaster's department. He was involved in the Baltic and Stockholm military ventures of 1807 and 1808. At Copenhagen he worked closely with and impressed Arthur Wellesley† (later the duke of Wellington) who sponsored his professional career thereafter. He was dispatched to Portugal as quartermaster-general to the army commanded by Generals Burrard and Dalrymple, served in the same capacity under Moore and lost both him and Anstruther at Corunna. In April 1809 he was made quartermaster-general under Wellesley in the Peninsula. After initial mutual doubts and reserve, they developed a close and confidential relationship. Murray aspired to the rank of brigadier-general, but felt he was being held back by the commander-in-chief, Sir David Dundas. He wrote to Hope, 14 May 1811, that he considered this request 'no very exorbitant one', as his 'avocations ... embrace some of the most important branches of the service' and he was 'the first officer who has held that situation in the British army upon such an enlarged and permanent scale'. He was given the rank the following month, along with the governorship of Edinburgh Castle at £400 per annum. In late 1811 he broke his collar bone while hunting and got leave to return to Britain, where he discovered that he had been promoted to major-general, a rank incompatible with his Irish deputyship. He was made Irish quartermaster-general and, to Wellington's chagrin, resigned his Peninsular army post. Wellington, unhappy with his replacement, James Willoughby Gordon*, enticed Murray to return to army headquarters in March 1813, and henceforth his reputation as the duke's 'very able' right hand man was assured.[4] In December 1814 he was appointed lieutenant-governor of the Upper Province of Canada, and he arrived in Quebec on 2 Mar 1815. News of the renewal of war in Europe brought him back, but he did not reach London until after Waterloo. In November 1815 he was made chief of staff of the Allied army of occupation and quartermaster-general of the British army. He served as such for three years, living in style in Paris and Cambrai. The mischievous radical Whig Thomas Creevey* was his dinner guest in the summer of 1818, when he described Murray as 'all politeness and good manners', but '*feeble*, though they say excellent in his department'.[5] Wellington, master-general of the ordnance in Lord Liverpool's administration from 1817, looked after Murray, who received regimental colonelcies in 1817 and 1823 and was made governor of the Royal Military College in August 1819. In February 1824 Wellington secured his appointment as lieutenant-general of the ordnance, with 'a further provision to be made for ... [him] hereafter'. His request to be sworn of the privy council on the strength of his 'previous services' since 1809 was turned down.[6] He was assured of a seat in the Commons for his native county, having obtained the backing of the dominant Atholl interest for the vacancy created by the impending restoration of the Tory sitting Member to a forfeited peerage. The Perthshire Whigs had no one to put up against him, and as one of them recalled in 1831, they were 'glad to obtain' him, even though he was 'an opponent in politics', for he was 'supposed to be one of the most liberal of his party' and, 'though but a small proprietor in the county, had claims to the respect and gratitude of his countrymen by successful military services'. After his unopposed return, 6 Apr. 1824, Murray declared:

> At a time when so many wild theories were abroad, when so many dangerous principles, with regard to remodelling or reforming constitutions, were agitating the minds of men and shaking nations to their foundation, he considered it incumbent upon him to avow his warm attachment to the glorious constitution of this country, to uphold which, in its purity, should always receive the most strenuous exertion of his heart and hand.[7]

He was in the ministerial majority against Brougham's motion condemning the prosecution of the Methodist missionary John Smith in Demerara, 11 June 1824.

A fortnight later a murky aspect of Murray's private life was exposed to public scrutiny when Lieutenant-General Sir James Erskine brought an action for £20,000 damages against him for crim. con. with his wife. The case for Erskine was that by forming a clandestine sexual liaison with Lady Erskine in Paris Murray had destroyed a happy marriage and betrayed a friend and fellow officer. The Erskines had separated, at the instigation of Sir James, in 1819, and thereafter Murray and Lady Erskine had lived together incognito at various locations in England. In April 1822 their bastard daughter Georgina had been born at Finchley, Middlesex. According to the prosecution, they had planned to procure a divorce for Lady Erskine under the Scottish law whereby a man who had not cohabited with his wife for four years could be sued for 'adherence' and ultimately divorce, but Erskine thwarted this scheme by taking his wife back under his roof. In Murray's defence it was argued that he and Erskine had never been friends and that no criminal congress had occurred until after Erskine had abandoned his wife in 1819. The jury found for Erskine, but damages were set at only £3,500, which partially vindicated Murray's honour. However, a clerical constituent was sorely troubled by these revelations and felt that he could not in conscience vote for Murray at the next election, when he was expected to have a Tory rival.[8] Erskine brought divorce proceedings in late 1824, but he died before they were completed, 3 Mar. 1825, which left Murray and Lady Erskine free to marry (he at the age of 43) eight weeks later. The stigma of her conduct made Lady Louisa *persona non grata* in some respectable circles.[9]

On 25 Feb. 1825 Murray, who was described at this time as possessing a face notable for 'a pleasing and happy combination of intelligence, sweetness and spirit, with regularity, beauty and a noble cast of features', presented a Scottish distillers' petition for reduction of the duty on spirits and voted for the third reading of the Irish unlawful societies bill.[10] A week later Wellington had him moved from the ordnance to command of the forces in Ireland, but his successor Sir William Henry Clinton* was required to engage to vacate the ordnance for him should the impending divorce proceedings prove a serious embarrassment in Ireland.[11] Murray spent much of the next three years there, but he was in the Commons to present a Perthshire agriculturists' petition against any interference with the corn laws, 2 May 1825.[12] On 17 June he bore testimony to the 'military character and services' of Sir Robert Wilson*, who had been dismissed from the army for his involvement in the disorder at the queen's funeral in 1821, but endorsed the crown's 'full and entire possession of all its present authority over the officers of the army'. He divided for the duke of Cumberland's annuity, 6 June 1825. He defended the grant to Kilmainham Hospital for army pensioners, 6 Mar., opposed the abolition of flogging in the army as 'inconsistent with sound policy', 10 Mar., and presented constituency petitions against interference with the Scottish banking system, 17, 21 Mar. 1826.[13] At the general election that summer he was returned unopposed for Perthshire: he 'disavowed being actuated by feelings of party spirit', reiterated his support for the 'purity' of the existing constitution and promised to resist any unwarranted diminution of agricultural protection.[14]

When Wellington resigned from the command of the army on the formation of Canning's ministry in April 1827 Murray assured him of his undiminished personal attachment. There was speculation in the summer that Canning might offer him the office of secretary at war or perhaps the army command. Canning did seriously consider the latter option, but it was not taken because it was feared that Murray's appointment, for all his 'good reputation', would offend senior general officers.[15] He congratulated Wellington on his resumption of the army command after Canning's death, observing that the duke's 'being avowedly unconnected with the [Goderich] ministers is no disadvantage' and that 'the less of party politics there is supposed to be at any time in the commander-in-chief the better it will be ... for the public service'. The Goderich ministry was preparing to recall him from Ireland and restore him to the ordnance and give him 'a government' at the end of 1827, but their resignation in January 1828 meant that he remained in place when Wellington became prime minister.[16] He did not go to London until 18 Apr. 1828.[17] He presented petitions in favour of the Scottish salmon fisheries bill, 5 May, and for continued agricultural protection, 13 May. That day and on 22 May he warmly supported the grant of pensions to Canning's family, observing that 'we are not the deputies of a penurious and narrow-minded race' but 'sit here as the representatives of a magnanimous, a liberal and a generous nation'. When filling the vacancies occasioned by the resignation from the government of the Huskissonites in late May 1828, Wellington initially earmarked Murray, 'as able and respectable a man as can be found in Parliament', as he told Lord Dudley, for the war secretaryship, with a seat in cabinet, but in the end offered him the colonial secretaryship, which Murray was foolish or vain enough to accept.[18] Some Whigs muttered about 'military' government, and the appointment received some criticism on this ground in the House, 30 May.[19] Ministerialists, however, had high hopes of him. Mrs. Arbuthnot thought he would

> make an excellent colonial secretary. He is very clever, an excellent man of business, a very good speaker and, from having been in Canada, knows that colony (which is now so important) well and, in short, is in every respect well qualified. He is also quite unpledged, a new man who has never mixed up in any party squabbles and who can do his duty without looking to one side or the other.

Lord Ellenborough, a member of the cabinet, believed that

> a better man could not have been found. He is able; a good man of business; a good speaker (as far as he is known), and he brings a high established character into the service of the country. He is, besides, a Catholic. My expectation is that next session he will be the most efficient man in the ... Commons.

Lord Anglesey, the Irish viceroy, told Wellington that 'you have a very superior man in ... Murray. I wish he had fallen to my lot here'.[20] He was quietly re-elected for Perthshire without attending the formalities.[21]

It soon became clear that Murray was out of his depth. The colonial office senior clerk Henry Taylor recalled that his handsome 'countenance and natural stateliness and simple dignity of demeanour were all that can be desired in a secretary of state, if to look the character were the one thing needful', but that, conscious of his own unfitness for the post, he presided remotely over two 'years of torpor'.[22] Treated by Wellington, who took his expert advice from Lord Bathurst and Goulburn, as a barely competent senior clerk, he was soon overwhelmed by the mass of material which confronted him and left as much as possible to his under-secretaries. One of these told Greville two years later that 'he had never met with any public officer so inefficient as he'.[23] On 23 June 1828 Mrs. Arbuthnot noted that had had 'not quite learnt his new duties', for on the 20th he had taken his seat 'dressed more *a la militaire* than the ... Commons quite liked, with a black stock, etc., and, having done so, he went off to dine with Esterhazy although his own business was coming on'. She reflected that he would 'soon learn that the House takes precedence of dinners and do very well, I make no doubt'.[24] In the event, Murray fell well short of expectations as a general debater, as Lord Palmerston*, one of the Huskissonites, predicted; 'he makes an elegant speech upon preparation, and with practice would make a useful debater, but it is too late in life for him to take up this exercise with hopes of excelling in it'.[25] On 1 July he secured leave to introduce a bill to continue the Slave Laws Consolidation Act for a year and explained it to Hume, who on the 4th flustered him by pressing for information on the cost of the crown colonies, which he did not have to hand. He justified the office of lieutenant-general of the ordnance as important and useful. He opposed a call for abandonment of the Canadian military defences, 7 July, and next day defended the governor of New South Wales, Sir Ralph Darling, against a charge of 'oppression and cruelty'. Ellenborough hoped Murray would blossom as a debater next session, but for the moment recorded the 'uniform' view that 'he is pleasing, and will be popular, but he has *no power* as a speaker'.[26] He gave an assurance that ministers had 'every desire to allay the irritation subsisting in the Canadas' and had no wish to 'uphold defects in the existing system of government, or to shield misconduct in its administration', 14 July. Next day he claimed to share the anxiety of Thomas Fowell Buxton that native South Africans should be properly treated, but observed that as the responsible minister he was obliged to consider the interests of all classes of that community. On 25 July 1828 he said that the cabinet was 'fully pledged to adhere to the resolutions of 1823' on the amelioration of West Indian slavery as the best means of doing justice to all parties concerned.

In early January 1829 Mrs. Arbuthnot wrote that Wellington now considered Murray 'a failure because he is so indolent and allows his under-secretaries to do all the business and govern him'. She added, however, that he was 'a gentlemanlike, honourable man, very desirous of serving the duke, and will, I dare say, improve'.[27] In the House, 20 Feb., he argued that 'any plan of economy, founded upon ... relinquishment' of colonies would 'materially deteriorate the station of Great Britain in the political scale of the world': he insisted on the need for a large military force in the West Indies, said caution must prevail on slavery abolition and explained that ministers were eager to 'secure the Canadas by making them dependent upon an extension of their own population'. He defended the Royal Military College against Hume's carping, 20 Feb., and on the 23rd told him that while he was keen to be rid of Sierra Leone as soon as possible, it would be inhumane to abandon the colony precipitately. He announced that the Canadian legislature had resolved to make the evidence of slaves admissible in court, 4 Mar. 1829. In July 1828 he had expressed to Ellenborough his 'fears' that Catholic emancipation would be 'delayed till the Catholics have gone so far as to make it impossible'. Ellenborough thought he 'put several points on the Catholic question extremely well' when he and Herries met him in the cabinet room, 20 Jan. 1829, and he made contributions to the cabinet's discussions of the details of the relief bill and the accompanying disfranchisement measure.[28] His speech in support of emancipation, 5 Mar., when he drew on his experiences in Ireland to argue that it was 'the most certain means of confirming the tranquility, of increasing the prosperity, and of extending the power of the empire', received praise from all sides. Ellenborough thought he 'spoke admirably' and Mrs. Arbuthnot 'beautifully', while the radical Whig Member John Cam Hobhouse reckoned that he had delivered 'one of the most affecting and effective speeches ever heard', containing some 'finished eloquence of the highest character'. Greville found the Whigs at Brooks's 'in great admiration' of his performance.[29] He presented petitions in favour of emancipation, 16, 30 Mar., opposed an attempt to amend the bill, 24 Mar., and welcomed the Edinburgh pro-Catholic petition, 26 Mar. He of course voted for emancipation, 6, 30 Mar. He defended various colonial grants and the Newfoundland fisheries bill, 6 Apr., and the Swan River settlement bill, 10 Apr., 1 May. On 14 May he asserted that Canada lacked an 'aristocracy ... which in this country is so important for the support of the constitution'. He told Brougham that the government did not plan to legislate immediately to make slaves' evidence admissible as this could be done more effectively as part of a general reform of colonial judicatures on the basis of the pending report of commissioners of inquiry, 25 May. He said ministers would 'assist' any practicable scheme of emigration, but could not 'afford to go to any expense for this purpose', 1 June. He assured Fowell Buxton, incorrectly, that the Mauritius slave trade had been suppressed, 3 June. On 5 June he met a motion for information on Canada with a general defence of ministerial policy, but admitted that plans to legislate in a 'conciliatory' spirit that session had been dished by the tardiness of the select committee in reporting. In mid-May the Whig Lord Althorp* heard that Murray was 'giving great satisfaction in his colonial management', at least as far as his associates Henry Labouchere* and Edward Smith Stanley* were concerned. In August the Irish Whig Thomas Spring Rice* thought he was 'deserving of every confidence' on the issue of the Mauritius slave trade, but five months later Fowell Buxton, after a series of meetings with him, was 'heartily angry' at his refusal to give 'a final answer' on the subject. Greville, while admitting that he knew 'nothing' of Murray personally, wrote that he was 'popular in his office, but has neither the capacity nor the knowledge of [William] Huskisson*', his predecessor.[30] In September 1829 he was appointed governor of Fort St. George, Inverness, which brought him £141 a year until his death.[31]

Murray, who was reported to have said not a word during his and Wellington's interview with aggrieved representatives of the West India interest in January 1830, was one of Sir Thomas Lawrence's pall bearers on the 21st. He was 'very quiet' during a cabinet discussion on slavery in the crown colonies a few days later; Ellenborough thought that although he was 'a very sensible man', he was 'overawed by the duke, having been under him so long'.[32] According to Ellenborough, after a cabinet on 7 Feb. Murray 'expressed his surprise the duke should cling to the hope of reclaiming the Ultra Tories', alienated by Catholic emancipation, for he 'would not get' them and they 'were not worth having'; and three weeks later Hobhouse was told that Murray and Wellington had said in private that 'the wishes of most individuals in either House were of the most liberal tendency, but they felt they had obstacles at Windsor and from their partisans'.[33] In the House, 19 Feb., he denied Labouchere's assertion that the Canadas were being 'governed upon a garrison system' and opposed cuts in the army establishment. On 22 Feb. he claimed that 'a system of reduction has been for some time in operation' and that economies in colonial expenditure could go no further. Next day, having voted with his colleagues against transferring East Retford's seats to Birmingham, 11 Feb., and Lord Blandford's reform scheme, 18 Feb., he opposed the enfranchisement of Birmingham, Leeds and Manchester, professing willingness to give 'representatives to the great towns' as disfranchisements occurred, but refusing to increase the numbers of the House for that purpose. He admitted that cost was a major stumbling block to implementing colonial judicial reforms, 4 Mar. He approved Wilmot Horton's emigration scheme, 9 Mar., but insisted that government could not fund it. When the cabinet discussed Goulburn's proposal for an income tax, 14 Mar., he 'said nothing' and was 'understood to go with the [hostile] majority'.[34] He denied that distress was widespread or severe in Scotland, 15 Mar. He divided against Jewish emancipation, 5 Apr., 17 May. He presented constituency petitions for the Perth navigation and Tay ferries bills, 26 Apr., 3 May. On 29 Apr. he obtained leave to introduce a bill to establish a fund for defraying the costs of the administration of justice in Canada, and on 4 May one to amend the law relating to the election of members of the legislative assembly of Lower Canada. The latter became law on 16 July 1830 (11 Geo. IV & 1 Gul. IV, c. 53), but the latter, after being committed for substantial alteration on 14 June, lapsed on 2 July 1830. He opposed Labouchere's resolutions censuring ministerial policy on Canada, 25 May. He was against abolition of the Irish lord lieutenancy, 11 May, and in passing refuted Hume's charge that the inhabitants of the colonies felt 'degraded by being placed under a delegated authority'. That day he resisted and defeated by 82-29 a motion for inquiry into the state of Newfoundland. He said there was no 'system of favouritism' in the government of New South Wales, 21 May, defended the grant of £120,000 for that colony, 11 June, and said that Darling had no case to answer over the punishment of two soldiers, 17 June, 8, 9 July. He thought the establishment of a representative system at the Cape would be 'extremely inexpedient', 24 May, and opposed inquiries into Ceylon, 27 May, and Sierra Leone, 15 June. On 30 Apr. he had admitted to Fowell Buxton and Spring Rice in private that 'slave trading to a *vast extent* had prevailed at Mauritius', but opposed the appointment of a select committee as 'unnecessary'.[35] He stood by the 1823 amelioration resolutions when Brougham proposed the immediate abolition of slavery, 13 July, and on 20 July 1830 said that he could give no pledge for abolition of the African coastal slave trade because treaties with foreign powers were involved. A few days later it was reported that the new queen, Adelaide, was 'very rude to ... Murray, who brought his little girl to be presented to her; saying afterwards that it was very painful but necessary'. It was 'thought rather unfortunate' that her husband's bastard Miss Fitzclarence 'should have been standing by her at the time'.[36]

Murray's future at the colonial office became the subject of intense speculation during the 1830 session. In April Ellenborough was told by Sir Henry Hardinge* (whom he suspected of aspiring to that place) that Murray 'does not do the business well' and would 'be very well satisfied to be master-general' of the ordnance, though Ellenborough doubted this.[37] Wellington was aware of Murray's deficiencies in office and debate and would have liked to move him to a military post more suited to his talents; but he got angry with Mrs. Arbuthnot when she badgered him on the need to strengthen the ministry's front bench team in the Commons. Ellenborough dismissed Lord Rosslyn's notion that Murray would make 'an excellent governor-general' of India because he 'would be too indolent'.[38] Greville thought he was 'silly' to say that he wished the French king had made a fight of it in response to the July Revolution.[39] He was returned unopposed and *in absentia* (pleading pressure of official business) for Perthshire at the general election of 1830.[40] When Mrs. Arbuthnot again raised the issue of recruiting 'speakers' for the Commons, Wellington lost his temper, but admitted that 'in the department, as a man of business', Murray was 'woeful'. By the end of September 1830 Wellington had decided to offer his office to the Palmerston and to compensate Murray with command of 'the Blues and a promise of the first thing that falls vacant', but the negotiations came to nothing.[41]

On the address, 3 Nov. 1830, Murray declared against repeal of the Irish Union and denied that the king's speech held out the prospect of military interference against the revolting Belgians. (He told Hobhouse the same in private a few days later.)[42] On reform, he said that he was 'willing to listen ... to the propositions that may be brought forward respecting it by others' and conceded that, while the 'great principles' of the constitution must remain inviolate, 'any particular detached portion of our system' might 'from time to time undergo modification'. When his statement that he was 'perfectly willing that reform should take place' evoked opposition cheers, he reacted by saying that if Members thought he was going 'further' than he had intended, he was sure that 'too great an extension of the franchise' would be dangerous and that 'a respectable and powerful aristocracy' was essential to 'secure this country against those changes and convulsions that have happened in other countries'. This speech, coming after Wellington's uncompromising declaration against all reform in the

Lords the previous evening, caused a stir and created an impression that ministers were divided on the issue. Mrs. Arbuthnot thought that Murray '*did not mean*' to express any opposition to the duke', but that 'what he said was so ill-judged that it had the effect', while Ellenborough and Goulburn, who attributed the lapse to Murray's' 'want of habit of speaking', believed that he 'had done much injury'. A Scottish observer reported that while speaking he had 'looked more as if a letter of his name had been transposed than ever'.[43] Murray denied that Protestant soldiers serving abroad were compelled to attend Catholic religious services, 15 Nov. 1830, when he was in the ministerial minority on the civil list. He duly resigned with his colleagues and went into opposition as one of the more prominent members of the mainstream of the Tory party under Peel's somewhat distant leadership.[44] In the House, 13 Dec. 1830, he defended his and the late government's record on slavery abolition, observing, without apparent irony, that he had 'always supposed ... that to abstain from any extraordinary activity in the measures to be carried into effect with respect to the colonies was a merit rather than a defect'. He added that precipitate emancipation would 'merely afford a sanction to the commission of murder ... plunder and devastation'.

Murray was named to the select committee on the Rideau canal, which he considered a project 'of importance', 10 Feb. 1831. He presented a petition of Perth merchants and manufacturers for repeal of the duty on printed calicoes, 16 Feb., and met deputations of ship owners and wine merchants disgruntled with other aspects of the Grey ministry's incompetent budget.[45] On 18 Feb. he said there was no significant difference between their proposed Canada bill and his own of 1830 and attacked them for creating unreasonable expectations of what they would achieve on retrenchment and reform: 'It does not appear that they are as sanguine ... now, when in office, as they were when out of it'. He welcomed their bill to facilitate emigration for poor families, 22 Feb. He spoke briefly against the English reform bill, 18 Mar., and on the 22nd voted against its second reading after asserting that the Irish bill would 'excite as much dislike in its details, as the Scottish bill has excited in Scotland'. On 25 Mar. he conceded that 'a large proportion of the people of Scotland' favoured the measure, but insisted that 'the wealth and influence of the country' were hostile, being particularly alarmed by the proposal to enfranchise tenants, which he said would damage the agricultural interest by encouraging landlords to shorten leases and lead to the creation of fictitious votes. He argued that the public salaries committee had shown a bias towards naval over army officers and defended the Cambridge University anti-reform petition, 30 Mar., maintaining that its signatories were 'men possessing s great variety of knowledge, who, though not hostile to reform', were 'decidedly opposed to revolution':

> One of my chief objections to ... this measure is, that if it be carried into effect, and out of it a reformed Parliament should arise, all those who wish for still further changes will be enabled to put forward this strong argument, that the reform was effected in a House of Commons in which the people were not represented, many of the Members giving their votes under the influence of interested motives.

On 14 Apr. he presented but dissented from a petition from the presbytery of Dunblane for Scotttish clergymen to be allowed to vote. In passing, he stated his view, which became a recurrent theme of his, that the larger Scottish counties (including Perthshire) were entitled to two Members each and Scottish towns of over 22,000 inhabitants (including Perth) to separate representation. He also mooted the notion of enfranchising the Scottish universities to give the church a voice and objected to a ministerialist's description of the Scottish counties under the present system as 'rotten'. Before dividing for Gascoyne's wrecking amendment to the reform bill, 19 Apr., he said that the effect of reform would be to 'subject the people, to a dangerous degree, to the influence of those plausible harangues which have so often deceived and misled them' and, mischievously, quoted Fox's dictum that the 'united wisdom' of the ages would never be able to devise 'even a tolerable constitution'. Next day (when he 'seemed to think ministers would go out')[46] he claimed that the Scottish measure 'as it now stands, has hardly any approver in Scotland', where even its supporters found fault with details. At the ensuing general election he offered again for Perthshire as a man not averse to 'prudent ameliorations of our political system', but he did not specifically mention the reform bills. He was present at the Perthshire annual general meeting, 30 Apr. 1831, when nothing was said about reform. The Perthshire Whigs had no one to put up against him and he was returned unopposed, professing support for 'prudent' and 'moderate' reform, but hostility to disruptive change which threatened the beneficial 'influence of property'. His lengthy speech of thanks, which was reproduced in *The Times*, ended with a fanciful and faintly ludicrous depiction of the 'ship of state', with 'monarchy at the helm, to guide her in her course, with aristocracy ... as ballast, to keep her steady in a troubled sea, and with the favouring breath of the people to fill the sails'.[47]

On the second reading of the reintroduced English reform bill, 5 July 1831, Murray, following Macaulay, denounced it as 'a measure, the tendency of which is likely to give rise in this country to those dangerous and revolutionary convulsions with which we have seen other nations so much shaken', and predicted the emergence of another Cromwell, an allusion to lord chancellor Brougham, who was supposed to be the author of a pamphlet advising the Lords to accept reform. Greville heard that Murray's effort was considered 'not bad', while Ellenborough thought it was 'capital'.[48] Next day, when he voted against the bill, he paid tribute to the drowned Sir Joseph Yorke* in moving a new writ for Reigate and had an angry exchange with Brougham's brother William over his Cromwell remark. He voted for use of the 1831 census to determine the borough disfranchisement schedules, 19 July, against the partial disfranchisement of Chippenham, 27 July, and in minorities of 17, 38 and 29 to preserve existing voting rights, 27 Aug., retain the vote for non-resident freemen, 30 Aug, and allow freeholders of the four sluiced boroughs to continue voting there, 2 Sept. He argued that Clitheroe was entitled to keep both Members, 28 July, protested against the decision to proceed with the bill on Saturday, 30 July, and told Lord John Russell that the measure could not 'be final, because it contains the seeds of its own destruction', 5 Aug. Murray, who, according to Ellenborough, considered the vote to enfranchise Greenwich, 3 Aug., as 'the worst sign of the times, and the clearest proof of the disgraceful slavery of the House of Commons', endorsed the prayer of a Perth petition for the city to be given a Member of its own, 6 Aug., and reiterated his accusation that Scotland had been unfairly treated and its people 'trampled upon and abandoned' by ministers.[49] He squabbled with Russell over the enfranchisement of Whitehaven and Huddersfield and denied that opposition Members were guilty of 'impropriety' in fighting the details of the bill. He claimed to represent 140,000 people, however small the Perthshire electorate might be, 10 Aug., when he complained of the proposed annexation of a detached portion of the county to the new combined constituency of Clackmannan and Kinross. He opposed the division of English counties and objected above all to the enfranchisement of the metropolitan districts as a step too far towards democracy, 11 Aug. He thought there was much merit in Hume's proposal that Members should be allocated to the colonies, 16 Aug. After a shooting excursion to Peel's Staffordshire home at the end of August,[50] he pressed Althorp, the leader of the House, to act justly by the Scottish counties, 13 Sept. He divided against the third reading, 19 Sept., and passage, 21 Sept. 1831, of the English reform bill.

Murray explained on 25 July 1831 that as colonial secretary he had been reluctant to abandon Sierra Leone because he 'looked upon it as the only chance of introducing civilization to Africa', but he conceded that it had cost an enormous amount of money. He also justified his policy towards Canada and defended the Rideau canal scheme. He accused ministers of following a muddled policy on Belgium and demanded an assurance that British interests would be safeguarded, 12 Aug.; he 'evaded the question' when Russell asked him privately which of the fortresses he thought could be 'spared', 31 Aug.[51] He was sure that Lescene and Escoffery deserved their grant of compensation for their expulsion from Jamaica, 22 Aug. He presented Perthshire petitions against the use of molasses in brewing and distilling, 24 Aug., and said that during his time in Ireland the Dublin Castle under-secretary Gregory had been 'strictly impartial', 29 Aug. He voted for inquiry into the effects of renewal of the Sugar Refinery Act on the West India interest, 12 Sept. He denounced the Scottish reform bill on its second reading, 23 Sept., as even more 'dangerous' than the English: 'I never was an enemy to all reform; and I have ... been ready to admit of the expediency of some modification in the Scottish system ... But I do object to the utter abandonment of the principle of representation which has ever existed in that country'. At the same time, he took up his theme that if Scotland was to have reform, it ought to receive fair treatment, with more Members and separate representation for the larger towns. He presented a petition from the freeholders of Ross-shire against its proposed amalgamation with Cromartyshire, 28 Sept. On 3 Oct. he said that this was just about acceptable, but he condemned the merger of Elginshire and Nairnshire and, in particular, the separation of the Culross area from Perthshire to form part of Clackmannan and Kinross, seemingly the product of 'caprice' rather than 'sound judgement'. However, he welcomed the decision to give Perth a Member of its own. Next day he proposed that Perthshire and seven other Scottish counties with populations in excess of 100,000 should have two Members each, but was beaten by 113-61. Ellenborough found him 'much elated' by the defeat of the English reform bill in the Lords, and on 10 Oct. 1831 suggested him to Hardinge as a possible leader of the Commons in a putative 'provisional government to carry reform'.[52] Opposing Lord Ebrington's confidence motion that day, he said the country was 'in a situation of very considerable difficulty' but not 'in an awful crisis'. He accused ministers of having turned to reform to revive their declining popularity after their ruined budget and failure to implement significant cuts in expenditure, and their supporters of indulging in 'inflammatory' language.

Murray voted against the second reading of the revised English reform bill, 17 Dec. 1831, and the principle of schedule A, 20 Jan. 1832, when he presented a Perthshire Tories' petition against the Scottish measure. He voted against government on the Russian-Dutch loan, 26 Jan., 12 July; he spoke at some length against the transaction, 20 July. He criticized the division of English counties, 27 Jan., and, still professing to be 'a friend to reform', said that the additional Members given to Scotland fell well short of her due entitlement. That day, at the request of Charles Grant*, president of the board of control, he accepted nomination to the renewed select committee on the East India Company, but he refused to have anything to do with the military subcommittee.[53] He supported the prayer of a petition from Argyllshire against the transfer of the Cowal district to Buteshire, 3 Feb., and protested at the English bill's effective disfranchisement of freemen who were on service away from their constituencies with the army or militia, 7 Feb. He supported the opposition motion for papers on relations with Portugal, 9 Feb., but was in the majority against Hunt's motion for information on military punishments, 16 Feb. Next day he defended against Hume's attack his own part in establishing the Swan River settlement and protested that it was not his fault that it had become 'a convict colony'. He was credited with a vote in the majority against an attempt to limit the duration of small borough polls, 26 Feb., but on the 28th he divided against the enfranchisement of Tower Hamlets after condemning it as unnecessary and dangerous and avowing that 'the power of the democracy overturned the constitution of Athens and destroyed the liberties of Rome ... and overthrew ... all order and civil government in France'. He presented and endorsed constituency petitions against the malt drawback bill and voted against it, 29 Feb., as he did again, 2 Apr., when he complained that it would penalize the small distillers of the Highlands for the benefit of Lowland and Irish producers of inferior whisky. He disapproved of the substitution of marines for regular troops in garrisons, 16 Mar. He voted against the third reading of the English reform bill, 22 Mar. He presented petitions from Perthshire ecclesiastical bodies against the government's Irish education scheme, which he said infringed 'the inalienable privilege of all Protestants to be ... instructed in the whole of the sacred volume', 16 Apr. He spoke in the same sense, 8 June, but on 5 July 1832 welcomed the Irish secretary's assurance that reading the Bible was not to be part of the scheme.

In the crisis of May 1832, when Wellington tried to form a ministry to carry a measure of reform, Murray remained loyal to the duke and, according to Ellenborough, was willing under duress to become leader of the Commons, although he was 'very reluctant' to do so.[54] In the rowdy debate of 14 May, he denied that it would be 'inconsistent' in men such as himself to take office to carry reform and accused Russell of having in the past 'expressed himself hostile to those very principles upon which he had since framed his reform bill'. He argued that 'the only line which it became the House to follow was to support the crown'. The Whig Denis Le Marchant† thought his speech was 'feeble', and Murray himself perceived that the 'effect of the debate ... was fatal to the formation of a government'.[55] He attacked the Scottish reform bill in his usual terms, 21 May, but applauded the decision not to separate Cowal from Argyllshire. On reform in general, he said that 'the people have been deluded into the expectations of blessings which no reasonable man anticipates can result' and 'have been industriously kept in a state of violent excitement'. He admitted that the Perthshire pro-reform petition of December 1831, only now brought up by the lord advocate, 23 May, was respectably and numerously signed, but contended that it did not express intelligent county opinion. He supported the government's temporizing amendment to Fowell Buxton's motion for slavery abolition, 24 May, and was named to the select committee on the issue, 30 May. He was appointed to that on Irish outrages next day. He divided against the second reading of the Irish reform bill, 25 May. His renewed proposal to give the eight most populous Scottish counties two Members each was defeated by 168-61, 1 June. He supported Hume's motion to preserve the rights of superiority holders for their lives, 4 June, but it was not pressed. He derided the unification of Orkney and Shetland for electoral purposes, 6 June, but admitted that he had changed his mind on the issue of excluding Scottish clergymen from the franchise, largely because he had found them generally indifferent to the matter. He presented Perthshire petitions against the hypothec bill and for a reduction in the duty on fire insurances, 14 June. Next day he failed by 54-24 to prevent the 'dismemberment' of Perthshire and supported unsuccessful amendments against the junctions of Ross-shire with Cromartyshire and Elginshire with Nairnshire and for the removal of Kilmarnock from the Ayr district. On 27 June he welcomed the abandonment of the proposed property qualification for Scottish burgh

Members and helped to persuade ministers to drop the county qualification also. He still believed that it was ridiculous to link Orkney and Shetland, but he could not support Traill's amendment against it because it involved the loss of a burgh seat. He supported the grants for Sierra Leone and the Society for the Propagation of the Gospels, 23 July. Next day he again opposed the abolition of corporal punishment in the army as 'unsafe'. He dismissed De Lacy Evans's motion for a reduction of the army to the level of 25 Jan. 1831 as idiotic, 26 July. He gave his 'cordial concurrence' to the vote of thanks to Manners Sutton on his retirement as Speaker, 30 July 1832.

Murray stood for Perthshire at the 1832 general election but was beaten by a Liberal peer's son. He regained the seat at a by-election in May 1834, was appointed master-general of the ordnance in Peel's first ministry, but lost his seat at the 1835 general election a month later.[56] He stood unsuccessfully for Westminster in 1837 and Manchester in 1839 and 1841, when he was again placed at the ordnance by Peel. Sir James Robert George Graham* observed of his performance on the hustings in 1839 that he was 'better suited to the Horse Guards than to popular assemblies; for when pressed he makes dangerous concessions to political adversaries, and wants that high courage of resistance in the conflict of opinion, which so eminently distinguishes him in the field'.[57] Widowed in 1842, and ravaged by 'a lengthened illness', he died three weeks after resigning with Peel in July 1846. By his will of 5 Jan. 1846 he settled £26,000 and his Belgrave Square house on his daughter, now the wife of Lieutenant Henry George Boyce.[58]

[1] See S.G.P. Ward, 'Gen. Sir George Murray', *Jnl. of Soc. for Army Hist. Research*, lviii (1980), 191-208. [2] *Oxford DNB*, from par. reg. of Sunninghill, Berks. [3] Ward, 'Murray', 191. [4] Ibid. 192-202; S.G.P. Ward, *Wellington's Headquarters*, 25, 29, 41-49, 52-55, 57, 60-62, 64, 106, 109-11, 118, 120-1, 125, 140, 142-52, 155-8, 163, 165, 166, 188-9; Holland, *Further Mems.* 180. [5] Ward, 'Murray', 202-3; *Creevey Pprs.* i. 279. [6] Wellington mss WP1/785/13, 17; 786/20, 21; *Prince of Wales Corresp.* viii. 3438. [7] *Perthshire Courier*, 19, 26 Mar., 9 Apr. 1824; Add. 51836, Glenorchy to Holland, 1 Aug. 1831. [8] Ward, 'Murray', 203; *The Times*, 24, 27 July 1824; NAS GD51/1/198/21/71, 72. [9] *The Times*, 10 Feb. 1825; Ward, 'Murray', 203-4. [10] Ward, 'Murray', 206; *The Times*, 26 Feb. 1825. [11] Wellington mss WP1/815/1; Ward, 'Murray', 204. [12] *The Times*, 3 May 1825. [13] Ibid. 7, 18, 22 Mar. 1826 [14] *Perthshire Courier*, 22 June 1826. [15] Wellington mss WP1/889/5; 908/13; *Canning's Ministry*, 331, 343, 363, 394; *Arbuthnot Jnl.* ii. 128-9. [16] Wellington mss WP1/895/47; 899/9; 920/28. [17] *Perthshire Courier*, 24 Apr. 1828. [18] Wellington mss WP1/933/11, 14; 935/49. [19] *Lady Holland to Son*, 86; *Russell Letters*, i. 67-68, 89; Broughton, *Recollections*, iii. 273 [20] *Arbuthnot Jnl.* ii. 188-9, 191; *Ellenborough Diary*, i. 122, 123, 133, 134; Wellington mss WP1/934/29. [21] *Perthshire Courier*, 19 June 1828. [22] *Taylor Autobiog.* i. 117. [23] D.M. Young, *Colonial Office*, 110-15; P.J. Jupp, *British Politics on Eve of Reform*, 80, 82, 85-86, 119; *Greville Mems.* ii. 11. For Murray's correspondence with Wellington on colonial subjects see *Wellington Despatches*, iv. 570-1, 629-30, 638, 642; v. 70-71, 79-80, 603-9; vi. 41, 48-50, 156-7, 206-10, 444-5; Wellington mss WP1/948/11, 38; 950/2; 978/6; 1022/23; 1034/11; 1035/60; 1044/20; 1045/4; 1050/2; 1135/6. [24] *Arbuthnot Jnl.* ii. 195. [25] Southampton Univ. Lib. Broadlands mss PP/GC/TE/201. [26] *Ellenborough Diary*, i. 156, 159. [27] *Arbuthnot Jnl.* ii. 229. [28] *Ellenborough Diary*, i. 176, 295, 305, 347, 375, 377. [29] Ibid. i. 381; *Arbuthnot Jnl.* ii. 250; Broughton, *Recollections*, iii. 309; *Greville Mems.* i. 265. [30] *Althorp Letters*, 142; *Buxton Mems.* 226, 228; *Greville Mems.* i. 304. [31] *Perthshire Courier*, 1 Oct. 1829; *Extraordinary Black Bk.*(1832), 556. [32] *Greville Mems.* i. 362.; *Ellenborough Diary*, ii. 176. [33] *Ellenborough Diary*, ii. 187; Broughton, iv. 11. [34] *Ellenborough Diary*, ii. 212. [35] *Buxton Mems.* 228-9. [36] *Howard Sisters*, 128. [37] *Croker Pprs.* ii. 58; *Ellenborough Diary*, ii. 220-1. [38] *Arbuthnot Jnl.* ii. 365-6, 372-3; *Ellenborough Diary*, ii. 290, 297; *Greville Mems.* ii. 11. [39] *Greville Mems.* ii. 24. [40] *Perthshire Courier*, 15, 29 July, 19, 26 Aug. 1830. [41] *Arbuthnot Jnl.* ii. 381, 389, 396; *Lieven Letters*, 249, 254. [42] Broughton, iv. 57. [43] *Arbuthnot Jnl.* ii. 396; *Lieven Letters*, 264; *Ellenborough Diary*, ii. 414, 416; *Baring Jnls.* i. 68; Parker, *Peel*, ii. 167; *Greville Mems.* ii. 54; NAS GD157/25508/1-3. [44] *Three Diaries*, 23, 41, 46, 50, 54, 55, 58; N. Gash, *Sir Robert Peel*, 7. [45] *Three Diaries*, 55, 58. [46] Ibid. 81. [47] *Perthshire Courier*, 28 Apr., 5, 12 May; Add. 51836, Glenorchy to Holland, 1 Aug.; *The Times*, 19 May 1831. [48] Broughton, iv. 120; *Greville Mems.* ii. 159; *Three Diaries*, 100. [49] *Three Diaries*, 114. [50] Parker, *Peel*, ii. 188. [51] *Three Diaries*, 126-7. [52] Ibid. 145, 148-9. [53] Ibid. 187, 189. [54] Ibid. 250-1; *Croker Pprs.* ii. 163; Ward, 'Murray', 205; Wellington mss WP1/1224/2; *Wellington Despatches*, viii.306. [55] *Three Diaries*, 255-6. [56] *Creevey's Life and Times*, 403. [57] *Arbuthnot Corresp.* 212. [58] *Gent. Mag.* (1846), ii. 424-6, 660.

D.R.F.

MURRAY, William David, Visct. Stormont (1806–1898).

ALDBOROUGH	1830–1831
NEW WOODSTOCK	1831–1832
NORWICH	1832–1837
PERTHSHIRE	1837–18 Feb. 1840

b. 21 Feb. 1806, 1st s. of David William, 3rd Earl of Mansfield, Mdx., and Frederica, da. of Most Rev. William Markham, abp. of York. *educ.* Westminster 1816-22; Christ Church, Oxf. 1823. *m.* 8 Apr. 1829, Louisa, da. of Cuthbert Ellison*, 1s. *d.v.p.* 1da. *suc.* fa. as 4th earl of Mansfield, Mdx. 18 Feb. 1840; KT 13 June 1843; *suc.* grandmo. Louisa, *s.j.* countess of Mansfield, Notts., as 3rd earl of Mansfield, Notts. 11 July 1843. *d.* 2 Aug. 1898.

Ld. of treasury Dec. 1834-Apr. 1835; ld. high commr. to gen. assembly of Church [S] 1852, 1858-9.

Ld. lt. Clackmannan 1852-*d.*

'Silver-tongued' William Murray (1705-93), the 1st duke of Newcastle's political henchman, became lord chief justice in 1756 and was created Lord Mansfield. His marriage was childless and in 1776 he was promoted to the rank of earl with a special remainder (on the mistaken assumption that a Scottish peer could not take an English peerage other than by inheritance) to

Louisa Cathcart (1758-1843), the wife of his nephew David Murray, 7th Viscount Stormont (1727-96), a Scottish representative peer who was lord president of the council in the Coalition and under Pitt from 1794 to his death. In 1792, after a ruling which removed this misapprehension, Mansfield received a new patent as earl of Mansfield, Middlesex, with remainder to Stormont, who duly succeeded to this peerage the following year, when his wife became countess of Mansfield under the 1776 creation.[1] Their eldest son David William Murray (1777-1840), who was noted for his 'sleepy manners', never held political office, but he emerged during the 1820s as one of the leaders of the diehard Ultra Tories utterly opposed to Catholic emancipation. He was active in their attempts to thwart the formation of Canning's ministry in 1827, when he incurred the king's anger with his speech in the Lords, 2 May, in which he impugned the sincerity of George's attachment to the Protestant constitution.[2] He was unhappy with the duke of Wellington's junction with Huskisson in January 1828, being 'strongly for *fixed* principles, and a pure ministry of one sort or the other'.[3] Catholic emancipation infuriated him but did not, as it did other Ultras, make him a supporter of parliamentary reform, against which he resolutely set his face. He continued to aim at the overthrow of the Wellington ministry, and in Sir Richard Vyvyan's* approach to Lord Palmerston* in October 1829 he was named as the likely 'head' of an Ultra government. In June 1830, however, he resisted the blandishments of the 4th duke of Newcastle and Lord Winchilsea for him to take the lead of the revamped Ultra party. Mansfield, who thought the duke of Richmond should lead, welcomed the prospect of co-operation between Ultras in Lords and Commons, though he had 'no expectations that it will prevail'.[4]

After leaving Oxford Stormont, Mansfield's eldest son, toured Europe, and he attended the coronation of Nicholas I in Moscow in the summer of 1826. Three years later he consummated 'an old and long attachment' by marrying 'that enticing looking female Miss Ellison'.[5] At the general election of 1830 Newcastle, who expected him to 'turn out to be something out of the common way', returned him for Aldborough.[6] Ministers of course numbered him among the 'violent Ultras' and he duly helped to vote them out of office on the civil list, 15 Nov. Stormont, whose father now thought that the Ultras might be able to hold the balance of power,[7] was named to the select committee on the reduction of official salaries, 9 Dec. 1830. He joined in objections to the proposed tax on steamboat passengers, a threat to the economy of the Western Highlands, 17 Feb., and called for action to be taken over the forged signatures on the Carrickfergus election petition, 22 Feb. 1831. He aligned himself with that section of the Ultras, led in the Commons by Inglis and Wetherell, which was opposed to parliamentary reform in principle, and on 2 Mar. he condemned the Grey ministry's reform bill outright: 'reform appears to me to be revolution, concession [to be] spoliation, and, in time, religion must end in atheism'.[8] He made much of the hostile petitions from Cambridge University, Edinburgh and London and voted against the second reading, 22 Mar. A week later he and Wetherell deputed John Herries* to seek a reconciliation with Peel, under whose leadership they wished to see opposition co-ordinated, but their approach was rebuffed.[9] Stormont demanded that adequate returns be furnished to explain the statistical basis of the Scottish reform bill, 25 Mar., when he also threatened to join Hume in supporting a reduction in civil list salaries. He pressed ministers to clarify their intentions as to the enfranchisement of large towns, 13 Apr., and, attacking the 'absurdity' and 'injustice' of the disfranchising schedules, 15 Apr., accused them of political bias in the selection of doomed boroughs. He was consulted on the form of Gascoyne's wrecking amendment and spoke in support of it, 18 Apr., when he voiced his fear that the bill would facilitate a large influx of Irish Catholic Members bent on repealing the Union. He was in the majority against the bill the next day. When the king arrived in the Lords to dissolve Parliament, 22 Apr. 1831, he found Stormont's father on his feet delivering a furious denunciation of ministers.[10]

Newcastle settled that Stormont should 'change places' with Sadler, whose re-election for Newark was extremely doubtful; but at the last minute Stormont pulled out of the arrangement, to the intense annoyance of the duke, who blamed Mansfield's 'most selfish' intervention. Aldborough went to Sadler and Stormont found a berth at Woodstock, where he came in on the Blenheim interest after a token contest.[11] On 21 June 1831 he was given 'a hard slap' by Sir James Graham, a member of the cabinet, who, recalling his speech of 2 Mar. in which he had quoted *Coriolanus* to 'prove that crows would sit in a reformed Parliament', commented that 'in an unreformed Parliament daws may peck at characters they cannot destroy'. Stormont retorted with a condemnation of the dissolution and an attack on pledged reformers as 'fawners on the base multitude'; but an opponent dismissed this reply as 'silly'.[12] He was 'amongst the most obstreperous of the minority' when Russell unveiled the reintroduced reform bill, 6 July. He was one of the 'principal actors' in the obstructive all-night opposition to the bill, 12

July, when, disclaiming 'factious motives', he declared his determination 'to teach a lesson to the other side' and repeatedly divided the House for adjournment.[13] He wanted to know 'the fixed and precise rule we are to act upon' concerning the inclusion of parishes within boroughs, 15 July, and voted for use of the 1831 census as a basis for disfranchisement, 19 July. He presented a Woodstock petition against the bill, 20 July, and pleaded for the borough, 'a very rising and prosperous town', to be allowed to keep one Member, 26 and 27 July, when he voted against the partial disfranchisement of Chippenham. Protesting against the proposal to use Saturdays to expedite the bill, 5 Aug., he claimed to be 'nearly worn out' by his 'constant attendance'. Yet when Peel subsequently informed a party meeting that he was not prepared any longer to stay in London to fight the bill clause by clause, Stormont was one of those who were 'dissatisfied with this and prepared to go on interminably on the present system'.[14] He pressed for information on the French invasion of Belgium, 6, 9, 11, 12, 17 Aug. He claimed that improper government influence was being exercised at the Dublin by-election, 20 Aug., and voted in censure of ministers for their alleged interference there at the general election, 23 Aug. He was a teller for the minority against the disfranchisement of Downton, 14 Sept., when he called for additional county Members to be given to Scotland. He voted against the passage of the reform bill, 21 Sept. He divided against the second reading of the Scottish bill, 23 Sept., and on 27 Sept. defended superiorities, which were 'as much legal property as land'. After the defeat of the reform bill in the Lords, where Mansfield was among its 'most prominent opponents', Lady Holland named Stormont as one of those who 'may be gratified by seeing the blood of their countrymen', having 'expressed a wish to have a *fight* with the people'.[15] In the House, 12 Oct. 1831, he denied that the bill's opponents were 'enemies to freedom' and deprecated attempts to present them as such to the public.

Stormont voted against the revised reform bill in the divisions on its second reading, 17 Dec. 1831, going into committee, 20 Jan., and the enfranchisement of Tower Hamlets, 28 Feb. 1832. He voted for the Vestry Act amendment bill, 23 Jan., and against government on the Russian-Dutch loan, 26 Jan. He objected to the admission of a petition from the Political Union against making the payment of rates a qualification for the vote, 2, 6 Feb. He defended a Barnet petition condemning the reform bill against allegations of chicanery in its promotion, 10 Feb. Soon afterwards John Croker* noted that Stormont was one of the Ultras who were now 'very cordial' in their attitude towards Wellington and Peel, though he seemed by implication to set little store by his parliamentary talents.[16] Stormont voted against the third reading of the reform bill, 22 Mar. He was in minorities against the malt drawback bill, 2 Apr., and for inquiry into smuggling in the glove trade, 3 Apr. On 16 Apr. he persuaded the House to take notice of a breach of privilege by a firm of solicitors, who had written and circulated a letter casting aspersions on the members of the Commons committee which had thrown out the Sunderland harbour bill. He initiated proceedings against them and the printer of their letter, 7 May, when they were let off with an admonishment. On 10 May Stormont made his London house in Jermyn Street available for an opposition meeting, attended by Peel, to decide how to meet Lord Ebrington's motion of confidence in the outgoing ministers. In the House, 14 May, he had Burdett chastised by the Speaker for calling the bill's opponents in the Lords 'a violent and virulent faction'. After the ensuing debate, which effectively put paid to any hopes of a Tory ministry being formed to carry a moderate bill, he was one of Peel's dinner guests. The following morning he was among the throng of opposition Members who gathered at the Carlton Club, where he made a last ditch attempt to rally support for such a government. He then went with Ellenborough to see Wellington, who assured him that the game was up. He was one of the committee of five appointed to manage the opposition general election campaign in Scotland.[17] On 21 May he called on ministers to punish those 'pests of society' responsible for press attacks on the monarchy, but he got no satisfaction. He voted against the second reading of the Irish reform bill, 25 May, and the Russian-Dutch loan, 12 July 1832. After the general election in December, when he was successful at Norwich in a notoriously corrupt contest, he lamented that 'nothing can be worse than the prospects of this country'.[18]

Stormont remained on reasonably cordial terms with Peel, who strongly urged him to take junior office in his first ministry in December 1834. Mansfield made some difficulties, but Peel sweetened him with a vacant green ribbon, and Stormont took a seat at the treasury board.[19] Four months after his electoral triumph in Perthshire in 1837 he was devastated by the sudden death of his wife at the age of 28. After this blow he 'virtually abandoned public life' and 'withdrew a great measure from social functions', though he did not become entirely reclusive. He succeeded to the two earldoms in 1840 and 1843 and died at Scone Palace in August 1898.[20]

[1] *Oxford DNB*; *HP Commons, 1754-90*, iii. 189. [2] *Countess Granville Letters*, i. 107; G.I.T. Machin, *Catholic Question in English Politics*, 96, 104; *Colchester Diary*, iii. 466, 472-5, 492, 497; *Geo. IV Letters*, iii. 1325-6; *Canning's Ministry*, 288, 296. [3] *Colchester Diary*, iii. 542. [4] Machin, 175-6, 181, 184; *Palmerston-Sulivan Letters*, 232-3; Mansfield mss box 110/5, notes, 5, 6 June 1830 (NRA [S] 776). [5] Mansfield mss ser. 2/2350, Stormont to Lady Mansfield, 9 Aug. 1826; *Shelley Diary*, ii. 192, Add. 52017, J. Townshend to H.E. Fox, 27 Dec. 1827. [6] Nottingham Univ. Lib. Newcastle mss Ne2 F3/1, 245. [7] Mansfield mss box 110/8, Mansfield to Knatchbull, 9 Dec. 1830. [8] B.T. Bradfield, 'Sir Richard Vyvyan', *EHR*, lxxxiii (1968), 732; D.G.S. Simes, 'Ultra Tories in British Politics' (Oxf. Univ. D. Phil. thesis, 1975), 479, 481, 483-4. [9] *Arbuthnot Jnl.* ii. 416. [10] *Greville Mems.* ii. 138-40. [11] Newcastle mss Ne2 F4/1, 17; Notts. Archives, Tallents mss, Newcastle to Tallents, 23 Apr. 1831; *VCH Oxon.* xii. 404-5. [12] *Baring Jnls.* i. 88. [13] Broughton, *Recollections*, iv. 117; Hatherton diary, 13 July [1831]. [14] *Peel Letters*, 134. [15] *Holland House Diaries*, 64; *Lady Holland to Son*, 120. [16] *Croker Pprs.* ii. 151. [17] Ibid. ii. 154, 166; *Three Diaries*, 257-8, 266. [18] N. Gash, *Politics in Age of Peel*, 169; Mansfield mss ser. 2/2350, Stormont to Lady Mansfield, 27 Dec. 1832. [19] *Three Diaries*, 308, 340; Add. 40405, ff. 181, 310; 40406, ff. 78, 131; 40407, f. 32; Mansfield mss box 82, Stormont to Mansfield, 16 Dec.; ser. 2/1344, to Lady Mansfield, 16 Dec. 1834. [20] *Ann. Reg.* (1898), Chron. pp. 185-6.

D.R.F.

MUSGRAVE, Sir Philip Christopher, 8th bt. (1794–1827), of Edenhall, Cumb.

PETERSFIELD	27 June 1820–25 Mar. 1825
CARLISLE	2 Apr. 1825–16 July 1827

b. 12 July 1794, 1st s. of Sir John Chardin Musgrave, 7th bt., and Mary, da. of Rev. Sir Edmund Filmer, 6th bt., of East Sutton, rect. of Crundale, Kent. *educ.* Eton 1805; Christ Church, Oxf. 1813. *m.* 21 Oct. 1824, Elizabeth, da. of George Fludyer† of Ayston, Rutland, 1 da. *suc.* fa. as 8th bt. 24 July 1806. *d.* 16 July 1827.

The Musgraves had been established in Cumberland since the thirteenth century and could boast a long parliamentary tradition. Latterly, this Member's grandfather Sir Philip Musgrave had sat for Westmorland, 1741-7, and a kinsman, George Musgrave, was Member for Carlisle, 1768-74. An interval in the family's service had then occurred, so that when Musgrave offered for a vacancy at Carlisle in March 1816, the 'young fox hunting baronet', who was evidently also a devotee of the turf, was attacked as an interloper.[1] Election squibs portrayed 'young Muzzy' as the naive instrument of his mother's ambition and denounced his alleged connection with the 1st earl of Lonsdale, whose interest the family had traditionally opposed. After six days he conceded defeat.[2] At the Westmorland general election of 1818 Musgrave gave his interest to Lonsdale's candidates in their contest with the Whig Henry Brougham*, despite an earlier declaration of neutrality.[3] For this Lord Thanet later branded him 'a contemptible rat'.[4] Brougham avenged himself by seconding Musgrave's opponent at another Carlisle by-election in May 1820, when observers found it difficult to credit his professions of independence, given the strong support he received from Lonsdale's partisans, and although he fought under his own colours, this was revealed as a sham by subsequent correspondence.[5] He was defeated after a seven-day poll, but was soon afterwards returned on a vacancy for Petersfield on the interest of Hylton Jolliffe*, a distant relative.[6]

An irregular attender, Musgrave was described by a radical commentary of 1825 as having 'voted with ministers', but this was not always the case.[7] He was in their majorities against economies in revenue collection, 4 July 1820, and censure of their conduct towards Queen Caroline, 8 Feb. 1821. Unlike Jolliffe, he voted against Catholic relief, 28 Feb. 1821, 1 Mar., 21 Apr., 10 May 1825, and removal of Catholic peers' disabilities, 30 Apr. 1822. On 15 Mar. 1821 he spoke against inquiry into a petition protesting at the intervention of a military force during the Carlisle election, in which he asserted 'much rioting' and intimidation of his voters had taken place, and read documents that were supposed to prove this, but in such a low voice that 'a great part of the House ... could not have understood their contents'. He divided against repeal of the additional malt duty, 3 Apr. and a motion for economy and retrenchment, 27 June. He voted against disqualifying ordnance officials from voting in parliamentary elections, 12 Apr. 1821, inquiry into the right of voting in parliamentary elections, 20 Feb., and reform of the Scottish representative system, 2 June 1823, and of Edinburgh's representation, 13 Apr. 1826. He divided for mitigation of the punishment for forgery, 23 May 1821. He voted against more extensive tax reductions, 11, 21 Feb., but for a gradual lowering of the salt duties, 28 Feb., and a reduction of the admiralty lords, 1 Mar. 1822. He was back in the ministerial lobbies against abolition of one of the joint-postmasterships, 13 Mar., and inquiry into the conduct of the lord advocate in Scotland, 25 June 1822. He divided against inquiries into coronation expenses, 19 June 1823, and the prosecution of the Methodist missionary John Smith for inciting slave riots in Demerara, 11 June 1824. He voted for the second reading of the Irish insurrection bill, 14 June 1824.

When another vacancy occurred at Carlisle in March 1825, Lord Lowther* thought Musgrave 'the best candidate who could be started'.[8] At the nomination he admitted to being a supporter of ministers in general and, 'after the exhaustion naturally attendant on a long, but just and necessary war', an admirer of their foreign policy in particular. He was returned unopposed.[9] He presented a Carlisle petition for a revision of the corn laws, 24 Apr. 1825.[10] He voted against the disfranchisement of Irish 40*s*. freeholders, 26 Apr. Presumably it was the interests of factory owners in his new constituency which prompted him to speak against a measure to restrict the number of hours worked by children in cotton mills, 16 May, though he wished to render effectual the regulatory Act of 1819. He voted for the duke of Cumberland's annuity bill, 30 May, 6 June 1825. He presented petitions for the abolition of slavery from Edenhall, 27 Feb., and Carlisle, 1 Mar. 1826.[11] According to a subsequent election speech, he divided against a motion to consider the state of the corn laws, 18 Apr. 1826.[12]

On 9 May 1825 Musgrave had written to the ordnance office for details of planned provision for barracks at Carlisle, doubtless with the disorder that had marred the 1820 by-election in mind.[13] His worst fears were realised during his canvass at the 1826 general election, when hostile questioning on his attitude to reform and the corn laws erupted into violence. He was forced to barricade himself inside a house, whence he was rescued by military intervention at the cost of three lives. Musgrave himself 'received several severe blows, but almost miraculously, escaped without loss of blood', though an obituary later recorded that the incident had 'produced a serious effect upon his health'. At the nomination he conceded the necessity of a considered modification of the corn laws, citing his isolated wayward vote on the salt tax as an example of his willingness to oppose ministers when necessary, and affirmed his opposition to Catholic emancipation and support for the abolition of slavery in the West Indies. He was returned after a three-day poll, but at the behest of his wife did not venture again upon the hustings and declined to attend the chairing and a celebratory dinner.[14] Lonsdale evidently paid a proportion of his election expenses and Musgrave voted for the earl's candidates in Westmorland, where he qualified by right of his Hartley estate.[15] On 19 Feb. 1827 he endorsed a Carlisle petition for an alteration of the corn laws.[16] He voted against Catholic relief, 6 Mar. 1827. In response to a petition presented by his Whig colleague Sir James Graham protesting at the military intervention during the Carlisle election, 3 Apr., he 'lamented the consequences' of their action, but denied that a civil police could have maintained order, though he admitted that the establishment of such a force would be of benefit there.[17] He had already corresponded on this subject with William Nanson, the town clerk, and the home secretary Peel had evidently sought the views of the borough Members.[18] They were given leave to bring in the Carlisle police bill, 14 Mar., but Musgrave played no further part in its progress through the House. It is probable that he was already suffering from the 'painful and protracted illness' which ended in his death, *s.p.m.* and intestate, in July 1827. The same complaint, 'consumption, or a general decline', had caused the deaths of his father and an aunt, and the fatalism which this engendered was said to have accelerated his own demise. An obituarist praised the 'plainness and sincerity' of his manners but admitted that as a politician, he had been of a 'retiring disposition'. His daughter Elizabeth Mary, born the previous year, stood to inherit 'a large fortune' from his wife, to whom his personal estate of £25,000 passed, but she died in 1844.[19] The baronetcy and Edenhall, which Musgrave had 'entirely rebuilt', and other entailed family properties in Cumberland, Durham and Westmorland reverted to his brother, the Rev. Christopher John Musgrave (1798-1834), who was succeeded in turn by his next brother George Musgrave (1799-1872).[20]

[1] *Carlisle Election for 1816*, pp. 47, 62. For his ownership of racehorses see *Carlisle Patriot*, 29 Sept., 6 Oct. 1826. [2] *Carlisle Election*, 87-88, 98-99, 117; *The Times*, 12 Mar. 1816. [3] Brougham mss, Musgrave to M. Atkinson, 22 Oct. 1817, 13, 19 Feb. 1818; *Address to Freeholders ... connected in interest with Sir Philip Musgrave* (1818). [4] Add. 51571, Thanet to Lady Holland, 26 Mar. 1820. [5] *The Times*, 4 Apr. 1820; Lonsdale mss, Lowther to Lonsdale, 23, 31 July 1827. [6] *The Times*, 5 June 1820; H.G.H. Jolliffe, *Jolliffes of Staffs.* 174, 233. [7] *Black Bk.* (1823), 173; *Session of Parl. 1825*, p. 477. [8] Lonsdale mss, Lowther to Lonsdale, 23 Mar. 1825. [9] *Carlisle Patriot*, 9 Apr. 1825. [10] *The Times*, 25 Apr. 1825. [11] *Carlisle Patriot*, 4 Mar.; *The Times*, 2 Mar. 1826. [12] *Carlisle Patriot*, 9 June 1826. [13] Cumbria RO (Carlisle), Musgrave mss D/Mus/A1/19. [14] *The Times*, 9, 13, 15 June; *Carlisle Patriot*, 9, 16 June 1826, 20 July 1827. [15] Musgrave mss A1/20, W. Nanson to Musgrave, 2 June, 22 July, 25 Aug. 1826; *Westmld. Pollbook* (1826). [16] *The Times*, 20 Feb. 1827. [17] *Carlisle Patriot*, 6 Apr. 1827. [18] Ibid., 12 Jan.; Musgrave mss A1/20, Nanson to Musgrave 21, 22 Feb. 1827. [19] *Carlisle Patriot*, 20 July 1827; IR26/1137/1363. [20] PROB 11/1448/658; P. Musgrave, *Notes on Musgrave Fam.* 164.

H.J.S./P.J.S.

MUSGRAVE, Sir Richard, 3rd bt. (1790–1859), of Tourin, nr. Cappoquin, co. Waterford.

CO. WATERFORD	1831–1832
CO. WATERFORD	1835–1837

b. 6 Jan. 1790, 1st s. of Sir Christopher Frederick Musgrave, 2nd bt., of Tourin and Jane, da. of John Beere of Ballyboy, co. Tipperary. *educ.* Trinity, Dublin 1807. *m.* 29 July 1815, Frances, da. of William Newcome, abp. of Armagh, 5s. *suc* fa. as 3rd bt. Sept. 1826. *d.* 7 July 1859.

Musgrave's uncle and namesake, a collector of excise for the port of Dublin and the author of an anti-Catholic *History of the Irish Rebellion of 1798*, had sat for Lismore in the Irish Parliament, 1778-1800. On his death in 1818 his Irish estates and baronetcy had passed to his younger brother, Musgrave's father, whom Musgrave succeeded in 1826.[1] Richard Sheil* observed that Musgrave, who had joined the Catholic Association in 1826, was 'in every political respect' the 'exact opposite' of his celebrated uncle:

> He is a man of views as enlightened as his manners are bland ... who possesses an understanding as clear and vigorous as his purpose is pure and sound. He is beloved by the people, respected by the gentry, the model of a country gentleman, a kind neighbour ... and ... an 'honest man!'[2]

At the 1826 general election Musgrave assisted Thomas Wyse* and other Association activists in their campaign to oust Lord George Thomas Beresford from county Waterford and on the hustings proposed his successful opponent, Henry Villiers Stuart.[3] He became the first president of the County Waterford Liberal Club in August 1828, was unable to preside at a grand dinner for Wyse that November owing to the death of his infant daughter and at the end of the year signed the Protestant declaration in support of Catholic emancipation.[4] On 24 Jan. 1829 he 'spoke at considerable length of his conviction that ... emancipation must be speedily conceded' and would bring 'peace and independence' at a county meeting in support of Lord Anglesey, the recalled Irish viceroy.[5] Following Villiers Stuart's vacation of his seat that June, he was solicited to stand against Beresford by the Liberals, or independents as they were now known, but declined.[6] He assisted Daniel O'Connell's* candidacy for the county in the 1830 general election and 'promised to propose him', although in the event he was not required to perform this role.[7] On 6 Apr. 1831 he chaired a county meeting in support of O'Connell's re-election and the Grey ministry's reform bill, which he believed would 'afford the country the best remedy against revolution'. 'You have the Musgraves with you and no man dare oppose their wishes in this county', an informant advised O'Connell that day.[8] At the dissolution Musgrave tentatively stepped forward as O'Connell's replacement following his decision to stand elsewhere, only to withdraw 'in consequence of the disunion' created by the appearance of a third reform candidate. A 'fine hubbub among the reformers' ensued, following which he was 'selected' at a meeting and persuaded to offer again in a cleared field. At the nomination he promised to 'assist in defeating those who have always been hostile to the liberties of the people' and announced that once reform had passed, 'I shall consider myself at liberty to resign'. He was returned unopposed.[9]

Musgrave voted for the second reading of the reintroduced English reform bill, 6 July, at least twice against the adjournment, 12 July, and gave steady support to its details, though he was in the minorities for the disfranchisement of Saltash, 26 July, and against the division of English counties, 11 Aug. 1831. He divided for the bill's third reading, 19 Sept., its passage, 21 Sept., for the second reading of the Scottish bill, 23 Sept., and Lord Ebrington's confidence motion, 10 Oct. In his maiden speech he condemned the grant to the Kildare Place Society, alleging that their agents made 'Catholic children read the Bible', 15 July. He presented constituency petitions in similar terms, 20 July, 12, 15 Aug., and one for repeal of the Irish Vestry Acts, 22 July. He voted for a reduction of civil list pensions, 18 July, and against the grant for the Society for the Propagation of the Gospels in the colonies, 25 July. On 11 Aug. he moved and was a minority teller for printing the Waterford petition for disarming the Irish yeomanry, whose 'inhumanity' in the Newtownbarry massacre had made their abolition 'necessary for the peace'. He divided with ministers on the Dublin election controversy, 23 Aug. He was in the minority of 24 against the truck bill, 12 Sept. He opposed delaying the Pembrokeshire writ, explaining that the election committee on which he had served had found no evidence of bribery, 26 Sept. He denied that the Catholic clergy were opposed to 'religious education' and defended the grant to Maynooth College that day. He divided for inquiry into the conduct of the Hampshire magistrates during the arrest of the Deacles, 27 Sept. That month he assisted James Grattan in preparing an abortive bill for Irish poor relief.[10] He presented and endorsed a constituency petition urging the Irish ordnance survey to be 'speedily' extended to county Waterford, 14 Dec. 1831, and was appointed to the select committee on Irish tithes next day.

Musgrave divided for the second reading of the revised English reform bill, 17 Dec. 1831, and again gave general support to its details. He voted for printing the Woollen Grange petition for the abolition of Irish tithes, 16 Feb., and brought up constituency petitions in similar terms, 1 Mar., when he warned that enforced collection would 'lead to the most calamitous consequences', and 13, 20 June 1832. He denounced the government's tithes resolutions as 'premature', 13 Mar., and voted accordingly, 30 Mar. He defended the conduct of anti-tithes campaigners and refuted claims that their grievances were 'generally exaggerated', 10 Aug. He called for the Irish Subletting Act to be 'totally repealed' rather than modified, adding that such 'legislative experiments' demonstrated 'a great ignorance of the local circumstances of Ireland', 20 Feb. He voted for inquiry into the Peterloo massacre, 15 Mar. He divided for the third reading of the reform bill, 22 Mar., but was absent from the division on Ebrington's motion for an address calling on the king to appoint only ministers who would carry the measure unimpaired, 10 May. He voted for the second reading of the Irish bill, 25 May, but was in the minorities for O'Connell's motion to extend the Irish county franchise to £5 freeholders and the enfranchisement of £30 tenants on leases of 19 years, 18 June. On 13 June he protested that the Dungarvan boundary commissioners had 'exceeded their instructions' and restricted the boundaries 'so as to form a nomination borough'. (Their recommendations were overturned by a select committee.) He voted against the government's temporizing amendment on the abolition of slavery, 24 May. He divided for a tax on absentee landlords to provide permanent provision for the poor, 19 June, and for coroners' inquests to be made public, 20 June. He was granted a month's leave on account of family illness, 9 July 1832.

At the 1832 dissolution he retired from county Waterford. He was elected unopposed as a Liberal in 1835 and stood down in 1837. Thereafter he was active in the local repeal campaign and in 1843 publicly resigned his commission of the peace in protest at the Peel administration's dismissal of magistrates who had attended repeal meetings. He died at Whiting Bay, county Waterford, in July 1859, and was succeeded in the baronetcy by his eldest son Richard (1820-74).[11]

[1] *Oxford DNB*; *Hist. Irish Parl.* v. 333-4. [2] R. Sheil, *Sketches, Legal and Political* ed. M.W. Savage, ii. 338. [3] *Dublin Evening Post*, 22, 27 June 1826. [4] F. O'Ferrall, *Catholic Emancipation*, 222; *Dublin Evening Post*, 15 Nov. 1828. [5] T. Wyse, *Hist. Catholic Association*, ii. p. ccxxvi; *Dublin Evening Post*, 31 Jan. 1829. [6] PRO NI, Primate Beresford mss D3279/A/4/33, 35; *Waterford Mail*, 23 Sept. 1829, 24 Feb. 1830. [7] *O'Connell Corresp.* iv. 1693; PRO NI, Pack-Beresford mss D664/A/155. [8] *Waterford Mail*, 9 Apr. 1831; *O'Connell Corresp.* iv. 1796-7. [9] *O'Connell Corresp.* iv. 1804; *Waterford Mail*, 7, 11, 14 May 1831. [10] *O'Connell Corresp.* iv. 1838. [11] *The Times*, 5 July 1843; *Gent. Mag.* (1859), ii. 200.

P.J.S.

MYDDELTON BIDDULPH, Robert (1805–1872), of Chirk Castle, Denb. and 35 Grosvenor Place, Mdx.

Denbigh Boroughs	1830–1832
Denbighshire	1832–1834
Denbighshire	1852–1868

b. 20 June 1805, 1st s. of Robert Myddelton Biddulph† of Burghill and Crofton Hall, Worcs. and Charlotte, da. of Richard Myddelton† of Chirk Castle. *educ.* Eton 1820; Christ Church, Oxf. 1822. *m.* 31 May 1832, Frances, da. of William Owen of Woodhouse, Salop, 3s. (1 *d.v.p.*) 3da. *suc.* fa. to Burghill 1814; mother to Chirk Castle 1843. *d.* 21 Mar. 1872.

A.d.c. to Queen Victoria 1869-*d.*

Ld. lt. Denb. 1841-*d.*; col. Denb. militia 1840-*d.*

Myddelton Biddulph's father, a Foxite Whig, was one of the Biddulphs of Ledbury and had made his fortune, estimated to be worth £70,000 a year, in the service of the East India Company and as a partner in the London bank of Cocks, Biddulph and Company. He had taken the name of Myddelton on his marriage to a co-heiress of the Chirk Castle estate in 1801. Defeated in Herefordshire in 1802, he had used his wealth and the Chirk Castle influence to come in for Denbigh Boroughs, so thwarting the ambitions of his wife's brother-in-law Frederick West†, and intensifying the sisters' acrimonious legal battle for control of the estate and the constituency, which their heirs were groomed to represent.[1] Despite attempts at containment, dynastic spending in the Boroughs escalated after the tripartite division of the estate in 1819, for the Wests strove to return their son for Denbigh Boroughs before Myddelton Biddulph came of age. His father had died when he was nine, and it fell to his mother to 'preserve the interest' without dissipating their fortunes.[2] In 1824 he was rumoured to be preparing to raise the Myddelton interest in Denbighshire with William Hughes* of Kinmel Park, but his mother would not spend. He joined Brooks's, 22 June 1825, proposed by Hughes and Sir Francis Burdett*, and in November announced that he would stand for Denbigh Boroughs at the next election.[3] However, when it was called in June 1826, a pro-West returning officer deliberately scheduled the nomination so that he was a week too young to stand, and he spent his 21st birthday campaigning for his nominee Joseph Ablett of Llanbedr Hall in the violent and financially exhausting contest which terminated in a dual return, decided in West's favour.[4] Lord Forester, whose beautiful daughter Isabella he courted in 1828, thought him 'a very gentlemanlike young man, rather too young to be married' and noted that although 'a great gamester', he was determined to add Chirk Castle and an uncle's estate to his father's fortune, of which he was said to have lost £80,000 in 1827 to the Ansons. Lady Williams Wynn, who understood that 'no more than £2,000 a year' was to be settled on the couple, predicted that they would go abroad immediately, as 'many I believe thought her too good for our young Taffy lord of the castle, who is not I think at present very popular'. Nothing came of the proposed match.[5] Myddelton Biddulph approved the Chirk Castle property sales, land exchanges and increased coal mining and quarrying, but his mother, besieged by bailiffs in August and September 1829 on account of their debts, had to give up her town house and go abroad, leaving their financial affairs in the capable hands of her brother-in-law, the Ledbury banker John Biddulph.[6] He had recently negotiated a marriage settlement between Myddleton Biddulph and Elizabeth Palmer, whose father Captain Palmer now called off the match.[7] Myddelton Biddulph threatened another contest in Denbigh in 1830, but in the event West stood down 'to avoid further ruinous expense' and he came in unopposed, proposed by their 1818-26 Member, John Wynne Griffith of Garn, and seconded by Ablett.[8] At Michaelmas, with his brother Thomas Myddelton Biddulph (1809-78) in attendance, he chaired his first Denbigh corporation dinner.[9]

The Wellington ministry listed him among their 'foes' and he divided against them on the civil list when they were brought down, 15 Nov. 1830. He presented anti-slavery petitions from Denbigh and Holt, 11 Dec. 1830. As a magistrate, he stood joint bail for the Chirk Bridge colliers tried for breaking the peace during the troubles in the North Wales coalfield that month. He also offered to pay for their defence when they were brought to trial.[10] After seeing him on 13 Feb. 1831, John Biddulph observed:

> I think it a most fortunate circumstance his coming into Parliament. It will in all probability give his mind a new direction and in time throw him into a new class of society. Unfortunately, he has *no [London] home*.[11]

He presented a petition from Chirk for the ill-fated Ellesmere and Chirk road bill, 18 Mar. He divided for the Grey ministry's reform bill at its second reading, 22 Mar., presented favourable petitions from Holt and Denbigh, 28 Mar., and voted against Gascoyne's wrecking amendment, 19 Apr. 1831. In view of his support for reform, which he considered 'equally indispensable to the future security of the monarchy as it is to the liberty and independence of the subject', he was acclaimed and returned unopposed for Denbigh at the general election that month.[12] He voted for the reintroduced reform bill at its second reading, 6 July, against adjournment, 12 July, and generally for its details, except on the case of Aldborough, 14 Sept. 1831. He divided for the bill's passage, 21 Sept., and Lord Ebrington's confidence motion, 10 Oct. He apparently did little to assist Griffith and their Denbigh friends, who wanted Abergele and Llanrwst included in the reformed Denbigh Boroughs constituency to offset domination by Wrexham, and declared for the second seat conceded to Denbighshire, 19 Sept., having promised his interest in the Boroughs to John Madocks of Glan-y-wern.[13] He did not divide on the revised reform bill at its second reading, 17 Dec. 1831, but he voted against amending it by introducing a £10 urban poor rate franchise, 3 Feb., for its voter registration provisions, 8 Feb., to leave Helston in Schedule B, 23 Feb., and to enfranchise Tower Hamlets, 28 Feb 1832. In common with other Welsh Members, he cast a protest vote to grant Merthyr separate enfranchisement instead of Gateshead, 5 Mar. He divided for the bill's third reading, 22 Mar., and Ebrington's motion calling on the king to appoint only ministers who would carry it unimpaired, 10 May 1832. He divided with government on the Dublin election controversy, 23 Aug., the Liverpool writ, 5 Sept. 1831, and the Russian-Dutch loan, 12, 16, 20 July 1832. His marriage in May 1832 strengthened his ties with the politically important Whig families of Lloyd, Owen and Mostyn.

Myddelton Biddulph rarely deigned to acknowledge his Denbighshire friends in London, but he sought them out in the county, where his inability to speak Welsh placed him at a disadvantage with natural Liberal supporters during his canvass, and defeated the Ultra Lloyd Kenyon* to come in with Sir Watkin Williams Wynn* at the December 1832 general election.[14] Accused of inactivity, he attributed his inattention to parliamentary duties to 'inflammation of the eyes', which frequently confined him to a dark room. He lost to a Conservative at the January 1835 election[15] and failed to return Thomas for Denbigh Boroughs in 1837 and 1841. He contested Denbighshire again in 1847 after succeeding Williams Wynn to the lord lieutenancy and as militia commander, and his mother to Chirk Castle and half her £30,000 fortune. Although defeated in 1847, when opposition to the Maynooth grant was the cornerstone of his campaign, he succeeded in 1852, retaining the seat until 1868, when his personal support for the established church, 'Adullamite Whig' principles and failure to condemn '*y sgriw*' (politically motivated evictions) cost him Liberal support.[16] He died at his London home in

Grosvenor Place in March 1872 and was buried at Chirk.[17] He was succeeded there by his eldest son Richard (1837-1913), left his town house to his wife and provided annuities, marriage settlements and life insurance for his remaining children and dependants. His brother Thomas retained a life interest in the Burghill estate which he barred Roman Catholics from inheriting.

[1] *HP Commons, 1790-1820*, ii. 495; iii. 205-6. [2] *The Times*, 15 Apr. 1819; NLW, Chirk Castle mss C/74-78; E/3460-2; F/4790, 4809, 6298, 7487, 11402, 11405-11406; NLW, Garn mss (1956), C. Biddulph to J.W. Griffith, 4, 22 Feb. 1820, J. Copner Williams to same, 7 June 1825. [3] NLW ms 2794 D, R. Smith to H. Williams Wynn, 15 Nov. 1824; NLW ms 2795 D, Lady Williams Wynn to same, 19 Oct., 3 Nov. 1825. [4] *Chester Courant*, 11, 18, 25 Apr., 20, 27 June; *N. Wales Gazette*, 13, 20, 27 Apr., 29 June; *The Times*, 19 Apr., 9 June; *Cambrian*, 17 June, 1 July 1826; NLW ms 12870 D; Chirk Castle mss F/5968, 9541. [5] NLW, Aston Hall mss C.323, 324; Rutland mss (History of Parliament Aspinall transcripts), Forrester to Rutland, 29 Jan., 6 Feb.; NLW ms 2796 D, Lady Delamere to H. Williams Wynn, 20 Mar., Lady Williams Wynn to same, 15 May 1828. [6] Chirk Castle mss E/2593, 2598, 2599, 2611, 3520 (i) and (ii), 3061; Herefs. RO, diaries of John Biddulph of Ledbury [Biddulph diary] G2/IV/5/55-57, 14 Aug. 1829-12 Aug. 1830. [7] Biddulph diary G2/IV/5/56, 17 Aug.-14 Sept. 1829. [8] *Chester Courant*, 13, 20 July, 3, 10 Aug.; *Chester Chron.* 6 Aug. 1830. [9] *Chester Courant*, 5 Oct. 1830. [10] NLW ms 2797 D, Harriet to F. Williams Wynn, 1 Feb. 1831; Chirk Castle mss E/3070, 3076. [11] Biddulph diary G2/IV/5/58, 13 Feb. 1831. [12] *Chester Courant*, 26 Apr., 3, 10, 31 May; *Morning Chron.* 3 May; *Chester Chron.* 6 May; *Spectator*, 7 May; *Caernarvon Herald*, 7 May 1831. [13] *Chester Courant*, 20, 27 Sept.; *Caernarvon Herald*, 24 Sept., 1 Oct. 1831; NLW ms 2797 D, Sir W. to H. Williams Wynn, 10 July 1832; UCNW, Mostyn of Mostyn mss 7872. [14] Garn mss (1956), W. to G. Griffith, 15 Feb.; Mostyn of Mostyn mss 7875, 7877-80; NLW, Wynnstay mss L 936-41, 1043; *Chester Chron.* 27 July, 17 Aug., 27 Oct., 28 Dec.; *Chester Courant*, 11, 25 Sept. 1832; Chirk Castle mss C/87; NLW ms 2727 D, Sir W. to H. Williams Wynn, 10 July, 21 Nov. 1832; NLW, Coedymaen mss 231, 234; Add. 40403, f. 119; *N. Wales Chron.* 1 Jan. 1833. [15] *N. Wales Chron.* 24 June 1834; *Caernarvon Herald*, 3 Jan. 1835. [16] *Byegones* (1880), 41; Wynnstay mss L/1041, 1042; PROB 11/1992/84; IR26/1664/73; F. Price Jones, 'Politics in 19th Cent. Denb.' *Trans. Denb. Hist. Soc.* x (1961), 183-90; K.O. Morgan, *Wales in British Politics, 1868-1922*, p. 23; *Yr Herald Cymraeg*, 5 Dec. 1868. [17] *N. Wales Chron.* 30 Mar., 6 Apr. 1872.

M.M.E.

NEALE (formerly BURRARD), Sir Harry, 2nd bt. (1765–1840), of Walhampton, nr. Lymington, Hants.

LYMINGTON	1790–1802
LYMINGTON	1806–1807
LYMINGTON	1812–24 Mar. 1823
LYMINGTON	1832–1834

b. 16 Sept. 1765, 1st s. of Col. William Burrard, gov. Yarmouth Castle, I.o.W., and 2nd w. Mary, da. of Dr. Joseph Pearce of Lymington. *educ.* Christchurch g.s. *m.* 15 Apr. 1795, Grace Elizabeth, da. and coh. of Robert Neale of Shaw House, Melksham, Wilts., taking name of Neale by sign manual 8 Apr. 1795, *s.p. suc* fa. 1780; uncle Sir Harry Burrard†, 1st bt., of Walhampton as 2nd bt. 12 Apr. 1791; KCB 2 Jan. 1815; GCB 14 Sept. 1822; GCMG 1824. *d.* 7 Feb. 1840.

Entered RN 1778, lt. 1787, cdr. 1790, capt. 1793, r.-adm. 1810, v.-adm. 1814; c.-in-c. Mediterranean 1823-6; adm. 1830.

Groom of bedchamber 1801-12, (Windsor) 1812-20; ld. of admiralty Jan.-Sept. 1804, Feb. 1806-Apr. 1807.

Lt.-col. Lymington vol. inf. 1803-5; riding forester, New Forest 1813-20; recorder, Lymington 1824.[1]

Neale enjoyed royal favour for his part in quelling the mutiny at the Nore in 1797 and his naval career always took precedence over Parliament.[2] At the 1820 general election he was returned again for his local borough of Lymington, where his family's influence had long been dominant. A lax and silent attender, for whom there is no trace of activity for 1820, when present he continued to give silent support to the Liverpool ministry. He voted against repeal of the additional malt duty, 3 Apr., and reduction of the grants for the adjutant general's office, 11 Apr., and miscellaneous services, 9 May 1821. He divided against more extensive tax reductions, 11, 21 Feb., and abolition of one of the joint-postmasterships, 13 Mar. 1822. Next year he relinquished his seat on his appointment as commander-in-chief in the Mediterranean. In 1824 he presided over the blockade and subsequent bombardment of Algiers, imposed in response to an outrage committed on the British consulate. In the ensuing negotiation the Algerian dey agreed to abide by the terms of an 1816 treaty on consular rights and European slavery, but refused to accept the reinstatement of the British consul, Hugh McDonell, claiming that his personal safety could not be guaranteed.[3] John Croker*, the admiralty secretary, was critical of Neale's failure to insist on this, and the chilly response to Neale's exculpatory dispatch led him to believe that others in authority shared this view.[4] When William Shaler, the American consul in the city, referred in print to the 'tameness exhibited by the British admiral in the negotiations', Neale took up his pen to explain that McDonell was 'personally objectionable to the dey, and not without sufficient reason'. With the benefit of hindsight, an obituarist was inclined to compare Neale's command favourably with that of his more bellicose successor, Sir Edward Codrington.[5]

On Neale's return from sea he was presented with a congratulatory address from 40 Lymington tradesmen, 11 May 1827.[6] Judging from the votes of his nominees, it appears that he swallowed the Wellington ministry's concession of Catholic emancipation in 1829. In a letter apparently written at the following year's dissolution, Neale advised one of the Members that the 'circumstance of the times' dictated that he must resume his seat, 'much against my inclination'. Nothing came of this, but he opposed the Grey ministry's reform bill through his nominees and sought Peel's recommendation for the return he made at the 1831 general election.[7] That October he urged his friend Sir Thomas Byam Martin not to blight his chances of an honour by actively opposing the revised reform bill, which in a modified form it might be 'desirable to pass', but defended the role of the bishops in the rejection of the previous bill:

> People in the violence of party spirit seem to forget that ... bishops ought also to exercise spiritual influence ... in order that they may be a wholesome check when a temporal preponderance is likely to overbalance and to endanger the church ... If they are to be debarred the exercise of all political influence, what power can they have in the state to stem the tide of levelling principles that would overturn the church?[8]

Although the enlargement of Lymington by the Boundary Act was far from detrimental to Neale's interest, he could no longer simply nominate the Members, a consideration which seems to have led him to contest the borough as a Conservative at the 1832 general election. His local prestige was sufficient to guarantee his return, a point acknowledged by his opponents when they lampooned him as 'his imperial majesty, the king of Lymington'.[9] His return to Westminster, however, was considered an obstacle to his appointment to the command at Portsmouth, which he had been offered in August 1832 by Sir James Graham, the first lord of the admiralty, in recognition of his 'distinguished services and high character in the profession'. After an angry correspondence Neale declined it rather than relinquish his seat, which he held until the next dissolution. The family historian postulates that the alleged conflict of interest was invented by Graham, and stemmed from the active support given by Neale to the victorious Conservative candidate at the 1832 South Hampshire election. According to Croker, William IV, at whose behest the original offer had been made, invited Neale to spend a week with him at Brighton, 'to show the fellows and the world his real sentiments'. Neale, who had also enjoyed the friendship of the duke of York, acted as a pall bearer at the king's funeral.[10]

Neale died at Brighton in February 1840, when the baronetcy and residue of his estate passed to his brother, the Rev. George Burrard (1769-1856), rector of Shalfleet, Isle of Wight. The only large bequest contained in his will was one of £2,000 to his widowed sister Marianne Rooke.[11] Two hundred Lymington inhabitants spontaneously attended his funeral and, at a meeting shortly afterwards, a fund was started to raise a monument to him. The Queen Dowager Adelaide was among the subscribers, and the 76-feet-high obelisk, designed to serve as a navigational aid for sailors in the Solent, was completed two years later.[12]

[1] Hants RO 27M74/DBC5. [2] *Gent. Mag.* (1840), i. 540-2. [3] R.L. Playfair, *Scourge of Christendom*, 288-305; S. Burrard, *Annals of Walhampton*, 131; *Martin Letters* (Navy Recs. Soc. xix), 78-82. [4] *Martin Letters*, 85-91; Add. 41367, f. 234. [5] W. Shaler, *Sketches of Algiers* (1826), 212; Neale, *Reply to Erroneous Statements and Unwarranted Reflections* (1826), *passim*; *Gent. Mag.* (1840), i. 541. [6] Hants RO 27M74/F88. [7] Ibid. F102, Neale to Boyd [?1830], to Peel [Apr. 1831]. [8] Add. 41368, f. 206. [9] C.P. Jones, *Hist. Lymington*, 141-5. [10] Burrard, 131-50; *Croker Pprs.* ii. 199-200 [11] PROB 11/1924/189; IR26/1557/159. [12] *Gent. Mag.* (1840), i. 542; Burrard, 151-4.

H.J.S./P.J.S.

NEEDHAM, Hon. Francis Jack (1787–1880), of Mourne Park, nr. Newry, co. Down.

NEWRY 6 Mar. 1819–1826

b. 12 Dec. 1787, 1st s. of Hon. Francis Needham†, 12th Visct. Kilmorey [I] (later 1st earl of Kilmorey [I]), and Anne, da. and coh. of Thomas Fisher of Acton, Mdx. *educ.* Eton 1802. *m.* (1) 7 Jan. 1814, Jane (*d.* 25 July 1867), da. of George Gun Cuninghame of Mount Kennedy, co. Wicklow, 3s. (1 *d.v.p.*) 1da.; (2) 20 Nov. 1867, Martha, da. of John Foster of Lenham, Kent, *s.p.*; 1s. illegit. *styled* Visct. Newry and Morne 1822-32; *suc.* fa. as 2nd earl of Kilmorey [I] 21 Nov. 1832. *d.* 20 June 1880.

Ensign 2 garrison batt. [I] 1813, half-pay 1814; capt. commdt. Newry inf. 1813.

Sheriff, co. Down 1828-9.

Despite their Irish title, the Needhams, originally from Cheshire, continued to reside largely in England, mostly at Shavington, Shropshire. In 1806 the 11th Viscount Kilmorey, this Member's uncle, inherited the Newry estates of the family's junior branch, the Nedhams, several of whom had represented the borough in the Irish Parliament. Thereafter his brother, Francis Jack's father, returned himself for Newry, consolidated the interest there and usually lived at the rebuilt Mourne Park.[1] His father having succeeded as 12th Viscount, Needham was brought in for Newry as an anti-Catholic supporter of Lord Liverpool's administration in early 1819.[2] He was again returned unopposed at the general election of 1820, when his brother Francis Henry briefly offered as the Tory candidate for Huntingdonshire.[3] On 5 July 1820 it was given in as an excuse for his defaulting the previous day that he had had a 'severe fall from his horse'. He paired against censuring ministers' conduct towards Queen Caroline, 6 Feb., and voted against repealing the additional malt duty, 3 Apr. 1821. Lord Newry, as he became in January 1822 on his father's promotion to an earldom, divided against more extensive tax reductions to relieve distress, 11 Feb., and abolition of one of the joint-postmasterships, 13 Mar. In August 1822, with five man servants, he rowed the 118 miles from Oxford to London in 18 hours to win a considerable wager.[4] He brought up petitions from Newry chamber of commerce for inquiry into the duties on East and West Indian sugars, 15 Apr. 1823, and from the landholders of the north of Ireland against the warehoused wheat bill, 11 May 1824.[5] He was granted a month's leave on account of another 'severe accident', 17 Feb., but was present to vote for the duke of Cumberland's annuity bill, 10 June 1825. Although he had previously been described as a frequent attender, no trace of parliamentary activity has been found for the 1826 session.[6] At the dissolution that year, when he promised to continue to defend the borough's interests, he retired in favour of his more assiduous brother-in-law John Henry Knox.[7]

In July 1826 Lord Londonderry, Down's leading Tory proprietor, advised his son Lord Castlereagh, the new county Member, that 'you cannot pay too much court to the Kilmorey quarter ... As old Kilmorey is stricken in years, I recommend you making up to Newry in every possible way. I like them all very much and we are very good friends'.[8] Writing from Wynyard, his seat in county Durham, in November 1829, Londonderry reported about the nascent Down Independent Club to Lord Downshire, with whom he controlled the county representation, that 'Newry treats it here as quite a joke'; he attended the county contest in support of Castlereagh and Downshire's brother Lord Arthur Hill* the following summer.[9] Having succeeded to his father's title and estates (including personal wealth sworn under £40,000 in the province of Canterbury) in November 1832, he remained a minor figure on the Conservative side of Down politics. But he declined to interfere in the Newry election the following month, when he prevented Francis Henry Needham from standing.[10] In 1834 he explained his reluctance to participate in Irish contests, stating that

> it was my father's pleasure, and I must not dispute it, so to devise by his will that the interests of the Irish estate should be greatly divided, and to throw obstacles in the way of its deriving any efficient advantages from its produce. I am but an agent for the trustees.[11]

Kilmorey, who was described by Dyott as 'a gentlemanlike man', thereafter travelled extensively abroad and conducted a scandalous private life. Having separated from his wife in 1835, he lived openly for a decade with his young ward Priscilla, daughter of Captain Sir William Hoste of the navy, with whom he had a son, the army officer Charles Needham (1844-1934).[12] 'Black Jack' or 'the Wicked Earl', as he was remembered in the family, died in June 1880, at his then residence of Gordon House, Isleworth, Middlesex. On the 24th he was buried in the mock Egyptian mausoleum which he had had constructed for Priscilla after her death in 1854 (it survives in the garden of 275 St. Margaret's Road, Twickenham).[13] His eldest son Francis Jack, Viscount Newry (1815-51), Conservative Member for Newry, 1841-51, had predeceased him and he was therefore succeeded as 3rd earl of Kilmorey by his grandson Francis Charles (1842-1915), Conservative Member for Newry, 1871-4.[14]

[1] NRA 40684; M. Bence-Jones, *Guide to Irish Country Houses* (1988), 218; *Hist. Irish Parl.* v. 339-41. [2] *HP Commons, 1790-1820*, iv. 653; *Black Bk.* (1823), 179. [3] Fitzwilliam mss, Maltby to Milton, 3, 5 Mar. 1820. [4] PRO NI, Kilmorey mss D2638/D/3. [5] *The Times*, 16 Apr. 1823, 12 May 1824. [6] *Session of Parl. 1825*, p. 477. [7] *Newry Commercial Telegraph*, 6 June 1826. [8] PRO NI, Londonderry mss D654/B4/2. [9] PRO NI, Downshire mss D617/C/12/418; *Newry Commercial Telegraph*, 20 July 1830. [10] *Gent. Mag.* (1833), i. 80-81; *Oxford DNB*; PROB 11/1811/95; IR26/1327/27; *The Times*, 15 Dec. 1832. [11] Downshire mss C/12/547. [12] *Dyott's Diary*, ii. 183; NRA 40684. [13] *Newry Telegraph*, 22, 24, 26 June 1880; *Guardian*, 21 Sept. 2000, 'Space' supp. p. 14. [14] *The Times*, 22 June, 31 July 1880.

S.M.F.

NEELD, Joseph (1789–1856), of Grittleton House, nr. Chippenham, Wilts.; Kelston Park, Som., and 6 Grosvenor Square, Mdx.

GATTON	8 Mar. 1830–1830
CHIPPENHAM	1830–24 Mar. 1856

b. 13 Jan. 1789, 1st s. of Joseph Neeld (*d.* 1828), attorney, of 31 Norfolk Street, Strand and Mary, da. of John Bond of Hendon, Mdx. *educ.* Harrow 1803; ?I. Temple. *m.* 1 Jan. 1831, Lady Caroline Mary Ashley Cooper, da. of Cropley Ashley Cooper†, 6th earl of Shaftesbury, *s.p.*; 1 da. illegit. *suc.* to fortune of over £600,000 by will of gt.-uncle Philip Rundell 1827. *d.* 24 Mar. 1856.

Gov. Harrow 1828; high steward, Malmesbury 1842-*d.*

Neeld's origins are obscure, though it is known that his grandfather, Joseph Neeld of Chobham, Surrey, married Mary Burchitt in 1754. Their son Joseph, who became an attorney in London, married Mary, the daughter of John Bond and his wife Susannah Rundell, 29 Mar. 1788.[1] Joseph Neeld junior, the eldest of their eight children, followed his father into the law, being formally apprenticed to him, 20 Jan. 1805. He had a practice at 12 Essex Street, Strand, but in the mid-1820s he moved to 12 Paper Buildings, where, since he was sometimes described as being 'of the Inner Temple', he was possibly studying for the bar under his friend Henry Hall Joy, of that address.[2] Neeld was a great-nephew of Philip Rundell, head of the firm of Rundell, Bridge and Rundell, goldsmiths, of Ludgate Hill, who died on 17 Feb. 1827. He had accumulated enormous wealth from nothing by 'steady gains and continual parsimony', and by his will, dated 4 Feb. 1827, he left the bulk of it to his 'esteemed friend' Neeld, who, according to Charles Greville, had 'taken care of him for the last fourteen years'. Rundell's personalty was sworn above £1,000,000, and it was generally assumed that Neeld had come into at least £900,000, though his share was actually £660,230.[3] His father, who died the following year at his then address, Gloucester Place, Portman Square, felt it was unnecessary to provide for him, and so left his property, including personal wealth sworn under £18,000, in trust for his youngest son, John.[4] Neeld made considerable investments in East India and Bank stock, and in land in London, Wiltshire and elsewhere. In 1828 he bought from his friend Colonel John Houlton the Grittleton estate, which he extended and made his principal residence.[5] By 1829 he had also purchased many of the houses in Chippenham, including about half the burgages which conveyed the right of voting, from its former patrons.[6]

He bought a parliamentary seat at Gatton from Sir Mark Wood†, and took his place in the Commons, 11 Mar. 1830. It may have been on that occasion that he was introduced to the home secretary Peel behind the Speaker's chair, and received 'an earnest shake of the hand'.[7] He made no known speeches during this period. At the Wiltshire Society meeting, 19 May, he claimed that he had

> always taken an interest in all that related to Wiltshire. He had now taken root in the county and he hoped to flourish there, and that the time was not far distant when he should have the honour of representing a borough in that county.[8]

He voted against abolition of the death penalty for forgery, 7 June. He canvassed Chippenham at the general election that summer, but had to inform the bailiff, 26 July, that he was still labouring under a severe illness, 'a circumstance which he particularly laments at the present moment'.[9] He was thought certain to be elected on his own interest with his chosen partner, Philip Pusey*, though Thomas Gladstone*, who considered standing on the popular interest, had heard that there was evidence of bribery which might be used against him.[10] On the hustings, 30 July 1830, he

> rose and looked 'unutterable things'. He promised to be a faithful representative and a good landlord; and then he thumped the rail and then he looked again. He apologized to the freemen that he could not say as much as he wished, from ill health, and sat down evidently exhausted with – thumping the rail.

His influence was challenged by an independent candidate and a riotous crowd, but he and Pusey shared a majority of the votes and were duly returned. He attended the Bath election the following day.[11]

He was, of course, listed by the Wellington ministry among their 'friends', but he was absent from the division on the civil list, 15 Nov. 1830. He brought up a reform petition from his constituency, 11 Mar., but voted against the second reading of the Grey ministry's reform bill, 22 Mar., and for Gascoyne's wrecking amendment, 19 Apr. 1831. Although an opposition was again raised, Neeld was sure of being returned at the subsequent general election, this time, after having apparently abandoned Pusey, in tandem with his brother-in-law, Henry George Boldero. Proposed as an opponent of the bill, 30 May, but not of reform as such, he spoke against monopolies and unnecessary taxation and promised to remain independent of party. Despite having to stand another contest, he managed to preserve his interest intact.[12] He voted against the second reading of the reintroduced reform bill, 6 July, and for his colleague's amendment to postpone consideration of the partial disfranchisement of their constituency, 27 July. In August he signed the Wiltshire declaration against reform. He divided against the passage of the bill, 21 Sept., and the second reading of the Scottish reform bill, 23 Sept. He was absent from the division on the second reading of the revised reform bill, 17 Dec. 1831, but voted against the enfranchisement of Tower Hamlets, 28 Feb., and the third reading, 22 Mar. 1832. He voted for Waldo Sibthorp's amendment concerning Lincoln freeholders, 23 Mar. His only other known votes were against government on the Russian-Dutch loan, 26 Jan., 12 July 1832.

According to one account of his marriage, Neeld 'laid siege to the heart of the daughter of a sinecurist Tory lord; and set up for a most magnanimous Tory himself'. It was to involve him in no little notoriety. Under the headline 'Delicate Discovery', the *Satirist*, 8 May 1831, reported that Lady Caroline Neeld had recently been taken ill and delivered of 'a little stranger', much to the consternation and humiliation of her husband of four months. It further alleged that she had had an affair with a Guards officer shortly before their wedding, was entitled under their marriage settlement to £10,000 a year in the event of a separation, for whatever reason, and that Neeld, whom the authors would not have thought was 'over-encumbered with brains, were we not assured to the contrary', had been thoroughly imposed upon. He was reluctant to pursue the editor through the courts, a fact which his wife's family held against him, but he did file a criminal information against him, 23 May. By July the couple had separated, and Lady Neeld sued for restitution of her conjugal rights, alleging that he had left her within weeks of the marriage. In a letter to her, 14 July, he complained of her numerous calumnies, which had made him withdraw 'from that style of living which otherwise I should have adopted', and warned her to stop her 'extravagant and vexatious expenditure'. He agreed to resume cohabitation, but towards the end of the year she sued for divorce on the grounds of cruelty. It was said, for example, that he had

> used every means in his power to vex and harass his said wife; that he grossly abused her; that he frequently treated her with sullen silence and 'pretended' contempt; that he abused her family, and said they were a set disgraceful to be connected with, and declared that he would bring her down 'lower, lower, lower still'.

The suit was defeated, but a formal separation was agreed, 17 May 1832, and the scandal no doubt hindered his political career.[13]

Neeld offered again for Chippenham at the 1832 general election, when he spoke in favour of lower taxation, tithe commutation and the abolition of slavery. His contribution to the town's prosperity was recognized and he was returned at the head of the poll, but he had to relinquish one seat to a reformer for the duration of the Parliament.[14] He thereafter reasserted his control and continued to represent Chippenham, as a staunch Conservative and Protectionist, until his death in March 1856.[15] His only child (with a French woman), Ann Maria (c.1812-89), to whom he must already have conveyed Kelston, had married William Inigo Jones in 1844.[16] The residue of his large estate passed in trust to his brother John (1805-91), who sat as a Conservative for Cricklade, 1835-59, and Chippenham, 1865-8, and was created a baronet in 1859.

[1] Cricklade Mus. 938, Neeld ped.; *Gent. Mag.* (1788), i. 365. [2] TNA CP5/226/21; *Bentham Corresp.* ix. 114. [3] *Gent. Mag.* (1827), i. 563-4; *Greville Mems.* i. 168-9; PROB 11/1722/127; IR26/1138/177; F.M.L. Thompson, 'Business and landed élites in 19th cent.', in *Landowners, Capitalists and Entrepreneurs*, 147. [4] *Gent. Mag.* (1828), ii. 649; PROB 11/1750/32; IR26/1203/6. [5] WCA D.Misc.112; *VCH Wilts.* xiv. 109, 171; *Gent. Mag.* (1856), i. 527. [6] Wilts. RO, Keary mss 415/272; Wilts. RO, Neeld mss 1305/45-77, 320; Wilts. RO, Ross mss 1769/52; *The Times*, 11 Aug. 1831. [7] *The Times*, 11 Aug. 1831. [8] *Salisbury Jnl.* 24 May 1830. [9] Wilts. RO, Chippenham borough recs. G19/1/38, 43. [10] St. Deiniol's Lib. Glynne-Gladstone mss 195, T. to J. Gladstone, 26, 28 June; *Devizes Gazette*, 1 July 1830. [11] *Keenes' Bath Jnl.* 2 Aug. 1830. [12] Hants RO, Carnarvon mss 75M91/L14/12; *Salisbury Jnl.* 4 Apr.; *Bath Gazette*, 3 May 1831. [13] *The Times*, 24 May, 26 Nov., 6 Dec.; *Devizes Gazette*, 1 Dec. 1831; J. Badeni, *Wilts. Forefathers*, 69-72; PROB 11/2231/314. [14] *Devizes Gazette*, 7 June, 13 Dec. 1832. [15] *Gent. Mag.* (1856), i. 527-8; *The Times*, 26 Mar. 1856. [16] Badeni, 72-73; IGI (Wilts.); *Gent. Mag.* (1844), ii. 424.

S.M.F.

NEVILLE, Hon. Richard (1783–1858), of Billingbear, Berks.

THIRSK	6 Feb. 1805–1806
SALTASH	19 Feb. 1807–1807
BUCKINGHAM	1807–1812
BERKSHIRE	1812–28 Feb. 1825

b. 26 Sept. 1783, 1st s. of Richard Aldworth Neville[†] (afterwards Griffin), 2nd Bar. Braybrooke, and Catherine, da. of George Grenville[†] of Wotton, Bucks. *educ.* Sunbury 1791; Eton 1796; Christ Church, Oxf. 1801 (MA Magdalene, Camb. 1811). *m.* 13 May 1819, Lady Jane Cornwallis, da. and coh. of Charles Cornwallis[†], 2nd Mq. Cornwallis, 5s. (2 *d.v.p.*) 3da. *suc.* fa. as 3rd Bar. Braybrooke 28 Feb. 1825 and took name of Griffin as owner of Audley End, Essex in compliance with will of distant cos. John Griffin Griffin[†], 1st Bar. Braybrooke (*d.* 1797). *d.* 13 Mar. 1858.

Recorder, Saffron Walden; high steward, Wokingham.

Capt. Berks. militia 1803.

Pres. Camden Soc. 1853-*d.*

Neville, 'a very gentlemanlike, good kind of man',[1] was a nephew of Lord Grenville and first cousin of the odious 2nd marquess (later 1st duke) of Buckingham, from whose political line he had steadily diverged since 1812. When he stood again for Berkshire at the general election of 1820 he 'authorized' local newspapers to contradict a report that he was disinclined to support the recently circulated petition of county agriculturists for relief from distress by means of enhanced protection. For the third successive election he and his Whig colleague Charles Dundas were taken to a poll by a radical reformer, but his seat was never in danger.[2] Buckingham and his small squad of Members coalesced with the Liverpool ministry in December 1821 but Neville, a member of Brooks's since 1817, continued to act with the Whig opposition, though he was, as previously, a very lax attender.

He voted against government on the civil list, 5 May, and the appointment of an additional Scottish baron of exchequer, 15 May 1820. Next day he presented and declared his support for Berkshire petitions for inquiry into agricultural distress.[3] He was given ten days' leave, 30 June 1820. He did not attend or send an excuse to the Berkshire county meeting in support of Queen Caroline, 8 Jan.,[4] but he voted in censure of ministers' conduct towards her, 6 Feb. 1821. He voted for Catholic relief, 28 Feb. He divided with opposition on the state of the revenue, 6 Mar., army reductions, 14 Mar., and repeal of the additional malt duty, 21 Mar., for which he paired, 3 Apr. He took another period of leave, 30 Apr., but he attended to vote for economy and retrenchment, 27 June 1821. He voted for more extensive tax reductions to relieve distress, 5, 11 Feb., relaxation of the salt duties, 28 Feb., admiralty economies, 1 Mar., and abolition of one of the joint-postmasterships, 13 Mar., 2 May 1822. However, he joined the largely ministerial majority against inquiry into the board of control, an attack on his Grenvillite kinsmen, 14 Mar.[5] He voted for inquiry into diplomatic expenditure, 15 May, but the following day divided with ministers against a specific attack on the recent appointment of Buckingham's (and his) cousin Henry Williams Wynn† as envoy to Switzerland. Buckingham commented:

> Neville, by voting *for* the first question which included the second, a little did away the merit attending his second vote. But we must not look too closely. It will not however pave the way for his brother's mitre.[6]

(His brother George, master of Magdalene College, Cambridge, rose no higher in the church than dean of Windsor.) Neville did not attend the Berkshire county meeting called to support parliamentary reform as a remedy for distress, 27 Jan. 1823, explaining by open letter that he was 150 miles away; but he supported the prayer of the petition when Dundas presented it, 27 Feb.[7] His last known votes were for parliamentary reform, 24 Apr., 2 June 1823. He was granted two weeks' sick leave, 17 Feb. 1825, but his father's death removed him from the Commons before its expiry.

As a peer he took up residence at Audley End, which he considerably improved. He supported Catholic emancipation and reform, but from 1834 sided with the Conservatives. He had keen historical and literary interests and was president of the Camden Society from 1853 until his death. His amateurish and bowdlerized edition of *Pepys' Diary* (the manuscript of which had been in the care of Magdalene since 1724, and had been laboriously deciphered and transcribed by John Smith, an impoverished sizar of St. John's) was published in 1825. Braybrooke produced slightly improved editions in 1848-9 and 1854, but he omitted from them his earlier lukewarm acknowledgement of Smith's contribution. He wrote a *History of Audley End* (1836) and edited the *Private Correspondence of Lady Jane Cornwallis* (1842) and the *Autobiography of Sir John Bramston* (1845).[8] Three weeks before his marriage in 1819 his aunt Lady Williams Wynn had written to her son:

> You will find Neville, with his 'young ideas on love-making' still only beginning to shoot. He takes the thing as yet very quietly, makes a morning call on his love, eats his dinner at his father's ... and hops across at ten o'clock for the close of the day ... Neville says that to talk of the smallest pretensions to beauty in his bride would be absurd, but that she is fresh and clean-looking 'Which is enough for him'. I fancy he has expressed so generally among his own set, his unfavourable opinion on her appearance, that it is much best to profess at once entirely to abandon that ground, and rest on the interior.[9]

Fifteen years later Lord Lyttelton visited Audley End:

> Lord and Lady Braybrooke received us most cordially, and the evening passed very agreeably in that very magnificent huge old mansion ... The conversation throve unceasingly. Lady Braybrooke *ne tait pas* and ... [he], rather a shy man in mixed company, was wondrous agreeable and flowing too in talk, and they both did the honours of their house in the simplest and heartiest way imaginable.[10]

In the last four years of his life he lost 14 near relations, including his wife and two sons who were killed within a week of each other in the Crimea. He died in March 1858 and was succeeded in the peerage by his sons Richard Cornwallis Griffin (1820-61) and Charles Cornwallis Griffin (1823-1902).

[1] Salop RO, Weld-Forester mss 337, Sir W. Williams Wynn to Forester, 10 June 1822. [2] *Reading Mercury*, 7, 21, 28 Feb., 7, 14, 21 Mar. 1820. [3] *The Times*, 17 May 1820. [4] Ibid. 9 Jan. 1821. [5] NLW, Coedymaen mss 629. [6] NLW ms 2794 D, Sir W. to H. Williams Wynn [15 May 1822]; Buckingham, *Mems. Geo. IV*, i. 325, 328-9; Bucks. RO, Fremantle mss, Buckingham to Fremantle, 19 May 1822. [7] *Reading Mercury*, 3 Feb.; *The Times*, 28 Feb. 1823. [8] *Oxford DNB sub* Griffin. [9] *Williams Wynn Corresp.* 235. [10] *Lady Lyttelton Corresp.* 274-5.

D.R.F.

NEWARK, Visct. *see* **PIERREPONT, Charles Evelyn**

NEWBOROUGH, 2nd Bar. [I] *see* **WYNN, Thomas John**

NEWMAN, Robert William (1776–1848), of Sandridge, nr. Dartmouth, Devon.

BLETCHINGLEY 28 Dec. 1812–1818

EXETER 1818–1826

b. 18 Aug. 1776, at Oporto, 1st s. of Thomas Newman, merchant, of Oporto, later of Bath, Som. and Sarah, da. of John Page, merchant, of Oporto and London. *m.* 21 Sept. 1813, Mary Jane, da. of Richard Denne of Meriteau House, Winchelsea, Suss., 4s. 5da. (1 *d.v.p.*). *suc.* fa. 1802; uncle Lydston Newman of Belmont, Devon 1829; *cr.* bt. 17 Mar. 1836. *d.* 24 Jan. 1848.

Sheriff, Devon 1827-8.

Newman, who came from a very old Dartmouth mercantile family with extensive interests in Newfoundland fisheries and the Portuguese wine trade, inherited £1,000 and a 19 per cent share of his father's estate in 1802.[1] He was again returned for Exeter in second place in 1820, with lukewarm support from the chamber, after claiming to be 'firmly attached to the principles of our glorious constitution' but 'perfectly unconnected with any political party'.[2] He was a regular attender who continued to vote with the Whig opposition to Lord Liverpool's ministry on most major issues, particularly for economy, retrenchment and reduced taxation. He divided for parliamentary reform, 9, 10 May 1821, 25 Apr. 1822, 20 Feb., 24 Apr., 2 June 1823, 26 Feb. 1824. However, he differed from the bulk of the Whigs by pairing against Catholic claims, 28 Feb. 1821 (having been given six weeks' leave on account of illness in his family on the 13th); he voted against removing Catholic peers' disabilities, 30 Apr. 1822, and relief, 1 Mar., 21 Apr., 10 May 1825. He seldom spoke in debate, but maintained that the Irish church was not averse to tithes reform, 5 July 1820, expressed his 'general concurrence in the principle' of Parnell's bill on this subject, 10 May 1821, and also wished to see the English system 'brought under the consideration of Parliament', 4 Mar. 1822.[3] He seconded Lord Ebrington's motion on distress and reform at the Devon county meeting, 5 Apr. 1821, arguing that economy and retrenchment were essential but that ministerial control of the Commons 'clearly showed that without ... reform the country could not be safe'.[4] He attended the county meeting on distress, 1 Feb. 1822, when he claimed that 'excessive taxation' was largely to blame and declared that 'retrenchment, to an extraordinary extent, might be effected in the military, naval and civil establishments, without endangering the state'. He explained to the Commons that the resulting petition was less numerously signed than might have been expected as many impoverished farmers were unable to travel to Exeter, 25 Feb., and he testified to the severity of the depression in Devon, 4 Mar. 1822.[5] He was present at the county reform meeting, 11 Apr., and supported the resulting petition, 2 June 1823.[6] He presented an Exeter petition complaining of the severity of Henry Hunt's* imprisonment, 14 Mar., and voted to remit his sentence, 24 Apr. 1822.[7] He divided against repeal of the usury laws, 27 Feb. 1824. He supported petitions for repeal of the 'unjust and partial' coal duties, 29 Mar. 1824, and presented others for repeal of the assessed taxes, 28 Feb. 1825, and of the house and window taxes, 7 Mar. 1826.[8] In presenting a South Devon petition for the maintenance of agricultural protection, 28 Apr., he warned that precautions were needed to prevent circumvention of the Corn Importation Acts, 2 May 1825.[9] He presented an Exeter petition condemning the trial of the Methodist missionary John Smith in Demerara, 28 May,[10] and voted in this sense, 11 June 1824, and to condemn the Jamaican slave trials, 2 Mar. 1826. He belatedly joined Brooks's Club, 4 June 1825.

In August 1825 Newman announced that he would not offer at the next general election, although he denied that his decision was 'in the slightest degree influenced by recent circumstances' in Exeter, where there were moves to force another expensive contest. He took consolation in the fact that while he had sometimes differed from his constituents, 'the views I entertained have of late, in many instances, been sanctioned by the measures of government'.[11] He had purchased an estate at nearby Mamhead in 1823, and six years later he inherited from his uncle real estate near Dartmouth and a half-share in properties in Dartmouth, at Coryton, near Tavistock and in Newfoundland, and seven-elevenths of the personalty, which was sworn under £16,000.[12] He delivered a 'most animated address' to the county reform meeting, 16 Mar. 1831, when he seconded the petition in support of the Grey ministry's bill, declaring that 'the constitution was deformed, and needed to be reformed' and that the proposed measure represented 'a moral revolution'.[13] He was awarded a baronetcy by Lord Melbourne's government in 1836. He died in January 1848 and was remembered as a 'constant and munificent benefactor of the public institutions of Exeter and its neighbourhood'.[14] He was succeeded by his eldest son, Robert Lydston Newman (1822-54), who was killed at Inkerman, and then by his second son Lydston Newman (1823-92).

[1] The personalty was sworn under £5,000 (PROB 11/1393/458; IR26/75/200). [2] *Alfred*, 29 Feb., 14 Mar. 1820. [3] *The Times*, 11 May 1821, 5 Mar. 1822. [4] *Alfred*, 10 Apr. 1821. [5] Ibid. 5 Feb.; *The Times*, 26

Feb., 5 Mar. 1822. [6] *Alfred*, 15 Apr. 1823. [7] *The Times*, 15 Mar. 1822. [8] Ibid. 1 Mar. 1825, 8 Mar. 1826. [9] Ibid. 29 Apr. 1825. [10] Ibid. 29 May 1824. [11] *Alfred*, 9 Aug. 1825. [12] W. Hoskins, *Devon*, 431; PROB 11/1757/369; IR26/1204/320. [13] *Western Times*, 19 Mar. 1831. [14] *Gent. Mag.* (1848), i. 435.

T.A.J.

NEWPORT, Sir Simon John, 1st bt. (1756–1843), of New Park, co. Waterford.

WATERFORD 7 Dec. 1803–1832

b. 24 Oct. 1756, 1st s. of Simon Newport, merchant and banker, of Waterford and Elizabeth, da. of William Riall of Clonmel, co. Tipperary. *educ.* Eton 1768-74; M. Temple 1770; Queen's, Oxf. 1773; L. Inn 1779; King's Inns 1780, called [I] 1780. *m.* 1 Oct. 1784, Ellen, da. of Shapland Carew, MP [I], of Castleborough, co. Wexford, *s.p. cr.* bt. 25 Aug. 1789; *suc.* fa. 1817. *d.* 9 Feb. 1843.

Chan. of exch. [I] Feb. 1806-Mar. 1807; commr. of treasury [I] Apr. 1806-Mar. 1807; PC [GB] 12 Mar. 1806, [I] 25 July 1806; comptroller gen. of exch. [UK] Oct. 1834-Sept. 1839.

Dubbed the 'Nestor of the Irish Whigs' by Richard Sheil*, Newport, who had joined Brooks's, sponsored by Lord Fitzwilliam, 11 June 1812, was considered by Lord Holland to be 'the best informed and most upright Irish politician (with the sole exception of Grattan) that we have had in Parliament since the Union'.[1] A small, asthmatic 'old man', noted for his gentlemanlike and agreeable manner, he remained an extremely active, if not very prominent, member of the moderate Whig opposition, despite increasing infirmity.[2] 'Your constitution is not like that of any man I know, and I have known you to get health and spirits from increasing exertions', observed his friend William Plunket* after a particularly severe asthma attack in 1821.[3] His frequent (sometimes daily) speeches were 'principally confined to Irish affairs' and 'characterized by good sense', but as George Agar Ellis* once griped, he 'goes rather too much into detail'.[4] 'If Sir John Newport be not a man of the very first-rate ability, his talents, and still more his industry and information are such as to command respect', noted *The Times* in 1829.[5] Although he continued to vote against the Liverpool ministry on most major issues, especially economy, retrenchment and reduced taxation, he maintained close personal connections with some of its senior figures, and had lifelong friendships with the former prime minister Lord Grenville, whose seat at Dropmore he regularly visited, and Richard, 1st Marquess Wellesley, Irish viceroy, 1821-8, who in a letter of 1840 about his 'early obligations' to Newport declared, '*You* are the foundation of my public character' and 'were to me what my father might have been'. In reply, Newport recounted how, 'under Mrs. Young's great tree at Eton, the brotherhood, for such it truly was, of Wellesley, Grenville and Newport commenced, and lasted undiminished even to the latest years ... through every vicissitude of political life'.[6]

At the 1820 general election Newport was again returned unopposed for his native Waterford under the terms of an 1818 compact between his family and the other leading members of its corporation carving up the local patronage. On the hustings he gave an 'animated speech' justifying his political conduct and reiterated his 'determination to support' Catholic emancipation.[7] He condemned the appointment of an additional Scottish baron of exchequer, 2, 15 May, and demanded an inquiry, 4 May 1820. He was appointed to the select committee on Irish election expenses, 3 May, and pressed for more time to be allowed for Irish election petitioners to enter into recognizances, 25 May. He advocated reduction of the Irish viceroy's household allowances, 17 May. He called for the transfer of Grampound's seats to Yorkshire, 19 May. He spoke against the introduction of a system of Irish poor laws, but conceded the necessity of 'some temporary measure' of relief, 7 June. On 12 June he criticized the 'extremely oppressive' customs duties imposed on Ireland at the Union and pressed for their annual reduction by one per cent. That day he was granted a week's leave on account of the death of his only brother William, head of the family's Waterford bank, who, following the disastrous run on their notes in May, had committed suicide, 6 June, precipitating the bank's total failure. Although he repudiated any personal liability, Newport later contributed at least £5,000 towards numerous local compensation claims.[8] He demanded measures to redress the deficiency of Irish education, 28 June. On 30 June he argued and moved successfully for a clause to be added to the Irish chancery bill preventing masters in chancery from sitting in Parliament. He welcomed the government's Irish tithes bill as a 'conciliatory measure', which would 'allay much of the discontent', 5 July. Next day he was a minority teller against the third reading of the female offenders bill. He objected to the use of public funds for repairs to Westminster Abbey, citing its 'scandalous and disgraceful' neglect by the dean and chapter, 12 July. He contended that encouraging breweries in Ireland would 'root out the pernicious system of drinking spirits', 14 July. Reporting from Dropmore that November, Grenville's brother Thomas Grenville† noted:

> He has lately had several grievous misfortunes which have pressed heavily upon him; he was very much attached to his wife (who was by the bye as disagreeable and vulgar a woman as I ever saw) but he was very fond of her and she died; then his brother failed as a Waterford banker, shot himself and left ... Sir John to settle the embarrassments of the house as he could; he had then no relation left but a nephew in the dragoons, and he is rendered incapable by a paralytic seizure at 35. Sir John is come to end his asthmatic days in England.[9]

Writing to Holland, 4 Dec. 1820, he added, 'Newport is ... much out of spirits' but 'says all is quiet in Ireland'.[10]

Newport condemned the removal of Queen Caroline's name from the liturgy, 26 Jan., and spoke and voted steadily in the opposition campaign on her behalf, deprecating the 'entanglement of political prejudices' and 'established religion', 13 Feb. 1821. He protested that an address to the king in the *London Gazette* complaining of the 'insolence' of the opposition was a breach of privilege, 1 Feb., and secured the concurrence of the House next day. (He had been appointed to the select committee on privileges, 24 Jan.) That February he spoke regularly against the Irish estimates and repeatedly berated ministers for their failure to produce detailed accounts. He warned the House that if they 'refused' to disfranchise Grampound 'they would inflict a greater injury upon their own character in the eyes of the people, than could be effected by any other means', 12 Feb., and voted in favour of Leeds becoming a scot and lot borough if it received Grampound's seats, 2 Mar. He divided for parliamentary reform, 9 May 1821, 25 Apr. 1822, 24 Apr. 1823, 27 Apr. 1826, reform of the Scottish electoral system, 2 June 1823, and of Edinburgh's representation, 26 Feb. 1824, 13 Apr. 1826. On 22 Feb. 1821 he condemned the military dispersal of a county meeting by the Dublin sheriff as a 'gross outrage' and voted for inquiry. He voted for Catholic claims, 28 Feb. 1821 (as a pair), 1 Mar. 1825, 21 Apr., 10 May 1825, and moved the order of the day for going into committee on the relief bill, 23, 27 Mar. 1821, when he drew attention to the lack of 'invidious distinctions' of religion abroad. On 29 Mar. Joseph Phillimore* informed the marquess of Buckingham that he had been 'shut up all the morning with Sir John Newport *and co.* on the subject of the clauses relating to the securities', and that to counter the anticipated opposition to the third reading, he was going to meet Newport at Lord Castlereagh's* 'to consider the propriety of some alterations which have been suggested as expedient'.[11] Newport paired for repeal of the additional malt duty, 21 Mar., 3 Apr. He endorsed a petition complaining of the interference of Lord Westmorland in the Lyme Regis election, denouncing the existing resolutions against peers' involvement as 'a mere farce', 12 Apr. He spoke and voted for repeal of the Blasphemous and Seditious Libel Acts, 8 May. Next day he moved and was in the minority for a 'string of resolutions' condemning the 'excessive' delays of the commission of inquiry into the courts of justice.[12] He spoke in favour of a local assembly for Newfoundland, 28 May. Criticizing the Irish budget, 1 June, he warned that 'taxation, augmented beyond a certain extent' would 'produce not an increased but a diminished revenue'. On 13 June he was a teller in the minority of 13 for a motion to allow Catholics to hold senior positions in the Bank of Ireland. He welcomed inquiry into abuses in Irish revenue collection, 15 June. On 20 June 1821 he was sent 'to sleep in the gallery' by a debate on the burning of Hindu widows and was unable to ask an intended question about the duke of York's association with Orange lodges.[13] That December Henry Brougham* observed that whilst at Dropmore Newport had 'passed some time with Wellesley', who had just accepted the Irish viceroyalty, and had 'come back in the highest glee'.[14]

Newport gave a 'gloomy account' of the state of rebellion in Ireland at Holland House, 2 Feb. 1822, when he told Sir James Mackintosh* that he 'believed that Lord Liverpool is about to resign, that the duke of Wellington, who is said to be a convert to Catholic emancipation, is to succeed him, and that Catholic emancipation is to be carried'.[15] He refused to endorse the government's 'repressive' Irish insurrection bill unless accompanied by an inquiry into the causes of the unrest, 5 Feb., and spoke and voted against it that day and 7 Feb. Next day, however, he cautioned against any modifications that would make it 'inoperative'. 'I confess myself a little surprised at the conduct of some of the Irish Members ... especially Newport', Goulburn, the Irish secretary, complained to Wellesley that day, noting that he had previously 'voted for the ... Act in times which he admits to have not so much required extraordinary exertion'.[16] On 13 Feb. Newport dissented from an opposition motion for inquiry into Sir Robert Wilson's* dismissal from the army, citing the 'fatal error of a former period' of bringing the army and committees of the House 'into too close a communication'. He welcomed and was appointed to the select committee on agricultural distress, 18 Feb. He implored ministers not to treat demands for retrenchment as 'idle, unfounded clamour' and spoke and voted for abolition of one of the joint-postmasterships, 13 Mar., 2 May. He supported calls for an inquiry into the public accounts,

14 Mar., and was appointed to the ensuing select committee, 18 Apr. He asserted that 'no time ought to be lost' in introducing another measure of Catholic relief, 29 Mar., but privately 'admitted that the question ... could not now be agitated with advantage' that year at a meeting of the Commons' 'friends of emancipation' with Canning, Charles Williams Wynn and Plunket, the newly appointed Irish attorney-general, 16 Apr.[17] Next day Agar Ellis described how Newport 'came and detailed to me some of his plans for a commutation of tithes and other ameliorations in Ireland'.[18] On 22 Apr., in a speech described by Williams Wynn as 'very poor' and by Mackintosh as 'feeble', he moved for an address to the king urging the necessity of an inquiry into the causes of Irish disturbances, observing that he had 'never risen under feelings of greater embarrassment' on account of 'not being favoured' on this occasion with Plunket's support. (Shortly beforehand, Mackintosh had observed that he was 'very anxious' because of the 'expectation' that he was to be 'attacked by his old friend', who in the event turned his fire elsewhere.)[19] After a 'long debate' and assurances from Plunket that measures for Irish relief were in hand, he agreed not to press his motion to a division, adding that he had not intended 'any reflection' upon the present Irish government and had the 'fullest confidence' in Wellesley, 'but it did not necessarily follow that he must place the same implicit confidence in all the other members of the cabinet'.[20] Reporting to Wellesley, Richard Wellesley* commented:

> Newport repelled in the strongest terms the accusation of any intention to impute blame to the present government of Ireland, and he told me privately that he was very sorry to hear that great pains were taken to impress you with an opinion that he had intended to cast some reflection on your government and I really believe that the fear of incurring this charge was one of his principal motives for not pressing his proposed address to a division.[21]

He denounced the 'dreadful' imposition of tithes on Irish potatoes and demanded their commutation, warning that their collection would produce 'tumult and insurrection', 15 May. 'Newport ... sees his way very clearly' but 'I doubt his being fully aware of the obstacles', Plunket advised Holland, 18 May.[22] On the 21st he obtained leave to introduce a bill making Irish landlords contribute to the parochial assessments of their tenants, which went no further. He welcomed proposals to repeal the window and hearth taxes, 24 May. He spoke and voted for reception of the Greenhoe petition for parliamentary reform, 3 June, and against the aliens bill, 5 June. He complained that the Irish constables bill would 'drive many of the most respectable magistrates out of the commission' and divided against its second reading, 7 June. He protested that the Irish tithes leasing bill 'only put off that evil day' of payment rather than offering commutation, 13 June, and was in the minority for his own amendment for a proposed inquiry to examine alternative sources of funding for the Irish church, 19 June. He urged the necessity of measures to employ the starving population of Ireland, 17 June, and argued and was in the minority of 37 for his own amendment to limit the duration of the Irish repressive legislation, 8 July 1822.

On 4 Jan. 1823 Lord Donoughmore reported hearing from Newport on the Catholic question, which its supporters 'all agree ... should be brought on as soon as possible' and 'disposed of before the commencement of the spring circuits'.[23] Newport called for the suppression of all Irish secret societies, 5 Mar. He congratulated ministers on their Irish tithes compensation bill, believing it would 'do great good' in alleviating the Irish church's 'unwarrantable encroachment' on the poor, 6 Mar. 'I have always wanted to see the abuses of the Irish church in good hands. They are not so in Newport's', remarked the duke of Bedford next day.[24] On 21 Mar. Newport, hitherto an outspoken protectionist, announced his conversion to free trade, by which Irish commerce 'would be greatly improved'.[25] Concerned at obstructing 'the course of justice', he voted with ministers against the production of papers on the supposed plot to murder Wellesley, 24 Mar., and was widely expected to support Plunket's controversial use of *ex-officio* informations against the Orangemen alleged to have been involved and oppose Brownlow's censure motion on 15 Apr. (At Dropmore Williams Wynn had 'found him much alarmed' that the 'great body of opposition' would 'vote against Plunket from personal animosity'.)[26] 'I am surprised that Newport ... should be disposed to support Plunket in his unconstitutional conduct about the Dublin rioters', Bedford carped to Holland, 27 Mar.[27] He argued and was in the majority for the compromise motion for inquiry into the conduct of the Dublin sheriff, 22 Apr., and put frequent questions to witnesses during its sittings next month, when he repeatedly reproached the Orangemen for refusing to reveal their 'rules and regulations'. He welcomed improvements to the Newfoundland judicature, 25 Mar. On 10 Apr., in what became a regular hobby horse, he moved and was a minority teller for a 'just and true valuation' of the Irish first fruits fund, which would lessen the 'need for public grants to the Irish church' and the burden of its church rates. He was in the minority of 19 against the grant for Irish churches and glebe houses next day. He called for a reform of Irish education grants, 11 Apr., and moved but eventually withdrew a resolution for inquiry into a nondenomination education system, 25 June. He was in the minority of 14 (as a teller) for a clause in the Irish county treasurers bill preventing the reappointment of insolvent collectors, 2 May. He reaffirmed his opposition to renewal of the Insurrection Act without a 'full inquiry' into Irish disturbances and divided accordingly, 12 May, 24 June. On 21 May he urged the necessity of Irish tithe reform, which Bedford privately doubted his ability to promote, noting that Irish churchmen 'have a perfect horror of Newport and look upon him as their most determined enemy'.[28] On 27 May he welcomed the Irish joint tenancy bill, observing that 'nothing had brought greater misery to Ireland than the subdivision of land among such a large multitude of tenants'. He demanded inquiry into the excessive fees charged by the Irish chief baron, Standish O'Grady†, 13 June. He objected to calls for the abolition of the Irish viceroyalty, asserting that nothing would be 'more injurious' and 'degrading' to the people of Ireland, 25 June. He voted to refer the Catholic petition against the administration of justice in Ireland to the grand judicial committee, 26 June. He obtained leave for a bill to enable Catholics to make gifts and grants for charitable purposes, which went no further, 3 July 1823.[29] That December he was 'warned off' going to Dropmore whilst Liverpool visited.[30]

Newport spoke and was a minority teller for his own motion for information on the legality of Catholic burials, 6 Feb. 1824. 'If Newport would have left it alone it would have been best, but having mooted it ... we must deal with it', remarked Williams Wynn.[31] He seconded a motion for leave to introduce a bill to prevent Irish landlords from seizing unharvested crops in settlement of rental arrears and welcomed another to compel the residence of the Irish clergy, 16 Feb. He recommended extending the jury laws consolidation bill to Ireland and spoke and voted for returns on Catholic office – holders, 19 Feb. Speaking for reform of Edinburgh's representation, 26 Feb., he warned that the 'Irish Parliament had accelerated its own downfall by separating itself from the feelings and interests of the people they professed to represent, and it was not improbable that in the case of England the same cause would lead to the same effect'. That day he demanded an 'extensive amendment' of the 'mischievous' Irish Church Rates Act. He complained that the survey and valuation of Ireland was taking too long, 27 Feb., and was appointed to the ensuing select committee, 10 Mar. He praised ministers for their recent tax cuts, 5 Mar., but advocated further Irish reductions, 12 Mar. He spoke and divided against the grant for Protestant Irish charter schools, 15 Mar., and on the 25th moved successfully for an inquiry into Irish education. Next month he was part of the Irish delegation to Robinson, chancellor of the exchequer, which pressed unsuccessfully for a five-year extension of the Irish linen bounties.[32] He feared that the bill to amend the Irish Tithes Composition Act would merely 'augment all the evils' of the original measure, 3 May. Next day he spoke and was in the minority of 33 for an advance of capital to Ireland. He endorsed a petition against Orange lodges, towards which the government should 'declare its hostility', 4 May, and had such petitions referred to the inquiry on the state of Ireland, 10 June. He moved the second reading of the Irish Royal Mining Company bill but withdrew it in the face of objections, 6 May. He voted for inquiries into the Irish church that day, and the state of Ireland, to which he was appointed, 11 May. He welcomed proposals to repeal the leather tax and urged their extension to Ireland, 17 May. On the 25th he reintroduced his motion against the 'improper collection' of Irish first fruits revenues and again was a minority teller for inquiry. He argued and was a minority teller for his own amendment to the Irish clergy residence bill prohibiting pluralities, 27 May. He feared that an abolition of the Irish butter trade regulations would encourage 'every description of fraud' by butter makers, 31 May. He denied that repeal of the Test Acts would endanger the Protestant church, citing the example of their brief suspension in Ireland before the Union, 4 June 1824.

Newport attacked ministers for their 'system of coercion' towards Ireland, 4 Feb. 1825. He cautioned against suppression of the Catholic Association, citing the 'fearful dangers' of attempting to stifle discontent and the lesson of the American war of independence, 15 Feb., and voted accordingly that day and 21, 25 Feb. He presented petitions in the Association's support and divided for it to be heard at the bar of the House, 18 Feb., and was one of the Members who met the deputation of its leaders, 20 Feb.[33] He welcomed a bill to alter the Irish Subletting Act, 22 Feb. That day he obtained leave for a bill to amend the levy of church rates in Ireland, stressing the burden of taxation imposed by a Protestant minority and the necessity of allowing Catholics to attend financial vestry meetings, which was read a third time, 13 June. After a number of amendments by the Lords, which in his absence were accepted by the Commons, it received royal assent as 6 Geo. IV, c. 130, 6 July. Writing to Holland from Milford Haven, where had been 'detained' by another 'asthmatic attack', 17 July 1825, Newport protested that the bill had been

> most artfully passed through several of its stages at unreasonable hours and finally, although I had again and again announced to Goulburn my intention of laying before the House ... my decided opposition to it, the last stages were delayed until circumstances had compelled me to quit London, and then it was expedited on its progress ... I shall most certainly take an early opportunity of urging ... next session the reconsideration of the entire subject.[34]

True to his word, on 16 Feb. 1826 he protested at the Lords' removal of the 'principal clauses' limiting expenditure and enabling parishioners to appeal against burdensome rates, and unsuccessfully moved a series of resolutions condemning their actions. He spoke in favour of the Liverpool and Manchester railway bill, saying it was the duty of the legislature to 'increase the facilities of conveyance', 2 Mar. 1825. During the negotiations over the Catholic relief bill that month, he agreed to introduce the accompanying bills for provision for the Catholic clergy and regulation of the Irish freeholder franchise.[35] On 26 Mar., however, Agar Ellis reported that he had been 'obliged to give up ... bringing forward the question of the elective franchise, in consequence of being so abused by some of his own friends', and that he believed the relief bill and 'measures connected with it' would 'all fail in consequence of the foolish dissensions among the Whigs'.[36] He defended the franchise bill as a material 'aid' to the 'more important one of emancipation', 22 Apr., denied that it would 'disfranchise one single individual' as it 'preserved existing rights to all', 26 Apr., and argued that it would 'put down fictitious votes', 12 May. He defended the inclusion of the Catholic oath in the relief bill, 6 May, and following its third reading stood in for Sir Francis Burdett, who had absented himself, and took it up to the Lords, 11 May.[37] He was appointed to the select committee on the Irish linen trade, 14 Apr. That day he obtained leave for a bill to limit Irish church pluralities and abolish episcopal unions, noting the existence of some parish unions that were 'forty miles long'. (It was introduced, 20 May, but made no progress.) He welcomed the assimilation of Irish and Scottish spirit duties, 22 Apr., and a proposal to unify Irish and English currencies, though he feared that it might cause 'alarm', 12 May. He supported the production of papers submitted to Wellesley on religious animosities, 26 May. He successfully moved for legal action to be taken against the abuses in Irish charter schools that had been revealed by the education commissioners, 9 June 1825, when he was in a minority of 23 for the abolition of naval flogging.

Newport declined to attend the Association dinner for the 'friends of civil and religious liberty', 2 Feb. 1826.[38] He approved ministerial proposals to suppress the circulation of Irish small notes, which from his 'personal knowledge' were injurious to 'both the recipients and the issuing banks', 13 Feb., and was named to the ensuing select committee, 16 Mar. He welcomed inquiry into Irish tolls and customs levied by corporations, 16 Feb., and was appointed to it, 21 Feb. He secured papers on Irish education grants, 7 Mar., was in the minority of 19 for his amendment to reduce the grant to Protestant charter schools, 20 Mar., and denied Protestant claims that the Catholic church 'absolutely refused the Bible to its members', saying that they 'merely objected' to its use by young persons 'without note or comment', 14 Apr. In a day of much activity, even by his standards, 9 Mar., he moved and was in the minority for bringing in a measure to disfranchise non-resident Irish borough voters, introduced a bill with Spring Rice to alter Irish local jurisdictions (which passed later that session), and obtained leave to reintroduce his bill against the formation of further episcopal unions, which again lapsed after its first reading, 17 Mar. On 13 Mar. he congratulated ministers on their 'considerable' tax reductions, hoping they would be carried 'still further'. Resuming his call for the proper use of Irish first fruit revenues, 21 Mar., he ignored protests by Goulburn that it had already been 'under discussion four different times', vowed to persist with it 'as long as he had a seat in this House' and was a minority teller for his motion for inquiry. 'He seems to pursue the church establishment in every way and in every place', Sir Robert Inglis* informed the bishop of Limerick that month.[39] On 25 Apr. he moved unsuccessfully for abolition of the 'tyrannical' power of Irish parish vestries to collect church rates from neighbouring parishes without a church. He called for the relief of distressed manufacturers, 2 May 1826.

At the 1826 general election he was again returned for Waterford unopposed. On the hustings he declared that 'increasing years were making him somewhat feeble, and he could not be expected to be as active as before, but in zeal for the benefit of his constituents he would yield to none'. He concluded by appealing for the Catholic question to be forwarded with 'temperance' as well as 'firmness'.[40] In late August 1826 he spoke in similar terms at an Association dinner in Waterford attended by Henry Crabb Robinson, who described him as an 'old man ... in full possession of his faculties', with a countenance that was 'sharp, even somewhat quizzical'.[41] He argued against the impressment of seamen, 13 Feb. 1827. He was appointed to the select committee on communications with Ireland, 21 Feb. He supported a motion for inquiry into electoral bribery, saying that 'some alteration was absolutely necessary', 26 Feb. He berated George Dawson, Member for county Londonderry, for his 'intemperate remarks' against the Catholic Association, 2 Mar. Next day he attended a meeting at Norfolk House to assess the strength of support for Catholic claims, for which he duly voted, 6 Mar.[42] He contended that a reduction of the Irish tobacco duties would result in 'increased consumption' and 'augmented' tax revenues, 26 Mar. That month Goulburn informed his wife that he intended to 'combat Newport' and 'take an opportunity of paying him off for some of those absurd speeches which he had made in my absence'.[43] On 3 Apr. Newport secured papers on the use of Irish first fruits and obtained leave to reintroduce his bill amending the levy of Irish church rates, noting the unfair burden imposed on Catholic taxpayers. 'Newport indulges us ... with his annual resolution about the building of churches', Goulburn commented to Wellesley beforehand.[44] The bill was read a first time, 16 May, but withdrawn, 1 June. He moved unsuccessfully for inquiry into the Irish estimates, 5 Apr. 1827. Following the appointment of the pro-Catholic Canning as prime minister later that month, Newport took a seat on the third row on the treasury side of the Commons, 1 May. Next day he asserted that the Irish Catholics would 'never be satisfied until they were placed on an equality with the people of England'. He recommended that Penryn's seats be transferred to an unrepresented wealthy town and voted for its disfranchisement, 28 May. He welcomed the appointment of the finance committee, which would result in a diminution of public expenditure, 1 June, and proposals to repeal the corn law, 18 June. On news reaching Ireland of Canning's death in August, Newport agreed with Holland in approving of the 'cordial acquiescence' of Lord Lansdowne, the home secretary, in the succession of Lord Goderich as premier and the continuation of William Lamb as Irish secretary, who he believed had 'gained much credit by his readiness of access and conciliating manners, in both of which qualities (exclusive of his narrow minded bigotry) Goulburn was pointedly deficient'.[45] He disagreed with those who thought the Whigs should leave office following the provocative appointment of John Herries* as the new chancellor, informing Holland, 9 Sept., that Lord Duncannon*

> tells me that many of our friends feel and express great dissatisfaction. One in particular wrote him that he supposed Peel would be the next person introduced into the cabinet. Was there ever more exaggerated prejudice than that of not seeing the distinction between Peel and Herries?[46]

In October 1827 Sir James Macdonald* informed Lansdowne that Goderich was 'warmly disposed towards Newport' becoming Irish vice-treasurer on the retirement of Sir George Hill*, who was anxious to leave office, but nothing came of it.[47]

After the collapse of the ministry, Newport told Holland that he and Duncannon had 'for some time' believed 'that poor Goderich ... was so absolutely deficient in the nerve and firmness of a statesman as to be wholly unsuited to take the lead in times like the present, and that the fabric disjointed by his vacillation must soon fall to pieces', 15 Jan. 1828.[48] Remarking on the duke of Wellington's appointment as premier, 6 Feb., he opined that the 'qualifications of a statesman and a general have seldom been united in the same individual', but promised to judge ministers 'by their acts'. He presented and endorsed petitions for Catholic claims, 12, 21 Feb., 18 Mar., and voted thus, 12 May 1828. He secured papers on the 'mismanagement' of the Irish admiralty court, 12 Feb., brought up and endorsed petitions against its 'abuses', 18 Feb., 2 May, and welcomed the government's announcement of an investigation by the Irish commissioners, 22 Apr., when he withdrew his tabled motion for inquiry. (On 2 Feb. John Croker*, the admiralty secretary, had advised Peel, again home secretary, that '*something* must be done' about Newport's motion as 'the matter properly belongs to the government and should not, I think, be left in the hands of an opposition Member'.)[49] Newport obtained papers on the operation of the Irish Vestry Acts, 12 Feb., and Irish corn exports, 15 Feb. That day he was appointed to the finance committee, apparently against the advice of Herries, who had informed Peel that he 'preferred [Spring] Rice to Newport because I think he is less mischievous and may be more useful'. 'I confess I am a little uneasy about the composition of the committee', Wellington told Peel a few days later, naming Newport as one of the members who were 'likely' to vote for Lord Althorp to be its chairman.[50] Newport defended the committee's slow progress, 24 Mar., insisting that the production of a 'hasty report' would be misleading to both Parliament and the country, 16 May. He resumed his protests against the taxation of Irish Catholics for the rebuilding of Protestant churches, 19 Feb., secured papers on Irish unbeneficed curates, 26 Feb., and demanded abolition of the Irish Vestry Act, by which bishops could tax 'to any extent they think proper' for church maintenance, 20 Mar. He voted for repeal of the Test Acts, 26 Feb. Next day he supported a motion for inquiry into the salaries of the Irish militia, in which 'very great reforms were required'. He opposed the Killiney chapel bill, 4 Mar., complaining that the money advanced would have to be repaid by parochial taxes, 14 Mar. He endorsed a petition against Irish Protestant education societies next day and welcomed the select committee on Irish education grants, to which he was appointed, 11 Mar. He advocated inquiry into parliamentary representation, 11 Mar., and voted to disfranchise East Retford in favour of a large unrepresented town, 21 Mar., 27 June. He welcomed a bill for the registration of English freeholders, without which 'it would be perfectly impossible to go through a contested election' in Ireland, 25 Mar., suggested that the bribery oath in the Manchester enfranchisement bill be included in a 'general measure of reform', 28 Mar., and called for the disfranchisement of all non-resident borough electors, 15 May. On 18 Mar. he opposed the passengers regulation bill, fearing it would restrict Irish emigration. He supported a bill to render Irish lessors liable for parish and county assessments, 20 Mar., and voted accordingly, 12 June. He condemned ministers for failing to abolish the office of the keeper of the general register of hornings in Scotland, 21 Mar., and demanded an inquiry prior to their filling up the vacancy, 28 Mar. He welcomed bills for the lighting, cleansing and watching of Irish towns, 25 Mar., and the correction of abuses in Irish public offices, 27 Mar. On 2 Apr. he ridiculed government proposals to lower the duty on cards and dice rather than articles of 'great public interest' and supported a bill amending the laws relating to testators and executors. That day the newly appointed Irish viceroy Lord Anglesey told Holland, 'I wish I had my little Sir John Newport at my elbow ... He was adverse to my going [to Ireland] but that was under an impression that my government might be considered by the Catholics as likely to be hostile to them, whereas the very reverse is the case, and ... I wish you would take the trouble to reconcile him'.[51] Newport attacked the 'great and unnecessary expense' of the new post office building and the 'impropriety' of using departmental funds without parliamentary approval, 15 Apr. He secured accounts of Irish revenue collection that day. He feared that the friendly societies bill would damage benefit societies, 17 Apr. He warned against 'interested parties' being appointed to the select committee on the Irish stock exchange bill, to which he was added, 6 May. Reiterating his opposition to the introduction of Irish poor laws that day, he drew attention to the difficulty of ensuring 'the fair distribution of poor rates'. On 22 May he spoke in support of the proposed grant to the family of Canning, to whom the country were 'indebted' for his stand against the Holy Alliance. He deplored the post office's rejection of the Liverpool Steam Navigation Company's offer to transport mail from Liverpool to Dublin, 30 May, and condemned the 'public expense' of their separate steam packets, 6, 25 June. He presented and endorsed a petition against the collection of Irish tithes by the episcopal courts, 2 June. He insisted that some measure was 'absolutely necessary' to alleviate Irish distress, 5 June. He obtained information on financial abuses in the Irish police, 12 June, and presented and endorsed a petition against the misuse of their funds, 20 June. He spoke in support of the small debts bill, 23 June. On 24 June 1828 he moved unsuccessfully for an inquiry into Irish church pluralities.

Following Anglesey's recall Newport chaired a Waterford meeting in his support, 15 Jan. 1829.[52] In the House, 6 Feb., he expressed 'joy' at the Wellington ministry's concession of emancipation and urged the Catholic Association to dissolve immediately 'without waiting for any legislative acts'. He presented favourable petitions, 16 Feb., and voted thus, 6 Mar., when he praised Peel for putting the 'interests of the country first' and defended the Irish franchise bill as a necessary sacrifice, and 30 Mar. (as a pair). He divided for O'Connell to be allowed to take his seat unimpaired, 18 May. Next month Wellington received an anonymous application from the 'people of Ireland' for an honour to be bestowed upon Newport, who was 'renowned for his adherence to his political conscience' and since the failure of his family's bank had 'been on the verge of financial ruin'.[53] No other parliamentary activity for Newport has been found for the rest of that year, of which he later recalled: '1829. Very ill of fever and asthma nearly whole session'.[54] He presented a constituency petition against the monopoly of the East India Company, 22 Feb. 1830. He warned that increases in Irish spirit duties would 'revive illicit distillation', 23 Feb. He voted for the enfranchisement of Birmingham, Leeds and Manchester that day, and paired for the transfer of East Retford's seats to Birmingham, 5 Mar., and parliamentary reform, 28 May. On 4 Mar. he revived his campaign against Irish church pluralities, but agreed to withdraw his motion for inquiry. He attended a meeting of '*the party*' at Althorp's, 6 Mar., but 'objected strongly' to the issue of 'some sort of communication' announcing they were acting together for a reduction of taxation, in which the others 'agreed with him'.[55] He voted steadily with the revived Whig opposition for economy and tax cuts thereafter. He was appointed to the select committee on the Irish poor, 11 Mar. He criticized the 'annoying' tax on Irish seaborne coals, 17 Mar., and presented and endorsed a Dublin petition for its abolition, 30 Mar. He opposed calls for repeal of the Union, warning that it would lead to a 'speedy destruction of one of the countries, and ultimately to that of the other', 22 Mar. He voted for Jewish emancipation, 5 Apr. He presented and endorsed petitions against the proposed increase of Irish stamp duties, 7, 26 Apr., 6, 27 May, and berated ministers for failing to provide more details, 28 Apr., and attempting to 'clog' the freedom of the Irish press, 17 May. He secured papers on the advances made by the Irish first fruits commissioners, 27 Apr., and unsuccessfully reintroduced his motion for their proper implementation, regretting that at present 'neither my health nor my strength' enabled him to speak 'at great length', 18 May. He argued and voted for amendment of the Irish Vestry Act, 27 Apr., and brought up a petition for its repeal, 25 May. He called for the estimates to be referred to a select committee, 3 May, and recommended revising the allowances of retired public officers, 14 May. That month he was entrusted by the Irish Members with presenting their resolutions against tax increases to Wellington and Goulburn.[56] He supported calls for the removal of Sir Jonah Barrington from the Irish admiralty court for embezzlement, 25 May. He secured papers on the drawback on soap and candles, citing the damage to Irish manufacturers, 27 May 1830.

At the 1830 general election it was rumoured that he would retire from Waterford, where the recently 'opened' corporation had renounced any further involvement in the representation. In the event, however, he offered again, stressing his 26 years' political service and opposition to O'Connell's campaign for repeal of the Union. 'For God's sake will nobody rid us of this nominee', protested the *Waterford Mail*, adding, 'Little Johnny is an alderman and he is at the very bottom of those humbug new rules ... of the corporation ... He is an excursive patriot and disdains to point to any services he ... has performed near home'. Attempts to get up an opposition came to nothing, however, and he was again returned.[57] On 3 Nov. 1830 he implored ministers to redress the grievances of Ireland, complaining of the delays to Irish legislation caused by the dissolution. Next day he presented and endorsed a petition for the abolition of slavery. He recommended that copies of the estimates be given to every Member, 8 Nov., and was appointed to the select committee on the Irish poor, 11 Nov. He of course had been listed by the Irish agent Pierce Mahony† as a 'contra' and by the ministry as one of their 'foes', but he was absent from the crucial division for inquiry into the civil list (to which he was nevertheless appointed) 15 Nov. On 19 Nov. he asserted that O'Connell's repeal campaign would have the 'most lamentable consequences' and recalled the system of 'misgovernment' carried out by the Irish Parliament. He acknowledged that on this issue he was 'opposed' to a respectable portion of his constituents, 6 Dec., and dissented from their favourable petitions, which he presented, 8 Dec. 1830, 11 Feb. 1831. On 9 Dec. 1830, in what Sir John Walsh* considered 'a feeble speech', he moved but agreed to withdraw a 'string of resolutions' for reform of the 'grossly defective' Irish grand jury system.[58] Sending Lansdowne details of his proposals, which included more regular meetings and a limited period of service and property qualification for grand jurors, 25 Dec., he explained that he had acted

> rather with the object of eliciting discussion than any idea of taking on myself the task far too heavy for me ... of planning or carrying through the necessary reforms ... I withdrew [the resolutions] on Althorp's declaration that the subject was under consideration of the government ... and on Peel's objection to coming to a vote upon them without their remaining for a time before the House ... In almost every county of Ireland the inequality of the assessment is severely felt and ... I consider it vicious in its foundation.[59]

He was appointed to the select committee on reducing the salaries of office-holders, 9 Dec., and secured information on the Irish civil list, 15 Dec. He called for repeal of the Irish seaborne coal tax, 17 Dec. 1830, 8 Feb. 1831. On 20 Dec. 1830 he rebutted criticism of the Grey ministry's Irish appointments, remarking on the 'hardship that an administration but three weeks in existence should be thus arraigned'.[60] 'Little Newport was charming. I wish we had a dozen such, so honest and so clever and so *bold*', observed William Ord*.[61] He implored ministers not to 'resist the wishes of the people' over parliamentary reform, citing Wellington's recent fall 'from popularity', 21 Dec. 1830, and presented a petition for additional Irish Members, 4 Feb. 1831, when he announced his conversion to the secret ballot. Regretting that he could no longer speak at length owing to 'age and increasing infirmities', 2 Mar., he contended that reform was essential to prevent revolution and recommended the enfranchisement of all householders. On 14 Mar. he reintroduced his resolutions for the proper use of Irish first fruits, and after agreeing to modifications by Smith Stanley, the Irish secretary, successfully moved for inquiry. He supported proposed amendments to the Irish Vestry Act and secured an inquiry into the Irish prerogative courts, to which he was appointed, 16 Mar. He dismissed allegations that the ministry's plan of reform was 'corporate robbery', noting Waterford corporation's willingness to 'waive' their privileges for the 'public benefit', 19 Mar., paired for the second reading of the English bill, 22 Mar., when he welcomed the destruction of the 'close borough system', and presented a favourable constituency petition, insisting that reform afforded the best means to preserve the Union, 29 Mar. He countered denials that close boroughs had been 'bought and sold', detailing their barter in marriage settlements, 18 Apr. 1831, and paired against Gascoyne's wrecking amendment next day.

At the ensuing general election he again defied local expectations that he would retire and stood for re-election as a supporter of the 'whole' reform bill, regretting that 'advanced age and infirm health' would 'wholly disable' him from attending in person. Following the last minute withdrawal of an opponent he was returned unopposed, with his nephew William Newport, 'a barrister', acting as his representative.[62] 'He is 75', reported Sheil that month, 'but his heart still beats with a vigorous passion for his country, though I am sorry to perceive that his hand has begun to tremble and his fine eyes have lost their lustre'.[63] Passing on an application from Newport, Grey observed to Anglesey, 'There is really nothing that would give me more pleasure than to have it in my power to do anything that might be for the service of good old Newport', 17 May 1831.[64] On 12 June Newport sent Holland a copy of a 'little statement' he had prepared for Duncannon on the first fruits question, which he hoped would be printed for those Members who 'would want patience to go through the details', adding:

> The bishop of Cork is dead and this vacancy would afford as I think a signal opportunity for Lord Grey to commence an admirable reform of the Irish church establishment, by uniting the diocese with Cloyne ... and appropriating the revenues either to the first fruits fund or other public uses. I anxiously wish that ... the cabinet would consider this well before you decided on filling it up.[65]

He cautioned against discussing the Newtownbarry massacre prior to inquiry, 23 June, but spoke and voted for printing the Waterford petition for disarming the Irish yeomanry, 11 Aug. 'It is lamentable that even Newport ... divided against government', observed Holland.[66] He paired for the second reading of the reintroduced English reform bill, 6 July, and gave generally steady support to its details (usually as a pair). He paired for the bill's passage, 21 Sept. He called for a reform of Irish education, 15 July, defended the grant to Maynooth College, 5 Aug., 26 Sept., and after being prevented by 'a severe attack' of asthma from attending the House, wrote to congratulate Smith Stanley on his announcement of the new plan of Irish education, which he promised to assist 'as far as health and age will allow', 10 Sept.[67] He contended that it was 'quite time' to suppress Orange processions, 18 July. He obtained information on the Irish admiralty court, 21 July. On the 27th, in an acknowledged volte face, he conceded the necessity of 'permanent provision' for the Irish poor, though he remained concerned about giving a 'premium to idlers', 26 Sept. He secured papers on the progress of the revaluation of Irish first fruits, 9 Aug. He welcomed the appointment of lord lieutenants to Irish counties, 20 Aug., and defended the selection of Henry Villiers Stuart* for county Waterford, stressing his non-political credentials, 6 Oct. He divided with ministers on the Dublin election controversy, 23 Aug. He protested that under the Irish Vestry Act the building of churches had become a 'complete job' and demanded its repeal, 29 Aug. He opposed calls for the abolition of the Irish lord lieutenancy, 31 Aug. He welcomed the establishment of an Irish board of public works, 16 Sept. On 19 Sept. he was discharged from further attendance of the select committee on malt drawback, to which he had been appointed, 5 Sept. That month he and O'Connell, acting as a 'deputation from the Irish Members', met with ministers to demand additional Irish representatives and other improvements to the Irish reform bill, which they had jointly agreed in a paper.[68] He renewed his call for the repeal of the drawback on English soap sold in Ireland, 11 Oct., and commended the bankruptcy court bill as 'economical and efficient', 14 Oct. On 17 Oct. 1831 he disputed complaints by Hunt* that Ireland was subsidized by England and failed to pay her 'fair share of taxation'.

Newport was appointed to the select committee on Irish tithes, 15 Dec. 1831. He was absent from the division on the second reading of the revised English reform bill, 17 Dec. 1831, but presented and endorsed a favourable constituency petition, 23 Jan., and paired for the enfranchisement of Tower Hamlets, 28 Feb., and the third reading, 22 Mar. 1832. On 10 Feb. a colleague postponed his tabled motion on Irish first fruits on account of his 'indisposition'. That month Holland noted that Newport and others 'of our best Irish friends' were satisfied that Smith Stanley's Irish tithes legislation was 'safe'.[69] Newport supported calls for a full inquiry into Irish education, 2 Mar., but rejected claims by the Protestant proselytiser James Gordon that the new plan was 'purely exclusive and Catholic', 8 June. He presented a Waterford petition for repeal of the Irish Vestry Act, 8 May. He spoke in support of Lord Ebrington's planned motion for an address calling on the king to appoint only ministers who would carry reform unimpaired, 9 May, and paired accordingly next day. On 22 May he was appointed to the select committee on the Bank of England's charter. He paired for the second reading of the Irish reform bill, 25 May, having given Smith Stanley advance warning that he was 'much indisposed with asthma ... in addition to a cold and cough', but complained that the Irish 40*s*. freeholders 'in fee' should have been restored to the 'same privileges' as their English counterparts and that the proposed 'mode of registration' was 'highly defective', 13 June.[70] He agreed with other Irish Members that the £10 household qualification was 'too high', but appealed for the Irish measure to be allowed to pass 'contemporaneously with the English and Scottish bills', as its 'great point' was the 'abolition of nomination boroughs', 18 June. That month, in what the *Morning Chronicle* deemed a 'valuable contingent to the history of corruption', Newport published a pamphlet on the state of Irish borough representation before the Union dedicated to Grey. 'On the eve of terminating my political life', he wrote, 'I offer to public inspection a document connected with its commencement'.[71] Citing his imminent retirement 'from Parliament and England' and 'strong and direct claims' on government, Holland, at Newport's request, that month pressed Anglesey for a deputy clerkship at the Irish hanaper court for his nephew William, only to learn that the position had already been filled and was not in his gift. On 25 June Holland reported that Newport had 'called, not without some chagrin, natural enough, that his nephew's claim ... has been hitherto neglected. Few deserve more from the Whigs than Newport. None can have got less, and the old man feels it'.[72] 'I was really touched at the parting visit of ... poor little Newport this morning', he wrote to Anglesey that day:

> He hardly means to return to England again and it is at least a painful consequence of retrenchment if it be not some reproach upon us all that so able, steadfast and honest a member of our party should retire to poverty in his old age without having been able to procure an employment however small for his only nephew and I believe heir, if he has enough to entitle those who come after him to any such appellation.

'You ought to know that dear little Johnny *has not* been overlooked', Anglesey corrected, 1 July, observing that he had 'already ... at his request, appointed one of his nephews to the situation of stipendiary magistrate, worth £500 a year, and another relation to a living of more than £300 a year'.[73] In Newport's last known spoken intervention, 2 July, he doubted that legislation would prevent frauds in the sale of flax or corn seeds used for sowing. He was granted six weeks' leave on urgent business that day. Following his return to Ireland, 17 July, he advised Holland that his 'strong conviction' against the tithes system had been 'decidedly confirmed':

> Depend on it the landed *proprietors* of the country *cannot* if they *would* and *will not if they could* generally undertake the perilous responsibility of the collection of either the tithe or its substitute ... The settlement can in my mind only be effected by the state becoming paymasters of the church and indemnify itself by a land tax during the continuance of the outstanding bishop's leases so as to provide for existing interests of bishops and clergy. This is I believe *now* practicable. How *long it will remain so* I cannot so easily foresee, but in this as in former instances procrastination will I fear prove the curse of Ireland.[74]

Writing in similar terms to Lansdowne, with whom he claimed to have acted 'in perfect unison' for 'so many years', 30 Sept. 1832, he explained that in his resignation address to his constituents:

> I felt myself bound ... to impress on my countrymen my conviction of the unjustifiable and perilous extent to which O'Connell and other agitators desire for their own depraved and selfish objects to commit the people of Ireland ... to ... wild and ruinous proceedings.[75]

At the 1832 dissolution he duly retired from Waterford on account of 'advanced age and infirm health', and in the ensuing election publicly supported the unsuccessful candidature of Thomas Wyse* against a local Repealer.[76] Shortly after the accession of Lord Melbourne as premier in 1834, he was appointed to the newly created comptroller-generalship of the exchequer, a salaried auditorship which he retained until 1839, when he retired with a pension of £1,000. (He was reportedly 'ready and eager to retire' in November 1838, having come close to death through illness the previous month.) He resigned his seat on Waterford corporation, 5 Nov. 1834.[77]

Newport died in February 1843, aged 87, the 'infirmities natural to an advanced age' having had 'so gradual an effect on his constitution' that his friends 'scarcely noticed the slow but sure symptoms of decay'. He was succeeded in the baronetcy by his brother's only surviving son, the Rev. John Newport (1800-59).[78]

[1] R. Sheil, *Sketches, Legal and Political* ed. M.W. Savage, ii. 339; Add. 51783, Holland to C.R. Fox, 28 June 1823. [2] *Black Bk.* (1823), 179; *Session of Parl. 1825*, p. 477; *Life of Campbell*, i. 398. [3] D. Plunket, *Life, Letters, and Speeches of Lord Plunket*, i. 394. [4] Northants. RO, Agar Ellis diary, 17 Apr. 1822. [5] *The Times*, 11 Nov. 1829. [6] Wellesley to Newport, 28 Feb., with reply, 23 Mar. 1840, cited in Plunket, ii. 131-3. [7] *PP* (1835), xxxiv. 149; T. Power, 'Electoral Politics in Waterford City, 1692-1832', in *Waterford Hist. and Society* ed. W. Noland and T. Power, 254; *Ramsey's Waterford Chron.* 21 Mar. 1820. [8] *The Times*, 13 June, 28 July 1820; W.P.

Burke, 'Newport's Waterford Bank', *Jnl. Cork Hist. and Arch. Soc.* (1878), iv. 279, 284. [9] Add. 75962, Grenville to Spencer, 30 Nov. 1820. [10] Add. 51534, f. 83. [11] Buckingham, *Mems. Geo. IV*, i. 145. [12] HLRO, Hist. Coll. 379, Grey Bennet diary, 9 May 1821. [13] Lonsdale mss, Beckett to Lord Lowther, 20 June 1821. [14] Lansdowne mss, Brougham to Lansdowne [n.d.]. [15] Add. 52445, ff. 25-26. [16] Add. 37298, f. 158. [17] NLW, Coedymaen mss 633; Buckingham, i. 314; Add. 51586, Tierney to Lady Holland, 16 Apr. 1822. [18] Agar Ellis diary, 17 Apr. 1822. [19] Coedymaen mss 636; Add. 52445, f. 78. [20] *Arbuthnot Jnl.* i. 157; *The Times*, 23 Apr. 1822. [21] Add. 37315, Richard Wellesley to Wellesley, 25 Apr. 1822. [22] Add. 51832. [23] TCD, Donoughmore mss D/28/8. [24] Add. 51667, Bedford to Lady Holland, 7 Mar. 1823. [25] *HP Commons, 1790-1820*, iv. 666. [26] Add. 40329, f. 62; Buckingham, i. 446; Harewood mss Har/GC/85, Williams Wynn to Canning, 7 Apr. 1823. [27] Add. 51663, Bedford to Holland, 27 Mar. 1823. [28] Add. 51663, same to same, undated. [29] *O'Connell Corresp.* ii. 1012. [30] Add. 51574, Abercromby to Holland, 30 Dec. 1823. [31] Buckingham, i. 314. [32] Agar Ellis diary, 8 Apr. 1824. [33] *O'Connell Corresp.* iii. 1172. [34] Add. 51832, Newport to Holland, 17 July 1825. [35] Brougham mss, Mackintosh to Brougham, 17 Mar. 1825; Lonsdale mss, Long to Lonsdale, 23 Mar. 1825. [36] Agar Ellis diary, 26 Mar. 1825. [37] *The Times*, 12 May 1825; TNA 30/29/9/2/30. [38] *O'Connell Corresp.* iii. 1278. [39] TCD, Jebb mss 6396/249. [40] *The Mail*, 10, 17 June 1826. [41] *Crabb Robinson Diary*, i. 34; *O'Connell Corresp.* iii. 1337. [42] *Canning's Ministry*, 40. [43] Surr. Hist. Cent. Goulburn mss Acc 304/66A, Goulburn to wife, 14 Mar. 1827. [44] Add. 37305, f. 53. [45] Add. 51833, Newport to Holland, 15 Aug. [1827]. [46] Add. 51833. [47] Lansdowne mss, Macdonald to Lansdowne, 21 Oct. [1827]. [48] Add. 51834. [49] Add. 40320, f. 1. [50] Add. 40395, ff. 219, 221; 40307, f. 50. [51] Add. 51567, Anglesey to Holland, 2 Apr. 1828. [52] *Dublin Evening Post*, 24 Jan. 1829. [53] Wellington mss WP1/1024/5. [54] NAI, Newport mss M. 483/17. [55] Add. 56554, ff. 71-72. [56] *O'Connell Corresp.* iv. 1672, 1677. [57] *Waterford Mail*, 3, 7, 14 July, 7 Aug. 1830. [58] NLW, Ormathwaite mss FG/1/6. [59] Lansdowne mss. [60] *The Times*, 21 Dec. 1830. [61] Add. 51569, Ord to Holland, 21 Dec. 1830. [62] *Waterford Mail*, 9, 13, 27 Apr., 7 May 1831. [63] Sheil, ii. 339. [64] PRO NI, Anglesey mss D619/28A-B/57. [65] Add. 51836, Newport to Holland [12 June 1831]. [66] *Holland House Diaries*, 28. [67] Derby mss 920 Der (14) 128/1. [68] A. Macintyre, *The Liberator*, 32; *O'Connell Corresp.* iv. 1836; *Holland House Diaries*, 94. [69] *Holland House Diaries*, 130. [70] Derby mss 920 Der (14) 128/1, Newport to Smith Stanley [n.d.]. [71] *Morning Chron.* 12 June 1832; *The State of the Borough Representation of Ireland in 1783 and 1800*. [72] *Holland House Diaries*, 195. [73] Anglesey mss 27A/165, 167, 168; 27B/110-12. [74] Add. 51837, Newport to Holland, 17 July [1832]. [75] Lansdowne mss, Newport to Lansdowne, 30 Sept. 1832. [76] Macintyre, 56. [77] Walpole, *Russell*, i. 308, 312; *Holland House Diaries*, 389; Newport mss M. 482/7. [78] *Gent. Mag.* (1843), i. 653; *Oxford DNB*.

P.J.S.

NICHOLL, Sir John (1759–1838), of Merthyr Mawr, Glam. and 26 Bruton Street, Mdx.[1]

PENRYN	1802–1806
HASTINGS	1806–1807
GREAT BEDWYN	1807–18 Aug. 1821
GREAT BEDWYN	11 Feb. 1822–1832

b. 16 Mar. 1759, 2nd s. of John Nicholl (*d.* 1773) of Llanmaes, Glam. and Elizabeth *née* Havard. *educ.* Cowbridge sch. 1766; Bristol 1773; St. John's, Oxf. 1775, BCL 1780, DCL 1785; L. Inn 1775. *m.* 8 Sept. 1787, Judy, da. of Peter Birt of Wenvoe Castle, Glam., 1s. surv. 3 da. (1 *d.v.p.*). kntd. 31 Oct. 1798; *suc.* Edward Powell to Tondu, Glam. 1771. *d.* 26 Aug. 1838.

Adv. doctors' commons Nov. 1785; king's adv. Oct. 1798-Jan. 1809; dean of ct. of arches and PCC judge 1809-34; PC 6 Feb. 1809; admiralty ct. judge 1833-*d.*, holding his other offices *in commendam*; vicar-gen. to abp. of Canterbury 1834-*d.*

Lt.-col. commdt. St. Giles and St. George's, Bloomsbury vol. inf. 1803.

An expert on admiralty, ecclesiastical and international law, Nicholl had been brought into Parliament as a government supporter in 1802, and had been returned for Great Bedwyn since 1807 on the interest of the Bruce family, Barons Ailesbury. Nothing had come of his aspirations to represent his native Glamorgan, where he had purchased and improved the Merthyr Mawr estate and was a generous benefactor to the new county town of Bridgend, but he exerted considerable influence in the county and Cardiff Boroughs. Like his friend and mentor, the admiralty judge Sir William Scott*, Nicholl's high church principles and reputation as an astute parliamentarian and effective speaker carried weight beyond his college of St. John's, and he was considered a likely candidate for one of the Oxford University seats. His speech on proposing Charles Abbot for the Speakership in 1812 was considered a masterpiece, and he had been the leader of the Commons Lord Castlereagh's choice to nominate the government candidate Charles Manners Sutton as Abbot's successor in 1817. An erstwhile Pittite, he tended to combine his ministerialist sympathies and scholarly expositions of orders in council with vociferous opposition to parliamentary reform and Catholic relief and promoting legislation against clandestine marriages.[2] He habitually devoted time to 'regular study and fireside reading', preferring to 'leave the management of domestic concerns and family accounts' to his wife.[3]

Nicholl was at the privy council meeting, 30 Jan. 1820, which issued the proclamation of George IV, and he attended George III's funeral and interment.[4] At the ensuing general election he was returned without incident for Great Bewdyn; and in Glamorgan he backed the victorious Margam candidate, Sir Christopher Cole, on whose behalf he had negotiated with the 6th duke of Beaufort's son, Lord Granville Somerset*, and the 2nd marquess of Bute's brother, Lord James Crichton Stuart*.[5] After returning to London on 14 Apr. Nicholl, who according to the 1820 *Black Book* received £5,000 a year from his offices, had meetings with his patron the 2nd Baron Ailesbury, Lord Harrowby, the duke of Montrose, his nephew John Dyneley, Sir Thomas Neave, and the new Member for

Cardiff Boroughs, Wyndham Lewis; and he attended Castlereagh's eve of session briefing on the 26th.[6] Diary entries indicate that he was now regular in his attendance and support for Lord Liverpool's administration. According to a radical publication of 1825, he 'attended occasionally and voted with ministers'. He frequented the Welsh Club, and was named to the select committee on the administration of justice in the Principality, 1 June. He spoke briefly and without his customary clarity on Phillimore's Marriage Act amendment bill, 2 June, and, having supported a similar measure in 1819, he was sorry to see it defeated in the Lords for want of government support.[7] The Welsh judge Robert Casberd† and Cole and his family were among the guests at Merthyr Mawr during the recess, which Nicholl as usual devoted to private study and his Glamorgan interests.[8] The earl of Westmorland and John Luxmore, bishop of St. Asaph, had kept him informed of developments in the Queen Caroline case; and after returning to London, 1 Nov. 1820, he attended the Lords proceedings, and conferred with Ailesbury, Sir Henry Halford, Montrose and the chancellor of the exchequer Vansittart.[9] He was at Castlereagh's pre-session meeting, 22 Jan. 1821, and attended those held by the Speaker, 27 Jan., Liverpool, 29 Jan., and Westmorland, 16 Feb. He voted against censuring government's handling of the queen's case, 6 Feb., and it may be inferred from his diary that he was in the majorities against the restoration of Caroline's name to the liturgy, 26 Jan., 13 Feb.[10] He paired against Catholic relief, 28 Feb., sought in vain with Scott to have the bill reprinted and deferred until after the Easter recess, 16, 19 Mar., and took pleasure in its Lords' defeat, 17 Apr.[11] He was not in the government majority against the malt duty repeal bill, 3 Apr., although the treasury secretary Arbuthnot had requested his attendance and vote.[12] He went to Cowbridge for the Glamorgan quarter sessions, 1 May, and returned to London for the debate on Irish tithes on the 10th only to find it postponed.[13] He divided with his fellow placemen for the Clarence annuity bill, 8, 25 June, and probably (as Sir G. Nicholl) on economy and retrenchment, 27 June 1821.

Nicholl's attention now focused on the forthcoming by-election for Oxford University, where Scott's elevation to the peerage as Baron Stowell had produced a vacancy. It soon emerged that should he stand and fail, Ailesbury, who refused to return his only son John Nicholl† in his place, might not bring him back in for Bedwyn.[14] Furthermore, his rival Richard Heber*, who had declared tactically against Catholic relief, was the chancellor of the University Lord Grenville's candidate and had the premier and the home secretary Lord Sidmouth's support.[15] On 16 July John Whishaw informed Lady Holland that Nicholl, to whom 'nothing can be objected but his temporary connection with the Whigs in 1806, which he has redeemed by an undeviating opposition to them when out of office', had

> the chancellor and Sir William Scott, doctors' commons, his own college of St. John's, All Souls College, Corpus, all the leading people connected with Christ Church, such as Lloyd, Goodenough, and Bull, etc. (the dean excepted, who belongs to Heber), Queen's and Magdalen Colleges and the greater part of the residents.[16]

His committee, chaired by the bursar designate of St. John's, Thomas Wintle, was soon active and secured promises of some 740 votes, but Nicholl delayed applying for the Chiltern Hundreds until 18 Aug. He vacated at Great Bedwyn, 20 Aug., only two days before the Oxford poll. He predicted that it would end on the 23rd, when, if unsuccessful, he proposed canvassing Bedwyn to deter any rivals.[17] He was 208-205 ahead on the first day, but was overtaken on the second and retired, trailing by 519-612, 23 Aug. Informing Ailesbury of the outcome, he estimated that 100 of his supporters had paired and a further 120 were unaccounted for.[18] As Ailesbury turned down his request to canvass Bedwyn, he returned via Abingdon to Merthyr Mawr, where letters of congratulation and pledges of future support awaited him.[19] Ailesbury's letter of 29 Aug. left Nicholl in no doubt that if re-elected he would not again be free to vacate Bedwyn to stand for Oxford. He was not formally offered Bedwyn until he had been to Oxford for discussions, 31 Oct.-2 Nov., and assured Ailesbury and Lord Jersey in writing, 3, 4 Nov., that the master of St. John's 'understands that upon no future occasion could I become a candidate'.[20] His time that autumn was largely taken up with plans for his son's marriage to Cole's stepdaughter Jane Harriet Talbot, which took place at Penrice, 14 Dec. 1821.[21]

Nicholl attended Lord Londonderry's eve of session briefing, 4 Feb. 1822. The Bedwyn writ was moved on the 5th, and, after a busy social round, which included engagements at the Travellers' Club, and the Bedwyn by-election, he resumed his seat, 15 Feb.[22] He divided with government against more extensive tax cuts, 21 Feb., but not against the proposed abolition of one of the joint-postmasterships, 13 Mar. On the 23rd he met Vansittart and attended the Speaker's levee. He was in the minority against Canning's bill to relieve Catholic peers, 30 Apr., and probably voted against its committal, 10 May. Later that day he turned down a request from Vansittart asking him to take a leading part in the

Commons campaign against it, as he had done in 1817, because

> my time (like yours) has been lately so much occupied by official business as not to have left me leisure to look into the matter with the care necessary to render any useful assistance. I must also frankly add, that a certain part of the House is so little disposed even to allow, much less to listen to 'impartial discussion' upon the subject, that I really have not nerves sufficient to encounter such an audience.[23]

Nicholl, who had also ceased to contribute to debates on parliamentary reform, delivered his judgment in the Sapha *v.* Atkinson case, 5 June, and sat through the debate on Irish tithes on the 13th, but was not listed in the majority against inquiry, 19 June 1822.[24] Towards the end of the session he was particularly busy in doctors' commons, and he also had separate meetings with Bute and Crichton Stuart, whom Bute proposed bringing in for Cardiff Boroughs at the next election in place of Wyndham Lewis. During the recess, part of which he spent on the continent, Lewis solicited his support on the same matter.[25]

Nicholl was at the Speaker's reception, 8 Feb., attended the debates on ordnance reductions, 19, 20 Feb., Lord John Russell's parliamentary reform resolutions, 20 Feb., and the revenue, 21 Feb., and moved the third reading of the Marriage Act amendment bill, 4 Mar. 1823. Writing on the 11th to his son in Rome, he noted that he had

> attended rather regularly since the term was over. We have had some interesting debates, which ended very triumphantly on the part of ministers ... Canning has hitherto been very prudent, judicious, and conciliatory in leading, and if he proceeds on the same course and is not hurried off his guard by temper, matters will go on well, and he will gain in the confidence of the House. He has an excellent second in Peel, and some circumstances which came out in the discussion on Wednesday on the subject of Orange lodges in Ireland strongly impressed the House with an opinion of Peel's judgement and caution, whilst secretary in Ireland. The attack upon the Orange lodges was evidently intended to throw down the apple of discord among the administration on account of their differing opinions on the Catholic question, but it went off without producing of the expected embarrassment. It fully appeared that the object of the whole government here is to promote *conciliation*. I still doubt however whether some of the late measures of the Irish government have been calculated to produce that effect. They have tended to gratify the Catholics but to irritate the Protestants, and irritation in either party must lead to anything but *conciliation* ... The Protestant party in Ireland is too strong to be put down by the government.[26]

He was in the government's minority against inquiry into the prosecution of the Dublin Orange rioters, 22 Apr., and was included on the select committee on trade legislation on account of his expertise. Speaking on the Irish tithes composition bill, 30 May, he said that he was not against its committal, but did object to the inference in the preamble 'that a similar measure would be expedient for England', and it was accordingly amended. So powerful was his defence of the rights of property and his criticism of those who assumed that the church's holdings were public assets at the disposal of the state, that the chancellor of the exchequer Robinson had to intervene to try to allay his doubts over the bill, which received royal assent, 19 July.[27] He voted against inquiry into chancery delays, 5 June 1823. He had recently undertaken additional work on behalf of the Society for the Propagation of the Gospels and the Society for the Propagation of Christian Knowledge, and during the recess he waited on Bute at Cardiff Castle, and attended county functions.[28] Feeling that the return of his son and daughter-in-law from their European tour marked the start of a new and possibly final stage in his own life, he reminded them of the importance he attached to professional advancement, connections, and domestic happiness, for which he recommended 'unreserve' as the 'surest basis'.[29] Proffering 'advice' to Cole's stepson Christopher Rice Mansel Talbot* when congratulating him on gaining a first at Oxford, 24 Dec. 1823, he digressed into politics and observed:

> The old distinctions of Whig and Tory so far as principles are concerned no longer exist. Divine right, passive obedience and non-resistance are doctrines quite extinct. We are all old Whigs. Political parties are now divided rather into men and measures than any great differences by principles, except perhaps a few ultras and radicals, and you may recollect my stating to you an opinion that you would do wisely to abstain very cautiously from committing yourself to any party or set of men, until you had a full opportunity by considerable experience of forming a deliberate judgement which set of measures generally pursued or recommended by contending parties were upon the whole most conducive to the real interests of the country. For if once you became a party man, you were no longer quite as independent, and perfect independence should in no degree be sacrificed but on most mature consideration guiding the judgement.[30]

Nicholl was on the steering committee prior to the founding of King's College, London early in 1824, and the master of the rolls Sir Thomas Plumer requested his opinion on the cases of Reynolds *v.* Richards, Alexander *v.* Allen and White *v.* Lequense, the last requiring expertise in Channel Island law which only he and Stowell could provide.[31] The Catholic question was not considered that session, and Commons proceedings now occupied little space in Nicholl's diary, which contains brief reports of the debate on Wrottesley's abortive proposal for a decimal currency, 25 Feb., and the home secretary Peel's speech on the introduction of treadmills in prisons, 26 Feb., a matter of local concern in Glamorgan. He voted that day against bringing in a bill to reform the representation of Edinburgh. He entertained the bishop of Llandaff, William van Mildert, and Crichton Stuart, who was canvassing Cardiff Boroughs, at Merthyr Mawr during the recess, and, fearing the likely impact of the struggle for the 'towns' on county politics, he cautioned Cole and Talbot accordingly.[32] Nicholl attended Canning's dinner and speech, 2 Feb., and recorded details in his diary of the debates and proceedings on San Domingo, 3 Feb.; the Irish unlawful societies bill, 10, 11, 14, 15, 18, 21 Feb.; the budget, 28 Feb.; Catholic relief, 3 Feb., 1 Mar., 21, 27 Apr., 2, 6 May; the attendant Irish franchise bill, 26, 27, 29 Apr.; the game laws, 10 Mar.; the corn laws, 28 Apr.; chancery delays, 31 May, 7 June, and the St. Olave tithe bill, 6, 13 June 1825. He considered Seymour Conway's justification of the Irish unlawful societies bill, 15 Feb., 'admirable' and 'conclusive', and kept notes of the speeches made on its second and third readings, 21, 25 Feb., when he apparently left without voting. He paired with Canning against the Catholic relief bill after hearing much of the debate, 1 Mar., and with Sir Thomas Mostyn, when out of town 'on visitation', 10 May. He thought Canning's speech at its second reading, 21 Apr., 'very brilliant', and Peel's reply 'very able ... but in parts not so successful and free from heaviness as some of his former speeches'. He chose not to divide on the Durham railway bill, 4 Mar., and discouraged raising opposition in the Commons to the Irish church rates bill. He was at the privy council meetings that considered East India Company appeals, William Rough's prosecution of the printer John Murray, the Jersey case, Guernsey regulations, and the duke of Buckingham's application to become governor-general of India, but had to be excused attendance on 4 June because of illness.[33] Opposing the St. Olave tithe bill, 6 June, he reminded the House that although the parish had offered to pay the present owner £1,800 a year, a successor would receive only £1,200. He thought privately that the measure was only carried that day by the accident of many opposition Members being present on account of the duke of Cumberland's annuity bill.[34] He divided for the latter, 6, 10 June, having paired, 9 June, before going to the Mansion House dinner. He considered Dr. Lushington's speech against inquiry into chancery delays, 7 June

> mainly candid ... doing justice to the course the lord chancellor [Eldon] had pursued, yet ... engaging not to stretch for full investigation in order to remedy the evil by ascertaining what the cause of it was on the constitution or the administration of the court ... Brougham violent in his attack against persons giving the chancellor credit for suavity of manners in order to abuse him in every other respect.[35]

Before leaving on 7 July 1825 for Glamorgan, where his advice had been sought on the dispute generated by the appointment of a non-lawyer, William Bruce Knight, as chancellor of Llandaff, he excused himself from that day's privy council meeting on the Douai College case, having submitted his 'opinion that no compensation was necessary for British subjects'.[36] He signed the petition for the Dyffryn Llynfi railway bill, which he later opposed

> only upon the statement that on account of error in the former petition the time for presenting the petition would be lost and that it was neither to preclude me from opposing parts of the bill, nor make me responsible in any degree for the costs of soliciting the bill.[37]

Nicholl had retained a high profile at St. John's College meetings;[38] and on 24 Jan. 1826, when he was busy electioneering in Glamorgan, he received a letter from the dean Michael Marlow informing him of Heber's intended resignation and urging him to declare his candidature immediately to 'pacify or prevent opposition'.[39] Being tempted to do so he consulted his son, Ailesbury, Casberd and Wintle, 25 Jan. He decided against offering when he realized that it was Heber's intention to retire immediately without waiting for a dissolution; but he delayed until the evening of the 27th, when it was widely reported that he would be opposed by the solicitor-general Wetherell because Oxford would not take another Christ Church man, before informing Marlow of his decision.[40] Writing on 28 Jan. to the dean of Christ Church, Peel observed, 'Nicholl's difficulty I apprehend arises from the certainty that if he vacated, he would never be returned again' for Great Bedwyn.[41] His decision, though widely accepted, posed a dilemma for the University, and he received further offers of support. His son and their friends joined Thomas Grimston Bucknall Estcourt's* committee, 3 Feb.[42] At the Speaker's dinner on the 4th Nicholl sat next to Sir George Warrender* and Peel.[43] His court was then considering the case of Dew *v.* Clarke and Clarke, on which his judgment on the will of the alleged lunatic Ely Stott established a precedent in case law.[44] Country banks and their notes were a major issue in Glamorgan following the collapse of the Neath and Swansea banks, and Nicholl attended the Commons debates on small notes, 18, 25 Feb.[45] Votes to receive the report on the president of the board of trade's salary, 10 Apr., and against reforming the Edinburgh representation, 13 Apr., were the only ones reported for him that session, when the protracted Brinco and Westmeath divorce cases again took up his time.[46] He retained his Bedwyn seat at the general election in June 1826, and was now asked to establish diocesan committees for the Society for the Propagation of Christian Knowledge, and drawn into the controversy surrounding the proposed Glamorgan turnpike.[47]

Nicholl heard Canning's speech at the pre-session dinner, 20 Nov. 1826.[48] When Goulburn sought his opinion on the movement to debar Irish prerogative court judges from private practice, 13 Jan. 1827, he drew parallels between their work and his own and stressed that he was only able to perform his duties as dean of the arches and of the peculiars, for which he received £50 a year, because he earned between £2,000 and £3,500 as a judge.[49] He attended a private meeting, 19 Jan., and the debates on Catholic relief, 5, 6 Mar., when he divided against it. As an 'immense majority against Mr. Whitmore's motion' to lower the pivot price of corn to 50*s.* was 'not in doubt', he came away before the division, 9 Mar.[50] He spent much of the period of political uncertainty following Liverpool's stroke on leave on urgent business. During Canning's short-lived ministry, he saw the 1827 benefices registration bill, which had originated in the Lords, through the Commons at the archbishop of Canterbury's request, and announced plans for more extensive legislation, 1 June.[51] He wrote to Harrowby on the 19th complaining of slowness, 'fatigue' and 'great labour', and asked to be relieved 'from the normal business of the privy council', attending only when admiralty and ecclesiastical court cases were considered. Acquiescing, Harrowby added cases 'from our Norman Isles' to the list, 'as you are now the only person who is at all conversant with their peculiar systems, and we shall be quite at sea without you'.[52] Finding government 'in nearly as great a state of embarrassment as when Mr. Canning was forming his administration', Nicholl was keen to 'discuss politics' with Ailesbury in August 1827, following Canning's death, and apparently concurred in his patron's belief that the Whigs would resign and their 'old friends' be brought back in.[53] Joseph Phillimore* subsequently blamed Nicholl for barring him from serving as king's advocate in the Goderich ministry.[54]

A draft application among his papers indicates that Nicholl himself sought the post when the duke of Wellington, as the new premier, appointed his nephew Herbert Jenner at the duke of Clarence's request in January 1828.[55] He was listed in the government minority against repealing the Test Acts, 26 Feb., but wrote in his diary: 'Came away before [the] division – *motion* carried by a majority of 44'. He paired against Catholic claims, 12 May. The 1828 benefices registration bill was placed 'under his protection', 24 June, but he failed to prevent its deferral.[56] Hume was expected to present a petition of complaint on 15 July against the prerogative court of Canterbury and its judge Nicholl, who 'came specially for the occasion' and expressed annoyance at its deferral until the 17th, after his intended departure from London for the summer.[57] The petition, with its list of vituperative charges of wrongdoing, nepotism and overcharging, was ostensibly from a disappointed suitor, the exciseman William Peddle, and dealt with the several judgments and costs awarded against him since 1821 in a case he had pursued in the interest of his wife, a beneficiary by one of two wills left by her godfather Evan Evans. Nicholl's judgments of 13 Dec. 1821 and 1 July 1824 had favoured the rival claimant, and he had refused to hear Peddle's recent complaints. In Nicholl's absence, lawyers on both sides of the House spoke in his defence, among them Lushington, who bore 'testimony to the unspotted purity of his judicial conduct', Daniel Whittle Harvey, who stressed that his decisions had been confirmed on appeal by three common law judges, and the attorney-general Wetherell, who compared Nicholl 'leaving his character behind him' to Sir Peter Teazle in Sheridan's comedy *The School for Scandal*.[58] Congratulating Nicholl afterwards, one of his staunchest defenders, Richard Hart Davis, observed:

> Nothing could have gone better than the debate of last night. The justification was so complete that even Harvey ... was bound to allow that there was not the slightest ground for imputing blame to you. In fine, the petition was not allowed to lie upon the table, and Hume was obliged to eat his words. If he had divided the House, he would not have had more than one, or at the most two, to support him. You did perfectly right to go into the country, first as showing no courtesy to ... [Hume], and lastly as giving your friends more liberty of speech than if you had been present.[59]

Lord Colchester and the new archbishop of Canterbury William Howley made similar remarks.[60]

Van Mildert, now bishop of Durham, was among the churchmen who looked to Nicholl to oppose

Catholic relief when it was conceded by Wellington in 1829.[61] Presenting the archdeacon and clergy of county Durham's unfavourable petition, 12 Feb., he announced that his own views were unchanged, 'but he could not join with some of those who had held the same sentiments in imparting blame and in charging a sort of apostasy' to Peel. He added:

> If he [Peel] could justify the change of course and produce such a measure as the gracious speech from the throne recommended, 'a measure consistent with the full and permanent security of our establishment in church and state', the present petitioners asked no more. He despaired of seeing such a measure; but he trusted that those who entertained the same opinions would calmly, but firmly watch the progress of the measures, and endeavour, as far as lay in their power, to preserve (as the petition prayed) the Protestant constitution inviolate.

He was 'by no means convinced of the propriety of removing Mr. Peel from the representation of the University', and reluctant to declare for his opponent Sir Robert Inglis* at the ensuing by-election.[62] He presented and endorsed, at Ailesbury's request, the mayor and corporation of Marlborough's petitions against concessions, 27 Feb.[63] and others from the archdeacons and clergy of London and Middlesex and the deaneries of Braughing, Dunmow, Harlow and Hedingham, 3 Mar. He divided against emancipation, 6, 18, 23, 30 Mar., as the patronage secretary Planta had predicted. Nicholl was included on the select committee that investigated the affairs of the Irish admiralty court and its absentee judge Sir Jonah Barrington, 7 Apr., and was summoned by lord chancellor Lyndhurst to a meeting of the privy council on the jurisdiction of the court at Bombay, 14 May.[64] At the request of Peel and the church commissioners, he drafted and introduced a bill 'to regulate the duties, salaries and emoluments of the officers, clerks and ministers of certain ecclesiastical courts in England', which, after some delay, caused largely by poor attendance, received royal assent, 19 June.[65] It had been approved by Lyndhurst and doctors' commons and attracted support from both sides of the House; but Hume used it to launch a personal attack on Nicholl and the fee structure of his court, and Nicholl required assistance from Peel and Phillimore to fend off the challenge, 11, 12 May, 3 June.[66] Dissatisfied with Nicholl's assertions that fees had to be regulated by the archbishop of Canterbury and bishop of London, approved by the privy council, and printed in the *London Gazette*, Hume ordered further returns of emoluments, 5 June, including those in the Brinco case. Planta offered Nicholl 'a vote out', but it proved unnecessary.[67] During the recess his daughter Katherine married Luxmore's son Charles, the dean of St. Asaph, whom Nicholl had appointed to the living of Bridgend.[68] The family's joy was checked by Lady Nicholl's death, 1 Dec. 1829.[69]

Nicholl did not vote on Lord Blandford's reform schemes, 2 June 1829, 18 Feb. 1830, and apparently stayed away when the East Retford disfranchisement bill was considered, 11 Feb., 5, 15 Mar.; but he paired against the proposed enfranchisement of Birmingham, Leeds and Manchester, 23 Feb. 1830. Consulted on 8 Apr. by Peel, prior to the concerted opposition attack over the Terceira 'blunder', he ruled that in law

> the duty of a neutral government to prevent 'fitting and equipping' in a neutral port, by either belligerent, is strongly insisted upon, together with the right of stopping vessels so fitted and equipped from sailing; and if, I recollect, it is maintained that if such a vessel should get to sea, make a capture and bring it back into the neutral state, it would be the duty of the neutral to seize the captured vessel, and restore it to the owner. The fallacy of the argument in the Lords seemed to be the attempt to consider the turning away the vessel from Terceira as a separate transaction instead of keeping it connected with, and as a continuation of, the circumstances that had previously taken place in this country. For perhaps it must be admitted that out of those previous circumstances alone arose the right of preventing the vessels proceeding to that island.[70]

Nicholl did not speak, nor did he divide with opposition when their resolutions were defeated by 191-78, 28 Apr. He voted against introducing a two-year mandatory probation period before permitting licensing for on-consumption under the sale of beer bill, 1 July, and against a proposed reduction in judges' salaries, 7 July 1830. Before the dissolution precipitated by the death of George IV, he was called on to discuss his political views afresh with Ailesbury, who had found it difficult to adjust to post-emancipation Toryism and anticipated opposition at Marlborough. He recalled that when first recommended to Bedwyn

> the only stipulation required of me was that I should not go into a systematic opposition to the king's government. This accorded with my own feelings and loyalty to the crown, founded on a strong conviction. In the times we were living our admirable constitution was exposed to more risk of being overbalanced by the increased weight of the democratic branch of it than by the influence of the crown. In this opinion I still remain and I believe your lordship does not differ. As a firm friend to the constitution both in church and state, I have always been decidedly opposed to Catholic emancipation and to parliamentary reform, but now Roman Catholic emancipation is carried it seems to me prudent to submit to the experiment with a good grace, and to make the best of things as they are, at least for the present.[71]

Following separate discussions with Ailesbury and Sir Henry Halford, Nicholl waited 'unofficially' on Wellington at Apsley House, 15 July, when it was understood that 'the treasury neither excited nor approved the interference in the Marlborough election'. Nicholl had let it be known that he, and by implication Ailesbury, hoped 'that by conciliatory steps, the Tories who had opposed the bill might be brought back to the support of the government'.[72] He was not in the House when Estcourt defended him and the church commissioners from further criticism by Hume, 17 July 1830.

Returned again for Bedwyn, Nicholl apparently declined to propose Manners Sutton as Speaker in the new Parliament.[73] He was naturally included among the Wellington ministry's 'friends', and he divided with them when they were brought down on the civil list, 15 Nov. 1830. He kept his place under Lord Grey's administration and was granted a fortnight's leave, 23 Nov., following Katherine's death in childbirth.[74] The sentence of separation he passed in the Mytton case, 27 Nov., set a precedent by recognizing a wife's right to divorce her husband for cruelty and adultery;[75] and on 23 Dec. 1830 he delivered a further judgment in the Grindall case, in which he distinguished between the effects of temporary lunacy and the infirmities of old age in a testator.[76] Fearing that reform '*must* be granted', Ailesbury sought Nicholl's 'opinion as to the course *most* prudent for *us* to pursue on this occasion' and asked him to take his second son to the debate on the ministerial measure, 1 Mar.[77] It proposed taking a Member from Bedwyn, and Nicholl voted against it at its second reading, 22 Mar., and paired for Gascoyne's wrecking amendment, 19 Apr. 1831. He was returned for Bedwyn at a cost of £300 at the ensuing general election and sought support for his son John in Glamorgan, where, backed by the 'great absentee and Tory interests', he had declared his candidature for the county's proposed second seat.[78] Nicholl voted against the reintroduced reform bill at its second reading, 6 July 1831. Though granted a month's leave on urgent business, 16 Sept., he found time to vote against its passage, 21 Sept., and to congratulate Ailesbury on his vote and the bill's rejection by the Lords.[79] He divided against the revised bill at its second and third readings, 17 Dec. 1831, 22 Mar. 1832, and with opposition on the Russian-Dutch loan, 12 July. His son had withdrawn his candidature for Glamorgan, and instead was put forward by Bute and the Conservatives for the reformed Cardiff Boroughs constituency, which he represented, 1832-52.[80] Having retired from the Commons at the 1832 dissolution, Nicholl was, as Dyneley predicted, 'gratified' to see John elected despite the high cost (over £2,000).[81]

Nicholl's connections, experience and outstanding legal skills served him well. Despite his advancing years and increasing deafness, accusations of nepotism and the aspirations of younger men, he was made a judge of the admiralty court in 1833 and retained his influence in the church courts while the Liberals were in office.[82] Where his judgments were later qualified, as in the Westmeath divorce case or Swift *v.* Kelly, they were invariably praised for showing 'an intimate knowledge of the authorities, a capacity to state clearly the facts of a case, and an equal capacity to deduce from the authorities and to apply to the facts the relevant principles and rules of law'.[83] He died in August 1838 at Merthyr Mawr and was buried in the parish church. The bishop of London, Charles Blomfield, one of many eminent churchmen and politicians to offer their condolences wrote:

> He was the friend of nearly all the good and great; and I never heard of his having an enemy. If, as is probable, he was aware, even for a short time, of his approaching end, it must have been a consolation to him to reflect that the energies of his mind were employed in the service of his country and of the church up to the last.[84]

His will, dated 13 Sept. 1830, was proved under £140,000 and executed by his son, who inherited the estate in fee simple, with all household effects and portraits. He made bequests to his daughters and 15 grandchildren, and a trust fund administered by the judge William Adam† and the king's proctor Iltyd Nicholl provided for his unmarried daughter Mary Anne (*d.* 1844).[85]

[1] Draws on Nicholl's papers among the privately held Merthyr Mawr mss, seen with the owner's consent at Glam. RO. Nicholl's diaries for 1816-28 and 1830-38 [F/2/1-21] are fullest for 1824-6. For his legal career see Sir W. Holdsworth, *Hist. English Law*, xiii. 691-6 and B. Hutton, 'Sir John Nicholl', *Legal Wales: its past and its future* ed. T.G. Watkin, 89-100. [2] *Gent. Mag.* (1838), ii. 546-7; *Cambrian*, 1 Sept.; *Glam. Mon. and Brecon Gazette and Merthyr Guardian*, 1 Sept. 1838; *HP Commons,1790-1820*, ii. 500; iv. 667-9. [3] Merthyr Mawr mss L/205/7. [4] Nicholl diary, 30 Jan., 16 Feb. 1820. [5] Merthyr Mawr mss CO/153/1-20; Nicholl diary, 5 Mar.-12 Apr.; NLW, Vivian mss A124; H.M. Williams, 'Geographic Distribution of Pol. Opinion in Glam. Parl. Elections, 1820-1950' (Univ. of Wales M.A. thesis, 1951), 21; *Cambrian*, 4, 11, 25 Mar. 1820. [6] Nicholl diary, 12-28 Apr. 1820. [7] Ibid. 28 Apr.-9 June 1820; Merthyr Mawr mss L/204/7; *Session of Parl. 1825*, p. 477. [8] Nicholl diary, 18 July-30 Oct. 1820. [9] Ibid. 1 Nov.-14 Dec.; Merthyr Mawr mss L/204/7; L/209, Luxmore to Nicholl, 14 Oct. 1820. [10] Nicholl diary, 20 Jan.-16 Feb. 1821. [11] Merthyr Mawr mss L/209, Redesdale to Nicholl, 18 Apr. 1821. [12] Ibid. L/204/5. [13] Nicholl diary, 17 Apr.-10 May 1821; *CJ*, lxxvi. 329. [14] Merthyr Mawr mss L/204/43, 44, 47; Wilts. RO, Ailesbury mss 9/35/109, Nicholl to Ailesbury, 14, 15, 20 Aug. 1821. [15] Merthyr Mawr mss L/179, Marlow to Nicholl, 5 July; *Althorp Letters*, i. 115; Ailesbury mss 1300/5753; Add. 52011, Stuart

Wortley to H.E. Fox, 25 July 1821. [16] Add. 51659. [17] Nicholl diary, 19 July-20 Aug.; Merthyr Mawr mss L/204/33, 45, 46; Ailesbury mss 9/35/109, Nicholl to Ailesbury, 14, 15, 20 Aug. 1821; TNA E197/1, p. 288. [18] *The Times*, 27 Aug.; Merthyr Mawr mss L/204/45; Ailesbury mss 9/35/109, Nicholl to Ailesbury, 24, 25 Aug., Pleydell Bouverie to same, 24 Aug. 1821. [19] Merthyr Mawr mss L/204/27, 26-33, 37, 38, 42; Nicholl diary, 25-27 Aug. 1821. [20] Merthyr Mawr mss L/204/34-36, 40, 41; Ailesbury mss 9/35/109, Nicholl to Ailesbury, 1 Sept., 3 Nov.; Nicholl diary, 31 Oct.-4 Nov. 1821. [21] Nicholl diary, 25 Sept.-11 Oct., 14-17 Dec.; Ailesbury mss 9/35/109, Nicholl to Ailesbury, 3 Nov. 1821. [22] Nicholl diary, 4-16 Feb. 1822. [23] Ibid. 30 Apr., 10 May 1822; Merthyr Mawr mss L/205/36, 37. [24] *The Times*, 17 May, 6 June; Nicholl diary, 13 June 1822. [25] Nicholl diary, 6 Apr.-31 Oct. 1822; Merthyr Mawr mss L/205/5. [26] Nicholl diary, 8 Feb.-11 Mar. 1823; Merthyr Mawr mss F/51/4. [27] *CJ*, lxxviii. 485. [28] Merthyr Mawr mss L/204/15, 16; L/209, Van Mildert to Nicholl, 20 Sept. 1822; Nicholl diary, 11 July-31 Oct. 1823. [29] Merthyr Mawr mss F/51/1, 5, 6. [30] Ibid. L/205/7. [31] *Gent.Mag.* (1824), i. 544;Merthyr Mawr mss L/205/17-20. [32] Merthyr Mawr mss F/51/7; Nicholl diary, 18 Aug.-30 Sept. 1824. [33] Nicholl diary, 2 Feb.-4 June; *The Times*, 21 Feb., 1 Mar.; TCD, Jebb mss 6396/226, Inglis to Jebb 15 June 1825. [34] Nicholl diary, 6 June 1825. [35] Ibid. 6-14 June 1825. [36] Merthyr Mawr mss L/206/15-20; L/209, Nicholl to Harrowby, 6 July 1825. [37] *Cambrian*, 29 Jan.; Nicholl diary, 16 Feb. 1825; E. Ball, 'Glamorgan: A Study of the Co. and the Work of its Members, 1825-1835' (Univ. of London Ph.D. thesis, 1965), 101. [38] Nicholl diary, 18, 25 Apr. 1825. [39] St. Deiniol's Lib. Glynne-Gladstone mss 194, T. to J. Gladstone [Jan.]; Bodl. Hughenden Dep. D/I/D/171; Merthyr Mawr mss L/206/35, 37; Nicholl diary, 21-24 Jan. 1826. [40] Merthyr Mawr mss L/206/21, 24-25; Nicholl diary, 24-27 Jan. 1826; Add. 40342, f. 297; 40385, ff. 109, 114; Bucks. RO, Fremantle mss D/FR/138/12/3B. [41] Add. 403432, f. 303. [42] Ibid. f. 305; Add. 40385, ff. 132, 173; Nicholl diary, 29 Jan.-2 Feb. 1826; Merthyr Mawr mss L/206/22, 23, 26, 28, 30, 32, 36, 37. [43] Nicholl diary, 4 Feb. 1826. [44] *The Times*, 24 Jan., 3, 10 Feb. 1826; *Report of Judgement Dew v. Clark and Clark* ed. J. Haggard, *passim.*; Holdsworth, xiii. 692. [45] Nicholl diary, 18, 25 Feb. 1826. [46] *The Times*, 22 Apr. 16 June 1826. [47] Merthyr Mawr mss F/52/3; L/205/9-12.; Nicholl diary, 2-10 Oct. 1826. [48] Nicholl diary, 20 Nov. 1826. [49] Merthyr Mawr mss L/209, Goulburn-Nicholl corresp. 13, 16 Jan. 1827. [50] Nicholl diary, 19 Jan.-9 Mar. 1827. [51] Merthyr Mawr mss L/204/22; *CJ*, lxxxii. 468, 473-4, 517, 558. [52] Merthyr Mawr mss L/206/10-11. [53] Ailesbury mss 9/35/109, Nicholl to Ailesbury, 31 Aug.; Merthyr Mawr mss L/209, Ailesbury to Nicholl, 4 Sept. 1827. [54] Add. 51813, Phillimore to Holland, 18 Nov. 1830. [55] Merthyr Mawr mss L/209, Nicholl to Peel, 25 Jan. 1828; Wellington mss WP1/915/62, 67. [56] Merthyr Mawr mss L/204/23; *CJ*, lxxxiii. 537. [57] *CJ*, lxxxiii. 541. [58] *The Times*, 3 July 1824, 16-18 July 1828. [59] Merthyr Mawr mss L/209, Hart Davis to Nicholl, 18 July 1828. [60] Ibid. L/209, Colchester to Nicholl, 21 July 1828; L/205/29. [61] Ibid. L/205/15; L/209, Luxmore to Nicholl, 8 Jan. 1829. [62] Ibid. L/205/2. [63] Ibid. L/205/40, 41; *Bath Chron.* 19 Mar. 1829. [64] Merthyr Mawr mss L/206/8. [65] *CJ*, lxxxiv. 291, 307, 311, 319, 326-7, 340, 344, 348, 372, 379-80, 389, 399. [66] Wellington mss WP1/1034/1; Merthyr Mawr mss L/206/9. [67] Merthyr Mawr mss L/206/9. [68] Ibid. L/205/32, 42; L/206/2-5; *Gent. Mag.* (1829), ii. 270. [69] Merthyr Mawr mss F/157; L/205/16, 33; *Gent. Mag.* (1829), ii. 648. [70] Merthyr Mawr mss L/205/24. [71] Ibid. L/184/2. [72] Ibid. L/209, secret memo. 1830. [73] Ibid. L/206/12. [74] *Gent Mag.* (1830), ii. 571; Merthyr Mawr mss L/209, Manners Sutton to Nicholl, 6 Dec. 1830. [75] *The Times*, 29 Nov. 1830. [76] *Report of Judgement in Case Grindall v. Grindall* (1831), *passim.* [77] Merthyr Mawr mss L/209, Ailesbury to Nicholl, 25 Feb. 1831. [78] Vivian mss A344; *The Times*, 25 Apr.; *Cambrian*, 30 Apr.; *Mon. Merlin*, 14 May; Merthyr Mawr mss L/209, Ailesbury to Nicholl, 3 June 1831. [79] Merthyr Mawr mss L/209, Ailesbury to Nicholl, 12 Oct. 1831. [80] NLW, Bute mss L75/83; NLW, Penrice and Margam mss 9239, Talbot to Llewellyn, 26 June 1832; Merthyr Mawr mss F/52/21-27; F/55/15-18; Cardiff Pub. Lib. Bute estate letterbks. iii. 20-25, 43-48; *The Times*, 11, 22 Oct. 1832. [81] Merthyr Mawr mss F/55/2; L/209, Dyneley to Nicholl, 10 Oct. 1832. [82] Merthyr Mawr mss L/206/13; Add. 51813, Phillimore to Holland, 23 May 1833, 28, 30 Sept., 1 Oct. 1834, 11 Oct. 1837; Brougham mss, same to Brougham, 27 May 1833. [83] *Greville Mems.* iii. 91, 209, 217, 376, 484; Holdsworth, xiii. 691. [84] Merthyr Mawr mss F/58/1-17. [85] PROB 11/1902/658; IR26/1495/721; Merthyr Mawr mss F/152, 155, 158/3; *The Times*, 19 Oct. 1838.

M.M.E.

NIGHTINGALL, Sir Miles (1768–1829), of Redgrave Hall, Botesdale, Suff. and 29 York Place, Portman Square, Mdx.[1]

EYE 1820–17 Sept. 1829

b. 25 Dec. 1768. *m.* 13 Aug. 1800, Florentia Maria, da. of Sir Lionel Darell†, 1st bt., of Ancaster House, Richmond Hill, Surr., *s.p.* KCB 4 Jan. 1815. *d.* 17 Sept. 1829.

Ensign 52 Ft. 1787, lt. 1789, capt. 1794; maj. 121 Ft. 1795; lt.-col. 119 Ft. Sept., 38 Ft. Oct. 1795; lt.-col. 51 Ft. 1802; brevet col. 1803; lt.-col. 69 Ft. 1806; maj.-gen. 1810; c.-in-c. Java 1813-15; lt.-gen. 1814; c.-in-c. and member of council, Bombay 1816-19; col. 6 W.I. Regt. 1815; col. 49 Ft. 1820-*d.*

Nightingall's military and parliamentary careers were furthered by the Cornwallis family. No conclusive proof of his parentage has been found, but he may have been a descendant of the London merchants and salters William and Miles Nightingall who traded in Love Lane and Fore Street in the 1760s. He entered the army in 1787 and in 1788 was sent to Madras, becoming in 1790, following his service at the capture of Dindigul and siege of Palicatcherry, brigade major of the king's troops in India. During the Mysore war he was appointed aide-de-camp to Colonel Nesbitt (1792) and the 1st Marquess Cornwallis (1793), serving with distinction at Pondicherry, Bangalore and Seringapatam. He returned to England with Cornwallis as brigade major of the eastern district, volunteered for the West Indies and was present at the capture of Trinidad in 1797. He became an extra aide-de-camp to Sir Ralph Abercromby† at Puerto Rico and inspector of the foreign corps before ill health brought him back to England in October; but he returned and was deputy adjutant-general in the capture of San Domingo in 1798. Sent home with dispatches, he undertook confidential missions for General Sir Thomas Maitland† in 1799 and served as assistant adjutant-general on the Helder expedition before joining Cornwallis in Ireland. He was Maitland's deputy-lieutenant at Quiberon Bay in 1800. He married the East India Company chairman's daughter that year 'agreeable to her own inclinations but with my consent' (Sir Lionel Darell), although their settlement had to be delayed pending decisions on his East Indian fortune; and after a period as quartermaster-general of the eastern district he attended the 1802 Amiens peace conference as Cornwallis's military private secretary. Appointed quartermaster-general of the East Indies in 1803, he served at Agra and Leswarree before returning to Calcutta in 1805 as military private secretary to Cornwallis as governor-general. Sent to England in February 1807, he undertook a secret mission to Cadiz before serving as a brigade commander under Wellington at the battles of Rolica and Vimiero in 1808, for which he was mentioned in dispatches and received a medal and the thanks of Parliament. In December 1808 he was made commander-in-chief of New South Wales, but ill health prevented him taking up the appointment. After holding brigade commands at Hythe and Dover he returned to the Peninsula in 1810, and in 1811 commanded the first brigade at the battle of Fuentes d'Onoro, where he was wounded in the head. He was placed in command at Java in 1813 and knighted in January 1815. Despite opposition from the East India Company directors, he was posted to Bombay later that year.[2] He returned overland to England in the summer of 1819 and settled briefly at Ancaster House, which his father-in-law had bequeathed to his unmarried children with provision that £1,050 a year be set aside to 'entertain' his married children there.[3] He now wrote to Wellington and others to press his claim for a medal in recognition of his service at Fuentes de Onoro, which was refused because he had not been 'engaged with the enemy with musket'.[4] During his command in Bombay his regiment had been disbanded and he did not receive a new one until the death of Sir Alexander Maitland in February 1820 created a vacancy in Princess Charlotte of Wales's.

His return for Cornwallis's family seat at Eye at the 1820 general election came about unexpectedly following the corporation's rejection of the sitting Member, the 2nd marquess's brother-in-law, Mark Singleton.[5] Nightingall advanced Cornwallis £6,000 and agreed to reside at his mansion, Brome Hall, as 'tenant-at will' liable for 'all rates and taxes' and to take over the 'family's financial obligations to the corporation and townspeople'.[6] Resisting Cornwallis's attempts to reimburse him, he requested '£200 per annum to me during my life and to Lady Nightingall during her life should she survive me'.[7] He later rented George St. Vincent Wilson's mansion, Redgrave Hall, purchased the land of the manor of Westhorpe (where Cornwallis also had an interest) from the Reilly family, and resided periodically at Brome for the hunting.[8] Dismissed as a generally silent Tory with little command of patronage,[9] he voted against Catholic relief, 28 Feb. 1821, 30 Apr. 1822, 1 Mar., 21 Apr., 10 May 1825, and the Irish franchise bill, 26 Apr. 1825; against parliamentary reform, 9 May 1821, 26 Feb. 1824, including the proposed disqualification of civil officers of the ordnance from voting in parliamentary elections, 12 Apr. 1821, and with the Liverpool government on the Queen Caroline affair, 6 Feb. 1821. He divided with them on the revenue, 4 July 1820, 6 Mar. 1821, but against them for the repeal of the additional malt duty, 21 Mar. 1821. He voted with government against more extensive tax relief, 11, 21 Feb. 1822. Making his only reported speech in the committee on the mutiny bill, 12 Mar., he defended army officers against Hume's allegation that they were akin to crown slaves and said that 'they had the interests of the constitution at heart as much as any set of men in the country'. He voted against abolishing one of the joint-postmasterships, 13 Mar., and inquiry into Irish tithes, 19 June, and the conduct of the lord advocate towards the Scottish press, 25 June 1822. He continued to vote steadily with government on taxation, 3, 10, 18 Mar., the Foreign Enlistment Act, 16 Apr., chancery delays, 5 June, the currency, 12 June, and the Scottish juries bill, 20 June 1823. He became a founder member and vice-president of the Suffolk Pitt Club that summer.[10] Nightingall was at Brome early in 1824 for the by-election at which the new patron Sir Edward Kerrison became his colleague, and seems to have attended the House less frequently thereafter.[11] He voted in a minority of 28 for a 15-day adjournment between the regular annual licensing day and the issue of new licences under the alehouse licensing bill, 12 May 1825. The sudden death of Sir Frederick Henniker thwarted opposition to his return at the general election of 1826.[12]

Nightingall's name was on a list of 'more senior officers' prepared when Sir George Murray* was considered as a possible commander-in-chief in June 1827, but he was no longer a serious contender for preferment.[13] He cast his customary votes against Catholic relief, 6 Mar. 1827, 12 May 1828, and voted against repeal of the Test Acts, 26 Feb. 1828. The Wellington ministry's patronage secretary Planta anticipated that he would vote 'with government' for Catholic emancipation in 1829, but his loyalties remained untested, for he was granted a month's leave of absence because of ill health, 20 Feb., and is not known to have attended subsequently. He died at Gloucester Spa in September 1829.[14] By his will, dated 8 Aug. 1829 and proved under £40,000, he left everything (including his Suffolk and London properties and East India stock) to his wife (*d.* 1863), with reversion to her Colville Darell nephews.[15]

[1] Draws on Nightingall's obituary in *United Services Mag.* i. (1830), 195. [2] PROB 11/938/168; 1400/888; *Oxford DNB*; *HP Commons, 1790-1820*, iii. 568-9; *Cornwallis Corresp.* ii. 298, 417, 455; iii. 231, 236, 285, 379, 384, 418; *Wellington Despatches*, iii. 81-83, 92, 181; C.H. Philips, *E.I. Co.* 197. [3] J. Hanson, *Route of Sir Miles Nightingall Overland from India*; PROB 11/1400/888. [4] Wellington mss WP1/629/12; 630/2. [5] *Bury and Norwich Post*, 8, 15 Mar.; *Suff. Chron.* 11 Mar. 1820. [6] Cent. Kent. Stud. Darell mss U24/C15, Nightingall to Cornwallis, 3 Apr. 1820, same to Wyatt, 18 Jan. 1821, accts. of Brome, Culford and Ship[pen]ham estates, 1821-3; Suff. RO (Ipswich), Henniker mss S1/2/8/1.11. [7] Darell mss C15, Nightingall to Wyatt, 18 Jan. 1821, accts. of Brome, Culford and Ship[pen]ham estates, 1821-3. [8] Darell mss C15, Wyatt to Sydney, 31 Aug., 28 Sept., F. Howe to Sydney, 26 Nov. 1823; Suff. RO (Ipswich) FB/132/C2/1; G2/3; *Suff. Coll.* ff. 199-203; White, *Suff. Dir.* (1844), 341, 348. [9] Henniker mss S1/2/8/1.12. [10] *Ipswich Jnl.* 9 Aug. 1823. [11] Ibid. 24 Jan., 7, 14, 21, 28 Feb. 1824. [12] Henniker mss S1/2/8/1.12, 13, 15; 8/2.3. [13] Wellington mss WP1/908/13. [14] *Gloucester Jnl.* 19 Sept.; *Ipswich Jnl.* 26 Sept. 1829. [15] PROB 1762/602; BL OIOC mss Eur.G.102 (probate Nightingall (1829) and wife (1863)); *E.I. Reg.* (1829), i. 556.

M.M.E.

NOEL, Sir Gerard Noel, 2nd bt. (1759–1838), of Exton Park, Rutland.

MAIDSTONE	1784–4 July 1788
RUTLAND	15 July 1788–3 May 1808
RUTLAND	9 May 1814–25 Feb. 1838

b. 17 July 1759, o.s. of Gerard Anne Edwards of Welham Grove, Leics. and Lady Jane Noel, da. of Baptist, 4th earl of Gainsborough. *educ.* Eton 1770-4; St. John's, Camb. 1776. *m.* (1) 21 Dec. 1780, Diana (*d.* 12 Apr. 1823), da. and h. of Sir Charles Middleton, 1st bt. (afterwards 1st Bar. Barham), whom she suc. as 2nd Baroness 17 June 1813, 12s. (4 *d.v.p.*) 6da. (2 *d.v.p.*); (2) 4 May 1823, Harriet (*d.* 11 Aug. 1826), da. of Rev. Joseph Gill of Scraptoft, Leics., *s.p.*; (3) 11 Aug. 1831, Isabella, wid. of Evans Raymond of Milton, Kent, *s.p. suc.* fa. to Welham 1773; uncle Henry, 6th earl of Gainsborough, to his estates 8 Apr. 1798 and took name of Noel by royal lic. 5 May 1798; fa.-in-law as 2nd bt. by spec. rem. 17 June 1813. *d.* 25 Feb. 1838.

Capt. Rutland militia 1779-94; col. Rutland fencibles 1794-9; lt.-col. commdt. Rutland vols. 1800, maj.-commdt. 1803.

High steward, Camden 1798; sheriff, Rutland 1812-13.

Justifiably confident of his return for Rutland on the Gainsborough interest at the 1820 general election, the quixotic and unpredictable Noel wrote to assure the premier Lord Liverpool, 28 Feb., of his readiness to support the 'strongest measures' in the 'present crisis of affairs', even to the extent of 'proclaiming martial law':

> It may not be irksome ... to receive assurances of determined support during this anxious period ... and I trust that the motive of public safety will be so apparent to all better minded persons, that popularity will result from the boldest measures of precaution.

Failure to act decisively, he warned, would induce him to 'pass a heavy censure upon government'. He wrote again to Liverpool in early March to seek naval patronage for his third son.[1] On the hustings, Noel, whose Foxite past was far behind him, declared his 'determination of supporting ministers'. He was returned unopposed, as he was throughout this period. He immediately issued an address in which he wrote that 'we must laugh at men calling themselves Whigs ... who would seat Papists in Parliament, put them at the head of the army and navy, and at the council board of our monarch'.[2] Yet he voted in the opposition minority against the appointment of a green bag committee to investigate Queen Caroline's conduct, 26 June 1820. In August he published a letter of 'remonstrance', addressed to Liverpool, in which he observed that as a long-serving and independent Member, who had generally supported ministers, he could not contemplate the 'monstrous' bill of pains and penalties without feelings of 'disgust' and 'astonishment'. He condemned the 'enormous growing expenses of the trial' and declared it his 'paramount duty' to 'interrupt and thwart the enactment of this bill in every stage'.[3] He tried to do so in the Commons, 18 Sept., when he declared that ministers had as much regard for the House as a huntsman for his hounds and voted in the minority of 12 for the prorogation of Parliament. On 17 Oct. he objected to the proposed adjournment at this 'critical period' and now condemned the House as a 'pack of hounds' at the beck and call of ministers, but at length withdrew his amendment to extend the sitting to the following day. His conspicuous support for the queen, to whom he presented a Stamford loyal address, enraged some of his leading county supporters, but he set them at defiance.[4] In late December 1820 Lord Lonsdale reported that Noel had made a 'short' visit to two prisoners held for blasphemy and sedition in Oakham gaol:

> He has given out that he entered Oakham *incognito*, lest his appearance should call forth the acclamation of the people, and he should be embarrassed by the attention they would show him. He has had addresses presented to him by the villages of Exton and Whitwell, both of them his own property.[5]

He paired for the opposition censure motion, 6 Feb., and for the proposal to restore the queen's name to the liturgy, 13 Feb. 1821. He voted to deplore the Allies' revocation of the liberal constitution in Naples, 21 Feb., and for inquiry into the conduct of the sheriff of Dublin, 22 Feb. He paired against Catholic relief,

28 Feb., but was apparently reckoned a likely supporter of the relief bill at its report stage, 26 Mar.[6] He voted to make Leeds, proposed for enfranchisement in place of Grampound, a scot and lot borough, 2 Mar. He was given a week's leave to attend to urgent private business, 13 Mar. He voted for economy in the army medical service, 16 Apr. He was granted a fortnight's leave on account of ill health, 18 May, but was present to vote for reduction of the duke of Clarence's annuity, 18 June 1821. His attendance seems to have lapsed thereafter.

On 8 Apr. 1823 Noel wrote to advise the home secretary Peel of his intention of supporting the petition of Mrs. Olivia Serres, who claimed to be the daughter of the duke of Cumberland. Peel replied, with the king's approval, that he must exercise his 'own discretion' as to the 'propriety' of drawing her claim to the attention of the House.[7] (Noel's wife of 42 years and at least 18 pregnancies died four days later, but he remarried within four weeks.) In the House, 18 June, he moved for a select committee to consider Mrs. Serres's petition and vowed to 'pursue this lady's claim to the death':

> To give judgement against any person without knowing why, would be still further to prove the necessity of the parliamentary reform sought for by the people ... The constitution, had been his watchword ... and if it had been corrupted through neglect the blame lay somewhere. Where there was a grievance it ought to be remedied.

Undaunted by Peel's exposure of Mrs. Serrers's imposture, Noel initially persisted in his demand for inquiry, but at length decided not to divide the House. He voted in the minorities for inquiry into naval patronage and the coronation expenses, 19 June 1823. His only other known votes in this Parliament were for repeal of the usury laws, 27 June 1823, for the Irish unlawful societies bill, 25 Feb., against Catholic relief, 1 Mar., 10 May, and for the grant to the duke of Cumberland, 2 June 1825.

Returning thanks for his re-election in 1826 (when he was absent from the hustings because his second wife was dying) Noel, who had not yet 'recruited his purse sufficiently', following the serious derangement of his financial affairs in 1816, to 'resume any parade' of the county, deplored the clamour against Lord Exeter's influence at Stamford and denied that the aristocracy enjoyed undue influence in elections.[8] When the lord lieutenancy of Rutland fell vacant soon afterwards Liverpool told Peel that Noel, who had applied for it, was 'entirely out of the question', and he nominated Exeter.[9] Noel paired against Catholic relief, 6 Mar. 1827. He presented constituency petitions against the Malt Act, 24 Mar., and the revised corn duties, 25 Apr. 1828. He again paired against Catholic relief, 12 May. Curiously, he was a guest at the annual Westminster purity of election dinner, 26 May.[10] On 23 June he voted in the opposition minority for inquiry into the alleged misapplication of funds in the refurbishment of Buckingham House, but he voted with the Wellington ministry against reduction of the salary of the lieutenant-general of the ordnance, 4 July 1828. The following day he presented a Rutland petition for additional protection for sheep farmers and breeders. Planta, the patronage secretary, thought he would side 'with government' for their concession of Catholic emancipation, but he presented hostile petitions, 16 Mar., voted against the measure, 18, 27 Mar., and paired likewise, 30 Mar. 1829. At the Rutland county meeting called to petition for relief from distress, 27 Feb. 1830, he endorsed its petition, despite the inclusion of an amendment in favour of parliamentary reform. Declaring his willingness to take charge of the petition he spoke of his determination 'to submit to any inconvenience [rather] than lose the principle of supporting the yeomanry' of Rutland;[11] but it was his colleague Sir Gilbert Heathcote who presented the petition, and Noel is not known to have spoken or voted during that session. He was granted three weeks' leave to deal with urgent private business, 8 Mar. 1830. Two months later he privately urged the prime minister to reconsider the delay in the payment of money due to Baron de Bode.[12]

At the general election of 1830, he claimed that he had voted against Catholic relief in accordance with his constituents' wishes, though 'his own feelings were enlisted in favour of the measure'. He said that he was 'decidedly against' parliamentary reform, which 'might merge into revolution', but conceded that if his constituents thought the current system an evil of 'such a monstrous magnitude, he believed he should help to relieve them from it'. He acknowledged that there had been 'something wrong' in the recent election at Stamford, where Exeter had repelled a reformer's challenge by dubious means, but insisted that 'every lord near a town ought to do his duty by that town'.[13] Ministers listed him as one of their 'foes', but he was absent from the division on the civil list which brought them down, 15 Nov. 1830. He presented a petition for the abolition of slavery, 19 Nov. 1830. He voted for the second reading of the Grey ministry's reform bill, 22 Mar., and against Gascoyne's wrecking amendment, 19 Apr. 1831. At the ensuing general election he deplored the 'extraordinary manner' in which the measure had been opposed, condemned the 'unconstitutional resistance' with which the anti-reformers had 'deprecated the dissolution' and declared himself a 'staunch friend' to the bill, 'fully approving the honest declarations of the men now in power'. At a celebratory dinner he reiterated his enthusiasm for reform and promised to call ministers to account should they show 'a disposition to escape from their pledges'.[14]

Noel voted for the second reading of the reintroduced reform bill, 6 July, and steadily for its details, though he was in the minority for the disfranchisement of Saltash, 26 July 1831. He interrupted his attendance to marry for the third time, at the age of 72, in the second week of August. He divided for the passage of the reform bill, 21 Sept., and Lord Ebrington's motion of confidence in the ministry, 10 Oct. He was credited with a vote in Hunt's minority of six for repeal of the corn laws, 15 Sept. He was absent from the division on the second reading of the revised reform bill, 17 Dec. 1831, but was present to vote for its details, 8, 21, 23, 28 Feb., and its third reading, 22 Mar. 1832. On 12 Feb. 1832 he rejoined Brooks's, almost 40 years after his original admission. He voted to amend the Vestry Act, 23 Jan., and divided with government on relations with Portugal, 9 Feb. He was absent from the division on the address asking the king to appoint only ministers who would carry undiluted reform, 10 May. He voted in a minority for an amendment to the boundaries bill designed to prevent Exeter's domination of Stamford, 22 June. He paired on the government side for the divisions on the Russian-Dutch loan, 12, 20 July, and voted with them in person, 16 July 1832.

Noel continued to sit for Rutland until his death in February 1838. His brief will of 27 Nov. 1837 was proved under £18,000.[15] He had transferred his longstanding claim to a peerage to his son and heir Charles Noel† (1781-1866), who had become Baron Barham in succession to his mother in 1823; he was created earl of Gainsborough in 1841.

[1] Add. 38383, ff. 147, 255. [2] *Drakard's Stamford News*, 24 Mar. 1820. [3] Noel, *The Queen's Letter to the King*, 7-8. [4] *Drakard's Stamford News*, 6, 27 Oct., 3, 17 Nov.; *Nottingham Rev.* 20 Oct. 1820. [5] Add. 38288, f. 343. [6] Buckingham, *Mems. Geo. IV*, i. 143. [7] Add. 40299, ff. 202, 203. [8] *Drakard's Stamford News*, 2, 23 June 1826. [9] Add. 40305, f. 205. [10] Add. 56552, f. 101. [11] *Boston, Louth, Newark, Stamford and Rutland Champion*, 2 Mar. 1830 [12] Wellington mss WP1/1114/7. [13] *Boston, Louth, Newark, Stamford and Rutland Champion*, 10 Aug. 1830. [14] Ibid. 3, 10, 31 May 1831. [15] PROB 11/1894/264; IR26/1494/285.

S.R.H.

NOLAN, Michael (?1765–1827), of 23 Bedford Square, Mdx.

BARNSTAPLE 1820–Feb. 1824

b. ?1765, 1st s. of Edward Nowlan of St. Peter's, Dublin and w. Florinda.[1] *educ.* Trinity, Dublin 3 Jan. 1780, 'aged 16', BA 1784, LLB 1787; L. Inn 1784, called 1790. *m.* Martha Carter Nolan, *s.p.*[2] *d.* 26 Dec. 1827.

KC 7 Dec. 1818; bencher, L. Inn 1819; c.j. Brecon circ. 1824-*d.*

Nolan's father, who styled himself Nowlan, was called to the Irish bar in 1769 and later appointed a commissioner of bankrupts; the date of his death has not been found. Nolan was admitted an attorney in the Irish court of exchequer in 1787, but it was at the English bar that he made his way as a special pleader on the home circuit. He had a taste for analytical writing and in 1795 produced an updated edition of *Strange's Reports of Chancery Cases.* The following year he was permitted to deliver a series of lectures at Lincoln's Inn on the municipal law of England, for which he published an extensive *Syllabus*,[3] and he contributed to the supplement to *Viner's Abridgement of Law and Equity* (1799-1806). He made something of a name for himself with his *Treatise of the Laws for the Relief and Settlement of the Poor* (1805), a digest intended to aid those responsible for administering the poor laws; it enjoyed considerable success and was revised and enlarged three times. He took silk in 1818. At the general election that year he was mentioned as a possible candidate for the venal borough of Barnstaple. In 1819 he was one of the counsel employed by Barnstaple corporation and the London out-voters to argue their case before the Lords against the bill to extend the borough's franchise. It was later said that he had given his services gratis, and in June 1819 he was reportedly one of the aspirants to the vacant seat there. At the general election of 1820, after the bill had been defeated, he was returned unopposed as a defender of the status quo at Barnstaple, and was said to be 'friendly to the present government'.[4]

He was a fairly regular attender who indeed gave general support to Lord Liverpool's ministry. He defended the king's bench proceedings bill and was a majority teller for going into committee on it, 20 June 1820. He condemned Newport's attempt to exclude Thomas Ellis from the House as 'an act of injustice of the deepest dye', 30 June. He divided against economies in revenue collection, 4 July 1820. He voted in defence of ministers' conduct towards Queen Caroline, 6 Feb. 1821. He dismissed Martin's proposal to allow persons on capital charges to be defended by counsel, 26 Feb., seeing no need to change 'the most humane system of jurisprudence that ever existed in any country in the world'. He opposed the forgery punishment mitigation bill, 23 May, maintaining that 'the sense of the country was that forgery ought to be punished with death'. According to a Tory Member, he spoke 'with great acuteness and force'.[5] He presented but dissented from a Nottinghamshire petition against Catholic claims, 28 Feb., although he did not vote on the issue later that day.[6] He divided with ministers on the additional malt duty, 3 Apr., the barracks estimates, 28 May, the duke of Clarence's grant, 18 June, and retrenchment, 27 June. However, he voted in the minority for inquiry into the currency, 9 Apr. He divided against the disfranchisement of ordnance officials, 12 Apr., and parliamentary reform, 9 May 1821. He voted against more extensive tax reductions, 11, 21 Feb., and repeal of the salt duties, 28 June 1822. He divided against inquiry into Irish tithes, 19 June, and the motion censuring the lord advocate's conduct towards the Scottish press, 25 June, and for the aliens bill, 19 July. He voted in the minority for investigation of the Calcutta bankers' claims on the East India Company, 4 July 1822.

He played a conspicuous part during the 1822 session in attempts to reform the poor laws. He opposed Scarlett's poor removal bill, 31 May, arguing that it took away that 'great stimulus to industry', the pauper's fear of removal. He was added to the select committee on poor returns, 10 June. In seeking leave to introduce his own poor law amendment bill, 10 July, he explained that it sought to reduce the intolerably heavy burden of poor rates by returning to the original spirit of poor law administration under the statute of 1601. The problem lay in maladministration of laws which, 'from being originally wise and useful, have been recently perverted into an instrument the most pernicious and destructive to the independence of the lower classes of society'. He proposed to strengthen the Act of 1819, chiefly by enhancing the power of vestries and extending the scope of inquiry into whether a claimant was idle or deserving to all his family, and he wished to empower authorities to hire out the unemployed poor to work; all of this would necessitate keeping detailed lists of the impotent and able-bodied poor and their circumstances. Incidentally, he advocated a 'well-regulated system of colonization' to deal with overpopulation. He maintained that his object was not to oppress the poor but to 'promote their comfort ... preserve their true spirit of independence ... cherish their domestic virtues [and] chase away every lure to laziness and dissipation'. The bill was given its first reading, 24 July 1822, before the close of the session. Nolan had his speech published to increase awareness of his scheme, and sent a copy to the home secretary Peel, to whom he wrote:

> I am anxious so far as lies in my power to ease government of the labour and possible unpopularity of a task, which either they or some individual like myself must soon undertake. But even if under immediate impressions you should deem it worthy of further consideration, I shall not feel disappointed if after discussion you should think it ought to be given up. I will add that the bill has been generally circulated throughout the country, and that so far as I can judge from the large correspondence which it has brought upon me, its principal provisions are not disapproved.

The bill was reintroduced, 27 Mar., but set aside at the report stage, 27 June 1823.[7]

Nolan divided against parliamentary reform, 20 Feb., 2 June 1823. He voted with government for the sinking fund, 3 Mar., against repeal of the Foreign Enlistment Act, 16 Apr., and against inquiries into the prosecution of the Dublin Orange rioters, 21 Apr., and delays in chancery, 5 June. He divided in the minorities to refer the silk bill to a select committee, 9 June, and against the Irish tithes composition bill, 16 June. That March he had solicited the living of Bradworthy, Devon for the son of a constituent. Nothing was done, and four months later he wrote to the patronage secretary to the treasury, Lushington:

> A letter I have just received convinces me that it is not less for the interest of government than my own that my request should be complied with ... Considering the priority of my application and the proximity of the vicarage to the place I represent, I do think my claim entitled to preference over those which I am given to understand are made for the presentation.

This expression of 'warm interest' did the trick, as Liverpool told him.[8] In September 1823 Nolan applied to Peel for the vacant puisne judgeship on the Chester circuit. The decision on this appointment was postponed, at Liverpool's insistence, until ministers gathered in London at the end of the year. Peel then favoured giving it 'at once' to Nolan, who had 'given a very steady and useful support to the government and ... is the best qualified of the candidates'. Liverpool and lord chancellor Eldon preferred Thomas Jervis, for reasons of expediency, but Nolan was promised the next vacancy.[9] On 25 Feb. 1824 he obtained leave to reintroduce his poor law amendment bill. It was presented by William Thompson the next day, when Nolan was informed by Peel that he was to fill the place on the Welsh bench made vacant by the retirement of William Wingfield.[10] He was obliged to seek re-election at Barnstaple, but faced strong opposition from two other candidates and was pushed into second place behind the brewer Frederick Hodgson.[11] At the general election in 1826 he considered, but thought better of, standing for Bridgwater, and tried again at Barnstaple, where he finished a poor third.[12] He died in December 1827 and left estates in counties Kilkenny and Meath to his wife, while his property at Geraldstown, near Naas eventually passed to his younger brother, the Rev. Frederick Nolan (?1781-1864), vicar of Prittlewell, Essex; his personalty was sworn under £5,000 and resworn under £7,000 in 1828.[13]

[1] IGI (Ireland) [2] PROB 11/1736/91. [3] *LI Black Bks.* iv. 66-68. [4] *HP Commons, 1790-1820*, ii. 104-5; *Alfred*, 14 Mar. 1820; *The Times*, 10 June 1826; Add. 38458, f. 310. [5] Dorset RO D/BKL, Bankes' jnl. 128 (23 May 1821). [6] *The Times*, 1 Mar. 1821. [7] Add. 38294, f. 172; 40354, f. 327. [8] Add. 38293, f. 52; 38295, ff. 200, 228; 40362, f. 101. [9] Add. 38195, ff. 153-5; 40304, ff. 150, 208; 40359, f. 307. [10] Add. 40362, f. 101. [11] *The Times*, 9-11 Mar. 1824. [12] Ibid. 25 May, 10, 13, 14 June 1826. [13] PROB 8/221; 11/1736/91; *Gent. Mag.* (1864), ii. 788-91.

D.R.F./T.A.J.

NORTH, Frederick (1800–1869), of Hastings Lodge, Hastings, Suss. and Rougham, nr. Swaffham, Norf.

HASTINGS	1831–1837
HASTINGS	10 May 1854–1865
HASTINGS	1868–29 Oct. 1869

b. 2 July 1800, 1st s. of Francis Frederick North of Hastings and Rougham and Elizabeth, da. of Rev. William Whitear, rect. of All Saints, Hastings and Ore, Suss. *educ.* Harrow 1808-18; St. John's, Camb. 1817; I. Temple 1821. *m.* 16 June 1825, Janet, da. of Sir John Marjoribanks, 1st bt.*, wid. of Robert Shuttleworth of Gawthorpe Hall, nr. Burnley, Lancs., 2s. (1 *d.v.p.*) 2da. *suc.* fa. 1821. *d.* 29 Oct. 1869.

Mayor, Hastings 1826-7, 1828-9, 1830-1.

North was a direct descendant of the Jacobite Roger North (1653-1734), attorney-general to Queen Mary of Modena and author of the *Lives* of his eminent elder brothers, who bought the Rougham estate for 8,000 guineas in 1690. His eldest son and namesake had 'a vile temper' and maltreated his son Fountain North (1749-1810), who ran away to sea and, on succeeding to the estate, had the mansion house reduced to the size of a farmhouse. He settled at Hastings and divided his time between there and Hampstead, Middlesex, where he built a house 'with a flat roof, bulwarks, and portholes, like a man of war's deck, on which he used to pace up and down, firing off cannon from it on all great occasions and birthdays'. His son Francis Frederick North also lived at Hastings, where he married the daughter of a local clergyman.[1] He too was cantankerous and his eldest son Frederick, who was bullied at Harrow, spent most of his university vacations at Rougham, 'in preference to his uncongenial home'. He travelled desultorily on the continent, returned in 1821 to train for the bar and succeeded his father, who died aged 43, later that year.[2] He did not persevere with the law and in 1825 he married an attractive widow, who brought him a delicate stepdaughter Janet, bore him four children and, according to their elder daughter Marianne North, 'enjoyed nothing' during her 'dreary life'.[3]

North resumed residence at Rougham, in what had been the laundry of the old house, but spent the winters at Hastings, where he became a leading member of its closed corporation.[4] His mother's sister was married to Edward Milward, who dominated the borough's affairs and, as the government's election agent, returned both its Members. During North's third term as mayor in the summer of 1830 he faced attempts, inspired by the recent example set at Rye, to assert the right of inhabitant ratepayers to the freedom and thereby to the parliamentary franchise. On four occasions at courts of record in June and July he rejected, with Milward's blessing, some 160 such claims.[5] At the ensuing general election the ratepayers put up two candidates against Milward's nominees, both of whom held office in the Wellington ministry. As returning officer, North refused to receive any of the votes tendered for the reformers and returned the ministerialists on the strength of the votes of a handful of freemen.[6] The reform movement at Hastings accelerated and in mid-March 1831, soon after the introduction of the Grey ministry's scheme, North accepted a public invitation from 50 inhabitants, none of them members of the corporation, but many of them Milward's cronies, to stand for the borough as 'a resident gentleman of independent views' when the measure became law. The leaders of the reforming inhabitants, who had adopted prospective candidates of their own, denounced North as his uncle's 'tool' and dismissed his professed conversion to liberal principles as a manoeuvre designed to perpetuate the corporation's hegemony under a reformed electoral system. When Parliament was dissolved after the defeat of the reform bill, 19 Apr. 1831, the corporation offered to return one of the ratepayers' candidates with North, who pledged himself to support the measure 'because it would promote the prosperity of the country', though on other issues he would follow 'the dictates of his conscience'. The compromise was accepted and he came in unopposed.[7]

At a Battle reform dinner, 20 June 1831, North declared that more mischief had arisen from maladministration of the poor laws than from the laws themselves.[8] He voted for the second reading of the reintroduced reform bill, 6 July, and for most of its details, though he was in the minority against the disfranchisement of Downton, 21 July, and his attendance seems to have lapsed during August. He was in the opposition majority against the issue of a new writ for Liverpool, 5 Sept. He divided for the third reading, 19, and passage of the reform bill, 21 Sept., the second reading of the Scottish measure, 23 Sept., and the motion of confidence in ministers, 10 Oct. 1831. He voted for the second reading of the revised reform bill, 17 Dec. 1831. He was in the ministerial majorities for its details, 3, 8, 21, 23 Feb., but he divided against enfranchising Tower Hamlets, 28 Feb. 1832. He voted for the third reading, 22 Mar. He divided in defence of government's Portuguese policy, 9 Feb. He voted for the address asking the king to appoint only ministers who would carry undiluted reform, 10 May, and the second reading of the Irish bill, 25 May, and against a Conservative amendment to the Scottish bill, 1 June. He is not known to have spoken in debate in this period, but he presented Hythe and Seaford petitions against the sewers bill and secured a return of the number of persons serving in the navy as punishment for smuggling offences, 24 May. On 18 June he obtained information concerning the election of corporate officers on the Sabbath. He voted in favour of a tax on the property of absentee Irish landlords, 19 June, and public inquests, 20 June 1832.

At the general election of 1832 North successfully contested Hastings, where he inherited Milward's interest on his death the following year. He won the seat again in 1835, but retired on account of poor health in 1837.[9] Three years later he wrote to a friend from Gawthorpe Hall, where he was keeping an eye on his stepdaughter's inheritance:

> Old Roger [North] would have taken an interest in his grandson's present occupations, for I am becoming a perfect collier, having descended from 'a Parliament man' and a pretty active magistrate, to being a sort of unsalaried agent and coal viewer. I cannot bear to be unemployed.[10]

In 1842 Janet Shuttleworth married the educationalist James Kay, who added her name to his own and was created a baronet in 1849. Between 1847 and 1850 North travelled extensively and adventurously in Europe with his wife and daughter Marianne, who later achieved fame as a painter of the world's flora. (Her works are housed in a special gallery, erected at her own expense, in the Royal Botanic Gardens at Kew.)[11] North regained the Hastings seat in 1854 and became a supporter of the ballot.[12] After his defeat in 1865 he toured Egypt and Syria with Marianne, for whom he was 'from first to last the one idol and friend of my life'. For his part, she was 'the main link that binds me to life'.[13] He came in again for Hastings in 1868, was taken ill in Austria the following summer and returned home to die at Hastings Lodge in October 1869, 'after a last three days of exhaustion and sleep'.[14] He was succeeded by his only surviving son Charles North (1828-1906), a barrister.

[1] Marianne North, *Recollections of a Happy Life* ed. J.A. Symonds, i. 1-2; *Farington Diary*, xv. 5264, 5271, 5274; *Oxford DNB sub* Marianne and Roger North. [2] PROB 11/1651/680. [3] North, *Recollections*, i. 3-5, 29-30. [4] Ibid. i. 8-10. [5] J.M. Baines, *Historic Hastings* (1963), 50-51; *Brighton Guardian*, 9, 23 June, 7, 21 July 1830. [6] *Brighton Guardian*, 4 Aug. 1830. [7] *Hastings Iris*, 26 Mar., 9, 23, 30 Apr. 1831. [8] Ibid. 25 June 1831. [9] *The Times*, 4 July 1837. [10] Add. 32502, ff. 247, 251. [11] North, *Recollections*, i. 13-26; *Oxford DNB*. See *A Vision of Eden. The Life and Work of Marianne North* (1980); L. Ponsonby, *Marianne North at Kew Gardens* (1990). [12] *Dod's Parl. Companion* (1855), 243; (1857), 255. [13] North, *Recollections*, i. 5; *Vision of Eden*, 235. [14] North, *Recollections*, i. 37-38 and *Some Further Recollections*, 231.

D.R.F.

NORTH, John Henry (?1788–1831), of 31 Merrion Square, Dublin.

Plympton Erle	11 Mar. 1824–1826
Milborne Port	9 July 1827–1830
Drogheda	1830–30 Sept. 1831

b. ?1788, o.s. of Richard North of Guilford House, Tyrellspass, co. Westmeath and w. Lucinda Gouldsbury. *educ.* Trinity, Dublin 6 June 1803, aged 15; King's Inns 1805; M. Temple 1808, called [I] 1809. *m.* 28 Nov. 1818,[1] Letitia Dorothy, da. of Rt. Rev. William Foster, bp. of Clogher, *s.p. d.* 30 Sept. 1831.

KC [I] 1824; judge of ct. of admiralty [I] 1830-*d.*

North, whose father, the brother of Ulysses North of Newcastle, Westmeath, died soon after his birth, received his early education under the supervision of his maternal uncle Ponsonby Gouldsbury, the 'wealthy and exemplary' vicar of Tullamore, Meath. He gained a reputation for brilliance at Dublin University and rose rapidly at the Irish bar as 'an eloquent pleader', enhancing his standing with a speech, 5 Feb. 1823, on behalf of two of the defendants charged by *ex-officio* information with conspiracy to murder the Irish viceroy. Lord Lansdowne was 'much pleased' to meet him in Dublin later that year, and found him 'as modest and sensible in private as he is said to be eloquent and spirited in public'.[2] He admitted about this time that 'the acquisition of a seat in Parliament' had 'been long a favourite object'. In 1819, having married into the prominent Protestant Foster family, who had an interest at Drogheda, he had expressed to his wife's cousin Thomas Skeffington a wish to stand for that borough at the next opportunity. Skeffington advised against this, because of the heavy expense involved, and North made no move in 1820. On a vacancy two years later, however, he was persuaded to make a bid for the borough by his wife and her impetuous sister Harriet, Countess de Salis, to whom he had apparently given '*carte blanche*' to act for him. He possessed the means to finance the election thanks to 'the generosity of a kind relative'. Unfortunately, Skeffington was already committed to another candidate and North had to withdraw amid some embarrassment. His brother-in-law John Leslie Foster* commented that the women 'seem really to have taken leave of their senses'.[3] Late in 1823 the foreign secretary Canning regretted that he had not presently the means of bringing North into the Commons, but three months later he was returned for Plympton Erle on the 2nd earl of Mount Edgcumbe's interest.[4]

He took his seat on the ministerial side of the House and delivered his eagerly anticipated maiden speech, 29 Mar. 1824, when he defended the Kildare Place Society for the education of the Irish poor, of which he was a founder member, and criticized the Irish Catholic clergy for obstructing its work. The backbencher Hudson Gurney described 'North's debut' as 'fluent, and in the main with a very sensible view of things, but *very set* and *got up*. We shall see whether he will be *ready for occasion* and whether he can drop fine flowers and quotations'. The junior minister Wilmot Horton thought the speech was

> very Irish, partaking in voice of Rice and young Grattan, much animation, antithesis, great ease, fluency, and power of expression; no shade of the lawyer, and a speech of promise, wanting perhaps the deep earnest tone that tells so much in Parliament when it can be adequately sustained, and which is the great characteristic of Plunket's eloquence.[5]

Despite this success the prime minister, Lord Liverpool, and Canning chose Leslie Foster in preference to North for membership of the commission on Irish education.[6] North opposed the proposal to allow defence counsel in felony cases to address the jury on evidence, 6 Apr., arguing that it would 'change the sober floor of a court of justice into an arena for two ingenious combatants to display their strength and agility'. He voted for the usury laws repeal bill, 8 Apr. He spoke at length against the opposition's call for inquiry into the state of Ireland, 11 May, urging ministers to take steps to ensure that the Catholic clergy were 'very much raised in the scale of society', and commending their initiatives on tithes, petty sessions and free trade. In a peroration which was loudly applauded, he appealed to the Irish gentry to 'banish all those invidious distinctions of party by which Ireland had been so long degraded, impoverished and debased', but also called for English bigotry to be set aside. Lord Grenville considered the speech to be 'one of great ability', adding that 'certainly a part of its use will be still further to open men's minds on what is passing in Ireland'.[7] North divided against the motion condemning the trial of the Methodist missionary John Smith in Demerara, 11 June 1824. He had attached himself to Canning, who was 'quite pleased to see him' in London for the opening of the 1825 session.[8] He voted for the usury laws repeal bill, 8 Feb. That day he condemned the attitude of the Catholic Association towards an alleged violation of the Marriage Acts, which was 'of a piece with the whole of their conduct'. Canning wanted him to speak in the debate on the bill to suppress the Association, 11 Feb.,[9] but the chance did not arise until the resumed proceedings on 14 Feb., when, as a 'friend to the Catholics of Ireland', he welcomed the bill, which would relieve them from 'the odium which they might incur by the violence and folly' of the Association. One Member, hearing him for the first time, noted that 'he went through the whole subject and with a very considerable eloquence and perspicuity'.[10] At Canning's request he gave up the Cavan assizes and stayed in London for the postponed debate on Catholic relief, 1 Mar.,[11] but in the event gave only a silent vote for it. Of his speech in favour of the relief bill, 19 Apr., Daniel O'Connell*, who resented his attack on the Association and was jealous of his professional success, remarked that it was 'in itself rather a good one, but it made no impression on the House and in fact was a total failure. He is gone as a public speaker in the House. Both parties equally disregard him'.[12] He divided for the bill, 21 Apr., 10 May 1825. He voted against the motion condemning the Jamaican slave trials, 2 Mar., and spoke in defence of the Irish chief justice Lord Norbury, 5 May 1826. Two months before the dissolution he canvassed Dublin University on reports that the sitting Member Plunket was about to become Irish chancellor, provoking Croker, the secretary to the admiralty, who had long coveted the seat, to follow suit. In fact, Plunket was not elevated and came in unopposed at the general election that summer, while North failed to find a berth.[13]

On the formation of Canning's ministry in April 1827 there was speculation that North would be made Irish solicitor-general, but nothing came of it. Plunket resigned his seat in anticipation of a peerage and Croker immediately offered for the vacancy. Canning tried to deflect North with the offer of Bletchingley, 'without contest or expense', but he declined and insisted on opposing Croker. They were joined by an Orange candidate in what proved to be a turbulent contest, ending in victory for Croker.[14] Two months later North was returned for Milborne Port by the 1st marquess of Anglesey, a cabinet minister, who told the Whig Lord Holland that he was 'glad to hear ... you approve of North's being brought in. If it does not alarm the king, which it need not, I dare say some good will be gained by it. At all events don't fear my want of forbearance'.[15] North took his seat, 7 Feb. 1828. On 25 Feb. he defended the recently passed Irish Landlord and Tenant Act which, if modified as he suggested, would end 'the minute subdivision of property' in Ireland, 'the grand evil by which that country had been so long afflicted'. He was absent from the division on repeal of the Test Acts, 26 Feb. He voted with the Wellington ministry against inquiry into delays in chancery, 24 Apr., but had qualms about details of the home secretary Peel's offences against the person bill, 5 May. In voting for Catholic relief, 12 May, he detected 'something in the state of party as it at present exists, that would cause this measure to be now viewed most peculiarly as one of grace and favour ... not as the triumph off one party over another, but as the triumph of truth over error'. He opposed Grattan's assessment of lessors bill, 12 June, voted for the usury laws amendment bill, 19 June, and objected to the attempted reduction of the grant for the Royal Cork Institution, 20 June 1828. Curiously, in February 1829 Planta, the patronage secretary, listed him among the 'doubtfuls' on Catholic emancipation, when in fact he was being consulted by senior ministers in their deliberations on the details of their proposed settlement of the question. His objections to the prohibition of the assumption of titles by Catholic bishops were overruled.[16] He made a set speech in support of emancipation, which he believed would 'give security, general content and satisfaction to all who care for the protection of our institutions ... complete the hitherto imperfect union with Ireland' and insert 'the keystone of the great arch of the policy of the empire', 6 Mar. George Agar Ellis* thought this was 'a good speech' in an otherwise dull debate.[17] He spoke briefly in favour of the measure, 13, 23 Mar., and voted for it, 30 Mar. He divided for the Irish franchise bill, 26 Mar. 1829. Later that session, when he applied for some military patronage, the Irish secretary Leveson Gower endorsed his claim, knowing him to be an 'excellent man' who 'during our late difficulties ... has rendered service in the ... Commons to an extent which would render him worthy of any favourable attention'.[18] Surprisingly, that autumn Sir Richard Vyvyan* listed him among those supporters of emancipation whose sentiments were 'unknown' regarding a putative Ultra administration. He divided against proposals for parliamentary reform, 11, 18, 23 Feb. 1830. He justified recent *ex-officio* prosecutions for libels on Wellington, 2 Mar., and called for delay in proceeding with the Irish Subletting Act amendment bill, 5 Mar. He was granted a month's leave for urgent private business in Dublin, 12 Mar. At this time Leveson Gower pressed for his appointment to the vacant place of Irish third serjeant, arguing that he had 'a superior claim ... over all other candidates', both in terms of 'undoubted professional fitness' and his 'great sacrifice and ... eminent service to government, incident to parliamentary attendance'. In the event, North was unwilling to take the post, for reasons 'founded on his present tenure of his seat' (Anglesey had gone over to the Whigs), but Leveson Gower nevertheless made him 'a complimentary offer of the serjeantcy' and secured his appointment to the Irish ecclesiastical commission of inquiry.[19] He defended Galway corporation against charges that they were obstructing Catholics from claiming the vote, 29 Apr., and opposed the Galway franchise bill as an infraction of municipal rights, 25 May. He clashed with O'Connell over the Irish vestry laws, 29 Apr., but welcomed his proposal that Irish Catholic priests should be permitted to solemnize mixed marriages, 4 May. On 12 May he responded to O'Connell's accusation that government had suppressed evidence in the trial of the Doneraile conspirators by declaring that a 'manly, kind and generous feeling' was 'springing up in Ireland', thanks to the 'wise legislative measure adopted last year', and that it would 'soon be out of the power of any man to heat the national atmosphere to the temperature of a furnace, merely that a political salamander may find his proper element to breath in'. He voted against Jewish emancipation, 17 May 1830. Soon afterwards, being obliged to vacate Milborne Port at the dissolution 'from his connection with government', North made 'a furious canvass' of the College against Croker. Ministers were powerless to stop him but assured Croker of their 'exclusive support'. As the general election approached it became clear that while North had no chance, his persistence in 'the vanity of standing' was likely to let in the Orangeman Lefroy. In what was presumably an attempt to buy him off, he was appointed to the vacant judgeship of the Irish admiralty court just after the dissolution in July. He then ostensibly withdrew from the university contest and offered for Drogheda, where he was opposed by O'Connell's son. He stressed his steady support for Catholic relief, claiming that this was not inconsistent with his opposition to the Galway franchise bill, and deplored 'agitation', whose 'season is no more'. However, in a move which Croker and Peel found 'inexplicable' and 'perfectly unaccountable', and for which he himself furnished no convincing justification, he appeared at Trinity College on election day and went to a poll. He finished bottom, but his intervention dished Croker, who lost to Lefroy by three votes. He returned to Drogheda, where he easily beat O'Connell after a contest that reputedly cost him between £5,000 and £10,000.[20] His opponents petitioned against his return alleging, among other illegalities, that he was disqualified by his judgeship and his wife's possession of a crown pension (of which no confirmation has been found), but he survived the challenge.[21]

Ministers of course listed North among their 'friends', but he was absent from the crucial civil list division, 15 Nov. 1830; he later said he would have supported them had he been present.[22] He objected to the increasing expense of printing petitions, 25 Nov. He obtained leave to introduce a bill to extend the provisions of the Act of 1780 abolishing sacramentary tests to Protestants of the Irish church, 2 Dec. 1830, but never did so. He prophesied practical difficulties in the revaluation of Irish church property liable to the first fruits levy, 14 Mar. 1831. He promised 'strenuous opposition' to the Galway franchise bill, 3 Feb., and secured returns to bolster his case against it, 9 Feb. That day he objected to Hunt's allegation that Irish juries were sometimes packed, but agreed with him next day that the regulation of Fisherton gaol, which permitted the governor to intercept a prisoner's written defence, was a breach of solicitors' confidentiality. He urged Lord Grey's ministry to drop their proposed tax on steamboat passengers, which would hit the Irish poor, 14 Feb., and claimed that they had abandoned their plan to tax transfers of funded property 'on the distinct ground of its being a violation of the national faith'. He voiced fears over some ministerial pronouncements on Ireland, which seemed to encourage violence and threaten the Union, 18 Feb., when he strongly objected to Sugden's proposals to extend the 1736 Mortmain Act to Ireland. On 7 Mar. he delivered a prepared attack on the government's reform scheme, a 'malignant measure' which, as far as Ireland was concerned, would overturn the 1829 settlement safeguarding the Protestant establishment. Of the plan as a whole he warned that 'it will not be a final measure' but 'only the first of those steps which will lead us day after day in our progress from our ancient institutions'; it was 'the first abyss in the revolutionary hell that is yawning for us'. The Whigs Lord Durham and William Ord* thought the speech 'very Irish' and 'without much effect', and its apocalyptic tone amused the cartoonists.[23] On the other hand, Hudson Gurney considered it the 'best speech' of the night, Henry Bankes* described it as 'very brilliant' and 'delivered with much spirit and animation', Thomas Gladstone* thought it 'extremely eloquent, but he went much too far', and Maria Edgeworth judged it 'the best and plainest speech he ever made', though he was much inferior in 'power' to Thomas Macaulay* as an orator.[24] He divided against the English bill's second reading, 22 Mar., condemned the potential destruction of 'Protestant interests in Ireland', 29 Mar., and spoke and voted for Gascoyne's wrecking amendment, 19 Apr. 1831, when he predicted that reform would ensure the mass return of Irish borough Members 'deeply involved in the principles of agitation'. At the ensuing dissolution the Irish administration were 'greatly in hopes of being able to spring a mine to blow up North for Drogheda', where he was opposed by the 'whole bill' sitting Member Thomas Wallace. Claiming to support 'temperate and constitutional' reform of 'existing abuses', he stood by his declared hostility to the bill and defied expectations by defeating Wallace after a bitter contest. In returning thanks, he rejoiced in the 'triumph ... of reason over rashness, of sound principles over doctrines dangerous and pernicious, of our ancient laws and glorious constitution over revolutionary madness and Jacobin innovation'. He denied Wallace's allegation that he had once been an advocate of reform, declaring that he had been 'bred as a politician in the school of Mr. Burke' and had entered Parliament on the invitation of Canning, whose 'confidence' in him had rested largely on 'our agreement ... on this very subject'. His victory, which owed much to the Protestant clergy and non-resident voters, was subsidized to the tune of £3,000 from the opposition election fund.[25]

They did not, as it turned out, get their full money's worth. North voted against the second reading of the reintroduced reform bill, 6 July, to use the 1831 census for the purpose of scheduling boroughs, 19 July, and to postpone consideration of Chippenham's inclusion in schedule B, 27 July 1831. It was surely not he, but the reformer Frederick North, who voted for Sudbury's partial disfranchisement, 2 Aug. Two days later he explained that he had 'taken no part' in the debates on the bill because he regarded it as 'a mere temporary measure', which would 'only last until displaced by the constitution of 1832 or 1833'. He voiced doubts about the proposed registration machinery, 2, 3 Sept., but ministers ignored his suggested improvements. He divided against the third reading, 19 Sept., and the bill's passage, 21 Sept. He defended the Irish attorney-general against O'Connell's attack over the Castle Pollard incident, 11 July. He agreed with O'Connell in calling for repeal, rather than modification, of the Irish Subletting Act, 5 Aug. He gave credit to the Irish administration for their vigorous enforcement of the rule of law, 10 Aug., but wished they would introduce 'some system of well-digested poor laws' rather than the reform bill. He voted against them on the Dublin election controversy, 23 Aug., when he replied to O'Connell's strictures on recent appointments of Irish crown prosecutors. On the Irish education grant, 9 Sept., he sketched the history of the Kildare Place Society, which had been better off when unsupported by government, and confessed that 'the interest I once felt on the subject of national education has died away'. When O'Connell called for lay appropriation of Irish church property, 14 Sept., North deplored the emptiness of the government front bench and promised a 'manly, persevering and honourable struggle' by the Irish Protestants against such spoliation. He welcomed in principle the government's bill to make the Irish penal code less sanguinary and promised his 'humble assistance in ... committee' to render it 'as perfect as possible', 22 Sept. He voted against the sugar and truck bills, 12 Sept. 1831.

North died at the end of September 1831 from 'violent inflammation of the lungs', after 'a very few days illness'. It was said that 'the extraordinary fatigue of parliamentary duty' had 'preyed upon a constitution weakened by the studious labours of his life'. One admiring obituarist wrote that he had been

> enough before the public during the last year, to give proof of what his splendid talents might have effected had he been longer spared ... His oratory was copious, brilliant and, best of all, correct; his speeches resembled high-wrought academic effusions, stately, orderly and chaste; with little of that ardour and impetuosity of passion characteristic of the Irish school. His intellect was singularly sound and clear; vigorous, cautious and comprehensive. The power of attention was under his absolute control; and whatever was capable of demonstration, was within his grasp.

A memorial inscription in St. Mary's, Harrow-on-the-Hill, probably composed by his wife, lamented that he had 'sunk beneath the efforts of a mind too great for his earthly frame, in opposing the revolutionary invasion of the religion and constitution of England'. According to *The Times*, however, his opposition to reform came 'as much from gratitude [to Wellington], perhaps, as from conviction', and his parliamentary career had 'not [been] of so splendid a nature as his friends had anticipated'.[26]

[1] IGI (Dublin). [2] *Gent. Mag.* (1830), ii. 378; (1831), ii. 466; Rev. R.J. M'Ghee, *Sermon on death of J.H. North* (Dublin, 1831), 9; J.H. North, *Speech in King's Bench, 5 Feb. 1823* (Dublin, 1823); W.H. Curran, *Sketches of Irish Bar*, i. 208-33; Add. 51687, Lansdowne to Holland, 10 Aug. 1823. [3] PRO NI, Foster mss D562/3404, 4616-22. [4] *Canning Official Corresp.* i. 131-3, ii. 364-5. [5] Gurney diary, 29 Mar. 1824; TNA 30/29/9/6/18. [6] Add. 40304, f. 240. [7] NLW, Coedymaen mss 403. [8] Foster mss D207/73/118. [9] Ibid. 73/119. [10] Merthyr Mawr mss F/2/8, Nicholl diary, 14 Feb. 1825. [11] Foster mss D207/73/121. [12] *O'Connell Corresp.* iii. 1168, 1205. [13] Add. 37304, f. 115; 40319, f. 171; *The Times*, 3 Apr., 31 May 1826. [14] *Canning's Ministry*, 213; *Croker Pprs.* i. 372; Lincs. AO, Tennyson mss H1/85, Herries to Tennyson, 30 Apr.; *Dublin Evening Post*, 24 Apr., 3, 15 May 1827. [15] Add. 51567, Anglesey to Holland, 25 July 1827. [16] *Ellenborough Diary*, i. 348-50, 374-5, 385. [17] Northants. RO, Agar Ellis diary, 6 Mar. 1829. [18] NAI, Leveson Gower letterbks., Leveson Gower to Somerset, 14 May 1829. [19] Ibid. Leveson Gower to Scarlett, 5 Mar., to Singleton, 5, 13, 16 Mar. 1830. [20] Ibid. Leveson Gower to Singleton, 15 June, 30 July; Add. 40320, ff. 154, 156, 161, 163, 166, 168, 170, 172; 51813, Phillimore to Holland, 14 July; *Dublin Morning Post*, 8 July, 3, 4, 6 Aug.; *Drogheda Jnl.* 31 July, 7, 14 Aug.; *The Times*, 14 Aug. 1830. [21] *Dublin Morning Post*, 17 Aug. 1830; *O'Connell Corresp.* iv. 1702. [22] *Drogheda Jnl.* 7 May 1831. [23] Grey mss, Durham to Grey, 7 Mar.; Add. 51569, Ord to Lady Holland, 7 Mar. 1831; M.D. George, *Cat. of Pol. and Personal Satires*, xi. 16608. [24] Gurney diary, 7 Mar.; Dorset RO D/BKL, Bankes jnl. 173 (7 Mar.); St. Deiniol's Lib. Glynne-Gladstone mss 197, T. to J. Gladstone, 8 Mar. 1831; *Edgeworth Letters*, 488. [25] PRO NI, Anglesey mss D619/28C, Anglesey to Grey, 30 Apr.; *Drogheda Jnl.* 7, 10, 14 May 1831; *O'Connell Corresp.* iv. 1800; *Three Diaries*, 138. [26] *Gent. Mag.* (1831), ii. 466-7; *The Times*, 1 Oct.; *Drogheda Jnl.* 4 Oct. 1831.

D.R.F./T.A.J.

NORTHCOTE, Henry Stafford (1792–1850), of the Pynes, nr. Exeter, Devon and 25 Portland Place, Mdx.

HEYTESBURY 1826–1830

b. 18 Mar. 1792, 1st s. of Sir Stafford Henry Northcote, 7th bt. (*d.* 1851), of the Pynes and Jaquetta, da. of Charles Baring of Larkbear, nr. Exeter. *educ.* Christ Church, Oxf. 1810. *m.* (1) 13 Nov. 1815, Agnes Mary (*d.* 9 Apr. 1840), da. of Thomas Cockburn of Bedford Hill, Surr., 4s. (2 *d.v.p.*) 2da.; (2) 6 Jan. 1846, Catherine, da. of Thomas Robbins of Pilewell, nr. Lymington, Hants, *s.p. d.v.p.* 22 Feb. 1850.

Northcote was the first member of this ancient Devon family to sit in the Commons since his celebrated seventeenth-century ancestor Sir John Northcote, 1st baronet, and his rather less conspicuous, but more typical relation Sir Henry, the 5th baronet, who represented Exeter, 1735-43.[1] His father, who succeeded to the baronetcy in 1770, married the eldest daughter of Charles Baring, the younger brother of Sir Francis Baring†, the founder of that family's commercial fortunes. Northcote, who took his degree in 1813, married the pious and amiable daughter of the Scottish former Madras civil servant Thomas Cockburn, but he did not share her Evangelical religious outlook.[2] In December 1824 Cockburn, who described Sir Stafford Northcote as 'one of the most attached friends of the government', informed the duke of Wellington, the lord lieutenant of Hampshire, that Northcote had lived at Malshanger in that county since 1818, and recommended his appointment as a magistrate.[3] Yet, apart from his London house, his address was usually given as the Pynes in contemporary directories.

At the general election of 1826, when his father proposed the Tory Sir Thomas Dyke Acland* for Devon, Northcote was returned unopposed for Heytesbury, presumably as the paying guest of the patron, Sir William A'Court†.[4] He voted against Catholic relief, 6 Mar. 1827, and the second reading of the corn bill, 2 Apr. He divided against repeal of the Test Acts, 26 Feb., and Catholic relief, 12 May 1828. He was listed by Planta, the Wellington ministry's patronage secretary, as 'opposed to the principle of the bill', but voted with government for Catholic emancipation, 6, 30 Mar. 1829. He divided against transferring East Retford's seats to Birmingham, 11 Feb., Lord Blandford's reform scheme, 18 Feb., and the enfranchisement of Birmingham, Leeds and Manchester, 23 Feb. 1830. His only other known votes were against Jewish emancipation, 17 May, and for Knatchbull's amendment prohibiting the sale of beer for on-consumption, 21 June. He made no known speeches in the House, which he left at the dissolution in 1830, and he is not known to have sought another seat. He seconded the nomination of Acland for the county at the ensuing general election and proposed the Conservative Sir John Buller Yarde Buller† for Devon South in January 1835, when he deprecated

> that spirit of party which would ascribe to an honest man placing confidence in the present government a wish to impede any great measure of reform which might be necessary and beneficial to the maintenance and improvement of our admirable constitution. It cannot but be the sincere wish of every true Conservative to apply such remedies to the defects of our constitution as might best meet the case. But ... let it not be attributed to him for a fault, if he tread with caution the very thin border which separates liberty and licentiousness.[5]

Thereafter he was not usually active in local politics.

On his death in 1831 the society painter James Northcote, who claimed a (spurious) connection with the Devon Northcotes, left them his collection of literary items and pictures relating to the family.[6] Henry Northcote, two of whose sons died in 1831, lost his wife in 1840, but later remarried, to the daughter of a West India planter who had settled in Hampshire. She was also the sister of the wife of his uncle, Stafford Charles Northcote, rector of Upton Pyne.[7] In early 1850 Northcote's life was despaired of and he died in February, leaving his estate to his eldest son Stafford Henry (1818-87), who succeeded his grandfather as 8th baronet, 17 Mar. 1851.[8] As Conservative Member for Dudley, Stamford and Devon North, he had a distinguished career, holding high ministerial office under Benjamin Disraeli† and Lord Salisbury, and was created earl of Iddesleigh in 1885.

[1] C. Worthy, *Life of Earl of Iddesleigh* (1887), 3-10, and *Devonshire Wills*, 441-7; *The Times*, 21 Jan. 1887. [2] *Life, Letters and Diaries of Earl of Iddesleigh* ed. A. Lang, i. 5-6, 25, 30-35, 46-50. [3] Wellington mss WP1/807/26; 824/3. [4] *Alfred*, 20 June, 11 July 1826. [5] Ibid. 10 Aug. 1830; *Western Times*, 17 Jan. 1835. [6] Add. 42524, f. 12; PROB 11/1788/411; *Gent. Mag.* (1831), ii. 102-6; *Oxford DNB*. [7] Devon RO, Northcote mss 51/24/15; IGI (Devon); M. Robbins, *Gleanings of Robins or Robbins Fam.* 45. [8] *Life of Iddesleigh*, 83, 87; *Western Times*, 2 Mar. 1850, 22 Mar. 1851.

S.M.F.

NORTHEY, William (1752–1826), of Box Hall, Wilts. and Woodcote, Epsom, Surr.

NEWPORT 1796–19 Jan. 1826

b. 7 Aug. 1752,[1] 1st s. of William Northey† of Compton Bassett and Ivy House, Wilts. and 2nd w. Anne, da. of Edward Hopkins† of Coventry, Warws. *educ.* Eton 1763-7; Queens', Camb. 1771; M. Temple 1771. *unm.*[2] *suc.* fa. 1770; cos. William Northey to Woodcote 1808. *d.* 19 Jan. 1826.

Commdt. Box vol. inf. 'during the war'.[3]

Northey, who had sat for Newport since 1796 on the interest of the 2nd and 3rd dukes of Northumberland, was returned unopposed in 1820. In accordance with the views of his patrons he had moved away from the Whig opposition and from 1818 gave general support to Lord Liverpool's ministry, although he was an increasingly lax attender as well as a silent Member. He paired against Catholic relief, 28 Feb., and repeal of the additional malt duty, 3 Apr. 1821. He voted against relieving Catholic peers of their disabilities, 30 Apr. 1822, and Scottish parliamentary reform, 2 June 1823. He again paired against Catholic relief, 10 May

1825. No other trace of parliamentary activity has been found. He died in January 1826, 'aged 73'.[4] He left his estates in Surrey and Wiltshire to his brother the Rev. Edward Northey, canon of Windsor, and an annuity of £400 to a Mrs. Louisa Wiseman; the probate valuation is not available.[5]

[1] IGI (Wilts.). [2] The marriage attributed to him in *HP Commons, 1790-1820*, iv. 678, was almost certainly that of his second cos. William Northey (1737-1808): see *Gent. Mag.* (1795), ii. 613; PROB 11/1466/679. [3] *Gent. Mag.* (1826), i. 177. [4] *Genealogist* (n.s.), x. 178. [5] PROB 11/1709/103.

H.J.S.

NORTON, Hon. Charles Francis (1807–1835), of Wonersh, Surr.

GUILDFORD 1831–1832

b. 4 Feb. 1807, 3rd s. of Hon. Fletcher Norton† (*d.* 1820), bar. of exch. [S], and Caroline Elizabeth, da. of James Balmain, commr. of excise; bro. of Hon. George Chapple Norton*. *m.* 29 Dec. 1831, Maria Louisa, da. of Maj.-Gen. Sir Colin Campbell, lt.-gov. of Portsmouth, 1s. 1da. *d.* 20 Oct. 1835.

Ensign 52 ft. 1826, lt. 1827, capt. 1831.

No details of Norton's education have been found, but his upbringing would have been in Edinburgh, where his father's legal appointment had taken him. Every Sunday Fletcher Norton, a devout Anglican, treated his family to 'a sermon selected from the works of the best of the English and Scotch divines'.[1] At the age of 13 Norton received a one-seventh share of the residue (valued at £7,438) of his father's estate, and he subsequently joined the army; his regiment was stationed in Nova Scotia during the period of his service.[2] At the general election of 1831 he offered for Guildford, where his eldest brother, who had succeeded an uncle as 3rd Baron Grantley, possessed an interest. Whereas his brother was strongly opposed to the Grey ministry's reform bill, Norton campaigned as a supporter of the measure and was returned with another reformer after a four-cornered contest.[3]

He divided for the second reading of the reintroduced reform bill, 6 July, and steadily for its details, except the inclusion of Guildford in schedule B, which he opposed by vote and in his only recorded speech, 29 July 1831. He argued that the town's population was 'respectable and increasing' and supported its petition to retain two Members by expanding the boundary, the case for which he regarded as unanswerable. He voted for the bill's passage, 21 Sept., the second reading of the Scottish bill, 23 Sept., and Lord Ebrington's confidence motion, 10 Oct. He was in the minority for O'Connell's motion to swear in the 11 members of the Dublin election committee, 29 July, but voted with ministers to prosecute only those found guilty of bribery, 23 Aug. On 5 Nov. he was granted the precedence afforded to the younger sons of peers by letter patent. He divided for the second reading of the revised reform bill (by which Guildford kept both its Members), 17 Dec. 1831, steadily for its details and for the third reading, 22 Mar. 1832. He voted for the address asking the king to appoint only ministers committed to carrying an unimpaired measure, 10 May, and against the Conservative amendment for increased Scottish county representation, 1 June. He voted against government on the Russian-Dutch loan, 26 Jan., was absent from the division on this issue 12 July, but voted with ministers, 16 July. He divided with them on relations with Portugal, 9 Feb. 1832. He stood again for Guildford at the general election later that year, but was defeated by one of his Conservative rivals from the previous contest.

Norton resumed an active military career, the prospects for which had not been harmed by his marriage in 1831 to the daughter of Sir Colin Campbell, then lieutenant-governor of Portsmouth, his regimental depot. His wife, according to Benjamin Disraeli†, was 'more beautiful even than the three [Sheridan] sisters', one of whom, Caroline, had married his brother George. In the conflict attendant on Caroline's unhappy union it appears that Charles Norton, along among his family, 'brought his influence to bear always on the side of conciliation and peace'.[4] He became assistant military secretary to his father-in-law, following the latter's appointment as governor of Nova Scotia, and it was there that he died suddenly in October 1835, 'in consequence of drinking cold water, whilst overheated in the pursuit of moose deer'. Administration of his estate was granted to his widow, and the personalty was finally sworn under a paltry £450.[5] His son, Charles Grantley Campbell Norton (1835-1921), also pursued an army career.

[1] *Gent. Mag.* (1820), ii. 856. [2] PROB 11/1646/418; IR26/877/907; Sir H. Newbolt, *Oxon. and Bucks. Light Infantry*, 158. [3] *County Chron.* 3 May 1831. [4] *Disraeli Letters*, i. 243; A. Acland, *Caroline Norton*, 65. [5] *Gent. Mag.* (1836), i. 445; PROB 6/214/19.

H.J.S.

NORTON, Hon. George Chapple (1800–1875), of Garden Court, Middle Temple, Mdx.

GUILDFORD 1826–1830

b. 31 Aug. 1800, 2nd s. of Hon. Fletcher Norton† (*d.* 1820), bar. of exch. [S], and Caroline Elizabeth, da. of James Balmain, commr. of excise; bro. of Hon. Charles Francis Norton*. *educ.* Winchester 1813-15; M. Temple 1820, called 1825. *m.* 30 July 1827, Caroline Elizabeth Sarah, da. of Thomas Sheridan, 3s. (2 *d.v.p.*). *d.* 24 Feb. 1875.

Commr. of bankrupts 1827-31; metropolitan police magistrate, Whitechapel 1831-44, Lambeth 1845-67.

Recorder, Guildford 1830-*d.*

Norton's grandfather Sir Fletcher Norton was renowned for his success in legal practice and in collecting government appointments, which earned him the nickname of 'Sir Bull-face Double Fee'; he was ennobled as Baron Grantley in 1782.[1] Norton's father held from 1776 the post of baron of the exchequer in Scotland, which brought him emoluments of £2,865 and led him to be lampooned as a pampered sinecurist.[2] According to an obituary notice, Norton attended Edinburgh University, but his name does not appear in its roll of graduates.[3] On his father's death in 1820 he received no specific provision other than a one-seventh share of the residue (valued at £7,438) of the estate.[4] In 1822 his elder brother succeeded their uncle as 3rd Baron Grantley and thus acquired an electoral interest at Guildford. Norton canvassed the borough in the autumn of 1825 and secured an unopposed return at the general election the following summer.[5]

In the House he generally acted in accordance with his family's Tory traditions. He divided against Catholic relief, 6 Mar., before being granted leave to go the home circuit, 22 Mar. 1827. He opposed Canning's ministry by voting against the bill to regulate the Coventry magistracy, 11, 18 June 1827. He divided against repeal of the Test Acts, 26 Feb., and Catholic relief, 12 May 1828. He voted with the duke of Wellington's ministry against inquiry into delays in chancery, 29 Apr., and reduction of the salary of the lieutenant-general of the ordnance, 4 July 1828. In February 1829 Planta, the patronage secretary, listed him as one who was 'opposed to the principle' of Catholic emancipation. When a friendly petition from Guildford was presented, 2 Mar., he stated that he anticipated a counter-petition 'from persons of equal respectability', and he presented a hostile one from a London Baptist chapel, 9 Mar. Nevertheless, he voted for emancipation, 6 Mar. 1829. He divided for Knatchbull's amendment to the address on distress, 4 Feb., but against Lord Blandford's parliamentary reform scheme, 18 Feb., and the enfranchisement of Birmingham, Leeds and Manchester, 23 Feb. 1830. He voted with ministers against Lord Palmerston's motion condemning British interference in Portugal, 10 Mar., and for the grant for South American missions, 7 June. He presented a petition from Guildford magistrates for an amendment to the sale of beer bill to prohibit consumption on the premises, 10 May, and voted accordingly, 21 June. He divided for the abolition of the death penalty for forgery, 24 May, 7 June, and reform of the divorce laws, 3 June 1830. At the dissolution that summer he found himself opposed at Guildford by two former Members and came bottom of the poll. In October 1830 he was elected recorder of the borough and, at the general election the following spring, he solicited support for his brother Charles, who was standing as an advocate of the Grey ministry's reform bill.[6] His own return to Parliament was barred by his appointment as a stipendiary magistrate for Whitechapel, at an annual salary of £1,000.

In July 1827 Norton had contracted his fateful marriage to Caroline Sheridan, a granddaughter of Richard Brinsley Sheridan†, who won renown as a writer, wit and beauty and provided the model for the heroine of George Meredith's *Diana of the Crossways*.[7] He had first proposed to her some three years earlier, when she was 16 and he, according to Caroline's biographer, was

> a briefless barrister of about 25, well made, though not tall, good looking, and with a fine ruddy complexion; but rather slow and lazy, and late for everything, till he at last gained the cognomen ... of the "late George Norton".

He even managed to be late for the wedding ceremony.[8] By his subsequent account, he then 'loved her to madness', a feeling that was never reciprocated by his wife, whose family were apparently misled as to the extent of his fortune and prospects. The couple were poles apart both in temperament and in their political views. Helped by an appointment as a bankruptcy commissioner, which may have been secured for him by his mother-in-law, Norton set up home at Storey's Gate, Birdcage Walk, where Caroline held court to a circle of Whig admirers, including the duke of Devonshire.[9] In 1830 Georgiana Ellis wrote that if Caroline 'were not conceited and affected, she would be a very delightful as well as a very singular person', and noted how in her conversational sallies, 'her poor husband is constantly brought in, in a very ridiculous manner'. But observers were unaware of the fact that, according to her own later account, Caroline suffered violent mistreatment 'from the earliest period of our marriage ... such as is brought before the police courts'. Her writing, which she began to supplement their slender income, contains much internal evidence of her unhappy plight.[10] She was characteristically vituperative in describing Norton's election defeat at Guildford to her sister:

> With that mixture of sanguine hope, credulity and vanity which distinguishes him, he assures me that, although thrown out, he was the most popular candidate; that the opponents are hated, and that all those who voted against him did it with tears. I swear to you this is not exaggerated, but what he says and believes ... I am sorry, not because I ever hoped to see him an orator, but because, after all, it is something lost, one of the opportunities of life slipped through one's fingers.[11]

His appointment as a stipendiary magistrate was arranged by the home secretary Lord Melbourne, at the behest of Caroline, who made the best use of her Whig connections in the expectation that bankruptcy commissioners would not survive the Grey ministry's retrenchment plans; she later claimed that it was only with the greatest reluctance that he was persuaded to surrender the latter position. In July 1831 Melbourne had to issue a gentle admonishment, through Caroline, after an unseemly row among London magistrates, who 'tell me ... that Norton does not go to his office early enough'.[12] Melbourne later assisted in obtaining a letter patent, granted 5 Nov. 1831, which entitled Norton to the form of address of the son of a peer: thus, in his wife's words, was he 'made Honourable'. He evidently hoped for further preferment and appears to have entirely subjugated his own political views to this end. Frustration in this ambition, and the resulting financial difficulties, put further strain on the marriage, and Caroline briefly left him in 1833 after a fight while she was pregnant, and again in 1835. Her novel *The Wife and Woman's Reward*, written that year after an excruciating trip abroad, depicted a mean, insensitive boor which was so plain in its origin as to draw a rebuke from Melbourne, now prime minister, who had become her intimate.[13] In 1836 the couple finally parted and Norton, determining on divorce, rashly sued the premier for crim. con. The case naturally excited great interest and, initially, some sympathy for the supposed cuckold, but afterwards Lady Holland judged that feeling against 'the somewhat indelicate and unguarded language and manners of Mrs. Norton' was outstripped by 'the disgust felt at the meanness ... spite and ... cruelty of the whole Norton family'. Melbourne was acquitted without leaving the dock, and the patent unreliability of the witnesses and flimsiness of the evidence offered aroused suspicions that Norton, egged on by Grantley, was merely a pawn in a Conservative plot to discredit the prime minister. The ludicrous construction placed on Melbourne's notes to Caroline by the prosecution counsel inspired Dickens's portrayal of the court case in *The Pickwick Papers*.[14] Yet Norton had no qualms about retaining his seat on the magistrates' bench secured for him by Melbourne, until he was able to retire with a pension. More remarkably, he exonerated his wife from all charges in a vain attempt to win her back, blaming the legal action on his advisers.[15]

Norton's financial worries were eased in 1836 by his inheritance of Kettlethorpe Hall in Yorkshire, along with an income, from Margaret Vaughan, a distant relative. This later became the subject of innuendo from his wife. The couple formally separated in 1848, prior to which Caroline had successfully campaigned for a change in the law governing her access to the children. In 1853 they met in court again over a debt she had incurred owing to Norton's refusal to pay her allowance as agreed. When the court found for him on a technicality, there followed a protracted washing of dirty linen in public as the feud continued in the columns of *The Times*.[16] Norton died in February 1875, a few months before his childless elder brother, thus depriving Caroline of the chance of a title, as she tartly observed.[17] The Kettlethorpe estate passed to his only surviving son, Thomas Brinsley Norton (1831-77), who succeeded shortly afterwards as 4th Baron Grantley.

[1] *Oxford DNB*. [2] M.D. George, *Cat. of Personal and Pol. Satires*, x. 13601. [3] *Law Times*, lvii (1875), 349. [4] PROB 11/1646/418; IR26/877/907. [5] *County Chron.* 11 Oct. 1825. [6] Ibid. 12 Oct. 1830; *Brighton Herald*, 30 Apr. 1831. [7] See *Oxford DNB*; A. Acland, *Caroline Norton*; J.C. Perkins, *Life of Mrs. Norton*. [8] Perkins, 10; *Chrons. Holland House* ed. Lord Ilchester, 218. [9] Perkins, 14-19; *Lady Holland to Son*, 45; *The Times*, 24 Aug. 1853; Add. 46611, f. 50. [10] *Howard Sisters*, 178; *The Times*, 2 Sept. 1853; Perkins, 16, 21; Acland, 35, 42-43. [11] Perkins, 29-30. [12] Ibid. 32-38; *The Times*, 2 Sept. 1853; Torrens, *Melbourne*, i. 423-5. [13] Torrens, i. 424; Perkins, 40, 43, 52-55, 59-64, 71-72, 76. [14] Perkins, 80-96; Acland, 90; *Holland House Diaries*, 344; *Greville Mems.* iii. 290-3; *Extraordinary Trial!* [BL 1508/1657]. [15] Perkins, 38, 101-2. [16] Ibid. 75-77, 130-47, 156, 171, 230; Acland, 195-6; *The Times*, 20, 24 Aug., 2, 8-10, 17, 24 Sept. 1853. [17] Perkins, 295.

H.J.S.

NOWELL, Alexander (1761–1842), of Underley Park, Kirkby Lonsdale, Westmld. and Wimpole Street, Mdx.[1]

WESTMORLAND 1831–1832

b. 19 Nov. 1761, 3rd s. of Ralph Nowell (*d.* 1781) of Eccleston, Lancs. and Coverhead, Yorks. and Sarah, da. of Thomas Whitaker of Holme, Lancs.[2] *m.* (1) at Dinapore, 6 Jan. 1793, Maria Theresa (*d.* 21 Mar. 1824), da. of Thomas Kearnan of London, wid. of Lt.-Col.

Henry Watson, chief engineer, E.I. Co., *s.p.*; (2) 5 Apr. 1825, Charlotte, da. of James Farington of Shawe Hall, Lancs., *s.p. d.* 17 Nov. 1842.

Cadet, E.I. Co. (Bengal) 1782; ensign 6th Eur. Batt. 1785, 2nd Eur. Batt. 1790, ret. 1792.[3]

Nowell was of the Gawthorp Hall branch of the family and a descendant thereby of the Lancashire Royalist Roger Nowell of Rede, who raised a regiment for the protection of Charles I. He entered the East India Company's army shortly after his father's death, but failed to rise above the rank of ensign and resigned in October 1792 to become an indigo manufacturer at Tirhut. Three months later he married Maria Theresa, the widow of the Company's former chief engineer Henry Watson.[4] Although unprovided for in Watson's will, she had secured the right to administer his valuable dockyard property in Calcutta and benefited also by the wills of her brothers Thomas (*d.* 1803), an officer in the East India Company's service, and Peter (*d.* 1811), a London attorney.[5]

Nowell returned to England with a fortune in 1805, bought a house in Wimpole Street and contested Liskeard unsuccessfully with another East India Company candidate, Joseph Childs, at the general election of 1806. He liaised with the 1st earl of Lonsdale and Sir James Graham* during the long campaign to clear the name of the Madras civil servant Robert Sherson, who in 1816 named his son Alexander Nowell Sherson in gratitude. He supported the Lowther interest, the Yellows, in Westmorland, where in February 1808 he paid £10,560 for the Underley estate, then worth £170 a year.[6] He added to it neighbouring Lowfields, Deansbiggin, Mansergh Hall and Belle View and built a Gothic mansion and racing stables, financed from his inheritance under the will of Maria Theresa (on which limited probate under £12,000 was granted on 24 May 1824) and £10,000 settled on his kinswoman Charlotte Farington of Shawe Hall, Lancashire on their marriage in April 1825.[7] His hopes of coming in that month for Carlisle, where Graham's death had produced a vacancy, were dashed by Lonsdale's preference for Sir Philip Musgrave.[8]

Possibly as a stalking horse for Sir Thomas Hesketh, Nowell was put in nomination for Lancashire at the general election of 1826, when others affiliated to the Lowthers declined to oppose the indolent Tory John Blackburn. On the hustings he stressed his Lancashire ancestry and experience in the camps and armies of India, but declined to make electoral promises. His pre-poll retirement was attributed to a reluctance to spend and to collusion.[9] The *Bolton Express* added that his supporters were lower class and very few were freeholders, and the *Blackburn Mail* that Nowell was 'unknown' and had 'neglected to declare his principles'.[10] That summer he pursued a boundary dispute with his neighbour, the Lowther Member for Cockermouth William Wilson Carus Wilson, who had been one of Blackburne's principal supporters.[11] The Lowthers blocked Nowell's candidature for Carlisle at the 1827 by-election.[12] 'Mortified' at being passed over by them for Westmorland in 1831, he stood against them as a supporter of the Grey ministry's reform bill. An agreement secured his unopposed return *in absentia* with the anti-reformer Henry Lowther.[13] Afterwards, his Whig proposer, William Crackenthorpe of Newbiggin, informed lord chancellor Brougham, who had thrice contested Westmorland unsuccessfully, that 'a gentleman who has taken very little stake in the politics of these parts, and that against the interest, which we have espoused, has by a lucky chance been returned the representative of this county with no other claim certainly than that he lives in it and has pledged himself to support that great measure'.[14] Writing to Brougham, 14 May 1831, Nowell endorsed the Lowthers' claim to one Westmorland seat and lobbied for amendment of the 1830 Beer Act's on-consumption provisions and renewal of the East India Company's charter.[15]

He was not an assiduous attender, but he divided for the reintroduced reform bill at its second reading, 6 July, consistently for its details and for its third reading, 19 Sept., and passage, 21 Sept. 1831. He voted for the second reading of the Scottish reform bill, 23 Sept., and for Lord Ebrington's confidence motion, 10 Oct. In his only reported speech, he defended the decision of the Pembrokeshire election committee, on which he sat, to recommend issuing a new writ, 26 Sept. He paired for the revised reform bill at its second reading, 17 Dec. 1831, and divided steadily for its details, 20 Jan.-5 Mar. 1832. He divided with government on the Dublin election controversy, 23 Aug., the Liverpool by-election writ, 8 Sept. 1831, and the Russian-Dutch loan, 26 Jan. 1832. Probably on account of a business visit to the East Indies, no further votes by him are recorded.[16]

Bereft of party support, Nowell did not stand for Parliament again and passed his later years in Wimpole Street and at his Yorkshire estate of Netherside, near Skipton, where he died without issue in November 1842, predeceased in January that year by his second wife.[17] His will, dated 20 July 1842 and proved under £5,000, was resworn at £7,000, 31 Oct. 1844, to take account of Indian property. He entrusted his entire estate, valued in September 1840 at £120,000, to his agent Richard Sylvester Cahill of Brighton, who, for £300 a year, finalized the sale of Underley (authorized by Nowell in agreements of 1 Dec. 1840, 20 July 1842) for £99,000 to his tenant, the Conservative Member for Westmorland, William Thompson*.[18] Nowell's niece Margaret (*d.* 21 Oct. 1861) and her issue succeeded to Netherside, Rede and his remaining property. As her husband, the Rev. Josias Robinson of Swinton-in-Craven, Yorkshire (*d.* 20 May 1843), had directed, she assumed the name and arms of Nowell by royal licence, 1 Nov. 1843, 'in order to testify her grateful and affectionate respect to the memory of her uncle'.[19]

[1] Dates relating to the purchase and sale of the Underley estate are as specified in the Underley deeds (Cumbria RO (Kendal) WD/U/Boxes 28 and 30) and correct those given in A. Pearson, *Annals of Kirkby Lonsdale and Lunedale*, 56-58, and J.D. Marshall and J.K Walton, *The Lake Counties*, 106. [2] IGI (Lancs.). [3] BL OIOC L/MIL/9/255; 10/1. [4] V.C.P. Hodson, *Officers of Bengal Army*. [5] *Gent. Mag.* (1786), ii. 996-8; PROB 11/155/249; 1686/312; *Mems. of William Hickey* ed. A. Spencer, iii. 145-6, 269-71; *E.I. Co. Dir.* 1799-1805. [6] Add. 29190, ff. 9-12; Cumbria RO (Kendal) WD/U/28/1. [7] PROB 8/217; IR26/1013/550; *Gent. Mag.* (1825), i. 365; Pearson, 56-58; W. Whellan, *Hist. Cumb. and Westmld.* (1860), 889. [8] *Carlisle Patriot*, 26 Mar., 2 Apr.; *The Times*, 28 Mar. 1825. [9] *The Times*, 30 May; *Manchester Guardian*, 3, 10, 17, 24 June; Lonsdale mss, Holmes to Lowther, 13 June, Nowell to Lonsdale, 14 June; *The Times*, 19 June 1826. [10] *Bolton Express*, 14 June; *Blackburn Mail*, 21 June 1826. [11] Cumbria RO (Kendal) WD/CAT (Addl.) A2354. [12] J.R. McQuiston, 'The Lonsdale Connection and its Defender', *Northern Hist.* xi (1975), 168. [13] Brougham mss, Nowell to John Wakefield, 1 May, J. Brougham to Atkinson, 12 May, Crackenthorpe to same, 15 May; *Wordsworth Letters* ed. A.G. Hill (1979), v (pt. 2), 384; *Westmld. Advertiser*, 7 May; Lonsdale mss, Lonsdale to Lowther, 16 May 1831. [14] Brougham mss, Crackenthorpe to Brougham, 30 May 1831. [15] Ibid. Nowell to Brougham, 14 May 1831. [16] *The Times*, 5 Oct. 1832. [17] *Gent. Mag.* (1842), i. 223; *Leeds Intelligencer*, 19 Nov. 1842. [18] PROB 11/1972/838; IR26/1622/807; Cumbria RO (Kendal) WD/U/Box 30/1; Marshall and Walton, 106. [19] PROB 11/1987/720; IR26/1654/706; *The Times*, 18 Nov. 1843, 1 Jan. 1859.

M.M.E.

NUGENT, 2nd Baron [I] *see* **GRENVILLE, George**

NUGENT, Sir George, 1st bt. (1757–1849), of Westhorpe House, Little Marlow, Bucks.

BUCKINGHAM	1790–1802
AYLESBURY	1806–1812
BUCKINGHAM	1818–1832

b. 10 June 1757, illegit. s. of Hon. Edmund Nugent† (*d.* 1771) of Gosfield, Essex.[1] *educ.* Charterhouse; R.M.A. Woolwich. *m.* 15 Nov. 1797, Maria, da. of Cortlandt Skinner, att.-gen. of New Jersey, 3s. (1 *d.v.p.*) 2da. *cr.* bt. 28 Nov. 1806; KB 1 Feb. 1813; GCB 2 Jan. 1815. *d.* 11 Mar. 1849.

MP [I] 1800.

Ensign 39 Ft. 1773; lt. 7 Ft. 1775; capt. 57 Ft. 1778, maj. 1782; lt.-col. 97 Ft. 1783, half-pay 1783-7; lt.-col. 13 Ft. 1787; a.d.c. to ld. lt. [I] 1787-9; lt.-col. 4 Drag. Gds. 1789; capt. and lt.-col. 2 Ft. Gds. 1790; col. 85 Ft. 1794; maj.-gen. 1796; command at Belfast 1798; adj.-gen [I] 1799-1801; lt.-gov. and c.-in-c. Jamaica 1801-6; lt.-gen. 1803; col. 62 Ft. 1805; col. 6 Ft. 1806; c.-in-c. India 1811-13; gen. 1813; command Bengal 1813-14; f. m. 1846.

Capt. and kpr. St. Mawes Castle 1796-*d.*

Nugent's public career was effectively ended by the death of his uncle, the 1st marquess of Buckingham, in 1813, but he transferred his allegiance to the 2nd marquess, head of the Grenvillite faction, who returned him for his borough of Buckingham in 1818. The possessor of a sinecure governorship worth £109 a year, he unsuccessfully solicited the Irish command from the Liverpool ministry in 1819.[2] He came in again for Buckingham at the general election of 1820. Nugent was a poor attender, whose only known vote in the first two sessions of the new Parliament was for Catholic relief, 28 Feb. 1821. At the Buckinghamshire quarter sessions in October 1821 he voted in the Tory majority of magistrates against placing official advertisements in the 'radical' *Buckinghamshire Chronicle*.[3] He was one of the 11 Members attached to the government in January 1822 by Buckingham, who was rewarded with a dukedom. He duly voted with ministers against more extensive tax reductions, 11, 21 Feb., and, at Buckingham's behest, against abolition of one of the joint-postmasterships, 13 Mar.;[4] but he was in the protectionist minority of 24 for a 40*s.* duty on wheat imports, 8 May 1822. The following month he presumably supported the aliens bill, as Buckingham desired.[5] His aspirations to an Irish peerage (he owned land in counties Dublin and Meath) were not favourably regarded by Buckingham, who in August 1822, when a ministerial reshuffle was in prospect after Lord Londonderry's*suicide, pressed his confidant William Fremantle* a junior member of the government, to promote Nugent's claims to the Irish command, which would 'liberate me from his and his little intriguing wife's constant worries about his impracticable and senseless peerage'. Fremantle pointed out that Nugent's rank as a general was 'now too high' for this post.[6] In January 1823 Buckingham complained to his friends that the prime minister had in some way slighted Nugent, but the matter was smoothed over by the duke's representative in the cabinet, Charles Williams Wynn.*[7] Nugent divided with government against parliamentary reform, 20 Feb., 2 June, on the sinking fund, 3 Mar., and against repeal of the Foreign Enlistment Act, 16 Apr., and inquiry into the prosecution of the Dublin Orange rioters, 22 Apr. 1823. Buckingham and his son Lord Chandos* were anxious for him to oppose Lord Cranborne's bid to relax the game laws in March 1823.[8] On 2 Feb. 1824 he presented a Buckingham petition for the abolition of slavery.[9] No recorded vote has been found for that session. His absence from the division on the opposition call for inquiry into the disturbed districts of Ireland, 11 May, which he had not considered to be 'of importance', irritated the duke; and Fremantle observed in the autumn that 'he seldom attends the House'.[10] He was a guest at the 'Stowe junket' to celebrate the baptism of Chandos's first son in June 1824.[11] His last known votes in the 1820 Parliament were for Catholic relief, 1 Mar., 21 Apr., 10 May 1825. In February 1826 Fremantle reported that Nugent 'has no reserve with me in speaking of the rash and foolish ... conduct' of Buckingham and Chandos over the former's wish to be made governor-general of India, which had alienated Lord Liverpool, and 'seems amazingly out of temper with them'.[12]

Buckingham returned him again at the 1826 general election, having told Fremantle that 'he never attends, but I cannot break his old heart and refuse him the continuance of his seat as long as he chooses to twaddle with it'.[13] He was a reluctant steward at county dinners in honour of the anti-Catholic Chandos's re-election in August, when he was amused to find himself reported in the local press to have changed his mind on the question. He helped to promote a similar gathering at Great Marlow, which lay close to his Westhorpe home, in September 1826.[14] He privately predicted that the duke of Wellington's appointment as commander-in-chief after the death of the duke of York in January 1827 would be 'very unpopular with the army'.[15] He was present to vote for Catholic relief, 6 Mar. Having paid over £1,000 for his elder son's army promotion and still seeking recovery of £1,222 owed him for timber by one William Norton, he was short of money, as he told his son-in-law Sir Thomas Fremantle* (William's nephew) when he refused to pay a share of the legal costs of drawing up the marriage settlement:

> Living up to my income, and denying myself a great many comforts, which a man of my age, who has served long in unpleasant situations and bad climates, generally requires at the close of his life, I cannot meet any extra and unforeseen expenses ... Having given as large a portion to my daughter as I could well afford, there the expense and diminution of my income must end, in justice to my other children, as well as Lady Nugent's and my own comforts.[16]

The duke made him act as chaperone to Sir Thomas when he replaced William Fremantle as Member for Buckingham in May.[17] He was asked to be prepared to 'run up' to Westminster to oppose a threatened oblique attack on Catholic claims in June 1827.[18]

That summer he went with his wife to German and Swiss spas, before wintering at Naples. He left his affairs in the hands of Sir Thomas Fremantle, who managed by means of a lawsuit to recover some of the money owed by Norton.[19] Nugent was not present to vote for Catholic relief, 12 May, but he was in the Wellington ministry's majority on the ordnance estimates, 4 July 1828. When Bernard Morland, Member for St. Mawes, fell seriously ill later that year, Buckingham, who had been abroad for 18 months, ludicrously made the 71-year-old Nugent leader of his tiny rump of personal followers in the Commons.[20] On 7 Feb. 1829 he received a letter written by Buckingham in Rome on 21 Jan. in which he expressed himself 'strongly in opposition to government', having interpreted the sudden recall of the Irish viceroy Lord Anglesey as 'drawing the sword ... against the Catholic claims'. Nugent, who was instructed to consult Buckingham's uncle Lord Grenville, assumed that the ministerial decision to concede emancipation would induce the duke to direct his Members to 'support government in every way, consistently with any line his friends took during the last session, as in the case of East Retford'. He kept Fremantle informed and, having compared notes with East, Member for Winchester, and learned that Buckingham had written favourably to Wellington, resolved that his friends must 'all meet and understand one another ... [so] that we may act together' in support of ministers. On 16 Feb. he called on Wellington as Buckingham's spokesman to assure him of the duke's support.[21] While he was perturbed by Chandos's furious opposition to emancipation and determination to promote hostile meetings in defiance of his father's wishes, Nugent assumed that once the question had been disposed of Chandos would rally to ministers and 'we may then go on smoothly together'. Anxious to keep out of the Grenvilles' family squabble and looking to the long-term welfare of the Tory interest in Buckinghamshire, he, like Fremantle, declined to attend the anti-Catholic meeting promoted by Chandos at Buckingham on 21 Feb. He told the duke's Whig brother Lord Nugent*, who wanted them to support the pro-Catholic cause, that 'in all other respects I have constantly been of what is called Tory principles' and that 'in all other political questions I should probably agree with ... [Chandos] in principles (as I think his father would also)'.[22] He voted silently for emancipation, 6,

30 Mar., and in June 1829 asked Wellington to expedite his younger son Charles's entry to the Grenadier Guards.[23] In April 1830, backed by Buckingham, he renewed his application for an Irish peerage to clear the slur of his illegitimacy, which had deprived him of his grandfather's earldom of Nugent and a large fortune. Wellington turned him down and also refused his bid for the vacant governorship of Plymouth in June 1830.[24] Nugent's only known vote in the 1830 session was against Jewish emancipation, 17 May. He was 'ordered to attend' the funeral of George IV, and 'being the senior officer was close to ... [William IV] in the procession and heard the whole of his conversation with that little chatterer Prince George'. In mid-July 1830 he expected Buckingham to be in the cabinet 'ere long'.[25]

After his return for Buckingham at the subsequent general election ministers counted him among their 'friends', and he was in their minority on the civil list, 15 Nov. 1830. On the 17th he presented a constituency petition for the abolition of slavery. At the end of 1830 he was prominent in organizing precautions at Marlow against further outbreaks of machine breaking, swearing in 'a great number of special constables' and seeking to 'assemble a mounted constabulary force of 50 men'.[26] On 19 Mar. 1831 he presented and endorsed the petition of Buckingham corporation protesting against the borough's inclusion in schedule A of the Grey ministry's reform bill, despite having a population of over 2,000. He voted against the second reading, 22 Mar., and for Gascoyne's wrecking amendment, 19 Apr., 1831, when he presented another hostile petition from Buckingham corporation. Returned for the last time for the borough at the ensuing general election, he voted against the second reading of the reintroduced reform bill, 6 July, the partial disfranchisement of Chippenham, 27 July, and the passage of the measure, 21 Sept. 1831. He was in the Tory opposition's majority against issuing the Liverpool writ, 5 Sept. He was absent from the division on the second reading of the final reform bill, 17 Dec. 1831, but divided against going into committee on it, 20 Jan., the enfranchisement of Tower Hamlets, 28 Feb., and the third reading, 22 Mar. 1832. His only other known vote was against government on the Russian-Dutch loan, 26 Jan. 1832. He retired at the dissolution following the passage of the Reform Act.

Nugent's wife died in 1834; her perceptive journals of her experiences in Jamaica and India were posthumously and privately published in 1839.[27] Nugent boasted to the Conservative prime minister Peel in 1844, when successfully soliciting a customs place for a relative, that he had 'contributed essentially' to the return for Great Marlow of his tenant Hampden in 1841.[28] He died, aged 91, at Westhorpe House in March 1849.[29] By his will, dated 29 July 1847, he created a trust fund of £10,000 for the benefit of the younger children of his sons. He left his Irish property to Charles and his Buckinghamshire estates to his elder son and successor in the baronetcy, George Edmund (1802-92).[30]

[1] His mo.'s surname was probably Fennings, the name with which he attended Charterhouse (*Oxford DNB*). [2] J.J. Sack, *The Grenvillites*, 37, 45-48; Add. 38278, f. 273; 38280, f. 53; *HP Commons, 1790-1820*, iv. 680. [3] Bucks. RO, Fremantle mss D/FR/46/9/9. [4] Ibid. 46/10/18. [5] Ibid. 46/12/77. [6] Ibid. 51/5/16; Buckingham, *Mems. Geo IV*, i. 373. [7] Sack, 197; Buckingham, i. 416. [8] Fremantle mss 46/11/78. [9] *The Times*, 25 Feb. 1824. [10] Buckingham, ii. 73-74; Fremantle mss 138/14/2. [11] *Williams Wynn Corresp*. 317. [12] Fremantle mss 138/16/18. [13] Ibid. 46/11/118; 46/12/90. [14] Ibid. 138/16/2,3,5; 138/18/12. [15] Ibid. 138/21/1/2. [16] Ibid. 138/26/13, 17. [17] Ibid. 46/9/2. [18] Ibid. 46/9/2; 138/28/5. [19] Ibid. 139/9 *passim*. [20] Sack, 216. [21] Add. 59004, f. 40; Fremantle mss 139/10/13, 14, 17; Wellington mss WP1/996/18. [22] Fremantle mss 139/10/14, 17, 21; R.W. Davis, *Political Change and Continuity*, 76. [23] Wellington mss WP1/1027/14. [24] Ibid. WP1/1107/12; 1111/22; 1120/21. [25] Fremantle mss 139/14/29. [26] Ibid. 139/14/72. [27] *Oxford DNB*. [28] Add. 40538, f. 26. [29] *Gent. Mag.* (1849), i. 540-1. [30] PROB 11/2093/376; IR26/1846/259.

D.R.F.

O'BRIEN, Sir Edward, 4th bt. (1773–1837), of Dromoland, co. Clare.

CO. CLARE 1802–1826

b. 17 Apr. 1773, 1st s. of Sir Lucius Henry O'Brien, 3rd bt., MP [I], of Dromoland and Anne, da. of Robert French, MP [I], of Monivea, co. Galway. *educ.* R. Sch. Armagh; Trinity, Dublin 1791. *m.* 12 Nov. 1799, Charlotte, da. and coh. of William Smith of Cahermoyle, co. Limerick, 5s. 7da. (3 *d.v.p.*). *suc.* fa. as 4th bt. 15 Jan. 1795. *d.* 13 Mar. 1837.
MP [I] 1795-1800.
Lt.-col. Clare militia.

Ultimately descended from the great medieval chieftain Brian Boroimhe (Boru), O'Brien's cadet branch of this ancient Clare family sprang from a younger son of Morrough O'Brien, who surrendered the kingship of Thomond to Henry VIII in 1543 and whose eldest son was the ancestor of the marquesses of Thomond.[1] As with the three former holders of his baronetcy, which had been granted to his great-great-grandfather in 1686, O'Brien, who first sat for the family borough of Ennis on succeeding to his father's extensive estates and electoral interests in 1795, represented his native county for many years.[2] According to Richard Sheil's* description of him, he was a striking Irish character who had a studied resemblance to his earliest forebear:

> He is squat, bluff and impassioned. An expression of good nature, rather than good humour, is mixed up with a certain rough consciousness of his own dignity, which in his most familiar moments he never lays aside, for the Milesian predominates in his demeanour and his royal recollections wait perpetually upon him. He is a great favourite with the people, who are attached to the descendants of the ancient indigenous families of the county and who see in Sir Edward O'Brien a good landlord as well as the representative of Brian Boru.[3]

While not sharing the exasperating piety of his wife, who busied herself with supporting local Protestant schools, he devoted himself to the promotion of his estates, the rebuilding of Dromoland and his family's parliamentary ambitions.[4]

A life-long supporter of Catholic relief and a ministerialist since 1807, he was an almost silent supporter of Lord Liverpool's Tory government, though he had occasion to resent its neglect of his demands for county patronage.[5] In 1819, when he was in conflict with the Irish secretary Charles Grant* over this, he expressed to his wife the hope that 'I shall not again have to complain of a continuance of a system which would have driven me into opposition'; and by this time he had also declared that 'London and Parliament has [*sic*] lost all of their charms for me and I now only remain in for the purpose of holding it open for my son'.[6] Relieved not to be opposed at the general election of 1820 by the childless Lord James O'Bryen (the 2nd marquess's brother and heir), he confided to his wife his delight that 'nothing is likely to interrupt the harmony that subsists between the Thomonds and our family, as each day makes it more probable that our sons will ultimately represent their house'.[7] No other challenge materialized and he was returned unopposed on his own interest with his colleague William Vesey Fitzgerald; with him, as at future elections, he co-operated over the choice of the Member for Ennis, where he occasionally served as provost.[8]

Writing en route to England, 29 Apr. 1820, O'Brien consoled his wife, who hated to be separated from him, that 'I shall either remain at home next year or take you with me and after that I shall take the matter very easy, whether I ever attend Parliament or not'. On 9 May he wrote to her that

> I am sure I shall never be able to give a close attendance in the House of Commons again. Indeed I entered it yesterday without a single feeling of either interest in the proceedings or pleasure at finding myself in a situation, the ambition of so many and the cause of such immense expense.

He was obliged to remain in London to divide with ministers that month, though on the 16th he informed his wife that, as he did not like the defence made by the lord advocate over the appointment of an additional baron of exchequer in Scotland, he had left the House before the division on this the previous night.[9] Nomination to the protracted committee on the Callington election and fears of a lengthy inquiry into the Queen Caroline affair, which he considered too sordid to merit a public airing, led him to despair of being able to return home early that summer, especially as he was again involved in negotiations with ministers over personal patronage.[10] It is unlikely that he attended the Commons in the autumn of 1820 or, having moved the loyal address to George IV at the Clare county meeting in January 1821, whether he was present during the following session, as no evidence of parliamentary activity has been traced.[11] Evidently recovering from illness, he travelled with his eldest son Lucius to Scotland that summer, but returned to Dublin for the royal visit in August 1821, when he observed that if the king failed to grant Catholic claims, 'he will disappoint very high raised hopes'.[12]

Having journeyed as far as Leicester, 28 Feb. 1822, he decided that the persistence of a cold would preclude his parliamentary attendance and so returned to Ireland. During the following two months he stayed at Dromoland, conscientiously and humanely assisting with local relief efforts, a duty which he judged to be incumbent upon him as a resident country gentleman, and corresponding with ministers about the devastating effect of the prevailing famine.[13] In the House, 29 Apr., he overcame the objections of Peel, the home secretary, to make an emotional, indeed tearful, but effective appeal for government intervention to relieve distress.[14] Perhaps dissatisfied with government's response, he divided for abolition of one of the joint-postmasterships, 2 May, but on the 8th he boasted to his wife that 'I am congratulated on all sides as being the cause of drawing public attention to the subject'.[15] He thanked the English for their generous subscriptions, 16 May, but urged further relief measures, 17 June. He spoke and voted for Newport's amendment to Hume's motion for inquiry into Irish tithes, 19 June, but sided with ministers against repeal of the salt duties, 28 June. He remained in London to help supervise the central committee's relief activities until the beginning of July 1822, when a county meeting in Clare passed resolutions thanking him for his endeavours and vindicating him from malicious charges of hoarding and profiteering.[16] At a Clare county meeting in January 1823 he moved the address congratulating the lord lieutenant, Lord Wellesley, on escaping unharmed from the Dublin theatre riot and he signed the requisition for another on agricultural distress, which he presumably attended that month.[17]

O'Brien probably missed the 1823 session as in early May Lucius, who was hoping that his father would soon fulfil his promise to relinquish his seat to him, reported to a friend that he 'has been prevented going to London hitherto by the state of his health which has been very precarious from liability to inflammation in the chest'.[18] He does not appear to have visited Westminster again until the end of May 1824, when what he described as 'a great variety of causes', including a brief attendance in Parliament, rendered a short trip necessary.[19] He was present to vote several times against the Irish unlawful societies bill in February 1825 and commented to his wife in an undated letter that month that 'I am remarkably well given the many late nights we have had'; on the 26th he noted that 'I am quite satisfied that as an independent Member I took the better line', especially as he had nothing to lose by alienating the in any case hostile Irish secretary Goulburn.[20] He divided for Catholic relief, 1 Mar., and although desperate to return home, continued to live in a very retired fashion at his lodgings for the satisfaction of doing so again, 21 Apr., 10 May, and in order to cast his vote against the second reading of the related Irish franchise bill, 26 Apr. By 11 May 1825, when he told his wife that the Catholic measure was bound to fail in the Lords, he was awaiting only the completion of the bonded corn bill to enable him to depart, and on the 14th he assured Lady O'Brien, whom he had kept informed of his efforts to secure the smooth transfer of the representation to Lucius, that 'I am heartily tired of Parliament and both hope and believe that I shall never have another session to attend'.[21]

From Dromoland, he wrote to Canning, the foreign secretary, 28 Oct. 1825, that having for the previous 20 years 'given a liberal and independent support to His Majesty's ministers', he would welcome government's endorsement of his plan to return Lucius for Clare and his second son William for Ennis at the next election:

> The politics of myself and my sons being in perfect unison with the liberal and enlightened views you have uniformly advocated both in and out of Parliament, I have thought it not unbecoming me to state these circumstances and to point out how you may attach two young *independent* men to your interest in the new Parliament.[22]

Declining to attend Daniel O'Connell's* dinner to the Friends of Civil and Religious Liberty early the following year, he emphasized his 'uniform and zealous support' for Catholic claims.[23] Electoral arrangements took him to London in the spring of 1826, though it is not clear that he participated much in the Commons: on 2 May he explained to his wife, with whom he was intending to travel abroad, that 'I do not feel the least interest in a parliamentary life and shall be glad to be released from the trouble of it', while on the 12th he recorded that 'several people in the House last night congratulated me on the prospect of our Clare election going off quietly'.[24] Once retired from public life he began a programme of drastic economies, particularly at Dromoland, and later that year he vowed to 'mortify the flesh like an anchorite' in order to restore his financial position.[25]

Although, perhaps because of his money worries, O'Brien nominated the ministerialist Thomas Frankland Lewis at Ennis, he secured the unopposed return of Lucius for Clare at the general election of 1826, and he was thanked for his exertions in their cause by the Catholics of his county at a meeting that summer.[26] On vacating Ennis and obtaining a partial refund of the sale price in April 1828, Frankland Lewis noted that O'Brien was 'not on the best credit', and the latter certainly complained of the 'considerable sacrifice' involved in bringing in William for the borough that month.[27] The new Member, who had just joined the Catholic Association, was more progressive than his father, whom he later described as being at this time 'one of the class called liberal Conservatives'; but O'Brien was proud of the advancement of both his sons and that month he related to his wife that the Commons 'is only suited to young men and I hope ours will be able to discharge their duties with credit to themselves, although I confess I am not sanguine enough to expect that either will be able to distinguish themselves'.[28] On behalf of himself and his sons, O'Brien backed Vesey Fitzgerald and condemned the activities of the Catholic agitators at the Clare by-election in June 1828. He proposed his former colleague on the hustings, but, in Sheil's words, while he 'stood aghast, Father Murphy marched into Ennis at the head of his tenantry and polled them to a man in favour of Daniel O'Connell', so provoking him to lament the breach between landlords and their freeholders; William later denied the O'Connellite charge that his father had retaliated by ejecting those who were in arrears with their rent.[29] Stressing his family's long parliamentary service and his sons' commitment to government, especially given its introduction of Catholic emancipation, he unsuccessfully applied to the prime minister, the duke of Wellington, for a peerage in March 1829.[30] Like the other leading Clare proprietors, he refused to interfere in or even attend O'Connell's re-election that summer, when the O'Gorman Mahon* wrote to his fellow prospective candidate William Macnamara* that had the latter taken the seat (in 1826), 'we should have no longer been exposed to the nausea resulting from those periodical doses, labelled with the pestle and mortar impress of concoction in the big spacious rat cage yclept House of Dromoland'.[31] Criticisms of his neglect of the state of Ennis were made at a meeting called to promote lighting it with gas, a project which he endorsed, 6 Nov. 1829.[32]

Despite a rumour that O'Brien would stand himself, he again put forward the ineffective Lucius for Clare at the general election of 1830. As provost, he oversaw William's re-election for Ennis, but illness forced his retreat from the proceedings at the county election and a few days into the poll, which Lucius lost, he was refused permission to enter the contest as a security for him.[33] This grievance was included in the election petition which he prepared, at a cost of £1,000 on top of the £800 he had already spent, although it was apparently as the result of another that the O'Gorman Mahon was unseated early the following year.[34] O'Brien, who had been actively electioneering that winter and had chaired a meeting of magistrates on the prevailing unrest in the county, 24 Feb., stood at the by-election in March 1831 as a rather grudging supporter of the Grey ministry's reform bill.[35] Despite the efforts of Lucius, who represented him on the hustings, to assert his reform principles, O'Brien, who was described by the lord lieutenant Lord Anglesey as 'a pitiful fellow', had effectively left his declared change of views too late. He was defeated by Maurice O'Connell in a short contest (which cost him another £1,000), and in a printed valedictory address he blamed his defeat on the agitation practised against him and stated that he was too old and infirm to fight further electoral battles.[36] Having reportedly refused to stake more money on the election, this defeat was thought to mark the end of the O'Briens' electoral interests in Clare.[37] Neither he nor Lucius offered for the county at the general election of 1831, when he displaced William, it was said because of his pro-reform vote, from Ennis in favour of Vesey Fitzgerald.[38] If, as was reported, it was intended to have him created Lord Dromoland that year, nothing transpired to this effect.[39] Still unwilling to put up the necessary cash, the increasingly ill-tempered O'Brien was angry when William gave up his prospects in Ennis on the eve of the 1832 general election and humiliated when, partly as a result of his own stubbornness over the representation of Ennis, Lucius was defeated in Clare at the next one. William's Liberal politics he perceived as a provocation, and in January 1835, when he was elected for county Limerick, O'Brien admitted to him that he was 'easily agitated and sometimes irritable', but quavered that he was 'too old to turn democrat'.[40]

In spite of his failing health, O'Brien more or less completed the rebuilding of Dromoland and, having predicted that year that he would expire at the same age as his father (64), he died, murmuring 'His mercy endureth forever', in March 1837, when his title and estates were inherited by Lucius.[41] According to his daughter-in-law's brother, the poet Aubrey de Vere, 'it was as an Irish chief that Sir Edward O'Brien was regarded by the masses in Old Thomond, and I have seen no other who reminded me so much of one'; he was the model for King Eochaid in his poem 'Legends of St. Patrick'. De Vere recalled that 'his stature was low and his eye of the paler Irish blue, his accost abrupt but friendly, his questions innumerable, his sympathies ready and he harboured malice against none', and observed that he 'had a great love for his country; but much of its noisier political life he regarded as more often a mixture of the game and the jest than as the serious expression of political convictions'.[42]

[1] See D. O'Brien, *Hist. of O'Briens* (1949); I. O'Brien, *O'Brien of Thomond* (1986). [2] *HP Commons, 1790-1820*, ii. 632-4; iv. 681. [3] R.L. Sheil, *Sketches of Irish Bar* (1854), ii. 288. [4] G.R. O'Brien, *These My Friends and Forebears*, 99-105, 109-10; *Recollections of Aubrey de Vere*, 77-79. [5] *O'Connell Corresp.* ii. 561; Wellington mss WP1/168/22; *Black Bk.* (1823), 180; A.P.W. Malcomson, *John Foster*, 258. [6] Add. 40296, ff. 45-46, 70-71; 40297, f. 52; NLI, Inchiquin mss T23/2970, O'Brien to wife [endorsed 1818]; 2971, same to same, 18, 20 Mar. 1819. [7] Ibid. T23/2972, O'Brien to wife, 16, 17, 21 Feb. 1820. [8] *Dublin Weekly Reg.* 12, 26 Feb., 25 Mar. 1820. [9] Inchiquin mss T23/2972. [10] Ibid. T23/2973, O'Brien to wife, 27 May, 6, 8, 13 June; 2974, same to same, 10, 24 June 1820. [11] *Dublin Weekly Reg.* 20 Jan. 1821. [12] Inchiquin mss T24/2980, O'Brien to wife, 26 July, 3, 17, 20 Aug. 1821. [13] Ibid. T20/2976, O'Brien to wife, 28 Feb., 18, 25 Mar., 11, 13 Apr.; *Dublin Evening Post*, 9 Apr. 1822; Add. 37299, ff. 74, 78, 80; 40324, f. 33; 40345, f. 222; 40346, f. 145. [14] *The Times*, 30 Apr. 1822; Sheil, ii. 288. [15] Inchiquin mss T24/2976. [16] Ibid. T24/2977; Add. 75937, Lady to Lord Spencer, 13 May; *Dublin Evening Post*, 4 June, 4, 6, 9 July 1822; K. Sheedy, *Clare Elections*, 130-3. [17] *Dublin Evening Post*, 7, 18, 30 Jan. 1823. [18] Hants RO, Calthorpe mss 26M62/F/C642. [19] Inchiquin mss T24/2978, O'Brien to wife, 27, 31 May, 2 June 1824. [20] Ibid. T24/2979; 3626. [21] Ibid. T24/3625, O'Brien to wife, 22, 23 Feb., 4, 7 Mar.; 2979, same to same, 11, 30 Mar., 27 Apr., 11, 14 May; 3626, same to same, 18, 22 Mar., 17 Apr., 6 May 1825. [22] Harewood mss WYL250/8/87. [23] *O'Connell Corresp.* iii. 1280. [24] Inchiquin mss T25/3627, O'Brien to wife, 26 Apr., 2, 6, 12, 15, 16, 18 May 1826. [25] Ibid. T25/3628, O'Brien to wife, 9, 18, 25 Nov.; 2981, same to same, 19 Dec. 1826; G.R. O'Brien, 115-17. [26] *Dublin Evening Post*, 20, 22, 29 June, 18 July 1826. [27] NLW, Harpton Court mss C/600; R. Davis, *Revolutionary Imperialist*, 24. [28] NLI, Smith O'Brien mss 449/3399; 10515 (4), Smith O'Brien to unknown, 25 Sept. 1844; Inchiquin mss T25/2982, O'Brien to wife, 9 Jan. 1827; T26/2983, same to same, 28 Apr., 2 May, 4 June 1828. [29] Inchiquin mss T26/2983, O'Brien to wife, 13, 17 June; *Clare Jnl.* 30 June, 3, 7, 10 July 1828; Sheil, ii. 283, 289; Davis, 30-32, 88-90. [30] Wellington mss WP1/1004/11. [31] *Dublin Evening Post*, 30 May, 1 Aug. 1829; D. Gwynn, *O'Gorman Mahon*, 99. [32] *Clare Jnl.* 9 Nov. 1829. [33] Ibid.

12 July, 5, 12, 16 Aug. 1830. [34] *Clare Jnl.* 30 Sept.; NLI, Stacpoole Kenny mss 18889 (15), W. to J. Macnamara, 11 Nov. 1830; Inchiquin mss T14/4893. [35] Gwynn, 121, 137; *Clare Jnl.* 28 Feb., 10, 17 Mar.; *Dublin Evening Post*, 19, 22 Mar. 1831. [36] *Clare Jnl.* 21, 24 Mar.; Derby mss 920 Der (14) 119/2, Anglesey to Smith Stanley, 27 Mar.; 121/1/2, Gosset to Earle, 26 Mar. 1831; PRO NI, Anglesey mss D619/28C, pp. 89-91; Sheedy, 832-4. [37] Stacpoole Kenny mss 18889 (16), W. to J. Macnamara, 26 Mar.; (17), same to same [23 Mar.] 1831. [38] Smith O'Brien mss 449/3398; *Clare Jnl.* 12 May 1831. [39] Davis, 55. [40] R. Sloan, *William Smith O'Brien*, 33, 40-41; Sheedy, 176-9. [41] I. O'Brien, 156-7, 196; G.R. O'Brien, 120-2; *Recollections of Aubrey de Vere*, 79-80; *Clare Jnl.* 16 Mar. 1837; *Gent. Mag.* (1837), i. 546; Inchiquin mss T18/3214/A1518. [42] *Recollections of Aubrey de Vere*, 77, 80, 357.

S.M.F.

O'BRIEN, Lucius (1800–1872).

Co. CLARE 1826–1830

Co. CLARE 1847–1852

b. 5 Dec. 1800, 1st s. of Sir Edward O'Brien*, 3rd bt., and Charlotte, da. and coh. of William Smith of Cahermoyle, co. Limerick; bro. of William Smith O'Brien*. *educ.* Welling, Kent ?1809; Harrow 1813; by Rev. Percy Scott, Harborough Magna, Warws. ?1818; Trinity Coll. Camb. 1819; Trinity, Dublin 1835. *m.* (1) 21 Feb. 1837, Mary (*d.* 26 May 1852), da. of William Fitzgerald of Adelphi, co. Clare, 1s. 5da. (2 *d.v.p.*); (2) 25 Oct. 1854, Louisa, da. of Maj. James Finucane of Ennistimon, co. Clare, 2s. 5da. *suc.* fa. as 5th bt. 13 Mar. 1837; 9th cos. 3rd mq. of Thomond [I] as 13th Bar. Inchiquin [I] 3 July 1855. *d.* 22 Mar. 1872.

Rep. peer [I] 1863-*d.*

Sheriff, co. Clare 1835-6, ld. lt. and custos rot. 1843-*d.*

O'Brien, the eldest of the nine surviving children of the Member for Clare, 1802-26, grew up in the largely unrestricted and, as his sister Harriet remembered it, happy family life at Dromoland, though he was considered the serious one of the family and another sister, Grace, once wrote that 'poor Lucius seems to be left out because he cannot or does not enter into that same union of mind'.[1] Like his next younger brother William, he was educated in England and was visited periodically during the parliamentary season by his father, who in 1813 found him 'most amiable and lovable'.[2] Sir Edward took him into the Commons, 18 May 1819, and the following day reported to his wife that Lucius, who 'was much pleased with the debate', was 'a most excellent young man and the more I see of him the more am I perfectly satisfied with both his understanding and his heart'.[3] A year later he found the studious Lucius doing well at Cambridge, where he kept himself 'rather retired from too numerous an acquaintance', and thought him set to be 'a credit and a comfort' to his parents.[4] Travelling with him on a fact-finding trip to Scotland in the summer of 1821, his father commented that he was 'a most excellent companion, sensible, intelligent and anxious to do anything in his power to meet my wishes', and that 'his character for life is already decided and I think he will improve most rapidly'.[5]

Lucius ably seconded Sir Edward's lobbying for governmental relief, both in Clare and London, during the dearth the following year and William Wilberforce*, writing to Lord Calthorpe, 23 Oct. 1822, observed that he 'seems quite filled with youthful zeal for the improvement of Ireland' and, if brought into Parliament by his father, 'I really think he will be a public blessing'. However, his intended entry into the Commons was put off, and although, as Lucius informed Calthorpe, 2 May 1823, he did 'not yet despair of being able to prevail on him to give me his seat before the next session, as he has not assigned any reason for refusing me now', he was made to wait for the dissolution.[6] He was elected a burgess of his father's tame corporation in Ennis, 24 June 1824, and later filled the office of provost.[7] Invited into the chamber to hear George Canning and Henry Brougham's speeches on the suppression of the Catholic Association, presumably on 15 Feb. 1825, Lucius was by that year designated to succeed Sir Edward, who during the passage of the bill to disfranchise the 40*s.* freeholders that spring, continually urged that he take care to preserve the family interest in their native county.[8] Amid speculation about possible challengers, Lucius, who returned to Clare with Sir Edward at the end of May 1826, was elected unopposed with the other Member, William Vesey Fitzgerald, at the general election that summer, when he declared that he would follow in his father's pro-Catholic politics.[9]

O'Brien went over to Westminster in January 1827, and the following month his father related that he 'writes highly delighted with his situation and I hope will apply himself to his parliamentary business. It will be a great source of occupation to him, as well as being the means of introducing him to the best society in England'.[10] He presented pro-Catholic petitions from his county, 21 Feb., and voted for Catholic relief, 6 Mar.[11] He divided for the duke of Clarence's annuity bill, 16 Mar. He was listed in the minority of five against the charge of treating on the Berwick election committee, which reported on the 19th.[12] He voted for Brownlow's motion for information on the Orange procession and Lisburn magistrates, 29 Mar., and Newport's for a select committee on the Irish miscellaneous estimates, 5 Apr. He was in the majority which carried the disfranchisement of Penryn against the wishes of the new prime minister, Canning, 28 May, but divided with ministers for the grant to improve water communications in Canada, 12 June 1827. He voted for repeal of the Test Acts, 26 Feb., and, after bringing up further Clare parochial petitions in their favour, 20, 28 Mar., 2 May, for Catholic claims, 12 May 1828. Having pressed his father to the step, he was delighted when his brother William Smith O'Brien was brought in for Ennis in April, though, as an almost entirely silent Member, he was quickly overshadowed by him in the House.[13] He divided in the minorities for information on civil list pensions, 20 May, and the Irish assessment of lessors bill, 12 June, but with the Wellington administration against reducing the salary of the lieutenant-general of the ordnance, 4 July. He moved the Clare writ, 12 June, and, having presumably followed his father's lead in backing the newly appointed president of the board of trade, Vesey Fitzgerald, in the ensuing contest, was said to have been entrusted with the petition against Daniel O'Connell's return the following month.[14] He signed the Irish Protestants' declaration in favour of Catholic relief in the autumn of 1828 and attended the Irish Protestants' pro-Catholic gathering in Dublin in January 1829.[15]

Early that year he was listed by Planta, the patronage secretary, as likely to be 'with government' on this, and he duly voted for emancipation, 6, 30 Mar. The Irish secretary Lord Francis Leveson Gower acknowledged his family's assistance to ministers that session, but turned down his patronage request on behalf of a relative, 17 June.[16] He had missed the division on O'Connell being allowed to take his seat, 18 May, and as this was in breach of the promise he had apparently made to recognize the validity of his colleague as a Member, he was pilloried by O'Connell at his re-election in Clare, 30 July 1829.[17] It was probably in relation to him that the O'Gorman Mahon*, who had ambitions of his own in the county, commented at that time that 'of dunces and grave-looking and dumb mutes, Clare has [had] more than enough for a century to come. Ireland requires regeneration – by none such can it be effected'.[18] An inactive ministerialist, O'Brien divided against the enfranchisement of Birmingham, Leeds and Manchester, 23 Feb. 1830. His only other known votes were for Jewish emancipation, 17 May, and against abolition of the death penalty for forgery, 7 June. He insisted that he was opposed to the increased Irish stamp and spirit duties, although he was criticized in May for failing to attend a meeting of Irish Members on this, and, unless it was his brother, he presented the hostile Clare petition, 2 July.[19] He defended his family's parliamentary seat, with government backing, at the general election of 1830, when he refused to accept pledges for tax reductions and parliamentary reform; but unlike his more progressive brother, whose return for Ennis he silently witnessed, he was defeated in the county contest by two local liberal candidates.[20] The attempt cost him, or his father, over £800, and another £1,000 was spent pursuing a petition.[21] However, on the O'Gorman Mahon being unseated, Lucius, who might have started, made way for Sir Edward to stand again for Clare at the by-election in March 1831. He spoke in favour of his absent father on the hustings, where he committed him to supporting the Grey ministry's reform bill, and shared in the subsequent ignominy of the family's electoral rout.[22]

O'Brien did not offer at the general elections of 1831 and 1832 and was defeated in 1835, but he was Protectionist Member for Clare in the 1847 Parliament. A quiet, bookish man, with a penchant for versifying and antiquarianism, he succeeded to the baronetcy in 1837 and thereafter refurbished Dromoland and improved the surrounding estates.[23] His extensive genealogical researches eventually substantiated his right to his distant cousin's Irish barony of Inchiquin, a claim which was confirmed, 11 Apr. 1862, by the House of Lords, to which he was elected the following year as a Conservative representative peer.[24] He died in March 1872, when his peerage was inherited by his eldest son, Edward Donough (1839-1900).[25]

[1] Rev. T.T. Carter, *Harriet Maunsell: A Mem.* 1-6; G.R. O'Brien, *These My Friends and Forebears*, 101-2. [2] R. Sloan, *William Smith O'Brien*, 12. [3] NLI, Inchiquin mss T23/2971. [4] Ibid. T23/2973, O'Brien to wife, 21, 25 May 1820. [5] Ibid. T24/2980, O'Brien to wife, 26 July, 3 Aug. 1821. [6] Ibid. T24/2976, O'Brien to wife, 18 Mar., 11 Apr., 8 May 1822; K. Sheedy, *Clare Elections*, 132-3; Hants RO, Calthorpe mss 26M62/F/C86, C642. [7] *PP* (1825), xxii. 214. [8] Inchiquin mss T24/3626, O'Brien to wife [Feb.], 15 July; 3625, same to same, 4, 7, 14 Mar.; 2979, same to same, 11, 30 Mar. 1825. [9] Ibid. T25/3627, O'Brien to wife, 18, 29 May; *Dublin Evening Post*, 15, 27, 29 June 1826. [10] Inchiquin mss T25/2982, O'Brien to wife, 9 Jan., 15, 19 Feb. 1827. [11] *The Times*, 22 Feb. 1827. [12] St. Deiniol's Lib. Glynne-Gladstone mss 277, Gladstone to Huskisson, 24 Mar. 1827. [13] R. Davis, *Revolutionary Imperialist*, 24. [14] Inchiquin mss T26/2983, O'Brien to wife, 13 June; *Dublin Evening Post*, 10 July 1828. [15] *Dublin Evening Mail*, 8 Oct. 1828; Davis, 33. [16] NAI, Leveson Gower letter bks. [17] NLI, Stacpoole Kenny mss 18889 (13), W. to J. Macnamara, 24 May 1829; *O'Connell Corresp.* iv. 1581, 1593, 1595, 1599; Sloan, 19-20. [18] D. Gwynn, *O'Gorman Mahon*, 100. [19] *Clare Jnl.* 17 May; *Dublin Evening Post*, 25 May 1830. [20] Leveson Gower letter bks. Leveson Gower to Hart, 7 July; *Clare Jnl.* 15, 22 July, 5, 12, 16, 19 Aug. 1830; Davis, 46-47. [21] Inchiquin mss T14/4924. [22] Derby mss 920 Der (14) 121/1/2, Gosset to Smith Stanley, 10 Mar.; *Clare Jnl.* 21, 24 Mar. 1831. [23] D. O'Brien, *Hist. of O'Briens*, 236-8; G.R. O'Brien, 127-30. [24] G.R. O'Brien, 149-50, 160, 165; *LJ*, xciv. 159-60. [25] *Clare Jnl.* 25 Mar.; *The Times*, 26 Mar. 1872.

S.M.F.

O'BRIEN *see also* **SMITH O'BRIEN**

O'CALLAGHAN, James (1743–1836), of Heighington, nr. Darlington, co. Dur.

TREGONY	1806–1812
TREGONY	1818–1826

b. 17 Oct. 1743,[1] 2nd s. of Thomas O'Callaghan of Shanbally, co. Tipperary and 1st w. Sarah, da. of John Davies of Carrickfergus, co. Antrim. *m.* (1) Hannah (*d.* 31 Mar. 1817, aged 50),[2] *s.p.*; (2) 29 Sept. 1827, Margaret, da. of Capt. James Simpson of Barnard Castle, co. Dur.,[3] *s.p. d.* 14 Feb. 1836.

Ensign 63 Ft. 1772, lt. 1775; capt. 10 Ft. 1778; capt. (half-pay) 88 Ft. 1783, ret. 1796.

Capt. co. Dur. supp. militia 1797; maj. co. Dur. militia 1805, lt.-col. 1805-16.

O'Callaghan, whose elder brother Cornelius had been created Baron Lismore in the Irish peerage in 1785, was a soldier who had fought at Bunker Hill and later served in the West Indies.[4] He was put up again for Tregony in 1820, at the age of 76, by his Durham neighbour the 3rd earl of Darlington, and he and the latter's son were returned after a contest; they survived a subsequent petition.[5] He was a silent Member who continued to vote regularly with the Whig opposition to Lord Liverpool's ministry, particularly on economy and tax cutting motions. He divided for Catholic relief, 28 Feb. 1821, 21 Apr., 10 May 1825, and parliamentary reform, 18 Apr., 9 May 1821, 20 Feb., 25 Apr. 1822, 24 Apr., 2 June 1823. He was granted three weeks' leave to attend to urgent private business, 9 Mar. 1821, and another three weeks on account of ill health, 19 Feb. 1823. Old age eventually interfered with his parliamentary attendance, and his only recorded votes in the 1824 session were for inquiry into the state of Ireland, 11 May, and proper use of Irish first fruits revenues, 25 May. He was allowed a month's leave owing to 'domestic affliction', 21 Feb. 1825. His last known vote was for repeal of the window tax, 17 May 1825. He retired at the dissolution the following year.

He married for a second time at the age of 83, and died in February 1836. One local newspaper accorded him this flowery tribute:

> He has for many years resided at Heighington, surrounded by a social and highly respectable society to which he was much attached, and by which he was greatly beloved. His conduct throughout his life was marked by the noble sentiments of a soldier, the courtesy and hospitality of a gentleman, and, above all, the real traits of a Christian. Few men have died more lamented, and none more deservedly. Long after his sepulchred remains, shrouded in general respect, shall have mouldered to the earth her due, will his memory survive embalmed in the public breast.[6]

He left all his property to his wife; his personalty was sworn under a meagre £600.[7]

[1] Lodge, *Peerage of Ireland*, vii. 245. [2] *Gent. Mag.* (1817), i. 378. [3] Ibid. (1827), ii. 365. [4] *Newcastle Jnl.* 20 Feb. 1836. [5] *West Briton*, 3, 10 Mar. 1820; Lincs. AO, Tennyson D'Eyncourt mss T d'E H108/34. [6] *Durham Chron.* 19 Feb. 1836. [7] PROB 8/229; 11/1866/503.

D.R.F.

O'CONNELL, Daniel (1775–1847), of 30 Merrion Square, Dublin and Derrynane, Iveragh, co. Kerry.[1]

CO. CLARE	5 July 1828–21 May 1829
CO. CLARE	30 July 1829–1830
CO. WATERFORD	1830–1831
CO. KERRY	1831–1832
DUBLIN	1832–31 Mar. 1836
KILKENNY	17 May 1836–1837
DUBLIN	1837–1841
CO. CORK	1841–15 May 1847

b. 6 Aug. 1775, 1st s. of Morgan O'Connell of Carhen, Cahirciveen, co. Kerry and Catherine, da. of John O'Mullane of Whitechurch, Mallow, co. Cork. *educ.* Reddington sch. Cove, Cork 1790; English Coll. St. Omer 1791, Douai 1792; Chevalier Fagan's acad. The Strand, Westminster 1793; L. Inn 1794; King's Inns 1795, called [I] 1798; G. Inn 1796. *m.* 24 July 1802, Mary, da. of Thomas O'Connell, physician, of Tralee, co. Kerry, 6s. (2 *d.v.p.*) 5da. (2 *d.v.p.*). *suc.* fa. 1809; uncle Maurice O'Connell to Derrynane 1825. *d.* 15 May 1847.

Patent of precedence [I] Oct. 1831.

Ld. mayor, Dublin 1841-2.

Gov. National Bank of Ireland 1834-*d.*

O'Connell was by far the most prominent Irishman in the Commons from February 1830, when he was finally allowed to take his seat, death having removed 'old Harry Grattan', whom he considered his country's leading man '*next to myself*', just after the general election of 1820.[2] Arguably, he was one of the greatest of all Members in this period, at least in terms of his hugely significant role in the attainment of Catholic emancipation in 1829. Yet it was not his activities in the House, early on at least, that won him lasting fame as an MP, so much as the simple fact of his election for Clare in 1828, his candidacy as a Catholic heavyweight being an act of such stupendous audacity that his triumphant victory was to signal the capitulation of the Protestant governing élite.[3] Certainly, for his ambitions were high and his reach almost unlimited (except in Ulster and the far West), he dominated Irish politics in the first half of the nineteenth century to an extent which was unmatched in Britain, save perhaps for the statesmanship of his antithesis and arch adversary Robert Peel*, with whom, for nearly four decades, he contended for the destiny of Ireland. Tall and deep-chested with a frank and good-humoured countenance, O'Connell was a physically imposing and theatrically seductive character. Bold, eloquent and committed, he was instantly recognizable as a public figure by his broad featured face, with its snub nose, wide mouth, 'potent' but 'crafty' eyes, and strong forehead, which, according to the poet Aubrey de Vere, was 'well adapted for thinking purposes, but better still, apparently, for butting against opponents or pushing his way through them'.[4] Acclaimed and beloved, by turns, as a Kerry clan chief, 'the Councillor', a national folk hero, one of the ablest of Catholic agitators, 'the Liberator', a leading advocate for repeal of the Union and 'the moral king of Ireland',[5] O'Connell had many identities. Nevertheless, his purpose was always to advance the interests of Ireland by promoting any form of legal and peaceful pressure that could be brought to bear on Parliament. Conscious since childhood that he would one day, as he put it, 'write my name on the page of history', he long envisaged a parliamentary career and, even though he had to wait till his mid-fifties to obtain a seat, it was to the Commons, ideally in some relocated and reformed version, that he looked as the summit of his hopes for the salvation of his country.[6]

Although it was in the context of listening to their reports of the parliamentary deeds of Grattan and the Patriots that the young O'Connell once startled his adult relatives by asserting that 'I'll make a stir in the world yet', his birth into a minor Catholic gentry family on the remote Iveragh peninsula was an inauspicious beginning for a would-be politician.[7] Fostered out to a peasant couple till the age of four, he was imbued with the language and traditions of the then still vibrant Gaelic culture, and ever afterwards he displayed a deep love for the common people, whose ways were second nature to him, even if he was unsentimental about the gradual abandonment of the Irish tongue.[8] Soon afterwards he left the house of his father, a farmer and storekeeper, to live at Derrynane as the adopted heir of his childless and idiosyncratic uncle Maurice, who, in a reference to the headgear which he habitually adopted in order to avoid the hat tax, was known as Hunting Cap. The head of an old established family, as well as a trader and smuggler, Hunting Cap epitomized the survival mentality of a Catholic chieftain, who, during the long era of the Penal Laws, was prepared to barter conspicuous prosperity for the comparative benefit of being left in undisturbed possession of his semi-lawless fastness. O'Connell, who retained a burning consciousness of his forebears' elevated status, undoubtedly shared his uncle's gift for pragmatism and resourcefulness, but, although for many years he had to accommodate himself to his patron's iron law, he clashed with him temperamentally, and in nothing more so than in his rejection of this characteristic Catholic form of demeaning compromise.[9] His father, a dependant junior partner in his business activities, had no influence over Hunting Cap, but O'Connell found a constant protector in another uncle, their brother Daniel Charles, Count O'Connell, who, reflecting the family's long and fruitful connections with the continent, had risen to be a general and peer in France.[10] Having been educated by the hedge-schoolmaster David Mahony and, at Reddington school, by Father James Harrington, O'Connell, who was something of a child prodigy and may at one point have been intended for the priesthood, travelled to northern France in 1791 with his brother Morgan (*d.* 1797). After a false start at Louvain, he spent ten months at the English College at St. Omer, where he was noted for his outstanding abilities, and another five at Douai, before finally escaping in January 1793 to rejoin Count O'Connell, himself an émigré in London, who installed him in a short-lived institution run by their relative Christopher Fagan.[11] The terrifying experience of fleeing republican France – he embarked at Calais on the day that the news arrived of Louis XVI's execution – never left him, and it was later said that he arrived in England 'half a Tory'.[12]

Quite the opposite picture emerges, however, from O'Connell's patchy journal, which he commenced in 1795, shortly after beginning to study at Lincoln's Inn. In it, along with accounts of his occasionally timorous misgivings and generally unadventurous activities, are mundane expressions of youthful good intentions, including the confession that 'I remain in general too long in bed' and the wish 'to get entirely rid of all propensity to falsehood'. But this private record also reveals that O'Connell, who acquired a detestation of tyranny through attending the treason trials in 1794 and found himself in the mêlée from which an attack was made on the king's coach the following year, developed an extensive radical philosophy. So much was this the case that in December 1795 Count O'Connell had to speak forcefully to him 'of my folly in being a democrat, of my absurdity in displaying my political opinions'.[13] In January 1796 he noted, after reading Mary Wollstonecraft, that 'surely the judgment of the one sex ought to be as unshackled as that of the other', and commented, of her husband William Godwin, whose principles of moral force and popular accountability he adopted as his own, that his *Inquiry Concerning Political Justice* (1793) 'has enlarged and strengthened my understanding, and infused into my mind a serenity never before enjoyed'.[14] In addition, his exposure to Deist authors, notably Thomas Paine, appears to have resulted in a profound religious crisis and the loss, temporarily at least, of the Catholic foundations of his faith.[15] Despite his Enlightenment rationalism, however, O'Connell, who was allowed to complete his qualifications by eating one term's dinners at Gray's Inn before transferring to the King's Inns in Dublin in 1796, retained an emotional patriotic streak which, at base, was an expression of what he called his 'meditative piety'.[16] His reaction to the threatened French landing at Bantry Bay in December 1796 was to exclaim that 'I love, from my heart I love, liberty ... Liberty is in my bosom less a principle than a passion'. The following month, when he rushed to enlist in the Dublin lawyers' artillery corps, he reiterated that 'I would, and I trust I will, serve man. I feel, I really feel, the sacred and mild warmth of true patriotism', adding, 'Oh, ETERNAL BEING, Thou seest the purity of my heart, the sincerity of my promises'.[17] Remarkably, O'Connell, who had attended at least one debate at Westminster (it was from Pitt, he later observed, that 'I learned to throw out the lower tones at the end of my sentences') envisaged entering the Irish Commons, in spite of the entrenched Protestant monopoly of its membership.[18] On 28 Jan. 1797 he wrote:

> I have been this day thinking on the plan to be pursued *when I come into Parliament*. If to distinguish myself was the object of my exertions that would be best done by becoming a violent oppositionist. But as it will be my chief study to serve my country, moderation will be a proper instrument for that purpose. Moderation is the character of genuine patriotism, of that patriotism which seeks for the happiness of mankind.

Having been present in the chamber, 20 Feb. 1797, he recorded that

> I too will be a Member. Young as I am, unacquainted with the ways of the world, I should not even now appear contemptible. I will steadfastly and perseveringly attach myself to the real interests of Ireland. I shall endeavour equally to avoid the profligacy of corruption and the violence of unreasonable *patriotism*. Of real patriotism moderation is the chief mark.[19]

Transposed to Westminster, such statements would not have seemed entirely out of place over 30 years later.

O'Connell, whose sojourns in London and Dublin had equipped him with the learning, debating skills and confidence required for a legal career, soon came perilously close to jeopardizing his future through a thoughtless miscalculation. Influenced by his friend Richard Newton Bennett, he, by his own confession, became briefly a member of the United Irishmen in 1798.[20] According to the probably over zealous government informer Francis Higgins, who told an implausible story about him proposing to surrender his corps' arms to the rebels, 'Connell [*sic*] ... is one of the most abominable and bloodthirsty republicans I ever heard. He is open and avowed in the most daring language'.[21] Considered to be in danger of arrest because of his association with insurrectionary elements (and the tearing out of several pages from his journal may have originated in these same fears), he left Dublin hurriedly by boat in June 1798 for Derrynane, where he spent the summer recuperating from a nearly fatal chill; he afterwards expressed his revulsion at the bloody and futile Rebellion.[22] He had been called in May that year, but did not start to practise until 1799, when he became (for a while) a freemason; he was an instant success at the bar and in 1800 he earned over £400.[23] To the disapproval of Hunting Cap, who would have preferred him to keep a low profile, O'Connell made a dramatic political debut by speaking against the proposed legislative Union with Britain at a Dublin Catholics' meeting, 13 Jan. 1800.[24] Adopting what became his habitual practice, he wrote out the heads of his speech beforehand, but, as he later recollected, 'my face glowed and my ears tingled', until he was able to get into what was to become his usual self-assured rhythm.[25] Taking the unconventional line that Irish Catholics should oppose the Union, which was intended as a prelude to emancipation, by putting their country before their religious interests, he declared that 'if the alternative were offered him of Union or the re-enactment of the penal code in all its pristine horrors ... he would prefer without hesitation the latter, as the lesser and more sufferable evil'.[26] This extravagant formulation afterwards allowed him to claim, what was largely true, that repeal was always the focus of his political opinions, even if he rose to prominence through the campaign for Catholic relief. There was no doubting his sincerity, however, as, by his own avowal, 'it was the Union which first stirred me up to come forward in politics', and, maddened by the bells of St. Patrick's Cathedral pealing it in, 1 Jan. 1801, he 'vowed, on that morning, that the foul dishonour should not last, if *I* could ever put an end to it'.[27]

As if to tempt disaster at the hands of his secretly rather admiring uncle, O'Connell contracted a clandestine and improvident marriage in 1802 with the undoubted love of his life, the Catholic daughter of his Protestant third cousin, Thomas O'Connell. Mary, who bore the trying circumstances of their early married life with quiet fortitude, quickly established herself as O'Connell's principal psychological prop, and in her roles as family manager, political wife and emotional confidante she frequently had to draw on immense reserves of patience and courage.[28] The strength of their relationship and the stability that this brought to O'Connell's hectic lifestyle can be gauged from the sometimes conflictual but always demonstrative nature of their letters, which survive in large numbers for periods, notably during the circuit, when they were apart.[29] As he wrote to her in 1809, by which time she had influenced him back into an at least nominal observance of his religion:

> Darling, if anybody were to read our *love letters* they would perhaps laugh at us, but we have the happiness to know that instead of exaggerating any feeling the difficulty is to find expressions sufficiently strong to describe those affections which we really entertain for each other. At least, sweet love, it is literally so *with me*, for from my soul I do *so* doat [*sic*] of you.[30]

For all Mary's worth, however, once Hunting Cap had been told in 1803, he disinherited O'Connell in favour of his younger brothers John (of Grenagh) and James (of Lakeview), and although the rupture was partly reversed in 1805 and their relations had been fully restored by about 1809, it had a permanent impact on his ever fraught financial situation.[31] As a flourishing barrister, O'Connell's income rose steeply in the first few years after his marriage, reaching nearly £4,000 by 1813, and from 1809, when he inherited Carhen and began to acquire other small estates, he benefited from rents of at least £2,000 a year.[32] However, he exhibited almost no control over his expenditure and was reckless in incurring liabilities, which Hunting Cap blamed on 'the softness and facility of your disposition', especially while vacationing among his own people in Iveragh.[33] As a result, he constantly lived in a frantic blizzard of unpaid bills and temporary expedients, a debilitating state of affairs which was exacerbated by the purchase of a Dublin home at 1 Westland Row in 1805 and 30 Merrion Square in 1809.

O'Connell, who condemned the pointless violence of Emmet's rebellion in 1803, when he enrolled in the Kerry yeomanry, became involved in the revived campaign against Catholic disabilities in November 1804, drafting the petition that was adopted the following year. Noted in 1806 by William Gregory, later the Irish under-secretary, to be 'impatient for emancipation, ambitious, very warm', he reacted against the inaction of the supposedly pro-Catholic Grenville administration that year by urging another petition, 17 Feb. 1807, when he was defeated by John Keogh, the Dublin merchant who led the still mostly aristocratic and conservative Catholic Committee. The following year he not only obtained approval for such a petition against Keogh's resistance, but by heading the furious opposition to the proposed royal veto over Catholic episcopal appointments he combined the people and the bishops under his banner against Grattan and other moderate pro-Catholic sympathizers.[34] He gained experience as an official at elections in Kerry and Clare, and of the technicalities of organizing petitions to Parliament, and added to his reputation in early 1810 by deputizing as secretary to the Committee.[35] He spoke successfully at a meeting of Dublin freemen and freeholders, of which he was one, 18 Sept. 1810, when he again placed wider national concerns ahead of narrow sectarian considerations to argue against the Union on the grounds of Ireland's recent economic decline and the loss of its sovereign dignity.[36] He later remarked that 'thenceforth do I date my first great *lift* in popularity. Keogh saw that I was calculated to become a leader ... The course he then recommended was a sullen quiescence. But I saw that agitation was our only available weapon'. He confirmed his predominance later that year by securing a petition and a resolution to extend the Committee's effectiveness via a rudimentary, and potentially illegal, form of national organization, and, as he afterwards boasted, thereafter 'I *was* the leader'.[37]

Making the struggle one where his professional expertise would enable him to concentrate power in his own hands, he provided legal advice to Lords Ffrench and Fingall in countering attempts by police magistrates to break up the gatherings chaired by them in February and December 1811, and that year and the next, the Irish administration having decided to suppress the Committee, he assisted as counsel in the partially successful defences made against government prosecutions.[38] He raised his profile further by publishing a pamphlet, *Historical Account of the Laws Respecting Roman Catholics* (1811), and, admitting to his wife that 'I actually *rave* upon these subjects', from this time began to speak frequently at local Catholic meetings, especially in the assize towns on his Munster circuit.[39] Increasing the political temperature, he damned the prime minister Spencer Perceval† for attempting to promote a regency limiting the powers of the supposedly sympathetic prince of Wales at a Catholic aggregate meeting in Dublin, 8 Mar. 1811, and at another, 18 June 1812, he condemned the prince (now regent), for failing to fulfil his apparent pledge to support emancipation and allowing the new premier Lord Liverpool to treat it as an 'open' cabinet question. In Limerick, 24 July, for the Catholics' county meeting, he promised to stand for the borough in order to open its corporation if the current Catholic relief bill passed, and at a like gathering in county Dublin, 14 Nov. 1812, he hailed the success of pro-Catholic candidates at the recent general election.[40] Settled in his own opinions, he reacted angrily against Grattan's relief bill of 1813 and, by his categorical resistance to the quite mild ecclesiastical securities proposed in it, he ruthlessly provoked the secession of most of the older generation of supporters of upper class origin from the short-lived Catholic Board (1812-14), 29 May. Keeping up the pressure for petitions to the Commons, he set out his programme for popular, but peaceful and constitutional, agitation in favour of Catholic claims, 15 June 1813.[41]

Confirmation of O'Connell's role as the Catholic champion emerged in three adversarial arenas. In 1813 he was a defence barrister in the highly contentious political trial of John Magee, the Protestant proprietor of the pro-Catholic *Dublin Evening Post*, who was alleged to have printed a seditious libel on the duke of Richmond, the retiring lord lieutenant. His speech on behalf of Magee, 27 July, was an unprecedented exercise in sustained insolence and bitter invective and, in printed form, it achieved high notoriety. In it he treated the lord chief justice William Downes with defiance, demolished the Irish attorney-general, the much hated Orangeman William Saurin, who was prosecuting, with a devastating personal attack, and provided the jurors and other Protestant auditors with a wholesale indictment of the entire system of Ascendancy discrimination against the majority Catholic population. Peel, the Irish secretary, who on 29 May had been described by O'Connell as 'Orange Peel', 'a raw youth, squeezed out of the workings of I know not what factory in England', commented that in his four-hour declamation, O'Connell had taken the 'opportunity of uttering a libel even more atrocious than that which he proposed to defend'.[42] At numerous Catholic meetings the following year he maintained a rigid hostility to securities, including by his famous pronouncement against papal approval for the veto that 'I would as soon take my politics from Constantinople as from Rome', and in January 1815, when he declared that 'I am sincerely a Catholic but I am not a Papist', he defeated the attempt by his rising professional rival Richard Sheil* to promote a petition for relief accompanied by securities.[43] His own petition for unqualified emancipation found no favour with Grattan and his parliamentary friends, but by at that time forming a Catholic Association, a forerunner of the more famous organization of the same name, O'Connell had effectively seized control of the Catholic lobby in Ireland.[44] That year O'Connell, who was sensitive to charges of having hitherto avoided the duelling ground, was required to defend himself with arms. On 1 Feb. he fought John Norcot D'Esterre, a publicity seeking Dublin common councillor and rabid Orangeman, who objected to O'Connell's description of his corporation as 'beggarly'; D'Esterre died of his wound, and O'Connell, who was privately filled with remorse, was hailed as a hero. Later that summer, having chosen to take exception to Peel's critical comments on him in May, especially as having been made under the protective cover of parliamentary privilege, he provoked a challenge from him; but somewhat farcically, given the elaborate preparations that were made, the duel was never allowed to come off since first Mrs. O'Connell alerted the authorities in Dublin and then O'Connell was apprehended in London on his way to meet Peel abroad. These experiences influenced him strongly in favour of adhering to the growing humanitarian trend away from the practice of duelling, even though his refusal to honour challenges (his second son Morgan O'Connell† sometimes substituted for him) was criticized as ungentlemanly by his political opponents.[45]

By the mid-1810s O'Connell had become the acknowledged head of his co-religionists in Ireland. Employing his maxim of 'being always in the right', he had displaced their 'natural leaders', who symbolized mutual jealousies and disunity, and, by politicizing the bishops and promoting the aspirations of middle class professional Catholics like himself, he had brought the grievances of his fellow countrymen into the mainstream of British politics.[46] In doing so he developed coherent religious, nationalist and radical philosophies, which would continue to be the basis of his campaigns in the cause of Irish liberty.[47] Aptly summarizing his ideological views, he stated at a dinner held for him in Tralee, 24 Oct. 1817, that 'my political creed is short and simple: it consists in believing that all men are entitled, as of right and justice, to religious and civil liberty'.[48] In terms of religion, O'Connell's Catholic faith, for by now (possibly confirmed by some sort of 'conversion' experience in 1816) he had become genuinely devout, lay at the heart of his political thought; he had unequivocally identified himself with Catholic interests since at least 1813.[49] Yet he always insisted that he neither wished to deny the beliefs of others, appealing rather for perfect freedom of religious conscience, nor to create a Catholic ascendancy, arguing instead for the total separation of church and state, while he also, without ever alienating Rome, opposed the temporal powers of the papacy.[50] Following from this, and as part of his instinctively territorial conception of Irishness, O'Connell had an inclusive notion of nationality, which would naturally embrace participation by moderate members of other denominations. His constant appeals for co-operation by liberal Protestants, as well as the example of his personal friendship with and employment of them, were meant to be (and were) sincere; but inevitably the weight of unresponsiveness increasingly influenced his thinking in the direction of a more exclusively Catholic sense of nationhood so that, for example, in July 1826 he proffered the definition that 'the Catholic people of Ireland are a nation'.[51] As it had been since 1800, the focus of this quasi-nationalist sentiment was repeal of the Union, although he was careful never quite to commit himself to what this might mean in practice. Indeed, he relied on it more as a slogan to encapsulate his demand for Ireland to be accorded equal treatment within the United Kingdom, to which he could then add his repeated taunt that government neglect of Catholic grievances, such as those against the Orange Order, would only strengthen the attractiveness of his position.[52] However, just as O'Connell's advocacy of repeal fell short of any desire for separation or independence from Britain, so his radicalism never encompassed republicanism, a fondness for monarchy being part of the eighteenth-century hangover in his political make-up.[53] But in contemplating the restoration of an Irish Parliament, he envisaged the kind of reforms, such as the abolition of nomination boroughs or the introduction of the ballot, which marked him out as an advanced liberal on the English model; unsurprisingly, perhaps, he and his counterparts across the Irish Sea found it practically impossible to work together.[54] In other respects, his radicalism amounted to an amalgam of Godwinite universalism, which involved the extension of civil rights to Jews, slaves and women as well as the encouragement of democratic movements overseas, and Benthamite Utilitarianism, which, except for his professional interest in the adoption of a legal code, was enthusiastically ethical rather than narrowly doctrinal in character.[55] A paternalist landlord and social conservative, he espoused a strict interpretation of *laissez faire* economics, which, in his disapproval of the restrictions placed on entry to trade guilds (he was not against unions as such) occasionally brought him into conflict with his working class constituency.[56]

In relentlessly restating his ideas and arguments, O'Connell, whose *modus operandi* seems to have been that by simply declaring his desires often enough he would will into existence the overwhelming public support required to obtain them, helped to raise Catholic assertiveness to a new level.[57] Despite the distinctly unpromising circumstances of the mid-1810s, in other respects he was assisted by the comparative openness of the Catholic masses to millenarian enthusiasm and their already increasing tendency towards greater sociability, including participation in political forms of organization.[58] He personified the strength of this enhanced self-belief and in defending Catholic interests he identified himself personally with his followers, so that, as Balzac put it, he 'incarnated a whole people'.[59] In appearance and style, he ably filled the part of a popular leader: a bear of a man, although he struggled against his increasing corpulence and hid his baldness beneath a black wig, his robust health, boundless vitality and aggressive self-confidence inspired great loyalty.[60] Unceasingly industrious ('activity is with me a habit', he once said), he usually rose early and stayed up late in order to work, while the middle of his days were spent at the Four Courts and his late afternoons at political meetings or dinners.[61] Even on holiday in Iveragh, he gave most of his time to studying or correspondence and on those days that he did devote to his favourite pastime, hunting on foot with dogs, he still devoured the newspapers and dispensed summary justice among his tenants.[62] Visible and accessible, he was attended by a hoard of admirers during his swaggering daily march through the Dublin streets and, perhaps indicating his penchant for martial airs and dress as well as a studied insolence of manner, it was said of him that 'there was sedition in his very walk'.[63] Deemed (in the composite article written by Sheil and Curran) to have infused an 'intensely national sensibility' into all he did and to be 'the most competent barrister at the Irish bar', where as a Catholic he was not permitted to take silk, he benefited from the most amazing popular reputation as 'the Councillor'. This was due partly to his meticulous care and versatile fluency in court, though he could not always stifle a temptation to flippancy and was sometimes just too voluble. But more especially it arose from his genius at cross-examination (with his intuitive understanding of the Irish character, he boasted that he could break any witness's testimony within five minutes) and his skill in winning over the most hostile of juries.[64] Even if his clients were often Protestants, his renown grew from the perception that he was unrivalled in defending Catholics from discriminatory prosecutions, and, as John Mitchel, the Young Irelander, later observed, in a wider sense, 'O'Connell took all Ireland as his client'.[65] Peel once paid him an unlikely backhanded compliment by remarking that, 'if I wanted an efficient and eloquent advocate, I would gladly give up all the other orators providing I had with me this broguing Irish fellow'.[66]

Speaking in court, O'Connell was usually sensible and workmanlike, but at public meetings his oratory more closely reflected his cerebral and corporeal strengths, being powerful, spontaneous, lucid and provocative, as well as frequently rough, vigorous and irregular, but nonetheless masterful and compelling. Commentators agreed that his success lay in the beautiful sonority of his voice, the honest directness of his appeal and the moving vivacity of his style, his face seeming to reflect every inspired emotional impulse of his passing thoughts.[67] As the French visitor Prosper Duvergier de Hauranne observed:

> *Avec lui, on sent la pensée naître et se développer; on la voit, pour ainsi dire, se revêtir d'une forme sensible; et les mots, les gestes, l'accent, tout se produit à la fois et par un seul effort. Il menace, et son corps entier semble suivre le défi qu'il lance à Angleterre; il plaisante, et avant que la plaisanterie soit sur ses lèvres, une gaîté expansive anime déjà ses traits. Je ne connais pas d'orateur qui donne autant l'idée d'une profonde conviction.*[68]

More critically, Lord Teignmouth judged that

> he seemed to converse aloud. He hesitated occasionally, but as his pauses invariably preluded the word best adapted to convey his meaning, it was shrewdly suspected that he employed them to conceal the study of his diction ... He would sometimes, when he deemed himself bound to exhibit more warmth than he really felt, act his part by impassioned grimace, bitter language and the convenient trick of twisting his wig. But it would be a mistake to suppose that O'Connell always elaborated in his speeches. On the contrary he was often evidently unprepared, rambling on, sometimes discursively, in his own easy way, so that his audience would have been wearied but for his occasional bursts of eloquence, flashes of wit, tart replies and keen sarcasms.[69]

Compared favourably with the shrill niceties of Sheil's measured delivery, O'Connell's effectiveness at mass meetings was undoubted: one old farmer commented that his 'voice you'd hear a mile off, and it sounded as if it was coming through honey'.[70] The parliamentary reporter Samuel Carter Hall remembered that at such a pre-emancipation gathering in Kerry, 'I was not near enough to hear what he said, but I could note how he was "rollicking" – in words; and for him how easy it would have been to evoke an appalling storm!'[71] It was this tremendous demagoguery that made him so potent a folk hero in long-surviving Irish oral tradition. There were several other elements to this – the supposedly miraculous circumstances of his birth, the evidence of his youthful brilliance and the premonitions of his greatness, as well as the mythical stories of his astonishing sexual prowess and his superhuman ability to cheat death – but at base his genius was perceived to lie in his private and professional gift of the gab, in his verbal trickery and guile, his silver-tongued ingenuity, his wit and repartee and, above all, in his courageous vocal championing of the downtrodden native Irish.[72] This process of developing a cult of personality, which began early in his career, was also reflected in the self-conscious manipulation of his own portraiture, by which the fresh-faced barrister of the *Dublin Magazine*'s image in 1813 was turned into John Gubbins's carefully crafted representation of 'the Catholic leader' a decade later.[73]

By contrast, contemporary caricaturists, in their crude and anti-Catholic cartoons, seized on O'Connell's negative qualities, from which there was much political capital to be made.[74] Although occasionally intemperate in his otherwise loving family life and mostly given to treating men with a kind and easy charm, he was known to be excessively rancorous in his political hatreds and in speaking he readily resorted to commonplace personal abuse, even of his supposed allies.[75] Aware of this handicap, he once blustered that 'it was not *irritation*, it was *calculation*', meaning that, by provoking and ridiculing his enemies or rivals, he aimed to deflate their pomposity and undermine their apparent invincibility.[76] One constant insult, although he always rejected later offers of official employment, was the charge that he was a 'trading politician', causing trouble only in order to raise his own price. Being in the habit of saying that he was 'the best-abused man in the British dominions', he claimed not to mind such scurrilous attacks, which often came from hostile newspapers, since 'I knew the scoundrels were only *advertising* me by their abuse'.[77] Nevertheless, he alienated many in the political establishment with his hyperbole, superiority and vanity, and most damaging of all was the general perception of his characteristic disingenuousness or dishonesty. At one level this merely amounted to harmless hypocrisy: after being praised by O'Connell for his *Sheridan*, which the writer knew O'Connell had privately criticized, Tom Moore noted the occasion in his journal as 'a signal instance of that inconsistency for which he is so remarkable'.[78] At another level, however, his artful mendacity disgusted potential friends and disaffected long-standing allies. On the eve of his admission to Parliament, it struck the Westminster radical Whig John Cam Hobhouse* that O'Connell, who had shaken hands with William Cobbett† after describing him as a scoundrel, was 'a strange compound and did not know his station', on hearing which the English Catholic leaders the duke of Norfolk and Edward Blount* exclaimed, 'What, you found that out only now?'[79] Perhaps most observers, giving him credit for his talents, overlooked this trait as a carryover from the typical Kerryman's doublespeak, the complex mentality of being deliberately evasive in the public sphere of English overlordship while utterly forthright in the private circles of Catholic solidarity.[80] Certainly, it was naive of liberal minded statesmen to suppose, after hearing him ooze conciliation in their drawing rooms, that he would not go out to continue breathing fire in meetings and newsprint. In addition, such pragmatism seems to have been a product of his tactical legal brain. Just as every case drew forth his narrow concentration on obtaining a favourable verdict, so each day's pressing issue forced him into pragmatic short term measures, whether that of unfairly quashing conflicting opinions or of temporarily justifying himself by a breathtaking sleight of hand.[81] In some ways, what was surprising about O'Connell was not this streak of essential realism but the uniformity of his long term strategies, and yet the weaknesses in his personality rendered him vulnerable throughout his career.[82]

Never was this more true than in his personal nadir of 1816-17, when he might easily have disappeared from public life. The initial disaster was the long feared bankruptcy in 1816 of the Killarney merchant James O'Leary, for whom O'Connell, against the warnings of Hunting Cap, had given security for up to £8,000. O'Connell was only saved from consequential insolvency, and the likelihood of being again disinherited, by his brother James, who, risking his own financial and family standing, masterminded a rescue package and managed to keep their uncle in ignorance of the whole episode. Nevertheless, within a year James was estimating that O'Connell's debts amounted to over £20,000 and that the necessary interest payments could only be met by sizeable economies, even though his brother's legal income was on average at least £5,000 per annum.[83] One consequence was that Mrs. O'Connell, who was devastated by the loss of trust implicit in her husband's secret involvement with O'Leary, was dispatched with her children to live cheaply in England, on the pretext of her recent ill health. Alone in Dublin at this time, it is possible to speculate that O'Connell may have been unfaithful, although, apart from jealous hints made by Mary to her probably innocent husband about his later visits (in 1823) to their daughters' governess, Mary Jane Gaghran, there is no evidence of any such indiscretions.[84] Ellen Courtenay's story (later published as a political smear) that in early 1817 O'Connell inveigled her into making repeated visits to the largely empty house in Merrion Square in order to seduce her, may not have been wholly implausible. However, the allegation that he raped her, that 'he sunk the man in the brutality of the monster', as she put it, is impossible to verify. Moreover, her account is so full of inconsistencies, including a claim that the son (Henry Simpson) supposedly resulting from their liaison was born on 4 Nov. 1818 (unless this was a misprint for 1817), that her version has usually been dismissed as a fantasy or an unsuccessful blackmail attempt.[85] Inasmuch as her case appeared to fit the popular tradition of O'Connell as a womaniser, it has come to be accepted that this was a stereotypical folkloric attribute and hence meaningless in its application to any historical individual. Most tellingly of all, the O'Connells' openly loving relationship continued throughout their marriage and any persistent infidelity on his part would appear to have been inconceivable. Nevertheless, one historian has suggested that such a close bond between them may not have prevented O'Connell from being unfaithful and that Mary's letter to him from Clifton, 14 July 1817 (including her statement that '*We* will, love, shortly be married 15 years and I can answer that I never had cause to regret it. I have, darling, experienced all the happiness of the married state without feeling any of *its* misery'), which is usually cited as evidence of her unquestioning affection for him, could be read, in its pleading to be allowed to return to his side rather than to have to move to France, as a sign of tension possibly relating to some undisclosed marital crisis.[86] Whatever the real truth of this affair, O'Connell's unending money troubles, including the unwise pre-emption of his long-lived uncle's wealth and an unfortunate reduction of his landed rentals, remained a destabilizing factor in his marriage, and the enforced but largely futile retrenchment exercise of having his family reside at various places in France and at Southampton in the early 1820s marked another low point in the couple's relationship.[87]

O'Connell, who in September 1817 felt that Ireland was 'most wretched – fever – poverty – party spirit and *want of animation*', showed great persistence: he continued to oppose securities through what was reconstituted that year as another Catholic Board. The following year, referring to agitation against the window tax, he commented that this '*little Parliament* is of infinite value and will habituate the people to form an organ to express the public sentiment on affairs of greater moment'.[88] In a fit of wild optimism during the winter of 1818, he vowed that 'if I petition alone, I *will* petition' for the claims of the Catholics, and wrote the first of his series of new year letters addressed to them, 1 Jan. 1819, which was designed, he recorded, solely 'to show that it was possible to call the Catholics together without introducing one irrelevant or irritating topic'.[89] He was instrumental in persuading Thomas McKenny, the lord mayor, to hold a full-scale pro-Catholic meeting of Dublin Protestants in February 1819, which brought him back into contact with Grattan, one of the city's Members; following the failure of Grattan's relief bill that year, he again pressed for a petition to be arranged.[90] Forever attempting to find other avenues through which to raise his popularity, he took a growing interest in the controversial subject of education, dramatically resigning as a member of the Kildare Place Society in February 1820 to protest against the inability of Catholics to control their children's religious studies.[91] He was active at the general election that spring, including as agent to William Wrixon* in Mallow, and during the Dublin by-election in June he eulogized the deceased Grattan and supported the candidacy of his son and namesake (Henry Grattan II*).[92] He addressed the Spanish American freedom fighter Simon Bolivar, whose title of 'the Liberator' he borrowed, 'in the cause of liberty and national independence' in April, on sending his son Morgan to fight for him in the Irish legion. Displaying his unquenchable appetite for institutional innovations, the following month he suggested the foundation of a Society for Parliamentary Information, but nothing came of it.[93] In July he offered to stand as recorder of Limerick in place of Henry D'Esterre, his victim's brother, who had been censured in the borough election report, though no vacancy in fact arose.[94] He sought an appointment as Irish attorney-general to Queen Caroline, whose cause he advocated at the officially dispersed county Dublin meeting in December 1820, but his application was ultimately stifled by her English law officers, Henry Brougham* and Thomas Denman*.[95] Vexed by his lack of progress, he used his annual address, 1 Jan. 1821, to advocate parliamentary reform, declaring that 'an unreformed Parliament will not grant us relief' and that it was 'worse than useless to petition a Parliament of *virtual* representatives for liberty'; Sheil, who rejected giving priority to reform over relief, delivered a ferocious public riposte, to which he replied in kind, and William Conyngham Plunket*, who had taken over Grattan's mantle as Commons spokesman for the Catholics, privately damned him as a revolutionary.[96] Exasperated by the restrictions in Plunket's proposed relief measure that session, which was defeated in the Lords, he repeated his frequently made call for Catholic unity in April 1821, contending that 'even the vetoists must admit that *securities* do no good because we are kicked out as unceremoniously with them as without them'.[97]

O'Connell, who was obsequious in leading the Catholic deputation to George IV during the 'conciliation' visit in August 1821 and effusive in welcoming the appointment of the pro-Catholic Lord Wellesley as lord lieutenant in January 1822, remained utterly undaunted by the task of winning emancipation, telling a new acquaintance that year: 'no matter; we will persevere and no doubt we shall one day or other carry it'.[98] His prospects began to look brighter as Plunket, the new Irish attorney-general, seemed willing to compromise over securities, and Wellesley, who invited him to the Castle, held out the prospect of restraining the Orangemen, but he failed to persuade the former to introduce another relief bill that session and his high-handed public letter calling on the latter to prevent the dressing of the Dublin statue of William III in Orange colours in July had a counterproductive effect.[99] Calling the Orange theatre attack against Wellesley, 14 Dec. 1822, providential for the future of the Catholics, he presented their loyal address to him that month, as he did one from Kerry in January 1823, when he imagined that, with peaceful pressure rendering emancipation imminent, he might soon be able to take silk and even enter Parliament. He canvassed prominently for the pro-Catholic Henry White in his successful bid to represent county Dublin in February and the following month he confided to his wife from Tralee the 'secret that I have already commenced my canvass to represent this county', since, if the Catholics were emancipated, there would be 'little doubt of my getting into Parliament if I choose'.[100] Buoyed by these advances, in April he and Sheil, with whom he had become reconciled earlier in the year, mustered the Catholics for an aggregate meeting, 10 May, when his resolution for the establishment of the Catholic Association was adopted. It met for the first time, 12 May, and moved into rooms above a Catholic bookshop at 4 Capel Street, 13 May 1823.[101]

Sidelining aristocratic figures like Lord Killeen* and Sir Edward Bellew and keeping such extremists as Eneas MacDonnell and Jack Lawless firmly in their place, O'Connell quickly put his stamp on the Association, which he dominated from the start.[102] Boasting to his wife in May 1823 that he had secured the admission of Protestants as members of what his detractors immediately dubbed the 'Popish Parliament', he showed that he was himself comfortable with mimicking this nomenclature by joking that, 'you see, we have in our little Parliament set the Protestants a good example' in theirs.[103] Much more than simply a vehicle for forwarding petitions for general relief, the Association's aim, O'Connell declared, was not to force on the Commons the annual farce of a debate on Catholic claims, but to agitate all Catholic grievances, including by seeking redress via the right to petition on specific matters. In innumerable speeches, he therefore advocated the appointment of a Catholic chaplain at Dublin's Newgate gaol, impartiality in the administration of justice, alteration of church rates, enforcement of the law against disorderly Orange processions, provision of Catholic burial grounds, commutation of tithes and the opening of Protestant corporations.[104] By carrying his suggestion for the free admission as members of all Catholic priests in June, he provided himself with a ready made national organization. Early in 1824, when he contemplated petitioning for relief and attending the Commons as counsel in support of it and other matters, he pushed through the incredibly dynamic innovation of the 'Catholic rent'.[105] Within a few months this had created a massive second tier of members, each contributing a penny a month to the Association's central funds. As he set out in February in his visionary report on the 'rent' scheme, of which he became the secretary, the expected income of £50,000 a year would be used mainly to fund legal aid for Catholics and support for sympathetic newspapers, as well as for education of the poor, provision of priests for America, church and school buildings, and the expenses of parliamentary lobbying.[106] All of these furnished useful propaganda, but in terms of getting his own message across the most important was his granting of limited subsidies to friendly papers and his fostering of at least intermittently good relations with Michael Staunton of the *Morning Register* (while Richard Barratt, who took over the *Pilot* in 1828, was more loyal).[107] Only about £20,000 was raised in the first year of operation, but the 'rent' had a profound effect in radicalizing the Catholic population, whose demands, through the return of 'grievance letters', could now be channelled back to the Association, so giving it a kind of quasi-representative legitimacy. From November 1824, when it began to use a chamber with two sets of facing benches in the Corn Exchange on Burgh Quay, the conscious imitation of the Westminster model became even more marked. As von Pückler-Muskau recorded (in November 1828):

> The room is not very large, and [is] as dirty as the English House of Commons. Here too every man keeps his hat on, except while he is speaking; here too are good and bad orators, but certainly occasionally less dignified manners than there. The heat was suffocating and I had to sit out five hours, but the debate was so interesting that I scarcely remarked the annoyances. O'Connell was undoubtedly the best speaker. Although idolized by the greater number, he was severely attacked by several, and defended himself with equal address and moderation; on the other hand he assailed the government without reserve, and in my opinion in too strong expressions. It was easy to perceive that much intrigue and several firmly united parties, whose minds were made up beforehand, were to be found here, as in other bodies of the like kind, and consequently that the discussion was often only a sort of sham fight.[108]

For all that the Association was O'Connell's power base, it consumed much of his energy and time, although, in having to sit through painfully tedious and callow harangues, he was at least preparing himself for the drudgery and futility of much of Westminster politics.[109]

O'Connell, who at the Dublin dinner in his honour on 3 July 1824 had promised to continue his 'intemperate' struggle on behalf of the Catholics, was now, for all that his violence estranged the moderate minority among them, pre-eminent in their cause.[110] Yet his position was far from invulnerable. Later that year the anxious administration decided to suppress the Association and its head, who had begun a new round of agitation that month, was arrested for using seditious language, 20 Dec. 1824, having four days earlier declared that 'if Parliament will not attend to the Roman Catholic claims, I hope that some Bolivar will arise to vindicate their rights'. Peel, the home secretary, was determined to prosecute, but the king pointed out the inconsistency of punishing him for holding up 'the conduct of Bolivar to the imitation of the people of Ireland, at the very moment at which we are going to make a treaty with Bolivar', to recognize his authority in the newly independent Columbia. Plunket's indictment was in any case thrown out, 3 Jan. 1825, but the affair delayed that session's parliamentary lobby, which concerned O'Connell because of its likely expense and his concomitant loss of legal earnings.[111] The death of the 97-year-old Hunting Cap, 10 Feb., at last brought him security in the form of Derrynane, but his spendthrift habits only increased, so, despite receiving a third share of his uncle's personalty of about £45,000, his dangerously exposed financial situation remained much the same.[112] That month he left Dublin with the members of the Catholic deputation, who, as he confidently informed his wife, would create a sensation by making 'speeches *at* those who speak against us in Parliament'.[113] His motives were distrusted by most of them, however, and Sheil, who described him as a 'political opium-eater', intoxicated by his own mob oratory in Ireland, recounted that he 'seemed half English at Shrewsbury' and in London succumbed to the blandishments of the Whig and Catholic grandees who fêted him during his stay. Regarded by most English politicians as a dangerous incendiary, he was stared at as a curiosity on his appearing in the Commons, with the quality of whose debates he was less than impressed, on 18 Feb., when Brougham failed to obtain permission for him to speak as counsel against the Irish unlawful societies bill, and again on 1 Mar., when he attended for Burdett's Catholic relief motion.[114] He improved his political reputation by his respectful, if occasionally fiery, performances before the select committees on the state of Ireland in the Commons, 25 Feb., 1, 4 Mar., and the Lords, 9, 11 Mar., although his disavowal of the utility of the 40*s*. franchise would soon rebound upon him in Dublin.[115] (The unnecessary misunderstanding that arose over the apology which he made to Peel, about their former quarrel, the following month showed the impossibility of pleasing both his Irish supporters and his English contacts.)[116] Delighted by the constant attention lavished on him at meetings in the City, of which he became a liveryman, and elsewhere, as well as at dinners in high society, where he won plaudits, he was convinced that opinion was moving in favour of emancipation, even among Members; admitting his vanity, he boasted to Mary that 'I have not the least fear of being *looked down on* in Parliament'. In the course of numerous conferences and by a steady attendance at Westminster, he joined the principal Whigs in drafting and promoting a Catholic bill, whose promising prospects were destroyed by the duke of York and Liverpool's opposition to it in the Lords in May.[117] The failed gamble of giving a pragmatic endorsement to the measure's two 'wings', state payment of the Catholic clergy and disfranchisement of the 40*s*. freeholders, earned him scathing rebukes from English radicals like Cobbett and damaging condemnation from extremists and rivals in Ireland, which for a while looked likely to overwhelm him.[118]

However, even before leaving London in late May 1825 he envisaged the setting up of a nominal 'New' Catholic Association to evade the provisions of what he called the 'Algerine Act', under which the old one had been suppressed, and this was done in July, effectively as a non-political version of the same organization. That autumn he fought a rearguard action to reassert his authority over the movement, shrewdly backpedalling over his support for the 'wings', for example at provincial meetings in Limerick, 24 Oct., and Carlow, 15 Dec. 1825.[119] In January 1826 he held a 14-day meeting of the Association, the maximum duration for which it could be temporarily reconstituted for political purposes, and he organized a high profile dinner in honour of the Protestant friends of religious liberty, 2 Feb.[120] A petition in his own name, alleging the incompetence of the aged and deaf chief justice of common pleas in Ireland, Lord Norbury, who had long been his *bête noire*, was presented by James Scarlett, 5 May.[121] Active and influential in several counties during the general election that summer, he spent most of his time campaigning prominently in county Waterford, where Thomas Wyse* engineered the tenants' revolt which led, with the support of the priesthood, to the anti-Catholic magnate Lord George Beresford* being defeated by his liberal Protestant challenger Henry Villiers Stuart. O'Connell was nominated as a candidate in order to speak on the hustings, and, according to Wyse, he might himself have been elected had he not withdrawn, as previously arranged.[122] Keeping just ahead of his supporters in recognizing the potential of the 40*s*. freeholders as a devastating electoral force, he now abandoned his former indifference to them and, in his letter to the Catholics of Ireland, 10 July, he proposed the resuscitation of the 'rent' to form a relief fund for evicted or browbeaten voters. That month he also created the Order of Liberators, a uniformed quasi-military corps of proven Catholic agitators, of which he became the president; the first of its members were installed in Waterford, 30 Aug. 1826, when he spoke at the Munster provincial meeting.[123] His mastery re-established, he was watched warily by the administration, though Henry Goulburn*, the Irish secretary, reported to Peel that 'I apprehend his policy to be to keep up irritation and hostility to the highest possible pitch short of actual violence, and to hope by intimidation to carry everything he looks for'.[124] The journalist Henry Crabb Robinson, who visited him in his fiefdom that month, thought O'Connell 'vehement – all but seditious' in his language in Waterford, but recorded him as saying in conversation that 'I never allow myself to ask whether an insurrection would be right, if it could be successful, for I am sure it would fail'.[125] Yet by the turn of the year he was ever more convinced, Wellesley's policy being merely 'calculated to cajole and tranquillize the Catholic population by a partial redress of their grievances', that '*temperateness*, *moderation* and *conciliation* are suited only to perpetuate our degradation', whereas what was needed was to 'rouse in Ireland a spirit of *action*' in favour of unqualified emancipation.[126]

Yet Liverpool's incapacitation early in 1827 encouraged O'Connell to hope for concessions from a potentially more sympathetic prime minister. In public speeches and private letters, mostly to his friend the knight of Kerry*, he urged Lord Lansdowne to come forward with the moderate Whigs or at least to join the pro-Catholic foreign secretary George Canning* in his protracted attempts to form an administration that spring. Having threatened Irish ministerialists with being deemed enemies if they backed Peel, the duke of Wellington and other leading Protestants against Canning, he reacted furiously on receiving the news in Ennis of the defeat of the latest relief motion, 6 Mar.; at the meeting he hastily arranged for the establishment of a Liberal Club for county Clare on the 11th, he secured a resolution denouncing any Irish Members who continued to adhere to the existing ministry. He began fomenting another petitioning campaign, but, on the advice of the knight and others, reluctantly agreed to postpone it to ensure that moderate opinion would not be deterred from rallying behind Canning's nascent coalition.[127] So much did he welcome this development, indeed, that he countenanced Lansdowne entering office without a stipulation to make emancipation a cabinet question, arguing for men in preference to measures, since 'measures would necessarily follow if there were in England a presiding spirit endowed with common sense and common honesty'.[128] Nevertheless, within weeks of Canning's accession in April, he started to voice impatience at the delays in removing senior Orangemen like Lord Manners, the lord chancellor, complaining that by swift government intervention the 'Orange faction in Ireland could be made to crumble like a rope of sand'. In June he damned the new Irish secretary William Lamb's* private message to him that '*I must for a time be worse than Peel*, but when we can we will do all the good we can', as proof of 'what flimsy materials the new cabinet is composed'.[129] The following month, pleading for the personal favour of a patent of precedence that would raise his rank and income at the Irish bar, he argued that 'to do me this simple act of justice would be received by *all* the Catholics of Ireland as a proof that the system of making the practical exclusion go beyond the legal prohibition is to be at an end'.[130] However, following the disaster of Canning's death in August, he continued to be disappointed by his successor Lord Goderich's inability to deliver alterations in Irish policy and personnel (though Manners was replaced by Sir Anthony Hart), let alone emancipation; he also failed to obtain his patent, about which he was bitterly resentful. Thomas Spring Rice*, regretting O'Connell's attack on the government in Cork that autumn, lamented that he should continue

> to play this fast and loose uncertain game, never adhering to any opinion steadily and manfully and giving the impression that he is swayed by principle rather than by passion. By such a shifting and incomprehensible course he deprives his hostility of all real power and his support of all grace and dignity.

O'Connell forwarded his plans for upholding Catholic education and resisting Protestant proselytization, while at the same time usually suppressing the initiatives of his colleagues, though he was subtle enough to make, for instance, Lawless's 'Rent Sunday' system of monthly rent collection and Wyse's pyramidal structure of local liberal clubs into ideas which he could represent and control as his own. Having spent much of the year dealing with challenges to his restrained stance, he reasserted his position at the vanguard of the emancipation cause by encouraging the holding of simultaneous parish gatherings and participating notably at the 14-day aggregate meeting in Dublin in January 1828.[131]

On the appointment of Wellington as premier that month, O'Connell concurred in the Association's resolution to oppose all future ministerial candidates in Irish elections. He attempted to have this rescinded after the new government had shown some evidence of good intentions by acquiescing in the repeal of the Test Acts, which he fervently supported. But, disillusioned with the Whigs and aware that there was 'an *under swell* in the Irish people which is much more formidable than any sudden or *showy* exhibition of irritation', he continued to urge the introduction of emancipation without restrictions, though he was tempted to retreat to his moderate position during the minor ministerial crisis in May 1828.[132] When, as a result of the secession of the Huskissonites, William Vesey Fitzgerald was appointed president of the board of trade in June, O'Connell induced the Association to try to find a local liberal Protestant to oppose his re-election for Clare, even though he was a pro-Catholic, and took a lead in the initial agitation against him. According to Patrick Vincent Fitzpatrick, son of the Catholic publisher Hugh Fitzpatrick, it was Sir David Charles Roose, sheriff of Dublin, who first suggested O'Connell's candidacy to him and this idea, triggering a memory of Keogh's having once contemplated forcing the issue by having a Catholic returned for a close borough, led to Fitzpatrick making his famous outburst, 'Good heaven, the Catholics are emancipated!' He took the proposal to O'Connell, but found him 'for some time quite disinclined to make the experiment', though on 24 June he and Frederick William Conway, editor of the *Dublin Evening Post*, persuaded him to draft an address, which was printed that day; Haverty's 1846 painting of this scene was said to have captured O'Connell's characteristic 'triumphant glance'. Even then, he hesitated until Fitzpatrick, who soon became his financial manager, offered to obtain the necessary funds.[133] The lord lieutenant, Lord Anglesey, who reckoned that O'Connell, although liable to change his opinions and tactics from one day to the next, knew he was the only man who could carry it and that, even then, he was 'pretty well convinced that all opposition to Vesey Fitzgerald is hopeless, unless some great crisis is produced', made preparations for the convulsion that was thought likely to accompany his expected success.[134] In fact, enforcing his aphorism that violently retaliating to acts of provocation would only strengthen the hand of their opponents, O'Connell – ably seconded by his acolytes in the Association and a small army of priests – masterminded a peaceful repeat of the county Waterford victory two years earlier. On the hustings, where his effortless command over the vast crowd was in itself an awesome show of strength, he was cruel in his destruction of the dispirited Vesey Fitzgerald and uncompromising in his demands, which he encapsulated in the watchword, 'O'Connell, the Catholic cause and old Ireland'. He afterwards told Benjamin Disraeli† that he 'did not sleep for two nights previous to the Clare election; not a single wink. He felt that everyth[in]g was [at] stake, and that if he failed, he had made himself ridiculous for life'. Yet, within a week he had polled two to one against his opponent among the freeholders, who readily answered his appeal to desert their landlords, and, despite the raising of objections against his eligibility, had been returned to Parliament as a self-acclaimed radical reformer. His first act, it was reported, was to frank letters to Wellington, Peel, Goulburn and another notable anti-Catholic, Lord Eldon.[135]

The Clare election victory, which confirmed O'Connell's status as a folk hero, marked a turning point in Anglo-Irish relations, as he and many English observers, not least Wellington and Peel, realized only too well.[136] To the relief of government, who decided not to make any immediate move to dislodge him, he did not try to take his seat during the brief remainder of the session, instead glorying in his triumph in Dublin, where, speaking at the Association, 10 July 1828, he asked, 'What is to be done with Ireland? What is to be done with the Catholics? One of two things. They must either crush us or conciliate us. There is no going on as we are'.[137] Unaware that senior ministers, fearing electoral annihilation and even violent upheaval in Ireland, had understood the consequences of his return and were beginning to contemplate conceding relief, O'Connell, who was unwilling to repeat the mistake he had made in 1825 of relaxing agitation, kept the pressure on them; some believed him incapable of controlling the popular forces he had unleashed, but he assured Anglesey, who rather prided himself on having got O'Connell's measure, of his 'extreme anxiety that the public peace should be preserved'.[138] Thus, he supported the burgeoning development of county liberal clubs and anti-Brunswick activities, particularly by personal interventions in Sligo and Cork, and the Association's enforcement of pledges on parliamentary candidates (for emancipation, repeal of the Subletting Act and parliamentary reform). He wished to continue the electioneering fever, for instance by putting up a Catholic to fight county Galway, where a vacancy was expected, and by attempting to open the rotten borough of Tralee, where Vesey Fitzgerald was thought likely to stand.[139] Henry Hunt* criticized him for backing off from a confrontation with Parliament, but O'Connell, whose advanced reformist principles were expressed in a series of admiring letters to Bentham at this time, was in fact sailing close to the wind.[140] In his best martial style, he declared in Clonmel, 25 Aug., that he could raise enough Tipperary boys to 'drive the Orange army into the sea', so exploiting a palpable sense of almost unrestrained 'moral insurrection', and the following month he encouraged Lawless in his insensitive Catholic 'mission' to Ulster, blithely indifferent to the sectarian strife that such a provocation was to produce.[141] Under scrutiny, however, he did call off the unrest in county Tipperary by an address, 30 Sept., and also came out against the divisive practice of 'exclusive dealing' (boycotting) against Protestants.[142] In October 1828 he considered, but did not pursue, the idea of suing the Ultra duke of Newcastle for libel, after being accused by him of fomenting sedition.[143] In January 1829, when he at last managed to galvanize the Irish liberal Protestants, led by the duke of Leinster, into meeting in support of the Catholics, he orchestrated further agitation against the ominous recall of the now unequivocally pro-Catholic Anglesey.[144]

In an otherwise positive appraisal of O'Connell at the turn of the year, Greville claimed that 'to accomplish any particular object he cares not to what charges of political inconsistency he exposes himself to'.[145] This was a prescient comment, for Brougham now learnt through O'Connell's usual London intermediary, Bennett, that he and the other Irish Catholic leaders were 'ready to go *very far indeed* in order to meet the disposition, which they seem not at all to question the duke of Wellington has, for granting emancipation on terms!!!'[146] O'Connell told the Association that he was determined to go to London to take his seat, 23 Dec. 1828, but postponed this in late January in order to give his detractors a chance to pursue a petition, and set out, after writing a circular letter explaining to Members the grounds of his claim, on 6 Feb. 1829.[147] From Shrewsbury, 8 Feb., he issued an address welcoming the announcement of emancipation in the king's speech, but he advised the Association against immediately dissolving itself, which it nonetheless did. Although he had informed the knight of Kerry that he would be one of the '*plus prononcés*' of the Whigs in Parliament, some of whom considered that it was technically possible for him to take his seat, he soon agreed to their request to postpone his attempted entry to the House so as not to risk damaging the prospects for emancipation.[148] According to Hobhouse, who noted that he was 'fool enough to canvass for Peel', on the home secretary's offering himself for re-election at Oxford University in February, O'Connell said that 'in his public capacity he was obliged to oppose the 40*s*. [freeholders] bill, yet privately he cared little about the matter'.[149] He did, however, at first refuse Brougham's request to endorse the Whigs' support for their proposed disfranchisement, telling his wife that 'they *trapped* me before' and, in any case, 'you do not think that I could ever turn my back on the poor fellows in Clare?' Furthermore, he was suspicious that Brougham should happen to have called on him on 3 Mar. 1829, at just the time when he would have felt reluctant to alienate any Whigs who might be appointed to his election committee that day; this, however, reported in his favour three days later.[150]

On 6 Mar. 1829 O'Connell recorded his delight over the terms of the relief bill, 'no veto – no payment of clergy – no ecclesiastical arrangements', and was dismissive of all other minor securities except the proposed £10 county franchise, though he admitted to his wife that 'the £10 will really give more power to the Catholics. I must however support the freeholders'. He called for petitions against the ensuing franchise bill, and secured one against considerable resistance at the *Thatched House Tavern* meeting of Irishmen, 7 Mar.[151] Yet, realizing that he had little support either from Irish Catholics or English reformers, he was forced to abandon this class of voters, just as he had to submit to the suppression of the Association, which he decided should be turned into Catholic reading rooms as a temporary rallying point, under the new or 'worse than Algerine Act' (or Proclamation Act), which he promised to try to overturn. He likewise won credit for not pressing his own case, which was raised in the Commons by Charles Jephson, 12 Mar., and Grattan, 23 Mar., although there had been suggestions that the emancipation bill could be made retrospective or could include him specifically by name, which would have been popular.[152] Already concerned with how to achieve just treatment for Ireland, he witnessed the giving of the royal assent by commission to the Emancipation Act, 13 Apr. 1829, and on the 14th, which he styled 'the first day of freedom!', wrote to congratulate Edward Dwyer, the secretary of the now defunct Association, on

> one of the greatest triumphs recorded in history – a bloodless revolution more extensive in its operation than any other political change that could take place. I say *political* to contrast it with *social* changes which might break to pieces the framework of society. This is a good beginning and now, if I can get Catholics and Protestants to join, something solid and substantial may be done for all. It is clear that, without gross mismanagement, it will be impossible to allow misgovernment any longer in Ireland.

Confessing that he wished he was in Dublin to 'laugh at the corporators', he insisted on there being no 'insolence of triumph' shown.[153] The wretched George IV, who on seeing him attend his first levée after emancipation, growled, 'O'Connell! God damn the scoundrel', reportedly moaned that 'Oh, the duke of Wellington is king of England, O'Connell is king of Ireland and I suppose I am only considered as dean of Windsor'.[154]

After receiving guardedly positive responses from ministers in April 1829 about their attitude towards his being seated, O'Connell, who seems briefly to have contemplated submitting himself for re-election in Clare under the old franchise or retreating to a borough, persisted in his promise to attempt to take his seat, not least because he was determined to begin 'an *immediate* active part in the proceedings'.[155] As he set out in a printed legal argument for the benefit of Members, 9 May, he still believed the (to some doubtful) proposition that, through an omission in the Act of Union, his sitting without taking the oaths could at most be considered a misdemeanour carrying a £500 fine, and that, now the emancipation bill had been passed, he could in any case (as was widely credited) claim protection from its provisions.[156] On being introduced by Lords Duncannon and Ebrington, 15 May, a nervous O'Connell refused to take the oath of supremacy and, at the second time of asking by an unyielding Speaker, had to leave the chamber. Brougham moved that he should be allowed to state his case at the table, but Peel opposed this and the debate was eventually adjourned over the weekend.[157] On the 18th it was agreed that O'Connell could be heard at the bar and he duly gave an assured performance, delivering a 'good and judicious' statement, which persuaded at least some Members, such as the future Speaker John Evelyn Denison, that there was sufficient doubt to justify allowing him in.[158] However, Nicholas Conyngham Tindal, the solicitor-general, ably assisted by the ambitious Scarlett, moved that, having been returned before the Emancipation Act, he could not sit unless he took the oath of supremacy, and this was agreed by 190, including 24 Irish Members, to a mostly Whig minority, headed by Brougham, of 116. When the Speaker invited O'Connell, who had listened to the debate under the gallery, to return to the bar, he demurred and, in Edward John Littleton's* words, 'actually left the House, with the most consummate insolence', an embarrassment which Peel covered by recourse to the procedural pretext that no Member could swear an oath after 4pm.[159] When it was tendered to him on the 19th, O'Connell stated that 'I see in this oath one assertion as to a matter of fact which I know is not true, and see in it another assertion as to a matter of opinion which I believe is not true; I therefore refuse to take this oath'. He was again ordered to withdraw, and Tindal moved for a new writ to be issued, which met strong opposition. After Rice had briefly attempted to have the Emancipation Act amended to take account of O'Connell's case, the writ was agreed, 21 May 1829, subject to a delay necessitated by the requirement to have all Irish county freeholders reregistered.[160] O'Connell's exclusion, depicted in one of the first of many parliamentary cartoons concerning him, was considered an act of personal spite on the part of ministers, though Peel later justified the decision as essential to the success of emancipation as a whole.[161]

O'Connell, who was blackballed by the Cisalpine Club of English Catholics, 12 May, but elected to Brooks's, 27 May 1829, was furious at the government duplicity which he blamed for his defeat, but took comfort from his triumph as a parliamentary orator. Declining the possibility of Tralee, which was again vacant, or a temporary berth in an English borough, he made strenuous preparations for his expected re-election for Clare. He issued what became known, from its litany of desired Irish reforms, as the 'address of the hundred promises', 25 May, when he spoke in much the same sense at the Westminster dinner in honour of Burdett. He wrote to Bentham, 28 May, that, once returned, 'then for Utility – Utility: Law – Church – Finance – Currency – Monopoly – Representation – How many opportunities to be useful'. At Anglesey's instigation, he forbore to raise repeal during the election, which he rather hoped would be contested, so as to raise his standing further, but it was at the forefront of his thoughts.[162] Having quarrelled furiously with the family of his colleague Lucius O'Brien and most other Clare landlords, he was in the end returned unopposed as an opponent of administration, 30 July, when, after the recent violence of his electioneering speeches, he was credited with attempting to lower the political temperature in Ireland.[163] In a reverential letter to Bentham, he boasted of having declared himself a 'Benthamite' in Ennis, promised to base his conduct on the 'greatest happiness principle' and stated that 'you have now one Member of Parliament *your own*', though within a year relations had cooled between them.[164] He likewise offered his parliamentary services to the Catholic bishops, as the representative of their interests, and the Jewish lobby, as an advocate for their emancipation, and, a resolute enemy to colonial slavery, he reportedly rejected the non-aggression pact held out by the West India planters in the House.[165] Supportive of the English reform movement generally – a London Radical Reform Association was formed in imitation of the Catholic Association in July – he the following year advised Thomas Attwood† to employ his ideas of moral force and mass membership in setting up the Birmingham Political Union, as he did for the organizer of the precursor to the Dublin Trades Political Union.[166] Long convinced of the need for trusted parliamentary agents in London, he renewed his efforts to set up an institutional link between Ireland and Westminster, which led (in January 1830), to the establishment in Dublin, under Dwyer, of the Parliamentary Intelligence Office, a 'species of reading room and temporary headquarters of agitation'. In the meantime, he contented himself with sending for parliamentary papers to read during a vacation at Derrynane in October, when a nasty coach accident might have ended his career.[167] Intending to devote himself to Parliament and now in receipt of enough money from what became an annual national tribute for personal and political expenses (amounting to £30,000 in its first full year and averaging £12,000 a year from 1831 onwards), he mostly gave up his practice at the bar. However, having answered an urgent call for assistance, he travelled all night to arrive in court in Cork on the morning of 26 Oct., when, in one of his most celebrated legal performances, he destroyed the crown's case, presented by the Irish solicitor-general John Doherty*, against those involved in the conspiracy to murder landlords at Doneraile.[168] Having controversially offered his services as an election agent to the Beresfords in county Waterford earlier that year, as a brief experiment in non-sectarian co-operation, in December 1829 he was drawn into a fracas there about a by-election, in which he canvassed for the unsuccessful John Barron the following month.[169] According to Pierce Mahony†, who broke with him over this affair, O'Connell, who was also involved in the county Limerick contest and had quarrelled with his supporters in Clare and Dublin, had lost popularity through pressing his repeal ideas and 'reduced himself to the leader of the mere mob and the mischievous meddling part of the clergy'. By comparison, Sheil, who was made a king's counsel the following year and was later given a parliamentary seat, was promoted by successive ministers as a counterweight to him in representing respectable Irish Catholic opinion.[170]

O'Connell, one of the first ever Members to have a considerable extra-parliamentary following, used a series of public letters and a Dublin dinner in his honour in January 1830 to promise unremitting activity in the House, where, according to popular mythology, he quickly exploited his native cunning to outwit his enemies.[171] On top of the many predictions that as a mob orator he would fail in the Commons, Wellington judged that should he 'be vulgar or violent in Parliament, nobody will listen after the first day', but added that, if he was moderate in his language and behaviour, 'he will be listened to, and his influence will be greater than ever'. He was, indeed, aware that he had to attune his delivery to its sensibilities, including for brevity, and, though it took time, he slowly won his critics over.[172] If anything, speaking from 'the second bench of the opposition', near to Hume's habitual seat, he rather underpitched his commonplace maiden speech against the address, 4 Feb. 1830, arguing for famine relief for Ireland and various legal and parliamentary reforms.[173] He walked out for the division with a curious new associate, the Tory free trader Michael Thomas Sadler, in voting for Knatchbull's amendment that day, and the next, instead of carrying out his stated intention of moving for an inquiry into agricultural distress, he formally seconded and acted as a teller for Lord Blandford's amendment.[174] Despite apparently joining a radical London dining club and belonging to Edward Davies Davenport's* clique of reformers, he largely acted alone at this time, having few supporters among the Irishmen.[175] Yet, dubbed 'the Member for Ireland' by Cobbett, he was a host in himself, and, claiming to have quickly grasped 'the tone and temper of the House', which he considered to be full of 'folly and nonsense', he duly fulfilled his promise to bring forward Irish business. He began to present innumerable petitions on many subjects, supporting others as requested, to busy himself with all sorts of minor legislation, about which he corresponded with various Irish advisers, and to intervene frequently and repetitively on anything that caught his attention, notably procedural, privilege, legal and especially religious questions.[176]

He dwelt on Irish agricultural distress, 8, 12 Feb., but made reasonable suggestions about government bills, 11, 16, 24 Feb., and was thanked by Peel for his 'temperance and moderation' in commenting on his intended judicial changes, which O'Connell reverted to on 9 Mar. 1830. He acted as a minority teller, a task he regularly performed, for Hume's amendment to adjourn proceedings on supply, 11 Feb., objected to the Irish yeomanry grant, 22 Feb., and divided steadily in the renewed opposition campaign for economies and lower taxation that session. At his own request, he was appointed to the select committee on vestries, 16 Feb., but a month later Hobhouse complained that he had only attended its proceedings for a total of 90 minutes.[177] Calling himself a radical reformer, 11 Feb., O'Connell voted for transferring East Retford's seats to Birmingham, and again, 5, 15 Mar. In what Littleton, who noted that the House considered him 'tame and harmless', thought his first major outing, O'Connell supported Blandford's reform motion, 18 Feb., when he condemned the influence of government or aristocratic patrons over at least 400 Members.[178] He divided for the enfranchisement of Birmingham, Leeds and Manchester, 23 Feb. He introduced an amendment to the East Retford bill for vote by ballot, which he said was essential to secure freedom of election, 5, 15 Mar., when it was defeated by 179-21. A leading figure in London radical circles, he chaired a mass meeting to establish the Metropolitan Political Union, 8 Mar., speaking in favour of the ballot, shorter parliaments and universal suffrage.[179] He voted for information on Portugal, 10 Mar. He made a prosaic blunder over moving the adjournment of Davenport's motion on the state of the nation, 18 Mar., and on its resumption, 23 Mar., he urged consideration of the distressed economic condition of Ireland.[180] Back in Dublin for Easter, he failed in his attempt to establish an improvement society, a cover for his repeal activities, and was unable to end damaging electoral differences with his friends in Clare, where it was believed that he had made 'a bad fight' of it in the Commons.[181] In April 1830 Peel, who agreed with the duke of Northumberland, the lord lieutenant, that O'Connell did not deserve promotion among with the first batch of Catholic KCs, quipped that 'he is so great a blackguard and so low at present that I should be unwilling to see him in possession, not of a silk gown, but of a legitimate grievance from the refusal of it'.[182] O'Connell, who continued to speak frequently, failed in his attempt to amend the Irish Vestry Act, on the ground of financial mismanagement by Protestants, being defeated by 177-47, 27 Apr. The following day, when he paired for censuring the affair at Terceira, he was 'treated with derision' at Brooks's on being made to own that his 'game' was 'dissolution of the Union', at least according to Lord Francis Leveson Gower*, the Irish secretary.[183] The complaints he levelled against the inadequacies of the law and the increased Irish stamp and spirit duties, 29 Apr., he repeated several times in the first days of May. During this time he squabbled discreditably over criminal cases with Doherty, especially on the 10th, when he began what he termed his 'serious attack' over the Doneraile conspiracy, and the 11th, when Joseph Planta*, the patronage secretary, observed that he was 'proceeding merrily in his work of *self-destruction*'.[184] Alleging serious irregularities in the gathering and presentation of crown evidence at the Cork trials, he moved ('feebly', according to Lord Howick*) for the production of papers on this, 12 May, but was 'operated on' by Doherty, in the words of Leveson Gower, whom O'Connell, in replying 'very forcibly', dubbed a 'shave-beggar'.[185] Attacked for not acting as he would at public meetings, O'Connell said:

> I admit that I thought a different conduct would be proper in this House; that I struggled and easily brought myself to adopt one; and for this I have been taunted, insulted and ridiculed. In future they shall have no cause to complain of me ... I will in future take my stand on the station to which they have forced me.

He was defeated by 75-12 and, despite his more vigorous approach, shortly afterwards Leveson Gower rated him 'the most insignificant man it has been my lot to meet with' in Parliament.[186] He spoke and voted for repeal of the Irish coal duties, 13 May 1830, when he lamented that the House 'entertains no sympathy for the people of Ireland'.

O'Connell made what Richard Monckton Milnes† called 'an energetic, but not well pointed' speech for Jewish emancipation and voted in the minority for this, 17 May 1830.[187] He divided for abolition of the death penalty for forgery, 24 May, 7 June, and sided with opposition on Canada, 25 May, and Ceylon, 27 May. Moving for leave for a bill to secure 'an effectual and radical reform of the abuses of the Commons', 28 May, he advocated the creation of a more representative and responsible legislature founded on triennial parliaments, a taxpayer franchise and the ballot. He failed in his appeal to the reformers in the House, which he blamed on Russell's more moderate proposals, dividing only 13 against 319, while Russell's motion, which followed, saw the minority rise to 117, including O'Connell, against 213. Following a late attendance the night before, he overslept and had to apologize for his absence from the committee on the Clyde navigation bill, 4 June, when, as he frequently did, he objected to the introduction of poor laws to Ireland. Endeavouring to end the grievance of Catholics bearing the cost of building new Protestant churches, he moved for the total repeal of the Irish Vestry Act, 10 June, but Rice obtained an amendment for its alteration against him by 141-17. He spoke and voted against the administration of justice bill as insufficient to improve the law's intelligibility, efficiency and cost, 18 June. Finding himself isolated and without party support when Trant condemned him for calling for a run on the banks in Ireland, 24 June, he haughtily remarked that he 'totally disclaimed the authority of the House over any acts of his that were done out of it' and insisted that he had the right to address the Irish people in print. To Doherty, who challenged his encouragement of mass protests and disparagement of Irish bank notes, he, as he afterwards wrote to Bennett, 'taunted him very successfully upon his sore point – his ignorance', and 'flung off the attack upon me gaily and with sufficient contempt for all parties concerned in it'.[188] By this time it was said of him that he 'shines more particularly in reply', but Vesey Fitzgerald, who noted that Doherty seemed to be the only Member courageous enough to stand up to him, commented to Peel that 'I know not which disgusts the most, the ruffian's craven cowardice in the House of Commons or the malignant and the mischievous baseness with which he serves agitation out of it'.[189] He complained of Irish distress, 30 June, and excessive expenditure and taxation there, 2 July, and opposed the Irish arms bill, especially in view of government's neglect of Irish problems, 3, 5 July 1830.

In early July 1830 Mary O'Connell reassured her youngest son Daniel that his father, who 'goes through great fatigue' and 'is now going to bed when formerly he used to be getting up', had several offers of county seats at the forthcoming general election.[190] As yet, not least because he retained a curious hope of being able to share its seats with Vesey Fitzgerald, this included Clare, where Tom Steele, one of the architects of the victory two years earlier, rallied supporters to his camp against the O'Briens and other interests. But, as gradually emerged, O'Connell had apparently spoilt his chances by imprudently promising to make way for both William Nugent Macnamara*, the liberal Protestant who had been originally suggested in 1828, and another of his former henchmen, the O'Gorman Mahon*, with whom he had reportedly made up after a quarrel the previous year. Unwilling to undergo a risky contest, he therefore abandoned Clare, though not without a dangerous confrontation with the O'Gorman Mahon during his procession into Ennis, 18 July, and turned elsewhere.[191] Active in promoting electioneering efforts for reformers and anti-ministerial candidates in many counties, he might have had an opening in Kerry, but for the candidacy of William Browne*, and could have stood in Cork, Galway, Louth, Meath or Wexford, or for Drogheda, where he unsuccessfully brought forward his eldest son, Maurice, but he instead chose county Waterford, where his prospects were considered to be good.[192] Having justified his parliamentary conduct and offered for the county, which he acclaimed for having first kindled the spirit of 'democratic liberty', as a wide-ranging reformer, he was introduced as a national hero on the hustings and urged that good order and moderation be displayed, especially towards his Protestant opponent, Beresford. On a plea of preventing bad feeling, he withdrew the following day, but this forced the unlucky third candidate, Wyse (who, however, came in for county Tipperary), to retire in his favour rather than to leave the Liberator stranded without a seat; he was returned unopposed. He vindicated what looked like an electoral compromise with the Beresfords and promised to renew his parliamentary exertions in two letters to the people of Waterford, while he also directed an address to Wellington calling for sittings at Westminster to terminate by 9 pm.[193] Content with having got the elections 'triumphantly over', he turned his attention to the renewal of the O'Connell tribute and, partly with an eye to its receipts, maintained a high profile that autumn. Unable to attend the Dublin meeting welcoming the recent French revolution, 15 Sept. 1830, his public letter on this subject to his son-in-law Christopher Fitzsimon† enthusiastically welcomed the political changes as a model for 'the severance of the church from the state'; later that month he was congratulated on this visionary statement by the French nobleman Montalembert, who paid homage to him at Derrynane and found him 'really great, without any affectation, but I think also with particularly high ideas'.[194] Equally a supporter of the uprising by the Belgians against Dutch rule, he later boasted of having gained three votes in the election for their new king that year.[195]

Agreeing with Staunton, whom he exhorted to 'AGITATE! AGITATE! AGITATE!', that repeal of the Union should be the focus of their attention, he now contemplated establishing a new movement and raising more funds, since money was always necessary 'to keep in due operation the springs of popular excitement'. Starting at Killarney, 7 Oct. 1830, he spoke at a series of local meetings organized for petitioning against the Union, including at Waterford on the 15th, and attempted to form the Irish Society for Legal and Legislative Relief as a repeal association.[196] This was proclaimed, 18 Oct., by the new Irish secretary, Sir Henry Hardinge*, whom O'Connell described at a Dublin dinner as 'that paltry contemptible little English soldier', 22 Oct.; he refused to meet Hardinge's subsequent challenge, replying to him that, in referring only to his public role, he had spoken 'as he would of any other man who trampled on the liberties of Irishmen'. His extremism over the highly contentious repeal issue lost an apparently nervous and disconcerted O'Connell many supporters (including his brothers) in Ireland, where the liberal Protestants signed up to the 'Leinster declaration' against repeal, and led to him being partially ostracized in society on his return at the end of the month to London, including at Brooks's.[197] Listed by ministers among their 'foes', he was present for the king's speech debate, 2 Nov., of which he recorded that

> there never was yet any man so beset as I was when I went into the House and, during the first speeches, every allusion to me of an unkind nature was cheered. Although Peel attacked me directly, he sat down amid rapturous applause. I got up at once. They at first were disposed to slight me but I rebuked them with indignation and certainly took my wicked will of them fully and to my heart's content. I cannot be a judge of my own speaking but I know that I threw out in my old Association style. I also know that the result was most cheering for me for the men who had been standing off from me before, and were not only cool but hostile, became of a sudden most cordial in their manner and confidential in their declarations. One perceives a change of this description better than one can describe it, and the change was complete.[198]

His powerful appeal for ending the Union was certainly a revelation: James Joseph Hope Vere* commented that with his rapid, telegraphic style, O'Connell 'cleaned his stomach in a more perfect manner than he has ever yet done', and Howick noted that day that O'Connell, 'for the first time made me understand how he has acquired so much influence in Ireland as a speaker'.[199] Unleashing his vitriolic streak, which frequently involved him in irate exchanges, on the 5th he referred to 'the present incompetent and imbecile administration', which angered the House, and on the 9th, when he presented and endorsed the Waterford inhabitants' petition for repeal and quarrelled with Doherty, George Robert Dawson and Littleton, he hailed the abuse thrown at him 'as my richest reward, as my highest encomium'. George Agar Ellis* described him as 'railing in a most blackguard way at everybody about the Union' that day, and Hope Vere observed that 'I never saw in the House such a storm', but he earned grudging respect from an unlikely quarter in that Sir Henry Bunbury*, who had formed 'a very mean estimate' of him, now considered him

> a fellow of formidable powers; coarse, but acute, wily and dexterous; dealing in calumnies, and showing occasionally very bad taste, but possessing great command of forcible language and the crushing grip of a giant when he has an advantage over an opponent.[200]

He moved for the total repeal of the Irish Subletting Act, 11 Nov., and, according to Wyse, 'spoke with energy and was listened to with attention', but Sir John Benn Walsh recorded that 'his paradoxical and quibbling speech was well answered by Doherty'; having expressed his regret that a negative decision would only create greater unease in Ireland, O'Connell was not surprised to be defeated (by 150-24).[201] He divided for Parnell's amendments for reducing the duty on wheat imported to the West Indies, 12 Nov., and against ministers on the civil list, which precipitated their resignation, 15 Nov. 1830.

With his popularity increasing in Dublin, where he encouraged the holding of 'repeal breakfast' gatherings and was searching for a permanent meeting place, and the expected change of government at Westminster, where the failure of Irish Members like Wyse to come to his support laid them open to criticism at home, O'Connell was confident that this was an advantageous moment to advance the cause of repeal, and he told Dwyer that 'I think some good may be done in the House or rather through the House. I am determined to *stick* to it as long *as I can*'.[202] He stated in a printed address to the people of Ireland, 17 Nov. 1830, that Lord Grey's ministry 'will not do Ireland any one solid or substantial service' and, despite the reappointment of Anglesey as viceroy, at once suspected that little would change in terms of personnel; he cited the retention of Doherty, with whom he clashed in the House on the 19th. Continuing to sit on the opposition benches and present, as he wrote, 'constantly from its sitting to its rising', he made incessant pleas for a variety of Irish reforms, as well as for repeal, until leaving town in the middle of the following month.[203] During that time the prime minister undoubtedly regarded O'Connell with insurmountable distrust, but Anglesey, whose efforts to placate him (including by pressing for the removal of his Commons 'master', Doherty, to the bench) he largely misjudged, represented the more amenable wing of the administration; this included Duncannon, who in talking to Hobhouse about Ireland, remarked that 'O'Connell was all powerful there and ought to be appeased'.[204] Although the exact details of the discussions are unclear, Anglesey, both in at least two private interviews with O'Connell in London and indirectly through Duncannon, certainly made him offers of official employment that winter, presumably in order to rein him in, but nothing came of this. It seems not impossible that he might have agreed to take the Irish mastership of the rolls (or another judicial position), although this would have excluded him from popular politics; reports then (as a year later) that he would be dispatched to India appear to have been wishful thinking.[205] He remained supportive of Anglesey and privately clarified his attitude by stating, 26 Nov., that 'I intend to give the new administration as strong support in all their useful measures as any independent man can give without committing myself in any degree as a ministerial Member', while on 7 Dec. he informed his go-between, Bennett, that he wanted 'for myself *nothing* – for Ireland much', adding a list of 12 desired Irish reforms.[206] For his part, Anglesey, who agreed to the home secretary Lord Melbourne (as Lamb had become), sanctioning an approach to him by Wyse in late December 1830, thought that 'it would be the cheapest purchase ever made, to obtain O'Connell *at any price*', since otherwise '*he, and not the government*, will rule Ireland', but believed that he 'is desperately committed, and bent upon the repeal, and from that he will never recede', as he 'is flying at higher game than a judgeship, and he is secure of a better income from the deluded people than *any government* can venture to give *any person* whatever'.[207]

O'Connell, who had briefly considered organizing a celebratory welcome for Anglesey, was himself greeted with remarkable scenes on his return to Ireland as a determined proponent of repeal, 18 Dec. 1830; it was a display which outshone the arrival of the lord lieutenant on the 22nd and which, the crowd having dispersed quietly at his bidding, gave a displeased William IV 'the most striking proof of the influence he has acquired over a portion of the lower classes'.[208] With the hearty concurrence of Grey, Anglesey, who for a while feared actual rebellion, prevented a mass military-style demonstration of the Dublin trades by a proclamation on the 26th, to which O'Connell immediately added his approval in order to maintain his authority over his supporters. Reflecting the general horror felt at his now unmasked 'course of ambition', Greville commented that, in his tussles with Anglesey, he had 'a moral power and influence as great in its way, and as strangely acquired, as Buonaparte's political power was'.[209] The following month, intent on foiling his increasingly isolated opponent, the exasperated viceroy issued a series of proclamations to meet the rapidly escalating crisis created by 'the Pacificator', a title briefly adopted at the establishment of his instantly suppressed General Association of Ireland, 6 Jan. 1831, by O'Connell, who spoke provocatively for repeal and even urged a run on the banks.[210] The agitation culminated with the arrest of an outraged O'Connell at home, 18 Jan., by one Farrell, whom his son John O'Connell† described as 'a venerable specimen of the old school of constables'; he insisted on being paraded on foot through the streets, but later allowed himself to be released on bail, since, as his wife commented the following day, had he been confined to Newgate, 'the Castle would have been torn down last night the people were so indignant'.[211] Ministers were at first divided about the wisdom of such an action, especially as O'Connell wriggled expertly to gain the advantage, by continuing to manipulate public opinion in his favour, making speculative approaches to such leading liberal figures as Lords Cloncurry and Meath and instigating a troublemaking (and very nearly successful) opposition to the return of Duncannon, now a junior minister, for county Kilkenny in February. Yet the arrest effectively forced O'Connell to lower his demands and enabled some sort of secret negotiation to take place, via Bennett, between him and government, although neither side would admit to having initiated it. Whatever the outcome of those obscure proceedings, and despite the ensuing furore nothing concrete emerged about them, O'Connell, whom ministers reckoned a coward, appears to have been frightened into making a tacit compromise, bartering ameliorative measures for Ireland in exchange not so much for the vanity of his own freedom, though that was certainly at stake, as for the practical necessity of being able to pursue his repeal campaign unhindered at some later date.[212] Therefore, to the surprise and dismay of those who, like Sheil, thought him 'fallen indeed', O'Connell pleaded guilty to the first 14 counts against him (of conspiring to evade the Proclamation Act), 12 Feb. 1831, when the other 17 counts (of offences under the recent proclamations) were dropped. Judgment was deferred to allow him to undertake what he called his duty to his constituents in returning to Parliament, where his case had already been raised (for example, on the 8th).[213]

The Irish secretary, Edward Smith Stanley, who gave his version of these events in the Commons, 14, 16 Feb. 1831, privately boasted that he envisaged nothing above 'a very piano tone' from his defeated and deceitful Irish enemy, but O'Connell, albeit that he was expected to fail in their forthcoming parliamentary duels, in fact thereafter became almost his opposition shadow, quizzing and baiting him at every turn.[214] Intending to lambast Smith Stanley on resuming his seat, 18 Feb., he confined himself to opposing Britain's interference in the internal affairs of Belgium and then left the chamber – 'evidently striking', according to Thomas Gladstone* – and so missed hearing Sir James Graham, first lord of the admiralty, denounce him as an Irish demagogue. Apparently with the House behind him, he disparaged Graham over this, 21 Feb., when he furiously denied that Ireland was in a state of insurrection, bitterly opposed the Irish yeomanry grant and divided for reducing the size of the army.[215] In untypically pessimistic mood, 22 Feb., he wrote to Bentham that

> my first mistake consisted in entertaining a high opinion of the moral worth and intellectual power of the House of Commons and I shaped my course mildly and gently in order to propitiate the opinions of men whom I respected. You have a right to despise rather than pity me for this gross mistake. The consequences are a shipwreck of my parliamentary fame and the great difficulty I now have to assert a power which perhaps would have been conceded to me had I asserted myself strongly in the first instance. Under these circumstances I am ashamed to call myself your disciple.[216]

Aiming to be 'tame and quiet but distinct' in explaining his part in the negotiations, which he claimed amounted only to a procedural arrangement over the trial, 28 Feb., he ended up delivering an onslaught against the government's continued repression of the subjugated Irish that day, but he at least found himself restored to his customary equanimity. As he wrote to his wife:

> I really was triumphant. It is impossible for any one to conceive what a partial auditory I spoke amidst, and yet I enforced silence and I may say compelled silence. I gave Stanley some very hard knocks and Lord Anglesey still more, and I have not done with them. In short, sweetest, my mind is at ease.[217]

He pleaded for leniency for Jacob Alexander, who from the gallery had yelled, 'That's a lie', at his assertion that he would not spill one man's blood to effect political change, and he magnanimously secured his discharge, 2 Mar. 1831.

Delighted by the ministry's parliamentary reform proposals, which he commended to the Irish in priority to repeal, he failed to catch the Speaker's eye during the several days of debate that followed Russell's statement, 1 Mar. 1831, but nonetheless soon detected a marked change of attitude towards him in the House. Fearing, as he confided to his wife, that 'I have literally the less chance of speaking well because I am puffed up with the vanity of thinking that I can and will do so', while also amazed at times at 'my being so absurd as to feel nervous in the rascally House', he finally had the chance to make a strong speech in support of the 'large, liberal and wise' bill, which he described as generous and effectual, on the 8th. He particularly welcomed the removal of aristocratic, corporate and Protestant interests from boroughs, though he argued that Ireland deserved more seats and ought to have a bigger county electorate. He was widely congratulated, including by his supporters in Dublin, and Greville recorded that he was 'vehemently cheered by the government, Stanley, Duncannon and all, all differences giving way to their zeal'.[218] Otherwise confining himself to interjections on minor matters, O'Connell, who did not pursue the list of reforming suggestions proffered to him by Bentham when they met on the 20th, backed ministers over reform, 19 Mar., when he stated that his desire for radical changes was secondary to his support for the bill, and again, on voting for the second reading, 22 Mar., when, with studied moderation, he remarked that he only 'looked to the repeal of the Union as a means of obtaining good government' for Ireland.[219] He approved of the Irish reform bill, though not without expressing some reservations, including over the definition of the £10 qualification, 24 Mar., and advocated reductions in the civil list and Irish official pensions, 25, 28 Mar. His son Maurice's successful return for Clare in late March was thought likely, in demonstrating his electoral influence, to deter ministers from seeking a dissolution, but Grey was already hopeful that his 'disposition for conciliation' would prevent him exploiting an election 'to throw all Ireland into confusion', and even Smith Stanley, who was adamant that he should be brought to judgment, conceded that his 'playing good boy' merited a fair response.[220] Melbourne argued that, the question being 'now brought to issue whether O'Connell or the king's lieutenant is to govern Ireland', he had to return to court, but he reported to Anglesey in early April that the cabinet had decided to allow him to apply for sentencing to be postponed, as the most it could do to assist him.[221] Stating that 'nobody has regretted more than I have done the course Mr. O'Connell has taken' and ruling out further attempts at mediation, Grey communicated this to Burdett, adding:

> I acknowledge that he has rendered good service on the reform bill, and that on many previous occasions his conduct in the House of Commons has been such as to encourage the hope that he would abstain from the pernicious courses in which he has been engaged. But these expectations have been as constantly followed by disappointment, his measures to excite in the people of Ireland a spirit of the bitterest hostility not only to the government but to the people of England – the Saxons, as he calls them – having always succeeded, as in a regular course, to his more moderate conduct in Parliament.[222]

He, in his own words, 'spoke often and *rather well, ipse loquitur* ... on various topics', including the Irish juries bill, 12 Apr., when he unsuccessfully divided the House (by 44-10) against increasing the allowance for emergencies. He differed over reform with Sugden, 13 Apr., Hunt, 14 Apr., and Edward Synge Cooper, 18 Apr., and on the 19th he earned the Speaker's rebuke on telling North that he had promoted the bill at home, not as a means to repeal, but so as to win justice for Ireland and to strengthen the institutions of monarchy, church and Lords. He spoke and voted against Gascoyne's wrecking amendment that day, which precipitated a dissolution, and on 21 Apr. 1831 he threw out the prospect of the number of Irish reformers rising from 59 to 80. Macnamara privately commented on the 23rd that 'O'Connell has changed his tone in the House very much and I tell you there is no man more attended to by the ministers than he is'.[223]

Well might O'Connell bear Moore's trenchant criticisms of his having prematurely agitated the repeal question 'with the most perfect candour and good humour', during their conversation on 23 Apr. 1831, because at the ensuing general election, during which no one could be unaware that ministers had made an unsavoury alliance with their untrustworthy new associate, he commanded his supporters to put that issue aside in favour of parliamentary reform.[224] Writing with his comments about numerous constituencies, notably Dublin and various southern counties, to one of his government contacts, Duncannon, for whom he secured a free run in county Kilkenny, he disclosed that his own plans to oust the Beresfords in county Waterford, where he may not have been sure of success, had given way to a desire to contest Kerry, which he had originally destined for his brother John.[225] Suspected of having broken a promise to stand by the Beresfords and to be in some doubt of winning his native county – a requisition from county Tipperary was prepared as a fallback – he ostensibly entered in order to attack someone more worthy of his powers, the knight of Kerry, who opposed reform and had most of the territorial interests behind him. After a convoluted struggle, the knight, distraught at the injustice inflicted on him, withdrew and a jubilant O'Connell, who benefited from government backing, was returned unopposed with his young acolyte, Frederick Mullins.[226] In the course of his campaigning in Dublin, Leinster and especially Munster, he also secured the re-election of Maurice O'Connell after turbulent scenes in Clare, where he blamed the Terry Alt outrages on his erstwhile friend the O'Gorman Mahon, while at the same time courting their support.[227] Overall, he may have obtained the return of the roughly 20 to 30 Members whom Charles Arbuthnot*, the former treasury secretary, had feared he would be able to nominate and thereafter formed his loose connection in the Commons.[228] Grey, who was satisfied with the Irish results and welcomed O'Connell's own success, since he was 'much less mischievous in Parliament', agreed with his cabinet colleagues that, 'after all that had passed during the elections', the dropping of the prosecution against him was 'upon the whole advantageous'. The Irish law officers therefore connived at O'Connell escaping punishment under the Proclamation Act, which, since it lapsed at the dissolution of Parliament, essentially meant that he had been acquitted. Anglesey commented that he had 'little faith in his good intentions', but believed O'Connell had learnt that 'he cannot attempt to rule here with impunity' and that, having seen his attempt to quiet Clare fail, he knew that he had 'not sufficient power over the people to subdue their bad passions'.[229] Newcastle, who had predicted that O'Connell would make the government look 'ridiculous and contemptible', spluttered with rage at this development, writing in his diary that 'thus it is with these rascals: the only true policy is to treat such men *as the law directs*'.[230] Although given his usual rousing reception at a Dublin reform dinner, 31 May, O'Connell was reportedly met without much enthusiasm, 5 June, on entering Ennis, where he acted as counsel for most of those prosecuted at the ensuing special commission, about which he had an interview with Anglesey and Smith Stanley, 11 June 1831.[231]

Convinced by such encounters that the Irish administration intended only 'to do good to Ireland *provided* it be in subserviency to English interest', O'Connell prepared to bring what he called the 'case of Ireland' before the House.[232] In the new session, when he was again extremely active (including in attempting to advance several Irish legal bills), he developed more fully into a parliamentarian both strategically, by using displays of alternating support and hostility to wring concessions from the Whig ministry, and tactically, by exploiting Irish controversies to weaken the sinews of Ascendancy domination.[233] He had hoped ministers would replace the Speaker and, according to one newspaper report, had he arrived in time to be sworn, 14 June 1831, he might have disrupted Manners Sutton's unopposed reappointment that day.[234] After illness had hampered him on the 21st, he spoke in favour of the address, 22 June, though he urged support for Belgian and Polish insurgents, advocated measures to relieve Irish agricultural distress, a theme to which he regularly reverted, and explained the circumstances of his release (as he did on the 27th). He expressed his regret at the heavy loss of life at Newtownbarry, 23 June, and on the 27th put up stiff resistance to the grant for the Irish yeomanry, whom he held responsible for this and other affrays, the subject of several forthright interventions by him that year (for example, on 18 July). He objected to the changes, particularly over the leasehold franchise, made in the Irish reform bill, 30 June, and gave notice that he would move for the restoration of the 40*s*. county franchise, 1 July, when he pounced on Smith Stanley's draconian arms bill.[235] He voted for the second reading of the reintroduced English reform bill, 6 July, at least twice against adjourning the proceedings on it, 12 July, and usually for its details. Conscious that, as the cabinet minister Lord Holland wrote to Anglesey, 'not only as a speaker but as a politician in the House, he rises in estimation with many on whom we ought to depend', ministers tried to mollify O'Connell, who, though generally sympathetic to them, constantly complained of excessive expenditure and sided with opposition against grants for professorial salaries, 8 July, and civil list services, 18 July. Thus, he was received by the chancellor Lord Althorp* to discuss the Irish bill, 11 July, when, in the Commons, he supported the case made for the former king's stationer Sir Abraham Bradley King to receive compensation (which he secured for him later that session).[236] He clashed with James Edward Gordon, a totemic Protestant bigot, in what he claimed were inadequately reported debates on Irish tithes, 12 July, the Kildare Place Society, 14, 15 July, the Maynooth grant, 19 July, 5 Aug., and Orange toasts, 9 Aug. He supported the disfranchisement of Aldeburgh, 15 July, and although he did not fulfil his privately stated desire 'to attack each of the boroughs in schedule A as the case arises', he often thereafter made brief contributions to the reform debates, and he divided in the minority against Saltash retaining one seat, 26 July 1831, when ministers allowed its transfer to schedule B.[237]

O'Connell, who was a minority teller for his own motion for swearing the original Dublin election committee, 29 June, and for Cressett Pelham's amendment to postpone issuing the new writ, 8 Aug., was furious at ministers' negligence in conceding a rerun of a contest in the Irish capital, about which he busied himself in August 1831. Claiming that 'there is a fatality about them touching Ireland which pervades their every act', he was particularly incensed by the decision to rearm the yeomanry early that month, and, as the premier noted, he 'said a few words in his usual false and Jesuitical tone' against this as part of an Irish delegation to Grey on the 12th. More than ever convinced of the growing popularity of a local legislature, he informed Dwyer that 'a domestic Parliament, an absentee *rate, an arrangement* of church property – these are the *sine qua non* of our assistance'.[238] Holland's fears of O'Connell leading an invigorated band of repealers into open hostility were realized on his denouncing government inaction over distress and Orange outrages, 10 Aug., after which the Commons clerk John Rickman recorded that his 40-strong 'squadron of Irish devils' were 'now at the service of the present opposition'.[239] The following day he not only again attacked Smith Stanley over the yeomanry and divided for printing the Waterford petition for its disarmament, but also spoke and voted against the division of (English) counties into what he said would become 'nomination' districts. As Smith Stanley had foreseen, although he put it down to O'Connell's personal animus against Lord Kenmare in Kerry, O'Connell criticized, largely alone and unsuccessfully, 15, 20 Aug., the creation in Irish counties of lord lieutenants who would have excessive and partisan powers. With Anglesey reassured that he had prevented a bid by O'Connell to assert his moral authority over the yeomanry and magistracy, Althorp and Smith Stanley reached a compromise with him on the 18th, when he may have voted in the majority for Chandos's amendment to enfranchise £50 tenants-at-will. Hardinge reported to Mrs. Arbuthnot later that day that on Vyvyan's motion on Belgium, O'Connell was 'very insolent, for the double object of praising the Belgians ... and also for the purpose of showing the government how useful he can be in attacking Tories', but he apparently 'quailed' under Peel's broadside against repeal; he made a lengthy statement vindicating his opinions on Belgium, 22 Aug. 1831. Concerned at O'Connell's mischief in embroiling ministers in 'endless and hazardous conflicts', Holland speculated that he could be neutered by taking a legal office in England, but Anglesey, who thought the attempt hardly likely to work, replied that they would just have to make 'the best fight they can against him in the House of Commons'.[240]

He voted with government in both divisions on the controversial Dublin election, 23 Aug., and kept up a stream of mainly supportive suggestions in the committee on the reform bill late that month, but again condemned misdemeanours by the yeomanry, 26 Aug., when Holland judged him 'a ready and powerful speaker but though pleasing, not so pleasing as I had expected', and 31 Aug. 1831, when he pummelled Smith Stanley and others with a barrage of Irish grievances.[241] It may have been at about this time that Brougham, now the lord chancellor, who despaired of Althorp's diffident Commons management, mocked that 'I expect any day to see O. come forward and offer his services to the majority, to lead them on and carry the measure of the country'.[242] In a letter to the *Pilot*, O'Connell explained that he had (on 29 Aug.) missed the vote on Sadler's motion for an Irish poor law, which he opposed, because of a severe headache, and regretted that the ridiculously late hours of the House were partly to blame for the recent deaths of his friends Alexander Dawson and the O'Conor Don.[243] On 5 Sept. he was named to the select committee on the malt drawback, which later that month he complained occupied his days, as the chamber did his nights.[244] He again angrily defended the Catholic church and himself from the aspersions of Gordon, 9 Sept., when, in Littleton's words, he 'all but embraced' Smith Stanley, whose plan for national education he hailed as guaranteeing non-sectarian Bible instruction.[245] He spoke and voted against the truck bill, 12 Sept., and although he divided for inquiry into the renewal of the Sugar Refinery Act that day, he stayed away to allow it to pass under a deal between government and the radicals, 28 Sept.[246] He raised the Doneraile conspiracy, 19, 27 Sept., and reluctantly agreed that there was a case for extending poor laws to Ireland, 26 Sept., when he made a long defence of the Maynooth grant. He voted for the third reading, 19 Sept., and passage of the reform bill, 21 Sept., and attended the meeting of independent Members who agreed to back the government even if the measure was lost in the Lords; he was present to see Russell deliver it to the upper House 22 Sept., when Wellington gleefully noticed that the muffled 'hear, hear' he emitted at the bar, in itself decided the bishop of London to vote against the measure.[247] Despite an illness which kept him from sitting late in the House, he found time to encourage Irish reform petitions and to consult with ministers about the 'very, very bad' Irish bill, for which he kept notice of an impending call in force, despite objections from English Members (especially on 27 Sept.) until 5 Oct. He privately believed that the peers were 'mad, stark mad, to dare to fly in the face of popular sentiment and popular indignation', and was less surprised than gratified by the reform bill's defeat because, 'in short, the game is up and the Tories must be put down'.[248] He therefore rallied strongly to the defence of ministers on Ebrington's confidence motion, for which he divided, 10 Oct. John Heywood Hawkins*, who averred that his particularly good speech that day showed that he was 'now one of the most powerful orators in the House', witnessed O'Connell demonstrating 'his own abusive style' in giving Sir Charles Wetherell a drubbing, 13 Oct. 1831.[249]

O'Connell confided to Barrett, 5 Oct. 1831, the strictly private communication that 'I COULD be [Irish] attorney-general – in one hour', an idea which, when rumours emerged about it later that month, was dismissed as preposterous, given his recent trial, by the Irish liberal Lord Donoughmore.[250] Grey certainly authorized an offer to be made to O'Connell at this time through one of his closest supporters, James Doyle, bishop of Kildare and Leighlin, who afterwards reported that 'my application to him was more successful than I anticipated, but finding how isolated the proposal was made to him, I fully agreed with him that it should be rejected'. In other words, O'Connell, who vented his frustration with ministers by lamenting to Duncannon that the Irish administration was seen to be 'as essentially anti-Irish and Orange as it was in the days of Peel and Goulburn', declined to be seduced by the thought of taking judicial office or a knighthood.[251] If Mrs. Arbuthnot is to be relied on, the project was actually thwarted by Smith Stanley, who, already vexed by O'Connell's having escaped justice earlier in the year, threatened to resign from the cabinet, whose moderate wing, according to Holland, could therefore only obtain permission for Anglesey to make an amicable approach to him. It then emerged that he would be willing to accept the patent of precedence which he had refused at the end of the previous year and to which he was fully entitled by his professional expertise. In late October he was accordingly granted seniority as a king's counsel in Ireland after the attorney and solicitor-generals and the first and second serjeants but ahead of the third serjeant, the recently promoted Catholic Michael O'Loghlen†, and he took his place as such in chancery, 4 Nov.[252] Although Smith Stanley remained wary, others were willing to give him the benefit of the doubt and, as Anglesey explained to Melbourne, who took exception to an anti-Union speech made by him in late October:

> He has a hard game to play, and we must not expect immediate and cordial support and the sudden abandonment of questions which he has been advocating. Such a course would not be advantageous to us in any way and it would disable him from rendering service to the government. It is important that he should appear to come round rather from conviction than by bribe. In the mean time, it has been fully made known to him that what he obtains he must earn.[253]

However, Anglesey's confidence that he was 'riding his race well' had collapsed by the middle of November 1831, when Holland recorded that 'O'Connell has again run out of his course, scurrilously abusing Mr. Stanley and disparaging Lord Anglesey in a letter to the newspapers, without provocation'. The king, who had been 'not indisposed to propitiate O'Connell for the sake of quiet in Ireland', remarked that 'the gloss was not off his silk gown before he began flinging dirt and kicking up dust to defile it'.[254]

O'Connell was, indeed, beset by more extreme challengers to his position that autumn, for the Dublin Trades Political Union, of which he was a member, had quickly risen to prominence as a working class organization with a strong repeal agenda. It required all his powers of guile and intimidation to subvert it, by November 1831, into the National Trades Political Union, with a broader social base and a wider reform remit, and even then he felt forced to found the National Political Union, a moderate reform association for the promotion of Irish interests, in order to absorb its potentially more dynamic rival.[255] Grey took note of O'Connell's fresh scheme, but, guessing that 'he is too cunning, and knows too well what he is about, to expose himself by any proceeding obviously contrary to law', decided to leave him undisturbed, especially as his return to Westminster would 'prevent his giving this new association the consistency, and to the public feeling the impulse, which he alone can give them'.[256] William Holmes* was alarmed that 'O'Connell is playing the devil with Stanley. I really believe he wishes to have him assassinated', but the Irish secretary, who dismissed these personal attacks as 'not very decorous, but I think very harmless', reported from Dublin that O'Connell was 'in very low circumstances, and bent upon obtaining another tribute ... and upon the whole his influence, vast as it is, is *rather* I think diminished', so that he had 'no fear but we shall have a quiet winter here'.[257] Yet, determined to maintain his leadership of the repeal cause, O'Connell announced in the National Political Union, 23 Nov., that its affairs were more important to him than attending the pre-Christmas session of Parliament, and he duly remained in Dublin during the following month as a mark of his resentment against the continued ministerial indifference towards Ireland. His presence in London was repeatedly urged by the radical Leslie Grove Jones† and by Duncannon, who was persuaded, not least by the frequent diatribes which he received in reply to his letters, that O'Connell should, and could, have been won through taking office.[258] It was understood that giving him the rolls would have pleased the Irish Members, who Smith Stanley felt were nevertheless 'rather beginning to abjure' him, and Holland lamented that he had not been secured by the offer of the Irish solicitor-generalship. However, Anglesey was confident that O'Connell's conduct in having repaid ministers' generosity with a vain and unnecessary resort to ruthless demagoguery, for example by falling out ferociously with Doyle, would lower his professional standing and his political reputation at Westminster, so much so that he would be worthless as a member of the government.[259] Mrs. O'Connell, who noted the success of 'the real Dan' ale produced at their son Daniel junior's brewery, protested that her husband was 'if possible more popular than ever' that winter, but Grove Jones, expressing an English perspective and challenging his tactics and motives in agitating for unrealisable radical reforms, warned him that 'you are evidently losing your consequence and ... will have to fight your battle over again in the House of Commons'.[260] Grey, refusing to countenance further relations with him, was praised by the king for stating in the Lords, 15 Dec. 1831, that he would have been glad to employ a man of O'Connell's calibre, but that no offer would be made to someone who acted in the way that he had done.[261]

O'Connell, who paired for the second reading of the revised reform bill, 17 Dec. 1831, failed to muster more than six Irish Members, including his son Maurice, in Dublin early the following month.[262] On his way to London, he addressed large reform meetings in Wolverhampton, 19 Jan., and Birmingham, 20 Jan., and he resumed his seat, 23 Jan. 1832, when he divided for partially disfranchising the 30 boroughs in schedule B.[263] He insisted, as he was frequently to do, that Ireland should receive equal treatment under the proposed reform legislation, but was supportive of the English bill that day, leading Grey to observe that he was once again on his best behaviour.[264] He vehemently aired his hostility to Irish tithes, 23, 24 Jan., and the following day was seen, in Campbell's description, 'fuming about there being no House, and saying that it is a manoeuvre to defeat his motion' to add a Catholic, Killeen, to Smith Stanley's exclusively Protestant select committee on this; at Lord Milton's* request, he withdrew it the following month, so avoiding what Rice termed, 'a most awkward discussion'.[265] Taking 'the opportunity of wreaking his vengeance' on ministers, he excoriated them over the Russian-Dutch loan, 26 Jan., when he sided with opposition but saved the government by sending Maurice and seven or eight other Irish Members out of the House before the division.[266] He was named to the select committee on the East India Company, 27 Jan., and served on the subcommittee on its judicial affairs during the session.[267] As active as ever, notably over petitions relating to Irish parliamentary and other reforms, he also participated frequently in matters of lesser and non-partisan interest, and, for instance, was listed in the minority for inquiry into the glove trade, 31 Jan. He headed a 'grand onslaught of Irish Members' against tithes, 8 Feb., about which he soon boasted that he had put ministers on the back foot, but, primed by Littleton, he gave them able assistance in speaking and voting against the production of information on Portugal, 9 Feb.[268] He called for the creation of peers to ensure the passage of the reform bill through the Lords, 10 Feb., praised some of its beneficial features, 16 Feb., when he divided for printing the Woollen Grange petition for the abolition of Irish tithes, and voted for going into committee on it, 20 Feb. He left London at the end of the month, but not without leaving behind him a loose following of Irishmen, whom Littleton called 'a stout little phalanx, sitting below the treasury benches, next the bar'.[269] He entrusted Maurice O'Connell with the responsibility of countering Smith Stanley's tithe proposals the following month and missed the division on the third reading of the reform bill, 22 Mar. 1832.

His return was partly due to professional commitments, and the fact that he hinted at resuming his practice at the bar may have been an indication of financial problems. He might also have desired to lie low on account of Ellen Courtenay's public revelations. She had approached the O'Gorman Mahon and Hunt the previous year, when O'Connell had privately rejected her charges with 'contemptuous defiance', pointing out that such a calumny 'would have been worth any money in Ireland at any time during the last 20 years, that is, if it had the least face of probability'. Having failed to exact anything from him then, she now issued her *Narrative*, dated from the Fleet Prison, 27 Feb. 1832, claiming that his refusal to honour his supposed promise of financial assistance had reduced her to bankruptcy. However, the fact that it was published from the offices of the scurrilous *Satirist* newspaper in The Strand marked it out as a sordid piece of sexual blackmail, and, as even his most hostile opponents refused to exploit it, for which he was grateful, O'Connell's standing was left largely untouched by the scandal. He always treated the story as a derisory fabrication: according to his investigations, she was 'an elderly strolling actress', of some other name, who in 1817 had been employed in the Isle of Wight and had never had a child.[270] In any case, he was given rousing popular receptions, including at Tralee, 11 Mar., Cork, 18 Mar., Cashel, 29 Mar., and Athlone, 2 Apr., and in his numerous speeches generated further excitement not only for reform, but also repeal. Back in England by the end of April, he extended his high public profile further, for instance by speaking in early May in Bath, where he floated his (rarely revealed but possibly significant) musings on the development of a federalist solution to Ireland's status within the United Kingdom, and by addressing a series of five public letters to 'the reformers of Great Britain', 22 May-11 June.[271] Despite Burdett's disgust at having to listen to 'such stuff', he was, Hobhouse thought, 'the hero of the evening' at the Westminster reform dinner, 27 June 1832, when he made a speech 'about the echoes of liberty resounding from the peaks of the Andes to the banks of the Barrampooter'.[272]

Having, among his usual plethora of daily comments, touched on reform, 7, 9 May, he leant his full support to (and voted for) Ebrington's motion for an address calling on the king to employ only ministers who would carry the bill unimpaired, 10 May 1832, declaring that it was a question 'between liberty and despotism of the very worst kind, the despotism of a sordid oligarchy'. His backing was crucial in ensuring the reinstatement of the Grey ministry that month, but from Brooks's on the 17th he reported that although he had tacitly allowed repeal 'to stand over for a fitter season', he intended to raise its cry the moment the English reform bill had passed.[273] He spoke and voted for Buxton's anti-slavery motion, 24 May. The following day, rebutting claims that he envisaged Ireland's separation from Britain and the elevation of the Catholics over the existing Protestant ascendancy, he gave guarded praise to the Irish reform bill, for whose second reading he divided. However, dubbing it a 'conservative' measure, despite the laudable effect it would have in reducing the number of rotten boroughs, he criticized both county and borough electorates as too small to be viable under their respective £10 freeholder and householder franchises, and attacked the retention of Ireland's inadequate system of registration.[274] He threatened to oppose Irish supplies at every stage if more liberal measures were not forthcoming for his country, 31 May, when he objected strongly to the appointment of a select committee on the recent outrages there; the following day he presented a petition to this effect from the inhabitants of Dublin, for whom he had already developed into almost a virtual representative. In early June Anglesey wrote despairingly to Holland that 'a vast number of Irish Members detest O'Connell, and would willingly detach themselves from him, if *we* gave them the chance, but we do not'.[275] O'Connell brought up the National Political Union's petition for more equitable treatment to be accorded to Ireland, 6 June, when he unsuccessfully attempted to throw out Alexander Baring's bill to exclude debtors from Parliament (by 72-29). He stepped up his opposition to the Irish bill, partly in anger at Smith Stanley's sneering, 13 June, stating that it failed to fulfil its intentions to extend the franchise and end nomination, and was of a piece with government's general neglect of just Irish demands. He was defeated on moving for the enfranchisement of 40*s*. freeholders in fee (acting as a teller for the minority of 73 to 122) and of 40*s*. freeholders for lives (without a division) that day, as he was on proposing that the vote be given to Irish £5 freeholders (being teller for the minority of 44 to 177), 18 June, when he also spoke and voted for Mullins's attempt to enfranchise £30 rent-payers on 19-year leases. His constant interventions on the 18th were marked by an extraordinary acerbity, particularly towards Smith Stanley and Philip Crampton, the Irish solicitor-general, who both attacked him for refusing to fight duels, and his retort against the latter had to be retracted after the Speaker intervened. On 19 June, when he disagreed with Sadler's motion for the introduction of poor laws to Ireland as futile in the face of market forces, Hunt maliciously abused him over the Ellen Courtenay affair, although, as Cobbett congratulated him that day, at least 'the evidence of rage in your enemies ... proves that you are working with effect'.[276] In a foretaste of his future bitter clashes with *The Times*, he complained, as a breach of privilege, that it had misreported him in order to suggest that he had abandoned his pledge to his constituents over poor relief, 20 June, but he withdrew this charge, 22 June, explaining that the reporter in question had apologized for his accidental inaccuracy.[277] He voted for requiring coroners to hold medical qualifications and for inquests to be held in public, 20 June 1832.

He sided with opposition on the boundaries of Whitehaven and Stamford, 22 June, and divided for a system of representation for New South Wales, 28 June 1832. He welcomed Smith Stanley's announcement of the reinstatement of the 'beneficial interest' test as the technical basis of the £10 county qualification, 25 June, but called for the adoption of the new method of registration envisaged for England, largely because of his suspicions about the overworked and partisan assistant barristers who were responsible for the supervision of this process in Irish counties.[278] Concerned that corporations would simply levy rates to disfranchise their opponents, he divided for Sheil's amendment against electors being liable to pay their municipal taxes before being allowed to vote, 29 June, and, determined that they should be forced to admit Catholics, he divided for the Tory Frederick Shaw's amendment to preserve the voting rights of Irish freemen along the lines of the English bill, 2 July; he continued to make numerous suggestions for improving the Irish reform bill, 4, 6, 9, 18 July.[279] Apart from the party processions bill, which he voted against as unnecessary, 25 June, and referred to on proclaiming that he would urge Catholics not to retaliate to Orange provocations, 29 June, he devoted most of the rest of the session to the vexed question of tithes. He gave notice that he would move for a call on this, 28 June, but seemed to hesitate on Smith Stanley announcing the following day that he would only press on with one of his three additional bills, and dropped the threat of a call, 2 July. He unsuccessfully divided the House against the discussion on the second report of the select committee (149-25), 5 July, but nonetheless got it postponed because of the lateness of the hour, which led Greville to note that 'O'Connell and the Irish Members debate and adjourn just as they please, and Althorp is obliged to give way to them'.[280] Stating that he had no intention of opposing the tithes composition bill (and he was not named in the Irish minority for postponing the subject for that session), 13 July, he damned government for failing to fulfil its promises to Ireland (for example, to carry the Irish jury bill) and posed the question, 'if Ireland had a Parliament of its own, I ask could the present system of tithes exist for an hour?'[281] On 20 July, when he menaced Smith Stanley with future impeachment proceedings and condemned Sugden's assertion that Ireland was in a state of insurrection, he declared, with characteristic bravado, that 'in the next Parliament we shall have the nomination boroughs out of this House, and, if I have a seat in it, the Irish people shall have justice'. Probably suffering from exhaustion, he took no further part in Parliament that year, but returned to Derrynane, where he soon recovered what he called his 'pristine elasticity of animal sensation', issued seven public letters on the Irish reform bill and began re-agitating the public mind.[282] Graham seems to have been quite wrong in his reliance on gossip that O'Connell would be admitted to the privy council with a view to making him attorney-general for Ireland that summer, as Grey, disgusted by the 'vulgar violence' of his renewed repeal campaigning, believed him little better than a revolutionary. Indeed, the prime minister later lamented that 'if I had thought that the result of the reform bill was to be the raising of a new Rienzi, and to make his dictatorship and the democracy of towns paramount to all other interests of the state, I would have died before I would have proposed it'.[283]

In September 1832 O'Connell informed Fitzpatrick that his political life was henceforth to be devoted to repeal or the obtaining of 'a local and domestic legislature', and not long afterwards he explained:

> My plan is to restore the Irish Parliament with the full assent of Protestants and Presbyterians as well as Catholics. I desire no social revolution, no social change ... In short, salutary restoration without revolution; an Irish Parliament, British connection; one king, two legislatures.[284]

Never reliably secure in any seat that he occupied, he left Kerry to be returned for Dublin, where nothing came of his intended alliance with a Conservative Repealer, at the general election of 1832.[285] He established a family connection at Westminster by securing the return of his sons Maurice for Tralee, Morgan for Meath and John for Youghal (while Daniel junior entered the Commons in 1846), as well as his brother-in-law William Francis Finn for county Kilkenny and his sons-in-law Fitzsimon for county Dublin and Charles O'Connell for Kerry (until 1834, when he was replaced by O'Connell's nephew Morgan John O'Connell). Furthermore, through the spectacular effectiveness of the repeal pledge, he created the nucleus of an Irish party of 35 to 40 Members, and was soon seen swaggering about the House at the head of the ragged banditti which had already become branded as his 'Tail'.[286] A parliamentary Goliath, his striking presence and forthright delivery made him, according to Francis Jeffrey*

> indisputably the greatest orator in the House: nervous, passionate, without art or ornament; concise, intrepid, terrible; far more in the style of the old Demosthenic directness and vehemence than anything I have heard in this modern world, yet often coarse and sometimes tiresome.[287]

Greville, who commented that 'it would not be very easy to do him perfect justice', wrote that

> history will speak of him as one of the most remarkable men who ever existed; he will fill a great space in its pages; his position was unique ... To rise from the humblest station to the height of empire like Napoleon is no common destiny.

He concluded that 'it is impossible to question the greatness of his abilities nor the sincerity of his patriotism'.[288] However, Lord Hatherton (as Littleton became), who agreed that 'history possesses no parallel to his career' and that 'it is difficult to say whether the savage or the patriot more predominated in his character', finally judged that it was impossible not to be struck by his dishonest conduct and 'not to feel that he was a faithless friend and an ungenerous foe'.[289] As Sydney Smith, memorably summing up the curious mixture of the execrable and the admirable in all that he stood for, once ventured, 'The only way to deal with such a man as O'Connell is to hang him up and erect a statue to him under the gallows'.[290]

His greatest feat was, without question, Catholic emancipation, not least because, in the words of Fingall, here classing himself with the 'criminally cowardly' aristocratic leadership

> we never understood that we had a nation behind us – O'Connell alone comprehended that properly, and he used his knowledge fitly. It was by him that the gates of the constitution were broken open for us; we owe everything to his rough work.[291]

But, despite such accolades, O'Connell, alluding to the inadequacies of his associates, was resentful that 'I never will get half credit enough for carrying emancipation because posterity never can believe the species of *animals* with which I had to carry on my warfare with the common enemy'.[292] His bitterness reached a crescendo in his printed letter to the Catholic peer Lord Shrewsbury, who had publicly attacked his receipt of the financial testimonial:

> For more than 20 years before emancipation, the burthen of the cause was thrown upon me. I had to arrange the meetings, to prepare the resolutions, to furnish replies to the correspondence, to examine the case of each person complaining of practical difficulties, to rouse the torpid, to avoid the shoals and breakers of the law, to guard against multiplied treachery and at all times to oppose, at every peril, the powerful and multitudinous enemies of the cause. To descend to particulars: at a period when my minutes counted by the guinea, when my emoluments were limited only by the extent of my physical and waking powers, when my meals were shortened to the narrowest space and my sleep restricted to the earliest hours before dawn, at that period, and for more than 20 years, there was no day that I did not devote one to two hours, often much more, to the working out of the Catholic cause. And *that* without receiving or allowing the offer of any remuneration, even for the expenditure incurred in the agitation of the cause itself.[293]

In the end, at least in his own analysis, backbreaking grind eventually provided him with the opportunity to best the victor of Buonaparte, and this – for, despite his protestations of non-violence, he was apt to encourage excitement and was epitomized in popular poems and songs as a warlike hero – he obtained by the threat of a barely contained military and social upheaval.[294] As O'Connell told Shrewsbury, Wellington

> *did* emancipate the Catholics, but he emancipated them because (as he himself avowed) emancipation was no longer to be resisted. We had our moral Waterloo, my lord, and our victory was more useful, if not more glorious. We chained the valiant duke to the car of our triumph and compelled him to set us free.[295]

Many, like Count O'Connell, admired him greatly for this crowning achievement, but also, like the later lord lieutenant Lord Clarendon, damned him for continuing to further the politics of extremism.[296] Yet, dismissing the lure of a quiet retirement into judicial office and ever seeking to emulate Washington, he later recorded that in the aftermath of emancipation

> I dreamed a day-dream – *was* it a dream? – that Ireland still wanted me; that ... the benefits of good government had not reached the great mass of the Irish people, and could not reach them unless the Union should be either made a reality or unless that hideous measure should be abrogated.[297]

There followed the two further stages of his career: the later 1830s, during which, making himself influential by alternately wooing and wounding his Whig ally Melbourne, he partly succeeded in bringing greater justice to Ireland; and the early 1840s, during which, rerunning the mass agitation of the 1820s in the form of the Repeal Association, he failed to wrest an independent Parliament from Peel.[298] Whether seen as the 'political Frankenstein' of the anglicized John Doyle's cartoon of 1831 or in the much more widespread and potent Irish image of him as the bearer of the 'cap of liberty' or Irish crown, O'Connell demonstrated an overall continuity in his life's work in that he always engaged in rectifying grievances – religious or constitutional – in order that such reforms would themselves breed further demand for changes and improvements.[299] Yet with his imprisonment in 1844, his physical and mental deterioration (due to the brain tumour which was caused by an infection following the operation on his piles in 1845), his break with the Young Irelanders in 1846 and his despair over the Famine in 1847, O'Connell's last years, which revealed the failure of his hopes, were agony to him. 'Killed, I should think, by the death of O'Connellism', as John Stuart Mill† surmised, with both insight and cruelty, early that year the ailing O'Connell departed on a last journey to Rome.[300] He died, at Genoa, in May 1847.[301] Like Moses, with whom he was very often compared in Irish folk tradition, he gave his people new laws, but did not live to see the promised land. Nevertheless, according to William Ewart Gladstone†, who admitted that he had shared the fearful prejudice against him in the early 1830s, but had even then recognized him to be 'the greatest popular leader whom the world had ever seen', he was an 'ethnagogue', the leader of a nation.[302] In addition to being a prophet of European Liberal Catholicism and a model of moral force persuasiveness, O'Connell's genius lay in being an Irish originator (with the contemporary American, Andrew Jackson) of mass participatory politics and, as is now acknowledged, a major contributor to Ireland's eventually independent and democratic constitutionalist tradition.[303]

[1] The main source for what follows are O'Connell's private letters, as taken from his descendant M.R. O'Connell's *Corresp. of Daniel O'Connell*, 8 vols. (1972-80), which replaced W.J. Fitzpatrick's two vol. edn. of 1888. His public letters and extra-parliamentary speeches were partially printed in John O'Connell's *Select Speeches of Daniel O'Connell* (1865 edn.), which is largely a reworked version of his *Life and Speeches of Daniel O'Connell* (1846), although neither work took his father's career beyond 1825. There are many lives, but the standard biography is now Oliver MacDonagh, *Hereditary Bondsman: Daniel O'Connell, 1775-1829* (1988) and *Emancipist: Daniel O'Connell, 1829-47* (1989), which was reprinted in one vol. as *O'Connell* (1991). Seán O'Faoláin, *King of the Beggars* (1970 edn.) is still admired for its evocative force. A good brief introduction is *Daniel O'Connell* (1998 edn.) by Fergus O'Ferrall, whose *Catholic Emancipation: Daniel O'Connell and the Birth of Irish Democracy, 1820-30* (1985) is the best account of the emancipation campaign. For his parliamentary following, see J.H. Whyte, 'Daniel O'Connell and the Repeal Party', *Irish Hist. Stud.* xi (1958-9), 297-316, and A. Macintyre, *The Liberator: Daniel O'Connell and the Irish Party, 1830-1847* (1965). The 20th-century historiographical rehabilitation of O'Connell, after decades of condemnation inspired by his nationalist successors (for which see D. McCartney, 'Changing Image of O'Connell', in *Daniel O'Connell: Portrait of a Radical* ed. K.B. Nowlan and M.R. O'Connell, 19-31, and M.R. O'Connell, 'Collapse and Recovery', in *Daniel O'Connell: The Man and his Politics* ed. M.R. O'Connell, 53-60), has mainly been in the form of articles, or collections of them, as indicated in this and later endnotes. [2] W J. O'N. Daunt, *Personal Recollections of Late O'Connell*, i. 51. [3] J.C.D. Clark, *English Society*, 397-8. [4] *Recollections of Aubrey de Vere*, 109. [5] S. C. Hall, *Retrospect of a Long Life*, i. 244. [6] Daunt, i. 49. [7] W. Fagan, *Life and Times of O'Connell*, i. 81-82. [8] M. Tierney, 'Politics and Culture: O'Connell and Gaelic Past', *Studies*, xxvii (1938), 353-68; G. Murphy, 'Gaelic Background', in *O'Connell: Nine Centenary Essays* ed. M. Tierney, 1-24; J.A. Murphy, 'O'Connell and Gaelic World', in *O'Connell: Portrait of a Radical*, 32-52. [9] MacDonagh, *Hereditary Bondsman*, 4-5, 7-8, 15-16; M.R O'Connell, 'O'Connell and his Fam.', in *O'Connell: The Man and his Politics*, 89-99. [10] See Mrs. M.J. O'Connell, *Last Colonel of Irish Brigade*. [11] T. Wall, 'Louvain, St. Omer and Douai', in *O'Connell: Nine Centenary Essays*, 25-50. [12] MacDonagh, *Hereditary Bondsman*, 26, 28. [13] A. Houston, *Daniel O'Connell: His Early Life and Jnl.* 68, 93, 141, 169; J. O'Connell, *Life and Speeches of O'Connell*, i. 10-11; Daunt, i. 258-60. [14] Houston, 102, 107; MacDonagh, *Hereditary Bondsman*, 41-42. [15] C.P. Curran, 'Religious Aspects of O'Connell's Early Life: His Deistic Tendencies', *Studies*, xviii (1929), 20-32. [16] *O'Connell Corresp.* viii. 3380. [17] Houston, 155, 174. [18] Daunt, i. 144-5. [19] Houston, 193, 202. [20] Daunt, ii. 99; MacDonagh, *Hereditary Bondsman*, 54-55. [21] *Revolutionary Dublin* ed. T. Bartlett, 227; R.B. McDowell, *Ireland in Age of Imperialism and Revolution*, 564. [22] Houston, 64, 216, 220, 222-3, 236; Daunt, i. 48-49, 117, 205. [23] Houston, 242; MacDonagh, *Hereditary Bondsman*, 66-67. [24] *O'Connell Corresp.* viii. 3378. [25] Daunt, i. 203-4. [26] *Select Speeches*, i. 9. [27] Daunt, i. 202-3. [28] See E.I. Bishop, *World of Mary O'Connell*. [29] H. Mulvey, 'Corresp. of Daniel and Mary O'Connell', *O'Connell Corresp.* i. pp. xix-xxx. [30] Ibid. i. 237, 247. [31] Ibid. i. 84, 107, 155, 164, 208, 306, 309. [32] M.R. O'Connell, 'Income and Expenditure', in *O'Connell: The Man and his Politics*, 13-17. [33] *O'Connell Corresp.* i. 337. [34] MacDonagh, *Hereditary Bondsman*, 94-100; *Mr. Gregory's Letter-Box* ed. Lady Gregory, 37. [35] *O'Connell Corresp.* i. 188, 189, 192, 215, 219, 261, 265, 271; viii. 3386. [36] *Select Speeches*, i. 15-24. [37] Daunt, i. 271-3. [38] MacDonagh, *Hereditary Bondsman*, 106-8. [39] *O'Connell Corresp.* i. 342. [40] *Select Speeches*, i. 43-49, 69-79, 91-105, 107-16. [41] Ibid. i. 164-213. [42] Ibid. i. 166, 240-304; F. Griffith, 'O'Connell's Most Famous Case', *Éire-Ireland*, ix. 2 (1974), 90-106; Parker, *Peel*, i. 104. [43] O'Ferrall, *O'Connell*, 35. [44] MacDonagh, *Hereditary Bondsman*, 131. [45] Parker, i. 185-202; J. Kelly, *'That Damn'd Thing Called Honour'*, 222, 242-7, 261-4, 277-8; *O'Connell Corresp.* viii. 3426. [46] Daunt, i. 25; ii. 149; Fagan, i. 229. [47] This paragraph is partly based on O. MacDonagh, 'O'Connell's Ideology', in *A Union of Multiple Identities* ed. L. Brockliss and D. Eastwood, 147-61. [48] *Select Speeches*, ii. 51. [49] *O'Connell Corresp.* ii. 624; MacDonagh, *Hereditary Bondsman*, 157-8; O'Faoláin, 81-82. [50] M.R. O'Connell, 'Religious Freedom', in *O'Connell: The Man and his Politics*, 30-40. [51] O'Ferrall, *Catholic Emancipation*, 144. [52] M. Tierney, 'Repeal of Union', in *O'Connell: Nine Centenary Essays*, 151-70; K. B. Nowlan, 'Meaning of Repeal in Irish History', *Historical Stud.* iv (1963), 1-17. [53] M.R. O'Connell, '18th-Cent. Background', in *O'Connell: The Man and his Politics*, 41-52. [54] F. D'Arcy, 'O'Connell and English Radicals', in *World of Daniel O'Connell* ed. D. McCartney, 54-71. [55] See, e.g., C. Kinealy, 'The Liberator: O'Connell and Anti-Slavery', *History Today*, lvii. 12 (2007), 51-57; M. O'Dowd, 'O'Connell and the Lady Patriots: Women and O'Connellite Politics', in *Politics and Political Culture in Britain and Ireland* ed. A. Blackstock and E. Magennis, 283-303. [56] J. Lee, 'Social and Economic Ideas of O'Connell', in *O'Connell: Portrait of a Radical*, 70-86; M.R. O'Connell, 'Lawyer and Landlord', in *O'Connell: The Man and his Politics*, 107-11. [57] O'Faoláin, 330. [58] T. Bartlett, *Fall and Rise of Irish Nation*, 268-9, 311-26. [59] O'Faoláin, 39. [60] For his appearance and character, see D. O'Connell, 'My Father as I Remember Him', *Temple Bar*, cxviii (1899), 206-22; J.J. Horgan, 'O'Connell – The Man', in *O'Connell: Nine Centenary Essays*, 270-302. [61] O'Faoláin, 115; *O'Connell Corresp.* iii. 1081, 1430; Daunt, i. 157. [62] Daunt, i. 158-68; Fagan, i. 445-70. [63] MacDonagh, *Hereditary Bondsman*, 117; K.F. Roche, 'Revolution and Counter-Revolution', in *O'Connell: Nine Centenary Essays*, 51-53. [64] R.L. Sheil, *Sketches of Irish Bar* (1854), i. 73-97; W.H. Curran, *Sketches of Irish Bar* (1855), i. 154-82; *Recollections of Aubrey de Vere*, 112; M. R. O'Connell, 'Lawyer and Landlord', 100-7. [65] O'Faoláin, 117-18. [66] F. Griffith, 'Contemporary Opinion of O'Connell's Oratory', *Éire-Ireland*, vii. 3 (1972), 24-28. [67] Ibid.; O'Faoláin, 135-8; *Recollections of Aubrey de Vere*, 112-13; Hall, i. 242-3. [68] *Lettres sur les Elections Anglaises* (1827), 174-5, 177-8. [69] Lord Teignmouth, *Reminiscences of Many Years*, ii. 219. [70] *Mr. Gregory's Letter-Box*, 39. [71] Hall, i. 244. [72] G. Ó Tuathaigh, 'Folk-hero and Tradition', in *World of O'Connell*, 30-42; D. Ó Muirithe, 'O'Connell in Irish Folk Tradition', in *Daniel O'Connell: Political Pioneer* ed. M.R. O'Connell, 72-85; R. uí Ógáin, *Immortal Dan*, *passim*. [73] *O'Connell: The Man and his Politics*, 8; F. O'Ferrall, 'Daniel O'Connell ... Changing Images', in *Ireland: Art into History* ed. R. Gillespie and B.P. Kennedy, 92-94. [74] M.D. George, *Cat. of Pol. and Personal Satires*, ix. 11898, 12073. [75] *Scottish Whig in Ireland* ed. H. Heaney, 37-38; Lord W.P. Lennox, *Drafts on My Memory*, ii. 51; *Croker Pprs.* iii. 307; M.D. Jephson, *Anglo-Irish Misc.* 188-90; Hall, i. 246. [76] Daunt, i. 56; Fagan, i. 111; MacDonagh, *Hereditary Bondsman*, 98. [77] Daunt, i. 36, 129. [78] *Moore Jnl.* iii. 906. [79] Add. 56554, f. 19. [80] O'Faoláin, 21, 41, 44, 47, 77-78, 80-82, 112-14, 249, 253-4. [81] MacDonagh, *Hereditary Bondsman*, 188. [82] Lee, 74; Roche, 81. [83] *O'Connell Corresp.* ii. 600, 611, 683; iii. 1100; M.R. O'Connell, 'Income and Expenditure', 17-19; MacDonagh, *Hereditary Bondsman*, 89-90, 152-7, 187. [84] Ibid. ii. 526, 528, 1061, 1063; MacDonagh, *Hereditary Bondsman*, 182-5, 301. [85] E. Courtenay, *Narrative ... of Most Extraordinary Cruelty, Perfidy and Depravity Perpetrated against her by O'Connell* (1832), 7-12, 30; D. Gwynn, *Daniel O'Connell and Ellen Courtenay* (1930), 1-24. [86] *O'Connell Corresp.* ii. 709; Bishop, 40-49, and Bishop, 'Was O'Connell Faithful?', *Éire-Ireland*, xxxi. 3 & 4 (1996), 58-75. [87] *O'Connell Corresp.* ii. 950, 952-4, 958, 991, 1050, 1053, 1057; iii. 1087-9, 1101; viii. 3396; M.R. O'Connell, 'Income and Expenditure', 19-24; MacDonagh, *Hereditary Bondsman*, 191-200. [88] *O'Connell Corresp.* ii. 711-12, 719, 744. [89] Ibid. ii. 752, 754, 756, 762. [90] MacDonagh, *Hereditary Bondsman*, 165-7. [91] T. Corcoran, 'O'Connell and Popular Education', *Studies*, xviii (1929), 211-24; J.

Coolahan, 'Primary Education as Political Issue in O'Connell's Time', in *O'Connell: Education, Church and State* ed. M.R. O'Connell, 87-100. [92] *O'Connell Corresp.* ii. 820, 823; *Select Speeches*, ii. 72-75. [93] *O'Connell Corresp.* ii. 837, 841. [94] Fagan, i. 248-50; *Select Speeches*, ii. 83. [95] *O'Connell Corresp.* ii. 869-70, 875, 881, 885-6, 904; *Select Speeches*, ii. 84-90. [96] *Select Speeches*, ii. 90-110; D. Plunket, *Life of Lord Plunket*, i. 405. [97] *O'Connell Corresp.* ii. 895, 898, 901. [98] E.A. Smith, *George IV*, 197; *Wellesley Mems.* iii. 318, 324-5; *Speeches and Public Letters of the Liberator* ed. M. F. Cusack, ii. 570. [99] *O'Connell Corresp.* ii. 930, 932, 949, 954a; *Select Speeches*, ii. 171-4; *Wellesley Mems.* iii. 319, 364. [100] *O'Connell Corresp.* ii. 982-3, 988, 990, 992, 996, 999, 1004. [101] Ibid. ii. 1013; *Select Speeches*, ii. 189-205. [102] For this paragraph, see O'Ferrall, *Catholic Emancipation*, 34-79. [103] *O'Connell Corresp.* ii. 1023. [104] See *Procs. of Catholic Association* (1825), *passim*. [105] *O'Connell Corresp.* iii. 1074, 1080, 1082, 1110, 1119, 1123a. [106] *Select Speeches*, ii. 269-92. [107] A. Aspinall, *Politics and the Press*, 319-25; B. Inglis, 'O'Connell and Irish Press', *Irish Hist. Stud.* viii (1952), 1-27. [108] *Tour ... by a German Prince*, ii. 117-18. [109] Daunt, i. 42. [110] *Select Speeches*, ii. 367-71; Buckingham, *Mems. Geo. IV*, ii. 199. [111] *Select Speeches*, ii. 430-64; *O'Connell Corresp.* iii. 1142, 1144, 1151; Wellington mss WP1/807/30; 808/17. [112] *Dublin Evening Post*, 15 Feb. 1825; *O'Connell Corresp.* iii. 1159, 1277, 1291, 1388, 1424; M.R. O'Connell, 'Income and Expenditure', 24-28; MacDonagh, *Hereditary Bondsman*, 201-4. [113] *O'Connell Corresp.* iii. 1161, 1168. [114] Ibid. iii. 1169, 1172-3; Sheil, ii. 201, 207; Gurney diary, 18 Feb. 1825. [115] *PP* (1825), viii. 48-85, 107-33; ix. 123-71; *Colchester Diary*, iii. 372. [116] Parker, i. 202-4. [117] *O'Connell Corresp.* iii. 1173-92, 1203-11, 1216-36; Sheil, ii. 221-3. [118] O'Ferrall, *Catholic Emancipation*, 94-95, 103-5, 108. [119] Ibid. 105-7, 110-13; *O'Connell Corresp.* iii. 1239-40, 1253, 1269-71. [120] *O'Connell Corresp.* iii. 1275, 1278. [121] Ibid. iii. 1096; viii. 3397; *CJ*, lxxxi. 328; *The Times*, 6 May 1826. [122] *O'Connell Corresp.* iii. 1308, 1312, 1314, 1319-22; O'Ferrall, *Catholic Emancipation*, 120-1, 124-5, 131-2, 134, 140-2. [123] O'Ferrall, *Catholic Emancipation*, 143-8; *O'Connell Corresp.* iii. 1325, 1334, 1337, 1345; *Collection of Speeches of O'Connell and Sheil* (1828), 1-20. [124] Parker, i. 417. [125] *Crabb Robinson Diary*, ii. 24-33. [126] *Geo. IV Letters*, iii. 1407; *O'Connell Corresp.* iii. 1354. [127] *O'Connell Corresp.* iii. 1358-60, 1364, 1370, 1372, 1374, 1376, 1378, 1380-2, 1384, 1386; MacDonagh, *Hereditary Bondsman*, 232-5. [128] Lansdowne mss, Knight of Kerry to Lansdowne, 21 Apr., O'Connell to former, 24 Apr. 1827. [129] *O'Connell Corresp.* iii. 1387, 1389, 1392-4, 1397. [130] Lansdowne mss, O'Connell to Knight of Kerry, 30 July 1827. [131] Brougham mss, Rice to Brougham, 1 Oct. 1827; *O'Connell Corresp.* iii. 1407, 1413, 1419, 1431-2, 1438-9, 1445, 1448; MacDonagh, *Hereditary Bondsman*, 237-47. [132] MacDonagh, *Hereditary Bondsman*, 247-8; *O'Connell Corresp.* iii. 1453, 1457, 1460. [133] Daunt, ii. 257-61; *O'Connell Corresp.* viii. 3206. [134] *Paget Pprs.* ed. Sir A.B. Paget, ii. 394-5; Mq. of Anglesey, *One-Leg*, 200-1; *Peel Mems.* i. 131, 135. [135] H.R. Addison, *Recollections of Irish Police Magistrate*, 68-69; *Clare Jnl.* 3, 7, 10, 14 July; *Dublin Evening Post*, 3, 5, 8, 10, 12 July 1828; *Disraeli Letters*, i. 324. [136] Uí Ógáin, 31-32, 75-76, 86-87; T. Wyse, *Hist. Sketch of late Catholic Association* (1829), i. 390-8; Ashley, *Palmerston*, i. 181-2; *Peel Mems.* i. 105-6, 115-17, 123-7. [137] Wellington mss WP1/940/14; 941/7, 12; *Peel Mems.* i. 140, 143-4; *Ellenborough Diary*, i. 156, 162-3; MacDonagh, *Hereditary Bondsman*, 255-6. [138] *Arbuthnot Jnl.* ii. 197-8; *Baring Jnls.* i. 57; Add. 40325, f. 171. [139] O'Ferrall, *Catholic Emancipation*, 202-3, 210-11, 215-16, 218-19, 223-4; *O'Connell Corresp.* iii. 1483-5; Add. 40322, f. 278; 40334, f. 246. [140] J. Belchem, *'Orator' Hunt*, 191-3; J.E. Crimmins, 'Bentham and O'Connell', *HJ*, xl (1997), 360-2, 368-744; *O'Connell Corresp.* iii. 1488; viii. 3404, 3407-10. [141] *Tour ... By a German Prince*, i. 333-4; ii. 130; G. Owens, '"A Moral Insurrection": Faction Fighters, Public Demonstrations and O'Connellite Campaign, 1828', *Irish Hist. Stud.* xxx (1997), 513-41; F. O'Ferrall, 'O'Connell and Cooke: Conflict of Civil and Religious Liberty in Modern Ireland', *Irish Rev.* i (1986), 20-27. [142] *O'Connell Corresp.* iii. 1493, 1501. [143] *Unrepentant Tory* ed. R.A. Gaunt, 61, 62, 354. [144] MacDonagh, *Hereditary Bondsman*, 263-5. [145] *Greville Mems.* i. 224-5. [146] NLS mss 24748, f. 76. [147] *Dublin Evening Post*, 24 Dec. 1828, 29 Jan., 7 Feb. 1829. [148] Ibid. 12, 14 Feb., 12 Mar.; Grey mss, Durham to Grey, 4 Feb. 1829; *O'Connell Corresp.* iv. 1513a, 1517, 1519. [149] Add. 56553, ff. 149, 152. [150] *O'Connell Corresp.* iv. 1525-9. [151] Ibid. iv. 1529-34. [152] Ibid. iv. 1535-40; *Greville Mems.* i. 251-2, 266, 280; *Ellenborough Diary*, i. 384-5. [153] P. Rogers, 'Catholic Emancipation', in *O'Connell: Nine Centenary Essays*, 148-50; *O'Connell Corresp.* iv. 1544, 1546, 1550a, 1551-2. [154] Daunt, i. 130; *Colchester Diary*, iii. 612. [155] Add. 40308, f. 170; *O'Connell Corresp.* iv. 1550, 1552, 1558-60; viii. 3411. [156] Add. 40397, ff. 101, 121; *The Times*, 11 May 1829; *O'Connell Corresp.* iv. 1561-6. [157] *CJ*, lxxxiv. 303; *Althorp Letters*, 143; Broughton, *Recollections*, iii. 320-1; D. Howell-Thomas, *Duncannon*, 139. [158] *CJ*, lxxxiv. 311; *Moore Jnl.* iii. 1208; Northants. RO, Agar Ellis diary, 18 May; Nottingham Univ. Lib. Ossington mss Acc. 636, Denison diary, 29 May 1829. [159] Hatherton mss, Littleton to Leigh, 19 May 1829. [160] *CJ*, lxxxiv. 314, 325-6. [161] George, xi. 15760, 15770; *Greville Mems.* i. 293; *Peel Mems.* i. 308. [162] *O'Connell Corresp.* iv. 1566, 1569-73, 1577-8, 1581; viii. 3412; Add. 56554, f. 19; PRO NI, Anglesey mss D619/32A/3/1/149. [163] *O'Connell Corresp.* iv. 1585, 1593-5, 1598-9; *Greville Mems.* i. 306-7; *Dublin Evening Post*, 11, 30 June, 21, 30 July, 1 Aug.; Grey mss, C. Grey to Grey, 4 Aug. 1829; Wellington mss WP1/1037/5. [164] *O'Connell Corresp.* viii. 3413, 3416-17; Crimmins, 374-83. [165] *O'Connell Corresp.* iv. 1597, 1604; viii. 3414; D.C. Riach, 'O'Connell and American Anti-Slavery', *Irish Hist. Studies*, xx (1976-7), 4, and 'O'Connell and Slavery', in *World of O'Connell*, 175-85. [166] *O'Connell Corresp.* iv. 1604, 1640, 1710; M. Brock, *Great Reform Act*, 58-59. [167] *O'Connell Corresp.* iii. 1490; iv. 1608, 1610, 1614, 1628a; viii. 3415-16; J. O'Connell, *Recollections and Experiences*, ii. 81-83. [168] MacDonagh, *Hereditary Bondsman*, 274-5, and *Emancipist*, 8-16. [169] *O'Connell Corresp.* iv. 1583-4, 1588, 1624, 1626, 1629-30; *The Times*, 23 Nov., 10, 23, 30 Dec. 1829; *Weekly Waterford Chron.* 2, 30 Jan. 1830. [170] Anglesey mss 32A/3/1/254; Add. 40327, f. 97a; Gash, 623-4. [171] *Dublin Evening Post*, 5, 7, 12, 28 Jan. 1830; uí Ógáin, 33-36, 83-85, 154-6, 225, 238. [172] Broughton, iv. 8; Buckingham, ii. 403; J.A. Roebuck, *Hist. Whig Ministry*, i. 82; Daunt, i. 278; M.D. Petre, *Lord Petre*, 313; Macintyre, 18. [173] R. Irish Acad. Foster mss 23 G 39/4; *Dublin Evening Post*, 6, 9 Feb.; Add. 51585, Holland to Fox, 7 Feb.; PRO NI T2534/2, North to MacDonnell [Feb.] 1830; *Greville Mems.* i. 370; *Taylor Pprs.* 314. [174] *Ellenborough Diary*, ii. 183; *Arbuthnot Jnl.* ii. 332. [175] Add. 56554, f. 63; JRL, Bromley Davenport mss, 'mem.' 1828. [176] O'Ferrall, *O'Connell*, 77; *O'Connell Corresp.* iv. 1637, 1639, 1651, 1653-4, 1658. [177] Add. 35148, f. 49. [178] Keele Univ. Lib. Sneyd mss, Littleton to Sneyd, 24 Feb. [1830]. [179] *London Radicalism* ed. D.J. Rowe (London Rec. Soc. v), 1-2; *O'Connell Corresp.* iv. 1647. [180] NAI, Leveson Gower letter bks. Leveson Gower to Singleton, 20 Mar. 1830. [181] *Dublin Evening Post*, 30 Mar., 8 Apr. 1830; *O'Connell Corresp.* iv. 1668, 1670. [182] Add. 40327, f. 145; 40338, f. 121; R. B. McDowell, *Public Opinion and Government Policy in Ireland*, 140. [183] Leveson Gower letter bks. Leveson Gower to Singleton, 29 Apr. 1830. [184] *O'Connell Corresp.* iv. 1674; Add. 40400, f. 170. [185] Grey mss, Howick jnl. 12 May; Leveson Gower letter bks. Leveson Gower to Singleton, 13 May 1830. [186] Leveson Gower letter bks. Leveson Gower to Lees, 23 May 1830. [187] Reid, *Monckton Milnes*, i. 95. [188] *O'Connell Corresp.* iv. 1683-4. [189] M.W. Patterson, *Burdett and his Times*, ii. 471; Add. 40323, f. 153. [190] *'My Darling Danny': Letters from Mary O'Connell to her Son Daniel* ed. E. I. Bishop, 28-29. [191] *Dublin Evening Post*, 8, 22 July 1830; *O'Connell Corresp.* iv. 1678-9, 1684, 1687, 1689-9, 1692; Fagan, ii. 47-49. [192] *Dublin Evening Post*, 13, 15, 27, 31 July 1830; *O'Connell Corresp.* iv. 1692-4, 1696; viii. 3420; PRO NI, Pack-Beresford mss D664/A/153-5. [193] *Weekly Waterford Chron.* 17, 24, 31 July, 14 Aug., 4, 11, 25 Sept. 1830. [194] *O'Connell Corresp.* iv. 1707-9; J. Hennig, 'Continental Opinion', in *O'Connell: Nine Centenary Essays*, 251-3. [195] Daunt, i. 108; ii. 10. [196] *O'Connell Corresp.* iv. 1716. [197] Ibid. iv. 1720a, 1721; PRO NI, Fitzgerald mss MIC639/13/7/98, 99; Add. 40313, f. 129; 56555, f. 33; *Unrepentant Tory*, 128; *Ellenborough Diary*, ii. 397, 402, 409; *Corresp. of Joseph Jekyll* ed. A. Bourke, 252. [198] *O'Connell*

Corresp. iv. 1722. [199] Ibid. iv. 1722-3; Hopetoun mss 167, f. 177; Howick jnl.; *Life of Campbell*, i. 483. [200] *O'Connell Corresp.* iv. 1725; Agar Ellis diary; Hopetoun mss 167, f. 183; *Bunbury Mem.* 155. [201] NLI, Wyse mss 15024 (8), Wyse to O'Donnell, 14 Nov. 1830; NLW, Ormathwaite mss FG1/5, p. 130. [202] *O'Connell Corresp.* iv. 1723-4, 1728, 1736; viii. 3422; Wyse mss 15024 (1), Coppinger to Wyse, 26 Nov. 1830. [203] *O'Connell Corresp.* iv. 1726-7, 1738; *Dublin Evening Post*, 20 Nov. 1830; *Croker Pprs.* ii. 78. [204] E.A. Smith, *Lord Grey*, 289-91; Anglesey, 245; Add. 56555, f. 64. [205] MacDonagh, *Emancipist*, 42-43; *O'Connell Corresp.* iv. 1729-30, 1737, 1744, 1751; *Life of Campbell*, i. 497; Monypenny and Buckle, *Disraeli*, i. 389; *Three Diaries*, 33; *Smith Letters*, ii. 546-7. [206] *O'Connell Corresp.* iv. 1732-3, 1740. [207] *Melbourne Pprs.* 167-70; Anglesey mss 29B, pp. 4-15; 33A/74-76. [208] *O'Connell Corresp.* iv. 1735-6; *Dublin Evening Post*, 21, 23 Dec. 1830; *William IV-Grey Corresp.* i. 28-29. [209] Anglesey mss 28A-B/28, 32, 36; 28C, pp. 19-21; 29B, pp. 16-23, 39-40; *Dublin Evening Post*, 28, 30 Dec. 1830; *O'Connell Corresp.* iv. 1744; L.G. Mitchell, *Lord Melbourne*, 114, 135; *Greville Mems.* ii. 98, 107. [210] *Dublin Evening Post*, 1, 13, 15 Jan.; Add. 51568, Anglesey to Holland, 2 Jan. 1831; *O'Connell Corresp.* iv. 1748, 1751, 1762; *Jekyll Corresp.* 264. [211] J. O'Connell, *Recollections and Experiences*, i. 65-69; *'My Darling Danny'*, 34; Anglesey, 247-8. [212] Le Marchant, *Althorp*, 288; *Melbourne Pprs.* 173-4, 177-8; Anglesey mss 27B, pp. 1-8; 28A-B/37; 28C, pp. 53-57; 31D/15; *O'Connell Corresp.* iv. 1757-8, 1764; *'My Darling Danny'*, 12-13, 37-40; MacDonagh, *Emancipist*, 45-46. [213] *Greville Mems.* ii. 115-16; *Moore Jnl.* iv. 1380, 1384; *O'Connell Corresp.* iv. 1751a, 1765, 1767; *Dublin Evening Post*, 22 Jan., 12 Feb. 1831. [214] Anglesey mss 31D/18-20; *Creevey Pprs.* ii. 219. [215] *'My Darling Danny'*, 44-45; St. Deiniol's Lib. Glynne-Gladstone mss 197, T. to J. Gladstone, 19 Feb. 1831; *Three Diaries*, 58. [216] *O'Connell Corresp.* viii. 3423. [217] Ibid. iv. 1768, 1775, 1777; viii. 3424. [218] Ibid. iv. 1778, 1780-4, 1787, 1790-1; MacDonagh, *Emancipist*, 46-47; *Greville Mems.* ii. 127. [219] Crimmins, 383-4. [220] Wellington mss WP1/1179/32; Anglesey mss 28A-B/46; 31D/30, 35, 36. [221] *Melbourne Pprs.* 179-81. [222] Patterson, ii. 586-7. [223] NLI, Stacpoole-Kenny mss 18889 (18), W. to J. Macnamara, 23 Apr. 1831. [224] *Moore Jnl.* iv. 1391; *Greville Mems.* ii. 140, 142; *Dublin Evening Post*, 26 Apr. 1831. [225] *O'Connell Corresp.* iv. 1793, 1799, 1800-6; Anglesey mss 28C, pp. 113-14. [226] D. Gwynn, *O'Gorman Mahon*, 110-11; Anglesey mss 28C, pp. 109-11; Wellington mss WP1/1184/9, 24, 31; Fitzgerald mss 14/7/26; *Western Herald*, 10, 14, 17, 19 May; Derby mss 920 Der (14) 124/3, knight of Kerry to Smith Stanley, 30 May, 7 June 1831; *O'Connell Corresp.* iv. 1810. [227] Derby mss 125/12, O'Connell to Gosset, 6 May; *O'Connell Corresp.* iv. 1808-9, 1811; *Clare Jnl.* 9, 19 May; Grey mss, Smith Stanley to Grey, 21 May 1831. [228] Add. 40340, f. 261; Macintyre, 43. [229] Derby mss 117/5, Grey to Smith Stanley, 18, 27 May 1831; Anglesey mss 28C, pp. 106-8, 118-19. [230] *Unrepentant Tory*, 137-8, 154. [231] *O'Connell Corresp.* iv. 1816, 1818a; Derby mss 125/4, Barrington to Smith Stanley, 5 June 1831; Anglesey mss 31D/41. [232] *O'Connell Corresp.* iv. 1820. [233] MacDonagh, *Emancipist*, 60-64 and 'O'Connell in House of Commons', in *World of O'Connell*, 43-53. [234] *O'Connell Corresp.* iv. 1815; *Dublin Evening Post*, 18 June 1831. [235] *O'Connell Corresp.* iv. 1822; Le Marchant, 326. [236] Anglesey mss 27A/122; *O'Connell Corresp.* iv. 1826, 1902, 1907. [237] *O'Connell Corresp.* iv. 1828, 1830, 1834. [238] Ibid. iv. 1831-4; Anglesey mss 28A-B/71; *Dublin Evening Post*, 16 Aug. 1831. [239] *Holland House Diaries*, 27; O. Williams, *Life and Letters of Rickman*, 288. [240] Anglesey mss 27A/131; 27B, pp. 42-46; 31D/52; Aberdeen Univ. Lib. Arbuthnot mss. [241] *Holland House Diaries*, 40. [242] NLS mss 24748, f. 120. [243] *Dublin Evening Post*, 13 Sept. 1831. [244] *O'Connell Corresp.* iv. 1836. [245] Hatherton diary. [246] *Three Diaries*, 138. [247] *Holland House Diaries*, 58; Wellington mss WP1/1197/13. [248] *O'Connell Corresp.* iv. 1835-7, 1839. [249] Ormathwaite mss FG1/5, p. 209; Cornw. RO, Hawkins mss 10/2172, 2174. [250] *O'Connell Corresp.* iv. 1837; TCD, Donoughmore mss E/375. [251] *O'Connell Corresp.* iv. 1839, 1842; W. J. Fitzpatrick, *Life of Dr. Doyle*, ii. 334-5. [252] *Arbuthnot Jnl.* ii. 433; *Holland House Diaries*, 68, 69; Patterson, ii. 596; *O'Connell Corresp.* iv. 1843; *Dublin Evening Post*, 8 Nov. 1831. [253] Grey mss, Smith Stanley to Grey, 23 Oct.; Derby mss 117/5, reply, 24 Oct. 1831; Anglesey mss 27A/136; 29B, pp. 91-92. [254] Anglesey mss 27A/138; 27B, p. 58; *Holland House Diaries*, 72, 78. [255] F.A. D'Arcy, 'Artisans of Dublin and O'Connell', *Irish Hist. Studies*, xvii (1970), 221-43, and 'National Trades Political Union and O'Connell', *Eire-Ireland*, xvii. 3 (1982), 7-16. [256] *Dublin Evening Post*, 17, 22 Nov. 1831; *William IV-Grey Corresp.* i. 436. [257] Arbuthnot mss, Holmes to Mrs. Arbuthnot, 18 Nov.; Lansdowne mss, Smith Stanley to Lansdowne, 18 Nov.; Grey mss, same to Grey, 18 Nov. 1831. [258] *O'Connell Corresp.* iv. 1849-51, 1853-4, 1861-3; *Holland House Diaries*, 86. [259] Hatherton diary, 21 Nov. 1831; Anglesey mss 27A/139-41; 27B, pp. 65-71, 80-84; 31D/77; Derby mss 119/3, Anglesey to Smith Stanley, 8 Jan. 1832; Fitzpatrick, ii. 283, 336, 342, 364-72. [260] *'My Darling Danny'*, 17, 68, 70, 76, 80; *O'Connell Corresp.* iv. 1863, 1873. [261] *William IV-Grey Corresp.* ii. 45-46, 54-55, 149. [262] Derby mss 119/3, Anglesey to Smith Stanley, 11, 13 Jan. 1832. [263] *O'Connell Corresp.* iv. 1867, 1872. [264] *William IV-Grey Corresp.* ii. 149. [265] *Life of Campbell*, ii. 4; Add. 51573, Rice to Lady Holland [Feb. 1832]. [266] *Three Diaries*, 184-5. [267] *PP* (1831-2), xii. 7. [268] *Three Diaries*, 191; *Raikes Jnl.* i. 12; Hatherton diary, 5 Feb. 1832. [269] Hatherton diary, 8 Mar. 1832. [270] MacDonagh, *Emancipist*, 65, 70, 78-79, 142; Gwynn, *O'Gorman Mahon*, 127-32; *O'Connell Corresp.* iv. 1848, 1852, 1871, 1890, 1900; Courtenay, 13-27. [271] MacDonagh, *Emancipist*, 65-72, 85, 255; *O'Connell Corresp.* iv. 1876-7, 1880, 1882, 1894; *Speeches and Public Letters*, ii. 458-515. [272] Add. 56557, f. 2. [273] *O'Connell Corresp.* iv. 1893. [274] Macintyre, 31-36. [275] Anglesey mss 27B, pp. 106. [276] Derby mss, Anglesey to Smith Stanley, 23 June 1832; *O'Connell Corresp.* iv. 1897. [277] *O'Connell Corresp.* iv. 1898; *Hist. of 'The Times'*, i. 311-14. [278] K.T. Hoppen, 'Politics, the Law, and Nature of Irish Electorate', *EHR*, xcii (1977), 756-8, 765; *O'Connell Corresp.* iv. 1899a. [279] *O'Connell Corresp.* iv. 1905. [280] *Greville Mems.* ii. 308-9. [281] *O'Connell Corresp.* iv. 1912. [282] Ibid. iv. 1911, 1919; MacDonagh, *Emancipist*, 1, 76-77; *Letters of O'Connell on Reform Bill* (1832), 3-42. [283] Sir James Graham mss (IHR microfilm XR 80), 2, Graham to Smith Stanley, 29 July 1832; G.M. Trevelyan, *Lord Grey of Reform Bill*, 357; Smith, 296, 322. [284] *O'Connell Corresp.* iv. 1921; v. 1957. [285] Ibid. iv. 1914-16, 1920-1, 1925, 1929, 1945; *Dublin Evening Post*, 11, 13, 27 Dec. 1832. [286] Add. 51688, Lansdowne to Holland, 23 Dec. 1832; *Greville Mems.* ii. 350, 354, 361; *Three Diaries*, 314; Whyte, 297, 299, 300, 316; Macintyre, 43-44, 69-70, 147-51, 301-2 and 'O'Connell and British Politics', in *O'Connell: Portrait of a Radical*, 87, 92, 94-95. [287] [J. Grant], *Random Recollections of Commons* (1837), 313-28; T. de V. White, 'English Opinion', in *O'Connell: Nine Centenary Essays*, 211. [288] *Greville Mems.* v. 449-50. [289] Hatherton diary, 25 May 1847. [290] *Oxford Dict. of Quotations*; *Moore Jnl.* iv. 1560. [291] Fagan, i. 162. [292] *O'Connell Corresp.* vi. 2621. [293] D. O'Connell, *Observations on Corn Laws* (1842), 66-67. [294] D. Griffin, *Life of Gerald Griffin*, 414-16; Daunt, i. 28, 111, 285; ii. 8-9; uí Ógáin, 101-3; M. R. O'Connell, 'O'Connell, Young Ireland and Violence', in *O'Connell: The Man and his Politics*, 61-88; O'Ferrall, *Catholic Emancipation*, 285-6. [295] D. O'Connell, *Observations on Corn Laws*, 34. [296] Mrs. M.J. O'Connell, ii. 294-5; *Recollections of Aubrey de Vere*, 114; E.A. Day, *Mr. Justice Day of Kerry*, 223; Maxwell, *Clarendon*, i. 278. [297] D. O'Connell, *Observations on Corn Laws*, 67-69. [298] See, especially, K.B. Nowlan, *Politics of Repeal*. [299] J.N. McCord, 'Image in Ireland: Cartoons of HB', in *O'Connell: Political Pioneer*, 57-71; G. Owens, 'Visualizing the Liberator: Self-Fashioning, Dramaturgy and the Construction of O'Connell', *Éire-Ireland*, xxxiii. 3 & 4 (1998), 103-30; K.T. Hoppen, 'Riding a Tiger: O'Connell, Reform and Popular Politics', in *Reform in Great Britain and Ireland* ed. T.C.W. Blanning and P. Wende, 121-43. [300] L.A. Williams, *O'Connell, British Press and Irish Famine*, 229-39; *Mill Works*, xiii. 710. [301] *The Times*, 24 May 1847; *Gent. Mag.* (1847), ii. 93-97; *DNB*; *Oxford DNB*. [302] W.E. Gladstone, 'O'Connell', *19th Cent.* xxv (1889), 151-2. [303] V. Conzemins, 'Place of O'Connell in Liberal Catholic Movement of 19th Cent.', in *World of O'Connell*, 143-9; P. Joannon, 'O'Connell, Montalembert and Birth of Christian Democracy in France', in *O'Connell: Political Pioneer*, 98-109; G.F.

Grogan, *Noblest Agitator: O'Connell and German Catholic Movement, passim*; *O'Connell: The Man and his Politics*, 137; O'Ferrall, *Catholic Emancipation*, 277-8 and 'Liberty and Catholic Politics', in *O'Connell: Political Pioneer*, 35-56; O. MacDonagh, 'Contribution of O'Connell', in *Irish Parliamentary Tradition* ed. B. Farrell, 160-9; M. Robinson, 'O'Connell, a Tribute', in *Hist. Ireland*, v (1997), 26-31.

S.M.F.

O'CONNELL, Maurice Daniel (1803–1853).

CO. CLARE	23 Mar. 1831–1832
TRALEE	1832–1837
TRALEE	12 Mar. 1838–18 June 1853

b. 27 June 1803, 1st s. of Daniel O'Connell* and Mary, da. of Thomas O'Connell, physician, of Tralee, co. Kerry; bro. of Daniel O'Connell†, Morgan O'Connell† and John O'Connell†. *educ.* Miss Everina Wollstonecraft's sch. Dublin 1810; Edward Whyte's sch. Dublin 1813; Clongowes Wood Coll. 1815; private tutors; Trinity, Dublin 1819; King's Inns 1821, called [I] 1827; G. Inn 1824. *m.* 29 Sept. 1832, Mary Frances, da. of John Bindon Scott of Cahircon, co. Clare, 2s. 2da.; ch. illegit. *suc.* fa. 1847. *d.* 18 June 1853.

Dir. National Bank of Ireland 1834.

Maurice, the Liberator's eldest son, was too weak a character to bear the full weight of his parents' loving devotion. As their extensive correspondence makes plain, he, even more than their younger children, was the constant subject of their deepest anxieties and consuming aspirations. Taken shortly after his birth to his paternal grandfather's house at Carhen in remote county Kerry, he was doted on by his family, but, in accordance with the old tradition, was fostered out.[1] O'Connell reported to his wife, about a visit to him in 1805, that their two-year-old son

> is as like you as two eggs – and has all that sauciness of temper and disposition. He is a wonderful favourite and the most affectionate little villain in the world. His temper is certainly hasty, but he is never for one moment sulky or sullen and I already perceive that there would be little difficulty in bringing him into proper discipline.

Later that summer she responded in kind with news that

> our dear Maurice is perfectly well. He is much attached to me though he sometimes calls me a bitch and desires me go to Tralee to Dada Dan. His nurse was to visit him yesterday and anything to equal his delight to see her I never saw. He kissed every bit of her and made her take out her breast and press it to his own.[2]

In 1809 O'Connell detected in Maurice 'an ardour and a distinctness which please me much', qualities which he prized 'because they are I know through life the sources of the only genuine pleasures – of those pleasures which alone render life worth having'. Yet he soon came to worry about his son's misbehaviour, bidding his wife to be more peremptory with him, and to fear that his gifts would be thrown away in idleness.[3] Mary Wollstonecraft's sister Everina, who ran the boys' school that he attended in Hume Street, Dublin, commented in 1811 that it was 'a pity a boy of such talents should be so sheepish and careless', and by 1813, presumably in order to improve his education, he had been put under the care of Edward Whyte, who had an establishment in Grafton Street.[4] In early 1815 he was sent with his brother Morgan to the newly opened Jesuit college at Clongowes Wood in county Kildare, where their father expected them to imbibe 'principles of Catholic faith and national feeling'. O'Connell criticized what he described to Maurice as 'a loose and rambling turn in your mind', and could not forebear to urge him to greater efforts, but the rector, Father Peter Kenney, rated him highly and informed his father in 1817 that 'if *you* and we conform him to steady habits of application, we shall get him to do anything. God has given him very ample talents. Exertion and cultivation will make him a solid and conspicuous scholar'.[5] He displayed a certain unctuous religiosity, for example in April 1816, when his mother wrote to O'Connell that he 'thanked God with his hands clasped for your *conversion*', or again in June 1818, when he expressed his gratitude to her for 'that love and tenderness with which you watched over my childhood'. Mary O'Connell took a maternal pride in his development at Clongowes, although in a letter to her husband, 1 Apr. 1820, in which she recognized that Maurice was still very young, she complained that he and Morgan were formerly nice mannered boys, but that now it was 'almost impossible to get them to divest themselves of the vulgarity they acquired at *that* college'.[6]

Having been assisted by a tutor, Maurice studied at Trinity College, but his father found him unconscionably idle as well as dilatory in the observance of his religious duties, and was not surprised by his taking only a reasonably good degree.[7] O'Connell, who already employed him in running minor political errands and was glad to have his company during his wife's absence abroad, took him to the Castle on the presentation of the Catholics' congratulatory address to Lord Wellesley, the lord lieutenant, in December 1822, and evidently envisaged a career for him at the bar.[8] Yet in 1823 he was distraught about Maurice's 'fidgets' or 'shocking and foolish gesticulations': he confided to his wife, who pitied him this restless disorder, that he 'actually has got a trick of lolling out his tongue round his lips which is childish and absurd in its appearance', and he doubted whether she would 'think it useless to go to the expense of giving him any profession'.[9] However, Maurice mastered his bad habits, at his father's insistence, and, having finally been to mass, was dispatched to join his mother in France for a short time. His uncle James O'Connell, writing to Daniel in November 1823 to argue that Maurice should be provided for during his intended residence at the inns of court, observed that he was 'blessed with a good constitution and with talents that ensure success at the bar if he applies but ... I have reason to know he thinks he will have a large landed property. It is cruel not to undeceive him'. An allowance of £200 a year was granted by his great-uncle, Maurice O'Connell of Derrynane, early in 1824, when Maurice began to keep his terms at Gray's Inn.[10] His father berated him for his procrastination and profligacy, but his mother, who benefited from seeing him frequently at her then residence in Southampton, interceded several times on his behalf and attempted to soothe her husband. She wrote to him in February that Maurice, who assured her he was diligent in his studies, 'is every day improving in his appearance and manners. He is certainly a very fine young man. He will, I think, darling, resemble what you were when I first knew you'; and in April 1824 she noted that her son was 'quite domestic in his habits and very good in every sense of the word'.[11]

Increasingly seen as one of O'Connell's deputies, in December 1824 either Maurice or more likely Morgan (who several times acted in this capacity) fought a duel with Maurice Leyne, a barrister who had insulted their (non-duelling) father in the Four Courts.[12] Early the following year O'Connell left him in Dublin to get up Catholic petitions and, from London, asked his wife to 'tell Maurice I trust to his prudence and care of everything', though he added that 'a little law reading and a little earlier rising would do him no harm'. He was proud of Maurice's speech in the Catholic Association condemning its suppression and attacking John Doherty*, 15 Feb., though he commented that 'he should not imitate his father's faults by being so personal'. Maurice wrote to him in defiant mood, 18 Mar., that the Association 'met today for the last time. A glorious day for Ireland'.[13] The following month he acted as secretary to his father's Catholic deputation to Westminster, attending a royal levée and parliamentary debates on Catholic relief; on 22 Apr. O'Connell related to his wife that the previous day Maurice 'was near getting us put out of the House of Commons by flinging himself over banisters and down a flight of steps to show his agility. Luckily it was not noticed'.[14] Maurice, who spoke at the Kerry Catholics' meeting in August, was in October described by John Boyle, editor of the *Cork Freeholder*, as 'a whelp we understand of extraordinary impertinence', a slur which aroused his father's amused irritation.[15] In November 1825 O'Connell again trembled for his son's future, despondently commenting to his wife that 'you see he attends to nothing useful', and in March 1826 he begged him to concentrate on his legal training.[16] The diarist Henry Crabb Robinson, who visited O'Connell at his recently inherited residence of Derrynane that summer, noted that Maurice 'has talents and high spirits. He is coming to the bar, but will do nothing there. He is aware that he will be one day rich'.[17] He was called in early 1827 and that spring his father initiated him into going the Munster circuit, during which he spoke at Catholic gatherings in Ennis, 11 Mar., and Limerick, 21 Mar.[18] However, he soon gave up what little practice he had.[19]

In late 1827 O'Connell appointed Maurice as the national secretary of churchwardens, a crucial position within the revamped organization for the collection of the Catholic rent.[20] He continued to play a minor role in the Catholic Association, to which, for instance, he was said to have made a talented speech, 26 Jan. 1828.[21] In June he canvassed for O'Connell in his successful contest against William Vesey Fitzgerald* in Clare, where he qualified as a freeholder in order to vote. At the Association, the radical Jack Lawless commended the 'most excellent and praiseworthy conduct' during the by-election of Maurice, who, in his father's absence, presided at the Clare Liberal Club dinner in Ennis, 22 July 1828.[22] He chaired a meeting in Tralee of the committee for the opening of that borough, 28 Jan. 1829, and transmitted its thanks to Nicholas Philpot Leader*, for his support.[23] In February he followed his father's line in wishing to postpone the immediate dissolution of the Association, which was expected to have taken place on the government's concession of Catholic emancipation. The following month he accompanied O'Connell on his abortive journey to take his seat at Westminster; he was reported to have been a social success in the capital, and he spoke at the *Thatched House* meeting in opposition to the disfranchisement of the Irish 40*s*. freeholders, 7 Mar.[24] He was again active in his father's successful re-election campaign that summer, when he escaped charges of incitement for having encouraged mob violence against a rival candidate, Toby Glascock.[25] Late in 1829 O'Connell, in the course of a furious row with the Beresfords in Waterford, threatened to start Maurice for that county.[26] The following year, when there was some mention of an election agent being found for him in Kerry, he evidently suffered a long bout of illness. He used his indisposition as an excuse for not being inveigled into fighting a duel, on his father's behalf, with William Nugent Macnamara* in county Clare in July 1830.[27]

Although one local supporter had warned O'Connell that, unlike himself, his untried son would not be an acceptable candidate, Maurice was brought forward at Drogheda at the general election of 1830, when he was again linked to an attempt to open Tralee. In his address he claimed reflected glory from his father's role in the attainment of emancipation and declared himself 'a radical reformer of every public abuse'.[28] He vigorously attacked his opponent John Henry North, who was also contesting Dublin University, especially as a supporter of the duke of Wellington's ministry, but trailed behind him in the five-day poll and finished 105 adrift. His brother-in-law Christopher Fitzsimon†, who blamed his defeat on a shortfall in the number of registered freeholders, consoled O'Connell that Maurice, who promised to petition against North's non-resident freemen voters

> has throughout acquitted himself in the most satisfactory manner and has given proof of talent that even surprised his friends. All that is wanting is to induce him to exert his powers and I trust such will be the effect of his visit to Drogheda.[29]

He spoke at a dinner in his honour in Cahirciveen, Kerry, 15 Sept., and his petition against North's return was presented, 16 Nov. 1830.[30] He, of course, took his father's side over his arrest and prosecution early the following year and at one point informed Richard Newton Bennett, O'Connell's intermediary with the Grey administration, that he would not negotiate with ministers unless the charges were dropped.[31] In line with his father's trouble-making opposition to the re-election of Lord Duncannon, the newly appointed Whig minister, in county Kilkenny, in February 1831, he made there what William Gosset*, the Irish under-secretary, described as 'a most inflammatory speech, if *not quite*, very near treason'.[32]

Despite being hopeful of the Drogheda committee's deciding to seat Maurice, O'Connell was not disheartened by its judgment against him, 3 Mar. 1831, especially as he expected the passage of parliamentary reform to open many potential constituencies to him. In fact, although he would not have countenanced Maurice standing against William Richard Mahon, the brother of the O'Gorman Mahon*, the recently disqualified Member, he had him put up for Clare, with the Mahons' backing, at the by-election that month.[33] There was little enthusiasm for him and he was reported by Lord Anglesey, the lord lieutenant, to be 'rather a croaker', but he spoke enthusiastically for radical reform and the eventual repeal of the Union, and vituperatively attacked his reluctantly pro-reform challenger, the former Tory Member Sir Edward O'Brien*, whom he defeated by nearly 200 votes.[34] In the Commons he opposed the Ennis Member William Smith O'Brien's motion relating to disturbances in their county, 13 Apr., arguing, with passion and at length, that the economic distress and related unrest had been provoked by the exploitative and irresponsible local gentry and the indifferent and bungling Irish administration. He was congratulated on his 'able and forcible manner' by Frederick Trench, and although the Tory *Clare Journal* defended the landlords against the effusions of their 'boy Member', a liberal political commentator called his maiden speech 'exceedingly promising'.[35] He divided against Gascoyne's wrecking amendment to the English reform bill, 19 Apr. 1831. He stood again for Clare at the ensuing general election, when his father persisted in fielding him in order to keep out the O'Gorman Mahon, whom he blamed for the prevailing agrarian insurgency; he had ministerial backing as a reformer but was expected to lose.[36] Having objected to the imposition of an Insurrection Act and promised to continue to work for the amelioration of Irish grievances, he was nevertheless returned behind Macnamara, after a severe contest against the O'Gorman Mahon, whose brother William insulted him in speaking on the hustings and then struck him in the street in a vain attempt to provoke him into fighting a duel.[37]

Maurice, who naturally followed his father's political lead and sometimes deputized for him, was reasonably active in the Commons, often presenting Irish petitions and raising minor matters of concern. He intervened during the debate on the address to indicate that Clare was now calm, 21 June, but commented on the state of his county, 11, 15 July, 31 Aug. He voted for the second reading of the reintroduced reform bill, 6 July, at least twice against adjourning the proceedings on it, 12 July, and steadily for its details (twice by pairing), though he was in the minority against the proposed division of English counties, 11 Aug. He divided against the grants for professorial salaries at Oxford and Cambridge, 8 July, and civil list services, 18 July, but defended the one for Maynooth College, 19 July. He was listed in the minority on his father's motion for swearing the original Dublin committee, 29 July, and voted against censuring the Irish government over the Dublin election, 23 Aug. He divided for making legal provision for the Irish poor, 29 Aug., called for the disbandment of the Irish yeomanry, 31 Aug., 9 Sept., and broadly welcomed the appointment of lord lieutenants in Irish counties, 6 Oct. He was in minorities against the quarantine duties, 6 Sept., and for inquiry into how far the renewal of the Sugar Refinery Act would affect the West India interest and against going into committee on the truck bill, 12 Sept. He belittled the Evangelical Tory James Edward Gordon, 9 Sept., and twitted the radical Henry Hunt, 15, 29 Sept. He voted for the passage of the reform bill, 21 Sept., the second reading of the Scottish bill, 23 Sept., and Lord Ebrington's confidence motion, 10 Oct. 1831.

He missed the division on the second reading of the revised reform bill, 17 Dec. 1831, but voted for the partial disfranchisement of 30 boroughs in schedule B, 23 Jan. 1832, again generally for its details and for the third reading, 22 Mar. On 26 Jan. he and seven or eight other Irish Liberals were sent out of the House by O'Connell, who had spoken against the Russian-Dutch loan, in order to prevent government being accidentally defeated on this issue.[38] He divided for a select committee on distress in the glove trade, 31 Jan., and information on Portugal, 9 Feb., and spoke and voted for Hunt's motion for inquiry into Peterloo, 15 Mar. He praised the much improved Irish subletting bill, 20 Feb., but criticized Philip Crampton, the Irish solicitor-general, over the Irish judicial system, 28 Feb., and came down against the inclusion of Ireland in the anatomy bill, 11 Apr. He voted for printing the Woollen Grange petition for the abolition of Irish tithes, 16 Feb., and joined Charles Brownlow in arguing (and voting) that the Irish secretary Smith Stanley's tithe proposals should be postponed until his select committee had completed its full report, 8 Mar.; O'Connell, who was in Ireland, commented that Maurice's speech was as usual 'miserably reported'. Retorting to Smith Stanley's slighting remarks about the smallness of the minority on the 8th, he declared on 27 Mar. that the question was 'not between a minority and a majority in that House, but between a minority and a majority of the people of Ireland', but also condemned the Irish Members who had missed the vote. He drew a sneer from Smith Stanley by suggesting that the subject had been brought forward because of the absence of his father, who afterwards wrote to his wife that Maurice 'was perfectly right throughout and ... really spoke excellently'.[39] He voted against the first two resolutions that day, and the resulting tithes arrears bill, 6, 9 Apr. He again spoke at length against the exaction of ruinously high tithes before the introduction of any conciliatory measures, telling Crampton that 'you wish to enforce a harsh law on the people without at the same time doing what you admit to be an act of justice', 9 Apr., and he protested against the third reading of the bill, predicting further widespread and violent resistance to the payment of tithes, 16 Apr. 1832.

He probably paired for Ebrington's motion for an address calling on the king to appoint only ministers who would carry the reform bill unimpaired, 10 May, but was absent from the division on the second reading of the Irish bill, 25 May 1832. From London, O'Connell instructed his factotum Patrick Fitzpatrick in Dublin to 'explain to him how impatient I am for his arrival here', 30 May, but Maurice was not prominent at Westminster the following month.[40] He gave an ironic cheer against Lord Althorp, the leader of the House, while supporting O'Connell's motion for restoring the Irish 40*s.* franchise, 13 June, but missed the division on his motion to extend the vote to £5 freeholders, 18 June. He attacked the Tory Frederick Shaw for opposing the Irish party processions bill, 14 June, but turned against it as unnecessary for the maintenance of public order, 25 July, when he sided with the minority against its committal. He divided for requiring coroners to have medical qualifications and for inquests to be held in public, 20 June. He voted for establishing a system of representation for New South Wales, 28 June, and Shaw's amendment to preserve the voting rights of Irish freemen, 2 July, and spoke against transferring Ennis's seat to county Clare and limiting Dublin University's franchise to its MAs, 9 July. He justified the efforts of Irish Members to delay the passage of the government's tithe legislation, 10 July, and spoke and voted for postponing the topic to the reformed Parliament, 13 July 1832.

Maurice, whose parents had frequently tried to interest him in rich or well-connected heiresses, eloped, to O'Connell's initial fury, by boat from her father's house on the Shannon with the daughter of a wealthy Tory Protestant landowner. He married her in a Catholic ceremony at Tralee, 29 Sept., and again, according to the rites of the Protestant church in Kenmare, 1 Oct. 1832; but the couple separated in early 1841 and he apparently thereafter fathered more than one illegitimate child.[41] Despite fighting a duel with Arthur Blennerhassett of Ballyseedy that month, he was returned as a repealer for Tralee after a brief contest at the general election in December 1832 and he held the seat, almost uninterruptedly, for the rest of his life.[42] One of the members of O'Connell's small family party, he was lackadaisical in politics and never as close to him as were his brothers. According to James Grant, in the Commons, where he was largely silent and careless of his appearance, he often sat affectionately hand in hand with his father, who once remarked in an off-hand fashion that 'the "pledge" worked a miracle on Maurice. People won't believe that he is Maurice at all now'.[43] He evidently struggled under his father's constant embrace and shortly after his death in 1847, when he inherited the encumbered Derrynane, he commented on being denied permission to spend money on a yacht by his executors that 'I have been too long trained to suppress and sacrifice my own feelings, in order to give way to my dear father's wishes and orders, to suffer much from my struggle against them at present'.[44] Perhaps under the influence of a congestion in the brain which was to kill him a few hours later, in mid-June 1853 he apparently told Charles Gavan Duffy† that he had disapproved of the break between O'Connell and the Young Irelanders in 1846, a rupture which he blamed entirely on his brother John's pernicious influence over their ailing father.[45] Remembered for his conciliatory manners and moderate politics, he was succeeded by his elder son Daniel (1836-1919), a naval officer and architect.[46]

[1] O. MacDonagh, *Hereditary Bondsman*, 8, 78-80 and *Emancipist*, 6; E.I. Bishop, *World of Mary O'Connell*, 73; *O'Connell Corresp.* i. 96, 124, 144; viii. 3381. [2] *O'Connell Corresp.* i. 151, 154. [3] Ibid. i. 233, 325-6, 442. [4] Ibid. i. 278, 415. [5] Ibid. ii. 508, 545, 595, 641, 715. [6] Ibid. ii. 624, 830; Bishop, 74-75. [7] *O'Connell Corresp.* ii. 813, 855-6, 955, 963, 990, 1005. [8] Ibid. ii. 649, 958, 983, 990. [9] Ibid. ii. 1009-11, 1022, 1032, 1036. [10] Ibid. ii. 1036, 1042, 1053; iii. 1075-6. [11] Ibid. iii. 1087-8, 1092-3, 1095, 1102-4, 1109, 1121. [12] D. Gwynn, *The O'Gorman Mahon*, 38-39, 111-12. [13] *O'Connell Corresp.* iii. 1168, 1170-1, 1173-4, 1184, 1194. [14] Ibid. iii. 1204, 1207, 1211. [15] Ibid. iii. 1254; *Dublin Evening Post*, 13 Aug. 1825. [16] *O'Connell Corresp.* iii. 1258, 1298. [17] *Crabb Robinson Diary*, ii. 31. [18] *O'Connell Corresp.* iii. 1366, 1372, 1375; *Dublin Evening Post*, 15, 17, 31 Mar. 1827. [19] MacDonagh, *Emancipist*, 5. [20] MacDonagh, *Hereditary Bondsman*, 240. [21] *Dublin Evening Post*, 26 Jan. 1828. [22] Ibid. 28 June, 1, 3, 15, 26 July 1828. [23] PRO NI, Leader mss D3653/16/3/37. [24] *The Times*, 14 Feb. 1829; *O'Connell Corresp.* iv. 1516, 1528-9, 1533. [25] *Clare Jnl.* 8 June; *The Times*, 11, 13 July 1829. [26] PRO NI, Hill mss D642/243; *Warder*, 9, 12 Dec. 1829. [27] *O'Connell Corresp.* iv. 1635, 1652, 1689. [28] Ibid. iv. 1667; *Clare Jnl.* 26 July; *Dublin Evening Post*, 31 July 1830. [29] *Drogheda Jnl.* 3 July, 3, 7, 10, 14 Aug. 1830; *O'Connell Corresp.* iv. 1701-2. [30] *Dublin Evening Post*, 28 Sept. 1830. [31] *O'Connell Corresp.* iv. 1764. [32] Derby mss 920 Der (14) 121/1/2, Gosset to Smith Stanley, 24 Feb. 1831; *'My Darling Danny'* ed. E.I. Bishop, 44. [33] *O'Connell Corresp.* iv. 1778, 1780, 1782, 1787; viii. 3424. [34] *Dublin Evening Post*, 17, 24 Mar.; *Clare Jnl.* 21, 24 Mar.; Derby mss 119/2, Anglesey to Smith Stanley, 21 Mar.; 121/1/2, Gosset to same, 22 Mar., to Earle, 26 Mar. 1831. [35] *Clare Jnl.* 21 Apr. 1831; F.B. Hamilton, *Picture of Parl.* (1831), 64; *'My Darling Danny'*, 53-54. [36] *O'Connell Corresp.* iv. 1800, 1809; Wellington mss WP1/1184/24; Grey mss, Smith Stanley to Grey, 9 May 1831. [37] *Freeman's Jnl.* 26 Apr.; *Clare Jnl.* 28 Apr., 9, 16, 23, 26 May; *Dublin Evening Post*, 21, 24, 26 May 1831; *O'Connell Corresp.* iv. 1811, 1813-14. [38] *Three Diaries*, 184. [39] *O'Connell Corresp.* iv. 1876, 1881; *'My Darling Danny'*, 89. [40] *O'Connell Corresp.* iv. 1895a. [41] Ibid. i. 96; iii. 1407-8, 1428; iv. 1549, 1550a, 1552; MacDonagh, *Hereditary Bondsman*, 276 and *Emancipist*, 6-7, 77-78, 215-16; M.R. O'Connell, *Daniel O'Connell: The Man and his Politics*, 93-94. [42] *Kerry Evening Post*, 3, 21 Nov., 1, 15 Dec. 1832. [43] [J. Grant], *Random Recollections of Commons* (1837), 327-8; *Recollections of Aubrey de Vere*, 110. [44] MacDonagh, *Emancipist*, 309-10. [45] Sir C.G. Duffy, *My Life in Two Hemispheres*, i. 174-5; O'Connell, 114-15. [46] *Dublin Evening Post*, 21 June 1853; *Gent. Mag.* (1853), ii. 201.

S.M.F.

O'CONOR, Denis, the O'Conor Don (1794–1847), of Belanagare and Clonalis, co. Roscommon.

CO. ROSCOMMON 25 July 1831–15 July 1847

b. May 1794, 1st s. of Owen O'Conor* of Belanagare and Jane, da. of James Moore of Mount Browne, co. Dublin. *educ.* Trinity, Dublin 1813; L. Inn 1817; King's Inns 1817; continental tour.[1] *m.* 27 Aug. 1824, Mary, da. of Maurice Blake of Tower Hill, co. Mayo, 2s. 5da. *suc.* fa. as O'Conor Don 12 June 1831. *d.* 15 July 1847.

Ld. of treasury July 1846-*d.*; PC [I] ?1846.

O'Conor, who was educated as a barrister and travelled extensively in Europe in the early 1820s, supported the pro-Catholic agitation in Roscommon led by his father, the O'Conor Don, later that decade and assisted in his return for the county, following the granting of emancipation, in 1830.[2] He moved the resolution for repeal of the legislative Union with Britain at a county meeting, 14 Jan., and seconded one in favour of parliamentary reform at another, 16 Apr. 1831.[3] On the death of his father in June, less than a month after he had regained his seat at the general election, he not only succeeded to his ancient title and large estates, but, as heir to his father's patriotic reputation, was the obvious choice of the county's liberal Catholics for the representation. Nothing in the end came of a challenge from the recently defeated Tory candidate and the new O'Conor Don, who declared himself in favour of reform and economies, was returned unopposed at a by-election in July 1831.[4]

He voted for the enfranchisement of Greenwich, 3 Aug. 1831, and thereafter generally divided for the details of the Grey ministry's reintroduced reform bill. However, on 11 Aug., when he presented a petition from the burgesses of Galway complaining about its franchise, he was in minorities for printing the Waterford petition for disarming the Irish yeomanry and against the proposed division of English counties. He voted for Pelham's amendment to adjourn the debate on issuing the Dublin writ, 8 Aug., but with government in two divisions on allegations of bribery and misconduct at the recent election there, 23 Aug. He divided for making legal provision for the Irish poor, 29 Aug., and against committing the truck bill, 12 Sept. He voted for the third reading, 19 Sept., and passage of the reform bill, 21 Sept., the second reading of the Scottish bill, 23 Sept., and Lord Ebrington's confidence motion, 10 Oct. He spoke for the Maynooth grant, 26 Sept., and criticized the appointment of the Orangeman Lord Lorton as lord lieutenant of Roscommon, 6 Oct. 1831. The O'Conor Don, who attended a gathering of Irish Members about their reform bill in September and signed the requisition for a Roscommon reform meeting that winter, voted for the second reading of the revised reform bill, 17 Dec. 1831, to go into committee on it, 20 Jan. 1832, and again steadily for its details.[5] He divided against amending the Vestry Act, 23 Jan., and recommitting the anatomy bill, 27 Feb., and with ministers against producing information on Portugal, 9 Feb. He supported the prayer of his county's reform petition, 3 Feb., and the following day he joined Brooks's, sponsored by Ebrington and Lord Duncannon*. Having voted to postpone the debate on Irish tithes, 8 Mar., he condemned the government's bill as coercive and ineffective, 13 Mar., 26 July, and was in hostile minorities, 13, 24 July. He spoke and voted for the third reading of the reform bill, 22 Mar., and on 11 May expressed his regret at missing the previous day's division on Ebrington's motion for an address calling on the king to appoint only ministers who would carry it unimpaired. He divided for the second reading of the Irish reform bill, 25 May, but with O'Connell to extend the Irish franchise qualification to £5 freeholders, 18 June, and with Sheil against requiring electors to pay their municipal taxes before they could vote, 29 June; he presented petitions for the Irish measure to be as extensive as the English, 2 July, and commented on the former, 6 July. He stressed the seriousness of the agricultural distress in Roscommon in giving evidence to the select committee on the state of Ireland, 14 June, and voted for making permanent provision for the Irish poor by a tax on absentees, 19 June.[6] He was in the majority for making coroners' inquests public, 20 June, and the minority for establishing a system of representation for New South Wales, 29 June. His only other known votes were with government for the Russian-Dutch loan, 26 Jan., 12 and (by pairing) 20 July 1832.

An active Member, the O'Conor Don kept his brother and agent Edward, who married his wife's sister, closely informed of his parliamentary and constituency endeavours. In August 1832 it was feared that his exertions, especially on the subject of tithes, had impaired his health, and he possibly contemplated retreating to an English borough. However, he was returned unopposed as a Repealer at the general election that year and held his seat for the rest of his life.[7] An 'ardent and consistent Liberal', he was appointed by Lord John Russell* to the treasury board in July 1846, but died a year later.[8] His sons Charles Owen (1838-1906), author of the *O'Conors of Connaught* (1891), and Denis Maurice (1840-83), a London barrister, were respectively Liberal Members for counties Roscommon, 1860-80, and Sligo, 1868-83.

[1] *O'Conor Pprs.* ed. G.W. and J.E. Dunleavy, pp. xvi, 99, 121-4. [2] Ibid. 179, 182; *Roscommon and Leitrim Gazette*, 22 Oct. 1825; *Dublin Evening Post*, 20 June 1826; *Roscommon Jnl.* 9 Aug. 1828. [3] *Roscommon Jnl.* 22 Jan., 16, 23 Apr. 1831. [4] Ibid. 17, 24 June, 22, 29 July 1831. [5] *O'Conor Pprs.* 197; *Dublin Evening Post*, 24 Dec. 1831. [6] *PP* (1831-2), xvi. 32-36. [7] *O'Conor Pprs.* pp. xxii, 169, 174, 181-2, 189; *Roscommon Jnl.* 3, 31 Aug., 14, 21 Dec. 1832. [8] *Roscommon and Leitrim Gazette*, 31 July 1847; *Gent. Mag.* (1847), ii. 434.

S.M.F.

O'CONOR, Owen, the O'Conor Don (1763–1831), of Belanagare and Clonalis, co. Roscommon.

Co. Roscommon 1830–12 June 1831

b. 6 Mar. 1763, 1st s. of Denis O'Conor of Belanagare and Catherine, da. of Martin Browne of Clonfad, co. Westmeath. *m.* 20 June 1792, Jane, da. of James Moore of Mount Browne, co. Dublin, 2s. 5da. *suc.* fa. 1804; kinsman Alexander O'Conor as O'Conor Don 12 Dec. 1820. *d.* 12 June 1831.[1]

O'Conor was descended from the ancient kings of Connaught through a younger son of Sir Hugh O'Conor Don (1541-1632) of Ballintubber Castle, sometime Member for county Roscommon. His grandfather Charles O'Conor (1710-91) was a noted antiquary and his father Denis and uncle Charles (1736-1808) of Mount Allen, as heirs to one of the oldest and most extensive Irish landholding families in the province, participated in the Catholic agitation of the late eighteenth century. Owen, who served as a Volunteer in 1782 and was one of the Roscommon delegates to the Catholic convention in 1793, was also active in this campaign and probably became involved with the United Irishmen. However, except for his remark to Wolfe Tone in January 1793 that he was prepared for extreme measures, he steered clear of revolutionary activity, unlike his radical cousin Thomas (of Mount Allen), who in 1801 emigrated to New York; it was there that his son Charles (1804-84) became a prominent Democrat lawyer.[2] After the Union, which O'Conor opposed, he joined in the renewed movement for Catholic relief, regularly serving in the delegations sent to lobby ministers in London; the extent of his commitment can be gauged by the large number of requisitions, resolutions, addresses and letters relating to local and national meetings that remain scattered throughout his surviving papers. In 1810 his brother Charles (1764-1828), a Catholic priest and polemicist (who wrote the memoirs of his grandfather and was librarian at Stowe), dedicated *Columbanus's Third Letter* to him, and in 1813 the Catholics of Roscommon presented him with a silver cup in recognition of his services. During that decade he became increasingly close to Daniel O'Connell*, who valued him for his integrity, straightforwardness and perseverance. Writing to O'Conor, as he often did, to encourage his presence at a crucial gathering, 15 June 1819, O'Connell stressed 'the utility of your honesty, conciliatory temper and admitted respectability'.[3]

Denis O'Conor's fourth cousin Dominick O'Conor (*d.* 1795) had left Clonalis to his wife (*d.* 1814) and then to Owen as future head of the family. This was disputed by Dominick's younger brother Alexander, who succeeded him as the O'Conor Don and had delusions of establishing himself as a self-styled monarch in a rebuilt Ballintubber Castle; he and his next brother Thomas, who predeceased him, were described by Skeffington Gibbon as 'men of high and noble birth, but from their eccentric, secluded, pecuniary difficulties and habits, hardly known beyond the walls of the smoky and despicable hovels in which they lived and died'. After protracted litigation that reduced the value of the property, O'Conor purchased Clonalis outright in 1805, and on Alexander's death in December 1820 he inherited the headship of the Don part of the old Catholic clan of the O'Conors. The following month he wrote a letter to the press to dismiss rival claims to this title, which the king, however, refused to recognize as an official designation through the issuing of supporters to his armorial bearings.[4]

By the early 1820s the O'Conor Don was one of the most influential of the older generation of reformers in the Catholic Association. For instance, in early 1821 his attendance in Dublin was considered by O'Connell as essential for ensuring Catholic unity on the divisive issue of the proposed royal veto on episcopal appointments, and later that year it was largely at his insistence that the Catholics' national address to George IV on his visit to Ireland was confined solely to uncontentious expressions of loyalty.[5] He continued to play a leading part in the regular petitioning by his co-religionists in Roscommon, where he gave his considerable electoral interest in support of the pro-Catholic county Members. At the general election of 1826, when he seconded Arthur French*, he condemned the unopposed return of the apparently hostile Robert King, and he chaired a meeting of the county's Catholics that summer, when it was proposed to present him with a piece of plate in gratitude for his unceasing exertions on their behalf.[6] In the latter half of 1828, when he became president of the Roscommon Independent Club, he played a prominent part at Catholic gatherings in his own and neighbouring counties, and he apparently extracted a promise from King that he would vote for relief.[7] Early the following year O'Connell congratulated him on their eventual success in the struggle for emancipation, commenting that 'no gentleman had a more useful or honourable share in this contest than you had and that at times when we were abandoned by many of the highest names'.[8] He chaired a celebratory meeting of the Friends of Civil and Religious Liberty in Roscommon, 8 June 1829, and opposed the efforts of King's father Lord Lorton to suppress unrest by invoking the Insurrection Act in the county that winter.[9]

The O'Conor Don, who spoke against the introduction of poor laws to Ireland and the increased Irish stamp and spirit duties at county meetings, 30 Mar. and 12 June 1830, agreed to offer at the general election that summer, when he pledged to support a range of radical reforms and to devote the rest of his life to the Irish cause. Nothing in the end came of a threatened Tory opposition and, benefiting from the able assistance of his sons Denis and Edward as agents, he was returned unopposed as the first Catholic to represent Roscommon since his ancestor Sir Hugh.[10] Listed by Pierce Mahony† among the 'neutrals' and by ministers among their 'foes', he voted against government in the division on the civil list that led to the duke of Wellington's resignation, 15 Nov. He divided in the minority for O'Connell's motion for repeal of the Irish Subletting Act, 11 Nov., and the following month, at a meeting of Irish Members, concurred with his decision to introduce their own reform bill.[11] On 4 Dec. he joined Brooks's, sponsored by Lords Althorp* and Duncannon*. He argued that the proposed inquiry into agricultural distress and the game bill should be extended to Ireland, 6, 7 Dec., and spoke in defence of the grand jury system, 9 Dec., and the landed interest, 17 Dec. He presented petitions against the grant to the Kildare Place Society, 10, 16 Dec. 1830, 15, 29 Mar. 1831, when he brought up two others from the Catholics of Kilteeven for repeal of the Irish Vestries Act and abolition of tithes. He declared himself in favour of repeal of the Union at a Roscommon meeting, 14 Jan., and was later thanked by the rope makers of Dublin for his statement that the English were not competent to legislate for Ireland.[12] He voted for the second reading of the Grey ministry's reform bill, 22 Mar., when (as on 29 Mar., 18 Apr.) he said that the Irish welcomed reform, and against Gascoyne's wrecking amendment, 19 Apr. He blamed the unrest in county Clare on the prevailing distress, 13 Apr. 1831.

According to the letters that the O'Conor Don sent home from London, he apparently threw himself into its parliamentary and social life and complained so much of weariness that his family feared for his health.[13] He travelled to Roscommon for the general election of 1831, when he and French defeated a Tory anti-reformer, but died at Belanagare in the middle of June, his death being attributed to the effect of changed habits of life and over zealous attention to constituency interests at his advanced age.[14] His title, estates and parliamentary seat were inherited by his elder son Denis, to whom O'Connell wrote later that month:

> The death of my most respected and loved friend, your father, was to me a severe blow ... How little does the world know of the value of the public services of men who like him held themselves always in readiness without ostentation or parade but with firmness and sincerity to aid in the struggles which nations make for liberty ... I really know no one individual to whom the Catholics of Ireland are so powerfully indebted for the successful result of their contest for emancipation ... His was not holiday patriotism ... No, in the worst of times and when the storms of calumny and persecution from our enemies and apathy and treachery from our friends raged at their height he was always found at his post.[15]

[1] *The Times*, 17 June 1831. [2] C.O. O'Conor, *O'Conors of Connaught*, 308, 312, 314, 316-18, 321-4; *Life of Tone* ed. T. Bartlett, 199-200; L. Gibbons, 'Republicanism and Radical Memory: The O'Conors, O'Carolan and the United Irishmen', in *Revolution, Counter-Revolution and Union* ed. J. Smyth, 211-37. [3] O'Conor, 324-8; *O'Conor Pprs.* ed. G.W. and J.E. Dunleavy, pp. xv-xvi, 83-190, *passim*; G. Costigan, 'Tragedy of Charles O'Conor', *AHR*, xlix (1943-4), 32-54; *O'Connell Corresp.* i. 338, 504; ii. 571, 754, 757, 772, 803, 839; O. MacDonagh, *Hereditary Bondsman*, 164-7. [4] O'Conor, 328; *O'Conor Pprs.* 77, 138; S. Gibbon, *Recollections* (1829), 85-87; *Dublin Evening Post*, 16 Dec. 1820, 13, 25 Jan., 1 Feb. 1821; Add. 37300, f. 322. [5] *O'Connell Corresp.* ii. 901, 907-8; MacDonagh, 175. [6] *Dublin Evening Post*, 24 Jan. 1822, 22 June, 15 July 1826. [7] *Roscommon Jnl.* 9 Aug., 13 Sept., 11 Oct., 15 Nov., 6, 13 Dec. 1828, 3 Jan. 1829; *O'Conor Pprs.* 166. [8] *O'Connell Corresp.* iv. 1531. [9] *Roscommon Jnl.* 13 June, 12, 19 Dec. 1829. [10] Ibid. 3 Apr., 12, 19 June, 24 July, 14, 21 Aug. 1830; *O'Conor Pprs.* 180, 182; O'Conor, 328. [11] R.B. McDowell, *Public Opinion and Government Policy*, 153. [12] *Roscommon Jnl.* 22 Jan. 1831; *O'Conor Pprs.* 160. [13] *O'Conor Pprs.* 182, 186. [14] *Roscommon Jnl.* 7, 20 May, 17 June; *Dublin Evening Post*, 26 May, 14 June 1831; O'Conor, 328. [15] *O'Connell Corresp.* iv. 1821.

S.M.F.

O'FERRALL, Richard More (1797–1880), of Balyna House, Enfield, co. Kildare.

Co. KILDARE	1830–1847
Co. LONGFORD	21 Apr. 1851–1852
Co. KILDARE	1859–1865

b. 1797, 1st s. of Ambrose More O'Ferrall of Balyna House and Anne, da. of John Bagot of Castle Bagot, co. Dublin. *educ.* Stonyhurst 1809-13; Downside. *m.* 28 Sept. 1839, Hon. Matilda Southwell, da. and coh. of Thomas, 3rd Visct. Southwell, 1s. 1da. *suc.* fa. 1835. *d.* 27 Oct. 1880.

Ld. of treasury Apr. 1835-Aug. 1839; sec. to admiralty Oct. 1839-June 1841; sec. to treasury June-Sept. 1841; PC 22 Nov. 1847.

Gov. Malta 1847-51.

O'Ferrall's family possessed a 'large property' in county Kildare. Unlike his brother John he declined to enter Dublin University on account of his strict Catholicism. An early member of the Catholic Association and associate of the influential Catholic bishop of Kildare and Leighlin, Dr. James Doyle, in February 1825 he was one of the deputation that went to Westminster to urge the case for emancipation.[1] At a meeting in its support in county Longford, where his family also owned property, 14 Nov. 1828, he denounced the 'annual farce of petitioning a hostile tribunal' and accused 'the middle class of Protestants' of being the 'dupes of their lords, who seek to maintain their monopoly in church and state to enrich their families'. The following month he helped to establish the Longford Independent Club.[2]

At the 1830 general election he came forward for an unexpected opening in county Kildare with the backing of the local Independent Club, citing his support for reform and retrenchment and opposition to the Irish Subletting Act and the 'odious and vexatious monopoly' of the East India Company. At the nomination he refuted the charge of an opponent that he was 'intemperate' and a 'wild theorist'. 'You will have an efficient Irish colleague in Richard O'Ferrall, he is pretty sure of success', Robert Cassidy informed Thomas Wyse*, 12 Aug. After a two-day contest he was returned in second place.[3] In September 1830 he was one of 15 Members who signed a Dublin requisition for a meeting in support of the French revolution.[4] He voted for repeal of the Subletting Act, 11 Nov. and reduction of West Indian wheat import duties, 12 Nov. He had of course been listed by the Wellington ministry as one of their 'foes', and he voted against them on the civil list, 15 Nov. On 20 Nov. he joined Brooks's, sponsored by the duke of Leinster and Lord Essex. That month he was named by Daniel O'Connell* as a 'proper person' to present petitions against the grant to the Kildare Place Society.[5] On 6 Dec. he presented one for repeal of the Union, but doubted that it would 'afford a remedy' and advocated 'general reform' and more measures 'to relieve the distresses of Ireland'. His comments were condemned by O'Connell, but he spoke again in similar terms, 11 Dec. 1830, when he complained that Ireland had not received the attention from governments that she had 'a right to expect' and had been passed over for additional representatives. He 'spoke like a sensible and fluent English country gentleman', recorded Denis Le Marchant†, adding to James Abercromby* that he made

> a considerable impression, especially as amidst his expression of very determined feelings he alluded to O'Connell in by no means a laudatory manner and assured government that the influential classes of society in Ireland were guided by very different principles and quite independent of his control. The subject once started, people in the lobbies and rooms were all talking of it, and I saw some who did not treat it as a slip, and what must somehow or other be corrected.[6]

On 22 Feb. 1831 O'Ferrall wrote to advise James Emerson of Belfast that he would support the extension of Littleton's truck bill to Ireland, but that 'some Irish Members think it would be injurious and prevent the employment of weavers' and that 'those interested' should send petitions to Parliament.[7] He sympathized with Catholic hostility to the Kildare Place Society, which used the Scriptures 'contrary to the feelings or even the prejudices of the people', 14 Mar. He presented another petition for repeal, 16 Mar. He voted for the second reading of the Grey ministry's reform bill, 22 Mar., and against Gascoyne's wrecking amendment, 19 Apr. 1831.

At the ensuing general election he offered again as an 'unflinching advocate' of the reform bill and its extension to Ireland, and 'every measure of economy and retrenchment'. A threatened opposition came to nothing and he was returned unopposed.[8] On 27 June 1831 he presented two petitions for draining Irish bogs and obtained leave to introduce an embankments bill for removing obstacles from rivers. He steered it through the Commons and, after amendment by the Lords, it received royal assent, 20 Oct. (1 & 2 Gul. IV, c. 57). He asserted the 'positive right' of Ireland 'to receive assistance by way of grant', 30 June. He voted for the second reading of the reintroduced reform bill, 6 July, gave steady support to its details, and divided for the third reading, 19 Sept., and its passage, 21 Sept. He divided for the second reading of the Scottish bill, 23 Sept., and Lord Ebrington's confidence motion, 10 Oct. On 14 July he denounced the 'system of proselytism' carried on by the Kildare Place Society, with which he had ceased to co-operate after finding that 'unless the poor were protected by a gentleman of their own persuasion, their religious principles were interfered with'; he presented petitions against giving it further grants, 5 Sept. He was in the minority for a reduction of the civil list, 18 July. He welcomed the introduction of lord lieutenants for Irish counties, as the country had suffered 'very badly under the present regulations', 25 July. He voted against disqualification of the Dublin election committee, 29 July, and the issue of a writ, 8 Aug., and with ministers on the controversy, 23 Aug. On 5 Aug. he defended the conduct of Maynooth College, which was inspected twice a year, and called for a 'liberal system of education' to be adopted throughout Ireland. That day he presented and endorsed petitions against the additional drawback on Irish malt, which enabled Scottish distillers to 'sell their whisky in Ireland at a price 20 per cent lower'. He divided in favour of printing the Waterford petition for disarming the Irish yeomanry, 11 Aug. He advocated reform of the law respecting marriages in Catholic chapels in England, the illegality of which induced husbands to 'desert their wives', 12 Aug. On 19 Aug. he spoke and voted against the Irish union of parishes bill, as it would force Catholics to support the construction of Protestant churches. He argued and divided for legal provision for the Irish poor and demanded that a third of Irish church revenues be conferred on the 'destitute', 29 Aug. He welcomed proposed reforms to the Irish grand jury system, 16, 29 Sept. He voted for inquiry into the conduct of the Hampshire magistrates during the arrest of the Deacles, 27 Sept. 1831.

O'Ferrall regretted that ministers had 'departed from the principle of giving additional Members to Ireland' and warned that this would lead to 'political agitation' and the 'commission of acts that both England and Ireland deplore', 12 Dec. 1831. He paired for the second reading of the revised reform bill, 17 Dec. 1831, again supported its details, and divided for the third reading, 22 Mar. 1832. He voted for the address calling on the king to appoint only ministers who would carry it unimpaired, 10 May. He voted for the second reading of the Irish bill, 25 May, but was in the minority of 61 for an increase in the Scottish county representation, 1 June. He divided for O'Connell's motion to extend the Irish county franchise to £5 freeholders, 18 June, welcomed the enfranchisement of 20 year leaseholders, 25 June, and voted against the liability of Irish electors to pay municipal taxes before they could vote, 29 June. On 18 July he advocated the division of Irish counties into polling districts, explaining that in 'long and narrow' Kildare the expense of bringing voters to the poll was 'very great'. That day he demanded that the 'degradation' of swearing an oath against the pope at the poll be dispensed with. On 9 Feb. he voted with ministers on relations with Portugal. He divided in favour of printing the Woollen Grange petition for the abolition of Irish tithes, 16 Feb., brought up similar petitions, 31 Mar., 9 July, 7 Aug., and voted against the Irish tithes bill, 8 Mar., and steadily thereafter. He feared it would provoke 'constant war and constant tumult', 13 Mar., considered that 'the representatives of the people' were 'bound to resist the passing of a law' based on 'imperfect information and *ex parte* evidence', 2 Apr., and was a minority teller against its second reading, 6 Apr. On 27 Feb. he protested that the anatomy bill would create 'a premium for murder in my own country', as there would be an 'open market' for bodies, and voted against it. He welcomed the new plan of Irish education, 6 Mar., and attacked the tactics of its opponents, observing that it had been 'well received by all the Catholics' and 'a great portion of the Protestants, and that ought to be sufficient', 28 June. On 3 Apr. he welcomed the Catholic marriages bill, as the present laws were a 'disgrace to the statute book'. That day he unsuccessfully pressed Smith Stanley, the Irish secretary, for correspondence relating to the dispatch of troops to Kildare at the time of anti-tithe meetings, which was 'very likely' to aggravate the 'excitement and irritation ... already too prevalent in Ireland'. He called for the 'greatest caution' and the 'immediate attention of the legislature' to Irish outrages, 23 May, and was appointed to the select committee on the disturbances, 30 May. He presented and endorsed a petition and was a minority teller against the bill to transfer King's County assizes from Philipstown to Tullamore that day. He voted for a tax on absentee landlords to provide permanent provision for the Irish poor, 19 June, and spoke in similar terms, 10 July. He divided with government on the Russian-Dutch loan, 12, 16, 20 July. On 23 July he denounced a Protestant tract of the 'most offensive and disgusting kind' written by James Gordon*, saying that it contained the 'grossest misrepresentations of the Catholic tenets', which he would 'not have thought it worthwhile' to notice, had Gordon not last year made some assertions against Maynooth, which 'I have been blamed for not answering'. Denouncing the 'inoperable' tithes bill the next day, he observed that 'we are placed in a difficult situation between the government on the one hand and our constituents on the other', and urged the House to 'remember the Stamp Act', with its 'precisely similar proceedings', by which 'America was lost to England'. On 2 Aug. 1832 he promised to 'resist its operation by every means in my power, short of force'. He was in the minority of ten for the reception of a petition for abolition that day.

At the 1832 general election O'Ferrall was re-elected after a contest against two other Liberals. He declined the Grey ministry's offer of a lordship of the treasury in June 1834, but on Lord Melbourne's return to power in April 1835 took office.[9] He retired from county Kildare in 1847 and was appointed governor of Malta by the Russell administration, but in 1851 he resigned in protest at their ecclesiastical tithes bill, which opposed the creation of a Catholic hierarchy in England. He came in on a 'chance vacancy' for county Longford in April 1851 but did not stand for re-election the following year. He sat again for county Kildare from 1859 until 1865, when he retired from public life. O'Ferrall died at Kingstown, near Dublin, in October 1880.[10] He was succeeded by his only son Ambrose (1846-1911), who in April 1880 unsuccessfully contested county Kildare as a Liberal.

[1] *Oxford DNB*; *Stonyhurst Biog. Dict.* i. 483; *Dod's Parl. Companion* (1846), 217; *Dublin Evening Post*, 24, 27 July 1830. [2] *Dublin Evening Post*, 29 Nov., 2 Dec. 1828. [3] Ibid. 22, 29 July, 14, 21 Aug. 1830; NLI, Wyse mss 15024 (4). [4] *O'Connell Corresp.* iv. 1709. [5] Ibid. 1731, 1733, 1738. [6] *Three Diaries*, 168; NLS mss 24762, f. 49. [7] PRO NI, Emerson Tennant mss D2922/C/1A/3. [8] *Dublin Evening Post*, 26 Apr., 10 May 1831. [9] *Three Diaries*, 381. [10] *Oxford DNB*; *The Times*, 30 Oct. 1880.

P.J.S.

OFFLEY *see* **CUNLIFFE OFFLEY**

OGILVY, Hon. Donald (1788–1863), of Clova, Forfar.

FORFARSHIRE 3 Oct. 1831–31 Jan. 1832

b. 27 May 1788, 3rd but 2nd surv. s. of Walter Ogilvy of Clova (*d.* 1819) and Jean, da. of John Ogilvy, MD, of Balfour and Murkle; bro. of Hon. William Ogilvy*. *m.* 8 Feb. 1815, Maria, da. and coh. of James Morley of E.I. Co. 3s. (1 *d.v.p.*) 4da. (3 *d.v.p.*). *d.* 30 Dec. 1863.

Cadet, E.I. Co., 1804; ensign 16th native inf. Bengal 1806, lt. 1808, res. 1814.[1]

Maj. E. Forfar militia 1809; col. Forfar and Kincardine militia 1828-57.

Ogilvy's father, the self-styled 5th earl of Airlie, an advocate, had succeeded his insane nephew David to Cortachy Castle and family estates in Forfarshire and Perthshire in 1812 and initiated the proceedings which led to the reversal by Act of Parliament in 1826 of attainders imposed on the Jacobite 3rd earl in 1715 and Lord Ogilvy in 1745, so confirming Ogilvy's elder brother David as 4th earl of Airlie.[2] Intended with his brothers for a military career, Ogilvy entered the East India Company's army in 1804. After failing to rise above the rank of lieutenant, he settled with his wife, the daughter of a former East India Company writer, at the Balbengo estate, near Fettercairn, and from 1820 at Clova.[3] At the general election of 1830, when his family were recovering from whooping cough at his brother William's residence, Airlie Castle, he contributed to Airlie's bid to boost his political influence and become a representative peer by contesting Perth Burghs, where he was unexpectedly defeated by John Stuart Wortley.[4] He petitioned urging the Lords to reject the provost of Dundee's petition against its disfranchisement as a burgh, 8 Nov. 1830, and had Stuart Wortley unseated, 11 Dec. 1830, but with his own eligibility to stand at the ensuing by-election in doubt, William was substituted for him. He was defeated, but returned in March 1831 on petition, so unseating the Grey ministry's lord advocate Francis Jeffrey.[5] The Ogilvys failed to return a Member at the 1831 general election and their conduct at the Forfarshire meeting on 16 May, when Donald Ogilvy proposed a petition for 'safe reform' and criticized the Scottish bill's provisions for county representation (a £10 householder vote and the enfranchisement of £50 copyholders), spawned an acrimonious public correspondence with Jeffrey and the Whig reformer Douglas Gordon Hallyburton of Pitcur, whom Ogilvy narrowly defeated at the Forfarshire by-election in October.[6]

Before being unseated on petition, 31 Jan. 1832, he voted against the revised English reform bill at its second reading, 17 Dec. 1831, and committal, 20 Jan., and against government on the Russian-Dutch loan, 26 Jan. 1832.[7] Writing on 4 Jan. 1832 to Airlie, he denied reports that he had suggested 'taking the *sense of the county*' on reform and described his quandary over his future candidature:

> I am most anxious to let my friends in Forfarshire know that under an extended constituency I would not again come forward, but I hesitate to tell them, which it would in fact be doing, that the government reform bill will be carried, as *I just learn* that the king is to create as many peers as these rascally ministers choose ... It would look like giving in, even before the Scotch bill was before us ... My opinion is that I have nothing to do but to let some of the party (*ours*) know my intentions and it is for them to judge of the candidate they would wish to succeed me.[8]

He started, but eventually declined the Conservative nomination for Forfarshire at the 1832 general election and did not stand for Parliament again.[9] He died in Aberdeen in December 1863, predeceased by his wife and at least four of their seven children. An obituarist wrote that 'being of a quiet and retiring disposition, his life was marked by few incidents requiring notice'.[10] His second son Donald (1824-85) succeeded to Clova, which he then occupied under an 'act of settlement' of 28 Oct. 1856. Ogilvy's will of that date and attendant codicils and settlements were disputed by Donald and his unmarried sister Dorothea, the major beneficiary by a revoking order and settlement of 15 Apr. 1861, before the court of session in January 1864. Administration was granted to Donald at Aberdeen sheriff's court, 9 Mar. 1864.[11]

[1] BL OIOC L/MIL/9/113, 258. [2] *Gent. Mag.* (1812), i. 594; NAS GD16/34/375; *Perthshire Courier*, 22 June 1826; *Bonnie House of Airlie* ed. K. Thomasson, 27; *LJ*, lviii. 382. [3] *Gent. Mag.* (1815), i. 274; NAS SC1/37/53. [4] NAS GD16/34/387/7, W. Ogilvy to Airlie, 23 Apr., D. Ogilvy to same, 8 July; 16/40/52; *Perthshire Courier*, 22, 29 July, 26 Aug.; *Stirling Advertiser*, 13 Aug. 1830. [5] *The Times*, 9 Nov., 15, 16 Dec. 1830, 13 Jan., 1 Feb., 28 Mar. 1831; Brougham mss, Hallyburton to Brougham, 25 Aug. 1830; NAS GD16/34/387/7, W. Ogilvy to Airlie, 18 Feb. 1831. [6] NAS GD16/34/387/8/12-17; 40/57; 41/1093; NAS GD224/525/18/1-6; *Dundee, Perth and Cupar Advertiser*, 19 May, 6 Oct.; *Perthshire Courier*, 26 May, 2 June, 15 Sept., 6 Oct.; *The Times*, 28 June 1831. [7] *The Times*, 25, 31 Jan. 1832. [8] NAS GD16/34/387/8/60-61x. [9] *Dundee, Perth and Cupar Advertiser*, 2 Aug., 27 Dec.; *The Times*, 13 Aug. 1832. [10] *Gent. Mag.* (1864), i. 266. [11] NAS SC1/36/54; 37/53.

M.M.E.

OGILVY, Hon. William (1793–1871), of Airlie Castle, Forfar.

PERTH BURGHS 28 Mar. 1831–1831

bap. 19 Sep. 1793,[1] 5th but 3rd surv. s. of Walter Ogilvy of Clova (*d.* 1819) and Jean, da. of John Ogilvy, MD, of Balfour and Murkle; bro. of Hon. Donald Ogilvy*. *unm.* *d.* 10 Apr. 1871.

Ensign 52 Ft. 1811, lt. 1812; capt. Cape regt. 1815, half-pay 1817-26.

The youngest son of the self-styled 5th earl of Airlie, Ogilvy joined the navy as his father intended, but 'an aversion to this profession caused him to give it up' to pursue a military career, like his brothers David, John (*d.* 1809) and Donald.[2] He fought with distinction in the major battles in the Peninsula (for which he received a medal with seven clasps) and at Waterloo, where his regiment suffered heavy casualties. After being promoted to the rank of captain he took half-pay. In 1826, when the reversal by Act of Parliament of attainders imposed in 1715 on the Jacobite 3rd earl of Airlie, and in 1745 on Lord Ogilvy, confirmed his brother David, of Cortachy Castle, as 4th earl of Airlie, Ogilvy retired from the army and resided at his family's subsidiary seat, Airlie Castle.[3] Although no public speaker, he assisted his brothers politically in Forfarshire, where Airlie became lord lieutenant in 1828, and contested the venal Perth district of burghs on their interest in January 1831, after Donald's petition against his defeat there in 1830 had resulted in the election being voided.[4] His address declared:

> I have, for some considerable time, been fully satisfied of the necessity of parliamentary reform and a reform in the borough system; and in reference to these measures, I am fully prepared to go as far as will satisfy the reasonable expectations of the country. I am also fully satisfied of the imperious necessity for economy and retrenchment in every department of state, and of as extensive a reduction in taxes as is consistent with the welfare of the country.

This guaranteed him the support of Forfar, the returning burgh, where the new provost William Smith was a committed reformer, and he also, albeit by dubious means, secured the Cupar vote.[5] His opponent, the Grey ministry's lord advocate Francis Jeffrey, could depend on Perth, St. Andrews and Dundee, which had recently appealed to the Lords against its disfranchisement by the court of session. Jeffrey's return, 13 Jan. 1831, was doubtful from the outset.[6] Ogilvy's petition against admitting the Dundee vote was delayed in transit by a blizzard, but Jeffrey's supporters failed to secure its rejection because it arrived after the session had commenced, 10 Feb.[7] He wrote optimistically to Airlie on the 18th from his London house at 31 Bury Street, St. James's:

> I have only yet twice taken my seat under the gallery, but am going down as soon as I can finish this. I do not think the ministers are at all in an enviable position, they seem absolutely afraid to allow a division of the House to take place on any question. I was there last night when Lord Chandos's proposal to disfranchise Evesham [came on] and they agreed to his motion notwithstanding that they said it interfered with their own plan of reform.[8]

The rejection on 3 Mar. of Ogilvy's plea to the Lords requesting to be admitted as a respondent in legal proceedings involving the corporation of Dundee had no direct bearing on the outcome of his petition to the Commons, where a committee belatedly appointed on the 22nd (after Jeffrey had brought in the Scottish reform bill and voted for the English measure), ruled in his favour and amended the return, 28 Mar.[9] John Macpherson Grant, son of the former Sutherland Member, observed that Ogilvy 'seemed highly pleased with his success, temporary as it most probably is, for I presume he will not be returned again for the Forfar Burghs'.[10] He divided for Gascoyne's amendment, which wrecked the English reform bill, 19 Apr. 1831, and stood down at the ensuing dissolution.[11]

Although mocked in the Liberal press throughout for his 'poor speech delivery' and as an unworthy opponent of Jeffrey, Ogilvy was unstinting in his efforts on behalf of his brothers in Forfarshire. His right to be enrolled as a freeholder when Donald was returned for Forfarshire in October 1831 was the only claim of its kind undisputed.[12] He never married and died suddenly and apparently intestate in April 1871 at Loyal, the Perthshire mansion near Alyth he had built 20 years previously. He was recalled as a lifelong Conservative who had quietly assisted his brothers at elections and political meetings in Forfarshire and Perthshire.[13]

[1] IGI (Forfar). [2] *Ann. Reg.* (1871), Chron. p. 148. [3] NAS GD16/34/375; *Perthshire Courier*, 22 June 1826; *Bonnie House of Airlie* ed. K. Thomasson, 27; *LJ*, lviii. 382. [4] *Perthshire Courier*, 22, 29 July, 26 Aug.; *Stirling Advertiser*, 13 Aug. 1830. [5] *Fife Herald*, 21 Oct., 11 Nov.; *Dundee Perth and Cupar Advertiser*, 18, 25 Nov., 23, 30 Dec.; Stair mss (History of Parliament Aspinall transcripts), J.A. Murray to Sir J. Dalrymple, 22 Dec. 1830. [6] *Perthshire Courier*, 30 Dec. 1830, 13, 20 Jan. 1831; *The Times*, 15, 16 Dec. 1830, 13 Jan., 1 Feb., 28 Mar. 1831. [7] St. Deiniol's Lib. Glynne-Gladstone mss 197, T. to J. Gladstone, 11 Feb. 1831. [8] NAS GD16/34/387/8/3. [9] *LJ*, lxiii. 282, 301; *Dundee, Perth and Cupar Advertiser*, 24, 31 Mar.; *The Times*, 28, 29 Mar. 1831. [10] Macpherson Grant mss 361. [11] *Dundee, Perth and Cupar Advertiser*, 5 May 1831. [12] NAS GD224/525/18/2; 580/3/1/19; *Dundee, Perth and Cupar Advertiser*, 6, 13 Oct. 1831. [13] *Perthshire Courier*, 18 Apr. 1871.

M.M.E.

OGLE, Sir Charles, 2nd bt. (1775–1858), of Worthy, nr. Winchester, Hants and 4 Belgrave Square, Mdx.

PORTARLINGTON 1830–1831

b. 24 May 1775, 3rd but 1st surv. s. of Sir Chaloner Ogle, 1st bt., of Worthy and Hester, da. and coh. of Rt. Rev. John Thomas, bp. of Winchester. *m.* (1) 22 Apr. 1802, Charlotte Margaret (*d.* Sept. 1814), da. of Gen. Hon. Thomas Gage, 1s. 2da. (1 *d.v.p.*); (2) 4 Sept. 1820, Letitia (*d.* 13 Nov. 1832), da. of Sir William Burroughs†, 1st bt., of Castle Bagshaw, co. Cavan, 1s.; (3) 10 Apr. 1834, Mary Anne, da. of George Cary of Tor Abbey, Devon, wid. of Sir John Hayford Thorold, 10th bt., of Syston Park, Lincs., *s.p. suc.* fa. as 2nd bt. 27 Aug. 1816. *d.* 16 June 1858.

Entered RN 1787, midshipman 1791, lt. 1793, cdr. 1795, capt. 1796, r.-adm. 1819, v.-adm. 1830, adm. 1841.

C.-in-c. N. America 1827-30, Portsmouth 1845-8; adm. of the fleet 1857-*d.*

Ogle's naval pedigree was impeccable. His great-uncle Sir Chaloner Ogle, Member for Rochester, 1746-50, had died admiral of the fleet, 11 Apr. 1750, while his father was created a baronet for his naval services and died as most senior admiral, 27 Aug. 1816. Ogle appears to have been intended for Winchester School, but he entered the navy in 1787, serving off the coast of Africa and in home waters. In 1793 he was made lieutenant in the *Vengeance*, as part of the fleet sent to subjugate the French West Indies, where he distinguished himself by capturing two schooners off Martinique, 6 Feb. 1794, and a few days later by taking Pigeon Island, which enabled the British to anchor at Fort Royal Bay and supply their army. He subsequently commanded the divisions of seamen put ashore at Port Negro to assist in Martinique's final conquest and at Guadaloupe, where on 12 Apr. 1794 he was conspicuous in the storming of Fort Fleur d'Epee. The following month, at the age of 19, he was appointed acting captain of the *Assurance*, supposedly the youngest man ever to hold such a post. He saw active service on the Jamaica station before being transferred to the Mediterranean, where he commanded numerous frigates; his elder brother Major Thomas Ogle was killed at Aboukir Bay in 1801. From 1805 he was employed chiefly in the Channel and home stations, until September 1816, after succeeding to his father's baronetcy and Hampshire estate. (By his father's will, dated 14 Apr. 1808 and proved under £90,000, he inherited personal property valued at £76,229.)[1] He became a flag officer in 1819 and was commander-in-chief on the North American station from April 1827 until July 1830.[2]

At the general election that summer Ogle stood for Norwich with a large purse and the backing of the corporation, who had been unable to secure a local candidate, prompting jibes that he was a political 'ogle eye'. Following his defeat he was returned unopposed for Portarlington as the paying nominee of its spendthrift patron, the 2nd earl of Portarlington.[3] He was listed by the Wellington ministry as one of their 'friends', but was absent from the crucial division on the civil list, 15 Nov. 1830. Ogle, who is not known to have spoken in debate, voted against the second reading of the Grey ministry's reform bill, 22 Mar., and for Gascoyne's wrecking amendment, 19 Apr. 1831. At the ensuing dissolution he retired. On 22 Feb. 1835 he informed the new premier Peel that he had 'obtained some information relative to the malt tax' and requested 'a five minute conversation'. Two days later he again pressed for an interview 'without loss of time'.[4] He died as admiral of the fleet at Tunbridge Wells in June 1858.[5] He was succeeded in the baronetcy by his elder son Chaloner (1803-59).

[1] PROB 11/1584/492; IR26/686/812. [2] *Gent. Mag.* (1858), ii. 189; J. Marshall, *R. Naval Biog.* i. 709-13; *The Times*, 9 Aug. 1796, 18 June 1858; *Oxford DNB*. [3] *Norf. Chron.* 10, 17, 24, 31 July 1830. [4] Add. 40415, ff. 105, 159. [5] W. O'Byrne, *Naval Biog.* ii. 831; *Gent. Mag.* (1858), ii. 190.

P.J.S.

O'GORMAN MAHON *see* **MAHON, James Patrick**

O'GRADY, Standish (1792–1848), of Mount Prospect, co. Limerick.[1]

Co. Limerick	1820–1826
Co. Limerick	2 Feb. 1830–3 May 1830
Co. Limerick	1830–1834

b. 26 Dec. 1792, 1st s. of Standish O'Grady (later 1st Visct. Guillamore [I]), c.b. exch. [I], of Cahirguillamore and Rockbarton and Katherine, da. of John Thomas Waller of Castletown. *educ.* Westminster by 1809; Trinity, Dublin 1809. *m.* 16 Oct. 1828, Gertrude Jane, da. of Hon. Berkeley Paget*, 6s. 4da. *suc.* fa. as 2nd Visct. Guillamore [I] 21 Apr. 1840. *d.* 22 July 1848.

Ensign 7 Drag. 1811, lt. 1812, capt. 1815, half-pay 1816; capt. 18 Drag. 1819, half-pay 1821; maj. (half-pay) 1825; maj. 24 Ft. 1827; lt.-col. (half-pay) 1829, col. 1842; a.d.c. to Victoria 1842-*d*.

O'Grady, whose ancient Irish family had long been resident in county Limerick, was the son and namesake of a Dublin barrister of wit, diligence and superiority, who was called in 1787 and, having come to the attention of his neighbour Lord Clare, the Irish lord chancellor, became a king's counsel ten years later. In early 1803 he was considered a possibility for the vacant Irish attorney-generalship and Clare's successor Lord Redesdale wrote to Addington, the prime minister, that he, 'five or six years hence, would be the man you would wish to place in the post, but [he] has not yet the years, the experience or the weight of character one would wish to find for such an office'. Nevertheless, and despite not being in Parliament, he was chosen and duly led the state prosecutions of Emmet and his fellow rebels that year. In 1805 he succeeded Viscount Avonmore as chief baron of the Irish exchequer and he held this senior judgeship for the following 25 years.[2]

O'Grady attended Trinity College, Dublin, like his father, but entered the army and served in the last stages of the Napoleonic Wars. He distinguished himself leading the rear troop of the 7th Hussars in their retreat, under constant attack by French lancers, to Genappe, 17 June 1815, when he was warmly praised by his commanding officer Lord Uxbridge†, who was shortly to be created marquess of Anglesey. He fought at Waterloo the following day, afterwards writing to his father that 'the 7th had an opportunity of showing what they could do if they got fair play. We charged 12 or 14 times, and once cut off a squadron of cuirassiers'.[3] He obtained his captaincy on 20 July and, of course, received a Waterloo medal, but he joined the half-pay list in May 1816. This was apparently because his father, who had already clashed with Clare's family on electoral matters, wished him to stand for county Limerick at the next opportunity.[4] In September 1817 O'Grady senior recorded that 'we have been on the alert and since my return from circuit Standish has registered near 400 *new* freeholders which must make some sensation in his favour', and that December he purchased much of Lord Courtenay's vast estates.[5] O'Grady junior duly offered at the general election of 1818, when it was considered curious that he should oppose Richard Fitzgibbon*, whose late father, Clare, had done so much to advance his own father's career, and that the chief baron should act inappropriately by voting, as a non-resident freeman, for his son-in-law John Vereker* in the city contest. He claimed to be standing on the supposedly independent principles of his uncle John Waller, who had sat for the county, 1790-1802, but trailed throughout the week-long poll, after which he promised to renew the attempt.[6] He did not petition, but the parliamentary proceedings which ended in the disgrace of Fitzgibbon's colleague Windham Henry Wyndham Quin gave him the chance to stand again at the general election of 1820.[7] Illness prevented him canvassing and Charles Grant*, the Irish secretary in the Liverpool administration, called him 'a decided oppositionist', so he had to suffer another severe contest, during which his brother Waller O'Grady, a barrister, joined him as a candidate. However, he was elected in second place, behind Fitzgibbon, and claimed his victory as a triumph for the independents.[8]

He voted for Hume's motion on the civil list, 3 May, against the appointment of an additional baron of exchequer in Scotland, 15 May, the aliens bill, 1 June, and for economies in revenue collection, 4 July 1820. The following day he wrote to Henry Grattan II* to explain that he had not hurried on the Dublin writ following his father's death the previous month.[9] He divided against omitting Queen Caroline's name from the liturgy, 23 Jan. 1821. He echoed his colleague's call for the relief of agricultural distress in their county, 19 Feb., and several times that session sided with opposition in favour of reduced expenditure, including on what he called superfluous or unnecessary items in the army estimates, 30 Mar., 6, 30 Apr., 2 May.[10] He voted for Catholic claims, 28 Feb., and on 2 Apr. denied that the Catholic priests' petition from Limerick against securities was representative of Irish opinion. He divided to repeal the Blasphemous and Seditious Libels Acts, 8 May, and to reform the Scottish county representation, 10 May. Evidently prepared to defend the charges levelled against the chief baron in the 9th report of the commissioners of inquiry into the Irish courts of justice, 14, 18 June, he made what Henry Grey Bennet* called 'a good speech', albeit that he became somewhat emotional, in vindicating his father from the accusations of charging excessive fees which were raised by Thomas Spring Rice, the Limerick Member, 22 June.[11] He 'cheerfully acquiesced' in the appointment of a select committee on this, to which he was named, 26 June, but called for further inquiry to clear his father's name on the presentation of its report, 3 July.[12] Leaving the 18th Dragoons, which he had joined two years earlier, he again became a half-pay officer in November 1821.

Perhaps because of the delicate position in which his father was placed by the continuing parliamentary inquiry into his conduct as a judge, O'Grady apparently showed a greater tendency to back ministers in the following two sessions. Speaking from experience, having been involved in attempts to suppress violent unrest in his county, he spoke at length for the Irish insurrection bill, 7 Feb. 1822, although he did hint that day that he would support conciliatory measures and on 4 Mar. he complained that two regiments had been disbanded at Limerick at the height of the disturbances. He divided against more extensive tax reductions to relieve distress, 11, 21 Feb., although he voted to reduce the number of junior lords of the admiralty, 1 Mar. He was named to the select committees on Irish grand jury presentments and Limerick taxation, 23 May. He backed the Irish tithes leasing bill, despite what he saw as its inadequacies, 13 June, but voted for inquiry into tithes on the 19th. The chief baron's case was put off for that session, 4 July 1822, and it may have been over this that O'Grady apparently fought a duel with James Grattan* early that month.[13] He secured a congratulatory address to the lord lieutenant Lord Wellesley at the Limerick county meeting, 6 Jan. 1823, when he was praised for his pro-Catholic stance.[14] He divided to take off £2,000,000 of taxes, 3 Mar., but against abolishing the tax on houses under £5, 10 Mar., and the assessed taxes, 18 Mar. He voted for repealing the Foreign Enlistment Act, 16 Apr., and to recommit the silk manufacture bill, 9 June, but against inquiry into the legal proceedings against the Dublin Orange rioters, 22 Apr. He presented and endorsed the Limerick corporation's petition against Rice's bill to regulate the borough, 6 May 1823.[15]

Rice having again raised the allegations against the chief baron, 12 Feb., O'Grady was appointed on 19 Mar. to another select committee on this, which reported, 16 May 1823.[16] With government reluctant to pronounce on the matter, O'Grady agreed to have it postponed, provided this would not detract from his father's reputation, 13 June, and delivered a substantial speech in justification of his father's conduct, 17 June, when he claimed that the judge had only been concerned to bring order into the proceedings of his court, had been acting on established legal usage and had merely transgressed, if at all, in the most trivial of cases. His candid declaration of his belief in his father's innocence was greeted with cheers, and Rice, who attempted to have the chief baron summoned to give evidence, was hindered in his attempt to secure a series of censure motions that day and 2, 3, 8 July. O'Grady, who otherwise confined himself to making minor observations, insisted that the matter should be settled that session, 9 July 1823, when (if he voted at all) he was presumably in the majority of 38 (to 16) for Scarlett's resolution that, as exchequer fees had recently been abolished, no further proceedings should be taken against the chief baron.[17] The affair nearly led to a duel between Waller O'Grady and Rice early the following year. Referring to the reprehensible 'fee increasing system' still existing in Ireland, Daniel O'Connell* later condemned O'Grady senior, whom he thought to be entering his dotage, for being 'distinctly convicted of it by a parliamentary commission [although] the honourable House did of course deal leniently with him'.[18]

No evidence of parliamentary activity by O'Grady has been traced during the 1824 session. He voted for the Irish unlawful societies bill, 15, 25 Feb., and praised the zeal of Limerick magistrates in ending outrages there, 22 Feb. 1825.[19] He voted for Catholic relief, 1 Mar., 21 Apr., 10 May, and argued for the disfranchisement of the Irish 40*s.* freeholders in order to give proper weight to the more substantial landowners, 9 May. He sided with ministers for the grant to the duke of Cumberland, 30 May, 6 June. Somewhat inaccurately, one contemporary source wrote of him that year that he 'attended frequently, and voted in general with the opposition; talks a good deal'.[20] During electoral speculation that autumn, when he became a major, he was considered vulnerable to a challenger, Thomas Lloyd*; O'Grady senior applied to Goulburn, the Irish secretary, for government support, but O'Connell gleefully remarked that his son's impending defeat was widely welcomed because it was 'terrific to think how the chief baron made the court of exchequer subservient to his county electioneering purposes'.[21] He did not sign the requisition for the abortive pro-Catholic county meeting in October 1825, declined to attend the O'Connellite dinner to the friends of civil and religious liberty in Dublin, 2 Feb., and unsuccessfully opposed the petition against the suppression of small Irish bank notes at a county Limerick meeting in April 1826.[22] He does not seem to have been present at Westminster that year.

His vote to suppress the Catholic Association and his failure to attend the Catholics' provincial meeting in Limerick in October 1825 partly accounted for his unpopularity at the general election of 1826, when he offered on the basis of his parliamentary conduct and stressed that he supported Catholic relief, but was suspected of being 'illiberal'. He trailed behind Fitzgibbon and Lloyd throughout the ensuing contest and protested that his defeat was caused by the aristocratic interests arrayed against him.[23] A petition was lodged on his behalf, but the committee found against him the following year. His name was first in the list of three local gentlemen forwarded to the Castle that autumn, yet he was passed over for the office of sheriff of county Limerick in early 1827. This was probably because he had joined the 24th Foot, which was garrisoned at Limerick, at the beginning of February.[24] Unlike Lord Norbury, the decrepit Irish chief justice of common pleas, who received an earldom, O'Grady senior failed in his bid to profit from the legal arrangements entailed by the appointment of Canning's administration that year; Wellesley reported to the new premier, 12 June 1827, that their negotiation was at an end because the chief baron was 'unwilling to resign until a peerage could actually be conferred upon him, and also *until some very extensive pecuniary demands* of his lordship on the government could be adjusted'.[25] Late the following year O'Grady married Gertrude Paget, whose father had once served in the 7th Dragoons and had only recently left the Commons and the treasury board. Her uncle was Anglesey, the new lord lieutenant, who thought O'Grady 'a sharp, useful fellow'.[26] He returned to the half-pay list, with the rank of lieutenant-colonel in April 1829.

On the death of Lloyd in December 1829 O'Grady offered again as an independent for county Limerick, with the significant endorsement of O'Connell, and fought a severe contest against an aristocratic interloper from Tipperary, James Hewitt Massy Dawson*.[27] O'Grady, who was grateful for the backing of Anglesey, though the latter was not viceroy at this time, faced the tacit opposition of the Wellington government and what he described as the 'banded lords' of the county on the hustings, 25 Jan. 1830, when he expressed his approval of emancipation and his displeasure at the disfranchisement of the 40*s.* freeholders. Despite being ill, he was active during the five-day poll, which he headed by 215 votes, many of which were from tenants who deserted their landlords in his favour.[28] His near namesake and, presumably, close relation, Standish Stamer O'Grady, a young barrister, was killed in a duel early that year.[29] He took his seat, 2 Mar., and his only major speech that session was in arguing for Irish proprietors to live and spend on their estates as a means of improving the condition of the poor, 9 Mar. He sided with opposition in its renewed campaign for economies, 22, 25, 26 Mar., and voted for Jewish emancipation, 5 Apr., and to condemn the affair at Terceira, 28 Apr. Massy Dawson's petition had alleged violence and intimidation by O'Grady's supporters, but it was the complaint that his Catholic voters had not been properly qualified that led to him being unseated, 3 May 1830. He subsequently issued a defiant address to the county and forced a guarded private apology from Lord Francis Leveson Gower, the Irish secretary, for the Irish administration's having been forced to act publicly against him.[30]

Perhaps sensing his electoral weakness, Massy Dawson eventually withdrew before the general election of 1830, so allowing O'Grady to be returned unopposed.[31] He was listed by Planta, the patronage secretary, among the 'bad doubtfuls' and 'opposition' was annotated against his name. He spoke against repeal of the Union, 9, 19 Nov., 11 Dec., but voted for O'Connell's motion to repeal the Irish Subletting Act, 11 Nov. Having left the chamber to dine, he was shut out of the division on the civil list, which precipitated Wellington's resignation, 15 Nov. He defended the Irish church establishment, 18 Nov., the quality of the Irish magistracy, 15 Dec., and his father's record as a judge, 20 Dec. 1830. Although said to be back 'at his tricks', the chief baron retired that month at the request of Anglesey, the reinstated lord lieutenant, and was granted his much coveted Irish peerage, 28 Jan. 1831.[32] O'Grady voted for the second reading of the Grey ministry's reform bill, 22 Mar., and against Gascoyne's wrecking amendment, 19 Apr. As no one else started, he was again returned unopposed with Fitzgibbon at the ensuing general election, when he clarified that he had been in opposition during the previous decade but now supported the ministerial programme of peace, retrenchment and reform. He was foreman of the grand jury for the Limerick special commission on agrarian rioting late that spring, but was back in London by mid-June 1831.[33]

He voted for the second reading of the reintroduced reform bill, 6 July 1831, at least twice against adjourning proceedings on it on the 12th and steadily for its details. He divided for printing the Waterford petition for disarming the Irish yeomanry, 11 Aug., but for the Irish union of parishes bill, 19 Aug., and with government in both divisions on the Dublin election, 23 Aug. He objected to the new Irish lord lieutenants being given the power to appoint county clerks of the peace and urged the creation of an Irish commission of works, 15 Aug. He advocated the introduction of a system of poor laws to Ireland, but declined to support Sadler's resolution on this as inadequate, 29 Aug. He voted for the passage of the reform bill, 21 Sept., and Lord Ebrington's confidence motion, 10 Oct. Reckoned to be a liberal Member and a tolerably good speaker, his poor attendance record was criticized by the radical William Carpenter that year.[34] He evidently missed much of the following session, as he was absent from the second, 17 Dec. 1831, and third readings of the revised reform bill, 22 Mar., and Ebrington's motion for an address calling on the king to appoint only ministers who would carry it unimpaired, 10 May, although he is known to have paired for the enfranchisement of Tower Hamlets, 28 Feb. 1832. However, he voted for the second reading of the Irish bill, 25 May 1832, and commented on the qualification of freeholders in counties, 6 July, and the right of election at Trinity College, 9 July. His only other known vote was with government for the Russian-Dutch loan, 12 July.

In August 1832 he wrote to one constituent that illness had kept him from the House, but that he hoped to present and endorse the Fedamore petition against Irish tithes before the end of the session (which he apparently failed to do).[35] In November Lord Dunraven, as Wyndham Quin had become, commented that 'I have no desire to see Col. O'Grady unseated – I have already punished his pocket ever too severely for the run he made to throw me out in 1818', and, despite an O'Connellite challenge, he was again returned for his county as a Liberal at the general election in December 1832.[36] He left the Commons two years later and, having inherited his father's title and estates in 1840, was appointed one of Queen Victoria's aides-de-camp in 1842. He died in July 1848, when he was succeeded as third Viscount Guillamore by his eldest son Standish (1832-60), a naval officer, three of whose brothers later came into the peerage.[37]

[1] *CP*, vi. 219 gives him the middle name 'Darby', which was a common one in the family. [2] *Later Corresp. Geo. III*, iv. 2746, 2748; F.E. Ball, *Judges in Ireland*, ii. 244, 248-9, 336; *Oxford DNB*. [3] H.T. Siborne, *Hist. War in France and Belgium*, 166-7; H.T. Siborne, *Waterloo Letters*, 130-6; Mq. of Anglesey, *One-Leg*, 130; *DNB*. [4] *HP Commons, 1790-1820*, ii. 667-8. [5] *Scully Pprs.* ed. B. MacDermot, 583; *The Times*, 25 Dec. 1817. [6] *General Advertiser and Limerick Gazette*, 16 June, 3, 7, 10, 14 July; *Dublin Evening Post*, 23 June, 9, 11 July 1818. [7] *HP Commons, 1790-1820*, ii. 668. [8] Add. 38458, f. 298; *General Advertiser*, 15, 29 Feb., 21, 24, 28, 31 Mar., 4, 7 Apr. 1820. [9] NLI, Grattan mss 27805. [10] *The Times*, 20 Feb., 7 Apr. 1821.

[11] Ibid. 15, 19 June 1821; HLRO, Hist. Coll. 379, Grey Bennet diary, 101. [12] *The Times*, 4 July 1821; *CJ*, lxxvi. 475-6, 499; *PP* (1821), viii. 465-86. [13] *The Times*, 6 July 1822. [14] *Dublin Evening Post*, 11 Jan. 1823. [15] *The Times*, 7 May 1823. [16] *PP* (1823), vi. 1-10. [17] *CJ*, lxxviii. 393, 402, 448, 451, 467, 470. [18] *O'Connell Corresp.* iii. 1092, 1095; viii. 3407, 3433. [19] *The Times*, 23 Feb. 1825. [20] *Session of Parl. 1825*, p. 478. [21] *Dublin Evening Post*, 15, 22 Sept. 1825; Add. 40331, f. 237; *O'Connell Corresp.* iii. 1253. [22] *Dublin Evening Post*, 6 Oct. 1825; *Limerick Chron.* 12 Apr. 1826; *O'Connell Corresp.* iii. 1278. [23] *Limerick Chron.* 10, 24, 28 June, 1, 5 July; *Dublin Evening Post*, 15, 27, 29 June, 4, 8 July 1826. [24] *Limerick Chron.* 6 Dec. 1826, 20 Jan., 10 Feb. 1827. [25] *Canning's Ministry*, 320, 327, 332, 368. [26] Anglesey, 361. [27] *Dublin Evening Post*, 19, 29, 31 Dec. 1829, 2 Jan.; *Limerick Evening Post*, 5, 15, 22 Jan. 1830; Add. 40338, f. 21. [28] PRO NI, Anglesey mss D619/32A/4/8; *Limerick Evening Post*, 26, 29 Jan., 2, 5, 12 Feb.; *The Times*, 2 Feb. 1830. [29] *Dublin Evening Post*, 20, 23, 25 Mar. 1830. [30] *Limerick Evening Post*, 7 May; NAI, Leveson Gower letterbks. Leveson Gower to O'Grady, 14 May 1830. [31] *Limerick Evening Post*, 13 July, 3, 6, 10 Aug. 1830. [32] Anglesey mss 29B, pp. 12-15, 23; 33A/78. [33] *Limerick Evening Post*, 3, 10, 13, 31 May, 17 June 1831. [34] F.B. Hamilton, *Picture of Parl.* (1831), 71; [W. Carpenter], *People's Bk.* (1831), 337. [35] *Limerick Herald*, 9 Aug. 1832. [36] NLI, Smith O'Brien mss 427/185; *Dublin Evening Post*, 20, 27 Dec. 1832. [37] *Limerick Chron.* 26 July 1848; *Gent. Mag.* (1848), ii. 317; *DNB*; *Oxford DNB* (which neglects to mention that he was an MP).

S.M.F.

O'HARA, Charles (1746–1822), of Nymphsfield and Annaghmore, co. Sligo.

CO. SLIGO 1801–19 Sept. 1822

b. 26 Apr. 1746, 1st s. of Charles O'Hara, MP [I], of Annaghmore and Lady Mary Carmichael, da. of James, 2nd earl of Hyndford [S]. *educ.* Christ Church, Oxf. 1763; M. Temple 1765, called [I] 1771. *m.* 1780, Margaret, da. and h. of John Cookson, MD, of Yorks., 1s. 3da. *suc.* fa. 1776. *d.* 19 Sept. 1822.

MP [I] 1776-1800.

Commr. of treasury [I] Apr. 1806-Apr. 1807.

Sheriff, co. Sligo 1785-6, gov. 1789-*d.*

Capt. commdt. Corran and Liney cav. 1796.

O'Hara, the leading proprietor in county Sligo, had been repeatedly pressed to make way for his son Charles King O'Hara by the county's other leading families, but fearing a challenge to his electoral supremacy he refused. He was again returned unopposed at the 1820 general election, almost 44 years after he had first entered the Irish Parliament.[1] He had acted with the Whig opposition, except on Catholic relief, from 1807, but, for all his observation to his son in 1818 that 'the duties of a Member ... is a very important trust', he is not known to have voted or spoken in debate after May 1816.[2] He died in September 1822, having struggled all his life to overcome the problems posed by his heavily encumbered estates. Charles King O'Hara declined for financial reasons to come forward at the ensuing by-election.[3] He in turn devised the estates to his nephew Charles William Cooper (1817-98), who sat for the county as a Conservative in the 1859 Parliament and took the name of O'Hara in 1860.

[1] NLI, O'Hara mss 338, C. to C.K. O'Hara, 6 June 1818. [2] Ibid. [3] Ibid. 20316, Verschoyle to C.K. O'Hara, 20 Sept. 1822.

D.R.F./P.J.S.

O'HARA, James (1796–1838), of West Lodge, co. Galway.

GALWAY 1826–1831

b. 1796, s. of James O'Hara, recorder of Galway, of Lenaboy, co. Galway and Margaret, da. of Richard Moore. *educ.* Trinity, Dublin 1811; King's Inns 1815, called [I] 1819. *m.* 15 Apr. 1823, Anne, da. of Hon. and Most Rev. Power Le Poer Trench, abp. of Tuam, 2s. 4da. *suc.* fa. 1838. *d.* 23 Dec. 1838.

Recorder, Galway 1819-26, 1831-*d.*; sheriff, co. Galway 1835-6.

Commr. of bankrupts [I], fisheries [I] 1829.

O'Hara's family came originally from county Sligo, so he may have been distantly related to Charles O'Hara*, its representative for nearly 40 years. His grandfather, another James, married the daughter of Robert Shaw (perhaps the former Galway Member of that name) in 1744 and from that time onwards the family occupied a prominent place in the offices of the corporation. An O'Hara held the position of town clerk from 1757 until at least the 1830s, and this Member's father (*b.* 1748), who graduated at Trinity, Dublin in 1768 and was called to the Irish bar in 1771, was its recorder, 1772-3, and again from 1774.[1] Following in his father's footsteps, O'Hara was elected recorder in 1819 and at the general election of 1820, when he acted as assessor, he apparently threatened with imprisonment any Catholic tradesmen who presented themselves to vote against the Tory patron James Daly's* nominee.[2] In 1823 he received plaudits for opposing the establishment of an Orange lodge and suppressing partisan disturbances.[3] That year he married the granddaughter of the 1st earl of Clancarty; her father and uncle, the 2nd earl, were prominent among the Protestant Tories in county Galway.

At the general election of 1826, when a contest was expected between Daly's nominee and a candidate to be put up by the powerful independent interest, O'Hara emerged as a last minute compromise, his unexceptionable character and good legal stewardship making him acceptable to all parties. He staked his claim to being unattached, distancing himself from the dominant interest by promising to open the corporation, and defeated an ostensible challenger in a fierce contest; it was soon suspected, however, that his loyalties secretly lay with Daly, who had been anxious to neutralize a potential challenge to his authority in the borough in order to safeguard his county seat.[4] A petition against him was not pursued. O'Hara was the assessor in the violent county contest that year and gave evidence to the subsequent election committee, 23 Mar. 1827, when he denied that he or the other officials had shown any partiality to Richard Martin (who was unseated).[5] He signed the requisitions for meetings of the pro-Catholic Protestants of the county and town of Galway in the autumn of 1826, when he apparently handed the recordership back to his father, and at the borough gathering (on 15 Sept.) he moved the resolution in favour of Catholic claims.[6] He brought up the ensuing town petition, 2 Mar., and voted for Catholic relief, 6 Mar. 1827.[7] He was granted six weeks' leave on account of his wife's illness, 10 Apr., and returned early from Parliament to be with her.[8] That winter he was active in promoting improvements in the town and took the opportunity to underline his independent and pro-Catholic principles, though during the following one he had to defend himself against criticisms of having failed to make progress on the development of the port or to alter the composition of the corporation.[9] He divided for repeal of the Test Acts, 26 Feb., and Catholic relief, 12 May 1828, and signed the Irish Protestant declaration in favour of the Catholics that autumn.[10] He voted for emancipation, 6 Mar., and, after returning to Galway, paired for it, 30 Mar. 1829.[11]

Although he had been attacked for being too close to Daly and declining to contribute to the national subscription to Daniel O'Connell* that year, he was warmly applauded for supporting the legislative campaign for enfranchising the borough's Catholic tradesmen at a meeting in Galway, 30 Aug., and for stating that he would honour his election pledges at another, 25 Oct. 1829.[12] He chaired other gatherings on the subject of the Galway franchise bill, 10 Jan., 11, 12 Apr. 1830, although when this was raised in the Commons, he confined himself to saying, in what amounted to almost his only known speech, 4 Mar., that 'I think the great object we should have in view is the promotion of peace and happiness by the union of all classes in society; and I shall be ready to vote for any measure calculated to promote that union'.[13] O'Hara, who divided against the enfranchisement of Birmingham, Leeds and Manchester, 23 Feb., brought up petitions to extend the franchise at Galway, 10 Mar., 26 Apr. He was reported to have voted against O'Connell's bill to alter the Irish vestry laws, 27 Apr., but was listed in the minority for repeal of the Irish coal duties, 13 May. Having attended a meeting of the Irish Members who were opposed to the increased Irish spirit and stamp duties, he presented other petitions from his constituents against them, 11, 17 May 1830.[14]

Having secured the passage of the Galway docks bill, if not of the franchise measure (which was defeated in the Lords), he offered again on the basis of his record at the general election of 1830, when he denied the allegations of his opponent, the former Member Valentine Blake†, that he was a creature of the corporation and declared in favour of limited parliamentary reform.[15] After ugly scenes on the hustings, where he denied that he would resort to polling non-resident freemen, he led throughout the contest, and even received a modest endorsement from O'Connell. He promised to maintain an independent line, but plumped for Daly in the county contest.[16] Listed by Pierce Mahony† as 'pro-government' in his analysis of the Irish results and by ministers among their 'friends', he was credited with voting in their minority on the civil list, 15 Nov.; conflicting newspaper reports had it that he intended to side with opposition, but had been shut out.[17] On 6 Dec. 1830 he raised no objection to extending the period in which recognizances could be entered into for the petition against his return, the proceedings on which he survived the following year. He signed the requisition for the county Galway reform meeting in January and voted for the second reading of the Grey ministry's reform bill, 22 Mar., and against Gascoyne's wrecking amendment, 19 Apr. 1831.[18]

It was initially believed that he would persist at the ensuing general election, or, if not, that his kinsman John, the town clerk, would offer in his place. However, boasting that the independence of the town had been secured, he gratefully retired back into private life, leaving the seat free for an advanced reformer.[19] He probably resumed the recordership later that year and thereafter played little part in politics, although he proposed Daly's Conservative son Denis for the borough at the general election of 1837.[20] Only narrowly surviving his father, whose death occurred on 22 Nov. 1838, he died a month later, when he was remembered for his disinterested attitude to politics. He was succeeded in his estates, including Lenaboy, by his elder son James (1832-1903), an army officer, while the recordership passed to his cousin William O'Hara of Nile Lodge.[21]

[1] *Burke Irish LG* (1904), 458; J. Hardiman, *Hist. Galway* (1820), 230. [2] *CJ*, lxxxii. 95; lxxxvi. 115. [3] *Galway Weekly Advertiser*, 11 Jan., 28 June 1823. [4] *Connaught Jnl.* 29 May, 12, 15, 19, 22 June; *Dublin Evening Post*, 27, 29 June, 11 July 1826. [5] *PP* (1826-7), iv. 962-5. [6] *Connaught Jnl.* 17 Aug., 11, 18 Sept. 1826; *Galway Weekly Advertiser*, 17 July 1830. [7] *The Times*, 3 Mar. 1827. [8] *Connaught Jnl.* 23 Apr. 1827. [9] Ibid. 1, 12, 22, 26 Nov. 1827, 15, 29 Dec. 1828, 5, 15 Jan. 1829. [10] *Dublin Evening Mail*, 8 Oct. 1828. [11] *Connaught Jnl.* 30 Mar. 1829. [12] Ibid. 26 Feb., 5 Mar., 25 June, 17, 31 Aug., 26 Oct. 1829. [13] Ibid. 7, 11, 14 Jan., 12, 15 Apr. 1830. [14] Ibid. 10 May; *Freeman's Jnl.* 15 June 1830. [15] *Connaught Jnl.* 31 May, 14, 21, 28 June, 5, 8, 19, 26 July; *Galway Weekly Advertiser*, 17 July 1830. [16] *Connaught Jnl.* 2, 5, 9, 12, 16, 21 Aug. 1830. [17] Ibid. 25 Nov., 13, 16 Dec. 1830. [18] Ibid. 20 Jan. 1831. [19] Ibid. 25, 28 Apr., 2, 9 May 1831. [20] *PP* (1835), xxvii. 521; *Galway Weekly Advertiser*, 5 Aug. 1837. [21] *Galway Patriot*, 28 Nov. 1838, 2, 9 Jan. 1839.

S.M.F.

OMMANNEY, Francis Molyneux (1774–1840), of Norfolk Street, Strand, Mdx.

BARNSTAPLE 1818–1826

b. 4 Oct. 1774,[1] 2nd s. of R.-Adm. Cornthwaite Ommanney (*d.* 1801) of Millbank Row, Mdx. and Martha, da. of Henry Manaton of Kilworthy, nr. Tavistock, Devon. *m.* 16 Oct. 1801, Georgiana Frances, da. of Jeremiah Hawkes of Cecil Street, Strand,[2] 7s. (1 *d.v.p.*) 2da. kntd. 17 May 1820. *d.* 7 Nov. 1840.

In 1819 Ommanney assumed sole control of the London naval agency founded by his uncle Edward, who had given him a start in life. The following year he stood again for Barnstaple, where he had been successful in a notoriously corrupt contest in 1818, and was returned unopposed. He was known to be 'friendly' to Lord Liverpool's ministry, and he received a knighthood shortly after the election.[3] He was an active and conscientious, if rather pompous Member, whose unsophisticated approach to the art of debating provided the House with a number of comic interludes. He supported the insolvent debtors bill, 5 June 1820. He maintained that the lords of the admiralty had abrogated their 'duty ... to the country in reducing the navy so low', 9 June. His observations on Hume's notice of a motion regarding the private property of George III were cut short by the Speaker, 3 July.[4] Next day he voted against economies in revenue collection. He approved of the East India volunteers bill, 11 July 1820.[5] He voted in defence of ministers' conduct towards Queen Caroline, 6 Feb. 1821. He divided with them on the ordnance estimates, 16 Feb., the state of the revenue, 6 Mar., the additional malt duty, 21 Mar., 3 Apr., and the duke of Clarence's grant, 18 June. He ignored cries for a division to oppose economies at the admiralty, 4 May.[6] He voted against Catholic relief, 28 Feb., and parliamentary reform, 9 May. He divided against the forgery punishment mitigation bill, 23 May, and objected to abolishing the capital penalty for forgery of country bank notes, 31 May.[7] He supported a drastic reduction in the compensation offered to General Desfourneaux for losses incurred in the capture of Guadeloupe, 15, 28 June, and spoke against the extra post bill, 29 June 1821.[8]

He divided against more extensive tax reductions, 11 Feb., and abolition of one of the joint-postmasterships, 13 Mar. 1822. He declared that he would support the 'repeal of all taxes that peculiarly affected the poor', 28 Feb., and voted for gradual reduction of the salt duties. However, he voted against their total repeal, 28 June, when he complained that government economies had reduced many civil servants to a state of beggary. He divided against removing Catholic peers' disabilities, 30 Apr., inquiry into Irish tithes, 19 June, and the motion condemning the lord advocate's conduct towards the Scottish press, 25 June. He voted against the Calcutta bankers' claim for recovery of debts from the East India Company, 4 July. He voted for the Canada bill, 18 July, and the aliens bill, 19 July 1822. He divided against parliamentary reform, 20 Feb., 2 June 1823, when he dissented from the Devon petition on the subject. He voted against further tax reductions, 3 Mar., repeal of the duty on houses valued at under £5, 10 Mar.,[9] and inquiry into the currency, 12 June. He divided against repeal of the Foreign Enlistment Act, 16 Apr., and inquiries into the prosecution of the Dublin Orange rioters, 22 Apr., and delays in chancery, 5 June. He voted against repeal of the usury laws, 27 June. On 14 Mar. he moved to add £1,000 to the admiralty estimates to provide for an extra junior lord, but found no support. He also drew attention to the hardship suffered by the widows of assistant naval surgeons, and was called to order after accusing the admiralty secretary, Croker, of lying.[10] In the debate on the system of naval promotions, 19 June, he recommended that these should be made strictly according to seniority and referred amid mounting laughter to the case of his own father, who had been 'greatly ill-used and exposed to the most galling and heart-breaking neglect'. At the end of his speech his audience was hysterical, and he failed to find a seconder for his amendment. Next day, in a 'low and indistinct' tone of voice, he offered some explanation of this outburst and admitted having said that a man who broke 'sacred promises' deserved 'the name of a reptile'. He then moved for information on the recent incidence of piracy in the Caribbean, with a view to securing 'some public regulation of reward' for naval officers and crews who captured or destroyed pirate vessels, a subject on which he had previously written to the prime minister. At the foreign secretary Canning's suggestion the motion was deferred until 23 June 1823, when it was agreed to. Ommanney raised the subject again, 6 Feb. 1824, securing an address to the king for a return of information. This was presented and printed, 15 June 1824, and in the following session government carried a measure (6 Geo. IV, c. 49) based on Ommanney's ideas.[11]

He voted against the production of papers regarding Catholic office-holders, 19 Feb. 1824. He welcomed an increase in the navy estimates, 16 Feb., and presented a Barnstaple petition for repeal of the coal duties, 23 Feb.[12] He again divided against the usury laws repeal bill, 27 Feb., yet voted to go into committee on it, 8 Apr. He was responsible for more farce in committee on the county courts bill, 26 Mar., when he moved to compensate the receiver of king's bench for lost emoluments. Although it was pointed out that no such office existed (he had confused it with the clerkship of the outer treasury), he threatened to divide the committee, only to withdraw in confusion; it was suggested that he ought to compensate the House for wasted time.[13] He favoured relieving clerks in civil departments of government from hardship caused by the Superannuation Act, 13 May.[14] He seconded an unsuccessful motion to refer the marine insurance bill to a select committee, 3 June, and raised a laugh by moving an amendment to make it inoperative until the year 2000; he was defeated by 33-12. He voted against the motion condemning the prosecution of the Methodist missionary John Smith in Demerara, 11 June, and for the Irish insurrection bill, 14 June 1824. He divided for the Irish unlawful societies bill, 25 Feb., and against Catholic relief, 1 Mar., 21 Apr., 10 May 1825. He afforded the House further amusement, 6 May, by declaring that the 'homage' paid to papal bulls was 'contrary to the second commandment, which prohibited idolatory'. He voted against the Irish franchise bill, 9 May. He divided for the financial provision for the duke of Cumberland, 6, 10 June. He opposed Hume's proposal to end flogging in the navy, 9 June 1825, with the observation that thanks to his repeal of the combination laws 'every town in the kingdom swarmed with insubordinate workmen standing out against their employers'. He complained of the low pay of admiralty clerks and again spoke of the problems experienced by assistant-surgeons' widows in securing pensions, 21 Feb. 1826. There was ribald laughter when he alluded to the 'protection' which he had personally given to two such women.[15] He defended the government's plan to give the president of the board of trade a ministerial salary and argued against the alternative proposal to merge the office with that of treasurer of the navy, 6, 7 Apr. He had something to say on the funding of exchequer bills, 17 Apr. He divided with the majority against the spring guns bill, 27 Apr.[16] It is unclear whether it was he or Lord Oxmantown who voted against Russell's resolutions on electoral bribery, 26 May 1826. He was initially expected to stand again for Barnstaple at the general election that summer, but he withdrew before the poll and found no way back into Parliament.[17]

Ommanney died in November 1840. His son Octavius carried on the naval agency, which in 1862 amalgamated with a firm of bankers and naval agents to become Hallett, Ommanney and Company; it had disappeared by the turn of the century.

[1] IGI (Surr.). [2] IGI (England). [3] Add. 38458, f. 310. [4] *The Times*, 4 July 1820. [5] Ibid. 12 July 1820. [6] Ibid. 5 May 1820. [7] Ibid. 1 June 1821. [8] Ibid. 16, 29, 30 June 1821. [9] Ibid. 11 Mar. 1823. [10] Ibid. 15 Mar. 1823. [11] Ibid. 20, 21 June 1823, 7 Feb. 1824; Add. 38293, f. 43; 38294, f. 300. [12] *The Times*, 24 Feb. 1824. [13] Ibid. 27 Mar. 1824. [14] Ibid. 14 May 1824. [15] Ibid. 22 Feb. 1826. [16] Norf. RO, Gunton mss 1/21. [17] *The Times*, 27 May, 5 June 1826.

D.R.F.

O'NEILL, Augustus John Henry (*b.* 1792), of Bunowen Castle, co. Galway; 8 Leinster Street, Dublin, and 19 Grosvenor Street West, Mdx.

KINGSTON-UPON-HULL 1826–1830

b. 23 June 1792, 1st s. of John David Geoghegan (afterwards O'Neill) of Bunowen Castle and Gertrude, da. and coh. of Robert Fetherston of Whiterock House, co. Longford. *educ.* Trinity, Dublin 1807. *m.* Jan. 1829, Elizabeth, da. of Robert Baring Bellamie of Sandford House, Som., 1s. 1da. *suc.* fa. 1830.

According to a contemporary, O'Neill 'could not be called a good looking man, he had dark staring eyes, rather pale complexion and slightly pitted with the smallpox, with hair having a tendency to curl'.[1] He had a distinguished background, being paternally descended from the Irish monarch of the fourth century, Niall of the Nine Hostages. The senior branch of the family had expired in the reign of Charles I and it had been the desire of successive generations of the Geoghegans, as heads of the family, to assume the name of O'Neill. It was only when O'Neill's father became accountant-general to the exchequer in Ireland that the family felt confident they would reclaim the title. George III accepted John Geoghegan's application in 1808 and the family assumed the name of O'Neill.[2] When the mayor of Hull inquired of O'Neill's background in 1826, the marquess of Clanricarde declared him to be 'a gentleman of a very old family, great respectability and considerable property ... chiefly in the county of Galway'.[3] O'Neill's father was in fact a close friend and political ally of Henry Grattan I*.

Little was known of O'Neill when he made a speculative visit to Hull shortly before the 1826 general election. The *Hull Rockingham* declared that it knew nothing of him: 'We suspect that he does not know all who may be useful to him in his electioneering campaign, or he would not have presented himself as *third man*, when neither a first nor second has entered the field'. He had in fact invited the burgesses to sign a requisition requesting him to stand. Between 500 and 700 did so, and ten days before the nomination he made his appearance. The rumour in the town was that he had come to Hull to contest a seat as a result of a wager struck at his London club. The truth of this is unknown, but he pursued an active campaign, taking care to cultivate the wives of the freemen, an observer describing him as 'one of the very best canvassers I ever met'. According to another witness

> he had a fair display of jewelry, which he took good care to show. His manners were very volatile, and to look at the man, a keen observer would say that he really could not make up his mind to imagine that he was firm in his statements for there was a flightiness of manner about him. He looked as wild and harum-scarum as an untrained colt, yet, he was possessed of sufficient *suaviter in modo* to carry his point.

He quickly established his popularity with the lower order of freemen and in his published address, in which he described himself as a relative of the earl of Antrim and Sir George Fetherston*, cited his support for free trade and a revision of the corn laws, and his hostility to Catholic emancipation. After an acrimonious contest, in which he boasted of connections that would benefit the people of Hull and promised that a ship of 800 tons would be built there if he was elected, he was returned at the head of the poll. At the declaration he described his victory as that of the 'independent freemen' over 'powerless Whiggism', while the *Hull Packet* attributed his success 'to an active and assiduous canvass, and to his frequently addressing the public'.[4]

Soon after entering the House, O'Neill had some dealings with John Cam Hobhouse* concerning his collection of Byron's works.[5] He voted against Catholic claims, 6 Mar. 1827, 12 May 1828, and brought up a hostile constituency petition, 6 June 1827. He was unable to attend the Dublin election committee owing to illness, 26 Mar.[6] He spoke and divided against the disfranchisement of Penryn for corruption, arguing that the evidence of 1807 and 1819 was irrelevant, 28 May, and spoke in similar terms against the disfranchisement of East Retford and 'this too rapid progress of reform', 11 June 1827. He campaigned steadily against both bills thereafter, asking whether any Member could 'lay his hand on his heart and in the face of his country declare that he has not expended a single shilling in these practices?', 14 Mar., and whether 'the honest freeman is to be deprived of his privilege because his neighbour has abused it?', 2 June 1828. He voted against the Coventry magistracy bill, 18 June 1827. He seconded Sir James Graham's unsuccessful motion in favour of the Wakefield and Ferrybridge canal bill, 3 Mar. 1828. He was in the minority (as a pair) for repeal of the prohibition of the use of ribbons at elections, 20 Mar., and protested that proposals to shorten the duration of polls would prevent many outvoters from polling, 23 May. He was in the majority against reducing the salary of the Wellington ministry's lieutenant-general of ordnance, 4 July. He presented a petition from Irish kelp traders for the tax to be maintained on imports of alkalis and gave notice that he would bring forward a motion concerning their grievances, 8 July. This he did, 15 July, but he withdrew it after receiving assurances from ministers. He divided with government on the silk duties, 14 July 1828. O'Neill was, of course, listed by Planta, the patronage secretary, as 'opposed' to their concession of Catholic emancipation. He presented and defended hostile petitions, 9 Feb., 10, 12 Mar., and voted accordingly, 6, 18 (as a pair), 23, 27, 30 Mar. 1829. On 26 Feb. he unsuccessfully moved for returns indicating the number of petitioners on both sides of the issue, in order to gauge the strength of feeling. Next day he clashed with his colleague Daniel Sykes, who had presented a favourable Hull petition, demanding to know 'How many signatures?', and, when told, insisting that the majority in Hull were opposed to further concessions. Following the home secretary Peel's introduction of the measure, 5 Mar., O'Neill accused him of misleading the country and declared, 'I dare ministers to a dissolution; they know they could not carry the measure if the present Parliament were dissolved'. On 27 Mar. he explained that 'the greatest objection I feel to the present bill is that it affords to the Catholics the power of legislation on all matters connected with our church, whilst we are not permitted to interfere in the most trifling degree with theirs'. He divided against Daniel O'Connell being allowed to take his seat unhindered, 18 May. He obtained returns of the number of borough electors, 25 May. On 2 June he seconded and was a minority teller for the Ultra Lord Blandford's motion for parliamentary reform, which he argued would result in better protection against the Catholic party. He presented a Galway petition complaining of misapplication of money granted for public works, 5 June. In his last known activity in the House, he was in the minority for the abolition of colonial slavery, 13 June 1829.

During the early months of 1830 O'Neill's health faltered and he suffered a further blow when his father died that April. The *Hull Rockingham* of 10 July reported various rumours that his arrival in the town was imminent but doubted them. William Denison*, advising Gilbert John Heathcote* on his pretensions to Hull, informed him, 16 July, that 'O'Neill, not having paid his bill, cannot stand'. He was also suspected of being involved in a gambling scandal. Nevertheless, he issued a statement professing an intention to return, citing his 'adherence to the cause of Protestant ascendancy', his defence of the voters of East Retford and his attempts to 'narrow the power of the great, and extend that of the people'. Summing up his politics, he declared, 'though returned on what is called the Tory interest, I neither did, nor could, give a regular support to government'. Although his election committee reformed to draw up a formal requisition to him, very few signed it, and no one of any great consequence in the town. As a result O'Neill retired at the 1830 dissolution.[7]

He returned to politics in the 1840s, trying to secure a quay for Bunowen and offering Peel, as premier, his services and advice on Irish matters. Reconciled to Catholic emancipation, he apologized to Peel for the criticisms he had made of him in 1829 and was granted an interview with him in the autumn of 1844, when he declared his intention of returning to the House.[8] A convert to O'Connell's campaign for repeal of the Union, in April 1845 he seconded William Smith O'Brien's* address to the county electors of Down, defending Peel's policy, thanking him for the Maynooth grant, but insisting that only repeal would solve Ireland's problems. In the autumn of 1846 he was disappointed at not being offered the chance to contest Clonmel or Dungarvan at by-elections, even though he was willing to contribute up to £1,000 to the expenses. He bitterly attacked O'Connell over this at a meeting of the Repeal Association, for which he was widely applauded.[9] O'Neill never did return to the House. His last known public act was to deny some accusations made against him in 1853 (when he was in London) by a witness to the commissioners investigating the corrupt practices at Hull elections. He denied that a peer had sent him £1,000 during his election and that his total election costs exceeded £12,000, maintaining that they had been no higher than £4,700. He had sold his Irish estates, but his movements after August 1853 are unknown.[10]

[1] *Hull Celebrities* ed. W. Gunnell, 449. [2] *Liber Munerum Pub. Hiberniae*, iii. 103; *Mss Sources Hist. Irish Civilisation*, ed. R. Hayes, ii. 247. [3] Hull Central Lib. Wilson-Barkworth mss, Clanricarde to W.W. Bolton, 1 June 1826. [4] *Hull Rockingham*, 20, 27 May, 10, 17 June; *Hull Advertiser*, 12 May, 16 June; *Hull Packet*, 10 June 1826; *Hull Celebrities*, 449. [5] Add. 36463, f. 317. [6] *The Times*, 27 Mar. 1827. [7] *Hull Rockingham*, 10 June, 10, 24 July 1830; Lincs. AO, Ancaster mss XIII/5/5b. [8] Add. 40551, ff. 145-52; 40565, ff. 356-60; 40574, ff. 63, 67, 127; 40578, ff. 73-94. [9] *Dublin Evening Packet*, 29 Apr. 1845; *O'Connell Corresp.* viii. 81, 124, 218. [10] *PP* (1854), xxii. 927; Add. 40574, f. 63.

M.P.J.C.

O'NEILL, Hon. John Bruce Richard (1780–1855), of Tullymore Lodge, co. Antrim.

CO. ANTRIM 1802–25 Mar. 1841

b. 30 Dec. 1780, 2nd s. of John, 1st Visct. O'Neill [I] (*d.* 1798), of Shane's Castle, co. Antrim and Henrietta, da. and h. of Charles Boyle, Visct. Dungarvan, MP [I], 1st s. of John, 5th earl of Cork [I]. *educ.* Eton 1793. *unm. suc.* bro. as 3rd Visct. O'Neill [I] 25 Mar. 1841. *d.* 12 Feb. 1855.

Ensign 2 Ft. Gds. 1799, lt. and capt. 1800; capt. 18 Drag. 1804; maj. 19 Drag. 1807; lt.-col. Chasseurs Britanniques 1808; lt.-col. 19 Drag. 1810; brevet col. 1814; lt.-col. 2 Ft. Gds. 1816; maj.-gen. 1825; lt.-gen. 1838; gen. 1854.

Constable, Dublin Castle Apr. 1811-*d.*; vice-adm. Ulster.

Rep. peer [I] 1843-*d.*

O'Neill's grandfather and father had both represented the family borough of Randalstown in the Irish Parliament, and the latter had subsequently sat for county Antrim before being raised to the peerage as Baron (1793) and Viscount O'Neill (1795). Killed during the Rebellion in 1798, he was succeeded by O'Neill's elder brother Charles Henry St. John, who was given an Irish earldom at the time of the Union, became a representative peer in 1801 and was grand master of the Orange Order. It was on his interest that O'Neill had sat for Antrim since 1802.[1] He was again returned at the general election of 1820, when nothing came of an expected challenge.[2] An Irish placeman like his brother, he continued to give sporadic and silent support to the administration of Lord Liverpool, whose offer of a marquessate was declined by Lord O'Neill in July 1820.[3] No trace of parliamentary activity has been found during the 1820 session, but he voted against censuring ministers' conduct towards Queen Caroline, 6 Feb. 1821. An Orangeman and sometime member of the committee of the grand lodge, he divided against Catholic claims, 28 Feb. 1821, and the Catholic peers bill, 30 Apr. 1822.[4] He voted against more extensive tax reductions to relieve distress, 11 Feb. 1822, and repeal of the assessed taxes, 18 Mar. 1823. His brother failed in his application to ministers to have him appointed custos rotulorum of Antrim in 1822.[5]

O'Neill sided with opposition for information on the plot to murder the Irish lord lieutenant, 24 Mar. 1823, and was apparently ready to resign his place in order to vote for Brownlow's intended motion on the use of *ex-officio* informations against the Orangemen implicated in the affair.[6] That did not come to a division, but he voted for inquiry into the legal proceedings against the Dublin Orange rioters, 22 Apr. He presented the county Antrim anti-Catholic petition, 16 Apr., when he voted against repeal of the Foreign Enlistment Act, and he paired against parliamentary reform, 24 Apr.[7] On 3 Sept. 1823 Thomas Wallace I*, a junior minister, reported to John Herries* from Dublin that he had heard of a

> *serious* representation made or to be made to Lord Liverpool by some of the *Irish Members against* the system of reform now happily proceeding in this country on the ground of its interfering with the patronage, the continuance of which in its full extent was a condition of their support in carrying the Union and threatening that if it is persisted in they will withdraw their assistance from government ... I am told too it is to be presented by Col. O'Neill ... Lord L. will know how to deal with it and with pretensions of such incomparable absurdity.[8]

He divided for the Irish unlawful societies bill, 25 Feb., and against Catholic relief, 1 Mar., 21 Apr., 10 May, and the Irish franchise bill, 26 Apr. 1825. He was promoted major-general in May, but in October 1825 ministers declined to promise a peerage to Lord O'Neill with a special remainder to him.[9] Despite having apparently been inactive or absent during the 1826 session, O'Neill was returned for Antrim at the general election that year, when a contest was again avoided.[10]

He attended an Antrim county meeting to agree an address of condolence on the death of the duke of York, 6 Feb. 1827, and that month signed the Irish Protestants' anti-Catholic petition. Bringing up the county's anti-Catholic petition, 2 Mar., his colleague MacNaghten stated that he was absent through illness but supported its plea.[11] He paired against Catholic relief, 6 Mar., and complained about the unequal treatment accorded to Orange processions, 11 Apr.[12] Lord O'Neill, who approved but did not follow the resignation of the anti-Catholics from Canning's new government, again unsuccessfully applied to ministers for a promotion in the peerage as marquess of Ulster.[13] Unless it was Augustus O'Neill, Member for Hull, O'Neill voted against the Coventry magistracy bill, 11 June 1827, and he may have divided for Fyler's amendment in the committee on the Customs Acts which was carried with government support, 14 July 1828. He again voted against Catholic relief, 12 May. Offended by the curt refusal of the new prime minister, the duke of Wellington, to consider his renewed application for a peerage, Lord O'Neill hinted in August to Peel, the home secretary, that he might take the 'most painful' step of separating himself from government. Peel commented that 'as he has a great name in the north of Ireland, I think his resignation would have a bad effect', but Wellington would not relent.[14] One of the vice-presidents of the Ulster Brunswick Club in September 1828, John O'Neill was elected president of the club at Ballymena and was the first signatory of its anti-Catholic petition, which was got up in January 1829.[15] Listed by Planta, the patronage secretary, as 'opposed to the principle' of ministers' emancipation bill, he voted against them, 6 Mar. He apparently tendered his resignation, but this was refused by Wellington, who also turned a blind eye to Lord O'Neill's hostile votes that session.[16] He divided against the bill, 18, 27, 30 Mar., the related franchise bill, 19, 20 Mar., and to exclude Catholics from Parliament, 23 Mar. 1829.

O'Neill was granted one month's sick leave, 5 Mar. 1830, and must have missed most or all of that session. He offered again at the dissolution in July, when his brother's adroit switch of allegiance from Lord Hertford to Lord Donegall was considered enough to ensure his return with the latter's son, Lord Belfast.[17] Complaining that neither of the O'Neills had attended Parliament since the settlement of the Catholic question and that they had continued to stir up religious unrest in Ireland and were now opposing government in Antrim, Wellington ordered them both to be dismissed. Lord O'Neill, who was duly removed from his office as joint Irish postmaster-general, angrily rebutted these charges, stating that he had been commanded to attend his official duties in Dublin and that his brother had succumbed to gout at Cheltenham and so had also been unavoidably absent, but Wellington was unforgiving.[18] However, partly because of the nature of O'Neill's tenure as constable of Dublin Castle and the receipt of a report that he would support government, his removal was delayed pending any further vote with opposition.[19] He was returned for county Antrim at the head of the poll after a contest, during which he confirmed that his inactivity had been caused by indisposition, and at a dinner in his honour in Belfast on 12 Oct. he promised to make up for it in the following session.[20] Although he was counted as 'pro-government' in Pierce Mahony's† analysis of the Irish elections, he was listed by ministers among the 'violent Ultras' and was absent from the division on the civil list which led to their resignation, 15 Nov. 1830. In February 1831 he signed the requisition for an Antrim county meeting against repeal of the Union.[21]

Aware of the need to maintain popularity in Belfast, he came round to supporting parliamentary reform and promised to support the Belfast and county petitions in its favour.[22] He duly voted for the second reading of the Grey ministry's reform bill, 22 Mar., and against Gascoyne's wrecking amendment, 19 Apr. 1831. He offered on the basis of these votes at the ensuing general election, when another attack of gout nearly prevented him from being present, but he was elected unopposed.[23] He voted for the second reading of the reintroduced reform bill, 6 July, and steadily for its details (pairing during August), and he paired for its passage, 21 Sept. He was disappointed in his aspirations for a coronation peerage that month, while his brother declined the offer of a marquessate, as it would not have had a special remainder to him, and the following month abstained on the reform bill in the Lords.[24] Grey concluded that Lord O'Neill had 'been gained by the enemy', and Lord Anglesey, the viceroy, exclaimed 'would to God that I could dispossess' him, but he was eventually confirmed as lord lieutenant of Antrim that autumn.[25] O'Neill paired for the second reading of the revised bill, 17 Dec. 1831, and voted for schedules A and B, 20, 23 Jan., against giving the vote to all £10 ratepayers, 3 Feb., and for the third reading, 22 Mar. 1832. His only other known votes that session were with government for the Russian-Dutch loan, 26 Jan., and against the production of papers on Portugal, 9 Feb. He presented three petitions against the ministerial plan of national education in Ireland, 23 Mar., and in his absence on account of ill health, Lord Belfast brought up two more in favour of the Kildare Place Society, 18 Apr. 1832.[26]

That month, when he applied to ministers for a military or colonial position, the duke of Richmond commented that 'he is a real Irishman and expects a reward' and that Lord O'Neill 'only supported the government to secure either a peerage or employment for his brother'; nothing came of it.[27] In an address dated 1 Oct. he stated that he had supported reform because 'it was the only means of averting that general disorder which menaced England at that moment', but he distanced himself from government and, explaining that his recent absences were caused by a family tragedy, he was elected as a Conservative for county Antrim after a contest at the general election in December 1832.[28] He sat until he succeeded to his brother's viscountcy and Antrim estates in 1841.[29] The last of the celebrated line of the O'Neills, he died in February 1855, when his titles became extinct.[30] He was succeeded by his second cousin twice removed (the nephew of Sir Arthur Chichester*), the Rev. William Chichester (1813-83), prebend of Christ Church, Dublin, who changed his name to O'Neill and was created Baron O'Neill [UK] in 1868. His eldest son Edward (1839-1928) was Conservative Member for Antrim, 1863-80.[31]

[1] *Hist. Irish Parl.* v. 406, 408-11; *HP Commons, 1790-1820*, iv. 691. [2] Eg. 3261, ff. 51, 57; *Belfast News Letter*, 24 Mar. 1820. [3] *Black Bk.* (1823), 180; Add. 38283, f. 198; 38289, f. 269; 40296, ff. 45-46. [4] PRO NI, Leslie mss MIC606/3/J/7/21/4. [5] Add. 37299, f. 271; 40347, f. 303. [6] Buckingham, *Mems. Geo. IV*, i. 446. [7] *The Times*, 17 Apr. 1823. [8] Add. 57401, f. 149. [9] Add. 40382, ff. 102, 104. [10] *Belfast Commercial Chron.* 21 June 1826. [11] Add. 40392, f. 5; *Belfast News Letter*, 9 Feb., 16 Mar. 1827. [12] *The Times*, 12 Apr. 1827. [13] Add. 40393, f. 231; PRO NI, Hill mss D642/A/13/8-11. [14] Add. 40397, ff. 226, 248; Wellington mss WP1/947/31; 950/14; 984/7. [15] *Belfast Guardian*, 30 Sept.; *Belfast News Letter*, 24 Oct. 1828, 2, 9, 30 Jan. 1829. [16] G.I.T. Machin, *Catholic Question in English Politics*, 174 [17] *Belfast News Letter*, 9 July 1830; Eg. 3261, f. 248. [18] Wellington mss WP1/1126/31; 1131/20, 31; 1133/32, 40; 1134/13, 14; 1135/2; 1137/21, 34, 51; 1138/62; Add. 40388, ff. 241, 256; 40401, ff. 91, 93, 94, 96, 115, 118, 123, 143. [19] Wellington mss WP1/1140/28; Add. 40313, f. 45. [20] *Belfast News Letter*, 13, 17 Aug., 15 Oct. 1830. [21] Ibid. 11 Feb. 1831. [22] Ibid. 25 Mar., 26 Apr. 1831; PRO NI, Emerson Tennent mss D2922/C/1/3. [23] *Belfast News Letter*, 29 Apr., 24 May 1831. [24] W. Suss. RO, Goodwood mss, Richmond to O'Neill, 11 Sept., to Lord O'Neill, 11, 25 Sept., to Grey, 25 Sept. 1831; M. Brock, *Great Reform Act*, 233-4. [25] Derby mss 920 Der (14) 117/5, Grey to Smith Stanley, 18 Sept.; 119/1/2, Anglesey to same, 18 Sept. 1831. [26] *Belfast Commercial Chron.* 24 Apr. 1832. [27] Goodwood mss, Richmond to Grey, 21 Apr., to Goderich, 23 Apr. 1832. [28] *Belfast News Letter*, 5 Oct., 28 Dec. 1832, 4 Jan. 1833. [29] *Gent. Mag.* (1841), i. 535. [30] *The Times*, 14 Feb.; *Belfast News Letter*, 14 Feb. 1855; *Gent. Mag.* (1855), i. 521-2. [31] *DNB*; *Oxford DNB*.

S.M.F.

ONSLOW, Arthur (1759–1833), of Send Grove, nr. Guildford, Surr.

GUILDFORD 1812–1830

b. 3 Aug. 1759, o.s. of Arthur Onslow, collector of customs, of Childwall, Liverpool, Lancs. and Alice, da. of Stephen Sumersett.[1] *educ.* Trinity Hall, Camb. 1775-6; M. Temple 1775, called 1780. *m.* (1) 9 Apr. 1793, Mary (*d.* 14 May 1800), da. of Francis Eyre of Hassop, Derbys., *s.p.*; (2) 13 June 1801, Pooley, da. of Sir George Onslow† of Dunsborough House, Surr., wid. of Sir Francis Samuel Drake, 1st bt., *s.p.* *suc.* fa. 1807. *d.* 8 Oct. 1833.

Commr. of bankrupts 1781-1800; sjt.-at-law 16 June 1800; king's sjt. 1816; chairman, Surr. q.sess. 1807; recorder, Guildford 1819-30.

Lt. Guildford vol. inf. 1803; capt. Liverpool custom house vols. 1804.[2]

Onslow, whose father's customs post was said at his death in 1807 to be 'one of the most lucrative offices under the government', was the residuary legatee of his estate, which amounted to over £26,000.[3] Onslow's second marriage to a distant cousin brought him Send Grove, 'a handsome mansion', and closer links to the ennobled Surrey branch of the family, which paved the way for his return for Guildford in 1812. It also proved financially advantageous, for in 1826 he won a case to establish his late wife's right to a half-share in the personalty of her first husband, which came to £9,100, in addition to her £15,000 marriage settlement.[4] As a lawyer, according to the family historian, Onslow 'acquired a considerable reputation in the court of common pleas and on the home circuit', but a less partial biographer, recalling his 'tall and slender' and 'gentlemanly, if not majestic appearance', assessed him as 'highly respectable ... though by no means one of the first class'. A contemporary at the bar lampooned his ponderous delivery and occasional misplaced emphasis in the epigram:

The heavy tongu'd blow
Of Serjeant Ons-low.[5]

He came in for Guildford for the third time in 1820.

He was a regular attender who continued to give general support to Lord Liverpool's ministry, although he occasionally displayed his independence. He voted in the minority against the appointment of an additional Scottish baron of exchequer, 15 May 1820. On 14 June he claimed to have the support of Birmingham chamber of commerce for a change in standing orders to subject all trade regulation bills to the scrutiny of a select committee before they received a first reading. This proposal was itself referred to a committee, which reported on 23 June, and the standing order was adopted after he had spoken in its favour, 5 July.[6] (Three years later he was appointed to a committee to reconsider it, as it was evidently found to be too restrictive, and it was duly rescinded, 30 May 1823.) When, in the debate on the Queen Caroline affair, 18 Sept. 1820, he suggested the introduction of a bill to permit the Commons to examine witnesses under oath, Creevey accused him of acting as an *agent provocateur* for a government intent on restricting rights of inquiry. Yet he divided against the omission of the queen's name from the liturgy, 23, 26 Jan., 13 Feb., arguing that it should not be treated as a matter for 'party spirit', 23 Jan., and that it was an 'illegal act', 31 Jan. 1821. On the other hand, he voted in defence of ministers' conduct towards the queen, 6 Feb. Four days later he reportedly seconded Stuart Wortley's motion accusing the *Morning Chronicle* of a breach of privilege, 'out of compassion, as for at least two minutes no one ... seemed inclined to do so'; he vainly urged the mover to withdraw.[7] In presenting a Guildford petition in support of the queen, which also called for action on parliamentary reform, 12 Feb., he agreed that 'a wholesome reform was necessary', and later that day he spoke in favour of transferring Grampound's seats to Leeds. However, he voted against the disfranchisement of ordnance officials, 12 Apr., and condemned Lambton's general reform plan as 'more obnoxious' than universal suffrage, 18 Apr., arguing that aristocratic influence in elections to the Commons was not excessive and trusting that 'great property, high character and amiable manners would always maintain their influence on that House'. He opposed repeal of the Blasphemous and Seditious Libels Act in the belief that 'the disposition to excite the people to tumultuous meetings still existed in full force', 8 May, and in the debate on Peterloo, 15 May, he denied that the yeomanry constituted a 'political soldiery'. As a champion of the legal establishment and its officials he defended Justice William Draper Best† (his former colleague at Guildford) for fining a defendant for contempt of court, 23 Feb., 19 Apr. He dismissed a petition from an inmate of Lancaster gaol complaining of ill-treatment as 'a foul and infamous calumny', 7 Mar., and 'saw no reason' for the strictures passed on the commissioners inquiring into the state of the English courts, 9 May. On 12 Apr. he introduced a bill to make a university degree a condition of admission for attorneys and solicitors, which stemmed from a select committee on which he had served; the bill gained royal assent, 8 June (1 & 2 Geo. IV, c. 48). Although his first wife had been a Catholic, he continued to divide against relief, 28 Feb. He voted against repeal of the additional malt duty, 3 Apr., but for inquiry into the currency, 9 Apr. He supported relaxation of the Navigation Acts, 25 June 1821.

Onslow's primary interest was in securing the repeal of the usury laws, a cause he had espoused since 1816. These laws, which regulated the level of interest rates, were routinely evaded but, as with his earlier successful campaign to remove the apprenticeship laws from the statute book, he ran into strong opposition, chiefly from the landed interest. Having stated his intention of reintroducing a repeal bill, 7 July 1820, he did so on 12 Apr. 1821, when he cited Bentham as an authority against the control of interest rates. The bill made no further progress and he consented to its withdrawal, 8 June.[8] Another bill, to regulate the acceptance of bills of exchange, was introduced on 12 Apr., and, after amendment by the Lords, gained royal assent, 2 July 1821 (1 & 2 Geo. IV, c. 78). He welcomed the prospect of the regulation of annuities, by which the usury laws were frequently avoided, 30 May 1822.[9] When, after delays, he again brought forward his repeal bill, 22 Apr. 1823, he gave a potted history of his previous endeavours. The House finally divided by 38-15 to enter into committee, 17 June, but the bill was defeated at the report stage by 26-21, 27 June 1823. Onslow reintroduced it, 11 Feb., and having extolled the benefits of 'full, fair and open competition in the money market', he carried the second reading by 120-23, 16 Feb. 1824. After repeated postponements he secured the bill's recommittal by 74-58, 8 Apr. 1824, but opponents then divided the House four times on details and finally defeated it by 67-63 on the timing of its future consideration.[10] The indefatigable Onslow tried again, 8 Feb. 1825, in the hope that the prevailing spirit of free trade would make the time ripe for his measure. When his opponents tried unsuccessfully to force a division on the first reading, he was urged by his allies to abandon conciliation. The lesson he gave to the House on the principles of competition, 17 Feb., was to no avail, and the second reading was lost by 45-40. In reintroducing the bill again, 15 Feb. 1826, he asserted that had its provisions already been in force, 'the late panic and its attendant distress would have been much mitigated'. Frustrated again by postponements, he was mollified by the home secretary Peel's promise to consider the issue as part of a general review of fiscal policy, and agreed to withdraw the bill, 17 Apr. 1826. The government did not adopt the measure, and Onslow left its promotion thereafter to others.

He divided against more extensive tax reductions, 11, 21 Feb., and abolition of one of the joint-postmasterships, 13 Mar. 1822. However, he protested against the tax on coals, 20 Feb.[11] He voted against relieving Catholic peers of their disabilities, 30 Apr., and for the aliens bill, 19 July 1822. He divided against Hume's tax-cutting amendment, 3 Mar. 1823. He voted against repeal of the Foreign Enlistment Act, 16 Apr., and inquiries into the prosecution of the Dublin Orange rioters, 22 Apr., and delays in chancery, 5 June. He tried to thwart discussion of Scottish parliamentary reform by raising a procedural point, 2 June 1823. Early in 1824 his bid to be considered for legal promotion was not taken seriously by ministers: Henry Hobhouse, under-secretary at the home office, described as 'very impudent' his letter to lord chancellor Eldon 'showing his readiness to take the vacant mastership in chancery and insinuating that he would not take the Welsh judgeship if it were offered to him'.[12] He gave encouragement to an attempt to reform the bankruptcy laws, 18 Feb., and spoke in favour of the aliens bill, 2 Apr. He voted against the motion condemning the prosecution of the Methodist missionary John Smith in Demerara, 11 June 1824. He divided for the Irish unlawful societies bill, 25 Feb., and against Catholic relief, 1 Mar., 21 Apr., 10 May (paired), and the Irish franchise bill, 26 Apr. 1825. He opposed Hume's resolutions on the Irish church establishment, 14 June.[13] He voted for the financial provision for the duke of Cumberland, 30 May, 6, 10 June. He opposed a local measure of tithe commutation because it 'interfered with the vested interests of the church', 6 June.[14] He declared that elderly judges were 'neither deaf nor peevish', 17 June 1825. He voted to maintain the salary of the president of the board of trade, 10 Apr. 1826. He divided against reform of Edinburgh's representation, 13 Apr., but for Russell's resolutions against electoral bribery, 26 May, although he did not think the problem was widespread. He denied that the blasphemy laws interfered with freedom of opinion, 17 Apr. 1826. He was again returned unopposed for Guildford at the general election that summer.

Onslow's subsequent parliamentary activity was less conspicuous, probably owing to incipient blindness.[15] In response to a petition, he maintained that provision for Deists and other non-Christians to swear oaths in court already existed, 29 Nov. 1826. He divided against Catholic relief, 6 Mar. 1827. In his familiar role as defender of the legal establishment, he attested to the 'great talents and unimpeachable integrity' of Eldon and the efficiency of the bankruptcy commissioners, 13 Mar. He was granted leave to go the circuit, 16 Mar. 1827. He voted for repeal of the Test Acts, 26 Feb., and against Catholic relief, 12 May 1828. He endorsed calls for his fellow king's serjeant William Rough to be compensated for his wrongful suspension as president of the supreme court of Demerara, 15 May. That day he denied that the lower orders would be hurt by repeal of the usury laws, the promotion of which had by then passed to Chales Poulett Thomson. Instancing Guildford, he argued that borough magistrates would not resent sharing responsibility for alehouse licensing with the county authorities, 21 May. He warmly welcomed the Wellington ministry's statement of intent to act against slavery, 25 July 1828. In February 1829 Planta, the patronage secretary, predicted that he would side with government for Catholic emancipation, but he was granted leave to go the circuit, 6 Mar.

1829, and no record of any parliamentary activity for that session has been found. His final oratorical flourish was a defence of the grant for new churches, 8 June 1830, when he blamed the dissolution of the monasteries for the failure to construct new churches and for the problems of pluralism and non-residence. He also attributed the alleged poverty of the Irish church to a tithe commutation measure carried by that country's Parliament. He voted in the minority to postpone on-consumption in beerhouses, 1 July 1830. He retired at the dissolution that summer, owing to a 'total loss of sight'.[16]

William IV, on his accession, granted Onslow precedence before other king's serjeants, and he continued to attend court with his accustomed diligence and punctuality until his death in October 1833.[17] While a legal biography speculated that his 'considerable practice' must have made him a wealthy man, it is apparent that an unspecified financial calamity had befallen him. In leaving small legacies to the sons of his cousin, Francis Allison of Liverpool, his will noted that 'had not circumstances over which I had no control much reduced the fortune I once possessed, I would have left them much more substantial marks of my regard'. Send Grove passed to his brother-in-law, the Rev. Arthur Onslow. He left the residue of his estate to his barrister nephew Richard Onslow, 'whom having lived with me from his earliest infancy ... I regard with the same affection as though he had been my own son'; his personalty was sworn under £600.[18]

[1] Surr. Hist. Cent. 173/1/5, 4th earl of Onslow, 'Hist. Onslow Fam.' v. 1444. [2] Ibid. v. 1445. [3] *Gent. Mag.* (1807), ii. 1081; PROB 11/1474/134; IR26/132/192. [4] Onslow, v. 1442-3; H.W. Woolrych, *Eminent Serjeants-at-Law*, ii. 774; *The Times*, 3, 14 July 1826. [5] Onslow, v. 1451; Woolrych, ii. 802-4; J. Grant, *Bench and Bar*, ii. 26, 28. [6] *The Times*, 6 July 1820. [7] HLRO, Hist. Coll. 379, Grey Bennet diary, 33. [8] *The Times*, 9 June 1821. [9] Ibid. 31 May 1822. [10] Ibid. 31 Mar., 9, 10 Apr. 1824. [11] Ibid. 21 Feb. 1822. [12] Add. 40360, f. 82. [13] *The Times*, 15 June 1825. [14] Ibid. 7 June 1825. [15] Woolrych, ii. 801. [16] *Gent. Mag.* (1834), i. 227. [17] J.H. Baker, *Order of Serjeants-at-Law*, 61; Grant, ii. 26-27; *The Times*, 10 Oct. 1833. [18] Grant, ii. 25; Onslow, v. 1403; PROB 11/1823/651; IR26/1334/659.

H.J.S.

ORD, William (1781–1855), of Whitfield Hall, Northumb. and 17 Berkeley Square, Mdx.

MORPETH	1802–1832
NEWCASTLE-UPON-TYNE	1835–1852

b. 2 Jan. 1781, 1st s. of William Ord of Fenham, Newminster Abbey and Whitfield Hall and Eleanor, da. of Charles Brandling† of Gosforth Park, Northumb. *educ.* Eton 1793; Trinity Coll. Camb. 1798. *m.* 1 Jan. 1803, Mary, da. of Rev. James Scott of Itchen Ferry, Hants, rect. of St. Lawrence, Southampton, 1s. *d.v.p. suc.* fa. 1789. *d.* 27 July 1855.

Ord's estates, the product of the fortuitous marriages and investments of his great-great-grandfather, the Newcastle attorney John Ord (*d.* 1703), and his descendants, included Benwell colliery, property in Newcastle and the Newminster Abbey interest in the borough of Morpeth, where in 1802 he had successfully challenged the Howards, earls of Carlisle, for the second seat that he retained unopposed for the next 30 years.[1] A well-connected Whig and supporter of Catholic relief and moderate parliamentary reform, he was a thick and thin attender, whose vote could be depended on. He rarely spoke in debate, but he was a popular figure at Grillion's, Brooks's and on the back benches, where his astute semi-private asides sustained his colleagues.[2] One of them, Frederick Cavendish Ponsonby, who like John Fazakerley* and John William Ward*, the future earl of Dudley, wrote to him from abroad for information on domestic politics, noted: 'There is no person in whose sound judgement and correct information I have more reliance than yours, nor to whose foresight of effects to spring from existing causes I give greater credit'.[3]

Ord divided steadily with the Whig opposition on all major issues in the 1820 Parliament, and fairly regularly with his stepfather Thomas Creevey and the 'Mountain' for economy, retrenchment, reduced taxation, a reduction in capital offences and to end military flogging. He voted to make Leeds a scot and lot borough under the Grampound disfranchisement bill, 2 Mar. 1821, for reform, 9, 10 May 1821, 25 Apr. 1822, 20 Feb., 24 Apr., 2 June 1823, 26 Feb. 1824, 13, 27 Apr. 1826, and in condemnation of electoral bribery, 26 May 1826. He divided for Catholic relief, 28 Feb. 1821, 1 Mar., 21 Apr., 10 May 1825. A radical publication of that session noted that he 'attended regularly, and voted with the opposition'.[4] He did so in condemnation of the indictment in Demerara of the Methodist missionary John Smith, 11 June 1824, and of the Jamaican slave trials, 2 Mar. 1826; and, having opposed the 1815 corn law from the outset, he divided to consider its reform, 18 Apr. 1826. Ord visited North Wales and the Lake District with his wife in the summer of 1821 and France, the Rhineland and Switzerland during the 1825 recess, keeping meticulous journal records of both tours.[5] He chaired the local committee for the Hexham road, and its construction under the 1821 and 1828 Acts greatly improved the approach to his mansion at Whitfield, which the Newcastle barrister James Losh considered 'one of the most comfortable residences I have seen'.[6] A suggestion that he might be prepared to return a paying guest for Morpeth and stand on the Whig interest for Northumberland when a by-election seemed likely in March 1824 was not tested.[7] When the county polled in February 1826 he gave his interest to the victor, his cousin Matthew Bell, an anti-Catholic Tory, having first pledged support for Lord Grey's son Lord Howick*, whom he seconded when he stood unsuccessfully at the general election in June 1826.[8] Of his own unopposed return, the 'liberal' *Tyne Mercury* commented, 'Mr. Ord is a staunch Whig and Morpeth is one of the most rotten boroughs in the kingdom'.[9]

In a rare speech, 7 Dec. 1826, he defended his friend John Thomas Biggs, the former chief justice of Trinidad, whose delayed report on the conduct of Lord Charles Somerset† as governor of the Cape of Good Hope was the subject of a complaint by Hume. He voted against the grant for the duke of Clarence, 16 Feb., and for Catholic relief, 6 Mar., a 50*s.* pivot price for corn imports, 9 Mar., and inquiry into the allegations against Leicester corporation, 15 Mar. 1827. In April he briefed Fazakerley on the new prime minister Canning's cabinet appointments.[10] He divided against government for the Penryn disfranchisement bill, 28 May 1827. Congratulating Lord Lansdowne, a close friend since their Cambridge days, on his appointment as home secretary, he wrote:

> I dare say I was more glad than you were to see that you had received the seals. I can tell you your appointment and your carrying our good friend [Thomas] Spring Rice* with you gives great satisfaction to the best people in these parts and you know Newcastle is a very liberal enlightened and criticizing place.[11]

He was at Whitfield, where Lord Althorp*, Edward Davenport*, and Dudley were among his hunting guests, when Canning died.[12] He deemed the Navarino victory 'a scrape'.[13] He cast a handful of votes against the duke of Wellington's ministry in 1828: for repeal of the Test Acts, 26 Feb., against sluicing the franchise at East Retford, 21 Mar., for a fixed 15*s.* duty on corn imports, 29 Apr., and against the Buckingham House grant, 23 June. He voted for Catholic relief, 12 May. Reviewing the political situation in a letter to Fazakerley, 3 Oct. 1828, he observed: 'Wheat rising in England and Papists rising in Ireland are formidable circumstances, to say nothing of Brunswick Clubs'. He later wrote disparagingly to him of the anti-Catholic duke of Northumberland's appointment as Irish lord lieutenant. Party through George Tierney* to the Whigs' pre-session plans to try to effect Catholic emancipation in 1829, Ord was listed by the patronage secretary Planta in February as 'opposed to securities', but he divided for the measure 6, 30 Mar., and to permit Daniel O'Connell to sit without swearing the oath of supremacy, 18 May.[14] He voted to transfer East Retford's seats to Birmingham, 5 May, and against the grant for the marble arch, 25 May. His Newcastle influence increased after he renegotiated the Town Moor lease with the corporation in December 1828, and he presented their petitions in support of the Newcastle-Carlisle railway bill, in which he had a proprietorial interest, 19 Mar. 1829. He also brought up the report on the South Shields railway bill that day and successfully moved the third reading of the Scotswood (Tyne) bridge bill.[15] He took a keen interest in the education and career of his only son William Henry, a barrister and former president of the Cambridge Union, and initially opposed his marriage on 8 Dec. 1829 to Frances Vere Lorraine, daughter of the failed Northumberland banker Sir William Lorraine of Kirkhale.[16] He divided for the Ultra Sir Edward Knatchbull's amendment to include reference to distress in the address, 4 Feb., and to enfranchise Birmingham, Leeds and Manchester, 23 Feb. 1830. He was a notable absentee when the 'old Whigs' met at Althorp's rooms, 3 Mar., but he divided with the revived Whig opposition on most major issues that session, including for Jewish emancipation, 5 Apr., 17 May, reform, 28 May, and the abolition of capital punishment for forgery, 24 May, 7 June.[17] He supported the sitting Whig Sir Matthew White Ridley when a contest threatened at Newcastle at the general election in July 1830, and he criticized the ministry and called for economy, retrenchment, civil and religious liberty, and a mild and constitutional reform in his election speech at Morpeth. His son backed the independent Thomas Wentworth Beaumont* for the county.[18]

Henry Brougham* and the Scottish lawyer Thomas Kennedy* were among the prominent Whigs who sought Ord's opinion on reform before Parliament met. He informed both that unless there was a sudden and unlikely change in the political situation, he was too short of money to return to London before the January session, and anticipated that Wellington would do 'anything rather than go out and will thus disarm opponents'.[19] He was naturally listed among the ministry's 'foes' and he voted to bring them down on the civil list, 15 Nov. 1830. He was disappointed to find his loyalty unrewarded when Grey formed his ministry.[20] He took a keen interest in the Newcastle reform meeting which his son addressed, 21 Dec. 1830, and was a requisitionist for the Northumberland reform meetings of 2 Feb. and 16 Mar. 1831.[21] In his regular reports to the Hollands on debates and ministerial performance, he attributed the former chancellor Goulburn's erudite reply to Althorp's budget speech to prior briefing by an informant within the treasury, 11 Feb., and deemed the performance of Peel (whom he personally disliked), when the reform bill was introduced, 1-3 Mar., 'too solemn and pompous' and inferior to that of the Irish secretary Smith Stanley.[22] He divided for the bill at its second reading, 22 Mar., brought up a favourable petition from Newcastle and a hostile one from Morpeth, which stood to lose a Member, 28 Mar., and was pleased to see this restored, 18 Apr. He divided against Gascoyne's wrecking amendment, 19 Apr. 1831, but he was not surprised to see it carried. At the ensuing general election he supported Howick's successful candidature for Northumberland and came in for Morpeth as previously.[23]

Ord voted for the reintroduced reform bill at its second reading, 6 July, against adjournment, 12 July, and divided steadily for its details and for its third reading, 19 Sept., and passage, 21 Sept. 1831. He voted for Lord Ebrington's confidence motion, 10 Oct. His letter of 13 Sept. to Fazakerley had predicted the bill's defeat in the Lords, but he remained convinced that the anti-reformers were deluded in their assumption that the 'country are become indifferent to the bill'. He recommended creating peers to carry it and, having sought the honour for himself, complained that half the peerages awarded at the coronation went to 'quite disreputable people ... without any claim that I can see'.[24] Despite receiving tactical advice from his son, a boundary commissioner, on the criteria applicable to Morpeth, he failed to prevent its demotion to schedule B in the revised reform bill, which 'on the whole' he thought 'much improved'.[25] He voted for its second reading, 17 Dec. 1831, when, as he had expected, ministers had a 'very good division', and on the 29th, after consulting Lansdowne at Bowood, he declared jointly with Beaumont for Northumberland South at the first post-reform election. He had rejected this option three months previously when 'sounded' by the recorder of Morpeth James Losh.[26] He divided steadily for the reform bill's details and for its third reading, 22 Mar. 1832. He intervened to counter Croker's criticism of the boundaries designated by his son for Appleby, 23 Feb. When in May a ministry headed by Wellington was contemplated, he authorized his Northumberland committee to canvass and voted for the address calling on the king to appoint only ministers who would carry the reform bill unimpaired, 10 May.[27] He divided for the Irish reform bill at its second reading, 25 May, and against a Conservative amendment to the Scottish measure, 1 June 1832. He sent Brougham further information on Appleby ahead of its consideration in the Lords.[28] He divided with government on the Dublin election controversy, 23 Aug. 1831, the Russian-Dutch loan, 26 Jan., 12 July (for which he paired, 20 July), and Portugal, 9 Feb. 1832. He was named by them to the select committee on West Indian slavery, 30 May 1832.

Friends and colleagues were stunned by Ord's defeat at the 1832 general election, when, standing as a Liberal he finished in third place behind Bell after a bitter contest. During it the alleged links of his son (who came in for Newport, Isle of Wight) with Thomas Attwood† and the Northern Political Union were severely criticized.[29] Ord successfully contested Newcastle in 1835 and topped the poll there in 1837 and 1847. His retirement through ill health in 1852 was marked with a civic banquet and tributes to his 'straightforwardness ... consistent maintenance of liberal opinions' and 'unswerving attachment to the cause of civil and religious liberty' over 50 years.[30] He died at Whitfield in July 1855, predeceased in 1838 and without issue by his son, and in 1848 by his wife.[31] His will, dated 10 Apr. 1854, was proved in the provinces of Canterbury and York and executed by the Rev. John Alexander Blackett, the husband of his niece Ann Jane (*née* Hamilton), to whom he bequeathed his estates in trust. As required, they took the additional name of Ord. He provided financially for his sister Eleanor, brother-in-law the Rev. Thomas Scott and sister-in-law Charlotte Bigge, and made his daughter-in-law (*d.* 1874), since 1851 the wife of Sir Edward Blackett of Halton Castle, Northumberland, his residuary legatee.[32]

[1] Northumb. RO, Blackett-Ord (Whitfield) mss NRO324/D/27; O/1/20-37; Tyne and Wear Archives, Benwell estate recs. I/89-100; R. Welford, *Men of Mark 'Twixt Tyne and Tweed*, iii. 235; *HP Commons, 1790-1820*, iv. 674-5. [2] Blackett-Ord mss A/65; *Cockburn Letters*, 437-8; D. Rapp, 'The Left Wing Whigs: Whitbread, the Mountain and Reform, 1808-1815', *JBS*, xxi (1982), 42-66; *HP Commons, 1790-1820*, iv. 674-5. [3] Blackett-Ord mss A/28, Ponsonby to Ord, 18 Nov. 1822; A/33, Ward to same, 26 Oct.; A/35, Fazakerley to same, Aug. [Dec.] 1821, Oct. 1823, Apr. 1824. [4] *Session of Parl. 1825*, p. 478. [5] Blackett-Ord mss A/10, 15; Add. 52011, Eleanor Fazakerley to H.E. Fox, 7 Aug. 1825. [6] *CJ*, lxxvi. 200; lxxxiii. 375; Blackett-Ord mss A/81, 83; *Tyne Mercury*, 2, 16, 30 Sept. 1823; *Diaries and Corresp. of James Losh* ed. E. Hughes (Surtees Soc. clxxiv) [Hereafter cited as *Losh Diaries*, ii], 96. [7] Northumb. RO, Ridley (Blagdon) mss ZRI 25/45, Bigge to Ridley, 1 Mar. [1824]. [8] Creevey mss, Creevey to Miss Ord, 16 Feb.; Grey mss, Ord to Howick, 24 Feb.; Blackett-Ord mss A/67; *The Times*, 12 June; *Newcastle Chron.* 17 June 1826. [9] *Tyne Mercury*, 13 June 1826. [10] Duke Univ. Fazakerley mss, Ord to Fazakerley [17 Apr. 1827]. [11] Lansdowne mss, Ord to Lansdowne, 21 July [1827]. [12] Le Marchant, *Althorp*, 224. [13] Add. 51569, Ord to Lady Holland, 10 Nov. [1827]. [14] Fazakerley mss, Ord to Fazakerley, 3 Oct. [1828] [1829]. [15] Tyne and Wear Archives MD/NC/2/11, Newcastle-upon-Tyne common council minutes, 23 Dec. 1828; Blackett-Ord mss

A/81. [16] Blackett-Ord mss A/29, 36; O/38, 39; *Losh Diaries*, ii. 90; S. Holliday, 'Lorraines of Kirkhale', *Northern Hist.* xxxvi (2000), 73-82. [17] Castle Howard mss, Sir J.R.G. Graham to Morpeth [3 Mar. 1830]. [18] Ridley (Blagdon) mss 25/59, Stable to Ridley, 31 May, Bigge to same, 5 June; *Tyne Mercury*, 20 July 1830. [19] *Cockburn Letters*, 236-7; Brougham mss, Ord to Brougham, 12 Sept. 1830. [20] Blackett-Ord mss A/36, W.H. Ord to fa. [Nov. 1830]. [21] Ibid. same to same, 23, 25 Dec. 1830; *Tyne Mercury*, 1, 8 Feb. 1831. [22] Add. 51569, Ord to Lord and Lady Holland, 23 Dec. 1830-4 Mar. 1831. [23] Add. 51569, Ord to Lady Holland [18 Apr.], to Holland [19 Apr.], 1 May; *Tyne Mercury*, 26 Apr., 3 May 1831. [24] Add. 51569, Ord to Holland, 1 Aug.; Fazakerley mss, Ord to Fazakerley, 13 Sept. [1831]. [25] Blackett-Ord mss A/36, W.H. Ord to fa. Sept.-Oct. 1831; *Cockburn Letters*, 365-8. [26] Add. 51569, Ord to [?Holland, 16 Dec.]; Blackett-Ord mss A/36, W.H. Ord to fa. 18 Sept. 1831; *Cockburn Letters*, 366; *Losh Diaries*, ii. 107, 135. [27] *Newcastle Chron.* 12, 19 May 1832. [28] Brougham mss, Ord to Brougham, 27 May 1832. [29] Blackett-Ord mss A/35, Fazakerley to Ord Dec.; A/42, Grote to Ord, 25 Dec.; A/43, Ebrington to same, 25 Dec.; A/68; Northumb. RO, Middleton mss ZM1/S/77/5/9; BMO/B/28; *John Bull*, 24 June, 1 July, 30 Dec.; *Newcastle Chron.* 22 Dec.; Add. 51688, Lansdowne to Holland [Dec. 1832]. [30] Blackett-Ord mss A/69-71, 75; *The Times*, 10 Sept. 1852; *Public Dinner to Ord* (1852). [31] *Gent. Mag.* (1855), ii. 319-20; Blackett-Ord mss A/57. [32] *Newcastle Chron.* 27 July 1855; PROB 11/2218/720; IR26/2043/875; Blackett-Ord mss B/18-20.

M.M.E.

ORMSBY GORE (formerly **GORE**), **William** (1779–1860), of Porkington, Oswestry, Salop and Woodford, co. Leitrim.

Co. Leitrim	1806–1807
Caernarvon Boroughs	1830–1831
Shropshire North	1835–1857

b. 14 Mar. 1779, 1st s. of William Gore, MP [I], of Woodford and Frances Jane Gorges, da. and h. of Ralph Gore, MP [I], of Barrow Mount, co. Kilkenny, wid. of Sir Haydocke Evans Morres, 2nd bt. *educ.* Eton 1796; M. Temple 1796; Merton, Oxf. 1797. *m.* 11 Jan. 1815, Mary Jane, da. and h. of Owen Ormsby of Willowbrook, co. Sligo and Porkington, 3s. (1 *d.v.p.*) 2da. *d.v.p.* Took name of Ormsby before Gore by royal lic. 14 Oct. 1814; *suc.* fa. 1815. *d.* 4 May 1860.

Lt. 1 Drag. Gds. 1800, capt. 1802, maj. 1802, brevet maj. 1813; half-pay 86 Ft. 1815; capt. 88 Ft. 15 Sept., sold out 29 Sept. 1829.

A.d.c. to ld. lt.[I] 1802-6; gent. of privy chamber 1815.

Trustee, linen board [I] 1807.

Sheriff, Salop 1817-18, Caern. 1820-1; mayor, Oswestry 1823-4; hered. mayor Criccieth ?1827.

His marriage in 1815 brought Ormsby Gore, who had lost his county Leitrim seat in 1807 on account of an anti-Catholic backlash, a controlling interest in the Ormsbys' estates in Ireland, Shropshire and North Wales, where, under a private bill enacted on 8 June 1821, he profited by adopting a policy of judicious land enclosures and exchanges, always paying due attention to quarrying enterprise and mineral rights.[1] The 4,000-acre Porkington estate gave him considerable influence in Oswestry and interests in Shropshire and Montgomeryshire. Clenennau, a 3,997-acre estate in Eifionydd, was the former seat of the Owens of Brogyntyn, who had controlled Criccieth, a contributory borough of Caernarvon, and they were the largest landowners in Llanfihangel-y-Pennant and Penmorfa in Caernarvonshire and Llanfihangel-y-Traethau in Merioneth.[2] As sheriff of Caernarvonshire, Ormsby Gore presided at the court of great sessions and convened meetings in April and December 1820 to petition for repeal of the coastwise coal duty and adopt a loyal address to George IV, following the withdrawal of the bill of pains and penalties against Queen Caroline. He attended neither meeting, but as an ardent anti-Catholic Tory he joined the Menai Pitt Club and chaired its annual dinner in September 1821.[3]

Documents from Llŷn had been taken to Porkington, where the Ormsby Gores pursued their interest in genealogy and antiquities and prepared a family pedigree in consultation with Sir Thomas Phillips, who in March 1827 was asked to obtain copies of the charters of Criccieth and of Broniarth, near Welshpool. Brogyntyn had controlled the hereditary mayoralty of Criccieth and Ormsby Gore now assumed it in the right of his wife, making the Dolgellau attorney William Williams his deputy.[4] North-west Wales was a hotbed of anti-Catholicism, and in December 1828 Ormsby Gore, who was already a committed Brunswicker in Oswestry and Shropshire, established and presided over a meeting of the club at the *White Lion*, Criccieth, with the Merioneth Member Sir Robert Williames Vaughan as vice-president.[5] Plans were already afoot to oust the Irish lord lieutenant Lord Anglesey's pro-Catholic son Lord William Paget as Member for Caernarvon Boroughs; and in January 1829 Ormsby Gore created 114 new burgesses at Criccieth (over half of them absentees from Dublin and Oswestry) and pressed his own and the Brunswickers' cause in the weekly *North Wales Chronicle*. He was also responsible for forwarding most Caernarvonshire, Denbighshire and Merioneth anti-emancipation petitions to Lords Eldon and Kenyon for presentation.[6] In February 1829 he sounded Sir Thomas Mostyn*, as mayor of Pwllheli, about contesting Caernarvon Boroughs, and asked the Pagets' agents for access to the Caernarvon burgess rolls. He moved the address at a late anti-Catholic meeting in Caernarvon, which urged the king to refuse to sanction emancipation, 11 Apr., when, drawing on his Irish and parliamentary experience, he said that if returned again, he would vote for triennial parliaments, so that ministries which changed their policies, as the duke of

Wellington's had done, could be more readily brought to account.[7] He arranged to be gazetted as on full-pay in November 1829 in order to sell his army commission.[8] He canvassed Caernarvon Boroughs at the dissolution in 1830. Although initially weak in the Paget stronghold of Caernarvon, his rallying cry of 'No Popery' appealed to the lower orders and he was returned unopposed following the late withdrawal of Sir Charles Paget*.[9]

Ormsby Gore was described on the Wellington ministry's lists as a 'moderate Ultra' who had applied for patronage, and he divided with them on the civil list when they were brought down, 15 Nov. 1830. He presented his constituents' petitions for the abolition of West Indian slavery, 10 Nov. His speeches on agrarian distress condemned the practice of supplementing agricultural labourers' wages from the poor rates and drew heavily on his experience as a Shropshire magistrate, 6, 8 Dec. Heeding bipartisan constituency pressure to secure reductions in the duties on slate, coal and culm carried coastwise, he reminded the House when a petition from Boston was brought up of Lord Castlereagh's* Union Act pledge, and promised to legislate for repeal of this 'most partial and oppressive tax' should others fail to do so, 8 Dec. 1830. He attended the Caernarvon meetings in January 1831 which petitioned for their repeal, and was subsequently credited with ensuring that the exemption conceded in April covered slate as well as coal.[10] He presented a petition for and brought in a new Ffestiniog railway bill, 7 Mar., but it was opposed locally and by William Bankes, Lord Palmerston and other directors and shareholders of the Welsh Slate Copper and Lead Mining Company in the House, and failed on a technicality.[11] He regarded the issue of first fruits in Ireland as one of church disestablishment, 14 Mar., presented a Brechin lawyers' petition for repeal of the duty on Scottish attorneys' certificates, 15 Mar., and others from Caernarvon and Oswestry, whose prayer compared the case for reform with that for Catholic emancipation in 1829. He shied from supporting them but conceded that some reform was necessary:

> The representation of the country requires some reform ... I am not prepared to say that I can go to the length of the [Grey ministry's] measure ... [and will feel] at liberty in the course of its progress through its different stages, to adopt any line of conduct which I may consider best calculated to promote the interests of the country.

The bill threatened to disfranchise Criccieth, but it attracted strong popular support in Caernarvon, and Ormsby Gore was well aware of the risk he took by voting against its second reading, 22 Mar.[12] Before doing so, he cited Blackstone, Burke and Bacon, and claimed that he was for reform, but not this particular bill, and criticized its dependence on the 1821 census and meagre provision for Glamorgan. He asked why Criccieth, a royalist stronghold during the Civil War with a charter dating from the reign of Edward I, had been singled out for disfranchisement as it had 120 £10 houses, and blamed the Pagets.[13] He voted for Gascoyne's wrecking amendment, 19 Apr. 1831.

Ormsby Gore was narrowly defeated in Caernarvon Boroughs (where his Criccieth voters were rejected) by the reformer Sir Charles Paget at the ensuing election, when he was ridiculed as an Irishman and praised as a good constituency Member.[14] His opponents estimated that the election cost him over £10,000, plus £3,000 in stamp duty.[15] Almost all the new Criccieth burgesses had been disfranchised by the time the borough was reinstated as a contributory of Caernarvon in the revised reform bill. He maintained a high profile in the constituency, which fêted him at a Caernarvon dinner in July 1832, bought a town house at 66 Portman Place and joined the Carlton Club.[16] Abandoning Caernarvon Boroughs, in December 1832 he chose to stand as a second Conservative for Shropshire North, where, amid talk of a coalition, he was nudged into third place by the Liberal John Cotes.[17] He declined Thomas Assheton Smith II's* offer of the Vaynol interest in Caernarvonshire in 1835 and was returned for Shropshire North, holding his seat as a Conservative until his health failed in 1857, when he was succeeded in the representation by his eldest son, John Ralph Ormsby Gore (1816-76), the former Member for Caernarvonshire and future Baron Harlech.[18] Ormsby Gore died at Porkington in May 1860 and was buried at Selattyn.[19] His will confirmed his marriage settlement of 6 Jan. 1815 and was accordingly administered by his widow (*d.* 1869) with William Watkin Edward Wynne† of Penniarth and Charles Kynaston Mainwaring as trustees. His second son, William Ormsby Gore (1819-1904), who sat for county Sligo, 1847-1852, and county Leitrim, 1858-1876, succeeded his brother that year as 2nd Baron Harlech.

[1] *HP Commons, 1790-1820*, iv. 40-41; *LJ*, liv. 471. [2] NLW, Aston Hall mss 138-41, 350, 351; NLW, Powis Castle mss 8729; *N. Wales Gazette*, 21 Dec. 1826. [3] UCNW, Porth-yr-aur mss 229; *N. Wales Gazette*, 6, 13 Apr., 9, 30 Nov., 7, 21 Dec. 1820, 13 Sept. 1821; *Shrewsbury Chron.* 14, 28 Apr., 22 Dec. 1820. [4] NLW, Brogyntyn mss 2817; Bodl. Phillips Robinson mss b.115, ff. 123-6; b.121, ff. 214-16; b.124, ff. 96-100; b.127, ff. 99-105; c.417, f. 202; c.422, ff. 16-21; c.425, ff. 186-9; c.440, ff. 139-45; c.452, f. 134; d.117, ff. 134-40; W.O. Gore, *Mss at Porkington*; *PP* (1838), xxv. 249-51. [5] *Shrewsbury Chron.* 21 Nov.; *N. Wales Chron.* 18, 25 Dec. 1828, 1 Jan. 1829. [6] Brogyntyn mss, uncatalogued 1947 deposit, Criccieth borough recs.; *N. Wales Chron.* 22 Jan., 12 Feb., 12, 19, 26 Mar. 1829. [7] UCNW, Mostyn of Mostyn mss 7451; UCNW, Plas Newydd mss v. 245; *N. Wales Chron.* 2, 9, 16 Apr. 1829. [8] Phillips Robinson mss c.425, f. 188. [9] Ll. Jones,

'Sir Charles Paget and Caernarvon Boroughs, 1830-32', *Trans. Caern. Hist. Soc.* xxi (1960), 85-91, 103-112; *N. Wales Chron.* 8, 15, 22, 29 July, 5 Aug.; *Shrewsbury Chron.* 6 Aug. 1830; Porth-yr-aur mss 12561. [10] *N. Wales Chron.* 20 Jan. 1831, 17 July 1832. [11] *CJ*, lxxxvi. 291, 339, 346, 401, 413, 480, 504-5, 533; J.I.C. Boyd, *Ffestiniog Railway*, i. 20-25; *Caernarvon Herald*, 23 Apr. 1831; J. Gordon Jones, 'Ffestiniog Slate Industry', *Jnl. Merion. Hist. and Rec. Soc.* vi (1969-72), 50-54. [12] *Caernarvon Herald*, 5 Mar. 1831. [13] D.A. Wager, 'Welsh Politics and Parl. Reform, 1780-1832', *WHR*, vii (1974), 437-8. [14] Jones, *Trans. Caern. Hist Soc.* xxi. 91-94; Plas Newydd mss i. 572, 583, 593, 598, 603-5, 616, 630; *N. Wales Chron.* 5 Apr., 10, 17 May; *Caernarvon Herald*, 7, 14 May; *Chester Chron.* 20 May 1831; Ll. Jones, 'Edition of Corresp. of 1st mq. of Anglesey relating to General Elections of 1830, 1831 and 1832 in Caern. and Anglesey' (Univ. of Liverpool M.A. thesis, 1956), 506; K. Evans, 'Caernarvon Borough', *Trans. Caern. Hist. Soc.* viii (1947), 62-63. [15] Plas Newydd mss i. 616, 617, 627. [16] R.G. Thomas, 'Politics in Anglesey and Caern. 1826-52' (Univ. of Wales M.A. thesis, 1970), 70; *Chester Courant*, 11 Oct. 1831; *N. Wales Chron.* 3, 17 July; *Caernarvon Herald*, 14 July 1832; Phillips Robinson mss c.440, f. 141. [17] Phillips Robinson mss c.440, ff. 143-5; Plas Newydd mss i. 73, 76; iii. 3564, 3587, 3589, 3734-80; *Caernarvon Herald*, 4 Aug.; *Shrewsbury Chron.* 14, 21 Dec. 1832; *VCH Salop.* iii. 311-12, 319. [18] Brogyntyn mss, uncatalogued 1947 deposit, Assheton Smith-Ormsby Gore corresp. 6, 13 Apr. 1834; uncatalogued 1955 deposit, Ormsby Gore to Lloyd Edwards, 18 Mar., to W. Wynne, 23 Dec. 1836; *VCH Salop*, iii. 319-21. [19] *Oswestry Advertiser*, 9 May; *Salop Conservative*, 12 May 1860.

M.M.E.

OSBORN, Sir John, 5th bt. (1772–1848), of Chicksands Priory, Beds.

BEDFORDSHIRE	15 Sept. 1794–1807
COCKERMOUTH	21 July 1807–June 1808
QUEENBOROUGH	1812–1818
BEDFORDSHIRE	1818–1820
WIGTOWN BURGHS	21 Mar. 1821–Jan. 1824

b. 3 Dec. 1772, o.s. of Sir George Osborn, 4th bt.†, and 1st w. Elizabeth, da. and coh. of John Bannister. *educ.* Westminster 1781-6; Christ Church, Oxf. 1790. *m.* 14 Sept. 1809, Frederica Louisa, illegit. da. of Sir Charles Davers, 6th bt.†, 5s. 3da. *suc.* fa. as 5th bt. 29 June 1818. *d.* 28 Aug. 1848.

Ld. of admiralty Oct. 1812-Feb. 1824; commr. of audit 1824-*d.*

Capt. Beds. yeomanry 1797, Beds. vols. 1803-5; col. Beds. militia 1805.

Osborn, who had regained his county seat in 1818 through the default of one of his opponents, stood again in 1820, heedless of his substantial election debts. He was alleged to have created the impression that if he was returned in 1818 he would resign his office at the admiralty; and his failure to do so lost him support, as did attacks on him in *The Times*, where he was denounced as a placeman whose professions of 'independence' were manifestly bogus and who had no right to occupy a county seat. Yet he bragged of his connection with a government which had defeated French tyranny and revolutionary doctrines. His two Whig opponents stood firm on this occasion and, despite the interference of government on his behalf and financial assistance from leading county Tories, he was beaten into third place amid public recriminations with the Whigs.[1] Four months later Osborn admitted to a friend that he had little chance of being able to pay his share of the costs or settle his election debts; and it was not until 1831 that the latter were paid off.[2]

A year elapsed before government created an opening for him by providing Lord Galloway's brother, who sat for his group of Scottish burghs, with a customs place. As 'one of the treasury phalanx', Osborn naturally voted unswervingly with his colleagues in office;[3] and he was a ministerial teller in at least 27 divisions in this period. He voted against criminal law reform, 23 May 1821, and the removal of Catholic peers' disabilities, 30 Apr. 1822. He was 'disposed' to support Richard Martin's bill for the prevention of cruelty to horses, 1 June 1821.[4] On 22 Feb. 1822, before he submitted the navy estimates, he clashed with Hume over a blatant case of government pensions held in plurality. He had the worst of the exchange and Hume raised a laugh against him by observing that he 'could not doubt, after the specimen which the House had received of ... [Osborn's] arithmetical abilities, that the navy estimates would be admirably expounded'.[5] He extolled the reduced estimates, 1 Mar., as evidence of the 'disposition of government to reduce, in a considerable degree, the public expenditure'; and he replied to Hume's criticism of the cost of the dockyard improvements at Sheerness, 22 Mar. 1822. When detailing the following year's estimates, 14 Mar. 1823, he stressed the 'prudent reductions' which had been made in the dockyards and boasted that the navy 'was never in so efficient a state as it was at the present moment'.

Osborn surrendered his office and seat in Parliament in return for a place in the audit office early in 1824 and remained there for the rest of his life. His salary was £1,200 a year but, with his large family and accumulated election debts, he had difficulty in making ends meet. In September 1842, harking back to his devoted support of Pitt some forty years earlier, he asked Sir Robert Peel to find a civil service place for his second son, who was proving too delicate for the army:

> It would in a great measure relieve me from a great load of anxiety; and would indemnify me for a great deal of vexation I have suffered, and tend materially to the comfort of the few years that may remain to me.

Peel could not oblige him.[6] Six months later, on the retirement of Francis Larpent from the head of the audit commission, Osborn, tentatively advancing his own pretensions to the post, but correctly suspecting that Sir William Herries would be promoted over his head, sought provision for his son as compensation for this disappointment

> in consideration of my long standing in this office, and of having spent nearly fifty years in parliamentary and civil service ... If Lord Liverpool's health had been spared for a very little longer time [in 1827] I should have received an appointment in addition to that which I now hold. But these are not days for pluralities.

Peel again dashed his hopes:

> I must claim an unfettered right to make that selection for the appointment in question, which I may deem most advantageous for the efficient conduct of the business of the department and I cannot admit the claim which you urge for consideration in some other way in the event of your not succeeding Mr. Larpent ... The civil patronage of the government is so totally inadequate to meet even a small portion of the claims upon it that I cannot hope to have the pleasure of finding suitable employment for your son.[7]

Osborn died in August 1848 and was succeeded in the baronetcy and family estates by his eldest son George Robert (1813-92).

[1] Add. 38458, f. 283; 51676, Lord G.W. Russell to Holland, 13 Mar.; *The Times*, 9, 17, 21, 22 Mar. *Cambridge and Hertford Independent Press*, 4, 11, 18, 25 Mar.; Beds. RO, Russell mss R 767, Bedford to Brown, 22, 26 Mar. 1820. [2] Beds. RO, Wrest mss L 30/11/204/9; Beds. RO M 8/11, 12, 14, 16, 19. [3] *Black Bk.* (1823), 181. [4] *The Times*, 2 June 1821. [5] Ibid. 23 Feb. 1822. [6] Add. 40516, ff. 106, 108. [7] Add. 40525, ff. 333, 335.

D.R.F.

OSBORNE, Lord Francis Godolphin (1777–1850), of Gogmagog Hills, nr. Stapleford, Cambs.

HELSTON	30 Mar. 1799–1802
LEWES	1802–1806
CAMBRIDGESHIRE	16 Mar. 1810–Oct. 1831

b. 18 Oct. 1777, 2nd s. of Francis Godolphin Osborne†, 5th duke of Leeds (*d.* 1799), and 1st w. Lady Amelia Darcy, da. and h. of Robert, 4th earl of Holdernesse. *educ.* Dr. Glass's sch., Greenford 1783;[1] Christ Church, Oxf. 1795; northern European tour 1797-8. *m.* 31 Mar. 1800, Hon. Elizabeth Charlotte Eden, da. of William Eden†, 1st Bar. Auckland, 5s. (2 *d.v.p.*) 1 da. *d.v.p. suc.* cos. Francis, 2nd Bar. Godolphin, to Gogmagog Hills and Farnham Royal, Stoke Poges and Upton cum Chalvey, Bucks. 1785; *cr.* Bar. Godolphin 14 May 1832. *d.* 15 Feb. 1850.

Commdt. Stapleford vols. 1803; capt. Cambs. militia 1831.

High steward, Cambridge 1836-*d.*

Osborne's inherited stake in Cambridgeshire consisted of a substantial house built within the ramparts of the Iron Age fort at Wandlebury, four miles south-east of Cambridge, together with some surrounding land.[2] A Foxite Whig, who had come in for the county by a coup at the expense of the Hardwicke interest in 1810, he offered for the fourth time in 1820. Rumours of a disturbance came to nothing and Osborne, who on the hustings expressed his contempt for attempts to label him 'a Jacobin' or 'a Radical', was returned, at a reported cost of £2,000, with the ministerialist sitting Member Lord Charles Manners, brother of the 5th duke of Rutland. When accused later in the day of 'professing atheism', Osborne retorted that 'the path he had followed led neither to place nor employment, but to sarcasm in Parliament and obloquy out of it'.[3] For a county Member and adherent of opposition, Osborne was not particularly active in the House in this period, largely because his health, despite his comparative youth, was unreliable. Yet he was reasonably assiduous when fit, and in any case, so strong was his electoral position as the representative of the independent freeholders and Whigs of Cambridgeshire, that he received little local criticism.

Osborne voted against government on the civil list, 5, 8 May, the appointment of an additional baron of exchequer in Scotland, 15 May, the aliens bill, 1 June, and economies in revenue collection, 4 July 1820. He voted against Wilberforce's compromise resolution on the Queen Caroline affair, 22 June. On 21 Aug. he condemned the bill of pains and penalties and, in protest against the 'mock' trial, which would 'convert that House into a judicial tribunal', moved an address for the prorogation of Parliament; he withdrew it when Tierney, the Whig leader, raised practical objections.[4] 'Some of our parliamentary friends', he told Tierney, suggested that he should 'repeat' his motion for an address when the House reconvened on 18 Sept:

> Much as I dislike personally intruding myself on the attention of the ... Commons, yet I feel so strongly on this subject that I should certainly concur in the propriety [of] so doing, provided no person more eligible or no other mode of proceeding more expedient should be pointed at.[5]

In the event, he merely questioned Lord Castlereagh on ministers' intentions regarding the royal divorce and voted in the minority of 12 for Hobhouse's call for a prorogation. He was the prime mover behind a requisition for a Cambridgeshire county meeting to appeal to the king to dismiss ministers for failing to relieve distress and sanctioning proceedings against the queen. He secured the prestigious Whig signatures of the duke of Bedford, Lord Tavistock*, Lord Dacre and Lord Fitzwilliam, to whom he explained, 27 Dec. 1820:

> My object was and is to address the king to remove his ministers ... but in order to obtain respectable signatures both of residents and non-residents and likewise to obtain their attendance ... I thought it better to throw out more than one inducement ... The dismissal of the ministers is the old constitutional remedy for general distress, which we all admit to prevail, but such is the difference of opinion on some of the leading political subjects that now occupy the public mind, that I thought myself justified in endeavouring to awake the feeling of each interest in order to bring them to coincide in one general resolution.

As it happened, illness prevented Osborne from attending the meeting, 16 Jan. 1821, when Dacre stood in for him; but he was voted thanks for his parliamentary conduct.[6] He took almost no part in the opposition campaign on the queen's behalf early in 1821: he presented and vouched for the respectability of the Cambridge petition for the restoration of her name to the liturgy, 6 Feb., but only paired for the censure motion on ministers later that day.[7] He was absent from the division on Catholic relief, 28 Feb. He voted for repeal of the additional malt duty, 3 Apr., and presented the Cambridgeshire petition for parliamentary reform, 17 Apr., though he had not attended the meeting which adopted it. No other trace of parliamentary activity has been found for 1821: leaves of absence for a month because of ill health, 5 Mar., 30 Apr., would appear to explain why.

Osborne was in the opposition minorities on the treatment of Alderman Waithman* and for reduction of the salt duties, 28 Feb. 1822; he pleaded attendance for the latter as his excuse for not appearing at the county meeting on agricultural distress that day.[8] He presented a petition from the agriculturists of the Isle of Ely calling for retrenchment and reform, 2 Apr. He did not attend the county reform meeting, 4 Apr., when radical elements carped at his absence and tried unsuccessfully to take the petition out of his hands. He duly presented it, 3 May. He also presented petitions from Holdsworth, Devon for reduced taxation and currency reform, 6 May, and from Cambridge for revision of the criminal code, 8 May.[9] In what was evidently another relaxed session for him, he voted for parliamentary reform, 25 Apr., economies, 2, 15 May, and inquiry into the government of the Ionian Isles, 14 May, and against the aliens bill, 14 June 1822. He wintered abroad, but returned in time to attend the county meeting of 14 Feb. 1823, which adopted a radical petition calling for reform, repeal of the taxes on necessities of life, abolition of unmerited pensions and sinecures, reduction of the army and public salaries, the abolition of tithes, a redistribution of ecclesiastical revenues, the sale of crown lands and a levy on funded property. When confronted with this, he boasted of being 'one of the oldest reformers present', but dissociated himself from the spoliation of legitimate lay and church property. He presented the petition without comment, 27 Feb., along with two similar ones from Cambridge parishes.[10] His only known votes this session were against the grant for the Royal Military College, 10 Mar., for repeal of the Foreign Enlistment Act, 16 Apr., inquiries into the prosecution of the Dublin Orange rioters, 22 Apr., and the state of Ireland, 12 May, and parliamentary reform, 24 Apr., and to abolish the death penalty for larceny, 21 May. He presented a Chatteris anti-slavery petition, 30 Apr., and on 16 May 1823 presented and endorsed one from a Yorkshire magistrate against the practice of putting remand prisoners on the treadmill. Peel, the home secretary, brushed aside his request that women should be exempted from this punishment.[11]

Osborne apparently went abroad again later in the year, and he was presumably with his wife at The Hague in March 1824, when Lady Granville described her as follows:

> She knows everybody, every custom, every shop, every royalty, and every drug. She seems excellent and amiable, bearing wretched health with exemplary patience; but ... she is tiresome, in a fever about trifles, and talking incessantly about nothing. With great confusion in her own ideas, and always taking hold of mine by the wrong end.

Lady Granville subsequently warmed to her as a 'very good, friendly and amiable' woman, whose 'worried, fidgety, bewildered manner' gave a bad first impression.[12] Osborne's perfunctory recorded activities in the 1824 session consisted of votes against the aliens bill, 2 Apr., for inquiries into Ireland and its church establishment, 6, 11, 25 May, and for repeal of the assessed taxes, 10 May; and the presentation of petitions against slavery, 1 Apr., the Combination Acts, 4 May, and the Beer Acts, 12 May, and for inquiry into the case of the prosecuted Methodist missionary John Smith.[13] He was a little more active in 1825, when he divided against the Irish unlawful societies bill, 21 Feb. He was a defaulter on a call of the House, 28 Feb., but attended and was excused the next day, when he voted for Catholic relief, as he did again, 21 Apr. He voted against the Irish franchise bill, 26 Apr. He voted for repeal of the window tax,

17 May, and against the duke of Cumberland's grant, 27, 30 May, 2, 6 June. He was in Hume's minority of 37 for inquiry into the Irish church, 14 June, and the small minorities for liberal amendments to the combination bill, 27 June. He presented petitions from Guisborough and Ely for repeal of the assessed taxes and in favour of the county courts bill, 2 Mar.; and on 28 Apr. presented 68 parish petitions from Cambridgeshire and Buckinghamshire (where he held inherited property in the Windsor area) against alteration of the corn laws.[14] At the Cambridgeshire meeting to support the abolition of slavery, 7 Mar. 1826, Osborne said that if ministers were sincere, which he doubted, 'much more good might be done by them than all the petitions'. Written criticism by one freeholder that he should have been in the House to support Hume's attack on the standing army was answered by a friend with a reminder that in 1822 he had been found fault with for giving precedence to parliamentary attendance. He presented the petition, 14 Mar.[15] His only known votes were against the president of the board of trade's salary, 10 Apr., for parliamentary reform, 13, 27 Apr., and in the protectionist minorities, which also included Manners, against the emergency admission of foreign corn, 8, 11 May 1826.

Although rumours of an opposition, aimed chiefly at Manners, were rife as the 1826 general election approached, Osborne took few active steps to prepare for a contest. Yet when sounded by Lord Hardwicke, the lord lieutenant, who was considering a bid to reassert his electoral interest in the county, as to whether he would step down if a serious third candidate started or was nominated, he replied that, despite appearances to the contrary, he had every intention of standing his ground and contesting the issue, though on 'a system as little expensive as possible'.[16] In the event Samuel Wells, the radical Huntingdon attorney, nominated Henry Adeane*, who had stood against the Rutland interest in the borough in 1818, but on the morning of the election had turned down a request to put him in nomination from a radical group among the county independents. While Adeane declined the nomination, on the pretext that he was pledged to do nothing that would endanger Osborne, Wells persisted and forced a contest intended to cause the Manners family as much inconvenience and expense as possible. Osborne, who midway through the affair publicly acceded to a request that he release Adeane from his pledge, of which he denied all knowledge, was in no danger. He was irritated by the sham contest, but was put to no expense and finished comfortably in second place behind Manners, who polled mainly plumpers. At the same time, one commentator thought that his votes for Catholic relief in 1825 had 'materially weakened his interest'. He stood by his support for emancipation, declaring that the issue 'resolves itself into a matter of political expediency between Whig and Tory, and not all the sophistry that can be urged on the other side, nor all the learning of the university, can controvert it'. On agricultural protection, he stated his continued support for the existing corn laws and promised to resist 'the attempt that will undoubtedly be made in the ensuing Parliament, to deprive you of that protection, as cultivators of land, to which you are entitled under the pressure of taxation of various sorts'.[17]

On neither issue did Osborne deliver. Although he presented the county petition against alteration of the corn laws, 26 Feb., he was not in the minority against the corn bill, 2 Apr. 1827.[18] Nor did he vote in the division on Catholic relief, 6 Mar: it was said that he had 'stayed away on purpose'.[19] On 27 Mar. he presented the petition of Hardwicke and the conservators of Bedford Level corporation complaining of the excessive fees charged for the drafting and passage of drainage bills.[20] When publicly challenged by Wells, he admitted that he had encouraged Thomas Fryer, the sheriff at the time of the 1826 election, to petition the Commons, 6 Apr., to take steps to prevent such 'vexatious' proceedings, which penalized genuine candidates.[21] Osborne, whose pro-Catholic Tory brother, the 6th duke of Leeds, was appointed master of the horse in Canning's ministry and rewarded with a vacant garter under an arrangement made before the change of government, voted for chancery reform, 22 May, and the disfranchisement of Penryn, 28 May. He presented several Cambridgeshire petitions for repeal of the Test Acts, 25 May, 6, 7, 19 June, and a county brewers' petition for reform of the regulations governing their trade, 7 June 1827.[22]

He voted for repeal of the Tests, 26 Feb. 1828, and presented petitions for it that day and 5 Mar. He was unwell during April,[23] and only paired for Catholic relief, 12 May. He was present to divide with the opposition to the Wellington ministry on civil list pensions, 20 May, the archbishop of Canterbury's registrar, 16 June, the Irish estimates, 20 June, and the cost of improving Buckingham House, 23 June. He presented petitions from Cambridgeshire farmers against the importation of foreign wool, 19 May, and from Eversden for the abolition of slavery, 19 June, 1828. He was again conspicuous by his absence from proceedings on the Catholic question in 1829, when his brother supported and his nephew Lord Carmarthen, Member for Helston, opposed emancipation. A defaulter on a call of the House, 5 Mar., he is not known to have voted on the issue; but he did present favourable petitions, 11 Mar., and voted for O'Connell to be allowed to take his seat unimpeded, 18 May. Although he feared that he was addressing 'an unwilling audience', Osborne voiced his 'decided opposition' to Warburton's anatomy regulation bill, 15 May; and three days later, when he suggested that it would be 'rendered nugatory by the humanity of individuals', he secured seven votes to 36 for his bid to kill it. He voted to reduce the grant for the marble arch sculpture, 25 May, and was one of the minority of 40 who supported Lord Blandford's parliamentary reform scheme, 2 June 1829.

With the state of the king's health promising a general election, the 1830 session was Osborne's most active of this or the previous Parliament. His was the first signature on the requisition of 2 Jan. for a county meeting to consider agricultural distress and petition for repeal of the beer and malt taxes and alteration of the licensing system. At the meeting, 22 Jan., he reproved Maberly, the eccentric vicar of Kingston, for his rant against Catholics and fundholders, argued that 'the distresses of the country were owing to excessive taxation and, observing that 'the great portion of his income was derived from the public funds', called for retrenchment to preserve the public credit. A motion that he and Manners be 'instructed' to support the petition and promote its object was carried.[24] Osborne voted for the amendment to the address, 4 Feb., and the next day, when he was prevented from presenting the Cambridgeshire petition by the protraction of other business, gave notice that after Easter he would move for repeal of the beer and malt duties. (He thought reform of the licensing laws a subject better suited to a select committee.) On 8 Feb. he presented and endorsed the county petition, together with one from the Ely area praying for a reduction of taxes on necessities and remodelling of the poor laws. He declared himself satisfied with Goulburn's advance notice of his budget statement, 2 Mar., and no more was heard of his threatened motion, though he did present several petitions for repeal of the beer and malt duties, 4 May. He voted for the introduction of the East Retford disfranchisement bill, 11 Feb., but for the transfer of its seats to Birmingham, 5 Mar. He voted for inquiry into the Newark petition alleging improper electoral interference by the duke of Newcastle, 1 Mar. He presented a petition for repeal of the tobacco duty, 30 Mar. He divided with the reviving Whig opposition for a reduction of taxes, 15 Feb., and admiralty economies, 22 Mar., and against the Bathurst and Dundas pensions, 26 Mar. He paired for the divisions on the salary of the lieutenant-general of the ordnance, 29 Mar., and inquiry into crown lands revenues, 30 Mar. He presented a Wisbech merchants' petition for mitigation of the penal code, 31 Mar., but paired against abolition of the death penalty for forgery, 7 June. He was against Jewish emancipation, 5 Apr. The following day he spoke and voted against the third reading of Lord Ellenborough's divorce bill, of which he had 'strong suspicions'. On the introduction of Wallis's divorce bill, 4 May, he explained his 'strong objections' to the present state of the law, which unfairly favoured the wealthy. He gave notice that next session he would propose a regulation to force all parties seeking divorce by statute to state 'some special reasons' to the House. He voted to reduce the grant for public buildings, 3 May. Poor health prevented him from presenting the Ely petition in favour of the sale of beer bill, 21 May.[25] He took a month's sick leave, 25 May, but was present to vote for cuts in diplomatic expenditure, 7, 11 June. He was one of a handful of Whigs who divided with government against a fixed duty on imported sugars, 21 June 1830.[26]

When he offered again for Cambridgeshire at the subsequent general election, Osborn claimed, somewhat implausibly, to have 'advocated the peculiar interests of this agricultural county with success'; and on the hustings he bragged that he had exerted himself last session to secure repeal of the beer tax and a change in the licensing system. He declared himself to be 'a friend to reform', reiterated his support for the corn laws and welcomed the emancipation of Dissenters and Catholics. He shrugged off Wells's jibes at his brother's household office and, in response to his direct question, pledged himself to support repeal of the malt tax, though he doubted if the state of his health would allow him to take the initiative.[27] This time Adeane, who had been disowned by Wells, accepted a requisition to stand. According to Manners and others, Osborne was 'very indignant at Adeane's behaviour'. Certainly there was much mutual hostility between them at first, but as it became clear that the Rutland interest was in trouble, a practical coalition developed which relegated Manners to third place. Near the end of the contest, Osborne asserted that his position at the head of the poll gave the lie to accusations that 'he slept at his post and that he neglected the private interests of the county'. He claimed to have preserved its 'independence' and 'beat the administration of the country'. He said that there had been so much chicanery, particularly by Hardwicke, who backed Adeane, as to make him 'almost sick of elections'. Some years later the daughter of Professor George Pryme, one of the leading Whig independents, recalled the chairing of Osborne and Adeane:

> Every now and then, when the populace pleased, the procession stopped, and the chairs were tossed up as far as the bearers could reach, amid loud huzzas. I recollect the look of discomfort at such times on Lord F. Osborne's face, as he sat in his peculiar, stiff, stately manner, dressed in a green coat and top boots.[28]

Osborne did not attend the Wisbech celebration dinner, 8 Oct. 1830: according to his spokesman, he stayed away because he did not wish to become involved in any 'personal triumph' over Manners, whom he respected as an individual.[29]

Osborne presented a number of anti-slavery petitions, 3, 4, 10, 16 Nov., and Wisbech petitions for repeal of the coal duties, 15, 22 Nov. 1830. He voted to scrap the Irish Subletting Act, 11 Nov., and against government on the civil list, 15 Nov. On 6 Dec. 1830 he was given three weeks' leave to attend to his magisterial duties in Cambridgeshire, where the 'Swing' disturbances were troublesome. He warned Warburton that he would resist his anatomy bill if he reintroduced it, 9 Feb. 1831. Later that day he presented the petition of the inhabitants of Shelford, his neighbours, calling for tax reductions, abolition of the game laws, select vestries and tithes, reform of Parliament and election by ballot. As he had told the petitioners beforehand, it was 'the first petition I have ever presented ... to which I have not been prepared to give my cordial support'. In a discussion on tithes, 16 Feb., he called for 'a fair commutation'.[30] He presented a Royston petition for parliamentary reform, 14 Feb. At the county meeting called to endorse the Grey ministry's reform bill, 18 Mar., he said that it 'had his entire approbation'.[31] He presented favourable petitions from Haddenham, 19 Mar., and Soham, 18 Apr., and voted silently for its second reading, 22 Mar., and against Gascoyne's wrecking amendment, 19 Apr. He presented petitions against slavery, 28 Mar., 13 Apr., and the general register bill, 28 Mar. On Tower's divorce bill, 13 Apr., he again declared his objection 'on principle' to such measures 'passing as a matter of course'. He did not oppose its report stage, 21 Apr. 1831, because of the 'extraordinary state of excitement' prevailing in the House, but called for urgent tightening of the law.

Unlike Adeane, who had reservations about details of the bill, Osborne had no difficulty in presenting himself as its unconditional supporter at the 1831 general election. When Manners came forward as a moderate reformer and farmers' friend, Osborne dismissed him on both counts, arguing that the bill as it stood would strengthen rather than harm the landed interest. Manners's bid collapsed, and Osborne and Adeane were unopposed; but Osborne was too ill to attend the formal proceedings. In his address of thanks he forecast that the bill would

> strengthen the king upon his throne ... [and] enable the aristocracy to shine with pure and uncontaminated lustre, and, limited to its constitutional duties, again to become a rampart round the throne, and a guardian of the people's rights; obliterating I trust from our memories and even our language the odious epithet of boroughmongers.[32]

He voted for the second reading of the reintroduced reform bill, 6 July, and was a steady supporter of its details in committee. Unlike Adeane, he voted with ministers against the enfranchisement of £50 tenants-at-will, 18 Aug. He voted against the issue of a writ for Dublin, 8 Aug., and with government on the controversy over the last election there, 23 Aug. When he repeated his objections to the 'farce' of divorce bills, 11, 19 July, Whittle Harvey advised him to address the king to draw the attention of the commission on the ecclesiastical courts to the problem. On 17 Aug. Osborne, reporting that he had found that it was not possible to proceed in this way, said that 'I almost begin to despair of being able to effect any good on this subject'. As a basis for others to work on, he suggested that divorce bills ought to be made public measures, started in the Commons and referred to select committees. On the presentation of a Gloucestershire petition for repeal of the corn laws, 22 July, he argued that 'unless protection be afforded to the agriculturalist, corn cannot be grown in this country'. He presented a Cambridgeshire petition against distillation from molasses, 2 Aug., and saw the Eau Brink drainage bill through its third reading, 17 Aug. He voted for the passage of the reform bill, 21 Sept. About a week later he let it be publicly known that he intended to immediately retire from the Commons, claiming that his health was unequal to the duties of a county Member. He had already tipped off his friend, neighbour and fellow-reformer Richard Townley, who won the ensuing by-election against Hardwicke's nephew.[33] In his last known act as a Member, Osborne voted for the motion of confidence in the Grey ministry, 10 Oct. 1831.

He had already been talked of as a candidate for the peerage, though when he retired he denied that this was on the cards.[34] He was, in fact, regarded as being 'in a manner promised'; and the elevation of himself and the veteran Whig Charles Dundas* were the only exceptions which William IV would admit to his veto on the ennoblement of commoners in the mass creations sought by Lord Grey to secure the passage of the reform bill through the Lords. The cynical Edward Littleton* believed that the peerage had been promised to Osborne principally to gratify Lord Granville, whose bastard daughter by Lady Bessborough Osborne's eldest son had married in 1828.[35] Early in April 1832 it was reported that Osborne had 'fully expected to be a peer last week', but had been frustrated by the king's latest contretemps with Grey. In the event, the barony of Godolphin of Farnham Royal was conferred on him as the gift of the king to his outgoing ministers at the beginning of the political crisis of May 1832.[36] Osborne, who lost his married daughter in 1838, his younger son in 1846 and his wife in 1847, died of 'a gradual decay of nature' at Gogmagog Hills in February 1850.[37] By his will, dated 9 July 1847, he confirmed the generous provisions made for his two surviving younger sons in his marriage settlement. In a cocidil of 14 Feb. 1850 he left £1,000 to a Mrs. Susan Gazelle Giles, 'now residing with me at Gogmagog Hills'. His Cambridgeshire and Buckinghamshire estates, together with a cottage and land at Tron Dinas, Denbighshire, bought in 1824, passed to his eldest son and successor in the peerage, George Godolphin (1802-72), who became 8th duke of Leeds on the death of his cousin in 1859.[38]

[1] *Heber Letters*, 19. [2] *VCH Cambs.* viii. 153, 227, 230-1. His property qualification was hardly 'of the slightest', as stated in *HP Commons, 1790-1820*, iv. 701. [3] *Cambridge and Hertford Independent Press*, 12, 19, 26 Feb., 11, 25 Mar.; Dorset RO, Bankes mss, Mrs. Henry Bankes's diary, 20 Mar. 1820. [4] *The Times*, 22 Aug. 1820. [5] Hants RO, Tierney mss 55. [6] Fitzwilliam mss 102/1; *Cambridge and Hertford Independent Press*, 6, 13, 20 Jan. 1821. [7] *The Times*, 7 Feb. 1821. [8] *Cambridge and Hertford Independent Press*, 2 Mar. 1822. [9] *The Times*, 3, 6 Apr., 4, 7, 9 May 1822. [10] Ibid. 15, 28 Feb.; *Cambridge and Hertford Independent Press*, 8, 15, 22 Feb. 1823. [11] *The Times*, 1, 17 May 1823. [12] *Countess Granville Letters*, i. 262-3, 268. [13] *The Times*, 2 Apr., 5, 13, 25 May 1824. [14] Ibid. 3 Mar., 29 Apr. 1825; *VCH Bucks.* iii. 229, 310, 316. [15] *Cambridge and Hertford Independent Press*, 11, 18 Mar.; *The Times*, 15 Mar. 1826. [16] Add. 35691, ff. 142, 144. [17] *Cambridge and Hertford Independent Press*, 10, 17, 24 June, 1, 8 July; *The Times*, 1 July 1826. [18] *The Times*, 27 Feb. 1827; C.H. Cooper, *Annals of Cambridge*, iv. 553. [19] Add. 56550, f. 143. [20] *Cambridge and Hertford Independent Press*, 17, 31 Mar. 1827. [21] Ibid. 14, 21, 28 Apr., 5 May 1827. [22] *The Times*, 26 May, 7, 8, 20 June; *Cambridge and Hertford Independent Press*, 9 June 1827. [23] *Cambridge and Hertford Independent Press*, 26 Apr. 1828. [24] Ibid. 9, 23 Jan. 1830. [25] Ibid. 29 May 1830. [26] Grey mss, Howick jnl. 21 June [1830]. [27] *Cambridge and Hertford Independent Press*, 10, 17, 24, 31 July, 7, 14 Aug. 1830. [28] Rutland mss (History of Parliament Aspinall transcripts), Manners to Rutland, 25 July; *Cambridge and Hertford Independent Press*, 14, 21 Aug.; *The Times*, 14 Aug. 1830; G. Pryme, *Autobiog. Recollections*, 188. [29] *Cambridge and Hertford Independent Press*, 9, 16 Oct. 1830. [30] Ibid. 5, 12, 19 Feb. 1831. [31] Ibid. 19 Mar. 1831. [32] Ibid. 30 Apr., 7, 14 May 1831. [33] Ibid. 1, 8 Oct. 1831. [34] Add. 37726, f. 189; *The Times*, 1 Oct. 1831. [35] *Holland House Diaries*, 98, 110; *Grey-William IV Corresp.* ii. 71, 113; *Three Diaries*, 178, 253; Add. 76369, Althorp to Brougham, 7 Jan.; Hatherton diary, 19 [Jan. 1832]. [36] Aberdeen Univ. Lib. Arbuthnot mss 3029/1/2/47; *Grey-William IV Corresp.* ii. 335, 397, 399. [37] *Gent. Mag.* (1850), i. 432; *The Times*, 18 Feb. 1850. [38] PROB 11/2113/356; IR26/1866/170.

D.R.F.

OSBORNE, Francis Godolphin D'Arcy, mq. of Carmarthen (1798–1859), of 16 Bruton Street, Mdx.

Helston 1826–1830

b. 21 May 1798, 1st and o. surv. s. of George William Frederick, 6th duke of Leeds, and Lady Charlotte Townshend, da. of George Townshend†, 1st Mq. Townshend. *educ.* privately by John Page, fellow of Brasenose, Oxf.;[1] Christ Church, Oxf. 1815. *m.* 24 Apr. 1828, Louisa Catherine, da. and coh. of Richard Caton, merchant, of Baltimore, USA, wid. of Sir Felton Elwell Hervey Bathurst, 1st bt., *s.p. styled* mq. of Carmarthen 1799-1838; *summ.* to the Lords in his fa's barony as Lord Osborne 2 July 1838; *suc.* fa. as 7th duke of Leeds 10 July 1838; took name of D'Arcy before Osborne by royal lic. 6 Aug. 1849. *d.* 4 May 1859.

Cornet 10 Drag. 1817; ensign (half-pay) R.W.I. Rangers 1820; lt. (half-pay) 10 Drag. 1821, lt. (full-pay) 1823; capt. army 1825; capt. 2 Life Gds. 1826; ret. 1828.

Col. N. York militia 1846-*d.*

Carmarthen's father, who was summoned to the Lords in his mother's barony of Conyers in 1798 and succeeded as 6th duke of Leeds the following year, took little active part in politics, but he abandoned his father's Foxite allegiance and went over to Pitt; his younger brother, Lord Francis Godolphin Osborne*, remained true to Whig principles. Leeds was a favoured crony and trusty drinking companion of George IV, and was sometimes the worse for wear in public: in March 1828, according to Thomas Creevey*, he and the king 'got so drunk as to be nearly speechless', and the following year Lady Granville encountered him in the royal entourage at Ascot races, 'drunk as a fish [and] quite incoherent', though she observed that 'scarlet strawberries in private conversation are very agreeable to meet with occasionally'.[2] Carmarthen travelled in France in the summer of 1816 and again in 1825, while his desultory army career took him to Ireland in 1824. In 1826 he was one of the young men who accompanied the duke of Devonshire on his lavish mission to represent Britain at the coronation of the new tsar.[3] Two years later he 'deeply mortified' his father, so Lady Holland reported, by marrying the profoundly stupid American-born widow Lady Hervey Bathurst, sister of Lord Wellesley's second wife, who was nine years his senior. Lady Williams Wynn had earlier commented of her that 'never was there ... so great a Bicky, though some people say ... much of it is assumed as *naïvété*', and, according to Lady Holland, it was held that she 'wanted six qualifications, youth, beauty, character, fortune, birth, sense'. Lady Holland thought the only consolations for the duke were the 'improbability' of his daughter-in-law producing any children and the fact that his younger son, Lord Conyers George Thomas Osborne, who in that event would inherit the title after Carmarthen, was 'a very fine young man ... just what such a father would be proud of'.[4]

At the general election of 1826 Carmarthen had been returned for Helston on his father's controlling interest, and he subsequently received a formal request for attendance from Canning, the leader of the Commons in Lord Liverpool's ministry.[5] He made no mark in the House, and is not known to have uttered a syllable in debate. He divided against Catholic relief, 6 Mar., and for the duke of Clarence's annuity, 16 Mar. 1827. In May 1827 his father became master of the horse in Canning's coalition ministry and, in keeping with an arrangement concluded before the demise of Liverpool's government, received one of the three vacant garters; the duke remained in his post under Lord Goderich and the duke of Wellington.[6] Carmarthen voted against repeal of the Test Acts, 26 Feb. 1828. However, he and his father were at odds over Catholic relief: whereas he paired against it, 12 May, the duke voted for it in the Lords, 10 June. He divided with Wellington's administration on the ordnance estimates, 4 July 1828. In February 1829 Planta, the patronage secretary, predicted that he would side 'with government' for Catholic emancipation, but in fact he voted or paired against it, 6, 18, 30 Mar. (His father gave his proxy to Wellington when he had to leave London in February and loyally voted for emancipation, 4, 10 Apr. 1829.)[7] His only other known trace of parliamentary activity is his pairing against abolition of the death penalty for forgery, 7 June 1830. He retired from the Commons at the dissolution that summer.[8]

Carmarthen, who subsequently gravitated towards the Whigs, succeeded to the dukedom in July 1838, only eight days after being summoned to the Lords in his father's barony of Osborne. He inherited the settled family estates at Hornby Castle, near Bedale, Yorkshire, and in Cornwall. However, other real estate and the bulk of the personalty, which was sworn under £60,000, went to his brother-in-law, Sackville Walter Lane Fox*, whom the old duke had evidently treated almost as a son.[9] As 7th duke of Leeds he joined Brooks's Club in 1841 and supported repeal of the corn laws. He died of diphtheria in May 1859. It was reported that not long before his death he had been received into the Roman Catholic church, but that on his last evening he expressed a wish to be given Holy Communion by the local Anglican clergyman.[10] His brother having been accidentally killed in 1831, aged 18, while wrestling at Christ Church, his title and estates devolved on his cousin, George Godolphin Osborne (1802-72), the eldest son of Lord Francis. The baronies of Darcy and Conyers passed to his nephew Sackville George Lane Fox (1827-88), who became 12th Baron Conyers.

[1] Eg. 3508, f. 36. [2] *Creevey Pprs.* i. 156; *Countess Granville Letters*, ii. 42. [3] Eg. 3385B, ff. 167, 169; 3508, ff. 1, 3, 35, 36. [4] *Lady Holland to Son*, 82; *Williams Wynn Corresp.* 200-1. [5] *West Briton*, 9, 16 June 1826; Eg. 3508, f. 37. [6] *Geo. IV Letters*, iii. 1273-4; *Canning's Ministry*, 269; *Colchester Diary*, iii. 491; Wellington mss WP1/887/49. [7] Wellington mss WP1/995/10; 996/6. [8] *West Briton*, 16 July 1830. [9] *Gent. Mag.* (1838), ii. 208; PROB 11/1903/706; IR26/1491/768; Add. 40406, f. 123; 40409, f. 79. [10] *Gent. Mag.* (1859), i. 642-3.

D.R.F.

OSSORY, earl of *see* **BUTLER, John**

OTWAY CAVE, Robert (?1796–1844), of Stanford Hall, Leics. and Castle Otway, co. Tipperary.

LEICESTER	1826–1830
CO. TIPPERARY	8 Aug. 1832–1832
CO. TIPPERARY	1835–29 Nov. 1844

b. 1 Mar. 1796,[1] 3rd but 1st surv. s. of Henry Otway of Castle Otway and Sarah, da. and h. of Sir Thomas Cave, 6th bt., of Stanford Hall, sis. and sole h. of Sir Thomas Cave†, 7th bt., of Stanford. *educ.* Eton 1808; Christ Church, Oxf. 1815. *m.* 23 Oct. 1832,[2] Sophia, da. of Sir Francis Burdett, 5th bt.*, *s.p. suc.* fa. to Castle Otway 1815 and took additional name of Cave by royal lic. 12 Mar. 1818. *d.* 29 Nov. 1844.

Capt. Leics. yeomanry 1818.

Otway Cave's maternal ancestors had long been prominent in Leicestershire politics: his grandfather Sir Thomas Cave, 3rd bt., and uncle Sir Thomas Cave, 5th bt., sat for the county in the eighteenth century. His mother, who had inherited Stanford Hall from her brother in 1792, and with him took the additional name of Cave in 1818, became *suo jure* Baroness Braye in 1839 after establishing her somewhat tenuous claim as coheir to the title, in abeyance since 1557. Otway Cave was 'highly distinguished for classical proficiency' at Eton and Oxford.[3] He showed an early interest in county politics and made a favourable impression on the Tory Member George Legh Keck, but was rejected as his prospective seconder at the contested general election of 1818 as this might have exposed him to awkward questions without a transfer of property from his mother's estate. He went to Paris in the autumn of 1819 and from there to Italy, but was in Leicester to second the successful nomination of Legh Keck for the county in March 1820.[4] He appears to have spent the next few years abroad. Charles Longley, the future archbishop of Canterbury, corresponded with him at Vienna on the Catholic question, 3 June 1822, and 'regretted much' that he was 'not coming home this year'. Another correspondent complained of his 'continental blindness', 6 Apr. 1823: 'while poetry instead of politics fill your mind you will never be the man you ought – speeches instead of verses!'. A proposed marriage to a 'princess' in Geneva in September 1823 came to nothing. At this time his rent roll stood at £3,500, and his potential inheritance, besides his Irish paternal property, was worth £10,810 per annum. On leaving Europe he stated his intention of residing in Ireland since, as he explained to a French friend, 'the state of that country grows daily worse'.[5] In the event he continued to nurse his political interests in Leicestershire. Longley, reviewing a proposed election address, 30 Jan. 1825, advised him to modify some of its content: there was a danger of alarming his 'more timid neighbours' by appearing to advocate 'some indefinite and sweeping reform in ecclesiastical matters'; the general effect of the whole 'stamps you decidedly liberal in your politics', which was a declaration 'you cannot avoid making whenever you offer yourself to the suffrages of your neighbours', and it was inadvisable to satirize the 'prevailing principles and practice' of the gentry, since this was likely to prove 'offensive to many of your Leicestershire squires'.[6] He was admitted to the Whig pantheon of Brooks's Club, 19 Feb. 1826, sponsored by Sir Francis Burdett and Sir Ronald Ferguson*, but secured the support of Lord Howe and Charles Godfrey Mundy on condition of remaining 'neutral with respect to the Catholics'. His friend George de Lacy Evans* assured him that this 'intermediate course' would 'smooth your way to the county and at all events secure your seat for the town', and would make his election 'more certain' and relieve him from heavy expenses:

> Hereafter when you are more independent in point of fortune you may be disposed to change your mind ... I doubt whether it will be necessary for you to tell your committee more than that you are to be strongly supported by these persons, and that finding the opinion of your constituents so strongly opposed to the Catholics, you would certainly not give a vote in opposition to their wishes.[7]

He offered for Leicester at the general election of 1826 and declared his admiration for the 'liberal line of policy' recently espoused by the Liverpool ministry's foreign secretary Canning. Given his willingness to compromise on the Catholic question, he was more acceptable to the Tory corporation than his rival, the reformer William Evans*. A coalition was proposed to exclude Evans and return Otway Cave with Charles Abney Hastings*, the corporation candidate. 'In the purity of his intentions', according to William Gardiner, he initially rejected this proposition, but, when pressed by his friends, he conceded that it was the only way of avoiding defeat. His equivocation over the Catholic question left him open to satire: Thomas Macaulay* called him a knight of 'partly coloured armour', and his public pledge not to vote for emancipation earned him the reputation of a turncoat. He repudiated 'malevolent and unfounded insinuations' that he had sold himself to the corporation. On the hustings he declared that on this question he had deferred to the majority opinion of the electors. After a fierce contest he and Abney Hastings were returned ahead of Evans and another anti-corporation candidate. At the celebration dinner he spoke of the corporation's 'zealous and friendly exertions' which had enabled him to 'continue the arduous struggle'; but it was at their insistence that he had coalesced with them, as promoters of Abney Hastings, and their demand for additional election expenses subsequently turned him into their most implacable critic in the House.[8] One report put Otway Cave's costs at £30,000, while William Fremantle*, convinced that he was 'likely to ruin himself at Leicester', had tried to persuade him to pull out a month before the election.[9]

He did not vote in the division on Catholic relief, 6 Mar. 1827. He defended the corporation's conduct against Sykes's call for inquiry, denying that they had 'gone to hedges and highways to select honorary freemen' for the 1826 election, 15 Mar., and he received the unanimous thanks of the corporation for his defence of their interests, 20 Mar.[10] He presented a petition calling for a machine tax from the operative sawyers of Leicester, 22 Mar.,[11] and voted in Hume's minority of 16 for a significant relaxation of the corn laws, 27 Mar. He divided for the disfranchisement of Penryn, 28 May. He presented a petition for repeal of the Test Acts, 6 June, and spoke against the Coventry magistracy bill, 8 June.[12] He questioned Peel's defence of the duke of Wellington against charges of interference with government on the question of preventing the release of foreign corn from bond, 18 June; but had a petition from his constituents censuring Wellington's conduct ruled to be unacceptable, 29 June.[13] He rode out the storm over election expenses and denied knowledge of the 'secret agreement' entered into by his friends, 15 Dec. 1827. He dismissed the corporation's demand for an additional £4,000 as being contrary to the letter of that deal.[14]

He voted for repeal of the Test Acts, 26 Feb., but again stayed away from the division on Catholic relief, 12 May 1828. He divided for the transfer of East Retford's seats to Birmingham, 21 Mar. He voted for attempts to modify the corn laws, 22, 29 Apr., arguing that the Wellington government's measure would tax the 'poor and industrious to fill the pockets of the rich and idle'. On 14 May he moved that the corporation of Leicester be summoned to account for failing to submit a return of their expenditure in accordance with his resolution of 26 Mar.: his object was to show that the new town gaol was 'totally unnecessary' and that its construction would 'saddle the inhabitants with an enormous and oppressive amount of taxation'. He denounced the 'glaring absurdity and futility' of the excuses offered by the mayor but accepted the home secretary Peel's assurances that the accounts would be produced. On 10 June he obtained leave to bring in a bill to restrain corporations from the political use of municipal funds, the 'malversation' of which he deemed a 'flagrant violation of the rights and privileges' of the House. He outlined his own dispute with the corporation over additional election expenses and criticized the 'grievous' rate they had imposed on his constituents. He deplored Abney Hastings's 'want of courtesy' in attempting to present a petition against him on the corporation's behalf, and vilified Legh Keck, whose alleged support of it was at variance with those 'frank and honourable feelings' he had 'so pompously professed' on the Penryn election bill. He warned against the House of Lords becoming an 'insuperable barrier' to reform and dismissed complaints that the bill had been brought in covertly. An attempt to kill it was defeated by 35-10, 8 July, and it passed its third reading, 10 July, but was defeated on its second reading in the Lords, 17 July. Otway Cave voted against the grant for the Society for the Propagation of the Gospels, 6 June, and the Irish assessment of lessors bill, 12 June, and for reduction of the grant to the Royal Cork Institution, 20 June. He supported a motion condemning the misapplication of public funds in the refurbishment of Buckingham House, 23 June, and voted against an excise license for retailers of cider, 26 June. He voted for inquiry into Irish church pluralities, 24 June, and spoke of the country's 'strong feeling of hostility' towards the additional churches bill, 30 June. He voted against a proposal to name and exclude the corrupt voters of East Retford, 24 June, and the modified disfranchisement bill, 27 June, and unsuccessfully moved that the franchise be retained by the freemen in preference to the enfranchisement of freeholders of the hundred of Bassetlaw, 30 June. He presented a petition from his constituents against the Leicester borough rate, 16 July, and in the absence of ministers agreed to delay his proposal to refer it to a select committee. Next day he denounced this 'unjust tax' as one of the 'worst cases of tyranny and petty oppression' ever brought before Parliament. He refuted Peel's charge that he was motivated by party feeling, but was required by the Speaker to apologize for impugning Peel's honesty. He withdrew his proposal but successfully moved for amended returns of the corporation's expenditure, 22 July. He presented and endorsed an anti-slavery petition, 25 July 1828, observing that it was as futile to expect a change in the attitude of the West India proprietors as to hope for 'constitutional freedom from Dom Miguel, or for Catholic emancipation from the present ministry'. He announced his intention of bringing in a bill next session to declare free 'all children born of slave parents' in British dominions after 1830.

Otway Cave was feted and addressed as the *enfant perdu* of oligarchy by the Leicester Friends of Civil and Religious Liberty, 25 Nov. 1828, when, returning thanks, he endorsed their condemnation of the corn laws, but said that as long as 'landowners make the men who make the laws' he saw 'little prospect of their repeal, or even of their amelioration'. He denounced the 'ignorant rapacity' of landlords and warned of 'dreadful acts of retribution, when a starving and despairing population shall be driven to insurrection'. In an allusion to the failure of his corporate funds bill, he condemned the 'crying and monstrous abuses' associated with such bodies:

> Bad as was the political morality of the Lower House, no man of any note could latterly be found in it with the effrontery to stand up to their defence. It was quite otherwise amidst the hereditary legislators.

He spoke of his 'anxious desire' to see a library and mechanics' institute established at Leicester: 'tyrants alone have cause to dread the march of intellect'. He advocated parliamentary reform and the establishment of national associations to oppose the Brunswick clubs. He insisted that he had no wish to see a repetition of the Peterloo massacre, but the time had arrived

> when every Englishman possessed of a heart, should come straight forward and unite and associate ... They should make the table of the House of Commons ring from side to side with long, loud, and deep imprecations against the feudal barbarity of the game laws ... the scandalous monopoly of accursed corn laws, but above all ... against the abuses of this rotten borough system, which have made the House of Commons ... a mere

taxing machine, and nothing better than a branch and excrescence of the House of Lords.[15]

Despite his ostensible neutrality on the Catholic question he received the plaudits of the Catholic Association for his 'splendid services' to that cause in England.[16] At a Leicester meeting, 4 Feb. 1829, he renounced his pledge not to vote for emancipation and offered to resign his seat, but the gathering endorsed his decision.[17] He presented petitions in favour of emancipation, 6, 24 Feb., and questioned whether 'the general feeling of the country was hostile' to it, 16 Feb. He condemned the hostile Bristol petition as a 'gross abuse of the right of petitioning', 26 Feb., objected to a similar one from Clifton because it was 'signed by a large portion of charity children', 27 Feb., and denied that the petition presented by Legh Keck spoke the 'sense of the county of Leicester', 3 Mar., when he alleged that Legh Keck had compromised his independence by accepting patronage from the Goderich ministry. The same day he presented a number of petitions on behalf of Daniel O'Connell* and said that to accompany relief with disfranchisement of the Irish 40*s*. freeholders would justify 'even the forcible resistance of Irishmen'. He presented a further petition in favour of emancipation from the Society of the Friends of Civil and Religious Liberty, 11 Mar., and duly voted for the measure, 6, 30 Mar. He was astonished that Tennyson should consider postponing his motion on the disfranchisement of East Retford as an accommodation to government, 5 May, and he voted for the issue of a new writ, 2 June. He divided against O'Connell's exclusion from the House for refusing to swear the oath of supremacy, 18 May. He presented several Irish petitions in support of the Subletting Act and for the introduction of a system of poor laws. He voted for a fixed duty on corn imports, 19 May, and presented and supported two anti-corn law petitions from Leicester, 2 June, when he also successfully moved for the printing of the return of expenditure submitted by Leicester corporation (though Abney Hastings prevented the publication in them of individual names) and voted for Lord Blandford's motion to extinguish rotten boroughs as a measure of reform, even though Blandford himself intended it to prevent the increase of Catholic power in the House. He attended the Westminster purity of election anniversary dinner, 25 May (and again, 23 May 1830).[18] He was actively engaged in the extra-parliamentary anti-slavery campaign and submitted his resolutions designed to secure the freedom of slave children, 4 June 1829, but was unable to find a seconder. He gave notice of his intention to renew this motion, 19 June, but was warned by a correspondent that it would be side-tracked by the appointment of a select committee to consider West Indian slavery only.[19] He obtained an order for amended returns from Leicester corporation, 22 June, and presented a petition from his constituents calling on the House to restrain them from levying a crippling borough rate, 24 June. At the same time, he took the opportunity of 'utterly disclaiming' the behaviour of 'the opposition side of the House', who seemed determined to impede 'all important business' and stifle 'every inquiry into abuses'. He asserted that the government's foreign policy, culminating in the Terceira incident, was a 'stain on the honour, and a prejudice to the interests, of this country, that all the victories of our armies never can wash away'. He gave ministers due praise for the accomplishment of Catholic emancipation, but said they had done nothing since to ameliorate distress. Alluding to the defeat of his corporate funds bill, he alleged collusion between 'the leading persons of both sides of the House' and accused 'some opposition Members' of intriguing for office. In August he chaired and addressed a Leicester reform dinner.[20] On 15 Sept. 1829 a dinner was held in his honour at Clonmel, county Tipperary, and O'Connell, though unable to attend, wrote to one of the organizers that the House did not contain 'a man of more pure, honourable, and patriotic mind': Otway Cave was 'one of the most unaffectedly honest public men in the British dominions', who if he became the representative of Tipperary would 'cause the magistracy to be purged, or at least expose the delinquencies which the improper part of them may commit'.[21] He was gaining a reputation as 'a Tipperary radical' and, in the eyes of ministers, a potential trouble maker.[22]

Otway Cave appears to have missed the first three weeks of the 1830 session, but was present to vote in the minority of 25 who divided for Harvey's proposal to prevent Members from voting in committee on bills in which they had a vested interest, 26 Feb. He voted for inquiry into the Newark petition complaining of the duke of Newcastle's electoral interference, 1 Mar., to give East Retford's seats to Birmingham, 5 Mar., and to abolish the offices of treasurer of the navy, 12 Mar., and lieutenant-general of the ordnance, 29 Mar. He presented a petition from Leicester complaining of distress, 16 Mar., and observed that the proposed reduction of beer duties 'would only be prospectively beneficial', whereas the problem was 'urgent' and required a 'direct remedy'. The same day he presented a petition from Carrick-on-Suir for repeal of the Irish Vestry Act, and he voted for O'Connell's motion for a bill to amend it, 27 Apr. He voted for an explanation of British foreign policy in Portugal, 10

Mar., and in condemnation of the violation of sovereignty in the Terceira episode, 28 Apr. He divided for Jewish emancipation, 5 Apr., 17 May, against the grant for the Royal Military Academy, 30 Apr., and to abolish the lord lieutenancy of Ireland, 11 May. He presented petitions from Sussex against the sale of beer bill and from Leicestershire complaining of distress and calling for parliamentary reform, 4 May. At the Westminster meeting called to petition against renewal of the East India Company's charter, 8 May, he moved the first resolution against its 'most mischievous monopoly'.[23] He presented anti-slavery petitions, 12, 17 May, when he also presented petitions for mitigation of the punishment for forgery, reform of the Marriage Act and a revision of the law of landlord and tenant. He divided in the minority of 12 for inquiry into the preparation of criminal cases for trial in Ireland, 12 May, and voted for a re-evaluation of Irish first fruits in order to prevent 'additional charge on the people', 18 May. He presented petitions censuring the 'wasteful expenditure' of Londonderry corporation, 21 May, gave notice of motions to prevent the misappropriation of corporate funds for electioneering purposes, 27 May, 11 June, and spoke in the debate on Irish corporations, 16 July. He voted for reform of the divorce laws, 3 June, paired in favour of abolition of the death penalty for forgery, 24 May, and voted thus, 7 June, and opposed increased recognizances for publishers and printers, 6, 9 July. He defended the efforts of the inhabitants of Rye to protect their harbour from despoliation by neighbouring landowners, 27 May, and condemned the introduction of troops by the magistrate, arguing that the borough patron wished to 'keep the people as poor and as dependent as possible', for 'if they were in comfortable and affluent circumstances, they might prove a little troublesome in the assertion of their rights'. On 16 July he repeated the allegation that the petition of Rye corporation against the Commons election committee's decision in favour of a ratepayer franchise there (which had secured the seat for de Lacy Evans, 17 May) was supported by the treasury. He supported inquiry into the administration of justice among slaves in the colonies, 13 July, and pledged himself to 'disprove the many false assertions that have been made on the subject of colonial slavery'. He trusted that at the forthcoming general election all electors would 'vindicate their national character' by supporting abolitionists irrespective of party considerations. He presented anti-slavery petitions, 16, 20 July, when he stated his intention of taking the issue further in the next session and confirmed that he had no confidence in ministers in consequence of their foreign and domestic policies.

He was a rumoured candidate for Hastings and Hertford in the weeks before the general election of 1830, but nothing came of the latter speculation.[24] He declined an invitation to stand for county Tipperary as an 'independent', since in an unreformed Parliament it was impossible for 'popular representatives' to have a beneficial impact on Irish affairs. He repudiated violence and pledged himself to assist in the recovery of Irish 'lawful rights' from the 'road-jobbing and ruffian magistrates who first robs you, and then tramples upon you, or from the cess ... you pay for ... the support of a faction against a nation'. He did not seek re-election at Leicester and declined to be put in nomination by the 'really independent electors', since he was already under an 'obligation' to the disgruntled ratepayers of Hastings, where he was defeated by the treasury nominees.[25] His subsequent petition against the return was unsuccessful. In his address to the Leicester electors, 2 Aug. 1830, he condemned the 'filthy and contaminating petty factions' of government and commended the ballot as the 'only sufficient check on the undue and immoral influence of wealth'.[26] At the general election of 1831 he was proposed as a candidate for Leicestershire by his future father-in-law Burdett, but he withdrew when Thomas Paget* refused to give way.[27] He made a futile bid to overthrow the Buckingham interest at St. Mawes.

Otway Cave maintained his interest in the appropriation of Irish church revenues, the anti-slavery movement and the reform of municipal corporations. He was returned unopposed for Tipperary on a vacancy, 8 Aug. 1832, and was sworn in on the 16th, the last day of the unreformed Commons. In October O'Connell was 'sure' of his allegiance to the repeal pledge, but he did not stand at the general election of 1832.[28] On his marriage to Sophia Burdett that autumn he received a portion of £30,000. He was returned again for Tipperary in 1835, determined to defy the Conservatives or 'any opponent of any party to the popular cause' and held the seat until his death, in his mother's lifetime, in November 1844.[29] On Lady Braye's death in 1862 the barony again fell into abeyance until it was restored to her only surviving daughter Henrietta Wyatt Edgell and her issue in 1879.

[1] IGI. [2] *Gent. Mag.* (1832), ii. 472. *Burke PB* erroneously gives 23 Oct. 1833. [3] *Gent. Mag.* (1845), i. 665. [4] Leics. RO, Braye mss 23D57 3524-6; *Leicester Jnl.* 17 Mar. 1820. [5] Braye mss 3528-32. [6] Ibid. 3542. [7] Ibid. 3536. [8] *Leicester Jnl.* 5, 12 May, 2, 9, 16, 23, 30 June 1826; W. Gardiner, *Music and Friends*, ii. 627; *Leicester Borough Recs.* vii. 403-4. [9] *Baring Jnls.* i. 46; Bucks. RO, Fremantle mss D/FR/138/16/7. [10] *Leicester Borough Recs.* v. 474. [11] *The Times*, 23 Mar. 1827. [12] Ibid. 7, 9 June 1827. [13] Ibid. 30 June 1827. [14] Braye mss 3464, 3465. [15] Ibid. 3502; *Leicester Chron.* 28 Nov. 1828. [16] Braye mss 3510. [17] *Leicester Chron.* 7 Feb. 1829 [18] Add. 56554, f. 17; *Nottingham*

Rev. 28 May 1830. [19] Braye mss 3512, 3513, 3513d. [20] *Leicester Chron.* 8 Aug. 1829. [21] *O'Connell Corresp.* iv. 1606. [22] Add. 40327, f. 55; PRO NI Pack-Beresford mss D664/A/102, Meara to Primate Beresford, 7 Oct. 1829. [23] Add. 56554, f. 96; *The Times*, 10 May 1830. [24] Hatfield House mss 2M, Nicholson to Salisbury, 29 Apr. 1830; NLW, Ormathwaite mss G37, f. 3. [25] Braye mss 3491, 3492, 3511. [26] *Leicester Jnl.* 6 Aug. 1830. [27] Ibid. 13 May 1831. [28] *O'Connell Corresp.* iv. 1929. [29] Braye mss 3513; *Gent. Mag.* (1845), i. 201; PROB 11/2010/19; IR26/1700/33.

S.R.H.

OWEN, Sir Edward William Campbell Rich (1771–1849), of Deal, Kent.

Sandwich 1826–20 Mar. 1829

b. 19 Feb. 1771 at Campobello, Nova Scotia, 1st illegit. s. of Capt. William Owen, RN, of Shrewsbury and Campobello and Sarah Haslam of Manchester.[1] *educ.* Chelsea. *m.* (1) 16 Dec. 1802, Elizabeth, da. of John Cannon of Middle Deal, *s.p.*;[2] (2) 28 Feb. 1829, Sarah Selina Elizabeth, da. of Capt. John Baker Hay, RN, *s.p. suc.* fa. 1778; KCB 2 Jan. 1815; kntd. 14 May 1816; GCH 24 Oct. 1832; GCB 8 May 1845. *d.* 8 Oct. 1849.

Midshipman RN 1786, lt. 1793, cdr. 1796, capt. 1798, r.-adm. 1825, v.-adm. 1837, adm. 1846.

Col. marines 1821; c.-in-c. W.I. 1822-4; surveyor-gen. of ordnance May 1827-Mar. 1828; member, council of lord high admiral Mar.-Sept. 1828; c.-in-c. E.I. 1828-32; clerk of ordnance Dec. 1834-Apr. 1835; c.-in-c. Mediterranean 1841-5.

Owen came from a very old Welsh family. His grandfather, David Owen (1700-77) of Cefnhafodan and Llangurig, Montgomeryshire, had four surviving sons. The eldest, Owen Owen (1723-89), was sheriff of the county in 1766 and founded the Glansevern branch of the family. The third son Edward Owen (?1728-1807) was educated at Oxford (where on his matriculation his father was described as 'pleb.'), became rector of Warrington, Lancashire and master of the local grammar school and published, among other works, verse translations of Juvenal and Persius.[3] David Owen's youngest son William, the father of this Member, was born in about 1735 and entered the navy. He served at Guinea and in the West Indies, and in 1754 went to India, where he saw much action, was wounded in the body and had his right arm blown off at Pondicherry in 1760. He obtained a small disability pension and lived at various places in England before settling at Shrewsbury. In 1766 he went to Nova Scotia as private secretary to the new governor, his friend Lord William Campbell†, a son of the 4th duke of Argyll. In May 1767 they toured Cape Breton and Prince Edward Island, and Owen visited New York and Boston. On 30 Sept. 1767, the day before he returned to England, he received confirmation of the grant to him and his three nephews (the sons of his eldest brother) of Passamaquoddy Outer Island in the Bay of Fundy. He visited France and Belgium in August 1768 and two months later was blinded in one eye and facially disfigured in an election brawl at Shrewsbury. In August 1769 he formed a company, composed mostly of Liverpool merchants but including his uncle the Reverend Edward Owen, to settle and administer Passamaquoddy. On 7 Apr. 1770 Owen and a party of 38 people sailed from Liverpool, reaching Passamaquoddy, which Owen renamed Campobello in honour of his benefactor, on 4 June 1770. Among the travellers was one Sarah Haslam, Owen's housekeeper; and with her he had an illegitimate son, who was born in February 1771. He was baptized at Halifax, on Owen's way back to England, 21 June 1771, and was named after Campbell and Owen's other close naval friend, Captain Sir Thomas Rich†. Soon afterwards Owen received a grant of three small neighbouring islands.[4] He returned to Shrewsbury, where he served as mayor in 1775, but established Sarah and his son in a household near Manchester.[5] In his will, dated 6 Aug. 1772, he devised all his property, which included two farms near Llanidloes, Montgomeryshire, and his share in Campobello, to Edward: 'in consideration of the tender age of my son' and 'the unhappy predicament of his illegitimate birth, which deprives him of the comfort, consolation, connections and rights of kindred', the bequest was entrusted to the Rev. Owen, his nominated guardian and tutor. He was to be trained for the navy, in which his godfathers Campbell and Rich had promised to start him; and his mother was to be given 'such pecuniary aid' as the Rev. Owen 'may from time to time judge she may want or by her conduct deserve'. In September 1774 Sarah Haslam, who was later known as Sarah Bagshaw, gave birth to another son of William Owen, who was christened William Fitzwilliam Owen. In a codicil to his will, 8 July 1776, Owen devised to him purchased property in Bedfordshire and Huntingdonshire. Owen, who composed two narratives of his travels and adventures, succeeded in reviving his naval career in 1777, when he was promoted to commander and returned to India. He wrote a second codicil to his will, 9 Aug. 1778, when in command of the *Cormorant*, with 'our little squadron in a line and the enemy to windward also formed'. He survived that encounter, but died in an accident at Madras when on his way home with dispatches later in the year.[6]

Edward Owen was already under the professional care of Rich, and was borne on the books of various ships from 1775 until his actual entry to the navy in

1786. After coming of age he made over his interest in Campobello to his younger brother, who followed him into the service under Rich's aegis. William Fitzwilliam Owen achieved distinction as a naval surveyor and founded the West African island colony of Fernando Po in 1827. He became sole proprietor of Campobello in 1835, developed quirky religious views, expounded in his *Quoddy Hermit* (1841), and died at St. John, New Brunswick in 1857.[7] Edward Owen was 'very well spoken of' in senior naval circles on account of his services during the first phase of the French wars. After his marriage in 1802 he took up residence at Deal. On the renewal of hostilities in 1803 Owen, who was credited by Lord St. Vincent with uncommon 'intelligence and firmness', emerged as the most active officer of the Dungeness squadron.[8] Commanding the *Immortalité*, he conducted a series of harassing operations off the French coast: he inflicted heavy losses on part of the invasion flotilla in July 1804 and supervised a rocket attack on Boulogne in 1806.[9] He played conspicuous parts in the Walcheren expedition in 1809 and the landing at South Beveland in 1813.[10] He was captain of the *Royal Sovereign* yacht from 1816 until 1822, when he took the naval command in the Caribbean. From Barbados, 23 Mar. 1823, he commented to Sir Thomas Cochrane that 'the king's speech is exactly what we had a right to expect, and cannot be disfigured even by all the froth of Mr. Brougham'.[11] He received the thanks of the assembly and merchants of Jamaica for his success in curbing piracy. On his return to England in October 1824 he accepted the offer of Lord Melville, first lord of the admiralty in the Liverpool ministry, to keep his ship, the *Gloucester*, and made himself available for further sea service, though he observed that 'whether I am likely to be so called on in the few years work which yet remains in me I have not the least idea'.[12]

Owen was reported to have broken his collar bone in a fall from his gig, 15 Apr. 1826.[13] At the general election that year he was invited to stand for Sandwich, where he had taken a 'warm interest' in the projected new harbour. His offer to step aside for Melville's son was turned down and he came in unopposed on the government interest.[14] In debates on the navy estimates, 12, 13 Feb. 1827, he argued that impressment and corporal punishment could not safely be abolished. He voted against Catholic relief, 6 Mar., and with the disintegrating ministry for the duke of Clarence's annuity, 16 Mar. He was appointed surveyor-general of the ordnance in Canning's administration on the recommendation of Croker, secretary to the admiralty, who rated him 'a very good man of business', but considered him 'removable with very little difficulty, as a professional command would always be an honourable retreat for him'. His re-election for Sandwich was untroubled.[15] He defended the grant for Canadian canal communications, 14 May, 1 June, and voted for it, 12 June.[16] He presented a petition from Bethnal chapel for repeal of the Test Acts, 7 June, and again upheld impressment and denied the prevalence of 'arbitrary punishment' in the navy, 22 June 1827.[17]

Owen, who remained at the ordnance in the administrations of Lord Goderich and the duke of Wellington, presented more petitions for repeal of the Test Acts, 21 Feb., but voted against that measure, 26 Feb. 1828. He presented a Sandwich maltsters' petition for repeal of the Malt Act, 25 Feb. Soon afterwards Clarence, lord high admiral since May 1827, secured Owen's appointment as a member of his four-man council (that is, as a lord of the admiralty). There was no problem with his re-election, despite a technical 'blot', as Croker noted, whereby it might have seemed to precede his appointment.[18] Owen, who admitted he was 'young in the forms of the House', fell foul of the Speaker in his attempt to raise objections to new clauses inserted into the Dover and Sandwich harbour bill, 31 Mar., but a compromise was reached. He was of course in the ministerial majorities on chancery delays, 24 Apr., the ordnance estimates, 4 July, when he justified from personal experience the need for a lieutenant-general in peacetime, and the silk duties, 14 July. He voted against Catholic relief, 12 May, and for the usury laws amendment bill, 19 June. In his official capacity, he defended the scale of naval shipbuilding, 16 May, the royal yachts, 19 May, and the pay of colonels of marines, 20 May. He supported the Marylebone vestry bill to 'restore peace and quiet to the parish', 6 June; presented a Sandwich petition against the clause of the alehouse licensing bill which permitted outside interference in the jurisdiction of Cinque Ports magistrates, 17 June; carried amendments to exempt the Ports from the measure, 19 June, and presented a Deal petition for the abolition of slavery, 27 June. He justified the grant for military works in Canada as a necessary precaution against American invasion, 7 July 1828.

Wellington ignored Clarence's request that Owen be made a privy councillor, 11 July 1828, when he also demanded the dismissal of Sir George Cockburn* from his council for writing a letter of remonstrance against his assumption of an unauthorized military command. In the ensuing wrangle, which ended in Clarence's resignation, Owen was used by him as an intermediary and messenger. He was the only one of the council who would not have resigned had

Cockburn been removed: he 'admitted that the duke was in the wrong', but thought that Cockburn should have voiced rather than written his protest. At the same time, he conceded that 'in general, affairs at the admiralty were not conducted as the law and the patent ... required they should be'; and he claimed that he had been about to say as much to Clarence when the argument broke out.[19] On the reconstitution of the admiralty board under Melville in September 1828 Owen retired, ostensibly because it would 'not be convenient to him at present' to seek re-election at Sandwich, and was appointed to the naval command in India.[20] In the House, 9 Feb. 1829, he defended Captain Walpole's part in the Terceira incident. He married for a second time at St. Martin-in-the-Fields at the end of the month. As the patronage secretary Planta predicted, he voted 'with government' for Catholic emancipation, 6 Mar., before vacating his seat and sailing for India on 24 Mar. 1829.[21]

He remained there for three years and returned in time to stand for Sandwich at the 1832 general election. Although the reformed constituency included Deal, he was heavily defeated by the Liberal sitting Members.[22] Owen, who acquired and moved to a Surrey property at Windlesham, near Bagshot, was appointed clerk of the ordnance in Peel's first ministry, even though he made it clear that he had 'no hope' of success at Sandwich at the impending general election. Against his better judgement he contested the borough, but finished in third place by 16 votes. Although his initial hopes of securing the seat by petition were dashed, and he remained out of Parliament, he kept his office, at Peel's request, until the government fell in April 1835.[23] Owen's last command, at the age of 70, was in the Mediterranean, 1841-5. His insistence on having with him his wife, who was widely thought to be insane, caused some disquiet at the admiralty; but he acquitted himself well during the Morocco crisis in 1844.[24] On 13 Jan. 1848 he replied in a frail hand to W.R. O'Byrne's request for details of his career by referring him to the official records, and with the comment that 'after 60 years of varied service' he had 'neither health or memory enough to be the recorder of his own adventures'.[25] He died at Windlesham in October 1849.[26] By his will, dated 24 May 1839, he devised Windlesham and the two Montgomeryshire farms to his wife, with remainder to his brother William's 'acknowledged daughters' Portia and Cornelia. He left a property at Gravel Walk, Deal, bought from William, to a former servant, Mary Rigden, and disposed of other small properties in the town in accordance with the terms of his first marriage settlement. The residue of his estate was to be divided between his wife and nieces. Codicils of 24 June 1847 and 11 Aug. 1849 dealt with the consequences of his sale of some of his Deal properties to the South Eastern Railway Company, a purchase of land at Ringwould, near Deal and his relinquishment of his claim on the house of his first wife's brother.[27] After his widow's death Windlesham passed to his niece Cornelia, the wife of Captain John Robinson, who took the additional name of Owen.[28]

[1] PROB 11/1053/213. [2] A.J. Willis, *Canterbury Marriage Lics. 1781-1809*, p. 262. This marriage is overlooked by *Oxford DNB*. [3] E. Hamer and H. W. Lloyd, *Hist. Llangurig*, 81, 100-2; *Mont. Colls.* iii. 233; *Gent. Mag.* (1807), i. 488; *Oxford DNB sub* Edward Owen. [4] Hamer and Lloyd, 103-10; *Narrative of American Voyages and Travels of Capt. William Owen* ed. V.H. Paltsits, pp. x-xi, 121, 151, 160, 163-5; *Mont. Colls.* xvi. 239-58; E.H. Burrows, *Capt. Owen of African Survey*, 1-25. [5] *Shrewsbury Burgess Roll* ed. H.E. Forrest, 222; H. Owen and J.B. Blakeway, *Hist. Shrewsbury*, i. 536. [6] PROB 11/1053/213. [7] *Oxford DNB sub* William Fitzwilliam Owen; Burrows, 217; *Owen Narrative*, 163-5. [8] *St. Vincent Letters* (Navy Recs. Soc. lv and lxi), i. 129; ii. 377, 399. [9] *Oxford DNB*; Add. 41080, f. 94; *Keith Pprs.* (Navy Recs. Soc. xcvi), iii. 2-3, 16, 37, 41, 57-58, 72-74, 84-85, 110-11, 118-19, 127, 129; *Markham Corresp.* (Navy Recs. Soc. xxviii), 128-33, 145, 150-2; *Barham Pprs.* (Navy Recs. Soc. xxxix), iii. 152, 169, 173, 180. [10] Add. 37291, f. 195. [11] NLS mss 2267, f. 177. See also ibid. ff. 181, 193, 195, 215, 231, 245, 247. [12] NLS mss 2268, f. 38. [13] *Kentish Gazette*, 21 Apr. 1826. [14] *Kent Herald*, 25 May, 8, 15 June 1826; Keele Univ. Lib. North mss N111/1-5. [15] *Canning's Ministry*, 156; *Croker Pprs.* i. 388; *Kent Herald*, 10, 17 May 1827. [16] *The Times*, 15 May, 2 June 1827. [17] Ibid. 8, 23 June 1827. [18] Wellington mss WP1/925/6; *Kent Herald*, 13, 20 Mar. 1828. [19] *Wellington Despatches*, iv. 520, 524-5, 528, 537, 622, 628-9; Wellington mss WP1/942/12; 944/18; 945/3; 947/37; 950/29; 951/5; 954/12; 956/23; 958/36. [20] *Wellington Despatches*, v. 7, 19-20, 65-66, 77; *Arbuthnot Corresp.* 116. [21] *Kent Herald*, 19, 26 Mar. 1829. [22] Ibid. 1 Nov., 13 Dec.; *Kentish Observer*, 13 Dec. 1832. [23] *Wellington Pol. Corresp.* i. 605; Add. 40407, f. 91; 40408, f. 167; 40409, ff. 196, 256, 258; 40410, f. 246; *Kent Herald*, 4, 25 Dec, 1834, 8 Jan. 1835. [24] *Oxford DNB*. [25] Add. 38049, f. 235. [26] *Gent. Mag.* (1849), ii. 647. [27] PROB 11/2107/144; IR26/1877/48. [28] *Owen Narrative*, 166.

D.R.F.

OWEN, Hugh Owen (1803–1891), of Williamston and Llanstinan, Pemb.

PEMBROKE BOROUGHS	1826–Feb. 1838
PEMBROKE BOROUGHS	22 Feb. 1861–1868

b. 25 Dec. 1803, 1st s. of Sir John Owen, 1st bt.*, and 1st w. Charlotte, da. of Rev. John Lewes Philipps of Llwyncrwn, Llangynin, Carm. *educ.* Eton 1817; Christ Church, Oxf. 1822. *m.* (1) 12 Apr. 1825, Angelina Cecilia (*d.* 4 Sept. 1844), da. of Sir Charles Morgan*, 2nd. bt., of Tredegar, Mon., 5s. (4 *d.v.p.*) 4da. (3 *d.v.p.*); (2) 28 Oct. 1845, Henrietta Fraser, da. of Hon. Edward Rodney, 1s. 3da. *suc.* fa. as 2nd. bt. 6 Feb. 1861. *d.* 5 Sept. 1891.

Lt.-col. commdt. Pemb. militia 1830; col. R. Pemb. artillery militia 1872-5; a.d.c. to Queen 1872-*d.*

Hugh Owen Lord, as he was first known, could trace his descent from the Anglesey nobleman Hwfa ap Cynddelw to the Owens of Orielton, who had a long tradition of parliamentary and military service in Pembrokeshire.[1] He was named after his cousin Sir Hugh Owen†, 6th bt., whose estates and political influence his father inherited without the baronetcy in 1809, when they also took the name of Owen. His father came in for Pembroke Boroughs on the Orange Orielton interest that year, and the county in 1812, where he defeated the heir of the county's leading Whig or Blue, the 1st Baron Cawdor of Stackpole Court.[2] A two-election agreement between them gave the Blues the less prestigious Pembroke Boroughs seat, while Owen was under age, and he was raised to assist with estate business and join his father (who was created a baronet in 1813 and county lord lieutenant in 1823) in Parliament.[3] In April 1825 he married the youngest daughter of the Monmouthshire Member Sir Charles Morgan, thereafter leasing Williamston and a house in Pall Mall. His income derived mainly from the interest on £10,000 settled on his bride and £10,000 invested in the Morgan estates, including collieries in Monmouthshire.[4] In the Pembrokeshire coalfield, the Owens were developing a colliery at Landshipping and the Llandykevan quarry.[5] At the 1826 general election he came in unopposed for Pembroke Boroughs, where the 2nd Baron Cawdor refused to back the sitting Blue John Hensleigh Allen in a contest against him.[6] He admitted his youth and inexperience and, in his only statement of policy, claimed that he supported religious toleration, but not Catholic relief.[7] He voted accordingly, 6 Mar. 1827. His father was 'mortified' at his 'old and constant opponent' Cawdor's promotion to an earldom in August 1827, and promised the home secretary Peel his own and Owen's 'warm and steady support' when the duke of Wellington became prime minister in January 1828.[8]

Owen paired against Catholic relief, 12 May, and his father informed Wellington, 24 May 1828, that they were both 'constant supporters of ... government in Parliament'.[9] In February 1829 the patronage secretary Planta expected them to vote 'with government' for Catholic emancipation. Owen presented hostile petitions, 13, 16 Mar., and only paired for the measure when his father voted for its third reading, 30 Mar. 1829. Following his mother's death, 1 Sept. 1829, he deputized for his father at the Pembrokeshire meeting to consider the justice commission's recommendations for abolition of the Welsh courts of great sessions, which threatened Haverfordwest's assize town status, 6 Oct. 1829. Disagreeing with Cawdor and Allen's pro-abolition stance, Owen said that like his father, he was for retaining the separate Welsh jurisdiction, but would represent the views of the meeting, whatever they might be.[10] He presented an unfavourable petition from Pembroke, 17 May, and in his father's absence, 27 May 1830, argued that while there was scope for reform, it was his wish, 'and the wish of many other gentlemen, that our sessions should be held in future where they are at present held'. He voted against the bill's recommittal, 18 June (his father was a teller). In August, after the change was enacted, he signed the Pembrokeshire grand jury's memorial regretting it.[11] He voted against Lord Blandford's parliamentary reform scheme, 18 Feb., and divided against Jewish emancipation, 17 May, and the Galway franchise bill, 25 May 1830. His return at the general election in August was unopposed, and in September he was given the command of the Pembrokeshire militia.[12]

Ministers listed Owen among their 'friends', but, like his father, he did not vote when they were brought down on the civil list, 15 Nov. 1830.[13] Family finances were precarious, and in November it was decided that Owen should reside at Llanstinan, which his father had been unable to sell or let. The 3,800-acre estate was valued at £12,000 and worth about £1,000 a year.[14] Though not involved in Pembrokeshire's anti-slavery meetings, he presented their petitions, 2, 6 Dec. 1830. Following the death in February 1831 of the Orielton agent, he negotiated post-enclosure land exchanges for Newport common.[15] He received ten days' leave on urgent private business, 7 Mar. Like his father, he divided against the Grey ministry's reform bill at its second reading, 22 Mar., and for Gascoyne's wrecking amendment, 19 Apr. 1831.[16] Nothing came of rumours that Allen would contest Pembroke Boroughs at the ensuing general election, but the Blues, with Owen's Eton friend Robert Fulke Greville of Castle Hall as their candidate, challenged his father in the county, where he topped the poll after a long, bitter and expensive contest.[17] During it and pending the outcome of Greville's petition, the local and national press made much of Owen's inattention to his parliamentary duties and speculated that his father was negotiating to return one of his supporters, John Mirehouse of Brownslade, for Pembroke Boroughs in his place, as a paying guest.[18] Toeing his father's political line, Owen divided for the reintroduced reform bill at its second reading, 6 July, the enfranchisement of Greenwich, 3 Aug., and the bill's passage, 21 Sept. 1831, but his conversion to reform was said to be 'cosmetic' and his votes minimal.[19] The Pembrokeshire election was declared void, 23 Sept., and on the 28th Owen was awarded five weeks' leave 'on the public service' to canvass for his father at the second election. Sir John won, but had to sell properties in Pembroke and borrow from Owen to pay his bills.[20] Owen divided for the revised reform bill at its second reading, 17 Dec. 1831, the enfranchisement of Tower Hamlets, 28 Feb., and the third reading, 22 Mar. 1832. He was 'absent in the country' when the House divided on Lord Ebrington's motion for an address calling on the king to appoint only ministers who would carry the reform bill unimpaired, 10 May 1832.[21]

From June until September 1832, Owen canvassed Pembroke and Tenby and attended to militia and yeomanry matters. He placed a notice in the *Welshman*, 13 July, to quash false reports that he was standing down or making way for John Jones*, and nothing came of threatened opposition to his return in December 1832.[22] He held the seat until obliged by his father to vacate for Sir James Graham* in 1838.[23] He came second to Sir John in a three-man contest in 1841, and afterwards sought refuge abroad from his creditors.[24] Hopes of financial recovery were shattered by the 1844 Landshipping colliery disaster.[25] Like his father, who sold most of their estates, Owen married twice and had two families to provide for on little more than land settled on his second wife and their children. When his debts permitted, he lived at Cranmore, near Midhurst, Sussex.[26] By recourse to chancery proceedings, interdependent conveyances, mortgages, remortgages and life insurance policies, he was able to clear his debts to stand for Pembrokeshire in January 1861, but he was defeated.[27] He succeeded his father in the baronetcy and as life-tenant of Orielton, Tasmania, the following month and as Liberal Member for Pembroke Boroughs.[28] He lost the seat in 1868. During the 1870s he conveyed their portions under his marriage settlements (some £3,000 each) to his children; and in January 1882 he made a pre-decease tax settlement of £82 4*s*.5*d*.[29] The Varsity Club raised a subscription for him late in 1890 when, 'enfeebled' and after experiencing 'much variety of fortune', he gave up Cranmore and moved to Barnes, where he died in September 1891, leaving everything to his widow.[30] The baronetcy passed to his son Hugh Charles Owen (1826-1909), of Goodwick, near Fishguard.

[1] H. Owen, *Owen and Perrin Fam. Hist.* (1981), 143, 148B. [2] NLW ms 1074 C, esp. f. 52. [3] Ibid. 6106 D, f. 129; F. Jones, 'Owen of Orielton', *Pemb. Hist.* v (1974), 11-32; R.G. Thorne, 'Pemb. Elections of 1807 and 1812', ibid. vi (1979), 13; Add 38297, f. 357; 38298, f. 10; Add 40359, ff. 100, 145, 184-6, 205. [4] NLW, Williams and Williams Haverfordwest mss 6133; *Gent Mag.* (1825), i. 365. [5] Bodl. Clarendon dep. 372, bdle. 2, 374 and *passim.*; *Cambrian*, 7 Mar., 25 May 1825. [6] Carm. RO, Cawdor mss 2/209. [7] *Cambrian*, 3 Dec. 1825, 4, 18 Feb., 9, 16, 23 June; *Carmarthen Jnl.* 10 Feb., 8, 22 June 1826. [8] Add. 40306, f. 284; 40395, f. 92. [9] Add. 40307, f. 135. [10] *PP* (1829), ix, *passim*; Cawdor, *Letter to ... Lyndhurst*; *Carmarthen Jnl.* 24 Apr., 11, 25 Sept. 9 Oct.; *Cambrian*, 10 Oct. 1829. [11] *Carmarthen Jnl.* 3 Sept. 1830. [12] Ibid. 9, 16, 23, 30 July, 6 Aug. 1830. [13] *Carmarthen Jnl.* 26 Nov. 1830. [14] Clarendon dep. 372, bdle. 5, Harvey to Foster Barham, 26 Aug., 28 Sept., 8 Nov. 1830; Thorne, *Pemb. Hist.* vi (1979), 13. [15] Clarendon dep. 372, bdle. 6, Harvey to Foster Barham, 26 Feb. 1831. [16] *Carmarthen Jnl.* 1, 8, 15 Apr.; *Cambrian*, 9 Apr.; *Seren Gomer*, xiv (1831), 155; Clarendon dep. 372, bdle. 6, Harvey to Foster Barham, 23 Apr. 1831. [17] D. Williams, 'Pemb. Elections of 1831', *WHR*, i (1960-3), 42-52; *Cambrian*, 16, 23, 30 Apr.; *Carmarthen Jnl.*, 29 Apr. 1831. [18] NLW ms 6099 E; *The Times*, 3, 10, 14 June; *Carmarthen Jnl.* 10 June; *Cambrian*, 11 June 1831. [19] *Carmarthen Jnl.* 23, 30 Sept., 7, 14 Oct.; *The Times*, 15 Oct. 1831. [20] Jones, *Pemb. Hist.* v. 32. [21] *Seren Gomer*, xv (1832), 26-27, 157, 189. [22] NLW, Highmead mss 3154; *Carmarthen Jnl.* 7, 14, 21 Dec.; *Welshman*, 14, 21 Dec. 1832. [23] NLW, Eaton Evans and Williams mss 289, 5810; Add. 40486, ff. 227-31. [24] *Carmarthen Jnl.* 2, 9 July 1841. [25] *Welshman*, 24 June, 5, 12 Aug., 2 Sept. 1842; D.J.V. Jones, *Rebecca's Children*, 90. [26] Eaton Evans and Williams mss 9863, 9864; Williams and Williams Haverfordwest mss 6885-7, 9367, 21933-5, 25715, 25716. [27] Williams and Williams Haverfordwest mss 1992, 25717, 25718; *Welshman*, 21 Dec. 1860; *Haverfordwest Telegraph*, 2, 9, 16, 23, 30 Jan.; *Pemb. Herald*, 4, 11 Jan. 1861. [28] H. Owen, *Old Pembroke Fams.* 115; *Haverfordwest Telegraph*, 13, 20, 27 Feb., 6, 13 Mar. 1861; D. Miles, 'Lord of Orielton, 1781-1852', *Jnl. Pemb. Hist. Soc.* xiv (2005), 21-30. [29] Williams and Williams Haverfordwest mss 6888, 6889, 17148, 25718-25. [30] *Pemb. Herald*, 2 Jan., 11, 18 Sept. 1891.

M.M.E.

OWEN, Sir John, 1st bt. (1776–1861), of Orielton, Pemb.

Pembroke Boroughs	13 Sept. 1809–1812
Pembrokeshire	1812–23 Sept. 1831
Pembrokeshire	24 Oct. 1831–1841
Pembroke Boroughs	1841–6 Feb. 1861

b. 1776, 1st s. of Joseph Lord of Pembroke and Corbetta, da. of Lt.-Gen. John Owen† of Bath, Som. *educ.* I. Temple 1794, called 1800. *m.* (1) 12 Dec. 1800, Charlotte (*d.* 1 Sept. 1829), da. of Rev. John Lewes Philipps of Llwyncrwn, Llangynin, Carm., 1s. 4da.; (2) 21 Oct. 1830, Mary Frances, da. of Edward Stephenson of Farley Hill, Berks., 3s. 2da. *suc.* fa. 1801; cos. Sir Hugh Owen†, 6th bt., to Orielton and took name of Owen 23 Aug. 1809; *cr.* bt. 12 Jan. 1813. *d.* 6 Feb. 1861.

Mayor, Pembroke 1813, Tenby 1821.

Gov. Haverfordwest Castle 1812, Milford Haven 1821; ld. lt. Pemb. 1823-*d.*

Owen, a lawyer by profession, had assumed the leadership of the Orange or Tory interest in Pembrokeshire on inheriting Sir Hugh Owen's estates. After demonstrating Orielton's continued superiority in Pembroke Boroughs, in 1812 he had succeeded, where his cousin had failed, in taking the prestigious county seat. To retain it unopposed, in 1816 he came to an arrangement for the next two elections with the county's leading Blue or Whig, John Campbell†, 1st Baron Cawdor of Stackpole Court, whose nominee was to represent Pembroke Boroughs unopposed during the same period.[1] The arrangement endured, but Owen's debts and commitments were so pressing by 1820 that he had to sell the manor of Lamphrey for £35,000 and properties in the parishes of Llanstinan and Penally for another £15,245.[2] His return at the general election that year (the last under the pact) was unopposed.[3] Hitherto, Owen's support for Lord Liverpool's administration, whose patronage he requested for his many relations, had been tempered by his readiness to oppose policies contrary to his constituents' interests, and he had acquired a reputation as a lax local Member.[4]

Owen, as a coal owner, had instigated the petitions against the coastwise coal duties that he presented and endorsed, 26 May, 6 June 1820.[5] He was appointed to the 1820-1 select committee on the administration of justice in Wales conceded to Cawdor's heir John Frederick Campbell, who, with their Member for Pembroke Boroughs, John Hensleigh Allen, urged the abolition of the Welsh judicature and courts of great sessions. Differing from them, and aligning with the West Wales Reds, Owen sponsored a bill to make the cost of levying fines and suffering recoveries in Wales comparable to that in the court of common pleas, which he carried through its first and second readings, 4, 5 July. Its third reading was postponed and had not taken place when the bill was mistakenly taken to and read for the first time in the Lords, 12 July. When returned to the Commons, 13 July, it was repeatedly deferred and timed out.[6] His younger brother Edward Lord (*b.* 1781) had speculated in land in Tasmania on their behalf, and Owen wrote to Liverpool, 7 Nov. 1820, seeking a government appointment for him there, but to no avail.[7] He divided with government against censuring their handling of Queen Caroline's case, 6 Feb., and on retrenchment, 27 June 1821, and was criticized in the Welsh language periodical *Seren Gomer*'s review of votes cast by Welsh Members for his absence from the division on the second reading of the additional malt duty repeal bill, 3 Apr., because Pembrokeshire's barley growers so resented the tax.[8] Although absent from the division on 28 Feb. 1821, he remained staunchly anti-Catholic, opposed all concessions, 30 Apr. 1822, 30 June 1823, 1 Mar., 21, 26 Apr., 9, 10 May 1825, and brought up and endorsed hostile petitions from Pembroke, 4, 10 May 1825.[9] He supported the successful Red candidate John Jones, his erstwhile nominee for Pembroke Boroughs and a vehement opponent of the Campbells, at the Carmarthen by-election in June 1821, when his opponent was Sir William Paxton†, a Whig with a substantial interest in the borough of Tenby.[10] In October 1821 Owen welcomed George IV to Pembrokeshire on his return from Ireland.[11] Like many Pembrokeshire landowners, he had difficulty letting land in 1821-2 on account of agricultural distress.[12] He divided for the government's relief proposals, 21 Feb., but for lower salt duties, 28 Feb. 1822.[13] In May he waited on the financial secretary to the treasury Lushington, with Jones, to lobby against taxing 'agricultural horses occasionally used to draw lime and coal'. He divided with government against inquiry into the currency, 12 June.[14] On 17 Oct. 1822 he wrote to the home secretary Peel with the other Pembrokeshire Members to support the magistrates' memorials against the proposed withdrawal of the Milford Haven-Waterford steam packet service. He did not present the petition adopted by the Pembrokeshire gentry that month for a tithe commutation scheme until 8 May 1823.[15] He voted against investigating chancery arrears, 5 June. In September 1823 he failed to obtain a Welsh judgeship for his 'cousin Sir William Owen (attorney-general on the Carmarthen circuit)'. He had informed Liverpool that he was 'particularly anxious to please [Owen] as he has the old title of my family with a very small fortune'.[16] However, in November ministers recommended him in preference to Cawdor and Richard Bulkeley Phillips Grant Philipps* for the county lord lieutenancy made vacant by Lord Milford's death.[17] Owen's vote for the Irish insurrection bill, 14 June 1824, is the only evidence of his attendance that session. In October, John Harvey, Joseph Foster Barham's* Pembrokeshire agent, noted that 'Sir John Owen and the trustees of [Milford's heir] Mr. Grant Philipps are negotiating some exchanges in Morvil parish Castlemartin, and it is expected that some part of the Llanstinan estate must come into value'; but no quick settlement was reached.[18] Having received a month's leave on urgent private business, 17 Feb. 1825, in March Owen became a director of the Pembrokeshire Slate and Iron Company, which had Jones as chairman and assets 'of £50,000 in 2,000 £25 shares', and caused 'a little *bustle* about Narberth'. According to Harvey, 'their principal object seems to have been the quarries on Sir John Owen's estates'. He cautioned Foster Barham against investing in the concern without a 'scientific survey' and predicted that the venture would fail unless served by a new railroad to Owen's colliery at Landshipping.[19] Plans to operate the latter in conjunction with the mines of the Morgans of Tredegar featured in the marriage settlement that Owen negotiated in April 1825 for his eldest son Hugh and the Monmouthshire Member

Sir Charles Morgan's daughter.[20] Owen applied again to Peel for favours,[21] and in the closing months of 1825 he introduced Hugh to the corporations of Pembroke and Tenby as a prospective parliamentary candidate and encouraged gentry intervention to restore confidence in the Haverfordwest bank, Phillips and Company, which suspended payment, 21 Dec. 1825.[22] Allen campaigned hard to keep his seat and the Grevilles of Castle Hall spent money at Milford, but Cawdor raised no opposition to Hugh Owen Owen's election for Pembroke Boroughs in 1826, and Owen's own election passed off quietly.[23] When he confirmed his anti-Catholic politics at the dinner afterwards,[24] according to *The Times*, the sheriff, Peel's kinsman Jonathan Haworth Peel of Cotts, called for a meeting one year hence to defray Owen's election expenses and bring him in 'free, in the true sense of the word'. It did not take place.[25]

Owen commanded the Castlemartin yeomanry cavalry, last deployed during the French invasion of 1797, to suppress a corn riot in Fishguard in January 1827, when agriculture and quarrying were depressed and his own venture temporarily closed.[26] He voted against Catholic relief, 6 Mar., and received a month's leave on urgent private business, 16 Mar., after serving on an election committee. The quarry reopened, but Harvey observed that 'few countesses [slates] are made' and 'I do not calculate that the produce as yet pays the expense'. Industrial disputes at the quarry persisted and his brother Edward Lord's return from Tasmania also posed financial problems.[27] Though glad to secure a commission in the dragoons for a constituent in August 1827, Owen could not hide his resentment at Cawdor's promotion to an earldom. He wrote to Peel:

> It is certainly mortifying to me to find that after opposing him for more than 15 years at a considerable sacrifice of money, ease and comfort, and after beating him out of every chance of political interest in this county, he is rewarded by his friends with more than he could reasonably have expected if by success he had done them any service, and at the same time by the elevation of my opponent in the scale of rank and consequence my difficulties in contending with him are proportionately increased. It is almost enough to induce me to give up the contest in despair, but I will nevertheless persevere in maintaining the influence of the right party in this county; hoping that by similar exertions in the other parts of the kingdom, the government will be restored to those in whom we confide and trusting that on their return to power they will not think it either wise or just to permit all the weight of permanent rank in this country to continue so exclusively on the side of their opponents.[28]

He offered Peel, on his return to office in January 1828, the 'warm and steady support both of my son and myself', and promised that he 'would not on any account be absent from the House when any subject of consequence to the government is likely to be brought forward'. However, he remained bitter at Cawdor's elevation.[29] He presented a petition, 21 Feb., and voted for repeal of the Test Acts, 26 Feb., when he brought up a petition from Pembrokeshire maltsters for repeal of the 1827 Malt Act. He wrote again to Peel, 2 Mar., supporting Jones's applications for legal preferment, but to no avail.[30] As a patron of the St. David's Benevolent Society, he brought up several petitions against the friendly societies regulation bill from small Pembrokeshire societies, 2 May.[31] He presented others that day from Haverfordwest and Pembroke opposing Catholic relief (against which he voted, 12 May), and from the gentry, merchants and landowners of Tasmania for an elective assembly and trial by jury. Forwarding to Sir George Murray* Owen's request that his brother be made registrar of the supreme court in New South Wales, 24 May, Peel added: 'He with his son have been constant supporters of ... government in Parliament. It would be very desirable to oblige Sir John Owen when a favourable opportunity may offer'. His many nominations that summer for vacancies in the Welsh courts, whose abolition Peel had already decided on, were immediately rejected.[32]

In February 1829, the patronage secretary Planta expected Owen and his son to vote 'with government' for Catholic emancipation, but opinion in Pembrokeshire remained hostile despite Cawdor's efforts to obtain favourable petitions.[33] Owen presented unfavourable ones, 12 Mar., and delayed voting for the measure until its third reading, 30 Mar. The bells were rung at Pembroke on his return from Parliament.[34] He could not attend the Pembrokeshire meeting on the proposed abolition of the Welsh judicature, 6 Oct. 1829, on account of his wife's death, but he let it be known that he was against the proposed change although he would accede to the views of the meeting. (They adopted an unfavourable petition.)[35] Presenting it, 9 Mar. 1830, he claimed that most of the gentry and freeholders were among its 1,900 signatories and that abolition would not, as others claimed, assist commerce, and would more than double legal costs. He also confirmed the Pembrokeshire magistrates' opposition to the prospect of transferring assize business from Haverfordwest to Carmarthen and joined in the clamour (which succeeded) to postpone the bill's committee stage to give magistrates at the spring assizes an opportunity to express their views.[36] He presented further hostile petitions before the bill's second reading, 27 Apr., and countered the attorney-general's arguments that Wales was short of suitable persons to serve as sheriff and that the Welsh had requested the change. Opposing the bill's recommittal as a minority teller, 18 June, he agreed that it might 'improve the administration of justice in England [but] I do not think it is a reason why the interests and advantages of ... Wales should be sacrificed to it'. He also pointed to the numerous hostile petitions on the table of the House as more reliable testimony to the views of Wales than the evidence of 'a few chairmen of quarter sessions and some few other individuals' before the 1828 law commission. He voted against Lord Blandford's reform scheme, 18 Feb., and enfranchising Birmingham, Leeds and Manchester, 23 Feb., and presented a petition from Narberth that day complaining of agricultural distress. He divided against Jewish emancipation, 17 May 1830.

He encountered no opposition in Pembrokeshire at the general election in August.[37] It was reported that month that he had turned down his political ally John Mirehouse of Brownslade's offer to lease the quarry, but he was indeed short of money and 'endeavouring to sell Llanstinan for £13,000 ... with the tithes'. He failed to do so, partly because he tried to include Cilgerran in the sale for an additional £4,000. Harvey estimated that Llanstinan, to which Hugh Owen Owen moved in November, was worth £12,000 and Cilgerran grossly overpriced.[38] Ministers listed Owen among their 'friends', but he was absent from the division on the civil list which brought them down, 15 Nov. 1830. He presented petitions against slavery 'from almost every church of Dissenting Christians throughout the county of Pembroke', 9 Dec.[39] He had married again in October 1830, and three daughters were wed within the year. Three weeks' leave on urgent private business were granted to him, 11 Feb. 1831, after serving on an election committee (Perth Burghs), when his affairs were complicated by the death of Mr. Thomas, the Orielton agent.[40] He divided against the Grey ministry's reform bill at its second reading, 22 Mar., and was annoyed at not being consulted when Pembrokeshire met to petition in its favour, 5 Apr.[41] On the 9th he issued a 'long exculpatory address to his constituents' explaining his anti-reform vote. He said that he was 'not an advocate of corrupt practices which I have never resorted to myself', that the census returns of 1821 had no bearing on the current population, and that the county freeholder franchise was inadequately protected. He added that he would be voting against the bill and for Gascoyne's wrecking amendment, as 'I have also a decided objection to the reduction which is proposed in the number of our representatives'.[42] He divided accordingly, 19 Apr. At the ensuing general election he was opposed by the reformer, Robert Fulke Greville of Castle Hall, who was backed by the Blues.[43] After meeting a deputation of his Pembrokeshire friends, Owen declared in his election address, 27 Apr., that he was an 'advocate of a real and complete reform which shall put an end to all undue influence in the representative system of the kingdom, though I cannot be the supporter of a bill which falsely assumes this character', and hurried home to canvass.[44] He already had debts of £67,000.[45] Harvey wrote that his 'attempts to show he is a true reformer [have] lost him some powerful friends whilst others are as easily satisfied with the explanations'.[46] Although he was taunted as 'a turnaround' and a 'true disciple of the Peel school', Charles Poulett Thomson's* prediction that Owen would 'go to the wall' proved inaccurate, and he defeated Greville in a long, costly and acrimonious contest.[47] Greville petitioned, alleging partiality and misconduct by the sheriff. Owen was repeatedly criticized in the press for abuse of church patronage to procure livings for relatives and making the unpopular John Hunter Humphreys vicar of St. Mary's, Tenby. Much was also made of his dealings with Mirehouse, who was accused of creating voters by means of verbal promissory leases, of his votes against the property tax and on Catholic relief and his absence from the division on the civil list. He was alleged to have obtained more livings from government than he had cast votes for them on major issues.[48]

Generally acting with Hugh, he divided for the reintroduced reform bill at its second reading, 6 July, and committal, 12 July, to enfranchise Greenwich, 3 Aug., and to combine Chatham, Rochester and Strood, 9 Aug. 1831. Milford Haven had been removed from the Haverfordwest constituency and made a contributory of Pembroke Boroughs, a decision popularly attributed to ministers' desire to counter Owen's influence in Pembroke and Tenby with Greville's at Milford, and when the new groupings were considered, 10 Aug., Owen reinforced the anti-reformers' argument that the change was politically motivated by asking why the Pembroke Boroughs had not been left alone when Pembroke and Tenby together had over 500 £10 houses. Later that day he voted against making Merthyr Tydfil, Wales's largest town, a mere contributory of Cardiff. His amendment to give Pembrokeshire a second county Member like Carmarthenshire, Denbighshire and Glamorgan was rejected without a division, 14 Sept. He voted for the bill's passage, 21 Sept., and the second reading of the Scottish reform bill, 23 Sept. Assisted by Charles Williams Wynn, he had successfully contrived to postpone consideration of Greville's petition against his return to 4 Aug. He based his case on postal delays between London and Pembrokeshire. Deferring matters further, he also claimed that the sitting Member had less opportunity to prepare his case than the petitioner, and explained that the sheriff could not prepare his own defence properly until after the summer assizes. On 23 Sept. the committee voided the May election and criticized the sheriff.[49] Owen's recent pro-reform votes had been well received, but during the campaign opponents stressed his inattention to its details, and Greville alleged that he would revert to his old colours when the bill ran into difficulty in the Lords. He was again lampooned as a quondam Whig and reformer and for his pro-Catholic vote in 1829.[50] Urging him to 'march with the times' and 'support a reform bill similar if not more liberal than the last', as he had promised, *The Times* attributed his success in October by 1,531-1,423 to the support of Tory squires and the clergy and the assessor's decision to accept the votes of £30 leaseholders and 'verbal promissory voters'.[51] The parties accumulated debts of some £22,000, and Owen sold property in St. Mary's and St. Martin's, Pembroke, and Monkton for £11,000 in December 1831 and borrowed a further £12,000 in 1832.[52] He had a motion criticizing the censure passed by the election committee on the sheriff and the assessors deferred, 12 Dec. He divided for the revised reform bill at its second reading, 17 Dec. 1831, steadily for its details, and for the third reading, 22 Mar. 1832. He voted for the address calling on the king to appoint only ministers who would carry it unimpaired, 10 May, and divided for the Irish reform bill at its second reading, 25 May. He was absent when party allegiance was tested on the Russian-Dutch loan, 26 Jan., 12, 16 July, but had forwarded recent patronage requests to the colonial secretary Lord Goderich.[53] He brought up petitions against the three commotes road bill, 2 Apr. 1832.

By late June 1832 Owen was back in Pembrokeshire attending to yeomanry matters and canvassing. Allen intended challenging him at the general election, but in September ministers decided that as Owen had 'supported government as readily and constantly as any man in the House', they could not put up a candidate against him.[54] The *Carmarthen Journal* announced that 'the reform bill has worked wonders in Pembrokeshire in forwarding the political interest of Sir John Owen'.[55] His failure to vote for Foxwell Buxton's motion for a select committee on colonial slavery (24 May 1832), however, rankled and the *Welshman* complained that he had never atoned for his failure to support the 1824 campaign on behalf of the Methodist missionary John Smith, indicted for encouraging slaves to riot in Demerara.[56] Owen was returned unopposed on the Conservative interest as a 'constitutional reformer' favourable to agricultural protection and sat unopposed until 1841, when he made way for Cawdor's son. At the same election, he outpolled Hugh and a third candidate to come in for Pembroke Boroughs, which in 1838 he had made available to Sir James Robert George Graham*. He retained the seat for life, but his later years were dominated by litigious financial crises, which obliged him to spend most of his time on the continent. The plate and most of the contents of Orielton were sold in 1842, and Owen moved to Taynton House, near Newent in Gloucestershire, but the 5,800-acre estate remained unsold until purchased by Mark Anthony Saurin of Cilwendeg in 1857.[57] Owen's numerous patronage requests, mainly to Peel, were rejected.[58] He was given a triumphal welcome in Pembrokeshire during Hugh's canvass for the county seat in January 1861, but soon became 'hopelessly ill', and he died at Taynton in early February.[59] Obituarists recalled that he had confined himself to Welsh subjects in Parliament. A Tory 'up to 1845', he supported the Maynooth grant, repeal of the corn laws and Lord Derby's 1852 budget. He opposed the 1859 reform bill and switched from Conservative to Liberal to retain his seat that year.[60] Hugh succeeded him in the baronetcy and as Member for Pembroke Boroughs but, with most of the family property sold, there was little left to inherit. Owen's widow eventually received an annual income of about £500.[61]

[1] NLW ms 6106 D, f. 129. [2] F. Jones, 'Owen of Orielton', *Pemb. Hist.* v (1974), 32. [3] *Carmarthen Jnl.* 3, 10, 17 Mar., 7 Apr. 1820. [4] R.D. Rees, 'Parl. Rep. S. Wales 1790-1830' (Univ. of Reading Ph.D. thesis, 1962), 428; R.G. Thorne, 'Pemb. Elections of 1807 and 1812'; *Pemb. Hist.* vi (1979), 13; *HP Commons, 1790-1820*, iv. 702-3; *The Times*, 9 May 1831. [5] *Carmarthen Jnl.* 14, 21 Apr. 1820; *CJ*, lxxv. 241, 279. [6] *The Times*, 5 July 1820; *CJ*, lxxv. 445-7; *LJ*, liii. 293, 296. [7] Add. 38323, f. 105. For an account of the Tasmanian branch of the family see D. Miles, 'Lord of Orielton, 1781-1852', *Jnl. Pemb. Hist. Soc.* xiv (2005), 21-30. [8] *Seren Gomer*, iv (1821), 154, 252. [9] *The Times*, 5, 11 May 1825. [10] *Carmarthen Jnl.* 29 June, 6, 13 July 1821. [11] Ibid. 12 Oct. 1821. [12] NLW, Lucas mss 3083, 3086, 3087. [13] *Seren Gomer*, v (1822), 91, 124. [14] *Carmarthen Jnl.* 10 May 1822. [15] Add. 40352, f. 72; *Carmarthen Jnl.* 20 Sept. 1822; *The Times*, 9 May 1823. [16] Add. 38576, f. 10. [17] Add. 38297, f. 357; 38298, f. 10; 40359, ff. 100, 145, 184-6, 205. [18] Bodl. Clarendon dep. 372, bdle. 2, Harvey to Foster Barham, 30 Oct 1824, 18 June 1825. [19] *Cambrian*, 7 Mar. 1825; Clarendon dep. 372, bdle. 2, Harvey to Foster Barham, 25 May, 5 July 1825; 374, bdle. 2, *passim*. [20] NLW, Williams and Williams Haverfordwest mss 6133. [21] Add. 40383, ff. 104-6. [22] Ibid.; Lucas mss 1232; *Cambrian*, 3, 31 Dec. 1825, 7 Jan. 1826. [23] *Cambrian*, 4, 18 Feb.; *Carmarthen Jnl.* 9 June 1826; Rees, 303, 427. [24] *Cambrian*, 24 June 1826. [25] *The Times*, 28 June 1826. [26] Clarendon dep. 372, bdle. 2, Harvey to Foster Barham, c. 20 Jan. 1827; *Carmarthen Jnl.* 19, 25 Jan., 20 Apr. 1827. [27] Clarendon dep. 372, bdle. 2, Harvey to Foster Barham, 9 June, 7 July 1827; Miles, 28.

[28] Add. 40306, f. 284; 40394, f. 225; *Carmarthen Jnl.* 14 Sept. 1827. [29] Add. 40395, ff. 92-94. [30] Add. 40396, f. 13. [31] *Carmarthen Jnl.* 15 Feb., 7 Mar.; *Cambrian*, 23 Feb. 1828. [32] Add. 40307, f. 135; 40397, ff. 231-5; Wellington mss WP1/943/8; 945/5; 949/30; 952/6; 958/13; M. Escott, 'How Wales lost its judicature: the making of the 1830 Act for the Abolition of the Courts of Great Sessions', *Trans. Hon. Soc. Cymmrodorion* (2006), 135-59. [33] *Carmarthen Jnl.* 6, 13, 20, 27 Mar.; *Cambrian*, 7, 21 Mar. 1829; NLW ms 6099 E. [34] *Carmarthen Jnl.* 26 June 1829. [35] Ibid. 11, 25 Sept. 8 Oct.; *Cambrian*, 26 Sept., 9 Oct., 6 Dec. 1829. [36] *Carmarthen Jnl.* 9 Feb. 1828, 12 Mar., 2 Apr. 1830. [37] Clarendon dep. 372, bdle. 5, Harvey to Foster Barham, 15 June, 10 July; *Carmarthen Jnl.* 9, 16, 23, 30 July 1830. [38] Clarendon dep. 372, bdle. 5, Harvey to Foster Barham 26, 28 Aug., 28 Sept., 8 Nov. 1830. [39] *Carmarthen Jnl.* 26 Nov. 1830. [40] Clarendon dep. 372, bdle.6, Harvey to Foster Barham, 26 Feb. 1831. [41] D. Williams, 'Pemb. Elections of 1831', *WHR*, i (1960-3), 42 and *passim.*; *Carmarthen Jnl.* 8 Apr.; *Cambrian*, 9 Apr. 1831. [42] *Morning Chron.* 26 Apr.; *Carmarthen Jnl.* 15 Apr. 1831; NLW ms 6099 E; Pemb. RO D/CT/457. [43] Clarendon dep. 372, bdle. 6, Harvey to Foster Barham, 23 Apr. 1831. [44] *Carmarthen Jnl.* 29 Apr., 6 May; *Cambrian*, 30 Apr., 7 May 1831. [45] F. Jones, *Pemb. Hist.* v. 32. [46] Clarendon dep. 372, bdle. 6, Harvey to Foster Barham, 9 May 1831. [47] *Carmarthen Jnl.* 13, 20, 27 May, 3 June; *The Times*, 14, 19, 26, 28, 31 May; *Cambrian*, 21, 28 May 1831. [48] *Carmarthen Jnl.* 3, 10, 17 June; *The Times*, 3, 10, 14 June; *Cambrian*, 4, 11, 18 June 1831; D. Williams, *WHR*, i. 48. [49] *The Times*, 17 Sept.; *Carmarthen Jnl.* 23 Sept. 1831. [50] *Carmarthen Jnl.* 30 Sept., 7, 14 Oct; *Cambrian*, 8, 15 Oct.; *The Times*, 15, 17, 18, 20 Oct. 1831; NLW mss 6099 E; Pemb. RO D/CT/462. [51] *Cambrian*, 22 Oct.; *Carmarthen Jnl.* 28 Oct.; *The Times*, 24, 25 Oct. 1831. [52] F. Jones, *Pemb. Hist.* v. 32. [53] Add. 40880, f. 35. [54] *Carmarthen Jnl.* 22, 29 June, 6 July, 17 Aug.; *Welshman*, 17, 24 Aug.; NLW, Highmead mss 3153, 3154; Sir James Graham mss (IHR microfilm XR 80), 2, bdle. 14, Graham to C. Wood, 8 Sept.; Add. 51724, Althorp to Holland, 9 Sept. 1832. [55] *Carmarthen Jnl.* 16 Nov. 1832. [56] *Welshman*, 14 Sept., 16 Nov. 1832. [57] NLW, Eaton Evans and Williams mss 289, 5810; Williams and Williams Haverfordwest mss 1992, 9367, 21933, 25715; *Welshman*, 21 Dec. 1832, 24 June, 5, 12 Aug., 2 Sept. 1842; Miles, 21. [58] Add. 40486, ff. 227-31; 40516, ff.110-12; 40518, ff. 39-41; 40524, ff. 315, 319; 40544, ff. 276-8; 40547, ff. 122-4; 40555, f. 250; 40557, ff. 374-6; 40559, ff. 210-14; 40570, ff. 325-9; 40589, f. 368. [59] *Haverfordwest Telegraph*, 2, 9, 16, 23 Jan.; *Pemb. Herald*, 4, 11 Jan.; *Carmarthen Jnl.* 11, 25 Jan., 8 Feb. 1861. [60] *Haverfordwest Telegraph*, 13, 20, 27 Feb.; *Welshman*, 15 Feb.; *Gloucester Jnl.* 16 Feb. 1861; M. Cragoe, *Culture, Politics, and National Identity in Wales, 1832-1886*, p. 63. [61] IR26/2263/274.

M.M.E.

OXMANTOWN, Lord *see* **PARSONS, William**

PAGET, Hon. Berkeley Thomas (1780–1842), of 15 Portman Street, Mdx.

ANGLESEY	1807–1820
MILBORNE PORT	1820–1826

b. 2 Jan. 1780, 6th but 5th surv. s. of Henry, 1st earl of Uxbridge (*d.* 1812), and Jane, da. of Very Rev. Arthur Champagné, dean of Clonmacnoise; bro. of Hon. Arthur Paget†, Hon. Sir Charles Paget*, Hon. Edward Paget†, Henry William, Lord Paget†, and Hon. William Paget†. *educ.* Rugby 1793; Christ Church, Oxf. 1797. *m.* 22 Nov. 1804, Sophia Askell, da. of hon. William Bucknall, 4s. (1 *d.v.p.*) 3da. *d.* 28 Oct. 1842.

Cornet 7 Drag. 1798; lt. 11 Drag. 1800; capt.-lt. 7 Drag. 1800; capt. W.I. regt. 1800; capt. 7 Drag. 1803, maj. 1805, ret. 1809; a.d.c. to duke of York 1803-9.

Ld. of treasury June 1810-June 1826; commr. of excise 1826-*d.*

Paget was the extravagant and immoral youngest son of a peer, whose financial problems were not solved by his marriage to a woman with a reputed fortune of 'at least £30,000', his appointment in 1810 to a junior ministerial post worth £1,600 a year, and an undisclosed 'portion' from his father's estate received before the latter's death in March 1812.[1] He had lamented to his brother Arthur in January 1812 that his greatest wish was to 'establish myself in the *country* free from Parliament and place', but that his salary was 'of the greatest consequence'.[2] Tied by necessity to a political career, he sat in three Parliaments for Anglesey on the family interest and was likewise returned for Milborne Port at the general election of 1820.

As 'one of the treasury phalanx', he of course supported Lord Liverpool's ministry when present, but he is not known to have spoken in debate.[3] He was absent from the division on Catholic relief, 28 Feb. 1821, but was reportedly averse to it at this time.[4] He divided against relief, 1 Mar., 21 Apr., 10 May 1825. His real purpose in politics was to obtain a more secure and remunerative berth, and on several occasions his name was mentioned in connection with possible vacancies. According to the Grenvillite Charles Williams Wynn*, he accepted the offer of a place at the audit board in January 1822 but was obliged to forego it as his brother Lord Anglesey feared the loss of the Milborne Port seat at a by-election.[5] In March 1824 Anglesey wrote directly to the king to press Paget's claim to the governorship of Madras, which would 'make his fortune', but the rumoured vacancy did not materialize.[6] The following month Canning's calculations included moving him to the excise board, as he was known to want 'a more lucrative office and one if possible for life!'[7] Nothing came of this, and in the autumn of 1825 Anglesey was considering bringing him forward at the next general election either for Caernarvon boroughs or Anglesey.[8] In the event, he retired at the dissolution in 1826 and shortly afterwards procured a place at the excise board, which was reportedly worth only £1,200 per annum in 1832.[9] He died at Hampton Court Palace, where he had been residing, in October 1842, and left all his property to his wife.[10]

[1] *Williams Wynn Corresp.* 75; PROB 11/1533/253. [2] *Paget Brothers* ed. Lord Hylton, 234-6. [3] *Black Bk.* (1823), 181; *Session of Parl. 1825*, p. 479. [4] HLRO, Hist. Coll. 379, Grey Bennet diary, 44. [5] Buckingham, *Mems. Geo. IV*, i. 275, 280. [6] *Geo. IV Letters*, iii.

1154. [7] Harewood mss, Canning to wife, 4, 6 Apr. 1824. [8] UCNW, Plas Newydd mss ser. I, Anglesey to Sanderson, 18 Sept., Sanderson to Paget, 18 Oct. 1825. [9] *Extraordinary Black Bk.* (1832), 558. [10] *Gent. Mag.* (1842), ii. 674; PROB 8/235; 11/1971/767.

S.K./T.A.J.

PAGET, Hon. Sir Charles (1778–1839), of Fair Oak, Rogate, Suss.

Milborne Port	12 June 1804–1806
Caernarvon Boroughs	1806–1826
Caernarvon Boroughs	1831–6 Mar. 1833
Caernarvon Boroughs	23 May 1833–1834

b. 7 Oct. 1778, 5th s. of Henry, 1st earl of Uxbridge (*d.* 1812), and Jane, da. of Very Rev. Champagné, dean of Clonmacnoise; bro. of Hon. Arthur Paget†, Hon. Berkeley Thomas Paget*, Hon. Edward Paget†, Henry William, Lord Paget† and Hon. William Paget†. *educ.* ?Portsmouth naval acad. to 1790. *m.* 7 Mar. 1805, Elizabeth Araminta, da. and coh. of Henry Monck of Foure, co. Westmeath, 4s. (1 *d.v.p.*) 6da. (1 *d.v.p.*). KCH 19 Oct. 1819; kntd. 3 Dec. 1822; GCH 3 Mar. 1823. *d.* 29 Jan. 1839.

Entered RN 1790, midshipman 1793, lt. 1797, cdr. 1797, capt. 1797, r.-adm. 1823, v.-adm. 1837; capt. royal yacht 1819-21; c.-in-c. Cork 1828-31, N. America 1837-*d.*

Groom of bedchamber 1822-37.

Paget had used his prize money as a naval captain to purchase his Sussex estate and raise a family, and had attended the regent as captain since 1819 of the royal yacht.[1] His sense of loyalty to his brothers was strong, and to safeguard their political influence he combined his career as a sailor and courtier with parliamentary duties, travelling to London by 'regulator' coach when required and staying at Uxbridge House. In 1820 he was again returned on his brother the marquess of Anglesey's interest for Caernarvon Boroughs, where he was well liked despite his periodic absences from the House and silent pro-government votes.[2]

Paget was required on the *Royal George*, which he brought successfully through severe gales off Dungeness in September 1820, and had little time for parliamentary concerns that session.[3] He voted in defence of the Liverpool government's conduct towards Queen Caroline, 6 Feb., and against repealing the additional malt duty, 3 Apr. 1821. A captain of the royal yacht, he played a prominent part in the ceremonies which marked George IV's sojourn at Anglesey's mansion, Plas Newydd, on his way to Ireland in August 1821; and he was with the king when news arrived of the queen's death.[4] Relinquishing the command of the *Royal George*, 27 Dec., he took charge at Portsmouth of his own yacht, *Apollo*, and was substituted for his brother Edward as a groom of the bedchamber, 30 Jan. 1822. He encountered no opposition at the ensuing by-election, voted as ministers directed, and was said 'always to have kept himself above the level of a good deal of the Court society and to have been always respected' as a placeman.[5] Commanding the *Royal George* again that autumn, he encountered a hurricane off Land's End, of which the king wrote, 'nothing, I believe, but the undaunted presence of mind, perseverance, experience and courage of Paget preserved us from a watery grave'.[6] He was accordingly knighted in December 1822, and promoted rear admiral of the blue, 9 Apr. 1823. He presented the Caernarvon licensed victuallers' petition against excise licenses, 1 Apr. 1824.[7] He had to cancel a dinner engagement with Anglesey and the home secretary Peel the following month because his customary place on the regulator had not been booked.[8] Paget (as previously, 23 Mar. 1821, according to Henry Grey Bennet*) divided for Catholic relief, 1 Mar., 21 Apr., 10 May, and presented his constituents petitions against it, 18 Apr. 1825.[9] A radical publication of that session noted that he 'attended occasionally and voted with ministers'.[10] Never one to delight in his parliamentary duties, in March 1825 he had written to his brother Arthur:

> Damn the ... Commons and H. Brougham more especially, whose twitching cursed ugly mug I could with pleasure have basted when after a second night's debate he chose in the face of almost all his own party to move an adjournment. I only hope the three hours speech he is going to favour the House with will be over before I reach it, which to secure shall first go to see the fool in *Belles Stratagem*. So, you see my dear fellow, about half my time is on the box of the regulator. I came down yesterday and go up again tomorrow, but I have not quite settled whether I shall return home and go up again, or stay for the oath on Friday.[11]

Anticipating a dissolution in September 1825, and with his household office worth £1,200 a year secure, he authorized the use of a draft resignation address attributing his decision to differences with his constituents on the Catholic question.[12] A local campaign to oust their ally, the pro-Catholic Member for Caernarvonshire Sir Robert Williams, was under way, and Anglesey, aggrieved, wrote to his second son Lord William Paget*, 18 Sept. 1825:

> At the most ticklish moment, when a false movement might produce a contest, if not endanger the representation of the borough of Caernarvon, my brother Charles chooses to withdraw himself. This I consider very selfish, and very ill timed, and very unkind, inasmuch as it [faces] me with the risk of an immense expense merely to save himself the occasional journey to Caernarvon, where I

generally take him, and a few trips from Fair Oak Lodge to London by regulator coach.[13]

By the dissolution in May 1826, arrangements were in place to bring William in for Caernarvon Boroughs and Sir Charles, who had recently suffered a 'violent palpitation of the heart', authorized the use of a resignation address similar to that of the previous autumn, and concentrated on his duties at court.[14]

Shortly after the death in November 1827 of his third son Horatio, a midshipman on the *Talbot*, which saw action at Navarino, Paget was appointed commander-in-chief at Cork, liaising with Anglesey as the Wellington ministry's Irish lord lieutenant.[15] The duke of Clarence, as lord high admiral, demanded that Paget should replace Sir George Cockburn*, with whom he had quarrelled, as a member of his council in July 1828 and 'if possible, be returned to Parliament before the session is concluded', but Wellington rejected the proposal.[16] Paget gave strong personal support to Anglesey following his dismissal from Ireland for adopting policies which Wellington considered too independent and conciliatory, and officiated at his leave-taking, 22 Jan. 1829; but he retained his command at Cork, whence he welcomed the passage of Catholic emancipation and congratulated Anglesey on his speeches in the Lords.[17] In May 1829 he publicly defended Anglesey's daughter Lady Agnes Byng against the slanderous attacks of James Smith Barry, for which the Protestant extremist Gerard Callaghan* was ultimately held responsible.[18] Before the dissolution in 1830 Anglesey asked Paget to stand again for Caernarvon, where the debt-ridden William had proved highly unpopular. He initially agreed and a canvass of the leading gentry showed that his personal standing remained high, giving him a fair prospect of success against the Ultra William Ormsby Gore*.[19] However, fears that Thomas Assheton Smith II* of Vaenol would capitalize on his absence in Ireland and Portsmouth, where he had to attend a court martial, and news of gentry defections (4 July) induced him to request Anglesey's permission 'to withdraw from Caernarvon and abstain from coming into Parliament', which was granted, 7 July.[20] He had explained that he needed his household salary and could not be expected to vote against his brother Berkeley or the king, nor could he support 'Wellington and his present cabinet, after, not only their outrageous treatment of you, but their utter incompetence to conduct the affairs of the nation'.[21] Hopes of using the election machinery already in place to return another candidate proved illusory and to counteract the 'considerable dissatisfaction' caused by his retirement and Ormsby Gore's unopposed return, Paget wrote personally to his leading supporters 'with *something like an explanation* accompanied by an expression of thanks'.[22]

Early in 1831 Paget tried to further his errant nephew William's naval career (he secured him the commands of the *Pearl*, *Winchester* and *North Star*) and to heal the breach between him and his father.[23] Anglesey had returned to Dublin as the Grey ministry's Irish viceroy, and Paget briefed him on the role the navy might play in containing an Irish rebellion.[24] His political and household obligations were no longer in conflict and at the dissolution following the ministerial reform bill's defeat Anglesey wanted him for both county Louth, where his candidature had been requested in 1829, and Caernarvon Boroughs.[25] Without him the Pagets stood little chance of regaining the latter, for which he announced his candidature from the *Semiramis* in Cork harbour, 24 Apr.[26] He carried Caernarvon 'gallantly', but the contest against Ormsby Gore proved costly and difficult.[27] Paget's call for parliamentary reform, lower taxes, and the 'king and constitution' had popular appeal, but he had lost gentry support, and suffered by arriving late because of his naval duties.[28] Learning during the campaign that Anglesey's eldest son Lord Uxbridge* was likely to be made a peer, so vacating the Anglesey seat to which Sir Richard Bulkeley Williams Bulkeley* aspired, he wrote in confidence to the marquess:

> If Sir Richard Bulkeley Williams ... feels a disposition to come forward for the county, there can be no doubt that with your support he would carry it, and my conviction is, that you would, looking both to the present and *the future*, do well to give him your interest, provided he will engage to return any friend or relative of yours for *Beaumaris*. If that arrangement is made, and I am beat at Caernarvon, I would not object to come in for Beaumaris; but on the other hand, if you will not let go the county I must at once candidly and honestly tell you that no inducement could engage me to come forward. The various things which are required of me even as a Member for a borough are only undertaken by me on the present occasion to meet your anxious wish that I would do so. But I too well know what will be required of me as the representative of this county (in which I am a stranger, and very unpopular on account of my steady support of the *Catholic question*) to offer myself, and this very day Holland Griffith has denied me his support, giving the *above* reasons for his doing so, the conceding of which question he conceived has been the primary cause of *this fatal reform bill* being brought forward.[29]

Paget secured a narrow victory at the poll,[30] and presented a pro-reform petition from Bangor, a contributory designate of Caernarvon, 25 June. He divided for the reintroduced reform bill at its second reading,

6 July, and regularly until early August for its details. He paired to unite Rochester, Chatham and Strood, 9 Aug., and against giving borough electors county votes, 17 Aug. He divided for the bill's third reading, 19 Sept., and passage, 21 Sept. He had recently consulted Anglesey's son-in-law the duke of Richmond, the postmaster-general, about a petition from the Petersfield area against 'changing the line of the Portsmouth mail'.[31] A medical certificate supported his successful application for a month's leave because of illness, 23 Sept., but he went to the House to divide for Lord Ebrington's confidence motion, 10 Oct. 1831. He voted for the revised reform bill at its second reading, 17 Dec. 1831, steadily for its details, and for its third reading, 22 Mar. 1832. He was on board the *Emerald* cruising at the mouth of the Shannon early in May;[32] but he returned to vote for the address requesting the king to appoint only ministers who would carry the reform bill unimpaired, 10 May. Alarmed at the prospect of Wellington returning to office and a dissolution, he wrote to Anglesey, 11 May, of his

> repugnance to again coming in to Parliament and to entreat you to absolve me from doing so. I could not support the duke's ... government and I cannot afford to lose my groomship of the bedchamber, which of course I should have to resign if I did not vote for the new government.[33]

When the crisis passed, he paired for the second reading of the Irish reform bill, 25 May, and against a Conservative amendment to the Scottish measure, 1 June. He divided with government on Portugal, 9 Feb. and military punishments, 16 Feb., and paired with them on the Russian-Dutch loan, 12, 16 July 1832.

Paget failed to attend Caernarvon's reform celebrations after the bill was enacted.[34] Realizing that Caernarvon would be hard to hold, the Plas Newydd agents asked him to lobby the chancellor of the exchequer for lower duties on coal, metal ores and slate, 30 June 1832.[35] Claiming to be 'ignorant of and inefficient in all matters concerning the interests of the place and above all a perfect noodle if there is any matter to be brought forward in the House connected with the trade and general interests of the Principality',[36] he asked Richmond, who was in London, to deal with Caernarvon business.[37] Anticipating that his opponents at a forthcoming dinner to Ormsby Gore would draw unfavourable comparisons between the 'placeman' and the 'local' Member, he issued a letter in July claiming:

> Though I may not possess the power of advocating the interests of my constituents by my set speeches in the House ... I shall, nevertheless, so long as I have the honour of being their representative, prefer voting in support of their local interests to any other consideration whatever'.[38]

He consistently rejected proposals to bring his sons into Parliament, fearing that it would disrupt their careers, but remained party to family discussions on post-reform representation, campaigned against Wellington's son Lord Douro* in Hampshire, and reluctantly agreed to stand for Caernarvon Boroughs at the 1832 general election.[39] His non-residence and delayed and perfunctory personal canvass augured against his return, and only a direct approach from Anglesey in Dublin, following Plas Newydd's surprise victory at Caernarvon's bailiwick elections, prevented him from standing down.[40] His opponents tried to dissuade Nonconformists from being 'bribed' to support him because he opposed colonial slavery and had allegedly voted to abolish Irish tithes, and claimed that a vote he had reputedly cast for the Irish education bill was one 'to expel the Bible from Ireland ... in utter defiance of the principles and feeling of his Protestant constituents'. His victory (later upheld on petition) was described by *The Times* as a triumph against 'a combination of pseudo-aristocrats and ultra-radicals'.[41]

Paget stood down at the dissolution in 1834 and retired from the household in 1837 to command the fleet in North American and West Indian waters. He accompanied Lord Durham to Canada in 1838 and died of yellow fever at sea off Jamaica in January 1839. He was buried in Bermuda.[42] His will, dated 20 June 1836, was proved under £25,000. In it he asked his executors (his brothers Berkeley and Edward, and friend John Frederick Fitzgerald, formerly de Roos) to repay his debts and become guardians of his children, and entrusted the Fair Oak estate with its stock and household contents to his widow (*d.* 1843) for life.[43]

[1] *Oxford DNB*. [2] UCNW, Plas Newydd mss i. 202, 203; *N. Wales Gazette*, 9, 16 Mar. 1820. [3] Rev. E.C. Paget, *Mem. Hon. Sir C. Paget* (1913 edn.), 84. [4] *N. Wales Gazette*, 9, 16, 23 Aug. 1821. [5] Paget, 85; Plas Newydd mss i. 204-8; *Caernarvon Advertiser*, 9, 16 Feb. 1822. [6] Paget, 82, 91. [7] *The Times*, 2 Apr. 1824. [8] Add. 40365, f. 94. [9] HLRO, Hist. Coll. 379, Grey Bennet diary, 44; *The Times*, 19 Apr. 1825. [10] *Session of Parl. 1825*, p. 479. [11] Add. 48405B, f. 123. [12] G.I.T. Machin, 'Catholic Emancipation as an Issue in North Welsh Politics, 1825-1829', *Trans. Hon. Soc. Cymmrodorion* (1962), 85-86; Paget, 86. [13] Plas Newydd mss i. 215 (copy). [14] Ibid. i. 221-6, 317, 318; Ll. Jones, 'Sir Charles Paget and the Caern. Boroughs, 1830-32', *Trans. Caern. Hist. Soc.* xxi (1960), 86-87; *Paget Brothers* ed. Lord Hylton, 312; Add. 48405B, f. 127. [15] Paget, 88, 92. [16] Wellington mss WP1/941/11, 14; *Arbuthnot Jnl.* ii. 197. [17] PRO NI, Anglesey mss D619/32/A/3/8, 61; *Dublin Evening Post*, 13, 17, 22 Jan. 1829. [18] Anglesey mss 32/A/3/126; *Dublin Evening Post*, 7 May 1829; Mq. of Anglesey, *One Leg*, 222-3. [19] Plas Newydd mss i. 376, 379, 386, 388-91, 393, 394, 397, 402-5, 407, 409, 411, 422, 425, 426, 430, 432, 488, 494. [20] Ibid. i. 394, 395, 398, 410, 433,

439, 443, 444. [21] Ibid. i. 466. [22] Add. 38758, f. 198; 51568, Anglesey to Holland, 17 July; Plas Newydd mss i. 441, 446, 474, 476, 478, 480, 486, 488, 449, 494 ii. 218; *Chester Courant*, 20 July, 10 Aug. 1830. [23] Sir James Graham mss (IHR microfilm XR 80), 1, bdle. 4, Graham to Smith Stanley, 6 Jan. 1831; Lord William Paget mss (held privately at Plas Newydd) 7M/644G/3/124, 130, 153, 154 (1 and 2), 156 (1 and 2). [24] Anglesey mss 32G, p. 14. [25] Ibid. 32/A/3/1/214, 218, 219; Plas Newydd mss i. 565. [26] Plas Newydd mss i. 567, 568; *Caern. Herald*, 30 Apr. 1831. [27] Add. 51568, Anglesey to Holland, 3 May; Anglesey mss 27B/15, 18; *Caern. Herald*, 7, 14 May; *Seren Gomer* (1831), 191; Jones, *Trans. Caern. Hist. Soc.* xxi. 91-94. [28] Plas Newydd mss i. 572, 578, 583, 585, 591-3, 595, 635; vii. 289. [29] Ll. Jones, 'Edition of Corresp. of 1st mq. of Anglesey relating to General Elections of 1830, 1831 and 1832 in Caern. and Anglesey' (Univ. of Liverpool M.A. thesis, 1956), 507. [30] *Chester Chron.* 20 May 1821. [31] W. Suss RO, Goodwood mss 1520, ff. 132, 149; 1450, f. 127. [32] Ibid. 648, f. 85; Paget, 88. [33] Ibid. 1435, f. 138; Jones, thesis, 515. [34] Plas Newydd mss iii. 3673. [35] Ibid. i. 618; iii. 3585, 3659-61, 3666, 3667; Jones, *Trans. Caern. Hist. Soc.* xxi. 92-95. [36] Plas Newydd mss iii. 3539. [37] Goodwood mss 1459, f. 504; 1521, f. 206. [38] *Caernarvon Herald*, 14 July 1832; Plas Newydd mss iii. 3588. [39] Plas Newydd mss i. 73; iii. 3589, 3592, 3593, 3596, 3675; vii. 307; Goodwood mss 1436, ff. 362, 370, 371; 1460, f. 123. [40] Plas Newydd mss ii. 366; iii. 3576, 3578, 3580, 3606, 3610, 3612, 3620, 3623, 3568-70, 3625, 3629, 3633, 3705, 3736. [41] *N. Wales Chron.* 18, 25 Sept.; *The Times*, 19 Oct., 15 Dec. 1832, 5 Jan. 1833; Jones, *Trans. Caern. Hist. Soc.* xxi. 97-98; T.M. Bassett, 'Y Bedyddwyr yng Ngwleidyddiaeth Sir Gaernarfon, 1832-1868', *Trans. Caern. Hist. Soc.* xlii (1981), 129-34. Plas Newydd mss vii. 309-22. [42] *Gent. Mag.* (1839), i. 657; Paget, 103. [43] PROB 8/232; 11/1915/525.

M.M.E.

PAGET, Henry, earl of Uxbridge (1797–1869).

ANGLESEY 1820–1832

b. 6 July 1797, 1st. s. of Henry William Paget†, 1st mq. of Anglesey, and 1st w. Lady Caroline Elizabeth Villiers, da. of George Bussy Villiers†, 4th earl of Jersey; bro. of Lord William Paget* and half-bro. of Lord Alfred Henry Paget†, Lord Clarence Edward Paget† and Lord George Augustus Frederick Paget†. *educ.* Westminster 1807-12. *m.* (1) 5 Aug. 1819, Eleanora (*d.* 3 July 1828), da. of John Campbell† of Shawfield, Argyll, 1s. 2da.; (2) 27 Aug. 1833, Henrietta Maria (*d.* 22 Mar. 1844), da. of Sir Charles Bagot† of Hanover Square, Mdx., 2s.; (3) 8 Mar. 1860, Ellen Jane, da. of George Burnand of Trewin Water, Welwyn, Herts., *div.* w. of W.J. Bell, *s.p. styled* earl of Uxbridge 1815-33; *cr.* Bar. Paget 15 Jan. 1833; *suc.* fa. as 2nd mq. of Anglesey 29 Apr. 1854. *d.* 7 Feb. 1869.

Cornet 7 Drag. 14 July 1814, lt. 21 July 1814, capt. 1817; capt. 1 Life Gds. 1820, maj. 17 June 1823; brevet lt.-col. 5 Aug. 1823; half-pay unattached 1827; brevet col. 1838.

State steward to ld. lt. [I] 1828-9; ld. in waiting 1837-9; PC 22 May 1839; ld. chamberlain of household May 1839-Sept. 1841.

Ld. lt. Anglesey 1854-*d.*

Paget was the heir to extensive family estates and political influence in Anglesey, Caernarvonshire, Dorset, Somerset, Staffordshire, Wiltshire and Ireland. Like others of his family, he attended Westminster School, where his particular friends were Lord Lichfield and Sir Francis Grant. While there he gained a reputation as an excellent athlete, cricketer, horseman and 'crack shot', and lost a few front teeth in a holiday riding accident.[1] His soldier father's affair with Henry Wellesley's† wife Charlotte, for whom he left his wife in 1809, caused a great scandal, and after they divorced the following year his father married Mrs. Wellesley and his mother married the 6th duke of Argyll.[2] Paget joined his father's regiment in 1814, tended him in Brussels after he lost a leg at Waterloo, and took the courtesy title of Lord Uxbridge when he was created marquess of Anglesey for his gallantry, 4 July 1815.[3] Ignoring parental disapproval, at Altyre in Scotland in August 1819, and again at St. George's, Hanover Square, 8 Feb. 1820, he married the beautiful Eleanora Campbell, daughter of the writer Lady Charlotte Bury (lady in waiting to Queen Caroline) and his mother's niece by her second marriage.[4] He had been too young to contest Anglesey on the family interest when he accompanied his uncle Berkeley Paget* to his election in 1818, but was returned there in 1820, when his wife's presence 'added much to the interest of the scene'.[5] Nothing came of a rumour that he would stand for Staffordshire.[6]

Uxbridge remained a serving army officer and, as a radical publication of 1825 noted, he 'attended very seldom and voted with ministers' in his first Parliament.[7] He divided with the Liverpool government on the Queen Caroline affair, 6 Feb. 1821, but the issue must have caused him unease, for his mother-in-law had been a witness for the queen, and his father had been threatened by a mob after supporting the bill of pains and penalties in the Lords.[8] He divided with ministers against the malt duty repeal bill, 3 Apr. 1821. On 13 Feb. 1822, making his maiden speech on Sir Robert Wilson's* dismissal from the army for forcing a way through the City at the queen's funeral, he demonstrated the weakness of the inquest evidence used against Wilson, for a 'number of men were ready to go up in a body before the coroner and swear that he, Uxbridge, was the man who shot one of the persons who fell, when it was notorious that he was more than 200 miles from the spot at the time'. He voted against abolishing one of the joint-postmasterships, 13 Mar. 1822, and repealing taxes on houses rated below £5, 10 Mar. 1823. He wrote to the home secretary Peel, 8 Feb. 1824, supporting the application of his wife's brother-in-law, Sir William Gordon Cumming*, for the lord lieutenancy of Nairnshire, but to no avail.[9] His votes to outlaw the Catholic Association, 25 Feb., and against Catholic claims, 1 Mar., 21 Apr 1825, were welcomed in North Wales, but his general neglect of local interests and absence from the county races he should have stewarded in August 1825 encouraged plots to oust him at the next election.[10] It was a time of marital crisis, and he and his wife planned to separate. One observer reported: 'She is to live with her brother Mr. Campbell. Their respective tempers is the reason assigned to the public. I fancy she has been very common lately. Henry Vyner I hear is the favourite'.[11] His father already faced problems managing his interests in Caernarvonshire and its Boroughs, and to ease matters he informed his North Wales friends:

> Uxbridge will start for Anglesey where he *deserves* to be kicked out. My friends there are really most kind in tolerating him, for he has sadly neglected them. I hope, however, they will continue to tolerate him in the hope of reformation. ... He really did mean to pass this autumn there, and will still go, but I believe he did not like to appear in public whilst the business of the separation of himself and his wife was in the height of *buz* and therefore he has rather delayed his journey there.[12]

Uxbridge indeed attended the Beaumaris Hunt week in November with his brother William and uncle Berkeley, and he was the chief mourner at his brother Arthur's funeral in January 1826.[13] The strategy succeeded. He presented Anglesey's petition in favour of the usury laws repeal bill, 15 Apr. 1826, and came in unopposed, at a cost of £388 10*s*., at the general election in June. Afterwards he joined his regiment at Loughborough, where they had been 'halted on account of the riots at Leicester'.[14]

He and his brother William, who had come in for Caernarvon Boroughs, voted against Catholic relief, 6 Mar. 1827. He was excused attendance later that month on account of his wife's illness – an excuse which, though genuine, provoked much laughter.[15] His father declined joining in the party forming against Canning, but Uxbridge voted against the corn bill, which they disliked, 2 Apr. Sir Richard Hussey Vivian*, in an endeavour to influence Anglesey, now suggested offering Uxbridge, who lived beyond his means, a position in the royal household; but nothing materialized.[16] He went to Beaumaris as comptroller of the hunt in November 1827, presented his constituents' petitions for repeal of the Test Acts, 25 Feb. 1828, and divided with the Wellington ministry against the measure the following day.[17] Anglesey, whom they appointed lord lieutenant of Ireland that month, made Uxbridge his steward. He was unopposed at the ensuing by-election.[18] It was erroneously reported that it was Uxbridge, not his pro-Catholic brother-Catholic William, who attended a Catholic Association meeting, 19 Apr. 1828.[19] Their differing views on the issue were confirmed when Uxbridge divided against and William for relief, 12 May.[20] Retrospectively, Anglesey wrote to Uxbridge, 9 Aug. 1831:

> So far from wishing to control your and your brother's opinion upon the great question of emancipation, a subject upon which I was peculiarly interested, I allowed you both to quit me, without ever ascertaining what course you meant to pursue.[21]

He paid more attention to politics after his wife died in July 1828, and spent more time at his mother's cottage at Halnaker, which was conveniently close to his brother-in-law the 5th duke of Richmond's seat at Goodwood, where he kept his best racing horses.[22] Ministers anticipated his opposition to the principle of the Catholic emancipation bill, and this proved popular in Anglesey, whose hostile petitions he presented, 16 Feb., 18 Mar. 1829.[23] He referred on the former occasion to his 'serious regret' at Wellington's conversion, alleging that he had 'deceived both Catholics and Protestants', and complained at the underhand measures used to procure Anglesey's dismissal from Ireland, especially the use made of his correspondence with Dr. Curtis. Opposing the relief bill, 6 Mar., and backed by Sir Richard Vyvyan, he criticized Peel for deserting the principles he had professed when refusing to serve under Canning; but Peel retaliated by pointing to William and Anglesey's 'conversion'. Uxbridge again defended his father and criticized Members who had broken election pledges on emancipation, 9 Mar. He presented anti-Catholic petitions from several places in Ireland, 3, 13 Mar., opposed adjourning the debate on securities, 24 Mar., and explained when the Irish freeholders' qualification was considered, 26 Mar.:

> I opposed this bill because I considered it altogether unnecessary. We have been told that this forty shilling franchise has been used to promote the success of an ulterior object – emancipation. But now as that object is about being attained, the inducement for such an abuse of the franchise will no longer exist; and I therefore conceive that this bill is quite needless and that there is not the least necessity for interfering with the existing state of the elective franchise in Ireland.

He opposed the measure to the last, 27, 30 Mar., and voted against permitting Daniel O'Connell to sit without taking the oath of supremacy, 18 May 1829. Expressing Anglesey's opinion, he said that the master-general of the ordnance should not be expected to combine his duties with those of the lieutenant-general, and voted against the opposition amendment to abolish the latter post, 29 Mar. However, aware that in doing so he differed from his political friends, he stated that he still had

> no hesitation in expressing my decided hostility to His Majesty's government, from a conviction of its inefficiency, and a general disapproval of its policy, both internally and in regard to our foreign relations; and I am determined to give my feeble aid in forcing upon them every measure of economy and of retrenchment which may be consistent with the well-being of the state; but on the present occasion I must (although very reluctantly I own) give them my support.

He was omitted from Vyvyan's October 1829 list predicting Members attitudes towards a Tory realignment, but was nevertheless among the hard core of Ultras in the Commons who now chose to abstain or vote with the Whig opposition. He divided for Knatchbull's amendment criticizing the failure of the address to notice distress, 4 Feb. 1830, and steadily with the revived opposition until 14 May. He presented his constituents' petitions against the government's proposals to abolish the Welsh courts of great sessions and judicature, 4, 14 May 1830.[24] His father, who almost died in June following a particularly severe bout of the *tic douloureux* to which he was prone, prepared a long letter advising him on family, estate and constituency matters, but it was not needed.[25] Uxbridge's return for Anglesey at the general election was a formality.[26]

Ministers listed him as one of the 'violent Ultras', but he did not divide on the civil list when they were brought down, 15 Nov. 1830, although he had been in the House earlier that evening to present a petition from Holyhead's Baptists against colonial slavery. He presented further anti-slavery petitions, 8 Dec. 1830, 13 Apr. 1831, and others from the vicarage of Clare, requesting equal trading rights for Galway's Catholics and Protestants, 11 Feb., and from Rahoon, Galway, seeking additional parliamentary representation, 13 Apr. In February he intervened to free his brother William from custody in Portsmouth, where, after being honourably acquitted at a navy court martial, he was immediately imprisoned for debt.[27] He voted for the Grey ministry's reform bill at its second reading, 22 Mar., and against Gascoyne's wrecking amendment, 19 Apr. Richmond had informed Anglesey, 22 Mar., that Uxbridge and their brother-in-law George Byng 'attend most constantly and are very eager, and if O'Connell attacks you, Uxbridge will give it to him'.[28] He certainly rushed to defend Richmond, when the Tory Sir Henry Hardinge criticized Lord Grey for briefly considering him, 'a mere army captain', for the post of master-general of the ordnance, 13 Apr. 1831.[29] His was the only house in Grosvenor Street whose windows were not smashed by the mob when the reform bill was lost, and at the ensuing general election he worked to maintain his absent father's political influence, corresponded regularly with him, and canvassed Caernarvon Boroughs, where, after a difficult contest, his uncle Sir Charles Paget, who arrived late, defeated the anti-reformer William Ormsby Gore*.[30] Uxbridge's return for Anglesey was assured despite rumblings of discontent from anti-reformers. However, plans to raise him to the peerage to strengthen the ministry in the Lords heralded a series of delicate negotiations with Sir Richard Bulkeley Williams Bulkeley* of Baron Hill on the county's future representation.[31]

In the meantime, Uxbridge remained in the Commons, where he presented Llangefni's petition to become a contributory borough of Beaumaris, 25 June 1831. He voted for the reintroduced reform bill at its second reading, 6 July, and to disfranchise Appleby, 19 July, but chose not to vote on the schedule B disfranchisements. He voted to enfranchise Greenwich, 3 Aug., and to give Gateshead separate representation, 5 Aug., and paired for the enfranchisement of Chatham, Rochester and Strood, 9 Aug. On the Dublin election controversy, 8 Aug., he denied Hunt's allegations that Anglesey was implicated in corruption and called for an inquiry 'to convince the world' that his father was 'guiltless of the very gross charge thus made against him'. Gratified, Anglesey responded, 9 Aug., with suggestions for his next speech:

> I see you have been fighting manfully in my cause, and have cleverly exposed your adversary. I only regret you had not one more worthy of you than Citizen Hunt ... I will endeavour to sketch what you might say, only saying it in your own way ... That so decided an advocate was I ever for freedom of opinion and action, that very early in life, when the late earl of Uxbridge, your grandfather, as a king's friend, asked me if I would have any objection to join him in the support of a government which had replaced Mr. Pitt, I immediately declined, and begged to go out of Parliament, as I could not abandon the person I had supported, and would not oppose my father's wishes, and that I therefore went out. ... That it is well known I placed the learned Member now sitting for Drogheda [John Henry North] in a borough (which you might say, by the by, I without the slightest reluctance abandoned to its fate upon principle) for the express purpose of supporting the late Mr. Canning's administration. That subsequent events produced an entirely different course of politics between that ... Member and myself; but that it had never occurred to me to make even the slightest attempt to influence ... [his] vote ... That I have not an agent upon any property who will not vouch that in the various applications made for my interest, my invariable answer has been, 'Let these tenants know to whom I give the preference, but let every one vote as he pleases'.[32]

Uxbridge spoke as directed on Gordon's censure motion, 23 Aug., and before dividing with ministers to defeat it, he added his own defence of Anglesey's private secretary Tuyll, whom the opposition sought to summon to testify at the bar of the House. Lord Holland, who knew of the activities of the 'active and *guilty* Baron', informed Anglesey, 'I heard much of the debate but not Uxbridge's speech, which handsomely and successfully sustained the only weak point, viz., Baron Tuyll's indiscretion'.[33] In September Uxbridge went to Doncaster races with Byng and they were conspicuously absent from the division on the reform bill's passage, 22 Sept.[34] He voted for Lord Ebrington's confidence motion, 10 Oct, and as 'a Tory turned reformer' was pressed by Lord Hatherton to speak at the Staffordshire county meeting, which considered the bill's Lords' defeat and carried an address to the king expressing confidence in the ministry. Moving the address of thanks to the sheriff, Uxbridge admitted that he was 'a comparative stranger' despite his close connections with the county and welcomed the unanimous support for the bill, offering reassurance that it was only temporarily lost.[35] Disappointed not to be made a peer, he remained in Staffordshire, where the hunting was good, instead of attending the coronation.[36] He divided for the revised reform bill at its second reading, 17 Dec. 1831, steadily for its details, except the schedule B disfranchisements, and for its third reading, 22 Mar. 1832. He voted for the address requesting the king to appoint only ministers who would carry the bill unimpaired, 10 May. He divided with government on the Russian-Dutch loan, 26 Jan., 16 July, and paired, 12 July 1832.

Uxbridge, who was too short of money to go to Newmarket, attended to his absent father's election business in the autumn of 1832.[37] Uncertainty concerning his elevation to the Lords and Anglesey's unwillingness to spend made negotiations for Caernarvon Boroughs and Anglesey particularly difficult, for Sir Charles Paget was ever the reluctant candidate, and there could be no suspicion of a pact.[38] Furthermore, to his annoyance, Anglesey objected to his becoming a peer if this meant forfeiting the county. Arrangements to bring in Frederick Paget for Beaumaris and Bulkeley for Anglesey were, however, proceeded with; and it was agreed that Uxbridge would be called up as Baron Paget of Beaudesert, the titles Baron Burton and Baron Cannock having been rejected. His hopes of becoming a groom of the bedchamber were now quickly dashed.[39] He took his seat in the Lords in January 1833. Uxbridge and his daughters Constance and Eleanora held court appointments under the Liberal administrations early in Victoria's reign, but the queen was said to consider him intemperate and it was rumoured that he kept a mistress.[40] He had been forced to admit to his father before he remarried in August 1833 that he owed £110,000;[41] and in September 1842, with debts of £60,000 and a shortfall of some £3,500 in estate income, he was convicted for failing to keep up payments on seven annuities he had issued. Anglesey was called as a witness.[42] Most of the Pagets' Irish and West Country property had been sold to cover debts before he succeeded as 2nd marquess in 1854. He died intestate at Beaudesert in February 1869 and was buried with his first two wives in Lichfield Cathedral. Probate was granted as 4th marquess to his son Henry William George Paget (1821-80), Liberal Member for North Staffordshire, 1854-7.[43]

[1] *Staffs. Advertiser*, 20 Feb. 1869; *Paget Brothers* ed. Lord Hylton, 86. [2] Mq. of Anglesey, *One Leg*, 89-104, 109-14; *HP Commons, 1790-1820*, iv. 709-10. [3] W. Suss. RO, Goodwood mss 599, f. 6. [4] Anglesey, 161-2; *Lady in Waiting*, i. 346. [5] NLW, Aston Hall mss 5727, 5728; UCNW, Plas Newydd mss i. 8-22; *N. Wales Gazette*, 16, 23 Mar. 1820. [6] Hatherton diary, 15 May 1820. [7] *Session of Parl. 1825*, p. 488. [8] Anglesey, 163-4. [9] Add. 40361, f. 56. [10] Plas Newydd mss i. 212, 213, 218, 223-6, 245, 250, 251, 264, 288, 289; *N. Wales Gazette*, 14 July, 1 Sept. 1825. [11] Add. 52017, J.R. Townshend to H.E. Fox, 6, 30 Aug. 1825. [12] Plas Newydd mss i. 215 [13] Ibid. i. 221, 229, 230, 262, 289, 296, 298, 301; *N. Wales Gazette*, 12 Jan. 1826. [14] Plas Newydd mss i. 25, 343; *N. Wales Gazette*, 8, 15, 23 June 1826. [15] *The Times*, 30 Mar. 1827. [16] *Geo. IV Letters*, iii. 1315. [17] *N. Wales Chron.* 8, 29 Nov. 1827. [18] Ibid. 28 Feb., 27 Mar., 3, 10 Apr. 1828; Plas Newydd mss vii. 265-7. [19] Wellington mss WP1/926/6, 13. [20] *Dublin Evening Mail*, 14 May 1828. [21] PRO NI, Anglesey mss D619/32G, p. 127. [22] *Gent. Mag.* (1828), ii. 92; *Staffs. Advertiser*, 13 July 1828; Plas Newydd mss i. 744. [23] *N. Wales Chron.* 26 Feb., 12 Mar., 16 Apr. 1829. [24] Plas Newydd mss i. 739, 759. [25] Anglesey, 234. [26] Plas Newydd mss i. 31, 32; vii. 267-80. [27] Lord William Paget mss (privately held at Plas Newydd) 7M/644G/2/76, 78 (1); 3/127, 128, 137-9; Anglesey, 294. [28] Goodwood mss. [29] Anglesey mss 28C, p. 1. [30] Ibid. 27B/14, 15, 18; 28/A/53; Plas Newydd mss i. 558, 566, 578-81, 591, 595, 597, 604; vii. 290, 291; Ll. Jones, 'Edition of Corresp. of 1st mq. of Anglesey relating to General Elections of 1830, 1831 and 1832 in Caern. and Anglesey' (Univ. of Liverpool M.A. thesis, 1956), 508, 512. *Caernarvon Herald*, 20 Apr., 7, 14 May 1831. [31] *Caernarvon Herald*, 30 Apr., 14 May; Anglesey mss 27A/114-16, 121; Add. 51568, Anglesey to Lord Holland, 23 May 1831, Plas Newydd mss i. 44, 45, 49, 50, 53, 57, 60-64, 69, 71, 73, 588-92; iii. 3561, 1590, 3603, 3675; vii. 287, 305, 355. [32] Anglesey mss 32G, p. 127. [33] Ibid. 27A/131; 27B/33. [34] Ibid. Smith Stanley to Anglesey, 22 Sept. 1831. [35] *Staffs. Advertiser*, 15, 22, 29 Oct.; Hatherton diary, 18, 21 Oct. 1831. [36] Goodwood mss 1455, f. 493; 1499, f. 190. [37] Ibid. 1436, f. 315. [38] Plas Newydd mss i. 78, 80, 637; iii. 3592, 3599; Ll. Jones, 'Sir Charles Paget and Caern. Boroughs, 1830-1832', *Trans. Caern. Hist. Soc.* xxi (1960), 95, 98-102. [39] Plas Newydd mss i. 74; iii. 3591, 3593; Goodwood mss 1436, ff. 306, 315, 327, 328, 340, 342, 347, 348, 402. [40] *Greville Diary* ed. P.W. Wilson, ii. 206; Anglesey, 309-10. [41] *Holland House Diaries*, 239; *Three Diaries*, 356. [42] *Ann. Reg.* (1842), Chron. p. 337; Anglesey, 310. [43] PROB 11/2194/508; *Illustrated London News*, 20 Feb.; *Staffs. Advertiser*, 20 Feb. 1869.

M.M.E.

PAGET, **Thomas** (1778–1862), of Humberstone Hall, nr. Leicester, Leics.

LEICESTERSHIRE 1831–1832

b. 30 Dec. 1778, o. s. of Thomas Paget, banker, of Ibstock, Leics. and Mary, da. of William Clare of Ibstock. *m.* 18 Feb. 1807, Anne, da. of John Pares of The Newarke, Leicester and Hopwell Hall, Derbys., 2s. *suc.* fa. 1814. *d.* 25 Nov. 1862.

Mayor, Leicester 1836-7.

Paget's Unitarian father was a noted cattle breeder who turned to banking in Leicester in partnership with the Pares family. Paget joined the firm on coming of age, married the sister of Thomas Pares, the future Member for the borough, in 1807 and succeeded to his father's partnership in 1824. He quickly sold out and established the bank of Paget and Kirby in 1825.[1] He became active in Leicester politics as a supporter of 'peace, reform and religious liberty', and at the 1812 general election joined in the unsuccessful radical bid to overturn the corporation's interest by putting up the reformer William Roscoe†.[2] He chaired the Leicester dinner held to celebrate the Liverpool ministry's abandonment of the bill of pains and penalties against Queen Caroline, 29 Nov. 1820, when Sir Francis Burdett* was the guest speaker.[3] A persistent critic and opponent of the corporation and its jobbery, he opposed in 1822 a proposed improvement bill because it was to be financed from the rates rather than corporation funds, and in a series of letters to the local press vilified the corporation as 'a polypus, who lies dead and silent in its native water'. That year he published a *Letter to David Ricardo* 'on the true principles of estimating the extent of the late depreciation in the currency', for which he was denounced by William Cobbett† as 'an empty headed coxcomb'.[4] On 29 Apr. 1824 he was nominated to the committee of St. Martin's vestry, who were pressing for inquiry into the borough's rates.[5] He chaired the Leicester meeting called to petition in support of Catholic emancipation in February 1829, and censured 'boroughmongers' for inciting popular prejudice against it.[6]

At the general election of 1830 Paget, prompted and backed by his fellow dissidents in the borough, came forward for the county in opposition to the interest of the Tory 5th duke of Rutland, whose brother Lord Robert Manners had occupied one seat for almost 24 years. He was not quite accurately described to Lord Holland as 'a Whig ... of the old school',[7] but he received support from the independent Whig county landowners Charles March Phillipps* and Robert Otway Cave* (another critic of corporation corruption and profligacy). In his two-hour speech at the nomination, he was said by a sympathetic reporter to have 'electrified the freeholders in one of the finest bursts of eloquence ever heard in Castle Yard'. He called for abolition of the 'injurious' monopolies of the corn laws and the East India Company's charter, dismissed the 'nostrums' of currency reformers, advocated the immediate abolition of slavery and revision of the criminal code, applauded the 'glorious' revolution in France and declared his support for such a measure of parliamentary reform, including the secret ballot, as would 'give the ... Commons ... the efficient control of the public purse'. He trailed his opponents throughout the contest, but finished a respectable third, having received a vote from 40 per cent of those who polled. In his final speech from the hustings he observed that 'the aristocracy had now found that the people had knowledge, and the power to exercise it', and urged 'perseverance'.[8] At a radical reform dinner in Nottingham, 9 Nov., he portrayed himself as 'the champion of the democracy of Leicester', refuted clerical calumnies that he was 'an infidel and a revolutionist' and argued that reformers such as himself were the only persons who could avert a calamitous upheaval.[9] Chairing a meeting to promote the independence of Leicestershire, 26 Nov., he 'rejoiced in the fall' of the Wellington ministry as 'the death blow to a Tory domination, here, and to the Holy Alliance abroad', and expressed 'confidence in the disposition of the new [Grey] ministry to do good'.[10] He presided and spoke at a Leicester reform meeting, 26 Dec. 1830. At the 1831 general election he offered for the county as a supporter of the ministerial reform scheme, denouncing the 'borough mongers' who had prospered from the corrupt old system, in contrast to the plight of the working classes of, for example, Hinckley, where he had seen 'children walking without stockings, with scarcely a rag to cover them their mothers equally ill fed, ill clothed, with every mark of care, their fathers struggling with patient resignation'. He again denied that he was 'a man of no religion, who regards not the obligations of Christianity': 'I am of the religion of my fathers, for hundreds of years'. Burdett, a Leicestershire landowner, who wanted to see his friend Otway Cave in the county seat, privately denounced Paget as 'a blackguard' and 'a pendant to [Henry] Hunt*'. There were public accusations that Paget had tricked Otway Cave into supporting him in 1830 and calls from Burdett and his associate George De Lacy Evans* for him to step aside now, but he stood firm and, with Rutland's brother having pulled out, he came in unopposed with March Phillipps. He proclaimed that 'the path I have chosen to pursue will not be very smooth' and hoped that his constituents would 'not expect too much from one individual'. He applauded the end of 'ducal influence' in the county and promised to support the ministerial reform scheme and seek improvements to it, but not to 'weaken' it, and to oppose 'all unnecessary expenditure of the public money'.[11]

Paget voted for the second reading of the reintroduced reform bill, 6 July 1831, and divided steadily for most but not all of its details. He was in the minority for the disfranchisement of Saltash, 26 July. On 30 June he had given notice that he would move an instruction to the committee against the proposed division of counties. He advocated this 'crotchet' at a party meeting at Lord Althorp's*, 11 July, and duly voted in the minority on the issue, 11 Aug.[12] He voted with other radicals for the disfranchisement of Aldborough, 14 Sept. He divided for the third reading, 19, and passage of the bill, 21 Sept. He condemned the misapplication of corporate funds, 27 June, and alluded to Leicester corporation's record of trying to 'smother the elective franchise'. He favoured 'equalizing the operation' of the poor laws, 28 June. He wanted relaxation of the 1830 Sale of Beer Act, because it confined the trade to the 'lowest description of dealers', 30 June. On 1 July he approved the import duty on Russian tallow, called for repeal of that on soap, as 'injurious to both health and industry', and complained of the deficiencies in public accounts, recommending their presentation in a 'simple and intelligible manner'. He was in small minorities against the grants for university professors' salaries, 8 July, civil list services, 18 July, and the Society for Propagation of the Gospels in the colonies, 25 July, and next day demanded the 'utmost economy' in every branch of expenditure. He was in minorities for swearing the Dublin election committee, 29 July, and postponement of the new writ, 8 Aug., but he sided with government in the division on the controversy, 23 Aug. He voted for printing the Waterford petition for disarming the Irish yeomanry, 11 Aug. He advocated reform of the game laws, 8 Aug., and sought amelioration of the penal clauses in the government's bill, 2 Sept. He said he was prepared to swallow the Lords' amendments to secure the measure, 30 Sept., but he was listed as one of the three Members who divided against them. On 15 Aug. he deplored the number of clerical magistrates appointed by lord lieutenants and questioned the 'propriety of extending an imperfect system to Ireland'. He voted for inquiry into the effects of renewing the Sugar Refinery Act, 12 Sept., when he expressed his 'unqualified opposition' to Littleton's bill to abolish truck payments and was a teller for the hostile minority. He was named to the committee on the measure the next day and endorsed a petition calling for compensation for wrecked threshing machines, being convinced that machinery 'which shortens labour eventually creates employment'. He initially approved the general register bill as likely to be of the 'greatest advantage' in facilitating transfers of landed property, 20 Sept.; but on 7 Dec. he complained that it was so arcane that 'none but a professed lawyer can understand it'. He was in the minority of 12 for postponing consideration of the grant for the refurbishment of Buckingham House, 28 Sept., but on 11 Oct., the day after voting for Lord Ebrington's motion of confidence in the ministry, he defended their general economic policy and attributed unemployment to a 'deficiency of capital' and, above all, to 'the borough mongering system, the greedy cupidity, the avarice of the rapacious monsters who have preyed on the vitals of the country'. He refuted charges that the trades procession to St. James's had been the work of a 'bloody minded mob', 12 Oct. He welcomed lord chancellor Brougham's attempt to improve bankruptcy administration, 14, 17 Oct. 1831.

Paget divided for the second reading of the revised reform bill, 17 Dec. 1831, and supported the bulk of its detailed provisions, but was in minorities against the enfranchisement of £50 tenants-at-will, 1 Feb., for the enfranchisement of all tax-paying householders, 2 Feb., and for Hunt's proposal that election expenses should be met out of corporate funds and county rates, 15 Feb. 1832, when he predicted that as it stood the measure would exclude from the House all but 'the superfluously rich, or the adventurous poor'. He supported the prayer of a Stamford petition against the imposition of the £10 franchise on former scot and lot boroughs, 19 Mar. He divided for the third reading, 22 Mar. He called for summary relief for hapless litigants in chancery, 20 Jan., and spoke and voted for a reform of select vestries, 23 Jan. When the government seemed to be facing defeat on the Russian-Dutch loan, 26 Jan., some of their supporters persuaded Paget to move the adjournment of the debate on a flimsy pretext, but the ploy failed, and he was in the narrow ministerial majority in the division on the loan.[13] Next day he reiterated his now 'determined' hostility to the general register bill. He was named to the committee on the bill, 22 Feb., and on 6 Mar. repudiated allegations of partiality in the nominations to it and objected to the addition of more county Members. He voted with ministers on relations with Portugal, 9 Feb., but against them for printing the Woollen Grange petition for the abolition of Irish tithes and (with Hunt) for information on military punishments, 16 Feb., and inquiry into the Peterloo massacre, 15 Mar. He divided for the address asking the king to appoint only ministers who would carry undiluted reform, 10 May, and, when endorsing the Loughborough petition for supplies to be withheld until it was secured, 17 May, rejoiced 'at the prospect of the present ministers continuing in power'. He had said as much in a public letter to the petitioners the previous day, noting that the 'tyranny' of 'oligarchy' had 'at last been overthrown' without damage to the fabric of society.[14] He voted against a Conservative amendment to the Scottish reform bill, 1 June. He voted to make inquests public, 20 June, to suspend army flogging, 19 June, for a system of representative government in New South Wales, 28 June, and for a reduction in the barracks grant, 2 July. On the boundaries bill, 22 June, he was in small minorities on the cases of Whitehaven and Stamford. On 9 July he argued against 'interference with the currency' and defended the payment of wages out of the poor rates. He again divided with government on the Russian-Dutch loan, 12, 16, 20 July 1832.

Paget retired from Parliament at the dissolution of the last unreformed Parliament, but he remained a prominent figure in Leicester radicalism. He was elected to the reformed corporation, 26 Dec. 1835, and appointed mayor, 1 Jan. 1836, the first of seven to be chosen from the Unitarian body. He balked at the extremism of the Chartists.[15] He was senior partner in the bank until his death in November 1862, when he was succeeded by his eldest son, Thomas Tertius Paget (1807-92), Liberal Member for Leicestershire South, 1867-8, 1880-6.

[1] W. Gardner, *Music and Friends*, i. 243; ii. 722-3; *Gent. Mag.* (1863), i. 381; R. Sayers, *Lloyds Bank*, 280, 350. [2] R. Greaves, *Leicester Corporation*, 101, 114; *Morning Chron.* 21 Oct. 1812. [3] *Leicester Jnl.* 1 Dec. 1820. [4] Ibid. 25 Jan., 8, 15, 22 Nov. 1822. [5] *Leicester Borough Recs.* vii. 292. [6] *Leicester Jnl.* 20 Feb. 1829. [7] Add. 51835, Goodwin to Holland [Aug. 1830]. [8] *The Times*, 11 Aug.; *Leicester Jnl.* 13, 20, 27 Aug. 1830 [9] *Nottingham Rev.* 12 Nov. 1830. [10] *Leicester Chron.* 27 Nov. 1830. [11] Ibid. 30 Apr., 7, 14, 21, 28 May 1831; Add. 36466, f. 331. [12] Hatherton diary, 11 July [1830]. [13] Ibid. 26 Jan. [1832]. [14] *Nottingham Rev.* 25 May 1832. [15] Greaves, 125; H. Hartopp, *Leicester Mayors*, 194; A. Herman Thomas, *Great Meeting*, 49; *Gent. Mag.* (1862), i. 382.

S.R.H.

PAGET, Lord William (1803–1873), of Plas Newydd, Anglesey.

CAERNARVON BOROUGHS	1826–1830
ANDOVER	1841–1847

b. 1 Mar. 1803, 2nd s. of Henry William Paget†, 1st mq. of Anglesey (*d.* 1854), and 1st w. Lady Caroline Elizabeth Villiers, da. of George Bussy Villiers†, 4th earl of Jersey; bro. of Henry Paget, Lord Uxbridge* and half-bro. of Lord Alfred Henry Paget†, Lord Clarence Edward Paget† and Lord George Augustus Frederick Paget†. *educ.* Westminster 1813-16. *m.* 22 Jan. 1827, Frances, da. of Lt.-Gen. Francis, Bar. de Rottenburg, 3s. (2 *d.v.p.*). *d.* 17 May 1873.

Entered RN 1817, midshipman 1823, lt. 1823, cdr. 1825, capt. 1826; capt. vice-regal yacht 1827-9; half-pay 1833, ret. 1846.

Paget was named after his father's sailor brother William, who had died in 1794. Like most of his family, he attended Westminster School, leaving in December 1816 to join the navy shortly after his fourteenth birthday as a first class volunteer on the *Glasgow*, 1 Apr. 1817. He served on her in the Mediterranean, the home station and the West Indies before being made a lieutenant, 18 Apr. 1823. His father, an eminent soldier and courtier who had been created marquess of Anglesey in recognition of his gallantry at Waterloo, feared that his promotion might have been delayed because of his own lack of favour.[1] Paget served briefly on several ships and was posted to South America, where he was made commander of the *Fly*, 20 Apr. 1825, for her return voyage to England.[2] When a dissolution was anticipated that autumn his father suggested him for Caernarvon Boroughs, where an anti-Catholic candidate was sought to replace Sir Charles Paget. Anglesey now described William as 'a nice lad, shy, but sensible [with a] lot of engaging manners', and added that as the inhabitants of Caernarvon considered it 'a port hardly second to Liverpool', a 'naval character [would be] the most proper person to represent it'. Lord William's candidature was not advertised, but in November he accompanied his brother, Lord Uxbridge, and uncle, Berkeley Paget*, to North Wales for the necessary introductions.[3] Next month he was made commander of the *Philomel*, then fitting for the Mediterranean, and he was on his way to Lisbon when Parliament was dissolved in May 1826. The admiralty was asked to help, but it proved impossible to bring him back in time for his election, 15 June, at which Berkeley Paget deputized. Plas Newydd agents drafted the addresses, the tone of which lent credence to the popular belief in North Wales that Sir Charles was standing down 'in a gentlemanlike manner' because of his pro-emancipation views, while William's anti-Catholic views coincided with their own. When the *Philomel* arrived at Caernarvon, 28 June 1826, Paget was admitted to the freedom of the borough and presided over a second round of entertainments, so increasing the cost of his election to over £1,020.[4]

He was made a post captain, 18 Oct. 1826, and spent much time in Bath wooing Fanny, the daughter of General de Rottenburg, a veteran like Anglesey of the 1809 Walcheren campaign. He married her in January 1827 despite his father's objections.[5] In Parliament, he presented a petition from Caernarvon and divided with Uxbridge against Catholic relief, 6 Mar. 1827.[6] He voted against the spring guns bill, 30 Mar., and after serving on the Denbigh election committee, he was awarded a week's leave, 3 Apr. In May, when corporation activists took him to task for failing to contribute towards the defeat in committee of the Caernarvon improvements bill, he responded with a spirited address blaming others.[7] Relations with his father remained strained, and he owed his £1,200 a year appointment as captain of the vice-regal yacht, the *Royal Charlotte*, during Anglesey's Irish lord lieutenancy to the duke of Clarence, who informed the marquess, 6 Nov.:

> As Lady William Paget is far advanced in her state of pregnancy and your Lordship is a man of gallantry, I am sure you, my excellent and old friend, will approve my having this day signed the commission.[8]

She was seriously ill following their eldest son's birth, and Paget subsequently claimed that de Rottenburg's £1,000 loan to provide her with a carriage and £120 allowance towards their expenses had encouraged him to live lavishly in Ireland,[9] where he soon courted controversy by visiting a Catholic Association meeting, 19 Apr. 1828, with Anglesey's secretary Baron Tuyll, Sir Hugh Adenyl, the Rev. Caesar Otway and Lord George Hill*.[10] On 15 Apr. the premier, the duke of Wellington reminded Anglesey

> how liable such a step is to misconstruction both here and in Ireland, how much it will be exaggerated beyond its real importance and how many unfounded influences will be drawn from it ... I am very much afraid that the presence of persons so high in your household and so entirely in your confidence will be considered by the Roman Catholics as a sanction of their proceedings and, what is still worse, will give great offence to the Protestants and incite in them feelings of suspicion and distress, if not of alienation and enmity.

Replying, 29 Apr., Anglesey acknowledged that it was 'an unfortunate occurrence and I have felt it much, but there is no use grumbling about it'.[11] Paget, though apparently under no pressure to espouse Anglesey's growing conviction that emancipation was essential to the pacification of Ireland,[12] announced his own 'conversion' when a relief bill was proposed, 9 May 1828:

> I am persuaded that if the Catholics of Ireland were placed on a footing of equality with their Protestant brethren, they would speedily forget and forgive all the injuries which they have endured; and would exhibit as much loyalty and good conduct as any other class of the community. I ... shall vote in favour of a cause, the success of which I honestly and conscientiously feel and believe to be intimately connected with the peace and prosperity of Ireland and the well-being of the empire at large.

John Croker* thought his words 'very well conceived and delivered with modesty and taste' and Edward Littleton* considered the speech 'most useful'; while others regretted that 'the noise in the House and the lowness of the Hon. Member's voice prevented our catching the purport of his first sentence'.[13] The Catholic press welcomed his vote for concessions, 12 May, but Protestant papers sought to discredit him by stressing his past differences with his father, Caernarvon's attempt to oust him for allegedly breaking an election pledge, and Uxbridge's continued opposition to emancipation.[14] On the 17th he returned to Dublin whence Anglesey announced that as an elected Member was 'the representative of the people of the empire, not of his electors merely ... he will not and he ought not to vacate his seat'.[15] He stayed away from the Caernarvon meeting that called for his resignation, 27 May, and, refusing to comply, issued an address confirming his belief that the removal of civil and religious disabilities was essential. He implied that his critics were in the minority and reiterated Anglesey's arguments concerning a Member's local and national responsibilities.[16] Speakers at the Catholic Association meeting, 29 May, vilified the burgesses of Caernarvon and suggested introducing a resolution thanking Paget and inviting him to stand for an Irish county. Daniel O'Connell considered 'the advocacy of their claims by Lord William Paget ... one of the most important incidents in the Catholic cause'. The resolution was carried, 11 June, but by then they had received Paget's letter stating:

> I cannot consider myself entitled to the thanks of the Roman Catholics as a *distinct body*. Whilst I am anxious that in discharging my duty as an independent Member of Parliament, consulting for the general interests of the empire at large, I wished to forward that important question which in my conscience I believe to be as much for the interests of the Protestants as of the Catholics.[17]

Asked by the O'Gorman Mahon* to stand at the county Clare by-election, 'he very properly said he would never take another step but by ... [Anglesey's] sanction and that he was sure ... [he] should object to that'.[18] On 19 June 'Lord William and the Ladies Paget' sailed for England, whence he returned after the Clare election, but in time for the Kingstown regatta, at which he was accused by the Protestant press of permitting the

Sabbath to be broken.[19] Paget remained unpopular in Caernarvon where, at the Michaelmas dinner, 29 Sept., he refused to drink to any but his own interpretation of 'the Protestant Ascendancy', bravely proclaiming:

> I must and will, upon all vital questions be unfettered. I will fearlessly and conscientiously support or oppose any and every measure as I shall believe it to be for the good of the empire, without for an instant allowing party or local attachments to influence my conduct'.[20]

The marquess's agent John Sanderson thought it the best speech heard in Caernarvon and arranged for it to be printed in the *North Wales Chronicle*; while the *Dublin Evening Post* reported, 'this rash young man has again rushed into print and wantonly forced himself once more upon public notice'. It did little to improve his prospects of a second unopposed return.[21] Paget's visit to the Catholic Association was mentioned in dispatches as a contributory factor in Wellington's decision to dismiss Anglesey in December 1828. He took part in the ensuing round of entertainments, attended his father at the official leave taking, 22 Jan. 1829, and accompanied him back to Beaudesert.[22] He congratulated him on his pro-emancipation speech in the Lords, 5 Feb., and the patronage secretary Planta predicted later that month that he would vote 'with government' for emancipation without insisting on additional securities.[23] However, despite reports to the contrary in the North Wales press, Paget did not vote on emancipation in 1829.[24] The Catholic Association incident was discussed again in May, when the Lords considered Anglesey's departure from Ireland and the attendant correspondence was printed.[25]

Paget had been accumulating more debts than he could discharge from his patrimony of £10,000 since at least the autumn of 1825, and in March 1829, when the consequences of his extravagant lifestyle could no longer be avoided, his father was informed. He rejected a suggestion that he should live rent free at Druids Lodge on the Plas Newydd estate, and instead took High Beeches, Waltham Forest, spending £1,300 on furnishings.[26] On 22 July he wrote:

> More than one execution is on the point of being put upon my property, poor and scanty, God knows as it is. ... Under these circumstances and after many thoughtful days and sleepless nights I do not hesitate to say that I feel no alternative is left to me but that of giving up my seat in Parliament and surrendering my person, when, if it appears that I am in fact totally bereft of property, I shall be ready and am indeed fully prepared to pay in my person whatever penalty the law may deem me liable to and thenceforward be exempt from my present hourly vexations.[27]

Anglesey, who liked to blame de Rottenburg for William's plight and conduct,[28] was furious to be thus forced to intervene and informed Sanderson, 23 July:

> I have long doubted Lord William Paget's feelings of honour and am therefore scarcely surprised at the circumstances you announce ... I will merely say that he is the worthy son-in-law of such a man as his father-in-law and that he has ably profited by the lessons he probably got from a scoundrel in Dublin who very narrowly escaped hanging and with whom I found him clearly connected. ... [Druids] would not have answered his purpose ... He can ... keep his seat till the first dissolution when he *ought* to go abroad and hide himself. Of course I would not, if I could again, return him to Parliament, and if after the present relief he chooses again to play the rogue, he must incur the penalty.[29]

With £20,000 needed to reimburse London, Dublin and Anglesey traders and pay off navy debts in Dublin, London, Plymouth and Portsmouth, Anglesey judged William to be 'irretrievably ruined, for his character is gone'; and he resolved to 'speak openly of him and throw myself and my family and this degraded young man at the mercy of the admiralty'.[30] He dismissed a requisition, 13 Sept., for William to stand for county Louth with the endorsement, 'I take no part in regard to Lord William Paget's remaining or again becoming a representative of the people'. Grange and Carlingford's address thanking him for his support for emancipation was not acknowledged.[31] Meanwhile, Paget's stepmother Lady Anglesey was annoyed that while £10,000 was being raised for him and a trust established, he was 'at his country house and coming up to London constantly, just as if nothing had happened'.[32] When appointed to command the *North Star* in December 1829, he immediately threatened to resign both his posting and his seat to force a better financial settlement.[33] He resorted to the same tactic in April 1830, shortly before his ship sailed for the West Indies, to try to secure £300 a year for his wife during his absence.[34] Sanderson replied, 19 Apr:

> Neither your privilege of Parliament, nor your rank in the public service, nor even your highly honoured name would protect you from the consequences of hostile proceedings by those of your creditors who hold dishonoured drafts ... In short, my dear Lord William, ask yourself the question whether the result might not be expulsion from Parliament, a suspension from the service and possibly a criminal process.[35]

While his debts continued to mount and legal action threatened, the trustees (Lord Forbes, Captain Hart and Sanderson) made repayment of Irish creditors their priority.[36] It was agreed that Paget's allowance from Lord Anglesey should be 'increased to enable him to live on naval half-pay; he was to go abroad, but not to a capital city, sell his carriages and horses, and ordered to give up certain of his friends'.[37] Early in June 1830, Anglesey, thinking himself close to death,[38] dwelt on the pain 'my unfortunate William' had caused in a farewell letter to Uxbridge, but hopes that he would 'reform and entitle himself to this indulgence' [a further £10,000] proved short-lived.[39] Caernarvon welcomed his retirement at the general election, when, for the first time in 50 years, the seat passed out of Paget control – a just reward for Lord William's 'ratting in the last Parliament'.[40]

The *North Star*'s voyage was marred by the death of a ship's boy, William Heritage, who threw himself overboard rather than face the dozen lashes ordered by Paget as punishment for his carelessness with the ship's water. Courts of inquiry at Bermuda and Halifax absolved Paget, and when a new inquiry was ordered at Portsmouth in January 1831, he rejected it as 'offering me a third loophole', and elected to be tried by court martial. His acquittal with honour, 7 Feb., did much to heal the breach with Anglesey, who had returned to Ireland as the Grey ministry's lord lieutenant, and received good reports of William's conduct from Grey, Lord Holland and the first lord of the admiralty, Sir James Graham.[41] William had already asked Sir Charles Paget, the duke of Argyll, and his brother-in-law, the postmaster-general the duke of Richmond, to intervene to secure him a posting to the West Indies and command of the *Westminster*, claiming that Admiral Colpoys had offered Lady William a home 'should she decide to come out'. He added in his letter to Sir Charles, 1 Feb:

> Loving Lady William however and my darling boy as I do, I cannot but feel my absence from them and from him particularly at his interesting age. But I love them too well to drag them about the ocean with me.[42]

With prosecutions then pending, he proved hard to assist, and no sooner did he step ashore than he was arrested for debt, forcing Uxbridge to intervene to pacify his creditors before he could put safely to sea again, 28 Feb.[43] Sir Charles had 'not a word to say in extenuation of Lord William's extravagance' but felt 'it is not inconsistent in me to continue on the most affectionate footing with him', and to facilitate the proposed move to Bermuda or Halifax, he persuaded Graham to give Paget the command of the *Winchester*, 10 May 1831.[44] Paget's wife did not sail for the West Indies. Her father died at Portsmouth, 24 Apr. 1832, and in September she and her mother left for Brussels, confident that Paget would join them.[45] He brought the *North Star* back to England, was paid off with the rest of her crew in September 1833 and sought refuge in Brussels.[46] While away, he had turned frequently to Richmond for patronage and free mailing and invoked Richmond and Uxbridge's names when creditors loomed. He was briefly thought of as a possible successor to Uxbridge as Member for Anglesey.[47] His father dismissed the idea, and Sanderson advised, 7 July 1831, that

> Lord William must be aware that a return to Parliament, although securing to him for the time freedom from arrest, would tend to increase the irritation of his creditors and I cannot omit to call to his recollection that there are some circumstances in this case which might render a public disclosure extremely detrimental to himself.[48]

Between 1830 and 1840 Paget's debts cost his family £26,916. The 1830 settlement was substantially revised in 1836, following his imprisonment in the Marshalsea, and again in 1840, when, after fighting against Don Carlos in Spain, he returned to Britain to escape creditors at Pau.[49] Though pledged to live abroad, he remained in England until 1846, and was returned to Parliament in 1841 as Liberal Member for Andover. From pecuniary motives, he regularly and dishonestly abused his family connections, and in December 1843 brought an unsuccessful action for crim. con. against the earl of Cardigan for alleged adultery with his wife.[50] An additional £15,000 was added to his trust fund under the terms of his father's will, proved in July 1854 and January 1855.[51] He died in Boulogne in May 1873 after a long illness.[52]

[1] *Paget Brothers* ed. Lord Hylton, 308. [2] W.R. O'Byrne, *Naval Biog.* ii. 850. [3] UCNW, Plas Newydd mss i. 262, 277, 283, 284, 289, 298, 301, 303, 307. [4] O'Byrne, ii. 850; Plas Newydd mss i. 24, 314-16; *N. Wales Gazette*, 8, 15, 23 June, 6, 13 July 1826; G.I.T. Machin, 'Catholic Emancipation as an Issue in North Welsh Politics, 1825-1829', *Trans. Hon. Soc. Cymmrodorion* (1962), 85-86. [5] O'Byrne, ii. 850; Lord William Paget mss (privately held at Plas Newydd) 7M/644G/21, Vivian to Anglesey, 25 Jan. 1827; Mq. of Anglesey, *One Leg*, 235. [6] *The Times*, 7 Mar. 1827. [7] *N. Wales Gazette*, 31 May, 7, 14 June 1827. [8] Lord William Paget mss 644G/21. [9] Ibid. 644G/1/1-4. [10] Ibid.; *Patriot*, 21 Apr.; *Dublin Evening Mail*, 23 Apr. 1828. [11] Wellington mss WP1/929/6, 13. [12] PRO NI, Anglesey mss D619/32G, p. 127; Machin, *Trans. Hon. Soc. Cymmrodorion* (1962), 86. [13] *Croker Pprs.* i. 419; Anglesey mss 31B/1; *Patriot*, 12 May 1828. [14] *Dublin Evening Mail*, 12, 14, 28 May; *Patriot*, 14, 26, 28, 30 May; *N. Wales Chron.* 22, 29 May; *Dublin Evening Post*, 23, 31 May 1828. [15] *Dublin Evening Post*, 17 May 1828; Plas Newydd mss vii. 2004. [16] *Dublin Evening Mail*, 28 May; *N. Wales Chron.* 29 May, 12 June; *Dublin Evening Post*, 9 June; *Cambrian*, 21 June 1828; Machin, *Trans. Hon. Soc. Cymmrodorion* (1962), 86-89. [17] *Dublin Evening Post*, 31 May, 3, 5, 14, 16 June; *N. Wales Chron.* 26 June 1828. [18] Anglesey mss 26C, pp. 48-51; Machin, *Catholic Question in English Politics*, 121; *Paget Pprs.* ed. A. B. Paget, ii. 395; Add. 51567, Anglesey to Holland, 1 July 1828. [19] *Dublin Evening Post*, 21 June; *Dublin Evening Mail*, 30 July 1828. [20] *N. Wales Chron.* 2 Oct.; *Dublin Evening Post*, 3 Oct.; *Shrewsbury Chron.* 10 Oct. 1828;

Machin, *Trans. Hon. Soc. Cymmrodorion* (1962), 90. [21] *Dublin Evening Post*, 3 Oct. 1828; Plas Newydd mss i. 1891, 1893, 1901; vii. 2009-11; Machin, *Trans. Hon. Soc. Cymmrodorion* (1962), 90-92. [22] Wellington mss WP1/966/17; Anglesey, 202-17; *N. Wales Chron.* 22 Jan. 1829. [23] Anglesey mss 32/A/3/64. [24] *N. Wales Chron.* 12, 26 Mar. 1829. [25] *The Times*, 5 May; *Dublin Evening Post*, 9 May 1829. [26] Lord William Paget mss 644G/1/3-7, 24, 55-9. [27] Ibid. 644G/1/14. [28] Ibid. 644G/3/132. [29] Ibid. 644G/1/14A. [30] Ibid. 644G/1/8-13, 19-21, 24, 26-34; 19A, 19E. [31] Ibid. 644G/1/25A; *Shrewsbury Chron.* 13 Nov. 1829; Anglesey mss 32/A/3/1/208, 210-12, 228. [32] Lord William Paget mss 644G/1/35(2). [33] Ibid. 644G/1/39-55; Anglesey mss 32/A/1/251. [34] Lord William Paget mss 644G/1/2/96, 97, 108. [35] Ibid. 644G/2/109. [36] Ibid. 644G/1/62, 62A; 2/81-95; 3/118-23, 150; 19D; Anglesey mss 32/A/1/251. [37] Anglesey, 236. [38] Plas Newydd mss i. 381; *Arbuthnot Jnl.* ii. 362. [39] Lord William Paget mss 644A/116; Anglesey, 232. [40] Plas Newydd mss i. 379, 395, 410; Add. 51568, Anglesey to Holland, 22 July; *Chester Courant*, 10 Aug. 1830. [41] Lord William Paget mss 644G/3/124, 124A, 127-30; W. Suss. RO, Goodwood mss 1433, f. 145; *The Times*, 9, 10, 14 Feb.; *Caern. Herald*, 12 Feb.; *United Services Mag.* (1831), i. 418; Anglesey mss 27/A/100; 28/A/43; Anglesey, 292-3. [42] Lord William Paget mss 644G/3/124; Goodwood mss 1433, f. 145. [43] Lord William Paget mss 644G/3/125, 127, 137-40, 141B (1), 142, 150-2. [44] Ibid. 644G/3/153, 154, 156 (1-2); Anglesey mss 32/G; O'Byrne, ii. 850. [45] Wellington mss WP1/1243/9; *Gent. Mag.* (1832), i. 562; Plas Newydd mss i. 636. [46] O'Byrne, ii. 850; Lord William Paget mss 644G/4/160; Anglesey, 294. [47] Goodwood mss 1433, f. 157; 1434, ff. 388, 421, 430; 1435, f. 160; 1449, f. 74; 1509, f. 153; 1656, ff. 12, 161; 1657, f. 347; Lord William Paget mss 644G/4/161; 19E. [48] Plas Newydd mss i. 45, 46. [49] Lord William Paget mss 644G/4/160-7; 644G/21. [50] Anglesey, 313-17; Lord William Paget mss 644G/21; *Ann. Reg.* (1844), Chron. pp. 21-25. [51] PROB 11/2194/508; Goodwood mss 1786, f. 1369. [52] *The Times*, 22 May; *Illustrated London News*, 31 May; *Ann. Reg.* (1873), Chron. p. 140.

M.M.E.

PAKENHAM, Hon. Hercules Robert (1781–1850), of Pakenham, co. Westmeath.

CO. WESTMEATH 27 Feb. 1808–1826

b. 29 Sept. 1781, 3rd s. of Edward Michael Pakenham, 2nd Bar. Longford [I] (*d.* 1792), and Catherine, da. of Hercules Langford Rowley, MP [I], of Summerhill, co. Meath. *educ.* Armagh; Caius, Camb. 1799. *m.* 25 Dec. 1817, Hon. Emily Stapleton, da. of Thomas, 2nd Lord Le Despenser, 6s. 3da. CB 4 June 1815; KCB 19 July 1838. *d.* 7 Mar. 1850.

Ensign 40 Ft. 1803; lt. army 1804; lt. 95 Rifles 1804, capt. 1805; maj. 7 W.I. Regt. 1810; lt.-col. army 1812; lt.-col. 26 Ft. 1812, 2 Ft. Gds 1814; half-pay Portuguese service 1817-37; col. army 1825; a.d.c. to the king 1825-37; maj.-gen. 1837; col. 43 Ft. 1844-*d.*; lt.-gen. 1846.

Trustee, linen board [I] 1826.

Pakenham, a veteran of the Peninsular war whose sister was married to the duke of Wellington, continued to sit for county Westmeath on the interest of his brother Thomas, 2nd earl of Longford, an Irish representative peer. Like Longford, who received a British peerage in 1821, he continued to support the Liverpool ministry, but he was a lax attender.[1] He voted in defence of their conduct towards Queen Caroline, 6 Feb., and against Catholic relief, 28 Feb. 1821. He took a month's leave, 7 May, but was present to vote for the duke of Clarence's grant, 18 June, and against retrenchment, 27 June 1821. Early the following year he proposed Lord Beauchamp* in the county Antrim by-election.[2] His next known votes were not until 1823, when he divided with ministers on the assessed taxes, 10, 18 Mar., but against them on the legal proceedings against the Dublin Orange rioters, 24 Mar. (He did not vote in the related division of 22 Apr. 1823.) No trace of activity has been found for 1824. Next session he voted for the suppression of the Catholic Association, 15, 25 Feb., and was in the majority against the usury laws repeal bill, 17 Feb. By now he had become a convert to Catholic relief, for which he voted, 1 Mar., 21 Apr., 10 May. 'Many people have become converts who were most adverse', Lord Palmerston* noted after the second vote, citing Pakenham and adding, 'their change results perhaps less from their own individual connection, than from a change of opinion among the Protestants of Ireland whom they represent'.[3] Pakenham was later said to have spoken for it during this session, but if he did so his words escaped the notice of the reporters.[4] His last recorded vote was for the duke of Cumberland's annuity, 10 June 1825.

At the 1826 general election Pakenham, who had been elected for Westmeath on an anti-Catholic ticket, abandoned his seat amidst reports that he had been 'discarded' by his brother and the 'high Protestant interest', which he tried to deny. He was 'the victim of the vote he gave ... in favour of emancipation', declared the Catholic press.[5] He later took up residence at Langford Lodge, county Antrim, where at Wellington's prompting he supported and proposed Edmund McDonnell in opposition to an Ultra Tory at the 1830 general election, to cries of 'why doesn't Pakenham stand!'.[6] In February 1831 he joined other leading Antrim residents in signing a requisition for a county meeting against repeal of the Union.[7] He refused to support McDonnell's attempt to offer again at that year's general election, on the grounds that it would have 'created much excitement in the county, have given infinite annoyance to the late Members and terminated in defeat', and was himself pressed to offer as a Conservative by Wellington in October 1832.[8] Rumours of his candidacy, however, came to nothing at that year's general election, when he again proposed McDonnell and on the hustings denounced the Grey administration's Irish policies.[9] In 1842 he unsuccessfully solicited an Irish bishopric from Sir Robert Peel, the premier, for his brother Henry.[10] As commander of the south – western district, his last active employment, he drew the attention of government in 1844 to the decrepit armament and 'defenceless condition' of Portsmouth arsenal.[11] He died 'suddenly' at Langford Lodge in March 1850.[12] Four of his sons followed him into the army and two of them were killed in action: Edward, Conservative Member for county Antrim since 1852, at Inkerman in 1854, and Robert at Lucknow in 1857. Edward was replaced in the county seat by his brother Thomas, who sat until 1865.

[1] Add. 38383, f. 375; 38283, f. 390; 40298, f. 42; *Black Bk.* (1823), 181; *Session of Parl. 1825*, p. 479. [2] *Belfast News Letter*, 15 Jan. 1822. [3] Southampton Univ. Lib. Broadlands mss PP/GC/TE/171. [4] *The Times*, 6 June 1826. [5] *Dublin Evening Post*, 10, 17 June; Brougham mss, Abercromby to Brougham, 12 July 1826. [6] Wellington mss WP1/1130/8, 54; *Belfast News Letter*, 13 Aug. 1830. [7] *Belfast News Letter*, 11 Feb. 1831. [8] Durham CRO, Londonderry mss Lo/C/117(29); Wellington mss WP1/1236/4. [9] *Northern Whig*, 1 Nov. 1832; *Belfast News Letter*, 28 Dec. 1832. [10] Add. 40511, ff. 398, 400. [11] *Von Neumann Diary*, ii. 195; Add. 40554, ff. 463-9. [12] *The Times*, 11 Mar. 1850; *Gent. Mag.* (1850), i. 532-33.

P.J.S.

PALK, Sir Lawrence Vaughan, 3rd bt. (1793–1860), of Haldon House, nr. Exeter, Devon.

ASHBURTON 1818–1831

b. 24 Apr. 1793, 1st s. of Lawrence Palk† of Haldon and 2nd w. Lady Dorothy Elizabeth Vaughan, da. of Wilmot Vaughan, 1st earl of Lisburne [I]†. *educ.* Eton 1808; Christ Church, Oxf. 1812. *m.* (1) 9 Dec. 1815, his cos. Anna Eleanora (*d.* 25 Jan. 1846), da. of Sir Bourchier Wrey, 7th bt., of Tawstock, Devon, wid. of Edward Hartopp of Little Dalby, Melton Mowbray, Leics., 3s. 2da.; (2) c. 1848,[1] Phillipine Anne Victoire, 1da.[2] *suc.* fa. as 3rd bt. 20 June 1813. *d.* 16 May 1860.

Capt. 2 Devon militia 1813; ensign E. Devon militia 1835.

Palk inherited his father's property in Ashburton and Torquay and the residue of his personal estate, which was sworn under £70,000 in 1813. He carried on his father's urban development project in Torquay, although the Ashburton estate had to be heavily mortgaged to provide the capital and he was left with 'scarcely enough ready cash to provide ... a suitable income'.[3] In 1818 he returned himself for Ashburton, where he was the joint lord of the manor, and he was unopposed at the next three general elections. He was an occasional attender who continued to give silent support to Lord Liverpool's ministry.[4] He was granted three weeks' leave on account of family illness, 14 June 1820. He voted in defence of ministers' conduct towards Queen Caroline, 6 Feb. 1821. He divided against Catholic relief, 28 Feb. 1821, and the removal of Catholic peers' disabilities, 30 Apr. 1822. He voted against repeal of the additional malt duty, 3 Apr. 1821, more extensive tax reductions, 11 Feb. 1822, and Scottish parliamentary reform, 2 June 1823. He divided against Catholic claims, 1 Mar., 21 Apr., 10 May, and the Irish franchise bill, 26 Apr. 1825. He voted for the duke of Cumberland's annuity, 6, 10 June 1825. At the general election of 1826 he nominated the Tory Member for Devon, Edmund Pollexfen Bastard.[5] He was granted three weeks' leave, having served on an election committee, 21 Mar. 1827. He divided against Catholic relief, 6 Mar. 1827, 12 May 1828. He attended the Devon county meeting, 16 Jan. 1829, when he sat with the supporters of the Protestant cause.[6] The following month Planta, the Wellington ministry's patronage secretary, predicted that he would side 'with government' for emancipation, but he voted steadily against it, 6, 18, 23, 27, 30 Mar. He divided for Lord Duncannon's registration amendment to the Irish freeholders bill, 20 Mar. 1829, and against Lord Blandford's parliamentary reform motion, 18 Feb. 1830.

After the 1830 general election Palk was listed among the 'moderate Ultras', but with the additional note that he was a 'sincere friend' of ministers; he indeed voted with them in the crucial civil list division, 15 Nov. 1830. He divided against the second reading of the Grey ministry's reform bill, 22 Mar., and for Gascoyne's wrecking amendment, 19 Apr. 1831. At the ensuing general election he was challenged by the independent interest at Ashburton, and though he 'admitted some reform to be necessary' his refusal to pledge support for the bill 'cost him his seat'; he came bottom of the poll after a contest lasting six days.[7] In September he put his Ashburton estate on the market, but legal complications delayed its sale until 1845. Meantime, he continued to develop his Torquay property, from which his family 'made a second great fortune'.[8] He resided latterly at Versailles. He died in May 1860 and was succeeded by his eldest son Lawrence Palk (1818-83), Conservative Member for South Devon, 1854-68, and East Devon, 1868-80, who was created Baron Haldon in 1880.

[1] IGI (pedigree resource files). [2] According to Dod's *Baronetage* (1860). *Burke PB* names 2da. with his 1st w., but his will refers to three. [3] PROB 11/1546/378; IR26/589/558; H. Hanham, 'Ashburton as a Parliamentary Borough, 1640-1868', *Trans. Devon Assoc.* xcviii (1966), 231, 240. [4] *Session of Parl. 1825*, p. 479. [5] *Trewman's Exeter Flying Post*, 15 June 1826. [6] *Western Times*, 17 Jan. 1829. [7] *Trewman's Exeter Flying Post*, 5, 12 May 1831. [8] Hanham, 240-1; W. Hoskins, *Devon*, 500-2.

T.A.J.

PALLMER, Charles Nicholas (1772–1848), of Norbiton Place, Surr.

LUDGERSHALL 26 June 1815–23 June 1817
SURREY 1826–1830

bap. 11 June 1772, at St. Dorothy, Jamaica, 1st s. of Charles Pallmer of Cold Harbour, Jamaica and Jane Peters, da. of Nicholas Bourke of Clarendon, Jamaica. *educ.* L. Inn 1796. *m.* 2 June 1808, Maria Francis, da. and h. of Francis Dennis (whose wid. Mary bought the Norbiton estate in 1797), wid. of Hugh Ingoldsby Massy, *s.p. suc.* fa. 1787; William Thompson to Jamaica estates 1817. *d.* 30 Dec. 1848.

Maj. of brigade, W.I. 1805.

Crown solicitor in Jamaica 1806; bailiff, Kingston-upon-Thames 1820; sheriff, Surr. 1822-3; commr. of lunacy, Mdx. 1828-9.

Pallmer belonged to a West Indian planter family and owed his links with Surrey to his wife, who brought him his mansion near Kingston. He embellished it and extended the accompanying estate 'to an area of about 300 acres', comprising 'an arable and sheep farm, a dairy farm, pleasure grounds, grotto, kitchen garden, grapery and other adjuncts of an attractive character'.[1] Lord Liverpool was a near neighbour and connection: in 1820 Pallmer wrote on behalf of Kingston corporation to congratulate the prime minister on the failure of the Cato Street conspiracy and offer thanks to Providence for 'the preservation of a life so inestimably useful to their country'.[2] They subsequently corresponded on such matters of local interest as the construction of a new bridge over the Thames.[3] During his first brief stint in the Commons Pallmer had been primarily a spokesman for the West India interest. He was a prominent figure in the West India Planters and Merchants' standing committee, which he chaired from 1818-20, and which he served thereafter as deputy to his cousin Charles Rose Ellis*, invariably featuring in the deputations sent to ministers to argue the West Indian case.[4] Ellis, on learning of his imminent ennoblement in June 1826, apparently considered returning Pallmer in his stead for Seaford at the general election. Liverpool was also keen to find a seat for him, but his acceptance of an invitation to stand for Surrey caused some embarrassment to the premier, as the Member at whom the contest was aimed was a government supporter. To the Whig 2nd Earl Spencer Pallmer meantime wrote that he was 'well aware ... that neither property nor any pretensions of my own' entitled him to ask for support, but if elected 'I shall trust to show myself in my principles not altogether unworthy of your lordship's approbation'.[5] On the hustings he made light of his West Indian proprietorship by boasting of the 1,000 slaves on his plantation who had converted to Christianity. Though he praised a number of Whig luminaries, he declared his 'decided preference' for ministers. He declined to be pledged on Catholic relief (which he had opposed in 1816), but admitted to a 'present bias' against it. With the support of manufacturing and commercial interests, he was returned in second place after a five-day poll.[6]

He had expressed the hope to his constituents that he might 'endeavour to act in some degree as a mediator between the legislature of this country and the West Indian planter'. He accompanied the planters' deputations to lobby Huskisson, the president of the board of trade, for the admission of sugar to distilleries in October 1826, and to discuss the sugar duties with Robinson, the chancellor of the exchequer, in March 1827. Four months earlier he had been in the delegation to the colonial secretary Lord Bathurst to urge compensation for slave owners once the order for abolition was enforced.[7] He spoke regularly in the House on West Indian and commercial matters. He defended the tax advantages enjoyed by West Indian over East Indian sugar, 23 Mar. 1827.[8] While admitting that justice in the West Indies was 'in general badly administered', 12 June 1827, he denied that Jamaicans of mixed race were peculiarly victimized and set his face against 'too sudden changes' in the system. He moved for trading accounts of West Indian produce, 5 Mar., and after lobbying ministers he presented a petition from the planters and merchants for a reduction in sugar duty, 21 Apr. 1828.[9] He argued that cheaper sugar might palliate the famine in Ireland, and that the revival of West Indian prosperity would provide a greater market for British manufactures. His suggestion for a clause to introduce the principle of reciprocity of duties to the corn importation bill was accepted, 23 May. He favoured the repeal of that part of the Foreign Enlistment Act which he deemed an interference with shipping interests, 3 July 1828. In January 1829 he led a delegation to the prime minister, the duke of Wellington, to lobby for a reduction in sugar duties.[10] He moved for accounts of imports and exports of rum, sugar and coffee, 24 Mar., and spoke in favour of the West India Docks bill, 14 Apr. 1829. That month Pallmer and Ellis, now Lord Seaford, resigned their official positions on the West India committee after an organizational coup at a general meeting. Although this implied criticism of their leadership, the committee acknowledged Pallmer's 'prompt and assiduous support of the colonial interest both in and out of Parliament'.[11] He briefly condemned the government's 'infatuated' policy towards the West India interest, 1 Mar. 1830. At a meeting of concerned Members, 2 June, he proposed the motion for a representation to be made 'in the strongest possible terms' to Vesey Fitzgerald, the president of the board of trade, for some measure of relief 'without loss of time'; the remedy suggested was an experimental reduction of the sugar duties in Ireland. The usual philanthropic gloss was put on this, and it was commended to ministers with the argument that if the expected increase in consumption took place, no loss of revenue would result.[12] Denouncing their response as 'very unsatisfactory', 14 June, Pallmer put the scheme to the House, 1 July, and saw it defeated by 68-38. Having complained about the punitive duties on West Indian rum, 7 Apr., he supported Huskisson's attempt to lift them, 5 July 1830.

On wider issues there was a streak of liberalism in Pallmer's philanthropic interests and his sympathy for measures of parliamentary reform. He expressed support for Lord Althorp's resolutions against electoral bribery, 22 Nov. 1826, and his motion for inquiry into the procedure for taking county polls, 15 Mar. 1827, when he detected an 'auspicious' mood in the House for 'beneficial measures' of this kind. He voted that day for inquiry into Leicester corporation, and explained on the 16th that he suspected malpractice in the creation of freemen. Yet he divided with Canning's ministry against the disfranchisement of Penryn, 28 May, and regulation of the Coventry magistracy, 18 June. He voted against Catholic relief, 6 Mar. He divided for the Clarence annuity bill, 16 Mar., and praised the duke and duchess for their 'domestic virtue and hospitality', 22 Mar. Though he voted for the spring guns bill next day, he believed that the right to set them should be retained by the owners of market gardens, 'a species of property especially subject to depredation, from being so near town', 17 May. He divided for information regarding delays in chancery, 5 Apr. He voted for the grant for Canadian waterways, 12 June. On 14 May he urged the importance of the moral reform of prisoners, a concern which he had shown in his attempt at the Surrey quarter sessions to secure daily instruction for prisoners, and in his patronage of the Surrey Refuge for the Destitute (for 'discharged prisoners ... desirous to forsake their depraved course of life') and the Surrey Asylum for the employment and reformation of discharged prisoners.[13] He introduced a bill to consolidate the law on savings banks, 22 May, when he lauded them as 'giving the benevolent rich the means of encouraging the prudence of the industrious'; it foundered at the report stage. He promised a bill to regulate lunatic asylums, 8 June, but nothing more was heard.[14] Similarly, he appears to have abandoned his intended bill to regulate jurors' recognizances, 14 June 1827, after the home secretary Sturges Bourne promised a government measure the following session.[15] He presented petitions for repeal of the Test Acts, 7, 19 Feb., and voted accordingly, 26 Feb. 1828. In presenting an anti-Catholic petition, 8 May, he declared that tranquillity in Ireland should not be bought 'at the price of the discontent of England'; he divided against relief, 12 May. He unsuccessfully moved for the extension of Penryn into the neighbouring hundreds, 24 Mar., and maintained that the guilt of '15 or 16 individuals' did not justify the borough's disfranchisement, 7 June. On 19 June he reintroduced his savings banks amendment bill, for which he had apparently secured backing from Wellington's ministry; he replied to minor objections, 27 June, 3, 8 July, and after amendment in the Lords it gained royal assent, 28 July (9 Geo. IV, c. 92). He voted against reduction of the salary of the lieutenant-general of the ordnance, 4 July 1828. In February 1829 Planta, the patronage secretary, listed him as one who was 'opposed to the principle' of Catholic emancipation. He confessed to having 'painful misgivings' about the anticipated concession, 20 Feb., presented hostile petitions, 26, 27 Feb., 3 Mar., and divided against emancipation, 6, 18, 23, 27, 30 Mar. Prior to the vote on the 6th he had divided the House against resumption of the debate, to allow more time for petitions, but was defeated by 205-76. Three days later his conduct attracted comment from Althorp and others about his earlier evasiveness on the issue, prompting him to affirm his 'solemn and sincere conviction' that the Protestant constitution would be endangered by the government's proposals. He admitted to occasional irregularities in the collection of signatures for anti-Catholic petitions, but insisted that they represented the majority view. On 19 Mar. he presented another petition from London and Westminster, to which he claimed 113,000 signatures were attached, and, anticipating the imputations that would be cast on its respectability, he sniped at the 'dogmas and declamations of those who arrogantly call themselves "the intellectual"'. At a county meeting two days later he outdid even his rabidly anti-Catholic predecessor, George Holme Sumner, in condemning the government's bill as 'idolatrous worship of the demon of fear' and a 'sacrifice upon the altar of unhallowed tranquillization'; Liverpool, he maintained, would not have remained in office to pass such a measure. He made no reply to John Maberly's* demand that he suggest an alternative means of pacifying Ireland, but along with the meeting's petition against emancipation he presented another for the establishment of a poor relief system in Ireland, 26 Mar.[16] Either he or

Charles Fyshe Palmer voted for the transfer of East Retford's seats to Birmingham, 5 May. His attempt to legislate against bull baiting fell at the first hurdle, 12 May, when his motion to repeal the existing Cruelty to Animals Act failed by 73-28. His bill to tighten the regulations on new buildings gained a first reading, 5 June 1829, too near the end of the session to make any further progress.

Although Pallmer's name does not appear in the lists compiled in the autumn of 1829 by the Ultra Tory leader Sir Richard Vyvyan*, his disillusionment with Wellington's ministry became apparent during the 1830 session. He divided for Knatchbull's amendment to the address on distress, 4 Feb. While professing continued admiration for the premier and for Peel, the leader of the Commons, he considered their proposed tax reductions to be inadequate, 19 Feb., and suggested that Members' 'abused privilege' of franking letters be abolished. He voted with the Whig opposition for military economies, 19, 26 Feb., 1 Mar., a revision of taxation, 25 Mar., and against the Bathurst and Dundas pensions, 26 Mar. He attended a county meeting on distress, 19 Mar., and spoke in support of the resulting petition, 23 Mar., when he called for the substitution of duties on fuel and candles with a 'fair and equal tax upon property'. That day he presented a petition from the labourers on William Cobbett's† Barn Elms farm complaining of distress and protesting at schemes for emigration.[17] He divided against the East Retford bribery prevention bill, 11 Feb., and for the enfranchisement of Birmingham, Leeds and Manchester, 23 Feb. On 28 May he voted for Russell's reform resolutions and conspicuously featured in the minority of 13 for O'Connell's motion for universal suffrage, triennial parliaments and the ballot; he did not explain his apparent conversion to the cause of radical reform. He divided for Jewish emancipation, 17 May, abolition of the death penalty for forgery, 24 May, 7 June, and against increased recognizances in libel cases, 9 July 1830. He retired at the dissolution that summer, citing to his constituents 'the state of my health and the consciousness of my utter inability to do justice to the duties incumbent on your representative'. On the hustings he endorsed the reformer John Ivatt Briscoe* and observed that 'great as were the duke of Wellington's merits ... there were others as capable of conducting the government of the country'.[18]

The background to Pallmer's sudden retirement emerged shortly afterwards. Reports appeared in the press during March 1831 that several West Indian houses had stopped payment, on account of the disappearance of a major creditor. The *Observer* referred to the culprit, none too obliquely, as the person who, 'from being an attorney of no great eminence in Jamaica rose, by his suavity and pliancy of manner, to be the "hail fellow" of Lord Liverpool and the recognized of the highest in the land', and who had 'spent £20,000 in obtaining the representation of a metropolitan county'. Seaford informed Lord Granville with obvious consternation, 1 Apr., that

> Pallmer, whom I believed to be one of the best ... of men, suddenly left England about a month ago, leaving debts to an enormous amount, contracted under circumstances of the most discreditable nature, and involving some of his most intimate friends and nearest connections in very serious losses. He had obtained from me, among many others, the loan of about £7,000, under assurances which have proved not only fallacious, but treacherous.[19]

Pallmer was listed as a bankrupt in the *London Gazette*, 26 Apr. 1831, where, presumably to allow him the protection of the bankruptcy laws, he was described as a 'ship owner, dealer and chapman'. The *Observer* thereupon expatiated on his fall from grace:

> Ten or twelve years ago this person launched forth on the world with the reputation of possessing a large income from West India property ... Whatever that income might have been in prosperous times, it soon sunk in the same proportion as that of other proprietors, and Mr. Pallmer's pride proving greater than his integrity, he continued spending some £8,000 or £10,000 a year long after his estate was wholly unproductive. The result of the system under which he raised the necessary supplies is a debt of £100,000 due to the firm with which he was connected. It is said that the ex-Hon. gentleman has written from Paris to say that everyone will ultimately be paid. On such a subject a little trading slang may be excused: 'we wish they may get it'.

He appears to have surrendered to his creditors *in absentia* and returned to Jamaica.[20] He died in Boulogne-sur-Mer in December 1848.[21] By his will, executed in Jamaica in 1837, he left his entire estate, 'with the full concurrence of my most dearly beloved and excellent wife', to his sister, Eliza Parker. She renounced probate and administration was granted to John Parkinson of 60 Lincoln's Inn Fields, a creditor; the personalty was sworn under a nominal £20.[22]

[1] E.W. Brayley and E. Walford, *Surr.* 236. [2] Add. 38283, f. 286. [3] Add. 38299, ff. 349, 360, 369, 371; 38300, f. 259. [4] Inst. of Commonwealth Stud. M915/3/4, 4/1. [5] Add. 38301, ff. 213, 231; 40305, f. 186; 76135, Pallmer to Spencer, 11 June 1826. [6] *Baldwin's Weekly Jnl.* 17, 24 June; *County Chron.* 20 June 1826. [7] *Baldwin's Weekly Jnl.* 17 June 1826; Inst. of Commonwealth Stud. M915/4/1. [8] *The Times*, 24 Mar. 1827. [9] Inst. of Commonwealth Stud. M915/4/1. [10] Wellington mss WP1/994/2. [11] Inst. of Commonwealth

Stud. M915/4/1. [12] Ibid. 11/7. [13] *The Times*, 11 Jan., 15 Nov. 1826, 15 May 1827, 9 May 1828. [14] Ibid. 9 June 1827. [15] Ibid. 15 June 1827. [16] Ibid. 23 Mar. 1829. [17] *County Chron.* 23 Mar. 1830; *Cobbett's Rural Rides* ed. G.D.H. and M. Cole, iii. 1016. [18] *County Chron.* 6 July; *Baldwin's Weekly Jnl.* 7 Aug. 1830. [19] *Observer*, 13 Mar. 1831; TNA 30/29/9/5/78. [20] I. Duffy, *Bankruptcy in Industrial Revolution*, 22; *Observer*, 1 May 1831; *Surr. Arch. Colls.* vii. p. xliii. [21] IR26/1880/836. A monumental inscription cited in *Caribbeana*, iii. 333, gives his date of death as 30 Sept. [22] PROB 11/2124/912; IR26/1880/836.

H.J.S.

PALMER, Charles (1777–1851), of Brock Street, Bath and Albany, Mdx.

BATH	2 Feb. 1808–1826
BATH	1830–1837

b. 6 May 1777, 1st s. of John Palmer† of Bath and 1st w. Sarah Mason. *educ.* Eton 1791-3; Oriel, Oxf. 1793. *m.* 14 Feb. 1823, Mary Elizabeth, da. of John Thomas Atkyns of Hunterscombe House, Bucks., niece and coh. of John Atkyns Wright†. *s.p.m.s. suc.* fa. 1818. *d.* 17 Apr. 1851.

Cornet 10 (prince's own) Drag. 1796, lt. 1797, capt. 1799, maj. 1805, lt.-col. 1810; brevet col. 1814; lt.-col. 23 Drag. Nov. 1814, half-pay Dec. 1814; maj.-gen. 1825.

A.d.c. to prince regent 1811-25.

Palmer's family were long established in Bath and had played a prominent role in that city's development in the eighteenth century. His grandfather, a prosperous brewer and tallow chandler, founded the Theatre Royal and his father, a driving force behind the development of the mail-coach system in the 1780s, served on the corporation and secured the parliamentary representation in 1801. He was 'groomed for a gentleman's life', originally pursued an army career (serving in the Peninsula), and moved in the highest social circles, including the regent's, 'for which his agreeable manners ... amiable disposition and ... attainments, admirably qualified him'.[1] In 1808 he replaced his father as Member for Bath and ten years later inherited his interests in the Bath and Bristol theatres and some adjoining properties, along with a quarter-share of the residue of the estate, which was sworn under £7,000.[2] He joined Brooks's Club, 7 May 1816. At the general election of 1820 he was returned unopposed for Bath with Lord John Thynne after the recorder, the 1st Marquess Camden, who had wanted to turn him out in favour of a lawyer to sit as a 'stopgap' until his son came of age, was deterred by the threat of a petition against such 'unconstitutional' interference. In his speech of thanks to the corporation, Palmer boasted that his voting record proved his 'independence of all parties but that of the constitution and my country'.[3]

He was a fairly regular attender and continued to act with the Whig opposition to Lord Liverpool's ministry on all major issues, including parliamentary reform, 31 May 1821, 25 Apr., 24 June 1822, 24 Apr., 2 June 1823, 26 Feb. 1824, 13, 27 Apr. 1826. He was absent from the division on Catholic relief, 28 Feb. 1821, but voted for it, 1 Mar., 21 Apr., 10 May 1825. He expressed no opinion on the charges laid against Queen Caroline, 26 June 1820, but condemned the 'unmanly' conduct of ministers in excluding her name from the liturgy, as 'derogatory to the honour of the crown' and 'a most improper act on the part of men who complained of the revolutionary principles, infidelity and disaffection ... that were prevalent in the country'. On 9 July 1823, the last day of that session, he moved for production of the instructions sent to the ambassador in Madrid regarding the French military intervention in Spain. Asserting that the 'crooked policy' of ministers did not represent the views of the British people and that invasion was the policy of the Bourbon regime, not of the French people, he looked forward to Britain declaring war 'for the liberties of France' and joining hands with the French people to protect Spain's independence. He said he had no wish to take the sense of the House and the motion was negatived without discussion.[4] In the debate on the address, 4 Feb. 1824, he spoke under the 'strongest feelings of shame and indignation', denouncing British neutrality towards Spain and the whole 'system' of ministerial policy based on national self-interest, which had made Britain 'the enemy of the whole human race'. He warned that France and the Holy Alliance were preparing to strike against Britain 'at any moment'. He regarded the Aliens Act, 12 Apr., as another 'measure of that weak and dishonourable policy' that had 'aggravated the danger of the country' and ruined its character: 'of all the dupes upon earth, he considered John Bull to be the greatest'. He presented Bath petitions for repeal of the assessed taxes, 24 Feb., 18 Mar., and inquiry into the trial of the Methodist missionary John Smith in Demerara, 31 May 1824.[5] In a wide-ranging speech on the address, 4 Feb. 1825, he attacked the foreign secretary, Canning, 'the enemy of his country', whose foolish 'half measures' had left Britain 'degraded and despised'. He dismissed his free trade principles as an attempt to 'patch an old coat with new cloth' and argued that it was essential to tackle the problem of the national debt, 'the root of the evil, which nothing but reform could cure'. He regretted that in the peace settlement of 1815 ministers had 'conspired with the powers of Europe against the liberties of the people, solely to prevent reform in the abuses of their own governments', and demanded Catholic emancipation. He presented Bath petitions for repeal of the house tax, 8 Feb., and all assessed taxes, 3 Mar.,[6] and expressed his support for 'all motions for relieving the burthens of the people', 17 May. Declaring an interest as the owner of a French vineyard in the debate on the wine duties, 22 Mar., he warned of the dangers of French and Portuguese trading monopolies and advocated equalizing the duties on foreign wines. He was averse to the duke of Cumberland's annuity bill, 10 June 1825, but felt honour bound to support it as he had previous grants for the royal dukes. During the debate on reform, 27 Apr. 1826, he defended Bath corporation, describing it as 'the only example of a close borough alike independent of the crown, the administration and the aristocracy of the country', and praising its members for 'not availing themselves of their unconstitutional power to promote their private interest'. Despite this flattery, which was suspected of being calculated, he lost his seat at the general election that summer, polling four votes fewer than Lord Brecknock, Camden's son, a result that was reportedly 'viewed with disgust by the inhabitants'.[7]

Palmer offered again for Bath at the by-election in February 1829 occasioned by Brecknock's appointment to office, but the outcome was a tie, and when another poll was held the following month he was defeated by two votes.[8] However, he regained the seat by the same margin at the general election of 1830, benefiting from changes in the corporation's personnel and divisions among his opponents over Catholic emancipation. He was hailed by a local newspaper as 'a universal favourite with the citizens', who had 'maintained the character of an independent English gentleman' and consistently advocated economy, retrenchment and reform.[9] The Wellington ministry regarded him as one of their 'foes', and he duly voted against them in the crucial civil list division, 15 Nov 1830. He presented two Bath anti-slavery petitions that day, and one for repeal of the house and window taxes, which was 'much more numerously signed than any other [previously] presented on this subject', 23 Dec. 1830. He presented a Bath petition for repeal of the game laws and four parish petitions for parliamentary reform, 19 Mar. 1831. He divided for the second reading of the Grey ministry's reform bill, 22 Mar., and against Gascoyne's wrecking amendment, 19 Apr. 1831. At the ensuing general election he was returned unopposed for Bath with Thynne, after Brecknock withdrew from the contest, but his success was thought to be due rather to 'personal regard' for him among corporation members than 'approbation of his political principles'.[10] He divided for the second reading of the reintroduced reform bill, 6 July, and voted steadily for its details in committee and its passage, 21 Sept. He used the debate on the Scottish bill, 4 Oct., to address the reform issue generally, describing the 'rotten system of the late Tory government' as 'worn out' and welcoming the 'fortunate events' that had 'combined the crown, the government, and the people in the same just cause'. He accepted the division of counties as a 'necessary compromise', personally favoured the ballot as the only protection against 'undue influence' and concluded that no Member could 'seriously believe' that the 'present glorious measure' would be a final one. He voted for Lord Ebrington's confidence motion, 10 Oct. He was in the minority to allow the eleven Members chosen for the Dublin election committee to be sworn, 29 July, but after its report he voted with ministers to punish only those guilty of giving bribes, 23 Aug. He divided for the second reading of the revised reform bill, 17 Dec. 1831, and for its details. He defended the conduct of the political unions, which had 'stood forward ... in defence of the constitution' and protected the country from the potentially 'dreadful effects' of the Lords' rejection of the bill, 20 Mar. 1832. He endorsed the principle that 'every man who contributes to support the government, either in his person, property or labour, is entitled to a vote', and observed that 'there will be no honest means of preventing universal suffrage but to relieve labour from taxation'. He voted for the third reading, 22 Mar., and Ebrington's motion for an address asking the king to appoint only ministers committed to carrying an unimpaired measure, 10 May, and presented three Bath petitions to withhold supplies until the Lords passed it, 25 May. He divided with ministers on the Russian-Dutch loan, 12, 16, 20 July 1832.

Palmer was returned at the head of the poll for the greatly enlarged Bath constituency in 1832 and sat as an advocate of 'Whig principles' until his defeat in 1837.[11] His final years were blighted by the disastrous consequences of his 'immense' investment in his Bordeaux estate, which placed him in the hands of the 'usurers' and obliged him to sell the Bath theatre and 'pass through the insolvent court'. At last he became 'a mendicant in the streets of London, shunned where he once was courted'.[12] He died in April 1851 and no will or grant of administration has been traced.

[1] R.S. Neale, *Bath, 1680-1850*, p. 299; *Gronow Reminiscences*, i. 139. [2] PROB 11/1609/470; IR26/759/1112. [3] *Bath and Cheltenham Gazette*, 8, 15 Mar. 1820. [4] A. Mitchell, *Whigs in Opposition*, 174. [5] *The Times*, 25 Feb., 19 Mar., 1 June 1824. [6] Ibid. 9 Feb., 4 Mar. 1825. [7] *Keenes' Bath Jnl.* 29 May, 12 June; *Bath and Cheltenham Gazette*, 13 June 1826. [8] *Keenes' Bath Jnl.* 16 Feb., 16 Mar. 1829. [9] Ibid. 19 July, 2 Aug. 1830. [10] Ibid. 25 Apr., 2 May 1831. [11] *Dod's Parl. Companion* (1833), 147. [12] *Gronow Reminiscences*, i. 139-43.

T.A.J.

PALMER, Charles Fyshe (?1771–1843), of Luckley House, Wokingham; East Court, Finchampstead, Berks., and Ickwell Old House, nr. Biggleswade, Beds.[1]

READING 1818–1826

READING 26 Mar. 1827–1834

READING 1837–1841

b. ?1771, s. of Charles Fyshe Palmer of Luckley, East Court and Ickwell and w. Lucy Jones of Celyn, Flints.[2] *educ.* Eton 1779-86;[3] ?Wadham, Oxf. 19 Nov. 1789, aged 18. *m.* 25 Nov. 1805, Lady Madelina Gordon, da. of Alexander, 4th duke of Gordon [S], wid. of Sir Robert Sinclair, 7th bt., of Stevenson, Haddington, *s.p. suc.* fa. 1807. *d.* 24 Jan. 1843.

Palmer's skeletal physique and great height amused Mary Russell Mitford, who wrote that 'three or four yards of brown thread would be as like him as anything, if one could contrive to make it stand upright'. She thought him 'a good sort of man', though, as a liberal, she had qualms about the £200 pension which his aristocratic wife enjoyed. She complained soon after his return for Reading, where his Berkshire estates and advanced Whig politics were electoral assets, at the contested election of 1818 that he had 'the worst fault that a franker can have; he is un-come-at-able. One never knows where to catch him. I don't believe he is ever two days in a place – always jiggeting about from one great house to another'.[4] Certainly, as brother-in-law to three dukes and a marquess, and the possessor of polished, if rather stiff manners, he moved easily in high society. He joined Brooks's on 20 Dec. 1819, sponsored by Lord Holland and Lord John Russell*, the son of his brother-in-law the 6th duke of Bedford, of whose electoral interests in Bedfordshire, where he also owned inherited property, he was a staunch supporter. He offered again for Reading at the general election of 1820, claiming to have fulfilled all his pledges. At the nomination, when he, the radical Whig John Monck and the Tory John Weyland* were put forward, he denied having voted systematically against government, instancing his support for them on the resumption of cash payments, against an attempt to increase the duty on coals and 'on several other occasions'. He boasted of his resistance to heavy taxation and the coercive legislation adopted after Peterloo. (He had attended and addressed the county protest meeting, 14 Nov. 1819.)[5] On parliamentary reform, of which he was a long-standing advocate, favouring triennial parliaments and a householder franchise, he said that he

> would not support the scheme of annual parliaments and universal suffrage, because he thought all the advantages proposed might be obtained without the danger which appeared to him in that measure. He viewed the Manchester proceedings as having done more mischief to the cause of substantial reform than could be remedied for years.

He was curiously reticent about affirming his support for Catholic relief. After a six-day poll, he beat Weyland into third place by only five votes. Proclaiming the victory of electoral purity and independence, he called for other boroughs to follow Reading's example and so produce 'a useful House of Commons, though he could not promise ... a good one till ... reform was effected'.[6]

Palmer was a conscientious attender, who voted steadily with the advanced wing of the Whig opposition to the Liverpool ministry. Although he was no orator (he was reported as saying in 1821 that 'he could not speak in the House of Commons and durst not attempt it') he was not afraid to intervene in debate.[7] He presented the petition of Reading agriculturists and tradesmen complaining of distress, 19 May,[8] and demanded economies at the Royal Military College, 2 June. He was one of the minority of 12 who voted for a prorogation, 18 Sept. 1820. The previous month he had attended the trial of his friend Major John Cartwright at Warwick.[9] At the Reading meeting in support of Queen Caroline, 7 Dec. 1820, he declared that her 'assailants ... had done more to degrade the kingly dignity than all the radical meetings which had been held for the past 50 years', but he thought that 'a change of ministers without a change of system would be worse than useless': 'the present men were undoubtedly leagued with foreign powers; and, under the present system, he feared English liberty could not exist'. He took the same line at the Bedford meeting, 29 Dec. 1820, when he 'utterly denied that he was a party man'. He also addressed the Berkshire county meeting, 8 Jan. 1821, but was handicapped by a cold.[10] He presented and endorsed Reading and Tilehurst petitions demanding the dismissal of ministers and economical and parliamentary reform, 26 Jan. He complained on 8 Feb. that he had been kept off the commission of the peace for Wiltshire, on whose borders he lived, on account of his 'known political conduct and principles'.[11] He divided for Catholic relief, 28 Feb., 1 Mar., 21 Apr., 10 May 1825. He voted for Leeds to be made a scot and lot borough if it received Grampound's seats, 2 Mar., and spoke for an amendment to the disfranchisement bill, 19 Mar. 1821.[12] He was one of the stewards of the City reform dinner, 4 Apr., when he detailed the attempts being made at Reading to eliminate electoral corruption.[13] Supporting Lambton's reform motion, 17 Apr., he warned that if change was not implemented, 'a tremendous convulsion would ensue'. He missed the division in the fiasco of 18 Apr., but voted for Russell's motion, 9 May, and for reform of the Scottish county representation, 10 May. He was an assiduous supporter throughout the session of economy, retrenchment and reduced taxation. He advocated referral of the Liverpool petition for recall of the Austrian loan to the committee on agricultural distress, 14 Mar., and presented a Biggleswade agriculturists' petition calling for a reduction of taxation, 3 Apr.[14] He demanded to know why the Bedfordshire yeomanry cavalry had tripled in size in the last year, 16 Apr. He was a severe critic of the grant to the duke of Clarence, which he opposed to the bitter end and denounced as an 'abominable' waste of public money, 25, 29 June. He spoke and voted for reception of Broadhurst's petition complaining of conditions in Lancaster gaol, 7 Mar., and on 15 May brought up a petition from a victim of Peterloo and pressed for inquiry, for which he divided next day.[15] On Lord Althorp's county courts bill, 15 Mar., he dismissed a suggestion that their business could be thrown on the quarter sessions, which were already overburdened. He advocated a fresh approach to the problem of smuggling prevention, after the failure of expensive coercive methods, 13 Apr. He said that the plan for an extra post was 'impracticable', 10 May. He saw no merit in the poor relief bill, arguing that rates might easily be diminished under the existing regulations, 24 May; asserting that 'farmers had never paid their labourers sufficient to enable them to support their families', 8 June;[16] and insisting that the laws, 'the chartered rights of the poor', ought not to be tinkered with, 2 July 1821.

At the Reading meeting promoted by the local radicals to pay tribute to Joseph Hume for his parliamentary exertions in the cause of 'economy, retrenchment and reform', 14 Jan. 1822, Palmer received a vote of thanks, with Monck, for supporting him. In response, he damned with faint praise Hume's campaign for economical reform, which however admirable, seemed likely to fail, just as Burke's had. The essential requirement, he argued, was 'a measure of [parliamentary] reform, on a plan much less limited than that pursued' by Hume, who in this respect was only 'a moderate reformer'. He admitted that he had occasionally differed with Monck, but stressed the importance, to compensate for the want of triennial parliaments, of holding regular public meetings to allow popular opinion to be expressed and brought to bear on Members. At the anniversary dinner of the Reading Purity of Election Association two days later he condemned the Constitutional Association, advocated 'reform of an efficient but temperate description' and exhorted extreme radical reformers to settle for what was attainable.[17] On one of his own pet subjects, the 'excrescence' at Sandhurst, he called for savings there, 20 Mar.,[18] and on 28 Mar. he spoke for Hume's attempt to reduce its grant and acted as a teller for the minority of 15. He dismissed Burgess's claims for remuneration for his extra post plan, 2 Apr., when he was a teller for the majority against inquiry, and on 22 July 'objected to the inhumanity of the scheme as it affected the horses'.[19] Yet he was a teller for the majority against the cattle ill-treatment bill, 24 May. He was one of the leading requisitionists of the Bedfordshire county reform meeting, 20 Apr., when he attacked the Grenvillites, who had recently joined the government, complained of the great increase in ministerial patronage and, as well as triennial parliaments, advocated an increase in the number of county Members and the disfranchisement of rotten boroughs, claiming the blessing of Pitt for such a scheme.[20] On the presentation of the meeting's petition, 25 Apr., he denied the allegation of Macqueen, Tory Member for East Looe, that it had been packed with reformers and misrepresented in the press.[21] He voted for Russell's reform motion later that day. He presented and supported the prayer of a Reading petition against the 'present oppressive system of licensing public houses', 1 May, entreated Bennet not to give up the compulsory clause of his licensing bill, 24 May, was a teller for the majority for the measure, 27 June, and expressed regret that the Lords had expunged its two key clauses, 30 July.[22] He presented a Reading petition in favour of Brougham's beer retail bill, 17 July.[23] On 26 July 1822 he asked ministers to extend to agriculturists the full benefit of the reduction of stamp duties.

At the anniversary dinner of the Purity of Election Association, 16 Jan. 1823, Palmer applauded the progress which the reform cause had made locally, but attacked the 'blameable timidity' of country gentlemen in Parliament and censured the Members for close boroughs who sustained ministers in power. He attended the county reform meeting, 27 Jan., but told his audience that their petition would be ignored by the Commons as it stood. He spoke briefly in support of it there, 27 Feb.[24] He questioned the utility of the yeomanry and criticized the Sandhurst establishment as before, 7, 10 Mar.[25] He voted for parliamentary reform, 20 Feb., 24 Apr., the production of information on Inverness elections, 26 Mar., and reform of the Scottish electoral system, 2 June. He asked ministers to relax the beer duties 'a little more', 21 Mar.,[26] and said that 'with certain modifications' the beer duties bill would be an improvement on the existing law, 12 May; but he voted against its report stage, 13 June. He sought leave to introduce a bill to enable public brewers to retail small quantities of beer for off-consumption, 28 May, but withdrew his motion in the face of official hostility. He questioned the chancellor about the scope of the current regulations, 8 July.[27] He spoke and voted against Onslow's bill to repeal the usury laws as 'most ruinous to the agricultural interest', 17 June. He supported the prayer of a Lancashire petition for curbs to be placed on magistrates' powers to levy county rates, 10 July 1823.[28] Palmer was slightly less assiduous in his attendance in 1824, when he seem to have been absent for short periods in March and early April. He voted for reform of Edinburgh's representation, 26 Feb. He presented a petition for repeal of the assessed taxes from Reading, 17 Mar., and advocated the imposition of a tax on 'the barking curs which infested every town and village in England', 18 May.[29] He presented a petition from Reading licensed victuallers against the existing system of excise licenses, 2 Mar., welcomed the beer duties bill as 'a very great improvement', 6 Apr., and presented favourable Reading, Newbury and Sonning petitions, 21, 24 May, when he said that he 'anticipated more good to the mechanics, tradesmen and to the mass of the people, than from any other measure that could be introduced', for the retail breweries, which it sanctioned, were 'calculated to break down the abuses' of the current brewers' monopoly.[30] He opposed Curteis's mariners' apprentices settlement bill as a source of aggravation for magistrates, 17 May, but supported Hume's motion for returns of committals and convictions by justices, 27 May 1824.

Palmer welcomed Stuart Wortley's bill to amend the game laws, 17 Feb. 1825, attributing increases in poaching to the low level of labourers' wages. He spoke and was a teller for the minority for Hume's motion for a return of clergymen holding municipal offices, 17 Mar., when the House was counted out. On 24 Mar. he supported Hume's motion for inquiry into the organization of the Indian army, which he said was riddled with 'discontent'. The same day he opposed Martin's bill to prevent maltreatment of animals, feeling that he had already gone too far with his interference on this subject; he was a teller for the hostile majority. On 22 Feb. he obtained leave to introduce a bill to empower quarter sessions to effect transfers or exchanges between counties of insulated parcels of land for the more convenient administration of justice. It got a second reading, 25 Apr., but at the home secretary Peel's request he had it printed to allow time for local inquiries. He secured a return of all parishes and townships which extended into two counties, 30 June.[31] He was an opponent of the Newbury improvement bill and the Berkshire and Hampshire canal bill. He wished the labourers' wages bill to be given a second reading so that it could be discussed in detail, 2 June 1825.[32] In September, when an early dissolution was expected, the local Tory newspaper reported that despite Palmer's public assertion that he intended to stand, his electoral position was weak and under serious threat from Edward Wakefield, who had started for the borough on the Blue, or Tory, interest earlier in the year. According to the same source, he 'passed a high and extraordinary eulogium' on the Liverpool ministry 'for the liberal and enlightened policy which they had pursued' in recent years at the mayor's inaugural dinner, 3 Oct. 1825.[33]

On the navy estimates, 17 Feb. 1826, Palmer argued that ministers should ascertain the effects of the alteration in the currency, which by its depreciation had inflated public salaries, before levying taxes. He divided with Hume and nine others for an amendment to the promissory notes bill, 27 Feb., and the following day spoke at some length against that 'ill-timed, injudicious' measure, elaborating his argument that unless public expenses were reduced, there could be no safe return to a metallic currency. He denied being an advocate of high prices, but contended that

> if corn were not kept up to a certain price, starvation must ensue amongst the agricultural classes. Ministers had a really difficult task to perform ... they must have low prices for the manufacturers, and they must have high prices for the other classes. But, under these circumstances, they were not justified in the unbounded extravagance of their expenditure. If the difficulty was to be met, it could only be by the most rigid economy.

He was one of the minority of nine against the third reading of the bill, 7 Mar. On 21 Feb. he endorsed the prayer of a Reading silk weavers' petition for protection against foreign imports, blaming government policy for their distress;[34] but he was persuaded not to vote for Ellice's motion for inquiry into the trade, 24 Feb., by the 'powerful' speech of Huskisson, president of the board of trade. He presented a Reading petition for the abolition of slavery, 20 Apr.[35] He voted for Newport's proposal to get rid of non-resident voters in Irish boroughs, 9 Mar., and, supporting Russell's bill to curb electoral bribery, 14 Mar., he argued that 'if the House did not reform itself from within, it would ultimately be reformed from without'. He voted for reform of Edinburgh's representation, 13 Apr., but seems to have missed the division on Russell's general reform motion, 27 Apr. He was present to support the resolutions against bribery, 26 May 1826, when, in response to Gurney's assertion that all Members paid for their seats in one way or another, he denied ever having done so.

Palmer stood again for Reading, as did Monck, at the general election of 1826, when the Blues produced a second man, George Spence, to run with Wakefield.[36] Palmer issued a new edition of his *Letter to the Electors* of 1818, updated to cover the issues of slavery, the corn laws and Catholic emancipation.[37] At the nomination, he boasted of his support for reform, retrenchment, reduced taxation, the abolition of slavery and an open beer retail trade. He denied having voted 'to place the Catholics in power', explaining that he had voted for concession of their claims 'for the purpose of conciliating and relieving the great body of the Irish people'. He praised the 'far more liberal principles' applied by the present ministers to their commercial policy, said that he had supported their recent opening of the ports, and insisted that 'low-priced corn and high taxes were incompatible'. Wakefield withdrew from the contest on the fourth day, in order to improve Spence's chances of beating Palmer for second place, and this he managed to do, by four votes in a poll of over 1,000.[38] Palmer was seated on petition, after a scrutiny of disputed votes by the election committee, 26 Mar. 1827. Four days later he was granted a week's leave on account of ill health. On 12 Apr. he supported the fledgling Canning ministry's corn bill, which he said was 'framed upon strict principles of impartiality', and expressed general support for the administration. In an address to his constituents, he proclaimed that 'the cause of rational liberty is daily adding to the number of its advocates'; and his reinstatement in the seat was lavishly celebrated in the town, 18 Apr.[39] In the House, 4 May, he called for full investigation of the allegations against Lord Charles Somerset's† conduct as governor of the Cape, 17, 30 May, 29 June.[40] He voted for the creation of a separate bankruptcy jurisdiction, 22 May, and for the disfranchisement of Penryn, 28 May. He presented Dissenters' petitions for repeal of the Test Acts, 15 June.[41] At the Reading mayoral dinner, 1 Oct. 1827, he rejoiced in the 'great change' in politicians' views on economy and retrenchment and remarked that 'I have lately found myself, rather unexpectedly I confess, sitting on the same benches with ... ministers, voting with them on important public questions'.[42]

He voted in Hume's minority of eight for naval economies, 12 Feb. 1828. He supported the petition of Reading Dissenters for repeal of the Test Acts, 25 Feb., and voted for that measure the following day. He denounced the 1827 Malt Act as 'injurious to the revenue, hurtful to the maltsters, and prejudicial to the landed interest' and presented a Newbury petition for its repeal, 27 Feb. Later that day he welcomed Acland's bill to improve the regulation of divisions of counties, though he wished its scope to be extended to cover other problems affecting county magistrates; he was named to the committee on the measure, 5 Mar. He voted for the transfer of East Retford's seats to Birmingham, 21 Mar., and on the Penryn disfranchisement bill, 24 Mar., called for a shortening of the duration of polls in all constituencies. He accordingly supported the principle of Davies's borough polls bill, 31 Mar., when he cited Reading in 1826 as an example of how the current law was frequently abused. He was named to the committee on the bill, 2 Apr., but on 23 May complained that ministers had rendered it 'ridiculous' and useless. He voted for inquiry into chancery delays, 24 Apr. He called for protection against common informers on the subject of sales of excisable liquor to be extended to retail brewers, 30 Apr., and the following day voted for the establishment of efficient control over proceedings by the crown for the recovery of excise penalties. On 19 June he obtained leave to introduce a bill to amend the Beer Duties Act so as to prevent informers from plaguing retail brewers. He introduced it, 24 June, but on the 26th set it aside for another one, of which John Wood, Member for Preston, took charge. Palmer presented petitions for Catholic relief, 24, 29 Apr., 8 May, and voted for it, 12 May. He sought to puncture Macqueen's inflated claims for the significance of the Bedfordshire petition for greater agricultural protection, 25 Apr. He voted for information on civil list pensions, 20 May, against the small notes bill, 5 June, for various economies, 6, 20 June, 7 July (though not for reduction of the salary of the lieutenant-general of the ordnance, 4 July), and against the additional churches bill, 30 June. He voted for inquiry into the Irish church, 24 June, and for the corporate funds bill, 10 July. He again blamed inadequate wages for destitution among agricultural labourers, 23 May. On 19 June he presented a Wallingford petition in favour of the alehouses licensing bill and, as a member of Bedford corporation, asserted that they did not consider the measure a violation of their rights. He wanted retail brewers to be allowed to remain open until ten at night for the convenience of agricultural labourers, 8 July. At the Reading mayoral feast, 6 Oct. 1828, he commented on the current 'absence of all party feeling' in national politics and 'the confidence generally felt by the public' in the duke of Wellington's ministry, from which he expected further liberalization.[43]

Palmer moved the address for a return of sheriffs' fees and allowances, 6 Feb., and called for further economies at Sandhurst, 20 Feb. 1829, though he regretted the recent removal of one of its surgeons, who also treated the poor of the neighbourhood. Presenting the Reading petition against Catholic claims, 26 Feb., he said that it was sparsely signed and that local opinion on the issue had 'changed, very materially, within the last few years'. He presented and dissented from an intemperate anti-Catholic petition from Alfold, 17 Mar., and duly voted for emancipation, 6, 30 Mar., and for O'Connell to be allowed to take his seat unhindered, 18 May. He voted against the silk trade bill, 1 May. He was prepared to go into committee on Slaney's labourers' wages bill, even though he thought it would do no good in the prevailing distress, 4 May; and on 15 May he denounced it as a serious threat to employment. Either he or Charles Pallmer, Member for Surrey, voted for the transfer of East Retford's seats to Birmingham, 5 May. He was shut out of the division on Lord Blandford's reform proposals, 2 June 1829. He voted for the amendment to the address, 4 Feb., and on 12 Feb. 1830 urged ministers to tackle distress which, as a magistrate, he knew to be at a level which 'baffles all description'. He voted for reductions in the estimates, 19 Feb., 1, 9 Mar., a revision of taxation, 25 Mar., to abolish the Bathurst and Dundas pensions, 26 Mar., and for inquiry into the management of crown lands revenues, 30 Mar. He voted for the transfer of East Retford's seats to Birmingham, 11 Feb., 5 Mar., against the disfranchisement bill and to incorporate the ballot in it, 15 Mar., and for Blandford's reform scheme, 18 Feb., the enfranchisement of Birmingham, Leeds and Manchester, 23 Feb., investigation of the allegations of electoral interference at Newark against the duke of Newcastle, 1 Mar., and for Russell's reform motion, 28 May. He secured the appointment of a select committee on the expenses attending the office of sheriff, 9 Mar., when he complained of the 'hardships, inconvenience, expense and great responsibility' attached to it. On 20 May, anticipating its report, he said that it was desirable that sheriffs should be allowed to pass their own accounts. He was in O'Connell's small minority for reform of Irish vestries, 27 Apr., and voted for abolition of the lord lieutenancy, 11 May, and repeal of the Irish coal duties, 13 May. He voted against the grant for public buildings, 3 May, to reduce the salary of the assistant secretary to the treasury, 10 May, for information on privy councillors' emoluments, 14 May, and inquiry into the government of Ceylon, 27 May, and to reduce the grants for South American missions, 7 June, and consular services, 11 June. He voted for Jewish emancipation, 17 May. He asserted that in practice tithes amounted to more than a tenth of rents, 18 May. That day he supported Hume's attempt to reduce the salaries of the new judges appointed under the administration of justice bill, which he opposed, 27 May, because it would 'give anything but satisfaction to the Welsh counties'. He voted against it, 18 June. He divided for abolition of the death penalty for forgery, 7 June, and against any increase in recognizances under the libel laws, 6 July. Unlike Monck, he was a supporter of the sale of beer bill, and he presented Reading and Henley petitions in favour of it, 11 May 1830.

He defied the expectations of some by standing again for Reading at the 1830 general election, when Monck retired and recommended in his room Dr. Stephen Lushington*, the eminent civilian, and the Blues put up Charles Russell, the second son of Sir Henry Russell, a former Indian judge, of nearby Swallowfield, whose first son, Henry Russell, another nabob, had taken an active part for Spence in 1826. Palmer made his usual statements of policy on the hustings, adding that while he had 'not supported' government for his first six years as a Member, he had since often 'voted with them' as they had adopted 'a system having for its object the welfare of the country'. He eventually finished top of the poll, with Russell in second place; and he reiterated his intention of supporting government 'so long as a due regard to the rights of the people and a provident expenditure of the public money is continued'.[44] He was one of the five Members who attended the London dinner to celebrate the French revolution, 18 Aug., when he gave the toast to 'purity of election and equal representation'.[45] Ministers of course listed him as one of their 'foes', and Wellington declined to interfere in support of Lady Madelina's request for an army commission for a protégé.[46] At the mayoral dinner, 2 Oct. 1830, Palmer applauded their 'promptitude' in recognizing the new French government, but expressed alarm at 'the revolutionary principles which had lately shown themselves in Brussels'.[47] At the Reading meeting called to petition for repeal of the assessed taxes, 12 Oct., he suggested that in the current climate of opinion 'petitions will be listened to'. He attributed unrest to 'oppression', which was the sole cause of 'revolution', in the shape of heavy taxes and harsh penal laws:

> The misery and distress of the agricultural labourers is constantly on the increase, and unless Parliament insist on an effectual reduction of the taxes it will go on increasing, for the farmer, whilst he has so many calls upon him ... cannot employ the labourers, and they are forced to go to the parish ... The expenditure of every farthing of the public money calls for the severest and closest scrutiny,

> and until the amount is seriously curtailed, the country can never be placed in comfortable circumstances ... Let us prevent revolutionary movements occurring here, by timely representations of our grievances and discontents to Parliament.[48]

He condemned slavery as 'unchristian and inhuman' at a Reading abolitionist meeting, 21 Oct., when he also attended the town reform meeting, called for reform to avert 'a terrible convulsion' and declared his support for the ballot, to which he had been converted by his experience of intimidation at Reading.[49] He voted to reduce the duty on wheat imported to the West Indies, 12 Nov., and against government on the civil list, 15 Nov. He presented Reading petitions for the abolition of slavery, 16 Dec. 1830, and repeal of the assessed taxes, 21 Feb. 1831. He was given a fortnight's leave on account of the disturbed state of his neighbourhood, 30 Nov. 1830.[50] He spoke for reform and the ballot at the county reform meeting, 17 Jan., and at the town meeting, 31 Jan. 1831.[51] He was reported as predicting in early March, when he was given a week's leave because of illness in his family (on the 9th), that the ministerial reform bill would 'miscarry'; but at the Reading meeting to endorse it, 14 Mar., when he complained of the 'bitter, rancorous hostility' of the Tory opposition, he commended it as 'the means of restoring happiness and prosperity to the country'.[52] On the presentation of the county reform petition, 22 Mar., he disputed the allegation of his namesake, the county Member, that there was 'a latent spirit of dissatisfaction' with the bill in Berkshire. He then presented the Reading petition, and later that day he voted for the second reading of the bill. He presented a Maidenhead petition for the proposal to tax steamboat passengers, 14 Apr., and when the county Members presented petitions for repeal of the Beer Act, 18 Apr., he argued that it had made cheaper beer more widely available and done no 'evil'. He voted against Gascoyne's wrecking amendment to the reform bill, 19 Apr. 1831. At the ensuing general election he was returned unopposed as a supporter of the measure with Russell, who had taken the same line. On the hustings he said that the bill was 'founded on reason, and a perfect regeneration of the English constitution':

> He ... should take it cheerfully, as presented by ministers, rather than endanger the whole by cavilling about the clauses. He was now a ministerial man, and while the government was conducted on liberal principles, as at present, doing away with all their patronage, and distinguishing their measures not for individual but the public good, so long would they have his support, but nothing would induce him to deviate from the pledges he had given to his constituents.[53]

Palmer voted for the second reading of the reintroduced reform bill, 6 July 1831, and was a steady supporter of its details in committee, though he took a pair for 8 and 9 Aug. He voted twice with ministers on the Dublin election controversy, 23 Aug. He opposed the use of molasses in brewing, by which 'the trade will again be thrown into the hands of the drug manufacturers', 20 July; and on the presentation of more petitions against the Beer Act, 23 Aug., he again defended the measure, which had provided the poor with 'a wholesome, nourishing beverage, instead of the abominable stuff that used to be very generally sold in the public houses', and benefitted the agricultural interest by raising the price of barley. He presented a Reading petition in favour of the measure, 16 Sept., along with one from local retail brewers and beer sellers asking to be put on the same footing as licensed publicans. He opposed the highways bill, 3 Aug. On 22 Aug. he spoke strongly for compensation to be given to Lescene and Escoffery for their removal from Jamaica in 1823, which he described as 'the grossest act of perfidy and injustice ever committed under the sanction' of a British government, even though his brother-in-law the duke of Manchester had been governor. He called for a reduction of the duties on Cape wines, 7 Sept., and on 16 Sept. sought to excuse the conduct of the Hampshire magistrates in the case of the Deacles. He voted for the passage of the reform bill, 21 Sept., and for the second reading of the Scottish measure, 23 Sept. At the mayoral dinner in Reading, 3 Oct., he confined himself to hoping that the Lords 'would do their duty' after mature deliberation. He voted for the motion of confidence in the Grey ministry, 10 Oct., and, like his colleague, was unable to attend the Reading radical meeting of the following day to consider the current crisis.[54] At the town meeting to honour Monck for his public services, 22 Nov. 1831, Palmer counselled moderation, arguing that further 'riots and tumults' would embarrass the ministry and that as 'enlightened men', the Lords 'must ultimately fall in with the wishes of the people'.[55]

He voted for the second reading of the revised reform bill, 17 Dec. 1831. He seems to have been a little less assiduous than previously in his attendance at the committee stage, for his name appears on the ministerial side in only five of the ten divisions for which lists have been found. He defended the proposal to give three Members to some counties, including Berkshire, 27 Jan. 1832, suggesting that it would break the monopoly enjoyed by 'men of large property' and provide openings for those 'whose talents would be devoted to the public service'. He had something to say on the clause dealing with the compilation of lists of eligible borough voters, 8 Feb. He voted for the third reading of the bill, 22 Mar. After its rejection by the Lords, he voted for the address asking the king to appoint only ministers who would carry it unimpaired, 10 May. At the Reading meeting of 14 May he advised the electors to 'trust no man further than you can see him. if ... [he] does not pledge himself to support enfranchisement, disfranchisement, and the £10 qualification ... reject him'. He said that he did not entirely despair of seeing the Conservatives carry a full reform, and criticized Grey and his colleagues for giving up the fight.[56] In the House later that day, however, he said that

> the general impression in the country is, that there has been a juggle, and that Lord Grey has been cajoled ... There is at the moment an excitement throughout the country which must be allayed soon, or it will burst out into a species of violence that I will not take upon me to describe.

On 21 May he welcomed the Scottish reform bill, recalling how his uncle, Thomas Fyshe Palmer, a Unitarian minister, whom he claimed to have visited in the hulks in 1794, had been transported for advocating reform. He attributed the change in opinion since those dark days to Tory 'misgovernment', excessive taxation and interference with the currency. He voted for the second reading of the Irish bill, 25 May, and against any increase in the Scottish county representation, 1 June, and again applauded the triumph of reform in Scotland, 27 June. He subscribed £20 towards the cost of the Reading celebrations of the passage of reform in July.[57] He voted with ministers on the Russian-Dutch loan, 26 Jan., 20 July (pairing on 12 July), relations with Portugal, 9 Feb., and the navy civil departments bill, 6 Apr., but was in the minority in favour of a reduction in the salary of the Irish registrar of deeds, 9 Apr. 1832.

On 14 Feb. 1832 Palmer got permission to bring in a bill to regulate and reduce the expenses of the office of sheriff, explaining that 'I intend to make that which is now avoided by country gentlemen an object of ambition'. He introduced it, 23 Feb., and after its second reading, 7 Mar., it was referred to a select committee. It passed the Commons on 20 July, when Palmer defeated an attempt to expunge the clause ending the procession of sheriffs to meet assize judges, but made no further progress. He praised the Oundle system of empowering select vestries to provide work for the able-bodied poor, 17 Feb. He presented petitions from Reading and Leighton Buzzard in favour of the bill to regulate children's factory hours, 10 Apr., and a Reading Dissenters' petition against the death penalty for non-violent crimes against property, 8 May. On 7 May he deplored the 'general cry' which had been got up against beer shops, merely because a few had given cause for complaint, and appealed for the Sale of Beer Act to be given a fair trial. He therefore opposed a proposal to introduce an amendment bill, which he dismissed as a bid to restore the brewers' harmful monopoly, 31 May; he was a teller for the hostile majority. He showed that he had misunderstood the object of Campbell's bill to reform the law of dower, 8 June. He sought confirmation of the exemption from tax of agricultural carts used to carry domestic coals on their return from market, 29 June 1832.

Palmer was returned unopposed for Reading at the general election of 1832, but he fell foul of the local radicals in 1835. He recovered the seat in 1837 and retired from Parliament at the next dissolution.[58] He died in January 1843. By his terse will of 4 Oct. 1832 he left all his property to his wife.[59]

[1] See J.M. Bulloch, 'Charles Fyshe Palmer', *N and Q*, clx (1931), 399-401; W. Lyon, *Chrons. Finchampstead*, 128. [2] *N and Q*, clx. 463; E. Hasted, *Kent*, ix. 572-3; Northill (Beds.) par. reg. [3] *The Times*, 28 Nov. 1831; *Eton Coll. Reg. 1753-1790*, p. 406. [4] *Life of Mary Russell Mitford* ed. A.G.K. L'Estrange, ii. 31, 35; *Letters of Mary Russell Mitford* (ser. 2) ed. H.F. Chorley, i. 56. [5] *The Times*, 16 Nov. 1819. [6] Ibid. 29 Feb., 4, 11-17 Mar.; *Reading Mercury*, 21 Feb., 13 Mar. 1820. [7] *The Times*, 5 Apr. 1821. [8] Ibid. 20 May 1820. [9] *Cartwright Corresp.* ed. F.D. Cartwright, ii. 186, [10] *The Times*, 11, 30 Dec. 1820, 9 Jan. 1821. [11] Ibid. 9 Feb. 1821. [12] Ibid. 8 Mar. 1821. [13] Ibid. 4, 5 Apr. 1821. [14] Ibid. 15 Mar., 4 Apr. 1821. [15] Ibid. 8 Mar., 16 May 1821. [16] Ibid. 9 June 1821. [17] Ibid. 16, 19 Jan. 1822. [18] Ibid. 21 Mar. 1822. [19] Ibid. 23 July 1822. [20] Ibid. 22 Apr. 1822; Buckingham, *Mems. Geo. IV*, i. 289. [21] *The Times*, 26 Apr. 1822. [22] Ibid. 2 May, 31 July 1822. [23] Ibid. 18 July 1822. [24] Ibid. 18, 28 Jan., 28 Feb. 1823. [25] Ibid. 8, 11 Mar. 1823. [26] Ibid. 22 Mar. 1823. [27] Ibid. 9 July 1823. [28] Ibid. 11 July 1823. [29] Ibid. 18 Mar., 19 May 1824. [30] Ibid. 22, 25 May 1824. [31] Ibid. 1 July 1825. [32] Ibid. 6 May, 1, 3, 11 June 1825. [33] *Berks. Chron.* 17, 24 Sept., 8 Oct.; *Reading Mercury*, 26 Sept. 1825. [34] *The Times*, 22 Feb. 1826. [35] Ibid. 21 Apr. 1826. [36] *Reading Mercury*, 13 Mar., 3 Apr.; *The Times*, 11 May 1826. [37] *Berks. Chron.* 6 May; *Reading Mercury*, 8 May 1826. [38] *Reading Mercury*, 19, 26 June 1826; Bodl. MS. Eng. lett. c. 159, f. 47. [39] *Reading Mercury*, 16, 23 Apr. 1827. [40] *The Times*, 18, 31 May 1827. [41] Ibid. 16 June 1827. [42] *Reading Mercury*, 8 Oct. 1827. [43] Ibid. 13 Oct. 1828. [44] Ibid. 12 July, 9, 16, 23 Aug.; *The Times*, 20 July, 3-7, 9-13 Aug. 1830. [45] Add. 56555, f. 13; *The Times*, 19 Aug. 1830. [46] Wellington mss WP1/1138/12. [47] *Berks. Chron.* 9 Oct. 1830. [48] *Reading Mercury*, 18 Oct. 1830. [49] *Berks. Chron.* 23 Oct.; *Reading Mercury*, 25 Oct. 1830. [50] Bodl. MS. Eng. lett. c. 160, f. 241. [51] *Reading Mercury*, 24 Jan., 7 Feb. 1831. [52] Bodl. MS. Eng. lett. c. 160, f. 91; *Reading Mercury*, 21 Mar. 1831. [53] *Reading Mercury*, 25 Apr., 2 May 1831. [54] *Berks. Chron.* 8 Oct.; *Reading Mercury*, 17 Oct. 1831; Bodl. MS. Eng.lett. d. 153, ff. 209-14. [55] *The Times*, 28 Nov. 1831. [56] Bodl. MS. Eng. lett. d. 154, f. 101; *Reading Mercury*, 21 May 1832. [57] Bodl. MS. Eng. lett. d. 154, f. 113. [58] N. Gash, *Politics in Age of Peel*, 284-91. [59] *Reading Mercury*, 28 Jan. 1843; PROB 8/236 (15 Feb. 1843); 11/1975/127.

D.R.F.

PALMER, Robert (1793–1872), of Holme Park, Sonning, nr. Reading, Berks. and 6 Charles Street, Berkeley Square, Mdx.

BERKSHIRE 30 Mar. 1825–1831

BERKSHIRE 7 June 1832–1859

b. 31 Jan. 1793, 1st s. of Richard Palmer of Hurst and Holme Park and Jane, da. of Oldfield Bowles of North Aston, Oxon. *educ.* Eton 1805; Trinity Coll. Camb. 1810. *unm. suc.* fa. 1806. *d.* 24 Nov. 1872.

Sheriff, Berks. 1818-19.

Palmer's ancestors had settled in the parish of Hurst, six miles east of Reading, by 1600. His grandfather Robert Palmer, a London attorney, prospered as the long-serving principal agent to the dukes of Bedford. He bought Hurst Lodge in 1742, and subsequently acquired property on the nearby manors of Sonning, Berkshire, and Sonning Eye, across the river in Oxfordshire. He died 21 Jan. 1787 at his London house in Great Russell Street, reputedly 'possessed of £45,000 a year freehold, and at least £60,000 in mortgages and in the stocks'. He was succeeded by Richard Palmer, his only son with his second wife Charlotte Wakelin (his first marriage had been childless), who was born in 1768.[1] In 1795 he bought Sonning House and its estates from Admiral Rich. He demolished the existing house the following year, and built a new one, Holme Park. He died 29 July 1806, a week after making his will, by which he provided his wife with an annuity of £400, in addition to her entitlement under their marriage settlement, and left £15,000 between his younger sons Richard (1795-1874) and Henry (1799-1870), who both entered the church, and their five sisters. His personalty was proved under £45,000.[2] The principal beneficiary was his eldest son Robert, who was then a 13-year-old boy at Eton. Soon after he went to Cambridge, where he did not graduate, his uncle Charles Bowles told Farington that on coming of age he would have '7 or £8,000 a year besides money'.[3] It was reported that at the 'treat' which he gave on attaining his majority, 31 Jan. 1814, 'Mr. Foster of Woodley, having drunk rather too much, was laid by to refresh, but was soon afterwards found to be dead'.[4]

In December 1816 Palmer turned down an invitation from the Tory corporation of Reading to stand for the borough at the next general election; and the home secretary Lord Sidmouth, who lived at nearby Woodley, declined to intervene with him, though he professed to be 'confident that the town ... could not have a worthier representative'.[5] At the county meeting to petition against the renewal of the suspension of habeas corpus, 10 June 1817, Palmer was one of the three members of the local Pitt Club who 'held up their hands against it'.[6] He attended the county meeting to address George IV, 8 Mar. 1820, and later that day he nominated for re-election the Grenvillite Whig sitting Member Richard Neville, observing as he did so that it was a duty to posterity to hand down a constitution 'improved if possible, but certainly not deteriorated'.[7] On Neville's succession to the peerage at the end of February 1825 Palmer offered for the county, ostensibly in response to a requisition got up by the leading Tory squires. He was threatened with an opposition from the radical reformer William Hallett, who had contested Berkshire at the three previous general elections. (In 1818 Palmer, as sheriff and returning officer, had been personally inconvenienced by Hallett's vexatious protraction of the poll to its maximum duration.) In the event Hallett, who was too ill to appear in person, withdrew at the last minute. At the nomination Palmer claimed that

> he came forward politically a perfectly independent man; by independence, he meant that he was not particularly attached or bound to any public party ... or biased by any party feeling. Nevertheless ... when he considered the present unexampled state of the prosperity of the country, in all the branches and relations of its trade, commerce and manufactures, coupled with the gradual and material reduction of the public burdens, and the confident anticipation of their speedy and still further diminution – in a word, when those who had so efficiently and with such advantage to the country held the reins of government, he ... thought such ministers, under whose wise and able administration these results had been obtained, were justly entitled to his support as well as that of the country at large.

At the same time, he reserved his right to exercise independent judgement on specific issues.[8] In a favourably disposed newspaper, he was fancifully described as being

> of a lofty stature, and gifted with a fine manly figure. His countenance is marked and expressive, and his eye intelligent. His voice is sufficiently powerful for the purposes of oratory, but he does not strike the observer as a practised speaker. His manner is both modest and resolute; in it may be remarked a strong feeling of independence, guided by genuine English caution.[9]

He presented the petition of Wallingford corporation against Catholic relief, 18 Apr.,[10] voted accordingly, 21 Apr. (but not on 10 May), and was in the minority against the disfranchisement of Irish 40*s.* freeholders, 26 Apr. 1825. He presented a petition from Wokingham against alteration of the corn laws, 25 Apr.[11] He voted with the Liverpool ministry to go into committee on the duke of Cumberland's annuity bill, 6 June, and was listed in the majority for the third reading on the 10th; but he wrote to *The Times* to assert that he had not been in the House on the second occasion and that he had voted in the minority on 6 June for Brougham's amendment to restrict the grant to £3,000.[12] In 1826, he divided with government on the Jamaican slave trials, 2 Mar., and the salary of the president of the board of trade, 10 Apr. At the general election he was returned unopposed with the veteran Whig sitting Member Charles Dundas. On the hustings, he replied to criticism that by his vote of 10 Apr. he had supported 'a great ministerial job' and 'a measure for increasing the influence of the government in the House of Commons': he repudiated such an inference, insisting that he had merely voted for adequate remuneration, as originally proposed by opposition, for a deserving individual minister, Huskisson. He was also anxious to dispel the notion that he was hostile to the interests of agriculture. Without going in detail into the question of the corn laws, he warned that ministers were certain to make 'some alteration' in them next session:

> Nor, indeed, have I heard any gentleman contend, that, under the existing state of the country, they ought to remain the permanent law of the land. I think that, if those principles of free trade which Parliament have thought proper to adopt (and be it remembered that they were adopted before I took a seat in that assembly) are to be persevered in, the same principle must be extended to the article of corn, taking care, at the same time, that a fair and sufficient protection be secured to the agriculturists of this country.

He suggested that before Parliament met the local agriculturists might confer and then inform himself and Dundas of their views by deputation. He reiterated his hostility to Catholic relief, and proclaimed himself 'an unfettered man', who would 'maintain his seat upon independent principles'.[13]

In February 1827 he felt obliged to give a written public explanation of his comments on free trade and protection, which had caused disquiet in the farming community. He denied having advocated repeal of the corn laws or expressed approval of free trade doctrines, and said that he had only intended to apprise the agriculturists of 'what I conceived would be the probable result of the deliberations of Parliament upon this question', so that they could give it due consideration. He promised to treat all petitions with 'attention'.[14] He presented one from Maidenhead against alteration of the corn laws, 27 Feb., together with others from Wallingford against the importation of foreign wool and from the farmers of north Berkshire for repeal of the Weights and Measures Act.[15] On the second reading of the corn bill, 2 Apr., he acknowledged the deficiencies of the Act of 1815, but said that as the representative of 'a very large class of persons engaged in agricultural pursuits', who believed that 'a great part of the poor lands must be thrown out of cultivation by the permission to import foreign corn', he felt it his 'duty' to oppose the measure from his conviction of 'the utter ruin which must fall upon the agriculturists'. On 26 Feb., having been primed by the Tories of Wallingford, he gave details of the 'flagrant bribery and corruption' practised there by the Whig sitting Member William Hughes, which highlighted the 'total inefficacy' of the existing Bribery Act. He therefore supported Lord Althorp's motion for the establishment of a select committee to consider petitions alleging electoral bribery; but later in the debate he expressed a preference for Williams Wynn's suggestion that the time limits governing the presentation of such petitions be extended. He rubbed Dundas's Whig nose in the dirt of Wallingford corruption, 19 Mar.[16] He voted against Catholic relief, 6 Mar. On 28 May 1827 he voted against the disfranchisement of Penryn, but for Althorp's bill to curb the expense of elections.

Palmer, who was appointed to the finance committee, 15 Feb., voted for repeal of the Test Acts 'as an act of kindness and conciliation' which posed no threat to the established church, 26 Feb. 1828. He secured a return of information on redeemed land tax, 5 Mar. He presented an anti-Catholic petition from the clergy of the archdeaconry of Berkshire, 25 Apr., and voted against relief, 12 May. He presented a petition against the alehouses licensing bill, 30 Apr., and on 19 June objected to a clause which seemed to demean borough magistrates. He said that Stuart Wortley's bill to legalize the sale of game would not put an end to poaching, 13 June. He presented Vale petitions for increased protection against foreign wool, 1 July, and one from Reading victuallers against the beer bill, 8 July. He was not in the Wellington ministry's majority on the ordnance estimates, 4 July 1828. Planta, the patronage secretary, submitted Palmer's name to the home secretary Peel as a possible mover or seconder of the address at the opening of the 1829 session, but he was not selected.[17] Planta was in any case 'doubtful' as to how he would vote on Catholic emancipation, though he numbered him among those who would, 'when the principle is carried, support the securities'. Presenting four hostile petitions from Berkshire, 16 Feb., Palmer stated that while he concurred in their contention that the concession of Catholic claims would endanger the Protestant establishment, he was prepared in these 'totally different' circumstances to listen with an open mind to what ministers had to propose, as he was 'in the habit of looking up with confidence' to them. He hoped, though with little optimism, for a satisfactory settlement of the issue. He presented a petition from Reading against emancipation, 26 Feb., but voted to consider the ministerial scheme, 6 Mar., explaining three days later that he felt 'there is no choice left to us ... but to come to the adjustment of this question'. At the same time, he feared the worst from the Irish Catholics' opposition to the bill to disfranchise 40*s.* freeholders and reserved his right to oppose the relief bill if he concluded that it would not bring peace to Ireland. He presented favourable petitions from Dorset, 16 Mar., and probably voted for the third reading of the bill, 30 Mar. He presented a petition from the archdeaconry of Berkshire against the annual Maynooth grant, 9 Apr. He voted in the minority against the grant for the Marble Arch, 27 May, and presented a Berkshire wool producers' petition for protection, 27 May 1829.

Palmer spoke and voted for Knatchbull's amendment to the address, 4 Feb. 1830, when he deplored ministers' failure to admit the full extent of the 'very great distress' which prevailed. His stand on this issue was said to have given 'great satisfaction' at the Reading corn market two days later.[18] On 18 Feb. he supported the prayer of the Berkshire agriculturists' petition, presented by his colleague, for repeal of the beer, malt nd hops taxes. He thought this a more practical soluion to their problems than currency reform, though e believed that the resumption of cash payments had used much hardship. Later that day he voted against ord Blandford's parliamentary reform scheme, as he d the enfranchisement of Birmingham, Leeds and anchester, 23 Feb. He voted against government the Bathurst and Dundas pensions, 26 Mar., and grant for Windsor Castle improvements, 3 May, n Goulburn, the chancellor, complained that ner and other country gentlemen had acted thus bily' 'with a view to their elections'.[19] He was rted to have been a dinner guest of Wellington, 4 [0] He presented Maidenhead petitions for mitigaf the death penalty for forgery, 5, 27 Apr., but t vote for that measure, 7 June. He voted against emancipation, 5 Apr., 17 May. He argued e sale of beer bill went 'a great deal too far', 4 ecured an amendment to it, 3 June, and voted ers to modify its impact, 21 June, 1 July. On 4 expressed regret that Lord Stanley had withis bill to deal with the removal of Irish and vagrant paupers, a 'serious evil' in Berkshire, roved Sturges Bourne's suggestion that parishes be empowered to assist at their own discretion. He voted against going into committee on the administration of justice bill, 18 June. On 30 June 1830 he divided in the opposition minority in the first division on a regency, but was 'driven away' from the second by Henry Brougham's 'violent' speech.[21]

At the Berkshire meeting to vote condolences and congratulations to William IV, 24 July 1830, Palmer, who was reported to be 'not popular in the county', responded to Whig and radical demands for notice to be taken of distress by saying that 'no man felt more for the privations of the labouring classes than he did', and that he would be 'ever ready to take charge of any petitions to the House of Commons on the subject, and to advocate to the utmost of his powers, any measures that might be calculated to afford relief'.[22] There was no opposition to the return of himself and Dundas at the general election, when he explained his pragmatic support for Catholic emancipation. His cautious comments on the question of slavery, which he seemed to some of his audience to be defending, created dissatisfaction, and he had subsequently to issue a public explanation of his views, in which he insisted that abolition must be accompanied by 'a due consideration of the interests of the West Indian proprietors'. On parliamentary reform, he substantiated his claim that he was 'always ready to remove practical corruption wherever it was detected' with an assertion that he had voted for the transfer of East Retford's seats to Birmingham, though his name appears in none of the surviving division lists on that issue. He professed to favour the enfranchisement of unrepresented 'commercial towns' at the expense of 'corrupt boroughs', but considered that 'radical reform', especially the ballot, would produce 'universal confusion': 'he was, therefore, a moderate reformer, but an objector to extensive innovation'. He boasted of the achievements of the finance committee in reducing public expenditure and called for tax remissions and inquiry into the civil list, though he was not sure that significant savings could be made in the latter. He asserted that the present corn laws provided 'an inadequate protection' against a poor harvest, and promised that on this subject he would 'be found a faithful expositor of their local sentiments'.[23] According to Charles Russell, the new Member for Reading, he gave a 'gentlemanly and unpretending' speech at the visitation feast of the grammar school in October 1830.[24]

Palmer, whom ministers listed among their 'friends', approved Williams Wynn's proposal to do away with various antiquated oaths required to be sworn by Members before taking their seats, 4 Nov.

1830, and called for a general reduction of the 'enormous number' of unnecessary oaths imposed on public officers and for an end to 'all civil disqualification in consequence of religious belief'. He voted against government on Parnell's motion for the appointment of a select committee on the civil list, to which he was named, 15 Nov. He was given a month's leave, 30 Nov. 1830, on account of the 'disturbed state of his county'. Russell reported that he 'very sensibly' said that 'against the fires' enrolling a yeomanry 'would be of no avail', and that he 'employed men to watch very vigilantly at night' and recommended his tenantry to do likewise, 'undertaking to share the expense with them'.[25] He was a member of the grand jury for the special commission which tried rioters at Reading at the end of December 1830, when he had 'much conversation upon the subject of reform' with the foreman, Sir John Walsh of Warfield, Member for Sudbury.[26] He attended the Berkshire reform meeting, 17 Jan. 1831, and, while insisting on his right to act as he saw fit, and suggesting that the country's problems were not solely attributable to the defects of the representative system, said that he would welcome any 'practical and rational reform', specifically the enfranchisement of large manufacturing towns, and that he would present the petition. Under pressure to support it in the House, he said that he would comply 'so far as its prayer was for practical, rational and effectual reform'.[27] He was as good as his word when he presented it, 8 Feb., and he went on to observe that

> having heard that the [Grey] government are unanimous in opinion as to the plan about to be proposed, and liking the constitution of the government, I entertain a sanguine hope that the plan will be such as this House may adopt, without endangering the structure of the constitution.

He presented a petition from the West Indian proprietors of Berkshire praying for fair compensation if slavery was abolished, 10 Feb. At the county meeting called to endorse the ministerial reform bill, 16 Mar., he admitted that he found himself 'in a situation of some difficulty', having expressed his support for 'rational and practical reform' and expected from an administration containing three former Canningites a moderate measure, but now being confronted with one which he considered to be 'much too sweeping': it 'went at once, and too extensively, to objects, which even if necessary, should be gradually sought'. He particularly objected to the proposal to disfranchise many boroughs which were not tainted by corruption, and argued that the bill, which failed to tackle the problem of bribery, was the thin end of the radical reform wedge. He approved, however, the proposals to do away with corporation boroughs as such and to enfranchise 50*s.* copy and leaseholders in the counties. In deference to his constituents' strong feelings in favour of the bill, he promised not to oppose its second reading, but made it clear that he would try to have it significantly modified in committee.[28] After Dundas had presented the Berkshire petition, 22 Mar., he admitted that his own had been the only dissentient voice at the meeting and reiterated his opinion that the bill went much further than the 'substantial' measure of reform which he was prepared to swallow. In accordance with his promise, he voted for the second reading later that day. He declined to support Hume's amendment to reduce the civil list grant by £12,000, 25 Mar., arguing that it was intended 'only for a contingency fund', but he reflected that the select committee seemed to have laboured 'for very little purpose indeed'. On Benett's motion to suspend the issue of the Liverpool writ, 29 Mar., he aired his view that the reform bill as it stood would not curb bribery and promised to propose a clause requiring succes[sful] candidates to swear that they had not resorted [to] it. He presented a petition against the Kennet navi[ga]tion bill, 13 Apr., and others from Berkshire aga[inst] the Sale of Beer Act, which he said had encour[aged] the labouring poor to waste their time and mon[ey in] drinking, 18 Apr. 1831. The following day he vot[ed for] Gascoyne's wrecking amendment to the reform [bill].

Palmer sought to retain his seat at the [...] general election, but he was up against it f[...] start, when he effectively left it up to th[...] to determine whether or not he should [...] Dundas was joined by another unreserved [...] and Palmer's statement that although he co[...] the whole length' of the government schem[e ...] friend to a substantial but at the same ti[me ...] measure, such as would extend the elect[...] where it can be shown to be necessary, [...] abuses', cut no ice with the overwhelmi[ng] majority. His withdrawal from the con[test ...] determined in consultation with his l[...] ers, was announced at the nominatio[n ...] 1831, and in an address the followin[g ...] that 'the force of public opinion', [...] his former supporters shared, had [...] admit defeat. Walsh thought that [...] retired, reserved man, caring v[...] representation of the county, an[d ...] trouble', had thrown in the towel [...] of his opponents acknowled[g...] honesty.[29]

It was expected that Dundas would be made a peer, and Palmer indicated in the autumn of 1831 that he would in that case stand for the county.[30] Yet in January 1832 Walsh reported that, reticent as ever, he seemed unwilling to incur the expense of a contest. A meeting of leading Tories, 25 Jan., failed to agree on starting a subscription for him, but set on foot a preparatory canvass. Palmer was 'very general in his expressions about politics [and] declared that he never would come in as the tool of any party, which watchword gave him an opportunity of evading all declarations about politics'. He did, however, 'say that he should oppose the reform bill on the second [sic] reading'. In view of this, Walsh was 'rather surprised' in March by Palmer's expression of his 'perfect willingness' to become a member of the Carlton Club. Walsh, who saw him as 'an important acquisition', was quick to put the necessary measures in train so as 'to fix him'.[31] Palmer duly offered when Dundas's peerage was ratified in May 1832. Denying the allegation that he was 'an enemy to the principle of reform', he stated his belief that

> a measure of reform, embracing the principal features of the bill now in progress, namely the abolition of nomination boroughs, the proportionate enfranchisement of important towns, together with an extension of the elective franchise, is necessary to afford satisfaction to the country.

Challenged by reformers to clarify his views and to state categorically whether he would support the current bill 'unimpaired in all its essentials', he replied in a public letter of 17 May, when the reform ministers had been reinstated, that while he could not make such a pledge, 'in direct contradiction of my former and present opinions, as to some of the details of that measure, and especially of the qualification clause', he would not oppose the passage of the bill, in the unlikely event of its returning to the Commons. The reformers rallied behind Hallett.[32] Palmer excused himself from attendance at the county meeting to address the king and petition the Lords in support of the bill, 25 May, on the ground that he had 'caught so bad a cold during my canvass, that I am totally unable to speak a word audibly'. At the nomination, he denied being a Tory stooge, stressed that as reform was now safe those who had deserted him the previous year could safely return to their allegiance, and claimed that he had not voted for Gascoyne's amendment with the intention of killing the reform bill, which he had wished to go into committee. He had no objection to inquiry into the possibility of an equitable commutation of tithes, but he was opposed to any 'spoliation'. On the opening day of the election, he argued that the corn and poor laws were issues of more immediate importance to the agricultural interest than was reform, but observed that misguided Tory resistance to any change in 1830 (from which he absolved himself) had done much to precipitate the crisis. He boasted of his constant attendance and unfailing support for reductions on the 1828 finance committee, and his vote against the Wellington ministry on the civil list. He was reported to have lapsed three times into a lengthy and unaccountable silence.[33] During the seven-day poll Palmer, who flatly denied a charge that he had in fact voted for East Retford to be thrown into the hundreds, rather than be disfranchised for the benefit of Birmingham, observed that when the reform bill had been

> passed, and there shall no longer be any ground for objecting to our system of representation, I trust that there will arise in the country a strong and influential Conservative party, which will be always ready to stand by the throne, by the altar and by the people. There is a party in the state ... which may be distinguished under the title of levellers, men, who, under the specious sound of reform, are ready to pull down the institutions which they have neither the intelligence nor the virtue to admire. If the time will ever come when these men will endeavour to carry their designs into execution, I shall be found one of the Conservative party, and I have no doubt that in this county, as well as throughout England, that party will have the predominance.

After his comfortable victory over Hallett, in a contest which attracted considerable national attention, he declared that the basic issue had not been reform, but 'whether the gentry and yeomanry of this county should have the liberty to return a Member ... of their own choosing, or whether they should submit to the dictation of the political unions'.[34] In the House, 28 June 1832, he requested government action to reduce the 'incredible annual expense' incurred by Berkshire in dealing with transient Irish paupers. He approved of Burrell's labourers employment bill, 9 July, arguing that it was 'better that a man should be employed and earn his livelihood, than that he should be paid out of the parish rate for doing nothing'. He voted against government on the Russian-Dutch loan, 12 July. He called for an end to the squabble over Lord Brougham's offensive remarks about Sir Edward Sugden*, though he thought Brougham owed an apology, 27 July. He endorsed the principle of the bribery bill, 30 July 1832, but thought it required more careful consideration than the House was able to give it at that late stage of the Parliament.

Palmer topped the poll for Berkshire at the 1832 general election and sat for the county until his retirement in 1859. Left to his own devices, he might well have followed Peel on repeal of the corn laws in 1846, but rampant protectionism among his farming constituents gave him little choice but to oppose it.[35] A long-serving chairman of Berkshire quarter sessions, he died a bachelor in November 1872.[36] By his will, dated 10 May 1849, he left all his real estate except a farm in Essex, which he devised to his brother Henry, to his brother Richard, rector of Purley, Berkshire. He bequeathed £5,000 each (doubled by a codicil of 5 Mar. 1862) to Henry and his surviving sisters Elizabeth, Susanna Caroline and Laura Frances. After Henry's death in 1870 he made over the Essex property to Richard, his residuary legatee (18 Jan. 1871). He left a total of £4,000 in three per cent consols to form a trust fund for the inmates of his almshouses at Sonning, and £2,000 to provide coals for the deserving poor of the parish. On the Rev. Richard Palmer's death the estates passed to his sister Susanna, and she was succeeded in 1880 by her nephew the Rev. Henry Golding, son of her sister Charlotte, who took the name of Palmer.

[1] *VCH Berks.* iii. 249; N. Gash, *Politics in Age of Peel*, 304; *Gent. Mag.* (1787), i. 94; PROB 11/1149/738. [2] *VCH Berks.* iii. 204, 213, 514; E.W. Dormer, 'Bishops' Manor at Holme Park', *Berks. Arch. Jnl.* xxxviii (1934), 177-83; A. Perkins, *Bk. of Sonning*, 7, 101, 104; PROB 11/1449/738; IR26/115/132. [3] *Farington Diary*, xi. 3845. [4] [W. Turner], *Reading 70 Years Ago* ed. P.H. Ditchfield, 11. [5] Ibid. 60; Devon RO, Sidmouth mss, Sidmouth to Simonds, 16 Dec. 1816. [6] *Reading 70 Years Ago*, 67. [7] *The Times*, 9 Mar. 1820. [8] *Berks. Chron.* 5, 12, 19, 26 Mar.; *Reading Mercury*, 7, 14, 21, 28 Mar.; *The Times*, 25, 31 Mar. 1825. [9] *Berks. Chron.* 2 Apr. 1825; Add. 28673, f. 365. [10] *Berks. Chron.* 30 Apr. 1825. [11] *The Times*, 26 Apr. 1825. [12] Ibid. 14 June; *Berks. Chron.* 18 June 1825. [13] *Berks. Chron.* 3, 24 June; *The Times*, 21 June 1826. [14] *Berks. Chron.* 10, 17, 24 Feb., 3 Mar. 1827. [15] *The Times*, 28 Feb. 1827. [16] Ibid. 20 Mar. 1827. [17] Add. 40398, f. 85. [18] *Berks. Chron.* 13 Feb. 1830. [19] Add. 40333, f. 101. [20] *Berks. Chron.* 10 Apr. 1830. [21] Grey mss, Howick jnl. 11 July [1830]. [22] *Berks. Chron.* 31 July 1831; NLW, Ormathwaite mss FG1/5, p. 10. [23] *The Times*, 9 Aug.; *Reading Mercury*, 9, 16 Aug. 1830. [24] Bodl. MS. Eng. lett. c. 160, f. 205. [25] Ormathwaite mss FG1/5, p.135; Bodl. MS. Eng. lett. c. 160, ff. 232, 241. [26] Ormathwaite mss FG1/5, pp. 149-50. [27] *Reading Mercury*, 24 Jan. 1831. [28] *The Times*, 17 Mar. 1831; Bodl. MS. Eng. lett. d. 153, f. 107; Surr. Hist. Cent. Goulburn mss Acc 304/67B, Goulburn to wife, 17 Mar. 1831. [29] *Reading Mercury*, 25 Apr., 2, 9, 16 May 1831; Add. 28671, f. 124; Ormathwaite mss FG1/5, p. 181; Warws. RO, Throckmorton mss CR 1998/Tribune/folder 16/28, 30, 31; Gash, 300-2. [30] Bodl. MS. Eng. lett. d. 153, f. 174; *Reading Mercury*, 10, 17, 24, 31 Oct., 7 Nov. 1831. [31] Ormathwaite mss FG1/6, pp. 5, 6, 9, 10, 52. [32] *Berks. Chron.* 12, 19 May; *Reading Mercury*, 14, 21 May; *The Times*, 23-25 May 1832. [33] *The Times*, 26, 29 May, 1 June 1832. [34] Ibid. 2, 4-9 June 1832; Ormathwaite mss FG1/6, pp. 79, 80, 83, 84, 87. [35] Gash, 317-18. [36] *The Times*, 26 Nov. 1872.

D.R.F.

PALMERSTON, 3rd Visct. [I] *see* **TEMPLE, Henry John**

PARES, Thomas (1790–1866), of Kirby Frith and Ulverscroft Cottage, Leics. and Hopwell Hall, Derbys.[1]

LEICESTER 1818–1826

b. 30 Oct. 1790, 1st s. of John Pares, hosier and banker, of The Newarke, Leicester and Agnes, da. and coh. of Adam Lightbody of Liverpool, Lancs. *educ.* Eton; Trinity Coll. Camb. 1808; L. Inn 1808, called 1818. *m.* 19 May 1821, Octavia, da. of Edward Longdon Mackmurdo of Upper Clapton, Mdx., 3s. surv. 4da. *suc.* uncle Thomas Pares to Kirby Frith 1824; fa. to Hopwell Hall 1833. *d.* 26 Apr. 1866.

Sheriff, Derbys. 1845-6.

Pares, the conventionally educated son of a Nonconformist Leicester hosiery manufacturer and banker, who evidently did not practise after his call to the bar, was returned unopposed for the borough in 1820, having ousted the corporation candidate in 1818. In his address he promised his continued 'undeviating endeavours to protect ... liberties, and guard against every increase in the public burthens or improvident use of the public money'.[2] He had been admitted to Brooks's Club on 11 Feb. 1819, and he continued to vote with the Whig opposition to the Liverpool ministry on most major issues, at least up to 1825. In early July 1820 he complained to his sister of the 'unwearied attention' he was obliged to give to his parliamentary duties:

> I am almost run off my legs by hard work and ... of the last 27 hours, 22 have been passed in the House of Commons. The truth is I am on ... [the Grantham] election committee ... Six or seven hours is the usual period of our confinement and when [to] this occupation of the morning, late night sittings in the House are added, it is difficult (if not impossible) to find time for one's ordinary meals and rest.

But there were compensations, as when the committee unseated a ministerialist, 11 July, thus giving 'a death blow to the influence of one of the corruptest corporations in the kingdom'. The Queen Caroline affair 'engages all the attention of everybody', he told his sister, 25 July 1820, but 'of her innocence I am sorry to say not even the Whigs themselves seem to entertain very much strong conviction'. He joined in the parliamentary attack on ministers' conduct towards her, but, curiously, did not vote for the opposition censure motion, 6 Feb. 1821. He approved making Leeds, proposed for enfranchisement in place of Grampound, a scot and lot borough, 2 Mar. He was twice granted six weeks' leave to attend to urgent private business, 7, 14 May (he got married on the 19th), but was present to vote for parliamentary reform, 9 May 1821, as he subsequently did on 25 Apr., 3 June 1822, 24 Apr., 2 June 1823, 26 Feb. 1824, 27 Apr. 1826. He was an occasional voter for economy, retrenchment and reduced taxation in 1821 and continued to muster for significant divisions on these issues in 1822. He voted in condemnation of Sir Robert Wilson's* dismissal from the army, 13 Feb. 1822, and observed that 'such a manifest determination on the part of the Tory Members to support and whitewash all the acts of administration right or wrong indiscriminately, must speak volumes in favour of reform'. He voted for Catholic relief, 28 Feb. 1821, 1 Mar., 21 Apr. (when he thought Canning's 'capital' speech did 'more than justice to the liberal spirit of the times'), 10 May 1825. He divided for inquiry into the Irish government's legal proceedings against the Dublin Orange rioters, 22 Apr. 1823, but

> did not much like the company ... [since] the result may be the discomfiture of the more liberal half of the cabinet and a consequent triumph to the less liberal one ... I should not wonder if our late success against ministers is ... objected to as a convincing proof that the H. of C. is not so corrupt as we aver it to be.

He voted against the Irish insurrection bill, 24 June 1823, and for inquiry into the state of Ireland, 11 May 1824, but was reluctant to criticize the government's Spanish policy and could not support Lord Nugent's motion, 17 Feb. 1824. He presented petitions for the abolition of slavery, 9, 17 Mar. 1824,[3] and voted to condemn the indictment of the Methodist missionary John Smith for inciting rebellion among the slaves in Demerara, 11 June 1824, and the Jamaican slave trials, 2 Mar. 1826. He was granted a fortnight's leave because of the illness of a close relative, 15 Feb. 1825. Pares backed his ministerialist colleague Mansfield in supporting the Leicester petition against the wool duties, 9 May 1820, and presented petitions against the Marriage Act, 6 May 1822, and for repeal of the malt duties, 14 May 1823.[4] He welcomed the chancellor of the exchequer's speech on the financial state of the country, 23 Feb. 1824, and abstained from the division on the reduction of the assessed taxes, 3 Mar. 1825, since he approved wholeheartedly of government's plans. He gave evidence to the select committee on artisans and machinery (of which he was a member), 23 Mar. 1824.[5] He applauded Peel's speech on the amelioration of the criminal code, 9 Mar. 1826, which, together with the financial speeches of Huskisson and Robinson, 23 Feb., 13 Mar., he felt formed 'a capital specimen both of the talent and the liberal opinions of those by whom we are now governed'. He approved the government's legislation to regulate country banks early in 1826 as a 'very great improvement ... [from which] the public will derive infinite advantage'.

Pares retired from Parliament at the dissolution in 1826, but did not relinquish his political interest. He supported the candidature of the reformer William Evans* at Leicester in 1826.[6] Thomas Babington Macaulay*, Evans's counsel, acknowledged Pares's civility and assistance and described him in an election *jeu d'esprit* as the 'good and gentle knight of the Frith'.[7] He was active in local politics throughout the 1830s. The Whig Thomas Spring Rice*, writing to his fellow minister Lord Holland in 1831 (when Pares declined an invitation to stand for Leicester with Evans at the general election), described him as a man of 'public spirit and perfect integrity' who could be depended on to supply 'all local knowledge' regarding the administration of Wigston's hospital in Leicester.[8] He acted as a director of Pares's Leicestershire Banking Company, some time after it had been converted into a joint-stock company in 1836, but appears to have preferred the life of a country gentleman on his estates in Leicestershire and Derbyshire. He owned considerable property in Charnwood Forest and built the 'elegant but unostentatious' residence of Ulverscroft Cottage.[9] He died in April 1866.

[1] Based, unless otherwise stated, on Pares's letters to his sister Mary, 1820-6, in Pares mss (Derby Local Stud. Lib.). [2] *Leicester Jnl.* 3, 10, 17 Mar. 1820. [3] *The Times*, 10, 18 Mar. 1824. [4] Ibid. 7 May 1822, 15 May 1823. [5] *PP* (1824), v. 267. [6] *Leicester Jnl.* 2, 9, 16, 23, 30 June; Pares mss, Pares's election scrapbk. [1826]. [7] *Macaulay Letters*, i. 212; Pares mss, Macaulay to Pares [1826]. [8] Add. 51573, Rice to Holland, Sat. [1831]; *Nottingham Rev.* 6 May 1831. [9] C.J. Billson, *Leicester Mems.* 24-25; R. Potter, *Hist. Charnwood Forest*, 150.

S.R.H.

PARKYNS, George Augustus Henry Anne, 2nd Bar. Rancliffe [I] (1785–1850), of Bunny Park, Notts.

MINEHEAD	1806–1807
NOTTINGHAM	1812–1820
NOTTINGHAM	1826–1830

b. 10 June 1785, o. s. of Thomas Boothby Parkyns†, 1st Bar. Rancliffe [I], and Elizabeth Anne, da. and h. of Sir William James†, 1st bt., of Eltham, Kent. *educ.* Harrow 1799. *m.* 15 Oct. 1807, Lady Elizabeth Mary Theresa Forbes, da. of George, 6th earl of Granard [I] and 1st Bar. Granard [UK], *s.p.* legit. *suc.* fa. as 2nd Bar. Rancliffe [I] 17 Nov. 1800; grandfa. Sir Thomas Parkyns as 4th bt. 17 Mar. 1806. *d.* 1 Nov. 1850.

Cornet 10 Drag. 1801; lt. 15 Drag., half-pay 1803-9.

Equerry to prince of Wales.

Provincial grand master of freemasons, Leics. 1812-*d.*

Rancliffe, whose family came from Nottinghamshire, was an Irish peer, the title having been awarded to his father, Member for Stockbridge and Leicester, when his chief, the 3rd duke of Portland, joined Pitt's wartime coalition in 1794. Like the 1st baron before him, Rancliffe was an aristocratic buffoon, whose intermittent parliamentary zeal in the advanced Whig cause had to compete for attention with his life as a society drone.[1] Constrained by the derangement of his financial affairs, he did not stand for Nottingham, which he had represented since 1812, at the general election of 1820, but was indefatigable in his support for his successful replacement, Thomas Denman. He exclaimed that he 'wished to God that he possessed such talents for the purpose of advocating that gentleman's cause' and, although ill health prevented him from attending the celebratory dinner in honour of the Members, he basked in their triumph and claimed to have laid the foundation of the Whig ascendancy in Nottingham.[2] In early 1822, as George Agar Ellis* recorded, he suddenly 'turned his wife out of doors at Paris on account of an intrigue she has had with M. de Mossion [or Morton] – foolish enough – he should have done it sooner, if at all, as it has now been going of for some three or four years'.[3] Although living a retired life in the country, Rancliffe was never far from the political stage; for instance, he was one of the Tory duke of Newcastle's Nottinghamshire opponents who in March 1823 got themselves put on the grand jury, which he would have chaired had he not been disbarred as a peer from so doing.[4] Presiding at a Nottingham dinner that September, he saluted Denman's conduct as one of Queen Caroline's law officers and praised the radical Sir Francis Burdett*: 'Talk not of the duke of Wellington and his bloody achievements, but give me the man who sticks by the people, who fights their battles and who, with their assistance, will conquer'. Addressing the Nottingham festival of Oddfellows in October 1824, he toasted the sitting Members and hailed the Whig corporation as the champion of independence there.[5]

He came forward again for Nottingham on Denman's retirement at the general election of 1826, declaring his political principles to be 'unchanged as they were unchangeable'. Hostile to the slave trade and food price increases, he favoured sweeping reforms in order to abolish wasteful expenditure and sinecures; above all, he singled out frequent Parliaments and a full and 'fair representation of the people' as imperative measures. Finding himself hard pressed, despite receiving Denman's support, he requested the presence of Burdett, but was instead offered his colleague John Cam Hobhouse*, to whom Lord Holland, the recorder, explained that

> they are in great want of spirit and oratory at Nottingham and no way occurs to them of supplying it so well as by your appearance there. I do believe that Lord Rancliffe's election and what I consider of more consequence, a friendly vote in the House of Commons and the future ascendancy of the good cause at Nottingham, depends on some such exertion.[6]

After a turbulent contest, he was returned with Joseph Birch ahead of an anti-corporation candidate. Acknowledging the support of the out-voters, he stated his opposition to the corn laws and slavery, and announced that it was his intention to endeavour to repeal the 'abominable bill' which allowed county magistrates to interfere in the policing of the town. At his election dinner, he declared himself a radical, deprecated the conduct of his opponent, and hailed the corporators of Nottingham as 'staunch friends of the people'.[7]

As previously, Rancliffe voted for Catholic relief, 6 Mar. 1827. He sided with opposition against the duke of Clarence's grant, 2, 16 Mar., and on the 22nd spoke against the bill's third reading, although he finally decided not to divide the House or to do anything that might be 'considered ungracious'. He denied that his Protestant constituents opposed Catholic relief and boasted of his popular support as an advocate of civil and religious liberty, 23 Mar. He divided in the minorities to relax the corn laws, 9, 12, 27 Mar., and to prohibit the use of spring guns, 23 Mar. He confirmed that the practice of electing honorary freemen had prevailed to some extent at Nottingham, 15 Mar., but, disapproving of this, he voted in the minority for inquiry into the conduct of the corporation of Leicester. Having served on an election committee, he was granted three weeks' leave to attend to urgent business, 29 Mar., and was given another week's furlough, 2 May. On 22 May he divided for ending chancery jurisdiction in bankruptcy cases, and, possibly because he objected to the new prime minister's antipathy to parliamentary reform, he registered several hostile votes against the Canning ministry that session. He spoke and voted for the disfranchisement of Penryn, 28 May, and presented and endorsed Leicester and Nottingham petitions, for reform and repeal of the Test Acts respectively, 6 June.[8] He condemned the Coventry magistracy bill as an 'invasion of the rights of corporations', 7 June, and voted in the minority against it, 18 June. He was one of the 11 who opposed the grant to improve Canadian water communications, 12 June. He alleged that many Nottingham electors had been deterred from voting for fear of losing their places, 14 June. His friend, the Irish poet Tom Moore, who liked his repartee and thought him 'a good fellow', was horrified by the 'bad company' he kept, on visiting him at Bunny in October 1827.[9]

He brought up a Nottingham Dissenters' petition for repeal of the Test Acts, 26 Feb. 1828, when he voted accordingly. He was listed in the minority for absolving William Leadbeater of culpability in giving false evidence before the East Retford disfranchisement committee, 7 Mar. In seconding the motion for inquiry into chancery administration, 24 Apr., he spoke of his wish to see the reform of those 'heavy abuses by which the court is at present unhappily distinguished'. He voted to loosen protection for corn producers, 29 Apr. On 19 May he denied that, as a landowner, he would favour the transfer of East Retford's seats to the hundred of Bassetlaw: 'I take an independent view of the subject, for, instead of wishing that the franchise be transferred to any part of the county of Nottingham, where I might perhaps have some interest, I shall vote that it be given to Birmingham'. On 2 June 1828 he deferred his motion for repeal of the Nottingham Peace Act and reiterated that it was his intention to vote for the disfranchisement of East Retford, irrespective of 'whether the franchise goes into the hundred or not'. He voted for Catholic emancipation, 12 May 1828, 6, 30 Mar. 1829. He brought up the favourable Nottingham petition, 9 Mar., when he denied that a hostile petition (presented a month earlier) was representative of his constituents' opinions. He repeated his zealous support for reform, but questioned the necessity of the Irish franchise bill, 20 Mar. 1829. He again divided to transfer East Retford's seats to Birmingham, 5 Mar., and for parliamentary reform, 28 May 1830, when he was also in the minority for O'Connell's radical resolutions. He urged relief for distressed manufacturing districts, including his own, 15 Mar., and paired against the Bathurst and Dundas pensions, 26 Mar. Declaring his support for 'any motion by which the public expenditure may be diminished', 3 May, when he voted to reduce the public buildings grant, he divided to decrease the salary of the assistant secretary of the treasury, 10 May, to abolish the viceregal court in Ireland, 11 May, and to lower consular expenditure, 7, 11 June. He voted for Jewish emancipation, 17 May, and against the death penalty for forgery, 7 June 1830.

Ostensibly disillusioned with politics, but in reality fearing another expensive contest, Rancliffe wrote to apprise Denman of his decision not to stand at the general election that summer. He offered his backing to Denman, whom Brougham deemed a 'good attender' by comparison, and proposed his eventual colleague Sir Ronald Ferguson on the hustings.[10] Disregarding assurances of support, he informed his constituents, 3 July 1830, that

> I am not so sanguine as to suppose that, in the event of another contest, perfect political purity will be found to exist – it does not in the majority of persons returned to Parliament ... I am disgusted with the House of Commons, God knows.

Stressing the importance of electoral independence, he continued:

> In times like these it becomes the duty, as it always is of every man, to vote for those who will act perfectly independent and, by their endeavours, bring back the House of Commons to what it ought to be, *the real representation of the people*, which it now is not. Let everyone keep this in mind. The time is fast approaching when your suffrages (*I wish they were universal*) will be called forth. Use what you have with discretion.[11]

Unable to attend the Nottingham meeting to celebrate the revolution in France, 23 Aug., he trusted that the French example would teach the people of England to 'prevent further inroads being made on our constitution', but appealed for clemency and an end to bloodshed. On 9 Nov. 1830 he presided at the Nottingham radical reform celebration and, reiterating his belief in the aristocratic domination of the Commons, advocated a 'full, fair and free representation of the people', as well as the ballot and a free press. The following evening he chaired a dinner at Wymeswould, Leicestershire, and urged the freeholders there to persist in the cause of independence. As a peer, he could not be supposed to wish for revolution, but he argued that the influence of the nobility deprived the people of a voice in Parliament.[12]

Rancliffe attended the meeting of Nottinghamshire freeholders in Mansfield, 17 Mar. 1831, approving their petition in support of the Grey administration. Having read the Commons debates, which he considered devoid of argument, he 'thanked God he was not there to hear them', but implored the voters to stand firm in their support for the reform bill.[13] When Parliament was dissolved that spring, he warned the Nottingham electors not to be 'deceived by the promises of moderate reform' and warmly anticipated the end of the boroughmongering system, providing they held fast to the king and his ministers.[14] Addressing the Nottingham meeting in the midst of the reform bill riots, 10 Oct. 1831, he seconded the motion attesting to the people's zeal for reform, but deprecated violence and called for calm, deeming the 'righteousness of their cause' their best weapon.[15] At the general election the following year, he proposed the Whig minister Lord Duncannon* and he endorsed the candidature of Hobhouse at the by-election in July 1834. Boasting of his early triumph in the cause of reform, he was proud to have been branded a republican and confident that he had laid the foundation of the Whig triumph in Nottingham. This was already a familiar refrain and, along with his views on the necessity of church reform, was one which he never tired of repeating.[16] He remained an active figure in Nottingham politics and as late as 1839 was badgering Hobhouse, president of the board of trade, for patronage on behalf of the editor of the *Nottingham Mercury*, whose services in the Whig cause he deemed worthy of recognition.[17] He was accused of interfering by 'thumbing' (intimidation), an allegation he strenuously denied, at the Nottingham election of 1841, and was observed by Newcastle regaling his friends, in his usual voluble style, after the successful visit of Queen Victoria to Nottingham in December 1843.[18] At the election of 1847 he supposedly voted for the Chartist Feargus O'Connor†, and in June of the following year he made his last public appearance, when he presided at a meeting to establish a branch of the people's league to advocate universal suffrage in Nottingham; only over the repeal of the corn laws did he abandon his life-long espousal of the liberal cause.[19] On Rancliffe's death in November 1850 the *Nottingham Review* reported that

> without professing eloquence, he had a happy talent of catching as it were the very thoughts of his hearers and blending them in his speech with admirable point and humour, so as to preserve amongst his audience good temper and discretion, though at the same time convincing them of the justice of their cause.[20]

Recognized as 'a Whig, and something more', as well as a 'good party man', the press paid tribute to his sound views, but considered him 'neither fitted by natural endowments, nor acquired attainments, nor yet by the habits he cultivated, for the post of a leader'.[21] According to Thomas Macaulay*, he was 'popularly and well known as a gentleman of considerable gifts, as convivial, witty, and as a giver of amusements of various sorts'.[22] His Irish peerage became extinct, but although the baronetcy devolved on his cousin, Thomas George Augustus Parkyns (1820-95), Rancliffe devised his life interest in the family estate to Mrs. Harriett Burtt (later Forteath), his mistress for over 35 years, whom he had established at Bunny 'in the teeth of the county and to the confusion of all decorum' in 1834. According to his nephew, Sir Horace Rumbold (1829-1913), a diplomat, Rancliffe had long been under her influence and 'very pardonably felt that a good income and an old family estate at his free disposal, made him a veritable *oncle d'Amérique*'. An attempt in 1861 to contest the will collapsed in court, and the estate remained alienated until 1910, when it was immediately divided and sold.[23]

[1] *HP Commons, 1790-1820*, iv. 721-3; M.I. Thomis, *Politics and Society in Nottingham*, 157-8; A.C. Wood, 'George, Lord Rancliffe', *Thoroton Soc.* lviii (1954), 65-68, 78. [2] Wood, 76; *Nottingham Rev.* 10 Mar., 11 Aug. 1820. [3] Northants. RO, Agar Ellis diary, 23 Mar. 1822; *Fox Jnl.* 107; *Moore Jnl.* ii. 549. [4] *Unhappy Reactionary* ed. R.A. Gaunt (Thoroton Soc. rec. ser. xliii), 42. [5] *Nottingham Rev.* 26 Sept. 1823, 1 Oct. 1824. [6] Add. 36462, ff. 271, 275. [7] *Nottingham Rev.* 9, 23 June, 7 July 1826. [8] *The Times*, 7 June 1827. [9] *Moore Jnl.* ii. 431; iii. 1062-3. [10] T. Bailey, *Annals Notts.* iv. 368; Add. 51813, Rancliffe to Denman, 28 June; 51835, Ferguson to Holland, 30 July; Brougham mss, Brougham to Denman [?3 Sept. 1830]. [11] *Nottingham Jnl.* 10 July 1830. [12] *Nottingham Rev.* 27 Aug., 12 Nov. 1830. [13] Ibid. 18 Mar. 1831. [14] *Lincoln and Newark Times*, 4 May 1831. [15] *Nottingham Rev.* 14 Oct. 1831. [16] *Nottingham Pollbook* (1832), pp. ix-xi; Wood, 78. [17] Add. 36470, f. 181. [18] *The Times*, 13 May 1831; *Unhappy Reactionary*, 32. [19] Wood, 78. [20] *Nottingham Rev.* 1 Nov. 1850. [21] *The Times*, 2 Nov. 1850; *Gent. Mag.* (1850), ii. 654. [22] *Nottingham Jnl.* 15 Mar. 1861. [23] *Gent. Mag.* (1850), ii. 654-5; H. Rumbold, *Recollections of a Diplomatist*, i. 97-98; ii. 75-76; *CP*, x. 730; Wood, 78-81.

S.R.H./S.M.F.

PARNELL, Sir Henry Brooke, 4th bt. (1776–1842), of Abbeyleix and Rathleague, Queen's Co.

QUEEN'S CO.	5 Apr. 1802–1802
PORTARLINGTON	1802–18 Nov. 1802
QUEEN'S CO.	17 Feb. 1806–1832
DUNDEE	17 Apr. 1833–1841

b. 3 July 1776, 2nd s. of Sir John Parnell, 2nd bt.†, MP [I] (*d.* 1801), and Letitia Charlotte, da. and coh. of Sir Arthur Brooke, 1st bt., MP [I], of Colebrook, co. Fermanagh; bro. of William Parnell Hayes*. *educ.* Eton 1791-3; Trinity Coll. Camb. 1794; L. Inn 1797. *m.* 15 Mar. 1801, Lady Caroline Elizabeth Dawson, da. of John, 1st earl of Portarlington [I], 3s. 3da. *suc.* fa. to estates 1801; bro. John Augustus as 4th bt. 30 July 1812; *cr.* Bar. Congleton [UK] 18 Aug. 1841. *d.* 8 June 1842.

MP [I] 1797-1800.

Commr. of treasury [I] Apr. 1806-Apr. 1807; sec. at war Apr. 1831-Feb. 1832; PC 27 Apr. 1831; treas. of navy 22 Apr. 1835-Dec. 1836; paymaster-gen. 14 May 1835-July 1841.

Capt. Maryborough inf. 1802.

Parnell had joined Brooks's, 23 June 1807, sponsored by Lord King, with whom he was considered by his Cambridge contemporary William Lamb* to be 'half mad and only eager to overthrow the Church and put up the Dissenters'.[1] A staunch advocate of Catholic claims, who in 1820 was reported to be 'on more friendly terms with Mr. [Henry] Brougham* than any other Irish Member', his 'connection with the Whig party', as he explained to William Huskisson*, had originated in 1805 with the marquess of Buckingham, who required 'as a condition of his giving me his interest in the Queen's County that I should vote for what was then called the prince's party'. However, 'in consequence of disapproving generally of the management of the proceedings of the party', in 1819 he had asked Lord Duncannon* not to send him 'any more notes for attendance', and since then had 'not received any'.[2] Thereafter he took an independent line in support of free trade, retrenchment and reduced taxation, voting with the Whig opposition to the Liverpool ministry on most major issues and serving on most of the financial and trade committees of the period. (A commentary of 1823 erroneously described him as 'an absentee in 1821 and 1822', adding that 'formerly this Member was laudably active in questions of economy, but latterly he has abandoned the field to Mr. Hume'.)[3] His other chief interest was roads, particularly schemes in Ireland and the improvement of the Holyhead road, for which he drafted much of the legislation, assisted by Thomas Telford.[4]

At the 1820 general election Parnell offered again for Queen's County on the 'popular interest', citing his support for tax reductions and his part in the passage of the recent Irish Election Act, which he had privately urged Lord Liverpool to push through before the dissolution, 22 Feb 1820.[5] Following criticism of the Act by an opponent, the Catholic press came to his defence as 'one of the most efficient' Irish Members. He was returned in second place.[6] He called for 'fuller investigation' of the civil list, 2, 3 May. On 17 May he advocated abolition of the Irish viceroyalty and the introduction of lord lieutenants of counties, 'after the English system'. He spoke regularly in similar terms throughout this session. He contended that the ten per cent duties on Anglo-Irish trade were a 'violation' of the Union, 14 June, when he was a minority teller for his own motion for inquiry, which failed by 30-66. He campaigned steadily for repeal of the duties thereafter, acting as a minority teller against their renewal, 10 July 1820, and securing agreement from the chancellor of the exchequer for the appointment of a select committee, 19 Apr. 1821. He welcomed the report recommending their abolition, 21 Feb., and their eventual repeal, 24 June 1823. He was a majority teller for the Irish court of chancery bill, 3 July 1820. He condemned the Irish tithes system for its 'oppression' of poor tenants and obtained leave for a bill to relieve them and 'secure the interests of the clergy', 5 July. He criticized the conduct of the Bank of Ireland during 'the late general distress' and called for the cessation of its monopoly, 2 Feb., 11 Apr. 1821, when he berated ministers for their 'departure from the sound principles of political economy'. He of course voted for Catholic relief, 28 Feb. 1821, 1 Mar., 21 Apr., 10 May 1825. He divided for the transfer of Grampound's seats to Leeds, 2 Mar., reform of the Scottish representation, 10 May 1821, parliamentary reform, 24 Apr. 1823, and reform of Edinburgh's representation, 13 Apr. 1826, but against the disfranchisement of non-resident Irish borough electors, 9 Mar. 1826. On 5 Apr. 1821 he was a minority teller for his own motion to equalize the timber duties, which was rejected by 54-15. He joined the Political Economy Club, 25 June 1821.

Parnell later claimed that early in 1822, following Buckingham's junction with government, he was 'offered a seat in the Irish cabinet', but had 'proposed a condition which was not agreed to, namely the granting to the Catholics what is called the minor concessions'.[7] No details of the offer have been found, although on 19 Feb. Buckingham advised his confidant William Fremantle*, who had taken office at the board of control, to 'be as civil as you can to Parnell, who is *my* recruit'. On 10 Mar. he asked Fremantle, 'Have you had any communication with Parnell and what he is doing?', but Fremantle replied that 'he will not commit himself until he finds which party prevails'.[8] On 7 Feb. Parnell acknowledged the necessity of the Irish insurrection bill but called for an investigation of the causes of 'tumult and disorder'; he was in the minority to limit its duration, 8 July. He attended the meeting of the 'friends of emancipation' at Plunket's, 16 Apr., when it was decided not to bring on the Catholic question that year.[9] On 22 Apr. he advocated a general commutation of Irish tithes and payment of the clergy, adding that no measure 'for the improvement of Ireland would ever avail, unless the complete emancipation of the Catholics was made the foundation of them'. He welcomed the government's Irish tithes leasing bill, 13 June, but wanted 'a more general remedy' for the 'chief evil of the system', namely 'the manner in which tithes were too frequently collected'. He criticized the Irish constables bill, 7 June 1822. On 11 Mar. 1823, in a speech which won over Ricardo but which he complained 'the papers very much misrepresented', Parnell suggested that opposition objections to 'a new sinking fund' could be obviated by placing it 'out of the reach of ministers' and allowing the commissioners to grant long annuities.[10] He voted against Hume's amendments to the national debt reduction bill, 5, 13 Mar., but was in the minority to limit government borrowing, 17 Mar. He was a minority teller for his own motion for inquiry into Irish disturbances, which was defeated by 39-88, 24 June, when he argued that the Catholics, 'being deprived of representation by persons of their own persuasion', were also 'deprived of the fundamental security of English liberty' which 'belongs to them as their birthright'. Next day he demanded that ministers give Ireland the 'whole of the English constitution' and 'get rid of the separate executive government' of the viceroy. He spoke and voted for referring the Catholic petition on the administration of Irish justice to a grand committee, 26 June. Brougham, who had brought forward the motion, explained to Daniel O'Connell* that he 'was ably supported' by Parnell.[11] In December 1823 he was reported to be in Paris.[12]

On 27 Jan. 1824 the Catholic bishop of Kildare, Dr. James Doyle, informed O'Connell of Parnell's request for assistance with the drafting of a bill to enable Catholics to endow their religious and charitable institutions in the same manner as Protestant Dissenters, and urged him to give his 'zealous co-operation' to 'a man who in all times and vicissitudes has been our steady and uncompromising friend'.[13] On the advice of the Irish attorney-general Plunket, however, Parnell withdrew his notice of the bill as the 'interpretation of the law restricting money for the endowment of Catholic institutions had now changed', 9 Mar. He called for a full investigation of the Bank of England's charter, 19 Feb., and welcomed proposals to assimilate the currency of England and Ireland, 25 Feb. 1824, 13 May 1825. He advocated total repeal of the '300 regulations' governing the Irish linen trade, 19 Mar. 1824. He endorsed a petition for repeal of the usury laws, 31 Mar., for which he voted, 8, 17 Feb., and spoke, 8 Apr. On 7 May he commended the budget for its 'reform of fiscal and commercial regulations in preference to the repealing of direct taxation', but warned that it was 'absurd' to suppose that a sinking fund of £5,000,000 a year could ever be effectual in reducing a debt of £800,000,000. In a speech which was later published, 11 May, he stressed the need to find a permanent solution to distress in Ireland, where the population was increasing, and seconded and was a minority teller for Lord Althorp's motion for a select committee on Irish disturbances, to which he was appointed, 11 May. He called for repeal of the Act regulating the Irish butter trade, 28 May. On 20 Nov. 1824 Goulburn, the Irish secretary, reported to Peel, the home secretary, that Parnell viewed the Catholic Association with 'considerable apprehension' and had ascertained '(how he attained his knowledge was not stated) that the Association had determined in the event of any measures directed against them to carry on their proceedings by means of weekly meetings in the several Catholic chapels'.[14] Four days later Parnell urged Buckingham to 'use every exertion in persuading government, before it is too late, to conciliate the Catholics', for if emancipation

> is not granted next session, and such a system of executive government established in Ireland as shall give the Catholics the full benefit of it ... the present commotions of the public mind will end in another general rebellion. By connecting with emancipation a provision for the Catholic clergy, the giving of a large share of public situations to Catholics, the abolition of forty shilling freeholds, and a general plan of education on a principle satisfactory to Catholic feelings, I feel quite confident that the commotion would subside, and the whole country become perfectly tranquil and extremely flourishing.

Buckingham sent this letter to Charles Williams Wynn* and Fremantle and was 'rather anxious that the king should see it, if it could be managed without a *direct* communication'. On 27 Jan. 1825 Parnell wrote again of the 'expediency of attempting to get the Catholics of their accord to put down their Association', since 'a special Act of Parliament' would be 'evaded' and 'lead to great violence and to systematic rebellion'. He spoke in similar terms against suppression of the Association, 4, 10 Feb., when, as Fremantle informed Buckingham, he 'went into the whole history of the Catholic question, and was not heard by the House; but his speech was probably meant for publication and will have its effect'.[15] It appeared later that year. On 25 Feb. O'Connell reported that Parnell had accompanied him on a visit to the bishop of Norwich and was 'the principal person who examined' him before the select committee on the state of Ireland, to which he had been appointed, 17 Feb.[16] Doyle told the committee that Parnell was one of the 'most bountiful contributors' to the construction of a local Catholic chapel.[17] 'The efficiency of the inquiry', the Catholic press later observed, was 'mainly owing to Sir Henry's exertions'.[18] On 22 Feb. he obtained leave to introduce a bill to 'put a stop to the practice of subletting farms' without a landlord's consent, which had caused 'much poverty and misery'. It was postponed, 30 June 1825, but subsequently taken up by Goulburn, 10 Mar. 1826. (It received royal assent as 7 Geo. IV, c. 29, 5 May 1826). He moved for papers on the Irish butter trade, in which the 'greatest corruption prevailed', 15 Mar., and presented a petition for repeal of the regulations, 22 Apr. 1825. His *Observations on the Irish Butter Acts* appeared later that year. On 22 Mar. he warned that if poor laws were introduced to Ireland, 'before a few years passed the whole rent of the landlords would be swallowed up'. He advocated gradual repeal of the Irish linen and wool duties, 25 Mar., but withdrew his motion for a committee on the linen trade on discovering that ministers intended to appoint their own, to which he was named, 14 Apr. He supported the Irish franchise bill 'as it was connected with the measure so likely' to bring 'peace and prosperity' to Ireland, 26 Apr., and insisted that the Catholic oath was 'harmless', 6 May. Pointing to the 'numerous protecting duties' that had been omitted from the customs consolidation bill, 17 June, he declared that it 'time to reconsider the old system of sacrificing every one who was not a landlord to the interests of the landlords'. On 17 July 1825 he complained to Herries, secretary to the treasury, that the proposed letting of Dublin docks would 'give a monopoly to the lessees' and 'create a restriction in the trade of Dublin that was never contemplated', and that he would attempt to get it 'reconsidered' next session.[19] He called for abolition of the Bank of England's monopoly, enlarged partnerships for London banks and repeal of the usury laws, 14 Feb. 1826. He was appointed to the select committee on promissory notes, 16 Mar., and was one of the 'dissentients' who opposed Peel's report against reform of the Scottish banking system.[20]

Shortly before the 1826 general election Lord Stanhope warned Parnell that in the event of a contest in Queen's County he would only support him if he would 'strenuously and steadfastly support the present corn laws'.[21] He offered again as 'a friend of civil and religious liberty' and was returned unopposed.[22] He denied that the tariff reforms of 1825 had established a system of free trade as the country still suffered from 'high protecting duties', 30 Nov. 1826, insisted the agricultural interest had 'nothing to fear' from free trade, 9 Mar., and condemned the cultivation of inferior land which resulted from import restrictions, 27 Mar. 1827. He voted for Catholic relief, 6 Mar. 1827, 12 May 1828. He voted for information on the conduct of the Lisburn magistrates during the Orange procession, 29 Mar. 1827. Following the formation of Canning's ministry, Parnell was reported to be one of the Irish Members 'loud in their protestations' against Lord Lansdowne for making his acceptance of office conditional on the appointment of a pro-Catholic Irish viceroy.[23] On 23 Apr. he privately advised Lansdowne of his 'great anxiety' for a coalition with Canning, which

> every circumstance serves to justify ... without stipulating for the Catholic question, or laying any stress on any minor difficulty that may exist. I feel quite confident that the Catholics will approve of any arrangement which will ... keep the old ministers from returning to power; and that the shortest way of carrying their question is to have these situations filled either by decided friends or more liberal opponents. I am extremely sorry to find so many of the opposition objecting to a divided cabinet, but I hope your lordship will persevere, and do all that you can to keep out the high Tory party.[24]

After the formation of Lord Goderich's ministry, 18 Sept. 1827, Parnell asked Huskisson, the colonial secretary, when he 'might expect to hear the result' of Goderich's communication with Lansdowne with respect to his being given office:

> The extract I read to you ... from Lansdowne's letter, shows that he leaves me at full liberty to continue to act as to the Whig party as I have hitherto done. His continued friendship since 1819, and his recommendation of me to Mr. Canning are proofs that he is not influenced by any strong party feelings. The other leading members of the opposition have acted towards me in a very different manner.

Two days later Huskisson replied:

> You must in some way have misunderstood me. It was not my intention, at either of our interviews, to state that Lord Goderich would under any circumstances communicate with Lord Lansdowne on the subject of his wish that the public should have the benefit of your talents ... but that in ... filling future vacancies ... it must in reference to your claim be a matter of communication between Lord Lansdowne and Lord Goderich.

Huskisson also told him that Lansdowne had given Goderich 'a memorandum to him from Canning, of his anxious desire to see you in the active service of government'. In response Parnell admitted that he had 'not correctly' understood 'what you said to me at our second interview'.[25] His *Observations on Paper Money, Banking and Overtrading*, urging abolition of the Bank's monopoly, was published that year.

He presented five petitions for Catholic claims, 4 Feb. 1828, and a steady stream thereafter. He was one of the 'reformers' considered for the finance committee by the Wellington ministry and was appointed, 15 Feb.[26] That day Edward Littleton* noted that following the objections of Herries and Huskisson to each other's choice for chairman (Sir Thomas Acland and Althorp respectively), Sir Matthew Ridley had been 'applied to' but declined, so that 'I suppose Sir Henry Parnell will be chosen'.[27] Expressing his unease with the committee's composition the following day, Wellington warned Peel that the 'friends of the late government' and 'even Parnell would vote for Althorp to be chairman', which would be a 'triumph over our friends and supporters'. On 17 Feb. Peel explained to

Althorp that in requesting Sturges Bourne, Ridley and finally Parnell to take the chair, he had been 'influenced not solely by a sense of their qualification', but 'by the impression that I was taking the course ... most free from embarrassments'.[28] Parnell was elected chairman next day.[29] Describing his subsequent examination 'for near three hours before the finance committee', John Croker* observed, 'Parnell is a pedant, thinking of nothing but political economics, and of them very confusedly'.[30] In the House he defended the committee's failure to report on the army and navy estimates, 17 Apr., 16 May, when he denied a 'want of diligence' and contended that they had been 'obliged' to postpone their report owing to great 'difficulties'. The following day the whip Holmes privately complained:

> The committee of finance have now sat nearly three months and have done nothing, and the longer they sit the more confused they get. Their chairman, Sir Henry Parnell, would be more usefully employed in trundling a barrow full of broken stones on the Holyhead road, than where he is. I really believe the government put him and Hume on the committee to retard all the proceedings.[31]

That month John Stuart Mill informed Parnell that he had considered the draft of his work *On Financial Reform* and could 'not see that it is possible to lay down the principles of political economy more broadly', adding that 'a great service' would be 'rendered to the country, if you can induce the committee to concur with you in reporting in such decisive terms'.[32] Parnell defended the Irish Subletting Act, admitting 'the share he had had in its progress', 19 Feb. He voted for repeal of the Test Acts, 26 Feb. He criticized grants to Protestant establishments in Ireland as 'acts of hostility committed against the religious feelings ... of the great mass of the people', 28 Feb. On 6 Mar. he moved for a copy of the Treaty of Limerick, declaring that the enactment of the penal laws against Catholics was a 'direct violation' of the compact which had been entered into between the Irish nation and William III. He moved for information on importation to demonstrate the 'benefits of reducing tariffs', 1 Apr. Speaking as a 'private Member' against the navy estimates, 16 May, he unsuccessfully moved for the abolition of the coastal blockade. On 18 May Lord Ellenborough recorded that Parnell had suggested the appointment of a committee to consider how British Catholics were affected by the existing laws as 'a proper preliminary to the discussion of the question', which would 'last long enough' to make a decision 'impracticable this year'.[33] He denounced the Scottish bank notes restriction bill as 'one of the most uncalled for pieces of legislation ever brought before the House', 5 June, and, contending that the security of a paper currency derived from the solvency of the issuing bank rather than the 'quantity of metallic currency circulating with it', advocated a complete review of the banking system, 16 June. He was in the minority of 24 against the Irish small notes bill that day. He called for reform of the Irish butter trade, 7 July, deplored increasing taxation to support a sinking fund of £3,000,000, 11 July, and was a minority teller against the customs bill, 14 July. On 21 Sept. Lord Anglesey, the Irish viceroy, wrote to upbraid Parnell for inaccurately stating that 'I had expectations of the Catholic question being granted if the leaders could be prevailed upon to restrain the meetings'.[34] In November 1828 Brougham informed Lord Holland that the 'account Parnell gives of Ireland is alarming beyond measure. He believes the government *must* come into some terms'.[35]

On 20 Feb. 1829 Parnell expressed dismay at the ministry's failure to reappoint the finance committee, declaring that if they had known this, 'their reports would have been made on the army and navy' and that 'immense' savings in colonial expenditure still remained to be considered. He pressed for naval reductions, 27 Feb. That month he privately told O'Connell that there was to be 'no veto, nor any attack or interference with the discipline of the Catholic church' in the ministry's emancipation scheme, for which he voted, 6, 30 Mar., and spoke, 18 Mar., when he said that the influence of the Catholic clergy over the people had been 'greatly exaggerated'.[36] He presented numerous favourable petitions. On 22 Mar. he forwarded a letter to Peel from Doyle, which he endorsed, suggesting that the terms of the bill prohibiting the wearing of habits should be modified to exclude clerical dress, and that the suppression of religious societies should be confined to the Jesuits.[37] He waived his objections to the measure to disfranchise 40*s.* freeholders rather than impede emancipation, 26 Mar. He voted for allowing O'Connell to take his seat unhindered, 18 May. He moved for accounts of the public works loan commissioners, 31 Mar. 1829, 5 Feb. 1830. On 1 May 1829 he commended the Liverpool ministry's relaxation of trade restrictions, without which there would have been 'a most injurious obstruction in the way of the employment of capital', and argued that 'all that is now wanting to secure the future prosperity of trade is the complete freedom of it'. He was later observed acting as chairman of a committee of the Society for the Propagation of Useful Knowledge, formed to publish a work illustrating the 'propriety' of Huskisson's 'alterations in the commercial policy of the country' before the meeting of Parliament, 2 Dec. 1829.[38] That month he wrote to Anglesey from

Ireland of 'several circumstances which prove beyond all doubt the benefits already derived from settling the Catholic question'.[39]

Parnell was one of '28 opposition Members who supported the address', 4 Feb. 1830, but thereafter he generally spoke and voted with the revived opposition for reduced taxation and retrenchment.[40] That year he published and began distributing to leading figures his *On Financial Reform*, which contended that 'the passage of merchandise from one state to another ... ought to be as free as air and water' and denounced the supporters of protection as 'among the greatest enemies of mankind'.[41] (A second edition appeared in 1832.) On 26 Feb. he defended his book's attack on the navy board's 'trifling reductions', but admitted the 'impropriety' of claiming that a revived finance committee would have censured their conduct. Explaining that the committee's draft report on tax reductions formed part of the work, he pressed ministers to 'revise and alter the system of taxation' and remove 'all obstructions ... in the way of industry', 25 Mar. He divided for the transfer of East Retford's seats to Birmingham, 11 Feb., but not for the enfranchisement of Birmingham, Leeds and Manchester, 23 Feb., or Russell's motion for parliamentary reform, 28 May. He welcomed amendments to his Subletting Act, but denied O'Connell's allegation that its operation had driven 'many paupers off their small tenements', 16 Feb. On 18 Mar. Wellington was sent a copy of a letter from Thomas Joplin to Parnell explaining the difficulties faced by joint-stock banks, and two days later Parnell was one of nine Members who urged the necessity of inquiry into the banking system at a private interview with Wellington and Goulburn, the chancellor of the exchequer.[42] He voted for Jewish emancipation, 5 Apr., 17 May (as a pair), when he presented a favourable petition. He was appointed to the select committee on superannuations, 4 May. On 11 May he resumed his campaign against the 'positive evil' of the Irish viceroyalty. He feared that the additional duties on newspapers would check 'the habit of reading', 17 May. He voted for the forgery punishment mitigation bill, 24 May, 7 June. He argued that the government's repeal of the beer tax was not 'of the greatest benefit to the public interest' and wished that 'some other taxes might have been selected', 3 July. On 6 July 1830 Stanhope told him that his opinions on 'several public questions' were now 'so different' from his own that he could no longer support him in Queen's County.[43]

At the 1830 general election Parnell stood again, stressing his part in 'carrying a number of measures of the greatest importance to the welfare of Ireland' and his 'constant attention' in 'every session'. Attempts to organize an opposition came to nothing.[44] He was listed by the Irish agent Pierce Mahony† as 'neutral' but by Planta, the ministry's patronage secretary, as one of their 'foes'. On 2 Nov. 1830 he denied that there was widespread support in Ireland for repeal of the Union, which would entail 'general and universal ruin'. He condemned proposals for additional duties on raw materials entering the West Indies as an unwarranted abandonment of free trade, 12 Nov., and was a minority teller for his own amendment to reduce West Indian wheat import duties, which failed by 39-136. That day he disputed the ministry's purported saving of £88,000 on the civil list and gave notice that he would propose an inquiry. On 15 Nov. he moved to refer the civil list to a select committee, declaring that Members 'just returned ... with professions of economy fresh on their lips' should not 'consent to vote away so large a sum' and sanction such 'extravagant expenditure', and that for the sake of 'the national tranquillity and the security of the monarchy', the household expenses should be made distinct from other charges. The motion (for which he and Althorp were tellers) was carried by 233-204, with the support of disaffected Ultra Tories. The Whig Lord Howick noted that 'Brougham ... wanted Parnell to put off naming his committee, but we raised such a cry ... that we made him go on', and he was named as chairman of the committee that day.[45] The following day the ministry resigned and Lord Grey took office. In private Parnell conjectured:

> In case an offer is made me of a situation in the new administration, on what grounds ought I to make up my opinion as to accepting it? I have proposed ... plans of reforms of the finances in my book, which have been approved of by the public. In order to put the finances in a sound state it is indispensable that these plans should be sooner or later adopted.

On 18 Nov. Parnell recorded that he

> called on Althorp and told him that relying on his opinion that he and Grey would adopt fuller measures of retrenchment and economy ... I would accept the office of the secretary of the treasury. He replied that he feared he had yesterday made a mistake, that Grey had told him he meant only to offer me a seat at the treasury board. I immediately replied that I would not accept ... Althorp behaved very badly in not letting me know sooner.[46]

In a 'note' to Althorp that evening he wrote that having 'taken so earnest a part in all matters of finance, I could not accept of any other office but that of chancellor of the exchequer, so pray do not give yourself any further trouble about me', but in private he wondered 'what to do if now offered the office', 21 Nov.[47] Althorp's version of events, as recorded by John Hobhouse*, was that 'he wanted Parnell to be chief lord commissioner of the treasury', which he had declined, saying 'there was only one place he could take, and that was chancellor of the exchequer. "Now", said Althorp, "to write this to the chancellor of the exchequer was a little too much"'. 'An appointment was offered to him, but he refused it as beneath his pretensions', Denis Le Marchant† later recorded, adding that 'these seemed to many of the party rather extravagant'.[48] Subsequent rumours that 'civic Harry', as he was now called by the press, would become vice-treasurer of Ireland proved incorrect, whereupon *The Times* expressed surprise at his exclusion from office, which 'is by many considered the most serious blot in the ministerial arrangements of Lord Grey'.[49] Lord Darnley informed Holland, 18 Jan. 1831, that he 'fully concur[red] in Doyle's opinion of Parnell, who, if not chancellor of the exchequer, ought ... to have been secretary in Ireland, a country which he knows ... better and with less prejudice, than any one'.[50] Another commentator noted that there had been 'a loud cry against Grey's rapacity and folly in thrusting *ten* members of his own family into high situations, and neglecting such men as Sir Henry'.[51] On 12 Dec. 1830 *John Bull* observed that Parnell

> still keeps his former seat on what is called the opposition bench ... forming no part of that administration which *his motion* has produced, not that he had not an offer, but as he tells everybody, they offered him a sinecure ... Ye Gods! only think of the Whigs, the retrenching Whigs, offering a sinecure ... to the chairman of the committee of finance!!

He pressed for further information on the civil list, 7 Dec., and was appointed to the select committee on salary reductions, 9 Dec. Next day he advocated a 'strict examination' of the English banking system. On 25 Jan. 1831 Lord Seaford reported a conversation with Parnell, in which he had insisted that the Whigs could have 'gained completely' the support of O'Connell 'by some advance in his profession', but that 'being passed over' had 'exasperated him and drawn him to the cause which he has now adopted'. 'If Parnell's version is correct', Seaford reflected, 'it was a great blunder not [to] have bought off O'Connell ... But Parnell is not quite to be trusted, for *he* feels *himself* to have been, if not passed over, not sufficiently considered'.[52] On 4 Feb. Parnell announced his 'decided objections' to the salaries of the household officials and berated the government for not abiding 'by the opinions expressed by them before they became ministers' and their 'want of strict and severe' economy. The Tories, Ellenborough commented, were 'much delighted', believing it had 'damaged' ministers 'very much', but Le Marchant thought that Parnell's 'motives were too open to suspicion' for his speech 'to have any injurious effect'.[53] He was appointed to the select committee on the East India Company that day. He welcomed Althorp's decision not to resist his motion for another committee on the public accounts, to which he was appointed, 17 Feb. On 25 Feb. he rejected as a 'complete misapprehension' Althorp's claim in his budget speech of 11 Feb. 1831 that his book had provided the 'authority for selecting the particular taxes' which he proposed to reduce, declaring, 'I never said anything which could justify any one of the taxes he proposes to lay on', and was sad to see 'the new government adopting the same scale of expenditure as the old one'. Even Mill, however, later accepted that 'ministers were luckily guided in their remission of taxes by Sir Henry Parnell's book'.[54]

On 4 Mar. 1831 Holland recommended Parnell for the office of secretary at war, made vacant by Williams Wynn's resignation over parliamentary reform, as he 'would be useful and above all is most hazardous and injurious to us out of office'. Grey agreed, but feared that 'what is passing in the civil list committee would make it very disagreeable to the king'. The following day he told William IV's secretary Sir Herbert Taylor* that Parnell's 'present activity is a good deal excited by discontent at having nothing' and 'we should put an end to all difficulties on his part, like those which have taken place respecting the civil list, by his appointment'.[55] On 7 Mar. Parnell recorded that Althorp had offered him the post, at which he was 'much flattered', but having

> formed so decided an opinion with respect to the scale of the public expenditure which he had proposed this session ... I had no hesitation in declining to accept it. Lord Althorp said that his determination was to reduce the expenditure in every possible way, and that in point of fact he did not believe there was any real difference of opinion between us ... to which I replied, that if he should make his future arrangements so as to be decidedly calculated to secure retrenchment, I would willingly take office and help him. I then mentioned my intention to oppose the regranting of the civil list pensions, and the colonial bill and the timber duties, and I strongly urged Lord Althorp to make some change about the civil list pensions, so as not to have any such obstacle in the way of the success about reform.[56]

On 11 Mar. he duly condemned the colonial trade bill as too protectionist and 'similar to the one submitted last year' and expressed his hope that 'reform would introduce a greater proportion of men than at present who understand such questions'. He voted for the second reading of the reform bill, 22 Mar. Two weeks later he was appointed secretary at war, to the approval of the Irish secretary Smith Stanley, who informed the reappointed viceroy Anglesey, 31 Mar., 'I am sure it has pacified the Irish *Members*, and hope it will the Irish people. He is well qualified for the place, which I always wished him to have taken at first'.[57] 'With a view to Ireland, to the conciliation of many of our friends, and the removal of much formidable and industrious enmity, it is a good appointment', remarked Holland, but 'I am afraid it will not be very popular in the army'.[58] Hobhouse commented that 'he is a much better man *there* than I should have been, but I am a better man in the House, at least as far as speaking goes'.[59] Privately recording his 'reasons for taking office', Parnell cited 'the certainty after the debate on the second reading of the reform bill that all prospect was removed of Peel's coming to an arrangement with the moderate Whig reformers' and 'the necessity of taking a part' in shaping the government's financial policy, adding

> if Peel had quitted the Ultra Tories and distinctly agreed to abolish the nomination boroughs ... a sufficient reform could have been secured, and a coalition [formed] with him in strong government for carrying on financial and legal reforms.[60]

On seeking re-election Parnell, anticipating that his support for the Union might provoke opposition, asked O'Connell to endorse him, explaining that he had 'abstained from accepting office until the government' had proved itself 'on the reform question' and he 'could feel confidence in their good intentions' towards Ireland, and warning that 'if the friends of reform fall out with me on account of any other question, I may cease to represent the Queen's County'. O'Connell declared in his favour and he was returned unopposed.[61] He was not back in time for the division on Gascoyne's wrecking amendment, 19 Apr. 1831.[62]

At the ensuing general election he stood as a 'thorough-going' reformer and was returned at the head of the poll.[63] That month it was reported to Wellington that Parnell and Althorp favoured 'a plan for the reduction of the army', which Hume would shortly bring forward.[64] On 3 June 1831 Parnell notified Althorp that his 'moderate schemes of retrenchment' in the army were being 'resisted' by the commander-in-chief Lord Hill, and recommended the appointment of an army board. Althorp agreed to 'talk to Grey about this as about stopping the recruitment of the army', but suggested that 'at present the only thing to do is to vote the army estimates exactly as they stand'.[65] In the House, 25 June, Parnell assured Hume that the reappointment of the public accounts committee was 'under consideration'. He secured a select committee on the militia estimates, 30 June. He defended the work of the Holyhead road commissioners, 1 July. He voted for the second reading of the reintroduced reform bill, 6 July, against the adjournment, 12 July, and of course gave steady support to its detailed provisions, although on 26 July he was one of those who 'voted against the government' in a division on Saltash in which 'no one knew what he was to do', after which the patronage secretary Ellice 'went home in a rage'.[66] That month, when it was rumoured that Lord Spencer was dying, Ellenborough noted that 'the persons talked of' as Althorp's replacement at the exchequer were '[Smith] Stanley, Rice and Parnell', of whom 'they all say Rice is the ablest, Parnell very dull, but Stanley of course will have it'.[67] Contemplating whom to appoint Irish secretary in the 'event of [Smith] Stanley going to the exchequer', Anglesey later warned that Spring Rice 'would not do' and 'neither would Parnell'.[68] He spoke against renewing the grant to the Kildare Place Society, 22 July, and presented hostile petitions, 12 Aug. He voted against disqualification of the Dublin election committee, 29 July, and with his colleagues on the issue, 23 Aug. He denied that his Subletting Act had failed but admitted that some of its provisions required 'further consideration', 5 Aug. On 24 Aug. 1831 Holmes reported that Parnell and Sir James Graham had 'carried their point of preventing a burst [of artillery fire] at the coronation', thereby making 'all the naval and military furious'.[69] That month Parnell, whom Duncannon had requested should 'occasionally' talk to the Irish Members during his absence, began a campaign to 'procure offices of trust' for some of the leading Irish Catholic Members.[70] On 18 Aug. Althorp relayed and endorsed to Le Marchant Parnell's conviction that 'there is no chance or hope of governing Ireland [until] O'Connell, Sheil and the leaders of the discontented party are provided for'.[71] The following month Parnell informed Lord Brougham that with 'O'Connell ... Sheil, Wyse and O'Ferrall in office, and the priests paid, Ireland would at once be quiet, whereas if things go on as at present, every one of them will be in opposition'. On 11 Oct. he added that Anglesey was 'most anxious to make an arrangement' and willing to offer O'Connell the 'attorney-generalship if nothing else would do', and that 'I can undertake to say that if O'Connell gets office, he will use his utmost exertions to assist government in every way ... The only difficulty Anglesey feels is with respect to Lord Grey.

Cannot you assist in removing it?' On 15 Oct. Parnell reported that he had urged on Grey 'in the strongest manner, the necessity of giving office to O'Connell', who was 'willing to take the solicitor-generalship'.[72] A few days later, at Parnell's request, an offer was apparently conveyed to O'Connell through Doyle, but he rejected it on 'finding how isolated the proposal of office was'.[73] Parnell, however, continued to insist that O'Connell could be gained. Lord Melbourne, the home secretary, observed to Anglesey, 18 Dec. 1831, that

> Parnell, having pressed upon me in the most urgent manner the necessity of gratifying O'Connell, I desired my brother to communicate to him ... what had passed between O'Connell and you ... and your conviction that it was hopeless to entertain any further expectation of conciliating him. He said that, whatever had passed, he was of a different opinion ... that he was certain he would immediately accept any direct offer was made [including] the master of the rolls.[74]

He voted for the third reading, 19 Sept., and passage of the reform bill, 21 Sept., and the second reading of the Scottish bill, 23 Sept. 1831. On 2 Oct. he submitted to Althorp his recommendations for army reductions, against which he alleged there was 'so powerful a coalition of military men in support of every useless and extravagant expense'. Informing Grey of his plans, 20 Oct., he declared that it would not be 'consistent with what I felt to be my duty on this subject, to propose to the House ... in the estimate of next year a vote, which shall leave the management of the clothing of the household cavalry in the hands of the colonels of regiments'.[75] He dismissed calls for an inquiry into the previous administration's proposed use of the Tower of London in the event of civil unrest, 4 Oct. He endorsed the policy of half-pay for officers in receipt of civil salaries, which had been recommended by the finance committee and saved £73,000 a year, 7 Oct. He voted for Lord Ebrington's confidence motion, 10 Oct. On 2 Dec. it was reported that the various points which Grey had conceded in his discussions with Lord Wharncliffe on the subject of reform were 'disapproved by Althorp and Parnell, and the negotiations in consequence fell through'.[76] Writing later that month, however, Wellington noted that Parnell had 'said to a friend "We must succumb"'.[77] He voted for the second reading of the revised reform bill, 17 Dec. 1831, again gave steady support to its details, and divided for the third reading, 22 Mar. 1832.

On 9 Dec. 1831 Parnell reminded Althorp that he had 'been constantly occupied during the last eight months in making the strictest investigation into every item of the army estimates' and urged the cabinet to approve his reductions:

> When I accepted office I distinctly gave you to understand it was my intention to act fully and strictly on the principles I had publicly avowed ... If it is postponed you must not hold me responsible for any inconvenience that may follow from my resigning my office while the reform bill is in progress.[78]

Later that month Greville noted that Parnell had caused 'something like a *tracasserie* of an official kind' in Paris, at which Grey was 'indignant', by negotiating 'about the mails' without the sanction of the duke of Richmond, the postmaster-general, who was 'very angry' and 'told me that if he had mentioned it to the king, he was sure he would have insisted upon Parnell's being dismissed'. Describing Richmond's 'great aversion' to Parnell, Greville recalled that

> Hume had given notice of a motion against the post office just when Parnell took office, and as he went to Ireland to be re-elected he wrote to Hume to urge him to bring it on. Hume brought the letter to Richmond, who was indignant ... He contented himself at the time with speaking to Althorp, who spoke to Parnell.[79]

On 26 Jan. 1832 Parnell was absent from the majority in support of ministers on the Russian Dutch loan. 'Our secretary at war would not vote on Thursday! Is this to be borne'?, noted Holland:

> It is pretty clear that he is looking out for popular grounds to resign. His conduct in office has been far from friendly to the government or even meritorious in his department. Not Grey only, but Althorp, who has great personal regard for him and estimates his talents and principles of political economy very highly, agrees he should be dismissed.[80]

On 30 Jan. Althorp, having asked Parnell to call on him and found him out of town, wrote 'to say what is most disagreeable':

> If the division ... had been against us, there would have been no possibility of our remaining in office another day ... I understand Duncannon told you as much, but still you went away and did not vote ... Under these circumstances my colleagues are, and I am sorry to say with myself, unanimously of opinion that you ought to resign your office. I can assure you I never was more annoyed by any political event than I am by being obliged to write you this letter. For a great many years you and I have acted cordially together. We have much the same objects in view. We differ very little about the means of obtaining them ... When you accepted office I felt that your knowledge of business and your power of application would supply that in which I am most deficient, and I looked forward to being able together to affect great good. But

> it is quite impossible for any government to exist if the members of it are not prepared to resist a vote of censure on their colleagues. Every man ought to agree to a vote of censure if he thinks the ministry deserve it ... but then he certainly ought not to continue associated with such a ministry. This is the state of the case, and I need not tell you that I write to you with the deepest regret.

Parnell replied the following day that he had 'no hesitation in taking the course you intimate', and thanked Althorp for having 'entertained the various suggestions' he had made while in office.[81] Privately he observed:

> I repeatedly apprized between 7 June and this date, that I could not hold office if Lord Hill remained commander-in-chief. I gave him my plans of estimates in a letter (9 December 1831) saying I would resign unless ... reductions in the household guards were conducted. In January 1832, having received Lord Hill's estimates, I wrote to Lord Grey to say I would not agree to them and that we could not go on together.[82]

Calling him an 'honest man', 31 Jan., Ellenborough observed that

> the Grey faction are much annoyed, as they think he goes out to avoid being smashed when the whole government is, and to have free scope for his attacks against the budget ... [He] had long been on cool terms with the government. He wished to deprive officers and soldiers on furlough of their pay, and to make reductions quite impossible. They found him impractical and they never liked him. He had often been absent and rarely sat with them.[83]

'Good riddance', commented Greville, 2 Feb., adding, 'he wrote an excellent book on finance, but he was a very bad secretary at war, a rash economical innovator, and a bad man of business in its details'.[84] They 'do wisely to turn out Parnell', remarked the duke of Bedford, 7 Feb. 1832.[85] Writing to Anglesey a few days later Richmond observed:

> Parnell was quite unfit for his office. He seldom went near it, and was too much of a radical. Pamphlet writers do not in general make good executive officers. He was turned out for not having voted with the government, but *entre nous* I believe he would have resigned upon the army estimates unless we had agreed to reduce the army, which is impossible. All his plans for saving expenditure were theories and would have been serious grievances to the army.[86]

Out of office, Parnell resumed his campaign against the army and navy estimates, demanding greater parliamentary control, 13 Feb., and accounting reforms, 17 Feb. 1832. On 28 Mar. he contrasted his successor Hobhouse's 'very small amount of reductions' with his own refusal to 'depart from the principles which I formerly professed', explaining that he had submitted proposals for an annual saving of £600,000 to Hill, which had been ignored, and that he 'could not continue to hold office unless I was supported, as I conceived I ought to be, by the government'. On 17 Feb., however, he privately offered Brougham another reason for his departure:

> I discontinued writing to you in consequence of a communication I had with Althorp early in December, from which I came to the conclusion that there was not any chance of having O'Connell and other Catholics appointed to office as long as the cabinet existed in its present form. This circumstance chiefly led me to determine to take the first opportunity of getting rid of my office.[87]

He endorsed a petition for the abolition of Irish tithes, 16 Feb., presented numerous others, 13, 26 Feb., and spoke and divided against the Irish tithes bill, 8 Mar., when it was reported that Smith Stanley had 'set up Parnell famously', and 30 Mar., 2 Aug.[88] Commenting on his revived opposition, 10 Mar., the backbencher John Hawkins contended that 'on Sir Henry's part, it was most probably pique and wounded vanity. He is a pragmatical coxcomb, who did all sorts of mischief in his office, and the ministry were right glad to be rid of him'.[89] He presented and endorsed a petition for military assistance following the disturbances in Queen's County, rejecting charges of 'inconsistency' with his campaign for reductions, 31 Mar. On the address calling on the king to appoint only ministers who would carry reform unimpaired, 10 May, he was one of twelve 'who might have voted if they had thought proper, having been present during the debate, but left the House and did not vote'.[90] He demanded inquiry into the banking system, 22 May, and was appointed to the select committee on the Bank's charter, 23 May. That day he gave notice that he would move for inquiry into the disturbed state of his county, but following remarks by O'Connell, 31 May, Wyse carried an amendment broadening its aim to investigation of the causes of these events and the laws for the suppression of outrages in Ireland, to which Parnell was appointed (as chairman). Commenting on the episode, 25 June, Daniel Egan observed to O'Connell that 'Sir Henry is a great fox and as all his measures have had the appearance when first broached of being for the good of Ireland and ultimately being rather curses than benefits, he must be well watched'.[91] He voted for the second reading of Irish reform bill, 25 May, but was in the minority of 21 for an amendment against the liability of Irish electors to pay municipal taxes before they could vote, 29 June. He paired with ministers against a Conservative amendment to increase the Scottish county representation, 1 June. On 29 June he charged the post office with incompetency, recounting that in Paris the previous November he had 'found every disposition to facilitate the project of a daily communication between the two capitals'. On 4 July he refuted O'Connell's claim that at a meeting of 28 Members in February he had agreed to a resolution advising ministers to adopt the English system of voter registration in Ireland. The following day he welcomed Althorp's decision to postpone consideration of the Bank's charter until the next session. He was credited with a vote against government on the Russian-Dutch loan, 12 July, but his name was absent from the lists in *The Times* and *Mirror of Parliament*.[92] He voted for inquiry into admissions to the inns of court, 17 July. He welcomed the ministry's new proposals for army reductions, which accorded 'very much with those I suggested', 26 July 1832. Urging the necessity of pushing retrenchment 'to the greatest possible extent' the following day, he warned of the 'vast expense' of maintaining the colonies and hoped that the 'first practical benefit we shall receive from parliamentary reform will be an effective retrenchment'.

At the 1832 dissolution Parnell retired from Queen's County after finding that 'the repeal cry' had lost him 'the support of all the Catholic voters'.[93] In 1833 he was elected unopposed as a Liberal for Dundee, where he sat until retiring in 1841. His *Treatise on Roads*, drawing on his experience at Holyhead, was published in 1833 and ran to a second edition in 1838. In the second Melbourne administration he served as treasurer of the navy and paymaster-general, in which office he continued to pursue 'many severe and impracticable schemes of reduction'.[94] Observing that he had 'spoken very little of late' and that 'his reputation is suffering in consequence', James Grant wrote in 1837:

> Parnell is a respectable but by no means a superior speaker. He has a fine clear voice, but he never varies the key in which he commences ... He delivers his speeches in much the same way as if he were repeating some piece of writing committed to memory in his schoolboy years. His gesticulation is a great deal too tame for his speeches to produce any effect. He stands stock-still, except when he occasionally raises and lets fall his right hand. Even this he does in a very gentle manner. What he excels in is giving a plain, luminous statement of complex financial matters. In this respect he has no superior; I doubt if he has an equal in the House.[95]

In August 1841 he was elevated to a United Kingdom barony, much to the consternation of Graham, the home secretary in the new Peel administration, who thought it a 'high crime and misdemeanour' on the part of the retiring ministry.[96]

In June 1842 Parnell committed suicide by hanging himself in his dressing room at Cadogan Place, Chelsea, having 'for two months been in a low, desponding state of mind' and 'under medical treatment'. By his will, proved under £7,000, the residue of his estate passed to his second son Henry William, his eldest son and successor in the barony John Vesey (1805-83), having 'renounced' it.[97]

[1] *Melbourne Pprs*. 28. [2] *O'Connell Corresp*. ii. 873; Add. 38751, f. 15. [3] *Black Bk*. (1823), 182; *Session of Parl. 1825*, p. 479. [4] M. Hughs, 'Telford, Parnell and Great Irish Road', *Jnl. of Transport Hist*. vi (1964), 199-209; Add. 40357, f. 202; 57418, f. 183; Inst. of Civil Engineers, Telford mss T/SW/63, Eaton to Telford, 21 Mar. 1824. [5] Add. 38283, f. 102. [6] *Dublin Evening Post*, 11, 25, 28, 30 Mar., 1 Apr. 1820. [7] Add. 38751, f. 15. [8] Bucks. RO, Fremantle mss D/FR/46/10/15, 18; Buckingham, *Mems. Geo. IV*, i. 297. [9] Fremantle mss 46/10/56; Buckingham, i. 314; Add. 51586, Tierney to Lady Holland, 16 Apr. 1822. [10] Add. 20032, f. 32. [11] *O'Connell Corresp*. ii. 1035. [12] Brougham mss, Wakefield to Brougham, 17 Dec. 1823. [13] *O'Connell Corresp*. iii. 1083, 1108. [14] Add. 40330, f. 207. [15] Buckingham, ii. 160-1, 198-200, 210; Fremantle mss 46/11/111/1, 2. [16] *O'Connell Corresp*. iii. 1175-6. [17] *PP* (1825), viii. 198. [18] *Dublin Evening Post*, 9 Apr. 1831. [19] Add. 57418, f. 116. [20] Nottingham Univ. Lib. Denison diary, 19 May 1826. [21] Cent. Kent. Stud. Stanhope mss U1590 C199/2, Stanhope to Parnell, 29 May 1826. [22] *Dublin Evening Post*, 17, 27 June 1826. [23] Wentworth Woodhouse mun. Milton to Fitzwilliam, 20 Apr. 1827. [24] Lansdowne mss. [25] Add. 38751, ff. 15, 24, 66. [26] Add. 40395, f. 221. [27] Hatherton diary. [28] Add. 40307, f. 5; 40395, f. 244. [29] Keele Univ. Lib. Sneyd mss SC17/37. [30] *Croker Pprs*. i. 407. [31] NLW, Powis mss 142, Holmes to Powis, 17 May 1828. [32] Southampton Univ. Lib. Congleton mss 13/21, Mill to Parnell, 1 May 1828. [33] *Ellenborough Diary*, i. 108. [34] Mq. of Anglesey, *One-Leg*, 373. [35] Add. 51562. [36] *O'Connell Corresp*. iv. 1517. [37] Add. 40399, ff. 68-70. [38] Add. 38758, f. 52. [39] PRO NI, Anglesey mss D619/32/A/3/1/269. [40] *The Times*, 6 Feb. 1830. [41] Congleton mss 32/5; *On Financial Reform* (1830), 3, 13, 79. [42] Wellington mss WP1/1102/13; Add. 38758, f. 138. [43] Stanhope mss C199/2. [44] *Dublin Evening Post*, 27 July, 14 Aug. 1830. [45] Grey mss, Howick jnl. 16 Nov. 1830. [46] Congleton mss 29, ff. 65-76. [47] Ibid. 15/5; 29, f. 76. [48] Broughton, *Recollections*, iv. 196; Le Marchant, *Althorp*, 271. [49] *The Times*, 24 Nov. 1830, 7 Feb. 1831; *The Age*, 5 Dec. 1830. [50] Add. 51572. [51] Add. 34614, f. 119. [52] TNA 30/29/9/5/76. [53] *Three Diaries*, 46; Le Marchant, 272. [54] *Newspaper Writings by J. S. Mill* ed. A. Robson and J. Robson, xxiii. 612. [55] Grey mss. [56] Congleton mss 29, f. 87. [57] Anglesey mss 31D/37. [58] TNA GD30/29, Holland to Granville, 14 Apr. 1831. [59] Broughton, iv. 98. [60] Congleton mss 29, ff. 101-2. [61] *O'Connell Corresp*. iv. 1794; *Dublin Evening Post*, 19 Apr. 1831. [62] *The Times*, 21 Apr. 1831. [63] *Dublin Evening Post*, 5, 12, 17 May 1831. [64] Wellington mss WP1/1184/1. [65] Congleton mss 31/1. [66] Hatherton diary, 26 July 1831. [67] *Three Diaries*, 110. [68] Anglesey mss 27/B, Anglesey to Holland, 3 Sept. 1831. [69] *Arbuthnot Corresp*. 148. [70] Brougham mss, Duncannon to Brougham [Aug. 1831]; *Holland House Diaries*, 41. [71] *Three Diaries*, 117. [72] Congleton mss 34/3, Parnell to Brougham, 23 Sept., 15 Oct.; Brougham mss, same to same, 11 Oct. 1831. [73] *O'Connell Corresp*. iv. 1837. [74] *Melbourne Pprs*. 168-9. [75] Congleton mss 34/1. [76] *Von Neumann Diary*, i. 265. [77] Wellington mss WP1/1205/18. [78] Congleton mss 34/1, 5. [79] *Greville Mems*. ii. 231. [80] *Holland House Diaries*, 120-1. [81] Add. 75941; Congleton mss 34/1. [82] Congleton mss 29, f. 102. [83] *Three Diaries*, 187. [84] *Greville Mems*. ii. 246. [85] Add. 51671, Bedford to Lady Holland, 7

Feb. 1832. [86] W. Sussex RO, Goodwood mss 1486, pp. 159-61. [87] Congleton mss 34/3. [88] UCNW, Mostyn mss 265, Mostyn to fa. 9 Mar. 1832. [89] Cornw. RO, Hawkins mss 10/2185. [90] *The Times*, 14 May 1832. [91] *O'Connell Corresp.* iv. 1899. [92] *The Times*, 14 July 1832. [93] Congleton mss 34/3, Parnell to Brougham, 19 Dec. 1832. [94] *Gent. Mag.* (1842), ii. 203. [95] [J. Grant], *Random Recollections of Commons* (1837), 239-40. [96] *The Times*, 14 Aug. 1841; *Arbuthnot Corresp.* 227. [97] *Gent. Mag.* (1842), ii. 204, 677.

P.J.S.

PARNELL HAYES, William (?1777–1821), of Avondale, co. Wicklow.[1]

Co. WICKLOW 12 Aug. 1817–2 Jan. 1821

b. ?1777, 3rd s. of Sir John Parnell, 2nd bt.[†], MP[I] of Rathleague, Queen's Co. and Letitia Charlotte, da. and coh. of Sir Arthur Brooke, 1st bt., MP [I], of Colebrook, co. Fermanagh; bro. of Sir Henry Brooke Parnell, 4th bt*. *educ.* Eton; Trinity Coll. Camb. 25 June 1794, aged 17. *m.* 1 Oct. 1810, Frances, da. of Hon. Hugh Howard, MP [I], of Bushy Park, 4th s. of Ralph, 1st Visct. Wicklow [I], 1s. 1da. *suc.* fa. to Avondale estate, formerly the property of Samuel Hayes, MP [I] (*d.*1795), and took additional name of Hayes 1801. *d.* 2 Jan. 1821.

In 1817 Parnell, a cultivated and intelligent man but a political innocent, had written to the Irish secretary Robert Peel* who, not for the first time, had disappointed his hopes of a more enlightened approach to the economic and social problems of Ireland:

> I have been rather unfortunate in my applications to you, so much so that I think some explanation is due to myself for having made them. I have always been miserable at the state of Ireland and have felt something of a personal gratitude to those who seem to wish her well, however they may have mistaken the means. I was a friend to Lord Hardwicke though his government was detestable and to the duke of Bedford though his was not much better, but both intended well. But in your good intentions there appeared more warmth and vigour, and though I could not approve of your administration, which seemed to have the vice common to all of receiving the Irish in a state of pupillage and keeping them so, yet I was so far captivated as to attempt to urge you to the adoption of those measures which can alone confer lasting honour on an Irish administration, those which tend to raise the lower orders in this country from the degradation into which they have been driven down. What was intended kindly ought not to be charged to interference or indiscretion. But though sanguine I am not quite absurd, and in future my good wishes shall be equally warm without being quite so troublesome.[2]

In the introduction to his polemical novel of Irish rural life, *Maurice and Berghetta; or the Priest of Raherty*, published in 1819, Parnell declared that he 'scarcely remembers the time, when a passion for his native country, and a painful commiseration of the deplorable state of the peasantry in Ireland, were not the strongest feelings in his breast'. This book, which he dedicated to 'the Catholic priesthood of Ireland', whose 'merits have always appeared to me equal to their privations', was savaged by a Tory journal as 'mischievous and absurd' and Parnell was portrayed as 'a child playing with fire-arms; an innocent who, by way of giving light to his neighbours, sticks his farthing candle into a barrel of gunpowder'. His sincerity was never in doubt, but he found it hard to shake off his reputation as an impractical theorist.[3]

At the 1820 general election Parnell, who had joined Brooks's in 1816, offered again for county Wicklow on the combined interest of Lord Fitzwilliam, Lord Carysfort and his father-in-law's family. He was returned unopposed.[4] He continued to act as an independent opposition Member, voting against the Liverpool ministry on the civil list, 8 May, the additional Scottish baron of exchequer, 15 May, military expenditure, 16 May, 14 June, and the aliens bill, 1 June, 7 July, but deprecating the Whigs' attacks on the turncoat lawyer Charles Warren*, 1 June. He criticized the protective Irish Union duties, 2 June, spoke and voted for his brother's motion for inquiry into them, 14 June, and supported his attempt to shorten their existence, 7 July.[5] After an appeal to the House on the hardships suffered by Irish paupers under the system whereby they were arbitrarily arrested and transported back to Ireland, 7 June, he obtained information on the subject. A week later he secured leave to introduce a bill to confine the landing of repatriated vagrants to designated ports and require arrangements for their reception. It received little support and, after a nominal second reading on 10 July, was set aside.[6] Parnell welcomed the advance of £1,500,000 for the relief of problems caused by Irish bank failures, 16 June, and objected to the vote of £60,000 for Millbank penitentiary, 19 June. On 28 June 1820 he spoke against calls from the government back benches for coercive legislation to quell disturbances in the west of Ireland. Two days later he called for the establishment of an eye hospital in Dublin, but was told that there were no funds.[7]

The failure of Parnell's Irish paupers bill, together with that of an earlier attempt to protect children employed in Irish cotton factories, was seized on by the *Quarterly Review* in its attack on his response to the ridicule of his novel in *A Letter to the Editor of the Quarterly Review* (Dublin 1820):

> Whether advanced in a bill or in a novel, in sad reality or fantastic fiction, his theories are the wildest ... the most impracticable, and the most idle even if they could be put into practice, that we have ever witnessed ... We have thought it advisable to endeavour ... to render his follies innocuous, and to enable our readers to form a fair judgement of what they may expect from any future attempt at domestic or general reform by this amiable but weak, this well-intentioned but extravagant gentleman.[8]

Others dealt more kindly with him after his early death in January 1821, when he had just had some success in his efforts to raise funds to improve the education of the Irish Catholic poor. 'No man was more amiable in private life ... and even his opponents admitted that, as an honest public man, he had no superior', observed *The Times*. 'Had Mr. Parnell lived', conjectured another obituarist, 'the attention which he was in the habit of giving in Parliament to Irish affairs would have been productive, ere long, of lasting benefits to his country. Time only was wanting to enable him to give effect to those plans, which had been his constant study from his earliest years, for relieving Ireland from her grievances, and for ameliorating the condition of all classes of her people, in wealth, in manners, and in morals'.[9] His only son, John Henry Parnell (1811-59), was the father of Charles Stewart Parnell (1846-91), the ill-fated champion of Irish home rule, on whom William's writing and example may have had a strong posthumous influence.

[1] See R.F. Foster, *Charles Stewart Parnell*, 16-29. [2] Add. 40269, f. 354. [3] *Quarterly Rev.* xxi. (1819), 471-86. [4] *Dublin Evening Post*, 7 Mar. 1820. [5] *The Times*, 8 July 1820. [6] Ibid. 11 July 1820. [7] Ibid. 20 June, 1 July 1820. [8] *Quarterly Rev.* xxiii. (1820), 373. [9] *The Times*, 11 Jan. 1821; *Gent. Mag.* (1821), i. 86.

D.R.F.

PARSONS, John Clere (1760–1826), of Hampstead, Glasnevin, co. Dublin.

KING'S COUNTY 1818–July 1821

b. 29 Jan. 1760, 2nd s. of Sir William Parsons, 4th bt. (*d.* 1791), MP [I], of Birr Castle, nr. Parsonstown, King's Co. and Mary, da. and h. of John Clere, MP [I], of Kilburry, co. Tipperary. *educ.* Trinity, Dublin 1778; M. Temple 1781; King's Inns 1785, called [I] 1792. *m.* Nov. 1805, Mary Anne, da. of William Moore, 3s. 2da. *d.* 1 May 1826.

KC [I] 1815; commr. of insolvent ct. [I] 1821-*d.*

Parsons had been returned for King's County on the family interest in 1818 to strengthen the hand of his elder brother Lawrence, 2nd earl of Rosse, in his quest for a United Kingdom peerage, and to act as 'trustee' for Rosse's eldest son, a minor. He came in again in 1820 on the same terms. A very lax attender, who had never been required to do more than go to Westminster 'a month in the year at snatches', he is not known to have voted or spoken in this period. He made way for his nephew as soon as he came of age in 1821, having at the same time secured promotion to the Irish bench, for which his brother had pestered successive governments on his behalf since 1803. In 1822 Rosse described him as 'a liberal, unsuspecting man' who 'had been all his life friendly to every concession to the Catholics'.[1] He died on the circuit at Roscommon in May 1826.[2]

[1] PRO NI, Rosse mss D/4/12; D/14/2; D/20/3; Add. 40297, ff. 34-35. [2] Rosse mss F/21, commonplace bk.

P.J.S.

PARSONS, William, Lord Oxmantown (1800–1867).

KING'S COUNTY 30 July 1821–1834

b. 17 June 1800, 1st s. of Lawrence Parsons†, 2nd earl of Rosse [I], of Birr Castle, nr. Parsonstown, King's Co. and Alice, da. of John Lloyd, MP [I], of Gloster, King's Co. *educ.* Trinity, Dublin 1819; Magdalen, Oxf. 1821, hon. fellow 1862-*d. m.* 14 Apr. 1836, Mary, da. and coh. of John Wilmer Field of Heaton Hall, nr. Bradford, Yorks., 6s. (2 *d.v.p.*) 1 da. *d.v.p. styled* Lord Oxmantown 1807-41; *suc.* fa. as 3rd earl of Rosse [I] 24 Feb. 1841; KP 4 Jan. 1845. *d.* 31 Oct. 1867.

Rep. peer [I] 1845-*d.*

Pres. Brit. Assoc. 1843-4, R. Soc. 1848-54; visitor, Maynooth Coll. 1845-*d.*; chan. Dublin Univ. 1862-*d.*

Ld. lt. King's Co. 1831-*d.*

Col. King's Co. militia 1834.

Oxmantown's father had been a prominent opponent of the Union in the Irish House, where he had represented Dublin University, 1782-91, when he succeeded to the family's seat for King's County, but on taking his place at Westminster he became a supporter of the Addington and Pitt ministries and was rewarded with office in the Irish treasury in 1805. In 1807 he succeeded to his uncle's earldom of Rosse and in 1809 was elected an Irish representative peer and appointed Irish joint-postmaster general, a non-resident sinecure worth £1,500 a year with a 'great deal of patronage attached to it', which he held under successive governments until his resignation on the fall of the Wellington administration.[1] In March 1820 it was reported that a 'conspiracy' had been detected to assassinate Oxmantown and his father on account of their attempts to preserve the tranquility of King's County, and that a 'party of military and constables' had been sent to protect them.[2] At his father's desire he matriculated in February 1821 at Magdalen College, Oxford, where he took first class honours in mathematics. On coming of age later that year he stood on the family interest for a vacancy for King's County, where his supporters hoped 'those abilities which he has displayed in his collegiate courses, both in Dublin and in Oxford, will, before long, recommend his lordship to one of the highest eminences to which a great statesman may laudably aspire'. Threats of opposition came to nothing and he was returned *in absentia*.[3] He seconded a motion at a county meeting for an address to the king on his arrival in Ireland, 9 Aug. 1821.[4] A radical commentary of 1823 noted that he had shown 'no trace of attendance in the last three sessions', but two years later he was reported to have 'attended frequently, and voted with ministers', though he often took an independent line.[5] His first recorded vote was with the Liverpool ministry against reform of the Scottish representation, 2 June 1823. He divided against inquiries into chancery delays, 5 June, and the currency, 12 June, but was in the minorities against the beer duties bill, 13, 17 June 1823, and the grant for repairs to Windsor Castle, 5 Apr. 1824. On 3 May he complained that the Irish tithes bill was 'too much in favour' of the 'extortionate clergyman'. He was in the minority to condemn the trial in Demerara of the Methodist missionary John Smith, 11 June 1824. He divided for suppression of the Catholic Association, 15 Feb. 1825. He was granted a month's leave on account of ill health, 25 Feb. He warned that alteration of the corn laws would result in a 'complete dependency' on foreign corn, 'throw much of our tillage lands out of cultivation, and thereby diminish the numbers of that hardy population of agricultural labourers', 28 Apr. He voted for Catholic relief, 10 May. He divided for the duke of Cumberland's annuity bill, 30 May, 6, 10 June 1825. On 3 Apr. 1826 he promised his father that he would inquire about what had 'really' been said 'against the post office' by Sir John Newport from 'any Members I may know who were in the House at the time', but on 7 Apr. he reported that he had 'not been able to ascertain that Newport made any charge' other than manifesting 'some impatience at the report of the commissioners not yet being out'.[6] He voted with ministers for the report on the salary of the president of the board of trade, 10 Apr., against reform of Edinburgh's representation, 13 Apr., and against Russell's resolutions to curb electoral bribery, 26 May 1826.

At the 1826 general election he offered again as a supporter of Catholic emancipation and was returned unopposed.[7] He voted for Catholic relief, 6 Mar. 1827, 12 May 1828, and presented favourable constituency petitions, 28 Apr., 6 May 1828. On 25 Sept. he warned Gregory, the Irish under-secretary, of a likely 'conflict of the most serious nature' at the 'well armed' town of Shinrone, King's County, where Denis Egan, a member of the Catholic Association, intended 'with a very large mob to pass through', and asked 'what course the magistracy should pursue'. The following day Lord Francis Leveson Gower, the Wellington ministry's Irish secretary, offered a 'sufficient military force for the prevention of any illegal assemblage in your lordship's area', but also recommended 'warning the leaders and their deluded followers' in a way that should 'by no means ... assume ... a tone of entreaty or deprecation, which might compromise the dignity of the civil authority and the government'. On 29 Sept. Oxmantown informed Leveson Gower that Egan had complied with the wishes of the magistracy and that the 'display of military force had a powerful influence on deterring the people from assembling'.[8] He signed the Protestant declaration got up in Dublin in favour of Catholic relief the following month.[9] In February 1829 Planta, the Wellington ministry's patronage secretary, predicted that he would vote 'with government' for emancipation, but he was absent from the division of 6 Mar. He presented favourable constituency petitions, 24, 30 Mar., when he divided for the bill's third reading. Speaking against the introduction of an Irish poor law, 7 May, he denied that 'money paid to the poor' was 'not a loss'. On 2 June 1829 he added that 'no greater cruelty' could be inflicted on 'the peasantry of Ireland, than to persuade them that they will be supported without industry', since 'when they are told that they will be provided for by law, they will then yield to the inactivity natural to all'. He presented and endorsed a counter-petition from Clara, King's County that day against one for the introduction of poor laws 'signed by nobody of the least respectability', and commended another hostile constituency petition, hoping that 'Ireland may not have inflicted upon it a system from which England has already suffered so much', 26 May 1830. He spoke against the disfranchisement of East Retford, saying that he had always been 'opposed to parliamentary reform', 2 June, and divided for the issue of a new writ, 4 June 1829. He was granted three weeks' leave to attend the assizes, 10 Mar. 1830. He contended that as soon as an Irish curate received his curacy, he should 'at the same moment, receive his license ... instead of being left, as he is at present, in a state of dependency upon his rector, differing but very little from that of a servant upon his master', 27 Apr. He was 'decidedly hostile' to Hume's proposal to abolish the office of Irish lord lieutenant, as it would 'greatly increase absenteeism', which was 'one of the greatest evils that can exist in a country', 11 May. He voted for repeal of the Irish coal duties, 13 May. He divided against Jewish emancipation, 17 May, but for abolition of the death penalty for forgery, as 'a less severe punishment would operate more beneficially', 24 May. He introduced a bill to facilitate summary proceedings before Irish magistrates, 28 May, and was appointed to the committee on it the following day, but it went no further. He was in the minority for reducing the grant for South American missions, 7 June 1830.

At the 1830 general election Oxmantown offered again, professing 'perfect independence' from party, and was returned unopposed.[10] He was listed by ministers as one of their 'friends', but he was absent from the crucial division on the civil list, 15 Nov. 1830. Both he and his father signed the declaration against repeal of the Union in early March 1831.[11] On 10 Mar. he argued that it would be 'detrimental' to Ireland to permit the continued cultivation of tobacco. He voted for the second reading of the Grey ministry's reform bill, 22 Mar., but was absent from the division on Gascoyne's wrecking amendment, 19 Apr. 1831. At the ensuing general election he stood as a 'decided and uncompromising supporter' of reform and topped the poll.[12] He voted for the second reading of the reintroduced reform bill, 6 July, but only gave sporadic support to its details, usually as a pair. He presented a petition from Maryborough, Queen's County, against alteration of the Irish distillation regulations, 17 Aug. He was granted leave on account of ill health for ten days, 12 Sept., and a fortnight, 26 Sept., and was absent from the division on the reform bill's passage, 21 Sept. He paired for the second reading of the revised bill, 17 Dec. 1831, but is not known to have voted for any of its details and was absent from the division on the third reading, 22 Mar. 1832. He voted for the address calling on the king to appoint only ministers who would carry reform unimpaired, 10 May, the second reading of the Irish bill, 25 May, and against a Conservative amendment to the Scottish bill, 1 June. He divided for the Liverpool disfranchisement bill, 23 May. He welcomed a bill to transfer the King's County assizes from Philipstown to Tullamore that day and was a majority teller for its second reading, 1 June. He was appointed to the select committee on Irish disturbances, 31 May, and presented a petition from the sheriff of King's County for a renewal of the Insurrection Act, 15 June. He warned that 'the introduction of the poor laws into Ireland would ... decrease the rate of wages [and] increase ... the influx of the Irish peasantry into this part of the kingdom' and voted against a tax on absentee landlords to provide permanent provision for the poor, 19 June. He presented and endorsed the petition of a 'most respectable man' who had been dismissed from the Dublin post office for exposing fraud, saying he had been 'most harshly treated', 4 July 1832.

At the 1832 general election Oxmantown offered again and was narrowly returned in second place as a Liberal. He retired at the 1834 dissolution in order to concentrate on his significant experiments with large astronomical telescopes, which he had begun in 1827. In the early 1840s, after succeeding his father in the peerage, he constructed a 'monster' telescope at his Birr Castle residence at an estimated cost of £20,000. Known as the 'Leviathan of Parsonstown', it was the largest in existence for over six decades. He sat in the Lords as a 'moderate Conservative' representative peer from 1845.[13] Oxmantown, a progressive landlord and philanthropist, died at Monkstown, County Dublin, in October 1867.[14] *The Times* remarked of his political career that 'though he shrank from the prominence of a parliamentary debater, he occasionally spoke on subjects on which he felt it due to his constituents to express his opinion'.[15] He was succeeded by his eldest son Laurence (1840-1908), a Conservative Irish representative peer from 1868.

[1] *HP Commons, 1790-1820*, iv. 728-9; Add. 40296, f. 48; Wellington mss WP1/1152/21. [2] *The Times*, 6, 9 Mar. 1820. [3] *Dublin Evening Post*, 21, 31 July, 4, 7 Aug. 1821. [4] Ibid. 14 Aug. 1821. [5] *Black Bk.* (1823), 181; *Session of Parl. 1825*, p. 478. [6] PRO NI, Rosse mss D/22/21-22. [7] *Westmeath Jnl.* 8 June; *Dublin Evening Post*, 10, 20, 27 June 1826. [8] Add. 40335, ff. 165-6, 212. [9] *Dublin Evening Post*, 7 Oct. 1828. [10] Ibid. 27 July, 14 Aug. 1830. [11] Ibid. 5 Mar. 1831. [12] Ibid. 3, 5, 10, 12, 19 May 1831. [13] *Oxford DNB*; *The Times*, 2 Nov. 1867. [14] *Gent. Mag.* (1867), ii. 813. [15] *The Times*, 2 Nov. 1867.

P.J.S.

PATTEN *see* WILSON PATTEN

PAXTON, William Gill (1788–1850), of 11 Buckingham Street, Strand, Mdx.; Watford Place, Herts., and Henbury House, nr. Wimborne, Dorset.

PLYMPTON ERLE 17 Feb. 1821–1826

b. 2 Apr. 1788,[1] o. legit. s. of Archibald Paxton, wine merchant, of Buckingham Street and Watford Place and Harriet, da. of William Gill, alderman and ld. mayor of London, of Wraysbury House, Bucks. and Yeovany Hall, Mdx. *educ.* Harrow 1801; Merton, Oxf. 1805; L. Inn 1806. *unm. suc.* fa. 1817. *d.* 3 May 1850.

Sheriff, Dorset 1828-9.

Paxton was descended from a Berwickshire family with a tradition of service in the Presbyterian ministry. His grandfather John Paxton, a burgess of Edinburgh, was employed there for many years by Archibald Stewart†, a wealthy wine merchant and Member for the city, and later became a partner in the business which Stewart transferred to London in 1747. His father Archibald assumed sole control of the firm in the early 1780s and later formed a partnership with Stewart Marjoribanks*, a grandson of Archibald Stewart, who had married his illegitimate daughter Eleanor; he married the daughter of an 'immensely rich' partner in the London stationary business of Wright, Gill and Dalton of Abchurch Lane, purchased an estate at Watford and served as sheriff of Hertfordshire in 1799.[2] One of Archibald's brothers was Sir William Paxton†, who sat in the Commons as a Whig, 1803-7. William Gill Paxton and his father were briefly partners in the short-lived banking house of Paxton, Cockerell and Traill, which William opened in 1813. He was the residuary legatee of his father's estate, which was sworn under £80,000,[3] and continued the wine business, initially in partnership with Marjoribanks. In 1820 he added a Dorset estate to his holding of landed property.[4] The following year he was returned on a vacancy for Plympton Erle on the Treby interest, presumably by purchase.

He was an occasional attender who gave general but silent support to Lord Liverpool's ministry. He divided against Catholic claims, 28 Feb., repeal of the additional malt duty, 3 Apr., parliamentary reform, 9 May, and abolition of the death penalty for forgery, 23 May 1821. He voted against more extensive tax reductions, 11 Feb., abolition of one of the joint-postmasterships, 13 Mar., removal of Catholic peers' disabilities, 30 Apr., and for the aliens bill, 19 July 1822. He divided for the Irish glebes grant, 11 Apr., and against repeal of the Foreign Enlistment Act, 16 Apr., and inquiries into the prosecution of the Dublin Orange rioters, 22 Apr., and delays in chancery, 5 June 1823. He voted for the Irish insurrection bill, 14 June 1824, and the Irish unlawful societies bill, 25 Feb., and against Catholic claims, 1 Mar., 21 Apr. 1825. He voted in the minority for the Leith docks bill, 20 May, but with government for the duke of Cumberland's annuity, 10 June 1825. He retired from Parliament at the dissolution in 1826. He served as sheriff of Dorset in 1828 but sold out of the county two years later.[5] He remained at the head of the wine business until his death in May 1850 when, in accordance with the instructions in his will, it was sold to George Tanqueray and Company.[6]

[1] *Ex inf.* A.J. Paxton, correcting *Burke LG*, which gives 1789. Other information kindly supplied by Mr. Paxton on the antecedents and immediate family of this Member has been incorporated in this biography. [2] Add. 35510, f. 10; 47556, f. 73; PROB 11/1305/257; *Gent. Mag.* (1798), i. 264-5; *Farington Diary*, viii. 2893. [3] PROB 8/210 (22 Nov. 1817); 11/1598/593. There was at least one illegitimate son, John William Paxton, who had a successful career with the East India Company in Bengal. [4] J. Hutchins, *Dorset*, iii. 353. [5] Ibid. [6] PROB 8/243 (3 June 1850); 11/2115/461.

D.R.F.

PAYNE, Peter (1762–1843), of Knuston Hall, nr. Higham Ferrers, Northants.[1]

BEDFORDSHIRE 1831–1832

bap. 17 Mar. 1762,[2] 4th but 2nd surv. illegit. s. of Sir Gillies Payne, 2nd bt., of Roxton and Maria, da. of John Keeling, farmer, of Potton, Beds. *educ.* Hackney; Queens', Camb. 1779; I. Temple 1779. *m.* 21 Aug. 1789,[3] Elizabeth Sarah, da. of Samuel Steward of Stourton Castle, Staffs., 3s. (1 *d.v.p.*) 4da. *suc.* fa. to property at Tempsford, Beds. and Sandy Point, St. Kitts 1801. *d.* 23 Jan. 1843.

Payne was descended from a family which had settled in the Caribbean island of St. Kitts in 1654, as royalist fugitives from Cromwell. His grandfather Charles Payne (*d.* 1744) received a large grant of land from the crown as reward for his part in the expulsion of the French, and profited from shrewd land purchases, sharp rises in the price of sugar and an advantageous marriage to Janet McArthur, the daughter and heiress of a former president of St. Kitts council. He was knighted in 1728 and created a baronet in 1737, and at his death was one of the richest planters on the island, with an additional estate on Nevis. His eldest surviving son, Sir Gillies Payne, whose elder brother Abraham died without male issue in 1738, was born in St. Kitts in 1720, but educated in England, at Hackney, Queens' College, Cambridge and the Middle Temple. The death of one brother, the bankruptcy of another, and the death of his mother put the entire West Indian property in his hands by 1767. A handsome, coarse-fibred, licentious man, he took up residence in Bedfordshire, initially at Roxton, and formed a liaison with a local farmer's daughter, whom he passed off in the county as his wife, though it is almost certain that they never married. With her he had numerous bastards, of whom the two elder surviving males were John Payne, born in about 1754, and Peter, born in 1762. Six years later Sir Gillies, who returned occasionally to St. Kitts, bought the 1,200-acre estate of Tempsford, seven miles east of Bedford on the River Ouse, where he built an imposing new mansion house in Palladian style. He had no difficulty in integrating into the upper echelons of county society, serving as sheriff in 1771. He was described in 1778 as 'a strong North American partisan', and he supported the petitioning movement for economical and parliamentary reform in the early 1780s. On John's marriage to Elizabeth Campbell of Blunham in 1788, he settled on him an annuity of £500, charged on one of his two plantations at Sandy Point in St. Kitts. She died in childbirth, and in 1792 John married the heiress of Monoux of Wotton, having in the interim been granted by his father a year's rent charge from Tempsford. At the general election of 1790 he unsuccessfully contested Bedford as a supporter of Pitt's ministry, and his subsequent petition was rejected.[4]

Peter Payne was educated more or less in his father's footsteps. On his marriage to a Staffordshire woman in 1789, his father provided him with an annuity of £400, charged on the Nevis estate and that of St. Thomas Middleground, St. Kitts. Sir Gillies Payne died in 1801, when John succeeded to the bulk of the family estates and assumed the baronetcy. By his father's will of 14 Feb. 1794 and its codicil of 1 July 1796, Peter received the old mansion house at Tempsford and some surrounding land, the plantation of St. Anne, at Sandy Point and an annuity of £100.[5] He did not question John's right to the baronetcy, and after his brother's sudden death in May 1803 he became the trustee of his property and the guardian of his children, of whom the eldest son, Charles Payne, assumed the baronetcy and joined the army, serving in the Peninsula. In 1808 Peter Payne, a lifelong devotee of hunting, left Bedfordshire and moved to the vicinity of Birmingham, explaining to his friend Samuel Whitbread, the maverick advanced Whig Member for Bedford, whose politics he greatly admired:

> It was of great importance that my daughters should have some instruction which their mother could not give them; schools and governesses disagreed either with our habits or our means. In the little village of Solihull we found in the midst of decent society masters tolerably qualified to give the instruction we desired under their mother's eyes.

For several years he lived mostly at Winson Green.[6]

Sir Gillies Payne had left a troublesome legacy, with many claims on the West Indian estates and difficulties in fulfilling the provisions of his will, despite the sale of the Nevis property. In 1815, when his nephew Sir Charles Payne had come of age, Peter persuaded him to make over to him for life the other Sandy Point plantation, in return for a payment of £2,200 and renunciation of his annuity. Sir Charles soon became enmeshed in financial difficulties, which led him to mortgage all his English property, and in 1824 to put Tempsford on the market. It was bought the following year by William Stuart, Tory Member for Armagh, and a cousin of the 2nd marquess of Bute. Peter Payne, never slow to feather his own nest, extracted from Stuart in return for his own stake in the property a payment of £200 and a life annuity of £100. In order to safeguard his right to vote at the next county election, the completion date of the purchase was delayed, Stuart meanwhile being legally recognized as Payne's nominal tenant. In 1827 Sir Charles Payne agreed to become responsible for the payment of one fifth (£20) of his uncle's annuity, making over to Stuart £666 in three per cent consols for this purpose.[7] In 1826 Payne, who had recently moved to Knuston Hall in Northamptonshire, aimed another blow at his nephew by claiming, after a silence of 25 years, that he was entitled to the baronetcy as his father's first legitimate son, resting his case on a supposed surreptitious marriage between his father and mother in 1761. Although no documentary evidence could be produced, a chancery judgment of 7 June 1828 ludicrously ruled that Payne was the eldest son born in wedlock and was therefore the third baronet. However, this finding was reversed by the lord chancellor in January 1829, when the issue of the legitimacy of Payne and his late brother John was directed to be tried. Neither side pursued the matter in Payne's lifetime, but he continued to style himself a baronet, though he never registered himself as such with the heraldic authorities.[8]

He had become politically active in the Midlands after his move to Birmingham. His occasional letters to Whitbread between 1808 and the latter's death in 1815 reveal that he regarded himself as an honest Foxite, albeit of advanced reforming views, who felt betrayed by the trimming conduct of the leaders of the party, notably Lord Grey and George Tierney*, during and after their brief and ill-starred coalition in government with the Grenvillite Whigs. Borrowing a phrase of Buonaparte, whom he admired, he denounced them as 'shopkeeping politicians' who had compromised their principles on the Catholic question and, above all, peace, both in power and in their subsequent 'plastic opposition', thereby forfeiting the support and trust of the people.[9] Thus on 1 Oct. 1809 he wrote that

> the conduct of the Grenvillites and Foxites in office reminds me of two physicians called in to a sick person who laboured under a mortal complaint upon which the physicians disagreed, but being employed and liking the fees, they determined to let that proceed as usual, lest their disagreement upon it should disgust their employer. They therefore set about looking for the little sores of the patient's body, which he did not even know he had,

and took great credit for their cure – the slave trade sore, the Scotch judicature sore and so on – leaving the decline by which the patient was dying to be treated in the same ineffectual way as heretofore. I do not know exactly what to make of the Burdettites. This I know, that if any new administration is formed not guided by the principles you are guided by, Burdett and his party may play the devil with it. That party has a party among the people, a strong party, a *sensible* party, though not of the highest condition. The calamities of the day will daily increase that party. A new administration will have no party among the people. Your principles only can meet the calamities from without and the discontents within, supported by calmness, liberality towards opponents, upon principle and firmness.[10]

Again, on 9 Apr. 1813, when he blamed the war with America largely on British provocation, he argued that the Liverpool ministry had 'but one really vulnerable point about it', against which everyone but Whitbread had ceased to strike:

> If once it is admitted that its wars are just, all their other faults and incapacities will be overlooked by the people, because they have no reason to think their opponents more virtuous, or more able, and because the private judgement of the community is lost in its resentment against foreign aggression. What an eternal foothold would the Foxites have had, if they had adhered with you to their original ground of opposition, what a pyramid of guilt, crowned with Moscow in flames, might they not have pointed out to the people. But the presence of royalty confounded all honest and wise principle in them, its waves washed piece by piece the foundation on which they stood away, and they sank into the corruption which surrounded them.[11]

Payne, who became friendly with Samuel Parr and John Cartwright, composed pamphlets on these and related themes, though none of the following seem to have been published: *England and the Cause of Europe's Subjugation* (1810); *The Character and Conduct of British Ministers in War and Negotiation* (1810) and *Mr Pitt the Grand Political Delinquent* (1812).[12] He was active in the Birmingham campaign for repeal of the orders in council, in support of which he published in 1812, under the pseudonym of Philagathos, *Seven Short and Plain Letters, to the Inhabitants of Birmingham*. He distrusted the Tory activist Richard Spooner*, whom he suspected of playing a double game.[13] In February 1814 he deplored to Whitbread the assumption that the destruction of Buonaparte was a *sine qua non* of peace; and a year later observed that although he had lost his empire, 'I continue his friend and admirer as before. He is great in his fall'.[14] In 1819 he stood bail for Cartwright on his indictment for sedition as chairman of the Birmingham meeting to elect a 'Member of Parliament', and wrote an apparently unpublished *Letter to Lord Erskine in Defence of the Whigs*. He also wrote on slavery and the education of women.[15]

Payne was intermittently active in Bedfordshire politics in the 1820s. At the general election of 1820, when his residence was given as Sherbourn, Northamptonshire, he voted for the two Whig candidates, while his nephew plumped for the unsuccessful Tory.[16] At the county meeting called to express support for Queen Caroline, 12 Jan. 1821, he seconded the petitions and spoke powerfully for parliamentary reform.[17] He did so again at the county reform meeting, 20 Apr. 1822, when he declared that until the system had been purified, it was 'not an honour at all' to have a seat in the Commons, and called on the people to force reform on the House.[18] At the general election of 1826 he nominated Pym, one of the Whig sitting Members, and spoke in support of the other, Lord Tavistock, the duke of Bedford's son, who stood on purity of election principles.[19] He was a leading requisitionist for the county meeting to petition for repeal of the malt tax, 16 Feb. 1830, when he stated his approval of the principle, but said that it would achieve little, given the size of the national debt, and moved alternative resolutions ascribing the country's problems to 'the corrupt state of the Parliament' and the sins of successive ministries since 1793. He was prevailed upon to drop them for the sake of unanimity.[20] At the general election in August 1830 he nominated Tavistock.[21] He advocated triennial parliaments and the ballot at the Bedford town reform meeting, 17 Jan. 1831.[22] At the general election precipitated by the defeat of the Grey ministry's reform bill just over three months later, Payne, now in his seventieth year, was persuaded to stand with Tavistock as a second 'good reformer' in an attempt to turn out Stuart, who had been returned in 1830 but had caused great offence by opposing the bill. A Bedford committee worked for him and Tavistock jointly, and the latter sought a contribution from the Loyal and Patriotic Fund for Payne, who was 'without a shilling in his pocket'. At the nomination, he said that he had agreed to come forward, despite his advanced years

> because he felt the time was now arrived, for which he had been looking for the last 50 years ... Before, he thought himself a little man, but strengthened as he was by the confidence of the people, he now felt himself to be a giant ... He was a friend of the constitution ... He wished the king to possess his prerogative, and the Lords theirs, but he was determined the people should have theirs.

In response to a jibe that he possessed no property in the county, he retorted that he was a freeholder and 'possessed ... far more than a legal freehold'. He was returned in second place, well ahead of Stuart.[23]

Payne made no mark in the House, where he is not known to have spoken in debate, though he presented Woburn and Ridgmount petitions for reform of the penal code, 30 Aug. 1831, and one from Leighton Buzzard in favour of the London and Birmingham railway bill, 22 Mar. 1832. He divided for the second reading of the reintroduced reform bill, 6 July, was a steady supporter of its details, and voted for its passage, 21 Sept. 1831. He voted for the second reading of the Scottish bill, 23 Sept., and the motion of confidence in the Grey administration, 10 Oct. He sided with them twice on the Dublin election controversy, 23 Aug. He voted for the second reading of the revised reform bill, 17 Dec. 1831, to go into committee on it, 20 Jan., and for schedule B of the borough disfranchisement, 23 Jan. 1832; but his wife's illness, which ended in her death, 23 Apr., seems to have interfered with his attendance that session.[24] He voted against Wason's attempt to limit polling in boroughs with under 1,200 electors to one day, 15 Feb., but was in Hunt's later minority of four in favour of paying the cost of erecting hustings and booths out of corporate funds. He paired for the enfranchisement of Tower Hamlets, 28 Feb., but voted in person for the third reading of the reform bill, 22 Mar. His bereavement was given as the reason for his absence from the division on Lord Ebrington's motion calling on the king to appoint only ministers who would carry the measure unimpaired, 10 May. He divided with government on the Russian-Dutch loan, 26 Jan., 20 July, but was in minorities for O'Connell's attempt to extend the Irish borough franchise to £5 householders, 18 June, and a tax on Irish absentee landlords, 19 June. He voted to make coroners' inquests public, 20 June 1832.

At the Bedford dinner to celebrate the enactment of reform, 27 June 1832, Payne announced his intention of retiring at the dissolution on account of his age. He spoke at the Biggleswade reform dinner, 16 July. He was subsequently persuaded to stand at the general election in December, but he was narrowly beaten into third place by Stuart, who spent heavily to secure his revenge. The influence of Tory landlords on Chandos tenants-at-will was also thought to have been instrumental in the defeat of Payne, whose advocacy of repeal of the corn laws in a pamphlet that year would not have aided his cause.[25] Six weeks after his defeat he addressed to the reformers of Bedfordshire from Leamington a *Letter on the Ballot, Triennial Parliaments and the Ministers*, in which he argued that the Reform Act, for all its virtues, had 'not placed the new electors in a state of safety from the unlawful interference of the rich'. He never joined Brooks's, and on the subject of party wrote that while he might be told that he had been 'a good party man' (a label which he disclaimed) in voting for reform

> if I had continued in Parliament, I should have separated from those who continued leagued on *party* views, confident that they would not assist in rendering the bill *generally* beneficial; and confident that it is union, not party, that effects public good ... Party has reduced a powerful monarchy to a weak one, a happy people, to a discontented people, has made the rich, richer, and the poor, poorer, and filled each with fear and hatred of the other ... Party has never had any fixed political principles.

He declared himself to be one of 'the party of the people'.[26]

Payne ended his days in Bedfordshire, for in 1835 he bought Blunham House, near Tempsford.[27] The following year Emily Shore, who lived at Potton, wrote:

> Sir Peter Payne and his daughters called. Sir P. is a remarkably healthy old man ... He was naturally very delicate, and says he never knew what good health was till he was sixty years of age. He attributes his present good health and strength to his constant hard exercise and his great temperance. He never drinks anything but a single glass of wine in soda-water; he eats scarcely any meat, and lives principally upon pudding.[28]

Payne died of a disease of the bladder in January 1843.[29] By his will, dated 4 Dec. 1841, he directed that his Blunham property be sold to pay specified debts amounting to about £3,360, with the residue going to his daughter Laura. He made a distribution among his children of shares in the Birmingham canal navigation. He also ordered the sale of all his other disposable real estate.[30] His elder surviving son, Charles Gillies Payne (?1794-1870), assumed the baronetcy, as did Payne's nephew, the Rev. Coventry Payne (c.1795-1849), who succeeded his brother Charles in the main family estates in Bedfordshire and the West Indies in 1841, and his descendants. The dispute was given further airings in the second half of the nineteenth century, but nothing was ever settled in law, and the published authorities eventually deemed the title to have become extinct on the death of Sir Gillies Payne.[31]

[1] See A. O'Shaughnessy, *A Planter Family and the Decline of the West Indian Sugar Industry: The Payne Estates of St. Kitts* (Beds. RO Cfls. 180) and 'A Gentleman Radical: the Life of Sir Peter Payne', *Beds. Mag.* xv (1975-7), 338-44; *Oxford DNB*. [2] IGI (Beds.), confirming *CB*, v. 82. *DNB* and *Oxford DNB* incorrectly give his year of birth as 1763. [3] IGI (Staffs.). [4] O'Shaughnessy, *Planter Fam.* pp. iv, 1-22; V.L. Oliver, *Hist. Antigua*, iii. 7-9, 10. [5] O'Shaughnessy,

Planter Fam. 22-24; *Beds. Mag.* xv. 338-9; Beds. RO BS 1443; PROB 11/1359/481. [6] O'Shaughnessy, *Beds. Mag.* xv. 339; Beds. RO, Whitbread mss W1/2443, 3210, 4187. [7] O'Shaughnessy, *Planter Fam.* 36-38; Beds. RO, Wynne mss WY 998/5, 33; Beds. RO BS 1459/1-3; 1461. [8] O'Shaughnessy, *Planter Fam.* 37-38; *CB*, v. 82; *Oxford DNB*; Payne's printed letter to Bedfordshire in support of his claim, 15 Jan. 1829 (Beds. RO HI 220). [9] Whitbread mss W1/2480, 2557. [10] Ibid. W1/2483. [11] Ibid. W1/3930. See also ibid. W1/2444, 2480, 2501, 2522, 4187, 4209. [12] *Oxford DNB.* [13] Whitbread mss W1/4209, 4237, 4241. [14] Ibid. W1/2569, 4260. [15] *Life of Cartwright*, ii. 169; *Oxford DNB.* [16] *Beds. Pollbook* (1820), 20. [17] *The Times*, 13 Jan. 1821. [18] Ibid. 22 Apr. 1822. [19] *Herts Mercury*, 1 July; *Cambridge and Hertford Independent Press*, 8 July 1826. [20] *Herts Mercury*, 6, 13, 20 Feb. 1830. [21] Ibid. 14 Aug. 1830. [22] *Cambridge and Hertford Independent Press*, 22 Jan. 1831. [23] Ibid. 30 Apr., 7, 14 May; Beds. RO, Russell mss R 767, J.H. Fisher to C. Haedy, 2 May; Add. 36466, ff. 368, 370; Add. 51786, Holland to C.R. Fox, 2 May 1831. [24] *Cambridge and Hertford Independent Press*, 18 Feb. 1832. [25] Ibid. 30 June; *The Times*, 28 Aug., 12 Oct., 25 Dec. 1832; *Russell Letters*, iii. 25. [26] Copy in Beds. RO Z 231/7/2. [27] Beds. RO X 336/44. [28] *Jnl. of Emily Shore* (1891), 156. [29] *Gent. Mag.* (1843), i. 94; O'Shaughnessy, *Beds. Mag.* xv. 344. [30] Beds. RO X 447/1, 3; PROB 11/1977/202; IR26/1652/133. [31] *Oxford DNB*; O'Shaughnessy, *Planter Fam.* 40-42; Beds. RO Cfls. 180, *Payne Baronetage* (1863).

D.R.F.

PEACH, Nathaniel William (1785–1835), of Bownham House, nr. Stroud, Glos.; Ketteringham Hall, Wymondham, Norf.; Hyde, Dorset, and 13 Savile Row, Piccadilly, Mdx.

CORFE CASTLE	8 Feb. 1828–25 Feb. 1829
TRURO	6 Mar. 1829–1832

bap. 14 Sept. 1785, 1st s. of Nathaniel Peach of Bownham and Julia Maria, da. of William Keasberry of Bath.[1] *educ.* Shrewsbury 1799; L. Inn 1814. *m.* (1) c. 1806, Elizabeth (*d.* 5 July 1809), da. of John Goodman of Oare, Wilts., 1s. 2da. (1 *d.v.p.*);[2] (2) 14 July 1824, Harriet, da. of John Thomas Atkyns of Huntercombe House, Bucks. and his cos. Mary, da. of Edward Atkyns of Ketteringham, *s.p.*[3] *suc.* fa. 1788.[4] *d.* 29 Aug. 1835.

Peach was descended from one of the leading clothier families of the Stroud valleys. His father, the son of Benjamin Peach of Westbury, was in partnership with John Ridley of Rooksmore, but following his death in 1788, at the age of 39, his capital and stock in trade in the business were withdrawn over a period of three years, according to his instructions. The estate was left unadministered and a fresh grant of probate was made to Peach, the residuary legatee, in 1809.[5] By then he had already married, produced three children and lost his wife. He made a belated entry to Lincoln's Inn in 1814, but did not persevere with the law. In 1824 he married the heiress of the Ketteringham estate, about ten miles from Norwich. She was dead within a year, but the property gave Peach a stake in the county. He was invited to stand for Norwich in harness with Jonathan Peel* in 1826, but thought better of it.[6] In February 1828, having also acquired a property in Dorset, he was returned on a vacancy for Corfe Castle on the Bond interest, and was commended by George Bankes* to Robert Peel, leader of the Commons in the duke of Wellington's ministry.[7]

He was apparently a silent Member. He divided against Catholic relief, 12 May 1828. In February 1829 Planta, the patronage secretary, listed him as one who was 'opposed to the principle' of Catholic emancipation. Shortly afterwards he transferred to Lord Falmouth's borough of Truro to replace a supporter of concession.[8] He duly voted against emancipation, 18, 23, 30 Mar. 1829. That autumn Sir Richard Vyvyan*, the Ultra Tory leader, numbered him among those Tories who were 'strongly opposed to the present government'. He divided against Lord Blandford's parliamentary reform scheme, 18 Feb. 1830. However, he voted against ministers on relations with Portugal, 10 Mar., and the Bathurst and Dundas pensions, 26 Mar. He chaired the committee on Muskett's divorce bill, 28 Apr., and the same day dealt with the withdrawal of the Highgate School estate bill. He divided against Jewish emancipation, 17 May. He was in the minorities for amendments to the sale of beer bill, 21 June (as a pair), 1 July 1830. He was returned for Truro at the general election that summer after an attempt to open the borough failed; he survived a subsequent petition.

The ministry regarded Peach as one of the 'violent Ultras', and he was absent from the crucial division on the civil list, 15 Nov. 1830. Opposition to the Grey ministry's reform bill restored him to his old allegiance. He divided against the second reading, 22 Mar., and for Gascoyne's wrecking amendment, 19 Apr. 1831. He came in again for Truro at the ensuing general election, after a token contest. He voted against the second reading of the reintroduced reform bill, 6 July, and at least twice for adjournment motions, 12 July. He divided against the bill's passage, 21 Sept., and the second reading of the Scottish bill, 23 Sept. He was named as a defaulter prior to the division on Lord Ebrington's confidence motion, 10 Oct. That autumn he played an active part on the opposition side in the Dorset by-election.[9] He voted against the second reading of the revised reform bill, 17 Dec. 1831, the enfranchisement of Tower Hamlets, 28 Feb., and the third reading, 22 Mar., and paired against the second reading of the Irish bill, 25 May 1832. He divided against ministers on the Russian-Dutch loan, 26 Jan., and paired against them, 12 July. He voted against the malt drawback bill, 2 Apr., and for the Liverpool disfranchisement bill, 23 May 1832.

Peach, who was a member of the committee formed by the Conservatives in May 1832 to manage the forthcoming elections in England, stood for East Norfolk in December, when he made a point of attacking the government's aggressive policy towards Holland. He and his colleague were defeated by two Liberals.[10] In December 1834 he asked the new premier, Peel, with whom he was evidently on cordial terms, to appoint his son-in-law Christopher Pemberton, a treasury clerk, as one of his private secretaries; Peel said he would have complied, but for a prior claim. Three weeks later Peach wrote to Peel's brother William, expressing an interest in the joint-secretaryship of the board of control and declaring that 'in spite of Lord Ellenborough's assurance that 12 hours will be daily necessary for the due performance of the duties of the office ... there is no appointment I should prefer'. William Peel* noted that 'Peach comes into Parliament' and 'deserves *well* of the party', adding that 'his complexion is *Indian*, but perhaps *fronto nulla fides*'. In the event, he obtained neither a seat nor office, though he worked for the successful Conservative candidate in East Norfolk.[11] He died in August 1835.[12] He left all his freehold property to his only son William Nathaniel Peach, who sold the Ketteringham estate the following year for £80,000; after settlement of a contingent chancery suit, his personalty was finally sworn under £35,000.[13]

[1] IGI (Glos.); PROB 11/1167/315. [2] *Glos. N and Q*, iv. 354; *Gent. Mag.* (1809), ii. 784. [3] *Gent. Mag.* (1824), ii. 271; Add. 39781, f. 317. [4] *Gent. Mag.* (1788), i. 468. [5] T.D. Fosbrooke, *Glos.* i. 272; *Trans. Bristol and Glos. Arch. Soc.* xxviii (1905), 362; lxi (1945), 136; lxxiii (1954), 220, 225; PROB 11/1167/315. [6] J. Hunter, *Hist. Ketteringham*, 51, 53; *The Times*, 30 May 1826; Add. 40387, f. 56. [7] Add. 40395, f. 44. [8] *West Briton*, 13 Mar. 1829. [9] *Arbuthnot Corresp.* 149; *Three Diaries*, 134, 138. [10] *Three Diaries*, 266, 291; *The Times*, 19, 24 Dec. 1832. [11] Add. 40404, ff. 315, 317; 40408, f. 65; *Wellington Pol. Corresp.* ii. 781. [12] *Gent. Mag.* (1835), ii. 444. [13] PROB 8/228/584; 11/1852/564; IR26/1397/564; Hunter, 53.

D.R.F.

PEACHY, William (?1763–1838), of Derwent Island, Cumb. and Worthing, Suss.

YARMOUTH I.O.W.	21 Mar. 1797–1802
TAUNTON	1826–1830

b. ?1763, o.s. of William Peachy of Gosport, Hants and Elizabeth, da. of Henri Portal of Freefolk Priors, Whitchurch, Hants. *educ.* Trinity, Oxf. 13 Nov. 1781, aged 18, BCL 1790, DCL 1813; I. Temple 1784. *m.* (1) 12 Sept. 1803, Emma Frances (*d.* Madeira, 2 Mar. 1809), da. of Thomas Charter of Lynchfield House, Bishop's Lydeard, Som., *s.p.*; (2) 10 Mar. 1812, Susannah, wid. of James Henry of Hopewell, Jamaica, *s.p. suc.* fa. 1790.[1] *d.* 21 Nov. 1838.

Capt. Wilts. militia 1791, 1798; lt. 10 Drag. 1794; capt. 120 Ft. 1795; maj. (with army rank) 2 R. Manx fencibles 1795-8; maj. (half-pay) 108 Ft. 1798-1813; lt.-col. 1800; col. 1810; maj.-gen. 1813; lt.-gen. 1825.

Peachy, a soldier in name only, had literary tastes and was a close friend of the poet and historian Robert Southey*. By the time Southey settled at Keswick in 1803 Peachy was in possession of a house on Derwent Island, at the northern end of Derwentwater, where he generally resided in the summer months; Southey's son recalled him as one of their 'most friendly and hospitable neighbours'. He was noted for mild eccentricity and unquenchable garrulousness. Southey told a friend in 1806:

> The Colonel has sent me half a collar of brawn and a little barrel of pickled sturgeon. This cost me a letter of thanks, which again produced such an answer! I wish you had seen it: he writes just as he talks – world without end, Amen! However he is a good-natured *homo*, if ever there was one.

On one occasion he had 'a narrow, though ludicrous escape' after capsizing a skiff on Derwentwater, being rescued by his servants, who towed him in 'like a Triton, waving his hat round his head, and huzzaing as he approached his own shores'. When his first wife died of consumption Southey, who particularly admired her, composed her epitaph and William Lisle Bowles commemorated her in execrable elegiac verse, beginning:

> How mournful, as she sunk resigned and meek
> Sat the last smile upon her pallid cheek.[2]

In 1812 Peachy married a West Indian widow whose two sons, James and Charles Edward Henry, were subsequently placed at Rugby. His new wife bore a striking physical resemblance to the first Mrs. Peachy and, as her health was delicate, they spent much of the next 14 years in travel, mainly around Britain, but with occasional excursions to Europe. In 1825 he 'commenced poet' and Southey, the principal victim of his dreadful efforts, commented that 'the longer he lives the queerer he grows, which is one sort of merit in my eyes'.[3]

He shared the reactionary political views of Southey's mature years. In his absence, Southey subscribed his name to the Cumberland loyal address of October 1819, and in February 1821 they congratulated one another on 'the abatement of the queen's-fever'. Above all, they were at one in their rooted hostility to Catholic relief, and in the autumn of 1825

Peachy canvassed Taunton (five miles from his late wife's family home) under the aegis of the prominent anti-Catholic Sir Thomas Lethbridge, Member for Somerset. Southey congratulated him on his 'fair prospects', which he hoped would 'give us one good vote in the ... Commons, at the expense of some fatiguing attendance for yourself'. At the general election of 1826 Peachy disclaimed any party allegiance and pronounced himself 'a tried and invariable friend to my king and my country', as well as a supporter of the settlement of 1688, which had delivered Britain from 'the fangs and the despotism of the tyrant James II'. His main platform was resistance to Catholic relief and, after a turbulent contest, he was returned in second place behind another anti-Catholic. Southey noted that in Keswick 'they say he has got in through bribery and corruption; and the wicked remark has been made that a lile lad would make as fit a parliamentarian'.[4]

Re-entering the House after an interval of 24 years, Peachy duly voted against relief, 6 Mar. 1827. Southey, rejoicing in its defeat by four votes, remarked, somewhat fancifully:

> It is amusing enough to think that my neighbour Peachy's election for Taunton decided the Catholic question in the ... Commons for this session. They would have had two Members for that place, if he had [not] taken it into his head to serve his country in Parliament; there would have been two votes lost to the church and as many gained to the Catholics – making just that difference which turned the scale.

In presenting a Taunton petition against relief, 15 May 1827, Peachy argued that there was 'a wide difference ... between giving men religious liberty and political power': his watchword was *nolumus leges Anglicae mutari*.[5] He divided against repeal of the Test Acts, 26 Feb., and Catholic relief, 12 May 1828. He voted with the Wellington ministry against inquiry into delays in chancery, 24 Apr., and reduction of the salary of the lieutenant-general of the ordnance, 4 July 1828. That session Southey exhorted him to oppose a clause introduced by the Lords into the offences against the person bill, which empowered judges to have murderers hung in chains rather than dissected: 'pray remember that you are a great traveller, that Mrs. Peachy has a natural abhorrence of such abominable sights, and that you have olfactory organs'.[6] In February 1829 Planta, the patronage secretary, of course listed Peachy among those Members 'opposed to the principle' of Catholic emancipation. He voted for Inglis in his victory over Peel at the Oxford University by-election.[7] He divided against the government's bill, 6, 18, 23, 27, 30 Mar. He presented and endorsed a hostile petition from Taunton, 16 Mar., and insisted that 'the Catholics held tenets which render them unfit to participate in political power in a Protestant state', 27 Mar. He supported inquiry into distress in the silk industry, to which Taunton was 'completely prey', 14 Apr., observing that 'free trade' had 'not answered the expectations of those who advocate it ... I hope they will recognize their error'. That autumn Sir Richard Vyvyan*, one of the Ultra leaders, counted him among those Tories who were 'strongly opposed to the present government'. He divided for Knatchbull's amendment to the address on distress, 4 Feb. 1830. He voted against parliamentary reform schemes, 11, 18, 23 Feb., but divided against ministers for admiralty reductions, 22 Mar., and inquiry into the state of Newfoundland, 11 May. He voted against Jewish emancipation, 5 Apr., 17 May, but for abolition of the death penalty for forgery, 7 June 1830. At the general election that summer, deprived of support from the renegade Lethbridge, he was defeated at Taunton by two Whig reformers and petitioned unsuccessfully to void the return of one of them. It was rumoured that he would try again in 1831, but had he done so it would have been fruitless.[8]

Peachy had taken up residence at Worthing by 1828, but continued his 'ubiquitarian movements', as Southey called them, until his death in November 1838. An obituarist commended his 'high sense of honour ... integrity of conduct ... benevolence and ... literary attainments', and Southey's son wrote that 'with him departed the open hand and kind heart of a true English gentleman'.[9] Having left his father's estate unadministered, he devised his own estates in Hampshire and Wiltshire to his only surviving stepson, James Henry (1803-84); his personalty was sworn under £70,000 and resworn under £60,000.[10]

[1] *Gent. Mag.* (1790), ii. 672; PROB 11/1196/438. [2] *Southey Letters* ed. J.W. Warter, i. 286, 357; ii. 155; *New Southey Letters* ed. K. Curry, i. 392; ii. 497; *Southey Corresp.* ed. C.C. Southey, v. 121-2; A.M. Broadley and W. Jerrold, *Romance of an Elderly Poet*, 52-53, 64-65, 125. [3] *Southey Letters*, iii. 483; *New Southey Letters*, ii. 41, 303; Add. 28603, ff. 5, 21, 23, 25, 33, 45, 47. [4] Add. 28603, ff. 45, 69, 71, 73; *New Southey Letters*, ii. 202, 306; *The Times*, 8, 28 Oct., 4 Nov. 1825, 2, 5, 9, 15, 16, 21-23, 26 June 1826. [5] *New Southey Letters*, ii. 311; *The Times*, 16 May 1827. [6] Add. 28603, f. 77. [7] Add. 28603, f. 81. [8] Add. 28603, f. 83; *The Times*, 20 July, 10 Aug. 1830, 29 Apr. 1831. [9] *New Southey Letters*, ii. 250; Add. 28603, f. 88; *Gent. Mag.* (1839), i. 96; *Southey Corresp.* v. 122. [10] PROB 8/232; 11/1905/49.

D.R.F./T.A.J.

PEARSE, John (1759–1836), of 41 Lothbury, London; 98 Long Acre; 4 Craig's Court, Charing Cross, Mdx., and Chilton Lodge, nr. Hungerford, Berks.

DEVIZES 1818–1832

bap. 19 Dec. 1759, 1st surv. s. of Nicholas Pearse, Blackwell Hall factor, of 41 Lothbury and Woodford, Essex and w. Sarah. *m.* 31 Jan. 1787, Anne, da. and coh. of John Phillimore, silk merchant, of 15 New Broad Street, London, 3s. (1 *d.v.p.*) 3da. (1 *d.v.p.*).[1] *suc.* fa. 1795. *d.* 21 July 1836.

Dir. Bank of England 1790-1, 1793-5, 1796-8, 1799-1802, 1803-6, 1807-8, 1812-28, dep. gov. 1808-10, gov. 1810-12; manager, Sun Life Office 1788-*d.*; dir. Sun Fire Office 1791, manager 1823-*d.*; gov. Van Dieman's Land Co. 1829-*d.*

Capt. commdt. Hungerford vols. 1798, 1803; capt. Bank of England supp. vols. 1803.

Pearse and his brother Brice were the senior partners in J. and B. Pearse and Company, and operated as Blackwell Hall factors at 41 Lothbury and as army clothiers at 98 Long Acre. He continued in business in this period, enjoying lucrative contracts through his connection with the duke of York, the commander-in-chief, and served as a director of the Bank of England until 1828.[2] He lived near the Wiltshire border, at Chilton Lodge, which he rebuilt.[3] He voted for Charles Dundas* and Richard Neville* against the radical William Hallett at the Berkshire election of 1818, but he apparently played little part in the affairs of that county.[4] He was more active in Wiltshire, where he regularly attended meetings of the Devizes Bear Club and the Wiltshire Society, especially after his election for Devizes in 1818, when he came in as the surprise choice of the corporation. He stood again at the general election of 1820, stating that, although he was 'advanced in years', he was 'young in Parliament', and stressing that 'my situation in life is such that I can have nothing to ask'. He answered criticisms of his having opposed economies and the resumption of cash payments by recommending the 'judgement of practical men in political considerations' against those economists who were 'only scientifically acquainted with these subjects', and was again returned with Thomas Grimston Estcourt, against a popular local candidate.[5] On resumption, he had previously confided to Sir John Sinclair† that 'Parliament seems to have gone wild on this measure and will not, I fear, come to its senses in due time'.[6] A supporter of the Liverpool administration, including on opposition motions for economies and tax reductions, he made no impact on the House except as a spokesman for the Bank of England.

He vindicated the Bank's conduct over the issuing of exchequer bills, 31 May, and spoke against reducing the size of its public balances, 13 June 1820. He denied the respectability of the Devizes petitioners in support of Queen Caroline, 24 Jan. 1821, but did not vote in the division on the opposition censure motion on this affair, 6 Feb. He muttered something about agricultural distress, 8 Feb., and moved for a return of the number of bank notes in circulation, 20 Mar., to show, 'together with the prices of gold, that the currency had no reference to the distresses of the country'. On 19 Mar. he expressed his surprise that those, like David Ricardo*, who had advocated the resumption of cash payments in 1819 should now object to it, and he opposed going into committee on it, 9 Apr., because he was 'convinced that it was the political events in Europe, and not the report of the committee of 1819, which had brought about the state of things so much complained of'. He confirmed that the Bank would issue sovereigns instead of bank notes, 26 Mar., 12 Apr., partly as a precaution against forgery, which he claimed the Bank was doing everything it could to prevent, 9 Apr., and for which he wished the death penalty to be retained, 4 June.[7] He decried country bankers' alarm about the Bank cash payments bill, 13 Apr., when he employed his usual argument that the Bank had been restrained in pursuing its own profits and had amply repaid the confidence of the public. He divided against disqualifying civil officers of the ordnance from voting in elections, 12 Apr., parliamentary reform, 9 May 1821, and inquiry into the right of voting in parliamentary elections, 20 Feb. 1823.

Pearse defended the policy of the Bank in comparison with the high interest rates charged by the Bank of Ireland, 8 Mar. 1822, when he stated that

> although a director, he had no great interest in the profits of the Bank; for to confess the truth, he had not much more Bank stock than was necessary to give him a qualification. Indeed, upon seeing the effects of the war, he had made it a point of honour not to increase his stock beyond the amount which he possessed upon first entering into the direction.

On 1 Apr. he 'contended that overproduction was the real cause of the distress, and that the rate of interest had always been governed by the price of the funds'. He spoke in justification of the Bank's monopoly, 31 May, and rebutted Ricardo's allegations that it had purchased too much gold, 12 June, asserting that as between 1797 and 1817, 'the Bank had never forced an issue, so neither had there ever been any depreciation in the value of their notes, with reference to the price of gold'. He commented privately that the suicide of Lord

Londonderry* that summer had occasioned 'universal dismay in London' as 'a great national loss'.[8] In his constituency, 30 Sept. 1822, he remarked that radicalism

> was on its deathbed and its chief heroes were fast sinking into decay. The lower classes, who had been made the dupes of these political itinerants, were returning to their former sober and religious habits, and again manifesting their love of our excellent constitution.[9]

Pearse, who made an interjection on behalf of the Bank on 18 Apr., voted for inquiry into the legal proceedings against the Dublin Orange rioters, 22 Apr. 1823.[10] Thomas Creevey* reported to Miss Ord, 12 May 1823, that the foreign secretary Canning

> says the king is violent for [the Irish attorney-general William] Plunket* from thinking that the duke of York interferes with the division on Tuesday [22 Apr.] and giving as his proof, Pearse, the Bank director, voting against the government which he knows he would never have done but at the instigation of the duke of York.[11]

Pearse defended the £4,000,000 balance held by the Bank, 19 Feb. 1824 (and again, 23 Feb. 1825). He voted against the abolition of flogging, 5 Mar., and spoke and voted in the minority against the exportation of long wool, 21 May.[12] He divided against condemning the trial of the Methodist missionary John Smith in Demerara, 11 June. He voted for the Irish insurrection bill, 14 June 1824, and the Irish unlawful societies bill, 25 Feb. 1825. As he had on 28 Feb. 1821, 30 Apr. 1822, he divided against Catholic relief, 1 Mar., 21 Apr., 10 May, and he voted against the related Irish franchise bill, 26 Apr. 1825. He assisted in the passage of the Devizes improvement bill and contributed £1,000 towards the cost of its implementation. At the mayoral dinner, 30 Sept. 1825, he spoke in praise of ministers and expressed the hope that his conduct towards his constituency had assured his re-election.[13]

Rebutting the attacks made on the Bank for its role in the recent financial crisis, 2 Feb. 1826, he stated that it had 'acted with the utmost prudence and consideration in the whole of the late tremendous convulsion', and a week later he argued that its privileges were well deserved, considering the 'eminent services performed by the Bank for the public, when that corporation had stood in the gap, and effected what, upon emergencies, legislative interposition would have failed to accomplish'. He spoke in defence of the Bank's charter and against the establishment of a rival bank in London, 13 Feb., when he also argued (as he did on the 20th) that it was the excessive issuing of bills of exchange, not of notes, which had led to the speculative panic. He advocated the establishment of a commission to issue exchequer bills on behalf of the government, as in 1793, in order to provide additional relief and restore confidence, 14, 15, 23 Feb. He informed John Beckett* of the decision to form one before it had been officially announced, supported it in the House on 28 Feb., and was asked a technical question about it by Peel, the home secretary.[14] He objected to the regular publication of the quantity of Bank issues, 24, 27 Feb., and defended its ability to control note issue, 7 Mar. He made other short speeches on the Bank in relation to merchant law, 8 Mar., electoral bribery, 14 Mar., the petitions of Elizabeth Pridham, 15 Mar., 2 May, and forged notes, 14 Apr.[15] His voted against condemning the Jamaican slave trials, 2 Mar., and for receiving the report on the salary of the president of the board of trade, 10 Apr. Business in the House had kept Pearse away from the by-election in Devizes in February, but he attended with his new colleague, George Watson Taylor, at the general election that summer, being returned unopposed. On 9 June 1826 he claimed that he had a long connection with the town and promised to act on its behalf, while remaining free to exercise his own judgement.[16] He was elected a free burgess of the borough, 23 Jan., and sworn, 4 June 1827.[17]

He voted against Catholic relief, 6 Mar. 1827, 12 May 1828. He was given a week's leave of absence, 23 Mar. 1827, on account of illness in his family. Brought to order by the Speaker, 30 May, the following day he managed to speak in mitigation of the offence of a fellow director, a letter of whose had been unintentionally sent round as a Bank circular. He denied that there were any prevailing circumstances which might force the Bank to suspend cash payments, 14 June, and insisted that it would act with 'perfect fairness and equity', 29 June.[18] He voted in the majority for the grant to improve water communications in Canada, 12 June. 'In allusion to the late political changes', 4 June, he commented in Devizes that 'without looking to the right hand or to the left, he should give his vote in Parliament for those measures which he conceived would be most conducive to the interests of the country'.[19] During the formation of Lord Goderich's ministry in August, he told John Herries*:

> I am not a fellow to pay compliments, but I will venture to say, if you will take the chancellorship of the exchequer, it will tend more to raise the funds and give financial confidence than the restoration of poor Canning's life.[20]

Writing to William Huskisson* from Ireland, which he found in a flourishing state, save for the 'Catholic, intrusive and arbitrary clergy', he commented, 30 Sept. 1827, that

> as I see a preponderance in the cabinet, of those who have entertained and put in practice principles that have saved the country in dangerous times, I augur well of the arrangements that have been made, and that at any rate radicalism will be kept down.[21]

He presented petitions for repeal of the Test Acts from Devizes Dissenters, 25 Feb., but voted against this, 26 Feb. 1828. He was one of the minority of nine who divided against repealing the Act which prohibited the use of ribbons at elections, 20 Mar., and he recommended investigation of the wool trade, 28 Apr. 1828.

In February 1829 Walter Long† informed Thomas Henry Sutton Bucknall Estcourt*, the son of Pearse's former colleague, that he had entered his name on their putative Wiltshire anti-Catholic declaration, 'which he will not quarrel with us about'.[22] Planta, the Wellington ministry's patronage secretary, listed him as 'doubtful', and he duly voted against emancipation throughout March, telling the House on the 30th that he had 'great confidence' in ministers and would have approved a limited measure, but that he could not surrender his judgement on such an important question. His comment that the majority of the people were against concessions to the Catholics brought an angry retort from a correspondent of the *Devizes Gazette*, 9 Apr. On 4 Dec. 1829 Lord Lansdowne described Pearse to Lord Holland as being among those who were 'quite malignants' in their attitude towards the Wellington administration.[23] He voted against Jewish emancipation, 5 Apr., 17 May 1830. Following the death of his second son, 28 Apr., he was unable to attend the Wiltshire Society dinner, 19 May, where he had been due to preside.[24] At the ensuing general election he was returned without incident, having stated on the hustings that he would work for all the inhabitants, vote for 'every measure which has a tendency to a rational reform of abuses, and to promote an economical expenditure of the public money', as well as looking to protect the Protestant ascendancy. At the mayoral dinner, 29 Sept. 1830, he said that the 'leaning of my political feelings is to support the king's government', but added that 'I have no party connection. No man can despise more than I do, a mean, subservient adulation of the minister, or deprecate more a restless, systematic opposition'.[25]

He was listed by ministers among their 'friends' and sided with them on the civil list, 15 Nov. 1830. He was granted a fortnight's leave on account of the disturbed state of his neighbourhood, 2 Dec., and in a letter to Bucknall Estcourt senior, 10 Dec. 1830, noted that his exertions against the 'Swing' rioters had made him ill. He was, however, optimistic:

> At this season, fortunate in that respect, the farmers have great crops and the funds are daily rising, and I anxiously fear will rise still higher. The advantages which the farmers will thus enjoy will much exceed the expense they will incur by the increased wages, and it is yet to be proved whether the increase of wages will not diminish the poor rates to a great extent.[26]

Despite poor health, which might have obliged him to retire from the House, he attended and voted against the second reading of the Grey ministry's reform bill, 22 Mar. 1831.[27] He signed the Berkshire declaration against it,[28] and presented and endorsed the anti-reform petition of the corporation of Devizes, 18 Apr. 1831, when he praised the borough for its electoral purity. The following day he voted for Gascoyne's wrecking amendment. Forced to defend himself against the Devizes reformers at the subsequent general election, he declared:

> I am ready to give my sanction to any *well-digested* measure of reform, and should have voted for a specific motion on the subject, which would have been brought forward by Sir Richard Vyvyan [the Ultra leader], in case the ministerial measure was lost.

He objected to the reduced representation of England, the sweeping nature of the bill, and the 'domineering and dictatorial' manner in which it had been introduced, but he was again elected unopposed.[29]

He voted against the second reading of the reintroduced reform bill, 6 July, and at least four times for adjourning the proceedings on it, 12 July, when he was noted as leaving the House before the seventh and last division. He divided for using the 1831 census to determine the disfranchisement schedules, 19 July, and to postpone consideration of the partial disfranchisement of Chippenham, 27 July. He announced that he would vote against the removal of one seat from Guildford, 29 July, and for Campbell's amendment to exclude weekly tenants and lodgers from the franchise, as their inclusion would amount 'almost to universal suffrage', 25 Aug., but his name appears in neither of the partial minority lists for these divisions. He was one of the signatories of the Wiltshire declaration against reform.[30] He divided against the passage of the bill, 21 Sept., and the second reading of the Scottish reform bill, 23 Sept. He voted against the second reading of the revised reform bill, 17 Dec. 1831, the enfranchisement of Tower Hamlets, 28 Feb., the third reading, 22 Mar., and the second reading of the Irish reform bill, 25 May 1832. He voted in the majority for Baring's bill to exclude insolvent debtors from Parliament, 27 June, and in the minority for establishing a system of representation for New South

Wales, 28 June. His only other known vote was against government on the Russian-Dutch loan, 12 July. In his last reported speech, 22 May 1832, he urged that a 'commanding preponderance of practical men', not of 'philosophers and political economists, whose obstinacy and perverseness are known by experience to be unequalled by any other description of persons', be appointed to the secret committee on the renewal of the Bank of England's charter.

Such was his popularity in Devizes, it was believed that if he had changed his mind on reform, he would have been returned at the general election of 1832, but by early June he had positively declined to stand again.[31] In February 1835 he informed Peel that, at his age, he did not think it desirable to continue with the fatigue of the Commons, but he wished his ministry well.[32] He died suddenly, on the point of recovering from an illness, in July 1836. Despite his 'high conservative opinions', the obituary in the *Devizes Gazette* praised him for having established a national school in the town, and recorded that he was a 'noble, manly character – honest, generous, frank and social', whose chief delight was 'in doing good'. As requested, he was buried at Chilton Foliat, in a family mausoleum done in the 'heaviest Grecian' style.[33] By his will, dated 24 July 1835, he left the bulk of his estate, including personal wealth sworn under £40,000, to his eldest son John (*b.* 1789).[34]

[1] IGI (London). [2] *HP Commons, 1790-1820*, iv. 739; Wellington mss WP1/880/13; 881/33; 1036/21; *The Times*, 11 Aug. 1831. [3] Reading Univ. Lib. Hist. Farm Recs. BER 36, summary guide, 28. [4] *Berks. Pollbook* (1818), 22. [5] *Devizes Gazette*, 16, 23 Mar. 1820. [6] *Mems. of Life and Works of Sir John Sinclair* ed. J. Sinclair (1837), ii. 314. [7] *The Times*, 9 Feb., 21, 27 Mar., 13 Apr., 5 June 1821. [8] Wilts. RO, Ailesbury mss 9/35/117. [9] *Devizes Gazette*, 3 Oct. 1822. [10] *The Times*, 19 Apr. 1823. [11] Creevey mss. [12] *The Times*, 22 May 1824, 24 Feb. 1825. [13] *Devizes Gazette*, 6 Oct. 1825. [14] Lonsdale mss, Beckett to Lowther, n.d. [1826]; Add. 40385, f. 309. [15] *The Times*, 9, 16 Mar., 3 May 1826. [16] *Devizes Gazette*, 2 Mar., 15 June 1826. [17] Wilts. RO, Devizes borough recs. G20/1/22. [18] *The Times*, 31 May, 30 June 1827. [19] *Devizes Gazette*, 7 June 1827. [20] *Mem. of Public Life of Herries* ed. E. Herries, i. 227. [21] Add. 38751, f. 90. [22] Glos. RO, Sotheron Estcourt mss D1571 X114. [23] Add. 51687. [24] *Gent. Mag.* (1830), i. 475; *Salisbury Jnl.* 24 May 1830. [25] *Devizes Gazette*, 5 Aug., 30 Sept. 1830. [26] Sotheron Estcourt mss X63. [27] Ibid. E411, Salmon to Bucknall Estcourt, 17, 20 Mar. 1831. [28] *The Times*, 9 Apr. 1831. [29] *Devizes Gazette*, 5 May 1831. [30] Ibid. 11 Aug. 1831. [31] Ibid. 24 May, 7 June 1832. [32] Add. 40415, f. 243. [33] *Devizes Gazette*, 28 July 1836; N. Pevsner, *Buildings of England: Wilts.* (1963), 151; *Oxford DNB*. [34] PROB 11/1867/564; IR26/1429/492; IGI (Berks.).

S.M.F.

PECHELL *see* **BROOKE PECHELL**

PEEL, Edmund (1791–1850), of Bonehill House, Tamworth and Hednesford Lodge, Cannock Chase, Staffs.

NEWCASTLE-UNDER-LYME 1831–1832

NEWCASTLE-UNDER-LYME 1835–1837

b. 8 Aug. 1791, 3rd s. of Sir Robert Peel†, 1st bt. (*d.* 1830), of Drayton Manor, Staffs. and 1st w. Ellen, da. of William Yates, calico printer, of Springside, Bury, Lancs.; bro. of Jonathan Peel*, Laurence Peel*, Robert Peel* and William Yates Peel*. *educ.* Harrow 1805. *m.* 2 Jan. 1812, Emily, da. of John Swinfen of Swinfen, Staffs., 3s. *d.* 1 Nov. 1850.

Peel briefly held a junior commission in the navy before he married and settled at Bonehill, which he initially leased from his father but subsequently bought outright. By 1825 his father had advanced him £60,000 of his personal fortune, and he received an additional £75,000 on Sir Robert Peel's death in 1830.[1] He was the only one of the six Peel brothers to show any taste for the business on which the family's wealth was founded, and he operated calico printing mills at Fazeley, Staffordshire and in Lancashire.[2] In October 1824 he declined to become involved in a scheme to put up one of the younger Peels for Newcastle-under-Lyme, having at that time 'particular reasons for not wishing to have any parliamentary connection' with the borough.[3] There was a notion of his standing for Leicester on the corporation interest in 1826, when it seemed possible that he might obtain a seat, 'perhaps for life', at a modest cost; but it came to nothing.[4] His support for Catholic relief, which was unique in his family, ruled him out as a candidate for Norwich on 'the Tory interest' at the same election; and when his eldest brother Robert, the home secretary, asked the premier Lord Liverpool if a government seat could be provided for Edmund, it proved to be too late.[5]

Peel took Robert's side over his rift with Canning in 1827, when he wrote:

> It has been my misfortune to differ from you in opinion on one subject. I feel at this moment that on every other there is *no* sacrifice I would not make, nor any exertion I would not employ to meet your wishes and advance your views.[6]

He was reported in November 1827 to have been invited to stand for Newcastle at the next election, but when he was 'sounded' on this by a local man, 'like a discreet politician he maintained the most impenetrable silence'.[7] At the general election of 1830 he did intervene at Newcastle, where the Huskissonite John Evelyn Denison* was up against two candidates on the 'Blue' or independent interest. Peel, who declared his support for free trade, relaxation of the corn laws and an end to the East India Company's monopoly, had high hopes of success, and was surprised to find himself bottom of the poll after the first day. He refused Denison's offer of 'terms of accommodation' and persevered, but his alleged heavy expenditure in 'buying votes' only secured him third place behind the 'Blue' candidates. Both Denison and William Huskisson* suspected that he had been instructed by ministers to ensure that Denison was defeated, even if he could not win himself. They consoled themselves with the reflection that Peel, who they thought had been 'infamously imposed upon', would 'have leisure to reflect on the folly of such a game, when he comes to pay his bills'. He was reckoned to have spent between £7,000 and £8,000, though in 1834 he himself admitted to a total outlay of about £9,500 at that and the next two Newcastle elections.[8] He continued to cultivate the borough and came forward in 1831, despite being in an 'infirm state of health' as a result of 'a serious accident'. He again espoused free trade 'as opposed to the dark and secret workings of base monopolies'. He claimed to have 'ever been an advocate for the reform of abuses, and the reduction of the public burthens'; and he welcomed the Grey ministry's reform bill's proposed extinction of rotten boroughs, enfranchisement of large industrial towns and extension of the franchise to £10 householders. At the same time, in harmony with the widespread feeling of resentment in Newcastle, he condemned its intended denial of the freeman franchise to future generations. He topped the poll, with the greatest number of votes ever obtained in the borough.[9]

Ministers may have expected Peel to support reform.[10] If so, they were disappointed, for on 5 July 1831 he delivered his maiden speech against the reintroduced bill, which he said could not be 'carried without the greatest injustice to those who have long enjoyed the elective franchise, and without some danger of disturbing too suddenly the existing and well-tried institutions of the country'. He voted against the second reading the following day, and was in the opposition minorities for use of the 1831 census as a basis for disfranchisement, 19 July, and against Chippenham's loss of a Member, 27 July. On 4 Aug., however, he voiced his 'approbation of the plan of giving representatives to populous towns and districts', as embodied in schedule C, though he thought that Stoke-upon-Trent was entitled to an additional Member. He opposed the exemption of Scottish factories from the limitation of children's working hours, 27 July. He presented the petition of Newcastle apprentices for preservation of their franchise, 17 Aug., was in the minority of 17 for the retention of existing voting rights, 27 Aug., and on 31 Aug. vainly proposed an amendment to preserve the vote in perpetuity for resident freemen by birth, servitude and marriage. When the Irish secretary Smith Stanley remarked that he had stood at Newcastle 'with an assurance that he was a reformer', Peel retorted that 'I did directly the reverse; for I was returned for Newcastle after giving the most distinct declaration that I would oppose this bill'. He voted against its third reading and passage, 19, 21 Sept. 1831. Thereafter his attendance and his resistance to reform lapsed. He was absent from the division on the second reading of the revised bill, 17 Dec. 1831, and was credited with having paired in favour of its third, 22 Mar. 1832. He divided with the ministerial majority for the address asking the king to appoint only ministers who would carry undiluted reform, 10 May, and was voted thanks for this action at a meeting of Newcastle reformers, 16 May.[11] When he presented their petition for supplies to be withheld until the reform bill was carried, 22 May, he explained:

> I ... have no hesitation in stating, that if the reform bill should pass into a law, it ought to be carried by its original promoters, rather than by those who have been its opponents; for in the one case I think it very possible that a satisfactory arrangement may take place, while on the other, there can be no arrangement whatever.

He voted against government on the Russian-Dutch loan, 12 July 1832.

Peel was easily beaten at Newcastle at the 1832 general election, but he was successful there under the auspices of his brother's first ministry in 1835. He remained an advocate of free trade, but was alarmed by Chartism and the movement to reduce factory working hours, and by 1844 was 'getting out of his own trading concerns as fast as he could'.[12] For most of his adult life he was 'miserably afflicted with the gout', mainly as a result of 'partaking to excess of the luxuries of the table'.[13] He died in November 1850, four months after Robert.[14]

[1]PROB 11/1772/396. [2]N. Gash, *Secretary Peel*, 63; Add. 40401, f. 238; 40513, f. 359; 40605, f. 382; *VCH Staffs.* ii. 219. [3]Add. 40605, f. 277. [4]Add. 40381, ff. 342, 345; 40386, f. 276; Gash, 404. [5]Add. 40305, ff. 176, 178; 40385, f. 333; 40386, f. 241. [6]Add. 40393, f. 258. [7]Add. 52447, f. 119; Derbys. RO, Gresley of Drakelow mss D77/36/5. [8]Add. 38758, f. 222; 40393, f. 258; 40408, f. 67; Nottingham Univ. Lib. Ossington mss OsC 75, 76; Gash, 636; *Staffs. Mercury*, 17, 31 July, 7 Aug. 1830. [9]*Staffs. Mercury*, 23, 30 Apr., 7 May 1831. [10]See Brougham mss, Ellice to Brougham, Wed. [?4 May 1831]. [11]*Staffs. Mercury*, 19 May 1832. [12]Add. 40408, f. 67; 40409, ff. 144, 306; 40426, ff. 387, 429; 40427, f. 41; 40513, f. 359; *Peel Letters*, 254-5. [13]*Dyott's Diary*, ii. 229, 288. [14]PROB 8/244 (21 Jan. 1851); 11/2126/61.

D.R.F.

PEEL, Jonathan (1799–1879), of Marble Hill, Twickenham, Mdx.

NORWICH 1826–1830

HUNTINGDON 1831–1868

b. 12 Oct. 1799, 5th s. of Sir Robert Peel†, 1st bt. (*d.* 1830), of Drayton Manor, Staffs., and 1st w. Ellen, da. of William Yates, calico printer, of Springside, Bury, Lancs.; bro. of Edmund Peel*, Laurence Peel*, Robert Peel* and William Yates Peel*. *educ.* Rugby 1812. *m.* 19 Mar. 1824, Lady Alicia Jane Kennedy, da. of Archibald, 12th earl of Cassilis [S], 5s. (1 *d.v.p.*) 3da. (1 *d.v.p.*). *d.* 13 Feb. 1879.

2nd lt. Rifle Brigade 1815; lt. (half-pay) 95 Ft. 1818; lt. 71 Ft. 1819; capt. (half-pay) 2 W.I. Regt. 1821; lt. and capt. 1 Ft. Gds. 1822; brevet maj. (half-pay) 1825; maj. 69 Ft. 1826; lt.-col. 53 Ft. 7 June 1827, half-pay (unattached) 9 Aug. 1827; brevet col. 1841; maj.-gen. 1854; lt.-gen. 1859; ret. 1863.

Surveyor-gen. of ordnance Sept. 1841-July 1846; sec. of state for war Feb. 1858-June 1859, July 1866-Mar. 1867; PC 26Feb. 1858.

Peel, guided by his eldest brother Robert, entered the army and was unpropitiously commissioned as a second lieutenant three days before Waterloo. His father reflected in 1817 that 'promotion in time of peace cannot be very rapid, consistent with a due regard for economy': his subsequent promotions were by purchase.[1] He was with the Rifle Brigade in Ireland in 1818. On his marriage in 1824 his father settled on him £60,000 of the £106,000 earmarked as his personal fortune. This sum was later increased by £29,000, so that he inherited a further £75,000 on his father's death in 1830.[2]

Late in 1824 he and Robert considered the possibility of his engaging himself to stand for Newcastle-under-Lyme as an opponent of Catholic relief at the next general election. They failed to obtain satisfactory financial guarantees and, deciding that it would be foolish to 'embark on the uncertainty which the present prospect affords', they eventually gave up all thought of the enterprise.[3] In 1826 the leaders of the ministerialist Orange and Purple interest at Norwich, where one of the sitting Members on the rival Blue and White interest had unexpectedly decided to retire, approached Robert Peel with an offer to bring in one of his brothers without opposition. Edmund was ruled out by his pro-Catholic views and Robert, having ascertained that £1,500 would probably cover all contingencies, accepted on behalf of Jonathan, who may otherwise have been in line for a seat on Lord Falmouth's interest. Sir Robert Peel gave his blessing:

> I am anxious to see ... [Jonathan] in Parliament if it can be effected at an expense not exceeding £1,500. I should object to some situations as not affording employment enough for a young man wishing to have his time occupied. Norwich is a manufacturing town of considerable consequence, and ... the business to be done requires constant attendance. As we wish to avoid being involved in a contested election, and Norwich being notorious in favour of one, should Jonathan feel himself called to give up all prospect of being one of the Members, could you afford him hopes of getting a seat recommended by government? If the invitation of voters be of that respectable kind that will almost secure him a seat, it is to be hoped that your brother will, by attention to his duties, make its continuance easy to him afterwards.

Peel, who declared his rooted opposition to Catholic relief and parliamentary reform, remained on tenterhooks to the end, as his opponents made frantic efforts to find a third man. He was prepared to go to a poll, his father having authorized the necessary expenditure, but a late bid to mount an opposition collapsed.[4]

Peel, who, with Robert, was admitted to the freedom of Norwich, immediately began to involve himself conscientiously in constituency business. In October 1826 he secured his temporary restoration to full pay in a bid to enhance his prospects of promotion. At the beginning of 1827, anticipating the duke of Wellington's appointment as commander-in-chief, he wondered if Robert could ask the duke to make him one of his aides-de-camp, which 'would relieve me from the necessity of moving about with my regiment and would be a sure step to promotion'. Nothing came of this, but he was promoted to lieutenant-colonel in June.[5] He presented Norwich petitions against Catholic relief, 26 Feb.,[6] and divided against the proposal, 6 Mar. 1827. He voted against the spring guns bill, 30 Mar. It was thought that he might speak in defence of Robert's refusal to serve under Canning, but he held his tongue.[7] He presented a Norwich Baptists' petition for repeal of the Test Acts, 6 June 1827,[8] but voted against that measure, 26 Feb. 1828. He presented petitions complaining of the 1827 Malt Act, 21 Feb., 7 Mar., voted against Catholic relief, 12 May, and was in the Wellington government's majority on the ordnance estimates, 4 July 1828.

Peel felt unable to follow Robert in his volte face on Catholic emancipation and, without giving him any warning, impulsively declared in the House, 9 Feb. 1829, that it would overturn the constitution, yet fail to pacify Ireland.[9] In explanation he wrote to his brother:

> I have had the misfortune to take a very different view from yours ... and in consequence of the very *recent* and *very decided* opinion I have given on the Catholic question

> (in answer to a letter requesting me to present the petition of the clergy of Norfolk) I thought it necessary to declare my opinion publicly, as I felt that remaining silent would lead everybody to suppose that I had changed it ... I ... hope that as soon as this unfortunate question is settled ... all difference of opinion between us will have *ceased* and in the meantime ... [I] assure you that no political event whatever can ever alter those feelings of affectionate regard I have ever entertained for you.

He was mortified when Robert, who was deeply hurt, suggested that he had deliberately 'selected an opportunity of declaring my difference of opinion from you, that should have the effect of giving weight and colour to attacks upon you, that were personally hostile and offensive'. In his defence, he tried to prove 'how *unintentional* any unkindness on my part has been'. It seemed possible that he would resign his seat in pique, but his father-in-law Lord Cassilis intervened to soothe the ruffled feelings on both sides.[10] Peel presented several anti-Catholic petitions, 19, 26 Feb., 9, 18, 24, 27 Mar. On 6 Mar. he spoke and voted against emancipation, likening it to an attempt to apply to religion the same free trade principles which had proved so damaging to industry and commerce. He called for a general election on the issue, the outcome of which 'would at least prove to the Roman Catholics that the public opinion of this country is entirely adverse to granting them political power'. The Whig Member George Agar Ellis thought it a 'good' speech, while another backbencher noted that it was 'done with great feeling and so perfectly in the tone of a gentleman'.[11] He voted against the relief bill, 18, 30 Mar., but paired for the divisions of 23, 27 Mar. 1829.

Peel, who was appointed to the select committee on the East India Company, 9 Feb., was not permanently alienated from the government, and he voted with them against parliamentary reform proposals, 18 and (as a pair) 23 Feb. 1830. He accused the advocates of economy of never being satisfied, 2 Apr., and voted with ministers on the grant for South American missions, 7 June. He divided against Jewish emancipation, 17 May. He condemned the subscription fraud exposed by the committee on the Birmingham and London Junction Canal bill, of which he was a member, 18, 20 May. He endorsed a Norwich petition for abolition of the death penalty for forgery, 17 Mar., and presented a similar one himself, 4 June; but he was credited with pairing against the proposal, 7 June 1830. At the general election he stood again for Norwich, where he was challenged by two opponents of government, who were set up by disaffected weavers to promote parliamentary reform and reduced taxation. In response to this Peel, of whom it was said that he had at least been useful in forwarding the scheme to link Norwich to the sea by canal, merely promised to support 'every requisite reduction'. He denied having opposed the principle of the sale of beer bill, and boasted of his resistance to the attempt to curb the distribution of colours at elections. He and his colleague Ogle were comfortably beaten, to the delight of Robert Peel's political opponents. Lord Holland reported gleefully that a Norwich clergyman 'preached the Sunday after the election on the following text out of 2 Samuel, ch. 1, v. 26: "I am distressed for thee, my brother Jonathan"'.[12]

At the general election of 1831 Peel was returned, after a token contest, for Huntingdon, which the Dowager Lady Sandwich had placed at the disposal of opposition. On the hustings he admitted that unyielding resistance to parliamentary reform was no longer tenable and professed himself to be 'a moderate reformer', in favour of enfranchising large towns and having 'the constituency of the country generally increased'. However, he objected to the wholesale disfranchisement of small boroughs proposed in the Grey ministry's reform bill, which he thought likely to lead to universal suffrage, the ballot and the spoliation of church property.[13] He was a less than dedicated attender in the 1831 Parliament. He voted against the second reading of the reintroduced reform bill, 6 July, was in the minority against the partial disfranchisement of Chippenham, 27 July, put the case for Huntingdon to retain two seats, 29 July, and voted against the third reading and passage of the bill, 19, 21 Sept. He was a defaulter, 10 Oct., when the motion of confidence in the government was carried. He voted against the second reading of the revised reform bill, which reinstated Huntingdon as a two Member borough, 17 Dec. 1831. He was in the minority against the enfranchisement of Tower Hamlets, 28 Feb., expressed his 'objection to the whole of the disfranchising principle' of the bill, 2 Mar., and voted against its third reading, 22 Mar. 1832. His only other known votes were against government on the Russian-Dutch loan, 26 Jan., 12 July 1832. He criticized the magistrates who had dealt with the Nottingham riots, 31 Jan., 1 Feb., thinking that 'a great deal of mischief had arisen from the tone of certain speeches which had been made by them'. He refuted Hume's allegation that a cavalry trooper had been disciplined for voicing subversive political views, 3 July 1832.

Peel was returned again for Huntingdon in 1832 and, without opposition, at the next eight general elections. He served in his brother's second ministry and, with some success, as a cabinet minister under Lord Derby, before resigning in protest at Benjamin

Disraeli's† reform scheme in 1867. He was best known as a racehorse owner on a grand scale, whose greatest triumph was his victory with Orlando in the notorious 1844 'Running Rein' Derby. He died in February 1879.[14]

[1] N. Gash, *Secretary Peel*, 40, 63; Add. 40245, f. 11; 40264, ff. 17, 313; 40267, f. 153; 40279, ff. 32, 110. [2] PROB 11/1772/396; Add. 40401, f. 238. [3] Add. 40369, ff. 64, 107, 108, 234; 40370, ff. 45, 178, 182, 233, 285, 287, 293; 40371, f. 35; 40372, ff. 101, 144, 186. [4] Add. 40386, ff. 241, 249, 257, 269; 40387, ff. 12, 14, 17, 54, 59b, 78, 88, 90; Gash, 404; *Norwich Mercury*, 6, 20, 27 May, 3, 10, 17 June 1826. [5] Add. 40388, ff. 115, 117, 297; 40391, ff. 13, 55, 40392, f. 80; 40394, f. 77. [6] *The Times*, 27 Mar. 1827. [7] *Geo. IV Letters*, iii. 1327. [8] *The Times*, 7 June 1827. [9] Northants. RO, Agar Ellis diary, 9 Feb.; Grey mss, Howick jnl. 9 Feb. [1829]. [10] Add. 40398, ff. 138, 213, 215, 217, 219, 250. [11] Agar Ellis diary, 6 Mar.; Gurney diary, 6 Mar. [1829]. [12] *Norwich Mercury*, 3, 10, 17, 24, 31 July; *Ellenborough Diary*, ii. 333; Add. 38758, f. 222; Howick jnl. 31 July; TNA 30/29, Holland to Granville, 1 Sept. 1830. [13] *Huntingdon, Bedford and Peterborough Gazette*, 30 Apr., 7 May 1831. [14] *Oxford DNB*.

D.R.F.

PEEL, Laurence (1801–1888), of 43 Park Street, Grosvenor Square, Mdx.[1]

COCKERMOUTH 16 Feb. 1827–1830

b. 28 June 1801, 6th s. of Sir Robert Peel†, 1st bt. (*d.* 1830), of Drayton Manor, Staffs. and 1st w. Ellen, da. of William Yates, calico printer, of Springside, Bury, Lancs.; bro. of Edmund Peel*, Jonathan Peel*, Robert Peel* and William Yates Peel*. *educ.* Rugby 1812; Christ Church, Oxf. 1819. *m.* 20 July 1822, Lady Jane Lennox, da. of Charles Lennox†, 4th duke of Richmond, 4s. (2 *d.v.p.*) 2da. (1 *d.v.p.*). *d.* 10 Dec. 1888.

Commr. bd. of control Feb. 1828-Feb. 1830.

Laurence was the youngest and least talented, but perhaps the most personally attractive of the Peel brothers. He entered Christ Church 15 years after Robert, the eldest, but never threatened to emulate his academic brilliance.[2] He became fast friends there with the Whig Lord Holland's son, Henry Edward Fox*, who was informed by their college contemporary Robert Vernon Smith* in July 1821 that Peel intended to stay in Oxford until August, '*compelled* by a prudent horror of Sir Robert's wrath'.[3] Notwithstanding his family's Tory politics, Peel became a welcome guest at Holland House, where early in 1822 Fox found him 'less formal than before' and looking 'quite handsome'.[4] When he left Oxford in March 1822 Robert, recently appointed home secretary in Lord Liverpool's ministry, took him into the office as his unpaid private secretary, though in practice he had virtually nothing to do.[5] Peel seems to have flirted with homosexuality at Oxford, but in the summer of 1822, just after coming of age, he married the daughter of the late duke of Richmond, Robert's former chief in Ireland. Fox thought it 'odd', for she was 'not pretty, nor with any great attraction but extreme good-nature'; indeed, she was 'too old and ugly'. But Peel was 'in the most tearing spirits' and 'happy beyond measure' at the prospect; and when Fox visited them at Fulham later in the year he found them 'as happy as the day is long'. She, having 'caught some of his sarcasm', now revealed herself to be 'clever', and he, as ever, was 'very kind and pleasant'.[6] Lady Holland deemed them 'agreeable and good hearted' and liked them 'uncommonly'.[7] On his marriage Peel's father settled on him an annual income of £2,000, with £800 a year to go to Lady Jane in the event of his death. Complications arose in 1826 when, on attaining the age of 25, he became entitled to £60,000 of the £106,000 which Sir Robert had allotted as his personal fortune. Peel, who had been ill and was taking the cure at Tunbridge Wells, was in some financial trouble, having exceeded his allowance for a London house by taking on one at 11 Connaught Place which was too big for his needs. His good relations with his father were momentarily threatened but Robert, who loaned him cash to tide him over his immediate difficulties, interceded and supervised a satisfactory settlement of the problem. The bond of the marriage settlement was annulled, about £47,000 of Laurence's portion was invested to provide £2,000 a year, and he was given control of the remaining £13,000. He disposed of the Connaught Place house and moved to more suitable premises off Grosvenor Square. On the death of his father in 1830 he received such an additional sum as raised his portion, like that of his four older brothers, to a total of £135,000.[8]

In January 1827 Lord Lowther*, a lord of the treasury, recommended Peel to his father, Lord Lonsdale, as a suitable Member 'for the next session' for their borough of Cockermouth, where a vacancy was pending: 'He will [be] a steady fellow and a good attender, and go in and out, just as you please. It will be paying a compliment to [Robert] Peel at a cheap rate'.[9] The latter was 'much pleased' by the offer, as was Laurence when he told him of it:

> I am quite at a loss how to express my thanks to you for the additional proof ... of your willingness to interest yourself in my welfare. When Jane spoke to you some time back about my getting into Parliament, it was entirely without my knowledge or concurrence; and though I should never have consented to her troubling you with the subject, I could not, when informed of the circumstances several weeks afterwards, blame her for it, as her only motive was to contribute by that means to the

> restoration of my health, and my future happiness. There is nothing, I am convinced, which will be of such service to me, or afford me a more interesting occupation than a constant attendance in the House of Commons during the approaching session; and I trust it is unnecessary for me to add ... that I shall do everything in my power to prevent your having cause to regret the favour you have conferred upon me, and be ready and anxious at all times, and upon all occasions, to be directed entirely by your advice, and to act in conformity with your principles, which so far from being at variance with my own feelings, would be the line I should wish to pursue, even were I unbiased by any ties of relationship or gratitude.[10]

For all his pious good intentions, Peel was an undistinguished Member, who is not known to have spoken in debate. He voted against Catholic relief, 6 Mar., and for the spring guns bill, 23 Mar. 1827. John Robert Townshend met him in the House that year and told Fox that 'I like [him] of all things, though I think sometimes one sees marks of the *Jenny*'.[11]

In January 1828 Peel excitedly relayed to Robert's wife the 'excellent news' that the Goderich ministry had collapsed.[12] He became an unpaid member of the board of control in the duke of Wellington's administration (Robert was again home secretary) after receiving another 'sessional lease' of his seat, which he was 'very anxious to keep', though ready to surrender if required.[13] He presented petitions against the 1827 Malt Act, 22 Feb., 26 Mar., voted against repeal of the Test Acts, 26 Feb., and Catholic relief, 12 May, and was in the government majorities on chancery delays, 24 Apr., and the silk duties, 14 July 1828. It was rumoured that he might be promoted or placed on the ministerial pay roll, and Lowther, worried by the evident drift of ministers towards the concession of Catholic relief, advised his father not to be 'very accommodating' about re-electing Peel, as 'there is no occasion to surrender your sword, and make yourself incapable of any resistance should that time arrive'.[14] When it did, in February 1829, Peel was expected to follow his brother's line, though Lowther claimed to know that he was 'anxious to have ... [Lonsdale's] wishes expressed to him to vote against him'. In the event he voted for emancipation, 6, 30 Mar. He offered to resign his seat, but the Lowthers, wishing to keep their options open in case of 'any political changes', allowed him to keep it 'at least for the present'.[15] Peel, who was listed by the Ultras in October 1829 among 'present government connections who will be hostile to a new one', left the board of control in February 1830. He was inconspicuous in the House in the ensuing session and at the dissolution was turned out of Cockermouth for an opponent of government.

Soon afterwards he removed to Brighton, where he and his wife devoted themselves to the promotion of charitable and religious causes. He continued to take a lively interest in Robert's career at the summit of politics, and during his first ministry offered suggestions on his scheme of church reform.[16] He died at his house at 32 Sussex Square, Brighton, in December 1888, having provided handsomely for his surviving children.

[1] Not to be confused with his cos. Sir Lawrence Peel (1799-1884), c.j. Calcutta, 1842-55 (*Oxford DNB*). [2] N. Gash, *Secretary Peel*, 63, 404; Parker, *Peel*, i. 291. [3] Add. 52011, Stuart Wortley to Fox, 31 Jan., 5 June; 52059, Smith to same, 6 July [1821]. [4] *Fox Jnl*. 92, 103; *Lady Holland to Son*, 20. [5] Add. 40605, f. 220. [6] Add. 52059, Smith to Fox, 6 July [1821]; *Fox Jnl*. 120, 123, 125-8, 149. [7] *Lady Holland to Son*, 28. [8] *Fox Jnl*. 126; PROB 11/1772/396; *Gent. Mag*.(1830), i. 557; Add. 40401, f. 238; 40605, f. 132; 40606, ff. 197, 203, 206, 214, 218, 222, 224, 236. [9] Lonsdale mss, Lowther to Lonsdale, 7, 17 Jan. 1827. [10] Add. 40391, ff. 98, 101, 141; 40607, ff. 61, 63. [11] Add. 52017, Townshend to Fox, 29 July 1827. [12] Add. 40395, ff. 7, 9. [13] Lonsdale mss, Lowther to Lonsdale, 26, 29 Jan. 1828. [14] Ibid. same to same, 5, 7 July 1828. [15] Ibid. same to same, 9, 12, 15 Mar., Lowther to Peel [c.12 Mar.] 1829. [16] Add. 40412, ff. 42, 45; 40487, f. 350; 40519, f. 237; 40540, f. 309; 40548, f. 179; 40555, f. 110; 40598, f. 76.

D.R.F.

PEEL, Robert (1788–1850), of 12 Stanhope Street and 4 Whitehall Gardens, Mdx. and Drayton Hall, Fazeley, Staffs.[1]

CASHEL	15 Apr. 1809–1812
CHIPPENHAM	1812–6 June 1817
OXFORD UNIVERSITY	10 June 1817–20 Feb. 1829
WESTBURY	2 Mar. 1829–1830
TAMWORTH	1830–2 July 1850

b. 5 Feb. 1788, 1st s. of Sir Robert Peel†, 1st bt., of Drayton Manor and 1st w. Ellen, da. of William Yates, calico printer, of Springside, Bury, Lancs.; bro. of Edmund Peel*, Jonathan Peel*, Laurence Peel* and William Yates Peel*. *educ*. by James Hargreaves, curate of Bury, until 1798; Rev. Francis Blick, vicar of Tamworth, Staffs. 1798-1800; Harrow 1800-4; Christ Church, Oxf. 1805; L. Inn 1809. *m*. 8 June 1820, Julia, da. of Gen. Sir John Floyd, 1st bt., of Mansfield Street, Mdx., 5s. 2da. *suc*. fa. as 2nd bt. 3 May 1830. *d*. 2 July 1850.

Under-sec. of state for war and colonies June 1810-Aug. 1812; chief sec. to ld. lt. [I] Aug. 1812-Aug. 1818; PC [GB] 13 Aug. 1812, [I] 5 Sept. 1812; commr. of treasury [I] 1814-17; sec. of state for home affairs Jan. 1822-Apr. 1827, Jan. 1828-Nov. 1830; first ld. of treasury and chan. of exch. 10 Dec. 1834-18 Apr. 1835; first ld. of treasury 3 Sept. 1841-6 July 1846.

Capt. Manchester regt. militia 1808; lt. Staffs. yeoman cav. 1820; rect. Glasgow Univ. 1837-8.

When George III died in January 1820 Peel, 'a remarkably good-looking man', tall, red-haired and fastidiously dressed, was a week short of his 32nd birthday.[2] He was heir to most of the great wealth which had accrued from the Lancashire and Staffordshire cotton textile manufacturing business founded by his grandfather and expanded by his formidable Pittite father, who had received a baronetcy in 1800, and to the substantial Staffordshire estate at Drayton, near Tamworth. (Peel himself had no personal involvement in the firm.) Having entered Parliament as an Oxford prodigy at the age of 21, he already had over eight years' experience of efficient office in the Tory ministries of Spencer Perceval† and Lord Liverpool, which had instilled in him the conception of ministers as servants of the crown and won him a high reputation for diligence, probity, administrative efficiency and 'business habits of the first order'. He had also proved himself to be an accomplished parliamentary debater.[3] He had served for six years in the demanding post of Irish secretary, which had enhanced his pessimistic and cynical view of human nature and contempt for the avarice and self-seeking of irresponsible backbench politicians. It had also had a direct bearing on his emergence as the Commons leader and 'spokesman' of 'the intolerant faction', as the Whig Sir James Mackintosh* called him,[4] who were implacably opposed to Catholic emancipation. This was symbolized by his prestigious position as one of the Members for Oxford University since 1817, and had been reinforced in 1819 by his support for an increase in the allowance for the anti-Catholic duke of York and resistance to Grattan's renewed relief motion. Despite having been out of office for eighteen months, Peel, who had acquired a personal following, was in a potentially strong position given the divided state of the ministry and its supporters on the question. Yet he was intelligent enough to perceive that emancipation could not be resisted indefinitely and that he had to some extent put himself into a false position.[5] His urbane manners concealed an irritable temperament and keen sense of superiority over less able men. His intelligence, though considerable, was of the mechanical kind, with 'not the slightest pretension to genius'.[6] A devotee of logic, he lacked creative imagination and, beneath his self-centred and often pompous exterior, was acutely aware of this deficiency; dogmatism was his refuge on many issues.[7] Lady Holland, a partisan opponent, likened him in 1821 to 'a boy brought up at a small academy, who has been considered a sort of prodigy with great assistance in private from the master'.[8]

A week before his unopposed return at the general election of 1820, Peel became engaged to the beautiful Julia Floyd. From his sister Mary's home at Bognor, 23 Mar., he wrote to his friend John Croker*, secretary to the admiralty, about the unsettled state of public affairs:

> Do not you think that the tone of ... public opinion is more liberal than the policy of the government? ... that there is a feeling ... in favour of some undefined change in the mode of governing the country? ... Can we resist for seven years reform in Parliament ... And if reform cannot be resisted, is it not more probable that Whigs and Tories will unite, and carry through moderate reform, than remain opposed to each other?[9]

He married Julia in early June and had impregnated her by the beginning of August. He largely 'kept aloof from Parliament' in the 1820 session, but was present on 12 July to criticize the Irish chancery bill. On 28 June Edward Littleton* noted an apparent attempt by James Daly* and 'the Peel faction' to persuade Charles Grant, Peel's successor as Irish secretary, to renew the Insurrection Act, with the aim of increasing 'the weakness of the government at this moment of vacillation in their councils'.[10] Before going to the continent with Julia in September, despite the indifferent health which had bothered him for a year or so, Peel commented to Croker that the Queen Caroline affair was a 'very formidable ... ingredient in the cauldron which has been bubbling for some time', and that ministers had made matters worse by omitting her name from the liturgy, which had 'degraded her'.[11] During November, when they had to abandon the prosecution of the queen, to the fury of the king, there was speculation that Peel was likely soon to be back in office.[12] On Canning's resignation from the board of control in protest at the hounding of the queen in December 1820, Lord Liverpool, prompted by George IV, invited Peel to replace him. It came as no surprise when he declined, on the pretext that he disapproved of ministers' initial treatment of Caroline and, while not inclined to 'take a hostile part against the government', wanted to be free to act 'unfettered by any official connection'. According to the patronage secretary Charles Arbuthnot*, who had it from Liverpool, he 'expressed a great disregard for office generally', but seemed not to rule it out for the future.[13] The radical Whig Sir Robert Wilson* commented that Peel 'positively refuses to embark in the foundering Tory vessel'.[14] The Grenvillite Charles Williams Wynn* observed:

> It is perfectly true that his irritability, and a certain arrogance which the want of family and connection renders

> less tolerable, have during the last two years rendered the House (particularly the ministerial men) less favourably disposed to him, but still he combines advantages of general character in the country, of talents and habits of business which place him higher than any man in the House.

In response to his leader Lord Buckingham's denigration of Peel, Williams Wynn wrote:

> He cannot supply the effect of one of Canning's glittering speeches ... [but] he combines greater advantages ... than any other man in the House. Talent, independent fortune, official habits and reputation, and, above all, general character ... have ... disposed more men to follow and more to unite with him than any person ... I do not deny the objections arising from want of family and connection, the irritability he has shown of late ... but ... you can name no one who has not greater difficulties to encounter, and fewer advantages to assist him.[15]

Peel left the House before the division on Hamilton's motion condemning the omission of the queen's name from the liturgy, 26 Jan. 1821, when his brother William voted with opposition.[16] On Lord Tavistock's motion censuring ministers' conduct, 5 Feb., he deplored the liturgy slight and the denial to her of a palace and a navy ship to bring her to England, but said he could not have concurred in Hamilton's motion because 'it was of an intricate and indistinct character, and ... would have prejudged the question'. He argued that the Commons should not 'stand shivering in every fitful breeze of popular feeling', criticized the queen's advisers and declared his support for the government's handling of the affair after their early blunders; he voted in their majority on the 6th. The radical Whig Member Henry Grey Bennet thought his speech was 'prosy and pompous', and his fellow 'Mountaineer' Thomas Creevey that it was 'as feeble as be damned'.[17] Von Neumann heard that it was 'very fine', Lady Granville judged it 'a very useful one for the government, but not in any way striking', and Mrs. Arbuthnot noted that he spoke 'powerfully and well'.[18] Williams Wynn subsequently detected 'symptoms of some understanding' between Lord Castlereagh (later Londonderry), the pro-Catholic foreign secretary and leader of the House, and Peel, the 'most decisive' being Peel's 'abandonment of Pitt's old Hill Fort ... and returning to his former position in the rear of the treasury bench'.[19] From there he backed a call for repeal of the Irish Union trade duties, 16 Feb., and opposed inquiry into the conduct of the sheriff of Dublin in calling in troops to break up a pro-queen meeting, 22 Feb. On 28 Feb. he led the opposition to Plunket's motion to consider Catholic relief, which he said would 'not harmonize contending and conflicting feelings' in Ireland. Mrs. Arbuthnot perceived that he 'certainly did not oppose the consideration of the subject so stoutly as he did last year', and Buckingham thought Plunket had 'driven' him 'off his ground' with his pre-emptive strike.[20] Williams Wynn had earlier guessed that Peel was 'not ill-inclined to back out of the Catholic question'; and Grey Bennet recorded in his diary:

> Peel, in reply, was bad and weak, evidently labouring under the weakness of his case, and showing an inclination to back out as soon as he could: no spirit or zeal, and very different in tone, sentiment and manner from what he exhibited last time ... His speech was good as to diction, choice of words and clearness of exposition, but very poor in knowledge, and exhibiting no power of thought or strength of mind.[21]

Peel voted in the minority and opposed the subsequent relief bill, though in the prevailing mood of 'great forebearance', 16 Mar., he conceded that the exclusion of Catholics from power was 'an evil' and said that if the measure became law he would strive to reconcile Protestants to it.[22] His amendment to extend the designated exclusions to the privy council and judicial offices was rejected by 163-120, 27 Mar. He spoke against the third reading, 2 Apr. He favoured a £20 householder franchise for Leeds if it received Grampound's seats, because a wider scot and lot one would lead to 'an abstraction of the people from their habits of industry', 2 Mar. On 19 Mar. he insisted that the 1819 select committee on bank restriction, which he had chaired, 'could have come ... to no other conclusion' than recommending the resumption of cash payments. He was in the ministerial majority against repeal of the additional malt duty, 3 Apr. 1821.

The Grenvillite Joseph Phillimore* thought that Peel's line on the Catholic relief bill indicated that he was 'paving the way for a junction with government', but he believed that he had not 'gained ground by his conduct' and had 'lost rather in the estimation of the House'.[23] Arbuthnot sounded Londonderry on the notion of Peel's becoming chancellor of the exchequer in the room of Nicholas Vansittart, who would move to the board of control (temporarily held by Charles Bragge Bathurst). Londonderry would not hear of it, arguing that it would enable Peel, who 'had never done anything to entitle him to so high a place', to threaten his own supremacy as leader. While this was largely fatuous, concealing personal animosity and paranoia, Liverpool evidently took Londonderry's side.[24] Yet in early May 1821, according to Mrs. Arbuthnot, Liverpool tried to persuade Londonderry to acquiesce in such an arrangement, for which Canning was said to be 'extremely anxious'. Liverpool got nowhere, and Londonderry additionally satisfied the duke of Wellington, master-general of the ordnance, that 'it would never do'. Lord Melville, first lord of the admiralty, evidently took the same view.[25] Liverpool now considered renewing the offer of the board of control, but when he saw Peel on 30 May he merely invited him to take unspecified cabinet office. Peel, who told Croker that 'it was done in a strange, shuffling, hesitating sort of way', had little doubt that the board of control was intended and 'gave an answer as vague as the application'. Arbuthnot told his wife that Peel

> expressed himself well-disposed towards the government, but stated that, from the state of his health, office was not a matter of much anxiety or importance to him ... He said his eyes were so bad that he could not read at all at night and very little in the day time, and that consequently he was much incapacitated for business. He said, however, as he was going away, that he should like to know what changes were to be made and what office offered to him before he made a more decisive answer.[26]

To a letter from Lord Bathurst, the colonial secretary, pressing him to join the government, Peel replied, 1 June, that 'many considerations induce me to prefer ... idleness to the occupations of public life', but that hostility to the ministry was not one of them: 'I shall never persuade myself to exchange Cannon Row [the location of the East India office] for Lulworth [his rented holiday home in Dorset] as a summer residence'. Bathurst interpreted this as a rejection of 'the particular office', while Wellington thought Peel would accept something 'if his friends endeavour to prevail upon him or are neutral'.[27] Peel informed Croker that he was inclined to bring Liverpool to the point and that he did not want the board of control, partly because he had already refused it 'when the government was in danger' and felt that 'it might look shabby to take it now', and, more importantly, because he did 'not think he could be of use', having 'no taste or turn for debate unless when obliged by his office to take part in it'. Croker urged him not to reject any return to office, though he suspected that Liverpool was merely trying to keep Peel 'under his lee' in case 'some hitch' occurred in his preferred plan to recruit Canning, which the king was resisting. On 4 June Peel, whom Croker had tried to 'convince ... that, if not in government, he would soon be in opposition', saw Liverpool and 'verbally and positively refused' the board of control. He told Croker that he believed that Liverpool was

> playing a game, and ... not quite a fair one. When Peel said he came to decline the India board, Lord L. said hastily, 'And *anything else* I should offer?' Peel begged to say that, when anything else should be offered, it would be time enough to decide on it ... He thought Lord L. was peevish and embarrassed.[28]

Croker, who reckoned that Peel would not settle for less than the exchequer or the home office, and the Speaker Manners Sutton, an adherent of Peel, agreed that while they would have liked him to take the board of control, they could not blame him for turning it down 'upon his own view of the awkwardness in which he thinks an office without parliamentary business would place him'.[29] Liverpool, reporting Peel's refusal, 'in which his health bore the principal part', to the king, who was wrongly reported to be 'angry' with Peel, commented that his 'consequence' would not have been diminished by acceptance.[30] Canning told Wellington that 'it was a bad thing not having ... Peel, as he would be trying to make a party of young men against the government'; but Mrs. Arbuthnot thought Canning was judging Peel by his own devious standards.[31] In the House, Peel opposed Maxwell's slaves removal bill, 1 June, and deplored the repeal of the tax on husbandry horses, 18 June, when he voted to include arrears in the duke of Clarence's grant. He was named to the select committee on the ninth report of the Irish judicial commission, 26 June, and voted against Hume's call for retrenchment, 27 June 1821.

The king's reluctance to see Lord Sidmouth removed from the home office and refusal to accept Canning's return to the cabinet continued to block Peel's way during the summer.[32] In the second week of November 1821, when he was at Lulworth with Julia, now two months pregnant again after the birth of their first child in April, Croker informed him that on the king's recent return from Hanover there had been a 'complete and cordial' reconciliation with Liverpool and that the premier was almost certain to offer him the home office as part of a general reshuffle to bring in the Grenvillites and send Canning to govern India. A fortnight later Liverpool duly did so, and Peel accepted with alacrity.[33] He was sworn in on 17 Jan. 1822. The Tory Henry Bankes* considered his appointment 'most judicious' and sure to 'give the government great strength in debate, where alone they want it'.[34] Von Neumann wrote that Peel

> is a young man of many accomplishments, clever and learned, a good orator and full of ambition. He has consistently refused second-rate places, knowing very well that they would be obliged to turn to him on account of his oratorical gifts ... It is not impossible that one day ... [he] will be first lord of the treasury.[35]

Mackintosh considered Peel's 'accession ... as a step to a higher Toryism and consequently to a more undistinguishing resistance to all novelties' and was unsure whether or not to press on with his parliamentary campaign for reform of the criminal law.[36]

In fact Peel showed willingness to co-operate cautiously in some of this work. When unsuccessfully opposing on a technicality Mackintosh's motion for early consideration of reform of the criminal law, 4 June 1822, he explained that he was planning or hoping to bring in measures to establish a 'vigorous preventive police', improve prison discipline and regulate transportation; but he assured Mackintosh of his support for the principle of his motion. He had on 14 Mar. 1822 secured the appointment of a select committee to investigate the policing of the metropolis, where crime was increasing. Although he himself chaired it, its report, presented on 17 June 1822, was a disappointment, declaring against 'improvements in police, or facilities in detection of crime'.[37] On prison reform, he had more immediate success. He left the government-approved consolidation and reform measure inherited from Sidmouth in the hands of William Courtenay; it passed the Commons but was thrown out by the Lords. In 1823 Peel convinced lord chancellor Eldon of the bill's importance, and it was reintroduced and became law as 4 Geo. IV, c. 64: it established common gaols in every county or riding, in London, Westminster and 17 provincial towns, financed from local rates and administered by local justices, answerable to the home office. It also prescribed a system of discipline. Peel's Acts of 1823 (4 Geo. IV, c. 47) and 1824 (5 Geo. IV, c. 85) respectively dealt with transportation of convicts and extended the home office's authority to a further 150 small gaols.[38] On the wider question of legal reform and mitigation of the criminal code, Peel made some careful progress in his first spell at the home office. In October 1822 he initiated a process of reform of the Scottish courts, leaving the work to the Scottish professionals. A modified juries bill, based on the measures introduced by the Whig Thomas Kennedy, became law in 1825 (6 Geo. IV, c. 22), as did one regulating the sheriff and burgh courts (6 Geo. IV, c. 23). On 21 May 1823 Mackintosh proposed nine resolutions for mitigation of the criminal code, which included the abolition of the death penalty for forgery, various types of larceny, and stealing of farm animals, and of a number of obsolete statutes. Peel was unwilling to accept a commitment to general resolutions and successfully moved the previous question, but not before, in a long and well – prepared speech, he had indicated how far the government was prepared to go in reform: capital punishment would be abolished for several common law misdemeanours and for larceny in shops and on canals, but not from dwelling houses, and the punishments for forgery would remain unaltered. By the end of the 1823 session five bills abolishing the death penalty for these offences, empowering judges to withhold it in all capital convictions except murder and ending the practice of burying suicides on the highroad were on the statute book (4 Geo. IV, cc. 46, 48, 52-54). Peel was motivated not so much by humanitarian zeal as by a desire to streamline and rationalize the criminal law in order to make it more efficient and to ensure that it was applied with greater certainty and consistency. It is now clear that while he simplified the criminal law, it was applied no more leniently under his aegis than previously, and that the significant mitigation of its severity was carried out by the Liberal ministries of the 1830s.[39] In March 1825 Peel introduced a bill to consolidate into one 85 statutes governing the empanelling of juries and to reform qualifications, appeals and selection procedures. It became law as 6 Geo. IV, c. 50. On 9 Mar. 1826 he secured leave to bring in a bill to consolidate the laws relating to theft and one to make the administration of criminal law more efficient. The latter became law as 7 Geo. IV, c. 64, but the former, on which Peel had second thoughts arising out of the close connection between malicious destruction of property and theft, he set aside for review until the next session.[40]

As home secretary, Peel's days were filled with a demanding plethora of business, including the maintenance of law and order: there were serious outbreaks of unrest in various manufacturing districts in 1822, and strikes by textile workers and colliers in the west of Scotland, Lancashire and the Midlands, and London and north – east shipwrights in late 1824. In 1825 Peel, who used troops where necessary, brought in a bill to repeal parts of Hume's half-baked 1824 Combinations Act in order to prevent the abuse of power by unions and protect individual employers and workers.[41] There was above all the continuing problem of Ireland, to which Peel paid close attention. He had friends and reliable allies in Henry Goulburn*, the new Protestant Irish secretary, and William Gregory, under-secretary at Dublin Castle; but the lord lieutenant, the quixotic, vainglorious and idle pro-Catholic Lord Wellesley (Wellington's brother), proved difficult and frustrating to work with. Mounting sectarian tension and, from 1823, the rise of the Catholic Association under Daniel O'Connell* and Richard Sheil*, dominated Peel's Irish correspondence.[42] The accelerating campaign for Catholic emancipation, the dominant single issue of the 1820s, had particular relevance for Peel, whose position within the reconstructed Liverpool ministry was a paradoxical and awkward one. While he generally supported in cabinet the more liberal foreign and trade policies pursued by Canning, Frederick Robinson* and William Huskisson*, and endorsed by Liverpool, and thus was emphatically one of the progressive group within the government, who subscribed to contemporary *laissez faire* economic doctrines, he was still 'Orange Peel', the acknowledged leader of the reactionary Protestants. On the Catholic question he was isolated among Commons cabinet ministers, though he had the support of Liverpool and Wellington.[43] The Whig George Tierney* thought in January 1822 that 'we shall soon see some attempt made by Peel and his partisans to counteract Wellesley's operations'; while Mackintosh noted that Peel was 'said to be haughty, passionate, and ill tempered, and to be in the highest degree thin skinned – a quality sure to make an English minister miserable'.[44]

Peel's well-intentioned attempt to bring forward his brother William by offering him the home office under-secretaryship backfired, and he appointed George Dawson*, his brother-in-law.[45] On the eve of the 1822 session he anticipated most 'trouble' from 'the country gentlemen and agriculture'.[46] Securing the appointment of a select committee (on which he did not sit) on agricultural distress petitions, 18 Feb., he defended the 1819 Bank Act (already known as 'Peel's Act'), dismissed a return to a paper currency and said that no legislation could effectively relieve distress. He spoke in the same terms, 17 Apr., 13 May, when he replied to Alexander Baring's condemnation of the 1819 settlement as 'iniquitous', 12 June, 10 July, defeating Western's motions for inquiry into the currency. He was against reduction of the salt tax, 28 Feb., arguing that there was no scope for remissions without a breach of public credit. He opposed inquiry into the assault on Alderman Robert Waithman* at the queen's funeral, 28 Feb., and defended the organization of that event, 6 Mar. On 13 Mar. he deplored the proven acts of cruelty in Ilchester gaol, but insisted that his enquiries had convinced him that Henry Hunt* was being well treated there; and in what the radical Whig Member John Cam Hobhouse described as 'a poor pompous speech, calculated for the days of French terror', he opposed Burdett's call for a remission of Hunt's sentence, 24 Apr.[47] The Tory backbencher Edward Bootle Wilbraham commented to Lord Colchester, 2 Apr., that Peel was 'of the greatest use in Parliament, and saves Lord Londonderry and Van[sittart] much speaking and explanations, as he is concise and clear in what he says'.[48] Peel opposed as too vague Newport's motion on the state of Ireland, 22 Apr., when he declared his support for education 'without reference to ... religion' and hostility to interference with tithes. On 30 Apr. he presented his constituents' petition against Catholic claims before giving his 'decided negative', in what the Whig George Agar Ellis* thought an ineffective speech, but which Mackintosh reckoned was 'dextrous and cunning', to Canning's bill to relieve Catholic peers. The Hollands' son Henry Fox*, who heard it, reckoned it was 'good in some parts', but went on, 'his manner is odious, and it is impossible not to hate him'. Mrs. Arbuthnot thought he performed 'very ably'.[49] He spoke against the second reading, which was carried by 235-223, 10 May,[50] but did not divide the House against the third, 17 May. According to Lady Spencer, after the government's defeat by disgruntled country gentlemen on the abolition of one of the joint-postmasterships, 2 May, Peel took a strong line in cabinet in favour of stout resistance to pending Whig motions criticizing diplomatic expenditure, which were attacks on the Grenvillites, who had joined the ministry as part of the reshuffle of January 1822. She claimed to know that Peel 'declared that if the question [of Henry Williams Wynn's† appointment to the Swiss embassy, 16 May] was lost, he would resign; that it was impossible to go on losing ground every day in Parliament and allowing the opposition to gain their objects ... that he did not covet office at any time, but much less under such disgraceful circumstances'. He got 'the better' of Londonderry, who wanted a more conciliatory approach. Charles Williams Wynn, president of the board of control and head of the Grenvillites in the Commons, wrote approvingly of Peel to Buckingham:

> Peel shows ... more spirit and good judgement ... than any man in the cabinet ... He has lately taken a much bolder and more decided tone both in Parliament and cabinet, and I have little doubt means to run for the lead of the ... Commons. It appears to me very probable that his object is to break up the government, in the expectation that it will be impossible for the opposition to substitute anything which can stand three months, and that he may then mould and form it at his pleasure. He has ... spoken to me of the advantage which would result from our retiring, and the certainty that we must return to power within three months. Does he think that period would be sufficient for opposition to pass the Catholic question?[51]

Peel said that the Greenhoe reform petition was couched in 'insulting' language and must therefore be rejected, 3 June, and on the 14th alleged that the Kent reform meeting had been dominated by William Cobbett† 'because he had not been manfully resisted' by the Whigs and said that Burdett and Grey Bennet were undermining public credit with their demands for a reduction of the interest on the national debt. Hobhouse considered his speech proposing renewal of the Aliens Act, 5 June,'very wretched', and remarked that 'he has been lately very flippant, and particularly to Burdett'.[52] Peel replied contemptuously to Denman's implied questioning of his motives in rejoining the ministry. He supported Goulburn's Irish constables bill, 7 June; said that the prospect of famine in Ireland took the problem of aid 'above the ordinary rules of financial calculation' and explained the government's efforts to implement relief measures, 17 June; opposed Hume's call for reform of Irish tithes, 19 June, and endorsed the Irish insurrection bill, 8 July. He opposed Brougham's motion alleging an increase in crown influence, 24 June 1822. Next day he defended the conduct of the lord advocate Sir William Rae* in the Borthwick affair.[53]

In mid-July 1822 Williams Wynn reported to Buckingham that Peel and Bathurst were 'strongly' of opinion that the government would be well rid of Canning, if, as seemed likely, he went as governor-general to India. He had also heard that Peel had vouchsafed the view that 'things would not go on well until they had got rid of the Grenvilles'; but he did not believe this, 'as he is far too cautious to commit himself by such a speech', though 'the coldness and reserve of his manner to me make me think that the opinion ... is not unlikely to be entertained by him'. Buckingham's acolyte William Fremantle* observed that Canning was wanted by 'no part of the government', for they 'find the strength and power of Peel have completely answered their purpose, and with more popularity and feeling of the House than the other would have done'.[54] Peel was obliged (with Julia) to accompany the king on his visit to Scotland, 10-30 Aug. When the news arrived on the 14th of Londonderry's suicide he was the one to inform George, on board his yacht in the Forth. Five days later the king told him that he had already written to Liverpool to tell him that he wished the arrangement for Canning to go to India to be effected forthwith. Peel declined to commit himself on the question of the leadership of the Commons (which the king may have pressed him to take, as chancellor of the exchequer); and on his return to London, 1 Sept., when he found Liverpool sure that the position must be offered to Canning, he made clear his perfect willingness to acquiesce in whatever was decided, though he laid what Bathurst thought was significant stress on his 'ill health' (his eyes were troubling him again, and he was weary) as a bar to his own appointment. Croker encouraged him to believe that he could conduct the business of the House without Canning or with Canning in opposition; but even had he wanted to, Peel knew that he could not reasonably object to the promotion of Canning, who was by some way his senior in parliamentary experience. The king was stubborn for a few days, but his objections to Canning were overcome by Liverpool and Wellington; and on 8 Sept. 1822 it was finally arranged that Canning would become foreign secretary and leader of the Commons.[55] There was some surprise in Whig circles, where Tierney had been confident that Peel would be made leader; Henry Brougham had hoped that the choice would fall on 'the damaged prig', 'the low miserable Spinning Jenny', whom he was confident of besting in debate, and Lord Essex had observed that 'some of the high bred country gentlemen won't like to pull on Peel's *cotton stockings every day*'.[56] James Macdonald* commented that 'although Peel has got through his first session pretty well, it has been by selecting his occasions of coming forward, and sometimes even pettishly declining to do so when against the grain: it would be therefore very nervous work for Liverpool to risk the whole fate of the ministry on such an experiment as Peel himself'.[57] If Peel did feel any chagrin at having been robbed of the second position in the ministry by an accident of timing, he kept it well hidden; and to Goulburn he wrote that 'that which has been done is the best that could be done', though he anticipated 'much perplexity and debate' when the Catholic question came again before Parliament with himself and Canning on opposite sides.[58] Lord Palmerston*, the secretary at war, thought Peel had 'behaved ... in the handsomest possible manner'; but William Henry Lyttelton† reported to Canning's friend Bagot a theory 'amongst the *exoterics* that Peel, whose early prudence and premature worldly wisdom made him always peculiarly odious in my eyes, looked with his habitual caution upon the dangerous honour of leadership and declined it'.[59] Peel was at Sudbourne in October 1822, when Lord Hertford told Croker that he was 'in great force but strikes me as being very thin, I am sure two stones lighter'.[60]

In January 1823 Liverpool countenanced a proposal from Canning that he should be allowed to occupy the house in Downing Street customarily used by the chancellor of the exchequer, if the prime minister did not want it. According to Henry Hobhouse, the premier failed to realize how much this was 'calculated to excite ... Peel's jealousy', as it would imply that Liverpool regarded Canning as his natural successor. When this was pointed out to him, the idea was abandoned.[61] The Whig leader Lord Grey heard of 'dissensions in the cabinet' and that 'Peel and his friends ... talk without reserve against both Wellesley and Plunket', the Irish attorney-general, who had created a potential source of difficulty by prosecuting *ex-officio* Dublin Orange rioters involved in an attack on the viceroy. An Irish Member observed that Peel was 'the real lord lieutenant' and that none before Wellesley had had 'so little power', largely because 'there never was before a secretary of state ... who was the leader of a party of Irish Members in the ... Commons'.[62] To his colleagues Peel made clear his exasperation with Wellesley's inefficiency and capriciousness, and Mrs. Arbuthnot noted in late February that he had told Wellington that 'he must really retire from office for he cannot bear the way in which things are going on in Ireland', and that Wellington intervened with Liverpool to stop this 'nonsense'. Williams Wynn, however, found him 'in general more fair, more manly, and more statesmanlike in his views than I had at all hoped', while Fremantle heard that despite the denigration of Wellesley by 'every hanger-on and agent of the Protestant part of the government', Peel 'behaves very well indeed, and is perfectly moderate and well-judging upon the whole question'.[63] On the address, 4 Feb., he defended ministerial non-intervention in the Franco-Spanish conflict and held out hopes of tax remissions. Creevey, who speculated that he and Canning could not go on together much longer, claimed that he 'could scarcely make himself heard'. After his brief intervention on the case of the Irish chief baron O'Grady, 12 Feb., the Whig John Lambton* told Grey that Peel had already 'shown himself utterly incompetent for the situation of leader, even if Canning were out of the way, and has fallen, as I expected always he would, much lower in public estimation'.[64] On 20 Feb. he opposed Lord John Russell's motion for information on the borough franchise, which would 'prejudice the question of parliamentary reform'. He told carping agriculturists, 26 Feb., that on the currency he 'maintained every opinion on the subject which he had advanced in 1819'; he gave his 'unqualified negative' to Western's motion for inquiry, 12 June. According to Agar Ellis, he 'got into a passion' when opposing Hume's motion for inquiry into the Irish church, 4 Mar., and was 'very well' answered by the knight of Kerry.[65] Sir John Nicholl*, who thought Peel had been an 'excellent second' to Canning so far that session, was pleased with his performance against Abercromby's motion for the suppression of Orange lodges, 5 Mar., when he avoided any Protestant acerbity.[66] He refuted Brougham's allegation that ministers were guilty of 'apathy' on agricultural distress and deplored Hume's 'charges vaguely brought forward' against Sir Thomas Maitland† for his government of the Ionian Isles, 24 Mar. That day he opposed Barry's motion for information on the prosecution of the Dublin rioters. On 26 Mar. he confirmed that he had advised the king not to release the blasphemous libeller Mary Ann Carlile and argued that Hamilton had made out 'no case' for his charge of irregularity in the crown warrant for Inverness council elections. Williams Wynn reported that Peel had 'with great difficulty' kept Dawson from resigning over Plunket's *ex-officio* prosecutions, and that at a meeting of government supporters before the debate on Brownlow's motion for papers (which in the event was withdrawn after the debate), 15 Apr., he 'distinctly stated that if the result ... was to be an opinion on Plunket's conduct, he should not hesitate one moment in giving his heartfelt and sincere opinion in favour of the proceeding he had adopted'.[67] On 17 Apr. he appealed to Brougham and Canning to draw a veil over their furious row on the Catholic question. On the 22nd, responding to Williams Wynn's statement on the 17th that he and the Grevillites had come into office in 1822 on being given a pledge that Ireland would be governed fairly, Peel, perceiving an implied censure of the previous Irish regime, said that the administration of justice had been 'impartial' in his time in Dublin and that he would not have entered the ministry in 1822 had he conceived that any of his colleagues thought otherwise. Next day he wrote privately to Williams Wynn to the same effect. This episode created a minor crisis, which Liverpool and Wellington nipped in the bud.[68] Later on the 22nd Peel opposed Burdett's successful motion for inquiry into the prosecutions. He stated on 25 Apr. that the current wages of Manchester cotton weavers were such that they could 'live in comparative comfort'. A few days later Creevey recorded the observation of Canning's acolyte John William Ward* that 'Peel was lower and lower every day, quite incompetent', and no support at all for Canning.[69] On 29 Apr. Peel opposed Macdonald's 'severe criminatory resolution' on British policy towards Spain, arguing that it would make it appear to Europe that the House 'condemned the policy of neutrality, and were advocates of war'. Next day he opposed as 'a dangerous experiment' Grey Bennet's motion for the abolition of whipping for minor offences. He defended continuation of the Irish Insurrection Act as 'a necessary' but 'only a temporary' measure, 12 May. He supported the Irish tithes composition bill, which, if it 'should not produce universal harmony and conciliation', would do 'much substantial good'. He was, as Henry Bankes told Colchester, 'partly disposed to accede' to Lord Nugent's bill to put British Catholics on the same footing as Irish. At a small meeting of Protestant Tories at Bankes's, Peel stated that he and Liverpool were willing to allow British Catholics to vote in parliamentary elections, but not to exempt them from the Test Acts. He said as much in the House, 28 May, when Nugent got leave to introduce his bill.[70] On the second reading, 18 June, he raised further objections to details, notably its dispensing with the oath of supremacy for office-holders. (Lord chancellor Eldon had recently told Colchester that 'he would undertake in a quarter of an hour to satisfy ... Peel that he does not understand' the bill; Colchester asked himself, 'Why do they not talk together?')[71] The measure was divided into two, and Peel supported the enfranchisement bill, 30 June, having concluded that there was no 'danger' in it. He defended the Irish insurrection bill and opposed inquiry into disturbances there, 24 June; dismissed Hume's motion for abolition of the lord lieutenancy, 25 June, and spoke against Brougham's bid to refer the petition of Irish Catholics complaining of biased administration of justice to the judicial commission, 26 June. Fremantle told Buckingham that 'Canning does nothing in the House, and I think suffers Peel to take completely the lead'; and a fortnight later he reported that Peel and Robinson, now chancellor of the exchequer, had risen much beyond ... [Canning] in estimation as general speakers and men of business'. Yet on 21 July 1823, Williams Wynn reckoned that Peel 'continues very glum and sulky'.[72] According to Henry Hobhouse, Peel at this time was 'resolved ... to resign his office' if the king, influenced by Lady Conyngham and Sir William Knighton (whom Peel distrusted, and who disliked Peel) persisted in his bid to obtain a reprieve for a convicted forger sentenced to death.[73]

Peel was obliged to go to London from Lulworth, where Julia, expecting their third child, was unwell, on departmental business in mid-August 1823, when he inspected the progress of his new town house, building in Whitehall Gardens, and hid from his prospective neighbour 'Chin' Grant*, a great bore. He was reassured, Arbuthnot told Bathurst, to find that Canning 'was *not making way* with the king', but Arbuthnot saw that he 'has great suspicions of Canning, and it annoys him not a little that Lord Liverpool should be under such subjection to him'.[74] In early October, according to Mrs. Arbuthnot, her husband spoke at Windsor with the king, who praised Robinson, but 'said Peel *had not heart enough for him*!!'.[75] Later that month Williams Wynn wrote to Buckingham:

> I am quite alone in town, for every one of my colleagues, with the exception of Peel, is absent, and you know that he hath no particular pleasure in communicating with me more than is necessary to avoid any public rupture, besides which he is at present otherwise engaged, as his wife is just brought to bed ... Since writing the above I have seen Peel, who gives me a very encouraging account of the success of the tithes bill.[76]

At this time, according to Mrs. Arbuthnot, Peel 'talked very confidentially' to her husband 'about Canning': 'He appeared to have the worst possible opinion of him, said he had no objection to do business in cabinet with him and that they were civil together in the ... Commons, but that he was the sort of person he should be very sorry to have a *tête à tête* with'.[77]

On the address, 6 Feb. 1824, Canning, goaded by Brougham, affirmed his undiminished support for Catholic relief, which prompted Peel to declare his unabated hostility, 'with some display of bad temper', as Fremantle thought.[78] He opposed Curwen's motion for papers on the criminal justice of the Isle of Man, 18 Feb., and Grattan's for information on Catholic office-holders, 19 Feb. On 24 Feb. he replied to and secured the withdrawal of Williams's motion for inquiry into chancery delays and defended Eldon personally. The speech was a great success, but Peel was not blind to the problems of chancery administration, and soon afterwards he set up a commission of inquiry, in which he took a close personal interest, trying to force it to reach a coherent conclusion.[79] He opposed Martin's motion for the appointment of a select committee on the curbing of cruel sports (as he did all Martin's attempts to legislate on this and related issues), 26 Feb.: his view was that it would result in partial and inappropriate legislation, and that 'the growing intelligence and refinement of the country' would put a stop to these 'evils' (11 Mar. 1825). On 1 Mar. 1824 he made what Fremantle considered an 'admirable speech' in opposition to Abercromby's motion accusing Eldon of a breach of privilege in court, which 'in the early part ... caught the House and carried it with him', though his case was a flimsy one.[80] He contended that contrary to the prayer of silk workers' petitions, 5 Mar., prohibition had harmed that industry, and it was essential to put commerce on 'sound principles'. He said that acquiescence in Lord Althorp's call for information on Irish ribbon societies would set a 'fatal' precedent, 11 Mar. He denied that ministers were temporizing on the abolition of slavery, 16 Mar. He got leave to introduce the aliens bill, defeating two opposition obstructive amendments, 23 Mar. On 25 Mar. he expressed his support for the Irish education commission and restricted the remit of Russell's proposed select committee on the payment of wages from poor rates. He challenged Hume to demonstrate how savings could be made in the military establishments of Guernsey and Jersey, 2 Apr., and endorsed the granting of an additional £500,000 for the building of new churches,

9 Apr. He supported the bill brought into amend the 1823 Irish Tithes Act, 3 May. He opposed William Maberly's motion for an advance of capital to Ireland, 4 May, and Althorp's for inquiry into the state of that country, 11 May, supporting Goulburn's amendment to confine the investigation to the disturbed areas and arguing that ministers had done their best to improve the magistracy and the police and stop illicit distillation. A week later Williams Wynn told Buckingham that at a cabinet meeting Peel, like Liverpool, Wellington and Huskisson, looked 'extremely ill and invalid'.[81] He thought Stuart Wortley's game bill had merit, but urged him to withdraw it for the session and carried this by 120-103, 31 May. He defended the treatment of the unrepentant and provocative blasphemer Richard Carlile in Dorchester gaol, 11 June. On 14 June 1824 he justified renewal of the Irish Insurrection Act. About a week earlier Wellington had consulted him about the Irish militia, and, as the duke told Mrs. Arbuthnot, 7 June

> he took the opportunity of letting out his discontent with the state of affairs, particularly in Ireland, of declaring his repentance that he had ever accepted the ... [home office] and that it would be much better if the four persons concerned in the Irish government were of the Catholic opinion rather than that they should be divided ... I think his feeling is more one of disgust at what passes in Parliament and at his being obliged to be silent when he hears Papists praised and Orangemen abused than it is with anything serious. I ... endeavoured to convince him that if he was out of office his own prudence and sense of duty would induce him to be silent upon such occasions ... I ... urged him to put himself as he ought manfully at the head of Irish affairs and to suggest the measures which his own good sense might suggest to get the better of the evil which is now an impending Roman Catholic rebellion, and to confide in the support of his colleagues; and that as to his inferiors, he must remove them ... if they don't implicitly obey his directions. I fairly *scolded* him, but I don't think I made much impression or did much good, excepting that I hope he will not take any important step without first consulting me.[82]

Peel was not in the best of mental and physical condition at this time, as Plumer Ward told Buckingham, 4 July:

> Lord Maryborough ... thought that ... [Peel] would not be long an object of speculation ... It is certain that he is a very shadow, and there are great fears of his lasting. His looks at present are those of a scarecrow, but this is owing partly to an operation ... upon his eye, the small veins of which he was persuaded to have cut in order to remove a tumour, instead of which the blood has extravasated, and he looks as if he had been in a row in St. Giles's. People, however, say he is only too fond of his wife ... Many ... agree with Lord Maryborough, and place him *hors de combat* as to futurity.

Two weeks later Ward wrote of Peel's supposed jealousy of Robinson's success as chancellor: he 'is, they say, evidently moody and ungracious with his colleagues; in fact in ill health ... The subalterns have noticed a sort of indifference of manners, by no means concealed, on the part of Peel towards Canning'. Yet when he related Canning's complaint in September of 'personal impropriety and unkindness' towards him in cabinet from the Protestants, he stressed that Canning 'always excepts Peel, who, he says, though he has opposed him, has always done it in a fair, open, manly manner'.[83] It was at about this time, according to Denis Le Marchant†, writing seven years later, that Peel told his Oxford tutor Dr. Charles Lloyd that he

> considers a revolution at no great distance – not a bloody one and perhaps not one leading to a republic, but one utterly subversive of the aristocracy and of the present system of carrying on the government. He thinks we may get on quite well after this change as before, but he considers it inevitable.[84]

On 19 Nov. 1824 the king, agitated by the growing influence of the Catholic Association and thinking that his own stance on emancipation was being misrepresented, warned Peel that if things continued as they were he would no longer tolerate leaving the question open in cabinet. As commanded, Peel showed this potentially destructive letter to Wellington, who favoured ignoring it, whereas Peel felt that they must either show it to Liverpool or return it to the king. Arbuthnot persuaded the duke that it was vital to inform the premier, and, after Wellington had contacted Knighton, the king instructed Peel to put the letter into Liverpool's hands. When he did so, Liverpool agreed with him that it was best to take no notice of it; but to ensure that the situation was kept under control Peel secured an audience with the king and successfully asked him not to say anything which would upset the existing state of affairs when he saw Liverpool. There the matter rested.[85] Alerted by Goulburn at the end of October to the pressing need to curb the Association, Peel considered the problem and consulted colleagues, but was initially frustrated by Wellesley's failure to say whether or not he thought legal action might be taken. Eventually Wellesley pronounced in favour of referring the question to the select committee on the disturbed districts. Peel dismissed this option, preferring a vigorous executive measure, and from 14 Dec. 1824 until 20 Jan. 1825, when the draft was laid before the cabinet, he worked on it with Goulburn, Plunket and the English law officers. The strain under which he was working was noticed on 2 Jan. by Charles Long*, who told Lord Lonsdale that 'judging from his manner it is impossible to suppose anything but that the state of ... [Ireland] annoys him much'; but he was in a better mood the following week.[86]

On the address, 4 Feb. 1825, Peel asserted that the continued existence of the Association was 'not consistent with the popular principles and liberties' of parliamentary government. He spoke in support of the bill to suppress it, 10 Feb., when he drew a distinction between the Catholic and Constitutional Associations. Fremantle thought he 'did very well', as did Bankes, and Nicholl reckoned that his low-key speech was 'excellent, varied in manner, good in matter'.[87] There was a curious episode on 15 Feb., when Canning, proclaiming that his devotion to the Catholic cause had cost him 'the first wish of his heart, the representation of Oxford [University]', 'laid hold of Peel's shoulder awkwardly, and wished him "a long possession of the mistress he had lost"'. Peel, according to Hobhouse, 'apparently not prepared for the familiar wishes of his colleague, shrugged his shoulder and looked uncomfortable'.[88] Nicholl liked his 'animated and excellent speech' against Brougham's motion to allow the Association to be defended by counsel at the bar of the House, 18 Feb., but Hobhouse recalled how he 'got into a lamentable scrape' by denouncing the Association member Hamilton Rowan, a former United Irishman, as 'an attainted traitor'. In reply Brougham, supplied with information by O'Connell and Sheil, who were under the gallery, pointed out that Rowan had been pardoned and appointed a magistrate:

> Never did minister get such a whipping ... Peel looked so red and so silly ... and we so ... cheered ... [Brougham], that a bystander would have thought the opposition certain of a majority; yet when ministers came to divide, after the exposure of their secretary, they had a majority of 222 ... to 89.

Hobhouse recorded that at the end of the debate 'Peel actually came up to Brougham and told him he was much gratified by his speech' and that Burdett explained this 'scarcely credible' act by surmising that Peel 'was so stunned and stupefied by the blow, that he scarcely knew what he said or did'. Wilson, who 'never saw a being, a thing so prostrated as Peel', attributed it to 'false taste'. Subsequent enquiries by Peel revealed that Rowan had not been made a magistrate, and he threw this information back in Brougham's face on the third reading of the bill, 25 Feb.[89] On 1 Mar. Peel opposed Burdett's motion to consider Catholic claims. The motion was carried by 13 votes, and a relief bill was brought in. Peel recorded his hostility to it, 22 Mar., but reserved his opposition for the second reading. Meanwhile he discussed by letter with Gregory and others in Ireland the proposed securities or 'wings', namely the disfranchisement of the Irish 40*s.* freeholders and payment by the state of the Catholic priests. He told Gregory that while there was 'apathy' in the country at large about emancipation, he was 'not prepared to make any compromise'. On balance, he concluded that these measures would harm rather than safeguard Protestant interests, and he told the House as much, 28 Mar.[90] He presented several anti-Catholic petitions, including one from Bolton Dissenters, 18 Apr., and the synod of Glasgow, 19 Apr. Agar Ellis thought he spoke 'tolerably' well against the second reading of the relief bill, 21 Apr., when he said that it 'diminished the security of our Protestant establishments, and thereby threatened the foundations of civil and religious liberty'.[91] Opposing the Irish franchise bill, 26 Apr., he stated that he was 'reluctant to begin his career as a parliamentary reformer by disfranchising, almost without examination, a large portion of the electors' of Ireland. He maintained that payment of the priests had been similarly under researched, 29 Apr. On 10 1825 May he spoke against the third reading of the relief bill, which was carried by 248-227. Meanwhile, there had developed a serious crisis in the cabinet, for, as Liverpool had feared, on 29 Apr. 1825 Peel, feeling completely isolated on the front bench, where Canning, Huskisson, Robinson and Williams Wynn all supported emancipation and seemed to him to be 'leaguing with the most factious of the opposition', tendered his resignation to Liverpool. Discussions, negotiations and arm-twisting continued for over two weeks, with Liverpool threatening to resign if Peel did and advise the king to send for Canning, though he was willing to stay in office if Peel relented. Wellington and, decisively, Bathurst, worked on Peel and weakened his resolve, arguing that he would wreck the government entirely, ruin his reputation as a statesman and fatally undermine the Protestant cause. In a last turn of events following the bill's rejection by the Lords, 17 May, Canning tried to persuade Liverpool to end cabinet neutrality on the Catholic question. At the decisive discussion, 24 May 1825, Peel insisted that he would resign rather than compromise. Canning got no support from the pro-Catholic ministers, and two days later he gave way. Peel agreed to stay in office at least until a new Parliament had given a verdict on the issue.[92]

On other issues in the 1825 session, Peel defended the grant for the Irish linen board, 18 Mar., secured an increase in London police magistrates' salaries, 21 Mar., agreed to go into committee on William Smith's Dissenters' marriages bill, 25 Mar., and persuaded Peter Moore to drop his measure to repeal the Bubble Act, 29 Mar. He acquiesced, as prearranged, in Hobhouse's motion for leave to introduce a bill to shorten children's hours of cotton factory labour, 5 May, but on 16 and 31 May voiced doubts about it and recommended Hobhouse to confine it to 'making his [Peel] father's bill operative'.[93] That day he supported the government's resolutions on judges' salaries, but on 20 May he opposed Brougham's motion to make puisne judges immoveable. He said that Alderman Wood's London tithes bill 'attacked private rights', 17 May, got rid of Spring Rice's motion for copies of correspondence with Wellesley on religious animosities, 26 May, and supported the grants for the duchess of Kent and duke of Cumberland, 27, 30 May. On 28 May he reluctantly attended the Pitt Club dinner, where his health was drunk with acclaim.[94] On 31 May he replied to Williams's criticisms of chancery administration and denied that the appointment of the commission, which had not yet reported, was 'a mere parliamentary manoeuvre to stifle effective inquiry'. He opposed and defeated Burdett's motion for production of the commission's existing evidence, 7 June, but Burdett carried motions for information on arrears and bankruptcy commitments, 30 June, 5 July. Eldon was 'offended', but Peel told Liverpool that he could not resist such motions indefinitely unless the commissioners' report was completed and laid before Parliament. By the end of February 1826 his pressure had had the desired effect, and he then initiated legislation. A chancery regulation bill was brought in in May 1826, but it was overtaken by the dissolution. (He was reported in June 1825 to have 'offended' Eldon by taking this 'reforming ground'.)[95] He backed Canning's resistance to Hume's motion for inquiry next session into the Irish church and tithes, 14 June 1825. In late July, when Peel was holidaying near Margate, the king vindictively inconvenienced him by changing at the last minute the date of a privy council meeting, observing to Knighton that he hoped this would be 'a useful lesson to him for the future'.[96]

During the financial crash of late 1825, Peel discussed the currency problem with Thomas Attwood†, who was recommended to him by Sir Robert, and, although he had no faith in the small note circulation which they advocated, he took Attwood to see Liverpool and Robinson. Keen to seize the opportunity of rationalizing the banking system, he played a leading part in the cabinet deliberations of January 1826 which produced bills banning the issue of new notes under £5 and authorizing the establishment of joint-stock banks beyond 65 miles from London and of branches of the Bank of England.[97] He endorsed these in the House, 13 Feb., arguing that 'to stand gazing at the bank in idle expectation, now that the river was passable, would be an irreparable mistake'. Abercromby judged this speech to be 'about the best I ever heard him make' and that he and Huskisson had outshone Canning and Robinson.[98] On 17 Feb. Peel reported to Wellington, who was abroad:

> We carried our [banking] measure through the ... Commons very triumphantly ... Great surprise was very generally felt ... for it was supposed that the country bankers had a great influence in the House and would exert it. The opposition supported the measures very fairly, with the exception of Baring and one or two of the commercial Whigs. Hume will give as much trouble as he can on the estimates, but I think we have every prospect of an easy session. It is quite clear that the Catholic question will not be brought on ... I trust we shall hear less than usual about Ireland ... The House seemed quite satisfied with the assurances which we gave about the measures recommended in the two reports of last year. The opposition in the ... Commons seems particularly slack.[99]

He supported the promissory notes bill, 20, 27 Feb., 7 Mar. He successfully opposed Hume's attempt to abolish the volunteer corps, 3 Mar. That day he informed Wellington that Canning and Huskisson had spoken effectively on the silk trade, but that ministers had been 'placed in a very unpleasant predicament' on the question of an issue of exchequer bills, for which there was a clamour in commercial circles, and had been rescued by the Bank's offer to lend money on deposit of goods. He also explained that, alarmed by Liverpool's apparent threat, echoed by Canning in the House, to resign if the government was defeated on this, he had gone to the premier and 'told him I thought him very wrong in using such language, that if he resigned when the country was in a crisis of financial difficulty ... he would lose all the credit he had gained' and that 'the country would right itself in two or three months, that the man who succeeded him would get all the credit, and he personally all the blame'. He had added that if Liverpool went, he would follow suit. He remained convinced that ministers had been 'right in refusing' to issue bills 'and that had we had consented, we should have defeated our other measures, and not impossibly have had to answer for another bank restriction'.[100] His speech detailing his criminal laws and administration of justice bills, 9 Mar., greatly impressed Tierney, who derived 'infinite satisfaction' from the notion that Eldon 'very much disapproves of what he is doing'.[101] Abercromby, surveying 'the strangest times I have ever seen', perceived Peel's uncomfortable position within the Tory party:

> The only friends that Canning and Huskisson have are a few of the Whigs. The Tories hate what they vote for, and their embarrassment is greatly increased by Peel being pledged to Huskisson's measures ... I always expect that the Tories will trip up any ministry who attempt to act upon liberal policy, and yet it is very difficult to do it, unless the king should die and the duke of York ... reign. Then it would turn upon Peel, who I hear does not feel at ease, although it is quite in his character, being pledged, to go through with it. The greatest proof he gives of his sense is in showing that he is perfectly aware that he has not talents to play a difficult or doubtful game, and that he can only win by steadiness and show of principle that confidence which he has *not* the genius or the talents to command.[102]

Williams Wynn observed that many of the government's supporters were disgruntled with 'our *liberal* and *conciliatory* measures', but that they were made powerless by 'the knowledge that ... [they] have not in their ranks a singe individual of weight and ability to stand forward' in the Commons, and that 'the person whose opinions on the Catholic question would naturally point him out for that purpose, is upon every other subject ... disposed to participate to the fullest extent in the line of policy adopted by his colleagues'.[103] On 20 Mar. Peel spoke against Spring Rice's motion affirming the principle of non-denominational education in Ireland and defended the activities of the Kildare Place Society. He vindicated the president of the board of trade's ministerial salary, 6 Apr., and on the 20th secured leave for the aliens registration bill. Next day he rejected Spring Rice's additional clause to the Irish church rates bill intended to empower Protestant vestries to raise money for maintaining Catholic and Presbyterian churches. He was against George Lamb's proposal to allow defence by counsel in felony trials, 25 Apr. Mrs. Arbuthnot recorded at this time that her husband had recently found Peel suspicious of the motives behind Canning's visit to the Whig Lord Lansdowne at Bowood:

> He is generally dissatisfied with the state of affairs, but then he is generally a great *frondeur*. He does not care for office, and every other word with him is always, 'If they want my office, let them take it. I don't want it'. In this he is sincere, but he is now more than usually irritated. Having refused to enter into intrigues with the king and Knighton, the king has quite cut him and never sees him; Lord Liverpool never sees him because he never sees anybody when he can possibly help it; so ... Peel is left entirely to the duties of his department.[104]

On 1 May he explained how he had sent troops to restore order in the distressed manufacturing areas, but at the same time expressed sympathy and admiration for those who were suffering patiently and urged the wealthy to reach into their pockets. He fully endorsed the government's emergency proposals to open the ports to bonded and foreign corn, 5, 12 May. Creevey commented:

> If a good Ultra Tory government could be made, Canning and Huskisson must inevitably be ruined by this daring step. You never heard such language as the old sticklers apply to them; and, unhappily for Toryism, that prig Peel seems as deeply bitten by 'liberality', in every way but on the Catholic question, as any of his fellows.[105]

He replied to Williams's motion on chancery administration and praised Eldon, 18 May. On 26 May 1826 he advocated the postponement of Russell's resolutions condemning electoral bribery until next session, but they were carried by the Speaker's casting vote. He also brought up and defended the report of the select committee on the Scottish and Irish banking systems, which he had chaired, and which he had brought to recommend no significant change.[106] According to Mrs. Arbuthnot, he was 'still more angry' than Wellington at the peerages which Canning obtained for his friends Charles Ellis* and James Stuart Wortley*:

> He told Arbuthnot ... that he quite felt for the state of degradation into which Lord Liverpool was fallen ... but that he had no words to express his contempt and abhorrence of ... Canning ... [whose] conduct this session in staying away whenever unpleasant subjects ... were to be discussed was quite pitiable, and that his dirty intrigues with the king and Knighton were disgusting ... Peel *almost* said he would not remain in a government of which ... Canning was the head, but he said he made it a rule never to make up his mind until the time came. The king wanted to make ... Peel believe that he had attended to his interests, meaning the Protestant cause, in these ... peerages; but ... Peel turned off the conversation and would not discuss the subject with him.[107]

He politely declined a fanciful invitation to allow himself to be nominated for Westminster as the champion of the Protestant cause, and was again returned unopposed for the University.[108]

He told Lord Liverpool, 9 July 1826, that while he was 'well aware of the immense importance of making every possible reduction in the estimates next year', he considered it 'absolutely necessary to maintain a very strong military force in the manufacturing districts', where continued unemployment was breeding discontent.[109] In mid-August he was busy in Whitehall, and told Julia that 'the absence of all those I wish to see on the state of crops in Ireland keeps me in constant occupation, as I am obliged to write to them all instead of settling the business in conversation'.[110] The appalling state of Ireland, where the Catholics had scored some notable successes in the elections and 'party animosities never were higher', was his main concern. As well as directing Goulburn to give him accurate details of the actual and potential military and police forces at the disposal of the government, he indicated to John Leslie Foster*, 3 Nov., that he was becoming resigned to the inevitability of Catholic emancipation, though he still could not persuade himself that it would end sectarian violence. Asking Foster to try to ascertain the 'whole truth respecting Irish popery and its adjuncts', he commented, 'When I see it inevitable, I shall (taking due care to free my motives from all suspicion) try to make the best terms for the future security of the Protestant'. But he assured Sir George Hill*, who feared that ministers were allowing the revived Catholic Association to run amok in the hope of persuading English Members of the necessity for a settlement to end the chaos, that he was 'no party to any preconcerted forbearance towards the ... Association' and knew 'nothing of compromise': 'I am as unfettered on the ... question, as able to offer unqualified opposition to further concessions, as I ever was at any period of my life'.[111] When the cabinet decided in December to divert troops from Ireland to the Portuguese expedition, Peel calmed the agitated Goulburn with assurances of support for any emergency measures he might have to adopt; and after several weeks of frustration waiting for Wellesley and the Irish law officers to supply accurate information as a basis for deciding whether to prosecute the Association, he was relieved to find the balance of opinion firmly against such action.[112] In the House, 22 Nov. 1826, he opposed 'not the principle but the expediency' of Althorp's resolutions condemning electoral bribery. He expressed sympathy for the distressed weavers of western Scotland, 5 Dec., but declined to raise 'false hopes' of government aid. He advised Hume against 'precipitate' legislation to end the ban on the export of machinery, reminding him of the mess created by his hasty intervention on the Combination Acts, 6 Dec. Next day he called for consideration of the tricky question of subsidized emigration to be shelved until the select committee's report and evidence were to hand and persuaded Hume to drop his motion for information on Lord Charles Somerset's† conduct at the Cape. On 9 Dec. Abercromby wrote to Lord Carlisle:

> I am very much struck with the industry and good sense of Peel ... On all the topics, whether it be emigration, machinery or corn laws, he is always ready to take his part with promptitude, decision and good knowledge of what has been said or written ... He bids fairly to be the minister of England, more so than any of his competitors, the Catholic question once got over; and then I think his tone and principles will be on a level with the age.

On 13 Dec. 1826 Abercromby reported the striking 'cordiality' with which Peel had the previous night 'cheered' Brougham's reply to Canning's exposition of the Portuguese issue.[113] At Sudbourne at Christmas Peel told Arbuthnot that he was 'very much disgusted' with Robinson's expressed desire to retire from the exchequer, but said that if he was pressed to take the office

> he would undertake it for the very reasons that made Mr. R. decline it, namely that there were difficulties, which he should not the least mind; that otherwise he should certainly prefer his present office ... Peel told Arbuthnot he was quite certain the king did not care a farthing for Canning ... and only valued him as the greatest and best jobber to do his dirty work. He said that a short time ago he was with the king, who said to him, 'Ah, Peel, what a misfortune it was that I had not a private conversation with you and misunderstood your sentiments before you left Edinburgh [in August 1822]. All the misfortunes that have happened since would have been avoided'.[114]

After the death of the duke of York, 5 Jan. 1827, Peel was 'heart and soul' for the successful effort to have Wellington appointed his successor as commander-in-chief, despite the king's 'monstrous' attempt to renege on a promise.[115] After attending the funeral at Windsor, 20 Jan., he went with Wellington to Stratfield Saye, where he told Arbuthnot of his suspicions that Canning (who had fallen ill) disapproved of the appointment, was hoping to get Liverpool to persuade Wellington to quit the cabinet and was even 'in some sort of communication with some of the opposition'.[116] Holland, noting a mounting 'clamour' against Canning, remarked that 'unless Peel is earnestly and eagerly with him on all other points but that of the Catholics, I should think his power ... is very precarious'.[117] On 7 Feb., the day before Parliament reconvened, Peel sent Huskisson a letter from distressed handloom weavers attributing their 'unmerited distress' to 'the discovery of the power loom', and reflected that he had 'better tell them the truth in the kindest manner in which I can', that technological progress could not be arrested, though their suffering was 'very lamentable, and I fear very irremediable'.[118] Canning's illness had made Peel acting leader of the House, and on 12 Feb. he moved the address of condolence on the death of York: 'not in very good style, weakish, and thin blooded', thought John Evelyn

Denison*, while Greville deemed his performance 'poor and *jejeune*'.[119] He acquiesced, with 'certain reservations', in the renewal of the emigration select committee, 15 Feb. Next day he defended the proposed grant to the duke of Clarence, and he voted thus, 16 Mar. Mrs. Arbuthnot recorded in mid-February that Liverpool and Peel were again talking of being 'driven out' on the Catholic question and that Peel was 'perfectly sincere and would be glad to go', knowing that time was on his side for a return to office 'in a more agreeable position than his now is in the government'.[120] Liverpool's incapacitating stroke on 17 Feb. took the matter out of his control and changed the political landscape. After a cabinet deliberation, Peel went to Brighton to see the king and Canning, who was recuperating there; and it was agreed to give no public indication that the premier's recovery was out of the question and to continue with business in the normal fashion.[121] On 21 Feb. Peel, disclaiming party prejudice, agreed to a full inquiry into the allegations of electoral interference against Northampton corporation. (His brief dealings with a deputation from the borough who had invited him to recommend his brother Jonathan as a government candidate gave the committee's Whig members some ammunition.)[122] He got leave to reintroduce his bills to amend, simplify and consolidate the criminal laws on a basis of 'reason and common sense', together with one abolishing benefit of clergy, 22 Feb. They became law that session as 7 & 8 Geo. IV, cc. 27-31. He opposed Althorp's proposal to establish a permanent select committee to consider all election petitions alleging bribery, 26 Feb., and next day, endorsing the attorney-general Sir John Copley's bill to separate bankruptcy from chancery administration, defended Eldon against Whig attacks. He presented and endorsed petitions against Catholic relief from his constituency and the Protestant noblemen, gentry and landowners of Ireland, 2 Mar., and on the 6th spoke in his usual terms against Burdett's motion to consider Catholic claims. Agar Ellis thought he 'spoke tolerably well, but heavily', while Denison judged that he performed 'poorly'. The anti-Catholic Sir Robert Inglis* enjoyed his 'lecture' to Plunket on the danger of stirring popular passions in Ireland, but Hobhouse assessed the speech as 'unfair and affectedly candid'.[123] The motion was unexpectedly defeated by four votes, but any pleasure which Peel might have felt was subsumed in the uncertainty created by the unresolved problem of the succession to Liverpool, for which he and Canning were widely seen as the main contenders. On 9 Mar., according to Mrs. Arbuthnot, he told her husband that he 'did not care one straw about office, and that ... when he spoke ... on the Catholic question, he did so in the firm belief that he should resign next morning', but that the result of the division had in some ways strengthened Canning's hand.[124] On 8 Mar. he defended the government's adjustment of the corn laws against protectionist complaints. On the 12th he refuted Wood's assertion that ministers had been 'bullied' by the landed interest to overprotect barley and replied to Hobhouse's rant; and on 19 Mar. he saw off Newport's motion for a fixed duty on foreign flour by 152-116. He opposed inquiry into supposed electoral malpractice by Leicester corporation, 15 Mar., when the Whig Member Lord Howick told his father Grey that his speech was 'so exceedingly unfair and so well answered that the feeling of the House was entirely changed', and there was loud cheering from the opposition benches when the motion's defeat by only 24 votes was announced, which made Peel appear 'very angry'.[125] He said that the charge that the Kildare Place Society was trying to convert Catholics to Protestantism was 'grossly exaggerated', 19 Mar. When Russell asked him if he would support repeal of the Test Acts, 23 Mar., he refused to answer, for 'sufficient unto the day was the vote thereof'. He was inclined to set up a commission of inquiry into the laws of real property, 27 Mar., said an 'experiment by a partial operation' of legitimizing the sale of game might be beneficial, 28 Mar., and opposed the motion for information on the Lisburn Orange procession, 29 Mar. He justified the calling out of the military to restore order at the Carlisle election, 3 Apr., when he urged Newport to withdraw his resolutions on the laws concerning the rebuilding of churches in Ireland and enshrine them in a bill, indicating that he was not averse to the notion of exempting Catholics from unfair burdens. That day he persuaded Hume to confine his proposed inquiry into the laws of imprisonment for debt to the limits set by previous investigations. He opposed Whittle Harvey's motion for information on chancery administration, 5 Apr. 1827, and next day defended against Trench's tirade the decision not to prosecute the Catholic Association. A week later, when Hobhouse noted that he 'seated himself on the corner of the treasury bench, but ... did not look at all tranquil or magnanimous',[126] he resigned from the home office, having, along with his cabinet colleagues Wellington, Eldon, Westmorland, Bathurst and Melville, declined to serve in Canning's new ministry. He did so, essentially, because he did not trust Canning personally, even though the Catholic question was to be left open in cabinet and the king had given him a personal guarantee that it would not be pressed as a government measure. While he would have been willing to remain in office with Canning under a reputable 'Protestant' peer (he had rejected Canning's offer of the foreign secretaryship with a peerage), he argued that he could not act under a premier whose personal views were notoriously favourable to Catholic claims, especially at the home office, where he would wish to remain, with ultimate responsibility for Ireland: he wished above all to preserve his 'character as a public man'. In truth, he was still trapped in the strait jacket of his increasingly uncomfortable position as the champion of the Tory anti-Catholics.[127] The episode caused a breach between Peel and Croker, who remained in as secretary to the admiralty; it was patched up in the autumn, but their relations were never again as cordial as before.[128]

In mid-April 1827 Goulburn urged Peel to 'take some opportunity of having it distinctly known why you declined continuing in office', as 'the activity of Canning's friends has created a general opinion even among some of the country gentlemen that your decision was part of a cabal against Canning and the king'. Mrs. Arbuthnot also noted this development.[129] Lord Londonderry reported that Wellington had told him that he and Peel wished 'to remain as the great Tory party ready for the king to fall back on'; but the Whig Lord Tavistock* did not believe that Peel 'will ever incur the fearful responsibility of shutting the door for ever upon the Catholics, and thus driving Ireland into rebellion, by taking the reins of a government *exclusively* Protestant'.[130] In the House, 1 May, Peel made a statement of his reasons for resigning, which he assigned to the incompatibility between his and Canning's views on the Catholic question. He defended himself and his fellow seceders, especially Wellington, against the charge of intrigue. Mrs. Arbuthnot thought 'nothing could be more triumphant or more perfect', and Agar Ellis considered it 'a good and temperate speech'; but the duke of Rutland commented that the peroration boasting of his achievements in office was 'too much trumpeting forth of his own public services'.[131] Tavistock's father the duke of Bedford considered it 'in some respects a manly and straightforward statement' but also 'an able and an artful one', in that it had conceded that emancipation was 'nearer its accomplishment by the appointment of the coalition ministry': 'it *clenches the nail*, and leaves Canning without retreat'.[132] On 3 May, however, Peel made what Canning reported to the king as 'a violent attack upon the supporters of the ministry', specifically Brougham and Burdett, who had criticized him for his opposition to reform and seized on his 'propensity to self-praise'. Canning thought he had thrown away 'all the moderation which he had professed ... on the first night', and Hobhouse that it 'showed the Peelites and Peel himself resolved upon opposition'.[133] On 7 May Peel opposed, with ministers, Gascoyne's motion for inquiry into the shipping interest.[134] The staunch anti-Catholics Lords Colchester, Kenyon and Mansfield and Inglis, who thought Peel had been utterly 'wrong' in resigning, wanted to move a resolution in the Lords in support of the 'Protestant constitution', but Peel talked Mansfield out of it.[135] When Tavistock criticized the Tory opponents of the ministry, 11 May, Peel denied being 'one of a factious and rancorous opposition', but said he could not place confidence in the government until its final composition and policies were known, even though it seemed unlikely that it would promote reform or repeal the Test Acts. Canning thought Peel's tone was 'greatly moderated', but the Whig Charles Richard Fox* commented that although he had 'declined twice being head of the opposition' he 'still sits with his brother-in-law Dawson and his own brothers close to him, all of whom are loudly and outrageously violent'.[136] Hobhouse and Huskisson, a member of the cabinet, agreed that 'Peel had been let off very easily' for his devious conduct, and Littleton informed his friend William Leigh, 19 May, that

> Peel is *feeding* his forces, consisting of no matter what complexion, provided they differ with the government. While he is professing neutrality in the House, he is doing all he can covertly to organize an opposition. But I really do not see what he will find to quarrel about, he is so pledged by his past conduct.[137]

Peel did not oppose the introduction of the Coventry magistracy bill, 22 May, but on 18 June he spoke and voted in the minority against its third reading. He presented but dissented from the prayer of petitions from Norwich weavers and manufacturers for legislation to fix local wages, 31 May, when he endorsed the attorney-general Sir James Scarlett's refusal to repeal the Newspaper Stamp Duty Act, but remarked on the absence of some ministerial Whigs who had opposed it in 1819. On 18 June he opposed Western's protectionist resolutions on the corn laws and supported Canning's proposal to admit warehoused corn as a temporary expedient, but, as Mackintosh saw it, on the anniversary of Waterloo 'worked himself into a paroxysm of enthusiasm for Wellington', whose amendment in the Lords had forced Canning to abandon the original bill, reproving Alexander Baring for his attack on the duke.[138] On 22 June he presented a bill, which was subsequently set aside for future consideration, to facilitate the recovery of small debts in county courts. On 14 July 1827, just returned from the country 'in high spirits', according to Arbuthnot, he concurred in Wellington's decision not to obey the king's summons for a talk: 'Peel ... is now convinced that the duke's conduct upon the corn bill has been productive of great good, and ... that we must have a systematic opposition next session, and keep no terms with the government'.[139]

Peel was shocked by Canning's premature death, 8 Aug. 1827, but, anxious to avoid 'the appearance even of being in the way', he brought forward by a day his departure with his family to Maresfield in Sussex (rented from the Shelleys). Kept informed by Arbuthnot, Sir Henry Hardinge* and others of the negotiations for the formation of a patched-up coalition ministry under the hapless Lord Goderich, he wrote to Arbuthnot, 17 Aug.:

> I have long foreseen that the Catholic question must place me in the position in which I am at present. If Lord Liverpool had lived, the great probability is that he and I would have been out of office at this time. I do not at all regret either that the king did not send for me after Canning's death; still less ... that I have received no communication from Lord Goderich. It would not have been an easy matter for the duke of Wellington and for me to form under existing circumstances a strong government in the ... Commons ... I should think it not improbable that the king had made my exclusion from office a *sine qua non* on the appointment of ... Goderich. It is very natural in a man, and particularly when that man is a king, to hate another who declines to trust him.

He thought that as a soldier Wellington could not 'with propriety' have refused the king's offer to resume the command of the army, and insisted that 'I view all that passes with very great complacency ... quite satisfied that no course of action would either be justifiable or successful that was not founded on public principle'.[140] Billy Holmes* and Lord Lowther* lamented that 'a regular Tory opposition cannot be formed, because there is no leader', and Peel, the only feasible one, 'though able, honest and high-minded', was 'too selfish, too proud and haughty in his manner to have a personal following', and, being without 'good manners or any courtier-like character', was 'disliked by the king'.[141] In mid-November Peel had 'a long political conversation' with Colchester, to whom he expressed his abhorrence of the wanton destruction of the Turkish fleet at Navarino and remarked on 'the incongruous composition of parties in the present administration, which rendered its duration impossible'; but when Colchester encouraged him to 'put himself at the head of an army of observation' and told him that 'the country would think itself safe ... if *he* were the leading minister in the Commons, and ... Wellington head of the government', he 'listened in silence and with much complacency', and then 'professed, very unaffectedly, to disclaim all ambition for power, or the common appendages of office, but did not disclaim such a situation if really called upon by the country'.[142] In early December 1827 Peel and Huskisson exchanged conciliatory messages, brokered by Littleton, expressing mutual satisfaction that Huskisson's reported statement that he would resign if Peel entered the ministry was a fiction.[143] At the end of the year Mackintosh was under the impression (probably mistaken) that 'Peel confidently assures his followers of his speedy and triumphal restoration'.[144]

On the collapse of the Goderich administration in early January 1828, the king turned to Wellington, who on the 9th summoned Peel to London. In the ensuing discussions he insisted on placing the new ministry on as broad a basis as possible, convinced that an exclusively Protestant government could not stand and also anxious to secure some able backing in the Commons, which he was designated to lead as home secretary: 'I cannot undertake the business of the ... Commons without more assistance than the mere Tory party ... would afford me', he told Julia, to whom he confided that 'my heart is set upon home and not upon ambition'. He made clear to close friends his contempt for the 'blockhead' Tory extremists: 'I care not for the dissatisfaction of the Ultra Tories. This country ought not, and cannot, be governed on any other principles than those of firmness ... combined with moderation.' After the successful termination of painful negotiations with Huskisson and the leading Canningites, who agreed to join the ministry, Peel asked the Irish under-secretary Gregory:

> What must have been the inevitable fate of a government composed of Goulburn, Sir John Beckett, Wetherell, and myself? Supported by very warm friends, no doubt, but no [more] than warm friends, being prosperous country gentlemen, fox-hunters ... most excellent men, who will attend one night, but who will not leave their favourite pursuits to sit up till two or three o'clock fighting questions of detail on which ... a government must have a majority. We could not have stood creditably a fortnight.[145]

Mrs. Arbuthnot blamed Peel, 'whose fault is not being courageous in the ... Commons [and] wishes to surround himself with all the speakers', for the inclusion of the hated Huskissonites, and thought Wellington at bottom shared her repugnance to the arrangement; but Croker told Hertford that the duke had admitted that 'what Peel said is perfectly true – that those who are for forming an exclusive ministry, expect that I am to go into the House of Commons with *half a party* to fight *a party and a half*'.[146] On 23 Jan. 1828 the king had a long interview with Peel in which, he informed Knighton, he 'had given a very strong lecture respecting his conduct both as to the past, as well as to the future, and which ... [Wellington] not only *highly* approved of, but was delighted at it'.[147] Peel entertained 32 prominent supporters of the ministry in the 'very handsome' picture gallery of his house on the eve of the session to give them a preview of the king's speech.[148]

At the home office, Peel continued his work of legal reform. His bill of 1828 for the recovery of small debts ran into problems over the compensation of holders of patent officers in the higher courts, and he abandoned it for the session, 23 June. He referred the question to the common law commission set up on Brougham's initiative in 1828, and on 18 Feb. 1830, in a review of the direction which legal reform might take, he got leave for a measure to regulate the fees of patent office-holders. He subsequently supported Brougham's plan to reform local jurisdictions. In May 1828 he brought in two bills, inherited from his predecessor Lord Lansdowne, to change the method of receiving evidence (allowing Quakers and Moravians to give evidence on affirmation and other relaxations) and to consolidate the laws governing offences against the person. They became law as 9 Geo. IV, cc. 31 and 32. By his consolidating Acts, 1825-8, 278 statues were repealed and their surviving provisions enshrined in eight Acts.[149] On 18 Feb. 1830 Peel outlined a number of measures to promote further rationalization, relating to the laws governing justices of the peace, the coinage and forgery offences, of which the latter, the subject of long discussions with the attorney-general Scarlett, William Gregson, the legal draftsman, and a few senior judges, was the most important. The bill which Peel introduced on 1 Apr. 1830 reduced the tangle of existing legislation to four clauses, one of which specified the offences for which the death penalty was to be retained: forgery of negotiable securities, bank notes, wills involving personal estate, the great seal, privy seal and sign manual. Brougham, Mackintosh, Russell and others pressed for a greater mitigation of penalties and were backed by a strong petitioning movement from bankers and company directors, but Peel would not give way, as he declared on 24 May. On the third reading, 7 June, in a thin House, Mackintosh carried by 13 votes an amendment replacing transportation for the death penalty for all forgery offences except that of wills. Peel was annoyed, but the cabinet decided to let the measure go to the Lords as it was. There the amendment was successfully opposed by lord chancellor Lyndhurst and others, so that the bill was passed into law as 11 Geo. IV & 1 Gul. IV, c. 66.[150] Peel's most lasting achievement in his second spell at the home office was the establishment of a rationally organized metropolitan police force for London, where crime was increasing at a frightening rate. On 28 Feb. 1828 he secured the appointment of a select committee, whose report recommended a restructuring of the police; and on 15 Apr. 1829 he brought in a bill to unite all the existing forces under one authority and meet costs from local taxation. It became law on 19 June 1829 as 10 Geo. IV, c. 44, setting up a force with jurisdiction within a ten-mile radius from Charing Cross (except the City), initially under the supervision of two magistrates and a receiver. It set the pattern, as Peel wished, for the establishment of similar forces in large towns in the rest of the country over the next 25 years.[151]

In the House, 12 Feb. 1828, Peel warned against divesting the lord chancellor of 'political consequence' when Taylor moved for information on chancery administration. He opposed and secured the withdrawal of Hobhouse and Burdett's motion for a vote of thanks to Admiral Codrington for Navarino, 14 Feb. In cabinet the previous day he had spoken 'of the absolute necessity of reducing expenditure, as we have no surplus and cannot impose taxes', and got Melville to concede that there might be scope for reductions in the number of seamen. In moving the appointment of the finance committee (on which he did not himself sit), 15 Feb., he reviewed the state of the finances 'as they really are', as his cabinet colleague Ellenborough noted, and gave an assurance of ministers' desire to promote economy in public expenditure. He had persuaded Sir Henry Parnell, a Whig, to chair the committee, and Littleton, who was also a member (and on 17 Feb. witnessed Peel being seized with an alarming 'fit of the whooping cough' at Sir Thomas Lawrence's house in Bedford Square, where 'his countenance was full of disappointment' at the portrait of Huskisson) 'thought it "a fair one"'.[152] He sarcastically thanked Waithman for his unwitting endorsement of the wisdom of appointing it, 22 Feb., and on the 25th explained that it had been impossible to include army and navy officers without making it too unwieldy. On 18 Feb. he claimed to know nothing of 'any secret influence' which might have brought down the Goderich ministry.[153] Next day he welcomed 'Bum' Gordon's bill to regulate lunatic asylums and made suggestions for its improvement. Agar Ellis thought he 'spoke wretchedly' when 'most foolishly' opposing Russell's motion for repeal of the Test Acts (his view was that 'there was no practical grievance' and that it was best to 'continue this sort of quiet'), which was carried by 44 votes, 26 Feb. The cabinet reached no immediate decision on how to respond. On 28 Feb. Peel urged the

House to adopt some measure short of full repeal, and, when this was rejected, to postpone further consideration for a few days. Lord Milton accused him of trying to wreck his opponents' success by obstruction. Peel lost his temper, retorted that he would now refuse any postponement and stalked out of the House to eat his dinner. When informed that Sir George Warrender, a ministerialist, was attacking him, he returned to the chamber and said that he had no intention of voting on the question. His petulant behaviour did him no good.[154] When the cabinet renewed discussion of the problem, he appeared to be 'indifferent', but after consultation with the two archbishops and several bishops he came up with an alternative declaration binding the taker not to injure the Church of England, which was adopted by the cabinet. At the prelates' request, Peel reluctantly agreed to propose this himself, and he did so on 18 Mar. 1828, when he successfully moved the insertion of the declaration, which Russell later described as 'useless and feeble', in the bill. In doing so, according to Canning's nephew Lord George Cavendish Bentinck*, he 'disgusted and enraged many of his followers' among the 'High Tories', who had attended in the expectation of a fight being made. Rutland complained that Peel was 'speaking too much for popularity' and that the declaration 'must furnish a most embarrassing precedent for the Catholic question', and Croker deemed it 'another step to Catholic emancipation'; but Bedford remarked that 'Peel behaves most handsomely'.[155] The measure went through the Lords with only a minor change to the wording of the declaration, which Russell accepted.[156]

Peel said that Irish Catholics had no claim on Parliament by the Treaty of Limerick, 6 Mar. 1828. He opposed as 'impracticable' Sykes's motion for inquiry into the franchise in boroughs with a county jurisdiction, 11 Mar., and persuaded him to bring in bills to deal with individual towns, such as Kingston-upon-Hull. That day he observed that unless the existing system of Irish education could be improved, it was best not to tinker with it. On Greene's tithes commutation bill, 'pregnant with injustice to the Church of England', he moved and carried by 81-29 an instruction to the committee to consider limiting the duration of agreements to tax stipends. On 15 Mar. Mrs. Arbuthnot recorded the first in a litany of criticisms of Peel as leader of the House and the Tory party:

> There never was such folly as ... [his] anxiety to have speakers on the treasury bench, and he enjoys now the full consequence of his sacrifices; not one of the Canning party have said five words since the session began ... The same cowardice and want of confidence in himself makes him court the liberals, and in point of fact he is more liberal than any of them. He is for giving up everything, and as the duke is anything but a liberal or a coward, he is for fighting everything, and it produces very unpleasant discussions in the cabinet and, what is still worse, Mr. Peel is daily losing ground in the opinion of the public.

Two days later she commented that 'the Tory party find him ill tempered and cowardly' and 'we hear from everyone that he offends everybody by his arrogance'.[157] While this was to a large extent dictated by Mrs. Arbuthnot's reactionary Toryism and partiality for Wellington, there was clearly a serious problem. Hobhouse heard from a friend of the premier that he was 'sensible he had got together a very poor cabinet, especially in the Commons', and blamed this on Peel's stipulations of January.[158] Ellenborough recorded that 'Peel does not much like his position in the Commons. He is not sufficiently well supported. He will fight anything, but then, he says, if he is defeated, he will resign'. Peel told Croker that 'the country gentlemen complained if ministers yielded, complained more if ministers were in a minority, but would not take the trouble of attending to put them in a majority'.[159] Colchester thought there was 'amongst the Members ... a general feeling of dissatisfaction at the wavering and unsettled state of the House ... without sufficient authority in the leading minister'.[160] Peel's quick temper, sulkiness, arrogance and coldness made matters worse. Wellington and John Herries* told Mrs. Arbuthnot that in cabinet on 19 Mar. he was 'in such a furious passion that he became as pale as death, and that really it was impossible to argue any question with him'. On 23 Mar., she wrote, Arbuthnot and Bathurst called on Peel, who had been 'so cross they did not either like to encounter him alone':

> He was very sulky when they first went in, and at last began talking of the House ... and his own position there, which he said was painful and distressing to him ... He said he was anxious to take a high tone and to fight the liberal principles, but that, all the time a debate was going on, his colleagues on the treasury bench were urging him to give up every point that was at all contested by the liberals ... In the meantime not one of them will say a word ... Holmes was on the same story, bitterly complaining of ... Peel's conduct which, he says, disgusts the Tories in the House to such a degree that they will not stay and vote ... He ended yesterday with Mr. A. and Ld. Bathurst by having talked himself into good humour; and one cannot but feel that his position must be very painful with such colleagues, but then why would he have them? ... Already the Tories are beginning to suspect ... Peel of acting unfairly by the duke, and of adopting this low tone out of jealousy. This is very unjust, for ... Peel is an honest, honourable, upright man; all his faults proceed from a want of political courage.[161]

From a Whig perspective, Holland was sure that Peel, 'if he in some degree disarms hostility by an appearance of moderation, loses ... authority and influence in the House'; and Bedford agreed that he had 'not the *calibre* necessary to lead the ... Commons in such times as these', but praised him as 'an honest man' who was 'hardly dealt by, by the disciples of Canning. If he acts ill, you say he is intolerant; if he acts well, he is hypocritical!'.[162]

Peel's peevishness owed something to the tensions within the cabinet. There was a potentially destructive wrangle over the proposed corn bill, with Wellington, Aberdeen, Bathurst and Ellenborough wishing to incorporate the duke's successful amendment of 1827 or increase duties and Huskisson and his associates, but also Peel, Goulburn and Melville, favouring the adoption of a modified version of Canning's original measure of relaxation. Peel worked for compromise and, after an initial stalemate, persuaded Wellington to drop his warehousing proposal and Huskisson to accept a higher rate of duties than in the 1827 measure. The continued intransigence of Charles Grant*, president of the board of trade, threatened to destroy the coalition, but Peel continued to promote conciliation and, after many frustrations, succeeded at the last minute in preventing the resignations of Huskisson and Grant. Their colleague Palmerston, secretary at war, commented in private that 'Peel is so right-headed and liberal, and so up to the opinions and feelings of the times, that he smoothes difficulties which might otherwise be insurmountable'.[163] After Grant had moved the corn resolutions, 31 Mar., Peel made clear his own preference for a permanent settlement to prevent fluctuations in imports and prices, with a duty rather than a prohibition, forming 'an equitable adjustment ... calculated to secure the interest of all parties'. He thought the 'agriculturists were well satisfied', but Hobhouse fancied that he enjoyed Huskisson's discomfiture in trying to justify his abandonment of Canning's proposal.[164] Peel saw off protectionist amendments, 25 Apr., and Hume's for a fixed duty, 29 Apr. He persuaded Wilbraham to drop his motion instructing the law commissioners to consider the county palatine courts of Chester, and with many misgivings acquiesced in Warburton's for the appointment of a select committee on the study of anatomy, 22 Apr. He opposed inquiry into chancery administration, 24 Apr. He presented his constituents' petition against Catholic relief, 29 Apr., and on 9 May spoke against Burdett's motion, which was carried by six votes on 12 May, when he was said to have been 'much annoyed by the division'. Croker thought he 'made a good argument on the Treaty of Limerick', but reflected that 'one might as well, at this time of day talk of Noah's flood'; and Hobhouse noted that he talked, 'as usual, a good deal of his own purity'.[165] Mrs. Arbuthnot asserted that Peel, 'the most short-sighted politician I ever knew', acted with 'his usual shabbiness' on the grant for Canning's widow and son by trying to persuade Wellington to let him decide on whether to confer it for two lives, as the Huskissonites wished, 'according to the feeling shown by the House'.[166] In the event, 13 May, he supported the pension and denied Althorp's insinuation that it represented 'some compromise between the members of the present administration'. He opposed Otway Cave's motion to summon the municipal leaders of Leicester to the bar of the House for failing to produce requested information, 14 May. On 16 May 1828, when Hume and John Maberly raised objections to the navy estimates, Croker claimed that he 'whispered to Peel, whose act it was', of 'the folly, as we before saw the cowardice', of putting them on the finance committee, which had made them 'more troublesome than ever': 'he was very little pleased with the remark ... But it is the turn of his mind to get over adversaries by concession. He always gives more importance, and weight even, to a public enemy than to his own supporters'.[167]

On 12 Mar. 1828 Peel raised in cabinet the problem of what to do about the proven corrupt boroughs of Penryn and East Retford. They settled on the line that provided there were two boroughs to be dealt with, one should have its seats given to a large unrepresented manufacturing town and the other be thrown into the neighbouring hundreds. He put this arrangement to the House, 21 Mar., indicating his preference for giving Penryn's seats to a large town and sluicing East Retford. Huskisson stated his wish to transfer the representation even if only one borough was available. When the opposition in the Lords to the transfer of Penryn's seats to Manchester forced Lord Carnarvon, who was handling the bill, to give notice that he would drop the proposal, considerable confusion arose in the cabinet and the Commons. Following inconclusive discussions on 17 and 18 May, it was decided on the 19th, the day of the resumed debate on the East Retford bill, that the government would stick to the original plan until the Lords reached a final decision on Penryn. Peel went to the House under the impression that Huskisson and his associates agreed with this. In the debate, both he and Huskisson were charged with inconsistency in advocating the sluicing of East Retford rather than the transfer of its seats to Birmingham, even though the Penryn to Manchester proposal wás known to be a dead letter. While Peel stuck to his guns, despite a mauling from Edward Smith Stanley, Huskisson became increasingly uncomfortable and perplexed. Peel refused his request for an adjournment, and when the division was called Huskisson stayed in the chamber with Palmerston to be counted among the minority for transfer to Birmingham. Peel was taken aback, but said nothing. In the early hours of 20 May Huskisson wrote a letter of resignation to Wellington, which was clearly only meant as a step towards apologizing and patching things up. But Wellington, sick of the Huskissonites' intransigence, took it at face value, showed it to Peel, who agreed with him, and laid it before the king. In the exchanges and interviews which ensued, as Palmerston and Lord Dudley tried to persuade the duke that Huskisson had not meant to resign, but merely to place his office at Wellington's disposal, Peel made no serious effort to mediate and prevent the entirely avoidable breach. He was out of patience with Huskisson and his associates, though he remained on good personal terms with Palmerston, who, with Dudley, Grant, William Lamb* and a few others joined Huskisson in resigning about a week after the East Retford fiasco.[168]

The secession worsened Peel's position in the House. He pressed Wellington to fill as many of the vacancies as possible with Members of the Commons, but the promotion of Sir George Murray, and John Calcraft to the front bench offered little prospect of effective assistance in debate. Ellenborough, who feared that Smith Stanley would 'terrify him', thought Peel took this too far, and told him to his face that 'I thought he had managed ill, that he had united the opposition, and made a weak government'. Mrs. Arbuthnot again bemoaned his 'arrogance and ill temper', which discouraged his juniors from speaking for fear that they would incur his displeasure by blundering, and alleged that 'he is detested by all the young men, and the House is ... under his management, in a more wild, disorderly state than I ever remember'.[169] When Huskisson delivered his explanation of his resignation, 2 June 1828, Peel followed him with his own account, professing regret at the breach, but denying any 'paltry subterfuge' by himself and Wellington, insisting that it had not been caused by any difference of policy or principles and promising to 'persevere to the last' in 'the spirit of moderation' in which the ministry had been formed. Hobhouse considered this 'one of the best speeches I ever heard him make. He was temperate and firm, and at the same time that he spared Huskisson, did not forget what was due to the duke of Wellington and himself'; but Bankes could 'not recollect to have ever seen ... Peel so much ruffled and nettled'.[170] Lamb conceded that Peel had spoken 'in a very fair, moderate and conciliatory tone' and had no doubt of the sincerity of him and Wellington, only fearing the latter's 'high opinions and strong prejudices', which could be exploited by such as Harriet Arbuthnot.[171] On East Retford, Peel said that if the Lords decided to sluice Penryn, he would 'redeem ... [his] pledge' to give the seats to a manufacturing town. The following day the Huskissonite Lord Binning* informed Sir Charles Bagot that 'in the Commons Peel [is] losing ground and at a discount, suspected by the Ultras, his friends, and not having conciliated the liberal Tories or the Whigs, disliked by the young men, and having shown upon various occasions that his temper was too strong for him'.[172] On 5 June Peel confirmed to Brownlow what he had told him in private, that an advance of public money to promote employment in Ireland was undesirable, and that absentee landlords ought to contribute, but he approved of the principle of Foster's proposal to encourage bog drainage. Later that day he opposed inquiry into the currency and bank restriction, defeating Graham's motion by 154-49; he resisted Hume's wrecking amendment to the Scottish notes bill, 16 June. When Burdett urged the government to take up Catholic relief next session, 12 June, Peel said that the question remained open in the cabinet and his own views were unchanged. He supported Stuart Wortley's game bill, without much hope that it would 'produce all the effects anticipated', 13 June, and opposed Taylor's call for inquiry into alleged misappropriation of public funds for the refurbishment of Buckingham House, 23 June. Next day he persuaded Wilmot Horton to lay aside for the time being his emigration scheme. On 27 June he declared his support for throwing East Retford into the hundred of Bassetlaw, now that the Penryn to Manchester proposal was no longer feasible, and responded heatedly to Tennyson's accusation that ministers had used the issue as a pretext to get rid of the Huskissonites, in 'a base ... compact'. The exchange ended amicably after Tennyson's apology. He insisted that nothing had been 'done by the British government calculated to imply the slightest approbation of the course pursued by Dom Miguel' in Portugal, 30 June. He defended the Foreign Enlistment Act and refuted a suggestion that Pitt's first ministry had pledged to carry Catholic emancipation as a *quid pro quo* for the Union, 3 July. He had clashed in cabinet with Wellington over the office of lieutenant-general of the ordnance, which he and Goulburn were willing to sacrifice in deference to a pending opposition motion. Ellenborough, who took the duke's side, wrote in his diary:

> Whatever I say against his opinion annoys him. He answers captiously ... Perhaps I did not meet him with

enough cordiality, but he does not suit me. I get on better with all the other members of the government than with him. The duke seemed much annoyed at Peel's indisposition to fight the question.

(A month later Ellenborough showed Peel some pictures at a cabinet dinner at his house and elicited in him 'a cordiality of manner', which led him to conjecture that 'he is only rather a proud, touchy man, and that the least attempt at management would make him very cordial'.) Mrs. Arbuthnot wrote that Peel 'runs sulky and talks of resignation', and wished the duke would 'take him at his word'. Peel eventually agreed to contest the point in the House, but Ellenborough remarked that he 'certainly has not the character suited to the leader of a party, or to the command of a popular assembly', and Mrs. Arbuthnot claimed that he was 'very sullen and cross' and that 'the duke abused him to me a good deal and said no man ever had such a confounded temper'.[173] Peel duly defended the office, 4 July, when the opposition motion was crushed by 202-95. He justified the grant for Canadian water defences, 7 July; defended the government's superannuation allowance proposals, 8 July; supported Fyler's amendment to alter the silk trade regulations in order to keep faith with interested parties, 14 July; opposed inquiry into the Leicester ratepayers' allegations against the corporation, 17 July; endorsed Huskisson's motion for information on tariff negotiations with the United States, advocating 'a commercial intercourse with all nations in a spirit of friendly co-operation, and on principles of sound and liberal policy', 18 July, and refuted Fowell Buxton's allegation that Wellington was reneging on the 1823 pledge concerning the amelioration of slavery, 25 July 1828.

On 15 Aug. 1828 Bathurst wrote to Arbuthnot that Peel would never

be a good head of a party. He is undoubtedly the first man in the House of Commons, and his influence, backed by a good character and a large fortune, must always be very considerable; but he seems to want that cordiality of manner, and that elevation of mind, one of which wins the affections, and the other commands the respect, of a popular assembly; and without one of these qualities no man can long be a formidable leader in the ... Commons.[174]

Bathurst was speculating whether Peel would resign and lead an opposition to the concession of Catholic emancipation, which it was accurately rumoured that Wellington had decided could no longer with safety be resisted. Peel was facing the biggest crisis of his career so far, the resolution of which liberated him from his increasingly irksome obligations to the Protestant diehards, though at a painful short – term cost to himself, the Tory party and the government. He shared Wellington's worries over the implications of O'Connell's election victory in county Clare in July 1828, which not only defied the authority of the government but confirmed the mounting influence of Catholic voters in Ireland, under the influence of the priests and the Association. In a memoir composed in the last years of his life, Peel described the problem not as a threat of imminent civil and sectarian conflict in Ireland, which could have been met with force, but as a long-term challenge to British power there: 'the real danger was in the peaceable and legitimate exercise of a franchise [in which] was involved a revolution in the electoral system of Ireland – the transfer of political power ... from one party to another'.[175] When in August 1828 Wellington told him that he had decided that emancipation must be conceded, Peel broadly agreed, but throughout the discussions which occupied much of their time during the next five months his position was that his only honourable course would be to resign from office and support emancipation as a private Member. However, when Wellington's bid in early January 1829 to win over the senior clergy, which was made partly in the hope of undermining the king's objections, failed, Peel concluded that as no other ministry could hope to carry the measure through the House, he could not abandon Wellington for the sake of his own political consistency and thereby endanger the government. He told Wellington of this decision on 17 Jan. 1829.[176] He confirmed it to the cabinet later that day, when he submitted a plan for the settlement of what he said was now 'a question of detail'. Ellenborough thought he had 'acted nobly as well as wisely', and later wrote him 'a note to tell him ... so', at which he 'was much pleased'.[177]

As Peel worked out the details of the relief bill and its accompanying measure to disfranchise the Irish 40*s*. freeholders and raise the county qualification to £10, he 'spoke of the thunderclap the announcement in the king's speech would be, and the very doubtful effect of it on public opinion'. Ellenborough reflected that he 'must expect to have strong things said against him', as 'the high Protestants, misled by the recall of Lord Anglesey [the Irish viceroy], imagine the government is Protestant'.[178] On 31 Jan. he informed Croker, who was pleased but feared he would 'individually lose some of the public confidence', of his 'conversion', and showed him the relevant documentary evidence, as he did two days later to Lord Lowther*, a member of the government, to whom he 'enumerated all his difficulties in having a divided government upon the state of Ireland'. Lowther, taken aback, was 'not convinced', and, observing to his father Lord Lonsdale that the king, Wellington and Peel had 'wheeled around, grounded upon the opinion that the government cannot meet the systematic opposition in Ireland and the ... Commons', complained that 'it is hard to be thrown over so suddenly after maintaining a good fight for the whole of my parliamentary life'. Croker reckoned that many of Peel's dinner guests summoned to hear the king's speech, 4 Feb., 'did not believe' in stories of his *volte face* until they heard it from his own lips.[179] He had decided to resign his seat for the University and stand for re-election, which Croker thought was 'a democratical and unconstitutional proceeding'.[180] On the address, 5 Feb., Peel confirmed and explained the decision to concede emancipation and his own role in the deliberations of the past six months. Croker wrote that he was 'only cheered by the opposition, as Canning used to be in 1827'. For the Whigs, Hobhouse recalled it as 'a lame speech', and that 'we could not help smiling to hear from his mouth arguments which he had so often opposed'. Greville, who was present, thought Peel 'was very feeble, and his case for himself poor and ineffective'; but Littleton conceded that after 'seventeen years of uncompromising opposition to the question' he had 'a difficult task', though it was impossible to forget his declaration of 1 May 1827 of his sole reason for declining to join Canning's ministry. Agar Ellis also found his performance 'lame', while John Denison wrote:

> Peel made a pitiful exhibition. His conduct has naturally created no measured disgust in the minds of his whole party. I think he has more to undergo than his touchy temper and his thin skin can endure. I think him myself a very disagreeable man. He did not attempt to produce one word of argument that did not apply in full force two years ago.[181]

At the Speaker's dinner, 7 Feb., according to Croker, Peel

> made a joke about old [Ebenezer John] Collett, who, not knowing Peel's conversion, had written to him to say he was hastening up to support the good old Protestant cause. This gaiety shows that Peel is sincere and cordially converted, but in a moment he seemed to recollect himself, and looked very grave and almost discomposed at his own mirth, and sat silent and frowning the rest of the evening.[182]

Many of the Tories were outraged by what they considered as a betrayal by Peel, whose brother Jonathan 'declared himself an anti-Catholic' on 9 Feb., when Peel, 'apparently unmoved', ignored him and said that in time 'justice' would be done to the purity of his and Wellington's motives. (The episode did hurt Peel, but Jonathan assured him that he had not intentionally set out to wound him.)[183] Mrs. Arbuthnot, who was now singing Peel's praises for acting so 'handsomely' by the duke, witnessed his clash with Henry Bankes and Sir Edward Knatchbull, 10 Feb., when he secured leave to introduce a bill to suppress the Catholic Association; like most observers, she thought he had the better of the exchanges. His speech on the bill was essentially moderate, designed, as Hobhouse perceived, to 'please the Whigs', and it certainly had this effect on Creevey, who conceded that 'Peel makes a great figure'. Littleton had concluded that Peel 'has done himself great honour, and ... should be stoutly supported'; and Lord Sandon* felt that he 'seems to fight his battle well and deserves infinite credit, though not for the quickness of his view into the seeds of things'.[184] Peel presented Oxford University's anti-Catholic petition, 13 Feb., and insisted to Gascoyne that the situation in Ireland had demanded action, 17 Feb. On 26 Feb. polling began in the University by-election, where Inglis, sustained by the support of country clergymen, beat Peel by 755-609. Ellenborough noted at the close, 28 Feb., that Peel was 'perfectly indifferent, and ... has shown himself *a great man* by his equanimity in all that has taken place'.[185] He was quickly accommodated at Westbury, where the patron and Member, Sir Manasseh Masseh Lopes, made way for him. Holmes represented him at the formalities, 2 Mar., when there was a demonstration of anti-Catholic anger. He was sworn in next day and gave notice for the 5th of a motion to consider Catholic relief.[186] By then the king, who had been worked on by his brother Cumberland, seemed about to throw a spanner into the works by behaving erratically and threatening to withhold his consent. Matters reached a head on 4 Mar., when Wellington, Lyndhurst and Peel were summoned to Windsor, where an unsatisfactory interview took place, in which Peel told George that he would resign if he would not endorse the measure. It was thought at one point that he and his colleagues were out, but the king, influenced by Knighton and the Conynghams, was brought to his senses and the crisis averted at the eleventh hour.[187] The four-hour speech in which Peel, addressing a House 'crammed to suffocation', moved to go into committee to consider emancipation, 5 Mar., was considered by Ellenborough, Hobhouse and Greville and others as 'by far the best he has ever made'. He declared that he was yielding to 'a moral necessity which I cannot control', but, while he was not especially optimistic about the future prospects of tranquillity in Ireland, he expressed a hope that the measure would at least encourage a more harmonious spirit. Greville thought the speech was 'full of his never-failing fault, egotism, but certainly very able, plain, and statesmanlike, and the peroration very eloquent'. It was 'enthusiastically' received by the Whigs, who liked the simplicity of the plan, and the motion was carried by 188 votes on 6 Mar.[188] On the 10th Peel introduced the relief and freeholders bills, which he defended against Brownlow. On the second reading of the relief bill, 18 Mar., he replied to the 'personal charges and invective' levelled against him by Sir Charles Wetherell, the attorney-general (who was about to be dismissed) and proved that he had been guilty of a breach of cabinet confidence; 'he was bursting with passion', Greville wrote, 'but restrained himself'. He denied any personal involvement in the 'inhuman cry' against Canning and paid tribute to him, Fox, Grattan, Plunket and veteran champions of emancipation. This part of his speech made Lady Bathurst 'a little sick', for 'those prodigious encomiums upon his dear departed friend Canning is [*sic*] too great humbug'.[189] On 19 Mar. he said the freeholders bill would 'raise up a real, substantial and independent yeomanry in Ireland'. He refused to accept Lord Duncannon's amendment to make the measure 'prospective', 20 Mar., and on the 26th successfully opposed George Moore's attempts to allow Protestant 40*s*. freeholders to continue to vote and to raise the qualification to £20. (He privately argued to Londonderry that this would give 'an undue influence to the town in county elections, and materially diminish the power of the landed aristocracy'.)[190] Supporting the third reading of the relief bill, 30 Mar., he stated that 'it does not always follow that the pilot is bound to steer the same course to guard the ship from danger', and ended with a quotation from Cicero: '*Neque enim inconstantis puto*'. It was carried by 320-142, to the accompaniment of loud cheering. The freeholders bill was passed later that night. Next day Peel and nearly 100 Members took the relief bill to the Lords. Hobhouse wrote that 'to see Peel with a Catholic emancipation bill in his hand was not to be conceived within the possibilities of chance, but there he was'.[191] There were a few minor difficulties with the Lords and the king, but the measure received royal assent (which Peel described to Croker as its '*most difficult* stage') on 13 Apr.[192] Mrs. Arbuthnot recorded that two days later he was 'in very good humour ... [and] very happy at the Catholic bill having passed and, I think, disposed if possible to make a junction with the Grey party'.[193] Charles Grant thought 'the effect ... has been to shake all trust in public men and confound all notions of right and wrong' and reported that 'the general notion' was that 'Peel's character' would 'never recover'.[194] Lowther told his father, 24 Mar. 1829, that 'many people' believed that Wellington and Peel 'have contrived to separate themselves from their old and staunch supporters' and would 'resign when the bill passes the Lords'.[195] The independent Whig Sir Robert Heron* reflected that he had always thought that Peel was 'really favourable to the question, and that his opposition arose merely from the selfish views and narrow calculations of a feeble mind; but the opponents relied upon him, and his happily timed desertion contributed much to weaken their defence'.[196] The young Richard Monckton Milnes† reckoned that his father was 'too hard on Peel

> who, in his miserable lack of genius, has enough of sound sense ... [and] must have perceived that by remaining in place he vacated that stronghold in which he had rested invincible for so long, his ostentatious honesty, his integrity of principle. Now, is it probable he would have thrust himself forward with the poor covering of his own ability into the pelting storm of irritated popular feeling, unless he had believed himself able not only to justify himself to his own heart, but to come forth with good report again before men?[197]

Brougham was not disposed to blame Peel, as some did, 'for not giving sufficient thanks to the opposition', but was 'a little spleened at both him and others giving the *chief* part of carrying the question to Canning'. He and Wilson agreed that Peel was 'far more to be trusted' than Wellington 'for liberal courses'.[198]

Peel warned Hume that he would resist any renewed motion for 'the spoliation of church property' in Ireland, 2 Apr. 1829. He acquiesced in Hobhouse's motion for an inquiry into select vestries, 28 Apr., as a means of checking wasteful expenditure, but dissented from his other allegations against them and call for their abolition in London. In cabinet he raised the 'difficulties' in which Britain might be placed by her 'moral obligation towards the Greeks' and argued that a select committee on the East India Company, pending renewal of its charter, should be conceded: Ellenborough, president of the India board, thought he was 'for free trade, and *unreasonable* towards the Company'. He was against extending the deadline set for abolition of the Brazilian slave trade by six months, because, as Ellenborough saw it, he 'does not like awkward questions in the House'.[199] There on 4 May he agreed with Slaney that the practice of paying wages out of poor rates was pernicious, but recommended a careful approach to the problem. He supported the sluicing of East Retford, 5 May, and opposed the Ultra Lord Blandford's reform scheme, 2 June, dismissing his argument that free trade had been advanced and Catholic emancipation carried by a corrupt and unrepresentative Commons. He said that any attempt to regulate wages by legislation would do more harm than good to the workers, 7 May. He acquiesced in Hobhouse's proposal to obtain the names of the owners of cotton factories employing children, 19 May, but asked him not to make it an annual ritual and said that on a recent visit to some Lancashire mills he had been pleased by the good conditions in the larger ones, though he admitted that there were abuses in the smaller. While maintaining in the Commons and in official correspondence his line that legislation could do nothing to relieve distress in the manufacturing districts, and making sure that disorder was not allowed to get out of control (as he explained in the House, 2 June), in the late summer he clandestinely sent home office agents to Lancashire to investigate distress and gave them authority to relieve the worst cases.[200] On 15 May he argued that O'Connell was not entitled to be heard in support of his case for taking his seat without swearing the oath of supremacy, but on the 18th he announced that he had changed his mind and proposed that he should be heard at the bar. He subsequently voted against his being allowed to take his seat unimpeded.[201] In the aftermath of the Edinburgh Westport murders, he supported the anatomy bill to protect 'the lower classes of society', 19 May. Responding to some captious resistance by Hume to the ecclesiastical courts bill, 21 May, he complained:

> I have been entirely employed from nine o'clock yesterday morning, and am kept here until three o'clock ... It is too hard upon ... ministers to be thus obstructed by the opposition of one ... Member, and that opposition ... the most vexatious within the memory of the House.

He supported the Maynooth grant next day. When Rae dropped his controversial Scottish gaols bill for the session, 27 May, Peel exhorted Scottish burgh Members to consider its proposals 'on general principles' and disregard their constituents' hostility. Agar Ellis thought his reply to Mackintosh's motion on Portugal, 1 June, was 'but a sorry apology for the disgraceful conduct of our government in maltreating the ... refugees'.[202] On 4 June he waved aside Attwood's currency nostrum and denied reports that he had used his influence to procure a large grant of land in New South Wales for one of his brothers, explaining that the recipient was in fact his second cousin Tom, who had been legitimately granted the Swann River holding by the colonial office. On 12 June 1829 he opposed the clamour of the Ultra Sir Richard Vyvyan and others for inquiry into manufacturing distress, arguing that 'the unequal distribution of wealth', though an 'evil', was 'unavoidable'. An outbreak of disorder in Ireland during the marching season and evidence of sectarian bitterness thereafter engaged the attention of the cabinet, where Peel, who sent some troops from Scotland, advocated the creation of an efficient police force, to be paid for by the landowners. In a letter to John Leslie Foster* he suggested the possibility of setting up an Irish education board to supervise national education and ways in which the religious schism might be got over in teaching; but Foster's reply was not encouraging. At least by the end of the year the country, apart from Tipperary, was more or less tranquil.[203]

In the summer of 1829 Brougham, on the northern circuit, noted the undiminished 'fury' of 'the provincial Ultras' with Peel; and in parliamentary circles Vyvyan, Knatchbull and the disaffected Ultras were fantasizing about coalition ministries with Whigs and Huskissonites.[204] Peel, buoyed by the initial success of his new police, was full of 'pride, pomp and ceremony' at Drayton in mid-October, according to General Dyott.[205] Despite the ministry's obvious weakness in debating talent and, given the fractured state of parties, potentially in numbers in the Commons, Wellington made no move to strengthen or broaden it. Tom Grenville† mused in September that perhaps the duke was 'so well satisfied with his House of Lords that he will leave Peel to shift for himself with his Commons in the same unsatisfactory manner which distinguished the last session'; and in late December Abercromby (the beneficiary the following month of act of 'rare generosity towards a political opponent' by Peel, who recommended his appointment as lord chief baron of the exchequer) surmised that Peel, 'the person most concerned in that matter ... must have changed his nature as well as his conduct on the Catholic question if he is [indifferent] in respect of maintaining a single-handed war against all against the host of assailants who may attack him'.[206] The illness of his friend and 'bottle-holder' William Vesey Fitzgerald, which forced him to resign as head of the board of trade before Parliament met, was seen, especially in Whig circles, as a 'great loss' to Peel, who seemed now to be 'nearly alone' on the government front bench. (But according to Mrs. Arbuthnot, Vesey Fitzgerald had complained in October of 'Peel's coldness and bad management and said it was impossible to get on unless some of the speakers on the other side were brought upon the treasury bench'.)[207] Yet neither Wellington nor Peel, who a week before Parliament met told Ellenborough that he had 'apprehensions' about 'the state of the country' and that 'the authority of the duke alone kept things quiet', seemed unduly worried.[208] On 4 Feb. 1830 he opposed Knatchbull's amendment to the address condemning the omission of any reference to distress in the king's speech, defended ministerial foreign policy and said 'rash experiments with the currency' would do no good. Mrs. Arbuthnot, deploring the small majority, wrote the first of many denunciations of Peel's management deficiencies with which she punctuated her commentary on the session:

> The mode he has ... will never do. He is always complaining that nobody speaks and that the whole weight falls upon him and, sure enough, not one man in office uttered a word except a few sentences from ... Goulburn. And why is this? Because ... Peel's system is to place confidence in no one. He will not let the official men know what the intentions of government are; they therefore cannot speak with safety and, if one does speak and says anything the least indiscreet, instead of backing and encouraging them he leaves them in the lurch to the tender mercies of the opposition and rather takes part against them. The consequence is, those who can speak *won't* and those young men who might be inclined to try, *dare not*.[209]

Ellenborough thought the tone he adopted when stalling on the question of his embarrassing leaked letter to Sir John Malcolm*, 5 Feb., was 'too apologetical', and after discussions with him and the chairs of the East India Company concluded that he 'did not seem to have looked much into the subject'.[210] Holland reckoned he had spoken 'with his usual mediocrity' in the opening days, but Lady Granville felt that 'if Peel is not alarmed and does not refuse to wade through the dirt of the session' the ministry would survive.[211] He secured the appointment of the East India Company select committee, 9 Feb., and tried to dispel suspicions that it would produce a whitewash. After supporting the sluicing of East Retford, 11 Feb., he expressed a hope that 'I shall not hear the name of this borough again'. He successfully defended the 1819 currency settlement against Graham's attack, 12 Feb., when his hint that ministers would dissolve if defeated seemed to Ellenborough to 'have had a good effect', though Lord Durham (Lambton) commented that it 'affected no one as it is quite notorious ... [they] would lose in that event'.[212] Even Mrs. Arbuthnot liked his speech against Hume's motion for tax reductions and a return to 1797 salary levels, 15 Feb., when he 'alluded strongly to the factious opposition of the Ultra Tories caused by his conduct on the Catholic question', for which he did not repent. Abercromby commented that the treasury bench in the Commons was 'Peel, and Peel alone, without even a decent second'. He interpreted the speech as an indication that ministers wished to court the Whigs without admitting them to high office. Holland now conceded that Peel, 'left as he is entirely to himself ... improves in spirit and speaking'.[213] On 18 Feb. he opposed Blandford's reform scheme, stating that he would never be a party to such a 'wholesale depreciation of the elective franchise'. Yet after he had opposed Russell's motion for the enfranchisement of Birmingham, Leeds and Manchester and Sandon's amendment to commit the House to the principle of transferring the franchise from corrupt boroughs to large towns, 23 Feb., Littleton thought he saw in his display 'the germ of another Catholic question':

> Peel, who has always been shy of committing himself on reform, was remarkably temperate, and said nothing that will make it dishonourable in him to take another line hereafter. My firm belief is that if he were prime minister, you would see a reform carried by him, and grounded on a basis that would disarm, for a century at least, any attempt on the part of the country for more extensive change.

Mrs. Arbuthnot, too, thought he 'does not oppose reform ... with any sort of energy'.[214] In reply to Gascoyne's explanation that he had withdrawn his support from the government because of its espousal of free trade doctrines and concession of emancipation, 23 Feb., Peel said that 'a minister should neither make himself the tool of a party, nor ... by courting popular applause, too much lose sight of the interests of the country'. He opposed inquiry into the duke of Newcastle's eviction of recalcitrant tenant electors at Newark, maintaining that 'property ... should always enjoy an influence in this House', 1 Mar. He again supported the sluicing of East Retford, 5 Mar., when he opposed O'Connell's motion for adoption of the secret ballot. He endorsed the ministerial amendment to Newport's motion for a commission on the Irish church and dismissed the 'impudent sarcasms' of the Ultra Trant, 4 Mar. Having told Ellenborough that he was 'disposed to take a high tone, and thinks men will follow him better when he does than when he temporises', he opposed Stewart's motion for information on the board of control's alleged interference with the Bombay judicature, 8 Mar.[215] He spoke against Palmerston's motion for information on relations with Portugal, 10 Mar. Agar Ellis thought he 'made a dextrous speech, but his case is so bad a one, that it was uphill work for him', but Grey reckoned that he had 'made rather a good case for himself against his old colleagues'.[216] He conceded the appointment of a select committee on the Irish poor to Spring Rice, 11 Mar., but declared his opposition to the introduction of English poor laws. On 12 Mar., 'excited more than usual', as Hobhouse recalled, he dismissed the opposition motion attacking the recent appointment of a treasurer of the navy as 'a proposition to visit with condemnation and censure those by whom this appointment was made'. He was particularly effective in criticizing Huskisson (who had once held the office), and Grey thought he 'had much the best of it'. Mrs. Arbuthnot wrote that his speech was 'so excellent that many voted with us who intended to be against us, and we carried our question by above two to one':

> Holmes and ... Hardinge told me it was quite astonishing how much ... Peel improved in speaking and in his management of the House, and ... if he went on in the spirited way he has done ... we should soon have a good stout party. It is a pity he makes himself so unpopular, for he can be very agreeable when he likes it, and he is really very good and amiable, but his manners are quite odious. He asks immense parties of the ... Commons to dinner every week and treats them so *de haut en bas* and is so haughty and silent that they come away swearing they will never go to his house again, so that his civilities do him harm rather than otherwise.[217]

Peel, who opposed Hume's motion for army reductions and forced him to explain his 'wild and senseless' encouragement of resistance by force to excessive expenditure, 22 Feb., was very keen on the adoption of a 'modified property tax' to enable the government to reduce the burden of taxation 'on the industry and the comforts of the labouring poor'. He argued his case in cabinet, saying that he wished to 'reach such men as Baring, his father, Rothschild and others, as well as absentees and Ireland', but 'most fairly', in Ellenborough's words, accepted his colleagues' majority opinion against the proposal.[218] He announced this to the House, 19 Mar., when opposing Davenport's motion for inquiry into the state of the nation. Like Herries, he believed that the Commons was 'in favour of an income tax' and that there must be one next year, and Ellenborough thought he 'rather unwillingly' agreed in cabinet, 24 Mar., to oppose Poulett Thomson's motion for inquiry into a revision of taxation the following day.[219] He did so forcefully enough, securing a majority of 167-78. He said that the Bathurst and Dundas pensions were 'not a job got up for the purpose of serving the sons of cabinet ministers', 26 Mar., but the case was a poor one, and ministers were placed in a minority of 18 against their abolition. He endorsed the ministerial Scottish judicature bill, 1 Apr., and next day answered Russell's questions about Greece. Three days later John Allen commented to Charles Fox that in Brougham's absence on the circuit Peel 'has been gaining ground ... and having no one to support him and no very formidable rival to oppose him has put forth his strength and acquired apparently more confidence in himself than he ever possessed before'.[220] Arbuthnot told Lord Cowley that although he had 'had terrible difficulties to encounter', Peel had 'done a great deal better this session then he ever did before, and he has risen amazingly in public estimation'.[221] His father was dying at Drayton, and Peel visited him in the first week of April, so missing the debate and division on Robert Grant's motion for leave to introduce a Jewish emancipation bill, which was unexpectedly carried by 18 votes.[222] He opposed O'Connell's motion for a bill to allow Irish Catholics to vote on church rates at vestry meetings, 27 Apr. He defended the conduct of the government on the Terciera incident, taken so that 'we may not be fooled, gulled, bullied, cheated, deceived into hostilities', 28 Apr. On 3 May 1830 he was summoned urgently to Drayton, but he arrived at midnight to find that his father had died a few hours earlier. By his father's will he inherited all the entailed estates in Staffordshire, Warwickshire and Lancashire, and a very handsome fortune.[223]

During his absence Croker wrote that the government had been left 'not only without a general to lead us' in the Commons, but even without one fighting man; for he is himself *our host*':

> I am quite aware of the extreme difficulty of going on in the ... Commons without help, but I much doubt whether Peel wishes for any ... I do not think he will change that feeling – for *such* it is, rather than an opinion – till he shall begin to feel the *personal* pressure of adverse debate. He has not yet been *attacked*, and his single speech has every night, supported the whole debate on our side.[224]

A month earlier Hardinge, who complained that Peel was 'cold and never encourages anyone' (a refrain later echoed by John Stuart Wortley*), had suggested to Ellenborough that Wellington would not 'remain in office above a year more, and that Peel will then be minister'. On 9 May Wellington, according to Mrs. Arbuthnot

> repeated more positively than ... ever ... his determination to quit office. He said that ... Peel complained that he could not go on in the House of Commons with the government constituted as it is, that not one of the ministers says a word ... and that he must have more assistance. The duke says that ... every office in the ... Commons has been filled by Peel himself, that he says himself he cannot join with Lord Grey and that, if he looks to the Huskisson party, which he suspects, he, the duke, cannot and will not be a party to such a junction ... He said he had not the proper weight and influence that, as head of the government, he ought to have, that the members of the cabinet had no respect or deference for him; that, if he gave an

> opinion, it was unattended to, whereas anything ... Peel said was immediately considered as law.

She claimed that Wellington 'was determined to write to Peel in a few days and resign the government into his hands'; she implored him not to do so. The duke did agree not to resign, but he composed a memorandum suggesting that Peel was better equipped and placed than himself to form a strong government. He seems not to have sent it to Peel, who must, however, have been aware of such speculation in Tory circles.[225]

He made his first appearance in the House as a baronet on 17 May 1830, when he said that Birmingham was not, as Davenport would have it, in a 'state of extreme suffering and depression' and opposed the second reading of the Jewish disabilities removal bill, which was thrown out by 228-165. Brougham claimed that Peel's speech was 'as great a failure as could be' and was cheered by 'only a few hacks'.[226] On 24 May (when Mrs. Arbuthnot wrote that he had resumed business 'as usual, sour and dissatisfied', and that he was blatantly courting 'the Liberals') he gave what Agar Ellis considered a 'shuffling' reply to Russell's question about the resignation of Prince Leopold.[227] He spoke against Labouchere's resolutions on Canada, 25 May, and defended the sending of troops to Rye to restore order, 27 May. On the 28th he argued that O'Connell's plan for the adoption of the ballot and universal suffrage would 'overthrow every valuable institution' and, opposing Russell's more moderate reform scheme, insisted that 'the popular voice' was able to exert its 'due and legitimate influence' in the House as things stood. He opposed inquiry into the divorce laws, 3 June, Attwood's currency reform motion, 8 June, repeal of the Irish Vestry Acts, 10 June, and reductions in the colonial estimates, 14, 15 June. After a cabinet dinner next day he spoke to Ellenborough

> with much *ennui* of his position in the Commons ... that it really was not worth any man's while to be there for so many hours every night. The sacrifice was too great. He said the radicals had brought the House into such a state that no man could do business but themselves. He seemed not well, and thoroughly out of humour.

This was partly a reaction to the success of Mackintosh's amendment to his forgery punishment bill on 7 June: John Campbell II* reported that 'Peel declares himself so disgusted with the House of Commons, that it is doubtful whether he will sit there again'.[228] He opposed and defeated by 182-144 Huskisson's motion for a reduction in the sugar duties, 21 June, but privately was not certain that the ministerial arrangements would answer; they were in fact abandoned.[229] He supported Littleton's truck abolition bill, 23 June. At the swearing in of Members after the death of the king, 28 June, he wore 'the Windsor uniform', in which Tom Macaulay* likened him to 'a good boy's beau ideal of human happiness, the reward of doing as you are bid and shutting the door after you'.[230] He favoured making provision for a regency and prolonging the session, but was overruled in cabinet. Ellenborough recorded that he was 'put out of humour' by this: 'He sees all the difficulties of our position, and does not meet them with energy and *élan*. He certainly is not an agreeable person to transact business with, but he is a very able man'. When Ellenborough went with Lord Rosslyn to show Peel the Lords' address on the king's death, 29 June, he 'hardly looked up' from his reading, 'hardly took any notice of us or it' and 'seemed really ill, and quite broken down'.[231] Later that day he presented William IV's message about the death of his brother and the dissolution. Ellenborough had alerted Wellington to his apparent illness, but the duke merely observed that Peel 'did not like the position he stood in in the House' and that 'no government was ever beaten by its enemies, but many have been by their friends'.[232] He moved the address in answer to the message next day and explained what legislation would be persevered with. An inebriated Brougham denounced ministers as the 'fawning parasites' of Wellington, for which Peel demanded an explanation. Brougham blustered, but, according to Hobhouse, Peel, who physically prevented Hardinge from creating a scene, 'with infinite skill and coolness said he had no doubt that Brougham did not allude to him', suggested what he had really meant to say and brought the episode to a close; he was generally thought to have humiliated Brougham.[233] He defended various grants, including the one for Windsor Castle, 2 July. On 6 July he opposed Robert Grant's motion on the regency, which was crushed by 247-93.[234] He got rid of Hume's attempt to reduce judges' salaries, 7 July, and on 13 July 1830 told Lord Killeen that there would be no advance of money to relieve Irish distress and successfully opposed as too binding Brougham's bid to pledge the House to consider the immediate abolition of slavery in the next session.[235]

At the beginning of July Stuart Wortley and Hardinge told Ellenborough that 'there must be a change' in the Commons, where Peel was in desperate need of support. Hardinge, who 'talked again of making Peel first lord of the treasury and chancellor', had spoken to Wellington on the matter, and the following day Arbuthnot, presumably at Wellington's behest, wrote to Peel of Wellington's 'admiration of the great efforts and display which you have made' and wish to 'consult ... your wishes alone in all that relates to the ... Commons':

> You will gratify him ... beyond all measure if you will state to him fully and most openly what your feelings are upon the subject. That strength must be obtained for you in the ... Commons part of the cabinet is necessary, not only for your own comfort and relief, but also to enable you to protect the king ... You have done wonders, but impossibilities cannot be expected of you ... I know very well that the duke is now holding the government with a strong feeling that it should come hereafter into your hands, and that he has a deep sense of what he owes to you for your immense exertions.[236]

According to Mrs. Arbuthnot, when she and her husband raised the problem with the duke on 14 July, he

> put himself into a furious passion, said he would not meet ... Peel about it for that it was all his own fault and his own bad management and that, if he turned these people out and took whoever ... Peel chose, he should have him coming in a fortnight's time with exactly the same complaints ... I said all that he complained of in ... Peel was perfectly true; but ... that now he positively had cause; that the whole of this session the treasury bench in the ... Commons had been a disgrace ... The duke said he knew it would never do till he retired and Peel had the head. I [said] he was really talking rank nonsense, for ... he knew perfectly well Peel could not go on a day without him. He has no party in the country and, in spite of his talents, is the most unpopular man in it.

Wellington, who had seemingly given up his intention of handing over the reins to Peel, mellowed subsequently, and on 16 July talked to Arbuthnot and Peel about the situation. Mrs. Arbuthnot wrote:

> They seem to have settled to do nothing at present. Peel said ... Palmerston, who we have had a sort of intimation would be glad to return, would be too discreditable and unsafe ... It is curious ... considering the sacrifices the duke made to please Peel in forming the government to have men who could speak, to find that literally nobody utters except himself ... but ... if Peel knew how to encourage, the official people would inform them and make them speak ... but he won't ... I am persuaded that he has a strong feeling of jealousy about anyone approaching him in speaking.[237]

She condemned Peel as 'a nasty sour-tempered creature' when he failed to thank Wellington for reinstating Wilson in the army 'to please him'.[238] He turned down an offer of 'a quiet seat ... without trouble or expense' from the duke of Northumberland, having already arranged to replace his brother William at Tamworth. He dissociated himself from the action of some of William's supporters in starting him in the hope of turning out the Whig Townshend, with whom he was returned unopposed. On the hustings he defended the concession of Catholic emancipation.[239] He felt partly responsible for the defeats of his brothers Edmund and Jonathan at Newcastle-under Lyme and Norwich, which intensified his dissatisfaction and ill humour; and Hardinge got the impression in early September 1830 that he was 'much depressed' and 'vigilantly looking out for an honourable pretence to withdraw'.[240]

According to Dyott, Peel at Drayton in mid-August said 'how joyously he looked forward to becoming settled as a country gentleman'. He observed in Brougham's return for Yorkshire a sign that 'the lawyers were getting the upper hand in the ... Commons by frightening the country gentlemen, bullying the government, and paid by the commercial and monied interest'. He considered it 'most unexpected and unaccountable'; but 'what he thought equally so was the outrageous conduct of the deputation from the Birmingham Political Union in their daring attempt to overawe the nomination ... at Warwick'.[241] He felt 'most strongly' that the exiled French king should be allowed to stay in England as a political refugee, but not 'if intrigues were allowed by him'. In mid-August he advocated the immediate recognition of Louis Philippe as the surest way of helping to stabilize the new regime and avert war. Six weeks later, at a cabinet meeting on the Belgian crisis, the Dutch king having asked his allies to join in crushing the revolt, he argued that the foreign secretary Lord Aberdeen's draft letter to the British ambassador in Paris was a virtual invitation to use force, and suggested changes to make it more anodyne. He produced next day a superior version, which was duly adopted.[242] As analyses of the election returns indicated the potential weakness of the ministry in a fragmented Commons, Peel, having been sounded by Arbuthnot on Wellington's behalf, agreed that it was necessary to consider how they could strengthen themselves, preferably through a junction with the Huskissonites. Like Wellington and Huskisson, he attended the opening ceremony of the Liverpool and Manchester railway, 15 Sept., partly with a view to opening negotiations. He witnessed Huskisson's fatal accident, which put things on hold.[243] In some respects, however, it removed an obstacle, and, again prompted by Arbuthnot, Peel on 22 Sept. hosted at Drayton (a 'frightful' house, Mrs. Arbuthnot thought) the prearranged conference with him, Wellington, Aberdeen, Goulburn and Holmes to discuss their options. They decided to make an initial approach to Palmerston alone, offering him the colonial secretaryship. Palmerston indicated that he could not singly join the government as it stood, implying that places must be found for Charles Grant, Lord Melbourne and others. Wellington suggested to Peel that Herries, master of the mint, might be asked to step aside, but Peel, who valued Herries's financial expertise, successfully resisted this, and the negotiation stalled in the second week of October.[244] By then Peel had declined an invitation from some Liverpool Tories to stand there in Huskisson's room.[245] Towards the end of the month Greville had some talk with Arbuthnot, who lamented that there was 'nothing like intimate confidence' between Peel and Wellington and criticized Peel's 'indisposition to encourage other men in the ... Commons'. When Wellington decided to make another approach to Palmerston at the end of October, Peel, who seemed to Arbuthnot to be 'in good heart and spirits', was not keen on the recruitment of the idle Grant, and wanted Robert Wilmot Horton* to be brought in. The negotiation foundered, 30 Oct. 1830, when Peel agreed perfectly with the duke that ... we must make up our minds to fight the battle as we are'.[246]

In cabinet, 25 Oct. 1830, Peel read letters from magistrates and manufacturers of Manchester which gave 'an alarming account' of the state of the area, where colliers were on strike and mills had been stopped. Anxious to avoid a spread of conflict and unsure of the adequacy of the local military force, he counselled non-resistance by the authorities. The 'Swing' disturbances in the southern agricultural districts prompted Peel, who believed that they were 'in many cases perpetrated for stock-jobbing purposes', to send police officers and troops to the worst affected area and place General Dalbiac in overall command.[247] On 31 Oct. he proposed the insertion in the king's speech of 'a paragraph referring to the disturbed state of the country', which he concocted next day: it declared determination to punish sedition and expressed 'a firm reliance on the loyalty of the great body of the people'.[248] On the address, 2 Nov., he denied that the speech had 'charged the people with disaffection'; admitted that there was local distress, but said that people were 'not in a starving condition'; defended the ministry's foreign and Irish policy, and declared that repeal of the Union would be lunacy. Agar Ellis reckoned that he 'spoke feebly', but Ellenborough wrote that he was 'very much cheered'. Next day he accused Hume of trying to 'dictate to me the manner in which I ought to transact the business ... [of] my department' and, at the Speaker's behest, recommended that in future upstairs committees should meet at eleven o'clock rather than noon and the House assemble at three rather than four, in order to expedite public business. After a cabinet dinner that day he voiced his disgust at the failure of any other minister to back him up on the address.[249] Campbell, remarking on 'the degraded state of the House of Commons', where Peel was 'quite a second-rate performer and his colleagues ... much below mediocrity', understood that he and Wellington were 'both desirous of retiring'; but Peel himself a year later dismissed as a fiction the story related by Croker, who had it from Arbuthnot, that he had told the duke in November 1830 of '*his fixed determination* not to continue in office beyond the approaching Christmas'.[250] After Wellington's declaration in the Lords against all reform, 2 Nov., Peel next day told the Commons that while he thought a 'moderate' scheme might be introduced 'with advantage', he could 'not see the bounds to which the limitation is to be fixed' and there was therefore 'little prospect of the adoption of any such system of reform as I could consider safe'. Mrs. Arbuthnot commented that Wellington opposed reform because he 'honestly' feared it, whereas Peel did so 'from feeling that *he* would be thought shabby if he lent himself again to a measure he had hitherto opposed'.[251] On 5 Nov. Peel told Kenyon that he had no intention of appointing an inquiry into agricultural distress and crossed swords with Hume, to whose rant for tax reductions he retorted that Hume had 'the vulgar opinion of the motives of public men ... that they are influenced only by a desire of emolument, and that they are utterly regardless of the interests of the public'. He also reproved Hume for using 'expressions which may tend to inflame and excite the minds of the misguided people to whom he alludes, when he has characterized the whole population of England as being a people in a starving condition' and spoken of 'the day of vengeance'. Reports from the City authorities that the traditional lord mayor's day dinner for the king and his ministers, 9 Nov., would probably see major disorder prompted Wellington and Peel (who had both received death threats) to cancel the visit. In the House, 8 Nov., Peel, 'looking very pale', explained and defended this decision. Ellenborough heard that he 'did admirably', but Hobhouse recalled that 'the excuse was very ill received'.[252] Peel stayed at the home office until midnight on the 9th to oversee the precautions and counter measures against disorder.[253] Next day he responded tartly to Brougham's complaint that he had not been in his place at three o'clock, but he acquiesced in the introduction of Brougham's bill to establish courts of local jurisdiction. On 9 Nov. he told Ellenborough that the terms of Brougham's pending reform motion 'did not signify', for it was a question of 'reform, or no reform', and 'he never would undertake the question'; and in cabinet the following day he reported that he had told the vacillating king that 'by opposing all reform in the first instance the government would be able to make better terms afterwards'.[254] He was for opposing Parnell's motion for inquiry into the civil list, and did so on 12 Nov. In cabinet on 14 Nov., according to Ellenborough

> he said he was satisfied that, whatever might be the division on reform, the question was carried ... If the county Members did [vote for it], and it was thrown out by the representatives of Scotch and English boroughs, it was impossible to stand much longer ... I cannot understand his reasoning; if he thinks reform must be carried, surely it is better to vote a general resolution, and to fight the details. By objecting to the general resolution, we shall probably be turned out ... It seems to me that obstinacy, and the fear of being again accused of ratting, lead to this determination to resist when resistance is, in his own opinion, fruitless.[255]

On 15 Nov. Peel assured Holme Sumner that he was spending at least four hours every day trying to identify and bring to justice the perpetrators of the 'abominable' rural riots, and had a tetchy exchange with Hume, whom he again accused of inciting disaffection. After the ministerial defeat on the civil list by 233-204 (which Le Marchant believed he had considered 'absolutely impossible') he remained silent when Hobhouse asked him if he and his colleagues intended to remain in office.[256] In talks with Wellington, he agreed that it was better to go out immediately rather than meet Brougham's reform motion, and on the 16th they and the other leading ministers put their resignations into the king's hands. That afternoon, as Hobhouse remembered, Peel entered the House, 'looking very pale indeed, and talked with the Speaker' before announcing the resignations in a matter of fact way.[257]

Peel, 'completely broke down', as Mrs. Arbuthnot saw it, 'by the fatigue and wear of mind consequent upon having no help' in the Commons for so long, was '*delighted* at having so good an opportunity for resigning'.[258] He told Henry Hobhouse that

> it was much better that ... this should happen than that we should continue to administer the government in difficult times without the requisite support. I personally could not have long continued to discharge the rapidly increasing duties of the home office and the business of the ... Commons. Our own party saw no injustice in requiring the same persons who did the effective business of the government should also do the mere drudgery of attendance in the House ... and remain three or four hours every night with a miserable attendance. Four cabinet ministers have sons in the Commons ... But on the night which terminated the official existence of their fathers, *not one* ... voted ... Can I personally regret the end of such a government?[259]

Greville perceived that Peel, with his 'youth (for a public man), experience, and real capacity for business', could afford to 'form his own plans and avail himself of circumstances'.[260] On 22 Nov. he and his former colleagues took their seats on the opposition benches, from where he insisted that during the 'Swing' disturbances 'every species of civil, military and legal aid' had been 'promptly despatched to the local magistracy'.[261] At meetings soon after his resignation he had, according to Hardinge, given 'a damping answer' to request that he should take the lead in opposition. Croker elaborated:

> He announced that he meant to retire into private life, to give no opposition and not to lead the party – in short, to be his own unfettered man. We did not much like that ... However, on this reaching the duke, he has announced that he means to keep the *party together*. This, I hope, will warm the cold caution of Peel into some degree of party heat; but if he won't lead us, there are others who will ... make the attempt.

In truth, the Tories could not do without Peel; and Ellenborough assured Hardinge that he would 'be in opposition in a fortnight, as soon as he recovered his health and his spirits'.[262] A week after his resignation his brother William reported that he 'thinks an attentive opposition desirable, and will not desert those who have looked up to and supported him'; and Croker found him 'much more cordial and zealous' than at first.[263] At a meeting with Wellington, Aberdeen, Ellenborough and others, 27 Nov., he explained that his

> great fear was that we should not be able *to keep them in*. He had little doubt of being able to turn them out. He wished them to disembarrass us from the question of reform. He said he would make no declaration, but his wish was never to be obliged to come into office again. The fear was they should dissolve ... which would bring on the most imminent danger of revolution in England and rebellion in Ireland.

A month later Thomas Gladstone* heard that Peel's 'private opinion is that the revolution is not very far distant'.[264] He favoured inquiry into the state of the disturbed rural districts, 6 Dec., and opposed the subsidization of Irish public works, 9 Dec. He was named to the select committee on the reduction of salaries, 9 Dec., but said next day that he would rather give evidence to than sit on it. He welcomed Littleton's bill to abolish truck payments, 13, 14 Dec. On 13 Dec. he warned abolitionists in the House against exciting among colonial slaves 'expectations of speedy benefits which it will not be in our power to confer'; Gladstone told his father, a slave owner, that he was 'much pleased with Peel's speech last night. He is the best speaker *I* have yet heard in the House'.[265] On 16 Dec. he 'carried the feeling of the House with him completely' on the suspension of the Evesham writ, on which ministers dithered. This, thought Greville, 'proved that he has more consideration out of office than any of the ministers, and much more than he ever had when he was in. Men are looking more and more to him, and if there is not a revolution he will assuredly be prime minister'. Lyndhurst agreed, but confirmed that Peel's relations with Wellington, whose 'little cabinet (the women and toad eaters) hate' him, were strained and that there had never been 'any real cordiality between them'. Russell dismissed the episode as 'a sham fight, which does not signify one farthing'.[266] On 20 Dec. 1830 Peel intervened in a row provoked by Dawson's 'injudicious' attack on the Irish appointments to deplore retrospective attacks on the Wellington ministry for their supposed indifference to distress and lecture their successors to the effect that they would soon find that 'they have been too precipitate in pledging themselves to effect reforms and retrenchments which they will find themselves unable fully to realize'. At the same time, he professed general moderation, welcomed the government's determination to uphold the Union and, as John Hobhouse thought, 'spoke equivocally of the conduct of the French'. His remarks on the 'covert design' of some sections of the press 'to degrade and lower all the constituted authorities' and 'subject this country to ... the tyranny of an ungovernable mob' provoked a heated exchange with Hume. Hobhouse considered it 'a strange speech, half reproving his friends for indiscreet attacks on the new ministry and half attacking those ministers'. Tories were generally pleased with it, but Lord Carlisle, a member of the ministry, heard that it was 'too self-denying for some of his eager friends'. Russell condemned him in private as 'a most atrocious fellow'.[267] Holland, however, took Peel seriously, as he told the Irish viceroy Lord Anglesey, 3 Jan. 1831:

> The conduct of Peel is so judicious and skilful that I am not sure it does not suppose something formidable behind. It is implied if not asserted that his line is distinct from Wellington's. He does not mean to oppose reform but to propose some more moderate plan of his own and many of his partisans affect to be confident of carrying it and thereby forcing the present ministers to resign or dissolve.[268]

The latter speculation was well wide of the mark.

Peel went to Drayton for Christmas and kept out of the activities of the party veterans who sought to organize for opposition and promote the Tory cause in the press. He poured cold water on the second project, prompting Herries to recommend to his coadjutors a suspension of 'all operations whatever until we have carefully reconsidered the subject'. Croker wished he 'would lead us with vigour and firmness'.[269] In January 1831 he entertained Charles Ross*, Sir George Clerk*, Croker, Murray, Herries and Holmes at Drayton, where he was having a new house built, but he resisted Croker's attempt to 'pledge himself, like the duke, against all parliamentary reform': 'though he will oppose anything, he will pledge to nothing', and 'said, good humouredly, that he was sick with eating pledges'. At the end of the month, when he declined to attend a party meeting at Statfield Saye, pleading 'his wife's illness and business with his architect and gardener', Croker, who thought he 'would not venture to what would look like a political *reunion*', treated Ellenborough to a bitter outburst about Peel's

> wish to remain alone, unconnected with others, of his selfishness, etc. He exaggerated a good deal, but still there was a *fond* of truth. In fact Peel does think chiefly of himself, and has not the manner or the character to become a popular leader of a party.[270]

Herries, who had 'made no impression on him with respect to the press', reported to Mrs. Arbuthnot, 26 Jan. 1831, that Peel was 'much as usual, extremely circumspect in all that he says and does', but was 'acting very imperfectly the character of a country gentleman indifferent to office and politics'. (Peel 'made himself very agreeable' as the host of a party of neighbouring squires five days later.)[271] Herries believed that he was

> much more hearty in the anti-ministerial cause than he acknowledges to others or even avows to himself ... I think he is very well disposed, and will pursue a firm and prudent line in the ensuing session. He is more of an anti-reformer than I expected to find him. But he must cultivate his party with more warmth or he will lose it. The younger Tories will not cling to a cold and over cautious leader; the less so, to one who is suspected, more than he ought to be, of an inclination towards liberalism.[272]

Peel's failure to attend the opening day of the new session, 3 Feb. 1831, put a 'damp' on the Tory activists,[273] but his subsequent performances considerably raised his stock in the House. On 8 Feb. he declared his determination to 'support the king's government in every extremity of preserving inviolate the Union'; Lord Camden notified him of the king's approval.[274]

The leaked news of the ministerial budget made him, according to Ellenborough, 'most indignant', so that he 'now speaks of this *revolutionary* ministry. He was walking with Holmes before the debate and made himself so hot by his excitement that he was obliged to change his clothes before he went to the House', 11 Feb. There he looked 'as black as thunder' before speaking.[275] He welcomed the proposed repeal of the duty on seaborne coals, but criticized that on steamboat passengers and urged Althorp to drop the controversial tax on transfers of funded property, which was 'at variance with public honour, public morals and sound policy'. He had his wish, but on 28 Feb. he regretted the decision to tax raw cotton rather than printed calico. On 18 Feb., supporting the army estimates, he made what Ellenborough deemed 'a capital speech' on economy and retrenchment, extolling the Wellington administration's record, observing that the new ministers were becoming increasingly aware of the difficulty of fulfilling promises and exhorting them not to be goaded by the taunts of radicals into going too far on reform. Smith Stanley, the Irish secretary, admitted privately that Peel had spoken 'very well', though in truth '*too* well', by '*showing* at the same time, *not saying*, that the moment he was a little less frightened about the prospects of the country, we should have in him a formidable and dangerous opponent'. Gladstone commented that 'the more I see of Peel, the more I regret that he is not leading the House with efficient fecklers. He seems to me to stand *alone* for the combination of leader's points'. When Ellenborough, who suspected that the removal of Brougham from the Commons had given Peel 'a feeling of security', so that he 'speaks better' and was 'now pre-eminent there', congratulated him on the speech, it '*thawed* him and he spoke glowingly of the debate'.[276] When Lord Chandos's motion for reduction of the sugar duties threatened to leave ministers in a minority on 'a question of public credit', which would have precipitated a resignation crisis, 21 Feb., Peel baled them out by persuading Chandos to withdraw.[277] On 28 Feb. he presented without comment two petitions for Scottish and general reform. Gladstone told his father, 1 Mar., that Peel had 'risen in the estimation of the House. Opposition has brought him out, and he has acted with temper and moderation'.[278] Ellenborough noted that Lord Dacre 'admitted that Peel had been rising greatly' and that 'a government might go on under him'. Hardinge also thought 'a better government could be formed under Peel than under the duke, but he wishes the duke to be restored for the *session* and then give up to Peel'; but Ellenborough believed that

> Peel would succeed best in the present state of public affairs. Hardinge thinks Peel keeps himself rather aloof from the duke, that he knows no ministry can be formed without him, and feels indignant at the conduct of the Ultra Tories and resolved to make them come on their knees to him.[279]

Greville wrote:

> The exultation of the opposition is unbounded, and Peel plays with his power in the House, only not putting it forth because it does not suit his convenience; but he does what he likes, and it is evident that the very existence of the government depends upon his pleasure. His game, however, is to display candour and moderation, and rather to protect them than not, so he defends many of their measures and restrains the fierce animosity of his friends, but with a sort of sarcastic civility, which, while it is put forth in their defence, is always done in such a manner as shall best exhibit his own authority and contempt for their persons individually. While he upholds the government, he does all he can to bring each member of it into contempt, and there they are, helpless and confused, writhing under his lash and their own impotence.[280]

The tables were about to be turned.

At a meeting of Commons Tories at Peel's house, 20 Feb. 1831, and of commoners and peers at Apsley House a week later, it was decided not to oppose the introduction of the ministerial reform scheme.[281] When its sweeping and shocking scope was revealed by Russell, 1 Mar., Peel sat silent amid the uproar, but according to Hobhouse 'looked serious and angry, as if he had discovered that the ministers, by the boldness of their measure, had secured the support of the country'. Le Marchant claimed in retrospect that Peel 'sat pale and forlorn, utterly at a loss how to act. His countenance at times looked convulsed. The workings within him were evidently beyond his control. He was completely mastered'.[282] Yet the argument that Peel was paralyzed and missed the chance of defeating reform by dividing the House against the proposal is nonsense.[283] At the close of the debate he sought confirmation from Russell that the proposed uniform £10 householder borough franchise meant that scot and lot voters were to be disfranchised after the expiration of current lives. There was intense speculation about his response to the scheme, which some thought would determine its fate.[284] He spoke on 3 Mar., following Palmerston, the foreign secretary, a reluctant reformer. He declared his opposition to the scheme *in limine*, deploying the customary arguments in defence of the existing system, but asserted that as a private individual he would have been willing to support 'certain alterations ... founded on safe principles'. He accused ministers of practising 'vulgar arts of government' by starting an auction for popular support in which they would eventually be outbid by others more radical still, and said that by bringing forward the proposals at a time of national excitement they had 'lighted three hundred brands, and scattered through the country discord and dismay'. His effort was loudly cheered, and most Tories liked it, though, significantly, Wetherell and the Ultras appeared 'angry' at his profession of support for some measure of reform. Hobhouse later conceded that it was 'a most effective address ... in favour of the present system', but was surprised when he read it objectively to 'find that there was so little in it'. The reformer Sir Henry Bunbury* thought that 'as a specimen of eloquence and oratorical effect, it was splendid; but his arguments were more captivating than solid'. The ministerialist William Ord* judged it 'too solemn and too pompous' while Charles Russell*, a reformer, described it as 'magnificent', but consisting 'more of moral invective than of dry argument'.[285] Peel opposed going into committee on the timber duties, 18 Mar., when ministers suffered a defeat.[286] He presented anti-reform petitions from Cambridge and the Isle of Ely, 21 Mar., but 'took flight' from the debate on alleged breach of privilege by *The Times* provoked by Inglis.[287] Although Peel, who was reported to believe that 'the *Movement*' for radical reform had begun, was determined to divide as strongly as possible against the second reading of the English reform bill, the opposition seemed divided and confused. The breach with the Ultras, some of whom, such as Chandos, Knatchbull and Vyvyan, preferred an amendment in favour of a moderate reform scheme, with which Peel would have no truck, persisted, leading Robert Clive*, for one, to complain 'bitterly' to Greville

> of the bad tactics and want of union of the party, and especially of Peel's inactivity and backwardness in not having rallied and taken the lead more than he has; he is in fact so cold, phlegmatic, and calculating that he disgusts those who can't do without him as a leader; he will always have political but never personal influence.

Croker found him 'sore perplexed', perhaps because 'his conscience tells him that he is the primary source of all the mischief'.[288] In the event, the second reading was met with a direct negative, and Peel did not speak. According to Macaulay, 'the jaw of Peel fell' when the result of the division, a one-vote majority for the measure, was announced.[289] On 24 Mar. he delivered what Hobhouse considered 'the speech he ought to have made on the English bill', ostensibly replying to the ineffectual lord advocate Francis Jeffrey on the Scottish measure, but arguing that the scheme overall would damage the legitimate influence of the aristocracy and could not possibly be a final settlement, and arguing that by invoking the king's name in support of reform ministers had dangerously raised the stakes.[290] The following day, when he agreed to act on Ellenborough's suggestion of setting up 'an *election committee* with a view to the dissolution', he made good capital out of the discrepancies and inaccuracies in the 1821 census figures used as the basis for disfranchisement.[291] But for all his pre-eminence in the House, he remained subject to Tory complaints of 'his coldness, incommunicativeness and deficiency in all the qualities requisite in a leader, particularly at such a time'; and Campbell thought he was 'very much cast down, for he cannot stem the torrent'.[292] Mrs. Arbuthnot wrote, 29 Mar.:

> Peel feels very strongly that the king, having so far sanctioned the measure ... has rendered it very difficult for any minister to prevent all change in the representation. Our difficulties in opposing reform are, however, all aggravated by Peel's character ... The Conservative party ... know he will yield some points on reform, and the consequence is they all have their own crotchets, all want to gain popularity with their constituents by advocating at once that which, from Peel's nature, they feel will be yielded sooner or later ... Peel, saying he does not wish to return to office while he enjoys the discomfiture of ministers ... treats all the Tory party with arrogance and insolence, affects to consider himself as an *individual* and not the leader of the party, and has hitherto positively rejected all the advances of the Ultra Tories. He told Arbuthnot that he knew ... they wanted to reunite themselves with us, and that he was determined never to consent to; and yesterday, when ... Herries went to him, deputed by Wetherell and Lord Stormont* to express their desire and that of their party to be led and directed by him, all he repeated twenty times over was, 'These are the fellows who turned us out three months ago'. 'Very true' ... Herries said, 'now they want to get you back, and if we are to save the country, you must take them'. Peel threw his chin in the air, said if a government was to be formed they would expect places and he could not throw over those who were with him before, he did not want to return to office.[293]

Yet Goulburn found Peel 'in good heart, determined to resist the bill most manfully and to do all that may be most likely to effect its rejection', when he returned to London on 12 Apr.[294] That evening he supported the civil list grant against Hume's amendment for a cut. Next day he ascertained from Althorp that he would allow a division on the reform bill's proposal to reduce the number of English Members. He subsequently explained to Croker that whereas other contemplated amendments seemed unlikely to succeed, which would put the anti-reformers on the back foot:

> I think we shall beat them on that question ... Give us another month, and there is an end of the bill, positively an end of it. It could never be carried except by the dread of physical force ... One month hence, if the bill is still in suspense, there will be an enforced natural union between aristocracy and disfranchised population, against a vulgar privileged 'Pedlary', as in a letter I have ... received, a farmer, trembling for the fate of the corn laws, calls the new voters.[295]

On 15 Apr. Peel opposed Fowell Buxton's motion to commit the House to the immediate abolition of slavery, recommending a cautious approach in accordance with the 1823 resolutions.[296] He evidently gave some credence to reports that the king had refused to dissolve Parliament in the event of the reform bill's defeat, and he spoke forcefully in support of Gascoyne's amendment against the proposed reduction in the number of English Members, 19 Apr., when he asserted that he would not propose an alternative 'safe' reform scheme 'because I am certain that if I did, I should be taunted with adopting that course as a means of getting back into office', and said that the ministerial proposals held out 'the melancholy prospect of seeing the interests and affairs of this great country committed to misrule and anarchy'.[297] The amendment was carried by eight votes, and Peel, according to Ellenborough, who thought he would be willing to form a government if sent for, seemed to 'think that the majority was decisive against the bill'.[298] When the dissolution was announced in the House, 21 Apr., Peel, who Hobhouse noted 'preserved his temper, but looked exceedingly foolish', called it unjustified and a threat to public order, especially in Ireland.[299] Next afternoon, in a hot and excited chamber, as the guns signalled the king's approach, Peel got possession of the House, 'completely lost his temper' and produced a torrent of furious, semi-incoherent invective against ministers who had already shown 'more incapacity, more unfitness for office, more ignorance of their duties, more deplorable imbecility than ever was exhibited'. He predicted that if the reform scheme was enacted 'there will be established one of the worst despotisms that has ever yet existed. We shall have a Parliament of mob demagogues'. He was cut short in mid-rant by the arrival of Black Rod. Hobhouse recalled that this performance had

> completely unmasked him: all his candour, all his moderation, all his trimming, shifty policy disappeared, and he displayed his real vexation, and true feelings of disappointment and rage in a harangue of sound and fury, signifying nothing but his own despair, and hatred of those who had overreached him by calculating on the good sense of the people, and the firmness of the king, with more accuracy than himself ... He was doing harm to himself, and injuring the character of the country ... I was more sorry than angry; I could scarcely have supposed such an incident possible. But Peel was not the only over-excited performer on that day

He had apparently recovered his equanimity by the time he arrived in the Lords.[300]

Peel was re-elected for Tamworth in 'perfect tranquillity'.[301] He interrupted his canvass to go to London to consult Hardinge as to how he should react to Hobhouse's reported reference to his 'debased' exhibition at the prorogation and allegation that he had subscribed large election funds in a bid to deceive the people. Peel wrote a firm request for an explanation, which took Hobhouse aback; but the affair was settled with the cool counsels of Hardinge and Dacre.[302] A notion of his being put up for Liverpool in harness with Gascoyne came to nothing.[303] He was not surprised by the reformers' sweeping successes at the general election, which seemed to guarantee the reform scheme's passage through the Commons.[304] He remained isolated and self-absorbed, and frankly told Wellington on 24 May 1831 that he was 'much disinclined to be a party to any distinct proposition of reform', as there was 'a clear distinction between mitigating the evil of the bill in committee and originating a scheme of reform', quite apart from the fact that no plan he could endorse would be accepted by the new House.[305] He begged off the Pitt dinner at the end of the month, discountenanced the proposed eve of session opposition dinner intended to promote reconciliation with the Ultras and refused to have his name attached to circulars for an early attendance.[306] He was extraordinarily sensitive to current press allegations that his tactics on the first reform bill had been intended to facilitate his own return to power; and he told Croker, 28 May:

> I detest the thought of office, and am *not* ready to join O'Connell in effecting my return to it. If the Tory party is gone to pieces, I doubt whether the new Parliament is to blame ... There are two parties among those who call themselves Conservatives: one which views the state of the country with great alarm ... sees a relaxation of all authority, an impatience of all that restraint which is indispensable to the existence ... of all government [and] is ready to support monarchy, property and public faith ... Another party ... by far the most numerous ... has the most presumptuous confidence in its own fitness for administering public affairs ... would unite with O'Connell in resisting the Irish coercion law ... sees great advantage in a deficit of many millions, and thinks

> the imposition of a property tax on Ireland and the aristocracy a Conservative measure ... and which, never having dreamt ... of the question how they could restore order, prefers chaos to the maintenance of the present government. Now to this latter section I do not, and will not belong. I will not play that game, which, played by the Ultra Tories against us, is the main cause of present evils. A radical and a republican avowed are dangerous characters; but there is nothing half so dangerous as the man who pretends to be a Conservative, but is ready to be anything, provided only he can create confusion.[307]

A week later he wrote confidentially to Goulburn in broadly the same terms, expressing his willingness to 'co-operate with any persons of any party in resistance to the bill', in principle or detail, but his refusal to 'form a party connection with the Ultra Tory party', adding that 'I would not abandon any one opinion I entertain in order to conciliate Ultra ... support ... I [also] feel a want of many essential qualifications which are requisite in party leaders, among the rest personal gratification in the game of politics, and patience to listen to the sentiments of individuals whom it is equally imprudent to neglect and an intolerable bore to consult'. He observed that he had 'no wish to slight the offers of new party adherents, or to offend those who make them', but would be 'very cautious in contracting any new party engagements.[308] Mrs. Arbuthnot noted that Peel, who was already giving thought to the problem how the Lords would react to the reform scheme, 'appears to hate everybody and everybody hates him, but he showed consummate ability and powers of speaking of the highest order during the late ... session, and it is not possible for anyone to lead but him, but he is cross-grained, timid, afraid of committing himself, afraid of having followers and a party for fear they should be a clog upon him in any future arrangements'.[309] Smith Stanley heard that 'Peel throws cold water upon the notion of an opposition to everything *a tort et a travers*, and that the Ultras are ... very angry with him'. Yet Arbuthnot told Lord Farnham that with an opposition able to muster over 250, 'a vast deal may be done'.[310]

At a pre-session meeting Peel 'recommended moderation very earnestly' on the address, arguing that there should be no amendment provided it did not imply 'approval either of the reform bill, or the dissolution'.[311] On 21 June 1831 he retrospectively condemned the latter and the appeal to popular support, and suggested that ministers now seemed to be retreating from the full extent of their original plan. Hobhouse recalled it as a typical effort, 'professing candour and moderation, but losing no opportunity of saying sly and injurious things to his opponents'.[312] He was 'temperate', as Creevey saw it, on the motion for leave to reintroduce the English reform bill, 24 June, but Hobhouse, who thought he looked 'a little uncomfortable' under Russell's attack on 'moderate reformers', reckoned that he was 'half-angry' and 'spoke out most decisively against the bill'.[313] Peel told Robert Clive, who was unhappy with the decision to divide against the second reading, that it would be impossible to prevent someone from forcing a division and that 'no successful opposition could be made to a bill of this kind, if there was that acquiescence in the principle of it, which must be inferred from consent to the second reading'.[314] Opposing this, 6 July, he pointed out that since the present government came to power, more people had died in clashes with the military than during the whole of his time at the home office. He reiterated his objections to the measure, ridiculed the hasty changes made to some of its details, notably the mechanics of the £10 franchise and, repelling Macaulay's taunts of inconsistency the previous day, insisted that he had always 'opposed reform upon principle, because I was unwilling to open a door which I saw no prospect of being able to close'. It was reckoned an impressive effort, but the second reading was carried by 367-231.[315] Holland considered that so far Peel 'plays his cards artfully and is much more adventurous in debate now ... Brougham is not there to check his pride, than he was wont to be'; but he expected that Smith Stanley and perhaps Macaulay would 'soon learn the art of keeping him in order, for in different ways I think both are his superiors or were destined to become so'.[316] On 11 July Peel outraged many Tories by walking out of a debate on the wine duties in the middle of a speech by Herries. He compounded matters the following night when, after speaking in support of Appleby's right to be heard by counsel against its proposed disfranchisement, for which opposition had mustered in strength, he went away at midnight from the adjournment wrangle, observing that he would be 'no party to anything like a vexatious opposition', leaving a dwindling 'rabble' to force repeated divisions until eight in the morning.[317] Ellenborough lamented that 'no party can be kept together unless they are well and gallantly led', and Wellington thought his behaviour was 'inexplicable' and 'complained much that the party could neither do with him, nor without him'. Althorp told his father that Peel had 'acted very shabbily' towards his followers: 'He cannot lead an opposition party; he has not decision enough for it, and he has now lost all hold upon them'. Ellenborough got Ross and Hardinge to try to persuade Peel to 'say something to tranquillize the party', but he was unaccommodating, and indicated to Lord Mahon* that he was 'exceedingly annoyed' by the conduct of those who had persisted with the obstruction. Walking to the House on 13 July, he met Littleton, who 'reported ... the lamentations about his absence'. He replied, 'Parties are likened to serpents in which the heads are moved by the tails. Now I do not choose to be moved by the tail. I shall take my own line, and act for myself'.[318] That evening he mocked 'the inconceivable absurdity' of using outdated and inaccurate 1821 census figures to determine borough disfranchisement, when the 1831 census was almost to hand, and predicted that reform would send to the Commons 'an undue proportion' of 'men of popular habits' at the expense of those of 'retired ... literary and philosophic habits'. At a meeting at Chandos's, 19 July, he proposed the appointment of a committee of 11 'to direct the movements' of the party; but two days later George Bankes* moaned to Ellenborough that 'Peel's dinners do harm. He asks by Holmes's list, and his manner is not conciliatory'. At Croker's on the 23rd he seemed to Ellenborough to be 'very low about public affairs' and of opinion that opposition would have 'done better in the Commons to have made the discussion [on the disfranchisement schedules] shorter and taken only the great points'; he perceived that 'the majority will vote *blindly* for the bill'.[319] Yet he continued steady attendance, though the opposition to the details and technicalities of the bill was effected mainly by Croker, Wetherell, Sugden and a few others. On 22 July, to the disgust of Creevey, who though 'nothing could be more low', he made much of the defection of 40 reformers on the case of Downton the previous evening. Littleton reported to a friend:

> We march slowly in the reform bill. All sorts of unfair tricks are practised to clog and defeat it ... Peel affects to dislike it, but never tells his friends privately not to delay it. This is always his way, and gets him the character of a Jesuit. He wishes to defeat the bill and upset the government.

Mackintosh admitted, however, after Peel had robustly questioned Palmerston about the problem of the Belgian frontier forts, 27 July, that 'Peel has undoubtedly risen and ... has converted more people than will dare to confess it. We are certainly outspoken in daily speaking'.[320] On 27 July Peel made what Ellenborough thought 'a capital speech', in which he argued, with the aid of a map, that the disfranchisements would damage the agricultural interest, to support his motion to allow all the schedule B boroughs to retain two Members; he was defeated by 182-115.[321] When Althorp on 29 July proposed at short notice that the House should sit next day, a Saturday, to compensate for the loss of Monday, 1 Aug. on account of the ceremony to mark the opening of the new London Bridge, Peel responded 'in a fury', but to no avail. He ostentatiously stayed away.[322] At the ceremony, which he attended 'in his barge with his name in large letters', he was 'much hissed, but not otherwise ill treated'.[323] Russell accused him of changing his view on the enfranchisement of large manufacturing towns since 1828, 2 Aug., but Peel retorted that Althorp, Palmerston and other ministers had for years been hostile to reform. Next day he made what Hobhouse conceded was 'a good speech' against giving Members to the metropolitan districts, which would 'create a new order of men in this House, who will alter in character and increase in power with each successive election'; he was in a minority of 188 to 295.[324] He supported Littleton's motion to give Stoke two Members and Milton's to do likewise for the schedule D enfranchisements, 5 Aug. On 9 Aug. he deplored O'Connell's provocative comments on recent Orange outrages in Ireland. He urged ministers to set up an objective inquiry, 10 Aug., and next day opposed printing the Waterford petition for disarming the Irish yeomanry. At the behest of some of the party, he reluctantly opposed the proposed division of counties, which was likely to benefit the landed interest, 11 Aug., but left the House before the division, in which government had a majority of 109.[325] Hardinge reported to Arbuthnot, 17 Aug., that although ministers seemed to be in trouble, both at home and abroad, Peel thought 'they are not ready for the *coup de grace*, and certainly until the foreign policy is more fully developed and reform has become more unpalatable, it would be desirable to allow them to consummate their own defeat and disgrace'. Hardinge liked his 'most admirable bitter speech' against ministerial policy on French aggression towards Belgium, 17 Aug., when he clashed with and got the better of O'Connell and Hume, 'evincing more than ever ... [his] complete mastery over the House'.[326] But Peel was weary of the constant attendance and late hours in 'that infernal place' and late hours, and was aching for Julia, whom he told on 22 Aug. that he had 'hinted to the [Charles Street] committee that I cannot go on staying here to fight the tedious battle, and that they must choose some other leader if the House is to go on sitting much longer'. Having failed to get a straight answer that evening from Althorp about an adjournment, he went on the morning of the 23rd to Charles Street

> and told the persons assembled there that I could not continue in town, that in my opinion there is very little use in protracting the debates and that I could not remain here to conduct the battle. I found several people ... dissatisfied with this and prepared to go on interminably in the

> present system. Others were disposed to agree with me ... We parted not in very good humour. I said I should stay a few days longer, and would then go into the country, and come back for the third reading.[327]

In the House that day, he 'went away with many of his followers' before the division on the motion of censure on the Irish government's alleged interference in the Dublin election.[328] On 25 Aug. he welcomed Althorp's statement that the French army had left Belgium. He reiterated his determination to 'abandon the bill to its fate' and next day, inviting Goulburn to Drayton for shooting the following week, observed that 'I see no reason why we should labour to perfect the machinery by which a principle of which we disapprove is to be effected. But we should labour in vain, for the majority is now become unassailable by reason'.[329] He stayed to support his brother Edmund's vain attempt to preserve resident freemen's voting rights, 30 Aug. 1831, and then went to Drayton.

There he told Dyott that he thought the reform bill would be rejected by the Lords, but 'could not answer' his question as to whether that would 'throw out the ministry'.[330] He was anxious to get the bill to the Upper House as soon as possible, fearing that 'the danger to the Lords would be increased in dark long nights of winter, and with workmen thrown out of employment'.[331] He returned to London on 15 Sept., and in the Commons next day questioned the wisdom of empowering Irish grand juries to spend money on improvement projects. His speech against the passage of the reform bill, which closed the debate, 21 Sept., was widely praised. Lowther and Greville considered it the 'best ... he ever delivered', Ellenborough thought it 'splendid' and 'unanswerable', and Campbell reckoned it 'very good' and such as 'would have made you hesitate about carrying *this bill* into a law'. Hobhouse recalled that it was 'thought a very brilliant speech, foretelling the downfall of the monarchy and many uncomfortable events', but he judged that Peel failed in his effort to 'be smart upon Macaulay', who had accused the late ministry of abandoning their responsibilities. Greville, however, wrote that he had 'cut Macaulay to ribbons'.[332] He defended the Hampshire magistrates who had arrested the Deacles, 27 Sept., dismissed De Lacy Evans's motion for information on the preparations made by the Wellington ministry to preserve public order in November 1830, 4 Oct., and next day approved the imprisonment of the Rev. Robert Taylor for blasphemy. On 10 Oct., when Hardinge told Ellenborough that 'Peel would be rather cut in pieces than have the responsibility of bringing in a measure of reform' following the bill's rejection by the Lords, he opposed the motion of confidence in the ministry, accusing Macaulay, O'Connell and Sheil of trying to incite 'the rabble' against Wellington and the Tory peers. He seemed, however, to be below his usual form: the reformer John Hawkins had 'never heard ...[him] at such a disadvantage', and Littleton recorded that 'Peel's countenance was dejected in the extreme. An allusion of Macaulay's to his having bowed his head into the dust, when he recanted his error on the Catholic question, seemed to *combler* him with suffering. His speech was one of almost unconditional surrender'.[333] 'Not quite easy' at his children being alone at Drayton, 'with Birmingham political unions on one side, and Derby and Nottingham on the other', Peel went there on 12 Oct., and wrote to Croker next day:

> If there are any persons dreaming that either an anti-reform or a moderate reform government could at this time stand one hour in the present House of Commons, the division of ... [the 10th], but far more the feeling manifested in the debate, must ... dissipate the delusion. The greatest misfortune, accompanied with the greatest disgrace, that could befall any of us anti-reformers would be the attempt under present circumstances to originate reform in any shape. I never will. Dissolution would make bad worse ... [and] in the present state of the three kingdoms would be a rapid step in advance towards utter ruin.[334]

There was 'an absurd report' in London on 31 Oct. that 'Peel had killed himself'.[335] Disgusted but not surprised by 'the progress of our moral contagion', which he considered 'the inevitable consequence of a king and government hallooing a ten-pound mob against the House of Commons, in the stupid belief that they could have the hunt to themselves', he favoured the formation of 'quiet unostentatious associations for the sole purpose of defence against unprovoked aggression ... and *concerted* resistance to any aggressive demonstration of force on the part of reforming mobs'.[336] He returned what his critics described as a 'stiff, dry and reserved' answer, 23 Nov., to the Tory 'Waverer' Lord Wharncliffe's 'very vague and unsatisfactory' letter inviting him to endorse and join in the attempt to find a compromise solution to avoid a mass creation of peers to force reform through the Lords. He did not think ministers would make meaningful concessions.[337] He urged the party organizers to secure a good muster for the start of the new session and was 'stout-hearted' before leaving Drayton and 'not in bad spirits' when he arrived in London, still believing that the reform crisis would end in 'a coalition between the higher and the lower classes'.[338] On the address, 6 Dec. 1831, he made what Mahon considered a 'powerful' speech reviewing ministerial foreign and domestic policy and warning them to take heed of the fate of France between 1789 and 1792.[339] He described the changes made to the revised English reform bill, 12 Dec., as 'a complete answer to the calumnies ... about the factious delays of those who sought to introduce those very modifications', but, 'at the top of his anger, and voice', promised determined opposition to the second reading. His bitter tone was 'disavowed' by Baring, Clive, Chandos, Sandon, Warrender and other more conciliatory Tories, and he was said to have left the chamber 'evidently chagrined at his position'.[340] On 15 Dec. he acquiesced in the appointment of a select committee on Irish tithes (to which he was named), advised ministers to produce 'a specific plan' and welcomed their professed intention of upholding the property rights of the church. Holland interpreted this as 'artfully' trying to 'sow dissension between the government and the Catholics'; but Stanley believed that he would 'go along with us, and having already the load of the rotten boroughs hanging to his skirts, has no idea of augmenting the weight by the addition of the tithes'.[341] On the second reading of the reform bill, 16 Dec., Macaulay delivered a 'caustic' personal attack on Peel, strong enough 'to blister a rhinoceros', in which, responding to Peel's taunting of ministers for incorporating the Tories' suggestions into the new bill, he reminded him of his recantation on Catholic emancipation and the support which the Whigs had then given him. Hobhouse noted that Peel 'looked as if sweating blood. I never saw him so scalded, not even in the days of Brougham'. Next day Peel 'showed he had been touched to the quick' by spending half an hour in giving what Hobhouse considered an 'unnecessary' vindication of his conduct on the Catholic question. Ord thought he had produced nothing but 'the old and stale encomiums upon himself, and which were no answer at all to the really unanswerable attack ... and which he had richly earned ... This was really satisfactory to me, who have been long sick of ... [his] pompous self-conceited and affected candour'. Greville saw it as another example of Peel's 'egotism, with which he is so much and justly reproached'. Peel made no attempt to defend Croker from Smith Stanley's humiliating attack (which he seems to have inwardly relished), and ended his speech with a declaration that he would oppose the bill as 'the first step' to the establishment of a republic.[342]

Peel supported the foundation of the Conservative Carlton Club in early 1832.[343] Believing the reform bill to be 'replete with mischief and trickery', he went to London in mid-January 'resolved to place himself firmly at the head of the constitutional party', as Ellenborough put it.[344] In an 'angry speech', he backed Croker's objections to going into committee on schedule A without full information, 20 Jan.;[345] and on the 23rd, after being interrupted by a deranged onlooker in the gallery, supported Goulburn's amendment against schedule D and moved one of his own, which was negatived. Earlier that day he got Althorp to dispute Hume's 'doctrine' that the Irish clergy's legitimate right to tithes was a dead letter; and he divided with Althorp and Smith Stanley against Hobhouse's vestry reform bill. On 26 Jan. he spoke and voted against government (who at one point seemed to be heading for defeat) on the Russian-Dutch loan, but Hobhouse believed that his declaration that even if the censure was carried 'he should not think himself precluded from paying the money ... gave an excuse to the economical Members to vote for ministers'. Smith Stanley felt that he was 'evidently alarmed at the probability of a victory'; and according to Sir John Walsh*, Peel said he was not sorry that ministers survived, for 'as none of the money votes or the Mutiny Act had passed, we should have been unable to have formed a ministry, and they must have returned to office with added power'.[346] He now supported the division of counties, 27 Jan., though his suggestion that if all urban freeholders were excluded from the counties they might all return four Members was rejected; he 'good naturedly' allowed Ellice to whip him into the ministerial lobby as he was leaving for dinner.[347] On 1 Feb., when he welcomed retention of the Chandos clause enfranchising £50 tenants-at-will and spoke for Mackworth Praed's unsuccessful bid to confine urban freeholders to the boroughs, he approved of the restriction of factory hours for children, but not of any of the other details of Sadler's regulation bill; he was added to the committee on it, 28 Mar. In response to the 'Waverer' Harrowby's letter of 4 Feb. suggesting that the Conservative peers should give the reform bill a second reading and try to amend it in committee, Peel contended that the only sensible course (though he admitted that there were strong arguments on the other side) was to try to throw it out, regardless of the threat of peerage creations:

> My great object ... for the last six months has been to vindicate the authority and maintain the character of the House of Lords ... [as] the institution most exposed to danger from the short-sighted folly of the times, and also the institution which, if it remain erect in character, is most likely to serve as a rallying point for the returning good sense and moderation of the country ... Why have we been struggling against the reform bill in the Commons? Not in the hope of resisting its final success ... but because we look beyond the bill ... [and] know the nature of popular concessions, their tendency to propa-

> gate the necessity for further and more extensive compliances. We want to ... teach young inexperienced men charged with the trust of government that, though they may be backed by popular clamour, they shall not override on the first springtide of excitement every barrier and breakwater raised against popular impulses; that the carrying of extensive changes in the constitution without previous deliberation shall not be a holiday task; that there shall be just what has happened – the House sick of the question, the ministers repenting they ever brought it forward, the country paying the penalty for the folly and incapacity of its rulers. Mine is a melancholy view, as it excludes the prospect of success. It excludes, however, participation in the crime, and gives to the present House of Lords the honours of determined though fruitless resistance.

Harrowby showed Peel's letter, which was not well received by his followers, to Greville, who considered it 'an able production, well expressed and plausibly argued, with temper and moderation', but, seizing on its essential 'contradiction', he deemed it 'neither statesmanlike nor manly to throw up the game in despair, and surrender every point ... in order to preserve the consistency of himself and his own party'. He suspected that this was 'not his real feeling, and that he promises himself some personal advantage from the adoption of such a course'.[348] In a conversation with Littleton, 5 Feb., Jeffrey 'expressed his great admiration of Peel's powers of debate', but Littleton thought that 'the coolness of a practised gambler' was 'not ... quite a correct description of his manner, as coolness, though frequently well acted by him, is not his characteristic. But still, ill-tempered and vehemently excited as he frequently is, he seldom loses his judgement'.[349] On 6 Feb. Peel, reviewing the national finances, observed that the small surplus was 'alarming' and that 'the prospects of the country ... are most melancholy'. Later, he welcomed the preservation of resident freemen's voting rights, as proposed by his brother the previous year. He seemed to Littleton to be 'dreadfully out of temper, as he always is now', when he spoke against government on relations with Portugal, 9 Feb., and 'winced' under Smith Stanley's reply.[350] He took credit for prompting Grey's declaration on the enforcement of the payment of Irish tithes, but resisted Duncannon's desire for a pledge in the committee's report that 'the name and character of tithes should be done away'. In the House, 14 Feb., he criticized Grey's most recent pronouncement holding out the prospect of a permanent provision for the clergy, because it would raise false hopes and 'preclude enforcement of the law'. Anxious to back the government as far as possible on this question, he supported going into committee on the ministerial resolutions and opposed Brownlow's attempt to postpone consideration of the report, 8 Mar., when, according to Littleton, he 'well taunted' the Irish Members 'with their insincerity'. On 13 Mar. he made what Greville considered an 'excellent' speech, 'smashing Sheil, taking high ground and a strong position, but doing nothing towards settling the question', in support of the resolutions, subject to receiving an assurance that the law would be upheld and the property of the church safeguarded.[351] He was against a major reconstruction of the House – 'our debates should be carried on in this ancient apartment' – and argued that the cost of enforcing the cholera prevention bill should not fall on the parishes, 14 Feb. 1832. Next day he welcomed the concession of empowering the privy council to assist impoverished parishes.

On 21 Feb. 1832 Croker told Hertford that although Peel shared Wellington's sense of the potential 'danger' after the enactment of reform, he '*feels*, or *seems to feel* it, infinitely less. It does not affect his *spirits*, though I think it does his *judgement*. He is very reluctant to attend the House, and anything like a bold course he entirely rejects'. Two weeks later Croker noted that although Peel 'seems very stout-hearted, and in good health, and makes every now and then a display against the bill ... he seems ... inclined to consult his own personal ease, and people are not satisfied with his sincerity, but I really believe it is only the weariness of being eternally defeated, and the conviction that no good is to be done'. Princess Lieven confirmed that unlike Wellington, he 'does not believe that everything is lost, but even thinks that it will be quite possible to have a tolerable government in England'.[352] Peel, who assured Lord Malmesbury that if the English reform bill was 'bad enough', the Irish measure was 'in itself an Irish revolution as far as the transfer of power from Protestant to Roman Catholic and from the proprietors of land to the mob is concerned',[353] showed plenty of spirit when claiming that comments by Althorp on the case of Petersfield proved that ministers accepted that the reform bill could not be a final settlement, and opposing the enfranchisement of Tower Hamlets, 28 Feb. He was concerned that multiple occupancy of houses in some boroughs would put the franchise in 'hands in which it cannot properly be confided', 4 Mar. He mocked the 'lopsided mathematics' which determined that Whitby should be enfranchised and Doncaster ignored, 9 Mar. He argued that if Merthyr was to be given its own Member, the seat should be taken from Gateshead rather than Monmouthshire, 14 Mar. Next day he dismissed Hunt's motion for a retrospective inquiry into Peterloo. Opposing the third reading of the reform bill, 22 Mar., he predicted that the new system, 'established upon the £10 enfranchising principle, will make it impossible for any government to refuse to yield to popular demands', accused ministers of having 'put rancour in our hearts and sown dissensions in our homes' and concluded with a self-righteous vindication of his own conduct. Littleton judged it 'a very eloquent speech, the most so I ever heard from him, though by no means effective in argument', and noticed 'the extreme deference with which he treated Macaulay'; and Hawkins reported that he 'was unable to give a satisfactory answer' to Macaulay's 'perfectly just' attack.[354] Peel backed Vyvyan's criticism of the government's foreign policy, 26 Mar., and next day urged caution before sanctioning Ewart's proposal to abolish the death penalty for non-intimidatory stealing from dwelling houses, for 'as civilization increases, the facility for the commission of crime increases more rapidly than the facility for the prevention of it'. He supported the anatomy bill, 11 Apr., called for a generous grant for the National Gallery, 13 Apr., and urged recognition of Dom Miguel as the legitimate ruler of Portugal, 16 Apr. 1832.

After the Lords had given the reform bill a second reading by nine votes, Peel told Croker that 'I now see nothing left ... but a strenuous concerted effort on the part of all those who deprecate such a reform ... to mitigate the evil of it'. Having kept out of the Conservative peers' tactical deliberations, 'thinking the Lords might be jealous, and fearing to differ from the duke', he 'approved most cordially' the plan, disclosed to him by Ellenborough, to seek a reduction in the number of disfranchisements and enfranchisements, restrictions on the £10 franchise and the exclusion of urban voters from the counties.[355] During the crisis which followed the defeat of the bill in committee and ministers' resignation, 7-14 May, Peel consistently refused to form or take office in an administration pledged to carry a wide measure of reform. He said so to Lyndhurst, the king's emissary, to William IV himself and Croker. He did, however, suggest that Speaker Manners Sutton might become titular head of such a ministry. In the House, 10 May, he opposed as 'unconstitutional' the motion asking the king to appoint only ministers who would carry undiluted reform, but he cut an unusually 'feeble' figure, as Hobhouse thought, and was 'roughly' handled by O'Connell. Next day he said, in reply to Tom Duncombe's question, that he had not been invited to take office. (This was not strictly true.) In the fiasco of a debate which spelled the end of the project to form a Conservative reform ministry, 14 May, 'in a very subdued manner' he tried to damp the excitement generated, insisted that he did not want office and praised the 'sense of public duty' which had prompted Wellington to try to rescue the king from the mess.[356] Later that night, after talks with Croker, Goulburn, Hardinge and others, he went with Manners Sutton to Wellington and persuaded him to inform the king that no alternative government was feasible and that he would withdraw his opposition to the bill to avoid the creation of peers.[357] He was mightily relieved to be out of the scrape, and told Ellenborough that 'the Tory party would have been disgraced by accepting office to carry the reform bill after all that had been said by them against it'. But he was widely criticized in the party for cowardice, selfishness (Baring 'supposed that Peel, as usual, thought chiefly of Peel', Littleton observed that 'his prudence is always more conspicuous than his generosity or courage' and 'his talent is eminently fitted for turning things to his own account', and Ellenborough that he 'wants moral courage, and has not a great mind') and disloyalty to Wellington. He was suspected in some quarters of having put up Manners Sutton as a stooge whom he would replace when reform was out of the way.[358] More importantly he and Wellington, whose relations had been strained since November 1830, were now virtually alienated, a state of affairs which lasted for two years. In his explanatory speech in the Lords, 17 May 1832, Wellington made 'a sort of covert attack upon Peel', to which he replied in the Commons the following evening, when he regretted their temporary separation, but defended his own conduct. According to Hobhouse, Althorp's 'humiliating testimony' to his honour 'made poor Peel look very foolish and sulky; he did not acknowledge Althorn's civility, but blushed, and fidgeted, and was silent'.[359]

On 21 May 1832 Peel challenged Denman's assertion that the sincerity with which libellous opinions were expressed should protect the authors from prosecution. He supported the government's temporizing amendment to Fowell Buxton's motion for the abolition of slavery, 24 May, when Howick, accusing him of ratting on the 1823 agreement, threw his recantation on the Catholic question in his face. Peel retorted that 'to affirm the principle of the extinction of slavery, before we possess the means of carrying our intentions into effect, is fraught with danger'. Opposing the second reading of the Irish reform bill, 25 May, he asserted that it would 'undermine the security of he established church ... diminish the influence of property' and strengthen the repeal movement. On the Lords' amendments to the English bill, 5 June, he said that the peers had 'consented to this bill under a menace'; accused ministers of whipping up popular excitement from the outset and recalled Russell's 'whisper of a faction' comment; said that reform would seal the fate of the corn laws; urged ministers to suppress the unions, who if left unchecked would establish a 'degrading and oppressive tyranny; reminded Russell of his assertion in 1827 that the people had become so 'indifferent to reform' that he would never again propose it, and defended the Wellington government's attempt to reform Irish tithes. He wanted working men's unions regulated, 14 June, when he acquiesced in the introduction of the ministerial bill to suppress Irish party processions, provided it was even-handed, and said that if Orange parades were to be outlawed, so too must be the roving gangs, 'led by priests', who were impeding the collection of tithes. At this time he dined with Lady Cowper, who told her brother that

> he did not seem very desponding at the state of affairs, said nobody could tell how things would turn, they might be better than he expected, or much worse than he feared. He said ... that the present government must stay in, and that if they tried to resist the radicals, they should have his support. One thing he said must be done, without which no government could stand ... was to curb the licence of the press.[360]

He clashed peevishly with O'Connell and Hume on the Irish reform bill, 18 June, accusing the latter of justifying the use of physical force to overawe Parliament. On 20 June he seconded the address to the king condemning the attack on him at Ascot races, but blamed this and the recent assault on Wellington on the 'intemperate language of the press and speeches in Parliament' by the likes of Hume. Hobhouse wrote that he was 'very bitter, but ... made no figure at all', and others reckoned that the castigation which he received from Smith Stanley put him in his place.[361] He had Walsall replaced by Lichfield as the nomination venue for the new South Staffordshire constituency, 22 June. He accused Jeffrey of giving in to pressure from the unions to abandon the proposed property qualification for Scottish county Members, 27 June, when he spoke and voted for Baring's bill to exclude insolvent debtors from Parliament. He deplored any hasty action on behalf of Poland, 28 June. He urged Irish Protestants to behave themselves on the 12th of July, 29 June, supported the introduction of the Irish tithes bill, 10 July, and endorsed Russell's condemnation of the illegal 'conspiracy' against collection, though he dissented from his views on Irish church reform in general, 13 July. He spoke and divided against ministers on the Russian-Dutch loan, 12 July. He described Hume's bill to ban the recorder of Dublin from sitting in the Commons as 'an act of oppression' and voted accordingly, 24 July. He was inclined to give lord chancellor Brougham the benefit of the doubt over the 'provisional' appointment of his brother to a chancery sinecure due for abolition, 25 July, but on the 27th joined in the condemnation of Brougham's offensive personal attack on his accuser Sugden. That day, in his last Commons speech in this period, Peel said that he did not consider the financial state of the country to be 'so lamentable as many persons would suppose', though a deficit was undesirable, and observed that reform was 'not calculated to produce an increase in the revenue'. He called for a swift settlement of the currency problem and criticized aspects of the government's foreign policy. He went to Drayton a few days later, having warned the minister Sir James Graham that the Conservative peers intended to throw out the tithes bill on the second reading and said that it would not surprise him to see O'Connell appointed Irish attorney-general before the next session.[362] On 10 Aug. 1832 he wrote to Croker from Drayton, where his new house was 'rising before the windows of the old', that to 'read of the House sitting till three o' clock, and abortive attempts to amend the reform bill in the present session' gave him 'no feelings but that of satisfaction that I am a hundred miles from the scene of contention'.[363]

In November 1831 Horace Twiss* had given the following assessment of Peel to Littleton:

> The best man of business and best debater in England, but always thinking of his reputation and his outward character, content to 'dwell in decencies', never decided and courageous, thinking more of getting well through a business into which he had been led by circumstance, than bold and decided in his pursuit and assertion of great principles and worthy objects. With great *show* of affability and condescension (which is always offensive when seen through, especially in a 'new man'), he was in reality selfish, cold, and unconciliatory ... [Twiss] doubted whether his conduct on the Catholic question, and on ... reform, would not throw him out of office for some years.[364]

Yet early in the first reformed Parliament, to which Peel was returned unopposed for Tamworth, Poulett Thomson perceived that his 'prodigious superiority over everybody in the House was so evident ... that he must draw men's minds to him'. Greville, no admirer of Peel at this stage of his career, wrote that he had 'hitherto been encumbered with embarrassing questions and an unmanageable party', but that 'if his great experience and talents have a fair field to act upon, he may yet, in spite of his selfish and unamiable character, be a distinguished and successful minister'.[365] So he became, but not without irreparably splitting the Conservative party on repeal of the corn laws. He died, aged only 62, in early July 1850, of internal injuries sustained in a fall from his horse on Constitution Hill. His death, which Campbell described as 'a very heavy blow to the Whigs', was nationally mourned.[366] He was succeeded in the baronetcy and estates by his eldest son Robert Peel (1822-95), Conservative Member for Tamworth, 1850-80.[367]

[1] The standard biography is the two-volume work by N. Gash: *Mr Secretary Peel* (1961) and *Sir Robert Peel* (1972). As correctives to its Conservative bias, see D. Beales, 'Peel, Russell and Reform', *HJ*, xvii (1974), 873-82; B. Hilton, 'Peel: a Reappraisal', ibid. xxii (1979), 585-614; and I. Newbould, 'Sir Robert Peel and the Conservative Party', *EHR*, xcviii (1983), 529-57. T.A. Jenkins, *Sir Robert Peel* (1999) is an excellent concise and candid survey of Peel's political career. [2] [J. Grant], *Random Recollections of Commons* (1837), 108-9. [3] Ibid. 109; *Shelley Diary*, ii. 21. [4] *Mackintosh Mems.* ii. 347. [5] Jenkins, 2, 11-15. [6] Grant, 116. [7] Hilton, 585-9. [8] *Fox Jnl.* 62-63. [9] *Croker Pprs.* i. 170. [10] Hatherton diary, 28 June; *The Times*, 13 July 1820. [11] *Peel Letters*, 42; *Croker Pprs.* i. 176-7. [12] Bucks. RO, Fremantle mss D/FR/51/5/5; *Arbuthnot Jnl.* i. 52. [13] *Croker Pprs.* i. 175, 184; *Arbuthnot Jnl.* i. 55-56; *HMC Bathurst*, 490-1; Add. 38288, f. 386; 40304, ff. 4-5; Buckingham, *Mems. Geo IV*, i. 93, 95, 100; *Colchester Diary*, iii. 202. [14] Add. 30123, f. 233. [15] NLW, Coedymaen mss, Wynn to Lord Grenville, 26 Dec. 1820; Buckingham, i. 102. [16] Broughton, *Recollections*, ii. 140. [17] HLRO, Hist. Coll. 379, Grey Bennet diary, 13; *Creevey Pprs.* ii. 12. [18] *Von Neumann Diary*, i. 50; *Countess Granville Letters*, i. 205; *Arbuthnot Jnl.*, i. 69. [19] Buckingham, i. 121-2. [20] *Arbuthnot Jnl.* i. 80; Fremantle mss 46/12/134. [21] Buckingham, i. 102; Grey Bennet diary, 28. [22] Buckingham, i. 132. [23] Ibid. i. 142-3. [24] *Arbuthnot Jnl.* i. 82; J.E. Cookson, *Lord Liverpool's Administration*, 308-9. [25] *Arbuthnot Jnl.* i. 90, 92, 94. [26] Ibid. i. 97; *Croker Pprs.* i. 187. [27] *HMC Bathurst*, 497-8. [28] *Croker Pprs.* i. 187-90. [29] *Hobhouse Diary*, 62; *Croker Pprs.* i. 191. [30] *Croker Pprs*, i. 190-1; Parker, *Peel*, i. 299-300; *Arbuthnot Jnl.* i. 100. [31] *Arbuthnot Jnl.* i. 101. [32] *Hobhouse Diary*, 65; *Arbuthnot Jnl.* i. 102; Buckingham, i. 173; *Croker Pprs.* i. 213; Cookson, 313. [33] *Croker Pprs.* i. 217-18; Add. 38195, f. 104; *Geo. IV Letters*, ii. 969; *Arbuthnot Jnl.* i. 130; *Hobhouse Diary*, 81. [34] *Hobhouse Diary*, 85; *Colchester Diary*, iii. 242. [35] *Von Neumann Diary*, i. 90. [36] Lansdowne mss, Mackintosh to Lansdowne, 28 Dec. 1821. [37] Gash, *Secretary Peel*, 312-14. [38] Ibid. 314-18; Jenkins, 29-30. [39] Gash, *Secretary Peel*, 326-4; Jenkins, 26-29; Beales, 879-80; Hilton, 'The Gallows and Mr. Peel', in *History and Biography* ed. T.W. Blanning and D. Cannadine, 92-97, 109-10; V.A.C. Gatrell, *Hanging Tree*, 554-65, 568-9, 576-8. [40] Gash, *Secretary Peel*, 334-9. [41] See ibid. 344-51. [42] See ibid. 367-95. [43] See Jenkins, 34-41. [44] Grey mss, Tierney to Grey, 23 Jan. 1822; Add. 52445, f. 31. [45] Gash, *Secretary Peel*, 296-7; Add. 40605, ff. 121, 125, 127, 129. [46] PRO NI, Hill of Brook Hall mss D642/A/14/22; Gash, *Secretary Peel*, 300-1. [47] Broughton, ii. 182-3. [48] *Colchester Diary*, iii. 251. [49] Northants. RO, Agar Ellis diary, 30 Apr. [1822]; Add. 52445, f. 83; *Fox Jnl.* 114; *Arbuthnot Jnl.* i. 161. [50] Buckingham, i. 323. [51] Add. 75937, Lady to Lord Spencer, 13 May 1822; Buckingham, i. 325-6; *Arbuthnot Jnl.* i. 162. [52] Broughton, ii. 187. [53] NLS mss 3895, f. 28. [54] Buckingham, i. 350-1, 353. [55] *Hobhouse Diary*, 95; *Croker Pprs.* i. 227-32; *Greville Mems.* i. 127; Buckingham, i. 365-6, 371; *Arbuthnot Corresp.* 27, 28; Add. 38575, f. 32; 38743, f. 197; 40319, f. 57; 40349, f. 187; 40351, f. 13; Wellington mss, Wellington to Mrs. Arbuthnot, 31 Aug., 2, 3, 6 Sept. 1822; Gash, *Secretary Peel*, 301-7; Jenkins, 25. [56] Bessborough mss, Tierney to Duncannon, 14 Aug., Brougham to same [19 Aug.]; Add. 51586, Tierney to Lady Holland [30 Aug., 4 Sept.]; 51596, Essex to same, 16 Aug. 1822; *Creevey Pprs.* ii. 44-45. [57] Lansdowne mss, Macdonald to Lansdowne, 18 Aug. [1822]. [58] Gash, *Secretary Peel*, 307. [59] Powis mss (History of Parliament Aspinall transcripts), Palmerston to Lord Clive, 13 Sept. 1822; Bagot, *Canning and Friends*, ii. 134. [60] Add. 60286, f. 278. [61] *Hobhouse Diary*, 101-2. [62] Grey mss, Grey to Holland, 22 Jan. 1823; TCD, Donoughmore mss F/13/73. [63] *Arbuthnot Jnl.* i. 219-20; Buckingham, i. 432, 434-5. [64] *Creevey Pprs.* ii. 62; Creevey mss, Creevey to Miss Ord, 21 Feb.; Grey mss, Lambton to Grey, 13 Feb.; NLS, Ellice mss, Grey to Ellice, 23 Feb. 1823. [65] Agar Ellis diary, 4 Mar. [1823]. [66] *Fox Jnl.* 157; Merthyr Mawr mss F/51/4. [67] Buckingham, i. 448, 451 [68] *Arbuthnot Jnl.*, i. 229; Buckingham, i. 457; Parker, i. 342-3; Gash, *Secretary Peel*, 401. [69] *Creevey Pprs* ii. 69. [70] *Colchester Diary*, iii. 280-1; Dorset RO D/BKL, Bankes jnl. 145. [71] *Colchester Diary*, iii. 289. [72] Buckingham, i. 469, 475, 479. [73] *Hobhouse Diary*, 104; *Arbuthnot Jnl.* i. 255. [74] *Peel Letters*, 46-47, 53; *HMC Bathurst*, 542-3. [75] *Arbuthnot Jnl.* i. 262. [76] Buckingham, ii. 11-14. [77] *Arbuthnot Jnl.* i. 271. [78] Buckingham, ii. 42. [79] Gash, *Secretary Peel*, 323-4; Agar Ellis diary, 24 Feb. [1824]. [80] Buckingham, ii. 53. [81] Ibid. ii. 78. [82] Arbuthnot mss; *Arbuthnot Jnl.* i. 321. [83] Buckingham, ii. 99, 105-6, 126. [84] *Three Diaries*, 118. [85] Parker, i. 349-51; Add. 40300, ff. 17, 21; 40306, ff. 72-81; *Arbuthnot Jnl.* i. 356-8; *Wellington Despatches*, ii. 345-6. See Gash, *Secretary Peel*, 401-2. [86] Gash, *Secretary Peel*, 388-92; Parker, i.345-9, 354-7; Add. 40330, ff. 310, 372; Lonsdale mss. [87] Buckingham, ii. 209-10; Bankes jnl. 152; Merthyr Mawr mss F/2/8 (10 Feb. 1825). [88] Broughton, iii. 88. [89] Merthyr Mawr mss F/2/8 (18 Feb. 1825); Broughton, iii. 88-90; Add. 30124, f. 139; Grey mss, Tierney to Grey, 21 Feb. 1825. [90] Add. 40334, ff. 118, 135, 140; 40372, f. 189; Parker, i. 369-70; Gash, *Secretary Peel*, 413-16. [91] Agar Ellis diary, 21 Apr. [1825]. [92] *Arbuthnot Jnl.* i. 381, 392-4, 397-8, 400-1; *HMC Bathurst*, 579-82; Broughton, iii. 98; *Peel Letters*, 69; *Arbuthnot Corresp.* 67, 68; *Hobhouse Diary*, 115; Gash, *Secretary Peel*, 417-20; Jenkins, 42-43. [93] Broughton, iii. 98-99. [94] *Peel Letters*, 69. [95] Gash, *Secretary Peel*, 324-6; Castle Howard mss, Abercromby to Morpeth, 24 June, 5 July 1825; Wellington mss WP1/849/5. [96] *Geo. IV Letters*, iii. 1207-8. [97] Gash, *Secretary Peel*, 354-6; Wellington mss WP1/849/5. [98] Castle Howard mss, Abercromby to Carlisle, 15 Feb.; Add. 51574, same to Holland, 16 Feb. [1826]. [99] Wellington mss WP1/850/9. [100] Ibid. WP1/851/3. [101] Add. 51584, Tierney to Holland, 12 Mar. 1826. [102] Add. 51574, Abercromby to Holland, 7 Mar. [1826]. [103] Buckingham, ii. 300. [104] *Arbuthnot Jnl.* ii. 21. [105] *Creevey Pprs.* ii. 100. [106] Nottingham Univ. Lib. Denison diary, 4, 19 May; Add. 51659, Whishaw to Lady Holland, 14 May 1826. [107] *Arbuthnot Jnl.* ii. 28-29. [108] Add. 40387, ff. 71-76. [109] Add. 40305, f. 192. [110] *Peel Letters*, 89. [111] Parker, i. 414-27; Jenkins, 45. [112] Gash, *Secretary Peel*, 397-9; Parker, i. 427-32. [113] Castle Howard mss. [114] *Arbuthnot Jnl.* ii. 69-70. [115] Ibid. ii. 72; *HMC Bathurst*, 627; Parker, i. 433-7; *Wellington Despatches*, iii. 551-3. [116] *Peel Letters*, 91-99; *HMC Bathurst*, 627. [117] Lansdowne mss, Holland to Lansdowne, 31 Jan. 1827. [118] Add. 38748, f. 242. [119] Denison diary, 12 Feb. [1827]; *Greville Mems.* i. 168. [120] *Arbuthnot Jnl.* ii. 79. [121] Parker, i. 448-51; *Canning's Ministry*, 1-10. [122] Add. 40392, ff. 152, 154. [123] Agar Ellis diary, 6 Mar.; Denison diary, 6 Mar.; TCD, Jebb mss 6396/275; Broughton, iii. 174-5; Grey mss, Howick to Grey 7 Mar.; Derby mss 920 Der (14) 2/3 (6 Mar. 1827). [124] *Arbuthnot Jnl.* ii. 87. [125] Grey mss, Howick to Grey, 16 Mar. 1827; *Macaulay Letters*, i. 219. [126] Broughton, iii. 183. [127] For Peel's part in the negotiations of March and April 1827 see *Canning's Ministry*, 21-23, 27-28, 51-56, 60, 66, 73-74, 77, 95, 101-2, 114, 116, 124; Parker, i. 452-68; Twiss, *Eldon*, ii. 589-92; *Geo. IV Letters*, iii. 1296, 1304-6, 1311; *Arbuthnot Jnl.* ii. 89, 98, 103; *Hobhouse Diary*, 127-8; *Colchester Diary*, iii. 477, 482-3; Gash, *Secretary Peel*, 429-36; Jenkins, 44-45. [128] See Gash, *Secretary Peel*, 442-4; *Croker Pprs.* i. 374 [129] Add. 40332, f. 319; *Arbuthnot Jnl.* ii. 108-9. [130] Rutland mss (History of Parliament Aspinall transcripts), Londonderry to Rutland, 16 Apr.; Lonsdale mss, Lowther to Lonsdale, 23 Apr.; Add 76380, Tavistock to Althorp, 25 Apr. 1827. [131] Denison diary, 1 May; *Arbuthnot Jnl.* ii. 113; Agar Ellis diary, 1 May [1827]; *Shelley Diary*, ii. 156. [132] Add. 51663, Bedford to Holland, 5 May [1827]. [133] *Geo. IV Letters*, iii. 1322; Agar Ellis diary, 3 May; Denison diary, 4 May [1827]; Broughton, iii. 191. [134] St. Deiniol's Lib. Glynne-Gladstone mss 123, Gascoyne to J. Gladstone, 9 May 1827. [135] *Colchester Diary*, iii. 490, 497-8, 503-4; Jebb mss 6396/279, 280. [136] *Geo. IV Letters*, iii. 1328; Add. 52058, C. to H. Fox, 13 May 1827. [137] Broughton, iii.

193; Hatherton mss. [138] Add. 52447, f.82; Broughton, ii. 204-5. [139] *HMC Bathurst*, 640. [140] Arbuthnot mss, Peel to Arbuthnot, 10 Aug. 1827; *Arbuthnot Corresp.* 87, 91; *HMC Bathurst*, 643. [141] *Arbuthnot Corresp.* 89; Lonsdale mss, Lonsdale to Lowther, 6 Sept., reply, 7 Sept. 1827. [142] *Colchester Diary*, iii. 526-9. [143] Hatherton mss, Huskisson to Littleton, 4 Dec., Littleton to Peel, 6 Dec., reply, 9 Dec. 1827. [144] Add. 52447, f. 129. [145] *Croker Pprs.* i. 402, 404; *Peel Letters*, 103-7; Add. 38754, f. 80; 40334, f. 197; Parker, ii. 26-36; *Peel Mems.* i. 11-18; Gash, *Secretary Peel*, 451-7. [146] *Arbuthnot Jnl.* ii. 158-60; *Croker Pprs.* i. 404 [147] *Geo. IV Letters*, iii. 1480. [148] *Croker Pprs.* i. 406 [149] See Gash, *Secretary Peel*, 477-8. [150] See ibid. 478-87. [151] See ibid. 487-507; Jenkins, 30-31. [152] *Ellenborough Diary*, i. 32, 33; Hatherton diary, 15 Feb. [1828]; Add. 40307, f. 50; 40395, f. 244. [153] Broughton, iii. 246. [154] *Ellenborough Diary*, i. 39, 43, 45; Broughton, iii. 246; Fitzwilliam mss, Milton to wife, 29 Feb. 1828. [155] Russell, *Recollections*, 58; Nottingham Univ. Lib. Portland mss PwH 147; Rutland mss, Rutland to Mrs. Arbuthnot, 28 Mar.; *Croker Pprs.* i. 412; *Colchester Diary*, iii. 553, 555; Add. 51669, Bedford to Lady Holland [26 Mar. 1828]. [156] See Gash, 460-5. [157] *Arbuthnot Jnl.* ii. 170-2. [158] Broughton, iii. 254. [159] *Ellenborough Diary*, i. 63-64; *Croker Pprs.* i. 413. [160] *Colchester Diary*, iii. 553-4. [161] *Arbuthnot Jnl.* ii. Ii. 173-7. [162] PRO NI, Anglesey mss D619/27A/14; Add. 51663, Bedford to Holland, 31 Mar. 1828. [163] *Ellenborough Diary*, i. 51-52, 58, 69, Add. 38755, f. 269; *Arbuthnot Jnl.* ii. 178; Ashley, *Palmerston*, i. 132. [164] Cent. Kent. Stud. Stanhope mss U1590 C355, Pusey to Mahon, 8 Apr. 1828; *Ellenborough Diary*, i. 74, 80; Broughton, iii. 257; Gash, *Secretary Peel*, 465-9. [165] *Ellenborough* Diary, i. 105; *Croker Pprs.* i. 418-19; Broughton, iii. 260. [166] *Arbuthnot Jnl.* ii. 186. [167] *Croker Pprs.* i. 418. [168] *Croker Pprs.* i. 409-11, 420; *Ellenborough Diary*, i. 63-64, 106, 112-13; Broughton, iii. 270; *Wellington Despatches*, iv. 449-72; Ashley, i. 149-62; Gash, *Secretary Peel*, 469-75. [169] *Ellenborough Diary*, i. 124, 126, 129-30; *Arbuthnot Jnl.* ii. 187, 189-90. [170] Broughton, iii. 276; Bankes jnl. 164 (2 June 1828). [171] Anglesey mss 31A/77. [172] Bagot mss (History of Parliament Aspinall transcripts). [173] *Ellenborough Diary*, i. 154-5, 156, 157, 175; *Arbuthnot Jnl.* ii. 196. [174] *Arbuthnot Corresp.* 108. [175] *Peel Mems.* i. 116-17. [176] See *Peel Mems.* i. 1-297; *Wellington Despatches*, v. 61 76, 80-81, 87, 92, 252-68, 324-6, 356-82, 413; Parker, ii. 46-81; *Colchester Diary*, ii. 579; *Croker Pprs.* i. 427-8; *Ellenborough Diary*, i. 171, 182, 200, 284, 293; *Arbuthnot Jnl.* ii. 200-2, 206-7, 210, 224, 228-31; *Arbuthnot Corresp.* 108; *Greville Mems.* i. 216, 238; Fitzwilliam mss, Scarlett to Milton, 30 Oct. 1828; Gash, *Secretary Peel*, 520-50; Jenkins, 49-51. [177] *Ellenborough Diary*, i. 299-300; *Peel Mems.* i. 296; *Colchester Diary*, iii. 595. [178] *Ellenborough Diary*, i. 308, 311-13, 347-51; *Arbuthnot Jnl.* ii. 233, 235-6; Add. 40323, f. 31. [179] *Croker Pprs.* ii. 7-8; Lonsdale mss, Lowther to Lonsdale, 2, 4, 5 Feb. 1829. [180] *Croker Pprs.* ii. 7, 9; Add. 40398, ff. 174, 188, 237; 51584, Tierney to Holland [3 Feb.]; 52011, Stuart Wortley to H.E. Fox, 8 Feb. 1829. [181] *Croker Pprs.* ii. 8; Broughton, iii. 302; *Greville Mems.* i. 249; Hatherton diary, 5 Feb.; Agar Ellis diary, 5 Feb.; Harrowby mss, Denison to Sandon, 6 Feb. 1829. [182] *Croker Pprs.* ii. 8. [183] Add. 40398, ff. 146, 148, 167, 169, 220, 250; Agar Ellis diary, 9 Feb.; Lonsdale mss, Lowther to Lonsdale, 10 Feb. 1829; *Greville Mems.* i. 250; Broughton, iii. 303. [184] *Arbuthnot Jnl.* ii. 239-40; Broughton, iii. 303-4; *Croker Pprs.* ii. 9; *Creevey Pprs.* ii. 195; Hatherton mss, Littleton to wife, 10 Feb.; Harrowby mss, Sandon to Harrowby, 12 Feb. 1829. [185] Broughton, iii. 306; *Ellenborough Diary*, i. 366; Add. 40398, f. 313; Gash, *Secretary Peel*, 560-4. [186] Add. 40320, f. 117; 40399, ff. 25, 27; Gash, *Secretary Peel*, 564-5. [187] *Arbuthnot Jnl.* ii. 243-4, 247-8; *Ellenborough Diary*, i. 376; *Wellington Despatches*, v. 482-519 *Peel Mems.* i. 349-50; Gash, *Secretary Peel*, 565-70. [188] *Greville Mems.* i.265; Broughton, iii. 308; *Ellenborough Diary*, i. 380; *Von Neumann Diary*, i. 198; *Arbuthnot Jnl.* ii. 249; *Lady Holland to Son*, 98; Agar Ellis diary, 5 Mar. [1829]; Gash, *Secretary Peel*, 570-6; Jenkins, 50-51. [189] Broughton, iii. 311; *Greville Mems.* i. 274 *Ellenborough Diary*, i. 405; Keele Univ. Lib. Sneyd mss, Lady Bathurst to Sneyd [19 Mar. 1829]. [190] Add. 40399, ff. 77, 79, 86, 90. [191] Broughton, iii. 314-15. [192] *Ellenborough Diary*, ii. 2, 9; *Croker Pprs.* ii. 14. [193] *Arbuthnot Jnl.* ii. 269 [194] NAS GD23/6/746/121/1. [195] Lonsdale mss. [196] Heron, *Notes*, 175. [197] Reid, *Monckton Milnes*, i. 60-61. [198] Add. 30115, f. 92; 51562, Brougham to Holland, Wed. [?8 Apr. 1829]. [199] *Ellenborough Diary*, ii. 25, 30, 37, 47. [200] Gash, *Secretary Peel*, 601-3. [201] Hatherton mss, Littleton to Leigh, 19 May 1829. [202] Agar Ellis diary, 1 June [1829]. [203] *Ellenborough Diary*, ii. 64, 68, 73, 78-79, 87, 134, 136; Parker, ii. 115-39; Add. 40308, ff. 209, 211, 217, 250; 40327, f. 76; 40337, ff. 40, 49, 61, 74, 92, 123, 181, 212; *Wellington Despatches*, vi. 31, 37-38, 52, 60, 198, 253-4; Gash, *Secretary Peel*, 603-8. [204] Add. 51562, Brougham to Holland, Sunday [?July], Wed. [?5 Aug.], Sat. [?22 Aug.], Mon. [?24 Aug.]; Cornw. RO, Vyvyan mss, Knatchbull to Vyvyan, 26 Aug. 1829. [205] *Croker Pprs.* ii. 17-20; *Peel Letters*, 116-17; *Dyott's Diary*, ii. 64. [206] Add. 51534, Grenville to Holland, 8 Sept.; 51574, Abercromby to same, 20 Dec. 1829; NLS acc. 10655, memo. [207] *Creevey Pprs.* ii. 146; Add. 51534, T. Grenville to Holland, 14 Jan.; 51580, Carlisle to Lady Holland, 7 Jan.; 51785, Holland to C.R. Fox, 11 1830; Northumb. RO, Middleton mss ZMI/S/77/3/1. [208] Add. 51785, Holland to C.R. Fox, 18 Jan. 1830; *Ellenborough Diary*, ii. 177. [209] *Arbuthnot Jnl.* ii. 331. [210] *Ellenborough Diary*, ii. 184. [211] Add. 51785, Holland to C.R. Fox, 7 Feb. 1830; *Countess Granville Letters*, ii. 57. [212] *Ellenborough Diary*, ii. 195; Grey mss, Durham to Grey, 13 Feb. 1830. [213] *Arbuthnot Jnl.* ii. 334; Bessborough mss, Abercromby to Duncannon, 16 Feb.; Add. 51785, Holland to C.R. Fox, 20 Feb. 1830. [214] Sneyd mss, Littleon to Sneyd, 24 Feb. [1830]; *Arbuthnot Jnl.* ii. 342. [215] *Ellenborough Diary*, ii. 198. [216] Agar Ellis diary, 10 Mar.; Grey mss, Grey to Howick, 14 Mar. 1830. [217] Broughton, iv. 12; Grey mss, Grey to Howick, 15 Mar. 1830; *Arbuthnot Jnl.* ii. 344-5. [218] *Arbuthnot Corresp.* 131; *Ellenborough Diary*, ii. 199; 203, 213, 215; *Arbuthnot Jnl.* ii. 335, 343, 345. [219] *Ellenborough Diary*, ii. 215, 216. [220] Add. 52176. [221] *Arbuthnot Corresp.* 134. [222] *Peel Letters*, 119-20; *Arbuthnot Jnl.* ii. 349; Add. 40400, f. 154. [223] *Croker Pprs.* ii. 57; *Peel Letters*, 121-2; *Ellenborough Diary*, ii. 236; Broughton, iv. 20. Gash, *Secretary Peel*, 627-9. [224] *Croker Pprs.* ii. 58. [225] *Ellenborough Diary*, ii. 220; Broughton, iv. 25; *Arbuthnot Jnl.* ii. 355-6, 358; *Wellington Despatches*, vii. 106-8; Gash, *Secretary Peel*, 633-5; Jenkins, 54. [226] Broughton, iv. 22; Add. 40607, f. 137; NLS mss 24748, f. 89. [227] *Arbuthnot Jnl.* ii. 358-9; Agar Ellis diary, 24 May [228] *Ellenborough Diary*, ii. 270, 274-5; *Life of Campbell*, i. 470 [229] *Ellenborough Diary*, ii. 274. [230] *Macaulay Letters*, i. 275. [231] *Ellenborough Diary*, ii. 280-1, 288-9. [232] Ibid. ii. 291-2. [233] Broughton, iv. 35; *Ellenborough Diary*, ii. 295, 297; *Arbuthnot Jnl.* ii. 366; Creevey mss, Sefton to Creevey, 2 July 1830. [234] Agar Ellis diary, 6 July [235] *Ellenborough Diary*, ii. 307. [236] *Ellenborough Diary*, ii. 297-8; Add. 40340, f. 223. [237] *Arbuthnot Jnl.* ii. 372-3, 378. [238] Ibid. ii. 374. [239] Add. 40327, f. 185; 40401, f. 70. [240] TNA 30/12/7/6; *Ellenborough Diary*, ii. 360. [241] *Dyott's Diary*, ii. 86-87. [242] *Ellenborough Diary*, ii. 334, 378, 380; Gash, *Secretary Peel*, 638-40. [243] Add. 40301, f. 175; 40340, f, 230; 40401, ff. 127, 140, 179. [244] Add. 40320, f. 236; *Arbuthnot Jnl.* ii. 389-91; Powis mss 173; Hatherton mss, Palmerston to Littleton, 12 Oct. 1830; Bulwer, *Palmerston*, i. 362-3. [245] *Peel Letters*, 125; Parker, ii. 162-3. [246] *Greville Mems.* ii. 51-52; *Arbuthnot Jnl.* ii. 392-5; Bulwer, 363-4. [247] *Ellenborough Diary*, ii. 400-1, 406, 432; *Arbuthnot Jnl.* ii. 396; Gash, *Secretary Peel*, 647-8. [248] *Ellenborough Diary*, ii. 409-10. [249] Agar Ellis diary, 2 Nov. [1830]; *Ellenborough Diary*, ii. 413-14; Add. 52453, f. 194. [250] *Life of Campbell*, i. 483; Parker, ii. 171-2. [251] *Arbuthnot Jnl.* ii. 398. [252] *Ellenborough Diary*, ii. 415, 418-21, 424-5, 427; Broughton, iv. 62-63. [253] Parker, ii. 168-9; Gash, *Secretary Peel*, 649-51. [254] *Ellenborough Diary*, ii. 426, 428. [255] Ibid. ii. 432-3 [256] *Three Diaries*, 1-2. [257] Broughton, iv. 67-68; *Life of Campbell*, i. 487-8. [258] *Arbuthnot Jnl.* ii. 401, 403. [259] Add. 40401, f. 292. [260] *Greville Mems.* ii. 66, 77-78. [261] Broughton, iv. 70-73. [262] *Ellenborough Diary*, ii. 441; *Life of Campbell*, i. 488; *Croker Pprs.* ii. 77-78. [263] *Greville Mems.* ii. 66; *Croker Pprs.* ii. 79-80. [264] *Three Diaries*, 27; Glynne-Gladstone mss 196, T. to J. Gladstone, 21 Dec. 1830. [265] Glynne-Gladstone mss 196. [266] Ibid. T. to J. Gladstone, 17 Dec. 1830; *Greville Mems.* ii. 91, 93-94; Add. 51655, Mackintosh to Lady Holland [18 Dec.]; 51680, Russell to same, 20 Dec. 1830.

[267] Broughton, iv. 78; *Three Diaries*, 37; Ward, *Letters to 'Ivy'*, 366; Add. 51534, T. Grenville to Lady Holland, 21 Dec.; 51578, Carlisle to Holland, 21 Dec.; 51659, Ord to Lady Holland, 21 Dec.; 51677, Russell to Holland [22 Dec. 1830]. [268] Anglesey mss 27A/90. [269] Aberdeen Univ. Lib. Arbuthnot mss, Herries to Mrs. Arbuthnot, 3 Jan.; Add. 57370, f. 69; Lonsdale mss, Croker to Lowther, 2 Jan. 1831. [270] *Croker Pprs*. ii. 97, 99, 101; *Three Diaries*, 43. [271] *Dyott's Diary*, ii. 104. [272] Arbuthnot mss. [273] Goulburn mss 67B, Goulburn to wife [5 Feb. 1831]; Anglesey mss 31D/13. [274] *Three Diaries*, 48; Add. 40402, f. 11. [275] *Three Diaries*, 50; Add. 51569, Ord to Holland [11 Feb. 1831]. [276] *Three Diaries*, 54; Anglesey mss 31D/20; Glynne-Gladstone mss 197, T. to J. Gladstone, 19 Feb. 1831. [277] Add. 34614, f. 119; Glynne-Gladstone mss 197, T. to J. Gladstone, 22 Feb. 1831; *Three Diaries*, 56-57; *Croker Pprs*. ii. 108. [278] Glynne-Gladstone mss 197. [279] *Three Diaries*, 59, 61. [280] *Greville Mems*. ii. 118. [281] *Three Diaries*, 13, 57; *Croker Pprs*. ii. 108. [282] Broughton, iv. 87; *Three Diaries*, 13. [283] *Three Diaries*, 13; Broughton, iv. 93; Gash, *Sir Robert Peel*, 13-14. [284] *Greville Mems*. ii. 123; Parker, ii. 176; *Three Diaries*, 62; Glynne-Gladstone mss 197, T. to J. Gladstone, 3 Mar. 1831. [285] *Three Diaries*, 14-15, 63; Broughton, iv. 89-90; *Bunbury Mem*. 159-60; *Greville Mems*. ii. 125; *Life of Campbell* i. 506; Add. 51569, Ord to Lady Holland [4 Mar.]; Glynne-Gladstone mss 197, T. to J. Gladstone, 4 Mar; Rutland mss, Mrs. Arbuthnot to Rutland [4 Mar. 1831]; Bodl. MS. Eng. lett. d 153, f. 76. [286] Glynne-Gladstone mss 197, T. to J. Gladstone, 19 Mar. 1831; *Croker Pprs*. ii. 112. [287] Add. 51573, Spring Rice to Lady Holland [21 Mar. 1831]. [288] Bagot mss, Maryborough to Bagot, 11 Mar; Kenyon mss, L. to Lord Kenyon, 19 Mar.; *Three Diaries*, 66, 70; Parker, ii. 179-80; *Greville Mems*. ii. 131; *Croker Pprs*. ii. 112. [289] Broughton, iv. 96; *Macaulay Letters*, 10. [290] Broughton, iv. 97; Glynne-Gladstone mss 197, T. to J. Gladstone, 25 Mar. 1831. [291] *Three Diaries*, 72. [292] *Greville Mems*. ii. 135; Broughton, iv. 99; *Life of Campbell*, i. 509. [293] *Arbuthnot Jnl*. ii. 415-16. [294] Goulburn mss 67B, Goulburn to wife, 12 Apr. 1831. [295] *Croker Pprs*. ii. 114-15. [296] Glynne-Gladstone mss 198, T. to J. Gladstone, 19 Apr. 1831. [297] Broughton, iv. 102; Glynne-Gladstone mss 198, T. to J. Gladstone, 20 Apr. 1831. [298] *Three Diaries*, 82-83. [299] Broughton, iv. 103. [300] Le Marchant, *Althorp*, 307; *Greville Mems*. ii. 137-8; Broughton, iv. 105-6; Glynne-Gladstone mss 198, T. to J. Gladstone, 22 Apr. 1831; *Life of Campbell*, i. 511-12. [301] *Peel Letters*, 128-9. [302] Parker, ii. 182-4; Broughton, iv. 110-12; Add. 40313, f. 145; 40402, ff. 21-31. [303] Glynne-Gladstone mss 224, G. Grant to J. Gladstone, 23 Apr. 1831. [304] Add. 40402, f. 43; Gash, *Sir Robert Peel*, 18. [305] Parker, ii. 186. [306] Add. 57402, ff. 84, 87. [307] *Croker Pprs*. ii. 116-17. [308] Parker, ii. 170-1, 187; R. Stewart, *Foundation of Conservative Party*, 58-59; Gash, *Sir Robert Peel*, 19. [309] *Arbuthnot Jnl*. ii. 422-3. [310] Anglesey mss 31D/42; NLI, Farnham mss 18602 (2), Arbuthnot to Farnham, 2 June 1831. [311] Cent. Kent. Stud. Stanhope mss U1590 S4, Peel to Freshfield, 18 June; Le Marchant mss, Althorp to Le Marchant, 21 June 1831. [312] Broughton, iv. 115. [313] *Creevey Pprs*. ii. 233; Broughton, iv. 117. [314] Powis mss 178. [315] Broughton, iv. 119-20; *Three Diaries*, 100; *Greville Mems*. ii. 159. [316] Anglesey mss 27A/122. [317] *Three Diaries*, 104; *Greville Mems*. ii. 163-5; Lonsdale mss, Croker to Lowther, 11 July [1831]; Anglesey mss 31D/46. [318] *Three Diaries*, 104, 106; Broughton, iv. 122; Berks. RO, Pusey mss D/Ebp C1/45, Mahon to Pusey [July]; Le Marchant mss; Hatherton diary, 13 July [1831]. [319] *Three Diaries*, 108-9. [320] Creevey mss, Creevey to Miss Ord, 23 July; Hatherton mss, Littleton to Leigh, 26 July; Add. 51655, Mackintosh to Lady Holland, 28 July [1831]. [321] *Three Diaries*, 113. [322] Broughton, iv. 125; Hatherton diary, 29, 30 July [1831]. [323] *Holland House Diaries*, 21; Hatherton diary, 1 Aug. [1831]. [324] Broughton, iv. 127. [325] Hatherton diary, 11 Aug. [1831]. [326] *Arbuthnot Corresp*. 147; Arbuthnot mss, Hardinge to Mrs. Arbuthnot, 19 Aug. [1831]. [327] *Peel Letters*, 130-4. [328] Anglesey mss 31D/57. [329] *Peel Letters*, 134-6; Parker, ii. 188. [330] *Dyott's Diary*, ii. 115. [331] Add. 40402, f. 102; NLW, Ormathwaite mss FG 1/5, p. 199. [332] Lonsdale mss, Lowther to Lonsdale, 22 Sept. 1831; *Three Diaries*, 133; *Life of Campbell*, i. 521, 526; *Greville Mems*. ii. 203. [333] *Three Diaries*, 147, 150; Cornw. RO, Hawkins mss 10/2172. [334] *Greville Mems*. ii. 209; Parker, ii. 189. [335] Add. 51590, Dover to Lady Holland, 1 Nov. 1831. [336] *Croker Pprs*. ii. 137. [337] *Croker Pprs*. ii. 139; Parker, ii. 194-6; *Holland House Diaries*, 84; *Greville Mems*. ii. 215; Sheffield Archives, Wharncliffe mss, Peel to Wharncliffe, 23 Nov., Harrowby to same, 25 Nov. 1831; Arbuthnot mss 3029/1/2/37; Powis mss 182. [338] Lonsdale mss, Croker to Lowther, 1 Dec. 1831; Parker, ii. 196-7; *Three Diaries*, 162. [339] Stanhope mss C318/2, Mahon to Lady Stanhope, 7 Dec. 1831. [340] Broughton, iv. 154-5; *Three Diaries*, 167-8; *Greville Mems*. ii. 229; *Holland House Diaries*, 93; Hatherton diary, 12 Dec.; Add. 51573, Spring Rice to Lady Holland [12 Dec. 1831]; NLS mss 24762, f. 49. [341] *Holland House Diaries*, 96; Anglesey mss 31D/77. [342] *Holland House Diaries*, 97; Hatherton diary, 17 Dec. 1831; *Three Diaries*, 170, 172; Broughton, iv. 156-7; *Cockburn Letters*, 365-6; *Greville Mems*. ii. 242. [343] Gash, *Sir Robert Peel*, 25; Stewart, 72-73. [344] *Dyott's Dairy*, ii. 122-3; *Three Diaries*, 175. [345] Add. 51573, Spring Rice to Lady Holland, 20 Jan. [1832]; Hawkins mss 10/2178. [346] Broughton, iv. 163; *Three Diaries*, 189; Ormathwaite mss FG 1/6, p. 15. [347] Hatherton diary, 28 [Jan. 1828]. [348] Parker, ii. 198-202; *Holland House Diaries*, 127; *Greville Mems*. ii. 250-2. [349] *Three Diaries*, 189. [350] Hatherton diary, 9 Feb. [1832]. [351] *Three Diaries*, 193, 195, 199; Hatherton diary, 8 Mar. [1832]; *Greville Mems*. ii. 271. [352] *Croker Pprs*. ii.151, 153; *Lieven-Palmerston Corresp*. 35. [353] Hants RO, Malmesbury mss 9M73/G2536/6. [354] *Three Diaries*, 213; Hawkins mss 10/2190; Add. 52058, C. R. to H. E. Fox [c. 23 Mar. 1832]. [355] *Croker Pprs*. ii. 175; *Three Diaries*, 236-7. [356] Broughton, iv. 222, 225; *Three Diaries*, 253. [357] See Gash, *Sir Robert Peel*, 28-35; *Three Diaries*, 247-58, *Croker Pprs*. ii. 153-69, 177-81; *Greville Mems*. ii. 293-4, 303. [358] *Holland House Diaries*, 178; *Lady Holland to Son*, 137; *Greville Mems*. ii. 293-4, 303; *Three Diaries*, 253, 256, 258, 260-2; Broughton, iv. 228. [359] *Greville Mems*. ii. 91, 94; iv. 233. [360] *Lady Palmerston Letters*, 194. [361] Broughton, iv. 243, 248; *Holland House Diaries*, 193; Hatherton diary, 20 June [1832]. [362] Sir James Graham mss (IHR microfilm XR 80), 14, Graham to Smith Stanley, 29 July 1832. [363] *Croker Pprs*. ii. 188. [364] *Three Diaries*, 157. [365] *Greville Mems*. iii. 18-19. [366] *Life of Campbell*, ii. 281. [367] *Oxford DNB*.

D.R.F.

PEEL, William Yates (1789–1858), of Bonehill Cottage, Tamworth, Staffs.

BOSSINEY	12 June 1817–1818
TAMWORTH	1818–1830
YARMOUTH I.O.W.	1830–1831
CAMBRIDGE UNIVERSITY	1831–1832
TAMWORTH	1835–1837
TAMWORTH	1847–13 Dec. 1847

b. 3 Aug. 1789, 2nd s. of Sir Robert Peel†, 1st bt. (*d*. 1830), of Drayton Manor, Staffs. and 1st w. Ellen, da. of William Yates, calico printer, of Springside, Bury, Lancs.; bro. of Edmund Peel*, Jonathan Peel*, Laurence Peel* and Robert Peel*. *educ*. Harrow 1802; St. John's, Camb. 1806; L. Inn 1812, called 1816. *m*. 17 June 1819, Lady Jane Elizabeth Moore, da. of Stephen, 2nd earl of Mountcashell [I], 4s. 9da. *d*. 1 June 1858.

Commr. bd. of control June 1826-June 1827; under-sec. of state for home affairs Jan. 1828-July 1830; ld. of treasury July-Nov. 1830, Dec. 1834-Apr. 1835; PC 20 Dec. 1834.

Maj. central Staffs. militia 1813.

Peel, a tall and strikingly handsome man, never fulfilled the promise of his boyhood or escaped from the shadow of his elder brother Robert.[1] On his marriage in 1819 (when his hopes of a quiet honeymoon at Burford Bridge were dashed by an invasion of 'a noisy crowd of their acquaintances'), his father settled £64,000 on him. On Sir Robert Peel's death in 1830 he received a further £71,000.[2] He was returned unopposed for Tamworth on the family interest in 1820 and 1826. He drew attention to himself by voting with opposition against the appointment of an additional Scottish baron of exchequer, 15 May 1820, when Robert stayed away.[3] He supported the call for remission of the prison sentences imposed on the Members Masseh Lopes and Swann for electoral bribery, 11 July 1820. He again raised eyebrows as one of the 'most remarkable' of the 'deserters' who voted with opposition against the omission of Queen Caroline's name from the liturgy, 26 Jan. 1821. By doing so he gave the impression that Robert, who was once more absent, was of the same mind, though Huskisson reckoned that the latter was genuinely unwell and claimed to 'have no influence' over William.[4] He endorsed a Birmingham merchants' petition for inquiry into distress, 8 Feb., but this was the end of his rebellion, if such it was, against the Liverpool ministry. He voted against Catholic relief, 28 Feb., and with government for the duke of Clarence's grant, 18 June, and against economical reform, 27 June. He favoured a large reduction in the compensation paid to Desfourneux, 28 June 1821.[5]

Five months later Robert Peel, out of office since 1818, agreed to enter the cabinet as home secretary. He made to William what he subsequently described as 'an unequivocal offer' of the under-secretaryship:

> I said the mere official duties were light; that the parliamentary duties would be by far the heaviest, and also of the greatest importance to me. I dare say I said what I feel, that the parliamentary under-secretary would be like my right hand to me ... I said the performance of these duties must be difficult at first, that nothing but experience could render them less so, but that experience would. I declared my readiness to do anything in my power to make them easier.

William, who was under pressure from his father to better himself, took umbrage at the reference to his inexperience and peremptorily declined the post, to which Robert appointed his brother-in-law George Dawson*. As a result, William fell foul of his father who, as he told Robert

> accused me of having broken my pledge to him, and went on to say that I had shuffled through life, that I had given up the church, the law and now politics; that I had lost one of the finest opportunities that ever was offered to a young man, and desired me to state my grounds for such conduct. There was one remark he made which I cannot omit, which was that 'He thought my not being appointed to the office ... was so great a reflection upon me that I could not attend Parliament'.

His attempt to explain the reasons for his refusal led his father to round on Robert; and lengthy explanations were required before the hurt feelings on all sides were soothed.[6]

On 11 Feb. 1822 Peel opposed the opposition call for extensive tax reductions to relieve distress:

> He believed that ministers were quite as anxious to relieve the distress of the country as those who dealt in nothing but assertion and complaint. He was glad that reductions were about to be made from the highest offices to the lowest, as he was convinced that such economical arrangements would tend to remove the evils complained of.

He voted silently to the same effect, 21 Feb., and divided against abolition of one of the joint-postmasterships, 13 Mar., and repeal of the salt duties, 28 June. He spoke and voted against Canning's bill to relieve Catholic peers, 10 May 1822. He voted against parliamentary reform, 20 Feb., 2 June, and inquiry into chancery delays, 5 June 1823. He 'entirely approved' government's 'neutrality' on the French invasion of Spain, 30 Apr. He objected to Lord Cranbourne's sale of game bill, 2 June, because it would concentrate game in the hands of large landowners. Like his brother, he supported Lord Nugent's Catholic franchise bill, 30 June 1823, but he warned that he 'would not go one iota beyond its provisions, in the way of concession'. He opposed inquiry into bear-baiting, 26 Feb. 1824, when he voted against reform of Edinburgh's representation. He presented a Tamworth petition for repeal of the duty on excise licenses, 5 Mar.,[7] and welcomed the remission of duties on raw silk, 8 Mar. He opposed Stuart Wortley's attempts to amend the game laws, 11 Mar., 31 May 1824, 7 Mar. 1825. He voted with government on the case of the Methodist missionary John Smith in Demerara, 11 June 1824. He was an enthusiastic advocate of the Liverpool and Manchester railway project, 2, 11 Mar. 1825,[8] 6 Apr. 1826. He favoured repeal of the usury laws, 8 Feb. 1825. He voted for the Irish unlawful societies bill, 25 Feb., and against Catholic relief, 1 Mar., 21 Apr., 10 May. When opposing the relief bill, 19 Apr., he declared that 'the longer he lived the more danger he saw in granting to the Catholics emancipation', and that 'he would never consent to entrust them with political power': the measure would not solve the problems of Ireland, which lay in 'the want of a resident gentry, the want of capital, the want of commerce, and of moral and religious education'. He presented a petition against alteration of the corn laws and voted against the Irish franchise bill, 26 Apr.[9] He was in the ministerial majorities for the duke of Cumberland's grant, 30 May, 6, 10 June 1825. He presented and endorsed a Tamworth petition for the gradual abolition of slavery, 1 Mar. 1826.[10] He supported Littleton's proposals for reform of the 'unjust and disgraceful' regulations governing private bill committees, 19 Apr., 28 Nov. 1826.

In December 1825 Robert Peel sounded Lord Liverpool on the possibility of promoting Dawson to make room for William. Nothing came of this, but in June 1826 Robert secured his appointment as a commissioner of the board of control. Informing their father, he observed that 'the duties are very important and may be made, by the exertion of the individual appointed, of great consequence'; and he professed to have 'not the slightest doubt that William will be a most useful public servant'.[11] Peel, who thought that the general election had 'proceeded in a manner favourable to the Protestant cause', had little chance to justify Robert's faith. He voted against Catholic relief, 6 Mar., and for the duke of Clarence's annuity, 16 Mar., and was a government teller in the division against inquiry into the mutiny at Barrackpoor, 22 Mar. 1827. On 4 May he explained why he had 'some reasons differing from those' of Robert for resigning his office on Canning's accession to power:

> Independent of the feeling which they had in common upon the Catholic question, he saw no reason for confiding in the government ... He admired ... [Canning's] talents ... and he had no fear, while he was assisted by the cooler heads and more regulated minds of the ministers who had now left him; but, when he saw him surrounded by a crowd of visionary theorists, of political economists, and the professors of what were called the liberal principles of the present day, he could not look without alarm at the dangers to which the country was exposed ... The government gave no sufficient security for the Protestant establishment.

He was at one with Robert in disclaiming any intention of offering 'rancorous and factious opposition', 11 May. He supported Wood's bill to legalize the sale of game, 7 June 1827.[12] He was privately contemptuous of the Goderich ministry, and in December 1827 played a part in the exchanges which presaged a reconciliation between his brother and the Huskissonites.[13] When Robert returned to the home office under Wellington in January 1828 he took William with him as under-secretary.[14]

Peel voted against repeal of the Test Acts, 26 Feb., and Catholic relief, 12 May 1828. He was a ministerial teller in the division on civil list pensions, 20 May. As his brother preferred personally to handle the bulk of departmental business in the House, there was little for him to do in that line. He opposed Rumbold's proposal to institute coroners' inquests on the deaths of confined lunatics, 1 Apr., and explained why the militia estimates could not be readily reduced, 30 Apr. He was outraged by Dawson's Londonderry speech of 12 Aug. 1828 calling for a final settlement of the Catholic question. Unlike Robert, he had had no inkling that Dawson's opinions on the issue had changed:

> I know of no plea but insanity which can justify his conduct ... I would rather see my wife and children in a workhouse and break stones on the highway for the rest of my days than ... have been guilty of such mean, time-serving apostacy ... As George Dawson, 'citizen of the world' or ... Member for Londonderry he had a right to say what he pleased, but as secretary to the treasury he had in my opinion no right to make the speech he did, unless he received the sanction of the duke of Wellington. But if the government had come to the resolution that Catholic emancipation was to become a cabinet measure, was a Derry dinner the occasion upon which they wished their intentions to be proclaimed to the world? Objectionable as Dawson's speech is as coming from the secretary to the treasury, I consider it as most unjustifiable as coming from your brother-in-law.[15]

Yet when, six months later, Robert told him that he had decided to stay in office to help carry emancipation, William pledged his support.[16] The opponents of relief reckoned that he was in fact mortified by his brother's conversion and, to make his point, ostentatiously absented himself from London; but he put his seat at Robert's disposal in case he was turned out of Oxford University, and in the House, 12 Feb. 1829, announced his support for 'concession accompanied by securities' as the only means of averting civil war in Ireland, though he admitted to some misgivings.[17] He presented a Staffordshire petition against relief, 19 Feb., and on 2 Mar. brought up one from Tamworth against any measure which endangered the church, but claimed to believe that the bill, 'far from destroying, will tend to preserve our Protestant constitution'. He voted silently for it, 30 Mar. 1829.

Peel was in the government majorities against parliamentary reform proposals, 11, 18, 23 Feb. 1830. On 23 Mar. he spoke at unusual length against inquiry into distress, dismissing calls for a return to 'a depreciated paper currency' and arguing that ministers had 'only to proceed in the good work of reduction and retrenchment, and the country will be finally righted'. He was now an enthusiast for Catholic emancipation, which he said had pacified Ireland and 'exceeded even the most sanguine expectations'. He refuted allegations that the country was possessed by 'a revolutionary spirit' or had lost confidence in the ministry. He voted against Jewish emancipation, 17 May, divided with his brother against the Galway franchise bill, 24, 25 May, handled the second reading of the militia ballot suspension bill, 25 May, and replied to complaints of the increase in rates under the new Police Act, 15 June. Shortly before the general election of 1830, when he made way at Tamworth for Robert and came in for Yarmouth on the Holmes interest, Peel transferred to the treasury in order to 'escape the confinement of the home office and see more of his family'.[18] In October there was a fleeting notion of his standing for the Liverpool seat made vacant by Huskisson's death.[19]

Peel was in the ministerial minority on the civil list, 15 Nov. 1830, and resigned with his colleagues. Soon afterwards he sought to dispel the idea that Robert wished to withdraw from politics and leave the new opposition to fend for itself.[20] He took leave to attend to urgent private business, 30 Nov. 1830. He was in 'high spirits' at the Grey ministry's discomfiture in the debate on the civil list, 4 Feb. 1831.[21] He advocated repeal of the duty on printed calico, 11 Feb. On 7 Mar. he attacked the ministerial reform bill, which he said was 'replete with danger in principle, and injustice in its operation', and likened its authors to doctors practising a policy of 'kill and cure'. Refusing to be cowed by the threat of a dissolution, he called on

> every man who respects church property, who is opposed to the vote by ballot, annual parliaments, and universal suffrage ... to reject this unconstitutional measure, which, if carried into effect, must end in the overthrow of the monarchy, and the annihilation of existing rights and privileges.

He complained of the plan to preserve Lord Lansdowne's borough of Calne as a two-Member constituency while depriving Tamworth of a seat, 14 Mar. He voted against the second reading of the measure, 22 Mar., but only paired for Gascoyne's wrecking amendment, 19 Apr. By the last week of March it was known that in the event of a dissolution he intended to stand for his university, among whose members, especially the rural clergy, there was widespread alarm over the bill, as Peel pointed out in the House to Lord Palmerston, one of the sitting Members, 22 Mar. 1831. At the general election, though initially handicapped by gout, he came forward with Goulburn, a fellow opponent of reform, against Palmerston and his colleague Cavendish. While he professed to be 'not averse to the consideration of a comparative measure of reform', he grounded his appeal for support on his conviction that

> those classes of the community which are most distinguished for intelligence and capacity to form a sober and dispassionate judgement on public affairs are adverse to the extreme change in our representative system which has been proposed by ... government.

He and Goulburn were comfortably returned.[22]

Peel joined in the chorus of outrage at the offensive language of a Stockport workers' petition against the reform bill presented by Hunt, 1 July 1831. He defended the grant for Oxford and Cambridge professors' lecturing allowances, 8 July 1831 (and again, 13 Apr. 1832). He voted against the second reading of the reintroduced reform bill, 6 July, and was in the opposition minorities for use of the 1831 census to determine the disfranchisement schedules, 19 July, and against the partial disfranchisement of Chippenham, 27 July. On 24 Aug. he condemned the £10 borough franchise as the 'most objectionable' feature of the bill: it would 'give to the democratic influence of this country an unfair, unjust, and undue preponderance'. The 'intelligent portion of the people', he claimed, now recognized the measure as 'the commencement of a series of revolutionary and democratic operations, the conclusion of which must be the overthrow of all the established institutions'. He voted against the third reading, 19 Sept., and passage of the bill, 21 Sept. In a discussion on Irish tithe reform, 6 Oct. 1831, he argued that the Irish Protestant clergy were 'well entitled' to protection.

Peel voted against the second reading of the revised reform bill, 17 Dec. 1831, going into committee, 20 Jan., the enfranchisement of Tower Hamlets, 28 Feb., and the third reading, 22 Mar. 1832. He spoke against the division of counties and the urban freeholders' county vote, 27 Jan., and supported an unsuccessful attempt to raise the householder qualification in larger boroughs, 3 Feb. He approved the government's proposal to advance money for the relief of Irish clergymen impoverished by the campaign to withhold payment of tithes, 13 Mar., but deplored their failure to act resolutely against this threat to the church. He advised them to abandon their scheme for mixed education in Ireland, 16 Mar.; but it is not clear whether it was he or Robert who voted against the Irish education grant, 23 July. He voted against government on the Russian-Dutch loan, 26 Jan., 12 July, and was in the minority against the malt drawback bill, 2 Apr. He voted against the second reading of the Irish reform bill, 25 May, but on 13 June welcomed, on behalf of 'the Protestant interest', the proposal to give Dublin University an additional Member. He agreed with several Irish Catholic Members that a Glasgow petition against the Maynooth grant was too offensively worded to be printed, 10 July; but three days later he condemned their threat to withdraw support from the government in protest against their interim measure to deal with the problem of tithes. He acknowledged the Irish secretary Smith Stanley's genuine concern for the integrity of the Protestant establishment but, prophetically, suggested that

> his power is not equal to his wishes. It is well known that the government, for the last eighteen months, have been controlled by political unions and associations, and I know that those bodies have no very strong feeling in favour of the church. It is proposed that this subject should stand over until a reformed Parliament; but ... I have no confidence in a reformed Parliament; and I think that it is not only desirable, but absolutely necessary, that the question should at once be settled. I would appeal to any man, in or out of this House, who is possessed of property, whether landed or colonial, or embarked in manufacturing or commercial pursuits, if he feels that property equally secure now, as he did before the reform bill was introduced?

Peel had grown 'more and more anxious to retire from Parliament', and did so at the dissolution in December 1832.[23] He re-entered the Commons as a junior member of his brother's first ministry in 1835, but increasingly 'dreadful' attacks of gout compelled him to give up his seat in 1837.[24] He made a brief reappearance in the House in July 1847, but the death of his wife the following September broke his heart and removed him from public life. He came through a serious illness in 1848 and led 'a secluded life' until his death at his then residence at Baginton Hall, Warwickshire, in June 1858.[25]

[1] N. Gash, *Secretary Peel*, 39, 81. [2] *Von Neumann Diary*, i. 37-38; PROB 11/1772/396; IR26/1236/289; *Gent. Mag.* (1830), i. 557. [3] *Williams Wynn Corresp.* 243. [4] Broughton, *Recollections*, ii. 140; Add. 38742, f. 171; Lonsdale mss, Lowther to Lonsdale, 27 Jan.; Macpherson Grant mss 361, Macpherson Grant to Lady Stafford, 27 Jan. 1821. [5] *The Times*, 29 June 1821. [6] Gash, 296-7; Parker, *Peel*, i. 303-4; Add. 40605, ff. 121-31. [7] *The Times*, 6 Mar. 1824. [8] Ibid. 12 Mar. 1825. [9] Ibid. 27 Apr. 1825. [10] Ibid. 2 Mar. 1826. [11] Gash, 404; Add. 40305, ff. 156, 159; 40386, f. 257; 40606, f. 186. [12] *The Times*, 8 June 1827. [13] Parker, i. 23-24; Add. 40394, f. 271. [14] Add. 40395, f. 62. [15] Add. 40397, f. 157. [16] Add. 40398, f. 73. [17] Lonsdale mss, Lowther to Lonsdale, 10 Feb.1829; Add. 40398, f. 138. [18] Gash, 636; *Ellenborough Diary*, ii. 323; Lansdowne mss, Empson to Lansdowne, 9 Aug. 1830. [19] Add. 40401, ff. 235, 238, 245. [20] Gash, 669. [21] *Three Diaries*, 45, 46, 49, 60, 72. [22] *Palmerston-Sulivan Letters*, 248-9; *The Times*, 27 Apr., 3, 4, 7 May 1831. [23] Add. 40403, f. 159. [24] *Dyott's Diary*, ii. 191, 229, 254, 288, 352. [25] Add. 40609, ff. 142-331; *Gent. Mag.* (1858), ii. 191.

D.R.F.

PEIRSE, Henry (1754–1824), of Bedale and Hutton Bonville, Yorks.

NORTHALLERTON 1774–14 May 1824

bap. 2 June 1754,[1] 1st s. of Henry Peirse† of Bedale and w. Anne Johnson (otherwise Masters). *educ.* Eton 1764-70; Pembroke, Camb. 3 July 1771, aged 17; grand tour 1775. *m.* 16 Aug. 1777, Hon. Charlotte Grace Monson, da. of John, 2nd Bar. Monson, 3da. (1 *d.v.p.*). *suc.* fa. 1759. *d.* 14 May 1824.

Peirse returned himself again for Northallerton in 1820, as he had done all his adult life. He was one of the largest landed proprietors in the North Riding and in 1820 bought back the Hutton Bonville estate, which his family had sold in 1785.[2] Described by Robert Peel* as 'a decided Whig', he was a fairly regular attender who continued to vote with the opposition to Lord Liverpool's ministry.[3] He divided for parliamentary reform, 9 May 1821, 25 Apr. 1822, 24 Apr. 1823, and Catholic relief, 28 Feb. 1821. He voted against the appointment of an additional Scottish baron of exchequer, 15 May, for economies in revenue collection, 4 July, and against the barrack agreement bill, 17 July 1820. He divided against Wilberforce's resolution calling for a compromise solution to the Queen Caroline affair, 22 June, and the secret committee on the queen's conduct, 26 June 1820. He voted to restore the queen's name to the liturgy, 23, 31 Jan., 13 Feb., and censure ministers' conduct towards her, 6 Feb. 1821. He divided for the motion condemning the conduct of the Allies towards Naples, 21 Feb., inquiry into Peterloo, 16 May, and Hume's economy and retrenchment motion, 27 June. However, he voted against the forgery punishment mitigation bill, 23 May 1821. He divided for more extensive tax reductions, 21 Feb., and repeal of the salt duty, 23 June 1822. He voted for reduction of the junior lords of the admiralty, 1 Mar., abolition of one of the joint-postmasterships, 13 Mar., 2 May, inquiry into diplomatic expenditure, 15 May, and reduction of the cost of the Swiss embassy, 16 May 1822. He divided for inquiry into the prosecution of the Dublin Orange rioters, 22 Apr. 1823. His last known vote was against repeal of the usury laws, 27 June 1823. Taciturnity characterized his near 50 years in the House: he made no known speech. Peirse died in May 1824 and left Bedale and Hutton Bonville to his surviving daughters Mary Anne and Henrietta, the wife of Sir John Poo Beresford*, respectively. His personalty was sworn under £7,000 and under £25,000 in the province of York.[4]

[1] IGI (Yorks.). [2] *VCH Yorks. N. Riding*, i. 402. [3] Add. 40305, f. 124. [4] PROB 11/1693/701; IR26/1014/751.

M.P.J.C.

PELHAM *see* CRESSETT PELHAM

PELLEW, Hon. Pownoll Bastard (1786–1833), of Canonteign, nr. Chudleigh, Devon.

LAUNCESTON 1812–9 Mar. 1829

b. 1 July 1786, 1st s. of [Capt.] Edward Pellew†, 1st Visct. Exmouth, of Flushing and Trefusis, nr. Falmouth, Cornw. and Susannah, da. of James Frowde of Knoyle, Wilts. *m.* (1) 1 Oct. 1808, at Madras, Eliza Harriet (*div.* July 1820), da. of Sir George Hilaro Barlow, 1st bt., gov. Madras, 2s. 1da.; (2) 15 Apr. 1822, Georgiana Janet, da. of Mungo Dick of Pitcarrow House, Forfar, 3s. 2da. (1 *d.v.p.*). *suc.* fa. as 2nd Visct. Exmouth 23 Jan. 1833. *d.* 2 Dec. 1833.

Lt. RN 1802, cdr. 1804, capt. 1806; naval a.d.c. to William IV 1830-2.

Capt. S. Hams yeomanry 1820.

Pellew, the son of a dashing and distinguished naval officer who was created Baron Exmouth in 1814 and made a viscount two years later, was returned unopposed for Launceston for the third time in 1820 on the 3rd duke of Northumberland's interest.[1] An almost silent Member and poor attender, he continued to support Lord Liverpool's ministry. He voted in defence of their conduct towards Queen Caroline, 6 Feb., and against repeal of the additional malt duty, 3 Apr. 1821, and was against more extensive tax reductions, 11 Feb. 1822. He divided against Catholic relief, 28 Feb. 1821, and the removal of Catholic peers' disabilities, 30 Apr. 1822. He was named as a defaulter, 28 Feb. 1825, but attended next day to vote against Catholic relief. He presented three hostile petitions, 18 Apr.,[2] divided against the relief bill, 21 Apr., and paired against it, 10 May. He voted against the Irish franchise bill, 26 Apr. 1825. He was again returned unopposed for Launceston at the general election of 1826.[3]

Responding to a direct appeal for information, he was 'understood to state that his father had always represented the *Indefatigable* to him as a very good ship', 12 Feb. 1827.[4] He divided against Catholic relief, 6 Mar., and was granted one month's leave having served on an election committee, 26 Mar. 1827. On the formation of the duke of Wellington's ministry in January 1828 he informed Peel, the leader of the Commons, that he would give his 'most decided support to any administration in which you take a place ... although my own wishes would have placed you at the head of the present cabinet'.[5] He voted against repeal of the Test Acts, 26 Feb., and Catholic relief, 12 May 1828. In February 1829 Planta, the patronage secretary, listed him as being 'opposed to the principle' of Catholic emancipation. However, his patron had been appointed lord lieutenant of Ireland and, after presenting three anti-Catholic petitions, 9 Mar. 1829, he resigned his seat. He was actively involved in the effort to reorganize Devon Toryism after the election defeat in 1830.[6] Having succeeded to his father's peerage in January,[7] he died in December 1833 and was succeeded by his eldest son Edward (1811-76); his personalty was eventually sworn under £12,000.[8]

[1] C.N. Parkinson, *Edward Pellew, Visct. Exmouth*, 399-400. [2] *The Times*, 19 Apr. 1825. [3] *West Briton*, 16 June 1826. [4] *The Times*, 13 Feb. 1827. [5] Add. 40395, f. 155. [6] W. Devon RO, Bastard mss 74/281, Pellew to Bastard, 5 Sept. 1830. [7] He was the residuary legatee of the estate, which was eventually sworn under £90,000 (PROB 11/1811/80; IR26/1319/103). [8] PROB 11/1827/84; IR26/1351/70.

T.A.J.

PEMBERTON, Thomas (1793–1867), of Lincoln's Inn and 3 Spring Garden Terrace, Mdx.[1]

RYE 1831–1832

RIPON 1835–13 Mar. 1843

b. 11 Feb. 1793, 1st surv. s. of Robert Pemberton (*d.* 1804), barrister, of Serle Street, Lincoln's Inn and Margaret, da. and coh. of Edward Leigh of Bispham, Lancs. *educ.* Dr. Horne's sch., Chiswick 1800-9; L. Inn 1811, called 1816. *unm. suc.* cos. Sir Robert Holt Leigh†, 1st bt., of Hindley Hall to life interest in his Lancs. estates and took additional name of Leigh by royal lic. 10 Mar. 1843; *cr.* Bar. Kingsdown 28 Aug. 1858. *d.* 7 Oct. 1867.

KC 1829; bencher, L. Inn 1829, treas. 1842; att.-gen. to prince of Wales 1841-3; PC 10 June 1843; chan. of duchy of Cornw. 1843-61; member, jud. cttee. of PC 1843.

Pemberton's father, a descendant of Sir Francis Pemberton (1625-97), chief justice of the common pleas, was earning about £2,000 a year at the chancery bar at the time of his death in 1804, but he had been unable to save any substantial sum and left his widow with only £500 a year to support herself and five children. Thomas, the eldest son, had to give up all hope of progressing from his preparatory school to Westminster and Oxford, which might have led him reluctantly into the church via a living at the disposal of a family friend. He left school at the age of 16 and spent a year in a solicitor's office before becoming a pupil in the chambers of his maternal uncle Edward Cooke, a chancery barrister. When he was called to the bar in 1816 he was earning a 'pittance of £100 or £150' by drawing equity pleadings for solicitors. Forty years later he wrote:

> All my earliest years were gloomy and joyless, and I cannot remember one, hardly indeed a month in the course of them which I would willingly live again, whereas there is hardly one year (if indeed there be one) since my twenty-fourth which I would not gladly repeat ... No doubt, however, it is to this period, however little agreeable in itself, that I am indebted for much of my consequent success ... I learned to consider indefatigable labour as the indispensable condition of success; pecuniary independence as essential alike to virtue and to happiness; and no sacrifices too great to avoid the misery of debt.

He initially took work on the northern circuit and as a parliamentary counsel, but he concentrated on the chancery bar, where his rise was unusually rapid: before he was 30 he had a professional income of £3,000 a year. He travelled widely in Europe in the vacations. He obtained a silk gown in 1829 and thereafter divided the practice of the rolls court with his friend and rival Henry Bickersteth. In 1830 he successfully conducted a minor case on behalf of his mother's cousin Sir Robert Holt Leigh, who in gratitude made him heir to his estates in the Wigan area.[2]

Pemberton had parliamentary ambitions and at the general election of 1831 became one of three king's counsel who were 'brought in to oppose the [Grey ministry's reform] bill'.[3] He was approached about standing for Rye by his former pupil Cecil Fane, brother-in-law of Charles Arbuthnot*, the former Tory election manager, who led him to expect a quiet return on the Lamb interest with the sitting Member Pusey, at a cost of £2,400. But the election was marked by serious disorder, as the patron's opponents, frustrated by the recent reversal of a decision on the right of election in their favour, and provoked by intimidatory tactics, strove to prevent the return of two anti-reformers. Pemberton, having narrowly escaped physical assault, gave up the contest and returned to London, only to learn that as a result of a compromise he had been elected with one of his radical opponents, Pusey being unacceptable.[4] In 1859 he wrote:

> I shall never forget the night in which, after so much excitement, I found myself a Member of Parliament. I threw myself on my knees and earnestly prayed ... that I might be enabled to perform faithfully and successfully the duties which belong to that position.

He voted against the second reading of the reintroduced reform bill, 6 July 1831, and divided steadily against its details. He presented a Rye petition for repeal of the duty on marine insurance, 1 July, but remained silent in debate for two months, as he later recalled:

> Of one ordinary failing of my profession, an eagerness to speak more often than the audience is disposed to listen, I could not be accused. I think nobody ever felt more nervous or more unwilling to open his mouth than I did, although I believe I did not show it much in my manner after I had once begun ... I remained silent so long that some of the party rather reproached me, and said that it was expected of me to speak.

He eventually did so on 20 Aug. 1831, when he attacked the government's proposal to allow certain borough freeholders a vote in county elections to counterbalance the effects of the Chandos amendment enfranchising tenants-at-will. He was 'greatly delighted' with his performance, but chagrined to find that it was 'hardly noticed' in the newspapers.[5] He voted in condemnation of the Irish government's alleged interference in the Dublin election, 23 Aug., criticized the arrangements for the registration of voters under the reform bill, 2 Sept., and divided against the issue of a new writ for Liverpool, 5 Sept. After voting against the third reading of the reform bill, 19 Sept., he opposed its passage:

> I am not blind to the defects ... of the constitution, but I would rather keep it such as it is, with all its theoretical imperfections, and all its practical blessings, than cast it away, and gamble for a new one in the lottery of revolution.

Lord Lowther* and Charles Williams Wynn* numbered it among several 'admirable and unanswerable' and 'good and effective' speeches against the bill, and Pemberton himself recollected that it had gained him 'a good deal of credit'.[6] He was in the minority against the passage of the bill, 21 Sept., and voted against the second reading of the Scottish reform bill, 23 Sept. He sought to expose the deficiencies of the bankruptcy court bill, 13 Oct., ridiculing its portrayal as a testament to lord chancellor Brougham's genius. Pemberton was not present for the division on the second reading of the revised reform bill, 17 Dec. 1831, but he voted against going into committee on it, 20 Jan., and the enfranchisement of Tower Hamlets, 28 Feb. 1832. Speaking against the third reading, 19 Mar., he opted for the 'danger of rejecting' it in preference to the 'certain evil of passing' it and appealed to the Lords to throw it out. He was in the hostile minority, 22 Mar. He voted against government on the Russian-Dutch loan, 26 Jan., 12 July, and the Irish reform bill, 25 May, 2 July. In June 1832 he was one of seven lawyers who sent a written protest to Brougham over the hasty passage of four real property law bills.[7]

Recalling his speech on the reform bill, Pemberton wrote that 'there is nothing so intoxicating ... as the success of a speech in the House of Commons, and no effort of which the reward is so out of all proportion to the merit'. In his own case, its effects were felt not in rapid professional advancement, which he eschewed, but in

> the alteration which it made in my social position, in the introduction into society to which I had not been accustomed, and for which, in truth, I was not very fit. I had neither the animal spirits nor the conversational talents which make men popular in company, nor the easy indifference which an early familiarity with it is, perhaps, necessary to produce. I was always, and still remain, shy and taciturn, and like no place so well as my own chimney-corner.

A founder member of the Carlton Club, he spent £800 on a two-day canvass of Taunton at the 1832 general election, but gave it up as a lost cause. He returned to Westminster in 1835 as Conservative Member for Ripon, but lacked the will to rise to the top in politics. He declined (through 'moral cowardice', as he later reflected) Peel's offer of the solicitor-generalship in 1834, which would probably have set him on the road to the great seal; and, diffidently distrusting his judicial abilities, he preferred to remain master of the chancery bar than to take a seat on the bench. His inheritance from Leigh in 1843 was reduced to a life interest in the Wigan estates, the baronet having in the interim fathered an illegitimate son and remaindered the property to him. It nevertheless made Pemberton financially secure and prompted him to retire from Parliament and the bar. He subsequently became a member of the judicial committee of the privy council, which he dominated for some 20 years, and in that capacity exercised his considerable talents to accomplish much valuable work. His attention to duchy of Cornwall affairs made him a friend and admirer of Prince Albert.[8] Greville, commenting on one of his judgments in 1857, wrote:

> Its publication will give the world in general some idea of his great ability, with the extent of which few are acquainted. It is a very singular thing that in such times as these, and when there is such a dearth of able men and so great a demand for them, that he should voluntarily condemn himself to a state of comparative obscurity, and refuse to take the station in public life which it would be difficult to find any other man so well qualified to fill.[9]

In 1858 he accepted a peerage, which became extinct on his death as a bachelor in October 1867. According to an obituary, he combined a 'remarkable clearness and precision of intellect' with a 'fastidious refinement, which removed him altogether from the common pursuits of fame and power'.[10]

[1] Based, unless otherwise stated, on his privately printed *Recollections* (1868), from which extracts were published in *Edinburgh Rev.* cxxix (1869), 40-68. [2] *Oxford DNB.* [3] *Life of Campbell*, i. 517. [4] *Hastings Iris*, 23, 30 Apr., 7 May 1831. [5] *The Times*, 22 Aug. 1831 confirms this claim. [6] Lonsdale mss, Lowther to Lonsdale, 22 Sept. 1831; NLW, Coedymaen mss 220. [7] Brougham mss, memo. [June 1832]. [8] *Oxford DNB.* [9] *Greville Mems.* vii. 279-80. [10] *Gent. Mag.* (1867), ii. 674-6.

D.R.F.

PENDARVES *see* WYNNE PENDARVES

PENLEAZE, John Story (?1786–1855), of Beech Cottage, Southampton and Bossington, nr. Stockbridge, Hants.

SOUTHAMPTON 1831–1832

SOUTHAMPTON 2 Apr. 1833–1834

b. ?1786, 1st. s. of James David Penleaze of High Cliff, nr. Christchurch, Hants and w. Ann. *educ.* Magdalen, Oxf. 1804; L. Inn 1803, called 1812. *m.* 15 June 1814, Mary Ann *née* Bowden of St. George's, Westminster, Mdx.,[1] ?2s. ?illegit. *suc.* fa. 1819. *d.* 12 Apr. 1855.

Consul, Amsterdam 1840-41, Barcelona 1841-54.

Penleaze's ancestry and origins remain obscure, though it is possible that his grandfather was James Penleaze, the Middlesex magistrate who died in Church Street, Spitalfields, 9 Sept. 1783.[2] His father was listed as a surgeon at his Hampshire address in an 1808 directory and left a substantial fortune at his death, 3 June 1819. Penleaze received a bequest of 3,000 guineas and a reversionary interest in the remainder of the personal estate of about £16,000 in total, which came his way on the death of his mother in 1823. (His younger brother, Robert Philip Penleaze, had been cut off with a shilling.)[3] He evidently disposed of High Cliff, the 'unpretentious' residence of his father, and purchased the Bossington estate before 1826, by dint of which he qualified for admission to the Hampshire bench.[4] He was called to the bar, but there is no evidence that he practised. He may have been the John Penleaze recorded as living in Greek Street, Soho, in 1811, though by the time of his marriage three years later he was resident in the parish of St. James's, Westminster. He was described as a bachelor, but it is clear that he already had at least one son, though the identity of the mother has not been established.[5] The Oxford University register entry for John Penleaze (*d.* 1879) indicates that he can have been born no later than 1809 and that he was his father's second son, but of older siblings, one of whom was referred to in an obituary notice, no record has been found.[6] A parish register for Bossington contains the baptism, 14 Sept. 1831, of a John Penleaze, his son with 'Mary', presumably his wife, but this is not noted as an adult baptism and if it refers to another child, he has not been traced thereafter.[7]

Penleaze was elected a burgess of Southampton, 8 Sept. 1826, and became deputy bailiff and a member of the borough council, 30 Sept. 1828, by which time he had presumably acquired his residence in the town.[8] In Bossington he assumed the mantle of a paternalist squire, giving dinners to the inhabitants in the winters of 1827 and 1828. On the latter occasion, his gift of blankets and stockings to the poor was reported as an example of his 'well known generosity'.[9] He was installed as senior bailiff of Southampton, 6 Oct. 1829, but resigned on becoming a candidate for a vacancy there two months later.[10] He adopted the same colours and inn headquarters as the late Member, a Whig, and in a wordy address proclaimed himself 'the strenuous friend of civil and religious liberty' and a supporter of the gradual abolition of slavery.[11] A London journalist's profile of him as 'a red hot supporter of Catholic emancipation' was disputed by a hostile local newspaper, which asserted that he had been 'as staunch a churchman as Mr. Peel, ratted with him, and signed the petition in favour of Catholic emancipation and, some folks say, turned again'.[12] Faced by a wealthy opponent, he withdrew after a canvass, but when his supporters insisted on putting him in nomination, he returned from London to appear on the hustings. Widely censured for this about-turn, he was soundly defeated after a six-day poll, which reputedly cost him about £4,500.[13]

Penleaze did not redeem his pledge to try again at the 1830 general election, by when he had resigned his burgess-ship, stating his intention to move away.[14] Evidently he did not do so, for he featured in a town delegation to lobby support for a proposed London to Southampton railway early in 1831, and when he spoke in favour of parliamentary reform at a town meeting, 25 Apr., it was as a resident.[15] By this time he had already accepted an invitation to offer again as a supporter of the Grey ministry's reform bill at the forthcoming general election, in spite of having developed, by his own admission, 'habits of retirement not very congenial with public life'. On the hustings he declared himself reconciled to the absence of a provision for vote by ballot in the bill, by which he insisted he would 'stand or fall'. After a four-day poll he was returned in tandem with the veteran Whig Arthur Atherley, who had advised Lord Holland, 24 Apr., that he was 'in some respects objectionable', but 'would do for the occasion'. Penleaze had disavowed all expenditure 'not legal and actually necessary' in his initial address, and his largesse fell so short of expectations that he was burnt in effigy by a thirsty mob.[16] Unabashed, he proclaimed his victory as 'a triumph which almost overwhelms me with its vastness', and in a rambling speech at a celebratory dinner, 26 May, included a touching tribute to his wife, who 'like himself ... had no pretensions to noble birth, but ... had a noble mind, because she had a heart open to the distresses of her fellow creatures'.[17] On 17 May 1831 he had applied to the duke of Wellington, the lord lieutenant of Hampshire, for a deputy lieutenancy, which he was evidently never given.[18]

A jaundiced commentator on his earlier attempt to enter the Commons had predicted that 'if he could not speak better in the House that he does out of it [he] would ... add another name to the glorious 658 who on all occasions confine themselves to the scriptural text of Aye and Nay'.[19] This was more or less accurate, for he proved to be a largely silent, yet reliable supporter of the Grey ministry. He voted for the second reading of their reintroduced reform bill, 6 July 1831, and gave steady support to its details. On 9 July he was admitted to Brooks's. He was in both government majorities on the Dublin election controversy, 23 Aug., but in the minority for the introduction of an Irish poor law, 29 Aug., of which he made much at the next general election.[20] On 1 Sept. he wrote to *The Times* to advertise his presence in both the majorities against preservation of the electoral privileges of freemen the previous day, saying that he had been 'present at every division on the reform bill (with one exception, when I paired off) and voted with ministers'. He divided for the bill's passage, 21 Sept., the second reading of the Scottish bill, 23 Sept., and Lord Ebrington's confidence motion, 10 Oct. 1831. At a reform meeting in Southampton four days later he opined that the bill might be modified to satisfy its opponents without sacrificing its 'efficacy and spirit', and excused his failure to contribute to debate. It was, he explained, 'his fixed determination to do so whenever he apprehended it would be productive of good', but in view of the delaying tactics adopted by the opposition, he considered that the ministry was at present best served by his silent support.[21]

He voted for the second reading of the revised reform bill, 17 Dec. 1831, and again gave steady support to its details. On 2 Feb. he presented a Southampton petition for a general drainage system, which he endorsed, presciently enough, with reference to the cholera epidemic, and called for a survey of 'the abodes of the poorer classes ... to see that their health is preserved by a due attention to cleanliness'. He divided for the third reading of the reform bill, 22 Mar., and the address calling on the king to appoint only ministers who would carry it unimpaired, 10 May. His steady conduct was praised in his absence at a Southampton meeting, 14 May.[22] Speaking in support of the resulting petition for withholding supplies until the bill was passed, 22 May, he warned that though 'the necessity of resorting to violent measures is for the present averted ... we must remember that we have "scotched the snake and not killed it"'. He voted with ministers on the Russian-Dutch loan, 26 Jan., 12, 16, 20 July, relations with Portugal, 9 Feb., and military punishments, 16 Feb. He was in the minority for a select committee on colonial slavery, 24 May, and divided to make coroners' inquests public, 20 June 1832.

At the 1832 general election he offered again for Southampton, boasting of a peerless record of Commons attendance, though he was obliged to admit that he had compromised his views in support of the ballot.[23] He was narrowly defeated, but seated on petition after a subscription had been raised to subsidize him.[24] The existence of financial difficulties may also be inferred from the contemporaneous sale of his Bossington estate, which fetched £23,000 at auction. (Penleaze won a subsequent court case confirming the obligation of the purchaser, one Elwes, to pay off a £6,000 mortgage, 7 Aug. 1833.)[25] In the House he continued to be classed as a reformer, but he abruptly retired on the eve of the 1834 dissolution, citing his age and ill health.[26] Afterwards he appears to have lived for a time at Exeter in Devon, where his son John, a clergyman, had lately acquired the living of Black Torrington.[27] In 1840 he took up the first of two European consular postings granted by the Melbourne ministry, which seem to have been acts of charity. He returned from Spain in December 1854 to consult a doctor in London, who advised him to go immediately to stay with a relative. He went to Hereford, where his son held an additional curacy, and died there 'in the full possession of his faculties, without suffering', in April 1855. Tribute was paid to his 'warm hearted character, charitable disposition and social excellencies' by the Southampton lodge of freemasons, to which he had belonged before becoming a Member.[28] No will or grant of administration has been found. A year before his death, his son had vainly sought a living in the south of France from Lord Brougham, which suggests that despite his denial of financial motives, he expected no patrimonial windfall.[29] Whether as a result of his father's expenditure on elections, or from some other cause, it seems fairly certain that he did not receive one, and at his own death, 24 June 1879, his personal estate was valued at £450.

[1] *Reg. St. George, Hanover Square*, iii. 85. [2] *Gent. Mag.* (1783), ii. 806. [3] PROB 11/1618/343; IR26/795/685. [4] *VCH Hants*, v. 84; Hants RO Q27/3/250. [5] *Reg. St. George, Hanover Square*, iii. 85. [6] *Hants Independent*, 21 Apr. 1855. [7] IGI (Hants). [8] *Southampton Corporation Jnls. 1815-35* ed. A. Temple Patterson, 43, 46. [9] *Salisbury Jnl.* 8 Jan. 1827, 11 Feb. 1828. [10] *Southampton Corporation Jnls.* 49; *Portsmouth Herald*, 20 Dec. 1829. [11] *Hants Advertiser*, 19 Dec. 1829. [12] *The Age*, 20 Dec.; *Hants Advertiser*, 26 Dec. 1829. [13] *Hants Advertiser*, 2, 16 Jan. 1830; Temple Patterson, *Hist. Southampton*, i. 152-3. [14] *Hants Advertiser*, 12 Dec. 1829; *Southampton Corporation Jnls.* 49. [15] Temple Patterson, i. 167; *Hants Advertiser* 30 Apr. 1831. [16] *Hants Advertiser*, 2, 9 Apr., 7, 14 May 1831; Add. 51836. [17] *Hants Advertiser*, 7, 28 May 1831. [18] Wellington mss WP4/3/4/24, 5/1/3. [19] *The Age*, 20 Dec. 1829. [20] *Hants Advertiser*, 15 Dec. 1832. [21] Ibid. 15 Oct. 1831. [22] Ibid. 19 May 1832. [23] Ibid. 15 Dec. 1832 [24] *The Times*, 14, 21 Dec. 1832; Temple Patterson, i. 172-4. [25] *The Times*, 8 Aug. 1833 [26] *Dod's Parl. Companion* (1833), 3rd edn., 149; Temple Patterson, i. 174. [27] Hants RO Q27/3/250. [28] *Salisbury Jnl.* 4 Jan. 1830; *Hants Advertiser*, 21 Apr.; *Hants Independent*, 21 Apr. 1855. [29] Brougham mss, Penleaze to Brougham, 22 Apr. 1854.

H.J.S./P.J.S.

PENNANT *see* DAWKINS PENNANT

PENNEFATHER, Matthew (1784–1858), of New Park, co. Tipperary.

CASHEL 1830–8 July 1831

b. 1784, 2nd but 1st surv. s. of Richard Pennefather†, MP [I], of New Park and Anna, da. and h. of Mathew Jacob, MP [I], of St. Johnstown, co. Tipperary. *m.* 1814, his cos. Anna, da. of Daniel O'Connor of Ballybricken, co. Cork, 2s. 2da. *suc.* fa. 1831. *d.* 1858.

Sheriff, co. Tipperary 1826-7.

Pennefather's father, Member for Cashel, 1818-19, owned 'extensive estates' in county Tipperary and was patron of the close borough of Cashel, which he invariably sold to government in return for offices for his family, who were later denounced by Daniel O'Connell* as the 'plundering Pennefathers and their bigotted gang'.[1] At the 1830 general election Pennefather was returned by his father. A few weeks later he proposed John Hely Hutchinson I* in the county election.[2] He was listed by the Wellington ministry as one of their 'friends', but this was subsequently queried and he was absent from the crucial division on the civil list, 15 Nov. 1830. He was granted a month's leave on account of the illness of a 'near relation', 25 Nov. 1830. Following the accession of the Grey ministry, Lord Anglesey, the Irish viceroy, informed the premier, 7 Feb. 1831, that a government nominee could be seated for the 'market price' at Cashel, which Pennefather was 'ready to vacate', but that the 'severe illness of the proprietor' would 'cause a few day's delay'. That day, however, Smith Stanley, the Irish secretary, heard 'that Pennefather will not part with Cashel'.[3] He remained in place and voted against the second reading of the ministerial reform bill, 22 Mar., and for Gascoyne's wrecking amendment, 19 Apr. 1831. He returned himself again at the ensuing general election and shortly thereafter succeeded his father as proprietor.[4] He divided against the second reading of the reintroduced reform bill, 6 July 1831. Two days later he resigned his seat in order to accommodate the anti-reformer Philip Pusey as a paying guest. The Irish Reform Act destroyed the family's electoral control of Cashel, for which he stood unsuccessfully as a Conservative in 1835. He died in 1858.

[1] *The Times*, 24 May 1831; *O'Connell Corresp*. v. 2255. [2] *Tipperary Free Press*, 18 Aug. 1830. [3] PRO NI, Anglesey mss D619/28C/66-67; 31D/14. [4] *Tipperary Free Press*, 21 May; *The Times*, 24 May 1831.

P.J.S.

PENRHYN, Edward (1794–1861), of The Cedars, East Sheen, Surr.

SHAFTESBURY 1830–1832

b. 16 Sept. 1794, 1st s. of Rev. Oswald Leycester, rect. of Stoke-upon-Tern, Salop, and 1st w. Mary, da. of P. Johnson[1] of Timperley, Cheshire. *educ.* Warrington; Eton 1808; St. John's, Camb. 1813; M. Temple 1818. *m.* 16 Dec. 1823, Charlotte Elizabeth, da. of Edward Smith Stanley, Lord Stanley*, 2s. 2da. Took name of Penrhyn in accordance with the will of his fa.'s 1st cos. Baroness Penrhyn 1816; *suc.* fa. 1846. *d.* 6 Mar. 1861.

Chairman, q.s. Surr. (Kingston-upon-Thames) 1845-*d.*

Edward Leycester, whose father Oswald (*bap.* 21 Mar. 1752)[2] was the fifth son of Ralph Leycester of Toft (1699-1777), was the much younger first cousin of Ralph Leycester (1763-1835), Member for Shaftesbury, 1821-30.[3] The Rev. Oswald, who lost his wife in 1812 and afterwards married Eliza, daughter of Charles White of Manchester, was a fellow of King's, Cambridge, 1772-86, and later became vicar of Harlington, Bedfordshire, and Hodnet, Shropshire. Edward followed him to Cambridge, where he was a scholar and president of the Union Society. During his childhood he had visited his fierce relation Anna Susanna, Lady Penrhyn, at Penrhyn Castle, Caernarvonshire, and his sister Maria recalled (in the *Memorials* prepared by her husband) that the 'Ladies of Llangollen' perhaps played a part in his future prospects:

> Lady Eleanor Butler was short and fat, but Miss Ponsonby was tall and thin, and used often to be supposed to be a man in disguise. They had a romantic attachment for each other, and had forsaken their own families to be more entirely together ... It was they who first told Lady Penrhyn that my handsome brother Edward was like her, and it is said they thus gave her the first idea of making him her heir; but I believe that which really made her do so was her amusement when her young cousin in riding home had not enough money left to pay a turnpike gate and was obliged to leave his handkerchief in pawn with the toll collector.[4]

Lady Penrhyn had been widowed in 1808, when the West India merchant and Irish peer Lord Penrhyn, formerly Richard Pennant, Member for Petersfield and Liverpool, left the Penrhyn estate to George Hay Dawkins Pennant, Member for Newark and New Romney. But Lady Penrhyn (who died on 1 Jan. 1816) retained a considerable fortune, and by her will, dated 11 June 1814 (in which she also provided pensions of £45 each for her six horses), she left the residue of her personal estate, which was sworn under £120,000, to Edward Leycester, provided that he changed his name to that of her late husband's extinct title.[5] Penrhyn, as he was now known, entered the Middle Temple in 1818, but does not appear to have been called. Later that year he travelled on the continent, and the following year he went to Scotland. He married a granddaughter of the 12th Earl of Derby in 1823 and settled in East Sheen. In 1826 he became the first chairman of the Richmond board of guardians of the poor, and thereafter was active in Surrey affairs.[6]

When Ralph Leycester retired from Parliament at the general election of 1830, Lord Grosvenor brought forward Penrhyn as one of his candidates at Shaftesbury, where the independent interest provoked a spirited contest. On the hustings he insisted that he was unshackled and spoke in favour of economies, parliamentary reform, religious toleration, the abolition of slavery and free trade, except in corn. He came top of the poll, but like Grosvenor's other nominee was roughly handled during the postponed chairing.[7] He attended on the opening day of the session, in company with Sir John Benn Walsh, 2 Nov.[8] He was listed by the Wellington ministry among the 'good doubtfuls', but he divided against them in the division on the civil list which brought them down, 15 Nov. 1830. He voted for the second reading of the Grey ministry's reform bill, 22 Mar., and against Gascoyne's wrecking amendment, 19 Apr. 1831. At the ensuing general election Penrhyn, who advised Grosvenor's agents on the management of the borough but was well respected there as a reformer, was re-elected for Shaftesbury after another contest against the popular party.[9] He voted for the second reading of the reintroduced reform bill, 6 July, at least twice against adjourning the proceedings on it, 12 July, and steadily for its details, though he divided for Lord Chandos's amendment to enfranchise £50 tenants-at-will, 18 Aug. He voted against printing the Waterford petition for disarming the Irish yeomanry, 11 Aug., and censuring the Irish government for interference in the Dublin election, 23 Aug. He divided for the passage of the reform bill, 21 Sept., and Lord Ebrington's confidence motion, 10 Oct. 1831.

He was appointed to the select committee on Irish tithes, 15 Dec. 1831, and, in his only known parliamentary speech, defended ministers on this subject, 27 Mar. 1832. He divided for the second reading of the revised reform bill, 17 Dec., and wrote to Lord Westminster (as Grosvenor had become) on 24 Dec. 1831 that 'I think the House of Commons will not show much fight on the amended reform bill'.[10] He again divided steadily for its details, and voted for its third reading, 22 Mar. 1832. He sided with ministers on the navy civil departments bill, 6 Apr. He voted for Ebrington's motion for an address calling on the king to appoint only ministers who would carry the reform bill unimpaired, 10 May, and for the second reading of the Irish bill, 25 May. His only other known votes were with government for the Russian-Dutch loan, 26 Jan., 12, 16, 20 July. On 4 June he informed Westminster that 'I should not hesitate to avail myself of the opportunity of standing again' for Shaftesbury, which was reduced to one seat by the Reform Act, but the patron was wary of offering any further overt influence.[11] His opponent, the Liberal John Sayer Poulter, denounced him as 'nothing in this place but the friend of close boroughs, and a complete ultra-Tory', and at the general election in December 1832 beat him by 318 votes to 210, largely because he was unpopular with the new electors from the recently added parts of the enlarged constituency.[12] Penrhyn, who succeeded his father in June 1846, died a respected country gentleman in March 1861. His sister recorded that 'short was the warning, but it found him ready; and so blessed was the close of his outwardly blameless life, so ripened was he for his heavenly inheritance, that it took away the "sting of death"'.[13] He presumably left the bulk of his estate to his elder son Edward Henry Leycester (1827-1919), an officer in the Royal Surrey militia, and provided for his three other children.

[1] His identity has not been traced. [2] IGI (Cheshire). [3] *Burke Commoners* (1833), i. 73-75; G. Ormerod, *Cheshire*, i. 507. [4] A.J.C. Hare, *Memorials of a Quiet Life* (1884), i. 3-4, 7, 10-11. [5] PROB 11/1580/276; IR26/685/409. [6] Hare, i. 22, 26, 30-31, 56; C.M. Rose, *19th Cent. Mortlake and East Sheen*, 111. [7] *Hist. Shaftesbury Election 1830*, pp. 12, 29, 41-43; *Dorset Co. Chron.* 22 July, 12 Aug., 9 Sept. 1830. [8] NLW, Ormathwaite mss FG/1/5, p. 126. [9] Grosvenor mss 9/11/48; *Dorset Co. Chron.* 5 May 1831. [10] Grosvenor mss 9/12/47. [11] Ibid. 9/12/48, 49; *The Times*, 28 June, 2 July 1832. [12] *Sherborne Jnl.* 19 July, 13, 27 Dec.; *Dorset Co. Chron.* 29 Nov., 13 Dec. 1832. [13] *Gent. Mag.* (1846), ii. 215; (1861), i. 467; Hare, ii. 406, 409-10.

S.M.F.

PENRUDDOCKE, John Hungerford (1770–1841), of Compton Chamberlayne, Wilts. and 35 Curzon Street, Mdx.

WILTON 1 Feb. 1821–1837

b. 23 Jan. 1770, 1st s. of Charles Penruddocke† of Compton Chamberlayne and Anne Henrietta, da. of Wadham Wyndham of Fyfield, Wilts. *educ.* Harrow 1785; New Coll. Oxf. 1789. *m.* 3 Oct. 1792,[1] Maria Anne, da. of John Pearse of Standen, Wilts., *s.p.*[2] *suc.* fa. 1788. *d.* 25 Dec. 1841.

Lt. Hindon troop, Wilts. yeoman cav. 1799; lt.-col. commdt.

Sheriff, Wilts. 1817-18; mayor, Wilton 1818-19.

Penruddocke belonged to a leading Wiltshire gentry family, which had been settled at Compton Chamberlayne, 'a commodious mansion, seated in a luxuriant part of the county', since the sixteenth century, and he was a descendant of the royalist Colonel John Penruddocke, who was beheaded for treason at Exeter in 1655.[3] His father, who was anti-government Member for Wiltshire from 1770 until his death in 1788, left him the property and the residue of his estate in trust, after provision had been made for his other children.[4] Through inheritances from his mother and wife, he held other land in Berkshire and Wiltshire, where he was a magistrate and militia officer.[5] He was elected a member of the corporation of nearby Wilton in October 1816, and the following month he signed the entry in the minute book for the return of Lord FitzHarris* at a by-election.[6] As sheriff of Wiltshire, he chaired the county meeting at Devizes in March 1817, which was called to congratulate the regent on surviving an assassination attempt. At the insistence of the radical Henry Hunt*, he agreed to remove it from the town hall and 'took up his station upon the steps of the market cross, where he was surrounded by such a gang of desperadoes as never disgraced a meeting of highwaymen and pickpockets in the purlieus of St. Giles's'. Amid rowdy scenes, Penruddocke, who, according to Hunt, 'looked ready to faint with shame at what he was about to do, dissolved the meeting, and ordered the Riot Act to be read ... and immediately gave orders for me to be taken into custody'. He had the 'mortification' of witnessing Hunt's escape.[7]

In 1818 Penruddocke again refused the honour of offering for the county, which he had declined in 1812 on the retirement of his idle relation, Henry Penruddocke Wyndham. Instead, at the general election that year he split for the sitting Member Paul Methuen† and the Tory interloper William Long Wellesley* against the agriculturist John Benett*, while at the by-election in 1819 he voted for the unsuccessful candidate John Dugdale Astley*, against Benett.[8] In late 1819 he signed the requisition against the holding of a county meeting on Peterloo.[9] His name appears in the Wilton minute book under the return of the sitting Members FitzHarris and Sheldon at the general election of 1820.[10] A few months afterwards, Methuen wrote, in an undated letter to Lord Ailesbury, that

> Penruddocke is laid up with the gout, but from what I hear he certainly will start for the county if there is a requisition sent to him, whenever there is another election, and really in the present uncertain aspect of affairs I think such a contingency by no means improbable at no very distant period ... All I hope is, we may all get over Her Majesty the queen with our lives and property safe.[11]

However, nothing ever came of his county aspirations. He attended a meeting of the local gentry in Salisbury, 30 Jan. 1821, which agreed a loyal address to the king.[12] Two days later he was returned unopposed on a vacancy for Wilton by its patron the 11th earl of Pembroke, the Tory lord lieutenant, and paid £153 in expenses.[13]

In the House, where he made no known speeches during this period, he was an inconspicuous general supporter of the Liverpool ministry. He voted in defence of their conduct towards the queen, 6 Feb. 1821. As Lord Sidmouth, the home secretary, predicted to the Devizes Member Thomas Grimston Estcourt, 28 Feb., Penruddocke voted against Catholic relief that day.[14] He was listed as voting with opposition for repeal of the additional malt duty, 21 Mar. He divided against disqualifying civil officers of the ordnance from voting in parliamentary elections, 12 Apr., parliamentary reform, 9 May, and Hume's motion for economy and retrenchment, 27 June 1821. He voted for reducing the number of junior lords of the admiralty, 1 Mar. 1822, but otherwise apparently always sided with ministers.[15] He divided against inquiries into Irish tithes, 19 June, and the conduct of the lord advocate relative to the press in Scotland, 25 June 1822. He signed the list of corporators present at the election of Edward Baker as his colleague for Wilton, 6 Jan. 1823.[16] He voted against repeal of the Foreign Enlistment Act, 16 Apr., and reform of the Scottish representative system, 2 June. He divided against repeal of the usury laws, 27 June 1823, 17 Feb. 1825. He voted against condemning the trial of the Methodist missionary John Smith in Demerara, 11 June 1824. He divided against Catholic relief, 1 Mar., 21 Apr., and the Irish franchise bill, 26 Apr. 1825. He voted against resolutions to curb electoral bribery, 26 May 1826.

He was returned unopposed for Wilton at the general election of 1826. He was granted one month's sick leave, 7 Mar., and voted against the Penryn election bill, 7 June 1827. He paired against Catholic claims, 12 May, and voted with the Wellington ministry against reducing the salary of the lieutenant-general of the ordnance, 4 July 1828. In February 1829 he was listed by Planta, the patronage secretary, as 'opposed to the principle' of the ministry's Catholic emancipation bill. He commented in a letter to Estcourt's son Thomas Henry Bucknall Estcourt* that 'I am not very well pleased with government on this occasion. As the Catholics have bullied them they will be more dissatisfied than ever unless they get all they possibly can'. He added that 'I am now confined to the house as the cold weather has brought on the complaint in my leg'. In fear of their conduct being shackled, he raised a scruple against Members signing the Wiltshire anti-Catholic address, but he did in fact do so.[17] He was named as a defaulter on this question, 5 Mar. 1829, and the order for his attendance was discharged, 9 Mar., when he was given three weeks' leave because of illness. He cast no known votes that session. He voted against Jewish emancipation, 17 May, and abolition of the death penalty for forgery, 7 June 1830.

The 12th earl of Pembroke having had him returned at the general election later that year, he was listed by ministers among their 'friends', but he was absent from the division on the civil list, 15 Nov. 1830. He was granted leave for three weeks because of illness in his family, 23 Nov. 1830, and again, 7 Feb. 1831, as well as on the grounds of the ill health of a near relation (for two weeks), 25 Feb., and urgent private business (for one week), 14 Mar. These absences were probably all occasioned by the fatal illness of his wife, who died on 5 Apr. Penruddocke, who had refused to sign Lord Radnor's requisition for a county meeting on parliamentary reform,[18] voted against the second reading of the Grey ministry's reform bill, 22 Mar., but was apparently not present for the division on Gascoyne's wrecking amendment, 19 Apr. He was left undisturbed at Wilton at the ensuing general election. He paired against the second reading of the reintroduced reform bill, 6 July, and was absent from the division on postponing consideration of the partial disfranchisement of Chippenham, 27 July. The following month he signed the Wiltshire anti-reform declaration.[19] He was given another month's sick leave, 12 Sept., and paired against the passage of the bill, 21 Sept. He also paired against the second reading of the revised bill, 17 Dec. 1831, but was present to vote against its third reading, 22 Mar. 1832. His only other known vote in this Parliament was against government on the Russian-Dutch loan, 12 July 1832. He was returned by Pembroke for the one remaining seat at Wilton at the general election in December 1832 and sat as a Conservative until his retirement in 1837. Penruddocke died in December 1841, leaving his estate to his great-nephew Charles (1828-99).[20]

[1] IGI (Berks.). [2] According to an uncorroborated source, in 1837 he married one of his first wife's Pearce cousins (*Grove Diaries* ed. D. Hawkins, 25). [3] Sir R.C. Hoare, *Wilts.*, Dunworth, 81; Addenda, 63-64; J.E. Nightingale, *Mems. Wilton*, 154-5; *Oxford DNB*. [4] PROB 11/1176/106. [5] *VCH Berks.* iv. 196; *VCH Wilts.* xiii. 63. [6] Wilts. RO, Wilton borough recs. G25/1/22, ff. 286, 288, 289. [7] H. Hunt, *Mems.* iii. 464-70; *Salisbury Jnl.* 24 Mar. 1817. [8] *HP Commons, 1790-1820*, ii. 411; *Wilts. Pollbook* (1819), 6. [9] *Devizes Gazette*, 4 Nov. 1819. [10] Wilton borough recs. G25/1/22, f. 298. [11] Wilts. RO, Ailesbury mss 9/35/100. [12] *Salisbury Jnl.* 5 Feb. 1821. [13] Wilts. RO, Penruddocke mss 332/270. [14] Glos. RO, Sotheron Estcourt mss D1571 F215. [15] *Black Bk.* (1823), 184. [16] Wilton borough recs. G25/1/22, f. 306. [17] Sotheron Estcourt mss X114, Penruddocke to Bucknall Estcourt, Long to same, Feb. 1829. [18] Wilts. RO, Radnor mss 490/1376, Radnor's diary of events, 1830-1. [19] *Devizes Gazette*, 11 Aug. 1831. [20] *Gent. Mag.* (1842), ii. 428-9.

S.M.F.

PEPYS, Charles Christopher (1781–1851), of 13 New Square, Lincoln's Inn, Mdx.

HIGHAM FERRERS	14 July 1831–26 Sept. 1831
MALTON	30 Sept. 1831–20 Jan. 1836

b. 29 Apr. 1781, 2nd s. of Sir William Weller Pepys, 1st bt. (*d.* 1825), of Wimpole Street, Mdx. and Ridley Hall, Cheshire and Elizabeth, da. of William Dowdeswell† of Pull Court, Worcs. *educ.* Harrow 1795-7; Trinity Coll. Camb. 1797; L. Inn 1801, called 1804. *m.* 30 June 1821, Caroline Elizabeth, da. of William Wingfield† of Lincoln's Inn, 7s. (1 *d.v.p.*) 9da. (3 *d.v.p.*). kntd. 26 Feb. 1834; *cr.* Bar. Cottenham 20 Jan. 1836; *suc.* elder bro. Sir William Weller Pepys, 2nd bt., in the baronetcy (1801) and to Ridley and Tandridge Park, Godstone, Surr. 5 Oct. 1845; cos. Hon. and Rev. Sir Henry Leslie, 3rd bt., rect. of Wetherden, Suff., in the baronetcy (1784) 9 Dec. 1849; *cr.* earl of Cottenham 11 June 1850. *d.* 29 Apr. 1851.

KC 24 Aug. 1826; bencher, L. Inn 1826, treas. 1837; solicitor-gen. to Queen Adelaide Nov. 1830-May 1832; solicitor-gen. Feb.-Sept. 1834; master of rolls Sept. 1834-Jan. 1836; PC 1 Oct. 1834; member, jud. cttee. of PC 1834; first commr. of great seal Apr. 1835-Jan. 1836; ld. chan. Jan. 1836-Sept. 1841, July 1846-June 1850.

Pepys came from the same old Cambridgeshire family to which the celebrated diarist belonged. His grandfather William Pepys, a youngest son, established a banking house in Lombard Street, London in about 1729, but died aged 45 in 1743. With his second wife Hannah Weller he had two sons, of whom the younger, Lucas Pepys (1743-1830), became one of George III's physicians and received a baronetcy in 1784. The elder son William Weller Pepys (1741-1825), the father of this Member, was a master in chancery, 1775-1807, and was made a baronet in 1801. A man of learning and refinement, 'well known in polite circles' as one of the 'steadiest abettors' of Elizabeth Montagu and the Bluestockings, he was characterized by Hannah More as 'the true high priest of conversation' and twitted by Horace Walpole for 'having a nose longer than himself'. In 1781 Dr. Johnson admitted to Mrs. Thrale that she had extolled Pepys 'with such disproportion' that he had been provoked to 'lessen him, perhaps more than he deserves'. Pepys held liberal views and, as Walpole noted, was 'not a little infected with ... the French disorder' in 1791, when he pronounced the Revolution to be 'one of the most wonderful and most important events in the history of mankind'.[1] Over 30 years later Maria Edgeworth described him as 'a most agreeable, lively, polite old gentleman, who tells delightful anecdotes of Mrs. Montagu, Sir Joshua Reynolds, Burke and Dr. Johnson, with whom he lived in former days'.[2]

Pepys doted on his three sons with the daughter of the Rockinghamite politician Dowdeswell, and took great pains over their education at home before sending them to school. The eldest, William Weller Pepys (1778-1845), succeeded to the baronetcy, but suffered from poor health and made no mark in public life. The youngest, Henry Pepys (1783-1866), took holy orders and became bishop of Worcester in 1841. The second, this Member, was at Harrow with Lord Althorp*, whose memories of him were recorded, and perhaps embroidered, by his friend and biographer Denis Le Marchant†:

> A stout, sturdy, thickset boy, of blunt speech and cold disposition, aiming at no distinction, making few friends, and exhibiting no traces of the peculiar discipline to which paternal care had subjected him. His proficiency in scholarship was respectable, but unaccompanied by a spark of genius. No one could say that he was clever; some of his schoolfellows pronounced him dull. His dark, searching eyes, massive forehead, and expressive lips, refuted the charge; and he had an air of independence and determination which indicated an inward consciousness of superiority.

In 1797 his father was pleased to see that he was 'developing very fast those good qualities, which, I never doubted, would by time and opportunity, expand themselves', and the following year, hearing good auguries of his university examinations, had 'no doubt that I shall always have reason to be glad, that I indulged him in his request to pass some time at Cambridge'. At Lincoln's Inn he was a pupil of William Tidd and was advised for a time by Samuel Romilly†. Although his indulgent father rejoiced in his 'rapid and uncommon' success at the chancery bar, his progress there as an equity draftsman was in fact exceedingly slow. Yet in time he built up a large practice on the strength of his reputation as, in Le Marchant's words, 'a lawyer of sound, though not showy parts, and of indefatigable industry'.[3] He made a felicitous and fecund marriage, at the age of 40, in 1821, pocketed some £6,600 in bank stock by his father's will, and at last got his silk gown in 1826.[4]

Pepys, who by 1813 had become legal adviser and auditor to the 2nd Earl Fitzwilliam, was in the running for the post of solicitor-general in the Grey ministry in November 1830, but was passed over for Sir William Horne*, whom he replaced as solicitor-general to Queen Adelaide.[5] At the 1831 general election lord chancellor Brougham pressed Fitzwilliam's son, Lord Milton*, to return Pepys, as he was 'most essential to my [legal] reforms and a most useful man in all ways, as well as a most respectable', but subsequently advanced his own brother's claims instead. In July 1831 Milton placed the surplus seat at Higham Ferrers at Pepys's disposal, on condition that he ceased to audit the Fitzwilliams' accounts, though he was retained as their legal adviser for 'a regular annual fee' of 100 sovereigns.[6] According to Le Marchant, Pepys in return 'insisted on being left to his own discretion as to attendance in the House', in order to safeguard his professional livelihood, 'a privilege which he used with such freedom, as to lose in the eyes of his party all claims to the honours of his profession'.[7]

Certainly he cut an undistinguished figure in the Commons where, in the words of an obituarist, 'his unadorned oratory made but little impression'.[8] He voted steadily for the details of the Grey ministry's reintroduced reform bill in August, was in the ministerial majorities on the Dublin election controversy, 23 Aug., and the Liverpool writ, 5 Sept., and voted for the passage of the reform bill, 21 Sept. 1831. After transferring to Fitzwilliam's borough of Malton he voted for Lord Ebrington's motion of confidence in the ministry, 10 Oct., and in his maiden speech, 13 Oct., defended Brougham's bill to establish a separate bankruptcy jurisdiction. During the recess the opposition whip Holmes joked that Pepys was one of three men who were to 'draw lots for the office of solicitor-general'.[9] On 1 Dec. Pepys and other lawyers friendly to the reform bill met at Althorp's to rehearse their defence of it, but he did not subsequently trouble the House on the subject.[10] He voted for the second reading of the revised bill, 17 Dec. 1831, and steadily supported its details, though he was in the minority of 32 against the Chandos clause enfranchising £50 tenants-at-will, 1 Feb. 1832. He divided for the bill's third reading, 22 Mar. On the occasion of the government's embarrassment over the Russian-Dutch loan, 26 Jan., he was reported to have felt that 'we made our men feel the collar too much' and did not vote, but he was in the ministerial majorities on the issue, 12, 16, 20 July, and on relations with Portugal, 9 Feb.[11] He spoke and voted against Knight's Irish master of the rolls bill, 22 Feb. He voted for the address calling on the king to appoint only ministers who would carry reform unimpaired, 10 May, and the second reading of the Irish reform bill, 25 May 1832. Next month he was one of seven senior lawyers who protested to Brougham against the precipitate passage of four bills reforming real property law.[12]

At the 1832 general election Pepys was again returned unopposed for Malton. He became solicitor-general *faute de mieux* in 1834, and within two years, thanks to a fortunate concatenation of circumstances, attained the pinnacle of his profession, taking his title from Cottenham in Cambridgeshire.[13] Joseph Jekyll,† playing on that village's fame for its cream cheeses, joked that Pepys, 'being *bread* to the bar, naturally took to the *Rolls*, and is now turned into *Cheese*'.[14] Yet he soon belied his reputation for 'mediocrity' and, in the view of his cabinet colleague Lord Holland, proved to be 'in his judicial capacity the very best [chancellor] since Lord Hardwicke, and his senatorial and political, useful, straightforward, conciliatory, *acute*, and intrepid'.[15] John Campbell II*, Le Marchant and Lord Palmerston* also acknowledged his success, which was aided not a little by the welcome relief which his steady reliability offered after the unpredictable flashiness of Brougham.[16] Lord Melbourne, the premier, asked how he got on with his new chancellor, was reputed to have replied, 'Oh! capitally; I'm like a man who has broken for good with a termagant mistress, and married the best of cooks'.[17] Le Marchant, who regretted only his indifference to judicial reform, later remarked that

> the coldness of disposition and reserve which had characterized him at Harrow, clung to him through life. He concerned himself too little with the sympathies of others to do many generous actions, or have many friends ... He cared little for general society, and less for that of learned and able men. His conversation generally turned on the topics of the day, which he discussed with much shrewdness; and the downright view he took, both of men and things, was often enlivened by a vein of dry humour which gave much zest to his remarks.[18]

Pepys succeeded to both his father's and uncle's baronetcies, which became merged in his peerage. Failing health obliged him to relinquish his second tenure of the great seal in June 1850. He wintered in Malta, in the hope of recovery, but died in April 1851 on his way back to England at Pietra Santa, on his 70th birthday.[19]

[1] W.C. Pepys, *Genealogy of Pepys Fam.* (1952), 49-51; *Horace Walpole Corresp.* xi. 30-31, 243, 264; xxxi. 213, 228, 242-3; *Boswell's Life of Johnson* ed. G. Hill and L. Powell, iv. 65, 82, 487; *A Later Pepys* ed. A. Gaussen, i. 6-8. [2] *Edgeworth Letters*, 386-7. [3] Le Marchant, *Althorp*, 58-61; *A Later Pepys*, ii. 55, 203, 208, 211, 295, 330, 338, 348; Torrens, *Melbourne*, i. 47. [4] PROB 11/1700/335. [5] Wentworth Woodhouse mun. F107/263; *Life of Campbell*, i. 490, 492; Brougham mss, Pepys to Brougham, 25 Nov. 1830. [6] Add. 76371, Brougham to Althorp [11 May]; Fitzwilliam mss vol. 732, p. 35, Milton to Pepys, 8 June 1831. [7] Le Marchant, 61. [8] *The Times*, 8 May 1851. [9] *Life of Campbell*, ii. 2. [10] Hatherton diary, 1 Dec. [1831]. [11] *Three Diaries*, 197; Le Marchant, 391. [12] Brougham mss, memo. [June 1832]. [13] *Oxford DNB*; E. Foss, *Judges of England*, ix. 239-42; Campbell, *Lives of Chancellors*, viii. 110, 121, 424, 479; *Greville Mems.* iii. 335. [14] *Disraeli Letters*, ii. 475. [15] *Holland House Diaries*, 332, 346. [16] Le Marchant, 61-68; *Life of Campbell*, ii. 207; *Lieven-Palmerston Corresp.* 111. [17] Torrens, ii. 174. [18] Le Marchant, 67. [19] *Gent. Mag.* (1851), ii. 84-85.

D.R.F.

PERCEVAL, Alexander (1787–1858), of Temple House, Ballymote, co. Sligo.

CO. SLIGO 1831–6 Sept. 1841

b. 10 Feb. 1787, 2nd but 1st surv. s. of Rev. Philip Perceval of Temple House and Anne, da. of Alexander Carrol of Dublin. *educ.* by Dr. Austin, nr. Lucan; Trinity, Dublin 1803-7. *m.* 11 Feb. 1808, Jane Anne, da. of Col. Henry Peisley L'Estrange of Moystown, King's Co., 4s. 6da. (1 *d.v.p.*). *suc.* fa. 1800. *d.* 9 Dec. 1858.

Treas. of ordnance Dec. 1834-Apr. 1835; ld. of treasury 8-20 Sept. 1841; sjt.-at-arms to House of Lords 16 Sept. 1841-*d.*

Lt.-col. Sligo militia 1809-1851.

Perceval's ancestor George Perceval (1635-75) had settled in Ireland on acquiring the Temple House property by marriage; he was the second son of the parliamentarian Sir Philip Perceval (1605-47), through whom his family were distantly related to the earls of Egmont and Spencer Perceval†, the prime minister. Alexander Perceval's elder brother Philip died unmarried, leaving him to succeed to the family estates on the death of his father, whose will was proved in 1800. He assumed 'the quiet and enviable life of a country gentleman'.[1] On 29 Sept. 1814 he complained to Peel, the Irish secretary, about a proposed 'junction' between the Temple House corps of yeomanry, which he commanded, and another corps, observing that his was 'the only corps in the barony of Lieney, in which I am the only resident magistrate' and that such a union would be 'highly inconvenient'.[2] On hearing 'rumours' in August 1821 that he had declared himself 'conditionally a candidate' for county Sligo, his neighbour Charles King O'Hara, son of one of the sitting Members, sought to dissuade him from standing:

> I feel it due to the friendship that has ever existed between us ... to declare that I will not *in any measure* give my assistance in promoting what I conceive must lead to your ruin ... You *now* enjoy a great share of domestic happiness ... occupying yourself for the advantages of your family, your property, and your country, with an income which, though moderate, by your present managements is sufficient to supply every comfort to render you highly respected as a most excellent and valuable resident gentleman. Place you in Parliament and you at once renounce the very qualifications which formed your recommendation ... Your property, amply sufficient for your present wants, will ill supply the demands of an Irish county Member.[3]

Undeterred, when a vacancy occurred in 1822 Perceval came forward in opposition to a non-resident candidate, with the support of Owen Wynne, Tory Member for and patron of the borough of Sligo, who had 'known him from early infancy'. 'In politics he is exactly the man you would wish to assist, a steady supporter of government and a staunch Protestant', noted George Dawson*, under-secretary to Peel, now home secretary.[4] Repeated attempts to avert a contest came to nothing and, 'finding it was utterly impossible to prevail on him' to withdraw, O'Hara, after receiving an imploring private letter from Perceval's wife, agreed to give him his 'reluctant support' as a 'most intimate friend and neighbour' and an 'honest man, born and ever residing in the county ... whose time, purse and person are ever at its disposal'. A fierce contest ensued, in which Perceval was warmly supported by the Orangemen, but he conceded defeat on the seventh day.[5] Rumours that he would stand in 1826 came to nothing.[6] At the 1831 general election he came forward again, citing the 'same principles' as before and his opposition to the Grey ministry's reform bill. He was again supported by Wynne, for whose son he was rumoured to be acting as a seat warmer, and allegedly received £5,000 from the Tories' 'secret committee', with a promise of 'more if needed'. (On 6 May Charles Arbuthnot*, who was responsible for the opposition's election fund, informed Lord Farnham that he had been asked to assist Perceval and had given him '£1,000 beyond the sum named in the letter by Mr. Robinson'.) At the nomination he explained that he favoured an 'amendment' of the voting system, but was 'decidedly opposed' to the 'most obnoxious and destructive measure that the ministry have attempted to delude you with'. After a two-day contest he was returned in second place.[7]

In his maiden speech, 27 June 1831, he praised the Irish yeomanry for providing an 'effectual safeguard to the lives and property of the peaceable inhabitants'. He spoke regularly in similar terms thereafter. He voted against the second reading of the reintroduced reform bill, 6 July, at least three times to adjourn the debates, 12 July, for use of the 1831 census, 19 July, and against the inclusion of Chippenham in schedule B, 27 July. He divided against the bill's third reading, 19 Sept., and passage, 21 Sept., and the second reading of the Scottish measure, 23 Sept. He presented and endorsed Protestant petitions for the cessation of the Maynooth grant, 5 Aug., and voted accordingly, 26 Sept. He defended the 'purity' and 'impartiality' of the administration of Irish justice, 10 Aug. Next day he expressed his regret at the Newtownbarry incident but objected to the 'use of the words "massacre" and "slaughter"' to describe it, as the indictments against those involved had been withdrawn. He demanded a reform of the law of divorce as practised by the Catholic clergy, which was subject to the 'greatest abuses', 2 Sept. That day he denied being an Orangeman, saying 'I was never at an Orange meeting in all my life'. He questioned Smith Stanley, the Irish secretary, about the appointment of lord lieutenants of Irish counties, 7 Sept., secured returns on the subject, 9 Sept., and proposed the immediate removal of any who were 'not resident', 6 Oct., asserting that in Sligo there had been a 'direct violation' of the agreement by the ministry to appoint only 'local residents'. On being told by Smith Stanley that no Sligo appointment had yet been made, however, he withdrew his motion, disclaiming any 'party feelings'. He voted against the issue of the Liverpool writ, 5 Sept. He was in the minority of seven for Waldo Sibthorp's complaint against the *The Times* for a breach of privilege, 12 Sept. That day he divided against the truck bill. He was a minority teller against the Irish public works bill, 16 Sept. 1831.

Perceval paired against the second reading of the revised reform bill, 17 Dec. 1831, and voted against the enfranchisement of Tower Hamlets, 28 Feb., and the third reading, 22 Mar. 1832. He divided against the second reading of the Irish bill, 25 May, and was in the minority of 39 for preserving the voting rights of Irish freemen, 2 July. He defended the existing Irish registration system, 6 June, 6 July, and the qualification oath demanded of Catholics at the time of registration, 18 July. That day he argued against the division of the larger Irish counties into polling districts, saying 'I ... like to see all my enemies and if counties were thus cut up, it would be necessary to have a legal staff attending at all the polling places'. He voted against ministers on the Russian-Dutch loan, 26 Jan., 12 July. He objected to the fees charged to Irish magistrates on the renewal of their commissions by the Irish lord chancellor Plunket, 24 Jan., obtained information on the matter, 2 Feb., and contested the legality of these 'most odious, vexatious and oppressive exactions', warning that 'in consequence of the disagreement existing between the lord chancellor and the magistrates' some districts were now without a local commission of the peace, 7 Feb. 'Though not long in the House', a Conservative publication later recalled, he so 'boldly and energetically' attacked the fees that the lord chancellor had 'to refund every shilling'.[8] He condemned the appointment of a non-resident, Arthur Knox Gore, to the lord lieutenancy of Sligo, 7 Feb., and moved for returns of deputy lord lieutenants, 12 July. He brought up petitions against the new plan of Irish education, 7 Mar., presented numerous others thereafter, and protested that it was 'inconsistent with the first principles of the Christian religion', 20 June, and 'obnoxious to the feelings of Protestants', 5 July. He was in the minority of 17 against the Irish education grant, 23 July. He spoke against the Dublin coal trade bill, 7 and 9 Mar., when he contended that the 'vested rights' of the coal-meters were being abolished because 'they did not vote for the reform candidates' at the last election. He was a founder member of the Carlton Club that month. He spoke and was a minority teller against the second reading of the Catholic marriages bill, 3 Apr. He voted for the disfranchisement of Liverpool, 23 May. He welcomed inquiry into the disturbances in Queen's County that day, and was appointed to the committee on Irish outrages, 31 May. He spoke in support of Alexander Baring's bill to exclude insolvent debtors from Parliament, 30 May, and voted accordingly, 27 June. On 14 June he asserted that the Irish party processions bill banning parades was an 'insult to the Orangemen of Ireland', noting that a reform procession, bearing banners and tricoloured flags, had recently been permitted in Dublin. He was a minority teller against it, 25 June. He voted against a tax on absentee landlords to provide permanent provision for the Irish poor, 19 June. On the 29th he welcomed the clandestine marriages bill but recommended sterner measures against 'suspended Presbyterian clergymen', who 'for the most part' carried them out. That month he joined the Conservative Society of Dublin.[9] On 6 July he complained that at the last election one of his opponents had been proposed without 'the least chance of his being elected' and that 'as it was impossible to prove that he had authorized his proposers ... the sheriff could not recover one farthing of the expenses'. He demanded a speedy settlement of the Irish tithes question, warning that the clergy were 'almost in a state of starvation', 9 July. He called for legal provision for the recovery of tithes when a valuation had been prevented, 13 July, voted for the tithes composition bill next day, and denounced the 'atrocious conspiracy' which existed in Ireland for their 'destruction', 20 July. He approved the Irish magistracy's opposition to anti-tithes meetings, observing that unlike Orange gatherings, which were 'held to maintain the laws', these were 'held to destroy them', 20 July. Citing his membership of the Kildare Place Society and the Hibernian Bible Society, he insisted that in his own neighbourhood the Protestant catechism was 'not taught, nor is any religious instruction given', 23 July 1832. Next day he spoke and paired against the bill to disqualify the recorder of Dublin from Parliament.

Perceval was returned as a Conservative in 1832 and at the next three general elections. He held junior office in Peel's first ministry and assisted in the negotiations which resulted in the peaceful dissolution of the Orange Association of Ireland, of which he had been treasurer.[10] He was briefly a lord of the treasury in September 1841 before being appointed serjeant-at-arms of the House of Lords, which ended his Commons career. 'A Conservative of the purest order', he died at 28 Chester Street, London in December 1859, when his estates passed to his third son and namesake (1821-66).[11]

[1] *Index of Wills* [I] ed. A. Vicars, 372; *Portraits of Eminent Conservatives* ed. H. Ryall (ser. 2), 2-3. [2] Add. 40239, f. 122. [3] NLI, O'Hara mss 20316, O'Hara to Perceval, 26 Aug. 1821. [4] Ibid. election address; Add. 40352, f. 26. [5] O'Hara mss 20316, O'Hara to Webber, 13 Oct., same to Lorton, 11 Nov., Jane Perceval to O'Hara, 9 Nov.; 20331 (2), O'Hara to Lorton. 18 Nov.; *Roscommon and Leitrim Gazette*, 30 Nov., 7 Dec. 1822. [6] *Roscommon and Leitrim Gazette*, 17, 24 June 1826. [7] *Sligo Jnl.* 29 Apr., 6 May; *Dublin Evening Post*, 10, 12 May 1831; NLI, Farnham mss 18606 (1). [8] *Portraits*, 3. [9] Farnham mss 18611 (3). [10] *Greville Mems.* iii. 286; Add. 40424, f. 267; *Oxford DNB*. [11] *Portraits*, 3; *Gent. Mag.* (1859), i. 209; *The Times*, 13 Dec. 1858.

P.J.S.

PERCEVAL, Henry Frederick John James, Visct. Perceval (1796–1841).

EAST LOOE 3 Mar. 1826–1826

b. 3 Jan. 1796, o.s. of John, 4th earl of Egmont [I], and Bridget, da. of Lt.-Col. Glyn Wynn† of Glynllifon, Caern. *educ.* privately; Trinity Coll. Camb. 1814. *m.* Nov. or Dec. 1828, Louise Marie, da. of Count D'Orselet,[1] 1s. *d.v.p. styled* Visct. Perceval 1822-35; *suc.* fa. as 5th earl of Egmont [I] 31 Dec. 1835. *d.* 23 Dec. 1841.

Perceval's great-grandfather, the 2nd earl of Egmont, had served in the Bute, Grenville and Rockingham ministries, and his grandfather, the 3rd earl, was a half-brother of Spencer Perceval, prime minister from 1809 to 1812. His father succeeded as the 4th earl in 1822 but, from the highly publicized legal case over Perceval's will in the 1860s, it emerges that the family's finances were already in a state of crisis. Debts of some £300,000 had accumulated on the estate at Churchtown, county Cork, and the property at Enmore, Somerset, was also heavily encumbered. The barrister engaged to defend Perceval's will claimed that he was 'a man of education and refinement' whose 'feeling of disappointment ... on account of the enormous embarrassments on his property, led him to drink, and at an early period of his life he acquired habits of dissipation'; the opposing counsel blamed this fall from grace on neglect by his mother, who was portrayed as a scheming courtesan.[2] While Egmont enjoyed immunity from prosecution for debt by virtue of his seat in the Lords (as Baron Lovel in the British peerage), Perceval was 'obliged to roam abroad' in order to evade the family's creditors. It may well be that his parliamentary ambitions stemmed from a desire 'to be relieved from this vagabond kind of life'.[3] In the autumn of 1824 he announced his candidature at the next election for Penryn, where his mother had canvassed on his behalf, but in the event he was returned on a vacancy at East Looe in March 1826 on the interest of James Buller Elphinstone*.[4] No trace of parliamentary activity has been found, and it is not certain that he even took his seat. The nature of his regular pursuits can be inferred from a letter supposedly sent to him on 28 Apr. 1826 by Edward Tierney, the family's Dublin solicitor and land agent, entreating him to 'abandon his evil courses and his associates'.[5] At the general election that summer he contested Penryn, despite being served during his canvass with a writ, which was almost certainly for debt. Unable to compete against the long purses of his opponents in a borough renowned for its venality, he was defeated.[6]

Having thus compounded his financial difficulties, Perceval was declared an outlaw at some point in 1828 and fled abroad. Later that year he married the daughter of a French count in Paris, but evidently not under the auspices of the British consulate. The son born to them about four months after the marriage was apparently living in 1835, but predeceased his father; the fate of the mother has not been discovered.[7] On his father's death in 1835 Perceval inherited all his property, but the will was not proved until 1857, when the personalty was sworn under £16,000. Enmore had been sold in 1834 for £134,000 to pay off creditors, but no takers had been found for the Cork estates, which comprised 11,250 acres, because of the burden of debt on them.[8] Egmont took his seat in the Lords in February 1836, but afterwards lived under the alias of 'Mr. Lovell' at Burderop Park, Wiltshire. This property was purchased in the name of his companion, a Mrs. Cleese, with whom it seems he had previously resided at Hythe, Kent and whom he passed off as his sister. It was later claimed, admittedly by a lawyer with an axe to grind, that

> the earl was so drunk sometimes at Burderop that Mrs. Cleese was obliged to lock him up lest visitors should see him in that state. He occasionally took runs to London, where he could seldom be traced. He there visited a place called Smith's Hotel, at which he ... spent his time at the bar drinking with ostlers and cabdrivers, treating them, while himself in a state of wild intoxication ... On his return ... he frequently brought back his portmanteau full of brandy bottles. He drank to excess in the morning, and had acquired such a detestation of business that he signed papers without troubling himself with their contents.

On the other hand, a Wiltshire cleric considered him 'a thorough gentleman', whose 'conversation [was] above par, intelligent, quick, rather'.[9] An application to end his outlawry in 1838 ended in farce, when no evidence that he was still alive could be produced.[10] He decamped to Portugal in 1840, but after Mrs. Cleese's death he returned to England, where he died in December 1841.[11] Tierney was made sole executor and residuary legatee of the estate, exciting some comment, but it was not until 1857 that the will was finally proved (under £20,000) by Tierney's son-in-law and heir, the Rev. Sir William Lionel Darell.[12] In 1863 the will was belatedly contested by George James Perceval (1794-1874), Egmont's cousin and successor in the peerage. It was alleged that alcoholism had rendered Egmont completely dependent on Tierney, whose misleading valuation of the estates had induced him to draw up his will as he did. The evidence was inconclusive and an out of court settlement was reached, by which the Irish property was returned to the Egmont family on payment of £125,000 to Darell.[13] It was estimated that Tierney and his heirs had realized at least £300,000 from their stewardship of the estates, which were eventually sold by the 7th earl in 1889.[14] The 8th earl (1856-1910), a former sailor turned London fireman, upheld family tradition by being arrested for drunkenness in Piccadilly, 16 May 1902.[15]

[1] *Gent. Mag.* (1828), ii. 638. [2] *The Times*, 3, 5 Aug. 1863. [3] Ibid. 3 Aug. 1863. [4] *West Briton*, 5 Nov. 1824, 10 Mar. 1826. [5] *The Times*, 3 Aug. 1863. [6] *R. Cornw. Gazette*, 27 May, 3, 10, 17 June 1826. [7] *The Times*, 13 Apr. 1829, 5 Nov. 1838, 6 Aug. 1863; GL ms 10891; *Gent. Mag.* (1836), i. 425. [8] PROB 11/2251/372; IR26/2095/336; *The Times*, 24 Nov. 1831, 17 Apr. 1834; *VCH Som.* vi. 38. [9] *The Times*, 3, 4 June, 3, 4, 6 Aug. 1863. [10] Ibid. 5 Nov. 1838, 7 Nov. 1839. [11] Ibid. 27 Dec. 1841, 3, 4 Aug. 1863; *Gent. Mag.* (1842), i. 324. [12] *The Times*, 13, 25 Jan. 1842; PROB 11/2251/271; IR26/2095/349. [13] *The Times*, 4 June, 4-8 Aug., 17 Dec. 1863. [14] Ibid. 4, 8 Aug. 1863, 1 Oct. 1889. [15] Ibid. 17, 26 May 1902.

H.J.S.

PERCEVAL, Spencer (1795–1859), of Elm Grove, Ealing, Mdx.

ENNIS	1818–1820
NEWPORT I.O.W.	25 May 1827–1831
TIVERTON	1831–1832

b. 11 Sept. 1795, 1st s. of Hon. Spencer Perceval† of Elm Grove and Jane, da. of Lt.-Gen. Sir Thomas Spencer Wilson†, 6th bt. *educ.* privately by Dr. John Carey of Dean's Yard, Westminster; Harrow 1804-13; L. Inn 1812; Trinity Coll. Camb. 1813; continental tour 1817-18.[1] *m.* 3 July 1821, Anne Eliza, da. of Norman Macleod† of Dunvegan Castle, Skye, Inverness, 3s. 8da. (2 *d.v.p*). *suc.* fa. 1812. *d.* 16 Sept. 1859.

Teller of exch. 1813-34; under-sec. of state for home affairs Apr.-July 1827; clerk of ordnance Aug. 1828-Dec. 1830.

Vol. London and Westminster light horse 1819.

Perceval had displayed precocious oratorical talent at Harrow, where his preparations for speech day in

May 1812 were interrupted by news of the assassination of his father, the prime minister. In the wave of sympathy that followed, he obtained an exchequer tellership worth £2,700 a year, an annuity of £1,000 and a reversionary interest in his mother's allowance, becoming, as he later admitted to the House, 14 Feb. 1831, 'the very child and creature of the nation's bounty'. 'Pessy', as he was known by his family, had survived a life-threatening bowel disorder in early infancy to grow into 'a hearty child', and at his father's death he promised his mother 'as far as in me lies to imitate him'. Though there was little immediate evidence of this, he ultimately did more than enough to fulfil a paternal injunction to be 'a champion of true religion in a careless world'.[2] His interest in Scripture is first evident in his surviving correspondence from 1821, and between 1825 and 1830 he attended the annual multi-denominational conferences held at the Albury residence of his distant kinsman Henry Drummond†, where he met Edward Irving, the Scottish divine, under whose fanatical influence he eventually fell.[3] Yet for a while his interests were wide. He corresponded on the subject of free will with George Combe, the Scottish phrenologist, and was evidently impressed with his advocacy of the fashionable pseudo-science.[4] In June 1828, John Croker*, the admiralty secretary, described a 'dull enough' dinner party at Lord Farnborough's, at which Perceval was 'preaching craniology' and 'took my head in hand', and by feeling the 'bumps ... found that I was a lover of ghost stories, the only stories, if I know myself, which I do *not* care about!'.[5] Politically, Perceval showed liberal leanings in his support for Canning's ministry, repeal of the Test Acts and Catholic emancipation, but with the millenarian convictions that took hold of him after 1830 came increasing conservatism. His later parliamentary performances resembled that of a seventeenth century sectarian and after 1832 he found a fresh vocation as a leader of the proto-fundamentalist Catholic Apostolic Church.

Perceval, who did not stand at the 1820 general election, had exhibited an independent streak in the 1818 Parliament and his reputation with ministers was not enhanced during the trial of Queen Caroline in October 1820, when he was said to have been the supplier of a quotation from Milton's *Paradise Lost* which was used to effect by Henry Brougham*. In May 1821 Croker suggested him as a candidate for an under-secretaryship at the home office, but noted that it was 'without any expectation that he could be seriously thought of yet; his late unsteady conduct is not forgotten' and 'a place at one of the boards would suit him better'.[6] That July he married 'Nancy' MacLeod, the daughter of a Highland clan chief and the subject of a love poem he had written in 1809, to 'the lovely nymph who scarcely yet has seen/Revolving years to make her age thirteen'.[7] In October 1822 he announced his candidacy for a vacancy for Cambridge University, an ambition he had apparently cherished for some time.[8] Given his family background and earlier vote against Catholic relief, there was surprise when he was portrayed as a supporter of Catholic claims, while a less credible rumour circulated that he was also favourable to parliamentary reform. The duke of Bedford remarked acidly that 'the Whig interest must be at a low ebb ... if they cannot find a better candidate', and Perceval soon withdrew from a crowded field with the intention of coming forward at a future time.[9] This never transpired, though a letter from his brother-in-law John Norman MacLeod* implies that he may have vainly sought another seat at the 1826 general election.[10]

Following the formation of Canning's ministry in 1827 Perceval was appointed as an under-secretary to William Sturges Bourne at the home office. On 7 May he chastised Robert Peel for failing to distance himself from Tory attacks on the fledgling administration, whose patchwork composition was 'the result of your own secession', and opined that

> considerable advantage may be derived from an admission of the more moderate Whigs into office, to cast down that barrier which has hitherto appeared to forbid the hopes of their ever coming into power ... to take out of their mouths the language of opposition; to snatch their children from the education of opposition. These are things of no mean importance, and if effected without too great a sacrifice must tend to the benefit and support of our most valuable establishments.[11]

On Canning's personal recommendation, Perceval was returned on a vacancy for Newport, Isle of Wight at the end of May.[12] On 1 June he introduced a bill for the consolidation of Irish parishes and laid before the House details of convictions under the game laws. He voted against the bill to disfranchise the corrupt borough of Penryn, 7 June, and in favour of a grant for Canadian waterways, 12 June. He presented a report from the commission of inquiry into the state of education in Ireland, 18 June.[13] Writing next day to his sister Fanny, he warned her against forcing her antipathy to Canning's administration on their brother Dudley and questioned her rigid notions of political ideology, noting, by way of illustration, the difference between the principles of Pitt and those of the clubs which bore his name. Recalling his own defiance of Lord Castlereagh* over the seditious meetings bill in 1819, he observed, 'I was called a radical, cut by his lordship and his wife; the shoulders of my own kith and kin shrugged at my name. I had forsaken my father's principles! Beastly, senseless, cruel, cant'.[14] When Sturges Bourne surrendered the seals of the home office to the Whig Lord Lansdowne in July 1827, Perceval too lost his place.

He voted for repeal of the Test Acts, 26 Feb. 1828, but two days later supported Peel's call for an adjournment as evidence of the Wellington ministry's willingness to entertain the proposal. He was in the minority against charging a witness before the East Retford election committee with perjury, 7 Mar., and spoke against the Battersea enclosure bill, 31 Mar. In April he assisted in the Sudbury by-election campaign of his brother-in-law, who ungratefully remarked that 'except for his name he was of no great use'.[15] MacLeod was a rabid opponent of Catholic relief, but in line with his previously rumoured alteration in his views, Perceval voted in favour of the measure, 12 May, when he explained that he had given a hostile vote in 1819 in spite of a growing conviction of its practical necessity, but nonetheless sought to rescue diehard anti-Catholics from the imputation of bigotry and denounced the Catholic faith as 'a foul pollution of the word of God'. For this 'peculiarly piquant and useful' speech, Lord Seaford reported that there was 'much praise'.[16] Perceval presented a constituency petition against restrictions on the circulation of £1 notes, 3 June, and voted against ordnance reductions, 4 July 1828. He had been listed by Lord Palmerston* among the Canningite liberal rump that June and his appointment as a clerk of ordnance in August raised eyebrows. Lord Ellenborough, the lord privy seal, considered it a 'doubtful' decision, and the duke of Rutland uncharitably speculated that as 'a Saint, and the worst species of Catholic supporter', Perceval had secured office only 'because he is a rat from the other side'.[17] The duke of Wellington, however, commended Perceval to the king as 'likely to distinguish himself in the House'.[18] Defending the ordnance estimates for the first time, 2 Mar. 1829, he referred all detailed enquiries to Sir Henry Hardinge, the war secretary, and dismissed Hume's suggestions for economies out of hand. Presumably from the resonance of his name, he was chosen by the ministry to act as a teller for resuming the debate on Catholic claims, which passed by 206-73, 6 Mar., and he voted for the third reading of their emancipation bill, 30 Mar. Yet he swallowed the grant to the Catholic seminary at Maynooth only 'on the understanding that we are never again to be called upon to grant money for this purpose', 22 May. He sponsored the Hampstead Heath enclosure bill on behalf of his cousin Sir Thomas Maryon Wilson and answered objections, 3, 12 June, but eventually bowed to pressure to withdraw it, 19 June. He defended the introduction of admission charges to the Tower of London armoury, 22 June 1829.

Perceval voted against the transfer of East Retford's seats to Birmingham, 11 Feb., parliamentary reform, 18 Feb., and the enfranchisement of Birmingham, Leeds, and Manchester, 23 Feb. 1830. He defended government expenditure on arms manufacture, 25 Mar, and, with reference to the financial committee audit, the ordnance estimates as a whole, 29 Mar. Sir James Graham, who moved for a reduction, nevertheless congratulated him on his efforts to simplify the accounts. Perceval explained that the lack of significant economies in his departmental budget was due to a growth in its responsibilities, 2 Apr., when he again ridiculed Hume's proposed retrenchments, but acceded to his demand to discuss the salary grant under separate headings. That day he argued that the manufacture of musket barrels should remain in government hands for reasons of economy. He denied the existence of an overproduction of gunpowder, 5 Apr. On 30 Apr. he defended regimental grants and would have refused Hume's request to vote on the extraordinary estimates in sections, but for the intervention of Goulburn, the chancellor of the exchequer. He argued that the Commons should remain a Christian assembly and was a minority teller against the introduction of a bill for Jewish emancipation, 5 Apr., and voted against its second reading, 17 May, when his attempt to explain further was drowned out by an impatient House. He was in minorities against the Galway franchise bill, 24, 25 May. He voted for the grant for South American missions, 7 June, and was a government teller for an address to the king on arrangements for the dissolution, 30 June. In July 1830 he was offered a seat on the admiralty board, but opted to remain at the ordnance.[19]

At the 1830 general election Perceval was re-elected for Newport at the behest of ministers. He was, of course, listed among their 'friends' and he voted with them in the crucial division on the civil list, 15 Nov. The fall of the ministry deprived him of office and appears to have triggered his descent into political and moral panic. Ellenborough recorded how at a 'dinner at the duke's', 15 Dec. 1830, Perceval had given 'a frightful account of the atheism he had heard applauded in the morning at the Rotunda, where [Robert] Owen ... spoke'.[20] On 4 Feb. 1831 Perceval reminded the House of the importance of the oath of abjuration to the preservation of the Protestant ascendancy. Three days later he clashed with Hunt over his own proposal for a general fast. Privately, he advised John Hobhouse* that he 'believed such a supplication might bring down a special interposition of Providence in our favour, just as Nineveh was saved of old'. Hobhouse, conscious of 'how much we English are indebted to fanaticism for our liberties ... did not smile at this', but came to the conclusion that on such matters, Perceval was 'not of sound mind, although on all others perfectly rational'.[21] He presented petitions for 'a day of fasting, public humiliation and prayer', 8, 10 Feb. Introducing his motion for an address to the crown on the subject, 14 Feb., he warned that

> the whole country is in a complete state of disorganisation; all the elements of society appear to be loose and disjointed; there is no attachment on the part of the people to their rulers ... The ancient and venerable institutions of the country ... which were once the proud boast of every Englishman, are now viewed with disregard ... My conviction is ... that a scourge is going forth over all lands ... that great troubles, tumults, convulsions and struggles are about to take place all over the world, and that they are inevitable.

The culprit, he concluded, was 'the very essence of liberalism which walks abroad', and which 'has shown itself in the late French revolution most distinctly'. Lord Althorp believed that further discussion of the motion in the Commons would be constitutionally inappropriate, and Perceval, nonplussed, withdrew it. Some marks of impatience were exhibited during the speech, though Thomas Gladstone* informed his father that 'Perceval gained great credit for the manly manner in which he brought forward his *misplaced* and I think *foolish* motion'.[22] He was an implacable opponent of the Grey ministry's reform bill, but refuted claims that he belonged to 'a party opposing ourselves to light, intelligence and information', 3 Mar. On 9 Mar. he condemned the measure as 'the greatest act of folly ever committed by any minister' and 'a death blow to the monarchy', and in defence of his argument that it was 'revolutionary', insisted that 'the very foundation of all society rests upon the surrender, by men, of all their natural rights to the appointed leaders of the state'. Accordingly, he regarded the abolition of close boroughs as a misbegotten product of empirical reasoning, though he was prepared to concede that representation should be granted to large industrial towns. His concluding diatribe against the 'corrupt and unprincipled' daily press was answered the following day by the *Morning Chronicle*'s ironic report of his closing words of thanks to God, who had 'permitted him to defend the commission of bribery and corruption'. Stung by a charge that he had insulted his constituents, he later published the speech with an address to them.[23] He supported Inglis's complaint of a breach of privilege against *The Times*, 21 Mar. He voted against the second reading of the reform bill, 22 Mar., and for Gascoyne's wrecking amendment, 19 Apr. A contemporary caricature depicted him as a rat seated on a sack bulging with money, labelled with the name of his sinecure office.[24]

At the 1831 general election Perceval was returned for Tiverton by Lord Harrowby in place of his son Lord Sandon, who had supported the reform bill.[25] On discovering that his speech on the general fast had been 'made a matter of reproach against me', he arranged for it to be published for the edification of his new constituents.[26] He voted against the second reading of the reintroduced reform bill, 6 July, and, though happy with government assurances that the 'principle of fair discussion' would be maintained in committee, urged them to accede to demands for an adjournment and voted accordingly, 12 July. He divided for the use of the 1831 census to determine the disfranchisement schedules, 19 July, and to postpone consideration of the inclusion of Chippenham in B, 27 July. Two days later he used the speech of Gisborne, Member for Stafford, to prove that 'the House is not led by ministers in this wild and mischievous measure of reform, but is blindly following a popular cry'. He warned against using population as the determinant of representation, 'rather than ... those most important interests into which a great country like this is divided', 4 Aug., and voted against the passage of the bill, 21 Sept. He spoke and was a minority teller against the Maynooth grant, 26 Sept., when he described the amused reaction to his violent denunciation of Catholicism as 'proof of the degeneracy of the present Protestant race'. He criticized Lord John Russell for addressing Thomas Attwood's meeting in Birmingham following the Lords' rejection of the reform bill, but distanced himself from the intemperate attack on ministers made by Sir Charles Wetherell, 12 Oct. He voted against the second reading of the revised reform bill, 17 Dec. 1831, and going into committee on it, 20 Jan. 1832. He suggested that body snatching might best be prevented by a two-year suspension of all dissections, 17 Jan. 1832.

As promised, 6 Dec. 1831, Perceval revived his motion for a general fast, 26 Jan. 1832, in what Edward Littleton* described as a 'conscientious but crazy speech' lasting almost two hours. The public gallery was cleared for the first time in some 18 years at his behest, and with Bible in hand, he warned the Members present (who were few in number on his own side of the House) that the cholera epidemic was a 'pestilence' and that the day of judgement was at hand.[27] His performance was a gift to cartoonists, and despite the absence of reporters was widely published in newspapers, 'with the object of throwing ridicule', as he protested, 31 Jan. (After Hume and Warburton had admitted to providing transcriptions, he took the matter no further.)[28] A fast day was duly appointed by the government for 21 Mar., though Perceval called in vain for it to be brought forward 'now that the pestilential disease has reached London', 16 Feb. He was listed as a founder member of the Carlton Club in early March, but he had clearly lost faith in political opposition to the march of liberalism, and with the reform bill poised to obtain its third reading, unleashed his most alarming performance yet on a bemused Commons, 20 Mar. Ignoring Althorp's invitation to move an adjournment, he raged against the godlessness of the House and the 'mockery' made of the approaching fast day:

> Will ye not listen for a few moments to one who speaketh in the name of the Lord? I stand here to warn you of the righteous judgement of God which is coming on you, and which is now near at hand ... Twice have ye, the Commoners of England, refused to humble yourselves before your God. Mark! mark! how your God hath caused ye to show your contempt of him! Ye have in the midst of you a scourge of pestilence, which hath crossed the world to reach ye. Ye brought a bill into the House to retard its approaches, and ye refused in that bill to insert a recognition of your God. Ye would not make an acknowledgement of His providence, and yet ye cast His name out of your book. I told ministers it was not God they worshipped. The people is the God before whom they bow down in absurd and degraded worship.

At this juncture several colleagues urged Perceval to desist, and government and opposition managers conspired to arrange a mass exodus. After he had descanted on the imminence of the apocalypse and condemned the established church as corrupt ('She hath played the harlot with the stranger; and she has leant on the arm of flesh for her support'), he finally ran out of steam, and an adjournment was secured after the gallery was cleared. Not surprisingly, the speech drew much comment. Littleton described it as 'a dreadful exhibition of fanaticism', adding that Perceval was 'clearly labouring under temporary derangement', which he blamed squarely on the malign influence of Irving.[29] Robert Throckmorton* reported similar views and noted that 'he is looking quite thin and worn like a madman'.[30] A different view was taken by John Heywood Hawkins*, who had conjectured that Perceval was 'rapidly progressing towards the occupation of a straight waistcoat' after his performance in January, but now conceded that there was '*method* in his madness – he took good care to make just so frequent allusions to the reform bill as were sufficient to prevent the Speaker from calling him to order for deviating from the subject'.[31] At all events, he succeeded in delaying its third reading, against which he voted, 22 Mar. It was with a prescience not suggestive of mental illness that he identified the rock on which the ministry would eventually split on 30 Apr., when in response to his probing, Smith Stanley, the Irish secretary, expressed his personal opposition to the appropriation of Irish church revenues for lay purposes, but declined to speak for the government when pressed. He was in minorities against the second reading of the Irish reform bill, 25 May, the Russian-Dutch loan, 12 July, and the Irish education grant, 23 July. In his last known speech he branded Hume's petitioning efforts on behalf of convicted blasphemers as 'disgraceful' and emptied the House in the process, 15 Aug. 1832.

Perceval evidently made no attempt to re-enter the Commons after 1832. On 14 Dec. 1833 he was called as an 'apostle' of the nascent Catholic Apostolic Church, which adopted the primitive Christian model in both its hierarchy and its charismatic forms of worship.[32] Greville, who heard Perceval preach at Irving's church in Regent's Square around this time, was impressed with his delivery, but disappointed that at the point when 'he appeared about to touch on politics', he was interrupted by two women speaking in tongues and enjoined the congregation 'to hear the voice of the Lord'.[33] Miss Hall, the governess of his children, was another who 'sang in the spirit', but though she later admitted to faking her utterances, her master's ardour was undimmed. In August 1834 he offered Greville a homily on the ills of the 'backsliding' established church and subsequently risked arrest by sermonizing in the street.[34] Following the formal secession of the Church in 1836, Perceval presented to the king and various privy councillors its 'lesser testimony', which was essentially a litany of abuse against almost every piece of progressive legislation passed or considered in the previous decade. The Reform Act, it asserted, had 'laid the foundations of the present order of things in wrong and robbery' and in conjunction with repeal of the Test Acts and Catholic emancipation (both of which Perceval had supported), had 'revealed and consummated the sin of departing from God'. The French Revolution was the first act of Armageddon: 'Oh! England, thy judgement cometh upon thee like a whirlwind, and there is no escape'.[35] All this bore the unmistakable marks of Perceval's authorship, though as he told Lord Lansdowne, he was merely the instrument of Providence: 'I am aware that it is not well written; the composition is not perfect, but I was not permitted to alter it; I was obliged to write it as I received it'. The response of the privy councillors ranged from the polite interest of Lord Howick*, and the combative arguments of Lord Melbourne, to the more basic reaction of Smith Stanley, who simply 'turned him out at once'. Lady Holland was sufficiently concerned to station two servants at the door during the interview with her husband, with instructions to rush in if he was heard to scream.[36] In July 1838 Perceval and Drummond delivered the Apostolics' 'greater testimony' to the Pope, via Cardinal Acton.[37] In the division of Christendom among the 'restored apostolate', Perceval was allotted the tribe of Manasseh, and given the thankless task, in which he failed by some distance, of recruiting 12,000 to the flock in the unpromising territory of Italy.[38] Little else is known of his contribution to the shrouded proceedings of the sect and one of its historians notes that he 'does not appear to have been a man of outstanding personality, but was sincere and earnest, and no doubt played his part adequately in the apostolic counsels'.[39]

In October 1834 Perceval complained that the compensation for his abolished exchequer tellership, which amounted to the full annual salary for life, took no account of the loss of patronage, which had enabled him to provide for his brother Dudley, among others.[40] Evidently he had fully regained his outward composure by October 1839, when Eleanor Fazakerley incorrectly reported that he had 'quite recovered from his Irvingite delusions' and assumed, equally wrongly, that his plan to reside in Italy was for 'economy and education'.[41] More perceptive was the observation of Lady Granville, who encountered him in Rome in December 1842 and found him 'very agreeable and gay, but ... still as odd as ever in opinion'. She noted that in addition to his Italian mission, he was the 'angel' (pastor in charge) of a church in Southampton 'and goes over whenever Henry Drummond says he is wanted there'.[42] Perceval died at Melcombe Regis, Dorset in September 1859 'after a few hours illness, having joined his family on the previous day apparently in good health'.[43] Letters of administration were granted on 11 Oct. 1859 to his wife, the universal legatee under the terms of his will, dated 16 Oct. 1844, after Spencer Horatio Walpole, his brother-in-law and sole executor, had renounced probate. Denis Le Marchant† remembered him as 'a gentleman highly esteemed in private life, and of abilities that might have raised him to distinction, but for his religious fanaticism'.[44]

[1] Add. 49191, ff. 92-97. [2] Ibid. ff. 7-8, 37; 52 Geo. III, c. 67; D. Gray, *Spencer Perceval. The Evangelical Prime Minister*, 12, 45, 429-31, 456, 461, 463. [3] Add. 49191, ff. 101-9; R. A. Davenport, *Albury Apostles*, 21, 25, 32, 36; A.L. Drummond, *Edward Irving and his Circle*, 126, 133-5. [4] Add. 49191, f. 122; B. Hilton, *Age of Atonement*, 189-202. [5] *Croker Pprs.* i. 425. [6] Ibid. i. 187; *Greville Mems.* i. 133. [7] Add. 49191, f. 1. [8] *Cambridge Chron.* 1 Nov. 1822; Suff. RO (Bury St. Edmunds) 1641/13; Hervey mss 941/11a, Ryder to Bristol, 25 Oct. 1822. [9] Harewood mss, C. Williams Wynn to Canning, 2 Nov.; Add. 49191, f. 118; 51567, Bedford to Lady Holland [1 Nov. 1822]. [10] Macleod of Macleod mss 1061/5. [11] Add. 49191, f. 125. [12] *Canning's Ministry*, 336. [13] *The Times*, 19 June 1827. [14] Add. 40191, f. 124. [15] Macleod of Macleod mss 1062/13. [16] TNA 30/29/9/5/65. [17] Bulwer, *Palmerston*, i. 278-9; *Ellenborough Diary*, i. 204; Aberdeen Univ. Lib. Arbuthnot mss, Rutland to Mrs. Arbuthnot, 21 Sept. 1828. [18] Wellington mss WP1/945/19. [19] Ibid. WP1/1125/37; 1130/53. [20] *Three Diaries*, 35. [21] Broughton, *Recollections*, iv. 79. [22] St. Deiniol's Lib. Glynne-Gladstone mss 197, T. to J. Gladstone, 15 Feb. 1831. [23] *Speech of Spencer Perceval ... on the reform bill* (1831). [24] M.D. George, *Cat. of Pol. and Personal Satires*, xi. 16612. [25] *The Times*, 11 Aug. 1831. [26] *Speech delivered in the House of Commons ... by Spencer Perceval ... on moving an Address to the Crown for the appointment of a General Fast* (1831). [27] Hatherton diary, 26 Jan. 1832; Le Marchant, *Althorp*, 388-9. [28] George, xi. 16943, 17021, 17155, 17197. [29] Hatherton diary, 21 Mar. 1832. [30] Warws. RO, Throckmorton mss CR 1998/Tribune/folder 16/51 [22 Mar. 1832]. [31] Cornw. RO, Hawkins mss 10/2179, 2189. [32] G.C. Standring, *Albury and the Catholic Apostolic Church*, 11; Drummond, 134-5. [33] *Greville Mems.* ii. 425. [34] Ibid. iii. 73, 79; P.E. Shaw, *Catholic Apostolic Church*, 80; Drummond, 215. [35] H. Miller, *Hist. and Doctrines of Irvingism*, ii. 361-71. [36] *Greville Mems.* iii. 273-4, 276-7. [37] Davenport, 135-6. [38] Miller, i. 285-6. [39] Davenport, 111. [40] Add. 40409, f. 130. [41] Add. 52011, Eleanor Fazakerley to H. E. Fox, 23 Oct. 1839. [42] *Countess Granville Letters*, ii. 343. [43] *Gent. Mag.* (1859), ii. 653-4. [44] Le Marchant, 388.

H.J.S./P.J.S.

PERCY, Algernon George, Lord Lovaine (1810–1899), of 8 Portman Square, Mdx.

BERE ALSTON	1831–1832
NORTHUMBERLAND NORTH	1852–1865

b. 2 May 1810, 1st s. of George Percy, Lord Lovaine*, and Louisa Harcourt, da. of Hon. James Archibald Stuart Wortley Mackenzie† of Admaleish, Bute. *educ.* Eton 1826. *m.* 26 May 1845, Louisa, da. and coh. of Henry Drummond† of Albury Park, nr. Guildford, Surr., 2s. *styled* Lord Lovaine 1830-65, Earl Percy 1865-67; *suc.* fa. as 6th duke of Northumberland 21 Aug. 1867; KG 22 Feb. 1886. *d.* 2 Jan. 1899.

Ensign 76 Ft. 1829; lt. 1 Ft. Gds. 1831, capt. 1835, ret. 1837.

Comptroller, household of ld. lt. [I] 1834; ld. of admiralty Mar. 1858-Mar. 1859; PC 3 Mar. 1859; vice-pres. bd. of trade Mar.-June 1859; ld. privy seal Feb. 1878-Apr. 1880.

Capt. Northumb. militia 1842, maj. 1852, col. 1862, hon. col. 1874; ld. lt. Northumb. 1877-*d.*

Lovaine, an officer in the Guards, was returned for Bere Alston on his father's interest at the general election of 1831, despite a local attempt to raise an opposition to him. He 'avowed himself a moderate reformer, but declined answering any questions as to the extent to which he was disposed to reform'. It was subsequently alleged in a petition that he was still a minor on the day of the election and that his real birthday was about 29 May, but the petition was withdrawn.[1] He is not known to have spoken in debate in this period. He divided against the second reading of the Grey ministry's reintroduced reform bill, which proposed to disfranchise Bere Alston, 6 July 1831. He voted to use the 1831 census for the purpose of determining the disfranchisement schedules, 19 July, postpone consideration of Chippenham's inclusion in schedule B, 27 July, and preserve the voting rights of non-resident freemen, 30 Aug., and against the bill's passage, 21 Sept. He voted for the motion censuring the conduct of the Irish administration during the Dublin election, 23 Aug. He divided against the second reading of the revised reform bill, 17 Dec. 1831, the enfranchisement of Tower Hamlets, 28 Feb., and the third reading, 22 Mar. 1832. He voted against ministers on the Russian-Dutch loan, 26 Jan. 1832.

He unsuccessfully contested Exeter in 1841 and North Northumberland in 1847, but was returned for the latter in 1852 as a Protectionist and upholder of the 'essentially Protestant character of our constitution'.[2] He held junior office in Lord Derby's second ministry and, having succeeded as duke of Northumberland in 1867, was surprisingly appointed to the cabinet in 1878, a beneficiary of Disraeli's penchant for aristocratic administrators; one of his colleagues found him 'rather deaf and slow'.[3] He became a member of the Catholic Apostolic or Irvingite sect, which his father-in-law had co-founded.[4] It was said of him that 'nature had chosen perversely to mask his real qualities under a somewhat grim countenance and chilling manner'.[5] He died in January 1899 and was succeeded by his elder son Henry George Percy (1846-1918), Conservative Member for North Northumberland, 1868-85.

[1] *Plymouth Herald*, 7 May 1831; *CJ*, lxxxvi. 603-5, 663. [2] *Dod's Parl. Companion* (1852), 219. [3] *Cranbrook Diary* ed. N.E. Johnson, 353-4. [4] *Ann. Reg.* (1899), Chron. p. 127. [5] Maxwell, *Clarendon*, ii. 347-8.

T.A.J.

PERCY (afterwards GREATHEED BERTIE PERCY), Hon. Charles (1794–1870), of Guys Cliffe, nr. Warwick.[1]

NEWPORT 8 Feb. 1826–Mar. 1829

b. 4 Mar. 1794, 8th but 6th surv. s. of Algernon Percy†, 1st earl of Beverley (*d.* 1830), and Isabella Susanna, da. of Peter Burrell† of Langley Park, Beckenham, Kent; bro. of George Percy, Lord Lovaine*, Hon. Henry Percy*, Hon. Josceline Percy† and Hon. William Henry Percy*. *educ.* Eton 1805; Christ Church, Oxf. 1812. *m.* 20 Mar. 1822, Ann Caroline, illegit. da. of Bertie Greatheed (*d.* 1804), grandda. and h. of Bertie Bertie Greatheed of Guys Cliffe, 1da. Took names of Greatheed Bertie before Percy by royal lic. 10 Apr. 1826. *d.* 11 Oct. 1870.

Treas. Ionian Islands 1818-21; priv. sec. to sec. of state for war and colonies June 1821-Jan. 1826; comptroller of household to ld. lt. [I] Mar. 1829-Dec. 1830.

Sheriff, Warws. 1835-6.

Percy, the youngest son of the Pittite 1st earl of Beverley (the second son of the 1st duke of Northumberland), spent his childhood at Orwell Park, near Ipswich. Of his elder brothers, one entered the diplomatic service, one the church, two the navy and one the army. After his conventional education, during which he became a close friend of Ralph Sneyd, George Agar Ellis* and the 2nd earl of Clare, he evidently held a place in Princess Charlotte's household. In 1815 he visited the battlefield of Waterloo and spent some time in Paris. He led a largely aimless life, joining White's and indulging his literary and aesthetic tastes, until 1818, when, after making an unsuccessful application for the vacant secretaryship of the Cape, he secured the post of treasurer of the Ionian Islands, or, as he facetiously termed it, 'the Vansittartship of Corfu'; it was worth £800 a year.

For Percy, who felt that his cousin, the 3rd duke of Northumberland, might have exerted himself to 'obtain for me any reasonable thing, such as a commissionership of stamps, which would be a life provision', it was a question of *faute de mieux*. He sailed early in March 1819 and, after a brief stay at Gibraltar, which he liked, he arrived in Corfu on 25 Apr., dreading 'the prospect of my life there, beyond belief, and far beyond what common sense will justify'. His initial off-hand reception by the autocratic lord high commissioner Sir Thomas Maitland,† who set him to work to learn accounting, filled him with despair. Yet he was captivated by the beauty and tranquillity of Corfu. Preferring the company of such 'sensible reading men' as he could find to that of the 'drinking, smoking, whoring garrison *sparks*', he was horrified by the contempt shown by the British for the natives; he made an attempt to master modern Greek. He soon realized that his office, which afforded him no scope for initiative, 'cannot *possibly* give me an honour or reputation, nor indeed even habits of business', as Maitland interfered in everything. Although he was not particularly disappointed when the commissioner reduced his salary by £100, having budgeted before setting out for its not exceeding £700, he was at a low ebb by July:

> The pleasantest moments I have passed since I left England were on board ship ... but here, fixed, without occupation to employ, much less interest me, without a friend or even acquaintance for whom I feel other than perfect indifference, feeling the total neglect I experience, yet not wishing it otherwise, and added to all a trying, debilitating, unpleasant and unhealthy climate, certainly does not mark out Corfu as a chosen residence. The beauties of the country are cut off from me also, by the malaria reigning there. Add to all these, that the necessaries of life are all dear, and that the same manoeuvring and reckoning and economy is necessary, which has always hitherto annoyed me. Could I come as lord high commissioner at some future time I should like it, from the conviction I feel that in that situation so much good might be done that is now neglected; but with my situation, I have no power, however limited, neither have I means had I the power, and my *example* here is nothing.

Maitland's temporary absence and a three-week tour of the other islands in the company of Sir Frederick Adam, the military commander at Malta, who befriended him, not only removed Percy from the worst of the summer heat, but raised his spirits and 'entirely reconciled' him to residence at Corfu: 'under the influence of climate, blue devils, outraged self-sufficiency and neglected vanity, I have abused this place ... far beyond its deserts'. He tried to learn Turkish as well as Greek, and began to get on better with Maitland, who had 'spoken kindly of me in England', though he was for a while tormented by fear that his earlier disparaging remarks in letters home might come to the attention of the authorities. On British domestic politics, he feared that the 'hurry and precipitation' of the Liverpool ministry's handling of the aftermath of the Peterloo massacre had 'produced a feeling hostile to them and their cause amongst a considerable portion of otherwise well disposed persons', and he had little confidence that 'the powers that be were strong enough to support our constitution as it is'. At the same time, he could not 'bear those who truckle to the mob' and deemed himself 'a poor *creature* in politics, as I find myself always on the neutral ground, and unwilling to go heartily the length of either party'. He professed to favour a purge of the patronage system and the adoption by government of the 'new and more enlightened system' of 'commerce and political economy'. He anticipated nothing but trouble and embarrassment from the prosecution of Queen Caroline, which he considered an act of 'insanity': 'the cause of public morality will not gain, even state convenience is not consulted by it, but the bad effects are clear and palpable', he wrote on 18 Oct. 1820. He did not think that ministers could creditably remain in office, wondered whether a conservative Whig administration headed by Lord Lansdowne might be formed and told Sneyd:

> It is only to your private ear that I twaddle in this way in politics, and I am glad I am not in Parliament, for I fear I should give mortal offence if I were to the high Tories of my own family, for I find the blue part wearing away. I believe it may be attributed (if not to right reason) a little to the inherent contradictiousness of man, for I am sickened by the *super ultra* Toryism of the court here.

In June 1820 Percy had confided to Sneyd his matrimonial interest in Ann Caroline Greatheed, a 'little, fat, good humoured' young woman, whom he had first met at Grimsthorpe, Lincolnshire, the home of his uncle, the 1st Lord Gwydir and his wife Baroness Willoughby d'Eresby. Miss Greatheed was a connection of the latter, whose aunt Lady Mary Bertie, sister of her father, the 3rd duke of Ancaster, had married in 1747 Samuel Greatheed (*d.* 1765), the owner of a plantation in St. Kitts and of a house and estate at Guys Cliffe, near Warwick, which borough he had represented, 1747-61. Samuel Greatheed's only surviving son and heir Bertie Greatheed, born in 1759, was a member of the British literary coterie which was active at Florence in the mid-1780s. His blank verse tragedy, *The Regent*, was supported by his friends John Kemble and Sarah Siddons, but it flopped when put on at Drury Lane in 1788. In an interlude from his foreign travels, he unsuccessfully contested Leicester as 'Citizen' Greatheed in 1796. His only son and namesake, born in 1781, was a talented artist, who exhibited at the Royal Academy in 1802. In December that year his eccentric parents, who had withdrawn him from Eton after two years to educate him themselves, took him to Paris, so that he might study the masterpieces in the Louvre. They were detained on the resumption of hostilities in 1803, but allowed to go on parole to Germany, whence they moved to Italy. Bertie Greatheed junior died at Vicenza, 8 Oct. 1804, leaving an illegitimate daughter, Ann Caroline. She was brought up by her grandparents, who made her their sole heir.[2]

Therein lay not the least of her attractions for Percy, whose suit had been encouraged by the old Greatheeds.

He renewed it, propitiously, by letter from Corfu in 1820, though he typically fell prey to guilt over the 'tone of mercenary levity' in which he had introduced the subject to Sneyd. He became increasingly anxious to return to England to bring matters to a conclusion, but was initially frustrated when Lord Bathurst, the colonial secretary, to whom he owed his job, got wind of his wishes and intervened to forbid Maitland to give him leave of absence. Towards the end of 1820 Percy appealed directly to Bathurst, citing 'particular private reasons' for wanting to go home. The intercession of his eldest brother Lord Lovaine, a lord of the bedchamber (like Northumberland), emboldened him to persuade Maitland to write to Bathurst in his favour. He was optimistic at the close of the year, though reconciled to a delay while he acted as one of the commissioners appointed to try some state prisoners. Bathurst agreed to his leaving Corfu and offered him the position of his private secretary. Percy stalled, asking for the interval of his journey home to consider the offer; but he was inwardly resigned to accepting it, even though the salary was only £300 and Bathurst had ruled out any prospect of future permanent employment. As he told Sneyd, 'it would be folly to throw away a trump, which appears to offer itself'; and it was 'showing some decision of character to give up £500 at least, in the hand, for a hen in the bush'. Percy arrived in England at the end of May 1821 and a fortnight later began his work in Downing Street.[3] He was immediately 'bored and uncomfortable', perceiving that 'it is not to be in the slightest degree a situation of confidence, or that if it was, I have not the power of availing myself of it'. He rapidly became nostalgic for the 'peace and tranquillity' of Corfu, 'which I rashly left for smoke and gloom, cool acquaintances, and friends on the point of departure': 'I have been a prey to blue devils. I want the peace within, without [*sic*] which external accidents cannot have any permanent effects'. However, he needed the money, and he stayed in the job, nominally at least, for almost five years.

Shortly before Percy married Miss Greatheed in March 1822 Maria Edgeworth, who described her as 'a great and fat heiress' with an appropriately 'very large' head, reported that as 'the substance is all on her side, the family on his', they 'have been called *Quantity* and *Quality*, or better still, *Flesh and Blood*'. Sir James Mackintosh* described her as 'the giantess of seventeen' and Percy as 'a puny insect shivering in the breeze'.[4] Bertie Greatheed settled on the bride, subject to his wife's life interest, Guys Cliffe, property in Leamington, some Ancaster estates in Lincolnshire and the St. Kitts plantation.[5] Yet Percy remained short of ready cash and was alarmed at the old Greatheeds' extravagance, which seemed to threaten to impair the inheritance. In January 1823 he whined to Sneyd, who was in Rome, from Guys Cliffe:

> I foresee ruin, without comfort. Oh! that I could have retained for a couple of years my situation at Corfu ... My longing to get abroad is greater from the numerous obstacles, and from the pressure of such slight vexations, which like the ropes of the Lilliputians are scarce perceptible, and yet bind me hand and foot.

He and his pregnant wife (they had one child, Ann Barbara Isabella) were at Keele and Teddesley in November 1823. Observing that Mrs. Percy 'sings like a nightingale', Lady Granville reflected on 'how blessings are thrown away in this odd world'.[6] In August 1824 Bathurst gave Percy permission to make a foreign tour, provided he did not stay away too long and so invite censure. The following month he and his wife set off for Italy, hoping to rendezvous with Sneyd in Rome. In this Percy was frustrated, and he briefly considered returning home in October, especially as the prospect of a change at the colonial office suggested that it might be in his best interests to be on the spot. Caroline persuaded him to stay on and they reached Rome in November 1824, when Percy sent Sneyd a letter for Bathurst, which evidently staked his claim to the under-secretaryship currently held by Robert Wilmot*: if he got it, he surmized, 'I might hereafter really arrive at the great object of my ambition, the commissionership of the Ionian Islands'. As he anticipated, nothing came of it. At the turn of the year he wrote to Sneyd, who had advised him to go home without much further delay:

> Since I quitted Corfu I have not passed two months so happily, but my unfortunate disposition to brood over the discomforts of my situation, the dread of returning to England and the weekly accounts of great folly and extravagance in Warwickshire have conspired occasionally to poison my enjoyment ... I do not see the necessity of my punctual return ... My situation is too private, and much too insignificant, to be alluded to in Parliament; and it has been one of little pleasure, or respectability, and it is one of so little promise, that I am ready to retire from it at any moment. Indeed, with my present income, and my future prospects (owing to the selfish silliness of those who have the power and inclination to sport with our happiness) I cannot see any other prudent step, as I am convinced entire retirement is the only possible chance, I will not say of happiness, but of ease and economy. Even in my child I do not anticipate any happiness! If I insist, as in duty I ought to do, on my right as a parent, mine and all its future prospects must be the sacrifice.

Henry Fox*, one of the British residents with whom the Percys mixed, took a jaundiced view of him:

> Percy is a coxcomb, made more so by frequenting, admiring and imitating Agar Ellis and Sneyd and the set of pedantic fribbles. Whenever anything really his own does break out, it is more sensible and agreeable and even sometimes clever than one could at all attend from his finicky, affected manner and laboured, far-fetched language, which fatigues me horribly.

When he caught up with Percy in Naples in January 1825 Fox decided that he was 'devoid of any real character', beyond 'a little narrow-minded selfishness'. His wife's flirtatiousness evidently aroused jealousy in Percy, and Fox delighted in 'making him suspicious and on the watch', hoping thereby to help realize his prediction that 'that menage will some of these days go wrong'. Yet when reproved by Eleanor Fazakerley for his mischief-making, Fox disclaimed any intention of

> throwing a touch of discord between the *happy* couple ... I only regret and lament for her sake, poor little woman. Of him I have not half such a good opinion as I once had and he therefore bores me with his refined, exquisite aristocracy, which is in fact nothing but low, parvenu Smithson vulgarity that apes gentility.[7]

The Percys made their way to Paris (it was reported that he 'did not admire *anything*' on the Riviera), with the intention of proceeding immediately to London so that he could resume his official duties. Informed, however, by Wilmot that he had 'survived the estimates' and was not urgently required, he stayed in Paris to act as personal secretary to Northumberland during his lavish special mission to attend the coronation of Charles X. He was grateful to be housed and fed at the duke's expense, especially as he had recently 'lost £300 by my banker's neglect'. His wife, who became 'the duchess's woman', was said to be 'in great force, with all these lordships to flirt with'.[8] Shortly before Northumberland's arrival Percy learned of the death of his brother Henry, one of the Members for their father's pocket borough of Bere Alston. Reflecting that there was now a vacancy for himself or his brother Algernon, he told Sneyd that the previous year Beverley had offered to bring him in 'on condition that I supported ministers, voted against Catholics, and against reform, and in all doubtful questions referred myself to Lovaine'. He had pleaded the excuse that Bathurst did not then wish him to retire from the secretaryship and asked for the offer to be repeated on the dissolution. If it was made now, he thought

> on the above conditions I could not accept it. But I am ready *not* to vote on the Catholic question. On doubtful questions of course I must reserve myself to use my own discretion instead of Lovaine's, holding myself ready to lay down my seat whenever, or if ever, I felt obliged to dissent from his views, except in insulated questions of no moment ... You know my present poverty, the uncertainty of my prospects, the unbounded extravagance and the caprice of those on whom I depend. You also know the little prospect there is of my connection with Lord Bathurst ever being of the slightest advantage ... I am not insanely vain enough to have any ambitious views. I know my incapacity sufficiently. Indeed, if ever I had any energy, I have lost it. I am fretted into being a disappointed, unhappy man, bankrupt in my spirits, as well as a pauper in means.

Whatever advice Sneyd gave was academic, for, as Percy told him in July 1825, he received not a word about the vacancy, and it was through a stranger that he discovered that it had been filled by his cousin Percy Ashburnham: 'I wrote to Lovaine in consequence, but without any anger, and he has not been graciously pleased to answer my letter'. Eleanor Fazakerley heard that on his reappearance in London Percy was

> amazingly out of humour with England and everything English ... and that with the help of his Parisian tailor, he looked *so* French in Kensington Gardens, that it was quite ridiculous. His little *pinchy* figure would easily look like a Frenchman's.

He and his wife spent a peaceful late summer at Guys Cliffe (the old Greatheeds were in Scotland), their relationship now 'become quite smooth' after the strains evident earlier in the year.[9] On 22 Sept. 1825, when a dissolution was expected, Percy told Sneyd that he meant to decline his father's intended offer of a seat 'as there is not time for explanations which would be unavoidably necessary, and if I am to be brought in by favour, I had rather take the chance of the duke, than my father's borough, with its probably rapid reversion to Lovaine'. He had also, he said, 'very *reluctantly*' declined an invitation to stand for Warwick, where he was encouraged to expect success 'without opposition or any considerable expense', giving him 'a seat for life and *entirely independent*'. He did so partly because '*any* expense to me is *considerable*', partly because he did not know whether the absent Greatheed would approve. Percy formally resigned his secretaryship on 5 Jan. 1826. Ten days later Greatheed died, but Percy was 'not richer', in terms of access to ready money, as a result. Greatheed's personalty was sworn under £80,000, 1 Mar., but Percy calculated that the likely annual income from the inheritance after the death of Mrs. Greatheed, who immediately made a will leaving everything to Caroline Percy, would be the 'much reduced sum' of £5,000. On 10 Apr. 1826 Percy obtained royal licence to take the names of Greatheed Bertie before Percy, supposedly in accordance with a stipulation of Bertie Greatheed's will, though in fact this had directed that he should adopt only the additional name of Bertie: in practice, Percy styled himself Charles Bertie Percy.[10]

He was by then a Member of Parliament, having been returned in February by Northumberland on a vacancy for Newport. He observed that 'I come into Parliament at a strange moment, when all the cheers that animate Robinson and Canning are from the opposition benches, and those behind the treasury silent as the grave'; but he showed no initial disposition to make anything of his membership, as he told Sneyd, 2 Mar. 1826:

> When it was more inconvenient than I can possibly say, I was obliged to hurry down into Cornwall to dine and be elected. Private business forced me up to town, so I took my seat; but this session I do not mean to attend, as my private business is far more pressing in importance than my public duties.

He was returned again at the general election, a fortnight after the death of old Mrs. Greatheed, which involved him in an unequal struggle with 'the harpies of the legacy office'. A deficit of £14,000 on the estate had to be paid by the legatees, of whom Percy and his wife were the principals: 'I have been worried into a bilious attack', he informed Sneyd, 5 Aug., 'and evacuate without intermission from all possible orifices'. Mrs. Fazakerley later found him 'very conversible and cheerful', though still complaining of 'poverty'; she supposed that 'if they are now poor it will only be for a time, as I believe the fortune is very good'.[11] At the close of 1826 Percy, still embroiled with the taxmen, ruled out of the question taking a London house next year, 'perhaps ever'; but he made an unconvincing attempt to stop grumbling and count his blessings:

> I own my fault (I ought to say my guilt) in letting the rubs and irksomenesses of the present moment so often plunge me into despondency and repining, when I have every reason to be grateful. When I reflect what I am, and what I deserve, how ought I to overflow with thankfulness.

Dividing his time between his father's house at 8 Portman Square and Roehampton, where he deposited his wife and child, Percy showed his face in the House at the start of the 1827 session. On 13 Feb. he was named to the Leominster election committee, which, to his delight, lasted only three days. He correctly predicted that the ministerial crisis precipitated by Lord Liverpool's stroke would end in a coalition between Canning, as premier, and the Lansdowne Whigs. He did not wish to believe the assertions of 'those who are *fatuous* for Canning' that Peel was under his thumb:

> I *shudder* at the notion of Canning uncontrolled, notwithstanding his ultra prudence and discretion so bevaunted by [Edward] Littleton* ... The fulsomeness of his supporters so outrages common sense and decency as to drive moderate people beside themselves, and I find myself rapidly assuming a *deeper blue*, which had faded to a very light cerulean a short time ago.

He said that Plunket's violent pro-Catholic speech of 2 Mar. 'almost converted me into a *Protestant*'; but he did not vote in the division on relief, 6 Mar. A week later his wife told Sneyd that Percy 'would take a great interest' in Parliament, 'had he not hitherto attended it so uncomfortably'.[12] Percy voted for the duke of Clarence's annuity bill, 16 Mar. He was given a month's leave to attend to 'urgent business', 3 May 1827. After Canning's death he hoped that 'all political bitterness is for the moment buried' with him and that the Goderich ministry

> will fulfil the hopes that seem generally to attend its infancy. Most heartily do I wish that the bugbear of [Catholic] emancipation, which cannot be obtained and had better not be agitated during the reign, was not to deprive us of Peel's practical ability. With that addition I should augur well for the country, as far as one can augur well of so worn out and crackledown a concern.

By now he appears to have sorted out his finances, in that he had £42,000 invested, with a further £5,000 lying idle; but he still saw 'no practicability of taking a house in London' in 1828.

He was 'charmed' with the return to power of Wellington and Peel in January 1828, and fully approved the 'general complexion of the government', with the exception of Lord Ellenborough. He trusted that Huskisson's participation would guarantee 'the most rigid scrutiny' of the national finances, believing that 'the philosophy of political economy must be applied to taxation'. He told Sneyd that he would 'as usual, pass an uncomfortable "before Easter"' at Roehampton and in an hotel, and return to Guys Cliffe 'just at the time that public business in the House would occupy and amuse me'. He was a spectator in the Lords for the 'grand field day' of ministerial statements and recrimination, 11 Feb. 1828. He thought that Huskisson had a good deal of awkward explaining to do about his recent conduct, but saw no reason why, once this difficulty and the embarrassment of Navarino had been got over, 'the ministry should not stand', though he did 'not feel quite comfortable' with Huskisson's attitude. The explanations of Huskisson and Herries in the Commons, 18 Feb., satisfied him that neither had been guilty of any 'unfair dealing' in the break-up of the Goderich administration. Percy, who is not known to have uttered a word in debate, voted against repeal of the Test Acts, 26 Feb., but was an absentee from the division on Catholic relief, 12 May 1828.

In September he went with his family to tour the Rhine, and by the turn of the year they were at Le Mans. They had intended to stay there until March, but Percy accepted Northumberland's offer of the place of comptroller of his viceregal household in Dublin. He did not, of course, do so without misgivings:

> I did not like to say nay ... and have been *perfectly miserable* ever since. All my independence at an end; hustled and bored to death; no saunterings in summer at Guys Cliffe, but instead, parading a sham gold stick at a Brummagem court ... I suppose secretary is the post I ought to have ambitioned, but it would be a certain confinement. I am glad it has not been offered ... A very vulgar Irishman, *like the rest of his nation*, tells me I have a four-windowed house in the Castle yard and £1,200 a year at least. I do not believe a word of it. Besides, if I have, the d—d journeys across the Channel will eat up my salary.

Planta, the patronage secretary, listed him as a possible but unlikely mover or seconder of the address,[13] and numbered him among those who would vote 'with government' for Catholic emancipation. He was in Dublin when named as a defaulter, 5 and 10 Mar. 1829. His necessary re-election for Newport did not take place, for at Wellington's request to Northumberland, he made way for the president of the board of trade, Vesey Fitzgerald, who was without a seat after his defeat in Clare.[14]

Knowing Percy's self-confessed ability to 'extract the poison of life from any position in which I am placed', it can have come as no surprise to Sneyd that within a month of his arrival in Dublin he was complaining that 'I never was so miserable in all my life'. His post was 'something between an aide-de-camp and a house steward, without the intimacy of the former, or the confidence reposed in the latter'; and he was 'entirely disgusted with the place, the court, and more especially with myself'. His attitude mellowed as he discovered the 'picturesque beauty' of Ireland beyond Dublin later in the year. There was talk in May of his resuming his seat as soon as Vesey Fitzgerald was accommodated elsewhere;[15] and in December 1829 he supposed that he was to be

> returned again for Newport soon after the meeting, but I would readily delay the event till Easter, indeed if I did not think it dangerous, I should not mind to be out of Parliament a little longer, and to go abroad comfortably ... next autumn, for a year and a half; but I am not sure it would be prudent under my present circumstances with respect to this seat in Parliament and its patron.

Nothing came of this, and Percy was never again in the House, where he had so signally failed to make any mark.

He left Dublin with Northumberland on the fall of the Wellington ministry. By his father's will, proved in February 1831, he received £5,000, having been advanced the same amount against his portion some years earlier.[16] He was appalled by the Grey ministry's reform bills and the unrest which accompanied their progress through Parliament. He and his wife were in Italy and Switzerland for two years from late 1832 and they spent much time abroad during the following 20 years. Mrs. Fazakerley encountered them and their 'remarkably pleasant and popular' daughter in Lucerne in September 1845, when they were 'very prosperous' but pining, as she thought, for Italy.[17] Percy, the last survivor of the eight brothers, died at Alnwick, the residence of his nephew, the 6th duke of Northumberland in October 1870. By his brief will, dated 25 June 1865 and proved under £160,000 at Birmingham, 7 Dec. 1870 (so much for poverty), he left all his property to his wife, who survived him by 12 years.

[1] Based, unless otherwise stated, on Percy's letters to Ralph Sneyd, 1809-70 (Keele Univ. Lib. Sneyd mss SC11/205-83; 12/1-213). [2] 2 *Oxford DNB* (Greatheed Bertie); *Caribbeana*, v. 49-50; *Englishman in Paris* ed. J.P.T. Bury and J.C. Barry; *Farington Diary*, vi. 2111; *Berry Jnls.* i. 245, 435; ii. 240, 431-2, 435; *Gent. Mag.* (1804), ii. 1073, 1236. [3] Northants. RO, Agar Ellis diary, 1 June, 6 July 1821. [4] *Edgeworth Letters*, 369; Add. 52445, f. 69. [5] PROB 11/1710/151. [6] *Dyott's Diary*, i. 352; *Countess Granville Letters*, i. 235. [7] *Fox Jnl.* 197-8, 202; Add. 61937, ff. 1, 3. [8] Add. 52017, Townshend to Fox, 25 Apr., 11, 18 May 1825. [9] Add. 52011, Mrs. Fazakerley to Fox, 29 Aug., 31 Oct. 1825, 14 Jan. 1826; 52017, Townshend to same, 30 Oct. 1825. [10] Add. 52012, H. Greville to Fox, 9 Feb. 1826; PROB 11/1710/151; 11/1713/326; IR26/1082/93. [11] Add. 52011, Mrs. Fazakerley to Fox, 24 Nov. 1826. [12] Sneyd mss SC12/80. [13] Add. 40398, f. 85. [14] Wellington mss WP1/1002/18, 20; 1007/11, 17. [15] Ibid. 1018/22; 1022/10. [16] PROB 11/1781/67. [17] Add. 52011, Mrs. Fazakerley to Fox, 11 Sept. 1845.

D.R.F.

PERCY, George, Lord Lovaine (1778–1867), of 8 Portman Square, Mdx.

BERE ALSTON 29 July 1799–21 Oct. 1830

b. 22 June 1778, 1st s. of Algernon Percy†, 1st earl of Beverley, and Isabella Susanna, da. of Peter Burrell† of Beckenham, Kent; bro. of Hon. Charles Percy*, Hon. Henry Percy*, Hon. Josceline Percy† and Hon. William Henry Percy*. *educ.* Eton 1789-95; St. John's, Camb. 1797. *m.* 22 June 1801, Louisa Harcourt, da. of

Hon. James Archibald Stuart Wortley Mackenzie† of Admaleish, Bute, 3s. 2da. *suc.* fa. as 2nd earl of Beverley 21 Oct. 1830; cos. Algernon Percy as 5th duke of Northumberland 12 Feb. 1865. *d.* 21 Aug. 1867.

Ld. of treasury May 1804-Feb. 1806; commr. bd. of control Apr. 1807-May 1812; ld. of bedchamber Mar. 1821-Dec. 1830; capt. yeomen of the guard Jan. 1842-July 1846; PC 15 Jan. 1842.

Col. Percy vols. 1798, col. en second 1803; lt.-col. Northumb. militia 1804, col. 1804.

Lovaine, who continued to be returned unopposed for Bere Alston on his father's interest, enjoyed a temporary revival of his political fortunes in the early 1820s. He voted in defence of the Liverpool ministry's conduct towards Queen Caroline, 6 Feb., and against Maberly's resolution on the state of the revenue, 6 Mar. 1821. Later that month he was appointed to the household and thereafter he voted silently with government. He cast no recorded votes on the Catholic question. In 1824 Charles Williams Wynn*, president of the India board, who had met him at Spa, suggested that he might make a suitable governor of Madras, observing that 'he is very poor, and has more information and sense than the world gives him credit for'.[1] He was granted three weeks' leave on account of ill health, 17 Feb. 1825. After 1826 he relapsed into inactivity and gave no more recorded votes; in February 1829 Planta, the Wellington ministry's patronage secretary, listed him as one who would be 'absent' from the divisions on Catholic emancipation. He was counted among the ministry's 'friends' in September 1830, but had royal permission to spend the winter in Italy. He wrote to Wellington from Florence, 8 Oct. 1830, explaining that as he was anxious to support the government he had obtained his father's permission to 'place my seat at your disposal', although he stipulated that he should 'have the power of resuming the seat' after two years.[2] His father's death a fortnight later resolved the matter by removing him to the Lords.[3] He was considered for reappointment to the household by Peel in 1834, and was given a post by him in 1842. Although he tendered his resignation in 1846 over repeal of the corn laws, he was apparently dissuaded from carrying it out.[4] He succeeded his cousin as duke of Northumberland in 1865 and died in August 1867, when he was succeeded by his eldest son Algernon George Percy*.

[1] Buckingham, *Mems. Geo. IV*, ii. 165, 170-1. [2] Alnwick Castle mss Add F/176. [3] The will was proved under £250,000 (PROB 11/1781/67; IR26/1245/105). [4] *Wellington Pol. Corresp.* ii. 461; Add 40582, ff. 373-4, 377-9; Parker, *Peel*, iii. 308.

T.A.J.

PERCY, Hon. Henry (1785–1825), of 8 Portman Square, Mdx.

BERE ALSTON 1820–15 Apr. 1825

b. 14 Sept. 1785, 5th s. of Algernon Percy†, 1st earl of Beverley (*d.* 1830), and Isabella Susanna, da. of Peter Burrell† of Beckenham, Kent; bro. of Hon. Charles Percy*, George Percy, Lord Lovaine*, Hon. Josceline Percy† and Hon. William Henry Percy*. *educ.* Eton 1802. *unm.* 2 illegit. s. CB 22 June 1815. *d.* 15 Apr. 1825.

Lt. 7 Ft. 1804, capt. 1806; a.d.c. to Sir John Moore 1808-9; capt. 14 Drag. 1810; brevet maj. 1810; a.d.c. to duke of Wellington 1815; brevet lt.-col. 1815; maj. 14 Drag. 1820; ret. 1821.

Percy, who served in the Peninsula and became aide-de-camp to Sir John Moore at Corunna, was captured during the retreat from Burgos in 1812 and detained in France until the peace. In 1815, while on Wellington's staff at Waterloo, he was entrusted with the first dispatches bearing news of the victory. He reached London on the evening of 21 June and searched out the prince regent at a party at Mrs. Boehm's in St. James's Square; to the hostess's chagrin, his dramatic intrusion broke up the gathering.[1] This was the pinnacle of his fame, and as Member for the family borough of Bere Alston in the 1820 Parliament he was thoroughly anonymous. He is not known to have spoken in debate and his only recorded vote was with Lord Liverpool's ministry against the disfranchisement of ordnance officials, 12 Apr. 1821. Described by Thomas Creevey* as 'by far the best hand at conversation of the duke's young men',[2] Percy suffered a premature loss of health and died, aged 39, in April 1825. He left all his property to 'my two sons Henry and Percy'; the personalty was sworn under £1,500.[3]

[1] *Gent. Mag.* (1825), i. 567; Bagot, *Canning and Friends*, ii. 4; *Raikes Jnl.* iii. 47. [2] *Creevey Pprs.* i. 278. [3] PROB 11/1698/220; IR26/1056/242.

D.R.F./T.A.J.

PERCY, Hon. William Henry (1788–1855).

STAMFORD 1818–1826

b. 24 Mar. 1788, 6th s. of Algernon Percy†, 1st earl of Beverley (*d.* 1830), and Isabella Susanna, da. of Peter Burrell† of Langley Park, Beckenham, Kent; bro. of Hon. Charles Percy*, George Percy, Lord Lovaine*, Hon. Henry Percy*, and Hon. Josceline Percy†. *unm. d.* 5 Oct. 1855.

Entered RN 1801, midshipman 1802, lt. 1807, cdr. 1810, capt. 1812, r.-adm. (ret.) 1846.

Commr. of excise 1828-49.

Percy, whose active naval career ended under a slight cloud in 1815, continued to sit for Stamford on the interest of his kinsman Lord Exeter. At the 1820 general election he was again returned unopposed. 'By way of thanks', the local press mocked, 'he mumbled over his address in the week's *Mercury*, adding, satirically enough, that his re-election was a *proof* of the *satisfaction* his previous conduct had given to his *constituents*'.[1] A lax attender, when present he continued to give silent support to the Liverpool ministry. He voted in support of their conduct towards Queen Caroline, 6 Feb. 1821, and against criminal law reform, 21 May 1821 (as a pair), and tax reductions, 11 Feb. 1822. He divided against Catholic relief, 30 Apr. 1822, 1 Mar., 10 May 1825. He voted against inquiries into chancery delays, 5 June, currency reform, 12 June 1823, and the trial of the Methodist missionary John Smith for inciting slave riots in Demerara, 11 June 1824. On 2 Mar. 1824 he presented a petition for repeal of the coal duties.[2] He divided for suppression of the Catholic Association, 25 Feb., and the duke of Cumberland's annuity bill, 6, 10 June 1825. He was in the minority against the spring guns bill, 21 June 1825. Commenting on a report in the *Sporting Magazine* that he and his brother Algernon had shot a large amount of game, including 'several coots', that December, the local paper dryly observed:

> What a fine thing it is to have a *representative* who can shoot coots! and what a vast stock of useful information must the gallant captain have brought from the coot-pond to the great council of the nation.[3]

He voted against condemning the Jamaican slave trials, 2 Mar., and for maintaining the president of the board of trade's salary, 10 Apr. 1826. At that year's dissolution he gave up Parliament for an excise place, worth £1,200 a year, which had long been his object.[4] 'Percy retires', observed the local press, 'for which our townsmen "praise God and make no boast of it"'.[5] He died at 8 Portman Square, the London home of his eldest brother George, Lord Beverley, in October 1855.[6]

[1] *Drakard's Stamford News*, 10 Mar. 1820. [2] *The Times*, 3 Mar. 1824. [3] *Drakard's Stamford News*, 3 Feb. 1826. [4] Add. 38291, f. 1; 38299, f. 100. [5] *Drakard's Stamford News*, 26 May 1826. [6] *The Times*, 9 Oct. 1855.

D.R.F./P.J.S.

PERRIN, Louis (1782–1864), of 3 Granby Row, Dublin.

DUBLIN	1831–8 Aug. 1831
CO. MONAGHAN	1832–1834
CASHEL	1835–Aug. 1835

b. 15 Feb. 1782, s. of Jean-Baptiste Perrin (*d.* 1818), French language teacher, of Leinster Lodge, Athy, co. Kildare and w. Mary Daly.[1] *educ.* R. Sch. Armagh; Trinity, Dublin 1796; M. Temple 1804; King's Inns 1806, called [I] 1806. *m.* Apr. 1815, Hester Connor, da. of Rev. Abraham Augustus Stewart, vic. of Donabate, co. Dublin, 7s. (at least 1 *d.v.p.*). *d.* 7 Dec. 1864.

KC [I] 1827; bencher, King's Inns 1832; 3rd sjt. [I] 1832, 1st 1835; att.-gen. [I] Apr.-Aug. 1835; PC [I] 11 May 1835; 1st commr. municipal corporations [I] 1835; j.k.b. [I] 1835-60.

'Honest Louis Perrin', as Daniel O'Connell* dubbed him, was descended from a French Huguenot family, which eventually established itself in Ireland. His father, who for many years worked as a French tutor to the gentry, achieved some celebrity with his numerous and much reprinted textbooks, especially the *Grammar of the French Tongue* (1768) and *Fables Amusantes* (1772).[2] 'John' Perrin, whose younger son Mark (1792-1877) entered the church, died in 1818 and was buried in Palmerstown, county Dublin.[3] Louis, who was born in Waterford, was a scholar at Trinity when he took an active part in the defence of the rebel Robert Emmet in 1803, sitting close to his college friend during the trial and, on judgment being given against him, dramatically entering the dock to give him a last embrace.[4] Having qualified in 1806, he swiftly became eminent in criminal and revenue law, although his progress was impeded by the disgrace of one of his near relations, an attorney who was severely punished for professional misconduct, and by his own liberal views, which were at odds with the conservative character of the bar. A kindly, dark complexioned, somewhat solitary figure, who delivered his vigorous opinions in a slow and ponderous style, his manners matched his habitual bearing, being 'independent, abrupt and honest – a little curt, perhaps, but never purposely uncivil'. In 1831 Richard Sheil*, who commented that he was 'universally admitted to be the best common law lawyer of the Irish bar', described his frank but grave countenance as being marked 'by a certain republican homeliness, intimating a natural, careless manliness of taste and not without its peculiar dignity'.[5]

Perrin, who had long associated with liberal and Catholic barristers, was mentioned as a possible candidate for Dublin during the general election of 1830.[6] As O'Connell's leading counsel early the following year, his announcement of the Catholic leader's having changed his plea from not guilty to guilty caused general astonishment, 15 Feb.; O'Connell nursed a grudge against him for 'deserting ME on Blackburne's infamous attachment motion [the previous month], upon this paltry defence that I was not the person *nominally* attached', but forgave him because he was 'so superior to the great mass of his profession [and] he has so many good and excellent and amiable points about him'.[7] Described by the lord lieutenant, Lord Anglesey, as a penniless but 'very able, popular barrister' who would be a 'great acquisition' to the Grey administration, he was brought forward for Dublin with Robert Way Harty, the lord mayor, as a reformer at the general election of 1831, when the bar apparently contributed at least £3,000 to a subscription in his support.[8] On the hustings, 6 May, when he condemned the corruption of the corporation of Dublin and advocated a householder rather than a freeman franchise, he called for free trade, retrenchment, lower taxation, alteration of the jury laws and the abolition of colonial slavery. He was returned just behind Harty after a severe contest against the sitting Tory Members, a triumph which, as he declared, demonstrated the validity of reform as a palliative and not a threat to the constitution, and the primacy of the cause over the disadvantages of his lack of wealth, connection or station. Perrin, who was criticized for representing the perpetrator of the fatal shooting of a woman during the illumination on the 19th, again thanked the independent electors for his return at the joint celebratory dinner, 31 May 1831.[9]

It was reported in the Tory press that Perrin, who had incurred enormous expenses, had almost refused to go over to attend Parliament in protest at the Irish government's failure to pay them.[10] However, he of course voted for the second reading of the reintroduced reform bill, 6 July, at least twice against adjourning the proceedings on it, 12 July, against using the 1831 census to determine the boroughs in schedules A and B, 19 July, and steadily for the details. In his only reported speeches, he argued that the parties involved in the Castle Pollard affair should be allowed to institute private legal proceedings, 11 July, and that the yeomanry should be disarmed, or even suppressed, if no end was put to the Orange outrages in which it was involved, 18 July. He presented petitions from the Dublin wine merchants against higher duties on wine, 12 July, and from the 40*s.* freeholders of Balbriggan calling for the franchise to be restored to them, 15 July. Implicated in the widespread bribery at the election, he was unseated with Harty, 8 Aug., after which Smith Stanley, the Irish secretary, noted that 'poor Perrin is I hear very low, but ready to do every thing in his power to assist his successors'.[11] At one point during the renewed canvassing that month, he was 'of opinion that defeat was certain, and that it would be less prejudicial to the government to give it up at once'; but he continued to work for the unsuccessful reform candidates, including as one of their counsel during the by-election contest and at the subsequent election committee at Westminster.[12]

In August 1831 O'Connell commented that ministers were ashamed of their conduct on the Dublin election and that Perrin would be rewarded with a borough, as 'they will not be contented to leave him out of Parliament'.[13] The following month Anglesey, who opposed giving him a position on the bench because he would be needed in the Commons as a law officer, hoped he could be seated for the remainder of the Parliament for county Louth, where a vacancy had occurred, and wrote to Smith Stanley that 'we *want* this triumph over Dublin'.[14] He was publicly spoken of as a plausible candidate and went to Dundalk to gauge the lie of the land that month, but withdrew in order to clear the way for Sir Patrick Bellew.[15] Anglesey, who continued to believe that he was 'a most safe and judicious man', stated in October that he would have preferred him to Philip Crampton* as Irish solicitor-general.[16] O'Connell, whose extreme speech on the Union highly offended Perrin that month, was angered at his being put up for Dublin the following year because he declined to pledge in favour of its repeal. Ministers approached O'Connell with the offer of giving him a free run provided he brought Perrin in with him, but this was rejected. On O'Connell's late entry for Dublin, Perrin withdrew and instead won a seat as an advanced reformer for county Monaghan at the general election of 1832.[17] He became Irish third serjeant that year, when his brother Mark was apparently the moving force behind the radical Dublin newspaper, the *Plain Dealer*.[18] In 1835, after a brief spell as attorney-general for Ireland and having been chosen to head the commission on Irish municipal corporations, whose report was mainly his work, he was appointed a puisne judge of king's bench. He died, at his residence of Knockdromin, near Rush, county Dublin, in December 1864, 'one of the most able, upright and conscientious judges who ever sat on the Irish bench'. Of his sons, four were entered at King's Inns in Dublin, although Louis later became rector of Garrycloyne, county Cork; two others, including James, who fell at Lucknow in 1857, were army officers.[19]

[1] *King's Inns Admission Pprs.* ed. E. Keane, P.B. Phair and T.U. Sadleir, 399. [2] *Gent. Mag.* (1865), i. 123; F.E. Ball, *Judges in Ireland*, ii. 275, 349; R. Watt, *Bibliotheca Britannica* (1824), ii. 747u. [3] J. D'Alton, *Hist. Co. Dublin*, 394, 641; *Clergy of Dublin and Glendalough*, 968. [4] D. Plunket, *Life of Lord Plunket*, i. 218; *Oxford DNB*. [5] R.L. Sheil, *Sketches of Irish Bar* (1854), i. 313-14; ii. 361-6; *New Monthly Mag.* (1831), ii. 3-4; *Dublin Evening Post*, 14 July 1831. [6] *Freeman's Jnl.* 3 Aug. 1830. [7] *Greville Mems.* ii. 115-16; *O'Connell Corresp.* iv. 1921. [8] PRO NI, Anglesey mss D619/28C, pp. 105-8; *Freeman's Jnl.* 2 May; *Dublin Evening Post*, 3 May 1831. [9] *Dublin Evening Post*, 7, 14, 21, 24 May, 2 June; *Freeman's Jnl.* 24 May; *Dublin Evening Mail*, 25 May 1831. [10] *Dublin Evening Mail*, 30 May, 20 June 1831. [11] Ibid. 8, 10 Aug. 1831; Anglesey mss 31D/52. [12] Derby mss 920 Der (14) 121/2, Gosset to Smith Stanley, 18 Aug.; *Dublin Evening Mail*, 24 Aug., 26 Sept. 1831. [13] *O'Connell Corresp.* iv. 1833. [14] Derby mss 119/1/2, Anglesey to Smith Stanley, 4, 11, 13 Sept. 1831. [15] *Dublin Evening Post*, 3, 13 Sept. 1831. [16] Anglesey mss 27B, pp. 49, 56. [17] Derby mss 119/1/2, Anglesey to Smith Stanley, 24 Oct. 1831; *O'Connell Corresp.* iv. 1915, 1917, 1921, 1929; *Dublin Evening Post*, 1 Sept., 30 Oct., 13, 22 Nov., 6, 11, 13, 18 Dec.; *Newry Examiner*, 22 Dec. 1832. [18] Derby mss 117/7, Gosset to Melbourne, 20 June 1832. [19] *Dublin Evening Post*, 8 Dec. 1864; *Gent. Mag.* (1865), i. 123-4; *King's Inns Admission Pprs.* 399; *DNB*; *Oxford DNB*.

S.M.F.

PETERS *see* BURTON PETERS

PETERS *see* BURTON PETERS

PETIT, Louis Hayes (1774–1849), of 9 New Square, Lincoln's Inn, Mdx.

RIPON 15 May 1827–1832

b. 9 Nov. 1774, 3rd surv. s. of John Lewis Petit, MD (*d.* 1780), of Bloomsbury Square and Katherine Letitia, da. of Rev. James Serces, minister of French Chapel, St. James's, Westminster. *educ.* Newcombe's sch., Hackney; by Rev. Samuel Perlby; Queens', Camb. 1792; L. Inn 1791, called 1801. *unm. d.* 13 Nov. 1849.

Petit was of Huguenot stock. His great-grandfather Lewis Petit (?1665-1720), a member of the ancient Norman family of Petit des Etans, fled to England from Caen on the revocation of the Edict of Nantes. He served in the British army as an engineer, rose to the rank of brigadier-general and was appointed lieutenant-governor of Minorca in 1708. His son John Peter Petit, who married Sarah, daughter of John Hayes of Wolverhampton, occupied the manor of Little Aston, near that town, from 1743 to the early 1760s. He and his younger brother Captain Peter Petit, who lived with him, were noted for their extensive charitable activities in the neighbourhood. After John Petit's death his widow left Staffordshire and took up residence in London at Bloomsbury Square, where she died in 1766. That year their only son John Lewis Petit qualified as a doctor and commenced practice in London: he was physician to St. George's Hospital, 1770-4, and to St. Bartholomew's from 1774 until his death, 27 May 1780.[1] In his will, executed three days earlier, he devised his undivided moiety of the estate of Ettingshall Park, near Wolverhampton, to his eldest son John Hayes Petit. He made provision for the maintenance and education of his two younger sons, Peter Hayes and Louis Hayes Petit, until they came of age, and for their support from landed property thereafter. He also gave the following instruction:

> I desire my body may be opened [for medical science] if the distemper of which I may die shall not have rendered it so loathsome as to endanger the operator and that the sum of ten guineas shall be given to the person who shall perform the operation.[2]

Louis Hayes Petit, who was raised by his mother and maiden aunt Mary Anne Petit (*d.* 1808), was bred to the bar. He went the Oxford circuit and also attended the Chester assizes and Stafford and Worcester sessions. According to an obituary

> the uprightness and integrity of his character, the depth of his legal knowledge, the soundness and discrimination of his judgement, and the infinite pains he bestowed on all business in which he was consulted, caused him to be much sought after as an arbitrator.

It was reckoned that he would have attained 'the higher honours of his profession had he persevered in his legal career', but he gave it up in 1821, though he occupied his chambers in Lincoln's Inn for the rest of his life.[3] His unmarried brother Peter, lieutenant-colonel of the 35th Foot, died in 1809 at Deal of a wound received at Flushing. His mother died the following year having, like her husband, left her body for dissection. She bequeathed Louis £1,500 in bank annuities. His only surviving brother John, perpetual curate of Shareshill, Staffordshire, died in 1822, when the Ettingshall estate, which was now being extensively and lucratively mined for coal, iron ore and limestone, passed to his eldest son John Louis Petit.[4] In his will Petit's father had described Lancelot Shadwell of Beamish, Shropshire, one of the trustees of his property, as his 'cousin'. Shadwell's son Lancelot Shadwell*, a leading king's counsel, to one of whose sons Petit was godfather, managed the controlling electoral interest at Ripon of Miss Elizabeth Sophia Lawrence. It was presumably he who engineered Petit's return for the borough on a vacancy in May 1827, when the 'smallness' of Petit's election 'disbursements', which were said 'not to exceed ... £50', created 'considerable dissatisfaction'.[5]

Petit voted against the disfranchisement of Penryn for electoral corruption, 28 May, 7 June, the election expenses bill, 28 May, and the Coventry magistracy bill, 18 June 1827. He divided against repeal of the Test Acts, 26 Feb., chancery reform, 24 Apr., and Catholic relief, 12 May 1828. He presented a Ripon petition for repeal of the Act preventing the circulation of small bank notes, 9 June. He was in the Wellington government's majorities on the ordnance estimates, 4 July, and the silk duties, 14 July 1828. In February 1829 he was listed by Planta, the patronage secretary, as 'opposed' to the principle of Catholic emancipation, against which he duly divided steadily the following month. He was not, however, permanently alienated from the ministry and he voted with them against parliamentary reform, 18, 23 Feb., and for the grant for South American missions, 7 June 1830. He divided for Jewish emancipation, 5 Apr., 17 May 1830. After the 1830 general election, when he was again returned unopposed for Ripon, ministers listed him among their 'friends'. He voted in their minority in the crucial division on the civil list, 15 Nov. 1830, but like his colleague, Spence, he promptly transferred his support to the Grey ministry and its reform bill, for which he voted, 22 Mar., 19 Apr. 1831. Miss Lawrence evidently raised no objection, for he was again returned for Ripon at the ensuing general election and continued to support reform. He voted for the second reading of the revised bill, 6 July 1831, and gave steady support to its details, though he voted against the disfranchisement of Saltash, 26 July, and for Lord Chandos's amendment to enfranchise £50 tenants-at-will, 18 Aug. He was in the ministerial majorities on the Dublin election controversy, 23 Aug. He voted for the third reading and passage of the reform bill, 19, 21 Sept., and for the second reading of the Scottish bill, 23 Sept. On 4 Oct. 1831 Sir Charles Wetherell accused Petit, who, he sneered, 'never says anything', of interrupting, with a 'strange, ambiguous' and 'slumbrous' noise, his tirade against that measure's provision for the establishment of a court of appeal to determine the validity of voting claims. Forced to his feet, Petit protested his innocence of any conscious interjection and went on:

> I own that during my attendance in this House I have sometimes felt rather thankful that I possessed the gift of somnolency, and could indulge it without the risk of noise. If we involuntarily nod in the course of any of [Wetherell's] lengthy orations, can it be interpreted into an interruption? ... I should not have risen upon the present occasion except, perhaps, for the reason that the gentlest animal will turn when trodden upon.

He voted for Lord Ebrington's motion of confidence in the reform ministry, 10 Oct. 1831.

Petit divided for the second reading of the revised reform bill, 17 Dec. 1831, again supported its details, and voted for the third reading, 22 Mar. 1832. On 1 Feb. he dismissed Wetherell's objections to the clause enfranchising leaseholders. He voted for the address calling on the king to appoint only ministers who would carry it unimpaired, 10 May, and the second reading of the Irish bill, 25 May. He was a member of the committee to which the Scottish exchequer court bill was referred, 27 Jan. He divided with ministers on the Russian-Dutch loan, 26 Jan., 12, 16 and 20 July, and relations with Portugal, 9 Feb. He voted against Hunt's call for information on military punishments, 16 Feb., and spoke and voted in favour of public inquests, 20 June 1832. Soon afterwards Miss Lawrence, having 'turned violent Tory', gave him notice to quit the Ripon seat. He did not seek election to the reformed Parliament.[6]

Petit had bought property at Yeading, Middlesex, and a house in Tamworth Street, Lichfield, which was occupied by his widowed sister-in-law and her unmarried daughters. He had also acquired an estate at Merridale, in the vicinity of Ettingshall, which provided him with income from mineral rights. His remaining years were largely devoted to literary and philanthropic pursuits and, according to his obituarist, he became noted for 'his unostentatious benevolence, his sound judgement, his extreme consideration for the feelings of others, his uniform kindness'.[7] He died in his chambers in November 1849, having left careful instructions for the treatment of his corpse:

> If I die in my own chambers or my body is brought there after death I order and direct that as soon as the apothecary or medical man attending me in my last illness or called in upon the occasion of my decease shall declare that I am dead my corpse shall be forthwith removed from the place or bed in which I die or where it was placed and shall be laid out in the small bed in the room below stairs usually called the office, there to remain until it is put into its coffin and the coffin to remain in the same room till the funeral.

By his will, dated 28 July 1849, he left legacies to the amount of about £15,000 to relatives and friends. The bulk of his estate passed to his nephew and sole executor, the Rev. John Louis Petit (1801-68), the last male representative of the family, who made a name for himself as an authority on church architecture.[8]

[1] *Oxford DNB sub* John Louis Petit; *Misc. Gen. et Her.* n.s. iv. 13-15; D. Agnew, *Protestant Exiles* (1886 edn.), ii. 356-7, 407; H. Sanders, *Hist. Shenstone*, 185-6; S. Shaw, *Hist. Staffs.* ii. 52. [2] PROB 11/1066/332. [3] *Gent. Mag.* (1850), i. 91. [4] PROB 11/1503/705; 1511/265; 1661/452. [5] *Leeds Intelligencer*, 24 May 1827. [6] *Disraeli Letters*, i. 205. [7] *Gent. Mag.* (1850), i. 90-92. [8] PROB 11/2105/953.

D.R.F./P.J.S.

PETRE, Hon. Edward Robert (1794–1848), of Stapleton Park, nr. Ferrybridge, Yorks. and 17 Charles Street, Berkeley Square, Mdx.

ILCHESTER 1831–1832

YORK 1832–1834

b. 28 Sept. 1794, 3rd but 2nd surv. s. of Robert Edward Petre, 9th Bar. Petre (*d.* 1801), and 2nd w. Juliana Barbara, da. of Henry Howard of Glossop, Derbys. *m.* 21 July 1829, Hon. Laura Maria Stafford Jerningham, da. of George William, 8th Bar. Stafford, *s.p. d.* 8 June 1848.
Sheriff, Yorks. 1830-1; mayor, York 1830-1.

Petre came from an old and prominent English Catholic family, based at Writtle Park, near Chelmsford, Essex, whose peerage dated from 1603. His father's first wife was a niece of the 9th duke of Norfolk and his half-brother Robert, the 10th baron, married a sister of the 12th duke of Norfolk. His nephew William succeeded as the 11th baron in 1809. On his father's death in 1801 his mother was appointed as his guardian, and the will instructed Robert to settle on Edward the unspecified 'estates' which had been settled on him at the time of his marriage.[1] He was described by Sydney Smith as 'a sensible, good looking, pleasing man', although to some he was unkindly known as 'Petre the Cretur'.[2] He was a leading figure on the Turf, and the stable he kept with Rodes Milnes, the uncle of Richard Monckton Milnes†, won the St. Leger five times between 1822 and 1830. It was reported in 1827 that he was 'out of his wits with his Doncaster success', having won £15,000, and that he intended to celebrate with a 'grand ball' at Stapleton Park.[3] At the time of his marriage a bet was said to have been made 'that Petre's belly is bigger than his wife's this time next year'.[4] His racing connections may help to explain why he was the first Catholic sheriff to be appointed after emancipation, as George IV apparently declared that he was 'a d—d good fellow ... he had had some concerns with him *in racing* and he did not mind him'.[5]

Imbued with his family's Whiggish principles, he became a member of Brooks's Club at an unusually early age, 6 Apr. 1814. His first known appearance on a public platform was at the Yorkshire county meeting in January 1823, when he admitted that he was a 'recent convert' to parliamentary reform, but said he had been alarmed to 'see the arm of power extended' in order to 'oppress' the people. He was 'convinced that nothing short of a constitutional reform can restore that sympathy which ... ought to exist between the electors and their constituents, and be an effectual safeguard against a renewal of these destructive measures which have been so long pursued'.[6] He was the first president of the Auxiliary Catholic Defence Society, founded at York in 1828, which petitioned for emancipation.[7] He became an alderman of York in 1829, and offered for the borough at the general election the following year. His nomination speech dwelt mainly on the issue of religious freedom, and he argued that his Catholicism was a purely private matter, but he also declared that he had been 'brought up in the detestation of slavery', was 'a friend to a more fair representation of the people in Parliament' and would support 'every measure [to] promote economy and reduction of taxation', particularly the abolition of 'unmerited sinecures'. He withdrew after five days of polling, as the 'No Popery' cry raised against him was too strong.[8] While mayor of York he attended the meeting in January 1831 when a reform association was founded.[9] At the general election that spring he declined to stand again for the borough, as both sitting Members were supporters of the Grey ministry's reform bill,[10] but a vacancy arose at Ilchester where he was returned unopposed on Lord Cleveland's interest.

He spoke briefly to confirm the good conduct of the Yorkshire yeomanry, which had been 'highly instrumental in the preservation of good order', 27 June 1831. He voted for the second reading of the reintroduced reform bill, 6 July, and generally for its details in committee, but he was in the minority for the amendment to preserve the rights of freemen, 30 Aug. He defended the provision granting six Members to Yorkshire, which would 'give the different interests ... adequate representation', 10 Aug. He divided for the bill's third reading, 19 Sept., its passage, 21 Sept., the second reading of the Scottish bill, 23 Sept., and Lord Ebrington's confidence motion, 10 Oct. He hoped that the grant to the Kildare Place Society would be considered 'in the true spirit of Christian charity', 15 July. He condemned the behaviour of a Catholic priest in county Clare towards the Irish yeomanry as 'unworthy of any minister of God', 26 Aug. He protested at the language used by Gordon, Member for Dundalk, in relation to the Maynooth grant and the Catholic religion, 26 Sept., observing that 'we are not sent here to attack each other in consequence of some minor differences in points of faith, but to do justice to all men and ... promote the interests of all classes in the community'. He warned that rejecting the grant would 'alienate the minds of the people of Ireland'. He voted to punish only those guilty of bribery at the Dublin election and against the censure motion on the Irish administration, 23 Aug. He became a member of the Maldon Independent Club, the principal organization of the Essex Whigs, 21 Nov. 1831.[11]

He divided for the second reading of the revised reform bill, 17 Dec. 1831, its details in committee and the third reading, 22 Mar. 1832. He opposed Hunt's motion for inquiry into the Peterloo massacre, 15 Mar., arguing that it would 'not be wise, or necessary ... to rake up grievances of such long standing'. He voted for Ebrington's motion for an address asking the king to appoint only ministers committed to carrying an unimpaired reform measure, 10 May. He divided for the second reading of the Irish bill, 25 May, and against the Conservative amendment to increase Scotland's representation, 1 June. He voted with government on the Russian-Dutch loan, 26 Jan., 12, 16, 20 July, and relations with Portugal, 9 Feb. On the Irish tithes bill, 16 Apr., he expressed confidence in ministers, who were 'the friends of liberality, and of civil and religious liberty', and emphasized that he considered the English and Irish churches to be part of the law of the land. Regardless of his personal faith, he felt 'bound ... by the solemn engagement I have made to support the Protestant establishment', and would always endorse measures which he thought 'conducive to the welfare of the Protestant church'. He hoped the bill would 'soften down religious animosities and place the Protestant clergy upon a safer footing'. He refuted O'Connell's claim that prior to 1829 the English Catholics would have settled for less than full emancipation, 18 June. He complained about the offensive language used in a Glasgow petition against the Maynooth grant, 10 July, maintaining that 'we, who are Roman Catholics, are not parties to any such illiberal feelings towards Protestants'. He queried Gordon's use of the label 'Arian' to describe Irish Protestant clergymen who favoured non-denominational education, 23 July. He supported the Norfolk assizes bill, 23 May, arguing that Norwich was the obvious venue on the ground of population. He voted for the ministerial amendment to Buxton's anti-slavery slavery motion, 24 May, and to make coroner's inquests public, 20 June 1832.

Ilchester was disfranchised by the Reform Act, but Petre renewed his connection with York, where he was comfortably returned at the general election of 1832. He sat until his retirement in 1834 as 'a reformer, in general a supporter of the [Whig] administration', who advocated 'free trade ... the immediate abolition of slavery, the substitution of a property for the house and window tax, and the abolition of all monopolies'.[12] He stood unsuccessfully as a Liberal at Bridport in 1847. To a friend in the racing fraternity he was 'as kind-hearted, hospitable a man, as ever lived'.[13] He died in June 1848 and left all his property to his wife, apart from a few small bequests mainly to Catholic charities.[14]

[1] PROB 11/1360/485. [2] *Smith Letters*, i. 392; Lord W. P. Lennox, *Biog. Reminiscences*, ii. 145. [3] Reid, *Monckton Milnes*, i. 37; Lonsdale mss, Shelley to Lowther, 20 Sept. 1827. [4] Keele Univ. Lib. Sneyd mss SC 17/49. [5] *Arbuthnot Jnl.* ii. 330. [6] *Leeds Mercury*, 25 Jan. 1823. [7] A.J. Peacock, 'York in the Age of Reform' (Univ. of York Ph.D. thesis, 1973), 146. [8] *York Herald*, 31 July 1830. [9] *Leeds Mercury*, 8 Jan. 1831. [10] *Yorks. Gazette*, 30 Apr. 1831. [11] *Colchester Gazette*, 26 Nov. 1831. [12] *Dod's Parl. Companion* (1833), 150. [13] Lennox, ii. 145. [14] PROB 11/2078/576; IR26/1815/474.

T.A.J.

PHILIPPS, Richard Bulkeley Philipps Grant (1801–1857), of Picton Castle, Pemb.

HAVERFORDWEST	1826–1834
HAVERFORDWEST	1837–1847

b. 7 June 1801,[1] o.s. of John Grant of Nolton, nr. Haverfordwest and Mary Philippa Artemisia, da. and h. of James Child of Begelly House. *educ.* Westminster 1816-17. *m.* (1) 14 Oct. 1824, Eliza (*d.* 24 Mar. 1852), da. of John Gordon of Hanwell, Mdx., *s.p.*; (2) 8 June 1854, Lady Anne Jane Howard, da. of William, 4th earl of Wicklow [I], *s.p. suc.* cos. Richard Philipps†, 1st Bar. Milford [I], to Picton Castle 1823 and took name of Philipps by royal lic. 10 Feb. 1824; *cr.* bt. 13 Feb. 1828; Bar. Milford 21 Sept. 1847. *d.* 3 Jan. 1857.

Ld. lt. and custos rot. Haverfordwest 1824-*d.*, mayor 1829-30, 1831-2.

Lt. Pemb. yeoman cav. 1819.

Grant was born and spent his early childhood in Narberth, Pembrokeshire, moving to Yardley in 1812 following his mother's marriage to the Rev. Henry Gwyther. Although not heir to the Philipps baronetcy, he was groomed to succeed its holder, his mother's kinsman Lord Milford, a leader of the Blue or Whig party in Pembrokeshire (which he represented, 1786-1812) to the 20,000-acre Picton Castle estate, in preference to Rowland Philipps Laugharne of the Orlandon branch of the family. He was commissioned as a lieutenant in the Pembrokeshire yeomanry cavalry, 29 Dec. 1819, and shortly after he came of age in 1822 he was made a freeman and common councillor of Haverfordwest, where Milford retained a controlling interest.[2] He was at Picton Castle when Milford died, 28 Nov. 1823, and wrote immediately to inform ministers and to put forward his claim to the county offices thus vacated. Despite his professed support for Lord Liverpool's administration, which they had not anticipated, he was denied the county lord lieutenancy; but they granted him the less prestigious offices of lord lieutenant and custos of the county of Haverfordwest.[3] As directed in Milford's will, he received an annuity of £600 and took the arms and name of Philipps. He was to succeed to the life tenancy of the estate at the age of 25, and until then its administration was entrusted to John Hensleigh Allen of Cresselly, a Blue who represented Pembroke Boroughs on Lord Cawdor's Stackpole Court interest, and John Philipps Adams of Lydstep.[4] Both were corporators of Haverfordwest and adept at negotiating post-enclosure land exchanges on Philipps's behalf.[5] He expressed an interest in purchasing the late Sir William Paxton's† Middleton Hall estate in Carmarthenshire shortly before his marriage in October 1824; and when in 1825 Cawdor put Pembroke's contributory borough of Wiston up for sale, it was suggested that Philipps might offer £77-80,000 in order to strengthen his influence in that constituency.[6] He bought neither and embarked on extensive improvements at Picton Castle, which were completed in 1827.[7] William Henry Scourfield, who since 1818 had represented Haverfordwest with Milford's support, made way for him there at the 1826 general election and county Whigs and Blue favours were much in evidence when he was returned unopposed a few days after his 25th birthday.[8] He was keen to promote and expand coal mining on his estates and had recently reminded ministers of his attention to militia duties and lack of a title commensurate with his inheritance.[9]

Philipps voted against Catholic relief, 6 Mar., and the government's corn bill, 2 Apr. 1827.[10] His new chapel at Picton Castle was opened during the recess, and he supported the campaign for improved amenities at Haverfordwest, becoming the secretary and honorary vice-president of the savings bank there.[11] Lord Goderich granted his request for a baronetcy in November 1827, shortly after Cawdor's elevation to an earldom, and he was invested at a cost of about £260 in February 1828, when the duke of Wellington was the premier.[12] He presented petitions from Pembrokeshire for repeal of the Test Acts, 18, 19, 21 Feb., and voted accordingly, 26 Feb., but divided against Catholic relief, 12 May 1828. He spent the summer recess at Picton Castle. Returning there in December 1828, he had a lucky escape when his carriage lost a wheel on the bridge at St. Clears and was suspended precariously above the swollen river.[13] The patronage secretary Planta predicted that he would vote 'with government' for Catholic emancipation in 1829. Haverfordwest petitioned both ways, but remained predominantly hostile to the measure. Philipps probably voted against it, 6, 18 Mar., and certainly presented unfavourable petitions, 9 Mar. His support for the anti-Catholic cause was gratefully acknowledged in a spontaneous ceremony when he returned to Haverfordwest in April.[14] He spoke in favour of introducing drawback duties on silk, 1 May, and against relaxing restrictions on the use of the cadavers of murderers and poor felons for dissection, 15 May 1829. (In 1823, the removal of a pauper's body for anatomical research had caused a disturbance at Haverfordwest.)[15] As mayor of Haverfordwest, on 3 Oct. 1829 Philipps chaired a meeting and encouraged petitioning against the proposed abolition of the Welsh judicature and courts of great sessions; for, as Cawdor had suggested, it was envisaged that Pembrokeshire business would be dealt with in Carmarthen, so depriving Haverfordwest of its assize town status. Philipps clashed again with Cawdor on the issue at a noisy county meeting on 6 Oct. 1829.[16] When the administration of justice bill proposing the changes came before the House, Philipps presented and endorsed Haverfordwest's hostile petition, 6 May, and voted in the minority against the bill's recommittal, 18 June 1830.[17] A late government amendment left the assize structure almost intact when the change was enacted, 23 July. He divided against enfranchising Birmingham, Leeds and Manchester, 23 Feb., but with the revived Whig opposition against the Bathurst and Dundas pensions, 26 Mar. He voted against Jewish emancipation, 17 May.[18] He voted against the sale of beer bill's provisions for on-consumption, 21 June. Haverfordwest returned him unopposed at the general election in August 1830.[19]

Ministers listed Philipps among the 'good doubtfuls', but later amended the entry to 'enemy'. He was absent from the division on the civil list when they were brought down, 15 Nov., but presented petitions from Haverfordwest and north Pembrokeshire for the abolition of West Indian slavery, 21 Nov. 1830. He divided for the Grey ministry's reform bill at its second reading, 22 Mar., and against Gascoyne's wrecking amendment, 19 Apr., but failed to find an opportunity to present the Pembrokeshire reform petition entrusted to him (5 Apr.) before the dissolution, 23 Apr. 1831.[20] Even so, Carmarthen reformers feted him on his journey to Haverfordwest, where his reelection was certain. Opposing Sir John Owen* in the county, he canvassed for and nominated the reformer Robert Fulke Greville of Castle Hall, the purchaser of certain Milford estates whose interest in yachting he shared, and liaised throughout with Cawdor's and Lord Kensington's† friends.[21] He subscribed generously to Greville's cause, petitioned with him against Owen's return, and objected in Parliament, 8 July 1831, to the delaying tactics used to prevent the petition being heard. He was not called to testify before the committee which declared the election void, but they considered his conduct at the election and named him in their report.[22]

He voted for the reintroduced reform bill at its second reading, 6 July, and consistently for its details, including the enfranchisement of Merthyr as a contributory borough of Cardiff, which Welsh reformers criticized as inadequate, 10 Aug. 1831. He divided for the bill's passage, 21 Sept., the second reading of the Scottish reform bill, 23 Sept., and Lord Ebrington's confidence motion, 10 Oct. He adopted a lower profile during the second Pembrokeshire election when Owen again prevailed, but gave his interest and financial support to Greville as previously.[23] He divided for the revised reform bill at its second reading, 17 Dec. 1831, for the schedule A disfranchisements, 23 Jan., to retain Helston in schedule B, 23 Feb., to enfranchise Tower Hamlets, 28 Feb., and for the third reading, 22 Mar. 1832. He voted for the address calling on the king to appoint only ministers who would carry it unimpaired, 10 May 1832. Although his votes on the reform bills were well publicized, his views on its provision to make Fishguard and Narberth contributory boroughs of Haverfordwest and an earlier proposal to add Milford, Newport and St. Davids to the district are not known.[24] He divided with government on the Dublin election controversy, 23 Aug. 1831, information on Portugal, 9 Feb., and the Russian-Dutch loan, 12 July, but against them on the vestry bill, 23 Jan., for printing the radical Woollen Grange petition for the abolition of Irish tithes, 16 Feb., and against their temporizing amendment to Fowell Buxton's motion for a select committee on colonial slavery, 24 May 1832, a vote praised by his constituents and the Welsh Nonconformist press.[25] He reminded the House that as a select committee was still sitting, it was too soon to move any resolutions on factory regulation, 7 June 1832.

After a thorough canvass of the new Haverfordwest district constituency he was returned unopposed as a Liberal at the general election in December 1832.[26] In December 1834, Peel's kinsman, Jonathan Peel of Cotts, capitalized on Philipps's scant attention to his parliamentary duties and almost permanent absence on the continent and challenged him at Haverfordwest, causing him to withdraw and transfer his interest to Scourfield, the victor at the 1835 general election.[27] Dissatisfaction with Scourfield's politics induced Philipps to stand successfully against him in 1837, and despite allegations that he was 'a nonentity ... whose Whig label was as false as his adopted name', he retained the seat until he was elevated to the peerage in 1847 on Lord John Russell's* recommendation.[28] The previous year, he had petitioned the Lords unsuccessfully for leave to bring in a bill to overrule a directive in Milford's will which prevented him granting long leases to facilitate coal mining in Saundersfoot.[29] He died childless and intestate at Picton Castle in January 1857, and was buried at Haverfordwest with all the pomp due to a major landowner and freemason.[30] His stepfather wrote: 'Poor fellow, he has been cut off in the midst of his years without having done or enjoyed half the good he might have done'.[31] The peerage was extinguished by his death and, as stipulated in his late uncle Milford's will, the Picton Castle estate passed to his half-brother, the Rev. James Henry Alexander Gwyther (*d.* 1875), who took the name of Philipps. In February 1848 administration and a half share in his personal estate, worth between £45,000 and £50,000, was granted to his widow (*d.* 1909), who had married Thomas Joseph Eyre of Upper Court, co. Kilkenny.[32]

[1] *CP*. [2] M. Philipps, *Philipps of Picton Castle*, 26-27; NLW, Picton Castle mss 948; Pemb. RO D/RTP/HAM/175; *PP* (1835), xxiii. 371. [3] Add. 40359, ff. 100, 183-6, 205; Picton Castle mss 4731. [4] PROB 11/1681/96. [5] Pemb. RO D/RTP/HAM/175; Picton Castle mss 4793; Bodl. Clarendon dep. C.372, bdle. 2, Harvey to Foster Barham, 23 Oct 1824; NLW, Lucas mss 1174. [6] Pemb. RO D/RTP, Picton Castle Estate mss 1/84; Carm. RO, Cawdor mss 2/209; Clarendon dep. C.372, bdle. 2, Harvey to Foster Barham, 19 Oct. 1825; Add. 40359, f. 184. [7] Picton Castle mss 600; *Cambrian*, 6 Jan.; *Carmarthen Jnl.* 12 Jan. 1827. [8] *Carmarthen Jnl.* 26 May, 2, 16 June; *Cambrian*, 17, 24 June 1826. [9] Picton Castle mss 4098, 4728; Add. 40363, f. 103. [10] *Seren Gomer*, x (1827), 125. [11] Picton Castle mss 600; *Carmarthen Jnl.* 2, 23, Nov., 21 Dec. 1827. [12] Bucks. RO, Buckinghamshire mss, Goderich to Geo. IV, Nov. 1827; Picton Castle mss 4962, 4963. [13] *Carmarthen Jnl.* 8 Aug., 28 Dec. 1828. [14] *Cambrian*, 7, 21 Mar., 11, 25 Apr.; *The Times*, 10 Mar.; *Carmarthen Jnl.* 17 Apr. 1829. [15] *Carmarthen Jnl.* 13 June 1823. [16] *Cambrian*, 10, 17 Oct. 1829; *PP* (1829), ix. *passim*. [17] *Carmarthen Jnl.* 30 Apr., 7 May; *The Times*, 22 June 1830. [18] *Pemb. Herald*, 9 Jan. 1857. [19] *Carmarthen Jnl.* 16, 23, 30 July, 6 Aug. 1830. [20] *Seren Gomer*, xiv (1831), 155; *Carmarthen Jnl.* 8 Apr.; *Cambrian*, 9 Apr. 1831. [21] *Carmarthen Jnl.* 23 July 1830, 15, 22, 29 Apr., 6, 13 May; *Cambrian*, 23, 30 Apr., 7, 14 May 1831; D. Williams, 'Pemb. Election of 1831', *WHR*, i (1960-3), 42-52; Clarendon dep. C.372, bdle. 6, Harvey to Foster Barham, 11 June 1831. [22] NLW, Eaton Evans and Williams mss 4593; D. Williams, *WHR*, i. 52-55; *CJ*, lxxxvi. 608-9, 633, 688, 744, 843-4, 863-4; *The Times*, 17, 19 Sept. 1831; *PP* (1831), iv. 585. [23] *Carmarthen Jnl.* 29 Oct. 1831; Eaton Evans and Williams mss 5121. [24] *Seren Gomer*, xv (1832), 26-27, 157, 189; D.A. Wager, 'Welsh Politics and Parl. Reform, 1780-1835', *WHR*, vii (1974-5), 440-1. [25] *Greal y Bedyddwyr*, vi (1832), 252. [26] *Carmarthen Jnl.* 7, 14 Dec.; *Cambrian*, 15 Dec. 1832. [27] *Carmarthen Jnl.* 12, 19, 26 Dec.; *Welshman*, 19, 26 Dec.; *Cambrian*, 20 Dec. 1834; *The Times*, 6 Jan. 1835. [28] Pemb. RO D/RTP, Sir R.B.P. Philipps mss 5/33, 34; *Welshman*, 30 June, 7, 14 July, *The Times*, 5, 12, 13 July 1837; D. Jones, *Rebecca's Children*, 88; Picton Castle mss 4800. [29] Picton Castle mss 1557, 1749, 4116, 4562, 4563. [30] *Cambrian*, 2, 9 Jan. 1857; *Welshman*, 27 Jan. 1843, 16 Jan. 1857; Picton Castle mss 4643. [31] Picton Castle mss 2074. [32] Ibid. 1558; IR26/3293/101.

M.M.E.

PHILIPS, George (1766–1847), of Sedgley, nr. Manchester, Lancs.; Weston House, nr. Chipping Norton, Warws., and 111 Mount Street, Grosvenor Square, Mdx.[1]

ILCHESTER	1812–1818
STEYNING	1818–1820
WOOTTON BASSETT	1820–1830
WARWICKSHIRE SOUTH	1832–1834

b. 24 Mar. 1766, 2nd but o. surv. s. of Thomas Philips of Sedgley and Mary, da. and h. of John Rider of Manchester. *educ.* Miss Heywood's sch.; Blue Coat Hosp. Manchester; Dissenting schs. Pillington (Mr. Pope), Manchester (Mr. Ralph Harrison).[2] *m.* 16 Oct. 1788, his cos. Sarah Ann, da. of Nathaniel Philips of Hollinghurst, Lancs., 1s.; 1s. illegit.[3] *suc.* fa. 1811; *cr.* bt. 21 Feb. 1828. *d.* 3 Oct. 1847.

Lt.-col. commdt. 1st batt. 4 Manchester vol. inf. 1803.

At the beginning of his engagingly Shandyesque memoirs, Philips recorded that

> the more I reflect on my own history, the more I am inclined to think its character is much to be attributed to the circumstances of my situation in early life. My father had become a follower of John Wesley, and lived almost exclusively with the sect of Methodists at the time that they were much reviled and persecuted. His society was of course very inferior to that which his station in life entitled him to frequent. I was left much to the care of the servants. I slept with one of the men-servants who, in our house, were of a very inferior order. From such society it is unnecessary to say that nothing good or useful could be learned.[4]

Both his grandfather, John Philips, and his father were prosperous partners in silk and cotton manufacturing firms in Manchester, but personal and business quarrels dominated his early life. He had a poor relationship with his father, who deprived him of a good education and regarded him as a 'sort of evil genius of the family, destined to work its ruin'.[5] However, he studied hard in private to improve himself, and to

> keep my attention awake I drank green tea very copiously and used other means to prevent me from sleeping. The consequence was that I became so nervous that I trembled at the sight of strangers and was totally unfit for society. In this state I tried to go into some parties, to which I was invited, but I was so agitated on entering the room, that my whole frame was disordered and my teeth chattered in my mouth. After thus exposing myself, all that I could do was to quit the party, who of course would make me a town's talk. I was some years in recovering from this state.[6]

His autobiography also dwelt on his early lack of religious belief and hinted at many youthful indiscretions. Of particular note was an adulterous affair which he conducted in a shameless manner, openly walking arm-in-arm with his mistress in the streets of Manchester. A child, 'that she had after my connection with her', was secured an appointment in the East India Company's artillery corps. However, Philips, whose personality was much influenced by his religious upbringing, subsequently experienced a conversion to the kind of faith which he had found so lacking in his enforced chapel attendance as a boy, and he enjoyed a happy domestic life with his wife.[7] He also succeeded in extending his social circle and, as well as mixing with Dissenters and merchants, he moved amongst the élite of Manchester's legal, medical and literary society, and knew some of the country's leading Whigs.[8]

Philips equally regretted the arrogance and vanity which had led him into many political difficulties during his life. His father's branch of the family had been Whigs who sympathized with the revolutions in America and France. He recalled that

> young and eager and inexperienced as I was, it was not surprising that I should be led astray by wild, enthusiastic hopes of an unattainable perfectibility of rulers and subjects when even the wisest, and ablest men like Fox and Sheridan partook of the general delusion.

He belonged to reform clubs in Manchester and London, and reckoned that his greatest folly was to have written a pamphlet, *The Necessity for a Speedy and Effectual Reform in Parliament* (1793), which advocated universal (including female) suffrage and annual parliaments, generally prefiguring the demands of the Chartists. In his memoirs he acknowledged its vigour of style, but added that 'a more impracticable and utopian scheme never entered into any man's head'.[9] His ambition to enter the Commons resulted in minor intrigues at Steyning and Stafford, before, by his own account, he purchased a seat at Ilchester from Sir William Manners† for £5,000 in 1812. In 1818 he was elected for Steyning

> for which I lent the then [12th] duke of Norfolk £50,000 at a time when there was such a demand for money, and so little in the market, that his agent Mr. [Edward] Blount* could not find any person willing to advance that sum to the duke on the security which he had to offer.

Confusingly, and probably wrongly, Philips recorded that in conformity with his agreement with Norfolk, 'I represented under the duke's interest first Ilchester, and afterwards Steyning'.[10] He was a frequent speaker, and boasted that after having congratulated Sir Samuel Romilly on an anti-slavery speech, 'he said, "I intended to have spoken to you of your speech in terms similar to those you have applied to mine". I consider this as the highest compliment that my speaking in Parliament was ever honoured with'.[11] Although Philips always believed that the militia had acted wrongly in opening fire on an essentially peaceable crowd in St. Peter's Fields, Manchester, 16 Aug., he condemned his own actions in support of the radicals and acknowledged that his manner in bringing the matter before the House, 24 Nov. 1819, had subjected him to ridicule and injured his parliamentary reputation.[12]

In 1820 Philips probably decided to resign his seat at Steyning in favour of his son, George Richard, and he turned instead to Wootton Bassett, where he owned houses and land. He was elected there on the interest of Lord Bolingbroke, despite an opposition, a scrutiny and a petition.[13] As an entrepreneur and merchant capitalist, he was by then an extremely wealthy man; his friend Sydney Smith joked that he doubled his capital twice a week. He was a partner in a cotton factory at Salford with George Augustus Lee, who kept him informed on business affairs, but had many other diversified businesses.[14] Unsurprisingly for the man dubbed the 'Member for Manchester', the main themes of his numerous parliamentary speeches (including those made on the presentation of mercantile petitions) continued to be the promotion of the manufacturing interest, especially in Lancashire, and, following David Ricardo*, the removal of restrictions in all branches of trade, notably by repealing the corn laws. He later wrote that the economist Robert Torrens* had addressed a pamphlet to him, 'as the first person in Parliament who had placed those laws in a true light, and treated them on just and comprehensive principles'. He also became more vocal in support of religious and humanitarian concerns.[15] Although the parliamentary reporters rarely distinguished unambiguously between him and his son, the very uniformity of these interventions suggests that they were by him rather than by George Richard. He was a teller for opposition on the civil list, 3 May, and voted against the Liverpool administration on this, 5, 8 May. On the 19th he stated one of his favourite arguments, that

> it was impossible that any such protection, extended exclusively to one branch of society, should not injure not only itself, but the other branches also. He was of opinion that the agriculture, the commerce and the manufactures of the country had but one common interest. Whatever injured one must also be prejudicial to others.

Referring to the debate on agricultural distress, Sir James Mackintosh* recorded, 1 June 1820, that 'poor George Philips made two vain attempts to be heard last night, but was twice obliged to sit down. What enhanced the mortification was that [Henry] Brougham and others were patiently heard afterwards'.[16]

Philips, an active committeeman, continued to divide regularly for economies and retrenchment in this and the following three sessions, as well as with the Whig opposition on almost all major political controversies and legal, social and foreign policy issues. He signed a requisition for a Manchester meeting on the Queen Caroline affair, 23 Nov. 1820, and in the following session voted steadily in support of the opposition campaign on her behalf.[17] He condemned the proceedings at meetings in her favour in London, 2 Feb., and Cheshire, 9, 20 Feb., when he was a teller for the minority for inquiry into the conduct of the sheriff. Because he believed that the opinions of the country generally, and the manufacturing districts in particular, were not sufficiently represented in the House, he advocated parliamentary reform, 31 Jan., 12 Feb. He spoke for inquiry into Peterloo, 20 Feb., 15 May, and voted for this, 16 May, and repeal of the recent repressive legislation, 8 May.[18] He divided for parliamentary reform, 9 May, alteration of the Scottish county representation, 10 May, and the bill to secure the independence of Parliament, 31 May. He attended the inaugural meeting of the Whig Club for Cheshire and its neighbouring counties, 9 Oct. 1821, declaring that its foundation showed that the 'spirit of liberty is as much at variance with anarchy on the one hand, as with despotism on the other'.[19] He was one of the founders of the *Manchester Guardian* later that year.[20] Attending and speaking frequently in the Commons, he voiced the anti-protectionist views of the Manchester chamber of commerce and urged the abolition of the tax on raw silk, 20 Mar., and again supported the idea of free trade, 1 Apr. 1822. He defended the interests of the public creditor, 8 May, calling the possible return to a deflated paper currency 'worse than inexpedient'. He voted for Ricardo's motion for a 20*s.* duty on wheat, 9 May. Using his own specialist knowledge, he made a lengthy speech against excessive agricultural protection, 13 May, arguing that it was unjustified and created fluctuations and imbalances detrimental to the whole economy.[21] At the meeting of the Cheshire Whig Club, 9 Oct. 1822, he condemned ministers' illiberal foreign policy and advocated reducing the power of the crown and the nobility by increasing the influence of the numerous and virtuous middle class.[22]

Philips voted for parliamentary reform, 25 Apr. 1822, 20 Feb., 24 Apr., and for information on Inverness elections, 26 Mar. 1823. Arguing that domestic producers could very well compete in foreign markets, he spoke against regulation of the cloth trades, 21 Mar., and denied that Manchester cotton weavers, whose profits he claimed were higher than those of their employers, were injured by the introduction of machinery, 25 Apr. On 12 May he said that he 'saw no hope of effectual relief but from reduced taxation'.[23] In arguing for the unhurried passage of the bill to repeal the Spitalfields Act, 21 May, and in raising objections to the repeal of the combination laws, 27 May, he underlined his *laissez faire* principles. He spoke against the wool tax, 4 June, and on the silk manufacture bill, 9 June, declared that 'ministers deserved the highest praise whenever they had the manliness to break through any of the absurd regulations which fettered our commerce'.[24] He attacked the method of selecting the grand juries of Lancashire as prejudicial to the trials of the Manchester militia following Peterloo, 12 June 1823. While supporting efforts to reduce the duties on imported silks, 5, 9 Mar., he advocated their gradual diminution in order to minimize disruption to trade, but he gave an optimistic forecast of the improved prosperity of the domestic industry, 19, 22 Mar. 1824. He asked that restrictions be lifted on trade with Prussia and Ireland, 6, 13 Apr. He spoke against combinations, which he argued were the result of wages being too high rather than too low, 14 Apr., 3 June. He spoke for Catholic claims, 27 May, and divided in condemnation of the trial of the Methodist missionary John Smith in Demerara, 11 June 1824.[25]

Philips stated that merchants would invest in Ireland as long as tranquillity was preserved, 21 Feb. 1825, but that this would not long continue unless the Catholic question was settled. As he had on 28 Feb. 1821, he voted for relief, 1 Mar., 21 Apr., 10 May, when he condemned the 'hole and corner' anti-Catholic petition from Manchester as a distortion of the true state of opinion there. He admitted that he had changed his mind on the Liverpool and Manchester railway bill, 2 Mar., and was now convinced that canal transportation was just as, if not more, efficient. He opposed the cotton mills regulation bill to reduce the extent of child labour, on the grounds that the scheme was impracticable, 16 May. He repeated that to reduce their hours would be to risk throwing children out of employment altogether, 31 May. He promised Brougham that he would try to get additional subscribers to the Cheshire Whig Club, 3 Oct., and when presiding at its meeting, 10 Oct., he praised ministers for the improvements in commercial policy and their recognition of the new South American countries, but advocated reform and Catholic emancipation.[26] In November 1825 Mackintosh urged him to take a lead in promoting anti-slavery agitation in Manchester.[27] He spoke for ending colonial slavery, 1 Mar., and voted in condemnation of the Jamaican slave trials, 2 Mar. 1826. He criticized the system of supplementing the wages of agricultural labourers from the poor rates, 14 Mar.[28] He raised a query about the office of the treasurership of the navy on the grant of a salary to the president of the board of trade, 6 Apr., and voted against this, 10 Apr. He divided for altering the representation of Edinburgh, 13 Apr., and parliamentary reform, 27 Apr. He seconded and was a minority teller for a motion to consider the corn laws, 18 Apr., when he advocated a protecting duty of no more than 10*s.* or 12*s.*, denied that agriculture deserved an advantage over manufacturing industry and argued that their repeal would lead to general prosperity. He welcomed the announcement that bonded corn would be released in order to relieve distress, 1 May, and told the House not to dismiss the opinions of well informed and moderate manufacturers, 2 May 1826.

Not least because of the unpopularity of his pro-Catholic votes, Philips again faced a challenge at the general election that summer, but he was returned for Wootton Bassett after a contest and survived a petition.[29] He voted for Hume's amendment to the address complaining of distress, 21 Nov. 1826, and remarked that the 'great evil' of protection lay in its depriving Britain's competitors of the wherewithal to purchase her manufactures, 21 Feb. 1827. He argued that a figure of 50*s.* would give the landed interest sufficient protection and that 'any system of duty was preferable to prohibition', 9 May, when he voted for Whitmore's amendment to make this, not 60*s.*, the import price. He voted against increased protection for barley, 12 Mar., but said that he would vote for the second reading of the corn duties bill, 2 Apr., because it represented some improvement on the former laws. He urged the lifting of the East India Company's trading monopoly, 15, 22 May, and spoke for encouraging emigration as a way of affording relief in the current severe circumstances, 21 May.[30] He voted for Catholic relief, 6 Mar. 1827, 12 May 1828. He returned thanks for a toast to the manufacturing interest at a meeting of the Wiltshire Society, 16 May 1827.[31] He advocated transferring the elective franchise of Penryn to Manchester and thought that the right of voting should be in those rated to the poor at £15 or £20, 28 May 1827, when he voted for the disfranchisement of Penryn. The new premier, Canning, had apparently expressed a wish that Philips should be offered some distinction, and although Lord Dudley thought he would accept nothing less than a peerage, Lord Goderich followed Sydney Smith's suggestion and secured him the baronetcy which he was awarded early the following year.[32]

Philips presented petitions for repeal of the Test Acts, 21, 22 Feb., and voted for this, 26 Feb. 1828. He was named to the committee to prepare a bill to transfer Penryn's seats to Manchester, 31 Jan., and made interventions in its favour, 14, 24, 28 Mar. He voted against extending East Retford's franchise to the freeholders of Bassetlaw, 21 Mar., and spoke of the importance of giving the vote to manufacturing areas and the 'tranquillizing effect of popular representation', 19 May. He again advocated free trade in corn, 21 Apr., and expressed himself dissatisfied with Huskisson's explanation of government policy, 22 Apr., as the new system would provide neither relief for the poor nor a good return for farmers; he voted that day to make the pivot price 60*s*. not 64*s*. He divided for Catholic relief, 12 May, but probably missed the last month of the session visiting his sick friend Richard Sharp*. As in the previous two years, he attended the Cheshire Whig Club meeting, 9 Oct. 1828, when he praised the repeal of the Test Acts.[33] He spoke in favour of the suppression of anti-Catholic associations in Ireland, 13 Feb., but his speech criticizing the Manchester anti-Catholic petition, 2 Mar. 1829, was apparently misreported.[34] He brought up and endorsed pro-Catholic petitions from the Dissenters of Manchester and Cheshire, 10, 16 Mar., and voted for emancipation, 6, 30 Mar. He opposed a return to the old system of regulating the silk trade to relieve weavers, as any such changes would only serve to worsen their problems, 26 Feb., 7, 10 Apr. He spoke and voted in favour of a fixed duty on corn imports, 19 May, and defended the use of child labour, 19 May, and the level of wages, 28 May. He voted to transfer East Retford's seats to Birmingham, 5 May, and to allow Daniel O'Connell to take his seat unimpeded, 18 May 1829.

Either Philips or his son was one of the 28 opposition Members who divided in the ministerial majority against Knatchbull's amendment to the address, 4 Feb. 1830. He voted for a reduction of taxes, 15 Feb., and complained that no representative of the manufacturing interest had been appointed to the select committee on the renewal of the East India Company's charter, 16 Feb. He again divided in favour of transferring East Retford's seats to Birmingham, 5 Mar., and he paired for reform, 28 May. He voted for the production of information on Portugal, 10 Mar., and joined in the revived opposition campaign in favour of retrenchment and reduced taxation that session. He observed that the manufactures of Lancashire were improving despite the existing distress, that ministers' domestic policy was highly praiseworthy, though he favoured greater reductions, and that he would vote against a committee on the state of the nation, 18, 22 Mar. He paired for information on the affair at Terceira, 28 Apr., and Jewish emancipation, 17 May. He sided with opposition on the civil government of Canada, 25 May, and voted to abolish the death penalty for forgery, 7 June 1830. By the general election that year, Philips had sold to Lord Clarendon his interest at Wootton Bassett, where a Tory reaction had anyway made his return unlikely. One Manchester paper noted with regret his decision to retire, 'his health being unequal to the arduous duties which have of late devolved on the Members of the House of Commons'.[35]

In an undated anecdote in his recollections, Philips wrote that

> one day when [his son] George and Sharp and I were together, some circumstance occasioned our making a rude estimate of the cost of our seats in Parliament, which we calculated *then* to amount to at least £20,000. Sharp said, 'I hope you will let Lord Grey [the incoming prime minister] and the leaders of the party know the fact'. 'Why should I?' I replied. 'I want nothing from them, and will neither ask nor accept anything. Instead of blazoning the fact I would prefer concealing it, as it might be considered a culpable and wanton extravagance on my part rather than an act entitling me to credit'.

Whether or not illness or expense was a factor, he had come to realize that a reputation in Parliament could only be gained by harder work than was consistent with a tranquil domestic life, and so he quitted 'without any reluctance, when my son, and several friends, Sydney Smith among the rest, thought I was doing what I should infallibly repent of. They were mistaken. My judgement on the subject never changed'. About this time he moved to Weston, a magnificent mansion which he had recently had built at vast expense in the Holland House style, and which was much admired by Lord John Russell*. On a visit to this retreat in October 1830, Smith wrote that the 'evils of old age, gout and prolixity of narrative are invading the worthy and recent baronet'.[36]

Despite being a relative newcomer, Philips had immediately become active in Warwickshire politics. He seconded the candidacy of the reformer Francis Lawley* at both the nomination meeting, 3 Aug., and the county election, 6 Aug. 1830.[37] He signed the requisition for a county meeting on reform, and at it, 4 Apr. 1831, he seconded the resolution in favour of the ministerial reform bill, which he said 'would enable the people to have their rights fairly stated in the House of Commons'.[38] On the retirement of Dugdale Stratford Dugdale at the general election of 1831, Philips was urgently solicited to stand as a compromise candidate in order to keep out the Tory Sir John Eardley Eardley Wilmot and to prevent a split among the reformers. He reluctantly agreed, but to his delight another candidate emerged on the morning of the nomination meeting, 4 May, though, as he informed Brougham the following day, 'I had actually ended my speech in the county hall before they informed me that they would agree to support Sir Gray Skipwith'. He duly withdrew in Skipwith's favour, being widely praised for his honourable conduct, and, apparently present at the election at Worcester, he left it to his son to propose Lawley on his behalf, 10 May.[39] At another county meeting (the requisition for which he had again signed), 8 Nov. 1831, he moved the first resolution deploring the Lords' rejection of the reform bill and condemned the magistrates' decision to call out the military.[40] Much to the surprise of his family, and despite his own declaration that 'had he wished to have been returned to Parliament, could he not have been two years ago, and without a contest', he allowed himself to be nominated for Warwickshire South at the general election of 1832, when he was returned as a Liberal by a margin of only 13 votes.[41] As he recorded in his memoirs, at the dissolution in 1834 he was 'most happy to retire into private life, still interesting myself about public transactions, and events, as I continue doing at present'. He died in October 1847, being succeeded by his only legitimate child, George Richard Philips.[42]

[1] Largely based on Warws. RO MI 247, microfilm of Sir George Philips's mems., written in two notebooks, 1845-6; typed transcript at CR 1381; location of original unknown. See also D. Brown, 'From "Cotton Lord" to Landed Aristocrat: the Rise of Sir George Philips', *HR*, lxix (1996), 62-82. [2] Philips mems. i. 6-9. [3] Ibid. ii. 19. [4] Ibid. i. 2. [5] Ibid. i. 3-9, 56; F. J. Faraday, 'Selections of Corresp. of J. L. Philips', *Mems. and Procs. of Manchester Lit. and Phil. Soc.* (ser. 4), iii (1890), 13-14. [6] Philips mems. i. 15-16. [7] Ibid. i. 3, 17-22; ii. 13-76; Brown, 70-73. [8] Philips mems. i. 57, 74-102, 226-50, 278-98, 311-41. [9] Ibid. i. 112-18, 257-68, 363. [10] Ibid. ii. 107-11; Brown, 74-75. [11] Philips mems. i. 294. [12] Ibid. i. 20-21, 261-8. [13] Ibid. ii. 111-12; *Devizes Gazette*, 30 Mar. 1820. [14] *Smith Letters*, i. 366; R. Owen, *Life* (1857), 120-1; Shakespeare Birthplace Trust, Philips mss DR 198/1-10; Brown, 67-69. [15] Philips mems. i. 269-79, 307-9; *HP Commons, 1790-1820*, iv. 793-4; Brown, 75-78. [16] Add. 52444, f. 123; *The Times*, 1 June 1820. [17] *Cowdroy's Manchester Gazette*, 25 Nov. 1820. [18] *The Times*, 21 Feb. 1821. [19] *Manchester Guardian*, 13 Oct. 1821. [20] Brown, 74. [21] Philips mss DR 198/10. [22] *Manchester Guardian*, 12 Oct. 1822. [23] *The Times*, 13 May 1823. [24] Ibid. 5 June 1823. [25] Ibid. 7 Apr., 28 May, 4 June 1824. [26] Brougham mss; *Manchester Guardian*, 15 Oct. 1825. [27] Add. 52453, f. 109. [28] *The Times*, 15 Mar. 1826. [29] *Devizes Gazette*, 8, 22 June 1826. [30] *The Times*, 22, 23 May 1827. [31] *Devizes Gazette*, 24 May 1827. [32] Philips mems. i. 411-12; Bucks. RO, Buckinghamshire mss O100, Goderich to Geo. IV, Nov.; *London Gazette*, 21 Dec. 1827. [33] Philips mems. i. 413; *Manchester Guardian*, 14 Oct. 1826, 13 Oct. 1827, 11 Oct. 1828. [34] *Manchester Guardian*, 14 Mar. 1829. [35] Ibid. 17 July; *Devizes Gazette*, 8 July 1830; Philips mems. ii. 112-13. [36] Philips mems. i. 309-10, 351-2; ii. 113-21b; *VCH Warws.* v. 52; *Smith Letters*, ii. 520; Brown, 78-79. [37] *Warwick Advertiser*, 7 Aug. 1830. [38] Ibid. 2, 9 Apr. 1831. [39] Ibid. 7, 14 May 1831; Brougham mss; Philips mems. ii. 124-5. [40] *Warwick Advertiser*, 29 Oct., 12 Nov. 1831. [41] Ibid. 15, 22 Dec. 1832; Philips mems. i. 309-10; ii. 125-8. [42] Philips mems. i. 310-11; *Gent. Mag.* (1847), ii. 636; *Oxford DNB*.

S.M.F.

PHILIPS, George Richard (1789–1883), of 12 Hill Street, Berkeley Square, Mdx.

HORSHAM	1818–1820
STEYNING	1820–1832
KIDDERMINSTER	1835–1837
POOLE	1837–1852

b. 23 Dec. 1789, o. legit. s. of George Philips* and Sarah Ann, da. of Nathaniel Philips of Hollinghurst, Lancs. *educ.* Eton 1803;[1] Trinity Coll. Camb. 1808. *m.* 18 Nov. 1819, Hon. Sarah Georgiana Cavendish, da. of Richard, 2nd Bar. Waterpark [I], 3da. *suc.* fa. as 2nd bt. 3 Oct. 1847. *d.* 22 Feb. 1883.

Sheriff, Warws. 1859-60.

The 'beloved and excellent' son of a wealthy Manchester cotton merchant, Philips displayed an invariable 'filial affection' for the father who so influenced his personal and political career.[2] Also a Whig, he was elected to Brooks's, 30 Mar. 1816, and, very much in his father's shadow, to the House in 1818. This was probably under the same financial arrangement with the 12th duke of Norfolk that saw George Philips returned for Steyning.[3] His parents, 'to whom I am bound by every tie of duty, gratitude and affection', highly approved of the prospect of his marriage, and a separate establishment in London was supported by his father's liberality in the form of an annuity of £1,000.[4] He agreed with his father that the bloodshed at Peterloo would have been avoided if the crowd had been allowed to disperse peacefully. He wrote to his fiancée, 17 Sept. 1819, that 'when the late proceedings come before the notice of Parliament, I shall be in a pleasing state of unpopularity both with the violent Tories and the violent reformers', although he added, 1 Oct., 'thank God a more agreeable object occupies my mind so that I can look upon all local politics with philosophical composure'.[5] Most likely under the same agreement with Norfolk, he was brought in for Steyning at the general election of 1820, and his father continued to bear his heavy electoral expenses.[6] Judging by George Philips's comment that his son's tact and circumspection, which he attributed to his good education, led him to avoid speaking often or on unfamiliar subjects, it is probably fair to conclude that the vast majority of the ambiguously ascribed speeches in the parliamentary reports were made by him rather than by his almost silent son.[7]

Philips voted frequently for lower expenditure and taxation in the early 1820s and, like his father, was a steady opponent of the Liverpool ministry on most major issues.[8] He voted for Catholic claims, 28 Feb. 1821, 1 Mar., 21 Apr., 10 May 1825. He divided for parliamentary reform, 9 May 1821, 25 Apr. 1822, 20 Feb., 24 Apr. 1823, 9 Mar., 13, 27 Apr., and to curb electoral bribery, 26 May 1826. He attended the inaugural annual meeting of the Cheshire Whig Club, 9 Oct. 1821, and was occasionally present in subsequent years.[9] Possibly he, rather than his father, spoke and acted as a teller for the minority against the third reading of the Salford small debts bill, 13 May 1822. It may have been he who condemned the duties on salt and transfers of property, 11 June, and attributed all the country's troubles to the suspension of cash payments in 1797, 14 June 1822.[10] He was appointed to the select committee on artisans and machinery, 12 Feb. 1824, and the following day he informed his father that William Huskisson*, the president of the board of trade, had promised to be open-minded about the inquiry, though he himself believed that in most cases 'it will prove to be sound policy to adhere to the general principles of free trade'.[11] He was listed in the majorities of 41 against the Leith docks bill, 20 May, and of 55 for the St. Olave tithes bill, 6 June 1825. Any notion of a contest at Steyning was ridiculed in the local press, and Philips was duly returned at the general election.[12]

He voted for the amendment to the address, 21 Nov. 1826, and to make 50*s.* the import price of corn, 9 Mar. 1827. He was given a month's leave of absence on urgent business, 19 Mar. 1827. He disapproved of his father's acceptance of a baronetcy from the Goderich ministry.[13] He voted for repeal of the Test Acts, 26 Feb. 1828, and, as he had on 6 Mar. 1827, for Catholic relief, 12 May 1828. He sided with opposition for making 60*s.* not 64*s.* the pivot price of corn, 22 Apr., and on the misapplication of public money on Buckingham House, 23 June. He divided against extending the franchise of East Retford to the freeholders of Bassetlaw, 21 Mar., and against the bill to disqualify certain voters there, 24 June 1828. He voted for Catholic emancipation, 6, 30 Mar., and to allow Daniel O'Connell to take his seat unimpeded, 18 May 1829. He voted to transfer East Retford's seats to Birmingham, 5 May, and for the issue of a new writ and Lord Blandford's parliamentary scheme, 2 June. He divided in favour of reducing the hemp duties, 1 June 1829. Either he or his father joined 27 other opposition Members in voting with the Wellington government against Knatchbull's amendment to the address, 4 Feb. 1830, but he divided regularly in favour of retrenchment and lower taxation during the session. He was one of the Whigs who joined Lord Howick in voting against the East Retford bribery prevention bill, 11 Feb., and he again divided to transfer its seats to Birmingham, 5 Mar. He voted for the enfranchisement of Birmingham, Leeds and Manchester, 23 Feb., to refer the Newark petition complaining of the duke of Newcastle's electoral interference to a select committee, 1 Mar., and general parliamentary reform, 28 May. He divided with opposition on Portugal, 10 Mar., the Terceira affair, 28 Apr., Canada, 25 May, and Ceylon, 27 May. He voted for Jewish emancipation, 17 May, and it may have been he rather than his father (who paired), who presented and briefly endorsed the Manchester petition in its favour. He voted for abolition of the death penalty for forgery, 7 June, and may have spoken in favour of applying the grant for the Society for the Propagation of the Gospels more generally and not confining it to the use of the established church, 14 June 1830.

Having been returned again for Steyning at the general election, Philips was of course listed by ministers among their 'foes', and he divided against them on the civil list, 15 Nov. 1830. He voted for a reduction of the duty on wheat imported to the West Indies, 12 Nov., and presented a Glastonbury petition for repeal of the assessed taxes, 11 Dec. 1830, when he asked the new Grey ministry whether they had any intention of lifting what was universally considered an oppressive and vexatious tax. He voted for the second reading of the government's reform bill, 22 Mar., and against Gascoyne's wrecking amendment, 19 Apr. 1831. He was returned unopposed for Steyning with another reformer at the subsequent general election. In the absence of his father, he nominated Francis Lawley* at the Warwickshire election, 10 May, when he declared that he intended to vote 'for that great, and wise, and salutary question of parliamentary reform', and that

> whatever might be the consequence to himself of the disfranchisement of the borough of Steyning, which he then represented, he was quite certain that there was no action in his life which he should hereafter look upon with such feelings of satisfaction, as that act of political suicide which he was about to commit.[14]

Philips duly voted for the second reading of the reintroduced reform bill, 6 July, and at least twice against adjourning proceedings on it, 12 July. He insisted that the electors of Steyning had returned him in the full knowledge that he would support the bill and that it was therefore the last vote they would give, 26 July. Although it was said that his 'penchant' was for only a moderate reform, he continued to vote regularly with ministers on the bill's details, and he sided with them on the Dublin election controversy, 23 Aug.[15] He voted for the passage of the bill, 21 Sept., and Lord Ebrington's confidence motion, 10 Oct. He signed the requisition for a Warwickshire county meeting in favour of reform after its rejection by the Lords, and was thanked by the meeting for his role in supporting the measure, 8 Nov. 1831.[16]

He voted for the second reading of the revised reform bill, 17 Dec. 1831, again consistently for its details and for the third reading, 22 Mar. 1832. He divided for Ebrington's motion for an address calling on the king to appoint only ministers who would carry it unimpaired, 10 May, the second reading of the Irish bill, 25 May, and against increasing the county representation of Scotland, 1 June. He voted in the majority for going into committee on Baring's bill to exclude insolvent debtors from Parliament, 27 June. He divided with ministers for the Russian-Dutch loan, 26 Jan., 12, 16, 20 July, against the production of information on Portugal, 9 Feb., and for the navy civil departments bill, 6 Apr. He was appointed to the secret committee on the Bank of England's charter, 22 May. He was introduced at the newly enfranchised borough of Kidderminster in an anonymous address, 14 June 1832, as

> a man who has voted in every stage for the bill which has disfranchised the place for which he is a Member, who has been brought up a commercial man and is therefore well suited to represent a commercial town, and whose principles and conduct are approved by that illustrious statesman and patriot, Lord Holland.

Though thought certain to succeed, he was narrowly defeated at the general election in December. He was returned there as a Liberal in 1835, before switching to Poole for the remainder of his parliamentary career.[17] Unlike his father, who never quite threw off his business concerns, Philips devoted himself to those 'liberal pursuits which occupy my mind and never allow me a moment's ennui', becoming a genuine country gentleman in the process.[18] He died in February 1883, when the baronetcy, to which he had succeeded in 1847, became extinct.[19]

[1] Eton Coll. Lib. entry bk. (*ex. inf.* Mrs. P. Hatfield). [2] Warws. RO, MI 247, microfilm of Sir George Philips's mems. i. 1; Warws. RO, Philips mss CR 456/8, G. to G.R. Philips, 20 June 1842. [3] Philips mems. ii. 110-11; *HP Commons, 1790-1820*, iv. 794. [4] Shakespeare Birthplace Trust, Philips mss DR 198/29, 30, 33-36. [5] Ibid. DR 198/31, 32; Philips mems. i. 264-5. [6] Philips mems. i. 352-2; ii. 110-11; *Spectator*, 1 Jan. 1831. [7] Philips mems. i. 20-21. [8] *Session of Parl. 1825*, p. 480. [9] *Manchester Guardian*, 13 Oct. 1821, 15 Oct. 1825, 14 Oct. 1826. [10] *The Times*, 12 June 1822. [11] Philips mss DR 198/11. [12] *Brighton Gazette*, 8 June 1826. [13] Philips mems. i. 412. [14] *Warwick Advertiser*, 14 May 1831. [15] [W. Carpenter] *People's Bk.* (1831), 347. [16] *Warwick Advertiser*, 29 Oct., 12 Nov. 1831. [17] Ibid. 23 June 1832; Kidderminster election address [BL L.23.c.7.(93.)]. [18] D. Brown, 'From "Cotton Lord" to Landed Aristocrat: the Rise of Sir George Philips', *HR*, lxix (1996), 78, 80-81. [19] *The Times*, 27 Feb. 1883.

S.M.F.

PHILLIMORE, Joseph (1775–1855), of Doctors' Commons and Shiplake House, nr. Henley-on-Thames, Oxon.

ST. MAWES	17 Mar. 1817–1826
YARMOUTH I.O.W.	1826–1830

b. 14 Sept. 1775, 1st s. of Rev. Joseph Phillimore of Kensington, Mdx., vic. of Orton-on-the-Hill, Leics., and Mary, da. and coh. of John Machin of Kensington. *educ.* Westminster 1789; Christ Church, Oxf. 1793, BCL 1800, DCL 1804. *m.* 19 Mar. 1807, Elizabeth, da. of Rev. Walter Bagot, rect. of Blithfield and Leigh, Staffs., 7s. (2 *d.v.p.*) 2da. (1 *d.v.p.*). *suc.* fa. 1831. *d.* 24 Jan. 1855.

Adv. Doctors' Commons 1804; commr. for disposal of Prussian ships 1806, Danish ships 1807; judge of Cinque Ports 1809; regius professor of civil law, Oxf. Univ. 1809-*d.*; chan. diocese of Oxford 1809, of Worcester 1834, of Bristol 1842; member, bd. of control Feb. 1822-Feb. 1828; principal commr. French claims (under treaties of 1815 and 1818) 1833; admiralty adv. 1834-*d.*; commissary, St. Paul's 1834; pres. registration commn. 1836; judge, consistory ct. of Gloucester 1846.

Ensign, R. Marylebone vol. inf. 1803, lt. 1805, maj., lt.-col. 1807.

Phillimore, who was described by a fellow Oxford professor in 1826 as 'that everlasting meddler',[1] was an experienced and able civilian, with a reputation for eloquence. He was well connected but relatively impoverished, even though his wife's kinswoman Mrs. Fulke Greville Howard had settled £500 a year on her.[2] One of the Grenvillite parliamentary squad, he was again returned for St. Mawes by its head, the fat and odious 2nd marquess of Buckingham, at the general election of 1820; but he continued to take his political cue from Buckingham's cousin Charles Williams Wynn, Member for Montgomeryshire, a close personal friend since their university days.[3]

He joined Williams Wynn in voting against the Liverpool ministry on the appointment of an additional Scottish baron of exchequer, 15 May 1820. He is not known to have done so on any other occasion that session and, in accordance with Buckingham's wishes, he evidently sided with them for the appointment of a secret committee on Queen Caroline's case, 26 June.[4] He agreed that the duties of an Irish master in chancery were incompatible with membership of the Commons, but thought it only 'just' to give Thomas Ellis, the new Member for Dublin, a choice between the two, 30 June. He supported Williams Wynn's attempts to have Sir William Manners† punished for defying the order to appear before the Grantham election committee (of which Phillimore was a member), 5, 10 July. On the 12th, in the absence of its chairman, he secured by 66-60 the adoption of a resolution outlawing the practice of paying out-voters under colour of indemnification for loss of time, observing that if it was rejected, 'the House would open a door through which corruption would soon make alarming inroads'. His hobby horse was liberalization of the marriage laws. On 4 May he got leave to introduce a bill, essentially the same as the one which he had unsuccessfully promoted in 1819, to amend the Act of 1753 for preventing clandestine marriages. He carried its report by 47-23, 30 June, and saw it to a third reading, 3 July.[5] In a bid to ease its passage through the Lords, he discussed its details and possible amendments with Lord Holland. The 'wily' opposition of lord chancellor Eldon dished it, but Phillimore, heartened by Lord Liverpool's admission that 'considerable reform' was needed, was determined to persevere.[6] In mid-August 1820 he wrote to Buckingham dismissing Lord John Russell's* public appeal to William Wilberforce* to renew his bid to settle the royal quarrel, and observing that

> the queen's partisans mainly rely on the effect they can produce by their ... daily intimidation on the electors, hoping through their instrumentality to make the electors subservient to their plans ... At all events, the government will have received a shock in the control of the House of Commons, which, constituted as they now are, they never can recover. Never ... do I remember so general an idea that there must be a change of ministry.

He was commended by Buckingham for his speech in the House, 18 Sept., when he attacked the queen's supporters Sir Robert Wilson and Hobhouse for introducing 'an *ex-parte* statement' of her claims. During the trial he sent 'daily bulletins' to Williams Wynn in Wales.[7] Informing Buckingham at second hand of the rowdy scenes in the Commons on the prorogation, 23 Nov., he said that ministers, having 'done ... everything they ought not ... are irretrievably gone'; and at the turn of the year Sir Henry Hardinge* reported that Phillimore, who had continued to keep Williams Wynn abreast of developments in the saga, had told him that he 'considered the present ministers as too unpopular to be of any further service, and that he thought an administration of which Lord Grey ought to be the chief, indispensable to the well being of the state under present circumstances'.[8]

On the eve of the 1821 session Phillimore, believing that the king's right to exclude the queen's name from the liturgy should not be challenged by Parliament and that if she was given the rumoured £50,000 a year she ought to drop her insistence on having a palace, sought Buckingham's views on the best line for the Grenvillites:

> Our situation as a party appears to be more critical than it has ever been. The ministers have condemned themselves with great imbecility and indecision, and the opposition distinguished themselves by their violence and intemperance; and under these circumstances we are looked upon as a rallying point between the two extremes ... [Ministers] very much encourage the idea that we are to support them, and to take office at or about Easter; but this is a mere *ruse de guerre*.[9]

Phillimore did not vote for the motions for restoration of Caroline's name to the liturgy, but Buckingham's toady William Fremantle* complained to the marquess that he and Williams Wynn were 'decidedly disposed to the opposition'. Buckingham at first wished his Members to 'stay away' from the debate and division on the Whig censure motion, 6 Feb., reflecting that in any case Williams Wynn would 'follow his own whim and Phillimore will follow him'; but when his uncle Lord Grenville urged him to support ministers, he instructed Phillimore to 'attend and vote against' the motion. A report that Phillimore was to make an excuse of his wife's weakness after giving birth to their fifth son on the 5th proved false, and, like Williams Wynn, he duly voted with government.[10] He voted silently for Catholic relief, 28 Feb. 1821, and took an active part behind the scenes in the subsequent attempts of its leading supporters, including Lord Castlereagh, the foreign secretary, to draft legislation which would have a chance of success.[11] In the House, he played down the significance of a hostile petition from English Catholics, 16 Mar., and spoke in support of the amended oath and the proposed securities, 23, 28, 29 Mar.[12] He was given leave to introduce another Marriage Act amendment bill, 14 Mar., but did not do so.[13] He supported the compensation claims of American loyalists, 21 Mar. He voted against parliamentary reform, 9 May, but for mitigation of the punishment for forgery, 23 May. He was involved in successful legislation to amend the salvage regulations, guiding two bills into law, 2 July (1 and 2 Geo. IV, cc. 75, 76).[14] He endorsed and was a minority teller for Williams Wynn's motion, 31 May, for James Stephen to be heard on behalf of the slaves affected by Maxwell's removal bill, which he condemned the following day as 'unjust and oppressive'. Like Williams Wynn, he voted for inquiry into the administration of justice in Tobago, 6 June, but with ministers for the duke of Cumberland's grant, 18 June. He said that William Smith's proposed reforms of the laws governing Dissenters' marriages were 'calculated to destroy ... [the] reverence and sanctity' of ceremonies, 8 June, and reminded the House that Catholics were obliged to be married by the forms of the Anglican as well as their own church, 27 June.[15] He supported the appointment of Thomas Frankland Lewis* to the Irish revenue inquiry, 15 June. At the request of the dean of Westminster, he denied allegations that the fabric of the Abbey was being wastefully neglected, 2 July 1821.[16]

When serious negotiations began in December 1821 for a junction of the Grenvillites with government, Phillimore told Buckingham that although his dearest object was to replace Sir Christopher Robinson† as king's advocate, he would settle for a seat at the India board under Williams Wynn (having already satisfied himself that this would be compatible with his professional practice), on the understanding that he would be made judge of the admiralty court when the 76-year-old Lord Stowell died or retired. Buckingham, who thought he was jealous of Fremantle, did not urge his pretensions on Liverpool, but Williams Wynn took them up, arguing that his 'abilities and eminence in his profession are such as would render him infinitely more capable [than Robinson] of rendering useful service to the government both in and out of the House', and suggesting that a place at the admiralty would suffice for the moment. Liverpool paid lip service to Phillimore's 'claims for professional advancement', which would 'receive a most favourable consideration', but refused to commit himself on his suitability as king's advocate and could offer no immediate opening for him. Williams Wynn restated his claims and told the premier that he would be 'mortified' if Phillimore, his closest personal and political associate, was excluded from the arrangement.[17] In mid-January 1822 Liverpool reluctantly agreed to offer him a seat at one of the boards 'if he discontinued the practice of his profession', a condition which Williams Wynn, who believed that Liverpool had never forgiven Phillimore for voting for Grenville in the election for the chancellorship of Oxford University soon after being made regius professor, considered 'a mere contrivance to negative it'. He persevered, and Liverpool gave Phillimore a place at the board of control with no restriction on his professional pursuits.[18] Buckingham, who received a dukedom as his part of the bargain, organized his re-election for St. Mawes, though he had considered seeking a treasury seat for him so that he could accommodate his Buckinghamshire neighbour Sir Codrington Carrington*, who might otherwise pose a threat to his county interest. Williams Wynn scotched this notion, warning that in view of Liverpool's personal aversion to Phillimore, such a request might damage his prospects of future professional promotion.[19]

Phillimore, who affected to disbelieve opposition claims that they had reached 'an understanding' with disgruntled Tory backbenchers, voted with his new colleagues against more extensive tax reductions, 21 Feb. 1822.[20] According to Sir James Mackintosh*, he asked Lord Londonderry (Castlereagh) for permission to abstain on a motion of 28 Feb. for reduction of the salt tax, of which he had himself proposed the repeal in 1819. Londonderry 'positively refused' as the government was 'too much pressed', and Phillimore was 'fool enough to tell this and imprudent enough not only to vote but even to speak against' the reduction. Yet Buckingham assured him that he heard 'on every side praises of your speech, and that it had considerable effect, both personally in your favour, and to the advantage of the government'.[21] He was in the ministerial majority against abolition of one of the joint-postmasterships, 13 Mar. When Creevey, aiming at the Grenvillites, proposed inquiry into the board of control, 14 Mar., he accused Phillimore of self-serving inconsistency on the salt tax. Mackintosh thought it was 'very amusing to see Phillimore's friends in spite of themselves convulsed with laughter all around him'. He defended himself as best he could, but Hudson Gurney* considered it a 'wretched' performance.[22] Phillimore was named to the select committee on the Calcutta bankers' claims on the Nabob of Oude, for which he spoke, 4 July. After he had given notice in March of his intention to introduce a new Marriage Act amendment bill, to stipulate that marriages could only be annulled in future by a law suit, he was contacted by Lord Ellenborough who, with Holland and Lord Redesdale, had sketched a proposal which they hoped would get Eldon's support. As he explained when seeking leave to introduce his bill, 27 Mar., in a speech which he had published, Phillimore modified his scheme in deference to the peers' suggestions. He remained in close contact with Holland and Ellenborough during its passage through both Houses. Although Eldon raised difficulties and the bill was in fact comprehensively amended, he had to swallow it for the time being; it became law on 22 July 1822 (3 Geo. IV, c. 75).[23] Phillimore attended a meeting of seven leading supporters of Catholic relief, 16 Apr., when it was decided not to move it that session.[24] While he had misgivings about the wisdom of pressing Canning's bill to relieve Catholic peers, he endorsed it as 'a measure of retributive justice and Christian charity', 10 May, and concluded privately that its passage through the Commons would prove beneficial to the main question.[25] He expressed to Buckingham, who was critical of ministers' tolerance towards their fractious country gentlemen, his pleasure that they were to make the attack on Williams Wynn's brother's appointment as envoy to Switzerland a 'vital question'. This earned him a lecture from the duke, which was approved by Williams Wynn, on 'the absurdity of the distinction of *vital* and *indifferent* points'. After the comfortable government victory, 16 May, Phillimore explained to Buckingham that the moderate tone of their critics had left 'no opening for any of us'.[26] He voted for Mackintosh's plans for reform of the criminal code, 4 June. He was in the ministerial majorities on the lord advocate's dealings with the Scottish press, 25 June, the salt tax, 28 June, the Canada bill, 18 July, and the Irish estimates, 22 July. He supported Wilberforce's call for an address to the king outlawing the introduction of slavery to the Cape, 25 July. He presented a petition against the public house licensing system, 30 July 1822.[27] In the aftermath of Londonderry's suicide the following month Liverpool and Canning, his successor, proposed Williams Wynn's removal from the cabinet to the Speakership, in order to accommodate Canning's associate William Huskisson*. Buckingham threatened to sever his formal link with the ministry by obliging Phillimore and Fremantle to 'make their option at the beginning of the session between their official situations and their seats' unless he himself was given cabinet rank. The difficulty was smoothed over and Williams Wynn, who had no wish to create problems for Phillimore, stayed where he was.[28] Buckingham remained in ill humour and in January 1823, after the failure of an application for a naval promotion, he told Phillimore, whom he had used as his messenger to the admiralty, that he would not attend the opening of Parliament: 'It is early for the government to begin to mark its disinclination towards me, but this is a challenge which I shall always be ready to accept'.[29]

Phillimore was preoccupied with the damage inflicted by the Lords on his marriage bill, as he told Holland, 12 Dec. 1822:

> The general impression of my friends is that I am pledged ... to bring in some amendment ... and that it will be advisable that I should do so lest the ground should be occupied by an enemy to the principle of the bill, who might avail himself of the absurd clamour which has been excited to revert entirely to the ancient state of things. My own idea of the amendments necessary is limited to the abolition of many of the absurd, vexatious and ill-digested regulations introduced with respect to marriages by licence by Lord Redesdale.[30]

He got leave to bring in a measure for that purpose, 5 Feb. 1823. It was given a second reading, 14 Feb., but Phillimore had to set it aside when an amendment bill was sent down from the Lords two weeks later. He did not oppose it, because it repealed the obnoxious 1822 changes, but regretted that it was 'not a permanent and final regulation of the law', 19 Mar. It received royal assent on 26 Mar. (4 Geo. IV, c. 17).[31] Soon afterwards he was in communication with the English Catholic leader William Poynter about a measure to legalize Catholic marriages and baptisms. He presented Poynter's petition for such a bill, 12 June, and on 8 July introduced one, which was printed for consideration.[32] On 10 July he introduced a bill from the Lords to validate marriages solemnized by British army chaplains overseas, which became law on the 18th (4 Geo. IV, c. 91).[33] He was in the ministerial majorities of March 1823 on taxation and the sinking fund. On the 24th he opposed Barry's motion for papers on the prosecution of the Dublin Orange rioters and was a teller for the majority. A few days later Buckingham confided to Fremantle that at the next election he would turn Phillimore out of St. Mawes for Carrington.[34] He voted for the Irish glebe houses grant, 11 Apr., spoke and was a government teller against repeal of the Foreign Enlistment Act, 16 Apr., and was in the ministerial majority against inquiry into the Dublin prosecutions, 22 Apr. He voted against Scottish parliamentary reform, 2 June, and the Scottish juries bill, 20 June. He explained the prize money distribution bill, 17 June.[35] He was a teller for the minority against a proposal to consider the poor bill, 27 June, when he voted for repeal of the usury laws (as he did again, 8 Apr. 1824, 8, 17 Feb. 1825). He was a ministerial teller for the majority against an amendment to the East India mutiny bill, 11 July 1823.

He was not much in evidence in the House in 1824, when he voted against the production of information on Catholic office-holders, 19 Feb., reform of Edinburgh's representation, 26 Feb., and the prohibition of flogging, 5 Mar. That month Buckingham 'particularly' requested him to attend to oppose Stuart Wortley's bill to reform the game laws, assuming that 'your habits and pursuits have probably not led you to form a decided opinion upon it'. When Phillimore disclosed that he approved of the bill, Buckingham grumbled that 'I was in hopes to have had the assistance of my friends, whom I do not trouble often ... and still venture to hope that I shall not be deprived of yours'. Phillimore stood his ground. One of his sons wrote 50 years later that Buckingham 'could not forgive' him for his 'conscientious vote' on the bill.[36] On 13 Apr. he obtained leave for a new measure to liberalize the regulations affecting English Catholic baptisms, marriages and funerals, but it got no further than its second reading.[37] He divided with his colleagues in defence of the prosecution of the Methodist missionary John Smith in Demerara, 11 June, and for the Irish insurrection bill, 14 June 1824. Phillimore voted for the bill to suppress the Catholic Association, 25 Feb., and for Catholic relief, 1 Mar. 1825. He opposed and was a teller for the majority against Hume's motion for a return of Anglican clergymen on English borough corporations, 17 Mar., as he was for the majority against a call for information on the Bengal army, 24 Mar. He voted for the Catholic relief bill, 21 Apr., 10 May, when he was a teller for the majority, and said that the Irish franchise bill was 'calculated to do away a great abuse and to confer a lasting benefit on Ireland', 22 Apr. He was reported to be in 'the greatest dismay' over Buckingham's brother Lord Nugent's* assertion that the duke disapproved of the cabinet's decision to leave the relief bill to its fate in the Lords.[38] He dismissed a petition complaining of oppression by Irish tithe collectors, 9 May, when he was named to the select committee on James Silk Buckingham's grievances.[39] On the Indian judges bill, 13 May, he advised retention of the crown's power of dismissal. He divided for the duke of Cumberland's grant, 30 May, 2, 6, 10 June. He moved the rejection of the St. Olave tithes bill, 'a direct spoliation of private property', and was a teller for the minority, 6 June. The following day he was one for the majority against the production of information on an alleged job in Calcutta, and on 9 June he acted in the same capacity for the majority in favour of the naval improvement bill. He supported a clause of the universities police bill providing for the summary imprisonment of prostitutes, 20 June.[40] He voted for the spring guns bill, 21 June 1825. That day he replied with platitudinous civility to Buckingham's letter informing him that he would not be returned for St. Mawes at the next general election. In September Williams Wynn, with whom Buckingham had also broken off political relations, assured Phillimore that when a decision on the timing of the dissolution was made he would urge his claims for a seat on Liverpool, but reminded him that even treasury seats did not come entirely free of charge.[41] In March 1826 Lady Williams Wynn remarked that the exclusion of 'Philly' from Buckingham's 'parliamentary squad' would be 'a most serious misfortune to him'; and two months later the duke told Fremantle that he was 'Wynn's, not mine'.[42] Phillimore voted with his colleagues in defence of the Jamaican slave trials, 2 Mar., and the salary of the president of the board of trade, 10 Apr., and against Edinburgh reform, 13 Apr., and a resolution condemning electoral bribery, 26 May. He praised the education given to East India Company writers at Haileybury, 16 Mar. He acquiesced in the introduction of Sykes's bill to allow district freeholders to vote in county elections, but declined to pledge support, 26 Apr. He repudiated Silk Buckingham's charges against the Indian government, arguing that unrestrained freedom of the press would undermine British rule, 9 May, and was a teller for the minority against inquiry. He complained of Lord John Russell's tactics on this issue, 11 May 1826. At the general election the following month he was returned for Yarmouth on the Holmes interest, presumably under the auspices of the treasury. He still coveted Stowell's judgeship, but Williams Wynn advised him in August 1826 that 'his resignation seems an event as distant as at any time during the last five years'.[43]

Phillimore voted for Catholic relief, 6 Mar. 1827. He agreed to production of the papers on Doctors' Commons moved for by Hume, 14 Mar., but repudiated his criticisms. He divided for the duke of Clarence's annuity, 16 Mar., and was a teller for the majority against the furnishing of information on the mutiny at Barrackpoor, 22 Mar. He voted for the spring guns bill, 23 Mar. He was retained in his office by Canning, though one observer noted that it might soon provide 'a sop for some more valuable adherent'.[44] He voted with government against the disfranchisement of Penryn, 28 May, and for the grant for Canadian canals, 12 June. He defended the Coventry election committee, whose report had led to the bill to curb corporation interference in elections, 18 June. The following day he supported Smith's Dissenters' marriages bill. In the negotiations to settle Goderich's ministry after Canning's death he was promised the first available vacancy in 'one of the great civil law offices', so that Mackintosh could be given his place at the board of control; but when the duke of Wellington formed his ministry in January 1828 he discarded Williams Wynn and Phillimore, to the delight of the

Whigs.[45] At a cabinet dinner Phillimore was ranked third in 'fitness' for the post of king's advocate behind Herbert Jenner, who was duly appointed (Stowell having retired from the bench to permit Robinson's removal to the admiralty court) and the Whig Stephen Lushington, Member for Tregony. Fremantle told Buckingham that the 'unlucky' Phillimore had been 'ruined' by this turn of events.[46]

On 22 and 27 Feb. 1828 he obtained returns of information to underpin his planned motion for leave to introduce a bill to regulate the ecclesiastical jurisdiction of county courts, but they were so long in forthcoming that he had to give up the plan for that session. Supporting Brougham's motion for inquiry into the common law, 29 Feb., he suggested possible changes to ecclesiastical jurisdiction; and on 25 Apr. he argued that clergymen were not qualified to preside in those courts. He voted for repeal of the Test Acts, 26 Feb., and on the 28th said that it would accelerate the accomplishment of Catholic relief, for which he voted, 12 May. He voted against the extension of the franchise at East Retford to the hundred of Bassetlaw, 21 Mar., and was in the minority in favour of the bill to transfer its seats to Birmingham, 27 June. On the Penryn disfranchisement bill, 24 Mar., he saw no reason to restrict polls there to two days. He handled the bill from the Lords to indemnify witnesses before their Penryn inquiry, 2, 3 Apr., when he supported Williams Wynn's proposed reforms of the machinery for dealing with controverted elections. He was added to the select committee on borough polls, 15 Apr. He supported the claims on the East India Company of individuals injured by the malpractice of the registrar of Madras, 18 Apr. As he drifted into opposition, he voted in the minority of 58 for a lower pivot price for corn imports, 22 Apr. In May and July he introduced and saw through bills to cater for the incapacity of the terminally ill Liverpool as lord warden of the Cinque Ports (9 Geo. IV, cc. 37, 71). He suggested that the Irish admiralty jurisdiction could be incorporated into the English, 20 May. He supported the grant to Canning's family, 22 May. He offered amendments to the rights of executors bill, but had reservations about extending it to Scotland, 4 June. He conceded that the Marylebone vestry required reform, but thought that Sir Thomas Baring's bill would only confuse matters, 6 June. When Hume moved for information on the prerogative court, 4 June, Phillimore insisted that allegations of 'defects and delays of justice' were 'utterly unfounded'. However, on the 16th he condemned the bill allowing the archbishop of Canterbury, the Speaker's father, to insert a third life into the patent appointing his registrar as one which sought to 'perpetuate sinecures', and was a teller, with Hume, for the minority against the third reading. He got leave for a bill to regulate the office and give the efficient officials 'ample remuneration', 25 June, but Hume objected to it, 10 July, when it foundered. On 17 July, replying to the strictures of Hume and Harvey on the prerogative court, Phillimore said that in none was 'justice more diligently, more expeditiously, or less expensively administered'. Next day he assured Hume that reports of inflated fees for its officials were exaggerated. He voted for inquiry into the Irish church, 24 June. His attack on British support for Dom Miguel in Portugal led to a clash with Peel, 30 June. That day he spoke and voted against the additional churches bill, and he presented a hostile petition from St. Pancras, 3 July. He supported and was a teller for the minority for inquiry into Baron de Bode's claims, 1 July. He gave qualified support to the benefices resignation bill, 4 July. He voted against government on the corporate funds bill, 10 July, and the silk duties, 14 July 1828.

As he told his second surviving son, Robert Joseph, an Oxford undergraduate, he regarded the ministerial decision to concede Catholic emancipation as 'a great triumph to us who have for so many years struggled for this great measure'.[47] In the House, 23 Feb. 1829, he denied that it would infringe the Protestant constitution. After voting for Peel in the Oxford University by-election, he disputed claims, based on a petition presented by Buckingham's son Lord Chandos, that undergraduate opinion was hostile to emancipation, 2 Mar. He encouraged Robert to help get up a counter-petition, which he wished to present himself, but advised him to desist when the authorities intervened to quash it. He voted for emancipation, which he felt was granted 'in the true spirit of conciliation', 6 Mar. He called for extra protection for the Church of Scotland, 23 Mar., but Peel said it was not necessary. He voted silently for the third reading of the relief bill, 30 Mar., having failed to find a 'good opportunity' of speaking in an inattentive House. He thought it would be 'unjust' and 'pitiful' to exclude Daniel O'Connell for refusing to swear the oath of supremacy and voted accordingly, 18 May.[48] He was appointed to the select committees on the Irish admiralty court, 7 Apr., and claims on the Madras registrar, 5 May, when he voted for the transfer of East Retford's seats to Birmingham. The following day he welcomed a proposed bill to oblige Members appointed to Indian posts to vacate their seats, as he did Sir John Nicholl's plan to reform the ecclesiastical courts, 12 May, when he explained that his own scheme would have to be deferred because the information he had requested was still not to hand. He supported the third reading of Nicholl's 'useful' measure, 5 June. He announced on the 3rd that he would next session seek to regulate the ecclesiastical jurisdiction of county courts. He approved ministers' intention to deal with outstanding claims on the French government and urged special attention to de Bode's, 28 May. He voted for a reduction of the hemp duties, 1 June. On 5 June 1829 he praised Williams Wynn's improvement of the administration of justice in India.

Phillimore attended the debate on the address, 4 Feb. 1830, and took the view, which Williams Wynn endorsed, that 'the division [was] most alarming to government'. Three weeks later he doubted to his son 'whether they will survive the session'.[49] He voted for the transfer of East Retford's seats to Birmingham, 11 Feb. and 5 Mar., when, invoking the spirits of Chatham, Pitt and Fox, he said that refusal to enfranchise such large towns would 'amount to a species of infatuation'. (He did not, however, vote for Russell's motion to enfranchise Birmingham, Leeds and Manchester, 23 Feb.) He voted against government on Portugal, 10 Mar., the admiralty estimates, 22 Mar., taxation, 25 Mar., and the Bathurst and Dundas pensions, 26 Mar. He regretted ministers' 'vague and unsatisfactory' response to his question about de Bode's claims, 5 Apr., when he voted for Jewish emancipation, as he did again, 17 May. He spoke and voted in the minority of 16 against Ellenborough's divorce bill, 6 Apr. On the 28th he expressed concern over the effect of increased stamp duties on law suitors, before speaking at length against government on the 'act of insult and outrage' committed against Portugal at Terceira. He was a teller for the opposition minority which, he told his son, did not reflect their 'triumphant debate'.[50] He voted with them on the treasury estimates, 10 May, privy councillors' emoluments, 14 May, Irish first fruits, 18 May, the government of Canada, 25 May, the commercial state of Ceylon, 27 May, and the grants for diplomatic services, 7, 11 June, and for Prince Edward Island, 14 June. He paired for abolition of the death penalty for forgery, 24 May, voted for it, 7 June, and opposed a Lords' amendment to the bill, 20 July. On 3 June he proposed inquiry into the divorce laws with the aim of facilitating divorce on the ground of adultery by 'legal process in courts of competent jurisdiction'; his motion was defeated by 100-45. He secured returns of information on divorce cases, 15, 19 June. He reported at this time that 'government has sunk into such insignificance in the House of Commons some persons think Lord Grey will be prime minister'.[51] He condemned the Additional Churches Act for making the law 'a dead letter', 1 July, when he postponed 'indefinitely' his motion for reform of the ecclesiastical courts, which was now in the remit of the judicial commissioners. He spoke and voted against Hume's proposal to reduce judges' salaries, 7 July. On 9 July 1830 he divided against any increase in recognizances in libel cases.

Since the death of George IV Phillimore had been hunting for a seat at the impending general election. He received, he informed his son, 'several offers', but they were 'all too expensive or too hazardous'. One such was from Norwich, where he was invited to stand 'upon the Dissenting interest'; but Holland could not assist him, and in any case he shied at the estimated cost of £5,000, 'a sum which I cannot command and which (hampered as I am by a numerous family) I should not be justified in spending on such an object'. Arundel was too 'expensive and uncertain', an approach to Lord Grosvenor about Shaftesbury proved unavailing and he dismissed suggestions that he should apply to the duke of Devonshire, Lord Fitzwilliam or Lord Anglesey, whom he did not know, merely on the strength of his recent voting record. He told Holland in mid-July that he had

> little ... expectation of being returned ... I regret this exceedingly. There are several measures in progress and others likely to be introduced in which I take a deep interest. I have of late felt myself much less embarrassed in delivering my sentiments in the House than I used to be, and had just begun to think that my experience and information, such as they are, might not be without their use to those with whom I might act during the remainder of the present Parliament.[52]

In the last week of July he went (with his wife) on a fool's errand to Stafford, where he found the ground occupied and the likely costs prohibitive. Williams Wynn later told him that this excursion had deterred his friends on the circuit from alerting him to a possible opening for £500 at Worcester.[53] He conceived hopes of finding accommodation at Devonshire's borough of Knaresborough or at Bletchingley on the interest of William Russell*; but Williams Wynn thought they were unrealistic, and in early August Phillimore told his son that it was 'too late now to think of any borough till the meeting of Parliament, when it is just possible that some arrangement may be made'.[54] He made an approach to Tennyson, one of the Members for Bletchingley, in the hope of securing his nephew Russell's interest, but the change of ministry in November 1830 gave him further cause to lament his lack of a seat. He lost no time in telling Holland, a member of the new Grey ministry, of his pretensions to the post of king's advocate, citing seniority in his profession, his '*virtual*' possession of the place when the Goderich administration collapsed and the backing of the Huskissonite ministers Lord Palmerston* and Charles Grant*. Holland discouraged him, pointing out that if it was decided to remove Jenner, Lushington would have first claim on the government.[55] A suggestion by lord chancellor Brougham that there was a chance of a free return for Beverley came to nothing, and there was another disappointment over an unspecified borough in early December 1830.[56]

Phillimore, who seems to have been rather alarmed by the reform bill, failed to find an opening at the general election of 1831.[57] On 31 July his aged clergyman father died virtually penniless: the residue of personal estate sworn under £600 was less than £20.[58] Phillimore added *Reports of Cases in the Arches and Prerogative Courts of Canterbury, 1752-8* (1832-3) to his *Reports of Cases in the Ecclesiastical Courts, 1809-23* (1818-27). At the dissolution in late 1832 he received an invitation from 'electors ... of every shade and variety of party' to stand for Marylebone, where the attorney-general William Horne* was one of the candidates. He consulted Williams Wynn, who doubted

> whether a seat ... for a very large and extensive constituency and which consequently could not be vacated for office without much expense and hazard could be really desirable to you at the present moment ... I do not understand your scruples about [the Conservative William] Holmes's* assistance. In the present situation of politics it would be in vain to hope for success in such a place ... without committing yourself to a decided line with one party or the other. Holmes is the parliamentary agent and whipper-in on one side ... and if you wished to have Conservative support you must apply to the agent of that party. Still ... in the present unsettled state of politics you are much better situated and have a greater probability of office by remaining out of Parliament than by coming in ... You are I think personally much indisposed to Peel and the other heads of the Conservative party, while your principles would not allow you to support the present administration. Are you not then better where you are, than to be put under the daily necessity of steering between them and probably pleasing neither party?

Phillimore declined to involve himself, on the pretext, as he told Brougham, that his intervention would lead to Horne's defeat.[59] He saw the possibility of a seat for Oxford in March 1833, but it escaped him.[60] On Robinson's death that month he applied for the admiralty judgeship, worth £2,300 a year, and was furious when, despite having the support of Brougham and Holland, he was passed over for the decrepit Nicholl.[61] He did at least secure a place on the French claims commission. He renewed his bid to become king's advocate in late September 1834, but was 'astonished' when, after he had been led to believe that the place was his, John Dodson* was preferred to him; he rightly suspected Brougham of 'treachery'. After some acrimonious correspondence he was made admiralty advocate, and he held the post, which carried a nominal salary of £13 6*s*. 8*d*., until his death.[62] Within a month he applied to Wellington, in temporary charge of affairs pending Peel's arrival from Italy to form his first ministry, to have himself installed as king's advocate, and hinted that he would like a treasury seat. He got a dusty answer from Peel.[63] He remained short of money, and in 1837, still moaning that Brougham and Nicholl had cheated him out of the office of king's advocate, he plagued Holland again with his pretensions to the admiralty judgeship, which were never fulfilled.[64] He did, however, reach the bench of a minor ecclesiastical court in 1846.

He was devastated by the accidental death by drowning of his youngest son Richard, an Oxford undergraduate, in June 1843. Dr. Bliss of St. John's noted that he had been 'a youth of great promise, with all the abilities but more of steadiness than the Phillimores generally possessed'.[65] Phillimore, who failed in his bid to be made a privy councillor in 1853, died at his home at Shiplake in January 1855.[66] In his will, dated 22 Nov. 1852, he stipulated that he was not to be buried 'in a coffin cased in lead or of any other material which may arrest the progress of natural dissolution'. He left a London leasehold house at 62 Gower Street to his wife, with reversion to his only surviving daughter Mary. He divided £4,000 charged on the Shiplake estate by his marriage settlement between her and four of his five sons. Shiplake went to his wife for life, with reversion to his eldest son John George Phillimore (1808-65), a jurist and Liberal Member for Leominster, 1852-7. By a codicil of 12 Aug. 1853 he left ground rents and buildings at Kensington to his youngest surviving son Augustus (1822-97), a naval officer.[67] He was succeeded as admiralty advocate by Robert Joseph (1810-85), Liberal Member for Tavistock, 1853-7, who attained the honours which had eluded him, as queen's advocate (1862), judge of the admiralty court and a privy councillor (1867) and temporary judge advocate (1871), and was created a baronet in 1881.[68]

[1] Add. 40342, f. 305. [2] *Williams Wynn Corresp*. 229. [3] NLW, Coedymaen mss bdle. 29, Williams Wynn to Phillimore, 10 Apr. 1820. [4] Christ Church, Oxf. Phillimore mss, Buckingham to Phillimore, 21 June 1820. [5] *The Times*, 2, 5 May 1820; *CJ*, lxxv. 147, 159, 180, 207, 270, 379, 389. [6] Add. 51813, Phillimore to Holland, 11, 21 July, 2 Sept. 1820; *LJ*, liii. 251, 299, 320, 329; Buckingham, *Mems.*

Geo. IV, i. 56. [7] Buckingham, i. 66; Phillimore mss, Buckingham to Phillimore, 20 Sept.; Coedymaen mss bdle. 29, Williams Wynn to Phillimore [7, 12, 18 Oct., 2 Nov.] 1820. [8] Buckingham, i. 79-80; Coedymaen mss bdle. 29, Williams Wynn to Phillimore, 19, 21, 30 Dec.; Phillimore mss, Buckingham to Phillimore, 27 Nov. 1820; Cent. Kent. Stud. Camden mss U840 C530/6. [9] Buckingham, i. 109-11; Phillimore mss, Buckingham to Phillimore, 4, 17 Jan. 1821. [10] Buckingham, i. 115; Bucks. RO, Fremantle mss D/FR/46/11/45; 46/12/35, 36; Phillimore mss, Buckingham to Phillimore, 3, 8 Feb. 1821. [11] Phillimore mss, Buckingham to Phillimore, 11, 26, 30 Mar. 1821; Buckingham, i. 128-30, 141-2, 145-6. [12] *The Times*, 17, 30 Mar. 1821. [13] Ibid. 15 Mar. 1821; *CJ*, lxxvi. 166. [14] *CJ*, lxxvi. 347, 351-2, 371, 468, 489-90, 492; *The Times*, 23, 26 June 1821. [15] *The Times*, 9, 28 June 1821. [16] Ibid. 3 July 1821. [17] Buckingham, i. 253-5; Fremantle mss 46/12/24; Phillimore mss, Williams Wynn to Phillimore [17 Dec.], to Buckingham, 23 Dec. 1821; Add. 38290, ff. 176, 210, 222. [18] Buckingham, i. 273-5; Coedymaen mss 615, 618. [19] Phillimore mss, Buckingham to Phillimore, 27 Jan. 1822; Buckingham, i. 279, 281; *Hobhouse Diary*, 85. [20] Buckingham, i. 280-1. [21] Add. 52445, f. 64; Phillimore mss, Buckingham to Phillimore, 3 Mar. 1822. [22] Add. 52445, f. 66; Gurney diary, 14 Mar. 1822. [23] *CJ*, lxxvii. 144, 175, 290, 399-402, 446; *The Times*, 4 Apr., 21, 22 May, 13 July, 1 Aug.; Phillimore mss, Ellenborough to Phillimore, 16, 17 Mar., 28, 31 May, 16 June; Add. 51813, Phillimore to Holland, 8 Apr. 1822; Buckingham, i. 319, 343. [24] Fremantle mss 46/10/56. [25] Buckingham, i. 314, 319-20, 323, 328. [26] Buckingham, i. 324, 326, 327; Phillimore mss, Buckingham to Phillimore [12 May 1822]. [27] *The Times*, 31 July 1822. [28] BL, Fortescue mss, Buckingham to Grenville, 3 Oct. 1822; Fremantle mss 46/12/72; Add. 38743, f. 236. [29] Phillimore mss, Buckingham to Phillimore, 10 Dec. 1822, 3, 22, 29 Jan. 1823. [30] Add. 51813. [31] *CJ*, lxxviii. 7, 19, 24, 81, 116, 157, 165, 175, 376-7; *The Times*, 11, 15, 18 Feb., 18 Mar.; Phillimore mss, Mackintosh to Phillimore, 13 Mar. 1823. [32] *Colchester Diary*, iii. 282; *The Times*, 4, 9 July 1823; *CJ*, lxxviii. 451, 465. [33] *The Times*, 11 July 1823; *CJ*, lxxviii. 474, 479. [34] Fremantle mss 51/5/17. [35] *The Times*, 18 June 1823. [36] Phillimore mss, Buckingham to Phillimore, 16, 17 Mar. 1824, 19 June 1825. [37] *The Times*, 16 Apr. 1824; *CJ*, lxxix. 292, 303, 367, 456. [38] Buckingham, ii. 265. [39] *The Times*, 10 May 1825. [40] Ibid. 21 June 1825. [41] Phillimore mss, Buckingham to Phillimore, 19 June, reply, 21 June, Williams Wynn to Phillimore, 18 Sept. 1825; Fremantle mss 46/11/118; 46/12/56. [42] *Williams Wynn Corresp*. 347; Fremantle mss 46/12/90. [43] Phillimore mss, Arbuthnot to Phillimore, 6 June, Williams Wynn to same, 6 Aug. 1826. [44] *Canning's Ministry*, 269. [45] Add. 38750, f. 180; 51690, Lansdowne to Lady Holland, 16 Sept.; Bucks. RO, Buckinghamshire mss, Lansdowne to Goderich, 2 Sept., replies, 6, 13 Sept.; Fremantle mss 138/21/2/17; Aberdeen Univ. Lib. Arbuthnot mss, Hardinge to Mrs. Arbuthnot, 7 Nov. 1827; *Creevey Pprs*. ii. 140; Grey mss, Ellice to Grey [30 Jan. 1828]. [46] Phillimore mss, Fremantle to Phillimore, 22, 29 Jan. 1828; Wellington mss WP1/915/73; 916/2; 920/3; *Ellenborough Diary*, i. 14; Buckingham, ii. 370. [47] Phillimore mss, J. to R.J. Phillimore, 6 Feb. 1829. [48] Ibid. same to same, 23 Feb., 3, 5, 6, 31 Mar., 16 May 1829. [49] Coedymaen mss bdle. 29, Williams Wynn to Phillimore, 6 Feb.; Phillimore mss, J. to R.J. Phillimore, 22 Feb. 1830. [50] Phillimore mss, J. to R.J. Phillimore, 29 Apr. 1830. [51] Ibid. same to same, 9 June 1830. [52] Add. 51813, Phillimore to Holland, 14 July; Phillimore mss, Holland to Phillimore, 12 July, J. to R.J. Phillimore, 14 July 1830. [53] Phillimore mss, Mrs. E. to R.J. Phillimore, 26, 27 July, Williams Wynn to Phillimore, 1 Sept. 1830. [54] Ibid. Williams Wynn to Phillimore [1 Aug.], 9 Aug., J. to R.J. Phillimore, 3 Aug. 1830. [55] Ibid. J. to R.J. Phillimore, 17 Nov., Holland to Phillimore [19, 23 Nov.]; Add. 51813, Phillimore to Holland, 18, 20 Nov. 1830. [56] Add. 51813, Phillimore to Holland [?30 Nov.]; Phillimore mss, J. to R.J. Phillimore, 7 Dec. 1830. [57] Phillimore mss, J. to R.J. Phillimore, 15 Mar.; Add. 51813, Phillimore to Holland, 5 May 1831. [58] *Gent. Mag.* (1831), ii. 186; PROB 11/1789/480; IR26/1268/410. [59] Coedymaen mss bdle. 29, Williams Wynn to Phillimore, 28 Nov.; Brougham mss, Phillimore to Brougham, 6 Dec. 1832. [60] Add. 34571, f. 211. [61] Add. 51813, Phillimore to Holland, 24 Apr., 23 May; Brougham mss, same to Brougham, 27 May 1833. [62] Add. 51813, Phillimore to Holland, 28, 30 Sept., 2, 9, 13, 16 Oct.; Brougham mss, same to Brougham, 30 Sept. 1834. [63] Add. 40309, ff. 282, 284, 286; *Wellington Pol. Corresp.* ii. 516, 517, 538. [64] Add. 51813, Phillimore to Holland, 11, 29 Oct. 1837. [65] Add. 34575, f. 79. [66] Add. 43067, f. 29; *Gent. Mag.* (1855) i. 319-20. [67] PROB 11/2207/152; IR26/2041/84; W.P.W. Phillimore, *Genealogy of Fam. of Phillimore*, 231. [68] *Oxford DNB*.

D.R.F.

PHILLIPPS *see* MARCH PHILLIPPS

PHILLIPPS *see* MARCH PHILLIPPS

PHILLPOTTS, John (1775–1849), of Bear Land, Gloucester.

GLOUCESTER	1830–1831
GLOUCESTER	1832–1834
GLOUCESTER	1837–1847

b. July 1775, 1st s. of John Phillpotts of Langaren, Herefs. and Sibella, da. and h. of Samuel Codrington Glover of Bridgwater, Som. *educ.* Gloucester Coll. sch.; called, I. Temple 1822. *m.* 19 Sept. 1797, Sarah, da. of Thomas Chandler of Ashcroft House, Glos., 1 surv. s. *suc.* fa. 1814. *d.* 29 June 1849.

Mayor, Gloucester 1819-20.

Phillpotts's father sold his family estate in Herefordshire and bought a pottery and brick factory at Bridgwater, but moved in 1782 to Gloucester, where he became the landlord of the *Bell* Inn, the headquarters of the Tory True Blue Club, and land agent to the dean and chapter. His younger brother Henry (1778-1869) was the high church bishop of Exeter, 1831-69.[1] He practised as an attorney in Gloucester, serving as registrar to the dean and chapter, before being called belatedly to the bar in 1822, after which he went the Oxford circuit and Gloucester sessions. He had acted as agent for the Tory 6th duke of Beaufort in the Gloucestershire and Monmouthshire elections of 1812, but in 1816 he performed the same role for the victorious Whig candidate for Gloucester, Edward Webb, and two years later for Webb and Frederick Berkeley*.[2] He served as mayor of Gloucester and became an increasingly prominent figure in the city, helping to complete the vitally important Gloucester-Berkeley canal project, promoting the building of Worcester Street and a new cattle market and organizing the rescue of the Turner and Morris bank in the winter of 1825-6.[3] His enhanced local status encouraged his political ambitions, and there was pressure on him to offer for the city at the general election of 1826. He declined, but appeared on the hustings where he angrily repudiated accusations of disloyalty levelled against him by Webb's supporters and made it clear that he felt free to stand in future.[4] In evidence before the select committee on borough polls, 15 May 1827, he made several practical suggestions to help shorten the duration of contests.[5] At the general election of 1830 he offered for Gloucester, championing the cause of 'independence' and claiming that as a local man he could better represent the city's interests. His politics were ambiguous, for he could not see 'where the line of distinction' between Whig and Tory was to be drawn, but he confirmed his opposition to the game laws and support for retrenchment and tax cuts. He was returned in second place behind Webb, defeating the Tory sitting Member Cooper, and at a subsequent dinner he adopted a more radical tone, declaring that 'my cause shall be the cause of the *people*' and 'the aristocracy have too great an ascendancy', and welcoming the recent events in France.[6]

In the Wellington ministry's list of September 1830 Phillpotts was placed among the 'good doubtfuls', with the additional note that 'surely he will be a friend', which was presumably based on the impending announcement of his brother's appointment to Exeter.[7] Henry Brougham*, on the other hand, counted him as a gain for the Whigs. His vote with ministers in the crucial civil list division, 15 Nov., provoked outrage in Gloucester, where effigies of him were burned in the streets and accusations made that he had been influenced by his brother's appointment.[8] It is more likely that he was anxious not to offend ministers at a time when controversy raged over his brother's retention of the living of Stanhope. He defended Henry's position in the House, 17, 22 Nov., but ascertained from Lord Grey's new government that they would not permit such an act of pluralism, 15 Dec.; an alternative arrangement was later made.[9] He complained that the membership of the select committee on the reduction of salaries consisted of former and current ministers and others hostile to economy, 10 Dec. 1830. He presented Holderness and Gloucester petitions for tax cuts, 4, 9 Feb. 1831. He moved for the separation of pensions from the civil list, 25 Mar., claiming that he was trying to assist ministers in overcoming the vested interests of the aristocracy, 'the influential vampires of the state', which was essential at a time when the people were 'groaning under the weight of excessive taxation'. He explained that his earlier vote on the civil list had been determined by his wish to have the subject considered by a committee of the whole House rather than by a select committee. The motion was withdrawn for procedural reasons. He presented a Gloucester petition for reform and the ballot, 26 Feb., expressed his 'entire concurrence' in Gloucester corporation's reform petition the same day, and presented petitions from Gloucester and elsewhere in favour of the government's bill, 9, 28 Mar., 18 Apr. He voted for the second reading, 22 Mar., and against Gascoyne's wrecking amendment, 19 Apr. 1831. At the ensuing dissolution he announced that he would not stand again for Gloucester, where continuing anger over his civil list vote made his return doubtful, but his friends persuaded him to offer on the understanding that he would be put to no expense. He denounced the 'coalition' entered into by Webb and Berkeley 'for the purpose of crushing and putting him down', defended his parliamentary record and 'undeviating attention' to the interests of the city, claiming that 'he had never received a letter which was not answered by return of post', affirmed his support for the reform bill and 'urged the necessity of Gloucester being represented by two citizens'. He came bottom of the poll by a very large margin.[10]

Phillpotts was conspicuous at Gloucester reform meetings in 1832, and at the general election that year he was returned in second place behind Berkeley but ahead of a Conservative.[11] He held the seat, with one interruption, until his retirement in 1847, sustaining a 'reputation as a consistent politician of a somewhat ultra school', who favoured 'extension of the franchise [and] vote by ballot' and was 'one of the earliest advocates for ... repeal of the corn laws'. According to an obituarist, he was 'at all times bland, courteous and laboriously attentive to his duties' and 'had the art of inspiring his ... supporters with a very large amount of personal regard'.[12] He died in June 1849 and left his entire estate, including land at Porthgwidden, Cornwall, to his only child, the Rev. Thomas Phillpotts (1807-90), vicar of St. Feock, Cornwall.[13] His wife died shortly after him, but an election verse of 1830 claimed that he had turned her out of his house 'with a pair of black eyes', and local directories confirm that they had lived at separate addresses.[14]

[1] *Oxford DNB*; R. Shutte, *Life of Dr. Phillpotts*, i. 4-5. Phillpotts senior left all his property to his wife, whose will has not been found; his personalty was sworn under £3,500 (PROB 11/1557/369; IR26/1620/452). [2] *Gent. Mag.* (1849), ii. 205; *Gloucester Jnl.* 7 July 1849; Badminton mss Fm M 3/6/1; G. Goodman, 'Pre-Reform Elections in Gloucester City, 1789-1831', *Bristol and Glos. Arch. Soc. Trans.* lxxxiv. (1965), 148-50, 154-5. [3] *VCH Glos.* iv. 136-7, 153; *Gloucester Jnl.* 26 Dec. 1825, 9 Jan. 1826; Glos. RO, Counsel mss D6330, f. 21. [4] *Gloucester Jnl.* 29 May, 12 June 1826. [5] *PP* (1826-7), iv. 1128-32. [6] *Gloucester Jnl.* 3, 10, 31 July, 14 Aug. 1830. [7] Henry Phillpotts accepted the offer of a bishopric in July, which was confirmed as Exeter in Sept. (Wellington mss WP1/1127/5; 1140/27). [8] *Gloucester Jnl.* 20, 27 Nov., 14 Dec. 1830. [9] Shutte, i. 282-95. [10] *Gloucester Jnl.* 30 Apr., 7 May 1831. [11] Ibid. 21 Jan., 19 May, 14 July, 1, 15 Dec. 1832. [12] Ibid. 7 July 1849. [13] PROB 11/2096/538; IR26/1846/398. [14] Gloucester Pub. Lib. Glos. Coll. NF 10.16 (5).

T.A.J.

PHIPPS, Constantine Henry, Visct. Normanby (1797–1863), of 19 Grosvenor Street, Mdx.

SCARBOROUGH	1818–18 May 1820
HIGHAM FERRERS	11 Feb. 1822–1826
MALTON	1826–1830

b. 15 May 1797, 1st s. of Henry Phipps†, 1st earl of Mulgrave, and Martha Sophia, da. of Christopher Thompson Maling of West Herrington, co. Dur. *educ.* Harrow 1811-13; Trinity Coll. Camb. 1814. *m.* 12 Aug. 1818, Maria, da. of Sir Thomas Henry Liddell†, 6th bt., of Ravensworth Castle, co. Dur., 1s. *suc.* fa. as 2nd earl of Mulgrave 7 Apr. 1831; GCH 1832; *cr.* mq. of Normanby 25 June 1838; GCB 10 Dec. 1847; KG 19 Feb. 1851. *d.* 28 July 1863.

PC 30 May 1832; gov. Jamaica 1832-4; ld. privy seal July-Dec. 1834; ld. lt. [I] Apr. 1835-Apr. 1839; sec. of state for war and colonies Feb.-Aug. 1839, for home affairs Aug. 1839-Sept. 1841.

Ambassador to France 1846-52, to Tuscany 1854-8.

Capt. 1 batt. Hull militia 1816.

Normanby was in Florence, his favourite city and regular retreat, when Parliament was dissolved in 1820. Despite his recent defection to the Whigs (he had joined Brooks's Club, 3 Dec. 1819), he was returned for Scarborough in his absence on his Tory father's interest.[1] However, Lord Mulgrave had second thoughts and turned him out in May 1820 to make room for his own brother. This was highly inconvenient both to Normanby and the Whigs, for whom he was a prestigious recruit. When a vacancy arose at St. Ives in May 1821 he hoped to come in there, but Sir Christopher Hawkins* exerted his considerable influence for his own benefit and Normanby gave up the contest without going to a poll. He admitted to the duke of Devonshire that it was 'a cruel disappointment to me in the great object of my ambition', but added that 'I mean to put the best face I can upon it'. In another letter to Devonshire, 9 Aug., he remarked that he would 'not be at all surprised' if the death of Queen Caroline 'turned out the ministers before long, as it removes the only remaining awkwardness between the king and their opponents'.[2] It was reported in September 1821 that Lord Grosvenor intended to offer him one of the vacant seats for Shaftesbury, but nothing came of this. That December he addressed the annual meeting of the York Whig Club.[3] In January 1822, with William Plumer, Member for Higham Ferrers, at death's door, Henry Brougham* wrote to Lord Duncannon* advocating the return of 'the excellent Normanby' in his place, noting that 'you know he can't in all probability want it above a session'. Duncannon's influence with his kinsman Lord Fitzwilliam, the borough's patron, paid off, and George Tierney* was able to report to Lord Grey that 'we have a new recruit'. In thanking Fitzwilliam, Grey observed that

> I have not heard, for a long time, any news that gave me so much pleasure as your bringing in Lord Normanby ... He will be a most valuable addition to the sound and moderate party ... It is a pleasant thing to see a young man of such principles and talents placed in a situation both to acquire distinction for himself and to render, as I trust he will, useful service to the public.[4]

Normanby joined readily in the Whig opposition to Lord Liverpool's ministry, voting with them on all major issues, including parliamentary reform (on which he had apparently been in correspondence with Lord John Russell*),[5] 25 Apr., 24 June 1822, 20 Feb., 24 Apr., 2 June 1823, 26 May 1826. He divided for Catholic relief, 1 Mar., 21 Apr., and paired for it, 10 May 1825. Speaking in favour of reduction of the salt duties, 28 Feb. 1822, he argued that 'the sinking fund ... ought to be applied to the amelioration of the prevailing distress'. He gave notice of a motion for the abolition of one of the joint-postmasterships, 6 Mar., which he brought on a week later, when he declared that it was 'as clear a question of reduction as any which could be brought under the consideration of Parliament' and 'could not be productive of any distress or embarrassment'. The motion was rejected by 184-159, but he announced the next day his intention of reviving it. He did so in the form of an address to the king, 2 May, which was carried by 216-201. Harriet Arbuthnot recorded that 'Mr. Stuart Wortley and 40 other country gentlemen who, a month ago, voted against Lord Normanby and with us, turned round and supported him'. It was the high point of the Whig assault on ministers that session.[6] He spoke in favour of economies in the 'extravagant' cost of the embassy to the Swiss Cantons and was a teller for the minority, 16 May. On 15 Mar. Russell raised the question of a possible breach of privilege by Charles Arbuthnot*, the patronage secretary, who had written a letter asking a Member to attend in order to 'resist the dangerous practices' of Normanby and other Whigs. After a brief exchange Normanby indicated that he was willing to let the matter drop, the letter being a private one. He presented a York petition for remission of the radical agitator Henry Hunt's* prison sentence and supported a similar one from Bethnal Green, 28 Mar., when he expressed the hope that the House would support Burdett's forthcoming motion on the subject.[7] He presented a Whitby petition in favour of the Yorkshire polls bill, 29 Apr., but stated that he disapproved of the measure, which was 'contrary to the general wish of the county'; he repeated this opinion, 7 June 1822. His name was mentioned by Brougham as one who might move an amendment to the address at the opening of the 1823 session, but in the event he was not asked.[8] On 19 Feb. he asked the home secretary Peel what action had been taken as a result of his address on the postmastership, besides stopping the salary of one of the incumbents; Peel replied that there was little else to do, the main object having been achieved. He asked if ministers meant to retain the office of joint-postmaster in Ireland, 24 Feb.[9] Of the debate on Hume's motion condemning the peacetime appointment of a lieutenant-general of the ordnance, 19 Feb., Mrs. Arbuthnot recorded that 'Lord Normanby (whose father was master-general of the ordnance ... and whose uncles are both in the office) was not ashamed of abusing the whole office'; yet there is no evidence that he spoke or voted for it.[10] In March, Brougham, who wanted to press for British intervention in Spain (a subject on which the Whigs were divided), tried to recruit Normanby to his cause.[11] Supporting Russell's motion for parliamentary reform, 24 Apr. 1823, he declared that 'the demand for reform was now general, but the tone was moderate', and observed that 'the weapons of the people were the justice of their case and the determination with which they supported it'. The next day he sought to clarify his reference to Edinburgh, explaining that 'however respectable the individual may be who is sent to Parliament as the representative of so large a population, and is yet chosen by so very small number of electors ... [the] case affords one of the strongest instances that can be advanced of what has been styled the mockery of representation'.[12] He wintered in Florence and returned to condemn the aliens bill, a measure that was 'hostile to the principles of the British constitution' and which 'outraged all those feelings with which, as Englishmen, we are bound to sympathize', 12 Apr. 1824. He signified his intention of moving a hostile amendment, but there is no record of his doing so. He moved the passage of the spring guns bill and was a teller for the minority, 29 June 1825. At the general election of 1826 he transferred from Higham Ferrers to another of Fitzwilliam's nomination boroughs, Malton, where he replaced Duncannon.[13]

In the summer of 1825 Normanby became a subject of society gossip. John Stuart Wortley* wrote to Henry Edward Fox*, 24 Aug., that 'there is a new mysterious novel come out which I am convinced is Normanby's, except that it is very well written, with considerable talent, and very interesting, which exceeds my estimate of his powers'. The book was 'called *Matilda* and is in one volume'. Fox considered it to be 'horrid trash', but Sir James Mackintosh* admired the 'line of sturdy and moderate liberalism which runs through the book'. Normanby was indeed the author, and he turned his hand to other works of fiction in this period, publishing *Yes and No* (1828), *Clorinda* (1829) and *The Contrast* (1832). He also produced two companion editions, *The English in Italy* (1825) and *The English in France* (1828), which, though ostensibly works of fiction, were supposedly based on his own observations and opinions. Writing from Rome at the end of 1825, Fox reported that 'the Normanbys are at Florence trying to get up a theatre', in which venture 'they will I hear succeed but have more actors than audience'.[14]

As 'a warm friend to the Catholic cause', Normanby condemned the government for their attempts to put down the Catholic Association and deplored the 'continuance of a system so inefficient and so mischievous', 2 Mar. 1827.[15] He divided for Catholic relief, 6 Mar. He spoke in favour of the Wakefield and Ferrybridge canal bill, 16 Mar. On 30 Mar. 1827 he was a minority teller in the division on Tierney's unsuccessful attempt to postpone the committee of supply. He left for Florence at the end of the session but returned to England for the Doncaster races in September.[16] In the House, 29 Jan. 1828, he declared that he had no confidence in the duke of Wellington's ministry. Pointing out that he had 'not had an opportunity to commit [himself] by any pledge or assurance of support' to either of the preceding coalition ministries of Canning and Lord Goderich, he paid tribute to Canning and hoped that 'among the remnants of his political friends, some of them at least will not depart from the line of policy which he has marked out'. Two days later he asserted that of all the governments he had seen formed, Wellington's, 'from the mode of its construction, holds out the least prospect of a favourable consideration of the measures essential to the welfare of Ireland'. He took a leading role in the subsequent discussions concerning the part played by William Huskisson* and John Charles Herries* in the downfall of Goderich's ministry. An explanation had been widely expected on 15 Feb., but Huskisson and Herries, now colonial secretary and master of the mint respectively in Wellington's government, remained silent. Next day Normanby approached Edward Littleton* and asked him to inform Huskisson of his intention 'to call forth an explanation', as he 'thought it right the public should be satisfied whether [Huskisson] had obtained pledges from the duke [of Wellington] or not'. In compliance with Huskisson's request, Normanby promised Littleton that he would give the same notice to Herries. He duly put his question, 18 Feb., after emphasizing his independence and maintaining that he had 'never had any connection' with Canning. He wished to know 'two things ... the cause of the dissolution of [Goderich's] ministry' and 'the principle on which the present government was constructed'. In the opinion of one observer, his speech was 'long, ill arranged and tedious, but quite gentlemanlike in tone and manner, which prevented his questions, as so young a man, being offensive'. However, Littleton considered that Huskisson 'made a triumphant and most satisfactory answer'.[17] Herries also replied, but declined to enter into details. Normanby challenged Herries again, 21 Feb., tartly observing that he 'seems to be as incapable of understanding the questions put to him as he is of answering those questions in a way that can be understood by others'. He voted for repeal of the Test Acts, 26 Feb., and was a majority teller for Catholic relief, 12 May. He backed the reintroduced Wakefield and Ferrybridge canal bill, 3 Mar., presented a Malton petition for repeal of the stamp duties, 20 Mar., and supported the Battersea enclosure bill, 31 Mar. Acting contrary to his patron's interest, Normanby was a minority teller against extending the East Retford franchise to Bassetlaw freeholders, 21 Mar. He told the House that he was 'quite ready with my ... friends near me' to vote against the East Retford disfranchisement bill 'in any future stage', 2 June. He was a teller against the bill, 27 June, when he warned that 'nothing will be more likely to raise the cry of parliamentary reform, during any temporary distress, than the course which [ministers] are at present pursuing'. He voted against the grant to the Society for the Propagation of the Gospels in the colonies, 6 June, to condemn the misapplication of public money for building work at Buckingham House, 23 June, to reduce the salary of the lieutenant-general of the ordnance, 4 July, and against the grant for North American fortifications, 7 July 1828. That summer Normanby's name appeared in Lord Palmerston's* list of Canningites, though it was omitted from a similar list compiled by Lord Colchester.

Normanby was in Florence once more for the winter, and the looming crisis over Catholic emancipation provoked concern at his absence in Whig circles as the 1829 session approached. Lord George William Russell* promised Lord Holland that he would try to persuade Normanby and other Whigs to return to England, which they did not plan to do until Easter, and Lord Tavistock* criticized him for 'winning thousands at Doncaster to spend them in scenes and theatres abroad'.[18] In fact, his first reported appearance in the House was on 5 May, when he voted to transfer East Retford's seats to Birmingham, after explaining that 'I do not think we ought to view it as part of the general question of reform, [but] as a ... reformer I am anxious to take what I can get'. Alluding to the government's settlement of the Catholic question, he described the current session as 'the most glorious that has occurred during the present century'. He voted to allow Daniel O'Connell to take his seat without swearing the oath of supremacy, 18 May 1829. He divided for Knatchbull's amendment to the address on distress, 4 Feb. 1830. He spoke of the harmful effect of the government's foreign policy on Britain's reputation abroad, 'as being rather the friends of despotism than of the liberal party', 8 Feb., but he welcomed the neutrality that ministers proposed to adopt in future. He was again a minority teller for transferring East Retford's seats to Birmingham, 11 Feb., having urged that an example be made of the borough. He voted for Russell's reform motion, 28 May. He divided for Labouchere's motion on the civil government of Canada, 25 May, and against the grant for South American missions, 7 June, and paired against that for the consular services, 11 June. He voted to abolish the death penalty for forgery, 7 June. He remarked to Devonshire, 15 June, that ministers were 'rather in a mess about the chancery bill owing to our friend' lord chancellor Lyndhurst, who had altered it 'just as Brougham liked without consulting the rest of the government'. On the 23rd he reported that the recent opposition dinner at Brooks's 'went off beautifully' and had been attended by 'all that is most venerable and revered in Whiggism'; it 'did good and looked more like a revival of party than anything that has happened for some time'.[19] In his final speech in the Commons, 9 July, he attacked Sir James Scarlett (another of Fitzwilliam's Members), who had taken office under Wellington as attorney-general, over the libel law amendment bill, declaring that he would be 'the last person to whom I should be willing to trust any additional power which might be converted into a means of oppressing the press'; he voted against requiring increased recognizances. The death of George IV and the 'unconscious state' of his father led Normanby to write to Fitzwilliam's son in late June 1830 that, 'under the circumstances, I do not think it will be worth my while again to come into the ... Commons'.[20] Ironically, Scarlett replaced him at Malton at the ensuing general election.

Subsequent developments caused Normanby to regret his decision to retire. Shortly after the formation of Grey's ministry in November 1830 he wrote to Devonshire from Florence asking him to pass on his request for 'any appointment in Italy'. He maintained that of 'all the names I have heard mentioned' for the foreign secretaryship, there was 'not one who I do not flatter myself would further do me a kindness', and if it was Palmerston, 'he is a very old friend of mine from whom no former political differences ever estranged me'. Nothing came his way, and he solicited a peerage instead. Early in 1831 Lord Durham reported to Grey that

> I have received a letter from Normanby requesting me to speak to you on the subject of his being called up to the Lords by writ of summons ... May I suggest some reasons why this request might be complied with. It would not increase the peerage either in future or even at present, for Lord Mulgrave is in such a state of mental imbecility that he cannot take his seat. Lord Normanby might be very useful in the House ... [He] is not an orator but he can speak better than nine out of ten peers, and would be a regular attendant.[21]

In fact, his father's death in April 1831 obviated the need for such an arrangement, and the 2nd earl of Mulgrave soon made his debut in the Upper House. Lord Ellenborough, however, judged that 'he will never speak effectively'.[22] He was appointed governor of Jamaica in 1832 and later served in Lord Melbourne's ministries, though he failed to form a government of his own after Melbourne's temporary resignation in May 1839. He was promoted to a marquessate in 1838 and later became a diplomat. In his final years he was partially disabled by a stroke. He died in July 1863 and was succeeded by his only son, George Augustus Constantine Phipps (1819-90). An obituarist recalled that 'everybody liked him, nobody can well say why', and observed that 'in good nature and good humour, the pleasant manner, the cheery smile, the ready hand, there is an indeterminable charm'.[23]

[1] *Yorks. Gazette*, 11, 18 Mar. 1820. [2] Chatsworth mss 6DD/GPI/524, 536. [3] Bucks. RO, Fremantle mss, T.F. to W.H. Fremantle, 2 Sept.; *The Times*, 7 Dec. 1821. [4] Bessborough mss, Brougham to Duncannon, 17 Jan.; Grey mss, Tierney to Grey, 23 Jan.; Fitzwilliam mss, Grey to Fitzwilliam, 1 Feb. 1822. [5] P. Mandler, *Aristocratic Government in Age of Reform*, 61. [6] *Arbuthnot Jnl.* i. 161; A. Mitchell, *Whigs in Opposition*, 165. [7] *The Times*, 29 Mar. 1822. [8] Bessborough mss, Brougham to Duncannon, 23 Jan. 1823. [9] *The Times*, 20, 25 Feb. 1823. [10] *Arbuthnot Jnl.* i. 216. [11] Bessborough mss, Brougham to Duncannon, 2 Mar. 1823. [12] *The Times*, 26 Apr. 1823. [13] Castle Howard mss, Lady Carlisle to Lord Morpeth, 1 June 1826. [14] Add. 52011, Stuart Wortley to Fox, 24 Aug.; 52017, J.R. Townshend to same, 30 Aug.; 61937, Fox to Eleanor Fazakerley, 28 Dec.; Lansdowne mss, Mackintosh to Lansdowne, 15 Oct. 1825. [15] *The Times*, 3 Mar. 1827. [16] Hants RO, Paultons mss 10M55/326. [17] Hatherton diary, 16, 17, 18 Feb. 1828; Keele Univ. Lib. Sneyd mss SC12/86. [18] Add. 51599A, Lady Cowper to Holland, 28 Jan.; 51676, Lord G.W. Russell to same, 24 Feb. 1829; Blakiston, *Lord William Russell*, 180. [19] Chatsworth mss 1946, 1947. [20] Wentworth Woodhouse mun. G1/3, Normanby to Milton, 29 June 1830. [21] Chatsworth mss 2107; Grey mss, Durham to Grey, 28 Jan. 1831. [22] *Three Diaries*, 96. [23] *The Times*, 29 July 1863.

M.P.J.C.

PHIPPS, Hon. Edmund (1760–1837), of Mulgrave Castle, Yorks. and 64 Mount Street, Mdx.

SCARBOROUGH	19 Sept. 1794–1818
QUEENBOROUGH	1818–1820
SCARBOROUGH	30 May 1820–1832

b. 7 Apr. 1760, 4th s. of Constantine, 1st Bar. Mulgrave [I], and Lepell, da. of John Hervey†, Lord Hervey. *educ.* Eton 1771-3; St. John's, Camb. 1778-80. *unm. d.* 14 Sept. 1837.

Ensign 85 Ft. 1780; lt. 88 Ft. 1780; lt. 93 Ft. 1781, capt. 1782; a.d.c. to gov. Gibraltar 1782; half-pay 1783; capt. 1 Ft. Gds. 1784; a.d.c. to ld. lt. [I] 1784-7; lt.-col. 1 Ft. Gds. 1793, brevet col. 1796; maj.-gen. 1801, lt.-gen. 1808; col. commdt. 60 Ft. 1807-*d.*; gen. 1819.

Paymaster of marines Jan. 1810-12; clerk of deliveries at the ordnance Oct. 1812-Nov. 1830.

Phipps was left without a seat in 1820 as his brother, the 1st earl of Mulgrave, had resigned as master-general of the ordnance and was therefore unable to return him again for Queenborough. However, shortly afterwards, Mulgrave removed his son Lord Normanby, who had recently defected to the Whigs, from the family's seat at Scarborough and Phipps filled the vacancy. As a member of the ministerial phalanx he gave reliable, though silent support to Lord Liverpool's government, notably in the economy and retrenchment divisions of the early 1820s. It was stated in a parliamentary return of 1822 that his ordnance post was worth £1,043 per annum, but *The Times* alleged that the total emoluments for this and his duties as inspector of the military academy amounted to £3,100.[1] He paired for Catholic relief, 28 Feb. 1821, and voted for it, 1 Mar., 21 Apr., 10 May 1825. He presented Scarborough petitions for the abolition of slavery, 11 June 1823. He was returned unopposed for that borough at the general election of 1826.

He divided for Catholic relief, 6 Mar., and presented a Scarborough petition against the reciprocity of duties bill, 2 May 1827. He remained in his post for the duration of the coalition ministries of Canning and Lord Goderich, but cast no recorded votes for the former. Thereafter he gave loyal support to the duke of Wellington's government, though his attendance was much less frequent than in the previous Parliament. In his first known speech in this period, 25 Apr. 1828, he blamed the Catholic Association for 'much, if not all, of the disloyalty and disturbance which have been recently witnessed' in Ireland, and he deplored the absence of censure of its activities from the advocates of emancipation there; he concluded that 'it would be extremely dangerous to grant any further accession of political power' to the Irish. Nevertheless, he paired for Catholic relief, 12 May. He presented a Scarborough petition against restrictions on the circulation of small notes, 2 June 1828. As Planta, the patronage secretary, correctly predicted, he divided for the government's Catholic emancipation bill, 6, 30 Mar. 1829. He presented a petition from Scarborough seamen against the tax levied for the upkeep of Greenwich Hospital, 4 May 1830. He was returned quietly for Scarborough at the general election that summer.

The ministry naturally regarded him as one of their 'friends', and he voted with them in the crucial division on the civil list, 15 Nov. 1830. He resigned with the rest of the government and his office was subsequently abolished by Lord Grey's ministry. He was granted periods of leave on account of family illness (presumably that of his ailing brother), 22 Nov. 1830, 9 Feb. 1831. He presented a petition from Scarborough ship owners for protection from foreign competition, 1 Mar. In response to a constituency petition for parliamentary reform, 19 Mar., he maintained that it did not 'express the opinions of the majority of the inhabitants' and certainly 'not those of the corporation'. He voted against the second reading of the government's bill, 22 Mar., but was absent from the division on Gascoyne's wrecking amendment, 19 Apr. In the debate on the civil list, 28 Mar. 1831, he helped force the chancellor of the exchequer Lord Althorp to admit that Robert Ward's* auditorship of the civil list was not a sinecure. Later that day he welcomed the ministerial statement that the taxation of seamen for the upkeep of Greenwich Hospital would continue. Although his Whig nephew had succeeded as 2nd earl of Mulgrave, he was returned as usual for Scarborough at the 1831 general election. He was absent from the division on the second reading of the reintroduced reform bill, 6 July, and his only recorded votes on it were for use of the 1831 census in determining the disfranchisement schedules, 19 July, and against its passage, 21 Sept. 1831. He voted against issuing the Liverpool election writ, 5 Sept., and for inquiry into the effects of renewing the Sugar Refinery Act on the West India interest, 12 Sept. In the discussion surrounding proposals to allow half-pay for certain naval officers appointed to civil office, 7 Oct., he asked why they should receive preference over army officers, for whom no such privilege was being considered. He divided against the second reading of the revised reform bill, 17 Dec. 1831, the enfranchisement of Tower Hamlets, 28 Feb., the third reading, 22 Mar., and the second reading of the Irish bill, 25 May 1832. He opposed the general register bill, 8 Feb., claiming that in Scarborough it was 'objected to most strongly, particularly by the shipping, commercial and agricultural interests'. He voted against ministers on the Russian-Dutch loan, 12 July. He welcomed the plan to permit both army and naval officers to retain half-pay, under certain conditions, when appointed to civil office, 8 Aug., and expressed surprise at Joseph Hume's opposition, pointing out that 'no officer can accept an appointment unless with the consent of the treasury and the war office'. In his last known speech in the House, 15 Aug. 1832, he defended the action of troops during the recent disturbances at Clitheroe, claiming that they had not acted 'till called on' and had shown 'the greatest forbearance'. He remarked that the radical Member Henry Hunt 'seems to object to the military acting in any case, right or wrong'.

With Scarborough opened by the Reform Act, Phipps retired at the dissolution in 1832. He died at Venice in September 1837. According to Benjamin Disraeli†, he spoke 'with that peculiar voice which Phipps's only have'.[2] He divided his estate between the children of his beloved elder brother, except for Mulgrave, who received nothing; his personalty was sworn under £35,000.[3]

[1] *PP* (1822), iv. 51; *The Times*, 21 Feb. 1821. [2] *Gent. Mag.* (1837), ii. 530; *Disraeli Letters*, i. 333. [3] PROB 11/1885/737; IR26/1462/736.

M.P.J.C.

PIERREPONT, Charles Evelyn, Visct. Newark (1805–1850).

EAST RETFORD 1830–1834

b. 2 Sept. 1805, 1st s. of Charles Herbert Pierrepont†, 2nd Earl Manvers (*d.* 27 Oct. 1860), and Mary Laetitia, da. and event. coh. of Anthony Hardolph Eyre† of Grove Park, Notts.; bro. of Sydney William Herbert Pierrepont†, Visct. Newark. *educ.* by Rev. Thomas Trevenen Penrose; Eton 1817; Christ Church, Oxf. 1823. *m.* 16 Aug. 1832, Emily, da. of Edward John Littleton*, *s.p. d.v.p.* 23 Aug. 1850.

Capt. Holme Pierrepont yeoman cav.; maj. S. Notts. yeoman cav.

Newark, whose father's succession as the 2nd Earl Manvers in 1816 ended the family's 38-year occupation of one of the Nottinghamshire seats, spent his sickly early years at Thoresby Hall, under a private tutor, before going to Eton.[1] According to Edward

John Littleton, who visited him in November 1821, Manvers, a former naval officer who now represented the Kingston family, 'has at Thoresby a large cold house, with quantities of rooms badly aired and furnished', adding that 'a constant round of indiscriminate hospitality, and his amiable, open sailor like habits procure him a good name and influence in his neighbourhood'.[2] Manvers, who spent modestly on rebuilding Thoresby in the following decade, was an anti-Catholic Tory and had refused to allow Newark to serve as a page at George IV's coronation that year because the invitation had come from the royal mistress, Lady Conyngham.[3] Nothing came of a rumour that Newark would stand for his native county at the general election of 1826, when he was still just under age.[4] In January 1827 the duke of Newcastle, with whom Manvers was politically connected, described Newark, shortly after he had left Oxford with a first, as 'a good and amiable young man', who 'I trust will not be spoiled by the world when he goes into it'.[5] Manvers considered him as a possible candidate for East Retford, and obtained Newcastle's approval for this in April 1828, when it was expected that that borough would be thrown into the hundred of Bassetlaw.[6]

At the general election of 1830 Newcastle, aghast at John Evelyn Denison's* brief intervention, considered that Newark 'ought to be the representative', in the event of any vacancy for the county. None arose there, however, and Newcastle presumably responded favourably to Manvers' renewed application for assistance, since Newark duly offered for the now enlarged constituency of East Retford, ostensibly as an independent, although he stressed his support for economies. On the hustings, he repudiated the imputation that he had coalesced with his uncle, Granville Venables Harcourt Vernon*, and after his relation had withdrawn from the contest, he was returned ahead of Arthur Duncombe, Newcastle's nominee.[7] The local Whig newspaper, which counted him as a supporter of the duke of Wellington's administration, denounced the swagger of his acceptance speech, noting that he 'either must or ought to be aware that nursery tales are not always accounted as wit, nor is swearing to be taken for a sign of good sense'.[8] Ministers listed him among the 'moderate Ultras', and he duly voted against them in the division on the civil list which brought them down, 15 Nov. 1830. He was granted four weeks' leave on account of ill health, 25 Nov. 1830, and again, 14 Feb. 1831. He presented and endorsed the East Retford anti-slavery petition, 8 Feb., but made his maiden speech proper on the Grey ministry's reform proposals, 2 Mar.[9] He urged the necessity of winning over the middle classes 'for the preservation of the state' and disavowed the alarmism of the anti-reformers, stating that

> if I am reduced to the alternative of adopting this bill with all its provisions, and with its full destruction of all these boroughs, or of having no reform at all, my warm, though humble, support shall be given to the bill, even without my desiring one single letter of it to be altered.

He presented his constituents' favourable petitions, 21 Mar., and voted for the second reading of the bill, 22 Mar., and against Gascoyne's wrecking amendment, 19 Apr. 1831.

At the ensuing general election Newark stood as an avowed reformer and, repudiating claims of a coalition, was returned behind his uncle after a short contest against Duncombe.[10] He voted for the second reading of the reintroduced reform bill, 6 July 1831, and generally for its details. He complained bitterly when *The Times* listed him as having opposed the disfranchisement of Appleby, 19 July, since he had in fact paired with Sir John Walsh, just as he had done earlier that day against using the 1831 census to determine the disfranchisement clauses.[11] He urged revision of the game laws, 8 Aug. He divided in the minority for enfranchising resident borough freeholders, 17 Aug., but spoke in support of the government's amendment to place Aylesbury, Cricklade, East Retford and New Shoreham on the same footing as other boroughs, 2 Sept. He voted for issuing the Liverpool writ, 5 Sept. Deliberately silent hitherto, he delivered himself of a tirade against what he saw as the absurd and often contradictory arguments of the reform bill's opponents, 19 Sept. At Sir Robert Peel's expense, he ridiculed the assertion that the bill favoured the northern manufacturing districts to the detriment of a largely agricultural south, and he was bemused by the paradoxical inconsistencies in the anti-reformers' arguments, particularly over the division of counties, the £10 borough franchise and the project for colonial representation. He accordingly divided for the passage of the reform bill, 21 Sept., and Lord Ebrington's confidence motion, 10 Oct. 1831.

Newark voted for the second reading of the revised reform bill, 17 Dec. 1831, and again mostly for its details. However, he opposed the creation of one Member constituencies, whose new seats he would have preferred to see divided between a smaller number of extra two Member boroughs, 23 Jan., and repeated his objections, 14 Mar. 1832, when his alternative proposal was negatived without a division. He voted for the third reading of the bill, 22 Mar., and Ebrington's motion for an address calling on the king to appoint only ministers who would carry it unimpaired, 10 May. He welcomed the reinstatement of the government, 18 May, and urged Edward Ruthven not to hinder the progress of the Irish reform bill over the representation of Dublin, 25 June. He divided against the production of information on Portugal, 9 Feb., and, although he had cast a wayward vote on this on 26 Jan., sided with ministers for the Russian-Dutch loan, 16, 20 July. Since May he had been wooing Emily Littleton, and during discussions with her father, who made clear that she would not have a substantial dowry, he entered into 'much explanation respecting the state of his health, concerning which he had some cause of anxiety'.[12] The marriage was solemnized in August, when it was wrongly reported that his father was dying.[13] Manvers, who backed Newcastle's heir Lord Lincoln† for one of the county seats, again put Newark up for East Retford at the general election in December 1832, when he was narrowly returned as a Liberal after a contest.[14] He retired at the dissolution in 1834 and died, 'a poet of considerable merit', in August 1850.[15] His younger brother Sydney William Herbert (1825-1900), was Conservative Member for Nottinghamshire South from 1852 until succeeding as 3rd Earl Manvers in 1860.

[1] *Doncaster, Nottingham and Lincoln Gazette*, 30 Aug. 1850. [2] Hatherton diary, 3 Nov. 1821. [3] J.V. Beckett, *Aristocracy in England*, 332; *Arbuthnot Jnl.* i. 109. [4] *The Times*, 5 June 1826. [5] *Unhappy Reactionary* ed. R.A. Gaunt (Thoroton Soc. rec. ser. xliii), 14. [6] Ibid. 54. [7] Ibid. 65, 67-68; Nottingham Univ. Lib. Portland mss PwH 987; *Nottingham Jnl.* 31 July, 14 Aug.; *Doncaster, Nottingham and Lincoln Gazette*, 13, 20 Aug. 1830. [8] *Nottingham Rev.* 23 July, 13 Aug. 1830. [9] *Blackwood's Mag.* xxix (1831), 662. [10] *Nottingham Rev.* 6 May 1831; *East Retford Pollbook* (1831), 6-8. [11] *The Times*, 21 July 1831. [12] Hatherton diary, 21, 22 June [1832]. [13] Portland mss PwH 359. [14] *Unhappy Reactionary*, 94, 98. [15] *Gent. Mag.* (1850), ii. 432-3.

S.R.H./S.M.F.

PIGOTT, George Grenville Wandisford (1796–1865).

ST. MAWES 3 May 1830–1832

b. 10 Mar. 1796, 1st s. of William Pigott of Doddershall Park, nr. Aylesbury, Bucks. and Anne, da. of Rev. William King, rect. of Mallow, co. Cork. *educ.* Rugby 1808. *m.* (1) 26 Oct. 1822, Charlotte (*d.* 20 Mar. 1823), da. of Edward Beeston Long of Hampton Lodge, Surr., *s.p.*; (2) 30 Oct. 1838, Charlotte, da. of William Lloyd of Aston Hall, Salop, 1s. 1da. *suc.* fa. 1838. *d.* 4 Jan. 1865.

Ensign 14 Ft. 1812, lt. 1814, half-pay 1818; lt. 6 Ft. 1818; lt. 86 Ft. 1822; lt. (half-pay) 12 Drag. 1822-30.

Asst. poor law commr. 1845-62.

Lt.-col. Bucks. militia 1836-52.

Pigott's ancestors were established in Wales and the Marches soon after the Conquest, and settled at Chetwynd, Shropshire. During the eighteenth century the small Buckinghamshire estate of Doddershall, with its Tudor house, came into the family. Pigott's father inherited this property in 1802 and later became receiver-general of land tax for the county.[1] Pigott was named in honour of the family's powerful county neighbours, the Grenvilles of Stowe, with whom they were on friendly terms. In his desultory army career he served in the Mediterranean, at home and in Ireland. His first wife died at Torquay, 'of a rapid consumption', only five months after their wedding.[2] In March 1822, when it seemed that Lord Liverpool's ministry would send out George Canning* as governor-general of India, Richard Grenville†, 1st duke of Buckingham, sought to recommend Pigott for Canning's 'establishment or secretariat', explaining that

> my father in a manner left him as a legacy to me to provide for, being his godson. He has travelled much, speaks French, Italian and German fluently, has a remarkable talent for business ... most gentlemanlike manners, and will I am certain ... be a very valuable member of any man's family. But I will not send him so far off as India upon an uncertainty, or unless he could be sure of being well provided for.[3]

Nothing came of this, of course, but the following year Buckingham secured Pigott a position as an 'unsalaried but official' attaché to the Württemberg embassy, headed by his cousin Henry Williams Wynn†, who reported from Stuttgart in June 1824 that

> I continue to like Pigott as much as ever; he is a most invaluable person and I shall be, on my own account, very sorry when we are to part. I trust, however, that in the course of a year or two you will be able to get him an appointment. It is yet too early to make an application in his favour, as Canning [now foreign secretary] would not probably be able to attend to it.[4]

Pigott went as an attaché with Williams Wynn to Denmark in 1825 and remained there until early 1830, 'performing during the greater part of that time', as he later said, 'the duties of secretary of legation'. He then obtained from Lord Aberdeen, foreign secretary in the duke of Wellington's ministry, 'a formal acknowledgement of my claim to advancement, with a distinct promise of promotion as soon as *the few* engagements to which he was pledged were redeemed'. He subsequently stated that 'a serious accident' had put him out of contention for such vacancies as had immediately occurred.[5]

In May 1830 Pigott came in on a vacancy for Buckingham's borough of St. Mawes. He was sworn in, 10 May, and voted for Jewish emancipation, 17 May. He was in the minorities for amendments to the sale of beer bill, 21 June, 1 July 1830. He was returned again for St. Mawes at the general election that summer, surviving an attempt to open the borough and a subsequent petition.[6] Wellington's ministry numbered him among their 'friends', but he was absent from the crucial division on the civil list, 15 Nov. 1830, apparently owing to an attack of gout.[7] He divided against the second reading of the Grey ministry's reform bill, 22 Mar., and for Gascoyne's wrecking amendment, 19 Apr. 1831. He came in again for St. Mawes at the ensuing general election, after a token contest.[8] He obtained an order for information on duties levied by foreign countries on British and colonial exports, 28 June 1831. He divided against the second reading of the reintroduced reform bill, 6 July, and for use of the 1831 census to determine the disfranchisement schedules, 19 July. On the proposal to disfranchise St. Mawes, 26 July, he entered his 'protest against the gross injustice' of schedule A and insisted that St. Mawes was neither 'decayed' nor 'corrupt', maintaining that 'the influence which has prevailed there is the fair influence of property'. He voted next day against the partial disfranchisement of Chippenham. He supported the argument of Buckingham's son Lord Chandos against conferring an additional county Member on Buckinghamshire, 13 Aug., suggesting that an extra one for Great Marlow would be preferable. He voted to preserve the voting rights of non-resident freeholders at Aylesbury, 2 Sept. On 15 Sept. he proposed that the flourishing county towns of Dorchester, Guildford and Huntingdon, currently in schedule B, should be permitted to retain two Members each, but this was negatived without a division, which the Tory leaders had been keen to avoid.[9] (All three boroughs were fully reinstated in the final bill.) He divided against the bill's passage, 21 Sept. He voted against the issue of a new writ for Liverpool, 5 Sept., and for inquiry into the effects of the Sugar Refinery Act on the West India interest, 12 Sept. He divided against the second reading of the revised reform bill, 17 Dec. 1831, and going into committee, 20 Jan. 1832, after complaining that it was 'impossible, from the documents now in our hands, to decide what boroughs ought to be disfranchised'. He secured a return of the population, assessed taxes and inhabited houses of the English counties, 31 Jan. He contended that Midhurst rather than Amersham should be included in schedule A, 21 Feb. Two days later his argument that the 'most extraordinary' omission of yeomanry exemptions from the estimate of assessed taxes had unjustly condemned Helston to schedule B was dismissed by ministers. He voted against the enfranchisement of Tower Hamlets, 28 Feb. On the English county schedule, 9 Mar., he moved an amendment for houses and assessed taxes rather than population to be taken to determine which were to have four and which three Members: on this basis, the agricultural counties of Berkshire, Hertfordshire and Oxfordshire would receive an extra seat, at the expense of Cumberland, Durham and Northamptonshire. Ministers would have none of it, and Pigott did not divide the House. He questioned Lord John Russell's assertion that the reform bill had given a preponderance to the agricultural interest, 20 Mar., arguing that the reverse was the case and that, since a reformed Parliament was likely to vote for 'an entirely free trade in corn', the prospect loomed of 'the ruin of the whole existing race of landowners and farmers', as well as the abolition of primogeniture, the peerage and the church. He divided against the third reading, 22 Mar. He voted against government on the Russian-Dutch loan, 26 Jan., 12 July, and spoke at length against the 'miserable sophistry' of their attempts to justify it, 16, 20 July. He protested at their acquiescence in the French invasion of Spain, which might encourage France to attack Ireland, 13 Mar. He joined in the attack on Russia's treatment of Poland, 28 June. He supported an amendment to Warburton's anatomy bill to prohibit dissection in private houses, 11 Apr. He presented Buckinghamshire petitions for a majority of parish ratepayers to be authorized to adopt schemes for the employment of the able-bodied poor, 8 May, and defended this proposal as incorporated in Burrell's agricultural labourers bill, 9 July. He seconded Robinson's protectionist motion for inquiry into trade, 22 May, when he condemned the tariff reforms of the last ten years. He presented a petition against the proposed scheme of Irish national education and the Maynooth grant, 20 June 1832. His parliamentary career ended with the disfranchisement of St. Mawes.

Pigott remained a zealous promoter of the Conservative and protectionist cause in Buckinghamshire, where he supported Chandos's electoral campaign amongst the farmers in the autumn of 1832. At a dinner in Buckingham, 6 Oct. 1832, when his father spoke as 'a farmer to all intents and purposes', Pigott declared his preference for a sliding scale to a fixed duty on corn imports, but emphasized that above all protection should be adequate. He attacked the 'theoretical politicians' and 'political economists' in the government, who were determined to introduce free trade in corn. He subsequently published a *Letter on the Present Corn Laws*, calling for the relief of agriculturists from heavy local taxation, which was the real cause of high bread prices.[10] On Peel's accession to power in 1834 Pigott applied for a place, citing

Aberdeen's earlier promise of diplomatic promotion, which had been frustrated by his parliamentary opposition to the Grey ministry. He now sought 'employment' at home, as the 'temporary embarrassment' of his father's affairs, caused by 'the depreciation of landed property' and the loss of the receivership in 1831, 'renders my presence in England almost absolutely necessary'. Peel gave him no encouragement, and he vainly approached Wellington for a foreign post.[11] When he succeeded to the Doddershall estate in 1838 his father's personalty was sworn under a paltry £1,500.[12] The following year he published a copious *Manual of Scandinavian Mythology*. He again asked for a domestic office on Peel's return to power in 1841 and, through the intervention of Chandos (now 2nd duke of Buckingham), a cabinet minister, his name was placed on the list for diplomatic advancement, with a seniority equivalent to a record of unbroken service since 1823. However, he was advised that this 'concession' would probably turn out to be 'a barren one', and so it proved.[13] In November 1844 he begged Peel to make him an assistant poor law commissioner, claiming that he had applied for and received a 'written assurance' of such an appointment in 1834, but had been cheated of it by Lord Melbourne's return to office. He observed that

> as I have never been in a position to forego the advantages of a profession, and as my exertions through life have been rendered abortive in consequence of political opinions sincerely held by me and now triumphant, I feel certain that you will pardon my appealing to you on grounds which have proved sufficient in the cases of so many now holding office under you.[14]

He received the desired appointment the following year and served in that capacity for 17 years, marking his retirement with a pamphlet on *The Laws of Settlement and Removal*, in which he advocated abolition of the power of removal and the creation of a general relief fund by levies on the parishes according to their rateable value. He died in January 1865 and left the Doddershall estate to his only son William Harvey Pigott (1848-1924), a naval officer.

[1] P.C. Lipscomb, *Bucks.* i. 256, 405-11; *VCH Bucks.* iv. 96; *Pprs. from Doddershall* ed. G. Eland, 1; *Autobiog. of Joseph Mayett* ed. A. Kussmaul (Bucks. Rec. Soc. xxiii.), 25, 81, 83, 92. [2] *Recs. of Bucks.* iii. 147. [3] Bucks. RO, Fremantle mss D/FR/46/10/21/1. [4] Buckingham, *Mems. Geo. IV*, ii. 61-64, 88. [5] Add. 40408, f. 103; 40486, f. 149; 40551, f. 368. [6] *R. Cornw. Gazette*, 31 July, 7 Aug., 13 Nov., 25 Dec. 1830. [7] Fremantle mss 139/20/2. [8] *The Times*, 7 May 1831. [9] Add. 40402, f. 102. [10] *Bucks. Herald*, 13 Oct., 8 Dec. 1832. [11] Add. 40408, ff. 103, 105. [12] PROB 11/1898/476; IR26/1404/461. [13] Add. 40486, ff. 148-9. [14] Add. 40551, ff. 370-2.

D.R.F.

PITT, Joseph (1759–1842), of Cirencester, Glos.; Eastcourt House, Crudwell, Wilts., and 36 Great George Street, Mdx.[1]

CRICKLADE 1812–1831

bap. 27 Nov. 1759,[2] 4th but 2nd surv. s. of Joseph Pitt, carpenter, of Badgeworth, nr. Cheltenham, Glos. and w. Ann Golding of Brokenborough, Wilts. *m.* (1) 29 Aug. 1786, Mary (*d.* 1788), da. of Cornelius Robbins of Didmarton, Glos., 1s. *d.v.p.*; (2) Ann (*d.* 13 July 1792), da. of Andrew Daubeny of Bristol, *s.p.*; (3) Ann, da. of Joseph Orlidge of Bristol, 4s. 2da. (?1 *d.v.p.*).[3] *d.* 6 Feb. 1842.

Bailiff, Cirencester by 1790, steward 1793; high steward, Cricklade 1812-26; capital burgess, Wootton Bassett 1814-30.

Pitt, who came from an obscure family on the Gloucestershire and Wiltshire border, was one of the few first generation self-made men to enter Parliament during the early nineteenth century.[4] His paternal grandfather, Joseph Pitt of Brokenborough, married Elizabeth Brown at Malmesbury, 16 Sept. 1723. Their son Joseph, who was baptized 7 Oct. 1724, married Ann Golding and moved to Little Witcombe in the parish of Badgeworth, where they had four sons: John (*d.* 1 May 1776, aged 22); Isaac (*d.* 6 May 1808, aged 52); Joseph (*d.* 12 Feb. 1758, aged 14 days); and another Joseph, who was baptized in late 1759. This Joseph Pitt's first two wives died soon after their marriages, the second from swallowing some loose hairs from her toothbrush while pregnant. His third wife died, 11 July 1819, in Clarges Street, where he occasionally resided when in London.[5] His friend the Rev. Francis Witts wrote in 1825 that Pitt was

> one of those fortunate members of the legal profession, whom great sagacity, lucky opportunity and the skill of seizing on favourable circumstances have elevated from a very humble to a very prosperous situation in life. His enterprises as attorney, banker, speculator in land, and many other ways of gaining or losing fortunes, have been eminently successful.[6]

As a boy he 'used to hold gentlemen's horses for a penny', but he was bred to business by an attorney and established a successful practice in Cirencester.[7] It was there that he became a partner in the bank of Pitt, Gardner, Croome, Bowley and Wood, which had branches in Tetbury and Cheltenham, where he was a partner in the brewery of Gardner, Pitt and Company.[8] He was also a partner in the London bank of Bosanquet, Beachcroft, Pitt and Anderson.[9] Pitt invested speculatively in land, purchasing the manor of Minety, Gloucestershire, from Lord Rivers for

£21,000 in 1791, and the neighbouring estate of Eastcourt, which he made his principal residence, from the Earle family for £28,000 in 1807. Both properties were improved by the passage of Enclosure Acts (in 1811 and 1816 respectively), and the same was done (in 1801) at Cheltenham, where in 1800 he acquired a considerable area of agricultural land, known as the Marsh, to the north of the town, from the earl of Essex. His first contribution to the architecture of Cheltenham was the Royal Crescent of 1812, and in the early 1820s he began to develop his estate there as the new spa of Pittville.[10]

In 1812 Pitt sold his legal practice to Joseph Bevir and, although he used his services occasionally, he mostly relied on another Cirencester attorney, Joseph Randolph Mullings†. Pitt had long been connected with the householder borough of Cirencester, and as bailiff and returning officer, appointed by the patrons, the Earls Bathurst, he evidently had some influence over elections there. It was, however, for the enlarged freeholder borough of Cricklade, where he had purchased the lordship of the manor from the 2nd earl of Carnarvon the year before (and was to purchase the rest of his interest in 1815), that he was first returned to Parliament, at the general election of 1812. He was usually credited with the control of one seat on the ministerial interest, which he occupied himself until 1831. It was also in 1812 that he bought outright the patronage of the rotten corporation borough of Malmesbury from Edmund Estcourt, and he returned its two Members without any serious threat to his position until 1832. His interest at Wootton Bassett, a scot and lot borough, which he had acquired from James Kibblewhite in the early 1810s, did not last into the following decade, as his candidates were unsuccessful at the general elections of 1820 and 1826. Nevertheless, he had proprietorial control over more seats than any of the aristocratic boroughmongers of Wiltshire.

Pitt, who in late 1819 signed the Wiltshire requisition against the holding of a county meeting on Peterloo, was an almost silent general supporter of the Liverpool administration in the Commons, where he served on a fair number of select committees.[11] He was granted three weeks' leave on urgent private business, 22 June 1820. He divided with ministers against the motion censuring their conduct towards Queen Caroline, 6 Feb. 1821. He voted against Catholic relief, 28 Feb. 1821, 30 Apr. 1822. He divided against Maberly's motion on the state of the revenue, 6 Mar., and reducing the barracks grant, 28 May, but was listed as voting with opposition for repealing the duty on husbandry horses, 5 Mar., and the additional malt duty, 21 Mar. 1821. He voted against disqualifying civil officers of the ordnance from voting in parliamentary elections, 12 Apr., and parliamentary reform, 9 May. He was actively involved in the progress of the Malmesbury enclosure bill, which received royal assent, 8 June 1821, and he was probably involved in the passage of other pieces of local legislation.[12] He voted against abolition of one of the joint-postmasterships, 13 Mar. 1822. He sided with ministers against abolishing certain taxes, 12, 18 Mar., and repeal of the Foreign Enlistment Act, 16 Apr. 1823. He divided in the minorities for inquiry into the East Indian sugar duties, 22 May, and for recommitting the silk bill, 9 June 1823. He presented a petition from the licensed victuallers of Cheltenham against the beer bill, 11 May, and voted in the minority against going into committee on the beer duties bill, 24 May 1824.[13] Having voted against the usury bill, 17 Feb., he divided for the Irish unlawful societies bill, 25 Feb. 1825. He was not listed as voting on the Catholic question, 1 Mar., but divided against relief, 21 Apr., 10 May, and the second reading of the Irish franchise bill, 26 Apr. 1825. The foundation stone of his most grandiose project, the Pittville Pump Room, was laid on 4 May. His bank survived the financial crisis of late 1825, but only through the action of John Gardner, who made a very fast return journey to London to collect sufficient specie to prevent the branch from defaulting. Yet the crash spelt the end of the speculative boom, and the building operations at Pittville were soon said to be 'in abeyance'.[14] He was credited with an opposition vote against receiving the report on the salary of the president of the board of trade, 10 Apr., but he voted with ministers against reforming the representation of Edinburgh, 13 Apr. 1826.

Pitt, who divided in the protectionist minority against the corn bill, 2 Apr. 1827, voted against Catholic relief, 6 Mar. 1827, 12 May 1828. The duke of Wellington, the prime minister, visited Pittville in August 1828, and 'expressed himself in very high terms as to the beauty of this delightful spot, and the manner in which the property had been laid out'.[15] Although Pitt was listed by Planta, the patronage secretary, as likely to side 'with government' on Catholic emancipation, he wrote to Thomas Henry Bucknall Estcourt*, 6 Feb. 1829, that

> I lament extremely that Wiltshire and other counties were not more forward in signifying their desires. If they had, I think that that which passed last night in our House [the address confirming ministers' intention to propose emancipation] would not have taken place, and I fear that we shall now have increased difficulties to contend with,

> for you know how many persons are governed more by the opinion of others than their own. I ... concur with those who think that admitting Catholics to place and power [is] open to great danger to our church and state.

He signed the Wiltshire anti-Catholic declaration (as Walter Long† informed Bucknall Estcourt a few days later), and divided against emancipation, 6, 18 Mar. 1829.[16] He voted against transferring East Retford's seats to Birmingham, 11 Feb. 1830. He divided against Jewish emancipation, 17 May, and abolition of the death penalty for forgery, 7 June. At the Wiltshire Society dinner, 19 May, he declared that 'there was no man, not excepting the county Members, who felt more interest for the county of Wiltshire than he did'.[17] At about this time he sold his remaining property in Wootton Bassett to the 3rd earl of Clarendon, and he left the corporation in June 1830.[18]

A gala opening ceremony was held for the Pittville Pump Room, 20 July 1830, but Pitt stayed away, possibly because he was already disillusioned with an enterprise which he later claimed had cost him £40,000.[19] He was elected for Cricklade for the last time at the general election the following month, when he was unable to 'find an opening' for Thomas Gladstone*.[20] He was listed by ministers among their 'friends', but was absent from the division on the civil list, 15 Nov. 1830, which led to their resignation. He was granted a fortnight's leave because of the disturbed state of his neighbourhood, 25 Nov. 1830, and again, on urgent private business, 16 Feb. 1831. He voted against the second reading of the Grey ministry's reform bill, 22 Mar., and for Gascoyne's wrecking amendment, 19 Apr. 1831, which precipitated a dissolution. Pitt, who signed the requisition for the return of Lord Robert Edward Henry Somerset* for Gloucestershire, retired at the subsequent dissolution. In an address to the electors, 25 Apr. 1831, he declared that 'it has required much resolution to make me decline soliciting to be replaced in the honourable situation to which you elevated me, but I find its arduous duties beyond my strength, at my advanced age'.[21] The real reason for his withdrawal was said to be his increasing unpopularity and failing fortunes. However, he put up (and voted for) a supposed opponent of reform, the former Member Thomas Calley, who was elected with the other sitting Member, Robert Gordon, against another reformer after a sharp contest.[22] On 30 May he apparently attended the reform dinner in Malmesbury, where his interest, which was challenged that month, collapsed after the passage of the reform bill the following year.[23] Illness prevented him from presiding at the Wiltshire Society's annual dinner, 23 June 1831.[24] His influence elsewhere had been eclipsed, but he may have retained a partial interest at Cricklade for a few years.

Since the mid-1820s Pitt's speculative ventures had gone awry, not least because of the success of the rival spas in Cheltenham.[25] Witts noted of the Pittville Pump Room in 1830 that

> the spirited proprietor and projector ... who in the course of a long life has risen from the lowest rank of society to wealth and consequence, must, I fear, find this an unprofitable concern, less advantageous than if the money it has cost had been invested in three per cent annuities.[26]

His financial affairs became more and more encumbered, with crippling debts being only partially offset by the sale of some of his properties, for example of the manor of Malmesbury to Joseph Neeld* in 1840. He died in February 1842, 'highly respected by all who knew him'.[27] He was buried at Crudwell, where his monument bore the arms of the celebrated family of Pitt, to whom he was not known to be related. It was estimated that he owed £150,000 and that the interest payments on his mortgages came to £6,000 a year, compared to the mere £4,000 he received in revenue from the properties. Another Joseph Pitt, a fox-hunting parson, who was the only son of Pitt's estranged first son Cornelius (1787-1840), vicar of Rendcomb, began a suit in chancery, on behalf of himself and others, for the settlement of their claims against the estate. Though most had received substantial gifts during their father's lifetime, there was to be nothing more for Pitt's surviving sons: his heir Joseph (1796-1869), an attorney; William Gregson (1798-1846), the manager of the County of Gloucester Bank at Cheltenham, into which his father's bank had been merged; Charles (1803-74), vicar of Malmesbury; and George Hicks, an Indian judge. A ruling was eventually given in favour of the main claimants, especially Mullings, who had lent Pitt over £50,000, and thereby came to purchase and live at Eastcourt. Other properties were sold at auction in 1843 and 1845, Neeld purchasing the manor of Cricklade. The ill-fated Pittville Pump Room, never a great commercial success, was acquired by the town council of Cheltenham in 1890.[28]

[1] Based on R. Howes, 'Rise and Fall of Joseph Pitt', *Glos. Hist. Stud.* viii (1977), 62-72. [2] IGI (London). [3] Wilts. RO, Mullings mss 374/679. [4] *HP Commons, 1790-1820*, iv. 806; I. R. Christie, *British 'Non-Elite' MPs*, 18. [5] Cricklade Mus. mss 1051; IGI (Glos., Wilts.); *Gent. Mag.* (1792), ii. 768; (1811), ii. 93. [6] *Diary of Cotswold Parson* ed. D. Verey, 42-43. [7] *Life of Campbell*, i. 286. [8] Pitt's business correspondence can be found among the collections of his associates (Glos. RO D1388, D2025, D3495). [9] F.G. Hilton Price, *London Bankers* (1890-1), 19. [10] R. Howes, 'Joseph Pitt and Pittville', *Glos. Hist. Stud.* vi (1974-5), 58-61; R. Howes, 'Joseph Pitt,

Landowner', ibid. vii (1976), 20 24; S. Blake, *Pittville Pump Room* (unpaginated); R. Howes, *Pittville*, 5-9, 11-17, 19-25. [11] *Devizes Gazette*, 4 Nov. 1819; *Session of Parl. 1825*, p. 480. [12] *CJ*, lxxvi. 48, 115, 118, 125, 249, 336-7, 366, 426. [13] *The Times*, 12 May 1824. [14] E. Humphris and E.C. Willoughby, *At Cheltenham Spa*, 157-8; G. Hart, *Hist. Cheltenham*, 198; *Diary of Cotswold Parson*, 53. [15] Blake, *Pittville Pump Room*. [16] Glos. RO, Sotheron Estcourt mss D1571 X114. [17] *Salisbury Jnl.* 24 May 1830. [18] Warws. RO MI 247, Philips Mems. ii. 112; Wilts. RO, Wootton Bassett borough recs. G26/110/2. [19] Blake, *Pittville Pump Room*. [20] St. Deiniol's Lib. Glynne-Gladstone mss 195, T. to J. Gladstone, 26, 28, 29 June 1830. [21] *Gloucester Jnl.* 16 Apr.; *Devizes Gazette*, 28 Apr. 1831. [22] *The Times*, 9, 27 May 1831; *Cricklade Pollbook* (1831), 22. [23] J.T. Bird, *Hist. Malmesbury*, 160, 214, 229. [24] *Salisbury Jnl.* 30 June 1830. [25] Blake, *Pittville*, 25-43. [26] *Diary of Cotswold Parson*, 86. [27] *Gloucester Jnl.* 12 Feb. 1842. [28] Mullings mss 374/373, 679; Blake, *Pittville*, 45-48; Humphris and Willoughby, 156-60; Cricklade Mus. mss 1051; IGI (Glos.); *Diary of Cotswold Parson*, 43, 87; Sir R. Graham, *Fox-Hunting Recollections*, 43-45.

S.M.F.

PITT, William Morton (1754–1836), of Kingston House, nr. Dorchester, Dorset.

POOLE	1780–1790
DORSET	1790–2 Feb. 1826

b. 16 May 1754, 1st and o. surv. s. of John Pitt† of Encombe, Dorset and Marcia, da. of Mark Anthony Morgan of Cottlestown, co. Sligo. *educ.* Queen's, Oxf. 1772; L. Inn 1774. *m.* (1) 26 Oct. 1782, Margaret (*d.* 6 Nov. 1818), da. of John Gambier, lt.-gov. Bahamas, 1da. *d.v.p.*; (2) 16 Nov. 1819,[1] Grace Amelia, da. of Henry Seymer of Hanford, Dorset, 1s. 2da. *suc.* fa. 1787. *d.* 28 Feb. 1836.

Capt. Dorset militia 1778, maj. 1798, lt.-col. 1799-1712.

Despite his philanthropic endeavours, Pitt, a kinsman of the late prime minister, was an almost silent supporter of the Liverpool administration in the Commons.[2] He apologized for his recent absences, but, disproving rumours to the contrary, declared himself fit enough to continue as a county Member on offering again for Dorset at the general election of 1820; there being no likelihood of an opposition, he was returned unopposed.[3] In his last Parliament, his contribution to the House was slight, and no evidence of activity has been found for the 1820 session. He voted against condemning ministers' conduct towards Queen Caroline, 6 Feb., repeal of the additional malt duty, 5 Apr., reducing the grant for the adjutant-general's office, 11 Apr., and omitting the arrears from the duke of Clarence's grant, 21 June 1821. He divided against disqualifying civil officers of the ordnance from voting in parliamentary elections, 12 Apr., and parliamentary reform, 9 May 1821. He voted against more extensive tax reductions to relieve distress, 11, 21 Feb., reduction of the salt duties, 28 Feb. 1822, and repeal of the Foreign Enlistment Act, 16 Apr. 1823. In February he stayed neutral during the Dorset by-election, which he did not attend.[4] He defended the governor of Millbank penitentiary from interference by the committee of superintendence, of which he was himself a member, in the press in April, and gave oral and written evidence on this to a Commons select committee, 12, 16, 24 June 1823.[5] He corresponded on such topics with Peel, the home secretary, and was named with him to the select committee on prisons, 18 Mar. 1824.[6] He was 'inaudible' in speaking a few words on the game bill, 25 Mar. 1824.[7] He divided for the Irish unlawful societies bill, 25 Feb., and (as he had on 28 Feb. 1821 and 30 Apr. 1822) against Catholic relief, 1 Mar., 21 Apr., 10 May 1825.

That year he participated in attempts to provide relief for those affected by storms and shipwrecks on the Dorset coast.[8] Although Henry Bankes, Member for Corfe Castle, had despaired that Pitt 'seemed likely to resign his seat only with his life', he announced his retirement in September 1825, when a dissolution was expected.[9] He relinquished his seat at the start of the 1826 session, deeming this the most convenient time to pass on the seat to Bankes, who publicly praised him for his 'amiable, humane and benevolent' character and his studious devotion to county affairs.[10] Thereafter Pitt played little part in local politics, though he voted for Benjamin Lester Lester* and Henry Charles Sturt* in the Poole contest at the general election that year. In the two Dorset contests in 1831, he voted for the Tory Bankes and the Whig Edward Portman* at the general election in the spring, and for the anti-reformer Lord Ashley* in the autumn.[11] He died in February 1836, widely respected for being a man whose

> time and exertions were unremittingly devoted to the public good ... He passed through life distinguished by the possession of the purest virtues, and by the exercise of a diffusive philanthropy and extensive practical benevolence.[12]

By his will, dated 12 Jan. 1836, he provided for his wife's immediate necessities and left the bulk of his estate, which included personal wealth sworn under £10,000, to his only son William Grey Pitt (1821-67).[13]

[1] *Western Flying Post*, 22 Nov. 1819. [2] *HP Commons, 1790-1820*, iv. 824-6; *Black Bk.* (1823), 184-5; *Session of Parl. 1825*, p. 480. [3] Dorset RO, Anglesey mss D/ANG B5/26; *Western Flying Post*, 28 Feb., 20 Mar. 1820. [4] Dorset RO, Bankes mss D/BKL, Pitt to Bankes, 13 Feb.; *Western Flying Post*, 24 Feb. 1823. [5] *The Times*, 29 May 1823; *PP* (1823), v. 545-50, 567-73, 687-8. [6] Add. 40359, f. 49; 40360, f. 59; 40364, f. 83. [7] *The Times*, 26 Mar. 1824. [8] *Salisbury Jnl.* 17, 31 Jan.; *Dorset Co. Chron.* 21 Apr., 23 June, 7 July, 13 Oct. 1825. [9] *Dorset Co. Chron.* 29 Sept.; Bankes mss, Pitt to Bankes, 27 Sept. 1825; Bankes

jnl. 156 (16 Feb. 1826). [10] Bankes mss, Pitt to Bankes, 23 Dec. 1825, 20, 23 Jan.; *Dorset Co. Chron.* 9, 23 Feb. 1826. [11] Dorset RO, Poole borough recs. DC/PL S1660; *Dorset Pollbooks* (1831), 23; (Sept.-Oct. 1831), 39. [12] *Gent. Mag.* (1836), i. 663-4; J. Sydenham, *Hist. Poole*, 285-6. [13] PROB 11/1864/446; IR26/1428/368.

R.B.C./S.M.F.

PLANTA, Joseph (1787–1847), of Fairlight Place, nr. Hastings, Suss.

HASTINGS	21 Apr. 1827–1831
HASTINGS	1837–20 Mar. 1844

b. 2 July 1787, o.s. of Joseph Planta of the British Museum and w. Elizabeth Atwood of St. George's, Hanover Square, Mdx.[1] *educ.* Eton 1799. *m.* 10 Nov. 1831, Charlotte Augusta, da. of Christopher Papendick of Kew Green, Surr., page of back stairs in Queen Charlotte's household, wid. of Thomas Oom of Bedford Square, Mdx. and Ham Common, Surr., *s.p.*[2] *suc.* fa. 1827; GCH 1837. *d.* 5 Apr. 1847.

Supernumerary clerk, foreign office 1802-3, clerk 1803-17, assistant précis writer 1809-17, priv. sec. to sec. of state 1814-17, under-sec. 1817-27; sec. to treasury Apr. 1827-Nov. 1830; ld. of treasury Nov.-Dec. 1834; commr. bd. of control Dec. 1834-Apr. 1835; PC 20 Dec. 1834.

Planta's family originated in the Grisons region of Switzerland. His grandfather Andrea Guisseppe Planta was pastor of a reformed church at Castegna before he came to London as minister of the German reformed church in 1752. From 1758 until his death in 1773 he was an assistant librarian at the British Museum, in which post he was succeeded by his son Joseph (*b.* 1744).[3] In 1776 he, who had been educated at Utrecht and Göttingen, was promoted to the keepership of manuscripts, and in 1799 he became principal librarian. As such he was a reformer, who granted new facilities to the public and compiled part of the catalogue of printed books. An urbane and scholarly man, he published *An Account of the Romansch Language* (1776) and histories of the *Helvetic Confederacy* (1800 and 1821). He was paymaster of exchequer bills from 1788 to 1811, when he retired with a pension of £266 a year.[4] His father had been Italian tutor to Queen Charlotte, and his sister Margaret, who lived until 1834, was for many years the English teacher and personal attendant of the Princesses Augusta, Charlotte and Elizabeth.[5]

It was supposedly to the queen that the young Joseph Planta, an only child whose education was 'anxiously superintended' by his father, owed his appointment to a foreign office clerkship in 1802. Four years later Princess Augusta tried to 'procure his name to be set down for a second survivorship of clerk to the signet office', but the home secretary Lord Spencer would not oblige.[6] Planta developed a close friendship with his schoolfellow Stratford Canning*, cousin of the foreign secretary George Canning*, and succeeded him as précis writer in 1809. They toured the Lake District together in the summer of 1813. Planta accompanied Canning's successor Lord Castlereagh* to the peace congresses of 1813-15 and personally brought the Treaty of Paris to London on 23 Nov. 1815.[7] William Wilberforce* had met him earlier that year and thought him 'a highly pleasing man'.[8] He was promoted to the under-secretaryship in 1817 and attended the conference of Aix-la-Chapelle the following year.[9] In his letters to Stratford Canning, Planta, a supporter of Catholic relief, revealed his Tory ministerial bias: the Whigs were 'almost broken up as a party' in the Commons (15 Mar. 1821) and Queen Caroline's behaviour at the coronation had 'ruined herself and her cause for ever' (8 Aug. 1821); but 'the Grenvilles have been bought very dear' (14 Jan. 1822).[10] At that time he told his friend Charles Bagot that the recent 'reduction of our poor clerks, of which only a few years ago I was one, while we *political* gentlemen keep the whole of our emoluments, has been a bitter pill to me'. On 1 Aug. that year he wrote:

> Our Parliament is at length drawing to a close, and a more wearying, troublesome and disagreeable session they never had: Lord Londonderry [Castlereagh] is more tired in mind than I have seen him yet with parliamentary labour ... Economy is the stalking horse; everybody mounts it; every loose fish has something to say upon it, and both friends and foes are in a very ungovernable and unsatisfactory state. Whether this looseness of connection be the prevailing taste of the times, or whether it arise from the fault of the government, I am hardly prepared to say; but I am sure of this, that (to use my master's expression) it is the worst *feature* of the present times, and will make the country more difficult to govern by any means whatever ten or fifteen years hence, if some remedy be not found for it. Lord Londonderry is however in health better than for some years.

Less than a fortnight later Londonderry killed himself. The 'awful' and 'thoroughly unexpected' news met Planta on his way back to London from a brief holiday at his house near Hastings. He was 'absolutely overwhelmed and wretched', and feared that he would 'not be for a long time, the man I was'.[11]

Yet he had no difficulty in transferring his devoted loyalty to Londonderry's successor Canning. As he told Mrs. Arbuthnot early in 1823, when the office was 'working as hard as, or a little harder, than we possibly can', he was 'so happy to be again where he could talk *à coeur ouvert*: it put him in mind of old times'.[12] Later in the year Stratford Canning found him 'quite as grey and quite as fat as under the preceding dynasty – a fit type of the prosperity of his country and its venerable institutions'.[13] In November 1824 the duke of Wellington's confidante Mrs. Arbuthnot noted that her husband had

> heard in London that Mr. Planta had been talking to Mr. Herries* about the duke's hatred of Canning and lamenting it; but Mr. P. is become the *ame damnée* of Canning and appears totally to have forgotten the policy he learnt under poor Lord Londonderry. It shows how indiscreet Mr. C. is when his under-secretaries go about talking in this manner.[14]

Earlier that year Canning had tried to seize an opportunity to install Planta as patronage secretary to the treasury. The incumbent, Stephen Rumbold Lushington*, coveted the governorship of Madras, which was expected to fall vacant. Canning acquiesced in the premier Lord Liverpool's support of his pretensions in order to replace him with Planta, as he confided to his wife, 4 Apr. 1823:

> It is nearly as important to *me* to have a person upon whom I can rely in that office, as in my own department. Lushington has behaved perfectly well, but his connections are ultra and he is no way *mine*. Planta will be wholly so and will make the House of Commons much easier and pleasanter to me than it is.[15]

According to some ministerialists Liverpool, to whom Planta was said to be 'personally disagreeable' (though he denied this to Canning), objected to the arrangement, which 'would have caused great jealousy among the anti-Canningites, who would have felt that, in the event of an election, all the influence of the government would have been directed by Mr. C.'[16] The king, too, was reported in September to be 'very much alarmed about Planta becoming secretary of the treasury'; and he certainly tried to ensure that Lushington stayed where he was.[17] Four weeks later it was said that Planta seemed 'not a little sick' of Canning's suspected intrigues against his colleagues, which provided 'an additional reason for his sighing for the settlement of Lushington's question, and getting a snug berth at the treasury'.[18] Yet Charles Arbuthnot*, who had held that office for almost 14 years, could not

> think that Planta will either like the treasury or that he will be well suited for the office. I have long had a very sincere liking for him; but should we again come into trying times he will fail physically if not otherwise. I think the House of Commons would drive him wild. I am sure it drove me out of my senses, and I had had more intercourse with all sorts of mankind than he has. The office he is to fill requires great activity of body, and this he has not.[19]

Although Canning overcame Liverpool's objections to Planta, his transfer was blocked for months by the refusal of the directors of the East India Company to accept Lushington's appointment. In mid-October 1824 Canning, hearing that Sir Charles Stuart, angry at being recalled from the Paris embassy, would be pacified by the governorship of Madras, advised Liverpool to offer it to him in preference to Lushington:

> Could Madras be better disposed of? For you and me, it certainly could not, for it would save you all trouble about the peerage; and it would not only save the necessity of finding an employment for Stuart, but preserve to me my Planta, whom I know not how to replace, especially now that the change has been suffered to run on till within prospect of the meeting of Parliament. I verily believe too that Planta himself, though if the vacancy should occur he would feel it a point of honour not to forego it, would nevertheless be not ill-satisfied that the whole of the projected change should fall to the ground.[20]

Lushington was persuaded to withdraw his pretensions, so depriving Planta of his promotion. According to Mrs. Arbuthnot, he admitted to her 'his disappointment in not becoming secretary of treasury'. She thought he had been hoodwinked by Canning, who had convinced him that 'he had had nothing to do' with the abandonment of Lushington for Stuart. (In the event, Stuart declined to go to Madras because government refused his exorbitant personal demands, and no change took place in the governorship.)[21] Planta kept Stratford Canning informed of developments in the campaign for Catholic emancipation and Canning's 'increasing' influence in the cabinet. After the 1826 general election he reported that the new Parliament would have 'a greater majority on the part of ministers generally', but 'a small loss (some state it much greater than others) of supporters of the Catholic question'.[22] On 22 Nov. 1826 he told Canning that it had been

> settled that if all things remain as they are amongst the higher powers I am to walk over to the treasury in July next, Lushington then proceeding to govern Madras. The time of this change will suit me exactly ... With [my under-secretary's] pension under my arm I can walk where I please without fear and trembling ... But if these youths in the House of Commons are so boisterous, what a deal of whipping they will take, and what a job I shall have![23]

Liverpool's stroke created uncertainty in the political world, as Planta, who had recently recovered from a 'very bad' cough, told Stratford Canning, 23 Feb. 1827: 'My earnest hope is that I shall have in my next letter, to announce to you, that your cousin is, as he ought to be, at the head of affairs. How I shall rejoice to see the country governed by him for many years'.[24] When Canning formed his ministry in April Planta, who received a foreign office retirement pension of £1,000, duly succeeded Lushington as patronage secretary and Lushington's brother as Member for the treasury borough of Hastings.[25] His initiation into parliamentary and political life was less than happy. Arbuthnot reported in July that he was 'in despair' at the divisions between Canning and his Whig partners, who made difficulties about obeying summonses for attendance from Planta and the much more experienced chief whip William Holmes*. Observing, too, that Canning had 'not a grain of common judgement', he went on:

> Planta is more impressed with this than anyone. I had occasion to see him yesterday, and in the course of conversation he burst forth and exclaimed, 'My dear Mr. Arbuthnot, who will ever be able to give judgement to Mr. Canning? He will take the advice of one person today, of another tomorrow, and on the next day of a third'.[26]

Planta himself confessed to Stratford Canning, 11 July:

> Our difficulties will be very great indeed next session, more particularly in the House of Lords ... In the Commons we are strong – by the means of those that have joined us – but then how will they act, and will they not give us constant trouble? In short, to say that our prospects are clear and satisfactory is impossible; but if your cousin does but keep his health (of which there is every chance, for he is delightfully well now) I think he will in the end triumph over all opposition.[27]

Less than a month later he was attending Canning on his death bed at Chiswick; and, 'struck down to the dust by this dreadful and most unexpected blow', he lamented the loss of 'the *best friend* and *most worthy chief* that ever directed and presided over the exertions of a set of men, for the attainment of great and noble and good objects'.[28] He urged William Huskisson* to take office under Lord Goderich in order to ensure the perpetuation of Canning's principles.[29] Holmes told Arbuthnot, 22 Aug. 1827, that in the difficult negotiations for the formation of the ministry Planta had behaved with 'great candour and I may add manliness', even though he was 'quite sick of what is going on, and is very sick of the Whigs and I think ashamed of his new master'.[30] Planta lost his father, whose effects were sworn under £5,000, on 3 Dec. 1827.[31] Soon afterwards he became embroiled in the turmoil which led the wretched Goderich first to offer and then to withdraw his resignation, a step which Planta 'went down on his knees to implore' him not to take. After Goderich's final resignation in January 1828 Planta, at Huskisson's request, sounded him as to his disposition towards the Wellington ministry and reported back his desire to 'make himself useful' in the Lords.[32]

It was reported that Planta was to lose his job, but in fact Huskisson's terms for taking office with Wellington included his retention at the treasury, which was conceded.[33] Sir Henry Hardinge* thought it '*un peu fort*' and likely to infuriate Lord Londonderry, who had been prejudiced against Planta by stories that he had spoken slightingly of his benefactor, Castlereagh, after his death. Hardinge discounted these allegations and was sure that Planta would be 'faithful to the duke'.[34] He started badly, for his failure to send out notes for attendance until the evening before the division on repeal of the Test and Corporation Acts, 26 Feb. 1828 (though he had warned the home secretary Robert Peel* three days earlier of the need to secure a good attendance), contributed to 'a general idea it was not to be made a government question' and so to the ministerial defeat. Wellington was 'much annoyed'.[35] A month later Mrs. Arbuthnot recorded Holmes's complaints that Peel's attitude deterred backbenchers from attending, and described Planta's receipt of 'an impudent letter' from four well-connected Members

> calling him the shepherd who was continually crying wolf. Holmes wanted Planta to send the note back with a list of the sums pocketed by the families of these four gentlemen ... However, Planta is a good natured man and would not take any notice of it.[36]

Planta voted for Catholic relief, 12 May. After the debate on provision for Canning's family the following day Lord George Cavendish Bentinck* complained to Mrs. Canning that 'that wretch Planta, who was *pro tempore* in the chair, never contrived to see' the Whig Mackintosh, who had attempted to speak in its favour.[37] On 14 May, when he brought up the report, Planta echoed Huskisson's sentiments :

> It was a very great relief to his mind ... that the provision ... was not to be considered as commensurate with his high public character, or as a reward for his eminent public services. If it had been to be so considered, he confessed he should have thought the provision very inadequate indeed.

He then delivered a eulogy of Canning, which he subsequently published, to the aggravation of Wellington who, according to Lord Ellenborough, was 'very much dissatisfied' with Planta's '*mutiny*' on this occasion.[38] He was reckoned to have precipitated, perhaps inadvertently, Huskisson's rash resignation from the ministry after his wayward vote on the East Retford disfranchisement bill, 19 May 1828. He walked home from the House with Huskisson and allegedly 'held very strong language' and 'told him the only thing he had left to do was to resign'. Planta might have been expected to follow suit, but he balked at the prospect of losing his £3,500 salary, as Lord Seaford commented:

> The pecuniary sacrifice (without a provision on retirement, of which there would have been little chance, from the duke of Wellington, in case of a hostile resignation) would have been very inconvenient. And one must not expect and certainly ought not to recommend, such sacrifices. So Huskisson felt when Planta consulted him, and he told him frankly, and I am satisfied sincerely, that he did not wish anybody to make any sacrifice for his sake.

He feared, nevertheless, that Planta would 'find his situation very uncomfortable'; and Lord Binning* thought that he did 'not seem very happy'.[39] Certainly Planta, who defended the grant for South American missions, 30 May 1828, seems never to have been quite at ease at the treasury, especially after the Huskissonites' resignation. He was probably aware that Wellington did not rate him very highly and was particularly dissatisfied with his management of the press. He had had some experience of this work at the foreign office and, according to Arbuthnot, had once boasted that he had then succeeded 'in gaining over *The Times*'. Yet in February 1828 he shrugged off Huskisson's reproaches over attacks on him in the ministerial press: 'the newspapers I do from my heart *despise* (a fine quality you will say in your secretary of the treasury) and never, while I live, shall anything they say go between me and my rest'. In September 1828 Wellington complained to John Croker* that Planta did 'not attend' properly to the press, 'nor does he meddle with that degree of intelligence which might be expected from him'. Planta continued to lack confidence in this sphere of his business and was perpetually exasperated by the intransigence of supposedly friendly editors.[40]

In September 1828 he told Huskisson that his treasury colleague George Dawson*, Peel's brother-in-law, had 'astonished us all' with his Londonderry speech in favour of Catholic relief, and he anticipated a speedy settlement of the question.[41] When ministers took it up he supplied Peel with miscellaneous information and various analyses of the Commons, by which he calculated that only about 119 Members would vote against it, with 33 others 'doubtful'.[42] In the event, minorities of 160 and 173 opposed the introduction and second reading of the relief bill, 6, 18 Mar. 1829. He was alleged to have 'miscalculated twenty or thirty': in fact, the first minority included no fewer than 49 Members whom he had expected to side with government.[43] He dealt with some routine treasury business in the House, 6 May. At the end of August 1829 Sir Richard Vyvyan* told his fellow Ultra Sir Edward Knatchbull* that Planta was 'with us in spirit'; but he was deluding himself, for a few days later Planta acted as Wellington's emissary on a visit to Knatchbull at Mersham. He found the baronet susceptible to flattery and propitiation, if only because of his rooted fear of a Whig government, which Planta exploited.[44] On the eve of the 1830 session, when he was 'confined ... with a severe cold and cough', he told Thomas Frankland Lewis* that ministers wanted 'as much support [as] we can get together' and that he expected to 'hear very much indeed of the distress of the agriculturists', but thought that the 'pretty good account' they could give of Ireland was 'a great point' in their favour.[45] The government's success in the debate on supply, 12 Feb., was said to have cheered him and Holmes, who 'say the temper of the country gentlemen is much improved' and were 'quite in spirits again'. He was rightly confident of an easy government win on the same issue, 15 Feb.[46] Yet the session turned out to be another troublesome one for Planta, with the government short of debating talent and sometimes struggling to retain control of a fragmented and mutinous Commons. He was embarrassed by their defeat on the Jewish emancipation bill, 5 Apr., though others were held largely to blame for the poor attendance; and he was said to be 'bemoaning himself' after the failure to make a House on 19 July for consideration of the Lords' amendments to the forgery punishment mitigation bill, which had Peel 'in a pet'.[47] On 24 May 1830 he took the government line of denying the existence of an interdict laid down by Canning against any attack by Mexico and Colombia on Cuba, which might have obliged them to protect the former against current Spanish aggression.

During the general election of 1830, when he came in again for Hastings in defiance of an attempt to open the borough, Planta wrote to Peel lamenting ministerial failures in Cambridgeshire, Devon and Suffolk and seeking to ward off criticism of his management: 'I must repeat that these matters are utterly unmanageable by anything that can be done from hence. In such things as we can influence and in some degree control, we have not been unsuccessful'.[48] With most of the returns in he reckoned on a ministerial gain of 20 or 21 Members, making the composition of the House 368 government and 234 opposition; but these estimates were optimistic, for the ministry was patently weaker than it had been in July.[49] On 21 Sept. 1830 he wrote to Peel from Fairlight:

> Being aware that this is about the time when the duke of Wellington will visit you, I have been working hard at our new House of Commons, and Charles Ross* has very kindly and efficiently assisted me. I now send you the results of his labours, with my remarks upon them. I am anxious that you shall receive these calculations when the duke is with you; and as Holmes is also in your neighbourhood, he may run through the lists, and, with his approval or alteration, they will no doubt be very tolerably correct.[50]

His analysis was as follows: 311 'friends'; 37 'moderate Ultras'; 37 'good doubtfuls'; 24 'doubtful doubtfuls'; 188 'foes'; 25 'violent Ultras'; 23 'bad doubtfuls', and 11 'Huskisson party'. This was ominous, with government in a minority of the House, though Planta's further refinements indicated that even if all the disaffected groups acted together, ministers would still command a paper majority of about 30.[51] Meanwhile Huskisson's untimely death, following those of Castlereagh and Canning, might have made any politician hesitate before accepting Planta's personal loyalty. He wrote to a friend:

> It has been my peculiar lot to go through a succession of painful shocks, in the sudden withdrawal of those with whom I have been politically connected (or rather under whom I have served) as well as by the intimacy of private friendship, and Mr. Huskisson was the *survivor*, who, with respect to me, united these two qualities.[52]

He was the conduit through whom Lord Clive* transmitted to Wellington and Peel his views, which Planta endorsed, on the urgent need for the government to recruit the Huskissonites; and in mid-October 1830 he was summoned to London to discuss what was to be done about the *Courier* newspaper, 'which goes on from bad to worse'.[53] The defeat of the ministry by 233-204 on the civil list, 15 Nov. 1830, exposed some of the flaws in Planta's earlier calculations of their strength. Of those designated 'friends', 17 opposed them, as did 20 of the 'moderate Ultras', including six of the nine additionally marked by Planta as 'friends'. Fourteen of the 'doubtful favourables' were hostile, among them five of the 18 he considered to be 'generally friends'. Above all, new Members voted decisively against the government and only 15 English county Members rallied to them.[54] Planta resigned with his colleagues, but managed to secure an addition of £500 his 1827 pension. He was one of the fallen ministers who immediately formed a small committee to organize and direct the opposition to the Grey ministry, and he placed his London house at 10 Charles Street, St. James's Square at their disposal when required.[55] On 3 Mar. 1831, according to Ellenborough, he, Francis Bonham* and Holmes were predicting a comfortable majority against the ministerial reform bill, but they were wide of the mark. Planta, who was 'low' and 'timid' at this juncture, duly voted against the second reading, 22 Mar., and for Gascoyne's wrecking amendment, 19 Apr. 1831.[56]

At the ensuing general election he had to abandon Hastings, where the reforming tide was too strong for him, but he continued to be involved in attempts to organize the parliamentary opposition. In June 1831 the Charles Street house, which he had now vacated, was formally adopted as an office and meeting place for the party. This establishment, which earned its frequenters the name of 'the Charles Street Gang', was the progenitor of the Carlton Club, formed the following year.[57] Planta was evidently not a member of the committee formed by the Conservatives in May 1832 to manage the forthcoming elections, and he seems to have stepped back from politics for a time after his marriage to the widow Charlotte Oom, who brought him a stepson, Adolphus. On 21 Sept. 1832 he wrote to Stratford Canning:

> I entirely agree in what you say of the happiness of being out of the way of politics. They have become wicked and discouraging things since, in the person of your cousin, a great mind, high feelings and most exalted views were defeated by selfishness and through narrowness of mind, when a short-sighted obstinacy took the name of consistency, and private dislike that of public principle, and thus one of the best hearts and the greatest of minds was broken, and driven from this world long before its time.[58]

He nevertheless obsequiously pressed his claims on Peel for a place in any future Conservative government. He enjoyed this in Peel's short-lived first ministry, but it was not until 1837 (after a surprise defeat two years earlier) that he regained the Hastings seat. Henry Goulburn* discounted him as a candidate for the post of chief whip for the Conservative opposition, admitting his 'integrity and honour', but doubtful 'as to his possessing [at the age of 50] the activity and energy necessary'. He was passed over for office in 1841.[59] Planta, who was described by Captain William Dyott in 1835 as 'a very agreeable man', died in April 1847.[60] He had left all his property to his wife and given instructions, which appear to have been carried out, for the destruction of most of his papers.[61]

[1] She was possibly a da. of Thomas Atwood, sometime c.j. of Dominica and the Bahamas, who *d.* in k.b. prison, 27 May 1793 (Add. 35642, f. 49; *Gent. Mag.* (1793), i. 576; ii. 669). [2] *Reg. St. George, Hanover Square*, iv. 160; PROB 11/2054/350; *Gent. Mag.* (1826), i. 287; (1829), i. 462. [3] *Gent. Mag.* (1773), 155. [4] *Oxford DNB*; E. Edwards, *Founders of British Museum*, 516-26; *Gent. Mag.*

(1827), ii 564-5. [5] *Horace Walpole Corresp.* (Yale edn.), xliii. 445-6; *Prince of Wales Corresp.* i. 437. [6] *Gent. Mag.* (1827), ii. 565; *Geo. III Corresp.* iv. 3194. [7] S. Lane Poole, *Stratford Canning*, i. 72, 196; *Farington Diary*, xiii. 4460, 4707; Add. 38257, ff. 259, 261; *Geo. IV Letters*, ii. 619. [8] *Life of Wilberforce*, iv. 259. [9] Bagot, *Canning and Friends*, ii. 57, 59; Add. 38273, f. 307. [10] TNA FO352/8/4. [11] Bagot, ii. 123, 131; Bagot mss (History of Parliament Aspinall transcripts), Planta to Bagot, 1 Aug. 1822. [12] *Arbuthnot Jnl.* i. 209; Bagot, ii. 156. [13] Bagot, ii. 200. [14] *Arbuthnot Jnl.* i. 355. [15] Harewood mss. [16] *Arbuthnot Jnl.* i. 360; Buckingham, *Mems. Geo. IV*, ii. 103; Add. 38411, f. 240. [17] Aberdeen Univ. Lib. Arbuthnot mss, Wellington to Mrs. Arbuthnot, 1 Sept. 1824. [18] Buckingham, ii. 133. [19] Add. 38746, f. 32. [20] *Arbuthnot Corresp.* 60; *Canning Official Corresp.* i. 174-5, 176, 182-8, 200-2; C.H. Philips, *E. I. Co.* 251-3. [21] *Arbuthnot Jnl.* i. 360-1. [22] FO352/10A/3, Planta to S. Canning, 11 Mar. 1825; 13A/1, same to same, 14 Feb., 26 Apr., 4 Aug. 1826. [23] Ibid. 362/13A/1. [24] W. Yorks. AS, Leeds, Stapleton mss 47; *Canning's Ministry*, 30. [25] *Canning's Ministry*, 107A; *Geo. IV Letters*, iii. 1368. [26] *Canning's Ministry*, 340, 343; Parker, *Peel*, i. 492. [27] *Canning's Ministry*, 360. [28] Bagot, ii. 417-19; FO352/17A/3, Planta to S. Canning, 7, 10 Aug. 1827. [29] Add. 38750, ff. 9, 19, 30, 145, 270; FO352/17A/3, Planta to S. Canning, 23 Aug. 1827. [30] Add. 40340, f. 192. [31] PROB 6/203/294. [32] Add. 38752, ff. 212-15; 38754, f. 95. [33] Cent. Kent. Stud. Camden mss U840 C351/1, Gore to Camden, 12 Jan. 1828; Add. 38754, f. 215; 40395, f. 85. [34] *Arbuthnot Corresp.* 101, 103 [35] *Ellenborough Diary*, i. 42; Add. 40395, f. 277; 40397, f. 1. [36] *Arbuthnot Jnl.* ii. 176. [37] Harewood mss, Bentinck to Mrs. Canning, 14 May 1828. [38] *Ellenborough Diary*, i. 106-7. [39] Add. 40397, f. 1; *Ellenborough Diary*, i. 114; TNA 30/29/9/5/71; Bagot mss, Binning to Bagot, 2 June 1828. [40] A. Aspinall, *Politics and the Press*, 200, 212, 239-33; Add. 38755, ff. 28, 41, 43; 40399, f. 290; *Wellington Despatches*, v. 54-55; vi. 329; *Croker Pprs.* ii. 21-23. [41] Add. 38757, ff. 68, 87; FO352/22/2, Planta to S. Canning, 26 Oct., 18 Nov. 1828. [42] Add. 40333, f. 88; 40340, f. 222; 40398, ff. 1, 3, 33-35. 83, 85. [43] *Ellenborough Diary*, i. 363, 382, 384; G.I.T. Machin, *Catholic Question in English Politics*, 162, 172. [44] Cornw. RO, Vyvyan mss DD/V/BO/48, Vyvyan to Knatchbull, 31 Aug. 1829; Wellington mss WP1/1044/4; H. Knatchbull Hugessen, *Kentish Fam.* 188-9. [45] NLW, Harpton Court mss, Planta to Lewis, 16 Jan. 1830. [46] *Ellenborough Diary*, ii. 195; Grey mss, Ellice to Grey [15 Feb. 1830]. [47] Add. 40333, f. 88; 40340, f. 222; 40400, f. 170; Lonsdale mss, Beckett to Lowther, 19 July 1830. [48] Add. 40401, f. 130; Chatsworth mss, Brougham to Devonshire, 8 Sept. 1830. [49] Add. 40401, f. 125; R. Stewart, *Foundation of Conservative Party*, 54-55; N. Gash, *Secretary Peel*, 641-2. [50] Add. 40401, f. 179. [51] Ibid. ff. 182-95. [52] Add. 37048, f. 67. [53] Powis mss (History of Parliament Aspinall transcripts), memo. 10 Oct., Planta to Clive, 21 Oct. 1830; Add. 40401, f. 232. [54] *Three Diaries*, pp. xxi-xxiii; A. Mitchell, *Whigs in Opposition*, 245. [55] Add. 40405, f. 272; Stewart, 55, 68; *Three Diaries*, 32, 35, 46, 47, 52, 57. [56] *Three Diaries*, 62, 63, 76, 85; Add. 40403, f. 276. [57] Stewart, 72-73; Gash, *Politics in Age of Peel*, 395-7; *Three Diaries*, 93, 190; Aspinall, 329-30, 336, 459, 467. [58] Lane Poole, ii. 17. [59] Add. 40309, f. 372; 40333, f. 372; 40403, f. 274; 40405, f. 272. [60] *Dyott's Diary*, ii. 207; *Gent. Mag.* (1847), ii. 86-87. [61] PROB 11/2034/350.

D.R.F.

PLEYDELL BOUVERIE, Hon. Duncombe (1780–1850), of Clyffe Hall, Market Lavington, Wilts.

DOWNTON	1806–1807
SALISBURY	20 Feb. 1828–1832
SALISBURY	6 May 1833–1834

b. 28 June 1780, 2nd s. of Jacob Pleydell Bouverie†, 2nd earl of Radnor (*d.* 1828), and Hon. Anne Duncombe, da. of Anthony Duncombe†, 1st Bar. Feversham; bro. of Hon. Philip Pleydell Bouverie* and William Pleydell Bouverie, Visct. Folkestone*. *educ.* Harrow 1790; Portsmouth naval acad. 1793. *m.* 27 Dec. 1809, Louisa, da. of Joseph May of Hale House, Hants, 1da. *d.* 5 Nov. 1850.

Midshipman RN 1795, lt. 1799, cdr. 1801, capt. 1802; col. marines 1830-37; r.-adm. 1837; adm. supt. Portsmouth dockyard 1837-42; v.-adm. 1846.

Pleydell Bouverie served in the navy almost continuously until 1813, being involved in numerous successful skirmishes with enemy shipping.[1] He later admitted that he had seen no general action, 'having been detached by Lord Nelson with other frigates up the Mediterranean two or three days only before his memorable and last action', and had no 'distinguished services to boast of, or have recorded'.[2] His father, the 2nd earl of Radnor, briefly had him returned for his pocket borough of Downton, and, after the war, settled on him his estate at Clyffe Hall in his native county, where he became a magistrate and a deputy lieutenant.[3] His political opinions were not so advanced as those of his elder brother, Lord Folkestone, who sat on their father's interest for Salisbury, a corporation borough, but it was perhaps because of his Whig views that Radnor set his face against returning him to Parliament on Folkestone's attempted resignation in 1812, or later. In 1818 the corporation considered asking Radnor to replace Folkestone with his less objectionable brother, but nothing came of it.[4] He split for Thomas Calley* and Robert Gordon* for Cricklade, and (having nominated them) for Paul Methuen† and William Pole Tylney Long Wellesley* for Wiltshire at the general election of 1818, but proposed and voted for the Tory John Dugdale Astley* at the county by-election in 1819.[5] He may have been present with Folkestone to witness Queen Caroline's return to London in November 1820.[6] He signed the requisition for a Wiltshire county meeting on her case, 17 Jan. 1821, when he proposed a petition to the Commons in her defence, declaring that the charges against her had not been proved. He used his own experience to argue that the canvas sheeting employed on board her polacca would not have afforded enough privacy to deceive the crew.[7] In 1827 he approved Folkestone's plan to have him returned for the vacancy that would be created by the death of their father, but feared that

> from my not being much accustomed to business and my inability to speak, I shall be putting myself in a situation where comparison to my disadvantage will often be made; I also feel that my means will be but little adequate to fill the situation of representative of the city as I could

wish; but I think I ought to keep these feelings secret to myself and you, and that I should be wanting to myself, were I willingly to forego the chance of a situation which many people have considered me as likely to succeed to, and towards my attainment of which you, knowing all my defects, are willing to lend your powerful aid.

After Folkestone succeeded as 3rd earl in January 1828, Pleydell Bouverie was made a free citizen of Salisbury, and he was elected unopposed following a canvass, 20 Feb., when he promised to 'act independently, honestly and uprightly, to the best of my judgement'.[8]

He took his seat, 27 Feb., and was admitted to Brooks's, 16 Mar. 1828. It was probably he, and not his uncle Bartholomew Bouverie, Member for Downton, who presented the Salisbury maltsters' petition against the Malt Act, 18 Mar. He divided against extending the franchise of East Retford to the freeholders of Bassetlaw, 21 Mar. He presented Salisbury petitions in favour of Catholic relief, 2 May, and voted for this, 12 May 1828. That month he was appointed to the command of the *Windsor Castle*, and he was stationed in the Mediterranean for the next two and a half years.[9] In early 1829 he was listed by Planta, the Wellington ministry's patronage secretary, among those 'opposed to securities', but he gave no further votes on the Catholic question, and presumably was not present for the rest of that Parliament. Following the accession of William IV in 1830, he was promoted to a colonelcy of marines. His absence did not create problems with the corporation of Salisbury at the general election that year, when he was represented by his brother Philip and was returned unopposed.[10] His negotiations at Samos were criticized by the duke of Wellington, who asked Lord Aberdeen, the foreign secretary, 19 Oct., to inquire into the matter because Pleydell Bouverie appeared 'to have given up altogether the decision of the allied powers in conference in London and to have encouraged the Samians to resist it'.[11] He was listed by ministers among their 'foes', and was absent from the division on the civil list, 15 Nov. 1830, which caused their downfall. He attended the Wiltshire reform meeting, 25 Feb. 1831.[12] It was almost certainly he and not Philip who presented and cordially endorsed a petition from the inhabitants of Salisbury for election by ballot, 26 Feb., and one in favour of the Grey ministry's reform bill, 9 Mar.[13] He may have been the 'Mr. Pleydell Bouverie' who was granted one week's sick leave, 14 Mar.; but if so, he was present to bring up a reform petition from the inhabitant householders of St. Martin-in-the-Fields, 21 Mar., and to vote for the second reading of the reform bill, 22 Mar. He presented the Downton reform petition, 18 Apr., and divided against Gascoyne's wrecking amendment, 19 Apr. At the ensuing general election he was forced to canvass extensively among the mainly anti-reform corporators of Salisbury, where Wadham Wyndham, the Tory Member, and William Bird Brodie, a reformer, both offered, but his return was never really in doubt. He spoke in favour of reform, 30 Apr., and at a rowdy meeting was elected at the head of the poll, with Wyndham. He was anxious to rejoin his ship, but was dissuaded from this, apparently because it was shortly due home, which allowed him to discharge his final duties as its captain before the meeting of Parliament.[14] Prompted by Brodie, and to the annoyance of Wyndham, he offered to stand again once reform had passed, and a meeting was held in his support, 8 June.[15] He wrote to William Cobbett†, 12 June 1831, to deny the accusation that his family had connived in the return of an anti-reform Member for Salisbury.[16]

He voted for the second reading of the reintroduced reform bill, 6 July, at least twice against adjourning proceedings on it, 12 July, and against using the 1831 census to determine the boroughs in the disfranchisement schedules, 19 July 1831. He told the committee, 21 July, that Radnor, who actually wanted Downton to be abolished, was ready to submit to its decision. But, slightly out of step with his brother, he pointed out that the borough was entitled to retain one Member and that it might legitimately be preserved by being united with Wilton, and he voted against ministers on the question of its standing part of schedule A. For the same reason, he voted against the total disfranchisement of Saltash, 26 July. He otherwise divided steadily with government on the bill's details until 18 Aug., when he voted for Lord Chandos's amendment to enfranchise £50 tenants-at-will. He voted with ministers on the Dublin election, 23 Aug., and for the passage of the reform bill, 21 Sept., and the second reading of the Scottish bill, 23 Sept. He was given a fortnight's leave on urgent business, 26 Sept. He signed the requisition for a meeting in Devizes, 30 Sept., when he moved a petition to the Lords in favour of the bill. Although disagreeing with more radical remarks, he said that 'the people must at last trust to themselves; and probably there may be as little confidence to be placed in the Whigs, *as a body*, as in the Tories'. He no doubt attended the county meeting held in Devizes that day, and after the bill's defeat in the Lords he signed the requisition for a further meeting of the freeholders, 28 Oct., when he expressed his confidence that the ministry and the king would carry reform, and urged those present to subscribe to the costs of William Ponsonby's* petition against the result of the Dorset by-election.[17] He voted for Lord Ebrington's confidence motion, 10 Oct. He divided in favour of the second reading of the revised reform bill, 17 Dec. 1831, probably for both the disfranchisement clauses, 20, 23 Jan. 1832, and again for its details. Either he or Philip, now Member for Downton, was the 'H.P. Bouverie' who voted in the minority for the second reading of the vestry bill, 23 Jan. He divided against the production of information on Portugal, 9 Feb., and military punishments, 16 Feb., but with the minority for inquiry into Peterloo, 15 Mar. He was listed in the majority against the Sunderland (South Side) Wet Docks bill, 2 Apr. He voted for the third reading of the reform bill, 22 Mar., and paired for Ebrington's motion for an address calling on the king to appoint only ministers who would carry it unimpaired, 10 May. He wrote to Radnor, 13 May, that 'I don't mean to be absent from the House after my pairing is ended, *viz*, after tomorrow', and commented on Wellington's appointment as premier that

> it is quite astonishing, and impossible that the country can be satisfied that the duke should thus trip up Lord Grey's heels and deprive him of his well-deserved fame, even if he were to give so much reform as would satisfy them.[18]

He presented the Salisbury petition for supplies to be withheld until the bill was passed, 21 May. He divided in the minority of ten against the second reading of the Liverpool disfranchisement bill, 23 May, and for the second reading of the Irish reform bill, 25 May. His only other known votes were with ministers for the Russian-Dutch loan, 26 Jan., 20 July 1832.

Although he had initially intended to withdraw from politics after the passage of the Reform Act, he decided to contest Salisbury again at the general election later that year. In various addresses and speeches, he pledged himself to the ballot and shorter parliaments, and reiterated his reasons for voting against the disfranchisement of Downton, the earlier gift of a seat for which he was rumoured to have refused because of his difference of opinion with his father. He also promised to support economies and boasted that he had offered to resign his position as colonel of marines for the sake of retrenchment. After a bitter contest, Pleydell Bouverie, whom Denis Le Marchant† described as 'an excellent man', was seated on petition, but he left the House at the following dissolution and never sat again.[19] Of an 'erect figure and light and active step' until his last illness, he died in November 1850, being succeeded by his wife (*d.* 1852) and their only child Louisa (1811-98), the widow of Samuel Hay (1807-47), a younger son of the 17th earl of Erroll.[20]

[1] J. Marshall, *Naval Biog.* iv. 550-2; W.R. O'Byrne, *Naval Biog.* i. 103-4; *Gent. Mag.* (1851), i. 197-8; Countess of Radnor, *Cat. of Pictures in Collection of Earl of Radnor*, ii. 89. [2] Add. 38040, f. 165. [3] *HP Commons, 1790-1820*, iv. 826; *VCH Wilts.* x. 93. [4] Berks. RO, Pleydell Bouverie mss D/EPb O28, Radnor to Folkestone, 18 Aug. 1812; *VCH Wilts.* vi. 122; Longford Castle mss 30/7, Folkestone to corporation of Salisbury, 31 July 1827. [5] Pleydell Bouverie mss O11; *Late Elections* (1818), 403; *Salisbury Jnl.* 26 July 1819; *Wilts. Pollbook* (1819), 128. [6] *Creevey's Life and Times*, 134. [7] *Devizes Gazette*, 11, 18 Jan. 1821. [8] Longford Castle mss 30/7, Pleydell Bouverie to Folkestone, 6 Aug. 1827, 7, 8, 10 Feb.; *Salisbury Jnl.* 25 Feb. 1828; Wilts. RO, Salisbury borough recs. G23/1/7. [9] O'Byrne, i. 103-4. [10] Longford Castle mss 30/7, Boucher to Radnor, 1, 5, 16 June, 3 July; *Salisbury Jnl.* 2 Aug. 1830. [11] Wellington mss WP1/1148/40; *Wellington Despatches*, vii. 311. [12] *Salisbury Jnl.* 28 Feb. 1831. [13] Ibid. 7 Mar.; *The Times*, 27 Feb., 10 Mar. 1831. [14] *Salisbury Jnl.* 18, 25 Apr., 2, 9 May, 13 June; Wilts. RO, Radnor mss 490/1375, Pleydell Bouverie to Radnor, 19, 24-28, 30 Apr., 1 May, Boucher to same, 24, 26, 28 Apr., 3 May 1831; R.K. Huch, *The Radical Lord Radnor*, 117-19. [15] *Salisbury Jnl.* 16 May, 6, 13 June; Radnor mss 490/1375, Pleydell Bouverie to Radnor, 5 May, Boucher to same, 5, 13 May 1831. [16] *Pol. Reg.* 18 June 1831. [17] *Devizes Gazette*, 29 Sept., 6 Oct., 3 Nov. 1831. [18] Longford Castle mss 30/7. [19] Ibid. 30/7, Pleydell Bouverie to Radnor, 13 May, 13, 17 June; 36/3; *Salisbury Jnl.* 18 June, 1 Oct., 26 Nov., 3, 10, 17 Dec.; Add. 51688, Lansdowne to Holland, 23 Dec. 1832; *Three Diaries*, 288. [20] *Devizes Gazette*, 14 Nov. 1850; Radnor, ii. 90.

S.M.F.

PLEYDELL BOUVERIE, Hon. Philip (1788–1872), of Down Ampney House, Glos. and 36 Curzon Street and 11 Haymarket, Mdx.

COCKERMOUTH	1830–1831
DOWNTON	20 July 1831–1832
BERKSHIRE	1857–1865

b. 21 Oct. 1788, 5th s. of Jacob Pleydell Bouverie†, 2nd earl of Radnor (*d.* 1828), and Hon. Anne Duncombe, da. of Anthony Duncombe†, 1st Bar. Feversham; bro. of Hon. Duncombe Pleydell Bouverie* and William Pleydell Bouverie, Visct. Folkestone*. *educ.* Harrow 1797. *m.* 7 Nov. 1811, Maria, da. of Sir William Pierce Ashe A'Court†, 1st bt., of Heytesbury, Wilts., 1s. 4da. (1 *d.v.p.*). *d.* 23 May 1872.

Commr. of lieutenancy, London 1831-62; sheriff, Som. 1843-4.

Chairman, Grand Junction Canal Co. 1821-40; dir. Sun Fire Office 1824; dir. Sun Life Office 1824, chairman 1861-5.

Pleydell Bouverie began his banking career as a clerk in the office of Bosanquet and Company of 73 Lombard Street, London, and by 1811 he had entered a partnership with one Edmund Antrobus (*d.* 1827) at 35 Craven Street.[1] In 1820 the leading Whig barrister Henry Brougham* instructed an agent to pay a sum of money into their bank, apparently in connection with the opposition campaign on behalf of Queen Caroline.[2] Pleydell Bouverie's petition concerning the holders of navy five per cent stock was presented to the Commons, 7 Mar. 1822, by his eldest brother Lord Folkestone, Member for Salisbury.[3] In 1825 Antrobus retired and was replaced by Pleydell Bouverie's childhood friend, Henry Francis, youngest son of Charles Shaw Lefevre†. He maintained business and political connections with the Shaw Lefevres but, against his wishes, Henry Francis resigned as his partner in 1830.[4] By then the firm had moved to 11 Haymarket, and by 1832 it was known as Bouverie, Norman and Murdoch. He had a hand in other commercial concerns. In 1829, for instance, Edward John Littleton* sought his opinion as chairman of the Grand Junction Canal Company on the effect of the reduction of the duty on seaborne coal on inland trade.[5]

Pleydell Bouverie voted for the Whig Robert Gordon* for Cricklade at the general election of 1818, and may have been present with Folkestone to witness the queen's return to London in November 1820.[6] His Whig politics were not nearly so advanced as Folkestone's and he never joined Brooks's. Yet, as with his brother Duncombe, and much to his disappointment, his Tory father, the 2nd earl of Radnor, who controlled two seats at Downton and one at Salisbury, objected to bringing him into Parliament. When Folkestone succeeded to the earldom in 1828, he declined Alexander Powell's offer to resign Downton in his brother's favour, but he put the seat at his disposal at the general election of 1830.[7] Then, as part of the compromise whereby Brougham agreed not to challenge the Lowther interest in Westmorland, and in spite of Radnor's objections, Pleydell Bouverie arranged for Lord Lonsdale to bring him in for Cockermouth and for Radnor to return Brougham's brother James for Downton.[8] At the urgent request of the family's agent, he successfully represented Duncombe, who was absent on naval service, at the Salisbury election, 30 July.[9] He was listed by the Wellington ministry among their 'foes' and voted in the majority against them on the civil list, 15 Nov. 1830. He signed the requisition for a Wiltshire county reform meeting and was present at it, 25 Feb. 1831.[10] He was a regular but silent attender at the Commons, where it was probably Duncombe who presented reform petitions from Salisbury, 26 Feb., 9 Mar., and St. Martin-in-the-Fields, 21 Mar., though it might have been to him that one week's sick leave was granted, 14 Mar. He voted for the second reading of the Grey ministry's reform bill, 22 Mar., and against Gascoyne's wrecking amendment, 19 Apr. 1831.

He originally intended to stand for Downton at the subsequent general election, but instead started for Cricklade, where his family had a vestigial interest, and which was close to his residence at Down Ampney. He offered with Gordon as a 'zealous friend' of reform, but his prospects were damaged by the entry of the former Tory Member Thomas Calley and he was defeated after a lengthy contest.[11] Alleging sharp practice, he expressed his disappointment in an address, 14 May 1831:

> I came forward to afford you the opportunity of sending to Parliament two Members pledged to a defined plan of reform; I was willing to bind myself to that plan, because I thought its provisions just and reasonable – a plan which will give to the middling, intelligent, independent classes the power of selecting such persons to represent them and their interests, and to manage their affairs, as they approve.

He expounded these views at a reform dinner in Malmesbury, 30 May.[12] Much to Lord Brougham's annoyance, Radnor turned out James Brougham in order to provide Pleydell Bouverie with a seat for Downton, 20 July 1831, when his address was given as Nether Broughton, Leicestershire.[13]

Pleydell Bouverie, who may have been present to vote in the majority for the total disfranchisement of his constituency, 21 July 1831, divided steadily in favour of the details of the reintroduced reform bill. He voted in the minority for printing the Waterford petition for disarming the Irish yeomanry, 11 Aug., but with government on the Dublin election controversy, 23 Aug. He divided for Lord Chandos's amendment to enfranchise £50 tenants-at-will, 18 Aug., and in the minority for transferring Aldborough from schedule B to schedule A, 14 Sept. He voted for the passage of the bill, 21 Sept., and for Lord Ebrington's confidence motion, 10 Oct. That month he signed the requisition for another Wiltshire county reform meeting.[14] He voted for the second reading of the revised bill, 17 Dec. 1831, and possibly for the schedule B clause, 23 Jan. 1832. He may have been the 'H.P. Bouverie' who voted in the minority for the second reading of the vestry bill, 23 Jan. He divided with government against the production of information on Portugal, 9 Feb., but in the minorities against restoring the salary of the Irish registrar of deeds to its original level, 9 Apr., and for inquiry into colonial slavery, 24 May. He divided against giving the vote to all £10 poor rate payers, 3 Feb., and for the registration clause, 8 Feb. He voted for the total disfranchisement of Appleby, 21 Feb., and the enfranchisement of Tower Hamlets, 28 Feb., but against the partial disfranchisement of Helston, 23 Feb. He voted for the third reading of the bill, 22 Mar., Ebrington's motion for an address calling on the king to appoint only ministers who would carry it unimpaired, 10 May, and the second reading of the Irish reform bill, 25 May, and against increasing the county representation of Scotland, 1 June. His only other known votes were with government for the Russian-Dutch loan, 26 Jan., 12, 16, 20 July 1832.

His seat having been abolished by the Reform Act, he sought another one in the neighbourhood, but decided not to start for Cricklade, Wilton or one of the Wiltshire divisions. He refused to contemplate replacing Duncombe at Salisbury and, after a brief canvass, declined to stand a contest at Cirencester. Radnor wrote at the time that 'my brother's politics are the same as mine, except that he does not push his opinions so far: he is a reformer, but not as *radical as I*'.[15] He stood unsuccessfully as a reformer at Devizes in 1835 and, having established himself at Brymore Park, near Bridgwater, for Somerset West in 1847.[16] He deposited some of the papers of John Pym of Brymore in the British Museum, while others remained in the family.[17] In 1855 his firm merged with Ransom and Company, to become Ransom, Bouverie and Company of 1 Pall Mall East.[18] Having returned to the House as Member for Berkshire, in 1861 he wrote the *Vindication of a Churchman* in favour of the abolition of church rates. He died in May 1872, leaving the bulk of his estate to his only son, Philip (1821-90), who, like his son Henry Hales (1848-1925), was a partner in the family bank.[19]

[1] F.G. Hilton Price, *London Bankers* (1890-1), 20; *The Times*, 23 Apr. 1827; Countess of Radnor, *Cat. of Pictures in Collection of Earl of Radnor*, ii. 92. [2] *Geo. IV Letters*, ii. 847. [3] *The Times*, 8 Mar. 1822. [4] Brougham mss, Pleydell Bouverie to Brougham, 12 Dec. 1825; Hants RO, Wickham mss 38M49/7/166/1-9; F. Willson, *A Strong Supporting Cast*, 67-68. [5] Wellington mss WP1/1020/8. [6] Berks. RO, Pleydell Bouverie mss D/EPb O11; *Creevey's Life and Times*, 134. [7] Pleydell Bouverie mss O28, Radnor to Folkestone, 18 Aug. 1812; Longford Castle mss 30/7, Folkestone to corporation of Salisbury, 31 July 1827, same to Powell, 8 Feb. 1828. [8] Wilts. RO, Radnor mss 490/1374, Radnor's mem. 9 July, Pleydell Bouverie to Radnor, 10 July, Shaw Lefevre to same, Tues. [n.d.]; *Carlisle Jnl.* 7 Aug.; Lonsdale mss, Lowther to Lonsdale, 20 Aug. 1830; Willson, 74-75. [9] Longford Castle mss 30/7, Boucher to Radnor, 1, 5, 16 June, 3 July, Pleydell Bouverie to same, 19 June; *Salisbury Jnl.* 2 Aug. 1830 [10] Radnor mss 490/1376, Radnor's diary, 17 Dec. 1830, 26 Feb. 1831. [11] *VCH Wilts.* v. 220-1; Radnor mss 490/1375, Boucher to Radnor, 24 Apr., 13 May; Warws. RO, Throckmorton mss CR 1998/Tribune/folder 10/1; Creevey mss, Creevey to Miss Ord, 2 May; *Devizes Gazette*, 5, 19 May; *The Times*, 9 May 1831. [12] *Devizes Gazette*, 26 May, 2 June 1831. [13] Add. 76371, Brougham to Althorp [11 May]; Creevey mss, Creevey to Miss Ord, 16 May 1831. [14] *Salisbury Jnl.* 24 Oct. 1831. [15] Ibid. 17 Dec.; Longford Castle mss 30/7, D. Pleydell Bouverie to Radnor, 10, 12, 15, 19 June 1832; Radnor mss 490/1382. [16] *Devizes Gazette*, 18 Dec. 1834, 8 Jan. 1835; *Taunton Courier*, 18 Aug. 1847. [17] Add. 11692; *HMC 10th Rep.* vi. 82-98. [18] *The Times*, 5 Dec. 1855. [19] Ibid. 27 May, 10 Aug. 1872.

S.M.F.

PLEYDELL BOUVERIE, William, Visct. Folkestone (1779–1869), of Coleshill House, nr. Highworth, Berks.[1]

DOWNTON	25 Mar. 1801–1802
SALISBURY	1802–27 Jan. 1828

b. 11 May 1779, 1st s. of Jacob Pleydell Bouverie†, 2nd earl of Radnor, and Hon. Anne Duncombe, da. of Anthony Duncombe†, 1st Bar. Feversham; bro. of Hon. Duncombe Pleydell Bouverie* and Hon. Philip Pleydell Bouverie*. *educ.* Paris 1789; Edinburgh Univ. 1794; Brasenose, Oxf. 1795; continental tour 1797. *m.* (1) 2 Oct. 1800, Catherine (*d.* 17 May 1804), da. and h. of Henry Fiennes Pelham Clinton, earl of Lincoln†, s. of Henry, 2nd duke of Newcastle, 2da. (1 *d.v.p.*); (2) 24 May 1814, Anne Judith, da. of Sir Henry Paulet St. John Mildmay†, 3rd bt., of Dogmersfield, Hants, 2s. 3da. (1 *d.v.p.*). *suc.* fa. as 3rd earl of Radnor 27 Jan. 1828. *d.* 9 Apr. 1869.

Chairman, q. sess. Wilts. (Salisbury) 1815-35; recorder, Salisbury 1828-36.

Capt. Berks. militia 1803, Berks. vol. cav. 1805; lt.-col. R. Berks. militia 1812, res. 1817.

The political principles of Folkestone, a leading member of the extreme wing of opposition in the Commons, conformed more to those of an advanced Whig than to the radicalism with which he was usually identified. Originally returned for Downton on the interest of his father, the 2nd earl of Radnor, he came to prominence with his attacks on the Addington ministry's peace preliminaries. But it was as a member of the 'Mountain', in close connection with Samuel Whitbread†, Sir Francis Burdett* and the radical political writer William Cobbett†, that he made his reputation. An inveterate opponent of corruption, he played a major part in the campaigns against Lord Melville, Lord Wellesley and the duke of York, and was active in resisting the power of the crown and defending the liberty of the subject. Yet he was content to vote with the Whigs on a wide range of issues, notably for economies and tax reductions, and this practice he continued into the 1820s. His excoriating attacks on government stemmed not from a desire to see it remodelled, but from a wish to have it restored, by means of ameliorative reforms, to the purity it had attained in 1689. He saw himself as an exemplar of the type of enlightened and disinterested aristocratic leadership which, with the support of public opinion, validated by county meetings, could effect such alterations.[2] Thus, he was in favour of annual parliaments, but only in order to ensure the good behaviour of Members, and he opposed all other political reforms (though by 1818 there was already evidence that his views were becoming more advanced in this area).[3]

That he was depicted as a radical was not surprising considering that he eschewed any close co-operation with the Whigs, whom he thought 'just a few shades better than the Tories', and preferred to call himself a 'radical reformer' or 'ultra-liberal'.[4] It also arose from the novelty of an heir to a peerage denouncing the system of influence which had promoted his own family's interests, and the originality of his character. Intelligent and well informed, he could be rash in debate and stubborn in his opinions; his views on the currency question, for example, were typically brilliant and idiosyncratic. In addition, his high-minded moral stance had been considerably tainted by the revelation of his liaison with York's mistress, Mary Ann Clarke. Folkestone's behaviour made for an uneasy relationship with Radnor, a convinced Tory. Dismayed by his misfortunes, Folkestone had been willing to withdraw from politics at the general election of 1812, but was persuaded against it by Radnor's reproachful response that it would mean the end of the family's control over one seat at Salisbury, which Folkestone had occupied since 1802.[5] Sensitive to his father's position, his conduct in Parliament was sometimes muted, but he did, for instance, vote several times in favour of Catholic relief. Despite the unpopularity which this caused him in Salisbury, a corporation borough, and the threat of an opposition, he was returned at the general election of 1818 without having to stand a poll. He plumped for the Whigs Robert Gordon* for Cricklade and Paul Methuen† for Wiltshire that year, and for John Dugdale Astley* at the county by-election in 1819.[6] Following the Peterloo massacre, he emerged from a period of comparative obscurity to join in the opposition to the subsequent repressive legislation. Speaking in Salisbury at the following general election, 9 Mar. 1820, when he was again returned unopposed, he said that his actions had been 'completely justified by the effects which those measures had produced'.[7] He was admitted a burgess of Nottingham, by gift, 28 Aug. 1820.[8]

Folkestone spoke for printing George Dawson's petition against his ill treatment in Ilchester gaol, 31 May, the East India Company's volunteers bill, 19 June, and a petition from the freeholders of Hungerford and Newbury for shortening the duration of polls, which he presented, 27 June 1820.[9] He divided against Wilberforce's compromise motion on Queen Caroline, 22 June, and the appointment of a secret committee, 26 June, and criticized ministers' handling of the affair, 17 Oct. He was present in the crowd to witness the queen's return to London, 29 Nov. 1820, and was involved in the extra-parliamentary campaign on her behalf, including by signing requisitions for county meetings in Kent and Wiltshire.[10] As usual, he was particularly active in Berkshire, where he resided on his father's Coleshill estate, and, distanced from immediate paternal disapproval, was perhaps more at liberty to express his own opinions. He got up a requisition, and, permission having been refused, organized a meeting of freeholders, 8 Jan. 1821. These attempts to stir up respectable opinion did not entirely gain the approval of the Whigs, even of such an 'intimate friend' as Lord Althorp*. But he successfully moved his resolutions, in a speech which again roundly condemned the proceedings against Caroline, and also signalled a development in his thinking on reform:

> Unless the House of Commons were made to act in unison with the general feeling of the people, it were vain for the country to look for a redress of grievances by any change which merely embraced the substitution of one set of men for another in the affairs of the country. A reform in the representation of the people was therefore indispensable.[11]

Although his intended attack on ministers for closing the previous session without a speech from the throne was 'knocked on the head' by the discovery that there were precedents, Folkestone referred to it in speaking against the address, 23 Jan., when he complained about agricultural distress, the currency and the poor laws.[12] He also denounced government for failing to take notice of the expressions of public opinion in the queen's favour, and, dividing consistently against government on this issue, called for further inquiry, 24, 31 Jan. He moved for an account of official salaries, 15 Feb., acted as a teller for the minority for production of the ordnance estimates in detail the following day, and divided steadily in favour of retrenchment and lower taxation that session.[13] He spoke against an unconvertible paper currency, 19 Mar., but his statement that there should have been an alteration in the standard before any return to cash payments had been agreed was condemned by the minister Huskisson as amounting to a breach of faith with the public creditor. If so, it was a breach which Folkestone, defending his position, 21 Mar., 3 Apr., argued might be justified in certain circumstances. He stated that repeal of the additional malt duty would provide relief, 21 Mar. He voted to make Leeds a scot and lot borough if it received Grampound's seats, 2 Mar., and for parliamentary reform, 18 Apr., 9 May, and to secure the independence of Parliament, 31 May. Among other opposition votes that session, he of course divided in favour of repealing the Blasphemous and Seditious Libels Act, 8 May, and for inquiry into Peterloo, 16 May 1821.

Folkestone, who voted against the introduction of a bill to suspend habeas corpus in Ireland, 7 Feb. 1822, condemned this and the insurrection bill the following day, on the grounds that no evidence had been produced to prove their necessity and that they concentrated too much power in the hands of Wellesley, the lord lieutenant. He was a teller for the minority against going into committee on the former bill and divided against ministers several times in the committee on the latter, 8 Feb. When Creevey moved to curtail the powers of government, 27 Feb., he apparently sat beside him on the front bench.[14] He presented his brother Philip's petition concerning navy half per cent stock, 7 Mar.[15] He continued to side frequently with opposition, including for remitting the remainder of Henry Hunt's* gaol sentence, 24 Apr. Making what he called his first speech on reform, 25 Apr., he revealed that, prompted by the House's support for the recent coercive legislation, he had become persuaded that it was the only way of saving the country. He stressed that 'the reform he should advocate was not framed so as to establish a democracy; it was not meant to destroy the throne, but to support it'. Taking Canning to task, he denied that the people were happy under the present system, argued that the Commons had gained too much weight in the tripartite constitution, and pointed out that the electoral influence of the peerage had greatly increased. He made no specific recommendations, but praised Bentham's idea of 'annuality of election'. George Agar Ellis* commented that he spoke 'tediously' and Mrs. Arbuthnot recorded that it was a 'dull speech of two hours', while Charles Williams Wynn* noted that the House was 'extremely clamorous and inattentive to Folkestone (so much that he was obliged repeatedly to stop, in order to procure silence)'.[16] Ministers became restless when, employing tortuous logic, he asserted that they really wanted to create a republic, and Canning later answered his criticisms in detail. He attended the Kent county meeting on distress, 11 June.[17] He spoke and acted as a teller for the minority of four against the second reading of the small notes bill, 2 July 1822, when he complained about the renewal of the Irish Insurrection Act.

In late 1822 he participated in the campaign for promoting county meetings to petition the Commons, and took a lead in preparing the requisition for one in Berkshire. He attended the meeting at Abingdon, 27 Jan. 1823, when he congratulated the freeholders on having 'traced the depression of agriculture to its true source, the corrupt state of the representation of the people', and advocated extensive reform, which, contrary to what was said by the new foreign secretary Canning ('that great apostle of anti-reformers'), would prevent, not encourage, revolution.[18] He voted for parliamentary reform, 20 Feb., 24 Apr., and alteration of the Scottish representative system, 2 June. He presented a petition from Charles Andrew Thomson complaining of losses arising from changes in the value of money, 21 Feb., when he also criticized the budget for failing to address the problems of distress and the currency. He seconded Althorp's motion for repeal of the Foreign Enlistment Act, 16 Apr., and was a teller with him for the minority. His speech, which Agar Ellis termed 'violent and rather eloquent', was a lengthy attack on Canning's policy of non-intervention over the French invasion of Spain, which drew from the foreign secretary the stinging retort that 'never before did I behold so complete a personification of the character which I have somewhere seen described as "exhibiting the contortions of the Sybil without her inspiration"!', and the assertion that 'however I may have "truckled" to France, I shall never "truckle" to the noble lord'. The following day Brougham forced up Canning again by employing the term 'truckling' in another context, and Creevey reported that 'the House generally was *decidedly* against Canning, as it had been the night before upon his passion and low-lived tirade against Folkestone'.[19] Despite acknowledging his anger on that occasion, Folkestone returned to his theme, 30 Apr., describing the failure to defend Spain as a blow to the cause of freedom and a diminution of Britain's security and reputation abroad. He voted for inquiries into the legal proceedings against the Dublin Orange rioters, 22 Apr., and the state of Ireland prior to renewal of the Insurrection Act, 12 May. Having touched on the question of the currency in relation to Irish tithes, 30 May, he emphasized the need for the equitable adjustment of contracts affected by its alteration, 12 June 1823. Without a division, it was agreed to add this suggestion as an amendment to his colleague Western's motion for a select committee on cash payments, and he voted in the minority for this that day.

Although, as usual, he presented several Salisbury petitions, Folkestone was surprisingly inactive during the following session, when his only recorded vote was for repeal of the assessed taxes, 10 May 1824. Nor was he greatly involved in public business the following year, though he did divide for the usury bill, 8 Feb. 1825, and steadily against the Irish repressive legislation, as well as for Catholic relief, 1 Mar., 21 Apr., 10 May. He raised difficulties concerning the exchange of country bank notes for gold, 27 June, and the poor returns, 1 July 1825.[20] He complained about the lack of notice on going into committee on the Bank Charter and Promissory Notes Act, 10 Feb. 1826, when he stated that 'the existing evils arose, in great measure, from the immense quantity of paper money which was in circulation', and criticized the proposed financial changes because they would bring back distress and increase the sufferings of the poor. John Evelyn Denison* thought it a 'long and stupid speech' and Sir James Mackintosh* deemed him 'unseasonably acrimonious', but Agar Ellis reported that he 'spoke well, in the plain country gentleman style, and was worth hearing upon the subject of the past and present state of the lower orders'.[21] On 20 Feb. he presented and endorsed a petition from Cobbett ('who, he should make no scruple in saying was, in his opinion, one of the ablest men in the country') complaining of fluctuations in the currency, and objected to the clause in the promissory notes bill which allowed the Bank to continue to issue small notes in certain circumstances. He was involved in an argument over an account of the issue of small notes, 26 Apr.[22] He voted for parliamentary reform, 27 Apr., and to curb electoral bribery, 26 May. He was probably the 'my lord' depicted helping Cobbett to attack 'fraudulent paper money' in a cartoon dated 2 June 1826.[23] He apparently subscribed £50 to the fund for electing Cobbett for Preston at the general election later that year, when he was again quietly returned for Salisbury, despite differing in politics with some of the corporators.[24]

Creevey, who noted that 'Folky has been but a shabby fellow considering all our past hospitalities to him', praised him for his speech on 1 Dec. 1826, in which he belaboured ministers 'for calling Parliament together and then not telling the people what they meant to do'.[25] He brought up petitions from Folkestone and Blackburn for free trade in corn, 21 Feb. 1827. The latter called, among other things, for annual parliaments and universal suffrage, and he remarked that 'they were, he knew, heretical doctrines in that House; nevertheless he was happy to find they were gaining ground throughout the country'.[26] The following day he charged ministers with being supine in their handling of the currency. He voted against the grant for the duke of Clarence, 2, 16 Mar., for an import price for corn of 50*s.* not 60*s.*, 9 Mar., and to reduce this by 10*s.* by 1833, 27 Mar. He divided for Catholic relief, 6 Mar. His last recorded votes were for inquiry into the allegations against the corporation of Leicester, 15 Mar., and with the majority in favour of the disfranchisement of Penryn, 28 May. In expectation of his father's death, Folkestone had prepared a letter to the members of the corporation of Salisbury, 31 July 1827, assuring them of his wish to maintain the cordial relations between them and his family. By then, Radnor being in failing health, Folkestone had managed his affairs for some time.[27] He succeeded him as 3rd earl in January 1828, just before the opening of the new session of Parliament. He inherited personal wealth sworn under £80,000 and several estates, including Longford Castle, the continuing alterations to which he hated and had promised to tear down.[28]

He brought in his brother Duncombe to replace him at Salisbury, where his interest proved to be short-lived, and returned other reformers for Downton from 1830 until its disfranchisement two years later. He was, of course, active in support of the Grey ministry's reform measures both outside Parliament and in the Lords, where, as a liberal Evangelical Whig, he unsuccessfully introduced bills to reform the universities in 1835 and 1837.[29] According to James Grant, he displayed there the 'ultra liberalism of his opinions' and was 'the nearest approach to a perfect radical in the House'. He added that Cobbett had said that he 'was the only nobleman who understood the first principles of politics, and that his were the only speeches in the Upper House worth a moment's attention'.[30] Another commentator remarked on how his zeal often outweighed his discretion:

> At those times, or when he is pursuing his favourite theme of repeal of the corn laws, he pours forth an interminable flood of talk, a strange mixture of assertion, one sided reasoning and shrewd illustration, in which every now and then you hear an argument of singular sense and applicability or an idea of striking originality, but overwhelmed in a mass of what, without wishing to use an offensive term, we fear can only be described as twaddle.[31]

He never held public office. An earnest agricultural improver, he retired to Coleshill, where he died in April 1869. He left the bulk of his estate to his elder son Jacob (1815-89), who succeeded him as 4th earl of Radnor. His younger son, Edward Pleydell Bouverie (1818-89), was Member for the Kilmarnock Burghs, 1844-74, and held office in several Liberal administrations.[32]

[1] R.K. Huch, *The Radical Lord Radnor* (Minnesota Monographs in the Humanities vol. 10, 1977), the only biography, is thin and unreliable. [2] Ibid. 4-5, 8, 14-15, 20-21, 36-37, 41, 102, 166-9. Huch, wishing to have it both ways, states that this essentially Whiggish outlook nevertheless made Folkestone 'a radical by the standards of the time' (ibid. 8). See also *Oxford DNB*. [3] Huch, 50-53, 92-93; *Bentham Corresp.* ix. 158; D. Miles, *Francis Place*, 120-1. [4] Huch, 4, 15-16. [5] *HP Commons, 1790-1820*, iv. 826-32; Berks. RO, Pleydell Bouverie mss D/EPb O28, Radnor to Folkestone, 18 Aug. 1812. [6] Pleydell Bouverie mss O11; *Wilts. Pollbook* (1819), 68. [7] *Salisbury Jnl.* 13 Mar. 1820. [8] Pleydell Bouverie mss O38. [9] *The Times*, 20, 28 June 1820. [10] *Creevey's Life and Times*, 134; *Kentish Chron.* 2 Jan.; *Devizes Gazette*, 11 Jan. 1821. [11] Fitzwilliam mss 102/10, Althorp to Milton, 4 Dec.; *The Times*, 19 Dec. 1820, 9 Jan.; *Pol. Reg.* 13 Jan. 1821; Huch, 99-100. [12] HLRO, Hist. Coll. 379,

Grey Bennet diary, 1; *Creevey Pprs.* ii. 5. [13] *The Times*, 16 Feb. 1821. [14] *Creevey Pprs.* ii. 34. [15] *The Times*, 8 Mar. 1822. [16] Northants. RO, Agar Ellis diary; *Arbuthnot Jnl.* i. 159; Buckingham, *Mems. Geo. IV*, i. 290. [17] *Kentish Chron.* 14 June 1822. [18] *The Times*, 28 Jan. 1823; Berks. RO, Pryse mss, Folkestone to Pryse, 16 Dec. 1822; Huch, 103-4. [19] Agar Ellis diary; Gurney diary; Add. 40687, f. 1; *Creevey Pprs.* ii. 68. [20] *The Times*, 2 July 1825. [21] Nottingham Univ. Lib. Denison diary; Add. 52448, f. 23; Keele Univ. Lib. Sneyd mss SC8/79. [22] *The Times*, 27 Apr. 1826. [23] M.D. George, *Cat. of Pol. and Personal Satires*, x. 15128. [24] *Salisbury Jnl.* 12 June; *Devizes Gazette*, 6 July 1826. [25] Creevey mss, Creevey to Miss Ord, 10 Dec. 1826. [26] *The Times*, 22 Feb. 1827. [27] Longford Castle mss 30/7; Countess of Radnor, *Cat. of Pictures in Collection of Earl of Radnor*, ii. 79. [28] *Edgeworth Letters*, 294; PROB 11/1741/306; IR26/1173/270. [29] R. Brent, *Liberal Anglican Politics*, 28. [30] [J. Grant], *Random Recollections of Lords* (1836), 290. [31] G.H. Francis, *Orators of the Age* (1847), 229. [32] *The Times*, 12 Apr. 1869; J. Stratford, *Wilts. and its Worthies* (1882), 168; Radnor, ii. 93-96; *DNB*; *Oxford DNB*.

S.M.F.

PLUMER, William (1736–1822), of Gilston Park and Blakesware, Herts.

Lewes	21 Feb. 1763–1768
Hertfordshire	1768–1807
Higham Ferrers	1812–17 Jan. 1822

b. 24 May 1736, 2nd but o. surv. s. of William Plumer† of Blakesware and Elizabeth, da. of Thomas Byde of Ware Park. *educ.* Pembroke, Camb. 1752. *m.* (1) 12 July 1760, Hon. Frances Dorothy Cary (*d.* 3 Dec. 1761), da. of Lucius Charles, 7th Visct. Falkland [S], *s.p.*; (2) 9 Aug. 1791, his cos. Jane, da. and coh. of Rev. the Hon. George Hamilton, canon of Windsor, *s.p. suc.* fa. 1767. *d.* 17 Jan. 1822.

Plumer had the distinction of being the only Member of George III's first Parliament whose Commons career extended into the reign of George IV. He was almost 84 years old and physically decrepit when Earl Fitzwilliam again agreed to return him for the pocket borough of Higham Ferrers at the 1820 general election, after he had indicated that he 'should like to be allowed to work ... as long as the faculties of my mind continue sound and unimpaired'.[1] In a letter to Lord Holland apologizing for his absence from the contest in Bedfordshire, where he had a freehold, he explained that he had 'hesitated about offering' again, on account of being unable to attend in person, and reported:

> I have been confined by gout and some other serious evils of advanced age ever since the early part of October, and it is my own opinion, as well as that of my medical advisers (who by the bye are good politicians) that it might endanger my life, if I were to travel.[2]

Though reputed never to stay in the House after six o'clock,[3] he continued to act with his lifelong Whig friends, largely by pairing for important divisions, as he did on the Queen Caroline affair, 22 June 1820.[4] He was granted three weeks' leave on account of ill health, 27 June 1820. He was present to vote against the omission of the queen's name from the liturgy, 23 Jan., and for parliamentary reform, 18 Apr. 1821. He paired in the minority on the liturgy, 26 Jan., for repeal of the additional malt duty, 3 Apr., for Lord John Russell's reform proposals, 9 May, and for inquiry into the Peterloo massacre, 16 May 1821. He is not known to have spoken in debate in this period.

Plumer spent the last six months of his life quietly at Gilston. Writing to Lord William Cavendish Bentinck*, with whom he corresponded regularly, he hoped ministers would 'set about in earnest to economize and make retrenchments ... or we shall be actual bankrupts', 22 July; hailed the outcome of the Oxford University by-election as 'a complete discomfiture of the Tories', 26 Aug.; and deplored the summary dismissal of Sir Robert Wilson* from the army, though he delayed subscribing to Wilson's relief fund until ministers had been given a chance to justify their action, 25 Nov. 1821. On 24 Dec. 1821 he observed:

> I live in the midst of bankrupt farmers, and starving poor ... There must be a crisis, and what will be the consequence no man can foresee! ... Mrs. Plumer is just come to me, after having attended the distribution of two pounds of good ox beef, and a proper portion of bread each to 400 fellow creatures ... If we live till Xmas next, shall we have it in our power to do the like?[5]

Three weeks later he was struck down and 'carried to the bed' where he died a few days later. By his will, dated 18 Oct. 1817 and proved under £45,000, 9 Feb. 1822, he left £52 10*s.* to his 'much esteemed friend' Cavendish Bentinck and the rest of his estate to his widow. After a brief marriage to a naval officer, she married in 1828 the novelist Robert Ward*, who took the additional name of Plumer.[6]

[1] Wentworth Woodhouse mun. WWM F49/67. [2] Add. 51830, Plumer to Holland, 20 Mar. 1820. [3] Lonsdale mss, Lord Lowther to Lonsdale, 27 Jan. 1821. [4] *The Times*, 26 June 1820. [5] *Letters at Welbeck Abbey* (Roxburghe Club, 1909), 107-19. [6] *Gent. Mag.* (1822), i. 377; PROB 11/1653/94; IR26/920/112.

D.R.F.

PLUMER *see also* **WARD, Robert**

PLUMMER, John (1780–1839), of 32 Fenchurch Street, London and Fort Lodge, Margate, Kent.

HINDON 1820–1826

bap. 11 July 1780, 2nd but 1st surv. s. of Thomas Plummer†, merchant, of Camberwell, Surr. and w. Sarah. *m.* 6 Mar. 1810, Mary, da. of John Taylor of Tunbridge Wells, Kent, 3s. 5da. (2 *d.v.p.*).[1] *suc.* fa. 1818. *d.* 1 Oct. 1839.

Dir. W.I. Dock Co. 1815, London Marine Assurance 1817.

Plummer's family background is largely unknown, though his mother may have been one Sarah Oliver, who was baptized at St Anne's, Soho, 14 Jan. 1739, and married a Thomas Plummer in the same church, 31 Oct. 1768. Like his father and elder brother, Thomas William (*bap.* 17 Dec. 1776), who were both briefly Members of Parliament in the first decade of the nineteenth century, Plummer was a West India merchant with interests in shipping and insurance.[2] Though it is not clear when he entered the family business, he undoubtedly played a part in the firm, which was usually called Plummer, Barham and Plummer, and was based, successively, at 2 Fen Court, Fenchurch Street, 2 Philpot Lane, Thames Street, and, by 1816, at 32 Fenchurch Street. The West India Planters and Merchants' Committee added him to the committee for managing their rum establishment in Fenchurch Street, 12 May 1813, but the 'Mr. Plummer jnr.' mentioned as attending the committee's meetings for some years prior to this was probably his brother. This is also true of similar entries in the minutes of the Merchants' Committee, though he was specifically mentioned as being present on four occasions in 1814.[3] His business letters to Joseph Foster Barham*, who was a partner in the firm until 1815, when he made way for his brother John Foster Barham*, show that he was in charge of its administration by the mid-1810s.[4] This was before the deaths of his brother in 1817, when he was living in Abbeville, France, and, in 1818, of his father, who had also probably retired. Plummer inherited the latter's entire estate, including personalty sworn under £60,000.[5]

Since 1807 the family had acted as agents for the Jamaican estates of William Beckford† of Fonthill, who was often irritated by the attempts of the 'Plummer people', as called them, to impose some sort of order on his affairs. He controlled and occupied one seat at Hindon, the sale of which was identified as a possible source of revenue to set against his increasing debts. In 1817 he complained that his attorney had 'made me an offer of £4,000 a year if I will go to the continent and leave a certain faithful Mr. John Plummer to Member-ify in my place'. Two years later he wrote that 'without a severe rule about every kind of purchase, great or small, one will certainly fall under the rule of Messrs. Plummer, who, refusing to advance a penny more, will force the sale of [Fonthill]'.[6] At the general election of 1820 he yielded the representation of Hindon to Plummer, who agreed to pay all the electoral expenses, to underwrite mortgages to the value of nearly £35,000 and to settle other debts, and to increase the firm's annual payment to Beckford (out of the income on his Jamaican property) from £4,000 to £5,000.[7] On 11 Mar., a few days after being returned unopposed, Plummer rather misleadingly informed Foster Barham

> of the proposition Mr. Beckford was good enough to make me of occupying his interest at Hindon as he found it more convenient to himself to remain out of Parliament and in accepting which I assure [you that] my object is the hope of being useful to West India interests.[8]

A regular attender at the meetings of both the Merchants', and the Planters and Merchants' Committees from the early 1820s, his parliamentary activities were, indeed, largely concerned with the protection of his mercantile affairs.[9] Though basically a supporter of the Liverpool administration, he displayed little consistency in his voting behaviour.

He voted against the appointment of an additional baron of exchequer in Scotland, 15 May 1820. He divided with ministers against repeal of the additional malt duty, 3 Apr., and reduction of the adjutant-general's office and barracks grants, 11 Apr., 28 May, but was listed in the minority against them on the miscellaneous services grant, 28 May 1821. He voted against more extensive tax reductions to relieve distress, 11 Feb. 1822. He was appointed to the select committee on foreign trade, 25 Feb. (as he was again in the following two sessions), and in his first known speech, 1 Apr., he applauded the introduction of the foreign trade bill and warned that a famine threatened the West Indies. He sided with opposition to condemn Sir Robert Wilson's* removal from the army, 13 Feb., and for reduction of the salt duty, 28 Feb., 28 June. Although he was named in the majority against abolition of one of the joint-postmasterships, 13 Mar., he apparently voted in the majority for this, 2 May. He divided for criminal law reform, 4 June, and in condemnation of chancery delays, 26 June, but against investigation of the conduct of the lord advocate towards the press in Scotland, 25 June 1822.

Activated by motives of both humanitarianism and pragmatism, Plummer fully concurred in Foster

Barham's plans for ameliorating the condition of the slaves:

> I have long since discountenanced the unnecessary extension of labour in producing sugars and I should be happy to find that your idea of employing it in the cultivation of articles of provision frequently imported without occasion, or even in the products for exportation, was more generally adopted. It is certainly only in the diminution of expenditure, that West India property can now be preserved.

In early 1823 he was cheered by an upturn in the market, though he thought it 'more owing to political appearances than to any other cause', and considered that the possible appointment of a Commons select committee on East India sugar 'may do us good rather than otherwise'. Particularly assiduous in his attendance at the Planters and Merchants' Committee at this time, he was named to a committee to carry into effect its opposition to the expected anti-slavery motion in the Commons, 25 Apr. He was not a member of the delegation which waited on ministers at Fife House (Lord Liverpool's residence) in May, but he wrote that

> I do not think the reception was a very favourable one by ministers, as they admitted that though they should oppose Mr. [Thomas Fowell] Buxton's motion, they could not refuse to admit the propriety of looking eventually to abolition. If this was to be done upon the principle of adequate and simultaneous compensation it might be just, but they say you must prove a loss before we can listen to compensation. Justice so deferred may never be given. They do however (at least Mr. Canning did) admit that the surrender of the one day's labour is some sacrifice and express their readiness to give some bonus for it. I shall not be sorry if they do compensate a sacrifice it is in our own interest to make.[10]

He spoke briefly about the condition of apprentices on merchant vessels, 13 Mar., presented a petition from Nevis against repeal of the protecting duty on East Indian sugar, 22 May, and asked a question about the continuance of the trade in slaves between British colonies, 4 July.[11] He voted with government against limiting the sinking fund, 3, 13 Mar., repeal of the Foreign Enlistment Act, 16 Apr., inquiry into the legal proceedings against the Dublin Orange rioters, 22 Apr., and reform of the Scottish representative system, 2 June. He was in the minorities against Stuart Wortley's amendment approving British neutrality towards the French invasion of Spain, 30 Apr., though he had 'really intended to vote for the amendment', and against the committal of the usury bill, 17 June 1823.

He was, however, in the majorities for going into committee on the measure, 27 Feb., 8 Apr. 1824. He voted against the committal of the beer duties bill, 24 May. He was named to a deputation to ministers from the Planters and Merchants' Committee to ask for a reduction of the rum duty, 4 Mar., and was appointed to a committee to improve its internal finances, 5 Apr. (and again, 20 June 1825).[12] He attacked the marine insurance bill as a violation of the charters of those companies which monopolized the business, 17 May. He brought up petitions against the bill from one of these companies, London Marine Assurance, of which he was a director, 26, 31 May.[13] He spoke against it again, 27 May, as he did on 3, 14 June, when he was a teller for minorities against it in three divisions. He voted in condemnation of the trial of the Methodist missionary John Smith in Demerara, 11 June. He divided with ministers for the Irish insurrection bill, 14 June 1824. He had voted for Catholic relief, 28 Feb. 1821, and although he was in the hostile minority on 1 Mar., he did so again, 21 Apr., 10 May 1825. He spoke against the Mauritius trade bill, 3 June, when he was a teller for the minority in favour of the wrecking amendment, and three days later he said that it would be a 'very great act of injustice' to the West India interest to allow the entry of sugar from Mauritius.[14] He divided in the majorities for the duke of Cumberland's grant, 30 May, 6, 10 June, the St. Olave tithe bill, 6 June, and the spring guns bill, 21 June. His last known votes were against going into committee on the Bank Charter Acts, 13 Feb., for receiving the report on the salary of the president of the board of trade, 10 Apr., and against resolutions to curb electoral bribery, 26 May 1826.

In the early 1820s Beckford's financial position became untenable, not least because he was heavily in debt to his West Indian agents, who threatened to foreclose. His lawyer informed the duke of Hamilton, 3 Nov. 1821, of the

> absolute necessity for an early payment to Mr. Beckford's merchants of £30,000, towards reduction of the debt of £40,000 remaining due to them, without which, they have intimated their inability, during the depressed state of West India produce, to continue their present quarterly payments to Mr. Beckford, or the payment of the interest of the £50,000 part of the mortgages on the Fonthill estate (amounting in the whole to £70,000) which they have hitherto discharged and which has tended considerably to increase the balance due to them.

Even after the sale of some Jamaican estates to meet part of these liabilities, Plummer was still owed well over £12,500, and since this was the valuation put on the seat at Hindon, there was a possibility that he might have taken over the interest.[15] However, Beckford sold Fonthill in 1822, and so avoided letting it fall into Plummer's clutches. The electoral influence passed to Lord Grosvenor, and despite trying to come to an arrangement with him and the other patron of the borough, Lord Calthorpe, Plummer was left without a seat at the general election of 1826.[16] He is not known to have sought one elsewhere, and never sat in the Commons again.

Plummer and Wilson, as his company was known from the mid-1820s, was itself in an increasingly precarious position, and on 5 Nov. 1830 Plummer apologized to Foster Barham that 'the house is so poor that it cannot advance the £250 before the dividends'. On 24 Nov. he informed Beckford's attorneys of his 'apprehensions that our house cannot long continue its payments owing to the extreme pressure on its resources which the long continued and unceasing pressure of West India property has occasioned'. They were declared bankrupt at the start of December 1830, but, as had been hoped, Plummer and William Wilson became partners in a new firm led by Thomson Hankey, another West India merchant, at 7 Mincing Lane. They brought with them clients such as Beckford, so that within ten years most of the debts had been repaid.[17] Plummer remained a partner until his death in October 1839, at his then residence in Bedford Square, and was buried with his father and two of his daughters at Carshalton, Surrey. He divided his estate between his six surviving children, of whom the eldest, Thomas William, was born in 1812.[18]

[1] IGI (London, Surr.); *Gent. Mag.* (1810), ii. 753. [2] IGI (London); *The Times*, 7 Feb. 1825; *HP Commons, 1790-1820*, iv. 836-7. [3] Inst. of Commonwealth Stud. M915/2, 3. [4] Bodl. Clarendon dep. c. 361, bdle. 3. [5] PROB 11/1603/195; IR26/756/322. [6] *Life at Fonthill* ed. B. Alexander, 85, 125, 208, 306, 326. [7] Bodl. ms. Beckford. c. 30, f. 105b. [8] Clarendon dep. c. 361, bdle. 3. [9] Inst. of Commonwealth Stud. M915/2-4. [10] Ibid. M915/4; L.J. Ragatz, *Fall of Planter Class*, 411; Clarendon dep. c. 361, bdle. 3, Plummer to Foster Barham, 6 Sept. 1822, 17, 28 Feb., 13, 17 May, 18 Sept. 1823. [11] *The Times*, 14 Mar., 23 May, 5 July 1823. [12] Inst. of Commonwealth Stud. M915/4. [13] *The Times*, 27 May, 1 June 1824. [14] Ibid. 7 June 1825. [15] Ms. Beckford. c. 30, f. 114; c. 39, ff. 25, 27, 36, 56; *Life at Fonthill*, 326-31; B. Alexander, *England's Wealthiest Son*, 189-91, 286. [16] Clarendon dep. c. 362, bdle. 3, Plummer to Foster Barham, 21, 24 June 1825, 4 Mar. 1826. [17] Clarendon dep. c. 362, bdle. 3; c. 389, bdle. 7; ms. Beckford. c. 30, ff. 143, 148; *The Times*, 4 Dec. 1830, 16 Mar., 2 June 1840. [18] *Gent. Mag.* (1839), ii. 545; G.B. Brightling, *Carshalton*, 72-73; PROB 11/1917/646; IGI (Surr.).

S.M.F.

PLUNKET, William Conyngham (1764–1854), of Old Connaught, Bray, co. Wicklow.

MIDHURST 26 Jan. 1807–1807

DUBLIN UNIVERSITY 1812–1 May 1827

b. 1 July 1764, 4th but 2nd surv. s. of Rev. Thomas Plunket (*d.* 1778), Presbyterian minister, of Enniskillen, co. Fermanagh and Mary, da. of David Conyngham of Letterkenny, co. Donegal. *educ.* Trinity, Dublin 1779; King's Inns 1780; L. Inn 1784, called [I] 1787. *m.* 20 Oct. 1790, Katherine, da. of John McCausland, MP [I], of Strabane, co. Tyrone, 6s. 5da. (1 *d.v.p.*). *cr.* Bar. Plunket 1 May 1827. *d.* 4 Jan. 1854.

MP [I] 1798-1800.

KC [I] 1795; solicitor-gen. [I] Oct. 1803-Oct. 1805; bencher, King's Inns 1804; att.-gen. [I] Oct. 1805-May 1807, Jan. 1822-May 1827; PC [I] 6 Dec. 1805, [GB] 10 May 1827; l.c.j.c.p. [I] June 1827-Dec. 1830; ld. chan. [I] Dec. 1830-Nov. 1834, Apr. 1835-June 1841.

Plunket was described by Tom Macaulay* in 1831 as 'very ugly, but with a strong expression of intellect in his strong coarse features and massy forehead'.[1] The undisputed leader of the Irish chancery bar, with a steady income of about £6,000 a year, he was, as Richard Sheil* noted, one of the comparatively few lawyers who enhanced their reputations in Parliament, where his unique 'sustained intensity' and 'lucidity and closeness of reasoning' put him in the first rank of orators.[2] Henry Brougham* reflected that 'there never was a more argumentative speaker, or one ... more difficult to grapple with and answer'.[3]

In the 1818 Parliament Plunket, whose principal political interest lay in the peaceful promotion, in association with his hero and friend Henry Grattan I*, of the cause of Catholic emancipation, acted with the Grenvillite wing of the Whigs, though many of his oldest personal connections were with Foxites. His political instincts were essentially conservative, however, and in the emergency session of late 1819 he disgusted some of the leading Whigs by conspicuously supporting the Liverpool ministry's coercive legislation to deal with popular unrest in the aftermath of the Peterloo massacre. His immediate reward, thanks to the unbidden intervention of Lord Grenville, was a government assurance that the opposition which he had encountered in his Dublin University seat at the general election of 1818, when John Croker*, a junior minister, had run him close, would not be repeated on the next occasion. Plunket, who correctly surmised that Croker's acquiescence was 'very reluctantly' conceded, was gratified, as he told Grenville, to be relieved

> not only ... of ... any serious apprehension as to the result of a contest, but ... from a state of incessant contention with persons under the influence of bad and angry feelings, which ... had become so hateful to me that, independently of the injury done to the College, I began to apprehend that the return was too dearly purchased. I have great pleasure in assuring your Lordship that the course which has been adopted in Parliament affords very general satisfaction on this side of the water, and that in acting under my entire conviction of the soundness of your ... views, I have no reason to think that I have forfeited the approbation of any one individual whose good opinion was worth preserving.[4]

He was nevertheless given 'a great deal of trouble' by the persistence of rumours that Croker would stand at the general election of 1820, and asked his fellow Grenvillite Charles Williams Wynn* to try to secure from him an authoritative disclaimer. In the event, he was returned unopposed.[5] At the Dublin by-election necessitated by Grattan's death in June 1820 Plunket tearfully nominated Grattan's son (who was defeated) and publicly assumed his mantle as the Irish spokesman for Catholic claims, explaining that Grattan's object in pressing for emancipation had been

> to give strength to the Protestant connection, and security to the empire. It is the basis of liberty, and I shall therefore be ... [the Catholics'] advocate. They are not storming the constitution by wild theories and dangerous innovations, but are calmly, temperately and constitutionally seeking for their rights ... I am probably shortly to lay their claims before the legislature.[6]

In a brief visit to London the following month, he spoke retrospectively in support of the bill to exclude from Parliament Irish masters in chancery, one of whom, Thomas Ellis, had defeated young Grattan, 12 July; he privately thought Ellis's return had been 'shameful'.[7] On the 17th he drew attention to but did not present two petitions for relief, from the Catholic inhabitants of certain Dublin parishes and on behalf of the whole Catholic population of Ireland, and announced that in deference to parliamentary and public preoccupation with the Queen Caroline affair he would postpone a general motion until early the next session.

At the end of 1820 Brougham told Lord Holland and George Tierney* that he was confident that Plunket was 'decidedly against the ministers on the queen's business' and would 'take an active part' when Parliament met; and a story to that effect was still current, to the evident 'dismay' of government, in mid-January 1821.[8] In fact, while he thoroughly disapproved of the ministerial proceedings against the queen, he was alarmed by the encouragement given by many leading Whigs, notably Lord Grey, whose recent public attack on Grenville he deplored, to popular agitation on the subject. This worry was closely connected with his fear that Daniel O'Connell* was attempting to involve the Irish Catholics in the queen's cause and to entice them 'towards revolutionary movements, and to abandon all application to Parliament'. Grenville, whom he consulted, gave him discretion to remain in Ireland until he came over to move the Catholic question, and he took advantage of this dispensation, explaining to Sir John Newport* that it was best if he kept out of the queen's business:

> Feeling strongly, I should express without reserve what I feel. I know by some experience the intolerant construction to which such conduct would expose me, and I am quite certain that I should have the mortification of returning to this country with the hostility of both parties, without having reason to console myself by the conviction of having effected or contributed to any public good.

He noticed Grey's reported reference to him in the autumn as an apostate; reviewed and defended his political conduct since entering public life, claiming to have been consistent throughout; asked Newport to show this vindication to Holland and Lord Lansdowne, and declared that 'all intercourse and connection' between himself and Grey was at an end. Lansdowne, alerted by Newport, sought to mollify Plunket, assuring him that he had been misinformed about Grey's attitude and exhorting him not to rule himself out of participation in any future Whig ministry.[9] In reply, 29 Jan., Plunket bared his soul:

> I wrote to ... Newport with a mind deeply wounded, and with a temper ... much exasperated. Your ... letter ... has taken the sting out of everything which had excited or offended me ... I am perfectly satisfied that the expression [by Grey] reported to me has not been uttered deliberately or recently ... It is quite a relief to me to be convinced that, however I may have been opposed to a passing resentment in Lord Grey's mind, when my public conduct may have surprised or disappointed him, I have not to resent ... his continuing to harbour an opinion that my conduct has been swayed by unworthy motives ... I regret the warmth with which I expressed myself ... [and] any unpleasant feeling is dismissed from my mind ... On the proceedings against the queen, I ... have the misfortune, in some respects, to differ from ... Lord Grenville. Without pretending to know exactly his opinions, my own are ... that the proceedings ... have been unwise and impolitic, as in the course of the business the feelings of the people of England have been roused in no ordinary degree. But all this, so far as the queen is concerned, is a mere passing cloud ... In six months hence ... the matter will ... be important, only in so far as it may have given strength to the revolutionary party ... The terror of this

growing monster will ... determine the judgement of that portion of the community whom I consider as the public, and in whose confidence the claims of all parties, as well as the safety of all parties must rest ... The measures which a great portion of the opposition have been, for some time, pursuing do not address themselves to this portion of the people, and ... I do not see any immediate prospect of their doing so ... I do not mean to go over until the ... Catholic question calls me. It grieves me to anticipate that when I do, I cannot look for the probability of that co-operation in public measures which I should find so honourable and so desirable.[10]

On 28 Feb. 1821, after presenting several Irish Catholic petitions and paying tribute to Grattan,[11] Plunket moved to consider relief in committee of the whole House, making out the case in a long speech which Peel, the leading opponent of Catholic claims, later said was 'the most powerful and eloquent ... I ever heard in Parliament'. It was described by Sir Henry Hardinge* as 'inimitable' and by Brougham as 'the finest thing ever heard', while John William Ward* wrote that

I have not for many years heard such an astonishing display of talent. His style is quite peculiar; for its gravity and severity, I prefer it to all others of which I ever heard a specimen. If he had been bred in Parliament I am inclined to think he would have been the greatest speaker that ever appeared in it.[12]

The anti-Catholic Member Henry Bankes, however, thought the speech was 'more praised than it seemed to me to deserve, being inferior to some of his other very able exertions'.[13] Although Lord Bathurst, the colonial secretary, had told Lord Harrowby the previous day that 'opposition do not mean to make a great press to support Plunket's motion, as they think he is quitting them and they do not like he should have the credit of [a] powerful if not a successful division', it was carried by 227-221, the first pro-Catholic majority since 1813.[14] The following day Plunket moved resolutions to form the basis of a bill, which he was given permission to introduce. So little had he expected to succeed, that he had no detailed measure prepared, but with Williams Wynn and the Catholic lawyer Blake he drafted a general relief bill, which was framed to make the oath of supremacy palatable to Catholics, and one dealing with the twin securities of regulation of the intercourse between British and foreign Catholics and the royal veto on the appointment of Catholic bishops.[15] Plunket, who on 5 Mar. supported a renewed attempt to exclude Ellis from the Commons, introduced the bills on 7 Mar.[16] While the English Catholic laity were willing to accept all these proposals, the misgivings of the clergy forced Plunket to make considerable changes to the 'explanation' of the oath; but in the House, 16 Mar., he condemned the public opposition of the extremist Catholic Dr. Milner as 'only an act of undeviating, consistent bigotry', which was 'inaccessible to reason' and 'irreclaimable by experience'. Lady Holland, a spectator, thought this speech was 'as neat and witty as Canning himself could have made', and that in support of the successful second reading later that day he produced 'the most perfectly well reasoned, clear, distinct argument I ever heard ... and gave a conviction of his wonderful abilities and powers'.[17] Irish Catholic laymen were divided on the bills, with O'Connell, for example, hostile to the securities, and Sheil favourable to both measures. There was an attempt by the moderate Irish Catholic clerics, led by Doyle, bishop of Kildare, to effect a compromise, but many of the provincial priests proved to be implacably anti-vetoist.[18] On 23 Mar. Plunket received news of his wife's mortal illness and returned immediately to Ireland 'in a state of distraction', leaving the Catholic bills, which were subsequently amalgamated into one, in the hands of Newport, who steered it through the Commons. Despite his grief 'under the heaviest blow on this side the grave', he corresponded with Williams Wynn and Grenville on the problem of how in future to reconcile the Irish Catholics to the securities. He was prepared for the measure's rejection by the Lords, though he lamented that 'so decided a tone has been adopted by a certain portion of the cabinet' and thought it 'scarcely possible that the question can be left to meet another session in its present shape'. At the same time he was averse to Williams Wynn's notion of seeking a limited concession without securities:

This piecemeal course of proceeding seems to me not to have anything of statesmanship; it has no principle; it leads to the final accomplishment of the R. C. claims, but not in a course of conciliation and confidence, or with the prospect of binding up the question in a way calculated to promote public peace, or to afford security to our establishments.[19]

Before he returned to Ireland he was sounded by Lord Liverpool about joining the administration as Irish attorney-general. He was strongly tempted, but on Grenville's advice stipulated that he must be allowed a free hand as to the timing and method of dealing with the Catholic question. Williams Wynn informed Grenville's nephew Lord Buckingham, the active head of the Grenvillites, whom ministers were also courting, of his

conversation with Plunket ... about his views, and I am sorry to find him most disinclined – indeed I might say almost resolved – against taking any office which would

> fix him in England, and looking only to the attorney-generalship and great seal of Ireland, but thinking that he could, while in the former office, give considerable attendance in the House of Commons. He appeared to feel that there was no longer any obstacle to his taking office under the present government, as now constituted, and to be well disposed to accept the offer of the attorney-generalship of Ireland whenever they can make room for him, though he would much prefer coming in with us.[20]

In the summer, when the king's particular attentiveness to Plunket on his visit to Ireland did not pass unnoticed, Liverpool tried to have him installed as Irish attorney-general in the room of the long serving Saurin, a Protestant bigot. The Protestant lord lieutenant, Lord Talbot, made difficulties, and evidently did so in November, when Liverpool again raised the matter, which he had pressed on the Irish lord chancellor Lord Manners as one of urgency.[21] Soon afterwards Talbot and his chief secretary Charles Grant* were dismissed and replaced by Lord Wellesley, a pro-Catholic, and the Protestant Henry Goulburn*. Plunket was offered the attorney-generalship, on the understanding that he would have 'entire freedom of action and opinion' on the Catholic question, which was to remain an open one within the cabinet and be kept in such a state as would give neither side a preponderance. His appointment became an important factor in the concurrent negotiations with the pro-Catholic Grenvillites. To Buckingham he argued, conveniently, that the cause of emancipation would be advanced by their junction with government:

> That the ... question cannot, for any great length of time, be kept back, appears to me evident, but it seems equally clear that there is great occasion for caution, and much room for accommodation, as to the time of bringing it forward; nothing could be more injurious than the risking the loss of the vantage ground which we have taken possession of during the last session; and ... such might be the consequence of bringing the measure forward, without some better prospect of good sense and good temper on the part of the Roman Catholic clergy than they displayed on the late occasion. Of improvement in that quarter I am led to entertain some hopes, as well as on the part of those of the laity who were least manageable; and all these are arguments for delay. At the same time this should be certainly kept open for discussion, and above all, must not be liable to be considered as the result of contract or stipulation, especially with any portion of the government, which would undoubtedly tend to throw the Roman Catholic body into dangerous hands. Under these circumstances, and reserving this perfect freedom, I am quite disposed to attend in Parliament, and render what services I can to the general measures of administration.[22]

The problem of providing for Saurin, who eventually resigned without compensation, delayed the ratification of Plunket's appointment until January 1822. He was quietly re-elected for the university the following month, when he claimed to have accepted office 'without compromise of any principle whatever'.[23]

The Foxite Whig Lord John Russell* regretted the loss of Plunket, but reflected that 'he is not yet formidable – new, and provincial, and no gentleman, no character'.[24] O'Connell optimistically hoped that in office he would 'completely accede to our wishes and allow us to be emancipated without any of those restraints on our religion for which no civil rights could afford any compensation'.[25] In reality, by accepting office and exposing himself to the formidable difficulties which confronted all Irish ministers in this period, Plunket had effectively hamstrung himself as the champion of Catholic emancipation. He performed his general duties creditably enough, though he was betrayed on occasions by his impetuosity and want of cool judgement. He reached London in the second week of March 1822, bringing a surprisingly cheerful report on the state of Ireland.[26] He was present to vote with his colleagues against abolition of one of the joint-postmasterships, 13 Mar. Three days later, reporting to Wellesley on inconclusive discussions with Liverpool on tithes, he went on:

> The parliamentary storm has I think spent its force, and the exposition of the resources of the country has inspired very general confidence. The retrenchments adopted have also ... given satisfaction to the great portion of the public mind which is capable of listening to reason. I rejoice to think that there is some reason to look to returning tranquillity in Ireland, and that the alarmists cease to call for martial law, and begin to acknowledge the efficacy of the measures which have been resorted to.

Like Williams Wynn, who was now in the cabinet, he was averse to pressing the general question of Catholic relief in present circumstances, and was 'sorry to say that many of the opposition Members are desirous of bringing it forward this session. Such a course would, in my opinion, be ruinous, and I trust that we may be able to prevent it'.[27] When Canning gave notice, 29 Mar., of his plan to introduce a bill to relieve Catholic peers of their disabilities and pointedly drew his attention to it, Plunket, caught on the hop, blustered indecisively as to his attitude to the general issue being moved. Pressed by Tierney for an explicit statement, he said that while he had not finally decided, he was inclined to think that 'this was an unfavourable season for the discussion of this question'. Lord Holland's worthless son Henry Fox* commented that he 'made a very bad figure and lost more credit with the House than anyone ever did in so short a time. Nobody cheered, nobody supported him'.[28] Plunket was 'in great doubt' for several days, though he retained his own view, which he expressed plainly to an impatient O'Connell, and which was shared by Wellesley and Lord Londonderry*, the foreign secretary, that forcing the question that session would set it back many years. After consultations with Williams Wynn and Grenville, he concluded that Canning's measure should be supported as a step in the right direction, and that the wider question should be considered at a meeting of the leading friends of relief on 16 Apr. At that gathering, which was attended by Plunket, Williams Wynn, Canning, Newport, Tierney, Grant, Sir Henry Parnell* and the Grenvillite Joseph Phillimore*, it was decided to defer the question until the next session. Tierney, who was unhappy with the decision, told Lady Holland that he had taken 'special care' to ensure that 'the postponement should be Plunket's own act, and not a measure advised by the friends of emancipation, which was the point he wanted to establish'.[29] The Whig George Agar Ellis* noted that when he appeared at the levee, 19 Apr., with 'the new Buckingham rats', Plunket was 'seemingly ashamed of himself'.[30] He partially redeemed himself on the 22nd when, in the debate on Newport's motion for inquiry into the state of Ireland, he made mincemeat of Thomas Ellis for his anti-Catholic rant and gave an optimistic account of the prospects for Ireland under Wellesley's enlightened administration. Sir James Mackintosh, who told Fox that 'he would rather be six days under the lash of Brougham or the ridicule of Canning than ten minutes under Plunket's invective', recorded the scene:

> Plunket sprang upon his prey. I have never seen such a chastisement. He fixed his eye on Ellis and treated him with a degree of scorn, disgust and contempt which I scarcely thought possible from one man to another. The invective was worthy of Demosthenes. P[lunket] was really angry as well as desirous of making his first official speech as an advocate of the Catholics rather than as an adversary of his old friend [Newport]. His success was complete. We who had prepared groans for him received his speech with raptures of clamorous applause. Even our Mountaineers were delighted and began to suspect that he may be honest.[31]

Hudson Gurney* thought the attack was 'strong but very coarse; his words disjointed like broken bones; his sentences very incomplete. It is not eloquence but a style that fixes attention'. Phillimore felt that the speech was 'everything that could be wished, and set us quite right with the House as to Ireland'; but Agar Ellis, while acknowledging that Plunket spoke 'admirably', could not 'say his explanation of his own political conduct was equally successful'. Buckingham preferred Grant's speech as showing 'more real practical desire to remedy the grievances of Ireland', but he acknowledged that Plunket 'fights in fetters owing to his official situation'.[32] When Plunket supported Canning's Catholic peers bill, 30 Apr., Mackintosh noted that he 'spoke with great energy and maintained true principles of Whiggism on which, alas! he does not act'; and Agar Ellis thought he performed 'rather in a rambling manner'.[33] Plunket told Holland in mid-May that he could not see his way through the problem of a commutation of tithes.[34] He said as much in the House, 15 May, when he argued that it would trench on the rights of property and that 'much of the evil arose from the heavy exaction of rent, and not of tithes. If the landlords of Ireland were not prepared to lower their rents, in vain would any relief be sought through a commutation of tithes'. He stood by this argument, 20 May, commending Spring Rice's suggestion that tithes be levied on rents. He supported the government's tithes leasing bill, 13 June, but again raised the problem of property rights; and on the 19th he condemned some of the propositions advanced by Hume and Newport as 'nothing less than spoliation and robbery', though he conceded that the present system of tithe collection might be ameliorated.[35] On the Irish constables bill, 7 June, he said that 'a change in the police must be the first step towards the promotion of tranquillity'. He defended the continuation of the Irish Insurrection Act as 'a lamentable evil', 2, 8 July. He opened the ministerial defence of the aliens bill, 14 June, supported inquiry into the Calcutta bankers' financial claims, 4 July, and on 12 July welcomed Lords' amendments to Phillimore's marriage bill, which 'would do great good, by removing a system whose principal features were manifest injustice and gross cruelty'. He was in the ministerial majorities against inquiry into the lord advocate's dealings with the Scottish press, 25 June, and repeal of the salt duties, 28 June 1822.

Towards the end of the session Fox wrote that Plunket 'has quite fallen this year, and has behaved most shabbily in a true *Hibernian* manner. Everybody gives him up'. Buckingham was also evidently out of humour with him, for Williams Wynn commented:

> I think you quite right in your plan of writing a letter to Plunket to explain your general views with respect to Ireland. He must remember he is attorney-general, and from his character ought to be House of Commons minister for that country, besides being representative of that shabby body called Trinity College. He cannot conceal

> from himself the resolution of the Irish Members, and indeed of the House, to force the tithe question, and that the only thing in his power to determine is, whether the government will take the conduct and management of the business to themselves or leave it to the opposition'.[36]

Had Peel become leader of the Commons after Londonderry's suicide in August 1822 Buckingham, so he told the duke of Wellington, would have insisted on Plunket's admission to the cabinet.[37] At this time Croker, speculating to Peel on the support to be had in debate if Canning decided to go to India, observed that

> from Plunket, except on Irish affairs, I do not think much could be expected. I do not think he has either the versatility, information, or boldness necessary for a general debater; besides, I hear he is dissatisfied, and if he be sulky, nobody is *so* sulky. In short, if he and Goulburn manage Ireland and keep Spring Rice, Lord Wellesley and Kit Hutchinson in check, it is as much as can be expected; but I ought to add that some of our friends here, and particularly the peers, talk sanguinely of Plunket's assistance.[38]

He was said to be 'very unpopular' in Ireland in the autumn of 1822.[39]

Plunket, who told Williams Wynn in late November that Wellesley's 'system of government affords satisfaction to all reasonable people', still planned to bring on the Catholic question early in the next session, but he was distracted and delayed in his departure for London by the consequences of the Dublin theatre riot of 14 Dec. 1822, when disgruntled Orangemen threw wood and bottles at Wellesley's box. Plunket indicted the rioters, but the Dublin grand jury threw out the bills, and he then filed *ex-officio* informations. These proceedings outraged not only their partisans, but many Whigs, while Peel and other ministers were in private highly critical of Wellesley and Plunket, and even Williams Wynn thought that they had acted 'absurdly', though he agreed with Buckingham as to the necessity of supporting them in public.[40] Plunket professed utter confidence in the outcome of the trial and told Williams Wynn, whom he asked to give notice of the Catholic question for him on an early day, that reports of the 'insurrectionary state' of Ireland were unfounded. At the same time he complained of incessant headaches and of Wellesley's neglectfulness in correspondence with the home government. The rioters were acquitted, leaving the Orangemen 'quite triumphant and insolent', and Plunket with a peck of troubles.[41] When he arrived in London, fortified by O'Connell's blessing, 15 Feb. 1823, Williams Wynn found him 'harassed and fatigued to a great degree'. He deplored 'Wellesley being surrounded by a set of people totally incapable of assisting or advising him, and who merely carry rumours to irritate him', and confirmed the impression of 'the ascendancy of the Orange faction in every department of government'. At a meeting at his London base, 18 Feb., it was decided that 'in consequence of the very agitated state of Ireland, and the certainty that the debate, instead of relating to the Catholic question, would have turned wholly on the late proceedings in Dublin', it was best to postpone the Catholic question until after Easter. Plunket, backed by Canning and Newport, gave notice accordingly in the House later that day.[42] He was in the ministerial majorities against inquiry into the parliamentary franchise, 20 Feb., and repeal of the house tax, 10 Mar., and for the national debt reduction bill, 13 Mar. When Brownlow, the Orange Member for county Armagh, moved for information on the Dublin trials, 24 Feb., Plunket challenged his associate Sir John Stewart to make good his threat to censure the proceedings. He said that Hume's resolutions on the Irish church establishment were 'full of desperation and folly', 4 Mar., and blamed Protestant hostility for the reluctance of Catholics to serve in the yeomanry, 10 Mar. The following day Plunket, who according to Williams Wynn still looked 'wretchedly ill', privately congratulated Grenville 'on the prospect of the affairs of Ireland being steadily administered, on ascertained principles, and in a spirit of sincerity and moderation'. He agreed that placing a limitation on the number of emancipated Catholic peers and Members of Parliament would 'probably reconcile many persons to the measure, who now entertain apprehension of a Popish parliamentary invasion', but thought that as it was 'in point of principle objectionable', it should be implemented 'by declaring a willingness to yield to such a modification [rather] than by making it part of the original proposition'.[43] He was vexed by Wellesley's threat to resign unless he returned 'immediately' to Ireland to take stock of 'the dangers which are rising around us'.[44] On 24 Mar., claiming that he was 'desirous to show that the power which the Irish government possessed had not been influenced by malice or party spirit', he defeated a motion for the production of copies of the *ex-officio* informations by 48-32. He had no objection to furnishing copies of the prisoners' recognizances. The Whig James Abercromby* thought he had done himself great 'injury' with 'his feeble and injudicious speech', and feared that 'he may be in danger'.[45] He defended himself against aspersions on his conduct in the petition of the Dublin grand jury, 11 Apr. There was concern in government circles that a combination of Orangemen, anti-Catholic Tories and Whigs out for Plunket's blood, together with ministerialist abstentions, might carry Brownlow's censure motion on the informations. Ministers were not prepared to risk a direct negative, but decided to have the orders of the day moved by Courtenay, Member for Exeter. In reply to Brownlow, 15 Apr., in what Bankes described as a speech of 'admirable talent', Plunket vindicated his actions and contended that he had used 'sound discretion'. Williams Wynn reported to Buckingham:

> The triumph of Plunket was complete. He addressed a House evidently unfavourably disposed to him, and for the first hour we could scarcely raise a decent cheer to encourage him. It then became evident that he was making progress, and he proceeded till the applause fairly rung from every part of the House, and his adversaries, who had every reason to expect a majority, found it impossible even to venture on a division.

Agar Ellis considered it 'a most able and ingenious speech'. Plunket told Grenville:

> There is a very active party at work against me, but I trust matters are now in such a state as to secure me against them. Had the question been met by a direct negative, I believe we should have succeeded by a great majority. However, I have no right to complain, as I am convinced the support of ministers was cordial and sincere.

His personal success was confirmed when it emerged, as he smugly reported to the House, 2 May, that Saurin, a principal instigator of the attack, had himself used *ex-officio* informations during his attorney-generalship.[46] Plunket voted against repeal of the Foreign Enlistment Act, 16 Apr. Before he moved to consider Catholic relief the following day Burdett frankly accused him of treachery; and when he was called by the Speaker, Burdett and a dozen advanced Whigs and radicals left the House. His proposal got little support, and was defeated by 313-111 on an adjournment motion.[47] Next day he said that his future course on the question would be guided by the wishes of its supporters at large. As arranged with ministers, he abstained on Burdett's successful motion for inquiry into the conduct of the sheriff of Dublin in allegedly packing the grand jury with Orangemen, 22 Apr., when his enemy Thomas Creevey* thought he cut a 'wretched' figure. Lord Lansdowne commented that 'putting ability in speaking aside', Plunket had 'managed his own case with very little judgement, which I am sorry for, connected as it is with that of liberal policy in Ireland'.[48] He explained, 24 Apr., that he would not prosecute the sheriff unless directed by the House to do so.[49] He took a minor share in the questioning of witnesses and was himself briefly examined in his place, 9, 14 May. On the renewal of the Irish Insurrection Act, a measure of 'melancholy necessity', 12 May, he denied Lord Archibald Hamilton's charges of political inconsistency and betrayal of the cause of Catholic emancipation. At about this time he mistook the day on which he had been invited to dine with Goulburn and found Brownlow and other Orangemen there. He 'did not stay dinner', and was said to be 'angry at the secretary for giving countenance to his persecutors'.[50] He was in the ministerial majorities against Scottish parliamentary reform, 2 June, and inquiry into chancery delays, 5 June 1823, and on the 9th defended a clause of the Irish tithes composition bill. The following day, to the annoyance of Peel, the home secretary, and Goulburn, who were 'left to carry through the ... bill unassisted', he returned to Ireland, 'much out of spirits', as Williams Wynn told Buckingham, and 'anticipating all evil from the irritation of the two factions, and I fear from the want of energy and vigour' in Wellesley. Williams Wynn subsequently told Buckingham:

> You must not wonder that Plunket did not stop to visit you in his way. He has now been four months absent from Ireland, suffering all the while from vexation and indifferent health, which have produced the effect of making him low and hypochondriac about himself. He was convinced that nothing but the native breeze of the potatoes could revive him, and he was besides not a little uneasy as to the consequences of his absence upon his professional business, and very anxious again to see his family. Nothing else could, I will not say justify, but excuse his turning his back upon the tithe bill ... but he is thoroughly dejected, and often talks of the probability of his being obliged to retire.

Hobhouse of the home office reckoned that during the session Plunket had 'made shipwreck of the weight he possessed in the country'.[51]

In late August 1823 Goulburn informed Peel that Wellesley understood that Plunket would resign if Lord Farnham, who, as Member for Cavan, had been one of his Orange tormentors earlier in the year, was elected an Irish representative peer.[52] A month later, however, a report reached Williams Wynn that Wellesley and Plunket now took 'great satisfaction' in 'the improving state of Ireland'.[53] Prompted by Williams Wynn, he asserted in November that the tithes bill was working 'reasonably well' and that he had 'little doubt of its ultimate and not very remote success'; that while the 'reign of terror' was over, the 'system of insubordination' persisted, making it necessary to retain the Insurrection Act, and that Wellesley's 'good sense and temper' in communicating with the Catholic clergy had prevented a public squabble on the burials question:

> Depend upon it that if our government here is carried on without grudge or suspicion, and if the Roman Catholics are led to believe that we are disposed to deal with them fairly on the principles announced two years ago, we may indulge in every prospect of governing this country in such a way as not to create disturbance or annoyance to the ... government in England; but otherwise I cannot answer for it. I need not tell you that in speaking thus hopefully, I do not underrate the necessity of the final settlement of the great question, without which I am convinced the true foundations of tranquillity in Ireland never can be effectually laid.

In response to Buckingham's exhortation to secure 'the admission of the Roman Catholics to their fair proportion of the offices to which they are by law admissible', he admitted that 'various circumstances (and I freely own not sufficient to afford a satisfactory explanation) have concurred to prevent it hitherto', but gave assurances that Wellesley and Liverpool were determined to redress the balance:

> The Roman Catholics ... are on the whole in good humour, and strongly disposed to place confidence in ... [Wellesley's] government ... Their entire confidence in myself is not without its share in producing this disposition.

Yet Williams Wynn perceived in this a symptom of 'a want of energy' in Wellesley and Plunket, 'which must almost disqualify them for coping successfully with the exterior and interior enemies they have to deal with'.[54]

Williams Wynn pressed Plunket to go to London in time for Newport's Catholic burials motion of 19 Feb. 1824, on which subject ministers were all at sea; but as his doing so would have been 'attended with very serious inconvenience', Plunket persuaded Newport to postpone the matter. After his arrival, 1 Mar., he assisted the cabinet in deciding to take over the question and to introduce a bill to repeal obsolete regulations and empower the Protestant clergy to permit the performance of Catholic and Dissenting burials by their respective ministers. He introduced this, 23 Mar., and explained it at length, 29 Mar. It passed the Commons on 1 Apr. and, after amendment by the Lords, became law on the 15th (5 Geo. IV, c. 25). O'Connell publicly attacked it and privately damned Plunket, who was 'as bad as any of the king's ministers'.[55] On the Irish Catholic bishops' petition for improving the education of poor Catholics, 9 Mar., Plunket agreed that it should be founded on religion, but said that to make it 'rest on a moral basis alone was not only useless, but absolutely pernicious', and that the union of morals and religion should not be 'converted into an instrument of proselytism' by the establishment of separate Protestant and Catholic schools.[56] Plunket, who received another resignation threat from Wellesley and was the subject of a complaint from Lord Clancarty to Wellington of supineness in the face of Roman Catholic aggrandisement,[57] opposed Lord Althorp's motion for information on the ribbonmen, 11 Mar., arguing that the Irish administration were 'endeavouring honestly to discharge their difficult duties'. He came back from Ireland in early May, according to Williams Wynn, 'low and out of spirits, deeply impressed with the dangers threatening us from the Roman Catholics and the Orange Association, and desirous of stronger measures to put both down than can be hoped for from a divided and paralysed administration'.[58] He opposed Hume's attack on the Irish church establishment, 'the great bond of union between the two countries', 6 May, and Newport's motion on the Irish first fruits fund, 25 May, and amendment to the clergy residence bill, 27 May; but, objecting to Hill's Londonderry Cathedral bill, 10 May, he observed that the Irish Protestant clergy must recognize 'the necessity of entrenching themselves on public opinion by their good conduct'. When asked by O'Connell and a deputation from the Catholic Association to present their emancipation petition, he agreed to do so, while making it clear that he had no intention of bringing on the question that session. O'Connell threatened to wash his hands of him.[59] Plunket presented the petition, 31 May 1824, regretting its reference to attacks on Catholicism by members of the Protestant hierarchy, and announced that he and the leading friends of relief concurred in thinking that it would be 'unavailing and hopeless' to propose it at that stage of the session. In what Christopher Hely Hutchinson* considered a 'neat and ... excellent reply', he repudiated Brownlow's insinuation that he had 'neglected his duty' by not prosecuting the Catholic Association.[60]

In mid-September 1824 Lord Redesdale told Lord Colchester that Manners 'talks of resigning', but that ministers now had 'little disposition to make Plunket chancellor, fearing he would not be very manageable'.[61] A month later Plunket assured Holland that

> the appearances of tranquillity in ... [Ireland] become more promising. There is certainly a considerable share of agitation amongst the Roman Catholics, and a correspondent apprehension on the other side that the measure is advancing to a consummation. The alarm ... which grows out of this, many of them pass on themselves as a fear of insurrectionary movements ... for which, so far

as the Roman Catholics are concerned, there does not appear to me to be any rational ground.[62]

Williams Wynn believed in late November that Plunket, who was required to submit to ministers his professional opinion on the legality of the Catholic Association, was still of the opinion that it had not broken the law.[63] A fortnight later Plunket informed him that while there was 'a more violent degree of political agitation than I ever remember, and a stronger excitement and more general union amongst the Roman Catholic body', he was confident that 'insurrection, and combination for the purposes of insurrection, is put down'. At the same time, he conceded that the 'intimate union' of the Catholics, forged by the priesthood under the aegis of the Association, was a potential source of 'mischief', which required vigilance. Yet he remained sure that 'coercion alone will be ineffectual for any lasting good'. He wrote in broadly the same terms to Buckingham in January 1825, stating that 'all the rational friends' of emancipation in Ireland were against bringing it forward in the forthcoming session. He hoped that 'admonition and private remonstrance', rather than coercion, could be used to restrain the respectable Catholics.[64] Without consulting the home government, he instigated a prosecution of O'Connell for a recent speech at the Association; its failure was an embarrassment.[65]

On his slightly belated arrival in London Plunket, backed by Wellesley's representations, carried his argument in favour of a bill to put down the Association without mentioning it by name.[66] He would have answered Denman, 10 Feb. 1825, if the debate on Goulburn's motion to introduce the measure had not been adjourned. The following day he defended the bill and his own political conduct since 1813, claiming that the success of 1821 had convinced him that emancipation could be carried by a divided government and that the Whigs were incapable of forming a stable ministry. The wife of the Irish Member John North, a spectator in the ventilator, thought it 'a very fine' speech, though 'more an ingenious than a triumphant one'. The Grenvillite toady William Fremantle* told Buckingham that 'nothing could have been more effectual ... and nothing ever was more manly and convincing: it was an admirable defence of the consistency of his conduct, and identified him greatly with the Grenvilles'. But to the advanced Whig Member Sir Robert Wilson, 'his admissions both to the past and present were monstrous records of the want of all character and principle in the G[renvillite] party'.[67] Plunket supported the bill, 15 Feb., when he said that one of the evil consequences of the Association's activities was that they distracted the priests from parochial work, and 22 Feb., when he also opposed Hume's motion for Irish office-holders to be required to disclaim on oath membership of illegal societies. According to Edward Littleton*, Plunket's speech of 28 Feb. in support of Burdett's motion to consider Catholic relief, which Agar Ellis thought the only 'good' one and Gurney considered 'most excellent', being 'all sense, no flourish', made six converts, who were crucial to the majority of 13.[68] The next day Plunket complained that Brownlow had withheld a petition denigrating Catholic priests, and on the 24th he presented one for relief from the Protestants of Newry.[69] Left to himself, he would have shelved the question that session, but, as he told Wellesley, the success of Burdett's motion made him optimistic that, given the 'reasonable prospect of tranquillity' afforded by the Unlawful Societies Act, the chances of an early settlement of the issue were high. He stressed the importance of 'a firm quiet system of things' and of maintaining cordial intercourse with Catholic leaders.[70] At about this time the Whig duke of Bedford wrote to Lady Holland:

> Why do you imagine that I should be shocked at your enjoying Plunket's society? There is no one more agreeable, and nobody feels his good qualities more sensibly than I do ... I am told that he has made the most powerful, convincing and eloquent speech ever heard in favour of the Catholic claims ... To be sure as a politician he is something of a rogue, but perfect honesty is a very rare quality in his class of men.

Bedford subsequently wrote:

> I am glad that you have done me justice with respect to Plunket. You may recollect that [Lord] John [Russell] was not the only one amongst *your friends*, who thought they were breathing an infectious air by being in the same room with Mr. Plunket. I have always liked him, and always shall like him. All the harm I wish him is to see him out of office, and no longer insulted and trampled upon by such men as the chancellor and Peel.[71]

With Burdett and an accommodating O'Connell, who now thought him 'quite sincere in his desire to emancipate the Catholics in the most conciliatory manner possible', Plunket framed a relief bill and, dispensing with the veto, measures to provide for the payment of Catholic priests and to disfranchise Irish 40*s.* freeholders.[72] Returning from Ireland after Easter, he voted silently for the second, 21 Apr., and third readings of the relief bill, 10 May. On 6 May he opposed various amendments to it and clashed with Peel on the securities issue. Supporting the franchise bill, 26 Apr., he tackled Brougham and, according to the Grenvillites, gave him a 'thorough beating' in his 'most eloquent and brilliant' style.[73] He briefly endorsed the plan to make state provision for the Irish Catholic clergy, 29 Apr. On 5 May he got leave to introduce a bill to assimilate the Irish regulations governing the striking of special juries to the English, which was brought in by Goulburn later that day. He was very disappointed by the cabinet's decision to leave the relief bill to its fate in the Lords, where it was defeated, and was said to be 'greatly indignant' at lord chancellor Eldon's 'having made a joke of him and compared him to a Jesuit'.[74] On 26 May 1825 he professed confidence in the eventual success of the Catholic cause, which only 'the egregious folly of the Catholics themselves' could thwart, and said that no purpose would be served by his own resignation. He left for Ireland the following day 'in excellent spirits', according to O'Connell, who was convinced that he would soon be made Irish chancellor.[75]

The revival of the Catholic Association and renewed violence in Ireland in the autumn compelled Plunket to acquiesce in Canning's insistence on setting aside the Catholic question for the remainder of the current Parliament; but he argued that it must not be put into abeyance. As he wrote to Williams Wynn, 'if we can tide through the remainder of the present Parliament without spreading any sails, and I hope without the dangerous aid of steam, we may look for everything favourable at the commencement of the new one'. In mid-December he wrote to Canning:

> Abstracting myself from all angry feelings growing out of the gross provocation of these mob leaders ... I am more than ever sensible of the necessity and *urgency* of the measure, but its urgency must wait on its practicability, and that must depend on circumstances which no man can anticipate. Should it be brought forward in the first session I do not look to any possible state of things in which I would not support it strenuously, but I can readily suppose circumstances under which I should strongly advise against its being brought forward. At the same time ... I cannot shut my eyes to the danger of the question assuming this position, namely, that a measure principally and substantially affecting Ireland, passionately desired by all the Roman Catholics of Ireland, and sought for or acquiesced in by the majority of the Protestants of that country, still must be indefinitely postponed in deference to the feelings of the people of England ... I see no rational solution of these difficulties, but by carrying the question, and by carrying it soon.[76]

Plunket was as partial to jobbery as the next Irishman, and at the end of 1825 he persuaded Wellesley to agree in principle to give the vacant deanery of Clogher, worth over £1,000 a year, to his eldest son Thomas Span Plunket (1792-1866), who had been ten years a curate. He was, however, required to consult Goulburn, who vetoed the appointment as a gross job which would discredit the Irish government. This view was endorsed by Peel, who recalled that during his time as Irish secretary 'every official man, not content with the favour of government to himself, thought he had a right to quarter his family on the patronage of government'.[77] Plunket was summoned to England in late January 1826 to give his views on the legality of the revived Catholic Association.[78] He was little in evidence in the House that session. On 16 Feb. he opposed Newport's motion on Irish church rates and Spring Rice's call for inquiry into Irish tolls, but indicated that the government was preparing measures to amend the laws affecting bankrupts and landlord-tenant relations. He voted with his colleagues on the Jamaican slave trials, 2 Mar. On the 9th he opposed Newport's proposal to disfranchise non-resident Irish borough freeholders. Expectations that he was to become Irish chancellor encouraged North and Croker to canvass Dublin University at the end of that month; but there was no opposition to his return at the general election in June when, in response to some barracking, he said that any of his votes which had caused offence had been conscientiously given. He was 'handled very roughly by the students', who 'pitched him violently out of the chair and broke it to pieces'.[79]

In reply to Canning's questions, Plunket agreed, 10 Oct. 1826, that 'the golden opportunity is gone by' to implement the disfranchisement of Irish 40*s*. freeholders, and that although the payment of priests was perhaps still attainable, the prospects were less good than in 1825. He went on:

> If ... you ask me, am I as sanguine ... of the efficiency of the Roman Catholic measure, if carried, in tranquillizing Ireland, I candidly answer I am not, and every year more of a postponement renders me less so. I do at the same time seriously believe that the measure, if soon carried and honestly acted on, will give a fair chance of tranquillity ... Until this takes place the task of governing Ireland becomes every day more difficult.

While he was unsure as to the best technical way of proceeding in the forthcoming session and had 'an anxious desire to prevent this question pressing too heavily on the government', he was willing to take it up if ministers had no objections, for he was sure that 'things cannot long continue in their present state'. Canning made it clear that his colleagues would not make emancipation a government measure.[80] He advised against the prosecution of Sheil for his attack on the duke of York.[81] Persuaded by Canning that it was best to proceed by resolution followed by a bill (some Whigs considered this to be a 'juggle') he pondered in January 1827 the problems of paying the Catholic clergy and regulating intercourse with Rome. He arrived in London on 24 Feb., soon after O'Connell had publicly accused him of being the secret enemy of emancipation.[82] On 2 Mar. he presented the Irish Catholic bishops' relief petition, and later that day he clashed with Peel's brother-in-law George Dawson, a junior minister, on the trustworthiness of the Catholic population of Ireland. Robert Wilmot Horton*, another member of the government, deplored the 'discreditable' spectacle of these two 'firing red-hot shot into each other, at point-blank distance'.[83] Mackintosh heard from Lansdowne, 4 Mar., that Plunket, like Burdett, 'had great misgivings about the Catholic question and thought of delay'; but on 6 Mar. he spoke at length, to 'loud cheers', in favour of Burdett's unsuccessful motion, following and replying in 'magnificent' style to Copley, the master of the rolls. At a small meeting at the duke of Norfolk's, 8 Mar., he, Lansdowne, Holland and others decided to do nothing more on the subject until the ministerial uncertainty created by Liverpool's stroke had been resolved.[84] He spoke and voted for the duke of Clarence's grant, 16 Mar. He announced that a scheme for a common system of education had been approved by the Irish Catholic hierarchy, 19 Mar. He opposed Brownlow's motion for information on the 1825 Orange march at Lisburn, 29 Mar., and Newport's attack on the first fruits fund, 3 Apr. He presented a pro-Catholic petition from the Protestants of Fermanagh, 5 Apr.[85] Next day he told Lord Chandos that there was no intention to legislate further against the Catholic Association and repudiated Trench's accusation that he was holding a match to the Irish powder keg. On 11 Apr. 1827 he assured Dawson that there was no doubt that Orange societies were illegal.[86]

When Canning formed his ministry soon afterwards Plunket was expected to become Irish chancellor, but the king intervened to thwart this. In compensation Canning offered him the mastership of the rolls in England and a British peerage. He accepted, but the great hostility of the English bar to the appointment of an Irishman forced him to renounce it.[87] He took the peerage, but another month elapsed before ministers were able to persuade the 81-year-old Lord Norbury to vacate the Irish chief justiceship of common pleas for him.[88] When John Hobhouse* met him for the first time socially at this juncture, he was 'quiet, but every now and then gave vent to flashes of humour and joviality'; and in September 1827 O'Connell, who felt that Plunket had suffered a 'pitiable fall' into political 'oblivion', told Sheil that he had probably not 'thrown *cold water*' on his patent of precedence, for it was 'no part of his character to act with duplicity. He has neither the *good manners* nor the *bad heart* of Iago'.[89] Plunket made spectacularly fine speeches in favour of Catholic emancipation in 1829.[90] Although, in Greville's view, he had been a 'rash, hasty, and imprudent' judge, he was made Irish chancellor in the Grey ministry, and he continued in the office in the Melbourne administrations.[91] His deficiencies in legal learning led to many of his decisions being overturned on appeal, but he remained politically influential in the 1830s. He earned a well-deserved reputation for nepotism and jobbery, providing Thomas and his other five sons with plenty of good things in the church and the law. In 1832 it was reckoned that he and close relatives took almost £15,000 a year in public money, not including income from church preferment.[92] Ironically, he was manoeuvred out of his place in favour of John Campbell II* in the summer of 1841 in what Brougham described as 'the most gross and unjustifiable act ever done by party, combining violence and ingratitude with fraud'.[93] In retirement he travelled in Italy, but his last years were clouded by mental decay. He died at his home at Old Connaught in January 1854 and was buried in Mount Jerome cemetery, Dublin.[94] He was succeeded in the peerage by Thomas, who was bishop of Tuam from 1839 until his death, and then by his second son John Span Plunket (1793-1871), a lawyer. Brougham described Plunket during his lifetime as

> the greatest orator of the age. I place him quite on a level with Pitt, Fox, Chatham, and in many respects above them, and his eloquence has not one single Irish fault of taste in it. He is accused of want of firmness in council. I never saw it. He is charged with nepotism; he is an Irishman no doubt. He can be believed on his word though an Irishman.[95]

Russell remembered him as 'the most perfect orator' of the 1820s, who 'so restrained his brilliant fancy that it was ever ready to help, to adorn, to illustrate, while it was never used to eclipse or encumber his argument'.[96] Lord Ebrington*, comparing him as a speaker with his contemporaries, remarked that while 'all the others made you feel that they were doing their best, with him it seemed as if he was taking no trouble, and could do even better if he liked'.[97]

[1] *Macaulay Letters*, ii. 82. [2] *Gent. Mag.* (1854), i. 192-4; *Greville Mems.* vi. 307; R.L. Sheil, *Sketches of Irish Bar* (1854), 104, 114. [3] D. Plunket, *Life, Letters, and Speeches of Lord Plunket* (1867), i. 5. [4] Add. 58963, ff. 36, 38; NLW, Coedymaen mss 576; *Croker Pprs.* i. 157. [5] *Dublin Evening Post*, 3, 10 Feb., 16 Mar. 1820; Coedymaen mss 1043;

Add. 58772, f. 22. [6] *Dublin Evening Post*, 24, 27 June 1820. [7] Christ Church, Oxf. Phillimore mss, Plunket to Phillimore [?6 July]; *The Times*, 13 July 1820. [8] Add. 51562, Brougham to Holland [21 Dec.]; 51586, Tierney to Lady Holland [28 Dec. 1820]; Buckingham, *Mems. Geo. IV*, i. 110. [9] Add. 58963, ff. 40, 46; Plunket, i. 394-409. [10] Lansdowne mss, Plunket to Lansdowne, 29 Jan. 1821. [11] *The Times*, 1 Mar. 1821. [12] Hatherton diary, 6 Oct. 1838; Torrens, *Melbourne*, i. 163; Cent. Kent. Stud. Camden mss U840 C530/8; Add. 51564, Brougham to Lady Holland [8 Mar.]; Ward, *Llandaff Letters*, 279-80; Northants. RO, Agar Ellis diary, 28 Feb. [1821]; HLRO, Hist. Coll. 379, Grey Bennet diary, 28. [13] Dorset RO D/BKL, Bankes jnl. 124. [14] Harrowby mss. [15] *Hobhouse Diary*, 53-54; Twiss, *Eldon*, ii. 416; Buckingham, i. 124, 129. [16] *The Times*, 8 Mar. 1821. [17] *Lady Holland to Son*, 3. [18] G.I.T. Machin, *Catholic Question in English Politics*, 27-29; *O'Connell Corresp.* ii. 894, 902; W.J. Fitzpatrick, *Life of Dr. Doyle* (1880), i. 157-60; Plunket, ii. 75-79. [19] Buckingham, i. 141-2; *Lady Holland to Son*, 4-5; Coedymaen mss bdle. 17, Plunket to Williams Wynn, 4 Apr., 2, 11 May 1821; Add. 58963, ff. 54, 56; Buckingham, i. 156-7. [20] Buckingham, i. 135-6, 233; Plunket, ii. 85, 87. [21] Twiss, ii. 435; Add. 38290, ff. 88, 92. [22] *Croker Pprs.* i. 218; Plunket, ii. 85, 87-95; Buckingham, i. 233, 235-6, 240-3, 250-1, 253, 255, 262, 277; *Geo. IV Letters*, ii. 971, 973; BL, Fortescue mss, Buckingham to Grenville, 30 Nov., 2, 6 Dec., memo. 30 Nov., Williams Wynn to Grenville [4, 5 Dec.] 1821; Add. 38290, f. 155; 38743, f. 72; 40328, f. 1. [23] *Arbuthnot Corresp.* 26; Plunket, ii. 97; *Dublin Evening Post*, 19 Jan., 16 Feb. 1822. [24] Add. 51679, Russell to Lady Holland [Jan. 1822]. [25] *O'Connell Corresp.* ii. 930. [26] Buckingham, i. 294, 297. [27] Add. 37298, f. 312; Coedymaen mss bdle. 17, Williams Wynn to Plunket, 5 Feb. 1822. [28] *Fox Jnl.* 108. [29] Buckingham, i. 299, 304, 306, 308-12, 314-15; Plunket, ii. 100-2; *Wellington and Friends*, 21; *O'Connell Corresp.* ii. 949, 954a; Coedymaen mss 367-368, 630; bdle. 17, Plunket to Williams Wynn, 6 Apr.; Bucks. RO, Fremantle mss D/FR/46/10/26/1; 46/10/27, 28; Add. 51586, Tierney to Lady Holland, 16 Apr. 1822. [30] Agar Ellis diary. [31] *Fox Jnl.* 113; Add. 52445, f. 79. [32] Gurney diary, 22 Apr.; Buckingham, i. 318-19; Agar Ellis diary, 22 Apr.; Fremantle mss 46/10/31. [33] Add. 52445, f. 83; Agar Ellis diary. [34] Add. 51832, Plunket to Holland, 18 May 1822. [35] *The Times*, 21 May, 20 June 1822. [36] *Fox Jnl.* 126; Buckingham, i. 351-2. [37] Wellington mss WP1/718/20. [38] Add. 40319, f. 57; *Croker Pprs.* i. 230. [39] Bessborough mss, Abercromby to Duncannon, 14 Oct. 1822. [40] Coedymaen mss bdle. 17, Plunket to Williams Wynn, 29 Nov., reply, 4 Dec.; Add. 40353, f. 226; 51574, Abercromby to Holland [29 Dec.] 1822; Grey mss, Grey to Holland, 22 Jan. 1823; *O'Connell Corresp.* ii. 988, 990; Buckingham, i. 408-9, 414-18, 434; *Arbuthnot Jnl.* i. 219. [41] Add. 58963, f. 60; Coedymaen mss bdle. 17, Plunket to Williams Wynn, 26, 28 Jan. 1823; Buckingham, i. 420, 424, 427-8; TCD, Donoughmore mss D/37/5; Fremantle mss 46/11/68/2. [42] *O'Connell Corresp.* ii. 996; Buckingham, i. 429-30, 432-3; Donoughmore mss D/43/54; *The Times*, 19 Feb. 1823. [43] Buckingham, i. 442; Add. 58963, f. 64. [44] Plunket, ii. 135. [45] *The Times*, 25 Mar. 1823; Brougham mss, Abercromby to Brougham, 26 Mar. 1823. [46] Bankes jnl. 143 (15 Apr.); Buckingham, i. 447, 450-2; Agar Ellis diary, 15 Apr.; *Arbuthnot Jnl.* i. 227; Harewood mss, Williams Wynn to Canning and reply, 7 Apr.; Lonsdale mss, Lowther to Lonsdale, 12 Apr. 1823; Add. 37301, f. 14; 58963, f. 68; Plunket, ii. 110-24. [47] Agar Ellis diary, 17 Apr. 1823; *Colchester Diary*, iii. 279. [48] Add. 40355, f. 328; *Creevey's Life and Times* 178; PRO NI, Fitzgerald mss MIC/639/11/6/51, p. 104. [49] *The Times*, 25 Apr. 1823. [50] Add. 51586, Tierney to Lady Holland, 19 May [1823]; *Russell Letters*, i. 26. [51] Buckingham, i. 467-9, 473; *Hobhouse Diary*, 103. [52] Add. 40329, ff. 117, 129. [53] Add. 51534, T. Grenville to Holland, 22 Sept. 1823. [54] Coedymaen mss bdle. 17, Williams Wynn to Plunket, 1 Nov., reply, 18 Nov., Plunket to Buckingham, 6 Dec. 1823; Buckingham, ii. 19; Plunket, ii. 140-4. [55] Coedymaen mss bdle. 17, Plunket to Williams Wynn, 28 Jan., 10 Feb.; Buckingham, ii. 45, 48-49, 54-55; Add. 37302, ff. 145, 147, 163, 167, 171, 177, 217; *The Times*, 26 Mar. 1824; *O'Connell Corresp.* iii. 1119, 1121. [56] Plunket, ii. 147-50. [57] Ibid. ii. 145-6; Wellington mss WP1/788/12; 796/8. [58] Buckingham, ii. 71, 74. [59] *O'Connell Corresp.* iii. 1123a, b, 1124; Donoughmore mss F/13/91, 92. [60] Donoughmore mss D/43/62. [61] *Colchester Diary*, iii. 341. [62] Add. 51832, Plunket to Holland, 14 Oct 1824. [63] Buckingham, ii. 165; Add. 37303, ff. 11, 13; Wellington mss WP1/805/47. [64] Coedymaen mss bdle. 17, Plunket to Williams Wynn, 15 Dec. 1824; Buckingham, ii. 193-4. [65] *O'Connell Corresp.* iii. 1144, 1147, 1148; Add. 37303, ff. 109, 117, 121, 129, 130; Parker, *Peel*, i. 354-5; Lonsdale mss, Long to Lonsdale, 2 Jan.; Add. 51578, Morpeth to Holland, 10 Jan. 1825. [66] Buckingham, ii. 200-6; Coedymaen mss 410, 412. [67] Buckingham, ii. 208, 210-11; PRO NI D207/73/119; Add. 30124, f. 133; Plunket, ii. 168-77. [68] Agar Ellis diary, 1 Mar.; Gurney diary, 1 Mar.; TNA 30/29, Littleton to Granville, 7 Mar. 1825; Add. 70928, f. 119. [69] *The Times*, 2, 25 Mar. 1825. [70] Plunket, ii. 200-3. [71] Add. 51669, Bedford to Lady Holland [6, 8 Mar. 1825]. [72] *O'Connell Corresp.* iii. 1178, 1180, 1192; *Croker Pprs.* i. 280; Buckingham, ii. 229; Brougham mss, Mackintosh to Brougham, 16 Mar. 1825. [73] *O'Connell Corresp.* iii. 1204; Buckingham, ii. 243-4; Agar Ellis diary, 26 Apr. [1825]. [74] *O'Connell Corresp.* iii. 1218-20, 1228; *Arbuthnot Jnl.* i. 398. [75] *O'Connell Corresp.* iii. 1229, 1232, 1238, 1239. [76] Plunket, ii. 213-17, 220-6; Camden mss C202/11/12; Wellington mss WP1/832/13. [77] Add. 40332, ff. 5, 7, 11. [78] PRO NI D207/74/180; Add. 37304, ff. 33, 41, 45, 55. [79] Add. 37304, ff. 115, 117; 40332, f. 30; *Dublin Evening Post*, 8, 13 June 1826; NLI, Farnham mss 18602 (20). [80] Plunket, ii. 232-9. [81] *Geo. IV Letters*, iii. 1261; Add. 37304, ff. 230-4. [82] Plunket, ii. 241-3; Lansdowne mss, Plunket to Lansdowne, 19 Jan.; Wellington mss WP1/906/2; *Canning's Ministry*, 6, 32; Creevey mss, Creevey to Miss Ord, 10 Feb.; Lonsdale mss, Long to Lonsdale, 22 Feb. 1827; *O'Connell Corresp.* iii. 1367. [83] *Canning's Ministry*, 38. [84] Add. 52447, ff. 46, 55, 56; *Canning's Ministry*, 43. [85] *The Times*, 6 Apr. 1827. [86] Ibid. 12 Apr. 1827. [87] Plunket, ii. 244-6; *Canning's Ministry*, 180, 196, 198, 210, 249, 256; Wellington mss WP1/887/35, 41; *Hobhouse Diary*, 132; *Arbuthnot Jnl.* ii. 107; Coedymaen mss 195, 196; bdle. 17, Plunket to Williams Wynn, 7 Oct.; Add. 51833, same to Holland, 28 Aug. 1827. [88] *Geo. IV Letters*, iii. 1333, 1343; *Canning's Ministry*, 320. [89] Broughton, *Recollections*, iii. 194; *O'Connell Corresp.* iii. 1389, 1393, 1397, 1414. [90] *Greville Mems.* i. 256, 259, 283. [91] Ibid. ii. 87. [92] *Three Diaries*, 198; *O'Connell Corresp.* v. 2012, 2073, 2359; *Greville Mems.* iii. 23; Warws. RO MI 247, Philips Mems. i. 279; *Extraordinary Black Bk.* (1832), 562. [93] Plunket, i. 20-21; *Greville Mems.* iv. 386; *Macaulay Letters*, iii. 381. [94] *Oxford DNB*; Plunket, ii. 346-7; *Gent. Mag.* (1854), i. 165, 196; *Speeches of W.C. Plunket* ed. J.C. Hoey, p. xxiv. [95] Brougham mss, autobiog. fragment. [96] Russell, *Recollections*, 56. [97] Torrens, i. 265.

D.R.F.

PLUNKETT, Arthur James, Lord Killeen (1791–1869).

CO. MEATH 22 Feb. 1830–1832

b. 29 Mar. 1791, at Geneva, o. surv. s. of Arthur James Plunkett, 8th earl of Fingall [I], and Frances, da. of John Donelan of Ballydonnellan, co. Galway. *m.* 11 Dec. 1817, Louisa Emilia, da. of Elias Corbally of Corbalton Hall, co. Meath, 6s. (1 *d.v.p.*) 2da. (1 *d.v.p.*). *styled* Lord Killeen 1793-1836; *suc.* fa. as 9th earl of Fingall [I] and 2nd Bar. Fingall [UK] 30 July 1836; KP 21 Oct. 1846. *d.* 21 Apr. 1869.

PC [I] 31 Oct. 1834; ld. in waiting 1837-41.

Ld. lt. co. Meath 1849-*d.*

Killeen's father, a leading Catholic in the campaign for emancipation, succeeded to his family's Irish peerage and estates in 1793 and took an active part in suppressing the rebellion of 1798. Killeen joined

Brooks's, 19 May 1812, sponsored by Lord King. The following month, at a meeting of the Catholics of Ireland in Dublin, he proposed resolutions regretting the failure of the relief bill.[1] A founding member of the Catholic Association, many of whose preliminary meetings he chaired, 1822-3, he took custody of its funds on its dissolution in March 1825, Daniel O'Connell* explaining that

> the only legal disposal of the Catholic rent that can now be made is by vesting it in some one individual of such integrity and honour as to be a sufficient assurance of the faithful and delicate execution of the confidential character which such a donation naturally requires. It is perfectly plain that if Lord Killeen will accept this donation we shall have such an individual as we could desire.

In October O'Connell described him as 'the proper person' to 'be applied to with respect to any disposal' of the rent.[2] He attended a Meath meeting to petition against alteration of the corn laws, 21 Apr., and chaired one to promote Catholic claims, 30 Aug.[3] In November 1825 Lord Camden reported that it was 'the decided wish of the more moderate party amongst the Catholics, Lord Killeen at their head, not to have the Catholic question agitated this year and before the probable dissolution', for fear that 'if the Catholics are violent, the Protestants will also be so and the next Parliament chosen, will be less friendly', and that these feelings were known to Canning and Lord Harrowby and led to the cabinet's decision.[4] At the 1826 general election Killeen proposed the pro-Catholics Sir Marcus Somerville* in Meath and Richard Talbot* in county Dublin, where he appeared on a hustings for the first time.[5] He attended meetings of the revived Catholic Association, but was critical of O'Connell's plans for a mission to England to combat anti-Catholic prejudice at the end of 1827.[6] He presided over the Meath Liberal Club, established on 1 Oct. 1828 to counter an Independent one got up by 'Honest Jack' Lawless, and congratulated Leinster on its 'happy union of Protestants and Catholics' at a meeting of the province's 'friends of civil and religious liberty', 20 Oct. 1828.[7] He chaired Meath meetings in support of Lord Anglesey following his recall as Irish viceroy, 19, 26 Jan., and attended one for the 'friends of civil and religious liberty' at the Rotunda, Dublin, 20 Jan. 1829. James Naper reported to Lord Downshire, 5 Feb., that it was

> clear from the conduct of Lord Killeen, Mr. [Thomas] Wyse* and others of the Catholics that they felt as we all do, how much harm to the cause the violent members of the Association do, and how impossible it is to control them unless the Protestants will come forward and give their weight to those Catholics who ... oppose the violence we so much lament.[8]

At an Association meeting on 23 Jan. Killeen offered his services to O'Connell, saying that he would 'gladly attend him to London', but at another held on 7 Mar. he questioned the 'prudence' of his proposal to petition against the disfranchisement of the Irish 40*s.* freeholders. He was a member of the committee established for the O'Connell testimonial, 25 Mar. 1829.[9]

In November 1829 he came forward for a vacancy in Meath, prompting the duke of Wellington, the premier, to comment that if he 'would keep clear of radical Roman Catholic politics he would make a suitable Member', and Peel, the home secretary, to 'hope' that Naper would offer and defeat him. Wellington advised the duke of Northumberland, the viceroy, not to support him, but he obtained Anglesey's backing as a counter-weight to O'Connell, Charles Hare observing that his return might help to 'detach the real gentry from among the Roman Catholics, from the upstart pretenders'.[10] At the nomination Killeen declared that he was 'unpledged to any party' and would not support ministers unless convinced that their measures would benefit Ireland, and promised his support for reduced taxation and 'assimilating the laws and institutions of both countries'. A rumoured opposition came to nothing and he was returned unopposed.[11] He took his seat, 22 Mar., voted steadily for civil and military reductions from that month onwards, and divided for parliamentary reform, 28 May 1830. He presented petitions and divided for Jewish emancipation, 5 Apr., 17 May, when he argued that it would 'promote the principle of Christianity'. He was granted a week's leave on account of family illness, 25 Apr. He seconded and voted for a motion for repeal of the Irish coal duties, 13 May. He presented petitions against the increased spirit duties, 24 May, the assimilation of Irish stamp duties, 21, 24 May, and tax increases, 15 June. He agreed that the Irish Vestry Act required amendment, 10 June, and, after expressing 'some difficulty in knowing' which measure to vote for, was in the minority of 17 for O'Connell's repeal bill. He supported a petition against the compulsory attendance of British Protestant soldiers at Catholic services when overseas, as 'no man ought to be called upon to do any act against his conscience', 16 June. He voted against government changes to the libel law amendment bill, 9 July, and for the abolition of colonial slavery, 13 July. That month he applied through Lord Conyngham for ministerial support at the impending general election, which Wellington gave, commenting that 'there is no reason to disturb the existing Members'.[12]

He stood as a 'friend to parliamentary reform' who had 'endeavoured to pursue a course of strict independence' and was returned unopposed.[13] He welcomed the French revolution in a letter read to a Dublin meeting, 15 Sept. 1830.[14] He voted for repeal of the Irish Subletting Act, 11 Nov., saying that it ought 'not to have anything but a prospective operation on the contracts between landlords and tenants', and presented multiple petitions in the same terms, 6 Dec. 1830, 28 Mar. 1831. He divided for reduction of the duty on Irish wheat imports, 12 Nov. 1830. He had been listed by ministers as one of the 'doubtful doubtfuls' and an 'enemy', but by Pierce Mahony† as one of the 'neutrals', and he voted against them in the crucial division on the civil list, 15 Nov. That month O'Connell recommended that Irish petitions on education 'should be presented by independent Irish Members' such as Killeen, Wyse and More O'Ferrall.[15] Killeen implored the Grey ministry to introduce a vestry bill 'satisfactory to the country at large', 9 Dec. On 14 Dec. 1830 he defended the Union, which was 'calculated to promote the prosperity' of both countries, and predicted that its repeal would be 'made the touchstone of the support of most candidates' at the next election, when he might 'become the victim of this declaration'. On 8 Feb. 1831 the Meath landowner Lord Darnley advised Lord Holland against considering Killeen for the lord lieutenancy and recommended Lord Gormanston, who was

> one of the first ... to sign the declaration against the repeal of the Union (which neither Fingall nor his son have signed to this day) ... [and] therefore no *Jesuit*, or indirect abettor of O'Connell, which is more than I would venture to assert of others. In a word, I think the appointment of Lord Killeen would only add to the *blunders* already made by government in that land of *blunders*.[16]

Darnley's hostility was evidently not shared by ministers, for on learning of his death the following month the Irish secretary Smith Stanley informed Anglesey, the viceroy, that it had removed 'a difficulty' and he hoped 'to give the lieutenancy to Killeen, who is the right man'.[17] In the event, however, another candidate was appointed. Killeen presented Meath petitions for repeal of the Union, 16 Feb., when he urged the House to 'turn their attention to such measures as will remove the various grievances under which Ireland suffers', and 28 Mar. On 16 Feb. he presented petitions from the Protestants of Killashee, county Longford, for a general fast and from the brewers and distillers of Cork against the duties levied by the corporation. He regretted that O'Connell had not informed him of one from Navan, county Meath, for withholding public pensions, which he endorsed, 2 Mar. He called for a bill to enable the Irish to grow tobacco for their own use, 10 Mar., warned that distress had extended 'all over Ireland' and 'amongst the labouring classes' of Meath 'to a very alarming extent', 18 Mar., and presented a constituency petition for relief, 23 Mar. He voted for the second reading of the English reform bill, 22 Mar., and against Gascoyne's wrecking amendment, 19 Apr. 1831.

At the ensuing general election he again cited his support for reform and retrenchment and was returned at the head of the poll.[18] His father was given a United Kingdom barony in June 1831. He presented a Meath petition for an increase of Irish Members, arguing that 'their present number ... is by no means in proportion to the population of the country', 27 June. He voted for the second reading of the reintroduced reform bill, 6 July, at least twice against the adjournment, 12 July, and gave generally steady support to its details. He presented a petition from Drogheda ship owners against the Irish steam marine bill, 1 July. He secured an account of firearms registered in Ireland, 5 July. He presented several petitions against the grant to the Kildare Place Society, 14 July, arguing that it was of 'little or no benefit' since the 'people consider the terms on which it is bestowed' to be 'repugnant to their religious feelings'. As a trustee of Maynooth College, where he had spent some of his 'earlier years' as a student, 20 July, he demanded to know whether the petitioners of Portadown, county Armagh, objected to the continuance of its grant 'on religious grounds alone' or charged 'the trustees with any misconduct or misapplication' of its funds. He denied that the College exhibited any 'indisposition' to 'permit the study of the Scriptures' and claimed that it produced 'men of exceedingly high character' and priests 'of the most liberal disposition', 31 Aug. He divided against disqualification of the Dublin election committee, 29 July, and the issue of a writ, 8 Aug., and with ministers on the controversy, 23 Aug. He contended that 'nothing less' than total repeal of the Irish Subletting Act would 'satisfy the people', 5 Aug. He disliked the language of the Waterford petition for disarming the Irish yeomanry, 11 Aug., but voted for its printing nonetheless, explaining that although he had never heard of any misconduct in Meath, such a force was 'not suited' to Ireland. That month he was a spokesman for a deputation of Irish Members, including O'Connell, Sheil and Wyse, which, as Grey informed Anglesey, 16 Aug., threatened him with

> opposing the government, if their views of the policy fit to be pursued in ... Ireland were not adopted. The

> measure they pressed most was that of regulating the yeomanry, with a view to its gradual reduction, admitting, at least several of them and amongst others Lord Killeen ... that an immediate suppression ... was not to be expected. This, however, certainly is not to be admitted by O'Connell who, before the meeting, pressed for the immediate suppression; but gave it up on Lord Killeen's stating that he would not attend if this was insisted on ... With respect to their future conduct in Parliament I told them plainly that they might by going into opposition, very probably furnish the adversaries of the present government with the means of overturning it [and] that I should find much less difficulty in relinquishing than I had done in accepting my present office ... I thought it best to meet their threat.[19]

According to William Holmes*, the opposition whip, two days later Lord Althorp* and Smith Stanley met with the Irish Members and 'submitted a plan for reorganizing the Irish yeomanry', but 'the radicals with Lord Killeen at their head, refused any measure short of a total disbanding' and 'they separated, all parties abusing the government'.[20] Killeen denied acting 'as the creature' of O'Connell and argued that the 'angry feelings' excited by 'arming a party force, animated by religious feelings, against the other parts of the country' threatened the Union, 26 Aug. He presented and endorsed a Navan petition for abolition of the yeomanry, but advised that in some districts it would be necessary 'to replace them with some other species of force', 7 Sept. He was appointed to the select committee on civil government charges, 12 Aug. He welcomed the Irish lord lieutenants bill, 15, 20 Aug., and divided for legal provision for the Irish poor, 29 Aug. He presented and supported a Navan petition for the legalization of marriages performed by Catholic priests between Catholics and Protestants, 2 Sept. He was granted three weeks' leave on account of family illness, 17 Sept., was absent from the division on the reform bill's passage, 21 Sept., but was present to vote for Lord Ebrington's confidence motion, 10 Oct. At a county meeting, 28 Nov. 1831, he complained that he had just returned from one of 'the most arduous sessions of Parliament that could be remembered' in which 'nothing' had been done for Ireland, except 'some improvement' in education. O'Connell observed to Lord Duncannon* that he 'said just what I do'.[21]

Killeen voted for the second reading of the revised reform bill, 17 Dec. 1831, and for going into committee on it, 20 Feb. 1832, and again gave general support to its details. He divided for the third reading, 22 Mar., but was absent from the division on the address calling on the king to appoint only ministers who would carry reform unimpaired, 10 May. He presented and endorsed petitions for an increase in the number of Irish Members, 31 Jan., 15 Mar., obtained returns of the ten largest unenfranchised Irish towns, 27 Feb., and presented a Catholic petition for provision for the peculiar franchise of Galway, 15 Mar. He voted for the second reading of the Irish reform bill, 25 May, and against a Conservative amendment to increase Scottish county representation, 1 June, but asked 'why a measure equally efficient with that for England should not be passed for Ireland', 8 June. He called for the 'bad system' of Irish voter registration to be assimilated with that of England, 4 July. He welcomed the 'great convenience' of having three or four polling places in large counties, 6 July, but predicted that the proposed method of describing voter qualifications would prove 'exceedingly inconvenient' in Ireland, where 'many voters live in no street at all', 9 July, and objected to Catholics being obliged to take an oath on registering, while Protestants were exempt, 18 July 1832.

He voted with ministers on relations with Portugal, 9 Feb., but was in the minority for printing the Woollen Grange petition for the abolition of Irish tithes, 16 Feb. 1832. Next day he warned that the proposed subletting bill would fail to 'produce that satisfaction and concord in Ireland which is expected'. He voted against the Irish tithes bill, 8, 27, 30 Mar., 6 Apr., 13, 24 July, but denied that his opposition was 'factious', saying that it was activated by a wish to defeat a measure which would be 'disastrous to the popularity of the present government in Ireland', 13 Mar. According to Denis Le Marchant†, that month Sheil commented that his opposition to the ministry was 'quite different from Lord Killeen, Sir Patrick Bellew and others who have received favours', as 'the government have no claim upon us'.[22] Killeen presented a steady stream of petitions for the abolition of tithes over the ensuing months, arguing that the evidence they contained showed 'how obnoxious this mode of paying the clergy is', 15 May. He protested again against the bill, 9 Apr., asserted that 'the mode in which the tithe committee was formed was unwise', 29 June, and warned that the government, of which he was 'in general a supporter', was 'pursuing a most erroneous system' regarding tithes, which were 'useless, unjust and oppressive', 13 July. He argued against going into committee, 18 July, and condemned the dispersal of a 'highly respectable' anti-tithe meeting at Nobber, county Meath, by the magistrates, 20, 30 July. He presented a petition for the equalization of civil rights in Galway, 10 Apr. He condemned the remarks of James Gordon against the new plan of

Irish education, 19 June, and presented a favourable petition from Rathfeigh and Skreen, county Meath, 30 July. He welcomed the Catholic marriages bill, 3 July. He voted with ministers on the Russian-Dutch loan, 12, 16, 20 July 1832.

At the 1832 dissolution Killeen retired from the Commons. He succeeded to the peerage in 1836 and sat in the Lords as a Liberal.[23] In 1837 he was appointed a lord in waiting to Queen Victoria, who noted his attendance at her riding parties.[24] In December 1838 he assured a sceptical O'Connell that Lord Melbourne, the premier, was 'perfectly satisfied that no change of administration will take place during the ensuing session'.[25] He was appointed lord lieutenant of Meath in 1849 and died of a 'disease of the heart' at 47 Montagu Square, Marylebone, in April 1869. *The Times* commented that he was 'always regarded as one of the moderate party who adhered to Whig principles, and stood opposed to Ultramontane notions'. The family estates passed to his eldest son and successor in the peerage, Arthur James (1819-81).[26]

[1] *The Times*, 24 June 1812. [2] *O'Connell Corresp.* ii. 982, 1013; iii. 1186, 1189, 1251. [3] *Dublin Evening Post*, 21 Apr., 1 Sept. 1825. [4] Cent. Kent. Stud. Camden mss U840 C202/11/12. [5] *Dublin Evening Post*, 24, 29 June 1826. [6] *O'Connell Corresp.* iii. 1376, 1441, 1444. [7] *Dublin Evening Post*, 4, 21 Oct. 1828. [8] Ibid. 24, 31 Jan. 1829; PRO NI, Downshire mss D671/C/12/379. [9] *Dublin Evening Post*, 24 Jan. 1829; *O'Connell Corresp.* iv. 1533, 1549. [10] Wellington mss WP1/1059/7,9,32; Add. 40308, f. 262; PRO NI, Anglesey mss D619/32/A/3/1/231, 239, 258, 272. [11] *Carlow Morning Post*, 18 Feb., 1 Mar. 1830. [12] Wellington mss WP1/1124/11; 1130/22. [13] *Dublin Evening Post*, 3 Aug.; *Westmeath Jnl.* 26 Aug. 1830. [14] *O'Connell Corresp.* iv. 1626. [15] Ibid. iv. 1733. [16] Add. 51572. [17] Anglesey mss 31D/37. [18] *Dublin Evening Post*, 3, 17 May 1831. [19] Anglesey mss 28A-B/71. [20] *Arbuthnot Corresp.* 148. [21] *O'Connell Corresp.* iv. 1853. [22] *Three Diaries*, 211. [23] *Dod's Parl. Companion* (1859), 36. [24] *Girlhood of Queen Victoria* ed. Visct. Esher, ii. 120, 248. [25] *O'Connell Corresp.* vi. 2574. [26] *The Times*, 23, 24 Apr., 14 Aug. 1869.

P.J.S.

POLE, Sir Peter, 2nd bt. (1770–1850), of Wolverton, Hants.

YARMOUTH I.O.W. 16 Mar. 1819–1826

b. 20 Oct. 1770, 1st s. of Sir Charles Pole (formerly Van Notten), 1st bt., and Millicent, da. and coh. of Charles Pole† of Holcroft, Lancs. *m.* 24 Dec. 1798, Anna Guerherlmina, da. of Richard Buller of Cumberland Street, London, 4s. 5da. (1 *d.v.p.*). *suc.* fa. as 2nd bt. 18 June 1813. *d.* 30 Aug. 1850.

Pole, a London banker, continued to sit unopposed for the pocket borough of Yarmouth on the Worsley Holmes interest. A lax attender, who is not known to have spoken in debate, when present he continued to support the Liverpool ministry.[1] He voted against economies in revenue collection, 4 July 1820, and sided with ministers over their conduct towards Queen Caroline, 6 Feb. 1821. He divided against Catholic relief, 28 Feb. 1821, 30 Apr. 1822, 1 Mar., 21 Apr., 10 May 1825. He voted against repeal of the additional malt duty, 3 Apr. 1821, tax reductions, 11 Feb., abolition of one of the joint-postmasterships, 13 Mar. 1822, and Brougham's motion condemning the trial of the Methodist missionary John Smith for inciting slave riots in Demerara, 11 June 1824. He divided for the duke of Cumberland's annuity bill, 10 June 1825. Pole's firm, Pole and Company, which was 'among the most considerable in London', was the first casualty of the banking panic of December 1825, despite its reported yield of £40,000 per annum for the previous seven years. When a loss of confidence followed the boom of autumn 1825, the bank allegedly paid out £1,250,000 in a week, which dangerously weakened its reserves.[2] On 5 Dec. 1825 this was reported to the Bank of England's deputy governor John Richards, who was consulted, as he later explained, 'because the governor [Cornelius Buller] was particularly connected with the house of Pole and Co. by marriage and other circumstances of relationship'. Richards called a meeting of the Bank's governors the following day to approve a £300,000 loan to the firm, secured on Pole's property. Despite this, the bank was forced to suspend payment on the 12th and subsequently dissolved.[3] 'The shock given to public credit', observed the *Annual Register*, 'was *tremendous* as it was known that they kept accounts with forty-four country banks, several of whom, in all probability, would also stop payment'. According to one historian, 'the agitation of the City exceeded everything that had been witnessed for a century'.[4] The same month Pole divested himself of his interests in two London mercantile firms, including the family concern of Peter and Charles Van Notten.[5]

At the 1826 dissolution Pole, who evidently managed to save much of his personal fortune, retired. He sold Wolverton Park to the duke of Wellington in 1837 and inherited the Gloucestershire property of Todenham from his brother Abraham in 1844.[6] At his death in August 1850 he left estates in Hampshire, Gloucestershire, Northamptonshire and Kent. By his will, dated 10 Aug. 1846, these were divided respectively between his sons Peter (1801-87), who succeeded him as third baronet, the Rev. Richard (1802-93), who also inherited all his personal estate, Samuel (1802-63) and Edward (1805-79).[7]

[1] *Black Bk.* (1823), 185; *Session of Parl. 1825*, p. 481. [2] *The Times*, 13 Dec. 1825; J. Francis, *Hist. Bank of England*, ii. 9; *Gent. Mag.* (1825), ii. 557. [3] F.G. Hilton Price, *London Bankers*, 130; *PP* (1831-2), vi. q. 5006; J. Clapham, *Bank of England*, ii. 99-100. [4] *Ann. Reg.* (1825), 123; Francis, 9. [5] *London Gazette*, 13 Dec. 1825. [6] *VCH Hants*, iv. 270; *VCH Glos.* vi. 252. [7] *Gent. Mag.* (1850), ii. 547; PROB 11/212/763.

H.J.S./P.J.S.

POLE *see also* **WELLESLEY POLE**

POLE TYLNEY LONG WELLESLEY, Hon. William (1788–1857), of 39 Dover Street, Piccadilly, Mdx. and West Green, Hartford Bridge, Hants.[1]

ST. IVES	1812–1818
WILTSHIRE	1818–1820
ST. IVES	1830–1831
ESSEX	1831–1832

b. 22 May 1788, o.s. of Hon. William Wellesley Pole*, 1st Bar. Maryborough [UK], and Katherine Elizabeth, da. and coh. of Adm. Hon. John Forbes, MP [I]. *m.* (1) 14 Mar. 1812, Catherine (*d.* 12 Sept. 1825), da. of Sir James Tylney Long†, 7th bt., of Draycot Cerne, Wilts. (who in 1805 *suc.* her bro. James to the estates of Tylney, Hants and Wanstead, Essex, worth £1.5 million, plus £300,000 personalty), 2s. (1 *d.v.p.*) 1da.; (2) 10 Nov. 1828, Helena, da. of Col. Thomas Paterson, wid. of Capt. Thomas Bligh, 2 Ft. Gds., at least 1 illegit. s. *d.v.p.* Took additional names of Tylney Long by royal lic. 14 Jan. 1812 in contemplation of his marriage. *styled* Visct. Wellesley 1842-5; *suc.* fa. as 4th earl of Mornington [I] and 2nd Bar. Maryborough [UK] 22 Feb. 1845. *d.* 1 July 1857.

Gent. usher 1822.

Kpr. Epping Forest 1816, Waltham Forest 1835-45.

On hearing from Long Wellesley in 1811 of his engagement to the heiress Catherine Tylney Long (who, according to the cartoonists, found it 'impossible to resist such a *Pole*') his father had written:

> I trust ... you may continue to deserve the astonishingly good fortune you have met with ... If you will act up to the determinations you have formed, you will be all that your mother and I can wish you to be, and you cannot fail of making Miss Long happy.[2]

Long Wellesley, surely one of the most odious men ever to sit in Parliament, soon blighted those pious hopes. By 1818, when he was returned for Wiltshire at a reputed cost of £32,000 in borrowed money, he was on the verge of ruin, largely, though not quite entirely, as a result of his own extravagance. By his marriage settlement an income of £13,000 was secured to his wife as pin money. He had a life interest in those estates of which she had the fee, and there was a power reserved to them both to charge this property with £100,000 by way of mortgage. The estates themselves were protected by entail on his eldest son. The mortgage was duly raised, but it did not rescue Long Wellesley from his embarrassments.[3] He initially sought re-election for Wiltshire at the general election of 1820, when he had the support of the Liverpool ministry, of which his father and uncle, the duke of Wellington, were senior members. He lacked the resources to finance another contest and, humiliatingly, had to give up the attempt.[4] Soon afterwards he was 'obliged to quit the country with all his family or live in the king's bench'.[5]

He lived for about two years in Paris where, sustained by his wife's separate income, he moved in fashionable circles.[6] In July 1821 he pressed his father, who had just been created Lord Maryborough in the United Kingdom peerage, to make such a resettlement of his estates as would give him the power of leaving them to his wife and children and enable him to raise on them money to meet the interest charges on the debts arising out of his wife's estates. Maryborough swallowed his suspicions and authorized negotiations which ended, after some acrimony, in a compromise arrangement not altogether to Long Wellesley's liking.[7] In the spring of 1822 he returned to England to attend to his affairs having obtained, presumably through his father's political influence, a nominal court appointment to protect him against 'personal molestation'. In June the contents of Wanstead House, a palladian mansion of great magnificence, were sold for £41,000.[8] Soon afterwards Long Wellesley, still hounded by creditors, was forced to return to the continent. He placed his finances in the hands of trustees, headed by his father who, enjoining on him 'the strictest economy', warned him that it would take at least five years to settle his 'tremendous and complicated debts' and so facilitate his return to England. In 1823 Wanstead was sold for demolition for £10,000 and virtually all trace of it was obliterated. In August of that year Maryborough, reporting to Long Wellesley on the first year of the trust's operations, told him:

> If you persevere for only three years you may return here in affluence and credit far beyond anything we thought possible ... If you ... leave us to exercise our own discretion, you may return at the end of three years with all your debts paid or secured; with all your creditors satisfied ... with Mrs. Wellesley's diamonds saved; with Wanstead Park ... free for you to do with it as you please; with the farms on all your estates in perfect repair ... with no arrear due to any person whatever; and with a clear income of £13,000 a year.[9]

Long Wellesley had already dished this prospect by committing a fresh act of folly. At Naples in the summer of 1823 he began a blatant adulterous relationship with Mrs. Helena Bligh, a protégée (some said a natural daughter) of Wellington. She left her ailing husband and Long Wellesley contrived to have her taken into his own establishment. Their fornication continued intermittently through the winter and was resumed in Paris in June 1824, when Mrs. Long Wellesley, goaded beyond endurance, threatened her husband with separation unless he abandoned Mrs. Bligh, whom she was willing to pay off. She appealed for Maryborough's intervention but Long Wellesley, brazenly trying to exculpate his conduct and browbeat his wife, would have none of this. In July Mrs. Long Wellesley went to England with their three children, having agreed to follow Long Wellesley's instructions for their upbringing and education. When she discovered early in August that he had renewed his intercourse with Mrs. Bligh she let him know that it was an insuperable obstacle to any reconciliation and that if he came to England to bother her she would start divorce proceedings.[10] Long Wellesley, determined to set everyone at defiance, received a stinging rebuke from Maryborough, whom he was pestering to expedite his return from exile:

> If you come ... before your affairs were arranged, I see no possibility of preventing your being put into jail during the whole of my life ... My only wish is to endeavour to save you from destruction; and to do this, it is absolutely necessary that you should be sensible of your true situation. I vainly hoped I had made you so; but ... I see ... that you have relapsed into the same vain delusion which has led you on to your ruin ... The whole world approve of your wife's separation from you; and were you now to come to England and it were possible for you to remain out of jail you would be driven out of society ... [Mrs. Bligh] would be a monster among savages. Among civilized Christians she is an outcast. If you do not separate yourself from this abandoned, profligate wretch, you must share her fate.[11]

Long Wellesley finally alienated his father early in 1825 by ordering him to give up his trusteeship. This he did, resolving to have no further communication with his son, whose letters he returned unopened. Mrs. Long Wellesley had already decided to seek a divorce when, on 7 July 1825, Long Wellesley, who had been in London *incognito* with Mrs. Bligh for a fortnight, gained entry to her house and forced her to flee with their youngest child Victoria. The next day she filed a bill in chancery to make Victoria and her two elder brothers wards of court and served Long Wellesley with a citation for divorce. He returned to France with Mrs. Bligh, who on 22 Aug. 1825 gave birth to their illegitimate son. Meanwhile Mrs. Long Wellesley's health had collapsed and she died 'of a fever', aged 35, 12 Sept. 1825, after enjoining her unmarried sisters Dora and Emma to continue their protection of the children.[12]

Long Wellesley's repeated applications for custody were refused by the Misses Long, who claimed to have the support of his close relatives. When the dispute reached court, 5 Nov. 1825, lord chancellor Eldon ruled that Long Wellesley's residence in France justified refusal of custody. He then petitioned to have a proper scheme of education settled by the court and this matter, together with the appointment of guardians, was referred to the master in chancery.[13] Before the order could be acted on, Long Wellesley returned to England, contrived by some means to satisfy his creditors, and bought a house at Hall Place, Regent's Park, from where he wrote to Mrs. Bligh, 20 Dec. 1825:

> Everything is going on as well as possible ... Be patient, and I will pawn my life but I beat them all ... Do not imagine I am humbugged in any way ... I really am glad you are not with me. I am quite myself. I am acting without *impetuosity*. My mind is quite free from reflection, and I have so solidly *laid the basis* that the blow I give shall be *but one* and that a lusty one. All depends on your ... *absence* from me till *I get my children*. Then neither duke or devil can breach either you or me.[14]

On 4 Jan. 1826 he petitioned chancery for the custody and future management of his children. Numerous affidavits were filed for and against his claim and the case, which excited great public interest, dragged on throughout the year. In the prerogative court, 24 Feb. 1826, Long Wellesley challenged the validity of a testamentary paper signed by his wife five days before her death revoking, 'to serve the interests of my dear children', her will of 1 July 1815, in which she had disposed of a contingent remainder of certain lands in his favour and charged others with a payment of £50,000 to him. He was granted sole administration of her personalty and effects in preference to Maryborough and Thomas Windsor, the executors named in the original will.[15] Soon afterwards Mrs. Bligh came to London, settling at 10 St. John's Wood Road, and resumed her intercourse with Long Wellesley, who on 5 May 1826 was sued for crim. con. damages by her husband. His counsel managed to postpone the hearing until 1 Nov. 1826, when the sordid details already publicized in the chancery affidavits were given another airing. To a 'tumult of applause' the jury awarded Bligh £6,000. Long Wellesley was arrested for non-payment of the damages and was escorted by two sheriff's men to the office of his solicitor, where the necessary security was lodged. Three weeks later Bligh filed for divorce from his wife. He was granted a decree in the consistory court, 11 May 1827, but presumably died before he could proceed further.[16] The chancery case was resumed in January 1827, and on 1 Feb. Eldon pronounced judgment: although Long Wellesley had been 'unnecessarily traduced before the public' and 'much more than was true had been said of him', he stood condemned by the failure of his family to testify in his favour; by his 'most shameful' adultery with Mrs. Bligh, a common whore, which had been carried on even while his suit was in progress, and by 'exceedingly strong evidence' that he had in the past been guilty of 'most grossly improper conduct' towards his children, including coaching them in the art of blasphemous and obscene swearing. He was therefore deemed unfit to have custody of them, and the appointment of suitable guardians was referred to the master.[17]

Long Wellesley resolved to appeal against the judgment to the House of Lords and, in an effort to strengthen his hand, importuned Wellington, the temporary guardian of his children, to effect a reconciliation with Maryborough. Yet by persistently threatening to disclose scandalous 'family secrets' if Maryborough refused to support him he soon alienated Wellington too. He duly published his *Two Letters* to Eldon, 'with official and other documents, and additional notes', which went through three editions between 6 May and 1 Aug. 1827. This, as well as excusing his adultery and dismissing much of the affidavit evidence against him as perjured, sought to prove that his family and the Misses Long were as vicious and immoral as himself. His appeal to the Lords was rejected on 4 July 1828.[18] The duchess of Wellington and William Courtenay* were appointed guardians of the children in that year.[19] Meanwhile in June 1828 Long Wellesley had threatened to contest a vacancy for his former constituency of St. Ives, where he had evidently acquired property. He withdrew at the last minute but canvassed for a future occasion and distributed money before leaving.[20] In November 1828 he married Mrs. Bligh.

On 31 July 1829 Long Wellesley personally conducted before Lord Lyndhurst, Eldon's successor, his case against a chancery order forbidding him to see his children except in the presence of a third party. The solicitor-general, opposing him, made much of allegations that he had earlier abused his access to the boys at Eton. Lyndhurst saw no reason to rescind the order but gave Long Wellesley the right of reply, in which he claimed to have 'established, to the satisfaction of all impartial minds, that the false evidence by which I have been traduced, and robbed of my parental rights, was the offspring of malice'.[21] In August 1829 Wellington acknowledged Long Wellesley's acquiescence in the confirmed guardianship of the duchess, but warned him that if he persisted in making verbal threats against Wellington's life and supplying newspapers with libellous material, he would be prosecuted. Long Wellesley apologized.[22] Early in 1830, when he had taken up residence in Hampshire, he published a report of the recent court proceedings as an appendix to *A View of the Court of Chancery*, a further defence of his conduct masquerading as an exposition of the case for reform of chancery procedure. He was frustrated in his bid to take possession, as a tenant of chancery, of the house and estate of Draycot in Wiltshire, the property under entail of his elder son. His attempt to have the Misses Long's solicitor, one of his principal accusers, struck off also failed; and he was again before Lyndhurst on 3 Apr. 1830, when he was ordered to surrender to the guardians his younger son James, who had absconded from Eton to join him.[23] Soon afterwards he published *Illustrations of Chancery Practice*, dedicated to Jeremy Bentham, which purported to be 'a practical illustration of the evils of that secret system of judicature' prevailing in chancery, but was in fact a renewed attempt to discredit those whose evidence had condemned him.[24]

In March 1830 Long Wellesley, abetted by the radical Daniel Whittle Harvey*, started for Essex on a vacancy in opposition to the ministerialist Bramston, but on the day of nomination he made way for Henry Conyers, who had a prior claim. In a self-righteous explanation of his conduct, a feature of virtually every transaction in which he became involved, he 'declared himself a reformer' and advocated a radical redistribution of taxes.[25] Although at the general election four months later he was returned unopposed for St. Ives, he also contested Essex to the bitter end as 'an independent' and 'a practical reformer' who was 'attached to no party'. He recommended a redistribution of taxation, moderate parliamentary reform through an extension of the franchise and shorter parliaments, civil and religious liberty, the abolition of slavery, poor law reform and mitigation of the penal code. He was only just beaten into third place by the Whig Western and the Tory Tyrell, who coalesced to thwart him. He claimed to be 'virtually the representative of the county' with his preponderance of single votes and condemned 'the ultra-Tory and the ultra-Whig' as 'equally injurious to the interest of the country'. The election was reckoned to have cost him £23,000.[26]

His uncle's ministry numbered him among their 'foes' and, showing no lack of confidence on his return to the House, he used the debate on the address, 2 Nov. 1830, to lecture them on the need for wholesale changes of policy. One ministerialist sarcastically applauded his reappearance at Westminster 'with such a magazine of oratory', while another Member reported that his speech 'excited much laughter'.[27] He voted in the majority in the division on the civil list which brought the government down, 15 Nov., but deplored personal attacks on Wellington by the Whigs, 23 Nov., and rebutted criticism of his uncle Lord Cowley's diplomatic pension, 13 Dec. He advocated a cautious reform of tithes, 19 Nov., 21 Dec., and poor law reform, 6 Dec. He extolled the 'glorious manner' in which the second French revolution had expiated the crimes of the first, 10 Dec. He presented anti-slavery petitions, 10 Nov., 10 Dec., but on 13 Dec. said that caution and 'full and entire compensation to the colonists' were necessary if abolition was not to precipitate revolution. Surveying the question of distress among the labouring poor, 17 Dec., he touched on the encouragement of spade-husbandry and of clerical residence (on which he had moved for information to form the basis for 'a measure of great importance', 10 Dec.) and reform of poor law administration as possible palliatives. Yet he hoped that the Grey government would tackle the problem in its entirety rather than leave it to piecemeal individual initiatives. On 23 Dec. 1830 he supported the ministerial motion to adjourn until early February, being disposed, on the strength of what they had already done, to 'wait in silent confidence' for disclosure of their future measures. He opposed as 'a false humanity' Hunt's call for an amnesty for agricultural labourers convicted after the recent 'Swing' disturbances, 8 Feb. 1831. On 28 Feb. he presented petitions for parliamentary reform from Devizes and an Essex meeting which, in the absence of the county Members, he had attended and addressed.[28] As a self-confessed 'proselyte to reform', he welcomed the ministerial reform bill as a 'necessary and safe' concession to 'the spirit of the age', 7, 9 Mar. At the Essex county meeting in its support, 19 Mar., he pledged to stand again at the first opportunity and declared his 'intention of supporting the present ministry as a party man, so highly did he approve of the course they had adopted'.[29] He voted for the second reading of the bill, 22 Mar., and against Gascoyne's wrecking amendment, 19 Apr. He clashed with Tyrell over the strength of reforming sentiment in Essex, 13 Apr., and questioned the worth of a hostile petition from Devizes, 18 Apr. 1831. He stood for Essex at the ensuing general election, this time in alliance with Western. They were comfortably returned over Tyrell on a wave of reforming enthusiasm and at little expense, even though Long Wellesley did not appear in person during the campaign. His absence was variously attributed by his spokesman Sir Felix Agar to business commitments in Cornwall and illness, but in truth he was once more in hiding from creditors at Calais.[30] According to Mrs. Arbuthnot, 'the sheriff who returned him had his hands full of writs against him'.[31] He admitted as much when he arrived at Chelmsford for a belated celebration, but claimed that the debts were 'not of his own contracting'. He went on to praise Lord Grey and the reform bill, which was 'exactly suited to the times':

> No doubt, some time back a something more moderate reform would have been received, but he firmly believed that a less radical reform would not suit the exigencies of the times ... The basis of the bill was to represent property, locality, and influence possessed by locality.[32]

Yet he found some cause for complaint against the government for what he saw as their failure adequately to support his 'wishes and interests' at the election. Ellice, the patronage secretary, thought he had been 'wholly misinformed' but, anxious to placate him on account of his steady support in the Commons, gave him 'the most ample explanation', which seems to have smoothed things over.[33]

At the prompting of some Marlborough reformers Long Wellesley condemned the anti-reform petition presented by William Bankes, 24 June 1831, as the product of bribery and intimidation; and on 5 July he presented a counter-petition in support of the revised reform bill, for which he voted at its second reading, 6 July, and against an adjournment, 12 July. He then provided the House and the public with a diversion from the reform struggle by abducting his daughter from her aunts' residence near Godalming on 15 July. Summoned to appear before lord chancellor Brougham the following day, he admitted the deed but refused to surrender the child, and was placed under house arrest for contempt of court. Brougham informed the Speaker, as did Long Wellesley who, disputing the chancellor's right to commit, claimed the immunity of parliamentary privilege. The matter was referred to the committee of privileges, before which Long Wellesley appeared on 19 July. One of its members, Edward Littleton, recorded:

> The profligate dandy perfumed the room as he entered. We asked him a few relevant questions, and then he made a long speech, stating what had passed in court between him and the chancellor, and he concluded apparently greatly affected, and shedding tears, and then withdrew.

The question became a party squabble, with opposition lawyers eager to embarrass Brougham, but on 26 July, 'to the general surprise', the committee decided that privilege did not apply. Long Wellesley meanwhile had raised the issue in chancery, but after the adverse Commons verdict his leading counsel declined to argue the case of lack of jurisdiction, 28 July. His junior wished to do so and was allowed by Brougham to state it as *amicus curiae*, before the chancellor pronounced a judgement upholding the jurisdiction. Long Wellesley was not released until 22 Aug., after Victoria had been retrieved from France and restored to her aunts. He continued to dispute the question of his access to the children but, after a private hearing before the chancellor in December 1831, he was again left frustrated.[34]

The day after his release Long Wellesley voted in the government majorities on the Dublin election controversy. He voted for clause 22 of the reform bill, 30 Aug., and for its passage, 21 Sept., having the previous day supported it as 'a renovation of the constitution', despite misgivings over some of its details. He voted for the motion of confidence in ministers, 10 Oct. At the Essex reform meeting, 10 Dec., he attacked the bishops and declared:

> Reform must pass, and all he saw was a scramble for power. He cared not for the ministry: all he wanted was pure representation, which would give every reform – financial reform and taxation.

He then almost came to blows with Harvey over an alternative address, but Western interceded to restore peace.[35] He endorsed the meeting's petition in support of the 'improved' and revised reform bill, 14 Dec., and voted for its second reading, 17 Dec. 1831. He was in the government majority on the Russian-Dutch loan, 26 Jan. 1832, and voted steadily for the reform bill's details during its progress through committee. On St. Ives's loss of one Member, 23 Feb., he said he had received no instructions to defend the borough. He voted for the third reading, 22 Mar. He divided with government for the navy civil departments bill, 6 Apr. That day and on 16 Apr. he supported the coercive Irish tithes bill on the understanding that ministers planned, when order was restored, to reform the system; and on 14 June he observed that the abolition of tithes must be accompanied by compensation to the clergy. He voted for the address asking the king to appoint only ministers who would carry undiluted reform, 10 May, implored Wellington not to 'stain his honour' by taking office, 14 May, and spoke to the same effect in his constituency, 16 May.[36] He voted for the second reading of the Irish reform bill, 25 May, and against a Conservative amendment to the Scottish measure, 1 June. He divided for prompt action to abolish slavery, 24 May, against the exclusion of debtors from the House, 6 June, and to make coroners' inquests public, 20 June. He spoke and voted in defence of government on the Russian-Dutch loan, 16 July, and the Greek convention, 6 Aug. 1832.

Long Wellesley stood for the Southern division of Essex in coalition with his fellow reformer Barrett Lennard at the ensuing general election, when he again hid from his creditors at Calais and left his campaign in the hands of his wife and Agar. The intervention of a strong Tory agriculturist candidate destroyed the reformers' alliance and Wellesley was beaten into third place. As ever, public recriminations followed: Wellesley accused Lennard and Western of a breach of faith and was charged in return with having been the first to abandon the coalition in an attempt at self-preservation.[37] For the next dozen years he lived mainly in Brussels. Scandal continued to surround his name and it was not long before his second wife separated permanently from him. He published *Un Mot aux Belges* in 1839 and a sequel, on Europe and the Eastern question, the following year.[38] When applying unsuccessfully to Peel's new Conservative ministry in 1841 for a diplomatic posting for his elder son he boasted of 'having applied my parliamentary influence for the last seven years in support of Conservative principles, and I believe in various parts of England with no small degree of success'.[39] In *A Fourth Political Word* (1842) he surveyed British politics since 1828 and confirmed that he had 'become a convert' to Peelite Conservatism. His *Fifth Political Word* (1843) dealt with foreign policy, and in two editions of *The Irish Question* (1844) he advocated a concordat with Rome to keep Catholic agitators in check. On succeeding his father in the peerage in 1845 he returned to England and took his seat in the Lords. He backed Peel on Maynooth and repeal of the corn laws, though he reckoned himself a supporter of Lord Derby's Protectionist ministry in 1852.[40]

By then his affairs were again in chancery in a dispute with his wife and elder son over the terms of a trust deed of 1834. She, who was a frequent recipient of parish relief and sued *in formâ pauperia*, sought to enforce payment of an annuity of £1,000 which Long Wellesley, in defiance of several court orders, refused to concede. His son wanted execution of those provisions of the deed which involved the payment to him of substantial sums and the raising of £462,000 to meet encumbrances.[41] The matter was still unresolved when Long Wellesley died suddenly, while eating an egg, at the lodging house of Miss Louisa Brooks at Thayer Street, Manchester Square, in July 1857. He had been living obscurely in the area for about four years, apparently sustained in his penury by a weekly allowance of £10 from his cousin the 2nd duke of Wellington.[42] In his will, dated 21 Feb. 1854, he recorded his 'deepest obligation' to Miss Anna Temple of Bayswater (he had in 1852 tried to get promotion in the postal service for a Mr. Temple) for 'her unvarying kindness in supporting me in my present state of destitution, while I have the gravest cause of dissatisfaction with the members of my family for their ingratitude in leaving me to starve after having derived immense benefit from my prosperity'. He gave directions for the payment of a few small debts and made Miss Temple his residuary legatee for her life. A house which he owned in Savile Row was to be sold or let unless William Richardson, his executor, wished to occupy it, in which case he could do so rent-free. The entailed estates in Essex, Hampshire and Wiltshire passed to his elder and only surviving son William (*b.* 1813).[43] He, who died unmarried in Paris in 1863, when the barony of Maryborough became extinct and the earldom of Mornington devolved on the 2nd duke of Wellington, left them to his father's cousin Henry, 1st Earl Cowley, after revoking his original bequest in favour of his sister Lady Victoria Long Wellesley. She, who seems to have had a relationship of mutual affection with her miscreant father, was a notable supporter of charities, founded the church of All Souls in Eastbourne and died in 1897.[44]

While some of the more spectacular feats of iniquity and depravity which were credited to Long Wellesley were obvious fabrications, the reality was sordid enough. A censorious obituarist dismissed him thus:

> The mockery of heraldry was never more displayed than in the case of this most unworthy representative of the honour of the elder branch of the house of Wellesley ... A spendthrift, a profligate, and gambler in his youth, he became a debauchée in his manhood ... Redeemed by no single virtue, adorned by no single grace, his life has gone out even without a flicker of repentance; his 'retirement' was that of one who was deservedly avoided of all men.[45]

[1] See O. Barry, *Lady Victoria Wellesley*, 29-69; Lady Longford, *Wellington*, ii. 250-7. [2] M.D. George, *Cat. of Pol. and Personal Satires*, ix. 11744, 11747, 11844; Redbridge Local Hist. Lib. Long Wellesley mss, Wellesley Pole to Long Wellesley, 19 Nov. 1811. [3] *Gronow Reminiscences*, i. 63-64; *VCH Essex*, vi. 324-6; *Ann. Reg.* (1827), Chron. p. 297. [4] *HMC Fortescue*, x. 454; *Devizes Gazette*, 24 Feb., 9 Mar.; Add. 51830, Suffolk to Holland, 9 Mar. 1820. [5] Hatherton mss, Hyacinthe to Gerald Wellesley, 11 June 1820. [6] *Von Neumann Diary*, i. 79. [7] W. Long Wellesley, *Two Letters to Lord Eldon* (3rd edn. 1827), 8-10, 83-94; Long Wellesley mss, Maryborough to Long Wellesley, 9 Aug. 1821. [8] Northants. RO, Agar Ellis diary, 5 June [1822]; *VCH Essex*, vi. 326; *Essex Rev.* vii (1898), 213-14. [9] Long Wellesley mss, Maryborough to Long Wellesley, 16 Aug., 10 Sept. 1822, 25 Feb., 1 Aug. 1823. [10] *Ann. Reg.* (1827), Chron. pp. 297-8; Long Wellesley mss, copy corresp. of Long Wellesley, his wife and Maryborough, 21 June-19 Aug.; Hatherton mss, Hyacinthe to Gerald Wellesley, 29 Dec. 1824. [11] Long Wellesley mss, Maryborough to Long Wellesley, 2 Aug. 1824. [12] Ibid. F. Somerset to Long Wellesley, 17 Feb., Maryborough to Mrs. Long Wellesley, 15 Apr., 8 June; *The Times*, 12 July, 19 Sept.; Wellington mss WP1/827/14; Hatherton mss, Hyacinthe to Gerald Wellesley, 14 Nov. 1825; *Arbuthnot Jnl.* i. 412-13. [13] *Gent. Mag.* (1825), ii. 467; *The Times*, 4, 7, 8, 10 Nov. 1825. [14] Long Wellesley mss. [15] *The Times*, 25 Feb., 18, 20, 22 Mar., 19 Apr., 20-22 Nov. 1825; PROB 11/1710/19. [16] *The Times*, 6, 9 May, 15 June, 2, 6, 8, 15 Nov., 25 Dec. 1826, 12 May 1827. [17] Ibid. 3, 4, 12, 17-20, 23, 25, 26, 29, 30 Jan., 2 Feb., 10 Mar. 1827; *Ann. Reg.* (1827), Chron. pp. 299-310; George, x. 15442. [18] *Two Letters*, 99-131; *Geo. IV Letters*, iii. 1393; *LJ*, lx. 69-70, 600-1; *The Times*, 25, 26 Apr., 3, 8, 15 May, 5 July 1828; Wellington mss WP1/891/13. [19] Wellington mss WP1/942/4; 945/22. [20] J.H. Matthews, *Hist. St. Ives*, 361, 363. [21] George, xi. 15928; *The Times*, 1 Aug. 1829; Wellington mss WP1/971/4, 11; 974/10, 28; 998/4; 1006/2. [22] Wellington mss WP1/1042/27, 28. [23] *The Times*, 12 Mar., 5 Apr. 1830; Wellington mss WP1/1009/18; 1014/13; 1020/7. [24] Add. 33546, f. 414. [25] *The Times*, 8, 9, 12 Mar. 1830. [26] Wellington mss WP1/1129/35; *The Times*, 7, 9-14, 16-21, 23, 24 Aug. 1830; *Essex Election, Aug. 1830*; G. Caunt, 'Essex in Parliament', *Essex Jnl.* i (1966), 69-76. [27] Hopetoun mss 167, f. 177. [28] *The Times*, 1 Mar. 1831. [29] Ibid. 21 Mar. 1831. [30] Ibid. 21, 25, 28 Apr., 6, 7, 9-12 May 1831. [31] *Arbuthnot Jnl.* ii. 421. [32] *The Times*, 19, 26 May 1831. [33] Long Wellesley mss, Ellice to Grey [7 June], Grey to Long Wellesley, 7 June 1831. [34] *Ann. Reg.* (1831), Chron. pp. 301-5; *The Times*, 18, 21-23, 29 July, 6, 22, 31 Aug., 19 Sept., 23 Dec.; *CJ*, lxxxvi. 667-8, 699-701; Hatherton diary, 18-21, 23, 26 July 1831; *Holland House Diaries*, 6. [35] *The Times*, 12 Dec. 1831. [36] Ibid. 17 May 1832. [37] Ibid. 30 Oct., 24 Nov., 3, 15, 17, 18, 20, 28, 29 Dec. 1832. [38] *Wellington Pol. Corresp.* ii. 15, 398, 399, 423, 424, 643. [39] Add. 43238, f. 119. [40] Add. 35788, f. 104. [41] *The Times*, 12 July 1851, 28 Feb. 1852, 15 Mar., 16 July 1853, 20 Jan., 14, 28 June 1854, 12 June 1855, 6 June, 9 Nov. 1857. [42] Ibid. 4 July 1857; *Ann. Reg.* (1857), Chron. p. 316. [43] PROB 11/2259/766; Add. 35788, f. 104. [44] Barry, 108-20. [45] *Gent. Mag.* (1857), ii. 215-16.

D.R.F.

POLHILL, Frederick (1798–1848), of Howbury Hall, nr. Bedford and Burwash, nr. Battle, Suss.

Bedford	1830–1832
Bedford	1835–1847

b. 2 July 1798,[1] 3rd but 2nd surv. s. of Capt. John Polhill (*d.* 1828) of 52 Harley Street, Mdx. and Mary, da. of James Bennett of Walthamstow, Essex. *m.* 6 Jan. 1824,[2] Frances Margaretta, da. of Osmond Deakin (Dakeyne) of Old Hall, East Bridgeford, Notts., 3s. (2 *d.v.p.*) 2da. (1 *d.v.p.*). *suc.* bro. Thomas Polhill to family estates 1828. *d.* 20 Sept. 1848.

Lt. 4 Drag. Gds. 1814; lt. 1 Drag. Gds. 1815, capt. 1823, ret. 1829.

Polhill was descended from a family, possibly a branch of the Cornish Polwheles, long settled in Kent and Sussex. His grandfather, Nathaniel Polhill (1723-82), the son of William Polhill (1689-1765) of Burwash, prospered as a tobacconist at 35 Borough

High Street, Southwark, which he represented in Parliament as a Wilkite from 1774 until his death, and as a partner in the London bank of Langston, Polhill, Towgood and Amery at 29 Clement's Lane.[3] The year before his death he bought the Becher property of Renhold manor, which included Howbury Hall, about three miles north-east of Bedford.[4] On his death his property in Bedfordshire, Kent, Middlesex, Surrey and Sussex and the tobacconist's business passed to his eldest son Nathaniel, who followed him to the grave within three months. The settled estates then went to his infant son, another Nathaniel, while he left the Southwark business to his younger brothers Edward and Robert Polhill. (It was styled Polhill and Jones by 1821, and seems to have ceased trading by 1832.)[5] The young Nathaniel Polhill of Howbury did not live to come into formal possession of his handsome inheritance, for he died, 'aged 19', unmarried and intestate, 19 Apr. 1802, having apparently been 'confined for near six months to a bed of sickness ... and doomed, by the loss of a limb, to purchase the precarious chance of surviving a little longer'. Administration of his effects, which included personalty sworn under £60,000, was granted to his mother Ursula, who was by then married to one James Warre.[6] The entailed estates reverted to his uncle John Polhill, the younger son of the purchaser of Howbury and the father of this Member.

John Polhill entered the army in 1780 and attained the rank of captain in the 15th Hussars before his retirement in about 1793. With his wife Mary Bennett he had three sons: Thomas, baptized in January 1795, Charles, baptized a year later, and Frederick. Charles died in 1813.[7] The following year Frederick obtained a commission in a fashionable cavalry regiment. He joined his father and elder brother in signing the Bedfordshire loyal address to the king adopted to counter the local campaign in support of Queen Caroline, 15 Jan. 1821.[8] John Polhill, a subscriber of £500 to the election fund of the beaten Tory Sir John Osborn* in the 1820 county contest, and a supporter of the successful Macqueen in 1826,[9] died 3 Sept. 1828, when the family estates passed to Thomas. By his father's will of 14 June 1826 Frederick became entitled to the residue of his personal estate, which in total was sworn under £30,000. A trust fund of £2,000 was created for his wife, and the children of his marriage were given an interest in the proceeds of the eventual sale of John Polhill's London House in Cavendish Square, which was to take place after his widow's death.[10] When Thomas Polhill died, aged 33, at Bath, 15 Oct. 1828, only six weeks after his father, Frederick succeeded to all the family property, promptly retired from the army and threw himself into his new role as squire of Howbury.[11] At the county meeting called to petition for repeal of the malt tax and other remedial measures for agricultural distress in February 1830, he seconded the main resolutions, testified to the extent of distress from his personal experience as a magistrate, and observed that the recent king's speech suggested that the Wellington ministry neither knew nor cared much about it.[12] At the general election six months later he stood for Bedford, where the local independents, mostly Tories, challenged the interest of the Russell family of Woburn Abbey who, backed by a subservient corporation, had engrossed the representation with their fellow Whigs, the Whitbreads, for 40 years. They were now vulnerable, partly as a result of the blatant neglect of his parliamentary and constituency duties by Lord George William Russell, a son of the 6th duke of Bedford, who had sat there since 1812. He was ditched by the duke, and replaced by his brother Lord John Russell, the leading Whig advocate of parliamentary reform in the Commons. If the reports are to be believed, Polhill uttered barely a word on politics throughout the bitter contest, which occupied eight days at the polling booths and another three before the assessor. He dealt in the commonplaces of independence, promised to do all he could to encourage the local lace industry and claimed to be a friend of religious toleration and the advocate of tax reductions 'to all practical limits'. In the end, boasting that almost two thirds of his votes were plumpers, he beat Russell into third place by one.[13]

Ministers listed him as one of their 'friends', and he voted with them on the civil list, 15 Nov., though it was thought at first that he had been an absentee.[14] He presented a Stourport petition for the abolition of slavery, 10 Nov. 1830. At the Bedford reform meeting, 17 Jan. 1831, when opinion was unanimous for change, he pledged himself to support its petition, and observed:

> The present administration are Whigs, honest Whigs, and as such they shall have my support so long as they advocate the cause of the people; but should they forsake them, then I will forsake the ministry.[15]

On 22 Mar. he declared his support for the second reading of their reform bill, for which he voted later that day, though he complained that the proposed £10 borough voting qualification would disfranchise many poor electors, and said that one of £5 would be 'more useful and more just'. He voted against Gascoyne's wrecking amendment, 19 Apr. 1831. He was returned unopposed for Bedford at the ensuing general election, when he again criticized the £10 proposal and stated his objection to the increase in the number of

Irish Members, but 'cordially approved' of 'the bill in general': 'he was an advocate for reform, and that a reform was necessary, all must allow'.[16]

Polhill voted for the second reading of the reintroduced reform bill, 6 July, and at least twice against adjournment, 12 July 1831. He voted, so he claimed, against the disfranchisement of Downton, 21 July,[17] and also went against government on the partial disfranchisement of Guildford, 29 July, and an attempt to preserve the voting rights of freemen, 30 Aug; but he was in the ministerial majorities in the divisions on St. Germans, 26 July, Chippenham, 27 July, Greenwich, 3 Aug., Gateshead, 5 Aug., Rochester, 9 Aug., and the rights of borough freeholders and copyholders to vote in counties, 17, 20 Aug. On 26 July he gave notice of a motion for the adoption of voting qualifications, based on rates rather than rents, of £5 in boroughs in which the old franchise was in the inhabitant householders, of £10 in close boroughs and of £20 in the newly enfranchised schedule C boroughs. By the time he proposed this scheme, 24 Aug., he had abandoned the second part, but he argued for the creation of a separate schedule of 46 boroughs with a £5 qualification, citing the example of Bedford as a constituency in which the standard £10 franchise would disfranchise many electors, and boasting of the 'glorious event' of its liberation from Russell domination. Lack of support forced him to withdraw his amendment; and that for a £20 franchise in the new boroughs, which he supported with the comment that imposing a uniform qualification was 'pursuing the same plan as that of a man who wears the same clothing in China as he would in Russia', was negatived without a division. Polhill voted for the passage of the reform bill, 21 Sept., but not for the motion of confidence in the Grey ministry after its defeat in the Lords, 10 Oct. He voted against them in favour of proceeding with the Dublin election committee, 29 July. His only known votes on the revised reform bill were for the second reading, 17 Dec. 1831, against the enfranchisement of Tower Hamlets, 28 Feb., and for the third reading, 22 Mar. 1832. He was reported to have been one of the four supporters of the measure who voted against the address calling on the king to appoint only ministers who would carry the bill unimpaired, 10 May.[18] He voted against the second reading of the Irish reform bill, 25 May. He divided against government on the Russian-Dutch loan, 26 Jan., and paired the same way, 12 July. He presented a petition from the archdeaconry of Bedford against the proposed new system of education in Ireland, 17 July 1832. Reverting to his true colours, he stood for Bedford at the 1832 general election as a Conservative, but lost his seat to a Liberal by three votes and failed with a petition.

During the next few years Polhill, whom Bedford denounced as 'a profligate, unprincipled fellow', and Le Marchant described as 'very dissolute and ill conditioned', was assailed by financial and personal problems, as he went a long way towards squandering his inheritance.[19] In 1830 he had become a lessee of the Drury Lane and Covent Garden Theatres, a speculation which soon involved him in heavy financial losses. In December 1834, after the failure of an experimental reduction in admission prices, he made over his interest to the former manager Alfred Bunn, a lessee since the spring of 1833, though he remained responsible for the rent of the two establishments. While the statement of his enemy J.R. Planche that he admitted to having lost £50,000 in the venture was perhaps an exaggeration, he was being pursued in the courts for arrears of rent to the tune of £2,500 by 1836, as well as owing Bunn £600 for tradesmen's bills contracted before the transfer. One aspect of the compromise which his legal adviser sought to secure was his making over to the proprietors of the theatres a quarter of his half-share in the scurrilous Tory newspaper, the *Age*, which he had bought for £4,000 in about 1834, but was now reckoned to be worth no more than £2,800.[20] In a post-nuptial agreement of 28 July 1834 Polhill, who claimed to be worth £158,000, settled his various properties, which were mortgaged to the tune of £23,000, on his wife and children.[21] In 1835 he won back his Bedford seat, which he retained at the next two elections, in company with another Conservative. He formally separated from his wife in April 1836, preferring the attractions of one Mary Ann Jeans.[22] His financial problems continued.[23] On Peel's accession to power in 1841 Polhill, who reflected that he had 'always been more in the habit of granting favours than asking them', applied for employment, claiming to have been 'the chief instrument' in liberating Bedford from the Whigs and in subsequently securing the return of two Conservatives both there and for the county: 'the different struggles I have been engaged in, have materially crippled my means, and ... I am not the rich man I was'. Peel brushed him off, as he did on at least three subsequent occasions during his ministry, when Polhill's aspirations included the governorship of Van Dieman's Land and an ordnance place.[24] He did, however, stay loyal to Peel on the repeal of the corn laws. His Commons career ended with his defeat at the 1847 general election. He died at Ramsgate in September 1848.[25] By his will, dated 18 June 1848, he left household goods, railway shares and a life annuity of £100 to Mary Ann Jeans, with whom he was then living at 55 Stamford Street, Southwark. He gave legacies of £500 each to his illegitimate children with her, James Frederick Charles, Alexander Thomas and

Victorine. These and the annuity were to be paid from a trust fund of £4,000 recently created by a mortgage on the Howbury estate in the name of his only surviving legitimate son, Frederick Charles Polhill (1826-81), the residuary legatee. Polhill's personalty, which in fact yielded no residue, was sworn under a meagre £1,500.[26] His son and successor, who took the additional name of Turner in 1853, sat as a Conservative for Bedford in the 1874 Parliament.

[1] *Ex. inf.* Stephen Lees. [2] *Gent. Mag.* (1824), i. 176. [3] *Top. and Gen.* i. 180, 187-92; F.G. Hilton Price, *London Bankers* (1890-1), 124; *HP Commons, 1754-1790*, iii. 306. [4] *VCH Beds.* iii. 203, 215; *Pubs. Beds. Hist. Rec. Soc.* v (1920), 158; J. Godber, *Hist. Beds.* 397. [5] *Top. and Gen.* i. 191-2; PROB 11/1095/464; 1098/603. [6] *Gent. Mag.* (1802), i. 381; PROB 6/178 (12 May 1802). [7] IGI (London); *Top. and Gen.* i. 192-3. [8] *Northampton Mercury*, 20 Jan. 1821. [9] Beds. RO, Wrest mss L 30/11/204/9; *Herts Mercury*, 5, 19 Aug. 1826. [10] *Gent. Mag.* (1828), ii. 283; PROB 11/1748/668; IR26/1175/702. [11] *Gent. Mag.* (1828), ii. 381; PROB 6/204/256; *Herts Mercury*, 10 Jan., 31 Oct. 1829, 2 Jan. 1830. [12] *Herts Mercury*, 20 Feb. 1830. [13] *Russell Letters*, i. 141-2; ii. 261, 267; R.M. Muggeridge, *Hist. Late Contest for Bedford* (1830), 11, 15-16, 39, 55, 58-59, 80-81; *Oakley Hunt* ed. J. Godber (Pubs. Beds. Hist. Rec. Soc. xliv), 52. [14] *Herts Mercury*, 27 Nov. 1830; *Russell Letters*, i. 162. [15] *Northampton Free Press*, 25 Jan. 1831. [16] Ibid. 3 May 1831. [17] *The Times*, 22 July 1831. [18] Ibid. 14 May 1832. [19] *Russell Letters*, i. 158-9; *Three Diaries*, 287. [20] *Cambridge and Hertford Independent Press*, 4 June 1831; H.S. Wyndham, *Annals of Covent Garden Theatre*, ii. 80-81, 89-90; *Macready's Rems.* ed. F. Pollock, i. 337, 444; C.E. Price, *Madame Vestris and her Times*, 156, 183-4; A. Bunn, *The Stage: both before and behind the curtain*, i. 10, 55, 103, 108, 212-14, 221-3; J.R. Planche, *Recollections* (1872), i. 178, 191, 237; Beds. RO GA 2777, 2778. [21] Beds. RO GA 2773. [22] Ibid. 2776; PROB 11/2090/217. [23] Beds. RO GA 2779, 2785, 2787, 2791-8. [24] Add. 40487, ff. 127, 129; 40516, ff. 162-6; 40532, ff. 336, 338; 40571, ff. 155-61. [25] *Gent. Mag.* (1848), ii. 545. [26] PROB 11/2090/217; IR26 1845/144.

D.R.F.

POLLEN, Sir John Walter, 2nd bt. (1784–1863), of Redenham, nr. Andover, Hants.

ANDOVER	1820–1831
ANDOVER	1835–1841

b. 6 Apr. 1784, 1st s. of John Pollen of Redenham and 1st w. Louisa, da. of Walter Holt of Redenham. *educ.* Eton 1799; Christ Church, Oxf. 1803; L. Inn 1806. *m.* 9 Sept. 1819, Charlotte Elizabeth, da. of Rev. John Craven of Chilton Foliat, Wilts., *s.p. suc.* fa. as 2nd bt. 17 Aug. 1814. *d.* 2 May 1863.

Col. S. Hants militia 1827-53.

Pollen's great-grandfather John Pollen (c.1642-1719) sat for his local borough of Andover, 1689-95, as did his grandfather John Pollen (c.1702-75), a Welsh judge, 1734-54. His father, also named John Pollen (c.1740-1814), was granted a baronetcy by Pitt in 1795. He was a bencher of Lincoln's Inn from 1802, where Pollen was himself admitted, though he was never called to the bar. Both were commended by obituarists for assiduous performance of their duties as Hampshire magistrates.[1] On the death of his father in 1814 Pollen succeeded to the baronetcy and to the Redenham estate that had belonged to his maternal grandfather. He bought the neighbouring manor of Fyfield the same year and made further additions to the property by later purchases. He was the residuary legatee of his father's personal estate, which was proved under £10,000.[2]

In 1818 Pollen was reported to have considered reviving the family interest at Andover, which had lain dormant for some fifty years.[3] Prior to the 1820 general election, he was said by Lord Malmesbury to be engaged in a canvass of the borough 'with every chance of success'. After one of the sitting Members retired he was returned unopposed, topping the token poll of the corporation. Malmesbury had rated Pollen as a 'very desirable' candidate for a vacancy for Hampshire, and though he had declined to come forward, pleading an inadequate fortune, he did nominate the successful aspirant, John Fleming of Stoneham.[4] He chaired meetings of the Hampshire Pitt Club and when present in the House could generally be relied on to support the Liverpool ministry, though he demonstrated a degree of independence.[5] He is not known to have delivered a full speech before 1832. He was in the minority against the appointment of an additional Scottish baron of exchequer, 15 May 1820. He voted with ministers on the Queen Caroline affair, 6 Feb., but in favour of repeal of the additional malt duty, 21 Mar. 1821. He divided against Catholic relief, 28 Feb. 1821, 1 Mar., 21 Apr., 10 May 1825, and the removal of disabilities from Catholic peers, 30 Apr. 1822. He voted against more extensive tax reductions, 21 Feb., but for abolition of one of the joint-postmasterships, 13 Mar., 2 May 1822. He divided against repeal of the Foreign Enlistment Act, 16 Apr., and inquiry into chancery delays, 5 June 1823. On 23 Feb. 1824 he presented an Andover petition for repeal of the coal duties.[6] He voted against inquiry into the conviction of the Methodist missionary John Smith in Demerara, 11 June 1824. He divided for suppression of the Catholic Association, 25 Feb., and against the bill to disfranchise Irish 40*s.* freeholders, 26 Apr. 1825. He voted for the duke of Cumberland's annuity bill, 30 May, 6, 10 June 1825. He presented an Andover petition in support of a bill to facilitate recovery of small debts, 24 Feb. 1826.[7] He was in a protectionist minority for a select committee on silk trade petitions that day, and voted against the emergency admission of foreign corn, 8, 11 May 1826.

At the 1826 general election Pollen was returned unopposed. On 22 Sept. he moved resolutions against relaxation of the corn laws at a meeting of local landowners and farmers, warning that such a move would add to the privations of the rural poor. 'It is melancholy to see the poor devils with scarcely a rag to their backs', he remarked, adding, 'I really believe that they now suffer more than the manufacturing labourers'. The radical Henry Hunt*, who effectively commandeered the meeting, denounced Pollen's expressions of concern as a cloak for self-interest and detected condescension in his use of the term 'poor devils'. The speech, and that phrase in particular, also aroused the wrath of William Cobbett†, who hoped that 'the people are no longer to be deceived by such stupid attempts at disguising hypocrisy'.[8] Unabashed, Pollen presented Andover petitions against alteration of the corn laws, 16 Feb., 12 Mar., and voted against the government's corn bill, 2 Apr. 1827.[9] He presented a petition from Droitwich against the Malt Act of the previous session, 5 Mar., and from Andover for an end to restrictions on the circulation of small notes, 4 June 1828. He voted against Catholic relief, 6 Mar. 1827, 12 May 1828. On 19 Aug. 1828 the prime minister the duke of Wellington professed 'great respect' for Pollen, but was nonetheless unable to appoint his brother Richard, a barrister, to a vacant Welsh judgeship.[10] The latter was an Oxford contemporary of the home secretary Robert Peel and supported his re-election bid for the University following the ministry's announcement of its plans to concede Catholic emancipation.[11] But Pollen himself presented Hampshire petitions against the measure, 26 Feb., was listed by Planta, the patronage secretary, as 'opposed' to its principle, and divided accordingly, 6 Mar. 1829, though not subsequently, as far as is known. His vote against Jewish emancipation, 17 May 1830, was his only recorded parliamentary activity of that session.

At the 1830 general election Pollen offered again. A reported canvass gave him 'every certainty of success', but the anticipated opposition failed to materialise and he was returned unopposed.[12] He was listed by the administration as one of the 'moderate Ultras', but with the endorsement 'a sincere friend', and he was in their minority in the crucial division on the civil list, 15 Nov. 1830. On 25 Nov. he was granted a fortnight's leave 'on account of the disturbed state of his neighbourhood'. Apparently he had returned to Hampshire the previous day, too late to prevent extensive damage being done by three days of rioting, during which a deputy had been appointed to assume command of his militia troop, 20 Nov. 1830.[13] He voted against the second reading of the Grey ministry's reform bill, 22 Mar., and for Gascoyne's wrecking amendment, 19 Apr. 1831. At the ensuing dissolution he retired from Andover, where the corporation had joined the inhabitants in supporting the bill.[14] At the 1832 general election he supported Lord Porchester's* abortive candidacy for the Northern division of Hampshire.[15] He was in Italy at the dissolution in 1834, when his brother commenced a canvass on his behalf at Andover, and he was narrowly returned as a Conservative at the general election early in the new year.[16] After an unopposed election in 1837, he was defeated by a candidate of more liberal inclinations in 1841, when an unsympathetic newspaper denounced him as a 'confirmed and bigoted Tory of the old and intolerant school'.[17] He was still suffering the taunts of the 'Andover Rads' in 1843, when he decided to let Redenham for two years.[18] He apparently made no attempt to revive his Commons career thereafter.

Pollen's brother Richard died in 1838, and his son John Hungerford Pollen (1820-1902), who won fame as an artist and writer, converted to Catholicism in 1852. He was followed a year later by his elder brother Richard Hungerford (1815-81), the heir to Pollen's baronetcy. Pollen thereupon disowned his nephews, on whom he had hitherto doted. Though friendly relations were nominally restored later, in his will of 16 Apr. 1862 Pollen made membership of the established church an absolute condition for the inheritance of Redenham, described in 1859 as 'a large mansion, pleasantly situated in a finely wooded park of about 120 acres, near the borders of Wiltshire'.[19] His wife assumed a life interest in the property when Pollen died in May 1863, and was appointed sole executrix and residuary legatee. After her death, 2 Oct. 1877, Redenham passed, according to the terms of his will, to Pollen's great-nephew Richard Hungerford Pollen (1846-1918), who succeeded his father and namesake to the baronetcy four years later.[20]

[1] *Gent. Mag.* (1814), ii. 294; (1863), i. 791-2. [2] Wilts. RO, Pollen mss 2216/8,13,14; PROB 11/1560/530; IR26/621/773. [3] *Ipswich Jnl.* 16 May 1818. [4] Hants RO, Malmesbury mss, Malmesbury to Fitzharris, 22 Jan; 19 Feb.; *Salisbury Jnl.* 6, 13, 20 Mar. 1820. [5] *Cobbett's Rural Rides* ed. G.D.H. and M. Cole, iii. 1020; *Black Bk.* (1823), 185; *Session of Parl. 1825*, p. 481. [6] *The Times*, 24 Feb. 1824. [7] Ibid. 25 Feb. 1826. [8] Ibid. 25 Sept. 1826; *Rural Rides*, ii. 468. [9] *The Times*, 17 Feb., 13 Mar. 1827. [10] Wellington mss WP1/951/9. [11] Add. 40399, f. 17. [12] *Salisbury Jnl.* 7 June, 5 July, 9 Aug. 1830. [13] R. Foster, *Politics of County Power*, 79, 81; Wellington mss WP1/1154/47. [14] *Hants Chron.* 2 May 1831. [15] Wellington mss WP1/1229/24. [16] *Salisbury Jnl.* 8 Dec. 1834. [17] *Hants Independent*, 19 June 1841. [18] Add. 40617, f. 139. [19] A. Pollen, *John Hungerford Pollen*, 10, 245-6, 323; *White's Hants Dir.* (1859), 455. [20] Will of Sir Richard Hungerford Pollen, 3rd bt., proved 15 July 1881.

H.J.S./P.J.S.

POLLOCK, Jonathan Frederick (1783–1870), of Queen Square House, Guildford Street, Mdx.[1]

HUNTINGDON 1831–Apr. 1844

b. 23 Sept. 1783, 3rd s. of David Pollock (*d.* 1815), saddler, of Charing Cross, Westminster and Sarah Homeria, da. of Richard Parsons, recvr.-gen. of customs. *educ.* Vauxhall (Mr. Allan); St. Paul's 1800; Trinity Coll. Camb. 1802, BA 1806, fellow 1807, MA 1809; M. Temple 1802, called 1807. *m.* (1) 25 May 1813, Frances (*d.* 25 Jan. 1827),[2] da. of Francis Rivers of Spring Gardens, 7s. (2 *d.v.p.*) 5da.; (2) 7 Jan. 1834, Sarah Anne Amowah, da. of Capt. Richard Langslow of Hatton, 4s. (2 *d.v.p.*) 3da. kntd. 29 Dec. 1834; *cr.* bt. 2 Aug. 1866. *d.* 23 Aug. 1870.

KC 12 June 1827; bencher, I. Temple 1827, reader 1836, treas. 1837; chairman, law commn. 1831; king's att. and sjt. co. pal. of Lancaster Mar.-Dec. 1834; att.-gen. Dec. 1834-Apr. 1835, Sept. 1841-Apr. 1844; c. bar. exch. 1844-66; sjt.-at-law 15 Apr. 1844; PC 17 Apr. 1844; member, jud. cttee. of PC 1844.

Commissary, Camb. Univ. 1824-35; recorder, Huntingdon 1835-44.

Pollock was descended from a junior branch of the Pollocks of Balgray, Dumfriesshire. His great-grandfather David Pollock (c.1662-1743) was a yeoman of Spittal, Durham, whose son John Pollock (c.1705-50) settled in Berwick-upon-Tweed, where he became a burgess. John's eldest son David Pollock (1739-1815), a stern Presbyterian, set up in London as a saddler and secured the official custom of the royal family. In 1779 he married, in defiance of her parents, Sarah Parsons, 'a lady of remarkable energy and force of character'. Soon afterwards they were established in Down Street, Piccadilly, which remained the site of a branch of the business after their removal to free accommodation in the royal mews at Charing Cross. The enterprise enjoyed fluctuating fortunes and, with a large family to support, they were sometimes in difficulties.[3] One of their younger sons recalled that the 'connection with the royal family was unfortunate', for when the prince of Wales's debts were liquidated by the nation in 1795, Pollock, by the terms of the settlement, had ten per cent struck off the £3,000 owed to him, and no interest paid on it.[4] Of his five surviving sons, two besides this Member distinguished themselves in public life: the eldest, David Pollock (1780-1847), died as chief justice of Bombay; and the fourth, George Pollock (1786-1872), an officer of the East India Company's artillery, gained fame for his services in the Afghan campaigns of 1841-2.[5] The second son, William Pollock (1782-1816), entered the family business, while the youngest, John Henry Pollock (1792-1873), became registrar of Bristol court.

Frederick Pollock, the third son, was a sickly child, though he subsequently enjoyed robust health. By his own confession, he 'lost much time' and 'learned nothing' at a succession of private schools; and for almost 18 months before he went briefly to St. Paul's at the age of 16 he was '*at no school at all*'. Yet, encouraged by his mother, he was

> during that time ... scarcely ever without a book in my hand, and was reading everything that came in my way ... This course of education has been of great service to me, and has enabled me to meet the sort of encyclopaedic demands that are now [1862] made upon every educated man.

It was at Cambridge, where his third term was wrecked by a recurrence of illness, that he blossomed intellectually. He continued there his habit of miscellaneous study 'at all odd times – dressing, undressing, walking, travelling, waiting, etc.', which he believed served him better than would have 'dogged, unshrinking attention to ... an unattractive and even disagreeable or revolting pursuit'. At the end of his first year he was faced with the prospect of having to leave, because his father could no longer afford to maintain him; but his tutor, the Rev. George Tavel, who perceived his talent, generously agreed to subsidize him. Pollock, who was a member of the Cambridge Speculative Society, repaid his faith by emerging as senior wrangler in 1806.[6]

The financial independence conferred by a Trinity fellowship enabled him to take his chance at the bar. (He had originally been destined for the church.) He later wrote of 'the disgust I felt in leaving Cambridge and substituting Tidd for Newton and Coke for Sophocles', but he 'stubbornly faced the difficulty and mastered it'. He took chambers at 18 Serjeant's Inn, joined the Forensic Debating Society, where he met Leigh Hunt, and, after giving up his fellowship, went the northern circuit.[7] His initial progress was slow, as he lamented to a friend from Carlisle, 21 Aug. 1811:

> When I am not disposed to think pleasantly, I endeavour not to think at all and to shut myself up in a sort of tortoiseshell of apathy ... When I find myself spending in counties, where I have no connection and, of course, no employment, the produce of a precarious and almost accidental town business with no certainty ... that the income of the next year may not fall short of the necessary expenditure ... [and] when in addition to that I consider the situation of the rest of my family, I have little place for that *gaité de coeur* which once attended every pulsation and which is necessary to continue a correspondence on a journey supposed to be pleasurable.[8]

When his father died in 1815, leaving everything to his widow, his personalty was sworn under £450;[9] but

Pollock, who since his marriage had taken a house at 23 Bernard Street, Russell Square (he later moved to 25 Bedford Row), was able to report that his 'circumstances had very much improved during the last 18 months, he had certainly become solvent and perhaps something better'.[10] Through his friendship with the architect John Nash and Lord Yarmouth,* Pollock secured from the regent his mother's succession as royal saddler: the accommodation and the royal custom afforded her an annual profit of about £250 until her death in 1817, when her effects were sworn under £200 and the business was apparently wound up.[11]

Pollock's professional fortunes soon improved, and he built up an extensive practice both on the circuit and at Westminster, particularly in bankruptcy cases. He owed his success, in the words of an obituary

> not so much to any showy qualities or attractive powers as a speaker, for these he never possessed, as to ... [his] extraordinary reputation for industry and general ability ... supported and confirmed as it was by the accurate and extensive legal knowledge which he displayed.[12]

On one circuit he got himself into 'a serious scrape' by committing the 'high misdemeanour' of dining with an attorney, but his rise was not impeded.[13] He was 'reasonably contented' with the earnings of over £4,000 a year which he commanded in the early 1820s.[14] To his surprise, his application for a silk gown in 1824, which had the backing of the duke of York, was unsuccessful; but he was only mildly disappointed, reckoning that promotion would cost him 'in one direction at least £1,500 a year, with the chance only of improvement or indemnity in another'.[15] Politically, he was a man of the right, and in an outburst to his brother George, 8 Feb. 1824, he damned the Whigs:

> As a party they are in general very bad – selfish, proud, vain, haughty, conceited and incompetent ... Here and there talents are conferred on the most unamiable of them, and now and then some of the twaddling and inferior sort have something of the common kindness of human nature. But such a man as Fox, who had the brightest talents and the warmest benevolence, is not often to be met with anywhere. He was born a Tory and he died a Tory, and his Whiggism was the result of faction and disappointment; and after all Fox, their great boast, was deficient in businesslike ability and still more deficient in that consistency and integrity without which benevolence is useless and talent is mischievous.[16]

His first wife, who had been in a state of pregnancy for a total of nine out of the slightly less than 14 years of their marriage, died early in 1827, leaving him with 11 children. In the summer he obtained his silk gown.

In September 1827 Pollock was mentioned as a possible candidate for Cambridge University in the event of a vacancy, which did not materialize.[17] That month he had narrowly the better of a spectacular tussle on the circuit with the Whig, Henry Brougham*, but their professional rivalry and wide political differences did not impair their friendship.[18] On 30 Mar. 1829 he wrote to his eldest son from the circuit at York:

> My table groans with briefs ... As to my health ... I know very little more than that I eat, drink, and sleep, and am decently fit for business. I am rather tired of the circuit and shall be glad of some change, without being very particular as to its nature.

In November that year, when a vacancy arose on the bench, he professed to have 'no wish' for further promotion, which 'would much diminish my income, and I think would not add to my happiness', even though the salary and retirement pension were not to be sneezed at.[19] No offer was made to him. His name was again linked with the University representation at the general election of 1830, but the rumour was without foundation.[20] Soon afterwards he boasted that he had 'bagged more guineas in spite of the elections than on any former summer circuit'. That year he moved his London residence to a large house in Guildford Street.[21]

On 3 Nov. 1830 Pollock declined lord chancellor Lyndhurst's offer of a puisne judgeship, 'saying', it was later reported, 'he thinks the functions of an advocate more agreeable and more honourable'.[22] To his niece Eliza Alexander he explained:

> I mean ... to do everything in my power to justify the offer and the refusal ... I cannot refer my own decision to ambition or avarice, but to a prudent resolution not to sacrifice £3,000 a year for certainty and comfort. As to rank, and scarlet and ermine, and trumpets, and tipstaffs, and great dinners, and being called 'My Lord' in court and 'Sir Frederick' out of it, I will not say I have a contempt for it altogether, but a very considerable indifference not far removed from the same, and I mean to go on with the degree of wretchedness or happiness ... that belongs to my present condition till I see some better cause for change than is now before me.[23]

He expected the premier, the duke of Wellington, to 'have the Tories with him and a regular Whig opposition against him', but 'never dreamt' that he 'could have done so indiscreet a thing' as to make his declaration against all reform. Yet it was with 'enormous surprise' that he learned of the ministry's defeat, 15 Nov. 1830. Initially he thought Lord Grey might fail to form a government and so permit the establishment of an anti-reform administration under 'some middle, moderate or neutral man'. Alarmed by the 'Swing' riots, which he considered 'entirely owing to 15 years peace', he commented that 'the times are fearful enough' and 'no man who has a good coat can be sure he will keep it long'. Pollock, who met Sir Robert Peel* for the first time in December 1830, continued to believe that either the Grey ministry or the new Parliament would not survive for six months.[24] At a loss to conceive how ministers could 'unite in any common measure' of reform, he was confident that any 'great and violent' proposal would founder. The government's token reduction of pensions he considered 'a humbug'. Rumoured details of their reform scheme, which fell far short of the sweeping changes which they actually proposed, seemed to him to presage

> a reform which I fear will be a revolution if carried into effect, and in a few years will trample down all other than popular rights, will put an end to the aristocracy and all their rights, will pull down the church and the throne behind it. But I hope the existing Commons will be firm enough to resist much of this and will leave us something of the constitution worth fighting for.[25]

In March 1831 he accepted the chairmanship of the reconstituted commission of inquiry into the defects of the law, which brought him an additional £1,200 a year: '*butter for fish* with a vengeance', as 'my bag is larger and more stuffed than ever [and] my fees increasing'. He expected to make that year at least £2,400 more than in 1830.[26] He was one of the lawyers consulted by Brougham, the new lord chancellor, in the preparation of his scheme to reform bankruptcy administration.[27]

At the general election of 1831 Pollock stood with Peel's brother Jonathan for Huntingdon, which the Dowager Lady Sandwich put at the disposal of the Tory opposition. Like Peel, he presented himself as 'a moderate reformer', and expressed approval of some features of the reform bill: the enfranchisement of large towns, the wider county franchise, the abolition of totally rotten boroughs and the attempt to reduce the expense of elections. But he objected to the proposed reduction in the number of Members and was not prepared to swallow 'the bill, the whole bill and nothing but the bill', fearing that if it was 'carried immediately the result would be dangerous'. He denounced colonial slavery, but argued that its precipitate abolition would violate rights of property. 'In conclusion, he avowed himself as favourable to nothing but improvements, and the friend to everything that will improve'. The opposition of two reformers, who forced a token poll, was a mere nuisance.[28]

Pollock, one of the 'king's counsel brought in to oppose the [reform] bill', tried twice to speak in the debate on the second reading, but was not called.[29] He voted against the second reading of the measure, 6 July, and four days later arrived in York for the summer circuit (he was granted formal leave on 18 July) with 'as *base* a hoarseness as ever mortal man that lived by his lungs was annoyed with'. He was on the circuit, which was 'pleasant more than usual and profitable in a still higher degree beyond the average', until 29 Aug. 1831, and so missed the protracted debates on the details of the bill.[30] He was present to vote in the majority on the Liverpool election bribery scandal, 5 Sept., and against the passage of the reform bill, 21 Sept. In June 1831 the Whig Tom Macaulay*, who considered Pollock a boring speaker, had amused a party at Holland House with the tale of his dream, all too likely to come true, that he 'heard Pollock speak in the House of Commons, that the speech was very long, and that he was coughed down'.[31] In the event Pollock's début, in enthusiastic support of Brougham's bankruptcy court bill, 14 Oct. 1831, was politely received, as he told his son:

> I ... gave great satisfaction to Brougham and all his friends. I am glad I am no longer a silent Member. I should have been mortified if November had come and found me undelivered of my maiden speech. It was, however, a very trifling effort, delivered with a very hoarse voice. Still, some people have been very civil about it.[32]

Pollock divided against the second reading of the revised reform bill, 17 Dec. 1831. He supported attempts to regulate and encourage the study of anatomy, 17, 26 Jan. 1832, when he joined in the attack on ministers over the Russian-Dutch loan: the House could not 'sanction the payment of money on the equitable construction of a treaty, without being put into possession of the supposed circumstances under which that construction had been devised'.[33] On 7 Feb. he made suggestions for refinement of the provisions of the reform bill concerning the residential qualification for £10 householders. Next day he presented a Huntingdon petition against Campbell's bill to establish a general registry of deeds. His statement that he felt obliged by the outcry against the bill to oppose it, even though he personally thought it could be advantageously modified, led Campbell to accuse him of surrendering his own opinion to 'popular dislike'. This, he retorted, had a rich irony in the mouth of a supporter of the reform bill. On 20 Feb. Pollock focused his mathematical expertise on the calculations made by Lieutenant Drummond, at the behest of government, to arrive at a revised list of boroughs for disfranchisement. He maintained that Drummond had blundered by adding rather than multiplying the figures derived from the averages of the number of houses and the amount of assessed taxes in each, with the result that a number of boroughs were incorrectly placed on the scale of relative significance. Lord John Russell invoked the names of the leading mathematicians who had approved Drummond's method and Pollock rather feebly backed down, though the following day, when he argued that Appleby ought in justice to retain one Member, he repeated his reservations about the calculation. He voted against the enfranchisement of Tower Hamlets, 28 Feb., but only paired against the third reading of the reform bill, 22 Mar., when he was presumably away on the circuit. Two months later, when the crisis of May had ended in the Grey ministry's return to office, he wrote to his son that 'the Commons have in effect voted the king a cypher, and the House of Lords an obstruction to the public good'. He was inclined to criticize Peel for refusing to take office, but acknowledged the validity of his determination not to 'play over again the game of the Catholic question', though he thought 'a better excuse (if it be true and sincere) would be that half the bill would be as bad as the whole, as both would be fatal':

> I would not give a pin to choose whether I should take ten grains of arsenic or five only, when one or two would be a deadly blow ... I take a very different interest in public affairs from what I did. I may be in another Parliament, but I think scarcely a third. I consider the constitution is at an end. The revolution has begun and practically we are a republic.

Yet a fortnight later, in anticipation of the bill becoming law, he was more positive:

> I hope I have not so little sense and temper as to wish all the melancholy forebodings ... of our friends to be realized. I do not want to see the king dethroned, the church despoiled, the bishops driven from their seats among the peers, the peers themselves shorn of their honours, Lord Grey's coronet in the dust ... I rather (now that the affair is over) am disposed to make the best of it, and to hope that the next Parliament may be composed of men more intelligent, more wealthy, more *conservative* than the present.[34]

He spoke and voted against government on the Russian-Dutch loan, 12 July, and supported inquiry into the admission procedures of the inns of court, 17 July 1832, believing that rejected candidates should have the right of appeal against exclusion. After recuperating from the rheumatism and hoarseness which had dogged him on the summer circuit, Pollock sought re-election for Huntingdon, whence he wrote to his niece, 4 Dec. 1832:

> The dissolution ... took place yesterday. The king fired a proclamation at the Parliament ... and it expired without a groan. The old phoenix is dead and I am part of the ashes and I mean to rake myself together and endeavour to form part of the new bird. Perhaps I may vindicate to myself a better station that I filled before, and contribute to a brighter plumage. Good heavens, what stuff!![35]

Pollock, whom Benjamin Disraeli† denigrated as 'a weak man', served as attorney-general in both Peel's ministries.[36] In 1844, when he was reputedly earning £18,000 a year, he was appointed chief baron of the exchequer.[37] As such, according to his obituarist, 'he showed himself an excellent judge – sound, safe, sensible, able, and indefatigable, ever ready at his post, and inflexible in the discharge of his judicial duties'.[38] In 1834 he remarried and acquired 'a small portion' of 'the dull, stale, flat (but not unprofitable) soil of Hounslow Heath' at Hatton. His second wife bore him a further 12 children. He retired from the bench with a baronetcy, at the age of 82, in 1866. The following year he reflected that he could 'look round with leisure and calmness to see what I have done, and I am thoroughly contented and satisfied'.[39] His old friend Henry Crabb Robinson described him in his retirement as 'a capital talker, and a kind and generous man'[40]; while David Veasey wrote of 'his varied knowledge, his cheerfulness, his fund of anecdote and his wonderful animation'; he was often 'merry ... as a boy' even in old age.[41] His son Edward's contemporary Richard Webster found him alarming at first, but thereafter 'extremely kind, and always most genial'.[42] Pollock died in August 1870.

[1] See Visct. Hanworth, *Lord Chief Baron Pollock* (1929). [2] *The Times*, 26 Jan. 1827. *Oxford DNB* erroneously gives 27 Jan. [3] Hanworth, 1-6; *The Times*, 24 Aug. 1870. [4] Sir F. Pollock, *Personal Remembrances*, ii. 224-5. [5] *Oxford DNB*. [6] Hanworth, 7-15, Pollock, i. 58, 60; G. Pryme, *Autobiog. Recollections*, 54; *Palmerston-Sulivan Letters*, 10-11, 40, 47. [7] Hanworth, 16-17; Add. 38111, f. 359. [8] Hanworth, 33-34. [9] PROB 8/208; 11/1573/513. [10] CUL, Pollock mss (Add. 7564) C/2, Pollock to G. Pollock, 3, 16 Sept. 1815. [11] PROB 6/193/227. [12] *The Times*, 24 Aug. 1870. [13] Lord Kingsdown, *Recollections*, 24; *Macaulay Letters*, i. 208. [14] Pollock mss C/2, Pollock to G. Pollock, 8 Feb. 1824. [15] Ibid. C/2, same to same, 31 Oct. 1824. [16] Ibid. C/2. [17] Bucks. RO, Buckinghamshire mss, Lansdowne to Goderich, 17 Sept. 1827. [18] *Macaulay Letters*, i. 227; *Life of Campbell*, i. 448. [19] Hanworth, 43-44; Pollock, i. 25-26. [20] Add. 51578, Carlisle to Holland, 10 July [1830]. [21] Hanworth, 47; Pollock, i. 35. [22] Hanworth, 47-48; *Life of Campbell*, i. 485. [23] Pollock mss A/4, Pollock to E. Alexander, 4 Nov. [1830]. [24] Ibid. A/4, same to same, 1, 4, 9, [16], 17, 20 Nov., 6 Dec. 1830. [25] Ibid. A/4, same to same, 7 Feb. 1831. [26] Hanworth, 48; Pollock mss A/4, Pollock to Alexander, 12, 22 Jan. 1831. [27] Brougham mss, Pollock to Brougham, 21 Mar. 1831. [28] Hanworth, 68; Pollock, i. 33; Pollock mss A/4, Pollock to Alexander, 26 Apr., 2, 4 May; *Huntingdon, Bedford and Peterborough Gazette*, 30 Apr., 7 May 1831. [29] *Life of Campbell*, i. 517; Pollock, i. 34. [30] Pollock mss A/4, Pollock to Alexander, 10 July, 1, 14, 22, 30 Aug. 1831. [31] *Macaulay Letters*, i.

227; ii. 26. [32] Hanworth, 68-69. [33] *Three Diaries*, 184. [34] Hanworth, 69-70. [35] Pollock mss A/4, Pollock to Alexander, 4 Dec.; C/1, same to same, 16 Sept. 1832. [36] Monypenny and Buckle, *Disraeli*, i. 265. [37] *Smith Letters*, ii. 831. [38] *The Times*, 24 Aug. 1870. [39] Add. 47671, ff. 15, 29. [40] *Crabb Robinson Diary*, i. 288; ii. 395. [41] Hunts. RO Acc 4023, 'Reminiscences of David Veasey', pp. 96-98. [42] Lord Alverstone, *Recollections*, 11.

D.R.F.

PONSONBY, Hon. Frederick Cavendish (1783–1837).

Co. Kilkenny	1806–1826
Higham Ferrers	1826–1830

b. 6 July 1783, 2nd s. of Frederick Ponsonby†, 3rd earl of Bessborough [I] and 3rd Bar. Ponsonby [GB] (*d.* 1844), and Lady Henrietta Frances Spencer, da. of John Spencer†, 1st Earl Spencer; bro. of John William Ponsonby, Visct. Duncannon* and Hon. William Francis Spencer Ponsonby*. *educ.* Harrow 1792-9. *m.* 16 Mar. 1825, Lady Emily Charlotte Bathurst, da. of Henry Bathurst†, 3rd Earl Bathurst, 3s. 3da. GCMG 5 Nov. 1828; KCB 13 Sept 1831; KCH 1831. *d.* 11 Jan. 1837.

Cornet 10 Drag. Jan. 1800, lt. June 1800, capt. 1803; capt. 60 Ft. and a.d.c. to ld. lt. [I] 1806; maj. 23 Drag. 1807, lt.-col. 1810; lt.-col. 12 Drag. 1811; brevet col. and a.d.c. to prince regent 1814; half-pay 1820; inspecting field officer, Ionian isles 1824; maj.-gen. 1825; lt.-gen. 1831; col. 86 Ft. 1835, R. Drag. 1836-*d.*

Lt.-gov. Malta Dec. 1826-May 1835.

Ponsonby was a veteran of the Peninsula and Waterloo, where he was seriously wounded. Pierced by lance and sabre, ridden over by Prussian cavalry and left for dead on the battlefield, where he was twice plundered, he owed his recovery, according to Raikes, 'to the extreme tranquillity of his character, which was never ruffled by irritation or discontent'.[1] After convalescence, he resumed his parliamentary and military careers, despite paralysing injuries to his right arm which obliged him to mount a horse, according to a fellow officer, 'by an active spring which showed the accomplished cavalier'.[2] At the general election of 1820 he was again returned unopposed for county Kilkenny on the family interest. As a consequence of his vote for Denis Browne*, the corporation candidate for the borough, he was roughly treated by a mob during an attempted chairing.[3] There had been a notion of his being replaced by his younger brother William Ponsonby, but county opinion was apparently against this, which Lord Clare considered 'strange, for [George Agar] Ellis* is quite right in asserting that though an amiable man, Fred Ponsonby is the worst of all representatives, never going near his constituents or the House of Commons'.[4] When present Ponsonby, whose poor record of attendance was exacerbated by two postings to the Mediterranean during this period, continued to vote with the Whig opposition to the Liverpool ministry on most major issues, including economy, retrenchment and reduced taxation.[5] Unlike his elder brother Lord Duncannon, a rising star of opposition, he is not known to have spoken in debate. He warned Harriet Arbuthnot that 'the Whigs in a body would vote strongly' against a royal divorce, 9 Feb. 1820, and joined in the attacks on ministers over their conduct towards Queen Caroline early the following year.[6] During the subsequent civil unrest he was a witness to Lord Exmouth's armed defence of his house from a mob.[7] He divided for Catholic claims, 28 Feb. 1821, 1 Mar., 21 Apr., 10 May 1825. His pair for repeal of the additional malt duty, 3 Apr. 1821, was his last recorded vote for almost four years, during which time he was abroad. The trigger for this was the death of his mother on 14 Nov. 1821 in Florence, whence he wrote to his sister, Lady Caroline Lamb, 24 Jan. 1822, and thereafter he travelled in Italy and sailed to Malta and the Ionian Islands.[8] The need to remain abroad stemmed from his gambling debts, in settlement of which the duke of Wellington, who had taken an interest in his welfare since Waterloo, wrote on 21 Mar. 1822 to advise him to take a post in the Mediterranean 'at present, and to look to go to India hereafter when you will be a major-general', which will enable 'you in a few years to return with means to pay your debts':

> I cannot conclude this letter without urgently entreating you to recollect what it is that has obliged you to separate yourself from your family and friends, and to quit the most advantageous and agreeable position that ever fell to the lot of any man in England. I am afraid that you can go to no part of the world whether near or distant in which you will not find means and opportunities of getting into similar scrapes; and you may rely on it that their only result will be to occasion fresh and increased regret to yourself and sorrow to your family and friends and to none more than ... [myself].[9]

On 4 Dec. 1821 Wellington had written in similar terms to Duncannon, opining that in Ponsonby's case an immediate posting to India would resemble 'a species of banishment, and I am anxious to avoid it if we can tie him up from play. This last object was at one time effected, and I should think we might attain it again'. The signs were encouraging. On 22 July 1822 Ponsonby replied from the Ionian Islands that he had

> received the very kind letter you wrote to me about my coming to these Islands in preference to my going to India. I do not think I am very likely to get any employment, but I have been so kindly received by Sir T. Maitland, and my expenses are likely to be so very

> trifling, that I think the plan is likely to succeed, especially as I am sure, if anything can be done for me by him, it will. With respect to play, I am afraid few people would believe me when I say that I have quite given it up, but I feel I can speak confidently on the subject, and if there is any faith in man, I promise that your advice shall not be forgotten.[10]

With the assistance of Wellington, who exerted himself in settling the prior claims of more senior officers, Ponsonby eventually secured an appointment as inspecting officer of the Ionian Islands, 24 Jan. 1824.[11] In November 1822 he wrote from Corfu to William Ord* to ask for news of the funds and the prospects for parliamentary reform, adding that the 'people in these islands are *peaceable* and *satisfied in the highest degree*, and good reason they have for *everything* is improved and improving under British protection', but that he was 'sorry to see the Russells humbugged as they are by the Greek patriots as they call themselves, fellows who would be stoned to death by the people here if they were to venture here *unprotected* by the government which they calumniate'.[12] An enthusiastic field sportsman, in a letter thanking Wellington for his forthcoming appointment he boasted of killing seventy birds in three days, 25 Nov. 1823, but admitted that he would enjoy a day's shooting at Stratfield Saye.[13]

On 24 Sept. 1824 Harriet Arbuthnot reported that Ponsonby 'is just returned from Corfu after three years' absence and is, as usual, delightful'.[14] In November he exchanged views on cavalry manoeuvres with Wellington, who, according to Captain Gronow, had specifically exempted his regimental tactics from general criticism during the Peninsular war.[15] Back in the Commons he voted, 15 Feb., and paired, 25 Feb. 1825, against suppression of the Catholic Association. He presented a Kilkenny petition for Catholic relief, 10 Mar.[16] In February 1825 he had announced his engagement to a daughter of Lord Bathurst, the colonial secretary. Lady Holland, who suspected Henry Greville of having been the matchmaker, informed her son Henry Fox*, 7 Feb., that

> Ponsonby marries wretchedly. When he wrote to me to announce it, I could only say I knew he had met with good temper, and that was the most valuable ingredient for happiness. When Lord Bathurst was asked by the Bessborough family for the name of his solicitor he said he had forgot it. Shabby man, he will do nothing. She has only £4,000 in the world ... They will have with places and appointments about £1,400 per annum.

To Lady Holland's glee, the wedding featured an embarrassing hitch:

> At the altar he could not find the ring. After 20! minutes search, it was at the bottom of his pantaloon pocket. They were to dine on the road, and reach Cirencester for the hymeneal rites.[17]

The couple's finances were partly secured by a loan of £1,000 from Wellington, which was later repaid.[18] Duncannon also gave assistance, though he was anxious not to prejudice his own children's inheritance, reminding his wife that 'we know many people who have married on £1,500'. A more generous benefactor was Ponsonby's brother William, who, as Lady Holland recalled, at the instigation of his wife gave 'up his own fortune, saying they had enough, to poor Fred Ponsonby, who was deeply in debt'.[19] According to Raikes, Ponsonby had previously been bailed out by the 5th duke of Devonshire, his maternal uncle by marriage.[20]

The demands of Ponsonby's Mediterranean command prompted his retirement from Kilkenny at the dissolution in 1826.[21] His place was taken by Duncannon, for whom the 2nd Earl Fitzwilliam had already reserved a seat at Higham Ferrers, which was now offered to Ponsonby. He was returned *in absentia*, Duncannon reporting that he had 'decided not to come to England'. It was 'thought that he would be willing to retire' in favour of the seatless Lord John Russell, but this proved unnecessary.[22] Before the new Parliament assembled Ponsonby obtained, through Bathurst and the evident assistance of Wellington, an appointment as lieutenant-governor of Malta, despite the disapproval of the duke of York, who, according to a letter from Sir Herbert Taylor* to Wellington, 15 Dec., had no personal objection to Ponsonby, but felt slighted by Bathurst's having written directly to the king the previous day, saying that 'the interests of a dear daughter are at stake' and recommending his son-in-law as 'an individual highly distinguished by birth', whose 'liberality was known to have involved him in such insuperable difficulties, as not to allow him to live in England'. To ease the way for Ponsonby Bathurst had suggested that the post be downgraded from a full governorship, and the appointment was duly gazetted as a lieutenant-governorship, 22 Dec. 1826.[23] Before leaving for Malta Ponsonby voted for Catholic relief, 6 Mar. 1827.

Judging from his Maltese letterbook he was in post on 19 Mar. 1827, and it is therefore highly unlikely that he cast many of the votes attributed to him in the remainder of the Parliament, which were almost certainly those of William.[24] He appears to have divided for the disfranchisement of Penryn, 28 May 1827, but he was certainly back in Malta by September. He could not have voted for repeal of the Test Acts, 26 Feb. 1828, as he wrote a letter from Malta concerning its defence that day.[25] It is possible that he voted for ordnance reductions, 4 July 1828. He was present to vote for Catholic emancipation, 6, 30 Mar. 1829, when he presented favourable petitions from several places in Ireland and one from Higham Ferrers for the Warwick and Napton canal bill. Referring to the government's concession, King Leopold of Belgium observed to Ponsonby in a letter of 5 Mar. that he must have been 'very interested in the important events which have taken place in England', but it is curious that his subsequent letters to his uncle Earl Spencer made no reference to domestic politics.[26] He could not have divided for allowing Daniel O'Connell to take his seat unhindered, 18 May 1829, as he had written from Malta only the previous day.[27] For similar reasons it seems unlikely that he cast many of the opposition votes credited to him during the 1830 session, although he may have divided for Jewish emancipation, 17 May, making Irish first fruits nominal, 18 May, reductions in the civil government of Canada, 25 May, parliamentary reform, 28 May, and the forgery punishment mitigation bill, 7 June. It beggars belief that he was in the majority to abolish the civil list pensions paid to the son of Lord Melville and his brother-in-law William Lennox Bathurst†, 26 Mar. 1830. He retired from Parliament at the dissolution.

At Malta Ponsonby threw himself into his administrative work with gusto, but the only major incident of his posting was the destruction of the Turkish fleet at the battle of Navarino in October 1827, following which he wrote to congratulate the commander, Sir Edward Codrington, on 'the success of your late operations, which could not have succeeded except by the greatest decision in most critical circumstances'.[28] Codrington was criticised in some quarters for exceeding his remit, and in his defence cited Ponsonby among those who had shared his bellicose interpretation of government instructions.[29] Ponsonby's lieutenant-governorship was also marked by a long-running dispute with the kingdom of the Two Sicilies over the right of nomination to the vacant Catholic see of Malta, an issue on which the government stood firm.[30] On learning of his appointment Ponsonby had promised Wellington to 'not be as grand' as his profligate predecessor Lord Hastings and to live within his means, and had despaired of the likely opportunities for shooting.[31] Fox, who visited him in April 1829, found him living unpretentiously in a small house with a single servant, and was gratified that his host 'has acquired by his rapid rise no humbug and pomp of office, but is just as free and open as I remember him fifteen years ago':

> He is one of the simplest, most manly, unaffected men that I know, with very good sterling sense, a sweet temper, and with the manners and experience of a man that has seen much of the world and has profited by what he has seen. The extreme, patient good humour with which he submitted to all his sufferings during the battle of Waterloo and in his very slow recovery afterwards, are said to have been the means of carrying him through ... Since that day he has been unable to use the fingers of his right hand and now writes with his left; but he contrives with singular ingenuity to wield a racket or indeed clench anything with it. Lady Emily is just as she was before her marriage, very good-humoured, but with a silly giggling manner which often offends, though only meant to do so occasionally.[32]

According to Gronow, it was during his Maltese stint that Ponsonby met Baron de Laussat, a deputy from the Pyrenees and the French field officer, who, it transpired, had saved his life at Waterloo by plying him with brandy.[33] Another visitor was Benjamin Disraeli†, who, having heard from his travelling companion William Meredith that Ponsonby was 'a very nonchalant personage and exceedingly exclusive in his conduct to his subjects', boasted of how his wit had 'made our nonchalant governor roll off the sofa from his risible convulsions' at their first meeting in August 1830. He 'is a most charming fellow', he wrote to his sister, but 'his wife is very ugly and not very popular'. A monumental pillar, since destroyed in a storm, was later erected on the island in his memory.[34]

Ponsonby retired from Malta in October 1836, citing ill health.[35] His sudden death in January 1837 occurred at the *Wellesley Arms*, Murrell Green, near Basingstoke, as he was sitting down to a meal.[36] Raikes reported that 'the physicians long ago pronounced that the action of his heart was disordered, that he might live on for years, but that when the crisis came, he would die suddenly, as if by a pistol shot'.[37] His obituary in the *Gentleman's Magazine* tellingly made no reference to his parliamentary career and quoted a tribute from an unnamed friend:

> I have seen him in sickness, in danger, in difficulties, in prosperity, in society, alone with myself ... and I never knew his beautiful disposition vary from that perfect state in which his gentle and noble mind had fixed it.[38]

By the terms of his brief will, dated 20 May 1834 with a codicil of 19 May 1835, he left all his property to his wife, the sole executrix, to whom administration was granted. His will referred to £10,000 in the keeping of his brother William and another, unspecified, capital sum in the hands of his bankers, but Raikes reported that he had left his family only 'slender means of support'.[39] Wellington subsequently took an interest in furthering the army career of his son Henry Frederick (1825-95), who achieved prominence as private secretary to Queen Victoria.[40] His second son Arthur Edward Vallette (1827-68) also went into the army, while his third son Frederick John (1837-94), born posthumously, was champion tennis player at Oxford and entered the church. His widow died in a grace-and-favour apartment in Hampton Court, 1 Feb. 1877.[41]

[1] *Gronow Reminiscences*, i. 204; *Raikes Jnl.* iii. 104. [2] P.M. Collins, 'Col. the Hon. Frederick Cavendish Ponsonby', *Jnl. of Soc. for Army Hist. Research*, xlvi (1968), 1-5. [3] *Ramsey's Waterford Chron.* 28 Mar. 1820. [4] Keele Univ. Lib. Sneyd mss, Clare to Sneyd, 25 Mar. 1820. [5] *Black Bk.* (1823), 185; *Session of Parl. 1825*, p. 481. [6] *Arbuthnot Jnl.* i. 1-2. [7] *Greville Mems.* i. 95. [8] *Lady Bessborough and her Family Circle* ed. Lord Bessborough, 276. [9] Wellington mss WP1/703/13. [10] *Lady Bessborough*, 272-3, 279. [11] Wellington mss WP1/769/17; 770/3, 9. [12] Northumb. RO, Blackett Ord mss NRO 324/A/28. [13] Wellington mss WP1/776/7. [14] *Arbuthnot Jnl.* i. 341. [15] Wellington mss WP1/804/1, 3, 6; *Gronow Reminiscences*, ii. 3. [16] *The Times*, 11 Mar. 1825. [17] *Lady Holland to Son*, 38, 40. [18] Wellington mss WP1/1009/23; 1014/20. [19] D. Howell-Thomas, *Duncannon*, 106; *Lady Holland to Son*, 217. [20] *Raikes Jnl.* iii. 104. [21] *Wexford Evening Post*, 2 May 1826. [22] Add. 51724, Duncannon to Lady Holland, 10 Apr. [1826]; Walpole, *Russell*, i. 132. [23] Wellington mss WP1/867/25; 879/31; *Geo. IV Letters*, iii. 1272. [24] Bodl. (Rhodes House) MSS Medit S 19, on which the following deductions about his votes are based. [25] Ibid. f. 42. [26] J. Ponsonby, *Ponsonby Fam.* 266; BL, Althorp mss, Ponsonby to Spencer, 4 Feb., 8 Mar., 30 May, 22 June, 16 Nov. 1831. [27] Rhodes House MSS Medit S 19, f. 113. [28] Ibid., f. 20. [29] *Greville Mems.* i. 261. [30] Rhodes House MSS Medit S 19, ff. 6, 23, 120, 139; Wellington mss WP1/1037/11, 1042/6, 1080/1. [31] Wellington mss WP1/879/31. [32] *Fox Jnl.* 334-5. [33] *Gronow Reminiscences*, i. 204-5. [34] Ponsonby, 123-4; *Disraeli Letters*, i. 97-99. [35] Ponsonby, 227. [36] *The Times*, 16, 17, 18 Jan. 1837. [37] *Raikes Jnl.* iii. 106. [38] *Gent. Mag.* (1837), i. 545. [39] PROB 8/230; PROB 11/1873/111; *Raikes Jnl.* iii. 104. [40] Howell-Thomas, 260. [41] Ponsonby, 125.

P.J.S.

PONSONBY, Hon. George (?1773–1863), of Woolbeding, Suss.

CO. KILKENNY	12 Apr. 1806–1806
CO. CORK	1806–1812
YOUGHAL	1826–1832

b. ?1773, 4th s. of William Brabazon Ponsonby†, 1st Bar. Ponsonby [I] (*d.* 1806), of Bishop's Court, co. Kildare and Hon. Louisa Molesworth, da. of Richard, 3rd Visct. Molesworth [I]; bro. of Hon. Frederick Ponsonby†, John Brabazon Ponsonby† and Hon. William Ponsonby†. *educ.* Trinity, Dublin 7 Mar. 1791, aged 18; King's Inns 10 Dec. 1796, aged 23; L. Inn 1794, called [I] 1797. *m.* (1) 7 Apr. 1807, Sarah (*d.* 18 July 1808), da. of John Jacob Gledstanes of Annesgift, co. Tipperary, 1s. *d.v.p.*; (2) 11 June 1812, Diana Juliana Margaretta, da. of Hon. Edward Bouverie† of Delapré Abbey, Northants., 1s. *d.v.p.* 1da. *d.* 5 June 1863.

MP [I] 1796-8.

Ld. of treasury Nov. 1830-Nov. 1834.

Ponsonby, who had joined Brooks's, sponsored by Lord William Russell*, 7 June 1806, had unsuccessfully attempted to re-enter Parliament for county Cork in 1818 with the assistance of his brother-in-law Earl Grey and the 6th duke of Devonshire.[1] At the 1826 general election he was returned unopposed for Youghal, where Devonshire had recently regained control.[2] A regular but mostly silent attender, he acted steadily with his Whig friends. He presented Youghal petitions against alteration of the corn laws, 28 Feb., and for Catholic claims, 26 Feb. 1827, 15 Apr. 1828, for which he voted, 6 Mar. 1827, 12 May 1828.[3] He was in the minorities for information on the Barrackpoor mutiny, 22 Mar., and the Lisburn Orange procession, 29 Mar. 1827. He divided for the spring guns bill, 23 Mar. He voted for inquiry into chancery delays, 5 Apr., and was in the minority of 37 for terminating its jurisdiction over bankruptcy, 22 May. He divided for the disfranchisement of Penryn, 28 May 1827. He brought up a petition for repeal of the Test Acts and voted accordingly, 26 Feb. 1828. He divided against the grant for the Society for the Propagation of the Gospels in the colonies, 6 June, and in the minority of 21 against the Irish lessors bill, 12 June 1828. He voted for Catholic emancipation, 6, 30 Mar., and presented a favourable constituency petition, 26 Mar. 1829. He had been listed by Planta, the Wellington ministry's patronage secretary, as being 'opposed to securities', but on 26 Mar. he announced that he was 'prepared to give up' his 'strong objections' to the disfranchisement of the 40*s.* freeholders as it was 'part of the great measure for the conciliation and pacification of Ireland'. That day he presented but dissented from two hostile petitions. He voted for the transfer of East Retford's seats to Birmingham, 5 May 1829, 11 Feb. 1830, and for the issue of a new writ, 2 June 1829. He divided to allow Daniel O'Connell to take his seat unimpeded, 18 May 1829. In October 1829 the Ultra leader Sir Richard Vyvyan* numbered him among those who had voted in favour of emancipation whose attitude towards a putative coalition government was 'unknown'. On 22 Feb. 1830 he presented a petition from Youghal boat owners in support of the Irish fishing bounties. He divided for the enfranchisement of Birmingham, Leeds and Manchester, 23 Feb., and parliamentary reform, 28 May. He voted regularly with the revived Whig opposition for economy and reduced taxation from March. He spoke in favour of inquiry into the state of Newfoundland, 11 May, when he voted for abolition of the Irish viceroyalty. He presented petitions from Youghal merchants against the East India Company's monopoly and Irish stamp duty increases, 12 May. He divided for repeal of the Irish coal duties next day. He voted for Jewish emancipation, 17 May. He divided for abolition of the death penalty for forgery, 24 May, 7 June (as a pair), 20 July. He presented and endorsed a Youghal petition against an increase of Irish spirit duties, which he believed would promote 'illicit distillation', 15 June. He divided against the libel law amendment bill, 6 July 1830.

At the 1830 general election he was returned for Youghal after a brief contest.[4] He presented and endorsed constituency petitions for the abolition of slavery, 10 Nov. 1830, 30 Mar. 1831. He was of course listed by the Wellington ministry as one of their 'foes', and he voted against them on the civil list, 15 Nov. On Grey's accession to power he was appointed a lord of the treasury and at the ensuing by-election was returned unopposed *in absentia*.[5] Speaking in defence of the Union, 11 Dec. he asserted that there was 'no place on the face of the earth in which greater abuses existed than in Ireland under its own Parliament' and berated Irish Members for complaining that Parliament 'does no good', while the remedy for absenteeism, the cause of the 'misery which prevails', lay in their own hands. He brought up a petition against repeal, 22 Dec. 1830, and a constituency one for abolition of the window duties, 30 Mar. 1831. He voted for the second reading of the ministry's reform bill, 22 Mar., and against Gascoyne's wrecking amendment, 19 Apr. 1831. At the ensuing general election he was returned unopposed for Youghal on the 'same principles', having also started for county Londonderry, where it was said that he would have given the Tory candidate 'serious trouble' had he continued.[6] He voted for the second reading of the reintroduced reform bill, 6 July, at least twice against the adjournment, 12 July, and gave steady support to its detailed provisions, though he was in the minority for the disfranchisement of Saltash, 26 July. He divided for its passage, 21 Sept., the second reading of the Scottish bill, 23 Sept., and Lord Ebrington's confidence motion, 10 Oct. He voted against disqualification of the Dublin election committee, 29 July, and with his colleagues on the controversy, 23 Aug. He defended the operation of the game laws, insisting that a 'gentleman' would 'give his name and address at once' if apprehended, 8 Aug. He presented petitions from the Youghal Catholics against the grant to the Kildare Place Society, and the inhabitants for abolition of the death penalty for crimes against property, 9 Aug. On 31 Aug. he justified the expense of publishing Irish statutes in newspapers. He voted against the issue of the Liverpool writ, 5 Sept. 1831.

Ponsonby voted for the second reading of the revised reform bill, 17 Dec. 1831, was a majority teller for going into committee on it, 20 Feb. 1832, and again gave steady support to its details. He voted for the third reading, 22 Mar., and for the address calling on the king to appoint only ministers who would carry reform unimpaired, 10 May. He voted for the second reading of the Irish bill, 25 May, against an increase in the Scottish county representation, 1 June, and an amendment to prevent the dismemberment of Perthshire, 15 June. He divided for the Vestry Act amendment bill, 23 Jan. He voted with government on the Russian-Dutch loan, 26 Jan., 12, 16, 20 July, and relations with Portugal, 9 Feb. In a heated exchange with Hunt, 2 Apr., he denied that as chairman of the mutiny bill committee he had given an assurance that it would contain no clause relating to corporal punishment. He complained that insufficient notice had been given to his family and those 'with an interest' in the King's County assizes bill, 18 Apr., condemned the transfer of the assizes from Phillipstown to Tullamore, which had already been rejected by the Irish Parliament and would 'totally ruin an already poor town', and moved for a six month postponement but declined to divide, 23 May. He denied that his opposition was 'influenced by private considerations', 30 May, and was a teller for the minority of eight against the bill, which he contended violated Acts of 1570 and 1692, 1 June. He voted for the Liverpool disfranchisement bill, 23 May, and coroners' inquests to be made public, 20 June. He divided for the Irish tithes bill, 13 July, 1 Aug., and defended a military presence at an anti-tithes meeting at Blarney, county Cork, where the troops 'were merely at their station, the garrison being there', 2 Aug. 1832.

At the 1832 general election he abandoned Youghal, where it was anticipated that he would be 'turned out' by a Repealer, and offered unsuccessfully for Dublin University, rejecting Protestant assertions that he and his Liberal partner were 'foes' of the established church, which he argued required reform to 'conserve it', and stressing his opposition to repeal.[7] He never stood again and died at Woolbeding in June 1863. He was survived by his second wife, sole executrix and beneficiary of his will of 15 Apr. 1858, and his daughter Diana, who in 1842 had married Devonshire's nephew Edward Granville George Howard (1809-80), later 1st Baron Lanerton.[8]

[1] *HP Commons, 1790-1820*, iv. 862-3. [2] *Cork Constitution*, 8, 20 June; *Dublin Evening Post*, 10, 20 June 1826; L. Proudfoot, *Urban Patronage*, 284. [3] *The Times*, 27 Feb. 1827. [4] *Dublin Evening Post*, 12

Aug.; *Cork Constitution*, 17 Aug. 1830. [5] *Cork Constitution*, 9 Dec. 1830. [6] *Belfast News Letter*, 10 May; *Cork Constitution*, 16 May 1831. [7] Wellington mss WP1/123910; *Dublin Evening Post*, 22 Nov., 1 Dec. 1832. [8] *Gent. Mag.* (1863), ii. 112.

P.J.S.

PONSONBY, John George Brabazon (1809–1880).

BLETCHINGLEY	1831–July 1831
HIGHAM FERRERS	6 Oct. 1831–1832
DERBY	1835–16 May 1847

b. 14 Oct. 1809, 1st s. of John William Ponsonby, Visct. Duncannon*, and Lady Maria Fane, da. of John, 10th earl of Westmorland. *educ.* Charterhouse 1822-6. *m.* (1) 8 Sept. 1835, Lady Frances Charlotte Lambton (*d.* 18 Dec. 1835), da. of John George Lambton*, 1st earl of Durham, *s.p.*; (2) 4 Oct. 1849, Lady Caroline Amelia Gordon Lennox, da. of Charles Lennox†, 5th duke of Richmond, *s.p. styled* Visct. Duncannon 1844-7. *suc.* fa. as 5th earl of Bessborough [I] and 5th Bar. Ponsonby [GB] 16 May 1847. *d.* 28 Jan. 1880.

Précis writer, foreign office May 1833-Nov. 1834; master of the buckhounds May 1848-Feb. 1852, Dec. 1852-Feb. 1858, June 1859-Jan. 1866; PC 27 June 1848; ld. steward of household Jan.-July 1866, Dec. 1868-Mar. 1874.

Sheriff, co. Carlow 1838-9, ld. lt. 1838-*d.*

Ponsonby was born into the charmed Whig circle, although his mother, who bore 13 children in a little over 20 years, came from a resolutely Tory family. As he grew up he accompanied his authoritarian father Lord Duncannon, the opposition whip and organizer, on his frequent absences from the ancestral home in county Kilkenny. He apparently gave Duncannon some clerical assistance in his role in the drafting of the Grey ministry's reform bill in early 1831.[1] At that year's general election precipitated by the defeat of the measure Ponsonby was returned unopposed for Bletchingley on the Russell interest. He voted for the second reading of the reintroduced bill, 6 July, and at least twice against the adjournment, 12 July 1831, before vacating his seat to accommodate the secretary to the board of control. Three months later his father's cousin Lord Milton*, son of Earl Fitzwilliam, brought him in on a vacancy for Higham Ferrers. He was absent from the majority for Lord Ebrington's motion of confidence in the ministry, 10 Oct. 1831. He voted for the second reading of the revised reform bill, 17 Dec. 1831, gave steady support to its details, and divided for the third reading, 22 Mar. 1832. He voted with government on the Russian-Dutch loan, 26 Jan., and relations with Portugal, 9 Feb., but was in the minority for printing a petition for the abolition of Irish tithes, 16 Feb. He voted for the address calling on the king to appoint only ministers who would carry reform unimpaired, 10 May, and the second reading of the Irish reform bill, 25 May. He paired against a Conservative amendment to the Scottish measure, 1 June. Ponsonby, who is not known to have spoken in debate in this period, was added to the select committee on the East India Company, 1 Feb. 1832.

Higham Ferrers was disfranchised by the Reform Act and he did not find a seat at the 1832 general election. Overwork under Lord Palmerston's* punishing regime at the foreign office, where he laboured for 18 months as a précis writer from May 1833, and delayed reaction to his mother's untimely death in March 1834, contributed to his bizarre nervous breakdown when standing for Derby as a Liberal at the 1835 general election. He was nevertheless returned in second place, as he was again in 1837 and 1841.[2] He was devastated by the loss of his first wife to consumption after only 16 weeks of marriage in 1835.[3] He remarried 14 years later after succeeding his father to the earldom of Bessborough, but according to the family historian he lost the sight of one eye in the process

> by putting his head out of the train window on his honeymoon. Some people have said the accident was caused by his having suddenly turned round to embrace his bride, who, not expecting this sudden advance, was shielding her face with her small ... parasol, when most unluckily the point ... penetrated her husband's eye. This accident had the effect of making his lordship rather sharp-tempered, and he was held in much awe by the younger members of his family.[4]

As a peer he held household places in the Russell, Aberdeen and Palmerston administrations. He spent almost 16 years as master of the buckhounds and was reputed to have said, in a discussion of where to place 'a certain peer ... not overburdened with brains', that 'the buckhounds is the job for him!' Yet Benjamin Disraeli†, no sufferer of fools, commended his 'excellent sense and tact'.[5] He died childless at Bessborough in January 1880. He was succeeded as earl of Bessborough by his brothers Frederick George (1815-95) and Walter William (1821-1906), a clergyman.

[1] D. Howell-Thomas, *Duncannon: Reformer and Reconciler*, 80, 83-84, 189. [2] K. Bourne, *Palmerston*, 428; Howell-Thomas, 184-5, 187-9; P. Mandler, *Aristocratic Government in Age of Reform*, 75. [3] Reid, *Lord Durham*, i. 65; ii. 20-22, 27; *Lieven-Palmerston Corresp.* 113; Howell-Thomas, 190-2. [4] Sir J. Ponsonby, *Ponsonby Fam.* (1929), 151. [5] Ibid.; *Disraeli Letters*, v. 2216.

D.R.F./P.J.S.

PONSONBY, John William, Visct. Duncannon (1781–1847).[1]

KNARESBOROUGH	25 Mar. 1805–1806
HIGHAM FERRERS	15 June 1810–1812
MALTON	1812–1826
CO. KILKENNY	1826–1832
NOTTINGHAM	1832–19 July 1834

b. 31 Aug. 1781, 1st s. of Frederick Ponsonby†, 3rd earl of Bessborough [I] and 3rd Bar. Ponsonby [GB], and Lady Henrietta Frances Spencer, da. of John Spencer†, 1st Earl Spencer; bro. of Hon. Frederick Cavendish Ponsonby* and Hon. William Francis Spencer Ponsonby*. *educ.* Harrow 1790-8; Christ Church, Oxf. 1799; continental tour 1800, 1802-3. *m.* 16 Nov. 1805, Lady Maria Fane, da. of John, 10th earl of Westmorland, 7s. (2 *d.v.p.*) 6da. *cr.* Bar. Duncannon [UK] 19 July 1834; *suc.* fa. as 4th earl of Bessborough [I] and 4th Bar. Ponsonby [GB] 3 Feb. 1844. *d.* 16 May 1847.

PC 23 Feb. 1831; first commr. of woods, forests and land revenues Feb. 1831-July 1834, May 1835-Sept. 1841; sec. of state for home affairs July-Nov. 1834; ld. privy seal Apr. 1835-Jan. 1840; ld. lt. [I] July 1846-*d.*

Ld. lt. co. Carlow 1831-8, co. Kilkenny 1838-*d.*

Lt.-col. commdt. Marylebone vols. 1803; vice-pres. County Fire Office 1816.

Duncannon, 'the great manager' of Brooks's deemed by Greville to be 'addicted to politics', was closely connected with the inner circle of leading Whigs (though he married outside it), who included his cousins Lord Althorp* and the 6th duke of Devonshire, and his brother-in-law William Lamb*, later Lord Melbourne.[2] To 'atone for his silence' in debate he had become 'indefatigable in his attendance' and since 1815 had performed the duties of Whig whip, in which capacity, 'although his manners were cold, if not forbidding, and he had little of the address or dexterity which distinguished the Tory whipper-in, Mr. [William] Holmes*, he contrived, by the exercise of more honest arts, especially a great readiness to oblige ... to be eminently successful'.[3] He frequently acted as an opposition teller in divisions.

At the 1820 general election Duncannon was again returned unopposed *in absentia* for the 2nd Earl Fitzwilliam's borough of Malton.[4] 'The elections have gone very good' and in Scotland 'we are much better off than I expected', he advised Lord Grey next month, urging him to 'come up after Easter'.[5] He backed the opposition campaign in support of Queen Caroline later that year, although privately he considered it 'quite shocking to have the country put into such a state for such a person'.[6] According to his wife's kinswoman Mrs. Arbuthnot, 28 Sept. 1820, he was 'quite sure the bill of pains and penalties would last for years' in the Commons, for he 'could name at least twenty persons' who 'would impede the proceedings and do everything in their power to weary the House and get them to dismiss the bill'. He 'alarmed' her by predicting that ministers would 'divide very ill' with 'about 40 majority' against the motion condemning the omission of Caroline's name from the liturgy, 26 Jan. 1821, but in the event they obtained 101.[7] He appears to have assumed responsibility for writing all the opposition attendance notes from about this time, when George Tierney retired as leader, until the accession of a Whig ministry and the appointment of Edward Ellice* as patronage secretary in 1830.[8] He was a majority teller for Catholic claims, 28 Feb. 1821. Commenting on the relief bill's success, 23 Mar., the radical Whig Henry Grey Bennet* noted that 'several of our enemies' had decided to 'vote no more' and that 'Duncannon tells me he knows of many who have come to the same resolution'.[9] Duncannon and Holmes 'agreed that we should have a majority of 38 if the whole House were to attend', reported Joesph Phillimore* the following day.[10] Next month Duncannon unwittingly asked the duke of Norfolk to canvass the husband of his divorced wife, Lord Lucan, in support of the bill in the Lords. 'How awkward he must have felt when he remembered what a mistake he had made', commented Henry Fox*.[11] He voted for parliamentary reform, 9 May 1821, 25 Apr. 1822, 20 Feb., 24 Apr., 2 June 1823, 13, 27 Apr. 1826. He was part of the 'large party' of the Commons who dined with the queen at the lord mayor's, 21 June 1821.[12] He later blamed ministers for the disturbances at her funeral, telling Grey that 'never was there such short sighted folly' as when they 'determined that the City would not show the queen their marks of respect'. Thereafter he assisted the campaign to vindicate Sir Robert Wilson*, who he believed had not 'done anything that ought to subject him to the sort of language that the government are making use of against him'.[13]

Early in 1822 Duncannon implored Grey to 'be in town before Parliament meets', as all our friends 'look to you' and 'it will give general satisfaction if you will call them together, in fact it is the only possible means of having any meeting'.[14] On 15 Apr. Canning thanked him for 'clearing Tuesday 30th' for his motion to relieve Catholic peers.[15] On 13 July Hume informed him of his 'intention to oppose several of the grants in the supply' and requested that he arrange 'a full attendance'.[16] On 7 Oct. 1822, however, Lord Holland warned him that Hume's attacks on the funds were reconciling 'all Tories' and that '*entre nous*, I think it was the tone of your opposition ... at the beginning of last session, which saved the "*sinking fund*" and prevented the Whigs instead of Canning being sent for on Castlereagh's death', adding, 'your strong ground for contest is Ireland', for 'the more Canning can divert attention from thence to public credit and reform the stronger he will be'.[17] Writing in similar terms, 2 Mar. 1823, Henry Brougham* recommended 'a little more discretion' with respect to Hume's more 'absurd and untenable' propositions, explaining, 'I prefer addressing these suggestions to you, as [John] Lambton* (to whom I intended at first to write) is ailing and may not like the trouble of talking over the subjects'.[18] That month Althorp asked Brougham about 'some plan of a republican form of government for the opposition', concerning which 'Lambton and Duncannon, I believe, have written to you', saying, 'I think it rather a bad plan, but ... if you approve of it I shall not object'.[19] On 19 Mar. James Abercromby* recounted how Duncannon had shown him 'a long paper', the object of which was 'to unite the whole body ... opposed to ministers by means of a sort of dinner club', to which his reaction was that 'to unite 200 people in all points is hopeless, and if we can agree on leading questions ... it would be all that ... can be hoped'. A week later he saw that Duncannon had 'struck out of the paper ... some of the most objectionable passages' and observed, 'we shall see how far it is possible ... to extract from these dinners the means of establishing some plan that may give more effect to future operations'.[20] He presented a petition for the abolition of slavery, 4 June.[21] On 11 Aug. 1824 George Agar Ellis* encountered the Duncannons on their way to Bessborough and noted how 'this being their first visit to Ireland, they were in the midst of a most amusingly innocent surprise at the strangeness of the people and the country'.[22]

Urging Grey to come up, Duncannon insisted that 'no one' could 'so well expose the iniquitous conduct of the government', who were 'doing their utmost to put Ireland into rebellion' by suppressing the Catholic Association, 18 Feb. 1825.[23] On the 21st he and Tierney went 'over the list of the House with a view to the Catholic question' and correctly concluded that the measure would 'be carried'.[24] He presented a petition for relief, 23 Feb., for which he was a majority teller, 1 Mar., 21 Apr., 10 May.[25] From Ireland, 2 Sept. he advised Grey that the country

> never was so quiet as it is at this moment, and it can only be attributed to a decided union among the Catholics ... and a determination to put aside all minor grievances and quarrels for the purpose of prosecuting their claims ... They talk now only of the means of opposing the government, and ... they never will consent again to have the question clogged with any other measure.

On 2 Dec. 1825 he added that 'the Catholics are violent upon their intentions' and 'if [William] Plunket* should persuade the Association ... not to present their petition', it 'will give very general disgust'.[26] He declined to attend the Association dinner for the 'friends of civil and religious liberty', 2 Feb. 1826.[27] Finding that his brother Frederick had decided not to come to England at the impending dissolution, he told Holland, 10 Apr. 1826, 'I fear I must make up my mind to go over for some time to Ireland and stand for Kilkenny, where we shall have a contest'.[28] On 1 June Lady Carlisle reported that he had gone 'for six months' and that 'Lord Normanby is to come in for Malton instead of Higham Ferrers, in case the latter should be wanted for Duncannon'.[29] 'The opposition do not seem to be exerting themselves much and Lord Duncannon (their chief manager) is gone to Ireland', remarked Mrs. Arbuthnot, 10 June:

> Lady Duncannon and her eleven children are also gone, to her great joy, for he is become a great flirt and is encouraged in neglecting her by her own sister, Lady Jersey, who does all she possibly can to engross him entirely to herself ... In Ireland Lady Duncannon has her husband to herself and, as he is *au fond* very amiable and domestic, he devotes himself there to her and his children, and she consequently means to keep him there as much as she can'.[30]

At the general election Duncannon duly stood for county Kilkenny on the family interest as 'a friend to civil and religious liberty'. The newly formed independent club having got up an opposition, in case of failure Devonshire seated him at Bandon Bridge. After a five-day contest, however, he was returned in second place for the county, for which he chose to sit. At the declaration he promised not to be 'an absentee' and to 'come to Ireland every year'.[31] Next month he notified Holland that the Waterford election, at which he had 'been on the spot from the beginning', had been 'a very great triumph for the Catholics' and 'conducted much to their credit':

> I think, however, it has opened a new view of the state of Ireland as connected with the Catholic question, and not a very pleasing one to those who have property here, if that question is not speedily put to rest. The priests have tried their strength and succeeded against the landlords, and ... unless something is soon done ... the whole power, at present in the south of Ireland, will be in their hands.[32]

On 20 Aug. 1826 Lord Lansdowne reported finding the Duncannons

> living with no society but their numerous progeny. She is expecting hourly to be confined, he most usefully occupied with his own affairs, of which it is fortunate that

he has taken measure, for they have been cruelly mismanaged [although] with his excellent sense and determined will, he cannot fail to do much for himself and his family.[33]

He became a vice-president of Dr. Murray's Education Society for the free instruction of the poor founded at the end of that year.[34]

Commenting on rumours of a negotiation to bring Lansdowne into the Liverpool ministry, 22 Jan. 1827, Mrs. Arbuthnot noted that 'Duncannon says it is nearly concluded and, as he is not of Lord Lansdowne's party, he is against it'.[35] He brought up petitions for Catholic claims, 27 Feb., 10 Apr. Following Lord Liverpool's stroke, he was one of those who met at Norfolk House 'to go through the list of Members' and 'learn the strength of the unbending parties' for the forthcoming division on Catholic relief, for which he was a minority teller, 6 Mar.[36] He assured Grey, 29 Mar., that the vote reflected the 'present new turn of affairs' rather 'than the real state of the question' and that 'the majority was principally owing' to the fact that Members 'voted on the question of whether Peel or Canning should govern us'.[37] He was a minority teller for Tierney's amendment to withhold the supplies, 30 Mar., and inquiry into the Irish estimates, 5 Apr., and was reported to be 'bent on voting' for Lethbridge's motion asking the king to appoint an administration united on the Catholic question, which was withdrawn next day.[38] Following the appointment of Canning as premier, 12 Apr., Duncannon told Wilson, a Whig supporter of the new ministry:

Though we differ ... upon this subject, I do not think we do to as great a degree as you think, for I am decidedly of opinion that Canning's government is to be supported, if it is possible ... but I cannot go the length of saying that if a Protestant majority should be insisted on in the cabinet that I should think any great gain had been accomplished ... That one may be formed with a few Protestants in it, which will give us a hope of a better system of government, I allow ... but unless it is clearly understood how it is circumstanced in relation to ... [the Catholic] question, I do think it would be a complete dereliction of principle in opposition to give support ... I do not say that the ... question must be immediately forced upon them, or any step taken to prevent their going on, if it should appear that their government is formed on liberal principles, but if they have allowed themselves to be pledged against a question of such importance, I cannot express any great joy at the change.[39]

On 14 Apr. Sir James Macdonald* urged Lansdowne to accept office in a government 'formed *without any restrictions* on the Catholic question', saying that 'Duncannon, backed by Lord Sefton* and some of the most unlikely men, is of the opinion that nineteen in twenty so think. He tells me too that the opposition was computed by the late ministry at 220; but that it may be fairly taken at 200, he having 180 on his list to write notes to'.[40] The duke of Bedford complained, 22 Apr., 'I regret that such men as Duncannon and Ebrington can talk of giving an unqualified support to Canning, solely to deny the intolerant ministers from returning, of which I think there is no chance whatsoever, if the Whigs present an unbroken phalanx'.[41] Two days later Lord Binning* reported a 'schism among the Whigs' on the question of whether Lansdowne should enter the cabinet without the appointment of a pro-Catholic Irish government, with 'Grey, Tierney, Duncannon, and *they say* Holland being adverse'.[42] On the 26th Lansdowne, who had accepted office following the appointment of Lamb as Irish secretary, told Devonshire that 'Duncannon approves decidedly of the arrangement in its present form and enters exactly into my feelings about it'.[43] Three days later Charles Williams Wynn*, president of the board of control, informed Canning that he had ascertained 'that the charge of *malignancy* against Lord Duncannon was quite groundless and that he both he and his brother have been uniformly anxious and active to promote the junction', adding, 'he might therefore be advantageously taken into council'.[44] Describing the 'strange' scene in the House resulting from the new arrangements, Thomas Creevey* remarked that 'Duncannon now counts noses on the other side, and sits on the treasury bench', 6 May.[45] A few days later, however, it was noted by Lady Jersey that

Duncannon seems as much out of sorts as possible. To me he says *very little*, for it did so happen that at an early period of these transactions, upon my saying that I was sure that Canning as prime minister would *not* be at liberty to act as he might wish about the Catholic question, Duncannon told me that I was completely mistaken, that he *knew* the contrary to be the case, and that he did in consequence do all he could to promote the junction.[46]

He was in the majority against ministers for the disfranchisement of Penryn, 28 May, after which Mrs. Arbuthnot met him

and some others afterwards at Lady Jersey's and they were quite jumping for joy. However, true to the system, though Duncannon told me he had never been so pleased in all his life, he went the next morning to Mr. Planta and pretended he was excessively sorry and lamented it very much! However, Mr. Canning is too sharp to be deceived by such falseness.[47]

Following the defeat of the government's corn bill in the Lords, 2 June, Greville observed that Duncannon, who 'is entirely in the confidence of the moderate Whig party, says it is impossible the thing can go on in this way', and that if the peers in the household who had voted against ministers were 'not dismissed', it would 'be such a proof of the feebleness of government as will disgust all the Whigs and make their support very lukewarm'. On 17 June he reported that Duncannon had told him the Whigs were 'extremely dissatisfied' and 'want Canning to display his power by some signal act of authority', and that the refusal of Lord Manners, the staunchly Protestant Irish chancellor, to appoint Sir Patrick Bellew*, a Catholic, to the commission of the peace had 'so disgusted Duncannon that he was very near withdrawing his name from the commission, and if he had his example would have been followed by many others ... [but] Lord Spencer dissuaded him'.[48] Commenting on the ministry's difficulties, 6 July, Charles Arbuthnot* noted that Holmes had complained that the Whigs up to the very last day of the session 'would not consent to receive treasury notes, and that they never would attend unless they were summoned by Lord Duncannon'.[49] Later that month Duncannon did not find Ireland 'in so comfortable a state as he expected'.[50] Following the appointment of Lord Goderich as premier, under whom Lansdowne remained home secretary, Duncannon wrote to Abercromby, 19 Aug.:

> I never expected the king to surrender to [the] Whigs; as it is, I think Lord Lansdowne has decided rightly ... If the king will consent to certain measures, which from the temper of the times, and more particularly of Parliament, is absolutely necessary, retrenchment among the first, it may go on, otherwise I know in the Commons it cannot. You are not perhaps aware to what an extent the government would be deserted, if they did not appear when Parliament meets to be seriously engaged on this subject ... Do not think I am making difficulties, but I am bound to say what I know will happen.

On 31 Aug. he assured Lansdowne of his

> entire concurrence in what you have done. I am quite aware of the difficulties of your present situation, but as those difficulties increase, you have a right to expect the support of those who have forced them upon you ... For the sake of this country in particular I should deplore any change, if it is practicable to carry on the present government. The Catholics generally and notwithstanding all you may hear, are satisfied, and I am persuaded that if a change was now to take place that satisfaction would turn to complete despair ... Circumstances may occur to make it impossible for the present government to go on, but I do think the clamour of many of our friends most unreasonable and unfair. I would only ask them to witness the feeling expressed by the Tories in Ireland at the prospect of a change.[51]

'We owe all our misfortunes to a little faction at Brooks's, consisting of Brougham ... Wilson ... Burdett, and Duncannon', Bedford, who disapproved of the new arrangements, complained that month, adding, 'each had his own views, and it is no difficult matter to surmise by what their views were directed'.[52] On 9 Sept. Sir John Newport* assured Holland that Duncannon 'thinks very much as you do respecting this business, but tells me that many of our friends feel and express great dissatisfaction. One in particular wrote him that he supposed Peel would be the next person introduced into the cabinet'.[53] Explaining his support to Althorp a week later, Duncannon observed:

> I should have regretted that Lord Lansdowne had gone out on the appointment of [John] Herries* [to the exchequer] ... I cannot think the appointment of a man without weight in Parliament or political connections in the country was a good reason for retiring. I will in short support, not from approving, but from dreading the return of those who have been put out ... The generality of the Catholics are beginning to feel some confidence, notwithstanding the untoward appearance of some of the Irish appointments, and if Lord Anglesey is really coming [as viceroy] with a determination not to inquire into the religious opinions of any man the best results must be expected.[54]

Writing in similar terms to Holland, 29 Sept., Duncannon added that he remained opposed to asking the Catholics to halt their campaign:

> It is true that Ireland must be benefited by having a Catholic secretary and Lord Lansdowne as home secretary ... but ... I should deeply regret ... attempts ... by persons connected with the government to induce the Catholics to forgo their petition. To this at least I will not be a party, and be assured if successful at the present moment, it would be ruinous ... I have written to Althorp some time since, but have not heard from him. I fear from what I hear we do not agree.

Assuring Holland that the Catholics would support government 'if they find that the report industriously circulated here is not true (that the Catholic question is to be postponed)', 10 Oct., he continued:

> From Althorp I heard the other day; not a satisfactory letter. He talks of neutrality, which I confess from so sensible a person surprizes me, because in the present state of things it is impossible. Neutrality, as I have tried to explain to him, is in fact opposition, and if he succeeds in pursuing it, he does that which he dreads [and] makes the king powerful by weakening his government. I rather fear ... that Lords Tavistock* and Milton* have also taken this fancy of strict neutrality ... Does it not appear to you an odd way to accomplish their end?

Later that month he confirmed that 'Althorp, [Lord] Milton, etc., look at the present state of things in a very different light from us', having 'taken a line which must be fatal to any government formed like the present', and asked, 'are government taking any steps to ascertain who are friends and who foes? If they are not, no time should be lost ... [as] when Parliament meets it will be too late to do so and ... I know that six months ago this was not attended to'.[55] Relaying his remarks to Lansdowne, 2 Dec. 1827, Holland observed that Duncannon

> is a great oracle on such matters and ... it is right you should know what is said by so sincere and judicious a friend. You should impress on Huskisson as I did on ... Canning the necessity of unreserved and frequent communication with him on the state of temper of the House.[56]

That month Lady Caroline Lamb, in the final stages of a fatal illness, told Lady Duncannon that she never heard Duncannon's name 'without crying', as 'all the under people and Dr. Roe told me he was the person [who] spoke most severely against me and wanted me locked up in a madhouse, so that I feared his very name'. On 26 Jan. 1828 he was notified of her death.[57]

Following the appointment of Wellington as premier, Newport informed Holland, 15 Jan. 1828, that Duncannon had for 'some time' speculated that Goderich was 'wholly unsuited to take the lead' and 'that the fabric disjointed by his vacillation must soon fall to pieces'.[58] He was a majority teller for repeal of the Test Acts, 26 Feb., presented petitions for Catholic claims, 28 Feb., 15 Apr., and was a majority teller for relief, 12 May, after which he agreed with Sir Francis Burdett* and Brougham 'that the line to take was that of moderate satisfaction at the lowered tone of the enemy, and an expectation ... that if the Catholics persevere they must succeed'.[59] He was named by the cabinet minister Lord Ellenborough among those who 'would willingly act with the government if Lord Grey belonged to it', in a statement to Wellington, 28 May.[60] He successfully moved for the printing of papers on the grand jury and constabulary of county Kilkenny, 18 July. That month he advised Ellenborough that Daniel O'Connell* 'would not be quiet' following his return for county Clare.[61] On 6 Aug. Richard Sheil* informed O'Connell that Duncannon had ascertained from Holland that there were '*great doubts* as to ... your admissibility'.[62] Writing to Grey from Ireland, 16 Sept., Duncannon reported that the 'greatest expectations' had been raised by Wellington's rumoured intention to concede emancipation, but feared that the 'moment is gone for making such a measure' because the Association, whose power 'is at present beyond belief', had 'mixed up their question with parliamentary reform'.[63] On 27 Sept. he confronted O'Connell about demanding pledges from candidates in support of emancipation and reform:

> I differ from you, not because I object to the subjects alluded to or undervalue their importance, but because I think the first of such paramount consequence that the mixing any other matter with it weakens the first pledge ... You have now brought the Catholic question to that point that it must be successful unless it is marred by some unfortunate and unexpected circumstance ... Wellington ... will not easily extricate himself from what his speech fairly conveyed ... but ... if he was called on to name the means of relieving himself from some of the difficulty, he could not devise a more likely one ... than raising in his opponents' ranks a question like parliamentary reform. I would require a *positive* and *distinct pledge* from every Irish Member to oppose any government that does not make the Catholic question its object, but I would do this simply and in such a way that it could not be evaded ... I am actuated only ... by an anxiety to forward the Catholic cause, and by a conviction ... that the introduction of other matters must injure that cause.[64]

Visiting the Duncannons at Bessborough that autumn, Creevey admired their patronage of the nearby village of Piltown. On 23 Oct. he accompanied Lady Duncannon to a Munster provincial meeting of the friends of civil and religious liberty 'in an immense Catholic chapel' at Kilkenny where

> Duncannon was to be voted into the chair, and as he could not be so without making a speech, *she* was nervous to the greatest degree, public speaking being quite out of his line. However, he acquitted himself to ... the satisfaction of all; and upon my saying to her, 'Come! We are in port now: nothing can be better than this', she said, 'How surprised I am how well he is speaking!', and then, having shed some tears, she was quite comfortable ... It was a prodigious day for Duncannon for, with the exception of Power and Tighe, not one of the Protestant gentry present gave Duncannon a vote at the last election, nor did they ever attend a Catholic meeting before.

Describing the meeting to Grey, 9 Nov., Duncannon remarked that if Protestants 'in other places' had attended similar ones, 'there would have been much less of the violent language that has been so much complained of'. 'That [Wellington] will do something is probable', he added, 'but it is equally probable that he will push an adjustment that will give general dissatisfaction, I mean an alteration in the elective franchise'.[65] That month Mrs. Arbuthnot put Wellington 'on his guard' against further communication with Lady Jersey about the details of emancipation, as 'through Lord Duncannon, it all went to the Catholic Association'.[66]

Duncannon brought up petitions for repeal of the Irish Vestry and Subletting Acts, 26 Feb., 27 Mar. 1829. He presented petitions for Catholic emancipation, 26 Feb., 4 Mar., and voted accordingly, 6, 30 Mar. He had been listed by Planta, the patronage secretary, as 'opposed to securities' in late February, and with Althorp had seen Arbuthnot 'two or three times' to say 'they would oppose such a measure as would disfranchise the freeholders'.[67] On 4 Mar. Greville noted that Duncannon had declared that 'nothing shall induce him to support it, and he would rather defeat the whole measure than consent to it'.[68] Writing to Maurice Fitzgerald* from Ireland, 7 Mar., Lord Donoughmore observed:

> I was always aware that Duncannon would be outrageous on the subject of the 40*s*. freeholders. When he was in this country, I thought him inclined to go to lengths unbecoming a man of his rank. I am not intimate with him, but as far as I know him, I do not estimate highly his intellectual powers ... One must chose a lesser evil in order to avoid a greater ... If there be many persons of Duncannon's feelings in the ... Commons, who would vote against the general bill on account of the disfranchisement of the freeholders, it will at least have this bad effect, that it will not go up to the Lords in as triumphant a manner as was originally hoped.[69]

In his first known speech, 10 Mar., Duncannon announced his opposition to the disfranchisement bill. On the 18th he presented and endorsed a hostile petition, observing that it would have been 'much more agreeable' and consonant with his 'usual habits to have given a silent vote' against this 'most unjust' measure, but that he felt obliged to state his objections, since his opinions were 'exactly the reverse' of those of his 'usual political associates'. Next day he explained that he had agreed to the 40*s*. freeholder franchise being 'given up' in 1825 because it had not then been used in a 'constitutional manner', but argued that it had since been exercised legitimately and called for the safeguards against abuses of the new £10 franchise to be applied to the 'whole constituent body'. On 20 Mar. he moved for the committee on the bill to implement measures against the fraudulent registration of 40*s*. freeholders. 'Painful as it is to me, at all times, to stand up in the House', he declared, 'and much more painful, when it is to oppose those with whom I am accustomed to agree, I have made up my mind ... if the £10 freeholder can be made a *bona fide* freeholder by this Act, so can the 40*s*. freeholder'. His motion, for which he was a minority teller, was crushed by 220-20. On 26 Mar. he announced that he would desist from further opposition, but without abandoning his objections. 'Duncannon has resumed his sane senses', commented Althorp, 'although he will vote against the disfranchisement bill, but he admits that he hopes the whole measure will succeed'.[70] That day Duncannon 'begged' Henry Grattan not to move an amendment enabling O'Connell to take his seat, as it might be an 'impediment to the success of the measure'.[71] Following the passage of emancipation, Arbuthnot informed Peel, the home secretary, 15 Apr., that Duncannon had spoken about the ministry's 'thanks to the Whigs' and 'said what had fallen from you in our House and from the duke in his had been quite perfect, and so had been thought by those who did not wish to make mischief'.[72] They 'had a long conversation ... on the state of parties generally', recounted Mrs. Arbuthnot, in which Duncannon

> appeared to think there were many persons in the Houses of Lords and Commons who, if the Grey party became connected with the government, would join. He abused Lord Lansdowne most violently, said nobody ever had behaved so ill or so shabbily as he did when he joined Canning, that he completely left all his party in the lurch and gave up all their political objects and that they had all determined to oppose if the Canning government had met Parliament again. I don't pay much attention to what Lord Duncannon says as I think him about the most dishonest politician I know, and his connection with O'Connell and the Catholic Association is a disgrace to him.[73]

That day O'Connell reported that Duncannon had gone to see Vesey Fitzgerald, president of the board of trade, to ascertain whether ministers would continue to oppose his admission. Two days later Ellenborough saw Duncannon at Lady Jersey's talking 'big about O'Connell's power and, in the same sense in which he talked to Fitzgerald, wishing to induce the government to let him take his seat'.[74] On 15 May Duncannon, having 'fixed' a day for this 'grand experiment', guided O'Connell 'through the necessary forms in the steward's office' and presented him to the Speaker in the hope that he would be permitted to take his seat without swearing the old oath of supremacy.[75] This was refused, following which he obtained leave for O'Connell to be 'heard in support of his claims' that day and was a minority teller for allowing him to take his seat unhindered, 18 May. In his last known votes in this Parliament, he divided for the transfer of East Retford's seats to Birmingham, 5 May, and for the issue of a new writ, 2 June, and against the grant for the marble arch sculpture, 25 May. Congratulating O'Connell on his unopposed re-election for Clare, 4 Aug., he regretted that the 'very dangerous illness of Lady Duncannon after her confinement' had prevented him from writing sooner and declared, 'there is no one who is more sincerely rejoiced than I am at your triumph', as 'any other result ... would have disgraced this country, who must ever look to you as having mainly contributed to the great measure of Catholic emancipation'.[76] Giving Grey 'anything but a good account' of the government of the duke of Northumberland, the new Irish viceroy, 31 Aug., he acknowledged the 'visible improvement' in the 'quiet counties' since emancipation, but apprehended 'a new spirit' in others, in which the 'old system will be overthrown'. On 4 Nov. 1829 he warned that 'nothing can persuade the people they can have justice, they have so long been prosecuted by tithe proctors'.[77] That autumn Lord Francis Leveson Gower, the Irish secretary, reported finding him 'very eager' on the Irish grand jury laws, but 'not at all I think sweeping or irrational'.[78] No trace of parliamentary activity has been found for the 1830 session.

At the 1830 general election Duncannon offered again for county Kilkenny, stressing his support for emancipation, liberty of the press, tax reductions and economy. He was returned unopposed.[79] 'I see the papers talk of government losing 23 or 24 by the Irish elections', Agar Ellis informed Brougham, 15 Aug., adding, 'if you write to Duncannon, express to him the absolute necessity of his being in England in October so that he may take his measures betimes'.[80] Sending Brougham a 'rough statement' of the Irish returns, which were 'more against the government than in England', 27 Aug., Duncannon observed:

> You will ... see a very obstreperous set from this country. The people are for the first time looking to the conduct of their representatives and ... they will be very cautious of supporting government. There are many returned for England whose names I do not know, and I cannot therefore make out a list, and of Scotland I know little. Upon the whole I should say they have lost near 30 ... The great thing ... against them more than the actual return, is the spirit that has shown itself both in England and in Ireland.[81]

On 30 Aug. Russell reported having 'heard one bad thing for the ministry ... Duncannon is coming over to oppose them; he approves of the duke and Peel, but cannot support the ragged regiment of Goulburn and Twiss'.[82] He was of course listed by the Irish agent Pierce Mahony† as a 'contra' and by Planta as one of the ministry's 'foes', but he was absent from the crucial division on the civil list, 15 Nov. Following the appointment of Grey as premier, he was one of those who persuaded Brougham to accept the lord chancellorship.[83] That month, 'on account of his acquaintance with borough history and details, more especially in Ireland', he became one of the 'committee of four' responsible for the drafting of the reform bills.[84] It was later claimed by Russell that Duncannon had supported Lord Durham's proposal to adopt the ballot at the desire of Althorp, the chancellor of the exchequer.[85] Duncannon was a signatory to the committee's 'report on the state of the representation' submitted to Grey, 14 Jan. 1831, and the author of the Irish 'plan of reform', which was later taken up by Smith Stanley, the Irish secretary. In an 'explanation' of its clauses, 26 Jan., Duncannon recommended that in the boroughs the new householder franchise be raised from £10 to £12, as there was 'no regular mode of rating', and that the term of registry be reduced from eight to three years, as 'persons so often change their residence'.[86] Neither proposal was adopted. He 'did not think it right' for a minister (as he then was) to join the Irish Members who expressed concerns to Smith Stanley about the bill later that year, but privately he advised him: 'I agree with them entirely in two of their objections', on 'the question of value', where 'every sort of fraud will be practised', and registration, which 'I beg you to consider' taking 'at special sessions', as 'the greatest inconvenience is felt by the people' in the 'delay of county business at quarter sessions, and this of course will be much increased by the increase of registry'. On 3 June 1831 he urged Smith Stanley to ascertain what would 'be the effect of admitting leaseholders in the different counties ... particularly Tipperary', as 'my belief is that it will nearly double the number of voters in that county; I know it will in Kilkenny'.[87]

On 2 Feb. 1831 Agar Ellis, who had resigned as first commissioner of woods and forests, received 'a note from Duncannon to say he is appointed my successor', as which 'he will do very well'.[88] That day Duncannon assured Smith Stanley that he had 'no apprehensions' about his re-election, but Holland feared that it would 'not be convenient to vacate his county just now'.[89] 'I am much pleased with Duncannon's appointment', commented Bedford, 3 Feb., but 'I hope and trust Duncannon's *ci devant* friend O'Connell may not be able to do him any mischief'.[90] On 7 Feb. O'Connell notified Alexander Dawson* that

> Duncannon is a man for whom I have the highest respect ... but he is now 'one of my prosecutors' and as the ministry are determined to *crush* me, I must carry the political war into their quarters ... If the *prosecutions* be not forthwith withdrawn, I will be obliged to *give* Lord Duncannon a violent contest and perhaps a complete defeat ... I console myself for the feeling of ingratitude

> towards Lord Duncannon by giving this warn[ing] – *Valeat quantum*.[91]

Anglesey 'deplored' that he was 'not upon the spot' in the ensuing contest against a Repealer and feared he would be beaten because of a 'great dearth of money', 22 Feb. 'He has been living at his estate and done more good and acquired more influence than most Irish landlords', observed Greville, 'but O'Connell holds up his finger and not a soul dares support him'. A few days later, however, reports emerged of his probable success.[92] This would be 'a tremendous blow to the wretch O'Connell ... but above all it would be a signal and well deserved triumph' to the 'whole family', commented Creevey, 25 Feb.[93] After a six-day poll he was returned *in absentia*.[94] He and O'Connell reputedly 'met a week after as if nothing had happened' and 'understood one another better from that day'.[95] He introduced a departmental bill to alter the boundaries of the Forest of Dean, 11 Mar., which he guided through its second, 31 Mar., and third reading, 16 Apr. On 20 Mar. he urged Grey to 'press upon' Smith Stanley and Plunket, the Irish lord chancellor, the necessity of dropping the proceedings against O'Connell, as 'a slight punishment will only tempt him to do all the mischief he can', while 'a severe punishment would I know be considered by almost all those who are supporting your government as unjust'. 'I am aware of the difficulties of letting him off', he added, but it would 'give you a hold over him greater than you can in any other way obtain'. The charges were soon dropped, whereupon Duncannon assured Grey, 29 Mar., that O'Connell will offer the reform bill 'his entire support' and 'do his best to prevent the agitation of any other question'. [96] Shortly before the reform bill's introduction, Thomas Macaulay* had reported that Duncannon, 'who knows the House of Commons better than any other man it, Billy Holmes excepted', was 'quite confident of success', 7 Mar.[97] Following the ministry's defeat on the timber duties, however, Maurice Fitzgerald* told Wellington, 19 Mar., that Duncannon believed 'the division proves the reform bill will be defeated on the second reading' and 'will advise Grey', over whom he 'has great influence', 'to dissolve Parliament immediately'.[98] He was a majority teller for its second reading, 22 Mar., when Macualay related how 'the tellers scarcely got through the crowd, for the House was thronged up to the table ... but you might have heard a pin drop as Duncannon read the numbers'.[99] He presented a Kilkenny petition for the Irish bill, 30 Mar. On 7 Apr. he went 'through all the alterations' to the bill with Althorp, Lord Durham and Sir James Graham* and was observed by Herries 'sowing promises and threats in all directions to catch or nullify votes', in which 'hitherto, according to our accounts, he has had little success'.[100] He defended his department's plans for a new street to Waterloo bridge, 18 Apr. 1831. Next day he was a minority teller against Gascoyne's wrecking amendment to the reform bill: he had previously advised Greville that 'he did not believe the ministers would be beaten, but if they were they should certainly dissolve instantly', and that '*he* should have liked to dissolve long ago, but they owed it to their friends not to have recourse to a dissolution if they could help it'.[101]

At the ensuing general election Duncannon offered again for county Kilkenny, insisting that the election was only about reform, on which he rested his claims.[102] He had been advised by O'Connell, who was now supplying him with regular Irish election reports, that he had no need to 'think of the election or to come over', but, concerned at rumours of another opposition, he asked O'Connell for support, 27 Apr., explaining, 'I have talked so openly to you ... that I can have no difficulty in saying ... that I am anxious not to be taken away ... for a longer time than is necessary, as great exertions are needed here against the opposers of the bill'. O'Connell assured him that the repeal candidate had withdrawn, saying he '*put* the compliment on me of having declined in consequence of my letter to him, but I am too candid to do so by you'.[103] At the nomination Duncannon commended the reform bill for 'extinguishing non-resident voters' and 'annihilating the disgraceful system of borough nomination'. Pressed on the Irish measure, he declared that he saw 'no objection' to an increase of Members, but that 'they should also recall that 19 close Irish boroughs were to be opened, which would virtually increase the representation of the people'. He was returned unopposed.[104] 'Upon the whole the elections are going better than I expected', he informed Grey, 10 May 1831.[105]

On 23 June 1831 Duncannon introduced bills for repairs to Buckingham House garden wall and the construction of a new street to Waterloo bridge, and reintroduced the Dean Forest boundaries bill, which he defended at its second reading, 27 June. (It received royal assent as 1 and 2 Gul. IV, c. 12 on 2 Aug.) He clashed repeatedly with Hume over the costs of the wall bill, 28 June, but successfully guided it through the House to become law as 1 and 2 Gul. IV, c. 1 on 11 July. He rebutted criticism of the Waterloo bill, 8, 11 July, when he insisted that 'the woods and forests are now very differently managed to what they were formerly; not a shilling can now be laid out without the sanction of Parliament'. (It received royal assent as 1 and 2 Gul. IV, c. 29 on 27 Sept.) He was a government teller for the second reading of the reintroduced reform bill, 6 July, and in many of the subsequent divisions on its details. On 12 July he complained in debate that Irish tithes had been calculated in a 'way most favourable to the clergyman', with 'reference to the prices of grain in the seven years from 1814 to 1821'. He was a minority teller against disqualification of the Dublin election committee, 29 July, and voted with his ministerial colleagues on the controversy, 23 Aug. Warning Grey of how 'disinclined your *friends* in Parliament from Ireland are for coming here', 31 July, he blamed the 'unfortunate misunderstanding in all our Irish appointments, in every case putting in enemies and rejecting friends', and asked how 'can you hope to carry a Catholic population by such measures?'[106] He upheld complaints that Catholics had been excluded from the Kilkenny jury, 10 Aug., and next day divided in the minority for printing the Waterford petition for disarming the Irish yeomanry, saying that it was with 'extreme regret' that he differed from Althorp, but that he felt obliged to support the 'feelings of the people ... who consider that they suffer under unredressed wrongs'. Holland deemed it 'lamentable' that he 'voted against the government'.[107] On 11 Aug. Duncannon, at the behest of the Irish Members, who had given assurances that they were 'not actuated by any feeling of hostility', urged Grey to receive a deputation from them, but at their ensuing meeting they threatened to go into opposition unless there was a change in the government's Irish policy. By then Duncannon had taken his wife to Ireland following the death of their second son William on foreign naval service. 'I can easily get a pair' and 'have nothing that ... presses except Buckingham Palace, which Ellice will kindly undertake to do for me', he informed Grey, 14 Aug.[108] Declining Holland's offer of a retreat at Ampthill, 16 Aug., he insisted 'the best thing for us is to go altogether away'.[109] 'Duncannon goes to Ireland for six weeks and leaves the woods and forests, Waterloo bridge, reform and Buckingham House to take care of themselves', commented Holmes, 18 Aug., adding, 'I hear he is going to give up his office'.[110] Concerned at what might happen during his absence, Duncannon 'strongly' recommended to Brougham that Sir Henry 'Parnell* or some other person occasionally talks to the Irish Members ... They are easily managed with fair words and a little concession to their wishes goes a long way with them ... and I am always afraid of misunderstanding and consequent violence'.[111] On 30 Aug. Smith Stanley recommended that Duncannon's appointment as lord lieutenant of Carlow 'be put in immediate communication with the chancellor', as the 'magistrates want a hint in that county'. He was soon in place, to the approval of the Catholic press.[112] On 2 Sept. Althorp, contemplating the reshuffle that would follow his anticipated succession as Earl Spencer, advised Ebrington that although Duncannon's view of the state of Ireland was 'pretty correct', he did not think he 'would do for Irish minister', as it was 'impossible for an Irish county Member to steer a steady course in the present excited state of public feeling there'.[113] 'Duncannon in his present mood would be quite the other extreme' to Smith Stanley, concurred Holland, 'but his good sense and temper might make him steer a more even course, or he might be counterpoised by his lord lieutenant'.[114] Duncannon paired for the passage of the reform bill, 21 Sept., and was not listed in the majority for Ebrington's confidence motion, 10 Oct. 1831. Later that month Mrs. Arbuthnot recounted that there had been 'another *tiff* in the cabinet', in which Duncannon had 'prevailed upon Lord Grey to make O'Connell attorney-general for Ireland', but Smith Stanley had refused, threatening that 'if this appointment took place, he should resign'.[115]

Following the rejection of the reform bill by the Lords, Duncannon was listed by Lord Palmerston* as one of those who wished 'to make the bill more extensive and radical' rather than 'more moderate'.[116] On 16 Oct. he implored Grey to avoid a long prorogation and take vigorous measures with the Lords:

> The fears of the people and I am sorry to say of many of our friends are excited by certain speeches of yours and Althorp's, and a postponement till after Christmas would I know only confirm them. There is a very strong feeling that the £10 franchise is to be touched. I know ... that this cannot be, but you must make allowances for those who do not know you so well. Schedule A and the £10 franchise are in fact the bill, and no one of us could ever show our faces again, that in the slightest degree being altered ... I write strongly on this subject because I know that very little is wanting to bring on again all the questions of ballot, annual or triennial parliaments [and] universal suffrage.

Dismissing his notion of getting the bill through the Commons before Christmas as 'the most chimerical hope that was ever entertained', Grey replied, 28 Oct.:

> I can never receive any communication from you of this nature, without a feeling that it has been prompted by a sincere desire to assist ... but really government is pressed upon matters which it ought to belong to them to determine ... If in what you say about vigorous measures for carrying the bill through the ... Lords you mean a creation of peers ... I have no hesitation in stating ... that it is

impossible. Not less than 80 to 100 would do. This would be destructive to the ... Lords and almost equally to the ... Commons, from where the new peers must chiefly be taken, and how could you meet so many new elections? Really people talk of these things without having considered them.

Unabashed, Duncannon retorted:

What is to be gained by a long recess? The chance of converting those who, be assured, will disappoint you ... On the other hand, what is to be lost? The support of the whole people of this country, and with it, of those who have supported you in Parliament, to which I would add almost an equally great evil, the formation of societies and unions in ... almost every parish in England, which perhaps you may not find so easy to put down when the bill is passed ... It is not a very pleasing task for me ... but I should not be acting kindly by you if I did not tell you openly how great a discontent will be produced by a prorogation beyond Christmas ... When you adopted the decisive measure of dissolving the Parliament to carry the bill, I never doubted that for your own honour, your character, and the consistency of your measures, you must adopt an equally decisive measure in the Lords.[117]

On 21 Nov., two days after the decision to recall Parliament for 6 Dec., Edward Littleton* encountered Duncannon in Ellice's room, 'writing to O'Connell and the Irish Members', and was 'amused' by a letter he showed him from Hume, 'abusing him' for not having given a keeper's position at Hyde Park to a 'servant of his' who had held out for nine months for a higher salary.[118] Alarmed at reports that O'Connell would not attend, Duncannon vainly urged him to 'come over' and 'give us your powerful support' and 'ensure as much attendance as possible from other Irish Members', 28 Nov.[119] 'Duncannon ridicules the notion of having put O'Connell in a state of probation' and 'says he might have been fixed and saved', Holland remarked the following day, noting that Duncannon's preference was 'for vigorous measures and ten eldest sons being called up' to get the bill through the Lords.[120] Commenting on Althorp's reluctance to 'let his troops fight a little short' in the recalled Parliament that month, Brougham reported that 'Duncannon is in perfect despair. He and all others whose opinion is worth having say there never was a minute when Althorp could not beat the enemy by 70, and yet he and Graham are always taking it for granted they are in a minority'.[121]

On 9 Dec. 1831 Duncannon introduced bills for the amalgamation of the surveyor-general's office with that of the woods and forests and for a portion of the land revenues to be put towards the completion of Buckingham House, which should 'not be allowed to go into decay' after 'so much expense'. He saw them through the Commons and they received royal assent as 2 Gul. IV, cc. 1, 3, on 13 Feb. 1832. That month O'Connell informed him 'candidly' of his 'abhorrence' of Smith Stanley's Irish policy, citing his failure to consult one single Irish Member on the Irish reform bill and surmising, 'I have an idea that you ... are as rigidly excluded as I am ... Is this not insulting?' 'He must be insane', O'Connell added after hearing the terms of Smith Stanley's inquiry into Irish tithes, to which Duncannon responded, 26 Dec.:

I rejoice that you have made up your mind to be here on the first day of the session ... I must, however, disagree with you in the very severe censure you pass on the present Irish government ... You make no allowance for the situation in which they came into power and the difficulty of altering old habits and prejudices ... You may think Stanley's proposal does not go far enough but surely it will be a great advantage to relieve the people from tithe proctors, ecclesiastical courts and process servers ... With respect to the Irish reform bill, I regret as much as you can do that it does not give additional Members to Ireland and that some other alterations are not made in it, but I cannot shut my eyes to this, that it opens nineteen boroughs and gives a free election to the other towns and cities. This must counterbalance many defects ... I am sure you will use your talents and assiduity when you are here in improving rather than condemning generally measures that are in themselves good.[122]

Duncannon was a majority teller for the second reading of the revised English reform bill, 17 Dec. 1831, and for many of its details. Warning Grey of the country's dissatisfaction 'with the slow progress we are making' and that 'our friends are very clamorous in their complaints of having been hurried to London', where 'little or nothing has been done', he advocated 'the absolute necessity of sitting on Wednesdays, and from 12 to 6 on every Saturday, till the reform bill is passed', 3 Feb. 1832.[123] At dinner with Holland the following day he 'urged vehemently the manifold and forcible reasons for creating peers and the dangers of neglecting or even postponing that measure'.[124] He was a majority teller for the third reading, 22 Mar. That month Russell, on hearing Holland remark that a majority in the Lords on the second reading was 'literally certain', advised him to 'go over the list with Duncannon'.[125] Shortly before that division, 10 Apr., Duncannon predicted that the bill would be carried by 'but two' votes, but in the event it passed by nine.[126] He was 'apprehensive' about the success of Ebrington's address asking the king to appoint only ministers who would carry reform unimpaired, for which he duly voted, 10 May.[127] During the ensuing crisis he conferred with Agar Ellis about a 'strong address' calling on the king to create sufficient peers to ensure the bill's passage.[128] On 20 May he put the idea to Lord Howick* that 'again the occasion is afforded' of bringing O'Connell into government.[129] He was a ministerial teller in the divisions on the Russian-Dutch loan, 26 Jan., 12, 16, 20 July. During the debate on the first occasion Denis Le Marchant† recorded that Duncannon had taken him 'aside and said if we were to divide now we should be in a minority or something like it', but owing 'to Ellice and others canvassing' they got 'a small majority'.[130] He was a government teller in the division on their relations with Portugal, 9 Feb. He presented a petition for giving an additional Member to Kilkenny city instead of Dublin University, 21 Feb. He was in the minority against the Irish registry of deeds bill, 9 Apr. He was a majority teller for the second reading of Irish reform bill, 25 May, and divided against an increase in the Scottish county representation, 1 June 1832.

On 3 Jan. 1832 Holmes reported that Duncannon was 'very much alarmed about the state of Ireland' and 'talking of martial law'.[131] He voted against Hobhouse's Vestry Act amendment bill, 23 Jan. Commenting on Smith Stanley's threat to resign rather than allow any spoliation of the Irish church, Le Marchant observed that Duncannon 'is very unhappy' and says Brougham has 'been trying to get Lord Grey round to moderate measures', 26 Jan.[132] Urging the case for the abolition of tithes to Grey, 4 Feb., Duncannon recommended using the land tax and first fruits revenues to support payment of the clergy and alleviate the Catholic population from the cess, a 'tax more offensive and more odious to them than even tithe'. 'I do not think there would be so much difficulty as you seem to anticipate', he insisted, 8 Feb.[133] On the 14th John Croker* noted how Duncannon had opposed Smith Stanley 'point blank' in the tithes committee, but conjectured that they 'take opposite sides for the purpose of consolidating opposite parties and keeping their majority together', with Grey and Smith Stanley endeavouring 'to manage the moderates, and Duncannon and Ellice to keep well with the radicals'.[134] That day Ellenborough heard that Duncannon 'would not agree to the [tithes] report unless there was distinct pledge that "the name and character of tithes should be done away with"', which was '*impossible*', and there would therefore 'be a schism in the government'; but he then learnt that he had 'given in'.[135] He was in the minority for printing the Woollen Grange petition for the abolition of tithes, 16 Feb. On 30 Mar. he announced that he was 'prepared to support' Smith Stanley's Irish tithes coercion bill on the 'implicit' understanding that it was to be 'followed by a measure for the extinction of tithes', but warned that 'the people of Ireland never will be satisfied until that pledge is redeemed'. He voted accordingly, 14 July, 1 Aug., being, according to Greville, well 'aware of the false position in which the government is placed, pretending to legislate with a knowledge that their laws cannot be enforced'.[136] Following his arrival in Ireland later that month, he reported 'a bitter feeling against the government' and 'a most extraordinary state of excitement on the tithe question', which would damage his 'chance of being returned' at the next election.[137] On 10 Sept. he apologized to Grey for 'boring' him with another 'long scrawl' on tithes, but explained, 'I am anxious you should know my opinion' as 'you think me prejudiced to certain views', but 'such I assure you is not the case'. Feeling that he 'must allude' to his support of the tithes bill, he submitted a draft of his county Kilkenny election address to Grey, who made 'some alterations', which included changing his call for 'an entire alteration of the tithe system' and 'permanent reform in every branch of the church establishment' into support for 'a new system, whereby tithes might be extinguished' and 'reform of ... defects in the established church'.[138] On 7 Oct. he warned Holland that he had 'very little chance' on 'account of voting for the tithe bill'. 'Duncannon will be ousted', remarked Ralph Sneyd.[139] 'You had better retire immediately and either stand in Surrey or come in for Malton' as 'there is no good in your being beat in Kilkenny', advised Russell, 12 Oct. On 10 Nov. Althorp 'strongly' urged him to stand for Nottingham, where a ministerial candidate was wanted and the expense would be 'very trifling'.[140] Next day Grey offered him New Windsor, which the king had placed at his disposal. 'Windsor would do the best, but I leave it entirely to you', Duncannon replied, 14 Nov.[141] Learning of his retirement from Kilkenny, O'Connell wrote:

> I cannot venture to dispute the decision you have come to, *connected as you are with government* ... What a pity it is that *you* should be the victim of Lord Anglesey's want of intellect and ... Stanley's insane presumption, you, I will say, naturally the most popular person that ever belonged to the party of the Whigs; you, whom everybody esteems and respects; you, to whom the Catholics owe a debt of gratitude and in whose personal qualities everybody places unlimited confidence ... I have had an intimation from Nottingham that you were to stand for that city, and you will smile at hearing that I have been called on for your *character*. What a strange resolution! As if you were not yourself, although belonging to the nobility, a more sincere and practical reformer than any one member of this political Union.[142]

Duncannon was returned in second place for Nottingham as a Liberal at the 1832 general election. To the surprise of many, he was appointed home secretary on Melbourne's accession as premier in July 1834, when he was given a United Kingdom peerage in an attempt to strengthen the government in the Lords.[143] 'Who could ever have thought of him in such a station?', remarked Greville:

> His proper element seemed to be the House of Commons, where he was a bustling, zealous partisan and a very good whipper-in; but he cannot speak at all, and though a tolerably candid talker, his capacity is slender; he has no pretensions of any sort to a high office, and nothing but peculiar circumstances could put him in one.[144]

On Melbourne's return to office in 1835 he was made lord privy seal and resumed his post at woods and forests, where he oversaw the completion of Buckingham Palace and the National Gallery, various metropolitan improvements and the design of the new Houses of Parliament.[145] A street linking Pall Mall with the Strand bears his name. He continued to assist the Whigs in the management of their elections, in which he was considered a 'great authority' by Arbuthnot, who noted in 1841 that his predictions had nearly 'always been right'.[146] Appointed Irish viceroy in the Russell administration in 1846, the 'first resident landlord' to hold that office 'for a generation', his tenure was overshadowed by the famine. He died in harness of 'dropsy on the chest' less than a year later, 'his days having no doubt been shortened by his devotedness to its duties', according to Le Marchant, who added, 'often have I known the Whigs, especially whilst in opposition, saved from very serious blunders by his firm, and almost pertinacious remonstrances'.[147] He was 'of great use', Brougham recalled of his role in Grey's ministry, 'but more in private as an adviser in consultation than in public. He was really a very sensible, staunch and worthy man, but he was no orator'.[148] He was succeeded in the peerage by his eldest son John George (1809-80).[149]

[1] See D. Howell-Thomas, *Duncannon* (1992). [2] *Life of Campbell* i. 408; *Greville Mems.* v. 447. [3] Le Marchant, *Althorp*, 47-48. [4] *Yorks. Gazette*, 11 Mar. 1820. [5] Grey mss. [6] Howell-Thomas, 97. [7] *Arbuthnot Jnl.* i. 39, 66. [8] A. Mitchell, *Whigs in Opposition*, 39; A. Aspinall, 'English Party Organization', *EHR*, xli (1926), 398. [9] HLRO, Hist. Coll. 379, Grey Bennet diary, 44. [10] Buckingham, *Mems. Geo. IV*, i. 141-2. [11] *Fox Jnl.* 66. [12] Grey Bennet diary, 104. [13] Grey mss, Duncannon to Grey, 17 Aug. [n.d.], 25 Aug. 1821. [14] Grey mss. [15] Duke Univ. Lib. Ponsonby mss. [16] Ibid. [17] Bessborough mss F150. [18] Ibid. F52. [19] Add. 76369, Althorp to Brougham, 17 Mar. 1823. [20] Brougham mss, Abercromby to Brougham, 19, 26 Mar. 1823. [21] *The Times*, 5 June 1823. [22] Northants. RO, Agar Ellis diary. [23] Grey mss. [24] Ibid. Tierney to Grey, 21 Feb. 1825; Buckingham, ii. 216. [25] *The Times*, 24 Feb. 1825. [26] Grey mss. [27] *O'Connell Corresp.* iii. 1278. [28] Add. 51724, Duncannon to Holland, 10 Apr. 1826. [29] Castle Howard mss, Lady Carlisle to Morpeth. [30] *Arbuthnot Jnl.* ii. 30. [31] *Dublin Evening Post*, 17, 20, 23, 27 June 1826. [32] Add. 51724. [33] Add. 51690. [34] *O'Connell Corresp.* iii. 1441. [35] *Arbuthnot Jnl.* ii. 74. [36] *The Times*, 28 Feb., 11 Apr. 1827; *Canning's Ministry*, 40. [37] Grey mss. [38] Castle Howard mss, Holland to Carlisle [Apr. 1827]. [39] *Canning's Ministry*, 103. [40] Lansdowne mss. [41] LMA, Jersey mss 510/412. [42] *Canning's Ministry*, 233. [43] Chatsworth mss 1469. [44] *Canning's Ministry*, 272. [45] *Creevey Pprs.* ii. 116. [46] Add. 48406, f. 125. [47] *Arbuthnot Jnl.* ii. 123. [48] *Greville Mems.* i. 175-6, 178-9. [49] *Canning's Ministry*, 340. [50] *Russell Letters*, ii. 71. [51] Lansdowne mss. [52] Walpole, *Russell*, i. 135. [53] Add. 51833. [54] Add. 76380, Duncannon to Althorp, 16 Sept. 1827. [55] Add. 51724. [56] Lansdowne mss. [57] *Lady Bessborough and her Family Circle* ed. Lord Bessborough, 290-1. [58] Add. 51834. [59] NLS mss 24748, f. 115. [60] *Ellenborough Diary* i. 126. [61] Ibid. i. 162. [62] *O'Connell Corresp.* iii. 1479. [63] Grey mss. [64] *O'Connell Corresp.* iii. 1491. [65] *Creevey Pprs.* ii. 171-3, 182-3; Grey mss. [66] *Arbuthnot Jnl.* ii. 222. [67] Ibid. ii. 242. [68] *Greville Mems.* i. 263. [69] PRO NI, Fitzgerald mss MIC/639/13/7/9. [70] Add. 76369, Althorp to Brougham, 29 Mar. 1829. [71] *Greville Mems.* i. 280. [72] Add. 40340, f. 213. [73] *Arbuthnot Jnl.* ii. 267-8. [74] *O'Connell Corresp.* iv. 1552; *Ellenborough Diary*, ii. 20. [75] *Greville Mems.* i. 292; *O'Connell Corresp.* iv. 1562, 1569. [76] *O'Connell Corresp.* iv. 1596. [77] Grey mss; ibid. Howick jnl. 4 Sept. 1829. [78] NAI, Leveson Gower letterbks. M. 737/99-100, Leveson Gower to Peel, 6 Sept. 1829. [79] *Kilkenny Moderator*, 31 July, 14 Aug. 1830. [80] Brougham mss. [81] Ibid. [82] Add. 51680. [83] A. Aspinall, *Brougham and the Whig Party*, 187; Brougham, *Life and Times*, iii. 74, 76, 79. [84] Parker, *Graham*, i. 119; *Creevey Pprs.* ii. 264; Walpole, i. 165. [85] Brougham mss, Russell to Brougham, 15 Nov. 1837. [86] Grey mss, reform committee to Grey, 14 Jan., 'Duncannon's plan of reform', 'Heads of a bill', Duncannon to Grey, 26 Jan. 1831. [87] Derby mss 920 Der (14) 116/7, Duncannon to Smith Stanley [n.d.], 3 June 1831. [88] Agar Ellis diary. [89] PRO NI, Anglesey mss 27A/99, 31D/13. [90] Add. 51670, Bedford to Lady Holland, 3 Feb. 1831. [91] *O'Connell Corresp.* iv. 1764. [92] Anglesey mss 29B/61-63, 68, 69; *Greville Mems.* ii. 121. [93] Creevey mss, Creevey to Miss Ord, 25 Feb. 1831. [94] *Kilkenny Moderator*, 16, 19, 26 Feb. 1831. [95] Torrens, *Melbourne*, i. 360. [96] Grey mss. [97] *Macaulay Letters*, ii. 6. [98] Wellington mss WP1/1179/2. [99] *Macaulay Letters*, ii. 10. [100] Grey mss, Durham to Grey, 8 Apr. 1831; *Arbuthnot Corresp.* 145. [101] *Greville Mems.* ii. 137. [102] *Kilkenny Moderator*, 27 Apr. 1831. [103] *O'Connell Corresp.* iv. 1799-1802. [104] *Kilkenny Moderator*, 11 May 1831. [105] Grey mss. [106] Ibid. [107] *Holland House Diaries*, 28. [108] Grey mss. [109] Add. 51724. [110] *Arbuthnot Corresp.* 148. [111] Brougham mss. [112] Anglesey mss 31D/59; *Dublin Evening Post*, 4 Oct. 1831. [113] Devon RO, Earl Fortescue mss 1262M/FC 87. [114] Brougham mss, Holland to Brougham, 27 Oct. 1831. [115] *Arbuthnot Jnl.* ii. 433. [116] Southampton Univ. Lib. Broadlands mss PP/GC/RI/11. [117] Grey mss. [118] Hatherton diary, 21 Nov. 1831. [119] *O'Connell Corresp.* iv. 1850. [120] *Holland House Diaries*, 86. [121] NLS mss 24748, f. 120. [122] *O'Connell Corresp.* iv. 1862a. [123] Grey mss. [124] *Holland House Diaries*, 124. [125] Ibid. 149. [126] *Baring Jnls.* i. 94. [127] *Three Diaries*, 246. [128] Agar Ellis diary, 18 May 1832. [129] Grey mss. [130] *Three Diaries*, 196-7; Le Marchant, 391-2. [131] Add. 40402, f. 2. [132] *Three Diaries*, 186. [133] Grey mss. [134] *Croker Pprs.* ii. 150. [135] *Three Diaries*, 195. [136] *Greville Mems.* ii. 309-10. [137] Add. 51724, Duncannon to Holland, 18 Aug. 1832. [138] Grey mss. [139] Add. 51724; Keele Univ. Lib. Sneyd mss SC17/77. [140] Ponsonby mss. [141] Grey mss. [142] *O'Connell Corresp.* iv. 1849, where this letter has been incorrectly dated as 1831. [143] *Melbourne Pprs.* 205; *Holland House Diaries*, 260. [144] *Greville Mems.* iii. 60. [145] See Howell-Thomas, 198-248. [146] P. Salmon, *Electoral Reform at Work*, 45; *Arbuthnot Corresp.* 224. [147] *Gent. Mag.* (1847), ii. 82-3; Le Marchant, 50-52. [148] Brougham mss, autobiog. fragment. [149] *Gent. Mag.* (1847), ii. 82-3; Le Marchant, 50-52.

P.J.S.

PONSONBY, Hon. William Francis Spencer (1787–1855), of Canford House, nr. Poole, Dorset and 20 St. James's Square, Mdx.

POOLE	1826–26 Sept. 1831
KNARESBOROUGH	28 June 1832–1832
DORSET	1832–1837

b. 31 July 1787, 3rd s. of Frederick Ponsonby†, 3rd earl of Bessborough [I] and 3rd Bar. Ponsonby [GB] (*d.* 1844), and Lady Henrietta Frances Spencer, da. of John Spencer†, 1st Earl Spencer; bro. of Hon. Frederick Cavendish Ponsonby* and John William Ponsonby, Visct. Duncannon*. *educ.* Harrow 1795. *m.* 8 Aug. 1814, Lady Barbara Ashley Cooper, da. of Anthony, 5th earl of Shaftesbury, 4s. (2 *d.v.p.*) 1da. *cr.* Bar. de Mauley 10 July 1838. *d.* 16 May 1855.

Lt. Marylebone vols. ?1803; maj. commdt. R. Putney and Roehampton vols. 1806.

'Willy' Ponsonby was delicate as a child and became a curiously feckless young man, with a touch of his sister Caroline's tempestuous character. Aged six, on one of several childhood visits to the continent, his father reported that he was 'very entertaining and has mighty odd expressions. His great rage is at the present to go into a nunnery to see the nuns. He says he understands after he is seven they will not let him in'.[1] He attended Harrow, and according to Denis Le Marchant† 'was amiable and well-looking, and is remembered among his contemporaries for the fluency with which he could speak French'. He left to spend a short period in the navy, and in July 1800 travelled on board the ship of Lord St. Vincent, the commander-in-chief in the Channel, to have an opportunity of 'seeing service'.[2] In late 1804 he went to Russia as attaché to the ambassador, Lord Granville Leveson Gower†, his mother's lover. He wrote to Lady Bessborough, 3 May 1805, that Ponsonby, who was making good progress with his studies, was

> a nice and amiable boy; he has a degree of prudence and discretion of which I never saw the parallel, but he is very shy and reserved: I have the greatest difficulty in persuading him to go into society ... In point of health I think he is really better than when he left England, he looks stouter and more manly, and if he would but go to bed earlier and not get up so late, I doubt not but that his cheeks would become blooming. Upon this subject I have repeatedly talked to him ... I fear, however, not with much effect.[3]

On his return to England in late 1805, he was said to be 'in every way as much improved as possible' by his cousin Harriet Cavendish (who in fact became Leveson Gower's wife a few years later). She so far tolerated Ponsonby's boyish and ill advised attentions that her servant thought they would be married, the more so as she allowed Ponsonby 'to dangle after her wherever she went'. Harriet confided to her sister Lady Morpeth in November 1807 that 'I really do not know what to do about William, as he certainly *dangles after me* ... more than ever, yet so childishly that I cannot see any way of stopping it without an appearance of affectation and prudery', especially as 'he is so particularly touchy about anything he imagines to be an affront that I cannot change my manner to him in the least without his immediately taking it as an egregious offence'. Yet the following month she wrote of her relief, the difficulty 'having ended happily in exactly the difference of our *manière d'être* that I wished to accomplish, without quarrelling, arguing or going one step out of the common way to effect it'. Though she thought he was 'just as childish and "*sans conséquence*" in his manner as ever', she noted a conversation with Lady Sarah Spencer, in which the latter began 'the old story that he seemed quite a fool, and I my old defence that few people are so much the contrary'.[4] Though doted on by the family, he continued to be scorned as 'that object of everybody's compassion' by Lady Sarah Spencer, who commented in 1809 that 'I never saw so fine a lesson as he is to warn one against idleness', and called him 'a monument of empty languor'.[5]

Ponsonby, who had been a lieutenant in his eldest brother Lord Duncannon's Marylebone volunteers in 1803, succeeded his father to the command of the Royal Putney and Roehampton volunteers in November 1806.[6] In mid-1809 he travelled as a civilian in Spain, where he suffered sick headaches.[7] In 1811 Bessborough forlornly hoped that the appointment of the prince of Wales as regent would be the means of obtaining a diplomatic posting for his son.[8] Ponsonby was persuaded to travel with Harriet's brother, the 6th duke of Devonshire, to Ireland in 1812, and he assisted at the election for county Kilkenny of his ineffectual brother Frederick, who was abroad. Devonshire, who had wanted to bring him into Parliament for county Waterford, had to fall back on Youghal. Ponsonby duly issued an address, in which he stressed his family's Irish connections, but he was defeated by Sir John Keane, whom he failed to unseat on petition.[9] He may have been the 'young William Ponsonby' whose chances of succeeding to the county Londonderry vacancy were scuppered three years later.[10] In 1814 he married the 5th earl of Shaftesbury's only daughter and heiress, who according to Lord Alvanley was 'as stupid as a post'.[11] Caroline, now the wife of William Lamb*, wrote to Duncannon:

> I hope he is kind to her. She certainly suffers. Her situation is, I think, rather unpleasant, but I dislike saying all this in a letter, and indeed I never more will speak openly if you breathe this again, as I am convinced a spark might raise a flame.[12]

Even though his wife was Catholic, the freeholders of Kilkenny would not countenance his replacing his brother there at the general election of 1820.[13] Late the following year, during another prolonged family sojourn on the continent, he lost his infant son Henry, and shortly afterwards, to his immense grief, his mother, after which he took over much of the responsibility for the family's affairs.[14] Nothing came of the suggestion that he fill the vacancy created at Higham Ferrers in early 1822.[15] He took Caroline's side in her violent quarrels with her husband, and once wrote Lamb an abusive and interfering letter, after which his sister, Lady Cowper, recorded that Ponsonby was 'reckoned an ass and a jackanapes by everybody'. He was present at his sister's death in 1828, and was reconciled with Lamb.[16]

Among the properties left to his wife by her maternal grandfather Sir John Webb, in a trust over which Ponsonby took control, was the estate at Canford. He settled there in the mid-1820s, constructed a new mansion and contributed to several local improvements.[17] Exploiting his local influence, he canvassed the nearby borough of Poole in late 1824, when the Member John Dent was in poor health, and again a year later, when there were rumours of an imminent dissolution.[18] The leading Whigs wanted to bring him into Parliament, but he declined Lord Fitzwilliam's offer of the seat at Malton which Duncannon was planning to vacate.[19] At the general election of 1826, when Dent retired, Ponsonby told the electors that 'from my early habits and connections, and from my own sentiments, I am attached to the opposition'. He was elected in second place, behind the corporation's Member, Benjamin Lester Lester, and ahead of his wife's first cousin, the Tory local gentleman Henry Charles Sturt*.[20] He was made a free burgess of Poole, 5 July 1826.[21]

Ponsonby divided against the grant for the duke of Clarence, 16 Feb., 2 Mar. 1827. He reported to Caroline Lamb, 20 Feb., that 'everything continues in an extraordinary state', and doubted Canning's ability to succeed the stricken Liverpool as prime minister.[22] Since his brother Frederick was absent in Malta, the votes attributed to him during this Parliament were probably those of this Member, including for inquiry into allegations against the corporation of Leicester, 15 Mar., information on the Orange procession and Lisburn magistrates, 29 Mar., and Tierney's amendment to postpone the committee of supply, 30 Mar. He certainly voted for a select committee on the Irish miscellaneous estimates and information on chancery administration, 5 Apr. In late April he thought that Lord Lansdowne and the moderate Whigs would join Canning, behind whom, and beside Tierney and Burdett, he was found seated in the House by Mackintosh on 1 May.[23] He voted to consider separating bankruptcy jurisdiction from chancery (as 'Hon. F. Ponsonby'), 22 May, and for the disfranchisement of Penryn, 28 May. He wrote to Devonshire, 10 Aug., of the good effect on Canning of the 'unbending integrity and constitutional principles' of the Whigs, and opined that 'our good honest Whigs have been [too] long unconnected with the details of office'.[24] He reported to Lord Holland, 15 Dec. 1827, that

> we are all rather in dudgeon, at the gloomy view which ministers take of the Navarino business, and their desponding language generally, and complete submission to higher powers; if they do not pluck up a little spirit, it will go hard with them.[25]

He voted for repeal of the Test Acts, 26 Feb. 1828. He divided against extending the franchise of East Retford to the freeholders of the hundred of Bassetlaw, 21 Mar. As 'Hon. F. Ponsonby', he voted to make 60*s*. not 64*s*. the pivot price of corn, 22 Apr., and to impose a duty on corn of 15*s*., reducing to 10*s*. by 1834, 29 Apr. Unless it was Frederick, he again voted in condemnation of chancery administration, 24 Apr. He sided with opposition against the misapplication of public money on Buckingham House, 23 June, and for reduction of the salary of the lieutenant-general of the ordnance, 4 July. He was in the minority against Fyler's amendment in the committee on the Customs Acts, which was carried with government support, 14 July 1828. As he had on 6 Mar. 1827 and 12 May 1828, he voted for Catholic emancipation, 6, 30 Mar. 1829. He objected to Hobhouse's St. James's (Westminster) vestry bill in a letter to him, 26 Apr., and repeated his main criticism, that the matter would be better dealt with by a general bill, in the House, 21 May, when he successfully moved to have it thrown out.[26] He voted for allowing Daniel O'Connell to take his seat without swearing the oath of supremacy, 18 May, and reduction of the hemp duties, 1 June 1829. He divided for the enfranchisement of Birmingham, Leeds and Manchester, 23 Feb., parliamentary reform, 28 May, and (as 'Hon. F. Ponsonby') to transfer East Retford's seats to Birmingham, 5 Mar. 1830. He joined in the opposition campaign for economies and retrenchment during that session, including no doubt on several occasions when such votes were credited to Frederick. He divided for Jewish emancipation, 5 Apr., 17 May. Unless it was his brother, he voted for O'Connell's Irish vestries bill, 27 Apr.; it was certainly he who sided with opposition on Newfoundland, 11 May, and Canada, 25 May. He divided for abolition of the death penalty for forgery, 24 May, 7 June 1830.

As no opponent was willing to go to a poll, Ponsonby was returned unopposed for Poole at the general election of 1830, when he was given a hostile reception on the hustings. In September he agreed to pay for the building of a new library there, and he attended a dinner in honour of the members of the enlarged corporation.[27] Listed by ministers among their 'foes', he was absent from the division on the civil list, 15 Nov. 1830, which led to their resignation. During the debate on the Grey ministry's reform bill, Charles Arbuthnot* reported to Peel, the Tory Commons leader, 3 Mar. 1831, that Ponsonby had just told him ministers would say nothing until Peel had spoken, and

> that they expected to carry their measure, but that what he has seen in the House makes him doubt it. He told me that if the measure were not carried they were to go out. He owned to me that the measure alarmed him very much, but of course he will vote for it ... He asked me what was to happen if the measure were lost, for the mere broaching of it would render it impossible for any other set of men to govern the country.[28]

He duly divided in favour of the second reading of the bill, 22 Mar., and against Gascoyne's wrecking amendment, 19 Apr., which precipitated a dissolution. He was thanked for his reform vote at a meeting in Poole, 7 Apr., when he spoke in support of the unfranchised commonalty and the bill. Having pledged to continue to vote for it, he was returned unopposed at the general election.[29] He regretted differing with the Bankes family, but explained privately to them that his opposition to them in the county was caused by the overriding importance of the reform question.[30] He attended the Dorset nomination meeting, 6 May, when his band of supporters was involved in an affray with a party of Henry Bankes's* anti-reformers. He split for the successful candidates Portman and Calcraft and presided at a dinner in their honour at Blandford, 23 May 1831, when he declared that the bill was based on principles which 'were not built upon any theoretic speculations, and still less upon any feelings of animosity or dislike to our present institutions, but upon an anxious desire for their preservation'.[31]

He voted for the second reading of the reintroduced reform bill, 6 July, at least twice against adjourning proceedings on it, 12 July 1831, and steadily for its details. Calcraft's suicide, 11 Sept., created a vacancy for the county which Ponsonby instantly moved to fill, issuing a pro-reform address to the freeholders on the 13th, though, anticipating a contest, he soon evinced a desire to withdrew in favour of a stronger candidate.[32] On the same day he made a farewell address to his supportive constituents, in which he explained his decision, the invitation to stand for Dorset

> not merely holding out an object of justifiable ambition to me, but as involving a question of public duty; considering that I am called upon to take a lead in that party, which has so recently asserted its power, and redeemed the character of the county [*sic*] from the charge of being backwards in the independent spirits of the times.[33]

He returned to the House, and, having presumably been shut out with Burdett on the third reading, 19 Sept., he divided in favour of the passage of the bill, 21 Sept., and the second reading of the Scottish bill, 23 Sept. 1831; he resigned his seat on the 26th.

Supported by ministers, who were concerned that the victory of an anti-reformer would further weaken their prospects of carrying the bill in the Lords, he was expected to be returned unopposed, especially as Bankes declined to offer. But the late entry of Lord Ashley*, another of his wife's cousins, turned the election into a ferocious contest, in which Ponsonby was branded an Irish Catholic interloper, castigated for voting against Lord Chandos's clause to enfranchise £50 tenants-at-will and repeatedly outperformed by Ashley on the hustings. Although he rebutted the allegations against him, urged the cause of the people against an oppressive aristocracy and continually exhorted his supporters to even greater efforts, he trailed on most of the 15 days of the poll. He eventually lost by only 36 votes, though he complained that he had a majority of the votes tendered, and promised to petition on the ground of excessive delay in the processing of the disputed votes.[34] He commented to a supporter that, despite his disappointment, 'a feeling of satisfaction predominates both at the kindness which I have personally experienced, and my conviction that such a power as we have brought into the field cannot be suppressed'; he was, of course, included in the prospective membership of the planned Dorset Whig Club that winter.[35] Nothing came of rumours that Ashley would capitulate, or that the Tories would allow Ponsonby to be returned unopposed for the other seat if Portman persisted in his intention to resign, and in any case he ruled out such a possibility.[36] On 19 Mar. 1832 the committee, perhaps riled by his time-wasting tactics, decided against Ponsonby, who issued an address asserting that the anti-reformers had won a merely nominal victory.[37] His enormous expenses, possibly as high as £30,000, were presumably largely met by subscription, but he admitted to being 'pretty well cleaned out' by the affair.[38] There was a newspaper report that Ponsonby would be returned for Chester,[39] but he was in fact out of the House until June, when Devonshire brought him in on a vacancy for Knaresborough. He voted for the Irish tithes bill, 13 July, and with ministers for the Russian-Dutch loan, 20 July. On 28 July 1832, he told Tom Moore that 'the metropolitan elections, instead of taking the turn that he and others dreaded they would, were likely to be, if any thing, *too* aristocratical'.[40]

Although thanked for his pro-reform conduct at a meeting in Poole, 9 June 1832, he became unpopular there once it was known that the enlargement of the borough would effectively give him control over at least one seat, and he was charged with using his interest to secure the re-election of his replacement, Sir John Byng. He was himself invited to stand for the three Member county of Dorset, and despite his reluctance to risk another contest and his absence because of injuries sustained in a fall from his horse, he was elected unopposed as a Liberal, behind Ashley and William John Bankes*, at the general election in December 1832.[41] He sat until 1837, when he became a member of Brooks's Club. The following year he was awarded a coronation peerage, taking his title from a barony which had been in abeyance since 1415, and to which his wife was one of the heiresses. She died, 7 June 1844, three weeks after his father, and Lady Holland commented that

> whilst *herself*, she was a generous, sober minded soul; witness her making ... [Ponsonby] give up his own fortune, saying they had enough, to poor Fred Ponsonby, who was deeply in debt; then sheltering for upwards of 20 years Lord Bessborough, really reversing the position of parent and child.[42]

Ponsonby died in May 1855, 'a cultivated man and a perfect gentleman', who 'had even more than the usual kindly nature of his family'. Although he had had to sell Canford in the 1840s, he was remembered in Poole for his 'private kindnesses and public benefits'.[43] He left his estate to be divided between his three surviving children: Charles Frederick Ashley (1815-96), Liberal Member for Poole, 1837-47, and Dungarvan, 1851-2, who succeeded him as 2nd Baron de Mauley; Ashley George John (1831-98), who was Liberal Member for Cirencester, 1852-7 and 1859-65, and Frances Anna Georgiana (1817-1910), wife of the 9th Lord Kinnaird.[44]

[1] *Lady Bessborough and her Family Circle* ed. Lord Bessborough, 99-103. [2] Ibid. 118; Le Marchant, *Althorp*, 53. [3] *Leveson Gower Corresp.* i. 469; ii. 77, 79, 100, 115, 427-8. [4] *Letters of Lady Harriet Cavendish*, 168, 169, 171, 217, 220, 230-1, 249-50, 254-5, 263-4, 269, 273, 283. [5] *Lady Bessborough*, 168; *Lady Lyttelton Corresp.* 74-75, 103-4. [6] D. Howell-Thomas, *Duncannon*, 50-51; *Lady Bessborough*, 150. [7] *Lady Bessborough*, 187; B. Jenkins, *Goulburn*, 25-31. [8] Howell-Thomas, 89. [9] *Lady Bessborough*, 227-8; Add. 40222, f. 35. [10] *HP Commons, 1790-1820*, ii. 670. [11] *CP*, iv. 176. [12] *Lady Bessborough*, 240, 253-4. [13] Keele Univ. Lib. Sneyd mss, Clare to Sneyd, 25 Mar. 1820. [14] *Lady Bessborough*, 16, 261, 265, 267-72, 277; Howell-Thomas, 103, 106-7. [15] Bessborough mss, Brougham to Bessborough [17 Jan.]; Lansdowne mss, Holland to Lansdowne, 18 Jan. 1822. [16] *Lady Bessborough*, 285-6, 291; M. Villiers, *Grand Whiggery*, 366-8, 376-7, 379; P. Ziegler, *Melbourne*, 81. [17] *Lady Bessborough*, 285; J. Sydenham, *Hist. Poole*, 58-60; *Dorset Co. Chron.* 10 Nov. 1825, 3 Jan. 1828; Add. 51724, Ponsonby to Holland, 16 Jan. 1827. [18] Dorset RO, Lester-Garland mss D/LEG F23, f. 113; *The Times*, 9 Oct. 1824; *Dorset Co. Chron.* 22, 29 Sept. 1825. [19] Grey mss, Grey to Holland, 4 Sept. 1825; Fitzwilliam mss 125/1, Ponsonby to Fitzwilliam, 12 June [1826]. [20] *Dorset Co. Chron.* 1, 8, 15 June 1826. [21] Dorset RO, Poole borough recs. DC/PL CLA45. [22] *Lady Bessborough*, 287. [23] *Canning's Ministry*, 196; Add. 52447, f. 61. [24] P. Mandler, *Aristocratic Government in Age of Reform*, 61. [25] Add. 51724. [26] Add. 36465, f. 117. [27] *Dorset Co. Chron.* 8, 15 July, 5 Aug., 9, 30 Sept., 14 Oct. 1830. [28] Parker, *Peel*, ii. 176. [29] *Dorset Co. Chron.* 14 Apr., 5 May 1831. [30] Dorset RO, Bankes mss D/BKL, Ponsonby to G. Bankes, 4 May, to H. Bankes, 15 May 1831. [31] *Dorset Co. Chron.* 12, 26 May 1831; *Dorset Pollbook* (1831), 66. [32] Bankes mss, Ponsonby to Bankes, 13 Sept.; *The Times*, 17 Sept. 1831; *Three Diaries*, 136. [33] *Dorset Co. Chron.* 15, 22 Sept. 1831. [34] Ibid. 15, 22, 29 Sept., 6, 13, 20, 27 Oct.; *The Times*, 1, 19 Oct.; *Salisbury Jnl.* 24 Oct. 1831. [35] Dorset RO, Fox-Strangways mss D/FSI 332, Ponsonby to Ilchester, 26 Oct. 1831, Parry Okeden to same, 14 Jan. 1832. [36] Add. 51601, Lady Cowper to Lady Holland [Mar.]; *Western Flying Post*, 2 Apr. 1832. [37] *Dorset Co. Chron.* 22 Mar. 1832. [38] Dorset RO D793/1; D1379/1, 2; Beds. RO, Russell mss R766, Ponsonby to Russell, 22 Oct. [1831]; *Sherborne Jnl.* 19 Jan. 1832. [39] Southampton Univ. Lib. Broadlands mss SHA/PC/128; *Dorset Co. Chron.* 10 May 1832. [40] *Moore Jnl.* iv. 1479. [41] *Dorset Co. Chron.* 23 Feb., 14 June, 5 July, 23 Aug., 22 Nov., 20 Dec. 1832, 3 Jan. 1833; *Western Flying Post*, 20 Aug., 5 Nov. 1832. [42] *Lady Holland to Son*, 217. [43] *CP*, iv. 176; *The Times*, 19 May; *Poole and South-Western Herald*, 24 May 1855; *Gent. Mag.* (1855), ii. 92. [44] PROB 11/2215/597; J. Ponsonby, *Ponsonby Fam.* 180-1.

S.M.F.

PORCHER, Henry (1795–1857), of 57 Arlington Street, Mdx.

CLITHEROE 14 Aug. 1822–1826

bap. 9 Feb. 1795, at Fort St. George, Madras,[1] 3rd but 2nd surv. s. of Josias Du Pré Porcher† (*d.* 1820), E.I. agent, of Hillingdon House, Mdx. and Winslade House, Devon and Charlotte, da. of Adm. Sir William Burnaby, 1st bt., of Broughton Hall, Oxon. *educ.* Winchester 1803; Corpus, Camb. 1811. *m.* 6 May 1822, Sarah, da. John Pearse*, *s.p. d.* 19 Nov. 1857.
Dir. Bank of England 1825-42.

Porcher was of Huguenot stock. His family had reached England by way of the Carolinas. The junior branch specialized in the Indian trade, and Henry and his brothers, Thomas, George and Charles, were born in Madras, where their father was employed in the East India Company's civil service. Thomas served with the Company before joining the family's East India agency, and with Charles (later of Clyffe, Dorset) and George (afterwards rector of Maiden Erleigh, Berkshire) intended for the law and the church, it was Henry who joined the family firm in London following Thomas's death in 1812, becoming a partner on his father's retirement in 1816. Edward Fletcher and James Alexander* joined them that year and they subsequently traded as Fletcher, Alexander and Company of Devonshire Square.[2] His father, who ensured that Henry Porcher's name was given to an East Indiaman, relinquished the representation of Old Sarum in 1818 and died in 1820 worth about £150,000, of which Porcher inherited £10,000.[3] In May 1822 he married the daughter of a director and former governor of the Bank of England John Pearse*. Pearse's negotiations with Lord Brownlow and Earl Howe that summer concerning the purchase of the latter's Clitheroe tithes paved the way for Porcher's return for the borough in August on the Brownlow interest.[4]

He is not known to have spoken in debate. He voted with the Liverpool ministry against parliamentary reform, 20 Feb., 1 June 1823. He divided against Catholic relief, 1 Mar., 10 May 1825, and was correctly described in a radical publication that session as a Member who 'attended occasionally, and voted with ministers'.[5] He did so against repealing the assessed taxes, 10, 18 Mar., producing information on, 24 Mar., and inquiring into the prosecution of the Dublin Orange rioters, 22 Apr., and the currency, 12 June; but, like Alexander, he voted in the minority for investigating the duties on East and West Indian sugars with a view to their equalization, 22 May 1823. He divided against the usury laws repeal bill, 8 Apr., in defence of the indictment in Demerara of the Methodist missionary John Smith, 11 June 1824, and for the duke of Cumberland's annuity, 9 June 1825. He stood down at the 1826 dissolution.

The previous year he had become a director of the Bank, a position he held until 1843, when he also retired as one of the capital's deputy lieutenants. Fletcher, Alexander and Company traded until at least 1861, but it remains unclear how long Porcher, who in 1843 took a 21-year lease on Park House, Heckfield (part of the duke of Wellington's estate on the Berkshire-Hampshire border) remained a partner. He died near Heckfield in November 1857, following a fall from his horse. By his will, dated 17 May 1835 and proved 28 Jan. 1858, he left all his property to his wife.[6]

[1] BL OIOC N2/2/227. [2] *HP Commons, 1790-1820*, iii. 555-6; *London Gazette*, 13 Jan. 1816; *Burke LG* (1871), p. 1113. [3] PROB 11/1630/305; IR26/835/157. [4] *Gent. Mag.* (1822), ii. 272; Lancs. RO, Francis mss DDFr5/43. [5] *Session of Parl. 1825*, p. 481. [6] Museum of English Rural Life, Wellington Estate coll. 1371/2; BL OIOC, India Office Register IOR/L/L/2/1819; *Morning Chron.* 24 Nov. 1857; IR26/2143/42.

S.R.B./M.M.E.

PORCHESTER, Lord *see* **HERBERT, Henry John George**

PORTMAN, Edward Berkeley I (1771–1823), of Bryanston, Dorset.

BOROUGHBRIDGE	1802–1806
DORSET	1806–19 Jan. 1823

b. 31 Jan. 1771, 2nd s. of Henry William Portman (*d.* 1796) of Orchard Portman, Som. and Bryanston and Anne, da. of William Wyndham of Dinton, Wilts.; bro. of Henry Berkeley Portman†. *educ.* St. John's, Camb. 1788; grand tour. *m.* (1) 28 Aug. 1798, Lucy (*d.* 20 Mar. 1812), da. of Rev. Thomas Whitby of Portland Place, Mdx. and Cresswell, Staffs., 4s. 3da.; (2) 16 Mar. 1816, Mary, da. of Sir Edward Hulse, 3rd bt., of Braemore House, Hants, *s.p. suc.* bro. Henry 1803. *d.* 19 Jan. 1823.

Sheriff, Dorset 1798-9; lt. Dorset yeomanry 1798, 1803.

Portman, who came from an old Somerset family now settled in Dorset, retained his county seat as an independent at the general election of 1820, being returned unopposed.[1] He appears to have attended irregularly, possibly because of poor health. He voted against the appointment of an additional baron of exchequer in Scotland, 15 May 1820. On 28 June he obtained leave to introduce a bill to prevent unqualified persons from practising as conveyancers. It failed to get a second reading, 4 July, and he vowed to reintroduce it next session, but did not do so.[2] He was one of the county Members, 'generally more inclined to opposition', who voted with ministers against condemning the omission of Queen Caroline's name from the liturgy, 26 Jan. 1821.[3] He was granted two weeks' leave because of illness in his family, 19 Feb., but was present to vote against Catholic relief, 28 Feb. He divided with government on the state of the revenue, 6 Mar., but against them on the repeal of the additional malt duty, 3 Apr., the army estimates, 21, 28 May, and the duke of Clarence's grant, 8 June. He paired against the forgery punishment mitigation bill, 23 May 1821, but voted for criminal law reform, 4 June 1822. His only other recorded votes were for more extensive tax reductions to relieve distress, 11 Feb., abolition of one of the joint-postmasterships, 14 Mar., and repeal of the malt duties, 3 June 1822. He died, in Rome, in January 1823, while travelling with his family, whose delayed return home was expected by the British attaché William Fox Strangways to be 'very melancholy'. His remains were interred in the family vault at Bryanston in April.[4] By that time his son and namesake, who succeeded to his estates in Dorset, Somerset and Marylebone, and most of the personalty sworn under £80,000, had also taken over his parliamentary seat for Dorset.[5]

[1] J. Hutchins, *Dorset*, i (1861), 256, 263; *HP Commons, 1790-1820*, iv. 873-4; *Western Flying Post*, 6, 20 Mar. 1820. [2] *The Times*, 29 June, 5 July 1820; *CJ*, lxxv. 365, 377, 397. [3] Add. 38742, f. 171. [4] Add. 51342, Fox Strangways to Lady Ilchester, 30 Jan.; *Western Flying Post*, 17 Feb., 21 Apr. 1823. [5] PROB 11/1669/236; IR26/970/376; M. Portman, *Bryanston, Picture of a Fam.* 128-9.

D.R.F.

PORTMAN, Edward Berkeley II (1799–1888), of Bryanston, Dorset.

DORSET	26 Feb. 1823–1832
MARYLEBONE	1832–7 Mar. 1833

b. 9 July 1799, 1st s. of Edward Berkeley Portman I* and 1st w. Lucy, da. of Rev. Thomas Whitby of Portland Place, Mdx. and Cresswell, Staffs. *educ.* Eton c.1811; Christ Church, Oxf. 1817. *m.* 16 June 1827, Lady Emma Lascelles, da. of Henry Lascelles†, 2nd earl of Harewood, 4s. (1 *d.v.p.*) 2da. (1 *d.v.p.*). *suc.* fa. 1823; *cr.* Bar. Portman 27 Jan. 1837; Visct. Portman 28 Mar. 1873. *d.* 19 Nov. 1888.

Ld. lt. Som. 1839-64; commr. duchy of Cornwall 1840; councillor, duchy of Lancaster 1847; chairman, q. sess. Dorset 1861-82; councillor to prince of Wales 1863; ld. warden of the stannaries 1865-*d.*

Pres. European Life Insurance Co. 1823-8; pres. Philological Sch. 1835-*d.*; pres. R. Agricultural Soc. 1846, 1857, 1862.

Capt. Dorset militia 1821; maj. 1st Som. militia 1839.

Portman, who took a first class degree at Oxford in 1821, witnessed the death of his father, Member for Dorset, in Rome in January 1823, but the poor health of other members of the family prevented his immediate return to England.[1] Under his father's will, he succeeded to estates in Dorset, Middlesex and Somerset and £70,000 of his personal wealth.[2] Charlotte, daughter of Thomas Grove of Ferne, Wiltshire, noted in her diary that Portman had 'a very deserving eldest son left to inherit his vast property. But as my father says, we shall see now *what* he is when he acts for himself'.[3] In fact, the estates were burdened by debts and legal restrictions and it was several years before Portman, who devoted himself to agricultural pursuits and later benefited from the escalation of property values in the metropolis, was able to put his finances on a prosperous footing. He disposed of most of his Somerset estates and, except when staying in short-term residences in London, usually lived at Bryanston, near Blandford Forum in central Dorset, where he became active in local affairs.[4] As the Member for Corfe Castle, Henry Bankes, his father's former opponent, came forward to fill the vacancy for the county, Portman's sponsors among the leading gentry initially withdrew his pretensions, imagining that he would enter the Commons on the expected retirement of the other Member, William Morton Pitt. Yet, so great was the disapprobation of Bankes, an old Tory, that in the absence of any realistic alternative the freeholders preferred to return the inexperienced son of their late respected and independent Member. Bankes gave way after the show of hands was against him at the nomination meeting, 18 Feb. 1823, and Portman was elected in his absence eight days later. As Thomas Grosvenor, Member for Chester, commented, 'What a lucky fellow young Portman is: "one man's poison is another man's bread"'.[5] He wrote an address of thanks from Genoa and returned to Bryanston that spring.[6]

Unlike his father, Portman, who was assiduous in presenting county petitions and serving on select committees, sided almost unwaveringly with the Whig opposition to the Liverpool administration.[7] He voted for the first time, 24 Apr. 1823, in favour of Russell's motion for parliamentary reform, an occasion which he afterwards alluded to with satisfaction.[8] According to a later recollection, he was present for the debates on Spain at the end of that month.[9] He voted with ministers against the production of papers on Catholic office-holders, 19 Feb., but against them on reform of the representation of Edinburgh, 26 Feb. 1824, and on several other occasions that session. He made his first known speech against the silk bill, 5 Mar. He offered a suggestion on the county courts bill, 26 Mar., and voted to permit defence by counsel in felony cases, 6 Apr. He paired for inquiries into the state of Ireland, 11 May, and the trial of the Methodist missionary John Smith in Demerara, 11 June 1824, when he defended the county magistrates over the imprisonment of Richard Carlile in Dorchester gaol. He was granted one month's sick leave, 10 Feb. 1825. He gave his 'hearty concurrence' to the Catholic relief bill, 21 Apr., which he said was 'called for by imperious necessity' to ensure peace in Ireland; he voted for it that day, as he did again on 10 May 1825.

In September 1825, during speculation over a possible dissolution, he issued an address indicating his intention to stand again for the county at the next general election. He declined to attend a meeting of Dorset landowners in Blandford, 9 Jan. 1826, but expressed approval of their plans to form an Agricultural Association to promote protection.[10] He was elected to Brooks's, 15 Feb., sponsored by Lord Fitzwilliam and John Calcraft, Member for Wareham. He voted against receiving the report on the salary of the president of the board of trade, 10 Apr., and spoke in defence of British ship owners, 27 Apr.[11] With Sir Thomas Lethbridge, the Somerset county Member, he was a teller for the minority for a select committee on distress in the manufacturing districts, 2 May. He approved ministers' resolution to admit bonded corn, 4 May, but opposed the introduction of corn from abroad, 5 May, and abandoned his attempt to strengthen government proposals by fixing minimum and maximum prices, 12 May. As Bankes had replaced Pitt earlier that year, he was returned unopposed with him for Dorset at the general election in June, when he reiterated his desire to be independent.[12] Portman, who the previous year had published a pamphlet of *Rules, Regulations and Tables* for the constitution of a friendly society, was heavily involved in the establishment of one in Dorset in late 1826.[13]

He seconded the formal reappointment of Manners Sutton as Speaker, 14 Nov. 1826. He spoke in defence of agricultural protection, 1, 12 Mar., when he observed that 'the landed interest, by conceding that 60*s.* should be the minimum price, had conceded as much as they could concede'; but he distanced himself from the fears of other agriculturists over the corn bill, 2 Apr. 1827. He voted for Catholic relief, 6 Mar. He brought up, but dissented from, an anti-Catholic petition from Blandford, 13 Mar., when he asked ministers if they had any plans to ameliorate the condition of the poor in Ireland. He divided for Tierney's amendment to postpone the committee of supply, 30 Mar., and for inquiry into the Irish miscellaneous estimates, 5 Apr. On 2 May he expressed the hope that Canning's difficulties in forming his administration would not lead to the public being inflamed over religious issues. He presented and endorsed the Dorset landowners' petition against the importation of foreign wool, 28 May, when he failed to obtain a select committee on this, but stated his general approval of administration.[14] In June 1827 he made a surprising match with a daughter of the moderate Tory Lord Harewood. Her sister-in-law Lady Caroline Lascelles, who described Portman as 'very good-looking, and particularly gentlemanlike and pleasing', noted that 'they will not be very rich in the first instance, but in four or five years he will be in receipt of his whole fortune, which will then go on increasing. It is a very brilliant marriage altogether'.[15]

Portman was named on George Tierney's* list for the proposed finance committee in late 1827, and was one of the possible substitutes listed by John Herries* in February 1828, but he was not in the end appointed to it.[16] In December 1827 Huskisson, the colonial secretary in the Goderich ministry, approached him to move the address at the start of the session, in 'recollection of the cordial support which you gave to Mr. Canning's administration'; he declined, pleading pressure of private business.[17] Praised for his support of the wool industry in the county newspaper, he replied in a published letter of thanks, dated 24 Jan. 1828, for the present of some Dorset cloth, 'which I shall have very great pleasure in wearing as soon as possible at the market at Blandford, and in my place in the House of Commons'.[18] He was named to the drafting and second reading committees on the friendly societies bill, 21 Feb., 25 Mar., and the division of counties bill, 27 Feb., 5 Mar., and gave his support to these measures during the session. He voted for repeal of the Test Acts, 26 Feb., and Catholic relief, 12 May. In a lengthy speech on the corn laws, 22 Apr., he asserted that the planned alterations would offer insufficient protection to agriculture if the price of corn fell below 60*s.*, but he had to withdraw his wrecking amendment against the corn bill through lack of support. He stated that his stand was principled and was not simply for the sake of opposition, 25 Apr., when his amendment to substitute a level of duty which would increase by 2*s.* for every 1*s.* fall in price was defeated by 140-50. On 20 May his motion to remove London from the list of places used in calculating the corn averages was lost by 132-36. He voted for information on civil list pensions that day, and called for lower official salaries, 30 May. Late that month he privately informed the friendly societies lobby that he would take over the emasculated bill from its previous sponsor and reintroduce it in the following session.[19] In September 1828 he approached the duke of Wellington for a peerage, arguing that his health was not sound enough for the onerous duties of a county Member, but the prime minister refused his request.[20]

Portman presented pro-Catholic Dorset and Somerset petitions, 6 Mar. 1829, when he spoke and voted for emancipation. He obtained leave for his friendly societies bill the same day, and oversaw its passage that session. He divided for transferring East Retford's seats to Birmingham, 5 May. He made suggestions on the ecclesiastical courts bill, 12 May, and the metropolitan police bill, 15 May, and objected to the solicitor-general moving the county Clare writ immediately after Daniel O'Connell's refusal to take the oaths, 19 May. He urged ministers to make clear their intentions on the wool duties, 27 May, to lower the duties on tobacco, 1 June, and coastwise coal, 4 June (when he moved the third reading of the divisions of counties bill), not to alter the corn laws, 2 June, and to investigate abuses under the vagrancy laws, 19 June 1829. On 15 Feb. 1830 he obtained leave to introduce his paupers removal bill (to prevent southern counties incurring costs for passing paupers to the Channel Islands) and his general measure to permit the watching, lighting and paving of parishes (on which he secured a select committee on 26 Apr.), both of which passed that year. He voted for a reduction in taxation, 15 Feb., and the following day insisted, against ministers' denials, that distress was general in the country and that the malt tax ought to be abolished for 'we must take every means within our power to lower the taxation generally'. He paired for the enfranchisement of Birmingham, Leeds and Manchester, 23 Feb., and voted to transfer East Retford's seats to Birmingham, 5 Mar. 1830. Denis Le Marchant† later recorded an encounter between him and George Dawson*, secretary to the treasury:

> Their conversation turned on some recent defeat of the Whigs, when, Mr. Portman attempting to explain it, Mr. Dawson laughingly said, 'Oh, you are a mere bundle of sticks and will always be beaten'. This taunt rather excited Mr. Portman, while at the same time he felt its truth, and he reported Mr. Dawson's words to his friends.

As a result, with the other county Members Lawley and Wynne Pendarves, he was instrumental in setting up the meeting in early March 1830 at which Lord Althorp was chosen as leader of the Whig opposition in the Commons.[21] Thereafter during the session Portman regularly made interventions and divided (or paired) with them for lower taxes and expenditure. He made a long speech urging inquiry into the state of the poor, 9 Mar., and advocated assisted emigration, 23 Mar. He objected to allowing the sale of beer for on-consumption, 3 May, and the following day, in what Lord Howick* called 'a most absurd speech', moved (and was a teller for) an unsuccessful wrecking amendment against the second reading of the beer bill.[22] He conceded that his earlier assumptions about the number of government placemen were exaggerated, 14 May, but nevertheless divided with opposition for information on privy councillors' emoluments that day. He left London in late May 1830 because of his wife's illness.[23]

Portman chaired the meeting in Blandford, 27 July 1830, when it was agreed to implement the Watching Act there.[24] At the general election that summer he expressed support for John Cam Hobhouse's* aspirations in Middlesex and Edward Sanford's* in Somerset.[25] Boasting of his 'integrity and diligence' and advocating freedom of the press, peace, liberty and retrenchment, he was returned unopposed with Bankes for Dorset.[26] In the House, 9 Nov., he was twice rebuffed by Peel, the home secretary, when he asked whether government had any plans to relieve the distress of the labouring poor. Listed by ministers among their 'foes', he divided in the majority against them on the civil list, 15 Nov., which led to their resignation. He obtained leave to bring in a bill, which was unsuccessful, to consolidate the laws relating to highways, 17 Nov., when he was a teller for the minority for not considering election petitions until after the Christmas recess. He was given three weeks' leave because of the disturbed state of his county during the 'Swing' riots, 23 Nov. 1830. Always a benevolent landlord, he angered his neighbours by agreeing to raise wages to 10*s.* a week for day labourers, but was closely involved in the re-establishment of the county's yeomanry cavalry early the following year.[27] He opposed the Grey ministry for the first time, 7 Feb. 1831, when he urged them to make further reductions in the pension list. He opposed Hunt's motion in favour of an amnesty for the agricultural rioters, 8 Feb., and called for an overall reform of the poor laws, 16 Feb. He spoke for parliamentary reform, 26 Feb., and, having voted for the second reading of the reform bill, 22 Mar., declared that he would support it despite having reservations about some of its details, 23 Mar. He attended a dinner in Poole, 7 Apr., when he recommended reform in order to ensure that those elected had the 'fittest head' and not the 'longest purse'.[28] He spoke and divided against Gascoyne's wrecking amendment, 19 Apr., which led to a dissolution, and on 21 Apr. 1831 asserted that the electorate would judge the general election on the whole reform question.

Portman was popular as a reformer and was certain of being returned, while Calcraft, with whom he declined to join, stood against the anti-reformer Bankes. On all six days of the poll he was ahead of the other two candidates, to each of whom he gave £3,000 towards their costs. According to Grey, this curious gesture was designed 'to show his impartiality, being himself a reformer and supporter of government'. He was elected with Calcraft, which he hailed as indicative of the triumph of reform, and at a celebration dinner in Blandford, 23 May 1831, he promised the electors that 'give me but the opportunity of meeting you, and you may depend upon it, you will never find me wanting'.[29] However, Bankes recorded in his journal that Portman had desired that the poll should not be closed early on the day the contest ended

> as he hoped to avoid a public dinner, and the annoyance of sitting down surrounded by many of those who supported him, of whom he seemed much ashamed; and he expressed himself afterwards as being tired of the representation of the county, and solicitous to find some proper occasion of withdrawing from it, so that he might live more in the country, and perform those duties in which he might be more permanently useful. He may perhaps speculate upon a peerage, but I should otherwise rather consider him as fond of the business of the House of Commons in which he frequently takes a share.[30]

In the House, Portman, who again failed to carry his highways bill (introduced on 23 June), urged improvement of the corn laws, 24 June, and repeal of the malt duty, 30 June, and quibbled with O'Connell, 1 July, and Hunt, 8 July. He voted for the second reading of the reintroduced reform bill, 6 July, and steadily (sometimes by pairing) for its details. He made a fool of himself, 15 July, when, from 'the rear ranks' he shouted out 'Lyme Regis' in response to Croker's asking whether there were any nomination boroughs in schedule B, which allowed Croker to argue that similar cases in schedule A might retain one seat. Stating that he had made it a rule not to comment on individual Dorset boroughs, 6 Aug., he nevertheless intervened in the debate on Weymouth to rebut opposition statements that reform was unpopular in the county. He called for repeal of the settlement laws, 8 Aug., and on the 10th advocated a scheme to relieve poverty in Ireland by such an application of the poor laws 'as would make it the interest of the proprietors of the soil to improve the condition of those around them'. The cabinet decided to oppose the intended motion to enfranchise £50 tenants-at-will which, according to Lord Holland, Portman was responsible for;[31] in fact, it was in the hands of the Tories Colonel Sibthorp and Lord Chandos, and it seems unlikely that he voted for it on 18 Aug.[32] He divided for the third reading, 19 Sept., and passage of the bill, 21 Sept. Later that month he signed Lord Ebrington's circular for a meeting to decide how to act if the bill was defeated in the Lords, and he duly voted for Ebrington's confidence motion, 10 Oct. 1831.[33] Rumours that Portman would receive a coronation peerage were groundless because ministers feared to open the county.[34] This, however, occurred on Calcraft's suicide in September 1831, and in the ensuing contest Portman's sympathies were with the reform candidate William Ponsonby*, although in ordinary circumstances he would have remained neutral. Yet, in a letter to the anti-reformer Lord Ashley*, he expressed the unnecessary punctilio that he could not remain in Parliament if Ashley proved Dorset to be a 'weathercock county' by overturning the result of the May election.[35] Ashley made his communication public, which not only led to a bitter private correspondence between them, so that friends had to mediate to settle the quarrel, but obliged Portman to make a public declaration.[36] Therefore, on the second day of the poll he voted for Ponsonby and promised to resign if Ashley was elected, because of 'the manner in which the present opposition [to Ponsonby] has been conducted'.[37] One observer rightly commented that 'Portman has made himself a host of enemies by a foolish sort of letter which he wrote to Ashley, but I think the clamour will not outlast the election'. After Ashley's narrow victory, Portman, who was unfairly accused of turning a blind eye to the riotous attacks on anti-reformers that subsequently took place in Blandford, undertook not to resign his seat until the House had decided on Ponsonby's petition.[38]

He spoke for the revised reform bill, 12 Dec. 1831, but 'unluckily tried to clinch' the vote of Lord Clive, who had made a non-partisan speech in its favour, and, as Le Marchant reported, 'there was no cheering at this; every one anticipated what must happen; the moment there was an opportunity, up got Lord Clive to explain and the country gentlemen took care not to expose themselves to such suspicious commendations'.[39] Portman paired for the second reading, 17 Dec. 1831. That winter he was sympathetic to a mooted plan for the establishment of a Whig Club in Dorset.[40] By early February 1832 he was reported to be back in good health after having nearly died from taking a dose of the wrong medicine.[41] He commented on an improvement in the timing of polls, 11 Feb., the factories bill, 29 Feb., and the regulation of benefit societies, 2 Mar. He voted for the enfranchisement of Tower Hamlets, 28 Feb., and paired for the third reading of the reform bill, 22 Mar., having informed Smith Stanley, the Irish secretary, on the 11th that 'I have paired off with [William Stratford] Dugdale on *the* bill because my sister (his wife) is too ill for him to leave her'.[42] That month it was expected that he would be made a peer if creations were needed to carry it through the Lords.[43] Out of what Sir John Benn Walsh* termed 'sheer spleen at Ashley's success' in the Dorset election committee, he announced his intended resignation in an address, 26 Mar., but in the face of numerous requests to stay, including one from Ponsonby, his likely successor, he agreed (by a further address on 7 Apr.) not to disturb the peace of the county. This was much to the relief of the Whigs, but he was reviled in the Tory press, and Hunt's raising it in the House, 17 May, led to embarrassing explanations there.[44] He voted for Ebrington's motion for an address calling on the king to appoint only ministers who would carry the reform bill unimpaired, 10 May, and claimed that he had several Dorset petitions to present in its favour, 17 May. He opposed the cruelty to animals bill, 30 May, commented on a breach of privilege, 31 May, argued for the establishment of municipal police forces, 4 June, and urged reform of the poor laws, 20 June, when he spoke and voted for making coroners' inquests public. He divided with ministers for the Russian-Dutch loan, 12 July, and paired for it on the 16th, when he urged them to oversee the future passage of the highways bill, which he moved to put off for that session, 18 July 1832.

Although expected to continue to represent Dorset, he cited poor health as the reason for withdrawing, and instead offered for Marylebone, where he owned extensive properties and had been establishing an interest. He was elected there in first place as a Liberal at the general election of 1832, but retired from the Commons early the following year.[45] Portman, who received a peerage from the Melbourne government in 1837 and whose wife was a lady of the bedchamber to Queen Victoria, profited from his metropolitan estates to become one of the richest men in England, with an estimated income of about £100,000 in 1883.[46] He, of whom it was written that 'by his courteous and dignified demeanour he admirably sustained the exalted position to which he had been raised', died in November 1888. He left his estates to his eldest son William Henry Berkeley (1829-1919), Liberal Member for Shaftesbury, 1852-7, and Dorset, 1857-85, who succeeded as 2nd Viscount Portman. His second son Edwin Berkeley (1830-1921) was Liberal and Home Rule Member for Dorset North, 1885-92, and his third son Maurice Berkeley (1833-88) was a member of the Canadian Parliament.[47]

[1] Add. 51342, Fox Strangways to Lady Ilchester, 30 Jan. 1823. [2] PROB 11/1669/236; IR26/970/376. [3] *Grove Diaries* ed. D. Hawkins, 151. [4] *Dorset Co. Chron.* 22 Nov. 1888; T. W. Mayberry, *Orchard and the Portmans*, 5, 38, 40; M. Portman, *Bryanston, Picture of a Fam.* 129-32; Sir M. Nathan, *Annals of West Coker*, 419. [5] *Western Flying Post*, 17, 24 Feb., 3 Mar. 1823; Grosvenor mss 9/10/94; 11/40. [6] *Salisbury Jnl.* 31 Mar., 21 Apr. 1823. [7] *Session of Parl. 1825*, p. 481. [8] For example, *Dorset Co. Chron.* 12 May 1831; *Russell Later Corresp.* ii. 52. [9] Le Marchant, *Althorp*, 211. [10] *Dorset Co. Chron.* 29 Sept. 1825, 12 Jan. 1826. [11] *The Times*, 28 Apr. 1826. [12] *Dorset Co. Chron.* 8, 15, 22 June 1826. [13] *Western Flying Post*, 8, 15 July, 23, 30 Dec. 1826. [14] *The Times*, 29 May 1827. [15] *Howard Sisters*, 59, 72-75, 77. [16] Add. 38761, f. 269; 40395, f. 221. [17] Add. 38753, ff. 49, 51. [18] *Dorset Co. Chron.* 7 Feb. 1828. [19] *The Times*, 26 May 1828. [20] Wellington mss WP1/955/13; 963/4. [21] Grey mss, Howick jnl. 3 Mar. 1830; Le Marchant, 243; A. Mitchell, *Whigs in Opposition*, 226. [22] Howick jnl. [23] Wellington mss WP1/1114/11. [24] *Western Flying Post*, 12 July 1830. [25] Add. 36466, f. 167; Dorset RO, Fox Strangways mss D/FSI 332, Phelips to Ilchester, 4 July 1830. [26] *Dorset Co. Chron.* 29 July, 12 Aug. 1830. [27] Ibid. 2 Dec.; Fox Strangways mss 242, Portman to Ilchester, 24-29 Nov., 3 Dec. 1830. [28] *Dorset Co. Chron.* 14 Apr. 1831. [29] Ibid. 28 Apr., 5, 12, 19, 26 May; Derby mss 920 Der (14) 117/5, Grey to Smith Stanley, 11 May 1831; M. Brock, *Great Reform Act*, 200. [30] Dorset RO, Bankes mss D/BKL, Bankes jnl. 174. [31] *Holland House Diaries*, 12. [32] Portman's name is not in the surviving partial division lists, but during the Dorset by-election, he, like Ponsonby, was attacked for having voted against giving the franchise to farmers (*Dorset Co. Chron.* 6 Oct. 1831). [33] Hatherton diary. [34] *Dorset Co. Chron.* 8 Sept. 1831; *Howard Sisters*, 200. [35] Shaftesbury mss SE/NC/5/5. [36] This corresp. is in ibid. SE/NC/5. See DORSET. [37] *The Times*, 5 Oct. 1831; *Dorset Pollbook* (Sept.-Oct. 1831), 2. [38] Fox Strangways mss 332, Murray to Ilchester [7 Oct.], latter to Portman, 18 Oct., reply, 19 Oct.; Bristol Univ. Lib. Pinney mss, domestic box R, bdle. 5, Lady Smith to Frances Pinney [19 Oct.]; *Dorset Co. Chron.* 27 Oct. 1831. [39] *Lady Holland to Son*, 124; NLS mss 24762, f. 49. [40] Fox Strangways mss 332, Parry Okeden to Ilchester, 28 Dec. 1831, 14 Jan. 1832. [41] *Dorset Co. Chron.* 2 Feb. 1832. [42] Derby mss 128/10. [43] *Dorset Co. Chron.* 15 Mar. 1832; *Greville Mems.* ii. 283. [44] NLW, Ormathwaite mss FG/1/6, p. 48; Add. 51601, Lady Cowper to Lady Holland, Tues. [Mar.]; *Dorset Co. Chron.* 29 Mar., 5, 12 Apr.; *Western Flying Post*, 2 Apr. 1832. [45] *Dorset Co. Chron.* 5 July; Brougham mss, Horne to Brougham [25 Aug.]; *The Times*, 4 Oct., 11-13 Dec. 1832. [46] J.V. Beckett, *Aristocracy in England* (1988), 292. [47] *Dorset Co. Chron.* 22, 29 Nov.; *The Times*, 20 Nov. 1888, 25 Feb. 1889; *DNB*; *Oxford DNB*.

S.M.F.

POULETT THOMSON, Charles Edward (1799–1841), of 11 Suffolk Street, Pall Mall, Mdx.[1]

DOVER	1826–1832
MANCHESTER	1832–Aug. 1839

b. 13 Sept. 1799, 3rd s. of John Thomson (afterwards Buncombe Poulett Thomson), Russia merchant (*d.* 1839), of 7 Austin Friars, London and Roehampton and Waverley Abbey, nr. Farnham, Surr. and Charlotte, da. of John Jacob, MD, of Salisbury, Wilts.; bro. of George Poulett Scrope†. *educ.* Hanwell, Mdx. (Rev. Hannington) 1806; private tutors 1809-15. *unm. cr.* Bar. Sydenham 19 Aug. 1840; GCB 19 Aug. 1841. *d.* 19 Sept. 1841.

Vice-pres. bd. of trade Nov. 1830-June 1834, pres. June-Dec. 1834, Apr. 1835-Aug. 1839; PC 22 Nov. 1830; treas. of navy Dec. 1830-Dec. 1834.

Gov.-gen. Canada 1839-*d.*

Poulett Thomson's great-grandfather John Thomson (*d.*1746) was an Edinburgh banker. His only son Andrew Thomson entered the Russian trade and by 1755 was established in London at 7 Austin Friars. His firm, which had other premises at 32 Old Bethlem and an office in St. Petersburg, was styled Thomson and Peters by 1763, and Thomson, Peters, Bonar and Thomson by 1791. His principal partner in his later years was his nephew and son-in-law Thomas Bonar (the son of his sister Agnes and Andrew Bonar, who married his daughter Anne in 1779). He acquired property at Roehampton, fathered several illegitimate children, including the merchant, philanthropist and art collector John Julius Angerstein, and died, 'in his 84th year', 11 Feb. 1795.[2] By his will, dated 2 June 1790, he devised £13,000 to Bonar, £8,000 to his son-in-law Sir Joshua Vanneck, £4,500 between the sons of his daughter Elizabeth and John Hankey, and a life annuity of £300 to his daughter Agnes Ibbetson, plus £5,000 for any future husband and £3,000 for her children. In a codicil of 14 Feb. 1792 he left £15,000 to be invested for the equal benefit of the then six children of his only legitimate son John Thomson, his residuary legatee and active head of the business.[3] John Thomson, who bought the Waverley estate in about 1796, took the additional names of Buncombe and Poulett in 1814 as the heir and representative, through his mother Harriet Buncombe, of those Somerset families.[4] He had three sons and six daughters. His eldest son Andrew Henry, born in 1786, was a director of the Bank of England, 1824-33, as well as the eventual head of the firm, which, as Thomson, Bonar and Company, was operating from 10 New Broad Street Mews by 1811, 51 Old Broad Street by 1816, and 7 Austin Friars, again, from 1821 onwards. The second son George Julius (1797-1876) was educated at Harrow, Cambridge and Oxford, took the name of Scrope in 1821, made a name for himself as 'Pamphlet' Scrope, author of many tracts on geology and political economy, and was Liberal Member for Stroud, 1833-67.[5]

Their brother Charles Edward, John Thomson's youngest child, had a 'constitutional weakness' from birth and was always prey to 'continued and harassing infirmities'. He was a pretty boy and a favourite of George III, to whom the family were introduced at Weymouth in 1803: his brother claimed to recall the king forcing Pitt, to his immense embarrassment, to dandle and kiss the child before an audience of smirking courtiers. After a private education he was sent in 1815 to St. Petersburg to be trained for the family business, currently under the direction of his brother Andrew. He was introduced to high Russian society and acquired the 'peculiar charm of manner' and 'polished tone' for which he became noted. After recovering from a long illness he returned to England in the autumn of 1817 and then accompanied his doting mother and two youngest sisters on a tour of northern Italy and Switzerland. In the summer of 1818 he took the waters at Valdagno and Recora, before rejoining his family and wintering in Naples. The following summer he travelled home with his brother George, who had joined him in Italy, and spent the winter in the London counting house. Irked by this drudgery, and being fluent in French, German, Italian and Russian, he nurtured diplomatic ambitions, but all attempts to place him failed. He went back to St. Petersburg in April 1821, now entrusted with a share in the conduct and profits of the business. He visited Moscow and central Russia the following year, and in August 1823 went on a tour of the south-east which took him to Vienna for the winter. He went from there in the spring of 1824 to Paris to attend his dying mother. He subsequently returned to London and played his part in the business, which he took charge of when Andrew was away.[6]

Poulett Thomson, who had his fingers slightly burnt as a result of some South American mining speculations in the financial panic of 1825-6, developed 'strong opinions of a liberal character', in contrast to the Tory views of his father. He made the acquaintance of the leading Utilitarians and philosophic radicals, attended meetings of the Political Economy Club, where he became friendly with Lord Althorp* and took lessons in economics from John McCulloch.[7] He aimed at a parliamentary career, and was introduced by Bentham's confidant John Bowring, who later credited him with 'considerable sharpness and sagacity', to the radical Member Joseph Hume.[8] Hume put him in touch with a group of Dover voters resident in London who wished to remove the sitting Members. In September 1825, when a dissolution was expected, he canvassed the borough in coalition with James Morrison*, a wealthy London silk merchant, as 'professed friends to economy and retrenchment', whose object was 'to produce the greatest sum of happiness to our fellow men'. They disclaimed 'any party attachments' and expressed approval of 'the liberal commercial changes, and other political ameliorations' recently introduced by the Liverpool ministry.[9] By the time of the dissolution in 1826 Morrison had dropped out, but Poulett Thomson, disregarding the remonstrances of his father and brother, who feared both the cost of a contest and his distraction from the family business, stood his ground. He boasted of his ability to serve local maritime interests through his commercial connections, and at the nomination advocated parliamentary reform, including shorter parliaments, 'removal' of the corn laws and retrenchment. In response to the strong 'No Popery' cry which was raised against him, he proclaimed himself 'favourable to civil and religious liberty' and 'hostile in every case to the prostration of intellect, of Protestant or Catholic, to either a lord warden or a town clerk'. After an eight-day contest, which cost him rather more (at least £3,000) than he had led his brother to expect, he was returned in second place.[10] At a celebration dinner he attacked the government on the national debt, foreign policy and, retrospectively, post-war repression. He said that he was 'no rash innovator, no theoretical reformer', but an advocate of 'constitutional reform', who believed that 'it were better there were no representation at all, than that the shadow of it should be purchased by so much corruption, perjury, and iniquity of every kind'.[11]

Poulett Thomson voted in the minority of 24 for Hume's amendment to the address, 21 Nov. 1826. He divided against the duke of Clarence's annuity, 16 Feb., 2 Mar., and the garrisons grant, 20 Feb. 1827. He presented a Dover petition against the corn laws, 26 Feb., and voted to relax them, 9, 27 Mar.[12] He observed that prohibitory customs duties only encouraged smuggling, 13 Mar., and called for rationalization of the system of measuring quantities of grain, 23 Mar. He voted for Catholic relief, 6 Mar., inquiry into the electoral activities of Leicester corporation, 15 Mar., and the spring guns bill, 23 Mar., and to postpone going into committee of supply in view of the current political uncertainty, 30 Mar. He divided for inquiries into the Irish miscellaneous estimates and chancery delays, 5 Apr., and next day objected 'most strongly' to the clause of the corn bill sanctioning the prohibition of imports from countries which imposed high duties on British goods. As he put it, 9 Apr., when he seconded Warburton's wrecking amendment, it 're-enacted the old system of prohibition'.[13] His first major speech was in opposition to Gascoyne's motion for inquiry into the British shipping interest, 7 May, which he construed as an attack on the 'liberal principles of policy' in commercial matters espoused by Huskisson, president of the board of trade, and other ministers. The speech, which his friend John Hobhouse* thought 'excellent', was a success, and drew 'loud applause from both sides of the House'. Later in the debate Huskisson complimented Poulett Thomson on his 'acuteness and knowledge'.[14] The Tory backbencher Henry Bankes noted that Poulett Thomson 'surprised the House' with his 'very able, detailed and argumentative speech', and the Canningite Member John Denison considered it 'very good'.[15] Poulett Thomson voted for the disfranchisement of Penryn, 28 May, presented a Dover petition for repeal of the Test Acts, 31 May, supported the introduction of the East Retford disfranchisement bill, 11 June, and, on the Preston election bill, 14 June, endorsed Hume's advocacy of the ballot.[16] He was in the Canning ministry's majority for the improvement of water communications in Canada, 12 June. On 2 June 1827 he was admitted to Brooks's Club, sponsored by Althorp and Lord Duncannon*.

On the Wellington administration's budget statement, 12 Feb. 1828, he tried to exploit apparently contradictory statements by Huskisson and Peel on the scope of the finance committee, and went on:

> Ministers, he had no doubt, did not wish to keep up large military establishments, but they were in a great measure controlled by the aristocracy ... who returned a majority of the Members of that House, and who urged them to many measures to which they would otherwise be repugnant.

He had more to say on this theme, 22 Feb., though he was reluctant to support Hume's call for extensive reductions in the armed forces. He presented petitions for repeal of the Test Acts, 18, 21, 26 Feb., 17 Mar., and took pleasure in voting in the 'wholly unexpected' majority for it, 26 Feb. Two days later he wrote to his brother:

> Thanks for your congratulations on what you are pleased to call my success in Parliament. I wish it were greater, but still, if I am permitted to proceed, I trust I may improve upon it. To the justice of every one of your maxims I entirely subscribe. The speech which I made last year, which gained me what little credit I have, is the best illustration of the principal one. A man who tells the House *facts* with which the majority are unacquainted, is sure to be listened to, and a reputation for doing so will procure him attention upon other points on which he, perhaps, does not deserve it. But a parliamentary reputation is like a woman's. It must be exposed as little as possible. And I am so sensible of this, that I would willingly abstain from opening my mouth more than once or twice in a session. I have latterly been obliged to infringe this rule more than I wish, but it has only been in committees, which are parliamentarily *sans consequence*. I hope to have one or two occasions for a splash, but I shall not go out of my way for them. This, to be sure, is all sad manoeuvring. But still, it is a *means* to being useful hereafter and therefore must be submitted to ... Now and then it occurs to me that some ten or fifteen years hence, when I am broken in health, in constitution and in spirits, and disappointed in both fortune and ambition ... I shall envy your position, and regret the useless waste of time, health, and money of the present day.[17]

Poulett Thomson, who voted for the disfranchisement of East Retford, 21 Mar., and for relaxation of the corn laws, 22, 29 Apr., continued to build up his reputation as a proponent of Ricardian economics. He was unhappy with the passengers regulation bill, 18, 24 Mar., objected to protection of the British lead industry, 1 Apr., advocated free trade in corn and silk and opposed wage regulation, 21 Apr., and supported reform of the laws governing friendly societies, 22 Apr. He moved for inquiry into the Hibernian Joint-Stock Company, 24 Apr., but gave up the motion a week later. He was against inquiry into the wool trade, 28 Apr., and called for a speedy settlement of the problem of protection against foreign wool, 1 May. He presented petitions for Catholic relief, 5 May, and voted for it, 12 May. He opposed the provision for Canning's family on 'constitutional' grounds, 13 May, and was in the minority of 14 against it, 22 May. He voted for a return of civil list pensions, 20 May, and paired for Hume's motion for their reduction, 10 June. On 20 May he spoke at some length in support of his motion for leave to introduce a bill to amend the usury laws which, he said, impeded fair competition and contributed to commercial distress, crime and misery. He brought it in, 5 June, and saw it through a second reading by 52-40, 19 June, but was forced by the strength of hostile feeling to abandon it.[18] He voted against the archbishop of Canterbury's bill, 16 June, and later that day, admitting that he had voted with government against inquiry into the circulation of small notes, 3 June, he opposed the bill to restrict the circulation of Scottish notes in England. On 17 June, opposing Gascoyne's renewed attempt to secure inquiry into the shipping interest, he expressed dismay at the apparent willingness of Vesey Fitzgerald and Courtenay, the new heads of the board of trade, to turn back the clock on commercial policy:

> If those great questions ... are to be subjected to the clumsy examinations of those who do not understand them ... where ... are we to look for an end of their inquiries? Under such a system, the country must become the scene of the most ruinous fluctuations and changes ... The course of policy has been taken, from which there is no return.

He voted for various economies, 20, 23 June, 4, 7 July, inquiry into abuses in the Irish church and against throwing East Retford into the hundreds, 24 June, against the additional churches bill, 30 June, and for the corporate funds bill, 10 July. He exhorted ministers not to increase the duty on foreign gloves, 26 June, and tobacco, 30 June, and supported repeal of the Foreign Enlistment Act on commercial grounds, 3 July. He welcomed that aspect of the pilotage bill which safeguarded the rights of Cinque Port pilots wishing to work west of Gravesend, 10 July, when his motion to reduce the duty on Indian manufactured silk goods was carried by the casting vote of the chairman. He defended the alteration against the attacks of spokesmen for the silk industry, 14 July, but could not prevent its reversal by 37-34. He complained next day that he had been beaten by a resort to 'brushing in votes', and on 16 July made a bid to reinstate his amendment, but was beaten by 48-31. He quizzed the chancellor, Goulburn, on his budget statement and advocated reduced taxation and free trade, 11 July, and on the national debt bill, 17 July, called for a limitation on the surplus applicable to the sinking fund. In September 1828 he apparently refused an offer of office from the Wellington ministry.[19] The following month Edward Davies Davenport* asked Lord Holland if he thought Poulett Thomson might legitimately attend the Kent county meeting called to petition against Catholic relief as Member for and a freeman of Dover. Holland reckoned that his presence to support those hostile to the petition would be 'most useful' and that he could get away with it; but he does not seem to have turned up.[20] Reviewing possible Commons leaders for the Whig opposition in November 1828, Davenport commented that Poulett Thomson, 'with talents little inferior [to Althorp and Edward Smith Stanley] has every recommendation that candour and integrity can give him, but I suppose it would be said that he has not *station*'. Their notion of forming a dining club of Members keen to 'reform the abuses and economize the revenues of the state' came to nothing, partly because, as Davenport recalled, when Parliament met Poulett Thomson 'was always engaged when I proposed to bring our resolves into operation'.[21]

Poulett Thomson, just back from a stay in France, dismissed a Dover petition against Catholic claims presented by his colleague Trant as unrepresentative and presented favourable ones, 3 Mar. 1829. He spoke and voted for emancipation, 6, 16, 19, 20 Mar., but he differed from many of his political associates by approving the relief bill's suppression of Jesuit and other Catholic monastic institutions, which he felt would destroy 'the nucleus of that resisting power to the principles of civil liberty, of which we have seen so much, of late, in Europe'. He could not, however, go along with Vyvyan's attempt to deprive Jesuits of their privileges under the Act of 1791. He opposed the West India dock bill, 14 Apr., and objected to that company's proposed purchase of the city canal, 16 Apr., because it was 'of the highest importance to discourage monopolies of all descriptions'. He applauded Vesey Fitzgerald's resistance to Fyler's motion for inquiry into the silk trade, 14 Apr.:

> I am no rash theorist, I am not desirous of carrying a favourite principle into operation at the expense of existing interests; but I maintain that your only course is a gradual, a progressive, but a steady approach to a

> free system; and ... that the very essence of commercial and manufacturing industry, is freedom from legislative interference and legislative protection.

He supported, with minor reservations, the silk trade bill, 1, 7 May. He denounced the corn laws as 'a tax which was laid on the people in general for the benefit of a particular class', 7 May, and was in the minority of 12 for a fixed duty on corn, 19 May. Yet, as he privately indicated to a friend who pressed him to take a parliamentary initiative on free trade, he was conscious of the restraints on action:

> I like your doctrine very well, but you fall into the line of which my friends the Utilitarians are but too justly accused, and with which you, as with them, will go further to defeat the extension of your principles, than your reasoning will go to establish them. You, like them, begin every discussion by telling those who differ from you that they are d—d fools, not exactly the way to put them in an humour for cool argument. You seem besides to have formed a most erroneous judgment of the facility with which any improvement can be carried into effect. To propose, to legislate, and to act on your law, you seem to think follow one another as glibly as cause and effect. Why, God bless you, the majority of the House of Commons, ay, 600 of the 650 senators, are opposed upon principle to any change, be it what it may; and a whole session could be readily spent by them in considering whether they had better consider.[22]

(Denis Le Marchant† thought Poulett Thomson's lack of a conventional education, by depriving him of 'social intercourse with young men of the class and position amongst which he now found himself', caused him to rate their abilities 'too low'.)[23] He voted for the transfer of East Retford's seats to Birmingham, 5 May, and for Lord Blandford's parliamentary reform resolutions and the issue of a new writ for East Retford, 2 June. He condemned the 'absurdity' of raising exchequer bills to reduce the unfunded debt, 8, 11, 14 May. He wanted an assurance that no more money would be demanded for the completion of Buckingham Palace, and was in the minority in the subsequent division, 25 May. His attempt to reduce the hemp duties, 1 June, was beaten by 60-40. He called for better protection of Spitalfields silk manufacturers against the depredations of disgruntled weavers, 2 June, presented a petition for a commutation of tithes, 4 June, and denied that there was serious distress in the shipping industry, 12 June 1829. He spent part of the winter in Paris, where he extended his contacts with the leading French free traders and corresponded with the junior minister Robert Wilmot Horton* on the subject of subsidized emigration.[24]

Poulett Thomson had been assured by Huskisson in October 1829 that reports of distress in the north of England were 'grossly exaggerated';[25] but he voted for the Ultra Knatchbull's amendment to the address, 4 Feb. 1830, after deploring the government's apparent indifference to distress. Yet on the appointment of the select committee on the renewal of the East India Company's charter, to which he was named, 9 Feb., he defended ministers against Bright's charge of procrastination. Later that day he clashed with Attwood, whose call for currency reform he dismissed as 'nothing less than a fraud on all the creditors in the country'. He attributed distress to a combination of bad harvests and inept legislation and advocated 'a better distribution of the taxes' as a solution. On 16 Feb. he gave notice of a motion on this subject. He voted for the transfer of East Retford's seats to Birmingham, 11 Feb., 5, 15 Mar., Blandford's reform scheme, 18 Feb., and the enfranchisement of Birmingham, Leeds and Manchester, 23 Feb. He presented a radical reform petition from Dover, 26 Feb., and on 1 Mar. presented and proposed inquiry into the Newark petition accusing the duke of Newcastle of electoral malpractice as crown lessee; he was beaten by 194-61. When O'Connell moved to insert voting by ballot in the provisions of the East Retford bill, 5 Mar., Poulett Thomson, 'friend as I am to the system of ballot', pressed him to withdraw the proposal and reintroduce it as a substantive motion. He voted against government on the Bombay judicature, 8 Mar., British interference in Portugal, 10 Mar., and the treasurer of the navy's ministerial salary, 12 Mar. At the meetings of the reviving Whig opposition in early March he not only recommended a property tax to offset tax reductions, but even suggested a legacy duty. Both notions met with opposition, and a meeting on 16 Mar. decided not to endorse a property tax but to back Poulett Thomson's planned motion for inquiry into a revision of taxation. He brought it on, 25 Mar., despite having been 'for some days past so indisposed, as to be rendered scarcely able justly to treat the matter'. He detailed proposals for reductions of duties on raw materials and articles of common consumption amounting to about £7,000,000, at an estimated cost to the treasury of £1,000,000. His motion was beaten by 167-78, a disappointing outcome which some blamed on Althorp's advocacy of a property tax during the debate.[26] Le Marchant recalled Poulett Thomson's performance on this occasion:

> He was ... clever, and thoroughly conversant with business; as he proved ... by the comprehensive view he took of the fiscal policy of the country, and his exposure of the vicious character of many of the existing duties ... He

> wanted the fullness and depth, and, it must be admitted, the modesty of Mr. Huskisson, for he had a dogmatism of tone and manner ill-suited to his youthful appearance; but in a ready flow of words, an animated diction, and the advantage of voice and delivery, he was incomparably the superior.[27]

Lord Grey's son Lord Howick* thought the speech was 'very good', but Bankes deemed it 'tedious' and delivered 'in the tone and manner of a whining Methodist preacher'.[28] The '*ostentation* of doctrine in his reasoning', not to mention his background and active involvement in trade, made him suspect in the snobbish eyes of many leading Whigs, including Brougham and Grey, who privately dismissed his financial plans as 'the height of infatuation and folly'.[29] In April 1830 there was speculation that ministers were anxious to recruit him in order to strengthen themselves in commons debates.[30] Poulett Thomson, who told Howick that he did not subscribe to the theory that absenteeism impoverished a country,[31] joined in the ensuing opposition campaign for economy, retrenchment and reduced taxation. He questioned the need for so many clerks in the office of the surveyor-general of the ordnance, 2 Apr., and criticized the cost of treasury messengers, 14 May. He objected to Spring Rice's motion for repeal of the Irish coal duties as 'partial', 13 May, but was listed in the minority for it, though Howick thought he had 'voted against us'.[32] The scorn which he heaped on a Northumberland miners' petition for an increased duty on lead, 25 May, drew a rebuke from Sir James Graham, its Whig presenter, who observed that Poulett Thomson 'must be made of most inflammatory materials, since he warms so easily upon such a subject'; but he cordially supported Graham's motion to reduce the cost of South American missions, 11 June, when he observed:

> I am ready to allow ... government some credit for a disposition to economy, although that disposition has probably been stimulated by the prayers and petitions of the people; but it is too much to see them take to themselves the infinite credit which they do on the subject.

He spoke against inquiry into the shipping interest, 6 May, opposed a return to a silver standard, 8 June, and denounced government's proposals on the sugar duties as 'injurious to the country', 21 June. He was called to order for renewing his attack on them when there was no question before the House, 23 June, and he supported Lord Chandos's attempt to reduce the duty on West Indian sugar, 30 June. He voted for Jewish emancipation, 5 Apr., 17 May, abolition of the Irish lord lieutenancy, 11 May, inquiries into Newfoundland, 11 May, the civil government of Canada, 25 May, and the commerce of Ceylon, 27 May, and parliamentary reform, 28 May. He reintroduced his usury laws amendment bill, 6 Apr., carried its second reading by 50-21, 26 Apr., and saw it through committee, where he accepted various amendments to it, but it never received a third reading. He presented petitions against the Dover improvement bill, 3, 6 May. He called for a simplification of bankruptcy procedure, 14 May, voted for abolition of the death penalty for forgery, 24 May, 7 June, and spoke and voted against an increase in the recognizances required under the libel law bill, 9 July 1830.

At the general election that summer Poulett Thomson, having declined an invitation to stand for London, offered again for Dover. He had damaged himself in some quarters by supporting Catholic emancipation, and when he was quizzed at a meeting of London voters, 2 July, he expended so much nervous energy in defending himself that he collapsed and had to be assisted from the overheated room. He was returned easily enough after a rowdy contest.[33] He told John Fazakerley* that 'in vexation and annoyance the cost had been so high, that I really don't think a seat for 20 years would make me consent to undertake it again'. Yet a week later he informed Althorp that although he had 'paid dearly in fatigue, trouble and illness', he had the consolation of knowing that 'nothing can touch my seat ... as long as I choose to retain it'. Of events in France he wrote:

> What a glorious revolution! Does it not raise your admiration of the state of the public mind there and demonstrate the fruits of the complete change of feeling, of education, and of prejudice which has been brought about by the first great change of '89? ... As for interference by our government, that must certainly be out of the question, but surely these events cannot pass so near us without producing positive good. The day is gone by when people's fears can be excited as in '92 and '93 ... and if so, reform of our institutions will be called for too loudly for the duke or any government to refuse it.

His only anxiety, expressed earlier to Fazakerley, was that Althorp's diffidence might prevent him from doing justice to the question of 'a general reform' in the House, where he was the man best equipped to take it up.[34] Poulett Thomson went to Paris in October, but was in the House to give notice of his intention of moving for a reduction of the newspaper stamp duty after Christmas, 12 Nov., and to help to vote ministers out of office on the civil list, 15 Nov. 1830.[35] Thanks to Althorp (who reluctantly took the exchequer and, as a financial greenhorn, probably wanted an experienced man of business at his elbow), he was made vice-president of the board of trade in the Grey ministry, under Lord Auckland, an amiable nonentity with no practical expertise.[36] According to Greville, who thought him 'very good-humoured, pleasing, and intelligent, but the greatest coxcomb I ever saw, and the vainest dog, though his vanity is not offensive or arrogant', Poulett Thomson told him five years later that

> when Lord Grey's government was formed ... he was averse to take office, but Althorp declared he would not come in unless Thomson did also, and that, knowing the importance of Althorp's accession to the government, he sacrificed a large income and took the board of trade; that when this was offered to him, he was asked whether he cared if he was president or vice-president, as they wished to make Lord Auckland president if he (Poulett Thomson) had no objection. He said, provided the president was not in the cabinet, he did not care; and accordingly he condescended to be vice-president, knowing that all the business must be done in the House of Commons, and that he must be (as in fact he said he was) the virtual head of the office. All this was told with a good-natured and smiling complacency, which made me laugh internally.[37]

Poulett Thomson's 'sudden' elevation excited considerable surprise and no little alarm, for he was known as 'a radical merchant' of doctrinaire views. Greville described him, curiously, as 'an ultra political communist'; and Edward Littleton* observed that 'although a clever man', he 'is a merchant, and the greatest of purists and political economists, and at whose names every Tory turns red or pale, as rage or fever predominates'.[38] Le Marchant, who called him an 'attenuated muscadin', noted that 'the City people were violently opposed' to his appointment, which was 'very injurious to the government', for 'his manners and his love of great society had made him very unpopular in the mercantile circles'.[39] Lord chancellor Brougham, who many years later unfairly dismissed him as 'a City fop or dandy who wanted to dine in good society' and was 'absolutely worse than useless in debate', admitted early in 1831 that his appointment was 'most unpopular': 'people *will not* draw nice distinctions, and a City man told me ... his ... name is still on *tallow* and *timber* bills in the market and then they go to him as a minister on such questions'.[40] At the same time, the Tory Thomas Gladstone* thought his merchant father would 'approve' of Poulett Thomson's appointment.[41] He gave up his involvement in the family business, but when the writ was moved for Dover, where his re-election was untroubled, 22 Nov. 1830, Lord Lowther made a point of asking, to 'a loud and general cheer', for confirmation of his withdrawal, 'in consequence of the sensation which this ... appointment has created out of doors'.[42]

As a minister Poulett Thomson, whose appointment advanced the development of the board of trade along Benthamite and Ricardian lines, rarely spoke on anything but departmental business.[43] He uttered not a syllable in debate on the ministerial reform bills, for which he voted steadily, though he did present favourable petitions, 7 Feb., 18 Mar., 15 Apr. 1831. His return for Dover at the general election of 1831 was unopposed, but, according to a hostile press report, he was 'severely reprehended' by some London voters over the proposed disfranchisement of non-resident freemen.[44] He supported Littleton's bill to end the truck system, 14 Dec. 1830, because 'it is our duty to endeavour to confer the greatest possible benefit upon the people for whom we are called upon to legislate'; but he annoyed Littleton by forcing through an amendment allowing factory masters to provide cooked food on their premises, 12 Apr. 1831. He acknowledged the force of objections to the colonial trade bill, 17 Dec. 1830, and promised to modify it. Later that day he remarked that 'remonstrance and fair dealing' were more likely to effect a relaxation of American protectionism than harangues like that just delivered by Herries. He confirmed that it was intended to reduce the duty on barilla, 20 Dec. 1830, but on 7 Feb. 1831 had to admit under 'severe' Tory harassment that through 'hasty zeal' he had erred in issuing the order to do so without first notifying the House.[45] He was credited with 'the great part' of Althorp's ill-starred budget proposals, particularly the plan for a one and a half per cent tax on transfers of funded and landed property, which provoked 'uproar' in the City. It was reported that his brother Andrew said to him, 'Brother or no brother, we are foes in future'; and there was a malicious story that the removal of the duty on candles was 'a job for Tallow Thomson'.[46] On the other hand, his brother George later claimed that he had 'remonstrated' against the transfer duty in ministerial discussions.[47] Whatever the truth, there can be no doubt of McCulloch's intellectual influence on Poulett Thomson, and it is hard to believe that he did not have an important part in the framing of the budget.[48] According to Le Marchant, he was ready and willing to reply to Goulburn's attack on it, 11 Feb., but Althorp, expecting backbench support which did not materialize, stayed his hand.[49] When he did speak, 14 Feb., he deplored the enforced abandonment of the transfer duty, which had necessarily limited the scope for tax reductions; but he argued that even so 'we shall have a mutation of taxation' which would 'materially add to the comfort of the consumer, and to the increase of the revenue'. He moved the previous question against Waithman's motion for inquiry into commercial distress, 15 Feb., when Gladstone reckoned that 'he appeared to be perfectly at home on all the subjects before the House' and was said to have 'raised himself from a very low station'. Yet he subsequently observed that Poulett Thomson's 'manner' of speaking was 'very affected and petulant' and 'operates unfavourably upon his matter'.[50] He defended the budget proposals on the coal duties, 16, 17 Feb., and printed calicoes, 28 Feb. On 21 Feb. Chandos, proposing a reduction of the West Indian sugar duties, claimed the votes of Poulett Thomson and Charles Grant, president of the board of control, on the strength of their utterances in opposition. Poulett Thomson 'blustered through', as Lord Ellenborough put it, and opposed the motion, but Grant expressed his support in principle for the proposition.[51] The episode made Poulett Thomson even more anxious, as he told Althorp, to obtain 'the formal authority of cabinet' for his proposed amendment to the colonial trade bill, which Grant had intimated he would oppose.[52] He evidently secured this sanction, and he defended the amendment, 11 Mar., as 'a great improvement' which would relieve the West Indies while increasing protection for Canada. Ellenborough noted a malevolent tale, 24 Feb., that Poulett Thomson would 'probably be obliged to leave his office' because he 'finds he cannot have the mercantile profits in the house accumulate as he wished till his release', as 'the Petersburgh partner objects'.[53] In the House next day he sought to vindicate his holding the treasurership of the navy jointly with his principal office. Greville thought his speech in defence of the timber duties, 18 Mar. 1831, was 'very good ... clear and satisfactory'. Smarting after the ministerial defeat, he alleged that their opponents had planned a similar measure before they fell from power.[54]

Poulett Thomson, who in mid-May 1831 perceived 'a more promising aspect' in the money markets, was privately mocked by Macaulay for his 'ludicrous sort of flirtation' with Mrs. Marcet, a political economist 30 years his senior.[55] He secured the appointment of a select committee on the expediency of permitting the use of molasses in brewing and distilling as a means of relieving the West India interest, 30 June. He supported Althorp in debate on the customs duties, 1, 11 July. He expressed grave doubts about Hobhouse's cotton factories apprentices bill, 18 July, and in consultations with Littleton he again insisted on the inclusion in his truck bill of provision for cooked food to be given in part payment of wages.[56] Greville noted in June 1831 that as 'a trader', he was 'very much disgusted' with the measures for containing cholera by quarantine in which he was 'obliged to concur' as a privy councillor; he answered questions on the subject in the House, 18, 19 Oct.[57] He was in the government majority against the Irish union of parishes bill, 19 Aug., but four days later got himself into a scrape by ostentatiously remaining in the Commons library with Howick during the first division on the Dublin election controversy. Although they evidently mustered for the second, on the opposition censure motion, Brougham, 'almost frantic on the subject', demanded Poulett Thomson's 'head on a charger'. He was eventually mollified by Grey's intercession and 'promises of amendment'.[58] Poulett Thomson defended the government's treatment of the West Indian colonies and opposed Burge's motion for inquiry into the proposed renewal of the Sugar Refinery Act, 12 Sept. He did so again, 28 Sept., when, dismissing as specious the argument that it would encourage the foreign slave trade, he argued that 'we must be just before we are generous'. In view of the narrow defeats of these motions, however, he conceded an inquiry into the commercial state of the colonies, 6 Oct., though he held out scant hope of its hitting on a handy remedy for distress. Next day he offered, if the West Indians would drop their opposition to the Act, to renew it for six months only, with the promise of a review in the light of the committee's findings. On 12 Oct. 1831 he introduced a bill to permit the temporary importation of American flour to Barbados and St. Vincent in the aftermath of recent hurricane devastation.

Poulett Thomson, who was of course in the government majority on Lord Ebrington's confidence motion, 10 Oct., went to Paris on 2 Nov. 1831, partly with the intention of seeing if 'something may be brought to bear upon their commercial system'. In consultation with the French authorities he conceived the idea of setting up a joint commission to investigate commercial relations between the two countries and, by exposing 'the absurdities of the present system', to prepare the way for a thorough revision of the tariffs. He got permission from London to prolong his stay in order to set it on foot, but a hitch arose over his wish to make Bowring, who was on the spot compiling a report on French public accounts, one of the commissioners. Lord Palmerston*, the foreign secretary, was particularly hostile to the employment of Bowring, 'a theorist, and a jobber'; but Poulett Thomson threatened to wash his hands of the scheme rather than see it 'marred' and eventually got his way. Bowring was joined by George Villiers, a commissioner of customs, and Poulett Thomson left Paris on 3 Dec. 1831, having seen the first session of the commission, which in truth accomplished little, fairly under way.[59] In his letters to Althorp from Paris he expressed surprise and disappointment at the renewed outbreak of cholera. On the reform crisis, he wrote:

> I cannot believe that you will consent to *retrograde*. If you do, you are lost. Not *you* of the *government only* but the country, for if you lose the confidence of the people, which you must do unless you take measures, and those directly, for making sure of the reform bill, the battle will be between the Tories and the people, and chaos must ensue. Depend upon it, there must be in these times no faltering.

He admitted that

> the unions are indeed awkward things, but they are the necessary consequences of the folly of the Tories, and you can only check them by passing the bill or showing that you have the means and the determination to do it. Here you see we have made a batch of 36 peers in order to *destroy* the peerage. Cannot you make as many to save it?[60]

It was at this time that Greville, at a loss 'to understand the enormous unpopularity' of Poulett Thomson, who 'appears civil, well-bred, intelligent, and agreeable (only rather a coxcomb)', had it explained to him by 'a person who knows him well':

> He was originally a merchant, and had a quantity of counting-house knowledge. He became a member of a club of political economists ... [in which] there were some obscure but very able men, and by them he got crammed with the principles of commerce and political economy, and from his mercantile connections he got facts. He possessed great industry and sufficient ability to work up the materials he thus acquired into a very plausible exhibition of knowledge upon these subjects; and having opportunities of preparing himself for every particular question, and the advantage of addressing an audience the greater part of which is profoundly ignorant, he passed for a young man of extraordinary ability and profound knowledge, and amongst the greatest of his admirers was Althorp, who, when the Whigs came in, promoted him to his present situation. Since he has been there he has not had the same opportunities of learning his lesson from others behind the curtain, and the envy which always attends success has delighted to pull down his reputation, so that he now appears something like the jackdaw stripped of the peacock's feathers.[61]

On 15 Dec. 1831 Poulett Thomson moved the reappointment of the West Indian committee, acquiesced in the introduction of Sadler's bill to regulate the employment of children in factories and explained the precautions taken against cholera. Opposing Davies's motion for inquiry into the glove trade, 31 Jan. 1832, he admitted the existence of distress, but denied that it was caused by French imports. In a debate on the budget, 6 Feb., he replied 'admirably', as Thomas Spring Rice* thought, to opposition attacks on the government's handling of the economy. As Littleton saw it, he 'carried the war into the enemy's quarter' and 'wrung Peel's withers' by pointing out his failure to support in opposition the same liberal commercial policies which he had espoused in power.[62] Poulett Thomson was much concerned with the cholera prevention bill in the following weeks: he argued that it would be folly to end quarantine on the strength of a fashionable but unproven theory that the disease was not contagious, 23 Feb. He conceded an inquiry, suitably circumscribed, into the silk industry, 1 Mar., but warned that duties, far from being increased, would probably have to be lowered. He opposed reduction of the West Indian sugar duties, 7 Mar., and a renewed bid to obtain inquiry into the glove trade, 3 Apr. He naturally voted for the address asking the king to appoint only ministers who would carry undiluted reform, 10 May, though he was reported on their restoration to power to believe that 'they could not last three weeks'.[63] He ridiculed Robinson's protectionist motion for inquiry into trade, 22 May, and made a detailed defence of the liberalization of commercial policy since 1822, concluding that 'free trade has no existence in this country – it is a mere delusion to tell the people that it is the cause of distress'. He brusquely opposed Waithman's similar resolutions, 3 July. Poulett Thomson, who successfully contested a law suit brought against him by a former supporter, alienated by his pro-Catholic views, for alleged non-payment of expenses incurred at the 1826 Dover election, was busy with the customs duties bill and attendance on select committees during the last weeks of the 1831 Parliament.[64] The work took toll of his health, as he noted on 28 July:

> A week of the hardest possible labour. I have not returned from the House any day till three o'clock ... It is impossible to stand this. I find my body quite exhausted, and my mind equally worn out. All this week I have alternated between the bank and silk committees, and then the House. On ... [25 July] I carried my bill through the committee; was at it from five till two in the morning, nine mortal hours! ... I passed my bill today, thank God!

He resisted attempts to have daily returns of cholera cases published, 21, 26 July. He supported the forgery punishment bill, claiming that City opinion strongly favoured abolition of the death penalty, which made juries reluctant to convict, 31 July 1832.

At the close of the session he went on a two-month tour of the manufacturing districts of Derbyshire, Lancashire and Scotland.[65] He successfully contested both Dover and Manchester (where he did not canvass) at the general election of 1832 and opted to sit for the latter, which gave him an influential platform for promoting his free trade views. He became president of the board of trade and a member of the cabinet under Lord Melbourne, but the exchequer eluded him. His father died early in 1839, and in April that year his brother Andrew was accidentally drowned in the Thames near his residence at Great Marlow. (His personalty was sworn under £50,000, and the provisions of his will included an annuity of £50 for one Mrs. Maria White, *née* Black, of 45 Portman Place.)[66] Soon afterwards Poulett Thomson took on the governor-generalship of Canada. His appointment raised many eyebrows, not least in his own party, but he made a considerable success of the job, exhibiting a vitality and ruthlessness which enabled him to force through the contentious union of the two provinces.[67] His rewards were a peerage, long coveted, and a red ribbon. By the summer of 1841 he was 'almost done up, and very like an old foundered horse'; and, having sent in his formal resignation in July, he anticipated returning to Britain in mid-October. On learning of the Liberal defeat at the general election he wrote to Lord John Russell:

> I am too much broken in health to take much more than the interest of a spectator in the political struggle ... next session, and I shall not be at all sorry for the opportunity of trying by quiet and amusement to save the remains of my constitution; but I cannot but feel deeply anxious about the country and I am very gloomy about its prospects. The evil which ten years ago I predicted, if we did not liberalize our commercial policy, has fallen on it.[68]

On 4 Sept. 1841 he was thrown from his horse and sustained a severe injury to his right leg. Gangrene set in, and after lingering in agony for several days he died, 'just as his most sanguine dreams of ambition had been gratified'.[69] By his will, dictated to his secretary the day before, he bequeathed all his property to his surviving brother. He left legacies amounting to £2,600, including £500 for Russell, and devised an annuity of £800 for their joint lives to his 'housekeeper Amy Washer and to the child with which she is now big or of which she has lately been delivered'. (A note in the death duty register indicated that she, who became Amy Diamond and died in 1908, in fact had 'no child'.) The will was proved in Canada on 13 Oct. 1841 and in London on 1 Mar. 1842, when the personalty was sworn under £25,000. It was re-sworn at £30,000 the following year.[70]

Ironically, in view of the praise heaped on him by Poulett Thomson in 1831, Bowring wrote very sourly in 1853 of one of the men 'whom I have been instrumental in bringing into the field of politics':

> He was by no means a man of high capacity, or of remarkable steadfastness and soundness of opinion. Happily the tide of his interests rolled in the current of his knowledge ... His connection with that free-trade citadel [Manchester] ... gave Thomson an influential status in the government, in Parliament, and in the country. Yet he was not the man to conceive, and still less to undertake, anything essentially grand. His free trade schemes were puny, hesitating, and imperfect ... He was ever querulous, impatient, and unteachable when anything was suggested of a more comprehensive and embracing character than a policy founded on an instinct of self-preservation appeared to warrant ... He ... died at an age which might have opened to him very bright prospects, but perhaps he was not winged with strength for a higher flight than that to which he reached.[71]

On the other hand Greville, who had no dogmatic axe to grind, wrote a year after Poulett Thomson's death that he had been 'underrated', as his performance in Canada had proved him to be

> a man of first-rate capacity, with great ability, discrimination, judgement, firmness and dexterity ... He was always known as a man of extraordinary industry, but nobody knew that he had such a knowledge of human nature and such a power of acquiring influence over others as he evinced when he went to Canada ... This is something very like greatness; these are the materials of which greatness is made – indefatigable industry, great penetration, powers of persuasion, confidence in himself, boldness, firmness, and all those jumbled up with a finikin manner, and a dangling after an old London harridan.[72]

The 3rd earl of Malmesbury remembered him as 'a remarkably agreeable man'.[73] Davenport noted laconically that he 'got office, went asleep, got made a lord and died of an accident'.[74]

[1] See *Mem. of Life of Lord Sydenham* ed. his bro. George Poulett Scrope (1843); *Oxford DNB*. [2] *Gent. Mag.* (1795), i. 256; *Glenbervie Diaries*, i.238; *Farington Diary*, ii. 400, 645, 647. [3] PROB 11/1258/216. [4] *VCH Surr.* ii. 625. [5] *Oxford DNB*. [6] *Mem. Sydenham*, 1-11. [7] Ibid. 12-14; L. Brown, *Board of Trade*, 16-17; E.A. Wasson, *Whig Renaissance*, 106, 109-10; *Greville Mems.* ii. 75, 225-6. [8] Bowring, *Autobiog. Recollections*, 301. [9] *Mem. Sydenham*, 14-15; *Kentish Chron.* 9, 23, 30 Sept., 4 Oct. 1825. [10] *Mem. Sydenham*, 16-17; *Kentish Chron.* 28 Apr, 6 June; *Kentish Gazette*, 13, 20 June 1826. [11] *Kentish Chron.* 30 June 1826. [12] *The Times*, 27 Feb. 1827. [13] *Mem. Sydenham*, 17-18. [14] Ibid. 18-19; Add. 56550, f. 170. [15] Dorset RO D/BKL, Bankes jnl. 160; Nottingham Univ. Lib. Denison diary, 7 May [1827]. [16] *The Times*, 1, 12 June 1827. [17] *Mem. Sydenham*, 20-21. [18] Ibid. 21-22. [19] *Palmerston-Sulivan Letters*, 214, 215; Duke Univ. Lib. Fazakerley mss, Abercromby to Fazakerley, 16 Oct. 1828. [20] Add. 51834, Davenport to Holland, 18 Oct.; JRL, Bromley Davenport mss, reply, 20 Oct. 1828. [21] Add. 51834, Davenport to Holland, 18 Nov. [1828]; Bromley Davenport mss, memo. [1832]. [22] *Mem. Sydenham*, 35-36. [23] Le Marchant, *Althorp*, 237. [24] *Mem. Sydenham*. 36-37; R. Wilmot Horton, *Causes and Remedies of Pauperism* (1830). [25] Grey mss, Ellice to Grey [7 Oct. 1829]. [26] *Mem. Sydenham*, 37-38; Wasson, 169-70; Brown, 13; A.

Mitchell, *Whigs in Opposition*, 227-8; Le Marchant, 238. [27] Le Marchant, 237-8. [28] Grey mss, Howick jnl. 28 Mar.; Bankes jnl. 169 (25 Mar. 1830). [29] Le Marchant, 237; *Arbuthnot Jnl.* ii. 345. [30] Grey mss, Ellice to Grey, Monday [Apr. 1830]. [31] Howick jnl. 2 May 1830. [32] Ibid. 13 May [1830]. [33] *Althorp Letters*, 152; *Kent Herald*, 8 July, 5 Aug. 1830. [34] Add. 61937, f. 116; 76381, Poulett Thomson to Althorp, 14 Aug. 1830. [35] *Mem. Sydenham*, 40. [36] Brown, 17-18; P. Mandler, *Aristocratic Government in Age of Reform*, 112; Wasson, 188; Le Marchant, 263-4; *Mem. Sydenham*. 41; *Three Diaries*, 6, 21; *Greville Mems.* ii. 75. [37] *Greville Mems.* iii. 272-3. [38] Ibid. ii. 75, 263; Hatherton mss, Littleton to Wellesley, 19 Nov. 1830. [39] *Three Diaries*, 6. [40] Brougham mss, autobiog. fragment; Add. 76371, Brougham to Althorp, Friday [Feb. 1831]. [41] St. Deiniol's Lib. Glynne-Gladstone mss 196, T. to J. Gladstone, 22 Nov. 1830. [42] *Mem. Sydenham*, 42; *Kentish Gazette*, 26, 30 Nov. 1830; *Croker Pprs.* ii. 78. [43] Brown, 17-18. [44] *Kentish Gazette*, 29 Apr. 1831. [45] Glynne-Gladstone mss 197, T. to J. Gladstone, 7, 8 Feb. 1831. [46] *Baring Jnls.* i. 81; *Greville Mems.* ii. 116-17, 119; *Three Diaries*, 9, 50. [47] *Mem. Sydenham*. 44. [48] Brown, 46-47. [49] Le Marchant, 282. [50] Glynne-Gladstone mss 197, T. to J. Gladstone, 16-18 Feb. 1831. [51] *Three Diaries*, 56; Glynne-Gladstone mss 197, T. to J. Gladstone, 22 Feb. 1831. [52] Add. 76382, Poulett Thomson to Althorp, 22 Feb. 1831. [53] *Three Diaries*, 58. [54] *Greville Mems.* ii. 132. [55] Add. 76382, Poulett Thomson to Althorp, 11, 18, 21 May 1831; *Macaulay Letters*, ii. 39. [56] Hatherton diary, 25 July [1831]. [57] *Greville Mems.* ii. 155, 157. [58] *Three Diaries*, 122; *Holland House Diaries*, 39. [59] Add. 76382, Poulett Thomson to Althorp, [1], 7, 18, 21, 28 Nov., 2 Dec. 1831; Brown, 121; Mandler, 113; *Mem. Sydenham*, 47-48; Maxwell, *Clarendon*, i. 62-3. [60] Add. 76382, Poulett Thomson to Althorp, 11, 18, 21 Nov. 1831. [61] *Greville Mems.* ii. 222-3. [62] Add. 51573, Rice to Lady Holland, 6 Feb.; Hatherton diary, 6 Feb. 1832. [63] *Arbuthnot Corresp.* 167. [64] *The Times*, 16 July 1832. [65] *Mem. Sydenham*, 49-52. [66] *Gent. Mag.* (1839), i. 432, 667; ii. 670; PROB 11/1912/399. [67] *Mem. Sydenham*, 97-218. See A. Shortt, *Lord Sydenham* (1926), 59-363; P. A. Buckner, 'Thomson, Charles Edward Poulett' in *Dict. Canadian Biog.* vii.; P.A. Buckner, *Transition to Responsible Government* (1985); *Oxford DNB*. [68] *Letters from Lord Sydenham to Lord John Russell* ed. P. Knaplund, 19, 55 – 59, 68-69, 79-80, 87, 92, 137, 144, 151-4, 160-4. [69] *Mem. Sydenham*, 259-65; *Raikes Jnl.* iv. 177-9. [70] PROB 11/1960/205; IR26/1623/170. [71] Bowring, 301-2. [72] *Greville Mems.* v. 46-47. [73] Malmesbury, *Mems. of an Ex-Minister*, i. 135. [74] Bromley Davenport mss, memo. [1832, 1842].

D.R.F.

POWELL, Alexander (1782–1847), of Hurdcott House, Baverstock, Wilts. and 63 Montagu Square, Mdx.

DOWNTON 18 Dec. 1826–1830

b. 9 June 1782, o.s. of Francis Powell of Hurdcott and Salisbury and Anna Maria, da. and h. of Sydenham Burrough of Salisbury. *educ.* Exeter Coll. Oxf. 1800. *m.* 7 July 1807, Joanna, da. of Rev. George Henry Law, rect. of Willingham, Cambs., 3s. (1 *d.v.p.*) 4da. (1 *d.v.p.*). *d.* 25 Dec. 1847.

Sheriff, Wilts. 1818-19; mayor, Wilton 1829-30.

Powell was descended from a branch of the Powells of Pengethley, Herefordshire, which settled in Wiltshire in the mid-seventeenth century. His grandfather Alexander Powell (?1716-84) was active in the municipal affairs of Salisbury and an unsuccessful aspirant to the parliamentary representation in 1765. He was knighted in 1762 and served for many years as deputy recorder of the borough.[1] His first two marriages were childless, but with his third wife, Catherine, daughter of Edward Willes, bishop of Bath and Wells, he had an only surviving son Francis, who inherited his town house in Castle Street and his estate at Hurdcott, near Wilton. Francis Powell, who was educated at Oxford, outlived his father by less than two years and died, aged 27, in January 1786, having devised the Salisbury house to his wife and all his other real estate to his infant son Alexander.[2] This Member came into his inheritance in 1803, and on the death of his mother, herself an heiress, in 1825 he succeeded to farm lands at Ringwood, Hampshire, and Witham Priory, Somerset, and to property in Salisbury and Fisherton Anger, all of which she had purchased during her long widowhood.[3] His sister Anna Maria Selina married in 1802 Wadham Locke (1779-1835) of Rowdeford House, a Devizes banker who came in there as a Liberal in 1832, after an abortive bid in 1820.

Powell's own politics were Tory and he married a niece of the 1st Lord Ellenborough, whose son and successor was later a member of the duke of Wellington's cabinet. He chaired the Wiltshire county meeting which approved an address of congratulation and condolence to the new king, 30 Jan. 1821, but was not otherwise prominent in local affairs.[4] He signed the requisition for, but did not attend, the Salisbury anti-slavery meeting in January 1826, and that autumn was elected a burgess of Wilton.[5] On a vacancy in December 1826 he was brought in for Downton, as an unexceptionable country gentleman, by the 2nd earl of Radnor, whose unbending Toryism he was expected to ape.[6] He was an anonymous Member, not known to have spoken in debate and apparently lax in his attendance. He voted against Catholic relief, 6 Mar. 1827. He was listed in the majority of seven for the charge of treating on the Berwick election committee, which reported on the 19th; having served on this committee, he had been granted three weeks' leave on urgent business, 16 Mar.[7] Radnor died in January 1828, but the radical 3rd earl, despite Powell's offer to resign, did not immediately interfere with his electoral arrangements, giving credit to Powell for his honesty even though, as he wrote to him, 'on all great political points, two friends cannot be more opposed in opinion than you and I am'. Duly grateful, Powell promised him that

> as long as I continue in Parliament, it shall be my endeavour to act in an upright and independent manner, and as

much as possible to justify the favourable opinion your lordship has expressed of me. I assure you, I have never given any vote which at the moment I do not sincerely believe is for the good of the country.[8]

Powell was therefore left free to vote against repeal of the Test Acts, 26 Feb., and Catholic relief, 12 May 1828. He was listed by Planta, the Wellington ministry's patronage secretary, as 'opposed to the principle of the bill' in February 1829, when he signed the Wiltshire anti-Catholic declaration, and was one of the diehard opponents of emancipation in the Commons the following month.[9] His only other known vote was against abolition of the death penalty for forgery, 7 June 1830.

At the dissolution that summer, he amicably withdrew from Downton, where Radnor replaced him with a member of the opposition.[10] He seconded the nomination of the Tory John Benett* at the Wiltshire election in May 1831, and rendered the same service for his childhood friend Sidney Herbert†, another Conservative, at the Wiltshire South election in December 1832.[11] Powell, an obscure squire, died in December 1847, leaving most of his estate to his elder surviving son Alexander Pitts Elliot Powell (1809-82).[12]

[1] *Wilts. N and Q*, viii. 440; Sir R.C. Hoare, *Wilts*. Salisbury, 526, 527. [2] PROB 11/1095/441; 1117/28. [3] Ibid. 1139/114; 1707/33. [4] *Salisbury Jnl*. 5 Feb. 1821. [5] Ibid. 30 Jan., 6 Feb. 1826; Wilts. RO, Wilton borough recs. G25/1/22, f. 317. [6] *Devizes Gazette*, 21 Dec. 1826. [7] St. Deiniol's Lib. Glynne-Gladstone mss 277, Gladstone to Huskisson, 24 Mar. 1827. [8] R.K. Huch, *The Radical Lord Radnor*, 109; Longford Castle mss 30/7, Powell to Radnor, 6, 10 Feb., replies, 7, 8 Feb. 1828. [9] Glos. RO, Sotheron Estcourt mss D1571 X114, Long to Bucknall Estcourt [?11 Feb. 1829]. [10] Wilts. RO, Radnor mss 490/1374, Powell to Radnor, 4 July 1830; Huch, 111-13. [11] *Devizes Gazette*, 12 May 1831, 20 Dec. 1832. [12] *Gent. Mag.* (1848), i. 441.

S.M.F.

POWELL, William Edward (1788–1854), of Nanteos, Card.[1]

CARDIGANSHIRE 27 May 1816–14 Feb. 1854

b. 16 Feb. 1788, 1st s. of Thomas Powell of Nanteos and Elinor, da. of Edward Maurice Corbet of Ynysmaengwyn, Merion. *educ*. Westminster 1801-3; Christ Church, Oxf. 1804. *m*. (1) 4 Oct 1810, Laura Edwyna (*d*. 8 Sept. 1822),[2] da. of James Sackville Tufton Phelp of Cottrell House, Glam. and Coston House, Leics., 2s.; (2) 21 Apr. 1841, Harriet Dell, da. of Henry Hutton of Cherry Willingham, Lincs., wid. of George Ackers of Moreton Hall, Cheshire, *s.p. suc*. fa. 1797. *d*. 10 Apr. 1854.

Ensign 18 Drag. 1811, half-pay 1822; maj. R. Card. militia 1811, col. 1816, lt.-col. commdt. (with rank of col.) 1823-*d*.

Sheriff, Card. 1810-11; ld. lt. 1816-*d*.

His family's readiness to foster dynastic alliances and clever manoeuvring by his grandfather Corbet and agents John Benyon and Charles Morgan had enabled Powell, like his great-uncle Thomas Powell (c.1701-52), to secure the county seat, the lord lieutenancy and the office of custos despite his heavy debts and evidence of rampant neglect on the scattered 30,000-acre Cardiganshire estates he had controlled since coming of age in 1809.[3] He customarily divided his time between London, Bath and his Newmarket stud; and his habit of living beyond his means, together with the unabated profligacy of his mother's establishments and the web of debt, bonds and interconnected obligations of the Phelps and Powell families (his sister Ellen had married his brother-in-law Edward Tufton Phelp in 1811) brought threats of sequestration which by 1820 caused his Nanteos agents and his London solicitor Robert Appleyard to fear lest 'general exposure which the county is too over fond of' should cause him to lose his seat. Charges had been brought against him for non-payment of interest, his usurpation of newly enclosed land at Nanteos and rights to the Cwmystwyth lead mines were in dispute, and Powell himself threatened to take legal action against Aberystwyth corporation, who he claimed had usurped his powers as their manorial lord. Furthermore, friends of the Member for Cardigan boroughs Pryse Pryse were said to be scheming to get him the county seat. Powell was 'prevented by illness' from canvassing in person before the 1820 general election. By the time he reached Nanteos shortly before the nomination meeting the threat of opposition had evaporated and he was duly returned.[4]

Powell, who made no reported Commons speeches before 1832, could spare little time for his parliamentary duties in 1820. His agents, Adam Armstrong of Ty'nyrhyd and John Beynon of Newcastle Emlyn, and his solicitors Appleyard and John Hughes of Aberystwyth agreed that as an absentee who 'neither understands nor takes the least interest in farming', he should give up his loss-making home farm and let the mansion at Nanteos.[5] They persuaded him to do so to avoid financial ruin and Appleyard refused to prepare the case against Aberystwyth corporation until current costs had been met. It was dropped, and in May Appleyard and Armstrong were summarily dismissed.[6] The House granted Powell a month's leave to attend to urgent private business, 21 June 1820, and he now revoked previous powers of attorney and made John Edwards of Bloomsbury and William George Cherry of Buckland, Herefordshire (his wife's brother-in-law) the managing trustees of his estates in Breconshire, Cardiganshire, Carmarthenshire and Montgomeryshire.[7] As hitherto, Powell was roused to vote on relatively few issues, but generally divided with Lord Liverpool's government. He paired, 28 Feb. 1821, and voted against Catholic relief, 30 Apr. 1822, 1 Mar., 21 Apr., 10 May 1825. On Queen Caroline's case, he voted to include the queen's name in the liturgy, 23, 26 Jan., but against censuring ministers' handling of the affair, 6 Feb. 1821. He divided with them on the army estimates, 11 Apr., retrenchment, 27 June 1821, and proposals to alleviate agricultural distress, 11 Feb. 1822. Mortgage debts remained a problem. His wife, whom he seldom saw, became gravely ill and there were suspicions that her death in Exeter in September was at least part self-inflicted through abuse of 'violent medicines' and Powell's inattention to her needs.[8] He acknowledged having a mistress in London, Mary Selina Gennet of Britannia Street, Gray's Inn Road, and she is reputed to have borne him four children between 1816 and 1830, afterwards emigrating with them to New Zealand.[9] He divided against Scottish parliamentary reform, 2 June, and investigating chancery arrears, 5 June 1823, and repealing the usury laws, 17 June 1823, 27 Feb. 1824. His own finances remained precarious.[10] His mortgage debt alone in 1823 was £58,500, and his gross income of £8,106 no match for current demands. Sheriff's officers with distraint warrants arrived at Nanteos mansion in November 1824, and matters did not improve until he sold his unentailed Llanbrynmair (Montgomeryshire) estate for £18,250 in 1825 and negotiated a new £50,000 loan at three-and-a-half per cent to remortgage his entailed estates.[11] He voted to retain military flogging, 5 Mar. 1824, and to outlaw the Catholic Association, 25 Feb. 1825. When a dissolution was contemplated that autumn he went to Carmarthen to mark the laying of the foundation stone of Sir Thomas Picton's† memorial, attended the races, and chaired the Aberystwyth sessions and Cardiganshire great sessions.[12] Amid promises of continued support, his cousin Edward Lewes of Llanaeron reminded him that 'though *high in popular favour*, it is better by personal courtesy to "nip in the bud" any political coalition in persons who *would be great men*'.[13] He shared his constituents' fears of reduced protection for agriculture, and his wayward votes against the government's corn bill, 11, 18 May 1826, were commended at the general election that summer and his return was unopposed. Afterwards, he thanked his constituents for 'supporting an administration whose attention has been particularly directed to the improvement of the finances, the encouragement of the agriculture and the extension of the commerce of my country'.[14] Following a family quarrel, he dismissed Cherry and appointed James Hughes of Glanrheidol a Nanteos trustee, and was summoned to Calais, where his mother, a refugee from her creditors, suffered a stroke, 6 Sept. 1826. She died before he arrived.[15]

Powell divided against Catholic relief, 6 Mar. 1827. He received three weeks' leave on urgent business, 10 Mar., and voted against the corn resolutions, 2 Apr. 1827. Drawing on his Aberystwyth assets over the next two years, he issued 60-year land leases for the construction of gentlemen's houses in the Castle Field (Laura Place).[16] He presented the Cardiganshire maltsters' petition for repeal of the 1827 Malt Act, 18 Feb., and several for repeal of the Test Acts, 25 Feb., and voted thus on the 26th.[17] He brought up petitions opposing their repeal, 7 Mar., and against Catholic relief, 7 May, from the clergy of the Salisbury archdeaconry. He divided accordingly, 12 May, having also presented unfavourable petitions on the 8th from Cardiganshire's Welsh Calvinistic Methodists. He divided with the duke of Wellington's ministry against ordnance reductions, 4 July 1828. As their patronage secretary Planta predicted in February 1829, Powell opposed the concession of Catholic emancipation. He presented well-publicized hostile petitions from Cardiganshire and beyond on six separate occasions, 17 Feb.-27 Mar., and divided against the measure, 6, 18, 23, 28, 30 Mar. 1829.[18] On the 1st (St. David's Day), he had attended the 150th anniversary celebrations of the Society of Ancient Britons at the Freemasons Hall.[19] Despite some early support organized by Herbert Evans of Highmead, opinion in Cardiganshire soon turned against the justice commission's proposals to abolish the Welsh judicature and courts of great sessions, which recommended altering the assize districts prior to their incorporation into the English system and so partitioning Cardiganshire. At a county meeting at Aberaeron, 18 Nov. 1829, Powell, whose brother Richard (*d.* 1859) was chamberlain and chancellor of the court of great sessions in Carmarthen and the counties of Cardigan, Carmarthen and Pembroke, declared 'against any change', and he presented their unfavourable petition, 9 Mar. 1830.[20] John Hughes corresponded with him on the progress of the administration of justice bill, by which the change (excluding the amended assize districts) was enacted, and he voted in the minority against the bill's recommittal, 18 June 1830.[21] He voted against enfranchising Birmingham, Leeds and Manchester, 23 Feb. In a letter postmarked 3 July 1830, shortly after news arrived of George IV's death, Hughes reassured him that reports of opposition in the county from Lord Kensington's† son and from Herbert Evans in Cardigan Boroughs were 'neat inventions of the enemy'.[22] He said little about his politics when he was returned unopposed at the general election in August 1830, which coincided with his return to live at Nanteos.[23]

Ministers counted Powell among their 'friends' and he divided with them on the civil list when they were brought down, 15 Nov. 1830. He presented petitions for the abolition of colonial slavery from the Welsh Calvinistic Methodists of Aberaeron, Aberystwyth, Llanilar and Tregaron (where chapels had been built on his land), 25 Nov. 1830. He was granted three weeks' leave, 14 Feb., and a further nine days, 8 Mar. 1831 because of illness, and so missed the early debates on the Grey ministry's reform bill. Despite his previous reservations, he paired for it at its second reading, 22 Mar., so earning the approbation of the Cardiganshire reform meeting at Lampeter, 7 Apr. However, Kensington, who proposed the resolution of confidence in the sitting Members, made it known that he

> would have been better pleased if I had seen the name of the Member for the county in another place, but, as I have seen his explanation I will only say, that I hope and trust and believe, or I would not do what I am now doing, that Mr. Powell will support the bill of Lord John Russell, not by pairing off, but by expressing his own, as well as the sentiments of his constituents in favour of it; and by voting for it in every stage. It is by that, that he will deserve the confidence and support of the county.

Powell voted against Gascoyne's wrecking amendment, 19 Apr., presented Cardiganshire's petition in favour of the bill, 20 Apr. 1831, and was not opposed at the general election that month.[24]

He divided for the reintroduced reform bill at its second reading, 6 July, and, excluding his vote against the disfranchisement of Downton, 21 July, generally divided for its details. However, he failed to do so on the controversial amendments to award county votes to freeholders in cities corporate, 17 Aug., and to enfranchise £50 tenants-at-will, 18 Aug. He voted for the bill's passage, 21 Sept., and received a month's leave on the 30th to attend the sessions. He divided for the revised reform bill at its second reading, 17 Dec. 1831. He is not known to have voted for it subsequently, but he divided for the address asking the king to appoint only ministers who would carry it unimpaired, 10 May. He stayed away from Cardiganshire reform meetings but wrote to his constituents of his pleasure at giving them satisfaction by 'my humble support for the bill'.[25] He presented a petition for the three commotes road bill from the gentry, magistrates and inhabitants of Cardiganshire, Carmarthenshire and Pembrokeshire, 22 May, and divided against government on the Russian-Dutch loan, 12 July 1832.

There was speculation in August 1832 that Powell might resign at the dissolution in favour of Herbert Evans's stepson Delme Seymour Davies.[26] In the event he stood as a Conservative in December 1832 and retained the seat unchallenged until obliged to resign through ill health in February 1854. The peerage he aspired to eluded him,[27] and the Rebecca riots of the 1840s, which preoccupied him as lord lieutenant, were another 'sore trial to his patience'.[28] He died in April 1854 at his London home in Hyde Park Terrace, recalled as an opponent of church disestablishment, supporter of agricultural protection and a popular local benefactor, and was buried at Llanbadarn Fawr (Aberystwyth).[29] Nanteos mansion and the entailed estates passed in trust to his son William Thomas Rowland Powell (1815-78), Conservative Member for Cardiganshire, 1859-65. Powell's will underestimated by over £4,000 the amount that could be realized to honour family bequests, but arrangements were made for his second wife Harriet, who erected a memorial in Llanbadarn extolling his virtues, to receive £500 a year and her income under their marriage settlement.[30] The estate declined steadily until the male line of Powells became extinct in 1930.[31]

[1] Draws also on M.M. Escott, 'Parliamentary Representation: From the French Revolution to the Passage of the Reform Bill, 1790-1832', *Card. Co. Hist.* iii. ed. G.H. Jenkins and I. Gwynedd Jones, 387-97. [2] *Ann. Reg.* (1822), Chron. p. 291. [3] *HP Commons, 1715-54*, ii. 364; *HP Commons, 1790-1820*, ii. 486-7; iv. 875-6; D. Gorman, 'William Powell of Nanteos and Public Affairs in Early 19th Cent. Card.', *NLWJ*, xix (1995-6), 119-25. [4] R. J. Colyer, 'Nanteos: A Landed Estate in Decline', *Ceredigion*, ix (1980-4), 60-64; 'Agriculture and Land Occupation in 18th and 19th Cent. Card.', *Card. Co. Hist.* iii. 21; NLW, Nanteos mss L362-7, 370, 371, 929, 930, 5338; *Nanteos: A Welsh House and its Families* ed. G. Morgan, 122-3; *Carmarthen Jnl.* 18 Mar. 1820. [5] Colyer, *Ceredigion*, ix.65; Nanteos mss L368-71. [6] Nanteos mss L373, 376-9, 395. [7] Colyer, *Ceredigion*, ix. 65. [8] Nanteos mss L545. [9] *Nanteos* ed. Morgan 67-68, 75; J. Joel, *Nanteos* (1995). The alleged parallel family were Edward William (*b.* 1816), Frederick James (*b.* 1819) and Henry William (*b.* 1825), baptized together under the surnames of Gennet or Powell at St. Leonard's, Shoreditch, London, 15 Mar. 1829; and Emma Mary (*b.* 1830). [10] J. Barber, 'Tithe Unrest in Card. 1796-1823', *WHR*, xvi (1992), 190. [11] Colyer, *Ceredigion*, ix. 65-66; Nanteos mss L581-627, 926. [12] *Cambrian*, 20 Aug., 3, 10 Sept., 1 Oct. 1825. [13] Nanteos mss L936, 1180. [14] *Cambrian*, 24 June, 1 July 1826; Nanteos mss L5302. [15] *Nanteos* ed. Morgan, 70-71; Nanteos mss L1101, 1111. [16] *Nanteos* ed. Morgan, 71-73. [17] *Cambrian*, 1, 8 Mar. 1828. [18] *Carmarthen Jnl.* 16, 30 Jan., 6, 13, 20 Feb.; *Cambrian*, 21 Feb., 14, 21, 28 Mar. 1829. [19] *Cambrian*, 7 Mar. 1829. [20] W.R. Williams, *Hist. Great Sessions in Wales, 1542-1830*, p. 199; *Cambrian*, 7 Mar, 18 Apr., 14, 21 Nov.; *Carmarthen Jnl.* 4 Sept., 13, 20, 27 Nov. 1829, 12 Mar. 1830. [21] Nanteos mss L855-880, esp.

855, 857, 859, 861, 867. [22] Ibid. L879. [23] *Carmarthen Jnl.* 23, 30 July, 6, 13, 20 Aug.; *Cambrian*, 24, 31 July, 14 Aug. 1830; *Nanteos* ed. Morgan, 75. [24] *Cambrian*, 2, 16 Apr., 7, 14 May; *Carmarthen Jnl.* 12 May 1831; *Seren Gomer*, xiv (1831), 155. [25] *Seren Gomer*, xv (1832), 26-27, 157, 189; *Welshman*, 6 June 1832. [26] *Seren Gomer*, xv (1832), 251. [27] Add. 40401, ff. 174-5. [28] D. Williams, *Rebecca Riots* (1971), 10-11; *Nanteos* ed. Morgan, 83-90. [29] *Carmarthen Jnl.* 30 Nov. 1832, 6 Jan. 1833, 14, 21 Apr. 1854; *Welshman*, 14, 21 Apr. 1854; Colyer, 'Gentry and County in 19th. Cent. Card.', *WHR*, x (1980-1), 497-535; R.G. Thorne, 'Parliamentary Representation: From the First to the Third Reform Bill, 1832-1885', *Card. Co. Hist.* iii. 387-97. [30] PROB 11/2191/392; IR26/2007/488. [31] Colyer, *Ceredigion*, ix. 67-68; *Nanteos* ed. Morgan, 117-44.

M.M.E.

POWELL *see also* **KYNASTON POWELL**

POWER, Richard (?1775–1834), of Clashmore House, co. Waterford.

CO. WATERFORD 25 Apr. 1814–1830

b. ?1775, 1st surv. s. of Richard Power†, MP [I], of Clashmore House and Elizabeth, da. of Shapland Carew, MP [I], of Castleborough, co. Wexford; bro. of Robert Power*. *educ.* Trinity, Dublin 4 June 1792, aged 16. *m.* 1809, his cos. Dorothea, da. of Robert Shapland Carew† of Castleborough, 1s. *d.v.p.* 1da. *suc.* fa. 1814. *d.* 12 Mar. 1834.

On the death of his Whig father in 1814, Power had been seated in his place for county Waterford with the support of the 6th duke of Devonshire. He had joined Brooks's, sponsored by Lord Fitzwilliam, 24 Feb. 1815. At the 1820 general election he stood again. Talk of an opposition came to nothing and he was returned unopposed.[1] A regular attender, he continued to vote with the Whig opposition to the Liverpool ministry on most major issues, including economy, retrenchment and reduced taxation.[2] He voted for Catholic claims, 28 Feb. 1821, 1 Mar., 21 Apr., 10 May 1825, and presented a favourable constituency petition, 1 Mar. 1825.[3] He divided in favour of Leeds becoming a scot and lot borough if it received Grampound's seats, 2 Mar. 1821, and voted for parliamentary reform, 25 Apr. 1822, 24 Apr. 1823, 27 Apr. 1826. He brought up a constituency petition for additional duties on imported butter, 26 Apr. 1822.[4] During the rumours of an early dissolution in September 1825, Devonshire announced that he would have his 'undivided support' in the anticipated contest with a Catholic Association candidate, whom Power had already promised to 'assist' under the terms of a private 'minute of agreement', 25 Aug.[5] 'Power ... has formed a junction ... which he asserts he was forced into ... without the sanction or knowledge of the duke', an informant advised Peel, the home secretary, 2 Sept. 1825, explaining, 'the priests and Roman squires peremptorily told him he should be turned out if he hesitated, and he ... yielded'.[6] He declined to attend the Association dinner for the 'friends of civil and religious liberty', 2 Feb. 1826.[7]

At the 1826 general election he offered again with the exclusive support of Devonshire, citing his family's 'long and tried services'. He surreptitiously assisted the Association campaign against his anti-Catholic colleague Beresford, and was returned in first place.[8] He insisted that his Protestant constituents were 'decidedly in favour' of Catholic claims, 2 Mar., presented favourable petitions, 5 Mar. 1827, 28 Feb. 1828, and voted accordingly, 6 Mar. 1827, 12 May 1828.[9] In October 1826 he had signed a requisition for a county meeting against the appointment and conduct of 'certain magistrates' who had summoned 'additional military' assistance to deal with alleged disturbances.[10] He seconded his new colleague's motion for information on the matter, 16 Mar. 1827.[11] He was granted a month's leave on account of ill health, 29 Mar. 1827. He divided for repeal of the Test Acts, 26 Feb. 1828. He signed the Protestant declaration in support of Catholic emancipation at the end of that year.[12] At a county meeting, 19 Jan. 1829, he spoke and moved an address in support of the recalled Irish viceroy Lord Anglesey.[13] He presented a petition against the Wellington ministry's concession of emancipation, 10 Feb., but of course voted in its favour, 6, 30 Mar. In October 1829 the Ultra leader Sir Richard Vyvyan* numbered him among those who had voted thus whose attitude towards a putative coalition government was 'unknown'. He voted steadily with the revived Whig opposition from March 1830, including for parliamentary reform, 28 May. He presented a constituency petition against the proposed increase in Irish stamp duties, 8 June 1830.

At the 1830 dissolution it was rumoured that he would retire, it being noted by a Beresford agent that the resignation of his cousin and brother-in-law Robert Shapland Carew, Member for county Wexford, who had been 'certain of his return', 'may influence' him.[14] In the event, however, he offered again, referring to his conduct in 'four successive' Parliaments, but amidst complaints that he had yet to settle his 1826 election debts. Faced with a contest with Beresford and Daniel O'Connell*, he withdrew a fortnight before the nomination, protesting that after the 'long tried parliamentary conduct of my father and myself' he had been snubbed by promises of support which 'were only contingent on the safety' of O'Connell. 'I cannot admit that my claims should be considered as second to those of any other candidate', he declared, and 'I cannot reproach myself with having given one vote which I would wish to retract'. On the hustings he attacked O'Connell for his unscrupulous 'understanding' with the Beresfords and proposed the abortive candidature of Thomas Wyse* as his successor.[15] In April 1831 it was reported that he was 'still quite anxious to resume his seat' and 'likely' to be chosen by the independents as O'Connell's running mate, although he 'fears a contest'.[16] He declined to stand at the 1831 general election, citing the 'disunion and jealousies' among the reformers of Waterford. A last minute compromise among them, however, allowed his younger brother Robert to slip in unopposed with his backing.[17] Power died in London in March 1834, when the family estates at Clashmore devolved on his brother as the next male heir.[18]

[1] *Dublin Evening Post*, 29 Feb., 25 Mar. 1820. [2] *Black Bk.* (1823), 139; *Session of Parl. 1825*, p. 450. [3] *The Times*, 2 Mar. 1825. [4] Ibid. 27 Apr. 1822. [5] NLI, Wyse mss 15023 (1), Devonshire to Wyse, 9 Sept. 1825; NLI, Villiers Stuart mss 24682. [6] Add. 40381, f. 208. [7] *O'Connell Corresp.* iii. 1278. [8] *Southern Reporter*, 24 June, 4 July; *Waterford Chron.* 29 June 1826. [9] *The Times*, 3, 6 Mar. 1827. [10] Villiers Stuart mss 24690. [11] *The Times*, 17 Mar. 1827. [12] T. Wyse, *Hist. Catholic Association*, ii. p. ccxxvi. [13] *Tipperary Free Press*, 24 Jan. 1829. [14] PRO NI, Pack-Beresford mss D664/A/151, 155, 156. [15] *Waterford Mail*, 24, 31 July, 14 Aug. 1830. [16] *O'Connell Corresp.* iv. 1796. [17] *Waterford Mail*, 5, 14 May 1831. [18] *Dublin Evening Post*, 18 Mar. 1834.

P.J.S.

POWER, Robert (?1793–1842), of Whitechurch, co. Waterford.

CO. WATERFORD 1831–1832

b. ?1793, s. of Richard Power†, MP [I] (*d.* 1814), of Clashmore House, co. Waterford and Elizabeth, da. of Shapland Carew, MP [I], of Castleborough, co. Wexford; bro. of Richard Power*. *educ.* Trinity, Dublin 1 Oct. 1810, aged 17. *suc.* bro. Richard to Clashmore 1834. *d.* 30 Nov. 1842.

Power was described by Richard Sheil* in 1831 as a 'sharp, active, quick-sighted man, with shrewd sense and good faculties', who was 'likely to be a very useful Member'.[1] His father had sat as a Whig in the Irish Parliament for county Waterford, 1797-1801, and at Westminster, 1801-2, and from 1806 until his death in 1814, when he had been replaced by Power's elder brother Richard, Whig Member until 1830. Shortly before the 1831 general election Power was solicited to stand by the county independents, but on account of their 'disunion' he declined to run alongside any other candidate except Sir Richard Musgrave* or his brother John Musgrave. At the last minute his demands were met and he came forward as a 'sincere and staunch' supporter of the Grey ministry's reform bill, whose 'political conduct shall be guided by the example of my family'. He was returned unopposed.[2] He voted for the second reading of the reintroduced reform bill, 6 July, at least twice against an adjournment, 12 July, and gave general support to its details, although he divided against the division of English counties, 11 Aug. 1831. He voted against the grant for the Society for the Propagation of the Gospels in the colonies, 25 July. He divided against issuing the Dublin writ, 8 Aug., but with ministers on the election controversy, 23 Aug. He voted in favour of printing the Waterford petition for disarming the Irish yeomanry, 11 Aug. He divided against the Irish union of parishes bill, 19 Aug., and the issue of the Liverpool writ, 5 Sept. He was in the minority of 24 against the truck bill, 12 Sept. He voted for the third reading of the reform bill, 19 Sept., its passage, 21 Sept., the second reading of the Scottish bill, 23 Sept., and Lord Ebrington's confidence motion, 10 Oct. Before the appointment of the first lord lieutenants of Irish counties that month, Ellice, the treasury secretary, had advised Smith Stanley, the Irish secretary:

> Power came to me to ask whether there was truth in the report that a Beresford was to be appointed to Waterford ... He said he would never act as a magistrate, and he knew many others who entertain the same, if any of the Waterford [Beresford] family were appointed, but that he otherwise had no individual feeling to express about it.[3]

The post went to Henry Villiers Stuart*.

Power divided for the second reading of the revised reform bill, 17 Dec. 1831, and again gave general support to its details, but was absent from the division on the third reading, 22 Mar. 1832. He voted with ministers on the Russian-Dutch loan, 26 Jan., 12, 16, 20 July, and relations with Portugal, 9 Feb. In his maiden speech, 16 Feb., he expressed fear that the Dublin coal trade bill would 'destroy a number of vested rights which have existed for centuries' and urged that 'ample time' be taken for its consideration. He divided for printing the Woollen Grange petition for the abolition of Irish tithes that day, and against the government motion to consider them, 8 Mar., the Irish tithes resolutions, 27, 30 Mar., and the composition bill, 6 Apr., 13, 24 July. He voted with ministers on the navy civil departments bill, 6 Apr. He divided for Ebrington's motion for an address calling on the king to appoint only ministers who would carry the reform bill unimpaired, 10 May, and the second reading of the Irish bill, 25 May, but was in the minority for Daniel

O'Connell's motion to extend the county franchise to £5 freeholders, 18 June. He voted against a tax on absentee landlords to provide permanent provision for the Irish poor, 19 June, and for coroners' inquests to be made public next day. On 9 July 1832 he objected to Dublin University's charges for a Master's degree, conferring the vote, 'being put into the private pockets of the fellows for the benefit of no other individuals than themselves', saying it should be 'applied to any literary, religious or charitable purposes', and received an assurance that it would be used to fund professorships.

At the 1832 general election he offered again for county Waterford as a Liberal, refused to take O'Connell's repeal pledge and was narrowly relegated to third place. He succeeded his brother Richard to the family estates in 1834 and died in London in November 1842.[4]

[1] R. Sheil, *Sketches, Legal and Political* ed. M.W. Savage, ii. 338. [2] *O'Connell Corresp.* iv. 1804; *Waterford Mail*, 7, 11, 14 May 1831. [3] Derby mss 920 Der (14) 117/4. [4] *Gent. Mag.* (1843), i. 104.

P.J.S.

POWLETT (formerly **VANE**), **Hon. William John Frederick** (1792–1864), of Langton Grange, co. Dur.; Somerby, Leics. and 19 Curzon Street, Mdx.

WINCHELSEA	1812–10 July 1815
DURHAM CO.	1 Aug. 1815–1831
ST. IVES	21 July 1846–1852
LUDLOW	1852–1857

b. 3 Apr. 1792, 2nd s. of William Harry Vane†, 3rd earl of Darlington (*d.* 1842), and 1st w. Lady Catherine Margaret Powlett, da. and coh. of Harry Powlett†, 6th duke of Bolton; bro. of Henry Vane, Visct. Barnard* and Hon. Harry George Vane†. *educ.* Brasenose, Oxf. 1809. *m.* 3 July 1815, Lady Grace Caroline Lowther, da. of William Lowther†, 1st earl of Lonsdale, *s.p. styled* Lord William John Frederick Powlett 1827-64; took name of Powlett by royal lic. 20 Apr. 1813 in compliance with the will of his maternal grandmother Katherine, dowager duchess of Bolton (*d.* 21 Mar. 1809); *suc.* bro. Henry as 3rd duke of Cleveland 18 Jan. 1864 and resumed name of Vane by royal lic. 4 Mar. 1864. *d.* 6 Sept. 1864.

Returned by his father Lord Darlington for Winchelsea in 1812, Powlett had in 1815 been substituted for his elder brother Lord Barnard as Member for county Durham, where he was only occasionally resident. He had generally followed Darlington's Whig, pro-Catholic line, shared his reservations on parliamentary reform and had shunned public meetings. As directed by him, he voted for the repressive legislation introduced by Lord Liverpool's administration after the Peterloo massacre. Powlett's return for county Durham was severely compromised in 1820 by the Tory challenge to his Whig colleague John George Lambton*, who afterwards claimed the credit for ensuring that he was not defeated at the poll.[1] Drawing on this experience, in May 1821 Powlett ordered a thorough revision of the Durham land tax returns.[2] He shared his family's love of the chase and Turf and relied heavily on the social skills of his wife. Mrs. Arburthnot, writing in 1828, described her as 'very good hearted and amiable' and a 'clever agreeable person, very ugly, with red hair and a beautiful foot and leg, which she takes every opportunity of displaying'.[3] Powlett adhered with Darlington to the main Whig opposition in the 1820 Parliament. He was said to have 'attended regularly and voted with the opposition', but he spoke only occasionally and served on no major committees.[4] He supported the parliamentary campaign on behalf of Queen Caroline in 1821, when the death on 8 Jan. of his sister Louisa kept him away at the start of the session.[5] He divided for reform, 18 Apr. 1821, 25 Apr. 1822, 24 Apr., 2 June 1823, and in condemnation of electoral bribery, 26 May 1826. He voted for Catholic relief, 28 Feb. 1821, 1 Mar., 21 Apr., 10 May 1825. Supporting humanitarian reforms urged by the Whig opposition, he paired for abolition of the death penalty for forgery, 21 May 1821, presented and endorsed petitions for criminal law reform, 4 May 1821, 3 May 1822, and repeal of the Insolvent Debtors Act, 21 May 1823, and voted to end military flogging, 5 Mar. 1824.[6]

Although Powlett was a West India proprietor, he voted in condemnation of the indictment in Demerara of the Methodist missionary John Smith, 11 June 1824, and of the Jamaican slave trials, 2 Mar. 1826, and voiced support for Canning's 1823 resolutions when presenting abolitionist petitions, 4 Mar., 25 May 1824, 18, 20 Apr. 1826.[7] He qualified his vote for large tax remissions to assist the depressed farmers and landowners by stating that he meant it to apply only to 'taxes which it was practicable to reduce', 8 May 1822. He opposed inquiry into the currency, 12 June, and government expenditure on London Bridge, 16, 20 June 1823. Praising its instigator Lord Suffield, he spoke for the spring guns bill, 4 Mar. 1825. (He supported a similar measure, 23 Mar. 1827.)[8] He presented petitions for (25 Apr.) and against (28 Apr. 1825) corn law revision.[9] Darlington's electoral arrangements took up much of his time at the general election of 1826, when his return for county Durham was unopposed.[10] On the hustings he declared for

Catholic relief and against slavery, denied that the distress of the Sunderland ship owners derived from the relaxation of the navigation laws, praised the foreign secretary Canning for granting diplomatic recognition to the South American states and defended his recent (unreported) votes for the government's corn importation bill.[11]

Powlett was abroad in the summer of 1826 when reports first circulated of the failure of John Wilks II's* 'bubble' Cornwall and Devon Mining Company, of which he was a director. Keen to avoid seeing his name 'dragged before the public on a subject which I admit was a pecuniary investment', he sought advice from the Whig lawyer Henry Brougham, whom his father's had returned for Winchelsea. Acting on it, he delivered a robust defence of his conduct which was loudly cheered, when he was implicated with his fellow director Lord Palmerston* in a hostile petition from the company's shareholders, 9 Apr. 1827.[12] He divided for Catholic relief, 6 Mar., and inquiry into the allegations against Leicester corporation, 15 Mar., and presented petitions for corn law revision, 21 Feb., protection for shipping, 13 Mar., Catholic relief, 10 Apr., and repeal of the Test Acts, 30 May, 6 June 1827.[13] He had gone over to government with Darlington when Canning succeeded Lord Liverpool as premier and was expected to support the administration of Lord Goderich, to whom Darlington owed his promotion to the marquessate of Cleveland in October 1827. Like his father and elder brother, he refused to join the county in marking Wellington's visit that month; but, according to Thomas Creevey*, he defied Cleveland by insisting on exercising his right as county Member to attend the bishop of Durham's dinner for the duke.[14]

Commenting to Brougham on the incoming Wellington ministry, to which the Huskissonites adhered, 11 Jan. 1828, Powlett conceded the impossibility of forming an exclusively Whig government:

> Huskisson is essential to an administration and if his system and principles can be maintained I hope most devoutly we shall not be split. For a good strong government is so very desirable in the present state of things and with energy and firmness I have no doubt we shall conquer all our difficulties. I am only fearful Peel will be placed at the head, and then however fair and plausible his conduct may appear, we must know Ireland cannot be tranquillized.[15]

Toeing the family line, he refrained from deliberate hostility to ministers in 1828 and, according to their secretary at war, Sir Henry Hardinge*, he 'gave in a general adhesion' to them at the close of the session.[16] He presented favourable petitions, 19 Feb., 17 Mar., and voted to repeal the Test Acts, 26 Feb., and divided for Catholic relief, 12 May. He thought that East Retford deserved disfranchisement, and his votes against sluicing its franchise were reluctant ones, 21 Mar., 19 May. He expressed support for the division of counties bill (as a member of the select committee), 27 Feb., and for Stuart Wortley's abortive game bill, 13, 26 June. He presented petitions against the promissory notes bill, 20 May, 3, 13 June, and supported inquiry into the circulation of small bank notes, 3 June. Alluding to his 1825 vote for funding new churches, he endorsed the 'principle' but opposed the details of the additional churches bill, 30 June. He voted against the proposed government expenditure on the Royal Cork Institution that day, but divided in their majority against ordnance reductions, 4 July 1828.

Most constituency business devolved on Powlett after the Whig William Russell, whose candidature Cleveland had approved, became his colleague following Lambton's elevation to the peerage in February 1828 (as Lord Durham).[17] Representing the interests of the Aire and Calder Canal Company, he seconded and was a majority teller for the amendment by which the Wakefield and Ferrybridge canal bill was killed, 3 Mar. He presented petitions for the Tees navigation bill, 26 Mar., and secured its passage when the Lords returned it amended, 2 June. Despite his continued professions of support for free trade, he pressed for government intervention to assist the depressed lead mining areas, which Huskisson refused, 28 Mar. He repeated his demand when presenting further petitions, 28 Apr., and, finding that the returns he ordered, 20 May 1828, 17 Feb. 1830, confirmed the petitioners' claims, he vainly took up their cause, 16 Feb., 19 Mar., 4, 25, 26 May 1830. He opposed the Llanelli docks and railway bill, which was perceived as a threat to the North-East and Somerset coal trade, 26 Mar. 1828, and defended the Tyne coal owners against allegations of monopoly and price fixing, 9 May. He joined Huskisson in urging Isaac Gascoyne to withdraw his motion for inquiry into the depressed shipping trade, 17 June 1828.

As the patronage secretary Planta predicted, Powlett divided 'with government' for Catholic emancipation, 6, 30 Mar., and he commended its concession on introducing a favourable petition from Sunderland, 9 Mar. 1829. He voted to transfer East Retford's seats to Birmingham, 5 May 1829 (and again, 11 Feb. 1830); and when this was rejected he opposed the new writ and declared for sluicing, 7 May 1829.[18] He defended the crew of the Sunderland coal brig *Rosanna*, denied compensation by the admiralty after being sunk by a naval vessel, 22 May, and presented petitions for corn law revision and a tax on machinery to alleviate distress, 28 May, and against renewal of the East India Company's charter, 4 May 1829, 15 Mar. 1830. On 1 June 1829 he endeavoured to persuade Lord Grey to approve the ministry to whom, like Cleveland, he confirmed his adhesion, 17 Jan. 1830.[19] Asserting his independence, he voted to enfranchise Birmingham, Leeds and Manchester, 23 Feb., having first confirmed his opposition to any general undefined reform scheme and the disfranchisement of boroughs solely on population grounds. He added that he considered the enfranchisement of large towns 'constitutional' and the allocation of two Members to Gatton and Old Sarum 'monstrous'. He voted against Lord Blandford's reform scheme, 18 Feb., but for Lord John Russell's moderate resolution, 28 May. He cast a wayward vote against the Bathurst and Dundas pensions, 26 Mar. He presented petitions, 18 Mar., and voted to abolish capital punishment for forgery, 7 May, and divided for Jewish emancipation, 17 May. He presented petitions against the coastal coal duty, 24 May, and opposed the northern roads bill with the Lowthers, 5 June. He voted for the grant for South American missions, 7 June, and was instrumental on the 17th in securing the withdrawal, pending inquiry, of the bill abolishing the Greenwich Hospital levy, having presented and endorsed a favourable petition from Sunderland, 12 May. He voted against increasing securities under the libel law amendment bill, 6 July, and spoke and voted against Hume's amendment to reduce judges' salaries under the administration of justice bill, 7 July 1830. A belated attempt to force a contest for county Durham at the general election in August failed, and he was returned as a professed supporter of the ministry, 'but not a blind adherent to them'.[20] On the hustings he commiserated with those affected by the depression in the lead and shipping trades, defended his voting record and repeated that although he favoured enfranchising Birmingham, Leeds and Manchester, his support for reform 'went no farther'.[21]

Ministers included Powlett among the 'good doubtfuls' and he divided in their minority on the civil list, 15 Nov. 1830. He presented numerous anti-slavery petitions, 11, 15, 17, 23 Nov., and several for repeal of the coal duties, 16 Nov. 1830, criminal law reform, 9 Feb., and against the register of deeds bill, 9 Feb. 1831. He endorsed one from the Sunderland ship owners for amending the timber duties, 14 Mar., and reiterated their case for continued protection for the Canada trade, 15 Mar. Cleveland had declared for the new Grey administration in December 1830, and Powlett, as requested, signed the requisition for and attended the county Durham reform meeting, 1 Feb. However, like Thomas Henry Liddell, the former Canningite Member for Northumberland, with whom he had travelled there, he spoke against wholesale disfranchisement and for transferring single Members from small depopulated places to manufacturing towns and an extended franchise. He promised to present and endorse petitions from Durham and the county requesting the ballot, although his views were 'at variance with those of many other reformers', and did so, 9 Feb.[22] Presenting a Sunderland reform petition, 2 Mar., he said he welcomed its proposed enfranchisement under the ministerial bill, but not the disfranchisement of 60 boroughs 'at one blow' and the loss of 62 Members. He added that 'with the proposition for extending the elective franchise I entirely concur, and so far ... [government] may rest assured of my support'. He divided for the bill at its second reading, 22 Mar., brought up a favourable petition, 28 Mar., but voted with his brother Lord Darlington for Gascoyne's wrecking amendment, by which it was lost, 19 Apr. Unseated by his furious father, he resigned at the dissolution, 23 Apr. 1831, before the reformers' resolutions to turn him out at the ensuing general election could be effected.[23] His retirement notice warned of the danger of a precipitate reform introduced when the country was in an inflammatory state and he explained that he was 'not prepared to abandon' opinions 'recently declared in the face of the county'.[24]

He settled at the Powlett (Bayning) estate of Downham Hall, Norfolk, and unlike Darlington, who came in for Shropshire South as a Conservative in 1832, he did not stand for Parliament again in the lifetime of his father, whom Grey rewarded with a dukedom in January 1833. He came in for St. Ives as a Liberal Conservative in 1846 and Ludlow in 1852 on the interest of his brother, now 2nd duke, to whose titles and entailed estates he succeeded in January 1864. He died eight months later, recalled as a 'kind hearted man' much 'respected in racing circles'.[25] His will, which was proved in London, 29 Oct. 1864, provided for his widow (*d.* 1883), sister Caroline Vane Russell, nephews, nieces and servants. Most family property, including the Powlett estates worth £25,000 a year, had already been made over to his younger brother and successor as 4th (and last) duke, Harry George Vane (1803-91), Liberal Member for Durham South, 1841-59, and Hastings, 1859-64, and to their nephew Sir Morgan Vane (1809-86), whose son Sir Harry de Vere Vane (1854-1918) inherited the estates with the barony of Barnard when the dukedom was extinguished in 1891.[26]

[1] *Pprs. of Sir William Chaytor, 1771-1847* ed. M.Y. Ashcroft (N. Yorks. Co. RO Publications l (1993 edn.)) [hereafter *Chaytor Pprs.*], 34-35; Durham CRO, Strathmore mss D/St X/1/4/37, 41, 43; Lonsdale mss, Long to Lonsdale, 1, 11 Mar.; NLS, Ellice mss, Grey to Ellice, 20 Mar.; *Durham Co. Advertiser*, 25 Mar. 1820. [2] *Chaytor Pprs.* 47. [3] Lonsdale mss, Beckett to Lowther, 25, 26 Dec. 1823; *Arbuthnot Jnl.* ii. 201. [4] *Session of Parl. 1825*, p. 481. [5] Grey mss, Darlington to Grey, 16 Jan. 1821. [6] *The Times*, 5 May 1821, 4 May 1822, 22 May 1823. [7] Ibid. 5 Mar., 26 May 1824, 17, 19 Apr. 1826. [8] Ibid. 5 Mar. 1825. [9] Ibid. 26, 29 Apr. 1825. [10] Creevey mss, Creevey to Miss Ord, 29 Apr.; *The Times*, 30 May; *Durham Chron.* 3 June 1826. [11] *Durham Co. Advertiser*, 17 June; *Durham Chron.* 17 June 1826. [12] Brougham mss, Powlett to Brougham, 2 Feb. 1827. [13] *The Times*, 22 Feb., 13 Mar., 11 Apr., 31 May, 7 June 1827. [14] Aberdeen Univ. Lib. Arbuthnot mss, Hardinge to Mrs. Arbuthnot, 6 Oct. 1827; *Creevey Pprs.* ii. 131; *Durham Co. Advertiser*, 6 Oct. 1828. [15] Brougham mss. [16] Durham CRO, Londonderry mss D/Lo/C83/24. [17] Brougham mss, Cleveland to Brougham, 8 Jan. 1828. [18] *The Times*, 15 Feb. 1830. [19] *Creevey Pprs.* ii. 201; Grey mss, Howick jnl. 2 June 1829, Durham to Grey, 20 Jan. 1830; Wellington mss WP1/1086/5; 1090/40. [20] Lincs. AO, Tennyson d'Eyncourt mss 2Td'E H89/9, Russell to Tennyson, 6 Aug., C. to G. Tennyson, 12 Aug.; Grey mss, Durham to Grey, 17 Aug. 1830. [21] *Durham Chron.* 14 Aug. 1830. [22] Lonsdale mss, Lowther to Lonsdale, 12 Dec. 1830; Brougham mss, Cleveland to Brougham, 24 Jan.; *Durham Co. Advertiser*, 21 Jan., 4 Feb. 1831. [23] St. Deiniol's Lib. Glynne-Gladstone mss 198, T. to J. Gladstone, 20 Apr.; Stair mss (History of Parliament Aspinall transcripts), Murray to Dalrymple, 24 Apr.; *Durham Chron.* 29 Apr. 1831; Ashcroft, 158. [24] *Durham Co. Advertiser*, 29 Apr. 1831. [25] *VCH Salop.* iii. 338; *The Times*, 8, 14 Sept.; *Gent. Mag.* (1864), ii. 516-17. [26] *The Times*, 8 Feb., 14 Mar. 1864.

M.M.E.

POYNTZ, William Stephen (1770–1840), of Cowdray Lodge, nr. Midhurst, Suss. and Midgham, Berks.

ST. ALBANS	23 June 1800–1807
CALLINGTON	16 Apr. 1810–1818
CHICHESTER	18 Feb. 1823–1830
ASHBURTON	25 Feb. 1831–1834
MIDHURST	1835–5 Dec. 1837

b. 20 Jan. 1770,[1] 1st s. of William Poyntz, insp. of prosecutions in the exch., of Midgham and Isabella, da. and coh. of Kelland Courtenay† of Poundesford, Devon. *educ.* ?Eton 1780-6; Christ Church, Oxf. 1787; European tour 1789-90. *m.* 1 Sept. 1794, Hon. Elizabeth Mary Browne, da. of Anthony, 7th Visct. Montagu (who *suc.* her bro. George Samuel, 8th Visct., to the Cowdray estate 1793), 2s. *d.v.p.* 3da. *suc.* fa. 1809. *d.* 8 Apr. 1840.

Capt. Midhurst vol. cav. 1794, Suss. militia 1795; lt.-col. commdt. W. Suss. militia 1812.

Poyntz, whose marriage had brought him a substantial estate in Sussex centred on the ruined mansion of Cowdray, was described by the local historian as 'a remarkably handsome man, very tall, and with a clear and bright complexion'.[2] He had acted with the Grenvillite connection and was a cousin of the 2nd Earl Spencer, but he temporarily withdrew from public life in 1818. Three years earlier he had tragically lost his two sons in a boating accident. Henry Edward Fox*, who encountered the Poyntz family in 1825, found them 'dull but worthy, all of them devotionally mad and quite enthusiasts about religion', though Poyntz himself was 'a most amiable man, and it is impossible not to admire him for his benevolence and fortitude'.[3] In 1820 he declined an invitation to stand for Chichester and that November he decided not to offer again for the venal borough of St. Albans, where a by-election was pending. The following month George Tierney* regretted to learn that he had expressed a 'strong opinion' against organizing a county meeting in Sussex on agricultural distress.[4] He resumed his parliamentary career in February 1823 when he was returned for Chichester on the independent interest as an advocate of 'moderate reform ... toleration to all religions' and 'rigid economy in the public expenditure'.[5]

He voted with the Whig opposition to Lord Liverpool's ministry on all major issues, including parliamentary reform, 24 Apr., 2 June 1823. He divided for Catholic relief, 1 Mar., 21 Apr., 10 May 1825. He decried the 'unconstitutional severity' of the game laws and ascribed the prevalence of poaching to the 'miserable pittance' paid to labourers, 2 June 1823. He sympathized with a publican who had petitioned the Commons on being refused a licence by Chichester magistrates, 31 May 1825, but denied the inference of corruption.[6] It was said of him at this time that he 'attended frequently and voted with the opposition'.[7] He spoke in support of a Chichester anti-slavery petition, 16 Feb. 1826.[8] At the dissolution that summer it was whispered that he would contest Berkshire, but he came forward again for Chichester pledged to a 'moderate' measure of parliamentary reform, including triennial parliaments, Catholic relief, free trade and mitigation of the criminal law. He faced criticism of his failure to agitate locally for reform and denied an accusation that he had been at Newmarket when Lord John Russell's recent resolutions on this subject had come on, explaining that he had been visiting a sick relative and had travelled 60 miles to attend the division, only to miss it by ten minutes. He was returned in second place behind the Tory Lord John George Lennox, but ahead of a radical candidate.[9]

He divided against the grant to the duke of Clarence, 16 Feb., and for Catholic relief, 6 Mar. 1827. He voted against increased protection for barley, 12 Mar., and for the spring guns bill, 23 Mar. On 9 May he warned that the bill to transfer Sussex elections from Chichester to Lewes would give excessive power to the voters of Brighton, who though 'respectable persons' had 'no claim to choose a Member for the agricultural county of Sussex'.[10] He divided against Canning's ministry for the disfranchisement of Penryn, 28 May 1827. He shed few tears at the demise of Lord Goderich's ministry, writing to Lord Tavistock*, 11 Jan. 1828:

> And so they are all out. Heaven be praised; an Ultra Tory administration excepted, anything must be better ... than going on as we have since March, deluding the country by an imaginary government, and letting the k[ing] run riot in the manner he has. As our friends have seen that vacillation and want of firmness do not succeed, I hope they will now try the other extreme. I hear the duke of Wellington will if possible include Peel in the new arrangement, but I cannot think he can form a Tory administration.

In passing this letter to Lord Holland, Tavistock observed that it contained 'precisely the sentiments which I hear amongst all classes', though he claimed that at an earlier stage Poyntz had been well disposed towards the coalition ministries.[11] He divided for repeal of the Test Acts, 26 Feb., and Catholic relief, 12 May 1828. He opposed Wellington's ministry by voting against the extension of the East Retford franchise to Bassetlaw freeholders, 21 Mar. He similarly divided for further relaxation of the corn laws, 22 Apr., against restrictions on the circulation of Irish and Scottish small notes, 5 June, to condemn the misapplication of public money for building work at Buckingham House, 23 June, and against the additional churches bill, 30 June 1828. In presenting petitions in favour of Catholic emancipation, 9 Mar. 1829, he clashed with Lennox over the division of opinion on the subject in Chichester and the alleged use of scare-mongering tactics by anti-Catholic petitioners. He voted for the government's emancipation bill, 30 Mar. 1829. He divided for Lord Blandford's reform motion, 18 Feb., the enfranchisement of Birmingham, Leeds and Manchester, 23 Feb., the transfer of East Retford's seats to Birmingham, 5 Mar., and Russell's reform resolutions, 28 May 1830. He sided with the revived Whig opposition on all major issues that session. He voted for Jewish emancipation, 17 May, and paired for the abolition of the death penalty for forgery, 7 June 1830. Prior to the dissolution that summer he announced his retirement from Chichester's representation on account of his age, although an earlier letter to Spencer suggests that financial constraints may have influenced his decision.[12]

He was soon returned to the Commons on a vacancy at Ashburton, engineered by his son-in-law Lord Clinton, in February 1831.[13] He divided for the second reading of the Grey ministry's reform bill, 22 Mar., and against Gascoyne's wrecking amendment, 19 Apr. 1831. He topped the poll at Ashburton at the ensuing general election, helping to oust the Tory joint-patron Sir Lawrence Palk.[14] He voted for the second reading of the reintroduced reform bill, 6 July 1831, and steadily for its details. He divided against the total disfranchisement of Saltash, on which ministers had failed to provide a clear lead, 26 July. Next day he declared that Ashburton, which was set to lose one Member, possessed the strongest case of all the schedule B boroughs for a reprieve, but he did not force a division. He defended the proposed division of counties, with specific reference to the Isle of Wight, 16 Aug. He divided for the bill's passage, 21 Sept., the second reading of the Scottish bill, 23 Sept., and Lord Ebrington's confidence motion, 10 Oct. He voted to punish only those guilty of bribery at the Dublin election, 23 Aug. He divided for the second reading of the revised reform bill, 17 Dec. 1831, steadily for its details, and for the third reading, 22 Mar. 1832. He voted for Ebrington's motion for an address asking the king to appoint only ministers committed to carrying an unimpaired measure, 10 May, the second reading of the Irish bill, 25 May, and against increased county representation for Scotland, 1 June. He divided with ministers on relations with Portugal, 9 Feb., flogging in the army, 16 Feb., the Irish registry of deeds bill, 9 Apr., and the Russian-Dutch loan, 12 July 1832.

Poyntz was returned unopposed for Ashburton at the general election of 1832 and later sat for Midhurst, where the Cowdray estate gave him an interest. While out hunting in 1836 he fell and damaged his spinal cord, which rendered him subject to fainting fits. He died in April 1840, after 'four years in constant suffering', and his daughters sold the Cowdray estate to the 6th earl of Egmont.[15]

[1] Sir J. Maclean, *Hist. Fam. Poyntz*, 226. [2] S. Roundell, *Cowdray*, 106. [3] *Fox Jnl.* 179. [4] Add. 76033, Harrison to Spencer, 11 Nov.; Grey mss, Tierney to Grey, 13 Dec. 1820. [5] *Brighton Gazette*, 13 Feb. 1823; *I am, my dear Sir* ed. F.W. Steer, 35. [6] *The Times*, 1 June 1825. [7] *Session of Parl. 1825*, p. 481. [8] *The Times*, 17 Feb. 1826. [9] *Brighton Gazette*, 15 June 1826. [10] *The Times*, 10 May 1827. [11] Add. 51675, ff. 20-25. [12] W. Suss. RO ms. 22266; Add. 75991, Poyntz to Spencer, 5 Feb. 1830; *I am, my dear Sir*, 81. [13] *Arbuthnot Corresp.* 136. [14] *The Times*, 12 May 1831. [15] Maclean, 224-5; *VCH Suss.* iv. 77.

H.J.S./T.A.J.

PRAED *see* MACKWORTH PRAED

PRATT, George Charles, earl of Brecknock (1799–1866).

LUDGERSHALL	5 May 1821–1826
BATH	1826–4 Mar. 1829
BATH	11 Mar. 1829–1830
DUNWICH	1831–25 Jan. 1832

b. 2 May 1799, o. s. of John Jeffreys Pratt†, 1st Mq. Camden, and Frances, da. and h. of William Molesworth of Wembury, Devon. *educ.* Eton 1814; Trinity Coll. Camb. 1816. *m.* 27 Aug. 1835, Harriet, da. of Rt. Rev. George Murray, bp. of Rochester, 3s. 8da. *summ.* to Lords in his fa.'s barony as Lord Camden 8 Jan. 1835; *suc.* fa. as 2nd Mq. Camden 8 Oct. 1840; KG 19 Jan. 1846. *d.* 6 Aug. 1866.

Member of ld. high admiral's council Feb.-Sept. 1828; ld. of admiralty Sept. 1828-July 1829.

Capt. W. Kent militia 1817; lt. W. Kent yeoman cav. 1820; capt. Tunbridge Wells troop of yeoman cav. 1822, res. 1825, capt. 1831; maj. W. Kent yeoman cav. 1831, lt.-col. commdt. Apr. 1831.

Ld. lt. Brec. 1865-*d.*

Brecknock, whose grandfather had risen to eminence as lord chancellor and 1st Baron, later 1st Earl, Camden, and whose father had served in high office under Pitt and was created a marquess in 1812, never lived up to the expectations which were placed on him by the rest of the family. He showed a good deal of early promise, and was praised for the 'excellence of his disposition, his capacity, and his principles' by James Henry Monk of Trinity College, Cambridge, where he took his degree in 1819.[1] In the same year he visited Paris (before travelling on to Vienna), from where the diplomat Sir Charles Whitworth wrote to Camden that his 'behaviour and conduct are marked with good sense and propriety and his cheerfulness and obliging disposition make him, I assure you, a very acceptable addition to our society'.[2] In March 1821 George Spencer, a contemporary at school and university, reported that

> the Prattery are just come to town. Brecknock is much the same as ever, as good-natured, and the most sensible and clever of the family; but they have not melted him down at all. He constantly attends the debates in Parliament, and is, I suppose, educated as for prime minister by Lord Camden. He ... himself ... would rather be a good country gentleman.

Later that year he noted that the train-bearers at the coronation, of whom Brecknock was to be one, would be dressed up like 'monkeys', 'if anyone of his portly dimensions can be called a monkey'.[3] Before the general election of 1820 Thomas Grenville† informed Lord Grenville that Camden, whose family had a latent interest there, 'starts Sir W[illiam] Scott* for Bath as a *locum tenens* for Lord Brecknock, who is not of age till 2nd May', but nothing came of this plan.[4] In September Camden made him a deputy lieutenant of Kent, where he was lord lieutenant and had his principal estates.[5] Still a wealthy man, despite having relinquished the profits of his tellership of the exchequer, he took advantage of a vacancy at the 'snug borough' of Ludgershall in May 1821 in order to purchase Brecknock a seat.[6] True to his father's Tory credentials, Brecknock aligned himself with the Liverpool administration, in which his aunt's stepson, Lord Castlereagh*, was foreign secretary, and, except on the issue of Catholic relief, he invariably voted with ministers.[7] However, prey to indifferent health, he was evidently a very lax attender in the House, where he hardly ever spoke.[8] He voted against parliamentary reform, 9 May, the forgery punishment mitigation bill, 23 May, and various economies, 28 May, 18, 27 June 1821. He divided against inquiry into Irish tithes, 19 June, and repeal of the salt duties, 28 June. Castlereagh's half-brother and heir Lord Londonderry, writing to his wife, 29 Dec. 1822, fulminated against ministers and the support shown for them by Camden, whose object, he believed, was 'to get Brecknock into the treasury or admiralty'.[9]

Camden wrote to Robert Peel, the home secretary, 6 Feb. 1823, that as the new session was the first that Brecknock 'on account of being abroad has been able to form the intention of attending with that sort of regularity which would have authorized me to have requested your notice of him', they both wished him to be placed on a number of committees where he might gain information about public business. He added that the

> general disposition he has shown to support the government I conceive authorizes me, thus, to mention him to you, whilst on the other hand I venture to think, a young man in his situation, *entirely independent*, may upon some of the occasions to which I allude, be a useful person for the government to place upon committees.

Peel reacted favourably, and Brecknock was added to the select committee on foreign trade, courtesy of its chairman Thomas Wallace, 19 Feb., and those on the game laws, 17 Mar., and gas light establishments, 17 June.[10] He voted against inquiry into the borough franchise, 20 Feb., repeal of the Foreign Enlistment Act, 16 Apr., reform of the Scottish representative system, 2 June, and inquiry into the currency, 12 June 1823. In the following session he was again appointed to the select committee on foreign trade, 4 Mar., and voted against censuring ministers over the trial of the Methodist missionary John Smith in Demerara, 11 June 1824. Peel explained to Camden, 18 Feb. 1825, that it had not been possible to accede to his request to have Brecknock added to the select committee on the state of Ireland, but he was appointed to one on the export of machinery, 24 Feb.[11] He voted for the third reading of the Irish unlawful societies bill, 25 Feb., but for the second and third readings of the Catholic relief bill, 21 Apr., 10 May. He was in Dublin between October and December 1825, and may well have remained in Ireland for the early months of the following year, as no trace of parliamentary attendance or activity has been found for that session.[12]

In late 1824 it had been rumoured that Brecknock might be returned unopposed for Kent in place of the Tory Sir Edward Knatchbull if a vacancy were to be created by his elevation to the Lords, but no such opportunity arose.[13] Instead, with a dissolution expected, Camden attempted to re-establish his interest at Bath, a corporation borough, where he had sat until 1794 and still held the office of recorder. He attended the mayoral election with Brecknock, 14 Oct. 1825, and began to prepare the ground by canvassing support amongst the corporation.[14] After an election meeting, at which Brecknock was so barracked as an unpopular outsider by the unfranchised inhabitants that his speech was rendered inaudible, he succeeded against the independent candidate, Charles Palmer*, with another Tory, Lord John Thynne.[15] At a dinner to celebrate their success, 29 June 1826, he claimed to have been a 'sincere, honest and independent' Member, and that

> no man should exceed him in his attention to the support of the laws and constitution of his country; and though he generally approved of the measures of the present administration, still he was free to vote in any way that he thought best calculated to promote the commercial, and to cherish the agricultural, interests of the country.[16]

He attended and spoke at the mayoral dinner, 20 Oct.[17] Frederick Robinson, the chancellor of the exchequer, relayed a polite rebuff from Lord Liverpool to Camden's suggestion that Brecknock should enter office, 10 Aug. 1826, though acknowledging that he 'could not but be acceptable to any government, both on account of his family and connections, and on account of his excellent disposition'. He added:

> I cannot help thinking that it would be very desirable that Brecknock should make up his mind to try his hand at a speech next session. The House would certainly be disposed to receive him kindly, and even if the first trial did not satisfy himself, still that ought not to discourage him ... I really think it would be very useful to him, and I am sure that it would be gratifying to you to know that he could make such an effort successfully.[18]

He was added to the select committee on emigration, 19 Feb., and was appointed to one on communication with Ireland via Milford Haven, 21 Feb., but in other respects he remained inactive that session, his only known vote being for Catholic relief, 6 Mar. 1827.

Camden's applications for a position for his son reached a peak when the duke of Wellington was appointed prime minister in January 1828. The new premier responded positively, and the following month Brecknock was appointed to a place on the council of the duke of Clarence, the lord high admiral, despite some opposition from other interests within the administration.[19] Palmer declined to stand against him at the subsequent by-election for Bath, where he was again returned amid an upsurge of popular hostility. The local radical newspaper printed a pseudonymous account of how the

> worthy young representative assured his *30 constituents* that he would 'stick to the present administration as long as he lived'. This, with a few other such sublime sentences, which, from the modesty of the juvenile orator (he holding down his head when delivering his *long* speech of about three minutes' duration), were wholly inaudible, constituted the substance of the candidate's address to his constituents.[20]

He took his seat, 13 Feb., when Camden wrote to Peel to 'recommend him to your notice and protection, confident that if he chooses to take the trouble to be useful he has the capacity to be so'.[21] He voted with ministers against criticizing chancery administration, 24 Apr., and for the salary of the lieutenant-general of the ordnance, 4 July, and Fyler's motion on the silk duties, which was carried with government support, 14 July. He again divided in favour of Catholic relief, 12 May. He took the side of his senior colleague, Sir George Cockburn*, in his disagreement with Clarence, and informed Wellington, 15 July 1828, that he would resign if Cockburn was forced out of office.[22] As Robert Cavendish Spencer, Clarence's private secretary, wrote, his 'best friends could not have wished him to steer a course more perfectly *high minded*, *honourable* and *handsome* than the one he chose entirely for himself'.[23] By September it was Clarence who had been removed, as Lord Colchester recorded, because of an illegal assumption of power by his royal highness in sending orders to the admiralty, whilst he was at sea; and sending a ship of war to take soundings off the coast of Denmark. This was told me by Lord Camden, as stated by his son Lord Brecknock, who, in conjunction with the rest of the lord high admiral's council, tendered his resignation, as declining to be responsible for such acts.[24]

According to Lord Palmerston's* journal, when the admiralty secretary John Croker* informed the board that Clarence considered him the only member of it to have acted like a gentleman, 'Brecknock broke the silence, which he is supposed to have held since his first appointment, by an humble opinion that Croker might as well not have accepted a compliment at the expense of all his colleagues'.[25] The board was reconstituted under Lord Melville, and Brecknock was retained on it. He attended the dinner for the new mayor of Bath, 10 Oct., when his brief speech was described, not without irony, as 'expressive of the great qualifications he evinced for his high office'.[26] Despite his pro-Catholic votes, he was listed as sitting with the Brunswickers at the Kent anti-Catholic county meeting, 24 Oct. 1828.[27]

His new position necessitated another by-election at Bath in February 1829, where he was opposed by Palmer, and although expected to win, he only managed to tie. After the election had been declared void, he succeeded in a second turbulent contest: it was noted that he looked pensive in front of the threatening crowd, and that his countenance indicated 'but little of that refined feeling and manliness of character for which the English nobility have so often been conspicuous'.[28] He took his seat, 13 Mar., and voted for the third reading of the Catholic emancipation bill, 30 Mar. Despite what Lord Mahon* described as his 'sleek and rosy appearance', his continued ill health and the demands of his office forced him reluctantly to resign in July 1829.[29] He spent much of the rest of the year recuperating.[30] He was present on 11 Feb. to vote against transferring East Retford's seats to Birmingham, and on 8 Mar., when he was excused for his absence from the ballot for the Cork election committee, 26 Feb. 1830. He was granted leave for two weeks to attend the assizes, 15 Mar. He presented a petition from the mayor and magistrates of Bath against the death penalty for forgery, 11 May. He divided against Jewish emancipation, 17 May, and reducing the grant for missions to South America, 7 June 1830.

Aware of the unreliable and troublesome nature of his seat, Brecknock and his father had been looking for an alternative route into Parliament since the time of his retirement from office.[31] He nevertheless started again at Bath at the general election of 1830, when he stressed his connections with the city and his independent conduct, and stated that he had 'determined to stand the poll'. As he had expected, he was defeated by Palmer in a close contest.[32] Camden immediately sought out Wellington to press on him again their favourite scheme of having Brecknock called to the Lords in his barony during his lifetime. Wellington marshalled several arguments against the idea and instead offered to bring him into the Commons. Camden informed his son that

I then said, I could give him no answer, that you had a very honourable mind and though it might be agreeable to you to be in one or other House, yet you felt so strongly what is due to those who might place you there, that I was not sure how you would feel as to such a proposition, that you would not like to be at the command of [Joseph] Planta* or Billy [Holmes*].

The prime minister, nevertheless, promised him the next available seat, without any conditions attached about attendance, but his fall from office in November 1830 left Brecknock unprovided for.[33] He signed the Kentish declaration against parliamentary reform in April 1831.[34] He was doubtful about offering again for Bath at the general election and, though he briefly visited the constituency, he took his father's advice and, being very uncertain of success, he withdrew and returned to London before the poll.[35] This decision was eased by the fact that Camden had already found him a seat at Dunwich, purchased from Lord Huntingfield for £1,000 a year.[36] He voted against the second reading of the reintroduced reform bill, 6 July, and for using the 1831 census to determine the disfranchisement schedules, 19 July, and to postpone consideration on Chippenham, 27 July. He paired against the inclusion of Cockermouth and Dorchester in schedule B, 28 July, and divided against the bill's passage, 21 Sept. He was given a fortnight's sick leave, 7 Oct. 1831, and being too ill to attend, he retired from the Commons in January 1832, having arranged for his seat to be transferred to Lord Lowther.[37]

When Peel took office in late 1834, Camden renewed his solicitations, pleading that

you are aware that Lord Brecknock continued in the House of Commons as long as his health would permit. You are also aware that he had a very severe and long illness and only on that account yielded it. It has pleased God that Lord Brecknock has recovered from the long and severe illness he has sustained but yet his health is not so firm as to induce his friends to allow him to expose himself to the fatigue and late hours of the House of

Commons and he has felt the mortification of not being able to acquiesce in most honourable offers to come into Parliament. He is therefore left at his age without any connection with either House of Parliament.

Peel agreed to have him promoted to the Lords, and in return Brecknock pledged himself to be 'amongst the firmest of your supporters', though he later sided with the Liberals.[38] In the last years of his life he served as president of the Royal Archaeological and Camden Societies. He died, of heart disease, in August 1866, and was succeeded as 3rd Marquess Camden by his eldest son, John Charles (1840-72), Liberal Member for Brecon Borough, Feb.-Aug. 1866.[39]

[1] Cent. Kent. Stud. Camden mss U840 C247. [2] Ibid. C202/1; C268; C504/1. [3] Ibid. F162; *Lady Lyttelton Corresp.* 234, 236. [4] *HMC Fortescue*, x. 454. [5] Camden mss O266. [6] *Lady Lyttelton Corresp.* 235. [7] *Black Bk.* (1823), 140; Brougham, *1830 Result*, 11. [8] H.S. Eeles, *Lord Chancellor Camden and Fam.* 263-4. [9] Norf. RO, Blickling Hall mss. [10] Add. 40353, ff. 165, 167; 40354, ff. 216-17. [11] Add. 40373, ff. 186-9. [12] Camden mss C202/11/1-24. [13] *Kent Herald*, 30 Dec. 1824. [14] *Keenes' Bath Jnl.* 17 Oct. 1825; Camden mss C202/11/14. [15] *Keenes' Bath Jnl.* 12 June 1826. [16] Ibid. 3 July; *Bath Chron.* 6 July 1826. [17] *Keenes' Bath Jnl.* 23 Oct. 1826. [18] Camden mss C257. [19] Camden mss C266/7; C351/1; C528/12; Wellington mss WP1/913/8; 915/44; 920/4; Add. 40307, f. 29; Harrowby mss, Denison to Sandon, 6 Feb.; Lonsdale mss, Lowther to Lonsdale [Feb. 1828]. [20] *Keenes' Bath Jnl.* 4, 11, 18 Feb.; *Bath Gazette*, 5, 12 Feb. 1828. [21] Add. 40395, f. 222. [22] Wellington mss WP1/941/14; 942/1; *Wellington Despatches*, iv. 530-1; *Ellenborough Diary*, i. 163. [23] Camden mss C126/8. [24] *Colchester Diary*, iii. 583. [25] Bulwer, *Palmerston*, i. 298. [26] *Keenes' Bath Jnl.* 13 Oct. 1828. [27] *Kentish Chron.* 28 Oct. 1828. [28] *Keenes' Bath Jnl.* 16 Feb., 16 Mar. 1829. [29] Berks. RO, Pusey mss D/EBp C1/29; Camden mss C38/2A, 2B; Wellington mss WP1/1024/13; 1029/22; *Arbuthnot Jnl.* ii. 282. [30] Camden mss C127/1; C376/3; C442. [31] Ibid. C38/1. [32] *Keenes' Bath Jnl.* 2 Aug.; *Bath Gazette*, 3 Aug. 1830. [33] Camden mss C38/1; C202/3; C212/3; Wellington mss WP1/1129/10; 1131/52; 1143/13; 1155/4. [34] *Kentish Gazette*, 26 Apr. 1831. [35] *Three Diaries*, 85; Camden mss C202/5; *Bath Chron.* 28 Apr., 5 May 1831. [36] Camden mss C202/4; Wellington mss WP1/1182/23; *The Times*, 2 May; Lonsdale mss, Lowther to Lonsdale, 13 Dec. 1831. [37] Lonsdale mss, Lowther to Lonsdale, 13 Dec. 1831. [38] Camden mss O257; C250/3, 4; Add. 40408, f. 141. [39] *Gent. Mag.* (1866), ii. 403.

S.M.F.

PRENDERGAST, Guy Lenox (1773–1845), of 23 Grafton Street, Piccadilly, Mdx.

LYMINGTON 1826–July 1827

bap. 12 June 1773, 5th s. of Thomas Prendergast (*d.* 1807), attorney, of Dublin and Johnstown Park, Clonmel, co. Tipperary and Jane, da. of Samuel Gordon of Spring Garden, Waterford.[1] *educ.* Harding's sch., Trinity Place, Dublin.[2] *m.* (1) 16 Feb. 1800,[3] Dorothy Christina (*d.* 1821), da. of Rev. James Stephen Lushington of Rodmersham, Kent, 4s. (2 *d.v.p.*) 4 da. (1 *d.v.p.*);[4] (2) 2 July 1822,[5] Emma Eliza, da. of Dr. Alexander Grieve of St. Petersburg, physician to Tsar Alexander, 1s. 2da.[6] *d.* 21 Feb. 1845.

Writer, E.I. Co. (Bombay) 1793; factor and resident, Broach 1800; paymaster to troops at Goa 1801; jun. merchant and military paymaster, Surat 1803; judge and magistrate, Broach 1806; sen. merchant 1809; at home 1810; returned to India 1813; second judge of ct. of circuit and appeal, Surat 1814, chief judge 1816; member of council, Bombay 1817; out of council 1824; collector of customs and town duties and reporter general of commerce, Bombay 1825; at home 1826; res. 1829.[7]

Prendergast was baptized at Clonmel, near Newcastle, county Tipperary, where his ancestors had been feudal lords. His great-grandfather Jeffery Prendergast (*d.* 1734) had converted to Protestantism and his grandfather Thomas (1703-61) died in a duel fought over an accusation that his wife was a secret Catholic. Prendergast's father, also Thomas, may have been the man of that name who entered King's Inns, Dublin in 1755. He was described as an attorney in Prendergast's baptismal record and by 1784 was resident in Dublin. Here, according to the records of the East India Company, Prendergast was trained to 'good proficiency' in writing, figures and book-keeping. His eldest brother Thomas (1764-1804) sat in the Irish Parliament for Clonakilty, 1796-1800, and held the office of cursitor of the court of chancery in Dublin. Another brother, Francis (1768-1805), served as registrar of the same court, while Jeffery (1769-1856) was knighted in 1838 for military service in Madras.[8]

Prendergast's own service in India lasted 33 years and culminated in his appointment to the governing council of Bombay. He came home in 1826 and at that year's general election was returned unopposed for Lymington by its ministerialist patron Sir Harry Neale*, possibly on the recommendation of his first wife's brother Stephen Rumbold Lushington*, the treasury secretary. A very lax attender, he left little mark on the parliamentary records and made no known speech. He may have been the 'M. Prendergast' who was listed in the majority against Catholic relief, 6 Mar. 1827, as Michael George Prendergast generally voted in favour. He was in a minority of seven against the committal of the Irish agitator Thomas Flanagan to Newgate for forgery of signatures on a petition, 19 June 1827. If this was viewed as a transgression by his patron, it may account for his vacation of his seat shortly thereafter. He apparently made no attempt to revive his political career. He retired from the East India civil service on the annuity fund, 15 June 1829, and continued to hold more than £10,000 worth of Company stock until 1839. That year 'infirmity' prevented him from signing his will.[9] He died in February 1845, when his age was incorrectly given as 66.[10] By his will, dated 6 Apr. 1839, with a codicil of 3 Aug.

1840, his London house passed to his second wife, who according to family tradition was descended in the illegitimate line from the Empress Elizabeth of Russia. The residue was divided equally between his surviving children, who included Guy Lushington Prendergast (1806-87) and Charles George Prendergast (1812-51), both of whom served the East India Company in civil capacities.[11]

[1] BL OIOC J/1/14, f. 228; Add. 59850, f. 139; H.M. Vibart, *Life of Gen. Sir H.N. D. Prendergast*, 16. [2] OIOC J/1/14, f. 229. [3] Ibid. N/2/11, f. 651. [4] Ibid. N/3/4, f. 112; Add. 59850, ff. 142, 172-3. [5] OIOC N/3/6, f. 148. [6] Add. 59580, ff. 142, 173. [7] OIOC, 'Bombay Civil Servants, 1750-1858', p. 312. [8] Add. 59850, ff. 3, 138-41; OIOC J/1/14, ff. 228-9. [9] PROB 11/2014/232. [10] *The Times*, 22 Feb. 1845; *Gent. Mag.* (1845), i. 448. [11] PROB 11/2014/232; PROB 8/238; IR26/1716/168; 'Bombay Civil Servants', 311.

H.J.S./P.J.S.

PRENDERGAST, **Michael George** (*d.* 1834), of Ballyfair, co. Kildare and Eyrecourt, co. Galway.

SALTASH	19 Apr. 1809–1818
GALWAY	1820–1826
GATTON	1826–1830
WESTBURY	1830–1831

s. of Miles Prendergast of co. Galway. *m.* (1) 4 Aug. 1791, at Calcutta, Catherine Frances, da. of George Smith, ?*s.p.*; (2) Mar. 1811, Rosetta, da. and coh. of Sir Skeffington Smyth, 1st bt., MP [I], of Tinnapark, co. Wicklow. *d.* 1834.

Ensign, E.I. Co. (Madras) 1786, res. 1789; private merchant, Dacca, Lucknow; inspector of indigo 1807.

Prendergast, an obscure Irish nabob, apparently came from county Galway; according to the *Returns* he had a property there and in Kildare, but he probably lived at a succession of London addresses.[1] He purchased the life interest in a seat at Saltash in 1809, entering Parliament as a follower of the former governor-general of Bengal, Lord Wellesley. In 1818, by now a pro-Catholic supporter of the Liverpool administration, he brought in a ministerialist for Saltash and unsuccessfully contested Galway, where his brother-in-law James Daly*, the Tory county Member, controlled the corporation. At the general election of 1820 he defeated Valentine Blake†, who sat on the independent interest, as Daly's nominee and survived a petition. He again used his seat at Saltash, where he had also been returned, to provide for a government supporter.[2]

No evidence of parliamentary activity has been traced for the 1820 session, but he voted against censuring ministers' conduct towards Queen Caroline, 6 Feb. 1821. He divided for Catholic claims, 28 Feb. 1821, 1 Mar., 21 Apr., 10 May 1825. He voted against Maberly's resolution on the state of the revenue, 6 Mar., repeal of the additional malt duty, 3 Apr., other reductions in expenditure, 11, 12 Apr., 18 June, and Hume's motion for economy and retrenchment, 27 June 1821. He was granted ten days' leave on account of illness in his family, 15 May. He was entrusted with the Galway addresses to the king on his visit to Ireland in August 1821, when he was involved in the royal meeting at the Curragh as secretary of the Turf Club, and to Wellesley as the new lord lieutenant in January 1822.[3] He divided against more extensive tax reductions to relieve distress, 21 Feb., abolition of one of the joint-postmasterships, 13 Mar., and repeal of the salt duties, 22 June, but registered a wayward vote against the aliens bill, 19 July. He was a minority teller on the question of adding James Drummond to the select committee on foreign trade, when the House was counted out, 28 Feb. 1822.

Evidently still considering himself close to Wellesley, though the other county Galway Member Richard Martin ridiculed his pretensions in this respect, he induced the lord lieutenant to intervene with Charles Williams Wynn*, president of the India board, in relation to his long-standing claim for compensation from the East India Company that year. Williams Wynn, who found himself unable to countermand the hostile decision of the court of directors, commented in reply that Prendergast 'rather looks to a parliamentary interference to put the question in a way of legal decision and from the powerful support which he appears already to have secured, this will probably be the course most advisable for his interest'.[4] His petition on behalf of the Calcutta bankers Monohur Doss and Seetul Bahoo (widow of Duarcah Doss) for repayment of the massive loan they had made in 1787 to the nawab of Oude, a territory now in possession of the Company, was duly presented, 10 June, and, after he had stated that he had been willing to compromise as to half the outstanding sum, was referred to a select committee (by 82-39), at which he was allowed representation by counsel, 4 July 1822. The committee reported that it was unable to make further progress so late in the session, 29 July, when he again defended his claim, and no further parliamentary proceedings were initiated.[5] In August 1822 John Croker* considered him as one of the handful of Wellesley's Indian friends who would be likely to follow Canning into opposition if the latter was not appointed foreign secretary.[6] Prendergast, who was active in promoting Daly's abortive Galway tolls bill that session, voted against parliamentary reform,

20 Feb., and repeal of the Foreign Enlistment Act, 16 Apr. 1823.[7] He was in the majority against producing information on the Orange plot to murder Wellesley in a Dublin theatre, 24 Mar., and the minority against inquiry into the legal proceedings against the rioters arrested after the attack, 22 Apr. 1823. He was criticized in a Galway paper at the start of the year as a puppet and ministerialist, but he sided with opposition for information on Catholic burials, 6 Feb. 1824.[8] He divided against reform of the representation of Edinburgh, 26 Feb., condemning the trial of the Methodist missionary John Smith in Demerara, 11 June, and for the Irish insurrection bill, 14 June. He moved the successful wrecking amendment against the Irish corporations bill, 21 June 1824.[9] He voted for the grant to the duke of Cumberland, 30 May, 10 June 1825, and to receive the report on the salary of the president of the board of trade, 10 Apr. 1826.

Avoiding the power struggle that took place in Galway at the general election of 1826, Prendergast was brought in as a ministerialist paying guest for Gatton by Sir Mark Wood†. Assuming that the Lymington Member Guy Lenox Prendergast (who was not, it seems, a relation) was the 'M. Prendergast' listed in the majority against Catholic claims, 6 Mar. 1827, it was presumably he who paired in its favour that day. Writing from Brooks's, of which he was not apparently a member, he informed Wellesley of William Huskisson's* ambitions to succeed Lord Goderich as prime minister.[10] On 26 Jan. 1828 he promised Peel, the home secretary, to 'be in my place when Parliament meets, to witness the debut of a government [led by the duke of Wellington] from which this long agitated country may, and I confidently hope, will derive solid and permanent advantages'.[11] He voted with ministers against inquiry into chancery administration, 24 Apr., and terminating the salary of the lieutenant-general of the ordnance, 4 July. He divided for Catholic relief, 12 May 1828, and, having been considered by the patronage secretary Planta as likely to be 'with government', for emancipation, 6, 30 Mar. 1829. He voted against transferring East Retford's seats to Birmingham, 11 Feb., the enfranchisement of Birmingham, Leeds and Manchester, 23 Feb., and (with Daly) the Galway franchise bill, 25 May 1830. He divided against Jewish emancipation, 17 May. He voted for the grant to South American missions, 7 June, when he was in the minority against abolition of the death penalty for forgery, and against reducing judges' salaries, 7 July 1830.

With the death of the patron, the seat at Gatton was no longer available at the general election that summer, when Prendergast was returned unopposed for Westbury, which the proprietor Sir Manasseh Masseh Lopes* had earmarked for government supporters. Listed by ministers among their 'friends', he divided in their minority on the civil list, 15 Nov. 1830. However, he turned coat to vote for the second reading of the Grey ministry's reform bill, 22 Mar., and against Gascoyne's wrecking amendment, 19 Apr. 1831. Deprived of his seat at Westbury by Masseh Lopes's heir Sir Ralph Franco*, at the ensuing general election he was sent from London by the Reform Committee to contest Weymouth as a reformer; however, finding the ground occupied, he withdrew on the second day of the poll.[12] Encouraged by lord chancellor Brougham, he again came forward at a by-election for Weymouth in July as the government's candidate, despite having to pay out more than the £1,000 which he considered the usual price for a year's tenure in the Commons, and even though he expected to have to travel shortly to India. He was defeated after a severe contest by an anti-reformer and retired complaining that he was the popular choice but had been thwarted by the illegal activities of the entrenched interests. A petition was subsequently lodged on his behalf, but was not pursued.[13]

Having in the period 1826-30 made numerous applications to government to advance his claim against the East India Company, he was relieved when Charles Grant*, the president of the board, agreed to take up his case in 1831.[14] Yet, as he reported to Brougham and his brother James Brougham*, Grant's timidity and procrastination over the following two years only increased Prendergast's vexation and came close to wrecking his health. In a letter dated '2 am, Monday morning', 18 Nov. 1833, he wrote to Brougham:

> In a few words I take the liberty to submit to your lordship that Mr. Grant, by a system of inexplicable delay, is as effectually undermining my constitution and destroying my life, as if he administered limited doses of prussic acid or any other deleterious medicine to me, and so I have repeatedly intimated to him particularly within the last month ... I can assert sincerely and truly that I have not slept two hours in any 24 these six months past – I mean in my bed. That your lordship may never experience such nights or feelings as mine is my fervent prayer. It cannot last long.

Writing to James Brougham from his sickbed, 4 Dec., when he confided that his wife and friends had at last succeeded in raising some credit, he added:

> This is the first letter I have attempted to write for weeks past save one I inflicted on your incomparable brother one night when I was in such a state of mind that I was a fitter subject for St. Luke's [Hospital for Lunatics] than any other place.[15]

In January 1834 it was reported to Wellington that the government, in consequence of a pledge extracted from Grey by Wellesley on his resuming the Irish lord lieutenancy, were insisting that the directors honour his claim and had even issued a writ of mandamus to this end.[16]

However, Prendergast died, with his financial affairs still unsettled, sometime that spring, probably at his then residence at 2 Grove End Road, St. John's Wood. He was certainly dead by 29 Apr. 1834, when, on Lord Ellenborough raising the matter in the Lords, Brougham indicated that any settlement would now be too late. Ellenborough, who had secured the return of papers on the subject, 21 Feb., 10 Mar., returned to the attack against ministers on the affairs of Oude, 5 May, when Brougham, who stated that Prendergast had come to Wellesley's attention (over another large loan) while in Bengal and was in fact a member of opposition in the early 1820s, spoke at length in his defence.[17] Denying the notorious allegation that he had made a possibly illegal purchase of the Calcutta bankers' debts, he said that

> Prendergast was the commission agent of the Dosses, acting for them by power of attorney, and ... he richly deserved all that he ever entitled himself to; for in the course of my professional practice (it was in that way I first became acquainted with Mr. Prendergast ...) I never ... met with an individual who devoted himself so entirely to his duties as an agent. I verily believe that the notion of his being interested, as a principal, arose entirely from his devoting himself so heartily, body and soul, to the duties of the agency he had undertaken.

On 12 Aug. 1834 Grant was approached by the legal representatives of Prendergast's widow and children, who urged that he ensure the payment of compensation, since 'the adoption of any other course would be ruin to Mrs. Prendergast and her family, who, already left in a state of destitution, are utterly unable to attempt to recommence such an undertaking'; two months later the board replied that no further action would be taken.[18]

[1] He was said to have been a nephew of the 1st Visct. Gort and an inspector of the opium monopoly in Bengal (*Key to Both Houses* (1832), 416). [2] *Dublin Evening Post*, 17 Feb., 24 Mar., 1, 11 Apr.; *Dublin Weekly Reg.* 25 Mar., 15 Apr. 1820; *Black Bk.* (1823), 186; *HP Commons, 1790-1820*, iv. 882-3. See SALTASH. [3] *Dublin Evening Post*, 4 Aug., 1 Sept. 1821, 29 Jan. 1822. [4] Add. 37298, f. 342; 37299, f. 68. [5] *CJ*, lxxvii. 331, 402, 405, 472; *PP* (1822), v. 815; *The Times*, 30 July 1822. [6] Add. 40319, f. 57. [7] *Connaught Jnl.* 24 Feb., 10 Apr. 1823. [8] Ibid. 29 Jan., 2 Feb. 1824. [9] *The Times*, 22 June 1824. [10] Add. 37297, f. 373. [11] Add. 40395, f. 131. [12] *Dorset Co. Chron.* 5 May 1831. [13] Ibid. 26 May, 9, 16, 23 June, 28 July, 4 Aug.; Brougham mss, Prendergast to Brougham [1], 25 May, 8 [28] June, [July] 1831; Add. 36466, f. 405. [14] Add. 38412, ff. 237-40; Wellington mss WP1/910/2; 984/12; 1093/27; *Ellenborough Diary*, i. 253; C.H. Philips, *E.I. Co.* 283-4. [15] Brougham mss, Prendergast to Brougham, 15 Oct., 9 Nov. 1831, 3 Mar., 18 Nov., to J. Brougham, 23, 31, 7, 14 Sept., 4 Dec. 1833. [16] *Wellington Pol. Corresp.* i. 431. [17] *LJ*, lxvi. 32, 61; *PP* (1834), xliv. 101. [18] BL OIOC L/P&S/3/119, pp. 224, 227, 267.

S.M.F.

PRICE, Richard (1773–1861), of Norton Hall, Knighton, Rad.

NEW RADNOR BOROUGHS 18 Mar. 1799–1847

b. 13 May 1773,[1] 1st s. of Richard Price, attorney, of Norton Manor and Mary *alias* Margaret, da. of Charles Humphreys, attorney, of Pennant Hall, Mont. *educ.* Univ. Coll. Oxf. 1790. *unm. suc.* fa. 1797. *d.* 10 Apr. 1861.

Sheriff, Rad. 1794-5.

Lt.-col. Rad. vols. 1803, lt.-col. commdt. 1803, (militia) 1808.

A lifelong Tory who augmented his estates through the sale of crown estates and enclosure in Radnorshire, Price had been returned for New Radnor Boroughs in 1799 with the acquiescence of Edward Harley, 5th earl of Oxford, whose family's long-standing rivalry with the Lewises of nearby Harpton Court for control of the constituency he endeavoured to overcome.[2] As in 1812, his return at the general election of 1820 was opposed by Percival Lewis of Downton, whom he defeated by 207-59 after an eight-day poll. He celebrated his victory with a series of dinners in Rhayader in November.[3] Price's addresses made no political statements, but he was known to be an anti-Catholic supporter of Lord Liverpool's ministry.[4] A radical publication of 1825 correctly surmised that he 'appeared to attend seldom and to vote with ministers', but as he was regularly confused with the Whigs Robert Price and Pryse Pryse, some uncertainty regarding his parliamentary conduct persists.[5] His alleged votes with opposition on the Queen Caroline case, 22 June 1820, 6, 20 Feb. 1821, for reductions in military, 6 Apr. 1821, and diplomatic expenditure, 15 May, and inquiry into the Peterloo massacre, 16 May 1822, can safely be discounted; as can reports that he presented petitions from Carmarthenshire for improvements in the Welsh judicature, 25 May 1820, and from Kingburn for Catholic claims, 21 Apr. 1825.[6] He may have been the 'Mr. Price' who intervened briefly in support of the grant to the Opthalmic Institution, 2 June 1820, and backed the Newington select vestry bill, 5 Mar. 1821. He divided against Catholic relief, 28 Feb. 1821, 30 Apr. 1822, 21 Apr. 1825, and voted against reforming the Scottish representation, 2 June 1823. He probably also paired against the malt duty repeal bill, 3 Apr. 1821, and voted against repealing the salt duties, 28 June 1822, and for the Irish insurrection bill, 14 June 1824.[7] He was one of Radnorshire's few resident landlords and an active magistrate who encouraged the education of the poor and did not shirk from implementing the game laws and attending public meetings. In December 1825, he co-operated with Robert Price and Edward Rogers* of Stanage Park to allay fears concerning the Kington bank.[8] He had been pledged since 1812 to promote the return of Thomas Frankland Lewis* of Harpton Court for Radnorshire on Walter Wilkins's retirement, and authorized Lewis to say so when he was looking for a seat in 1826. Price seconded the elderly Wilkins's nomination at the general election that year and came in again for New Radnor Boroughs unopposed.[9]

A stalwart of Knighton races and the Knighton Association 'for the prosecution and bringing to justice of all persons committing felonies or other offences against our respective persons or property', he signed the resolution adopted at the Radnorshire sessions, 12 Jan. 1827, for legislation to improve the Hereford – Aberystwyth road, and was a member of the local committee for the Rhayader road bill, which received royal assent, 23 Mar. 1829. However, as with the 1828 Rhayader enclosure and 1829 Kington improvement bills, his involvement with it in the Commons cannot be verified.[10] With Thomas Wood*, he made representations to the home secretary Peel on behalf of Charles Hanbury Leigh†, who was anxious to avoid serving as sheriff of Breconshire in 1827.[11] He divided against Catholic relief, 6 Mar. 1827, and presented the Radnorshire wool producers' petition for protective tariffs, 28 May, and one from Ross for repeal of the Test Acts, 12 June 1827, which he divided against, 26 Feb. 1828.[12] He canvassed for and nominated Lewis at the by-election caused by Wilkins's death, 17 Mar. 1828. On the hustings Sir Harford Jones Brydges of Boultibrook, Radnorshire, and Kentchurch Court, Herefordshire, accused him of being party to a coalition to give the Tories control of both Radnorshire constituencies, which he found hard to deny.[13] The Wellington ministry's patronage secretary Planta listed him among those 'opposed to the principle' of Catholic emancipation in February 1829, but he divided for it, 30 Mar. He nominated Lewis for re-election after his appointment as treasurer of the navy, 1 Mar. 1830, when the major issues were the fate of the Welsh judicature and the location of the Radnorshire assizes.[14] Price did not attend the county meetings or comment publicly on the issue until the general election in August 1830, when he praised Lewis's role in saving the Presteigne assizes and refuted charges of his own inaction. His return was unopposed.[15]

The Wellington ministry counted Price among their 'friends', but he may well have divided against them on the civil list when they were brought down, 15 Nov. 1830.[16] He was granted three weeks' leave after serving on the Aberdeen Burghs election committee, 7 Feb. 1831. He voted against the Grey ministry's reform bill at its second reading, 22 Mar., and seconded Lewis's unsuccessful amendment to 'moderate' the pro-reform petition adopted at the Radnorshire meeting, 5 Apr. He divided for Gascoyne's wrecking amendment, 19 Apr. 1831, and in a short speech on the 21st he apparently denied that he had voted to defeat the bill, 'as others had done', and said that he hoped the government would not resign. Nominating Lewis at the general election in May, he professed continued opposition to 'the present reform bill'. His own return was 'a quiet affair'.[17] He divided against the reintroduced reform bill at its second reading, 6 July, and voted to make the 1831 census the criterion for English borough disfranchisements, 19 July 1831. He was criticized for playing no part in securing amendments to the clause establishing the new Radnor District constituency, 9, 10 Aug., 6 Sept., and was absent from the division on the bill's passage, 21 Sept.[18] He failed to divide on the second reading of the revised measure, 17 Dec. 1831, but voted against enfranchising Tower Hamlets, 28 Feb., and the third reading, 22 Mar. 1832.[19] He divided against government on the Russian-Dutch loan, 12 July 1832.

Price's return for the new Radnor District constituency in December 1832 was not opposed. He failed to secure Rogers's nomination for Radnorshire when Lewis resigned in 1834, and in 1842 was passed over for the county lord lieutenancy in favour of Sir John Walsh*, whose election for Radnorshire in 1840 he had helped to bring about.[20] He was 'father of the House' when he made way for Lewis in Radnor Boroughs in 1847. He died, aged 88, in April 1861. As he had willed, the Norton estate passed to his sister Margaret's son, Richard Green (1803-87), who assumed the name of Price as directed and represented Radnor Boroughs as a Liberal, 1863-9.[21]

[1] IGI (Herefs.). [2] P.D.G. Thomas, *Politics in 18th Cent. Wales*, 46-47; K. Parker, 'Parl. Enclosure in Rad.' and 'Sale of Crown Lands in Rad. in 19th Cent.' *Trans. Rad. Soc.* lxxiii (2003), 127-47 and lxxv (2005), 151-73. [3] *Shrewsbury Chron.* 10 Nov. 1820. [4] *HP Commons, 1790-1820*, iv. 488; *Hereford Jnl.* 9, 16 Feb., 8, 22 Mar.; *The Times*, 14-18, 21 Mar. 1820; D.R.Ll. Adams, 'Parl. Rep. Rad. 1536-1832' (Univ. of Wales M.A. thesis, 1969), 652-4. [5] *Session of Parl. 1825*, p. 481. [6] *The Times*, 26 May 1820, 6 Mar. 1821, 22 Apr. 1825. [7] *Seren Gomer*, iii (1820), 219; iv (1821), 92, 154, 189; v (1822), 124, 188; *The Times*, 12 Feb. 1821. [8] Herefs. RO Q/JC/4-8; X21; W.H. Howse, 'A Family Feud at New Radnor', *Trans. Rad. Soc.* xxviii (1958), 19; *Shrewsbury Chron.* 15 Feb. 1822. [9] NLW, Harpton Court mss C/281,

595, 597, 626; *Hereford Jnl.* 7, 14, 28 June 1826. [10] *Hereford Jnl.* 17 Jan. 1827, 14, 28 May, 16, 23 June 1828; *Carmarthen Jnl.* 27 Apr. 1827; *CJ*, lxxxiii. 376; lxxxiv. 46, 158, 354. [11] NLW, Maybery mss 6924-7. [12] *The Times*, 29 May, 13 June 1827. [13] Harpton Court mss C/597; *Hereford Jnl.* 26 Mar., 2, 9, 16 Apr.; *Cambrian*, 19 Apr. 1828. [14] *Hereford Jnl.* 22 Apr., 26 Oct. 1829, 10, 17 Feb., 3 Mar. 1830; *Cambrian*, 5 Mar. 1830. [15] *Hereford Jnl.* 17 Mar., 7 July, 18 Aug. 1830; Harpton Court mss C/399, 605-606. [16] Adams, 654. [17] *Hereford Jnl.* 13 Apr., 4, 18 May 1831; Harpton Court mss 2163; Adams, 470-1. [18] *Seren Gomer*, xiv (1831), 253; *Greal y Bedyddwyr*, vi (1831), 24. [19] *Seren Gomer*, xv (1832), 130, 189. [20] NLW, Ormathwaite mss FG1/7, pp. 203-4; Add. 40511, ff. 82-84. [21] *Gent. Mag.* (1861), i. 704; R.W.D. Fenn, 'Sir Richard Green Price of Norton Manor, 1803-87', *Trans. Rad. Soc.* lv (1985), 54-56.

M.M.E.

PRICE, Robert (1786–1857), of Foxley, Herefs.[1]

HEREFORDSHIRE 1818–1841

HEREFORD 31 July 1845–Feb. 1857

b. 3 Aug. 1786, o.s. of Sir Uvedale Price, 1st bt. of Foxley and Lady Caroline Carpenter, da. of George Carpenter†, 1st earl of Tyrconnel [I]. *educ.* Eton 1793-1802; Christ Church, Oxf. 1805; Edinburgh Univ. 1807-8. *m.* 8 July 1823, his cos. Jane Mary Anne, da. of Rev. Robert Price, canon of Salisbury, *s.p.* *suc.* fa. as 2nd bt. 11 Sept. 1829. *d.* 5 Nov. 1857.

Steward, Hereford 1845-*d.*

Price, who counted Lord Milton* and John Fazakerley* among his closest friends, had defeated another Whig, Sir George Cornewall† of Moccas Court, to come in for his native Herefordshire in 1818 with the anti-Catholic Tory Sir John Geers Cotterell.* A member of Brooks's and Grillion's, he generally divided with opposition, and readily expressed support for retrenchment and 'a limited and moderate reform of Parliament'. In his long parliamentary career, he was rarely sure of an uncontested return despite the close attention he paid to patronizing local causes, the Agricultural Society, race meetings, the Herefordshire Association in London, and county and city meetings. Knowing that some of his erstwhile supporters were pro-Catholic ministerialists, he issued a conciliatory canvassing address at the 1820 general election in which he acknowledged past and present political differences and reiterated his commitment to the county and to 'promoting the general welfare and preserving unimpaired the constitution of the state'.[2] Financial exhaustion rendered opposition unlikely when, on the hustings, he identified taxation and the repressive legislation introduced after Peterloo, which restricted petitioning and freedom of the press, as the most important issues in the last Parliament; and, as agreed at the agriculturists' meeting, 7 Feb., he urged the freeholders to petition for government action on poverty and distress.[3]

In the 1820 Parliament, which until 1824 Price attended assiduously (voting in most of the reported divisions), he divided consistently with the Whig opposition to Lord Liverpool's ministry on most major issues, including parliamentary reform, 18 Apr., 9, 10 May 1821, 20 Feb. 1822, 25 Apr. 1822, 20 Feb., 24 Apr., 2 June 1823, and Catholic relief, 28 Feb. 1821, 1 Mar., 21 Apr. (a vote commonly misattributed to Pryse Pryse), 10 May 1825, for which he also presented a petition from Kingsburn, 21 Apr. 1825.[4] He gave fairly steady support to the 'Mountain' on economy and retrenchment and was commended for doing so at the Hereford dinner for Joseph Hume*, 7 Dec., which he addressed and was instrumental in organizing, 7 Dec. 1821.[5] He supported the parliamentary and extra-parliamentary campaigns on behalf of Queen Caroline and presented or forwarded several Herefordshire addresses to her.[6] Presenting a petition from Leominster for the restoration of her name to the liturgy, inquiry into the Milan commission and an end to her prosecution, 1 Feb. 1821, he claimed that most of his constituents agreed with the petitioners on the liturgy question and expressed his disappointment at the outcome of the House's recent votes 'in direct opposition to the sentiments of nine tenths of the whole community'.[7] He voted to make Leeds a scot and lot borough under the Grampound disfranchisement bill, 2 Mar., and to disqualify civil officers of the ordnance from voting at parliamentary elections, 12 Apr. Before voting against government on the revenue, 6 Mar., he presented the Herefordshire agriculturists' petition for action on distress and condemned the taxes on working horses and malt as particularly harmful.[8] He voted to repeal the latter, 21 Mar., 3 Apr. When Hume was a guest at Foxley for the Hereford dinner, 7 Dec. 1821, they claimed publicly that they had been in general agreement on politics that session. Afterwards Price led the delegation that accompanied Hume to Monmouth, where the ruling anti-Beaufort party made them honorary freemen.[9]

Bringing up a radical distress petition from Ross, 15 Feb., he said that 'trifling reductions' were of no avail and called for the 'most rigid and severe economy throughout every department of the state'; but he now rejected the petitioners' demand for a 'reduction of the interest of the public debt' as unsound. On parliamentary reform, which the petitioners advocated, he added:

> I have never been of opinion that it would be advisable to make any immediate and comprehensive change in the whole system of our representation, in the nature as well as extent of our elective franchise; but at the same

time I have thought that it would be consistent with a sound, safe and wise policy to undertake a gradual and temperate reform of those abuses which in the lapse of time have crept into our representative system, and have disfigured ... our constitution ... Every succeeding year has confirmed me in my opinions and when I consider the number of petitions which have been laid upon the table of this House, and the great anxiety which prevails out of doors on this important subject, I cannot help thinking that such a reform would not only be of advantage to the country, but is due to the earnest wishes and repeated supplications of a suffering, but of a patient and loyal people.[10]

Supporting Althorp's resolutions criticizing the ministry's inadequate relief proposals, he countered Wolrych Whitmore's arguments and asserted:

Nobody in opposition said ... that the present low prices of agricultural produce were caused by the weight of taxation ... [only] that as an extraordinary stimulus, which had now ceased to operate, had been given to agriculture during the war, and as the cessation of it had rendered it necessary to look for some measures whereby the farmer might be enabled to grow his produce cheap, a remission of taxation appeared at once to be the most practicable and the most natural way of proceeding.

Intervening later, he endorsed Althorp's call for greater reductions and a temporary abandonment of the sinking fund, and called for an end to 'every useless place ... no matter what might be the parliamentary influence of the party who held it, or of any of his near relations'. Referring again to the Ross petition, he confirmed that he had had a change of heart, if not opinion, and was now prepared to dispense with the sinking fund for a short period as a 'conciliatory measure' to afford 'immediate relief' to the agricultural interest.[11] He presented another Herefordshire distress petition, 18 Mar., and in May forwarded the county's memorial for repeal of the agricultural horse tax to the treasury.[12] He presented favourable petitions, 27 Apr., 4 June, and voted to consider criminal law reform, 4 June 1822.[13] During the recess he stewarded the Bromyard races, and joined other Herefordshire Members in endorsing the Haw Bridge scheme.[14]

Possibly under duress, Price signed the unsuccessful requisition for a county meeting to petition for further action against distress, and attended that convened in lieu by the lord lieutenant Lord Somers, 17 Jan. 1823, when a petition based on proposals for abolishing the sinking fund, the placemen system, the hop duties and agricultural taxes, put to the meeting by the liberal Edmund Lechmere Charlton† after prior consultation with Edward Ellice* and Lord Grey, was adopted in preference to the original petition from the Hereford Pitt Club and the 'Norfolk petition' proposed by William Cobbett†.[15] Presenting it, 21 Feb., Price claimed that many had approved it to prevent Cobbett's being carried, while others 'who agreed in the prescriptive measures it suggested' had refused to sign 'from an objection to the unqualified censure which it cast upon the past conduct of ministers', and he warned that 'unless government altered its system' it risked alienating its supporters.[16] Presenting the 700-signature Cobbettite petition, 27 Feb., he expressed regret that 'such doctrines ... had received even the apparent sanction of so many respectable names' and called again for the 'strictest economy into every branch of the public expenditure'. The radical Lord Folkstone condemned his 'rash conduct' as a county Member in pronouncing 'such an unqualified judgement on the opinions of his constituents'. Price's comments in committee of supply, 10 Mar., were too quiet to be reported by the *Times*. On 8 July 1823 he married his cousin Jane, on whom his father settled £300 a year for her private use.[17]

In 1824 Price showed less commitment to opposition and cast only a handful of votes with them: on ordnance reductions, 27 Feb., the complaint against lord chancellor Eldon, 1 Mar., the window tax, 2 Mar. (and again, 17 May 1825) and Irish first fruits revenues, 25 May. He voted in condemnation of the indictment in Demerara of the Methodist missionary John Smith, 11 June, and possibly for the Irish insurrection bill, 14 June 1824. He presented a petition from Ross supporting the county courts bill, 24 May.[18] Endorsing the prospective Whig candidate for Hereford, Edward Bolton Clive*, at a party dinner, 30 Aug., he reaffirmed his commitment to retrenchment and reform; but he also expressed satisfaction with recent ministerial appointments, particularly that of Canning as foreign secretary.[19] On 29 Dec. 1824 he presided at the Hereford dinner in honour of three eminent and wealthy local radicals, the horticulturist Thomas Andrew Knight of Downton Castle, the merchant Benjamin Lloyd and Walter Wilkins*, whose nominations as Hereford freemen had been rejected by the corporation. Reports of Price's consequent exclusion from city functions proved unfounded.[20] He voted for hearing the Catholic Association at the bar of the House, 18 Feb., and against the bill outlawing them, 21, 25 Feb. 1825. He divided steadily against the grant to the duke of Cumberland, 27 May-10 June, and for inquiry into chancery arrears, 7 June 1825. He addressed and chaired meetings in Herefordshire throughout the 1825-6 banking crisis and did all he could to save the 'Whig' Hereford City and County

Bank.[21] Although appointed to bring in the Hereford railway bill, 23 Feb. 1826, there is no record of Price's attendance before the dissolution. Writing on 22 May 1826 to Milton from Foxley, where his mother lay terminally ill and his father's *Essay on the Picturesque* yielded a late friendship with the Ledbury poet Elizabeth Barrett (Browning), he noted:

> I had almost determined to make my appearance on the night of Lord John's motion on reform [28 Apr.], but it so happened that just at that moment, in addition to her usual state of suffering, my poor mother had to contend with an attack of fever which lasted some days, and made me really afraid of being absent ... I have been a very impartial observer of all your conflicts with the agriculturists from this distant quarter, and in some respects I am not sorry to observe them from a distance, since just at present it would not perhaps be politic to show the bearing of my mind too strongly on the corn question. The landed gentlemen must be prepared for a change of system, and prohibitory duties must cease in respect to corn, as they already have ceased on so many other articles of commerce. What is the precise amount of protection to which we are entitled is another question. I shall probably be for a higher duty than you would concede, though I do not carry my pretensions very far. I am rather inclined to [David] Ricardo's* plan of having a descending scale. ... I have not the least reason to apprehend any disturbance in this county, but the contest for the city will be very severe.[22]

His return in June was unopposed. On the hustings, he reaffirmed his support for retrenchment and moderate reform and expressed his gratitude to Canning 'for having broken asunder those ties which bound us far too closely to the more despotic governments of the continent' and recognizing newly independent states. He acknowledged his political differences with Peel, yet spoke highly of his abilities and legal reforms, which he maintained the opposition had helped to bring about.[23] At the city election he and his father split their votes between the pro-emancipation Tory Lord Eastnor* and Clive, and Price proposed the vote of thanks to the sheriff and officers.[24]

He continued to attend Parliament irregularly until after his father's death in 1829. When present, he tended to act with Clive. He divided for Catholic relief, 6 Mar., inquiry into the allegations against Leicester corporation, 15 Mar., and the spring guns bill, 23 Mar.; and voted to postpone supplies pending resolution of the succession to Liverpool as premier, 30 Mar., and to refer the Irish miscellaneous estimates to a select committee, 5 Apr. 1827. He did not apparently vote on the corn bill, but he was present at the agriculturists' meetings that petitioned against change.[25] He voted to disfranchise Penryn for electoral corruption, 28 May, and presented Herefordshire petitions for repeal of the Test Acts, 31 May, 7 June. He stayed away from the Hereford meeting that sent an address of support to Peel and the seceders who refused to serve under the pro-Catholic Canning as premier, but otherwise he adopted his customary high profile at constituency meetings.[26] Reflecting on the Canning and Goderich ministries in a letter to Milton, 4 Oct. 1827, he remarked:

> I should like to hear what Althorp says about the state of politics. I have always regretted that so much was done last session without any consultation with him, and without much with yourself; for it appears to me that both one and the other ought to have been consulted far earlier than Burdett, or many others who seem to have taken a lead in the new arrangements of last session; and that if you had been consulted much mischief might perhaps have been prevented. As matters are at present, I fear Lord Grey is separated for ever from the large body of Whigs, and that alone is a great evil. The loss of Canning, I suspect with you, will be grievously felt. He seemed to have made up his mind as to the course he was to pursue, and he had the energy and confidence in his own powers sufficient to carry his plan into effect. Our present premier, though very amiable, is of a different calibre, and moreover he is removed from the House of Commons where he would have been far more powerful than he is in his more dignified situation. Nevertheless, anything is better than having recourse again to the seceders, and I am very much of opinion that if we act wisely we shall not be *too* nice. I absolutely sicken at the thought of the return of Peel to power: if he were once fairly established in office again heaven knows [when] we should see the end of his reign: but you know my opinions of this great statesman, and I will say no more about politics.[27]

He claimed that he would have rejected the baronetcy awarded to his father in December 1827 as insufficient, had it been given 'directly to me', but consoled himself that the inferior honour placed him under less pressure to become an 'out and out' ministerialist. He was in any case 'perfectly prepared to give *fair* support to the [Goderich] government, firmly persuaded as I am that if we lose this administration we have very little hopes of ever getting a better'.[28] As the duke of Wellington succeeded Goderich as prime minister before Parliament reassembled in 1828, Price's allegiance was not tested.

In opposition, he voted, 26 Feb., and presented petitions, 28 Feb., 10 Mar., for repeal of the Test Acts, and divided against sluicing the franchise at East Retford, 21 Mar. 1828. He is not known to have voted on the corn question, but he divided for Catholic relief, 12 May. He presented an anti-slavery petition from Ross,

4 June, and voted against the ministry's expenditure proposals, 20, 23 June 1828. At the Hereford meeting, 24 Feb. 1829, Price spoke strongly but to little effect against the anti-Catholic petition adopted.[29] He voted for emancipation, 6, 30 Mar., and to permit Daniel O'Connell to take his seat without swearing the oath of supremacy, 18 May. That month he became a patron and founder member of the Hereford Association for superseding the use of climbing boys in chimneys.[30] He probably voted for Lord Blandford's reform resolutions, 2 June. He succeeded as 2nd baronet and inherited everything when his father died in September 1829, but Foxley with its picturesque grounds and mansion was already hopelessly encumbered.[31]

The Herefordshire Pitt Club resolved to take up the agriculturists' cause in September 1829, and at the Hereford Agricultural Society dinner, 8 Feb. 1830, Cotterell and Thomas Smythies took Price to task for failing to vote against government on the address, 4 Feb., and his previous support for free trade and currency reform. Responding, he said that he adhered to Wellington's view that abandoning the latter would only make matters worse, and that although he acknowledged that government had underestimated the scale and extent of the current depression, he could not support the Ultras' petition. This caused it to be abandoned and all others were entrusted to Cotterell.[32] In the House, Price voted for inquiry into Newark's petition of complaint against the duke of Newcastle's electoral influence, 1 Mar., and to transfer East Retford's seats to Birmingham, 5, 15 Mar. He divided steadily with the revived Whig opposition until 14 June, including for Jewish emancipation, 7 May, for which he also paired, 5 Apr., parliamentary reform, 28 May, and abolition of the death penalty for forgery, 7 June. Despite expressions of dissatisfaction and a challenge by an anonymous candidate, his return at the general election in August was unopposed, but he had to canvass assiduously. In Ledbury his fellow Whig John Biddulph, who accompanied him through that town, had to refuse him a bed for the night as his wife 'thought Lady P. had slighted her'.[33] On the hustings, Price expressed pleasure at the progress made in civil and religious liberty since 1826, but bemoaned the current levels of distress and the deterioration in foreign policy since Canning's death. He made it clear that although he wished to see colonial slavery abolished he would not, as the Quakers had requested, commit himself to support all measures against it. On reform, he reaffirmed his opposition to 'sudden and comprehensive change in the whole system, in the nature as well as in the extent of our elective franchise', annual parliaments and universal suffrage, and emphasized his commitment to reform as a remedial step to stop decayed boroughs returning Members while Birmingham, Leeds, Manchester and other large towns remained unrepresented.[34]

The administration counted him among their 'foes' and he divided against them on the civil list when they were brought down, 15 Nov. 1830. He presented many Herefordshire anti-slavery petitions 8, 12, 22 Nov.[35] On 11 Dec., assuming that he was the Member on the ministerial benches with 'a sneer on his countenance' alluded to by Robert Gordon, Price quipped: 'I have now discovered that it is as dangerous to smile as to speak in this House', and used the occasion to declare his confidence in the Grey ministry and Althorp as chancellor; but he refused to be drawn into condemning any pension arrangements, including the Irish ones criticized by Gordon, until the details were 'fully understood'.[36] To Milton, 15 Dec. 1830, he observed that his own finances required attention as a result of his purchase of a 'small house in Stratton Street' and the redemption of a mortgage to the 5th earl of Peterborough (*d.* 1814). On politics he commented:

> Our ministers are going on pretty well, but not without receiving every now and then attacks from quarters that ought to be friendly: Althorp bears it well, and puts down opposition by a conduct as plain and straightforward as that we used to see him display when sitting on the other side of the House.

Although he regretted the proposed increase in the army, he was prepared to 'trust to ministers' knowledge', and preferred 'even this addition to the regular forces, to calling in ... the yeomanry ... popular amongst the country gentlemen'.[37] He was not consulted over arrangements to counter the riots and incendiarism in Herefordshire that winter.[38]

According to Denis Le Marchant†, Price, a 'dull Herefordshire baronet', thought lord chancellor Brougham's oration on the state of his court, 22 Feb. 1831, 'prodigiously fine indeed' and reminiscent of 'Demosthenes or some of those fellows one reads of at school'.[39] Taken to task by 'Philalethes' in the *Hereford Journal*, he faced strong constituency pressure to prove his commitment to parliamentary and tithe reform. He announced on presenting reform petitions from Ross, Kington and certain Herefordshire freeholders, 26 Feb., that he 'entirely concurred' in their prayer. He again praised Ross for petitioning for the ministerial bill, and endorsed its claim to have its former seat restored should one like East Retford become 'available', 18 Mar.[40] He sent a letter of support apologizing for his absence on parliamentary business from the county reform meeting,

19 Mar. He presented and endorsed their petition in favour of the bill, adding that it 'would of itself ensure that all other requisite reforms in the administration of public affairs' were enacted, 21 Mar. He explained that Bromyard's petition for parliamentary reform, tax and tithe reductions, which he also presented that day, had been 'adopted before details of the bill were announced'.[41] He divided for its second reading, 22 Mar., and against Gascoyne's wrecking amendment, 19 Apr. In a letter read out at the Hereford reform dinner to Lechmere Charlton, the self-proclaimed local champion of the cause, 2 Apr., Price described his attempt to persuade ministers to revise their decision to deprive Leominster of a Member, or, alternatively, to create a new constituency for the Whig strongholds of Ledbury and Ross.[42] Leominster's reprieve was announced, 18 Apr. 1831, together with the decision award the county a third seat.

Price's return at the ensuing general election was assured, but, with other reformers in the field and the Tories active, a contest seemed inevitable until Lechmere Charlton made way for the Whig banker Kedgwin Hoskins, and Cotterell retired.[43] On the hustings he stressed the reformers' achievement in returning five supporters of the bill from Herefordshire, instead of the previous three, and countered allegations by the Tories, substantiated by cited extracts of his 1830 election speech, that his commitment to 'extensive reform' was recent and based on self-interest:

> I have always been of opinion that there were advantages in the present very varied form of our representation, which ought not to be abandoned except for the attainment of great and beneficial objects. The exercise of their franchise by persons in the very humblest class of society, by the lowest order of freemen, or even by those whose right arises from their boiling a pot the night previous to an election has never appeared to me as unattended with some good, however little disposed I might be to enlarge and extend such rights of voting. But when this bill was introduced it was clear to me that under existing circumstances we had to make our election; that it was not possible to put an end to all nomination by means of close corporations and by individuals, and not to give something of a counterbalance by establishing a constituency large in numbers indeed, but of which property would form an essential and necessary qualification ... At all former periods I have found the advocates of reform sitting on the opposition side of the House of Commons, with a government decidedly averse to the consideration of the question. In such a state of things it would have been most unwise to have attempted any great change; all that could be done was to introduce measures for a gradual amendment of the representative system. These measures were resisted; the transfer of the elective franchise from boroughs convicted of corruption to large unrepresented towns was not conceded; and whilst the people were becoming every day more anxious for reform, the administration were declaring their more determined opposition to it, even in its most mitigated shape. It was under these circumstances that a change of government took place ... The bill was introduced ... I considered it to afford a great practical remedy for a great and crying evil, and I should have been ashamed of myself if I had allowed any minor doubts and difficulties to have had weight with me, and to have prevented me giving it my most zealous and cordial support. ... In the very extent of the change there is safety, in the very comprehensiveness of the plan there is security for the future.[44]

He divided for the reintroduced reform bill at its second reading, 6 July 1831, and Littleton, who dined with him on the 10th, noted that 'as usual' the bill was the 'sole topic' of conversation.[45] He voted against adjournment, 12 July, and consistently for its details. He was criticized in the local press for failing to vote against government on Lord Chandos's amendment enfranchising £50 tenants-at-will, 18 Aug., for which there was strong constituency support.[46] He kept silent on the bill's details, but voiced support for the procedural reforms, including Saturday sittings, which hastened its progress, 29 July. He voted for the bill's passage, 21 Sept., and the second reading of the Scottish measure, 23 Sept. That day, as chairman of the Pembrokeshire election committee, he reported their decision voiding the election because of the 'culpable neglect ... partiality ... and inefficiency' of the sheriff and his officers. He raised no objection to printing the committee's report and evidence, and was a majority teller against suspending the new writ, 26 Sept.[47] He divided for Lord Ebrington's confidence motion, 10 Oct. At the county meeting, 5 Nov. 1831, which addressed the king commending the Grey ministry and the bill, following its rejection by the Lords, he suggested that the anti-reform clergy were acting contrary to their own interests, warned of the danger of treating agriculture and manufacture as enemies rather than interdependent and, cautioning against complacency, voiced his fear that as with emancipation, the Tories would try to introduce and take the credit for bringing about reform. When pressed, he and Hoskins now attributed the alleged shortcomings of the government's game bill to Lords' amendments.[48] Afterwards, he interrupted his holiday at Aberystwyth to write to the *Hereford Journal* to deny 'Philalethes's' allegations that his speech proved that he was an enemy of the established church.[49] Price voted for the second reading of the revised reform bill, 17 Dec. 1831, and 'left Herefordshire for the express purpose of voting' for its committal, 20 Jan. 1832, but, being 'delayed on the road', he 'arrived just after the divisions were over'.[50] He voted silently for its details and third reading, 22 Mar., and for the address requesting the king to appoint only ministers who would carry it unimpaired, 10 May. When its passage was assured, he intervened to object to inferences that the advocates of reform were opposed to a monarchy, and referred to an unpresented petition from Ross, calling for supplies to be withdrawn pending the bill's passage, as proof of 'the greatest interest felt' in its fate 'even in my quiet part of the country', 17 May. He voted for the Irish reform bill, 25 May, and paired, 1 June, and divided, 15 June 1832, against Conservative amendments to the Scottish measure. He divided with government in both divisions on the Dublin election controversy, 23 Aug. 1831, on the Russian-Dutch loan, 26 Jan., 12, 16, 20 July, relations with Portugal, 9 Feb., and the navy civil departments bill, 6 Apr. 1832. He advocated a combination of prompt government measures and self-help through charities to prevent the spread of cholera, 14 Feb. After moving the Lords' amendments to the metropolis bill, 24 May, he joined Clive in endorsing the Herefordshire anti-slavery petitions presented by Hoskins, but, whereas they voted for the immediate appointment of a select committee on colonial slavery, he expressed support for the government amendment postponing it, and so alienated many of his erstwhile supporters.[51] The appointment of Grey's brother Henry Grey as bishop of Hereford had reignited a controversy over absenteeism and pluralism in the diocese into which Price waded by recommending Clive's son-in-law Henry Wetherell for the vacant post of dean.[52] He suggested postponing consideration of the corn laws, on which he had 'not made up my mind', for 'full and fair discussion' next session, 1 June 1832.

Writing to Lord Holland, 20 Aug. 1832, Price attributed the 'considerable disinclination' of voters to register which then preoccupied him to the shilling fee and the '*newness* of the measure', but he was confident that it affected the parties equally, and correctly predicted that Hereford and the three Member county would return four reformers and one anti-reformer at the general election in December.[53] Criticized for putting party before constituency interests, he remained vulnerable to the last, but was spared a contest by the Conservatives' decision to field a single candidate.[54] He almost lost his seat to a Conservative in January 1835, and, conscious of the anger generated by his support for a fixed duty on corn, he retired rather than risk defeat in 1841.[55] His finances were already in disarray when he succeeded Clive as high steward and Liberal Member for Hereford in 1845, and overspeculation in railways and the iron trade, financed by 'a damaging series of mortgages', virtually bankrupted him.[56] His petition of 5 Oct. was gazetted, 19 Oct. 1855, and dismissed, 15 Apr. 1856, following the sale of the Foxley estates to the Conservative John Davenport†.[57] Price's resignation from Parliament was repeatedly called for, but delayed until Clive's son George (1806-80) could replace him in February 1857.[58] He died without issue in November 1857 at his London home in Stratton Street, so extinguishing the baronetcy, and was buried at the church he had rebuilt at Yazor.[59] He left everything to his wife.[60]

[1] Price's parliamentary conduct cannot be charted with certainty owing to some confusion in the records between him and Pryse Pryse, Whig Member for Cardigan Boroughs, Richard Price, Member for Radnor Boroughs, and George Rice Rice (later Trevor), Member for Carmarthenshire. [2] *Hereford Jnl.* 9 Feb. 1820. [3] Add. 38280, f. 12; Worcs. RO, Lechmere mss, Beauchamp to Sir A. Lechmere, 17 Feb.; *Hereford Jnl.* 16, 23 Feb., 8, 22 Mar. 1820. [4] *The Times*, 22, 25 Apr. 1825. [5] *Hereford Jnl.* 12 Dec. 1821. [6] *The Times*, 21 Nov., 15 Dec. 1820; *Hereford Jnl.* 10 Jan., 14 Mar. 1821. [7] *The Times*, 21 Nov., 15 Dec. 1820; *Hereford Jnl.* 10 Jan., 14 Mar. 1821. [8] *The Times*, 7 Mar. 1821. [9] Ibid. 14 Dec. 1821, 8 Jan. 1822. [10] TNA C110/96 (ii), Price to T. Jay, 3 Mar. 1818; *The Times*, 16 Feb.; *Hereford Jnl.* 20 Feb. 1822. [11] *The Times*, 22 Feb. 1822. [12] Ibid. 19 Mar.; *Hereford Jnl.* 29 May 1822. [13] *Hereford Jnl.* 17 Apr.; *The Times*, 5 June 1822. [14] *Hereford Jnl.* 5 June, 17, 24 July, 15 Aug. 1822. [15] *The Times*, 26 Nov., 6 Dec. 1822, 25, 28 Jan., 10 Feb. 1823; *Hereford Jnl.* 11, 18 Dec. 1822, 22 Jan. 1823; Grey mss, Ellice to Grey, 14, 21 Jan. 1823. [16] *The Times*, 26 Nov., 6 Dec. 1822, 10, 20, 22, 25, 28 Jan., 10 Feb. 1823; *Hereford Jnl.* 11, 18 Dec. 1822, 8, 15, 22 Jan. 1823. [17] *Gent. Mag.* (1823), ii. 368; Herefs. RO, Pateshall mss A95/ET/64. [18] *The Times*, 25 May 1824. [19] Ibid. 3 Sept. 1824. [20] *Hereford Independent*, 13 Nov., 11 Dec. 1824, 1 Jan., 1, 8 Oct. 1825; *Hereford Jnl.* 15 Dec. 1824. [21] Herefs. RO X21, notice of Kington and Radnorshire Bank, 20 Dec. 1825; *CJ*, lxxxi. 94; TNA C110/97, Price to T. Jay, Feb.-Apr.; *Hereford Jnl.* 15, 22 Mar., 19 Apr., 14 June; *Hereford Independent*, 15 Apr. 1826. [22] *Oxford DNB sub* Price, Sir Uvedale; Fitzwilliam mss 125/16. [23] *The Times*, 2 June; *Hereford Jnl.* 7, 14, 21 June 1826. [24] *Hereford Jnl.* 21 June 1826; Fitzwilliam mss, Price to Milton, 4 Oct. 1827. [25] *Hereford Jnl.* 7 Feb. 1827. [26] *The Times*, 1, 8 June; *Hereford Jnl.* 3, 24 Oct.; *Hereford Independent*, 20 Oct. 1827. [27] Fitzwilliam mss. [28] Ibid. Price to Milton, 8 Dec.; Add. 51687, Lansdowne to Holland, 8 Dec. [1827]. [29] *Hereford Jnl.* 25 Feb. 1829. [30] Ibid. 20 May 1829. [31] PROB 11/1768; IR26/1235/42. [32] *Hereford Jnl.* 16 Sept. 1829, 10 Feb. 1830. [33] Ibid. 7, 28 July, 4, 11 Aug.; Herefs. RO, diaries of John Biddulph of Ledbury [Biddulph diary] G2/IV/J/57, 21-22 July 1830. [34] *Hereford Jnl.* 11 Aug. 1830. [35] Ibid. 8, 15, 22 Nov. 1830. [36] According to *Parl. Deb.* (ser.3), i. 1022, Price merely 'concurred in ... [Gordon's] opinion that every government should be watched with the utmost vigilance'. [37] Fitzwilliam mss, Price to Milton, 15 Dec. [1830]. [38] *Hereford Jnl.* 1, 8, 15, 22, 29 Dec. 1830, 19 Jan. 1831. [39] *Three Diaries*, 10. [40] *Hereford Jnl.* 2, 9, 23 Feb. 1831. [41] Ibid. 23, 30 Mar. 1831. [42] Ibid. 6 Apr. 1831. [43] Biddulph diary, 20 Apr.-1 May 1831; Pateshall mss A95/V/EB/595; A95/V/W/a/130; *The Times*, 11 Apr.; *Hereford Jnl.* 27 Apr., 4 May; *Globe*, 30 Apr., 2 May 1831. [44] *The Times*, 9 May; *Hereford Jnl.* 11 May 1831. [45] *Three Diaries*, 102. [46] *Hereford Jnl.* 24 Aug. 1831. [47] *CJ*, lxxxvi. 844, 863-4, 866; *Carmarthen Jnl.* 23, 30 Sept.; *The Times*, 27 Sept. 1831. [48] *Hereford Jnl.* 19, 26 Oct., 2, 9 Nov.; *The Times*, 7 Nov. 1831. [49] *Hereford Jnl.* 16, 30 Nov., 14 Dec. 1831. [50] Ibid. 25 Jan. 1832. [51] Ibid. 8 Feb., 30 May, 6, 13, 20 June 1832. [52] Grey mss, Ellice

to Grey, 2 May; *The Times*, 2, 13, 25 June 1832. [53] Add. 51837. [54] Biddulph diary, 17 Sept., 27 Nov., 15, 18 Dec.; *Hereford Jnl.* 20 Dec. 1832. [55] *Hereford Times*, 14 Nov. 1857. [56] Ibid. 26 July, 2, 9 Aug., 27 Sept.; *The Times*, 26, 31 July, 1 Aug. 1845; Herefs. RO, schedule of privately held Foxley mss. [57] *London Gazette*, 19 Oct. 1855, 22 Jan., 8 Feb., 7 Mar., 15 Apr. 1856; Pateshall mss A95/ET/64. [58] *The Times*, 22 Oct., 31 Dec. 1855; *Hereford Jnl.* 16, 23 Jan., 6, 13 Feb., 13 Mar. 1856. [59] *Gent. Mag.* (1857), ii. 689; *Hereford Times*, 14 Nov. 1857. [60] PROB 11/2262/923; IR26/2110/1149.

M.M.E.

PRICE, Samuel Grove (1793–1839), of Knebworth, Herts. and 9 Gray's Inn Square, Mdx.

SANDWICH	1830–1831
SANDWICH	1835–1837

b. 17 June 1793, o.s. of Rev. Morgan Price, rect. of Knebworth and Letchworth, and Catherine, da. and h. of Samuel Grove of Taynton, Glos. *educ.* by Rev. Roberts; Eton 1808; Trinity Coll. Camb. 1810, BA 1815, fellow, Downing 1817, MA 1818; L. Inn 1813, called 1818; G. Inn 1823. *m.* 4 Dec. 1830,[1] Marianne, da. of William Page of 5 Fitzroy Square, Mdx., 2s. *suc.* fa. 1830. *d.* 17 June 1839.

There is some doubt as to the identity of Price's father, but he was probably the Morgan Price, son of Lewis Price of Prignant, Cardiganshire, who matriculated at Christ Church, Oxford on 10 Dec. 1768, aged 21. If so, he was turned 41 when he married in January 1789, just under a year after his institution as rector of Knebworth, Hertfordshire. His wife's inheritance at Taynton lay six miles from Gloucester, of which city he acquired the freedom in 1794; and he may have had a family connection with Morgan Price, a Gloucester timber merchant, who died in 1776 and whose descendants lived at Tibberton, adjacent to Taynton.[2]

Samuel Grove Price, an only child, left Eton with a high reputation as a scholar, which he enhanced at Cambridge. His contemporary Charles John Shore, president of the Union Society, recalled him as its 'principal Conservative speaker' and 'an ardent and chivalrous high Tory', who 'revered' and modelled himself on Burke 'as the denouncer of the French Revolution'. Although Price supposedly had 'a distaste for the law', he went the home circuit after his call to the bar and found occasional work as a parliamentary counsel.[3] He attended the Hertfordshire county meeting called to petition for parliamentary reform, 8 Feb. 1823, but was shouted down when he attacked reform as 'the euthanasia of the British constitution'.[4] To set the record straight, he published an expanded and improved version of his speech, in which he argued that there was no connection between 'the depression of the agricultural interest and the construction of the Commons' and predicted that reform, by upsetting the essential balance of the existing constitution, would lead, 'after a feverish and convulsive struggle, into an inconvenient and ill-digested republic':

> I confess that my views of the future are somewhat melancholy: I fear more from what is likely to fail within, than from what menaces us without. A rash, presumptuous, meddling spirit has usually preceded the downfall of every free state in the world. There is something, I fear, like this spirit abroad at present.

Price voted for the anti-Catholic William Bankes* at the Cambridge University by-election of 1822. In the uproar provoked in the Senate House in 1826 by a Whig attempt to have the bribery oath administered, he mounted the vice-chancellor's table and 'declared he had never been insulted in his life till this day'.[5] At the nomination for Hertfordshire that year, he intervened to attack the unopposed candidates for their support of Catholic relief; and at a dinner to celebrate the return for Hertford of the nominee of the 2nd marquess of Salisbury, 11 July 1826, he delivered a long anti-Catholic rant.[6]

Price was taken up by Salisbury, whom he may have known at Eton and who shared his extreme Tory views. In April 1827 he wrote at Salisbury's behest a piece for the *Herts. Mercury* in which he praised the retiring ministers and indirectly censured their successor Canning. Salisbury had 'never read a cleverer paragraph' and told him that 'if you can write in so formidable a strain as that which pervades this short essay, you have it in your power to render the cause you have espoused most essential service'.[7] The following March he composed for Salisbury's private amusement a spiteful and tasteless verse epitaph on Canning, which began:

> Sprung from a harlot, by a playwright got,
> Here George remains, in infamy, to rot;
> A wretch, condemned to everlasting fame,
> Without one virtuous tear to blot his name.[8]

He continued to act as Salisbury's go-between with the editor of the *Mercury*.[9] On 2 Nov. 1828 the Hertfordshire Whig Lord Dacre informed Lord Holland of

> various little, contemptible and hitherto most ineffectual attempts to excite the Brunswick mania in different parts of this county. At the sessions a pert barrister, of the name of Price, produced a species of declaration of faith – half political, half polemical – in the hope of obtaining priestly signatures. He did not get one. This Price is the instigator and organ of the intolerants. The fellow has no intellect, but he possesses great facility of

> loose declamation ... He is brought into contact with very many by attending the sessions as well at St. Albans as at Hertford. Thus, he is in a condition to produce some effect. Lord Salisbury is at Rome, and if here, he would not lend himself ... to the blandishments of the bigots.[10]

Like Salisbury, he was outraged by ministers' concession of Catholic emancipation in 1829, and he 'strained every nerve' to ensure the apostate Peel's defeat in the Oxford University by-election.[11] In March 1829 he came forward at the last minute to contest a vacancy for Sandwich, where Sir Henry Fane, surveyor-general of the ordnance and a pragmatic supporter of emancipation, was expected to come in on the government interest. Price, who had been invited to stand by a local anti-Catholic clergyman, was too late in the field to be anything but a nuisance, and he finished 220 behind Fane in a poll of 402.[12] He immediately declared his candidature for the next vacancy. At a meeting of the London freemen, 24 Apr. 1829, he attacked Wellington and Peel for their 'expediency' and condemned the 'new-fangled notions respecting our commercial policy, by which the strength of the nation had been reduced'. In a typically portentous peroration he

> declared himself to be a Tory ... He was a friend to civil and religious liberty, but did not agree that ... [it] would be advanced by altering the constitution ... We may prepare ourselves for a series of evils ... and ... a period of misery ... Let us hope that the new system of liberty will not cause sorrow and bloodshed.[13]

He duly stood for Sandwich at the general election of 1830 when, claiming to be 'unfettered by any party connection', he deplored emancipation and called for measures of 'just economy', enhanced protection and preservation of the constitution from 'the evils of an unlimited monarchy, an overbearing aristocracy or a violent democracy'. His ministerialist opponent withdrew on the eve of the election leaving Price, who suffered from a 'severe indisposition' immediately afterwards, to come in with the independent sitting Member.[14] He was to have been married on 24 Sept. 1830, but he was 'fetched from Sandwich, at the moment he was quitting that place for another, where he was to meet his destined bride', to attend his father's death bed at Knebworth that day; he was 'much cut up'. The wedding was postponed for ten weeks.[15]

Ministers listed Price among the 'moderate Ultras', but he was in their minority on the civil list, 15 Nov. 1830. At a Hertford election dinner, 24 Nov., he attributed distress to 'a want of general credit' and said that parliamentary reform was no solution. He explained that he had 'found fault' with Wellington's ministry 'for adopting too closely, and following with so much adherence, the opinions of the present [Grey] administration'; but that if forced to choose between them, he would opt for that of Wellington.[16] In the House, 10 Dec., he disclaimed 'any desire to embarrass the new government', but tried to do precisely that by asking whether they had sanctioned or acquiesced in the united trades' procession to St. James's, which he considered to have been illegal. When a Member called him to order for digression, the Speaker took his side, and Price rambled on, making particular play of the alleged flaunting of the tricolour, 'the signal of more crime, bloodshed, rapine, and destruction, than any other that has ever been raised in Europe'. Peel gave him little support. His intervention in a squabble over the corn laws, 11 Dec. 1830, earned him a rebuke from the chair for attributing expressions to another Member. He criticized petitioners against the burden of tithes in St. Giles, Cripplegate, 11 Feb., and attacked the proposed tax on steamboat passengers, 17 Feb. 1831. He ridiculed ministers' failure to execute in office promises of civil list economies made in opposition, 28 Mar., and on 30 Mar., disregarding protests at his prolixity, accused them of allowing Spanish liberal refugees to use Gibraltar as a base for insurgency. Price voted against the second reading of the ministerial reform bill, 22 Mar. In an exchange with his colleague Marryat, 25 Mar., he cited his own return as proof that Sandwich was not 'an appendage to the admiralty' and denounced in general terms the 'bill of pains and penalties', which would disfranchise at least half his constituents. On 30 Mar. he asserted that 'I do not wish to retain my seat in this House after the reform bill passes'. The same day Tom Macaulay, who had encountered him at Cambridge, wondered 'why did not the great Samuel Grove Price speak' in the debate on the second reading:

> He often came to the front rows, and sat making notes. Everybody expected him to rise, and prepared night-caps accordingly. But he always sneaked away. On my soul, I believe that he is a craven with all his blushes. Indeed if he is afraid, it is the best thing that I ever knew of him. For a more terrible audience there is not in the world.[17]

Price, whose 'accidental aid', according to the Rev. George Gleig of Ash, near Sandwich, enabled a meeting of local Tories to take 'much higher ground' than he had expected in declaring against reform, voted for Gascoyne's wrecking amendment, 19 Apr. 1831.[18] Two days later he protested against Dr. Lushington's assertion that the present corrupt Parliament deserved to be dissolved. There were cheers from the ministerial benches when he said that this was 'possibly ... even ... probably' the last time he would address the

House. Price, who claimed to be 'in infirm health', held up the 1830 revolution in France as an awful example, and quoted De Lolme, Hume, Addison, Bolingbroke and of course Burke in a wild diatribe against the bill. There was a laugh at his pronouncement that 'we are now standing in the eleventh hour of the constitution'; but, unabashed, he predicted that once embarked in 'the career of revolution', ministers would be 'hurried, with an accelerating velocity' into the 'abyss' of 'confusion, civil war, and ... a military despotism'.

Price, whose father had died intestate, with effects sworn under £200,[19] was in some trouble at Sandwich, where there was considerable support for the reform bill, despite its threat to the voting rights of freemen: 'the reformers', he wrote, 'are moving heaven and earth against me', for his speech of 21 Apr. had 'driven them frantic'. He was opposed by Marryat and Sir Thomas Troubridge*, a naval officer who stood on the government interest. Price managed to prevent any second anti-reform candidate, endorsed by Wellington in his capacity as lord warden of the Cinque Ports, being sent down to join him, and professed to be 'quite certain if I am left undisturbed'. Yet his appearance at Deal provoked a riot, which forced him to abandon his canvass, and he gave up on the third day, when he lagged 100 behind Troubridge.[20] In a long and defiant address, 7 May, he attributed his defeat largely to government influence, though he did acknowledge the strength of 'popular excitement' on reform. He denounced the politicians of all parties who, under the spell of those 'pretended philosophers, the political economists', had 'tampered with the agriculture, the commerce, the shipping of this country' and 'contracted the currency and limited that credit, without which the agricultural and manufacturing interests can never flourish'.[21]

Price returned to London with a letter of introduction to Wellington from Gleig, who wrote:

> At a crisis like the present, when above all things talent and a knowledge of the constitution are needed in the House of Commons, a vacancy ought to be made for Mr. Price at almost any cost.

Wellington replied that Price was 'one of those whom I should be most anxious to see in Parliament, if it should ever be in my power to take any steps upon such a subject'. In July 1831 the duke was in negotiation for an unspecified seat for Price, but this collapsed, to the great regret of Gleig, who hoped that 'some other opening may yet occur'.[22] Price remained active at Sandwich, which he continued to cultivate, and in Kent as an opponent of the reintroduced reform bill. He harangued meetings at Sandwich, 7 July, and Sittingbourne, 3 Aug., when he called it 'a decoy duck intended to lead us on to a revolution'.[23] With Gleig, he organized a Sandwich meeting to petition the Lords against the bill, 29 Sept.; he travelled from Cheltenham to address it.[24] On 7 Nov. 1831 he wrote to Gleig from his then London house at 20 Guildford Street, Russell Square:

> I am fortified to the teeth, in 'my castle'. I am determined to set the example of resistance to a turbulent and felonious mob at any risk of person, or personal misrepresentation ... You may depend upon my temper and forbearance, until forbearance shall be feebleness, and until the law shall justify more decisive measures. But my house shall not be invaded with impunity, whatever be the sacrifice. We do live in fearful times, but the firmness of the crew may bring weather-beaten ships to port. Dreadful is the example of Bristol, but it may be salutary ... We have been hitherto undisturbed, but there is a meeting of the *most* desperate Jacobins now, I am informed, in White Conduit Fields. Numerous ill-looking fellows have flocked to town, I have no doubt from Birmingham, etc. I expect something this afternoon or night, and am quite prepared. *You* would smile to see my arsenal.[25]

In January 1832 he assisted Salisbury and Lord Verulam in their promotion of a Hertfordshire address to the king calling for the suppression of political unions and applauding his reported refusal to create peers to carry the reform bill. Later in the year he drew up for Salisbury draft articles of impeachment against Lord Grey for his 'unconstitutional use' of the king's name and threats to create peers.[26]

The opposition whip Holmes pointed out to Wellington in November 1831 that Price, 'violent Protestant as he was', had 'voted with us on the civil list, and has ever since acted in concert with the Conservative party'.[27] His candidature for the reformed constituency of Sandwich at the 1832 general election had their backing, but he was beaten by the sitting Members.[28] Salisbury had him in mind as a candidate for Hertford after the election there had been declared void in April 1833, but subsequently set him aside for Wellington's younger son. (In the event, no new writ was issued until the dissolution in December 1834.) Price was one of the counsel employed by Salisbury in the libel suits of July 1833 against Thomas Duncombe* arising out of the Hertford election.[29] He was 'seriously ill' early in 1834, when he was living at Sunninghill, Berkshire, and he boasted to Salisbury of his 'most perfect hatred, contempt and aversion' to the Whigs, 'the vilest faction which the empire ever beheld'.[30] With his Conservative friends in power, he topped the poll at Sandwich in 1835, but he lost his seat again in 1837.

He was an enthusiastic supporter of Don Carlos in the Spanish civil conflict.[31]

An anonymous schoolfellow and uncritical admirer of Price credited him with 'a powerful and comprehensive mind' and a capacity for 'bold, manly and sincere' oratory.[32] Shore wrote of him:

> The sonorous and well-rounded sentences which had elicited the admiration even of his opponents at Cambridge wearied the House of Commons. His eloquence nevertheless was no less appreciated than his honesty. But he was an anachronism during the period of his parliamentary career ... Price was endowed with many excellent qualities, and beloved by a small number of attached friends.[33]

He died at Sunninghill on his forty-sixth birthday. By his brief will, dated 3 Apr. 1839, he devised all his property, which included that at Taynton, to his wife. His personalty was sworn under £1,500.[34] His surviving sons Lettsom Grove Price and Stanhope Grove Price went to Eton; and in 1870 the latter, a naval officer, took the name of Grove instead of Price after coming into possession of the Taynton property.[35]

[1] *Gent. Mag.* (1830), ii. 640. [2] Ibid. (1789), i. 86; R. Clutterbuck, *Herts.* ii. 380; J.E. Cussans, *Herts.* 'Broadwater', 26, 115; *Reg. Gloucester Freemen* ed. A.R.J. Jurica, 182, 208, 236; *VCH Glos.* iv. 127. [3] *Gent. Mag.* (1839), ii. 200; Lord Teignmouth, *Reminiscences*, i. 48. [4] *The Times*, 10 Feb. 1823. [5] Ibid. 15 June 1826; *Palmerston-Sulivan Letters*, 183. [6] *Herts. Mercury*, 17 June, 15 July 1826. [7] Ibid. 21 Apr.; Hatfield House mss 2M/Gen., Price to Salisbury and reply, 18 Apr. 1827. [8] Hatfield House mss 2M/Gen., Price to Salisbury, 16 Mar. 1828. [9] Ibid. Macqueen to Salisbury, 20 July, 11 Sept., 2 Nov., Sunday [Dec. 1828]. [10] Add. 51834. [11] Hatfield House mss 2M/Gen., Price to Salisbury, 4 Jan. 1829. [12] *Kent Herald*, 26 Mar., 2 Apr. 1829. [13] *Kentish Gazette*, 28 Apr. 1829. [14] Ibid. 2, 13, 20, 23, 27, 30 July, 10 Aug. 1830. [15] Hatfield House mss 2M, Nicholson to Salisbury, 24 Sept. 1830. [16] *Herts. Mercury*, 27 Nov. 1830. [17] *Macaulay Letters*, ii. 11-12. [18] Wellington mss, Gleig to Wellington, 9, 13 Apr. 1831. [19] PROB 6/207. [20] Hatfield House mss 2M/Gen., Price to Salisbury, 23 Apr.; Wellington mss WP1/1182/11; Gleig to Wellington, 22 Apr.; *Kent Herald*, 7, 14, 21, 28 Apr., 5 May 1831. [21] *Kentish Gazette*, 10 May 1831. [22] Wellington mss, Gleig to Wellington, 9 May, 21 Sept. 1831; WP1/1186/11; 1190/17; 1191/11, 14; 222/15, 16. [23] *Kent Herald*, 7, 14 July, 4 Aug. 1831. [24] Ibid. 29 Sept., 6 Oct. 1831. [25] Wellington mss WP1/1196/35; WP2/215/72. [26] *Herts. Mercury*, 7 Jan.; Hatfield House mss 2M, draft articles [1832]. [27] Wellington mss WP2/215/67. [28] Ibid. WP2/215/70; 222/85; Hatfield House mss 2M/Gen., Mahon to Salisbury, 7 Oct. 1832. [29] *Wellington Pol. Corresp.* i. 160, 196; V. Rowe, 'Hertford Borough Bill', *PH*, xi (1992), 90, 103-3; *Morning Post*, 13, 15 July 1833. [30] Hatfield House mss 2M/Gen., Price to Salisbury, 5 Mar. 1834. [31] *Wellington Pol. Corresp.* ii. 245; Add. 40407, f. 91. [32] *Gent. Mag.* (1839), ii. 200-1; Add. 40427, f. 394. [33] Teignmouth, i. 49. [34] PROB 8/232 (5 Sept. 1839); 11/1916/586. [35] *London Gazette*, 27 Dec. 1870.

D.R.F.

PRINGLE, Alexander (1791–1857), of Whytbank and Yair, Selkirk.

SELKIRKSHIRE 1830–1832

SELKIRKSHIRE 1835–23 Jan. 1846

b. 30 Jan. 1791, 1st s. of Alexander Pringle of Whytbank and Mary, da. of Sir Alexander Dick, 3rd bt., of Prestonfield, Edinburgh. *educ.* Selkirk; Trinity Coll. Camb. 1809. *m.* 12 Jan. 1830, his cos. Agnes Joanna, da. of Sir William Dick, 4th bt., of Prestonfield, 1s. *suc.* fa. 1827. *d.* 2 Sept. 1857.

Ld. of treasury Sept. 1841-Apr. 1845; principal kpr. of sasines [S] 1846-*d.*

The Pringles of Whytbank were descended from Robert Hoppringle, esquire to the 4th earl of Douglas (duke of Touraine), with whom he was killed at the battle of Verneuil in 1424. Whytbank was acquired later that century, and Yair was added to it by James Pringle (*d.* 1667), Member for Selkirkshire in the Scottish Parliament, 1628-33. Alexander Pringle, this Member's father, was born in 1747, entered the Madras civil service of the East India Company as a writer in 1776 and retired as a senior merchant in 1790, soon after succeeding his soldier brother John to Whytbank. He bought back the Yair estate, which had been sold to the duke of Buccleuch, and built a new mansion there. In 1812 he secured the patent office of chamberlain of Ettrick Forest.[1] His eldest son Alexander, the only one of his five sons not to enter the service of the East India Company, matriculated at Cambridge in 1809, but did not graduate. In July 1815 he accompanied Sir Walter Scott, who was sheriff of Selkirkshire and had mentioned Pringle and his father in the introduction to Canto II of *Marmion* in 1808, on an excursion to the field of Waterloo and Paris, along with his county neighbour and Cambridge contemporary John Scott of Gala and the advocate Robert Bruce. Pringle was described by Scott at the time as being 'about five feet six inches [with] light hair and eyes, round face, and slightly made'; he was generally known as 'little Pringle' in his adult life. At the beginning of September 1815 he and Bruce travelled to Switzerland.[2] He was in Florence in late 1818, and in April 1820 he served with the Midlothian yeomanry in quelling unrest in Glasgow, 'the land of the radicals', from where he reported to Robert Dundas of Arniston:

> We lead a life of constant uncertainty and expectation, which is abundantly interesting ... Every night brings some new event, and we are kept constantly on the alert ... We never know what we have to do the next hour ... I am living in capital quarters, the guest of the lord provost.[3]

He had a taste and talent for genealogy, on which subject he liked to baffle Scott (a distant kinsman) at his home at Abbotsford.[4] On the death of his father, who left personalty sworn under £3,000, in February 1827, he succeeded to the family estates.[5]

In May 1829 he informed the 5th duke of Buccleuch, who had come of age the previous year, that he intended to offer for Selkirkshire on the next vacancy and that he had three years earlier secured the approval for this plan of Buccleuch's uncle Lord Montagu, acting head of the family during the duke's minority. At the same time, he explained that his ultimate object was the sheriffship of a Scottish county, even though this would disqualify him from Parliament: 'I should certainly prefer being for a time in Parliament if I might thereby hope ultimately to obtain an office of superior emolument'.[6] He duly came forward for Selkirkshire in the room of the retiring sitting Member at the general election of 1830 and was returned unopposed.[7] The Wellington ministry listed him among their 'friends', and he was in their minority in the division on the civil list which brought them down, 15 Nov. 1830. He presented petitions for the abolition of slavery, 9, 22 Nov. 1830, 28 Mar. 1831. He alleged that a Dunbartonshire reform petition had been covertly got up, 26 Feb., and complained that the Grey ministry's Scottish reform scheme destroyed chartered rights, 19 Mar. He presented and endorsed the Selkirkshire freeholders' petition against the 'highly objectionable' proposal to unite it with Peeblesshire to return one Member and imputed 'partial and unworthy motives' to its authors, 22 Mar., when he voted against the second reading of the English bill. On 25 Mar. he defended the signatories of the Edinburgh inhabitants' anti-reform petition. A staunch churchman, he presented and supported a petition from the Bible Society of Edinburgh for the right to import bibles from England, 18 Apr. 1831. Next day he voted for Gascoyne's wrecking amendment to the English reform bill. At the ensuing general election he came in again unopposed for Selkirkshire, where two potential challengers, who were also anti-reformers, were persuaded to back down. A 'blow in the eye from my horse's head' did not materially hamper him.[8] On 15 May he wrote to Buccleuch welcoming 'the triumphant result of the Lanarkshire election', but deploring the violence which had marked it: 'It is quite a new feature in Scotland to bring up the mob and excite them to canvass the election, and we have on this occasion had some notable examples'.[9]

He divided against the second reading of the reintroduced English reform bill, 6 July, to the bitter end for an adjournment, 12 July (when his own motion mustered a minority of 24), for use of the 1831 census to determine the disfranchisement schedules, 19 July, against Chippenham's inclusion in B, 27 July, and to preserve the voting rights of freeholders of the four sluiced boroughs, 2 Sept. On 4 Aug. he opposed the 'revolutionary' creation of the new metropolitan districts as 'likely to introduce, ultimately, a division of the representation ... according to the mere rule of numbers', which would adversely affect Scotland. He had given considerable thought to the detailed proposals of the Scottish bill,[10] and said that the disfranchisement of the Anstruther Burghs was unfair, 6 Aug., and urged ministers to reconsider their treatment of the Scottish counties, 13 Aug. On the 27th he presented and endorsed a petition from Selkirk against the proposed inclusion of Falkirk in its district. He brought up another Selkirkshire petition against the merger with Peeblesshire and gave notice of a motion to oppose this, 3 Sept. He divided against the passage of the English bill, 21 Sept., and the second reading of the Scottish measure, 23 Sept. He wanted Scottish freeholders to be compensated for loss of superiorities and condemned the bill as a 'rash attempt to sweep away all our ancient laws, which will materially lessen the value of landed property in Scotland', 27 Sept. On 3 Oct. he spoke at some length against the measure, dwelling on the danger of introducing the 'uproar, riot, dissipation, corruption and confusion' of 'populous elections' to Edinburgh and Glasgow, where most of the new voters would 'belong to a low grade of society'. He professed willingness to accept a limited revision of the old system, but predicted that the bill as it stood would destroy the wholesome influence of the Scottish gentry. On 4 Oct. he denounced the ministerial decision to allow Selkirkshire and Peeblesshire to return a Member each by the expedient of removing the burghs of Selkirk and Peebles from the Linlithgow district and giving their qualified householders a county vote. He defended the Scottish yeomanry and damned the 'most unwise act' of their partial disbandment in 1827, 27 June. He was in the minorities of 11 for the Irish union of parishes bill, 19 Aug., and of 47 to terminate the Maynooth grant, 26 Sept. He voted to censure the Irish administration for interfering in the Dublin election, 23 Aug., to suspend the Liverpool writ, 5 Sept., and for inquiry into the effects of renewal of the Sugar Refinery Act on the West India interest, 12 Sept. He presented Scottish agriculturists' petitions against the use of molasses in brewing and distilling, 27 Aug., 3 Sept. He defended the grant for the Society for the Suppression of Vice, 5 Sept., called the appointment of the Rev. Sheepshanks as a parliamentary boundary commissioner 'a desecration of the holy office of a minister of the gospel', 13 Sept., and on 16 Sept. asserted that sympathy for the Deacles in their complaint against William Bingham Baring* had been got up by a 'reckless' press keen to traduce 'the characters of men whose virtues or public spirit have placed them in a prominent situation'. He opposed the bill to abolish the Scottish exchequer court, but was beaten by 95-31 in his bid to have the debate adjourned, 7 Oct. 1831.

Pringle voted against the second reading of the revised English reform bill, 17 Dec. 1831, the enfranchisement of Tower Hamlets, 28 Feb., and the third reading, 22 Mar. 1832. He divided against government on the Russian-Dutch loan, 26 Jan., 12 July. A motion to add him to the committee on the Scottish exchequer court bill was defeated, 2 Feb.; he said on 10 Apr. that it would 'do more to effect a change in the institutions of Scotland than anything ... since the Union'. He voted against the malt drawback bill, 2 Apr., and for the Liverpool disfranchisement bill, 23 May. He supported the prayer of Scottish petitions against the proposed system of interdenominational education for Ireland, 16 Apr., and criticized it from his staunch Protestant standpoint, 19 June, 5 July. He denounced the Scottish reform bill as 'an entire subversion of the ancient constitution', 21 May; protested against the arrangement for Peebles and Selkirk and called for an increase in the county representation, 1 June, and moved unsuccessfully to have the plan for the revamped burgh districts referred to a select committee, 15 June, when he asserted that ministers had engineered it 'to augment the power and influence of their own supporters'. On the third reading, 27 June, he accused them of truckling to the political unions and, while admitting the existence of defects in the old system, declared that 'the risk of ruin was greater than the prospect of effecting improvement'. He divided against the third reading of the Irish bill, 25 May, and to preserve freemen's rights, 2 July. He may have voted against the Irish party processions bill, 25 June. He supported the appointment of a select committee on infringements of the Sabbath and was named to it, 3 July. On the 13th he said that for the first time 'scenes of dissipation', produced by large scale treating, were occurring in the Scottish counties. He was given a month's leave to attend to urgent business, 20 July 1832.

Pringle stood for Selkirkshire at the general election in December, but lost to a Liberal by nine votes in a poll of 267. He blamed 'intimidation' and his opponent's influence over the householders of Selkirk and Galashiels, 'bound together by a reform club or political union', and anticipated, as he told Sir Robert Peel, 'much jobbing, combined with many reckless experiments ... and ... a serious check to the prosperity of Scotland'. He regained the seat in 1835, retained it in 1837 and came in unopposed in 1841.[11] He was described in 1838 as 'a man of some consideration among the Scotch Conservatives, though comparatively little known in the House', where his 'very respectable talents' as 'a calm and quiet speaker' usually gained him a hearing.[12] He was made a lord of the treasury in Peel's second ministry, but resigned in 1845 in protest at the decision to enhance the Maynooth grant.[13] He retired from Parliament in February 1846 after replacing the late William Dundas* as keeper of sasines. He died at Yair in September 1857 and was succeeded by his only child Alexander Pringle (1837-98).

[1] A. Pringle, *Recs. Pringles*, 229, 241-2. [2] Ibid. 242-4; J. Scott, *Jnl. of a Tour to Waterloo and Paris* (1842), 1, 11, 16, 44, 77, 193; Lockhart, *Scott*, 315, 321; *Cockburn Letters*, 419. [3] *Arniston Mems.* 99, 310-11. [4] *Scott Jnl.* 508. [5] PROB 11/1726/320; IR26/1139/527. [6] NAS GD224/581/4, Pringle to Buccleuch, 23 May 1829. [7] Pringle mss box 16, Pringle to J. Pringle, 16 June; NAS GD224/581/4, Pringle to Buccleuch, 10 June, 2 Aug.; *Caledonian Mercury*, 14 Aug. 1830. [8] NAS GD157/2978/14; 2981/10; GD224/581/4, Buccleuch to A. Eliott Lockhart, 26 Apr., reply, 29 Apr., Pringle to Buccleuch, 2 May; *Caledonian Mercury*, 30 Apr., 21 May 1831; *Scott Jnl.* 650. [9] NAS GD224/581/4. [10] Ibid. Pringle to Buccleuch, 17 June 1831. [11] Add. 40403, f. 174; 40410, f. 269; 40424, f. 125. [12] [J. Grant], *Random Recollections of Lords and Commons* (1838), ii. 226-9. [13] Parker, *Peel*, ii. 495; iii. 86, 425.

D.R.F.

PRINGLE, Sir William Henry (?1771–1840), of 17 Stratford Place, Mdx.

ST. GERMANS	1812–1818
LISKEARD	1818–1832

b. ?1771, 1st s. of Lt.-Col. Henry Pringle of 51 Ft. and Mary, da. of Rev. William Godley, DD, of Dublin. *educ.* by Rev. Richard Norris, Drogheda; Trinity, Dublin 16 May 1789, aged 17. *m.* 20 May 1806,[1] Hester Harriet Pitt, da. and h. of Hon. Edward James Eliot† of Bromfield, Clapham, Surr., 1s. 4da. *suc.* fa. 1800; KCB 2 Jan. 1815; GCB 19 Dec. 1834. *d.* 23 Dec. 1840.

Cornet 16 Drag. 1792, lt. 1793; capt. Ind. Ft. 1794; maj. 111 Ft. 1794; lt.-col. 4 Ft. 1799; capt. and lt.-col. 2 Ft. Gds. 1802; col. army and inspecting field officer of militia in Canada 1809; maj.-gen. 1812; on staff of Peninsular army 1812; col. R. Newfoundland fencibles 1814; col. 64 Ft. 1816; lt.-gen. 1825; col. 45 Ft. 1838-*d.*

Pringle, who had married William Pitt's† niece in 1806, served with distinction in the Peninsula and survived being shot through the body at Orthes in 1814. Nevertheless, Charles William Wynn*, president of the board of control, when reviewing potential candidates for the Indian command in 1825, wrote that he 'appears a very dull man, and never has been in any situation which enabled him to exhibit the sort of ability which is required'.[2] In the Commons, where he sat undisturbed for Cornish boroughs controlled by his wife's uncles, the 1st and 2nd earls of St. Germans, he was an occasional attender who continued to give silent support to Lord Liverpool's ministry. He divided against economies in revenue collection, 4 July 1820. He voted in defence of ministers' conduct towards Queen Caroline, 6 Feb. 1821. He divided for Catholic relief, 28 Feb. He voted against repeal of the additional malt duty, 3 Apr., and Hume's economy and retrenchment motion, 27 June 1821. He divided against more extensive tax reductions, 11, 21 Feb., and abolition of one of the joint-postmasterships, 13 Mar. 1822. He voted in defence of the lord advocate's conduct towards the Scottish press, 25 June 1822. He divided against repeal of the Foreign Enlistment Act, 16 Apr., and inquiry into the prosecution of the Dublin Orange rioters, 22 Apr. 1823. He voted for the Irish insurrection bill, 14 June 1824. The previous month he had obtained official permission to 'pass through the Horse Guards, on horseback occasionally', on his way to the Commons from his house just north of Oxford Street.[3] He divided for Catholic relief, 1 Mar., 21 Apr. (paired), 10 May 1825. On 15 Apr. he was one of three Members who confirmed that they had not heard the question put for the division on the Southwark paving bill, and whose names were subsequently added to the favourable minority. He voted for the financial provision for the duke of Cumberland, 30 May, 10 June 1825. It was said of him at this time that he 'attended occasionally and voted with ministers'.[4]

His only known votes in the 1826 Parliament were for Catholic relief, 6 Mar. 1827, 12 May 1828, the Wellington ministry's emancipation bill, 6, 30 Mar. 1829, and against the enfranchisement of Birmingham, Leeds and Manchester, 23 Feb. 1830. He paired against abolition of the death penalty for forgery, 7 June 1830. After his return for Liskeard at the general election that summer ministers reckoned him as one of their 'friends', and he duly voted with them in the crucial civil list division, 15 Nov. 1830. He divided against the second reading of the Grey ministry's reform bill, 22 Mar., and for Gascoyne's wrecking amendment, 19 Apr. 1831. He voted against the second reading of the reintroduced bill, 6 July 1831. In his only reported contribution to debate in 20 years, 29 July, he 'bore testimony to the intelligent character of the constituency of Liskeard', which was scheduled to lose one of its seats. He divided against the bill's passage, 21 Sept., and the second reading of the Scottish bill, 23 Sept. Opposition managers hoped at this time that he might be able to persuade his wife's notoriously feckless uncle Lord Chatham (Pitt's brother) to take his seat in the Lords and oppose reform; but if he tried he failed.[5] He was absent from the division on the second reading of the revised reform bill, 17 Dec. 1831, but voted against the enfranchisement of Tower Hamlets, 28 Feb., and the third reading, 22 Mar. 1832. He divided against ministers on the Russian-Dutch loan, 12 July 1832. He retired from Parliament at the dissolution in December.

Pringle died suddenly of 'disease of the heart' in December 1840. He left an inherited estate in county Armagh to his only son John Henry, and the remainder of his property to his wife, noting that 'almost all I am possessed of I have through her'; his personalty was sworn under £14,000.[6] His widow, who died in 1842, distributed £41,000 among their four daughters and left her inheritance of £5,000 from the 1st earl of St. Germans to John Henry; her personalty was sworn under £14,000 and the residue calculated for duty at £2,309.[7]

[1] *Gent. Mag.* (1806), i. 477. [2] Buckingham, *Mems. Geo. IV*, ii. 215. [3] Add. 40365, f. 124. [4] *Session of Parl. 1825*, p. 481. [5] Wellington mss WP1/1198/1. [6] *Gent. Mag.* (1841), i. 317; PROB 8/234; 11/1939/49. [7] PROB 11/1971/266; IR26/1622/734.

D.R.F.

PRITTIE, Hon. Francis Aldborough (1779–1853), of Corville, co. Tipperary.

CARLOW	21 Mar. 1801–30 June 1801
CO. TIPPERARY	1806–1818
CO. TIPPERARY	8 Apr. 1819–1831

b. 4 June 1779, 2nd s. of Henry, 1st Bar. Dunalley [I] (*d.* 1801), and Catherine, da. and coh. of Francis Sadleir of Sopwell Hall, wid. of John Bury of Shannon Grove, co. Limerick; bro. of Henry Sadleir Prittie, 2nd Bar. Dunalley [I]*. *educ.* Trinity, Dublin 1795. *m.* (1) 10 Sept. 1800, Martha (*d.* 10 Apr. 1802), da. of Cooke Otway of Castle Otway, co. Tipperary, wid. of George Hartpole of Shrule Castle, Queen's Co., 1 da.; (2) 16 July 1803, Elizabeth, da. of George Ponsonby† of Corville, co. Tipperary, 3s. 3da. *d.* 8 Mar. 1853.

MP [I] 1800.

Custos rot. co. Tipperary 1807, sheriff, 1838-9.

Prittie, who was almost certainly the 'Mr. Prittie' who had joined Brooks's, sponsored by Lord Bessborough, a cousin of his father-in-law George

Ponsonby, 29 June 1807, had sat for county Tipperary on the 'popular interest' from 1806 until 1818, when he had been ousted by the heir of a rival pro-Catholic family. The following year he had been re-elected unopposed on a vacancy.[1] At the 1820 general election he offered again with the additional backing of his elder brother Baron Dunalley, a supporter of the Liverpool ministry. 'Dunalley will now support his brother. The death of his wife, and the accession of George IV ... make a great influence in that family', noted Lord Hutchinson, 1 Feb. 1820. A last minute attempt by his former opponent, who had succeeded as 2nd earl of Glengall, to introduce another candidate came to nothing and he was returned unopposed.[2] A mostly silent Member, he continued, at least initially, to attend frequently and vote with the Whig opposition on most major issues, including economy, retrenchment and reduced taxation.[3] He was absent from the division on Catholic claims, 28 Feb. 1821, having been granted six weeks' leave on account of the 'death of a near relation' that day. He divided for parliamentary reform, 25 Apr. 1822, 20 Feb., 24 Apr. 1823. In May 1822 Lady Spencer described how, during the recent unrest in Ireland, 13 magistrates 'with Prittie at their head' had applied repeatedly to the Irish government for military assistance under the terms of the Insurrection Act without success, whereupon 'Prittie wrote singly to the Castle and threatened that if immediate attention was not shown to the application ... he would bring the case before Parliament; upon which he was instantly attended to and obtained the relief the district required'.[4] He was in the minorities against the Irish constables bill, 7 June, and the Irish insurrection bill, 8 July 1822, and voted for inquiry into the prosecution of the Dublin Orange rioters, 22 Apr. 1823. Urging his claims on the ministry for a representative peerage in July 1823, Dunalley informed Peel, the home secretary, that 'out of many obligations by which I think their support is due to me on this occasion, I consider it not the least to have sat opposite my brother now for some years in the House'.[5] There is no trace of parliamentary activity for Prittie in 1824, and his only known votes in 1825 were for the Catholic Association to be heard at the bar of the House, 18 Feb., and Catholic relief, 1 Mar., 21 Apr., 10 May. On 16 Oct. 1825 Lord Liverpool recommended him as a suitable candidate for the representative peerage and commented inaccurately to Lord Wellesley, the Irish viceroy, that 'his brother is in the House of Commons, and a very good friend of government'.[6]

At the 1826 general election Prittie stood again, regretting his colleague's resignation following the introduction of another candidate by Glengall, against whom he and a new candidate formed a coalition. On the hustings he denied allegations that he was an Orangeman, explaining, 'I am a Protestant but am friendly to my Catholic countrymen'. After an eight-day contest he was returned in first place.[7] He presented ten constituency petitions for Catholic claims, 2 Mar., and voted thus, 6 Mar. 1827, 12 May 1828.[8] On 10 January 1828 he informed William Lamb, the Wellington ministry's Irish secretary, of the death of the bishop of Killaloe and successfully recommended his 'friend' Richard Ponsonby for the vacancy.[9] He presented petitions against the Irish Subletting and Vestry Acts, 5 May 1828, 28 May 1830. Following Dunalley's election to the representative peerage in 1828, Glengall complained to Lord Anglesey, the Irish viceroy, at having been passed over, citing the large sums Dunalley had spent in 'returning his brother Mr. Prittie, who has uniformly supported his father-in-law *Mr. Ponsonby's politics*'.[10] He signed the Protestant declaration in support of Catholic emancipation at the end of that year and brought up 11 Tipperary petitions in favour of the ministry's concession, towards which he denied that his constituents were 'indifferent', insisting that 'both the Protestants and the Catholics' were 'alive' to its importance, 27 Feb. 1829.[11] He was absent from the division of 6 Mar., but voted for the third reading of the relief bill, 30 Mar. In October 1829 the Ultra Commons leader Sir Richard Vyvyan numbered him among those who had voted for emancipation whose attitude towards a putative coalition government was 'unknown'. He was granted a month's leave to attend the assizes, 5 Mar. 1830. He divided for the second reading of the Jewish emancipation bill, 17 May, and parliamentary reform, 28 May. He brought up a petition from Thurles against the assimilation of English and Irish corn spirit duties that day, commenting that it was 'only the prelude to a county petition', which he presented with others against increases in Irish stamp and tobacco duties, 10 June 1830.

At the 1830 general election he stood again for Tipperary, where Archdeacon Singleton predicted that he would be 'molested but not unseated'.[12] Criticized on the hustings for his failure to oppose Irish tax increases and support Daniel O'Connell's motion to repeal the Irish Vestry Act, he insisted that he had been 'in his place ... when the proposed taxes on stamps was brought forward and opposed them'. (No record has been found of this.) His alliance with his colleague against a popular challenger prompted the £50 freeholders to warn that if he persisted with such an 'unconstitutional and odious aristocratic coalition' they would 'strenuously oppose' him on 'future occasions'. After abandoning his colleague he was returned in first place, promising to perform his parliamentary duties with greater 'care and diligence'.[13] Reporting the prospect of a petition against the return by his defeated colleague in October, an agent of the new Member noted that 'Prittie as custos for this county is accountable for all the public records' and 'if through his negligence or connivance irregularities have occurred ... I should think the committee will be inclined to punish him ... and I should not be surprised if Prittie was unseated'. 'Prittie will not start' in the event of a new election, observed another commentator.[14] A petition was duly presented, 4 Nov. 1830, but it went no further. Prittie was listed by ministers as one of the 'good doubtfuls', with a supplementary comment, 'a friend, asks patronage', but he was absent from the crucial division on the civil list, 15 Nov. 1830. He presented petitions for the abolition of slavery, 23 Nov. 1830. He did 'not concur' with a petition he presented from the tradesmen of Clonmel for repeal of the Union, but conceded that it had been 'signed most respectably', 8 Feb. 1831. He voted for the second reading of the Grey ministry's reform bill, 22 Mar., presented a petition for the Irish measure from Tipperary's high sheriff, 13 Apr., and divided against Gascoyne's wrecking amendment, 19 Apr. 1831.

At the ensuing general election he offered as a reformer, having obtained the backing of Glengall and, through a neighbour Stephen Egan, a declaration of support from O'Connell saying 'Prittie is your first object'. In the face of hostility from both the Protestants and his former colleague, however, he resigned two days before the anticipated contest, citing his unwillingness to 'draw upon that sum of liberality from which I have always been so generously supplied' and the probability that the new Parliament would only last 'a few short months'. During his 25 years in the House, observed the *Clonmel Herald*, 'he was scarcely ever absent from his parliamentary duties'.[15] Prittie died as heir presumptive to his brother in 1853, leaving his eldest son Henry (1807-85) to succeed as 3rd Baron Dunalley the following year.[16]

[1] Add. 40357, f. 210. [2] TCD, Donoughmore mss F/13/26; *Dublin Evening Post*, 21 Mar. 1820. [3] *Black Bk.* (1823), 186; *Session of Parl. 1825*, p. 481. [4] Add. 75937, Lady to Lord Spencer, 13 May 1822. [5] Add. 40357, f. 210. [6] Add. 37303, f. 253. [7] *Southern Reporter*, 24, 27, 29 June 1826. [8] *The Times*, 3 Mar. 1827. [9] Add. 37305, f. 250. [10] PRO NI, Anglesey mss D619/32A/2/121. [11] T. Wyse, *Hist. Catholic Association*, ii. p. ccxxvi; *The Times*, 29 Feb. 1829. [12] Add. 40338, f. 223. [13] *Tipperary Free Press*, 18, 25 Aug.; *Clonmel Herald*, 18, 25 Aug.; *Southern Reporter*, 19, 26 Aug. 1830. [14] NLI, Wyse mss 15024 (2), J. Scully to Wyse, E. Scully to same, 16 Oct. 1830. [15] Wyse mss (6), J. Scully to Wyse, 2 May; (13), Fennell to same, 8 May, Quinlan to same, 12 May, Egan to same, 11 May; *Tipperary Free Press*, 7, 11 May; *Clonmel Herald*, 11, 14 May 1831. [16] *Gent. Mag.* (1853), i. 540-1.

P.J.S.

PRITTIE, Henry Sadleir, 2nd Bar. Dunalley [I] (1775–1854), of Kilboy, co. Tipperary.

CARLOW	1801–3 Jan. 1801
OKEHAMPTON	11 May 1819–May 1824

b. 3 Mar. 1775, 1st s. of Henry, 1st Bar. Dunalley [I], of Kilboy and Catherine, da. and coh. of Francis Sadleir of Sopwell Hall, wid. of John Bury of Shannon Grove, co. Limerick; bro. of Hon. Francis Aldborough Prittie*. *educ.* Trinity, Dublin 1792. *m.* (1) 10 July 1802, Maria (*d.* 15 Oct. 1819), da. of Dominick Trant of Dunkettle, co. Cork, *s.p.*; (2) 10 Feb. 1826, Hon. Emily Maude, da. of Cornwallis, 1st Visct. Hawarden [I], *s.p. suc.* fa. as 2nd Bar. Dunalley [I] 3 Jan. 1801. *d.* 19 Oct. 1854.

MP [I] 1797-1800; trustee, linen board [I] 1828; rep. peer [I] 1828-*d.*

Dunalley, an Irish peer, came in again for Okehampton in 1820 as the paying guest of Albany Savile*. He was an occasional attender who gave silent support to Lord Liverpool's ministry, though his younger brother remained, initially at least, in opposition. He voted in defence of ministers' conduct towards Queen Caroline, 6 Feb. 1821. He may have divided for Catholic relief, 28 Feb.[1] He voted with government on the state of the revenue, 6 Mar., and Hume's economy and retrenchment motion, 27 June. He divided against parliamentary reform, 9 May 1821. His name appears in none of the surviving division lists of the 1822 session, but on 16 May he was added to the select committee on Irish grand jury presentments, in which he took a special interest. Two months later he asked the home secretary Peel whether he should serve on a grand jury at the forthcoming assizes, but was told that the only precedent of an Irish peer with a seat in the Commons doing so was a doubtful one. Nevertheless, it appears that he was appointed, as he caused irritation in Dublin administrative circles by his 'impudent' request to be made foreman of the jury.[2] He voted against repeal of the Foreign Enlistment Act, 16 Apr., and inquiry into delays in chancery, 5 June, but he went against ministers with the combined majority for inquiry into the prosecution of the Dublin Orange rioters, 22 Apr. 1823. He coveted above all an Irish representative peerage, and on a vacancy in July 1823 he stated his claim to Peel:

> I have gone considerable lengths and made much personal sacrifice to support the present administration. Out of many obligations by which I think their support is due to me on this occasion I consider it not the least to have sat opposite to my brother now for some years in the House of Commons ... I feel it hard that I have been passed over, probably from not having friends who are connected with government to urge my claims ... I have

through life been very little absent from my country residence, and been always zealous to maintain the peace and assist the improvement of my part of Ireland ... Previous to [obtaining] my seat in the Commons I had applied for government support, at which time His Majesty was pleased to express that my return would be agreeable to him if consistent with ministerial views. I then took my seat with an implied feeling as I conceived that I should soon receive the support of government.[3]

He received no satisfaction on this occasion and vacated his seat in May 1824 for his late wife's brother. The following year Liverpool recommended him to the lord lieutenant of Ireland as a 'respectable' candidate who should be seriously considered for government support on the next vacancy in the representative peerage, his pretensions having been enhanced by the fact that his brother had largely lapsed from active opposition.[4] Dunalley achieved his ambition in 1828, to the 'surprise and mortification' of his rival in county Tipperary, Lord Glengall.[5] He went on to support the Grey ministry's reform bill. He died in October 1854 and was succeeded by his nephew, Henry Prittie (1807-85).

[1] According to *Parl. Deb.* (n.s.), iv. 1031, but not *The Times*, 5 Mar. 1821. [2] Add. 40348, ff. 39, 41; TCD, Donoughmore mss F/13/49. [3] Add. 40296, f. 17b; 40357, f. 210. [4] Add. 37303, f. 253. [5] PRO NI, Anglesey mss D619/32A/2/121.

D.R.F.

PROBY, Hon. Granville Leveson (1782–1868).

CO. WICKLOW 13 Feb. 1816–19 June 1829

b. 12 Nov. 1782,[1] 3rd s. of John Joshua Proby†, 2nd Bar. Carysfort [I], and 1st w. Elizabeth, da. of Sir William Osborne, 8th bt., MP [I], of Newtown, co. Tipperary. *educ.* Rugby 1792-8. *m.* 5 May 1818, Isabella, da. of Hon. Hugh Howard, MP [I], 4s. (2 *d.v.p.*) 4da. (2 *d.v.p.*) *suc.* bro. John Proby†, Lord Proby, as 3rd earl of Carysfort [I] 11 June 1855. *d.* 3 Nov. 1868.

Entered RN 1798, lt. 1804, cdr. 1806, capt. 1806, r.-adm. 1841, v.-adm. 1851, adm. (ret.) 1857.

Sheriff, co. Wicklow 1831-2.

Proby, whose active naval career had ended in 1816, when he had entered Parliament and joined Brooks's, continued to sit for county Wicklow on the combined interest of his father and Earl Fitzwilliam. At the 1820 general election he offered again, promising 'to bring passing events to the test of the most free and disinterested judgement', and was returned unopposed.[2] A lax attender, who tended to side with the Whig opposition when present (but cast no known vote for parliamentary reform), he was in their minority for postponing the motion for a secret committee on the Queen Caroline affair, 26 June 1820.[3] That day he was granted a fortnight's leave on urgent private business. No other trace of parliamentary activity has been found for that or the following session, beyond his being granted a further six weeks' leave on account of the illness of a near relation, 12 Mar. 1821. (The mental health of his elder surviving brother John, who succeeded to the earldom in 1828, had been precarious since 1817.)[4] Proby's lassitude evidently incurred the displeasure of his father, who in January 1822 lamented to Lord Grenville that of Proby's political views

I know nothing, nor have I courage to question him. You know how much his situation in Wicklow depends on Lord Fitzwilliam. But for two years he has not attended Parliament. I wished him much to attend the Catholic question, on his account, and my own. His not supporting it gives an impression as if I had abandoned a principle on which I have acted so long. And towards Lord Fitzwilliam it has the appearance of trying to make a party in the county independent of him ... Yet I think he would not vote against either me or you, and he feels strongly and expresses himself well, on the subject of Ireland.[5]

Thereafter Proby made a slightly greater impression, voting for reduction of the salt duties, 28 Feb., and the number of lay lords of the admiralty, 1 Mar. 1822. He voted against inquiry into the currency, 12 June 1823, but next day was in the minority of 20 against an increase in the barilla duty. He voted for repeal of the assessed taxes, 10 May, and the leather tax, 18 May, and to condemn the trial of the Methodist missionary John Smith for inciting slave riots in Demerara, 11 June 1824. On 2 Mar. 1825 he was ordered to be taken into custody after defaulting on a call of the House. He gratified his father's wishes by voting for Catholic relief, 21 Apr., and was appointed to the select committee on Irish prisons, 2 May 1825. No trace of parliamentary activity has been found for the 1826 session.

Early that year he had informed Fitzwilliam's son Lord Milton* that the registry for Wicklow had been neglected by all except their respective fathers, the effect of which had been to strengthen Fitzwilliam's hold on the county, and that he could 'truly say that the seat is not less agreeable to me because I owe it so much to his support'. He wished Lord John Russell* electoral success in Huntingdonshire, where his family had their English estate, but doubted his chances.[6] At the general election he was again returned unopposed: given his attendance record, the first words of his election address, 'Living entirely among you', carried an unconscious irony.[7] In his only known intervention in debate, 2 Mar. 1827, he insisted that the Protestants 'of property' in Wicklow were not averse to Catholic relief, for which he voted, 6 Mar. 1827, 12 May 1828. He divided for the disfranchisement of Penryn, 28 May 1827. He voted for repeal of the Test Acts, 26 Feb. 1828. He presented constituency petitions for the Wellington ministry's concession of Catholic emancipation, 2 Mar., and voted thus, 6, 29 Mar. 1829. That June he made way for his brother-in-law Ralph Howard. Thomas Grenville informed Lord Holland, 3 Sept. 1829:

> Proby resigned his seat ... because he is a devilish odd fellow who grudged the trouble of a journey to London, and therefore, as I hear, made a bargain with Lord Fitzwilliam that if [he] would consent to his brother-in-law replacing him now, he would on future occasions support Lord Fitzwilliam's nomination ... If Lord Carysfort should ever get well, it may create an awkwardness on this subject, because he probably would not think himself bound by his brother's agreement ... but this difficulty is not likely to occur.[8]

Thereafter, according to an obituarist, he was a 'firm supporter' of the Liberal party, but 'took no active part in politics'.[9] The reason for this may have been financial. His eldest son John Joshua Proby (1823-58) apparently wished to contest Wicklow at the 1847 general election, but Proby refused to back him, having only recently made provision for his daughter Emma Elizabeth's marriage. (John Joshua went instead to Rome to study painting, where he became the travelling companion of the writer and artist Edward Lear.) Proby and his unmarried daughters (his wife had died in 1836, after giving birth to their youngest son William), were reportedly active in providing relief during the Irish potato famine of 1846.[10] The succession to his brother's title and estate in 1855 eased his financial difficulties and as Lord Carysfort he considerably embellished Elton Hall, his Huntingdonshire seat.[11] He died there in November 1868.[12] His title and estates passed to his elder surviving son and namesake (1825-72), Liberal Member for county Wicklow, 1858-68.

[1] *IGI* (Lincs.). [2] *Dublin Evening Post*, 7 Mar. 1820. [3] *Black Bk.* (1823), 186; *Session of Parl. 1825*, p. 482. [4] *Lear in Sicily* ed. G. Proby (1938), 13. [5] BL, Fortescue mss. [6] Fitzwilliam mss, Proby to Milton [Jan. 1826]. [7] *Dublin Evening Post*, 6, 20 June 1826. [8] Add. 51534. [9] *The Times*, 6 Nov. 1868. [10] *Lear in Sicily*, 18-19, 24. [11] *VCH Hunts.* iii. 155, 157. [12] *The Times*, 6 Nov. 1868, 13 Jan. 1869; *Peterborough Advertiser*, 7 Nov. 1868.

P.J.S.

PROTHEROE, Edward (1798–1852), of Newnham, Glos. and 28 Charles Street, St. James's Square, Mdx.

EVESHAM	1826–1830
BRISTOL	1831–1832
HALIFAX	1837–1847

b. 1798, o.s. of Edward Protheroe† (*d.* 1856) of Bristol and Anne, da. of John Waterhouse of Wellhead, Halifax, Yorks. *educ.* Christ Church, Oxf. 1817. *unm.* Took name of Davis before Protheroe by royal lic, 21 Jan. 1845. *d.v.p.* 18 Aug. 1852.
Commr. for pub. recs. 1830-4.

Protheroe's father, the founder of an extensive industrial empire of collieries and iron works in the Forest of Dean, came from a prosperous family of bankers, West India merchants and local Whig politicians at Bristol, where he was Member, 1812-20. At the 1826 general election Protheroe offered for the open borough of Evesham as 'a Whig'. After a token contest got up by the independents, who accused him of attempting to forge an 'unnatural coalition' with the sitting Tory, he was returned in second place.[1] He voted against the Clarences' grant, 16 Feb., 2 Mar. 1827. He divided for Catholic relief, 6 Mar. 1827, 12 May 1828, and presented favourable petitions, 8 May 1828.[2] He voted for inquiry into electoral interference by Leicester corporation, 15 Mar., and for the spring guns bill, 23 Mar. 1827. He divided to withhold the supplies, 30 Mar., and for the disfranchisement of Penryn, 28 May. He was a majority teller for the Coventry magistracy bill, 11 June. He was considered for but not appointed to the finance committee in late November 1827.[3] He brought up multiple petitions for repeal of the Test Acts, 15 Feb., for which he voted, 26 Feb. 1828. The following day he joined Brooks's, sponsored by Lords Essex and Duncannon*. He obtained detailed accounts of the work of the public records commissioners, 19 Feb. 1828, 22 June 1829. He divided against extending East Retford's franchise to Bassetlaw, 21 Mar. 1828. He was appointed to the committee on the borough polls bill, 2 Apr. He divided for a reduction of corn duties, 22, 29 Apr., and inquiry into chancery delays, 24 Apr. He quizzed ministers over their intentions regarding 'alteration of the Trinidad laws', 16 May, and divided against them on the civil list, 20 May. He voted against the appointment of a registrar to the archbishop of Canterbury, 16 June. He divided for the usury laws amendment bill, 19 June, and the corporate funds bill, 10 July. He was in the minority against an amendment to the customs bill affecting the silk duties, 14 July 1828.

Protheroe divided for the Wellington ministry's concession of Catholic emancipation, 6, 30 Mar., and presented and endorsed petitions in its favour, 16 Mar. 1829. He secured returns of wills and administrations transmitted to the legacy office the following day. He was a regular speaker and presenter of petitions against proposals to relocate Smithfield cattle market, which he denounced as 'absurd and ludicrous', 14 May, and was a majority teller against the bill, 15 May. He welcomed the addition of a clause to the friendly societies bill prohibiting 'compulsory payments for entertainment' at meetings, 15 May. That day he endorsed the anatomy bill, explaining that the evidence taken before the committee had 'completely removed' his initial misgivings. He divided for allowing Daniel O'Connell to take his seat unimpaired, 18 May. He doubted that Buckingham House could 'be completed for the estimate now framed', 25 May, when he voted against the grant for the marble arch, but thought 'no fraud could be fairly imputed' to John Nash in his handling of crown leases, 19 June 1829. (He welcomed the report of the select committee vindicating Nash, 2 Mar. 1830.) He divided for Lord Blandford's parliamentary reform scheme, 2 June 1829. On 4 Feb. 1830 Protheroe proposed an amendment to the address on the need to alleviate distress, arguing that 'discontent from large masses' and the 'growing contempt in which the House is held' could only be dealt with by a 'decided retrenchment of expense, large reduction of taxation, and by a needful reform, commencing with our own House'. He withdrew it later that day, 'not from any doubt of the truth' of his assertions, but because it was 'the most expedient course', and voted for a similar amendment moved by Sir Edward Knatchbull. He was erroneously listed by *The Times* as one of the '28 opposition Members who supported the address'.[4] He divided to transfer East Retford's seats to Birmingham, 11 Feb., 5, 15 Mar., for reform, 18 Feb., 28 May, and for the enfranchisement of Birmingham, Leeds, and Manchester, 23 Feb. On 18 Feb. he presented and endorsed a petition from the females of Alcaster against the burning of Hindoo widows and secured confirmation that the Indian government intended to abolish the practice. He brought up another complaining of distress from Stow-in-the-Wold that day, and again urged ministers to 'promote retrenchments', 26 Feb. He quibbled with their estimates 8, 29 Mar., and divided steadily with the revived opposition for economy and retrenchment from March 1830.

Protheroe continued to press for improvements to the nation's public archives, securing returns on the work of the commissioners, 26 Feb., 4 Mar., 11 June, urging 'consideration of a measure for the collection and preservation of the different records scattered throughout this great city', 3 May, and complaining of the 'extraordinary want' of a building for 'keeping our testamentary records' and 'taking care of the records in Doctors' Commons' and the 'papers in Westminster Hall', 10 May 1830. On 24 May he accused the existing commissioners of 'the grossest blunders' in the printing of records and called for the appointment of an entirely new commission composed of 'competent persons of antiquarian taste and research' rather than 'bishops and great officers of state'. He was made a commissioner himself later that year. On 4 Mar. he spoke in support of a Galway petition complaining that Catholics were not permitted to be admitted as freemen and were thus denied the franchise. He called for the opening up of St. James's, 26 Mar., and Regent's Parks, 29 Mar., when he asserted that 'a comparison of our parks' with those 'on the continent does not tell in our favour'. He warned against any 'architectural expense' and 'extravagance' of 'external decorations' in the construction of the Pembroke dockyard chapel, 29 Mar. He divided for Jewish emancipation, 5 Apr., 17 May, endorsed favourable petitions from Bristol, 4 May, and argued for the admission of 'all religious denominations, to a participation of equal civil rights and privileges', 17 May. He voted for abolition of the Irish lord lieutenancy, 11 May. Citing the overcrowding of London's burial grounds, he recommended the removal of interments 'to a place distant from the metropolis', 13 May. Explaining that he wished to 'obviate objections to the church' and 'see the clergy discharge their duties properly', he urged that the 'stumbling-block of tithes ... be set to rights', 18 May, when he voted for the proper use of Irish first fruits revenues. He presented a petition from Neath for abolition of the death penalty for forgery, 24 May, and voted thus that day, 7 June, 20 July. On 10 June he rebutted attacks by the home secretary Peel on the parliamentary conduct of Joseph Hume. He presented a petition from the Forest of Dean collieries against the coal duties, 11 June 1830.

Protheroe had resolved to retire from Evesham at the 1830 dissolution and accept 'repeated applications' to come forward for an anticipated opening at Bristol, with 'assurances of support' from 'the tried friends' of his father.[5] Speaking in the House of his backing for the abolition of slavery, 13 July, he described how 'no sooner had I made known my sentiments' than 'I was threatened with a formidable opposition from the powerful body connected with the West Indian interest', and that 'I have been implored in consequence' to 'absent myself from the House this night'. This he refused to do, commenting:

> Those advisors little know the spirit by which my public conduct has been actuated if they imagine that any personal consequence to myself can possibly influence my attendance or my vote ... It will be a subject of lasting gratification to myself, that the last vote I shall have given in this Parliament, will be in favour of the rights of humanity.

He duly voted for the abolition of slavery that day, jeopardizing his prospects at Bristol. Instead of 'bowing to the inevitable', however, he ignored his advisors and stood his ground, declaring that 'not by expense, not by interest, not by popular tumult, but by *moral strength alone* shall the triumph be obtained' and resolving to 'expend nothing'. After a bitter contest, during which he stubbornly refused to concede defeat and was 'seriously injured' in a riot, he was beaten, falling 535 votes short of the 3,378 cast for his nearest rival.[6] Offering again at the 1831 general election with 'unchanged principles' and 'undiminished spirit', he declared his support for the Grey ministry's 'excellent plan of parliamentary reform' and pledged 'to vote for the bill, the whole bill, and nothing but the bill'. He was returned unopposed.[7] He divided for the second reading of the reintroduced bill, 6 July, at least twice against adjourning the debates, 12 July, and steadily supported its details, though he argued and voted for giving Stoke two Members, 4 Aug., and divided for the disfranchisement of Aldborough, 14 Sept. Denying reports that 'reform fever' had 'abated in Bristol', he claimed that it was only owing to his influence that his constituents had refrained from 'the strongest remonstrances on the subject of the delays which have retarded the progress of the bill' and called for all other business to stand over until it was passed, 27 Aug. He spoke and voted against Edmund Peel's amendment to preserve the electoral rights of freemen, 30 Aug., insisting that although he had 'been sent here to support the bill and the whole bill', he was 'left entirely at liberty with respect to its details'. He divided for the bill's passage, 21 Sept., the second reading of the Scottish bill, 23 Sept., and Lord Ebrington's confidence motion, 10 Oct. 1831.

Protheroe was appointed to select committees on the East India Company, 28 June, the House of Commons, 9 Aug., and the West Indian colonies, 7 Oct., 15 Dec. 1831. He called for accounts of the charity funds administered by corporations and details of their distribution in Bristol, 29 June. He encouraged John Cam Hobhouse to reintroduce his bill to open select vestries, which 'yields, in point of importance, only to the reform bill', 30 June. He presented and endorsed a Bristol petition for inclusion in the vestries bill, 28 Sept., and argued in its support, 30 Sept., 5 Oct., when he denounced the present system as a 'great injustice'. He warned of the 'evils which must arise' from the 'establishment of an unlimited number of beer houses in the agricultural districts', 30 June. He advocated repeal of the soap tax, 1 July. He called for 'some part of the new building in the British Museum' to be 'appropriated for records contained in the about to be demolished King's Mews', 8 July. Speaking on Irish education, he defended the role of Catholic priests, 15 July. He was in the minorities for civil list reductions, 18 July, and reappointing the original Members chosen to serve on the Dublin election committee, 29 July. Although 'pledged to support every measure of economy', he welcomed the grant to the duchess of Kent, 3 Aug. He secured returns of spirit duties, 5 Aug., when he presented two petitions from the Catholics of Galway for an equalization of their civil rights. He cautioned against delaying abolition of the game laws, 8 Aug. He was in the minority for printing the Waterford petition for disarming the Irish yeomanry, 11 Aug., but voted with ministers on the Dublin election controversy, 23 Aug. He secured accounts of Bristol's poor rate assessments, 19 Aug. He clashed with Henry Hunt over the conviction of Robert Taylor for blasphemy, 18 Oct., and presented a Bristol petition on the subject, 20 Oct. 1831. He voted for the second reading of the revised reform bill, 17 Dec. 1831, and for going into committee on it, 20 Jan., again gave steady support to its details, but was absent from the division on its third reading, 22 Mar. 1832. He divided for the address calling on the king to appoint only ministers who would carry it unimpaired, 10 May. He declared his intention to introduce a bill to alter the municipal government of Bristol, 14 Dec. 1831, but did not do so. He successfully moved the second reading of the Bristol drainage compensation bill, 17 May 1832. He divided against the government's temporizing amendment on the abolition of slavery, 24 May. No other votes have been found for that session. He presented a petition for the remission of a prisoner's sentence in consequence of a cholera outbreak at Bristol gaol, 24 July 1832.

At the 1832 general election Protheroe offered again for Bristol but was defeated in a contest involving two other Liberals and a Conservative. He missed being seated for Halifax by a single vote in 1835, but he was returned there in first place in 1837 and 1841, retiring at the dissolution of 1847. In September 1832 he published a *Letter ... to the secretary [of the Records Commission] on the continuation of Sir Francis*

Palgrave's edition of the Parliamentary Writs. He continued to campaign for improvements to the public records, particularly those relating to genealogy, and established a substantial archive on his maternal ancestors, now held by the British Library.[8] In 1845 he took the additional name of Davis in compliance with the will of Dame Mary Hill, widow of Mark Davis of Turnwood, from whom he 'inherited considerable property'. Protheroe died *v.p.* in August 1852, having been 'paralysed' for 'three years before his death'. By his will, dated 12 Oct. 1847, he left small annuities to friends, but the bulk of his estate and residue passed to his 78-year-old father.[9]

[1] *Worcester Herald*, 13, 27 May, 10, 24 June 1826. [2] *The Times*, 15 May 1828. [3] Add. 38761, f. 269. [4] *The Times*, 6 Feb. 1830. [5] Lincs. AO, Ancaster mss xiii/B/50; *Bristol Mercury*, 13 July 1830. [6] *Worcester Herald*, 17, 24 July; *Bristol Mercury*, 20 July, 3, 10 Aug. 1830. [7] *Bristol Gazette*, 28 Apr., 5 May; *Bristol Mercury*, 10 May 1831. [8] Add. 31006-21. [9] *Gent. Mag.* (1852), ii. 638-9; PROB 11/2159/721; IR26/1943/807.

P.J.S.

PRYSE, Pryse (1774–1849), of Gogerddan, Card. and Buscot Park, Berks.

CARDIGAN BOROUGHS	1818–1841
CARDIGAN BOROUGHS	18 Apr. 1842–4 Jan. 1849

bap. 1 June 1774, o. surv. s. of Edward Loveden Loveden† of Buscot and 1st w. Margaret, da. and h. of Lewis Pryse of Woodstock, Oxon. and Gogerddan. *educ.* Eton 1789-91; Christ Church, Oxf. 1792. *m.* (1) 20 July 1798, Hon. Harriet Flower (*d.* 14 Jan. 1813), da. of William, 2nd Visct. Ashbrook [I], wid. of Rev. the Hon. John Ellis Agar, *s.p.*; (2) 29 Apr. 1815, Jane, da. of Peter Cavallier of Guisborough, Yorks., 3s. *suc.* grandmo. Margaret Pryse to Gogerddan and took name of Pryse 24 Mar. 1798; fa. to Buscot 1822. *d.* 4 Jan. 1849.

Sheriff, Card. 1799-1800.

Ensign, Berks. militia 1794, capt. (vols.) 1794-6; lt. Oxf. yeomanry 1803.

Pryse, a committed Whig whose pedigree and 30,000 acres in Cardiganshire gave him a strong claim to the county seat, had overcome the tribulations of his father's divorce (from his third wife) and his own wife's tragic death and lived with his second wife at Gogerddan, whose administration Loveden had surrendered to him under threat of litigation. At the dissolution in 1820 it was widely reported that he would stand for Cardiganshire, so terminating an arrangement made in 1816 with the sitting Tory, the lord lieutenant William Powell, whose election he had condoned in exchange for support in the less prestigious Cardigan Boroughs, that had first returned him in 1818.[1] However, he again canvassed the Boroughs, where he had been a generous benefactor, and came in unopposed in 1820 at a personal cost of £169 15*s*.6*d*. His addresses and speeches called for further retrenchment and lower taxes.[2]

Pryse aligned in Berkshire with John Berkeley Monck* and the reformers and in West Wales with the Blues, while in the Commons he divided regularly and consistently with the main Whig opposition. Until 1823, he also supported the 'Mountain' and Hume's campaigns for economy and retrenchment, often voting in small minorities. He divided for parliamentary reform, 9, 10 May 1821, 25 Apr. 1822, 27 Apr. 1826. He paired for Catholic relief, 28 Feb. 1821, but subsequently abstained on the issue 'because he had no strong feelings of his own and was therefore prepared to concede a little to the views of his friends'. He wrote to correct a report in *The Times* that he had voted for relief, 21 Apr. 1825.[3] A radical publication that session noted that he 'attended frequently and voted with the opposition'.[4] Pryse, never a significant debater in the Commons, spoke 'in so low a tone of voice' on presenting a petition from Carmarthenshire for reform of the Welsh courts of great sessions, 25 May 1820, that *The Times*, which may have confused him and George Rice Rice, was 'not able to distinguish the object of it', and assumed it came from Caernarvonshire.[5] Queen Caroline's health had been drunk at proclamation celebrations that Pryse chaired at Aberystwyth in February, and he supported the 1820 and 1821 parliamentary and extra-parliamentary campaigns on her behalf and authorized celebrations at Gogerddan when her prosecution was abandoned in November 1820.[6] His efforts as a speaker for the Newington select vestry bill met with little success, 21 Mar., 16 May 1821.[7] He had a net income of some £6,000 a year from the Gogerddan estate, where he spent the 1821 recess, taking a keen interest in the home farm and the hunting, and also contributed £200 towards erecting a gallery at St. Mary's church, Cardigan.[8]

Loveden died, 6 Jan. 1822, and Pryse inherited a life interest in his 3,000-acre Berkshire estates at Buscot, Eaton Hastings and Farringdon.[9] These were mortgaged for £15,760 to his brother-in-law, the Rev. Samuel Wilson Warneford, and were charged with £1,000 annuities for his sister (Margaret Warneford) and half-sister Jane Loveden. Family correspondence and Pryse's letters to the solicitor Charles Deare, 1822-9, describe his problems in providing for his relations as his father had directed, even after letting Woodstock, selling bark and timber and taking out

£29,750 in mortgages.[10] It persuaded him to authorize trustees under his own will of 3 Dec. 1822 to sell mortgaged estates.[11] From Gogerddan, where he had reduced his rents to alleviate distress, he led the opposition in 1822-3 to the county's largest tithe owner, Col. John Palmer Chichester, who had extend the range of titheable goods, but the Lords decided in Chichester's favour, and the campaign lost momentum when Pryse and his family moved to Buscot in 1823.[12] In Berkshire as in Cardiganshire, he tended to keep aloof from the activities of the magistracy, but when Lord Folkestone* sought his signature on a requisition for a Berkshire reform meeting, Pryse was happy to provide it, 3 Jan. 1823, adding:

> Although I am not one of those who consider that a reform of the Commons House would act as a cure for all evils under which we are suffering, still I am not the less convinced of the expediency of such a measure, and feel fully satisfied that if properly regulated it would tend much towards ameliorating the condition of this oppressed country.[13]

His main concern in Parliament in 1823 and 1824 was the Llanfihangel Genau'r Glyn and Llancynfelyn enclosure bill, which affected much of the Gogerddan estate and amended previous parliamentary enclosures. Working closely with the Carmarthen and Carmarthenshire Members John Jones and Rice (both Reds) and his local agent James Morris, he secured its enactment, 17 June 1824, and subsequently corresponded with the office of woods and forests about Cyfoeth Y Brenin and draining Cors Fochno.[14] He voted for inquiry into the currency, 12 June, against the usury laws repeal bill, 17, 27 June 1823, and to permit defence by counsel in cases of felony, 6 Apr. 1824. The Welsh language periodical *Seren Gomer* praised him as the presenter of Aberystwyth's petition for the gradual abolition of negro slavery, 14 Apr., and for voting in condemnation of the indictment in Demerara of the Methodist missionary John Smith, 11 June 1824.[15] Possibly in response to Powell's increased involvement in the borough, he had 39 of his tenants admitted as burgesses of Cardigan, 27 Dec. 1824.[16] He voted against the proposed relaxation of the corn laws which his constituents opposed, 8, 11 May 1826, was unopposed at the general election in June, and paid £158 4*s*. for the customary entertainments.[17] He played no part in the proceedings resulting from the Myfenydd enclosure riots, although a critical petition of 12 June 1826 from the hundred of Ilar urged him to take action against the squire, Augustus Brackenbury.[18]

Pryse divided against the grant to the duke of Clarence, 16 Mar., and to delay supplies, 30 Mar., including the Irish estimates, 5 Apr., pending resolution of the succession to Lord Liverpool as premier, and voted against the corn bill, 2 Apr. 1827. He seems to have stayed away from the House for the next 22 months, but he was a frequent visitor to Wales and Bath, where Jane Loveden had settled. He arranged her move to the family's town house in Aberystwyth in March 1828 and oversaw plans for post-enclosure sales and the cultivation of Genau'r Glyn.[19] He assured Thomas Lloyd of Coedmore, the anxious proprietor of a weir on the Teifi, that 'the salmon bill has been floored for this session [1828]', and 'if it should be renewed next year, I shall be very happy to attend to any suggestions of yours respecting it'.[20] He held aloof from the petitioning for repeal of the Test Acts in 1828 and was similarly reticent on Catholic emancipation. Listed by the Wellington ministry's patronage secretary Planta in February 1829 as 'opposed to securities', he delayed voting for the measure until its third reading, 30 Mar.[21] When in July he sought patronage through Lord Dalhousie for a constituent (one of the Lloyds of Dôl-haidd), his Berkshire neighbour the earl of Kintore commended him as that county's '*ace of trumps*'.[22] He adopted a higher profile in Cardiganshire in the autumn of 1829, when Cardigan's future as an assize town was threatened by the law commission's endorsement of Lord Cawdor's proposals for abolition of the Welsh judicature and courts of great sessions and reorganization of assize districts. He did not, like several other Blues, sign the Cardiganshire gentry's favourable memorial promoted by Cawdor's agents, and when the county met in protest at Aberaeron, 18 Nov., he explained that he remained undecided on the matter and would fall in with his constituents' views.[23] His attendance early in 1830 was lax, but he divided steadily with the revived Whig opposition, 22 Mar.-6 July, including for Jewish emancipation, 17 May, and abolition of the death penalty for forgery, 7 June. He presented a petition from Cardigan against abolition of the great sessions and Welsh judicature, 27 Apr., and voted against the recommittal on 18 June of the administration of justice bill by which it was enacted, earning belated recognition in the *Carmarthen Journal* as one of its 'active opponents'. Herbert Evans of Highmead had confirmed Pryse's popularity at Lampeter in October 1829, but his strength in the Boroughs was nevertheless tested in 1830 by Edward Lloyd Williams, the barrister son of John Lloyd Wiliams of Gwernant. The proprietor of Peterwell, John Scandrett Harford, came from Gloucestershire to assess the situation, but Pryse had rushed to Cardiganshire to take a prominent part in celebrations marking the accession of William

IV and he avoided a contest at the ensuing general election.[24]

Ministers naturally listed him among their 'foes' and he divided against them on the civil list when they were brought down, 15 Nov. 1830. He presented and endorsed petitions against colonial slavery from the inhabitants of Aberystwyth and Cardigan and several Dissenting and Nonconformist congregations, 18 Dec. 1830, 30 Mar. 1831. He divided for the Grey ministry's reform bill at its second reading, 22 Mar., and against Gascoyne's wrecking amendment, 19 Apr., and brought up Aberystwyth's reform petition endorsing the bill the following day. A county meeting at Lampeter, 7 Apr., commended his conduct and his return at the general election in May was a formality. On the hustings, he promised consistent support for ministers 'on this vital question of parliamentary reform, and in all such measures as may appear to me likely to promote the general welfare of the country'.[25] He divided for the reintroduced reform bill at its second reading, 6 July, against adjourning its committee stage, 12 July 1831, and steadily for its details. He voted against granting borough freeholders county votes, 17 Aug., but cast a wayward vote (attuned to local interests) for the enfranchisement of £50 tenants-at-will, 18 Aug. He divided for the bill's passage, 21 Sept., the second reading of Scottish reform bill, 23 Sept., and Lord Ebrington's confidence motion, 10 Oct., but failed to attend the Cardigan reform meeting, 14 Nov.[26] He divided for the revised reform bill at its second and third readings, 17 Dec. 1831, 22 Mar. 1832. He was 'in the country' when the House adopted an address asking the king to appoint only ministers who would carry it unimpaired, 10 May, but later 'welcomed' the opportunity to present a similarly worded address from Cardigan.[27] He divided with government on the Dublin election controversy, 23 Aug. 1831, but against their temporizing amendment to Buxton's motion for a select committee on colonial slavery, 24 May 1832. He voted in the majority against suspending the Liverpool writ, 5 Sept. 1831, and was absent when party strength was tested on the Russian-Dutch loan, 26 Jan., 12 July 1832. He now received a gift of plate from his tenants in Genau'r Glyn and he was praised in the *Welshman* and *Greal y Bedyddwyr* as a supporter of reform and the campaign against colonial slavery.[28]

Pryse was returned unopposed for the new Cardigan Boroughs constituency in December 1832, when the arrival at the nomination of a lady in orange to await a second candidate caused a flurry of excitement.[29] He almost lost to a Conservative in 1841, when a double return was made but rescinded on petition, but held the seat for life.[30] He died in Carmarthen in January 1849 and was buried with his ancestors at Llanbadarn Fawr (Aberystwyth), recalled as a generous benefactor and for his opposition to the establishment of a county police force in Cardiganshire at the time of the Rebecca riots.[31] His Woodstock and Cardiganshire estates had been settled since 1846 on his eldest son, Pryse Pryse (1815-55), his successor as Liberal Member for Cardigan Boroughs, who later that year readopted the name and arms of Loveden. When he faced insolvency in October 1852 it was decided that his father (Pryse), whose will had provided generously for his widow and relations, had 'had no power to charge the real estate with payment of said £20,000' for the younger sons.[32]

[1] R.J. Colyer, 'Pryse Family of Gogerddan', *WHR*, ix (1979), 408-9; *HP Commons, 1790-1820*, iv. 457-8, 901-2; NLW, Nanteos mss L930. [2] *Cambrian*, 22 Jan., 11, 18, 25 Mar.; *Carmarthen Jnl.* 4 Feb., 17 Mar.; NLW, Glanpaith mss F164; Ceredigion Archives CDM/SE6/34; NLW, Gogerddan mss (uncatalogued), election bills Mar. 1820. [3] *The Times*, 25 Apr. 1825. [4] *Session of Parl. 1825*, p. 482. [5] *The Times*, 26 May 1820. [6] *Carmarthen Jnl.* 18 Feb., 1 Dec. 1820. [7] *The Times*, 22 Mar., 17 May 1821. [8] Colyer, 'Gogerddan Demense Farm', *Ceredigion*, vii (1972-5), 170-88; Gogerddan mss RA60-82; *Greal y Bedyddwyr*, v (1831), 192. [9] PROB 11/1657/265; IR26/916/433; Berks. RO D/ECr/E3. [10] Colyer, *WHR*, ix. 410-12; Gogerddan mss, Deare to Pryse, 5 Oct 1824; NLW ms 19001 C, *passim*. [11] PROB 11/2095/464; NLW ms 19001 C, f. 3. [12] J. Barber, 'Tithe Unrest in Card. 1796-1823', *WHR*, xvi (1992), 181-201. [13] Gogerddan mss, J. Gill to Mrs. Pryse, 22 May 1822; Pryse mss (History of Parliament Aspinall transcripts), Folkestone to Pryse, 16 Dec. 1822, reply, 3 Jan. [1823]. [14] *CJ*, lxxviii. 54, 159; lxxxix. 63, 191, 364, 435, 468, 504; Gogerddan mss, Pryse-Morris corresp. 17 Mar. 1823-4 July 1829; Colyer, 'Enclosure of Cors Fochno', *Ceredigion*, viii (1976-9), 181-92. [15] *Seren Gomer*, vii (1824), 189-90, 224-5; *The Times*, 15 Apr. 1824. [16] Ceredigion Archives CDM/44, 45; Gogerddan mss RB55. [17] *Cambrian*, 10, 24 June; *Carmarthen Jnl.* 23 June; Gogerddan mss, election bills, June 1826. [18] D. Jenkins, 'Rhyfel y Sais bach', *Ceredigion*, i (1950-1), 199-200; *Cambrian*, 8 July, 26 Aug., 21 Oct. 1826. [19] *Cambrian*, 22 Sept. 1827; Gogerddan mss, letters to Pryse from Jane Loveden, Richard Griffiths of Bishop's Castle, Thomas Morris and John Ball, 1827-8. [20] *Carmarthen Jnl.* 1, 22 Feb. 1828, 13 Feb. 1829; *Cambrian*, 1 Mar. 1828, 14 Feb. 1829; Gogerddan mss, Pryse to Tufnell, 19 June 1829; Carm. RO, Lloyd of Coedmore mss D/LL/865. [21] *Seren Gomer*, xii (1829), 155. [22] NLW, Penty Park mss 100. [23] *Cambrian*, 7 Mar., 18 Apr., 14, 21 Nov.; *Carmarthen Jnl.* 16 Oct., 13, 20, 27 Nov. 1829. [24] *Carmarthen Jnl.* 16, 23, 30 July, 6, 13 Aug. 1830; Pryse mss (Aspinall transcripts), H. Evans to Pryse, 19 Oct. 1829; *Cambrian*, 24, 31 July 1830; Bristol RO, Blaise Castle mss 28048/C3; Ceredigion Archives CDM/SE8/35. [25] *Cambrian*, 2, 16 Apr., 7, 14 May; *Seren Gomer*, xiv (1831), 155; *Greal y Bedyddwyr*, v (1831), 192; *Carmarthen Jnl.* 12 May 1831. [26] *Carmarthen Jnl.* 6 Dec. 1831. [27] Ibid. 30 Mar.; *Welshman*, 25 May, 6, 22 June 1832. [28] *Carmarthen Jnl.* 10 Feb.; *Welshman*, 25 May 1832; *Greal y Bedyddwyr*, vi (1832), 221-2, 252. [29] *Carmarthen Jnl.* 14 Sept., 7 Dec.; *Welshman*, 21 Sept., 21 Dec. 1832, 6 Jan. 1833. [30] *Carmarthen Jnl.* 22 Apr. 1842; *Ann. Reg.* (1849), Chron. p. 215. [31] *Carmarthen Jnl.* 12 Jan. 1849; Colyer, 'Gentry and County in 19th. Cent. Card.' *WHR*, x (1980-1), 500-02; A.L. Trott, 'Church Dayschools in 19th Cent. Aberystwyth', *Ceredigion*, ii (1952-5), 70-75; D.J.V. Jones, *Rebecca's Children*, 135; G. Jenkins, 'Hetwyr Llangynfelyn', *Ceredigion*, x

(1984-7), 25; R.G. Thorne, 'Parliamentary Representation: From the First to the Third Reform Acts, 1832-1885', *Card. Co. Hist.* iii. ed. G.H. Jenkins and I. Gwynedd Jones, 387-92. [32] PROB 11/2095/464; Colyer, *WHR*, ix. 412-13; IR26/1846/357.

M.M.E.

PUREFOY JERVOISE, George (1770–1847), of Herriard House, nr. Basingstoke, Hants and The Moat, nr. Britford, Wilts.

SALISBURY 17 Feb. 1813–1818

HAMPSHIRE 1820–1826

b. 10 Apr. 1770, 1st s. of Rev. George Hudleston Jervoise (afterwards Purefoy) of Britford, rect. of Shalstone, Bucks., and Mary, da. and coh. of Rev. Wright Hawes, rect. of Shalstone. *educ.* Westminster 1781-6; Corpus, Oxf. (as Purefoy) 1787. *m.* (1) 10 Apr. 1799, Elizabeth (*d.* 1821), da. and h. of Thomas Hall of Preston Candover, Hants, *s.p.*; (2) 18 Apr. 1837, Anna Maria Selina, da. of Wadham Locke† of Rowdeford, Wilts., *s.p.* Took additional name of Jervoise by royal lic. 17 July 1792. *suc.* uncle to Herriard 1794; fa. 1805. *d.* 1 Dec. 1847.

Capt. N. Hants militia 1794, lt.-col. 1798, col. 1800-11; sheriff, Hants 1830-1.

Jervoise resumed his family's original patronymic in 1792 at the behest of his uncle, Tristram Hudleston Jervoise, from whom he inherited the Herriard property two years later. He added to it by marriage and purchase, though in 1820 he was living at the Wiltshire residence which had formerly belonged to his father.[1] Evidently he took up the option in the latter's will to buy the Purefoy estate at Shalstone, Buckinghamshire, and he was sufficiently well off to be able to refuse a cash bequest in a codicil, which he believed to be a misdirection.[2] A double vacancy for Hampshire at the 1820 general election presented an opportunity for Jervoise, formerly Member for Salisbury, to resume his parliamentary career, but he apparently needed encouragement, and he publicly avowed his reluctance to incur the 'unknown expense' of a contest.[3] Lord Malmesbury considered him 'strange' and 'a poor person to represent us', though he admitted the antiquity of his family, which had produced several county Members.[4] Following the withdrawal of a third candidate he was returned unopposed, and on the hustings promised 'to watch with a jealous eye over the conduct of the government, with a view to maintain the just freedom of the empire'.[5] He had previously taken a Whiggish line in the Commons, but sympathetic squib writers emphasised that he was 'not a party man' and disavowed 'such violent opposition principles as many represent him of'.[6]

Jervoise was apparently an assiduous Member, but is not known to have delivered a full speech in the House. He voted steadily with the Whig opposition to the Liverpool ministry on most major issues, including economy, retrenchment and reduced taxation, and dismissed supplicants for government favour with a reminder that his 'independence' was inviolable.[7] Although he had divided for Catholic claims in 1816 and 1817 and offered a vague pledge to support religious liberty on the hustings in 1820, he voted against relief, 28 Feb. 1821, 1 Mar., 21 Apr., 10 May 1825, and the removal of disabilities from Catholic peers, 30 Apr. 1822. It is conceivable that he was responding to constituency pressure, for shortly after his return an anonymous anti-Catholic freeholder warned him that 'your re-election depends *entirely* on which side you vote on this most important question'.[8] He presented a petition from Fordingbridge and Basingstoke lawyers for regulation of the appointment of conveyancers, 19 May 1820.[9] At a Hampshire county meeting, 12 Jan., he expressed 'great satisfaction' with a petition in support of Queen Caroline, which he presented, 26 Jan. 1821, observing that its signatories were 'opposed to the unwise and dangerous acts of the present administration', yet 'as much attached to the soundest principles of religion and loyalty as any men in the kingdom'.[10] He presented four similar petitions the same day and another, from an Isle of Wight parish, 31 Jan.[11] At a meeting of his supporters in Portsmouth, 14 Mar., he was praised for his 'unremittant attention' to Parliament and the care he took to investigate subjects before giving a vote.[12] He divided for parliamentary reform, 18 Apr. 1821, 24 Apr. 1823, 27 Apr. 1826, reform of the Scottish representative system, 2 June 1823, and the representation of Edinburgh, 13 Apr. 1826. (At a dinner in Portsmouth, 14 Mar. 1823, a well-wisher 'particularly dwelt on his firm and continued support for reform in Parliament'.)[13] In July 1821 it was reported that he had donated a gallon loaf apiece to poor households in the Herriard district.[14] On 15 May 1822 he presented a petition from Hampshire tanners for repeal of the leather tax.[15] He presented a Portsmouth petition for easier recovery of small debts, 21 Mar.,[16] and on 12 May belatedly brought up the petition of a Hampshire meeting on agricultural distress which had taken place on 1 Mar. 1823.[17] He presented another county petition against the game laws, 23 May.[18] He was in the government majority against inquiry into the currency, 11 June, but voted against their beer duties bill, 17 June. He divided against repeal of the usury laws that day, 27 June 1823, 17 Feb. 1825. He presented a petition from Southampton victuallers against the duty on excise licenses, 4 Mar. 1824.[19] His speech at a county meeting on economic distress, 23 Apr., followed that of his ministerially inclined colleague John Fleming, whose eloquence he admitted he could not match, 'but he could say one thing, that he had proved himself by his *actions* instead of words'.[20] He presented the resulting petition for a repeal of assessed taxes with another in similar terms from Salisbury, 10 May.[21] He presented a petition from a Hampshire parish for inquiry into the prosecution of the Methodist missionary John Smith for inciting rebellion among slaves in Demerara, 28 May, and voted thus, 11 June 1824.[22] He presented a Southampton petition for suppression of the Catholic Association, 14 Feb., and one from a Hampshire parish against Catholic relief, 18 Apr. 1825.[23] For much of that session he was preoccupied with local business. He co-operated with Fleming over the Portsea paving and lighting bill and reported its progress to the House, 17 Mar.[24] Next day he presented a petition against the Portsmouth and Arundel canal bill and reported from the committee on the Gosport chapel bill, having been alerted to the latter by a constituent.[25] On 21 Mar. he introduced the Christchurch enclosure bill, on which he reported, 13 May; it received royal assent, 10 June 1825.[26] That September he announced that he would not stand again for health reasons, and his parliamentary activity appears to have diminished thereafter.[27] He presented a Basingstoke petition for the abolition of slavery, 21 Mar. 1826.[28]

At that year's dissolution Jervoise duly retired, and on the hustings his colleague paid tribute to his efforts.[29] As sheriff of Hampshire, his absence abroad in February 1830 delayed a county meeting on the assessed taxes.[30] He spoke in support of the Grey ministry's reform proposals at a similar meeting, 17 Mar. 1831, when he lamented that illness had forced his retirement from public life.[31] At the 1831 general election he proposed Charles Shaw Lefevre*, one of the reform candidates for Hampshire.[32] Jervoise died childless at Herriard in December 1847, and received only the briefest of obituary notices in the local press.[33] His Hampshire and Wiltshire estates passed to his sister Mary, and after her death, 30 May 1849, to her son Francis Ellis Jervoise (1809-81). Shalstone descended to his niece Sarah Anna Elizabeth Fitzgerald (1809-99), who by the terms of his will, dated 22 Nov. 1822, received a £22,843 half-share of the residue of his personalty. An equal portion was divided between Francis Ellis Jervoise and his sisters Mary, Caroline and Harriet. In a codicil of 10 Apr. 1847, Jervoise left instructions that the duty should be paid on small bequests to relations and good causes, which included hospitals in Winchester, Salisbury, Oxford and Aylesbury, and the poor of his several neighbourhoods.[34]

[1] *VCH Hants*, iii. 367, 370, 375, 387; Hants RO, Jervoise mss 44M69 G2/428/1; 448/1. [2] PROB 11/1436/50; IR26/107/192. [3] Jervoise mss G2/428/1-7, 458. [4] Hants RO, Malmesbury mss 9M73, Malmesbury to Fitzharris, 28 Feb., 4 Mar. 1820. [5] *Hants Telegraph*, 20 Mar. 1820. [6] Jervoise mss G2/449, 458. [7] Ibid. G2/446/1,2, 4-6; *Black Bk.* (1823), 167; *Session of Parl. 1825*, p. 470. [8] Ibid. G2/446/3; *Hants Telegraph*, 20 Mar. 1820. [9] *The Times*, 20 May 1820. [10] *Hants Telegraph*, 15 Jan. 1821. [11] *The Times*, 27 Jan., 1 Feb. 1821. [12] *Hants Telegraph*, 19 Mar. 1821. [13] Ibid. 17 Mar. 1823. [14] Ibid. 9 July 1821. [15] *The Times*, 16 May 1822. [16] Ibid. 22 Mar. 1823. [17] *Hants Telegraph*, 3, 31 Mar.; *The Times*, 13 May 1823. [18] *The Times*, 24 May 1823. [19] Ibid. 5 Mar. 1824. [20] *Hants Telegraph*, 26 Apr. 1824. [21] *The Times*, 11 May 1824. [22] Ibid. 29 May 1824. [23] Ibid. 15 Feb., 19 Apr. 1825. [24] Jervoise mss G2/466/3. [25] Ibid. G2/466/1, 464. [26] *CJ*, lxxxv. 520. [27] *Hants Telegraph*, 26 Sept. 1825. [28] *The Times*, 22 Mar. 1826. [29] *Hants Telegraph*, 19 June 1826. [30] Ibid. 1 Mar. 1830. [31] Ibid. 21 Mar. 1831. [32] *Portsmouth Herald*, 8 May 1831. [33] *Gent. Mag.* (1848), i. 107; *Hants Advertiser*, 4 Dec. 1847. [34] PROB 11/2067/40; IR26/1805/44.

H.J.S./P.J.S.

PUSEY, Philip (1799–1855), of Pusey, nr. Faringdon, Berks.

RYE	1 Mar. 1830–17 May 1830
CHIPPENHAM	1830–1831
CASHEL	16 July 1831–1832
BERKSHIRE	1835–1852

b. 25 June 1799, 1st s. of Hon. Philip Pusey of Pusey and Lady Lucy Sherard, da. of Robert, 4th earl of Harborough, wid. of Sir Thomas Cave†, 7th bt., of Stanford Hall, Leics. *educ.* Mitcham, Surr. (Rev. Richard Roberts) 1807;[1] Eton 1812; Christ Church, Oxf. 1817. *m.* 4 Oct. 1822, Lady Emily Frances Theresa Herbert, da. of Henry George Herbert†, 2nd earl of Carnarvon, 1s. 2da. *suc.* fa. 1828. *d.* 9 July 1855.

Pres. R. Agric. Soc. 1840-1, 1853-4.

The male line of the Pusey family, who had been settled at the north-west Berkshire estate of that name since the eleventh century, became extinct on the death of Charles Pusey in 1710. He bequeathed the property to his nephew John Allen, who was married to a sister of Jacob Bouverie, 1st Lord Folkestone, and took the additional name of Pusey. On his death without issue it was settled by his sisters on his wife's nephew Philip Bouverie, Folkestone's third son by his second marriage, who was born in 1746 and took the name of Pusey in 1784.[2] His first two sons, Philip and Edward, the future Regius Professor of Hebrew and leader of the Oxford Movement, were born within 14 months of one another. As their mother recalled, both were studiously inclined and 'clever; Philip had more talent, but Edward was the more industrious'.[3] At Eton and Oxford, which he left in 1819 without taking a degree, Philip's closest friend was Lord Porchester*, son of the 2nd earl of Carnarvon, with whose talented sister Emily he fell in love. Her family's Whig politics were in harmony with his own liberal, if rather undefined opinions at this time, in contrast to the inflexible Toryism of his father, who forbade an immediate marriage.[4] Pusey visited Paris and Rome and travelled with Porchester to Portugal and Spain, where they were captured by guerillas and were in danger of being shot as suspected constitutionalists until they established their identities. After close acquaintance with the Spanish peasantry, he concluded that they were 'the finest race of men we ever met with and would certainly afford excellent materials for a free state'; but he took a dim view of the 'upper orders'.[5] He returned to England in 1822 and, his father's objections having been waived, married Emily Herbert in the autumn.

Pusey was interested in theology and scriptural scholarship, and in December 1823 he told Edward that 'my great object of ambition now is to be able to write something in defence of religion'. A year later he contemplated 'a new arrangement of old matter with the hope of some new stuff of my own'; but nothing seems to have come of the project.[6] He and his wife, whose health was not robust, spent lengthy periods on the continent, especially favouring Rome, where they moved in intellectual circles and became friendly with Baron Bunsen.[7] Pusey, who joined Brooks's Club on 2 Dec. 1826, sponsored by his father-in-law and Lord King, the currency pundit, turned his mind to financial questions. He devoted a year to the composition of a book on political economy but, as he told his close friend Lord Mahon*, son of the 4th Earl Stanhope, he was

> preparing to publish it, when Lord Carnarvon suggested to me to write on political profusion, and I have since determined to lay my technical crotchets on the shelf. The science, if it can be called one, is so unpopular, that I do not wish to declare myself its votary. I agree with you that it is in very bad hands, but I own I think, though this is contrary to the resolution I have just expressed, that this is a reason the more for those who are honestly disposed, to engage in the science themselves and to endeavour to prevent it from becoming a tool of Jacobins. I am convinced that the doctrines of sound economical science are really ... extremely conservative.

Early in 1828 he published a 'little financial squib' in the form of *A Letter to the Earl of Carnarvon* on Peel's financial statement of 15 Feb., in which he argued that the national debt, far from diminishing since 1815 as Peel claimed, had in fact increased because of the failure to adjust the value of the currency at the end of the war: 'the first stroke of the mint hammer upon the new sovereign, was a blow which shortened the political existence of this country, at least, by half a century'. On learning that Stanhope considered it 'very clever and well written', he commented to Mahon that

> I think an acquaintance with him, is the best antidote to that intolerance towards those who prefer established institutions to supposed improvements, into which the friends of unlimited toleration, of whom I confess myself one, are in danger of falling. I believe that a violent Whig, and am certain that a violent liberal, is in reality far more impatient of contradiction, and therefore less tolerant, than most decided Tories.

On domestic politics, he judged that 'the only point of strength in the present cabinet is the iron firmness' of the duke of Wellington. He confided to Mahon that he was 'engaged in a negotiation for a seat in Parliament which I hope to bring to a satisfactory termination'.[8] In May 1828 he published *An Historical View of the Sinking Fund*, which advocated capital investment in Ireland, colonial expansion and reform of the poor rates as the best means of reducing the national debt.

The previous month he had succeeded his father, whose personalty was sworn under £140,000, to the family estates, but he did not take up permanent residence in Berkshire for another two years.[9] After suffering from a complaint of the trachea in the summer, he wintered in Rome, from where he told Mahon, 2 Jan. 1829, that 'my hopes of Parliament are again disappointed'.[10] A few months after his return to England in the spring, Porchester observed to Mahon that as far as coming into Parliament was concerned, Pusey, 'who is ready to offer *any* sum, cannot contrive it, but will ultimately I suppose'. In June he had 'two negotiations pending, one for an immediate occupancy, the other for a permanent arrangement, depending however upon the contingency of a dissolution'. The boroughs in question may have been the Cinque Ports of Rye and Seaford; and Pusey offered Mahon, who had rather fancifully suggested that he might try at the next general election to turn out one of the 'brace of violent radicals' currently sitting for Reading, first refusal of one if he himself was accommodated in the other. Nothing immediately came of this.[11] Pusey was then toying with 'a rambling survey of our financial condition, which appears to me more hopeful than the public has been led to imagine'; and he had it published in the November 1829 *Quarterly Review* (xl. 492-522) as 'The Finance Committee', after amending it in accordance with some judicious advice from Lockhart, the editor. Mahon, of course, was unstinting in his praise, but he reported that 'more competent judges', including Lord Goderich and Sir Henry Parnell*, had also 'spoken of it in very high terms of commendation'. His father, though impressed by its 'clearness of thought and comprehensiveness of style', considered it 'fallacious from viewing objects too much *en couleur de rose*'. Pusey was 'not desirous to be known as a contributor even to so respectable a review as the *Quarterly*', but neither did he 'have any strong desire of concealment'; a month later the piece was attributed in the *Morning Herald* to 'some ministerial or official personage'.[12] In March 1830 Pusey reviewed for the *Quarterly* (xlii. 505-36) Parnell's *On Financial Reform*, constructing an argument against its call for the abandonment of colonies to save money.

It was at that time that he entered the House after a contested by-election for Rye, where he stood on the established Lamb interest.[13] He was sworn in on 4 Mar. 1830 and the following day voted for the transfer of East Retford's seats to Birmingham. He divided against the emasculated disfranchisement bill, 15 Mar., and with the minority of 30 for inquiry into the management of crown lands revenues, 30 Mar. He was unseated on his opponent's petition, 17 May 1830, the day of the second reading of the Jewish emancipation bill, of which he disapproved.[14] In late June 1830 the Whig agent John Goodwin told Lord Holland that he had 'hopes' of finding a seat at the approaching general election for Pusey, who had professed willingness to 'do honour' to Fox's 'memory'.[15] There was speculation in Berkshire that he might stand for the county, but it is unlikely that he seriously contemplated doing so.[16] As it was, he successfully contested Chippenham, where he declared himself to be friendly to the Wellington ministry, in conjunction with and on the new interest of Joseph Neeld.[17] A joint project with Mahon to make an attempt on Seaford had proved to be a waste of time and money.[18]

Ministers listed him among the 'doubtful doubtfuls', but, like his brother, he had become alarmed by the increasing clamour for reform, and he voted in the government minority in the crucial division on the civil list, 15 Nov. 1830, and went into opposition to the Grey ministry. His wife told her brother Edward, 18 Dec., that Pusey

> says that the present ministers will quickly lose their popularity [and] will be torn to pieces by internal factions; that ... Peel rises each day in the ... Commons ... [and] is decidedly the leader, not Lord Althorp; that the ex-ministers from a sense of the country's danger mean to give the present ministry assistance in all moderate views, by which they will be able to check the wilder schemes ... and ... that before Parliament meets again a general war may absorb attention and postpone these hasty plans of reform.[19]

Pusey obtained the production of information on terminable annuities as a portion of the funded debt, 10 Dec. On 21 Dec. 1830 he moved for accounts of national expenditure and revenue, 1827-1830. When Hume objected to the expense of printing them Pusey explained that he wished to have them 'prepared in a particular way, so that at one view we shall be able to examine the finance accounts of the country'. From the government front bench Sir James Graham conceded that his scheme was 'most ingenious', and the motion was agreed to. He secured the insertion into these accounts of the various categories of civil expenditure, 7 Feb. 1831. He wished to question ministers on their foreign policy, with the object of advocating the need to close ranks with Prussia and Austria against France; but at the behest of Wellington and Goulburn, whom he consulted, and who did not wish to embarrass the government on this issue, he remained silent.[20] He presented a petition from Grittleton (Neeld's territory) calling for the establishment of a national fast day, 14 Feb. 1831.

In January 1831 Pusey, who was described at this time by his father-in-law as 'a decided Peelite',[21] composed for the benefit of Mahon, who was about to return from the continent to take up his duties as Member for Wootton Bassett, a review of recent political events entitled 'A Country with a Provisional Government', in which he expressed his unease at the composition of the Grey administration and the state of public opinion, especially on reform; it was never published.[22] He sent a letter to be read out at the Berkshire county reform meeting, 16 Mar., in which he argued that the ministerial reform scheme was 'rather an appeal from our reason and justice to our passions and interests', was admitted even by some of its supporters to be 'too sweeping' and had as its object the annihilation of the Tory party, to leave the king with 'nothing but a Whig ministry and a republican opposition'.[23] He voted silently against the second reading, 22 Mar. Between then and dividing for Gascoyne's wrecking amendment, 19 Apr. 1831, he rapidly composed and published *The New Constitution*, a detailed criticism of the bill, which he deemed to be 'rash, but not bold; its principle is concession to temper, not conviction of evil'. He conceded the need for 'moderate reform', but argued that the measure would 'go far to convert a free monarchy into a despotic republic'. The faithful Mahon deemed the pamphlet to be to be 'one of the ablest among the myriad on this question'; and Pusey's wife thought it was 'very good' and might 'go far to damage' the measure.[24] Pusey was one of the leading Berkshire landowners who signed a declaration against the bill, admitting the necessity for the enfranchisement of unrepresented large towns, the elimination of corruption and diminution of the cost of elections, but condemning the proposed reduction in the number of English Members and the £10 borough franchise. He also, at the instigation of Mahon, signed the Kent anti-reform declaration.[25]

His opposition to the reform bill was very unpopular in Chippenham, and he did not try again there at the general election of 1831, when he was confined to London by his wife's illness, though Mahon suggested eight months later that had he put his name forward he would have been returned.[26] He stood with the Tory lawyer Thomas Pemberton for Rye, where the decision on the right of election which had cost him the seat in 1830 had since been reversed. There was serious disorder, and so fierce was the independents' hostility to the attempted return of two anti-reformers that the patron was forced to concede them one seat. Pusey was unacceptable to the reformers and it was Pemberton who was returned.[27] Pusey, who was gaining a reputation as a rising man of the Tory opposition, was accommodated in mid-July 1831 at Cashel on the Pennefather interest, with the blessing of the party organizers in Charles Street. Shortly before or just after his return, he was miffed not to be invited to a meeting there. Mahon remonstrated on his behalf, and was assured by Holmes, the whip, that the oversight had been 'unintentional, owing to your present absence from the list of MPs, and that although the smallness of the room makes them very limited in number, you shall certainly be asked in future'.[28]

On the reintroduced reform bill he spoke and voted for Chippenham's retention of both seats, 27 July, and argued, 29 July 1831, that Dorchester and Guildford had similarly strong claims on the basis of property if not population. He secured a return of the 113 least populous boroughs according to the 1831 census, 2 Aug. On 24 Aug. he criticized the limitation of the borough franchise qualification to property held under one landlord, but was told that to allow multiple holdings would invite fraud. He voted in the minority of 29 in favour of permitting non-resident freeholders in boroughs previously thrown into the hundreds to retain their votes for life, 2 Sept. He voted against the passage of the bill, 21 Sept., and the second reading of the Scottish measure, 23 Sept. He again obtained public accounts on his own model, 13 Aug., when he was appointed to the select committee on the charges of civil government. He voted to censure the Irish government for interference in the Dublin election, 23 Aug., and to safeguard the West Indian sugar trade, 12 Sept. 1831. The following month he was invited to lend his 'zeal and abilities' to the Tory central committee for conducting the Cambridgeshire by-election.[29]

Pusey voted against the second reading of the revised reform bill, 17 Dec. 1831. At the start of the new year Mahon, who had been urging him to take up his pen again, exhorted him to cultivate an interest at Chippenham and to take the plunge with a major parliamentary speech in the spring, either on the details of the reform bill or, better still, 'finance': 'in that manner reputation for business may be combined with reputation for speaking'.[30] Pusey did not comply. He was in the government majority on the registration clause of the reform bill, 8 Feb. 1832, but divided against the enfranchisement of Tower Hamlets, 28 Feb., and the third reading, 22 Mar. 1832. He was with Wellington and other opposition grandees during the crisis of May, and he formed the opinion, from which Mahon dissented, that the party should several months earlier have taken up 'the line of moderate reform'. On the 16th he joined a small deputation of 'influential men ... in the ... Commons' who unsuccessfully entreated Peel to take office.[31] His only other recorded votes in 1832 were in the opposition minorities against the Russian-Dutch loan, 26 Jan., and the second reading of the Irish reform bill, 25 May, and the majority against the production of information on military punishments, 16 Feb. He was named to the select committee on the East India Company, 28 Jan., and secured a further return of national accounts, 5 July 1832.

Pusey was beaten in a contest for Berkshire at the 1832 general election, but was successful there in 1835 and held the seat for 17 years. A friend of Peel and William Gladstone†, he came to enjoy a high reputation as a thoughtful and intelligent backbencher.[32] He was one of the leading theorists and practitioners of agricultural improvement and a founder member and mainstay of the Royal Agricultural Society, whose journal he edited for many years. He found other outlets for his intellectual energies in journalism and hymn writing.[33] Bunsen, who spent some time with him in 1830, admired his 'extraordinary statesman-like judgement' and 'speculative talent and depth', and thought him 'a most *unique* union of a practical Englishman and an intellectual German'.[34] After the death of his wife in November 1854 he moved into his brother's rooms in Christ Church. Within a week he suffered a stroke, and he died from a second one in July 1855. By his brief will, he left his two daughters equal shares in his consolidated railway company stock, and all the remainder of his property to his only son, Sidney Edward Bouverie Pusey (1839-1911), on whose death without issue the Pusey estate passed to the Fletcher descendants of his married sister Clara.[35]

[1] H.P. Liddon, *Life of Edward Bouverie Pusey*, i. 9. [2] *VCH Berks.* iv. 473. [3] Liddon, i. 10. [4] Ibid. i. 2, 14, 27. [5] Ibid. i. 28, 50; *Oxford DNB*; Add. 51831, Porchester to Holland, 19 Dec. 1821; Bodl. Eng. Lett. d. 58, f. 4; Berks. RO, Pusey mss D/EBp C8/1, 2. [6] Bodl. Eng. lett. d. 58, ff. 6-8; Pusey mss C8/3-7, 15, 19. [7] Baroness Bunsen, *Mem. Baron Bunsen*, i. 264. [8] Pusey mss C1/7, 21; Cent. Kent. Stud. Stanhope mss U1590 C130/4, Mahon to Stanhope, 13 Apr.; C355, Pusey to Mahon, 8 Apr. 1828. [9] PROB 11/1742/373; IR26/1173/332. [10] Bodl. MS. Eng. lett. d. 58, f. 10; Stanhope mss C355; Pusey mss C1/39. [11] Stanhope mss C353, Porchester to Mahon, 10 June; C355, Pusey to same, 18 June 1829; Pusey mss C1/29, 36. [12] Stanhope mss C355, Pusey to Mahon, 18 June, 28 Nov. 1829; Pusey mss C1/4, 26. [13] Hants RO, Carnarvon mss 75M91/H2/1. [14] Pusey mss C1/35. [15] Add. 51835, Goodwin to Holland, 27 June 1830. [16] *Reading Mercury*, 7 June 1830. [17] British Library, Talbot collection, Pusey to Fox Talbot [June]; *Devizes Gazette*, 1 July, 5 Aug.; *Keenes' Bath Jnl.* 2 Aug.; *The Times*, 5 Aug. 1830; Pusey mss C1/15. [18] Pusey mss C1/43; Stanhope mss A122/1, Mahon's acct. bk. 1823-35. [19] Carnarvon mss F4/3. [20] Wellington mss WP1/1175/12, 15. [21] Carnarvon mss E4/93. [22] Pusey mss C1/13; F5/2. [23] *The Times*, 17 Mar. 1831. [24] Pusey mss C1/38, 44; Keele Univ. Lib. Sneyd mss, Mahon to Sneyd, 5 May 1831; Carnarvon mss L16/2. [25] N. Gash, *Politics in Age of Peel*, 301; *The Times*, 9 Apr.; *Kentish Gazette*, 26 Apr. 1831; Pusey mss C1/44. [26] Pusey mss C1/1; Carnarvon mss L3, H. Howard to Lady Porchester, 4, 25 May 1831; L14/12. [27] See RYE. [28] Pusey mss C1/45. [29] Ibid. C1/24. [30] Ibid. C1/1, 8. [31] *Three Diaries*, 260; Pusey mss C1/22; C2, Wellington to Carnarvon, 15 May 1832; Carnarvon mss H5/3, 4. [32] Gash, 304-6; Pusey mss C1/12, 18, 22, 25, 31, 40; Wellington mss WP1/1239/35. [33] Gash, 309-10, 311, 318; *Oxford DNB*; Sir E. Clarke, *Philip Pusey*, 7-16. [34] Bunsen, i. 504, 522. [35] *Gent. Mag.* (1855), ii. 319; PROB 11/2218/721; IR26/2043/793.

D.R.F.

PYM, Francis (1756–1833), of The Hasells, Biggleswade, Beds.

BEDFORDSHIRE	5 Feb. 1806–1818
BEDFORDSHIRE	1820–1826

b. 28 Oct. 1756,[1] 3rd but 1st surv. s. of William Pym of Radwell, Herts. and Elizabeth, da. and h. of Heylock Kingsley of The Hasells. *educ.* Charterhouse 1772-4; Trinity Coll. Camb. 1774. *m.* 21 May 1785,[2] Anne, da. of Robert Palmer of Holme Park, Berks., 5s. (1 *d.v.p.*) 2da. *suc.* fa. 1788. *d.* 4 Dec. 1833.

Sheriff, Beds. 1791-2; lt.-col. commdt. 2 Beds. vol. inf. 1803; capt. Beds. militia 1810.

Pym's prevarication and loss of nerve in 1818, when, fearing ruinous expense, he had run away at the last minute from a contest for the county which he had represented on the broad 'Whig interest' since 1806, so letting in a Tory, had angered many of the county's leading Whigs.[3] By the time of the 1820 general election, however, he had been forgiven, and he was 'started by the Whigs independently of the [6th] duke of Bedford', whose son Lord Tavistock occupied the other seat on the Woburn interest. Bedford observed to Lord Holland that having thus stirred things up, the Whigs must 'not suffer old Pym to run away again'. According to one report, at the nomination his 'feelings appeared to overpower him, and the few words he uttered were scarcely audible to those immediately around him'. After a hard-fought contest, he narrowly beat the Tory sitting Member into third place.[4] As during his previous membership of the House, Pym, who never joined Brooks's, was a lax attender, though he usually showed his face for the most important divisions. He evidently uttered not a word in debate in this Parliament.

He was present to vote with opposition on the civil list, 3, 5, 8 May, the appointment of an additional Scottish baron of exchequer, 15 May, army reductions, 14 June, and economies in revenue collection, 4 July 1820. He divided against Wilberforce's compromise resolution on the Queen Caroline affair, 22 June 1820. He attended the county meeting in her support, 13 Jan. 1821, but was reported as merely expressing his 'satisfaction' at being instructed to support its petition for redress and reform.[5] He voted for the restoration of Caroline's name to the liturgy, 23, 26 Jan., 13 Feb., and for the motion of censure on ministers' treatment of her, 6 Feb. He voted for Catholic relief, 28 Feb. 1821, as he did again, 1 Mar., 21 Apr., 10 May 1825. His only other known votes in the 1821 session were for inquiry into the state of the revenue, 6 Mar., a substantial reduction in the army, 14 Mar., repeal of the additional malt duty, 21 Mar., 3 Apr., and parliamentary reform, 9 May. On 21 Mar. he presented a Bedfordshire petition complaining of agricultural distress.[6] He was granted a month's leave to attend to urgent private business, 11 May 1821. He voted for more extensive tax reductions to relieve distress, 21 Feb. 1822, and went on to divide that session for detailed returns of the navy and ordnance estimates, 27 Feb., lowering of the salt duties, 28 Feb., admiralty reductions, 1 Mar., abolition of one of the joint-postmasterships, 13 Mar., inquiry into the board of control, 14 Mar., ordnance economies, 25, 27 Mar., against the public works grant, 29 Mar., and for cuts in diplomatic expenditure, 15, 16 May. He did not attend the county reform meeting, 20 Apr., when his eldest son apologized for his absence on 'unavoidable business', but indicated his support for its object;[7] and he duly divided for Russell's reform motion, 25 Apr. He voted for mitigation of the penal code, 4 June, and against the aliens bill, 5 June 1822.

Pym voted for abolition of the office of lieutenant-general of the ordnance in peacetime, 19 Feb., and against the national debt reduction bill and misapplication of the Barbados four and a half per cents,

17 Mar. 1823. He voted for reform, 20 Feb., 24 Apr. He divided for inquiries into the prosecution of the Dublin Orange rioters, 22 Apr., and chancery arrears, 5 June 1823. In 1824, he voted for reform of Edinburgh's representation, 26 Feb., reduction of the barrack grant, 27 Feb., and repeal of the window tax, 2 Mar., against the aliens bill, 23 Mar., for further inquiry into the findings of the Scottish judicial commission, 30 Mar., and in condemnation of the trial of the Methodist missionary John Smith in Demerara, 11 June. He voted against repeal of the usury laws, 27 Feb. He presented a Bedford petition for the abolition of slavery, 26 Feb, and one from Leighton Buzzard against a property tax, 8 Apr. 1824.[8] He voted against the Irish unlawful societies bill, 15, 18, 21 Feb. 1825. Towards the end of that session he turned up to vote against the duke of Cumberland's annuity, 6, 10 June, and for inquiry into chancery delays, 7 June.

In the autumn of 1825 an anti-Catholic Tory declared his intention of standing for Bedfordshire at the next general election. Tavistock offered again, albeit on strict purity of election principles, with no canvass or treating of voters; but Pym, after showing his usual 'want of decision', announced in December his resolution to retire rather than face a contest. Tavistock observed to a friend that he 'could not be brought to the post', even though he 'would have won in a canter'.[9] Pym presented Luton and Ramsdaile anti-slavery petitions, 27 Feb., 16 Mar. 1826.[10] He voted with opposition against giving the president of the board of trade a ministerial salary, 10 Apr. He presented a county petition against alteration of the corn laws, 1 Mar.,[11] and was in the protectionist minorities against the temporary admission of foreign corn, 8 May, and the corn bill, 11 May 1826. At the general election the following month he was nominated in his absence by the county Whigs, in a bid to keep out the Tory. His son, who represented him throughout the ensuing contest, explained that despite his well known aversion to standing, he would serve if elected. Although the Whigs subscribed for him, he was soon seen to have no chance, and he finished third in the poll; but Tavistock wrote that 'if old Pym had run straight I think he might have won our race this time'.[12]

Pym seems to have retired into private life, though his son, a Whig protectionist and enthusiastic supporter of church missionary work overseas, became increasingly active in county affairs and was talked of as a possible candidate in 1830.[13] Pym died in December 1833. By his will, dated 24 Aug. 1831, he left his wife an annuity of £200, in addition to her jointure of £10,000 under their post-nuptial settlement, which had set up a trust fund of £15,000 for their younger children. His personalty was sworn under £9,000, but the estate yielded no residue for his eldest son, Francis Pym (1790-1860), who succeeded him in the family estates in Bedfordshire and Hertfordshire, and an uncle to property in Cambridgeshire.[14] His two next sons, William Wollaston (1792-1852) and Robert (1793-1862), entered the church, while Charles (1797-1881), the youngest surviving one (John having perished at Waterloo), became an assistant tithe commissioner and took the name of Reading in 1870.

[1] E.L. Arrowsmith, *Charterhouse Reg. 1769-1872*, p. 306. [2] *Gent. Mag.* (1785), i. 402. [3] Add. 51662, Bedford to Holland, 4, 11 Aug., 27 Sept. 1818; *HP Commons, 1790-1820*, ii. 3-4. [4] *Althorp Letters*, 103; Add. 51662, Bedford to Holland, Tuesday [22 Feb.]; *Cambridge and Hertford Independent Press*, 26 Feb., 4, 11, 18, 25 Mar. 1820. [5] *The Times*, 13 Jan. 1821. [6] Ibid. 22 Mar. 1822. [7] Ibid. 22 Apr. 1822. [8] Ibid. 27 Feb., 9 Apr. 1824. [9] Ibid. 19 Dec. 1825; *Althorp Letters*, 127; Add. 36461, ff. 347, 385. [10] *The Times*, 28 Feb., 17 Mar. 1826. [11] Ibid. 2 Mar. 1826. [12] *Cambridge and Hertford Independent Press*, 8 July 1826; *Althorp Letters*, 130, 132; Add. 36462, f. 311. [13] Add. 35690, ff. 200, 201; *Gent. Mag.* (1860), i. 524; Bodl. MS. Eng. lett. c. 160, f. 134. [14] PROB 11/1826/44; IR26/1363/14; *VCH Cambs.* v. 51-52.

D.R.F.

RAE, Sir William, 3rd bt. (1769–1842), of St. Catherine's, Edinburgh.

ANSTRUTHER EASTER BURGHS	26 July 1819–1826
HARWICH	16 May 1827–1830
BUTESHIRE	1830–1831
PORTARLINGTON	1831–1832
BUTESHIRE	4 Sept. 1833–19 Oct. 1842

b. 14 Apr. 1769, 2nd s. of David Rae, Lord Eskgrove, SCJ (*d.* 1804), of Eskgrove and Margaret, da. of John Stuart of Blairhall, Perth. *educ.* Edinburgh h.s. 1779-82; Glasgow Univ. 1788; Edinburgh Univ.; adv. 1791. *m.* 9 Sept. 1793, Mary, da. of Lt.-Col. Charles Stuart, 63 Ft., *s.p. suc.* bro. Sir David Rae, 2nd bt., as 3rd bt. 22 May 1815. *d.* 19 Oct. 1842.

Ld. advocate June 1819-Nov. 1830, Dec. 1834-Apr. 1835, Sept. 1841-*d.*; PC 19 July 1830.

Sheriff, Orkney 1801-9, Edinburgh 1809-19; dir. (extraordinary), Bank of Scotland 1809-14.

Cornet Edinburgh vol. cav. 1797, capt. 1797-1810.

Rae, a tall man with 'a fine, thoughtful countenance' and 'strong' Scottish accent, was described by his friend Sir Walter Scott as 'sensible, cool-headed and firm'.[1] At the general election of 1820 he secured an unopposed return on the interest of Colonel Robert Anstruther† for the Anstruther Burghs, which he had successfully contested nine months earlier on his surprising appointment as lord advocate.[2] In the weeks before the elections he kept Lord Melville, the Liverpool ministry's Scottish manager, informed of developments, and found and encouraged friendly candidates for a few seats, including the Aberdeen, Haddington and Stirling districts.[3] Had the new reign led to the formation of a Whig ministry, he would have been compensated for the loss of his place with the additional barony of exchequer, which in the event went to Sir Patrick Murray†.[4] He initially took a relaxed view of the manifestations of unrest in Glasgow and the west of Scotland, but he was involved in the pre-emptive strike which flooded Glasgow with troops on 5 Apr. 1820. He wrote from there next day to the home secretary Lord Sidmouth:

> All has continued quiet ... I am satisfied that the radical gentlemen are completely frightened, and that we shall have no opportunity of bestowing upon them any of that description of chastisement which I came here in the hope of seeing inflicted. It now ... remains for us to augment this fear and confirm the confidence of the well-disposed, which has revived wonderfully since our arrival ... We proposed tomorrow to make a formidable search for arms, and to take many of those into custody with whom pikes or such like arms shall be found. A number of other arrests are taking place on stronger grounds, and we shall have abundance of examples to make in the way of trial. A commission of oyer and terminer for the trial of those accused of high treason ... ought not to be delayed.[5]

In the subsequent trials, held successively at Stirling, Glasgow, Dumbarton, Paisley and Ayr, 23 June-9 Aug. 1820, Rae led for the crown: 24 men were sentenced to death, but only three were executed.[6]

Rae was named to the select committees on the municipal government of the Scottish royal burghs, 4 May 1820, 16 Feb. 1821. In the House, 1, 4 May, he explained and defended Murray's controversial appointment, and on 15 May 1820, in what the Tory backbencher Henry Bankes considered a 'heavy and indifferent speech', replied to Lord Archibald Hamilton's censure motion, arguing that the position had been filled, contrary to the recommendation of the Scottish judicial commissioners, 'on a due consideration of the national contract at the Union'.[7] His description of Hamilton's attack on the Scottish lord clerk register Archibald Campbell Colquhoun* as 'unfounded and illiberal' earned him a rebuke from the Speaker. The motion was defeated by only 12 votes. Rae presented a constituency petition for restoration of Queen Caroline's name to the liturgy, 31 Jan. 1821.[8] He opposed Hamilton's motion for a copy of the order in council to the general assembly of the Church of Scotland on this issue, 15 Feb., when the radical Whig Henry Grey Bennet thought he 'replied in a very good manner, but gave up *all* the question by admitting that the clergy of Scotland could pray or *not* ... as they pleased, for the queen'.[9] Later that day he defeated by 59-22 an amendment to his resolution ordering compensation for clerks of the Scottish admiralty court; and on 1 May he asserted that the enabling bill 'did not contain a single objectionable clause'.[10] He voted against Catholic relief, 28 Feb. 1821, 1 Mar., 21 Apr., 10 May 1825. On 2 Apr. 1821 he defended the labours of the royal burghs select committee against Hamilton's criticisms, admitting that many of the petitioners' complaints had proved to be 'well founded', but dismissing the call for root and branch reform. The ministerialist lawyer Robert Grant* noted that Rae

> seems to have managed matters in the committee with address and ability, and to have brought them pretty nearly into a state that the committee are likely to make a very different report ... from that which was made by their predecessors ... [He] carried a resolution ... which puts an end to the hopes of the reformers so far as the reports of that committee are concerned.[11]

Rae had indicated his dislike of the Whig Thomas Kennedy's bill to reform the Scottish jury system, 16 Feb., observing that while 'a great practical evil must be shown before any innovation should be permitted', there was 'a general disposition in the present day to hunt out every hole and corner in our constitutional system to which some theoretical remedy might by possibility apply'. In early April he sent a copy of the measure and his own critical comments to the conveners of the Scottish counties and urged them to have the bill considered at the impending annual general meetings. A number of hostile petitions were sent to Parliament, and Rae's intervention was noticed there by the Whigs, but he claimed that he had only been laying the case before the public, 8, 18 May 1821.[12]

In December 1821 Melville asked Rae if he wanted to take the vacant barony of exchequer, but, while admitting that his claim 'could not with justice or propriety be resisted', strongly discouraged him from doing so, because his departure from office would 'at present be attended with public inconvenience'. Rae replied:

> The situation of a baron is one which I have long looked to, and if it passes me now, the chance of another opening is truly remote. On the other hand I have had full experience of your friendship, and government have so acted towards me that I should be most unwilling to take any

step contrary to their wishes or which might be attended with real public inconvenience. Having no family, I can venture to run greater risks than most other people, and if I do not get this situation I must somewhat change my views and look to what may happen to fall elsewhere. Under these circumstances and not knowing all the reasons which may influence you ... I am truly desirous to put myself entirely into your hands, and shall cheerfully accede to whatever arrangement you may deem most expedient.

He went to London to see Melville, who evidently raised serious objections to his suggestion of 'keeping the baron's gown unfilled up' for the time being, so that he could take it at the end of the next session, when the ticklish issue of his involvement with the virulent Glasgow Tory newspaper the *Beacon* had been disposed of. Rae acknowledged the awkwardness of these difficulties and, not wishing to expose himself to the charge that he was 'a judge elect who ought not to be in Parliament', advised Melville 'forthwith to give the gown to David Hume':

I shall then meet the *Beacon* question wholly unfettered, and with a feeling in the House, I should rather suppose, somewhat favourable to me. What the consequences ... may be to me hereafter cannot be foreseen, and is immaterial to be looked to. I have, however, seldom observed anyone suffer from following a straightforward course.

On 2 Jan. 1822 Lord Liverpool, the foreign secretary Lord Londonderry* and Sidmouth endorsed this decision and asked Melville to inform Rae of their sense of 'the propriety and handsomeness' of his conduct.[13]

In the House, 18 Feb. 1822, Rae failed to persuade Hamilton to withdraw his motion for a bill to abolish the inferior Scottish commissary courts, having one in preparation himself, and had it negatived. He introduced his measure on 3 Apr. but abandoned it on 3 June, when he admitted to Hamilton that the problem had turned out to require 'much consideration'.[14] On 20 Feb. he opposed Hamilton's motion for inquiry by committee of the whole House into the royal burghs and heralded his own 'comprehensive' bill, which would 'effect a remedy for the existing grievances without injuring any chartered rights or violating any article of the Union': he 'could not view any alteration in the constitution of them in any other light than of a parliamentary reform'. He brought in the bill, which sought to regulate the burghs' accounts and outlaw non-residence by magistrates, on 7 Mar. The latter provision provoked considerable opposition from the councils, especially those in the north, but Rae assured Lord Gower†, whose father Lord Stafford had a significant stake there, that 'the members of the town council were not intended by him to have been included, not being named in the former laws, and that he would endeavour to omit them'.[15] On 17 June it was resolved to divide the measure into two bills, one to regulate the accounts, the other to deal with non-residence. The former became law as 3 Geo. IV, c. 91. The latter passed the Commons, 19 July, when Rae and Lord Binning secured the addition of a clause requiring a majority of council members to be resident and defeated radical Whig amendments making residence obligatory and excluding revenue officers.[16] The bill foundered in the Lords. Rae allowed Kennedy to bring in his renewed Scottish juries bill, 5 Mar., but on 20 June he unsuccessfully opposed its second reading, which the new home secretary, Peel, supported.[17] The affair of the *Beacon*, which had been put out of business in the late summer of 1821 by exposure of the part played by Rae and other Tories as guarantors of its financial stability, had taken an embarrassing turn.[18] Its replacement, the *Sentinel*, had continued the practice of publishing savage personal attacks on individual Whigs, and one of these, James Stuart of Dunearn, had brought a libel action against Borthwick and Alexander, the publishers. In the course of this it had emerged that the author of one of the offending articles was Alexander Boswell*, who in late March 1822 was challenged by Stuart to a duel, in which he was fatally wounded. Stuart was tried for murder at Rae's instigation, but was acquitted. Meanwhile, the crown had also started proceedings against Borthwick for theft, at the instance of Alexander. He spent many weeks in prison on remand, but was released without trial after Stuart's acquittal. In the House, 25 June, the Whig James Abercromby moved for inquiry into the conduct of Rae and his deputies, especially in the proceedings against Borthwick. Rae initially denied all knowledge of the *Sentinel* and that he had signed a circular recommending it, but when Abercromby handed him the physical evidence he admitted his error, though he still claimed not to recall signing the paper. He subsequently confessed that he had subscribed £100 to the *Beacon* and acted as its guarantor. He defended the conduct of his deputies in prosecuting Borthwick, but took the ultimate responsibility on himself. The motion was defeated by 120-95, but Bankes recorded his impression of Rae's discomfort, observing that he 'appeared much agitated and confused, and unequal to his antagonist'. The Whig Member George Agar Ellis thought his 'answer was miserable'.[19] In a 'frequently' inaudible speech on 23 July 1822, Rae elaborated on his defence, maintaining that he would not personally have initiated the action against Borthwick, but again standing by his deputies and accusing Abercromby of failing to disclose the full scope of his motion, thereby forcing Rae to give in the first instance 'a very unsatisfactory reply'.[20] When Abercromby moved on 3 June 1823 that his conduct in the Borthwick affair had been 'unjust and oppressive', Rae insisted that he had 'acted upon pure and conscientious motives'. No minister spoke for him, and the motion was rejected by only six votes (102-96). The Whig George Tierney* commented that Rae would doubtless follow the 'precedent' set by the Irish attorney-general William Plunket* of 'not resigning in consequence of ill usage and being deserted by those who are bound to support you'; and the Edinburgh Whig lawyer Henry Cockburn reported that there was 'but one opinion, even among the enemy, as to its being an undeniable and signal defeat'. Henry Brougham* thought Rae must resign, but Cockburn expected him to be 'speedily made a judge'.[21] The junior minister Lord Lowther* had commented in March 1823 that Rae 'does not seem equal to his business', but he comfortably survived.[22]

In the late summer of 1822 Rae had let Melville know that he had 'not the slightest wish' to fill the vacant lordship of session. Under the aegis of Peel, he consulted during the recess with senior Scottish judges on proposed changes in the criminal law and made suggestions of his own.[23] On 26 Mar. 1823 he led the opposition to Hamilton's motion for a copy of the 1822 crown warrant authorizing a new Inverness council election after the suspension of the sett. He stressed that the warrant had been issued on the 'wise and sound discretion' of the privy council, and claimed that the local government of the burgh had 'considerably improved under the present management'; the motion was defeated by 49-31. He defended the Edinburgh authorities' intervention against the 'blasphemous' Free Thinkers Zetetic Society, 16 Apr. He opposed Hamilton's motion for reform of the Scottish county representation, claiming that the existing system was 'approved of by the people', 2 June. He had introduced on 27 Mar. a bill for the better granting of confirmations, regulating the commissary court of Edinburgh and altering the jurisdiction of inferior Scottish commissaries. 'With the view of preserving the consistorial law' and saving 'the public from heavy claims of compensation on the part of commissary clerks', as he explained to Peel, he decided 'not to propose the entire abolition' of the inferior courts.[24] The measure was divided into two, 28 Apr.: one dealing with confirmations, the other with the commissaries. Rae was forced to defer the third reading of the latter, 18, 19 June, when he accused Hamilton and other Whigs of being obstructive 'for no other purpose than to cast unpleasant personal reflections upon him'.[25] He secured the third reading of the bill, which transferred the commissaries' business to the sheriffs depute, by 56-21 on 30 June. The measures became law on 19 July as 4 Geo. IV, cc. 97 and 98. Rae divided the House against the second reading of Kennedy's renewed Scottish juries bill, 20 June 1823, but was in a minority of 42 to 47.[26]

In the autumn of 1823 he was involved in the Edinburgh deliberations of the Scottish judicial commission appointed by Peel.[27] When Hamilton moved to refer its reports to a committee of the whole House, 30 Mar., Rae accused him of trying to make him 'defend himself from the charge of having neglected his duty, by not giving effect to the recommendations of the commissioners'. He recapitulated recent changes to the Scottish courts, said (to Abercromby's satisfaction) that he wished to enable justices to take their share of criminal administration and sat down to 'loud and general cheering'. The motion was defeated by 124-76.[28] He disliked Kennedy's Scottish poor bill, 6 Apr., defended the existing system, 14 May, presented hostile petitions, 19 May, 3 June, and said that the measure had 'never received the slightest encouragement from any public body in Scotland', 26 May.[29] He thought Kennedy's revised juries bill was 'impracticable' and unnecessarily complex, 4 May. He anticipated 'heavy objections' to Hamilton's bill to amend the Small Debts Act for Scotland, which he considered too biased towards creditors, 10 June. On the 17th he endorsed Peel's decision to postpone the ministerial Scottish judicature bill until next session, a course which he had strongly advised behind the scenes.[30] Soon afterwards he was given leave by the treasury to go to Edinburgh until at least 28 July 1823 'to attend to personal and professional duties'; but on the 19th he asked Melville to excuse him from attendance for Abercromby's motion for reform of Edinburgh's representation a week later:

> I am in hopes that the ... case will not be treated as a Scotch question, but will be met by ... Canning [the leader of the House] on the general ground of its being a commencement to the introduction of parliamentary reform ... I should certainly not wish to quit Edinburgh at the present moment ... We are ... deeply engaged in taking measures for putting down by means of proceedings before the judiciary several shops whose atheistical publications are daily issued to a great extent ... You must be aware of the necessity as far as possible of discountenancing the practice of the lord advocate being required to attend in London during the whole sittings of Parliament. Though I should submit to this without grumbling, it is obvious that if once such a rule is estab-

> lished no lawyer of great professional practice could accept of the situation.[31]

He was evidently allowed to remain in Edinburgh.

In November 1824 Rae was very anxious to ascertain from Peel and Melville that he and the Scottish solicitor-general John Hope would be entrusted with the task of preparing the amended judicature bill, feeling miffed that it had been taken out of their hands in the previous session:

> If the same arrangement is to be persevered in, the only inference which the public can draw is that ... government have not that trust in their council which ... they ought to have. I am hopeful ... that no one can suppose for a moment that we would feel inclined to introduce any change into the bill ... inconsistent with the views and wishes of government.

He and Hope had also prepared 'a set of clauses' for inclusion in a planned ministerial measure to deal with jury selection; and he questioned Kennedy's fitness to handle the issue, even leaving aside his close connection with 'those whose unremitting object it is to make a run at the Scotch crown council'. Liverpool, Peel, Melville, lord chancellor Eldon and Lord Gifford came to a decision on the matter, but it is not entirely clear how this affected Rae.[32] He tried to get out of attending for a call of the House on 18 Feb. 1825, but Peel would not indulge him.[33] The Scottish jurors and judicature bills were originated in the Lords. Rae explained the latter on its second reading, 18 Apr., when Kennedy welcomed its concession of selection by ballot. It became law as 6 Geo. IV, c. 22. Rae thought John Peter Grant's bill to amend the Scottish wrongous imprisonment laws would cost too much to implement and do little good, 5 May. He was in the minority of 52 against the Irish franchise bill, 9 May. He denied any responsibility for the controversial Leith docks bill, 20 May, when he voted in the favourable minority of 15. He defended the Scottish shooting and stabbing bill, 20 June, and the Scottish partnerships bill, 22 June 1825. On 28 Feb. 1826 he brought in a bill to amend the Jurors Act, which became law as 7 Geo. IV, c. 8. He presented petitions against interference with the Scottish banking system, 14, 20 Mar.,[34] and was named to the select committee on the circulation of small notes, 16 Mar. That day he defended his conduct in the matter of the disfranchisement of Pittenweem (one of his constituent burghs) and objected to production of the information demanded by Hamilton.[35] On 21 Mar. he secured the appointment of a select committee on Scottish gaols, after detailing some of their deficiencies: 'in one case ... The gaoler was stone-blind and the gaol was managed by his daughter ... the blind gaoler could not give his eye to the prisoners, and as to the daughter, it might occur that the prisoners might be giving an eye for her'. He opposed reform of Edinburgh's representative system, arguing that extension of the franchise from the council to £5 householders, who were of the class of 'gentlemen's servants', would create chaos. He defended the Scottish bankers bill, 12 May 1826.[36]

At the general election a month later Rae was opposed and beaten in Anstruther Burghs by James Balfour, a wealthy nabob with a Fifeshire estate.[37] He remained in place on the formation of Canning's ministry in April 1827 (when Melville was one of the Tory seceders); it was noted that he could 'not afford to resign and wait' for the chance of a judgeship.[38] He was provided with a seat for Harwich on the treasury interest in May. He was in the ministerial minority against the Penryn disfranchisement bill, 7 June, and defended the Edinburgh bridewell bill, 11 June.[39] Abercromby, a supporter of the ministry, strove in vain to convince his leader Lord Lansdowne of the 'absolute necessity' of getting rid of Rae in order to erect 'a proper government standard' in Scotland.[40] He was retained in office by Lord Goderich, who in early September asked him to back the Whig Sir Michael Shaw Stewart* in the Lanarkshire by-election. Rae vouched for the willingness of the Tory candidate Charles Douglas*, a personal friend, to support the government if elected, and the premier and the colonial secretary William Huskisson* concluded that it would be 'prudent' for them to remain 'neutral', provided it was made clear to Rae that it must be a 'real' and not 'a *pretended* neutrality, operating covertly' in Douglas's favour. Tierney, a member of the government, was told by Shaw Stewart's backers that Rae was in fact 'most active in his exertion' for Douglas, and pressed Huskisson to intervene. Huskisson felt that Tierney had been misinformed, and explained to him the understanding reached between Goderich and Rae. Shaw Stewart won the contest.[41] Abercromby continued to agitate for Rae's removal and replacement by Hope, with Cockburn becoming solicitor-general. He believed that Rae was 'quite as impatient to be translated to a less conspicuous station as any of us are to see his place vacated', but he acknowledged that he was 'a poor man' with 'no resources in the profession', who could not 'be cast off without the promise of an early provision'.[42] Hope reckoned that Rae would not take a seat in the court of session, but that he still aspired to a barony of exchequer.[43] With the return to the cabinet of Melville under the duke of Wellington and Peel in January 1828 Rae was back in more congenial company.

He divided against repeal of the Test Acts, 26 Feb., and Catholic claims, 12 May 1828. He doubted the practicability of Graham's bill to facilitate the removal of Scottish paupers from English counties, 19 Feb., and did not think intelligent Scottish opinion was ready for the changes in the law of entails proposed by Kennedy, 6 Mar. On 10 June, however, he stated that the measure had been so much improved by the committee upstairs (on which he had sat) that it now 'merited the most dispassionate ... consideration'. On 14 Mar. he introduced a bill to establish an additional circuit judge at Glasgow, in response to a 'very considerable' increase in crime. He had it committed *pro forma*, 25 Mar., and sent copies to Scotland for consideration by the profession. The measure passed the Commons on 12 May and became law as 9 Geo. IV, c. 29. Rae did not want Spring Rice's rights of executors bill extended to Scotland, where its principle had been 'long in practice', 4 June. He brought in a bill to regulate and improve Scottish gaols, 6 May, but on the 15th said he would not press it 'against the feelings of the Members for Scotland'; he had it printed for circulation, 20 June. He opposed and defeated by 88-12 an amendment to add the River Thurso to the exemptions from the salmon fisheries bill, 23 June 1828. As expected, he sided with his colleagues for the concession of Catholic emancipation in 1829. On 24 Mar. he admitted that there was much hostility to it in Scotland, but as a member of the Church of England he declared that 'my friends north of the Tweed need not entertain any fear that the Church of Scotland, or their Presbyterian form of worship, is in the least danger'. He had his reintroduced (14 Apr.) gaols bill referred to a select committee, 8 May, but it continued to arouse fierce opposition from the burgh councils. He warned on 27 May that he would have to legislate on the problem next year, as the condition of its gaols was 'perhaps, the only part of the national establishment of which Scotland need be ashamed'. Next day he abandoned the bill and introduced a revised version as a basis for further inquiry. He had been leading counsel for the crown in the sensational murder trial of the Edinburgh body snatchers in December 1828, and on the anatomy regulation bill, 15 May 1829, he advised that prescribing too severe a punishment might lead to undeserved acquittals and that this should be left to the discretion of the courts. He joined in the defence of the ministerial proposals to give 'a very moderate addition' to judges' salaries, 21 May 1829.

When Rae belatedly discovered in mid-February 1830 that lord chief baron William Shepherd† had retired and was to be replaced by Abercromby (whom he did not blame personally), he was mortified. He complained to Melville that it looked like 'a job for a particular individual' engineered by lord chief commissioner William Adam† and lord chancellor Lyndhurst, and that it 'showed in how little estimation I am held by ... government':

> I have no *right* to be offended at the selection ... but I ... have some grounds to complain of the manner in which this arrangement has been conducted, as unkind to me and disrespectful to my office ... What has now occurred has greatly altered my feelings as to holding office. It has not been from pecuniary motives that I have so long continued advocate. I liked the duties, however laborious and responsible, and I thought it probable that ... this ... would lead to some respectable retirement for the close of life. This expectation is ended. The office which was the object of my ambition is to be passed by me like a shadow without my being allowed even to grasp at it; and if disposed (which I certainly am not) to commence with the duties of an ordinary Scotch judge at a time of life when my contemporaries are retiring from the bench on the score of infirmity and old age, the contemplated judicial arrangements would preclude the *possibility* of my ever attaining such a position ... It shall not, however, be said that I do anything from pique or from a wish to embarrass the government. But my course must be so guided that I may withdraw at the time and in the manner which may place me in the best point of view with those of my countrymen whose opinions I value.

Melville sent him a conciliatory but firm reply, observing that he had 'not viewed the subject' with his 'usual fairness and impartiality'. He dismissed Rae's conspiracy theories, said that he had personally proposed his nomination as lord chief baron, but had not been prepared to insist on it in the circumstances, which required the appointment of an English barrister, and assured him that he and other ministers held him in high regard. Having been delayed on his journey to London by his wife's illness, Rae accepted Melville's exoneration of Lyndhurst, but insisted that he had never acquiesced in the notion that the chief baron must be an English barrister, a principle of selection which 'necessarily went not only to exclude me, but my successors in office in all time coming, and even the whole members of the Scotch bar, from one of the honours of the profession'. He was, however, gratified by Melville's personal support.[44] On 1 Apr. 1830 he introduced the Scottish judicature bill, one part of the ministry's package of legal reforms, which aimed to unite jury trials in civil causes with the ordinary jurisdiction of the court of session and abolish two judges of the latter. He asserted that there was 'no hostility' to it in Scotland, 30 Apr., but had it committed and printed for amendment, 10 May. He presented favourable petitions from the profession, 27 May, 11

June. On 18 June he invited written suggestions for improvements, and he answered some criticisms on the third reading, 23 June. When the king's death three days later threatened its passage through the Lords, Rae told ministers he would resign if it was not carried before the dissolution.[45] He got his way, and the bill became law on 23 July as 11 Geo. IV & 1 Gul. IV, c. 69. Rae said that the death penalty for serious forgery offences had had a good deterrent effect in Scotland, but did not oppose its abolition, 13 May. He was in the Protestant minorities against the Galway franchise bill, 24, 25 May. He explained that he had been unable to prepare a satisfactory gaols bill for that session, 28 May. On 10 July he applied to Wellington for admission to the privy council in recognition of his work as the longest serving lord advocate since the Union. After some consideration, during which Peel noted that he had a 'strong' claim, he was sworn in on 19 July 1830.[46]

At the general election the following month he was returned unopposed for Buteshire by the 2nd marquess of Bute. He was in the ministerial minority on the civil list, 15 Nov. 1830, and duly resigned with his colleagues a few days later, having secured a civil list pension of £660 for his wife.[47] In the House, 2 Dec., he urged the Grey ministry to appoint his successor as soon as possible. (They picked Francis Jeffrey*, former editor of the *Edinburgh Review*.) On Kennedy's entails reform bill, 7 Dec. 1830, Rae professed to be 'anxious' for change, but suggested that legislation should begin in the Lords, where judicial expertise could be utilized. Next day he introduced a bill to alter the Scottish law concerning heritable enfeoffments. On 13 Apr. he brought in one to facilitate the transfer of heritable securities, but both measures were overtaken by the 1831 dissolution. Following Jeffrey in the debate on the ministerial reform scheme, 9 Mar., Rae said that 'a great alteration is proposed, for which no sufficient reason has been assigned'. Confining himself to the Scottish proposals, he objected to various details of the redistribution of seats, defended the existing county franchise, by which 'in the great majority of cases the largest landed proprietor in the county becomes ... its representative' and predicted 'excitement ... disorder and even bloodshed' at Edinburgh elections held under a £10 householder franchise. He asserted that the plan was only popular in Scotland because the people did not fully understand it, 19 Mar. He divided against the second reading of the English bill, 22 Mar. He presented and endorsed a petition against the proposed disfranchisement of Anstruther Burghs and one from Glasgow cotton manufacturers against the duty on raw cotton wool, 28 Mar. He voted for Gascoyne's wrecking amendment to the English reform bill, 19 Apr. 1831. Buteshire's return passed to Caithness at the ensuing general election, when Rae was accommodated with a seat for the Irish borough of Portarlington on the interest of the 2nd earl of Portarlington, financed from the Tory election fund.[48]

His comment on the riotous tendencies of lower class Scots had been widely noticed,[49] and in the House, 27 June 1831, he claimed that he had been 'very much misrepresented' and had merely observed that although they were 'orderly, peaceable and difficult to excite, yet when excited and formed into a mob', they had 'an extraordinary disposition to riot, and seldom separate without it'. Two days later he deplored Shaw Stewart's attempt to find excuses for the Lanarkshire election disturbances, which he had witnessed at first hand. He voted against the second reading of the reintroduced English reform bill, 6 July, for use of the 1831 census to determine the disfranchisement schedules, 19 July, against the partial disfranchisement of Chippenham, 27 July, and in a minority of 17 for the preservation of existing voting rights, 27 Aug. On 6 Aug. he protested again against the proposed disfranchisement of the Anstruther Burghs, pointing out that his own defeat there in 1826 proved that they were not in anyone's pocket. He suggested disfranchising instead Tain Burghs, given that the patron Lord Stafford had been left with his 'nomination county' of Sutherland. He divided against the passage of the reform bill, 21 Sept., and the second reading of the Scottish measure, 23 Sept., when he presented and endorsed a petition from St. Andrews for representation for the Scottish universities. On 3 Oct. he conceded that the original 'undigested and objectionable' Scottish reform bill had been materially improved, largely thanks to the suggestions of Tories, but he still found many faults in it and was convinced that it would bring an 'end for ever to the influence of the landed interests'. He also urged ministers to deal firmly with disorder to dispel the impression created by Jeffrey and others that they desired a strong demonstration of popular reform feeling. He wanted sheriffs to have the final say on disputed registration claims, 4 Oct. He was in the minority for inquiry into the effects of renewal of the Sugar Refinery Act on the West India interest, 12 Sept. In late July he had sent Wellington a memorandum criticizing lord chancellor Brougham's bill to reorganize the Scottish exchequer court, which he considered a botch and a job for Abercromby.[50] In the House, 6 Oct. 1831, he questioned the leader of the Commons Lord Althorp about the measure, expressed dismay at the proposed abolition of the entire court and pressed for further inquiry by commission. Next day he divided the House unsuccessfully (31 95) against the second reading. As a former sheriff of Orkney, he was consulted by its Member George Traill, who was seeking to secure separate representation for the county, and who considered his obliging letter 'stating the objections to the junction' with Shetland to be 'very valuable'.[51]

Rae was 'ordered up' to London in early December 1831 and was present to vote for the second reading of the revised English reform bill on the 17th.[52] He voted against the enfranchisement of Tower Hamlets, 28 Feb., and the third reading, 22 Mar. 1822. Named to the select committee on the new Scottish exchequer court bill, 27 Jan., he secured the adoption of an instruction widening its remit, 31 Jan., and supported Clerk's attempt to add six Members to it, 2 Feb. When he proposed unsuccessfully to refer the bill back to a select committee, 30 May, he complained that three quarters of the members of the first one had been 'direct adherents of the government' and argued that many of the court's important duties could be redistributed. On 15 Feb. he called for the cholera prevention bill to be extended to Scotland if this was legally feasible; but when Jeffrey introduced a specifically Scottish measure later that day, he said that it would be 'the commencement of a compulsory system of poor laws in the parishes of Scotland'. Yet next day he said that the bill had not been brought in soon enough, as it had 'been known for some weeks that the disease is raging in Scotland'. He remained of the view that the problem should have been left to the Scottish privy council. He voted against the second reading of the malt drawback bill, 2 Apr. He made practical suggestions for registration of Scottish £10 voters, 4 June, and on the 6th persuaded Jeffrey to agree to an amendment to the machinery whereby three sheriffs were to be appointed to rule on appeals. He spoke against the annexation of part of Perthshire to Kinross-shire and the junction of Cromartyshire with Ross-shire and Nairnshire with Elginshire, 15 June. He divided against government on the Russian-Dutch loan, 12 July 1832.

It was later written of Rae that

> as a speaker, he never achieved any eminence; but he made up for want of the higher powers of oratory by a careful attention to the points and bearings of the subject ... which he always argued with great skill, and, above all, with clearness and impartiality. His delivery was very careful, and his language particularly correct ... In proportion as he wanted fire, animation, and ambition in style, he made up for their absence by a steady, persevering adherence to fact, and to a common sense practical mode of reasoning, which was much better adopted to the nature of his subjects.[53]

He failed to find a seat at the 1832 general election, but he was returned again for Buteshire in September 1833. Peel valued his unspectacular abilities, and made him lord advocate in both his administrations. He died in harness at his home near Edinburgh in October 1842.[54]

[1] *Gent. Mag.* (1843), i. 313; Lockhart, *Scott*, vi. 140. [2] NLS mss 11, f. 14. [3] NLS mss 11, ff. 14, 17, 24. [4] NLS mss 11, f. 19. [5] G.W.T. Omond, *Lord Advocates of Scotland* (1883), ii. 258-61. [6] Ibid. ii. 261-3. [7] Dorset RO F/BKL, Bankes jnl. 117 (15 May 1820). [8] *The Times*, 1 Feb. 1821. [9] HLRO, Hist. Coll. 379, Grey Bennet diary, 20. [10] *The Times*, 2 May 1820. [11] NAS GD23/6/573/2. [12] *The Times*, 9, 19 May 1821; Omond, ii. 267; *Cockburn Letters*, 30-31. [13] NLS mss 11, ff. 115-25. [14] *The Times*, 4 June 1822. [15] Macpherson Grant mss 489, G. Macpherson Grant to Lady Stafford, 18 Mar., Gower to Macpherson Grant [22 Mar. 1822]. [16] *The Times*, 24 July 1822. [17] Add. 52445, f. 88. [18] NAS GD51/5/522. [19] Omond, ii. 272-82; Bankes jnl 138 (25 June); Northants. RO, Agar Ellis diary, 25 June 1822. [20] *The Times*, 24 July 1822. [21] Omond, ii. 282-3; Add. 51586, Tierney to Lady Holland, 6 June 1823; *Cockburn Letters*, 87; NLS mss 24749, f. 30. [22] Lonsdale mss, Lowther to Lonsdale, 18 Mar. 1823. [23] Add. 40339, ff. 39-46, 50, 52, 59. [24] Add. 40339, f. 67. [25] *The Times*, 20 June 1823. [26] Ibid. 21 June 1823. [27] Add. 40339, ff. 82, 95. [28] *The Times*, 31 Mar. 1824. [29] Ibid. 15 May, 4 June 1824. [30] Omond, ii. 287. [31] NLS mss 11, f. 139. [32] Add. 40317, f. 46; 40339, ff. 180, 193. [33] Add. 40339, ff. 200-4. [34] *The Times*, 15, 21 Mar. 1826. [35] Ibid. 17 Mar. 1826. [36] Ibid. 13 May 1826. [37] *Edinburgh Evening Courant*, 3, 12 June, 6 July; Add. 51800, Lauderdale to Lady Holland, 2 June [1826]. [38] *Cockburn Letters*, 153, 157-8. [39] *The Times*, 12 June 1827. [40] NLS mss 11800, f. 16. [41] Lansdowne mss, Goderich to Lansdowne, 6 Sept. 1827; Add. 38750, ff. 280, 283. [42] Add. 38751, f. 9; NLS mss 11800, ff. 23, 26. [43] Add. 38752, f. 176. [44] NLS mss 11, ff. 192-204; Bessborough mss, Abercromby to Duncannon, 16 Feb. [1830]. [45] Omond, ii. 297; Wellington mss WP1/1124/4; *Ellenborough Diary*, ii. 303. [46] Wellington mss WP1/1124/24; 1125/31; 1131/4. [47] *Extraordinary Black Bk.* (1832), 564; Hatherton diary, 24 Nov. 1831. [48] PRO NI, Wellington mss T2627/3/2/296, Arbuthnot to Wellington, 10, 17, 19 Aug. 1831. [49] *Cockburn Mems.* 8-9. [50] Wellington mss WP1/1190/16. [51] Orkney Archives, Balfour mss D2/3/14, Traill to J. Balfour, 11 Dec. 1831. [52] *Cockburn Letters*, 359. [53] *Gent. Mag.* (1843), i. 313. [54] *The Times*, 22 Oct. 1842; *Oxford DNB*.

D.R.F.

RAINE, Jonathan (1763–1831), of 33 Bedford Row, Mdx.

ST. IVES	1802–1806
WAREHAM	1806–1807
LAUNCESTON	8 May 1812–1812
NEWPORT	1812–14 May 1831

bap. 21 Jan. 1763, 2nd s. of Rev. Matthew Raine (*d.* 1807) of Hartforth, Yorks., rect. of Kirkby Wiske, and Esther, da. of William Varey of Cumb.[1] *educ.* Eton 1776-82; Trinity Coll. Camb. 1782, fellow 1789; L. Inn 1785, called 1791. *m.* 24 June 1799, Elizabeth *née* Price of Knightsbridge, Mdx., *s.p. d.* 14 May 1831.

KC 8 Mar. 1816; bencher, L. Inn 1816, treas. 1821; solicitor-gen. co. pal. of Durham 1821-3; c.j. N. Wales circuit 1823-1830.

Raine, the son of a clergyman,[2] owed his legal preferment and political career largely to the patronage of the 2nd and 3rd dukes of Northumberland, whose shifting political allegiances he had been obliged to follow. In 1820 he was returned for Newport for the third time, on the 3rd duke's interest, after the candidates on a rival interest withdrew.[3] He continued to attend occasionally and gave silent support to Lord Liverpool's ministry. He voted in defence of their conduct towards Queen Caroline, 6 Feb., and against Catholic relief, 28 Feb. 1821. Having been appointed solicitor-general to the county palatinate of Durham he was granted an unspecified period of leave to go the northern circuit, 7 Mar. 1821. He divided against more extensive tax reductions, 11, 21 Feb., was again granted leave to go the circuit, 6 Mar., but returned to vote against the removal of Catholic peers' disabilities, 30 Apr. 1822. In March 1823 Liverpool explained Raine's appointment as a Welsh judge to the foreign secretary Canning by observing that 'his station and standing in the profession afforded a better security that his nomination would be less likely to provoke an inconvenient motion in Parliament ... than that of any other person', although he had received 'a full explanation of the contingency to which the appointment might possibly be subject'. This was a reference to the controversy over Welsh judges being allowed to sit in the Commons. In the event Raine was re-elected for Newport, despite a strong local challenge, but it was around this time that he 'retired from practice at the common law bar'.[4] He divided against repeal of the Foreign Enlistment Act, 16 Apr., and inquiry into delays in chancery, 5 June 1823. He presented a Newport petition for repeal of the coal duties, 20 Feb.,[5] and voted against the abolition of flogging in the army, 5 Mar. 1824. He divided for the Irish unlawful societies bill, 25 Feb., and against Catholic relief, 1 Mar., 21 Apr., 10 May 1825. He was returned unopposed for Newport at the general election of 1826.[6]

He continued to divide against Catholic relief, 6 Mar. 1827, 10 May 1828. He was granted three weeks' leave 'on urgent business, having sworn off', 29 Mar. 1827, and presented a Burford petition for repeal of the Small Notes Act, 2 June 1828. In February 1829 Planta, the Wellington ministry's patronage secretary, listed him as being 'with government' on Catholic emancipation, which reflected the fact that Northumberland had recently been appointed lord lieutenant of Ireland. Raine dutifully voted for the emancipation bill, 6, 30 Mar. 1829. Shortly after his unopposed return for Newport at the general election in 1830 his judicial position was abolished, and he was compensated with an annual pension of £1,000.[7] The ministry regarded him as one of their 'friends', and he voted with them in the crucial civil list division, 15 Nov. 1830. He divided against the second reading of the Grey ministry's reform bill, 22 Mar., and for Gascoyne's wrecking amendment, 19 Apr. 1831. He was returned unopposed for Newport at the ensuing general election, but died suddenly in May 1831.[8] He left all his property, apart from a few small bequests, to his wife, and instructed that on her death (which occurred in 1843) it should pass to his sister Esther; his personalty was finally sworn under £60,000.[9]

[1] IGI (Cumb., Yorks.). [2] Who named his wife and daughter in succession as the residuary legatees of his estate, which was sworn under £5,000. Raine was to receive £600 from the sale of stock on his mother's death (PROB 11/1471/991; IR26/130/247). [3] *R. Cornw. Gazette*, 11 Mar. 1820. [4] Add. 38193, f. 190; 40311, ff. 13-15; *R. Cornw. Gazette*, 22, 29 Mar. 1823; *Gent. Mag.* (1831), i. 476. [5] *The Times*, 21 Feb. 1824. [6] *West Briton*, 9, 16 June 1826. [7] Ibid. 7 Aug. 1830; W.R. Williams, *Hist. Great Sessions in Wales*, 27, 118-19. [8] *West Briton*, 6, 20 May 1831. [9] PROB 11/1787/355; IR26/1268/244.

T.A.J.

RAMSAY, Sir Alexander, 2nd bt. (1785–1852), of Balmain, Fasque, Kincardine.

KINCARDINESHIRE 1820–1826

b. 14 Feb. 1785, 1st s. of Alexander Burnett (afterwards Ramsay), adv., of Crathes Castle and Elizabeth, da. and coh. of Sir Alexander Bannerman, 4th bt., of Elsick. *m.* (1) 1 Aug. 1811, Jane (*d.* Aug. 1819), da. and coh. of Francis Russell of Blackhall, 3s. (1 *d.v.p.*) 2da.; (2) 26 Dec. 1822, Elizabeth, da. of William Maule*, 4s. 3da. *suc.* fa. as 2nd bt. 17 May 1810. *d.* 26 Apr. 1852.

Ramsay was descended from a cadet branch of an old Kincardineshire family, the Burnetts of Leys. His father Alexander, the second son of Sir Thomas Burnett, 6th baronet (*d.* 1783), was born in 1757 and called to the Scottish bar in 1779. He was sheriff of Kincardineshire from 1783 until 1806, when he succeeded as the younger brother of the heir of line to the Balmain estates of his cousin, Sir Alexander Ramsay Irvine, 6th baronet, Member for the county, 1765-8. He took the name of Ramsay in March 1806 and on 13 May received a baronetcy from the Grenville ministry, who regarded him as a political ally. He settled at Fasque, where he built a grandiose house at a cost of £30,000.[1] At the general election in October 1806 he offered for the county on the independent interest, unaware of the intention of the Foxite party manager William Adam†, who had a stake there, to stand in a bid to strengthen the ministry. It was with great reluctance that Ramsay eventually yielded to pressure from Adam, the prime minister and the prince of Wales to leave the way clear.[2] On his death in 1810 he was succeeded in the baronetcy by his 25-year-old eldest son and namesake, the subject of this biography, who was soon seen as the head of the county's independent interest; but their lack of stomach for a contest deterred him from challenging the wealthy Melvillite newcomer George Drummond in 1812 and 1818.[3] When Drummond announced his retirement at the 1820 dissolution Ramsay (who had lost his wife only six months previously) declared his candidature 'without pledging myself to support any particular party in Parliament'. He had two ministerialist rivals, James Farquhar*, former Member for Aberdeen Burghs, and Colonel Hugh Arbuthnott*, brother of the lord lieutenant, the 8th Viscount Arbuthnott.[4] As Lord Arbuthnott (on behalf of his brother, who was detained in France by illness) and Farquhar vied for the support of ministers, who initially stayed neutral, Ramsay was in a strong position, especially as Arbuthnott made it plain that he would rather see him returned than Farquhar.[5] At the end of the first week of March Arbuthnott withdrew his brother, but insisted on supporting Ramsay against Farquhar. On the 6th Ramsay went from Edinburgh to Granton to see Charles Hope†, lord president of the court of session (whom he did not know personally) and, as Hope reported to Lord Melville, the Liverpool ministry's Scottish manager, assured him

> that his political principles had been much misrepresented; that when a very young man, he had been induced to preside at one of Fox's dinners here, which he regretted, as he was far from wishing to go with his adherents in this country; that under present circumstances at least, he certainly should support government in every measure necessary for preserving the country from the attempts of the seditious and disaffected ... In short, if you do not get a determined partisan, you will get at least a supporter in this time of need. But from his whole conversation, and from his volunteering to come down to me to explain himself, I have little doubt that he only requires to be courted a little, and when he goes up to Parliament, if you and the ministers show him proper attention ... you will secure him.[6]

Melville was angry with Arbuthnott and felt that Farquhar must now be openly supported, but he told the lord advocate Sir William Rae* that if Ramsay acted up to his professions in the House the affair would not end too badly, and advised him, if Ramsay seemed sure of success, 'not ... to carry our hostility to such an extent as to leave him scarcely any other alternative than throwing himself into the ranks of the enemy'. Rae, who believed and convinced Melville that Arbuthnott and Ramsay had been in cahoots from the outset, remained 'very doubtful of ... Ramsay's politics', but went along with this.[7] In the event Ramsay defeated Farquhar by 12 votes in a poll of 52.[8]

Although he never joined Brooks's, he voted with the Whig opposition in the House, but he was a virtual cipher there after Easter 1821. He divided against Wilberforce's compromise resolution on the Queen Caroline affair, 22 June, and the appointment of the green bag committee on her conduct, 26 June 1820. He was in the minorities for economies in revenue collection, 4 July, and against the aliens bill, 7 July 1820. His only known vote in the parliamentary campaign on behalf of the queen in early 1821 was to deplore the omission of her name from the liturgy, 23 Jan. He voted to condemn the Allies' suppression of liberalism in Naples, 28 Feb., for repeal of the tax on husbandry horses, 5 Mar., and of the additional malt duty, 21 Mar., 3 Apr., and for inquiry into the revenue, 6 Mar. He divided for Catholic relief, 28 Feb. He was given six weeks' leave on urgent private business, 12 Apr. 1821. His only other known votes were for the remission of Henry Hunt's* gaol sentence, 24 Apr., parliamentary reform, 25 Apr., abolition of one of the joint-postmasterships, 2 May 1822, and repeal of the assessed taxes, 10 May 1824. He was granted three weeks' leave on private business, 17 Feb. 1825. He is not known to have spoken in debate, but he presented a Kincardineshire landowners' petition calling for 'economy and retrenchment in the expenditure of government' to relieve agricultural distress, 12 Mar. 1822.[9] He announced his 'determination of retiring' in December 1824 and duly did so at the 1826 dissolution, when Colonel Arbuthnott replaced him.[10]

Ramsay, who married as his second wife in 1822 a daughter of the zealous Foxite William Maule, died in Baker Street, London in April 1852. He was succeeded by his eldest son Alexander (1813-75), Conservative Member for Rochdale, 1857-9.

[1] *Fam. of Burnett of Leys* ed. J. Allardyce (New Spalding Club), 96-97, 101-2. [2] *HP Commons, 1790-1820*, ii. 547. [3] Ibid. ii. 548-9. [4] *Aberdeen Jnl.* 9, 16, 23 Feb. 1820. [5] NLS mss 11, ff. 6, 11, 17, 22, 28. [6] NLS mss 11, f. 32. [7] NLS mss 11, ff. 39, 44, 55, 62, 79. [8] *Aberdeen Jnl.* 5 Apr. 1820. [9] *The Times*, 13 Mar. 1822. [10] NAS GD51/1/198/12/38.

D.R.F.

RAMSAY, William Ramsay (1809–1850), of Barnton House, Edinburgh and Sauchie House, Stirling.

STIRLINGSHIRE 1831–1832

EDINBURGHSHIRE 1841–12 June 1845

b. 29 May 1809, o.s. of George Ramsay of Barnton and Hon. Jean Hamilton, da. of Robert, 8th Bar. Belhaven [S]. *educ.* Christ Church, Oxf. 1828. *m.* 4 Aug. 1828, Hon. Mary Sandilands, da. of James, 10th Bar. Torpichen [S], 1s. *suc.* fa. 1810. *d.* 15 Mar. 1850.

Ramsay was 'still an infant' when he inherited his father's estates, which 'popularly conferred on him the distinction of "the richest commoner in Scotland"'. He was 'widely known on the Turf for a considerable number of years'.[1] In 1831 he was invited to offer for Stirlingshire on the Tory interest, which was being organized by a relative, Thomas Stirling of Airth, and he was returned ahead of a reformer. He declared his determination to 'uphold unimpaired the institutions of the country', said he was 'free and unfettered from any pledges whatever' and claimed to be 'friendly to a fair, liberal, safe and equitable reform', but 'decidedly opposed' to the Grey ministry's 'altogether too sweeping and irrevocable' scheme.[2] He divided against the second reading of the reintroduced English reform bill, 6 July, to postpone consideration of Chippenham's inclusion in schedule B, 27 July, and against the third reading, 21 Sept. 1831. He seconded the motion to reject the second reading of the Scottish bill, 23 Sept., maintaining that it was 'the duty of everyone connected with Scotland ... to stand forward and manfully defend those rights and privileges which we have hitherto enjoyed'. The ministerial plan seemed 'calculated to create fresh disturbances and raise fresh clamours for reform' and he denied that it had the support of the Scottish people, most of whom were 'entirely ignorant' of its 'real nature'. He asserted that he was 'bound to no party and I trust shall always be independent', but he regarded the bill as the 'death warrant of the constitution of Britain'. He presented a petition from voters in the parish of Alloa against its inclusion in Clackmannanshire, 3 Oct. He presented a Stirlingshire petition against repeal of the drawback on malt, 11 Oct. He paired against the second reading of the revised reform bill, 17 Dec. 1831, and voted against the enfranchisement of Tower Hamlets, 28 Feb., and the third reading, 22 Mar. 1832. No other votes are known, and in July 1832 he announced that he would not stand at the forthcoming general election.[3] He sat as a Conservative for Edinburghshire, 1841-5.[4] He died in March 1850 and was succeeded by his only son Charles William Ramsay (1844-65), who died unmarried.

[1] *Gent. Mag.* (1850), i. 666. [2] Wellington mss WP1/1184/7; *Stirling Jnl.* 13 May 1831. [3] *Stirling Jnl.* 20 July 1832. [4] M. Stenton, *Who's Who of MPs, 1832-1885*, p. 323.

T.A.J.

RAMSBOTTOM, John (1778–1845), of Clewer Lodge and Woodside, Windsor, Berks.

NEW WINDSOR 14 Mar. 1810–8 Oct. 1845

bap. 5 Apr. 1778, 1st s. of John Ramsbottom, brewer and banker, of Windsor and w. Molly.[1] *educ.* Eton 1791. *m.* 21 May 1799,[2] Sophia Augusta Pryor of Portland Place, Mdx.,[3] 2s. 2da.; 1 illegit. da. *suc.* fa. 1826. *d.* 8 Oct. 1845.

Cornet 16 Drag. 1798, lt. 1799, ret. 1803; maj. commdt. Clewer vols. 1803.

Dep. chairman, Hope Life Insurance Co. 1827-43.

Ramsbottom, a partner with his father and William Legh in the Windsor brewery and bank at Thames Street, was again returned unopposed for the borough on the independent interest in 1820.[4] He was secure for life in the seat, in which he had succeeded his uncle, Richard Ramsbottom, the founder of the family's fortunes, in 1810; his apparently casual attitude to parliamentary attendance made no difference. When present, he continued in the independent ways which he had pursued in the House since 1812. He voted against the Liverpool government on the appointment of an additional Scottish baron of exchequer, 15 May 1820. At a Windsor meeting to vote a loyal address to the king, 1 Dec. 1820, he objected to its reference to the press as 'mercenary and corrupt' and had it toned down.[5] He did not attend the Berkshire meeting in support of Queen Caroline, 8 Jan. 1821, but he voted for restoration of her name to the liturgy, 26 Jan., 13 Feb., and in censure of ministers' conduct towards her, 6 Feb. He did not vote in the division on Catholic relief, 28 Feb. On the Grampound disfranchisement bill, 2 Mar., he was in Lord Milton's minority in favour of vesting the Leeds franchise in the ratepayers rather than the £10 householders. He voted for army reductions, 14 Mar., repeal of the malt duty, 3 Apr., and a curb on pensions on the Barbados defence fund, 24 May 1821. He divided for more extensive tax reductions to relieve distress, 21 Feb. 1822, parliamentary reform, 25 Apr., abolition of one of the joint-postmasterships, 2 May, a cut in diplomatic expenditure, 16 May, and repeal of the salt duties, 28 June 1822. He did not attend the county reform meeting, 27 Jan. 1823, and his only known vote in the ensuing session was against the appointment of a lieutenant-general of the ordnance in peace-time, 19 Feb. He voted for the abolition of army flogging, 5 Mar., inquiry into the state of Ireland, 11 May, and against the beer duties bill, 24 May 1824. He voted with government for the Irish unlawful societies bill, 25 Feb., and the duke of Cumberland's annuity, 10 June 1825. He divided for Catholic relief, 1 Mar., 21 Apr.,

10 May 1825. In early December that year news that the London bank of Williams, Burgess and Williams, on which Ramsbottom and Legh drew, had stopped payment caused consternation in Windsor. According to Charles Knight, editor of the *Windsor and Eton Express*, Ramsbottom, a man 'of unimpeached credit', and Legh hurried to London to take his advice. While Legh was sent back to Windsor to forestall the anticipated closure of the bank, Knight and Ramsbottom scoured the City in search of funds to prevent a 'fatal run' on it. At the office of the brewery they found a modest sum awaiting deposit in the London bank. Knight recalled:

> We decided upon a plan of action, the artifice of which was justified by the necessity of the case. I took my seat in a postchaise with my treasure – something less than a thousand pounds – and was whirled to Windsor in a couple of hours by four horses. As I changed horses at Hounslow, or stopped at turnpikes, I proclaimed, 'funds for the Windsor bank'. The news spread down the road ... I drove triumphantly into the yard of the bank, amidst the hurrahs of a multitude outside, to whom I had proclaimed my mission. There was a meeting at the same time taking place at the town hall, at which my townsmen entered into resolutions declaring their opinion of the solvency of the firm, and the necessity of not pressing upon them in the hour of difficulty. The bank was saved.[6]

Ramsbottom's only known vote in the 1826 session was for revision of the corn laws, 18 Apr.

After his return at the general election in June 1826 he defended his support for Catholic claims, which he had given 'conscientiously, not having been instructed by his constituents to the contrary'.[7] On the death of his father later that year he inherited an equal share in his property, which included personalty sworn under £80,000, with his younger brother James.[8] He did not vote in the division on Catholic relief, 6 Mar. 1827. He presented a Windsor Dissenters' petition for repeal of the Test Acts, 6 June 1827.[9] He voted for that measure, 26 Feb., but only paired for Catholic relief, 12 May 1828. He divided against the proposal to extend the East Retford franchise to the neighbouring hundred, 21 Mar., and for a pivot price of 60*s*. rather than 64*s*. to regulate corn imports, 22 Apr. 1828. Planta, the Wellington ministry's patronage secretary, expected him to vote 'with government' in favour of Catholic emancipation, and he duly did so, 6, 30 Mar. 1829. He voted for the transfer of East Retford's seats to Birmingham, 5 May 1829, Lord Blandford's parliamentary reform scheme, 18 Feb., the enfranchisement of Birmingham, Leeds and Manchester, 23 Feb., and Russell's reform motion, 28 May 1830. He divided against government on the Bathurst and Dundas pensions, 26 Mar., and the salary of the lieutenant-general of the ordnance, 29 Mar. He voted for Jewish emancipation, 17 May. He was in the minorities for attempts to restrict the proposed opening of the beer trade, 21 June, 1 July 1830.

At the general election of 1830 Ramsbottom boasted that he had 'always voted independently' and declared that he was 'still an advocate for reform, for moderate and rational reform, such a reform as had been well commenced in the last Parliament, and would, he trusted, be equally well continued in the next'. Soon afterwards he visited the continent.[10] Ministers listed him as one of the 'bad doubtfuls', and he voted against them on the civil list, 15 Nov. 1830. He was not at the Berkshire reform meeting of 17 Jan. 1831, but he voted for the second reading of the Grey ministry's reform bill, 22 Mar., and against Gascoyne's wrecking amendment, 19 Mar. 1831. At the ensuing general election he and his colleague, Edward Smith Stanley, the Irish secretary, were returned free of expense as reformers. On the hustings Ramsbottom said:

> For some years the Commons ... had not received the entire confidence of the people because it was felt that whatever it represented it did not represent the nation ... The seats in that House were in the hands of an imperious, overbearing, and reckless oligarchy ... who would soon take the power out of the people's hands unless the people took it out of theirs.

After calling for demonstrations of support for reform to strengthen the hands of the king and his ministers, he asserted that

> I shall pursue the same independent and undeviating course which I have hitherto endeavoured to tread. I shall neither look to the right nor to the left; I shall support measures and not men. As long as the present administration continue to advocate liberal principles, and act for the benefit of the people at large, they shall have my warm ... support.

In the county election he exerted his local influence in support of the reform candidates, and on the hustings nominated the veteran Whig sitting Member, Charles Dundas.[11]

Ramsbottom voted for the second reading of the reintroduced reform bill, 6 July, and against the adjournment, 12 July 1831. He was criticized in the *Express* for his failure to vote against the opposition proposal to use the 1831 census as the basis for disfranchisement; but he redeemed himself by voting steadily for the details of the schedules in late July and August, and, in particular, by having the 'manly independence' to vote against ministers for the disfranchisement of Saltash, 26 July.[12] He did likewise on an attempt to have Aldborough totally disfranchised, 14 Sept. In his only known contribution to debate before 1832, responding to allusions to 'the influence which the royal patronage exercises over the borough of Windsor', 2 Aug., he said that Smith Stanley, even though a member of the government, would 'never' have been returned there if he had not been an enthusiastic reformer. He voted for the passage of the bill, 21 Sept., and the second reading of the Scottish bill, 23 Sept. He was in both ministerial majorities on the Dublin election controversy, 23 Aug. He voted for the motion of confidence in the reform ministry, 10 Oct. 1831, and a week later chaired the Windsor public meeting, held in defiance of the borough authorities' original veto, to demonstrate continued support for the king, the government and reform. He pointed out that the bill had been defeated in the Lords by the bishops and recently ennobled Tory peers, while the ancient nobility had taken the popular side. Replying to a vote of thanks for his parliamentary conduct, he welcomed and encouraged the inhabitants' evident determination to assert themselves despite recent surreptitious attempts from the Castle to stifle the expression of political opinion in Windsor.[13] He voted for the second reading of the revised reform bill, 17 Dec. 1831, was a fairly steady supporter of its details, and divided for its third reading, 22 Mar. 1832. He was in the majority for the motion for an address asking the king to appoint only ministers who would carry the measure unimpaired, 10 May. His only other known votes in this period were against government on the Russian-Dutch loan, 26 Jan. (he paired with them in the divisions of 12 and 20 July), and with them on relations with Portugal, 9 Feb. On 28 Feb. 1832 he presented a petition from the licensed victuallers of Windsor for relief from their liability to make restitution for losses of guests' property.

Windsor was contested at the next four general elections, but Ramsbottom's return at the head of each poll was never in doubt.[14] He joined Brooks's in 1837. At around that time he disposed of the brewery and bank to Nevile, Reid and Company, having suffered a serious 'reverse of fortune'.[15] He died at the Albany in October 1845. By his will, a brief memorandum dated 2 Mar. 1844, he left items of silverware to his sons and residuary legatees, John Richard Sneyd and Somerville, and his married daughters, Mary Sophia Harcourt Riley and Susan Sophia Letitia Orwyn. He left £1,000 to Sarah Townsend, his illegitimate daughter, with remainder to her daughter Sarah Matilda. Whether this money materialized must be doubtful, for Ramsbottom's personalty was sworn under a paltry £800, and the word 'insolvent' was appended to the assessment of his estate in the death duty register.[16]

[1] IGI (London); PROB 11/1747/606. He was baptized at St. Martin-in-the Fields, Westminster. [2] *Reg. St. Mary le Bone, Mdx.* vi. 70. [3] She may have been the Sophia Pryor, da. of Daniel and Susannah, who was *bap.* at St. George, Hanover Square, 27 Aug. 1777 (IGI). Ramsbottom's wife died, 'in her 27th year', in the spring of 1804 (*Gent. Mag.* (1804), ii. 691). [4] *The Times*, 8 Mar. 1820. [5] Ibid. 5 Dec. 1820. [6] C. Knight, *Passages of a Working Life*, ii. 40-42; *Berks. Chron.* 17 Dec. 1825. [7] *Berks. Chron.* 17 June 1826. [8] PROB 11/1719/654; IR26/1101/1182. [9] *The Times*, 7 June 1827. [10] *Windsor and Eton Express*, 31 July, 28 Aug. 1830. [11] Ibid. 23, 30 Apr., 7 May; Warws. RO, Throckmorton mss 1998/Tribune/folder 16/31, Throckmorton to wife [27 Apr.]; *New Windsor Election, 1831*, pp. 11, 15-16; *Berks. Chron.* 9 May 1831. [12] *Windsor and Eton Express*, 6 Aug. 1831. [13] Ibid. 15, 22 Oct. 1831. [14] N. Gash, *Politics in Age of Peel*, 375-8. [15] *VCH Berks.* ii. 409. [16] *Gent. Mag.* (1845), ii. 647; PROB 11/2028/937; IR26/1719/937.

D.R.F.

RAMSDEN, John Charles (1788–1836), of Buckden and Newby Park, Yorks. and 6 Upper Brook Street, Mdx.

MALTON	1812–1831
YORKSHIRE	1831–1832
MALTON	8 Mar. 1833–29 Dec. 1836

b. 30 Apr. 1788, 1st s. of Sir John Ramsden†, 4th bt. (*d.* 1839), of Byram, Yorks. and Hon. Louisa Susan Ingram Shepherd, da. and coh. of Charles, 9th Visct. Irwin [S]. *educ.* Harrow 1798-1805. *m.* 5 May 1814, Hon. Isabella Dundas, da. of Thomas Dundas†, 1st Bar. Dundas, 2s. (1 *d.v.p.*) 3da. (2 *d.v.p.*). *d.v.p.* 29 Dec. 1836.

Lt.-col. commdt. Halifax regt. militia 1813.

Ramsden, whose family could trace their ancestry back to the fourteenth century in Huddersfield, which they practically owned, was again returned by his kinsman the 2nd Earl Fitzwilliam for his pocket borough of Malton at the 1820 general election. A regular attender, who rarely spoke, he continued to vote steadily with the Whig opposition to the Liverpool ministry on most major issues, including economy, retrenchment and reduced taxation.[1] He was granted a fortnight's leave following a family death, 28 June 1820. He divided for Catholic relief, 28 Feb. 1821 (as a pair), 1 Mar., 21 Apr., 10 May 1825. He voted for repeal of the additional malt duty, 21 Mar. 1821. He was appointed to the select committee on woollen cloth, 28 Mar., argued for a postponement of the third reading of the woollen cloth bill, 13 June 1821, and presented a Huddersfield petition against the free import, storage and re-export of woollens, 25 Apr. 1822.[2] In his first speech, 18 Apr. 1821, he contended that parliamentary reform would remove 'that steady band of placemen who came down to the House ready to vote away the liberties of the people'. He voted accordingly that day, and again, 9 May 1821, 25 Apr. 1822, 24 Apr. 1823, 27 Apr. 1826, and for reform of the Scottish representation, 2 June 1823, and of Edinburgh's, 26 Feb. 1824. On 21 Feb. 1822, when he voted for more extensive tax reductions, he deplored the current agricultural distress, saying that he 'could not support any set of ministers unless they greatly lessened the expenditure and agreed to such a reform of the ... Commons as would ensure amongst its Members a sympathy with the distress of the country at large'. He brought up multiple petitions for relief from the West Riding of Yorkshire, 26 Apr. He spoke against the Yorkshire polls bill, 2 May, presented a hostile petition from the county's freeholders, 13 May, and on its second reading, 7 June 1822, declared that he could 'perceive no benefit which the bill was likely to produce, but was confident that its effects would be mischievous'.[3] During the rumours of a dissolution in the autumn of 1825 speculation grew about the allocation of the two extra seats that Yorkshire had gained at the next election. On 6 Dec. Ramsden assured Fitzwilliam's son Lord Milton* that 'though we are all now thrown into a feverish state, yet it will abate and when the day of nomination comes all will depend on who has the *best pluck*'. Adding that his 'electioneering devil has risen within me', he promised to support Milton's candidacy along with that of Lord Morpeth*, although he stressed that the latter would need the backing of his uncle, the duke of Devonshire, and derided the Tories for lacking any substantial property in Yorkshire.[4] On 27 Dec. 1825 Milton advised Lord Althorp* that if Morpeth declined to stand, Ramsden or George Strickland* of Boynton would be ready to replace him.[5]

At the 1826 general election, however, Ramsden was again returned unopposed for Malton. He voted against the duke of Clarence's grant, 16 Feb., and for Catholic relief, 6 Mar. 1827. He voted for a 50*s.* duty on corn, 9 Mar., and increased protection for barley, 12 Mar. He was in the majority to go into committee on the spring guns bill, 23 Mar., and voted to postpone the committee of supply, 30 Mar. 1827. He divided for repeal of the Test Acts, 26 Feb., and presented a petition to that effect, 4 Mar. 1828. He voted against the extension of East Retford's franchise to the hundred, 21 Mar. He presented petitions for the abolition of slavery from Malton, 30 May, and Huddersfield, 2 June 1828. He voted for the Wellington ministry's concession of Catholic emancipation 6, 30 Mar., and to allow Daniel O'Connell to take his seat unhindered, 18 May 1829. He presented a Malton petition for repeal of the assessed taxes, 1 May, and voted to reduce the grant for the marble arch, 27 May 1829. He brought up a Malton petition for abolition of the death penalty in all cases except murder, 17 Mar., and one from Huddersfield complaining of distress, 23 Mar. 1830, when he called for a reduction of public expenditure 'in every department of state'. He voted steadily with the revived Whig opposition for economy and reduced taxation from that month onwards. He voted for Jewish emancipation, 5 Apr., 17 May. He presented petitions from Shipley against renewal of the East India Company's charter, 7 Apr., and from Wakefield praying that the assizes be held there, 8 Apr. His son John William died on 22 Apr., but he was present to vote for abolition of the lord lieutenancy of Ireland, 11 May, repeal of the Irish coal duties, 13 May, and parliamentary reform, 28 May. One of his daughters, Frances Margaret, died in June 1830 and he was abroad by the time of the dissolution, when it was widely expected that Milton would retire in his favour.[6] The arrival of Henry Brougham*, however, complicated matters and on 20 July Thomas Tottie, Ramsden's lawyer, advised Milton:

> When Sir John Johnstone* and [George] Strickland were with me last Thursday, several names were mentioned as candidates ... Mr. Ramsden was one intended to be proposed by them. I have heard in other quarters that Mr. Ramsden is expected to remain abroad until the election is over, and that Sir John Ramsden has declared that he will be at *no* expense, whether there be any foundation to these rumours I do not know.[7]

Milton asked his friend Henry Gally Knight* to start a requisition in favour of Ramsden, but Gally Knight was busy contesting St. Albans and advised Milton to try someone in Yorkshire.[8] Strickland told a Whig meeting in York, 23 July, that 'no person had a greater claim to the representation of the county than Mr. Ramsden', but admitted that the prospect of returning Brougham was too good to miss. When Charles Wood* proposed Ramsden no one seconded him and Edward Baines, editor of the Whig *Leeds Mercury*, warned that if the meeting decided in favour of Ramsden 'there would be an inevitable split of the liberal interest'. Daniel Sykes*, a leading East Riding Whig, and Strickland then asked Wood to withdraw Ramsden's nomination. Thomas Dundas, nephew of Ramsden's wife and Member for York, read out an address and letter from Ramsden, but concluded by saying that if he had been present to gauge the sense of the meeting, he would have withdrawn. Wood complied and Brougham was selected as the second Whig candidate.[9] Ramsden, who had hoped to return to

England on 30 July, only arrived on 3 Aug. 1830. By the time he reached London he found that he had been re-elected for Malton.[10]

He was, of course, listed by ministers as one of their 'foes' and he voted against them in the crucial division on the civil list, 15 Nov. 1830. He divided for the second reading of the Grey ministry's reform bill, 22 Mar., for which he received an address of thanks from his constituents, and against Gascoyne's wrecking amendment, 19 Apr. 1831.[11] At the ensuing dissolution he offered for Yorkshire with the backing of Milton. The *Leeds Mercury* observed that he had

> long been known to the county as a consistent reformer, a friend of economy and a staunch supporter of civil and religious liberty. His character is unimpeachable and his connections are amongst the most distinguished ornaments of the Yorkshire aristocracy.

In his farewell address to the electors of Malton he reiterated his support for the reform bill and criticized the transfer of the Grampound seats to Yorkshire, instead of Leeds, and the failure to give East Retford's to Birmingham.[12] He canvassed the West Riding thoroughly but was prevented by illness from covering the rest of the county. At the nomination he declared that while he was a friend of 'that pure religion, in which I have been brought up', he was 'not blind to the necessity of some reform in the church establishment of England', and argued for a reform of the tithe system, greater equality in the income of the episcopal sees and an increase in the income of the lower orders of the clergy, citing his support for Catholic relief. He attacked the critics of the reform bill, condemned the corn laws, and called for the abolition of slavery.[13] He was returned unopposed with three other reformers. Writing to Milton, 13 May 1831, he declared, 'I am overpowered with surprise and honour at the task which so suddenly and with so little trouble has befallen me'. Believing that the Whigs would have everything in Parliament 'practically nearly as much our own way', he added that 'it is high time to divide the county, for human strength is not sufficiently gifted to bear such an extensive and still increasing canvass as is becoming the fashion.'[14]

Ramsden voted for the second reading of the reintroduced reform bill, 6 July, and gave generally steady support to its details, though he was in the minority against Downton's total disfranchisement, 21 July 1831. Next day he argued that Hedon should remain in schedule A instead, 'for I believe that a more rotten or corrupt borough does not exist in the whole country'. That day he claimed that a Huddersfield petition presented by the radical Henry Hunt demanding universal suffrage, annual parliaments and the ballot was a forgery. Following the announcement, 6 Aug., that in considering the terms for the enfranchisement of Huddersfield, ministers intended to include the entire parish, as most of the town was owned by one person, namely Ramsden's father, Ramsden observed:

> I can only say that this property was not bought for the purposes of electioneering, for it has been in my family for a period of upwards of three centuries ... The influence I may derive from the property I hold will not be very great. I think that the bestowing the franchise on the large manufacturing towns is a most wise and beneficial measure, and I should regret if the influence of property were so great in any of these places as to prevent the just expression of the wishes of the constituency ... If the inhabitants of Huddersfield should do me the honour of electing anyone connected with me, I should feel the greatest happiness, but this can never result from any power I possess, for this bill ... most properly and effectually prevents this.

He had previously urged Lord John Russell to confine the franchise to the town, however, and when it was clear that it would be extended to the parish he wrote to Milton to seek his help in altering the terms, 23 Oct. Arguing that if the boundary could not be restricted to the town only, the suburb of Lockwood would be a suitable addition, he explained:

> It would never do to take in more of [the hundred of] Aldmondbury than Lockwood, for I am sorry to say there is not to be found so riotous and radical a population as that parish ... It really will be very absurd and troublesome to have to canvass Marsden, eight miles from Huddersfield, and all the other townships in the parish which lie in a moorish wild country and full of the wildest inhabitants unconnected with Huddersfield.

He added that he was anxious that the returning officer in each place should be a 'fixed known person' and that 'Aldborough and Northallerton ought to be in Schedule A, or B at least'.[15] He voted with ministers on the Dublin election controversy, 23 Aug. He was given a month's leave on account of illness in his family, 29 Aug. He divided for the passage of the reform bill, 21 Sept., and for the second reading of the Scottish measure, 23 Sept. He was again given a further month's leave, 26 Sept. 1831, and a second daughter died soon afterwards. Ramsden was absent from the division on the second reading of the revised reform bill, 17 Dec. 1831, but gave general support to its details, though he was in the minority of 32 against enfranchising £50 tenants-at-will, 1 Feb. 1832. He voted with ministers on relations with Portugal, 9 Feb., and defended mill owners in a discussion on factory reform, 20 Feb. When Morpeth presented a Huddersfield petition against the influence of the Ramsdens and praying for its extension into a larger two Member constituency, 5 Mar., Ramsden again denied that his family had any improper or controlling interest. He divided for the reform bill's third reading, 22 Mar. He was in the majority for the motion for an address calling on the king to appoint only ministers who would carry it unimpaired, 10 May, and endorsed a number of petitions for withholding supplies until it passed, 22 May. He voted in favour of making coroners' inquests public, 20 June 1832.

On 4 Aug. 1832 he informed Milton that his prospects at Huddersfield were poor, despite having many promises. He also feared that he would not be returned for a division of the county due to the voters' apathy over registering.[16] His apprehension was well founded and he was defeated in a contest for the North Riding at the 1832 general election. He was returned on a vacancy for Malton in 1833 and re-elected in 1835. After a long illness, he died *v.p.* in December 1836.[17] By his will, dated 10 July 1835 and proved under £25,000, 13 July 1837, his London house and Yorkshire estates at Arncliffe, Buckden, Kettlewell and Weddon passed to his wife, with reversion to his only surviving son John William Ramsden (1831-1914), who succeeded to the baronetcy in 1839.[18] Sir John was Liberal Member for Taunton 1853-7, Hythe 1857-9, the West Riding of Yorkshire, 1859-65, Monmouth, 1868-74, the Eastern Division of the West Riding, 1880-85, and Osgoldcross Division of the West Riding, 1885-6. He served as under-secretary for war in Lord Palmerston's* first ministry, 1857-8.

[1] *Black Bk.* (1823), 187; *Session of Parl. 1825*, p. 482. [2] *The Times*, 14 June 1821, 26 Apr. 1822. [3] Ibid. 3 May 1822. [4] Fitzwilliam mss 123/7. [5] Add. 76379. [6] Hull Univ. Lib. Hotham mss DDHO/8/5; *Ellenborough Diary*, ii. 313. [7] Fitzwilliam mss. [8] Wentworth Woodhouse mun. G2/11. [9] *Leeds Mercury*, 24 July 1830; Add. 51578, Lady Carlisle to Holland [1830]; Castle Howard mss, Johnstone to Carlisle, 23 July 1830. [10] *Leeds Mercury*, 9 Apr. 1831. [11] Fitzwilliam mss, W. Allen to Milton, 29 Mar. 1831. [12] *Leeds Mercury*, 9 Apr. 1831. [13] Ibid. 23, 27 Apr., 7 May 1831. [14] Fitzwilliam mss. [15] Wentworth Woodhouse mun. G83/143b. [16] Ibid. G9/2. [17] *Gent. Mag.* (1837), i. 318. [18] PROB 11/1882/561; IR26/1462/472.

M.P.J.C.

REID, Sir John Rae, 2nd bt. (1791–1867), of 8 Broad Street Buildings, Finsbury Circus, London and Ewell Grove, Surr.

DOVER	1830–1831
DOVER	1832–1847

b. 2 Dec. 1791, 1st s. of Sir Thomas Reid, 1st bt., merchant, of 3 Angel Court, Throgmorton Street, London and Elizabeth, da. and h. of John Looker Goodfellow of Newbury, Berks. *educ.* ?Eton 1808. *m.* 9 Sept. 1840, Maria Louisa, da. of Richard Eaton of Stetchworth Park, Cambs. 2s 1da. *suc.* fa. as 2nd bt. 29 Feb. 1824; mo. to Ewell Grove 1829. *d.* 30 July 1867.

Dir. Bank of England 1820-47, dep. gov. 1837-9, gov. 1839-41.

Reid's grandfather James Reid (*d.* 1775), the son of John Reid of Kirkmahoe, was a prominent merchant of Dumfries. His sons Thomas and Joseph, born in 1762 and 1772 respectively, entered the London commercial world. In about 1790 Thomas became a partner with John Irving* in the West India trading house of John Rae in Angel Court. The firm, which extended its operations to the East Indies, became known as Reid, Irving and Company, and from about 1799 to 1838 occupied premises in Broad Street Buildings. Thomas Reid was elected a director of the East India Company in 1803 and served as its forceful chairman in 1816 and 1821. He acquired Surrey estates at Ewell and Woodmanstone and also owned a 'small landed property' at Greystone Park, Dumfriesshire.[1] In 1819, he deplored 'the infamous machinations of the disaffected', but at the same time urged the Liverpool ministry to relieve the 'serious and grievous distresses ... felt by the poor operatives in manufacturing and other districts' by repealing the taxes on leather, malt and salt and replacing them with one on '*realized* property, not meddling with capital in trade or professional income because they are in a state of transition'. He also advocated statutory wage regulation, 'for whatever Mr. Malthus and other philosophers may say, every man has a right to live'.[2] A year later he exhorted Lord Liverpool to counter the 'daily increasing' threat of sedition by 'calling out and encouraging volunteer yeomanry corps in much greater numbers' and to postpone Queen Caroline's trial until tranquillity had been restored.[3] He was in pursuit of a baronetcy from at least 1809, when he renewed his application after letting it lapse for a while in deference to the 'turmoil' caused by radical attacks on public 'profusion'. His ambition was not gratified until late 1823, and within four months he was dead, 'from the effects of a paralytic attack'.[4] By his will, dated 25 Aug. 1822, he left £1,000 and a life annuity of £2,500 to his wife; £10,000 to his brother; £20,000 to his daughter Harriet Lempriere; £7,000 to his grandson Charles Sandford, on whom he entailed his West Indian property, and £5,000 to Charles's brother Thomas. His personal estate was sworn under £400,000. He devised Woodmanstone to his younger son George Reid (1800-55) and the Dumfriesshire estate to the elder, John Rae Reid, who was only to take possession of Ewell Grove on the death of his mother (which occurred five years later). He considered that any comparative loss suffered by John on account of his mother's life interest would be 'amply' compensated for by 'the profits that have accrued to him from his having been so long a partner in the house of business'.[5]

At the general election of 1830 Sir John Rae Reid, a director of the Bank of England for ten years, stood for Dover with the backing of the premier the duke of Wellington in his capacity as lord warden of the Cinque Ports. Although he 'expressed his intention of standing upon independent principles, and would pledge himself to no party', it was clear that his politics were 'ministerial'. When smeared as 'a large slave holder', he issued an immediate denial, explaining that he had nothing more than 'a temporary interest as mortgagee of an estate in the West Indies'. He promised to give the abolition question his 'attentive consideration' when he judged that the time was ripe. He was returned in second place after a contest and survived a petition.[6] Ministers of course numbered him among their 'friends', and he was in their minority on the civil list, 15 Nov. 1830. Reid, who is not known to have spoken in debate, declined to support the Dover petition in favour of the Grey ministry's reform bill: the measure was, he told his constituents, 'of too sweeping a nature to receive his support', though he claimed to be 'friendly to reform' in principle.[7] He divided against the second reading, 22 Mar., presented a hostile petition from Dover out-voters, 15 Apr., and was in the opposition majority for Gascoyne's wrecking amendment, 19 Apr. 1831. At the ensuing general election he started again for Dover, but was forced to withdraw by what he admitted was a 'strong ... bias ... in favour of the measure of reform' among the electors.[8]

Reid continued to cultivate the borough and fought successful contests there in 1832 and at the next three general elections. His firm, which was located from 1838 at 16 Tokenhouse Yard and had a branch in Liverpool, failed for £1,500,000 on 17 Sept. 1847. While its assets were nominally greater than its liabilities, they were not very liquid, being mostly tied up in property in the West Indies and Mauritius; and it was over nine months before a dividend of 1*s.* 6*d.* was paid.[9] Reid died 'suddenly' in July 1867.[10] By his will, dated 4 Dec. 1855, 6 Nov. 1867, he confirmed the settlement of Ewell Grove on his male issue and devised to his daughter Louisa Wilde a life interest in its rents. He was succeeded in turn by his sons John Rae Reid (1841-85) and Henry Valentine Reid (1845-1903), on whose death the baronetcy became extinct.

[1] *Scott Corresp.* ed. C.H. Philips (Cam. Soc. ser. 3. lxxiv), 419; Philips, *E.I. Co.* 337-9; *Surr. Arch. Coll.* xlviii (1948), 14; PROB 11/1684/245. [2] Add. 38280, f. 108. [3] Add. 38287, f. 231. [4] Add. 38243, f. 123; 38296, ff. 341, 354; *Gent. Mag.* (1824), i. 646. [5] PROB 11/1684/245; 11/1752/106; IR26/113/1318; *Gent. Mag.* (1829), i. 285. [6] *Kent Herald*, 8, 22 July, 5 Aug. 1830. [7] *Kentish Chron.* 15, 22 Mar., 5 Apr. 1831. [8] *Kentish Gazette*, 26 Apr.; *Kent Herald*, 28 Apr., 5, 12 May 1831. [9] *Macaulay Letters*, iv. 335-6; *London Gazette*, 10 Aug. 1847, 5 May 1848; *The Times*, 18 Sept., 11 Oct. 1847; W. Marston Acres, *Bank of England from Within*, ii. 506, 625; *Overstone Corresp.* i. 394; D.M. Evans, *Commercial Crisis* (1849), pp. xxi-xxv. [10] *Gent. Mag.* (1867), ii. 391.

D.R.F.

REYNOLDS MORETON, Hon. Henry George Francis (1802–1853), of Lasborough, nr. Tetbury, Glos. and 15 South Audley Street, Mdx.

GLOUCESTERSHIRE 1831–1832

GLOUCESTERSHIRE EAST 1832–1834

b. 8 May 1802, 1st s. of Thomas, 4th Bar. Ducie, and Lady Frances Herbert, da. of Henry Herbert†, 1st earl of Carnarvon. *educ.* Eton 1814; Trinity Coll. Camb. 1820. *m.* 29 June 1826, Hon. Elizabeth Dutton, da. of John, 2nd Bar. Sherborne, 1s. (1 *d.v.p.*) 4da. *suc.* fa. as 2nd earl of Ducie 22 June 1840. *d.* 2 June 1853.

Ld. in waiting July 1846-Dec. 1847; charity estates commr. 1849.

Maj. N. Glos. militia 1835.

Reynolds Moreton, whose family had been established in Gloucestershire since the seventeenth century, was renowned as a 'follower of the hounds' and frequenter of 'fashionable circles'.[1] He joined Brooks's Club, 11 Feb. 1824, made his first public appearance in the county in 1826, when he nominated the sitting Whig Member Sir Berkeley William Guise, and repeated this service in 1830.[2] He took a prominent part in the county meeting on reform, 17 Mar. 1831, when he dismissed the 'silly ... groundless' claims that the Grey ministry's bill would undermine traditional institutions and maintained that its purpose was merely to 'correct the abuses which had crept into the government' and 'let the fabric of the constitution rest firm, fair, and glorious on the same solid basis in which it was at first reared'.[3] He accepted a requisition to offer at the ensuing general election in conjunction with Guise, and was returned unopposed after the retirement of the Tory sitting Member. He declared that he supported reform 'because the interests and pockets of the people have been too long at the mercy of those who have only represented their own interests', expressed confidence that once the bill was passed 'the country will be represented by men of integrity' and hoped 'the system of bribery will ... receive a death blow'.[4]

He confirmed Guise's opinion that it was desirable to re-establish local courts in the Forest of Dean, 27 June 1831. He divided for the second reading of the reintroduced reform bill, 6 July, and generally supported its details, though he voted against giving borough freeholders the right to vote in counties, 17 Aug., and for Lord Chandos's clause to enfranchise £50 tenants-at-will, 18 Aug., and the transfer of Aldborough from schedule B to A, 14 Sept. He divided for the bill's passage, 21 Sept., the second reading of the Scottish bill, 23 Sept., and Lord Ebrington's confidence motion, 10 Oct. He attended the county meeting to petition the Lords for reform, 28 Sept., when he advised against 'any act of disaffection' and promised that 'if this bill should not pass he would come down again immediately to ask his constituents to petition the throne for a creation of new peers'.[5] He voted in the minorities against the grant for Oxford and Cambridge professors' salaries, 8 July, and the quarantine duties, 6 Sept. He opposed Hunt's suggestion that restrictions should be placed on the right of small farmers to appoint gamekeepers, 8 Aug. He voted to punish only those guilty of bribery at the Dublin election and against the censure motion on the Irish administration, 23 Aug., and was in the minority for issuing the Liverpool writ, 5 Sept. He divided for the second reading of the revised reform bill, 17 Dec. 1831, supported its details, the third reading, 22 Mar., and Ebrington's motion for an address asking to king to appoint only ministers committed to carrying an unimpaired measure, 10 May 1832. On 22 June he moved an amendment to the boundaries bill against the 'very injudicious substitution' of Thornbury for Wotton-under-Edge as the nomination place for West Gloucestershire, and complained about the underhand way in which the change had been made; he was defeated by 83-54, acting as a teller. He voted with the minority that day for another amendment to the bill regarding Stamford's boundaries. He divided with ministers on the Russian-Dutch loan, 26 Jan., 12 July, and relations with Portugal, 9 Feb. He voted in the minorities to omit the reference to Providence in the Scottish cholera precautions bill, 16 Feb., and for inquiry into the Peterloo massacre, 15 Mar., dismissing the claim that too much time had elapsed since the event as 'no argument whatsoever. Murder was committed'. That day he presented a Gloucestershire woollen manufacturers' petition against the factory bill. He was presumably the 'Hon. H. Mortimer' who voted against postponing the Irish tithes bill, 13 July 1832.

At the general election later that year Reynolds Moreton was returned for East Gloucestershire in second place behind Guise, which he proclaimed a triumph for the 'cause of freedom and independence'.[6] He sat as an advocate of 'Whig principles ... in favour of the immediate abolition of slavery and the ballot' until his retirement in 1834.[7] He succeeded to his father's title and estates in 1840[8] and became an 'eminent agriculturist', promoting scientific methods of farming and stockbreeding, manufacturing new agricultural implements and advocating repeal of the corn laws. The 'man of pleasure' also became a 'lover of God', furnishing a fine 'example of spiritual regeneration'; he was a 'zealous promoter of temperance' and a 'prominent member of the Evangelical Alliance'.[9] He died in June 1853 and was succeeded by his son Henry John (1827-1921), Liberal Member for Stroud, 1852-3, and then by his fourth son Berkeley Basil (1834-1924).

[1] *Von Neumann Diary*, i. 239; *Gent. Mag.* (1853), ii. 87. [2] *Gloucester Jnl.* 19 June 1826, 7 Aug. 1830. [3] Ibid. 19 Mar. 1831. [4] Ibid. 23, 30 Apr., 7, 14 May 1831. [5] Ibid. 1 Oct. 1831. [6] Ibid. 21 July, 22 Dec. 1832. [7] *Dod's Parl. Companion* (1833), 141. [8] The will was proved under £70,000 (PROB 11/1937/829; IR26/1544/846). [9] *Gent. Mag.* (1853), ii. 87; Glos. RO D2698/2/27, 'The late earl of Ducie' (anon. pamphlet); J. Stratford, *Great and Good Men of Glos.* 319-34.

T.A.J.

RICARDO, David (1772–1823), of Gatcombe Park, Minchinhampton, Glos. and 56 Upper Brook Street, Grosvenor Square, Mdx.[1]

PORTARLINGTON 20 Feb. 1819–11 Sept. 1823

b. 18 Apr. 1772, 3rd s. of Abraham Ricardo (*d.* 1812), stockbroker, of Bury Street, London and Abigail, da. of Joseph Delavalle, tobacco merchant, of London. *educ.* Talmud Tora, Amsterdam 1783-5. *m.* 20 Dec. 1793, Priscilla Ann, da. of Edward Wilkinson, apothecary, of Bow, Mdx., 3s. 5da. (1 *d.v.p.*). *d.* 11 Sept. 1823.

Sheriff, Glos. 1818-19.

1st lt. Loyal Lambeth inf. 1798; capt. Tower Hamlets vols. 1803.

Ricardo was a short, weedy man with a squeaky voice. A Jew who had abandoned his faith for Unitarianism (though he was probably agnostic), and a retired stockbroker who purchased landed estates in four counties, he was the founder of the classical theory of political economy. He was a disciple of Bentham and a close friend of James Mill, who egged him on in politics; and during his short parliamentary career he was the leading spokesman of the Utilitarians on economic issues.[2] By 1820, he had to his credit, through his writings and his verbal evidence before the 1819 committee on the resumption of cash payments, the major single contribution to the decision to make gold ingots rather than coins the security for bank notes. In the wider sphere, his ideas on economic policy as set out in his *Principles of Political Economy* (1817), at the core of which was his labour theory of value, had a considerable influence on the thinking of ministers confronted with the task of managing the post-war national economy.[3] On the other hand, he was regarded by many politicians as a rigid theorist with little grasp of reality, an impression which his advocacy in December 1819 of a capital levy to pay off the national debt only strengthened.[4] An unshakeable conviction of the pressing need for radical parliamentary reform was at the heart of his political philosophy. A conscientious and diligent Member, with a record of attendance second to none, he sided on most issues with the advanced wing of opposition, though he regarded himself as independent.[5]

In early January 1820 Ricardo flattered himself that 'political economy is making progress in this country' and that 'every day correct principles advance'. His friend John Louis Mallet dined with him at this time and assessed his virtues and defects:

> It is impossible to be in company with Ricardo and not to admire his placid temper, the candour of his disposition, his patience and attention, and the clearness of his mind; but ... he meets you upon every subject that he has studied *with a mind made up*, and opinions in the nature of mathematical truths. He spoke of parliamentary reform and ballot as a man who would bring such things about, and destroy the existing system tomorrow, if it were in his power, and without the slightest doubt on the result ... It is this very quality of the man's mind, his entire disregard of experience and practice, which makes me doubtful of his opinions on political economy. His speech on paying off the national debt has very much damaged him in the House of Commons.

Ricardo dismissed as nonsense a report that he was to stand for Gloucestershire at the 1820 general election, when he came in again for Lord Portarlington's pocket borough, for which he had paid £4,000 for a four-year term, in addition to lending the proprietor £25,000 on mortgage at six per cent, in 1819. He thought that 'whether the ministers have a majority of 200, 100 or 50' would 'not ... in any degree affect the important questions about which the country should be most particularly solicitous', especially that of agricultural protection, on which he was determined to resist the expected demands of the country gentlemen for an increase.

Ricardo, whose married daughter, Fanny Austin, died the month after the election, seconded and voted for Hume's motion for civil list accounts, 3 May 1820.[6] He voted against government on the civil list, 5, 8 May; the additional Scottish baron of exchequer, 15 May; the aliens bill, 1 June, 7 July; inquiry into Anglo-Irish trade and reduction of the standing army, 14 June; the barrack establishment, 16 June, and economies in revenue collection, 4 July. On the London merchants' petition for a relaxation of restrictions on commerce, 8 May, the presentation of which he had anticipated with pleasure, he applauded its 'sound as well as liberal principles' and the countenance given to them by Robinson, president of the board of trade. While he admitted the obstacles to the attainment of more open trade, he said there was no reason to 'make every mischievous system perpetual' and called for a gradual progression towards commercial liberalism. At the same time, he questioned the validity of Robinson's reservations about the corn laws, arguing that agriculture was not uniquely burdened by taxes. Later that day he insisted that Alexander Baring had exaggerated the extent of the depreciation of the currency in consequence of cash resumption. He dismissed as misguided agriculturists' demands for increased protection, 12, 25 May: reducing the price of corn was 'the first step to that great remedy, the making labour productive'. He spoke at length in the same terms against Sumner's motion for inquiry into agricultural distress, 30 May, when he said that 'this would be the happiest country in the world, and its progress in prosperity would be beyond the power of imagination to conceive, if we get rid of the two great evils, the national debt and the corn laws'. Privately, however, he feared that no plan for discharging the debt would be taken seriously, for 'men do not like to make an immediate sacrifice for a future good'. His technical theoretical argument against the need for national self-sufficiency in corn production prompted Henry Brougham* to observe that Ricardo had addressed the problem 'as if he had dropped from another planet'.[7] He objected to export bounties as a 'bribe' to foreign merchants 'to take goods off our hands which we could not otherwise manufacture with profit', 25 May.[8] He advocated repeal of the Irish Union duties, 2 June, and welcomed government's proposals for their progressive diminution as a step in the right direction, 8 June. He approved the terms of Vansittart's loan contract to raise £5,000,000 by annuities, 9 June, but was generally critical of his policy of public borrowing, as he was again, 19, 21 June, when he deplored the 'alarming deficiency upon the consolidated fund'.[9] He opposed Maxwell's motion for inquiry into means of relieving distressed cotton weavers, 29 June:

He conceived the duty of government to be, to give the greatest possible development to industry. This they could only do by removing the obstacles which had been created ... If government interfered, they would do mischief and no good.

The session left him with a sense of frustration, which was heightened by Baring's pointed failure to name him to his select committee on foreign trade, 5 June, as he told his friend and acolyte John McCulloch:

You are mistaken in thinking that I could be of use in Parliament by bringing forward the question of free trade with France. In the first place I have not talents for such an undertaking, and in the second I am treated as an ultra reformer and visionary on commercial subjects by both agriculturists and manufacturers.

He confessed five weeks later that he was 'more than usually daunted by observing that on every point where an abuse is to be got rid of there are such powerful interests to oppose, who never fail of making the worse appear the better reason'.[10] In the late summer of 1820 his article for the *Encyclopaedia Britannica* on the 'Funding System' was published.[11]

Ricardo had voted with opposition in the divisions of 22 and 26 June 1820 on the Queen Caroline affair; and in the autumn he deplored the 'impolicy and inexpediency' of the government's prosecution of her, merely to gratify the 'resentment and hostility' of the king. After due consideration, he declined Mill's offer to promote his election as a director of the East India Company, which would

not contribute to my happiness. You are mistaken in supposing that because I consider life on the whole as not a very desirable thing to retain after 60, that therefore I am discontented with my situation, or have not objects of immediate interest to employ me. The contrary is the case ... I am led to set a light value on life when I consider the many accidents and privations to which we are liable ... I have already lost the use of one ear, completely, and am daily losing my teeth ... I have not ... seriously quarrelled with life; I am on very good terms with it, and mean while I have it to make the best of it; but my observation of the loss of esteem and interest which old people generally sustain ... convinces me that general happiness would best be promoted if death visited us on an average at an earlier period than he now does. If I were an East India director I should be kept from my family more than I now am. I should not be able to absent myself from London for six months together as I now do.

He rejoiced in the abandonment of the bill of pains and penalties and was full of 'indignation against all the queen's persecutors', who had forced her to set herself up as 'the rallying point of the discontented and disaffected'. While he did not seriously expect a change of government, he hoped the Whigs might be given a chance to show what they could do: if, as he anticipated, they failed to implement a significant measure of reform, at least 'the eyes of the public would be opened, and they would know that the means for good government must be sought in another direction and could only be obtained by their own strenuous exertions'. At bottom, the unreformed representative system was the chief obstacle to improvement:

What ministers, with the present constitution of the House of Commons, can succeed in sweeping away many of our commercial restraints, particularly the greatest, the restraints on the importation of corn? What ministers will dare to encounter our financial difficulties, in the only way in which they should be met, or will seriously commence the work of retrenchment in our expenses? We may probably find men who will remove the disabilities from the Roman Catholics, and make some amendments in our criminal laws, but this will be all.

Ricardo, who was 'exceedingly agreeable' to Maria Edgeworth when she met him at Christmas 1820, turned down a proposal from Lord Portarlington to extend the tenure of his seat in return for another cash payment and an increase in the loan. He attended the Gloucestershire meeting to express support for the queen, 30 Dec. 1820. He found its proceedings 'tame and insipid' and 'stoutly refused to second the address', which he thought did not go far enough; but having agreed to move thanks to Lords Ducie and Sherborne, he spoke

half a dozen sentences in favour of reform ... and endeavoured to impress on the meeting that most of our grievances were occasioned by the bad constitution of the House of Commons, and the little sympathy which did or could exist between such a body and the people. I was listened to with attention, and was cheered by the audience below the upper classes, and even amongst the higher ranks I am sure there were many agreeing with me.

Ricardo's politics were anathema to the duke of Beaufort, lord lieutenant of Gloucestershire, who kept him off the commission of the peace.[12]

He voted silently against ministers on the queen's case in January and February 1821. Curiously, his name did not appear in the list of those who divided for Catholic relief, 28 Feb., although he was present at the debate and expressed the private opinion that 'no reasonable man can apprehend danger to the United Kingdom' from conceding Catholic claims in Ireland; presumably there was an oversight on the part of the tellers or the reporters. He was a dedicated supporter of the opposition campaign for economy, retrenchment and reduced taxation throughout the session, though he was not listed in the minority for Hume's general motion of 27 June. He voted for repeal of the additional malt duty, 14 Feb., 21 Mar., 3 Apr., and on 5 Apr. spoke and voted for repeal of the tax on agricultural horses, 'not because it was in itself a bad tax, or pressed with peculiar hardship on the landed interest, but with a view of compelling the observance of strict economy in the administration of government'. He voted with opposition in support of the liberal movements in Naples, 21 Feb., and Sicily, 21 June, and for inquiry into the administration of justice in Tobago, 6 June. He divided for repeal of the Blasphemous and Seditious Libels Act, 8 May, inquiry into the Peterloo massacre, 16 May, and abolition of the death penalty for forgery, 25 May, 4 June 1821.

On the eve of the session Ricardo had told McCulloch that 'if the House will listen to me, and my courage do not fail me, I will take the first good opportunity of saying something on the injurious effects of the corn laws on the farmers'. He did so on the presentation of the Birmingham merchants' petition complaining of distress, 8 Feb., when he disputed Baring's contention that the alteration in the currency was to blame and argued against his call for the adoption of a bimetallic standard: 'the House listened to me with great attention', he thought, and the radical Whig Henry Grey Bennet* considered his speech 'a most able one'.[13] He said that the bill to regulate the corn averages would raise the import price and that the only remedy for distress was 'the total repeal of the corn laws', 26 Feb. On 7 Mar. he opposed the appointment of a select committee, which would 'look for relief to restrictions upon importation'. At the same time, he admitted the impossibility of moving to free trade overnight and suggested that a countervailing duty be imposed on imports to compensate domestic producers for any peculiar burdens of taxation which could be proved to exist. He was named to the committee, and in the ensuing weeks effectively exerted himself on it in support of free trade ideas. Ricardo, an economic optimist, thought that 'the generality of people', including the parliamentary opposition, 'undervalue the resources of a great nation'; and he clearly perceived his own role on the committee, where, as he told Mallet, he was given his head by most of the other members, who 'look upon him as a mere theorist, but ... are very civil and allow him to take his own course with a view to establishing his principles by evidence':

> I have worked very hard ... and I hope not without effect in correcting mistaken principles. We have had many farmers before us who have given a sad but I believe a true picture of the great prevalence of distress. These farmers ... were all for protecting duties, amounting almost to the prohibition of foreign corn. It was my business to show how little they were qualified to be advisers on this important question, by exposing their ignorance of the first principles which should guide our judgements.

He thought that he and Huskisson, a member of the board of trade, who gave him useful support, had successfully demonstrated the wrong-headedness of Attwood's currency theories, though Attwood himself came away with quite the contrary impression. He reported that the country gentlemen on the committee were 'all as dull as beetles, whilst Huskisson and Ricardo are as sharp as *needles* and as active as bees'.[14] In the House, 31 May, Ricardo exonerated the government and his fellow committee members from the charge of creating 'unnecessary delay' in the production of the report.[15] This document, which was drawn up by Huskisson, rejected the arguments that taxation or deflation was responsible for agricultural distress and recommended an open trade in corn subject to a moderate fixed duty, though it fell short of suggesting any immediate action to modify the corn laws in the manner desired by Ricardo. He was largely satisfied with it and with his own efforts in bringing it about, notwithstanding its definition of his notion of the countervailing duty as compensation for the differences between domestic and foreign production costs. He told McCulloch, 'It is better than could be expected, and I flatter myself there is enough of good about it to show the fallacies which we could not expunge from it'. He praised Huskisson, who was 'for establishing the trade on the most free and liberal foundation', but he noted that there was a basic difference between them: 'he would uphold agriculture permanently to its present height', while 'I would reduce it gradually to the level at which it would have been if the trade had been free'. Although the report was presented too late to be acted on that session, it effectively determined future government policy on the corn laws, and was strongly influenced by Ricardo's theory of diminishing returns, which led him to advocate decultivation of marginal land and free trade to stimulate foreign demand for British manufactures.[16]

He voted against renewal of the sugar duties, 9 Feb., and objected to the higher duty on East as opposed to West Indian produce, 4 May 1821. He opposed the timber duties, 9 Feb., 27 Mar.,[17] 5 Apr., when he argued that it was nonsense to 'take the worst timber at the dearest rate' for the sake of protecting the American trade: 'wrong notions of commercial policy had too long prevailed; and now that the country had begun to recognize sounder principles, the sooner they acted upon them the better'. Privately, he was not without hope that this 'stand for good principles' had been beneficial. He admitted that as long as the West Indian cotton trade was treated as a monopoly, government was bound to indemnify the producers for the restriction of their market, 25 June; but he 'complained altogether of the existence of the restrictive system'. At the close of the session he told one of his correspondents that he believed that ministers

> view these questions in their true light and would make great improvements in our commercial code if they were not thwarted and opposed by the narrow and selfish policy of the particular interests which are so powerfully exerted in the House of Commons to check improvement and support monopolies.

He spoke and voted for Maberly's motion for the remission of £2,000,000 in taxes, 6 Mar., and in passing attacked the sinking fund, as he did again when reviewing Vansittart's budget statement, 1 June 1821. On 23 June he advocated a supreme effort to get rid of the national debt.[18] The government's decision to comply with the desire of the Bank of England to scrap the plan to found the currency on ingots and to bring forward the time for the resumption of cash payments, in terms of gold coin, to May 1821, irritated Ricardo, and put him on the defensive against the currency reformers, as he was blamed for the consequences – an appreciation greater than that which he had predicted – of actions for which he was not personally responsible. He opposed Baring's call for further inquiry, 19 Mar.; told Attwood that 'if the Bank, instead of buying, had sold gold, as he recommended, the effect would have been very different from what it was at present', 9 Apr., and on the third reading of the cash payments bill, 13 Apr., again blamed the Bank for their mismanagement. In private, he hoped that the matter had now been laid to rest, but he remained scathing in his contempt for the authorities of the Bank:

> I very much regret, that in the great change we have made, from an unregulated currency, to one regulated by a fixed standard, we had not more able men to manage it than the present Bank directors. If their object had been to make the revulsion as oppressive as possible, they could not have pursued measures more calculated to make it so ... They are a very ignorant set.[19]

Ricardo welcomed Onslow's attempt to repeal the usury laws, which 'occasioned inconvenience, but did no good', 12 Apr. 1821. He supported Lambton's parliamentary reform scheme, 18 Apr., but regretted its omission of provision for the secret ballot, 'a greater security for the full and fair representation of the people than any extension of the elective franchise'. He voted for Russell's reform motion, 9 May, and for reform of the Scottish county representation the following day. He thought that Scarlett's poor laws amendment bill would benefit the poor by reducing the supply of labour below the demand, 8 May. He said that it was 'idle' to legislate against the ill-treatment of horses, as Martin proposed, 1 June, if the barbarities routinely perpetrated in hunting and fishing were to be ignored. He expressed willingness to support the grant of £6,000 a year to the duke of Clarence to put him on the same footing as his brothers, 18 June; but later that day he voted to reduce the sum by £2,500 and to omit any payment of arrears. In April 1821 he had become a founder member of the Political Economy Club.

At the end of August 1821, Ricardo commented to Mill that the Whigs

> are an inconsistent set of people – they are the loudest in their complaints of the bad measures which are pursued by government, and yet the opposers of every scheme which shall afford us a chance of obliging the government to pursue none but good measures. The only prospect we have of putting aside the struggle which they say has commenced between the rich and the other classes, is for the rich to yield what is justly due to the other classes, but this is the last measure which they are willing to have recourse to.

At the same time, he was 'startled at the extent' of Mill's proposition, in his essay on *The Liberty of the Press*, 'respecting the liberty to be allowed of exhorting the people by means of the press to resist their governors': 'I fear you would make the overturning of a government too easy, which would certainly be an evil, as well as the making it too difficult'. John Cam Hobhouse* had 'a violent argument' with him in October, disputing his tenet that 'to raise one man degraded another'.[20] Maria Edgeworth was his guest at a typically boisterous family gathering in November 1821, and was captivated by him:

> Mr. Ricardo with a very composed manner has a continual life of mind and starts perpetually new game in conversation ... I never argued or discussed a question with any person who argues more fairly or less for victory and more for *truth*. He gives full thought to every argument brought against him and seems not to be on any side of any question for one instant longer than the conviction of his mind is on that side. It seems quite indifferent to him whether *you* find the truth or *he* find it, provided it be found. One gets at something by conversing with him. One learns either that one is wrong or right and the understanding is improved without the temper being ever tried in the discussion ... He is altogether one of the most agreeable persons as well as the best informed and most clever I ever knew.[21]

Ricardo was invited to attend the Hereford dinner in honour of Hume, 7 Dec. 1821, when, in addition to pledging his continued support for Hume's crusade against 'every wasteful expenditure of the public money', he again stressed the crucial importance of the ballot in any measure of reform: 'it was nothing but mockery and delusion to pretend to give the right of voting to a man, if you prevented him from exercising it without control'. To one sceptical correspondent he explained:

> You will call all these proceedings by the name of 'Radical', but I believe that they are calculated to do much good – to increase the interest of the people in the affairs of government, and to make them better judges of what constitutes good and what bad government. At the same time this will be useful to our governors, and incline them to economy and forbearance.

Attacks on him by disgruntled agriculturists at a Monmouth meeting to give the freedom of the borough to Hume typified, he thought, the 'error' prevailing on the subject of the currency, which was given frequent expression by William Cobbett†, who denounced him as the 'Oracle'.[22]

Ricardo planned to 'enter with all my energies on my parliamentary duties' in the 1822 session; and he made an immediate mark by declining to vote for Hume's amendment to the address, 5 Feb., because he did not believe that high taxation was the cause of agricultural distress, which he ascribed to low prices caused by over-production. Of Ricardo's insistence that the pound 'has not varied ten years', the backbencher Hudson Gurney, a country banker, noted privately, 'Are these economists mad?'; and John Allen of Holland House dismissed him as 'the greatest fool in the world'.[23] Ricardo reiterated his opinions on agricultural protection, taxation and the currency in the debate on Brougham's motion for more extensive tax reductions to relieve distress, 11 Feb. Although he privately believed that Brougham had talked rubbish, he voted for the motion, on the grounds that some relief might be afforded by the repeal of certain taxes and that reductions in expenditure were intrinsically desirable. He was blamed in some Whig quarters for the opposition's poor showing in the division and their failure to attract the support of disgruntled Tory country gentlemen, many of whom were supposed to have been induced to side with ministers by his apparent approval of their policies. Yet John Whishaw thought that such criticism was largely unfounded:

> I think ... that, considering the audience whom he addressed, he spoke too much as a theorist, and in a manner likely to be misrepresented. But though his speeches may have served as pretexts, I cannot think that they operated as the true motives of many votes. Mackintosh represented the number thus influenced, or professing to be so, as nearly forty, but they were all willing to be satisfied with the measures of government, and would have found good reasons for being so if Ricardo had never opened his lips.[24]

He voted for Lord Althorp's similar motion, 21 Feb., and went on to divide steadily for economies and reductions. As he said on 20 Mar., he 'would not trust any ministers ... with a surplus revenue, and he should, therefore, join in any vote for a remission of taxes ... so long as a surplus revenue remained'. Ricardo, who believed that 'the evils of Ireland ... arise from misrule', voted against the suspension of habeas corpus and insurrection bills, 7, 8 Feb.; and later in the session he divided against the Irish constables bill, 7 June, for inquiry into tithes, 19 June, and, on the renewal of the insurrection bill, for an investigation of the causes of distress and to limit the duration of the measure, 8 July. He voted in support of Sir Robert Wilson*, 13 Feb., and Robert Waithman*, 28 Feb., over their roles in the disturbances at the queen's funeral, and for attempts to secure a remission of Henry Hunt's* gaol sentence, 22, 28 Mar., 24 Apr. 1822.

His principal concern was with the issue of agricultural protection, on which he had feared that 'some injudicious measures may be adopted, in consequence of the general prevalence of error'. On the motion to renew the select committee on agricultural distress, 18 Feb. 1822, he replied at length to his critics in a speech which excited 'loud and general cheering'. He felt that the House had 'listened to me with attention, and appeared to follow and understand my arguments', though he could not say the same for the newspaper reporters, who, he complained, had again put nonsense into his mouth. He was named to the committee, but felt that he would be 'able to do little good on it' in the current climate of agricultural opinion. The loss to him of Huskisson, who refused to attend, was partially compensated by the support he received from the free trader William Wolryche Whitmore. He continued to put forward his views in the House, 5, 14 Mar., but he became increasingly gloomy as the committee, which did not take evidence, proceeded with its deliberations:

> The answer to every proposal for the adoption of good measures ... is that the agriculture of the country is in a state of unparalleled distress, and that the committee was appointed for the purpose of affording it relief. I had no idea of being able to do any good now, in the way of making better laws, but I hoped to lay the foundation of

> a better system in future. In that hope I shall probably be disappointed ... the country gentlemen ... form themselves into a compact body determined to yield no point which has the least semblance to diminished protection.

In the House, 3 Apr., he strongly attacked the principle of the committee's report, which recommended that there should be an open trade below 70*s*. and above it a fixed countervailing duty to compensate the domestic producer for his higher production costs. Ricardo immediately rushed into print during the Easter recess with his pamphlet *On Protection to Agriculture*, which was in effect a minority report. According to Whishaw, it was 'much praised. The ministerialists, in particular, are much pleased with his doctrines, evidently because he says little against taxation'.[25] When the government proposals based on the report were put to the House, 29 Apr., Ricardo laid out his alternative scheme for a fixed 20*s*. duty to operate when prices attained 70*s*., to be reduced by 1*s*. a year until it reached its final level of 10*s*., and to be balanced by a 7*s*. bounty on exports. He spoke in his usual terms on the subject, 7 May, seeing himself as fighting 'the best battle I can against the country gentlemen'. When Huskisson abandoned his own proposals, Ricardo 'adopted those of them which laid down the correct principles, and added to them my own personal measure'; but on 9 May his scheme was rejected by 218-25. He made further hits at agriculturists who sought salvation in higher food prices, 10, 16 May, but told a correspondent that he felt unequal to the struggle against 'the fallacious arguments for monopolies':

> I do my best, but that is bad enough. It is difficult to express oneself in terms sufficiently familiar to be understood by those who either understand nothing on these subjects, or who have imbibed prejudices to which they obstinately adhere. I am a very bad speaker, and am sorry to say I do not improve. I have not one good supporter; there are some who understand the subject, but they are on the ministerial bench, and dare not always speak as they think.[26]

However, he approved the corn bill, 3 June, as an improvement on the former law, and welcomed Canning's proposal to allow foreign corn in bond to be ground into flour for export, for which he spoke and voted, 10 June 1822.

Ricardo complained of the unsatisfactory way in which Vansittart's accounts of the national finances were set out, 22 Feb.,[27] supported Maberly's motion for their simplification, 14 Mar., and was named to the select committee appointed on 18 Apr. 1822. He commended Vansittart's plan to convert the navy five per cents, 25 Feb. On 8 Mar. he attacked the directors of the Bank, who 'did not know what they were about', for their handling of the currency conversion and their involvement in the proposed loan of £4,000,000 in exchequer bills to help the agricultural interest; and he supported Hume's attempt to ensure that the Bank did not derive any profit from its management of the increased capital stock created by the five per cents conversion. He again criticized the Bank and threatened to oppose renewal of its charter, 31 May. In March he was encouraged by political activists in Liverpool to come forward for the borough when Canning vacated his seat to go as governor-general to India; but his first instinct to have nothing to do with it was endorsed by one of his local contacts.[28]

He voted silently for parliamentary reform, 25 Apr., 3 June, and spoke in its favour at the Westminster anniversary reform dinner, 23 May 1822.[29] He again voted for criminal law reform, 4 June. He was unshaken in his views on the sinking fund and the desirability of getting rid of the national debt, as he wrote to a friend, 25 Mar:

> While ministers have this fund virtually at their disposal they will on the slightest occasion be disposed for war. To keep them peaceable you must keep them poor.

He supported Hume's attempt to take the sum required to implement Vansittart's 'crooked' scheme to relieve the burden of naval and military pensions by granting contractors a fixed annuity of 45 years from the sinking fund, 3 May. On the same subject, 24 May, he said that while he was always prepared to give ministers credit where it was due, and that in trying to reduce taxes they had 'acted judiciously in listening to the general prayer of the people', he 'must decline concurring in any terms of excessive gratitude' for the modified pensions plan, whereby trustees were to manage a fund raised by exchequer bills on the sale of annuities: they were merely 'giving the people what was, in fact, their own money'. He again supported Hume's 'simple and easy' plan, 3 June, when he also voted for repeal of the salt duties. His only quarrel with the navigation bill, 20 May, 4 June, was that it did not go far enough; and he praised the efforts of Wallace, vice-president of the board of trade, to liberalize commerce.[30] Quoting Adam Smith to make his point, he scorned calls for higher protection for the Irish butter trade, 20 June, and next day urged ministers to open the silk trade by repealing the restrictive Spitalfields Acts. He voted against the aliens bill, 5 June, 1, 10 July. In a free trade speech before the court of the East India Company, 12 June, he said that he 'wished to see a House of Commons free from party, where the interest of the public would alone be considered, in which a deaf ear would be turned to all partial application'. Later that day he spoke at length against Western's motion for inquiry into the effects of the resumption of cash payments and contended that the Bank's 'mistake' in purchasing gold and abandoning bullion had 'materially affected the public interests'. Changing his emphasis from previous speeches, he now admitted that there were bound to be difficulties in the early stages of the transition; but he insisted that there could be no going back and called for an end to agitation on the subject. On 14 June he maintained that public creditors had not significantly benefitted from the change.[31] He voted in condemnation of the allegedly increasing influence of the crown, 24 June, and the lord advocate's dealings with the Scottish press, 25 June, and for inquiry into chancery delays, 26 June. He called into question Vansittart's optimistic financial forecasts and recommended repeal of the usury laws, 1 July. He opposed inquiry into the claims of the Calcutta bankers, 4 July. His last significant speech of the session was against Western's renewed attempt to reopen the currency question, 10 July 1822.

Two days later Ricardo set off for Switzerland, where he intended to take necessary 'rest and recreation' until September. In the event, his wife persuaded him to press on into Italy, and they went as far as Florence. They returned by way of Paris and reached London on 8 Dec. 1822. A week later, Ricardo was anticipating more clamour for relief from the agriculturists. At the end of the year, a disgruntled clergyman condemned him as one of the 'gang of Jew speculators and moneylenders and loanraisers', a 'set of vagrant countryless ragamuffins', who were doing untold damage.[32] Ricardo was 'astonished' by the success of Cobbett in carrying resolutions at the Norfolk county meeting for the cancellation of all debts, which would be 'used as an argument by the anti-reformers against the extension of the suffrage'. He was unable to attend the Herefordshire meeting, where Cobbett 'as usual asserted falsehoods respecting my opinions', and the deluded country gentlemen ascribed all their problems to 'the augmented value of the currency':

> I am rather singularly circumstanced – agreeing as I do with the reformers, on the subject of parliamentary reform, I cannot agree with them that taxation and bad government has been the cause of our present difficulties ... Still less can I support the doctrines of the new converts to reform, who attribute our distress to every cause but the right one, and who, not being governed by principle, will quit the cause of reform the moment that the times mend. I on the contrary am a reformer on principle.

He was inclined to think that British policy on the Franco-Spanish conflict, which he hoped to see end in the defeat of France and 'the establishing of *real* representative governments all over Europe', had been 'firm and judicious', for he was very much a pacifist. While he saw merit in the scheme which Robert Wilmot Horton* submitted to him to mortgage the poor rates to finance emigration, he disclaimed any special expertise on the subject:

> You know I am frequently reproached with being a theorist, and if those who so reproach me, mean that I am not conversant with the practical details of the subjects which have engaged my attention, they are right. The subject of the poor laws, for instance, is one intimately connected with the science of political economy, but nobody is so little acquainted with them, as forming a part of parish economy, as I am.[33]

As for the currency, he told Pascoe Grenfell*, who had communicated to him Lord Grenville's views, 19 Jan. 1823, that 'we now possess the best system ... that has ever been established in any country'.[34]

On the motion for the reappointment of the committee on foreign trade, 12 Feb. 1823, Ricardo again paid tribute to Wallace's work, though he regretted the 'obstacles' erected by vested interests which had rendered it less effective than it might have been. He repeated his praises, 21 Mar., when he welcomed the warehousing bill, based as it was on 'a sound and judicious principle'. Before the session, he had assessed Robinson, now chancellor of the exchequer, as 'a tolerable political economist' who was 'well inclined to liberal principles of trade', but whose notorious timidity would probably deter him from acting on 'enlarged views of policy'. On 18 Feb. he exhorted Robinson to be firm with the Bank over the renewal of its charter. On 21 Feb. he generally applauded Robinson's finance resolutions and flattered him as a talented 'expositor' of political economy; but he pointed out that he had overestimated the amount of money available to reduce the national debt by £2,000,000. He thought Maberly's alternative scheme to get rid of the debt through redemption of the land tax was theoretically feasible, but felt that his proposed remission of £7,000,000 in taxes went too far. He resurrected his own pet scheme for a capital levy to remove the debt at a stroke. He voted for the principle of Maberly's plan, with the proviso that the concomitant tax reductions should be set at £5,000,000, 28 Feb. He opposed the government's proposals for reduction of the debt, 3 Mar., when he criticized the currency fanatics;[35] 6 Mar., when he said that he 'did not ... think the national purse safe in the hands of ministers' and 'confessed his fear of the present Parliament, and its disposition to ministerial compliance'; 11 Mar., when he supported Hume's amendment to limit the sinking fund to the surplus of revenue over expenditure and denied Grenfell's assertion that his own nostrum was the 'wildest' idea of all, and 13 Mar. He spoke and voted against the naval and military pensions bill, 18 Apr., describing the related bargain with the Bank as 'a very improvident one for the country'. On 25 Feb. he was named to the select committee on commissioners of sewers in London, on which he was still 'busily engaged' at the end of April. He made his usual points about the effects of cash resumption on prices and the value of the currency and supported Whitmore's attempt to reduce the import price for corn to 60*s.*, 26 Feb. He voted against the appointment of a lieutenant-general of the ordnance in peacetime, 19 Feb., and divided for other measures of retrenchment in March. On the 13th he expressed strong reservations about the merchant vessels apprenticeship bill, which he thought would enable owners to reduce wages. His amendment to expunge the compulsory element, 24 Mar., was defeated by 85-6; and at Huskisson's request, he withdrew the wrecking amendment which he put forward on 18 Apr. 1823.

Ricardo voted for inquiry into the Irish church establishment, 4 Mar. 1823. He divided against Barry's motion for the production of papers on the alleged plot against the lord lieutenant, 24 Mar., but in the opposition majority for inquiry into the prosecution of the Dublin Orange rioters, 22 Apr., though there had been speculation that he would side with ministers in defence of the Irish attorney-general William Plunket*.[36] He divided for inquiry into the state of Ireland, 12 May. Soon afterwards he wrote to Maria Edgeworth:

> Your restless nation gives us a great deal of trouble in Parliament. The best amongst us do not know how to manage you, nor what course to take to give you the blessings of peace, order, and good government. You have been so long subjected to misrule as hardly to be in a fit state to be reclaimed by common means. Coercion and severity have proved of little use, and I hope the system of indulgence, kindness and conciliation will now be tried. If that system will not succeed I hope we shall get rid of you altogether.

He opposed aspects of the Irish tithes composition bill, 30 May, 6, 16 June; was added to the select committee on the employment of the poor in Ireland, 23 June; seconded Hume's motion to consider abolition of the lord lieutenancy, 25 June 1823, and the following day voted for reception of the Catholic petition complaining of the administration of justice in Ireland.

Ricardo attended the dinner in honour of the Spanish and Portuguese ambassadors, 7 Mar.; but in the House, 18 Mar. 1823, he denied that in so doing he had indicated a readiness to 'engage the nation in war' in support of the Spanish liberals and protested against ministers being condemned by sections of the opposition before they had had a chance to state their case. Mrs. Arbuthnot recorded Rothschild's story that Ricardo and John Maberly* had profited in the funds on the strength of their advance knowledge of Canning's statement of the British position on the matter; and Ricardo himself later confirmed at least the partial truth of the tale.[37] He condemned the coastwise coal duties, 21, 27 Mar., and on 18 Apr., at McCulloch's request, presented a Fifeshire petition for repeal of the equivalent duties on stone; 'neither the House nor the reporters paid much attention' to him on the latter occasion, but ministers shortly afterwards conceded the repeal.[38] Supporting Mary Ann Carlile's petition for release from prison, 26 Mar., he disputed the attorney-general's argument that no leniency could be exercised until she had recanted her blasphemy, deplored the activities of the Constitutional Association and declared that 'prosecutions ought never to be instituted for religious opinions ... however absurd and extravagant'. In reply to a correspondent who thanked him for this contribution, he remarked that he would extend toleration to atheists and that it was 'a disgrace to the age we live in, that a part of the inhabitants of this country are still suffering under disabilities imposed upon them in a less enlightened age'. He voted for inquiry into the parliamentary franchise, 20 Feb., and on 24 Apr. supported and was a teller for Russell's reform motion, though he believed that without the ballot it would be nugatory. He spoke in the same vein at the Westminster anniversary dinner, 23 May.[39] He voted for reform in Scotland, 2 June. He divided for the abolition of whipping as a punishment, 30 Apr., of the death penalty for larceny, 21 May, and of flogging in prisons, 7 July. He voiced his 'astonishment' that the Spitalfields Acts, 'an interference with the freedom of trade', should still be in force and warmly supported the bill for their repeal, 21 May, 9, 11 June, when he denied that Parliament was 'legislating to the injury of the working classes'. On the presentation of a Southampton petition complaining of agricultural distress, 12 May, he once more 'attributed all the evils of a fluctuating price of grain to the corn laws and urged a speedy revision of the whole system'.[40] He was named to the select committee on mercantile law, 15 May, and on the proposal to set up one on trade bills, 22 May, expressed his pleasure at 'this contest for the adoption of liberal principles'.

Later that day he supported equalization of the sugar duties, as he had in another speech to the East India Company, 19 Mar.[41] He spoke and voted for inquiry into the beer and malt duties, with a view to taxing malt only, 28 May. He opposed the beer duties bill as 'very unjust', 13 June, when he also objected to any increase in the duty on barilla. On 30 May he excited some surprise by expressing reservations about the introduction of machinery, which he now admitted might in some instances create difficulties. At the same time, he said that the tide of progress could not be resisted and suggested that the working classes could prevent serious unemployment by exercising better birth control. He voted in censure of the lord advocate on the Borthwick case, 3 June, and for investigation of chancery delays, 5 June. He applauded the 'enlightened views' incorporated by Huskisson, now president of the board of trade, in the reciprocity of duties bill, 6 June, 4 July. On 9 June he voted to abolish the Leeward Islands four and a half per cent duties, for inquiry into the expenses of the coronation and to reduce the expenditure on foreign embassies. He led the opposition to Western's call for inquiry into the currency, 11 June, in a long speech, over which he had taken considerable trouble.[42] He again supported repeal of the usury laws, 27, 28 June.[43] He voted against the grant for Irish churches and glebe lands, 1 July. Speaking in support of Hume's motion for unfettered discussion of religious issues that day, he cited the atheism of Robert Owen as proof that Christians had no monopoly on beneficence. According to Mallet, he had obtained Owen's ready agreement to the use of his name in this context earlier that day; but on witnessing from the gallery the outrage which Ricardo's statement excited in the majority of his audience, Owen's 'natural boldness forsook him and a desire for fair fame prevailed'. When Ricardo declined his hastily written request to withdraw the remark, Owen primed William Money to inform the House that he wished it to be known that Ricardo had misrepresented him. Ricardo told Mallet that he was 'very near stating to the House what had passed between him and Owen in the morning; but his good nature prevailed', and he merely explained that he had deduced Owen's non-belief from his writings.[44] He voted for the introduction of jury trials to New South Wales, 7 July, and the same day was a teller for the minority against the report stage of the Irish linen manufacture bill. His last reported speech in the House was a brief statement of his undiminished objection to this measure on the occasion of its passage, 9 July 1823.[45]

From his summer retreat at Gatcombe, Ricardo recalled that in the session just finished, 'besides the regular attendance which I always give to the House, I was obliged to be every day on some committee'. He took satisfaction in the 'more liberal spirit than heretofore' which had been shown in Parliament and hoped that further progress would be made towards 'getting rid of some of the absurd regulations which fetter commerce, till all shackles are removed'. He composed a paper detailing his plan for the establishment of a national bank, 'with a view to prove that the nation would lose nothing in profits by abolishing the Bank of England'. He continued, and concluded with an amiable agreement to differ, his long-running correspondence with Malthus on the theory of value. On 30 Aug. he wrote to Mill, who was planning to visit him in mid-September:

> The grand cause, good government, is always present to my mind, but I hope it will have a better champion in the House of Commons ... I am quite sure that the good cause is advancing, though at a very moderate step, and all we can hope to do in our time is to help it a little forward.

On 5 Sept. Ricardo began to suffer severely from earache, a complaint to which he was prone. He became seriously ill, appeared to rally when the abscess burst, but developed an infection of the mastoid and, after enduring 'a period of unspeakable agony', died on the 11th, aged 51.[46] Hume, shocked, as many were, by his wholly unexpected death, wrote to Hobhouse:

> I consider him to have filled a space in the public eye and in the House of Commons that no other man can fill, and I deplore his loss as a public calamity. To me the loss cannot be made up. I never knew an individual with so many valuable qualities. I know no one at present likely to take his place.

Lady Holland regarded him as 'a loss to the community, as he was a virtuous, upright man'. She found 'rather diverting' Lord Lauderdale's observation that he was 'a very good man, though he has often provoked me by the labour it cost me to decipher the most obscure style of writing I ever attempted to read'. Grenville, a great admirer of Ricardo, commented that he was

> a great loss both to the country and to government. The extreme candour and fairness of his mind and conduct contrasted very strikingly with the extravagance of his *political* opinions.[47]

Hume and Huskisson paid warm tributes to him in the House, 12 Feb. 1824. His *Plan for the Establishment of a National Bank* was published that month.[48] By his will of 4 Apr. 1820 Ricardo (of whom it had once been said that he had not been 'improperly influenced, as to the principle of population, by his intimacy with

Malthus') divided his real estate in Gloucestershire, Herefordshire, Worcestershire and Kent and his residuary personal estate between his sons: Osman (1795-1881), Liberal Member for Worcester, 1847-65; David (1803-64), Liberal Member for Stroud 1832-3, and Mortimer (1807-76), an army officer. He provided his unmarried daughters Berthia and Mary with £25,000 each and his surviving married daughters Henrietta and Priscilla with £10,000, in addition to their portions of £12,000. He left his wife £4,000 and a life annuity of the same amount. His personalty was sworn under £500,000, but the total value of his estate must have been between £675,000 and £775,000.[49]

An anonymous obituarist wrote that Ricardo's 'amiable disposition and conciliating manners' had combined with his 'profound knowledge of all the mysteries of commerce' to earn him the respect of the Commons.[50] His brother Moses, in an affectionate memoir, commented that 'to intellectual powers of the first order, he joined a candour, a modesty, a diffidence, which never allowed him to assume to himself a merit which he felt he did not deserve'.[51] Hobhouse wrote warmly of him a few days after his death:

> He was of unblemished integrity, both public and private ... In all the relations of private life he was kind, amiable, and engaging, as well as just and generous. He seemed free from every bad passion, and those who came within the sphere of his gentle but resistless influence felt that he was born for the consolation of those around him, and for the happiness of mankind.[52]

Mallet had this to say of him:

> No man was more open to conviction, and more ready to acknowledge an error. His great and only object was the discovery of truth; and he carried into conversation a degree of candour and modesty of manner which were not less remarkable than his extraordinary clearness and facility of elucidation ... Ricardo was a bold man ... because he reasoned thoroughly with himself, and carefully examined the opinions which he adopted. Whether he made sufficient allowance for disturbing causes, and for the preponderating influence which the passions of mankind often acquire over their own interests, may admit of doubt. His knowledge of mankind, and of political society, was chiefly acquired in books, and wanted the test of experience; but although he was a thorough reformer ... no man was less of a revolutionist in principle: he was, on the contrary, humane, considerate and just in all his views ... No one was less forward in asserting his opinions, or less impatient to speak: he never argued for purposes of victory, but always with good nature, simplicity and a most winning playfulness of manner.[53]

Sixteen years after his death, Brougham depicted him as

> a person of good information and great ability, though not overtopping all others in learning, nor entitled to be reckoned a man of genius. The originality of some speculations on political economy, in which he engaged, was, indeed, undeniable ... His speaking, his conduct, his manner, were all unexceptionable, and all suited to the man, his high station among philosophers, his known opinions on political affairs, his kindly nature, and his genuine modesty. There was something about him, chiefly a want of all affectation as well as pretension in everything he did or said, that won the respect of every party. His matter was ever of a high value ... His views were often abundantly theoretical, sometimes too refined for his audience, occasionally extravagant from his propensity to follow a right principle into all its consequences, without duly taking into account or practice the condition of things to which he was applying it ... Few men have ... had more weight in Parliament; certainly none who, finding but a small body of his fellow-Members to agree with his leading opinions, might be said generally to speak against the sense of his audience, ever commanded a more patient or even favourable hearing; and, as this was effected without any of the more ordinary powers of oratory or of entertainment possessed by others, it might be regarded as the triumph of reason, intelligence, and integrity over untoward circumstances and alien natures.[54]

Although few of the reforms for which Ricardo worked were implemented in his lifetime, the influence of his ideas on the formation of British public policy in the nineteenth century was immense. At the same time, his labour theory of value was taken up by a succession of radicals and transformed by them into the fundamental tenet of Socialism: his economic orthodoxy contained principles which were adopted by others to overturn his own assumptions about the natural order of society and to promote revolutionary ideas.[55]

[1] Based, unless otherwise stated, on *Works and Corresp. of David Ricardo* ed. P. Sraffa and M. H. Dobb, 11 vols. (Cambridge, 1951-73), vols. vii, ix and x. The most recent general biography is by D. Weatherall (1976). On Ricardo's economic theories see M. Blaug, *Ricardian Economics* (1958); M.J. Gootzeit, *David Ricardo* (1975); S. Hollander, *Economics of Ricardo* (1979) and *Legacy of Ricardo* ed. G.A. Caravale (1985). See also *David Ricardo. Critical Assessments* ed. J. Cunningham Wood (1985), which reprints the 1894 article, 'Ricardo in Parliament', by E. Cannan; B. Gordon, *Political Economy in Parliament* (1975); M. Milgate and S.C. Stimson, *Ricardian Politics* (1991), and T. Peach, *Interpreting Ricardo* (1993). [2] *Oxford DNB*. [3] See *Biog. Dict. of Modern British Radicals* ed. J.O. Baylen and N.J. Grossman, i. 404. [4] Gordon, 2-3; *Works*, v, p. xx; viii. 147. [5] *Works*, v, p. xix. [6] *The Times*, 4 May 1820. [7] Gordon, 82-86. [8] *The Times*, 26 May 1820. [9] Ibid. 22 June 1820. [10] Gordon, 89-90. [11] *Works*, iv. 143-200. [12] *Edgeworth Letters*, 226-7; *Works*, v. 469-70; viii. 326-31; *The Times*, 1 Jan. 1821; *Pol. Economy Club*, vi. 213. [13] HLRO, Hist. Coll. 379, Grey Bennet diary, 16-17. [14] *Works* vol. v, p. xxv. [15] *The Times*, 1 June 1821. [16] Gordon, 99-100; B. Hilton, *Corn, Cash, Commerce*, 104-7, 117, 124-6, 131, 134. [17] *The Times*, 28 Mar. 1821. [18] Ibid. 25 June 1821.

[19] Hilton, 90-95; Gordon, 102-13. [20] Broughton, *Recollections*, ii. 159. [21] *Edgeworth Letters*, 257-62. [22] *Works*, v. 471-4, 515-21; *The Times*, 14 Dec. 1821. [23] Harewood mss HAR/GC/83, J. Gladstone to Canning, 6 Feb.; Gurney diary, 10 Feb. 1822. [24] *'Pope' of Holland House* ed. Lady Seymour, 243-4; *The Times*, 13 Feb. 1822. [25] *Works*, iv. 201-70; *'Pope' of Holland House*, 249. [26] *The Times*, 11 May 1822; Hilton, 150-2. [27] *The Times*, 23 Feb. 1822. [28] *Works*, vol. xi, pp. xiii-xiv. [29] Ibid. v. 47-5; *The Times*, 24 May 1822. [30] *The Times*, 5 June 1822. [31] Gordon, 145-7. [32] *Heber Letters*, 302-3. [33] *Works*, vol. xi, pp. xv-xvi. [34] Add. 69082. [35] *The Times*, 4 Mar. 1823. [36] Buckingham, *Mems. Geo. IV*, i. 446. [37] *The Times*, 8 Mar. 1823; *Arbuthnot Jnl.* i. 221. [38] *The Times*, 22, 28 Mar., 19 Apr. 1823. [39] *Works*, v. 446-8; *The Times*, 24 May 1823. [40] *The Times*, 13 May 1823. [41] *Works*, v. 478-83. [42] Gordon, 180-1. [43] *The Times*, 28 June 1823. [44] *Works*, v. 331. [45] *The Times*, 10 July 1823. [46] *Gent. Mag.* (1823), ii. 376. [47] Add. 36460, f. 123; 38279, f. 64; 51654, Lady Holland to Mackintosh [22 Sept.]; 51700, Lauderdale to Lady Holland, 17 Sept. 1823, [48] *Works*, iv. 271-300. [49] *'Pope' of Holland House*, 180-1; PROB 11/1676/595; IR26/973/1313; *Gent. Mag.* (1823), ii. 376. [50] *Gent. Mag.* (1823), ii. 376. [51] *Ann. Biog.* (1824), 377. [52] Broughton, iii. 26. [53] *Pol. Economy Club*, vi. 207-9. [54] *Hist. Sketches* (ser. 3), 185, 188-90. [55] Gordon, 184; *Modern British Radicals*, i. 403, 406-8; Milgate and Stimson, 149-50.

D.R.F.

RICE (afterwards RICE TREVOR), Hon. George Rice (1795–1869), of Barrington Park, Glos. and Dynevor Castle, Carm.

CARMARTHENSHIRE	1820–1831
CARMARTHENSHIRE	1832–9 Apr. 1852

b. 5 Aug. 1795, 1st. s. of George Talbot Rice† (sometime De Cardonnel), 3rd Bar. Dynevor, and Hon. Frances Townshend, da. of Thomas Townshend†, 1st Visct. Sydney. *educ.* Westminster 1806-12; Christ Church, Oxf. 1812. *m.* 27 Nov. 1824, Frances, da. of Lord Charles Fitzroy† of Wicken, Northants. 4 da. (2 *d.v.p.*). Took name of Rice in lieu of De Cardonnel 4 Feb. 1817; *suc.* John Trevor, 3rd Visct. Hampden, to Bromham, Beds. 9 Sept. and took additional name of Trevor by royal lic. 28 Oct. 1824; fa. as 4th Bar. Dynevor 9 Apr. 1852. *d.* 7 Oct. 1869.

Lt.-col. Carm. militia and militia a.d.c. to Queen Victoria 1852-*d.*

The Rice (Rhys) family, who traced their descent from the Lord Rhys of Deheubarth, relied heavily on traditional loyalties and the evocative name of Dynevor to preserve their status as the first family and leaders of the Red or Tory party in Carmarthenshire. Rice's father (then known as De Cardonnel) had had to relinquish the county seat in 1793 on succeeding his mother in the peerage; but, by giving his interest to the Williamses of Edwinsford and subsequently Sir Robert Seymour† of Taliaris, he tried to keep it available for Rice at the first election after he came of age.[1] Sir James Williams's† display of pique at not being consulted before Seymour's sudden resignation at the dissolution in 1820 was overcome;[2] and, by persuading John Jones* of Ystrad (a Red) not to stand against the 1st Baron Cawdor's heir John Frederick Campbell* in Carmarthen, Dynevor ensured that Rice was returned for the county unopposed.[3] Any patronage requests were referred to Dynevor.[4]

Rice's father and grandfather had fostered the West Wales Reds' preference for reform rather than abolition of the Welsh courts of great sessions, and he was naturally named to the select committees on the issue, 2 June 1820, 21 Feb. 1821; it was the only one on which he made a major Commons speech before 1833. He divided with the Liverpool ministry against economies in revenue collection, 4 July, and could usually be relied on to vote with them in the 1820 Parliament, but some doubt remains concerning pro-retrenchment votes attributed to him on the estimates, 16 Feb., 15 Mar., 30 Apr. 1821.[5] Others credited to him for printing the Nottingham petition for the impeachment of ministers and inquiry into the conduct of the sheriff of Cheshire, 20 Feb. 1821, can be discounted. Lord Eldon summoned Dynevor to the Lords to vote for the bill of pains and penalties, 17 Aug. 1820, and Rice divided with ministers against censuring their handling of the Queen Caroline affair, 6 Feb. 1821.[6] He divided against Catholic relief, 28 Feb. 1821,[7] 30 Apr. 1822, 1 Mar., 25 Apr., 10 May, and against the attendant Irish franchise bill, 26 Apr. 1825. A radical publication of that session noted that he 'attended frequently and voted with ministers'.[8] He presented petitions from Carmarthenshire great sessions complaining of distress and calling for repeal of the salt duties, 24 Apr., and from the county's tanners for repeal of the leather tax, 29 Apr. 1822.[9] When the county met at Llandeilo to petition for government action on distress, 28 Jan. 1823, he strongly opposed the Unitarian George Thomas's resolution to include parliamentary reform in the petition's demands and helped to secure a compromise petition requesting repeal of the assessed taxes and a modified property tax.[10] His remarks on presenting it to the House, 17 Feb., could barely be heard, but they prompted Hume to ask if he would 'now support measures of economy, as he was not aware that they had yet had the benefit of a single vote from him'. Rice was cheered when he replied that

> he should continue to vote as hitherto upon measures as they came before the House. He did not conceive that he or any Member was called upon to pledge himself to a particular line of conduct during the session. The present was not the usual and regular mode of extracting information; and if ... [Hume] brought forward any motion of economy, he should, as before, exercise his discretion as to its fitness or otherwise.[11]

He voted against reform, 20 Feb. 1823. He presented petitions from Carmarthen for repeal of the coal duties, 23 Apr., and Carmarthenshire against the window tax, 11 May 1824.[12] He spent the recess in Gloucestershire, London and at Dynevor, where he was anxious to dissuade his guest, the Breconshire Member Thomas Wood, from taking his wife on electioneering visits. On 31 Aug. he informed his fiancée, 'I have never liked to increase popularity at the expense of my mother and sisters and vow I will not at yours'.[13] Early in September he accompanied his father to the sessions and meetings about the proposed Kidwelly canal, receiving word shortly thereafter that John Trevor, Lord Hampden, to whom he was related through his paternal grandmother, had died leaving him his encumbered estate at Bromham and a third of his personalty estimated at £150,000.[14] Hampden had only succeeded his brother Thomas Hampden† to the title in August, and Rice knew that 'the will was made at the instigation of the dowager Lady Hampden, who pressed it on as much as possible; and it was completed only the day before Lord Hampden's death'.[15] He had to change his surname to inherit and wrote to his fiancée:

> Now you must make up your mind to know me by another name too for I am to be Trevor for the future; that is, when the king shall give me leave. I have been changing my name often enough for one of my age. I was first De Cardonnel, then Rice and shall be Trevor ... I am to take the Trevor arms also.[16]

As Rice Trevor, he voted to outlaw the Catholic Association, 25 Feb., and presented his constituents' petitions against Catholic claims, 24 Apr., and corn law revision, 4 May 1825. He was named as one of those who had been unable to hear the question put before the division on the Southwark paving bill, 15 Apr.[17] He brought up anti-slavery petitions from Haverfordwest, 21 Mar., and Llanelli, 26 Apr. 1826.[18] With opposition pending, he had canvassed early, and at the 1826 dissolution promised his constituents that he would 'consult the welfare and interests of every class'. John Jones, a hardened Welsh-speaking politician who since 1821 had represented Carmarthen on the same interest, rallied their supporters and Rice Trevor was eventually returned unopposed, but his voting record was criticized and he found it difficult to 'explain and vindicate' his parliamentary conduct.

He divided against Catholic relief, 6 Mar., and, having served on an election committee, was granted a month's leave on urgent business, 23 Mar. 1827. His constituents petitioned strongly for repeal of the Test Acts and he may have brought up a favourable petition, 17 Feb., but he did not vote on the issue when it was opposed by the duke of Wellington's new ministry, 26 Feb. 1828. As urged by John Johnes of Dolaucothi, he introduced, 21 Feb., and did all he could to secure the passage of the Carmarthen roads bill.[19] On moving the second reading of the Llanelli railroad and docks bill, 26 Feb., he pointedly declared without foundation that he had no private interest in it beyond 'its having been represented to him to be one of public utility and from his being the Member of the county in which it was intended to take effect'. Despite opposition from Lord William Powlett, Tennyson and Waithman, who proclaimed it unnecessary, Rice Trevor's argument that the undertaking was justified because navigation in the Bury estuary was dangerous held sway and he carried the bill without a division. He presented anti-Catholic petitions from Calvinistic Methodist congregations in Carmarthenshire and other South Wales counties, 29 Apr., and divided against the relief bill, 12 May, and with government against ordnance reductions, 4 July 1828. Later that month he travelled to Carmarthen for the official opening of the memorial to Sir Thomas Picton†.[20]

Rice Trevor disagreed with the government's decision to concede Catholic emancipation in 1829 and felt obliged to explain his attitude. Bringing up a series of hostile petitions from Carmarthenshire, 9 Feb., he declared that he was

> ignorant of the nature of the measure which it is intended to submit to the House, and can therefore have no distinct notion of what securities may be proposed for the Protestant church establishment. If ... I should find that those securities are not sufficient to satisfy my mind, my vote shall be what it always has been on this subject.

Later that month the patronage secretary Planta predicted that he would vote 'with ministers' for emancipation; but he presented further unfavourable petitions, 27 Feb., 3, 10, 12, 16, 20, 30 Mar., and divided 6, 18, 30 Mar., and paired, 23, 27 Mar., against the measure. The fate of its courts and judicature had become a major political issue in West Wales following publication in April 1829 of a law commission's report advocating their abolition and redesigning the Welsh circuits.[21] Rice Trevor kept a low profile at the county meeting in Carmarthen, 24 Oct. 1829,[22] but presented its petition against altering the present system, 9 Mar. 1830, when, taking his father's line, he criticized the government's administration of justice bill by which the change was to be enacted. He suggested making alterations 'without destroying the system altogether' and was the first speaker to point out that Welsh justice was not 'some strange code' and differed from the English only in its 'mode of administration'. He raised objections to the proposed partitioning of Breconshire and Cardiganshire; claimed that the extra expense of the new courts would fall on a landed interest which was already hard pressed; and said he would wait to hear the attorney-general before 'pronouncing a positive opinion', but threatened opposition 'if the object ... should be to divide counties so as to form parts of different assize districts'. He spoke similarly and brought up further unfavourable petitions at the bill's second reading, 27 Apr., and presented another from the sheriff, magistrates, grand jury and clergy of Carmarthenshire, 28 Apr. He did not object to going into committee on the measure, 18 May 1830, and apparently waived his objections when a late amendment left the existing assize structure almost intact.

He voted with the Ultras to condemn the omission of distress from the king's speech, 4 Feb., but divided against Lord Blandford's parliamentary reform scheme, 18 Feb., and paired against enfranchising Birmingham, Leeds and Manchester, 23 Feb. 1830. He had a vested interest in the deliberations of the select committee on the coal trade in London and the south-east, to which he was appointed, 11 Mar. On the 18th he presented a private petition against the Breconshire roads bill. When the miscellaneous estimates were considered, 10 May, he spoke of the need for better communications with southern Ireland, despite greater expense. He voted against Jewish emancipation, 17 May, and amending the Galway franchise bill, 24 May, when he presented a petition from Stowe against the sale of beer bill.[23] Alarmed by the early success of the Whig Edward Bowles Symes of Brynhafod, who was manoeuvring against him in Carmarthenshire, on 1 July 1830 he requested the support of Johnes of Dolaucothi at the forthcoming general election, explaining that he was 'almost a constant prisoner to the house from my strain, the effects of which I have not yet got over'.[24] Illness forced him to remain in London until shortly before the nomination, at which he faced no more than a show of opposition from Symes, but he had to endure much heckling and questioning about his votes. He defended those on the Catholic question and the judicature as ones of conscience, reasserted his right to act independently, defended the corn laws and pointed to differences among the reformers. When criticized for failing to vote with the revived Whig opposition, he said privy councillors' emoluments were justified, but claimed that he would have voted against the Bathurst and Dundas pensions had he been present. He remained under pressure to support some measure of reform, and his statement of support for the gradual extinction of slavery did not go far enough for the Dissenters.[25]

The ministry listed Rice Trevor among their 'friends', and he spoke briefly on their behalf on the address, 3 Nov., and divided with them on the civil list when they were brought down, 15 Nov. 1830. He echoed Hobhouse's plea for better provision for the insane, 16 Dec., joined its presenter Lord James Crichton Stuart in endorsing Neath's petition for repeal of the coastwise coal duties, 17 Dec. 1830, and brought up another against West Indian slavery, 7 Mar. 1831. Aware that his views on reform were increasingly at variance with those of his constituents, he stayed away from county meetings, and presented but declined 'from a conscientious feeling of public duty' to endorse Carmarthenshire grand jury's petition for reform, 11 Mar.[26] He divided against the Grey ministry's reform bill at its second reading, 22 Mar., and for Gascoyne's wrecking amendment, 19 Apr. 1831. At the magistrates' dinner in Carmarthen afterwards he explained that he found the bill too sweeping, particularly in its provisions to enfranchise £10 householders and disfranchise boroughs which were not necessarily rotten, merely underpopulated. He stood down at the dissolution that month rather than feel obliged to support a bill 'most mischievous in its effects to the best interests of the country', and earned the respect of all parties by doing so.[27]

Dynevor continued to oppose reform in the House of Lords, and the Carmarthenshire Whigs criticized Rice Trevor for joining the 'Conservative Oak Reform Club at Gloucester in 1831 with Beaufort and other sinecurists'.[28] Standing as a Conservative, Rice Trevor, who always maintained that 'a pledged man is an automaton', and staunchly defended the rights of the established church and the agriculturists, topped the poll in the new two Member Carmarthenshire constituency in December 1832 and at each election until he succeeded his father to the peerage in 1852.[29] He died of paralysis at Great Malvern in October 1869, recalled for the part he played, as his father's deputy lieutenant, in quelling the Rebecca riots, and as the benefactor who restored Sir Rhys ap Tewdwr's tomb in St. Peter's church and helped to endow Carmarthen infirmary. He was buried in the family vault at Barrington Park, Gloucestershire.[30] Having no sons, he was succeeded in the peerage by his cousin, the Rev. Francis William Rice (1804-78), rector of Fairford, Gloucestershire, to whom he bequeathed £12,000 and the Dynevor Castle and Kidwelly estates. His other Welsh estates and Barrington Park were kept in trust for his grandson

Edward Rhys Wingfield (1849-1901), who was also to inherit the family town house in Prince's Gardens.[31]

[1] *HP Commons, 1790-1820*, ii. 488-91; iv. 139; v. 13, 123, 580-1. [2] Carm. RO, Dynevor mss 161/5, Williams to Dynevor, 17 Feb. 1820. [3] *Carmarthen Jnl.* 21 Feb. 1820. See JONES and CARMARTHEN. [4] Dynevor mss 154/5, 6. [5] *Seren Gomer*, iv (1821), 154 reported that John Hensleigh Allen was the only Welsh Member to vote with Hume on the ordnance estimates. This is confirmed in the version of Hume's speech of 17 Feb. printed in *The Times*, 18 Feb. 1822, and cited below. [6] Dynevor mss 161/3; *Seren Gomer*, iv. 93. [7] *Seren Gomer*, iv. 124, 154. [8] *Session of Parl. 1825*, p. 482. [9] *The Times*, 25, 30 Apr.; *Carmarthen Jnl.* 26 Apr. 1822. [10] *Carmarthen Jnl.* 31 Jan.; *The Times*, 3 Feb. 1823. [11] *The Times*, 18 Feb. 1823. [12] Ibid. 24 Apr., 12 May 1824. [13] NLW ms 21674 C, f. 12. [14] Ibid. ff. 13-14, 19, 22; PROB 11/1693/667. [15] *Gent. Mag.* (1824), ii. 465; PROB 11/1690/518; Dynevor mss 154/12. [16] NLW mss 21674 C, ff. 15, 22. [17] *The Times*, 22 Apr., 5 May 1825. [18] Ibid. 22 Mar., 27 Apr. 1826. [19] NLW, Dolaucothi mss L3838, 3839; *Cambrian*, 23 Feb. 1828. [20] *Carmarthen Jnl.* 1 Aug. 1828. [21] *Cambrian*, 7 Mar.; *Carmarthen Jnl.* 18 Apr. 1829. [22] *Cambrian*, 31 Oct. 1829. [23] Dynevor mss 160/13. [24] Dolaucothi mss L3840; *Carmarthen Jnl.* 30 July 1830. [25] *Carmarthen Jnl.* 13 Aug. 1830. [26] *Ibid.* 25 Mar., 1 Apr. 1831. [27] Ibid. 22, 29 Apr. 1831; Dolaucothi mss L3841; *Yr Efangylydd*, i (1831), 256. [28] NLW mss 11772 E. [29] Dolaucothi mss L1726, 3844-9; *Carmarthen Jnl.* 6, 13 July, 17, 24, 31 Aug., 28 Dec. 1832; Dynevor mss 161/4, 5. [30] D.J.V. Jones, *Rebecca's Children*, 69, 88-89, 223-4, 376; *Carmarthen Jnl.* 15 Oct. 1869. [31] *Illustrated London News*, 22 Jan. 1870.

M.M.E.

RICE, Thomas Spring (1790–1866), of Mount Trenchard, nr. Foynes, co. Limerick.

LIMERICK	3 July 1820–1832
CAMBRIDGE	1832–Aug. 1839

b. 8 Feb. 1790, 1st s. of Stephen Edward Rice of Mount Trenchard and Catherine, da. and h. of Thomas Spring of Ballycrispin, Castlemaine, co. Kerry. *educ.* Trinity Coll. Camb. 1809; L. Inn 1817. *m.* (1) 11 July 1811, Lady Theodosia Pery (*d.* 11 Dec. 1839), da. of Edmond Henry, 1st earl of Limerick [I], 5s. (1 *d.v.p.*) 3da. (1 *d.v.p.*); (2) 13 Apr. 1841, Mary Anne, da. of John Marshall*, *s.p. suc.* fa. 1831; *cr.* Bar. Monteagle 5 Sept. 1839. *d.* 7 Feb. 1866.

Under-sec. of state for home affairs July 1827-Jan. 1828; sec. to treasury Nov. 1830-June 1834; PC [I] 29 Apr. 1831, [UK] 5 June 1834; sec. of state for war and colonies June-Nov. 1834; chan. of exch. Apr. 1835-Aug. 1839; commr. on civil administration of army 1835-7, ecclesiastical duties and revenues 1835-7; trustee, Nat. Gallery 1835-*d.*; comptroller gen. exch. 1839-65; pres. Statistical Soc. 1845-7; chairman, commn. on decimal coinage 1855-9.

Chairman, Provincial Bank of Ireland.[1]

At one point nicknamed 'Jack [John] the Painter', after the radical dockyard arsonist James Aitken, whom he perhaps resembled, Rice was thought by Lord Donoughmore to be 'the least-looking shrimp, and the lowest-looking one too'; and Henry Edward Fox*, who commented that his unbearable manner of speaking was like that of 'an affected fine lady on the stage', exclaimed after their first meeting that 'a more conceited, chattering, provoking elf I never beheld'.[2] Yet he was highly esteemed by the Whig leaders, of whom he acknowledged Lord Lansdowne as his chief, and by political friends in all parties, for his conversational ease, his conciliatory kind-heartedness, his indefatigable industry and his unwarranted optimism.[3] A spry, quick-witted, voluble, little man, with a gift for hyperbole and the literary sensibilities of a poet, he was also one of the best-informed political economists of the Bowood circle and a member of the generation of devout liberal Anglican Whigs.[4] In the Irish context, he was at the forefront of a group of influential liberal Protestants, who provided an alternative to the popular Catholic movement associated with Daniel O'Connell* by furthering the cause of moderate and cross-sectarian reforms, particularly through an emphasis on Christian citizenship.[5] Yet it was considered a matter of regret, as expressed by Lady Holland, for instance, that his talents were not in the end quite sufficient to raise him out of the second rank of Westminster politicians, among whom he served a career of useful drudgery.[6]

Rice, whose family was Welsh in origin, was probably descended from Sir Stephen Rice (*d.* 1715), the Jacobite chief baron of the Irish exchequer. His grandfather Thomas purchased Mount Trenchard (formerly Cappagh) and married into the notable family of the knights of Kerry, while his father,[7] who had a small electoral interest in county Limerick, married an heiress from neighbouring Kerry, where he was appointed sheriff in 1792.[8] Avoiding the risk of what he much later described as the licentiousness of '*base society*', Thomas's early marriage, to the first cousin of his brother-in-law Sir Aubrey Vere Hunt, brought him a valuable connection in Lord Limerick, who had represented Limerick borough in the Irish Commons and now sat in the Lords as an (at this time still) anti-Catholic supporter of Lord Liverpool's administration. He toyed with the idea of entering the diplomatic corps and briefly enrolled at Lincoln's Inn, but by the 1810s he was evidently more interested in imbibing the liberal opinions of his Whig friend, the journalist William Empson.[9] He established his reformist credentials with a pamphlet, published in London in 1815, on the iniquities of Irish grand juries: in it, declaring himself 'unconnected with party [and] unperverted by personal animosities', he urged Irish Members to end the financial mismanagement and political partisanship of local government in their country.[10] This brought him into contact with the advanced Whig Francis Horner†, who was influenced by its arguments in questioning witnesses before the Commons select committee on the subject that year.[11]

Sidelining the former independent candidate John Tuthill, Rice offered for Limerick at the general election of 1818, when he had the backing of his father-in-law in standing against John Vereker, the son of his local rival Lord Gort, the borough's patron. He made great play of his hard-working character, his hostility to corporation abuses and his hopes for the commercial improvement of his native city, but was defeated by nearly 300 votes after a protracted contest. He promised a petition and, setting out his opinions on the duties, as well as the freedom of action, of a representative, was hailed as their champion by the friends of independence at a dinner in late July 1818.[12] His petition, which complained of the admission of non-resident freemen to the electorate of the county borough, was presented, 22 Jan., but was thrown out by the committee, which declined to take the usual course of accepting the pollbook evidence, 27 Feb. 1819. This decision was attacked in the Commons, 1 Mar., and again on the 5th, when Rice's own objections were brought forward in another petition.[13] A determined magistrate and grand juror, it was he who arrested Scanlan, the killer of the Colleen Bawn, in November 1819.[14]

Rice, who praised Croker's speech on Catholic relief on 3 May 1819, attended at Westminster on Irish electoral affairs that year and in 1820, when he again challenged Vereker at the general election. His increased assertiveness on the hustings gave him a stronger claim, especially as he was no longer entirely seen as simply Lord Limerick's nominee, but he finished in second place, 236 votes adrift.[15] He petitioned and, the committee having redefined the right of voting to exclude the non-resident freemen, was seated in place of Vereker, 3 July. He voted against the aliens bill, 7, 12 July 1820, his only recorded activity that session. He was triumphantly chaired through Limerick on the 20th and enthusiastically participated in further efforts to weaken the corporation's dominance that year.[16] He had been admitted to Brooks's in May and his close connection with the opposition Whig leadership was apparent by November, when O'Connell used him as a conduit to Henry Brougham* in his bid to be appointed one of Queen Caroline's law officers.[17] Rice's nephew Stephen Edward De Vere, whose association with him began in 1820-1, later recorded that 'from that time until his death he imparted to me, as I believe, all his political thoughts and actions [and] I saw his wonderful energy, straightforwardness and honesty'.[18]

'Spring Rice' as he now became universally known, presumably to distinguish him from the Welsh Tory George Rice (Trevor)*, became an extremely active, if not at first a very prominent, member of opposition from the beginning of the 1821 session, when he divided steadily in the Whig campaign on the queen's behalf. He voted for Catholic claims, 28 Feb., but indicated that he would support securities in order to obtain this, despite personally deeming them unnecessary, 28 Feb., 28 Mar., 2 Apr., and, to O'Connell's disgust, he presented and endorsed a petition to the contrary effect from the Catholic bishop and clergy of Limerick, 11 Apr.[19] Thereafter he spoke and voted with exemplary regularity, especially for economies and reduced taxation, as well as on legal matters, foreign policy and miscellaneous domestic controversies and, of course, Irish issues, occasionally serving as a teller. He was frequently appointed to select committees, including some on English social and economic affairs, and busied himself ceaselessly with minor Irish legislation, such as a measure concerning stealing from shops which he piloted through the Commons that year.[20]

A dedicated constituency Member, he often presented Limerick petitions, notably on commercial matters: for instance, those complaining of agricultural distress, 26 Feb., and of the obstacle posed by the corporation to investment in the city, 1 May 1821.[21] He brought up many others from Ireland, including for Catholic relief, in this period, and, as his reputation grew, not least as the opponent of other corrupt corporations, petitions from British reformers and radicals were increasingly forwarded to him for presentation. He divided for making Leeds a scot and lot, and not a £10 householder, borough, 2 Mar., and it was perhaps at this time, in relation to the disfranchisement of Grampound, that he told his Cambridge acquaintance George Pryme that 'it was said on that occasion among a few of his friends, "reform is now carried".'[22] He voted for parliamentary reform, 9 May, and to ensure the independence of Parliament by the exclusion of placemen, 31 May 1821. He divided silently for inquiry into the Scottish royal burghs, 20 Feb., and to condemn the present influence of the crown, 24 June 1822. He voted for Russell's reform motions, 25 Apr. 1822, 20 Feb. 1823, 27 Apr. 1826, and to amend the Scottish representative system, 2 June 1823, and the electoral franchise of Edinburgh, 26 Feb. 1824, 13 Apr. 1826.

In October 1821 he played a major part in restoring peace to county Limerick, but he questioned the propriety of addressing the king on this at a meeting of Irish landowners in London that winter.[23] Having voted for Hume's amendment to the address on distress, 5 Feb., he joined his equally dynamic friend Sir John Newport in refusing to endorse government's repressive legislation unless accompanied by an inquiry into the causes of the unrest, to the annoyance of the Irish secretary Goulburn, 7 Feb. 1822.[24] He divided against the Irish suspension of habeas corpus bill that day and on the 11th, and unsuccessfully moved amendments to the Irish insurrection bill (on retaining trial by jury and the appointment of justices in county boroughs), 8 Feb., when he was in the minority against its passage. He made what Sir James Mackintosh* described as 'a very powerful and eloquent answer' to Goulburn in an informative speech in support of Newport's motion on the state of Ireland, 22 Apr., and was damning in his criticisms of ministers for failing to sanction ameliorative Irish measures, 8 July.[25] He approved Goulburn's poor employment bill, 16 May, and expressed his gratitude for English generosity in relieving the victims of the Irish famine, 17 June, but he opposed the constables bill as ineffective, 7 June, and urged that greater alterations be made in the system of Irish tithes, for instance on 19 June 1822, when he was a teller for the minority for inquiry. By that summer he was said by his correspondent Maria Edgeworth to be 'one of the most distinguished men in the British Parliament', and O'Connell flattered him that there was 'no Irish Member who possesses near so much of the public confidence as you already do'.[26]

His raised standing in Ireland, which was recognized by his admission to the freedom of Dublin, 4 Jan. 1823, reflected his role in several vexed Irish parliamentary questions.[27] He led calls for the Irish chief baron, Standish O'Grady, whose son and namesake sat for county Limerick, to be censured for charging excessive fees, making what Henry Grey Bennet* described as 'a clear, convincing statement' of the allegations, 22 June 1821.[28] He was named to the select committee on this, 26 June, but Lord Londonderry, the foreign secretary, had further consideration postponed, 3 July 1821, and again, 4 July 1822.[29] Claiming to be disinterested in the outcome, Rice reintroduced the case, 12 Feb., secured another select committee, 19 Mar., and called on ministers to take it up, 16 May 1823. Failing this, he pursued it with increasing impatience, proposing nine resolutions, 13, 17 June, 2, 3, 8 July, and, although relieved to bring the matter to an end, he acted as a teller for the minority against Scarlett's motion, which he found unsatisfactory, declaring that no further proceedings would be taken against O'Grady, 9 July 1823. Apparently in consequence of this, the chief baron's son Waller grossly insulted Lord Limerick, leaving Rice, who took the affair with deadly seriousness, no choice but to issue a challenge to a duel, which was meant to take place near Dublin on 8 Feb. 1824. As George Richard Philips*, who deemed it a triumph for Rice, recounted: 'With true Irish dexterity the peace officers seized the seconds and *not* the principals, and for three or four days Rice was dodging the police, for he was determined that it should not be said that *he* had avoided fighting'. Waller O'Grady later apologized.[30]

Rice, who was also closely involved with the concurrent inquiry relating to the corporation of Dublin, chaired the select committee on Limerick local taxation, from which he reported in favour of remedial legislative action, 31 July 1822.[31] Having clashed with Gort at a meeting in Limerick about this, and on the city's address congratulating the lord lieutenant Lord Wellesley on escaping unharmed from the Dublin theatre riot at the turn of the year, he brought up his constituency's petition complaining of abuses in the corporation, 11 Mar. 1823, and oversaw the passage of the ensuing Limerick Regulation Act that session.[32] He praised government's Irish tithes proposals, 6 Mar., 21 Apr., but argued for changes to the grand jury presentments bill, 14 Mar., and, despite being broadly favourable to another insurrection bill, was a minority teller for Lord Althorp's amendment for prior inquiry into the state of Ireland, 12 May, when he complained that nothing had been done to increase employment of the Irish poor.[33] Having obtained Goulburn's acquiescence, 18 June, he was the first Member named to the select committee, 20 June, and presented his report, which urged direct public investment, 16 July 1823.[34] This formed the basis of Maberly's motion for an advance of capital to Ireland, to which Rice gave his full approval, 4 May 1824. He also chaired a handful of other committees, such as that on the survey and valuation of Ireland that year, and he was, of course, appointed to the significant inquiries on his native country, 11 May 1824, 17 Feb. 1825.[35]

He condemned the outrages perpetrated by Orangemen in a letter to Lansdowne, 1 Feb., as he did in the House, 12 Feb., 10, 24 Mar. 1823, when he was teller for the majority against the production of information on the theatre attack; he privately speculated that the replacement of Wellesley with an anti-Catholic might, by precipitating a crisis, actually lead to emancipation, although he admitted that this was not only 'a deep game, but a dangerous and perhaps a criminal one'.[36] He spoke and voted for Catholic relief, 17 Apr., and although he disapproved of Burdett's secession that day, he opined to O'Connell that 'it worked well for us, for we should not have had as good a division as we might have expected; and as it is that calamity was averted. *All I am confident* will yet be well with prudence. The quieter we are the better'.[37] He had been expected to support the Irish attorney-general Plunket's use of *ex-officio* informations on the Dublin Orange rioters against Brownlow's censure motion on the 15th, and, although he did not speak that day, he insisted, 22 Apr. 1823, when he was in the majority for inquiry, that the real issue was the perversion of justice by the Dublin sheriff and grand jury.[38]

As energetic as ever on a wide range of subjects in the following session, he (as he repeatedly did in subsequent years) spoke against the grant for Irish Protestant charter schools, 15 Mar., and for securing proper use of the Irish first fruits fund, 25 May, and he voted for Hume's motion for inquiry into the Irish church establishment, 6 May 1824. Back in Ireland late that summer to pick up election intelligence and forward Limerick business, he was credited with being one of the most efficient Irish Members, but O'Connell wrote sourly to his wife from Tralee, where Rice had sat on the grand jury, that he 'would have had a public compliment paid to him if I had not interfered. I am quite dissatisfied with him and his politics'.[39] This probably reflected Rice's doubts about the growing influence of the Catholic Association, which he felt would alienate moderate opinion on the Catholic question and make it less likely that a compromise could be reached with the leading Irish Protestants. Writing to Lansdowne, 8 Dec. 1824, he predicted that at the next election the Catholic tenants would desert their landlords in droves, which

> in most places will make the separation between the upper and lower orders greater than ever; between them will be opened that great gulf which cannot be passed; the violence and the animosities will be frightful, and if not arrested will make our condition more hopeless than ever.

Yet he also conceded that to attempt to suppress the Association would only worsen the situation.[40]

Thus, in early 1825, when there were apparently rumours that he would replace William Gregory as Irish under-secretary, he was active in the opposition's resistance to the Irish unlawful societies bill.[41] He opposed giving leave for the bill, not on the ground that the excesses of the Association were largely pardonable, but because it was rather by concession than by repression that Ireland was to be pacified, 14 Feb. He spoke and was a teller for the Catholics' leaders to be heard at the bar against it, 18 Feb., when he called for Catholic relief, and he moved the unsuccessful wrecking amendment against the third reading, basing his argument on the constitutional right of Irishmen to gather together in order to advance their interests, 25 Feb. He participated in the questioning of O'Connell that day, and was involved in the preparations for the presentation of the Irish Catholics' petition on 1 Mar., when, as on 21 Apr., 10 May, he of course voted for their claims.[42] He supported the related franchise measure as a salutary electoral development, 28 Mar., when he presented and endorsed the petition from his county's Catholics in favour of emancipation accompanied by securities, and 9 May, as well as the proposal for the state payment of Catholic priests, 29 Apr. He stated that he felt wretched at the defeat of the relief measure in the Lords, 18 May, and on the 26th made a long speech on moving for papers on the state of religious animosities in Ireland. He complained bitterly that nothing had been done to improve the country's condition, recommended that further evidence be produced to influence peers in favour of concession and advocated steps to prevent the increase of divisive sectarianism, but he acceded to calls not to force a vote, admitting that he had at least been able to provoke an extensive debate. One contemporary source sourly remarked that he had been 'very active, but not very profound' during the session.[43]

Rice, who was considered popular enough to be secure in his seat during electoral speculation that autumn, signed the requisition for a pro-Catholic county Limerick meeting (which the sheriff refused to authorize) and spoke in favour of emancipation at the Catholics' provincial meeting in Limerick, 24 Oct. 1825.[44] He was, nevertheless, convinced of the need to hold back agitation on the issue during the last session before a general election, and declined to attend the O'Connellite dinner to the friends of religious and civil liberty in Dublin on 2 Feb. 1826.[45] He had his first two articles, on Irish education and the sculptor Canova, published in the *Edinburgh Review* that winter.[46] He asked that the emergency banking regulations should be extended to Ireland, 15 Feb., and briefly called for a commission on Irish tolls and customs, 16 Feb. With Newport, he introduced a bill to alter Irish local jurisdictions, 9, 20 Mar., and secured its passage that session.[47] He strongly attacked the Protestant bias inherent in Irish religious education, 20 Mar., failed in his attempt to amend the Irish church rates bill to the advantage of Catholic and Presbyterian places of worship, 21 Apr., and was reluctantly drawn into a vindication of Catholic relief by George Robert Dawson's vitriolic attack on him, 28 Apr. 1826.

Early that year Rice exchanged a series of addresses with a rival, ostensibly independent, candidate at Limerick, Samuel Dickson, who, however, soon withdrew. Rice, who boasted of the reforms he had obtained and supported Catholic relief (on which he acknowledged he had not been pledged in 1820), alteration of the corn laws and further retrenchment, was therefore returned unopposed at the general election of 1826, when he seconded Richard Fitzgibbon* in the county contest.[48] He also attended the Mallow contest in support of his brother-in-law Lord Glentworth.[49] In his pastoral letter on the education of the Catholic poor that August, Bishop Doyle praised Rice, 'whose talents and whose zeal for the public interests have on this occasion, as on many others, placed him foremost among his countrymen'.[50] He gave notice of a motion, for after the Christmas recess, on the government of Ireland, 28 Nov. 1826, and informed Wellesley's secretary Colonel Merrick Shawe the following day that the real point behind it was to consider the substitution of a cabinet minister for the lord lieutenant in order to bypass the 'arts of *counteraction*' practised by the Irish administration. A week later he complained to Shawe that his intentions had been misunderstood ('my countrymen at large have a most ingenious faculty for misapprehension') and despaired: 'What a state our country is in. I think there is more real danger though *latent* than in [17]98 or 1803'.[51]

In January 1827 Rice published, as a letter addressed to Liverpool, his pamphlet in favour of *Catholic Emancipation*, which Wellesley admired and which Lansdowne, who had seen it the previous month, lauded as 'clear, striking and dispassionate'.[52] Unlike Lansdowne, in February Rice was among those Whigs who, not least because 'the safety of the Protestant establishment in Ireland requires Catholic emancipation', were for persisting with the planned motion for relief, despite Liverpool's recent stroke. He was involved in the planning for 5 Mar., including by informing the police about Raikes's challenge to Brougham, who might otherwise have been unable to attend.[53] His contribution, which, according to Charles Richard Fox*, was 'the speech of the night', was much admired, although George Agar Ellis* thought he had spoken only 'tolerably'.[54] He was a teller for the minority the following day and on the 7th, summoning Edward John Littleton* to take part in a Whig confabulation, confided that 'great interests in both countries – the very existence of Ireland – all in short is at stake. God forgive those whose follies and wickedness have overthrown our hopes *for a time* – but it is for a time only'.[55] He assumed an increasingly high profile that spring, for example on the allegations against Leicester corporation, 15 Mar., Brownlow's motion for information on the Orange procession and Lisburn magistrates, 29 Mar., and the Irish miscellaneous estimates, 5 Apr. 1827.

Rice voted in the minority for Tierney's motion to postpone the committee of supply, 30 Mar. 1827, but was clearly favourable to the appointment of the pro-Catholic Canning as prime minister the following month. He pressed O'Connell to show forbearance so as not to weaken the new premier's position among the Tories and, with Brougham, John Calcraft* and Lord Dudley, he was one of the 'principal performers' in the negotiations between Canning and the moderate Lansdowne Whigs.[56] Although said to be eager for office, he at an early stage declined Canning's offer to him, as an individual, of a seat at the India board, and it was recorded (in the account of his political life that he gave in 1843) that he did so 'on the grounds that as a party man he should go with his party'.[57] He told Canning that he would vote with government 'zealously and anxiously', but, even with his patron's blessing, he felt he had to make the painful decision to stand aloof as long as there was any prospect of an administration being formed in full co-operation with Lansdowne.[58] Much to the regret of O'Connell, who was intent on '*non-oranging* Ireland', he was therefore not in office during the initial stage of the new ministry.[59] Nevertheless, he took his seat behind Canning on the treasury side of the Commons, 1 May, and he heard the duke of Wellington deliver his hostile but 'admirable' speech in the Lords the following day.[60] He spoke several times, mainly on non-party topics, during the remainder of the session, for instance in favour of a select committee on Irish grand jury presentments, to which he was named, 6 June, and liaised with William Lamb*, the Irish secretary, on minor legislation.[61] He divided in the majority for the disfranchisement of Penryn, which Canning was forced to accept, 28 May, but sided with ministers for the grant for water communications in Canada, 12 June 1827.

By that time there were rumours that the king, already unhappy with the intended appointment of Lansdowne to the home office, would refuse Rice's nomination as under-secretary, not least because he was perceived, as Mrs. Arbuthnot recorded, as 'a most violent ultra Whig, who, among other pledges, has given notice of a motion for abolishing the lord lieutenancy'.[62] However, Canning, despite being furious about Rice's attempt to undermine his own pet scheme for the government of Ireland, named him to the post in mid-July 1827. Lord Londonderry, a disaffected Ultra Tory, believed this indicated that Lansdowne was '*omnipotent*' within the ministry, while the Whig Edward Ellice*, disappointed by the limited number of places offered to opposition, consoled himself with the observation that 'Lansdowne and Spring Rice will be something to the purpose'.[63] As he later acknowledged, Rice had no hesitation in accepting the under-secretaryship because, by becoming the *de facto* home office minister in the Commons, 'his position and status were thus permanently established'.[64] Writing to congratulate him on this promotion, the English Whig Edward Davies Davenport*, who believed 'that no greater boon could be conferred upon the half starved people of this and your native country', commented that 'you will have little trouble *in Parliament*; men *must* feel disposed to confide in you'.[65] The expectation that Rice would soon be 'intermeddling in everything' led to the retirement of the home office civil servant Henry Hobhouse, and even the more equable Lamb was not entirely pleased by his frenetic interest in Irish affairs, which included the compilation of a list of nine legislative proposals for the following session.[66]

Canning's death in early August 1827 found Rice in Limerick, where he just had time to inform O'Connell that 'it was *impossible* to form a no-popery administration' and that he imagined Lansdowne would become premier, before rushing back to London.[67] He was overoptimistic regarding his chief, but, as he wrote to Brougham on the 13th, by means of 'the firmness of some and the self denying moderation of others ... all *promises* to go well, and ... the good principle will survive and be transmitted forwards' under Lord Goderich. In particular, he was adamant that the Whigs should remain in office despite the provocative appointment of John Herries* as the new chancellor. In a letter of about this date, he wrote firmly to Brougham, with whom he differed over the handling of Barnes's hostile treatment of the ministry in *The Times* in early September, that the

> only real danger we have to encounter, unless from the pains that the old Tories take to make mischief and to create disunion [is] to suggest to some of us that we make undue sacrifice of dignity, and to others that they are establishing the supremacy of the Whigs, and to the country that the administration is composed of two sides that must eventually split like an ill built wall in a frost. This must be counteracted by frankness, confidence and good humour.[68]

He thoroughly approved of Lansdowne proffering his resignation, which was refused by the king, 1 Sept. 1827, because this gesture, by isolating the secessionist Tories, re-established the influence of the government. He informed Lansdowne that all his correspondents thought the same and he was confident that the ministry, being popular with the country, would be able to continue to pursue Canning's policies, such as retrenchment.[69]

To give an example of one of his initiatives, that autumn Rice recommended the ending of payments for the publication of proclamations in Irish newspapers, arguing that this practice 'has produced the degradation of the press without in any degree contributing to the power of the government'; Lamb was persuaded by his opinion, but left it to his successor to implement the change.[70] As a friend to Ireland, he had to deal with various patronage requests, the most awkward of which, such as for an overseas posting for Richard Newton Bennett, came from O'Connell, whose alternating public statements of support for, and hostility to, the ministry, Rice denounced as 'a shifting and incomprehensible course'. He also had to deal with O'Connell's frustration at not receiving a patent of precedence at the bar, and, following a misunderstanding between them in December, Rice pointedly informed him that 'at the very moment when you expressed so much of bitterness of feeling towards me and others and suggested so much more, I was actively, zealously and I hope usefully employed in advancing your object'; O'Connell's grateful and apologetic reply prevented their quarrel becoming permanent, as yet.[71] Overall, Rice's attitude to Ireland, especially his desire to see the Orangemen put down and sectarian outrages ended, chimed in with that of Wellesley, on whose retirement that winter he wrote to him of 'the deep sense I entertain as an Irishman of the great services you have rendered my country'.[72]

Rice, who was in communication with Lansdowne on police and lunacy questions, was well aware of the instability of the government in January 1828, and on the 15th, informing O'Connell that he expected to return to the opposition benches, he wrote from Whitehall that

> I came here that I might be of service to Ireland and, when that hope ceases, I shall quit office without at least the consciousness of having done or omitted any act that could compromise the great interests to which I am pledged ... A Tory and exclusive government cannot certainly claim any sympathy from me, should such a *monster* be formed, as I consider is most probable.[73]

He was given a hint that Wellington, the new prime minister, might ask him to stay on, but no direct offer was made, so he quitted the home office with Lansdowne, whose departure soon made life much harder for Lamb.[74] Lord Limerick regretted the loss of family influence caused by this resignation and, like Rice's father, who agreed that he should seek greater financial and political opportunities, urged him to accept the position of private secretary to Lord William Henry Cavendish Bentinck*, who was shortly to become governor-general of Bengal. He had apparently done so by the end of February, partly in 'despair of being able to do any real good in Parliament', and although his wife was against the idea, he was expected shortly to leave for India.[75] This was 'universally deplored', according to Joseph Jekyll†, who blamed Rice's father for making him live in penury, and so the Whig grandees, led by Lansdowne, who made a personal appeal to Stephen Rice, began a subscription to provide him with a sufficient income. Such a mark of importance and popularity seems to have had an effect, and Rice senior, to whom Rice wrote in early April 1828 that 'my stay in England has been considered of such value to the interests of Ireland than could have been looked for even of your parental partiality', secured his continuance in Parliament by raising his allowance, reportedly by £2,000 a year. Thanking him for this sacrifice, Lansdowne offered to contribute to any political expenses, such as future contests at Limerick, where Rice's apparent desertion was a cause of considerable unease.[76] It was perhaps in relation to these episodes that De Vere later commented about his uncle, that 'I was aware of his determination to abandon political life and sacrifice all his prospects, rather than forsake the old Whig principles of his career'.[77]

Rice, who indicated that he would support government measures to liberalize trade, 31 Jan., posed the awkward question whether ministers would renew the Irish Unlawful Societies Act that day and again, 12, 15 Feb., and vindicated the continued agitation in favour of Catholic claims, 5, 6 Feb. 1828. He divided for repeal of the Test Acts, 26 Feb., insisting on the 29th that Irish Catholics approved of this measure, and Catholic relief, 12 May, speaking in its favour, 6 Mar., 25 Apr., 12 June, 3 July. In drawing up the list of the finance committee, Herries observed that he 'preferred Rice to Newport because I think he is less mischievous and may be much more useful. Both of them would be too much, especially considering how much they act together'; but in the end it was Newport who was chosen as the Irish opposition Member.[78] Rice presented, but distanced himself from, the Limerick petition for repeal of the Irish Subletting Act, 19 Feb. He defended Lansdowne's decision to reduce the yeomanry corps, 25 Feb., 20 June, and referred to other home office business, 28 Mar., 2 Apr., 14 May. He fully supported the proposals of Peel, the home secretary, for a metropolitan police force, 28 Feb., being appointed to the select committee on this that day, and on 11 Mar. he secured another on Irish education, whose report in favour of the devising of a national system, written by himself, he presented, 19 May.[79] As on 20 Mar., when he successfully divided the House for the continued prohibition of the use of ribbons at elections, he remained active on many electoral, financial and Irish bills, perhaps most significantly on the corporate funds bill. He often worked in co-operation with ministers, for example personally lobbying Wellington on various Irish measures, and showed great persistence, for instance over his rights of executors bill, which, first introduced on 2 Apr., he did not get on to the statute book until two years later.[80] On the provision for Canning's family, which Wellington had at one point thought of placing in his hands, he made such a strong emotional appeal in its support, 14 May, that he had to apologize to several aggrieved Members, 20 May.[81] He referred disparagingly to the 'Bassetlaw bill', 2 June, spoke and voted against the additional churches bill, 30 June, and divided several times in favour of economies towards the end of the session. He discouraged Wilmot Horton, who mentioned him to Wellington among those who were happy to be quoted in favour of emancipation, from moving for an inquiry into the English and Irish churches, 8 July, but called on ministers not to leave Ireland in a dangerously restless state, 18 July 1828.[82]

He interpreted the speech by George Dawson*, the treasury secretary, at Londonderry in August 1828 as sufficient proof of ministers' intentions, and only hoped that emancipation would be granted swiftly, with grace and liberality, once Parliament reassembled in the autumn.[83] In June he received an address of thanks from the congregated trades of Limerick for rescuing the city from 'political non-existence' under a 'mercenary faction', so it was rather unfair of Donoughmore to tell Thomas Creevey* in October that Rice was

> very clever in conversation, tells his stories capitally, like a man of the world in great practice, without any vulgarity, and never overcharging them; but as for the interest he takes in Ireland – I am quite sure my old shoe feels as much.[84]

He was at first cautious of opposition launching a concerted attack at the start of the session in the new year, fearing that making a last ditch stand on emancipation would alienate many pro-Catholics in government, while concentrating on foreign policy was not an option because he thought the Whigs cared 'not a fig' about Greece and Portugal.[85] However, despite the recall of the pro-Catholic lord lieutenant Lord Anglesey, which he deprecated, he was quietly confident of Wellington accepting a relief bill with some securities and, as he wrote to Lord Milton*, 26 Jan. 1829, if

> Wellington does not pledge himself either to *introduce* or to *support* a measure of concession, I trust and believe that among our friends in the *House of Commons* there will be no difference of opinion with respect to the *duty* and necessity of immediate, earnest and systematic opposition. Any other course would be in my mind unintelligible to all and indefensible to many.[86]

The ministry's about-turn in favour of emancipation rendered such a proposal unnecessary. Rice explained that, with its avowed purpose obtained, he would willingly support the suppression of the Catholic Association, 12 Feb., and angrily insisted that the granting of Catholic relief was in no way intended to weaken the rightful place of the established church in Ireland, 6, 9, 10, 16 Mar. Conscious of how historic a decision it would be for his country, he, of course, voted for emancipation, 6 Mar. (and on the 30th), and rejoiced that it would create peace for the Protestants, 17 Mar. With Althorp, he had approached government with a request to make the related Irish franchise measure prospective in character, but, being 'ready to swallow anything to get emancipation', as Greville recorded, he strenuously advocated the abolition of the 40*s*. freehold franchise as its essential accompaniment, 20 Mar. (though he objected to details of this and other minor securities, 24, 26 Mar.)[87] In spite of having apparently taken offence at something attributed to O'Connell, he judged that his status was such as to merit his being seated for Clare; he was against pressing this, 23 Mar., but, having voted for allowing him to take his seat unimpeded, 18 May, he spoke forcefully, if unsuccessfully, for his own motion for amending the Emancipation Act in O'Connell's favour, 21 May.[88] As he was often to do, he argued against the introduction of poor laws to Ireland, 7 May 1829, contending that they were 'indefensible in principle, oppressive in practice, burdensome to the farmer and landowner, and injurious to the real interests of the lower classes', but he advocated a general inquiry into the issue of Irish economic relief. By that summer Rice was evidently disappointed that, as he had anticipated a year earlier, the way emancipation had been handled had neutralized its good effect, but, in reference to one (unidentified) issue, Wellington commented to Peel that 'we are travelling along the road which he recommends to us'.[89]

Rice, who encouraged O'Connell to study the parliamentary papers on the East India Company that autumn, asked the anti-slavery campaigner Thomas Fowell Buxton* what his plans were 'and what I ought to fag at during the recess', while offering him his 'best help, night and day, if necessary' on any intended committee on colonial slavery.[90] He busied himself with Limerick concerns, including the Mechanics' Institute and his own electoral position, in September 1829, when, despite the renewed calm, he expressed great dissatisfaction with the lackadaisical Irish secretary Lord Francis Leveson Gower* and the continued dominance of the old Ascendancy interest at the Castle.[91] He informed Vesey Fitzgerald, the president of the board of trade, on the 23rd that 'I never stood so well in Limerick, I may say with both parties', and would be safe in the event of an election, 'unless I should voluntarily make my bow and give way to an agitator', as 'I am not very much in love with the House of Commons and where the step could be taken honourably I do not think my friend Villiers Stuart's resolution [to retire] an unwise one'.[92] In a letter dated 4 Nov. to the knight of Kerry*, in which he contemplated writing a long printed address to Wellington on the state of Ireland, he speculated that, as 'the federal system of cabinet making is so utterly at a discount', it was unlikely that Huskisson would join the government.[93] Ironically, in December 1829, and again the following spring, there were rumours in the press that he was about to accept public office, so precipitating a by-election, but it was finally made clear that he had never intended to accompany Lord Clare, an ally in his struggles against the corporation of Limerick, to Bombay, of which he was to be the new governor.[94] John Croker* judged that his adhesion, like that of other Whigs, would only weaken Wellington, but included him in his list of a conjectured Huskissonite government.[95] Calling it 'a sound, reasonable, as well as learned and very agreeably written paper', Macvey Napier accepted his article on 'Mr. Sadler's School – Italian Economists' for publication in the January 1830 issue of the *Edinburgh Review*, after which Rice offered to send him an essay on 'the duties political and civil which remain to be performed in Ireland and for Ireland'.[96] In a long and cogent parliamentary analysis in a letter of the 9th to James Abercromby*, during which he regretted the enforced resignation on the ground of illness of Vesey Fitzgerald, he concluded that 'if my dissection of the House of Commons is just, it would appear that the *relative* strength of the government is increased, and that the *absolute* strength of all other parties is considerably diminished since the adjournment', and that Wellington would continue to 'endeavour so to poise the political balance as to make it incline either way at his will and pleasure', while trying 'in various ways to conciliate and to soften opposition'.[97] A month later Lord Limerick agreed with Rice that 'the ministry cannot stand as now constituted'.[98]

Rice admitted that it was really only the ministerial slip about distress that induced him to vote for Knatchbull's amendment to the address, 4 Feb., but he reverted to the problem of Irish distress, 12, 17 Feb. 1830. He raised a question about the East India Company, 5 Feb., and was named to the select committee on it, 9 Feb. As he had the previous year, he voted to transfer East Retford's seats to Birmingham, 11 Feb., 5, 15 Mar., and he divided for the enfranchisement of Birmingham, Leeds and Manchester, 23 Feb., and parliamentary reform, 28 May. He backed O'Connell's attempt to reduce the grant for Irish volunteers, 22 Feb., and joined in the renewed opposition campaign for economies and lower taxation that session, privately expressing to Althorp his horror at the idea of opposition supporting any proposal for the reintroduction of a property tax.[99] He threatened to move for an investigation into Irish education if the grants for it were left unaltered, 26 Feb., and, not for the first time, insisted that an inquiry into the Irish church could only be to its own benefit, 4 Mar. With government support, he carried his motion for a wide-ranging select committee on the Irish poor, which he intended as a means of making practical suggestions, 11 Mar.[100] A few days later he commented to John Rickman, a Commons clerk, that 'they must make a great effort in Ireland at agricultural improvements', and, treating his cynical response with characteristic courtesy, accepted the written evidence which Rickman gave him 'as a God-send at a dead lift'.[101] He chaired most of its meetings, proving himself a highly able questioner, to Doyle's satisfaction, and drafted its extensive reports, which, when they became available in print in October, Wellington promised to consider.[102] His assiduity in attending these committees prevented him from attending a rescheduled meeting with Sir John Benn Walsh*, who complained in his diary, 25 Mar. 1830, that 'there is always something mistaken, or blundered, in all engagements with Irishmen'.[103] Rice sided with opposition on Portugal, 10 Mar., and the affair at Terceira, 28 Apr. 1830. He voted for Jewish emancipation, 5 Apr. (when his name also appeared in the minority list) and 17 May. He supported Hume's motion for abolition of the Irish lord lieutenancy, not because he favoured it as such, but because he wanted to improve the efficiency and reduce the expense of the viceregal system of government, 11 May; opposition was split, with O'Connell and others hostile, but Rice persuaded them to divide, which they did by 229-115, and John Cam Hobhouse* considered this 'a very great minority for such a question'.[104] He was a teller that day, and again on the 13th for the minority (182-120) on his own motion for repeal of the Irish coal duties, which he considered a crucial economic issue. He played a major part in the parliamentary lobby against the increased Irish spirit and stamp duties that month, expressing his delight on the abandonment of this plan in a letter to the Limerick chamber of commerce, 15 June, and in the House, 2 July, when he complained about the mishandling of the Irish miscellaneous estimates and the loss of intended Irish reforms.[105] He spoke in support of Newport's resolutions on the Irish first fruits fund, 18 May, but condemned O'Connell's motion for repeal of the Irish Vestry Acts, preferring a forlorn amendment of his own for their alteration, 10 June. After much obstruction, he got his Galway franchise bill through the Commons, 25 May, but it was lost in the Lords. Among numerous other votes that session, he divided to end capital punishment for forgery, 24 May, 7 June, and he spoke and was a teller for reform of the divorce laws, another hobbyhorse, 3 June 1830.

Having been detained on parliamentary business, he arrived in Limerick, where a memorial to him was under construction, in time for the general election of 1830, when, faced with a challenge from Dickson, he emphasized his many years of service and advocated further economic and social reforms.[106] It was probably at this time that O'Connell, who placed his name on Rice's committee, made a speech in his favour as a Repealer; his nephew De Vere later recalled Rice's 'indignant chafing' at this action by O'Connell, who 'thought he could have tied him to the tail [political following]. He failed, and thenceforth he hated him ... there was no love lost between them'.[107] Identifying himself on the hustings as an independent, resident, honest and proven candidate, Rice was nevertheless subjected to a long contest, and was feared to be 'in jeopardy'. Yet he finished over 300 votes ahead of Dickson and was congratulated by Edward Smith Stanley*, who opined that 'it would have been a scandal to Ireland had you been thrown out, and I was glad to see the decisiveness of your victory at last'.[108] On 20 Sept. he confided to Dawson from Mount Trenchard that

> I have had some indisposition and many severe trials since the election. We lost a most beautiful and accomplished child, a daughter of my sister Lady De Vere, under our very windows, drowned while bathing. Immediately after [his eldest son] Stephen had the narrowest escape from fire and I burned both my hands so desperately as to lose the use of them for three weeks. I am not yet recovered though doing well. I am, however, grateful for the escape

I have had from greater calamities. What an awful event has been the death of Huskisson.

Unable to attend the Dublin meeting on the French revolution that month, he warned Dawson, not without surprising prescience, that

the time draweth near when the small games of parliamentary tactics will be as nothing when compared with the larger and more fearful questions that are arising and must arise. The *war of opinion* of which Canning spoke, and which I sincerely believe he was the only man who could have averted, is now begun. And if begun, think you that we insulars are in so satisfactory a state that the French cry will not find an echo on our shores. Depend upon it, times of no ordinary difficulty are approaching, to be met in my mind by one course only [of] acquiring through the means of large concessions, made *early and cheerfully*, a right to resist what is unreasonable and dangerous. You opposed us last year [23 Feb. 1830] on Lord J. Russell's motion in favour of the great unrepresented towns. You will have to swallow that and many larger matters before long.[109]

However, he thought the time was ripe for advantageous Irish improvements to be implemented and, convalescing in Limerick that autumn, he occupied himself with local affairs and, for example, chaired an anti-slavery meeting, 29 Sept.[110] In November 1830 two petitions were entered against his return, but were not pursued.

Rice, who was of course listed by ministers among their 'foes', was thought of as a possible opposition candidate for the Speakership if Manners Sutton retired.[111] He had lost some of his alarmism about the state of Ireland by the time of his speech on the address, 2 Nov. 1830, when he condemned O'Connell's repeal agitation out of hand and, much to the frustration of the knight of Kerry, turned the moderate Whigs 'on an adverse course' away from conciliation with Wellington.[112] He gave notice of a motion for repeal of the coal duties, 3 Nov., and secured the reappointment of his committee on the Irish poor, 11 Nov., although both these matters were overtaken by subsequent events. He voted to reduce the duty on wheat imported to the West Indies, 12 Nov., when he agreed that the Irish Subletting Act should be amended. He was privy to the preparations for Brougham's parliamentary reform motion and duly divided in the decisive majority for appointing a select committee on the civil list, to which he was named, 15 Nov.[113] It was initially thought that he would resume his position under Lansdowne at the home office in Lord Grey's new government;[114] but Lansdowne, now the lord president, whose prop (with Smith Stanley) Rice was supposed by Abercromby to be, obtained for him the Irish vice-treasurership, which he declined as a sinecure. Rice, the only Irishman in the new administration, was then offered the financial secretaryship to the treasury, which he accepted with the blessing of Althorp, the new chancellor and leader of the Commons.[115] Like his colleague Ellice, the patronage secretary, he did not have to stand for re-election, which was just as well as it was considered possible that he might have lost his seat.[116] He moved the writs for Althorp and the other new ministers, 22 Nov. 1830, and, in their absence, fielded much of the treasury business during the remainder of the pre-Christmas session.

He was courted over Irish education grants, in 'a confidential conversation', 25 Nov. 1830, by O'Connell, who, however, perhaps in relation to the dusted-off Irish proposals he had formulated in 1827, privately remarked: 'as to Spring Rice's "nineteen bills", they may all be dispatched in one word – *fudge*!'[117] George Pigott* reported that Rice 'began very well with the estimates', 6 Dec., but, succumbing to the pressures of office, he was non-committal on the topics of coal duties, 8 Dec., and Irish grand juries, 9 Dec. 1830, and soon demonstrated a reluctance to release official papers as parliamentary returns.[118] In a letter to Lansdowne on the 30th he made several suggestions about the Irish electoral system, including the enfranchisement of leaseholders and payers of local taxes, and stated that Limerick deserved a second Member.[119] According to Maria Edgeworth, he was confident of his colleagues' chances of success, in that 'though it requires nice steering, we shall get through', and in early January 1831 he informed her that ministers would choose their moment to make a dramatic strike against O'Connell.[120] He notified Grey that the Provincial Bank of Ireland, of which he was chairman, had 'stood the shock' of O'Connell's attempted run on it, and his hostility to repeal, as expressed in his reply to the Limerick cordwainers' request to present their repeal petition (which he did not bring up), 10 Jan., was given wider currency in a Unionist pamphlet published that month.[121] He devoted himself to the administrative detail of his post and, for example in relation to the admission of sugar to distilleries, the Orkney Member Traill commented that

I am much pleased with him. He is one of the ablest men connected with the ministry, and is so willing to receive information and so attentive to what is suggested, that it is very satisfactory to have such a person to treat with in matters of importance to our local interests.[122]

However, he was not unaware of the necessity of forwarding his constituents' patronage demands and, out of fear of 'treasury jobbing', Anglesey, the reappointed lord lieutenant, warned Smith Stanley, his chief secretary, 24 Feb., that Rice 'is a capital fellow and full of intelligence upon Irish matters, but he is Limerick all over'.[123] Doyle's pamphlet in favour of making legal provision for the Irish poor was addressed to Rice in March 1831 in recognition of his commitment to the cause, despite their acknowledged differences on the subject.[124] With Poulett Thomson, another junior minister, he took the credit for much of Althorp's first and rather disastrous budget in February 1831, although he was a late, and perhaps not sincere, convert to the idea of the controversial transfer tax.[125] This he defended on the 14th in the House, where, amid numerous contributions to debate, he stressed government's endeavours to make economies, 21, 28 Feb., 25, 28 Mar., and challenged O'Connell to put down a substantive motion on repeal, 28 Feb. Voicing '*ad deterrendum*' the hint that the king would grant a dissolution if the reform bill was lost, he sat through the debates on 21 and 22 Mar., scribbling the first of a series of laconic accounts of the proceedings for the delectation of Lady Holland.[126] He was a teller for the majority of one for the second reading, 22 Mar., and, in what he feared would be a 'doubtful' division, for the minority against Gascoyne's wrecking amendment, 19 Apr. 1831. The following day, when he clashed with the knight of Kerry over this in the chamber, he privately observed that the decision not to increase the number of Irish and Scottish seats 'will I very much apprehend lead to most formidable and calamitous consequences ... slackened support here and great and increasing discontent in Ireland'.[127]

Rice declined a requisition to stand for Liverpool, Gascoyne's constituency, at the general election of 1831, but made a good declamation in favour of the reform bill there on his way to Limerick, where the now completed statue of him had recently been placed on a tall pillar in Pery Square.[128] His friends mustered in his support, but once it became clear that neither Dickson nor Tuthill would stand, he was returned unopposed as a steadfastly reformist minister, who explained that he had joined the government in order to advance the best interests of Ireland.[129] He voted for the successful reformers Robert Way Harty and Louis Perrin in the Dublin contest and was the guest of honour at a public dinner in Belfast at the end of May 1831.[130] Back at Westminster, where one of his duties was to hold parliamentary dinners, despite the seriousness of the cholera epidemic that summer, he resumed his very constant attendance in the House.[131] He was frequently on his feet to handle routine government business, notably the proceedings in the committee of supply and on minor financial legislation, and, while making almost no significant speeches, he often intervened on petitions, returns, procedural and privilege questions. He of course invariably divided with his ministerial colleagues, except, as very often, when he was acting as a teller. The *Freeman's Journal* called him 'the legislator for Ireland' that year, and Denis Le Marchant† later stated that Rice, 'an excellent secretary to the treasury, was a ready speaker, and thoroughly conversant with Irish affairs'.[132]

Heading his letter to Lady Holland, 4 July 1831, '1st bulletin of the grand army', he noted that 'the thermometer stands in the House at 96 at the least and our reform quicksilver is equally high', while on the 27th, referring to the debacle about Saltash being transferred from schedule A, he reassured her husband that 'I think the accident of last night will not lead to the mischief that might have been feared ... We have got on our legs and people are in good humour again'.[133] He differed with Goulburn on Irish tithes, 12 July, and made a suggestion about tightening up the system of grants for colonial improvements, 25 July. His decision to retain his hat, because of a cold, while chairing the grand committee, 15 July, led to remonstrations from the floor and Littleton drew up a bogus list of precedents which enjoyed much success.[134] At the end of the month, Lord Ellenborough observed of the possible demise of Lord Spencer, which would have removed Althorp to the Lords, that the 'persons talked of for the exchequer are Stanley, Rice and Parnell. Of these they all say Rice is the ablest, Parnell very dull, but Stanley of course will have it'.[135] He spoke at length against Sadler's motion for an Irish poor law, 29 Aug. (and again, 19 June 1832), for the plan of national education in Ireland, of which he was in large part the architect, 9 Sept., and against Goulburn's amendment to the Irish public works bill, 16 Sept. 1831.[136]

On the death of his father, 20 Sept. 1831, Rice came into an annual income of about £8,000, or what he later described as 'the fortune of a comfortable Irish country gentleman and no more'.[137] That month Anglesey doubted that he would be a suitable Irish secretary: 'he has already too much to do with Ireland, even where he is. He is clever, and I like him; but he is *not liked*'.[138] As if to bear this out, Grey deemed him to have stepped out of line in expressing his mortification at not being consulted over who was to be appointed as lord lieutenant of county Limerick.[139] Despite being ill and dispirited, he was back at his post to see the reform bill reintroduced, 12 Dec. 1831, and later that month was heard dropping heavy hints in private that ministers would accept alterations to it in order to secure its passage through the Lords.[140] On its recommittal, 20 Jan. 1832, he informed Lady Holland that 'we make way but slowly and it almost looks like a recommencement of the botch of last session', while on the 24th he despondently pointed out that 'the bill consists of 53 pages: in three nights we have got through four'. He despaired of the grindingly slow progress on the second readings of the English and Irish reform bills in typically amusing letters to her, 20 Mar. and 22 May, and was of course prepared to resign with Althorp on the reform issue in early May 1832.[141]

In relation to the difficult debate on the Russian-Dutch loan, 26 Jan. 1832, he reported to Lady Holland that it 'was a very nervous moment. The keel scraped along the shingles for two mortal hours, and even when we floated downwards the water was very shallow. Still, we did float'. Given an opening by Dawson, he 'gallantly supported' Althorp, as Littleton noted, against Goulburn's censure motion on the state of government finances, 6 Feb., and his implicit attack on Lord Eldon for giving his son six public offices, 6 Mar., drew a rejoinder from him in the Lords, 12 Mar.[142] He spoke for Smith Stanley's Irish tithes resolutions, 27 Mar., and on 31 Mar. declared that it was not by legislative repression but by the determined resistance of the magistracy that unrest was to be quelled in Ireland, although he was prepared to concede a select committee on this, 23 May. It was about this time that he joined the Political Economy Club, and on 6 Apr. John Lewis Mallet recorded in his diary that he had met him the day before: 'a cheerful, agreeable, good-natured man, with whom I chatted on all sorts of subjects, and it was much the best part of the entertainment'.[143] Attacked by O'Connell on Frederick Shaw's motion for preserving the rights of Irish freemen, 2 July, Rice, according to one newspaper report, 'answered in a great passion and at the close of each sentence thumped the table with a very vehement gesture'; he returned to this subject on 3 Aug., promising that the unacceptable Lords' amendment would be altered sometime in future.[144] His only other major speech that session was for the grant for scriptural education, 23 July, when he repeated his arguments in favour of children of all religions being educated together except for religious studies. He was kept incessantly busy in attending the House right up to the prorogation, 15 Aug. 1832.

O'Connell's determination that Repealers should be returned for his constituency led Rice to seek a berth elsewhere, and he received offers from Manchester and Wolverhampton.[145] On the pretext of needing to reside closer to London, he therefore took leave from what he referred to as the now liberated borough of Limerick in a parting address, 26 June. At the suggestion of Ellice, he announced his candidacy that month for Cambridge, where he defended the government's record and was returned with the like-minded Pryme after a contest against a Conservative, at the general election in December 1832.[146] He was again considered the ministry's preferred candidate for the Speakership that year, but, despite his several times staking his claims, the chair always eluded him.[147] He therefore continued in office and joined the cabinet in 1834, having given the performance of his life on 23 Apr. that year in his speech repulsing O'Connell's repeal motion. As chancellor in Melbourne's second ministry he was considered a failure and he retired into an exchequer sinecure, with a peerage, in 1839. A capable speaker, if sometimes given to 'studied pompousness', he made few enemies in the House, where he was described by James Grant as 'somewhat of a dandy', having a 'prim appearance, both in manners and dress', although Maria Edgeworth was more struck by his 'inspiration-electrico look'.[148] Although he assisted in the development of liberal doctrines, he, by his own admission, never departed from the precepts of the Whigs throughout his career, once calling himself 'an old Foxite Whig'.[149] In a not entirely unjust attack, Benjamin Disraeli† (in his sixth Runnymede letter) addressed Rice as

> shrewd without being sagacious, bustling without method, loquacious without eloquence, ever prompt though always superficial, and ever active though always blundering, you are exactly the sort of fussy busybody who would impose upon and render himself indispensable to indolent and ill informed men of strong ambition and weak minds.[150]

He died in February 1866, his title and estates descending to his grandson, his late son Stephen's son, Thomas (1849-1926), 2nd Baron Monteagle. Several of his offspring obtained official employments, including another grandson, the diplomat Sir Cecil Arthur Spring Rice (1859-1918), who wrote the words to the hymn, 'I vow to thee, my country'.[151]

[1] Wellington mss WP1/1042/70. [2] *Creevey Pprs.* ii. 180; *Fox Jnl.* 94, 135. [3] M. Hurst, *Maria Edgeworth and Public Scene*, 46; *Taylor Autobiog.* ii. 209-13; *Scott Jnl.* 545; Lord Teignmouth, *Reminiscences of Many Years*, ii. 216; *Jerningham Letters* ed. E. Castle, ii. 396. [4] C. Knight, *Passages of a Working Life*, ii. 160; P. Mandler, *Aristocratic Government in Age of Reform*, 100, 113; R. Brent, *Liberal Anglican Politics*, 78, 135-6; B. Hilton, *Age of Atonement*, 237, 258; *Oxford DNB*. [5] See J. Ridden, "Making Good Citizens': National Identity, Religion and Liberalism among the Irish Elite, *c.*1800-1850' (London Univ. Ph.D. thesis, 1998), 7-13, 20, 167-75, 258-71, and 'Irish Reform between 1798 Rebellion and Great Famine', in *Rethinking the Age of Reform* ed. A. Burns and J. Innes, 271-94. [6] *Lady Holland to Son*, 178-9; S.C. Hall, *Retrospect of Long Life*, i. 210. [7] Not to be confused

with Stephen Henry Rice (*d.* 1831), asst. barrister of Kerry (*Limerick Evening Post*, 5 July 1831). [8] C.M. Murphy, 'Life and Politics of Thomas Spring Rice, 1st Baron Monteagle of Brandon' (Univ. Coll Cork M.A. thesis, 1991), 1-2; D.H. Burton, *Cecil Spring Rice*, 20-21; NLI mss 14119. [9] Murphy, 3-5. [10] T. Rice, *Inquiry into Effects of Irish Grand Jury Laws*, 3-4, 7, 89-90. [11] NLI, Monteagle mss 11140 (1), Horner to Rice, 27 June 1815; *Horner Pprs.* 9, 901. [12] *General Advertiser and Limerick Gazette*, 23, 30 June, 3, 10, 17, 24, 28, 31 July 1818; *HP Commons, 1790-1820*, ii. 668-9. [13] *CJ*, lxiv. 22-23, 171, 189; *PP* (1819), iv. 287-9. [14] Murphy, 6. [15] *Croker Pprs.* i. 131-2; *General Advertiser*, 22 Feb., 3, 10, 24 Mar., 11, 14 Apr. 1820. [16] R. Herbert, 'Chairing of Thomas Spring Rice', *N. Munster Antiquarian Jnl.* iv (1945), 133-42; *General Advertiser*, 7, 21 July, 1 Aug., 12 Sept. 1820. [17] *O'Connell Corresp.* ii. 869. [18] Monteagle mss A/30 (NRA 19437). [19] *O'Connell Corresp.* ii. 895. [20] *CJ*, lxxvi. 147, 168, 294, 383. [21] *The Times*, 27 Feb., 2 May 1821. [22] *Autobiographic Recollections of George Pryme* ed. A. Bayne, 89, 179. [23] *Dublin Evening Post*, 25 Oct., 8 Dec. 1821. [24] Add. 37298, f. 158. [25] Add. 52445, f. 78; Buckingham, *Mems. Geo. IV*, i. 318. [26] *Edgeworth Letters*, 402; *O'Connell Corresp.* ii. 973. [27] *Dublin Evening Post*, 7, 16 Jan. 1823; *O'Connell Corresp.* ii. 987-8. [28] HLRO, Hist. Coll. 379, Grey Bennet diary, 101. [29] *The Times*, 4 July 1821. [30] Ibid. 12-14, 17, 18 Feb. 1824; Monteagle mss A/2-13 (NRA 19437); Shakespeare Birthplace Trust, Philips mss DR 198/11; *O'Connell Corresp.* iii. 1092, 1095. [31] *PP* (1822), vii. 235-348. [32] *Dublin Evening Post*, 31 Dec. 1822, 2, 7, 11 Jan.; *The Times*, 12 Mar. 1823. [33] *The Times*, 15 Mar. 1823. [34] Ibid. 21 June 1823; *PP* (1823), vi. 331-529; B. Jenkins, *Era of Emancipation*, 208-9. [35] *PP* (1824), viii. 79-203. [36] Lansdowne mss. [37] *O'Connell Corresp.* ii. 1012. [38] Buckingham, i. 446. [39] Add. 37302, f. 350; 37303, ff. 1-5, 105; Lansdowne mss, Lansdowne to Rice, 2 Sept.; *Dublin Evening Post*, 9 Sept. 1824; *O'Connell Corresp.* iii. 1126. [40] Add. 37303, f. 75; Lansdowne mss. [41] Jenkins, 227. [42] *O'Connell Corresp.* iii. 1176, 1178. [43] *Session of Parl. 1825*, p. 482. [44] *Dublin Evening Post*, 8, 10 Sept., 4, 11, 27, 29 Oct.; Brougham mss, Rice to Brougham, 14 Oct. 1825. [45] NLW, Coedymaen mss 999, 1000; Jenkins, 234; *O'Connell Corresp.* iii. 1278. [46] *Edinburgh Rev.* xliii (1826), 194-224, 496-510. [47] *The Times*, 16 Feb., 21 Mar. 1826. [48] *Limerick Chron.* 25 Feb., 1, 22 Mar., 1, 12 Apr., 31 May, 7, 14, 17, 24 June 1826. [49] *Southern Reporter*, 15, 17 June; *Dublin Evening Post*, 17, 20 June 1826. [50] *Pastoral and Education Letters of Bishop James Doyle* ed. T. McGrath, 228. [51] Add. 37304, ff. 248, 281; E. Brynn, *Crown and Castle*, 71. [52] Add. 37405, f. 1; Lansdowne mss, Lansdowne to Rice, 30 Dec. 1826. [53] *Canning's Ministry*, 32, 40; *Creevey Pprs.* ii. 107-8; Hurst, 44. [54] Add. 52058, f. 7; 52447, f. 51; Northants. RO, Agar Ellis diary. [55] *Canning's Ministry*, 43. [56] *O'Connell Corresp.* iii. 1378; Add. 51584, Tierney to Holland [22 Apr. 1827]; *Canning's Ministry*, 241, 272. [57] *Creevey Pprs.* ii. 114; Monteagle mss A/26 (NRA 19437). [58] *Canning's Ministry*, 206. [59] *O'Connell Corresp.* iii. 1389, 1397-8. [60] Broughton, *Recollections*, ii. 189. [61] Add. 37305, ff. 117, 121. [62] *HMC Bathurst*, 638; *Arbuthnot Jnl.* ii. 129-30. [63] TNA, Ellenborough mss, Londonderry to Ellenborough, 10 Aug. 1827; *Canning's Ministry*, 340, 344. [64] Monteagle mss A/26 (NRA 19437). [65] Murphy, 33-34. [66] Parker, *Peel*, ii. 36; Torrens, *Melbourne*, i. 223-4, 247-8, 274-5, 287-8; Jenkins, 253-4; Monteagle mss 548, pp. 4, 17, 18, 26, 32, 35, 37, 57. [67] *O'Connell Corresp.* iii. 1407. [68] Brougham mss; NLS mss 24748, f. 30; Lansdowne mss, Rice to Lansdowne, 6-8 Sept. 1827. [69] Murphy, 36-37; Add. 37305, f. 169; Lansdowne mss, Rice to Lansdowne, 3, 11 Sept.; Fitzwilliam mss, Rice to Milton, 7, 11 Sept. 1827. [70] Torrens, i. 248-50; B. Inglis, *Freedom of Press in Ireland*, 185-6. [71] Brougham mss, Rice to Brougham, 1 Oct. 1827; *O'Connell Corresp.* iii. 1413, 1419, 1431, 1437-9, 1445, 1447. [72] Add. 37305, ff. 179, 204, 258. [73] Lansdowne mss, Rice to Lansdowne, 1, 6 Jan., reply, 2 Jan. 1828; *O'Connell Corresp.* iii. 1450; Hurst, 46, 48. [74] Monteagle mss A/26 (NRA 19437); Torrens, i. 304-5. [75] Murphy, 42, 46-48; Torrens, i. 305-6; Nottingham Univ. Lib. Portland mss PwH 146; Add. 38755, ff. 116, 141; Hurst, 48; *Corresp. of Lord William Henry Cavendish Bentinck* ed. C.H. Philips, i. 13, 17, 22, 25, 30. [76] *Corresp. of Joseph Jekyll* ed. A. Bourke, 178; Agar Ellis diary, 29 Feb., 1 Mar., 12 Apr.; Lansdowne mss, Lansdowne to Rice [Mar.], to S.E. Rice, 10 Mar., 11 Apr.; *Limerick Evening Post*, 14, 18 Mar., 1, 4, 15 Apr., 9 May, 3 June 1828; Murphy, 48. [77] Monteagle mss A/30 (NRA 19437) [78] Add. 40395, ff. 219, 221. [79] *PP* (1828), 223-8. [80] Wellington mss WP1/942/9; 1010/3; 1100/7; P. Jupp, *British Politics on Eve of Reform*, 160, 171 n, 177, 203. [81] *Ellenborough Diary*, i. 61. [82] Wellington mss WP1/978/13. [83] Brougham mss, Rice to Brougham, 20 Aug. 1828; Coedymaen mss 1003. [84] Monteagle mss A/15 (NRA 19437); *Creevey Pprs.* ii. 180. [85] Lansdowne mss, Lansdowne to Rice, 26 Dec., Smith Stanley to Lansdowne, 31 Dec. 1828; Jupp, 299. [86] PRO NI, Anglesey mss D619/32A/3/1/13; Fitzwilliam mss. [87] *Greville Mems.* i. 263-4; *Arbuthnot Jnl.* ii. 250. [88] *Greville Mems.* i. 266, 280; *O'Connell Corresp.* iv. 1513a, 1572-3. [89] Hurst, 48; Jenkins, 277; Wellington mss WP1/1042/70. [90] *O'Connell Corresp.* iv. 1610; viii. 3415; *Buxton Mems.* 225-6. [91] Lansdowne mss, Rice to Lansdowne, 1 Sept.; Monteagle mss 549, same to ?same, 23 Sept., to Vesey Fitzgerald, 23 Sept., to Goderich, 23 Sept., to wife, 23, 24 Sept., to Dawson, 28 Sept.; *Limerick Evening Post*, 29 Sept. 1829. [92] Monteagle mss 549. [93] PRO NI, Fitzgerald mss MIC639/13/7/24. [94] Lansdowne mss, Clare to Lansdowne, 23 Dec.; *Dublin Evening Post*, 29 Dec. 1829; *Limerick Evening Post*, 16 Mar., 6 Apr.; Grey mss, Ellice to Grey, 25 Mar. 1830. [95] *Croker Pprs.* ii. 58, 62. [96] Monteagle mss 13370 (1), Napier to Rice, 20 Dec. 1829; Add. 34614, ff. 268, 446; *Edinburgh Rev.* c (1830), 344-63. [97] NLS mss 24770, f. 39; Torrens, i. 327-8. [98] Monteagle mss 13370 (5), Limerick to Rice, 9 Feb. 1830. [99] Le Marchant, *Althorp*, 239. [100] Jupp, 163. [101] O. Williams, *Life and Letters of John Rickman*, 252-3. [102] W.J. Fitzpatrick, *Life of Dr. Doyle*, ii. 213; Add. 34614, f. 431; *PP* (1830), vii. 1-834; Wellington mss WP1/1144/8, 9. [103] NLW, Ormathwaite mss FG1/5, pp. 39-40. [104] Add. 56554, f. 98. [105] *Limerick Evening Post*, 4, 11, 21 May, 18 June 1830. [106] Ibid. 6, 9, 16, 23, 27 July 1830. [107] *Dublin Evening Post*, 22 July 1830; Monteagle mss A/29, 30 (NRA 19437). [108] *Limerick Evening Post*, 6, 10, 13, 17 Aug.; Add. 76381, Poulett Thomson to Althorp, 14 Aug; Monteagle mss 13370 (6), Smith Stanley to Rice, 26 Aug. 1830. [109] Monteagle mss 13370 (8); *Warder*, 4 Sept. 1830. [110] NLI, Wyse mss 15024 (7), Rice to Wyse, 9 Sept.; *Limerick Evening Post*, 21, 28 Sept., 1 Oct. 1830. [111] Hatherton mss, Palmerston to Littleton, 19 Nov. [Dec.] 1830. [112] Fitzgerald mss T3075/18/54; Derby mss 920 Der (14) 124/3, knight of Kerry to Smith Stanley, 7 June 1831. [113] Agar Ellis diary, 12 Nov. 1830. [114] *Croker Pprs.* ii. 77. [115] Add. 51575, Abercromby to Holland, 19 Nov. 1830; Monteagle mss A/26 (NRA 19437). [116] Fitzgerald mss MIC639/13/7/99; Murphy, 54. [117] *O'Connell Corresp.* iv. 1733, 1735. [118] Bucks. RO, Fremantle mss D/FR/139/14/73; *Cockburn Letters*, 280, 283. [119] Lansdowne mss. [120] *Edgeworth Letters*, 440, 467. [121] Grey mss GRE/B41/10/1; *Limerick Evening Post*, 14 Jan. 1831; *Ireland Vindicated ... by a True Whig*, 11-12, 48. [122] Orkney Archives, Balfour mss D2/8/9, Traill to Balfour, 5 Feb., 16 Mar. 1831. [123] Derby mss 119/2. [124] Fitzpatrick, ii. 275-6; *Pastoral and Education Letters of Doyle*, 26-27. [125] *Baring Jnls.* i. 81; *Three Diaries*, 9. [126] *Three Diaries*, 70; Add. 51573. [127] Add. 51573, Rice to Lady Holland [19, 20 Apr. 1831]. [128] *Dublin Evening Post*, 21, 28 Apr.; Hatfield House mss, Leigh to Salisbury, 27 Apr. 1831. [129] *Limerick Evening Post*, 26, 29 Apr., 3, 10 May; *Limerick Herald*, 5, 9 May 1831. [130] *Dublin Evening Post*, 17 May; *Limerick Evening Post*, 31 May 1831. [131] *Macaulay Letters*, ii. 46, 48. [132] Murphy, 62; Le Marchant, 489; *Dublin Evening Post*, 12 July 1832. [133] Add. 51573. [134] Hatherton diary. [135] *Three Diaries*, 110. [136] Monteagle mss A/30 (NRA 19437); Ridden, 'Irish Reform', 286-7. [137] *Limerick Evening Post*, 27 Sept. 1831; *Gent. Mag.* (1831), 381, 653; Murphy, 2. [138] Anglesey mss 27B, p. 52. [139] Derby mss 117/5, Grey to Smith Stanley, 18 Sept.; 8, Rice to same, 17 Sept. 1831. [140] Add. 51573, Rice to Lady Holland [12 Dec. 1831]; Bodl. MS. Eng. lett. d. 154, f. 46; Wellington mss WP1/1205/18. [141] Add. 51573; Lansdowne mss, Lansdowne to Rice [10 May 1832]. [142] Add. 51573, Rice to Lady Holland, 27 Jan., 6 Feb. 1832; *Three Diaries*, 190; *Holland House Diaries*, 153. [143] *Pol. Economy Club* (1921), 233, 360. [144] Murphy, 59-60. [145] *O'Connell Corresp.* iv. 1905; Hatherton diary, 31 May; Monteagle mss 13372 (1), De Vere to Rice, 12 June; (5) Hadfield to ?Fincham, 25 June 1832. [146] *Dublin Evening Post*, 30 June, 12 July; *The Times*, 30 June, 8 Aug., 6 Nov. 1832; *Pryme Recollections*, 186-9.

[147] *Croker Pprs.* ii. 185; Coedymaen mss, Williams Wynn to Phillimore, 28 Nov. 1832. [148] F.B. Hamilton, *Picture of Parl.* (1831), 80; [J. Grant], *Random Recollections of Commons* (1837), 208-12; *Edgeworth Letters*, 488. [149] Brent, 16, 39, 43; I. Newbould, *Whiggery and Reform*, 316; D. Southgate, *Passing of the Whigs*, 129. [150] B. Disraeli, *Whigs and Whiggism*, 261. [151] *Limerick Chron.* 8 Feb.; *The Times*, 9 Feb. 1866; *Gent. Mag.* (1866), i. 425-6; *DNB*; *Oxford DNB*.

S.M.F.

RICKETTS, Charles Milner (1776–1867), of 6 Park Street, Westminster, Mdx.

DARTMOUTH 4 Jan. 1820–1 Apr. 1822

b. 21 Apr. 1776, 2nd s. of George Poyntz Ricketts (*d.* 1800) of Midgham, Jamaica and Grove Place, Hants, gov. Tobago and Barbados, and Sophia, da. of William Watts of South Hill, Berks., gov. Fort William, sis. of Amelia, 1st w. of Charles Jenkinson†, 1st earl of Liverpool. *educ.* Westminster 1788. *m.* 8 Mar. 1800, Ellen Theresa, da. of Miles Prendergast of co. Galway, wid. of Sackville Marcus Taylor, 4s. (3 *d.v.p.*) 4da. *d.* 7 Sept. 1867.

Writer, E.I. Co. (Bengal) 1792; asst. to sec. to govt. Aug. 1792, to resident at Rangpur Nov. 1792, to opium agent at Bihar 1798; first asst. to commercial resident, Dacca 1798; jnr. merchant 1801; acting sec. to bd. of trade 1799, sec. to bd. 1802; commercial resident, Commarcolly 1801; jt.-inspector of opium 1805; snr. merchant 1807; sec. to govt. in public dept. 1811; dir. Bank of Bengal 1811; principal private sec. to gov.-gen. Nov. 1813, again Jan. 1817; ch. sec. to govt. 1815; member of council and pres. bd. of trade Dec. 1817; ret. Jan. 1819.

Consul-gen. at Lima 1825-30.

Ricketts had obtained a seat for Dartmouth on the Holdsworth interest through his cousin Lord Liverpool, the prime minister, who had done much to advance his successful career in India. He came in again at the general election of 1820, only nine weeks after his original return, but his incursion into British public life proved to be brief and unrewarding. He voted in defence of ministers' conduct towards Queen Caroline, 6 Feb. 1821. He divided against Catholic relief, 28 Feb. He voted with government against repeal of the additional malt duty, 3 Apr., the disfranchisement of ordnance officials, 12 Apr., and retrenchment, 27 June. He was granted ten days' leave owing to illness in his family, 15 May 1821. No other trace of parliamentary activity has been found and he vacated his seat early in 1822.

By then he was skulking on the continent, with his marriage in ruins. The exact cause of the breakdown is not clear, but it evidently did him no credit. His brother-in-law Michael George Prendergast*, one of the trustees of the Ricketts's deed of separation, wrote of his 'gross and unworthy conduct' and 'acts of insult and injury to my sister', and disputed Ricketts's plea that 'the *faux pas* with the girl he carried off was the only crime he ever committed against his marriage vows'. Ricketts kept in touch with Prendergast, who in October 1822 reported to Liverpool that there would be 'considerable difficulty' in persuading him to 'relinquish his views of political preferment in this country', which the premier had vetoed. Prendergast suggested that Ricketts might be surreptitiously sent back to India as private secretary to the new governor-general, Lord Amherst, on the understanding that he should resign this post 'as soon as a suitable office for a person of his rank in the service [became] vacant'. This, Prendergast hoped, would be the 'means ... of reconciling him to a meeting with his old friends and associates', which was desirable since 'his going out without the marked countenance of persons in power will make it more irksome to him to face society in Calcutta ... under the unhappy circumstances of his situation'. Liverpool would not countenance this ruse and Prendergast had to apologize for his 'indiscretion' in proposing it, though he still saw Ricketts's return to India as 'the surest mode of averting the never-ceasing conflicts which will be kept alive so long as he continues in Europe'.[1] Ricketts subsequently irritated Prendergast by publicly seeking to fix 'the entire blame of separation' on his wife and accusing the trustees of imposing punitive financial terms on him. Prendergast's threat in November 1823 to expose the unsavoury truth drew a conciliatory response, and Ricketts made known his anxiety to obtain 'office of some kind anywhere but in India', preferably a consulship in South America. Liverpool considered Ricketts, whom he presumed to have no Spanish, to be utterly unfit for such a sensitive appointment, and denied his allegations that he had encouraged him to expect employment at home when he returned from India:

> I had a conversation with him in which I was quite explicit. The truth is, India is not the road to office in this country. It would be unfair if it was so generally, for whatever disadvantages may attend an India life a person has the means of making a fortune there, which he has not now through civil office in this country ... I procured him an easy seat in Parliament ... and gave him thereby the opportunity of making himself known, and of forming English connections. Whether anything further would have resulted from this it is impossible for me to say ... but the road was certainly open to him and it is no fault of mine he has not been able to take advantage of it.

Ricketts again lapsed into bitterness and recrimination, forcing Prendergast to end their private correspondence. In 1824, claiming to have given 'close application to the Spanish language for the last year', he applied through his wife for consulships in Colombia, Cuba,

Mexico and Puerto Rico, but Liverpool still would not recommend him. In 1825, however, he was offered the consulship in Peru, worth £1,600 per annum, which he gratefully accepted.[2] He returned from Lima in 1827, but retained the consulship until January 1830; the remainder of his life is largely obscure. He died in September 1867.[3]

Liverpool could have been forgiven for regretting his connection with the Ricketts family, for two of Ricketts's sons caused him almost as much aggravation as did their father. The eldest, Charles Prendergast, had to be withdrawn from Sandhurst in 1818 after repeated brushes with authority. He subsequently made some progress in the army, but died as lieutenant-governor of Sierra Leone in 1828. Liverpool obtained a writership for the youngest, Dashwood Watts, in 1822, but he was expelled from Haileybury in 1824 after a series of misdemeanours culminating in profiteering in the sale of college books; he later made a career in the foreign service. Poyntz, the other son to survive infancy, was provided by Liverpool with a Bombay writership in 1820, but died in India four years later.[4]

[1] Add. 38411, ff. 101, 103, 109. [2] Add. 38298, f. 219; 38299, ff. 29, 38; 38475, ff. 17, 19, 94-108, 114, 117, 188, 192, 194, 199. [3] *Gent. Mag.* (1867), ii. 546. [4] Add. 38411, f. 113; 38474, ff. 238, 345; 38475, ff. 132-6, 140-6, 155-69.

D.R.F./T.A.J.

RICKFORD, William (1768–1854), of Green End, Aylesbury, Bucks.

AYLESBURY 1818–1841

b. 30 Nov. 1768, o.s. of William Rickford of Aylesbury and w. Elizabeth *née* Brookes.[1] *m.* 28 Sept. 1791, Mary, da. of John Vanderhelm of Amsterdam, 2s. *d.v.p.* 2da. (1 *d.v.p.*). *suc.* fa. 1803. *d.* 14 Jan. 1854.

Rickford was a native and lifelong resident of Aylesbury, and since 1803 had been head of its Old Bank, which he had founded with his father six years earlier. Once an ally of the Grenvilles of Stowe in local affairs, he had diverged politically from the head of that family, the increasingly alarmist 2nd marquess of Buckingham. In 1818 he had contested Aylesbury as an independent and came in with Buckingham's advanced Whig brother Lord Nugent, destroying the Whig Cavendish interest in the process. His local roots, ownership of Aylesbury property, resolute independence and judicious generosity with his wealth put him in a strong position; and at the general election of 1820 he was returned unopposed with Nugent after an interloper had given up.[2] He joined Nugent in presenting the Aylesbury address of loyalty to Queen Caroline on 16 Aug. 1820.[3]

In February 1823 Buckingham, now a duke in consequence of his coalition with the Liverpool ministry, claimed to know from their patronage secretary Arbuthnot that 'there was a letter extant in the treasury from Rickford after his first election offering his support to government "on consideration"', and reckoned that he had been given the recommendation to the local post office.[4] Whatever the truth of this, Rickford had voted regularly in opposition to government on all major issues in the 1818 Parliament, and he generally continued to do so in that of 1820, although he never joined Brooks's and was not a thick and thin attender. He divided for parliamentary reform, 18 Apr., 10 May (but not 9 May) 1821, 25 Apr. 1822, 20 Feb., 24 Apr. 1823, 9 Mar., 27 Apr. 1826. He was sometimes in the very small minorities who backed the campaign of the 'Mountain' for economy and retrenchment: for example on distress, 6 Apr., the navy estimates, 7 May, the Clarences' grant, 18 June 1821, revenue collection accounts, 12 Mar., the army estimates, 18, 20 Mar. 1822, 6, 7 Mar. 1826, the grant for embassies, 22 July 1822, the ordnance estimates, 27 Feb., and the Irish miscellaneous estimates, 15, 19 Mar. 1824. On two important issues he differed from the bulk of the Whig opposition. He voted against Catholic relief, 28 Feb. 1821, 30 Apr. 1822, 1 Mar., 21 Apr., 10 May 1825, and for the bill to suppress the Catholic Association, 25 Feb. 1825; and he favoured enhanced agricultural protection, voting in a minority of 36 against the proposed new corn duties, 9 May 1822, and against the emergency admission of warehoused foreign corn, 11 May 1826. He also voted against inquiry into the currency, 12 June 1823. He divided against abolition of the death penalty for forgery offences, 23 May 1821, but was in Hume's small minority for ending army flogging, 10 May 1826. He was no orator, in or out of the House. He said a few encouraging words at the Aylesbury meeting to petition for economy and reform, 29 Jan., and endorsed the petition in the House, 31 Jan. 1821, as he did a similar one, 25 Apr. 1822. At a meeting of local agriculturists, 9 Feb. 1822, he led the successful resistance to an amendment for reform, on procedural grounds.[5] He presented a petition against Catholic relief from Albrighton, Shropshire, 18 Apr. 1825.[6] On the promissory notes bill, 27 Feb. 1826, he opposed a Whig attempt to give the holders of £1 notes priority in the event of bank failures, observing that some Members seemed to think that the chancellor of the exchequer 'had not done sufficient to injure the country bankers, and came forward ... to assist him'. At an Aylesbury anti-slavery meeting, 19 Apr. 1826, he agreed to support its petition.[7] A bid to have his vote against the London water bill annulled on account of his ownership of shares in the Westminster Water Company was unsuccessful, 1 Mar. 1825.[8]

At the 1826 general election Rickford was returned unopposed for Aylesbury, though he did not adopt the 'purity of election' stance taken by Nugent.[9] On 20 Feb. 1827 he moved and was a teller for the minority of 15 for an amendment to deduct the £173 salary of the governor of Dartmouth Castle from the garrisons grant. He presented an Albrighton petition against interference with the corn laws, 21 Feb., and voted against the new corn bill, 2 Apr.[10] He divided with opposition against the Clarence annuity, 2 Mar., and for inquiries into the Irish estimates and chancery delays, 5 Apr. He voted against Catholic claims, 6 Mar., and for the spring guns bill, 23 Mar. He divided against Canning's ministry for separate bankruptcy jurisdiction, 22 May, and the disfranchisement of Penryn, 28 May 1827. Requested by Aylesbury Dissenters that month to support repeal of the Test Acts, he did so, 26 Feb. 1828.[11] He divided as usual against Catholic relief, 12 May, and presented another hostile Shropshire petition, 19 May. His only other recorded votes that session were against the Wellington ministry on crown control of excise penalties, 1 May, civil list pensions, 20 May, the cost of the Buckingham House improvements, 23 June, and the ordnance estimates, 4 July, and with them on the silk duties, 14 July. On 2 June he said that he had voted previously for the transfer of East Retford's seats to Birmingham, and strongly urged that if the borough was thrown into the hundred of Bassetlaw the franchise should be restricted to resident freeholders, in order to curb the creation of faggot votes, as Buckingham had done in the Aylesbury hundreds. At the Aylesbury dinner to celebrate Nugent's election, 28 May 1828, Rickford claimed the right to follow his conscience on the Catholic question.[12] In February 1829 Planta, the patronage secretary, listed him among Members 'opposed to the principle' of Catholic emancipation; and he took issue with Nugent in the House over the balance of opinion in Aylesbury and the hundreds, 16 Mar., and divided steadily against the measure that month. He was in the minority of 14 against the Maynooth grant, 22 May. He divided in a small minority against the silk bill, 1 May, and to transfer East Retford's seats to Birmingham, 5 May 1829 (as he did again, 11 Feb., 5 Mar. 1830) and to condemn the cost of the marble arch, 25 May 1829. Curiously, the Ultra leader Sir Richard Vyvyan* included him in October 1829 in his list of 'Tories strongly opposed to the present government' on account of the concession of Catholic emancipation; but he had nothing to do with the Brunswickers.[13] He voted for the amendment to the address deploring the omission of any reference to distress, 4 Feb., and at the Aylesbury protest meeting, 24 Feb. 1830, made much of this and explained that he had paired the previous evening for the enfranchisement of Birmingham, Leeds and Manchester.[14] He divided steadily against government that session with the revived opposition, and was in Russell's minority for reform, 28 May. On 23 Mar. he said that the low price of their produce made agriculturists 'utterly incapable of paying the burdens imposed upon them' and demanded 'some remedy'. He harped on a minor clerical error in the navy estimates until he was put down by ministers, 26 Mar. He presented and endorsed an Aylesbury publicans' petition against the sale of beer bill before voting against the second reading, 4 May; he also divided for the restriction of on-sales, 21 June. He voted against Jewish emancipation, 17 May, when he presented a Cashel petition against any increase in Irish newspaper stamp duties. He again voted against abolition of the death penalty for forgery, 7 June 1830.

Returned unopposed for Aylesbury at the general election in August, he could do no more on the hustings than express his gratitude, having been 'bled the day before'.[15] Ministers reckoned him as one of their 'foes', and he helped to vote them out of power on the civil list, 15 Nov. 1830. On the 11th he had presented a Buckinghamshire parish petition for the abolition of slavery. He divided for the second reading of the Grey ministry's reform bill, 22 Mar., and against Gascoyne's wrecking amendment, 19 Apr. 1831. At the ensuing general election, when an anti-reformer intervened, he offered as an 'independent' supporter of reform and economy. He took many of the second votes of the other two men and finished at the head of the poll. In the county election he split his votes between the reformer John Smith* and the Ultra Tory Lord Chandos*, Buckingham's son, whose championship of the Protestant cause and agricultural protection accorded with his own views; but he did not impose this line on his personal followers in the borough.[16] He voted for the second reading of the reintroduced reform bill, 6 July, and generally for its details, though he was in the minorities on the cases of Downton, 21 July, St. Germans, 26 July, and Aldborough, 14 Sept., and the majority for Chandos's proposal to enfranchise £50 tenants-at-will, 18 Aug. 1831. On 2 Sept. he secured from ministers an assurance that non-resident freeholders of the four sluiced English boroughs would be disfranchised. In reply to the Tory Wetherell's slurs on pledged reformers, 15 Sept., he boasted that his 2,000 constituents had left him to 'follow my own judgement' and pursue his 'independent line of conduct'. He voted for the passage of the bill, 21 Sept., and the second reading of the Scottish reform bill, 23 Sept. He divided with government on the Dublin election controversy, 23 Aug., but against them for inquiry into the state of the West India interest, 12 Sept., and to terminate the Maynooth grant, 26 Sept. He voted for the motion of confidence in the ministry, 10 Oct. At the Aylesbury reform dinner to honour him and Nugent, 17 Nov. 1831, he claimed that 'I have never attached myself to any party' and, stressing the 'absolute necessity for a reform', expressed his wish for such a measure 'as will be calculated to satisfy the reasonable expectations of the people'.[17]

Rickford voted for the second reading of the revised reform bill, 17 Dec. 1831, and generally for its details, though he divided against the enfranchisement of Gateshead, 5 Mar. 1832. He voted for the third reading, 22 Mar. He voted against government on the Russian-Dutch loan, 26 Jan., 12 July, but with them on British relations with Portugal, 9 Feb. He was in minorities for inquiry into distress in the glove trade, 31 Jan., to reduce the Irish registrar's salary, 9 Apr., and for a tax on Irish absentee landlords, 19 June. He divided for the address calling on the king to appoint only ministers who would carry reform unimpaired, 10 May, but was absent from the Aylesbury meeting to consider the crisis, 15 May, when a call of the House was expected.[18] He voted for the second reading of the Irish reform bill, 25 May 1832.

He topped the poll for Aylesbury at the general elections of 1832, 1835, and 1837 as a Conservative, having steadily diverged from Nugent and the Whigs on the questions of church reform and agricultural protection. He stood down, at the age of 72, in 1841.[19] He remained head of the Old Bank until about 1850, when his kinsman (through his sister's marriage) Zachariah Daniel Hunt took over. He died at his Aylesbury home in January 1854. His two sons had died young, and by his will of 5 Apr. 1852 he left the bulk of his property to his wife, with remainder to his only surviving child Elizabeth Harriet, the wife of Sir Astley Paston Cooper of Gadebridge, Hertfordshire.[20]

[1] They *m.* 15 Sept. 1765 at St. Mary's, Aylesbury (IGI). [2] R.W. Davis, *Political Change and Continuity*, 47, 55-57; G. Lipscomb, *Bucks.* i. 328; ii. 346; *HP Commons, 1790-1820*, v. 18; *The Times*, 7, 9, 13 Mar. 1820. [3] *The Times*, 17 Aug. 1820. [4] Bucks. RO, Fremantle mss D/FR/46/11/68. [5] *The Times*, 1, 8 Feb. 1821, 12 Feb., 26 Apr. 1822. [6] Ibid. 19 Apr. 1825. [7] *Bucks. Chron.* 22 Apr. 1826. [8] *CJ*, lxxx. 139. [9] *Bucks. Chron.* 3, 10, 17 June, 15 July 1826. [10] *The Times*, 22 Feb. 1827. [11] *Bucks. Chron.* 2 June 1827. [12] Ibid. 31 May 1828. [13] Davis, 77. [14] *Bucks Gazette*, 27 Feb. 1830. [15] Ibid. 7 Aug. 1830. [16] Ibid. 30 Apr., 7, 14 May 1831; *Bucks. Pollbook* (1831), 6; Davis, 96-97. [17] *Bucks Gazette*, 19 Nov. 1831. [18] Ibid. 19 May 1832. [19] Davis, 112-16, 124, 135, 146. [20] *Gent. Mag.* (1854), i. 321; PROB 11/2186/149; IR26/2006/157.

D.R.F.

RIDER, Thomas (1765–1847), of Boughton Monchelsea Place, nr. Maidstone, Kent.

KENT 1831–1832

KENT WEST 1832–1834

b. 20 Aug. 1765, 1st s. of Ingram Rider of Leeds, Yorks. and Margaret, da. of Ralph Carr of Cocken Hall, co. Dur.[1] *educ.* Charterhouse 1776; Univ. Coll. Oxf. 1783. *m.* 13 Dec. 1808, Mary Ann Elizabeth Pinnock,[2] *s.p. suc.* fa. 1805. *d.* 6 Aug. 1847.

Sheriff, Kent 1829-30.

The Riders of Essex, who had originally made their fortune in the City in Tudor times, acquired Boughton Monchelsea Place in 1685, on the marriage of Thomas Rider (*d.* 1698) to Philadelphia Barnham. He was succeeded by Sir Barnham Rider (*d.* 1728), whose son, Sir Thomas, willed the estate to his cousin Ingram, son of Sir Barnham's youngest brother, William, in 1785. Ingram is listed in the International Genealogical Index as having married an Ann Carr at Headingley, Leeds, 27 Feb. 1758. However, although no record of a subsequent marriage to Margaret Carr has been found, she is named by Hasted, the historian of Kent, as the mother of his large family. Ingram died, aged 72, 12 Oct. 1805, and by his will, dated 4 May 1804, he bequeathed his Kentish estates to his eldest son, and appointed his wife Margaret as the residuary legatee of his personal wealth, which was sworn under £10,000. Rider, who had been an exhibitioner at Charterhouse and had taken his degree in 1787, rebuilt the south range of the house in 1819 and made improvements to the park.[3]

In 1831 it was said that Rider had been active at county elections for 30 years.[4] He was almost certainly the 'Mr. Ryder' who seconded the nomination of the independent, Sir William Geary†, for Kent at the general election of 1812, when he also praised the patriotic and reformist views of the retiring Member, William Honywood.[5] He spoke in favour of the adoption of pro-reform candidates at the general election of 1818 and seconded the candidacy of the Whig, William Philip Honywood*, in 1820.[6] He was one of the Whigs who signed the requisition for a county meeting on the Queen Caroline affair, presumably after Lord Thanet had asked Lord Holland to forward it to him, 5 Dec. 1820. It was refused, but at the informal gathering, 18 Jan. 1821, Rider moved a petition complaining of agricultural distress.[7] He seconded the adoption of another such petition at a county meeting, 11 June 1822, when he argued that the problem was caused not only by the alteration of the currency and excessive taxation, but also by the lack of a reform in Parliament, which would make it more attentive to the needs of the people. He again seconded the nomination of Honywood at the general election of 1826.[8] He sat among the pro-Catholics at the stormy county meeting on emancipation, 24 Oct. 1828, and was named as a steward for the anti-Brunswick dinner on 22 Dec. 1828.[9] In proposing Thomas Law Hodges at the general election of 1830, he explained why Honywood had withdrawn and made an aggressive plea for further economies and various measures of reform, including triennial parliaments.[10] He was one of the magistrates involved in attempts to quell the 'Swing' riots in the autumn of 1830.[11] He chaired a reform meeting at Sittingbourne, 25 Feb. 1831, and his petition in its favour, on behalf of the freeholders of Kent, was presented to the House by Hodges the following day. In advocating reform at a county meeting, 24 Mar., he argued against retaining rotten boroughs on practical grounds or elevating ancient wisdom above human intellect, and stated that the Commons was

> intended to describe the third estate of the realm, elected by and from amongst the people; that any nomination by individuals or by the aristocracy in that House is an abuse not to be tolerated, and is one great cause of what we have suffered and are suffering.[12]

Before the dissolution in 1831 it was rumoured that Rider had been approached by the reformers of west Kent and might stand at the general election.[13] He agreed to come forward in an address, 26 Apr., though not to incur the ruinous expense of a contest against the sitting Member, Sir Edward Knatchbull, an Ultra. He united his cause with Hodges and together they conducted a successful canvass: for instance, at a meeting in Canterbury, 30 Apr., when he declared that

> he had no ambition to go into Parliament, but having attended a meeting at Sittingbourne [on 26 Apr.], and finding no one disposed to step forward in the cause of reform, he had done so. His friends had proposed to return him free of expense and so long as they desired, so long would he remain, even till the last man was polled.[14]

Knatchbull's withdrawal assured Rider's success and, on the hustings, 11 May, he noted that although the Grey ministry's reform bill was not perfect

> he took it as a definite measure, in preference to the vague and undefined which he had heard of only in words, but had never seen in practice. He took it as emanating from men of talent, of tried consistency and as sanctioned by a patriot king.

He was duly elected unopposed and without expense. He again advocated reform at dinners in Rochester and Cranbrook, 8, 10 June 1831.[15] He declined the corporation of Rochester's offer to make him an honorary freeman, on the grounds that his oath would require him to defend the privileges of the city generally and the rights of non-resident freemen in particular, which would conflict with his promise to support the reform bill. He was, however, admitted late the following year.[16]

Rider made no known speeches in the House in this period. He voted for the second reading of the reintroduced reform bill, 6 July 1831, at least twice against adjourning debate on it, 12 July, and fairly steadily for its details in committee. He voted against ministers on the division of counties, 11 Aug.; like Hodges, whose conduct he probably imitated, for Lord Chandos's amendment to enfranchise £50 tenants-at-will, 18 Aug.; and for the total disfranchisement of Aldborough, 14 Sept., when they had decided to leave it with one seat. He divided with them on the Dublin election, 23 Aug., and for the passage of the reform bill, 21 Sept. He voted for Hume's amendment to postpone the grant for the improvements to Windsor Castle and Buckingham House, 28 Sept. He signed the requisition for a county meeting on 30 Sept., when he again advocated reform and lower taxation.[17] He divided for Lord Ebrington's confidence motion, 10 Oct. He voted for the second reading of the revised reform bill, 17 Dec. 1831, to go into committee on it, 20 Jan. 1832, and again for many of its details. At a meeting in Maidstone, 5 Jan., he supported reduction of the malt duties and in the House he divided against the production of information on Portugal, 9 Feb.[18] Recommending him for a place on any government commission on his area of specialist interest, 19 Jan., Thomas Hyde Villiers* described him as 'an able writer and witness upon the poor laws, with ample magisterial connections'.[19] He divided for the reform bill's third reading, 22 Mar., Ebrington's motion for an address calling on the king to appoint only ministers who would carry it unimpaired, 10 May, and against increasing the county representation of Scotland, 1 June, but he voted against government on the boundaries of Whitehaven and Stamford, 22 June. Following a dispute over the management of Rochester bridge, Rider, who had previously served as assistant, 1822-7, and junior warden, 1824, was elected as its senior warden, 4 May 1832.[20] He was in the minorities in favour of appointing a select committee on colonial slavery, 24 May, and establishing permanent provision for the Irish poor by a tax on absentees, 19 June, but he was in the majority for opening coroners' inquests to the public, 20 June. He voted for the Russian-Dutch loan, 26 Jan., 20 July, and paired in its favour, 12, 16 July. He erected a commemorative cartouche in the entrance hall at Boughton Monchelsea to celebrate the success of reform. At a series of dinners in Kent late that summer he spoke in its praise, defended his conduct against his Tory critics and advocated further reductions in taxes and tithes.[21] He had promised to stand again whenever there was a general election, and he was duly returned in December 1832 for Kent West as a reformer who favoured the ballot, revision of the corn laws and the abolition of slavery.[22] He was defeated in contests for Kent West in 1835 and Kent East in 1837, and never sat again. He died in August 1847, his estate passing to his nephew, Thomas Rider (*b*. 1817), one of the sons of his brother, the Rev. Ralph Carr Rider, curate of Kentisbeer, Devon, and rector of Stoke, Kent.[23]

[1] E. Hasted, *Hist. Kent*, vi (1798), 563. [2] IGI (London). [3] Ibid. (Yorks.); Hasted, vi. 563; *Burke LG* (1846), i. 191; *Guide to Boughton Monchelsea Place* (1963); *Country Life*, 20, 27 June 1963; *Gent. Mag.* (1785), ii. 1010; (1805), ii. 981; PROB 11/1136/617; 1434/793; IR26/105/158. [4] *Maidstone Jnl.* 24 May 1831. [5] *Kentish Chron.* 16 Oct. 1812. [6] Ibid. 23 June 1818, 21 Mar. 1820. [7] Ibid. 2, 19 Jan. 1821; Add. 51571. [8] *Kentish Chron.* 14 June 1822, 23 June 1826. [9] Ibid. 9 Dec. 1828; *Report of Speeches at Kent County Meeting* (1828), 1-2. [10] *Maidstone Jnl.* 17 Aug. 1830. [11] *Maidstone Gazette*, 2 Sept. 1830. [12] *Maidstone Jnl.* 1, 29 Mar. 1831. [13] *Maidstone Gazette*, 19 Apr. 1831. [14] *Maidstone Jnl.* 26 Apr., 3 May; *Kentish Gazette*, 29 Apr., 3 May; *Kentish Chron.* 3 May 1831. [15] *Maidstone Jnl.* 10, 17 May, 14 June; *The Times*, 12, 28 May 1831. [16] Medway Archives and Local Stud. Cent. Rochester city recs. RCA/A1/6, 655, 659-61, 713. [17] *Kentish Gazette*, 27 Sept.; *Maidstone Jnl.* 4 Oct. 1831. [18] *Maidstone Jnl.* 10 Jan. 1832. [19] Grey mss GRE/B129/9C/2. [20] *Rochester Gazette*, 8 May 1832; *Traffic and Politics* ed. N. Yates and J. M. Gibson, 301. [21] *Country Life*, 20, 27 June 1963; *Kentish Gazette*, 22 June; *Kentish Chron.* 31 July; *Maidstone Jnl.* 17, 31 July, 14, 28 Aug., 18 Sept. 1832. [22] *Kentish Chron.* 8 May; *Maidstone Jnl.* 18 Dec. 1832; *Dod's Parl. Companion* (1833), 153. [23] *Gent. Mag.* (1847), ii. 436; IGI (Kent).

S.M.F.

RIDLEY, Sir Matthew White, 3rd bt. (1778–1836), of Blagdon, Northumb. and 1 Grafton Street, Mdx.

NEWCASTLE-UPON-TYNE 1812–14 July 1836

b. 18 Apr. 1778, 1st s. of Sir Matthew White Ridley, 2nd bt.†, of Blagdon and Heaton and Sarah, da. and event. h. of Benjamin Colborne of Bath, Som.; bro. of Nicholas William Ridley Colborne*. *educ*. Westminster; Christ Church, Oxf. 1795. *m*. 13 Aug. 1803, Laura, da. of George Hawkins, 6s. (1 *d.v.p.*) 6da. (1 *d.v.p.*). *suc*. fa. as 3rd bt. 9 Apr. 1813. *d*. 14 July 1836.

Capt. Northumb. supp. militia 1798; lt.-col. Loyal Newcastle vol. inf. 1803.

According to the Whig barrister James Losh, who compared him unfavourably with his younger brother Nicholas Ridley Colborne, Sir Matthew White Ridley was a man 'spoiled by prosperity ... his temper probably made irritable by some domestic grievances ... his faults ... those of an opulent man with moderate talents, labouring to be thought a person of consequence'.[1] A baronet with 30,000 acres in Northumberland and valuable commercial property in Newcastle-upon-Tyne, which his family had represented since 1747, he was also the senior partner in the Newcastle Old Bank of Ridley, Bigge and Company and had, as such, lobbied against the planned restriction of country bank notes under the 1819 Act. Politically a devotee of Lord Grey, with whom he corresponded on Northumberland politics, as Member for Newcastle since 1812, he had established himself as a regular and respected speaker against Lord Liverpool's administration and taken particular pride in his select committee work. He habitually annoyed his constituents, who accused him of meanness, by promoting measures favourable to his personal interests in agriculture and the Tyneside coal, glass-making and soap trades.[2] But, as he intended, his promise early in 1820 to present the Dissenters' petitions for revision of the Marriage Act (which he introduced, 4 May) and support for the Newcastle reform meeting of 26 Jan., chaired by his banking partner Charles Bigge, at which he declared for moderate reform, without the ballot, revived his popularity. The contest at Newcastle at the general election in March, when lord chancellor Eldon's nephew William Scott* was the third man, was directed against his colleague Cuthbert Ellison, and Ridley's return, after a short poll which cost him about £1,500, was assured.[3]

He remained a reliable spokesman for the main Whig opposition in the 1820 Parliament. When in London, he attended unstintingly and voted against administration in almost every major division, but family illnesses, foreign travel and his love of the chase tended to delay his return after the Christmas recess and to hasten his departure in the summer. He was especially active in the select committees on foreign trade (1820-4) and the business of the House.[4] A voluble defender of the country bankers and northern coal owners, he was a consistent advocate and promoter of petitions for the abolition of capital punishment for forgery and non-violent crimes, and favourable also to ending military flogging. He had been a founder of the

Blagdon Hunt,[5] and remained a regular speaker and teller against Richard Martin's bills opposing cruelty to animals, which, to the annoyance of his Newcastle critics, he regarded as matters for enforcement by magistrates and a waste of parliamentary time, 21 May 1823, 24 Feb., 11 Mar. 1825, 20 Apr. 1826. Where, as in the case of mad dogs, a legal loophole existed, he suggested legislating and making all dogs, except sheep dogs, taxable, 7 June 1830.[6]

On 12 May 1820 Ridley presented the Newcastle reformers' temperate petition and hailed it as a 'tribute to the middle class' and as a 'preliminary step in the successful progress of a constitutional reform'. Equivocal as yet in his support for the Newcastle freeholders' campaign and petitions for county or borough votes, 9 June, he refused to deal with similar requests couched in radical addresses to Queen Caroline, whose cause he supported purely from party loyalty, 29 Nov. 1820.[7] He approved the preamble and voted for a scot and lot franchise for Leeds under the Grampound disfranchisement bill, 2 Mar. 1821,[8] and for reform, 25 Apr. 1822, 2 June 1823, 26 Feb. 1824, 9, 13 Mar., 27 Apr. 1826, and was a teller for Russell's resolutions to curb electoral bribery, 26 May 1826. He considered the abortive division of counties bill 'unnecessary' and was pleased to see it killed by adjournment, 17 May 1823.[9] He divided for Catholic relief, 28 Feb. 1821, 1 Mar. (paired), 21 Apr., 10 May, and against the attendant Irish franchise bill, 26 Apr. 1825. He criticized the methods used to obtain signatures to hostile petitions, 16 Mar. 1821, and presented a favourable one from the Catholics of Cumberland, Durham and Northumberland, 21 Apr. 1825.[10]

Ridley welcomed Gascoyne's failure to have the agriculture committee selected by ballot and distanced himself from Henry Brougham and the Whig opportunists by whose votes it had been conceded, 31 May 1820. Elaborating, he said that, if present, he would have voted against it with the Whig leader George Tierney (30 May) and was prepared to back any proposition that confined its remit, in order to reduce tension between manufacturing and agriculture. Ever conscious of the importance of the admiralty, Trinity House and Greenwich Hospital votes in Northumberland, he made a point, as in the last two Parliaments, of quibbling over the navy estimates and proposed his annual amendment for a reduction in admiralty lords, to no avail, 9 June. He called for measures to cut the cost of turnpike trust renewals, 30 June 1820, 27 Feb. 1821. He recommended printing the radical Nathan Broadhurst's petition alleging ill-treatment in Lancaster gaol 'on principle ... whatever its merits', 5 July, and demanded an end to the 'great fraud' of the national lottery, 6 July 1820.

Contributing to the parliamentary campaign on behalf of the queen, and backed by her attorney-general Brougham, he warned of the danger of premature disclosures by secret committee members if their deliberations were adjourned, and substantiated his point by citing the garbled newspaper reports of the St. Omer negotiations, 12 June 1820. Harrying ministers preparatory to Brougham and Tierney's successful attacks, 6 July, he objected to confining proceedings to the Lords and to the government's decision to suspend rather than discharge the order for the green bag inquiry, 'so opening the way for further prosecutions' should the bill of pains and penalties fail. He added that had he known what ministers intended he 'might well' have divided against them, 22, 26 June. He voted against the prorogation proposed by the queen's radical partisans, 18 Sept., but threatened further opposition and made the chancellor of the exchequer Vansittart disclose that £20,000 had already been advanced for her defence.[11] After her prosecution was abandoned, he acted with Grey to call county meetings in Durham and in Northumberland (where the sheriff refused it), 'for though the innocence of the queen may not be proved to the conviction of everyone, it is too monstrous to say that she shall be liable to any further proceedings'.[12] His infant daughter Mary's death, 1 Jan. 1821, and second son Nicholas Henry's serious illness precluded his attendance at the Northumberland meeting, 10 Jan.;[13] but he testified in the House to the respectability of the signatories to their petition and demanded that the queen 'have the full benefit of her acquittal', 1 Feb. His failure to vote on the opposition censure motion, 6 Feb., was attributed retrospectively to the ill health for which on the 12th he had received ten days' leave.[14] He voted 'on principle' to print the radical Nottingham petition urging the impeachment of ministers for mishandling the affair, 20 Feb. He recommended the withdrawal of James Stuart Wortley's motion of complaint against the *Morning Chronicle*, 9 Mar. 1821.[15]

Pressing ministers on taxation (as he would again to less effect, 17 Mar. 1825), Ridley highlighted their tardiness in legislating to compound the assessed taxes on expiry of the 1819 Act and proposed doing so himself, 31 Jan., 22 Feb., before making way for the ministerial measure, 15 Mar. 1821. He protested at its deferral, 29 Mar., and his warning that it was 'hurried through ... with as many blunders and errors as ... the last bill' was loudly cheered, 13 Apr.[16] Drawing on his correspondence with the excise office, he sparred with the financial secretary to the treasury Stephen Rumbold Lushington over the glass duties, which were due to expire, 19, 21 Feb. (and intervened similarly to protect his commercial interests when they were reviewed in 1825, 1828, 1830 and 1832).[17] He praised the objectives but declined to endorse the protectionist principles of petitions against altering the timber duties that he introduced from South Blyth, 21 Feb., and Greenock, 26 Feb., but indicated that his silence did not signify acquiescence in the ministerial measure, 30 Mar. On 5 Apr., quoting the Tyne ship owners' claim that Canadian timber was 'less prone to dry rot' and their estimate that the proposed change would cost ship outfitters £150,000 annually in lost North American revenue, he eschewed Lord Althorp's amendment favouring Norway deals, likewise Sir Henry Parnell's for gradual equalization, and proposed another (defeated by 70-15) reducing the duty on colonial timber from 10*s.* to 5*s.* a load, and making 5*s.* the maximum concession for non-colonial imports.[18] Protesting that Northumberland interests were ignored, he opposed the appointment of the select committee on the additional malt tax in Scotland to which he was named, 12 Apr.[19] He endorsed Michael Taylor's bill to reduce steam engine emissions, 18 Apr., was locked out from the division on Grey's son-in-law John Lambton's reform proposals that day, and appears to have stayed away for the remainder of the session. At Durham assizes, 21 Aug. 1821, an out of court settlement was reached in a high profile test case for trespass brought against him by the bishop of Durham, Shute Barrington, for infringing manorial rights while hunting.[20]

Ridley defended Althorp's moderate resolutions criticizing the government's relief proposals, 21 Feb. 1822. He also made an issue of the rising cost of pensions for navy widows, 22 Feb., and highlighted an anomaly whereby the regulations for dispatching petitions by post were 'contained in an Act for laying an additional duty upon tea and coffee', 25 Feb.[21] He pressed for the production of detailed estimates, 27 Feb., and the gradual reduction proposed in the salt duty (a means of cutting production costs in his soap factories), 28 Feb. Making a bid to capture the disaffected agriculturists' votes, he pre-empted his planned motion of 7 Mar., moved directly for an address recommending a reduction from six to four in the number of junior admiralty lords, 1 Mar., and carried it by a resounding 182-128. Doing so, he poured scorn on the Tory Gooch's attempt to upstage him by reviving the malt question, and appealed directly to the country gentlemen to back the wider campaign for lower taxes. He also contrasted the 'recent' increase in admiralty lords (four in 1702 and 1709, five in 1714, 1717 and 1774 and six since 1785) with the sharp decrease since 1815 in naval personnel, and mollified the Whig 'Mountain' by portraying the trivial (£2,000) annual saving his reduction achieved as the removal of 'undue patronage'. By the 5th he had turned his attention to Greenwich Hospital expenditure.[22] He expressed qualified support for the government's pensions bill, 11 Mar., and opposed Hume's attempt to reduce funding for the Royal Naval College, 18 Mar.[23] Notwithstanding his critical votes for abolition of one of the joint-postmasterships, 13 Mar., 2 May, on the composition of the India board, 14 Mar., diplomatic expenditure, 16 May, and Henry Williams Wynn's† appointment to the Swiss embassy, 16 May, he refused to participate with his associates as a speaker, mover or teller, in the attack on the Grenvillite accession.[24] He insisted that the 4,820-signature Newcastle petition for clemency for Henry Hunt*, which imputed corruption to the House and was rejected, did not represent the inhabitants' views, 22 Mar.; but he did believe that the circumstances of Hunt's imprisonment merited Parliament's attention, and voted to receive petitions for remission of his sentence, 28 Mar.[25] He called for and was named to the committee on the vagrancy bill, 29 Mar., and, furnished with hostile petitions, he opposed Scarlett's poor bill, objecting especially to the speed with which removals were to be effected, 31 May.[26] His remarks at the second reading of the colonial trade bill, by which the navigation laws were relaxed, 6 May, were not reported, but after failing to delay it or obtain concessions for the Tyne ship owners (20 May), he opposed it to the last, because he was convinced that while taxes remained artificially high it would be impossible for British merchants to compete effectively in an open market, 4 June. He prevaricated similarly over the details of the consolidated Customs Acts, 5 June,[27] and considered the leather tax a 'bad choice' for repeal, 1 May, 15 May.[28] He endorsed the Newcastle merchants' complaint at the depreciation in the value of warehoused corn stocks following the return to the gold standard, 6 Mar., took charge of the successful Tyne tolls and Newcastle gaol bills, 2 May, and quizzed ministers that day on the likelihood of legislation for Bank of England charter banks. He complained that the residual 2*d.* duty on salt increased the cost of alkali used in glass manufacture, 11 June 1822, and joined in the clamour for its total repeal, 6 Apr. 1824.[29]

Ridley was host to the duke of Sussex during his visit to Newcastle in September 1822, and a trustee of the city's Literary and Philosophy Society Club, whose foundation stone the duke laid.[30] He dismissed as premature Grey's proposal for a Northumberland reform meeting in January 1823.[31] Appearing late for the session, he presented petitions against the house tax and Insolvent Debtors Act, 10 Mar.,[32] but explained on the 13th that he had no wish to see the latter abandoned. Backed by the political economist Ricardo, he endorsed the principle of government's warehousing bill as 'highly beneficial to the commerce of the country', although 'particular interests might be partially injured', 21 Mar.[33] He brought up petitions opposing the equalization of the East and West Indian sugar duties, 21 Mar., and for repeal of the coastwise coal duty, 28 Apr., and argued that retaining the tariff on wool encouraged importation of 'inferior' cloth, 4 June.[34] He did not vote, when defeat obliged ministers to concede inquiry into the prosecution of the Dublin Orange theatre rioters, 22 Apr., and took no part in it, but he was instrumental in persuading John Maxwell Barry to withdraw a breach of privilege motion alleging misreporting of their deliberations, 8 May. He voted to refer Catholic petitions on the administration of justice in Ireland to the law commission, 26 June 1823. He was an active member of the select committee on the game laws that session, and a majority teller for Stuart Wortley's bill, 11 Mar. 1824. (He opposed his next one because he thought it was unlikely to prevent poaching, 13, 24 June 1828, and supported Althorp's measure, 8 Aug., 2 Sept. 1831.) He was a majority teller against the spring guns bill, 29 June 1825.

The duke of Bedford was one of many surprised at Ridley's appointment in February 1824 as a Windsor Castle commissioner, responsible for its refurbishment, an office which although unpaid was portrayed by his Newcastle adversaries as a 'job'.[35] He defended expenditure on Buckingham House, 1 Mar., but was reluctant to vote an additional £13,000 that day for the Caledonian Canal. He asked the home secretary Peel to produce the report on Millbank penitentiary (and was duly added to that committee) next day. He also badgered the colonial under-secretary Horton over the distribution of the grant for the Society for the Propagation of the Gospels in the colonies and the religious persuasions of its recipients, until silenced by Joseph Butterworth, brandishing before him the resolutions of a Newcastle meeting condemning the indictment in Demerara of the Methodist missionary John Smith, 12 Mar. Ridley later justified his vote (11 June) against inquiry into Smith's case, which vexed his constituents, as one of confidence in Canning's November 1823 resolutions.[36] He voted to reduce the grant for Irish charter schools, after calling in vain for its postponement, 15 Mar. As a member of the select committee on private business, he rejected Hume's call for a ban on Members voting on bills in which they had a pecuniary interest, 27 May 1824, and subsequently endorsed the committee's view that the matter was best left to the integrity of individual Members, 23 Feb. 1825.[37] However, he conceded the case for a 'declaratory resolution' to guide Members' future conduct, 10 Mar. 1825. He objected to and was a majority teller against a proposal to ballot select committees for private bills, 19 Apr. 1826; but supported resolutions imposing similar restrictions on Members employed as parliamentary agents, 26 Feb. 1830.

Representing Tyne shipping and coal interests, Ridley called for a full inquiry into the coal duties and denied allegations made in the London petition that supply was rationed to inflate prices, 23 Feb. 1824. He headed the coal owners' delegation at meetings with the chancellor of the exchequer Robinson in March, when, contrary to Grey's prediction, ministers rejected their case for gradual repeal. Ridley referred to it, giving brief details, when presenting the Newcastle petition, 11 Mar., and again on the 26th. Protesting vehemently at the preference accorded to 'inland' coal, on which tariffs had been reduced from 7*s*. 6*s*. to 1*s*. a ton, while 9*s*. 4*d*. to 6*s*. 9*d*. a chaldron was still levied on coastwise coal, he threatened to move for equalization, 29 Mar.[38] Forcing divisions on resolutions proposed in the Tyne and Wear colliery owners' petition for free trade, 1 Apr., he failed (by 83-51) with a proposal to charge coastwise coal at 4*s*. 6*d*. a ton or 6*s*. a chaldron, and inland coal at 3*s*. and 4*s*. 6*d*.; (by 80-54) with another proposing a staged reduction of the duty by a further 2*s*. in 1825; and (by 73-60) with one for total repeal. He criticized the differential duties in the coal and linen bill, 5 Apr., and was a minority teller against it, 27 May.[39] His Newcastle coal (loading) bill, received royal assent, 28 May 1824.[40]

Ridley was appointed to the select committee on Ireland, 17 Feb. 1825 (having voted for inquiry, 11 May, to amend the clergy bill, 10 June, and for the Whig insurrection bill, 14 June 1824). Commenting on a hostile petition from the deanery of Bath and Wells, 15 Feb. 1825, he said that he 'certainly regretted some of the [Catholic Association's] proceedings ... not because they had done any injury to their Protestant fellow-countrymen, but because they were calculated to retard the progress of their own cause'. He voted against the ministerial bill outlawing the Association, 15, 21 Feb., but refrained from supporting Brougham's attempt to have their counsel heard, 18 Feb. He presented petitions and voted for repeal of the assessed taxes, 23 Feb. Quipping that the current elevation resembled 'a double stand on a race course like Doncaster', he defended government spending on additional official residences in Downing Street, 28 Mar. The recent good conduct of his Blyth colliers encouraged him to propose a select committee on workers' combinations, to which he was appointed, 29 Mar., and he backed petitions for repeal of the statutes outlawing them, 25 Apr., 3, 4 May, and remained a committed supporter of the repeal bill notwithstanding his differences on minutiae with its sponsor Hume and the president of the board of trade Huskisson, 16, 27 June.[41] He presented and endorsed a petition in favour of the St. Katharine's Docks bill from Newcastle chamber of commerce, 15 Feb., and opposed the Tyne and Weardale railway as a 'wild speculation', 4 Mar., preferring the Carlisle-Newcastle, for which he was the banker.[42] True to the Tyne ship owners' resolution, he joined in the vain clamour to exclude a clause from the private Isle of Dogs docks bill that allocated collier vessels particular berths and charged them supplementary fees, 23 Mar. 1825.[43] He consistently supported some relaxation of the corn laws (5 May 1820, 2 Apr. 1821, 28 Apr. 1825) and failed with an amendment to reduce the duties charged under the warehoused corn bill, 13 May 1825.[44] He approved of the proposed increase in judges' salaries, 16 May, and referred to his own 12-year chancery case as proof that inquiry into arrears was overdue, 7 June; but he disavowed his friends' 'useless' 'baiting' of Eldon that day, for which he and his brother were duly thanked.[45] He was a minority teller against the award to the duke of Cumberland, 9 June 1825.[46]

The Newcastle Old Bank weathered the 1825-6 crisis and was among those licensed (and gazetted) in November 1828 to print money on unstamped paper.[47] Ridley's preference for banks similar to his own, with few partners, was well known when, responding to the address, 2 Feb. 1826, he conceded the case for further regulation and defended the country bankers against imputations that they had contributed to the recent crisis. This he attributed to commercial distress, poor management and diminished confidence in the Bank of England. He estimated the number of country bank notes in circulation at between 3,500,000 and 8,000,000, cautioned against their precipitate withdrawal and explained that country bankers issued notes for the convenience of their customers rather than for profit. He confined his interventions on the government's promissory notes bill to a few brief technical points, 27, 28 Feb., and hailed it as a harbinger of lower prices and wages, 6 Mar.[48] He exercised similar restraint in discussions on the Bank charter bill, 21 Mar., 14 Apr. He was one of the predominantly Whig minority on the select committee on Scottish and Irish pound notes who remained dissatisfied with their report, but even so, he conceded that the immediate withdrawal of Scottish notes was inexpedient.[49] Breaking his 'silence' in a major speech, 26 May 1826, he objected to compelling country banks to lodge surety funds with the Bank, described the damage done by the government's letter to its directors and reaffirmed his confidence in English banking. He made clear his preference for a 'paper currency, upon a secure and solid basis, convertible into gold' to a metallic one, but considered paper more liable to overspeculation, hence his doubts about the Scottish concession. Defending English country bankers in general and the Newcastle banks in particular, he tabled a resolution and announced that in the next Parliament he proposed investigating the implications of retaining different currency systems in England and Scotland and of assimilating them. Having withdrawn his much postponed resolutions for revising and consolidating the statutes, he praised Peel's, in which he noted an anomaly on horse exports, 9 Mar. 1826; he revived the issue in 1830.[50] He sought additional information on government expenditure on public buildings, and criticized the 'overgenerous' award for Edinburgh University, 13 Mar. 1826. He opposed, as Tierney's seconder, the proposed increase in the president of the board of trade's salary to accommodate Huskisson, 7, 10 Apr. He voted for corn law revision, 18 Apr., to bring up the report on the government's importation bill 'without pledging himself to support it', 5 May, and divided against it, 11 May. To conciliate the shipping interest before the general election, he endorsed protectionist petitions from Sunderland, 17 Apr., and South Shields, 27 Apr.; and, using statistics for the port of London, where foreign tonnage had doubled since 1823, imports from Norway, Denmark and Russia were up by £343,151 and exports down by £290,000, he demonstrated the increasing uncompetitiveness of 'unprotected' British shipping, 13 May.[51] Certain it would be a casualty of the dissolution, he seconded Sykes's motion for a bill to redress the grievance of the unenfranchised Newcastle freeholders, 26 Apr. 1826.[52]

Ridley and his brother's correspondence with Grey when the retirement as Member for Northumberland of the Whig 'madman' Thomas Wentworth Beaumont was first anticipated in 1823 had fuelled Grey's ambition to bring in his son Lord Howick*; but they had vexed Grey by broaching the subject prematurely to the Tory 3rd duke of Northumberland, who opposed the scheme, and by confiding its details to Ridley's neighbour Sir Charles Monck†. Despite Ridley's formal declaration, 19 Mar. 1824, and early canvass for Howick, whom he introduced to the magistracy in 1825 and to the 'county' at a grand New Year ball at Blagdon in 1826, speculation that he sought the seat for himself or Monck persisted.[53] Accounting for this, Grey's brother-in-law Edward Ellice* explained that Ridley 'is afraid of his bank suffering, which keeps him back in public, in private they say he is very active' [for Howick].[54] He voted tactically for the anti-Catholic Tory Matthew Bell* against the Canningite Henry Thomas Liddell* when Howick started prematurely for Northumberland at the February 1826 by-election; and, giving a second vote to Bell, he proposed Howick when he finished a poor fourth there at the general election of 1826.[55] Attempts to jeopardize his own return, which he privately attributed to the Liddells and Beaumont, failed, and he came in unopposed with Ellison at a cost of £721. However, he was hard pressed on the hustings to defend his parliamentary conduct, and obligated to the shipping interest, who sought concessions on the reciprocity duties.[56] He objected to the publication in July, by Grey's agents, of correspondence showing his family's dealings with Beaumont. He also maintained publicly and privately that Lambton's sporadic intervention had undermined Howick's canvass. On 24 Oct. 1826, before Parliament met, the Tyne ship owners openly expressed dissatisfaction with Ridley and looked elsewhere for a spokesman.[57]

Family illness, for which he eventually took six weeks' leave, 8 Mar. 1827, kept Ridley away for most of the 1826-7 session, during which he cast no reported votes and the Tyne ship owners passed a resolution of dissatisfaction with his conduct, 5 Feb.[58] He approved the admiralty's decision to improve impressed seamen's conditions, 22 June 1827.[59] Responding to the new Wellington ministry's address, 4 Feb. 1828, he criticized the too cautious endorsement of Admiral Codrington's conduct at Navarino and praised him personally, although he could 'not support the treaty behind the battle'. He agreed with the decision to omit Ireland from the address, but he urged action on the Catholic question and expressed qualified support for administration 'if their measures are likely to promote the prosperity of the country'.[60] He countered Sir John Sebright's criticism of the Windsor Castle grant and defended the work of the architect and commissioners, 4 Feb., and intervened again to support ministers, 11 Feb. The compromise choice as chairman of the 1828 finance committee, 15 Feb., an appointment which governed his political conduct over the next three years, he warned that it was unrealistic to expect major expenditure cuts, 25 Feb., and gave a similar caveat when acknowledging John Calcraft's suggestions to the committee, 24 Mar.[61] Dismissing Calcraft's criticism of delays to their report, he referred to the 'obstacles and difficulties ... hourly thrown' in their way and steered the debate elsewhere, 16 May. He joined Althorp in pressing for the abolition of the office of lieutenant-general of the ordnance, as the finance committee had recommended, 4 July, but, differing from his 'friends', he thought government expenditure on Canada entirely justified, 8 July 1828.

He presented favourable petitions, 6, 22 Feb., and voted for repeal of the Test Acts, 26 Feb., and was prepared to accept a 'security declaration' to see it effected, 18 Mar. 1828. He wanted the stamp duty on receipts repealed, 19 Feb., and spoke pragmatically on the maltsters' differing opinions of the merits and demerits of the 1827 Act, 22, 27 Feb. He reviewed the testimony of the East Retford witness Fox in the same equivocal manner, 3 Mar. He preferred imprisonment to fines for offences under the Penryn disfranchisement bill, 24 Mar. Securing and chairing a select committee, 1 May, he embarked on a crusade to cut what he believed was the excessive cost of printing voluminous reports and petitions 'containing no useful or valuable information whatsoever' at Members' whims (23 May, 6, 20 June 1828, 1 Mar., 20 May, 7 June 1830).[62] He supported Graham's campaign against the small notes bill, 5 May, and spoke of government's 'mistake' in paying £28,000,000 in debts incurred in a paper currency in specie and of the impossible tax burden it imposed, 3 June 1828. He denied Frankland Lewis's assertion that the 'convulsion of 1825 was ... caused by the pressure of the country bankers on the Bank ... for gold', criticized their shoddy treatment by the Bank and reaffirmed his resolve to prove that the Scottish banking system was no better than the English. He endorsed the borough polls bill and made several allusions to Newcastle, whose favourable petition he presented, 10 Mar., when advocating inquiry into the franchise in counties corporate, 11 Mar. He found much to fault in Alexander Baring's tithes commutation bill, although he supported its principle, 17 Mar. He refuted charges made in justification of the Llanelli railroad and dock bill, that the northern coal owners were profiteering, 26 Mar., but deliberately refrained from opposing the Surrey land coal meters bill, 25 Apr., and a Sunderland petition making similar allegations, 9 May. In what Abercromby described as the 'meanest speech of the night', 13 May, he condemned the provision for Canning's family and maintained that 'his powers as an orator, great as they were, were frequently employed in dazzling rather than convincing the minds of his countrymen, and that they were sometimes employed in inculcating doctrines which were not becoming to the minister or the legislature'.[63] He condoned discussion of Sir Edward Knatchbull's resolutions, 24 Mar., and said that despite its poor provisions for taking averages, the ministry's corn bill afforded 'a fair and sufficient protection to the agriculturist', there being no prospect of a permanent measure for corn while the currency question remained unresolved, 25 Apr. He echoed calls for protection for wool, 28 Apr., and tobacco, 27 June, but perceived Gascoyne's inquiry motion on the decline of shipping as a cloak for an attack on the former president of the board of trade, the Canningite Charles Grant*, and a measure harmful rather than beneficial to the shipping interest. He declared his intention of dividing against it, despite constituency pressure to support it, and was glad to see it withdrawn, 17 June. He voted for inquiry into the Irish church, 24 June 1828. He left with his family on an extended tour of Italy the following month, of which he kept a journal.[64] Leading Whigs suggested summoning Ridley home from Rome to vote for Catholic emancipation in 1829, and he was one of several who returned in April, with a view to capitalizing on divisions between the Tories and the Ultras.[65] He presented and endorsed a petition from the architect John Nash, the designer of his £15,000 house in Carlton Terrace, for inquiry into his profiteering from crown land leases, 27 May 1829. (He thought it exonerated Nash and opposed further inquiry, 2 Mar. 1830). He was shut out of the division on Lord Blandford's reform resolutions, 2 June 1829. He presented a petition for inquiry into the 1819 Bank Act that day, but said it could achieve no useful purpose as 'the mischief is already done'. He objected to the Ultra Sir Robert Inglis's defence of soldiers dismissed for refusing to participate in Catholic ceremonies in Malta, 12 June 1829.

Ridley returned to the House in late February 1830, having deliberately held aloof from the Northumberland distress meeting instigated by Liddell, 15 Feb., whose petition he declined to support, 8 Mar.[66] He voted to transfer East Retford's seats to Birmingham, 5 Mar. Provoked by criticism of the banks, he attributed 'any difficulty' to the 'hasty and inconsiderate ... abolition of small note circulation' and insisted that distress was 'partial, temporary and passing', 8, 16, 25 Mar. He seconded the motion for and was appointed to the select committee on the London coal trade, 11 Mar., presented petitions for referral to it, 19, 22 Mar., but, to Howick's annoyance, divided with government against repealing the Irish coal duties, 13 May.[67] He was included on the select committee on superannuation, on which he had a bill prepared, 26 Apr.[68] He continued to press ministers on taxation, 5 Mar., 27 Apr., and, believing that individuals should finance their own education to lighten the burden on the state, he opposed government spending on the Royal Military College, 26 Feb., and the Woolwich grant, 30 Apr. Yet his speeches were mainly favourable to government, 26 Mar., 30 Apr., 3 May, and he became increasingly impatient with Hume's time-wasting tactics, 30 Apr., 3, 10 May. He refrained from casting a critical vote on Frankland Lewis's appointment as navy treasurer, an issue on which opposition were divided, 12 Mar.; but he disputed Lewis's claim that country banks could not supply the service with silver for wages, 22 Mar. He was selective in his support for the measures promoted by the revived Whig opposition which met in Althorp's rooms. He divided with them on the Bathurst and Dundas pensions, 26 Mar., the ordnance salaries, 29 Mar., the public buildings grant, 3 May, and the assistant treasury secretary's salary, 10 May, and for Jewish emancipation, 5 Apr., 17 May. He suggested halving the number of bankruptcy commissioners, 14 May. Before voting for returns of privy councillors' emoluments, 14 May, he defended his 1828 finance committee and criticized the manner in which their proposed reductions 'were more rapidly turned out, than they had been introduced into the House'. He countered Daniel O'Connell's case for postponing the administration of justice bill, 18 May. He opposed Slaney's poor bill, 15, 16 Mar., called for legislation against the truck system, 20 Mar., and suggested, as a member of the relevant committee, that their initial recommendations should be enacted forthwith without further referral, 3, 5 July. His bill abolishing the merchant seamen's levy (6*d.* a month) for Greenwich Hospital, first announced, 4 May, and supported on the 6th by a petition from its instigators, the Newcastle Merchant Seamen's Society, was repeatedly postponed and withdrawn, pending inquiry, 17 June. He suggested imposing a 10 pm closing time under the sale of beer bill, 3 June, and established that licenses would be issued by the excise office, not magistrates, 4 June. According to Howick, he left the House early to avoid voting on its on-consumption proposals, which his constituents opposed, 21 June.[69] He was a minority teller for an amendment introducing a two-year (probationary) delay before on-consumption licences could be issued, 1 July. (He afterwards opposed precipitate remedial legislation and recommended giving the Act a fair trial until after parliamentary reform was carried, 30 June, 24 Aug. 1831.) He persuaded Agar Ellis to postpone to the next Parliament his motion vesting the management of the Commons Library in the Speaker and a committee of four, 7 July 1830. He claimed that his vote against increasing recognizances under the libel law amendment bill was one of principle, unconnected with Lord Normanby's hostile campaign, 9

July. Clashing frequently with Hume and O'Connell, he condemned the practice of detaining prisoners in unseaworthy hulks prior to transportation, and defended General Darling's record as governor of New South Wales, 11 June, 8, 9 July 1830.

His agents had alerted Ridley on 30 May 1830 to the campaign to unseat him at Newcastle, where John Hodgson* of Elswick as third man was ready to poll at the general election. He now heeded criticism of his 'hauteur' and inattention to his constituents, corresponded with his agents daily and canvassed personally until the nomination. He categorically denied involvement in Ellison's retirement, 8 June.[70] His return was unopposed but not unchallenged, and replying to criticism that he had given 'a liberal vote now and then to save his credit' and none on reform, he attributed this to his unplanned absences from the House. He was also required to account for the vast sums expended on Windsor Castle, his defence of Nash and Darling, his failure to secure the repeal of the coal duties and the Richmond shilling, and his refusal to endorse the Northumberland distress petition. He promised to press for the extinction of all slavery.[71] In September 1830 the corporation voted their confidence in him for resisting the transfer of the customs house to Shields.[72] Ministers anticipated a 'fierce battle' with Ridley over access through his garden to the duke of York's monument in St. James's Park. His preference was that it should be by a flight of steps to Nash's design.[73]

The ministry listed Ridley among their 'foes' and he divided against them when they were brought down on the civil list, 15 Nov. 1830. Speaking on the 12th, he had urged repeal of the coastwise coal duty and reductions in the taxes on soap, candles, houses and windows, with a 'property tax to make good the difference'. Asked to manage election petitions, he tried, 15-17 Nov., but failed (by 156-95), to have all except double returns postponed until after Christmas, and regarded the adjournment caused by the 'Swing' disturbances, although he did not oppose it, as an unwelcome interruption to election committee ballots, 23 Nov. He resented and resisted postponing the decision on the Queenborough double return, 25 Nov. He took charge of the petition denying that the '*tricolore*' was among the banners at the London trades procession, 17 Dec. 1830, and rallied strongly in defence of the Grey ministry's budget, 7 Feb., 23, 25 Mar., and civil list proposals, 14 Apr. 1831. Arguing that it was not a case for the strict application of the 'rules of political economy ... and principles of free trade', he opposed a reduction in the barilla duties on behalf of the Newcastle alkali and glass producers, but stated that he had 'no wish to throw any impediments in the way, or occasion any inconvenience to the present government', 20 Dec. 1830, 7 Feb. 1831. For this, and for abandoning his superannuation bill in deference to ministers, he was rebuked by the Tory Portman, 7 Feb. 1831. Ridley pressed as hitherto for repeal of the coal duties, 8, 14 Dec. 1830, 7, 28 Mar., and the 'Richmond shilling', 12, 23 Feb. 1831, and claimed, when challenged at the general election in April, that he had mistakenly assumed that the latter had been conceded with the duties in March.[74] On the Irish coal trade bill, 28 Mar., he quoted extracts of the 1830 committee report to contradict allegations that the northern cartel kept the London market undersupplied, called for sales exclusively by weight and asserted that tax reductions would not push up pithead prices. He also opposed, 9 Feb., and presented petitions against the registry of deeds bill on his constituents' behalf, 28 Mar. Arbuthnot had suggested him for the East India select committee, but he was not appointed to it. He sought (as a committee member) to make some permanent provision for the Irish poor, 18 Mar. 1831.[75] He sent a letter of support to the Newcastle reform meeting of 21 Dec. 1830 and published a notice approving the extension of the franchise to inhabitant householders, although it would affect the 'privileges of some' at Newcastle, 24 Jan. 1831.[76] He presented and endorsed petitions for a general reform and in favour of the ministerial bill, 8, 23, 28 Feb., 2, 7, 18, 28 Mar., 18 Apr. He protested at the 'wearisome' language of its critics, 21 Feb., 3 Mar., and cautioned against permitting misgivings about the details of the government's scheme to defeat the 'great and essential measure', 2 Mar. Even so, according to Creevey, 'that goose Ridley was the only untractable hound with the exception of a growl or two from "Bum" Gordon' at the ministerial meeting at Althorp's where 'the necessity of not dabbling in any amendments' was urged, 17 Mar.[77] He divided for the reform bill at its second reading, 22 Mar., and against Gascoyne's wrecking amendment, 19 Apr. His personal preference, evident in the Newcastle merchants, bankers and manufacturers' petition which he presented, 23 Feb., was for enfranchising 'all households possessing sufficient property to give them an interest in the election of Members' and transferring the franchise from corrupt boroughs to the larger unrepresented towns. He opposed the ballot, 8 Feb., called for the separate enfranchisement of Gateshead, South Shields and Sunderland, 2, 25 Mar., and welcomed the modification of the bill to preserve certain freemen's rights, 29 Mar. His conduct was locally acclaimed and he was returned unopposed with Hodgson at the 1831 general election.[78]

On 14 June 1831 Ridley seconded Manners Sutton's re-election as Speaker and was praised in turn for his own 'high standing, station, and character in the House', where he intervened regularly on procedure and to regulate Members' language and conduct throughout the session. He divided for the reintroduced reform bill at its second reading, 6 July, and complained when *The Times* omitted him from its list.[79] He voted against adjourning its committal, 12 July, and to use the 1821 census to determine English borough representation, 19 July. He justified and voted in favour of the separate enfranchisement of Gateshead, 5 Aug. He cast a handful of wayward votes: against including Appleby in schedule A, 19 July, Sudbury in schedule B, 3 Aug., for Lord Chandos's clause enfranchising £50 tenants-at-will, 18 Aug., and to extend the franchise to borough copyholders and leaseholders in counties corporate like Newcastle, 20 Aug. He presented petitions against disfranchisement from Newcastle's Sunderland out-voters, 5 July, and certain other burgesses, 20 July, and voted in the minority for preserving freemen's rights, 30 Aug. Before doing so he explained that he considered their destruction of minor importance compared with securing the bill's passage; but he still believed that the 'life' provision for resident freemen should be permanent, 'as in large corporations it gives equal control to the mechanic and to the merchant over the Members whom they elect'. He was absent through illness when the bill was passed, 21 Sept., and applied in vain to Grey that day for a peerage.[80] He did not vote on Lord Ebrington's confidence motion, 10 Oct. At the Northumberland reform meeting, 12 Oct., he refused to pledge outright support for the 'rejected bill' without leaving room for 'improvement', criticized Monck's lurch to Toryism and defended the bench of bishops and Eldon, notwithstanding their votes.[81] He chose not to vote on the revised reform bill at its second reading, 17 Dec. 1831, but he divided for its committal, 20 Feb., and provisions for Appleby, 21 Feb., Helston, 23 Feb., Tower Hamlets, 28 Feb., and Gateshead, 5 Mar. 1832, when, to the acclaim of the Newcastle press, he disputed the anti-reformers' case for uniting it to Newcastle, to release a Member for Merthyr Tydfil or Toxteth.[82] After dividing for the bill's third reading, 22 Mar., he went to Newcastle, where he was fêted with his son at the mayor's dinner, 4 Apr., and elected and installed as president of the chamber of commerce the following day 'as a mark of approbation of his conduct'.[83] He voted for the address requesting the king to appoint only ministers who would carry reform unimpaired, 10 May, for the Irish reform bill at its second reading, 25 May, and against a Conservative amendment to the Scottish measure, 1 June. He criticized the anti-reformer Lord Dudley Stuart for quibbling over boundaries, 4 June, but intervened himself to object to the commissioners' proposal for adding suburban townships to Newcastle, 8 June. He voted against disqualifying the recorder of Dublin from Parliament, 24 July. He divided with government on the Russian-Dutch loan, 26 Jan., 12, 16 July, and paired, 20 July 1832.

Ridley defended Althorp's decisions to levy tariffs on coal exports to Europe and treat the colonies preferentially, 1, 8, 18 July 1831. He wanted consular salaries to be derived partly from fees, according to an agreed scale, and acknowledged the foreign trade committee's failure to resolve the matter, 25 July. He had commended the ministry's regency bill, 10 Dec. 1830, and, undeterred by the laughter he knew it would excite, he suggested that when Princess Victoria was officially declared heir presumptive, she should change her name to one 'more congenial to the feelings of Englishmen', such as Elizabeth, 3 Aug. 1831. He had repeatedly deferred his bill abolishing the Greenwich Hospital levy to make way for the reform bill, 28 Mar., 9 Aug. 1831, 13 Feb. 1832, and was bitterly disappointed when Graham as first lord of the admiralty refused concessions. His proposal was abandoned, 8 Mar. 1832, having being portrayed as an attack on the hospital and a means to 'put money into the hands of ship owners'.[84] Opposing the locally unpopular registry of deeds bill, he presented hostile petitions, 27 Jan., and condoned its second reading only 'on the clear understanding that the House is not pledged to the principle of the bill', 18 July. Following his appointment to the secret committee on the Bank's charter, 22 May, he spoke against including the currency question in their remit, warning that it would create uncertainty and 'excite expectations which would never be realized'. His several interventions on the coroners bill were brief and ineffective, 20 June, 6 July. He spoke and was a minority teller against amending the sheriffs' expenses bill, 20 July. He presented a petition for the South Shields and Monkwearmouth railway bill, 20 Feb., and assisted with one to refinance the Newcastle-Carlisle scheme, 13 Mar. Though of the committee, he avoided voting on the locally contentious Sunderland docks bill, 2 Apr. He waited until Kidson, the printer of their division list, had been found guilty of breach of privilege before speaking on his behalf, 7 May 1832.[85] He voted in the minority against the quarantine duties, 6 Sept. 1831, and called for public finance to combat cholera, 14, 15 Feb. 1832. He was in favour of proceeding with the customs duties bill so that a pro-forma could be printed, 13 July, and joined Hodgson in pressing for extended warehousing facilities under it at Newcastle customs house, 25 July 1832.

Ridley resisted the temptation to declare his candidature for Northumberland South at the general election of 1832, lest he forfeit Newcastle, where he topped the poll.[86] He had agreed to support Charles Williams Wynn in preference to the Whig Littleton for the expected vacancy in the Speakership, reserving himself 'if others should start'. His allegiance was not tested.[87] An increasingly unreliable supporter of Liberal reforms, he was returned in second place for Newcastle in 1835, and afterwards went over to the Conservatives.[88] He died suddenly of apoplexy while staying at Richmond, Surrey, in July 1836.[89] As stipulated in his will, dated 10 Jan. 1826 and proved under £35,000 in the province of Canterbury and £160,000 in that of York, he was succeeded in the baronetcy and to his estates, bank and businesses by his eldest son Matthew (1807-77), Conservative Member for Northumberland North, 1859-80. His youngest son George (1818-87) represented Newcastle as a Liberal, 1856-60. His daughters and younger sons all became estranged from his increasingly eccentric widow (*d.* 1864) and were provided for by trust, with £10,000 marriage portions reserved for the seven who were unmarried at his death.[90]

[1] *Diaries and Corresp. of James Losh* ed. E. Hughes (Surtees Soc. clxxi) [hereafter *Losh Diaries*, i], 190. [2] *HP Commons, 1790-1820*, ii. 311-12; v. 19-20; P. Fraser, 'Party Voting in the House of Commons, 1812-1827', *EHR*, xciii (1983), 764, 783. [3] Grey mss, Ridley to Grey, 11 Jan.; *The Times*, 31 Jan., 22 Feb., 5 May; *Tyne Mercury*, 1 Feb.; *Newcastle Courant*, 12 Feb., 11, 18 Mar. 1820; Northumb. RO, Ridley (Blagdon) mss ZRI25/39, 41; *Newcastle Pollbook* (1820), pp. vii-ix.; P.D. Brett, 'Newcastle Election of 1830', *Northern Hist.* xxiv (1988), 104, confuses Scott with his cousin William Henry John Scott, Member for Hastings. [4] Ridley (Blagdon) mss 25/42, 55. [5] Ibid. 25/51/1, 2. [6] *Newcastle Chron.* 17 June 1826. [7] *The Times*, 13, 26 May, 10 June 1820; Add. 36458, f. 109; Ridley (Blagdon) mss 25/37. [8] *The Times*, 3 Mar. 1821. [9] Ibid. 18 May 1823. [10] Ibid. 17 Mar. 1821, 22 Apr. 1825. [11] Brougham mss, Grey Bennet to Brougham [19 Sept. 1820]. [12] Ridley (Blagdon) mss 25/45, Grey to Ridley, 29 Nov.; Grey mss, Ridley to Grey, 30 Nov. 1820. [13] *Newcastle Chron.* 12 Jan.; *The Times*, 15 Jan. 1821; *Gent. Mag.* (1836), ii. 322. [14] *Newcastle Chron.* 16 Feb. 1821. [15] Ibid. 10 Mar. 1821. [16] Ibid. 1, 23 Feb., 16, 30 Mar., 14 Apr. 1821, 18 Mar. 1825. [17] Ridley (Blagdon) mss 25/40; *The Times*, 20, 22 Feb. 1821, 31 Mar. 1825. [18] *The Times*, 22, 27 Feb., 31 Mar. 1821. [19] Ibid. 3, 13 Apr. 1821. [20] Ibid. 27 Aug. 1821. [21] Ibid. 23, 26 Feb. 1822. [22] Ibid. 19 Feb., 1, 2, 6 Mar. 1822. [23] Ibid. 19 Mar. 1822. [24] BL, Althorp mss, Lord to Lady Spencer, 13 May 1822. [25] *The Times*, 23, 29 Mar. 1822. [26] Ibid. 1 June 1822. [27] Ibid. 7 May, 5, 6 June 1822. [28] Ibid. 2, 16 May 1822. [29] *CJ*, lxxvii. 45, 103, 115, 161, 241, 244, 292; *The Times*, 7 Mar., 3 May, 12 June 1822. [30] R.S. Watson, *Hist. Lit and Phil. Soc. Newcastle-upon-Tyne*, 83; Reid, *Lord Durham*, i. 158; *Losh Diaries*, i. 169-71. [31] Grey mss, Ridley to Grey, 14 Nov. 1822. [32] *The Times*, 11 Mar. 1823. [33] Ibid. 22 Mar. 1823. [34] Ibid. 22, 29 Apr. 1823. [35] Add. 51668, Bedford to Lady Holland [27 Feb. 1824]; Wellington mss WP1/790/21; 911/9; *Newcastle Chron.* 17 June 1826. [36] *The Times*, 12 June 1826. [37] Ibid. 24 Feb. 1825. [38] Ridley (Blagdon) mss 35/25; Grey mss, Grey to Ridley, 4 Mar.; *The Times*, 27, 30 Mar. 1824. [39] *The Times*, 6 Apr. 1824. [40] Ibid. 12 Mar.; *CJ*, lxxix. 361, 427. [41] *The Times*, 17, 28 June 1825. [42] Ibid. 16 Feb., 5 Mar., 29 Apr. 1825. [43] Ridley (Blagdon) mss 25/47; *The Times*, 7 Jan., 24 Mar. 1825. [44] Ibid. 26 Apr. 1820, 29 Apr. 1825. [45] Ridley (Blagdon) mss 25/61, Eldon to Ridley, undated. [46] *The Times*, 10 June 1825. [47] *London Gazette*, 18 Nov.; *Newcastle Chron.* 22 Nov. 1828. [48] *The Times*, 28 Feb. 1826. [49] Ibid. 18 Mar.; Nottingham Univ. Lib. Acc. 636, Denison diary, 19 May 1826. [50] *The Times*, 13 Apr., 4 May, 15 June 1824, 31 Mar. 1825; Ridley (Blagdon) mss 25/57. [51] Ridley (Blagdon) mss 25/45, notes and letters, 1824-6. [52] The following paragraph draws additionally on P. Burroughs, 'Northumb. Elections of 1826', *PH*, x (1991), 78-104. [53] Grey mss, Ridley to Grey, 25 Aug., 5 Sept., 14 Oct. 1823, 26, 27 Feb., 3, 11, 13, 16, 19, 24 Mar. 1824, 25 Sept., 10, 18 Nov. 1825, Tankerville to same, 8 Mar., Lambton to same, 16, 17 Mar. 1824, 20 Nov., 26 Dec. 1825; Ridley (Blagdon) mss 25/45, Grey to Ridley, 31 Aug. 1823, 28 Feb., 4, 6, 13, 18, 19, 21 Mar. 1824, 16 Sept., 14 Nov. 1825, Ridley Colborne to Beaumont, 18 Mar. 1824; *Tyne Mercury*, 14 Jan. 1826. [54] Grey mss, Ellice to Grey, 3 June 1826. [55] Ridley (Blagdon) mss 25/48, Grey to Ridley, 4, 6 Feb. 20 May, Liddell to same, 7 Feb., reply, 8 Feb.; Grey mss, Ridley to Howick, 4, 6, 7 Feb.; Northumb. RO, Middleton mss ZMI/B16/VI, Monck to Ridley, 15 Feb.; *Newcastle Chron.* 17, 24 June, 1, 15, 23 July 1826. [56] Northumb. election pprs. [BL J/8133.i.13.], ii. 573-83, 587-9, 673; *Durham Chron.* 18 Mar.; Ridley (Blagdon) mss 25/52 (election expenses 1826); 25/53, Ravensworth to Ridley, 4, 6 Mar., Liddell to same, 21 Mar.; *The Times*, 26 May, 2, 12 June; *Newcastle Chron.* 27 May, 10, 17 June; *Tyne Mercury*, 13 June 1826. [57] Ridley (Blagdon) mss 25/48, Ridley to Grey, 12, 26 July, Monck to Ridley, 21 July, Swinburne to same, 23 July and reply, 24 July; 25/53, bdle. Beaumont corresp.; *The Times*, 21 July; *Globe*, 22 July; *Newcastle Chron.* 23 July, 13 Aug.; Grey mss, Lambton to Grey, 17 Aug. 1826. [58] *Durham Chron.* 10 Feb. 1827. [59] Ridley (Blagdon) mss 25/54; *The Times*, 23 June 1827. [60] Add. 52453, Mackintosh to Allen, 2 Feb. 1828. [61] Add. 38761, f. 269; 40307, f. 50; 40395, ff. 219, 244; Keele Univ. Lib. Sneyd mss SC12/85; Grey mss, Ellice to Grey, 4 Feb.; Hatherton diary, 15 Feb. 1828; B. Hilton, *Corn, Cash, Commerce*, 247. [62] Ridley (Blagdon) mss 25/55. [63] Castle Howard mss, Abercromby to Carlisle, 17 May 1828. [64] Ridley (Blagdon) mss 28/8, 32/3. [65] Add. 51599A, Lady Cowper to Holland [28 Jan. 1829]; 60288, f. 122. [66] *Newcastle Chron.* 20, 27 Feb., 7 Aug. 1830. [67] Grey mss, Howick jnl. 13 May 1830. [68] *Newcastle Chron.* 7 Aug. 1830. [69] Howick jnl. 21 June 1830. [70] Tyne and Wear Archives, Ellison of Hebburn mss DF/ELL/A66, *passim*; Ridley (Blagdon) mss 25/59, *passim*; Brett, 101-23. [71] *Newcastle Chron.* 7 Aug. 1830. [72] Tyne and Wear Archives MD/NC/2/11 (Newcastle corporation minutes, pp. 565, 569). [73] Wellington mss WP1/1137/24, 35; 1141/27; 1143/53; 1182/10. [74] *Tyne Mercury*, 3 May 1831. [75] Add. 40340, f. 246. [76] *Newcastle Chron.* 28 Dec. 1830; *Durham Chron.* 29 Jan. 1831. [77] Creevey mss, Creevey to Miss Ord, 17 Mar. 1831. [78] Northumb. election pprs. ii. 773, 775, 787; *Tyne Mercury*, 26 Apr., 3, 10 May 1831. [79] *The Times*, 8, 9 July 1831. [80] Grey mss, Ridley to Grey, 21, 22 Sept., reply, 22 Sept. 1831. [81] *Newcastle Chron.* 15 Oct.; Ridley (Blagdon) mss 25/61, Eldon to Ridley, 21 Oct. 1831. [82] *Tyne Mercury*, 13 Mar. 1832. [83] Ibid. 10 Apr. 1832. [84] Ridley (Blagdon) mss 25/59, T. Smith to Ridley, 1 July 1830. [85] *Durham Chron.* 6, 13 Apr. 1832. [86] Northumb. RO, Blackett-Ord (Whitfield) mss 324/A/36, W.H. Ord to fa. 18 Sept. 1831; *Tyne Mercury*, 24 July; *Newcastle Courant*, 8-22 Dec. 1832; Ridley (Blagdon) mss 25/63-4. [87] NLW, Coedymaen mss bdle. 29, Williams Wynn to Phillimore [Dec. 1832]. [88] *Newcastle Chron.* 10 Jan. 1835; Add. 40415, ff. 219, 221; *Greville Mems.* iii. 219. [89] *Tyne Mercury*, 19, 26 July; *Gent. Mag.* (1836), ii. 221-2. [90] PROB 11/1866/506; IR26/1428/452; Ridley (Blagdon) mss 24/80; U. Ridley, *Cecilia*, 45-50.

M.M.E.

RIDLEY COLBORNE, Nicholas William (1779–1854), of West Harling, Norf.

Bletchingley	8 May 1805–1806
Malmesbury	1806–1807
Appleby	30 July 1807–1812
Thetford	1818–1826
Horsham	14 Feb. 1827–1832
Wells	5 May 1834–1837

b. 14 Apr. 1779, 2nd s. of Sir Matthew White Ridley, 2nd bt.† (*d.* 1813), of Blagdon and Heaton, Northumb. and Sarah, da. and event. h. of Benjamin Colborne of Bath, Som.; bro. of Sir Matthew White Ridley, 3rd bt.* *educ.* Westminster; G. Inn 1795; Christ Church, Oxf. 1796. *m.* 14 June 1808, Charlotte, da. of Thomas Steele† of Westhampnett, Suss., 1s. *d.v.p.* 4da. (1 *d.v.p.*). *suc.* mat. uncle William Colborne and took additional name of Colborne by royal lic. 21 June 1803; *cr.* Bar. Colborne 15 May 1839. *d.* 3 May 1854.

Ridley Colborne was returned again for his local borough of Thetford in 1820 on Lord Petre's interest. He was a regular attender and frequent speaker who continued to vote with the Whig opposition to Lord Liverpool's ministry on all major issues, including parliamentary reform, 9 May 1821, 25 Apr., 24 June 1822, 20 Feb., 24 Apr., 2 June 1823, 9 Mar., 13 Apr. 1826. He divided for Catholic relief, 28 Feb. 1821, 1 Mar., 21 Apr., 10 May 1825. He described the ill treatment of horses bill as 'wholly unnecessary' and complained that the House was 'too prone to legislation upon subjects which did not require it', 1 June 1821. He similarly spoke against the cruelty to animals bill, 14 June 1821,[1] and was a minority teller next day against the cattle protection bill. He questioned the need for legislation against bear-baiting and dog-fighting, 21 Feb. 1826, and asked if some of the sports of the higher orders should not be likewise prohibited. He called for a revision of the beer duties to permit a greater variety to be sold, 14 May, 3 June 1822.[2] He was convinced that the game laws were detrimental to the 'peace and happiness' of the lower orders, 13 Mar. 1823, but opposed legalization of the sale of game, 11 Mar. 1824, arguing that this would give poachers a 'certain market' and end the 'interchange of civilities' whereby landlords bestowed gifts of game in return for tenants' co-operation in its preservation. Unlike most Whigs, he opposed the bill to outlaw spring guns, 21 June 1825, as he considered them preferable to the 'well organized bands of armed men' otherwise used against poachers; he was a teller for the minority. He was persuaded to withdraw a clause to allow their use at night, 30 June 1825, but protested against the supposition that opponents of the measure were deficient in humanity. He voted against the third reading of the reintroduced bill, 27 Apr. 1826.[3] He maintained that publication of parliamentary debates, by 'subjecting men to the influence of public opinion', had 'done much towards a practical reform', 22 Apr. 1823. He presented petitions from Newcastle-upon-Tyne ship owners against the reciprocity of duties bill, 30 June 1823, and for repeal of the coal duties, 18 Feb. 1824;[4] both reflected family business interests. When presenting a petition against removal of the Norfolk lent assizes from Thetford to Norwich, 24 Feb. 1825, he argued that it was an interference with the royal prerogative; he corresponded with the home secretary Peel on the matter.[5] He put his faith in public opinion as a corrective for abuses in private bill committees, 19 Apr. 1826.

It was said of Ridley Colborne that he was 'better known to the world as a warm and active promoter and encourager of art' than as a Whig politician,[6] and his aesthetic interests were much in evidence during the 1820 Parliament. He supported the grant to the British Museum and approved its open access policy, 26 May 1820, though 'a system of economy should as far as possible be adopted'. He advocated a new building to house the museum, 16 Feb. 1821, 20 Feb. 1822.[7] He approved the amalgamation of George III's library with the museum's existing collection, 20 June 1823, when he observed that it was 'singular' that alone in Europe, Britain possessed no gallery for paintings. He praised Sir George Beaumont's† gift of paintings to the museum, 1 Mar. 1824. He suggested the Marlborough House site for a gallery to house the Angerstein collection of paintings (the basis of the National Gallery), 9 Apr. 1824. He spoke generally on the need for a more central location for a picture gallery than the British Museum, 25 Mar. 1825, when he recommended the purchase of Marshal Soult's art collection. He presented a petition for the encouragement of historical painting from the artist Benjamin Haydon, 23 Feb.,[8] and approved additions to the national collection, 19 Apr. 1826. Appointed to the select committee on Westminster public buildings, 24 Mar., he answered criticism of Sir John Soane's design for the new law courts by supporting the architect's assertion that his plans had been interfered with by that committee, 21 May 1824. He deplored the heavy expenditure on building work at Buckingham House, which was 'such a wretched site', 16 June 1825.[9] To his brother's suggestion that the design of public buildings be opened to competition, 17 Apr. 1826, he countered that senior architects 'would not have time to make such presentations'. He was left without a seat after the general election that summer, owing to the lapse of Petre's interest, but the 12th duke of Norfolk returned him on a vacancy for Horsham in February 1827 and he sat undisturbed until 1832.

He regarded continued objections to the duke of Clarence's grant as 'ungracious', 19 Feb. 1827. He divided for Catholic relief, 6 Mar. He questioned the use of solitary confinement at Millbank penitentiary, 10 Mar.[10] He opposed the Wakefield and Ferrybridge canal bill on behalf of the Aire and Calder Canal Company, whose service he claimed would be duplicated, and acted as a majority teller, 15 Mar. (and again, 3 Mar. 1828).[11] He voted for inquiry into the allegations made against Leicester corporation, 15 Mar., and for information regarding the conduct of the Lisburn magistrates, 29 Mar. He divided next day for Tierney's amendment to postpone the committee of supply, and for inquiry into the Irish miscellaneous estimates, 5 Apr. He joined Lord Althorp in offering 'a very handsome and disinterested support' to Canning's ministry, while admitting differences over reform and Catholic relief and remaining in opposition, 7 May; he also criticized the 'want of temper' shown by the Ultra Tories. However, he voted against the government for the disfranchisement of Penryn, 28 May. He accepted the need for a new Middlesex asylum, 13 June 1827, though he denied that conditions in the existing one were as bad as portrayed. He divided for repeal of the Test Acts, 20 Feb., and Catholic relief, 12 May 1828. After attending a meeting of backbenchers at Henry Bankes's house, 7 Mar., he supported the appointment of a select committee to investigate the public building department of the office of works, 24 Mar., arguing that it would be a restraining influence on extravagant expenditure.[12] He voted against extending East Retford's franchise to Bassetlaw freeholders, 21 Mar. He believed that election committee proceedings should remain behind closed doors, 3 Apr. He criticized the distinction drawn in Slaney's poor relief bill between the able-bodied and the sick poor, 17 Apr., observing that 'if an able-bodied man is refused relief, in 48 hours he becomes weak and helpless'. He believed the operation of the settlement laws made it imperative that the unemployed be provided with work or relief. He expressed concern at the casualization of labour, 21 Apr., preferring to see 'an attachment between master and servant'. He voted against the duke of Wellington's ministry for inquiry into civil list pensions, 20 May, to omit the salary of the governor of Dartmouth, 20 June, and to reduce that of the lieutenant-general of the ordnance, 4 July. He accepted the need for a grant for repairs at Windsor Castle, 6 June, but voted to condemn the misapplication of public money for building work at Buckingham House, 23 June. He withdrew his opposition to the game bill, 13 June, acknowledging that 'the country calls on us to make an alteration and will not be satisfied without it'; he nevertheless opposed an ambiguously worded clause on the property qualification, 10 July. He voted for inquiry into pluralism in the Irish church, 24 June, and against the additional churches bill, 30 June 1828. He divided for Catholic emancipation, 6, 30 Mar. 1829. He advised the House not to be too scrupulous when validating petitions, given the 'great division' of opinion on the subject, 12 Mar. Though he supported the disfranchisement of Irish 40*s*. freeholders, 18 Mar., he regretted the implication that relief was 'not granted as a boon, but as a matter of barter'. He opposed an amendment to apply emancipation retrospectively and thus allow Daniel O'Connell to take his seat, 21 May. He quizzed ministers over the renewal of the Assessed Taxes Composition Act, 16, 24 Mar. He regarded the proposed democratization of select vestries as a disincentive to the involvement of 'gentlemen' in local government, 28 Apr. He professed himself to be 'no greater admirer' of Buckingham House 'than any other Member', 25 May 1829, and while it was 'too late to interfere' he voted against the additional grant for the sculpture of the marble arch. He divided against Lord Blandford's parliamentary reform motion, 18 Feb., but for the enfranchisement of Birmingham, Leeds and Manchester, 23 Feb., and the transfer of East Retford's seats to Birmingham, 5 Mar. 1830. He acted with the revived Whig opposition on all major issues that session. He broadly accepted emigration as a means to relieve distress, 23 Mar., but was sceptical about a proposal to give magistrates the power to set a minimum wage, 6 Apr. He argued that consumption of beer rather than spirits would 'improve the morality and well being of the people', and considered the qualms felt over the removal of the beer duty to be unduly alarmist, 21 May. He voted for Jewish emancipation, 5 Apr., 17 May, and abolition of the death penalty for forgery, 24 May, 7 June. He favoured amending the Church Building Act to give surplus revenues to minor church officials, 20 May, 8 June 1830.

The ministry naturally regarded Ridley Colborne as one of their 'foes', and he voted against them in the crucial civil list division, 15 Nov. 1830. He gave lukewarm support to Lord Nugent's labouring poor bill, 19 Nov. He opined that the 'deluded peasantry' involved in recent agricultural disturbances should be tried by special commissions rather than by the magistrates who had committed them, 7 Dec. He considered it 'bad economy' to underpay government clerks, 9 Dec. 1830. He maintained that Parliament would never agree to a property tax, 17 Feb. 1831. He divided for the second reading of the Grey ministry's reform bill, 22 Mar., and against Gascoyne's wrecking amendment, 19 Apr. He voted for the second reading of the reintroduced bill, 6 July, and many of its details in committee, but he was against the disfranchisement of Downton, 21 July, and St. Germans, 26 July, and for the Chandos amendment to enfranchise £50 tenants-at-will, 18 Aug., and Hughes's amendment against giving county votes to urban copyholders and leaseholders, 20 Aug. He confessed his surprise at the initial omission of Horsham from the disfranchisement schedules, 19 July, but denied that any favouritism was involved and noted that the extended franchise would so reduce Norfolk's influence as to render his own re-election unlikely. He believed 'the country imperiously demands some reform', and while the government's proposals 'may not exactly suit my views, I think we were forced to take strong measures ... as nothing else would have satisfied the people'. He defended the disfranchisement of his patron's borough of Steyning, 26 July. He voted for the bill's passage, 21 Sept., the second reading of the Scottish bill, 23 Sept., and Lord Ebrington's confidence motion, 10 Oct. He drew attention to the decrepit condition of the National Gallery's temporary home in Pall Mall and expressed his 'hearty concurrence' with the grant for a new building, which would encourage further bequests, 1, 8 July. He spoke in favour of issuing the Dublin election writ, 8 Aug., acting as a majority teller. He voted to prosecute only those guilty of bribery at the Dublin election and against the motion condemning the Irish administration for exercising undue influence, 23 Aug. He divided for the second reading of the revised reform bill, 17 Dec. 1831, and for its details, except the enfranchisement of Tower Hamlets, 28 Feb. 1832. He voted for the third reading, 22 Mar., and the address asking the king to appoint only ministers committed to carrying an unimpaired measure, 10 May. He divided for the Liverpool disfranchisement bill, 23 May, and Baring's bill to exclude insolvent debtors from the House, 27 June. He voted with ministers on the Russian-Dutch loan, 26 Jan., 12, 16, 20 July. He favoured conferring additional powers on parish officers to combat the cholera epidemic and corroborated an anecdote which 'proved' the disease was contagious, 28 Mar. He renewed his opposition to the Norfolk assizes bill, 3 Apr., 23 May, 4 June. He defended lord chancellor Brougham against a charge of sinecurism, 27 July 1832.

The partial disfranchisement of Horsham by the Reform Act left Ridley Colborne without a seat. He unsuccessfully contested Wells as a Liberal in 1832 but was returned for that borough in 1834 and sat until his retirement in 1837. Raised to the peerage by Lord Melbourne's ministry in 1839, he was appointed to the fine arts commission in 1841 and to the metropolitan improvements commission the following year. He died in May 1854 and left his West Harling estate to his daughter Charlotte, the wife of Sir George Nugent*. He bequeathed eight paintings including two Rembrandts to the National Gallery, of which he had been 'a most active trustee' since 1831. According to a fulsome obituary, he was 'open-hearted' and 'of a nature singularly kind and conciliatory', and was

> one of those valuable members of society – a highly cultivated English country gentleman, enjoying the world's goods with gratitude to the giver of all good, but enjoying them at the same time for the welfare and enjoyment of others.[13]

[1] *The Times*, 15 June 1821. [2] Ibid. 4 June 1822. [3] Norf. RO, Gunton mss 1/21. [4] *The Times*, 1 July 1823, 19 Feb. 1824. [5] Ibid. 25 Feb. 1825; Add. 40356, f. 58; 40366, f. 27; 40372, f. 37. [6] *Gent. Mag.* (1854), i. 645. [7] *The Times*, 21 Feb. 1822. [8] Ibid. 24 Feb. 1826. [9] Ibid. 17 June 1825. [10] Ibid. 11 Mar. 1827. [11] Ibid. 16 Mar. 1827. [12] Northants. RO, Agar Ellis diary, 7, 24 Mar. 1828. [13] PROB 11/2192/438; C. Holmes and C. Baker, *Making of Nat. Gallery*, 28; *Gent. Mag.* (1854), i. 645.

H.J.S./T.A.J.

ROBARTS, Abraham Wildey (1779–1858), of 15 Lombard Street, London; 26 Hill Street, Berkeley Square, Mdx., and Roehampton, Surr.

MAIDSTONE 1818–1837

b. 1 Aug. 1779, 1st s. of Abraham Robarts† of North End, Hampstead, Mdx. and Sabine, da. of Thomas Tierney of Limerick; bro. of George James Robarts* and William Tierney Robarts*. *educ.* Rev. Thomas Horne's sch. Chiswick until 1794. *m.* 20 Jan. 1808, Charlotte Anne, da. of Edmund Wilkinson of Potterton Lodge, Tadcaster, Yorks., 4s. (1 *d.v.p.*) at least 3da. *suc.* fa. 1816. *d.* 2 Apr. 1858.

Writer, E.I. Co. (Canton) 1794-c.1801.

Robarts was the eldest of the four sons of Abraham Robarts, who sat for Worcester, 1796-1816, and the longest lived of the three that entered Parliament. Like his father, a wealthy merchant, he was a partner in the London banking firm known by 1820 as Curtis, Robarts and Curtis of 15 Lombard Street, whose senior partner, Sir William Curtis, was Tory Member for London. In 1816 Robarts received a considerable inheritance from his father, which included East and West Indian interests. His fortune was supplemented by the bequests he received on the deaths of his brothers (for each of whom he acted as executor): William, Member for St. Albans, in 1820; James, an East India Company employee, in 1825; and George, who had formerly sat for Wallingford, in 1829.[1] He seems to have settled in Hill Street in about 1820, and lived there for the rest of his life, though from 1827 he also rented, and later purchased, Lord Duncannon's* house at Roehampton.[2] Universally respected for his mild manner and patent honesty, he was first returned to Parliament for Maidstone in 1818, and was a frequent, but almost invariably silent, attender and voter. Like his brothers, he followed the line of their uncle, George Tierney, the Whig Commons leader, and he was elected to Brooks's, 23 Jan. 1819. However, perhaps because of his change of attitude towards the Catholics and his occasional doubts about the Whigs, ministers sometimes questioned his allegiance to opposition; he may occasionally have been confused with Wilson Aylesbury Roberts, a supporter of the Liverpool administration. He offered again at Maidstone at the general election of 1820, claiming to stand on independent principles, and was opposed by John Wells, who had been the unsuccessful government candidate in 1818, and the Whig socialite Richard Sharp*. After a contest which revealed Maidstone's partisan and venal character, Robarts was returned with Wells.[3] A petition alleging corruption against Robarts was presented, 11 May 1820, but was allowed to lapse.[4]

Robarts voted against government on the civil list, 3, 5, 8 May, the appointment of an additional baron of exchequer in Scotland, 15 May, and for economies in revenue collection, 4 July 1820. He divided with opposition on the Queen Caroline affair, 22, 26 June, and presented a Maidstone address to her, 30 Oct.[5] He does not seem to have endorsed the requisition for a county meeting on the subject, even though Lord Thanet sent it to Lord Holland, 5 Dec. 1820, with instructions to 'hand the paper to Tierney that he may get the Member for Maidstone to sign it'.[6] He was a silent participant in the campaign on her behalf early in 1821, and voted constantly with the Whigs for reduced expenditure and taxation that session. He divided against Catholic claims, 28 Feb., being one of only 12 of the Whig minority on the censure motion of 6 Feb. to do so.[7] He divided in favour of making Leeds, proposed for enfranchisement in place of Grampound, a scot and lot borough, 2 Mar., disqualifying civil officers of the ordnance from voting in parliamentary elections, 12 Apr., and parliamentary reform, 9 May. No doubt from professional considerations, he joined ministers to vote against the forgery punishment mitigation bill, 23 May 1821, but he took no part in proceedings on the Bank cash payments bill. He voted for Hume's amendment to the address, 5 Feb., more extensive tax reductions to relieve distress, 11, 21 Feb. 1822, and regularly for economies and related matters that year. He divided for inquiry into the Scottish royal boroughs, 20 Feb., parliamentary reform, 25 Apr., and to receive the Greenhoe reform petition, 3 June. He presented a petition from the Unitarians of Maidstone for a bill to legalize their form of marriage service, 17 Apr., but divided against the Catholic peers bill, 30 Apr.[8] He was listed in a handful of opposition minorities that session and, at a dinner held for him in Maidstone in August 1822, Lord Torrington declared that Robarts was 'guided by constitutional principles and not by violence or strong party prejudice'.[9]

He divided in favour of parliamentary reform, 20 Feb., 24 Apr., and alteration of the Scottish representative system, 2 June 1823. He voted for inquiries into the Irish church establishment, 4 Mar., and the legal proceedings against the Dublin Orange rioters, 22 Apr. He served his constituents by assisting in the passage of the bill to light Maidstone with gas, which he introduced, 13 Mar. 1823, when he presented a petition from the town's merchants, bankers and manufacturers for repeal of the Insolvent Debtors Acts.[10] As well as continuing to support economical reform, he cast several votes on significant legal and other questions in this and the following session. He presented a Maidstone victuallers' petition against their licenses, 5 Mar., and one from the town's inhabitants for the abolition of slavery, 11 Mar. 1824.[11] He was also involved with the bill to erect new markets there which passed that session. He voted for inquiries into the Irish church establishment, 6 May, and the state of that country, 11 May, and against the second reading of the Irish insurrection bill, 14 June 1824. He paired, 15 Feb., and divided against the Irish unlawful societies bill, 21, 25 Feb., and again for inquiry into the Irish church establishment, 14 June 1825. He voted for Catholic relief, 1 Mar., 25 Apr. When Wells presented an anti-Catholic petition from Maidstone, 26 Apr., he made what may have been his first major parliamentary speech, asserting that opinion in his constituency was predominantly pro-Catholic. He also declared that he had previously been averse to emancipation, but that after hearing Canning and Plunket's recent speeches

> his views had been entirely changed and he much regretted that he had ever voted against the Catholic claims. So firm were his sentiments upon the subject, that as long as he should have a seat in that House, no consideration whatever would induce him to withhold his support from

the measures intended to relieve the Catholics from their political disqualifications.

He duly voted for the relief bill's third reading, 10 May 1825. He divided against going into committee on the Bank Charter Acts, 13 Feb. 1826, but he was not listed in any of the known minorities on the promissory notes bill during that month. He voted for altering the representation of Edinburgh, 13 Apr. (as he had, 26 Feb. 1824), parliamentary reform, 27 Apr., and curbing electoral bribery, 26 May. Like George James Robarts he divided in favour of taking the corn laws into consideration, 18 Apr., and probably witnessed his brother's dramatic collapse in the House later that day. His last recorded votes that session were for inquiries into the state of the nation, 4 May, and the petition of James Silk Buckingham† on the liberty of the press in India, 9 May 1826.

Robarts offered again at the general election that summer, receiving cordial support at a meeting in Maidstone, 5 June 1826. However, the popularity of Wells, combined with the entry of the wealthy Wyndham Lewis*, led to expectations of a spirited contest: and one correspondent in the *Kentish Chronicle* of 9 June wrote that 'Mr. Robarts has every weapon to contend against that bigotry, ignorance and venality can wield and invent. The timely and vigorous perseverance of his friends will, however, secure his election'.[12] On the hustings, he spoke briefly in favour of civil and religious liberty, 10 June, and he was returned just behind Wells after a contest, in which he received a high number of plumpers despite his unwillingness to bribe. His success was celebrated at the annual fête he provided for his supporters at Gibraltar Fields, 23 Aug.[13] He voted against the address, 21 Nov. 1826, and the duke of Clarence's grant, 16 Feb., 2, 16 Mar., and for setting the import price of corn at 50*s.* not 60*s.*, 9 Mar. 1827. He divided for the production of information on the Irish government's handling of the Lisburn Orange procession, 29 Mar., the postponement of the committee of supply, 30 Mar., and the disfranchisement of Penryn, 28 May. He had been in the pro-Catholic minority, 6 Mar., and on presenting a petition from the Protestant Dissenters of Maidstone for repeal of the Test Acts, 8 June, he stated that they wished him to contradict Wells's false statement that the majority of them opposed Catholic claims.[14] He was presumably sympathetic to the short-lived Canning ministry, which Tierney joined, and, following Lord Goderich's appointment as prime minister, Thomas Spring Rice* reported to Lord Lansdowne, 9 Sept. 1827, that Robarts had written that 'I am glad, very glad that poor Canning's government is sustained, but I am not altogether satisfied with the *barking* of the Whigs. I should like to know what dog barked loudest'.[15]

Robarts divided for repeal of the Test Acts, 26 Feb., and Catholic relief, 12 May 1828. He voted against extending the franchise of East Retford to the freeholders of Bassetlaw, 21 Mar., for information on civil list pensions, 20 May, and for inquiry into the circulation of small promissory notes, 5 June. He cited urgent business as the reason for missing an anti-Brunswick dinner in Maidstone, but pledged his support for relief by letter, 21 Dec. 1828. At the meeting on the 23rd, one of his principal supporters, Charles Ellis, said that Robarts was the 'first gentleman that was *ever* returned from this town, at the same time avowing his sentiments to be favourable to Catholic emancipation'.[16] In February 1829 he was listed by Planta, the Wellington ministry's patronage secretary, as being opposed to securities, but was also marked among those 'opposition or doubtful men who, we think, will vote with the government on this question'. He again argued, 26 Feb., that a large proportion of his constituents were in favour of relief, and that its opponents would soon see that their apprehensions about the consequences of the bill were imaginary. He voted for considering Catholic claims, 6 Mar., and, having brought up favourable petitions, 11, 16 Mar., quarrelled with Wells on the 16th about the balance of opinion in Maidstone and their conduct at and since the election. He voted for the third reading of the emancipation bill, 30 Mar., and to allow Daniel O'Connell to take his seat without swearing the oath of supremacy, 18 May. His only other known votes in that session were for transferring East Retford's seats to Birmingham, 1 May, and the issue of its new writ and parliamentary reform, 2 June. In October 1829 he was listed by Sir Richard Vyvyan*, the Ultra leader, among those supporters of emancipation whose 'sentiments' on the notion of an alliance between Ultras and Whigs were 'unknown'. In January 1830 Planta reported to the premier that Robarts had sent in his support via William Yates Peel* and requested the government's 'notes' (the whip).[17] Yet he voted for Knatchbull's amendment to the address on distress, 4 Feb., and during the session regularly joined his Whig colleagues in voting for lower taxation and expenditure. He divided for transferring East Retford's seats to Birmingham, 11 Feb., 15 Mar. (pairing for this on 5 Mar.). He voted for parliamentary reform, 18 Feb., the enfranchisement of Birmingham, Leeds and Manchester, 23 Feb., and to refer the Newark petition complaining of electoral interference by the duke of Newcastle to a select committee, 1 Mar.; he paired for reform, 28 May. He divided for Jewish emancipation, 5 Apr., 17 May. He voted to abolish the Irish lord lieutenancy, 11 May, and for papers on the civil government of Canada, 25 May 1830.

With a dissolution looming, Robarts offered again at Maidstone at the end of June 1830 and engaged in some active canvassing. Wells retired, but was replaced by Alderman Henry Winchester, while two independents also entered.[18] Stressing his independence, 29 July, he declared that 'I consider myself as your old and tried servant, only temporarily discharged and anxiously hoping to be taken into your service again'. The following day he reiterated his support for civil and religious liberty, reform and retrenchment. After a heated contest at the general election, during which he was obliged to swear to land in the parish of Lillingstone, Buckinghamshire, as his property qualification, he was returned comfortably ahead of the rest of the field.[19] He was, of course, listed by ministers among their 'foes', and duly voted against them on the civil list, 15 Nov. 1830. At the request of his constituents, he presented their pro-reform petition, 18 Mar. 1831.[20] He voted for the second reading of the Grey ministry's reform bill, 22 Mar., and against Gascoyne's wrecking amendment, 19 Apr. A meeting in his interest at Maidstone, 13 Apr., had protested at his supporting a measure which would disfranchise the non-residents, but he offered again at the ensuing general election, declaring that he had voted for reform because it was a 'question of such *deep* and *vital* importance to the best interest of the country'.[21] In another campaign speech for reform, 1 May, he introduced the Whig banker Charles James Barnett as his colleague, and their success as reformers was considered certain.[22] At the election, 3 May, he opined that '*my whole energies, my paramount aim will be directed to support parliamentary reform*', and, having topped the poll with Barnett, he ridiculed his opponents for attempting to carry the seat against the torrent of public opinion.[23] He was too ill to attend the Kent reform dinner at Rochester, 8 June, but at the Inflexible Society's fête, 5 Sept. 1831, he attributed a 'very great part' of his success to their 'exertions and independence'.[24]

Robarts voted for the second reading of the reintroduced reform bill, 6 July, at least twice against adjourning proceedings on it, 12 July 1831, and steadily for its details. He paired against extending the county franchise to town freeholders, 17 Aug., and divided against censuring the Irish government for using undue influence in the Dublin election, 23 Aug. He voted for the third reading, 19 Sept., and passage of the reform bill, 21 Sept., and for Lord Ebrington's confidence motion, 10 Oct. He divided in favour of the second reading of the revised bill, 17 Dec. 1831, going into committee on it, 20 Jan., 20 Feb. 1832, and again usually for its details. He voted for its third reading, 22 Mar., Ebrington's motion for an address calling on the king to appoint only ministers who would carry it unimpaired, 10 May, and the second reading of the Irish bill, 25 May. At the Inflexible Society dinner, 13 Aug., he denied that he had tried to turn Maidstone into a close borough by dragging in Barnett with him, and claimed that he had 'sat up night after night, at the expense of my health and the sacrifice of all domestic comfort' in order to defend schedules A and B.[25] His only other known votes in this Parliament were with ministers for the Russian-Dutch loan, 26 Jan., 12, 16, 20 July, against information on Portugal, 9 Feb., and for the navy civil departments bill, 6 Apr. 1832. Although he had promised to take charge of a Maidstone petition against child employment in factories, it does not seem to have been presented.[26]

He was appointed to the committee of secrecy on renewing the Bank of England charter, 22 Mar. 1832. According to Charles Arbuthnot*, 14 June, Robarts and John Smith were the members of this committee who most feared being at the mercies of a reformed Parliament

> both having voted through thick and thin for the bill, and both so unwilling to be the victims of their own law that they yesterday in the committee told Lord Althorp [the chairman] that, if they were not given time to report, the Bank and the monied interest would be so alarmed that they would call in all their accommodations and close their accounts, which would cause the greatest confusion and embarrassment. Can you conceive such villainy as forcing upon the country a law which they themselves consider dangerous?[27]

After he had offered again at Maidstone, he apologized to his constituents, 9 July, for having to return immediately to London for this committee, which he called 'a subject of the most vital importance to the best interests of the country'.[28] By 24 July, as Sir John Beckett* informed Lord Lowther*, Robarts seemed to 'think they can get no further with examination of witnesses. They had Old [Nathan Meyer] Rothschild today. He gave very good evidence says Aby. That is, said I, evidence in favour of the Bank? *Yes!*'[29] On 12 Aug. Greville recorded that Commons business would soon be over, and that

> Robarts told me that the Bank committee had executed their laborious duties in a spirit of great cordiality, and with a general disposition to lay aside all political differences and concur in accomplishing the best results ...

He told me that the evidence all went to prove that little improvement could be made in the management of the Bank.[30]

He was again successful at the general election of 1832, being returned as a Liberal with Barnett against Lewis, despite refusing to engage in bribery.[31] On the eve of another such victory in 1835, Greville described him thus:

A reformer, and supports all Whig and reforming governments; but he does so (like many others) from fear. What he most dreads is collision, and most desires is quiet, and he thinks non-resistance the best way.[32]

He left Parliament in 1837, but continued to pursue his career in banking, becoming chairman of the committee of bankers, and also indulged his passion for paintings, mainly Dutch, of which he established a fine collection.[33] He died, after a brief illness, in April 1858, *The Times* obituary notice stating that 'no member of the financial world ever held a higher position or was more universally esteemed'.[34] His two eldest sons, Abraham George and Henry Christopher, both partners in his banking house, inherited the bulk of his estate.

[1] *Oxford DNB sub* Robarts fam.; PROB 11/1587/636; 1637/694; 1709/112; 1762/607; IR26/687/1139; 838/1431; 1206/635. [2] D. Howell-Thomas, *Duncannon*, 271. [3] *Kentish Chron.* 18 Feb., 3, 10 Mar.; *Maidstone Jnl.* 29 Feb., 7, 14 Mar. 1820. [4] *Maidstone Jnl.* 16, 30 May 1820. [5] Ibid. 7 Nov. 1820. [6] Add. 51571; *Kentish Chron.* 2 Jan. 1821. [7] G.I.T. Machin, *Catholic Question in English Politics*, 26. [8] *The Times*, 18 Apr. 1822. [9] *Maidstone Jnl.* 27 Aug. 1822. [10] *The Times*, 14 Mar. 1823. [11] Ibid. 6, 12 Mar. 1824. [12] Ibid. 9 June; *Maidstone Jnl.* 6 June 1826; Bodl. Hughenden Dep. D/II/C/1d, 13. [13] *Maidstone Jnl.* 13 June; *Kentish Chron.* 13 June, 25 Aug. 1826; J. Phillips, *Great Reform Bill in Boroughs*, 115. [14] *The Times*, 9 June 1827. [15] Lansdowne mss. [16] *Maidstone Jnl.* 23, 30 Dec. 1828. [17] Wellington mss WP1/1083/13. [18] *Maidstone Jnl.* 6, 13, 20, 27 July; *Kentish Gazette*, 13 July; *The Times*, 2 Aug. 1830. [19] *Maidstone Jnl.* 3 Aug.; *Kentish Chron.* 3 Aug. 1830. [20] *The Times*, 19 Mar.; *Maidstone Jnl.* 15 Mar. 1831. [21] *Maidstone Gazette*, 19 Apr.; *Maidstone Jnl.* 26 Apr. 1831. [22] *Maidstone Jnl.* 3 May; Brougham mss, Ellice to Brougham [2 May] 1831. [23] *Maidstone Jnl.* 10 May 1831. [24] Ibid. 14 June, 6 Sept. 1831. [25] Ibid. 14 Aug. 1831. [26] Ibid. 14 Feb., 6 Mar. 1832. [27] Aberdeen Univ. Lib. Arbuthnot mss 3029/2/1/31. [28] *Maidstone Jnl.* 10 July 1832. [29] Lonsdale mss. [30] *Greville Mems.* ii. 317. [31] *Kentish Gazette*, 29 June; *Maidstone Jnl.* 28 Aug., 18 Dec. 1832. [32] *Greville Mems.* iii. 133. [33] G.F. Waagen, *Galleries and Cabinets of Art* (1857), 158-65. [34] *The Times*, 5 Apr. 1858; *Oxford DNB*.

S.M.F.

ROBARTS, George James (?1782–1829), of Grosvenor Street, Mdx.

Wallingford 1820–12 Dec. 1826

b. ?1782, 2nd s. of Abraham Robarts (*d.* 1816) of North End, Hampstead, Mdx. and Sabine, da. of Thomas Tierney of Limerick; bro. of Abraham Wildey Robarts* and William Tierney Robarts*. *unm.* 2s. 1da. illegit. CB 1815. *d.* 16 Oct. 1829.

Cornet 23 Drag. 1803; lt. 10 (Prince's Own) Drag. 1804, capt. 1806, maj. 1811, brevet lt.-col. 1813; maj. 24 Drag. Nov. 1814, 9 Drag. Dec. 1814 (half-pay).

Robarts served in the Peninsula, distinguished himself in command of the prince of Wales's Hussars at Morales, 2 June 1813, and fought at Vitoria later in the month. On his return home he was promoted to lieutenant-colonel. He was the senior of the 24 officers of the regiment who in August 1814 signed a letter requesting a court martial on the allegedly reprehensible conduct of their colonel, George Quentin, in France the previous spring. Quentin was largely exonerated and, to mark the prince regent's displeasure, his officers were disbanded as a corps. Robarts was transferred to the 24th Hussars on 12 Nov. 1814. In the Commons, 23 Nov., his uncle George Tierney refuted an official statement, placed in the *Courier*, that in an earlier debate he had made light of Robarts's personal indebtedness to the regent for his promotion. Like the chief scapegoat in the affair, Colonel Charles Palmer, Robarts was placed on half-pay shortly afterwards.[1]

He received £6,107 from his wealthy father in his lifetime and on his death in 1816 inherited a further £33,893 plus £10,000 in trust.[2] He joined Brooks's in 1817 and bought five houses in the venal borough of Wallingford, which he unsuccessfully contested in 1818. He tried again at the general election of 1820, when some of the respectable electors formed an association to promote independence and root out corruption. He professed sympathy with their aims, came second in the poll and so joined two of his brothers in the House.[3] (The other son of Abraham Robarts, James Thomas, was a supercargo with the East India Company in Canton.) Robarts followed the family line and was a steady, though apparently silent adherent of the Whig opposition to the Liverpool ministry. He was a regular voter for economy, retrenchment and reduced taxation, favoured making Leeds, proposed for enfranchisement in place of Grampound, a scot and lot borough, 2 Mar. 1821, and divided for parliamentary reform, 9 May 1821, 25 Apr. 1822, 20 Feb., 24 Apr., 2 June 1823, 26 Feb. 1824. He led the Wallingford deputation which presented a supportive address to Queen Caroline, 22 Jan. 1821.[4] He was apparently a lukewarm supporter of Catholic relief: his only certain vote for it was on 1 Mar. 1825. His last recorded votes were against the president of the board of trade's ministerial salary, 7, 10 Apr., and for reform of Edinburgh's representation, 13 Apr., and relaxation of the corn laws, 18 Apr. 1826. That day, as Tierney told Lady Holland, 28 Apr., his family came 'very near losing' him:

> He was suddenly attacked in the House of Commons ... by loss of speech and for the four following days the physicians gave hardly a hope of his being likely to live. A favourable change has however taken place and he is now out of danger, though still attended by the doctors four times a day. The case is not paralytic but is connected with some pressure of the brain.

On 16 May Tierney wrote:

> My poor nephew is still in a very precarious state, but the physicians encourage us to hope that he will ultimately recover. I should have more confidence in them if they were able to say distinctly what was his complaint.[5]

He had come in for criticism in Wallingford for failing to pay the expected rewards to his supporters; and two months before the general election of 1826 (a few days before his seizure in the House) he was persuaded that his only chance of re-election lay in coalescing with the other veteran Whig sitting Member William Hughes, an enthusiastic briber. He was too ill to take any part in the campaign, and his brother-in-law John Maddox stood in for him. He was returned in second place, but he vacated his seat soon after the new Parliament met.[6] He survived in a state of vegetation for a further three years, but on 27 Aug. 1829 Tierney told Lord Holland that he

> cannot possibly last long. He is in as wretched a condition as can well be imagined, his bones through his skin and his faculties entirely gone. The physician who lives with him says that he cannot answer for him from day to day, at the same time that he may linger on for some weeks.[7]

He died in October 1829, 'aged 47'. On the 19th his brother Abraham, the only survivor of the four (William had died in 1820 and James in 1825, at Macao), told Lord Salisbury, to whom Robarts left his shooting equipment:

> The illness which led to this fatal event has been of such long duration, and was attended with so many distressing and melancholy circumstances, the termination of it can scarcely be considered otherwise than [as] a providential release from a miserable existence.[8]

By his will, dated 24 Nov. 1823, and proved under £70,000, he bequeathed £10,000 to Mary Ann Harben, who lived in a house he owned at 57 Welbeck Street; £10,000 each to their bastards Georgiana Charlotte and James George, and the same sum to another illegitimate child, George Francis Stuart Andrews. He commended the first two to the 'favourable notice' of his mother and sisters, trusting that they would 'have some feeling in consideration for the circumstances of their birth and do all in their power to make them respectable and happy in life'. His daughter received his Vitoria medal and a set of dental instruments looted from Joseph Buonaparte's carriage at that engagement.[9]

[1] *HP Commons, 1790-1820*, iv. 714; *Gent. Mag.* (1814), ii. 494, 577; *HMC Fortescue*, x. 393-4. [2] PROB 11/1587/636; *Oxford DNB*. [3] *Reading Mercury*, 6, 13, 20 Mar. 1820. [4] Ibid. 5 Feb. 1821. [5] Add. 51584. [6] *Berks. Chron.* 22 Apr., 3, 10, 17 June, 2, 9 Dec. 1826. See WALLINGFORD. [7] Add. 51586. [8] Hatfield House mss 2M/Gen. [9] PROB 11/1762/607; IR26/1206/635.

D.R.F.

ROBARTS, William Tierney (c.1786–1820), of Old Broad Street, London and 8 John Street, Berkeley Square, Mdx.

ST. ALBANS 26 Feb. 1818–9 Dec. 1820

b. c.1786, 4th s. of Abraham Robarts† (*d.* 1816) of North End, Hampstead, Mdx. and Sabine, da. of Thomas Tierney of Limerick; bro. of Abraham Wildey Robarts* and George James Robarts*. *unm. d.* 9 Dec. 1820.

Dir. Bank of England 1810-*d.*

Robarts was a prosperous London merchant and bank director, who had been given a total of £30,000 by his father.[1] At the general election of 1820 he fought his third contested election at St. Albans in two years. The support of Earl Spencer's family and, crucially, his wealth, again secured him the seat.[2] A nephew of George Tierney, the Whig leader in the Commons, and a member of Brooks's since 1817, he would have joined his brothers in the opposition ranks had he not been incapacitated by a debilitating illness soon after his return. He is not known to have spoken or voted in the new Parliament and on 21 June 1820 he took a month's sick leave. A false report of his death circulated in late September,[3] but Tierney reported to Lady Holland, 1 Oct. 1820:

> My nephew is I think much the same, quite a cripple, and notwithstanding he has an excellent appetite, hardly gaining any strength. I do not from all I can make out believe his life to be in any danger, but I own I can now see no chance of his getting well till next spring. A disorder, however, which nobody pretends to understand may take a sudden favourable turn, particularly when there is youth to assist.[4]

He was given 'very slender hopes of continuing' to breathe in early November 1820, but he lingered for four more weeks until his death at his mother's house in Lower Grosvenor Street.[5] 'It was', wrote Tierney, 'a happy release to himself, and, indeed, all possible hope being at an end, a relief to the family'.[6] This was not quite the last that was heard of him, for his shade was conjured to appear before the Royal Family during their 'Christmas gambols at Brighton', as Tierney complained to Lady Holland, 4 Jan. 1821:

> I wish they had chosen some other object for their amusement than poor W. Robarts, because if, as is not improbable, the story of the apparition should find its way into the papers, it may give much pain to his mother and family. I know of no picture of him by which the old deception could have been practised.[7]

By his will, dated 21 June 1820, and proved under £80,000 (later revalued under £120,000), he divided his estate among his siblings.[8]

[1] *HP Commons, 1790-1820*, v. 24. [2] Add. 76033, J. Harrison to Spencer, 25 Feb.; *County Chron.* 14 Mar. 1820. [3] Add. 76124, A. Ross to Spencer, 30 Sept. 1820. [4] Add. 51586. [5] Add. 76033, Harrison to Spencer, 7 Nov.; Grey mss, Tierney to Grey, 21, 25 Nov. 1820. [6] Grey mss, Tierney to Grey, 7, 13 Dec. 1820. [7] Add. 51586. [8] PROB 11/1637/694; IR26/838/1431.

D.R.F.

ROBERTS, **Wilson Aylesbury** (1770–1853), of Bewdley, Worcs.; Packwood, Warws., and 26 Dover Street, Mdx.

BEWDLEY 1818–1832

b. 23 June 1770, 1st surv. s. of Wilson Aylesbury Roberts, attorney and dep. recorder, of Bewdley and Packwood and Betty Carolina, da. and h. of John Crane of Bewdley. *educ.* Christ Church, Oxf. 1788; L. Inn 1790. *unm. suc.* fa. 1819. *d.* 28 Nov. 1853.

Bailiff, Bewdley 1809, 1812, 1815; sheriff, Worcs. 1837-8. Lt. Wolverley yeomanry 1803.

Roberts's ancestors were originally from Cornwall, but at the beginning of the eighteenth century his great-grandfather Henry settled in Droitwich and established an 'extensive salt works'. Thereafter his family benefitted from two fortuitous marriages: Roberts's grandmother was heir to the Packwood estates of her brother William Aylesbury, and his mother to the Bewdley properties of her uncle Thomas Cheeke. Roberts's father, a local attorney, became an increasingly 'influential member' of the close corporation at Bewdley, which had his son returned without opposition in 1818. On his death the following year Roberts inherited canal shares and local property worth approximately £60,000, and assumed control of the family interest.[1]

At the 1820 general election he was again returned unopposed by the corporation. A lax attender, whose votes were subject to confusion with those of Abraham Robarts, Member for Maidstone, when present he continued to give silent support to the Liverpool ministry. 'As this Member entertains some "philosophic doubt" on the utility of the House of Commons', jibed the *Black Book*, 'it is not surprising he is so remiss in his devotions at St. Stephen's'.[2] On 28 June 1820 he was excused attendance from the Berwick election committee after its chairman had verified a certificate from a surgeon who claimed to have found him 'in a state of bodily illness that rendered it impossible for him to attend'. He was absent from the division on Catholic relief, 28 Feb. 1821, but present to divide against it, 1 Mar., and in its favour, 21 Apr. 1825. He was listed in the minorities for repeal of the malt duty, 3 Apr. 1821, and reductions in naval expenditure, 7 May 1821, 22 Feb. 1822. He divided against parliamentary reform, 9 May 1821. He voted for the Irish insurrection bill, 14 June 1824, and suppression of the Catholic Association, 25 Feb. 1825. He was granted a month's leave on urgent private business, 28 Mar. 1825. At the 1826 general election Roberts was again returned unopposed.[3] He voted against Catholic claims, 6 Mar. 1827, 12 May 1828. On 13 Mar. 1827 he was granted six weeks' leave on urgent private business after serving on an election committee. He was one of the Members who presented multiple petitions for repeal of the Test Acts, 22 Feb., but he did not vote on this issue, 26 Feb. 1828. In February 1829 the Wellington ministry's patronage secretary predicted that he would vote 'with government' for Catholic emancipation, and he duly paired in its support, 6 Mar. 1829. He divided against parliamentary reform, 18 Feb. 1830. On 11 Mar. he was granted a month's leave on account of domestic affliction. He voted for Jewish emancipation, 17 May, and paired against abolition of the death penalty for forgery, 7 June 1830.

At the general election the following month he was re-elected unopposed.[4] He was listed by the Wellington ministry as one of their 'friends', but was absent from the crucial division on the civil list, 15 Nov. 1830. He voted against the second reading of the Grey ministry's reform bill, 22 Mar., and paired for Gascoyne's wrecking amendment, 19 Apr. 1831. At the ensuing general election he was again returned without opposition.[5] He voted against the second reading of the reintroduced reform bill, 6 July, but was absent from the divisions on Chippenham's inclusion in schedule B, 27 July, the passage of the bill, 21 Sept., and the second reading of the revised bill, 17 Dec. 1831. He was in the minorities against the enfranchisement of Tower Hamlets, 28 Feb., and the third reading, 22 Mar. 1832. He voted against ministers on the Russian-Dutch loan, 12 July 1832. At that year's dissolution he retired from Bewdley, where the operation of the Reform Act had destroyed the electoral hegemony of the corporation and 'rendered his re-election impossible'. The following year he withheld his father's accounts as deputy recorder from the municipal corporations commission.[6]

Roberts died at Bewdley in November 1853. By his will, dated 24 Feb. 1848, the bulk of his property passed to his 'natural son' Thomas Lloyd Roberts of Langley Farm, near Ludlow, Shropshire (*d.* 9 June 1922) and his 'lawfully begotten' grandchildren. He was buried at Dowles churchyard, Worcestershire, alongside his 'late companion' and 'trustworthy and faithful servant', James Lankester.[7]

[1] *Gent. Mag.* (1854), i. 322; *PP* (1835), xxv. 367; PROB 11/1617/294; IR26/794/539. [2] *Black Bk.* (1823), 188; *Session of Parl. 1825*, p. 482. [3] *Worcester Herald*, 17 June 1826. [4] Ibid. 24 July, 7 Aug. 1830. [5] Ibid. 30 Apr. 1831. [6] *Gent. Mag.* (1854), i. 322; *PP* (1835), xxv. 367. [7] PROB 11/2186/150; IR26/2006/163.

P.J.S.

ROBERTSON, Alexander (1779–1856), of 38 Broad Street Buildings, London and Hoe Bridge Place, Woking, Surr.

GRAMPOUND 1818–1826

b. 14 Feb. 1779, 4th but 3rd surv. s. of Rev. James Robertson, minister of Ratho, nr. Edinburgh and Jean, da. of Rev. Alexander Robertson, minister of Eddleston, Peebles.[1] (?)*m.* 1da.[2] *d.* 17 Dec. 1856.

Robertson told the House of Lords foreign trade committee, 20 June 1820, that he was involved in the China trade and had been to Canton nine times between his first visit in 1795 and his last in 1812. As a ship owner, he emphasized the importance of fully opening that market to private enterprise.[3] At the general election earlier that year he had came in again for the venal borough of Grampound, which was under sentence of death for corruption, but was granted a temporary reprieve by the intervention of the Lords.[4]

He was a regular attender who gave general support to Lord Liverpool's ministry, but he opposed them on specific issues and expressed strong views on commercial and financial questions. He was named to the foreign trade committee, 5 June 1820, and in the next four sessions. He divided against economies in revenue collection, 4 July 1820. He voted in defence of ministers' conduct towards Queen Caroline, 6 Feb. 1821. He divided against Catholic relief, 28 Feb. He was in the minorities for army reductions, 14, 15 Mar., on the Baltic timber duties, 5 Apr., and the composition of the Irish revenue commission, 15 June, and against the grant for the aliens office, 29 June. On the other hand, he voted with government against repeal of the additional malt duty, 3 Apr., for the barracks grant, 28 May, and against Hume's economy and retrenchment motion, 27 June. He divided against parliamentary reform, 9 May 1821. He voted against more extensive tax reductions, 11, 21 Feb., but was against government on the time limit for conversion of the navy five per cents, 8 Mar., and abolition of one of the joint-postmasterships, 13 Mar. 1822. He opposed repeal of the house and window taxes, 2 July, but thought 'it was impossible the country could go on under the present [financial] system' and said he 'looked with much apprehension to the consequences of some of the measures which had been adopted'. He presented a London merchants' petition for 'freer commercial intercourse' with India, 2 Apr.[5] On the government's corn law proposals, 9 May, he urged them to 'protect and advance commerce as the best mode of securing the welfare of all classes, and of giving the farmer a remunerating price'. He called on agricultural and commercial Members to unite to resist the navigation bill, which would hand the eastern trade on a plate to the Dutch, 23 May, 4 June.[6] He recommended repeal of the duty on foreign wool, which he considered to be prejudicial to British exports, 30 May.[7] He opposed currency reform, 10 July.[8] He divided against removal of Catholic peers' disabilities, 30 Apr., the Irish constables bill, 7 June, and investigation of the Calcutta bankers' grievances, 4 July 1822.

On 14 Feb. 1823 Robertson asserted that the 'one great cause' of distress was 'the system of credit' adopted during the French wars, when vast sums had been borrowed 'on ruinous terms'. The country was therefore 'completely in the hands of a great monied body in [the] metropolis' who could keep interest rates 'as high ... as they chose'. He stressed the need to support the landed interest, 'upon which ... the government must principally rely for its resources', 21 Feb. He traced and deplored successive governments' departure from the original principle and practice of the sinking fund, 3 Mar., and maintained that 'the system was an entire delusion, which threatened the ruin of the country and the subversion of the throne, for ... if the aristocracy ... were destroyed the other institutions ... could not stand'. However, he concluded that low interest rates were 'perhaps the only thing that could enable our merchants and manufacturers to cope with the markets and productions of other countries', and resolved to support the government's proposals for regulation of the fund, while urging the importance of securing 'just' rates of interest and a fixed amount of capital debt for repayment, in order to 'do away with stock-jobbing'; he duly voted with ministers later that day. He divided with them against repeal of the assessed taxes, 18 Mar., but spoke and voted against the naval and military pensions bill, 11, 14, 18 Apr. He approved the principle of the warehousing bill, 17 Mar., but complained that it exhibited 'unnecessary caution', 21 Mar.[9] He opposed interference with the law merchant, 15 May. He argued that the 'vested interests' of West India proprietors deserved preference over the 'interested attempts' of East India agents in respect to the sugar duties, 22 May, and pointed out 'several defects in the present commercial intercourse with India and the system carried on in our eastern colonies', 3 July.[10] He was a determined opponent of the reciprocity bill, protesting, 6 June, that it sacrificed the principle of protection for the sake of free trade dogma and would aggravate the distress of the shipping interest. He urged agriculturists to resist it, 23 June, 4 July, when he claimed that as a result of recent commercial measures, 'which had been acquiesced in by Parliament almost without deliberation', Britain's overseas trade had 'diminished within the last three years to the extent of 150,000 tons and 8,000 seamen'; he was a minority teller that day against the third reading. He voted in the minority on the silk manufacture bill, 9 June, and supported a petition for reduction of the hemp duties, 12 June.[11] He emphasized the 'high importance' of conciliating and cultivating the new South American states for the sake of potentially 'boundless trade', 8 July, and objected to 'the manner in which ministers had accommodated themselves to the unjust and injurious demands' of the European powers.[12] He divided against inquiry into the parliamentary franchise, 20 Feb., and reform in Scotland, 2 June. He voted against repeal of the Foreign Enlistment Act, 16 Apr., but criticized the government's feebleness in the face of French aggression against Spain, 29 Apr. He divided against inquiry into the prosecution of the Dublin Orange rioters, 22 Apr. Surprisingly, in view of his previous votes, he endorsed a petition from Irish Catholics for repeal of the penal laws preventing them from endowing religious institutions, 9 May.[13] Three days later he went further by supporting the Whig amendment for inquiry into the state of Ireland, declaring that 'all the troubles of Ireland arose from the persecution of the Catholic religion' and that renewal of the Insurrection Act was 'only throwing a firebrand amongst the already inflamed population'. He voted in the same sense, 24 June, when he recommended Catholic emancipation, the payment of priests and an equitable adjustment of tithes. He divided against inquiry into delays in chancery, 5 June. On 20 June 1823 he voted against treasury control over the appointment of the London Bridge engineer and in the Tory minority against the Scottish juries bill.

He voted for information on Catholic burials, 6 Feb., and spoke and voted for inquiry into the Irish church establishment, 6 May 1824. Next day, claiming that he 'belonged to no party', he complained of misrepresentation of his speech in the *Globe*, but, harried by the Speaker, he let the matter drop.[14] He divided for inquiry into the state of Ireland, 11 May, and voted in the minority (where he was listed as 'A. Robinson') against the insurrection bill, 14 June, after deploring 'the brutalizing policy of successive governments'. Yet he was averse to any 'concessions' to Protestant Dissenters, whom he stigmatized as 'sectarians', 17 June, declaring that 'it was necessary, for the safety of the established church, to withstand their growing influence'.[15] He reiterated his 'decided disapprobation of the whole system of reciprocity', which 'would be the ruin of the shipping interest', 13 Feb. He endorsed a London merchants' petition for repeal of the duty on foreign wool, 20 Feb., but voted in the minority against removing the prohibition on the export of long wool, 21 May. On the budget statement, 23 Feb., he welcomed the proposed tax remissions and ministers' professed determination to protect the sinking fund, and criticized the opposition, who 'talked as if they had never looked beyond the present hour'. He defended the planned reduction of silk duties, 4 Mar., but argued that no immediate relief would accrue to West Indian proprietors from remission of the duties on rum because of the 'great quantity now in bond', 8 Mar. He voiced his 'utter dissent' from the Westminster petition for the surplus on the sinking fund to be used for tax reductions, 12 Mar., and exhorted ministers to stick to a 'simple and straightforward measure', 7 May. He objected to the law merchant bill, which was backed by 'the monied men who were in the habit of making advances on goods', 17 May. He denounced the marine insurance bill as a greater threat to national interests than Fox's East India bill, 28 May, when the Speaker cut short his intemperate attack on the government's 'disastrous' commercial policy.[16] He was a minority teller against going into committee on the bill, 3 June, after defending Lloyd's and arguing that the measure, 'so far from breaking down monopoly ... would more than ever promote it, by condensing the power of money capital and placing the public interest at the entire disposal of the wealthy'. He condemned the surrender of Bencoolen to the Dutch as a severe blow to British trade, 17 June. He opposed the usury laws repeal bill with a tedious historical review of the subject, 27 Feb., and moved a wrecking amendment, which was defeated by 43-34; he again attacked the 'superficial' measure, 8 Apr. In his guise as 'A. Robinson' he voted to limit the aliens bill to one year, 12 Apr. He endorsed a Falmouth petition against the prosecution of the Methodist missionary John Smith in Demerara, 10 June, but divided in the ministerial majority next day. He spoke and voted in the minority for inquiry into naval impressment, 10 June 1824, though he doubted if it could be dispensed with.

He earned cheers when he attacked the Irish unlawful societies bill, 15 Feb. 1825, observing that 'the Catholic peasantry had been deserted by the landed gentry, Protestant as well as Catholic, and left unprotected against the oppressions of partial magistrates and all the exactions of unfeeling tithe collectors'. He believed that 'the only advisable measure by which they could put down the violence and discontent which now raged in Ireland would be by concession, not by coercion'; he again voted against the bill, 21 Feb. He divided silently for Catholic relief, 1 Mar., but confessed, 19 Apr., that 'in a political point of view' he was less inclined to indulge English and Scottish Catholics. While he voted for the principle of the relief bill, 21 Apr., he tried to insert a clause to prohibit Catholics from representing English and Scottish constituencies, 6 May. He divided for the bill's third reading, 10 May, but remarked that if it was to be 'coupled' with the disfranchisement of Irish 40*s.* freeholders, 'it was a question with him how far its supporters ... were bound to advocate it'. He remained hostile to Dissenters' claims, 25 Mar., 2 May, 21 June, as 'the Church of England was essential to the safety of the throne'. He again opposed repeal of the usury laws, 17 Feb. He defended the navy estimates against Hume's strictures, 21 Feb., but saw no valid reason for 'any augmentation of the army', 11 Mar., and spoke and voted with the minority for information on the Indian army, 24 Mar. He supported Hume's unsuccessful attempt to debar Members from voting on questions in which they had a direct pecuniary interest, 10 Mar. He approved the Canadian waste lands bill, 15 Mar. Next day he opposed the Peruvian Mining Company bill, arguing that 'all the speculations that were at present afloat ... particularly the mining speculations, afforded little chance of being successful'. He spoke and was a minority teller against the third reading of the Equitable Loan Company bill, 'an undue interference with the pawnbrokers', 24 Mar.[17] He welcomed Moore's proposal to legislate on joint-stock companies, 29 Mar., contending that the public were 'quite as much entitled to protection as any of the princes of the blood or the archbishop of Canterbury'. He suggested that 'the most effectual relief to be afforded to our colonies' would come from 'a total emancipation of the slaves', 18 Mar. Yet he supported the West India Company bill, 29 Mar., and attacked Fowell Buxton, 'the great champion of joint-stock companies', for opposing it 'on the ground of his ... excessive sympathy for the Negro population'. The Speaker intervened to end their recriminatory exchanges the following day. On 5 May he 'deprecated any reduction of the sinking fund in the present state of the world, when both France and the United States of America were endeavouring to reduce the public debt'. He considered the Indian judges bill to be 'unnecessary', 13 May. He was in the majority against the Leith docks bill, 20 May. Supporting Hume's call for the abolition of flogging in the navy, 9 June, he maintained that 'the want of discipline in the naval service more often arose from a want of qualification in the officers than from misconduct in the men'. Next day he voted with government for the duke of Cumberland's annuity bill. He lamented the 'great decrease' in British shipping as a result of erosion of the navigation laws, 22 June, and in attacking the ships registry bill next day, stated that he had 'always opposed the measures of ministers' in this area of policy. He believed that 'every branch of industry in this country ought to be protected', but 'the House would not do this and proposed rather to grind and oppress the people'; British trade 'was going to decay under the new regulations'. After being called to order for denouncing ministerial shipping policy during a debate on the combination bill, 27 June 1825, he warned that the latter would be 'attended with the most mischievous consequences to the workmen themselves', who, 'being enabled to extort ... any rate of wages they pleased ... would pass one half of their week always in idleness and contract the most dangerous habits of excess and intoxication'.[18] That autumn, while admitting that he had 'no right to ask any favour from government', he applied to the home secretary Peel for preferment in the Scottish church for his eldest brother James, minister of Livingston. Although Peel noted that he 'should not be sorry to have an opportunity of obliging Robertson', nothing came of it.[19]

In a ponderous diatribe during the debate on the address, 2 Feb. 1826, Robertson claimed to have predicted the 'unavoidable consequences' of 'open and barefaced spoliation ... by the machinations of joint-stock companies', and blamed the current financial crisis on the 'speculative and gambling system of commerce' encouraged by ministers. Attributing the country's problems to the £189,000,000 excess of exports over imports since 1815, he called for protection of domestic industry to ensure that capital was kept at home: he 'considered the doctrine of absolute free trade, as applied to this country, as the most vicious principle which had ever been adopted by thinking men'. His complaint of press misrepresentation of his speech was cut short by the Speaker, 6 Feb.[20] He maintained that only the banking system was keeping the country from total ruin and that the government's plan to restrict the circulation of small notes would undermine it, 9 Feb.; he divided in the minority on this question, 13 Feb. He recommended the establishment of branch banks and the encouragement of country banks to pay in gold, 27 Feb. He spoke and voted in the minority against the third reading of the promissory notes bill, 7 Mar., expressing fears that it would lead to a large influx of foreign bullion. He believed that 'a currency founded on a metallic basis' was essential, 26 May. He accused ministers of ruining the silk industry, 9 Feb., and voted for inquiry into its problems, 24 Feb. He 'strongly condemned the miscalled and delusive system of reciprocity' and deplored the 'union' between government and opposition to promote it, 14 Feb.; he returned to this theme, 22 Feb., 13 May. On the presentation of the London merchants' petition calling for an immediate issue of exchequer bills, 23 Feb., he declared that ministers had 'proved themselves unfit for their situations' and that 'their continuance in office was an embarrassment to the king'. He wanted the bill dealing with merchants' goods offered as security for exchequer bill loans to be 'general' rather than 'partial', 8 Mar.[21] He objected to the 'violent language' of a Staffordshire pottery workers' petition for revision of the corn laws, 2 Mar., and maintained that 'there could not be a greater grievance inflicted on the country than cheap bread', as the real need was for 'good rents, good profits and well-paid labour'. He reckoned that the emergency admission of bonded corn would entail 'ruin', 2 May, and suggested the alternative of buying it to feed to starving workers in the manufacturing districts. In recommending the imposition of a duty on foreign shipping, 17 Apr., he alleged that opposition, who had 'urged ministers to these experiments [in free trade], saw now sufficient reason for retracing their steps'. He dismissed Hume's call for inquiry into the state of the nation as 'delusive', posited as it was on the supposed need for tax reductions, 4 May. He declared that it was 'necessary, for the interests of the country, that the naval force should not be suffered to decline in any degree', 17 Feb.,[22] but four days later, complaining that no minister was present, he rejected the plea of the war in India as a 'totally inadequate' reason for maintaining it at the proposed level, and divided in Hume's minority. He also voted for large army reductions, 3 Mar., having concluded that ministers 'did not know what they were about'. He divided against the opposition motion condemning the Jamaican slave trials, 2 Mar. On 6 Apr. he alluded to the 'mysterious circumstances' surrounding the chartering in 1825 of the London Silk Company, headed by Alexander Baring*, who had subsequently emerged as a leading advocate of the proposal to give the president of the board of trade, Huskisson, an enhanced ministerial salary. He voted twice in minorities on this subject next day, but was apparently absent from the division of 10 Apr. He was presumably the 'R.C. Robertson' who divided against the resolutions condemning electoral bribery, 26 May 1826.[23]

The disfranchisement of Grampound came into effect at the dissolution in June 1826 and left Robertson without a seat. His unsuccessful candidature for Durham in February 1828, against the re-election of Sir Henry Hardinge, the secretary at war in the duke of Wellington's ministry, was nominal and involuntary.[24] John Cam Hobhouse* recorded in October 1830 that Robertson, 'a queer man', had expressed the opinion that 'I ought to *take a lead*' in the Commons against the government.[25] In July 1843 he offered Peel, as prime minister, information on the 'ill consequences' of current British policy towards Spain, having recently returned from a two-month stay in Madrid; he was taken seriously enough to be interviewed by the foreign secretary, Lord Aberdeen.[26] He appears to have remained active as a merchant until about 1851. He died in December 1856. By his will, he instructed that a trust fund be created for the benefit of his daughter Margaret Turnbull Robertson, an imbecile, and left the residue of his estate to his great-nephew, Alexander Robertson.[27]

[1] *Fasti Eccles. Scot.* i. 183. [2] PROB 11/2245/62. [3] *PP* (1821), vii. 37-43. Identical views were advanced in the 1820 tract, *Reflections on the Present Difficulties of the Country*, but internal evidence indicates that Robertson was perhaps not its author, as suggested in *HP Commons, 1790-1820*, v. 25. [4] *West Briton*, 10 Mar.; *R. Cornw. Gazette*, 11 Mar. 1820. [5] *The Times*, 3 Apr. 1822. [6] Ibid. 24 May, 5 June 1822. [7] Ibid. 31 May 1822. [8] Ibid. 11 July 1822. [9] Ibid. 18 Mar. 1823. [10] Ibid. 4 July 1823. [11] Ibid. 13 June 1823. [12] Ibid. 9 July 1823. [13] Ibid. 10 May 1823. [14] Ibid. 8 May 1824. [15] Ibid. 18 June 1824. [16] Ibid. 29 May 1824. [17] Ibid. 25 Mar. 1825. [18] Ibid. 28 June 1825. [19] Add. 40381, ff. 439-43; 40382, f. 43. [20] *The Times*, 7 Feb. 1826. [21] Ibid. 9 Mar. 1826. [22] Ibid. 18 Feb. 1826. [23] Ibid. 27 May 1826. [24] Ibid. 8, 9 Feb. 1828. [25] Add. 56555, f. 30. [26] Add. 43062, ff. 355, 357. [27] *Gent. Mag.* (1857), i. 251; PROB 11/2245/62; IR26/2107/62.

D.R.F.

ROBINSON, Sir Christopher (1766–1833), of Beddington, nr. Croydon, Surr. and 47 Bedford Square, Mdx.

Callington 1818–12 June 1820

b. 18 July 1766,[1] 2nd s. of Christopher Robinson, DD (*d.* 1802), rect. of Albury, Oxon. and Wytham, Berks., and 1st w. Elizabeth Bailey of Haseley, Oxon. *educ.* Charterhouse 1776; Univ. Coll. Oxf. 1782, Magdalen 1783, BA 1786, MA 1789, DCL 1796. *m.* 11 Apr. 1799, Catherine, da. of Rev. Ralph Nicholson, rect. of Dudcote, Berks., 3s. 2da. kntd. 6 Feb. 1809. *d.* 21 Apr. 1833.

Adv. Doctors' Commons 1796, treas. 1804-5; king's adv. 1809-28; chan. diocese of London and judge of consistory ct. 1821-8; judge of ct. of admiralty 1828-*d.*; PC 5 Mar. 1828.

Commr. for building new churches 1825.

Robinson, the editor of six well-regarded volumes of reports of admiralty court cases (1799-1808), a specialist in prize law and king's advocate since 1809, stood again for Callington on the increasingly precarious Clinton interest in 1820. He was returned after a contest, but was unseated on petition three months later, before he could make any mark in the new Parliament. It was subsequently alleged that these proceedings cost Robinson, who was never a wealthy man, £5,000 and that a promise of reimbursement by Lord Liverpool's ministry was not kept. In 1821 he succeeded his early patron Lord Stowell as chancellor of the diocese of London, and seven years later he again stepped into Stowell's shoes as judge of the admiralty court. He died from 'an effusion of water on the brain' in April 1833. An obituarist wrote of him:

> A thorough English gentleman in mind and manners, endowed with a graceful presence and a pleasing address, though slightly shaded by reserve, he carried into private life the same mild and conciliating demeanour which characterized him on the bench.[2]

His second son William Robinson (1801/2-70) was also an advocate and reporter on admiralty cases.[3]

[1] *Charterhouse Reg.* 319. [2] *Law Mag.* x. (1833), 485-8. [3] *Oxford DNB.*

D.R.F.

ROBINSON, Hon. Frederick John (1782–1859), of Nocton Hall, Lincs.[1]

Carlow 1806–1807

Ripon 1807–28 Apr. 1827

b. 1 Nov. 1782, 2nd s. of Thomas Robinson†, 2nd Bar. Grantham (*d.* 1786), and Lady Mary Jemima Yorke, da. and coh. of Philip Yorke†, 2nd earl of Hardwicke. *educ.* Sunbury, Mdx.; Harrow 1796-9; St. John's, Camb. 1799; L. Inn 1802; to France 1802. *m.* 1 Sept. 1814, Lady Sarah Albinia Louisa Hobart, da. and h. of Robert Hobart†, 4th earl of Buckinghamshire, 2s. 1da *d.v.p.* *cr.* Visct. Goderich 28 Apr. 1828; earl of Ripon 13 Apr. 1833. *d.* 28 Jan. 1859.

Private sec. to ld. lt. [I] 1804-6; sec. to embassy, Lord Pembroke's mission to Vienna 1807; under-sec. of state for war and colonies May-Nov. 1809; ld. of admiralty July 1810-Oct. 1812; PC 13 Aug. 1812; vice-pres. bd. of trade Sept. 1812-Jan. 1818; ld. of treasury Oct. 1812-Nov. 1813; jt.-paymaster-gen. Nov. 1813-Aug. 1817; sec. to Lord Castlereagh* at Congress of Chatillon 1814; pres. bd. of trade Jan. 1818-Feb. 1823; treas. of navy Feb. 1818-Feb. 1823; chan. of exch. Jan. 1823-Apr. 1827; sec. of state for war and colonies Apr.-Sept. 1827; first ld. of treasury 3 Sept. 1827-26 Jan. 1828; sec. of state for war and colonies Nov. 1830-Apr. 1833; ld. privy seal Apr. 1833-June 1834; pres. bd. of trade Sept. 1841-June 1843; pres. bd. of control May 1843-July 1846.

Capt. N. regt. W. Riding yeomanry 1803, maj. 1814-17. Dir. Greenwich Hosp. 1819.

Robinson was genial, clever, ambitious and idle. As the younger son of a peer who had died when he was four, he was financially dependent until his mother's death in 1830, which terminated the trust fund set up by his father, on handouts from her and his brother, his wife's inheritance and income from political office. He owed his rise through the ranks of the Perceval and Liverpool administrations as much to 'favour and stipulation' on the part of Lord Castlereagh*, his powerful patron, as to his talent.[2] As president of the board of trade, with a seat in the cabinet, from January 1818, and a thorough disciple of Adam Smith, he played an important part in the liberalization of ministerial commercial policy. Yet, as Lady Granville noted, 'his nerves were not made to be tried ... high', and he was 'not good at a pinch'.[3] His lack of a political nerve commensurate with his ambition ultimately covered him in humiliation and contempt. Nor did his abiding devotion to a querulous and neurotic wife equip him for the punishing demands of high office.[4]

At the general election of 1820 he was again returned unopposed for Ripon on the secure interest of his kinswoman Miss Lawrence. On the presentation by Alexander Baring of the London merchants' petition for the removal of restrictions on trade, 8 May 1820, he stated that 'the restrictive system of commerce in this country was founded in error', but was 'so deeply rooted' that reform must be gradual; denied that he and his colleagues looked 'more to their offices than to the interests of the people'; pointed out that a 'considerable relaxation' of the tariff structure had been effected since 1817; promised further revisions, and discounted giving additional protection to agriculture.[5] Despite suffering 'a degree of indisposition' he expanded on the last point when answering agriculturists' complaints, 30 May, in what the Tory backbencher Henry Bankes called 'an argumentative speech[6]: he blamed distress on the current low corn prices resulting from the inevitable post-war fall in demand. A procedural difficulty prevented him from then proposing, in a cynical move to fob them off, that the proposed select committee's remit be confined to an investigation of alleged frauds in taking the averages; but he carried this the following day, when he was duly named to the committee (as he was to its successors, 7 Mar. 1821, 18 Feb. 1822).[7] He did not oppose Littleton's motion for leave to introduce a bill to regulate labourers' wages, 1 June, but expressed 'great doubts' as to the wisdom of 'legislative interference' in such matters. Later that day he got into a tangle over the linen bounties, having apparently led Maberly, who wanted to consider their extension, to believe that his motion would not be resisted, which put him at cross purposes with Nicholas Vansittart, the chancellor of the exchequer. The motion was conceded, but Robinson thwarted Maberly's 'extraordinary' bid to instruct the committee to levy a duty on imported linen yarn. On its report, 30 June, he again strongly objected to this. Successfully opposing inquiry into cotton weavers' distress, 29 June, he observed that it was 'tolerably well known he was no advocate for parliamentary reform and he was the less so, because he was unwilling to convert the House into a college of disputants'. He dismissed Dr. Lushington's 'unmeaning rant' against the plans for the coronation, 3 July, and opposed reception of an individual's petition alleging that too many Members were returned by corrupt aristocratic influence, 15 July. There was speculation in December 1820 that he might be moved to the board of control to replace George Canning*, but nothing came of it.[8]

While Castlereagh dutifully told the king that Robinson's speech against Hamilton's motion condemning the omission of Queen Caroline's name from the liturgy, 26 Jan. 1821, when he led the government reply, was 'very good', other witnesses were less impressed. Stephen Lushington, the treasury secretary, thought it was 'animated', but felt that 'the latter part of the subject [he] left perhaps a little imperfect', and another observer reckoned that his 'most sorry' exhibition 'broke down'. The young Whig George Howard*, in the gallery, judged that he 'began very well indeed, and with a very good manner, but in the end fell into confusion, and concluded abruptly and higgledy-piggledy'. The Tory backbencher Edward Bootle Wilbraham complained in general terms that Castlereagh got little support in debate and, somewhat unfairly, that Robinson 'seems to do nothing but occasionally answer a question on trade'.[9] Robinson 'deprecated ... any attempt to abrogate' the 1819 currency settlement, 8 Feb., favoured the traditional remedy of sluicing the corrupt borough of Grampound, 12 Feb., and spoke briefly against the opposition motion on the government's failure to protect the liberal regime in Naples, 21 Feb. He announced a measure to regulate the method of striking the corn averages, 26 Feb., and, conceding the renewed inquiry into agricultural distress, 7 Mar., said it was now 'a question of feeling as well as of expediency', but set his face against interference with the sinking fund. He voted, as previously, for Catholic claims, 28 Feb., and supported the relief bill, 2 Apr., observing that Daniel O'Connell* and his like 'would always be dissatisfied'. He backed his deputy Wallace's defence of the government's timber duties proposals, 5 Apr., and on smuggling, 13 Apr., conceded the 'expediency of taking away many of the restrictions on the importation of French goods'. He replied to Hume's attacks on the navy estimates, 4 May. Meeting Grey Bennet's motion for a reduction of the number of placemen in the House, 31 May, he said it would 'destroy ... that just, reasonable, and natural influence, of which all statesmen and philosophers had admitted the necessity, in support of the supreme power of the state'. Grey Bennet thought it was 'a feeble, bad speech, as usual beginning well, but afterwards breaking down, and not at all touching the points in discussion'.[10] Robinson defended the appointment of Thomas Frankland Lewis* to the Irish revenue inquiry, 15 June 1821. In November Edward Littleton* recorded the complaint of William Huskisson*, commissioner of woods and forests and the most dynamic member of the board of trade, who was aggrieved at his continued exclusion from the cabinet, that he had been 'long engaged in rowing the boat, while the cabinet ministers sat idle in it, and instanced Lord Maryborough and Frederick Robinson, who sit there like dead weights, though the latter is a clever man'.[11]

Robinson objected to Hume's amendment to the address calling for economies and tax reductions, 5 Feb. 1822, 'because it went, with one sweeping censure, to condemn a whole system of finance as fallacious'. He carried by 234-126 resolutions embodying the ministerial case for a 'gradual progressive reduction of taxes' while upholding the integrity of the sinking fund against opposition's critical motion, 21

Feb. He was the government spokesman on the navy estimates, 1 Mar., and against abolition of one of the joint-postmasterships, 13 Mar., and opposed Curwen's call for an increase in the tallow duties and repeal of the candle tax, 20 Mar., when he remarked that 'if this was to be our rule of commercial policy, we might as well shut up shop at once'. In a major speech, 1 Apr., he sought leave to introduce two bills to open and regulate trade between British Canadian and West Indian colonies and the United States, and with Europe and the rest of the world. These measures (3 Geo. IV, cc. 44, 45), which significantly relaxed the navigation laws and greatly improved Anglo-American relations, were the crowning achievement of Robinson's period at the board of trade.[12] When opposing Lord John Russell's reform proposal, 25 Apr., he denied that he was 'an advocate for parliamentary corruption'. He tried to convince Hume that ministers were grappling with the knotty problem of consuls' fees, 7 May. On the agricultural committee's report that day he deplored Burdett's 'party invective' and reiterated his view that tax reductions and currency reform would not cure distress. Privately, he considered the amended corn bill to be virtually useless,[13] but he opposed a protectionist amendment to it, 3 June. He spoke briefly against the opposition motion criticizing diplomatic expenditure, 15 May, and vindicated ministers' decision to make it an issue of confidence. He thought legislation would not eradicate truck payments, 17 June, and thwarted an attempt to increase the duty on foreign butter, 20 June. The Whig Member Sir James Mackintosh reckoned that in reply to a wrecking amendment to the aliens bill, 1 July 1822, he 'answered well in manner but feebly though speciously in substance'.[14]

Robinson, a pall-bearer for Castlereagh after his suicide in August, was prominent in the subsequent jockeying for position among the ministerial Commons hierarchy. There was a school of thought that while he lacked 'readiness and nerve', his 'acuteness of mind and great natural eloquence of expression' could be made better use of if only he could be induced to 'boldly throw himself into the stormy current of debate', though this remained doubtful.[15] According to Hobhouse of the home office, Robinson 'put in his claim to succeed to the foreign office in preference to any other person except Canning'; and it was thought in Whig circles that if Canning declined to rejoin the ministry Liverpool was considering Robinson 'as leader of the House of Commons'.[16] In the event Canning took the foreign seals and the lead and persuaded Liverpool to try to arrange Vansittart's retirement from the exchequer and replacement by Robinson. While the obvious choice was Huskisson, Canning's protégé, it was known that Vansittart would not accept this, whereas he would probably be amenable to making way for Robinson as Castlereagh's 'favourite child in the House of Commons'. In the short term Canning envisaged Huskisson's taking over the board of trade and in the longer the exchequer, on the assumption that Robinson, who in effect was chosen as a sop to Vansittart and the country gentlemen, would soon find it too much for him.[17] When the proposition was put to Vansittart in December 1822 he acquiesced, but he warned Liverpool that care should be taken in 'making the overture to Robinson, who will be very apt to be nervous when it is first started to him', though he perceived that

> he is not without ambition, and I know (though not immediately from himself) that he has had the feeling of being superseded, which this offer, whatever may be its result, must of course remove. But I do not think the exchequer is the object he aims at, for I have occasionally talked with him in a loose way on the subject, and he has always expressed a great dread of the labour and confinement of the situation.

Liverpool was reasonably confident that Robinson, who was staying at Lulworth Castle with the home secretary Peel when the offer was made, would take the job, but his unhesitating and enthusiastic acceptance came as a surprise to Canning, Vansittart and Charles Arbuthnot*, who thought it 'indicates better nerves than we gave him credit for'. Robinson, who was sworn to secrecy for a few weeks until the contingent arrangements had been settled, learnt from Vansittart that the annual salary was about £5,300 and the patronage 'nothing', and that the Downing Street house 'wants painting very much'.[18] Lord Harrowby, president of the council, hoped Robinson would 'throw off his idleness and take pains to make himself master of subjects new to him'; and Charles Williams Wynn*, president of the board of control, felt that he would be 'a decided improvement' on Vansittart, 'both in manner and popularity with the House', and that although Liverpool 'must ... give the orders, and he obey', he was 'a man of sense and judgement, though perhaps deficient in energy'. William Fremantle* reckoned that while Robinson 'may not have been the fittest man, there is none other who would have done so well with Lord Liverpool, and he is a very popular man in the House of Commons'.[19] The Whig George Agar Ellis* noted that he had 'a high character for probity, and a fair one for talent'; and Bootle Wilbraham reflected that he was now 'in a situation in which he must speak, instead of a situation in which he was generally idle'.[20] However, the duke of Wellington, master-general of the ordnance, who had a low opinion of Robinson, thought his appointment 'very bad indeed', predicting that he would 'change his mind ten times a day'; and Lord Colchester observed that 'nobody thinks [it] will answer'.[21] His remaining in office after Castlereagh's death and replacement by Canning had put paid to the fanciful notion of Castlereagh's half-brother and successor, the 3rd marquess of Londonderry, of forming a 'third party'.[22]

As it turned out Robinson, who confided to his friend Lord Malmesbury, 3 Feb. 1823, 'God knows how one can get through the labour of such an office in such times and with such a House of Commons, but I am tolerably strong as to health, and hope therefore I may get through it *tant bien que mal*', was a striking success, at least for three years.[23] While Huskisson, his successor at the board of trade, was the prime mover behind the fiscal revolution of these years, Robinson ably assisted him and took much of the credit. He dismissed Hume's complaint about crown lands revenues, 14 Feb. In his first budget statement, 21 Feb. (the preparation of which may have made him nervously ill, but which he delivered 'with distinguished ability, and far exceeding expectations', according to Bankes),[24] he explained that of the £7,147,214 surplus, £5,000,000 would be applied to reduction of the national debt and the rest to facilitate extensive tax reductions in order to stimulate economic activity and consumption. While the radicals inevitably wanted more, his speech (which was marred in its effect by his subsequent admission that he had forgotten to mention his proposed plan to simplify the sinking fund) was received with 'unprecedented applause'. Its peroration on 'the wide, the unbounded prospect' which lay before the country, earned him the nickname of 'Prosperity Robinson'.[25] Speaking, of necessity, more often than previously, he grew in confidence during the session. He preferred his own to Brougham's measure to regulate the sale of beer, 28 Feb., when he opposed Maberly's call for more drastic tax remissions. He explained and steered through the national debt reduction bill the following month. On 10 Mar. he defeated Curwen's attempt to add repeal of the window and house taxes to his mitigation of the assessed taxes. He defended the warehousing bill and outlined plans for the beer duties and excise licences, 21 Mar. He brought in and defended a bill to rectify an omission in the 1822 Act dealing with the funding of naval and military pensions and explained the contract made with the Bank, 11, 18 Apr. He tried to pour oil on the troubled waters stirred by a clash between Brougham and Canning on the Catholic question, 17 Apr., and on the 29th vindicated, at length, British neutrality in the Franco-Spanish conflict. He opposed repeal of the tax on tallow candles, 21 May, transfer of the duty on beer to malt, 28 May, and inquiry into the coronation expenses, 11, 19 June. He defended his beer duties bill, 13 June, and the grant for the King's Library, 20 June, 1 July. In a statistical review of the finances next day, he asserted that public opinion was 'generally ... completely satisfied' with ministerial policy. He got rid of Hume's resolution on land tax collection, 8 July 1823. He had privately complained to the backbencher Hudson Gurney in June that 'the business of the country was become so enormous neither the government nor the Parliament could get through with it'.[26] Yet his parliamentary stock had risen 'in an extraordinary degree' by the end of the session. Fremantle reckoned that Robinson and Peel, the home secretary, had obtained a 'complete ascendancy' over Canning 'as general speakers and men of business'; and Hobhouse wrote that 'his manner of speaking is fervid and displays an appearance of manly candour, which predisposes his audience in his favour'.[27] In October 1823, however, Liverpool, ordering Lord Bathurst to get Robinson to come to London for a cabinet on the need to reinforce the West Indian army, was 'sorry to say that he loves his ease so much that he will never move if he has an option'.[28]

Robinson admitted the force of Hume's complaint about demands for arrears of legacy duty, 11 Feb., endorsed (after a change of mind) repeal of the usury laws, 16 Feb., and defended the Bank and its relations with government, 19 Feb. 1824. Opposing a call for information on Irish Catholic office-holders 19 Feb., he said 'there was no disposition to exclude' them on religious grounds. In his budget statement, 23 Feb., he explained that the £2,200,000 windfall from part repayment of the Austrian loan had created a healthy surplus, which he proposed to augment by redeeming the four per cent annuities at three and a half and by removing bounties from whale fishing and Irish linen exports. He offered no direct tax cuts, but outlined planned reductions of the duties on rum, coal, foreign wool and raw silk. He proposed substantial grants for the building of new churches, the repair and refurbishment of Windsor Castle and the establishment of a National Gallery. His speech, with its stirring description of a country blessed with 'comfort and content, prosperity and order, going hand in hand, and dispensing from the sacred portals of an ancient and constitutional monarchy, all their inestimable blessings', was enthusiastically cheered. Robert Wilmot Horton*, the colonial under-secretary, reflected that Robinson deserved his popularity, 'for he has no *hum* about him'.[29] Robinson's references to the Austrian loan repayment, which he explained to a captious Hume, 25, 26 Feb., as a 'Godsend', and to the emperor as a 'despotic sovereign', annoyed Wellington and sparked a minor diplomatic row.[30] He explained the grant for public building works, 1 Mar. Next day he successfully resisted opposition demands for repeal of the window tax and sale of the land tax. Fremantle reported that 'nothing could have been more favourable to him' than this debate, when his critics squabbled and 'the open and manly manner in which he again explained his objects, had the effect of rendering any other speech from the government quite unnecessary'.[31] He defended his proposals for the silk duties, 5, 18 Mar., when he declined to accept praise from opposition at Vansittart's expense; but in response to petitions he eventually agreed to defer the tariff reductions to 1826. He also compromised on repeal of the wool duties and linen bounties.[32] He carried the rest of his budget proposals, both remissions and grants, in the shape in which he had announced them. He failed to prevent the House voting to set up an inquiry into the cost of the new Westminster law courts, to which he was named, 23 Mar. He opposed calls for immediate repeal of the coal duties, 29 Mar., and revision of the legacy duties, 1 Apr. He again resisted inquiry into redemption of the land tax, 6 Apr., and a proposal to advance £1,000,000 to Ireland, 4 May, arguing that the removal of taxes and opening of trade would bring more permanent relief. He introduced resolutions for the regulation of savings banks, 7 May. He refused to countenance repeal of the remaining assessed taxes, 10, 13 May, and secured the defeat by 71-55 of a motion for repeal of the leather tax, 18 May, when he boasted that since he became chancellor he had implemented reductions to the tune of £4,500,000. He defended his beer duties bill against the attacks of monopolist brewers' spokesmen, 24 May, and explained the marine insurance bill, 28 May 1824.

Robinson was now seen by some inside observers on the pro-Catholic side as a possible premier in the event of Liverpool's retirement, though his natural ally Canning was perceived to have superior credentials. The duke of Buckingham told Lord Wellesley, the Irish viceroy, that he was 'the most popular of the ministers but holds aloof from all parties'. The anti-Catholic Peel was reckoned to be jealous of him, and Wellington continued to think him 'beyond his place in public opinion' and, according to an indiscretion by Arbuthnot, 'even asserted he was "a shallow fellow"'. Yet in September 1824 Canning complained to a friend that during the recent cabinet dispute over what line to take on the Catholic question, Robinson 'had shown no fight ... but had lost with both sides from indecision'. Wellington was now reckoned to be courting him.[33] In the House, 14 Feb. 1825, Robinson supported the bill to suppress the Catholic Association, 'the bane and curse' of Ireland. He duly voted to consider Catholic claims, 1 Mar., when he was excused for defaulting on a call of the House the previous day, and for the second reading of the relief bill, 21 Apr. In cabinet, where he continued to try to keep the peace, he put the case for introducing, without the king's consent, a bill to authorize payment of the Irish catholic clergy, but Liverpool put a stop to this, pointing out that it could lead to his impeachment.[34] Robinson voted silently for the third reading of the relief bill, 10 May, but, opposing a motion on the state of Ireland, 26 May, he sought to justify the question being kept an open one in cabinet.

His budget statement, 28 Feb. 1825, when he revealed a surplus of £443,528 and announced reductions of the duties on hemp, iron, coffee, wine, spirits and cider, was triumphalist in tone and received 'loud cheers'. He boasted, when opposing repeal of the assessed taxes, 3 Mar., that his proposals had gone down well in public opinion; and he stood by them when resisting a motion for inquiry into duty remissions on spirits, tobacco and tea, 10 Mar., not wishing matters to be taken out of the government's hands. He defended the army estimates, 11 Mar., items in the Irish miscellaneous estimates, 18 Mar., and the grants for new public buildings and the National Gallery, 28 Mar. He made a concession on the duties on Cape wines, 22 Mar. He opposed Hume's call for information on the Indian army, 24 Mar., as a covert attack on Lord Amherst. He expressed the government's willingness to have the general question of subsidised emigration investigated, 15 Apr., and outlined plans to regulate distilleries and the spirit duties, 22 Apr. Speaking against revision of the corn laws, 28 Apr., he said that ministers would not be goaded into meddling with them. He described the measure dealing with bonded corn as 'a boon' and vindicated its element of Canadian preference, 2, 13 May. He opposed motions for repeal of the beer duties, 5 May, and the window tax, 17 May. He denied Hume's allegation that the proposed increases in judges' salaries was 'a link in the chain of augmentation', 16 May; but he announced a decision to modify the scheme to place more emphasis on retirement pensions, 20 May. He spoke in defence of the grants to the duchess of Kent and the duke of Cumberland, 27, 30 May, 6, 10 June. In reply to Sykes's bid to secure reduction of the duties on soap and tallow, 7 June, he pointed out that £1,500,000 in taxes had already been got rid of that session; and when announcing a cautious remission of some coal duties, 17 June, he confessed to being 'afraid of having too many irons in the fire'. He refused to interfere with the newspaper stamp duty, 22 June, and defended the Deccan prize commissioners, who included his critics Wellington and Arbuthnot, 1 July 1825. Three weeks later he stayed at Dropmore with Lord Grenville, whose brother Tom found 'his manners and conversation extremely agreeable from the natural unreserved and unaffected tone in which he speaks of everything that occurs in society'. Despite appearing to be 'as strong as a horse', he was taken ill in the night.[35] In September 1825 John Croker* claimed to know that in the divisive cabinet discussion on whether or not to dissolve Parliament that autumn, Robinson, characteristically, was 'of both opinions'. In December he turned down (as he had that summer) an offer of Whig backing if he stood for Cambridge University; and nothing came of speculation by the leading Bedfordshire Whigs that he might be induced to stand for the county, where his aunt Lady De Grey owned property, to keep out a hated Tory parvenu.[36]

The commercial panic and financial crash of the winter of 1825-6 destroyed Robinson's vaunted prosperity and found him personally wanting in a crisis. In September he rejected John Herries's* advice to raise money by borrowing, to pay off exchequer bills, arguing that an increase in interest rates would be 'the most legitimate way of doing the thing'.[37] On 30 Nov. he told Lord Grenville, who had sent him correspondence with John Horne Tooke† on the subject, that while he agreed that the unrestricted issue of small notes by country banks was potentially dangerous and did not altogether absolve the government and the Bank from blame for 'our present embarrassment'

> much of *our* difficulty ... arises from ... the extreme difficulty in such a complicated system as ours has progressively become, of bringing practically to bear upon a sound theory, a clear and comprehensive view of those disturbing causes, which affect its application to the actual state of things. Ignorance, prejudice and interest are arrayed against us, and it is not every man who has nerves to apply the actual cautery, even where it may be pretty evident that that is the true remedy for the disease. The more indeed that I contemplate the irregular state into which the late war brought all our relations, political, commercial and financial, the more I feel my own incompetence to grapple all at once with such complicated difficulties; and yet I feel that they cannot be successfully grappled with at all, unless the mind is directed to the most enlarged and comprehensive view of them.[38]

In other words, he was baffled and indecisive; and when the crisis broke in December 1825 he, like most of his colleagues, was paralyzed. In the event, the financial community saved itself, and it remained for the government to try to prevent a repetition. In January 1826 Robinson and Liverpool, blaming the crash on rash speculation, persuaded the Bank to accept the withdrawal of small notes and to acquiesce in the establishment of joint-stock banks in the country.[39] In the House, 2 Feb., Robinson defended the ministry's general commercial and financial policy and thanked the Whigs for their 'important aid' in promoting it. Agar Ellis thought he spoke 'frankly and well'.[40] On the 9th he denied having discussed the formation of branch banks with the Bank authorities and expounded an analysis linking the crash to overexpansion resulting from a succession of poor harvests, which had collapsed when agricultural profits fell with the occurrence of a good season. John Denison* thought 'he did not speak well; instead of a grave calm statement, he was wordy and noisy, and laboured and strained at trifling points'.[41] His speech of 10 Feb. explaining the measures to end the circulation of small notes and permit the establishment of private joint-stock banks did his reputation no good. Agar Ellis considered it 'a manly frank performance' but perceived that he 'spoke rather as a man who is not quite certain of his own knowledge upon the subject'. Charles Ellis*, who heard only the last hour, which 'certainly was very stammering and laborious and unimpressive', told Lord Granville that Robinson had been 'very nervous and spoke much below himself' and was reckoned to have failed. Gurney thought it 'a very ignorant speech'. Greville wrote, 12 Feb., that Robinson

> is deemed to have made a very bad speech ... [He] is probably unequal to the present difficult conjuncture; a fair and candid man, and an excellent minister in days of calm and sunshine, but not endowed with either capacity or experience for these stormy times, besides being disqualified for vigorous measures by the remissness and timidity of his character. However ... he may well be excused for not doing that which the united wisdom of the country seems unable to accomplish.[42]

On 14 Feb. he refused to countenance an issue of exchequer bills, which many commercial Members were urging, and angrily told Wilson of London that if he thought ministers were 'such unskilful pilots in a storm, he ought not to have contributed to support them ... during fair weather'. Three days later he announced the government's willingness, after incessant badgering by Gurney and others, to compromise by allowing the Bank to issue small notes until October; and he formally secured this amendment to the notes bill, 20 Feb., when he denied any 'secrecy' or 'hidden motive' behind the concession. He reputation was further damaged, as Greville noted:

> Robinson is obviously unequal to the present crisis. His mind is not sufficiently enlarged, nor does he seem to have any distinct ideas upon the subject; he is fighting in the dark. Everybody knows that Huskisson is the real author of the finance measures of the government, and there can be no greater anomaly than that of a chancellor ... who is obliged to propose and defend measures of which another minister is the real though not the apparent author.[43]

Denison liked his speech resisting further demands for an issue of exchequer bills, 23 Feb., when he 'spoke pretty well ... very feelingly and with a show of his true honesty'.[44] He got rid of attempted amendments to the notes bill, 24, 27 Feb. George Tierney* thought that if Wilson's motion of the next day for an issue of bills was carried, as seemed at one moment likely, Robinson's position would be untenable.[45] In the event he averted disaster by revealing the government's decision to authorize the Bank to advance money to merchants on the security of their goods and, opposing Tierney's call for an issue, gave an optimistic view of the country's economic situation:

> All its sources of wealth, all the springs of its action, notwithstanding this superficial pressure, were in their pristine vigour. Although the leaves and branches of the tree had been shattered, its roots were firmly fixed, and they would shoot forth again with fresh beauty.

On 10 Mar. he treated as a direct censure of himself, which, if carried, would compel him to resign, Maberly's motion on the government's transactions with the Bank; it was withdrawn. His financial statement of 13 Mar., when he claimed that 'the violence of the storm has passed away', boasted that £27,522,000 in taxes had been remitted since 1816 and forecast a surplus of £714,579, was well received.[46] He secured the appointment of a select committee on Scottish and Irish small notes, 16 Mar.; and as a member of it he acquiesced in Peel's recommendation of no change.[47] He tried to justify the proposal to give the president of the board of trade a distinct ministerial salary, 6, 7, 10 Apr., when the majority fell to 11, forcing ministers to agree to combine the office with that of treasurer of the navy. On 17 Apr. he persuaded Onslow to postpone his usury laws repeal bill and moved resolutions to relieve the Bank from a portion of its advances. He favoured reform of private bill committees, 19 Apr. On 4 May he replied spiritedly and at length, but without support from Canning, Herries, Huskisson or Peel, to Hume's major attack on financial and economic policy. He endorsed the corn bill, 11 May, and assured agriculturists that this temporary relaxing measure would not prejudice consideration of the whole subject next session. He was returned unopposed for Ripon at the general election in June 1826. The following month Canning, discussing with Liverpool a way of avoiding the appointment of Lord Morley to the post office, suggested the possibility of making Robinson a peer and giving it to him, which he felt 'would not be disagreeable' to him, and replacing him at the exchequer with Lord Palmerston*. Liverpool was not prepared to create more peers so soon after an unpopular batch, and in any case pointed out that such a move 'would be considered at this time an admission of Robinson's failure' and would 'very much shake the confidence the country has in the government'.[48]

Robinson had been harassed by the state of his wife, who in March 1826 had suffered a nervous collapse and contracted religious mania.[49] In late August he was in correspondence with Peel about how to deal with defective crops of oats and potatoes and the funding of chancery reform. The next month he produced a memorandum recommending revision of the corn laws and the imposition of import duties on other produce as a means of raising money to subsidize emigration. His scheme was not taken seriously.[50] In late October he was dragged from a visit to his mother and aunt at Wrest, Bedfordshire, to his house at Blackheath by his wife's hysterical claim that she was at death's door. He found her perfectly well, but tragedy ensued when their mentally handicapped 11-year-old only child Eleanor fell ill with hydrocephalus and died after great suffering on 31 Oct. Lady Sarah took it very badly and on 3 Nov. Robinson, who was himself close to an emotional breakdown, wrote to the king asking leave to 'absent himself from the approaching *early* session of Parliament' in order to look after her at her parental home at Nocton, Lincolnshire. Permission was readily granted and Robinson's cabinet colleagues were supportive.[51] He commented to Huskisson that his absence from the meeting of Parliament might benefit the government:

> Hume and Maberly (who are our great financial questioners) will be disposed to hold their tongues when they find they cannot get answers; and I am quite satisfied that under the present circumstances of our money concerns, the less that is said about them the better. We could say nothing positive and nothing very satisfactory. In short it seems clearly to be the policy of the government to say and do as little as possible before Christmas.

He asked to be kept informed of the cabinet's deliberations on the corn laws, and 'cordially' acquiesced in their adoption of Huskisson's sliding scale scheme, which was preferred to his own. To Herries on 29 Nov. he confided his worries about escalating public expenditure and his leaning 'towards the idea of having a sinking fund without an accumulation of compound interest'.[52] In the 'rustic bedlam' of Nocton his wife, who was desperate for another child (he impregnated her in January 1827), was making his life a misery with her paranoia and violent fluctuations of mood.[53] On 14 Dec. 1826 he wrote to Liverpool asking to be removed to the Lords and given another office, on the ground that 'the return to Downing Street and the inevitable solitude arising from my constant attendance in the House of Commons may be more than ... [Sarah's] bodily health and strength would be equal to withstand'. Liverpool retorted that not only would he damn himself for ever in public estimation but also 'infallibly precipitate a crisis' which would destroy the ministry. Robinson agreed to remain where he was and to meet Parliament but, so he later told Peel, he made it clear that if he had not been moved by the end of the session he would retire altogether. The story got out, thanks to the Arbuthnots, who put it about that Robinson, 'the greatest political coward and the poorest creature in difficulties that ever lived', had taken fright at the prospect of having to explain a revenue deficiency to the House. Peel was supposed to be 'very much disgusted with such conduct'.[54]

Robinson, who participated in the planning of the ministerial agenda for the 1827 session,[55] explained the provision made for the Clarences and answered Maberly's criticisms of the finances, 16 Feb. He opposed abolition of the salary of the governor of Dartmouth Castle, 20 Feb. His name cropped up in the initial speculation following Liverpool's stroke on the 17th, but after suggesting an early meeting of the cabinet he kept himself in the background, hoping for a satisfactory reconstruction of the government and contemplating retirement.[56] He voted silently for Catholic relief, 6 Mar., and outlined the new corn duties scale, 8 Mar., by which time the notion of his becoming a peer and foreign secretary was gaining ground.[57] He repudiated Harvey's charges concerning excise prosecutions, 13 Mar., acquiesced in Lord Althorp's motion for inquiry into county polls, 15 Mar., and defended details of the corn bill, 19, 23 Mar. On the 26th he refused to answer Maberly's questions about the finances and in committee simply moved a vote of £200,000 for civil contingencies. Closing the debate on the opposition motion to withhold supplies, 30 Mar., he endorsed Canning's view that 'the public exigency required the formation of a new administration'. He opposed inquiry into the Irish miscellaneous estimates, 5 Apr., and spoke on behalf of the revenue commissioners on the case of the County Fire Office, 10 Apr. After the failure of his approach to Peel, Canning saw Wellington and suggested, from whatever motive, that they might both serve under Robinson as premier; but Wellington thought him 'hardly of calibre enough' and the idea was dropped.[58] On 10 Apr. Canning invited Robinson to join his ministry, and he agreed in principle. He was disconcerted by the wholesale anti-Catholic defections and it was not until the 14th that Canning informed him of his planned coalition with the Lansdowne Whigs, in which Robinson was to become colonial secretary and lead the Lords. 'Fearful and unconvinced', he wrote at length next day to Canning expressing his many worries about the instability of such an alliance, the folly of leaving parliamentary reform as well as Catholic emancipation an open question and the 'insuperable' problems likely to result from his being placed over Lansdowne's head in the Lords. Canning waved aside his fears and Robinson, who was additionally mortified to be accused by Londonderry of 'a dereliction of principle', agreed to the arrangement, which was made more palatable to him by the postponement of Lansdowne's admission to the cabinet. His creation as Viscount Goderich, 28 Apr. 1827, removed him from the Commons.[59]

He turned out to be a 'wretched' performer in the Lords, but far worse was to follow.[60] On Canning's death in August he accepted the king's commission to form a government. It lurched from crisis to crisis as 'Goody' Goderich, 'firm as a bullrush', plagued by his wife and little comforted by the safe birth of a son in October, presided with 'utter imbecility', in 'a kind of fool's paradise, convinced his conduct was perfect'. His feeble nerve gave way and he resigned in January 1828 after 146 days as premier, the weakest in British history and the only one never to meet Parliament.[61] Astonishingly, after almost three years in the political wilderness Goderich, despite this humiliation, was invited to join the Grey ministry as colonial secretary, which he did, conveniently setting aside his previous hostility to parliamentary reform. He was sidelined as lord privy seal and fobbed off with an earldom in 1833, and resigned the following year with Stanley and Graham over Irish church appropriation. He moved with them to Peel's Conservative party, formally joining it in 1836. Peel made him president of the board of trade (where William Gladstone†, the vice-president, soon formed a low estimate of his knowledge and competence) and in 1843 put him at the board of control, from which he resigned with Peel on his defeat in 1846. The last 20 years of his stressful life were marred by intermittent bouts of illness, and he died at Putney of pulmonary complications following influenza in January 1859.[62] His widow lived until 1867. He was succeeded in the earldom and the

Lincolnshire estates which had come to him through his marriage by his only son, George Frederick Samuel (1827-1909), who had a distinguished political career and was made marquess of Ripon in 1871.

[1] The only current biography is W.D. Jones, *'Prosperity' Robinson* (1967), a dull and uncritical assessment. [2] Add. 38743, f. 279. [3] *Countess Granville Letters*, i. 421. [4] Jones, 6-7, 49-52, 64-67; B. Hilton, *Corn, Cash, Commerce*, 173, 182-3. [5] Buckingham, *Mems. Geo. IV*, i. 21. [6] Dorset RO D/BKL, Bankes jnl. 117. [7] Ibid. 118 (31 May 1820); J.E. Cookson, *Lord Liverpool's Administration*, 222; Hilton, 102-3. [8] *Croker Pprs*. i. 184. [9] *Geo. IV Letters*, ii. 894-6; Castle Howard mss, Howard to Lady Morpeth [28 Jan. 1821]; *Colchester Diary*, iii. 201. [10] HLRO, Hist. Coll. 379, Grey Bennet diary, 93. [11] Hatherton diary, 20 Nov. [1821]. [12] *HMC Bathurst*, 517-18, 524-5; Jones, 83-87. [13] Jones, 68. [14] Add. 52445, f. 90. [15] Add. 40319, f. 57; *Croker Pprs*. i. 230. [16] Buckingham, i. 365; *Hobhouse Diary*, 95; *Arbuthnot Corresp*.; Castle Howard mss, Abercromby to Morpeth, 1 Sept. 1822; Add. 31232, f. 297. [17] Add. 38743, ff. 192, 217; 38193, f. 171; *Arbuthnot Jnl*. i. 194; *HMC Bathurst*, 537; Harrowby mss XIV, f. 123; Cookson, 382; Hilton, 166-9; Jones, 92-93. [18] Add. 31232, ff. 297, 299; 38193, f. 171; 38291, ff. 211, 216, 223, 225, 233, 241, 335; 40862, f. 83; 45063, f. 183; *Hobhouse Dairy*, 101; *Arbuthnot Jnl*. i. 199-200; Jones, 93-94; Hilton, 169. [19] *HMC Bathurst*, 538; Buckingham, i. 411, 417. [20] Northants. RO, Agar Ellis diary, 12 Jan. [1823]; *Colchester Diary*, iii. 273. [21] Add. 38291, f. 241; *Colchester Diary*, iii. 270. [22] Norf. RO, Blickling Hall mss, Londonderry to Lady Londonderry, 29 Dec. 1822, Hardinge to Londonderry, 24 Jan. 1823. [23] Hants RO, Malmesbury mss 9M73/G2543/3. [24] Bankes jnl. 141. [25] Jones, 98-101; *Hobhouse Diary*, 103. [26] Gurney diary, 18 June 1823. [27] Buckingham, i. 475; Bucks. RO, Fremantle mss D/FR/46/11/84; *Hobhouse Diary*, 103. [28] *HMC Bathurst*, 550. [29] Jones, 101-5; TNA 30/29/9/6/2. [30] *Arbuthnot Jnl*. i. 290-1. [31] Buckingham, ii. 51-52. [32] Jones, 103. [33] Buckingham, ii. 85, 99, 105, 127; Add. 37302, f. 302; Fremantle mss 51/5/22. [34] Lonsdale mss, Long to Lonsdale, 23 Mar. [1825]; *Arbuthnot Jnl*. i. 392; *Hobhouse Diary*, 115, 116; *Wellington Despatches*, ii. 564; Jones, 112-13. [35] Add. 51534, Grenville to Holland, 24 July 1825. [36] *Croker Pprs*. i. 282; Harewood mss, Canning to Robinson and reply, 2 Dec.; Add. 36461, f. 317; 51749, Holland to H.E. Fox 30 Dec. 1825, 18 Jan. [1826]. [37] Hilton, 213-14. [38] BL, Fortescue mss. [39] Hilton, 215-18; Jones, 114-17. [40] Agar Ellis diary, 2 Feb. [1826]. [41] B. Gordon, *Economic Doctrine and Tory Liberalism*, 48-49; Nottingham Univ. Lib. Denison diary, 9 Feb. 1826. [42] Agar Ellis diary, 10 Feb.; Keele Univ. Lib. Sneyd mss SC8/79; TNA 30/29/9/5/38; Gurney diary, 10 Feb. [1826]; *Greville Mems*. i. 156. [43] *Greville Mems*. i. 156-8. [44] Denison diary, 23 Feb. 1826. [45] Add. 51584, Tierney to Holland, 24 Feb. 1826. [46] Agar Ellis diary, 13 Mar. [1826]. [47] Add. 51659, Whishaw to Lady Holland, 14 May; Denison diary, 19 May [1826]. [48] Add. 38301, f. 261; 38568, f. 129. [49] *Miss Eden's Letters* ed. V. Dickinson, 100-1; Jones, 125-6. [50] Add. 40388, ff. 305, 325; 40389, f. 55; *Wellington Despatches*, iii. 432-7; Hilton, 282-3. [51] *Miss Eden's Letters*, 113-16; Lonsdale mss, Beckett to Lowther, 27 Oct. [1826]; *Geo. IV Letters*, iii. 1264. [52] Add. 38302, f. 103; 38576, f. 110; 38748, ff. 190, 192, 195; Jones, 129-30. [53] *Miss Eden's Letters*, 118-20, 122-4; Jones, 130-1. [54] Add. 38302, f. 113; *Arbuthnot Jnl*. ii. 66-67, 69; *Arbuthnot Corresp*. 79; *Lady Palmerston Letters*, 157; Parker, *Peel*, i. 476-7; Jones, 131-3. [55] Add. 38749, ff. 1, 5. [56] *Croker Pprs*. i. 364; *Canning's Ministry*, 3, 4, 9, 16, 31; Jones, 136-7. [57] *Canning's Ministry*, 48. [58] Ibid. 116; Jones, 137-8; Add. 51609, Holland to Adair, 15 Apr. 1827. [59] Parker, i. 476-7; *Canning's Ministry*, 125, 126, 142, 153, 176, 208, 240; *Hobhouse Diary*, 134; *Colchester Diary*, iii. 486; Jones, 138-42. [60] *Creevey Pprs*. i. 120. [61] Jones, 142-204; *Miss Eden's Letters*, 142, 156-7; *Croker Pprs*. i. 391, 392, 401; Bagot, *Canning and Friends*, ii. 427-8; *Countess Granville Letters*, ii. 1; Hilton, 243; Hatherton diary, 10 Feb. [1828]. [62] Jones, 237-79; *Gent. Mag*. (1859), i. 318-20.

D.R.F.

ROBINSON, Sir George, 6th bt. (1766–1833), of Cranford, Northants.; Stretton Hall, Leics., and 34 South Street, Grosvenor Square, Mdx.

NORTHAMPTON 1820–1832

b. 12 Jan. 1766,[1] 1st. s. of Sir George Robinson†, 5th bt., of Cranford and Dorothea, da. of John Chester of Covent Garden, Mdx. *educ*. Harrow 1775-9; Trinity Coll. Camb. 1783; M. Temple 1785. *unm*. *suc*. fa. as 6th bt. 10 Oct. 1815. *d*. 23 Nov. 1833.

Sheriff, Leics. 1818-19.

Robinson's father had inherited substantial estates in Northamptonshire and sat for Northampton as a Whig on his own interest, 1774-80. Robinson, who shared his politics and joined Brooks's, sponsored by the duke of Devonshire, 21 July 1806, sought to emulate him after succeeding him in 1815. That year the Whig William Hanbury, one of the sitting Members for Northampton, announced that he would not stand again. Rumours of a dissolution next year prompted Robinson, who had received an assurance from Hanbury that he would not oppose him, to canvass. Nothing came of this, but at the 1818 general election he came forward, having started an early campaign. After a 13-day poll against two ministerial candidates he was narrowly defeated, finishing 27 votes behind his nearest rival. His petition against the return was unsuccessful.[2] At the 1820 general election he offered again for Northampton against two ministerialists. On 13 Feb. 1820 Lord Althorp* informed his father Earl Spencer that he had 'very little doubt [Robinson] will be beaten again', but five days later reported that the other candidates had 'quarrelled', so that 'Robinson is likely to come in at last' as 'they both split their votes upon him'. He topped the poll.[3] An assiduous but mostly silent attender, Robinson was rarely out of the division lists and voted with the Whig opposition to the Liverpool ministry on most issues, including economy, retrenchment and reduced taxation.[4] According to an obituary:

> So strict was he to his parliamentary duties, that he never missed a single day without remaining to vote, or pairing off with an opponent; and he was even so scrupulous that he would not leave the House for a time without having adopted a similar precaution.[5]

He divided for Catholic claims, 28 Feb. 1821, 1 Mar., 21 Apr., 10 May 1825. He voted for making Leeds a scot and lot borough if it got Grampound's seats, 2 Mar., when he presented a Northamptonshire petition complaining of agricultural distress.[6] He attended the City dinner for parliamentary reform, 4 Apr., and on the 17th presented and endorsed a Northampton reform petition, declaring that 'every proposal for retrenchment had been negatived, and every ministerial job ... had been supported' by government, while 'the profusion of ministers had increased with the poverty of the country'.[7] He voted for reform, 9 May 1821, 25 Apr. 1822, 20 Feb., 24 Apr., 27 Apr. 1826, in protest against the influence of placemen, 31 May 1821, for inquiry into the Scottish royal burghs, 20 Feb. 1822, for reform of the representation of Scotland, 2 June 1823, and Edinburgh, 26 Feb. 1824, 13 Apr. 1826, and to exclude non-resident voters from the Irish borough franchise, 9 Mar. 1826. He presented Northampton petitions for repeal of the leather tax, 30 May 1822, 30 Apr. 1823, 23 Feb. 1824, and against the poor removal bill, 31 May 1822.[8] He was a minority teller to hear counsel on the equitable loan bank bill, 26 May 1824. He presented a Wellingborough petition supporting the county courts bill, 7 Mar. 1825.[9] At a Northampton meeting for reform of the corn laws, 21 Feb. 1826, he argued that there was 'nothing more detrimental than the fluctuating prices of agricultural produce' and that they ought to be 'placed on a more steady and regular footing'.[10] He presented the meeting's petition, 18 Apr., and voted for a review of the laws that day.[11] He presented petitions for the abolition of slavery, 28 Feb., and against the duties on East Indian sugar, 1 Mar. 1826.[12]

At the 1826 general election Robinson offered again for Northampton. After a violent contest against a Tory and a Whig convert, both of whom, according to Althorp, sought his assistance and feared 'his joining the other', he topped the poll, claiming that his victory was clear proof that his constituents were 'friends to the cause of toleration and religious liberty'.[13] On 21 Feb. 1827 he endorsed a petition protesting at the £1,000 spent by Northampton corporation supporting a rival candidate. He presented a Northampton petition for Catholic claims, observing that it was the first from the town, 2 Mar.[14] He voted for Catholic relief, 6 Mar., and for information on the Lisburn Orange procession, 29 Mar. On 6 June he presented multiple petitions from Northamptonshire for repeal of the Test Acts and stated that 'the majority of the Protestant Dissenters among his constituents were favourable to Catholic emancipation'. This prompted a response from John Jones, who denied that a majority of Dissenters approved of relief, to which Robinson replied that he had misheard and that he had been referring to his own constituents. After a few more exchanges the Speaker intervened, and although Robinson apologized 'for any use of expressions of a strong nature', he insisted that Jones had misconstrued his meaning.[15] He presented more petitions from Northamptonshire Dissenters for repeal of the Test Acts, 7, 11 June.[16] He divided for a 50*s.* rather than 60*s.* protecting duty on corn, 9 Mar. He voted for the spring guns bill, 23 Mar. He divided to postpone the committee of supply, 30 Mar., and for inquiries into the Irish estimates and chancery delays, 5 Apr. He voted to disfranchise Penryn and for the election expenses bill, 28 May 1827.

He presented Northamptonshire petitions for repeal of the Test Acts, 21 Feb., and voted accordingly, 26 Feb. 1828. He presented a constituency petition for religious toleration, 28 Apr., noting that it was signed by five Protestant Dissenting ministers. He presented another from Northampton's Unitarians for Catholic relief, 12 May, when he voted for that measure. He divided against throwing East Retford's franchise into its hundred, 21 Mar. He voted for a pivot price of 60*s.* rather than 64*s.* for corn imports, 22 Apr., and for a gradual reduction in duty to 10*s.*, 29 Apr. He voted for the Irish assessment of lessors bill, 12 June, against the appointment of a registrar to the archbishop of Canterbury, 16 June, in protest at the use of public money to renovate Buckingham House, 23 June, and against the additional churches bill, 30 June. He divided to reduce the salary of the lieutenant-general of the ordnance, 4 July, against the grant for North American fortifications, 7 July, and for the corporate funds bill, 10 July. He presented Northamptonshire petitions for the abolition of slavery, 8 July 1828. He presented petitions from Northampton's Baptists and Unitarians for Catholic emancipation, 12 Feb., 3 Mar., and voted thus, 6, 30 Mar. 1829. He divided for Daniel O'Connell to be allowed to take his seat unhindered, 18 May. His only other recorded votes of 1829 were for the transfer of East Retford's seats to Birmingham, 5 May, against the grant for the marble arch, 25 May, and to reduce the hemp duties, 1 June. He presented a constituency petition for repeal of the corn laws and greater economies in government expenditure, 28 May 1829.

Robinson resumed voting with his usual assiduity during the 1830 session, though he did not vote for Knatchbull's amendment to the address on the distressed condition of the country, 4 Feb. 1830. That month he contributed £35 to relieve the poor in his constituency.[17] He voted for the transfer of East Retford's seats to Birmingham, 11 Feb., 5 Mar. (as a pair), 15 Mar. He divided for Lord Blandford's parliamentary reform scheme, 18 Feb., the enfranchisement of Birmingham, Leeds and Manchester, 23 Feb., and Lord John Russell's reform motion, 28 May. He voted for tax cuts, 15 Feb., and military reductions, 19 Feb., 1 Mar., and divided steadily with the revived opposition for economy and retrenchment thereafter. He was in the minorities for referring the Newark petition accusing the duke of Newcastle of electoral malpractice to a select committee, 1 Mar., and for information on the interference of British troops in the internal affairs of Portugal, 10 Mar. He voted for Jewish emancipation, 5 Apr., 17 May. He divided for alteration of the Irish Vestry Act, 27 Apr., abolition of the Irish lord lieutenancy, 11 May, and proper use of Irish first fruits, 18 May. He voted for abolition of the death penalty for forgery, 24 May, 7 June 1830.

At the 1830 general election Robinson offered again for Northampton, citing his support for economy and retrenchment, Catholic emancipation and parliamentary reform, and regretting the failure to abolish colonial slavery. After another fierce contest he topped the poll.[18] He presented anti-slavery petitions from Northampton's Baptists and Unitarians, 5, 10 Nov. 1830. He was listed by the Wellington ministry as one of their 'foes' and he voted against them in the crucial division on the civil list, 15 Nov. On 6 Dec. he attended the Whig dinner to celebrate Althorp's re-election for Northamptonshire after his appointment as chancellor of the exchequer in the Grey administration.[19] He presented a constituency petition for repeal of the assessed taxes and a reduction in official salaries, 15 Dec. 1830, when he welcomed Althorp's stated intention to make economies and hoped that they would be 'effectual for the relief of the country'. He presented a Northampton petition supporting the ministry's anticipated reform bill, 14 Feb. 1831. Presenting another, 26 Feb., he explained that many of those who had signed the first 'were not satisfied with its prayer' and had got up a second, calling, among other things, for the introduction of vote by ballot, shorter parliaments, and an extension of the suffrage. Writing to the chairman of the meeting that had produced it, 28 Feb., he declared, 'Till I hear the plan proposed, and the debate tomorrow, I do not wish to pledge myself to any particular enactment, but I feel very much inclined at present to support election by ballot'.[20] Asked by the mayor to present a petition for the ministerial bill, Robinson replied, 16 Mar., 'I am much rejoiced to see the general satisfaction this great measure gives, and I hope it will be carried triumphantly'.[21] He brought up the petition, 19 Mar., and voted for the second reading of the reform bill, 22 Mar. A Northampton meeting, 28 Mar., unanimously passed a motion approving his votes on the civil list and reform.[22] He was unable to attend the county reform meeting, 13 Apr., owing to 'indisposition', but in a letter which was read out, stated that he was 'satisfied of the justice and expediency of the bill, and hoped by his vote on the third reading to assist in carrying it through the House'.[23] He divided against Gascoyne's wrecking amendment, 19 Apr. 1831.

At the ensuing general election Robinson, who had been in poor health for some time, apparently considered retiring but was persuaded by Robert Vernon Smith* to offer again as his pro-reform colleague. On the hustings he made much of the king's support for the bill, castigated boroughmongers and their nominees, who 'were always ready to vote for the raising of taxes, for it was on the taxes they lived', speculated that had reform been achieved earlier 'Mr. Pitt would not have been permitted to have entered into the last war', and dismissed fears of a reduction in the number of English Members, insisting that there would still be 'sufficient numbers left to do the business of the House'. Poor health prevented him attending every day, but he headed the poll throughout. A 15-day scrutiny, carried out at a defeated candidate's request, did not alter the result, and at the declaration Robinson reproved the 'rump of the Tory party', claiming that 'all their trickery had miserably failed'. A petition against his return was not pursued. He attended the county election dinner to celebrate the triumph of Althorp and Lord Milton, 23 May 1831, when he told the gathering that the 'court flies that had sucked the blood of the country for so long would be swept away', denounced Wellington's failure when prime minister to humble Dom Miguel, and condemned the foreign policy pursued by Lord Aberdeen.[24]

Robinson voted for the second reading of the reintroduced reform bill, 6 July, and gave steady support to its details, though he was in the minority for the total disfranchisement of Aldborough, 14 Sept. 1831. He voted with ministers on the Dublin election controversy, 23 Aug. He voted for the passage of the reform bill, 21 Sept., the second reading of the Scottish measure, 23 Sept., and Lord Ebrington's confidence motion, 10 Oct. He divided for the second reading of the revised reform bill, 17 Dec. 1831, again supported its details, and voted for the third reading, 22 Mar. 1832. He divided for the motion calling on the king to appoint only ministers who would carry the bill unimpaired, 10 May, for the second reading of the Irish measure, 25 May, and against a Conservative amendment to increase Scottish county representation, 1 June. He was listed as one of the stewards for the Northamptonshire reform dinner, 27 June, and although poor health prevented him attending, he sent a letter rejoicing 'in the triumph of the cause you meet to celebrate'.[25] He voted with ministers on the Russian-Dutch loan, 26 Jan., and as a pair, 12, 16 July, and on relations with Portugal, 9 Feb. He presented a petition from the freeholders and landed proprietors of Northampton against the general register bill, 7 Feb. He divided against restoring the salary of the Irish registrar to £1,500, 9 Apr. 1832.

In the autumn of 1832 the Northampton Whigs pressed Robinson to stand at the approaching general election. On 10 Nov., however, he notified them that 'as I have, on account of my health, declined attending any public meeting at Northampton for some time, you will not be surprised at my determining not to undertake the duty of attending the House of Commons in the new Parliament'. At a meeting of the Whig committee, 24 Nov. 1832, a resolution expressing 'deep regret' was passed and the chairman described Robinson as 'the greatest thorn in the flesh of the [Northampton] Tories which they had ever met with'.[26] His poor health persisted and he went to Hastings in search of a cure in early November 1833, after which he paid a short visit to his Northamptonshire home, before returning to London. His life was 'considered in imminent danger' by 18 Nov. and he died five days later.[27] By his will, dated 13 Apr. 1833 and sworn under £16,000, 4 Mar. 1834, he left £2,000 to his younger nephew Henry William Robinson, £250 to his niece Caroline Penelope Robinson, £100 each to the Leicester and Northampton infirmaries and smaller bequests to his great-nephews and nieces. His elder nephew and residuary legatee George Stamp Robinson (1797-1873) succeeded him in the baronetcy.[28]

[1] According to *Al. Cant.* pt. II, vol. v. p. 328, which states that *Harrow Reg.*, *CP* and *Burke PB* erroneously give 1765. [2] *HP Commons, 1790-1820*, ii. 301-2; J.C. Cox, *Recs. Northampton*, ii. 509; *CJ*, lxxiv. 87, 296. [3] *Althorp Letters*, 101-2. [4] *Black Bk.* (1823), 190. [5] *Gent. Mag.* (1834), i. 226. [6] *The Times*, 3 Mar. 1821. [7] Ibid. 18 Apr. 1821. [8] Ibid. 31 May, 1 June 1822, 1 May 1823, 24 Feb. 1824. [9] Ibid. 8 Mar. 1825. [10] *Northampton Mercury*, 25 Feb. 1826. [11] *The Times*, 19 Apr. 1826. [12] Ibid. 1, 2 Mar. 1826. [13] *Althorp Letters*, 127; Cox, ii. 510; *Northampton Mercury*, 3, 10, 17, 24 June 1826. [14] *The Times*, 3 Mar. 1827. [15] Ibid. 7 June 1827. [16] Ibid. 8, 12 June 1827. [17] *Northampton Mercury*, 13 Feb. 1830. [18] Ibid. 17, 31 July, 7 Aug. 1830. [19] Ibid. 11 Dec. 1830. [20] *Northampton Free Press*, 8 Mar. 1831. [21] Ibid. 22 Mar. 1831. [22] Ibid. 29 Mar. 1831. [23] Ibid. 19 Apr. 1831. [24] Ibid. 26 Apr., 3, 10, 31 May 1831, 1 Dec. 1832. [25] Ibid. 30 June 1832. [26] Ibid. 1 Dec. 1832. [27] Ibid. 23 Nov. 1833. [28] PROB 11/1829/168; IR26/1363/85.

M.P.J.C./P.J.S.

ROBINSON, George Richard (?1781–1850), of 5 John Street, Adelphi and Dorset Cottage, Fulham, Mdx.

WORCESTER	1826–1837
POOLE	1847–24 Aug. 1850

b. ?1781, ?*s.* of Richard Robinson, surgeon and mayor of Wareham, Dorset. *unm.* ?1 da. illegit. *d.* 24 Aug. 1850.

Chairman, Lloyd's 1834; gov. British American Land Co. 1834; dir. Bank of British North America 1836, Provincial Bank of Ireland 1838.

Robinson's father was almost certainly Richard, a surgeon and apothecary at Wareham and the town's mayor, 1806-7, 1810-11, connected 'by marriage' with the Garland dynasty of prosperous Newfoundland merchants who dominated the representation and corporation of neighbouring Poole, where Robinson was enrolled as a burgess in August 1804.[1] 'At an early age' Robinson went into the family's Newfoundland trade, then headed by Benjamin Lester, Member for Poole, 1790-6, and later by Lester's son-in-law George Garland, Member for Poole, 1801-6, who was in partnership with his brother Joseph, a London corn merchant, until 1805. Robinson then worked in Joseph's London office, before going to St. John's to take control of the Newfoundland operations of Hart, Eppes and Gaden, based at Woolbrook, of which he became a full partner in 1810, when his 'cousin' John Bingley Garland, brother of Benjamin Lester Lester, Member for Poole, 1809-35, joined the firm. By 1815 Hart, Garland and Robinson, as the company became after Gaden's death in 1811, was among the largest in the Newfoundland trade, and on Hart's retirement in 1822 Robinson became its senior partner. A ship owner and East India proprietor, he remained head of Robinson, Garland and Brooking until his death.[2] In 1827 *The Times* reported hearing from 'a correspondent on whose veracity we place the greatest reliance' that Robinson, 'the newly elected opulent representative for the city of Worcester', had 'eloped with Miss M. Read, the beautiful and accomplished daughter of a wealthy merchant residing at Poole', but no record of a marriage has been found.[3]

At the 1826 general election Robinson had stood for Worcester as an 'independent' entirely 'unconnected with party', claiming to have the support of the non-resident freemen of London, Birmingham and elsewhere. After a contest lasting one week he was returned at the head of the poll. At his dinner he declared his 'approval' of the Liverpool ministry and eulogised the foreign secretary Canning.[4] A regular attender, Robinson campaigned steadily for tariff reforms and on behalf of the shipping interest and the North American colonies, and was a strong advocate of Newfoundland's claim to a legislative assembly; his business partner John Bingley Garland was elected as the first Speaker of its short-lived House of Assembly in 1832.[5] On 5 Dec. 1826 Robinson denounced the 'fraudulent schemes' which had been pursued by joint-stock companies. He divided against the Clarences' grant, claiming to have hitherto 'usually voted with ministers', 16 Feb. 1827. He divided for Catholic relief, 6 Mar. 1827, 12 May 1828. He advocated revision of the corn laws, 9, 19 Mar., voted against increased protection for barley, 12 Mar., and demanded that agriculture be placed 'on the same footing as any other branch of commerce', 31 Mar. 1827. He voted for inquiries into electoral interference by Leicester corporation, 15 Mar., and the Irish estimates, 5 Apr. 1827. He seconded his colleague Thomas Davies's successful motion for the appointment of a select committee on polling that day, but disapproved of his bill to limit the duration of polls and provide multiple booths in the next session, fearing that it would 'abridge the freedom of election', 21 Feb., and presenting a hostile Worcester petition, 24 Mar. 1828. He was a minority teller against its details, 6 May, when he moved an amendment to extend the poll to ten days in order to accommodate out-voters, and 13 May 1828, when he threatened to 'take advantage of the forms of the House, to stop ... future progress'. In this he failed. He supported inquiry into the activities of the Devon and Cornwall Mining Company, 9 Apr., 15 May 1827. He voted for the disfranchisement of Penryn, 28 May, but against the Coventry magistracy bill, 11 June 1827.

Robinson was in the minority of 15 against the navy estimates, 11 Feb., and 'highly approved' of the composition of the finance committee, 12 Feb. 1828. He presented multiple petitions for repeal of the Test Acts, 25 Feb., and voted accordingly next day. He secured accounts of government expenses in Newfoundland, 29 Feb., 30 May, and called for a 'small naval force' to protect its fishing fleet, 19 May. He argued for hearing evidence on the East Retford disfranchisement bill, 3 Mar., and divided against extending its franchise to Bassetlaw, 21 Mar. He spoke in support of the steamboat passengers regulation bill, 4, 18, 20 Mar. He explained that he was favourable to the 'principle' of free trade but utterly opposed to its adoption until 'something like reciprocity' had been established with other countries, 1 Apr., and defended the notion of tariff retaliation against the United States, 18 July. On 22 Apr. he spoke and voted for an amendment to reduce the pivot price of corn. He supported repeal of the usury laws, 20 May, and voted thus, 19 June. He recommended the use of private packets in the place of post office steam vessels, 6 June. He called for the unification of Lower and Upper Canada, 16 June, for inquiry into the 'unjustifiable expenditure' on military works there, 7, 8 July, and for the interests of the British settlers to be better consulted, 14 July. On 17 June he argued at length for a 'fair and dispassionate inquiry' into the shipping interest, 'the prosperity or adversity of which may one day decide the fate of this country'. He divided to condemn the expense of improving Buckingham House, 23 June. He spoke against the corporate funds bill, 1 July, and voted accordingly, 10 July. He argued for restrictions on savings bank deposits, 3 July 1828.

Robinson secured returns on glove imports, 12 May 1828, 9 Feb. 1829, and endorsed Worcester petitions against foreign competition, 23, 26 June 1828, when he warned of its 'most detrimental effect on the trade'. He obtained returns on foreign silk imports, 24 June, and spoke and was a majority teller for an amendment to the silk duties that obtained government support, 14 July. A presenter of numerous petitions complaining of distress in that industry during the 1829 session, he deprecated further reductions in the duties, 10 Apr., and seconded the motion for an inquiry, 13 Apr., for which he was a minority teller, 15 Apr. He criticized the silk trade bill, 28 Apr., 4, 7, 8 May, when he protested that government 'refuse any protection to the manufacturer' yet 'give protection to the landed interest', and was a minority teller against it, 2 May. On 19 Feb. he dissented from a Worcester anti-Catholic petition presented by Lygon, the county Member, and declared his approval of the Wellington ministry's concession of emancipation and his intention to 'vote for the ultimate measure'. He was absent from the division of 6 Mar., but divided in its favour, 30 Mar. He refuted assertions that the colonies were 'a burden to the country', affirming their 'essential service' and 'material benefit', 20 Feb. He protested that the impressment of seamen operated 'most injuriously to the trade of the kingdom', 27 Feb. He welcomed the grant for the Society for the Propagation of the Gospels, which would encourage 'religion and morality throughout the colonies', 6 Apr. That day he condemned the Newfoundland fisheries bill and called for inquiry into the 'state of the island, that we may finally improve the system of its administration'. He voted for the transfer of East Retford's seats to Birmingham, 5 May, and against the grant for the marble arch, 25 May. He advocated inquiries into distress and the state of the shipping interest and secured returns on shipping in Newfoundland, 12 June 1829.

Robinson voted for Knatchbull's amendment to the address, 4 Feb., and although he declared that he had 'much confidence in the great skill of ministers', 8 Feb., he divided steadily with the revived Whig opposition for economy and retrenchment from March 1830. He wanted clarification of the state of trading relations between the United States and the West Indies, 5 Feb., deprecated 'admitting to a free commerce and trade, those foreign powers whose commercial policy may be hostile to us, and calculated to displace our own capital and manufactures', 9 Feb., and asked 'if the principles of free trade are to be acted on, why are they not extended to corn as well as gloves', 13 May. He continued to campaign for tax reductions, urging repeal of those which 'press most heavily on the industrious classes', 2 Mar., 12, 15 Mar., and protesting that 'scarcely one tax has been removed from the necessities of life, or from the articles which are used by the poor and industrious', 7 June. He welcomed the four per cent annuities bill but condemned the 'great public inconvenience' of stamp duties, 7 Apr., against which he presented and endorsed a Worcester petition, 4 May. He attacked proposals to reduce the duties on French wine to the Portuguese level, claiming that Portugal was a better importer of British goods, 25 Mar. He moved for copies of the instructions sent to the governor of Newfoundland, 29 Mar., and for a select committee on its government (which was defeated by 82-29), 11 May, when he declared that 'unless a better system is adopted, I, for one, shall advocate the right of the inhabitants of this colony to legislate for themselves'. He again urged the 'introduction of the representative system' into 'some of our colonies', 24 May. He deplored the 'constant refusal' of government to grant inquiry into the shipping interest, 2 Apr., warning that there had been a 'considerable falling off in the amount of British registered tonnage' as a result of owners being 'obliged, in order to obtain a British register, to build their vessels here of expensive materials' and pay high wages, 6 May. Robinson voted to transfer East Retford's seats to Birmingham, 11 Feb., 5, 15 Mar., and for the enfranchisement of Birmingham, Leeds, and Manchester, 23 Feb., called for 'some measure' to be carried by which 'the franchise might be transferred to certain large towns', 25 Mar., and voted for reform, 28 May. He was a majority teller for the usury laws repeal bill, 27 Apr. He concurred with a Worcester petition presented by Davies in favour of the forgery punishment mitigation bill, 26 Apr., for which he spoke, 13 May, and voted, 24 May, 7 June; he was twice a minority teller against the Lords' amendments to it, 20 July. He presented a Worcester petition against the insolvent debtors bill and urged the adoption of a more 'efficacious measure', 11 May. He voted for Jewish emancipation, 17 May. He argued and was a minority teller against Littleton's truck bill, 23 June, denounced it as 'prejudicial to the labouring classes of the people', 5 July, and spoke in the same sense, 8, 9 July. He voted for the abolition of colonial slavery, 13 July 1830.

At the 1830 general election Robinson offered again for Worcester, citing his support for 'every practical reduction in political expenditure' and claiming never to have 'mixed myself with any degree of party'. Denying allegations that he was 'an enemy to the poor', he defended his opposition to the truck bill. (He asserted that although it had made him 'unpopular', his opinion remained 'unchanged', 18 Nov., but then promised to support 'legislation on the subject if the House, after due deliberation, shall deem it necessary', 14 Dec. 1830.) Attempts to get up an opposition foundered and he was returned unopposed.[6] He resumed his calls for a review of taxation and an 'amelioration of the condition of the people', 3 Nov., contending that 'without inquiry, and without remedy, the state of the country can never be improved', 6 Dec. He condemned proposals to relax trading arrangements between the United States and the West Indian colonies as 'greatly injurious' to Britain and Canada, 8 Nov., and doubted that the timber trade between Canada and the West Indies would survive if the Americans were allowed to compete on an equal footing, 12 Nov. He had been listed by the Wellington ministry as one of their 'foes' and he voted against them on the civil list, 15 Nov. He denounced the 'injurious and oppressive' stamp duty levied on the admission of freemen, which deprived many 'of the exercise of the privilege of voting', 9 Dec. He presented numerous petitions for the abolition of slavery the following day. He objected to the colonial trade bill, 17 Dec., and its 'interference' with duties, 20 Dec. That day he presented numerous petitions alleging bribery at the recent Liverpool election. He criticized the Grey ministry's proposals for ambassadorial pensions, which they had 'regularly opposed' when in opposition, 10 Dec., condemned their proposed civil list as 'monstrous' and likely to induce 'odium and scandal', 23 Dec. 1830, and demanded a 'formal and grave investigation into the manner in which pensions have been granted', 4 Feb., and their revision, 28 Mar., 14 Apr. 1831. He approved of much of the budget, but quibbled with the proposed reductions of duties on French wines and foreign timber, 11 Feb., describing how the latter would have 'an injurious effect on the colonies', 14 Feb., 15, 18 Mar. He welcomed removal of the calico tax as a 'great advantage' to manufacturers, 28 Feb. Speaking as 'a commercial man', 15 Feb., he complained that recent governments had pursued a 'most ruinous and fatal' policy in their attempt 'to fortify a foreign trade ... in contradistinction to our colonial and home trade', which would not only 'lead to the downfall and abandoning of several of our colonies', but also 'sacrifice' the shipping interest, which had 'made us the greatest maritime nation in the world'. He contended that the introduction of a 'graduated property tax' would 'have the effect of relieving all branches of productive industry', 14 Mar. He voted for the second reading of the ministerial reform bill, 22 Mar., but insisted that he was not 'pledged to any of the details' and had merely expressed 'approbation of the principle', 21 Apr. He voted against Gascoyne's wrecking amendment, 19 Apr. 1831.

At the ensuing general election Robinson mocked calls for 'moderate reform' as the 'greatest bug-bear that ever was attempted to be put upon the people', declared himself 'an opponent of the free trade system ... while trade in corn remains shackled', and boasted of his support for 'those measures which I have thought calculated to relieve my constituents and the country from taxation'. He was returned unopposed.[7] He harassed ministers over the government of Newfoundland, 27 June, welcomed the appointment of a commission of inquiry into colonial establishments, 1 July, and announced that the people of Newfoundland had 'instructed' him to say that 'if you will grant them a local legislature, they will not again ask you for money', 25 July. He urged the introduction there of a 'constitutional legislative assembly' similar to those of other North American colonies, 13 Sept., but withdrew his motion for this after being assured of the appointment of a select committee early the next session. He attacked the report on the East India Company, alleging that the committee had 'strongly preconceived opinions', 28 June. He resumed his calls for a reform of taxation, 1 July, and campaigned steadily against the reduction of French wine duties. He spoke and was a minority teller for his own amendment to reduce the civil list, 18 July, but refrained from opposing the consular salaries in the hope that next year's settlement would be 'extremely small', 25 July. He believed that the Irish landed proprietor, 'who derives his property from that country, should contribute to the support of its poor', 15 Aug., and welcomed calls for the introduction of an Irish poor law, 29, 30 Aug. (when he was minority teller on the issue), 26 Sept., 11 Oct. He pressed repeatedly for information on the duties paid by British ships in foreign ports, condemning the 'tonnage and other duties' charged on vessels in France, 18 Aug., and arguing that the costs of quarantine should be paid by 'the community at large', 23 Aug., 6 Sept. He spoke and voted against issuing the Liverpool writ, 5 Sept., and moved and was a minority teller for withholding the Pembrokeshire writ until the evidence of the committee had been presented, 26 Sept. According to Littleton, at the coronation that month Robinson 'came with an *enormous* nosegay in his hand, which excited much laughter'.[8] He argued and divided for inquiry into the effects of renewal of the Sugar Refinery Act on the West India interest, 12 Sept. He denounced the 'extravagant outlay' on Buckingham House, 28 Sept., and next day opposed increasing the salary of the president of the board of trade. He welcomed the vestries bill, 30 Sept., and presented a Worcester petition against the sale of beer bill, 18 Oct. 1831.

Robinson voted for the second reading of the reintroduced reform bill, 6 July, dismissed any consideration of 'universal suffrage', 8 July, and divided at least twice against adjourning the debates, 12 July 1831. He spoke briefly in the bill's favour, 13 July, but bemoaned the 'angry altercations' on it and appealed for 'a tone of moderation' to be adopted, remarking that 'we must not, night after night, waste our time in debate on frivolous points', 20 July. He gave generally steady support to its details, defending the arrangements for his native Wareham, 26 July, and Stoke, 4 Aug., but voted against the proposed division of counties, 11 Aug., for Lord Chandos's amendment to enfranchise £50 tenants-at-will, 18 Aug., and to preserve the electoral rights of freemen, who made up all of his constituents, 30 Aug. He objected to 'only one day' being allowed for the erection of county polling booths and contended that 'every other question should be postponed until the reform bill has passed', 5 Sept. He divided for its passage, 21 Sept., the second reading of the Scottish bill, 23 Sept., and Lord Ebrington's confidence motion, 10 Oct. 1831, but explained the following day that in view of his line 'in opposition to the commercial policy' of the ministry, it should be clear that he supported it only 'in the cause of reform' and upon 'no other ground'. At the Poole by-election that month he lent his assistance to the ostensible reformer but otherwise Tory Charles Tulk*, rather than the ministerial candidate Sir John Byng*.[9] Robinson objected to an anti-reform petition from Worcestershire, 16 Dec. 1831, and voted for the second reading of the revised reform bill next day. He spoke and divided for going into the committee on it, 20 Jan., and again gave steady support to its details, though he spoke against altering the boundaries of 'ancient boroughs' where 'no occasion for complaint had ever arisen', 23 Jan. 1832. He defended the principle of the bill but again denied that he was 'pledged' to all its details, 20 Mar., and voted for its third reading, 22 Mar. He defended Lord Grey's resignation following the bill's defeat in the Lords and divided for the address calling on the king to appoint only ministers who would carry it unimpaired, 10 May, and presented a Worcester petition for withholding the supplies until it passed, 18 May. He paired against a Conservative amendment to the Scottish bill, 1 June, but complained that Ireland had 'not been treated fairly, either as regards the number of Members to be given ... or in the extension of the elective franchise', 18 June. Asserting that the 'commissioners were guilty of a mistake', he proposed an amendment to include Corfe Castle within the boundaries of Wareham, which was defeated by 122-55, 22 June 1832.

Robinson demanded immediate inquiry into distress, 6 Dec., and criticized the estimates, 9 Dec. 1831. He now voted against the vestries bill, 23 Jan. 1832. He argued and was minority teller against the anatomy bill, 25 Jan., 11 Apr., when he warned that legalizing the 'sale of human bodies' would 'facilitate and encourage the commission of murder'. He spoke and voted against ministers on the Russian-Dutch loan, 26 Jan., 12 July, asserting that its payment was 'unconstitutional' when the 'finances of the state are in a most deplorable condition', 6 Feb., and berating ministers for threatening to resign if they were 'not supported in this measure', 16 July. He criticized their handling of relations with Portugal, 17, 29 Feb. He called for the introduction of a 'modified property tax', 31 Jan., 27 July, and inquiry into how the 'whole system of taxation can be remodelled', 14 June. He pressed repeatedly for inquiry into the glove trade and was a minority teller on the issue, 31 Jan., 3 Apr., when he warned that if 'we allow foreign manufacture to take the place of our own ... we shall soon have to support half our population'. He presented a petition from Worcester's glove manufacturers complaining of their distress, 19 June, and petitions for inquiry into the silk trade from Sandbach, 3 Feb., and Macclesfield, 1 Mar. He opposed the sale of beer bill, 3 Feb., and presented and endorsed a hostile Northampton petition, 31 Mar. He welcomed the factories regulation bill, 10 Feb., and was appointed to the select committee on it, 17 Mar. He urged lifting the restrictions on vessels imposed during the recent London cholera scare, 20 Feb., stressed the 'direct benefit' to the shipping interest of hemp tax repeal, 2 Apr., and again deplored the 'manifest injustice' of French tonnage duties, 1 June. He welcomed the register of births bill, 22 Feb., and presented a favourable petition from Northampton Dissenters, 20 June. He voted for a reduction of the sugar duties, 7 Mar. He presented four Newfoundland petitions for a legislative assembly that day, and urged granting New South Wales 'the benefit of trial by jury' and voted for the introduction of a system of representation there, 28 June. He spoke for and was appointed to a select committee on petitions, 9 May. Maintaining his stance against free trade in commerce, he moved unsuccessfully for inquiry, 22 May, and warned that 'if a change is not soon made, it may end in the complete ruin of our manufactures', 3 July. On 19 June he divided to suspend flogging in the army, observing that corporal punishment was 'absolutely unnecessary for the maintenance of due discipline'. That day he voted for permanent provision for the Irish poor by a tax on absentee landlords. He insisted that the cost of improving the water supply of the metropolis should be met from 'local funds', 6 July. He supported the grant to the Society for the Propagation of the Gospels, 22 July. He was in a minority of 16 for Hume's motion to disqualify the recorder of Dublin from Parliament, 24 July. He condemned lord chancellor Brougham's appointment of his brother James Brougham* to a chancery sinecure as 'ill-advised', 25 July, 27 July. He called for 'additional security' to 'guard against the unconstitutional interference of peers in the election of Members', 6 Aug. He spoke and voted against the Greek loan that day, and argued that the Greek convention bill should 'make provision for the payment of their former debts', 10 Aug. He presented a Worcester petition for the abolition of Irish tithes, 11 Aug. 1832.

At the 1832 general election Robinson was returned for Worcester as a Liberal. He remained a prominent campaigner for tax reforms and retired in 1837.[10] He unsuccessfully contested Tower Hamlets as a Conservative in 1841 and was Peelite Member for Poole from 1847 until his death, 'aged 69', in August 1850. By his will, dated 1 July 1850, he directed that all his interests at St. John's and 'elsewhere in the Island of Newfoundland' be sold for the benefit of Louisa Matilda Peillon, his 'natural or reputed daughter, the wife of Lazuard Peillon, now or late living in or near Paris', and her children. He left annuities of £500 to his business partner Thomas Brooking, £100 to his godson George Thomas Brooking and £200 to his goddaughter Ellen Garland, daughter of his late partner. A sum of £7,000 was to be invested to provide for the poor of Wareham. He left instructions for his remains to be interred at Poole in the same vault as his mother and sister.[11]

[1] *Gent. Mag.* (1850), ii. 551; J. Hutchins, *Hist. Dorset*, i. 83; *Univ. Brit. Dir.* (1791), iv. 677; *Eighteenth Cent. Medics*, 508; Dorset RO, Poole borough recs. DC/PL CLA 43. [2] *Gent. Mag.* (1850), ii.

551; *Dict. Canadian Biog.* vi. 311-12; C. Cullingford, *Hist. Poole*, 123-4; D. Beamish, *Mansions and Merchants of Poole*, 115. [3] *The Times*, 23 Feb. 1827. [4] *Worcester Herald*, 27 May, 3, 10, 17, 24 June 1826. [5] Beamish, 119. [6] *Worcester Herald*, 3, 10, 17, 24, 31 July 1830. [7] Ibid. 30 Apr., 7 May 1831. [8] Hatherton diary, 8 Sept. 1831. [9] *Sherborne Jnl.* 13 Oct. 1831; Poole borough recs. DC/PL S1661. [10] *Raikes Jnl.* i. 175. [11] PROB 11/2156/591; IR26/1943/642.

P.J.S.

ROCHFORT, Gustavus (c.1784–1848), of Rochfort, co. Westmeath.

CO. WESTMEATH 1826–1832

b. c.1784, 3rd but 1st surv. s. of Gustavus Hume Rochfort* and Frances, da. of John Bloomfield of Redwood, King's Co. *m.* c.1806, his cos. Dorothea, da. of John Nixon of Carrick, 1s. 2da. (1 *d.v.p.*). *suc.* fa. 1824. *d.* 2 Feb. 1848.

Entered army 1798; lt. 68 Ft. 1799; capt. army 1802, 67 Ft. 1803; maj. 102 (later 100) Ft. 1811, half-pay 1818-*d.*; lt.-col. 1819; col. 1837.

Rochfort saw active service in the Caribbean, the East Indies and America. His two elder brothers were dead by 1812 and his welfare then became the chief object of his father, the importunate Member for county Westmeath, who was beleaguered with financial problems and a large family. Early in 1817 Rochfort senior sought the support of the Irish secretary Robert Peel* for his bid to have Gustavus considered for 'promotion and safety in the expected reduction of some regiments'. Peel obliged, but was unable to keep Rochfort off the half-pay list a year later. Both he and his father immediately solicited for him employment on full pay 'to enable me', as Rochfort pleaded, 'to support a wife and large young family'. Again Peel, on behalf of the Irish government, was sympathetic, but the military authorities held out scant hope of being able to accommodate Rochfort. His father continued to seek a civil or military appointment for him, but nothing had been done by the time he died early in 1824, leaving Rochfort with only a modest inheritance and his four younger brothers also very poorly provided for.[1]

Rochfort declined to come forward as his father's replacement at the ensuing by-election, despite the solicitations of 'numerous friends', but at the 1826 general election he offered on the 'high Protestant interest' with the backing of Lord Longford, who had dropped his pro-Catholic brother. He was returned after a gruelling contest.[2] A petition against his return alleging insufficient property qualification came to nothing.[3] He lost no time in acquainting ministers with his wants and in April 1827 solicited promotion for his clerical brother Henry.[4] He presented petitions against Catholic relief, 12 Feb., signed the hostile petition of Irish landed proprietors that month, and voted accordingly, 6 Mar.[5] On the formation of Canning's ministry he offered his 'support' to Peel, the leader of the Protestant party in the Commons, and received a non-committal but friendly reply: 'Your private friendship and esteem I shall be desirous to cultivate, even without any reference to politics'.[6] Rochfort voted against repeal of the Test Acts, 26 Feb., and Catholic relief, 12 May 1828. He was a founder member of the Brunswick Constitutional Club of Ireland formed later that year and spoke at the inaugural meeting of the Westmeath Brunswick Club, of which he was a vice-president, 25 Nov. 1828.[7] On the address, 5 Feb. 1829, he deplored the Wellington ministry's decision to concede Catholic emancipation and a week later denounced Peel and Wellington as traitors to those who had trusted them to uphold the Protestant cause:

> We may now be compared to an Orange with the *Peel* taken off; but the seeds of the fruit still remain, and will strike root downwards, I trust; so that from them, hereafter, may spring a tree that may extend its branches far and wide.

He presented numerous anti-Catholic petitions, 18, 23 Feb., 3 Mar., when he defended his brother-in-law Mervyn Archdall* against a charge of inciting Irish Protestants to physical violence against Catholics, and voted steadily against the relief bill, which he condemned as 'a subversion of the constitution', 23 Mar. He was in the minority of 16 for doubling the Irish freeholders' electoral qualification, 26 Mar. In October 1829 he was listed among the Tory Ultras who were 'strongly opposed' to the ministry. He voted against them on economies, 3 May, and repeal of the Irish coal duties, 13 May, but with them on the grant for South American missions, 7 June 1830. He voted against the second reading of the Jewish emancipation bill, 17 May, and paired against abolition of the death penalty for forgery, 7 June. He defended Westmeath grand juries against Daniel O'Connell's strictures, 21 June 1830.

At the 1830 general election he offered again for Westmeath and was returned after another contest.[8] He was listed by ministers among the 'moderate Ultras', with the observation, 'Asks for patronage. Don't give it'; and he duly helped to vote them out of office on the civil list, 15 Nov. 1830. He voted against the second reading of the Grey ministry's reform bill, 22 Mar., and for Gascoyne's wrecking amendment, 19 Apr. 1831. Reconciled to the Tories, at the ensuing general election he came forward as an anti-reformer, 'sufficient' party funds having been placed at his disposal.[9] A contest was averted at the last minute and he was returned unopposed, amidst reports that he had 'undergone a change' and given a 'sort of pledge' for reform.[10] If he did so, he broke it, for he attacked the reintroduced bill, 4 July, voted against its second reading, 6 July, and was in the minorities for use of the 1831 census to determine the redistribution schedules, 19 July, against the partial disfranchisement of Chippenham, 27 July, for the preservation of existing electoral rights, 27 Aug., and against the disfranchisement of Aldborough, 14 Sept. 1831. He voted against the bill's passage, 21 Sept., and the second reading of the Scottish reform bill, 23 Sept. He defended the magistrates of Westmeath in the context of the fatal affray at Castle Pollard, 11 July, as he did the grand jury which had acquitted the policemen consequently charged with manslaughter, 23 Aug. He also spoke up for the yeomanry involved in the Newtownbarry massacre, 9 Sept. He voted in censure of the Irish government over the Dublin election, 23 Aug., and paired against the Maynooth grant, 26 Sept. 1831.

Rochfort voted against the second reading of the revised reform bill, 17 Dec. 1831, and the enfranchisement of Tower Hamlets, 28 Feb., and dismissed as unrepresentative a favourable Westmeath petition, 9 Mar. 1832. He divided against the third reading, 22 Mar. He voted against ministers on the Russian-Dutch loan, 26 Jan. 1832. That day he presented and endorsed a petition against the proposed plan of Irish education, which was anathema to Protestants of all denominations, and demanded that goverment adopt a 'line of policy ... by which the Protestants of Ireland should be protected, and all unjust demands refused'. On 13 Feb. he expressed his 'infinite satisfaction' at Grey's recent declaration in the Lords of the government's intention of dealing severely with Irish disorder. When presenting a petition from the lord lieutenant and magistrates of Westmeath complaining of its lawless state, 15 Mar., he called for 'stronger measures' for the protection of life and property, though he insisted that he 'meant to cast no reflection upon the government'. On 20 Mar. he warned that Ireland was in a 'most alarming' condition and that 'the mob have, for some reason or another, taken it into their heads that ... government are disposed to favour their proceedings'. His last recorded votes were for the Liverpool disfranchisement bill, 23 May, and against the second reading of the Irish reform bill, 25 May. He was a founder member of the Conservative Society of Dublin established next month, and contested Westmeath as a Conservative at the 1832 general election, but was beaten into third place by two reformers.[11]

Soon after Peel became premier at the end of 1834 Rochfort wrote to him:

> From the kindly manner I have been always treated with by you, I am encouraged to hope for a kind attention to this letter. Indeed I once had a note from you which I shall ever prize, in it you were pleased to express the word *esteem* (which I have done nothing to forfeit) ... My claims have been acknowledged by the late ministry of the duke of Wellington. You well know my family represented Westmeath for 150 years, always supporting the true interests of the country, my father for 30 years, during which he gave his steady support to the several ministries on those principles which, thanks be to God, have rallied under you for the salvation of the Empire. My father's private affairs suffered from his constant attendance. His claims were repeatedly acknowledged but the intentions of the ministers were never accomplished. I myself zealously supported the same line. I don't think I missed a question on the reform bill, and but for the alteration in the ... bill of 1829, instead of six years I should *now be* the ninth year fighting under your banner. That registry deluged Ireland with false votes. I may add as a soldier I have received the approbation of my superiors.

What he wanted was civil employment for his 19-year-old only son and namesake, but Peel, overwhelmed with similar applications, could give him no hope. (He purchased a cornetcy for his son in the 4th Dragoon Guards in 1836 and a lieutenancy two years later.) Within a month of Peel's resumption of power in 1841 he solicited a civil or military appointment for himself, but was again disappointed.[12] In 1844 he bought Gustavus a troop. Rochfort died in February 1848 at Brighton and was buried at Hever. By his will, dated 21 Aug. 1840 with a codicil of 14 Oct. 1844, he left all his property to Gustavus, hoping that he 'may get more out of the estate than his father did', and instructed him to give his mother £500 plus interest and to 'take care she gets her pension'. His surviving daughter died in 1849. His son died unmarried in modest circumstances in 1855 and his widow, who had been living at Iping House, near Midhurst, Sussex, the following year. They too were buried at Hever.[13]

[1] Add. 40219, ff. 134, 157; 40220, f. 195; 40273, ff. 127, 240; 40296, ff. 54-55; 40414, f. 107; 40489, f. 81. [2] *Westmeath Jnl.* 12 Feb. 1824, 29 June, 6 July; *Dublin Evening Post*, 27 June 1826. [3] *CJ*, lxxxii. 32-33, 111-12. [4] Add. 40393, f. 161. [5] *The Times*, 13 Feb. 1827; Add. 40392, f. 3. [6] Add. 40394, ff. 36, 38. [7] *Westmeath Jnl.* 27 Nov., 4 Dec. 1828. [8] *Roscommon and Leitrim Gazette*, 14 Aug. 1830. [9] NLI, Farnham mss 18606 (1), Arbuthnot to Farnham, 4 May 1831. [10] *The Times*, 13 May 1831. [11] Farnham mss 18611 (3), T. Lefroy to Farnham, 4 June 1832. [12] Add. 40414, ff. 107, 109; 40490, ff. 291, 295. [13] *Gent. Mag.* (1848), i. 548; (1849), ii. 443; (1855), ii. 445; (1856), i. 666; PROB 11/2075/429, 2221/867.

D.R.F./P.J.S.

ROCHFORT, Gustavus Hume (c.1750–1824), of Rochfort, co. Westmeath.

CO. WESTMEATH 1801–30 Jan. 1824

b. c. 1750, o.s. of George Rochfort, MP [I], of Rochfort and his cos. Alice, da. of Sir Gustavus Hume, 3rd bt., MP [I], of Castle Hume, co. Fermanagh. *m.* July 1779, Frances, da. of John Bloomfield of Redwood, King's Co., 7s. (2 *d.v.p.*) 5da. (2 *d.v.p.*). *suc.* fa. 1786. *d.* 30 Jan. 1824.
MP [I] 1798-1800.
Sheriff, co. Westmeath 1796-7, gov. 1815-*d.*
Capt. commdt. Moyarshell yeomanry 1796.

For over 20 years Rochfort had bartered with successive governments for provision for his seven sons in return for his political support. Much had been done for them, but not enough to satisfy Rochfort, whose financial problems, originating in the Irish Parliament's refusal to countenance his claim to the £16,000 a year Hume estates, were exacerbated by a protracted and expensive lawsuit. He had been 'harassed by law', he told the Irish secretary Peel in 1818, and was anxious 'to get my sons assisted, as that will materially ... enable me to get through the difficulties brought on me by the schemes of others'. At the 1820 general election, when he came in again for county Westmeath on the family interest, his main objects were civil or military employment for his now eldest son Gustavus, a soldier on half-pay, and promotion in the church for his son Henry. In neither case had ministers, who were out of patience with his incessant importunity, been able to oblige him; and he had evidently complained to Lord Liverpool that 'he has had nothing done for him since Mr. Perceval's time' and had been deprived of 'all the county honours'.[1] Rochfort was largely a cypher in the 1820 Parliament, when he is not known to have spoken in debate. He voted with government against repeal of the additional malt duty, 3 Apr. 1821. On 11 Apr. 1821 he was given leave to attend the House of Lords as a witness before the committee of privileges on the Marchmont peerage claim. That year he foolishly turned down an offer of promotion for Henry 'from a misunderstanding as to the value of the parish'.[2] He was given renewed leave to attend the Lords, 30 Apr. 1822, when he paired against the bill to relieve Catholic peers of their disabilities. No other trace of parliamentary activity has been found.

Rochfort, who apparently had had to sell most of his Irish property, died in January 1824, leaving his five surviving sons 'very ill provided for'. It was in his name that at least three of them continued to obtrude their respective claims for relief on Liverpool's and later Conservative ministries, but to no avail.[3]

[1] Add. 40219, ff. 21, 76, 83, 130-6, 152, 153, 157; 40296, ff. 54-55; 40298, f.43. [2] Add. 40376, f.157. [3] *Gent. Mag.* (1824), i. 382; Add. 40376, f. 157; 40393, f. 161; 40414, f. 107; 40489, f. 81; 40490, f. 291.

D.R.F.

ROCKSAVAGE, earl of *see* **CHOLMONDELEY, George Horatio**

ROGERS, Edward (1781–1852), of Stanage Park, nr. Knighton, Rad. and 8 Charles Street, Mdx.

BISHOP'S CASTLE 16 June 1820–1832

b. 30 Sept. 1781, o.s. of Charles Rogers, merchant, of Cheapside, London and Harriet, da. of Robert Heptinstall of Hound Hill, Yorks. *educ.* Charterhouse 1793; Emmanuel, Camb. 1798; M. Temple 1797; I. Temple 1801, called 1807. *m.* (1) 21 Oct. 1807, Sarah Augusta (*d.* 28 Dec. 1816), da. of George Wolff of Balham House, Surr., Danish consul-gen. in England, 4s. *d.v.p.*; (2) 22 Nov. 1832, Eliza Casamajor, da. of Henry Brown of E.I. Co. civil service (Madras), *s.p. suc.* fa. 1820.[1] *d.* 20 Dec. 1852.
Capt. S. Salop militia 1811-12.
Bailiff, Ludlow 1825-6; sheriff, Rad. 1840-1.

Charles Rogers, this Member's father, was a younger son of the Rev. Edward Rogers of The Home, a direct descendant of Roger de Norbury, who had held property and influence in Ludlow and southern Shropshire in the fourteenth century. In partnership with Thomas Brown of Cheapside, whose son Benjamin married his daughter Mary in 1803, he prospered as an East India merchant. By 1800 he had retired to Ludlow, where he was made an alderman, and purchased Stanage Park, about 17 miles away on the Herefordshire-Radnorshire border, from Thomas Johnes†, who had relinquished his Radnorshire interests after coming in for Cardiganshire in 1796.[2]

Rogers, his only son, was born in London and was called to the bar shortly before his marriage. He settled briefly at Wigmore, Herefordshire, where his son Edward was born in 1810, served under the Clives in the Ludlow militia and apparently practised on the Oxford circuit.[3] His wife, who shared his mercantile background, died at Ludlow in 1816 at the age of 26, having borne him three further sons, none of whom survived to adulthood.[4] The deeper purse of the radical Member for Radnorshire, Walter Wilkins*, left Rogers with little prospect of a seat for that county, and he was one of the three squires who dissuaded Thomas Frankland Lewis* from risking a premature challenge there in 1812.[5] Amid speculation that he and his relations would assist the anti-Clive party at the general election of 1820, he acted as go-between in the negotiations which secured the withdrawal of the candidature of Edmund Lechmere Charlton† against the 1st earl of Powis's sons Lord Clive and Robert Henry Clive at Ludlow, and he contested Bishop's Castle on Powis's interest with the government whip William Holmes.[6] On the hustings he promised to 'act as my conscience and my judgement direct me ... in support of the present form of government'.[7] The Commons determined the ensuing double return in their favour, 16 June.[8] Rogers assisted in the passage of Lord Clive's estate bill (which received royal assent, 8 July 1820), so confirming his role as one of the Clives' men of business.[9] His cousin, the Rev. John Rogers of The Home, became bailiff of Bishop's Castle that Michaelmas, and Lord Clive replaced Rogers's ailing father as an alderman of Ludlow. The latter died, 31 Dec. 1820, leaving personal estate of £20,000 (resworn under £16,000, 23 Nov. 1821), and Rogers inherited Stanage Park, which had been rebuilt under the direction of the Reptons.[10]

No speeches by Rogers are reported before 1831. He divided steadily with the Tory Clives against Catholic relief, 28 Feb. 1821, 30 Apr. 1822, 1 Mar., 21 Apr., 10 May 1825, but differed from them by voting against the attendant Irish franchise bill, 9 May 1825. He divided against parliamentary reform, 9 May 1821, 20 Feb., 2 June 1823, 26 Feb. 1824, and his few wayward votes against the Liverpool and Wellington administrations tended to reflect local concerns. Nevertheless, strong popular support for Queen Caroline in Bishop's Castle and Ludlow did not deter him from dividing with government against a motion censuring their handling of her case, 6 Feb. 1821.[11] He brought in the abortive Ludlow paving bill, 16 Feb.[12] Unlike the Clives, he voted for reductions in the army, 14 Mar., 31 May, and for the additional malt duty repeal bill, 3 Apr., winning approval thereby in Radnorshire, where he was an active magistrate.[13] He voted against making forgery a non-capital offence, 23 May 1821. He became bailiff of Bishop's Castle that September and helped to secure the passage of the Bishop's Castle roads bill, which received royal assent, 15 May 1822.[14] He divided with government against more extensive tax reductions, 21 Feb., but voted to lower the duty on salt, 28 Feb., and to abolish one of the joint-postmasterships, 2 May. He divided against inquiry into the lord advocate's treatment of the Scottish press, 25 June. He was in the ministerial majorities against repeal of the Foreign Enlistment Act, 16 Apr., and inquiry into chancery delays, 5 June 1823; but, unlike the Clives, he divided against them for inquiry into the prosecution of the Dublin Orange rioters, 22 Apr. 1823. He voted against condemning the indictment in Demerara of the Methodist missionary John Smith, 11 June, and in the government's majority for the Irish insurrection bill, 14 June 1824. He was added to the select committee on salmon fisheries, in which Powis had a vested interest, 18 May, and appointed with Powis's sons to that on county rates, 19 Mar. 1824, 9 Mar. 1825, 2 Mar. 1826. He voted for the Irish unlawful societies bill, 25 Feb., and the duke of Cumberland's annuity, 10 June 1825. He promoted the abortive Ludlow and Severn railroad bill for Powis, and attended and addressed public meetings in Ludlow and Radnorshire following the collapse in February 1825 of Prodgers' Bank and that of Coleman and Wellings in March 1826. He was sworn in as high bailiff of Ludlow in October 1825.[15] His minority vote against empowering government to admit foreign corn, 8 May 1826, was his only recorded one that session. Notwithstanding criticism of his Cheapside connections and 'Pythagorean silence', his return for Bishop's Castle at the general election in June was not seriously challenged.[16] At Ludlow, where he was the returning officer, Lechmere Charlton forced a brief poll, which terminated in favour of the Clives, with a view to having the franchise and boundaries determined on petition.[17] Hurt by Lechmere Charlton's public denunciation of Ludlow corporation, Rogers challenged him to a duel near Bath, which 'terminated without bloodshed' 9 Oct. 1826.[18]

He voted against corn law reform, 2 Apr., and Catholic relief, 6 Mar. 1827, 12 May 1828, and divided with the Wellington administration against ordnance reductions, 4 July 1828. In February 1829 their patronage secretary Planta predicted that, like the Clives, he would divide 'with government' for Catholic emancipation, but he abstained. He cast votes against enfranchising Birmingham, Leeds and Manchester, 23 Feb., Jewish emancipation, 17 May, and reducing expenditure on the South American missions, 7 June 1830, when he divided against abolishing the death penalty for forgery. Rogers had been at the forefront of the Radnorshire magistrates' successful campaigns for parliamentary funding for the Hereford-Aberystwyth road and the new gaol and county hall at Presteigne, and he strongly supported their memorials and petitions against the 1830 administration of justice bill, which proposed transferring the assizes to Brecon or Hereford when the court of great sessions was abolished. He voted against the bill, 18 June.[19] His minority votes to restrict on-consumption under the sale of beer bill, 21 June, 1 July 1830, accorded with the prevailing opinion of the corporations of Bishop's Castle and Ludlow.[20] At the general election that month he was returned for Bishop's Castle with another Ludlow corporator,

Frederick Hamilton Cornewall of Delbury, the eldest son of the bishop of Worcester and a kinsman of the late countess of Powis.[21] Lechmere Charlton was belatedly 'bought off' at Ludlow,[22] and 'though labouring under considerable indisposition', Rogers hurried from there to Presteinge to support Frankland Lewis, whose election for Radnorshire he had tacitly supported at by-elections in April 1828 and March 1830.[23]

The Wellington ministry counted him among their 'friends', and he divided with them on the civil list when they were brought down, 15 Nov. 1830. Bishop's Castle was to be disfranchised by the Grey ministry's reform bill, and he voted against its second reading, 22 Mar., and for Gascoyne's wrecking amendment, 19 Apr. 1831. At the ensuing general election he came in for Bishop's Castle with a new Clive nominee, the anti-reformer and barrister James Lewis Knight, and supported Frankland Lewis in Radnorshire, where he was challenged by a reformer.[24] He divided against the reintroduced reform bill at its second reading, 6 July 1831. Presenting a hostile petition from Bishop's Castle, which he fully endorsed, 14 July, he claimed that ministers had 'decided to pass the bill without giving the parties aggrieved a chance of being heard in support of their claims' and asserted that his 'only consolation' was 'that to the last, my vote shall be given against a measure which I conceive to be unjust and oppressive'.[25] He voted to make the 1831 census the criterion for English borough disfranchisements, 19 July, and stayed on in London to monitor the bill's progress;[26] but, like Powis's other Members, he voted only against the partial disfranchisement of Chippenham, 27 July, and the bill's passage, 21 Sept. 1831. They did not divide on the second reading of the revised measure, 17 Dec. 1831, but voted against enfranchising Tower Hamlets, 28 Feb., and the bill's third reading, 22 Mar. 1832. Rogers also divided against the second reading of the Irish measure, 25 May. He paired against government on the Russian-Dutch loan, 12 July 1832.

Rogers, who married a granddaughter of Thomas Brown in November 1832, did not stand for Parliament again.[27] He remained an active magistrate and benefactor of the poor and was sheriff of Radnorshire during the Rebecca riots. He died at the Bath home of his nephew Benjamin Brown in December 1852 and was buried in the family vault in Brampton Bryan, having outlived his second wife and only surviving son, who had died unmarried in Geneva, 4 Dec. 1838, at the age of 28.[28] His unmarried sister Harriet thus became the main beneficiary under the wills of both Rogers and their mother (*d.* 1834), and she alone was empowered to open his papers. Stanage was placed in trust and reverted to the descendants of the Rev. John Rogers of The Home on Harriet's death in 1867.[29]

[1] *Burke LG* erroneously gives 1830. [2] R.C. Oliver, 'Three Early 19th Cent. Letters pertaining to Rad.' *Trans. Rad. Soc.* xlii (1972), 34-35; IGI (Surr.); P. Beesly, *Hist. Knight Fam.* 8. [3] IGI (London, Herefs., Surr.); *Gent. Mag.* (1807), ii. 976; H.T. Weyman, 'Members for Bishop's Castle', *Trans. Salop Arch. Soc.* (ser. 2), x (1898), 64-66. [4] Oliver, 36-37; IGI (Salop); *Gent. Mag.* (1816), ii. 627. [5] NLW, Harpton Court mss C/595; *HP Commons, 1790-1820*, ii. 510-11. [6] Salop Archives DA1/100/2, Bishop's Castle corporation minutes, 1713-1861, p. 266; Salop Archives, Ludford Park mss 11/1001; Salop Archives, Clive-Powis mss 552/22/67; *Salopian Jnl.* 1, 8, 15 Mar.; *Shrewsbury Chron.* 3, 10, 17 Mar.; *The Times*, 7 Mar. 1820. [7] *Shrewsbury Chron.* 10 Mar. 1820. [8] *CJ*, lxxv. 181-2, 316-17. [9] Ibid. 418, 423. [10] *Salopian Jnl.* 3 Jan. 1821; PROB 11/1640/104; IR26/875/126; Oliver, 35. [11] *The Times*, 20 Nov. 1820. [12] *CJ*, lxxvi. 77. [13] W.K. Parker, 'The Great Rebuilding', *Trans. Rad. Soc.* l (1980), 24. [14] *Shrewsbury Chron.* 19 Oct. 1821; Bishop's Castle corporation minutes, p. 270; *CJ*, lxxvii. 42-43, 267. [15] *Hereford Jnl.* 16 Feb. 1825; Salop Archives, Ludlow Borough LB2/1/7, pp. 399-419; *Shrewsbury Chron.* 14 Apr. 1826. [16] Clive-Powis mss 552/22/82-85 and uncat. 'A Burgess' to Rogers, 19 Nov. 1825; *Hereford Independent*, 25 Feb.; *Shrewsbury Chron.* 2, 16 June 1826. [17] Ludlow Borough LB7/1847. See LUDLOW. [18] *Salopian Jnl.* 18 Oct.; *The Times*, 19 Oct. 1826. [19] Parker, 21-33; *Hereford Jnl.* 20 Sept., 4, 11 Oct. 1826, 17 Jan. 1827, 2 Apr., 26 Oct. 1829, 10, 17 Mar., 27 Apr. 1830; Harpton Court mss C/399, 517, 596, 604-6; *CJ*, lxxxv. 211. [20] *Hereford Jnl.* 14 July 1830. [21] Ibid. 14 July; *Salopian Jnl.* 4 Aug. 1830; Clive-Powis mss 552/22/90-95; Bishop's Castle corporation minutes, p. 288. [22] NLW, Aston Hall mss C.599; *VCH Salop*, iii. 291. [23] Harpton Court mss C/597; *Shrewsbury Chron.* 13 Aug.; *Hereford Jnl.* 18 Aug. 1830. [24] Clive-Powis mss 552/22/97 and uncat. Clark to F. Allen, 25 Apr.; Bishop's Castle corporation minutes, pp. 292-3; Harpton Court mss 2163; *Hereford Jnl.* 13, 27 Apr.; *Salopian Jnl.* 4 May 1831. [25] *Salopian Jnl.* 20 July 1831. [26] Oliver, 34. [27] *Gent. Mag.* (1832), ii. 472; IGI (London, Surr.); BL OIOC J/1/12, f. 94. [28] *Gent. Mag.* (1839), i. 334; (1850), i. 225; *Hereford Co. Press and Salop Mail*, 22 Dec. 1838; *Hereford Times*, 1 Jan. 1853; W.C. Maddox 'Some Rad. Epitaphs', *Trans. Rad. Soc.* xxxv (1965), 65. [29] PROB 11/1834/431; 2171/311; IR26/1364/383; 1974/247.

M.M.E.

ROOPER, John Bonfoy (1778–1855), of Abbots Ripton Hall, Hunts.

HUNTINGDONSHIRE 1831–1837

b. 8 Aug. 1778, 1st s. of John Rooper of Berkhampstead Castle, Herts. and Abbots Ripton and Elizabeth, da. and h. of Thomas Bonfoy. *educ.* Rugby 1790; St. John's, Camb. 1797; L. Inn 1800. *m.* 15 June 1810, Harriet, da. and h. of William Pott of Gloucester Place, Portman Square, Mdx., 5s. (1 *d.v.p.*) 11 da. (at least 2 *d.v.p.*). *suc.* fa. 1826. *d.* 11 Mar. 1855.

Lt. Beachwood troop Herts. yeoman cav. 1805.

Sheriff, Cambs. and Hunts. 1845-6.

Rooper's great-grandfather John Rooper, deputy cofferer of the household to Queen Anne, obtained the lease of Berkhampstead in 1720 from the duchy of Cornwall, and his descendants renewed it several times during the eighteenth century.[1] Little is known of Rooper's early life, but some time before 1807 he travelled with one of Lord Erskine's sons to the United States, where, according to his nephew, he was fired with those 'strong liberal views which he carried throughout life'. In his own words, his 'principles were Whig ones, they were those in which he had been brought up'.[2] He was still abroad in 1807 when his father mismanaged the negotiations over the renewal of the Berkhampstead lease and was obliged to sell out. Rooper deeply resented the loss of the Hertfordshire property and, it was said, refused to speak to his father again. Abbots Ripton in Huntingdonshire, which had come to his father through his marriage to the niece and coheiress of Nicholas Bonfoy, sometime serjeant-at-arms to the House of Commons, became the family's residence.[3] By the time of his father's death in 1826 Rooper had already made a mark in Huntingdonshire politics. At the general election of 1820 he seconded Lord John Russell's nomination for the county and lamented the loss in the Lords of his bill to suspend the issue of writs to Grampound and other corrupt boroughs, which 'would not be lost in the minds of the people'. At a celebratory dinner in July he complimented the freeholders on their independence from 'political thraldom'. He denounced the Aliens Act, barrack system and the repression of free speech by military force. He was congratulated by Russell, who wished to see him elected to Parliament and predicted that 'giving utterance to such opinions as I know him to entertain ... there are not many who would distinguish themselves *more* for independence and for eloquence than he would'.[4] In March 1821 Rooper addressed the county meeting called to censure the Liverpool ministry: he condemned their conduct towards Queen Caroline as 'not only unjustifiable, but unconstitutional' and argued that parliamentary reform was 'absolutely necessary'.[5] He elaborated on this theme at the county reform meeting in March 1823, when he repudiated the argument that reform was synonymous with revolution: 'He did not wish to destroy, but to restore the constitution'.[6] He came into actual possession of the Ripton estates on the death of his mother in July 1824.[7] He was again active in Russell's support at the contested election of 1826, when he deplored the intrusion of the 'No Popery' cry and the bigotry of the 'old women' of the county. He won great applause for his comments on the corn laws, arguing that a stable market was more desirable than high prices.[8] He was one of the requisitionists of the Huntingdonshire agricultural meeting in October 1826.[9]

Rooper remained associated with the county's independents after Russell's defeat and, as Lord John was engaged elsewhere by 1830, emerged as their first choice to contest the county at the general election. He was encouraged to come forward by Lord Milton*, but he shied at the expense of a contest and refused to stand without a guarantee of financial indemnity. He told Milton:

> The more I think on the subject, the more I feel satisfied of the imprudence of my placing myself in a situation, I must, one day have incurred considerable expense to have maintained; the running into a contest would, with my family, have been little short of madness.

He could not be cajoled into standing even by a deputation of freeholders, 7 July 1830, but that day he informed Milton: 'I am to be nominated, not as a candidate, nor to be put into any expense, but if elected am pledged to serve'.[10] A subscription was opened and he was canvassed for with some degree of success as the 'farmer's friend'. He was nominated in opposition to the Montagu candidates, but although he appeared on the hustings and was by far the most popular candidate, he refused to accept the nomination. He defended his reluctance to come forward on the ground of his determination to maintain his integrity, and declared that a seat in Parliament 'might be purchased too dearly'. He welcomed the growing spirit of independence among the freeholders, adding that nothing remained for them but the election of a candidate of 'sentiments congenial with their own, or returning two Members who dared not and who would not vote as they ought'. In a reference to the July revolution in France, he condemned the conduct of Polignac's ministry and trusted that 'speedy and condign punishment would fall upon them'. He reaffirmed his Whig principles and commitment to the agricultural interest, but denied being under Milton's thumb. His supporters persisted on his behalf, but the cause was hopeless and he came bottom of the poll after a four-day contest.[11]

Rooper addressed the Huntingdon reform meeting, 2 Apr. 1831, when he represented the Grey ministry's reform bill as a compromise between extremes. He considered that the disfranchisement of nomination and corrupt boroughs was 'a pretty good sweep, but not more so than the country required', and he particularly welcomed the enfranchisement of industrial towns. He acknowledged the duke of Wellington's achievements, but said that even repeal of the Test Acts and Catholic emancipation were 'dust in the balance when weighed against his opposition to parliamentary reform, for in a reformed Parliament such evils could not for a moment have existence'.[12] Writing to Milton on the dissolution, 24 Apr., he remained as pragmatic as ever about the possibility of coming forward:

> The same motives which compelled me to resist becoming a candidate at the late election still exist; indeed are stronger, as I have an additional child to provide for. No nomination can succeed, neither is it fair merely for the purpose of putting our opponents to expense. You, I think, will enter into my feelings respecting subscriptions, agents unpaid and tradesmen injured in their business, though others will not.

He was aware of his increased popularity at Huntingdon, particularly among the tradesmen, and continued, 'I hear they mean to nominate me, at all events, for the borough, not with any view to success now but in case it should be thrown open'.[13] Nothing came of this. As a member of the county's independent committee he was a party to their initial agreement not to oppose Lord Strathavon, one of the county Members, in consequence of his support for reform. The independents, however, soon lost confidence in Strathavon, and shortly before the election they brought forward Rooper, whom they had guaranteed against expense, as an uncompromising reformer. Under normal circumstances, he told the freeholders, he would not have aspired to a seat in Parliament; but when so important a measure was brought forward by ministers and approved by the crown, it would have been improper for him to have demurred:

> The friends of the independence of the county had been so often taunted with the epithets of Jacobin and radical, that it would have been unworthy of him had he not afforded them an opportunity of evincing their loyalty ... He was not a moderate reformer; if reform was necessary let them have such a one as would effect some good.

He repudiated the assertion of Lord Mandeville, the senior county member, that reform was prejudicial to the agricultural interest, and headed the poll throughout the three-day contest. In returning thanks he pledged himself to a 'diligent attendance', and at his celebration dinner he boasted that his triumph had emancipated the county from aristocratic dictation.[14]

Rooper, who never joined Brooks's Club, voted for the second reading of the reintroduced reform bill, 6 July, and divided steadily for most of its detailed provisions, though he voted for the disfranchisement of Saltash, 26 July 1831. He is not known to have spoken in debate during this period, but he presented an anti-slavery petition, 25 June. He voted with government against charges of improper interference in the Dublin election, 23 Aug. He divided for the passage of the reform bill, 21 Sept., the second reading of the Scottish bill, 23 Sept., and Lord Ebrington's motion of confidence in the ministry, 10 Oct. He voted for the second reading of the revised reform bill, 17 Dec. 1831, and was again a reliable supporter of its details. He divided for its third reading, 22 Mar., and the second reading of the Irish measure, 25 May 1832. He was in the government majorities on the Russian-Dutch loan, 26 Jan., 12, 16, 20 July, inquiry into the number of British mercenaries serving in Portugal, 9 Feb., and rationalization of the civil administration of the navy, 6 Apr. He voted for the Irish register of deeds bill, 9 Apr., and to open coroners' inquests to the public, 20 June 1832.

Rooper represented the county until his defeat in 1837, when he retired to private life, from which he had emerged, it was generally believed, more out of deference to his friends than from any ambition of his own. According to a fulsome obituary he was 'the personification of that rare virtue political honesty', and 'there was in him no bending sycophancy, no double-faced policy, no subserviency'. He was 'thoroughly English', for 'no other land would have produced the bones and gristle of his mind'.[15] He died in March 1855, from injuries sustained after falling over the bannisters in the middle of the night.[16] In his will, dated 28 July 1854, he devised £5,000 to each of his three youngest sons, but made additional provision for his second son who held the family advowson. He had already settled £3,000 on each of his married daughters and he bequeathed the same sum to those who remained single.[17] He was succeeded in turn by his sons Bonfoy Rooper (1827-69) and the Rev. Plummer Pott Rooper (1828-81), rector of Abbots Ripton.

[1] W.H. Rooper, *Reminiscences of My Life*, 3-4; *VCH Herts.* ii. 167. [2] Rooper, 41; *Huntingdon, Bedford and Peterborough Gazette*, 7 Aug. 1830. [3] J.R. Rooper, *The Rooper Story*, 134, 144, 252-3; W.H. Rooper, 3-4. [4] *Huntingdon, Bedford and Peterborough Gazette*, 18 Mar., 5 Aug. 1820. [5] *Cambridge Chron.* 23 Mar., 6 Apr. 1821. [6] Ibid. 8 Mar. 1823. [7] *Huntingdon, Bedford and Peterborough Gazette*, 17 July 1824. [8] Ibid. 17 June 1826. [9] *Drakard's Stamford News*, 27 Oct. 1826. [10] Fitzwilliam mss, Day to Milton, 23 June, Rooper to same [3], 5 [7] July 1830. [11] *Huntingdon, Bedford and Peterborough Gazette*, 24 July, 7, 14 Aug. 1830. [12] Ibid. 8 Apr. 1831. [13] Fitzwilliam mss. [14] *Huntingdon, Bedford and Peterborough Gazette*, 7, 14 May 1831. [15] *Cambridge Chron.* 17, 24 Mar. 1855. [16] *Gent. Mag.* (1855), i. 419-20. [17] PROB 11/2211/28; IR26/2024/348.

S.R.H.

ROSE, Sir George Henry (1770–1855), of Cuffnells, nr. Lyndhurst, Hants.

SOUTHAMPTON	26 Aug. 1794–Feb. 1818
CHRISTCHURCH	6 Mar. 1818–1832
CHRISTCHURCH	1837–20 Mar. 1844

b. 3 or 5 May 1770, 1st s. of George Rose† of Cuffnells and Theodora, da. of John Duer of Fulham, Mdx. and Antigua. *educ.* Winchester 1781; L. Inn 1784; Geneva 1786-7; St. John's, Camb. 1788. *m.* 6 Jan. 1796, Frances, da. and coh. of Thomas Duncombe† of Duncombe Park, Yorks., 6s. (2 *d.v.p.*) 4da. (3 *d.v.p.*). *suc.* fa. 1818; GCH 1819. *d.* 17 June 1855.

Sec. of legation and chargé d'affaires, Berlin 1793-4; dep. paymaster-gen. 1804-6; spec. mission to USA 1807-8; minister plenip. to Bavaria 1814-15, to Prussia 1815-23; clerk of the Parliaments 1818-44; PC 6 Apr. 1818.

Capt. Christchurch vols. 1795, maj. commdt. 1798, lt.-col. commdt. 1806; lt.-col. commdt. S. Hants vols. 1803.

Metropolitan commr. of lunacy 1829.

The manner in which Rose's father, Pitt's chief treasury secretary, had obtained places for his two sons was, according to an 1820 radical commentary, 'one of the most impudent and selfish jobs recorded'.[1] Under this umbrella of patronage Rose, who had succeeded his father as Member for Christchurch (and its patron) in 1818, continued to pursue a lucrative, if undistinguished, diplomatic career. In 1822 his posting to the Berlin court commanded a salary of £7,500, while his sinecure office of clerk of the Parliaments brought him an additional £4,632. The crown emoluments thus enumerated were far in excess of those received by any other Member of the House, in which his attendance while a serving diplomat was inevitably very sporadic.[2] His political mentor was the foreign secretary Lord Castlereagh*, with whom he communicated in a private as well as an official capacity. In October 1819 his correspondence echoed alarmist sentiment at home in its portrayal of events in Germany, 'which had no less an object than the subversion of the whole of the existing government', and in its defence of press restrictions.[3]

It fell to Rose to give the news of the death of George III to the duke of Cumberland, who characterized their relations as 'most cordial and confidential'.[4] On 7 Feb. 1820 Rose requested leave of absence from Berlin to deal with matters arising from the death of his father and enable him to be resworn as clerk of the Parliaments, 'both to secure the post and to collect the emoluments of this session'. He had hoped to 'stand in person at Christchurch' at the general election, but in the event was absent from his unopposed return as his leave did not commence until 25 Apr.[5] He was present to vote with the Liverpool ministry against a motion for economies in revenue collection, 4 July, but was back in post by 5 Aug. He was evidently vexed by the failure of George IV's divorce bill in November 1820, when Cumberland assured his brother of Rose's unswerving loyalty.[6] In January 1821 he was troubled by 'lumbago in an extraordinary degree', but assured Castlereagh of his fitness for work.[7] He apparently visited England that July to attend a coronation dinner in his constituency, and he travelled to Hanover in October 1821 to be presented to George IV, reportedly at the latter's insistence.[8] It had long been rumoured that Rose wished to retire, a matter pointedly alluded to by Canning after his appointment as foreign secretary, 20 Sept. 1822. He offered no hope of the ambassadorship coveted by Rose, then on leave in England, who declared that he had no intention of surrendering his existing appointment.[9] According to Lady Holland, 25 Sept., this was already earmarked for Lord Clanwilliam, Castlereagh's nephew, who duly succeeded when Rose finally took the hint and resigned in December 1822. In the meantime, he had denounced Canning to Sir Charles Bagot, the ambassador at St. Petersburg, as 'utterly unprincipled', though he acknowledged his administrative talents.[10] Resettled in Hampshire, he pestered Peel, the home secretary, and the duke of Wellington with plans for the reorganization of his militia troop, and irritated the latter by hectoring him for approval of appointments.[11] Evidently a keen country sportsman, in 1830 a newspaper highlighted his fame as a dead shot by relating how he had killed a bird at a distance of 298 yards.[12]

Free to attend the House more regularly, Rose was in the ministerial minority against inquiry into the prosecution of the Dublin Orange rioters, 22 Apr., and their majorities against reform of the Scottish representation, 2 June, and inquiry into the currency, 12 June 1823. Before the last he visited his constituency, where he was greeted with 'a merry peal from the church bells'.[13] He voted against the Whigs' Scottish juries bill, 20 June. As a West India proprietor by inheritance, he testified to the moral improvement of the slave population that had resulted from the advance of Christianity and recommended that religious instruction should be made mandatory, lauding the efforts of missionaries from the Wesleyan and Moravian churches, 15 May 1823. That July he published *A Letter on the Means and Importance of Converting the Slaves in the West Indies to Christianity*, calling for similar Evangelical spirit to be shown by the resident clergy of the established church. In the

House, 16 Mar. 1824, he asserted that 'the cure for West Indian evils' lay in moral rather than legislative measures and stressed the need to replace 'concubinage' with marriage. He gave a silent vote against inquiry into the prosecution of the Methodist missionary John Smith for inciting riot among the slaves of Demerara, 11 June, but spoke again in glowing terms of Nonconformist missionaries, 15 June. As a Hampshire magistrate, he thought Lord Althorp's bill to reform the county courts 'most laudable', 26 Mar. 1824. Later he privately favoured Peel with his thoughts on the criminal code, which he admitted to be 'too bloody', but advised against its mitigation 'until we have some more efficient substitute for death than transportation'.[14] In the reorganization of the parliament office which took place in 1824, he was persuaded to relinquish his right to make all future appointments bar one, though he continued to draw a salary of £3,300.[15] He defended his late father from a charge of vote manufacturing in Southampton levelled by Monck, 12 May 1825. He voted against Catholic relief, 1 Mar., 21 Apr., 10 May, and the disfranchisement of the Irish 40*s.* freeholders, 26 Apr., 9 May. From personal acquaintance he defended the character of Cumberland, 30 May, and he was in the majorities for his civil list provision that day, 6, 10 June 1825. No trace of parliamentary activity has been found for 1826.

At that year's general election he was returned unopposed for Christchurch with his eldest son.[16] He voted against Catholic relief, 6 Mar. 1827, 12 May, and repeal of the Test Acts, 26 Feb. 1828. He congratulated Peel on his accession as leader of the Commons, 22 Jan. 1828, and in February presented him with a plan for the reform of consular services, which he claimed had been approved by Canning.[17] On 14 Apr. he chaired a meeting at Romsey, Hampshire, for replacing boy chimney sweeps with machinery.[18] He divided against inquiry into chancery delays, 24 Apr., and ordnance reductions, 4 July 1828. He had declined the offer of a baronetcy from the premier Lord Goderich in November 1827, and had been poised to advance a claim to be made a knight of the Bath when the administration fell.[19] On 13 June 1828 he renewed his application to Wellington, the premier, and took great umbrage at its brusque rejection. Writing to Peel, 12 Jan. 1829, he complained that while the Whig diplomat Robert Adair[†] had been made a privy councillor, he, who had 'for more than thirty-four years ... supported the Pittite administrations in Parliament by every means in his power', had long waited in vain for recognition of his services, and hinted that his future support in the Commons could not be counted on.[20] Wellington, pleading the volume of claims, remained unmoved, and while Rose thanked Peel for his efforts to mediate, 30 Jan., he plainly regarded his treatment as an insult.[21] He warned that the ministry's concession of Catholic emancipation would 'compromise the Protestant establishment in church and state', 13 Feb., and was listed by Planta, the patronage secretary, as being 'opposed' to the measure. He presented hostile petitions, 9 Mar., and voted against it at every opportunity, 6, 18, 23, 27, 30 Mar. On the 27th he voiced concerns about the proselytizing tendencies of the Catholic church and forecast that its communicants would form a disciplined parliamentary squad in the House. Desirous of ensuring Rose's future adherence, Goulburn, the chancellor of the exchequer, vainly revived his claim to the order of the Bath, 15 Oct. 1829, and reported him to be still further aggrieved by honours conferred upon other diplomats.[22] Rose voted against Jewish emancipation, 17 May, and commented that the recently abolished requirement of British soldiers to attend Catholic services abroad had been indefensible, 17 June 1830. He was in minorities for amendments to the sale of beer bill to restrict on-consumption, 21 June, 1 July 1830.

At the 1830 general election Rose was returned unopposed.[23] He presented a petition for the abolition of slavery, 3 Nov. 1830. Ministers listed him as one of the 'moderate Ultras', but he was in their minority in the crucial division on the civil list, 15 Nov. 1830. He voted against the second reading of the Grey ministry's reform bill, 22 Mar., and for Gascoyne's wrecking amendment, 19 Apr. 1831. He was returned again without opposition at the ensuing general election, and voted against the second reading of the reintroduced reform bill, 6 July, and the partial disfranchisement of Chippenham, 27 July. He defended the conduct of the Member William Bingham Baring, a colleague on the Hampshire bench, accused of using unnecessary force in the apprehension of two 'Swing' riot suspects of respectable status, 21 July, and looked forward to his triumphant vindication, 19 Sept. He recommended that the foreign office should regulate the consular fees charged to merchants, 25 July. On 16 Aug. he argued that a separate legislature for Ireland would inevitably lead to secession, and he voted to censure the Irish government for use of undue influence at the Dublin election, 23 Aug. As the mover of a private divorce bill, he agreed that the limited availability of this option was unjust, 17 Aug. On 19 Aug. he emphasized the need for legally trained, properly remunerated returning officers at future elections. He voted against the third reading of the reform bill, 19 Sept., its passage, 21 Sept., and the second reading of the Scottish bill, 23 Sept. Rose divided against the second reading of the revised reform bill, 17 Dec. 1831, and made a procedural intervention during discussion of the registration clauses, 8 Feb. 1832. He voted against the enfranchisement of Tower Hamlets, 28 Feb., and the bill's third reading, 22 Mar., when he warned of the detrimental effect of popular government on a decisive foreign policy and, in a reference to the current cholera epidemic, likened the clamour for reform to a 'moral pestilence'. The speech was privately published and a copy presented to John Wilson Croker*. He voted against the second reading of the Irish reform bill, 25 May. On 24 Jan. he called for British protection to be extended to the Vaudois, a proto-Protestant religious sect allegedly suffering persecution in France. He voted against ministers on the Russian-Dutch loan, 26 Jan., 12 July. He divided against the Irish education grant, 23 July, and was in the minority of eight against the grant to the Catholic seminary at Maynooth, in protest, he explained, at the withdrawal of financial backing from the Protestant Kildare Place Society, 27 July 1832.

At the 1832 dissolution Rose retired from Christchurch. He was re-elected there as a Conservative after a contest in 1837 and resigned his seat and clerkship in 1844.[24] In 1831 he edited *A Selection from the Papers of the Earl of Marchmont*, and contributed a preface, which was in part an apologia for the Act of Union. 'I have great suspicion of anything published by so intolerable a bore as Sir George Rose', noted the Whig George Agar Ellis* to Lady Holland.[25] *Scripture Researches* (1832) was the first of his several works on the Old Testament and the fate of the lost tribes of Israel, which included *The Spread of Circumcision* (1846), an inquiry into Egyptian circumcision, and *The Afghans, the Ten Tribes and the Kings of the East* (1852). In *The Churches of Luther, Calvin and England*, one of three religious tracts published in 1854, he sought biblical justification for the Reformation and likened Roman Catholics to worshippers of the golden calf of Babylon. Rose died in June 1855 at Sandhills, Mudeford, near Christchurch, which, along with Cuffnells, his principal residence, was sold. By his will, dated 13 Dec. 1851, he left £7,000 to religious and charitable institutions, including sizeable bequests to Protestant missions in Ireland, and made provision for his wife and the widow and child of his recently deceased eldest son.[26] His surviving sons included Hugh Henry Rose (1801-85), who pursued a distinguished military and diplomatic career and was ennobled as Baron Strathnairn in 1866, and William Rose (1808-85), who was knighted in 1867 and succeeded to his father's old office of clerk of the Parliaments in 1875.

[1] *Black Bk.* (1820), 73-74. [2] *PP* (1822), iv. 48-49. [3] Add. 42795, f. 152. [4] *Geo. IV Letters*, ii. 791, 798. [5] Add. 42795, ff. 183-7; *Salisbury Jnl.* 13 Mar. 1820. [6] *Geo. IV Letters*, ii. 882. [7] Add. 42795, f. 206. [8] *Salisbury Jnl.* 23 July 1821; Add. 42793, f. 142. [9] Add. 42794, f. 104; NLS mss 3797, ff. 155, 157. [10] *Lady Holland to Son*, 13; Bagot, *Canning and Friends*, ii. 140-1. [11] Add. 40358, f. 131; Wellington mss WP1/827/7; 832/2. [12] *Salisbury Jnl.* 11 Jan. 1830. [13] Ibid. 9 June 1823. [14] Add. 40382, f. 249. [15] Sir J. Sainty, *Parl. Office in 19th and 20th Cents.* 5; *Colchester Diary*, iii. 320-1; J. Wade, *Extraordinary Black Bk.* (1831), 478. [16] *Salisbury Jnl.* 12 June 1826. [17] Add. 40395, ff. 77, 289; 40396, f. 50. [18] *Salisbury Jnl.* 14 Apr. 1828. [19] *Geo. IV Letters*, iii. 1430; NLS mss 3797, f. 188. [20] Wellington mss WP1/936/25; 972/18; 975/13; Add. 40398, ff. 67, 99. [21] Add. 40308, f. 150; 40398, f. 107. [22] Wellington mss WP1/1051/10. [23] *Portsmouth Herald*, 30 July 1830. [24] *Gent. Mag.* (1855), ii. 198. [25] Add. 51590, Agar Ellis to Lady Holland, 27 Feb. 1831. [26] *Gent. Mag.* (1855), ii. 198-9; *White's Hants Dir.* (1859), 374; (1878), 334; PROB 11/2216/638; IR26/2043/773.

H.J.S./P.J.S.

ROSE, George Pitt (1797–1851), of Upper Kensington Grove, Mdx.

CHRISTCHURCH 1826–1832

b. 9 Jan. 1797, 1st s. of George Henry Rose* (*d.* 1855) and Frances, da. and coh. of Thomas Duncombe† of Duncombe Park, Yorks. *educ.* St. John's, Camb. 1815. *m.* 30 Apr. 1828, Phoebe Susannah, da. of Maj.-Gen. John Agmondesham Vesey, 1s. *d.v.p.* 19 Sept. 1851.

Cornet 15 Drag. 1822, lt. 1824, capt. 1826; capt. (half-pay) 9 Drag. 1837; out of service 1848.

Cornet S. Hants yeoman cav. 1815, lt. 1817, capt. 1820.

Rose was named after his godfather William Pitt†, under whom his grandfather George Rose† had served as a loyal lieutenant and prospered as a place hunter for himself and his family.[1] On the latter's death in 1818 Rose's father declined to return him for the resulting vacancy at Christchurch, the family's pocket borough, as he was 'young for his age' and he 'wished to keep him under his eye at Berlin', where he held a diplomatic post.[2] In October 1821 he was presented to George IV by the foreign secretary Lord Londonderry* on the king's visit to Hanover.[3] Next year he embarked on an army career, which appears to have been free of active engagement. At Hampton Court in 1828 he married the orphan daughter of a major-general and former aide-de-camp to the duke of Kent.[4]

At the 1826 general election Rose was returned unopposed for Christchurch with his father, whose Tory line he followed in the House.[5] He is not known to have delivered a full speech. He voted against Catholic relief, 6 Mar. 1827, 12 May 1828, and repeal of the Test Acts, 26 Feb. 1828. He divided with the Wellington ministry against ordnance reductions, 4 July. He was listed by Planta, the patronage secretary, as 'opposed to the principle' of Catholic emancipation in February

1829. Like his father, he voted steadily against it, 6, 18, 23, 27, 30 Mar., but, as Planta had also anticipated, he did not vote against the disfranchisement of Irish 40*s*. freeholders, 19 Mar. 1829. He divided against Lord Blandford's parliamentary reform motion, 11 Feb., the enfranchisement of Birmingham, Leeds and Manchester, 23 Feb., and Jewish emancipation, 17 May 1830. On 14 May he presented a petition for the building of a direct road from Waterloo Bridge to the British Museum. He was in minorities with his father for amendments to the sale of beer bill to prohibit on-consumption, 21 June, 1 July 1830. At the 1830 general election Rose was again returned unopposed for Christchurch. He was listed as one of the 'moderate Ultras' by ministers and was absent from the division on the civil list, 15 Nov. 1830. He voted against the second reading of the Grey ministry's reform bill, 22 Mar., and for Gascoyne's wrecking amendment, 19 Apr. 1831. After another unchallenged return at the ensuing general election, he voted against the second reading of the reintroduced reform bill, 6 July, and the partial disfranchisement of Chippenham, 27 July. He paired for a censure motion on the Irish government for using undue influence at the Dublin election, 23 Aug., and voted against the passage of the reform bill, 21 Sept., and the second reading of the Scottish bill, 23 Sept. He divided against the second reading of the revised reform bill, 17 Dec. 1831, the enfranchisement of Tower Hamlets, 28 Feb., and the third reading, 22 Mar. 1832. On 25 May he paired against the second reading of the Irish reform bill. He voted against ministers on the Russian-Dutch loan, 26 Jan. (as a pair), 12 July 1832.

At the 1832 dissolution Rose retired from Christchurch, which had been partially disfranchised. He apparently bided his time until the general election of 1841, when he was narrowly defeated as a Conservative at nearby Poole. On 25 Aug. he informed Peel, the new premier, of his impending petition against the return and requested a household appointment for himself or his wife, noting that his family had 'for three generations steadily and invariably supported Conservative governments' and that though the expense of his defeat had been 'great', the 'salary is not a consideration, but an employment in or near London is one'.[6] Explaining that he had been forced to abandon his petition on the advice of Lord Lyndhurst, 2 Sept., he outlined his qualifications to serve Prince Albert, observing that 'having served all my life in the light cavalry and acquired in Prussia a proficiency in German, I might ... be enabled to make the prince acquainted with our cavalry system'.[7] Subsequently he obtained an interview to explain 'some circumstances which it would be difficult to do in writing', but Peel could do nothing for him.[8] Undaunted, he submitted a dubious plan for an efficient reorganization of the cavalry, based on the establishment of regimental settlements on waste crown lands. By this means, he enthusiastically added, 'Protestant colonies might be founded in Ireland'. This was met with a polite rebuff, as was his request for assistance to obtain a grace and favour apartment at Hampton Court early the following year.[9]

Rose died *v.p.* and intestate at Winchester in September 1851.[10] His wife and son were allowed provision from a trust fund of some £22,000 in his father's will drawn up later that year and proved on 9 July 1855, in addition to an annuity settled on his wife in 1833.[11] Rose's only son George Ernest Rose, who followed him into the army, saw active service in the Crimea and acted as an aide-de-camp to his uncle General Hugh Rose during the Indian mutiny. He died at Calcutta, 'aged 27', in 1865.[12]

[1] *Salisbury Jnl.* 5 June 1826. [2] Hants RO, Malmesbury mss, Malmesbury to Fitzharris, 21 Feb. 1818. [3] Add. 42793, f. 142. [4] *Gent. Mag.* (1812), i. 189; (1828), ii. 465; Add. 40486, f. 190. [5] *Salisbury Jnl.* 12 June 1826. [6] Add. 40486, f. 190. [7] Add. 40487, ff. 130-3. [8] Add. 40488, ff. 250-2. [9] Add. 40492, ff. 47-52; 40499, ff. 209-11 [10] *Gent. Mag.* (1851), ii. 55. [11] PROB 11/2216/638; IR26/2043/773. [12] *Gent. Mag.* (1865), i. 661-2.

H.J.S./P.J.S.

ROSS, Charles (1799–1860), of 60 Portland Place, Mdx.

ORFORD 1 Oct. 1822–1826
ST. GERMANS 1826–1832
NORTHAMPTON 1832–1837

b. 6 July 1799,[1] o. s. of Maj.-Gen. Alexander Ross of Savile Row, Mdx. and Castlemilk, Dumfries and Barbara Evelyn Isabella, da. of Sir Robert Gunning, 1st bt., of Horton, Northants. *educ.* at home by Rev. Andrew Irvine;[2] Christ Church, Oxf. 1818. *m.* 7 Apr. 1825, Lady Mary Cornwallis, da. of Charles Cornwallis†, 2nd Mq. Cornwallis, 2s. (1 *d.v.p.*) 2da. *suc.* fa. 1827. *d.* 21 Mar. 1860.

Ld. of admiralty July-Nov. 1830, of treasury Dec. 1834-Apr. 1835; commr. of excise 1845-9, of audit 1849-*d.*

Commr. of lunacy 1828-35.

Ross's father, a youngest son, was born in Aberdeenshire in 1742 and entered the army in 1760. He served with distinction in America as aide-de-camp to the 2nd Earl Cornwallis, whose intimate friend he became. He was Cornwallis's secretary during his period as governor-general of Bengal from 1786 to 1793. On his return home in 1794 he was belatedly made an aide-de-camp to the king after Cornwallis had expressed displeasure at his omission from the original list. He accompanied the 2nd Earl Spencer, with whom he formed a close friendship, on their special mission to Vienna in August 1794: he 'went very unwillingly', as Cornwallis noted, 'as it was exceedingly inconvenient for his private affairs'. Cornwallis joined Pitt's ministry as master-general of the ordnance in January 1795 and six months later, to meet his need for 'a capable friend in one of the efficient offices', secured Ross's appointment as surveyor-general. Ross obtained the colonelcy of the 89th regiment, the 'least lucrative corps' in the army, in 1797. He landed the more rewarding command of the 59th in March 1801, when Cornwallis overcame his wish to resign from the ordnance with him and persuaded him to stay on under Lord Chatham.[3] He remained in the office until November 1804, when he was appointed governor of Fort George, Inverness. Cornwallis died in India a year later. Ross bought a Scottish estate in 1794, but had disposed of it by the time of his death, worth £20,000, in 1827, when he was the owner of a London house in Portland Place.[4]

Charles Ross, an only child, was barely of age when, in the autumn of 1820, his father sought Spencer's 'countenance' for his candidature for St. Albans, where a vacancy was expected, provided no one of Spencer's Whig opposition politics started. Spencer would not oblige, but when the opening occurred in December General Ross secured the neutrality of his son Lord Althorp*, in acknowledgement of having 'received so much kindness from him ever since I was a child'. Charles Ross's claim to be a local man was based on his father's residence for 'several years', presumably as a tenant, at the Garrard property of Lamer Park, five miles north-east of St. Albans. (Earlier in the century he had been in occupation of Russell Farm, on the Watford side of the borough.) Ross, who was seen as the 'Court' candidate, finished 20 votes behind Wright Wilson, another ministerialist, and 21 ahead of John Easthope*, an opposition man. When the latter threatened to petition, with every hope of voiding the election, Althorp, though unwilling in that event to support Easthope against Ross, half-heartedly tried to persuade the general to withdraw Charles and let him take his chance at the next general election.[5] In the event, no petition was forthcoming, presumably because the Rosses refused to leave the way clear for Easthope. In October 1822 Charles Ross was returned by the 3rd marquess of Hertford to fill the vacancy at Orford created by Lord Londonderry's suicide.

He proved to be a thoroughly reliable supporter of the Liverpool ministry, with whom he voted against parliamentary reform, 20 Feb., 2 June; on the sinking fund, 3, 13 Mar., and the assessed taxes, 10, 18 Mar.; and against repeal of the Foreign Enlistment Act, 16 Apr., and inquiries into the legal proceedings against the Dublin Orange rioters, 22 Apr., and the currency, 12 June 1823. At the end of the debate on chancery delays, 5 June, he moved an amendment to get rid of the subject, but was persuaded to withdraw it. He voted against inquiry the following day. He was in the majority against Onslow's usury laws repeal bill, 27 June 1823, but voted for his reintroduced measures, 27 Feb. 1824, 8 Feb. 1825. He divided against the production of information on Catholic office-holders, 19 Feb., and reform of Edinburgh's representative system, 26 Feb. (and again, 13 Apr. 1826), and the abolition of corporal punishment in the army, 5 Mar. 1824. He had been named to the select committee on the game laws, 13 Mar. 1823, and on 11 Mar. 1824 he 'warmly' supported Stuart Wortley's amendment bill which, far from diminishing 'the legitimate influence possessed by the country gentlemen over the lower classes', would increase it by removing 'one of the main sources of irritation'. He was named to several other select committees in this Parliament. He divided with ministers on the case of the Methodist missionary John Smith, 11 June, and for the Irish insurrection bill, 14 June 1824, and the Irish unlawful societies bill, 25 Feb. 1825. He divided against Catholic relief, 1 Mar., 21 Apr., 10 May, and the Irish franchise bill, 26 Apr., 9 May. He was in the government majorities for the duke of Cumberland's annuity, 6, 10 June. He was one of the minority against the spring guns bill, 21 June 1825. He voted with ministers on the Jamaican slave trials, 2 Mar., and the salary of the president of the board of trade, 10 Apr. On 26 Apr. he spoke at some length against Lord John Russell's reform scheme, a 'sweeping plan of alteration' which was 'fraught with fallacy, and replete with danger'; and he voted against Russell's resolutions on electoral bribery, 26 May 1826.

At the general election of 1826 Ross transferred to the pocket borough of the 2nd earl of St. Germans, whose eldest son was married to the sister of his wife, Cornwallis's granddaughter.[6] The following year he inherited a moderate fortune and the Portland Place house from his father.[7] He was appointed to the select committee on the electoral activities of Northampton corporation, 21 Feb. 1827. On 11 Apr. he presented the petition of some inhabitants alleging that their names had been added under false pretences to the original petition of complaint, but he did not fulfil his threat to move for inquiry.[8] He voted against Catholic relief, 6 Mar., and was a teller for the minority against the spring guns bill, 23 Mar. He advised Whitmore to drop his motion for inquiry into Indian trade, 15 May, and leave the matter in the hands of the Canning ministry. An opponent of the transfer of East Retford's seats to Birmingham, he saw no reason to depart from the traditional methods of purifying corrupt boroughs, 11 June; but he acquiesced in the second reading of the disfranchisement bill, 22 June, 'since all the proper amendments might be made in the committee'. He had by this time ingratiated himself with the Tory Commons leader Peel, to whom he wrote from Tunbridge Wells in August 1827 with news of the problems besetting the new premier Lord Goderich, whose conduct 'seems very singular and very weak'. Thomas Macaulay* scorned Ross as 'an ass' and was at a loss to know 'what Peel saw in him'; but by 1828, when Peel was restored to the home office under the duke of Wellington, they were on terms of mutual cordiality.[9]

Ross was one of the 'supporters' of the ministry considered for appointment to the finance committee, 10 Feb. 1828.[10] He voted against repeal of the Test Acts, 26 Feb., and Catholic relief, 12 May, and in the majorities on chancery delays, 24 Apr., and the ordnance estimates, 4 July 1828. He was forced to withdraw his motion for a return of the number of freemen recently created in several boroughs, 27 Feb., and his bid to introduce a bill to regulate such admissions with the object of reducing election expenses, 20 Mar., was thwarted. He cavilled at details of the Penryn disfranchisement bill, 24 Mar., and attacked Davies's 'very objectionable' borough polls bill and unsuccessfully divided the House against it, 15 May. He condemned Baring's bill to reform the Marylebone vestry, against which 'not a shadow of anything corrupt or illegal' had been proved, and was a teller for the hostile minority, 6 June. He was a stern critic of Otway Cave's bill to regulate the use of corporation funds, 10 June, 1, 8, 10 July, when he called it 'as unjust in its operation, as it was unconstitutional in principle'; he was a teller for the minority against its third reading that day. He was twice a teller for the anti-reform majorities in procedural divisions on the East Retford bill, 27 June 1828. In February 1829 Planta, the patronage secretary, predicted that he would side 'with government' for Catholic emancipation; but he evidently made himself scarce during the potentially embarrassing debates and divisions on it, though on 22 May he urged Members to agree to the current Maynooth grant, leaving it open to ministers to limit it as necessary in future. He raised practical difficulties in response to Hume's call for a return of Irish freemen, 7 Apr., and presented a Marylebone vestry petition against the metropolitan roads bill, 1 May. He was a teller for the majority for the West India Dock Company bill, 14 Apr. Named to the committee on select vestries, 28 Apr., he was a teller for the majority which threw out the St. James's, Westminster vestry bill, 21 May. He acted likewise for the majority against a proposed addition to the ecclesiastical courts bill, 5 June 1829.

Early in 1830, Mrs. Arbuthnot was unimpressed when Peel tried to persuade Wellington to appoint Ross a lord of the treasury:

> I rather hope he won't, for Mr. Ross, though to a certain degree clever, is a ridiculous man and I think the appointment would be laughed at. Mr. Peel only wishes it because he is a flatterer of his.[11]

The Whig Edward Ellice* commented that Ross, 'a decided Tory', had 'no one qualification that can be of the least use to his employers'.[12] Nothing came of this, nor of a report that he was to be made a lord of the admiralty, which, so Greville reckoned, occasioned 'much disgust'.[13] He was a teller for majorities against the transfer of East Retford's seats to Birmingham, 11 Feb., 5 Mar. 1830. He voted against Lord Blandford's reform scheme, 18 Feb., and the enfranchisement of Birmingham, Leeds and Manchester, 23 Feb. He did not see how Blandford's request for a return of Irish borough voters could be furnished, 18 Mar. He was a teller in six divisions for majorities for amendments to the St. Giles's vestry bill, 1, 2 Apr. When he obstructed Hobhouse's vestry reform bill the following month, Hobhouse complained to the minister Sir Henry Hardinge*, who 'called him an ass or some such name', but failed to talk him round.[14] He voted against Jewish emancipation, 5 Apr., 17 May. He presented the petition of Marylebone vestry against the Irish and Scottish poor removal bill, 18 May, and defended the administration of Millbank penitentiary, 21 May. He had been named to the select committees on the metropolitan police, 28 Feb. 1828, 15 Apr. 1829; and on 15 June 1830 he denounced vestry interference in police affairs. He voted with Peel against the Galway franchise bill, 25 May, and was in the government majority for the grant for South American missions, 7 June, when he also voted against abolition of the death penalty for forgery. On the dissolution in July 1830 he was appointed a lord of the admiralty. After his safe return for St. Germans he wrote to a friend from his office, where he was 'learning my business':

> Public affairs do not look brilliant. Though the elections on the whole have turned out well for government, we shall have plenty to do next session, France of itself affording ample cause for deep consideration.

He was reported to have been 'in his glory as chairman' of a Northampton Tory dinner in October 1830.[15]

Whether Ross had acted as an assistant whip before his appointment is not clear, but after the election he 'very kindly and efficiently assisted' Planta in producing their notably misleading analysis of the new House.[16] Curiously, he was an absentee from the division on the civil list which brought down the ministry, 15 Nov. 1830. He answered Hume's criticisms of the Marylebone vestry, 22 Nov., asked Hobhouse to postpone the second reading of his vestries bill, 14 Feb., and presented a hostile Marylebone petition, 17 Mar. 1831. He was disparagingly referred to by Greville in December 1830 as one of 'the refuse of society and of the House of Commons' who were the 'confidants, friends and parasites' of Peel. He was Peel's guest at Drayton the following month and was one of the 'Charles Street gang' of former ministers and party hacks who, in default of Peel's active involvement, sought to organize the Tory opposition to the Grey ministry and its reform bills. Though supposedly one of 'Peel's *âmes damnées*' and 'his devoted adherent', he apparently confided to Greville in March 1831 his view of Peel's 'deficiency in all the qualities requisite for a leader', but he did so 'with all kinds of regrets and endeavours to soften the picture'.[17] With his friends, he rejoiced in ministerial discomfiture on the civil list, 5 Feb.[18] He had backed Lord Chandos's bid to have the Evesham writ suspended, 16 Dec. 1830, and on 18 Feb. 1831 he supported his proposal to transfer its seats to Birmingham, though he remained hostile to 'a general measure of reform'. He felt privately that the opponents of reform had been 'thrown aback' by the audacity of the ministerial bill and, according to Lord Ellenborough, he remained 'low' in spirits for several days after its unveiling.[19] He voted against its second reading, 22 Mar., having been 'very confident' of defeating it, and for Gascoyne's wrecking amendment, 19 Apr., for which he had 'expected a majority of 16 or 17', instead of the actual eight. Next day he was reported to be 'in high spirits', believing that 'if the ministers did not go out, the bill was lost'.[20]

His hopes were dashed by the dissolution, but he retained his own seat. On 29 June 1831 he denied Hume's allegations that an opposition agent had infiltrated the *Republican* newspaper. He voted against the second reading of the revised reform bill, 6 July. He opposed the issue of the Liverpool writ, 8 July, 5 Sept., and demanded inquiry into the use of barracks to house supporters of the ministerial candidate at the Northampton election, 11 July. Two days later Ellenborough asked Ross, who he had recently discovered to 'have more *nous* than I supposed', to persuade Peel to be more accommodating towards Tory backbenchers. Ross spoke to Peel, but to little effect, and in turn complained to Ellenborough of 'bad attendance'.[21] He voted for use of the 1831 census for the disfranchisement schedules, 19 July, and against the partial disfranchisement of Chippenham, 27 July. He was an opposition teller for the divisions on the cases of Guildford, 29 July, and Sudbury, 2 Aug. On 22 July he argued for Minehead and Plympton being allowed to retain one Member and complained of 'the inconsistent and arbitrary manner' in which ministers had applied the disfranchisement criteria. He vainly pleaded for a reprieve for his own constituency, 26 July. He failed to persuade ministers to amend the measure in order to permit electors whose qualification was disputed to tender votes, 5 Sept. He voted against the passage of the bill, 21 Sept. According to Edward Littleton*, he was 'indefatigable' in his attempts to muster Tory members of the committee of privileges on the William Long Wellesley* affair, in an unsuccessful bid to overturn lord chancellor Brougham's ruling.[22] He presented petitions for the protection of Irish clerical income from tithes and against the vestries bill, 23 Aug., when he voted against government on the Dublin election controversy. He was a teller for the majority against a Lords' amendment to the lunatics bill, 26 Sept., and the minority against the issue of the Liverpool writ, 12 Oct. 1831.

Ross acted likewise for the minority against the second reading of the revised reform bill, 17 Dec. 1831, and voted against going into committee, 20 Jan., and the third reading, 22 Mar. 1832. He suggested alterations to some of its details, 11, 15 Feb. He was in the majority against the vestry bill, 23 Jan. He voted against government on the Russian-Dutch loan, 26 Jan., 12 July, the malt drawback bill, 2 Apr. and the glove trade, 3 Apr. His bill to regulate Scottish landlords' right of hypothec, introduced on 11 Feb., was thrown out on its second reading, 1 June. During the crisis of May, Ellenborough noted that Ross, who professed to believe to the very last that the Conservatives would be able to form a ministry to carry a moderate reform bill, 'would like to be secretary of the treasury in Planta's place, and he would do very well in it'. A moving spirit and original committee member of the Carlton Club, he was one of the seven men deputed by opposition to 'obtain information as to all the new boroughs' in England in preparation for the next general election.[23] He voted against the second reading of the Irish reform bill, 25 May. On the boundary bill, 7 June, he objected to the proposed division of Surrey; and the next day he questioned the need for so many polling places in Bedfordshire and criticized the union of Hythe with Folkestone. His attempt to embarrass ministers by moving a new writ for Aylesbury in anticipation of Lord Nugent's appointment as commissioner of the Ionian Isles was foiled, 24 July, and he was dressed down by Nugent himself the following day. He was in the minority of 20 against the crown colonies relief bill, 3 Aug., and obtained a return of Commons Speakers and their emoluments since 1688, 6 Aug. He was a teller for the majority against Evans's motion for a bill to remedy supposed problems created by the regulations governing the payment of rates as a prerequisite of electoral registration, 7 Aug. He objected to all the Lords' amendments to the lunatics bill, 9 Aug., was named to the committee appointed to consider the matter and reported its recommendation of a conference with the Lords, 10 Aug. 1832.

At the general election of 1832 Ross successfully contested Northampton, on the strength of his mother's family's property.[24] He continued his activities as an assistant opposition whip and, at Peel's pressing request, became a lord of the treasury in his first ministry.[25] Evidently his 'unfortunate' and 'objectionable manner' was a source of irritation to some backbenchers, but Lord Granville Somerset* thought his 'indefatigable activity' more than made up for it.[26] Ross, dismissed by John Stuart Mill as one of 'the hack official jobbing adventurer Tories', lost his seat at the 1837 general election.[27] He was in the field at Tiverton in 1841, but did not risk a poll, and spent the last 15 years of his life as a civil servant.[28] His elder son Captain Charles Cornwallis Ross was killed at Sebastopol, aged 28, in 1855. (He was the fourth of the great-grandsons of Cornwallis to perish in the Crimea in the space of ten months.)[29] In 1859 Ross published an edition of Cornwallis's *Correspondence*, which Macaulay told him to his face was 'full of interest', but privately considered to contain 'frightful blunders'.[30] Ross died in March 1860. He left his wife his London house and £1,500, in addition to an annuity of £3,000 secured by their marriage settlement. He bequeathed £70,000 to provide for his three surviving children. His son Alexander Ross (1829-88), a barrister, was Conservative Member for Maidstone from 1880 until his death.

[1] *Cornwallis Corresp.* ed. C. Ross, iii. 115. [2] Add. 38296, f. 139. [3] *Oxford DNB*; *Cornwallis Corresp.* i. 76, 80, 91, 142, 151; ii. 232, 235, 256, 273, 279, 284-6, 288, 292, 297; iii. 351, 536; *Windham Diary*, 63; *Burke Corresp.* v. 297, 301; *Geo. III Corresp.* ii. 1019, 1597, 1675; iii. 2376. [4] PROB 8/220 (22 Dec. 1827); 11/1734/719. [5] Add. 76124, Gen. Ross to Spencer, 30 Sept., 13 Dec., replies, 1 Oct., 12 Dec., Howarth to Spencer, 11 Dec., reply, 12 Dec., Duncannon to Spencer [11, 13 Dec.]; 75940, Althorp to Spencer, 25 Nov., 8 Dec. 1820; 76378, Althorp to Gen. Ross, 24 Jan. 1821; *Cornwallis Corresp.* iii. 514; *The Times*, 13, 19 Dec. 1820, 16, 18 Jan. 1821. [6] Add. 76134, Ross to Spencer, 10 Oct. 1825. [7] PROB 11/1734/719. [8] *The Times*, 12 Apr. 1827. [9] Add. 40394, f. 202; 40397, f. 137; *Macaulay Letters*, vi. 196. [10] Add. 40395, f. 221. [11] *Arbuthnot Jnl.* ii. 328. [12] Grey mss, Ellice to Grey [5 Feb. 1830]. [13] *Greville Mems.* i. 370. [14] Add. 56554, f. 94. [15] Bucks. RO, Fremantle mss D/FR/139/14/66, 67. [16] Add. 40401, f. 179; R. Stewart, *Foundation of Conservative Party*, 55. [17] *Greville Mems.* ii. 92, 126, 135; Stewart, 68-69; N. Gash, *Sir Robert Peel*, 7; *Three Diaries*, 35, 37, 41, 52, 54, 57, 93. [18] *Three Diaries*, 46. [19] Ibid. 62-63. [20] Add. 56555, f. 114; *Three Diaries*, 80-82. [21] *Three Diaries*, 45, 104, 106. [22] Hatherton diary, 20, 21, 26 July [1831]. [23] *Three Diaries*, 250, 256-7, 266; *Croker Pprs.* ii. 153. [24] *Arbuthnot Corresp.* 173. [25] *Three Diaries*, 291, 296, 306, 308, 315, 336, 340, 349; Add. 40406, ff. 108, 150. [26] *Wellington Pol. Corresp.* ii. 477. [27] *Mill Works*, xii. 345. [28] K. Bourne, *Palmerston*, 634. [29] *Gent. Mag.* (1855), ii. 666. [30] *Macaulay Letters*, vi. 196-7.

D.R.F.

ROSS, Horatio (1801–1886), of Rossie Castle, nr. Montrose, Forfar.

Aberdeen Burghs	1831–1832
Montrose Burghs	1832–1834

b. 5 Sept. 1801, o.s. of Hercules Ross of Rossie and Henrietta, da. of John Parish of Hamburg. *m.* 1 Dec. 1834,[1] Justine Henriette, da. of Colin Macrae of Inverinate, Ross, 5s. *suc.* fa. 1816. *d.* 6 Dec. 1886.

Cornet 14 Drag. 1820; ensign (half-pay) 59 Ft. 1823-39.

Hercules Ross, this Member's father, was described thus by Lawrence Hill in his 1788 survey of the Forfarshire electoral roll: 'A new proprietor. Very rich. Made his money by privateering in the West Indies'.[2] His early life remains obscure, but by the 1770s he had been 'long' resident at Kingston, Jamaica, where he had prospered as a merchant, carrying on 'very extensive business with the Spaniards'.[3] By 1779 he had become a close friend of Captain Horatio Nelson, who was serving in the Caribbean and whom he evidently helped out of a financial difficulty. He returned to Britain in 1782, and the following year bought the Scott estate of Rossie, near Montrose. He had a castellated house built there in 1800.[4] He married Henrietta Parish at North Leith on 18 Apr. 1785, and with her had three daughters and an only son, who was born 16 years later. Nelson, for whom he was named, readily agreed to become his godfather.[5] Hercules Ross had been consulted by Lord Grantham†, foreign secretary in the Shelburne ministry, on matters relating to the West Indies and the Spanish colonies, and in 1787 he placed his expertise at the disposal of Pitt's foreign secretary, Lord Carmarthen†.[6] He told William Wilberforce* that his 'testimony before the House of Commons', 1789-90, in support of abolition of the slave trade had earned him 'a plentiful load of abuse' and cost him 'all my West India connections'.[7] In late August 1805 (56 days before Trafalgar), he wrote to

Nelson of his hope that 'there still remains some great action to be achieved ... worthy of his fame' and that one day he would be able to introduce 'my boy Horatio ... as fine a fellow as can be imagined', to his godfather.[8] A story developed that when Horatio was six, his father got him to present colours to the Rossie regiment of yeomanry, but that when they fired a salute the boy fled in terror. His enraged father ordered a servant to fire a musket several times over his head daily. This, unsurprisingly, made him even more frightened; but one day the servant had him fire the gun at a sparrow, which he hit and killed. In that moment he found his metier.[9]

Hercules Ross died in December 1816, and Horatio was served as his heir general in the Rossie estate in March 1818. He joined the 14th Hussars in October 1820, but had no taste for barracks life and went on half-pay as an infantry ensign in November 1823. He was known thereafter as Captain Ross, though with what justification is not clear. Between 1825 and 1830 he became a notable figure in the world of sport, making and usually winning matches for large sums in steeple chasing, rowing and shooting. He excelled in the last, with both pistol and rifle. He slaughtered thousands of birds and animals for pleasure and to win wagers: in one particularly disgusting episode, he shot dozens of adult swallows as they hovered outside their nests when bringing food for their young.[10] In January 1830 he was one of a Whig shooting party at Woburn. His fellow guest Lord Howick* complained that the presence of him and George Anson* made life difficult for less skilful practitioners, for they were 'always put in the best places, shoot jealously and walk as if they were racing'.[11]

At the general election of 1830 Ross stood for Aberdeen Burghs (of which Montrose was one). In his address, he observed that as 'parties have of late been so confounded and mingled with each other', he would not call himself 'either Whig or Tory'; but he advocated the enfranchisement of large manufacturing towns, while denouncing 'schemes of universal suffrage, annual parliaments, etc.', a cautious application of free trade theories, the promotion of 'liberty and its blessings' abroad and the implementation of rigid economy and retrenchment in public expenditure. On this, he claimed that his views were 'quite as decided' as those of Joseph Hume, the popular radical sitting Member who had decided to stand for Middlesex. Hume gave Ross his blessing, but he was able only to secure the votes of Arbroath and Montrose, while his Tory opponent, Sir James Carnegie, who had Aberdeen and Inverbervie, won the decisive backing of Brechin.[12] On the introduction of the Grey ministry's reform scheme, which proposed to give Aberdeen a Member of its own and add Peterhead to the other four burghs, in March 1831, Ross attended Aberdeen reform dinners and announced his intention of offering for the new district as 'a sincere friend of reform and an admirer of the constitutional measure ... divested as it was of all revolutionary tendency'. On the dissolution which followed the defeat of the English reform bill, 19 Apr., he started for the existing district, claiming a well nurtured 'knowledge of trade' which qualified him to represent it. Support for the reform proposals was overwhelming, Carnegie, who had opposed them, gave up, and Ross was returned unopposed at Aberdeen amid celebratory scenes. Returning thanks, despite feeling unwell, he repudiated both 'moderate' and 'radical' reform and pledged himself, as 'a supporter of Whig principles', to back the government's 'middle course', whereby the franchise was to be confined to 'those who, from their station in life, must have had the means of acquiring a good education, and who, from the necessary qualification as to property, must have such a stake in the country as ... to make it their interest to preserve the constitution ... from revolutionary demagogues'. On other issues, he promised to ascertain his constituents' views before committing himself, but he advocated burgh reform and economy and retrenchment.[13]

Ross duly joined Brooks's Club on 30 July 1831. In the House, 27 June he endorsed the argument of William Maule, Member for Forfarshire, that the county's anti-reform petition did not reflect majority opinion and that many former local advocates of radical reform had received the ministerial scheme with 'unbounded satisfaction'. He divided for the second reading of the reintroduced English reform bill, 6 July, at least twice against the adjournment, 12 July, and generally for its details, though he was in the minority on the case of Saltash, 26 July. On 13 Aug. he brought up a petition from Arbroath complaining of delays in the bill's progress, but said that its language made him doubt whether it could be received. He nevertheless quoted its reference to 'frivolous and vexatious discussions', before the Speaker accused him of trying to air these views 'by a side-wind' and shut him up. He voted for the passage of the bill, 21 Sept., and the second reading of the Scottish measure, 23 Sept. He presented a petition from the council and householders of Forfar asking for the burgh to be substituted for Peterhead in the new Montrose district, 28 Sept. On 27 July he presented and 'cordially supported' a petition from Aberdeen woollen manufacturers against extension of the bill to restrict children's cotton factory hours to Scotland, where 'children were not hardly treated': if it was, it would 'facilitate the introduction of poor laws into Scotland, which were considered as a curse'. He conceded that some Glasgow cotton factories might need regulation, but argued that the woollen and flax trades did not. He was in the ministerial majority against the Irish union of parishes bill, 19 Aug. He presented a Montrose merchants and ship owners' petition for compensation for losses sustained by cholera quarantine restrictions, 6 Sept., when he divided in the minority of 20 against quarantine duties. He voted for the motion of confidence in the government after the reform bill's defeat in the Lords, 10 Oct. 1831.

Ross voted for the second reading of the revised reform bill, 17 Dec. 1831, steadily for its details, and for the third reading, 22 Mar. 1832. He divided with government on the Russian-Dutch loan, 26 Jan. (but not in July), and relations with Portugal, 9 Feb.; but he was in the minority of 51 for printing the Woollen Grange petition for disarming the Irish yeomanry, 16 Feb. Next day he presented and endorsed a Dundee merchants and manufacturers' petition for equalization of the duties on flax and a drawback on bonded hemp. He brought up and supported petitions from Aberdeen mill owners and Montrose textile manufacturers against the factories bill, 20 Feb., insisting that men who had invested heavily in such enterprises were entitled to consideration, while admitting, following discussions with masters and operatives, that children required humane protection. He was put on the committee on the bill, 16 Mar. He had been named to the select committee on malt drawback, 5 Sept. 1831; and on 29 Feb. 1832 he seconded and was a minority teller for Dixon's wrecking amendment to the second reading of the drawback bill, which he condemned as a ministerial concession to the 'clamour' of Irish distillers and the precursor of renewed smuggling and illicit distillation. When he opposed the motion to go into committee on the measure, 30 Mar, he said:

> I can hardly speak with temper of the conduct of government with regard to this bill. I have hitherto been one of their steady supporters; but ... my confidence in them is very much shaken ... They are about wantonly to ruin a great many individuals.

He was defeated by 74-36. His wrecking amendment to the third reading, 2 Apr., when he was again a minority teller, was beaten by 82-41. He rallied to ministers on the navy civil departments bill, 6 Apr. He was, however, a conspicuous absentee from the division on Lord Ebrington's motion for an address requesting the king to appoint only ministers who would carry undiluted reform, 10 May. According to Raikes, this prompted Hume to write to Ross's constituents alleging that he had 'deserted his duty to them, and was become lukewarm in the cause'. Ross gave him the lie, and Hume retracted.[14] His absence from the division did not pass unnoticed in the burghs, and he was later called to account for his 'equivocal' conduct'.[15] He presented Montrose petitions for supplies to be withheld until reform was secured and one from Arbroath council for the chief magistrates of burghs to be designated as returning officers, 23 May. He paired against a Conservative attempt to increase the Scottish county representation, 1 June. On 15 June he argued against the separation of Paisley and Port Glasgow and said that making Elgin the poll burgh for its district would cause inconvenience. He wanted ministers to retain the proposed property qualification for burgh Members, 27 June, when he voted for Baring's bill to exclude insolvent debtors from Parliament. He presented a Banff petition for Scottish burgh reform, 6 July. He was granted six weeks' leave on urgent private business that day, but was credited with a vote in the minority of 17 against the Irish education grant, 23 July 1832.

Ross successfully contested Montrose Burghs against another Liberal at the general election of 1832, but he was already on friendly terms with the Conservative leader Peel, and by the time of the 1835 election had transferred his political allegiance to him. He stood for Paisley, but was beaten by one of 'the enemies of the constitution', as he now termed Liberals and Radicals.[16] He sold the Rossie estate in 1845 and bought one near Stonehaven, Kincardineshire. After living a quiet laird's life with his family for about 18 years he came again to public notice in 1862 as the captain of the Scottish rifle-shooting team which competed against England for the Elcho shield; he continued to shoot with great skill well into his old age. He died at his shooting lodge in Inverness-shire in December 1886 and was succeeded by his eldest son, Horatio Seftenberg John Ross.[17]

[1] IGI (Scotland). [2] *Pol. State of Scotland, 1788*, p. 158. [3] Add. 28062, f. 202. [4] *Nelson Dispatches* ed. N.H. Nicolas, i. 29, 32, 59, 80, 97, 273; iv. 269, 280-1, 348-9, 488; v. 13, 38; A.J. Warden, *Angus*, iii. 144. [5] *Nelson Dispatches*, iv. 404, 487-8. [6] Add. 28062, f. 202. [7] *Life of Wilberforce*, i. 354. [8] Add. 34930, f. 253. [9] *Sportascrapiana* ed. C.H. Wheeler (1868), 54. [10] *Oxford DNB*; *Squire Osbaldeston: his Autobiog.* (1927), 69-72, 82-84, 94-104, 231, 234; *The Times*, 16 June 1830. [11] Grey mss, Howick jnl. 1 Jan. 1830. [12] St. Deiniol's Lib. Glynne-Gladstone mss 195, T. to J. Gladstone, 9 July; *Aberdeen Jnl.* 28 July, 4, 11, 18, 25 Aug. 1830. [13] *Aberdeen Jnl.* 9, 30 Mar., 6, 13, 27 Apr., 4, 11, 25 May 1831. [14] *Raikes Jnl.* i. 34-36. [15] *Aberdeen Jnl.* 18 July 1832. [16] Ibid. 26 Dec. 1832; Add. 40403, f. 103; 40420, ff. 16, 18; *Gladstone Diaries*, ii. 141; *Scottish Electoral Politics*, 222, 227-8, 259. [17] Warden, iii. 144; *Oxford DNB*.

D.R.F.

ROUSE BOUGHTON, William Edward (1788–1856), of Rous Lench, nr. Alcester, Worcs. and Downton Hall, nr. Ludlow, Salop.

EVESHAM 1818–23 Feb. 1819

EVESHAM 1820–1826

b. 14 Sept. 1788, o. s. of Sir Charles William Rouse Boughton† (formerly Boughton Rouse), 9th bt., and Catherine, da. and h. of William Pearce Hall of Downton Hall. *educ.* ?Westminster 1803-5; Christ Church, Oxf. 1806; European tour until 1813.[1] *m.* 24 Mar. 1824, Charlotte, da. and coh. of Thomas Andrew Knight of Wormsley Grange, Herefs., 3s. (1 *d.v.p.*) 5da. *suc.* fa. as 10th bt. 26 Feb. 1821. *d.* 22 May 1856.

Rouse Boughton, only son of the nabob and former Member, 1780-90, had been returned for the venal borough of Evesham as an 'independent' in 1818 but unseated on petition the following year. At the 1820 general election he offered again professing 'unchanged' principles and was returned unopposed.[2] A very lax attender, when present he generally voted with the Whig opposition to the Liverpool ministry on most major issues, including economy, retrenchment and reduced taxation, but not Catholic relief; he never joined Brooks's.[3] On 26 Jan. 1821 he presented and endorsed an Evesham petition in support of Queen Caroline, urging ministers 'to retrace their steps'. He was granted a month's leave on account of his father's death, 26 Feb., when he succeeded to the baronetcy and family estates, though his father's will was proved 'insolvent' at under £25,000.[4] He was absent from the division on Catholic relief two days later. He divided for reform of the Scottish representation, 10 May 1821, 2 June 1823, to reduce the number of placemen in the Commons, 31 May 1821, and for parliamentary reform, 25 Apr. 1822. According to Hudson Gurney*, he was one of several Members 'converted' by Sir Robert Wilson* to vote against his removal from the army, 13 Feb. 1822.[5] He divided for inquiries into the prosecution of the Dublin Orange rioters, 22 Apr., and Catholic petitions complaining of the administration of justice in Ireland, 26 June 1823. He divided for suppression of the Catholic Association, 25 Feb., and against Catholic relief, 21 Apr., 10 May, and the Irish franchise bill, 26 Apr. 1825. He was in Brougham's minority of 29 for making puisne judges immovable, 20 May 1825.

At the 1826 dissolution Rouse Boughton retired without explanation. He died in May 1856. By his will, dated 21 June 1846, he provided his five daughters with equal shares in £50,000 and left legacies of £100 to his two married sisters. The remainder of his estate passed to his elder surviving son and successor in the baronetcy, Charles Henry (1825-1906).[6]

[1] *Castlereagh Corresp.* ix. 11. [2] *Berrow's Worcester Jnl.* 17, 24 Feb., 2 Mar. 1820. [3] *Black Bk.* (1823), 140; *Session of Parl. 1825*, p. 452. [4] PROB 11/1640/127; IR26/850/177. [5] Gurney diary, 13 Feb. 1822. [6] PROB 11/2237/607; IR26/2055/906.

R.M.H./P.J.S.

ROWLEY, Sir Josias, 1st bt. (1765–1842), of Mount Campbell, Drumsna, co. Leitrim.

KINSALE 3 July 1821–1826

b. 1765, 2nd s. of Clotworthy Rowley† (*d.* 1805) of Mount Campbell and Letitia, da. and h. of Samuel Campbell of Mount Campbell; bro. of Samuel Campbell Rowley† and William Rowley†. *unm. suc.* bro. William Rowley to Mount Campbell 1812; *cr.* bt. 2 Nov. 1813; KCB 2 Jan. 1815; GCMG 22 Feb. 1834; GCB 4 July 1840. *d.* 10 Jan. 1842.

Entered RN 1777, midshipman 1780, lt. 1783, cdr. 1794, capt. 1795, r.-adm. 1814; c.-in-c. Ireland 1818-21; v.-adm. 1825; c.-in-c. Mediterranean 1833-7; adm. 1837.

Col. marines 1813.

Rowley's father, a younger son of Sir William Rowley (c.1690-1768), of Tendring Hall, Suffolk, Member for Taunton, 1750-4, and Portsmouth, 1754-61, who became admiral of the fleet in 1762, departed from the family tradition of naval service. He practised at the English bar from 1754, but in 1763 married an Irish heiress, as had his father. He established himself in Ireland, sat in the Irish Parliament as Member for Downpatrick, on the interest of his wife's sister's husband, the 20th Baron de Clifford, and with his first and third sons, William, an Irish barrister, and Samuel Campbell, who pursued a naval career, rallied to government after the outbreak of war. He opposed the Union but was nevertheless returned to the first United Parliament as Member for Downpatrick, although he never took his seat, for he was immediately made a commissioner of Union compensations. Samuel replaced him, thereby joining at Westminster William, who had sat for Kinsale since the Union, also on the de Clifford interest. William, who later managed that interest in both boroughs, left the House in 1802, when Samuel came in for Kinsale, where he sat until 1806. On the death of their father in 1805, William succeeded to his Leitrim estates.[1]

By then Josias Rowley, Clotworthy's second son, was an experienced naval officer. He began his career in 1778 under the immediate command of his uncle Joshua Rowley, who was created a baronet in 1786 and died in 1790. He served in the West Indies and the North Sea and, after achieving post rank in the early stages of the French wars, commanded ships in the East Indies, the North Sea and at the Cape. He took part in the battle of Cape Finisterre off the Spanish coast, 22 July 1805. At the end of that year he sailed to the Cape under Sir Home Popham†, with whom he subsequently went on the abortive expedition to South America, where he distinguished himself. In September 1809 he concerted with the commander of troops at Rodrigues a successful assault on the batteries at St. Paul's, on the Island of Bourbon; and he took part in the attack on the whole island, which ended in its capitulation, in July 1810. Two months later, in the *Boadicea*, he recaptured the *Africaine* and took the French frigate *Venus* and its prize, off Bourbon. In October 1810 he instituted the close blockade of Mauritius which led to its surrender, after the arrival of British reinforcements, before the turn of the year. He was sent home with the dispatches, and served on the *America* in the Mediterranean until the end of hostilities, being present at the reduction of Genoa. In November 1813 he was rewarded with a baronetcy.[2] On the death of his brother William the previous year he had succeeded to the family estates; but, as he explained to Robert Peel, the Irish secretary, in January 1818, asking for his nomination as sheriff of Leitrim to be annulled, he did not reside at Mount Campbell.[3] He was in any case about to take up his duties as commander-in-chief on the Irish station, where he served for the customary three years.

In July 1821 Rowley was returned unopposed on a vacancy for Kinsale, on the interest of his cousin, the 21st Baron de Clifford. In marked contrast to his Whig cousin Sir William Rowley, who had sat for Suffolk since 1812, he was a steady, though silent supporter of the Liverpool ministry.[4] He was in their majorities against more extensive tax reductions, 11, 21 Feb., abolition of one of the joint-postmasterships, 13 Mar., and repeal of the salt duties, 28 June 1822. He voted against Canning's bill to relieve Catholic peers of their disabilities, 30 Apr. 1822, and Catholic relief, 1 Mar., 21 Apr., 10 May 1825. He divided for the national debt reduction bill, 13 Mar., and against inquiry into the prosecution of the Dublin Orange rioters, 22 Apr., and Scottish parliamentary reform, 2 June 1823. On 26 May 1823 he presented a petition from the tanners of Kinsale for reduction of the duties on foreign bark.[5] He was in the ministerial majority on the case of the Methodist missionary John Smith, prosecuted for inciting a slave uprising in Demerara, 11 June 1824. He supported the repressive legislation for Ireland, 14 June 1824, 15, 25 Feb. 1825. He voted in favour of giving the president of the board of trade a ministerial salary, 10 Apr., when he presented a Kinsale petition for revision of the prison laws,[6] and against reform of Edinburgh's representation, 13 Apr. 1826. He retired from Parliament at the dissolution a few weeks later.[7]

In 1833 the Grey ministry appointed Rowley to the Mediterranean command, subsequently giving him a 'discretionary order' to comply with any request from Turkey, conveyed through Lord Ponsonby, the ambassador at Constantinople, for intervention against Russia. As foreign secretary in Peel's first ministry, the duke of Wellington decided that such powers were potentially dangerous and, at his instigation, the cabinet countermanded them in March 1835. They were only partially restored by the Melbourne ministry on their return to office.[8] On his retirement from active service in 1837 Rowley, who never married, took up residence at Mount Campbell, where he died, 'beloved and respected by all classes' in January 1842.[9] By his will, dated 12 Dec. 1841, he left all his personal property to his youngest brother, the Rev. John Rowley, who inherited the family estates on the death of Samuel Campbell Rowley without issue in 1846.[10]

[1] *HP Commons, 1790-1820*, v. 58-59. [2] *Oxford DNB*; *Gent. Mag.* (1842), i. 325-7; J. Marshall, *Royal Naval Biog.* ii. 622-35; Add. 37292, f. 284; 41513, ff. 18-21, 24. [3] Add. 40273, f. 219. [4] *Black Bk.* (1823), 190; *Session of Parl. 1825*, p. 483. [5] *The Times*, 27 May 1823. [6] Ibid. 11 Apr. 1826. [7] *Dublin Evening Post*, 10, 20 June 1826. [8] H. Temperley and L. Penson, *Foundations of British Foreign Policy*, 119-21; *Wellington Pol. Corresp.* ii. 89, 782, 1052, 1057, 1062, 1067, 1079, 1169. [9] *Gent. Mag.* (1842), i. 327. [10] PROB 11/1960/202; IR26/1619/203.

D.R.F./P.J.S.

ROWLEY, Sir William, 2nd bt. (1761–1832), of Tendring Hall, Suff. and 34 Lower Grosvenor Street, Mdx.

SUFFOLK 1812–1830

b. 10 Feb. 1761, 1st s. of Adm. Sir Joshua Rowley, 1st bt., and Sarah, da. and h. of Bartholomew Burton†, dep. gov. Bank of England, of Petersham, Surr. *educ.* Harrow 1774. *m.* 23 Mar. 1785, Susanna Edith, da. of Adm. Sir Robert Harland, 1st bt., of Sproughton, Suff., 5s. (3 *d.v.p.*) 6da. (1 *d.v.p.*). *suc.* fa. as 2nd bt. 26 Feb. 1790. *d.* 20 Oct. 1832.

Lt. and capt. 96 Ft. 1780, 3 Ft. Gds. 1782-6; lt.-col. commdt. Suff. vol. cav. 1798.

Sheriff, Suff. 1791-2.

Rowley was a pro-Catholic Whig and well-connected country gentleman of Irish descent, whose family had returned Members for Downpatrick and

Kinsale and produced five distinguished admirals. He had been kept waiting until 1812 to realize his ambition of representing Suffolk, where he commanded the yeomanry and had rebuilt Tendring Hall. As a silent but steady adherent of opposition, his votes generally cancelled out those of his colleague, the anti-Catholic Tory Sir Thomas Gooch, with whom he was returned 'by the oligarchy' for the third time at the 1820 general election.[1] He had recently held aloof from an attempt by Sir Henry Bunbury*, who aspired to the representation, to secure a county meeting to protest at the Liverpool ministry's response to Peterloo, but he declared on the hustings that he would continue to vote for retrenchment and against legislation which threatened 'the constitutional safeguards of the people'.[2] In the 1820 Parliament Rowley appears to have attended regularly and voted consistently with the Whig opposition to Lord Liverpool's ministry on most major issues, including parliamentary reform, 9 May 1821, 25 Apr. 1822, 27 Apr. 1826, and Catholic relief, 28 Feb. 1821, 1 Mar., 21 Apr., 10 May 1825. He also gave fairly steady support to the 'Mountain' and Hume's campaigns for economy and retrenchment and was commended accordingly by the *Bury and Norwich Post*.[3] He was appointed with Gooch to the select committees on agricultural distress, 7 Mar. 1821, 18 Feb. 1822, and the game laws, 13 Mar. 1823, and added to that on labourers' wages, 6 May 1824.

He voted against Wilberforce's compromise motion on Queen Caroline's case, 22 June 1820, and came under considerable pressure, agitated by Bunbury and the Bury St. Edmunds reformers that autumn, to assist the extra-parliamentary campaign on her behalf. He eventually agreed (24 Dec. 1820) to present a contentious address to her from freeholders in Suffolk's Lackford Hundred and he acted with her parliamentary partisans in 1821.[4] He 'regretted' the dismissal of Sir Robert Wilson* from the army for his conduct at the queen's funeral, 13 Feb. 1822.[5] A call of the House had kept him from the county meeting that called for a change of ministry and petitioned for parliamentary reform to alleviate agricultural distress, 16 Mar. 1821, and the tragic death of his 16-year-old nephew Henry Joshua Rowley prevented him from presenting their petition as requested.[6] In September 1821 he contributed to the success and attended the celebrations of his brother-in-law Sir Robert Harland, 2nd bt., who outpolled the duke of Wellington at the steward's election in Ipswich.[7] A bad cold prevented him from addressing the January 1822 county meeting which petitioned for reform and measures to alleviate distress, and he was again indisposed when Gooch presented their petition, 7 Mar.[8] In March and April he returned to Suffolk for a series of lieutenancy and magistrates' meetings to consider recent arson attacks and the agricultural committee's report.[9] He was toasted in his absence at the Suffolk Fox and reform dinner in August 1822, having sent them two fat bucks.[10] Rowley divided, albeit less assiduously, as hitherto with his colleagues in opposition for the remainder of the Parliament. He attended and agreed to present the reform petition adopted at the county meeting at Stowmarket, 4 Apr. but delegated it to its opponent Gooch, 24 Apr. 1823.[11] He presented one for repeal of the coastal coal duty, 30 May.[12] As chairman of the grand jury of the liberty of Bury St. Edmunds, he presented a memorial to the home office on the inconvenience of the shared assize system in Suffolk, to which Peel sent a non-committal reply, 9 July 1823.[13] He presented petitions for repeal of the excise licence duties, 11 May, and voted against the beer duties bill with his son-in-law, the brewer Charles Calvert, 24 May 1824.[14] He voted to condemn the indictment of the Methodist missionary John Smith in Demerara, 11 June 1824. He was a minority teller against the City of London water bill, in which his family had a vested interest, 1 Mar. 1825. He voted to repeal the assessed taxes, 3 Mar., and the window tax, 17 May, for inquiry into chancery delays, 7 June, and against the grant to the duke of Cumberland, 6, 9, 10 June 1825. A radical publication that session noted that he 'attended occasionally'.[15] He was in the minority for referring petitions from the distressed silk traders of London and Suffolk to a select committee, 24 Feb. 1826, and in May backed a deputation of Suffolk maltsters, who lobbied ministers for remission of the duty on malt.[16] He favoured some protection for corn growers, presented petitions from the owners and occupiers of Heyland and Cossford against any alteration in the corn laws, 17 Apr., and joined Gooch in opposing the government's proposals for releasing corn from bond (8, 11 May), a locally important general election issue. On the hustings at Stowmarket, 16 June, and Ipswich, 20 June, he stated only that his political opinions were unchanged, but his sponsors praised his votes against jobbing and taxes affecting the 'poor and middling classes' and he was spared the roasting given to Gooch before they were returned unopposed.[17] In December 1826 he was among the Whig duke of Norfolk's shooting guests at Fordham.[18]

Rowley voted for Catholic relief, 6 Mar. 1827, 12 May 1828. He was obliged to deny reports that he had voted for the financial provisions for the duke of Clarence in February 1827.[19] He divided for the production of information on the mutiny at Barrackpoor, 22 Mar., and for the spring guns bill, 23 Mar. He voted against Canning's coalition government for the disfranchisement of Penryn, 28 May 1827. On 26 Feb. 1828 he presented several Suffolk petitions for repeal of the Test Acts and voted for that measure. He presented his constituents' anti-slavery petitions, 22 May, 23 June 1828, when he voted against the Buckingham House expenditure. He divided for Catholic emancipation, 6, 30 Mar., and presented favourable petitions from Hadleigh and Stowmarket, 11 Mar. 1829. He attended the county agricultural distress meeting requisitioned by the Tories to petition for protection and retrenchment, 6 Feb. 1830, and briefly reaffirmed his commitment to reducing the taxes on malt and beer and removing those which affected 'the lower classes'.[20] No record of his parliamentary attendance that session survives before 12 Mar., when, as until 11 June, he voted steadily in person or paired with the revived Whig opposition. He did not vote on Jewish emancipation (5 Apr., 17 May), but paired for Lord John Russell's reform motion, 28 May, and for abolition of the death penalty for forgery, 7 June. He voted to amend the sale of beer bill to restrict on-consumption, 21 June, 7 July 1830. He retired, ostensibly on health grounds and in Bunbury's favour, at the dissolution that month. Critics condemned him as a Member who 'has voted and paired off and paired off and voted and at last surrenders up the county through the means of an advertisement'.[21] He took no part in proceedings at the ensuing election.

Rowley's eldest son William died without issue, 24 Oct. 1830, but the marriages of Joshua and Charles into the Moseley, Vanneck and Arcedeckne families perpetuated the family's close ties with the Whig hierarchy in Suffolk. He died in October 1832 at Tendring Hall, recalled as 'an undeviating supporter of the popular cause', and was buried in the family vault at Stoke-by-Neyland.[22] By his will, dated 25 Dec. 1830, which was proved under £25,000, Tendring passed with the baronetcy to his eldest surviving son Joshua Ricketts Rowley (1790-1857), a naval captain. He bequeathed a life interest in his London house in Wimpole Street to his widow and unmarried daughters and provided legacies for each of his children and his brother, the Rev. Joshua Rowley.[23]

[1] *HP Commons, 1790-1820*, ii. 366-7; v. 58-59; W.P. Scargill, *Peace of the County* (1830), 4-10. [2] *Mem. and Literary Remains of Sir Henry Edward Bunbury* ed. C.J.F. Bunbury, 85-86; *Suff. Chron.* 26 Feb., 18 Mar.; *Ipswich Jnl.* 18 Mar. 1820. [3] *Bury and Norwich Post*, 13 Feb. 1823. [4] *Suff. Chron.* 26 Aug.; *The Times*, 4 Sept. 1820, 5, 30 Jan.; *Bury and Norwich Post*, 3, 10 Jan., 7 Feb. 1821; Add. 38574, f. 232. [5] *The Times*, 14 Feb. 1822. [6] *Ipswich Jnl.* 17 Mar.; *The Times*, 21 Mar., 18 Apr.; *Gent. Mag.* (1821), i. 369. [7] *The Times*, 9 Sept., 4 Oct. 1821. [8] Ibid. 31 Jan., 8 Mar. 1822. [9] *Bury and Norwich Post*, 20 Feb., 10, 24 Apr. 1822. [10] *The Times*, 23 Aug. 1822. [11] *Ipswich Jnl.* 5 Apr.; *The Times*, 5, 7, 25 Apr. 1823. [12] *The Times*, 31 May 1823. [13] Add. 40357, f. 87. [14] *The Times*, 12 May 1824. [15] *Session of Parl. 1825*, p. 483. [16] *Bury and Norwich Post*, 10 May 1826. [17] Ibid. 7, 14, 21 June; *The Times*, 9 June 1826. [18] *The Times*, 9 Dec. 1826. [19] *Bury and Norwich Post*, 28 Mar. 1827. [20] Ibid. 3, 10 Feb. 1830. [21] Ibid. 16, 30 June, 14 July; *The Times*, 17 June; *Ipswich Jnl.* 10 July 1830. [22] *Suff. Chron.* 7 Aug. 1830, 27 Oct. 1832; *Gent. Mag.* (1830), ii. 476; (1833), i. 83. [23] *Suff. Chron.* 7 Aug. 1830, 27 Oct. 1832; *Gent. Mag.* (1830), ii. 476; (1833), i. 83; IR26/1331/89; PROB 11/1813/82.

M.M.E.

RUMBOLD, Charles Edmund (1788–1857), of Woodhall Park, Watton, Herts.

GREAT YARMOUTH	1818–1834
GREAT YARMOUTH	1837–1847
GREAT YARMOUTH	8 July 1848–1857

b. 11 Aug. 1788, 5th s. of Sir Thomas Rumbold†, 1st bt. (*d.* 1791), of Woodhall and 2nd w. Joanna, da. of Rt. Rev. Edmund Law, DD, bp. of Carlisle; half-bro. of William Richard Rumbold†. *educ.* Oriel, Oxf. 1806; Trinity Coll. Camb. 1808; European tour 1812-13. *m.* by 1834, Harriet, da. of John Gardner of Ashford, Kent, 3s. *d.* 31 May 1857.

In 1782, by means of a bill of pains and penalties, the Commons had unsuccessfully prosecuted Rumbold's father, whom he barely knew, for corruption as governor of Bengal, 1778-81. A breach between him and the sons of his first marriage, who resented their stepmother, subsequently left Rumbold heir with his siblings to the proceeds from the sale of his Hertfordshire estate and town house in Harley Street, in which his mother had a life interest. Not until her death in 1823 did the East India Company auditors rule that his father had died insolvent.[1] His mother's connection with the Lushington family of Park Place, Kent, into which her late sister Mary had married, had given him, through the Whig barrister Stephen Lushington*, an introduction to the venal borough of Great Yarmouth, which he contested successfully on the Whig or 'Blue' interest in 1818 and represented, with a single interruption, for almost 40 years at an estimated cost of £80,000.[2] At the general election of 1820 he stood jointly with Thomas William Coke I* of Norfolk's grandson George Anson, his colleague since 1819, narrowly defeating two Tories backed by the corporation, who dubbed the Members 'Death and the Devil'; Rumbold was the latter. On the hustings, he countered criticism of his anti-government votes against the oppressive measures enacted after Peterloo, with a robust defence of his opposition to the unpopular salt tax and, mindful of the importance of the Dissenters' votes, he promised to promote criminal law reform, civil and religious liberties, the fisheries and local commerce.[3] Noting the £8,000 bill, the Whig banker Hudson Gurney* commented that Rumbold, who at first also paid the Ansons' costs, would 'be imprudent ever again to face an opposition for Yarmouth'.[4]

An occasional contributor to debates, he served on several minor committees, before he was appointed to that on foreign trade in 1824. He made no major speeches, but was entrusted, as previously, with most constituency business, including petitions. He divided steadily with the Whig moderates on most major issues, and for economy and retrenchment, but took care, when 'directed', to represent the opinions of Great Yarmouth's leading Dissenting merchants and ship owners. He voted to disqualify civil officers of the ordnance from voting at parliamentary elections, 12 Apr. 1821, cast his first known votes for parliamentary reform, 9, 10 May 1821, and voted similarly, 25 Apr. 1822, 24 Apr., 2 June 1823, 26 Feb. 1824, 9 Mar., 13, 27 Apr. 1826. He divided for Catholic relief, 28 Feb. 1821, 1 Mar., 21 Apr., 10 May 1825. A radical publication that session noted that he 'attended regularly and voted with opposition'.[5] The 1820 Norwich Bridge and Norwich gas light bills were successfully entrusted to Rumbold.[6] He divided with opposition on the Queen Caroline case, 26 June, which he later informed William Lamb* and William Wilberforce* caused him 'much alarm', and he returned to London from Watton in September 1820 to hear the Lords proceedings, in which Lushington was the queen's third counsel.[7] He was a steward at the Norfolk Foxite dinner, 19 Jan., and steadily supported the 1821 parliamentary campaign on the queen's behalf.[8] He presented petitions from Great Yarmouth against the Hull poor rates bill, 19 Feb., and the extra post bill, 18 June 1821.[9] His votes to repeal the salt duties, 28 Feb., 3, 28 June, accorded with constituency interests and, stressing the inadequacy of a partial repeal, he spoke in support of the Cornish pilchard fisheries' petition, 11 June 1822, and presented and endorsed another that day from the principal fish curers of Great Yarmouth.[10] A regular guest of the Great Yarmouth banker John Brightwen and corn merchant and maltster Benjamin Dowson, he was for amending the corn laws and voted in Ricardo's minority of 25 for a 20*s.* fixed duty, 9 May 1822, and for corn law reform, 26 Feb. 1823, 28 Apr. 1825, 18 Apr. 1826. During the 1822 recess he was briefed on and asked to oppose the Norwich and Lowestoft navigation scheme, which threatened the commerce and corporation revenues of Great Yarmouth.[11]

Rumbold's mother died, 4 Jan. 1823, leaving personal estate sworn under £12,000 and a share in the £68,595 fortune, locked in chancery, of Caroline, the late wife of Admiral Sir William Sydney Smith[†]. As co-executor with his cousin, the barrister and Ceylon judge Edmund Henry Lushington, Rumbold sold the mansion at Watton, which his father had commissioned from Thomas Leverton, to his late half-brother's son, the disgraced East India merchant Sir William Rumbold (*d.* 1833). He accommodated his sisters in London and at Park Place, before purchasing the Preston House estate in the Hampshire parish of Condover, with its manor and advowson, from the executors of the insolvent London merchant John Blackburn[†].[12] He presented a petition against the reciprocities duties bill from the ship owners of Great Yarmouth, 27 June, and voted against its third reading, 4 July, having called in vain for it to be held over. He maintained that the 'shipping interest did not require protection, but they protested against an entire alteration'. He presented their petitions against the ships' apprentices bill, 15 Apr., and the duties on coastwise coal, 2 May 1823.[13] At Michaelmas his sisters accompanied him to Great Yarmouth for the corporation dinner and ball.[14] Rumbold was named to the select committee on foreign trade, 4 Mar. 1824. His 'few words' on the salt tax, 6 Apr., were 'totally inaudible in the gallery'.[15] He voted in condemnation of the trial in Demerara of the Methodist missionary John Smith, 11 June, having presented and endorsed his constituents' petition of complaint, 28 May. He presented their petition against the beer bill, 21 May 1824.[16] A keen linguist and antiquarian, he was informed on applying to the herald's office in November that his descent from the comptroller of the great wardrobe, William Rumbold of Fulham (*d.* 1667), was presumed and not proven.[17] He presented a petition for repeal of the assessed taxes from Harwich, 21 Feb., and one from Great Yarmouth against the coastwise coal duties, 24 Feb. 1825.[18] When a dissolution was anticipated that autumn, he hurried to Great Yarmouth, where the brewer Charles Barclay* had declared his candidature, and Stephen Lushington canvassed Coke, Thomas Fowell Buxton* and Lord Suffield on his behalf.[19] Speaking on the navigation laws and shipping, 13 May 1826, he used evidence supplied by the ship owners of Great Yarmouth to reinforce his argument that reductions in taxes and pilotage fees would make the industry more competitive, and expressed a hope that 'the alarm ... now felt by the ship owners would cure itself, or that [at] any rate it would be put down by some well considered measure in the next session'. He co-operated throughout with colleagues on the local committee against the Norwich and Lowestoft navigation bill and helped to secure its defeat by 25-20 in the select committee, 2 May.[20] He was rewarded with the freedom of Great Yarmouth, 15 May 1826.[21] Predictions that he and Anson would be unopposed at the general election in June proved incorrect, but their victory over the newly formed anti-Catholic 'Crimson interest' was assured.[22] At the Michaelmas dinner, he joined Coke in castigating the instigators of the vexatious opposition.[23]

Early in the new Parliament Rumbold was preoccupied with the revised Norwich and Lowestoft navigation bill, which Great Yarmouth again opposed, but his motions for its recommittal and amendment both failed, 21 Mar., and it received royal assent, 27 May 1827.[24] He divided against the payment to the duke of Clarence, 16 Feb., and for Catholic relief, 6 Mar., a 50*s*. pivot price for corn imports, 9 Mar., and inquiry into the allegations against Leicester corporation, 15 Mar., and the Lisburn magistrates, 29 Mar. He voted to refer the Irish miscellaneous estimates to a select committee, 5 Apr. He voted to disfranchise Penryn for electoral corruption, 28 May, and presented protectionist petitions from the merchants and ship owners of Great Yarmouth, 3 May, 7 June 1827.[25] Thomas Spring Rice* informed the Goderich ministry's home secretary Lord Lansdowne in September that, commenting on the ministerial changes following Canning's death, Rumbold, 'a most excellent and independent man' had said:

> I care not so long as Lord Lansdowne remains in. He and those who act with him ought to feel that whatever sacrifices to form may be made now, they will be amply compensated hereafter. Into his hands the conduct of affairs will fall hereafter, and in a very short time as large and strong confidence will be placed by the treasury in this administration as ever fell to the lot of a minister'.[26]

Rumbold voted for repeal of the Test Acts, 26 Feb., and Catholic relief, 12 May 1828. He presented the Great Yarmouth maltsters' petition for repeal of the 1827 Malt Act, 28 Feb. He voted against sluicing the franchise at East Retford, 21 Mar., and for the disqualification bill, 24 June. A member of the 1827 select committee on pauper lunatics, he moved a late amendment concerning coroners' inquests to the lunatic regulation bill, 1 Apr. 1828, but withdrew it rather than compromise the measure. On 22 Apr. he voted to amend the corn bill by lowering the pivot price from 64*s*. to 60*s*. He divided against the Wellington government on the Buckingham House expenditure, 23 June, and the ordnance estimates, 4 July 1828. He presented and endorsed petitions for Catholic emancipation, 11, 27 Feb., 4, 10 Mar., and divided thus, 6, 30 Mar. 1829. He voted to transfer East Retford's seats to Birmingham, 5 May. He opposed the grant for the marble arch sculpture, 25 May, and was appointed to, 27 May, and reported from, 19 June, the select committee to examine Nash's conduct in granting leases on crown lands. His attitude towards a projected coalition involving the Ultras in October 1829 was 'unknown'.

Rumbold was one of 28 'opposition Members' who voted against Knatchbull's amendment to include reference to distress in the address, 4 Feb. 1830, but he divided fairly steadily for retrenchment that session. He voted to transfer East Retford's seats to Birmingham, 11 Feb., 5, 15 Mar., to enfranchise Birmingham, Leeds and Manchester, 23 Feb., and for parliamentary reform, 28 May. He spoke against proceeding against Nash personally over the mishandling of the Buckingham House improvements, 2 Mar., but paired for inquiry into the management of crown lands, 30 Mar., and voted against the public buildings grant, 3 May. He divided steadily with the revived Whig opposition from March until 14 June, including for Jewish emancipation, 5 Apr., 7 May, and abolition of the death penalty for forgery, 24 May, 7 June, for which his constituents petitioned, 26 Apr., 17 May. He voted to consider abolishing colonial slavery, 13 July. Rumbold's attempt to extend the scope of the inquiry into the coal trade beyond London failed, 11 Mar., but he obtained returns on duties and drawbacks affecting textiles, which were of concern to the Great Yarmouth crepe manufacturers, 8 Apr. He presented several petitions against the Southwold Haven bill, which was promoted by the Suffolk Member Gooch and opposed by the corporation, but failed to secure its recommittal (by 54-22) or amendment (by 49-21), 3 May. As requested, he took charge of the Acle and Yarmouth road bill, which received royal assent, 3 May, and presented petitions against the sale of beer bill, 4 May, and renewal of the East India Company's charter, 6 May, and for retrenchment and lower taxes, 10 May, equalization of the duties on corn, spirits and rum, 19 May, and 'continuance of the fishery bounty', 21 May.[27] When a petition of complaint from London ship owners was presented, 6 May 1830, he stated that 'the shipping interest look entirely for relief to the reduction of taxes and the removal of the East India monopoly' and called on government to afford them immediate and effectual relief on both. He and Anson were opposed 'by almost the entire force of the corporation' at the general election in August, but to ministers' regret they defeated two Tories to retain their seats. On the hustings, Rumbold professed support for reform and retrenchment, praised Wellington for conceding emancipation, and drew attention to his own votes against slavery and for religious toleration.[28]

The ministry listed Rumbold as one of the 'bad doubtfuls' likely to vote with 'opposition' in the new Parliament; and he did so on the civil list when they were brought down, 15 Nov. 1830. He presented his constituents' petitions against slavery, 4, 19 Nov., 11 Dec. 1830, and for repeal of the coastwise coal duty, 9 Feb., secured the referral of their petitions against the Norwich and Yarmouth road bill to the committee that day, and presented one for parliamentary reform, 28 Feb. 1831. He was named as a defaulter, 14 Mar., but excused on account of illness, which also prevented him from voting for the second reading of the Grey ministry's reform bill, 22 Mar. He divided against Gascoyne's wrecking amendment, 19 Apr.[29] At the ensuing election 'a bad attack of gout' delayed his canvass at Great Yarmouth, where the freeman and out-voter disfranchisements which the bill proposed were a major issue, and during the poll he promised to try to secure concessions.[30] Afterwards, acting on financial and political grounds, he and Anson lobbied for the transfer of government patronage from Tory Harwich to Whig Great Yarmouth.[31] Rumbold's health problems persisted. He voted for the second reading of the reintroduced reform bill, 6 July, and against adjournment, 12 July, and using the 1831 census to determine borough representation, 19 July 1831. He divided fairly steadily for the bill's details, but, bowing to constituency pressure, on 30 Aug. he moved an amendment to grant non-resident freemen compensatory voting rights in their boroughs of residence, which he withdrew for want of support. He spoke highly of the Great Yarmouth out-voters, acknowledged his obligation to them and disputed Lord John Russell's claim that the £10 householder vote afforded them ample compensation. He voted for the bill's passage, 21 Sept., and Lord Ebrington's confidence motion, 10 Oct. He was in the minority for legislating for the relief of the Irish poor, 29 Aug. He divided for the revised reform bill at its second reading, 17 Dec. 1831, consistently for its details, for the third reading, 22 Mar., and for the address requesting the king to appoint only ministers who would carry it unimpaired, 10 May 1832. He divided for the second reading of the Irish measure, 25 May, and paired against amending the Scottish bill, 1 June. He voted for Alexander Baring's bill denying parliamentary privileges to debtors, 27 June. He apologized for his absence from the Great Yarmouth reform festival on 12 July and, responding to a summons from the leader of the House Lord Althorp, he divided with administration on the Russian-Dutch loan, 12, 16 July 1832.[32] Vetting Rumbold's application to become a Hampshire magistrate that winter, the Conservative John Fleming* informed Wellington, 'I am not aware of any objection to him, excepting his politics'.[33]

Rumbold was returned for Great Yarmouth after a contest at the general election of 1832.[34] He was defeated in 1835, but triumphed again in the Liberal interest in 1837. His defence of church rates and opposition to disestablishment cost him the support of the Dissenters, and following his defeat at the voided election of 1847 he allied increasingly with the Conservatives. Despite hostile speculation, he retained his seat until he retired through ill health in March 1857.[35] He died at Brighton two months later, survived by his wife (*d.* 6 Oct. 1877) and three sons, who with his unmarried sisters were the beneficiaries of his will, dated 17 Nov. 1846.[36]

[1] PROB 11/1212/593; H.D. Love, *Vestiges of Old Madras*, iii. 148, 224; BL OIOC D/151; *HP Commons, 1754-90*, ii. 381-4; *Oxford DNB sub* Sir Thomas Rumbold. [2] Norf. RO, Great Yarmouth boroughs recs.; Rumbold mss L14/4; *Hants Chron.* 13 June 1857. [3] *The Times*, 8 Feb., 13 Mar.; *Norf. Chron.* 26 Feb., 4, 18 Mar. 1820; *Diary and Journal of C.J. Palmer* ed. F.D. Palmer, 70; Norf. RO, Gurney mss RQG 572/3. [4] Trinity Coll. Camb. Dawson Turner mss DT2/K1/30, Gurney to Turner, 22 Mar. 1820. [5] *Session of Parl. 1825*, p. 483. [6] *The Times*, 6 May 1820. [7] *Wilberforce Corresp.* ii. 433; Rumbold mss L14/6. [8] *Norf. Chron.* 13, 20 Jan. 1821. [9] Rumbold mss L14/7-8; *The Times*, 20 Feb., 19 June 1821. [10] *The Times*, 12 June 1822. [11] Rumbold mss L14/9-12. [12] PROB 11/1673/436; IR26/971/817; Wellington mss WP1/555/32; 856/23; 857/1; C.H. Philips, *E.I. Co.* 225-7, 281; *Arbuthnot Jnl.* i. 286-7; *VCH Hants* iii. 373; iv. 205. [13] *The Times*, 16 Apr., 3 May, 28 June 1823. [14] Rumbold mss L14/14. [15] *The Times*, 7 Apr. 1824. [16] Ibid. 22, 29 May 1824. [17] C.J. Palmer, *Perlustration of Great Yarmouth*, i. 336; OIOC mss. Eur. Photo. Eur. 99. [18] *The Times*, 22, 25 Feb. 1825. [19] *Norf. Chron.* 3, 24 Sept., 1 Oct. 1825; Rumbold mss L14/22-23; Dawson Turner mss K2/D1/3, Brightwen to Turner, 31 Oct. 1825. [20] *Norwich Mercury*, 15, 22, 29 Apr., 6, 13, 27 May; *Norf. Chron.* 21 May 1825, 11 Feb. 1826; Norf. RO MC222/1. [21] Norf. RO, Yarmouth corporation Y/C19/17; *Norwich Mercury*, 13, 20 May 1826. [22] C.J. Palmer, *Hist. Great Yarmouth*, 235; *The Times*, 7 Apr.; *Norf. Chron.* 10, 17, 24 June; *Globe and Traveller*, 13 June 1826. [23] *Norf. Chron.* 7, 14 Oct. 1826. [24] Ibid. 2 Dec. 1826, 24 Feb., 17, 24 Mar., 25 May 1827; *CJ*, lxxxii. 13, 29, 44, 148, 305, 345, 459. [25] *The Times*, 4 May, 8 June 1827. [26] Lansdowne mss, Spring Rice to Lansdowne, 3 Sept. 1827. [27] *Norf. Chron.* 17 Apr. 1830; Rumbold mss L14/26. [28] F.D. Palmer, *Yarmouth Notes*, 6-7.; *Norf. Chron.* 3, 17, 24, 31 July, 7 Aug.; *The Times*, 13, 21 July 1830. See also GREAT YARMOUTH. [29] *The Times*, 25 Mar., 21 Apr. 1831. [30] *East Anglian*, 26 Apr., 3, 10 May; Palmer, *Yarmouth Notes*, 9-11; Dawson Turner, unpub. 'Yarmouth Misc.' [BL N. Tab. 201216], handbills, 22-30 Apr. 1831. [31] Grey mss, Duncannon to Grey, 26 May [1831]. [32] *Norf. Chron.* 14 July; *East Anglian*, 17 July 1832. [33] Wellington mss WP4/4/1/10-13. [34] *Norf. Chron.* 15 Sept.; *East Anglian*, 18, 25 Sept., 11, 18 Dec.; *The Times*, 13, 14, 18 Dec. 1832. [35] Palmer, *Hist. Great Yarmouth*, 236-42; Palmer, *Yarmouth Notes*, 54-5, 79-80, 121-4; Rumbold mss L14/29-33; *The Times*, 22 July 1847, 8 July 1848, 11 Mar., 6, 8 July 1852, 24 Dec. 1855. [36] *Gent. Mag.* (1857), ii. 101; PROB 11/2256/643; IR26/2109/686.

M.M.E.

RUSSELL, Charles (1786–1856), of 27 Charles Street, St. James's Square, Mdx.

READING 1830–1837

READING 1841–1847

b. 22 July 1786, 3rd but 2nd surv. s. of Henry Russell (*d.* 1836), commr. of bankrupts, of 9 New Square, L. Inn and 2nd w. Anna Barbara, da. of Sir Charles Whitworth† of Leybourne, Kent. *unm. d.* 15 May 1856.

Cadet, E.I. Co. 1800, ensign 1801, lt. 1803, capt. 1818, furlough 1817, ret. 1822.

Chairman, Great Western Railway 1839-55.

Russell's family originated in Worcestershire, and was related to the Russells of Strensham. In the late seventeenth century Michael Russell, whose father had been an active Parliamentarian in the Civil War, settled in Dover. His only surviving son, Michael Russell (1711-93), acquired property in the town and farms in Kent. With his wife Hannah Henshaw he had four sons, of whom the third, Henry Russell, born in 1751, was the father of this Member.[1] He was educated at Charterhouse, Queens' College, Cambridge and Lincoln's Inn, was appointed a commissioner of bankrupts in 1775 and associated with Dr. Johnson in his last years. In 1776 he married Anne Skinner of Lydd, but she died in 1780, and their son Henry a year later. In 1782 he took as his second wife Anna Barbara Whitworth, daughter of Sir Charles Whitworth, Member for various constituencies from 1747 to his death in 1778, and chairman of ways and means for the last ten years of his life. Her brother Charles Whitworth (1752-1825) was created an Irish peer in 1800 and a United Kingdom one in 1813, and was viceroy of Ireland, 1813-17. In 1782 Russell, who looked for patronage to the 3rd earl of Hardwicke, was appointed a puisne judge of the supreme court at Calcutta and knighted. He did well in Bengal, where he became friendly with William Hickey, who admired his 'superior talents as a deep-read lawyer' and recorded that his 'claret was always of the very best, while his dinners were execrable'. In 1805 Russell, who that year suffered a bad carriage accident which permanently damaged his right arm, successfully applied through Hardwicke to succeed Sir John Anstruther† on his pending retirement as chief justice of Bengal.[2] He was created a baronet, 10 Dec. 1812, retired on an East India Company pension of £2,000 at the end of 1813, returned home the following year and was made a privy councillor in 1816. He was said to have turned down Whitworth's offer of a seat for East Grinstead, where his wife had a controlling interest, but at the general election of 1820 he unsuccessfully contested the volatile borough of Colchester. That year he bought the Berkshire estate of Swallowfield Park, six miles south of Reading, near the Hampshire border. He had the existing house extensively altered, and seems to have spent most of his time at his London home at 62 Wimpole Street, where Ugo Foscolo, the Italian poet, was a regular guest. After his death in 1836 his personalty was sworn under £80,000.[3]

With his second wife Russell had five sons. The two youngest, Whitworth (1796-1847) and George Lake (1802-78), made careers in the church and the law respectively, while the other three were all provided with appointments in India. Henry (1783-1852), the eldest, obtained a writership with the East India Company in 1798 and occupied a variety of posts before being made resident at Hyderabad in 1810.[4] Francis Whitworth (1790-1852) also entered the civil service, in 1807, and was appointed second assistant to his brother in 1811. Both were educated at Charterhouse, but no record has been found of the English education of the second son, Charles Russell, the subject of this biography. Described by Hickey as 'a fine dashing youth',[5] he entered the Indian army in 1800 and served as an ensign and lieutenant in the 17th and 21st regiments of Native Infantry before being appointed to the command of the escort at Hyderabad in July 1810, when he also took temporary responsibility for the conduct of the business of the residency until Henry arrived from his previous post at Poona. He left India at the end of 1817, and on his way home visited St. Helena, where he was given a view of Buonaparte walking in front of his house, though he had declined to press for an interview on being told that he must address him as 'General'.[6] Back in England, he lived mostly in London, formally retired from the army in 1822 and became a proprietor of East India Company stock.

Russell was implicated with Henry, who retired as resident at Hyderabad in December 1820 and came home, in the scandal which broke at that time over the governor-general Lord Hastings's alleged corrupt partiality on behalf of the Hyderabad banking house of Palmer and Company, to whom in 1816 he had granted an exemption from the Act of 1797 prohibiting British subjects from lending money to the native princes. It emerged that Henry Russell had been involved in and profited from the firm's dealings with the nizam of Hyderabad; and his successor as resident, Sir Charles Metcalfe, discovered and revealed to the home government that the new loan of 1820 was fraudulent and fictitious. The affair was investigated by the East India Company, who in 1824 ordered the relevant papers to be printed. In response, Henry Russell published a *Letter to the Court of Directors*, in which he sought to vindicate himself and Charles from the allegations against them, complaining that these had originated in 'acrimonious party spirit' and that they had been given no chance to defend themselves. He did so when the matter was debated in the court in February 1825. To avoid a charge of peculation against Hastings, the court passed resolutions absolving him and, by implication, the members of the residency from acting corruptly, but endorsing earlier Company despatches censuring the encouragement of the dealings of Palmer and Company.[7]

Soon afterwards Henry Russell, who had married in 1816, as his second wife, a French aristocrat, Marie Clotilde Mottet de la Fontaine, moved from his quarters at Sutton Park, near Biggleswade, Bedfordshire, to Southern Hill, Reading, from where he kept an eye on the completion of the work at Swallowfield. There was a late approach for him to stand for Colchester at the general election of 1826, but his father would not sanction another contest, which there was no guarantee of avoiding. Charles offered to stand in his place, on the understanding that he would retire should there be a contest, if Henry thought it prudent for himself to keep a low profile until the Hyderabad affair, which it seemed might be raised in Parliament, had completely blown over; but he was 'not very solicitous about it', and kept the notion secret from their father. Henry vetoed involvement in Colchester, arguing that the risk of becoming embroiled in a ruinous contest was too great, and pointing out that Daniel Whittle Harvey, the sitting Member and local radical hero, who had attacked their father mercilessly in 1820, and since interested himself in the Hyderabad affair, would exploit it in order to 'defame' Charles and the rest of the family. Otherwise, he did not consider the Indian scandal a reason in itself for staying out of Parliament, and recommended Charles to take any offer of 'a close seat at a fair price'. Although Charles thought there was every chance of avoiding a contest at Colchester and that it was in Harvey's 'interest as much as ours to keep things quiet', he had to agree that it was best to keep away:

> Once entangled with Colchester, occasions of local politics and local patronage would be every day occurring to excite angry feelings and we should be involved from one end of the session to another in newspaper skirmishing. I remember thinking when I heard that Harvey was the author of those long dissertations on the Hyderabad question that one motive ... was to arm himself with weapons against us. Hang that rascal Metcalfe. How he is perpetually crossing our path.[8]

At the 1826 election, Henry and his wife, despite her advanced state of pregnancy, were very active in support of George Spence, the candidate of the Reading Blue or Tory party, a firm opponent of Catholic relief, who succeeded in defeating Charles Fyshe Palmer, the advanced Whig sitting Member, though he was turned out on Palmer's petition nine months later. Henry Russell's intervention was inspired by a desire to secure his own eventual return for the borough on the Blue interest, but Charles, who thought he had an awkward game to play, advised him to proceed cautiously and avoid being 'drawn into the town set', especially as he was a newcomer to the county.[9] At a celebration dinner, 19 July 1826, Henry professed his personal support for religious toleration, but answered criticism of his wife's having canvassed for an opponent of the claims of her fellow-Catholics by saying that she did not wish her children to suffer from revolution in England as her father had in France. He accused Fyshe Palmer and John Monck, the radical Whig returned with Spence, of having in the previous Parliament sought to obstruct a liberalizing government through factious opposition. Charles complimented him on the speech:

> I think you are rather above than below your audience, but it is a fault on the right side. The tone of a gentleman is always becoming and the blackguards, if they do not thoroughly understand it, are pleased to be thought to understand it ... I think you have very judiciously shown your opinions on the Catholic question and your coincidence with the liberal part of the administration.[10]

Charles Russell accompanied Henry on a tour of Flanders, Germany, Switzerland and France in the summer of 1827.[11] In January 1828 he went to Dover, his father's birthplace, to investigate the possibility of standing for the vacant seat, but he retreated, with few regrets, on finding that an anti-Catholic was required. In April he reported to Henry 'a very curious proposition' made to him by a stockbroker cousin of Abel Dottin, Member for Southampton, to purchase for £63,000 property in an unnamed borough, which would give command of 214 of the electors and thus of both seats. Even more 'extraordinary', the offer was coupled with one of a peerage on secret payment of an additional £40,000. Nothing, of course, came of this 'gross fudge'.[12] Later in the year he was in the Low Countries with Henry.[13] In June 1829 he received from the same source as the previous year an offer, for himself or Henry, of the seat for Leominster soon to be vacated by the outlawry of Rowland Stephenson. He was not convinced by the assurances he received that there would be no contest, and did not seriously pursue the matter.[14] In March 1830 Spence told him that Holmes, the government whip, had sounded him as to whether Henry 'wished to be in Parliament' and would support the duke of Wellington's ministry if he was.[15] It was Charles rather than Henry, whose indifferent health may have been a deterrent, who offered for Reading at the 1830 general election, when Monck unexpectedly retired and recommended as his successor Stephen Lushington*, the prominent Whig civilian. Henry acted as his chaperon and mentor throughout the ensuing contest, which cost them not far short of £6,500.[16] On the hustings Russell uttered the platitudes of independence, but addressed the allegations that he was the advocate of West Indian slavery and the 'promoter of monopoly' by the East India Company: he 'utterly abhorred' slavery, but its abolition required a balancing 'measure for the protection of British property'; and he had 'no tie to bind him' to the Company and its interests. After a protracted contest, prolonged by the referral of numerous disputed votes to the assessor, he narrowly beat Lushington into third place. Claiming that the Blues had 'rescued the borough from the intolerable burden which oppressed it', he declared that he would 'go to Parliament a free and independent Member'.[17] To Henry he offered

> my most grateful thanks for all your kindness during the election. Nothing but your assistance could have carried me through it ... I wish to God you had been fighting for yourself instead of for me. Your success would have been more easy and more certain and you would have made a much better use of it both for the public and your own family. I will not despair, however, of seeing us still side by side in the House.[18]

In a speech at the Blues' celebration dinner, 9 Sept. 1830, which was probably got up for him by Henry, he observed that while in many respects party differences were 'now scarcely perceptible', there remained important distinctions between Tories and Whigs on a variety of issues. In general terms

> they would rashly sweep away what they consider, and what we, perhaps, may consider, the evil, regardless of the good which must be carried with it. We would separate the evil from the good, and would even consent to endure the smaller portion of the evil, rather than expose to risk the infinitely larger portion of the good. The leading principle on which they proceed ... is practically a destructive principle. The leading principle on which we proceed ... is practically a conservative principle.

He claimed to be anxious to convince the more moderate Whigs, with whom he was content to share the representation, that 'we are no more enamoured than they are of a despotic power, but that we would only so temper our love of civil liberty, as to prevent freedom from degenerating into licence, anarchy and revolution'.[19]

The Wellington ministry listed Russell, who on 28 Sept. 1830 'saw old Talleyrand on his way to Portland Place through Regent Street', as one of their 'friends'. On 11 Oct. he met Planta, the patronage secretary, 'whose whole manner', he reported to Henry, 'was courteous and complimentary', as he 'said we had fought the battle gallantly and they felt very much indebted to us'.[20] The following day a Reading meeting, which Palmer attended but Russell did not, carried a petition for repeal of the house and window taxes and a resolution that the Members be requested to present and support it. Russell, observing to his brother that 'my troubles begin to thicken on me', thought it was 'hard under a declining revenue to force on a minister specific repeals of taxation', and said he would agree to present any petition entrusted to him and promise to support 'every measure of retrenchment which may be compatible with the safety of the state', but refuse to pledge himself to specifics 'until I see what measures are proposed by the government'. He was also requested by the local Quakers to attend an anti-slavery meeting, fixed for 21 Oct., but he was strongly inclined to stay away, plead a prior engagement in London and refer to his pronouncements on the hustings:

> I am aware that my answers in both these cases will be held to be evasive, but they are no more so than prudence requires and than all my declarations have invariably been. They must be so if I would go unfettered to these questions. If I acquiesce more fully or attend the meetings I shall gradually be drawn into the predicament of connecting myself with the radical and Dissenting party.

At his request, Henry drafted a letter of excuse to the anti-slavery meeting, which he had no difficulty in evading, even though he was in Reading only a day or two beforehand to speak at the visitation feast of the grammar school. He also stayed away from – indeed seems not to have remotely considered attending – a meeting in support of parliamentary reform, held on the same day as the anti-slavery one, and at which Palmer was present.[21] Unsure whether or not to speak on the assessed taxes petition whenever his colleague presented it, he sketched a short speech, which he wished to be 'sound in principle, and clear and precise, though unpretending, in language', for Henry to polish or rewrite as necessary:

> My scheme is to state the arguments in favour of a repeal of the taxes as strongly as I can; but to close my speech in

> such a way as to show that I am not ignorant of what are held to be the sound principles affecting the question and to leave myself at liberty to vote as future circumstances may suggest.

He did likewise on the subject of slavery:

> The two points I aim at are to keep the direction of the measure in the hands of government and to confine ourselves in the present stage to obtaining the more cordial co-operation of the colonial legislatures ... for the amelioration of the condition of the slaves, because I am satisfied that these are the most effectual steps which an honest and zealous emancipist could take to accomplish the ultimate extinction of slavery. ... I am afraid that in presenting a petition such as that signed at Reading I shall hardly be considered as supporting it in going no further than I am disposed to go.[22]

Russell, who took his seat and the oaths on 26 Oct. 1830, shared in the general opinion that the government acted foolishly in cancelling the royal visit to the City on 9 Nov. On the problem of distress, he believed that although it was 'severe' among 'parts of the agricultural population', it was 'by no means general'; and he was inclined to think that 'in the present state of the government and the country ... I shall be wise in saying as little as may be with my petitions'. On 13 Nov. he wrote to Henry:

> The government is evidently very hard pressed for speakers. Last night Planta watched an opportunity of getting next me and after some general conversation said, 'When do you intend to speak? We want very much to hear you'. I made all sorts of modest speeches when he urged me to speak on Tuesday [16 Nov.] on the question of parliamentary reform and added, 'You must try a rap at that fellow Brougham'. Of course I persisted in declining. It is a bad subject for a man representing a popular borough to begin upon, and I have not time now, even if I were so inclined, to prepare myself properly.[23]

He voted silently with ministers in the division on the civil list which brought them down, 15 Nov. As he had feared, a petition against his return alleging bribery and corruption was presented, 16 Nov.; but its promoters, anticipating an early dissolution after the change of government, did not persevere with it. This was 'a great relief' to him, though he remained anxious that his accounts should be promptly settled and that extreme care should be taken in 'making illegal payments', which might yet land him in trouble.[24] He soon had more pressing matters to worry about, for he was informed by the editor of the Tory *Berkshire Chronicle* that his vote with ministers on the civil list had 'occasioned disappointment at Reading'. Russell, who argued that it was 'absurd to call it a question of economy', for it had been one of 'whether the duke of Wellington or Lord Grey should be premier, and I should have been a coward and traitor if I had not voted as I did', authorized him to print a defence of his vote, after consulting Henry, if it was attacked in the liberal *Reading Mercury*. Nothing was done immediately, but it emerged that many of Russell's leading friends at Reading were 'grievously offended'. He thought they were being 'very unreasonable', and refused to repent of his vote, as he explained to Henry:

> It seems to me that after professing in every speech I made at Reading opinions favourable to the late ministry, I should have been guilty of the grossest inconsistency, if, on the first important division, before they had time to develop any of their plans, I had lent my hand to cut their throats. Even the opposition ... raised but little clamour about the amount of the civil list ... I know as a positive fact that the effect of the division ... was not generally foreseen, and that, if it had been, many who voted in the majority would have supported ministers.

At the same time, he was willing to go to Reading in person to attempt to pacify his critics, if Henry approved. In the event, after he had been denounced in the *Mercury* of 29 Nov., he and his brother decided to reply with a written defence in the *Chronicle*. Their original intention was to couple this with an attack on the new ministry, for which Russell thought there were 'good materials' in its aristocratic composition, Grey's nepotism and the removal of Brougham from the Commons, which hinted at backsliding on reform. When, however, Russell was told that 'the opinion of the necessity of economy and reform seems universal and prevails with both parties' in Reading, and that there was 'a desire to give a fair trial on these points' to the new government, he warned Henry:

> You see we must manage any attack on the present ministry cautiously. It is still ... open to us to say, though we do not feel implicit confidence in them, that we are willing to give them a trial. If we predict disappointment to the public expectation I do not think we shall prove false prophets. The blindness of those who swelled the majority to the effects of their votes seem to me a fair sort of hint for a newspaper.

He still contemplated making a speech on the assessed taxes, using material culled from the practical example of their effects in Reading to put forward a scheme for their modification. He thought that the article which Henry composed for the *Chronicle* of 4 Dec. was 'capital' and provided a 'complete' defence of his vote, though he agreed that when it had had time to take effect he should go down in person to make such explanations as were necessary. Both discounted the notion, urged on them by their chief agent, Alfred Compigne, that Russell should justify the vote in a public letter to the electors. As he put it to Henry:

> It is the adoption of a principle, from which I entirely dissent, that I owe a responsibility to my constituents for each individual vote; it may prove a very inconvenient and embarrassing precedent; and it commits me still further than I am committed to the present opposition and against the present government.

He was the less inclined to this course because he thought that he had done himself some good by his brief intervention, 10 Dec., in warm support of the prayer of a petition entrusted to him, perhaps mischievously, by 'the opposite party', led by Monck, endorsing Brougham's bill to establish local courts. He did not, however, read it to the House, because he 'did not approve of the vehement language in which it was couched'. He presented without comment a petition from the women of Reading for the abolition of slavery, 17 Dec. Asking his brother, 11 Dec. 1830, if there was any prospect of a Reading reform meeting, he commented:

> I had rather avoid attending if I can, but I suppose I will be required to show myself. My opinion has always been favourable to granting representatives to the large unrepresented towns, and for this, among other reasons, that I think it will prove the means of checking the torrent of reform.[25]

At the start of the new year Russell was busy trying to bring his election accounts to a final settlement and, alarmed by persistent reports of an early dissolution, he made plans to show himself in Reading. Henry advised him to accompany Monck and the town deputation to Lord Melbourne, the home secretary, with a petition pleading for clemency for the 'Swing' rioters sentenced to death at the recent Berkshire special commission, even if he did not wish to sign it himself.[26] He thought the signatories for the county reform meeting, 17 Jan. 1831, were 'few and scurvy', but he attended, with Palmer, and spoke, to the effect that reform was no longer a party measure and was about to be brought on by ministers, to whom he was happy to leave the details, 'on a firm conviction of its expediency'. He read extracts from a recent speech on the subject by Grey and said that he was prepared to support a 'temperate' measure of the type foreshadowed by the premier. Repeatedly called on to pronounce on the ballot, he said that such 'an innovation upon the constitution' 'would not lead to the results which the supporters of it expected'. Henry did not think that 'any substantial use' could be made of the argument which he privately advanced that the ballot would destroy beneficial 'social influences' and admit the 'evil' ones of 'such men as [William] Cobbett† and Carlile'. Russell, however, harboured notions of speaking on Warburton's promised motion on the subject, and Henry duly worked up a suitable speech based on his ideas.[27] On 26 Jan. Henry received a visit from Wellington, whose Hampshire house at Stratfield Saye was only a few miles from Swallowfield. He informed Charles that 'from his whole tone and manner, I am quite sure that your vote has been neither overlooked nor thrown away'. At the town reform meeting, promoted by the radicals, 31 Jan., for which Henry made a surreptitious muster of Blues, Russell, coached by his brother beforehand, reiterated his willingness to support 'a practical and substantial reform', so long as it was 'temperate and consonant with the principles and practice of the English constitution'. He flatly refused to countenance the ballot, an amendment for which was carried, and, replying to a personal attack, defended his vote on the civil list, saying that he had supported the late administration 'because he believed them friends to economy and peace' and that if the Grey ministry 'showed the same inclination to the two objects, he should give them the same support'. His brother produced a slightly improved version of his speech for insertion in the *Chronicle*; and he was pleased to learn that even some of the radicals conceded that he had performed well and with unsuspected ability.[28] Not without difficulty, Henry composed for him a speech on the ballot. Russell, who thought that ministers had made 'a false move' with their budget, particularly the proposed tax on transfers of funded property, was pleased with it, though he had to agree that the subject had become 'common and trite' and, thinking better of his plan, decided to remain silent 'unless the opening be very good'.[29] He gave his first impressions of the ministerial reform scheme to Henry, 2 Mar. 1831:

> It is gigantic in its dimensions, and it is impossible to contemplate such vast changes without anxiety and alarm. As regards the main point after all, however, the degree in which it will increase the democratic element of our constitution, it has some redeeming virtues.

These included the increase in the number of county Members and the proposal to exclude borough voters from counties, which would 'introduce into the House a phalanx of country gentlemen connected with the most solid property in the country'. He also liked the plans for a £10 householder borough franchise, getting rid of non-resident voters and shortening the duration of polls. Anticipating an early division, he urged Henry to make immediate soundings among their 'leading supporters' in Reading. Henry did so, and told him the following day that 'as far as you look to Reading, you must support the measure', which

> in its leading features, is popular among the most Tory of our friends. By supporting it, you will not displease any of your party, and you will conciliate several of the adverse party; by opposing it you will please nobody; you will exasperate all the adverse party, and alienate many of your own friends ... This ... is the unanimous opinion of all I have spoken to. For myself, I think it the beginning of revolution; but still I think it was inevitable ... It is desirable on every account that you should support it with a good grace.[30]

Russell, though still 'alarmed at the magnitude of the changes', thought that '*the government* having brought them forward, the country will never be satisfied till they are carried'; and he was therefore ready to support the bill 'on public ... as well as on personal considerations'. He was urged 'most vehemently' by Compigne to speak on it, but had 'great doubts of making any debut on such a question', fearing that 'the fall from such a height will be tremendous' and that it might be prudent to 'begin with less ambitious views'. He nevertheless sent for Henry's consideration the outline of a speech, which he admitted 'puts forward too much the objections to a measure which one intends to support'. Henry, observing that his speaking on the bill would only benefit him in Reading if he did so 'strongly and unreservedly in its favour', as 'anything like reluctant or qualified assent would only derogate from the merit which would be ascribed to even a silent vote in the affirmative', thought this line 'would never do':

> Your constituents would none of them thank you for doing what you proclaim you do against your judgement and inclination; and it would be truly said of you ... that you give your argument to one party and your vote to the other.

He advised Russell to give a silent vote for the second reading and to speak in committee, praising the bill's 'principle of raising the respectability of the electors' and arguing from that for an increase in the borough franchise to £12, or for the £10 qualification to be based on rates rather than rent. This, he contended, would have the added advantage in Reading of getting rid of that portion of the electorate which habitually held out for bribes and of damaging 'the radical party'; but he warned that he 'must not openly propose or advocate the change, for fear of giving offence to the parties who would be affected by it'. Russell, who asked Henry to try to get him off the hook with Compigne, was attracted by this idea, though he also composed a set speech on the principle of the measure for use should the occasion arise. His brother thought it admirable, but still felt that the case which it presented against the bill was stronger than that which it advanced in its favour; and, finding Compigne adamant in his view of the electoral advantages to be gained by a speech, he attempted to refine it. Russell, irritated by a further demand for money, complained to Henry that

> I have got amongst a set of cormorants, and, though I have not said it to a human being, I think I shall probably consult both my happiness and my interest by giving up Parliament. To be sure I have fallen on troubled times, but as yet I have experienced nothing but annoyance.

He also asked his brother to provide him with the outline of a short speech for the town meeting of 14 Mar. called to petition in support of the bill, and Henry obliged with an endorsement of its principle, 'framed ... according to what I think will please your hearers, those of our own, as well as of the adverse party'. Russell, who considered such meetings 'prodigious bores', told Henry, 10 Mar.:

> The ground on which I rest my vote is that the present bill, with great and alarming tendencies, yet has many securities; and that with the impulse which the measure has received from the authority of government, it is better to take it as it is and not wait till we shall get it on worse terms. This is my conscientious view, which is always a valid reason for presenting it. With respect to Reading, the honest truth is I am not over-solicitous about it. A seat in Parliament is not worth holding in such trammels, and under such odious and disgusting sacrifices as are constantly demanded from me.[31]

At the meeting he declared his unequivocal support for the bill, which was based on the 'combined principles of population and property; population, to infuse into the system the spirit of real and popular representation; property, to impart to it a character of stability and order'.[32] He did not in the event make a set speech on its second reading, but on 22 Mar., when Palmer presented the Reading petition, he 'forced on the House, which was very reluctant to listen to me', a 'few words' in support of it and the bill. His intervention escaped the notice of the reporters. Russell, who voted for the second reading later that day, could scarcely credit the rumours that there would be no dissolution even if the measure was defeated, for he could not see 'how Lord Grey is to carry on the business of the country with the present House' and thought that 'Peel would probably shrink from forming a new administration on the unpopular basis of a reform short of that now proposed'. His brother, who had all along regarded the bill with much greater alarm, and now claimed to perceive a rapid decline in enthusiasm for it, at first suggested that 'time only is wanted to defeat' it, and that if the king 'will but resist the demand for a dissolution Lord Grey must be driven out'; but he soon came to regard a dissolution as 'inevitable'.[33] Russell voted against Gascoyne's wrecking amendment, 19 Apr. 1831. At the ensuing general election he offered again for Reading, produced, as requested, a 'specific pledge in writing' of his intention to give his 'honest support' to the bill and was returned unopposed and by acclamation with Palmer. At the formalities, he reiterated his support for the measure on the grounds of 'that legitimate power given to property' and 'that influence conferred on those classes where influence ought to reside'. He reserved his right to support alterations and improvements, but denied that he did so 'in any covert spirit of hostility to the bill', citing his vote against Gascoyne's amendment as proof of his sincerity.[34]

He fell ill soon afterwards, but responded positively to Henry's warning in early June that one of the leading Blues felt that since the election he had allowed Palmer to steal a march on him in cultivation of the constituency.[35] He was, however, too unwell to attend the opening weeks of the new Parliament, obtained a fortnight's sick leave, 8 July, and did not resume his attendance until 26 July 1831.[36] His first known vote in committee on the reintroduced reform bill was for the partial disfranchisement of Sudbury, 2 Aug., though he confessed to Henry his belief that the hostile minority 'had much reason on their side'. He went on to vote fairly steadily for the details of the measure for the rest of that month, and was forced by his anxiety not to be absent from the debate on the borough qualification proposals, 'in which my Reading friends will take an interest', to miss his father's eightieth birthday celebrations on the 19th. Under 'urgent' pressure from Compigne to speak on the qualification clause, he did so, 24 Aug., when he supported that part of Polhill's amendment which sought to establish the parochial rate rather than rent as the test of value, arguing that it would remove a 'fertile source of fraud and litigation'. To Henry he wrote:

> I quite lost my head; and I fear that both my manner and matter must have seemed very confused. *Entre nous* I may say that I think it was a failure, but I trust that if not here I may have done myself good with my Tory friends, and no harm with my Whig friends, at Reading. And I must trust to the future to repair any mischief I may have done in the House to myself.[37]

He is not known to have opened his mouth again in debate in this period. He divided with ministers for the prosecution of those found guilty of giving bribes at the Dublin election, 23 Aug., but not against the subsequent motion of censure on the use of government influence. In September, fearing an early dissolution if the Lords rejected the bill, he got Henry to put in order their election accounts, which remained in an unsatisfactory state, so that they could prevent 'the wasteful and exorbitant expenditure' which had been foisted on them in 1830.[38] He was at dinner when the unexpected division on the third reading of the reform bill came on, 19 Sept., but he was present to vote for its passage two days later. He was 'not surprised' at his brother's report that the Reading meeting of 19 Sept. to petition the Lords to pass the bill was 'a failure', for he was aware that 'those in London even ... have been tame and thinly attended' and felt that 'this reaction of public opinion is beginning to produce its effect on the Lords'. At the annual Reading mayoral inauguration dinner, 3 Oct., he observed that 'whatever result might attend the present discussion ... the cause of legitimate reform had made great progress'.[39] Anticipating Lord Ebrington's motion of confidence in the ministry, he told Henry:

> If the reform question be made the ground ... or if it even occupy a prominent place amongst other grounds, I must vote for it *in redemption of my pledges*, for any course which could be interpreted into a shrinking from my promises would do me harm with both parties. If the reform question should not mentioned, and a resolution of confidence be proposed on general grounds, even then I think the utmost I could do would be to abstain ... and to take an opportunity of explaining at Reading that I did so because, though I could not give a vote which would embrace an approbation of the financial and foreign policy of the present ministry, yet that I could not give one which might be interpreted into a condemnation of their measures on the subject of parliamentary reform.

Henry, who as requested consulted Compigne, endorsed this line; and on 10 Oct. Russell duly voted for the motion, though he did not see 'what advantage' ministers derived from it, as it was 'generally understood that they retain their places' and obviously implied that they would 'at an early period bring forward the old measure with some modifications'. He was not sorry to receive notice of the Reading meeting called by Monck and the radicals to address the king in support of reform, 11 Oct., too late to be able to attend. Henry felt that if a similar county meeting was called, he would not be able to get out of it, especially if Palmer attended; but Russell thought it would be 'extremely awkward', as 'I could not avoid taking a decisive tone in supporting reform or I should be considered as a trimmer by the reformers; and if I did take a decisive tone I should offend many of the old Blue party'. Henry insisted that evasion, which would anger the radicals and dissatisfy the Blues, was not an option, for 'your aim must be to conciliate the reformers'; but in the event, to Russell's relief, no meeting took place.[40] He was unwell again later in the autumn, suffering from 'a deranged stomach, a dry hacking cough', and reporting that 'the secretions of my bowels are slimy and unhealthy'. He used his convalescence, as he slowly responded to treatment for a liver complaint, as an excuse to avoid attendance at the Reading dinner to pay tribute to Monck's public services, 22 Nov. 1831.[41]

Though still 'far from well', Russell, who, with Henry, was about to be plagued by the financial misdeeds of their brother Frank in India, was in the House for the opening of the new session. Of the changes to the reform bill, he wrote that they were 'literally nothing', and he was at a loss to know 'by what means Lord Grey proposes to carry it through the Lords'. He later informed Henry that 45 peers were to be made as soon as it passed the Commons, and that Grey had been 'troubled with the renewal of his vision of himself walking about with his head under his arm'.[42] He divided for the second reading, 17 Dec. 1831. He voted for the proposal to deprive 30 boroughs of one Member, 23 Jan. 1832, and the same day was in the majority against reform of select vestries. His vote against government on the Russian-Dutch loan, 26 Jan., apparently excited no interest in Reading.[43] He was added to the select committee on the East India Company's affairs, 22 Feb., the day after Henry gave evidence to its political and foreign subcommittee. He did so again, 30 Mar., and appeared before the military subcommittee, 19 Apr.[44] He voted with government in the reform committee divisions on Appleby, 21 Feb., Helston, 23 Feb., and Tower Hamlets, 28 Feb., and was present to vote for the third reading of the bill, 22 Mar.[45] He voted for the address calling on the king to appoint only ministers who would carry the bill unimpaired, 10 May; but, on the advice of Henry and Compigne, he stayed away from the Reading meeting called to consider the current crisis, 14 May. As his brother put it:

> The whole tone and character of the meeting, and the resolutions that will be moved, and probably adopted, are expected to be of the most violent description. Your entering into them cordially is out of the question; your entering into them partially will offend your friends, without satisfying your enemies; and your opposing them, perhaps the wisest as well as the manliest course, if you were compelled to attend, would exasperate a very powerful body of hostile and even neutral constituents, without pleasing the Tories a bit more than you would please them by staying away altogether.

As suggested by Henry, who thought that 'as long as you are to be essentially a Tory Member', there was no reason to dissemble the real reason for his absence, Russell wrote to the chairman stating that his votes provided 'the best proofs of his sincerity in the cause of reform'.[46] He voted for the second reading of the Irish reform bill, 25 May, and against any increase in the Scottish county representation, 1 June. He may have voted against ministers on the Russian-Dutch loan, 12 July 1832.

Russell was returned unopposed for Reading with Palmer at the 1832 general election, when he came out in favour of cautious reform of the church and the corn laws, but was evasive under questioning on the subjects of slavery, triennial parliaments and municipal reform. In the new Parliament he gravitated to the moderate Peelite Conservatives, and it was in those colours that he was elected in 1835 and narrowly defeated in 1837. He regained the seat in 1841, but lost it for the last time in 1847.[47] He was a forceful and successful chairman of the Great Western Railway in its formative years from 1839 until his retirement through ill health in August 1855.[48] He died by his own hand at his then London home in Argyll Street, off Oxford Street, 15 May 1856. (He was the second of the four Members for Reading in this period to take his own life, Spence having done so in 1850.) Evidence given to the inquest indicated that in his bedroom in the early hours he had shot himself in the mouth at the second attempt, after the pistol which he had first used had misfired. His valet, who testified that he had been suffering for the previous few days from chest pains, which had depressed him, found him alive but insensible at 6.45 in the morning, and he lingered until two in the afternoon with a bullet in his brain. A verdict of suicide under the influence of 'temporary insanity' was returned.[49] By his will and its six codicils, drawn up in February 1856, Russell left the residue of his estate to his nephew, Henry's son Charles, who had succeeded to the baronetcy and Swallowfield in 1852. He created a trust fund for the payment of various legacies, which included life annuities of £200 each to Mary Ann Watkins, a spinster, of Shepherd's Bush and her (and presumably his) daughter Jane Watkins, born in 1830. As the trustee of Mrs. Jane Monies, formerly Ellis, now confined in a Hoxton lunatic asylum, he left for her care and maintenance the rents and profits on a leasehold house in St. Pancras, together with such a sum as would provide her with £100 a year for life.[50]

[1]PROB 11/1239/614; C. Russell, *Swallowfield and its Owners*, 252. [2]Russell, 259; Add. 35643, f. 52; 35645, f. 135; *Hickey Mems*. ed. A. Spencer (1925), iv. 195, 211, 222, 232, 312-14; *Geo. III Corresp*. iv. 3163. [3]Russell, 254-8; *VCH Berks*. iii. 267; PROB 11/1859/187; IR26/1427/152. [4]Russell, 262-7. [5]*Hickey Mems*. iv. 260. [6]Russell, 286. [7]C.H. Philips, *E.I. Co*. 225-7; J.W. Kaye, *Life of Lord Metcalfe*, ii. 8-9, 11, 13-20, 41-94; *Oxford DNB sub* Hastings, F.R.; *The Times*, 12 Feb., 4 Mar., 27 May, 24 June 1824, 12, 19, 26 Feb., 2, 4, 17, 19 Mar. 1825; Bodl. MS. Eng. lett. c. 177, ff. 1-3. [8]Bodl. MS. Eng. lett. c. 159, ff. 38-43. [9]Ibid. ff. 32, 47, 51, 53, 68. [10]*Berks. Chron*. 29 July; *The Times*, 4 Aug. 1826; Bodl. MS. Eng. misc. c. 329, ff. 140-4; Eng. lett. c. 159, f. 118. [11]Bodl. MS. Eng. lett. c. 159, ff. 135, 139; c. 177, f. 150; Eng. misc. 329, ff. 96-125. [12]Bodl. MS. Eng. lett. c. 160, f. 7. [13]Bodl. MS. Eng. lett. c. 159, ff. 171, 173; Eng. misc. c. 329, ff. 128-35. [14]Bodl. MS. Eng. lett. c. 160, f. 83. [15]Ibid. f. 138. [16]*Reading Mercury*, 12, 19 July; *Berks. Chron*. 24 July 1830; Bodl. MS. Eng. misc. c. 329, ff. 234-318. [17]*Reading Mercury*, 26 July, 2, 9, 16 Aug. 1830. [18]Bodl. MS. Eng. lett. c. 160, f. 183. [19]*Berks. Chron*. 18 Sept. 1830. [20]Bodl. MS. Eng. lett. c. 160. ff. 191, 196. [21]*Reading Mercury*, 18, 25 Oct.; *Berks. Chron*. 23 Oct.; *The Times*, 26 Oct. 1830; Bodl. MS. Eng. lett. c. 160, ff. 199, 204, 205. [22]Bodl. MS. Eng. lett. c. 160, ff. 207, 210, 213, 218. [23]Ibid. ff. 210, 218, 223, 225. [24]Ibid. ff. 210, 218, 223, 225, 227, 232, 234, 239, 243, 247. [25]Ibid. ff. 236-59. [26]Bodl. MS. Eng. lett. d. 153, ff. 4-10. [27]Ibid. ff. 11, 14, 15, 18, 24; *Berks. Chron*. 22 Jan.; *Reading Mercury*, 24 Jan. 1831. [28]Bodl. MS. Eng. lett. d. 153, ff. 21, 27, 32, 34, 37; *The Times*, 1 Feb.; *Berks. Chron*. 5 Feb.; *Reading Mercury*, 7 Feb. 1831. [29]Bodl. MS. Eng. lett. d. 153, ff. 37, 39, 44, 48; Eng. misc. c. 329, f. 145. [30]Bodl. MS. Eng. lett. d. 153, ff. 68, 73. [31]Ibid. ff. 75-100. [32]*Windsor and Eton Express*, 19 Mar.; *Reading Mercury*, 21 Mar. 1831. [33]Bodl. MS. Eng. lett. d. 153, ff. 101-107. [34]*Reading Mercury*, 25 Apr., 2 May; *The Times*, 28 Apr.; *Berks. Chron*. 7 May 1831; Bodl. MS. Eng. misc. c. 329, ff. 222, 231. [35]Bodl. MS. Eng. lett. d. 153, ff. 113, 115. [36]*Reading Mercury*, 1 Aug.; *Berks. Chron*. 6 Aug. 1831. [37]Bodl. MS. Eng. lett. d. 153, ff. 121, 137, 144, 147, 153. [38]Ibid. ff. 163, 165, 169, 174, 181. [39]Ibid. ff. 183, 188, 190, 197; *Berks. Chron*. 8 Oct. 1831. [40]Bodl. MS. Eng. lett. d. 153, ff. 201-18. [41]Bodl. MS. Eng. lett. d. 154, ff. 2, 6, 8, 10, 16, 21, 26. [42]Ibid. ff. 26, 32, 55. [43]Ibid. ff. 71, 81. [44]*PP* (1831-2), xiii. 160-4; xiv. 10-16, 65-67, 162-74. [45]Bodl. MS. Eng. lett. d. 154, f. 90. [46]Ibid. f. 101; *The Times*, 16 May; *Reading Mercury*, 23 May 1832. [47]*Reading Mercury*, 10 Dec.; *The Times*, 11 Dec.; *Berks. Chron*. 15 Dec. 1832; *Dod's Parl. Companion* (1835), 119; (1843), 198. See also N. Gash, *Politics in Age of Peel*, 284-300, where, unaccountably, Russell is described as 'a West India proprietor' and the 'son of a West Indian nabob'. [48]E.T. MacDermot, *Hist. GWR*, i. 149-50, 399-401. [49]*The Times*, 17 May 1856. [50]PROB 11/2234/499; IR26/2075/601.

D.R.F.

RUSSELL, Francis (1793–1832), of 2 Charles Street, Grosvenor Square, Mdx.

TAVISTOCK 25 Oct. 1831–24 Nov. 1832

b. 7 Mar. 1793, 1st s. of Lord William Russell* (*d*. 1840) and Lady Charlotte Anne Villiers, da. of George Bussy Villiers†, 4th earl of Jersey; bro. of John Russell*. *educ*. Westminster; Christ Church, Oxf. 1810. *unm*. *d.v.p*. 24 Nov. 1832.

Ensign 2 Ft. Mar. 1811, lt. June 1811; lt. 7 Ft. July 1811, capt. 2nd garrison battalion and half-pay[I] 1814; capt. 57 Ft. 1816; capt. 52 Ft. 1817; brevet maj. 1819; capt. 12 Drag. 1819, half-pay 1821; brevet lt.-col. and inspecting field officer of militia, Nova Scotia 1821; capt. and lt.-col. Coldstream Gds. 1825-*d*.; a.d.c. to duke of York 1826-7.

Russell's mother died when he was 15, and his father, the younger brother of the 6th duke of Bedford, hitherto a keen politician in the family's Foxite Whig tradition, was driven by serious financial problems to adopt a nomadic existence to evade his creditors, though he retained his seat for Tavistock on the family interest until 1819. Russell joined the Peninsular army with the Royal Fusiliers in the summer of 1811, aged 18, and served with conspicuous gallantry at all the major engagements of the next three years. He was badly wounded at the storming of Badajoz in 1812.[1] Captain Gronow recalled his act of asinine bravery at the battle of the Pyrenees the following year:

> The French General ... sent an overwhelming force against Frank's regiment, which was posted against a mountain wall. The Fusiliers defended themselves with obstinate courage, but their colonel, for some reason which was never explained, declared it prudent to order a retreat, though his line was unbroken. Frank Russell, however, shouted out, 'Not yet, colonel', and with the colours of his regiment mounted the wall and cheered our men on; the French meanwhile renewing their attack with redoubled vigour. During this fierce struggle, however, our hero kept his position, till the fierce energy with which the French had been fighting began to cool: for Wellington had meanwhile broken Soult's centre, and the retreat of the French forces was ordered. Before Russell quitted his post of honour, Lord Wellington with his staff happened to pass by the wall, and saw Russell standing on the wall, holding the colours of his regiment, which were riddled with bullet holes. On the following day, when the gallant young officer's conduct was reported to our great commander, he exclaimed, 'Ah! there's nothing like blood'.[2]

At Waterloo Russell was aide-de-camp to the prince of Orange.[3] He had a period as inspector of militia in Nova Scotia in the early 1820s, and in 1825 obtained a lieutenant-colonelcy in the Coldstream Guards. The following year he was appointed one of the aides-de-camp to the duke of York, the commander-in-chief.[4]

Russell, a devotee of the Turf and a hopelessly addicted gambler, was a popular figure in fashionable society, for, in Gronow's words, 'his temper and disposition were eminently sociable, and he was noted for his kindness of heart'. He was also, as Gronow coyly put it, 'a great favourite with the fair sex', and had 'a pretty compliment' paid to him by the duchess of York, who 'presented him with a ring ... having for a motto, "None but the brave deserve the fair"'.[5] Greville recorded in 1820 that he had Lady Worcester on a string; and in 1824 the wife of his cousin Lord George William Russell* wrote to his father from Woburn Abbey:

> Your son *le beau Franzis* (as Alava calls him) was here – *l'air plus conquerant que jamais* – he looks at women and says 'how do you do' even, with a voice and glance accustomed to subdue. He has added to his manly attractions whiskers of dimensions hitherto unknown – not moustachios – but *les favoris*, they are black, bright, curled, thick, and garnish the whole face, which gives him the look of a *joli Sapeur*.[6]

In 1828, however, he was reported to be 'breaking his heart' for Isabella Forester.[7]

Russell, who had joined Brooks's in 1820, sponsored by his cousin Lord Tavistock* and his uncle the 5th earl of Jersey, entered the House for Tavistock in October 1831 when Lord Tavistock's young son found parliamentary life too much for his health. Bedford reported that 'the *Tavistockians* are much pleased with Francis'.[8] Sworn in on 7 Dec., he voted for the second reading of the revised reform bill, 17 Dec. 1831. He was a steady, though silent supporter of its details and voted for its third reading, 22 Mar. 1832. He voted for the address calling on the king to appoint only ministers who would carry undiluted reform, 10 May, and for the Scottish reform bill, 1, 15 June. He divided with ministers on the Russian-Dutch loan, 26 Jan., 12, 16, 20 July, relations with Portugal, 9 Feb., and against Hunt's motion for information on military punishments, 16 Feb. 1832.

Lady William was unintentionally prophetic when she told Russell's father at the time of his return that he 'has been dying to be in Parliament these many years', for he died, intestate and *v.p.*, 'of a rapid decline' in November 1832, just over a week before the dissolution.[9] Bedford told Lady Holland, 28 Nov., that he had been 'sadly affected' by Russell's death 'and all the melancholy circumstances attending it', but that he had 'the consolation of reflecting that no human skill or care could have saved him'.[10] To his son Lord George William Russell he wrote:

> Poor fellow! He was capable of better things than an inglorious life spent amongst Newmarket gamblers and blacklegs! He was a brave and high-spirited soldier, and had excellent abilities, besides many other good qualities; but the love of gambling wholly absorbed him, and I have no doubt that his losses preying on his mind accelerated the bodily disease which eventually carried him off, by total destruction of his lungs.[11]

Lord John Russell*, reflecting on his cousin's 'melancholy end', wished that 'he could have lived to act a better part in society', but observed that 'if he had one uncle to save him, he had a father and an uncle to lead him wrong'.[12] Russell left massive debts, reportedly in the region of £35,000.[13] Administration of his effects, which were sworn under £1,000, was granted to his younger brother John.[14]

[1] *Gent. Mag.* (1833), i. 84. [2] *Gronow Reminiscences*, ii. 198-9. [3] *Gent Mag.* (1833), i. 84; *HMC Bathurst*, 283. [4] *Russell Letters*, ii. 14; Add. 52017, Townshend to H. E. Fox, 30 Apr. 1826; *Greville Mems.* i. 159. [5] *Gronow Reminiscences*, i. 199-200; *Raikes Jnl.* i. 109; *Creevey Pprs.* ii. 74, 100, 167; *Greville Mems.* i. 217, 221, 294; *Von Neumann Diary*, i. 231, 240. [6] *Greville Mems.* i. 101; Blakiston, *Lord William Russell*, 114. [7] NLW, ms 2796 D, Lady Delamere to H. Williams Wynn, 20 Mar. 1828. [8] Blakiston, 243; Add. 51670, Bedford to Holland, 24 Oct., to Lady Holland, 31 Oct. [1831]. [9] Blakiston, 243; *Raikes Jnl.* i. 109; *Gent. Mag.*(1833), i. 84; *The Times*, 3 Dec. 1832. [10] Add. 51671. [11] *Russell Letters*, iii. 32. [12] Add. 51680, Russell to Lady Holland, 2 Dec. [1832]. [13] *Greville Mems.* ii. 352; *Miss Eden's Letters* ed. V. Dickinson, 216. [14] PROB 6/209/246.

D.R.F.

RUSSELL, Francis, mq. of Tavistock (1788–1861), of Oakley, Beds. and 18 Arlington Street, Mdx.

PETERBOROUGH	14 Mar. 1809–1812
BEDFORDSHIRE	1812–1832

b. 13 May 1788, 1st s. of John Russell†, 6th duke of Bedford, and 1st w. Hon. Georgiana Byng, da. of George, 4th Visct. Torrington; bro. of Lord George William Russell* and Lord John Russell*. *educ.* by Dr. Moore, Sunbury; Westminster 1801; by Rev. John Smith at Woodnesborough, nr. Sandwich 1805-6; Trinity Coll. Camb. 1807. *m.* 8 Aug. 1808, Lady Anna Maria Stanhope, da. of Charles Stanhope†, 3rd earl of Harrington, 1s. *summ.* to the Lords in his fa.'s barony as Lord Howland 15 Jan. 1833; *suc.* fa. as 7th duke of Bedford 20 Oct. 1839; KG 26 Mar. 1847. *d.* 14 May 1861.

PC 6 July 1846.

Ld. lt. Beds. 1859-*d.*

Lt. Beds. militia 1806-9, lt.-col. 1809; capt. Woburn yeoman cav. 1807.

With his friends Lords Althorp* and Milton* – like himself the heirs of prominent Whig grandees – Tavistock was one of the 'Young Whigs', who, inspired by a strong sense of moral purpose, with Evangelical overtones, an awareness of the obligations of their rank and the tenets and spirit of liberalism, sought to co-operate with and harness moderate progressive opinion in order to promote change. Imbued with a deep detestation of all that Pittism had come to stand for, they espoused parliamentary reform as a means of forging an alliance between the landed interest and the commercial and industrial middle classes: government and aristocratic predominance in it, they believed, could only rest safely on the confidence and attachment of the governed.[1] Tavistock, though less intellectually inclined than the other two, was further to the left politically: he had been a supporter and advocate of parliamentary reform since the time of the 'Talents' ministry; had acted with the Whig 'Mountain' in the House, to the dismay of some of the party hierarchy; and had flirted with the Burdettites during their electoral struggles with the Whigs in Westminster in 1818-19, though his innate Whiggism had ultimately proved to be stronger than his radical leanings. Yet, for all his undoubted cerebral interest in politics, his active participation had been spasmodic, with bursts of zeal and energy (as when he campaigned vigorously for inquiry into the Peterloo massacre and opposed the subsequent repressive legislation in 1819) punctuating periods of indolence and indifference. The same was true of his parliamentary and political career in this period, when wretchedly poor health, together with his passionate love of hunting (he was a dedicated but accident prone master of the Oakley, 1822-9) and the Turf, frequently removed him from the centre of affairs. While he could speak forcefully when necessary, he was not a natural or gifted orator, being basically diffident, as well as handicapped by the characteristic Russell lisp. He had his share of his family's oddity. He was something of a cold fish, apparently without humour, 'feeble' as a social conversationalist, and capable of inducing numbing boredom in those who did not share his enthusiasms. Miss Eden, a victim on one occasion, wrote, without rancour, of 'that slightly damaged article, his mind. It is a good old mind, too, in its little bald shell'.[2] His friend and Cambridge contemporary John Cam Hobhouse, Burdett's protégé as Member for Westminster, whose sometimes prickly relationship with him grew easier during the 1820s, noted in 1827 that Tavistock 'does not like company, but he does not like solitude either. He is a good man, but not a happy man. Who is?' He added that 'he every now and then appears above himself, and gives proofs of a vigorous mind'.[3] He was, as Denis Le Marchant† observed, 'remarkable for the soundness and coolness of his judgement', which gave him a useful role as a political negotiator, conciliator and adviser.[4]

At the general election of 1820 Tavistock stood again for Bedfordshire on the powerful family interest, declaring himself to be a 'friend to religious freedom, an advocate for parliamentary reform, and an enemy of corruption'. A second Whig started in opposition to the ministerialist sitting Member, precipitating an expensive contest. In his nomination speech, Tavistock denied that reformers were the promoters of 'sedition, rebellion and assassination', denounced the massive tax burden which Pittism had imposed on the country as the price of military victory and condemned ministerial endorsement of the authorities' actions at Peterloo. Althorp feared that he might be defeated, but he topped the poll comfortably enough, with the Tory in third place.[5] Before his own election came on, he had seconded the nomination of the Whig Robert John Smith* for Buckinghamshire, where part of the Russell estates lay.[6] At the levee in early May 1820 he was, according to Althorp, 'received very graciously' by the new king.[7] Tavistock was reported to be, like his father and Lord Holland, one of the Whigs 'most inclined to high popular principles' who were 'determined not to consent' to Henry Brougham's becoming party leader in the Commons.[8] He voted against government on the civil list, 5, 8 May, and the appointment of an additional Scottish baron of exchequer, 15 May 1820. He presented a petition from Bedfordshire agriculturists praying for relief from distress, 16 May.[9] He resisted Hobhouse's pressure on him to attend the meeting in support of the jailed demagogue Henry Hunt* later that month, pleading that he was 'so little in the habit of taking a lead in public matters' that it would not be congenial.[10] He may have been in the minority against the appointment of a secret committee on the conduct of Queen Caroline, 26 June. According to Sir James Mackintosh*, Tavistock's aunt Lady Bath

> expostulated very warmly with ... [him] on Lady T[avistock] leaving her name with the queen ... [Tavistock] first defended himself by urging the numerous presents and favours which Lady T. when going had accepted from the queen; but on being pressed about the queen's bad character, he said, 'I can no longer bear this sanctimonious morality. Is not Lady Charlotte Greville who is your most intimate friend known to be the duke of Wellington's mistress?[11]

He divided for economies in revenue collection, 4 July, and against the aliens bill, 7 July 1820.

At the Bedfordshire county meeting got up by his father to express support for the queen and petition for parliamentary reform, 12 Jan. 1821, Tavistock declared that

> nothing but meetings like the present could bring about any change in a system so long and so fatally pursued ... For the sake of their offices ... [ministers] were content to sacrifice their queen. They had now goaded the people almost to despair and risked a revolution ... It had long been his persuasion that no good could arise from a mere change of men without a temperate but effectual reform of Parliament.[12]

In a public exchange of letters with the lord lieutenant, Lord Grantham, he refused to sign the loyal declaration got up by the county Tories because it was 'of a party nature, intended as an indirect support of the king's ministers, and may be interpreted as a covert approbation of the late and present measures against the queen'.[13] When he presented the county meeting's petition, 26 Jan., he accused ministers of skulking away from the force of public opinion and exhorted them to 'pause before they drove the people to the last extremity of despair'. He voted for restoration of the queen's name to the liturgy, 23 Jan. He proposed to move a series of resolutions criticizing the proceedings against her, which most leading members of the Whig party felt should take precedence over Lord Archibald Hamilton's planned motion for an address calling on the king to restore the queen's name. Hamilton insisted on going first, but reluctantly agreed to move resolutions instead of an address. Tavistock gave him silent support, 26 Jan.[14] He brought on his own censure motion, 5 Feb., when he said that he would take office under no administration and called for a mass petitioning movement for 'such a change in the representation as might make the House of Commons no longer the obedient instrument of the servants of the crown, but render it the legitimate and invariable organ of public opinion'. After the resumed debate, 6 Feb., the motion was humiliatingly crushed by 324-178. Thomas Creevey* thought that Tavistock's performance had been 'infinitely below himself', but Lady Granville heard that he 'did pretty well'.[15] The Tory backbencher Henry Bankes reckoned his speech was 'feeble and embarrassed', but the 'Mountaineer' Henry Grey Bennet judged it 'good', with 'parts of it ... forcible and eloquent'.[16] He again voted with opposition on the liturgy question, 13 Feb. He only paired for Catholic relief, 28 Feb., though he presented a Bedfordshire petition in favour of the bill, 19 Mar.[17] He voted for repeal of the additional malt duty, 21 Mar., and paired in the same sense, 3 Apr. At the Cambridgeshire reform meeting of 13 Mar., which he attended with his father, who advocated triennial parliaments and the enfranchisement of unrepresented large towns, he moved the resolutions, reiterated his support for reform and condemned the high taxation which financed the spoils system keeping ministers in power, but argued that it was now 'perfectly useless' to persist with the queen's cause. His father told Lady Holland, 16 Mar., that his 'manly declaration ... pleased me much, and if all our Whig reformers would follow his example, some good might be done'.[18] Tavistock was listed as a steward of the City reform dinner, 4 Apr., but, after his outburst at Cambridge, he saw no point in attending, as he told Hobhouse:

> If the Whigs are determined not to give the country some pledge about reform, I for one shall feel very much disposed to give up politics altogether. The events of the last few years have made me indifferent to almost every other subject of a public nature.

He voted for his brother Lord John Russell's parliamentary reform motion, 9 May, and, with Milton, later had what Bedford described as 'an unsatisfactory interview' with Lord Grey 'on a plan of promoting the measure by the Whigs'.[19] He presented a petition for mitigation of the penal code, 7 May,[20] and voted for repeal of the Blasphemous and Seditious Libels Act, 8 May, in censure of the delay in the commission of judicial inquiry, 9 May, against sending the printer of *John Bull* to Newgate, 11 May, to reduce the ordnance estimates, 14, 31 May, for inquiry into Peterloo, 16 May, for a reduction in the number of placemen in the House, 31 May, and against including arrears in the duke of Clarence's grant, 18 June. Seconding Hume's motion for an address to the king for economy and retrenchment, 27 June, he praised Hume's efforts to reduce public expenditure, but regretted that he had been forced by ministerial intransigence to resort to

> bringing all these minute details of the estimates before the House. This was a new feature in ... [their] proceedings ... They appeared to be deviating widely from the common and ancient usage of Parliament; and he was not one of those who wished to see that House assume the functions of the executive government.

He told Hume that he was wasting his time, and made a personal declaration that after witnessing the drunken excesses which had marked the last Bedfordshire election, 'he should not consider himself as acting either an honest or consistent part, if he ever again spent a single shilling to obtain a seat in that House'.[21] He acknowledged that ministers had recently slightly softened their tone on the question of economy, but ended with a denunciation of the large standing army and the plans to ring London with troops for the impending coronation. Grey Bennet thought he had adopted 'too desponding a tone'.[22] He felt that Tierney and other party leaders had 'abandoned him' on this subject, and 'suffered Lord Londonderry to browbeat and misrepresent him', and he therefore returned to the charge, 10 July 1821, when he tried unsuccessfully to get Londonderry to say when the army, even more unnecessarily large in view of the death of Buonaparte, was to be reduced.[23]

He divided for more extensive tax reductions to relieve distress, 11, 21 Feb. 1822, but his next recorded vote of that session was for remission of Hunt's sentence, 24 Apr. He attended the Cambridgeshire reform meeting, 4 Apr., when his father spoke at length but he remained silent. At the Bedfordshire reform meeting, 20 Apr., he spoke in his usual terms, but admitted that so hopeless was it to attempt an opposition to ministerial majorities ... he [had] ceased to give a constant attendance in the House, since it was only in waste of time and health, but only on all great questions he felt it his duty to appear in his place.[24] When he presented the petition, 25 Apr., he conceded that 'as long as government, through the medium of taxation, retained its present extent of patronage, so long it might set public opinion at defiance', but insisted that among the 'respectable, intelligent and suffering middle classes of the community' there was 'a total want of confidence in Parliament, and a firm belief in the necessity ... of parliamentary reform'.[25] Later that day he voted for his brother's reform scheme. He was present to vote for abolition of one of the joint-postmasterships, 2 May, and cuts in diplomatic expenditure, 15, 16 May; against the aliens bill, 14 June; in condemnation of the influence of the crown, 24 June, and of the conduct of the lord advocate towards the Scottish press, 25 June; for inquiry into chancery delays, 26 June, and for repeal of the salt, 28 June, and window taxes, 2 July. He was in the minority of 36 against the revised corn duties, 9 May 1822. That month he approached Hobhouse with his fanciful notion of having Sir Francis Burdett installed as Whig leader in the Commons. Burdett professed to Hobhouse willingness to take on the role, and Tavistock claimed to have secured influential support for the scheme, but it came to nothing.[26]

Early in 1823 Tavistock fell seriously ill with a digestive complaint, which kept him away from Parliament for the entire session. He paired for his brother's reform motion, 24 Apr., and may well have done so for other divisions. In March Hobhouse, who wrongly thought that he had persuaded him to give up hunting, found him in 'a very precarious state of health indeed', and the following month his brother Lord George William Russell was shocked to find him 'a perfect skeleton'. He rallied with the arrival of spring and summer, though he remained, to the distress of his father, 'sadly wasted in bulk'.[27] In August, however, he suffered a relapse, and was for some weeks so ill that many gave him up for dead, as they did his father, who was also in a bad way.[28] With the aid of a milk diet, he recovered and put on weight, and by November 1823 was considered to be out of danger and on the mend. Lord George William observed that he 'will be an invalid for a long time, and will probably be obliged to give up hunting, or at least to take it in moderation'. Lady William reported to Tavistock's uncle, old Lord William Russell*:

> He weighs more, he loses no more, he sleeps better, he has an appetite, his spirits have returned – that he must look lean and haggard for a long time to come is but natural, *mais voilà où nous en sommes après en avoir été quittés pour la peur* for everyone thought him dying ... Although he is by no means an agreeable member of society he is an honest one – a good Whig – a good sportsman – a good landlord in prospective ... I felt very sorry ... though not affecting to be frantic with grief as his demise would have made no vacuum in my affections, never having exchanged above a hundred words with him ... and having, of course, no ideas in common.

Lord John was 'delighted', 'as he is the best, most kind-hearted, generous friend I have in the world'.[29]

Tavistock was *hors de combat* as far as Parliament was concerned for the whole of the 1824 session, from which the record of his pair for the division on Brougham's motion condemning the prosecution of the Methodist missionary John Smith in Demerara, 11 June, has survived. There were varying reports on the state of his health throughout the year, and in late October his father noted that he 'seems much more feeble and languid than he ought to be'. A month later Tavistock himself told Hobhouse that 'I have gained a little strength, and a little flesh since I saw you, but it is slow work'. He suffered a temporary setback in January 1825.[30] He was a defaulter on a call of the House, 28 Feb., paired for Catholic relief, 1 Mar., was ordered to be taken into custody for non-appearance the following day, and formally discharged on the 3rd.[31] He paired for the relief bill, 21 Apr., 10 May, but was present to vote against the duke of Cumberland's annuity bill, 6, 10 June 1825, when, leading the opposition to its third reading, he explained that while he could have swallowed a direct grant, he could not accept one which was notoriously to be used for a purpose other than that for which it was ostensibly granted. He concluded:

> He had witnessed with pleasure the wise and liberal policy which had recently been adopted by ministers, and especially by ... [Canning]. He was, therefore, at a loss how to express the astonishment he felt at seeing them risking the great popularity they had so justly acquired, by making themselves parties to a juggle like the present.

On 17 Oct. 1825 Tavistock, who was now back in the saddle, issued an address to the freeholders of Bedfordshire stating that in fulfilment of his pledge of 1821, he would neither canvass nor spend any money to secure his return for the county at the next general election, when it was up to the electors to choose him or reject him, on grounds of political principle, as they saw fit. He was 'full of eagerness' for what he saw as a personal attempt to advance the wider cause of reform by promoting the moral regeneration of the electorate. His father approved, thinking that it would 'have the most beneficial effect, ultimately';

but Tierney expressed reservations, 'in his usual way of croaking', and Lord John Russell commented that 'to use a metaphor that is appropriate, he hunts a fox by himself very well, but he does not run with the pack'.[32] Early in the new year Tavistock discussed prospects for the Catholic question with Althorp at Woburn Abbey. He was unsure whether to subscribe to James Silk Buckingham's *Oriental Herald*, on which he consulted Hobhouse, but he was in the majority for his brother's motion for inquiry into Buckingham's petition for redress of his grievances against the East India Company, 9 May 1826.[33] Tavistock, who complained of being 'far less well since he left the country', having 'lost 7lb in weight',[34] also voted for reform of Edinburgh's representation, 13 Apr., and Lord John's reform motion, 27 Apr., and resolutions condemning electoral bribery, 26 May 1826.

It had seemed for many months that Tavistock and Thomas Macqueen, a wealthy, anti-Catholic Tory, would walk over the course for Bedfordshire, for his Whig colleague Pym had announced his retirement in December 1825, and no replacement candidate could be found. At the last minute, however, the local Whigs in desperation subscribed to support Pym, who did not attend the election but indicated through his son that he would serve if returned. At the nomination Tavistock confirmed that 'latterly he had supported the measures of ministers, in consequence of Mr. Canning adopting a more liberal policy'. He called for an 'absolutely necessary' reduction of taxation, but stated that much as he approved of free trade in principle, he believed that an adequate protecting duty on corn 'could alone save the farmer from ruin'. He affirmed his support for Catholic claims and his determination to abide strictly by the terms of his October address. Widespread resentment of his refusal to spend any money led to angry scenes around the hustings, where he was so knocked about that he hardly appeared there after the first day, leaving friends and prominent supporters, including Althorp and Lord William Russell, to speak for him. He finished in second place, almost 250 votes behind Macqueen, with Pym a distant third.[35] It was revealed after the election that when he issued his address of 1825, Tavistock had written to Dr. Joseph Thackeray pledging to give £2,000, which would otherwise have been spent on promoting 'drunkenness and corruption', towards the new buildings planned for the county infirmary.[36] While the outcome of the election seemed to some, including Lord Holland, a humiliating rebuff for the 'Tavistock principle' (the more so as Lord John Russell was beaten into third place in Huntingdonshire, where he sought re-election on the same platform), Tavistock himself, as he told Hobhouse, considered that it had been 'more than satisfactory'. His father, too, professed to believe that 'the event will work well for Tavistock's plan of internal election reform, though I may not live to see it'. To Bedford's regret, Tavistock decided not to publish his election addresses and speeches: 'I must be content to be misunderstood and misrepresented, which is certainly a bore, but it can't be helped'. After further reflection on the election, he concluded that 'if I had spent £20,000 I should not have polled ten more votes', though he thought that a protracted canvass might have raised him in the poll. Yet he believed that a 'quite disheartening ... decline of public principle', whereby 'people are ready to vote for any man who will seek places in the excise and customs, writerships and cadetships, promotion in the army and navy, and preferment in the church', had been the main obstacle to the unqualified success of his experiment. Later in the year, refusing to be a party to a contemplated petition against Macqueen, he observed to Milton that if the electors were corrupt, the 'fault of having corrupted them' lay with himself and his former Tory colleague:

> If I have seen my error only lately it is no wonder they should not yet be reformed. It is a satisfaction, however, to me to reflect that the result of the late election was a more constitutional, a less drunken contest than was ever before known, and thereby a great reform, and a great good has been effected.[37]

Tavistock had 'a baddish fall' in the hunting field in mid-November 1826, when he was exercised about the choice of university for his hypocondriachal only son, whose education he closely and fussily supervised, and who was a source of constant worry for him.[38] On 19 Feb. 1827 he went to London in dreadful weather to speak and vote (to the annoyance of Holland) against the Clarence grant, 'one of the most indecent and most ill-timed propositions he ever remembered during his parliamentary experience'.[39] He was initially disinclined to go up to support Burdett's motion for Catholic relief, arguing to Hobhouse that there was no reason for the Whigs to 'take up that which is the business of government and ought to be a government measure', and that 'there can be no good reason for risking all our popularity and our chance of doing good, merely for the sake of keeping up a juggle between one set of ministers and another'. In the end, not wishing to be 'obstinate in this matter, or to stand aloof from my friends', he gave way, though he remained convinced that he was right, and that if Ireland was in 'such a wretched state' as Hobhouse claimed, it was 'more than ever the business of the ministers to take a decided line, and let us support or oppose their measures as we find them to be good or bad'. He duly voted in Burdett's minority, 6 Mar. 1827, but he subsequently wrote angrily to Hobhouse:

> Having sacrificed my own opinions and consistency, and the decided policy of my constituents, in deference to the wishes of others ... I beg you will take an opportunity of informing Burdett that I must follow my own course another time, though I cannot think that he will ever meddle with the subject again, till His Majesty thinks fit to call to his counsels a cabinet united on the subject. The farce supported by us, has existed for sufficiently long to open the eyes of everyone. Our *majorities* have been gradually growing smaller and smaller, till at length we have been left in a *minority*, with the country more against us than at any former period ... Every trick, and every kind of corruption was made use of at the general election to procure a majority against the Catholics, and this was more than connived at by Canning ... I am glad we are beat, because it will open people's eyes, and set the question at rest in its *present shape*.

He subsequently explained that while he did not doubt Canning's sincerity in wishing to carry the Catholic question provided he could stay in place, 'if he cannot have both, he had rather keep his place than lose both'.[40]

Tavistock, like Althorp and Milton, refused to join in the Whig coalition with Canning in April 1827, 'solely on account of my reform principles', as he told Holland, though he argued that 'moderate Whigs might without any violation of principle join him, and let us radicals stand by, and see fair play between such a government and the Ultra Tory opposition'. Anxious that there should be no conflict or misunderstanding between himself and Althorp, he reviewed the situation towards the end of the month, seeking to steer a middle course between the keenness to support the new ministry shown by such as Brougham and Sir Robert Wilson, who were 'so overjoyed at having got rid of the old high Tory faction, that they seem to be in great danger of losing sight of principle', and the overt hostility of Grey, who was 'perhaps too nice under all the circumstances of the case and expects too much'. As well as noting the fact that on the Catholic question the 'same game is to be played, with a new set of players, and with this difference only, that the principal performer is better disposed to our side', he argued that 'when policy and expediency are forgotten, *principle alone* is the test of men and parties'. He reminded Althorp that Canning, whom he deeply distrusted, had been 'the greatest enemy, the most violent libeller of parliamentary reform, and the sarcastic reviler of the Whigs and their principles'. He concluded:

> Our course should be to stand aloof, and to support Canning's measures when they are good, and in accordance with our own principles, but not to go one step further. No *general* support, no *confidence* in the minister, beyond the surface. Above all, let us avoid as much as possible doing anything that may give the least countenance to the Ultra Tory opposition ... I do not blame Lord Lansdowne, or any of our friends, for joining Canning ... and I am glad to have them in office instead of the intolerants ... All I wish is to be allowed to take my own line without quarrelling with my friends, or wishing to influence others.[41]

Accordingly Tavistock made a declaration of qualified support for Canning's ministry, on the basis of measures not men, 11 May.[42] He deplored the rancour of its opponents, who were exhibiting 'Toryism in its most hideous shape', and singled out Peel for criticism; but when Peel protested, and denied that he planned to raise any 'factious opposition', he readily withdrew his remarks. He voted for the disfranchisement of Penryn, 28 May. At the county meeting to petition the Lords to reject the new corn bill, 23 May, he defended the measure and asked the agriculturists 'whether it was not better now to adopt it, than to wait until it was forced upon them by the ferment of discontent among the manufacturing and commercial interests'. His father was in the Lords majority which threw it out, but at the dinner of the Bedfordshire Agricultural Society in the autumn they portrayed their difference of opinion on this subject as one of 'degree' only.[43] Tavistock presented county petitions for repeal of the Test Acts, 15 June 1827.[44]

When he heard, amid a gathering of jubilant Tories at Goodwood, of the appointment of the anti-Catholic Tory John Herries* as chancellor of the exchequer in the Goderich ministry, '*at the express desire of the king*', he wrote angrily to Althorp's father that in his opinion it had 'completed the downfall of Lord Lansdowne as a political leader, and the downfall of the Whigs, as a party'. It was widely reported that he, Althorp (who thought that Tavistock, normally a man of 'excellent judgement and certainly quite sane', was 'mad to think that I could be thought of as leader of the House of Commons') and Milton would 'go into decided opposition'. Lord John Russell, who met him at Goodwood, divined that he would not do so, but would 'think it his duty to watch the conduct of the government with '*the utmost jealousy and suspicion*'.[45] Tavistock was evidently courted by Holland and other Whigs favourable to the new ministry, but Bedford, who felt that they were in basic accord, warned that 'you will none of you get Tavistock over. He is too firmly fixed in the principles of his family, which are pure Whig without any admixture of Toryism, to be easily shaken'. In mid-September Tavistock, who had been lately 'engaged in politics so much more than I like', wrote to his brother Lord William:

> It so happens that from being one of the few neutrals, I have been talked to, or written to, by all parties. My father is more determined than ever against the government. I can see however no reason to change the course which I had determined to take at first. There have been faults on all sides ... Althorp takes the right line ... My father thinks I am taking Lord Grey's line. Certainly we both stand aloof to watch, but I suspect with very different dispositions – his hostile, and mine indulgent – he ready to strike a blow whenever he can, I willing to avert it if possible.[46]

He acted as a broker in abortive negotiations between Tierney and Althorp, and was one of the Whigs consulted by Lord John Russell before he sent Tierney a list of requirements for their neutrality, which the cabinet rejected. He was in favour of Althorp's accepting the chairmanship of the finance committee, provided he was allowed a free hand.[47] He broke his collar bone in a hunting fall in early December 1827, but spurned Hobhouse's renewed advice to give it up and was not out of action for long, claiming that 'my general health has suffered from the confinement'.[48]

Tavistock, who was reported to have declined a ministerial approach for him to 'propose a property tax' in the Commons and to have upset Brougham with a remark at Althorp's at the beginning of the new year, explained to his brother Lord William, 1 Jan. 1828, the principles on which he and the self-styled 'watchmen' were acting in relation to the present 'wretched administration':

> I can hardly think that they will stand a fortnight ... In your dread of a Tory administration (which I always considered as a bugbear so long as we were true to ourselves) you have set up a *Court* administration, the most completely subservient to the crown which has existed for a century and a half ... When I decided to form a little party with Althorp, I said to Tierney that it would serve to keep minds and principles together, that if matters turned out well there could be no harm done, that we should be of use to the government by giving our disinterested support, and service to the public by keeping a watchful lookout. But if on the other hand matters should take an unfavourable turn, those who too joined the administration would find us a rallying point to fall back on, and would be received with open arms. We have now reason to rejoice at having taken this course, and you will see that people will be flocking to our little standard every day.[49]

On the collapse of the ministry, which led to the cancellation of the meeting which he and Althorp had planned to organize the 'watchmen', he initially hoped that 'we may now all get together again (although Lord Lansdowne's blunders can never be quite repaired)' and 'the prospect is not encouraging'. But as the Wellington ministry was being formed, he told Hobhouse:

> *Our* course ... is clear, and always will be so long as we continue in the path of public principle. We have only to continue our offices as *watchmen*, and to guard the House not merely from the imbecility of 'hysterical housemaids', but also from the assaults of Tory commanders-in-chief, and the intrigues of subtle and wily lawyers. Whether it would be worthwhile to lend a hand in rallying the beaten army is another matter. For my part, I am sick of party, and when I reflect upon who and what our leaders were, and how they have treated us, I am not disposed to make any efforts to bring them back to us. The king and Canning (the natural and avowed enemies of the Whigs) have divided us and defeated us. If we go to the wars again it must be in guerilla parties.

He saw Brougham as 'the stumbling block' to any satisfactory reunification of the party: 'Let us wash our hands of the whole set ... I am more and more for acting alone, at least till we can find a leader in whom we can place confidence'.[50] In a correspondence with Holland on the rights and wrongs of the conduct of the Lansdowne Whigs during the previous nine months, he took a high moral line:

> It is better that the Tories should come back than that we should do wrong. The only *safe* course in politics (and I wish that it was more attended to) is to do what one thinks *right*, let the consequences be what they may. By following this course one always gets home at last, but if we are tempted by consideration of *policy* and *expediency* (however plausible they may appear) to deviate from the straight path of public principle, measures abandoned, and pledges unredeemed, will one day or other rise up in judgement against us (to the prejudice of public men, and the distrust of all political professions) when the objects which have tempted us astray are lost sight of, or forgotten. This is the rule which I have ventured to lay down for my own conduct, and it has hitherto kept me out of difficulties. At the same time I must agree with you that politics, at least *practical* politics, can only be considered as a choice of evils.[51]

Despite another fall on 21 Jan. 1828, he was, to his father's chagrin, 'hunting almost every day' at this time.[52] He had nothing to say for himself in the House that session, when he presented petitions for repeal of the Test Acts, 26 Feb., before voting for his brother's successful motion to that effect. He paired in favour of Catholic relief, 12 May, but voted in person against the provision for Canning's family the following day. A fortnight later Lord John reported to Lord

William that Tavistock was 'full of good sense, good feeling, and indolence about politics. The *pulverem Newmarkham Colligere* occupies much more of his thoughts than the state of the nation'.[53] He divided against the salary of the governor of Dartmouth, 20 June, and to reduce that of the lieutenant-general of the ordnance, 4 July, and presented a Luton petition for the abolition of slavery, 30 June 1828. Two months later he observed to Lord William that while Wellington would probably 'carry us through our present difficulties' in foreign affairs 'with safety and honour', the basic corruption of the political system urgently required drastic reform:

> I started in life a reformer, and every year's experience has confirmed me more and more in the opinion of my early days ... surely the conduct of our friends in Bedfordshire at the last election proved that public virtue is not extinct amongst *the people*.[54]

When attempting to persuade Lord William to return to England to fulfil his duties as Member for Bedford instead of idling away his time on the continent, Tavistock wrote:

> There are a set of discontented spirits, who will allow no merit to their native country ... I have no patience with them. Are we sent into this world merely to enjoy ourselves? to discharge no duties? to pass our time in ease? to degrade ourselves into selfish and sensual beings? making no exertions for the good of others and spending what we have among those who care not for us, our families or our country, so long as we spend amongst them those resources from whence we derive all the comforts and enjoyments we possess?[55]

Lord John, who wanted him 'to give up the fox with a small "f" to the Fox with a large one', reported that he was 'warm and right' as to the course to be taken on the Catholic question; and, indeed, Tavistock, who thought that 'on the whole' Wellington was 'the best minister we have had', suggested to his brother 'a plan to be adopted and pursued by us when Parliament meets', which he wished to be communicated to 'the big guns'. By early January 1829 he, Althorp and Brougham were 'quite decided' to 'call urgently [and] perpetually on the government for measures to settle Ireland'.[56] He did not go up for the meeting of Parliament, but was present on 10 Feb., when he 'warmly praised ministers' for their decision to concede Catholic emancipation, though he could have wished that it had 'not been introduced on terms which may tend to lessen its grace and dignity'.[57] Illness prevented him from taking any further share in the parliamentary proceedings on the question, for in late February he began to spit blood, to the alarm of his father, who could not 'but remember how frequently his poor mother had these haemorrhages, and how fatally they terminated'. He remained unwell for several weeks, and in the spring gave up the mastership of the Oakley. Lord William, who had come to England, found him 'in a precarious state and much worried about his hounds and the conduct of his neighbours'. There was talk of his going abroad in search of a warmer climate.[58] He paired for the third reading of the Catholic relief bill, 30 Mar. He was fit enough to present a petition from the magistrates and clergy of Redbournstoke detailing the desperate condition of local agricultural labourers, 25 May, having earlier drawn the problem to the attention of Peel, the home secretary, in a personal interview.[59] He was 'shut out' of the division on Lord Blandford's reform motion, 2 June 1829.[60]

Tavistock decided against going abroad and settled for a winter in Devon. In September 1829 he told Lord William that unless his health greatly improved, he would probably retire from Parliament before the next general election. On politics he wrote:

> It is easy, certainly, to find fault with the present government, but what is your alternative? Surely anything is better than the people with whom we are threatened [the Ultras] ... I am always more disposed to be an opposition than a ministerial man, but I cannot so soon forget what we owe to the duke. He has done for us and for Ireland what others have only talked of, and what no other man upon earth would have done. We owe him something for this, at least.[61]

He sold his London house in Arlington Street (soon afterwards he bought one in Carlton Terrace) and in November went with his wife to Torquay, with the intention of moving to Bedford's cottage at Endsleigh, near Tavistock, in the spring. Lord John reported on the 27th:

> Tavistock says he must as yet keep aloof [from the ministry, which his father wished to support]. Poor fellow, he must keep aloof the greater part of the session. Everyone says he looks very ill, but he is pleased with the climate of Torquay, and though he has been ailing has no fresh discharge from the lungs. It remains to be seen what is his strength of constitution.[62]

Tavistock, who was one of the Whig politicians named by Colonel Leslie Jones as potential leaders of his projected Reform Society, and commented to Hobhouse that 'nine tenths of our evils have sprung from the quackery and obstinacy of Pitt and George III', only gradually rallied and regained his strength, experiencing a number of setbacks.[63] He told Hobhouse that had he been present, he would have 'deserted Althorp for once' and been one of the opposition Members who voted with ministers against the amendment to the address: 'Political parties seem to have been strangely jumbled by the events of the last two years', he observed. Like his father, he thought Wellington's was 'the best administration we are likely to have *under existing circumstances*'. He would not, however, give it his confidence, though he thought that it ought to be supported when it produced 'good' measures:

> He must work them with miserable tools, but we have seen mischief enough done by strong governments ... Our rulers must now look to public opinion for support. They have no longer the power of carrying bad measures, even if they have the will ... I am for the duke, with his wings clipped, because I see nothing better to look to, but I should like to weed the stable, and to see some better cattle put into it.

When he learnt that Hume planned a motion for the abolition of the lord lieutenancy of Ireland, he passed on through Hobhouse his father's opinion, based on his own experience in 1806-7, that it was 'a useless office for all purposes of good, and of course mischievous and powerful for objects of corruption', and also drew Hume's attention to the 'great jobbery' of the Irish pension fund.[64] When he left Endsleigh at the beginning of April he was, according to Bedford, who had joined him there, 'full as well as I expected to find him, though very thin'. Lord John found him 'looking tolerably well': 'his strength and spirits seem quite returned'. Later in the month he was at Newmarket, looking 'surprisingly well', according to Lord John, but 'wretchedly ill' in the eyes of Mrs. Arbuthnot. On 28 May he made a point of attending the House to vote for his brother's parliamentary reform motion.[65] He paired for abolition of the death penalty for forgery, 7 June, and reduction of the consular services grant, 11 June. He presented a Bedfordshire petition calling for the poor to be provided with small allotments, 5 July 1830. Three days later, in a letter to Milton, he reflected on the 'very unsatisfactory, and to me, most painful state' of politics, in which he was trying to steer 'a middle line' between his father's support for the government and Lord John's overt hostility:

> You and I have seen evils enough done by strong administrations, and if we now have one that is too weak for evil, and yet strong enough to carry through any good measure that may be forced upon [them], we have surely changed for the better, although we may not admire the men who are so ready to lay their principles aside whenever they find that others of an opposite character are likely to be forced upon them.[66]

He claimed that he wished to retire 'on the plea of health' at the 1830 dissolution and actually drafted a letter announcing this, but he was prevailed on by his leading supporters to stand again. He told them that he would 'stay quietly at home, take my chance of being returned, and spend no money, or retire if they can find a more able-bodied candidate'. There was no opposition to his return with a new Tory, before which, resting again on his 'purity of election' principle, and denying the charge that his father sought to 'enslave' the county, he boasted that 'he never had given a vote which infringed on public liberty, caused the shedding of a single drop of blood, or added one shilling to the burdens of the people'. He felt that he had no option but to advise his wife to accept the queen's 'flattering' offer of a place in her household, even though it would 'interfere sadly with my habits of life'.[67]

Tavistock, who took his share in the task of trying to make the resentful Lord William see sense over his removal from the Bedford seat (which Lord John, his replacement, lost by one vote), visited Ireland in August 1830. From Newmarket in early October he wrote:

> I shall not be surprised at the duke of Wellington's proposing parliamentary reform, or anything that may be called for by circumstances of the times. There are two or three events for which we may bless our stars. First, that George IV is not on the throne of England. Secondly, that the duke of York is not alive to succeed him, and thirdly that the Catholic question was carried last year ... We shall have a strange, and I fear, a very stormy session of Parliament. Alas! I can look with perfect confidence on none of the present parties.[68]

He had 'another spitting of blood' in late October, and did not attend the opening of Parliament, but readied himself to go up for the anticipated showdown on reform, as he told Lord William:

> The times are serious, and it was my anxious wish to have given all the support in my power to the government, but alas, the duke of Wellington's determination to resist all reform, and to stand by the present corrupt representation at all hazards, makes it impossible to go with him. The boroughmongers have made earnest and successful remonstrances to him on this subject and he has taken his stand against the people. I dread the consequences of continued resistance to just demands: witness Ireland, and the two revolutions in France ... I have been satisfied for some time that the duke had no thoughts of moving reform or making it a cabinet measure ... From the neutrality I have hitherto observed ... both sides, the duke's and Lord Grey's, have written confidentially to me since the close of the last session ... In answer to your remarks on the unpopularity of the Whigs, I have only to observe that whenever they have appeared before the people in counties and cities they have been universally at the head of the poll.[69]

He was absent from the division on the civil list which brought down the ministry, 15 Nov. 1830. He told Hobhouse that he had defended him against criticism at Brooks's for pressing ministers to resign immediately afterwards; but Hobhouse noted privately that 'I know friend Tavistock very well, and am aware that, with all his good qualities, he is not ill read in the "school for scandal"'.[70] Tavistock, who presented Bedfordshire petitions for the abolition of slavery, 17 Nov., was consulted by Grey as to what office Lord John, in Devon for his election for Tavistock, would like in his ministry; and Wellington later told Lord Ellenborough that Tavistock and other prominent party men had 'overruled' Grey 'in almost every appointment he wished to make'. Yet Hobhouse noted, 21 Nov., that he was 'not pleased at ... John being left out of the cabinet' and had 'remonstrated with Althorp on the impropriety of appointing Lord Anglesey to Ireland instead of abolishing the office' of viceroy. A fortnight later, according to Hobhouse, Tavistock told him that he was 'going to Lord Althorp to propose that not less than 100 seats shall be remodelled by the proposed reform. He says that Althorp wants encouragement, as he stands almost alone in the cabinet'.[71] He also 'lost no time in speaking to Althorp, amongst other matters, about the game laws', and told Lord William, 6 Dec. 1830:

> My part has been to keep matters right and straight as well as I could, and in some respects I have succeeded. In Althorp I have an admirable coadjutor, and I think we have been of great assistance to each other. ... If the ministers act as I think they will, forced by Althorp and backed by Lord Grey, they will stand upon a rock. Otherwise they will be kicked out, with the execrations of all the country ... They are surrounded by difficulties, the most appalling on all sides, both at home and abroad, in Ireland and even in Scotland. I think they will reduce their own salaries, and abolish all useless offices ... We are in a dreadful state, on the eve, I fear, of a revolution, which would have broken out before this time if the people had not been pacified by the overthrow of the Wellington administration. You and I have long foreseen and foretold this state of things, for which we have been called radicals, theorists, alarmists and atheists.[72]

He was summoned by his father to Oakley to help deal with the 'Swing' disturbances later in the month, when he wrote to his brother:

> Eighteen months ago I told Sir Robert Peel that matters would soon come to this pass and that we should be obliged to establish night watches for the protection of our property. And he held me cheap at that time, and thought me I believe a croaking alarmist. This is the state to which England has at length been brought by a long course, half a century, of Tory misgovernment and extravagance and corruption, but this is not the worst, for it is not only the schoolmaster who is abroad but the revolutionists also, and we shall have a hard matter to escape anarchy. If the ballot is forced upon the legislature by the people, which I think more than probable, farewell to rational and peaceable liberty ... I am for the ballot and always have been ... but I never wished to see it come thus.[73]

At the Bedford reform meeting, 17 Jan. 1831, Tavistock spoke for change and defended his family against allegations that they had tried to impose an electoral tyranny on the borough. In particular, he challenged John Pulley, the prime mover of the opposition which had overturned their interest at the last election, to substantiate or retract slurs on the conduct of Bedford and his late brother, the 5th duke, made on the hustings and in print. He was forced to leave the room by the onset of another haemorrhage, but returned to advocate the ballot, for which he presented petitions, 7, 26 Feb. He was quite badly affected by his Bedford exertions.[74] He presented a Bedfordshire coal merchants' petition for repeal of the coal duties, 11 Feb. He thought that Althorp's budget had 'damaged him as a financier', but concluded that 'although it will shake his influence, it is a mere measure and not a principle'. He anticipated a significant measure of reform, and was contemptuous of the Tories who were now 'crying out for John's moderate reform (the large towns) after having made their stand against all such imposition in the East Retford case only last year'. He was in his place to hear his brother detail the reform bill to an astonished House, 1 Mar. In his last known speech in the Commons, 3 Mar., he indignantly repudiated Alexander Baring's assertion that the bill had been framed to preserve the Russell family interest, stating that he would personally support any motion for the disfranchisement of their pocket borough of Tavistock, even though it had a larger population than that of Bedford, and his father (so he expected the House to believe) had never interfered with the votes of his tenants there. He went on:

> The government of this country has for years been carried on on principles of most unjustifiable and wasteful extravagance ... Patronage has been kept up for the purpose of maintaining the influence of the crown, and that which was known by parliamentary influence, for the purpose of carrying on measures against the sense of the country. The people feel now, more fully than at any former period, that they have not their just influence in the legislative councils of the nation, and they naturally seek for that change which will give it to them ... I sincerely hope and believe that the measure will have that effect ... I hope it will curb the monopoly so

> long maintained by the higher orders, and give a fair expression of the sense of the middling classes.[75]

Poor health forced him to pair for the second reading of the bill, 22 Mar., and against Gascoyne's wrecking amendment, 19 Apr. 1831. According to the Tory Charles Arbuthnot*, Tavistock admitted that 'the Irish part of the question was a very difficult one', and that dependence on Daniel O'Connell's* fulfilment of his promise 'not to agitate Ireland' if the bill passed was 'a very sorry security'.[76] He was earmarked for elevation to the Lords in his father's barony, but no action was taken before the general election of 1831, when he stood again for Bedfordshire and was returned with a second reformer after a contest. On the hustings, where he asked to be allowed to keep his hat on because of his habitual cold, he declared that 'it was no longer a question between Whigs and Tories, but it was a question of reform, or consultation of the rights of the British nation, or of the continuance of corrupt power'. At the victory dinner, he proclaimed that 'reform is coming peaceably from within, and not with a vengeance from without'.[77] He voted for the second reading of the reintroduced reform bill, 6 July, and divided fairly steadily for its details (taking pairs for the divisions on St. Germans, 26 July, and Rochester, 9 Aug.) until mid-August, when he paired off until the third reading. Holland noted that he was 'disposed to lament though not to oppose the changes in county elections, and to approve though not to support Lord Milton's crotchets of either giving *all* leaseholders or *none* votes for the counties'.[78] He voted for the passage, 19 Sept., and third reading of the bill, 21 Sept., and for Lord Ebrington's motion of confidence in the ministry, 10 Oct., when Greville was at a loss to understand how he, Althorp and Milton, with their 'great stake in the country', could be so 'extreme' in support of reform.[79] Later that month he worked enthusiastically for the reformers in the hard-fought Cambridgeshire by-election, which he considered to be 'the most important election that ever occurred'. He was only a nominal chairman of the London committee, as he stayed in the country throughout the successful campaign.[80]

Tavistock, who was wrongly expected to be called to the Lords when Parliament reassembled, voted for the second reading of the revised reform bill, 17 Dec. 1831, and a week later told Arbuthnot, with whom he had developed a friendship:

> I have long ceased to take a very active part in politics, on account of my health, and it matters very [little] to anybody except my constituents and myself what I think and what course I pursue. I have been a reformer all my life, but I see that the question has now brought us into a position of no ordinary difficulty and danger.[81]

When Hobhouse was appointed secretary at war in February 1832 Tavistock, as well as advising him to preserve his health under the press of official business by 'taking a trot on the roughest bone-shaker you can get, for an hour, at least, every morning', encouraged him to make the economies in the administration of the army which the public expected:

> Whilst Ireland and the continent remain in this unsettled state I don't suppose that it will be possible to reduce the amount of the army – nay it may even be necessary to increase it – but surely there must be some way of simplifying the mode of managing it, and of making it less of a *jobbing* concern. All the departments have been hitherto made subservient to the interests of the few for the sake of parliamentary patronage, and the army has not escaped the curse. Reform, it is to be hoped, will put an end to that ... I would not bother with little penny-wise savings, which will only create discontent, make you many enemies, and do no good ... Therefore I say *begin* with your *grand scheme*, by which both the army and the country may be really benefitted.[82]

He told Hobhouse at the beginning of the month that he had 'paired till the third reading' of the reform bill; but he was listed in the ministerial majority for the enfranchisement of Tower Hamlets, 28 Feb. He duly paired for the third reading, 22 Mar. He voted for the address calling on the king to appoint only ministers who would carry the measure unimpaired, 10 May, and with government on a clause of the Scottish bill, 15 June. He paired on their side on the Russian-Dutch loan, 12 July, and went up to vote with them on the same issue, 16 July 1832. A week later Tavistock, whose elevation to the Lords was now fixed for the dissolution, announced his retirement from the county seat in a long retrospective address. He later told Lord William that he had turned down 'a most flattering and gratifying requisition' to stand again:

> I am satisfied with my decision. It is always something to time one's affairs well. I have the satisfaction now of making my bow, and taking leave of the country with the good feeling, and kind expressions of all, after having seen all our measures carried amidst the buffeting I have met with when they were less fashionable than they are now.[83]

He got himself into a minor scrape by voting at the Bedford election in December 1832, not being aware that the gazetting of his elevation to the Lords (which did not actually take place until the following month) had been published; the second reformer's margin of victory was three votes.[84]

He was never very active in the Upper House, but his close and affectionate relationship with his brother Lord John, to whom he acted as confidant, adviser and financial supporter, together with his equable and conciliatory temperament, gave him a role of sorts in high politics. He turned down offers of the Irish lord lieutenancy in 1839 and of cabinet office when Lord John was trying to form an administration in December 1845.[85] Perhaps his greatest achievement as duke of Bedford was his transformation, largely by dint of his own dedicated work, of the fortunes of the family's vast English estates, which he consolidated and rescued from the debt and decay which had spread under his sybaritic and negligent father. He was an agricultural improver and notably enlightened landlord. He made Woburn Abbey, which received a royal visit in 1841, a social centre for the Whigs. After staying there in 1842 Greville recorded that Bedford was

> well and wisely administering his estate and improving his magnificent palace in every way. I never saw such an abode of luxury and enjoyment, one so full of resources for all tastes. The management of his estates is like the administration of a little kingdom. He has 450 people in his employment on the Bedfordshire property alone, not counting domestic servants. His pensions amount to £2,000 a year. There is order, economy, grandeur, comfort, and general content.[86]

In 1850 the 4th earl of Clarendon wrote to his sister, who had recently been a guest at Woburn:

> I am sure by his letters he [Bedford] feels the 'greateth rethpecth' for you ... His appearance at your early breakfast was a compliment that I never heard of his paying to anybody, for at that hour he is always in a very old dressing gown, scribbling the illegible letters that will be the death of him ... He loves to think himself the centre to which information tends and from which advice radiates, and I have no doubt that in the course of a twelvemonth he does a great deal of good by smoothing down political and social asperities ... He never intentionally made an ounce of mischief in his life; but this vanity of good-nature and self-importance amount to mania, and will kill him. No man at his age, with a slender stock of health, can keep getting up through the winter at 4 or 5 in the morning, lighting his own fire and writing till 10 or 11 upon an empty stomach.[87]

He survived for another decade, dying at Woburn in May 1861, four years after his wife.[88] By his enormously long will, dated 7 May 1861, he left Lord John his Irish estates, plus a life interest in £15,000, and £1,000 for his wife. He was succeeded in the main family estates and the dukedom by his eccentric and reclusive only son.[89]

[1] On the 'Young Whigs' see E.A. Wasson, 'Coalitions of 1827 and Crisis of Whig Leadership', *HJ*, xx (1977), 587-606; 'Great Whigs and Parl. Reform', *JBS*, xxiv (1985); and *Whig Renaissance* (1987). They are also examined in P. Mandler, *Aristocratic Government in Age of Reform* (1990), 30-31, 87-96. [2] *Creevey Pprs.* ii. 321; Blakiston, *Woburn and the Russells*, 189. [3] Broughton, *Recollections*, iii. 166; Blakiston, *Lord William Russell*, 23. [4] Le Marchant, *Althorp*, 257-8. [5] *Cambridge and Hertford Independent Press*, 26 Feb., 18, 25 Mar. 1820; *Althorp Letters*, 103. [6] Add. 51662, Bedford to Holland, 10 Mar. [1820]. [7] *Althorp Letters*, 108. [8] Add. 52444, f. 110. [9] *The Times*, 17 May 1820. [10] Add. 36458, f. 311. [11] Add. 52444, f. 163. [12] Add. 51662, Bedford to Holland, 1 Dec. [1820]; *The Times*, 13 Jan. 1821. [13] *Northampton Mercury*, 27 Jan., 3 Feb.; *Cambridge and Hertford Independent Press*, 3 Feb. 1821. [14] *Creevey Pprs.* ii. 5; *Arbuthnot Jnl.* i. 65. [15] *Creevey Pprs.* ii. 12; *Countess Granville Letters*, i. 205; A. Mitchell, *Whigs in Opposition*, 156-7. [16] Dorset RO D/BKL, Bankes jnl. 123; HLRO, Hist. Coll. 379, Grey Bennet diary, 12. [17] *The Times*, 20 Mar. 1821. [18] *Cambridge and Hertford Independent Press*, 17 Mar. 1821; Add. 51667. [19] *The Times*, 4 Apr. 1821; Add. 47223, f. 34; 51663, Bedford to Holland, 14 June [1821]. [20] *The Times*, 8 May 1821. [21] Wasson, *Whig Renaissance*, 147, unaccountably states that Tavistock made this declaration during the debates on the Queen Caroline affair. He may well have spoken in the same sense at the Cambridgeshire meeting in Mar. 1821, but the press reports do not notice it. [22] Grey Bennet diary, 106-8. [23] Add. 51667, Bedford to Lady Holland, 10 July; *The Times*, 11 July 1821. [24] *Cambridge and Hertford Independent Press*, 6 Apr.; *The Times*, 22 Apr. 1822. [25] *The Times*, 26 Apr. 1822. [26] Add. 56545, ff. 5-7. [27] *Russell Letters*, i. 13, 16, 17, 25; Broughton, iii. 18; Blakiston, *Lord William Russell*, 82, 84, 90, 96-100; Add. 51586, Tierney to Lady Holland, 6 June; 51667, Bedford to same, 28 Mar., Fri. [20 June]; 51679, Lord J. Russell to same [?Aug. 1823]. [28] Blakiston, *Lord William Russell*, 106, 108; Add. 51586, Tierney to Lady Holland, 24 Aug., 23 Sept.; Bessborough mss, Brougham to Duncannon, Sat. [18 Oct. 1823]. [29] Blakiston, *Lord William Russell*, 110-11; Add. 51564, Brougham to Lady Holland, Thurs. [6 Nov.]; 51676, Lord G.W. Russell to same, 9 Nov., to Holland, Thurs. [Nov.]; 51679, Lord J. Russell to Lady Holland [24 Nov. 1823]. [30] *Russell Early Corresp.* i. 236; *Russell Letters*, i. 30b; ii. 41, 47; *Creevey Pprs.* i. 79; Add. 36460, f. 348; 51668, Bedford to Lady Holland, 26 Oct. [1824], Fri. [28 Jan. 1825]. [31] Wasson, 'The Old Whigs: Bedford, Fitzwilliam, and Spencer in the House of Lords, 1833-1861', *Lords of Parliament* ed. R.W. Davis, 117, incorrectly places this episode in 1824. [32] *Cambridge and Hertford Independent Press*, 2 Oct., 19 Nov.; *Herts Mercury*, 29 Oct., 5 Nov.; Add. 36461, ff. 281, 317; 51586, Tierney to Lady Holland, 24 Oct.; 51663, Bedford to Holland, 28 Oct.; 51679, Russell to Lady Holland, 9 Nov. [1825]. [33] Add. 36461, f. 385. [34] Add. 51668, Bedford to Lady Holland, 27 May [1826]. [35] *Herts. Mercury*, 10, 17, 24 June, 1, 8, 15 July 1826; *Althorp Letters*, 130. [36] Add. 51663, Bedford to Holland, Fri. [June]; *Herts. Mercury*, 15 July 1826. [37] Add. 36462, f. 311; 36463, f. 243; 51663, Bedford to Holland [2 July], 6 Oct.; 51675, Tavistock to Holland, 1 Aug.; 51784, Holland to C.R. Fox, 30 June; *Russell Letters*, i. 47, 49; Fitzwilliam mss, Tavistock to Milton, 3 Dec. [1826]; Wasson, *Whig Renaissance*, 147. [38] Add. 36463, ff. 42, 189, 243. [39] Add. 51663, Bedford to Holland, Tues. [20 Feb.]; 51784, Holland to C.R. Fox, 21 Feb.; *Cambridge and Hertford Independent Press*, 24 Feb. 1827. [40] Add. 36463, ff. 247, 260, 304, 307, 315; *Canning's Ministry*, 46, 49. [41] Add. 36463, ff. 361, 378; 51675, Tavistock to Holland, 13, 22 Apr.; Add. 76380, Tavistock to Althorp, 25 Apr. 1827; LMA, Jersey mss 510/416; *Canning's Ministry*, 112, 143; Wasson, *Whig Renaissance*, 137, 147-8, 150, and *HJ*, xx. 597-600. [42] *Geo. IV Letters*, iii. 1328. [43] *Cambridge and Hertford Independent Press*, 26 May, 9 June, 7 July, 13 Oct. 1827. [44] *The Times*, 16 June 1827. [45] BL, Althorp mss, Tavistock to Spencer, 15 Aug.; *Russell Early Corresp.* i. 258; *Arbuthnot Corresp.* 89; Add. 51677, Russell to Holland, 16 Aug.; Lansdowne mss, Holland to Lansdowne, 22 Aug., Tierney to same, 5 Sept. 1827. [46] Add. 36464, f. 95; 51663, Bedford to Holland, 9 Sept. [1827]; *Russell Letters*, i. 75; ii. 104-5. [47] Hants RO, Tierney

mss 61b, c; Add. 51724, Duncannon to Holland, 10 Oct. [1827]; Wasson, *Whig Renaissance*, 152-3; Le Marchant, *Althorp*, 226. [48] *Cambridge and Hertford Independent Press*, 15 Dec.; Add. 36464, f. 112; 51569, Burdett to Holland, 6 Dec. 1827; *Russell Letters*, ii. 222. [49] *Greville Mems*. i. 194; Broughton, iii. 232; *Russell Letters*, ii. 222-3. See also his letter to Holland, 8 [Jan. 1828] in Add. 51675. [50] Add. 36464, ff. 166, 176, 182; 51675, Tavistock to Holland, 10 Jan. [1828]; Wasson, *Whig Renaissance*, 155. [51] Add. 51675, Tavistock to Holland, 13, 15 Jan. [1828]. [52] *Cambridge and Hertford Independent Press*, 26 Jan.; Add. 51669, Bedford to Lady Holland, 6 Feb. [1828]; Blakiston, *Lord William Russell*, 153, 156. [53] *Russell Letters*, ii. 87. Mandler, 61 (giving the reference incorrectly as i. 87), wrongly associates this comment with Tavistock's attitude to politics in 1827 and implies that his professed scruples over parliamentary reform as an obstacle to supporting Canning were bogus. [54] *Russell Letters*, ii. 137-8. [55] Blakiston, *Lord William Russell*, 176. [56] Ibid. 174; *Russell Letters*, i. 105, 115-16; ii. 170; Add. 36464, f. 461; 51677, Lord J. Russell to Holland, Mon. [Jan.]; 76369, Althorp to Brougham, 2 Jan. 1829. [57] Add. 51677, Lord J. Russell to Holland, Tues. [3 Feb. 1829]; *Russell Letters*, ii. 182. Wasson, *Lords of Parliament*, 118, erroneously states that this was Tavistock's 'last speech in either House of Parliament'. [58] *Herts. Mercury*, 28 Feb., 4 Apr.; *Cambridge and Hertford Independent Press*, 7 Mar.; Add. 51669, Bedford to Lady Holland, Fri. [27 Feb. 1829]; *Oakley Hunt* ed. J. Godber (Pubs. Beds. Hist Rec. Soc. xliv), p. xii; *Russell Letters*, i. 118; ii. 179, 191, 194, 204; Blakiston, *Lord William Russell*, 189. [59] J. Godber, *Hist. Beds.* 417; *Herts. Mercury*, 25 July 1829. [60] *The Times*, 4 June 1829. [61] Add. 51669, Bedford to Lady Holland, 11 Aug. [1829]; *Russell Letters*, 128. [62] Add. 36466, f. 69; 47223, f. 47; *Russell Letters*, i. 132, 134-5; Blakiston, *Lord William Russell*, 202-3. [63] Fitzwilliam mss, Jones to Milton, 8 Dec. 1829; Wasson, *Whig Renaissance*, 162; Add. 36465, f. 349; 47223, f. 38; 51670, Bedford to Lady Holland, Wed. [? 6 Jan.], 14 Feb. [1830]. [64] Add. 36466, ff. 12, 23, 31; 47223, f. 38; 51670, Bedford to Lady Holland, 20 Feb. [1830]; *Arbuthnot Corresp.* 157. [65] Add. 51670, Bedford to Lady Holland, 1 Apr., Sun. [? 2 May]; 51680, Russell to same, 20 Apr. 1830; *Arbuthnot Jnl.* ii. 350. [66] Fitzwilliam mss. [67] Ibid. Tavistock to Milton, 5, 8 July; Devon RO, Earl Fortescue mss, Tavistock to Ebrington, 15 July; *Russell Letters*, i. 141-2; *Cambridge and Hertford Independent Press*, 7, 14 Aug. 1830. [68] Blakiston, *Lord William Russell*, 220-1; *Russell Letters*, i. 145-7, 148-50, 152-5; Add. 47223, f. 41. [69] Add. 47223, ff. 43, 45; 51670, Bedford to Lady Holland, Tues. [26 Oct. 1830]; *Russell Letters*, i. 151, 155-7; Blakiston, *Lord William Russell*, 222; *Arbuthnot Corresp.* 157, 200. [70] Broughton, iv. 70. [71] Walpole, *Russell*, i. 159-60; *Greville Mems.* ii. 68; *Three Diaries*, 42; Add. 56555, f. 62; Broughton, iv. 90. [72] *Russell Letters*, i. 161-3. [73] Ibid. ii. 299. [74] *Cambridge and Hertford Independent Press*, 22 Jan. 1831; Add. 51670, Bedford to Lady Holland, 20 Jan. [1831]. [75] *Russell Letters*, i. 166-8; Add. 51675, Tavistock to Holland [1 Mar. 1831]; Broughton, iv. 90. [76] Add. 40340, f. 261. [77] PRO NI, Anglesey mss D619/27A/14, 15; Add. 36466, ff. 327, 368, 370; *Cambridge and Hertford Independent Press*, 30 Apr., 7, 14, 21 May 1831. [78] Add. 47223, f. 47; *Holland House Diaries*, 29. [79] *Greville Mems.* ii. 207. [80] Beds. RO, Russell mss R766, W. Russell to C. Hardy, Wed. [19 Oct.], Lord J. Russell to same, 18, 19 Oct., Tavistock to W. Russell, 21, 23, 25 Oct. 1831. [81] *Cambridge and Hertford Independent Press*, 3 Dec. 1831; *Arbuthnot Corresp.* 157. [82] Add. 47223, ff. 49, 52, 57. [83] Earl Fortescue mss, Grey to Ebrington, 19 Aug.; *Cambridge and Hertford Independent Press*, 28 July 1832; *Russell Letters*, iii. 25. [84] Jersey mss 510/451, 452; *Cambridge and Hertford Independent Press*, 22 Dec. 1832. [85] See Wasson, *Lords of Parliament*, 117-18, 122-4, 125-6, 130-3 for a slightly exaggerated estimate of his political significance as a peer. [86] Ibid. 120-1; D. Spring, *English Landed Estate in 19th Cent.* 35ff.; Godber, 465, 469; Blakiston, *Woburn*, 194-6; *Lady Lyttelton Corresp.* 312-15; *Greville Mems.* v. 39, 347. [87] Maxwell, *Clarendon*, i. 320. [88] *Gent. Mag.* (1861), i. 697. [89] *The Times*, 10 Aug. 1861.

D.R.F.

RUSSELL, Lord George William (1790–1846).[1]

BEDFORD 1812–1830

b. 8 May 1790, 2nd s. of John Russell†, 6th duke of Bedford (*d.* 1839), and 1st w. Hon. Georgiana Elizabeth Byng, da. of George, 4th Visct. Torrington; bro. of Francis Russell, mq. of Tavistock* and Lord John Russell*. *educ.* by Dr. Moore, Sunbury 1800; Westminster 1803; by Rev. John Smith at Woodnesborough, nr. Sandwich 1805. *m.* 21 June 1817, Elizabeth Anne, da. of Hon. John Theophilus Rawdon† of Bolney Court, Oxon., 3s. 1da. *d.v.p.* GCB 19 July 1838. *d.* 16 July 1846.

Cornet 1 Drag. 1806, lt. 1806; capt. Canadian fencibles 1808, 81 Ft. 1808; capt. 23 Drag. 1808; maj. 102 Ft. 1813, lt.-col. 1814; maj. 42 Ft. (half-pay) 1815; maj. 8 Drag. 1824, lt.-col. 1824, half-pay 1828; lt.-col. 90 Ft. 1829; col. army 1830; half-pay 1831; a.d.c. to William IV 1830-7, to Victoria 1837-41; maj.-gen. 1841.

Special mission to Portugal 1832-4; minister plenip. to Wurttemberg 1834-5; envoy extraordinary and minister plenip. to Prussia 1835-41.

Although Russell was idle and diffident, he was far from untalented. He had shown himself to be a brave and resourceful soldier on active service in the Peninsula, and, like most of the Russells (of whose characteristic oddness he had his full share) he was genuinely interested in politics, though he lacked the confidence to open his mouth in Commons debate. Yet his parliamentary and military careers, and to a large extent his entire adult life, were blighted by his emotional subjugation to his ravishing, selfish, domineering wife, Bessy Rawdon. Her ascendancy over him, her preference for the social and intellectual milieu of the continental capitals to the standard domestic lifestyle of the English aristocracy, her innate Toryism and her prickly temperament spoiled Russell's relationship with his stepmother (his own mother had died when he was 11), threatened to cut him off from his father and brothers (of whom he was essentially very fond) and encouraged him to neglect his parliamentary duties and cast away his prospects in the army.[2]

At the beginning of this period the Russells, whose first son was born in November 1819 (after the death of a baby girl the previous year), were probably happier together than at any other time in their ill-starred marriage. Living in London on his half-pay, but with rooms always at their disposal at Woburn Abbey and a warm welcome assured at Holland House, where Lady William's intelligence was appreciated, they were popular in fashionable Whig society.[3] At the general election of 1820 Russell was returned again for Bedford, where he had sat on the family interest since 1812, without opposition. His father heard 'great commendations of the beauty' of his speech, and Russell himself told Lord Holland that 'my election went off very well'. He relished the prospect of the 'bitter, spiteful and passionate' contest which loomed for the county, where his elder brother, Lord Tavistock, was one of the sitting Members.[4] He was present to vote with opposition on the civil list, 5, 8 May, the appointment of an additional Scottish baron of exchequer, 15 May, the secret committee on Queen Caroline's case, 26 June, economies in revenue collection, 4 July, and the barrack agreement bill, 17 July 1820. With Bedford, Tavistock and his younger brother Lord John Russell (to whom he was always very close), Lord William (as he was always known) attended the county meeting in support of the queen, 14 Jan. 1821, but did not speak.[5] He voted for the restoration of her name to the liturgy, 23, 26 Jan., 13 Feb., and for the motion of censure on ministers' conduct towards her, 6 Feb. He presented the Bedford petition in her favour, 24 Jan.[6] He voted for Catholic relief, 28 Feb. He divided against government on the state of the revenue, 6 Mar., and for repeal of the additional malt duty, 21 Mar., pairing for the division of 3 Apr. He voted for reductions in the admiralty, 4 May, and ordnance establishments, 11, 14, 31 May. Although listed as a steward of the City reform dinner in April, he did not attend it;[7] but he voted for his brother's reform motion, 9 May, when he also divided in condemnation of the delay in the commission of inquiry into the judicial system. He voted for inquiry into the Peterloo massacre, 16 May, and for mitigation of the punishment for forgery, 23 May, 4 June 1821.

By then Lady William's relations with the duchess of Bedford had become uncomfortably strained, their frequent intercourse having served only to demonstrate their incompatibility and bring out their mutual antipathy. Lady William's health suffered, and on this pretext, in mid-June 1821 Russell took her and their son to Europe, where he stayed for almost two years. Their principal resorts were Spa, Frankfort, Vienna (late September), Venice (late October), Florence (February 1822) and Rome (October).[8] From Spa, 20 July 1821, he gave Holland the benefit of his views on the shortcomings of the high-minded Foxite Whigs, who

> attach too little importance to the intrigues that are carried on against you. You take the high ground of truth and publicity and look with contempt on all beneath, yet if the enemy mines you, you should countermine ... Why did the Holy Alliance request the king not to make the Whigs his ministers? Because they believe them to be the promoters of rebellion and discord, the enemies of kings, laws and order. The mischief of all this is, that it assists in keeping the Whigs out of office and Europe from enjoying the good you might do it. You are like gallant young troops fighting against veterans, who get behind walls and ditches and shoot you at their leisure ... Grey, yourself and others, with your superior talents and straightforward, open, liberal sentiments have been kept out and are likely to remain out, whilst such pitiful fellows as Castlereagh and the Doctor [Lord Sidmouth] govern England and spread their baneful policy.[9]

He evidently criticized in letters home the Whigs who rallied to support Sir Robert Wilson* after his dismissal from the army, which led his father to reproach him towards the end of the year:

> Tavistock and John tell me you are become quite an *Ultra-Tory*. You were once accused of being a *radical* ... I trust, however, that every son of mine will act steadily, uniformly, and invariably on the old Whig principles, and never lose sight of the solid rights of the people, the foundation on which our liberties and our government rest.

A month later Bedford wrote to him:

> There is one good symptom in your letter to John attacking the subscribers to indemnify ... Wilson ... that you are indignant at being called a Tory ... but your arguments to prove that you are not a Tory rather tend to show that you are one, and the violence of your abuse, and bitterness of your sarcasms against us poor Whigs, equals that of the *Courier* itself ... Your brothers are seriously unhappy at your change in politics, though I feel sure that you will come right again, when you once more breathe the atmosphere of your native land.

Nevertheless, the duke did not retract his earlier comment that Russell need not trouble to attend Parliament during the approaching session, 'if your wife's health requires a warmer and more genial climate than ours'. Indeed, he saw Lord William's apparent reaction against Whiggism as a good reason for staying away, 'as you are not likely to concur in the motions to reduce the public expenditure, and if you did not support Mr. Hume in his motions for retrenchment, your constituents would not receive you well if you ever asked for their votes again'.[10] By 26 Mar. 1822, however, Bedford was able to write that 'your politics are very good, and quite congenial to my own mind, so we will have no more disputes about Whig and Tory'.[11] Yet on 29 May Russell, writing from Florence, told Lady Holland of his dissatisfaction with the 'unintelligible' tactics of the Whig leaders in the Commons, who seemed to have 'yielded with the greatest modesty to the overpowering talents of the second bench', and such men as Hume, Grey Bennet and Colonel Davies:

> Is it not singular that the government should have brought the country to the present state, that it should be distrusted and abused by all parties, and disgraced day after day in the House of Commons, and yet that neither king nor nation should express the smallest desire to confide in the Whigs? Surely this must prove some radical error in their conduct.[12]

In June he addressed Lord John on his reported conversion to 'radical' reform:

> I ought to complain, for after converting me you have left me in the lurch; however, never mind, I will follow you. Whatever you propose, I will vote for. I will be radical again too, rather than have no reform, but I don't think you will now do *any good*. With the old jog trot plan you would have done a *little good* ... your coalition will never do. Oil and vinegar would sooner mix together than a radical and a moderate reformer.

That month his father told him that the reformers of Cambridgeshire were minded to put him up against the Tory sitting Member at the next general election..[13]

In May 1822 Russell informed Lady Holland that he and his wife were

> rather cogitating a longer stay on the continent, at least till Parliament meets next year. It has done Bessy much good, another mild winter might finish the cure, and an English winter might undo all that we have done. That is the best and strongest reason for our remaining here. Then there are a quantity of little ancillary reasons, domestic reasons, agreeable reasons, prudent reasons, idle reasons, etc., etc. If you did but know the worries that await us in our native land, pinches from poverty and pinches from our near and dear. Here we live in clover. This is the Paradise of small incomes.

Bedford was taken ill in the summer, and Russell's first instinct was to return home, but his father's apparent recovery reinforced his second thoughts, as he explained to Lady Holland, in confidence, 27 June 1822:

> I believe it is better to endeavour to fortify Bessy's health by passing part of our next winter on the continent, for unhappily the duchess has taken such a hatred for Bessy and myself, and has so poisoned my father's mind against us, that I fear our presence gives him no pleasure. This is a great source of unhappiness to me, for you know how I love my father. This is my real reason for not returning, but it is *entre nous*, and I beg it may go no further. However, if he should not get better, nothing shall prevent me from passing the winter with him.

In late August he received news that his father had suffered a stroke, and he immediately set off for England, reaching the duke's sick bed on 3 Sept. after eight days' hard travelling. Satisfied that his father was out of danger, he left London on the 19th, and was back in Florence with his grumbling wife on 2 Oct. 1822 (her 29th birthday).[14]

They planned to leave their winter quarters in Rome, where Russell was executing Bedford's commissions for purchases of sculpture for the gallery at Woburn, early in the new year, but delayed their departure when he received assurances that his presence would not be required in the Commons until after Easter. According to the Hollands' son Henry Fox*, who met them on their journey at Genoa at the end of March, Lady William was 'quite miserable at going home, and keeps no bounds about the duchess'.[15] In early April 1823, when they were expected in Paris, Bedford told Russell that Lord John was 'eager to get you over, that your name may appear in every division, to the comfort of your constituents, after your long truancy'. As it was, he arrived in England on 23 Apr., having left his wife with her widowed mother in Paris, and, as arranged, he hastened to London to vote for his brother's reform motion the following day.[16] He remained there for a couple of weeks, attending the House with his brother, but complaining to his wife, whom he was shortly to fetch over from Paris, of the vile weather, and the awkwardness of relations with the duchess. He pleaded with Bessy to make an effort to settle in England, but at the same time betrayed the weakness which she was to have no compunction in exploiting:

> You never yet saw anything like the state of the family – quarrellings, intrigues, repetitions, misrepresentings, etc. ... I trust you will be able to ... bear them all with indifference, looking upon the calumnies and intrigues of that ill conditioned madwoman, as unworthy of your anger or consideration, and the intentions of those who repeat them as either mischievous or foolish, and consequently to be despised or let pass by ... I know I am bringing you from the soft air, the sun, the charm, the indolence of Italy, to encounter the keen wind, the cold, the difficulties of England, and above all the differences, the intrigues, the wickedness that unhappily pervades my family. Nobody ... regrets ... more than I do the sacrifices I cause you to make ... for I know you to be a gentle, delicate, fine spun piece of texture whose mind is as ill calculated to encounter a difficulty or trouble, as your body is to resist the cold ... I believe as yet that it is my duty to urge you to live in your husband's country, yet if on this coming trial you again experience the sickness and worry you did before ... I will leave Parliament and the army, and go and spend and end my days in some southern climate with you – but for God's sake do not urge me too hastily to take this step, think what it is for a man to live out of his country, to waste his life in nothing, to sit down a nonentity for the rest of his being.[17]

He brought her to London in early June, her mood improved by the Hollands having placed Holland House at their disposal for a few weeks during their own absence in Paris.[18] Russell resumed his sporadic attendance of the House, voting for inquiry into the expenses of the coronation, 19 June, and for the Scottish juries bill, 20 June. He paired in favour of investigation of Catholic complaints against the administration of justice in Ireland, 26 June. On 3 July 1823 he presented a petition from Leighton Buzzard for relief from distress caused by the importation of foreign straw plait.[19] At this time Fox wrote of Russell and his wife:

> She is totally unlike anybody else I know. Her expressions are very peculiar and well chosen; she is accused by many of coldness and want of heart, I believe unjustly. She is certainly fond of William and of her delightful child. William is in my opinion by far the most amiable of the Russells; there is a warmth of heart and tenderness of manner that is delightful, nor is he at all deficient in understanding. His admiration and love for her is as just and great as it ought to be.[20]

For about nine months from July 1823 the Russells had Woburn more or less to themselves. Their comparative tranquillity was marred only by Lady William's miscarriage in August, which she soon got over, and their discovery later in the year that they had not sufficient funds to buy a London house. Lord Tavistock made part of his in Arlington Street available to them from March 1824.[21] In the Commons, Russell voted for reform of Edinburgh's representation, 26 Feb. 1824. He presented a Bedford petition for the abolition of slavery, 18 Mar.[22] At that time his father wrote to Lady Holland:

> I wish someone would take William in hand and *thrust him forward* a little. His talents are quite lost to the public. He went to our assizes, and in Tavistock's absence, took his place as foreman of the grand jury, and gave universal satisfaction by the manner in which he conducted the business. I know Holland has a good opinion of him. Why won't he take him in hand?[23]

After Easter, he voted against the aliens bill, 2, 12 Apr., and the grant for building new churches, 9 Apr. He was in the majority for repeal of the usury laws, 8 Apr. He divided for inquiries into the Irish church establishment, 6 May, and the state of Ireland, 11 May, and for a repeal of assessed taxes, 11 May, and in condemnation of the trial of the Methodist missionary John Smith in Demerara, 11 June 1824.

That summer there occurred a serious quarrel between the duchess of Bedford and Lady William, who stood accused of incivility and was barred from Woburn. Russell, blaming the affair on 'an act of hatred and revenge on the part of the duchess', whom he now regarded with open hostility, refused to go there without her, though he assured Lady Holland that he remained on the 'best of terms' with his father, despite the reprimand which he had received from him.[24] Earlier in the year he had accepted the offer of his wife's uncle, Lord Hastings, of a place on his staff as governor of Malta, but in the event he persuaded his father, who had some difficulty in raising the money, to obtain for him a full-pay majority in the 8th Hussars. Very soon afterwards he got command of the regiment, which was stationed at Dorchester, as lieutenant-colonel. Bedford, who bent over backwards to meet his wishes, professed to have 'no doubt of your conquering your natural indolence, and using the whole energies of your mind to get the regiment into good order'.[25] Lady William disingenuously told Lord Lynedoch, Russell's former commanding officer and a close friend, that she was 'much pleased' at this development:

> I have for seven years been urging him to do something. I hate idleness ... and have ever discouraged the notions he had (I believe only vague ones, but still he frequently has talked of them to me) of giving up Parliament and the army ... for my own propensities nothing could have been more propitious as I confess I dislike England ... It is entirely principle ... that makes me forgo the gratification of my inclinations in living abroad ... My object and constant pursuit since I married has been to *rehausser* Lord William in his own opinion, for he is too diffident, and from being kept like a frightened schoolboy under the thumb of an artful and vulgar minded woman for so many years, who wished to cow him, my task was not easy. Every friend of his and people whose opinion I value ... have spoken of his judgement as you do. Lord Holland puts it above that of both his brothers. What he wants is confidence in himself and I do think that his present situation will lead to it, independent of its professional advantages ... I have been in despair at his *desoeuvrement* hitherto, which has been greater in England than abroad, as here he actually did nothing but hunt all winter and lounge all summer ... I have not had fair play ... I am misrepresented because I scorn malapropos displays of sentiment and ethics.[26]

At the turn of the year Lady William, four months pregnant, reported to Bedford's brother, old Lord William Russell*, that her husband 'has shook off all his Russell indolence and slaves at his regiment, which was in a wretched plight and which he will gain great credit by putting in order'. (In August 1825 Bedford congratulated him on the 'favourable reports' he heard of the military authorities' 'high opinion' of his success in improving the regiment, and the following year the duke of Wellington warmly approved his proposals for changes in cavalry formations in the field.)[27] For his own part Russell fretted that it was 'a melancholy life for Bessy, the ornament and brightest flower of the brightest society of Europe, to be pent up in a small provincial town', though her current good health made her 'gay, amiable, original and amusing'. He thought that 'there will be nothing to do in Parliament', and that 'Ireland is all a bugbear'.[28] He was a defaulter on a call of the House, 28 Feb. 1825, but attended and was excused the next day, when he voted for Catholic relief, as he did again, 21 Apr., 10 May. He was present to vote for inquiry into chancery delays, 7 June 1825. After the birth of his second son that month he took a small cottage in Richmond Park for six months, while his regiment was quartered at Hounslow. In September 1825 he evidently made some sort of apology to his father for the incident of the previous year, which gave the duke 'the most heartfelt satisfaction'.[29] In January 1826 Russell, who shortly afterwards moved with the 8th Hussars to Brighton (which pleased his wife), appealed to his father for help with a debt of £1,000, and got a sympathetic response.[30] He was in the minority of 24 on the promissory notes bill, 20 Feb. Four days later Lady William denied Lynedoch's charge that she had bullied Russell into cutting down his hunting activities:

> It is a subject on which Lord William is sore as he dreads henpecking amazingly from its being in the family ... We all have our weaknesses, and I should say Lord William's peculiar one was that of such a dread of being led that he will not be advised ... Pray open your eyes and see whether I prevent him from hunting. He is constantly absent when there is anything of moment in the House of Commons and always because he is hunting. His elder brother writes volumes to him on the abuse of his constituents ... [He] is now at Woburn hunting and there is much going on in the House and many enquiries made after him ... he goes at least every ten days and I never really urge his return ... I think his friends and well wishers ought to be satisfied with his free agency; he has given up none of his former friends, he has not given up his profession, he is not gone out of Parliament and he does keep hunters ... He does not control me ... in anything for I am as free an agent as he is, and I do not see that there is any violent coercion on either side.[31]

Possibly with an eye to the approaching general election, Russell showed his face in the House for the divisions on the Jamaican slave trials, 2 Mar., the promissory notes bill, 7 Mar., the ministerial salary of the president of the board of trade, 10 Apr., reform of Edinburgh's representation, 13 Apr., and Lord John's reform motion, 27 Apr. 1826. His father exhorted him to 'take at least an useful, if not efficient part' when the Fen drainage bill came before Parliament: 'if you are not yet acquainted with the common routine business of the House of Commons, after so many years service, it is high time you should learn it'.[32]

Russell was returned unopposed for Bedford at the 1826 general election, when, observing that it was 'difficult to define the actual state of parties', he praised the recent liberalization of government foreign and domestic policies, though he called for further tax reductions and blamed ministers for the overspeculation and consequent commercial crash of the previous winter. He said that he was 'a friend to reform in Parliament' and would welcome 'every prudent measure for obtaining an effectual one', promised to resign his seat if a majority of the electors found his pro-Catholic views unacceptable, and declared his support for fair protection for British farmers against imports of foreign corn.[33] He did himself much good in Bedford, as well as raising his stock with his immediate family, by making a vigorous and lucid defence of the purity of election principles on which the temporarily indisposed Tavistock was contesting the county, 17 June 1826.[34] The following month, however, he received a lecture from his father, who was unable to meet his request for an additional £500 of ready money, having had to raise a similar amount for Lord John, and was shocked by his 'talk of quitting active service from inability to go on with it':

> I think after the credit you have gained in forming an excellent regiment out of a very bad one, you ought not, in justice to yourself, to think of going again on half-pay, nor ought you, in fairness to me, after the large sum of money I have paid to obtain for you the command of the 8th. You ought now to be in possession of a very fair and reasonable income ... and you should consider how many officers there are in command of regiments, with scarcely any private fortune, and little to live upon besides their pay and appointments.

Russell told Lady Holland in August that while 'we enjoy ourselves in Brighton, as indeed we do at most places, having light hearts, nice children and few cares', he was worried again about Lady William's health, and afraid that 'we shall be obliged to escape to the continent to avoid the butcher and baker': 'Indeed I believe Bessy never sees the steamboat leave the chain pier without longing to get into it and leave her clothes and servants to themselves'.[35] His reluctance to carry out the routine constituency duties expected of a Member for Bedford, such as attending the local races in late August (he eventually appeared for one day, under sufferance) also distressed his father, who complained to Lady Holland that 'he seldom writes, except to scold me for something I have done or left undone, so I am glad when I do not perceive his hand amongst my post letters': Bedford subsequently moaned about his maintaining his '*imperturbable* silence'. Russell for once attended the annual Bedford mayor's feast, 29 Sept., to the pleasure of his father, who did not, however, fail to tell him that his unexcused absence the previous year had caused offence. He had evidently offered to make way for Lord John, who had been defeated in Huntingdonshire at the general election, but the duke would not hear of it.[36]

Russell, who was reported by Tavistock to their father in October 1826 as having 'taken a very erroneous view of the corn question' by favouring a more open trade, joined in urging Lord John not to stay on the continent, as he threatened to do, but to return to Parliament to 'look after the rotten boroughs' and turn his attention to the desperate state of affairs in Ireland.[37] Russell voted for Catholic relief, 6 Mar., and for the opposition motion to delay voting the supplies until the ministerial uncertainty was resolved, 30 Mar. 1827. Bedford concurred in his view that Canning was 'forming a ministry of odds and ends, all he can catch or purchase'; but he deplored the Lansdowne Whigs' union with him, of which his sons took a more relaxed view. In mid-May he acknowledged Russell's 'very amiable and sensible letter', which gave 'the only clear *exposé*, and well argued apology for the late transactions I have yet seen', but warned him that his belief that the ministry would do good in Ireland would be 'disappointed, for there is no doubt that it is an understood thing between the king and Canning that the Catholic question is not to be carried'.[38] Russell, who attended the county meeting to petition the Lords for enhanced agricultural protection, 23 May,[39] voted for the disfranchisement of Penryn, 28 May 1827. In June he went with his regiment to Ireland, having evidently incurred his wife's very severe displeasure by some unknown transgression, for which she punished him by refusing to go with him immediately. At the end of July he begged her forgiveness:

> I feel so wretched ... My thoughts are incessantly with you and my boys ... I love you with all my heart and soul. I hope that when we meet again we shall part no more ... I ... am tormented by dreary, disagreeable thoughts. Dearest Bessy, pardon me. I am not as bad as you believe me to be, and with the help of God I will be better. How I wish we could live in peace and harmony together.

He remained somewhat at odds with his father over politics, though Bedford assured him that he had 'never heard your political conduct maligned or calumniated by anyone'. The duke reproached him for the 'splenetic bitterness' with which he attacked Lord Grey and wished him joy of his declared preference for Holland, who would 'swim you into foul waters'.[40] Russell sent Lord John his observations on the state of Ireland, 'a most curious country'; they were well received, though his brother quibbled with his assessment of Canning's successor, Lord Goderich, as 'a Tory'. Bedford accused him of being 'singular' in his admiration of Lord Lansdowne for joining the new ministry, and suggested that only he and old Lord William were now out of step with the rest of the family. Russell confided to Lady Holland that he could see no reason to condemn Lansdowne as 'weak', and that his own object, which would determine his conduct when the government met Parliament, was to 'exclude those horrid old Tories'.[41]

After two wretched months in barracks in Dundalk, Lady William became determined to visit her mother in Berne, and Russell, who was upset to see 'the most brilliant, the sweetest flower of Europe on such a dung-hill', gave in. Making what was probably the crucial mistake of his life, he used the state of her health to obtain three months' leave of absence from his regiment to accompany her. Exhorted by his father, anxious to secure family unity, to talk with Tavistock before deciding what political line to take on his return, and if possible to look to Lord Althorp* for a lead, he told Lord John, 24 Dec. 1827, that he might be home in time for the opening of Parliament, and hoped he might be able to go with the 'upright, well-intentioned' Althorp. In the event, he arrived in London on 12 Feb. 1828, 'looking well, and very "dapper"' as Lord John reported.[42] He attended the House to vote for his brother's motion for repeal of the Test Acts, 26 Feb., but his only other known vote that session was against extending the franchise at East Retford to the freeholders of Bassetlaw, 21 Mar. Five days earlier the arrival of a 'dreadful letter from Bessy' had, as he noted in his diary, 'overwhelmed my spirits'. He took to reading the Bible, 'with an intention of reading it through, two or three chapters a day', and reflected, 6 Apr., after a family gathering at Woburn, that 'politics is the only subject on which Englishmen talk with pleasure and eagerness, and it is the most important affair of life except for religion'. The following day, when he went to Laleham to meet Wellington, whose gossiping conversation disappointed him, he told his wife, in a letter chiefly about the problem of their sons' education, that 'I pass my time here much in reading and reflecting, I hope beneficially ... and indeed I feel my mind is adopting different views and sentiments'. He presented petitions against the friendly societies regulation bill, 1, 5 May. Three days later, on his 38th birthday, he wrote to Lady William.

> I pray to God that those years which He is graciously pleased to allot me in this world, may be spent in sincere repentance for the past and such an anxious desire to lead a life of goodness, as may induce Almighty God to pardon my past transgressions, and assist me to atone for my sins by upholding me in my intentions. But you, dearest Bessy, what am I to say to you? Alas, this is a black page without hope. Nothing, no nothing can restore your confidence, your love – God have mercy on me.

Clearly a deeply troubled man, he had hoped to vote on the Catholic question before returning to Switzerland, but its repeated postponement and adjournment meant that he sailed for the continent on 10 May, two days before the division.[43]

Settling his pregnant wife at Lausanne, Russell returned to rejoin his regiment in Ireland in mid-July 1828. On arrival in London he discovered that he could not afford to have a house built at Wimbledon, as he had been planning to do. After consulting Wellington and Lord Fitzroy Somerset* about his professional prospects, he indicated to his father, who was not a little irritated, that he was inclined to go back on half-pay. From barracks in Ireland, reflecting on his 'fatal sin' and admitting that 'had it not been for my own brutality you and my boys would have been with me', he informed his wife that he had decided to join a French expedition to fight the Turks in the Morea, and that he hoped to collect her in Switzerland and take her south with him. As he told Lady Holland (whose husband he now referred to as 'my political leader, the only statesman left who has the great noble manly views of Mr. Fox'): 'Lady William will probably be confined abroad. We cannot afford to live in England; besides, her health is better abroad and we have no house and little to do in England'. At Cheltenham, on his way to London, he met Wellington, who strongly advised him to forget the French project. He concurred and, after selling his commission for £5,000, settling his debts, and depositing surplus money with his father, he left for Lausanne on 28 Sept. 1828. He eventually found his wife at Berne, and at the beginning of the winter they migrated to Florence, where she was to be confined.[44] Russell's absence from the Bedford mayor's feast at the end of September 'excited much discontent', as it was reported to his father, who initially admonished him, though he took part of the blame on himself for having forgotten to urge him to delay his departure to attend. After Russell's explanation, however, he deemed his 'justification ample', and criticized Tavistock and the mayor for not having transmitted the apologies which Russell claimed to have sent to the latter. The duke went on:

> With regard to your going out of Parliament I can see no necessity for it whatever. If any unforeseen event should occur so as to prevent your future attendance, it will then be time enough to think of it, but I suppose there will be nothing to prevent your coming over after Lady William *est relevée de ses couches*, and there is seldom business of much importance till after Easter.[45]

Lord John, anticipating an important session, with the Catholic question coming to a crisis, was anxious that Russell should

> be here, for it will be a time to assert great and immortal principles ... I am quite uneasy to think you should be so far away. It exposes you either to a long journey, and a long separation from your family, or to your discontenting my father, Tavistock, your friends, and yourself by not doing your duty.

Bedford endorsed these sentiments, though he felt that he could not press Russell 'to stir till your wife is safe in her bed'. Yet at the end of 1828 Lord John informed his brother that in view of the prevailing uncertainty, 'you may as well wait at least for the report of the first day's debate'.[46] In January 1829 Lord John, who assured Russell that 'your perpetual complaints of the injustice with which your wife is treated in this country are totally unfounded', and Tavistock brought increasing pressure to bear on him in an attempt to prevent him from being permanently seduced from England. They pointed out the desirability of having his sons educated there, and reminded him of his political obligations and the threat which his absence was posing to the family interest at Bedford. In early February, when the Wellington ministry's concession of Catholic emancipation was confirmed, they, Bedford and Holland, who was 'asked to press you', insisted that he should go to England as soon as Lady William was safe. She gave birth to their third son on 20 Feb. Four days later Russell, whose diary indicates that he was finding her increasingly hard to live with, though he laid some of the blame on himself, wrote to Holland:

> You are right in thinking you have great influence over me, *politically*, no one except my good brother has more. When Aeolus let loose the *Luctantis ventos tempestatesque sonoras* which scattered and shipwrecked the Whigs, you were the plank to which I stuck – in the first place there is magic in the name of Fox, in the next place I like your views on our foreign policy. England should be the terror of the ambitious and the scheming, and the asylum of the oppressed ... in civil and religious freedom and all that concerns our domestic policy, we go hand in hand together. I liked Canning because he lifted us out of that

> foreign mud in which we had been grovelling ever since the peace, and because he was a friend to Ireland. In these two great virtues were swallowed up all his little vices. It does not do to look at a minister with a microscope.

He eventually left for England after christening his son, but arrived too late to vote on the Catholic relief bill.[47] He attended the House to divide for the transfer of East Retford's seats to Birmingham, 5 May 1829, the last known vote of his parliamentary career.

Russell paid £1,314 for the lieutenant-colonelcy of the 90th Foot, then stationed in the Ionian Islands. Just before returning to the continent in early June 1829, he was persuaded by Tavistock, against his own better judgement, to write to the alderman who had proposed him at the last election offering to resign his seat. Tavistock later claimed that the offer was declined, but that the leading supporters of the Russells suggested that he might make way for Lord John at the next general election. This notion evidently had little appeal for Russell, who was lectured sternly on the subject of Bedford later in the year by a worried Tavistock.[48] Russell rejoined his family in Florence in mid-June, before moving with them to Switzerland for the summer. In the autumn they returned to Italy, where Lady William took up residence in Rome, while Russell went to inspect his regiment. He remained there for four weeks, was offered by Adam, the high commissioner, the post of resident at Cephalonia and got two months' leave to return to Rome. Lord John, who had been with the Russells at Florence earlier in the year, gathered that his brother's professional prospects would be best served by his remaining with his regiment until it came back to England, and, taking a quite different line from Tavistock, advised him that he could probably stay away for all or most of the next session, provided he returned to England in the summer to safeguard his seat. Trying to persuade Lady William of the wisdom of this course, whether or not she decided to go to Corfu, he wrote:

> Never allow William to quit Parliament, army, etc., which in his last letter to me he talks of. Bedford will be quiet this year ... Give up all thoughts of Parliament this year – settle between Corfu and Rome as best you can with credit, for William must not lose his military reputation; come to England in August next year, and contrive to have the regiment here for the next winter so that William may vote in every important question that comes on.

As Russell had feared, his wife would have nothing to do with Corfu, and at the end of the year he turned down the offer of Cephalonia.[49]

Russell, who in January 1830 deplored to Lady Holland 'our pitiful foreign policy' and expressed the hope that her husband and Grey would form 'a cordial alliance', went back to Corfu in March. To Lord John he wrote, 1 Apr.:

> I like your line in politics, it is straightforward, principled and devoid of factious opposition. This great reduction of taxes puts me in good humour with the ministry, it is beyond our most sanguine hopes and will relieve the poor suffering peasantry, but I should not yet be satisfied, much more yet can still be reduced without hurting our respectability or efficient force ... I am for urging on the ministry, without turning them out. We shall not get so good a one to replace them.

His brother now urged him to resign his commission in June and come home, and pressed Lady William to accompany him and settle in England.[50] Russell returned to Italy on leave in June, missed his wife at Rome, and eventually ran her to earth at Genoa on 6 July. It was not a happy reunion, and their increasingly tempestuous relationship tortured Russell. He was furious when he was peremptorily notified by his father that at the general election occasioned by the death of George IV, Lord John was to stand in his place for Bedford, where the family interest was under serious attack, largely as a result of Russell's absenteeism: 'Your coming into the new Parliament is quite out of the question. You must stick to your profession where you are doing so well'. Lord John told him that all concerned were 'agreed that it would be folly for you to stand for Bedford again', for his defeat was certain; and the duke, who, without consulting him, secured him an appointment as one of the new king's aides-de-camp, assured him that when he left the army, but not before, 'I have no doubt that we shall be able to find you a seat in Parliament if such should be your wish'. Russell, who moved with his family to Geneva in early August 1830, remained sore for months over his summary ejection from Parliament; and his brother's defeat by one vote at Bedford only reinforced his astoundingly purblind argument, of which family and friends tried to show him the folly, that he himself would have won the seat.[51]

Lady William decided to accept the offer of a place in the queen's bedchamber, and Russell got another six months leave from his regiment in September 1830, but they remained in Switzerland all winter. Russell had plenty of advice, on both domestic and foreign politics, for his brother, appointed paymaster in the Grey ministry, and for Holland, the lord privy seal: he was particularly anxious that

> the Whigs should not fall into that error of which they are so commonly accused, of holding one language out of office and another in office ... You have promised us

> reform, economy and non-interference, and that is all we ask for; act up to your own motto, and the country will support you.

He had decided by February 1831 to go back on the half-pay list, a decision of which his father '*entirely*' disapproved: 'You are a good soldier, and no great politician, no farmer, no scientific pursuits'.[52] Russell, leaving his wife and children in Paris, arrived in England at the beginning of May, in time to assist with the Bedfordshire election, in which Tavistock and another reformer were successful. He told Lord John:

> You have raised a noble spirit in the country ... It is like a burst of spring after a severe winter. A few months ago we were all discontented, and none more discontented than myself, now we are all contented, and none more contented than myself ... There is a most extraordinary spirit abroad, not only in England but all over the world, and I don't think your colleagues are aware of it. The art is to lead this spirit and not let it lead you.

He confirmed his decision to revert to half-pay later in the month, and his father made him the offer of a return for Tavistock, where Lord John was about to vacate, having been returned for Huntingdonshire: 'it must be on one condition, viz. that you are not running over to Paris or elsewhere, while this great question is pending, but you must be at your post day and night, till the reform bill is safely through the Commons'. Russell 'hesitated', and before he came to a decision Bedford was pressed by the leading electors of Tavistock to accommodate John Hawkins, a young man who had made a splash with a speech in support of the reform bill and been turned out of his seat for Mitchell. When his father informed him of this Russell took the hint and 'desired to waive all claim'.[53] A few days later he told Holland:

> Madame de Flahaut wrote in a good natured wish to be of use to me, to suggest I should be employed in diplomacy. I have no desire whatever to be so employed. It is too intricate and unintelligible a science for my poor understanding. I might be proclaimed a liar and hypocrite all over Europe, like Lord Ponsonby, or duped like poor Lieven, and I have no wish to expose myself to be despised or laughed at without deserving either. If ever diplomacy is put upon a footing of straightforward open dealing upon principle, I shall be very glad to serve in it, but at present I feel no disposition to lose myself in its dark and tortuous ways.[54]

Less than two months after this outburst he went as private secretary to Sir Robert Adair† on his special mission to Brussels, thus embarking on the diplomatic career which occupied him for the next ten years and restored some point and self-respect to his life. His marriage, however, went from bad to worse, and was effectively destroyed by his embarrassingly blatant infidelity with a Jewish widow at Baden Baden in 1835, which shocked many who witnessed it.[55] Thereafter he and Lady William lived essentially separate lives, though there was no formal split. Russell, who turned down the offer of the government of Bombay in July 1841, was outraged to be recalled from Berlin soon afterwards by the new Conservative government, though he could not reasonably have expected to be left in place. The public quarrel which he picked with Lord Aberdeen, the foreign secretary, required the intervention of Charles Greville to settle it and restore their mutual good humour.[56]

Russell cut a sad figure in his last years. On 8 May 1845 he wrote: '55 alas, alas. Hair grey, teeth decaying, strength diminishing, memory failing and all the symptoms of old age; time to die'.[57] He left England for the last time that month to join his wife at Carlsbad, but was soon made miserable by her temper. He moved to Italy, while Lady William and their two youngest sons wintered in Vienna. He was taken seriously ill at Genoa in March 1846, and again in June, when his eldest son went to attend him. When Lady William, responding to an urgent summons, reached Genoa on 19 June 1846, she found Russell 'unconscious and speechless', but five days later he had made something of a recovery. It was only temporary, for he died at Genoa, 16 July 1846, the very day on which his younger brother, just installed as prime minister after Peel's fall from power, explained and defended his conduct in the Commons.[58] By his will, dated 2 Mar. 1844, he confirmed the trust fund provisions made a year earlier for his younger sons. He left his leasehold London house in Grosvenor Place to his eldest son, with permission for his wife to occupy it if she wished.[59] The weak health of Tavistock and his only son, Lord Russell*, had often seemed to put the dukedom tantalisingly within Russell's reach, but they both comfortably outlived him. However, his eldest son, Francis Charles Hastings Russell (1819-91), a suicide, succeeded his cousin as 9th duke of Bedford in 1872. The second son, Arthur John Edward (1825-92), was Liberal Member for Tavistock, 1857-85; and the third, Odo William Leopold (1829-84), had a distinguished diplomatic career and was created Baron Ampthill in 1881. Lady William, who became a Catholic in 1860, was a celebrated London hostess from 1850 until her death in 1874.[60]

[1] See G. Blakiston, *Lord William Russell and his Wife, 1815-1846* (1972), which draws in part on the privately printed *Letters to Lord G. William Russell* (1915-20). [2] Blakiston, 1-17. [3] Ibid. 46-47.

[4] *Cambridge and Hertford Independent Press*, 11 Mar.; Add. 51662, Bedford to Holland, 10 Mar.; 51676, Russell to same, 13 Mar. 1820. [5] *Northampton Mercury*, 20 Jan. 1821. [6] *The Times*, 25 Jan. 1821. [7] Ibid. 4 Apr. 1821. [8] Blakiston, 48-81; Add. 51676, Russell to Holland, 20 June, to Lady Holland, 18 Aug., 6 Oct. 1821, 29 May, 27 June 1822. [9] Add. 51676. [10] Blakiston, 59-60; *Russell Letters*, i. 4-5; ii. 1-3. [11] *Russell Letters*, ii. 6. [12] Add. 51676. [13] *Russell Early Corresp.* i. 225-6; *Russell Letters*, ii. 12. [14] Blakiston, 64-72; Add. 51676. [15] *Fox Jnl.* 159. [16] Blakiston, 72-82; *Russell Letters*, i. 10, 13, 15, 17; ii. 19; Add. 51667, Bedford to Lady Holland [13 Apr. 1823]. [17] Blakiston, 82-94. [18] Ibid. 94-102; Add. 51676, Russell to Holland [c.10 June 1823]. [19] *The Times*, 4 July 1823. [20] *Fox Jnl.* 168. [21] Blakiston, 103-14; Add. 51676, Russell to Holland [c.10 June], Thursday [Nov.], to Lady Holland, 9, 23 Nov. 1823. [22] *The Times*, 19 Mar. 1824. [23] Add. 51667, Bedford to Lady Holland, Tuesday [16 Mar. 1824]. [24] Blakiston, 113, 117-34; Add. 51668, Bedford to Lady Holland, 22 Aug. [1824]; 51679, Lord J. Russell to same, 12 Aug. [1824]. [25] Blakiston, 113, 116-17; *Russell Letters*, i. 30-40; ii. 42-43; Add. 51668, Bedford to Lady Holland, Wed. [27 Oct. 1824]. [26] Blakiston, 125-6. [27] Ibid. 128-9; *Russell Letters*, ii. 53; *Wellington Despatches*, iii. 353-4. [28] Blakiston, 131. [29] Ibid. 114, 131-4. [30] Ibid. 136; *Russell Letters*, i. 42-43. [31] Blakiston, 136-7. [32] *Russell Letters*, ii. 57. [33] *Cambridge and Hertford Independent Press*, 17 June 1826. [34] Ibid. 1, 8 July 1826; *Russell Letters*, ii. 59-60. [35] Blakiston, 138-40. [36] Add. 51669, Bedford to Lady Holland, 1, 5, 7, 21 Sept.; 51676, Russell to same, 20 Aug. [1827]; *Russell Letters*, i. 130-2. [37] *Russell Letters*, i. 51-52; *Russell Early Corresp.*, i. 252-3. [38] *Russell Letters*, i. 62-63; ii. 83-85. [39] *Herts. Mercury*, 26 May 1827. [40] Blakiston, 144-6. [41] *Russell Early Corresp.* i. 260-1; *Russell Letters*, i. 73-74; ii. 99-100; Blakiston, 147; Add. 51676, Russell to Lady Holland, 19 Sept. [1827]. [42] Blakiston, 147-8, 151-3; *Russell Letters*, i. 81-84; *Russell Early Corresp.* i. 269-70; Add. 51679, Lord J. Russell to Lady Holland, Sat. [5 Jan. 1828]. [43] Blakiston,157-66. [44] Ibid. 167-73; *Russell Letters*, i. 94; ii. 130-2; Add. 51676, Russell to Lady Holland, 20 Aug.; 51679, Lord J. Russell to same, Sat. [27 Sept.] 1828. [45] *Russell Letters*, ii. 154; Blakiston, 173. [46] *Russell Letters*, i. 104-5; ii. 156; Blakiston, 173-7. [47] Blakiston, 174-8; *Russell Letters*, i. 109, 112, 116; ii. 178-9, 181-2, 184; Add. 51676, Russell to Lady Holland, 24 Feb. [1829]. [48] Blakiston, 194, 198; *Russell Letters*, i. 153-4. [49] Blakiston, 189-204, 207-8; *Russell Letters*, i. 132-3; ii. 235; Add. 51676, Russell to Lady Holland, 4 Oct. [1829]. [50] Blakiston, 204-11; Add. 51676, Russell to Lady Holland, 9 Jan., 26 Feb. [1830]; *Russell Early Corresp.* i. 318; *Russell Letters*, ii. 239. [51] Blakiston, 209-21, 223; *Russell Letters*, i. 143, 145-7, 152-5, 158-9; ii. 251, 256-7, 260-8; Add. 51670, Bedford to Lady Holland [22 Aug.]; 51676, Russell to same, 30 July [1830]. [52] Blakiston, 221-31; *Russell Letters*, ii. 320-1, 325, 329, 334; *Russell Early Corresp.* i. 318; ii. 15-17; Add. 51676, Russell to Holland, 9 Jan., to Lady Holland [Mar.], 22 Apr. 1831. [53] *Russell Early Corresp.* ii. 19-20; *Russell Letters*, ii. 340-2; Add. 51663, Bedford to Holland, Tues. [31 May 1831]; Blakiston, 231-2. [54] Add. 51676, Russell to Holland, 7 June 1831. [55] Blakiston, 235-363; G. Huxley, *Lady Elizabeth and the Grosvenors*, 150-1; *Lieven-Palmerston Corresp.* 111. [56] Blakiston, 363-459; Add. 43238, ff. 66, 240, 242, 273, 281; 43239, ff. 17, 19; *Greville Mems.* iv. 434; v. ii, 41. [57] Blakiston, 507. [58] Ibid. 507-37; Add. 52010, Lady W. Russell to 4th Lord Holland, 24 June [1846]; Walpole, *Russell*, i. 432. [59] PROB 11/2047/923; IR26/1751/784. [60] Blakiston, 544.

D.R.F.

RUSSELL, John (1796–1835), of Upton House, nr. Kineton, Warws.

KINSALE 1826–1832

b. 10 July 1796, 3rd s. of Lord William Russell* (*d.* 1840) and Lady Charlotte Anne Villiers, da. of George Bussy Villiers†, 4th earl of Jersey; bro. of Francis Russell*. *educ.* Westminster 1806-8. *m.* 21 Aug. 1822, Sophia, da. of Col. George Kein Hayward Coussmaker of Marylebone, Mdx. (*s.j.* Baroness de Clifford, 1833), 1s. 2da. surv. *d.v.p.* 27 Apr. 1835.

Lt. RN 1815, cdr. 1822.

Russell, one of the four sons of the eccentric and impecunious Lord William Russell and a nephew of the 6th duke of Bedford, was commissioned a lieutenant in the navy a month after Waterloo. Little is known of his professional career, though he was supposed to have 'served many years' in the Mediterranean and other parts of the world.[1] In 1822 he made a financially rewarding marriage to Sophia Coussmaker, the eldest niece and co-heiress of the 21st Lord de Clifford.[2] By about this time he had a Warwickshire residence at Upton, where his maternal uncle, the 5th earl of Jersey, was lord of the manor.[3] On 16 Feb. 1823 he was admitted to Brooks's, sponsored by his cousin, Lord Tavistock*, and his brother-in-law, Henry Grey Bennet*. At the general election of 1826 de Clifford put him up for his Irish proprietary borough of Kinsale. There was no opposition to his return, but on the hustings one John Cranmer lectured him, as 'quite a stranger' who had only shown his face there the previous day, on the views of his constituents, which included hostility to any alteration of the corn laws and support for Catholic relief. In reply, Russell dealt in the contemporary cant of independence:

> He would not give any pledge as to his future conduct in Parliament, thinking he would best maintain the interests of his constituents by keeping his mind free and unshackled ... he would be happy to meet them again in due time, to give an account of his conduct, and he should always prize as his best reward, their approbation.[4]

In the House Russell, who presented constituency petitions for agricultural protection, 22 Feb., and Catholic relief, 4 May 1827,[5] took his family's Whig line; but before the reform crisis he was a markedly poor attender. He did not vote in the divisions on Catholic relief, to which de Clifford was opposed, 6 Mar. 1827, 12 May 1828. He voted to postpone going into committee of supply until the ministerial uncertainty was resolved, 30 Mar., and for the disfranchisement of Penryn, 28 May 1827. He was at Woburn Abbey with his father in early April 1828.[6] He voted with opposition on civil list pensions, 20 May, the grant for the Society for the Propagation of the Gospels in the colonies, 6 June, the archbishop of Canterbury's bill, 16 June, the spending of public money on Buckingham House, 23 June, the salary of the lieutenant-general of the ordnance, 4 July, and the grant for Canadian fortifications, 7 July 1828. As Planta, the Wellington ministry's patronage secretary, had anticipated, he was absent from the divisions on Catholic emancipation in 1829, when de Clifford opposed it by proxy in the Lords. His only other known vote in the 1826 Parliament was for Lord Blandford's parliamentary reform scheme, 18 Feb. 1830. He was returned without fuss for Kinsale at the general election of 1830.[7] Ministers of course listed him among their 'foes', but he was an absentee from the division on the civil list which brought them down, 15 Nov. 1830. On 7 Mar. 1831, in his only known Commons speech, he defended his cousin Lord John Russell* and the other framers of the ministerial reform bill against charges of unjustly and corruptly sparing Bedford's nomination borough of Tavistock from disfranchisement. He argued that the measure, which could not have been 'fairer' in its treatment of the electoral interests of the aristocracy of Ireland, and than which 'a better plan could not be devised', was not directed against 'just and proper influence' such as that exercised by Bedford at Tavistock on the strength of property ownership. The following day he was given ten days' leave of absence, but he was present to vote for the second reading of the bill, 22 Mar., and against Gascoyne's wrecking amendment, 19 Apr. 1831. On the dissolution, he offered again for Kinsale, issuing an address to the current electors (the freemen) urging them to sanction his 'honest vote' for reform, even though it would eventually destroy their own 'exclusive privilege'. As de Clifford himself favoured reform, there was no difficulty over his re-election.[8] He voted for the second reading of the reintroduced reform bill, 6 July, and was a steady supporter of its details in committee until the second week of August, though he was in the minority against the total disfranchisement of Saltash, 26 July 1831. His attendance subsequently fell away. He voted for the passage of the bill, 21 Sept., and the motion of confidence in the Grey ministry, 10 Oct. His only known votes on the revised bill were for the second reading, 17 Dec. 1831, the second borough disfranchisement schedule, 23 Jan., and the third reading, 22 Mar. 1832. He voted for the address calling on the king to appoint only ministers who would carry the bill unimpaired, 10 May, and for the Irish, 25 May, and Scottish reform bills, 1 June. He divided with ministers on the Russian-Dutch loan, 12, 16, 20 July 1832. He retired from the House at the dissolution in December.

Russell was master of the Warwickshire Hunt from December 1830 until poor health forced him to stand down at the end of the 1833 season. It was later written that he

> united the sound judgement and energy of the first rate sportsman with the conciliatory and polished manners of a gentleman, and ... was much beloved for his gentleness of deportment and excellent temper, which, though often tried in the field, was never ruffled.

One observer, however, carped that while he was 'a good judge of hunting, and particularly gentlemanlike in his demeanour', 'his men might have been better mounted, or at all events on horses better suited to the country'.[9] On 4 Mar. 1833 the barony of de Clifford, in abeyance since the death without issue of Russell's electoral patron the previous year, and in dispute between the children of his deceased sisters, was deemed by the Lords to have devolved on Russell's wife. Russell followed his two elder brothers to the grave in his father's lifetime, dying, after 'a short illness' in April 1835, aged 38. Raikes noted the tragic irony of the death, 'in the very prime of his existence' and only just embarked on 'his career of worldly prosperity', of the only one of Lord William's sons who was 'in affluent circumstances'.[10] Administration of his estate, which was sworn under £30,000, was granted to his widow, 8 Aug. 1835.[11] On her death, worth about £100,000, in 1874, the barony of de Clifford passed to their only surviving son, Edward Southwell Russell† (1824-77).

[1] C. Mordaunt and W.R. Verney, *Annals of Warws. Hunt*, i. 107. [2] Blakiston, *Lord William Russell*, 67. [3] *VCH Warws*. v. 145; Mordaunt and Verney, i. 70. [4] *Southern Reporter*, 8, 17, 22, 24 June 1826; Cent. Kent. Stud. Stanhope mss U1590 C191/1, Stanhope to Cranmer, 4 Apr. 1827. [5] *The Times*, 23 Feb., 5 May 1827. [6] Blakiston, 159. [7] *Constitution*, 17 July 1830. [8] *Southern Reporter*, 30 Apr., 7 May 1831. [9] Mordaunt and Verney, i. 97-107; 'Venator' [John Cooper], *Warws. Hunt*, 210-53; *Nimrod's Hunting Reminiscences* ed. A. Shaw Sparrow (1926), 141. [10] *Gent. Mag.* (1835), i. 669; *Raikes Jnl.* ii. 92. [11] PROB 6/211/152.

D.R.F.

RUSSELL, Lord John (1792–1878).[1]

TAVISTOCK	4 May 1813–28 Feb. 1817
TAVISTOCK	1818–1820
HUNTINGDONSHIRE	1820–1826
BANDON BRIDGE	19 Dec. 1826–1830
TAVISTOCK	27 Nov. 1830–1831
DEVON	1831–1832
DEVON SOUTH	1832–Apr. 1835
STROUD	19 May 1835–1841
LONDON	1841–July 1861

b. 18 Aug. 1792, 3rd s. of John Russell†, 6th duke of Bedford (*d.* 1839), and 1st w. Hon. Georgiana Elizabeth

Byng, da. of George, 4th Visct. Torrington; bro. of Francis Russell, mq. of Tavistock* and Lord George William Russell*. *educ.* by Dr. Moore, Sunbury, Mdx. 1800-1; Westminster 1803-4; privately by Dr. Edmund Cartwright 1804-5; by Rev. John Smith at Woodnesborough, nr. Sandwich, Kent 1805-8; Edinburgh Univ. 1809-12. *m.* (1) 11 Apr. 1835, Adelaide (*d.* 1 Nov. 1838), da. of Thomas Lister of Armitage Park, Staffs., wid. of her 2nd cos. Thomas Lister, 2nd Bar. Ribblesdale, 2da.; (2) 20 July 1841, Lady Frances Anna Maria Elliot Murray Kynynmound, da. of Gilbert Elliot Murray Kynynmound†, 2nd earl of Minto, 3s. (1 *d.v.p.*) 1da. *cr.* Earl Russell 30 July 1861; KG 21 May 1862; GCMG 25 Mar. 1869. *d.* 28 May 1878.

PC 22 Nov. 1830; paymaster-gen. Dec. 1830-Dec. 1834 (in cabinet from June 1831); commr. on civil administration of army 1833-4, 1835-7; sec. of state for home affairs Apr. 1835-Sept. 1839; ecclesiastical commr. 1835-7; sec. of state for war and colonies Sept. 1839-Sept. 1841; first ld. of treasury 6 July 1846-27 Feb. 1852, 3 Nov. 1865-6 July 1866; commr. on new bishoprics 1847; sec. of state for foreign affairs Dec. 1852-Feb. 1853, June 1859-Nov. 1865; in cabinet without office Feb. 1853-June 1854; ld. pres. of council June 1854-Feb. 1855; 4th charity commr. 1854-6; special mission to Vienna Feb.-Apr. 1855; sec. of state for colonies May-July 1855.

Rect. Glasgow Univ. 1846-7, Aberdeen Univ. 1863-6.

Capt. Beds. militia 1810.

At the start of this period the 27-year-old Russell, the runt of his strange aristocratic family, with a 'thin, diminutive figure and shrivelled countenance', had staked a claim to be the Foxite Whig spokesman for moderate parliamentary reform.[2] By its close he was probably the most popular politician in Britain, fêted as the chief author of the first Reform Act.[3] Yet in 1820 Russell, a proud, shy, insecure, sensitive and quick-tempered man, plagued by unreliable health and infected with his father's 'moving mania', which lured him frequently to the continent, was as much attracted to literature and history as to politics, although his abilities in those fields were pedestrian. He had not yet served out his political apprenticeship under Lord Holland, who found him a readier pupil than his own disappointing elder son.[4] At the general election of 1820 he abandoned his secure seat for the family borough of Tavistock to stand for Huntingdonshire, having been recommended by his friend Lord Milton* to the local independents who wished to break the dominant aristocratic Tory coalition. He canvassed successfully, made, so Milton heard, a 'very neat and judicious speech' at the county meeting, 4 Mar., and came in unopposed with the ministerialist sitting Member.[5] He appeared on the Westminster hustings in support of the Whig George Lamb*, 21 Mar.[6] Anticipating his appearance at the Middlesex election at the head of the Chelsea Pensioners who were to vote for Samuel Whitbread*, 27 Mar. 1820, George Agar Ellis* hoped he 'means to be dressed in the invalid costume', for he would 'make a capital withered little veteran'.[7]

Russell spoke and voted against the Liverpool ministry on the civil list, 3, 5, 8 May, when he tried to delay the report, and the appointment of an additional Scottish baron of exchequer, 15 May 1820. On 9 May he got leave to introduce his bill to disfranchise the corrupt borough of Grampound (to which ministers had agreed in principle before the dissolution) and give its seats to Leeds. On the second reading, 19 May, he expressed his preference for Leeds over Yorkshire and deplored the foreign secretary Lord Castlereagh's persistence in advocating throwing Grampound into its hundreds. Time ran out for the measure that session.[8] He 'stabbed with a polished dagger' Warren, the chief justice of Chester, 1 June, when arguing that Welsh judges should be excluded from the Commons.[9] He divided against the aliens bill that day, and the appointment of a 'green bag' inquiry into Queen Caroline's conduct, 26 June. At a constituency dinner, 28 July, he attached 'some blame' to her, but criticized ministers for involving Parliament.[10] On 3 Aug. he wrote a public letter (published in *The Times* two days later) to William Wilberforce*, enclosing a draft address to the king asking him to end proceedings by proroguing Parliament and urging him and other influential Tory backbenchers to persuade ministers to effect an amicable compromise. Wilberforce took a dim view of this and even Russell's father, the duke of Bedford, who had had no inkling of the letter, told him that he considered its publication impolitic, however 'admirable and ... unanswerable' its argument. In a preface to a subsequent issue Russell argued that it had been aimed against both diehard Tories and 'enraged demagogues', equally the 'enemies of liberty'.[11] Many Whig partisans were upset by his admission that the party was powerless to exert anything more than 'moral influence'; but he told his friend Tom Moore:

> My letter, though it pleased the people, was much blamed by our big wigs, who think our party ought to stand by, profess no principles, and hazard no opinions ... They are waiting to let ministers 'drown themselves', an ill-judged policy. The first thing needful in an opposition is to be 'honest men who will tell the truth *coute que coute*'.[12]

That month he somewhat smugly acknowledged his authorship of the trifling *Essays and Sketches of Life and Character*, dedicated to Moore, which Henry Fox* considered 'on the whole lively, full of knowledge, observation and wit'.[13] He encouraged Tierney, the

Whig leader in the Commons, to 'take a bold line' when the House met in October; and on the 17th, presenting and endorsing a Plymouth petition against the prosecution of Caroline, he condemned it as 'unwarranted and unprecedented'. He sympathized with Hume's call for the release of William Franklin, imprisoned for sedition, though a few weeks earlier he had been embarrassed by the unauthorized publication of his name as a steward of a 'Spanish dinner', which was 'evidently meant to encourage a revolt in the army', in the company of Henry Hunt* and 'Thistlewood's nearest and dearest'.[14] From late November until 1 Jan. 1821 he was in Paris, where he spent much time with Moore, to whom he suggested that 'the queen's business had done a great deal of good in renewing the old and natural alliance between the Whigs and the people'. When Lady Holland told him of his father's irritation at his sudden disappearance, he retorted that Bedford had 'no right to be *grieved* ... nor you to mention it', and that it was 'a pleasure to talk so little about the queen and politics of the parish as I do here'.[15] The day after his departure from Paris Gallois complained to Moore that he 'showed to so little advantage in society from his extreme taciturnity and still more from his apparent coldness and indifference to what is said by others'.[16]

Russell, who thought that the proliferation of loyal meetings had 'done more for us by creating a spirit than all we could do besides', spoke cogently, according to Fox, at the Bedfordshire county meeting, 12 Jan. 1821.[17] He voted in support of the opposition campaign on behalf of the queen, but spoke only tersely on the subject, 24, 26, 31 Jan. He presented, by request, a petition alleging a military outrage by the sheriff of Dublin at a pro-Caroline county meeting, 22 Feb., but his motion for inquiry was defeated by 124-90. He thought opposition produced a 'famous debate' to condemn the Allies' suppression of liberalism in Naples, 21 Feb., when he was a silent voter; but he asked Moore, 'What is an eloquent speech against a million men with whiskers, tight waists, and long swords?'[18] He reintroduced his bill to transfer Grampound's seats to Leeds, 1 Feb., and on the 12th promoted it as 'a safe, salutary and practical' measure of the sensible change which was 'the best means of guarding against the views of those who looked for reform through violence and mischief'; he saw off an attempt to sluice the borough into the hundreds. On 2 Mar. he successfully opposed Milton's amendment to give Leeds a scot and lot franchise; but when Stuart Wortley, the ministerialist Member for Yorkshire, carried by 148-94 a proposal to raise the householder qualification from £10 (a concession by Russell, who had wanted £5) to £20, he washed his hands of the bill, which Bedford thought had been made 'a perfect mockery'.[19] Not wishing to lose it, however, he endorsed the third reading, 19 Mar. Russell only paired for Catholic relief, 28 Feb. He was considered by the rising barrister John Campbell II* as 'the fittest person' to succeed the ailing Tierney as leader if he showed 'a moderate share of sense and talent'; but during the first half of March he was, as he told Lady Holland, if 'not really ill', certainly 'weakened, and worried, and made ill by London and the House of Commons'. After a fortnight's repose at Woburn Abbey he went to Holland House, 'still looking ill', as Bedford thought, and 'unfit for House of Commons air, and the hot rooms of London'.[20] He divided for repeal of the additional malt duty, 21 Mar., and paired for it, 3 Apr. At the Huntingdonshire county meeting to petition for a fair settlement for the queen and tax cuts, 30 Mar., he advocated 'retrenchment and a rational and constitutional reform'.[21] He was in three small minorities on the army estimates, 30 Apr., and divided sporadically for economy and retrenchment during the following fortnight. He voted to condemn the slow progress of the judicial commission, 9 May. Later that day he proposed inquiry into reform of the Commons by extending the franchise to deserving unrepresented large towns and establishing machinery for the disfranchisement of notoriously corrupt boroughs. His defeat by only 155-124 was considered 'a great division for reform' by the radical Whig Henry Grey Bennet*, while Bedford thought it 'grand'. On 11 May Russell was so hard on Castlereagh when supporting Bennet's allegation of a breach of privilege by *John Bull*, that the minister 'complained ... in private' to his eldest brother Lord Tavistock of his '*bitterness* towards him'.[22] He acquiesced in the Lords' amendment to give Grampound's seats to Yorkshire, 30 May, having told Lady Holland that 'the bill, your grandchild, after changing nurses several times, is now to be allowed to go alone, and I shall not disdain to own my progeny'.[23] Bedford was pleased with

> John's little beginning of a reform of Parliament. At all events, he has obtained an acknowledgement of the principle from both Houses, and the election of two Members by a rotten borough has been abrogated by a purely popular representation. This is an important point gained, as being the first step towards an efficient and salutary reform ... John would not be a bad parliamentary reformer, but he is too fond of an epigram or a sarcastic joke, which he thinks he can play off with effect upon the reformers.[24]

Russell paired for inquiry into Peterloo, 16 May, voted for Sir James Mackintosh's forgery punishment mitigation bill, 23 May, 4 June, when he joined in protests at ministers' devious attempts to defeat it, and divided to reduce the number of placemen in the Commons, 31 May, and in a minority of 27 for inquiry into the government of the Ionian Islands, 7 June 1821.

A week later he arrived in Paris, where he gave Moore a copy of his new publication, *An Essay on the History of the English Government and Constitution*, which compared the British favourably with continental systems of government and argued that 'its abuses easily admit of reforms consistent with its spirit, capable of being effected without injury or danger, and mainly contributing to its preservation' (pp. iii-iv). He had a flirtation, possibly more, with Madame Durazzo, and was reported to be 'looking pale and thin'. He returned to England in late September 1821.[25] He spent most of the autumn at Woburn, 'looking ill, but in good spirits', reading 'incessantly' and keeping his literary projects to himself.[26] On 22 Dec. he attended, with Brougham, Stephen Lushington* and Edward Ellice*, a small London meeting called by Hume to 'concert the time, place and best means of ascertaining the public feeling at a public meeting in favour of the Greeks'.[27] In Paris he had told Moore that he meant next session to 'bring forward a plan of reform', being 'displeased with the shilly-shally conduct of his party'; and in December 1821 he asserted to Lord Normanby* that reform should be made central to the party's political credo, for it had 'got into the people's marrow and nothing will take it out'. He informed Moore in early January 1822 that he planned to 'nurse myself this year, and perhaps the following' and would 'do little'; but, observing to Lady Holland that the prospects for opposition were good 'if we keep together', he insisted that '*reform*, moderate if you will, is indispensable': 'I am in my politics for reform and nothing but reform'.[28]

He 'brought a hornets' nest upon him' by writing two public letters to the yeomanry and farmers of Huntingdonshire in which he discountenanced agitation for enhanced agricultural protection and contended that the 'only safe remedies' for distress were 'retrenchment of the public expenses, the abolition of the sinking fund and the repeal of some of the most obnoxious taxes', to achieve which a reform of the Commons was essential. Mackintosh considered this 'an undistinguished attack on the application of reason to economy', executed with 'an air of levity and rashness which is very injurious to the character of a public man'; and Tierney remarked that he 'goes to press much too often, and greatly injures himself by it'.[29] Russell later admitted that he had 'deserved' the lashing which he received from the political economists in so far as he had provoked them, but he still believed that his only fault had been to 'let out too many truths at once'.[30] He stayed away from the Huntingdonshire meeting of 3 Apr. He voted for more extensive tax reductions, 11, 21 Feb., when he said that the 'great suffering and misery' of agriculturists was 'a proof of mismanagement on the part of government'. He divided silently and sporadically with his friends on major issues for a few weeks, but now felt that they were 'beat at the game of politics', as he told Moore:

> I hope to make something of reform by and bye. Meetings first must be held in most counties, but after all the country is flat and poor and dispirited, the country gentlemen base and servile, and these ministers have really established themselves in such a way that it will require king and country to unite very strongly to turn them out.[31]

On 15 Mar. he tried to embarrass Charles Arbuthnot, the patronage secretary, over his circular note summoning members to attend to resist the 'dangerous innovation' of abolition of one of the joint-postmasterships, but the Speaker took Arbuthnot's side and Russell was 'obliged to draw in his horns'.[32] Presenting the petition of the British agent Captain Romeo, who had been imprisoned and transported by the king of Naples, 25 Mar., he denounced the tyranny of the Holy Alliance. The prospect of his reform motion worried Grey and Lord Fitzwilliam, whose son Milton was the only person privy to its details, but Grey recognized that in the current climate of opinion it could hardly be suppressed.[33] Russell sat with Moore under the gallery before the time came for his motion, 25 Apr., when he spoke well for two and a half hours and was 'listened to throughout with the profoundest attention'.[34] Arguing that the Commons, where Members for small boroughs were disproportionately inclined to support government, no longer possessed 'the esteem and reverence of the people' and that stubborn resistance to reform in the face of dramatic changes in society would lead to disaster, he put the case for restorative reform to avert revolution. Specifically, he proposed to deprive 100 small boroughs of one Member and to transfer 60 seats to the counties and 40 to unrepresented large towns. Although defeated by 269-164, he secured the largest vote for reform since 1785 and had the satisfaction of seeing three millionaire converts in the minority for what represented an abandonment of gradualism by the Whig mainstream. As Lady Spencer observed, he had 'got the question into *his* hands and out of the violent Mountaineers'.[35] He was reported in May to be 'favourable' to Tavistock's fanciful notion of installing Sir Francis Burdett as leader of the opposition in the Commons.[36] Suffering 'occasional derangements from over fatigue and the bad atmosphere in the House of Commons',[37] he voted only intermittently for the rest of the session. He spoke and was in the minority of 35 for Hume's amendment to pay the deadweight pensions from the sinking fund, 24 May. He divided for reception of the Greenhoe reform petition, 3 June. On the Kent distress petition, 14 June 1822, he said that reform was 'wholly unconnected with the public debt', opposed a reduction of interest on the national debt except in extreme emergency and promised 'upon the first favourable opportunity' to renew his pressure for 'a just, necessary and constitutional reform'. A few days later he replied to Holland's observation that ministers were 'divided':

> So they always are, but we are much so, and have not the cabinet glue to keep us together. My notion is ... that they are so low in the country that we can make them do what they please as long as we are a little in the right, except about foreign politics, and there John Bull won't stand by us. The House of Commons, bad as it is, is become a sort of executive and legislative senate that governs the country half the year and with good attendance much good may be done to everybody but ourselves.[38]

'Much knocked up by the heat of London and the House', he had planned to go abroad, but his father's serious illness kept him in England for the rest of the year, 'following up his literary pursuits with laudable zeal'. He published a dreadful novel, *The Nun of Arrouca*, and a blank verse play, *Don Carlos*.[39] He noted that the marriage of Lord Mandeville*, the duke of Manchester's son, to a wealthy Huntingdonshire heiress probably meant that he would be turned out of his seat next time, but professed indifference. Yet in early October 1822 he publicly denied a report that he planned to step down and said he would stand a poll, though he was not prepared to spend illegally. Later that month he told Lady Holland, 'I mean to be a looker-on the greater part of next session. Whether I bring on my reform is doubtful, but I shall certainly do nothing else'.[40]

Russell thought the ministerial reshuffle of January 1823 would 'make the House of Commons pleasanter to attenders', but he was disgusted by the Irish attorney-general William Plunket's* use of *ex-officio* informations to prosecute the Dublin Orange rioters and wondered whether 'Ireland is to be left like Mahomet's limb hanging in mid-air between two lodestones, or whether Wellesley [the lord lieutenant] will force our statesmen to be honest in their own despite'.[41] His father regretted that he was 'led away' by the Whig 'great guns' to disregard Hume's attack on the appointment of a lieutenant-general of the ordnance in peacetime, 19 Feb., 'as he has a rising reputation to keep up, and such shabby conduct will do him some harm in the world, particularly among his constituents'.[42] Next day Russell, borrowing an idea from the 'Mountaineer' Creevey, moved for inquiry into the franchise and number of voters in the English and Welsh boroughs, suggesting that a mere 8,000 men returned a majority of the House. He was said to be 'exceedingly pleased with the result', a defeat by 128-90.[43] At the Huntingdonshire county meeting, 7 Mar., he argued that reform would 'restore rather than destroy the constitution' and denounced both his Tory colleague Fellowes's opposition to change and the extreme programme advocated by the radical Samuel Wells.[44] He approved Lord Duncannon's* plan to hold dinner meetings to promote opposition 'union', but told Brougham, whom he encouraged to assume the lead, that he saw it 'as a beginning of something else', and that there should be 'a committee of seven to ten Members to put business into some form previously to general meetings' and to act as 'a sort of cabinet'. Worried by the government's passivity towards the French invasion of Spain, he embarrassed Canning, the foreign secretary, with a mischievous question on the subject, 25 Mar.[45] Later that day he spoke and was a teller for the minority of 26 for information on diplomatic expenditure, having divided against the grant for colonial agents on the 24th. He spoke and voted for repeal of the Foreign Enlistment Act, 16 Apr., but was dissatisfied with his performance.[46] Bedford deplored the 'strange crotchet' which made him reluctant to back any motions condemning Plunket's prosecution of the Dublin rioters for fear of 'giving strength and countenance to the Orange faction';[47] but he voted silently for Burdett's successful call for inquiry, 22 Apr. Two days later, handicapped by 'a violent cold', he proposed his reform scheme of the previous year and mustered an impressive minority of 169 against 280.[48] He was one of the 22 Members who were shut in the House to form the minority on the Franco-Spanish conflict, 30 Apr. He divided for inquiries into the state of Ireland, 12 May, and the Newfoundland fisheries, 14 May, paired for abolition of the death penalty for forgery offences, 21 May, to condemn arrears in chancery business, 5 June, and in support of Irish Catholic complaints of judicial bias against them, 26 June, and voted for reform in Scotland, 2 June, to censure the lord advocate's treatment of the press, 3 June, for proper use of the Barbados defence fund, 9 June, and inquiry into the cost of the coronation, 19 June 1823. He abandoned a plan to visit Ireland with Moore that summer because both Bedford and Tavistock were ill. After performing some irksome constituency duties he confided to Lady Holland that 'I begin to be rather tired of county business, and if I could get honourably out of it should not be sorry to have the retirement of a rotten borough'. His brother George William's wife reported in September that the 'dear little manikin' was 'fat and flippant ... and does not think small beer of himself as usual'.[49] He went to Paris in pursuit of Madame Durazzo in November 1823 and wrote '*gai comme un pinson*' to his sister-in-law, confessing that 'he feels another man when he crosses the Channel, with all his patriotism'. He continued to take a keen interest in the situation in Spain, concluding that the French had 'conquered a desert', but 'sorry to see Canning so inferior to Castlereagh in stoutness and spirit'.[50]

Back in England in late January 1824, 'looking well and ... in good spirits, and ... rather eager for the opening of the parliamentary campaign', as his father thought, Russell told Moore:

> The Holy Alliance ... are the veriest curse after the plague that ever afflicted mankind ... I shall be in the House of Commons the first day, but we are likely to have a blank session. I saw leading Whigs in town. Tierney is at freezing point, Mackintosh rather below temperate; Lord Holland and Brougham alone are at blood heat.[51]

He divided for information on Catholic burials, 6 Feb., but three days later joked to Moore that the House 'is going to be shut up, and let to a great proprietor of asses; asses' milk is to be sold there'.[52] He was in the minority of 30 for papers on the Franco-Spanish war, 17 Feb., and on 18 Mar. made a motion of his own on the French evacuation, seeking to promote 'the glorious cause of humanity, of civilization, of science, of freedom' against the efforts of the Alliance to 'subdue in man all that connected him with a superior state of being, and to degrade him to a level with the brute creation'. Canning got the better of him with a comic masterpiece, and he shied from dividing the House.[53] He spoke and voted for the 'experiment' of reforming Edinburgh's representative system, 26 Feb., and divided for repeal of the window tax, 2 Mar., and, in a minority of 19, against the Welsh judiciary bill, 11 Mar. He attacked and was a minority teller against the aliens bill, 23 Mar., 12 Apr. He was named to the select committee on labourers' wages, 25 Mar., having acquiesced in the home secretary Peel's proposal to investigate this rather than the whole condition of the poor, as he had originally wished. He spoke and voted for postponement of the grant for Windsor Castle repairs until the details were disclosed, 5 Apr. He voted against the grant for building new churches, 9 Apr. He presented and endorsed a Separatists' petition for exemption from oaths of affirmation, 6 May, when he divided for inquiry into the Irish church establishment, as he did for investigation of the state of Ireland, 11 May, and proper use of Irish first fruits revenues, 25 May. On 14 June he opposed the Irish insurrection bill and urged ministers to grasp the nettle of Catholic emancipation. He said he would revive the reform issue next session, 17 May. He voted for repeal of the leather tax, 18 May, deplored the 'degrading' Test Acts, 4 June, and voted to condemn the prosecution of the Methodist missionary John Smith in Demerara, 11 June 1824. Russell, who tried to keep the peace between his stepmother and the William Russells that summer, was with the Durazzos at Bowood and Longleat in August.[54] Soon afterwards he went to Paris, and thence to Nice and Genoa, but he gave up a plan to stay in Italy for several months. He told Lady Holland that he hoped the Whigs would 'not take arms for the Catholic Association, who are grateful to none but the king and William Cobbett† for the support they have had from them'. The first volume of his *Memoirs of the Affairs of Europe from the Peace of Utrecht* appeared in 1824. (The second was published in 1829.)

Russell was in London to vote in a minority of 15 for information on the organization of the Indian army, 24 Mar. 1825. He disliked the proposals to disfranchise Irish 40*s*. freeholders and pay the Catholic clergy, 28 Mar., but was willing to swallow them to secure emancipation, for which he duly voted, 21 Apr., 10 May, and spoke, 6, 26 May. He attended and 'spoke well' at the annual Westminster purity of election dinner, 23 May.[55] He divided against the duke of Cumberland's annuity, 30 May, 19 June, to reduce judicial salaries, 17 June, and for the spring guns bill, 21 June 1825. The announcement that autumn of Mandeville's coalition with Fellowes for the anticipated general election threatened his seat. He reluctantly decided to stand his ground, but made clear his determination to spend no money (as Tavistock had in Bedfordshire) and, indifferent and torpid, resigned himself to defeat.[56] He gave up his planned autumn visit to Paris, being 'tired of travelling'. He had 'a sort of fit' at Tavistock's Bedfordshire hunting lodge in late November, when John Hobhouse, radical Whig Member for Westminster, a fellow guest, noted that he had 'a good memory and a happy recollection, which enables him to play a good part in conversation when roused to talk, which is seldom the case'.[57] At a constituency dinner, 23 Dec. 1825, he advocated reform of chancery and Parliament, condemned the Holy Alliance's suppression of Greek independence and bestowed 'liberal encomiums' on Canning's South American policy and the government's more enlightened attitude since 1823. He declined to commit himself to oppose relaxation of the corn laws and above all stressed the need for Catholic emancipation, in defiance of the 'No Popery' cry which his local opponents were raising against him.[58] He instructed Milton, to whom he left the appointment of a committee, to ensure that his agent understood that no money was to be spent except in drawing up canvassing lists, and irritated some of his supporters by refusing to canvass before Easter and by dashing off to Paris, where Lady Granville found him 'white as a sheet and smelling of ether', to see his father in late January 1826.[59]

He was in the House to vote in the minorities of 24 against the ministerial proposals to restrict the circulation of small bank notes, 20 Feb. 1826, and of 15 on the 'inordinate' navy estimates next day, when he seconded Hume's amendment. On the 24th, however, he opposed inquiry into the distressed silk trade, arguing that the ministry's estimable liberal commercial policy should not be impeded. He did not persist in his bid to reduce the grant for the volunteer corps, 3 Mar., but he continued to object to details of the army estimates and voted for the abolition of military flogging, 10 Mar. When Creevey sent him an advance copy of his *Letters to Lord John Russell* on the state of the borough representation, in which he contended that the ancient element of popular suffrage had been eroded over time, he replied that it was 'calculated to do good when money ceases to be uppermost in everyone's thoughts'. Creevey, who believed that 'my materials were much better than any he had ever produced', felt that he had 'gravelled' the 'conceited little puppy'; but he was miffed because 'little white-faced Lord John' gave him 'not a word of compliment' when they met in London.[60] On 2 Mar. Russell got leave to introduce a bill 'for the better discovery and suppression of bribery and corrupt practices in the election of Members'. The measure, which enhanced the powers of investigative select committees, had a second reading on 14 Mar. and made some progress in committee; but strong objections from the procedural pundit Charles Williams Wynn, a member of the cabinet, forced Russell to abandon it on 28 Apr. He urged ministers to alleviate the peculiar burdens of agriculturists before settling the corn law problem, 9 Mar., and said that their proposal for the emergency admission of bonded corn begged the question of a permanent solution, 2, 4 May.[61] He voted against the president of the board of trade's ministerial salary, 10 Apr., but refused to damn the government over the Burmese war before hearing their side of the story, 26 Apr. He divided to disfranchise Irish non-resident borough voters, 9 Mar., and for reform of Edinburgh's representation, 13 Apr., and presented and endorsed the Rye householders' petition for the franchise, 26 Apr., when he said that freeholders of counties corporate should have a borough vote. Next day he moved for general reform on the same basis as before, in what the Tory Member Henry Bankes thought a 'feeble' speech, but which Tierney considered 'very good'. Agar Ellis reckoned that he spoke 'indifferently'. The defeat by 247-123 was disappointing.[62] Russell voted for Hume's call for inquiry into the state of the nation, 4 May, and to reduce the salaries of Irish prison inspectors, 5 May. Next day he told Moore that 'it was evident I was not a Whig, for though my views were strongly on the side of liberty, they were not modified by those constitutionalities and legalities with which a Whig fenced round his principles'.[63] On 9 May he presented James Silk Buckingham's† petition complaining of the curtailment of press freedom in India and secured by 43-40 the appointment of a select committee. His 'broadside into the treasury' failed to prevent the government's addition of eight Members with offices or connections with the East India Company, 11 May.[64] On 26 May 1826, when he observed that he was 'by no means certain of having a seat in the next Parliament', he moved three resolutions for the prevention of electoral bribery. The House divided 62-62, but the Speaker gave his casting vote for the resolutions as merely declaratory.

Russell had been occasionally optimistic about his Huntingdonshire prospects, but knew that he was up against it. At the nomination he advocated revision of the corn laws and Catholic emancipation. He regarded his defeat by only 53 votes as a moral victory, which must 'sicken our enemies' and had laid a 'foundation' for future Whig success, though he was not prepared to stand there again himself. He commented to Holland that the Whigs'

> present situation is ... most unpleasant. We lose in opinion by supporting the liberal part of the ministry, and when we fight a battle in the elections we find the whole force of government at work to oppose us ... I am glad to be out of such a mess. Last session I voted with ministers even when I thought their measures imprudent and ill-timed, because I thought their general views sound and liberal. But I believe the only way is to say boldly what one thinks of their base compromise, and support nothing that is not undeniably a wise and well-timed measure.[65]

Russell, who was helped by his father out of some minor financial trouble, went to Paris and then to Switzerland, where he translated the fifth book of the *Odyssey* (published in 1827). He made a good impression on his erstwhile critic Fox, whose mother Lady Holland recorded this as a 'victory': 'he is essentially excellent, and a model for anyone to follow'.[66] Back in Paris, he contemplated a swift return home, but in the event reluctantly submitted to advice from his father, who had accepted Fitzwilliam's offer to return him for Higham Ferrers, to winter in Italy. While he did not relish missing 'any question of importance ... in Parliament', he admitted that he would be 'glad to avoid' the corn issue. He envisaged returning to England in March 1827 at the earliest, observing sourly to his brother George William that 'I don't quite know why people are so anxious for my being in Parliament', as 'they attend to me very little when I am there'.[67] He signified his handing over of the electoral bribery issue to Althorp in a public *Letter*.[68] His brother encouraged him to exert himself in the House to root out 'rotten boroughs', which were under his 'special guard', and to make himself 'master' of the Catholic question. The Higham Ferrers arrangement fell through, but the duke of Devonshire brought him in for his Irish borough of Bandon Bridge in December 1826.[69]

Russell returned to England in 'flourishing health' in February 1827, and on the 27th supported inquiry into electoral interference by Northampton corporation; he was named to the select committee. He backed Althorp's motion to improve the means of dealing with bribery, 26 Feb. At a meeting of leading Whigs convened after Lord Liverpool's stroke, he concurred in the general view that 'it was not their business to throw any difficulties in Canning's way'.[70] He voted for Catholic relief, 6 Mar., and on the 23rd repudiated the radical Whittle Harvey's charge that the Whigs gave it priority over the removal of Dissenters' disabilities. He subsequently gave notice of a motion to repeal the Test Acts. He was at odds with Bedford on the importance of pressing the Catholic question, which he considered 'a matter of life and death for the country'.[71] He was appointed to the select committees on county, 15 Mar., and borough polls, 5 Apr. He divided for information on the Lisburn Orange procession, 29 Mar., to suspend supply until the ministerial crisis was resolved, 30 Mar., and for inquiry into the Irish miscellaneous estimates, 5 Apr. He was at Holkham, Norfolk, over Easter (having bored himself rigid by watching a race at Newmarket, which he vowed never to do again as long as he lived), and explained to Lady Holland his belief that the Whigs' line was 'quite clear; to support Canning's government at all events for the present and keep out the old Tories'. He was sorry that 'one of our great talents, that of abusing each other, is exerted on this occasion in great perfection', and joked, 'How much better it would all be if we had a good honest cheap American republic!' He approved the Lansdowne Whigs' coalition with Canning and told Lansdowne that he would 'endeavour to support government generally, for your sake, and not for Mr. Canning's'.[72] Bedford disapproved of the junction, but, aware that Russell could not abandon his commitment to reform, which Canning opposed, but would have to surrender his seat if he did not support the new ministry, which Devonshire had joined, left it 'entirely to him to decide'. Yet he considered 'silly' and 'shabby and trimming' Russell's speech of 3 May, in which he argued that the Whigs had broken no pledges for reform by supporting Canning and said that as there now was 'a great lukewarmness on the subject throughout the country', he had no intention of embarrassing Canning by raising it.[73] In a return to gradualism, he indicated on 8 May his wish to have the seats of the venal borough of Penryn given to Manchester; and on the 28th he carried by 124-69 the disfranchisement of Penryn to facilitate this. He attended and addressed the rowdy Westminster anniversary dinner, 23 May.[74] On 7 June 1827 he stated that he had been reliably informed that Grampound had prospered economically since losing its seats. That day, as he had hinted on 11 May, he withdrew his notice of a motion for repeal of the Test Acts because the Dissenters' leaders had decided not to force the issue on the new ministry.

Russell spent part of the summer at Woburn, working on his European histories (his *Establishment of the Turks in Europe* came out in 1828), worrying vaguely about Canning's declining health and believing that he and those who thought like him would 'make together a very respectable Whig phalanx, supporting the ministers, and never framing a question with the Tories, but at liberty to go our own way when we please'.[75] In the initial negotiations for the formation of Lord Goderich's ministry after Canning's death, he took the view that it must be backed 'if foreign affairs and the Catholic question proceed as we wish', but felt that the proposed appointment of the anti-Catholic John Herries* as chancellor of the exchequer would make it impossible for Althorp, Tavistock, Milton and himself to give 'a cordial support', though unmitigated hostility was 'out of the question'. Only 'a near prospect of the Catholic question' being promoted would make him consider taking office, and he feared that Lansdowne was not resolute enough to safeguard Whig interests.[76] As he discovered more about the Herries affair he concluded that Lansdowne had been given no choice by the king but to stay in office, yet he remained convinced that the young Whigs could have 'no confidence' in Herries and 'must support the government when they are liberal, but measure our support by their actions'. At the Hollands' Bedfordshire home at Ampthill (where he arrived refreshed by sea breezes and the company of Lady Elizabeth Vernon at Ryde), 5 Sept., he told Tierney, a member of the government, as much, though he was 'a good deal annoyed by what has happened'.[77] In mid-September he aired his differences with Grey over the new ministry and the corn laws.[78] Soon afterwards, following consultations with Grey, Althorp, Tavistock and Milton, he sent Tierney a list of six propositions as 'hints of what, if done, would attach our Whig friends to the government and make them wish its continuance'.[79] Russell, who was nettled by a report, false as it turned out, that Lady Holland had said that his continuing his work on the history of Europe was unfair to the toiling Mackintosh, labouring with painful slowness in an adjacent field, decided against taking the risk of vacating Bandon Bridge to contest a possible vacancy for Huntingdonshire.[80] In mid-December 1827 he observed to Holland that there was no point in blaming Admiral Codrington for the destruction of the Turkish fleet at Navarino, that there were 'many and weighty' reasons to approve the Treaty of London, though it was worrying that 'Russia should have the means of commanding in the Mediterranean and of injuring if not destroying our commerce', and that on the Portuguese civil war ministers had 'done what under the circumstances was the only right and wise thing'. Domestically, he considered that Ireland was 'all in all' and that the grumbling Catholic leaders should be disregarded and the Catholic population attached to the British government by ministers showing themselves 'in earnest about the Catholic question', which would be better started in the Lords than in the Commons in the forthcoming session.[81] No verification has been found of a story of a 'fracas' between Russell and Lady Holland provoked by his answering her question as to why her husband was excluded from office with the comment that 'it is because no man will act in a cabinet with a person whose wife opens all his letters'. He told her in early January 1828 that he hoped soon to see Holland 'on the treasury bench *de plein droit*'.[82]

Russell was 'glad' at the final collapse of the Goderich ministry and pleased with the inclusion of the Huskissonites in the duke of Wellington's administration which replaced it.[83] In the House, 29 Jan. 1828, he protested against 'a style in affairs of business, which deals less in argument than declamation', expressed reservations about Wellington's suitability as a civil leader, urged him to deal decisively with the Irish problem and approved Navarino. Herries, discussing with Peel, the home secretary, the composition of the contentious finance committee, observed that if Russell was included he 'knows too little of the details of business to give much trouble'.[84] He was not appointed to it, but was named to the select committees on the metropolitan police, 28 Feb., criminal commitments, which he himself proposed, 5 Mar., and the poor laws, 22 May. He was one of the committee on the borough polls bill, 2 Apr. Since the previous summer he had been trying to orchestrate the campaign of the organized Dissenters for repeal of the Test Acts, for which he planned to move 'in spite of all changes of ministers'.[85] He presented several petitions, 5, 20, 26 Feb., when, in his second major speech, which Agar Ellis thought was delivered 'well and clearly', he proposed (using Fox's words of 1790) to go into committee to consider repeal. To his surprise and Peel's fury, he won by 237-193.[86] He carried the repeal without a division on 28 Feb. On 18 Mar. he acquiesced in Peel's substitution for the existing test of a declaration 'on the true faith of a Christian'; and he accepted the Lords' amendment to the bill, which received royal assent on 9 May (9 Geo. IV, c. 17). At the end of March he wrote to Moore:

> My constitution is not quite so much improved as the constitution of the country by late events, but the joy of it will soon revive me. It is really a gratifying thing to force the enemy to give up his first line, that none but churchmen are worthy to serve the state, and I trust we shall soon make him give up the second, that none but Protestants are.[87]

On 20 Feb. 1828 he reintroduced his bill to transfer Penryn's seats to Manchester, which had a second reading, 14 Mar., when he agreed to Peel's request that he postpone further proceedings until the comparable East Retford question had been disposed of; he spoke and voted against throwing that borough into the hundred of Bassetlaw, 21 Mar. Three days later he got the Penryn bill into committee by 213-34, after presenting a Manchester merchants and inhabitants' petition in its favour, but he was persuaded to drop the clause restricting polling to two days. He resisted and crushed by 120-1 a proposal to require the Manchester Members to foreswear bribery on taking their seats. The bill passed the Commons on 31 Mar., but foundered in the Lords. He presented a London petition against the friendly societies bill, 18 Apr., called for clarification of Peel's law of evidence bill regarding exemptions from oaths, 5 May, brought up a Bristol petition for Catholic relief, 8 May, and voted in the unexpected majority for that measure, 12 May. Shortly afterwards he went 'in a great hurry to Paris, to recruit health and strength'. From there he informed George William that while he did not anticipate a speedy concession of Catholic claims, 'if the Irish manage well the question is carried'. Learning of the Huskissonites' resignation from the ministry, he decided to return immediately: 'There is much to do and to see done. England never stood more critically. Common sense and liberal views may make her all-powerful; the reverse, ruin her at once'. He considered the patched-up government 'a bad, foolish ignorant ministry' and said he would be 'in despair' but 'for the belief that the Catholic question will break them up at Christmas'.[88] He and Holland were fêted at a dinner given by the Dissenting deputies.[89] On 23 June he said in the House that all outstanding war claims on the French should be investigated and spoke and voted against the use of public money for the improvement of Buckingham House. Next day he quizzed Peel on British relations with Portugal. On East Retford, 27 June, he moved an amendment, which was rejected by 89-18, to disfranchise the borough, leaving the choice of where to allocate the seats to the crown, failed with an amendment to rule out sluicing and was unable to commit Peel to support the principle of transferring the seats of corrupt boroughs to large towns. He presented a petition for the abolition of slavery, 4 July, when he voted for ordnance reductions, as he did again, 7 July, after deploring the waste of large sums on Canadian defences. His father noted 'on politics he is very sore', being 'quite under [the] *petticoat* influence' of Lady Hardy and 'threatens to take his name out of the Fox Club'.[90] On 8 July he gave notice of a motion for the 17th for an address to the king on the alarming state of Ireland, but the resulting 'clamour' against it on all sides forced him to withdraw it on 14 July, when he remarked that ministers 'cannot be insensible to the awful responsibility which the present state of Ireland imposes on them'. Privately, he could not 'blame [Daniel] O'Connell for being a little impatient after 27 years of just expectations disappointed' and suspected that Wellington, hitherto invincible, had 'now found a task that makes his cheeks pale, and his nights uneasy'.[91] On 17 July 1828 he brought up the report of the committee on criminal commitments and turned the subject over to Peel.

He decided against visiting Ireland that autumn, but events there and ministerial intentions on the Catholic question engrossed his thoughts, though he could not see through the 'political ... mist'.[92] Russell, who was reported to have had his proposal of marriage spurned by the youngest of the three Hardy sisters, failed to persuade Grey, Althorp and other opposition leaders of the wisdom of forming an association to promote pro-Catholic petitioning and counteract the Brunswick clubs.[93] However, acting on a hint from Lansdowne, he pressed on Brougham the importance of 'at least an attempt towards' securing unity among 'all who think right on the Catholic question' by agreeing 'not to support or take office under any ministry not favourable to the Catholic claims' and to 'make no personal exclusions against any who would agree to the first principle', and by sorting out the leadership problem. His personal preference in mid-December 1828 was for an amendment to the address and 'a division (however bad) the first day'; but he was ready to 'waive this opinion, if not the prevailing one', in favour of forcing ministers' hand with a substantive motion for relief. He hoped 'we shall be reasonable as to securities', for 'to put the Papist on the benches of Parliament is the main thing': 'if it be possible, *ne splittons pas*, this time'.[94] In early January 1829, when he drew up for Althorp two resolutions stating the urgency of conceding emancipation, he continued to preach the gospel of action and unity, arguing that 'we *must* form a party, and the more solid it is, the less people are left to bargain for themselves, the better'. He told Lansdowne:

> I see no medium in politics between not caring at all about public matters, or wishing to see them well conducted. And I consider the principle on which Huskisson professed to act last year, of stipulating for certain measures, without regard to the men who were to carry them into effect, as a most mischievous innovation on old established rules for the conduct of statesmen in this country ... I shall be ready when Parliament meets to join a party, I trust a very large one, to carry the Catholic question. And the further such a party will afterwards engage in defence of public liberty the better.

Yet he complained to George William that 'we have a sad want of leaders; Lord Grey does not come; Lord Holland is unwell, and unwilling to enter into battle; Lord Lansdowne is mysterious. Brougham likewise holds his tongue and is puzzled'.[95] He attended the anti-Catholic meeting in Devon (where Bedford owned much land), 16 Jan. He did not try to speak, but at the subsequent dinner of pro-Catholics, which produced a counter-petition, he invoked the authority of Fox, Pitt and Burke for supporting emancipation. He thought the affair 'by no means discouraging' and, still unsure of Wellington's intentions, predicted that 'peace or civil war [in Ireland] will be the consequence of this session'.[96]

Resolved to hear what ministers planned, he listened to the speech and address, 6 Feb. 1829, and, while he said that he would prefer the Catholic Association to be given the option of dissolving itself, welcomed the concession of emancipation with 'the most heartfelt joy'. 'Our party are delighted', he told his brother, and 'the moderate Tories ... as usual ... ready to yield a great deal of principle for a great deal of place'. He thought Peel's explanation was 'manly enough', but wished he had 'made it two years ago, when Canning was hunted to death for being what his pursuers are now'.[97] He presented and endorsed numerous pro-Catholic petitions from Protestant Dissenters, 10, 12, 24, 26 Feb., 9, 18, 30 Mar.; denied on 17 Mar. that most intelligent Scots or English Dissenters were hostile to emancipation, but was 'not much inclined to disagree' with the view that the Maynooth grant should be discontinued if public opinion proved hostile, and voted for relief, 6, 30 Mar. Relishing the 'mighty triumph' of the Whigs, he confessed to his sister-in-law that 'I am tired of my old [bachelor] ways, and should like to be settled quietly, but of that I see no prospect'.[98] On 4 May he presented petitions from the inhabitants of Rye for admission to the franchise and from Carnaby market against the friendly societies bill. Next day he spoke and voted for the transfer of East Retford's seats to Birmingham and said that next session he would propose 'a general measure' for the enfranchisement of large manufacturing towns at the expense of corrupt boroughs; he gave advance notice of this, 1 June, when he voted to reduce the hemp duties. He presented an Irish petition against the Subletting Act, 14 May, and spoke in favour of allowing O'Connell to take his seat unhindered, 19 May 1829, when he brought up the Canterbury freemen's petition complaining of their Tory Member Lushington's prolonged absence in India.

Russell, 'the most uncertain little fellow that ever lived', as Bedford put it, decided after much deliberation to go to Italy with George William. He stayed a few days at Genoa with Madame Durazzo, joined the William Russells at Florence in late June and went with them to Berne in September. After his departure for Paris in early October 1829, George William wrote to Lady Holland:

> I think he is determined to be married to somebody ... I dread his taking a rash step, which may embitter the latter part of his life ... I know nobody whose happiness is so likely to be influenced by marriage ... A foolish woman would thwart his fixed habits and make him wretched, but he is kind-hearted, easy, gentle, with a manly mind, and agreeable society that would make any sensible woman happy.

Bedford, however, thought he was 'cut out for an old bachelor'. He arrived in London, 'as sensible and amiable as ever', in Lady Holland's eyes, and resumed his courtship of '*la petite Hardy*'.[99] On foreign politics, he agreed with Holland that it was the business of Britain to prevent Russia and France from 'combining at her expense'.[100] He did not believe the Wellington ministry could survive without recruiting additional strength, but suspected that 'the duke after his fashion will make no resolution till it is quite necessary, and then surprise us by some new combination'. On 12 Dec. 1829, after ten days in London 'in fog, and snow, and cold and cough', he observed to George William that 'we have no plan of campaign for the next session; the ministry entirely depend on our resolves, on our want of faction, and love of place, for if we had either we should make short work of them. As it is, they will be treated as they behave'.[101]

On the eve of the 1830 session he observed to Devonshire that it was now 'quite clear' that no ministerial approach would be made to Grey:

> I should have been glad to have supported the men who carried the Catholic question, but as their measures abroad have been in my opinion bad, and there is no one in the cabinet in whose opinion I have any confidence, I shall not think it by any means necessary to give any vote or refrain from giving any vote, with a view to keep them in office.[102]

He informed Brougham that while it would be 'very unadvisable on our parts' to move an amendment to the address, he might 'be obliged to support' one (as he did the Ultra Knatchbull's, 4 Feb. 1830). On the ground that the government was 'rickety and unsafe', he proposed that the Whig opposition should promote 'commercial freedom, an honest currency, parliamentary reform, etc., without any reference to ministers'; 'that we should look at no long time hence to a co-operation' with the Huskissonites as 'men of official experience', stopping short of 'any formal junction of parties'; that 'none of us should take office without Lord Grey's being considered', and that 'we should declare ourselves early on foreign politics', as British 'conduct on Turkey has been folly, in Portugal wickedness'.[103] He did this in the House, 5 Feb., arguing that ministers had left Turkey 'a prey to Russia' and abandoned Portugal to Dom Miguel. He failed to obtain information on the situation in Greece, 16 Feb. He voted to transfer East Retford's seats to Birmingham, 11 Feb., 5 Mar., when he opposed O'Connell's amendment for the secret ballot. He considered much of the Ultra Lord Blandford's reform scheme to be nonsense, but divided for it, 18 Feb. On 23 Feb. he presented a

Sheffield petition for the franchise before proposing the enfranchisement of Birmingham, Leeds and Manchester, contending that the true 'danger' to the constitution lay in resisting 'all reasonable and rational reform'; he got 140 votes to 188. Grey's son Lord Howick* thought his speech 'was certainly a good one, but dreadfully deficient in animation'. His father commented:

> John did well with his reform motion, both in matter and manner, and his division was such as fairly to justify hopes of carrying it ultimately. I wish he would stick to these questions and others of home policy, in which he does so well, without *embrouilleing* himself with foreign politics; there, he becomes a little factious, and identifies himself too much with the Huskissonites, etc.[104]

Russell voted for reception of the Newark petition complaining of the duke of Newcastle's electoral interference, 1 Mar. With other Whigs, he voted in the majority against Hume's motion for extensive tax cuts, 15 Feb.[105] He presented petitions for modification of the 1829 Benefit Societies Act, 2 Mar. Next day he attended the opposition meeting of 27 who resolved to act together under Althorp's Commons leadership to campaign for reductions in expenditure and taxation.[106] He tried unsuccessfully to kill the Rother Levels bill, which threatened Rye harbour, 5 Mar., and on the 12th presented an inhabitants' petition against it, along with George De Lacy Evans's* election petition. He voted to restrict the grant for volunteers, 9 Mar. Despite claiming to be 'too unwell to speak', 10 Mar., he forcefully supported, in what Howick thought 'a goodish speech', Lord Palmerston's motion condemning British interference in Portugal, asserting that the government showed 'a disinclination to oppose tyranny and despotism'. John Allen thought he was almost the only opposition Member who took 'a proper interest in our foreign policy or at least' was prepared to 'express a proper opinion against it'.[107] Russell voted for economies and reduced taxation, 12, 22, 25, 29 Mar., and paired for inquiry into crown lands revenues, 30 Mar. On 16 Mar. he endorsed the Hertfordshire reform petition and, presenting a Dursley petition for tax cuts, applauded the government's own proposals as 'judicious', but urged a total revision of the tax system. He challenged the currency fanatics to put their case fairly before the House, 25 Mar., when he presented and approved a Sheffield printers' petition for reduction of the newspaper stamp duties. On the 29th he questioned ministers' sincerity on economy. Disliking their foreign policy and considering them 'not decisive enough at home', he felt that they were 'too weak'.[108] He spoke and was a majority teller for an amendment to the St. Giles's vestry bill, 1 Apr., and supported its third reading and was a majority teller next day, when he again expressed his 'distrust' of Wellington's foreign policy. He divided for Jewish emancipation, 5 Apr., 17 May, after declaring his 'hearty support' for it. He disliked Lord Nugent's employment of the poor bill, 6 Apr. During the Easter holiday he wrote to George William:

> My satisfaction with the present ministry ... is not very considerable. Lord Holland and I feel very strongly on foreign politics ... The ministry is so much at the mercy of the House of Commons, that I cannot imagine Peel's not seeking strength. It is to be sure very difficult to get, without admitting some equality of power ... The result is a tolerable government on all questions which debates can influence, but by no means so on all other questions.[109]

He presented petitions for abolition of the death penalty for forgery offences, 26, 27 Apr., 7 June, argued that transportation could be made an adequate substitute, 13 May, and voted for abolition, 24 May, 7 June. He voted against government on the Terceira affair, 28 Apr., called for a remonstrance to Spain over the attack on Cuba, 20 May, and interrogated Peel on the Greek situation, 24 May, 10 June. He was in the opposition minorities for repeal of the Irish coal duties, 13 May, and proper use of Irish first fruits revenues, 18 May, and on the government of Canada, 25 May. He was willing to acquiesce in the royal signature bill on ministerial assurances that the king was not insane, 28 May. Later that day he opposed O'Connell's radical reform scheme and moved as an amendment his own plan to transfer 100 seats from the smaller boroughs to the likes of Birmingham, Bolton, Brighton, Cheltenham, Halifax, Leeds, Manchester, Sheffield and Wolverhampton; he was defeated by 213-117. He reprimanded Goulburn, the chancellor of the exchequer, for calling Hume 'the enemy of religion' and presented and endorsed a petition to permit affirmations by persons with religious scruples, 8 June. He paired against the grant for consular services, 11 June, and voted against those for Nova Scotia and Prince Edward Island, 14 June, when he said that a system of emigration must be incorporated into any reform of the poor laws. On 30 June 1830 he spoke and was a minority teller for adjournment of the debate on the new king's message about a possible regency: however much he approved of some of ministers' measures, he had 'no confidence' in them overall, for 'their weakness has been conspicuously shown'.

Russell initially declined a chance to stand for Huntingdonshire at the general election that summer and reluctantly submitted to his father's decision to put him up for Bedford, which George William had outrageously neglected. When he attempted to get out of this to accept an invitation to try Huntingdonshire, he found it was too late, with a rich Tory in the field and his leading supporters insisting on his keeping his word. Publication of an extract from the second volume of his *Memoirs of the Affairs of Europe*, in which he had traduced Wesleyan Methodists as fanatics, damaged him.[110] Before the election, when he was still optimistic, he expressed to Holland his hope that in the new Parliament 'we Whigs shall be very moderate and at the same time firm. There seems to be no cause for regular opposition at present. But a large party combined for large objects must at least rule measures, and if ministers do not behave themselves have everything their own way'.[111] In the event Russell, who authorized some dubious financial transactions, was beaten by one vote. He privately claimed that 'at last I little cared how it ended', but in truth he was 'mortified', as his father perceived, and he gave vent to his anger in a parting address. He was, however, sure of a seat, for Lord Ebrington's return for Devon as well as for Bedford's borough of Tavistock meant that the latter would become available to him. 'Hankering after France' at the 'very interesting' moment after the revolution, he was invited to stand for Southwark on an unexpected vacancy. He felt 'some temptation', but soon decided against, ostensibly to avoid splitting the liberal interest. Bedford thought he was well out of it.[112] By 13 Sept. he was in Paris, where at Holland's behest he interceded with Louis Philippe and Lafayette to spare Polignac's life.[113] Back in England on 2 Oct., he predicted that while 'English politics are in rather an odd state, as usual', the next session would 'clear the air, and then we shall know what we are to have'. He wanted opposition to 'begin quietly'. He considered taking Holland's 'advice about publishing on reform, and had prepared more than half a pamphlet', but concluded in mid-October 1830 that it was 'better to wait, and let Brougham run riot as he pleases', reckoning that 'if ministers keep at peace, propose reform and reduce the civil list', he would 'give very few votes in opposition before Christmas'.[114]

Russell, who believed that 'while the ministry is too weak for any important measures, all moderate men are frightened at the violence of Brougham, and would scruple to lend themselves to a coalition with Ultra Tories to turn out a minister who has in many respects deserved well', encouraged Ebrington to consider moving an address asking the king 'to strengthen and extend the basis of his administration', but nothing came of this.[115] At a meeting of leading Whigs, which he did not attend, 31 Oct. 1830, Althorp announced that Russell intended to renew his motion for the enfranchisement of Birmingham, Leeds and Manchester, but the mood was for something more far reaching and it was agreed that Brougham, who produced a bolder but vague scheme of his own, should propose reform in the Commons on 16 Nov.[116] After Wellington's declaration against reform and the cancellation of the king's visit to the City Russell became convinced that the 'weak and unpopular' ministry 'must go out'. A rumour of opposition at Tavistock, which ended 'in smoke', obliged him to go there in mid-November. He returned to London on the 20th, having been informed by Bedford and Althorp that the ministry had fallen and that Grey wanted him to take office in his new administration.[117] A notion of making him under-secretary at the foreign office was set aside when Palmerston, a Member of the Commons, took the foreign seals. His health was not considered equal to the duties of the secretary at war, but he was offered and accepted the post of paymaster of the forces, a virtual sinecure with £2,000 a year and 'a very nice house at Whitehall, next to the Horse Guards', where he later installed a bath. His exclusion from the cabinet rankled, but he masked his disappointment under a façade of 'cheerfulness'. The Tavistock writ had been delayed to enable him to avoid the inconvenience of two elections, and he was returned *in absentia* on 27 Nov. 1830, having written to his sister-in-law the previous day:

> We put on our flag, peace, economy and reform. I trust we shall keep to these good and fair words. Neither foreign nor domestic affairs, however, look promising. The labourers have risen and are carrying on a servile war against the gentry ... The king behaves better than it was possible to expect.[118]

Russell, who had recently published a reprint of his 1819 *Letter to Lord Holland on Foreign Politics*, in which he argued that British influence should be used to 'prevent unjust aggression', uphold states' right to amend their internal institutions, promote international intercourse and preserve peace, welcomed Lord Chandos's bill to reform the game laws, 'a serious reproach to this country', 7 Dec. 1830. On the 9th he reproved Henry Bankes for trying to 'give a bad name to the government' before hearing details of its planned economies, though he cautioned against inflated expectations of their inquiry into public salaries. He endorsed the regency bill, 9, 10 Dec., when he defended the mass procession of the trades to St. James's to address the king. On 13 Dec. he repeated his warning against unrealistic expectations of economies, but attacked the Wellington ministry's 'obstinate resistance to reform', which had endangered the monarchy and aristocracy. He presented reform petitions from Tavistock, 15 Dec., and St. Ives, Huntingdonshire, 23 Dec., when he was a majority teller against printing Sir Harcourt Lee's petition against the oaths bill, and he did not resist Chandos's motion to suspend the Evesham writ, 'a sham fight, which does not signify one farthing', 16 Dec. 1830.[119]

By then he was involved in drafting the ministry's reform plan, as one of the ad hoc committee of four chaired by Lord Durham, the lord privy seal, and including also Sir James Graham, first lord of the admiralty, and Duncannon, commissioner of woods. (Russell had blocked the inclusion of the Ultra duke of Richmond, the postmaster-general.) After rejecting a minimum scheme submitted by Althorp, they worked from a more comprehensive plan swiftly drawn up by Russell, providing for 50 of the smallest boroughs to lose both seats and 50 more to lose one. Of these 150 seats he proposed to utilise only 82, giving six additional Members to London, two each to the 20 most populous counties and two each to 18 large towns. He envisaged the enfranchisement of long-term copy and leaseholders in the counties, of men qualified to serve on juries in existing boroughs and of £15 householders in new ones. After protracted discussions, the disfranchisement schedules were based on the 1821 census returns: 60 boroughs with under 2,000 inhabitants were to lose both seats (schedule A), 47 with between 2,000 and 4,000 were to lose one (schedule B), and Weymouth was to be reduced from four to two seats. Of the 168 seats thus liberated (Higham Ferrers, a schedule A borough, was a single Member constituency), 106 were redistributed, reducing the House by 62 Members to 596: 34 to the new towns, eight to London, five to Scotland, three to Ireland, one to Wales and 55 to the English counties. Russell reluctantly yielded to Durham and the others' wish to incorporate the ballot, but in return had the proposed £10 borough franchise raised to £20. When he visited his father at Woburn in mid-January 1831, he was 'completely *boutonné* as a minister ought to be' about the scheme.[120] On foreign affairs, he believed that despite the 'ill-timed and unreasonable' proposals of the French ministry, the chance of war with France was 'daily diminishing'; but Holland did not share his optimism and urged him to impress on Grey 'the necessity of peace, the consequences and impracticability of a war ... which ... would ... dissolve the ministry'.[121] When the reform plan was submitted to the cabinet in late January the ballot was rejected, to his relief, but the £20 borough franchise was retained. By mid-February Russell, who had been deputed to introduce the bill, had realized to his consternation that this franchise, 'a mark for all the noisy and turbulent advocates of popular rights', together with the emerging deficiencies of the 1821 census returns, would create risibly small electorates in many boroughs. He alerted Durham and the rest of the cabinet and, arguing that the two main objects of the reform were to 'satisfy the just expectations of the people' and, 'infinitely more important, to give a good political constitution to the nation', by placing 'the power of choice in men of property and intelligence, who will exercise it with honesty and discrimination', recommended a uniform £10 householder franchise. This was adopted, along with a plan to extend the boundaries of the smaller schedule B boroughs.[122]

Meanwhile in the House Russell had defended the ministerial proposals for the barilla duties, 7 Feb., called for revision of the way in which public money was spent on royal residences and endorsed the government's game bill, 15 Feb., and dismissed piecemeal reform at Evesham, presented a Huntingdonshire petition for repeal of the assessed taxes and brought up and endorsed one from London Dissenting deputies for Jewish emancipation, 17 Feb. 1831. He was named to the select committee on public accounts that day. On 1 Mar., 'very pale and subdued', he unveiled the reform bill to a packed House in one of the most dramatic episodes of British parliamentary history. His speech of over two hours contained little declamation, as he aimed to furnish 'a clear and intelligible statement' of the proposals. His recitation of the boroughs in schedules A and B caused 'an absolutely electrifying shock' and provoked uproar; many supporters of the government were 'very much astonished' and the Tory opposition were 'angry and shocked'.[123] When securing returns of population, houses and voters for the schedule A boroughs, 3 Mar., Russell dismissed Wetherell's sneer that this was 'posthumous legislation'. On 5 Mar. he joined his father at Brighton, looking well and 'in great spirits'. 'Sanguine' about the bill's chances, he returned to London on the 7th, 'refreshed by two nights quiet rest'.[124] Replying to the debate on 9 Mar., in what Tavistock considered 'one of the most splendid and animating speeches I have ever heard', he avowed that 'there is nothing mean, or timid, or cowardly, in a sacrifice of private and personal interests for the sake of the peace of the country'. Leave was given to introduce the bill. Two days later Russell wrote to George William:

> We have had complete success in the country with our reform measure, and although the House is bitter and furious, I have the greatest hopes of the division on the second reading. The strength of our case is that we have

> the king sincerely with us ... Neither are we to blame, though we have incurred odium, on other points. Peace and retrenchment have been kept steadily in view; Ireland now answers the helm and I trust will grow more and more prosperous.[125]

When he introduced the bill on 14 Mar. he corrected a blunder whereby the single Member borough of Bewdley had been placed in schedule B and rectified his omission to state that some 'large suburbs' would be joined to their towns to form new constituencies. After opposing Inglis's motion alleging a breach of privilege by *The Times*, 21 Mar., he moved the second reading of the bill and presented favourable petitions. Replying to the debate, 22 Mar., he said that the measure 'would not advance democracy, but it would make the constitution harmonize with the present state of the people'. Amid great excitement, the bill was carried by 302-301. On 25 Mar. Russell denied that part of the proposals for Wales had been framed to benefit the Whig Lord Cawdor and argued that use of the 1831 census to determine the disfranchisement schedules would have encouraged the officials of threatened boroughs to falsify their returns. Bedford commented that he had 'covered himself with honour, and raised himself on a pinnacle of imperishable fame'.[126] On 30 Mar. he criticized the Cambridge University anti-reform petition, pointing out that for years he and his associates had been frustrated in their attempts to introduce piecemeal reform, so that they were now driven to propose 'an innovation, which residents of colleges, sitting in their closets, may not, in the abstract, think it wisdom to make'. With Grey and other ministers he attended and addressed the Mansion House dinner, 4 Apr., when he stressed the king's complete confidence in the government.[127] Having become increasingly aware of discrepancies and errors in the population and other returns, he told the House on 12 Apr. that ministers had looked closely into the most serious cases and planned some changes accordingly. He added that if the Commons was strongly in favour of retaining 658 Members, government would give way, but that they would not violate schedules A and B. His personal wish was to distribute the extra seats among 'respectable towns' and the counties, rather than give them to 'all the manufacturing parishes of the north'.[128] On the 18th he detailed the alterations to the bill, after showing that Members for counties and large towns had voted overwhelmingly for the second reading. He admitted difficulties arising from the 1821 census, particularly its frequent failure to distinguish between boroughs and the parishes in which they lay, and proposed to transfer five boroughs from A to B, reprieve seven previously included in B, give a Member to seven new boroughs (including Wakefield, accidentally omitted before) and give a third Member to seven counties and one more to Glamorgan. While he had to admit that he had 'unluckily ... mislaid' the paper on which he had noted these changes, he calculated that they, together with five new Members each to Scotland and Ireland, would reduce the numbers of the House to 627. He explained adjustments to the county franchise and conceded that the sons and apprentices of existing qualified freemen would retain their voting rights. Warning that rejection of the bill would create immense problems for any new government, he moved to go into committee. Friendly observers thought he spoke 'beautifully' and 'admirably'.[129] For opposition Gascoyne, Member for Liverpool, moved an artful amendment to the effect that there should be no reduction in the number of Members for England and Wales. Closing the debate on 19 Apr. 1831, Russell defended the bill as an attempt to 'raise a bar to the accomplishment of the wishes of those who looked forward to more extensive and violent changes'. The amendment was carried by 299-291 and, after deliberations, ministers persuaded the king to dissolve Parliament.

Russell received invitations from several populous constituencies, including Lancashire. Holland wanted him to try Buckinghamshire, but Bedford vetoed this, and he opted to stand for Devon, with Ebrington. On his way to Exeter he was 'received with shouts of applause all along the road' and fêted in the towns he passed through. The witty parson Sydney Smith reported to Lady Holland that 'the people along the road were very much disappointed by his smallness. I told them he was much larger before the bill was thrown out, but was reduced by excessive anxiety about the people'.[130] From the elections as a whole he initially anticipated a government majority of '80 or 100', which would be 'good to pass the bill, and for nothing else'. (Like many others, he underestimated the strength of the reform tide, for the final majority was about 130.) Russell, who had already been seated for Tavistock as insurance, was returned unopposed with Ebrington.[131] From Devon he wrote to Holland, 1 May 1831, admitting his 'mortification' at being omitted from the cabinet in November and informing him that 'although I will never desert you while the difficulties of the reform bill press on you, and although I am far from wishing to occupy any other man's office, yet I shall take the first honourable opportunity to free myself from a situation I feel to be embarrassing and unpleasant'. The paymastership, he added, was 'awkward ... to a man who speaks, without a seat in the cabinet'. Holland, who had for several weeks been urging his admission, assured him that he and Grey were keen to take him in as soon as possible.[132] A fortnight later Bedford, apparently on his own initiative, strongly urged Grey to accommodate Russell before the new Parliament met, in order to remove him from his situation of 'a sort of *half-responsibility*' and to mark approval of the 'temper, good sense and judgement' with which he had handled the reform bill. Grey assured him of his anxiety to oblige, once a difficulty over the size of the cabinet had been overcome, though he pointed out that Russell had 'generally attended' cabinet meetings on the bill and that no 'material' changes had been made without consulting him. In the event Grey took Russell (and the Irish secretary Smith Stanley) into the cabinet in June 1831.[133]

Shortly before this Campbell had 'a long interview' with Russell, who 'talks like a man of sense and sees the difficulties and objections he has to encounter'.[134] On 24 June 1831 he reintroduced the reform bill, detailing minor changes to the schedules and arguing again that 'by extending to a great, and powerful, and enlightened people the right of having their legitimate representatives assembled within the walls of Parliament, we furnish the means for the future carrying on unimpaired of the constitution'. He made 'a good speech as his friends, and a dull one as his enemies say', according to Greville.[135] Before moving the second reading, 4 July, he dealt with an awkward question about the draftsman Gregson's supposed alterations of the provisions concerning quarterly urban rent payers.[136] On 6 July, when in closing the debate he denied having spoken earlier 'in a tone not only of exultation, but of irony', he also stated that prominent Irish Protestants living in England had advised Orangemen to abandon processions. The bill was carried by 367-231. On 9 July Russell was presented with the freedom of the City in a gold box.[137] In the fractious and protracted committee proceedings which occupied the next ten weeks, Althorp, as leader of the House, shared the brunt of the work with Russell, who in his old age recollected that these efforts caused him 'much labour, and considerable sacrifice of health'. John Fazakerley* was worried about this as early as 14 July, and next day Bedford observed that the aim of 'many' of the 'anti-reformers' seemed to be 'to kill John by wearing him completely out'. Between 11 and 23 Aug. he left the bill in Althorp's hands, but when he reappeared in the House he was still 'the picture of death'.[138] By and large Russell, who on 12 July got rid of a vexatious attempt to hear counsel on the case of Appleby and next day defended the decision to appoint boundary commissioners, acquitted himself creditably, but there were a number of scrapes along the way. The deficiencies of the population returns and the difficulty of distinguishing between parish and borough boundaries had created many anomalies, which were seized on by shrewd and persistent Tory critics of the bill, notably Croker and Wetherell. Russell nevertheless stood stubbornly by the 1821 population criteria for disfranchisement and repeatedly repudiated accusations of 'partiality' in the selection of doomed and reprieved boroughs. He defeated by 244-169 an attempt to have the 1831 census used, 19 July. On 26 July he and Althorp made a mess of things and allowed Saltash to be transferred from A to B, by 231-150.[139] On 2 Aug. he complained that 'every concession which has been made by ... ministers in reference to these two schedules has been met with taunts and reproaches, more particularly on the part of those who have themselves called for such concessions'. His declaration on 5 Aug. that the bill 'would not be final if it was not found to work as well as the people desired' was considered 'sufficiently impudent' by Greville.[140] Russell was laid up when Lord Chandos's amendment to enfranchise £50 tenants-at-will was carried against ministers, who decided to submit, 18 Aug.; but on the 23rd, when he reappeared in the House to put their case on the Dublin election controversy, he privately opined that 'reform goes on slowly but I think surely' and that 'Chandos has done us some mischief, but none that will essentially change the bill'.[141] He fended off bids to confine urban freehold voters to the boroughs, 27 Aug., when Tom Macaulay* thought he made 'a better speech than any ... for a long time', and to preserve all freemen's rights, 30 Aug. On the report, 13 Sept., he explained minor adjustments to the bill, defended the inclusion of the Members Littleton and Gilbert on the boundary commission and made what Macdonald considered 'a good spirited' reply to Vyvyan's apocalyptic 'prophecies'.[142] On the motion to pass the bill, which was carried by 345-236, 21 Sept., he declared that 'if you again delay [reform], the tempest must break in upon you, and your edifice will be swept away'. Next day he and Althorp and a large number of Members 'brought up the bill to a full House of Lords', where he expected the second reading division to be 'tremendously near'.[143] He voted silently for the second reading of the Scottish bill, 23 Sept., and next day was honoured with Althorp at a *Thatched House Tavern* dinner.[144] In the Commons, 4 Oct., he denied that in his speech of 21 Sept. he had abandoned his original position on the finality of the reform bill and dismissed the opposition case for an increase in the Scottish representation. After the heavy defeat of the English bill in the Lords, 7 Oct., Russell, who voted silently for Ebrington's confidence motion on the 10th, landed himself in trouble by including in his reply to a vote of thanks from a meeting of Thomas Attwood's† Birmingham Political Union the comment that it was 'impossible that the whisper of a faction should prevail against the voice of a nation'. He defended himself vigorously in the House, 12 Oct., insisting that 'the great part of the opponents of reform do belong to a faction' but claiming that he 'did not intend to say that the decision of the House of Lords is the whisper of a faction'. Grey was embarrassed and the king angered, and Russell was obliged to apologize to the latter for an expression 'written in the first moments of disappointment'. Bedford thought he had 'got well out of the scrape', though 'it was a most imprudent letter for a cabinet minister to write'. Russell was later reported to have subscribed £10 to the union.[145] He did some work in the Cambridgeshire by-election which returned a reformer in late October 1831.[146]

On the 20th Russell submitted to Grey, through Althorp, a budget of possible modifications to the reform bill, suggesting that schedule B could be drastically pruned and conceding that the 1821 census returns had been shown to be unreliable. He thought the controversial proposed increased representation for London might be given instead to adjoining counties. Grey was in broad agreement, but the subsequent negotiations with the 'Waverer' peers initiated by Palmerston, who wrongly believed that Russell 'in his heart thinks [the bill] goes much too far', came to nothing and collapsed at the end of November.[147] Meanwhile Russell worked on various plans to modify the measure, but as Bedford noted, he remained '*boutonné*', and rightly so, 'as cabinet ministers should not talk and chatter'. Littleton, the head of the boundary commission, called on Russell to ask for 'some principle ... [to] be laid down for our guidance', but found nothing decided. At a long interview with him on 11 Nov. Littleton was 'much amused at observing ... that the government had not yet settled their bill'. On the 27th he thought Russell was 'much dispirited' at the prospects in the Lords, after talks with Lord Essex, but was struck by 'the merriment with which he frequently makes admission of errors, which however they gallantly defended in the past'.[148] By 2 Dec. 1831 Russell was, according to Littleton, 'rather nervously anxious' about pressing on with essentially the same measure and 'vexed at little alterations that Althorp wished to make'. Lady Harrowby, whose husband was a leading 'Waverer', found him 'all moderation and candour ... mild and *doucereux*', but sick of Durham's erratic behaviour in cabinet.[149] Ministers had decided at the eleventh hour to abandon the 1821 census and devise new criteria for disfranchisement from calculations based on boroughs' number of houses and amount of assessed taxes. The statistics were hastily gathered through the home office, but the last nine reports did not reach Russell until 12 Dec. 1831, when he was due to introduce the revised bill, and his feverish work on them made him half an hour late at the House, 'looking very pale, and ... feeling very ill'. In a deliberately 'flat' speech, 'without pretensions to eloquence', he made a 'clear' statement of the changes: the House was to retain its current membership of 658; 56 boroughs were to lose both seats and 30 one, in a reduced and revamped schedule B; ten new towns were to be given a second Member, as was Monmouthshire, while Chatham was to be separated from Rochester; the borough freeman franchise was to be perpetuated for men resident within seven miles. The speech was praised as 'prudent' and 'judicious' by Russell's friends and family; but Greville considered it 'very feeble' and Hobhouse thought it was 'not well done'.[150] Later that day Russell told captious Irish Members that their country had been fairly treated in the reform scheme. He carried the second reading of the bill for England and Wales by 324-162, 17 Dec. Soon afterwards Bedford, surmising that he had 'burnt his fingers by the "whisper of a faction"', told Lady Holland that John 'hardly ever writes, and when he does, he does not commit himself by a single opinion or a single fact that may not be proclaimed at Charing Cross'.[151] Behind the scenes there was a ludicrous episode when, on 20 Dec. 1831, Russell gave the boundary commissioners 'a fresh set of instructions' concerning boroughs with less than 300 qualifying householders, which were to be extended into neighbouring parishes. When Littleton said that this 'complete *bouleversement*' of previous proceedings, which would necessitate more field work, could not be accomplished by the time Parliament reconvened on 18 Jan. 1832, Russell 'seemed annoyed, and rather ashamed of this tardy announcement', settled by the cabinet 'only this morning'. Next day Lord Melbourne, the home secretary, blamed Russell, who 'had not taken on himself sufficient authority' and 'ought to have decided better, or to have consulted us earlier'. A week later Littleton was 'excessively amused to find Lord John Russell had ordered his new instructions given to the commissioners on the 26th instant, to be dated the 24th of November, so that the lateness of the decision should not be discovered'.[152]

In the House, 17, 20 Jan., Russell had to admit to Croker that some of the information on individual boroughs was not yet to hand, but he comfortably carried the principles of schedules A, 20 Jan., and B, 23 Jan. 1832, when he said that 'the effect of reform will be not to give power ... to [the people's] excited passions, but to confer on them that power which the constitution meant they should have, and which has only been destroyed by abuse'. In a break from the reform debates, 26 Jan., he made a 'spirited speech' to help save the ministry from humiliation on the Russian-Dutch loan.[153] Next day he insisted on the division of counties and excluding voters in represented boroughs from the counties. He defeated bids to disfranchise all 40*s*. freeholders and to exclude unrepresented borough freeholders from the counties, 1 Feb., and defended the £10 householder franchise against Hunt's strictures, 2, 3 Feb. The 'whisper of a faction' affair was resurrected in early February when the Tory Sir Henry Hardinge accused him of having 'libelled' the Lords. He was not disposed to take issue with Hardinge personally, but at the end of the month wrote a 'frantic' letter to Wellington complaining of the matter having been raised again four months after he had denied applying the expression to the Lords. Wellington did not think he had much of a case, but the business seems to have been dropped.[154] Russell, who voted silently with his colleagues on the government's relations with Portugal, 9 Feb., and against Hunt's motion for information on military punishments, 16 Feb., and justified the army estimates, 17 Feb., continued with Althorp to steer the reform bill clause by clause through the House. When the condemned boroughs were considered one by one, 20 Feb., he defended the principle of the new criteria. The following day he conceded that there were some 'discrepancies', but he refused to meddle with the lists. On 28 Feb. he stoutly upheld against Peel's attack the proposed enfranchisement of Tower Hamlets and the other metropolitan districts (on which his father had tried unsuccessfully to get him to recant),[155] arguing that 'the apprehension that a democratic spirit will invariably come from these ... districts' was 'a mere childish imagination, derived from the terrors of the French revolution'. He was, however, made to squirm by Croker over the enfranchisement of Walsall (of which he privately disapproved), 9 Mar.[156] He remained silent in the third reading debate, 19-22 Mar., but on the 23rd, moving the passage of the bill, he declaimed:

> If Parliament refuses to entertain any measure of this nature, they will place in collision that party which ... opposes all reform ... and that which desires a reform extending to universal suffrage ... Much blood will be shed in the struggle ... and ... the British constitution will perish in the conflict.

He and Althorp 'led the way' when the bill was carried to the Lords, 26 Mar. 1832, and Denis Le Marchant† made the curious comment that Russell 'does not trouble himself much about politics'.[157]

The fate of the bill in the Lords had all along been the crucial factor. In early January 1832 Russell 'felt some but no insuperable objections' to a mass creation of peers to carry it, as 'a choice between two evils'. At the end of the month, in Brighton with Holland, he floated the 'more *constitutional*' notion of the Commons forcing the Lords to swallow the measure 'by voting the Mutiny Act for a short time, from month to month or fortnight to fortnight, only'. A week later Greville claimed to know that he had sent for Harrowby's son Lord Sandon* and 'entreated him to get something done by his father and his associates' to avert the necessity of creations. In early March he 'talked despondingly' to Littleton about the bill's chances, said Lansdowne, Palmerston and Melbourne were 'very slack' about it and was 'utterly at a loss to know who could fight the bill' in the Lords. In cabinet, 11 Mar., he expressed 'great distrust' of assurances that the measure would be given a second reading and 'suggested the propriety of an actual written declaration from the new converts or at least a direct personal assurance from each to Lord Grey'. When Durham threatened to resign over his colleagues' refusal to apply for a creation of peers at this juncture, Russell did likewise, which raised the spectre of the self-destruction of the ministry.[158] In the House, he handled some departmental business 2, 4 Apr. He divided for the navy civil departments bill, 6 Apr., and on the 18th said that after Easter he would present Dissenters' petitions in favour of the government's plans to reform Irish education. In cabinet, 3 Apr., Russell, who believed that lord chancellor Brougham was trying to wreck the government, 'questioned the policy' of the proposed memorandum to the king and 'would have preferred meeting the second reading [in the Lords] this week and advising the king according to the result but not pressing him on hypothetical or contingent cases'. Next day, thinking that prospects were 'gloomy', he said to Hobhouse that 'as the government had not carried their measure by force, they ought not to hesitate about concession', and that 'it would be foolish to go out because they were beaten on the number of boroughs, which Althorp thought ought to be the test'.[159] The second reading was carried by nine votes, 14 Apr., but when an opposition amendment to postpone consideration of the disfranchising clauses succeeded by 35, 7 May, Grey asked the king to create peers, and on his refusal the ministers resigned, 9 May. Russell of course voted for the address calling on the king to appoint only ministers who would pass reform unimpaired, 10 May. Two days later, talking to Littleton about stories that Grey had 'wilfully deceived the country', he observed that '"We cannot speak anything we are not permitted to speak on that subject, but we believed the king would create peers, and we therefore permitted others to believe it, and that will be our defence"'. His dignified but sarcastic speech in the House on 14 May, when he denied having become 'a radical reformer' and 'dashed with great vigour and felicity of illustration into a most severe scrutiny of the motives of the duke [of Wellington] and his adherents' – any administration formed by them, he said, would be one 'into which honour cannot enter' – was praised even by Greville as 'the best he ever made'.[160] Back in office with his colleagues, Russell voted silently for the second reading of the Irish reform bill, 25 May, and against a Conservative amendment to the Scottish measure, 1 June. He was named to the select committees on the Bank charter, 22 May, and the abolition of slavery, 30 May. When Peel taunted him with the 'whisper of a faction' episode, 5 June, he defended the government's recent conduct. Taking charge of the boundaries bill, on 7 June he explained it and in reply to Croker's observation that events in France should be 'a warning ... not to trust to the stability' of the reform settlement, said that the tyranny of the French king had justified the revolutionaries. On 14 June Littleton recorded that he and Drummond of the home office, anxious to finalize alterations in the measure, had run Russell to earth in a stable in King Street, where, 'with the groom's ink bottle and pen, and lying down on straw in one of the stalls', they completed the work.[161] Russell denied O'Connell's allegation of a 'secret compact' concerning the disfranchisement of Irish 40*s.* freeholders, 13 June, and spoke and voted against more opposition amendments to the Scottish reform bill, 15 June. He deplored the physical attack on the king and press libels of the royal family, 20 June, when he voted to open coroners' inquests to the public. Lady Cowper's observation that 'even little John' was 'frightened' at what the government had done on reform was wide of the mark: he looked forward confidently to the elections.[162] He opposed Alexander Baring's bill to exclude insolvent debtors from the House, 27 June, because 'it might become a party engine in the hands of the government or of a dominant party'. He pushed through the Lords' amendments to the boundaries bill, so that registration could begin, 9 July. He protested against Irish Members' obstructive opposition to the government's plans to revise tithes, 10, 12 July, when he accused O'Connell of trying to disturb the peace of Ireland and stressed the urgent need to improve Irish education in order to eradicate 'the state of ignorance ... which ... is the cause of the political and moral degradation of that country. He presented the promised Protestant Dissenters' petition on this subject, 17 July. When Macaulay dined with Russell, 'a bachelor, much against his will, I believe', at this time, he found that his official residence 'swarmed with women and children as if it had been a lying-in hospital', for his sisters-in-law and their broods were there.[163] Russell spoke briefly against the opposition's 'vote of censure' on the Russian-Dutch loan, 12 July, and divided silently on the 16th. He tried to defend Brougham in the fuss over his appointment of his brother to a chancery sinecure, 27 July. He explained the bribery bill, 30 July, 'omitted a great number of clauses', 7 Aug., and carried a resolution allowing 28 days for a formal complaint of electoral bribery to be lodged and the third reading of the amended bill, 9 Aug. On 7 Aug. 1832 he was a spokesman for ministerial foreign policy, especially on Poland. At the end of the month he told George William, 'We have finished the session well here and people are becoming satisfied. Trade is flourishing, etc. I am going to Ireland for a jaunt'.[164]

Russell, whose death from cholera was falsely reported in September, and who grew 'tired' of being 'drawn, hazzaed, cheered and hip hip hipped' during an election tour at that time, was returned with Ebrington for the Southern division of Devon after a contest at the general election in December 1832. Contrary to his reputed observation of 1831, that because of the boldness of the reform scheme the radicals 'would and must be amply satisfied without looking to any further encroachment', he anticipated the presence of a 'very numerous, and very formidable' band of 'Philo-Radicals', whom ministers would be obliged to 'conciliate', in the reformed Parliament.[165] His threat of July 1833 to resign from the cabinet in protest at Grey's endorsement of the failure of Smith Stanley's Irish church reform bill to incorporate the appropriation of surplus revenues to other purposes was a portent of many future storms in his long career at the centre of British politics.[166] In a 'Gallery of Illustrious Characters' in the 1831 Parliament Russell was described as

> not by any means a commonplace speaker ... [He] possesses a good deal of mannerism [and] ... is always pleasing ... His appearance is not effeminate, but it is more gentle than consists with a leader ... His language is scholar-like, but before ten sentences are uttered the idea of a morning gown, a pair of slippers, and a library table, involuntarily haunts your imagination ... [He is] one of the best employed lecturers in ordinary.[167]

In 1841 his under-secretary at the colonial office told Lord Hatherton that Russell was 'one of the most extraordinary men he had ever become acquainted with; the prominent qualities of his mind were truth and courage ... His firmness of decision ... was remarkable. In ordinary matters he seemed an ordinary person'.[168] Five years later, when Russell became prime minister for the first time, Campbell wrote of him:

> His manners are cold, and he not only takes no pains to please, but ... he sometimes has an air of *hauteur* and superciliousness which, although quite foreign to his nature, gives cause of offence. But in truth he is a very amiable as well as a very great man ... His talents are of a high, although I cannot say of the highest, order ... His information is copious, his reasoning is sound, and his sentiments are noble, but he is wanting in rapidity of thought and utterance ... Yet he is listened to in the House of Commons with uniform respect.[169]

Russell was never an easy colleague, for he was touchy and impetuous, and for a decade from 1850 he lost his way, behaving outrageously and irreparably damaging his reputation. After leaving the political arena, he admitted (in 1869) that he had 'committed many errors, some of them very gross blunders'; but he claimed credit for having had the country's interests 'at heart' as a believer in and proponent of rational progress.[170] He died at Pembroke Lodge, Richmond Park, of which he had been granted use by Queen Victoria in 1847, in May 1878. He was succeeded in his earldom by his grandson John Francis Henry (1865-1931), whose father John, Lord Amberley, Liberal Member for Nottingham, 1866-8, had predeceased Russell in 1876, aged 34.

[1] See S. Walpole, *Life of Lord John Russell*, 2 vols. (1889) and J. Prest, *Lord John Russell* (1972). [2] *Life of Campbell*, ii. 205; *HP Commons, 1790-1820*, v. 69. [3] *Pol. Mag.* (1831-2), 49; Prest, 46. [4] Prest, 17-24, 73-77; Walpole, i. 92-93; P. Mandler, *Aristocratic Government in Age of Reform*, 58. [5] *Cambridge Chron.* 25 Feb., 10, 17 Mar.; Wentworth Woodhouse mun. WWM F48/171; F49/68; Fitzwilliam mss, Maltby to Milton, 3, 5, 17 Mar. 1820. [6] Add. 56541, f. 18. [7] Keele Univ. Lib. Sneyd mss SC8/44. [8] Broughton, *Recollections*, ii. 128; Add. 51586, Tierney to Lady Holland [?4 June 1820]. [9] Add. 52444, f. 125. [10] *Huntingdon Gazette*, 5 Aug. 1820. [11] *The Times*, 5, 15 Aug.; *Life of Wilberforce*, v. 74-75; *Arbuthnot Jnl.* i. 32; *Shelley Diary*, ii. 103; Buckingham, *Mems. Geo. IV*, i. 60, 66; *Colchester Diary*, iii. 155; Add. 51659, Whishaw to Lady Holland [11 Aug.]; 51662, Bedford to Holland, 11 Aug. 1820. [12] Add. 51579, Morpeth to Lady Holland, 13 Aug. [1820]; *Russell Early Corresp.* i. 213. [13] Prest, 19; *Countess Granville Letters*, i. 163; *Fox Jnl.* 42-43. [14] Add. 51579, Morpeth to Lady Holland, 2 Oct.; 51679, Russell to same, 19 Sept. [Oct.] 1820. [15] *Moore Jnl.* i. 365-6, 368-9, 371, 373, 374; Walpole, i. 122; Add. 51662, Bedford to Lady Holland [14 Nov.]; 51679, Russell to same [18 Dec. 1820]. [16] *Moore Jnl.* ii. 415; Walpole, i. 122. [17] Walpole, i. 123; *Russell Early Corresp.* i. 217; *Fox Jnl.* 60 [18] *Russell Early Corresp.* i. 217. [19] Add. 51663, Bedford to Holland, 6 Mar. [1821]. [20] *Life of Campbell*, i. 396; Add. 51667, Bedford to Lady Holland [16 Mar.]; 51679, Russell to same [Mar. 1821]. [21] *Lady Holland to Son*, 4; *Huntingdon Gazette*, 31 Mar. 1821. [22] HLRO, Hist. Coll. 379, Grey Bennet diary, 76; Add. 51667, Bedford to Lady Holland, 13 May [1821]. [23] Add. 51679, Russell to Lady Holland, 24 May [1821]. [24] Add. 51663, Bedford to Holland, 14 June [1821]. [25] *Moore Jnl.* ii. 458-63, 466-71, 474, 479-88; *Fox Jnl.* 73-74; Blakiston, *Lord William Russell*, 49, 51. [26] *Lady Holland to Son*, 5; Add. 51667, Bedford to Lady Holland, Sunday [?25 Nov. 1821]. [27] Add. 36459, f. 183. [28] *Moore Jnl.* ii. 482; Mandler, 61; *Russell Early Corresp.* i. 219; Add. 51679, Russell to Lady Holland [Jan. 1822]. [29] *The Times*, 18, 22 Jan.; Add. 51667, Bedford to Lady Holland [Jan.]; 52182, f. 96; Grey mss, Tierney to Grey, 23 Jan. 1822. [30] Add. 38080, f. 10. [31] Ibid.; *Russell Early Corresp.* i. 223-4. [32] *Arbuthnot Jnl.* i. 151-2. [33] Grey mss, Grey to Holland, 9 Feb., Fitzwilliam to Grey, 24 Mar., 4 Apr.; Fitzwilliam mss, Grey to Fitzwilliam, 6 Apr. 1822. [34] *Moore Jnl.* ii. 557; *Arbuthnot Jnl.* i. 159; Blakiston, 63; Gurney diary, 25 Apr.; Northants. RO, Agar Ellis diary, 25 Apr. 1822; Dorset RO D/BKL, Bankes jnl. 136. [35] Prest, 29-31; J. Cannon, *Parl. Reform, 1640-1832*, p. 184; M. Brock, *Great Reform Act*, 44; Add. 75937, Lady to Lord Spencer, 13 May 1822. [36] Add. 56544, f. 6. [37] Blakiston, 63. [38] Add. 51677. [39] *Russell Letters*, ii. 12; *Russell Early Corresp.* i. 227; Blakiston, 74; Add. 51667, Bedford to Lady Holland [1 Nov. 1822]. [40] Add. 51679, Russell to Lady Holland [July] [c. 20 Oct.]; *The Times*, 5 Oct. 1822. [41] Add. 38080, f. 20; 51679, Russell to Lady Holland [Jan.], 28 Jan. 1823. [42] Add. 51667, Bedford to Lady Holland [23 Feb. 1823]. [43] Creevey mss, Creevey to Miss Ord, 21 Feb. 1823; Prest, 31. [44] *Huntingdon Gazette*, 8, 22 Mar. 1823. [45] Brougham mss, Russell to Brougham [23 Mar.]; Broughton, *Recollections*, iii. 17; Add. 51663, Bedford to Holland, 27 Mar. 1823; A. Mitchell, *Whigs in Opposition*, 36-37. [46] Add. 51663, Bedford to Holland [18 Apr. 1823]. [47] Ibid. same to same, Sun. [?23 Mar. 1823]. [48] Blakiston, 82; Agar Ellis diary, 24 Apr. 1823. [49] *Moore Jnl.* ii. 648, 652, 680-4; Add. 51679, Russell to Lady Holland [Aug. 1823]; *Russell Early Corresp.* i. 235; Blakiston, 96, 110. [50] Blakiston, 111; Add. 51667, Russell to Holland, 3, 24 Nov.; 51679, to Lady Holland [24 Nov.], 8, 15, 25 Dec. 1823. [51] Add. 51668, Bedford to Lady Holland [18 Jan. 1824]; *Russell Early Corresp.* i. 236. [52] Add. 38080, f. 24. [53] *Life of Wilberforce*, v. 217; Agar Ellis diary, 18 Mar. [1823]; TNA 30/29/9/5/22. [54] Blakiston, 118-21, 124; *Moore Jnl.* ii. 759-63. [55] Add. 56549, f. 124; *The Times*, 24 May 1825. [56] Fitzwilliam mss, Rooper to Maltby, 19 Sept., Maltby to Milton, 20 Sept.; Add. 51679, Russell to Lady Holland, 9 Nov.; Hunts. RO, Sandwich mss 21a/8, Russell to Mandeville, 22 Oct. 1825. [57] *Russell Early Corresp.* i. 238-40, 243; Broughton, iii. 122-3; Add. 51679, Russell to Lady Holland, 11 Oct., 28 Nov. 1825. [58] *The Times*, 26 Dec. 1825. [59] Fitzwilliam mss, Russell to Milton, 13 Jan., Maltby to same, 17, 23 Jan.; box 124/7, 12; *Russell Early Corresp.* i. 244-5; Add. 51679, Russell to Lady Holland, 16 Jan. 1826; *Countess Granville Letters*, i. 379. [60] *Creevey's Life and Times*, 225; *Creevey Pprs.* ii. 97-98. [61] Add. 51663, Bedford to Holland, 9 May [1826]. [62] Bankes jnl. 157; Add. 51586, Tierney to Lady Holland, 28 Apr.; Agar Ellis diary, 27 Apr. 1826; Prest, 31. [63] *Moore Jnl.* iii. 929. [64] Add. 51668, Bedford to Lady Holland [12 May 1826]. [65] *Russell Early Corresp.* i. 247, 248; Fitzwilliam mss, Russell to Milton, 23 June; Add. 51677, to Holland, 23 June [1826]. [66] Blakiston, 138-9; *Lady Holland to Son*, 51; Add. 51668, Bedford to Lady Holland [2 July 1826]; Walpole, i. 131. [67] Add. 51663, Bedford to Holland, 6 Oct.; 51669, to Lady Holland, 21 Sept.; 51679, Russell to same, 24 Sept. [1826]; Blakiston, 141; *Russell Letters*, i. 97-98; ii. 63. [68] E.A. Wasson, *Whig Renaissance*, 148; Walpole, i. 131. [69] Walpole, i. 131-2; *Russell Early Corresp.* i. 252-4. [70] Add. 51663, Bedford to Holland [22 Jan., 20 Feb.]; 51669, to Lady Holland [26 Jan. 1827]; *Canning's Ministry*, 31. [71] Add. 51669, Bedford to Lady Holland [6 Apr.]; Lansdowne mss, Russell to Lansdowne [c. 13 Apr. 1827]. [72] Add. 51679. Russell to Lady Holland [17], 22 Apr. 1827; *Canning's Ministry*, 301. [73] LMA, Jersey mss 510/416, Bedford to Lady Jersey, 1 May 1827; *Russell Letters*, i. 61, 62; Blakiston, 144. [74] Add. 56550, f. 177; *The Times*, 24 May 1827. [75] *Russell Letters*, i. 72; ii. 93; Add. 51679, Russell to Lady Holland, 27 July [1 Aug. 1827]. [76] Add. 51677, Russell to Holland, 16 Aug. 1827; *Russell*

Early Corresp. i. 214-15, 259; *Russell Letters*, i. 74-75; ii. 99, 104; *Moore Jnl.* iii. 1040. [77] Fitzwilliam mss, Russell to Milton, 6 Sept.; Blakiston, 146; Lansdowne mss, Tierney to Lansdowne, 5, 6 Sept.; Hatherton mss, Vernon to Littleton, 5 Sept. 1827. [78] *Russell Early Corresp.* i. 262-4. [79] Wasson, 152; Hants RO, Tierney mss 61a-e. [80] Add. 51669, Bedford to Lady Holland, 26 Oct.; 51677, Russell to Holland, 15, 20 Oct.; Fitzwilliam mss, Russell to Maltby [6 Nov. 1827]. [81] Add. 51677, Russell to Holland, 18 Dec. [1827]. [82] Broughton, iii. 230; Add. 51679, Russell to Lady Holland [5 Jan. 1828]. [83] Add. 51679, Russell to Lady Holland [8], 17 Jan. [1828]. [84] Add. 40395, ff. 219, 221. [85] Add. 51677, Russell to Holland, 14 Oct., 18 Dec. [1827]; 51679, to Lady Holland [8 Jan. 1828]. [86] Agar Ellis diary, 26 Feb.; Hatherton diary, 26 Feb. [1828]; Prest, 33-35. [87] *Russell Early Corresp.* i. 272. [88] Add. 51669, Bedford to Lady Holland [18 May]; 51677, Russell to Holland, 23 May [1828]; Blakiston, 165-6, 167; *Russell Letters*, i. 67-68, 89; ii. 128-9. [89] Prest, 35. [90] Add. 51669, Bedford to Lady Holland, 30 June [1828]. [91] *Ellenborough Diary*, i. 162; *Baring Jnls.* i. 57; *Russell Early Corresp.* i. 271-8. [92] *Moore Jnl.* iii. 1153-4; *Russell Letters*, ii. 135, 155; *Russell Early Corresp.* i. 281; Add. 51679, Russell to Lady Holland [27 Sept.]; Brougham mss, Russell to Brougham, 28 Sept. 1828. [93] *Lady Holland to Son*, 89; *Smith Letters*, i. 482; Add. 51600, Lady Cowper to Lady Holland [15 Dec.]; Blakiston, 174; *Russell Early Corresp.* i. 282-4; *Ellenborough Diary*, i. 266-7; Lambton mss, Grey to Durham, 2 Nov. 1828. [94] Brougham mss, Russell to Brougham, 26 Nov., 15 Dec. [1828]; *Russell Letters*, i. 104; Add. 51677, Russell to Holland, 25, 28 Dec.; 51679, to Lady Holland, 18 Dec. 1828. [95] Add. 51677, Russell to Holland, 2 Jan.; 76369, Althorp to Brougham, 2 Jan.; Lansdowne mss, Russell to Lansdowne, 4 Jan.; Brougham mss, to Brougham, 5 [Jan. 1829]; *Russell Letters*, ii. 178. [96] Add. 51663, Bedford to Holland [7 Jan.]; 51677, Russell to same [19 Jan.]; Blakiston, 182; *Russell Early Corresp.* i. 287; *The Times*, 19 Jan. 1829. [97] Add. 51677, Russell to Holland [3 Feb. 1829]; *Russell Letters*, ii. 181; *Moore Jnl.* iii. 1194. [98] Blakiston, 187-8. [99] Ibid. 191-2, 194-9, 201, 203; Add. 51680, Russell to Lady Holland, 7 July, 3 Aug., 23 Oct., 1829; 51670, Bedford to same [?6 Jan. 1830]; *Russell Letters*, ii. 213. [100] Add. 51677, Russell to Holland [23 Oct. 1829]. [101] *Russell Letters*, i. 133; iii. 218, 221; Blakiston, 202-3. [102] Chatsworth mss, Russell to Devonshire, 29 Jan. 1830. [103] Brougham mss, Russell to Brougham, 30 Jan.; Grey mss, Howick jnl. 3 Feb. [1830]; Mitchell, 219-20. [104] Howick jnl. 23 Feb.; Add. 51667, Bedford to Lady Holland [1 Mar. 1830]. [105] Howick jnl. 15 Feb. [1830]. [106] Castle Howard mss, Graham to Morpeth [3 Mar. 1830]. [107] *Howard Sisters*, 125; Howick jnl. 10 Mar.; Agar Ellis diary, 10 Mar.; Add. 52176, Allen to C.R. Fox, 4 Apr. 1830. [108] *Russell Letters*, ii. 234-5. [109] Ibid. ii. 239. [110] Fitzwilliam mss, Day to Milton, 23 June, Tavistock to same, 5 July; Blakiston, 211-12, 215; Add. 51385, Wilks to Holland, 27 July 1830; C.T. Flick, 'Bedford Election of 1830', *Beds. Hist. Rec. Soc.* xliv (1970), 162-6. [111] Add. 51677, Russell to Holland [26 July 1830]. [112] Add. 51670, Bedford to Lady Holland, 12 Sept.; 51677, Russell to Holland [6 Sept.]; 51680, to Lady Holland, 30 Aug. [1 Sept. 1830]; *Howard Sisters*, 142. [113] Add. 51677, Russell to Holland, 13, 17 Sept. 1830; Prest, 37; Walpole, i. 157; *Russell Early Corresp.* i. 305-6, 307-8. [114] Agar Ellis diary, 4 Oct.; Brougham mss, Agar Ellis to Brougham, 4 Oct.; Blakiston, 222; Add. 51677, Russell to Holland [18 Oct.]; 51680, to Lady Holland, 13 Oct. 1830. [115] Devon RO, Earl Fortescue mss, Russell to Ebrington, 20 Oct. [1830]. [116] Howick jnl. 31 Oct. [1830]; M. Brock, *Great Reform Act*, 115; Prest, 38; *Russell Letters*, i. 156; Blakiston, 224. [117] *Russell Letters*, i. 159; ii. 285-6; Add. 51680, Russell to Lady Holland [c. 15 Nov.]; Grey mss, Holland to Grey [20 Nov. 1830]; *Russell Early Corresp.* i. 312-14. [118] Grey mss, Holland to Grey [20 Nov. 1830]; Walpole, i. 159-60; *Russell Early Corresp.* i. 314-15; *Russell Letters*, i. 161; ii. 296-7, 306; *Greville Mems.* ii. 68, 84-85; Blakiston, 225; Prest, 38-40. [119] Add. 51680, Russell to Lady Holland, 20 Dec. [1830]. [120] Prest, 40-42; Cannon, 204-10; Brock, 136-8, 140-1; Russell, *Recollections*, 68-70; *Russell Letters*, ii. 315; *Three Diaries*, 42; Lansdowne mss, Grey to Lansdowne, 14 Jan.; Add. 51670, Bedford to Lady Holland, 20 Jan. [1831]. [121] Add. 51677, Russell to Holland, 26 Jan. [1831; *Russell Early Corresp.* ii. 11-13. [122] Hatherton mss, Littleton to wife, 3 Feb.; Add. 51663, Bedford to Holland, 4 Feb.; Lambton mss, Russell to Durham and memo, 13 Feb.; Sir James Graham mss (IHR microfilm XR 80), 1, Graham to Grey, 17 Feb. 1831; Brougham mss, Russell to Brougham, 15 Nov. 1837; Cannon, 211-12; Brock, 141-2; Prest, 42-44. [123] Add. 51675, Tavistock to Holland [1 Mar.]; St. Deiniol's Lib. Glynne-Gladstone mss 197, T. to J. Gladstone, 2 Mar. 1831; Broughton, iv. 87; *Baring Jnls.* i. 83-84; Le Marchant, *Althorp*, 297-8; *Lieven-Grey Corresp.* ii. 178; *Three Diaries*, 12-13, 61-62; *Greville Mems.* ii. 112-13; *Russell Letters*, ii. 326; Russell, 70-72; Prest, 44-46. [124] Add. 51590, Agar Ellis to Lady Holland, 7 Mar.; 51670, Bedford to same [6, 7 Mar.]; Agar Ellis diary, 6 Mar. [1831]. [125] *Russell Letters*, ii. 326, 329. [126] Ibid. ii. 334-5. [127] Cent. Kent. Stud. Gambier mss U194 C8/2; *The Times*, 5 Apr. 1831. [128] Parker, *Graham*, i. 109. [129] Add. 51569, Ord to Lady Holland [18 Apr.]; 51573, Spring Rice to Holland [17 Apr.]; 51576, Fazakerley to same [17 Apr. 1831]. [130] Derby mss 920 Der (14) 1166, Winstanley to Smith Stanley, 25 Apr. 1831; *Smith Letters*, ii. 534. [131] Add. 51663, Bedford to Holland [25 Apr.], Russell to Bedford, 29 Apr.; 51677, Holland to Russell [Apr.]; 51680, Russell to Lady Holland [May] [3, 6 May]; *Russell Early Corresp.* ii. 14-15; *The Times*, 3, 9, 12 May 1831; Blakiston, 231. [132] Add. 51677, Russell to Holland, 1 May; PRO NI, Anglesey mss D619/27A/106; TNA 30/29, Holland to Granville, 14 Apr. 1831; *Russell Early Corresp.* ii. 20-22. [133] Grey mss, Bedford to Grey, 19 May, reply, 22 May; Anglesey mss 28A-B/62; Prest, 46-47; Walpole, i. 169; *Greville Mems.* ii. 152. [134] *Life of Campbell*, i. 516. [135] *Greville Mems.* ii. 157-8; *Baring Jnls.* i. 88; Prest, 47-48. [136] *Three Diaries*, 99. [137] Broughton, iv. 121; *The Times*, 11 July 1831. [138] Add. 51576, Fazakerley to Lady Holland [14 July 1831]; Blakiston, 234; *Greville Mems.* ii. 175; *Peel Letters*, 132; *Lady Holland to Son*, 113; Prest, 50. [139] *Greville Mems.* ii. 171. [140] Ibid. ii. 181-2. [141] *Russell Letters*, ii. 373. [142] *Macaulay Letters*, ii. 91; Add. 61937, f. 125. [143] *Holland House Diaries*, 58; *Russell Letters*, i. 177. [144] Prest, 50. [145] *Greville Mems.* ii. 208-9; *Holland House Diaries*, 70; *Russell Early Corresp.* ii. 25-26; *Grey-William IV Corresp.* i. 387-8; Add. 51670, Bedford to Lady Holland, 18 Oct. [1831]; Prest, 51; *Three Diaries*, 155. [146] Beds. RO, Russell mss R766, Russell to Hardy, 18, 19 Oct. [1831]; *Russell Letters*, ii. 386-7. [147] Cannon, 225-6; Add. 76373, Althorp to Grey, 20 Oct.; Grey mss, Russell to Grey, 20 Oct.; Southampton Univ. Lib. Broadlands mss PP/GC/RI/11. [148] *Russell Letters*, ii. 286; Hatherton diary, 8, 11, 12, 27 Nov. [1831]; *Three Diaries*, 158-9. [149] Hatherton diary, 2 Dec. [1831]; *Greville Mems.* ii. 225-6. [150] Hatherton diary, 12 Dec.; *Three Diaries*, 167; *Holland House Diaries*, 97; NLS mss 24762, f. 49; Add. 51573, Spring Rice to Lady Holland [12 Dec.]; *Greville Mems.* ii. 229; Wilts. RO, Hobhouse mss 145/2/b, Hobhouse to wife, 13 Dec. 1831; Cannon, 228-9; Prest, 52. [151] Add. 51670, Bedford to Lady Holland [20 Dec. 1831]. [152] Hatherton diary, 19-21, 27 Dec. [1831]. [153] *Holland House Diaries*, 119. [154] Add. 51676, Ld. G. W. Russell to Holland, 3 Feb. [1832]; *Russell Letters*, iii. 8; *Three Diaries*, 203-4; *Wellington Despatches*, viii. 229. [155] Add. 51664, Bedford to Holland [27 Feb. 1832]. [156] Hatherton diary, 6 Mar. [1831]. [157] *Three Diaries*, 215; *Holland House Diaries*, 161. [158] Parker, *Graham*, i. 135; *Holland House Diaries*, 109, 121, 151, 154; *Greville Mems.* ii. 253; *Three Diaries*, 205; Hatherton diary, 6 Mar.; Agar Ellis diary, 13 Mar. [1832]; Prest, 52-53. [159] *Holland House Diaries*, 166-7; Broughton, iv. 210. [160] Hatherton diary, 12 May [1832]; *Three Diaries*, 255; *Greville Mems.* ii. 299. [161] Hatherton diary. [162] *Lady Palmerston Letters*, 193; *Russell Letters*, iii. 15, 17. [163] *Macaulay Letters*, ii. 152. [164] *Russell Letters*, iii. 23-24. [165] *Lieven-Palmerston Corresp.* 36; *Russell Letters*, iii. 26-27; Add. 51680, Russell to Lady Holland, 30 Aug., 13 Sept. [26 Nov.], 2, 8, 21 Dec. 1832; Earl Fortescue mss Add. 2/f. 20, Lady D. Harrowby to J. Fortescue [Feb. 1835]. [166] Walpole, i. 187-93; Prest, 56-59. [167] *Pol. Mag.* (1831-2), 48. [168] Hatherton diary, 4 Sept. 1841. [169] *Life of Campbell*, ii. 205-6. [170] Prest, pp. xv, 73-81; Russell, 221.

D.R.F.

RUSSELL, Matthew (1765–1822), of Brancepeth Castle, co. Dur. and 4 Park Street, Westminster, Mdx.

SALTASH 1802–19 Feb. 1807

SALTASH 26 Feb. 1808–8 May 1822

b. 24 Feb. 1765, o.s. of William Russell of Brancepeth and 1st w. Mary, da. and coh. of Robert Harrison, merchant, of Sunderland. *educ.* Univ. Coll. Oxf. 1781; L. Inn 1782. *m.* 23 Feb. 1798, Elizabeth, da. of George Tennyson† of Bayons Manor, Lincs. 1s. 1da. *suc.* fa. 1817. *d.* 8 May 1822.

Capt. Dur. militia 1792, maj. 1800; capt. Workington regt. Cumb. militia 1811.

Russell, who in 1817 inherited landed estates and colliery leaseholds in county Durham from his merchant father (whose personalty was finally sworn under £160,000), was reputedly 'the richest commoner in England', able to spend over £120,000 on rebuilding Brancepeth Castle.[1] His inheritance also included control of both seats at Bletchingley and one at Saltash, for which he had sat with one brief interruption since 1802; he was again returned there unopposed in 1820. There is no record of any votes or speeches by him and he may have carried out his threat of 1819 to withdraw support from Lord Liverpool's ministry, which he believed had neglected him. He was granted a month's leave for urgent private business, 23 June 1820, and again on account of illness, 13 Feb., 1 May 1821. He was presumably the Mr. Russell who presented a petition from Elsborough, Buckinghamshire, for relief from agricultural distress, 18 Feb. 1822.[2] He died three months later and his estates passed to his only son William, who was also returned for Saltash; his personalty was sworn under £120,000.[3]

[1] PROB 11/1594/386; IR26/720/608; H.C. Surtees, *Castle of Brancepeth*, 38-39. [2] *The Times*, 19 Feb. 1822. [3] PROB 11/1658/335; IR26/921/601.

R.M.H./T.A.J.

RUSSELL, William (1798–1850), of Brancepeth Castle, co. Dur.

SALTASH 22 May 1822–1826

BLETCHINGLEY 1826–28 Apr. 1827

DURHAM CO. 13 Feb. 1828–1832

b. 9 Nov. 1798, o.s. of Matthew Russell* and Elizabeth, da. of George Tennyson† of Bayons Manor, Lincs. *educ.* Eton 1811; St. John's, Camb. 1818. *unm. suc.* fa. 1822. *d.* 30 Jan. 1850.

Sheriff, co. Dur. 1841-2.

With a fortune derived from banking, trade and coal mines, Russell's family had purchased three borough seats at Bletchingley and Saltash and built interests at Great Grimsby and in the county and city of Durham. At the general election of 1820 the question arose of his possible candidature for Great Grimsby, where his uncle Charles Tennyson, one of the sitting Members, had 'not the slightest doubt' of his success. However, his father informed Tennyson that he had determined

> to write to William that I should not be justified in bringing him into Parliament at this time from my knowledge of his indolence, and indisposition to attend to anything in the form of business (the propriety of which I am sure you agree with me). Indeed, with his present frame of mind and all its bearings, it would be the worst step I could take for him, and most likely to be attended with ruinous consequences.

Tennyson advised his nephew that he must resolve 'to make Parliament a *business*', and Russell decided to bide his time until 'my father reposes greater confidence in me'.[1] In the event, following his father's sudden death in May 1822, when he inherited the family estates, Russell was able to return himself for Saltash.

He was a poor attender, who made no known speech in his first Parliament. He was apparently content to allow Tennyson, his borough manager, to act as his political representative. In September 1822 Tennyson, anticipating Canning's return to the foreign office, wrote to him offering to support Lord Liverpool's ministry and adding that 'I may venture from what I know of his sentiments to answer for my nephew Mr. Russell', whose important borough interests he alluded to. Tennyson indicated in a letter of April 1823 that they would have followed this line up to that point, had they not been 'detained in France until Easter', but despair of any change in foreign policy now led them to 'suspend the intention we had evinced of attaching ourselves to government', in favour of a policy of neutrality; they maintained their personal regard for Canning.[2] Russell divided for parliamentary reform, 24 Apr. 1823. He voted for reduction of the army, 23 Feb. 1824. His presence four days later in the minority against entering committee on the usury laws repeal bill perhaps stemmed from a procedural objection, as he was likely to have been the 'M. Russell' listed as voting for repeal, 17 Feb. 1825. He joined Brooks's Club, 9 May 1824. He divided for Catholic relief, 21 Apr. 1825. At the general election of 1826 he returned himself for Bletchingley.

Early in April 1827, according to a subsequent letter from Tennyson, Russell made an 'unqualified and unconcealed offer of support to Mr. Canning'. Later that month he temporarily resigned his seat, in favour of a member of Canning's government, so that he might travel abroad.[3] However, his plan to visit the eastern Mediterranean was curtailed by the outbreak of hostilities there, and in November 1827 he wrote from Naples that he intended to return home and resume his seat; Tennyson advised the prime minister Lord Goderich that his nephew's attitude towards government had 'somewhat changed' since Canning's death.[4] The need to reclaim one of his borough seats was obviated by a propitious vacancy in county Durham, for which he was returned unopposed in February 1828. He pledged support for Catholic emancipation, 'should the state of Ireland ... be such as to warrant [it]', and promised to attend to the shipping interest and promote measures to revive trade. He approved of the revision of the corn laws proposed by government in the previous session, and said he was willing to support the duke of Wellington's new ministry provided it continued with Canning's policies.[5] He took his seat, 11 Mar., and divided for Catholic relief, 12 May. He may have been the 'Capt. Russell' who was listed in the minority against the archbishop of Canterbury's bill, 16 June 1828, though no evidence has been found that he ever held military rank. That summer he reportedly 'declared himself against the government'.[6] He divided for Catholic emancipation, 6 Mar., and against requiring Daniel O'Connell to swear the oath of supremacy before taking his seat, 18 May 1829. He presented Stockton petitions in favour of a local railway bill, 18 Mar. 1829. He voted for his uncle's amendment to transfer East Retford's seats to Birmingham, 11 Feb. 1830. He presented a petition against the malt and beer duties, 26 Feb. On 1 Mar. he was named as a defaulter and ordered to attend the next day. In his stead appeared his medical attendant, who testified that he was 'in such a state of excitement as to render him unfit for any serious business'. Further light is shed on this episode, and on his poor attendance record generally, by Lord Durham's report to Lord Grey, 9 Mar., of rumours that 'Russell is a confirmed lunatic and under confinement, drinking having at last effected it'.[7] In fact, he resurfaced later in the session to vote for Jewish emancipation, 17 May, abolition of the death penalty for forgery, 24 May, 7 June, and reform of the civil government of Canada, 25 May 1830. Despite whispers against him in Durham, he was returned unopposed at the general election that summer.[8]

In August 1830 Durham informed Grey that, during an interval in which Russell 'happened to be sober', he had confided his belief that 'no good would ever come until the duke was turned out'. The following month Durham gathered that Russell and Tennyson were likely to wait and 'see how "the cat jumps"', but that they 'incline towards the Huskisson section'.[9] Ministers listed Russell among their 'foes' and, had he not been shut out of the lobby, he would have voted against them in the crucial civil list division, 15 Nov.[10] He presented anti-slavery petitions, 11 Nov., 8 Dec., and commended the repeal of the coastwise coal duty to Grey's ministry as a popular measure, 19 Nov. 1830. Early in 1831 he received generous remuneration for making two of his borough seats available to the premier.[11] Although the government's reform bill scheduled Bletchingley and Saltash for disfranchisement, Russell divided for the second reading, 22 Mar., and presented petitions in its favour, 28 Mar., 19 Apr. 1831, when he voted against Gascoyne's wrecking amendment. He was returned again for Durham at the ensuing general election. He presented a petition from the inhabitants of Stockton for parliamentary representation, 30 June. He paired for the second reading of the reintroduced reform bill, 6 July, but was listed as an absentee from many of the divisions in committee. He was granted three weeks' leave on account of ill health, 16 Sept., and again, 7 Oct. He divided for the second reading of the revised bill, 17 Dec. 1831, its details and the third reading, 22 Mar. 1832. He was absent from the division on the motion for an address asking the king to appoint only ministers committed to carrying an unimpaired measure, 10 May. He voted with government on the Russian-Dutch loan, 26 Jan., and relations with Portugal, 9 Feb., but was absent from the later division on the loan, 12 July. He divided in the minority for inquiry into distress in the glove trade, 31 Jan. He voted with the majority in a committee against the Sunderland wet docks bill, 2 Apr. 1832.

The division of Durham by the Reform Act weakened Russell's interest, and he did not stand again at the general election of 1832. Writing to Lord Melbourne the following year, he bitterly recalled 'the largest sacrifices of property' he had made for the Whig cause, for which he had 'never asked any but the slightest favours, not one of which has been granted'.[12] He continued the comprehensive rebuilding programme at Brancepeth Castle begun by his father, but he neglected Wallsend colliery, the fount of his wealth; it became prone to accidents and flooding and was eventually closed, contributing to the depletion of the family fortunes.[13] He died in January 1850. He left £5,000 to his 'adopted son' Alfred Joseph Riddell, while all his real estate passed to his only sister Emma, wife of Gustavus Frederick Hamilton, 7th Viscount Boyne, who took the additional name of Russell.[14]

[1] Durham CRO, Brancepeth mss D/Br/F294; Lincs. AO, Tennyson d'Eyncourt mss Td'E H108/15, 16, 18, 24. [2] Tennyson d'Eyncourt mss H1/87, 93. [3] Ibid. 105, 108. [4] Ibid. 109; Add. 38753, f. 4. [5] *Durham Chron.* 16 Feb. 1828. [6] Lonsdale mss, Lowther to Lonsdale, 5 July 1828. [7] Grey mss, Durham to Grey, 9 Mar. 1830. [8] *The Times*, 16 July 1830. [9] Grey mss, Durham to Grey, 17 Aug.; Brougham mss, Durham to Brougham, 7 Sept. 1830. [10] *The Times*, 18 Nov. 1830. [11] NLS, Ellice mss, Ellice to Russell, 25 Dec., reply 27 Dec. 1830; PRO NI, Anglesey mss D619/28A-B/36. [12] Tennyson d'Eyncourt mss H3/8. [13] Brancepeth mss F375; H.C. Surtees, *Castle of Brancepeth*, 11, 39; D. Bean, *Tyneside*, 164-5; W. Richardson, *Hist. Wallsend*, 240-2. [14] PROB 11/2212/313; IR26/1878/250.

H.J.S.

RUSSELL, William, Lord Russell (1809–1872).

TAVISTOCK 1830–Oct. 1831

TAVISTOCK 1832–1841

b. 1 July 1809, o.s. of Francis Russell, mq. of Tavistock*, and Lady Anna Maria Stanhope, da. of Charles Stanhope,† 3rd earl of Harrington. *educ.* Eton 1823; Christ Church, Oxf. 1827. *unm. styled* Lord Russell 1809-39; mq. of Tavistock 1839-61. *suc.* fa. as 8th duke of Bedford 14 May 1861. *d.* 26 May 1872.

Russell was an only child, doted on and worried about by his odd, Stanhope mother and, more particularly, by his father, the serious-minded heir of the 6th duke of Bedford. As a child he was sickly, with hypochondriacal tendencies, and, like his father, he never enjoyed robust health. Nor did he ever overcome his extreme shyness, reserve and lack of self-confidence, which provoked Lord Grey to describe him, when he was 25, as 'the most impenetrable person I ever met with'.[1] He appears to have been educated at home until, in a departure from the long family connection with Westminster, he was sent to Eton, when well turned 13. His uncle, Lord George William Russell*, whose wife had recently described him as 'a very gentlemanlike, pleasing lad, and well looking too', wrote approvingly to Lord Tavistock:

> A public school is what is necessary and is that which will add to his happiness hereafter and be a source of great satisfaction to yourself. I grant that the system of education is bad ... but it fits a boy to be a man, to know his fellow creatures, to love them, to be able to contend with the difficulties of life, to attach friends to him, to take a part in public affairs, to get rid of his humours and caprices and to form his temper and manners ... I can only rejoice that he is to have a public education. I am fully aware of the difficulties you have had to decide this question – an only child is an anxious care – but his being an only child makes public education more necessary, and I trust you will be rewarded for your decision by seeing him improve in health and strength.

Russell came home after his first term 'with a return of his cold, glandular swellings, etc., etc.', joining his father and grandfather on the sick list. 'We are a miserable family', commented Lord George William.[2] Russell was reckoned to be 'a very good, although not a first-rate scholar'.[3]

Tavistock agonized over the problem of his university education, being alarmed by 'very bad' reports of the current state of Cambridge, his own alma mater. He consulted his friend and Trinity contemporary John Cam Hobhouse* and eventually settled on Christ Church, Oxford, which seemed to be 'the least objectionable of all our English colleges, and has more advantages for a young *nobleman* than any other'.[4] When Hobhouse, who privately considered Tavistock's instructional 'system' for his son 'too strict', visited the family at Oakley in January 1827, he found Russell

> grown into a tall, full-made man ... Lord T. extremely anxious about him ... The boy understands him completely, and though now very docile and just what could be wished, may, very probably, turn out like other gay young men of his rank. He has good abilities, and apparently a very sweet and obliging disposition.

A conversational walk with Russell impressed Hobhouse:

> He spoke with great simplicity of the mode adopted by his father towards him, and told me he thought it too strict, though he was aware it arose entirely from his attachment and anxiety for him. In the course of our walk he made some very judicious reflections on men and manners, and even on politics, which I remarked, because it is of importance to the nation that the head of his house should be an honest and a right-judging man.[5]

When Hobhouse soon afterwards sent him 'a most formidable array of books' Russell, who was bound for Christ Church after the Easter vacation, thanked him diffidently:

> If I possessed your capacity to learn and your memory to retain, I might then hope to make myself master of them, but I greatly fear that my poor cranium does not contain half the sufficient quantum of brains. However, I must set at them ... I miss you very much in our pedestrian excursions.[6]

He attended his first grand London dinner, at Devonshire House, in July 1827.[7] At the end of the year his father told Hobhouse that he was 'doing very well at Oxford, much better, I believe, than we did at the other university, in as far at least as his constitution is concerned, and he has no turn, thank God, for play'. Twelve years later, just after succeeding to the dukedom, Tavistock noted that Russell

> never was in debt, and I am persuaded he never will be ... When he was at Oxford, he told me that if I wished him to keep out of debt, and not exceed his income, I had better take him away, on account of the extravagance he found established there and which it would be impossible for him to resist.[8]

In 1828 he was sent on a tour of the Fens with the auditor of the Bedford estates, William Adam, who reported to Tavistock that although he was open and frank, he showed a worrying lack of mental energy and ambition: 'It would be a great object to excite his curiosity and attention by making him acquainted with interesting subjects ... In his situation he must gain knowledge now or not at all'. Russell was in fact developing into a deep thinker, but his reflections on the misery and futility of the human condition only made him increasingly prey to morbid depression.[9] In early January 1829 he visited Paris with Lord Lynedoch.[10] Towards the end of the year he went to Rome, where he was taken under the wing of Lord and Lady George William, who had been encouraged by her brother-in-law Lord John Russell* to 'put him in the way of opening his understanding to the wonders of Italy. He is very well disposed'.[11] His father, who commented that 'a better or truer boy never existed', was pleased with the 'excellent accounts' which he received from Russell himself and the praise lavished on him by Lord George William. Privately, however, the latter thought that his nephew (whose tantalizingly delicate health stood between him and eventual succession to the dukedom), though 'a nice young man', had 'little in him – pity he is not more brought out, directed and better educated'.[12] On a lighter note, he reported to Lady Holland, who had formed a great liking for Russell, that he

> was disposed to admire a pretty little Spanish lady but probably did not kindle so quickly as Spanish eyes desire ... so she gave the preference to young L. Bonaparte, whom the indignant husband caught and cuffed and kicked downstairs, and has packed off his poor little frail wife to be shut up in a convent in Spain for life. Thus has tragically ended the little innocent *amour*, of which Russell might have been the hero; still it is as well not to be kicked by an enraged Don.[13]

Russell moved on to Naples in mid-February 1830.[14]

That summer, when he came of age and was admitted to Brooks's (7 July), the senior members of the family considered starting him at the approaching general election for Bedford, where, thanks largely to the neglect and absenteeism of the sitting Member, Lord George William, their interest was under serious threat. They decided to put up Lord John, but even so, only the chance of his discovering that a rival had stolen a march with a premature canvass, when he went to Bedford to announce that he had after all decided to stand for Huntingdonshire, prevented Russell from being thrown in at the deep end.[15] As it was he was nominated to replace his ailing great-uncle, Lord William Russell*, on the secure family interest at Tavistock. His fretting father committed him to the experienced care of the other Russell nominee, Lord Ebrington*: 'on every account I wish him to commence his political career there under your advice and direction. Pray have the kindness to take charge of him and to tell him how to act'. Lord John reported that Russell had gone to Devon 'rather alarmed at the new career he is about to enter on'; but he and Ebrington were returned without fuss.[16] After the election he spent much time with the Hollands, and his mother thanked Lady Holland, 27 Aug. 1830, for their 'great kindness' in this regard:

> He feels it too, and is sensible of the advantage it is to him to be with you and Lord Holland, and the agreeable society you always have. He writes us word that he is only surprised at your patience in hearing him, for that he is seized with terrible fits of shyness, and is so stupid and taciturn that he is persuaded you must find him a great bore.[17]

In October 1830 he was paraded at the annual Bedford mayor's feast as part of the Russells' attempt to rally their supporters after Lord John's narrow defeat.[18]

The Wellington ministry of course reckoned Russell among their 'foes'. Entrusted by his father, who was unwell, to the care and direction of Hobhouse, he voted against them on the civil list, 15 Nov. 1830.[19] He is not known to have spoken in debate in this period, but he presented petitions from a Gloucestershire congregation of Protestant Dissenters for the abolition of slavery, 22 Nov. 1830, and from Thorney, Bedfordshire, in favour of the reform bill introduced by his uncle, 19 Mar. 1831. He voted for its second reading, 22 Mar., and against Gascoyne's wrecking amendment, 19 Apr. 1831. He could not be 'prevailed upon' to stand for Buckinghamshire at the ensuing general election, showing what his grandfather perceived as 'unreasonable diffidence'; and it was for Tavistock that he was again returned without opposition, this time with Lord John.[20] Russell, who continued to frequent Holland House,[21] voted for the second reading of the reintroduced reform bill, 6 July, and against using the 1831 census to determine the borough disfranchisement schedules, 19 July 1831. He paired for the committee divisions on Greenwich,

3 Aug., Gateshead, 5 Aug., Rochester, 9 Aug., clause 15, 17 Aug. (and doubtless for all the others), and for the passage of the bill, 21 Sept. Two days later Lord Tavistock, as he informed his brother, proposed to Bedford that Russell

> should either accept the Chiltern Hundreds now, or retire from Parliament at the next general election. His health is not equal to the attendance he ought to give to his parliamentary duties. At some future time I hope he may be able to take his seat in a reformed Parliament.

It seems that late sittings brought on 'his headaches'; and, on medical advice, he vacated his seat after voting for the motion of confidence in the ministry, 10 Oct. 1831.[22]

A reluctant and terrified Russell was cajoled by the family elders into nominating Townley*, the reform candidate, at the formal opening of the Cambridgeshire by-election, on which much public attention was focused, 27 Oct. 1831. In the event, to the satisfaction of his father and grandfather, he spoke capably, criticizing self-styled 'moderate reformers' as hypocrites and denying that 'the friends of reform were in any respect the enemies of the farmers'.[23] A year later Bedford, though incredulous of 'a strange report' that Russell was to marry Lavinia Harcourt, observed that 'he would be better *of* marriage (as the Scots say), for it would give him rational pursuits, and draw him out of his snail shell, where he buries his talents in his own shyness and extreme diffidence'. Soon afterwards, when the sudden death of his replacement at Tavistock threatened to derange Bedford's arrangements, he 'gallantly, and with proper courage' agreed to stand there at the forthcoming general election. He topped the poll and held the seat without distinction until his retirement in 1841.[24] He was very much inclined, at least in the abstract, to radicalism (and, indeed, was wrongly thought by some to espouse republican doctrines), though he had a poor opinion of the current radical leaders.[25]

Russell never married, writing in 1841 that 'I shrink almost with a feeling of horror of uniting a young girl full of life to a semi-corpse'. He retreated even further into his carapace of shyness and morose introspection as he got older. Shortly after his retirement from the Commons he wrote to his father that

> the more wisdom a man has the more miserable he is ... I have little life in me now. Always and every day I am living rather as flogged along or upon pluck, than having anything approaching to enjoyment of life ... I think that few people have ever passed a much more unpleasant life than I have done ... I have often broken out into a cold sweat and felt sick at the stomach with misery ... Fancy a soul in hell, that gives a better idea of my sensations and existence than anything else.

The medical men ascribed this and similar tormented outbursts to 'deep hypochondria'; while Lord John Russell reflected that 'a bad stomach, Byron and Voltaire have been the cause of the mischief'.[26] Russell's father lamented his 'most extraordinary and morbid feeling of diffidence, which makes him think that he cannot be useful or agreeable to anybody'.[27] After succeeding to the dukedom in 1861, he became a complete recluse, only leaving his London house at 6 Belgrave Square to ride in a brougham with wooden shutters to visit his current mistress in Kensington.[28] He dropped dead in the hall of his house in May 1872.[29] By his will, dated 12 July 1870 and proved under £600,000, 13 June 1872, he left, among sundry legacies, a life annuity of £450 to Mary Ann Ryland of Leonard Place, Kensington, 'in testimony of my approbation of her long and faithful services to me'. He was succeeded as 9th duke of Bedford by his cousin, Lord George William's eldest son, Francis Charles Hastings Russell† (1819-91).

[1] Blakiston, *Lord William Russell*, 24-25; *Russell Letters*, iii. 314. [2] Add. 51681, Lady G.W. Russell to Lady Holland [n.d.]; *Russell Letters*, i. 11; Blakiston, *Lord William Russell*, 75-76, 88, 100. [3] *Russell Letters*, i. 44. [4] Add. 36463, ff. 42, 189. [5] Add. 56550, ff. 124, 125, 128; Broughton, *Recollections*, iii. 162-3. [6] Add. 36463, f. 262. [7] Broughton, iii. 207. [8] Add. 36464, f. 100; Blakiston, *Lord William Russell*, 432. [9] G. Blakiston, *Woburn and the Russells*, 201. [10] *Russell Letters*, i. 115. [11] Add. 36465, ff. 251, 349; *Russell Letters*, i. 135; Blakiston, *Lord William Russell*, 202. [12] Add. 47223, f. 38; *Russell Letters*, i. 43-44; Blakiston, *Lord William Russell*, 205. [13] Blakiston, *Lord William Russell*, 205; Add. 51669, Bedford to Lady Holland, 19 Aug. [1829]. [14] Add. 36466, f. 12. [15] Blakiston, *Lord William Russell*, 212, 214; *Russell Letters*, ii. 251. [16] Devon RO, Earl Fortescue mss, Tavistock to Ebrington, 15 July; Add. 51677, Russell to Holland [26 July]; *Woolmer's Exeter and Plymouth Gazette*, 7 Aug. 1830. [17] Add. 51675. [18] *Russell Letters*, i. 150. [19] Add. 47223, f. 43. [20] Add. 51663, Bedford to Holland [25 Apr.]; *Trewman's Exeter Flying Post*, 5 May 1831. [21] *Macaulay Letters*, ii. 21, 254. [22] *Russell Letters*, ii. 382; Add. 51670, Bedford to Lady Holland, 24 Oct. [1831]; Blakiston, *Lord William Russell*, 243. [23] Beds. RO, Russell mss R766, Peyton to W. Russell, 25, 26 Oct., Tavistock to same, 28 [Oct.]; Add. 51670, Bedford to Lady Holland, 31 Oct; *Cambridge and Hertford Independent Press*, 29 Oct. 1831. [24] Add. 51671, Bedford to Lady Holland, 5 Nov. 1832; Blakiston, *Lord William Russell*, 25, 449. [25] *Russell Letters*, iii. 47-48, 99, 198-9; Blakiston, *Woburn*, 205; *Greville Mems*. iv. 152. [26] Blakiston, *Woburn*, 204-6. [27] *Russell Letters*, iii. 314. [28] Blakiston, *Lord William Russell*, 25; Blakiston, *Woburn*, 206-7. [29] *The Times*, 28 May 1872.

D.R.F.

RUSSELL, Lord William (1767–1840).

SURREY	1 Jan. 1789–1807
TAVISTOCK	1807–18 Mar. 1819
TAVISTOCK	1826–1830

b. 20 Aug. 1767, 3rd and posth. s. of Francis Russell, mq. of Tavistock† (*d.*1767), and Lady Elizabeth Van Keppel, da. of William Anne, 2nd earl of Albemarle; bro. of Lord John Russell I†. *educ.* Loughborough House, Lambeth Wick;[1] Westminster 1778; Christ Church, Oxf. 1784. *m.* 11 July 1789, Lady Charlotte Anne Villiers, da. of George Bussy Villiers†, 4th earl of Jersey, 4s. (3 *d.v.p.*) 2da. *d.* 6 May 1840.

Ld. of admiralty Feb. 1806-Apr. 1807.

Capt. commdt. Streatham vols. 1803-4.

Russell, whose worsening eccentricities did not conceal from those who knew him well a generous spirit and a genuine interest in politics, continued the aimless and peripatetic mode of life which he had increasingly adopted after suffering the blows of his wife's early death in 1808 and the onset of seemingly intractable financial problems. In 1820 he was in Switzerland, where on an outing to Chamonay he 'amused' Lady Hardy and Miss FitzClarence

> by jumping and hopping about like the boys who were with us and when he took off his coat and capered about in his waistcoat holding his staff to jump over the *crevasses* and pieces of rock, I am afraid that Mary FitzClarence and I laughed most uncivilly but it was impossible to help it.

He outdid himself on a visit to Lady Hardy, one of the mature women with whom he liked to flirt, at Lausanne in September 1822:

> He was very absent always and had a trick of opening his mouth and putting his watch into it, as he walked up and down the room ... he told me he had lost his watch and was inclined to suspect his servant of having stolen it, but as this man was a most respectable one, and I was sure he had left it somewhere, I tried to dissuade him from these suspicions and said, of course in joke, 'Ah! you swallowed it in one of your absent fits.' He stopped short in his walk and said, 'Do you really think so? *It is possible*' – which most certainly it was not, as it had a gold chain and seal attached to it which could never have got down his throat even if his huge watch had, by *im*possibility. I made inquiries through my maid as to where his servant thought he had been and it seemed he had taken several warm baths at a questionable establishment in ... Lausanne, where it was not advisable for ladies to go and probably it had disappeared then and there.[2]

He had been in Florence the previous spring.[3] In January 1823 the wife of his favourite nephew and kindred spirit, Lord George William Russell*, reported that he was in Rome, flirting with Lady Westmorland, 'who sometimes sits up from 9 till 5 in the morning with him *tête à tête*, and at others tells him he is "like a bad nut, I crack you and find nothing in you."'[4] The following month he went '*en Pierrot*' to a fashionable ball, and he participated in amateur theatricals at Florence later in the year.[5] In 1823-4 he again wintered in Rome, where he made fine art purchases for his elder brother the 6th duke of Bedford, the head of the family.[6] He migrated in the spring to Florence, whence he wrote to Lord Holland on politics, 19 Apr. 1824:

> The cause of liberty is not at this moment rampant on the continent ... it has for some time been making retrograde movements, and those rapid ones. Still I am ... sanguine in belief that there is good working almost everywhere, to be brought to perfection sooner or later according to the understanding and common feeling that may be induced among persons who from talents or more adventitious circumstances, with right intentions, may be influentially placed in different parts ... I really think all looks well in England: public spirit improving, both in itself, and in its authoritative effect, and Canning well disposed to go with it and (if he finds it strong enough to keep him on his legs) to assist its right course. The case of Ireland is certainly one of tremendous difficulty, but there are some symptoms of attempting a better course towards her; and judging by the temper of the debates, I think we may be satisfied this will be the last year of the aliens bill.[7]

Lady Hardy found him 'as odd and absent as ever' at Lausanne in July 1825.[8]

At the general election the following year Russell was returned, rather surprisingly, by his brother for his former seat at Tavistock. In late October he was in Rome, whence he wrote to his nephew Lord John Russell*, urging him not to neglect his parliamentary duties for continental travel, as he seemed inclined to do:

> One is always apt to think the present the most critical of all times, but I am very sure that good men were never *more* wanted than now. We are to struggle for life or death in the new Parliament ... There are not wanting numbers indisposed to the ministry as it is now constituted, but there *is* wanting a right tone to the opposition – the House of Commons is what it always has been, and has been justly described like a pack of hounds, ready to follow the huntsman's call, and we have no one to lay them on the right scent. The opposition as it stands is a body of most discordant materials ... it is at least worth an effort to bring them together and draw them to one point. I hold it of first-rate importance that not a moment should be unnecessarily lost in announcing your reform bill – I mean the great plan – I don't meddle with the revolution ... The zeal of a convert is always strong, and I am impatient to show myself in the colours of my new faith.

After seeing his daughter Gertude, who had been forced into continental exile in 1825 with her sexually deviant husband Henry Grey Bennet*, he made his way to England in the new year.[9] He later wrote that he had 'flattered myself with a delusive hope, that I might effect arrangements that would enable me to keep my place in the House of Commons'; but, after an initial burst of activity, he became a virtual cypher, largely as a result of ill health.[10] He divided for Catholic relief, 6 Mar. 1827. He voted for inquiry into the allegations of electoral corruption against Leicester corporation, 15 Mar., for further information on the Orange procession at Lisburn, 29 Mar., to postpone the committee of supply until the ministerial uncertainty was resolved, 30 Mar., and for inquiry into the Irish miscellaneous estimates, 5 Apr. He voted for the spring guns bill, 23 Mar. To the distress of Bedford, who thought he had been 'talked over by Brougham and old Tierney', he generally approved of Canning's ministry.[11] (It is ironical that Canning described him privately as 'an acknowledged driveller' in politics.)[12] In the House, however, he took an idiosyncratic line. He was in the minority of 37 for the establishment of a separate bankruptcy jurisdiction, 22 May. That day he criticized the Coventry magistracy bill as 'hardly strong enough'. He voted in largely Tory minorities against it, 11, 18 June, when, claiming to be 'wholly unconnected with either party', he condemned it as introducing 'a principle highly dangerous to a free constitution, namely, that of non-responsibility in public offices'. He was in Lord John Russell's majority for the disfranchisement of Penryn for electoral corruption, 28 May. He presented a petition from Tavistock Unitarians for repeal of the Test Acts, 30 May.[13] He opposed Hume's motion for repeal of the Blasphemous and Seditious Libels Act, 31 May, admitting that to do so 'gave a seeming contradiction to that which had been the tenor of his whole life, the support of public liberty in its most extended sense', but singling out the measure as the only one of the Six Acts to which he was 'friendly'.[14] He failed in his attempt to have Forbes ruled out of order for introducing the question of the ballot into a debate on Preston elections, 14 June 1827.[15]

Bedford was deeply unhappy that Russell was 'induced to go as a mourner to the funeral of that political rogue and mountebank, Mr. Canning', and he received complaints from other Whigs over the incident.[16] The duke was implacably opposed to the Goderich ministry and Whig participation in it; and his son Lord Tavistock* had the impression in mid-September that Russell was 'less disposed than he was to support and give confidence'.[17] However, Russell wrote to Holland from Paris, 2 Oct. 1827:

> I never felt a clearer conviction of anything in my life than that it is imperiously the business of those who hold Whig doctrines at heart ... to give to the ministry as it now stands an active, though undoubtedly a conditional and guarded support ... I by no means imply that I think it satisfactorily constituted. God knows, far from it. There is abundance of unfitness in many parts of it. Many are out of it, one would wish in, and some in, one would wish out. No one can regret more cordially than I do, that Lord Grey was not a party to the first arrangement ... I am sure that as far as can depend on you, or indeed any who have ever acted with him, nothing will be wanted to keep up an opening for co-operation with him, should circumstances come about favourably for it ... some accession on the right side is indispensable to the character and stability of administration. *You* ought to be in an efficient office ... I am sure it is required and anxiously looked for, both at home and abroad, and at home not merely by those who have generally acted with and followed you and your friends, but by all the moderate men of any party ... any little exertions in my power to make, will always be at your command. I will be in my place without fail on the first day of the session. Unhappily for me, my nerves disqualify me from expressing myself in public, but if I fail, it is not for want of attentive and I will say dispassionate consideration, and I must do my best.

In January 1828, when he sent Holland 'a little book of poetry from Louis Buonaparte, with every sort of cordial assurance from him to you', he admitted that while he had 'certainly expected some upset', he had not reckoned on 'so complete a *bouleversement*' as had brought the duke of Wellington to power.[18] He presented petitions for repeal of the Test Acts, 18, 22 Feb., and voted for that measure, as proposed by his nephew, 26 Feb. He made a procedural point regarding membership of committees on private bills, 28 Feb. He voted against the scheme to extend the franchise at East Retford to the hundred of Bassetlaw, 21 Mar., and for inquiry into chancery delays, 24 Apr., and more effective control over crown proceedings for the recovery of excise penalties, 1 May. He presented petitions for Catholic relief, 5 May, and voted for it, 12 May. Soon afterwards he fell 'very ill with inflammation on the chest', but by the end of June 1828 he was better, having made 'a great rally'. He suffered a relapse in the autumn, however, and was for a while 'very seriously ill'.[19]

He did himself no good by 'shooting and acting' at Woburn Abbey in January 1829, and seems to have been unable to attend the House much for the first half of that session, though he was named to the Clare election committee which declared O'Connell duly elected, 3 Mar.[20] He was a defaulter on a call of the House, 5 Mar., but he claimed to have been present later that day to hear Peel's speech proposing the concession of Catholic emancipation, which, despite his inherent pessimism, tempted him to perceive 'a clearer horizon, than I have ever done before'.[21] There is no record of his having voted on the issue, but he divided in favour of O'Connell being allowed to take his seat without hindrance, 18 May. He voted for the transfer of East Retford's seats to Birmingham, 5 May, but on 2 June stated that he intended to vote for Fane's motion for the issue of a new writ:

> I have been anxious to throw the elective franchise into populous places, on proof of any delinquency ... I do not, however, consider East Retford as particularly delinquent, for nine-tenths of the Members of this House are returned avowedly by means of corruption ... If a practical opportunity were afforded of conferring the franchise on such a place as Birmingham, I should be most happy: that opportunity is hopeless now, and I vote for the issue of the writ, rather than the giving the right to the hundred.

Yet his name does not appear in the list of Fane's minority.

Russell returned to the continent later in the year, when his brother, believing him to be '*very* ill', was anxiously awaiting reports from his doctor in Munich.[22] On hearing more reassuring accounts of him in September 1829, Lord Tavistock commented that 'the farther he is removed from England the more eager he always is about politics. There cannot be a more honest and anxious minded politician'.[23] He was in Florence, 10 Apr. 1830, when he wrote to Holland to express his anger at the 'intolerable' conduct of 'many till then sound Whigs' in voting with an 'insincere' and disorganized government against the amendment to the address and supporting it merely 'because there is a *possibility* of a worse being formed in its place':

> Now this is very different from the doctrines I have always listened to. My only consolation is, it is some alleviation to my regret at leaving the field altogether. God knows my power to render assistance to the cause I am attached to and anxious to promote has been unavailing enough at all times. It is now absolutely nothing. My health is such that I very much doubt my being able even to take my place in the House during the whole session, but I am ... very earnest not to close my parliamentary life for ever, without two or three more votes if possible, and that they should be on such subjects as would bring the full spirit of our old principles the most clearly into action ... There appear now no leaders, and it would be vain boasting to offer myself as any man's follower, but I may at least say with peremptory confidence that if I ever give another vote it will be such as you might dictate.

He made his way painfully towards England, reaching Paris in early May, when he counselled Holland, with whose views he was largely in agreement, against being 'over apprehensive on imaginary grounds of consequences injurious to a good cause from your taking a more broad and distinct line on general measures':

> The public opinion I firmly believe would be right, if it were properly brought into action, and for evidence of that I will only recur to the short period of Canning's administration ... I have never known the feeling of the country so united and so strong from unity, as during that interval. And why? Was it from any popularity that attached to the man? On the contrary, no man was more generally obnoxious, or had made himself even bitter enemies in a greater variety of sources than he had; but it was the courage with which he came out and the manly sentiments he proclaimed that had almost a magical effect, and generosity became catching.

Although he lamented the 'terrible shabbiness and selfishness' of some of 'our own best friends', especially in their attitude to foreign affairs, he was pleased with what Holland had told him of Grey's 'general tone', and with the emergence of such 'good young ones' as Lords Howick* and Morpeth*. He was determined to attend to vote for the latter's motion for repeal of the banishment clause of the Libels Act, scheduled for 18 May, even though 'my doctors forbid me from entering the House'.[24] In the event, the motion was postponed; but Russell was present that day to vote for Newport's motion on Irish first fruits revenues, having paired for Jewish emancipation on the 17th. He paired for abolition of the death penalty for forgery, 24 May, and voted for it in person, 7 June. His only other known votes were for his nephew's parliamentary reform motion, 28 May, and reform of the divorce laws, 3 June 1830. His brother, whom he joined at Campden Hill at the end of June 'for change of air', pressed Lady Holland to get her husband or John Allen to 'look in upon him to cheer his solitude by talking a little *Whiggery* with him'. He retired from Parliament at the dissolution because of his continuing ill health.[25]

He elaborated on this decision in the course of trying to mollify Lord George William, who was angry at not being put up again for Bedford, even though he had shamelessly neglected both the constituency and his parliamentary duties for the best part of ten years. Russell said that if he had had his own way he would have vacated 'two or three years ago', when it had become clear that he was not capable of constant attendance, but that he had been persuaded to remain in for the sake of 'the election interests at Tavistock'. After the election (in which Lord John Russell was beaten by one vote), Russell wrote:

> We must have reform. The voice of the country, through the whole run of the late elections, has thundered retrenchment and reform ... In the early part of my life, I was a strenuous anti-reformer, though I never was hostile to the *principle* of reform; but it appeared to me as a measure impracticable, and extremely dangerous to its own professed end. The general call for it renders it now infinitely more easy of attainment; still, it is very far from being clear of difficulties. John has broached the outlines of a plan, preferable beyond measure to any that had before appeared, but would it satisfy the clamorous part of the public? I fear not. What we do want ... is a ministry of weight and capacity that would clap their shoulder to the wheel, in downright earnest, and fairly face the difficulties of the time, with their eyes open to everything around them. Retrenchment and reform should be carried into practice with responsibility attached to the execution, with reference to a whole and uniform system, not by piecemeal ... to save appearances, but with a real sincere desire of destroying the many-headed hydra that has been long unceasing in its activity to devour.[26]

He had 'strong confidence' in the intention and ability of the Grey ministry to deliver a 'sweeping' measure of reform and was delighted with the bill detailed by his nephew in March 1831: 'I think we are landed in safety from a storm as tremendous as ever state was engaged in'.[27] From the ministry he immediately solicited a legal appointment for his youngest and third surviving son William. (His second son, George, had died at the age of 30 in 1825.)[28] William was appointed attorney-general of the duchy of Lancaster court in 1833 and doubled as secretary to lord chancellor Cottenham from 1836 to 1839, when he was given the post of accountant-general of the court of chancery, which he held for 34 years. In June 1831, Russell reflected on matters personal and public:

> No pains were ever taken to correct my innate defects. They grew with my growth, but have not as a natural corollary decayed with my decay of strength. My sufferings from infirmity of health are sometimes very severe ... there never was a more critical period than the present ... the whole of the known world is in a state of ferment ... England ought to show the way ... I hope, and am inclined to believe we are in a right train at home, but it must be pursued vigorously and vigilantly. We must give content to our people, who deserve it, if ever people did, and we must hold out example for others to dress by.[29]

Russell, who was plagued with increasing deafness and had to wear a truss day and night, lost his sons Francis and John, both of whom were Members in this period, in 1832 and 1835. He continued his odd existence, passing back and forth between England and Europe. His sister-in-law reported from Woburn at Christmas 1838 that he 'chatters more and more to himself every day'.[30] He met a suitably bizarre end, for he was murdered in his bed (his throat cut from ear to ear and a napkin placed over his face) at his London house in Norfolk Street, Marylebone, in the small hours of 6 May 1840 by his Swiss valet, François Courvoisier, whom he had caught in the act of pilfering silver spoons and told that he would be dismissed in the morning. The case, as Greville noted

> excited a prodigious interest, and frightened all London out of its wits. Visionary servants and air-drawn razors or carving knives dance before everybody's imagination, and half the world go to sleep expecting to have their throats cut before morning.

Courvoisier, who might well have been acquitted for lack of evidence but for the fortuitous discovery during his trial of stolen plate which he had deposited at a Leicester Square hotel, confessed to the crime after he had been found guilty. He was executed before a large crowd on 6 July 1840.[31] On 12 Jan. 1841 administration of Russell's estate, which was sworn under £2,000, was granted to his son William.[32]

[1] J.H. Adeane, *Early Married Life of Lady Stanley*, 3. [2] J. Gore, *Nelson's Hardy and his Wife*, 67, 68, 75-76. [3] *Russell Letters*, ii. 4, 14. [4] Blakiston, *Lord William Russell*, 78-79. [5] *Berry Jnls.* iii. 330; Gore, 119. [6] *Russell Letters*, ii. 27-35, 37-40. [7] Add. 51681. [8] Gore, 129. [9] *Russell Early Corresp.* i. 249-52. [10] *Russell Letters*, ii. 255. [11] LMA, Jersey mss Acc. 510/416. [12] Blakiston, 28. [13] *The Times*, 31 May 1827. [14] *Geo. IV Letters*, iii. 1341. [15] *The Times*, 15 June 1827. [16] *Russell Letters*, i. 74; Lansdowne mss, Lady Holland to Lansdowne [?4 Sept. 1827]. [17] *Russell Letters*, ii. 104. [18] Add. 51681. [19] *Russell Letters*, i. 67, 100; ii. 88; Add. 51669, Bedford to Lady Holland, 30 June [1828]. [20] *Russell Letters*, ii. 188; *O'Connell Corresp.* iv. 1526; *CJ*, lxxxiv. 98. [21] *Russell Letters*, ii. 191. [22] Blakiston, 195-6. [23] *Russell Letters*, i. 128. [24] Add. 51681. [25] Add. 51670, Bedford to Lady Holland [?24 June 1830]; *Russell Letters*, ii. 251. [26] *Russell Letters*, ii. 253-60. [27] Ibid. ii. 301-5, 330-2; Add. 51681, Russell to Holland, 7 Dec. [1830]. [28] Brougham mss, Russell to Brougham, 22 Nov. [1830]; Add. 51681, same to Holland, 5 Dec. [1830], 6 Aug. [1831]. [29] *Russell Letters*, ii. 347-9. [30] Ibid. i. 284. [31] *Gent. Mag.* (1840), ii. 86, 204-5; *Greville Mems.* iv. 261-2; *Von Neumann Diary*, ii. 145, 146, 147-8; *Raikes Jnl.* iv. 13, 14, 18-20; Broughton, *Recollections*, v. 264, 266, 275-6; *Lady Lyttelton Corresp.* 298; *Disraeli Letters*, iii. 1075; *Ann. Reg.* (1840), Chron. pp. 229-45. See Y. Bridges, *Two Studies in Crime* (1959), 11-128. [32] PROB 6/217/221.

D.R.F.

RUTHVEN, Edward Southwell (1773–1836), of Oakley, co. Down.

DOWNPATRICK	1806–1807
DOWNPATRICK	1830–1832
DUBLIN	1832–31 Mar. 1836

b. 3 Nov. 1773,[1] 1st s. of Rev. Edward Trotter, LLD, of Oakley, preb. of Down, and Mary, da. of Very Rev. James Dickson of Dromore, dean of Down. *educ.* Trinity, Dublin 1787; Wadham, Oxf. 1790; M. Temple 1791. *m.* 12 Mar. 1794, Harriet Jane, da. of Francis Price, MP [I], of Saintfield, co. Down, 3s. 4da. *suc.* fa. 1777; took name of Ruthven 1801. *d.* 31 Mar. 1836.

Cornet, army 1800, 10 Drag. 1801-3.

Capt. Down militia 1793, Downpatrick yeoman inf. 1803.

This Member's originally Scottish family moved from Durham to Ireland in the seventeenth century, his great-grandfather Samuel Trotter being a dealer in skins and wools. His grandfather, John (?1698-1771) of Downpatrick, was agent to Lord de Clifford, which perhaps explains why one of his names was Southwell. His father, who married on 20 Dec. 1771, died on 8 July 1777, leaving him many houses in Downpatrick by his will, which was proved the following year; he was described by the resident diarist Aynsworth Pilson as a 'sensible good sort of man', who despite his 'considerable vanity' had 'an understanding very superior to his son and grandson who afterwards figured in Downpatrick'. His mother, whose father had been Member for Lisburn, 1759-76, remarried in 1792, to James Cumine of Killough, but died the same year. Pilson later recorded that the young Trotter 'was greatly indulged by his mother, which, superadded to a temper naturally self-willed, contributed much to his unhappiness through life'.[2] On 24 Jan. 1801 he was given royal permission to 'resume' the name of Ruthven, 'out of grateful respect to the memory of his paternal ancestors the Ruthvens', earls of Gowrie. A minor Down landowner, he allied himself with the dominant Whig interest of the 3rd marquess of Downshire and, having been returned for the open householder borough of Downpatrick in 1806, he supported the Grenville administration.[3] His brother John Bernard Trotter was appointed private secretary to the foreign secretary, Charles James Fox†, that year; he published the first biography of him in 1811.

Having lost his seat in 1807 and been defeated in 1815 and 1818, Ruthven offered again for Downpatrick at the general election of 1820, when the sitting Member withdrew. At the county election there he urged the local magistrates to maintain order and a few days later, despite thinking himself certain of success, he was defeated in the borough by his Tory opponent, John Waring Maxwell.[4] His eldest son Edward addressed the lord lieutenant Lord Wellesley in favour of reforming the government of Ireland, 7 July 1823, while he himself spoke at the Belfast reform meeting in November that year.[5] He proposed the Whig Lord Arthur Hill* for Down at the general election of 1826, when he did not offer for Downpatrick.[6] In late 1828 he and his son tried to wrest control of the Down races, leading the Rev. Charles Hamilton, vicar of Garvaghy, to complain to Downshire that 'I regret exceedingly the part which the Ruthvens have taken (so unsuitable for them and ungrateful to you)', adding that 'the son is a vain assuming, prating and scribbling creature, and I have often been astonished at the influence he exercises over his father's stronger intellect'.[7] Said by Pilson to have distinguished himself in the cause of Catholic emancipation, he spoke in its favour at the Down Catholics' meeting and the Downpatrick dinner to Daniel O'Connell* in early 1829.[8] That autumn, from an 'old grudge towards my family', as the leading Tory county proprietor Lord Londonderry put it, he was a major figure in the establishment of the Down Independent Club, which agitated against the predominating electoral interests.[9] He signed the requisition for and spoke at the county Down meeting against the increased Irish stamp and spirit duties, 19 May 1830.[10]

On Waring Maxwell's withdrawal at the general election of 1830, Ruthven, who claimed to be unconnected with any party, offered again for Downpatrick and was returned unopposed, described as a 'public spirited gentleman' of 'most independent and uncompromising principles'.[11] Having finally broken with Downshire, he supported the unsuccessful campaign of the former county Member, Mathew Forde, against Hill and Lord Castlereagh, Londonderry's son, in the county contest; he spoke in Forde's favour on the hustings, plumped for him and presided at the Downpatrick dinner in his honour, 16 Sept. 1830.[12] Regretting Ruthven's return, Downshire's law agent Thomas Handley commented to his employer that 'there will I fear be too many of his levelling class get in this time', and Planta, the Wellington ministry's patronage secretary, listed him among government's 'foes'.[13] In the Commons, where he was a frequent speaker on all manner of Irish concerns, he quickly earned a reputation as a bore; Tom Macaulay* privately denounced him as 'that stupid Irishman'.[14]

In a maiden speech, 3 Nov. 1830, he denied that Ireland sought independence from Britain. He objected to Hume's call for reducing army widows' pensions, 5 Nov., and, although usually a supporter of reduced expenditure and taxation, he on various later occasions opposed false economies. As in the debate on the state of the labouring classes, 9 Nov., he frequently advocated the extension of proposed measures to Ireland. He spoke and voted for repealing the Irish Subletting Act, 11 Nov., and was in the majority against ministers on the civil list, which led to their resignation, 15 Nov. He defended the Irish clergy, 18 Nov., and magistracy, 15, 23 Dec., and took a moderate stance on slavery, advocating compensation for planters, 23 Nov., 15 Dec., and on agricultural distress, opposing repeal of the corn laws, 2, 7, 17 Dec. He praised O'Connell's support for parliamentary reform, 9 Dec., but stated his disagreement with him over repeal of the Union that day and on the 11th. On 17 Dec. 1831 he engaged in the first of what became a long series of rancorous squabbles. He helped to secure the petition for radical reform at the Down meeting, 20 Jan. 1831, and signed the requisition for the county gathering against repeal of the Union in March, when he unsuccessfully applied to the new prime minister, Lord Grey, for the colonelcy of the Down militia.[15] Blaming the tithe system for economic distress, he moved for leave to introduce a bill to exempt small occupiers from payment of the tithe on potatoes, 22 Feb.; it was defeated by 133-1 when the O'Gorman Mahon divided the House. He suggested other means of relieving Irish distress, 10, 16, 18 Mar. He complained that ministers' reform proposals provided insufficient additional representation for Ireland, 9, 24, 29 Mar., but voted for the second reading of their English reform bill, 22 Mar. Although three times cautioned by the Speaker, he persisted in complaining about Londonderry's remark in the Lords that the Down petition had been got up by a 'rabble', 25 Mar.; he presented it on the 30th, after the county Members had refused to do so. He advocated alteration of the Irish jury laws, 12, 20 Apr., and reductions in the civil list, 14 Apr. He divided in the minority against Gascoyne's wrecking amendment to the reform bill, 19 Apr. 1831. He offered again for Downpatrick at the ensuing general election, when he easily saw off the challenge of a Scottish Tory interloper.[16] In the county contest, he seconded the nomination of the unsuccessful independent candidate William Sharman Crawford†, but attempted to placate the moderate freeholders by opposing radical changes and indicating that he would also vote for Hill, another reformer, against Castlereagh.[17]

Ruthven praised the address for promising to tackle Irish distress, 22 June, but criticized the use of molasses in British distilleries as depreciating the work of Irish labourers, 30 June, 26 July 1831. He divided for the second reading of the reintroduced reform bill, 6 July, at least twice against adjourning proceedings on it, 12 July, and thereafter generally for its details in committee, though he cast wayward votes for postponing consideration of the partial disfranchisement of Chippenham, 27 July, against the division of counties, 11 Aug., and for Lord Chandos's amendment to enfranchise £50 tenants-at-will, 18 Aug. He opposed the continuation of the grant to the Kildare Place Society, 18 July, when he had something to say on the role of the yeomanry in Orange processions, and the following day he defended the Maynooth grant. He justified the respectability, if not the sentiments, of the Belfast petition for repeal of the Union, 20 July. He was listed in the minorities for swearing the original Dublin election committee, 29 July, and against issuing a new writ, 8 Aug., but in government majorities in the two divisions on the controversy, 23 Aug. He called for the introduction of a form of poor laws to Ireland, 10 Aug., and voted for this, 29 Aug. On 11 Aug. he divided for printing the Waterford petition for disarming the Irish yeomanry, which he argued would relieve tension, 15, 26 Aug. He favoured the appointment of lord lieutenants in Irish counties, 15, 20 Aug., but was occasionally hostile to ministers, for instance in the committee of supply, 31 Aug. On 2 Sept. he proposed legalizing Catholic marriages (he introduced an abortive bill on this the following session), and he suggested alterations to the Irish administration of justice bill, 2, 15 Sept. He voted for the third reading, 19 Sept., and passage of the reform bill, 21 Sept., and for the second reading of the Scottish bill, 23 Sept. He clashed with Bateson, Member for County Londonderry, 26 Sept., and Castlereagh, 27 Sept., and was angered by the House's refusal to hear him, 4 Oct. He divided for Lord Ebrington's confidence motion, 10 Oct., and spoke generally for reform, 12, 17, 18 Oct. He was a teller for the minority against the ecclesiastical courts bill, 14 Oct. 1831.

Having missed the division on the second reading of the revised reform bill, 17 Dec. 1831, he called for an increase of Irish Members and defended the £5 householder franchise, 19 Jan. 1832, when he condemned the Union. He divided for the committal of the reform bill, 20 Jan., 20 Feb., steadily for its details and for the third reading, 22 Mar. He complained about the partisan composition of the select committee on Irish tithes, 23 Jan., when he voted for the vestry bill, but urged his countrymen not to react violently against the ministerial plan for Irish education, 26 Jan., 13 Feb. He sided with opposition against the Russian-Dutch loan, 26 Jan., and for inquiry into distress in the glove trade, 31 Jan., but with ministers against the production of information on Portugal, 9 Feb. He initially suggested that the anatomy bill should be extended to Ireland, 6 Feb., but voted for recommitting it, 27 Feb., and expressed his horror of it, 16 Mar., 11 Apr., 11 May. He declared for the total abolition of Irish tithes, 8 Feb., and gave guarded support to the Irish subletting bill, 20 Feb., and juries bill, 22, 28 Feb., when his amendment for juries in criminal cases to be chosen by ballot was negatived. He divided to postpone debate on Irish tithes, 8 Mar., and secured an adjournment on this, 13 Mar., presenting hostile petitions, 23, 30 Mar., 14 May. He led the protests against government's interim report on the subject, 27 Mar., when he was teller for the minority for his amendment to the first resolution for redistributing church revenues, and argued that conciliation not enforcement was the remedy for disorder in Ireland, 31 Mar. Having divided against the second and fourth resolutions, 27, 30 Mar., he moved (and was a teller for) the unsuccessful wrecking amendment against the second reading of the Irish arrears of tithes bill, 6 Apr., and again raised objections to it, 9, 16 Apr. He spoke for the ministerial education plan, 16 Apr., and, as he had promised its instigator Sharman Crawford, brought up the favourable Bangor petition, 18 Apr.[18] He voted for Ebrington's motion for an address calling on the king to appoint only ministers who would carry the reform bill unimpaired, 10 May, and, despite claiming that his native country deserved better, for the second reading of the Irish bill, 25 May. He was a teller for the minority against inquiry into the outrages in Ireland, 23 May, when he voted for the Liverpool disfranchisement bill, although in what he called a more moderate atmosphere on the 31st he accepted the need for a committee. He divided for Buxton's motion to abolish colonial slavery, 24 May. He remarked that Alexander Baring's bill to exclude insolvent debtors from Parliament did not go far enough, 30 May, 1 June. On 6 and 25 June he presented and endorsed Dublin petitions for it to receive two additional Members, which he failed to secure in the committee, 18 July. He supported various O'Connellite changes to the Irish reform bill, 13, 18, 25 June, 2, 9 July, and sided with him for amendments to it, 18, 19, 29 June and (as teller) 2 July. He attacked the Irish party processions bill, 14 June, and voted against going into committee on it, 25 June. He objected to Newry's extensive boundaries, 5, 9 July, and presented its petition to confine the borough to the limits of the town, 17 July. He divided for postponing the Irish tithes bill until the following Parliament, 13 July, justified the opposition to it, 18, 20 July, spoke and voted against it, 24 July, 1 Aug., and registered further protests, 2, 3, 6, 15 Aug. He voted for inquiry into the Inns of Court, 17 July, criticized the bribery at elections bill as ineffective, 30 July, and advocated independence for Greece, 8, 10 Aug. Reverting to one of his favourite ideas for bringing home to the Parliament in England the problems of Ireland, he gave notice, 24 July 1832, that in the following session he would move for a committee to meet in Dublin to investigate the true state of the country.

The Protestant Ruthven, who had for many months been cultivating a following in Dublin, was surprisingly adopted as a candidate by the National Political Union there after he had pledged himself to advocate repeal of the Union, and he was elected as a Repealer with O'Connell at the general election of 1832.[19] A large, slightly hump-backed figure, he increasingly infuriated the Commons by his persistence in moving the adjournment each evening, in an effort to end the practice of late sittings. According to James Grant, who commented that 'his manners are awkward in the extreme; he looks like a person newly imported from the country, and who has all his life been a working farmer', he 'cannot speak the English language at all; he often tries to correct himself, and stammers away at an extraordinary rate in the attempt, but he only in the end flounders the more deeply in the mire of bad English'.[20] Although careful with money, he had to sell his estates at Crossgar in 1827 and Oakley in 1831 and at his death, in March 1836, he retained almost no property in Down. Pilson observed that 'late hours accompanied by excess and perhaps a disturbed mind from his reduced circumstances probably combined to hasten his dissolution'. He was buried in Glasnevin cemetery, Dublin, 11 Apr. 1836, and although he had been returned for that city at the general election in 1835, he was posthumously unseated a few weeks later.[21] His estate, such as it was, passed to his widow (*d.* 16 Apr. 1846, aged 76) and son Edward of Ballyfan House, Kildare, the Repeal Member for that county, 1832-7.[22]

[1] *Clergy of Down and Dromore*, pt. ii, p. 60. IGI (Down) unaccountably gives a baptism date of 3 Oct. 1773 for Edward Southerland Trotter. [2] *Burke Irish LG* (1958), *sub* (Otway-) Ruthven; *Clergy of Down and Dromore*, pt. ii, pp. 59-60; *Index to Prerogative Wills of Ireland* ed. Sir A. Vicars, 461; PRO NI, Pilson 'Mems.' D365/7, pp. 24-30. [3] Pilson 'Mems.' p. 28; *HP Commons, 1790-1820*, ii. 645-6; v. 74-75. [4] *Belfast News Letter*, 24, 28 Mar. 1820; PRO NI, Ker mss D2651/3/36. [5] *Belfast News Letter*, 11 July, 25 Nov. 1823. [6] *Belfast Commercial Chron.* 28 June 1826. [7] PRO NI, Downshire mss D671/C/2/333/1; 75/81. [8] PRO NI, Pilson diary D365/3, 19 Aug. 1828, 2 Apr.; *Newry Commercial Telegraph*, 20 Feb.; *Northern Whig*, 23 Apr. 1829. [9] Downshire mss C/2/396/1; 12/418; 75/89. [10] *Newry Commercial Telegraph*, 14, 21 May 1830. [11] Ibid. 23, 27 July, 10 Aug. 1830; PRO NI,

Perceval-Maxwell mss D3244/G/1/67. [12] Pilson 'Mems.' p. 28; *Newry Commercial Telegraph*, 27 July, 17 Aug., 21 Sept. 1830; PRO NI T761/19. [13] Downshire mss C/1/618. [14] *Macaulay Letters*, ii. 73. [15] *Newry Commercial Telegraph*, 14, 25 Jan., 18 Mar. 1831; PRO NI, Anglesey mss D619/28A-B/48. [16] *Belfast News Letter*, 3, 10, 13 May 1831. [17] *Newry Commercial Telegraph*, 13, 17, 20 May 1831. [18] PRO NI, Sharman Crawford mss D856/D/20. [19] *Dublin Evening Post*, 21 Aug., 30 Oct., 1, 11 Dec.; *Newry Commercial Telegraph*, 7 Sept., 14 Dec. 1832; *O'Connell Corresp.* iv. 1917, 1921, 1925, 1929; J. Hill, *From Patriots to Unionists*, 351. [20] [J. Grant], *Random Recollections of Commons* (1837), 339-43. [21] Pilson 'Mems.' pp. 28-30; *The Times*, 1, 8, 14 Apr.; *Dublin Evening Post*, 2, 7, 12 Apr. 1836; *Gent. Mag.* (1836), i. 664-5; *DNB*; *Oxford DNB*. [22] Pilson 'Mems.' p. 29.

S.M.F.

RYDER, Dudley, Visct. Sandon (1798–1882), of 39 Grovesnor Square, Mdx.

TIVERTON	6 July 1819–1831
LIVERPOOL	21 Oct. 1831–1847

b. 19 May 1798, 1st s. of Dudley Ryder†, 1st earl of Harrowby, and Lady Susan Leveson Gower, da. of Granville Leveson Gower†, 1st mq. of Stafford; bro. of Hon. Granville Dudley Ryder*. *educ.* by Mrs. Braidwood, Hackney 1803-6; by Rev. Hooker, Rottingdean 1806; by Rev. Cross at Latton, nr. Harlow 1807-9; by John Thelwall at 1 Bedford Place, Mdx. 1809; by Rev. Gilbert Beresford at Trowbridge, later at Aylstone, nr. Leicester 1810-15; Christ Church, Oxf. 1816. *m.* 15 Sept. 1823, at Berne, Lady Frances Stuart, da. of John Stuart†, 1st mq. of Bute, 4s. (2 *d.v.p.*) 2da. *d.v.p. suc.* fa. as 2nd earl of Harrowby 26 Dec. 1847; KG 28 June 1859. *d.* 19 Nov. 1882.

Sec. to bd. of control Dec. 1830-May 1831; commr. for building new churches 1845; ecclesiastical commr. 1847-80; PC 31 Mar. 1855; chan. of duchy of Lancaster Mar.-Dec. 1855; ld. privy seal Dec. 1855-Feb. 1858.

Lt. Staffs. militia 1819, capt. 1826.

Sandon, who came from a prominent Tory family, was briefly tutored by the radical John Thelwall, of whom he recalled that 'he did not try to make us revolutionists, but we read much English history ... and he gave us a stout Whiggish tendency in regard to it ... I am still in English history a Whig'. His liberal Tory proclivities were reflected in his friendships at Oxford with the future Whig Members Edward Smith Stanley and Henry Labouchere.[1] He was still an undergraduate when he was returned for Tiverton on his father's interest, and he was again returned unopposed in 1820 with his uncle Richard Ryder.[2] He attended occasionally to support Lord Liverpool's ministry, in which his father was lord president, but he is not known to have spoken in debate in this Parliament. He divided against economies in revenue collection, 4 July 1820. He appears to have been inactive in 1821. He voted against more extensive tax reductions, 21 Feb., and abolition of one of the joint-postmasterships, 13 Mar. 1822. He voted against inquiries into Irish tithes, 19 June, and the conduct of the lord advocate in relation to the Scottish press, 25 June 1822. In January 1823 he wrote to his father from Rome expressing regret that his absence might have prevented him from being appointed Canning's foreign office under-secretary, 'a situation I should have liked particularly, as being one of much and regular occupation'.[3] He divided against the motion for information on Catholic office-holders, 19 Feb., and reform of Edinburgh's representation, 26 Feb., and for the usury laws repeal bill, 27 Feb. 1824. According to Canning, he went 'astray' by absenting himself from the division on the aliens bill, 2 Apr. 1824.[4] He appears to have been in Italy throughout the 1825 session, although at one point he was packed and ready to return to support Catholic relief, until his father notified him that he was not needed.[5] He voted to receive the report on the salary of the president of the board of trade, 10 Apr., and against reform of Edinburgh's representation, 13 Apr., and Lord John Russell's resolutions to curb electoral bribery, 26 May 1826. Russell identified him at this time as one of a group of industrious young Members, including Smith Stanley, John Evelyn Denison and John Stuart Wortley, who 'really attend to questions and give themselves trouble'.[6] He was again returned unopposed for Tiverton at the general election that summer.[7]

He divided for Catholic relief, 6 Mar. 1827. In his maiden speech, 23 Mar., he supported the spring guns bill, observing that landowners who wished to enjoy such an 'expensive and fatal luxury' should employ more gamekeepers. He denied that supporters of Catholic relief who had joined Canning's ministry, such as his father, had abandoned their principles, 25 May, arguing that while this was not the time to force the issue the new government was more likely than any other to remove the obstacles to a settlement. However, he made what was described as a 'very reforming speech' in favour of transferring Penryn's seats to Manchester and voted against ministers, 28 May.[8] He voted for the grant to improve water communications in Canada, 12 June. He supported the Coventry magistracy bill, 18 June, as proof had been given of the 'vice of the system' as well as of individuals. Whereas his father declined to serve in Lord Goderich's ministry, Sandon agreed to join it in November 1827 as a lord of the admiralty, an arrangement that was approved by the Whig Lords Lansdowne and Holland, although he admitted that he was 'only inclined to support [it] through dread of the worse consequences that might arise from the possession of power by [its] adversaries'.[9] His appointment had not been gazetted when the government collapsed, however, and he made it clear that he would not fill the same position in the duke of Wellington's ministry, explaining that 'in the present confusion of political parties I ... should be ... unwilling to find myself engaged to any particular course, and shall be glad to put myself completely at liberty to ... vote as occasion may arise'.[10] Edward Littleton* advised Peel, the new leader of the Commons, that 'the most important party' in the House consisted of 'a few young men', including Sandon, Stuart Wortley and Lord Eliot, who 'hang much together, and who though having different party connections [are] all united ... against high Tory principles'.[11] He voted for repeal of the Test Acts, 26 Feb., described them as 'one of the greatest scandals which ever disgraced' the statute book, 18 Mar., and opposed Lord Mandeville's Trinitarian amendment to the proposed new oath, 2 May 1828. He divided for Catholic claims, 12 May. He voted against extending the East Retford franchise to Bassetlaw freeholders, 21 Mar., and supported the transfer of its seats to Birmingham, 19 May, when his pressure on Huskisson to back this contributed to the latter's departure from the government.[12] He presented a Tiverton petition against the concurrent jurisdiction clause in the alehouses licensing bill, 28 Apr., supported the second reading in the hope that changes would be made in committee, 21 May, and spoke against the objectionable clause, which was rejected, 19 June. He said that his favourable impression of the additional churches bill had been 'considerably weakened' by the arguments he had heard against it, and advised that it be considered by a committee, 30 June. He divided with ministers against reducing the salary of the lieutenant-general of the ordnance, 4 July. He voted for the corporate funds bill, 10 July 1828. He was generally reckoned at this time to be a member of the Canningite or Huskisson party. In January 1829 he wrote to Denison that he suspected Wellington was personally 'well disposed to the Catholic question', but was prevented from acting by the obstacles in his way, notably 'the embarrassment as to the choice of materials for ... reconstruction' of the cabinet. He believed the duke had 'behaved too ill' towards the Huskissonites for them to rejoin his government, and speculated on a union between Wellington and 'Lord Grey and a few friends', cemented by 'common hostility to Canning and his memory'. He lamented the weak and disorganized state of the Huskissonites, observing of Huskisson, 'who can trust his judgement as a leader, even if his honesty be not doubted?'; and he urged the need for a 'clear and strong' line to be taken on the Catholic question.[13] He voted for emancipation, 6, 30 Mar., and condemned the clause relating to members of Catholic monastic orders as 'hostile to the principles of our free constitution', 24 Mar. He welcomed the Irish franchise bill, 26 Mar., arguing that the 40*s.* freeholders had abused their privilege and that many freeholds had been created by absentee landlords for political purposes, and he hoped it would encourage landlords to reside on their estates so that property might 'regain its due influence'. He called for Catholic emancipation to be extended to the colonies, 6 Apr., and supported the Maynooth grant, 22 May. He seconded Stuart Wortley's motion for a game laws amendment bill, 17 Feb. He approved of the bishops' leases bill, which would 'relieve [them] from a habit of gambling, inconsistent with the nature of their employment', 2 Apr. He voted to transfer East Retford's seats to Birmingham, 5 May, and to reduce the grant for the marble arch sculpture, 25 May. In June 1829 Wellington reportedly considered him for a vacant lordship of the admiralty, despite Mrs. Arbuthnot's complaint that he was a 'rank Canningite'.[14]

Sandon was absent from the opening of the 1830 session, but he wrote to Denison deploring the Huskissonites' hostile action against the government on the address, from which he could see no 'practical honest result', as it raised further barriers to their taking office with Wellington at a time when the formation of a 'mixed government' with the Whigs would be resisted by the king and the Lords. Shortly after his arrival in London he reported to his father that the political temperature had cooled, but there was still 'a good deal of discontent at the levity with which, both in public and private, the ministers ... have treated the general distress'. He regretted the recent conduct of his 'friends' and explained his own position:

> I sit at present near them, but not with them, and generally contrive to get [Sir Thomas Dyke] Acland to keep me company. I must be governed by circumstances for my own conduct, and should be much inclined to rally round the government on any attack dangerous to their existence, but to be rigorous on points of economy and free from all ties on ordinary occasions. Certainly the unpleasant part of the present government is its general motley composition and deficiency of talent equal to the times. It is however our only resource, so that we must be content, and I have no doubt it will do a great many excellent things.[15]

He divided against Lord Blandford's reform motion, 18 Feb., and the enfranchisement of Birmingham, Leeds and Manchester, 23 Feb., although this caused him 'considerable embarrassment' as the object was 'very highly desirable'. He maintained that any measure of reform should contain 'some principle of self-limitation', in order to prevent endless claims for similar treatment, and he proposed a 'middle course' by reviving Russell's old resolution that in all cases where boroughs were disfranchised for corruption their seats should be transferred to an unrepresented town or a large county; this was negatived. According to a Whig Member, his plan pleased neither the reformers nor the ministry, and 'between the two he had a fall, which everybody but himself foresaw'.[16] He voted again to transfer East Retford's seats to Birmingham, 5 Mar. From this point he seems to have participated more wholeheartedly in opposition attacks on the government. He voted to restrict the grant for the volunteers, 9 Mar., and inquire into a revision of taxation, 25 Mar., demanded inquiry into the grant for repairs to Windsor Castle, 3 May, and voted for retrenchment in the consular service, 7, 11 June. He condemned the government's conduct of foreign policy and was a minority teller for Lord Palmerston's motion regarding interference in the affairs of Portugal, 10 Mar. He denounced the affair at Terceira as 'a foul blot ... upon our national character', 28 Apr. He voted for Jewish emancipation, 5 Apr. He approved of the ministerial plan to defray the cost of administering justice in Canada, 29 Apr., but seconded Labouchere's resolutions regarding the civil government of that colony, 25 May, declaring that they were based on principles that had 'become so much axioms in the science of politics as to have been long since placed ... beyond dispute'; he was a minority teller. He opposed any reduction in the grant for erecting churches in the West Indies, 10 May, and argued that the grant to the Society for the Propagation of the Gospels in the colonies should not be ended immediately, 14 June. He voted for reform of the divorce laws, 3 June, and abolition of the death penalty for forgery, 7 June. He maintained that the labourers' wages bill was 'equally defensible upon the soundest principles of commerce and of common sense', 1 July 1830. At the ensuing general election he was again returned unopposed for Tiverton, with his brother Granville Ryder.

The ministry regarded him as a member of the 'Huskisson party'. He presented an anti-slavery petition from Sandon, 11 Nov. 1830. Next day he advised his father of the 'altered feeling' in the country with regard to reform, which was 'no longer the cry of the turbulent and disaffected' but extended to 'the most sober and peaceable classes', and of his belief that 'the current is too strong to be permanently resisted and ... early concession is better and more effective than late'. He divided against ministers in the crucial civil list division, 15 Nov., although one Tory Member noted that he 'did not seem to imagine ... it would lead to [their] resignation'. Nevertheless, he told his father that he welcomed their departure, as 'nothing is so bad as a government that does not make itself respected in such times as these'.[17] He was offered a position in Lord Grey's ministry, and was reassured on the subject of reform in an interview with the premier, whom he found to be 'decidedly against any such change as should insulate one House from the other or destroy that influence which enabled the three powers to move together'. He was satisfied that 'if something must be done, I believe it could not be trusted to firmer or more aristocratic hands'. He expressed a 'decided preference' for the proposed secretaryship to the India board (which he took), in view of the 'higher and more interesting topics' which it involved, felt alarm at the suggestion that he might become secretary at war, 'from the prominence of the situation and the strangeness of the subject', and would have been content to become clerk of the ordnance, for 'although the subject is as dry ... as can be ... I hope not to stay in it long and can easily move from that ... to something more in my own way'.[18] He was named to the select committee on the East India Company, 4 Feb., and said he saw no reason for maintaining the excessive emoluments in the Indian supreme court, 17 Mar. 1831. He welcomed the 'more liberal tone' adopted in the government's Canada bill, 18 Feb. In the debate on secondary punishments, 17 Mar., he held that solitary confinement was often 'productive of the best consequences' and that 'short punishments' generally had 'a wholesome effect upon the mind, whereas longer ones render it perfectly callous or indifferent'. He supported the truck abolition bill, 12 Apr., arguing that Parliament was bound to protect labourers who felt themselves to be 'the slaves of their employers'. He observed that 'many wise men have considered the ballot destructive of public liberty', 28 Feb., and divided for the second reading of the government's reform bill, 22 Mar., and against Gascoyne's wrecking amendment, 19 Apr. Two days earlier he had informed Grey that his support for the bill had alienated many of the corporation electors at Tiverton and that he would not be re-elected. It was impossible for him to 'fight an expensive and uncertain battle' in an open seat, given his father's 'decided disapprobation of the present measure', and he was unwilling to accept one from the government, as this would form 'an additional tie' when he 'already ... felt the discomfort of being fettered ... in the discussion of this ... vital question'. He therefore concluded that since he could not give a 'thorough approbation of the whole measure as it now stands', he should resign, a decision which he confirmed, 28 Apr. 1831.[19]

Sandon was out of the House until October 1831, when he was returned for Liverpool at a by-election, defeating a radical reformer with support from 'a singular mixture of ultra and moderate Tories, Whigs and moderate reformers'. He advocated the abolition of nomination boroughs, the enfranchisement of large towns and 'a liberal extension of the ... franchise founded on a combined consideration of property, education and numbers', but warned that the reintroduced reform bill contained 'considerable errors' and hoped ministers would make concessions in order to obtain a satisfactory settlement.[20] That autumn his father voted against the bill's second reading in the Lords and became a leader of the Tory 'Waverers' trying to effect a compromise, and Sandon entered into a lengthy correspondence with the Irish secretary Smith Stanley in a bid to promote that object. His kinsman Lord Wharncliffe, the other leading 'Waverer', learned that he had 'quite come to his senses ... since he was at Liverpool and that ... his opinions were now almost exactly the same as Harrowby's and mine'. Russell was privately adverse, however, to one of his suggestions, that borough residents should be excluded from county elections.[21] On the address, 7 Dec., Sandon repeated his call for a compromise, which he believed the Lords desired, and expressed approval of the government's policy towards Holland and Belgium. He commended the 'spirit of conciliation' shown in the revised reform bill, 12 Dec., particularly the removal of population as the sole criterion for disfranchisement and the preservation of freemen's voting rights, and hoped that a settlement could be reached without creating peers to effect it. A Whig observer thought that while 'this young lad's observations were more amicable to us than before ... the tone was far from cordial and the praise he gave the bill, such as it was, seemed wrong from him'.[22] He divided for the second reading, 17 Dec. 1831, and to go into committee, 20 Jan. 1832, when he welcomed the decision to adhere to the figure of 56 boroughs for schedule A. However, he criticized the proposal to include 30 boroughs in schedule B, 23 Jan., arguing that 'the free elections of moderately sized county towns ... influenced by the calm, enlightened and virtuous feelings of ... the little aristocracy of such places' was 'a most desirable element in our new representation', and that he would be 'sorry to see the whole House consist entirely of representatives of large popular bodies exercising ... a constant vigilant superintendence over every vote and action of their representatives'. He voted for the unsuccessful amendment to enfranchise £10 ratepayers, 3 Feb., but sided with ministers that day against raising the qualification in large boroughs to £15, and voted for the registration clause, 8 Feb. He divided against the enfranchisement of Tower Hamlets, 28 Feb., as he objected to the 'increased artificial preponderance of the metropolis over the remoter parts of the empire' and to a precedent 'involving the necessity of continual change'. He voted against the enfranchisement of Gateshead, 5 Mar., believing Merthyr Tydvil had a better claim. He divided for the third reading, 22 Mar. He initially approved of Lord Ebrington's motion for an address asking the king to appoint only a government committed to carrying an unimpaired measure, 10 May, although he felt it had been unnecessary for ministers to resign, but he later explained that he could not support the motion if it was understood to endorse the advice to create new peers; he therefore 'left the House without voting'.[23] He thought the constitutional crisis had 'arisen from misunderstanding and not from intention' and that the Lords meant to carry 'the whole of the essential parts of the bill', 14 May. He endorsed the substitution of Lichfield for Walsall as the nomination place for South Staffordshire, 22 June, as it was 'naturally the agricultural capital' of the constituency. He voted for Alexander Baring's bill to exclude insolvent debtors from Parliament, 27 June. He could not understand why the counties were omitted from the scope of the bribery bill, 6 Aug. 1832.

At a government meeting to settle the membership of the select committee on Irish tithes, 12 Dec. 1831, Lord Althorp, the leader of the Commons, objected to Sandon, as he 'always tried to steer a middle course and was full of crotchets'.[24] He condemned the conduct of Irish Members in encouraging resistance to the payment of tithes, 2 Apr., and expressed surprise at the opposition to the composition bill from Irish landlords when their English counterparts wanted a similar measure, 2 Aug. 1832. He presented a Liverpool petition against the plan for Irish education and argued that 'conciliation ... is only another word for collision', 16 Mar.; he divided against the education grant, 23 July. He presented a Liverpool corporation petition against the general register bill, 24 Jan., but hoped it could be amended, 2 Feb., and was named to the committee on it, 22 Feb. He intervened in defence of the corporation with regard to the Liverpool revenue buildings bill, 8 Feb. He pressed the government to 'proceed to ulterior measures' if the Brazilians did not immediately pay compensation for the seizure of British vessels, many of which came from Liverpool, 28 Feb., and again, 16 Apr., observing that there was a wider problem of inadequate protection for British property in the 'half-constituted' states of South America to which the British government showed 'peculiar tenderness'. He promised unrelenting opposition to the Liverpool franchise bill, 24 May, and moved its rejection, 4 July, claiming that it would inflict 'private injustice' on innocent freemen; it was later withdrawn.[25] He welcomed the proposed reductions in the customs duties, 15 June, and spoke on details of interest to his constituents, 25 July. He divided with ministers on the Russian-Dutch loan, 26 Jan., 12, 20 July, when he criticized those Members who 'on the eve of an election, and under the guise of economy, advocate an absolute breach of the national faith'. He warned that the motion for papers regarding Portugal was effectively a 'vote of censure', 9 Feb., and declared that he was 'still inclined to repose my faith in the good intentions of ministers'. He condemned the 'outrage upon national independence' committed by Russia against Poland, 18 Apr., said that Britain must protest to 'liberate our own honour from any participation in the guilt', 28 June, and feared that a conflict was 'fast approaching between the democratic and despotic states of Europe', 7 Aug. He reluctantly voted against ministers for reduction of the sugar duties, 7 Mar., as urgent action was needed to save the West India interest from ruin. He welcomed their measures to assist the planters, 23 Mar., but protested at the 'reckless' language of anti-slavery campaigners, which was 'calculated to sow the seeds of discord and tumult'. He acknowledged that slavery was 'a condition vicious in its source and origin' and 'productive of great evil both to slave and master', 24 May, but argued that ameliorative measures were required before abolition could take place. He applauded the proposal to issue exchequer bills for the relief of the West Indies, 29 June. He presented a Liverpool petition against the immediate abolition of slavery, 27 July, and urged Members to await the report of the select committee before pledging themselves to their constituents. He opposed the withdrawal of the grant for the civil establishment in Sierra Leone, 23 July, arguing that 'we have now the chance of gradually transforming the colony into a native state' and that 'if we abandon it, the barbarians will again take possession ... and put an end to all hopes of the civilization of Africa being effected through that colony'. He mentioned an expedition being organized 'by parties with whom I am closely connected, to penetrate into the interior of Africa by means of steam', which he hoped would help to facilitate this object. He supported a select committee on Sabbath observance (to which he was appointed), 3 July, although he recognized the need to balance the 'interests of religion and morality' against 'improper interference with the recreations of the poor'. He doubted whether there was a serious agricultural depression and did not consider 'the condition of the working classes ... so bad as is generally supposed', 27 July 1832.

Sandon had returned to the Conservative fold before the general election in December 1832, when he was returned for Liverpool in second place with support from the West India interest and the freemen voters. He was 'opposed to the ballot' and the immediate abolition of slavery and 'in favour of throwing open the trade to China'.[26] He declined Peel's offer of the colonial under-secretaryship in 1835, thinking it 'incompatible with his position at Liverpool', and was prevented from accepting the presidency of the board of trade in 1845 by the strength of his constituents' feeling against the Maynooth grant.[27] He retired from the Commons in 1847, and later that year inherited his father's title and landed properties and the residue of his personal estate, which was sworn under £60,000.[28] Having reluctantly supported repeal of the corn laws he temporarily gravitated to the Liberals and took office in Palmerston's first ministry, but he later rejoined the Conservatives. One female friend wrote that 'there is no one whose character is so delightful to people of all sects and ages. There is a simplicity about him quite peculiar to himself and his opinions on all grave subjects are so fixed and earnest and yet so moderate'. Anthony Panizzi, the librarian at the British Museum, who knew him as 'an excellent friend and supporter of [London] University', believed he was 'very honest and independent in his opinions'. Henry Goulburn* had 'never [seen] anyone to whom I have naturally a greater liking and respect', but Smith Stanley, while acknowledging that he was 'the cleverest of his contemporaries', thought this was 'ruined by his indecision'.[29] He died in November 1882 and was succeeded by his eldest surviving son Dudley Ryder (1831-1900), Conservative Member for Lichfield, 1856-9, and Liverpool, 1868-82, and then by his other son, Henry Ryder (1836-1900).

[1] Harrowby mss, 'Reminiscences by Dudley, 2nd earl of Harrowby', 7. [2] *Trewman's Exeter Flying Post*, 9 Mar. 1820. [3] Harrowby mss, Sandon to Harrowby, 25 Jan. 1823. [4] Harewood mss, Canning to wife, 4 Apr. 1824. [5] Add. 52011, E. Fazakerley to H.E. Fox, 21 Feb.; 52015, Lord D. Stuart to Fox, 26 June 1825. [6] Add. 51789, Russell to Lady Holland, 26 Mar. 1826. [7] *Alfred*, 20 June 1826. [8] *Canning's Ministry*, 317. [9] *Geo. IV Letters*, iii. 1425; Add. 51687, Lansdowne to Holland, 22 Nov.; Lansdowne mss, Holland to Lansdowne, 23 Nov. 1827; Harrowby mss, Sandon to Harrowby, 11 Jan. 1828. [10] Wellington mss WP1/913/40. [11] Hatherton diary, 29 Jan. 1828. [12] TNA 30/29/9/3/39. [13] Nottingham Univ. Lib. Ossington mss OsC 67a. [14] *Arbuthnot Jnl*. ii. 282. [15] Ossington mss OsC 73a; Harrowby mss, Sandon to Harrowby, 19 Feb. 1830. [16] Keele Univ. Lib. Sneyd mss, Littleton to Sneyd, 24 Feb. 1830. [17] Harrowby mss, Sandon to Harrowby, 12, 18 Nov.; NLW, Ormathwaite mss FG/1/5, p. 134. [18] Harrowby mss, Sandon to Harrowby, 19, 25 Nov.; Grey mss,

Sandon to Grey, 19, 25 Nov. 1830. [19] Grey mss, Sandon to Grey, 17, 28 Apr.; Harrowby mss, Sandon to Harrowby, 29 Apr. 1831. [20] *The Times*, 22, 24 Oct. 1831. [21] Derby mss 920 Der (14) 127/3; Sheffield Archives, Wharncliffe mss, Lord to Lady Wharncliffe [Nov. 1831]; Hatherton diary, 7 Dec. 1831. [22] NLS mss 24762, f. 49. [23] *The Times*, 12 May 1832. [24] Hatherton diary, 12 Dec. 1831. [25] Liverpool RO 328/PAR5/3, Mayor Sandbach to Sandon, 2 Feb. 1832, thanking him for his attention to this subject. [26] R. Stewart, *Foundation of Conservative Party*, 374; *The Times*, 13-15 Dec. 1832; *Dod's Parl. Companion* (1833), 157. [27] *Gladstone: Autobiog. Memoranda, 1832-1845* ed. J. Brooke and M. Sorensen, 42, 273. [28] PROB 11/2071/218; IR26/1805/155. [29] Add. 52011, E. Fazakerley to H.E. Fox, 14 Jan. 1826; Manchester New Coll. Oxf. Shepherd mss vol. vii. f. 87; Surr. Hist. Cent. Goulburn mss Acc 304/67A, Goulburn to wife, 9 Mar. [1826]; Hatherton diary, 1 Dec. 1831.

T.A.J.

RYDER, Hon. Granville Dudley (1799–1879), of 44 Grosvenor Street, Mdx.

TIVERTON	1830–1832
HERTFORDSHIRE	1841–1847

b. 26 Nov. 1799, 2nd s. of Dudley Ryder†, 1st earl of Harrowby (*d.* 1847), and Lady Susan Leveson Gower, da. of Granville Leveson Gower†, 1st mq. of Stafford; bro. of Dudley Ryder, Visct. Sandon*. *educ.* Durham House, Chelsea; Trinity Coll. Camb. 1823; L. Inn 1824 (readmitted 1835). *m.* 30 May 1825, Lady Georgiana Augusta Somerset, da. of Henry Charles Somerset†, 6th duke of Beaufort, 4s. (2 *d.v.p.*) 5da. (4 *d.v.p.*). *suc.* uncle Hon. Richard Ryder* to Westbrook Hay, Herts. 1832. *d.* 24 Nov. 1879.

Entered RN 1813, lt. 1819, half-pay list 1822, cdr. (half-pay) 1864.

Ryder, who was described as being 'clever, but deaf and very pompous', was an active committee member of the Evangelical Reformation Society.[1] His support for Catholic emancipation meant that the corporation of Tiverton, where his father was the patron, were unwilling to elect him in the place of his anti-Catholic uncle in 1827, and it was not until the general election of 1830, after the issue had been settled, that their objection was removed and they returned him unopposed with his brother Lord Sandon.[2] The duke of Wellington's ministry listed him as a member of the 'Huskisson party'. In November, Sandon wrote that his brother was 'perhaps ... rather more of a reformer than I am, but more anxious ... that the carrying of the question should not be the destruction of the ministry'. Though he was listed as voting against the government in the crucial civil list division, 15 Nov. 1830, according to Sandon he had voted the other way, 'agreeing in the views of the majority, yet thinking it a question of confidence, and that economy was just the one point on which they deserved it'.[3] In contrast to Sandon, a member of Lord Grey's ministry, Ryder divided against the second reading of their reform bill, 22 Mar., and for Gascoyne's wrecking amendment, 19 Apr. 1831. At the ensuing general election he was returned for Tiverton with the Evangelical Spencer Perceval, despite local manifestations of opposition, and reported to his father that 'we have great reason to be thankful for our escape, seeing that, in many places, the unpopular candidates have been very ill used'. He also expressed 'very great' satisfaction at Sandon's decision to resign from the government.[4]

He divided against the second reading of the reintroduced reform bill, 6 July, for use of the 1831 census to determine the disfranchisement schedules, 19 July, and for preservation of the voting rights of non-resident freemen, 30 Aug., and against the bill's passage, 21 Sept. 1831. He voted for the motion censuring the conduct of the Irish administration during the Dublin election, 23 Aug. He seconded Perceval's motion to abolish the Maynooth grant, 26 Sept., arguing that it was 'a complete anomaly in our parliamentary bounty' and that the college had failed to produce a 'liberal, tolerant, enlightened and loyal' priesthood. He wished to see 'the ascendancy of Protestant religious principles ... over the hearts and minds and lives of all my countrymen', but not in a vindictive spirit. He presented a petition from Westham and Hailsham complaining that Protestant office-holders in Ireland were being compelled to participate in Catholic church services, 12 Oct., when he also presented a Hemel Hempstead petition for suppression of the Indian pilgrim tax. He divided against the second reading of the revised reform bill, 17 Dec. 1831, and the enfranchisement of Tower Hamlets, 28 Feb., seconded the motion to add Ramsgate to Sandwich, 14 Mar., and voted against the third reading, 22 Mar., and the second reading of the Irish bill, 25 May 1832. He presented a Hemel Hempstead petition in favour of the factories regulation bill, 20 Mar. He divided against Baring's bill to exclude insolvent debtors from Parliament, 6 June. He voted for a permanent provision for the Irish poor by a tax on absentees, 19 June, and against the grant for Irish education, 23 July. He presented several petitions for better observation of the Sabbath, 28 June, 3, 16 July, when he condemned the 'pernicious and appalling' effects of the Sale of Beer Act on rural districts, where 'drunkenness, gambling and debauchery' were rife. He maintained that he was 'no enemy to the general principles of free trade', but said they were not applicable in all cases and hoped the reformed Parliament would prohibit the consumption of beer on the premises and establish a 'more efficient system of police'. He voted against ministers on the Russian-Dutch loan, 12 July 1832.

Ryder did not stand again at Tiverton, which had been opened by the Reform Act, but he was returned for Hertfordshire as a Conservative in 1841. He voted against repeal of the corn laws in 1846, before retiring the following year.[5] He had inherited landed property at Westbrook Hay, near Hemel Hempstead, from his uncle in 1832, and was the residuary legatee of the personal estate, which was sworn under £140,000.[6] He received £2,000 on his father's death in 1847.[7] He died in November 1879 and left Westbrook Hay to his eldest son, Dudley Ryder (1830-1911). His other surviving son, Granville Ryder (1833-1901), was Conservative Member for Salisbury, 1869-80.

[1] Add. 52017, f. 20; J. Wolffe, *Protestant Crusade in Britain*, 43-44. [2] Devon RO, Harrowby-Tiverton mss (xerox copy), xvi. 141; xvii. 43. [3] Harrowby mss, Sandon to Harrowby, 12, 18 Nov. 1830. [4] Ibid. G. Ryder to Harrowby, 6 May; *Trewman's Exeter Flying Post*, 5 May 1831. [5] *Dod's Parl. Companion* (1847), 237. [6] PROB 11/1808/720; IR26/1302/684. [7] PROB 11/2071/218; IR26/1805/155.

T.A.J.

RYDER, Hon. Richard (1766–1832), of Westbrook Hay, nr. Hemel Hempstead, Herts. and 37 Grovesnor Street, Mdx.

TIVERTON 26 Feb. 1795–1830

b. 5 July 1766, 2nd s. of Nathaniel Ryder†, 1st Bar. Harrowby (*d.* 1803), and Elizabeth, da. and coh. of Rt. Rev. Richard Terrick, bp. of London. *educ.* Neasden, Mdx. by Rev. Richard Raikes; Harrow 1780; St. John's, Camb. 1784; L. Inn 1788, called 1791. *m.* 1 Aug. 1799, Frederica, da. and h. of Sir John Skynner† of Great Milton, Oxon., l.c.b. 1777-87, 1 da. *d.v.p. suc.* 1st cos. once removed Thomas Ryder† to Westbrook Hay 1812. *d.* 18 Sept. 1832.

Dep. paymaster c. 1797-1800; solicitor to ordnance 1801-6, to bd. of control ?1804-6; second justice of S. Wales circuit 1804-7; commr. for nawab of Arcot's debts until 1806; ld. of treasury Sept.-Dec. 1807; PC 25 Nov. 1807; judge adv.-gen. Nov. 1807-Nov. 1809; sec. of state for home affairs Nov. 1809-June 1812.

Jt. registrar, consistory ct. of Canterbury bef. 1808, sole registrar 1813-*d.*; bencher, L. Inn 1811, treas. 1819.

Capt. Staffs. supp. militia 1797; vol. London and Westminster light horse 1798.

Ryder had been hopelessly out of his depth as home secretary in Perceval's ministry, and after his resignation in 1812 persistent ill health provided an additional reason for his retreat to the sidelines of politics. His wife had reputedly brought with her 'a fortune of £100,000', and he had inherited £2,000 and chambers in Lincoln's Inn from his father in 1803, in addition to the unspecified provision already made on his marriage.[1] In 1812 he inherited landed property in Hertfordshire from a cousin and was the residuary legatee of the estate, which was sworn under £10,000.[2] Though it was claimed in 1820 that he received £5,060 per annum from the tenure of various legal offices, most of this related to the post of judge advocate-general, which he had resigned in 1809.[3] He continued to sit for Tiverton on his brother Lord Harrowby's interest, and he attended occasionally to give silent support to Lord Liverpool's ministry. He voted in defence of their conduct towards Queen Caroline, 6 Feb. 1821. He paired against Catholic relief, 28 Feb., and the forgery punishment mitigation bill, 23 May. He voted against repeal of the additional malt duty, 21 Mar., 3 Apr. 1821. He divided against more extensive tax reductions, 21 Feb., abolition of one of the joint-postmasterships, 13 Mar., and repeal of the salt duties, 28 June 1822. He voted against the removal of Catholic peers' disabilities, 30 Apr. 1822. He divided against repeal of the tax on houses valued at under £5, 10 Mar., and inquiries into the prosecution of the Dublin Orange rioters, 22 Apr., and delays in chancery, 5 June 1823. However, he voted for the motion condemning the trial of the Methodist missionary John Smith in Demerara, 11 June 1824. He divided against the Irish unlawful societies bill, 25 Feb., Catholic relief, 1 Mar., 21 Apr., 10 May, and the Irish franchise bill, 26 Apr. 1825. He voted for the financial provision for the duke of Cumberland, 30 May, 6 June 1825. Ill health caused him to be absent for much of the next session, but he was present to vote against reform of Edinburgh's representation, 13 Apr. 1826.[4]

Following his unopposed return in 1826, Ryder became even less active and he was reportedly 'still suffering from his headaches'. It appears that he would have retired in favour of his nephew Granville Ryder* in 1827, but for the fact that the latter's pro-Catholic views made him unacceptable to Tiverton corporation.[5] He divided against Catholic relief, 6 Mar. 1827, 12 May 1828. In February 1829 Planta, the Wellington ministry's patronage secretary, listed him as an absentee, but after being twice named as a defaulter, 5, 10 Mar., he attended to vote against emancipation, 18, 30 Mar. 1829. He divided against Jewish emancipation, 17 May 1830. At the dissolution that summer he was able to make way for his nephew, now that the Catholic question had been settled.[6] He became increasingly infirm, owing to 'oppressive asthma', and died in September 1832 after an attack of influenza and 'three weeks in acute dropsy'.[7] He had no surviving children and left Westbrook Hay and the residue of his estate to Granville Ryder; his personalty was sworn under £140,000.[8]

[1] *Gent. Mag.* (1799), ii. 716. His father's will was proved 'at the upper value' (PROB 11/1396/630; IR26/77/74). [2] IR26/558/817; *VCH Herts.* ii. 223. [3] *Black Bk.* (1820), 440. [4] Surr. Hist. Cent. Goulburn mss Acc 304/67A, Goulburn to wife, 9 Mar. [1826]; Add. 40386, f. 145. [5] Goulburn mss 67A, Goulburn to wife, 20 Nov. 1826; Devon RO, Harrowby-Tiverton mss (xerox copy), xvi. 141. [6] Harrowby-Tiverton mss, xvii. 43a. [7] Duke Univ. Lib. Fazakerley mss, Sandon to Fazakerley, 18 Sept. 1832. [8] PROB 11/1808/720; IR26/1302/684.

T.A.J.